THE ELVIS
ENCYCLOPEDIA

THE ELVIS ENCYCLOPEDIA

ADAM VICTOR

OVERLOOK DUCKWORTH

NEW YORK • WOODSTOCK • LONDON

Photos on pages : ii, iv, 1, 5, 7, 8, 9, 14, 18, 21, 22, 23, 25, 26, 30, 31, 35, 39, 41, 45, 49, 51, 60, 61, 62, 63, 66, 68, 70, 73, 76, 77, 78, 79, 80, 81, 82, 83, 85, 86, 87, 91, 95, 96, 100, 101, 102, 103, 105, 106, 107, 110, 113, 123, 124, 126, 129, 131, 135, 136, 139, 141, 143, 145, 146, 148, 149, 151, 152, 153, 155, 156, 158, 159, 160, 161, 166, 166, 169, 171, 173, 176, 177, 181, 182, 183, 188, 189, 191, 193, 194, 195, 196, 197, 198, 201, 203, 205, 206, 207 208, 215, 216, 222, 223 225, 227, 232, 233, 235, 236, 237, 238, 239, 243, 244, 245, 247, 250, 235, 254, 257, 259, 260, 263, 265, 267, 269, 271, 272, 275, 279, 281, 284, 285, 287, 290, 291, 293, 295, 297, 300, 302, 303, 305, 307, 308, 311, 312, 314, 315, 317, 319, 320, 321, 322, 323, 325, 329, 331, 332, 334, 335, 337, 341, 344, 346, 349, 353, 355, 357, 359, 361,363, 365, 367, 371, 373, 374, 375, 377, 379, 381, 383, 385, 386, 387, 389, 390, 393, 397, 398, 400, 403 407, 408, 409, 410, 411, 413, 414, 416, 417, 420, 421, 422, 423, 424, 427, 431, 433, 434, 437, 439, 448, 449, 453, 456, 460, 463, 465, 466, 471, 475, 478, 479, 485, 491, 493, 495, 498, 499, 501, 502, 507, 512, 513, 515, 517, 520, 521, 522, 525, 527, 528, 529, 530, 535, 539, 541, 542, 548, 550, 560, 567, 571, 573, 578, 579, 580, 585, 587, 588, 591

Were provided by Paul Lichter's Elvis Unique Record Club

www.elvisunique.com

A website fit for a king!

This edition first published in the United States in 2008 by
Overlook Duckworth, Peter Mayer Publishers, Inc.

NEW YORK:
141 Wooster Street
New York, NY 10012

WOODSTOCK:
One Overlook Drive
Woodstock, New York 12498
www.overlookpress.com
[for individual orders, bulk and special sales, contact our Woodstock office]

LONDON
90-93 Cowcross Street EC1M 6BF
inquiries@duckworth-publishers.co.uk
www.ducknet.co.uk

Cataloging-in-Publication Data is available from the Library of Congress

Book design and type formatting by Bernard Schleifer

Photos on the following pages were provided by Photofest: 3, 13, 19, 24, 46,
55, 57, 63, 69, 71, 72, 74, 75, 86, 92, 108, 109, 117, 121, 125, 162, 167, 180,
185, 192, 200, 202, 211, 213, 219, 220, 221, 229, 268, 270, 277, 288, 315,
316, 372, 418, 420, 429, 445, 455, 458, 459, 473, 483, 489, 511, 513, 533,
544, 545, 549, 551, 552, 555, 557, 559, 561, 563, 565, 566, 567, 569, 577,
582, 589, 595, 596

Manufactured in China
1 3 5 7 9 8 6 4 2

ISBN 978-1-58567-598-2 US
ISBN 978-0-7156-3816 -3 UK

To Thomas Giulio

ACKNOWLEDGMENTS

ACKNOWLEDGMENTS FOR THIS BOOK COULD START AND END WITH ELVIS: his music, movies and enduring presence have inspired this book. As a work of reference *The Elvis Encyclopedia* necessarily owes a great debt to Elvis's friends, family, entourage members, fellow music professionals, girlfriends, journalists, and the millions of millions of fans for whom his music has been the beating heart of their lives. It is these people I have to thank for the books and memoirs that they have written, the documentaries they have made, the interviews they have given and the reminiscences they have shared, and which have served as source material for this encyclopedia. You will find all of these names and sources within the main body of the encyclopedia.

My specific thanks for working on this book go first and foremost to my publishers, The Overlook Press, who graciously tolerated a one year delay in my delivery of this book. Peter Mayer, Tracy Carns, Alex Young and, most hands on, Aaron Schelchter, found minimal solace in this late-delivering author's assertion that all of the milestone books on Elvis have come out a year after the anniversary they were commissioned to celebrate: Peter Mayer, for commissioning me, Tracy Carns for holding the reins, Alex Young for his initial editorial input, Aaron Schelchter for scouring the country for photographs and taking delivery of a frighteningly huge number of words and making sure that they all ended up in the right place, and Bernie Schleifer for his impeccable design.

I must thank Conor Deane for assisting me in the task of amassing and checking the all-important discographic information on Elvis. Perhaps most of all, I thank my family for putting up with my pretty much absenting myself from life for more years than I care to admit as I approached, one day at a time, the Sisyphean task of piecing together this outsized book.

To name names, my wife Patrizia (I have assured her that with this, I retire from the Encyclopedia-writing business), my mother Michelene (who also helped me with copy editing), my father (and agent) Ed, without whom this book would never have existed, and the many, many people, friends and family, who have had to put up with my obsession, constant citing of offbeat Elvis facts, and ever-present soundtrack of Elvis songs these past years.

INTRODUCTION

"He was the firstest with the mostest."
—ROY ORBISON

As I finish my outsized contribution to the vast body of Elvis literature, I smile at the thought that the written word is the least appropriate way of enjoying, experiencing or learning about Elvis. Elvis is simple: listen to him—nobody is better at conveying emotion through song than Elvis—or watch him—see video of his commanding stage performances or follow his progress on celluloid to appreciate his looks and charisma.

So why this King-sized book? Because after half a century of writing on Elvis, people still want to know more. *The Elvis Encyclopedia* is an attempt to bring together the myriad and kaleidoscopic details of Elvis's life within a single publication. This book is intended to serve as a kind of Elvis Central, a one-stop-shop for information on Elvis's music, life, achievements, likes and loves; the people who mattered in his life and about whom he cared; his motivations during the different stages of his career; his influences and who he influenced; what he said and what was said about him; all the events of his life and unprecedented afterlife; the impressions of the hundreds of people who lived part of their lives in proximity to him, and the millions of fans around the globe whom he touched. To borrow from an album title, this is *Elvis for Everyone*: for dedicated fans and for people discovering the Elvis cosmos for the first time.

The focus of *The Elvis Encyclopedia* is inevitably the United States. In the interests of brevity—this book is already longer than the Old Testament—we have kept to a minimum record release, book and documentary information for non-English speaking countries. We have endeavored to use broad categories where possible, to ensure that as well as serving as a reference resource, the book is an entertaining read. To leaven what can be dry information, the book includes thousands of quotes from Elvis, Elvis fans and Elvis's friends, many of which refer back to books written by these people.

We have done our utmost to check all of the facts in this book against the most reliable available Elvis resources. It is our sincere hope that any inaccuracies in this book are minimal.

A note about footnotes: reluctantly, for space considerations, we have had to dispense with them—it was the only way to get the contents of this book between two covers.

We sincerely believe that *The Elvis Encyclopedia* is the best ever Elvis reference resource in book form. Where *The Elvis Encyclopedia* does not provide information, pointers are given for follow-up reading, listening and viewing.

ABOUT THE AUTHOR

Elvis authors fall into one of three categories: insiders, outsiders and fans. I began this project as an outsider; I finish very much a fan. *The Marilyn Encyclopedia* provided me with the template for writing about the only other 20th century icon whose fame has so comprehensively transcended their mortal existence. Five years of full immersion in Elvis's music—like the majority of Elvis fans, I believe that with Elvis, it's about the music—and his movies, literature and lore leave me with a profound respect for the man's achievements. Along the way, I have enjoyed the pleasure of a voice capable of infusing incredible passion and emotion into any song, and come to an understanding of the myriad reasons why so many millions of people continue to be touched by Elvis. Elvis sincerely believed that his mission in life was to make a difference through song. This he achieved beyond his wildest dreams.

ABERBACH, JEAN AND JULIAN

The Austrian-born brothers were the force behind a music publishing company, Hill & Range, that had a lasting impact on the entire music industry by establishing the practice of setting up ad hoc subsidiary companies for their musicians. Their approach was so successful that at one stage, they represented 3 out of every 4 songs made in Nashville.

Julian went into music publishing after becoming keen on country music when he served in the military in Georgia during the Second World War, not long after fleeing Europe. He founded Hill & Range in 1943 in Los Angeles. Jean was song publisher Hill & Range's representative to Elvis for 22 years, though cousin Freddy Bienstock served as point man.

A great collector of art, Julian bequeathed his French paintings to museums following his death in 2004, two years after his brother Jean.

JEAN ABERBACH: "Elvis was the finest human being I ever met."

ACADEMIC STUDIES

The Elvis phenomenon has been fertile ground for academic investigation since the late Fifties, when his effect on young women and on race relations first became topics for college dissertations.

Much of the serious academic literature on Elvis has grown out of music criticism. Greil Marcus can lay claim to being a founding father of the genre with his extended essay on Elvis' music and cultural significance in his 1975 publication *Mystery Train*. Music critics Stanley Booth and Lester Bangs and musicologists Henry Pleasants and Charles Wolfe have done much to advance understanding about what Elvis did, how he did it and how nothing was ever quite the same again.

Elvis first became part of school curricula in the book *Meet Elvis Presley*, by Favius Friedman, published in 1971.

Academia proper came late to the party, only really putting Elvis in the context of cultural studies after his death. University of Memphis Professor John Bakke organized an Elvis conference in 1979; that year Patsy Hammontree taught a course on Elvis as a cultural phenomenon at the University of Tennessee.

Also in 1979, the University of Mississippi journal *Southern Quarterly* published a major collection of essays on Elvis by scholars and fans, which later appeared in book form as *Elvis: Images and Fancies*.

Academic conferences on Elvis have become more widespread since the Nineties. The University of Mississippi held the First Annual International Conference on Elvis Presley in 1995, which spawned the book *In Search Of Elvis: Music, Race, Art, Religion*.

In the fullness of time, Elvis and Elvis phenomenon have become a touchstone for articles and books ranging from socio-economic to geographical to psychoanalytic to historic, taking in cultural studies, musicology, movie criticism and women's studies. High-flying academics and cultural pundits from Clarissa Pinkola Estes to Abbie Hoffman have taken a shot at fixing Elvis' place in the cultural firmament. Others have preferred to examine his status as icon, the "religion" that has built up around him, and the significance of Graceland to our understanding of Elvis and the Elvis legend. The mystery surrounding Elvis' death was tackled notably by Serge Denisoff and George Plasketes in *True Disbelievers: The Elvis Contagion* (Transaction Publishers, 1995)

Books:

Dead Elvis: A Chronicle of a Cultural Obsession, by Greil Marcus, Doubleday, 1991.

The Elvis Reader: Texts and Sources on the King of Rock 'n' Roll, edited by Kevin Quain, St Martin's Press, 1992.

In Search Of Elvis: Music, Race, Art, Religion, edited by Vernon Chadwick, Westview Press, 1997.

Elvis: A Sociological Portrait, by Dorothy Arnall Leasman, Simon & Schuster Custom Publishing, 1998.

Elvis Culture: Fans, Faith, and Image, by Erika Lee Doss, University Press of Kansas, 1999.

Fortunate Son: The Life of Elvis Presley, by Charles L. Ponce de Leon, Farrar, Straus and Giroux, 2006

Elvis Religion: Exploring the Cult of the King, by Gregory L. Reece, IB Tauris, 2006.

ACTING

If there is one thing that Elvis failed to achieve in his career, it was being taken seriously as a dramatic actor. He was mustard keen on learning the trade, a humble listener to old pros in his early films, but soon after his return to the limelight after his time in the Army, his dreams of becoming a respected actor were spiked by his own incredible popularity: the Colonel made him Hollywood's highest earning actor for his travelogue/bikini pictures, and on the few occasions that Elvis landed a more toothsome film vehicle (his two 1960 pictures for Twentieth Century-Fox, and the last two feature films he made), box office returns were comparatively disappointing.

When Elvis first started out in the movies, a number of industry people were struck by his acting potential. His screen test for Hal Wallis at Paramount promised great things. Wallis's partner Joe Hazen commented soon after: "As a straight actor, the guy has great potentialities."

Before ever reporting to a movie set, Elvis studied the actors he admired most, notably method performers Marlon Brando and James Dean. Elvis surprised writer/director Hal Kanter on his first movie project, *Loving You*, with his observation that he didn't want to smile a lot in the movie, as it was experience that actors who appealed most to female fans—without doubt his demographic—rarely if ever smiled: "If I don't smile," he concluded, "I'm gonna get 'em." He also believed that dark-haired actors generally had longer careers than blond lead men.

Acting in the movies was a dream come true for Elvis. He reported for his first projects knowing not just his own lines but those of the other characters. Even before he did his first screen test for Hal Wallis, he publicly declared that he'd like to go somewhere like the Actor's Studio. Though he later said that he had no prior acting experience, fellow-students at Elvis' Humes High English class recall that Elvis was often assigned the lead roles in the Shakespeare plays they studied.

By Elvis' own admission, landing a movie contract was the biggest thing that had happened to him. In interviews he gave before starting work on his first picture, he declared that he would be disappointed if he wound up singing in his movies. Elvis was disappointed so many times that he wound up not caring. One, two, four, a dozen songs were shoehorned into the pictures because cross-promotion between movies and songs was a founding principle of the Colonel's strategy for his client.

Elvis was candid about his performance in his first film: "Pretty bad . . . I mean that's something you learn through experience. I think that maybe I might accomplish something at it through the years." The experience of playing a character so far removed from his own life prompted Elvis to seek projects closer to his own world. This too eased his unwitting passage into typecast movie history, and a future of repeating more or less plasticized, pre-

packaged versions of himself for a decade.

Walter Matthau, who knew a thing or two about acting and worked with Elvis on *King Creole*, described him as "an instinctive actor," and then went on to explain, "he was intelligent enough to understand what a character was and how to play the character simply by being himself through the means of the story."

Elvis believed that great acting was a matter of being natural. Tom Diskin gave Elvis a Stanislavsky book in 1958 so that he could read the father of method acting's views on the topic. However, none of Elvis' management team ever took advantage of the many drama coaches out in Hollywood.

It was not that he lacked the raw talent. Director George Cukor, who sat in on a day's filming on an Elvis picture in the early Sixties, declared, "He can do anything. He would be a dream to direct. His comedy timing is faultless."

On resuming his career after his stint in the Army, Elvis told a press conference that progressing as an actor remained his number one ambition.

Don Siegel, who directed him in *Flaming Star*, was favorably impressed by Elvis' performance and wanted to give the movie the tagline "Elvis Acts!" By the end of that key year for his career, 1960, with three movies in the can, Elvis' take on acting had modified to a belief that he wasn't yet ready for a properly dramatic role.

Biographer Elaine Dundy suggests that Colonel Parker actively prevented Elvis from pursuing a "serious" acting career by such expedients as dissuading film studios from sending Elvis scripts in advance. That way he would just turn up, shoot the scene he needed to shoot and go home, without becoming overly interested in the mechanics. For much of the Sixties, the biggest challenge for Elvis on a film set was what new pranks to invent and implement.

In the mid-Sixties, one of Elvis' directors suggested that he go study at the Actors Studio.

In a 1967 interview, Elvis admitted he still had plenty to learn about acting: "There isn't a day that goes by that I don't pick up on something from the other actors." He told cousin Billy Smith that he particularly admired the way that Valentino projected so much using just his eyes.

Paradoxically, Elvis finally got more of a chance to act at the very end of his film career, once it became clear that soundtrack sales were no longer the money-spinner that they had once been. *Charro!* (1969) was Elvis' first non-musical in almost a decade, and a movie he said he really enjoyed making. His final feature film, *Change of Habit*, saw an accomplished performance from a man who, by that time, was a veteran actor. Author Eric Braun describes this as "arguably the most sensitive performance of his career."

In the early Sixties, Elvis made more money acting than anybody else in Hollywood, thanks to the wily dealing of Colonel Parker, who ensured that in addition to his fees he commanded 50% of profits.

ELVIS SAID IN 1956: "All of my life, I've wanted to be an actor, though I never was in any school plays or recited a line other than the Gettysburg Address for my sixth-grade homeroom class."

ELVIS SAID IN 1957: "I was tryin' to act and when you start tryin' to act, you're dead."

ELVIS SAID IN 1972: "I had thought they would . . . give me a chance to show some kind of acting ability or do a very interesting story . . . They couldn't have paid me no amount of money in the world to make me feel some sort of self-satisfaction inside."

LA TIMES, 1956: "Elvis can act. So help me the boy's real good, even when he isn't singing."

RICHARD EGAN: "They seemed to put him in front of a backdrop and have him sing a song. He could do that easily but he had much more depth. He showed extraordinary ability to catch on."

HAL KANTER: "I think that given time and given better scripts and more retention and less reliance on money and on lyrics and on singing, he could have been a superb motion picture actor."

ANGELA LANSBURY: "Elvis was essentially a one-take actor. He liked to get his scenes in one take. It wasn't the kind of material that allowed him to show signs of unusual talent."

JUNE JUANICO: "They just would not take Elvis seriously as an actor, and that's a damn shame. That was his desire."

PHILLIP DUNNE: "He took to his part as if he'd been a dramatic actor all his life."

GENE NELSON: "Even with the kind of trivial dialogue we had, there were moments where he incorporated a great deal of thoughtfulness into his delivery."

BURGESS MEREDITH: "He has the natural talent that too few 'personalities' have. He is in essence, a totally natural actor."

DON SIEGEL: "Elvis could have become an acting, as well as a singing, star . . . he would have been much happier. You could see that he had a lot of layers, a lot of potential."

RED WEST: "He proved to me beyond any doubt that he had that certain presence that could bring out emotions in the audience."

MARLYN MASON: "He always knew his dialogue. He was never unprepared. He was as professional as anyone I'd ever worked with."

BILLY SMITH: "Heck, he was a good actor. He acted every day."

Michael St. Gerard in two outings as Elvis.

ACTORS WHO HAVE PORTRAYED ELVIS OR ELVIS-BASED CHARACTERS

Elvis has come in for the biopic treatment a fair few times, to varying degrees of critical acclaim and fan approval.

Aside from versions of his own rags-to-riches story which he played in several of his early movies, Elvis' meteoric rise and status as the undisputed king of rock 'n' roll was prime story material for Fifties movies starting with Tommy Sands—a singer managed by Colonel Parker when he took Elvis on—who took on the role of singer Virgil Walker in 1958 movie *Sing, Boy, Sing*, which was very much modeled on the Elvis story.

A year earlier, Rom Bigson played a character called Elvin Pelvin in an episode of Sgt. Bilko.

Jesse Pearson played the Elvis role in 1963 movie *Bye, Bye Birdie*. Ann-Margret did this picture immediately before hooking up with Elvis in *Viva Las Vegas* (1964).

Kurt Russell played Elvis in John Carpenter's 1979 TV movie *Elvis*, the first and in many people's opinion the most convincing portrayal of the King by an actor in a biopic, beating many hundreds of competitors at audition, and trumping the Colonel's preference, Sylvester Stallone. Randy Gray played little Elvis, Ronnie McDowell sang the songs, and Russell received an Emmy nomination. *Elvis* came out on DVD in 2007.

This Is Elvis (1981) featured the man himself and dramatizations from Johnny Harra, David Scott, Dana MacKay and Paul Boensh III. Ral Donner voiced the Elvis dialogue.

Don Johnson played Elvis in *Elvis and the Beauty Queen*, the 1981 TV movie about Elvis' relationship with girlfriend Linda Thompson.

Dale Midkiff was Elvis in *Elvis and Me* (1988). David Keith played a kidnapped Elvis in *Heartbreak Hotel* the same year.

Peter Wilcox has played Elvis in many US TV serials over the years, including "Valerie," "ALF" and more recently, "The Next Best Thing"; he has also sung Elvis songs as an impersonator.

Michael St. Gerard had an Elvis franchise in the late Eighties and early Nineties, playing the King in Jerry Lee Lewis biopic *Great Balls of Fire!* and *Heart of Dixie* (both 1989), 1990 mini-series *Elvis*, produced by Priscilla (once again with Ronnie McDowell providing the Elvis singing voice; young Elvis was played by Lucas Cain, teen Elvis by David Dunavent), and again in a 1993 episode of "Quantum Leap."

Rob Youngblood played Elvis in 1993 made-for-TV movie *Elvis and the Colonel: The Untold Story.*

Kurt Russell voiced Elvis in *Forrest Gump* (1994), though actor Peter Dobson and a guy called Elvis both played Elvis in that picture; Dobson returned to the role for 2007 movie *The Head Hunter.*

Val Kilmer was Elvis in Quentin Tarantino's *True Romance* (1993).

Rick Peters played Elvis in *Elvis Meets Nixon* (1997).

Harvey Keitel may or may not have been Elvis in 1998 movie *Finding Graceland.*

Ed Shifres played Elvis in 1999 movie *The King and Me.*

Bruce Campbell was Elvis in *Bubba Ho-Tep* (2002).

Tyler Hilton played Elvis in the 2005 Johnny Cash biopic *Walk the Line*, after auditioning for a role as a musician in Johnny Cash's band. Afterwards he said, "It felt real special being Elvis."

Irish actor Jonathan Rhys-Meyers won a Golden Globe in 2006 for Best Performance By an Actor in a Mini-Series or TV Movie for his interpretation of Elvis Presley in *Elvis* (2005).

Jason Alan Smith played Elvis in *Crazy* (2006), a biopic about guitarist Hank Garland.

Jack White of The White Stripes had signed to played Elvis in comedy *Walk Hard* (2007).

ACUFF, ROY
(1903-1992)

Early in his career Elvis said that Acuff was one of the singers he admired. Acuff returned the compliment by taking in one of Elvis' shows during his first engagement in Las Vegas in 1956. They shared a bill on a tour in late 1955.

Acuff started out singing hillbilly music and playing the fiddle with the Tennessee Crackerjacks in the early Thirties. With the Smoky Mountain Boys he was a regular at the Grand Ole Opry from 1938, while pursuing a successful movie career and founding Acuff-Rose Music Publishing, a firm that has been a powerhouse in country music ever since.

Acuff was the first ever inductee to the Country Music Hall of Fame in 1962.

The final song Elvis sang alive, "Blue Eyes Crying in the Rain," was an Acuff composition.

"ADAM AND EVIL"

Fred Wise and Randy Starr wrote this cautionary tale for Elvis to lay down at Radio Recorders on February 17, 1966 for the *Spinout* soundtrack. It has since appeared on the *Double Features* issue for the movie.

Alternates are on FTD releases *Out in Hollywood* and *Spinout*. Bootleg *Spin-in . . . Spinout* contains a dozen extra takes.

ADAMS, NICK
(B. NICHOLAS ALOYSIUS ADAMSCHOCK, 1931-1968)

Nick Adams turned down a potential minor league baseball career to pursue his acting dreams. He got his big break as a supporting actor opposite James Dean in *Rebel Without a Cause* (1955).

Elvis met Adams when he reported for work on his first movie *Love Me Tender*, in August 1956. Until his untimely death in September 1955, Adams had been a close friend of James Dean. He was also good friends with Natalie Wood, who Elvis dated that year. Adams and Elvis hit it off immediately. When Elvis flew back to Memphis after completing principle shooting on *Love Me Tender*, he took Adams along for the ride. Adams' talent for impersonating people made him fun to be around for Elvis. The story goes that this talent got him his break in the movies: his James Cagney impression persuaded director John Ford to cast him in *Mister Roberts* (1955).

For a while, Adams accompanied Elvis on tour and hung out with him in Memphis. Elvis introduced the actor to the crowd during one of his homecoming concerts in Tupelo in September 1956.

At one stage in the late Fifties, Adams was reported to be working on an Elvis biography with Colonel Parker.

Adams rushed to Memphis in the summer of 1958 to be with Elvis after his Ma Gladys died. Earlier that year he took a role in *Sing, Boy, Sing*, a 1958 movie loosely based on Elvis' life, playing . . . a sidekick to the singer. Colonel Parker, who was involved behind the scenes on this picture, continued to keep an eye on Adams' career through the Sixties.

Like Elvis, Adams studied the martial arts with Ed Parker.

Greil Marcus describes Adams as a "Hollywood Hustler" in his book *Last Train to Memphis*, while Elaine Dundy says that Colonel Parker actively encouraged Adams to become a member of Elvis' paid entourage so that the Colonel could use him as his eyes and ears.

Adams was nominated for a Best Supporting Actor Oscar in 1963 for *Twilight of Honor*; he also starred in (and created) 1959 TV series "The Rebel."

Elvis saw Adams in 1964, at a birthday party for the Colonel held on the MGM lot.

Adams took his own life with an overdose in 1968, the very same week that Lisa Marie was born.

NICK ADAMS: "He's the nicest person I've ever met in showbusiness. He's humble, he's a genuine friend."

ADVERTISEMENTS

Ask the Colonel and he would happily have told you (for a price): Elvis sells. With very few exceptions, the Colonel leveraged Elvis' selling power to sell Elvis and little else. For almost the entire Sixties, the Colonel succeeded in using movie soundtrack single releases to promote movies and then the associated soundtrack album.

B.C (before Colonel), a couple of weeks before releasing his second single "Good Rockin' Tonight," Elvis played to mark the opening of the Katz Drugstore on Lamar and Airways in Memphis.

The only commercial Elvis knowingly did was a radio jingle for Southern Made doughnuts, which went out in November 1954, with the lyrics "You can get 'em piping hot after four p.m.; you can get 'em piping hot. Southern Made Doughnuts hit the spot; you can get 'em piping hot after four p.m." The staff at the Louisiana Hayride would eat the doughnuts on stage, sending the audience out to the local concessionaire; on stage at the Hayride, Elvis performed beneath an advert for Lucky Strike cigarettes with the slogan "Be Happy, Go Lucky."

Elvis was already well-established on the tour circuit, having played to audiences several thousand strong, when in June 1955 he played a show at a Pontiac Showroom in Lubbock, Texas.

In 1956 Elvis recorded some short spots backed by his own songs for radio commercials cross-selling RCA Victrola record players, finished in blue denim and known as Elvis Presley Autograph models. Customers who shelled out the $45 for the de luxe model got all of Elvis' RCA-released songs into the bargain.

Elvis appeared in a 1957 TV commercial for the March of Dimes.

In 1958 Elvis parlayed a three-bedroom Stylemaster Mobile Home to live in offbase with his family while he was stationed at Fort Hood during his army service, in exchange for publicity shots of the Presleys in the unit. Meanwhile, Colonel Parker tried and failed to land Elvis a $100,000 product endorsement through William Morris—the figure frightened off Revlon, who had initially expressed an interest in Elvis fronting their Top Brass hair product.

Elvis appeared to endorse Coppertone tanning lotion in the *Ladies' Home Journal* in 1962, until the Colonel put a stop to the unauthorized campaign.

The Singer sewing machine company brought out a special Elvis album in 1968, timed to coincide with the NBC TV "Comeback" Special, sold only in its stores, and subsequently re-released by RCA as *Elvis Sings Flaming Star*.

In 1977, mere months before his death, Elvis reputedly agreed to put his name to a new line of hair care products his pal and hairdresser Larry Geller was launching.

In the third millennium, Elvis has been much more active in product promotion. Nike used the remix of Elvis' "A Little Less Conversation" for a TV commercial in 2002. The same track also appeared in a Coca Cola ad.

In 2004 Elvis fronted a commercial for Kingsmill bread.

His likeness has also been used for Energizer batteries, an NBA campaign and Pizza Hut.

EPE has been authorizing use of Elvis' likeness and songs more frequently since it was taken over by CKX.

In 2006, digital magic paired Elvis and Dolly Parton in an advert for Tennessee tourism. Also in 2006 Honda advertised a new version of its CR-V vehicle with a remix of "Burning Love."

Elvis song "Viva Las Vegas" was used in a 2007 Viagra commercial, without the blessing of EPE.

"AFTER LOVING YOU"

An Eddy Arnold tune that had also been a hit for Della Reese, Elvis recorded this song at American Studio on February 18, 1969. Joe Henderson recorded the song in 1962, which had originally been written by Eddie Miller and Johnny Lantz.

As well as Elvis' country rock recording from American, first released on *From Elvis in Memphis* in 1969, a home recording from 1966 appeared on 1997 album *Platinum: A Life In Music* and 1999 release *The Home Recordings*.

Elvis' American studio recording has since appeared on *From Nashville To Memphis*, *Artist Of The Century* and *The Country Side of Elvis*.

Felton Jarvis remixed the track for release on the *Guitar Man* album in 1980; this version was subsequently included on FTD issue *Too Much Monkey Business*.

Alternate takes from the original recording session are on *Suspicious Minds: The Memphis 1969 Anthology* and FTD release *The Memphis Sessions*.

AFTERLIFE

Brought up in the church, from his earliest years Elvis believed in an afterlife. After his mother's death, he took some little solace that they would meet up again in the beyond.

He could never have suspected that he would have such a spectacular and enduring afterlife here on earth.

Elvis' death merely planted a seed that has grown into a many-limbed tree of speculations that he is still alive, nostalgia, a geometric progression in the number of Elvis impersonators around the globe, and in time a navigable current of sociology—this would have amused Elvis—in which academic writers investigate the phenomenon of a dead man who earns close to $50 million a year.

PETER GURALNICK: "The cacophony of voices that have joined together to create a chorus of informed opinion, uninformed speculation, hagiography, symbolism, and blame, can be difficult at times to drown out, but in the end there is only one voice that counts. It is the voice that the world first heard on those bright yellow Sun 78s, whose original insignia, a crowing rooster surrounded by boldly stylized sunbeams and a border of musical notes, sought to proclaim the dawning of a new day."

Books:
Elvis After Elvis, by Gilbert B. Rodman, Routledge, 1996.

AFTERNOON IN THE GARDEN, AN

A 1997 BMG release of one of Elvis' Madison Square Garden shows from June 1972.

TRACK LISTING:
1. Also Sprach Zarathustra
2. That's All Right
3. Proud Mary
4. Never Been To Spain
5. You Don't Have To Say You Love Me
6. Until It's Time For You To Go
7. You've Lost That Lovin' Feelin'
8. Polk Salad Annie
9. Love Me
10. All Shook Up
11. Heartbreak Hotel
12. (Let Me Be Your) Teddy Bear / Don't Be Cruel
13. Love Me Tender
14. Blue Suede Shoes
15. Reconsider Baby
16. Hound Dog
17. I'll Remember You
18. Suspicious Minds
19. Introductions By Elvis
20. For The Good Times
21. American Trilogy
22. Funny How Time Slips Away
23. I Can't Stop Loving You
24. Can't Help Falling In Love

AGING

Elvis may have been the hottest thing to hit the music business in 1956; by 1960, there were plenty of people who were ready to write him off.

When Elvis returned to America after serving in the Army, a journalist asked him if, at 25, he was now too old for his teenaged fans. Elvis brushed the question off with a laugh: "I don't feel too old. I can still move around pretty good."

As he approached his thirtieth birthday, Elvis became more interested in spirituality, seeking out meaning and answers to metaphysical questions. He had no public engagements for almost two months after his thirtieth birthday, and the first time he returned to the recording studio, he was decidedly unenthusiastic.

As a thirty-year-old, Elvis was acutely aware of

the fate that had befallen other famous singers, who in later years carried on performing in lesser venues, a mere caricature of their former selves.

In his thirties, Elvis reputedly referred to his youthful exploits and bad boy behavior as his "spastic days." He also told people that he didn't expect to live much beyond forty.

If thirty was bad, forty was way worse. Elvis confided in Priscilla that he feared being a 40-year-old man "still shaking to Hound Dog." When the fateful day came, *National Enquirer* showed no mercy, running the headline "Elvis at 40: Paunchy, Depressed and Living in Fear."

ELVIS SAID IN 1966 "Everything's so dreamy when you are young. After you grow up it kind of becomes—just real."

ELVIS SAID IN 1976: "When I was twenty-one years old . . . my mind was just scattered to the four winds."

ELVIS SAID: "Every time I think that I'm getting old, and gradually going to the grave, something else happens."

T. G. SHEPPARD: "As Elvis got older, he was seeking and searching, and, therefore, in a strange way he became more religious as time went on."

STEVE DUNLEAVY: "He is one of the few Peter Pans who has managed not only to survive but to thrive."

JOE ESPOSITO: "Turning forty was a very hard time for him."

RAQUEL WELCH: "He was in a state of arrested development and never got to graduate. Colonel Parker always referred to him as 'The Boy' and kept him on a leash. They never allowed him to grow."

JUDY SPRECKELS: "I think he got as old as he wanted to get."

AGNEW, SPIRO T.
(B. SPIROS ANAGNOSTOPOULOS, 1918-1996)

Elvis met Vice President Spiro Agnew in Palm Springs in late 1970, and offered him a gift of a gold-inlaid .357 Magnum revolver. Though he refused the gift for legal reasons, when Elvis wrote to President Nixon later that year asking for a meeting, Agnew may have provided him with bona fides. Agnew was forced to resign in 1973 after an inquiry into tax irregularities from when he was a state governor.

"AIN'T THAT LOVING YOU BABY"

Though this rock'n'roller was recorded on June 10, 1958, it didn't see the light of day until 1964 owing to quality problems with the master. It finally earned release as the B-side to "Ask Me." The B-side reached #16 in the charts, running the A-side close. The song was first sung by Eddie Riff, and was written by Clyde Otis and Ivory Joe Hunter. Since its album debut on *Elvis' Golden Records Vol. 4*, the song has appeared on *Worldwide 50 Gold Award Hits Vol. 1*, *Essential Elvis Vol. 3*, *The King of Rock 'n' Roll* anthology and *Hitstory*.

Alternate studio versions have come out on *Reconsider Baby*, *Essential Elvis Vol. 3*, and *The King of Rock 'n' Roll*. All eleven takes from the original recording session are on FTD release *50,000,000 Million Elvis Fans Can't Be Wrong*; FTD release *Flashback* also features an alternate.

TOP: Elvis aboard an airplane (1968).

CENTER: Lisa Marie Presley's airplane bathroom.

BOTTOM: An inside view of Lisa Marie Presley's plane.

AIRPLANES

Elvis' first flight was on March 23, 1955, to an audition for the "Arthur Godfrey Talent Scouts" in New York, accompanied by band members Scotty Moore and Bill Black, and manager Bob Neal.

In his early career, Elvis spent plenty of time crisscrossing the South in small planes. One chartered flight, taking Elvis and his band to Nashville for a recording session from Amarillo in April 1956, included the pilot losing his way, refueling, and an engine cutting out. If the pilot hadn't succeeded in making an emergency landing (Elvis was instructed to remove sharp objects and get into the brace position), Elvis would have been remembered like Buddy Holly, the Big Bopper and other victims of mid-century air travel.

Back on *terra firma*, Elvis told the press "Man, I don't know if I'll ever fly again." Gladys wasn't too keen on his flying either. Rumors did the rounds that he had died in a plane crash around this time.

Before his Army service, Elvis only flew twice more, one of those times to get back to Memphis

in time to see his mother who was dying in hospital. He was taken up for a helicopter ride soon after by police buddies who wanted to cheer him up.

In March 1961, Elvis was taken for a ride over Graceland in a Piper Comanche, and for a spell took over piloting duties, but as a rule he traveled between Memphis and LA in a motor home or on his own greyhound bus. That changed when Elvis' procrastination at leaving Memphis for Hollywood made the gang so late that the only way to get to the studio on time was to fly—much to the surprise of a planeload of people, Elvis flew in standard class on a commercial flight. This was also a bumpy ride, but the next time he was late and had to take a small chartered plane from Memphis to Nashville, things went much more smoothly until the pilot put the plane through some acrobatic maneuvers, which Elvis loved so much he lost his fear of flying.

For years, the Colonel chartered aircraft to shuttle Elvis around between commitments. To begin with, Elvis borrowed the Holiday Inn corporate jet; later, he sometimes used the Playboy plane "Big Bunny."

On tour in the Seventies, Elvis would fly in to a town on one chartered plane as the Colonel took off for the next venue on other, to check that everything was ship shape for his boy. According to Marty Lacker, in 1971 Elvis spent close to half a million dollars on leasing a 12-seater jet and a pilot (who on one occasion hit the runway so hard that the plane bounced back into the air).

Elvis acquired his first jet in January 1975 when he bought a Boeing 707 that had been repossessed from financier Robert Vesco, who had fled the country to Costa Rica to avoid charges of embezzlement, illegal funding of Richard Nixon and cocaine smuggling. Elvis was less interested in the plane's previous uses than in keeping up with local musicians Charlie Rich and Jerry Lee Lewis, who had recently bought themselves private planes—though Elvis pulled out of the deal after only paying a down payment, after he was warned that the plane risked being seized if it touched down outside the US.

Elvis being Elvis, one wasn't enough. By April he had purchased a retired Delta plane, a 100-seat Convair 880 that he purchased sight unseen after sending Joe Esposito and Marty Lacker out to an aircraft park near Tucson. After Elvis had it totally refurbished, it cost him the best part of a million dollars—or as much as two million, depending on who's telling the story. Delta had mothballed the plane because it was particularly thirsty on fuel. Elvis couldn't wait for the plane to be ready, and went at least a dozen times to check on the refurbishment at an airport near Dallas. On one of these occasions he gave his ex-wife Priscilla a personal tour, and told her that she could use it whenever she wanted.

When it took to the air with its queen-sized bed, video system, de rigueur rock star gold-plated bathroom and TCB logo on its tail, the plane was renamed the *Lisa Marie*. Elvis took delivery of the aircraft in November 1975, the third in his fleet. George Klein remembers joking one day as they taxied to the runway at Memphis International, "Ladies and gentlemen, welcome to Presley Airlines . . ."

In July that year, Elvis bought a Grumman Gulfstream G-1 as a gift for the Colonel. The Colonel turned it down as an excessive extravagance he neither needed nor could afford.

That August Elvis put down a deposit on a Fairchild F-27, which was going to cost him $13,000 per month, but then changed his mind and bought an Aero Jet Commander outright for half a million dollars.

Before the month was out, Elvis arranged for the plane he had bought for the Colonel and the Jet Commander that he had only just bought to be sold, before acquiring a 15-year-old Lockheed JetStar for close to $1 million. At one point, Elvis actually owned five planes, and had four pilots on a retainer so that there was always someone to take

him up whatever time of day or night. One of the pilots was the wonderfully-named Milo High.

Before 1975 was out, Elvis had also acquired a 1966 Dassault Falcon jet, more as an investment than anything else, which he sold in July 1976. He bought another Lockheed JetStar to add to the fleet. Meanwhile, the FBI had begun investigating suspicious financial transactions involving the original JetStar leasing and refurbishment deal, in which an attempt was made to swindle Elvis and his father Vernon.

Elvis' two remaining planes, the *Lisa Marie* (call sign Hound Dog One) and *Hound Dog II*, are now parked opposite Graceland and are a favorite tourist side-trip for visitors.

ALABAMA

- Birmingham
Elvis' sole show here was at the Birmingham-Jefferson County Coliseum on December 29, 1976.

- Huntsville
Elvis began a 12-day tour with 5 shows in three days at the Von Braun Civic Center between May 30 and June 1, 1975 (featured prominently on FTD's 2006 album *Southern Nights*). He played here again on September 6, 1976.

- Jackson
Elvis performed at the National Guard Armory on October 27, 1955.

- Mobile
Elvis played the Ladd Stadium on tour with Hank Snow on May 4 and 5, 1955; on the second night Elvis had to outrun a gang of girls who chased him across the football field. He was on safer ground at Curtis Gordon's Radio Ranch, which he played on a bill with the house band for the last two nights of June, 1955. His October 27, 1955 morning show at the Vigor High School was suspended after half an hour by the school principal, after Elvis told a lewd joke. He played another gig at Curtis Gordon's Ranch Club on October 28, 1955.

Fifteen years passed before he next performed in Mobile, at the Municipal Auditorium on September 14, 1970. Elvis played the Mobile Municipal Auditorium at the start of a swing through the South and Mid-West, on June 20, 1973. He performed two shows at the Municipal Auditorium on June 2, 1975. He was at the Municipal Auditorium on August 29, 1976. Elvis' last performance in town was at the Municipal Auditorium on June 2, 1977.

- Montgomery
After a Talent Contest Final at the State Coliseum, Elvis earned $400 for a performance in a show with Roy Acuff, Kitty Wells and other artists on December 3, 1955.

There was considerably more money on the table when he returned for a show at the Garrett Coliseum on March 6, 1974, when Governor George Wallace was in the audience. Elvis next played the Garrett Coliseum on February 16, 1977.

- Pine Bluff
Elvis played the Convention Center for the last two dates of his September 1976 tour, on 7 and 8 of the month.

- Prichard
Elvis played two shows at the Greater Gulf States Fair on October 26, 1955.

- Sheffield
Elvis' show at the Community Center on January 19, 1955, was one of the most popular performances at the venue, according to the local

paper. He came back for more on August 2, 1955, in a show that included new Sun Records hopeful Johnny Cash, and returned once again for two shows on November 15, 1955.

- Tuscaloosa
The University of Alabama Field House hosted Elvis and the TCB band on November 14, 1971. He played the University of Alabama Memorial Coliseum on June 3, 1975 and August 30, 1976.

Elvis was made an honorary colonel of the state by Governor George Corley Wallace, who in 1974 declared a full "Elvis Presley Week."

ALBUMS

No exact figures exist on how many Elvis albums have been released. He brought out around 70 official albums during his lifetime, but taking other issues including budget releases, compilations and tie-ins the figure swells to anywhere between 150 and 400. What follows is a listing of all of Elvis' official RCA albums during his lifetime (with catalogue numbers) and significant post-1977 releases.

STUDIO:

LPM 1254	Elvis Presley (1956)
LPM 1382	Elvis (1956)
LOC 1035	Christmas Album (1957)
LPM 1990	For LP Fans Only (1959)
LPM 2011	A Date With Elvis (1959)
LSP/LPM 2231	Elvis Is Back! (1960)
LSP/LPM 2328	His Hand in Mine (1960)
LSP/LPM 2370	Something for Everybody (1961)
LSP/LPM 2523	Pot Luck with Elvis (1962)
LSP/LPM 3450	Elvis For Everyone (1965)
LSP/LPM 3758	How Great Thou Art (1967)
PRS 279	Singer Presents Elvis Singing Flaming Star and Others (1968)
LSP 4155	From Elvis in Memphis (1969)
LSP 6020	From Memphis To Vegas/From Vegas To Memphis (1969—2 album set reissued in 1970 as live album Elvis In Person At The International Hotel and studio album Back In Memphis
LSP 4429	Back in Memphis (1970)
LSP 4460	Elvis Country (I'm 10,000 Years Old) (1971)
LSP 4530	Love Letters from Elvis (1971)
LSP 4579	Elvis Sings "The Wonderful World of Christmas" (1971)
LSP 4671	Elvis Now (1972)
LSP 4690	He Touched Me (1972)
APL1 0283	Elvis [The Fool Album] (1973)
APL1 0388	Raised on Rock/For Ol' Times Sake (1973)
CPL1 0475	Good Times (1974)
APL1 0873	Promised Land (1975)
APL1 1039	Today (1975)
APL1 1506	From Elvis Presley Boulevard, Memphis, Tennessee (1976)
AFL1 2428	Moody Blue (1977)

MOTION PICTURE SOUNDTRACKS
(See also EPs)

LPM 1515	Loving You (1957)
LPM 1884	King Creole (1958)
LSP/LPM 2256	G.I. Blues (1960)
LSP/LPM 2426	Blue Hawaii (1961)
LSP/LPM 2621	Girls! Girls! Girls! (1962)
LSP/LPM 2697	It Happened at the World's Fair (1963)
LSP/LPM 2756	Fun in Acapulco (1963)
LSP/LPM 2894	Kissin' Cousins (1964)
LSP/LPM 2999	Roustabout (1964)
LSP/LPM 3338	Girl Happy (1965)
LSP/LPM 3468	Harum Scarum (1965)
LSP/LPM 3553	Frankie and Johnny (1966)

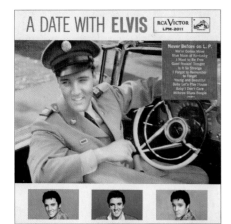

The album *A Date with Elvis*, released in 1959 during Elvis' service in the Army.

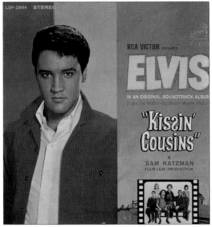

The cover of the soundtrack album for *Kissin' Cousins*. It was released shortly after the film debuted in 1964.

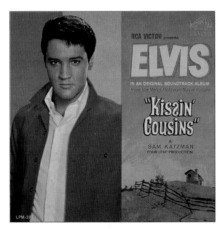

Rare U.S. LP. of *"Kissin' Cousins"* with the movie frame missing.

LSP/LPM 3643   Paradise, Hawaiian Style (1966)
LSP/LPM 3702   Spinout (1966)
LSP/LPM 3787   Double Trouble (1967)
LSP/LPM 3893   Clambake (1967)
LSP/LPM 3989   Speedway (1968)

From 1993 all of Elvis' soundtrack material was re-issued on the *Double Feature* series of CDs, initially in a 4 CD box set. See below under 'posthumous' for details.

LIVE ALBUMS
LPM 4088   NBC TV Special (1968)
LSP 4362   On Stage: February 1970 (1970)
LSP 4428   Elvis In Person At The
            International Hotel, Las Vegas,
            Nevada (1970)
LSP 4445   That's The Way It Is (1970)
LSP 4776   Elvis As Recorded At Madison
            Square Garden (1972)

VPSX 6089   Aloha From Hawaii Via Satellite
            (1973)
CPL1 0606   Elvis Recorded Live On Stage In
            Memphis (1974)
APL2 2587   Elvis In Concert (1977)

COMPILATIONS:
LPM 1707   Elvis' Golden Records (1958)
LPM 2075   Elvis' Gold Records Vol. 2 (1959)
LSP/LPM 2765   Elvis' Golden Records Vol. 3
               (1963)
LSP/LPM 2075   Elvis' Gold Records Vol. 4 (1968)
LPM 6401   Worldwide 50 Gold Award Hits
               (1970)
LPM 6402   Worldwide 50 Gold Award Hits
               Vol. 2—The Other Sides (1971)
CPL1 0341   Elvis: A Legendary Performer Vol.
               1 (1974)
CPL1 1349   Elvis: A Legendary Performer Vol.
               2 (1976)
APM1 1675   The Sun Sessions (1976)
APL1 2274   Welcome to My World (1977)

BUDGET RELEASES (ON RCA AND CAMDEN RECORDS):
CAS 2304   *Elvis Sings Flaming Star* (1969
            identical to *Singer Presents Elvis
            Singing Flaming Star and Others*
            from 1968)
CAS 2408   Let's Be Friends (1970)
CAS 2440   Almost in Love (1970)
CAL 2424   Elvis' Christmas Album (1970)
CAL 2472   You'll Never Walk Alone (1971)
CAL 2518   C'mon Everybody (1971)
CAL 2533   I Got Lucky (1971)
CAS 2567   Elvis Sings Hit Songs From His
            Movies Vol. 1 (1972)
CAS 2595   Burning Love And Hits From His
            Movies (1972)
CAS 2611   Separate Ways (1972)
CPM1 0818   Having Fun With Elvis On Stage
            (1974)
ANL1 0971   Pure Gold (1975)

Posthumous releases:
The following list is limited to albums and box sets with new or previously unreleased material and landmark issues. Consult one of the excellent Elvis discographies in book form or online for more detail and for information on the many other releases, greatest hits albums, special partner issues and non-US albums.

He Walks Beside Me (1978)
Elvis Sings for Children and Grown-Ups Too (1978)
Mahalo From Elvis (1978)
Elvis: A Legendary Performer Vol. 3 (1979)
Our Memories Of Elvis (1979)
Elvis Aron Presley (1980)
Guitar Man (1980)
This Is Elvis (1981)
Greatest Hits Vol. 1 (1981)
Memories Of Christmas (1982)
Elvis: A Legendary Performer Vol. 4 (1983)

An extremely rare Elvis Japanese EP.

Elvis: The First Live Recordings (1984)
Elvis: The Hillbilly Cat (1984)
A Golden Celebration (1984)
Elvis' Golden Records Vol. 5 (1984)
Rocker (1984)
Valentine Gift For You (1985)
Reconsider Baby (1985)
Always On My Mind (1985)
Return Of The Rocker (1986)
The Memphis Record (1987)
The Number One Hits (1987)
The Top Ten Hits (1987)
The Complete Sun Sessions (1987)
Essential Elvis - The First Movies (1988)
The Alternate Aloha (1988)
Elvis In Nashville (1988)
Essential Elvis—Stereo '57 (1989)
The Million Dollar Quartet (1990)
The Great Performances (1990)
Double Dynamite (1990)
Essential Elvis—Hits Like Never Before (1991)
Elvis Sings Leiber And Stoller (1991)
Elvis NBC TV Special (1991)
For The Asking (The Lost Album) (1991)
Collectors Gold (1991)
The King Of Rock 'n' Roll: The Complete 50s
   Masters (1992)
Double Features: Harum Scarum / Girl Happy (1993)
Double Features: Viva Las Vegas / Roustabout (1993)
Double Features: Kid Galahad / Girls! Girls! Girls!
   (1993)
Double Features: It Happened At The World Fair /
   Fun In Acapulco (1993)—all four also released as
   a box set
From Nashville To Memphis: The Essential 60s
   Masters (1993)
Double Features: Frankie And Johnny / Paradise,
   Hawaiian Style (1994)
Double Features: Spinout / Double Trouble (1994)
Double Features: Kissin' Cousins / Stay Away, Joe
   (1994)
Amazing Grace (1994)
If Every Day Was Like Christmas (1994)
Double Features: Flaming Star / Wild In The
   Country / Follow That Dream (1995)
Double Features: Easy Come, Easy Go / Speedway
   (1995)
Double Features: Live A Little, Love A Little /
   Charro / The Trouble With Girls / Change Of
   Habit (1995)
Walk A Mile In My Shoes: The Essential 70s
   Masters (1995)
Command Performances: The Essential 60's Masters
   II (1995)
Elvis '56 (1996)
Essential Elvis—A Hundred Years From Now (1996)
Great Country Songs (1996)
An Afternoon In The Garden (1997)
Loving You (1997)
Jailhouse Rock (1997)
King Creole (1997)
Blue Hawaii (1997)
G.I. Blues (1997)
Platinum: A Life In Music (1997)

A Spanish-release EP.

Memories: The '68 Comeback Special (1998)
Tiger Man (1998)
Essential Elvis—Rhythm and Country (1998)
Suspicious Minds: The Memphis 1969 Anthology (1999)
Tomorrow Is A Long Time (1999)
The Home Recordings (1999)
Sunrise (1999)
Artist Of The Century (1999)
Burning Love (1999)
Essential Elvis — Such a Night (2000)
That's The Way It Is (2000)
Peace in the Valley (2000)
Live In Las Vegas (2001)
Greatest Hits Live (2001)
Blue Suede Shoes Collection (2001)
The Country Side of Elvis (2001)
ELV1S - 30 #1 Hits (2002)
Today, Tomorrow and Forever (2002)
Elvis: Close Up (2003)
Elvis 2nd To None (2003)
Christmas Peace (2003)
Elvis '56 (2003)
Elvis at Sun (2004)
Love, Elvis (2005)
History (2005)
The Complete Million Dollar Quartet (2006)
Elvis Christmas (2006)

In 2006 BMG released six themed greatest hits albums: *Elvis Rock, Elvis Inspirational, Elvis Country, Elvis Movies, Elvis Live* and *Elvis R&B*.

Specialist label FTD has been releasing collectors' albums of previously unreleased material since 1999. See also discographies.

Book:

Elvis: The Ultimate Album Cover Book, by Paul Dowling, Harry Abrams 1996.

GOLD AND PLATINUM ALBUMS (81)

Elvis Presley - Gold
Elvis - Gold
Loving You - Gold
Elvis' Christmas Album (1957 Package) - Platinum x3
King Creole - Gold
Elvis' Golden Records, Vol. 1 - Platinum x6
50,000,000 Elvis Fans Can't Be Wrong (Elvis' Gold Records, Vol. 2) - Platinum
Elvis Is Back - Gold
G.I. Blues - Platinum
His Hand in Mine - Platinum
Something for Everybody - Gold
Blue Hawaii - Platinum x3
Girls! Girls! Girls! - Gold
Elvis' Golden Records, Vol. 3 - Platinum
Roustabout - Gold
Girl Happy - Gold
Frankie and Johnny - Platinum
How Great Thou Art - Platinum x2
Elvis, NBC TV Special - Platinum
Elvis' Gold Records, Vol. 4 - Gold
Elvis Sings Flaming Star - Platinum
From Elvis in Memphis - Gold
Elvis: From Memphis to Vegas, From Vegas to Memphis - Gold
On Stage, February 1970 - Platinum
Worldwide 50 Gold Award Hits - Platinum x2
Almost In Love - Platinum
Elvis' Christmas Album (1970 version) - Platinum x9
Elvis: That's the Way It Is - Gold
Elvis in Person at the International Hotel - Gold
C'mon Everybody - Gold
I Got Lucky - Gold
Elvis Country - Gold
Elvis: The Other Sides; 50 Gold Award Hits, Vol. 2 - Gold
You'll Never Walk Alone - Platinum x3
Elvis Sings the Wonderful World of Christmas - Platinum x3

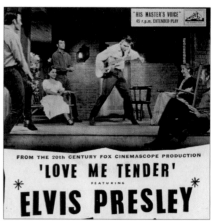

*Elvis * My Life* — rare U.S. special limited collectors edition.

Elvis Now - Gold
He Touched Me - Platinum
Elvis As Recorded at Madison Square Garden - Platinum x3
Elvis Sings Hits From His Movies Vol. 1 - Platinum
Elvis Sings Burning Love and Hits from His Movies, Vol. 2 - Platinum x2
Separate Ways - Platinum
Aloha from Hawaii - Platinum x5
Elvis, A Legendary Performer, Vol. 1 - Platinum x2
Elvis Recorded Live on Stage in Memphis - Gold
Pure Gold - Platinum x2
Elvis, A Legendary Performer, Vol. 2 - Platinum x2
From Elvis Presley Boulevard, Memphis, Tennessee - Gold
Welcome to My World - Platinum
Moody Blue - Platinum x2
Elvis in Concert - Platinum x3
He Walks Beside Me - Gold
Elvis, A Legendary Performer, Vol. 3 - Gold
Our Memories of Elvis - Gold
This Is Elvis - Gold
Elvis Aron Presley - Platinum
Memories of Christmas - Gold
The Number One Hits - Platinum x3
The Top Ten Hits - Platinum x4
Love Me Tender (1987 compilation) - Gold
Double Dynamite - Platinum
Elvis, The King of Rock 'n' Roll, The Complete 50's Masters - Platinum x5
Elvis, From Nashville to Memphis, The Essential 60's Masters I - Platinum
Elvis: His Greatest Hits (Readers Digest compilation) - Platinum
Blue Christmas - Gold
Elvis' Golden Records, Vol. 5 - Gold
Amazing Grace - Platinum x2
If Everyday Was Like Christmas - Platinum
Walk a Mile in My Shoes, The Essential 70's Masters - Gold
50 Years, 50 Hits - Platinum x2
Let's Be Friends - Platinum
Worldwide Gold Award Hits, Vol. 1 & 2 (club version) - Platinum
The Elvis Presley Story - Platinum x2
Elvis Gospel Treasury - Gold
The Complete Sun Sessions - Gold
Heart and Soul - Gold
It's Christmas Time - Platinum x2
The Rock 'n' Roll Era - Gold
The Legend Lives On - Gold
Platinum - A Life In Music - Gold
ELV1S 30 #1 HITS - Platinum x4
ELVIS 2ND TO NONE - Platinum

Love Me Tender — Britain HMV EP.

ALDEN, GINGER
(B. 1956)

Elvis met local beauty queen Ginger Alden with her two sisters when George Klein brought them round to Graceland in November 1976. Though Klein thought that Elvis would go for elder sister Terry, Elvis was immediately smitten by "Miss Traffic Safety" and "Miss Mid-South," or "Gingerbread" as he preferred to call her.

On their first date Elvis whisked Ginger off to Las Vegas in his plane, and stayed overnight after she got permission from her mother, conceded on the grounds that they were being chaperoned by Elvis' cousin Patsy and her husband Gee Gee Gambill.

Elvis called Ginger to join him on tour later that month. This did not go down well with previous long-term girlfriend Linda Thompson, who originally stood her ground after Elvis suggested she fly back to Memphis. When Linda did leave, she left for good.

With Ginger along to impress, on stage Elvis lifted his standards and performed with more energy and vigor than of late. Ginger told Elvis that she wanted to go home to see her family; Elvis persuaded her to stay by flying out her Ma, Pa, brother and sisters. Speculation soon appeared in the press that Elvis' gift of a Lincoln Continental might be an engagement gift.

Elvis told close friends that he saw his mother in Ginger's eyes. That he was falling very much in love became clear when within two months of meeting her, he had an engagement ring made for her, using the diamond from of his own TCB ring. The consensus among Elvis' inner circle is that the engagement was a spur of the moment thing, and he would not have gone through with the marriage. Ginger later claimed that the nuptials were all set for Christmas 1977.

Though Ginger spent a lot of time at Graceland with Elvis in the last months of his life, she never moved her stuff in—she would come over with what she needed in a small bag.

At Elvis' request, Ginger went on tour with him in 1977; without her, he was unwilling to fulfill his touring or recording commitments. When she complained of feeling lonely on the road with the Elvis circus, Elvis tried to fly her mother and/or her sisters in to keep her company rather than allowing her to return home to Memphis. He had his suspicions about what she was up to, confirmed by members of his security team who shadowed her movements. Elvis considered it a betrayal of trust that when she said she was going home, she was actually going out on the town.

Ginger left Elvis on tour in May to spend some time with her family. Though Elvis was beginning to be irked by how tightly she was tied to home, he let her go . . . and then picked her up on the Lisa Marie before the tour was out. It became increasingly clear to Elvis that he was not going to be able to "mold her" into the kind of caring woman he was looking for. Some of Elvis' friends have said that if Ginger had refused to accompany Elvis on the tour he was set to start the day he died, he had resolved to end the relationship.

It was Ginger who found Elvis face down on his bathroom floor on August 16, 1977. Ginger was at Elvis' funeral service; soon afterwards, she sold her story to the *National Enquirer*, reputedly for a six-figure sum.

In the Eighties and Nineties, Ginger landed some acting roles, including the 1980 movie *Living Legend: The King of Rock and Roll*, in which she played the girlfriend of an Elvis-like main character. She made a number of commercials, and a record for the Monument label.

In 1978, Ginger's mother Jo Laverne lost a law suit against the Elvis Estate regarding promises to pay off the family mortgage.

JOE ESPOSITO: "Ginger Alden looked a lot like Priscilla."

LARRY GELLER: "I liked Ginger very, very much; she was a very sweet lady. But I did not think Ginger was good for Elvis.... too inexperienced. They were just incompatible. And Elvis was dying."

DAVID STANLEY: "As far as loving Ginger and wanting to marry her, I think Elvis was so far gone and had missed reality bad. It was like he just said, 'I think I'll pick you. Here's a ring. Let's get married.' I don't think the feeling was mutual."

DR. NICHOPOULOS: "He was very wrapped up in her 'cause apparently something about her eyes or facial expressions reminded him of his mother.... Her behavior just kept him in emotional turmoil. I don't think he'd ever been faced with a female companion that he didn't have the upper-hand with; it really got to him."

ALI, MUHAMMAD
(B. CASSIUS MARCELLUS CLAY JR., 1942)

Elvis, Priscilla and a mess of pals watched the first Ali-Frazier bout in 1971 at a closed circuit event in the Ellis Auditorium in Memphis.

Ali won a light heavyweight gold medal at the 1960 Olympics in Rome and in a career spanning almost two decades earned the title "The Greatest." No other heavyweight boxer has bettered his record of three world heavyweight crowns. He may have achieved even more if he had not made a stand against being drafted into the Vietnam War, on the grounds that it was against his religion.

In Las Vegas in early 1973, Elvis was performing and Muhammad Ali in training for a title fight with Joe Bugner of England. Elvis gave Ali a studded robe with the words, "The People's Champion." It did not bring him luck when he wore it against Ken Norton that March, one of the few bouts he lost. The robe is now at the Muhammad Ali museum in his birthplace, Louisville, Kentucky.

Ali gave Elvis a pair of his boxing gloves, inscribed with "You're the greatest" and "To Elvis, my main man, from Muhammad Ali."

A longtime sufferer of Parkinson's disease, Ali is not only widely considered the greatest heavyweight the sport of boxing has ever known, he was crowned "Sportsman of the Century" by *Sports Illustrated* in 1999.

In 2006, Ali and Elvis were drafted onto the same team with CKX bought the rights to Ali's image.

DVD:
Elvis—Adrenaline '71

"ALL I NEEDED WAS THE RAIN"

A Sid Wayne and Ben Weisman number that Elvis recorded in Nashville for *Stay Away, Joe* on October 1, 1967. The song was first released on the *Singer Presents Elvis Singing Flaming Star and Others* (almost immediately re-released as *Elvis*

Sings Flaming Star. It is included on the *Double Features* reissue.

"ALL SHOOK UP"

Elvis' version of this song, which shipped in late March 1957, two months after he recorded it at Radio Recorders on January 12, came out as a single with "That's When Your Heartaches Begin" on the B-Side.

Elvis knew that this was #1 material the first time he heard it and insisted on take ten as his next single. After rocketing to the top of the charts it stayed at number one for eight whole weeks and sold almost 2.5 million copies.

Songwriter Otis Blackwell famously wrote the song after record executive Al Stanton came into his office at Shalimar Music shaking a bottle of Pepsi and challenged him to write a song inspired by the words "all shook up." David Hill released a version of the song in 1956 before Elvis took the song to the top. Vicki Young also released an "All Shook Up" that year, though this was a different song altogether.

For Elvis' version, the Colonel made sure that his boy got a slice of the royalties and a credit.

"All Shook Up" proved to be Elvis' second biggest hit in the US, staying on the charts for 30 weeks. It also delivered Elvis his first UK #1. Music commentators have stated that The Beatles added their hallmark "yeah, yeah, yeah" into their hit song "She Loves You" in homage to Elvis' inventive "yay-yay-yay."

The song saw its first album release on 1956 album, *Elvis*. It was one of the tracks recycled just before his return from the Army in 1960 on the *A Touch of Gold Vol. 3* EP. Mainstream US album releases include *Elvis' Golden Records Vol. 1*, *Worldwide Gold Award Hits Vol. 1*, *Pure Gold*, *Essential Elvis Vol. 2*, *The King Of Rock And Roll*, *Platinum: A Life in Music*, *Artist Of The Century*, *Hitstory* and *The Essential Elvis Presley*.

Elvis reprised the hit for his early-career medley on the NBC TV "Comeback" Special in 1968, and slotted it into his opening residency at the International Hotel in Las Vegas in 1969 (on the *From Memphis To Vegas* album). He went on to sing it hundreds of times during the Seventies. Live performances can be found on dozens of live

Elvis albums released over the years, starting with a 1961 performance (on *Elvis Aron Presley*) and running through to his 1976 show in Tucson (FTD release *Tucson '76*).

Versions from the 1968 Comeback special are on the original soundtrack release, *Memories: The '68 Comeback Special*, and FTD release *Burbank '68*, plus the usual bootleg suspects.

More live versions are on *Elvis in Person / Back in Memphis*, *That's the Way it Is* (and FTD release *The Way It Was*), and *Live in Las Vegas*. Other live recordings of the ever-popular hit are on *Elvis Aron Presley*, *Elvis: Close Up*, *An Afternoon In The Garden*, *Elvis As Recorded At Madison Square Garden* and *The Live Greatest Hits*.

FTD releases include *All Shook Up*, *Summer Festival*, *Elvis Recorded Live On Stage in Memphis*, *An American Trilogy*, *Elvis At The International*, *Live In LA*, *It's Midnight*, *Dragonheart*, *Dixieland Rocks*, *Writing for the King* and *Tucson '76*. The deluxe 2 CD edition of *ELVIS 30 #1 Hits* included a bonus rehearsal version from 1972 (also on FTD release *6363 Sunset*) in addition to the original studio recording.

ALL SHOOK UP

A 2005 live FTD release of Elvis' midnight Vegas performance on August 26, 1969, including the infamous "laughing" version of "Are You Lonesome Tonight."

TRACK LISTING:
1. Blue Suede Shoes
2. I Got A Woman
3. All Shook Up
4. Love Me Tender
5. Jailhouse Rock / Don't Be Cruel
6. Heartbreak Hotel
7. Hound Dog
8. I Can't Stop Loving You
9. Mystery Train / Tiger Man
10. Monologue
11. Baby What You Want Me To Do
12. Runaway
13. Are You Lonesome Tonight? (Laughing version)
14. Rubberneckin'
15. Yesterday / Hey Jude

Muhammad Ali with Elvis, May 12, 1974.

ALL SHOOK UP (MUSICAL)

A Broadway musical that melds a medley of Elvis songs with a loose interpretation of the plot from Shakespeare's *Twelfth Night*, which opened at the Palace Theater in the summer of 2005 with Cheyenne Jackson in the starring role.

"ALL THAT I AM"

Virtuoso guitar augurs well on this sweet-voiced Sid Tepper / Roy C. Bennett ballad that Elvis recorded at Radio Recorders on February 17, 1966 for Spinout. The song was sufficiently well regarded to merit release as the B-side to "Spinout" in September 1966. The B-side peaked at #41 in the charts, just one place lower than the A-side.

After appearing on the soundtrack LP release, the song came out on *Elvis Sings Sid Tepper & Roy C. Bennett*, *Command Performances*, the *Spinout Double Features* release, *Hitstory* and *Elvis at the Movies*. Alternate takes of the song appear on FTD releases *Out In Hollywood* and *Spinout*; many more are to be found on bootleg *Spin-in . . . Spinout*.

"ALLÁ EN EL RANCHO GRANDE"

A rare Spanish-language outing for Elvis, recorded during a rehearsal jam in July 1970 not officially released until *Walk A Mile In My Shoes* in the Nineties. The song was originally sung by Tito Guízar in 1936, and written by Silvano Ramos, E. Urange and J. Del Moral; Elvis' version had already appeared on bootlegs.

ALLEN, STEVE
(B. STEPHEN VALENTINE PATRICK WILLIAM ALLEN, 1921-2000)

"The Father of TV Talk Shows" and one of five American comedians to win a Lifetime Achievement Award at the original *American Comedy Awards* telecast, Steve Allen began his career in radio, moving a successful radio format onto the NBC TV network in "The Tonight Show" in 1953, which he hosted until 1957. He began hosting "The Steve Allen Show" in 1956, a variety showcase for up-and-coming singers that gave a break to Steve Lawrence, Sammy Davis Jr. and a number of talented comics. For decades a familiar face on TV panel shows and games, he was also a prolific composer, winning a 1963 Grammy for best jazz composition "The Gravy Waltz," wrote more than 50 books, earned quite a reputation as an actor, and is said to have written almost 8000 songs (including "This Could Be The Start of Something Big").

In the run-up to Elvis' appearance on Steve Allen's variety show on July 1, 1956—the second in a new series—the host came close to canceling his appearance altogether because of Elvis' allegedly scandalous antics on the Milton Berle show a month earlier. Allen assured the press that Elvis "will not be allowed any of his offensive tactics." Part of the host's plan to present Elvis as a more wholesome act was to dress him up in an establishment tuxedo. He also involved Elvis in a sketch which was less than flattering to American Indians, though he is unlikely to have known that Elvis' racial heritage included Cherokee blood.

ALLIED ARTISTS

In late 1963 the Colonel saw an advantageous bargaining position and struck a deal for a movie, *Tickle Me*, with this ailing studio. The deal guaranteed Elvis (and the Colonel) half of the entire budget plus a 50% share of profits. The Colonel kept costs down by recycling songs from past Elvis albums rather than recording new tracks—Elvis was perfectly happy with this arrangement. The comedy, packed with a bevy of pretty co-stars, did so well that it became the third highest-grossing film in the Studio's history (after *55 Days at Peking* and *El Cid*), and staved off the specter of bankruptcy for the formerly prominent studio, which under the name Monogram Pictures had been a Hollywood low-budget specialist since 1931. The studio finally went under in 1979.

"ALMOST"

A gentle Buddy Kaye / Ben Weisman ballad recorded on October 23, 1968 at United Artist Recorders in Los Angeles, initially for *The Trouble with Girls*, but first released in an alternate version on 1970 album *Let's Be Friends*.

Alternate takes have been released on *Today Tomorrow & Forever* and FTD issue *Silver Screen Stereo*; an undubbed version was included with the original on the *Double Features* compilation version. The song is sometimes referred to by the movie's original working title, *Chautauqua*.

"ALMOST ALWAYS TRUE"

Released on the *Blue Hawaii* album, Elvis recorded this Ben Weisman and Fred Wise track on March 22, 1961 at Radio Recorders. The song borrows the tune of traditional French song "Alouette." Two takes made it onto bootleg release *Behind Closed Doors*. An alternate take appeared on 2003 BMG box set *Elvis: Close Up*.

"ALMOST IN LOVE"

Elvis crooned this way through this slinky Rick Bonfa / Randy Starr ballad for release as the B-side to "A Little Less Conversation" on March 7, 1968, when he recorded it at Western Recorders for the movie *Live a Little, Love a Little*. When released as a single later that year, the tune climbed no higher than #95 in the charts.

The song became the title track of an album two years later. It has since appeared on *Command Performances* and the *Double Features* release for the movie.

ALMOST IN LOVE

A budget Camden album of reprised material released in October 1970 and released in March 1973 that initially sold 400,000 copies and peaked at #65 in the charts during an 18-week stay.

TRACK LISTING:
1. Almost In Love
2. Long Legged Girl (With The Short Dress On)
3. Edge Of Reality
4. My Little Friend
5. A Little Less Conversation
6. Rubberneckin'
7. Clean Up Your Own Back Yard
8. U.S. Male
9. Charro
10. Stay Away, Joe (replaced with Stay Away on the 1973 re-release)

ALOHA FROM HAWAII

The Colonel announced the first ever worldwide live satellite broadcast in July 1972, a month after Elvis' highly acclaimed Madison Square Garden concerts in New York. In the Colonel's words, "It is the intention of Elvis to please all of his fans throughout the world"—this broadcast was the closest the Colonel ever let Elvis get to his long-held desire to play outside North America.

Originally slated for the fall of 1972, the live concert broadcast was pushed back to early 1973 to prevent it from clashing with the release of MGM's live show documentary *Elvis on Tour*.

Producer/director Marty Pasetta persuaded Elvis to slim down to a decent performance weight. Pasetta also designed the stage jutting right out into the crowd, with the giant Elvis backdrop.

The concert took place on January 14, 1973, after a dress rehearsal on January 12. The event raised $75,000 for the Kui Lee Cancer Fund, though it cost $2.5 million to put on.

The estimated audience for this, the first ever worldwide TV broadcast, varies between 1 and 1.5 billion people in more than forty countries around the world. At the time, that was around a third of the world's population, more than watched the Apollo 11 moon landing in 1969. *Elvis Aloha from Hawaii* remains to this day the most-watched performance by an individual entertainer in the history of TV.

The 12:30 a.m. show was seen live in Australasia, Japan and the Far East. It was broadcast to European markets the next day, barring the UK, after the BBC refused to pay the price. Japan registered a record 37.8% share for the Elvis show. In the Philippines, 92% of the TV-viewing public at that time watched Elvis.

After the live broadcast was over and the audience cleared from the Honolulu International Center Arena, Elvis and the band re-emerged to record five extra songs for the US broadcast. When it finally aired on April 4, the show captured a commanding 57% audience share.

Larry Geller describes this event as the "last peak before the long free fall." John Wilkinson describes Elvis' performance as "the pinnacle of his career."

The broadcast was, incidentally, the one and only time that Elvis garnered a producing credit.

The more relaxed January 12 dress rehearsal was released as *The Alternate Aloha* in 1988.

Songs: Intro ("Paradise, Hawaiian Style;" "Also Sprach Zarathustra"); "See See Rider;" "Burning Love;" "Something;" "You Gave Me a Mountain;" "Steamroller Blues;" "My Way;" "Love Me;" "Johnny B. Goode;" "It's Over;" "Blue Suede Shoes;" "I'm So Lonesome I Could Cry;" "I Can't Stop Loving You;" "Hound Dog;" "What Now My Love;" "Fever,;" "Welcome to My World;," "Suspicious Minds;" "I'll Remember You;" "Long Tall Sally"/"Whole Lotta Shakin' Goin' On;" "An American Trilogy;" "A Big Hunk o' Love;" "Can't Help Falling In Love;" Closing Vamp

Performing in Honolulu for his
"Aloha from Hawaii" concert;, 1973

US version additions: "Early Morning Rain;" "Blue Hawaii;" "Hawaiian Wedding Song;" "Ku-U-I-Po" ("No More" was recorded but not used in the end).

LENGTH: 90 minutes (US version)

Directed by: Marty Pasetta

Produced by: Marty Pasetta (producer), Elvis Presley (executive producer), Ray Miller (producer special edition), Gary Hovey and Todd Morgan (executive producers special edition)

Film Editing by: Stephen McKeown, Steven Orland, Ray Miller (special edition)

Costume Design by: Bill Belew

FEATURING:
Elvis Presley
James Burton
Jerry Scheff
Charlie Hodge
John Wilkinson
Ronnie Tutt
J.D. Sumner
Kathy Westmoreland
Glen D. Hardin
Donnie Sumner

ADDITIONAL CREW:

Hal Alexander	assistant director
Ron Cates	assistant director
Bill Levitsky	sound
Bruce Buehlman	sound re-recording mixer (special edition)
Mark Kaim	sound recorder (special edition)
Andre Perreault	sound re-recording mixer (special edition)
Anthony Chickey	stage manager
John Freschi	lighting director
Joe Guercio	musical director
Danette Herman	technical director
Colonel Tom Parker.	production coordinator
George Parkhill	production coordinator
Mimi Seawell	assistant to producer
Jerry Smith	video
O. Tamburri	technical director
Bob Tribble	technical supervisor

DVD:

Elvis—Aloha from Hawaii (Deluxe Edition, 2004) is a two DVD remastered set of the rehearsal, broadcast concert, extra songs and bonus footage.

Book:

Elvis: Aloha Via Satellite, by Joe Tunzi, J.A.T. Publications, 1998.

ALOHA FROM HAWAII VIA SATELLITE (LP)

Elvis' first #1 album in 8 years, on the back of the world-girdling satellite TV broadcast concert from Honolulu, turned out to be the final #1 of his life. The double-LP soundtrack, on coordinated release around the world in February 1973, sold half a million copies in the US in its first two weeks, before going on to multi-platinum status. It remained in the US charts for exactly one year.

TRACK LISTING:
1. Introduction: Also Sprach Zarathustra
2. See See Rider
3. Burning Love
4. Something
5. You Gave Me A Mountain
6. Steamroller Blues
7. My Way
8. Love Me
9. Johnny B. Goode
10. It's Over
11. Blue Suede Shoes
12. I'm So Lonesome I Could Cry
13. I Can't Stop Loving You

14. Hound Dog
15. What Now My Love
16. Fever
17. Welcome To My World
18. Suspicious Minds
19. Introductions By Elvis
20. I'll Remember You
21. Long Tall Sally / Whole Lotta Shakin' Goin' On
22. An American Trilogy
23. A Big Hunk O' Love
24. Can't Help Falling In Love

The album has seen re-release with additional material in 1992 and 1998 (the extra tracks recorded after the show).

The Alternate Aloha, released in 1988, is a pre-concert dress rehearsal from August 13, 1973, in which Elvis is demonstrably more relaxed.

TRACK LISTING:
1. Also Sprach Zarathustra
2. See See Rider
3. Burning Love
4. Something
5. You Gave Me A Mountain
6. Steamroller Blues
7. My Way
8. Love Me
9. It's Over
10. Blue Suede Shoes
11. I'm So Lonesome I Could Cry
12. Hound Dog
13. What Now My Love
14. Fever
15. Welcome To My World
16. Suspicious Minds
17. Introduction by Elvis
18. I'll Remember You
19. American Trilogy
20. A Big Hunk O'Love
21. Can't Help Falling In Love
22. Blue Hawaii
23. Hawaiian Wedding Song
24. Ku-U-I-PO

The original release did not have the last two tracks or "Hound Dog."

DVD:

A DVD of the same name, released in 2000, includes the dress rehearsal, considered by many to surpass the concert itself. A 2004 version adds extra footage, the after-show songs recorded for broadcast in the US, and full versions of both concerts.

"ALOHA OE"

Elvis recorded this traditional Hawaiian song (meaning "farewell to thee") for the soundtrack of *Blue Hawaii* on March 21, 1961 at Radio Recorders. The song was written by Princess Kamekeha Liliuokalani in 1878, though it is sometimes stated that she wrote the song twenty years later, when in exile after the United States had taken over the islands. Before Elvis, Bing Crosby and Harry Owens both had hits with the song in the Thirties. *Elvis: Close Up* contains an alternative take of the song.

"ALONG CAME JONES"

Elvis greeted Tom Jones in his Las Vegas audience on August 18, 1970 with a line from this 1959 Leiber and Stoller song (initially released by The Coasters) before launching into "Hound Dog"—

the moment has been immortalized on bootleg *The Memphis Flash Hits Las Vegas*.

"ALRIGHT, OKAY, YOU WIN"

On September 29, 1974, Elvis sang this jazz standard, written by Sid Wyche and Mayme Watts and best known in a version by Peggy Lee, though it was first recorded by Ella Johnson in the mid-Fifties.

Elvis' version finally appeared officially in 2003 on FTD release *Dragonheart*.

"ALSO SPRACH ZARATHUSTRA" (2001 THEME)

In 1971, at the suggestion of orchestra director Joe Guercio (though Marty Lacker for one says that the idea was Elvis'), the singer strode out onto the stage to the strains of the opening section of this Richard Strauss piece, composed in 1896. Three years earlier the tune had been popularized as the theme to Stanley Kubrick's sci-fi masterpiece *2001: A Space Odyssey*.

Richard Strauss, a German conductor and composer who lived between 1864 and 1949, wrote the 30-minute symphonic poem *Also Sprach Zarathustra* after being inspired by philosopher Friedrich Nietzsche's book of the same name.

The opening notes graced Elvis' live acts ever after (the song is consequently on far too many live albums to list).

"ALWAYS ON MY MIND"

Elvis laid down this track on March 29, 1972 for RCA at their Hollywood studios, for release as the B-side of Red West's song "Separate Ways" later that year, in the immediate aftermath of his separation from Priscilla. Written by Mark James, Johnny Christopher and Wayne Carson Thompson, "Always On My Mind" was first recorded by Brenda Lee in 1971 in a version that was released before Elvis'.

Footage of the recording session when the track was laid down the song featured in 1981 documentary *This Is Elvis* (and on the accompanying album).

B. B. King once told an interviewer that this was his favorite song. Many international Elvis fans agreed, making the song a bit hit when it was released on their home markets—Willie Nelson's version outsold Elvis' in the US. In later years, the song also brought fortune to the Pet Shop Boys.

The song appeared on Elvis album *Separate Ways*. The song served as the title track for the eponymous 1985 memorial album, and can be found also on *Artist Of The Century, Burning Love, The Country Side Of Elvis, Elvis By The Presleys, Elvis Country, Elvis 2nd to None, The Essential Elvis Presley, Great Country Songs, The Great Performances, Walk A Mile In My Shoes, Hitstory,* and *Love Elvis*.

Alternate takes from the original sessions are on 1997 anthology *Platinum: A Life In Music* and FTD release *6363 Sunset*. A version from rehearsals for the *Elvis on Tour* documentary came out on 2005 FTD album *Elvis On Tour—The Rehearsals*.

A remixed version of Elvis' 1972 recording appeared on the official 2006 FIFA World Cup soccer album.

ALWAYS ON MY MIND

A maudlin 1985 release to mark what would have been Elvis' 50th birthday.

TRACK LISTING:
1. Separate Ways
2. Don't Cry, Daddy
3. My Boy
4. Solitaire
5. Bitter They Are, Harder They Fall
6. Hurt
7. Pieces Of My Life
8. I Miss You
9. It's Midnight
10. I've Lost You
11. You Gave Me A Mountain
12. Unchained Melody
13. Always On My Mind

"AM I READY"

Elvis recorded this ballad on February 16, 1966 at Radio Recorders for the *Spinout* soundtrack. Songwriters Roy Bennett and Sid Tepper based the song on traditional ballad "To A Wild Rose." "The song is included on *Burning Love and Hits from His Movies*, and on the *Double Features* album for the movie. Alternative takes are on *Collectors Gold*, *Elvis Sings Sid Tepper & Roy C. Bennett* and the FTD *Spinout* release.

"AMAZING GRACE"

Elvis recorded this gospel staple on March 15, 1971 in Nashville for release on the *He Touched Me* album. Reverend John Newton paired the lyrics he wrote to a traditional melody in the 1770s, some years after he renounced the slave trade and became a minister.

The song was subsequently used as the title track to a 1994 gospel compilation. It has since come out on the *Peace In The Valley* gospel compendium, *Christmas Peace*, *Ultimate Gospel*, *Elvis Inspirational*, and on 2001 four-track CD *America The Beautiful*.

The *Walk A Mile In My Shoes* compilation features a different take to the original release.

AMAZING GRACE

This double-platinum gospel compilation, originally released in 1994, is a compendium of Elvis' most heartfelt gospel works, plus previously unreleased material, some from the *Elvis On Tour* sessions and live performances.

TRACK LISTING: DISC: 1
1. I Believe
2. (There'll Be) Peace In The Valley (For Me)
3. Take My Hand, Precious Lord
4. It Is No Secret (What God Can Do)
5. Milky White Way
6. His Hand In Mine
7. I Believe In The Man In The Sky
8. He Knows Just What I Need
9. Mansion Over The Hilltop
10. In My Father's House
11. Joshua Fit The Battle
12. Swing Down, Sweet Chariot
13. I'm Gonna Walk Dem Golden Stairs
14. If We Never Meet Again
15. Known Only To Him
16. Working On The Building
17. Crying In The Chapel
18. Run On
19. How Great Thou Art
20. Stand By Me
21. Where No One Stands Alone
22. So High
23. Farther Along
24. By And By
25. In The Garden

26. Somebody Bigger Than You And I
27. Without Him
28. If The Lord Wasn't Walking By My Side
29. Where Could I Go But To The Lord

DISC: 2
1. We Call On Him
2. You'll Never Walk Alone
3. Only Believe
4. Amazing Grace
5. Miracle Of The Rosary
6. Lead Me, Guide Me
7. He Touched Me
8. I've Got Confidence
9. An Evening Prayer
10. Seeing Is Believing
11. A Thing Called Love
12. Put Your Hand In The Hand
13. Reach Out To Jesus
14. He Is My Everything
15. There Is No God But God
16. I, John
17. Bosom Of Abraham
18. Help Me
19. If That Isn't Love
20. Why Me Lord (live)
21. How Great Thou Art (live)
22. I, John
23. Bosom Of Abraham
24. You Better Run
25. Lead Me, Guide Me
26. Turn Your Eyes Upon Jesus / Nearer My God To Thee

The final five tracks were previously unreleased versions.

"AMEN"

Elvis sang this traditional song live more than five hundred times from 1970 to 1977, almost always in a medley with "I Got A Woman." The first time it appeared on an official release was on 1972 album *Elvis Recorded Live On Stage In Memphis*.

Other artists who have released the spiritual include The Impressions and Otis Redding. The biblical Hebrew word means "so be it" or "truly."

The song was included on 1972 live documentary *Elvis on Tour* (at Hampton Roads, Virginia). He reprised it during his final concerts, when it was filmed for *Elvis in Concert*. The song was also included on the *Elvis Aron Presley* collection.

Live performances from the Seventies are to be found on many FTD releases including *Takin' Tahoe Tonight*," *Closing Night*, *Elvis Recorded Live On Stage In Memphis*, *Live In LA*, *It's Midnight*, *Dragonheart*, *Big Boss Man*, *I Found My Thrill*, *Dixieland Rocks*, *Dinner At Eight*, *Tucson '76* and *New Year's Eve*.

AMBITION

The Elvis story starts with a little boy who promises his impoverished parents that when he grows up he will come good and banish their hardship.

Heedless of derision, as a junior high school student Elvis boasted to his classmates that he was going to sing at the Grand Ole Opry. To achieve this, he had to overcome deep natural shyness and conquer knock backs along the way: he was turned down by local Memphis bands including gospel group the Songfellows, and it took two self-paid records at the Memphis Recording Service before Sam Phillips asked him to come to the studio and show what he could do.

After Elvis achieved his initial ambition of a singing career, he revealed that his greatest ambition was to become a serious, dramatic actor. He was still saying this to the press in the mid-Sixties, long after it was evident that he was not going to get the roles to prove his acting credentials.

There was some solace—perhaps more for the Colonel than for Elvis—in the knowledge that for a spell he was Hollywood's highest-paid actor. Famously, not one of Elvis' films failed to make back the money it cost to shoot.

A burning ambition, whether it was playing as much football as he could, getting as far as he could in karate or breaking attendance records at major venues, was vital to the mental well-being of a man who ran on abundant reserves of nervous energy and needed constant challenge if he wasn't to sink into boredom or worse. The majority of biographers chart the beginning of his final decline after his last major challenge, the 1973 worldwide satellite broadcast, *Aloha from Hawaii*.

Elvis said in 1965: "I can never forget the longing to be someone."

Elvis said: "You gotta prove yourself, prove yourself, prove yourself."

AMERICA

Elvis, viewed by many as the scourge of Fifties American youth, demonstrated his patriotism at the height of his fame by humbly going into the Army in 1958 as an ordinary soldier.

When he returned to the concert stage in the Seventies, he showed his pride and patriotism by swathing himself in the flag; he pledged his allegiance to defending America to President Nixon in Washington in 1970.

Elvis remains a poster boy for the American dream, having risen from provincial poverty and obscurity to unrivaled fame and wealth.

The charitable works he pursued throughout his life included a benefit concert to build a monument for the *USS Arizona*, which was sunk by Japanese bombers at Pearl Harbor.

He proudly cited patriotism as the reason why he didn't shield his earnings from tax through tax shelters—this, at a time when the top tax bracket was 90%. No advisor could shake his belief that as an American, the government deserved its fair share of his income.

In the aftermath of 9/11, BMG released patriot-themed Elvis single CDs with "America The Beautiful," "An American Trilogy" and "If I Can Dream."

ELVIS SAID IN 1971: "This country has been great to me and if I can ever help it out in some way, I will wholeheartedly."

ELVIS WROTE IN 1977: "She is ours under God and thru liberty and freedom only as long as we fight for, respect and keep her free."

FRANK SINATRA: "I'm just a singer, Elvis was the embodiment of the whole American culture."

DAVE MARSH: "Elvis Presley was an explorer of vast new landscapes of dream and illusion. He was a man who refused to be told that the best of his dreams would not come true, who refused to be defined by anyone else's conceptions. This is the goal of democracy, the journey on which every prospective American hero sets out."

GREIL MARCUS: "When Elvis sings 'American Trilogy'... he signifies that his persona, and the culture he has made out of blues, Las Vegas, gospel music, Hollywood, schmaltz, Mississippi, and rock 'n' roll, can contain any America you might want to conjure up."

JOE ESPOSITO: "Elvis was a very patriotic person."

LARRY GELLER: "Elvis believed that if he could uplift himself—financially, emotionally, and intellectually—anyone could."

"AMERICA THE BEAUTIFUL"

Elvis' version of this song was released as the B-side of "My Way" posthumously. It was recorded during Elvis' December 13, 1975 show at the Las Vegas Hilton—the song was a highlight of his live shows during the bicentennial year of 1976 and beyond.

This lyrics to the song are a poem written by schoolteacher Katherine Lee Bates, inspired by her trip across the country in 1893, put to the tune of Samuel Ward's hymn "O Mother Dear Jerusalem."

Elvis' version of the song was also issued on his *Elvis Aron Presley* collectors' set. An alternate live performance from the same Las Vegas run came out on *Live In Las Vegas* in 2001. Another version is available on FTD release *Dinner at Eight*. An instrumental outtake from a Graceland recording session in early 1976 came out on FTD release *The Jungle Room Sessions*. There are rumors that Elvis recorded a disparaging version of the song at that session, which producer Felton Jarvis taped over with the next cut.

Over the years, there have been attempts to make this song the American national anthem instead of the "Star Spangled Banner" (a line of which Elvis slipped into "He's Your Uncle, Not You Dad," a soundtrack song from *Speedway*). A kazoo version of the tune featured in *The Trouble with Girls* (1969). The song also provided the title track for a patriotic release in 2001.

Perhaps the best-known version of the song is Ray Charles', though artists from Frank Sinatra to Boyz II Men have sung it.

AMERICA THE BEAUTIFUL

A four-track CD of this name came out in 2001 for The Red Cross Liberty Disaster Relief Fund.

TRACK LISTING:
1. If I Can Dream
2. America The Beautiful
3. Amazing Grace
4. If I Can Dream (Video)

"AMERICAN BANDSTAND"

In January 1959, Dick Clark produced a tribute to Elvis on his 24th birthday, including a telephone link-up with the birthday boy from his Army posting in Germany.

Elvis regularly topped popularity polls on this, the most popular music show on TV when he first started making music, though he never appeared; the Colonel would not agree to the derisory fee the show offered.

In August 1959, Dick Clark told Elvis in a telephone interview that his latest single, "A Big Hunk of Love," had gone gold.

The show first began on Philadelphia TV station WFIL-TV 1952, hosted by Bob Horn. Dick Clark took over in 1956, taking it to a national network TV slot on ABC-TV. The show remained a standard-bearer for pop music on TV in the United States until 1989 and spawned countless similar format shows around the globe, on which performers mimed to their latest hits (with the exception of Jerry Lee Lewis and B.B. King).

In 1979, Dick Clark produced *Elvis*, the first of many TV biopics about Presley.

AMERICAN SOUND STUDIO

Chips Moman's Memphis recording studio at 827 Thomas Street, located in a rat-infested building in a less-than-safe part of town, was the unlikely location for the Return of the King after his statement of intent on NBC-TV at the end of 1968. The local pest catchers were in the building on one of the days that Elvis was there, the first time that Elvis had recorded in his home town since leaving Sun Records. Neil Diamond and Dusty Springfield (*Dusty in Memphis*) also recorded at American around this time.

In three sessions (January 13 - 16, 20 - 23 and February 17 - 22) in 1969 Elvis laid down the songs that confirmed his return to passionate, rock-fuelled form after too many years of wan and uninspiring material. "Suspicious Minds" was Elvis' first number 1 hit in over five years. The sessions also yielded "In The Ghetto," "Kentucky Rain" and "Don't Cry, Daddy."

Founded by Chips Moman and Bob Crewe in 1964, American was driven by a house band with a harder edge than the Nashville players Elvis was used to. Boosted after Jerry Wexler of Atlantic funded the purchase of new equipment, over a three year period the studio managed a phenomenal 122 chart hits, and was instrumental in adding a Southern complement to the new soul sound.

American had a very strong and instantly recognizable rhythm section that Elvis wanted to try out—he was a fan of American artists The Boxtops and B. J. Thomas. At the recording sessions he worked with the house band of guitarist Reggie Young, bassists Tommy Cogbill and Mike Leech, drummer Gene Chrisman, and keyboard players Bobby Wood and Bobby Emmons. When Elvis was cutting tracks by night, the studio filled the day with Roy Hamilton's latest album, giving Elvis a chance to meet a man he had long admired.

Elvis was persuaded to eschew Nashville for American by pal Marty Lacker, who was working at American at the time. Lacker's suggestion was eagerly backed by long-term friend George Klein and producer Felton Jarvis.

Things began slowly as Elvis worked through the songs he was contracted to do for RCA. Everything clicked when he began to record tracks by American songwriters Mark James and Mac Davis. After the success of the January sessions, Elvis returned in February for more.

The resulting songs, credited with resurrecting Elvis' career, very nearly didn't see the light of day because of publishing wrangles. Moman was not prepared to buckle under to the Colonel's usual diktat. At a certain point, on Moman's advice Elvis threw the Hill & Range delegation out of the studio and just got on with what he did best: making music. Song arrangements were worked out there and then by Elvis and the musicians after hearing the demos.

The tracks Elvis recorded at American—for many, a pinnacle of his career—went through the most complex post-production process of any Elvis material so far. American Studio arrangers Mike Leech and Glen Spreen added layer upon layer of overdubs—including the famous "Memphis Horns," who had been in the studio during the recording session but laid down their parts later. Felton Jarvis then brought in Don Tweedy to add more overdubs in Nashville. All the while, ill-tempered negotiations continued between Elvis' management and Moman, who was determined to hold on to publishing and pro-

ducer rights, and was adamant that he should receive his credit. The songs came out but Elvis never recorded at American again.

Suspicious Minds: The Memphis 1969 Anthology, a double CD released in 1999, features all of the tracks released from the session plus extras, alternates and banter.

Elvis said on his way out the door: "We have some hits, don't we, Chips?" Moman replied, "Maybe some of your biggest."

"AMERICAN TRILOGY, AN"

Elvis first sang this medley of "Dixie," "The Battle Hymn of the Republic" and "All My Trials," arranged by Mickey Newbury, in Las Vegas in January 1972. The performance released as a single on Elvis' insistence in April 1972, with a B-side of "The First Time Ever I Saw Your Face," was from a February 16 show that year. The single struggled to sell 100,000 copies and failed to climb any higher than #66 in the charts, significantly lower than the #40 achieved a year earlier when released by Newbury himself.

The medley of Yankee and Confederate fighting songs plus a song of comfort and hope was a big crowd-pleaser whenever Elvis sang it live, which he did often from 1972 through to 1975. It appears on many live album and Elvis documentaries from the Seventies and on countless bootlegs, including *Elvis As Recorded At Madison Square Garden*, *Aloha From Hawaii Via Satellite*, *Elvis Recorded Live On Stage In Memphis*, *Elvis Aron Presley*, *Walk A Mile In My Shoes*, *Platinum: A Life in Music*, *Artist Of The Century*, *Burning Love*, *The Great Performances*, *The Live Greatest Hits*, *Elvis 2nd to None* and *Hitstory*.

It's also on *Elvis Aron Presley*, *This Is Elvis* (recorded at Hampton Roads, Virginia), *An Afternoon In The Garden*, *The Alternate Aloha*, *Live In Las Vegas*, *Elvis: Close Up*, and FTD releases *An American Trilogy*, *Summer Festival*, *Closing Night*, *Live In LA*, *I Found My Trill*, *Big Boss Man*, and *Dixieland Rocks*. A rehearsal version from 1972 has also done the rounds on bootlegs.

"All My Trials" is a traditional song covered by many-folk artists during the Sixties folk revival in the States.

AN AMERICAN TRILOGY

A 2007 FTD release of live material from Elvis' winter 1972 Las Vegas shows.

TRACK LISTING:
1. See See Rider
2. Proud Mary
3. Never Been To Spain
4. You Gave Me A Mountain
5. Love Me
6. All Shook Up
7. Teddy Bear
8. Don't Be Cruel
9. Hound Dog
10. Little Sister
11. Get Back
12. It's Impossible
13. It's Over
14. The Impossible Dream
15. A Big Hunk O' Love
16. An American Trilogy
17. Can't Help Falling In Love
18. Until It's Time for You to Go
19. Polk Salad Annie
20. One Night
21. Bridge Over Troubled Water
22. Lawdy, Miss Clawdy
23. I'll Remember You
24. Suspicious Minds

"AND I LOVE YOU SO"

When Elvis recorded this Don McLean ballad at RCA's Sunset Boulevard studios on March 10, 1975, he was looking directly at girlfriend Sheila Ryan.

Elvis' romantic take on the song—initially released by Don McLean on his debut album *Tapestry* in 1970, and a 1973 hit for Perry Como—first appeared on *Today,* one of Elvis' final albums. It's also on *Elvis Aron Presley* and *Love Elvis.*

Alternate takes may be found on 1997 album *Platinum: A Life In Music,* and FTD releases 6363 *Sunset* and *Today.*

Live performances have been released on *Elvis in Concert, Live In Las Vegas* and FTD concert issues *Big Boss Man, Live in L.A., Dinner At Eight* and *Tucson '76.*

"AND THE GRASS WON'T PAY NO MIND"

Elvis laid down this smooth Neil Diamond track on February 17, 1969 at American Studio in Memphis. It is on *Back in Memphis* (aka *From Memphis to Vegas / From Vegas to Memphis*) and *From Nashville to Memphis.* Diamond didn't record the song until after Elvis.

The track is included on *Suspicious Minds: The Memphis 1969 Anthology* and *Elvis Inspirational.* An undubbed master came out in 2001 on FTD album *The Memphis Sessions.*

ANDRESS, URSULA
(B. 1936)

Elvis' love interest in 1963 *Fun in Acapulco* was rumored to be a love interest offstage . . . little wonder that Elvis counted 1962 movie *Dr. No,* in which the Swiss Miss plays the original Bond girl, as one of his favorites. However, Sonny West has said that though Andress mercilessly pursued Elvis, he asked his entourage guys never to leave them alone—he had a rule that he was simply not interested in married women; at the time she was filming with Elvis, she was married to actor/director John Derek.

Other notable Andress vehicles after this, her first Hollywood foray, include quintessential Sixties zeitgeist comedies and Elvis favorites *What's New Pussycat* (Elvis liked the Tom Jones title song too) and the original *Casino Royale.* Andress's roll-call of romantic liaisons is something of an entertainment who's who of the decade, running to Ryan O'Neal, Warren Beatty and Jean-Paul Belmondo, as well as reputed dalliances with method actors extraordinaire James Dean and Marlon Brando.

Elvis' nickname for Andress was "Ooshie." After the movie was shot, she complained at how virginal she was forced to be, "just to please innocent little girls who make up Elvis' audiences."

URSULA ANDRESS: "At the beginning, I was not fond of him. You know, you judge people by what you read about them. But Elvis was adorable, so sweet, nice, and kind. We continued to be friends, and I saw him once or twice a year. But he was a troubled person."

"ANGEL"

In Nashville on July 2, 1961 Elvis recorded this Sid Tepper / Roy C. Bennett smoothie for *Follow That Dream* and the accompanying EP—Millie Kirkham does her best soprano angel impression. The song saw album release on later budget releases *C'mon Everybody* and *Elvis Sings for Children and Grown-Ups Too* (later re-released as *Elvis Sings For Kids*). It's also on *Elvis Sings Sid Tepper & Roy C. Bennett,* the anthology *Command Performances,* the *Double Features* release for the movie, and appears on *Elvis: Close Up.* An alternative take of the song is on *Silver Screen Stereo.*

ANGER

Elvis' temper was one of his legendary character traits. He is said to have inherited a ferocious temper from his Ma Gladys; when she got upset, objects started to fly and men much bigger than her had reason to cower. Elvis told friends a story about how she once had a disagreement with a farm owner for whom the Presleys were working at the time, picked up a heavy plowshare and smacked him in the head.

Early entourage members have said that he first time Elvis showed signs of anger was during the filming of *Jailhouse Rock* in 1957. Before then, friends and fellow musicians recall him as being unfailingly courteous and level-headed, always ready to muck in with others. On *Jailhouse Rock* he blew up when studio executives instructed backing band The Jordanaires to move away from Elvis so that he would stop singing the gospel songs he sang to warm up and get down to the day's business.

However, before then, at a 1955 concert, out of the blue Elvis decked a doorkeeper for not doing what he wanted when he wanted it. He apologized immediately and offered to pay the unfortunate victim's medical bills.

Rarely did Elvis turn his anger on people who were in a position of power over him—the legacy of his upbringing in which he was taught to respect authority.

Entourage members recall that once he blew up, almost always half an hour later he was back to normal.

In 1960, Elvis reputedly roughhoused Christina Crawford, Joe Esposito's girlfriend at the time, after she objected at Joe springing into action to light Elvis' cigar. Around that time Elvis pulled a gun on some guys in a car who flipped him the bird.

In 1962, Elvis drove right through the Graceland music gates because there was no one at the gatehouse to let him in early one morning.

In her memoir, Priscilla mentions occasions when she said something that so incensed Elvis that he pushed her or hurled an object at her—Gladys is said to have hurled things at Vernon back in the day. Sometimes Elvis would blow up because he felt somebody—or indeed everybody—needed to be taught a lesson. After the storm passed, Elvis regained his composure while everyone else remained in a state of agitation and subjugation. Priscilla nicknamed him "Fire Eyes" for his outbursts; former entourage members have gone on record that Elvis was sometimes violent to her.

Billy Smith remembers that from the mid-Sixties, Elvis was perfectly capable of trashing a room if he got mad about something.

In the Seventies, Elvis' temper flew out of control increasingly often as a result of his drug-prompted mood swings. In 1971 he stormed out of a Nashville recording session in anger that the backing singers kept fluffing their parts on a recording of "My Way."

Under the wrong circumstances, a throwaway comment by one of the guys might provoke a huge scene, usually after a delay. Red West tells of several occasion when Elvis waved a gun around in rage at a perceived lack of loyalty or insubordination. Even without firepower, Elvis had a vocabulary of insults that few men could equal (and very few in the entourage would dare challenge). When Elvis got really mad he would use his ultimate weapon and fire members of his entourage. Invariably they were rehired once he had calmed down . . . with the exception of Red and Sonny West, who after being fired in 1976 went on to write a tell-all book about Elvis. Indeed, they begin the book with what is generally considered to be Elvis' most extreme temper tantrum, when in 1973 he tried to get his bodyguards to kill Priscilla's lover, karate champion Mike Stone.

Elvis lashed out more and more as the Seventies wore on. Red West recounts an incident in Vail, Colorado, where Elvis decided in the middle of the night that he wanted to swap apartments with Jerry Schilling. When Schilling refused, Elvis tried to get Red West to use force on Schilling, and then pulled a gun. Soon afterwards, Schilling handed in his notice. By the end of 1976, the only long-term members of the entourage left were family; all the others had either left or been fired.

ELVIS SAID IN 1962: "When I am pushed to a certain point, I have a very bad temper, an extremely bad temper. So much to the point I have no idea what I'm doing."

PRISCILLA: "Because of the continuous pressures and problems in Elvis' life, all magnified by taking prescribed drugs, little things would set him off."

LARRY GELLER: "Elvis had a volatile temper, and anger built up inside him until he exploded in rage. Once he got started on something, he'd rant and carry on for hours... People were safe, only inanimate objects were in danger."

PRISCILLA: "You could sense the vibration when he was angry. The tension in the room mounted to flashpoint, and no one wanted to be around for the explosion. Yet, if anyone decided to leave, they automatically became the target for his rage."

MYRNA SMITH: "Elvis was easily angered due to the drugs he was taking."

MARTY LACKER: "Elvis was an impulsive guy. And when you mix impulse, temper, and pills, you're going to have some interesting situations."

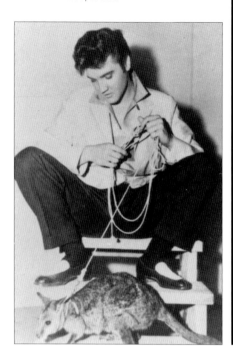

"ANIMAL INSTINCT"

A promising title for a tame Bill Giant / Bernie Baum / Florence Kaye song (one of very few Elvis songs to feature a flute, played by Rufus Long) recorded on February 26, 1965 in Nashville for *Harum Scarum*. The song didn't make it into the movie but was reinstated for the soundtrack album. It has since appeared on the *Double Features* album for *Harum Scarum*. Alternate takes are on the FTD soundtrack release.

ANIMALS

A stuffed version of Nipper, the RCA dog, featured on stage with Elvis at many of his Fifties shows. Scandal followed when Elvis picked up the dog during a show in LA in 1957 and simulated an amorous act. Elvis kept a little Nipper model in his bedroom in later years.

When the Presleys moved to Graceland in 1957, Vernon stocked the barns with pigs and chickens. That year Elvis drove out into the country, filled the back seat of a Cadillac with geese and brought them back to Graceland to keep the lawn trim. Elvis also kept a few donkeys he had been given in the drained Graceland swimming pool when he first moved in, until work was finished on the fence around the property.

Though the larger farm animals were gradually pensioned off, Graceland retained a henhouse for a supply of fresh eggs. At one time or another, Elvis also had goats and turkeys (one called Bow Tie).

Elvis donated a wallaby to Memphis Zoo after receiving it as a gift from Australian fans in 1957. He became a serial wallaby donator by repeating the gift in 1962.

His best-known pet was a cheeky chimp called Scatter, just one of several monkeys he owned.

Elvis was briefly a cattle rancher when he bought the Circle G ranch in Mississippi in 1967, after he started amassing a collection of horses. He sold the cattle to Winthrop Rockefeller, brother of Nelson.

For a while, he had a peacock in the Graceland grounds, until the bird started damaging the cars, after which it was given away. He also owned Mynah birds, one of which could say "Elvis! Go to hell."

The Graceland menagerie included mules at one time.

Snakes that happened to venture onto Graceland had a tough time. A maid remembers Elvis blazing away with a rifle at a tree after a snake was seen slithering up the trunk.

See also PETS

ANKA, PAUL
(B. 1941)

Canadian-born songwriter Paul Anka wrote "My Way," which Elvis first recorded in 1971 and often sang in the Seventies. Anka, who had hit songs in his own right ("Diana" was a #1 smash in 1957), more famously wrote for artists like Patti Page, Connie Francis, Frank Sinatra and Tom Jones. He visited Elvis on the set of *Viva Las Vegas* in 1963. Anka often saw Elvis perform in concert, from his first show in Vegas in the summer of 1969 onwards. When he took in Elvis' show in Lake Tahoe in August 1971, he received a telling off from the stage when Elvis accused him of talking while he sang.

Anka's work as an actor includes a small role in 2001 heist movie *3000 Miles to Graceland*.

ANN-MARGRET
(B. APRIL 28, 1941, ANN-MARGARET OLSSON IN SWEDEN)

Discovered by George Burns singing in a cabaret while still at Northwestern University, Ann-Margret sang as well as she acted, and was known in her early days as "the female Elvis."

Before working together, Ann-Margret had become a stable-mate of Elvis' at RCA. She even recorded her own version of "Heartbreak Hotel," though her recording career never took off like her acting career. Her place in pop culture was cemented in 1963, when she featured in *The Flintstones* as Ann-Margrock.

When Elvis and Ann-Margret met on the MGM lot during pre-production of *Viva Las Vegas* in the summer of 1963, they both said, at exactly the same time, "I've heard a lot about you." Over the next few years they went about discovering just how alike they were. News of their affair leaked off the set and into the press, at a time when Elvis had only recently succeeded in getting Priscilla Beaulieu to come and live with him in Memphis. That summer, Ann-Margret and Elvis went for motorbike rides together, hung out at Elvis' LA home, sang and danced on screen and off, and by all accounts had the most fun. It was all Elvis could do to dispel Priscilla's suspicions and put her off coming out to Hollywood. Elvis nicknamed Ann-Margret "Rusty Ammo," a pun on her character name in the movie, Rusty Martin— she called him "Lucky." The Swedish actress bought a pink Cadillac while she was seeing Elvis.

Entourage members recall that Ann-Margret was the only one of Elvis' girlfriends for whom he was not just willing but happy to head out into the world alone, without his usual retinue of pals.

While in England promoting *Bye Bye Birdie* that fall, Ann-Margret told the press that she was "seeing" Elvis. The press wrote that they were in love and might well soon marry. Priscilla's probing questions did not prevent Elvis from spending time with Ann-Margret while he was in LA— they were together at his home on the day that JFK was assassinated. Much to Priscilla's annoyance, Ann-Margret visited Elvis regularly on the set of *Girl Happy* in 1964.

Many Elvis memoirs state that Elvis made a reasoned choice between Ann-Margret, who describes Elvis as her "soulmate" in her autobiography, and the impressionable young Priscilla he had stashed away at home. His conviction that he would never marry a "career woman" was the deciding factor in his choice, though Ann-Margret was still an open issue in his life when, in December 1966, he finally decided to marry Priscilla. Larry Geller says that Elvis told him that Ann-Margret intimidated him because she wouldn't take orders and had a definite mind of her own. It has also been claimed that Elvis asked the Colonel to take over management of Ann-Margret's career, only to go cold on the idea when the Colonel told him he'd only have half the time to manage Elvis' career.

In June 1967 Elvis sent Ann-Margret a guitar-shaped bouquet for her opening night in Las Vegas. He repeated this eloquent gesture every time she performed in Vegas. He went to see there in July 1967, along with his dad and some of his pals. On May 8, 1967, just one week after Elvis married Priscilla, Ann-Margret married fellow actor Roger Smith.

Elvis and Priscilla saw Ann-Margret perform at the International Hotel in February 1971, when she followed on from Elvis' month-long residency.

Elvis had a pink round bed made and delivered to Ann-Margret.

Elvis called Ann-Margret in 1972 and asked her to come up and see him. She declined because she was a married lady who knew that one thing so easily leads to another. Billy Smith believes that Elvis actually proposed to her not long after his separation from Priscilla.

When she was in the audience on Elvis' final night in Vegas in February 1973, Elvis told Lamar Fike from the stage to leave a spotlight on her all night so that he could feast his eyes.

At a 1976 concert at the Sahara Tahoe, Elvis quipped that when he and Ann-Margret got married on camera in *Viva Las Vegas* it felt so real that "it took us two years to figure out we weren't."

Over the years Ann-Margret has been nominated for five Emmys and two best actress Academy Awards (*Carnal Knowledge*, 1972, and *Tommy*, 1975). She has also won five Golden Globes, and made the top ten of *Empire* magazine's 100 sexiest movie stars in 1995.

Ann-Margret was the only one of Elvis' leading ladies to go to his funeral in 1977, chartering a plane and canceling a Las Vegas show to do so.

In the eighties she lived up to her female Elvis moniker by performing regularly in Las Vegas, where she won the Las Vegas Entertainer of the Year Award. She has carried on acting into the new millennium.

ANN-MARGRET, on meeting Elvis: "We both felt a current, an electricity that went straight through us. It would become a force we couldn't control."

ANN-MARGRET: "Funny, Generous, giving, kind, loving. Gifted, so talented."

ANN-MARGRET: "What Elvis and I had remains between us. He has taken it to the grave. I will take it to my grave."

JOE ESPOSITO: "During the making of that movie, the two of them were having a great time."

LANCE LEGAULT: "Ann-Margret and Elvis got along great—two good-looking people just having a ball. They both sang. That broke the ice right there. They both liked to move... They dated, and you could just tell they really liked each other. It was all up on the screen."

BILLY SMITH: "Once you met Ann, you didn't forget her. She had the same effect on men that Elvis did on women."

RED WEST: "Ann-Margret was a nice lady and we all loved her, but there were others—so many others. He liked all of them."

PETER GURALNICK: "At one point he was so overwhelmed with his feelings for Ann-Margret and so guilty over his inability to do anything about them, that he even approached the Colonel for help."

LARRY GELLER: "Elvis and Ann-Margret were beautiful together; not only were they each very attractive, but they shared an energy and enthusiasm for life that made you feel happy for them."

LAMAR FIKE: "I think of all the women he went with, it was Ann-Margret he liked best of all. She was a sweetheart. They got along real well. But the relationship was doomed from the beginning 'cos Ann wasn't gonna quit the business, and Elvis had these old-fashioned Southern values, you know, 'a woman's place is in the home'."

MARTY LACKER: "This idea that Ann was the love of his life... if you ask me, Elvis didn't have one. I'm not sure he was capable of it."

Elvis and Ann-Margret in *Viva Las Vegas*.

Book:
Ann-Margret: My Story, by Ann-Margret and Todd Gold, Berkley, 1995.

ANNIVERSARIES

The anniversaries of Elvis' birth and death are landmarks in every fan's life. Major anniversaries bring retrospectives and a new crop of album releases, books, documentaries and anniversary concerts to mark Elvis' passing on August 16, 1977.

"ANY DAY NOW"

Elvis recorded this Burt Bacharach / Bob Hilliard song at American Studio on February 20, 1969—a hit for Chuck Jackson in 1962 and Ronnie Milsap who took it to the top of the country chart two decades later. The song was released as the B-side to "In The Ghetto" in April 1969, and may be found on *From Elvis in Memphis*, *Worldwide Gold Award Hits Vol. 2*, *From Nashville to Memphis* and *Suspicious Minds: The Memphis 1969 Anthology*.

An alternate take is on FTD release *The Memphis Sessions*.

"ANY WAY YOU WANT ME (THAT'S HOW I WILL BE)"

Elvis shoehorned extra passion into this track when he laid it down for RCA in New York City on July 2, 1956, a day after he appeared on the "Steve Allen Show." Written by Aaron Schroeder and Cliff Owens, RCA released the song as the B-side of "Love Me Tender" in September 1956—the Colonel tried but failed to get this song onto the *Love Me Tender* movie soundtrack.

The song spawned an EP release later in 1956, and later appeared on *Elvis Golden Records Vol. 1*, *Worldwide 50 Gold Award Hits Vol. 1*, *Elvis '56*, *Artist Of The Century*, *The King Of Rock And Roll*, and *Love Elvis*.

ANY WAY YOU WANT ME (EP)

One of two October 1956 EP releases from RCA as they put out everything Elvis they had in every available format. This one made it to #74 in the charts.

TRACK LISTING:
1.   Any Way You Want Me
2.   I'm Left, You're Right, She's Gone
3.   I Don't Care If The Sun Don't Shine
4.   Mystery Train

"ANYONE (COULD FALL IN LOVE WITH YOU)"

Bennie Benjamin, Sol Marcus and Louis DeJesus conspired to write this down-tempo ballad for Elvis to record on September 30, 1963 as part of the *Kissin' Cousins* soundtrack sessions at Radio Recorders. The song wound up on the cutting room floor but appeared on the original soundtrack album, as well as on the *Double Features* re-release.

"ANYPLACE IS PARADISE"

A Joe Thomas composition that Elvis recorded on September 9, 1956 at Radio Recorders, adding a blues touch to his second album, *Elvis*. It also appeared on EP *Elvis Vol. 2*. It has since been released on albums *The King Of Rock And Roll*, *Elvis '56* and *Artist Of The Century*.

"ANYTHING THAT'S PART OF YOU"

Elvis put his heart into this mellifluous Don Robertson ballad at RCA's Nashville studios on October 15, 1961. It came out as the B-side to "Good Luck Charm" in late February 1962 but rose no higher than #31 in the eight weeks it stayed on the *Billboard* charts.

The track had a run out on the *Elvis' Golden Records Vol. 3* album. It is also on *Worldwide Gold Award Hits Vol. 1, From Nashville to Memphis* and *Artist Of The Century*.

An alternate take was released in error on the *Elvis In Nashville* album in 1988. Alternates may also be found on *Today Tomorrow & Forever, Elvis By The Presleys*, and FTD release *Studio B: Nashville Outtakes, Long Lonely Highway* and *Something For Everybody*.

APPEARANCE

Practically every woman and quite a few men who met Elvis describe him as stunningly beautiful. His exotic blend of racial ancestries, steel-blue eyes, black-dyed hair and "firm but pliant lips" made nations swoon.

Hard as it may be to imagine today, when Elvis first became a source of national attention his long hair and particularly his sideburns were viewed by many as a threat, a sign of perilous moral decline and depravity. Early interviewers unfailingly questioned him about why he grew them, how long he'd been growing them, if he intended keeping them.. Whether he answered straight or with a joke—aged 21 Elvis told a reporter he'd been wearing sideburns for 28 years — the reason he had 'em was because he liked 'em.

Elvis created the first of his many, highly-recognizable looks as he metamorphosed from an unpopular acne-suffering school kid to the world's most popular performer and a lightning rod for sexual desire. He had the knack of standing out from the crowd as an untutored and observant kid; later, with clothes designers such as Bill Belew, he developed iconic styles (the leather-clad rock god of his '68 TV Special; the caped and bejeweled stage superhero of his Seventies shows). Even on the downslide, nobody did excess quite like Elvis.

According to Barbara Leigh, Elvis simply couldn't walk past a mirror without checking his reflection. It was important to Elvis that the woman he was with looked good too.

The Elvis who returned from the Army was altogether a smoother, more parent-friendly proposition. Gone were the menacing sideburns. The man who crossed the nation in his Army uniform had dutifully served America, unaware that his fate was to enrich a number of Hollywood studios by churning out pabulum fare.

Weight became an issue for Elvis soon after he returned from Germany. By the mid-Sixties, Paramount producer Hal Wallis told Colonel Parker his concerns that Elvis seemed to be letting himself go. Perhaps in a veiled reference to drug abuse, Wallis noted how puffy Elvis' face was on occasion, and that his hair had become very unnatural looking. The Elvis who looks out from the screen in many of his more forgettable movies is a thing of plastic.

Until his last few years alive, Elvis was able to shed excess weight when he needed to. The svelte Elvis who excelled in his 1968 NBC-TV Special and triumphed on stage in Las Vegas in 1969 and 1970 (immortalized in the *That's The Way It Is* concert documentary) was as fit and trim a 35-year old man as the world is likely to see.

The last time that Elvis had the conviction to pull off his weight loss trick was for his 1973 *Aloha from Hawaii* satellite broadcast. As Ronnie Tutt puts it, he would "jump into his phone booth" and turn into his own alter ego.

Elvis appears bearded in gritty Western *Charro!* (1969)—the sideburns were back by this time too, and stayed 'til the end.

Much has been made of how bad Elvis looked at the end. His unenviable collection of health conditions left him extremely bloated on some days; there were times during his final months alive when Elvis bore a striking resemblance to the puffed-up look of his mother Gladys in the weeks before her death.

Eyes:

Most often, Elvis' eyes are described as steel-blue in color, possessed of a captivating sparkle under long black lashes. In an early interview, Elvis described his eye color as greenish-blue. One journalist described them as "boudoir eyes."He refused to wear brown contact lenses for 1960 movie *Flaming Star*, in which the character he plays is an American Indian.

Girlfriend Juan Juanico fondly remembers his eyes: "They were dark blue, but it wasn't the color that stood out, it was this dreamy look he would get. It was pretty irresistible."

Countless Elvis girls have said that they could feel Elvis' magnetic gaze on them from a distance. Unfailingly, they'd turn round and melt.

Face:

Elvis' face has been compared with Michelangelo's David: a classic profile and a small, full-lipped mouth. Many have remarked on his androgynous features, very different from the lantern-jawed fashion for male beauty of the time, and not a million miles away from Rudolph Valentino's look.

His complexion was not without flaws: he suffered from youthful acne, and according to one entourage member, had pores "big enough to hide a tank in."

Elvis turned his need for prescription glasses to iconic advantage in 1970 by buying 6 pairs of customized goggles, another pair of silver goggles and special gold prescription glasses with his initials and a TCB lightning bolt on the frames. Thereafter he bought hundreds of pairs with TCB or EP insignia.

His scream-inducing lip curl served him well on stage and off it.

Body:

Elvis' body, an object of desire to many, was the unreconstructed Sixties version of the human form, before body-building became de rigueur for actors and much of the rest of the populace. Elvis spends much of his 1961 movie *Blue Hawaii* cavorting in swim trunks.

In the Seventies, Elvis studiously avoided exposing his body to the sun, though he did like to feel the rays on his face.

Elvis' skin reacted against chlorine, so had to use other means of keeping his pools clean.

Larry Geller says that cutting Elvis' hair was an exercise in patience as Elvis was constantly in motion, a study in kinetic energy.

What Elvis didn't like about his body was his neck—he thought it too long, which was why he favored high and turned up collars—and he thought his legs were on the skinny side, hence he didn't wear shorts if he could avoid it.

Elvis had a menagerie of personal tics and jitters. As well as being a lifelong nail biter, when he was nervous about meeting somebody—even after he had been a household name for a decade —he'd tap his fingers or his leg would start jiggling, in a muted version of his early stage moves.

For many years, Elvis had calloused knuckles from all of his karate practice and board breaking.

Elvis liked getting massages. Larry Geller would give him a massage after his concerts in the Seventies to help him wind down.

Towards the end, Elvis was reticent to uncover in public, even among friends and family on vacation in Hawaii.

See also HAIR, CLOTHES, COSTUMES.

ELVIS SAID (TO HIS OWN REFLECTION): "You handsome thing, you!"

PAUL SIMPSON: "The dyed hair, the make-up, even the eternally turned-up collars . . . were parts of a very conscious makeover by a man whose look represented almost as challenging a synthesis as his music."

HAL KANTER, 1957: "The young man with the ancient eyes and the child's mouth, a body as loose and unadorned and as unpredictable as a whip."

ANITA WOOD: "I have to say that Elvis was the most handsome man I'd ever seen before or after."

DR. NICHOPOULOS: "He could've weighed 100 pounds more and still been loved and admired by his fans, but you couldn't convince him of that. He still had that image of himself when he was more physical and thinner and more macho."

K.D. LANG: "He was the total androgynous beauty. I would practice Elvis in front of the mirror when I was twelve or thirteen years old."

BILL MEDLEY on Elvis, ca. 1968: "I thought he looked phenomenal . . . I would have had his children."

TONY BROWN: "When I met him it was like seeing the most beautiful human being."

LARRY GELLER: "Given how physically beautiful Elvis was and the pride he took in his appearance, it is surprising that vanity didn't arouse a greater awareness of and respect for his body."

PAUL SIMON: "I grew my hair like Elvis . . . once I went all over New York looking for a lavender shirt like the one he wore on one of his albums."

CAMILLE PAGLIA: "Presley, a myth maker, understood the essence of his own archetypal beauty."

LARRY GELLER: "Deterioration awaits all of us eventually. For Elvis, it took only a few short years for something so magnificent to evolve into a bloated, blotched caricature of itself."

JERRY SCHEFF: "I think that it very well could be that Elvis thought that he was a normal American man approaching middle age, and let himself go a little bit."

Elvis in the 50's

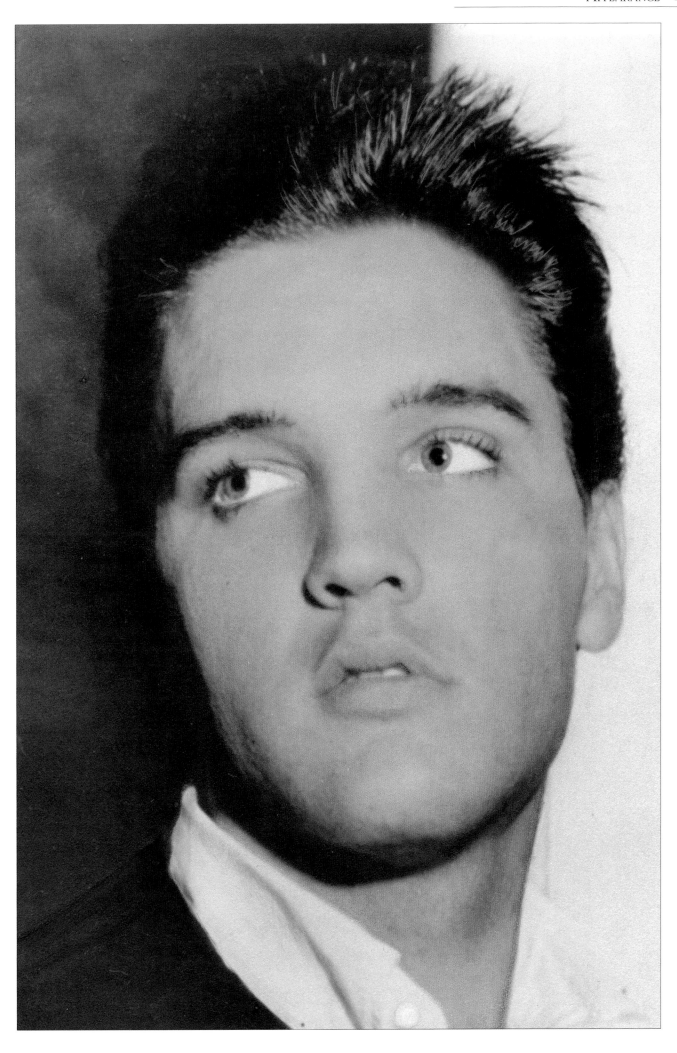

"APRON STRINGS"

Elvis' version of this track by George Weiss and Aaron Schroeder made a late debut on *Platinum: A Life in Music*, though it was recorded while Elvis called Bad Nauheim home, during his military service. Multiple versions are on bootleg album *Greetings From Germany*; one was released officially in 1999 on FTD release *In A Private Moment*.

ARDEN, TONI
(B. ANTOINETTE ARDIZZONE)

At his press conference before sailing for Germany in September 1958, Elvis announced that his favorite song was "Padre," by Toni Arden, known as "the little girl with the big voice." A major hit for her that year, Arden carried on recording into the Sixties. She started performing as a singer with big bands in the Forties, her own radio show in the Fifties, and appeared on many variety shows in the Fifties and Sixties. Arden covered Elvis' early Sun hit "I Forgot to Remember to Forget" in 1955.

"ARE YOU LONESOME TONIGHT?"

Recorded during an all-night session in Nashville in the early hours of April 4, 1960, this is generally credited as the only track Elvis ever recorded at the behest of Colonel Parker . . . it was Colonel Parker's wife Marie's favorite. To get the right feeling for the song, Elvis had the lights turned down low in Studio B, so low that according to engineer Bill Porter, at one stage he audibly knocks into the microphone stand.

When Elvis first heard the remastered version, he was furious that the volume of his voice had been raised to the detriment of the backing vocals, and threatened to re-record the whole thing.

Written by Lou Handman and Roy Turk, this Tin Pan Alley standard was first recorded by Vaughn Deleath in 1927, though before Elvis it was best known as a hit for Al Jolson. Elvis was likely more familiar with a 1950 version by Blue Baron and his orchestra.

The Elvis single sold more than two millions copies on release in November 1960, shooting up to #1 in the charts where it stayed for six weeks, backed with "I Gotta Know" on the B-side. It was a #1 in the UK for four weeks.

Elvis' version is not dissimilar to the version sung by the Blue Barron Orchestra in 1950. The voiced vocal is a loose adaptation of a Shakespeare passage from *As You Like It* (Jacques' "All the World's a Stage" soliloquy in Act II, Scene VII). Three of Elvis' unsuccessful Grammy nominations were for this song.

Elvis sang the song during the NBC TV Special recordings in June 1968. While not making it into the finished show, his performance appeared in 1974 on the *Elvis: A Legendary Performer Vol. 1* album.

A live version, recorded at the International Hotel in Las Vegas on August 26, 1969, features Elvis dissolving into uncontrollable laughter during Cissy Houston's soprano singing, supposedly because of something funny he spotted going on in the audience (though other versions of the tale are that he cracked up over a balding back up singer coming out on stage in a wig, or the singer tipping up his hairpiece after Elvis ad-libbed a humorous line about baldness). After circulating for years as a much-sought-after bootleg, Elvis' laughing version of this hit appeared on 1980 8-album collection *Elvis Aron Presley*, and was a top 40 hit in the UK two years later. The laughing version has also come out on *Elvis: A Legendary Performer Vol. 4*, *Collectors Gold* and more recently on FTD release *All Shook Up*. When he performed

the song live, which he only did a few dozen times during the Seventies, Elvis sometimes ad-libbed lines to keep the song fresh.

A laughter-free live version can be heard on *From Memphis To Vegas* (his first live performance in 9 years, as he reminds the audience, with Millie Kirkham warbling a harmony). The studio version first came out on LP *Elvis' Gold Records Vol. 3* and EP *Elvis By Request / Flaming Star EP*. It has since appeared on albums *Worldwide Gold Award Hits Vol. 1, A Golden Celebration, This Is Elvis, A Valentine Gift For You, From Nashville to Memphis, Platinum: A Life in Music, Artist Of The Century, ELVIS 30 #1 Hits, Hitstory, Love Elvis* and *The Essential Elvis Presley* among others.

Alternate studio versions from the original session have appeared on *Today, Tomorrow & Forever, Hitstory* and the 2005 FTD release of *Elvis Is Back!*

Dozens of live versions have been released over the years on official albums and countless others on bootlegs (some with a giggle or two). Live versions are on *Elvis In Person At The International Hotel, Elvis In Concert, Elvis Aron Presley* (live from 1961 and 1969), *A Golden Celebration, Collectors Gold, Memories: The '68 Comeback Special, Tiger Man, That's The Way It Is - Special Edition, Live In Las Vegas* and *The Live Greatest Hits*, and on FTD releases *Let Yourself Go* (from the NBC TV Special), *Elvis At The International, New Year's Eve*, and *Spring Tours '77*.

In the 1980s, UK playwright Alan Bleasdale wrote an Elvis stage show using this song as the show's title.

Elvis' "Are You Lonesome Tonight?" was inducted into the Grammy Hall of Fame in 2007.

"ARE YOU SINCERE"

Elvis rehearsed this Wayne Walker ballad, a #3 hit for Andy Williams in 1958, for Las Vegas in the summer of 1973. He recorded it in Palm Springs on September 23, 1973—in his pajamas—after RCA sent out a mobile studio to get his vocals.

The song appears on *Raised on Rock* and *Walk A Mile In My Shoes*, and was included on the 2006 *Elvis Country* compilation. Alternate takes without the backing vocals by Voice were later released officially on *Our Memories Of Elvis* and *Platinum: A Life In Music*. Further alternates are on the 2007 FTD *Raised On Rock* release.

The song was released as a posthumous single with B-side "Solitaire" in 1979, when it made it to #10 on the country chart.

Elvis in his signature Fringe Suit in Phoenix (9.9.70).

ARIZONA

- Apache Junction
Elvis spent time here in 1968 doing location shooting for *Charro!* (1969). In a fire that for the second time in its history destroyed almost the whole of Apacheland in 2004, the chapel where Elvis gets married in the movie was one of very few buildings to survive. At time of writing, there are plans to move the "Elvis Presley Memorial Chapel" to the nearby Superstition Mountain Museum.

- Phoenix
Elvis and the band played the State Fairgrounds Grandstand on June 9, 1956. He returned to the Coliseum with the TCB band on September 9, 1970. Elvis and the band returned to town at the start of his April 1973 tour, playing the Veterans Memorial Coliseum on April 22.

- Sedona
Location shooting on Elvis' 1968 movie *Stay Away, Joe* took place in Sedona, where Elvis was joined by five-month pregnant Priscilla and other entourage wives and girlfriends.

- Tempe
Elvis played the Arizona State University Activities Center at the start of his March 1977 tour (on March 23).

- Tucson
Elvis performed at the Rodeo Grounds on June 10, 1956. When he returned on November 9, 1972, he played the Community Center Arena. He last played the Community Center Arena on June 1, 1976 (released in 2000 on the FTD label).

ARKANSAS

- Aubrey
Elvis played the High School here on a bill with the Louvin Brothers on September 29, 1955.

- Augusta
Elvis played a show at the High School on February 2, 1955.

- Batesville
Elvis played the River Stadium at the 12th Annual White River Carnival on August 6, 1955, only to be accused of ruining the show and being unprofessional by promoter Ed Lyon.

- Bono

So many people thronged the High School Gym to see Elvis on September 6, 1955 that the floor gave way.

- Camden

On a Jamboree Attractions tour of the state, Elvis played the City Auditorium on February 21, 1955, and the Municipal Auditorium on August 4, 1955. Elvis returned to play two shows at the City Auditorium on November 16, 1955.

- Dermott

Elvis played Dermott High School on March 25, 1955 (entrance fee 50¢ for kids).

- El Dorado

Elvis played the High School Auditorium on March 30, 1955 and the Memorial Stadium on October 17, 1955.

- Forrest City

On September 5, 1955 Elvis headlined a bill with Johnny Cash, Bud Deckelman, Floyd Cramer and Eddie Bond at the St. Francis County Fair and Livestock Show Jamboree at the Smith Stadium. He was back at Forrest City High School Auditorium on November 14, 1955.

- Fort Chaffee

Elvis reported for his army service here in March 1958. From here, after receiving his regulation haircut in front of several dozen photographers, he traveled to his new station at Killeen, Texas.

- Helena

On December 2, 1954 Elvis played the Catholic Club in Helena with Jim Ed and Maxine Brown. Manager and DJ Bob Neal MC'd the night's entertainment. He played the club again on January 13, 1955, on March 8, 1955 and December 15, 1955.

- Hope

Elvis played Hope City Hall on February 22, 1955, and Hope Fair Park on May 5, 1955. After leaving this second show, his car caught fire en route to Texarkana.

- Jonesboro

Elvis played the Community Center on January 4, 1956, in a show sponsored by the Delta Beta Sigma Sorority.

- Leachville

Elvis played the Leachville High School Gym on January 20, 1955.

- Little Rock

Elvis and his band played the Robinson Auditorium on February 20, 1955, on a Jamboree Attractions tour on which he achieved, for the first time, top billing. He returned on August 3, 1955, on a four-day tour set up by Bob Neal towards the end of his tenure as Elvis' manager. Elvis and his band played the Robinson Memorial Auditorium on May 16, 1956 (portions of the concert are on 2000s boxed set *Today, Tomorrow & Forever*).

Elvis came through town in 1972, playing the T. H. Barton Coliseum on April 17.

- Marianna

Elvis played Futrell High School Gym most likely on January 14, 1955.

- Nettleton

Elvis played the High School in Nettleton in November 1954, in a show arranged by Bob Neal. Reportedly the entire audience numbered just 32.

- Newport

Elvis played the US Armory on March 2, 1955, and then squeezed in a 10 p.m. show at Porky's Rooftop Club that same night. He was back on July 21, 1955, at the Silver Moon Club, where he appeared again on October 24, 1955.

- Pine Bluff

Elvis took the High School Auditorium by storm on February 23, 1955. He passed through town on his way to play the Louisiana Hayride in December 1956, and stopped to have dinner with Jim Ed and Maxine Brown at the Trio restaurant.

- Swifton

A young Elvis played the High School with Johnny Cash on December 9, 1955, before doing a later show at the B&I Club.

- Texarkana

Elvis played one of his earliest gigs at the Municipal Auditorium here on November 24, 1954, with Tibby Edwards and Johnny Horton. He may also have played the Red River Arsenal nearby in the last few days of 1954. There is some uncertainty whether or not he was on the bill on May 20, 1955. He was late for his September 2, 1955 show at the Municipal Auditorium because of a car accident on the way, leaving local high school student Carl "Cheesie" Nelson to entertain the crowd. He gave two performances at the Municipal Auditorium on November 17, 1955, in a bill that featured Johnny Cash.

ARMSTRONG, LOUIS
(1901-1971)

Satchmo, short for "satchel-mouth" after his brass instrument blowing technique, was one of the jazz world's most famous voices and trumpet players and, like Elvis, a world-famous Southern boy from down the road in New Orleans. Armstrong's influence on development of jazz and mainstream music from the twenties onwards is without equal. Many of his recordings—"Wonderful World" for one—are as fresh today as when he laid the tracks down. His 1964 hit "Hello Dolly," recorded when he was 63, knocked The Beatles off the top of the US charts, and he remains the oldest recording artist to score a #1.

LOUIS ARMSTRONG IN 1957: "I'm definitely gonna do a record with him. You'd be surprised what we could do together. You ask me if I think he's good. How many Cadillacs was it he bought? That boy's no fool."

ARMY

Elvis' time in the Army was a watershed in his career. He'd had two years of national stardom—more than most performers could hope for—when he was faced with the stark reality of two years out of the public eye. Colonel Parker quickly recognized opportunity in adversity. Counseling Elvis to soldier rather than sing for the nation in Special Services as many other performers had done before in the past, he perceived Elvis' Army service as an excellent way to dispel the aura of scandal that had pervaded his boy's early career and take him into the mainstream.

Elvis went for his pre-induction checkup in early January 1957, before finding out his draft status. The Army beat the other armed forces to the huge publicity coup of drafting Elvis in part because they offered him a deferment that enabled him to complete shooting of his upcoming film for Paramount, *King Creole*.

Elvis is said to have made comments that he was hoping the draft would be repealed before it became his turn, but when the card came through the door, he was ready to do his duty. Jack Clement recalls that when Elvis stopped by at Sun Records to tell him, he seemed almost happy and relieved. However, fellow Sun artist Barbara Pittman recalls that he cried in her lap because of his upcoming

Greetings from Uncle Sam (Elvis holding his order to report for induction).

draft. Fans wrote in their thousands to the Pentagon and picketed recruitment offices to protest.

Elvis adopted the philosophy of keeping his head down and doing what he was told, just like any regular G.I. Joe. During his time in the Army he lived as close to a normal life as he ever would; on his one and only trip to Europe he made important new friends like Charlie Hodge and Joe Esposito, who were to remain in his entourage for the duration, and he met Priscilla there too.

Elvis reported for the draft on March 24, 1958, a day dubbed "Black Monday" for Elvis fans in the press. There was apparently a plan for a whole cohort of Elvis' pals to join the Army at the same time, so that they would all be sent off together. The plan failed when Lamar Fike, the only one who was prepared to carry it through, was told he needed to lose weight before he could enlist.

After four days of draft processing at Fort Chaffee, under sergeant Francis Johnson, Private Presley was transferred to Fort Hood, Killeen, Texas, home to General Patton's Second Armored Division ("Hell on Wheels"), where as he told Colonel Parker he enjoyed the "rough and tumble" of the obstacle course. He was much less upbeat in a letter to pal Alan Fortas, in which he lamented his homesickness and said he hated the training. Pal Eddie Fadal remembers Elvis distraught that his career would never survive his time in the Army. Instructor Bill Norwood recalls that when Elvis came to his house to call home, he would break down in tears. However, Elvis did enjoy certain privileges. For example, he could afford to slip fellow soldiers $10 to take his KP duty.

By the time he had completed basic training and was granted his first furlough in June 1958, Elvis had become a pistol sharpshooter and won a marksman's medal with a carbine. He was also acting assistant leader of his squad. Colonel Parker and Anita Wood picked up Elvis and two pals (Rex Mansfield and William "Nervous" Norvell) on May 31, 1958. He had time to go back to Memphis and fit in a recording session in Nashville and then it was back for his ten week Advanced Tank Training at Fort Hood in mid-June 1958. By now he had moved offbase into town, where he was joined by his Ma, Pa, Grandma Minnie Mae, and pal Lamar Fike, all of whom came down to try and cheer him up.

Colonel Parker was a regular visitor prior to Elvis' departure for Germany, reporting on his various negotiations, and trying to disabuse Elvis of his conviction that two years out of the limelight would be the end of him. Elvis repeatedly told pal Eddie Fadal, "It's all over . . . There's no way I can

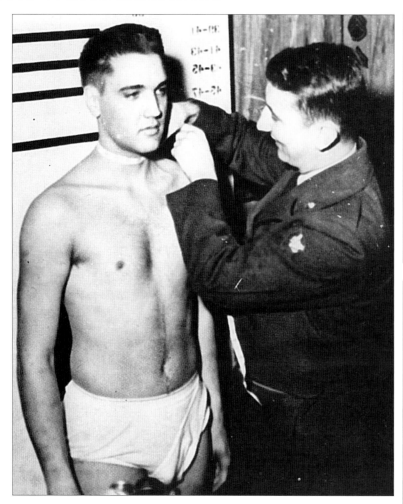

ABOVE: Elvis posing for army publicity photo. TOP, RIGHT: Elvis in uniform. CENTER: shining boots. BOTTOM RIGHT: posing for Army publicity photo.

come back and they're going to remember me."

Before the end of his tank training, Elvis had to seek emergency leave to visit his mother in hospital in Memphis. Permission was so slow coming that Elvis apparently threatened to go to Memphis with or without official consent to be at his dying mother's bedside. He arrived on August 12, 1958, several days after he had sent her back to Memphis to get treatment for her worsening health. His leave was extended to a total of 12 days after her death. It has been claimed that Elvis was offered a chance to cut short his stay in the Army after Gladys died but decided it was too important to serve his country.

A 1959 magazine cover highlighting Elvis Presley's time in the Army.

A couple of weeks after returning to his unit in Texas, Elvis was posted to the 3rd Armored Division (Spearhead) in Germany. The posting was not without at least the threat of danger, at a time when US defense analysts suspected that the Soviet Union was considering an invasion of nearby Hungary. Even without the Cold War threat, Germany in wintertime was anything but a soft posting.

Elvis left Fort Hood on September 19, 1958 for the Brooklyn Army Terminal in New York, and then before massed ranks of reporters and photographers at a Colonel-arranged press conference, walked up and down the gangplank onto the USS Randall, the ship taking him to Bremerhaven, Germany, more than half a dozen times with a borrowed duffel bag so that the photographers could get all the shots they wanted, while the band played a medley of Elvis hits including "Tutti Frutti." Despite the brave face, the party of friends who saw Elvis off from Fort Hood remember the day like a wake. On ship, Elvis took part in a show, playing piano in the band, but followed the Colonel's strict orders not to "debase your merchandise" by singing.

On arrival in Friedberg, Private Presley was once again offered a chance to join Special Services and give concerts. Once again he refused, expressing his desire to serve as a regular solider. He was assigned to the job of driving jeeps for the commanding officer of Company D, Captain Russell. However, in order to avoid perceptions of favoritism in driving an officer (and because the Captain was not best pleased with all the kafuffle that surrounded Elvis wherever he went), Elvis was reassigned to Reconnaissance Platoon Sergeant Ira Jones in Company C of the First Medium Tank Battalion of the 32nd Armor, under Lieutenant Taylor, stationed around 50 miles from the border with Communist East Germany, where Elvis served in the scout patrol unit. At the height of the Cold War, this was regarded as a combat soldier position.

Within a week of arrival, Elvis was allowed to live offbase at the Hilberts Park Hotel in Bad Nauheim, from where he commuted the 15 km to base early every morning. He was given this special dispensation because Vernon and Minnie Mae, his dependents, had joined him from the States. Soon they moved to more commodious surroundings at the Hotel Grunewald.

In November Elvis' company was sent to Grafenwöhr, close to the Czech border, for winter maneuvers, which included playing the role of aggressor to test tank battalion defenses. Later that month he received his promotion to private first class. Elvis returned to Bad Nauheim just before Christmas. Back home in the States, Colonel Parker had to field press questions about wild parties at Elvis' hotel, an image that did not fit with the gen-

Soldier Boy Elvis. A rarely seen photo of America's favorite G.I.

eral impression they were striving to convey.

Elvis, Vernon, Grandma Minnie Mae and his pals moved out of the staid Hotel Grunewald into a five-bedroom family home at 14 Goethestrasse in late January/early February 1959. Just like back in Memphis, Elvis' home was surrounded by a vigil of fans, and every evening he came out to chat and sign autographs. Also just like at home, Elvis had no shortage of potential girlfriends on hand. Elvis spent his three days leave in March 1959 traveling to Munich, where he met up with actress Vera Tschechowa and got some R&R at the local outpost of the Moulin Rouge. He even launched into "O Sole Mio" until a member of his entourage reminded him the Colonel did not want him singing in public for free.

Parker tried to shorten Elvis' exile by persuading the Army that Elvis would be more useful if he was brought back to the States to do recruiting work. Photos from this time show Elvis looking puffy and listless. His homesickness did not ease even after the "Over the Hump" party to celebrate passing the halfway mark of his Army term.

Bob Hope inquired whether Elvis would be willing to join his Christmas tour of the troops. Elvis felt he had to say no, because the Colonel did not want him playing for free.

In June 1959, Elvis was promoted to Specialist 4th Class. He celebrated with a two-week break: a couple of days in Munich looking up old (girl) friends, and then the best part of two weeks enjoying the delights of Paris with pals Lamar Fike, Charlie Hodge and Rex Mansfield. According to Charlie Hodge, in Germany Elvis turned down a trip out of the cold back to Miami because he didn't want to be treated differently to his fellow soldiers. In September, Elvis made the acquaintance of a very pretty, very young woman called Priscilla Beaulieu.

In October 1959, Elvis and his unit took part in the so-called "Big Lift" maneuvers at Wildflecken, just over the border from Switzerland. Soon afterwards, Elvis was readmitted to hospital for another bout of tonsillitis. The next time he was due leave, in January 1960, he traveled to Paris with pals Joe Esposito, Lamar Fike, Cliff Gleaves and new addition, karate instructor Jürgen Seydel. On his return he was promoted to acting sergeant, and then left on "Operation Winter Shield" maneuvers. He received his full promotion to sergeant soon after his return to base.

At the Army press conference called on the eve of Elvis' return from Germany to the US, his commanding officer awarded him a certificate of merit and praised his "cheerfulness and drive and continually outstanding leadership ability."

Elvis flew out of Germany on March 2, 1960, right into a snowstorm at McGuire Air Force base near Fort Dix, New Jersey, where the Army put on a welcoming party attended by Colonel Parker, Nancy Sinatra, Jean Aberbach and RCA personnel. Elvis was officially discharged two days later. He returned home by train with members of his entourage, the Colonel and Tom Diskin, waving to the many fans who gathered at stations along the way, in a dress uniform that sported an extra, unearned stripe added by mistake by a German tailor. He completed his military service with a full discharge in 1964 after serving as a standby reserve based in Memphis.

For his time in the Army, Elvis received a Good Conduct Medal and the 3rd Armored Division Certificate of Achievement for Faithful and Efficient Performance of Duty.

Friends noticed that the Elvis who returned from the Army was more mature and far keener to take care of business. George Klein noted, "He had a little harder side at first, but then he softened up . . . He had that Army hardness to him but it disappeared after a while, and he became Elvis again."

Elvis in Germany. This great candid captures Elvis in Germany during his two-year military obligation. Elvis wanted to be treated like any other soldier and in doing so he proved just how special he really was.

In 1970 Elvis' favorite movie was World War Two epic Patton, for which George C. Scott won an Oscar. Whether it was because he could identify with the tank commander, or it was the similarity in his own life as a leader of his immediate entourage and a man destined for greatness, Elvis watched this movie time and time again, learning the opening speech by heart.

ELVIS SAID IN 1958: "The army can do anything it wants with me. Millions of other guys have been drafted, and I don't want to be different from anyone else."

ELVIS SAID IN 1960: "People were expecting me to mess up, to goof up. They thought I couldn't take it, and I was determined to go to any limits to prove otherwise."

ELVIS SAID IN 1960: "The biggest thing of all was the fact that I did make it. I tried to play it straight like everybody else. I made a lot of friends that I would never have made otherwise. All in all it's been a pretty good experience."

WILLIAM J. TAYLOR: "I simply cannot forget that Elvis chose to serve in a combat unit. If others want to argue that he did so because his agent, Colonel Tom Parker, thought it would be good for public relations purposes, that's their opinion. But I don't believe it."

KEITH GIBSON (FELLOW PLATOON MEMBER): "I told Elvis I admired him for not getting into Special Services but staying a regular soldier and getting in the mud and the snow just like everybody else did. He asked for no favors and got none."

SERGEANT IRA JONES: "If I had to rate Elvis as a soldier, I'd rate him very high—the highest. He really knew the basics, and they say he'd done well in basic training at Fort Hood—caught on fast."

LAMAR FIKE: "The time in Germany was kind of a reprieve of sorts for Elvis. He just did his job, and that's all he really wanted to do. It was a two-year relief, really."

SENATOR ESTES KEFAUVER, TENNESSEE, MARCH 1960: "To his great credit this young American became just another G.I. Joe . . . I for one would like to say to him yours was a job well done, Solider." (Elvis carried a newspaper clipping of this speech in his wallet to his dying day).

LAMAR FIKE: "After the service, the biggest change, other than becoming harder, was that he became much more what people thought he should be."

Books:
Operation Elvis, by Alan Levy, Holt, 1960.
Soldier Boy Elvis, by Ira Jones, Propwash Publishing, 1992.
Private Presley: Elvis in Germany — the Missing Years, by Andreas Shroer, Oskar Hentschell, Michael Knorr and W.A. Harbinson, Boxtree Press, 1993 (republished as A Date With Elvis, Army Days Revisited in 2004.
Elvis in the Army: The King of Rock 'n' Roll As Seen by an Officer Who Served with Him, by Col. William J. Taylor Jr., Presidio Press, 1995.
Sergeant Presley—Our Untold Story Of Elvis' Missing Years, by Rex and Elisabeth Mansfield, ECW Press, 2002.
Sergeant Elvis Presley In Grafenwöhr, by Peter Heigl, Buch und Kunstverlag, 2007.

ARNOLD, EDDY
(B. RICHARD EDWARD ARNOLD, MAY 15, 1918)

Elvis liked listening to this smooth-voiced Southern gentleman country in his early teen years. One of the best-selling country artists of all time with 28 country #1 hits, "Eddy Arnold, known as the Tennessee Plowboy," was inducted into the Country Hall of Fame in 1966 after doing as much as anyone to take country music into the mainstream.

Arnold had a solo artist slot at the Grand Ole Opry from 1943. After he hired Colonel Tom Parker as his manager in 1945 (biographers have provided a spread of dates from 1942 to 1948 for this step up in the Colonel's career) he returned to the top of the country charts—"I'll Hold You in My Heart" was the best-selling single of the Forties—and forged a career in the new medium of television, becoming the first country star to host his own show. Arnold's success for RCA under the Colonel's tutelage is something Elvis will have been aware of when it was time to pick a new manager to take him national.

Elvis first met The Jordanaires backstage at an Eddy Arnold show in Memphis in 1954. Arnold was photographed with RCA executive Steve Sholes, Elvis and Colonel Parker at the time Elvis signed for the label.

After a fallow period from the mid-Fifties when rock'n'rollers like the Colonel's new boy had the run of the record charts, Arnold enjoyed a resurgence in the Sixties as more of a love song crooner.

Elvis covered quite a number of Eddy Arnold songs, including "How's The World Treating You" in 1956, "It's A Sin" in 1961, "You Don't Know Me" and "Just Call Me Lonesome" in 1967, "After Loving You" and "I'll Hold You In My Heart" in 1969, and "I Really Don't Want to Know" in 1970.

Arnold carried on performing well into his Seventies. He has released more than a hundred albums and sold in excess of 85 million records.

ALANNA NASH: "Nearly every major career move [the Colonel] guided for Arnold—a string of chart-topping records, the judicious use of early television, a foray into Hollywood movies, and even engagements in Las Vegas—served as a blueprint for Parker's plan with Elvis."

ART

The vast majority of art work Elvis has inspired over the years is by his adoring fans. Betty Harper, to name but one, has produced hundreds of Elvis portraits in charcoal, out of a total of more than 10,000 Elvis portraits to date.

Andy Warhol couldn't resist making prints of such an American Icon. He chose an image of Elvis Presley in cowboy getup, pistol pointed, taken from 1960 movie Flaming Star, to create single, double and multiple Elvii—he also shot a film, Elvis at Ferus, to document one show. Recently, Warhol's Silver and Red Elvises were part of the rights sold by the Warhol Foundation to Levi Strauss for use in a high-end denim collection.

Howard Finster, Elaine Goodman, Joni Mabe, Chris Rywalt, Danny Williams and Kata Billups have all used Elvis in their work. British artist Peter Blake used Elvis in his alphabet under "K for King."

In 1994, headline contributors Robert Arneson, Keith Haring, Edward Ruscha and Andy Warhol were some of the 108 artists who exhibited in the traveling show "Elvis + Marilyn: 2 x Immortal," a hit all over the world.

Not all Elvis exhibitions have gone off so smoothly. Fan protests in 1997 forced the removal of exhibits considered offensive to religious sensibilities from the "Elvis 20/20: Past and Future" show.

In 2002, artist Russell Young added a mug shot of Elvis to his collection from his "Pig Portraits" series.

A quirky 14x9 foot portrait of Elvis made out of 2,646 post-it notes made the news in 2005, designed by two creatives at a North Carolina public relations and marketing agency. Jeff Koons titled some of his 2007 paintings "Triple Elvis" and "Hulk Elvis."

Traditional Mexican velvet artists have had a very profitable line in Velvet Elvis pictures, despite objections from EPE. Elvis portraits are favored items for many collectors, and have been known to fetch large sums at auctions of Elvis memorabilia.

Elvis statues are to be found in Tupelo, Memphis, Las Vegas, Shreveport and Hawaii, and also in London, Bad Nauheim, Tokyo and Israel.

Like many performers, Elvis collected art by William Verdult.

An Elvis Presley International Art Show was one of the centerpieces of the 30th anniversary commemoration of Elvis' death in 2007. The "Living Elvis" exhibition ran in Melbourne, Australia, in 2007.

JONI MABE: "There's something so mysterious about him that I can't figure out . . . he's such a contradiction of himself all the time."

Books:

Elvis in Art, compiled by Roger G. Taylor, Elm Tree Books/Hamish Hamilton Ltd, 1987.

Elvis Is Everywhere, by Mark Pollard and Rowland Scherman, Clarkson Potter, 1991.

Elvis + Marilyn: 2 x Immortal exhibition catalog, ed. Geri DePaoli, Rizzoli International, 1994.

Everything Elvis, by Joni Mabe, Thunder's Mouth Press, 1996.

Elvis: The Record Covers of the King, by Paul Dowling, St Martin's Press, 1994.

Images of Elvis Presley in American Culture, 1977-1997: The Mystery Terrain by George Plasketes, Haworth, 1997 (on Elvis' iconographic influence post-death).

Elvis & Presley, by Robert Huber and Stephan Vanfleteren, Kruse Verlag, 2001.

The King, by Jim Piazza, Black Dog & Leventhal, 2005.

"ARTHUR GODFREY'S TALENT SCOUTS"

Cleveland Ohio DJ Bill Randle of WERE radio suggested to Elvis manager Bob Neal that an appearance on this radio and TV show would be the perfect springboard for Elvis' burgeoning reputation to spread nationwide, after Elvis played a live show in Cleveland, Ohio in February 1955. Elvis was undoubtedly aware of the show: one of his favorite gospel combos, the Blackwoods, featured and won the previous year.

In the meantime, Colonel Tom Parker contacted Harry Kalcheim at the William Morris Agency to arrange an audition for Elvis on March 23, 1955. Under the terms of the audition, if Elvis won, he would appear on Godfrey's morning TV show over the following three weeks.

In the 1950s, Arthur Godfrey (1903-1983) was arguably the biggest star on TV, with two top-ten prime time TV shows on CBS as television was becoming a mass medium. "Arthur Godfrey's Talent Scouts" was a live show that ran simultaneously on radio and TV from 1948 to 1958, and was just one of several TV shows he hosted at the time. The format was that various "scouts" presented their discoveries, and then the audience voted for their favorite via an "applause meter."

Hopefuls who got their big break on the show included Pat Boone, Tony Bennett, The Chordettes, Pasty Cline, The McGuire Sisters, Marilyn Horne and Carmel Quinn. Elvis' audition was a resounding failure, the last false step on his otherwise unstoppable march to stardom. In later years, he could commiserate with pals

Charlie Hodge and the Jordanaires, who won the show respectively in 1954 (with the Foggy Bottom Boys) and 1956.

ARTIST OF THE CENTURY

A 1999 3-CD compilation combining most of Elvis' hits with rarer material and a comprehensive information booklet

TRACK LISTING:
1. That's All Right
2. Good Rockin' Tonight
3. Baby Let's Play House
4. Mystery Train
5. Tryin' To Get To You
6. Heartbreak Hotel
7. Blue Suede Shoes
8. My Baby Left Me
9. Lawdy, Miss Clawdy
10. Hound Dog
11. Any Way You Want Me (That's How I Will Be)
12. Don't Be Cruel
13. Love Me Tender
14. Love Me
15. Anyplace Is Paradise
16. All Shook Up
17. Got A Lot O' Livin' To Do!
18. (Let Me Be Your) Teddy Bear
19. One Night
20. Jailhouse Rock
21. (You're So Square) Baby I Don't Care
22. Treat Me Nice
23. Don't
24. Santa Claus Is Back In Town
25. Trouble
26. Hard Headed Woman
27. Wear My Ring Around Your Neck
28. A Big Hunk O' Love
29. (Now And Then There's) A Fool Such As I

DISC: 2
1. Stuck On You
2. It's Now Or Never
3. Are You Lonesome Tonight?
4. A Mess Of Blues
5. Like A Baby
6. The Girl Of My Best Friend
7. Such A Night
8. Reconsider Baby
9. Surrender
10. Can't Help Falling In Love
11. That's Someone You Never Forget
12. Little Sister
13. (Marie's The Name) His Latest Flame
14. Anything That's Part Of You
15. Good Luck Charm
16. She's Not You
17. Return To Sender
18. (You're The) Devil In Disguise
19. Memphis Tennessee
20. It Hurts Me
21. Down In The Alley
22. Run On
23. Tomorrow Is A Long Time
24. Big Boss Man
25. Guitar Man
26. Tiger Man

DISC: 3
1. If I Can Dream
2. In The Ghetto
3. Suspicious Minds
4. Don't Cry, Daddy
5. I'll Hold You In My Heart
6. Stranger In My Own Home Town
7. After Loving You
8. Only The Strong Survive
9. The Wonder Of You
10. Polk Salad Annie
11. I've Lost You

12. You Don't Have To Say You Love Me
13. I Just Can't Help Believin'
14. Merry Christmas Baby
15. I'm Leavin'
16. An American Trilogy
17. Burning Love
18. Always On My Mind
19. Promised Land
20. For The Heart

"AS LONG AS I HAVE YOU"

A Fred Wise / Ben Weisman weepie recorded during the *King Creole* sessions at Radio Recorders on January 16, 1958 and released initially on volume one of the film EP and LP. It later came out on *Worldwide Gold Award Hits Vol. 2*.

The shorter version of the song used in the movie first saw release on *Essential Elvis Vol. 3* in 1991, which also includes the vinyl version. The twin versions are also on *The King Of Rock And Roll* anthology and on the 1997 *King Creole* reissue.

"AS WE TRAVEL ALONG THE JERICHO ROAD"

Elvis sang this song during *The Million Dollar Session* on December 4, 1956, until he ran out of words. The traditional gospel song, notably sung by Don and Marguerete McCrossman, is sometimes listed as "On The Jericho Road." It has since appeared on *The Complete Million Dollar Quartet* and *Peace In The Valley—The Complete Gospel Recordings*.

"ASK ME"

In the original Italian version, "Io," this song was Domenico Modugno's follow-up hit to "Volare." The English lyrics were crafted by Giant, Baum and Kaye. Elvis' first recording, on May 27, 1963, didn't satisfy him. His second stab at the song, on January 12, 1964, worked a dream, so much so that "Ask Me" supplanted his cover of Chuck Berry's "Memphis, Tennessee" in RCA's plans for the next single release, in September 1964 with B-side "Ain't That Loving You Baby" (recorded way back in 1958). "Ask Me" sold in sufficient numbers to make it to #12 in the charts, higher than any Elvis single for some time, selling 700,000 copies on initial release. In error, the French pressing of the single had only one of the stereo channels—fortunately the one with Elvis' voice.

The song later appeared on *Elvis' Gold Records Vol. 4* and *Worldwide Gold Award Hits Vol. 2*. It has since been released on *For The Asking (The Lost Album)*, and in a remastered version on *From Nashville to Memphis* and *Hitstory*.

The May 1963 version appeared many years later on *Collectors Gold*. Alternate takes from the 1964 session have appeared on box sets *Today Tomorrow & Forever, Elvis: Close Up* and FTD release *Studio B: Nashville Outtakes*.

ASNER, EDWARD
(B. 1929)

Best known for his long-running TV roles in "Mary Tyler Moore" and "Lou Grant" and still a hard-working actor, Asner landed one of his first ever movie roles in *Kid Galahad* in 1962. He also worked with Elvis in 1969 movie *Change of Habit*, co-starring Mary Tyler Moore, a year before he and MTM teamed up in her top TV show. He has won 7 Emmy and 5 Golden Globe awards, and in 2002 was given the Screen Actors Guild Life Achievement award.

ASSASSINATION ATTEMPTS

In his early career Elvis handled threats and episodes of violence from jealous boyfriends and husbands who wanted to get at him for turning their girls into baying, screaming slaves to his sex appeal.

Aside from this braggadocio, Elvis was the target of a number of bona fide death threats, including one during his Army service in Germany, when a Red Army soldier was reputedly planning to kill him.

Marty Lacker traces Elvis' obsession with guns to the Kennedy assassination, which filled Elvis with rage and fear for his own safety; it was at this time that he reputedly first told members of his entourage that if anybody assassinated him, he wanted the assassin killed before he had the chance to gloat.

In 1970, an anonymous source threatened to kill him while he performed at the International Hotel in Las Vegas. Extra security was put on by the hotel, and Elvis called in members of his entourage from far and wide to beef up the ring of protection around him. He made doubly sure that nothing would happen that night by performing with a pair of pistols in the boots. Bodyguard Sonny West recalls that after they event, they realized it was an extortion attempt, but at the time they took it deadly serious.

Threats to Elvis' life were telephoned in prior to concerts on other occasions too, including his record-breaking show at Pontiac, Michigan, on New Year's Eve 1975.

Elvis was shaken by the major political assassinations of the Sixties. The slaying in 1968 of Martin Luther King in Elvis' hometown and of Robert Kennedy in Los Angeles was one of the reasons why, unusually, he chose to close his NBC TV special with the powerful message song "If I Can Dream."

ASSEMBLY OF GOD CHURCH

See FIRST ASSEMBLY OF GOD

ASTROLOGY

Elvis was born at 4:35 a.m. on January 8, 1935, under the sign of Capricorn, with the moon in Pisces, indicative of a psychic temperament.

Capricorns are typically ambitious, perfectionists who persevere at what they're good at.

In Chinese astrology, Elvis was a dog.

In the mid-Sixties, as Elvis became increasingly interested in the esoteric and spiritual, Larry Geller had charts drawn up for Elvis and members of Elvis' family. One chart and commentary written for Elvis in 1965 pinpointed 1972 as a pivotal year, and suggested that he was "open to inspiration and inner guidance and a channel for the fulfillment of a social human need."

Jerry Hopkins' 1971 biography of Elvis featured an astrological chart and analysis. A number of astrology websites do likewise.

Elvis was particularly fond of astrology work *New Mansions for New Men*, written by Dane Rudhyar, and was known to own quite a number of prophecy books, including *My Life and Prophecies* by Jeane Dixon.

Books:
Elvis Aron Presley's Astrological Horoscope and Psychological Profile, Elvis Collectable Ltd., 1994

"AT THE HOP"

Though never officially released, a home recording of Elvis singing this 1957 Danny and the Juniors hit during his time in Germany has appeared on bootleg recordings including *Greetings From Germany*.

ATKINS, CHET
(B. CHESTER BURTON "CHET" ATKINS, 1924-2001)

Born in Tennessee, Atkins was a virtuoso country guitarist who for many years worked as a top producer for RCA in Nashville with acts ranging from Eddy Arnold to Jim Reeves, Connie Smith and Waylon Jennings.

RCA executive Steve Sholes signed Atkins to the label in 1947. He crossed over from one side of the studio to the other to become am RCA producer in the early Fifties.

In January 1956, Atkins was put in charge of Elvis' first recording session for his new label, and played on the session as well. Elvis and Atkins had already met; Elvis introduced himself to the famous guitarist backstage at the Grand Ole Opry in 1954. Though Atkins helped the band focus on their material, Elvis felt much less at ease with him than he had done with Sam Phillips at Sun. In consequence, Elvis recorded the bulk of his Fifties material for RCA in Los Angeles, with the exception of a session in New York in 1956 and another slipped in while on leave from the Army in June 1958, on which Atkins played guitar.

Atkins produced Elvis when he returned to Nashville to record in the Sixties, right up to 1966 when he handed over production duties to Felton Jarvis, who was more of a night owl and developed a lasting friendship with Elvis. Marty Lacker has suggested that Elvis decided he no longer wanted Chet Atkins working on his sessions after he caught him napping over the soundboard during a take.

Atkins was known for his finger-picking guitar style that became so popular he picked up the nickname "Mr. Guitar." He was a major influence in creating the "Nashville sound," which was a direct response to the flight of C&W fans to rock and roll. Together with Owen Bradley he developed a new style eschewing fiddles and steel guitar which restored the popularity of country music and led to a string of crossover hits that continues to this day.

In the Sixties, Atkins became vice president of RCA's country division, where he signed the first black Country singer, Charley Pride (who, incidentally, Elvis greeted from a Las Vegas stage in 1971, singing a line from his recent hit "The Easy Part's Over").

Atkins was the youngest ever inductee into the Country Hall of Fame, received 14 Grammy Awards and 9 Country Music Association Instrumentalist of the Year awards, and was named by Guitar Player Magazine as the most influential stylist.

CHET ATKINS: "He was the first to start the thing about rhythm . . . He was electrifying . . . I don't think there will ever be another like him."

CHET ATKINS: "Years from now, after I'm gone someone will listen to what I've done and know I was here. They may not know or care who I was, but they'll hear my guitars speaking for me."

"AUBREY"

Elvis did a version of this Bread hit in concert in September 1974, talking the words while his backing group Voice did the singing. It has never appeared on an official CD, though it is on bootleg *Desert Storm*.

"AULD LANG SYNE"

Elvis sang this traditional Scottish song (an old melody with words written by Robbie Burns, the title roughly translatable as "times gone by") at his Pittsburgh New Year's Eve concert on December 31, 1976. It appears on a number of bootlegs and FTD album *New Year's Eve*. The song is sometimes most aptly referred to as "the song that nobody knows"; the vast majority of people who sing it only know a line or two.

AUSBORN, CARVEL LEE "SLIM"
(B. 1926)

"Mississippi Slim., as he was better known, was the warm-up act for the Saturday WELO Jamboree talent show in Tupelo. Nine years older than Elvis, Ausborn also grew up in East Tupelo. Elvis used to ride up with this local celebrity to the radio station and watch him do his Saturday show "Singin' and Pickin' Hillbilly." Ausborn encouraged Elvis to stick with the guitar. He also taught Elvis chords after he got his first guitar. In some tellings of Elvis' childhood, Slim got Elvis onto the amateur hour slot too. He later went on to perform at the Grand Ole Opry.

Elvis' best friend at junior high school was James Ausborn, Carvel Ausborn's younger brother.

AUSTRALIA

Elvis' popularity in Australia has matched that of any other English-speaking country. The closest Elvis ever came to touring down under was when Elvis—The Concert traveled through in the 2000s.

Australia gave Elvis a wallaby in 1957. That year there were plans to take Elvis on tour to Australia just before and just after his time in the Army, inevitably stonewalled by the Colonel. Another offer, this one for $1 million, was turned down in 1974.

Australia has one of the world's most active Elvis fan club scenes; since the early Nineties the town of Parkes in NSW has been holding an Elvis festival to mark Elvis' birthday that draws up to 5,000 people.

AUTRY, GENE
(B. ORVON GENE AUTRY, 1907-1998)

"The Singing Cowboy" was America's archetypical Western balladeer in the Thirties. Autry began on radio, became a recording sensation, and launched into the movies with trusty steed Champion, becoming Hollywood's number one Western actor by the beginning of the Second World War. After the war, Roy Rogers gradually cornered the market for singing cowboys. Autry had his own TV show in the early Fifties, as Elvis was just starting out.

As a kid, Autry was one of Elvis' favorite Hollywood stars. Elvis never recorded Autry's biggest-selling record, "Rudolph The Red-Nosed Reindeer," but he did record a number of songs that had been a hit for Autry, including "Here Comes Santa Claus," "Blueberry Hill," "Frankie And Johnny," I'll Never Let You Go (Little Darlin')," "The Yellow Rose of Texas" and "Blue Hawaii."

"AVE MARIA"

This Johann Sebastian Bach melody, married to text from Luke 1:28, made it into a medley arrangement with "I Got A Woman" that Elvis performed in Las Vegas in the summer of 1970, and on a select few occasions up to 1972. It is on *The Hillbilly Cat Live* bootleg.

AWARDS

Arguably, no more popular entertainer has received less industry recognition than Elvis. Luckily for Elvis and his heirs, popularity and longevity are a function of the reaction of fans rather than industry peers.

From when he first became nationally-famous to when he went into the Army, Elvis won just about every popularity and record sales award going between 1956 and 1958. Even out of the limelight doing his Army service in Germany, he still topped the American Bandstand Popularity Poll for Favorite Male Vocalist and Favorite Record of 1958.

- Academy Awards

If Elvis had one unfulfilled ambition it was to reach the highest echelons of the acting profession. Colonel Parker may have had an unerring eye for making money, but over the years he turned down at least half a dozen movie projects that went on to garner Oscars, sometimes for the actors who took on roles originally offered to Elvis (see MOVIES ELVIS CONSIDERED OR WANTED).

The closest Elvis got to an Oscar was for *Roustabout* song "It's A Wonderful World," which was under consideration for a Best Song nomination.

- Grammy

Though nominated fourteen times, Elvis won just three Grammys, all for his gospel and spiritual songs. His first award, surprisingly, was 13 years into his singing career: the 1967 "Best Sacred Performance" award for his gospel album *How Great Thou Art*. He took the 1974 Grammy for "Best Inspirational Performance" with the live recording of "How Great Thou Art," released that year on the *Elvis Recorded Live On Stage in Memphis* LP, and also won for 1972 gospel album *He Touched Me*. Elvis did, however, receive a Grammy Lifetime Achievement award in 1971 (See NARAS, BELOW).

- Jaycee

In January 1971 Elvis picked up a Junior Chamber of Commerce Award as one of America's Ten Outstanding Young Men of the Year. His nomination was sponsored by pal and former Shelby County Sheriff Bill Morris. Fellow

A candid shot of Elvis with two awards he received in the 1960's.

honorees that year, all of whom were under 35, included the Boston civil rights activist Tom Atkins, Ronald Reagan's press secretary Ron Ziegler, and biophysicist Dr. Mario Capecchi.

Elvis remained very proud of this award, the only accolade he accepted at a public ceremony. Past winners included Orson Welles, John F. Kennedy, Howard Hughes, Reverend Jesse Jackson and Henry Kissinger.

The January 15, 1971 awards ceremony included a prayer breakfast, a press conference, a luncheon and then an 8 p.m. awards ceremony. Elvis and Priscilla attended them all, and threw their own Graceland reception for fellow award winners and Jaycee personnel, including a formal dinner.

At the Awards ceremony, held at the Ellis Auditorium in Memphis where Elvis had sung as a young man, Elvis made a speech that he agonized over for a long time: "When I was a child, ladies and gentlemen, I was a dreamer. I read comic books, and I was the hero of the comic book. I saw movies, and I was the hero in the movie. So every dream that I've dreamed has come true a hundred times.." A portion of the speech concludes 1997 commemorative box set *Platinum: A Life in Music*.

As with all of the achievements he held in highest esteem, the Jaycee award became something of a treasured talisman which Elvis took along with him wherever he traveled.

- NARAS *Lifetime Achievement*

In August 1971, Elvis was presented with a lifetime achievement award by Gene Merlino, Bill Cole and Chris Crosby, representing the National Academy of Recording Arts and Sciences (at the time the accolade was known as the Bing Crosby Award) "in recognition of his artistic creativity and his influence."

Only five music greats had won the award before Elvis: Bing Crosby, Frank Sinatra, Duke Ellington, Ella Fitzgerald and Irving Berlin.

Founded in 1957, NARAS is the music industry organization best known for holding the Grammy Awards.

- Other

In December 1956, Elvis was given the honorary title of "Louisiana Colonel" (the same honorific as Mr. Parker) by Louisiana Governor Earl K. Long.

In March 1961, Elvis was awarded a Tennessee Colonelship at the Tennessee State Legislature in Nashville. That same month he received the USS Arizona Award of Honor for his charity benefit concert to help fund a monument to the sunken battleship.

Elvis' one and only movie award was a Golden Laurel Award (for a male musical performance) in 1965 movie *Tickle Me*. He also won a Laurel Award second prize for *Girls! Girls! Girls!* and a third prize for *Viva Las Vegas* in the same category.

After the NBC TV Special, Elvis was named "Outstanding Male Singer" of the year by the *New Musical Express*.

After completing his third, attendance-record-smashing residency in Las Vegas in September 1970, the International Hotel presented Elvis with an unofficial but much appreciated award: a boxing champion-style gold belt encrusted with diamonds, declaring him to be an attendance champ. Elvis proudly wore the belt in public and private thereafter.

Elvis' haul of unofficial accolades include the countless polls that acknowledge him as the single

most important musician of the Twentieth century. In the Eighties, the Smithsonian Institute named Elvis as the most significant single influence on American music throughout history.

The 1972 *Elvis On Tour* concert movie won the Golden Globe for Best Documentary that year, the only one of his movies to win a top-tier award.

On stage during his infamous "rambling monologue" shows in the summer of 1974, Elvis read out a special lifetime membership award that he had been given by the International Narcotics Enforcement Officers Association. This was just one of many police badges—honorary and standard-issue—that he acquired during the Seventies.

Two months before he died, *Photoplay* magazine gave Elvis its Favorite Variety Star and Favorite Rock Music Star awards.

Elvis' minimal haul of movie awards includes the dubious distinction of Harvard Lampoon's "Worst Supporting Actor" award for *Love Me Tender* in 1956, and a "Sour Apple" award for "least co-operative actor" in 1966 (Bill Cosby took the most cooperative gong that year, but then he had better material).

Elvis received the W. C. Handy Award in 1984 from the Blues Foundation in Memphis for "keeping the blues alive" in his music.

Elvis is the only performing artist who has been inducted into the Rock 'n' Roll, Country and Gospel Halls of Fame.

To this day, he continues to top polls of entertainment legends and music industry figures.

AXTON, MAE BOREN
(1914-1997)

Axton's multi-talented life is best remembered, at least by Elvis fans, for her work co-writing Elvis' first single on RCA, "Heartbreak Hotel," though she had many other strings to her bow.

Originally from a well-known oil family, Mae worked for Bob Neal and then Colonel Parker as a publicist during Elvis' May and July 1955 tours of Florida. As is so often the case with Elvis' early years, there is debate about how much of a role she played in helping Elvis cement his career; it has been claimed that she actively got Elvis onto the Hank Snow tour of Florida, after Elvis' original manager Bob Neal asked her to intercede in order to prove to Elvis that he could manage his career just as well as Colonel Tom Parker. However, Snow's (and Axton's) close links with Parker at the time would indicate otherwise.

Axton met and greeted Elvis and his band when they arrived in Jacksonville in May 1955, finding him to be a paragon of politeness. That night, Elvis had his pink suit ripped off him by rioting female fans.

Axton held down a regular job as an English teacher at the High School in Jacksonville—where her husband worked too—as well as occasionally hosting radio and TV slots. On July 28, 1955 Mae interviewed Elvis in Jacksonville. On November 10, 1955, she caught up with Elvis at the Country Music Disc Jockey Convention in Nashville and played him the demo of "Heartbreak Hotel," which she had recently co-written with Tommy Durden—one of almost 200 songs she wrote.

Axton went to Miami in the spring of 1960 at the Colonel's invitation to attend the rehearsals and filming of Elvis' homecoming appearance on the "Frank Sinatra Show." She remained friends with the Presley family ever after.

Axton's son, Hoyt Wayne, had a successful acting career as well as writing songs, including "Never Been to Spain," which Elvis added to his live act in 1972.

"BABY I DON'T CARE"

Elvis recorded this Leiber/Stoller track on May 3, 1957 for *Jailhouse Rock* and the EP of the same name, after the instrumental track been laid down previously at Radio Recorders. On this song, Elvis made his recording debut on bass.

The song has since come out on *Worldwide Gold Award Hits, Vol. 2*, *I Was The One*, *Elvis Sings Leiber & Stoller*, *Essential Elvis Vol. 1*, *The King Of Rock 'n' Roll*, the 1997 *Jailhouse Rock* CD, *Artist Of The Century*,

Alternate versions of the song have appeared on *A Date with Elvis* (1959), *Out in Hollywood* (1999) and *Elvis: Close Up* (2003).

"BABY, IF YOU'LL GIVE ME ALL OF YOUR LOVE"

Joy Byers wrote this proposition of a song for Elvis to sing in *Double Trouble* at Radio Recorders on June 29, 1966.

Later releases are limited to *Maholo From Elvis* and the *Double Features* issue for *Double Trouble* (paired with *Spinout*). Alternate takes lurk on the 2004 FTD release for the movie.

"BABY LET'S PLAY HOUSE"

Recorded at Sun Studio in the first week of February 1955 and released on April 10, 1955 with "I'm Left, You're Right, She's Gone" as a B-side, this song was Elvis' fourth single: Sun 217.

The song was originally recorded by its author, Arthur Gunter, a year earlier, though the edgy, syncopated intro was all Elvis' doing. Gunter's bluesy song was, itself, based on Eddy Arnold earlier country #1, "I Want To Play House With You." A live version of this song was also released on August 20, 1955.

Elvis played this song on February 4, 1956 on his first national TV showcase, the Dorsey Brothers' "Stage Show."

Music critics cite this track as the apogee of everything Elvis and Sam Phillips achieved at Sun. When the single came out it spawned dozens of copycat attempts, but the biggest challenge it had across the South was from DJs pitting one side of this single against the other to see which one came out top in the charts. "Baby Let's Play House" was Elvis' first single to make it onto a *Billboard* chart, climbing to #10 on the Country chart. A number of other rock 'n' rollers made covers of the song, none quite rivaling the energy in Elvis' version, in which he ad libs a "pink Cadillac" for "religion" in Gunter's original's lyric "You may get religion but don't you be nobody's fool."

Elvis could not fail to reprise the song when he returned to live performing in the Seventies—there's even a rumor that he ran through the song with a view to including it in his 1968 NBC Comeback Special. *Platinum: A Life In Music* (1997) features a rehearsal in the run-up to his Las Vegas engagement filmed for *That's The Way It Is* in 1970. After its initial 1959 album release on *A Date with Elvis*, various recordings of the track have come out on a great many official albums and bootlegs, including *I Was The One*, *A Golden Celebration* (from Sun and from the Mississippi/Alabama Fair and Dairy Show in 1956, more recently released on independent issue *Tupelo's Own Elvis Presley*), *The Sun Sessions*, *The Complete Sun Sessions* (the master version on the original release under the tile, the master plus a live version on the 2006 re-issue), *The King Of Rock 'n' Roll*, *Sunrise*, the CD issue of *Elvis' Golden Records Vol. 1*, *Artist of the Century*, *Elvis at Sun*, *Elvis R&B* and the 2007 *The Essential Elvis Presley*. Early live versions are on *Elvis Raw*,

Good Rockin' Tonight and other Louisiana Hayride collections. A 1955 live version from Eagle's Hall in Houston has appeared on *Memphis Recording Service Vol. 2*.

"BABY WHAT YOU WANT ME TO DO"

Elvis sang this Jimmy Reed blues song to kick off his long live segment medley on the NBC TV Special in June 1968—to be specific, the 6 p.m. June 27 taping; it also rounds out the "Lawdy, Miss Clawdy" medley from the same show. As well as featuring on the tie-in album, the track has since appeared on *A Golden Celebration* (from both sessions that evening), *Memories: The '68 Comeback Special* and *Tiger Man* (which also has a second version from the proceedings).

Versions that failed to make it onto the final TV Special may be found on *Elvis Aron Presley*, *Elvis: A Legendary Performer Vol. 2* and *Collectors Gold*. Rehearsal versions are on *Memories: The '68 Comeback Special* (a double album on which five versions are presented), while an instrumental rehearsal version features on FTD release *Burbank '68*.

Elvis showcased the song in concert when he returned to performing in Las Vegas in 1969. Live versions from this engagement are on *Collectors Gold*, *Platinum—A Life In Music*, *Live In Las Vegas*, *Today Tomorrow & Forever*, and the 2007 *Viva Las Vegas*. It's also on FTD concert discs *All Shook Up* and *Elvis At The International*.

There are also rumors that "Baby What You Want Me To Do" was one of the tunes that Elvis enjoyed singing back home at Graceland with pals in the Sixties, after Reed's original version came out at the start of the decade. A bluesy jam version from Elvis' 1973 home recording at Sam Thompson's house was released in 2005 on *Elvis By The Presleys* and 2006 FTD issue *Made in Memphis*, after previously only being available on bootleg.

"BABY WHAT'S WRONG"

Elvis messed around with this 1962 Jerry Reed composition backstage before his 1968 NBC TV Special during a jam on "Peter Gunn." It's on bootleg *Complete Dressing Room Sessions*. The song has been notably covered by The Yardbirds and Eric Clapton.

BACK IN MEMPHIS

A 10-track album, issued in November 1970. The previous year this album formed half two-disc set *From Memphis to Vegas / From Vegas to Memphis*. Because it had already come out before, it failed to even make it onto the *Billboard* top 100 LPs (#183) and has the unwarranted distinction of being the worst-performing of any Elvis album released during his lifetime.

TRACK LISTING:
1. Inherit The Wind
2. This Is The Story
3. Stranger In My Own Home Town
4. A Little Bit Of Green
5. And The Grass Won't Pay No Mind
6. Do You Know Who I Am
7. From A Jack To A King
8. The Fair is Moving On
9. You'll Think Of Me
10. Without Love (There Is Nothing)

BACKSTAGE WITH ELVIS

A 2001 unofficial release on Memory Records, consisting of backstage conversations, banter and more between Elvis, his entourage and his musicians from time on the road in the Spring of 1972.

BACKING SINGERS

Much of the music Elvis grew up with involved choirs and harmonies; that's what his parents enjoyed. Long before he landed his first recording contract, he had a good idea who he wanted to do back-up vocals on his songs: he worked with The Jordanaires from 1956 until 1970. Over his career, Elvis worked with practically all of his male voice favorites (The Imperials and The Stamps), and even set up his own group, Voice, who he called when he felt like doing some home harmonizing.

Elvis also worked with outstanding female artists: sopranos Millie Kirkham and Kathy Westmoreland, and the backing band Aretha used, the Sweet Inspirations, who he signed sight unseen when he returned to performing in the late Sixties.

Along the way, many other voices joined with Elvis', in the studio and at home.

His love of intertwined voices was often the cause of the few disagreements he had with RCA about how his records were mixed. The record label and the Colonel wanted to push Elvis up in the mix, thinking that's what his fans paid for; Elvis wanted to hear the backing singers on the final acetate the way he heard them in the studio. He even sometimes deliberately shifted his mike so that the backing singers were at least partially on his own vocal track.

Seventies Elvis liked to bring his back-up singers into the limelight during his shows, over the years giving many of them a chance to shine. The Sweet Inspirations and sometimes Voice or the Stamps served as warm up acts. And of course, the back-up team could expect to be involved in his stage act pranks and japes.

JOE MOSCHEO: "Because his musical conception was so influenced by the quartet style, Elvis' career can almost be traced by tracking the backup singers he worked with at various times."

MAIN BACK-UP GROUPS

- *The Jordanaires (1956-1970)*
   Gordon Stoker, Neal Matthews, Hoyt Hawkins, Hugh Jarrett (up to June 1958, replaced by Ray Walker).

- *The Imperials (1966-1971)*
   1966: Jake Hess, Jim Murray, Gary McSpadden, Armand Morales, Sherrill Nielsen and Henry Slaughter
   1970: Terry Blackwood, Roger Wiles, Winnifred Brest, Jim Murray and Armond Morales
   1971: Terry Blackwood, Greg Gordon, Joe Moscheo, Jim Murray and Armond Morales

- *The Sweet Inspirations (1969-1977)*
   Emily (Cissy) Houston, Ann Williams, Myrna Smith, Estelle Brown, Sylvia Shemwell

- *J.D. Sumner & The Stamps Quartet (1971-1977)*
   J.D. Sumner and three of Ed Enoch, Ed Hill, Larry Strickland, Donnie Sumner, Bill Baize, Buck Buckles, Richard Sterban, Pat Brown, Dave Roland, Dave Rowland, Ed Hill, Ed Wideman

- Voice (1973-1975)

Donnie Sumner, Per-Erik (Pete) Hallin, Tim Baty, Sherrill Nielsen

Elvis worked with other backing groups on movie soundtracks and in the studio:

- THE KEN DARBY SINGERS (1956, *Love Me Tender*): Chuck Prescott, John Dodson, Rad Robinson

- THE SURFERS (1961, *Blue Hawaii*): Patrick Sylva, Bernard Ching, Clayton Naluai and Alan Naluai

- THE AMIGOS (1962–1963, *Girls! Girls! Girls!* and *Fun in Acapulco*): Jose Vadiz, Miguel Alcaide, Felix Melendes, Pedro Berrios, German Vega

- THE CAROLE LOMBARD QUARTET / TRIO (1963-1964, *Viva Las Vegas, Girl Happy*): Carol Lombard, Gwen Johnson, Jackie Ward and Marjorie Cranford.

- THE JUBILEE FOUR (1963-1964, *Viva Las Vegas, Girl Happy*): Bill Johnson, George McFadden, Jimmy Adams and Ted Brooks.

- THE MELLO MEN (1962-1965, *It Happened At The World's Fair, Roustabout, Paradise Hawaiian Style*): Thurl Ravenscroft, Max Smith, Gene Merlino, Bill Lee, Bill Cole

- THE BLOSSOMS (1968, *NBC TV Special, The Trouble With Girls, Change Of Habit*): Darlene Love, Jean King, Fanita James

- THE NASHVILLE EDITION (1970-1971, recording sessions): Dolores Edgin, June Page, Hurshel Wiginton, Joe Babcock

The following individual singers worked with Elvis over the years:

Jacqueline Allen (1961)
Lea Jane Berinati (1975-1977)
B.J. Baker (1968-1969)
Janie Fricke (1977)
Larry Bunker (1966)
Glen Campbell (1963)
Dolores Edgin (1966-1976)
James Glazer (1970)
Jeannie Green (1969-1973)
Mary Greene (1969)
Jack Halloran (1968)
Ron Hicklin (1968)
Charlie Hodge (1960-1977)
Ginger Holladay (1969-1975)
Mary Holladay (1969-1975)
Priscilla Hubbard (1967)
Millie Kirkham (1957-1975)
Marlyn Mason (1968)
Dorothy McCarthy (1961)
Ronnie Milsap (1969)
Sonja Montgomery (1969-1971)
Loulie Jean Norman (1961)
Sherrill Nielsen (1975-1977)
June Page (1966-1977)
Susan Pilkington (1969-1973)
Sandy Posey (1966-1977)
Virginia Rees (1961)
Temple Riser (1970-1977)
Sally Stevens (1969)
Myrna Smith (1976)
Ben Speer (1956)
Brock Speer (1956)
Gordon Stoker (1956)
Wendellyn Suits (1976)
Donna Thatcher (1969)
Jackie Ward (1969)
Kathy Westmoreland (1970-1977)
Hurshel Wiginton (1969-1976)
Kitty White (1958)
Eileen Wilson (1965)

BAHAMAS

Elvis and Priscilla and the Espositos, Gambills and Schillings traveled to Nassau in October 1969 for a two week vacation, on the recommendation of the Colonel, who said that they'd enjoy the gambling. The lure of the green baize was not enough to make up for incessant winds and strong rain, and the party returned home early from the Paradise Island Hotel where they were staying.

Lamar Fike has said that Elvis and Priscilla snuck off to the Bahamas for a few days on their own soon after their wedding.

BAKER, LAVERN
(B.DELORES WILLIAMS, 1929-1997)

A leading R&B lady of the Fifties, powerful-voiced LaVern Baker made her recording debut as "Little Miss Sharecropper" on RCA Victor in 1949 before moving to Atlantic. Elvis was an avid fan as he scored three million-selling hits at the time he was breaking through. She made it onto TV and the into the movies in the late Fifties.

Elvis covered a number of Baker hits: "Tweedlee Dee," "Shake A Hand," Seventies concert opener "See See Rider" (her last hit and the inspiration for Elvis' version) and Leiber and Stoller anthem "Saved." Both of them covered "Harbor Lights" (Elvis at his first professional recording session) and "Tomorrow Night." The duet Elvis recorded with Ann-Margret, "You're The Boss," that was cut from *Viva Las Vegas* had also previously been a Baker release.

Elvis appeared on a bill with Baker right at the start of his career in Cleveland, Ohio.

In 1961, mere months after Elvis released the song "Little Sister," Baker recorded an answer record titled "Hey, Memphis."

LAVERN BAKER: "He was fantastic . . . people didn't care if he was white or black, he was a good artist and they felt his music."

BALLADS

Elvis told a reporter in 1956, "I used to sing nothing but ballads before I went professional. I love ballads."

The first song Elvis paid to record at Sun in 1953, "My Happiness," was a ballad. Sun Records assistant Marion Keisker noted down on the label's files "Good ballad singer—hold." When Elvis was called back to Sun, the vast majority of songs he proposed to Sam Phillips were ballads. As he tried to wheedle that "something else" he'd glimpsed out of the promising young singer, Phillips later said he "didn't have the heart to stop him."

All of Elvis' Sun singles followed the formula of a rocker on one side and a ballad on the other. "I'll Never Let You Go" is a ballad until, close to the end, Elvis calls out "Weeeeeeeeeeelll" and Bill Black starts slapping the bass and the track metamorphoses into a rocker.

Perhaps because he had initially wanted to be a balladeer but was discouraged by Sam Phillips, Elvis felt a degree of insecurity with the genre until after his return from the Army in the early Sixties, when he continued to cut roughly as many ballads as rockers for RCA, most of them new songs written specially for him. Even during the soundtrack years, Elvis carried on singing ballads, though mostly for his own delectation at home among friends.

After Elvis returned to national touring in 1970, he gradually increased the ballad quotient in his shows. Many ballads lent themselves perfectly to the concert environment, gradually growing in intensity and culminating in huge and dramatic finales.

Greil Marcus writes that Elvis' ability to deliver a ballad with honesty was vital to maintaining his success after he lost the rebel energy that took him to the top in the first place (though he put it more eloquently than that).

ELVIS SAID IN 1956: "I like to sing ballads the way Eddie Fisher does and the way Perry Como does."

ELVIS SAID IN 1957: "To be truthful, I can't do ballads nearly as well as I can the other kind because I don't have the voice for it."

BAMFORD, A. V. "BAM"

Promoter "Bam" Bamford was a close friend of Colonel Parker's, and to begin with a dissenting voice against the Colonel's conviction that the sky was the limit for the boy. Initially, "Bam" would only book Elvis in areas he was unknown if the tour included bookings in Texas towns where he was already a hot property. On April 18, 1956 Elvis finally landed "100% top billing" on a Bamford-promoted tour, supported by Faron Young and Jimmy and Johnny.

BAND

Pop music has been much more about groups than individual singers. To make a noise in the world, Elvis needed help.

In the days when he was an unknown, Elvis tried hard to get into several bands. He failed auditions, was turned down point blank and told to go back to driving a truck. That didn't matter so much when he was living at Lauderdale Courts in Memphis, where he could play with Johnny Black (whose brother Bill played bass for the Starlite Wranglers), Lee Denson or Johnny and Dorsey Burnette.

When Elvis finally received his callback from Sun, he acquired a fully-formed band without even trying. On Sam Phillips' advice he tried out with guitarist Scotty Moore and bass player Bill Black and never looked back. When they started playing live immediately after "That's All Right (Mama)" hit the airwaves, they split the money 50/50: half to Elvis, half to the band. For the next year or so they strapped their instruments to a succession of jalopies and criss-crossed the South. Drummer D. J. Fontana joined the touring band a year after their first gig, while other Louisiana Hayride players occasionally helped Elvis out on tour, including pianists Leon Post and Floyd Cramer, steel guitarists Sonny Trammel and Jimmy Day, and drummer Joe Morris. Local musician Buddy Cunningham is said to have added percussion to some of Elvis' early Sun tracks.

In Scotty Moore's words, "At first Elvis was just one of the guys. We'd go out and get a hamburger, you know, just like most everybody did, till he became so recognizable that you couldn't even stop at a truckstop." By all accounts, they had a lot of fun, while suffering the obvious hardships you'd expect of any three guys living out of a car for weeks on end.

By the time Elvis signed for RCA, poised to crack the national market and on the brink of a film career, Elvis was traveling with his early entourage pals Gene Smith and Red West, and started flying between venues while the band drove. From May 1956, Elvis was staying in different hotels to his band. The Jordanaires started their fourteen-year collaboration with the King that year

When Elvis started recording for RCA in early 1956, he began working with an extended studio group of musicians. For his first recording session, in Nashville, the sound was supplemented by a backing group of Gordon Stoker, Ben Speer and Brock Speer, while instrumental work featured Chet Atkins on guitar, and over the next few months, Floyd Cramer, Shorty Long and Marvin Hughes taking turns on the piano.

Never a believer in paying musicians any more than he could get away with, the Colonel would not hear of raising the band members' pay. When Elvis was drafted into the Army in early 1958, Scotty, Bill and D.J. were still on the same pay as in late 1955: $200 dollars a week out on tour, $100 weekly as a retainer.

Elvis tried to land Scotty, Bill and DJ parts in *Love Me Tender* but music arranger Ken Darby turned them down because they didn't look "hillbilly enough." For the first time, Elvis worked with musicians he did not know (Vito Mumolo on guitar, Mike "Myer" Rubin on bass, Richard Cornell on drums, Luther Rountree on banjo, backing singers Rad Robinson, Jon Dodson and Charles Prescott, and accordion players Carl Fortina and Dom Frontieri). Not surprisingly, a new venue and unknown players left Elvis feeling uncomfortable. The next time he was in Hollywood for his Paramount picture *Loving You* he insisted on having his own band, augmented by LA-based guitarist Hilmer "Tiny" Timbrell and pianist Dudley Brooks, who played on many later soundtrack sessions.

By the time he did *Jailhouse Rock*, Elvis landed some bit parts for Scotty, Bill and D.J.

Early in the fall of 1957 tensions between the band and Elvis bubbled to the surface. At the end of a recording session at Radio Recorders in Santa Monica, Elvis failed to keep a promise to make time for the band members to record instrumental tracks they intended to release under the name "The King's Men," with Elvis on piano. Scotty Moore and Bill Black handed in a letter of resignation; D. J. Fontana refused to sign. An immediate replacement was found in top session guitarist Hank "Sugarfoot" Garland, while bassist Chuck Wigginton filled in for the Elvis Presley Youth Center benefit show in Tupelo. However, within a month Scotty and Bill were persuaded to return on improved terms of $250 per show, only a little above union scale.

Elvis' final recording session before he was drafted into the Army in early 1958 saw him working with a 14-strong band at Radio Recorders; his regulars were joined by a brass section hired by Paramount and second drummer Bernie Mattinson. These sessions were the last that Elvis played with the full complement of original band members.

When RCA lured Elvis to their new Nashville studio on furlough in June 1958, Elvis played with top talents Hank Garland and Chet Atkins on guitar, Bob Moore on bass, Floyd Cramer on piano, Buddy Harman on bongos, and old stalwarts D. J. Fontana and The Jordanaires.

Once he was back from the Army, Elvis picked up with the session musicians he worked with at recording sessions in Nashville, LA and Memphis, along with Scotty Moore and DJ Fontana. His Nashville studio band circa 1961 was Scotty Moore and Hank Garland on guitar, Bob Moore on bass, D.J. Fontana and Buddy Harman on drums, Floyd Cramer on piano, Boots Randolph on saxophone and backing vocals from The Jordanaires and soprano Millie Kirkham. The same personnel accompanied him to Hawaii for his benefit concert that year (Elvis jokingly presented them as "The Unwashables") and played on the *Blue Hawaii* soundtrack recording sessions. Hank Garland suffered a career-ending car crash in late 1961 and was replaced by top Nashville guitarists Harold Bradley and Grady Martin.

Elvis' records appeared without any mention of the personnel who played the instruments and worked the recording facilities. When RCA put it to the Colonel that some of the musicians wanted to get credit, Colonel Parker replied that it was his standard policy, and besides, Elvis was the real producer.

In the Sixties, Elvis' core players were supplemented by other instrumentalists and backing singers as the material required. For *Fun in Acapulco* in early 1963, it was trumpet players Rudolph Loera and Anthony Terran, percussionist Emil Radocchia and back-up singers The Amigos. On *Viva Las Vegas*, Elvis' studio band

swelled to a total of 32 musicians and back-up singers. The Colonel soon reigned back this profit-eating excess. By the *Kissin' Cousins* session later that year, the extras included Bill Justis on sax and Boots Randolph on the jug. More and more frequently as the Sixties wore on, Elvis took to overdubbing his own vocal part after the instrumental parts had been laid down.

By early 1968, the last time Elvis recorded in Nashville before launching into the next phase of his career, the studio line-up was Scotty Moore, Jerry Reed and Chip Young on guitar, Bob Moore on bass, D. J. Fontana and Buddy Harman on drumming duty, Floyd Cramer on piano, Pete Drake on pedal steel guitar, Charlie McCoy on harmonica and The Jordanaires providing backing vocals. His next recording session, for *Live A Little, Love A Little*, had only one player Elvis had worked with before, drummer Hal Blaine; on this session, Billy Strange added his trademark strings and horns.

Elvis reunited with original band members Scotty Moore and D.J. Fontana on his 1968 NBC TV Special in the informal, intimate segment, assisted by pals Charlie Hodge, Alan Fortas and Lance LeGault. The "Arena" segment band, put together by producer Bones Howe, was Tommy Tedesco, Mike Deasy and Al Casey on guitar, Larry Knechtal on bass and keyboards, Charles Berghofer on bass, Don Randi on piano, Hal Blaine on drums, John Cyr and Elliot Franks on percussion, Frank DeVito on bongos, Tommy Morgan on harmonica, and backing vocals by The Blossoms; Billy Goldenberg wielded the conductor's baton.

Later that year Elvis played with two almost completely unknown bands to him to lay down his soundtracks for *Charro!* (Tommy Tedesco, Ralph Grasso, Howard Roberts, Raymond Brown, Max Bennett, Carl O'Brian, Emil Radocchia and Don Randi) and *The Trouble with Girls* (Jerry McGee, Morton Marker, Robert Gibbons, Max Bennett, Frank Carlson, John Guerin, Don Randi, Buddy Colette, Roy Caton and Lew McCreary).

It was all change again for Elvis' at American Studio in Memphis in January 1969. Chips Moman and Felton Jarvis brought Elvis' sound bang up to date with the American House Band of Reggie Young on guitar (and sitar), Tommy Cogbill and Mike Leech on bass, Gene Chrisman on drums, Bobby Wood on piano, Bobby Emmons on organ, John Hughey on Steel Guitar and Ed Kollis on harmonica. Elvis cameo'd on guitar and piano, and later the Memphis Horns and a flock of female backing singers added to the richness of the sound on overdubs.

In 1969, when it was time to pull together a new touring band for his first month-long residency in Las Vegas, Elvis went through his little black book after long-time regulars Scotty Moore, D.J. Fontana and The Jordanaires all demurred. Elvis' initial thought was to go with the studio musicians he'd worked with so well at American Studio, but the ongoing feud between studio chief Chips Moman and the Colonel put paid to that idea.

The first name on the nascent TCB band sheet was guitarist James Burton, who Elvis had originally wanted for his 1968 NBC TV Special. Burton put together a core band of pianist Larry Muhoberac, drummer Ronnie Tutt, rhythm guitarist John Wilkinson and bass player Jerry Scheff. To supply his gospel needs, Elvis took on not one but two backup quartets, the Imperials and the Sweet Inspirations, with Charlie Hodge contributing backing vocals, guitar, scarves and water. Two band members, James Burton and John Wilkinson, never missed a show from the first Vegas gig onwards.

In 1970 Elvis returned to RCA's Nashville Studio B with a new band assembled by producer Felton Jarvis from musicians with whom Elvis had worked in the past: guitarists James Burton and Chip Young, bassist Norbert Putnam, drummer

Jerry Carrigan, pianist David Briggs, and multi-talented Charlie McCoy on harmonica and organ— the core of the famous Muscle Shoals rhythm section, plus the now customary quota of twenty or so musicians and backing singers for overdubs (the Jordanaires, the Imperials, and a horn section of George Tidwell, Don Sheffield, Glenn Baxter, Wayne Butler, Norman Ray, Skip Lane, Gene Mullins and William Puett). By this time, Glen D. Hardin had taken over on piano for live work.

Back out on the road at last in September 1970, Elvis toured with his Vegas band augmented by a male backing group formed by former Jordanaire Hugh Jarrett in substitution of The Imperials, who had a prior commitment. For the first time, Elvis toured with an orchestra directed by Joe Guercio.

The band that backed Elvis for concert documentary *That's The Way It Is* was essentially his live band, which followed him back into the Nashville studio in 1971 (with Eddie Hinton and Chip Young standing in for James Burton in the studio). This time, backing singers were kept out until the post-production stage in an attempt to speed up matters and cut down on distractions.

The first time that Elvis recorded in the studio with his full live band was at RCA's Hollywood studio in March 1972. This was also the first time that Elvis worked with J. D. Sumner and the Stamps in the studio.

Elvis' band members were paid by the Colonel, who discouraged them from "hanging out" with Elvis or visiting him backstage. One exception to this general rule was Voice, a vocal harmony group that Elvis put together initially for his friend Tom Jones, but ended up hiring himself. They were paid every month out of Elvis' account, and spent plenty of time round a piano with their employer, singing hymns and harmonizing whenever he wanted.

At Elvis' ill-fated Stax Studios sessions in July 1973 his band was a mix of live guys and studio musicians with whom Elvis had played either at American Studio or in Nashville, until the sessions overran and Stax house musicians Bob Manual, Johnny Christopher, Donald Dunn and Al Jackson took over. The December 1973 Stax session was far more productive with James Burton, Johnny Christopher and Charlie Hodge on guitar, Norbert Putnam on bass, Ronnie Tutt on drums, David Briggs and Per-Erik Hallin sharing piano and organ duties, and vocal back-up from J.D. Sumner and the Stamps plus Voice and female back-up singers Kathy Westmoreland, Mary Greene, Mary Holladay and Susan Pilkington.

In January 1974 the TCB band included, for the first time, back-up group Voice, and new arrival Duke Bardwell on bass. Voice served as Elvis' back-up until late 1975. Every now and then, Elvis might call up other band members and send a plane to whisk them over to Graceland if he wanted someone to hang out with.

Apart from band member substitutions necessitated by previous commitments (generally, according to band members, because the Colonel didn't tell them of upcoming tours in time), Elvis' stage band remained more or less stable until early 1976, when a number of long-serving band members found Elvis' erratic and impulsive behavior too much. Nashville-based player Shane Keister replaced pianist Glen D. Hardin for eight shows, and drummer Larrie Londin took over from Ronnie Tutt for a spell. At the last minute, James Burton had a change of heart and decided to stay.

On stage, Elvis delighted in playing his own little game, "Stump the Band," by stopping in the middle of a song and beginning one of his more obscure back catalogue hits. Unbeknownst to Elvis, the band had rehearsed practically every single song Elvis had ever recorded for this very eventuality.

Madison Square Garden Tour Photo Album.

Tour Photo

As Elvis found performing more of a struggle, the band members pulled through. They played and sang harder to help pull him through. Ronnie Tutt, who returned, said he even tried telepathy to get Elvis going.

By the end, in addition to Elvis' core band, he was touring with as many as twenty back-up singers, a 12-piece horn section and a rhythm section. Unlike in earlier years, the show was pretty much cast in stone. Every now and then Elvis decided to try some new material, but the few times rehearsals were arranged, the whole band would gather either at Graceland (on the racquetball court) or on the road, only for Elvis to pull a no-show.

On Elvis' last ever tour in 1977, the band was James Burton, John Wilkinson and Charlie Hodge on guitar, Jerry Scheff on bass, Ronnie Tutt on drums, Tony Brown on piano, Bobby Ogdin on keyboards, and a back-up vocals section of The Sweet Inspirations and J.D. Sumner and The Stamps, plus Sherrill Nielsen and Kathy Westmoreland, and Joe Guercio's orchestra. Regular drummer Ronnie Tutt had to pull out with three shows to go. He was replaced first by Jerome "Stump" Monroe, who usually played with the Sweet Inspirations, and then by Larrie Londin.

The TCB band has lived on long after he stopped singing. The Elvis—The Concert extravaganza has celebrated major Elvis anniversaries and toured (with Elvis on screen) to rapturous success around the world.

In 2006, an advert for BBC Radio 2 used footage of Elvis in his *Aloha In Hawaii* period in which he introduces a super group of the Sugababes, Marvin Gaye, Jimmy Page, Noel Gallagher, Keith Moon, Sheryl Crowe and Stevie Wonder.

ROCK AND ROLL HALL OF FAME

Elvis players inducted into the Rock and Roll Hall of Fame:

Chet Atkins
Hal Blaine
Floyd Cramer
Scotty Moore
James Burton

ELVIS SAID IN 1972: "It's like a new experience every day. The guy on the guitar will find a new lick, or the guy on the piano will find something, or the voices will add something. And I hear all this and it inspires me. I like it."

ELVIS SAID IN CONCERT IN 1976: "You know these musicians are all hand-picked from the bottom of the barrel . . . Only kiddin'!"

D.J. FONTANA: "I didn't leave Elvis' band because anybody was mad. Scotty didn't leave because anybody was mad. It was just one of those things; people wanted to do other things. Elvis understood that. People make him out to be a bad guy, and I really hate that."

JOHN WILKINSON: "He didn't know it, but we had rehearsed almost every single song he'd ever done. He wasn't aware of that. And we didn't tell him."

JERRY SCHEFF: "I think the reason he liked the band was that we sort of listened to each other, we listened to him, and we instinctively picked up on what should be there."

ERNST JORGENSEN: "Elvis always pushed himself to excel whenever he was recording with new players."

DVD:
The TCB Gang—The Way It Was (2006)

BAPTIST HOSPITAL, MEMPHIS

See HEALTH.

BARBITURATES

See DRUGS.

BARDOT, BRIGITTE
(B.1934)

In his pre-departure press conference before sailing for Germany in 1958, Elvis said that on furlough he'd like to make it to Paris to meet Brigitte Bardot. The boy tried: he had a glamorous poster of the French star up on the wall where he lived in Bad Nauheim, and during his time on the Old Continent one of his girlfriends, Margit Buergin, looked a lot like B.B. in his opinion.

The original "sex kitten" who later became known for her animal protection campaign, Bardot starred in many movies including *And God Created Woman* (1956) directed by then husband Roger Vadim. She also had a pop career.

BARDWELL, DUKE
(B. 1943)

Bass player Bardwell, long an Elvis fan and from a country background, toured with Elvis in 1974 after Ronnie Tutt put Elvis in touch with him (they had both worked with Jose Feliciano) until regular bass player Jerry Scheff returned in 1975. Elvis and Bardwell had something of a personality clash—Elvis said he didn't like his attitude, Bardwell didn't like being the butt of japes and pranks on stage. After Elvis' March 1975 recording session, all of Bardwell's bass lines were replaced in post-production (except on T-R-O-U-B-L-E, which RCA pressed as a single almost immediately). Bardwell went on to work with Emmylou Harris, Kenny Loggins and others.

"BAREFOOT BALLAD"

Elvis plays the hillbilly in this *Kissin' Cousins* track by Dolores Fuller and Lee Morris, complete with banjos, fiddle and jug. The band laid down the instrumentals on September 30, 1963, for which Elvis added vocals on October 20, 1963.

The song came out on the soundtrack LP and, in the Nineties, the *Double Features* issue.

BARHANOVICH, FRANK "YANKIE"
(? – D. 1987)

Mississippi promoter and business "Yankie" Barhanovich met Elvis in New Orleans in February 1955, when he was on tour with his daughter-in-law Ann Raye. He booked him for a number of shows in Biloxi later that year, including at the Keesler Air Force base.

BARRIS, GEORGE

LA's "Customizer to the Stars" and "King of the Kustomizers" worked on Elvis' "solid gold" 1960 Cadillac limousine and on his 1962 Dodge Motor

Home, but had a far more important role to play in Elvis' life when he and his wife Shirley offered to be chaperones to young Priscilla Beaulieu—the factor that persuaded her reluctant parents to allow her to fly to LA to spend some time with Elvis in 1962.

Elvis awarded Barris a king-sized commission in 1965, when he hired him to customize a secondhand Greyhound bus he had bought, and which he planned to use to shuttle between Memphis and LA.

Barris's firm, Kustom Industries, also worked on Elvis' unique Stutz Blackhawk, a car he bought in 1970. Over the years Barris's special vehicles have graced a great many films and won a great number of hotrod prizes.

BATCHELOR, RUTH
(1934-1992)

A journalist and critic on both sides of the Atlantic who with Bob Roberts co-wrote five songs for Elvis soundtracks in the Sixties ("Because Of Love," "Cotton Candy Land," "King Of The Whole Wide World," "Thanks To The Rolling Sea" and "Where Do You Come From"). Batchelor also released music on her own label, Femme Records. She founded the Los Angeles Film Critics Association and spent a spell as an entertainment reporter on "Good Morning America."

BAUM, BERNIE
(B.1929)

Hardworking songwriter who collaborated on soundtrack songs on more than a dozen Elvis movies as a staff writer for Hill & Range. With writing partners Florence Kaye and Bill Giant, he has credits on over forty songs Elvis sang.

"BE MY LOVE"

Elvis sang this Sammy Cahn / Nicholas Brodszky tune at home with pals in 1966.

"BEACH BOY BLUES"

Elvis as a poor Hawaiian beach boy . . . a fate that befell him in more than one movie. This one was *Blue Hawaii*, in a track written by Sid Tepper and Roy C. Bennett which Elvis recorded at Radio Recorders on March 23, 1961.

The track has since seen the light of day on *Elvis Sings The Blues*, *Command Performances* and the 1997 *Blue Hawaii* album reissue, which also features the movie version of the song (also available on *Elvis Chante Sid Tepper & Roy C. Bennett*).

"BEACH SHACK"

An upbeat Bill Giant / Bernie Baum / Florence Kaye song that Elvis recorded at Radio Recorders on February 16, 1966 for *Spinout*.

Several alternates are on the FTD *Spinout* release.

BEAN, ORVILLE

When Elvis was born in 1935, his father Vernon worked for dairy farmer Orville Bean, who had his spread on Saltillo Road. As was his customary practice, Mr. Bean lent Vernon $180 to build a house on Old Saltillo Road and move into with his new bride, Gladys. This house was where Elvis was born.

In 1937, Vernon, Gladys's brother Travis Smith and a man called Lether Gable were charged with altering a four-dollar check issued by Orville Bean which they had received in payment for a pig—adding a one before the four (or in some account a zero after the four) in order to better reflect the animal's value.

Bean ignored pleas from Elvis' great-uncle Noah Presley, a friend of his, who said he would pay twice the money back if Bean did not go ahead with the prosecution, instead preferring that Vernon be taught a lesson. Vernon was found guilty and sentenced to a three-year spell at Parchman Penitentiary.

In 1945, Vernon Presley bought a house from Orville Bean on Berry Street in East Tupelo. As had happened before, he found it impossible to keep up with payments. Vernon's friend Aaron Kennedy recalled that Bean operated in a tried-and-tested feudal fashion: "Orville Bean was a politician. He made his money by taking advantage of people and keeping them indebted."

Bean's daughter Oleta was Elvis' fifth-grade school teacher.

BEATLES, THE

The press may have cast them as bitter rivals, but the biggest selling musicians of the Fifties and Sixties were more inclined to be respectful friends than enemies. Entourage members recall that Elvis loved the hard-edged sound of the early Beatles.

When The Fab Four first came to America in 1964, their manager Brian Epstein boasted that they were "going to be bigger than Elvis Presley." This bravado contrasted with Elvis and the Colonel's public show of magnanimity: when The Beatles made their first appearance on "The Ed Sullivan Show," a telegram was read out on air from Elvis and his manager congratulating them on their appearance on the show, ending "hope your engagement will be successful and your visit pleasant." While they were in the States on this first trip, the boys from Liverpool took in Elvis' latest movie, Fun in Acapulco. The band would have met Elvis on this initial Stateside tour—Elvis is said to have invited them to Graceland—but they couldn't reconcile their schedules

Low-level negotiations in 1964 between Paramount and The Beatles management team explored the possibility of the Liverpudlians featuring in the finale of Elvis' next movie project.

Three days before their second Hollywood Bowl concert, The Beatles at last found time to meet their idol. Though it was meant to be secret, word had got out that the biggest names in pop were to congregate at Elvis' Bel Air home, and by the time The Beatles arrived at 10 p.m. on August 27, 1965, the place was thronged with reporters and fans.

Initially the atmosphere was subdued. The usually outspoken Beatles were uncharacteristically awestruck, and sat in silence on the floor opposite Elvis. Elvis broke the ice when he quipped: "Guys, if you're just going to sit there and stare at me, I'm going to bed." Elvis showed off his color TV, and then suggested they play some music. John Lennon later wrote that they started of with Cilla Black hit, "You're My World," Ringo, without a drum kit, had to make do with drumming away on the side of his seat. They also jammed through Chuck Berry and Little Richard numbers. No tape was running—at least no tape has ever surfaced, despite rumors

that somebody snuck one in—and no pictures have ever surfaced of this historic meet, after the Colonel ordered a strict photo embargo. Some reports cite that they also played their way through "I Feel Fine," "Hound Dog," "See See Rider" and "Johnny B. Goode." Managers Brian Epstein and Colonel Parker went off into a side room to play a little roulette (the Colonel brought along a wheel). Ringo played pool with various members of Elvis' entourage. George snuck off and smoked a joint with Larry Geller. At one stage Elvis and The Beatles went outside to admire E.'s car collection and compare notes about owning Rolls Royces. The fans clustered around the gate started a chanting competition for their heroes—Elvis, playing on home territory, won. When the host showed the Fab Four the sauna that Colonel Parker had given him, they discovered a fan who had somehow managed to evade security and sneak in to the house. She had to be hauled off Elvis and ejected. During the evening, Elvis and the Beatles compared fan and touring experiences. According to one account, a member of Elvis' entourage went out to the gate and picked a bunch of girls to come in and party. When the Beatles finally left at 2 a.m., they asked Elvis and his pals to join them. Elvis declined but some of the guys carried on partying.

Though many biographers have described the occasion as frosty, The Beatles asked Elvis if he wanted to join up as the fifth Beatle.

John Lennon passed on a message to Elvis through Jerry Schilling, or said it directly in other accounts, that The Beatles "would have been nothing" if it hadn't been for the King.

It has been reported that The Beatles planned a trip to Stax to record an LP in the spring of 1966, and that Elvis offered to have them stay at Graceland. The veracity of this claim is put into question by the fact that as a rule, Elvis did not invite anybody but family and entourage pals to stay.

In 1970, when Elvis visited the FBI headquarters on a quest to land a narcotics agent badge, Elvis is reported to have said that The Beatles' tours of the States encouraged the spread of a filthy, unkempt appearance and suggestive music. However, Elvis and John Lennon kept up a phone friendship in later years.

Elvis sang a number of Beatles hits on his return to touring. In the run-up to his 1970 Vegas summer engagement (see the re-edited Elvis: That's the Way It Is documentary). Elvis performed a rocking medley of "Little Sister" with The Beatles' "Get Back." He also sang "Yesterday" and "Hey Jude" in a slightly less successful medley treatment, and gave "Lady Madonna" a studio run-through. George Harrison composition "Something" made it into Elvis' Aloha From Hawaii Via Satellite set. Elvis declared that his favorite Beatles song was "I Saw Her Standing There"; he owned Beatles albums Rubber Soul and Revolver and their single "Going Slow,"

Elvis saw George and Ringo again backstage after Seventies concerts of his.

BILLY SMITH: "Elvis was very threatened by the Beatles, but he tried to hide it."

GEORGE KLEIN: "Elvis was very fond of John and Paul. But in later years he became closer to Ringo because Ringo used to come to Las Vegas to see him."

LARRY GELLER: "Elvis liked all the Beatles, but John was his favorite."

PAUL MCCARTNEY: "When we were kids growing up in Liverpool, all we ever wanted to be was Elvis Presley."

RINGO: "He was just like one of us, none of the old Hollywood show-off thing."

Book:
Elvis Meets the Beatles: The Untold Story of Their Tangled Lives, by Chris Hutchins and Peter Thompson, Smith Gryphon Ltd, 1994.

"BECAUSE OF LOVE"

Ruth Batchelor and Bob Roberts penned this sentimental ballad on March 27, 1962 at Radio Recorders for Girls! Girls! Girls!. Billy Fury took the song to #20 in the UK charts later that year.

More recently, the song has been available on the Double Features release and Command Performances.

BENNETT, ROY. C
(B. 1918)

The songwriting partner for many decades of Sid Tepper, Bennett provided Elvis with a prolific amount of material for movies. The duo wrote ballads and novelty songs for artists including Guy Lombardo, Eddy Arnold, Andy Williams, Dean Martin, Perry Como, Eartha Kitt, Frank Sinatra and Sarah Vaughn.

ROY C. BENNETT: "In my opinion, our ballads for Elvis' movies are among the best songs we ever wrote—songs such as Puppet On A String, Hawaiian Sunset, All That I Am, Am I Ready, Island of Love, Angel, Beginner's Luck and others."

BEAULIEU, PAUL AND ANN

Priscilla's step-father and mother did their best to chaperone their little girl safely but were no match for Elvis' charm, protestations of honorable intent and strategic moves.

Ann Beaulieu married her childhood sweetheart James Wagner, and bore him a daughter, Priscilla, by the time she was eighteen. Wagner died in an airplane accident when Priscilla was just six months old. Three years later she remarried Paul Beaulieu, with whom she had another four children.

Air force Captain Paul Beaulieu arrived in Wiesbaden, Germany with his wife and three children in mid-August 1959 from Bergstrom Air Force Base in Austin, Texas, to join the 1405 Support Squadron. Previously he had earned a degree in Business Administration in Texas, and was a veteran of the Second World War, serving with the Marines in Okinawa.

A month later, Mr. Beaulieu gave fellow airman Currie Grant the go-ahead to take Priscilla to meet Elvis, after checking up on his reputation with his commanding officer, who Captain Beaulieu knew.

After Priscilla had visited Elvis a few times, Captain Beaulieu summoned Elvis to his home to assess his intentions. Elvis turned up in uniform, with Vernon, and on his best behavior won over his future father-in-law, calling him Captain and Sir throughout. Beaulieu consented to Priscilla continuing to visit Elvis' place as long as Elvis personally brought her home, which he did, at least to begin with.

Paul and Ann did their best to get their little girl to carry on studying. This was no easy task as she mooned around the house, love struck, and her grades suffered as she battled a lack of sleep.

The situation did not improve as they might have hoped when Elvis returned to the States in 1960. He continued to call, and Priscilla continued to be distracted.

Priscilla's parents finally agreed to let their

then 17-year-old girl visit Elvis in Los Angeles in 1962, after he assured them that she would be staying not with him but with friends of his, the Barrises. They were bamboozled into believing this official version of events after receiving postcards with an LA postmark detailing Priscilla's daily activities—all of which she wrote before leaving Los Angeles to hit Las Vegas with Elvis.

The daughter who returned home after spending Christmas at Graceland with Elvis in 1962 was rebellious and intractable: all she wanted to do was to get back to Elvis' side. Paul and Ann could no longer harbor any illusions about the relationship between their daughter and the world's #1 entertainer when she told them that they were in love. After Elvis reiterated his "honorable intentions" to Captain Beaulieu, Priscilla's parents felt they could not stand in the way of her big chance at happiness.

In her memoir, Priscilla later said that one of the reasons why she tried so hard to make her relationship with Elvis work was to repay the faith and understanding her parents had shown her.

Captain Beaulieu met Elvis in March 1963 and was satisfied that Priscilla would be living with Elvis' father Vernon and second wife Dee Stanley round the corner from Graceland. They arranged for her to finish her education at a local Memphis Catholic school.

The Beaulieus returned to the States two years after Priscilla moved to Memphis, when her stepfather was transferred to Travis Air Force Base, near Sacramento. Priscilla reluctantly went to visit them, but balked at their request that she spend the weekends with them. When her folks came down to visit in LA, she moved some of her things into Charlie Hodge's bedroom and pretended it was hers. Even so, her parents quizzed her about Elvis' intentions.

The Beaulieus played a *deus ex machina* role in the majority of accounts of events leading up to Elvis and Priscilla's 1967 wedding. According to Marty Lacker, "In order to get Priscilla over here, Elvis had made promises to her stepfather and her mother—like, it's not just a one-night stand, I'm really serious about her—and they called him on it. He really didn't want to marry anybody."

At the wedding, the then Colonel Beaulieu announced, "Our little girl is going to be a good wife."

PRISCILLA SAID: "He was a firm believer in discipline and responsibility, and he and I frequently knocked heads."

BEAULIEU, PRISCILLA

See PRESLEY, PRISCILLA BEAULIEU

BEDFORD, ELOISE

Elvis' second and third grade (maybe even fourth and fifth grade) sweetheart from school in Tupelo. In a pattern that he was to follow for the rest of his life, Elvis grew bored of the relationship and found a new love . . .

"BEGINNER'S LUCK"

Soundtrack kings Sid Tepper and Roy C. Bennett wrote this smooth ballad for *Frankie and Johnny*, which Elvis recorded in Nashville on May 12, 1965.

An appearance on the soundtrack LP apart, "Beginner's Luck" has appeared on *Elvis Chante Sid Tepper & Roy C. Bennett* and the *Double Features* and FTD movie re-issues.

BELEW, BILL
(B. 1931-2008)

Costumer designer Bill Belew began working with Elvis on his 1968 NBC TV Special, and then made his costumes went he went back to touring. Belew's inspiration for Elvis' memorable skintight leather outfit for the Comeback special was the classic Fifties rebel look in a design that reproduced a denim shirt and jeans. It has also been said that the design mimicked ladies' leather opera gloves, which stick to the contours of the body once they heat up.

Southerner Belew had previously designed for Josephine Baker among others, and knew Steve Binder who was directing the NBC Special.

For Christmas 1968, Priscilla commissioned Belew to make some clothes for Elvis.

In early 1970 Belew designed an iconic Elvis item, the first of many stage jumpsuits, which he had manufactured by the IC Costume Company of LA. Belew also designed off-stage outfits for Elvis, and remained Elvis' designer until the end, assisted by Gene Doucette.

Elvis gave Belew a Mercedes Convertible with the license plate 2BBFREP.

BILL BELEW: "I spoke to Elvis and he said, 'I want something different. I don't want to go up there in a tuxedo, I don't want to wear a suit.' The first thing we did was a jumpsuit. It was comfortable and he liked that. The public just sort of identified with it. We tried new stuff, but whenever he went back to Vegas, it never quite worked."

PAMELA CLARKE KEOGH: "As Hubert de Givenchy and Coco Chanel were to Audrey and Jackie, Bill Belew was to Elvis."

BELL, FREDDIE

Elvis saw Freddie Bell and the Bellboys performing Big Mama Thornton's rhythm and blues song "Hound Dog" in Las Vegas in May 1956, and immediately thought it might work after him. It was this stint at the Sands Hotel that launched Freddie Bell and the Bellboys onto a wider stage, first TV shows, then movies, and ultimately foreign tours. Bell's version was reissued in 2007 by independent label *Memphis Recording Service* as *New York RCA Studio 1: The Complete Sessions*.

BELLMAN, EDDIE

Shoe-store owner Eddie Bellman was going steady with May Juanico, mother of June Juanico, with whom Elvis was romantically involved in the summer of 1956. Elvis spent a lot of time with Eddie and May, and got his parents to come along for some go deep-sea fishing. Elvis also put in a promotional appearance at the Biloxi clothing store where Eddie had his shoe store, in exchange for which Bellman and his colleagues presented Elvis with a Winchester shotgun. Home-shot footage of these times appeared in 2002 documentary *Elvis & June: A Love Story*

BENEFIT CONCERTS
See CHARITABLE WORKS

BERLE, MILTON
(B.MILTON BERLINGER, 1908-2002)

Showman Milton Berle was so popular in the early days of TV that he was dubbed "Mister Television"; he offered a compelling reason for people to buy into this still-novel technology.

Berle lived and breathed entertainment from an early age. Known as "The Boy Wonder" during his child performing days in Vaudeville and early "flicker" films, he was one of the first people ever to appear on television in an experimental 1929 TV broadcast. A jokesmith throughout his career, he earned a reputation for "borrowing" other performers' material and the nickname "The Thief of Bad Gags." However, his best-known nickname, reflecting his familiarity to households across America, was of course "Uncle Miltie."

The unchallenged ratings king of early TV from 1948 until his show was finally knocked off top spot in 1955, Berle's audience was so vast that there is anecdotal evidence that many theatre shows considered taking a night off on Tuesdays, when he was on air. In 1951, NBC signed him to an unprecedented 30-year contract for a stratospheric $6 million fee, but by June 1956 he was hosting the last of his weekly variety shows—as it happened, the second and final time that Elvis appeared.

In his long career Berle made many cameos in movies, including one with Marilyn Monroe in *Let's Make Love*. He also popped up on practically every popular TV franchise during the Seventies and Eighties. Berle was one of the first seven people to be inducted into the Television Academy Hall of Fame.

Elvis appeared on the "Milton Berle Show," broadcast from the USS Hancock in San Diego, on April 3, 1956. He earned $3,000 for the appearance. His second and last appearance was from Los Angeles on June 5.

Berle got into the habit of dropping in to say hello to Elvis on the Paramount set when he was filming *Paradise, Hawaiian Style* in 1965.

BERLIN, IRVING
(B.ISRAEL BALINE, 1888-1989)

One of America's most prolific and celebrated composers was born in Russia to parents who later immigrated to America. Berlin's vast catalog of theatre and movie songs include some of the most popular of all time, including "White Christmas," a hit for Bing Crosby that Elvis recorded for his first Christmas album in 1957.

Berlin wrote over a thousand songs in a marathon career, including "Alexander's Ragtime Band," "God Bless America" (of which Elvis sang one line at a 1976 concert in Fort Worth), "Puttin' on the Ritz," "Cheek to Cheek," "Let's Face the Music and Dance" and "There's No Business Like Show Business"—not bad going for a man who (like Elvis) never learned to read music. Nominated seven times for a best song Oscar, the only time he won was for "White Christmas" in 1942, the year he was there to present that very Academy Award.

Berlin was one of only five music industry figures to receive the National Academy of Recording Arts and Sciences Lifetime Achievement Award before Elvis.

BERMAN, PANDRO S.
(1905-1996)

A man who rose through the ranks from script clerk to director and then producer, and had the foresight to bring together Fred Astaire and Ginger Rogers on screen. Berman produced *Jailhouse Rock*, and also worked on a blockbuster

Elvis with "Uncle Miltie" on the "Milton Berle Show" June 6, 1956.

production of *The Brothers Karamazov*. Other Berman movies include *Top Hat*, *Blackboard Jungle* and *The Hunchback of Notre Dame*.

BERNERO, JOHNNY
(1931-2001)

Local Memphis drummer Johnny Bernero featured on the tracks Elvis laid down at Sun Records in early July 1955 including "I Forgot To Remember To Forget," "Tryin' To Get To You" and "I'm Left, You're Right, She's Gone," though for many years the credit went to D. J. Fontana. Much like Elvis, Bernero got his chance by dropping into Sam Phillips Sun Studio on lunch breaks from his day job at the Memphis Light Gas & Water company. After doing session work for a number of Sun acts, Bernero persuaded Phillips to record his own band, but the tracks weren't released until the late 1980s.

BERRY, CHUCK
(B. CHARLES EDWARD ANDERSON BERRY, OCTOBER 18, 1926)

Rock 'n' roll trailblazer Chuck Berry—sometimes dubbed the "Poet of Rock 'n' roll—is universally recognized as one of the most important songwriters, voices, guitarists and performers in the history of rock 'n' roll music, complete with his own stage act, the duck walk, that has been his trademark for half a century. In and out of trouble with the law, young Berry trained as a beautician before signing to Chess in 1955 and forging rock 'n' roll out of the rhythm 'n' blues he grew up with. He had a string of hits in the mid-1950s, and was a top touring artist for many decades, buoyed by the new wave of British artists that swept across America in the mid-Sixties and covered his back catalog.

No man with rock 'n' roll in his veins could fail to cover Chuck Berry's tunes. At one time or another Elvis did his own version of "Brown Eyed Handsome Man," "Johnny B. Goode," "Long Live Rock And Roll (School Days)," "Maybellene," "Memphis, Tennessee," "Promised Land" and "Too Much Monkey Business,"

Surprisingly, Berry didn't score a US #1 until his joke number "My Ding-a-Ling" in 1972.

BETWEEN TAKES WITH ELVIS

An unofficial release of backstage banter and between-takes reflections from Elvis, musicians and members of his entourage, all from 1972.

"BEYOND THE BEND"

Elvis recorded this breezy Ben Weisman/Fred Wise/Dee Fuller song for *It Happened at the World's Fair* at Radio Recorders on September 22, 1962.

In addition to the self-evident later issues in the *Double Features* and FTD series, alternate takes have appeared on *Collectors Gold* and the FTD *It Happened at the World's Fair* re-issue.

"BEYOND THE REEF"

Elvis laid down this Jack Pittman song, initially recorded in 1950 by Jimmy Wakely and Margaret Whiting, in Nashville on May 26, 1966, but it was never released in his lifetime, not even with a new instrumental track added in 1968.

The song first appeared in an overdubbed version on 1980 compilation *Elvis Aron Presley*. The original May 1966 recording, with harmonies by Charlie Hodge and Red West, first appeared on *From Nashville to Memphis* in the Nineties. FTD 2004 release *In A Private Moment* features a home recording from earlier in 1966; Elvis is also rumored to have tried out the song in late 1960. "Beyond The Reef" did earn a full release in the UK, as a single, with "It's Only Love" on the B-side.

BIENSTOCK, FREDDY
(B.1928)

Bienstock was the point man for Hill & Range (and a cousin of the company owners, the Aberbach brothers), who started in the music business in the stock room of Chappell & Co. Music—a company he took over four decades later.

Bienstock acted as the liaison who gave Elvis his first look at potential material for his upcoming recording commitments all the way through until 1968, after which he continued to work with Elvis through his own music publishing interests.

One story has it that Bienstock had a chance to manage Elvis right at the start of his career, when Bill Randle suggested he contact the hot young singer because he knew Elvis was looking for a manager.

Bienstock was born in Switzerland and emigrated to the US just before World War II. He met Elvis for the first time (or again—see story above) in New York in July 1956, at the session where Elvis recorded Hill & Range song "Don't Be Cruel."

In the summer of 1959 Bienstock and Jean Aberbach met Elvis and pals when they arrived in Paris for a two week sojourn. Bienstock also visited Elvis in Germany to take him demos for his first post-Army recording session.

Bienstock often sat in on Elvis' recording sessions, organizing the material and making sure that Elvis recorded the songs he was contracted to record rather than others for which Hill & Range did not own the rights. As the sixties wore on, Elvis became increasingly dissatisfied with the songs Hill & Range brought to him, and started casting his eye further afield for new songwriting talent.

Bienstock bought out Hill & Range's UK interests and set up his own company, Carlin, in 1966. In 1969, Bienstock co-founded The Hudson Bay Music Company with Jerry Leiber and Mike Stoller. By 1970 Bienstock was beginning to supply Elvis with new material on his own, while still working on behalf of Hill & Range. In 1972 the Colonel approached Bienstock about setting up their own publishing company to step in and take over from Hill & Range, which was about to cease trading.

Bienstock added the UK arm of Hill & Range to his burgeoning publishing empire, and continued to sign up promising new bands including a once little-known Irish combo called U2. He has remained in the music business ever since, and at the time of writing was a board member of ASCAP and the NMPA.

FREDDY BIENSTOCK: "For the first 12 years of his career, Elvis didn't look at a song unless I brought it to him."

ERNST JORGENSEN: "Throughout his relationship with Elvis, Freddy Bienstock always took notice of which songs caught the singer's attention, and even if they weren't chosen immediately he kept them around against the day when they might be useful."

"BIG BOOTS"

Sid Wayne and Sherman Edwards wrote this lullaby for Elvis to record for G.I. Blues on May 6, 1960 at Radio Recorders A slow version of the song (recorded on April 28 at RCA's Hollywood studios) came out on 1978 album Elvis Sings For Children (And Grown Ups Too)—later re-released as Elvis Sings For Kids. The fast version was used in the film and on the soundtrack album. Collectors Gold offered a discarded version from the April 28 session. Both versions plus an acoustic tryout are on the 1997 G.I. Blues CD, while Elvis: Close Up features a fast version alternate.

"BIG BOSS MAN"

Recorded in Nashville on September 10, 1967 and rushed out the door two and a half weeks later, this Al Smith / Luther Dixon classic had been a blues hit for Jimmy Reed in 1961. The song was actually originally called "Stack O' Dollars" when it was first released by Charley Jordan in 1930.

Accompanied by B-Side "You Don't Know Me," the return to blues reversed Elvis' sliding record sales as the single climbed to #38 in the charts and sold close to 350,000 copies. Incongruously, the track made its LP debut as a bonus to the Clambake soundtrack release. It has since appeared on Elvis Sings Hits From His Movies Vol. 1, Double Dynamite, Elvis Sings The Blues, Elvis' Golden Records Vol. 5, From Nashville to Memphis (which also has an alternate take), Artist Of The Century, Tomorrow Is A Long Time, and more recently the Clambake reissue from FTD, Elvis R'n'B, and The Essential Elvis Presley (2007 version).

Elvis recorded a second version of the song at Western Recorders for the R'n'B medley in his NBC TV Special on June 20, 1968. This version made it into the finished show and onto the tie-in album Elvis. Sixty-eight Special versions have since resurfaced on Memories: The '68 Comeback Special. Alternate takes from these sessions have appeared on Today Tomorrow & Forever and FTD album Let Yourself Go.

Elvis enjoyed performing this fans' favorite at live shows from 1973, hence its inclusion on many bootlegs releases and FTD live albums—"Big Boss Man" is of a handful of tracks that Elvis tried out as an alternative show opener to "See See Rider." Seventies live versions can be found on Live In Las Vegas and on FTD gigs Live In L.A., It's Midnight, Dragonheart, Big Boss Man, Southern Nights, New Year's Eve and Spring Tours '77.

BIG BOSS MAN

An FTD release of Elvis in Las Vegas, featuring a complete concert from March 30, 1975 and other live tracks from this period. Released in 2005.

TRACK LISTING:
1. Also Sprach Zarathustra
2. See See Rider
3. I Got A Woman / Amen
4. Love Me
5. If You Love Me (Let Me Know)
6. And I Love You So
7. Big Boss Man
8. It's Midnight
9. Promised Land
10. Burning Love
11. Introductions
12. More introductions incl. What'd I Say & School Days
13. My Boy
14. I'll Remember You
15. Let Me Be There
16. Hound Dog
17. An American Trilogy
18. Can't Help Falling In Love
19. You Don't Have To Say You Love Me
20. The Wonder Of You
21. Bridge Over Troubled Water
22. Little Darlin'
23. Hawaiian Wedding Song
24. Green, Green Grass Of Home
25. Fairytale
26. You're The Reason I'm Living

BIG D JAMBOREE

Elvis played this major country bash in Dallas, organized by promoter Ed McLemore, a number of times in 1955. The Saturday night radio broadcast on KRLD helped significantly to extend Elvis' reach.

"BIG HUNK OF LOVE, A"

A #1 success for the last single released during the long hiatus when Elvis was away in Germany on his Army tour of duty. The track shipped with B-Side "My Wish Came True" on June 23, 1959, a full year after Elvis recorded the Aaron Schroeder / Sid Wyche piano-led romp on June 10, 1959, during two weeks of furlough. Six weeks on the Billboard Hot 100 and a million sales proved that Elvis' fan base was secure despite his absence. Studio performances have since come out on Worldwide 50 Gold Award Hits Vol. 1, The King Of Rock 'n' Roll, Artist Of The Century and Hitstory among others.

The song was a regular in Elvis' Seventies repertoire, including during his 1972 performances in Las Vegas (the Elvis on Tour documentary and the Walk A Mile In My Shoes anthology) and the Aloha From Hawaii Via Satellite extravaganza.

Further live performances have appeared on The Alternate Aloha, the 1999 Burning Love CD, The Live Greatest Hits and Live In Las Vegas. There are others on FTD releases An American Trilogy, Writing For The King, Summer Festival, Closing Night and Takin' Tahoe Tonight!

Rehearsals of the song have appeared on FTD releases On Tour--The Rehearsals and Elvis 6363 Sunset.

Alternate studio takes may be found on Essential Elvis Vol. 3, The King Of Rock 'N' Roll, Platinum: A Life In Music and ELVIS 30 #1 Hits. FTD release 50,000,000 Million Elvis Fans Can't Be Wrong features four alternate takes.

"BIG LOVE, BIG HEARTACHE"

A Dee Fuller / Lee Morris / Sonny Hendrix ballad that Elvis recorded for the Roustabout soundtrack at Radio Recorders on March 3, 1964. The only official re-release has been on the Double Features CD, paired with Viva Las Vegas.

BIGGS, DELTA (NÉE DELTA MAE PRESLEY) (1919-1993)

Elvis' aunt on his father's side, who for many years lived at Graceland in a bedroom off the kitchen next to the Jungle Room. Aunt Delta moved in to Graceland in 1967 after her husband Pat died. Soon she was in charge of the day-to-day running of the household, and became a formidable presence at Graceland.

Aunt Delta seems to have been a prickly character. She liked her drink, was a heavy smoker and has been described as a woman who talked first and thought later.

On Christmas Day 1975, Aunt Delta got famously drunk and had a row with some of Elvis' pals—like Vernon, she believed that the entourage guys sponged off her nephew. She reportedly threatened to shoot an entourage member or two that night, when the party was on the Lisa Marie. Grandma Minnie Mae begged Elvis not to throw her out—this was not the only time Aunt Delta had caused a ruckus—to which Elvis couldn't say no.

Aunt Delta ended up being the last Presley to live at Graceland, outliving Elvis, Vernon and Minnie Mae. She refused to leave when Graceland was opened to public visitors in 1982. Over the years, one or two startled fans were told in no uncertain terms to clear off her property. She had few friends but constant company in a Pomeranian breed dog called Edmond that Elvis gave her. When Edmond I died, Edmond II replaced him. She died in 1993.

BILLY SMITH: "When it came to her personality, Aunt Delta was a whole lot like Vernon. She hated everybody."

BIGGS, PAT

When he was growing up, Elvis' uncle (the husband of Vernon's sister) Pat Biggs was the one person in the family who had money. In later years,. Elvis gave him some money to help buy a nightclub.

When he died in 1966, Elvis had the funeral arrangements taken care of and afterwards asked Aunt Delta to come and live with Graceland where her mother Minnie Mae already was.

BILLBOARD MAGAZINE

Billboard magazine was founded in 1894 as a bill posting rather than a music paper. Billboard Advertising, as it was originally called, began to focus on music when the recording industry cranked into gear in the teens. In 1940 the magazine introduced a short list of Best Selling Retail Records, the first in a long line of charts.

Editor Paul Ackerman reviewed Elvis' first single in the magazine's "Talent" section on August 7, 1954, describing the singer as "a potent new chanter who can sock over a tune for either the country or the R & B markets." He tipped Elvis and his new sound for success and marked him out as "a strong new talent."

By mid-November 1955, with Elvis' star most definitely on the rise, the magazine's Annual Disc Jockey Poll gave Elvis the year's accolade for "Most Promising C&W Artist."

See also RECORD SALES

Elvis signing authographs, 1956.

BINDER, STEVE

Binder was hired to direct Elvis' 1968 Comeback Special on NBC. Elvis knew and appreciated his work on the 1965 T.A.M.I show featuring Chuck Berry, James Brown, Marvin Gaye and the Rolling Stones, and his more recent Petula Clark Special.

Ten years younger than Elvis, Binder brought a breath of fresh air into the King's creative world. Binder had the imagination to convert what was conceived originally as a standard-issue Christmas TV special into a show unlike anything previously seen on TV, a one-man extravaganza presenting Elvis past, present and future.

Elvis and Steve hit it off the first time they met. When Binder rued the fact that he had great ideas but was constrained by the Christmas format, Elvis told him they could do whatever they wanted. Elvis was so enthusiastic at the prospect of cutting loose that for once Parker was unable to stamp his authority on proceedings, and Binder goes down in the annals of Elvis' career as one of very few men to get one over on the Colonel.

The Colonel could only re-establish his pre-eminence after the show was recorded: he changed his mind about hiring Binder to direct one of Elvis' upcoming feature films, and he issued orders that Binder not be admitted backstage at Elvis' triumphant first night in Las Vegas in the summer of 1969, even though Elvis was asking for him.

After Elvis' NBC show, Binder carried on producing music-based spectaculars and sports broadcasts.

STEVE BINDER: "I felt very, very strongly that the special was Elvis' moment of truth, and that the number-one requirement was honesty."

COLONEL PARKER (20 years later): "I don't think there was any producer could ever get the talent out of Elvis like Steve."

BIOGRAPHIES

Hundreds of Elvis biographies have been written, from Fifties fan pamphlets to Peter Guralnick's unsurpassable two-volume life portrait. What follows is a summary of some—but by no means all—landmark Elvis biographies.

The first Elvis biography to feature interviews with people who knew Elvis was *Elvis Presley Speaks!*, a 68-page booklet written by Memphis journalist Robert Johnson and published in 1956.

James Gregory's book-length collection of articles *The Elvis Presley Story* was popular with fans from 1960.

Jerry Hopkins' 1971 work *Elvis* was the best-regarded biography during Elvis' lifetime—even Elvis liked what he saw of it. UK fan club president Todd Slaughter published an Elvis biography while Elvis was still alive in 1977.

The most negative major biography, also titled *Elvis*, was written by Albert Goldman and published in 1981. Many Elvis fans refuse to read this book on principle, though it is by no means the only scurrilous account of Elvis' life and times.

In 1982 rock critic Dave Marsh published a well-regarded biography, *Elvis*, focusing very much on the man's musical heritage.

Peter Guralnick's two-volume biography *Last Train To Memphis* published in 1994 and *Careless Love, The Unmaking Of Elvis Presley* published in 1999, combines a non-judgmental approach with impressively rigorous research.

The first Elvis biography authorized by EPE is 2004 book *Elvis Presley: The Man. The Life. The Legend*, by Pamela Clarke Keogh, which contains rare photographs from the Elvis archives.

Priscilla and family worked on multimedia

project *Elvis By The Presleys*, published by Crown Publishers in 2005 alongside a DVD and CD.

For Elvis biopics, *see* ACTORS WHO HAVE PORTRAYED ELVIS.

BIRTH

Elvis Aron Presley was born at 4:35 a.m. on January 8, 1935. Surprisingly, accounts differ over whether Elvis was born half an hour before or half an hour after his stillborn twin brother, Jesse Garon. Though official documents and eye-witness accounts conflict, the likelihood is that Elvis came into the world half an hour after Jesse Garon.

The twins were delivered by midwife Mrs. Edna Robinson, who was joined later by Dr. William R. Hunt at the family home in East Tupelo after Vernon sent for him. Elvis weighed 5 pounds when he was born.

Years later, Vernon told Larry Geller that to save sickly little Elvis they put him in a shoe box and kept him warm in the oven. Vernon also told people that when Elvis was born, the shotgun shack in Tupelo was bathed in a mysterious blue light.

Concerted lobbying has been taking place for years to make Elvis' birthday or the date of his death a national holiday in the USA.

LAMAR FIKE: "Elvis used to say that Vernon knew when Elvis was conceived, because afterwards, he blacked out."

WHAT ELVIS DID ON HIS BIRTHDAYS

On his 11th birthday, Elvis' parents bought him his first guitar at the Tupelo Hardware Store. Elvis was disappointed; what he really wanted was a rifle (or a bicycle depending on the telling).

When he was 14, Vernon gave Elvis a book of cartoons by George Price.

Elvis played a Louisiana Hayride date on his 20th birthday.

For his 21st birthday, Elvis flew home to Memphis with Red West.

Elvis made it back to Memphis fro his "Ed Sullivan Show" appearance for his 22nd birthday.

Elvis celebrated his 23rd party by singing at a birthday bash in a Memphis hotel, and then went skating with 50 close friends.

Elvis was not in too much of a mood for celebration for his first birthday without his mother, in Germany to boot, for his 24th birthday.

Elvis threw a party for his 25th birthday at a club in Bad Nauheim, where he was living during his Army service in Germany. Priscilla Beaulieu was one of 200 guests.

Elvis celebrated his 26th birthday on the set of *Wild in the Country*, and received a plaque from the cast and crew engraved with the words "Happy Birthday, King Karate."

Elvis was at the Sahara Hotel in Las Vegas for his 27th birthday, where owner Milton Prell gave him a Sahara-shaped cake.

It was Graceland and no particular fuss for his 29th birthday.

He spent his 30th birthday on January 8, 1965 at Graceland, without making much of a fuss, with the usual birthday sheet cake decorated with a big music note.

On his 31st birthday Elvis hired out the Memphian Theater for a screening of *It's a Mad Mad Mad Mad World*.

His 32nd birthday was spent at home, enjoying his latest hobby, horse riding, and spending time with Jordanaire Gordon Stoker who stopped by

to say hi. Priscilla gave him a calendar pendant that year.

Elvis had his 33rd birthday at home, as usual going out to the Memphian Theater later on; his 34th was also an at-home affair.

Elvis was in Los Angeles with his family, preparing for his first Las Vegas engagement, for his 35th birthday.

For his 36th, Elvis went out to buy himself police paraphernalia.

Elvis was consoled by Joyce Bova at Graceland for his 37th birthday, a week after Priscilla told him she was leaving.

Elvis' 38th birthday was spent in Los Angeles, preparing for the journey to Honolulu and, a few days later, his *Aloha From Hawaii* show.

Elvis' 39th birthday was celebrated in Memphis as an official "Elvis Presley Day" celebration, including a mayoral march to Graceland. Jimmy Carter, then governor of Georgia, declared January 8, 1974 "Elvis Presley Day."

Elvis' 40th birthday held little cause for celebration. He holed up at Graceland with Linda Thompson, more or less secreted away as he recovered from a stomach ulcer, excess pills and a bout of depression. The next day the Colonel roused him by suggesting a benefit concert for the victims of the tornado that had devastated McComb in Mississippi.

Perhaps mindful of how miserable his last birthday had been, Elvis took off with a large cohort of friends and family to Vail, Colorado, for his 41st birthday in 1976. He didn't feel like partying, but invited Jerry Schilling and Myrna Smith round for cake.

Elvis' last birthday, his 42nd, was spent in Las Vegas (Palm Springs according to Jo Alden) with Ginger Alden, her sister Rosemary and various entourage pals. Dressed in a black suit and a blue silk shirt, Elvis handed out $100 bills to traveling wives and girlfriends after reading to them from his favorite spiritual books.

SHARING ELVIS' BIRTHDAY . . .

Charles Osgood (1933)
David Bowie (1947)
Graham Chapman (1941)
Robby Krieger (1941)
Ron Moody (1924)
Shirley Bassey (1937)
Stephen Hawking (1942)
Terry Sylvester (1947)
William Wilkie Collins (1824)
Yvette Mimieux (1939)

"BITTER THEY ARE, HARDER THEY FALL"

Elvis recorded this Larry Gatlin song at Graceland on February 2, 1976. It first came out on the *From Elvis Presley Boulevard, Memphis Tennessee* album. It was later released on *Always On My Mind*, CD re-releases of *Moody Blue*,

Alternates have appeared on FTD albums *The Jungle Room Sessions* and *Made in Memphis*.

BIXBY, BILL
(B. WILFRED BAILEY BIXBY, 1934-1993)

Years before he became mild-mannered David Bruce Banner, alter ego of "The Hulk," versatile actor Bill Bixby worked with Elvis on *Clambake* and *Speedway*. Bixby began his career on TV in "The Many Loves of Dobie Gillis" and scored his greatest successes on the small screen, before turning his hand to directing.

In his final years he presented a documentary

delving into the question of whether Elvis really died, and then directed TV biopic *The Woman Who Loved Elvis*, starring Roseanne Barr and Tom Arnold in 1993.

BLACK, BILL
(B. WILLIAM PATTON BLACK, JR., SEPTEMBER 17, 1926-1965)

Memphis-born Bill Black was the bass player in Doug Poindexter's Starlite Wranglers, an act on the Sun roster featuring guitarist Scotty Moore. On July 4th, 1954 Scotty asked Bill round to his place to put a young hopeful through his paces. The next day Bill, Scotty and that young hopeful went to Sun Records to show Sam Phillips what they could do. During a break from the repertoire they had agreed to run through, Elvis broke into an impromptu rendition of Arthur "Big Boy" Crudup hit "That's All Right." And that's the standard story of how Bill Black became a founding member of Elvis' first band, the Blue Moon Boys.

An alternative has it that Elvis knew Bill Black from as early as 1951, through his two younger brothers, with whom he went to Humes High, and who were neighbors of the Presleys at Lauderdale Courts. Johnny Black followed in his elder brother's footsteps and played bass in Fifties bands.

Bill Black, or "Blackie" to his friends, married young, served in the army and then found a succession of jobs in Memphis, including at Firestone Tires.

Before Elvis started doing well enough to give up the day job, Black earned his living working for a tire company, and had previously worked on the railways.

Bill Black's sound was an integral part of the live act, his slapped bass driving the rhythm alongside Elvis' vocal delivery. In the early years Black was a livewire part of the stage act, clowning around and helping to warm up audiences that had no idea who Elvis was. He'd also muck in and help sell Elvis photos at out of the way venues. Black toned down his stage antics by the time national fame came Elvis' way.

Black only played with Elvis a few times more after he and Scotty downed tools over their meager salaries in 1957. He had already left by the time Elvis did his last recording sessions before his Army service in January 1958, replaced by Jordanaire Neal Matthews and tuba player Ray Siegel.

Post-Elvis, Bill formed his own band, Bill Black's Combo, with Memphis players Carl McVoy, Jerry Arnold, Ace Cannon and Reggie Young. The Combo made its record debut on Hi Records with "Smokie," an instrumental that made it into the top 10 in 1959. The band scored a number of Top 40 singles over the next few years, including previous Elvis hit "Don't Be Cruel," with what they billed as their "untouchable sound." The Combo appeared on the "Ed Sullivan Show," and featured in Hollywood movie *Teenage Millionaire*. The Bill Black Combo toured with The Beatles on their first tour of the States in 1964, though by this time Bill himself was suffering serious health problems.

Black died of a brain tumor aged 39 in October 1965, leaving behind a wife and three daughters. Elvis did not attend his funeral because he feared his presence would overshadow the solemnity of the occasion. He told a local newspaper: "This comes as such a shock to me that I can hardly explain how much I loved Bill."

ELVIS SAID: "One of the best bass men in the business."

EDDIE BOND: "The slapping bass had been around for a long time, but they really made it dominate. It was almost like beating the drum."

SAM PHILLIPS: "Bill was one of the worst bass players in the world, technically, but man, could he slap that thing!'"

"BLACK BOTTOM STOMP"

Jerry Lee Lewis took it away with this Ferdinand "Jelly Roll" Morton song at the tail end of the *Million Dollar Quartet* session on December 4, 1956 at Sun Studios. By this time, Elvis had already left the building.

"BLACK STAR"

A Sid Wayne / Sherman Edwards collaboration that Elvis consigned to tape at Radio Recorders for *Flaming Star* on August 8, 1960. The song became surplus to requirements (for decades) when the movie title changed.

For "Black Star" so far, a debut on *Collectors Gold* in 1991, and a follow-up on the inevitable *Double Features* re-issue.

BLACKMAN, JOAN
(B. 1938)

Joan Blackman was Elvis' love interest in two early Sixties movies, *Blue Hawaii* and *Kid Galahad*. She was also a love interest off-screen, dating Elvis while he was making *Loving You* in 1957. She worked in many well-known Sixties TV series, and was still acting into the Eighties. She also starred opposite Jerry Lewis playing an alien in 1960 movie *Visit to a Small Planet*.

BLACKWELL, OTIS
(1932-2002)

A prolific singer and songwriter who spent his formative years listening to music at the Apollo and Savoy in New York—and Tex Ritter too—before starting a singing career at 16. Blackwell soon found that he could make more money writing songs than performing, and went on to write many of Elvis' early hits including "All Shook Up," "Ready Teddy" and "Return To Sender." When Blackwell wasn't writing the songs, he lent his voice to the RCA/Hill & Range demos from which Elvis chose what he wanted to record. Blackwell also wrote hits for Jerry Lee Lewis ("Great Balls of Fire") Ray Charles, Otis Redding, James Brown, The Who, Billy Joel, Dolly Parton and many more, occasionally under the pseudonym John Davenport.

Other notable Elvis Blackwells are "Fever," "One Broken Heart for Sale," "Easy Question" and "Paralyzed," one of three songs on which Elvis has a writing credit that's all to do with publishing royalties and nothing to do with songwriting.

Over his career, Blackwell songs are said to have sold around 200 million records.

Blackwell can be heard singing his own hits (and even some of the demos Elvis used) on 2003 album *They Called It Rock 'n' Roll*.

He has a rightful place in the Songwriters' Hall of Fame and the Nashville Songwriters Hall of Fame.

Otis Blackwell: "I used to sing all my own demos, and it just so happened that a lot of what Presley and Jerry Lee did sound alike. I thought that they did justice to the songs. They put the kind of feeling into it that I felt."

BLACKWELL, ROBERT "BUMPS"
(1918-1985)

A musician, songwriter and record producer instrumental in Little Richard and Sam Cooke's early career, Blackwell started out playing jazz in a band that featured then unknowns Ray Charles and Quincy Jones in Seattle. After moving to Los Angeles, Blackwell and his business partner bought out Little Richard's recording contract and started supplying him with hits, three of which Elvis covered in 1956 ("Long Tall Sally," "Ready Teddy" and "Rip It Up").

In later years, Blackwell produced Bob Dylan and Art Neville.

BLACKWOOD BROTHERS

The Blackwood Brothers quartet was a leading gospel group originally from Ackerman, Mississippi who young Elvis regularly saw at the First Assembly of God Church in Memphis. The original line-up of brothers Roy, Doyle and James Blackwood (with Roy's son R.W.) changed many times over the years, as you would expect of a band that in one form or another was still performing into the Nineties.

Gladys' favorite group relocated to Memphis in 1950 and put on a monthly gospel show called the All-Night Gospel Singing at the Ellis Auditorium. The Presley family often attended these shows; Elvis took girlfriend Dixie Locke along on one of their first dates. Elvis also regularly listened to the Blackwood's midday radio show on WMPS in Memphis.

The quartet was struck by tragedy on June 29, 1954, when R. W. Blackwood and Bill Lyles were killed in a plane crash in Alabama. Elvis, his parents and his girlfriend Dixie Locke all attended the funeral on July 2, 1954.

One year later, Elvis performed with the Blackwood Brothers and another favorite gospel quartet, The Statesmen, at a gospel picnic show to celebrate July 4, 1955, in Stephenville, Texas.

Elvis went to an All-Night Singing session on September 23, 1955. When James Blackwood found out that Elvis had paid for his own ticket, he sent him a courtesy refund.

On July 27, 1956, Elvis was back at an All-Night Singing event. This time he joined the group on stage and sang "Jesus Built My Every Need" and "You'll Never Walk Alone." The rare times Elvis was back home in Memphis during his frenetic early touring years he would try to get to the "singings" at Ellis Auditorium, listening from backstage until he came out and joined in. Then one day the Colonel told him that now he was a star, it wasn't right for him to sing without getting paid.

In August 1958, Elvis flew the Blackwood Brothers to Memphis from their concert tour in North Carolina for the sad honor of singing at his mother Gladys's funeral.

When Elvis recorded his first gospel album in 1960, he included Blackwood Brothers classics "In My Father's House," "Mansion Over The Hilltop" and "Known Only To Him."

Blackwood Brothers singer J. D. Sumner worked with Elvis regularly in the Seventies.

The Blackwoods won a total of eight Grammys, and were so synonymous with the gospel genre that James Blackwood became known as "Mr. Gospel Singer of America."

In 1977, James Blackwood (1919-2002) sang at Elvis' funeral.

BLACKWOOD, CECIL
(1934-2000)

Nephew of Blackwood Brothers founding member James Blackwood, Cecil lived in Lauderdale

Courts, not far from Elvis and his family when they first moved to Memphis. Cecil Blackwood ran a quartet for youngsters called the Songfellows, for which Elvis had an unsuccessful audition. Soon after, Cecil was drafted into the main group after two of its members were killed in a plane crash.

BLAINE, HAL
(B. HAROLD SIMON BELSKY, 1929)

Drummer and percussionist Blaine worked with Elvis on the Blue Hawaii soundtrack in early 1961 and subsequent movie soundtracks recorded in LA, right up to and including the 1968 NBC TV "Comeback" Special, including a cameo in Girls! Girls! Girls!

Blaine's stick work has given the rhythm to thousands of familiar songs; he seems to have worked on practically every recording made in Los Angeles in the Sixties and Seventies, including Sonny and Cher's "I Got You Babe," The Byrds' "Mr. Tambourine Man," The Mamas and the Papas "California Dreamin' ," Beach Boys classics "I Get Around" and "Good Vibrations," as well as multiple hits for Frank Sinatra, Phil Spector, John Denver, Simon and Garfunkel, The Carpenters and more, winning Grammy Record of the Year recognition every year from 1966 to 1971.

Not surprisingly, Blaine is in the Rock and Roll Hall of Fame.

BLAND, BOBBY "BLUE"
(B. 1930)

In the early Fifties, Beale Street blues legend Bobby "Blue" Bland cut singles for Chess that were actually recorded by Sam Phillips at Memphis Recording Service. After returning from his military service, Bland took up where he left off, scoring his first national hit with "Farther Up The Road" in 1957 and recording smooth-edged blues, gospel and soul right through to the Nineties.

"BLESSED JESUS (HOLD MY HAND)"

Elvis sang this Albert Brumley gospel track from the Thirties (with Jerry Lee Lewis doing the harmony) on December 4, 1956 during what has ever been known as the Million Dollar Quartet Session. Complete gospel anthology Peace In The Valley has the track too.

BLOSSOMS, THE

A backing group of Darlene Love, Jean King and Fanita James that worked with Elvis on his 1968 NBC TV Special and recorded on his final feature films (the group make a cameo in Change of Habit). Elvis is said to have approached them about backing him when he returned to live performance in Las Vegas, but they already had a booking. The Blossoms later backed Tom Jones in Vegas.

The Blossoms actually started out as a high school group in Los Angeles in 1954. In the early Sixties members of the group worked with Phil Spector as the Bob B. Soxx, before landing a regular slot on TV show "Shindig." They also had hits in the Sixties with "Son-in-Law" and later "Good, Good Lovin'."

"BLOWIN' IN THE WIND"

Elvis never succeeded in recording this 1962 Bob Dylan breakthrough hit on an official release, but a home-recorded version, with Elvis singing along to an instrumental record in 1966, has made it into the world on Platinum: A Life In Music and In A Private Moment. He is also said to have performed the song in at least one of his Seventies concerts, and is rumored to have recorded this and other Dylan songs at a May 1971 Nashville recording session, of which no trace thus far.

"BLUE CHRISTMAS"

Elvis first recorded this Billy Hayes / Jay Johnson track on September 5, 1957 at Radio Recorders for his inaugural festive LP, Elvis' Christmas Album (and EP Elvis Sings Christmas Songs). The song was originally a hit for Doye O'Dell in 1948—also famous for "Old Shep," the first song Elvis ever performed in public—and for Ernest Tubb in 1950.

When "Blue Christmas" was re- released as a single in early November 1964, backed by German song "Wooden Heart" from G.I. Blues, it made it to #1 spot but only on the specially-compiled Christmas charts but not leaving a dent on the Hot 100. In a case of seasonal déjà vu, the track was re-released in 1965 as the B-side to "Santa Claus Is Back in Town."

The studio version has since appeared on Elvis: A Legendary Performer Vol. 2, Memories Of Christmas, A Golden Celebration, If Every Day Was Like Christmas, Blue Christmas, The King Of Rock 'n' Roll, Christmas Peace and Elvis Christmas.

Elvis featured this, his "favorite Christmas song," in a NBC TV Special live segment medley recorded on June 27, 1968—the only festive song in what was originally intended to be an hour-long Christmas Special before producer Steve Binder had other ideas. Even this bluesy Christmas number was dropped from the 1969 repeat broadcast of the TV Special in favor of "Tiger Man."

Performances from the two shows Elvis recorded on June 27 appeared on the tie-in NBC TV Special album, and later on Elvis Aron Presley, A Golden Celebration, Memories: The '68 Comeback Special and Tiger Man. Alternates from this period are on FTD releases Burbank '68 and Let Yourself Go.

Live concert recordings from the Seventies have come out on Elvis by the Presleys and FTD releases Dragonheart, Dinner At Eight and Spring Tours '77.

BLUE CHRISTMAS

A 1992 8-track CD, reissued in 2006.

TRACK LISTING:
1. O Come, All Ye Faithful
2. The First Noel
3. Winter Wonderland
4. Silver Bells
5. Blue Christmas
6. Silent Night
7. White Christmas
8. I'll Be Home For Christmas

"BLUE EYES CRYING IN THE RAIN"

This was the last track Elvis completed on his February 7, 1976 Graceland recording session, his last ever. It was also the last song he is known ever to have sung, in the early hours of the morning on which he died.

Written by Leon Rose but first released by Roy Acuff and His Smokey Mountain Boys in 1947, when Elvis took it on the song had recently been a #1 Country hit for Willie Nelson. Elvis' version came out on the From Elvis Presley Boulevard, Memphis Tennessee album. According to some recollections, Elvis picked up and played bass on the song.

Later releases include The Country Side Of Elvis, CD versions of Moody Blue, and the 2006 Elvis Country release. Alternate versions are on The Jungle Room Sessions, released on the FTD label.

"BLUE HAWAII"

The title song to the film and album soundtrack of the same name had a long pedigree before Elvis took on the Lee Robin / Ralph Rainger composition at Radio Recorders on March 22, 1961. After the Blue Hawaii LP, Elvis' version has since appeared on Elvis in Hollywood, Mahalo From Elvis, Command Performances, Elvis Movies and Elvis at the Movies.

The Colonel was no doubt aware of the association with Bing Crosby, who first had a hit with the song after premiering it in 1937 picture Waikiki Wedding, as he repositioned Elvis for a long and successful mainstream movie career. Gene Autry and Billy Vaughn among others also had a hit with the tune.

Elvis returned to the song live immediately after his 1973 Aloha From Hawaii Via Satellite concert, when "Blue Hawaii" was added for the US version of the broadcast. This version didn't make it onto the concert album, but it did see the light of day on Elvis: A Legendary Performer Vol. 2 three years later, followed a decade and more later by The Alternate Aloha.

The Blue Hawaii 1997 re-release album features an alternate take from the 1961 studio session.

A 1966 home recording of the song from Graceland saw release on 1999 FTD album In A Private Moment.

BLUE HAWAII (LP)

Elvis' biggest selling album in his lifetime—and the soundtrack album with the most songs—raced to #1 on the Billboard Hot 100 and stayed there for 20 weeks, selling over two million LPs in its first year alone. Originally released in October 1961, the soundtrack album stayed in the charts for 79 weeks. It wasn't until 1977 that Fleetwood Mac's album Rumors eclipsed the length of time that Blue Hawaii hogged the #1 spot.

TRACK LISTING:
1. Blue Hawaii
2. Almost Always True
3. Aloha Oe
4. No More
5. Can't Help Falling In Love
6. Rock-A-Hula Baby
7. Moonlight Swim
8. Ku-U-I-Po
9. Ito Eats
10. Slicin' Sand
11. Hawaiian Sunset
12. Beach Boy Blues
13. Island Of Love
14. Hawaiian Wedding Song

A remixed 1997 re-issue includes previously unreleased takes and movie versions of "Can't Help Falling In Love," "Slicin' Sand," "No More," "Rock-A Hula Baby," "Beach Boy Blues," "Steppin' Out Of Line" and "Blue Hawaii."

BLUE HAWAII

Producer Hal Wallis was keen to put Elvis in a movie that showed how time in the Army changes

The movie poster for *Blue Hawaii* (1961).

a man, of course in the midst of bikini-wearing lovelies. Juliet Prowse was all set to land the co-star role until she asked for more perks than Paramount was willing to concede. Wallis was concerned enough about Elvis' physical condition to recommend a specific brand of suntan lamp before shooting. Elvis reported to Paramount on March 20, 1961. Three weeks of location photography on Hawaii commenced a week later. The movie took in many of top Hawaiian tourist attractions, including Waikiki Beach, Diamond Head, Mount Tantalus and Hanuana Bay.

To relax during shooting, Elvis and Red West held karate demonstrations and smashed boards to the point that Elvis' fingers suffered swelling. Producer Hal Wallis sent word to the actresses that they were not to attend parties with Elvis and his entourage because they were turning up for work looking worn out.

Before release, the movie was known as *Hawaii Beach Boy*. Three songs wound up on the cutting room floor: "La Paloma," "Playing With Fire" and "Steppin' Out Of Line."

Director Norman Taurog had previously directed Bing Crosby, who sang the original "Blue Hawaii" song in 1937 movie *Waikiki Wedding*.

Producer Hal Wallis made a cameo in the movie as a man walking down the street.

The Coco Palms hotel on Kauai, where the movie was shot, was built on the site where Kauai's last monarch, Queen Deborah Kapule, once lived.

Blue Hawaii opened in late November 1961, rising to #2 on the weekly Box Office Survey and earning more than twice its budget to become the 14th highest grossing movie of 1962 (it was #8 for 1961). The movie was nominated unsuccessfully for a best soundtrack album Grammy. No matter, it grossed as much as $14 million (up to $30 million in some estimations), three times Elvis' previous best earner *G.I. Blues*, and spawned Elvis' best-selling album of all.

ELVIS SAID: "In the movie we did a song called the Hawaiian Wedding Song. And it was so real that it took me 10 years before I realized I wasn't married to the chick."

CREDITS:
Paramount, Color.
Length: 102 minutes
Release date: November 22, 1961

TAG LINES:
Ecstatic romance...exotic dances...exciting music in the world's lushest paradise of song!
Elvis Presley rides the crest of the wave in *Blue Hawaii*.

Directed by: Norman Taurog
Produced by: Hal B. Wallis
Written by: Allan Weiss (story), Hal Kanter
Associate producer: Paul Nathan
Music by: Joseph J. Lilley
Cinematography by: Charles Lang Jr.
Film Editing by: Terry Morse
Art Direction by: Hal Pereira, Walter Tyler
Set Decoration by: Sam Comer, Frank McKelvy
Costume Design by: Edith Head

CAST:

Elvis Presley	Chad Gates
Joan Blackman	Maile Duval
Angela Lansbury	Sarah Lee Gates
Nancy Walters	Abigail Prentice
Jenny Maxwell	Ellie Corbett
Pamela Kirk	Selena (Sandy) Emerson
Darlene Tompkins	Patsy Simon
Christian Kay	Beverly Martin
Roland Winters	Fred Gates
John Archer	Jack Kelman
Howard McNear	Mr. Chapman
Steve Brodie	Tucker Garvey
Iris Adrian	Enid Garvey
Hilo Hattie	Waihila
Lani Kai	Carl Tanami
Jose De Vega	Ernie Gordon
Frank Atienza	Ito O'Hara
Tiki Hanelot	Ping Pong
Bobby Barber	Man in Beach Brawl
Tom Carroll	Beach Party Guest
Roger Clark	Lawyer
Sharon Lee Connors	Bit part
Lillian Culver	Matron
George DeNormand	Gen. Anthony
Veronica Ericson	Bit part
Lamar Fike	Extra
Bess Flowers	Maile's customer
Gregory Gaye	Paul Duval
Thomas Glynn	Man at Party
George Halas	Extra
Flora Hayes	Mrs. Maneka
Yolanda Hughes	Extra
Donna Juhl	Extra
Debra M. Kawamura	Extra
Gene LeBell	Extra
Robert M. Luck	Extra
Clarence Lung	Lonnie, Bartender
Tani Marsh	Dancer
Harold Miller	Maile's customer
Irene Mizushima	Waitress
Kate Murtagh	Woman at Party
Ngarua	Dancer
Patti Page	Extra
Rudi Polt	Extra
Robert Kenui Pope	Extra
Richard Reeves	Harmonica-playing Convict
Bella Richards	Extra
Michael Ross	Police Lt. Gray
Elsie Russell	Extra
Pat Tackenthall	Extra
Hal B. Wallis	Man Walking Down Street
Red West	Party Guest

ADDITIONAL CREW:

Nellie Manley	hair styles supervisor
Wally Westmore	makeup supervisor
Michael D. Moore	assistant director
Charles Grenzbach.	sound recorder
Philip Mitchell	sound recorder
Bill Wistrom	sound editor
John P. Fulton	special photographic effects
Barney Wolff	special effects
Farciot Edouart	process photographer
W. Wallace Kelley	photographer: second unit
Joseph J. Lilley	conductor
Warren Low	editorial supervisor
Jack Mintz	dialogue coach
Richard Mueller	color consultant
Charles O'Curran	musical number staging
Colonel Tom Parker	technical advisor

Plot:

Elvis plays newly demobbed G.I. Chad Gates, pondering what to do with himself now that he is back home in Honolulu after two years serving in Italy. After a lackluster welcome home party thrown by his well-to-do folks, Chad goes against Ma Sarah Lee Gates (played by Angela Lansbury) and Pa Fred (Roland Winters) and refuses to go into the family pineapple business. Elvis and girlfriend Maile (played by Joan Blackman) head off to celebrate her Grandma's birthday, a much more congenial event.

Maile gets Chad a job at the tour agency where she works, but on his first assignment Ellie (played by Jenny Maxwell), one of the teenage girls in his tour group, gets him into a fight at the

Elvis in a scene from *Blue Hawaii*, 1961.

night club where he sings. His dad has to bail him out of jail, and he finds himself out of a job.

Teacher Abigail (played by Nancy Walters) decides that she wants to keep Chad on anyway to take herself and her teenage girls round the island. Precocious teenager Ellie sneaks into Chad's hotel room, followed by the rest of the girls and soon after Abigail, who declares that she is in love (but not with Chad). Just then, Chad's girlfriend Maile tires of waiting for him in the lobby and comes upstairs to find him in the company of another woman. Before sorting things out with Maile, Chad has to rescue runaway girl Ellie and give her a good spanking.

After Chad and Maile reconcile, all that remains is the happy ending. Chad and Maile decide to get married. Father Fred agrees to help them start their own travel company (to be called Gates of Hawaii) on condition that Chad does some work for the family business. Even Sarah Lee cheers up when she learns that Maile is not low-born but actually a member of the Hawaiian royal family.

Songs: "Blue Hawaii," "Almost Always True," "Aloha Oe," "No More," "Can't Help Falling In Love," "Rock-A-Hula Baby," "Moonlight Swim," "Ku-U-I-Po," "Ito Eats," "Slicin' Sand," "Hawaiian Sunset," "Beach Boy Blues," "Island Of Love," "Hawaiian Wedding Song"

The Blue Moon Boys: Bill Black (left), Elvis (center), and Scotty Moore (right).

"BLUE MOON"

Elvis recorded several eerie takes of this Richard Rodgers / Lorenz Hart classic at Sun Records during his first summer as a recording artist—it was the one song he laid down on August 19, 1954. Sun never released it, though Elvis sang it live regularly in the year that he established himself across the Mid-South.

Within four months of signing Elvis, RCA issued the tune on his debut album, *Elvis Presley*, and during the rest of 1956 rolled out the track as the B-Side to "Just Because" (it was "Blue Moon" which charted highest, at #55) and on one of the *Elvis Presley* EPs they released that year.

Since the Fifties, the lunar song has appeared on *The Sun Sessions, The Complete Sun Sessions, The King Of Rock 'n' Roll, Sunrise, Elvis At Sun, Hitstory,* and most recently the FTD release of *Elvis Presley*.

Commissioned in 1933 for Jean Harlow to sing in MGM movie *Hollywood Party*, several sets of lyrics and a new title later—it originally came into the world as "Make Me A Star"—the song was covered by Benny Goodman, Billie Holiday, Frank Sinatra, Dean Martin, Tony Bennett, Ella Fitzgerald, Louis Armstrong and too many others to mention here. After Elvis, The Marcels had a million-selling #1 doo-wop version.

Alternate takes of Elvis recording the song have appeared on *The King Of Rock & Roll, Platinum: A Life In Music, Sunrise,* the 2006 *Complete Sun Sessions* issue (which has several outtakes) and FTD release *Let Yourself Go* (a rehearsal version from 1968 in a medley with "Young Love" and "Oh Happy Day").

BLUE MOON BOYS

Elvis' original band of Scotty Moore and Bill Black (later joined by drummer D. J. Fontana) was initially billed as the Blue Moon Boys when they first started touring. Bob Neal came up with the name, though it was soon dropped from publicity material when it became abundantly clear that "Elvis" was the only name they needed.

In late 1957, after falling out with Elvis' management over money, Scotty and Bill were ready to tour again under the name and had dates set

up, until Tom Diskin lured them back for a marginal increase in their money.

Book:
   The Blue Moon Boys: The Story of Elvis Presley's Band, by Ken Burke and Dan Griffin (foreword by Brian Setzer), published by Chicago Review Press, 2006.

"BLUE MOON OF KENTUCKY"

The B-side to Elvis' first single, "That's All Right (Mama)," was an improvised up-tempo version of the 1947 bluegrass standard by Bill Monroe, which Elvis recorded with Scotty Moore and Bill Black on July 6, 1954. Just like "That's All Right (Mama)," the song seemed to materialize out of thin air. Bill Black started the ball rolling when he began goofing around on bass and singing the Monroe song in a clownish falsetto.

Up until then, the trio had got nowhere with Elvis' favored ballads as they searched for something to back "That's All Right (Mama)." Sam Phillips was much more enthusiastic about this one, especially after they upped the tempo from the first mess-around.

When the single first came out, "Blue Moon Of Kentucky" had by far had he most airplay. Not only did Elvis sing it like it was a blues song, the band changed the whole tempo around; such a strikingly different reworking of an intensely familiar song primed people's curiosity about this new kid. On August 18, 1954, the song reached #3 on the *Billboard* Country and Western chart for Memphis, ultimately selling almost 20,000 copies.

The song was not released on LP until *A Date with Elvis* in 1959, by which time RCA had added even more reverb. Soon after, it followed on EP release *A Touch of Gold Vol. 3*. "Blue Moon Of Kentucky" has since appeared on compilations including *The Sun Sessions, The King Of Rock & Roll, Great Country Songs, The Complete Sun Sessions, Sunrise, The Country Side of Elvis* and *Elvis at Sun.*

A slower version recorded at that same session appeared years later on *A Golden Celebration.* Other versions and outtakes have been issued on *The King of Rock & Roll* and Sun compilations such as *The Complete Sun Sessions* (the most

recent version of which also has a live performance) and *Sunrise*. Early live versions feature on the many Elvis Louisiana Hayride compilations and early concert bootlegs; Elvis' debut Louisiana Hayride performance is on *Memphis Recording Service Vol. 1* (later Hayride performances are on Vol. 2).

A rehearsal version from 1968 appeared on FTD release *Burbank '68*.

"BLUE RIVER"

On May 27, 1963 Elvis recorded this Paul Evans / Fred Tobias song in Nashville. When it was finally released in late 1965 as the B-side to "Tell Me Why," the song struggled to #95 on the charts and dropped out a week later, but inevitably still went gold. Curiously, the French EP version of the song was stretched by an extra few seconds.

The track has since appeared on the *Double Trouble* soundtrack release as a bonus, on 1991 release *For The Asking (The Lost Album)*, on *From Nashville To Memphis* and on the FTD *Double Trouble* re-issue.

"BLUE SUEDE SHOES"

Elvis recorded this song the very month it was released by Carl Perkins, who wrote and recorded it at Sun Records just after Elvis' contract was transferred from the Memphis label to RCA. Perkins' version massively outsold Elvis' and became the first song ever to make it onto three separate *Billboard* charts: the Top 100, R & B and Country. And yet the song is eternally associated with the Elvis legend, still thriving half a century on, while Perkins is remembered (by those in the know) as a rockabilly pioneer.

Elvis recorded the song for RCA on January 30, 1956 at the company's New York recording facility on 155 E. 24th Street.

Before Elvis went into the studio, RCA man Steve Sholes assured Sam Phillips that Elvis' version would not be released as a single and would in no way harm Carl Perkins' career. Two months later Carl Perkins had a car accident that left him seriously injured, by which time Elvis had already performed the song on TV. According to D.J.

Fontana, after Elvis released the song, he donated all the money he made from it to Carl Perkins so that he could pay his hospital bills.

Perkins famously woke one night with the song in his head, after a concert where a guy told his girl what not to step on. Unable to find any paper at three in the morning, he wrote down the lyrics on a potato sack. Johnny Cash also claimed at least partial paternity for the song. In his version, he told Perkins that he'd heard an Air Force pal of his called C. V. White say to somebody "don't step on my blue suede shoes" and that there might be a song in it.

Elvis performed "Blue Suede Shoes" on TV three times during his breakthrough year of 1956: on the Dorseys' "Stage Show" (February 11, and March 17, 1956), and on "The Milton Berle Show" (April 3, 1956)—for hardened blue suede fans, these performances are collated on collectors' set *A Golden Celebration*, which sports a total of six different versions. He also picked this song for his March 1956 screen test for Paramount. He played the song live too, in Las Vegas with a one-off drum solo from D.J. Fontana (released years down the line on *Elvis Aron Presley, The King Of Rock & Roll, Live In Las Vegas* and *Today Tomorrow & Forever*), and at his Tupelo Homecoming Show on September 26, 1956 (on *A Golden Celebration* and *Tupelo's Own Elvis Presley*, released by Memphis Recording Service in 2007). The song was also part of Elvis' repertoire during his final Louisiana Hayride gigs (examples are to be found on various Hayride releases)

RCA did not break the letter of Sholes' agreement because they released "Blue Suede Shoes" in April 1956 (as the opening track) on the *Elvis Presley* EP and LP. They finally released it as a single in late August 1956, with "Tutti Frutti" on the B-side. Though the single failed to chart, the song had already made it to #20 on the main *Billboard* chart by dint of its EP release. The song rose to #9 in the UK on release.

In April 1960, Elvis re-recorded the song for a scene in which it plays on a jukebox in *G.I. Blues*.

He tried out several versions of "Blue Suede Shoes" for the NBC TV Special in June 1968 but it did not make it into the final broadcast. These recordings later surfaced on bootlegs and albums including *Elvis: A Legendary Performer Vol. 2, Collectors Gold, This Is Elvis, A Golden Celebration*, later releases of *Elvis NBC TV Special, Memories: The '68 Comeback Special, Tiger Man* and FTD release *Burbank '68*.

The live version Elvis sang during his first Las Vegas engagement in the summer of 1969 appeared on *From Memphis To Vegas* (aka *Elvis In Person At The International Hotel Las Vegas*). Further live versions from his return to the stage are on *Collectors Gold, Live In Las Vegas, The Live Greatest Hits*, the 2007 *Viva Las Vegas* release and on FTD discs *Elvis At The International, Writing For The King* and *All Shook Up*.

Other live versions feature in 1970 documentary *Elvis: That's The Way It Is*— the track did not make it onto the tie-in album released at the time but it is on *That's The Way It Is—Special Edition* and FTD release *The Way It Was*.

Elvis performed "Blue Suede Shoes" when he played Madison Square Garden in 1972 (released as *An Afternoon In The Garden*).

He sang the song for the *Aloha from Hawaii* satellite broadcast and the previous night's rehearsal (released as *The Alternate Aloha*).

Other Seventies versions available on official FTD discs include *The Impossible Dream, Summer Festival, Takin' Tahoe Tonight!, Dragonheart, Southern Nights, New Year's Eve* and *Spring Tours '77*.

The many later releases of the original studio recording include the *G.I. Blues* soundtrack album and the CD issue of *Elvis' Golden Records Vol. 1*. A selection of more recent releases includes *The Great Performances, The King Of Rock & Roll, Elvis '56, Artist Of The Century*, CD issues of *For LP Fans Only, Elvis 2nd to None, Hitstory* and 2007 release *The Essential Elvis Presley*.

FTD's 2006 re-release of Elvis' debut LP kicks off with the track. There's also a re-instrumented *Guitar Man* session version on FTD release *Too Much Monkey Business*.

In 2007, footage from Elvis' Paramount screen test appeared on the *Elvis #1 Hit Performances* 2-disc DVD issue.

BLUE SUEDE SHOES COLLECTION

A 2001 30-CD box set looking back over Elvis' career, including rare interview material

Amazing Grace: His Greatest Sacred Performances CD 1
Amazing Grace: His Greatest Sacred Performances CD 2
An Afternoon In The Garden
Best Of Artist Of The Century
Burning Love
Can't Help Falling In Love: The Hollywood Hits
Elvis Speaks! Interview CD
Essential Elvis Vol. 4-A Hundred Years From Now
Essential Elvis Vol. 5-Rhythm & Country
Essential Elvis Vol. 6-Such A Night
From Elvis In Memphis
If Everyday Was Like Christmas
Love Songs
Memories CD 1
Memories CD 2
On Stage
Pot Luck
Promised Land
Something For Everybody
That's The Way It Is-CD 1
That's The Way It Is-CD 2
That's The Way It Is-CD 3
The Complete 50's Masters CD 1
The Complete 50's Masters CD 2
The Complete 50's Masters CD 3
The Complete 50's Masters CD 4
The Complete 50's Masters CD 5
The Million Dollar Quartet
Tiger Man
Tomorrow Is A Long Time

An 11-disc DVD set with the same name came out in the UK in 2007, featuring his two early Seventies documentaries and a selection of motion pictures.

"BLUEBERRY HILL"

Elvis' version of this song, most famously recorded by Fats Domino in 1956 and written by Al Lewis, Larry Stock and Vincent Rose, was taped on January 19, 1957. It was issued on Elvis' third album, *Loving You*, and on EP *Just For You*.

Gene Autry originally sang the song in 1941 movie *The Singing Hill*, but Glenn Miller and his band (with singer Ray Eberle) was the first to take it to the top of the *Billboard 100*.

In his article on the Million Dollar Quartet session in December 1956, journalist Bob Johnson stated that Elvis began the session with this song, though it has yet to appear on any of the Quartet releases.

The song has since appeared on *Essential Elvis Vol. 2, The King Of Rock & Roll*, and on

Alternate versions from the original studio session have subsequently appeared on *Essential Elvis Vol. 2, Platinum: A Life In Music, Elvis: Close Up* (the master) and 2006 FTD releases *Flashback* and *Loving You*.

Elvis played the song on occasion live in 1970 (in a medley with "Lawdy, Miss Clawdy," 1974 and 1977. From 1974, the song made the cut on *Recorded Live On Stage In Memphis* in a medley with "I Can't Stop Loving You." A 1977 performance found its way onto FTD release *Unchained Melody*. FTD release *I Found My Thrill*

closes with a virtual medley of Elvis Seventies live performances.

BLUES

Biographers disagree whether teenaged Elvis snuck off to Beale Street juke joints to listen to the blues but even if he didn't, he heard it on the radio and had it in his soul.

Many Elvis fans rue the fact that so little of his vast output is out-and-out blues. And yet the passion and feeling that runs through blues is something that Elvis conveys in almost everything he sings.

Nuggets of blues are waiting to be found on many Elvis albums, even a few of the less promising soundtrack releases, an example being "Hard Luck" on *Frankie And Johnny*. Often at recording sessions Elvis and his band would launch into long blues jams, many of which have made it onto recent releases from the RCA/BMG vaults. At the Nashville sessions were Elvis laid down material for 1971 Christmas album *Elvis Sings The Wonderful World of Christmas*, the most relaxed and comfortable moment was when the band cut loose on "Merry Christmas Baby," that rarest of genre-hopping hybrids, a bluesy Christmas number. Though Elvis eased off doing all-out blues material far too early in his career for some, he continued to inject a blues sensibility into his later live material. And when he did pull out a blues number, for example "Reconsider Baby" at his 1972 Madison Square Garden engagement, illustrious fans like Robert Plant remembers "the hairs shot up on the back of my neck."

Over the years, RCA have released blues compilations: *Elvis Sings the Blues, Reconsider Baby* and *Elvis R'n'B*.

The Blues Foundation, based in Memphis, gave Elvis the W.C. Handy Award in 1984.

Elvis was inducted into the West Coast Blues Hall of Fame in 2004.

BILL DAHL: "Ever since the blues first developed from African-American field hollers, feeling has been the most essential ingredient."

B.B. KING: "He loved the blues, it was a pity he didn't do more."

JOE COCKER: "He was one of the greatest blues singers in the world. Give Presley a good blues number and he just sold it right."

MUDDY WATERS: "That boy made his pull from the blues, if he's stopped, he's stopped, but he made his pull from there."

Book:
Beale Black & Blue: Life and Music on Black America's Main Street, by Margaret McKee, Fred Chisenhall, Louisiana State University Press, 1993.

BOATS

Elvis was keen to buy a boat in his first flush of wealth, but his mother didn't like the idea at all.

Elvis bought a 16-foot 75 hp waterskiing boat in July 1960 for $3,000, in a fetching shade of powder blue, which he named *Karate* and used that summer on McKellar Lake in Memphis. Vernon bought some land by the lake around that time and built a cabin.

Elvis upgraded to a 21-foot Chris-Craft Coronado with a 325 hp Cadillac engine, a $9,000+ purchase, in June 1961. When he traveled to Florida to shoot *Follow That Dream* a couple of months later, pals Lamar Fike and Alan Fortas towed the boat behind Elvis' Cadillac limousine.

Elvis later owned an 18-foot Chris-Craft Cavalier, a '63 model he named *Hound Dog*.

Elvis never used the most expensive boat he bought: the *Potomac*, for which he paid $55,000. He gave the boat, which had belonged to President Roosevelt, to St. Jude's Hospital in Memphis for charity.

BODYGUARDS

Fan enthusiasm is one thing, all-out riots quite another. It soon became apparent that Elvis needed protection if he was to survive an evening onstage without being ripped to shreds by wild women or socked by some jealous guy. The police were only prepared to go so far, so Elvis drafted in cousins and school pals to serve as a security cordon.

For twenty years, Red West was the main man, aided and assisted by his cousin Sonny West, while other entourage members pitched in as required. Jerry Schilling, who came on board in 1964, was another formidable physical presence.

After the Charles Manson slayings in 1969, Elvis revised his security arrangements and beefed up security. Gun permits were not a problem once Elvis started his national collection of police badges.

In the early Seventies, when Elvis was the target of death threats and potential assassination attempts, Jerry Schilling and Red West were instructed to "neutralize" anybody who threatened Elvis with a gun before they could get off a shot. There was also tacit agreement among the bodyguards that if Elvis was assassinated, it was their job to make sure that the assassin did not live to tell the tale.

In later years, Elvis hired former policemen Dick Grob, assisted by Sam Thompson and David Stanley, to plan and map out security for his tours. At times Elvis also took along karate champion pals Ed Parker and Dave Hebler when he was on the road. Security arrangements extended to Lisa Marie, who was particularly vulnerable to kidnap threats on her frequent trips between Memphis and Los Angeles.

In their book *Elvis: What Happened?* Red and Sonny West say that Elvis had a "Robin Hood" streak and would sometimes send out his hired muscle to lean on people who had slighted his step-brothers; on one occasion, Elvis sent his guys to help a stranger he met in the street who told him a tale about how his wife had been beaten up by two local hoods.

During concerts, Elvis' bodyguards did double duty to keep audience members from getting crushed or stampeded, or, even worse, things happening to kids brought along to the show.

RED WEST: "Somebody somewhere said Elvis' security team was better than the President's. That made me feel good whether it was true or false, but we really worked at it. We worked at keeping him from getting hurt."

DAVE HEBLER: "If anyone was going to hurt him, they would have had to kill us to get to him. That was the relationship."

BON AIR CLUB, MEMPHIS

This was the first venue where Elvis ever performed, singing the two songs from his debut single "That's All Right" and "Blue Moon Of Kentucky." Fellow bandsmen Scotty Moore and Bill Black had a regular gig at the venue every Saturday with their band the Starlite Wranglers. Elvis played there three Saturdays in a row from July 17, 1954.

BOND, EDDIE
(B. 1933)

Two years Elvis' senior, in May 1954 Eddie Bond auditioned Elvis to join his band, The Stompers. Elvis was very upset when he was rejected; Elvis later claimed that Bond told him to "go back to driving a truck."

A popular Louisiana Hayride performer in the mid-1950s with his rockabilly sound, Bond also issued many popular country tracks, though he never got the national exposure Elvis did, and took considerably longer to get a record deal; Sam Phillips turned him down at Sun Records. Guitarist Hank Garland, later to play with Elvis, spent a spell with Bond's band in the mid-Fifties.

Elvis and Bond were on the same bill in Arkansas in September 1955, with Elvis headlining. Bond has continued to perform into the new millennium, and has had a successful career as a radio DJ.

BONJA, ED

A nephew of Tom Diskin's who started out as a tour manager for Elvis in the early Seventies and went on to be Elvis' official photographer up to the summer of 1975. He shot a number of concert pictures that featured on Elvis' Seventies live albums. In recent years he has been touring an exhibition titled "I Shot Elvis."

Book:
Elvis, Shot By Ed Bonja by Ed Bonja, Elvis Unlimited Productions, 2000

BOOKS ABOUT ELVIS

Rock idol, cultural phenomenon, template for global fame, fun-time guy, sex symbol, bad boy and life inspiration to many, Elvis has featured in countless books—countless here is not a figure of speech, people really have tried to count and come away with no better than best estimates. In her annotated bibliography *Infinite Elvis*, Mary Hancock Hines says that she verified 1700 Elvis titles, of which over 1000 are books. By 2007, this number had swelled to over 2000 books, of which at least one tenth were written in languages other than English. The world's largest online bookseller yields over 12,000 different results to a search on "Elvis Presley" (a number inflated by multiple editions and formats).

The first hardback book to be published about Elvis in the United States was *Operation Elvis* (1960), a book about Elvis' time in the Army rather than his music or movies. That year also saw publication of a the first paperback and the first book-length biography, James Gregory's *The Elvis Presley Story*.

Apart from Jerry Hopkins' 1971 biography *Elvis*, while he was still alive very few authors attempted to write the Elvis life story. The Colonel certainly wasn't going to authorize a biography, and the loyalty of the Memphis Mafia and family members who were close to Elvis meant that few people were willing to spill the beans.

The first breach in this ring of silence came a month before Elvis' death in 1977. *Elvis: What Happened?* by former entourage members Red and Sonny West and Dave Hebler, packed with prurient and salacious allegations about Elvis' life, was presented as a last ditch attempt to get him to change his ways before it was too late.

When Elvis died, fans bought books in their millions, publishers took note and what had been a trickle of literature about Elvis during his career, consisting mainly of publicity material and fanzines, became a flood that is yet to subside.

Since then, well over a hundred Elvis-related memoirs have been published by people who knew or met the man, however fleetingly, from his maids to his wife, school pals, Army buddies, long-term girlfriends, practically every member of the Memphis Mafia, fans, many relatives and some of the musicians with whom he worked. A small number of books, notably *Elvis: His Life and Music* by Timothy Frew, *Elvis Presley: A Life in Music* by Ernst Jorgensen, and *Elvis by the Presleys* were published with accompanying CDs.

Several of Elvis' friends have said that in the last years of his life he was considering writing an autobiography. Larry Geller says that he was keen to convey his deeply-held spiritual beliefs and reveal to the world the man behind the image. Jerry Schilling says that Elvis planned an autobiography, to be titled *Through My Eyes*, on which he wanted Schilling to collaborate. There's also always the chance that one day Elvis' diaries will turn up—a big ask as that would require having written them in the first place.

UNLESS OTHERWISE STATED, BOOK INFORMATION IN *THE ELVIS ENCYCLOPEDIA* REFERS TO ORIGINAL PUBLICATIONS RATHER THAN REPRINTS AND REVISED EDITIONS.

General information on books about Elvis may be found in the (partial) bibliography at the end of the *Encyclopedia*. Where relevant, book titles appear under encyclopedia entries. Apologies to readers who speak other languages; Elvis book guides, international fan clubs and the internet are all excellent sources of information about foreign-language titles.

ELVIS SAID IN 1960: "Maybe someday I will write a book."

GURALNICK: "Elvis Presley may well be the most written-about figure of our time."

JOAN DEARY: "In a lot of the books written about Elvis, people are trying to magnify their own importance in Elvis' life . . . But the fans can always spot a phony."

ERNST JORGENSEN: "Since August 16, 1977, hundreds of books have appeared, some seeking honestly to explain a popular phenomenon, many simply looking to cash in on that phenomenon or, more often than not, to place the writer at the center of Elvis' life."

BOOKS ABOUT ELVIS BOOKS:

Elvis: A Bio-Bibliography, by Patsy Hammontree, Greenwood Press, 1985.
The Printed Elvis—The Complete Guide to Books About The King, by Steven Opdyke, Greenwood Press, 199.9
Infinite Elvis: An Annotated Bibliography by Mary Hancock Hinds, Acapella Book, 2001.

A number of fan sites offer excellent "Elvis in print" sections.

BOOKS ELVIS READ:

The old adage never to judge a book by its cover has no corollary about not judging a reader by his books.

Larry Geller, who for years was Elvis' main supplier of reading material, estimates that Elvis read over a thousand books on philosophy, the esoteric and spiritual teachings. For many years, Elvis

A mega-rare 1956 candid photograph capturing Elvis at a gospel show in Memphis.
He is surrounded by police for his protection. This is one of the last times Elvis
would dare to go to a public event.

traveled with two trunks full of books (as many as three hundred) so that he could read when he felt like it away from Graceland.

Elvis was a lifelong and often voracious reader. Graceland archives include Elvis' library card from the Tupelo Public Library from when he was thirteen. This was despite the fact that the Church to which Gladys belonged, First Assembly of God, taught that no book other than the Bible should be read.

In fifth grade, Elvis learned by heart Alfred Lord Tennyson's poem "Crossing the Bar" and the Gettysburg Address.

For his 14th birthday, Vernon gave his son a book of George Price cartoons, bearing the inscription "May your birthday be sprinkled through 'n through with joy and love and good times too. Daddy."

Through his school years, Elvis read fairy tales and biographies of famous Americans and adventurers. Famously, in his youth Elvis loved reading comics. Once his career took off and he hit the road, other interests prevailed over reading anything but the occasional football magazine or concert review.

Elvis sought consolation after his mother's death with *Poems That Touch the Heart*, an anthology compiled by A. L. Alexander, given to him by a fellow soldier en route to his Army posting to Germany.

Tom Diskin presented Elvis with a Konstantin Stanislavsky book on acting for Christmas 1958.

In Germany, Elvis read Western novels, magazines and plenty of *Mad* comics.

On Elvis' bedside table in 1960 were *The Power of Positive Thinking* by Dr. Norman Vincent Peale, and *How to Live 365 Days a Year* by Dr. John A. Schindler.

Elvis told a reporter in 1962 that he often read medical texts, and also liked to read philosophy. He knew his way so well around the Physicians Desk Reference (PDR) that in later years he more than held his own when talking to medical professionals about prescription drugs.

In 1962 Elvis read and reread a book called *Leaves Of Gold, An Anthology of Prayers, Memorable Phrases, Inspirational Verse, and Prose*, edited by Clyde Frances Lytle.

In 1964 Elvis met Larry Geller, hairdresser by trade and spiritual seeker by vocation, and for the first time found a peer with whom to share his curiosity about weighty metaphysical questions. On Geller's advice, Elvis began to build up a library, starting *The Impersonal Life*, an anonymously-written book espousing the view that God resides in us all, *Autobiography of a Yogi*, *The Initiation of the World* (which Elvis insisted Priscilla read) and *Beyond the Himalayas*.

According to Geller, within a year Elvis had devoured a hundred books on religious, spiritual and supernatural topics, eagerly scribbling his thoughts and annotations in the margins. One of Elvis' favorites at that time was *Through the Eyes of the Masters: Meditations and Portraits*, by David Anrias.

In the summer of 1965 Elvis read Timothy Leary's book *Psychedelic Experience*, and Aldous Huxley's *The Doors of Perception*. Elvis handed these books round his entourage for reading and discussion, and not long afterwards had his one and only experimentation with LSD.

In 1966 Elvis' spiritual reading included J. W. Jupiter's *The Changing Condition of Your World* and Billy Graham Presents Man in the 5th Dimension. He also found a lifelong favorite in *Cheiro's Book of Numbers*, to which he often turned for guidance.

The majority of Elvis' book collection—purchased at the Bodhi Tree in Los Angeles by Larry Geller—came to a *Fahrenheit 451* end in a bonfire a little before his marriage to Priscilla. The Colonel was convinced that these new age books and magazines were a bad influence on his boy, while Priscilla was happy to see the back of this rival claimant on Elvis' time

when Elvis offered to sacrifice the books. They threw all the reading matter into an abandoned well behind Graceland, doused it in gasoline and set it ablaze. This would explain why so few of the many books he read and collected in the Sixties, and more interestingly his musings and scribblings in the margins, have made it onto the Elvis memorabilia and collectors' market.

Elvis was a lifelong fan of Kahlil Gibran, and knew significant chunks of *The Prophet* by heart.

In the early Seventies, Elvis read and enjoyed Ram Dass's book *Be Here, Now*. He also read a biography of Madame Blavatsky, founder of the theosophical society, whose face reminded Elvis of his mother. He read Herman Hesse's *Siddharta*, and Thomas Troward's *The Creative Process*.

To relax from such weighty fare, Elvis read books by J. Edgar Hoover, including *A Study of Communism* and *Masters of Deceit*.

It wasn't non-fiction all the way. Elvis was known to enjoy novels too; he was photographed in 1976 clutching a copy of *The Omen*.

Elvis liked being read to as well as reading. Girlfriend Sheila Ryan remembers reading to him until he fell asleep. On nights when sleep just wouldn't come, Elvis would sometimes retire to the reading chair in his personal bathroom.

When he died, Elvis was reading *The Scientific Search for the Face of Jesus* by Frank O. Adams (Psychical Aid Foundation, 1972).

We can only conjecture what Elvis would have thought about becoming such a popular character for fiction writers; the closest he came to writing a novel in his lifetime was playing a troubled writer in 1961 movie *Wild in the Country*.

ELVIS' BOOK PURCHASES IN 1963:

Antique Guns
East of Eden
Exploring Earth
Eyewitness History of World War II
First 100 Days of the Kennedy Administration
Giants of Medicine
Giants of Science
Good Night Mrs Calabash
Guns
Histories of 100 Events
Host's Handbook
I Owe Russia
I Take This Land
If I Knew Then
In Laws. Outlaws
Joke Dictionary
Jokes for the John
Lonely Life
Our Fifty States
Picture History of World War II
Right to Privacy
Strange People
The Whole Truth
Trail Guide
Transport to Disaster
Underwater
Vocabulary Builder
World Atlas
World Philosophy

ELVIS' FAVORITE BOOKS

A SELECTION BY LARRY GELLER (SOURCE: *If I Can Dream*, by Larry Geller et al.)

Adams, Frank: *The Scientific Search for the Face of Jesus*.
Alder, Vera Stanley: *The Initiation of the World; The Finding of the Third Eye; The Fifth Dimension; The Secret of the Atomic Age*.
Augustine, Saint: *The City of God*.

Bailey, Alice A: *The Light of the Soul; Initiation of Human and Solar; Glamour: A World Problem; The Reappearance of Christ; Esoteric Healing; From Intellect to Intuition; The Externalization of the Hierarchy*.
Bayne, Murdo Medowald: *Beyond the Himalayas*.
Benner, Joseph: *The Impersonal Life; Brotherhood; The Way to the Kingdom*.
Blavatsky, Helena Petrovna (Madame): *Isis Unveiled; The Secret Doctrine*.
Brunton, Paul: *Wisdom of the Overself; Hidden Teachings Beyond Yoga; In Search of Secret India; The Secret Path; Discover Yourself; A Hermit in the Himalayas; The Quest of the Overself*.
Brydlova, Bozema: *Ten Unveiled: The Brydlovan Theory of the Origin of Numbers*.
Bucke, Richard Maurice, M.D: *Cosmic Consciousness; The Lost Books of the Bible and the Forgotten Books of Eden*.
Cheiro (Count Louis Harmon): *Cheiro's Book of Numbers; When Were You Born? Cheiro's World Predictions; Fate in the Making*.
Collins, Mabel and C. Jinarajadasa: *Light on the Path*.
Dowling, Levi H.: *The Aquarian Gospel of Jesus the Christ*.
Eddy, Mary Baker: *Science and Health with the Key to the Scriptures*.
Fisher, Martin (trans.): *Gracian's Manual*.
Geller, Larry: *The New Age Voice* (magazine).
Gibran, Kahlil: *The Prophet; The Spiritual Sayings of Kahlil Gibran; Thoughts and Meditations*.
Goldsmith, Joel: *The Infinite Way*.
The Gospel According to Thomas
Gurdjieff, G. I .: *Meetings with Remarkable Men*.
Hall, Manly Palmer: *Man, Grand Symbol of the Mysteries; The Mystical Christ; The Phoenix; Twelve World Teachers; The Secret Teachings of All Ages; The Lost Keys of Freemasonry; Old Testament Wisdom*.
Heindal, Max: *The Rosicrucian Cosmo-Conception*
Heline, Corinne: *America's Invisible Guidance; Color and Music in the New Age; Music: The Keynote of Human Evolution; The Sacred Science of Numbers; New Age Bible Interpretation*, Vol. I.
Hodson, Geoffrey: *The Hidden Wisdom of the Holy Bible*, Vols. I and II
Holy Bible. Old and New Testaments, King James Version
Krishnamurti, J.: *You Are the World; The First and Last Freedom*.
Leadbeater, C. W.: *The Masters and the Path; The Inner Life; The Chakras*.
Long, Max Freedom: *The Huna Code in Religions*.
Mata, Sri Daya: *Only Love*.
Metaphysical Bible Dictionary.
Nicoll, Maurice: *The New Man*.
Ouspensky, P. D.: *In Search of the Miraculous; The Fourth Way*.
Percival, Harold: *Thinking and Destiny; Masonry and Its Symbols*.
Pike, Albert: *Morals and Dogma*.
Ramacharaka, Yogi: *Fourteen Lessons in Yogi Philosophy*.
Roerich, Nicholas: *Leaves of Morya's Garden*, Vols. I and II; *Agni Yoga; Aum; Brotherhood; Hierarchy; Heart; Fiery World*, Vols. I and II; *Infinity*, Vols. I and II.
Roerich, Helena: *Letters of Helena Roerich*, Vols. I and II.
Rudhyar, Dane: *New Mansions for New Men; Fire Out of the Stone*.
Russell, Walter: *The Secret of Light*.
Rutherford, Adam: *Pyramidology: The Science of the Divine Message of the Great Pyramid; Pyramidology: The Glory of Christ as Revealed by the Great Pyramid*.
Satprem: *The Adventure of Consciousness*.
Spaulding, Baird: *Life and Teachings of the Masters of the Far East*, Vols. I-V; *The Urantia Book*.
Waite, A. E.: *The Holy Kabalah*.
Yogananda, Paramahansa: *Autobiography of a Yogi; How You Can Talk with God; Science of Religion; Man's Eternal Quest*.
Yukteswar, Sri: *The Holy Science*.

RED WEST: "He always was quite self-conscious over the fact that he was not well read."

LARRY GELLER: "Although it hardly fit his public image as the King of Rock and Roll, Elvis was a voracious and careful reader."

LAMAR FIKE: "In our camp, the PDR was like a Bible . . ."

JERRY SCHILLING: "His copies of books were always ferociously dog-eared and margins were full of his own scribbled notes and questions. He loved to lose himself in a text, seeking out deeper meaning in words and ideas . . ."

DAVID BRIGGS: "Elvis was actually very well-read, and he could talk to you on any subject for hours at a time because all he did was read. History, religion—you name it, he knew it."

BOONE, PAT
(B.CHARLES EUGENE PATRICK BOONE, 1934)

The only singer to run Elvis close at the top of the charts in the mid- to late-Fifties was Pat Boone. Teenagers loved one or the other; Boone had the advantage of winning over many more parents with his non-threatening croonings of rock 'n' roll hits, many of which ("Long Tall Sally," "Tutti Frutti") Elvis also sang. Elvis had the lip-curling sneer, Boone the flashing white smile; Elvis dressed to kill, Pat Boone white buck shoes as his trademark. Boone's all-American image was completed by being a fifth-generation descendant of frontier hero Daniel Boone.

Born in Jacksonville, Florida on June 1, 1934, Boone got his big break on the *Ted Mack Amateur Hour* and then spent a year performing on the "Arthur Godfrey Talent Scouts" show, for which Elvis was turned down at the audition stage.

The press had them pegged as rivals but nothing could have been further from the truth. Elvis was magnanimous in his praise of his fellow singer, publicly acknowledging his admiration of Boone's way with a ballad. Elvis had been buying Pat Boone records since before he got his own break. The two of them also were on the same bill in Cleveland, Ohio in October 1955.

Elvis had first call on a song that became one of Boone's biggest hits, "Don't Forbid Me," which he sang with pals at Sun studios in what came to be known as the *Million Dollar Quartet*. Other major successes for Boone in the Fifties were "I Almost Lost My Mind" and "April Love."

Boone was still a chart success when Elvis returned to the States after his time in the Army. He hosted his own TV show, and starred in more than a dozen movies (including *April Love* and *Journey to the Center of the Earth*). Elvis and Pat Boone stayed in touch in Los Angeles; Boone would sometimes show up for Elvis' football games in Bel Air, and then famously be hauled off the park by his wife Shirley, daughter of singer Red Foley.

In 1963 Boone recorded an album of Elvis songs, entitled *Pat Boone Sings . . . Guess Who?*, after Colonel Parker could not be persuaded to waive a large fee for using Elvis' name on the cover of this tribute record. By this time Boone's record sales had started to decline as the new crop of British popsters colonized America.

In the Seventies Boone sang mainly gospel; he was inducted into the Gospel Music Hall of Fame in 2003.

In the Nineties Boone finally got rock religion when he released (tongue in cheek) album *In a Metal Mood: No More Mr. Nice Guy.*

PAT BOONE: "We were friendly competitors."

BOOTLEGS

Many thousands of bootlegs have circulated over the years, from poor-quality fan tapes of concerts to excellent soundboard recordings, with a healthy sprinkling of home recordings, banter, rehearsals, outtakes and alternates from studio sessions.

Though the Elvis bootleg market really took off in the Seventies when he returned to touring, bootlegs have been circulating since Elvis first started performing. Live recordings of early Elvis shows were a premium item. A show at the Grand Prize Jamboree in Houston in March 1955 included much of his early Sun work, while Fifties DJ promos and special publicity releases have long been popular on the specialty market.

Bootlegging picked up during Elvis' Sixties recordings sessions because in many cases no individual producer was making sure that a set procedure was followed and the material was all locked down.

Rich pickings for the bootleg set came from rehearsals and recordings of Elvis and Co. in the run-up to the 1968 NBC TV Special. When he returned to live performing in 1969, he started on a run of over a thousand shows, the majority of which have yielded some kind of bootleg. There was little RCA or the Colonel could do except release better quality live albums, and then in 1972 try to beat the bootleggers at their own game by bringing out *Elvis as Recorded at Madison Square Garden* just eight days after the end of his record-breaking run in the Big Apple.

The better concert recordings are soundboard recordings, though many of these were made onto cassette and therefore fall a little short in quality. Some sound recordists' private recordings have made it out through hidden channels over the years. Bootleggers have traditionally had a field day with various tapes of Elvis singing and jamming at home in Graceland, or Elvis and the band doing rehearsals before a Vegas season or a new tour.

Bootlegging is an international phenomenon that has spawned a parallel world of record labels such as Fort Baxter, Bilko, Memory Records, Captain Marvel Jr. Records, Famous Groove and King Records to name just a few.

The unofficial recordings listed in this Encyclopedia are here because they marked the first time that certain material became available. Completists will already know where to look; typing in "Elvis bootlegs" to an internet search engine yields a great deal of information too.

Landmark bootlegs include: *Please Release Me, The Hillbilly Cat Live, The King Goes Wild, The Dorsey Shows, Desert Storm, Opening Night '72, Spanish Eyes, Unsurpassed Masters, Whole Lotta Shakin' Going On,* and *As Recorded In Stereo '57 Vol. 2.*

Since 1999, official collectors' label FTD has been releasing significant amounts of previously unheard material from Elvis rehearsals, film shoots and more, in many cases improved and better-mixed versions of songs previously solely available on bootlegs. If you can't beat 'em . . .

JOAN DEARY: "The amount of bootlegging on Elvis—even today—is phenomenal."

Book:
Jailhouse Rock: The Bootleg Records of Elvis Presley 1970-1983, by Lee Cotten and Howard A. DeWitt, The Pierian Press, 1983.

CD BOOTLEGS—READ THROUGH THIS LIST AND IT'S LIKE SEEING ELVIS' LIFE FLASH BEFORE YOUR EYES!

24 Carat Gold
50's Movies Outtakes (Elvis Presley Vol. 5)
60 Million TV Viewers Can't Be Wrong
60th Anniversary Celebration
71 Summer Festival Vol. 1
71 Summer Festival Vol. 2
A Bright Midnight With Elvis
A Capital Performance - Madison
A Capital Performance - LMP
A Crazy Show At Lake Tahoe
A Damn Fine Show
A Day In Duluth
A Dinner Bell In Vegas
A Dinner Date With Elvis
A Dinner Date With Elvis - Re-issue
A Dream To Follow
A Hot Winter Night In Dallas
A Legendary Performer Vol. 3
A Legendary Performer Vol. 4
A Legendary Performer Vol. 5
A Legendary Performer Vol. 6
A Legendary Performer Vol. 7
A Legendary Performer Vol. 8
A New Live Experience

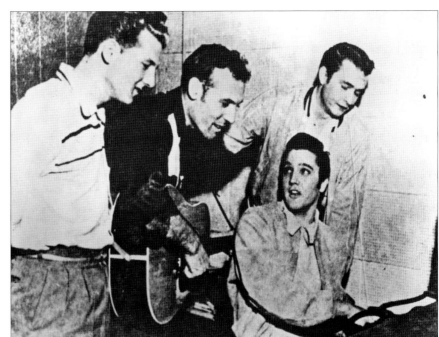

The Million Dollar Quartet.

A Night At The Sahara
A Pair Of Boots
A Private Moment With The King
A Profile (The King On Stage) Volume 1
A Profile (The King On Stage) Volume 2
A Thunder In The Night
Absent Without Leave
Across The Country Vol. 1
Adios, The Final Performance
All Shook Up
All That I Am
All Things Are Possible
America, The Beautiful
American Crown Jewels
American Rejects
America's Own
America's Own (Ampex)
America's Own Volume 2
An Afternoon In Nashville
And I Love You So—The King Rocks Milwaukee
...And The King For Dessert
And Then The Lights Went Down
Animal Instinct
Another Night In Tahoe
Another Opening Night
Anything That's Part Of You
As I Leave You
As Recorded In Stereo '57
As Recorded In Stereo '57 Vol. 2
Auld Lang Syne
Aztec King
Back At The Falls
Back In Portland
Back On The Mainland
Backstage With Elvis
Because Of Love Vol. 1
Because Of Love Vol. 2
Behind Closed Doors
Beltway To Largo
Better Than Ever
Big Boss Man At Lake Tahoe
Bilko's Gold Cut
Black Diamond
Blazing Into Darkness
Blue Hawaii Outtakes - Elvis Presley Vol. 3
Blue Hawaii Sessions Vol. 1
Blue Hawaii Sessions Vol. 2
Blue Hawaii Sessions Vol. 3
Blue Hawaii - The Complete Session Vol. 1
Blue Hawaii - The Complete Session Vol. 2
Blue Hawaii - The Complete Session Vol. 3
Blue Rainbow
Born To Give Us Fever
Breathing Out Fire
Bringin' The House Down
Broken Finger By Elvis
Burbank Sessions
Burning In Birmingham
Burning Vegas Down
By Request - More Kid Galahad Sessions
By Special Request
By Special Request, From Louisiana To Tennessee
C. C. Rider
Café Europa Sessions
Cajun Tornado
Camera And Microphone Rehearsals
Candid Elvis On Camera
Candy Bars For Elvis—Elvis Presley Vol. 1
Carry Me Back To Old Virginia
Caught In The Act
Celluloid Rock Vol. 1
Celluloid Rock Vol. 2
Charleston Rocks
Checkmate In Las Vegas
Chicago Beat
Chicago Illinois
Closing Night—February 23rd, 1970
Come What May
Coming On Strong
Command Performances And More
Conquering The Falls
Crying Time In Vegas
Cut' Em Down To Size
Cut Me & I Bleed
Cuttin' Loose
Dancin' With Elvis
Datin' With Elvis
Deep Down In Texas
Deep Down South
Desert Storm
Don't Think Twice
Down In The Alley

Double Dynamite
Drug Story
Early Recordings
Easy Come, Easy Go
Edge Of Reality
Electrifying!
El Goes El Paso
Elvis: The Cover Up
Elvis Among Friends
Elvis & Friends
Elvis At Full Blast!
Elvis At The Dome
Elvis Best
Elvis Diamonds
Elvis Goes El Paso
Elvis' Greatest Shit
Elvis In Girls! Girls! Girls!
Elvis Live "Unlicensed"
Elvis Mania Atlanta
Elvis Meets Presley
Elvis Meets The Beatles
Elvis On Tour
Elvis On Tour (re-issue)
Elvis Rocks Little Rock
Elvis Sails
Elvis' Second Night
Elvis Slips Into Austin
Elvis Uncensored
Especially For You
Eternal Flame (Lone Star)
Eternal Flame (Snowball)
Event Number 8
Explosion In Vegas
Fairy Tales
Fast Movin'
Fever Pitch
Film Session Outtakes—Elvis Presley Vol. 4
Finding The Way Home
Fire In Vegas
Flaming Star
Flip, Flop & Fly—Elvis In The Hilton Vol. 1
Fly T-R-O-U-B-L-E !
For Elvis Fans Only
For Movie Fans Only Vol. 1
For Movie Fans Only Vol. 2
For Movie Fans Only Vol. 3
For The Good Times
Forum Of Inglewood
Fried Bananas, Ice Cream And Gatorade—
    Elvis Presley Vol. 6
From Burbank To Memphis
From Burbank To Vegas
From Fans To Fans—Ann Arbor
From Fans To Fans—Savannah
From Sunset Boulevard To Paradise Road
From The Archives Vol. 1
From The Archives Vol. 2
From The Bottom Of My Heart Vol. 1
From The Bottom Of My Heart Vol. 2
From The Vaults Of RCA
From The Vaults Vol. 1 "In My Dreams"
From The Vaults Vol. 2 "Never Ending"
From The Vaults Vol. 3
From Union Avenue To Thomas Street 1954-1969
From Vegas To Macon
G.I. Blues Anniversary Edition Vol. 1
G.I. Blues Anniversary Edition Vol. 2
Get Down And Get With It
Girl Happy At The World's Fair
Girls Girls And More Girls !
Go Cat Go
Going Home
Good Times Never Seemed So Good
Goodbye Memphis
Green Green Grass Of Home
Greetings From Germany
Greetings From Saginaw
Guaranteed To Blow Your Mind
Guitar Man Sessions
Gyrating Asheville
Hang Loose
Happy New Year From Pontiac 1975
Have Some Fun Tonight
Hawaii USA
Hawaiian Oddities
Hello Memphis!
Her Masters Voice
Here I Go Again
Hey Baby Let's Rock It
Holding Back The Years
Home Made Recordings
Hometown Memphis

Hot And Tight
Hot Time In Miami
Howdy Houston!
Hurt
I Beg Of You
I Couldn't Live Without You
...I Did It My Way
I Don't Wanna Sing These Songs
I Got Stung
I Was The One
If You Talk In Your Sleep
I'd Like You To Meet Jack Lord
I'll Remember You
I'll Whoop His Ass!
In Dreams Of Yesterday
In My Way
Inherit The Wind
International Earthquake
International Heatwave
International Heatwave re-release
Intimate With Elvis
It's A Matter Of Time
It's Midnight In Vegas
Jailhouse Rock Man In Concert
Jailhouse Rock Sessions
Janis And Elvis
Just A Closer Walk To Thee
Just Pretend
Kansas City Blues
Keep Following That Dream
Keep The Fire Burning
Kicked It Up In Dallas
Kickin' Back And Forth
Kid Galahad Sessions
King Of The Neon Jungle
King Time In Abilene
Kiss Me Quick—Little Sister
Lake Charles (Turn Around, Look At Me)
Last Tango In Tahoe
Last Time In Portland
Las Vegas Dinner Show
Las Vegas Fever Vol. 1
Las Vegas Fever Vol. 2
Las Vegas Fever Vol. 3
Las Vegas Hilton Hotel
Las Vegas in Gypsy Style
Las Vegas Moonlight
Las Vegas Stage Show
Lawdy Miss Clawdy
Lean, Mean And Kickin' Butt
Legendary Rarities
Let Me Be There
Let Me Take You Home
Let's Be Friends
Little Darlin'
Live At The H.I.C.
Live At The International Volume 1—
    Time Stood Still
Live At The International Volume 2—
    In Dreams Of Yesterday
Live At The Lakeside
Live At The Omni
Live From Roanoke
Live In Dallas
Live In Lake Tahoe
Live In Las Vegas '73
Live In The 50's —Vol. 1
Live In The 50's—Vol. 2
Live In The 50's—Vol. 3
Live In The 50's—Vol. 4
Live In Virginia
Long Beach California 1972
Long Lost And Found Songs
Loose Ends—Vol. 1
Loose Ends—Vol. 2
Loose Ends—Vol. 3
Los Angeles California
Lost On Tour
Lost On Tour—The Sequel
Love Letters From Me To You
Love Letters From Nevada
Loving You
Loving You Recording Sessions
Loving You Sessions
Magic Moments
Make The World Go Away
Memories From Kalamazoo
Merry Christmas
Midnight Inspirations—A Night to Remember
Midnight Show
Moody Blue & Other Great Performances
More Pure Elvis

Movie Session Memories
Movin' Mobile
My, It's Been A Long Long Time
Nashville Sessions 1960 - 1961
Nashville Sessions 1961 - 1963
Nation's Only Atomic Powered Singer
Neon City Nights
Night Fever In Vegas
Night Rider 61—Studio B Sessions Vol. 3
No Fooling Around
Now—Or Never!
Not Too Sweet
O Come All Ye Faithful
Old Ones , New Ones And In Between
Old Times They Are Not Forgotten
On A April Fool's Day Vol. 2
Once Upon A Time
One Helluva Night
One Night
One Night At The Omni
One Night In Alabama
One Night In Portland
One Night Only!
One Night With You
Only The Songs Survive
On The Road Again
Opening Night 1969
Opening Night 1972
Original Film Music—Vol.1
Original Film Music—Vol. 2
Original Film Music—Vol. 3
Original Film Music—Vol. 4
Original Film Music—Vol. 5
Original Film Music—Vol. 6
Original Film Music—Vol. 7
Original Film Music—Vol. 8
Our Memories Of Elvis
Pearl Harbor Show
Perfect For Parties
Phenomenon
Philadelphia '77
Phoenix Over Tennessee
Pieces Of My Life
Portrait Of My Love
Presley At The Hilton
Pure Diamonds Vol. 1
Pure Diamonds Vol. 2
Pure Diamonds Vol. 3 (Gospel Greats And Stax)
Pure Diamonds Vol. 4 (From Nashville To
   Hollywood)
Pure Stage Power
Rags To Riches - Pittsburgh '76
Raised On Country
Raised On Gospel
Rare Elvis Interviews
Rarities
Release Me
Return To Lake Tahoe
Return To Long Beach
Riot In Charlotte
Rip It Up
Rockin' Against The Roarin' Falls
Rockin' Chicago Vol. 1
Rockin' Chicago Vol. 2
Rockin' The Northwest
Rockin' With Elvis Presley And Friends
Rockin' With Elvis April Fool's Day
Rockin' With Elvis New Year's Eve
Rockin' With The King April's Fool Day, Vol. I & II
Rough Cut Diamonds
Run On
Running For President
Sahara Tahoe Hotel
Season's Greetings From Elvis
Season's Greetings From Vegas
Send Me The Light... I Need It Bad!
Setting The Standard
Sheik Of The Desert
Shining in Portland
Showtime At The International
Since Cincinnati
Slippin' n' Slidin' With Elvis
Snowbird
Soldier Boy Is Back
Sold Out In Dixie!
Something Complete—Studio B. Sessions Vol. 2
Something For Everybody & Pot Luck
Something Old, Something New
Songs To Sing
Southbound
Spanish Eyes
Spin-In... Spinout

Spring Fever
Springtime In Nevada
Springtime In Saginaw
Stand By Me Vol. 1
Stand By Me Vol. 2
Standing Room Only
Stasera Resta Con Me
Stateline California
Stax Trax
Stay Away
Steamroller Blues
Steamrollin' Charlotte
Still Rocking The Nation!
Storm Over Portland
Stormin' Syracuse
Sunlight In Vegas
Surrender By Elvis—Studio B Sessions Vol. 1
Suspicious King
Suspicious Minds
Sweet Carolina
Take These Chains From My Heart
Tennessee Starlight
Thank You Very Much—Fort Baxter's Greatest Hits
That's All Right Anyway You Do
The '68 Comeback
The Alternate Aloha
The Alternate Golden Hits Vol. 3—
   The Little Sister Sessions
The Alternate Recordings
The Alternative Memphis
The Best Of Blue Hawaii Sessions
The Best Of G.I. Blues Sessions
The Best Of The Lost Binaural Takes
The Bicentennial Elvis Experience
The Brightest Star On Sunset Boulevard Vol. 1
The Brightest Star On Sunset Boulevard Vol. 2
The Cisco Kid Strikes Again
The Colonel's Collection
The Complete Bonus Songs 1960 - 1967
The Complete Burbank Sessions Vol. 1
The Complete Burbank Sessions Vol. 2
The Complete Burbank Sessions Vol. 3
The Complete Dressing Room Session
The Complete Follow That Dream Session (Angel)
The Complete Follow That Dream Session (Memory)
The Complete Frankie & Johnny Sessions
The Complete G.I. Blues Sessions Vol. 1
The Complete G.I. Blues Sessions Vol. 2
The Complete G.I. Blues Sessions Vol. 3
The Complete On Tour Sessions Vol. 1
The Complete On Tour Sessions Vol. 2
The Complete On Tour Sessions Vol. 3
The Complete Spinout Sessions
The Complete Wild In The Country Sessions
The Continuing Story Of Memory Records (1999-
   2004)
The Cream Of Culver City
The Eagle Has Landed
The Echoes Of Love Sessions
The Elvis Acetates Vol. 1—Fun In Acapulco
The Elvis Acetates Vol. 2—Girls! Girls! Girls!
The Event
The Eyes Of Texas Are Upon You
The Funny Side Of Elvis Presley
The Greensboro Concert
The Hampton Concert
The Hampton Roads Concert
The Hillbilly Cat Live
The Hollywood Sessions
The How Great Thou Art Sessions Vol. 1
The How Great Thou Art Sessions Vol. 2
The How Great Thou Art Sessions Vol. 3
The Jailhouse Rock Sessions
The King Of Entertainment
The King Rocks Tampa
The King Unadulterated Recordings
The King Will Never Die!
The Last Farewell
The Last Live Session
The Last Show
The Legend Lives On
The Legend Of A King
The Legendary Ed Sullivan Shows
The Lightning Storm In Florida
The Live Elvis
The Long Lost Home Recordings
The Lost Performances 1970 / 1972
The Lost Performances 1970 / 1972—Re-issue
The Lost Promo
The Man In White Vol. 1
The Man In White Vol. 2
The Man In White Vol. 3 - Get Dirty

The Man In White Vol. 4
The Memphis Flash Hits Las Vegas
The Midnight Hour
The Night When Elvis Sung When The Snow Is
   On The Roses
The Other Side Of Memphis
The Paradise Hawaiian Style Sessions Vol. 1
The Paradise Hawaiian Style Sessions Vol. 2
The Pot Luck Sessions Vol. 1
The Pot Luck Sessions Vol. 2
The Power Of Zhazam!
The Rehearsal For The Hampton Concert
The Request Box Shows
The Return Of The Tiger Man
The Roots Of Elvis
The Teen-Age Rage
The Unissued Elvis / 1956 - 1958
The Vegas Years Volume 1
The Thrill Goes On
The Unreleased Collection
The Winner Back In Vegas
There's A Whole Lotta Shakin' Goin' On
There's Always Him
There's Always Me Vol. 1
There's Always Me Vol. 2
There's Always Me Vol. 3
There's Always Me Vol. 4
There Goes My Everything
They Released Those Alternate Takes By Mistake
This Is Elvis
Tiger Man, An Alternate Anthology Vol. 1
To Know Him Is To Love Him
Tonight, 8:30 p.m....
Too Hot To Handle
Top Acts In Vegas Vol. 1
Top Acts In Vegas Vol. 2
Top Acts In Vegas Vol. 3
Top Acts In Vegas Vol. 4
Top Acts In Vegas Vol. 5
Top Acts In Vegas Vol. 6
Top Acts In Vegas Vol. 7
Tornado From Vegas
Totally Stung!
Trouble In Vegas—Elvis In The Hilton Vol. 2
True Love Travels On A Gravel Road
Trying To Get To Memphis
Trying To Get To You
Turning Up The Heat In Las Vegas
Tuscaloosa, Alabama
Tuscaloosa Night
Twenty Days And Twenty Nights
Ultra Rare Trax
Unchained Elvis
Unsurpassed Masters Box 1
Unsurpassed Masters Box 2
Unsurpassed Masters Box 3
Unsurpassed Masters Box 4
Unsurpassed Masters—Vol. 1
Unsurpassed Masters—Vol. 2
Unsurpassed Masters—Vol. 3
Unsurpassed Masters—Vol. 4
Vegas Birthday Show
Vegas Memories
Vegas Remembering
Vegas Showman
Vienna Woods Rock 'n' Roll—Vol. 1
Vienna Woods Rock 'n' Roll—Vol. 2
Vintage '55
Viva Las Vegas
Walk A Mile In My Shoes
Walk That Lonesome Road
Welcome Home Elvis
Welcome In Germany
Welcome In San Antone
We'll Keep You Happy
What A Wonderful Life
What Now My Love
When All Was Kool
When The Blue Moon Turns To Gold Again
Why Me, Lord ?
Wild In The Country Sessions
Wildcat
Wings Of An Angel (Angel Records)
Wings Of An Angel (German Records)
With A Song In My Heart
Whole Lotta Shakin' In Vegas—Elvis In The
   Hilton Vol. 3
Yesterday / Today
You've Lost That Lovin' Feelin'

"Bosom Of Abraham"

Elvis' June 9, 1971 Nashville recording of this Golden Gate Quartet gospel favorite (originally released as "Rock My Soul") appeared on Elvis' 1972 Grammy-winning gospel album, *He Touched Me*, a month after it featured as the B-side to the title track of the album.

The song has since appeared on gospel compilations *Amazing Grace, Peace In The Valley*, and *Ultimate Gospel*.

Rehearsal versions from March 31, 1972, when Elvis sang the song with Charlie Hodge and the Stamps for the *Elvis on Tour* documentary in a religious medley with "Lead Me, Guide Me," have appeared on gospel compilations *Amazing Grace* and *Peace In The Valley*.

Very occasionally, Elvis would sing the song live in the Seventies: a number of bootlegs list it as "Rock My Soul." The song was written by William Johnson, George McFadden and Ted Brooks, who had sung with Elvis as part of the Jubilee Four in the early Sixties.

Alternate takes from the original session have appeared on *Platinum: A Life In Music* and FTD releases *Easter Special* and *I Sing All Kinds*.

"Bossa Nova Baby"

Elvis recorded this upbeat Leiber and Stoller tune, released a year previously by Tippy and the Clovers, for the soundtrack of *Fun in Acapulco* at Radio Recorders on January 22, 1963. The transposition of a Brazilian musical form to the Mexican movie setting did not seem to bother anyone concerned.

When "Bossa Nova Baby" was released in October that year as a single, with "Witchcraft" on the B-side, it only made it as high as #8, despite selling almost 700,000 copies on initial issue.

The song has since appeared on *Worldwide 50 Gold Award Hits Vol. 1, Elvis In Hollywood, Elvis Sings Leiber & Stoller, The Top Ten Hits, Command Performances*, the *Double Features* reissue for the movie, *Elvis' Gold Records Vol. 4* (CD reissue), *Elvis 2nd to None, Hitstory, Elvis at the Movies* and *The Essential Elvis Presley*.

Platinum: A Life In Music features an alternate take of the song; the FTD *Fun in Acapulco* release includes multiple outtakes.

Elvis' movie performance is on the extended version of DVD collection *Elvis #1 Hit Performances*.

Bova, Joyce

Elvis met 24-year-old Joyce Bova in 1969 when he was performing in Las Vegas. A government employee at the time, and like Elvis a twin, they had an affair that lasted several years, notwithstanding her commitments as a staffer on the Armed Services Committee in Washington.

Their relationship lasted until 1972, and ran concurrently with Barbara Leigh (and of course, Priscilla). She met with Elvis during a May 1971 recording session in Nashville, and visited him in Las Vegas while he was performing at the Hilton in August that year. Elvis visited Bova in Washington in November 1971, and then before Christmas she made a flying visit to Graceland, after which Elvis flew back with her to Washington.

In 1994 Bova published a book about her experiences, *Don't Ask Forever: My Love Affair With Elvis* (published by Kensington Books), in which she recounted her whirlwind love affair, dalliance with drugs at Elvis' insistence, ensuing pregnancy and a secret (from Elvis) abortion.

"Boy Like Me, A Girl Like You, A"

A smooth-delivered ballad written by Sid Tepper and Roy C. Bennett for *Girls! Girls! Girls!*, recorded on March 27, 1962 at Radio Recorders.

It has since appeared on the usual *Double Features* and FTD releases for the film, and on *Elvis Sings Sid Tepper & Roy C. Bennett*

Alternates have appeared on *Today, Tomorrow & Forever* and the FTD *Girls! Girls! Girls!* release.

Bradley, C. W.

The Pastor at the Whitehaven Church of Christ, which Vernon attended, Bradley gave a eulogy at Elvis' funeral.

Bradley, Harold

Bradley was hired to back Elvis on guitar in Nashville in 1962, working on Pot Luck tracks and a few singles. He was in on Elvis' January 1964 recordings too, and played guitars on Nashville sessions in 1966 and 1967.

Brando, Marlon
(1924—2004)

Elvis greatly admired Marlon Brando's acting ability and cited him in an early interview as one of his favorites. In 1956, Elvis was introduced by Milton Berle on his TV show as "the Marlon Brando of Rock"; Jackie Gleason called him "Marlon Brando with a guitar."

Elvis was such a fan of Brando's rebellious characters that he knew chunks of his dialogue from *The Wild One* by heart. He met Brando at the commissary at Paramount in January 1958, when filming *King Creole*.

The role Elvis played in *Flaming Star*, half-American Indian Pacer Burton, was initially offered to Marlon Brando.

Brando is considered by many to be one of the greatest movie actors of all time, if not the greatest. He won two Oscars for best actor, for 1954 movie *On the Waterfront* and for *The Godfather* (1972), and was nominated a further six times.

Born in Omaha, Nebraska on April 3, 1924, Brando was a rebel from the start, showing very little ambition beyond digging ditches. He had grown up with the theater through his mother, who ran a local drama group, and leapt at the chance to go to New York and study the Stanislavsky method at the Actor's Studio. By 1946 he was voted the most promising young actor on Broadway. A year later he starred in the stage production of *A Streetcar Named Desire*, a role he reprised on film in 1951, and for which he received his first Oscar nomination, before becoming the archetypical on-screen rebel in a succession of hit movies.

Brando's career recovered from a Sixties slump as he returned to make craft-defining performances in the Seventies, including *The Godfather, Last Tango in Paris* and later in the decade, *Apocalypse Now*. By the Nineties he had became that oxymoron so beloved of the tabloid press, a "famous recluse," after weight problems and family tragedy involving his children Christian and Cheyenne.

MARLON BRANDO: "To grasp the full significance of life is the actor's duty, to interpret it is his problem, and to express it his dedication."

Brewster, W. Herbert
(1897-1987)

This well-known preacher, civil rights activist and gospel songwriter wrote many gospel classics including Clara Ward's "How I Got Over" and Mahalia Jackson's "Move On Up a Little Higher," which Elvis didn't sing on record but was happy to belt out at home. When he was 19, Elvis would sometimes skip Sunday school class at the Assembly of God Church and head on over to the Reverend's Church to hear him preach and listen to the gospel singing.

"Bridge Over Troubled Water"

Elvis recorded his version of this 1970 Simon and Garfunkel hit (the title song to their last studio album, the best selling single of 1970 and recipient of three Grammys) in Nashville on June 5, 1970. One of those songs that showcases what Elvis' voice can do even with an archly familiar tune (also covered by some of the greatest voices of the 20th century including Aretha Franklin and Eva Cassidy), Elvis' version was released on the *That's The Way It Is* album and features in the documentary of the same name. The song sounds live on disc because applause was overdubbed at the end; the version he did perform live on August 11, 1970 came out in 1997 on *Platinum: A Life In Music*. An alternate version from the same engagement was released on *Essential Elvis Vol. 4* in 1996.

The *Elvis on Tour* documentary features a powerhouse rendition that Elvis delivered in Greensboro, North Carolina in April 1972.

Elvis sang the song at his shows regularly from 1970 to 1974, and played it less frequently after, though sometimes to his own piano accompaniment. In addition to the many bootlegs available, live performances are on *Live In Las Vegas, That's The Way It Is—Special Edition, Elvis By The Presleys, Elvis Live*, and the 2007 *Viva Las Vegas* release. It's also showcased on FTD releases *One Night In Vegas* (also includes a rehearsal version), *An American Trilogy, Takin' Tahoe Tonight!, Closing Night* (while the band played "Suspicious Minds"), *Dragonheart, Big Boss Man, Dixieland Rocks, Southern Nights* and *Spring Tours '77*.

The studio version is on Seventies anthology *Walk A Mile In My Shoes*; more recently, the track also appeared on compilation *Elvis Inspirational*. In 2002, FTD released the raw first take from that June 1970 session on *The Nashville Marathon*. A rehearsal.

Brightest Star on Sunset Boulevard, Vols. 1 and 2

A Fort Baxter unofficial release from 1998 of Elvis' July 1970 rehearsal sessions.

Vol. 1
1. That's All Right
2. I Got A Woman
3. The Wonder Of You
4. I've Lost You
5. The Next Step Is Love
6. Stranger In The Crowd
7. You've Lost That Lovin' Feelin'
8. Something
9. Don't Cry, Daddy
10. Don't Cry, Daddy (Reprise)
11. You Don't Have To Say You Love Me
12. Polk Salad Annie
13. Bridge Over Troubled Water
14. I Can't Stop Loving You
15. Just Pretend

Elvis in one of his first television appearances on "The Steve Allen Show," 1956 singing his hit "Hound Dog."

VOL. 2

BRIGGS, DAVID
(B. 1943)

Pianist David Briggs first played with Elvis in Nashville in 1966, stepping in for regular keyboard player Floyd Cramer on the *How Great Thou Art* album recording session, much of it on organ (sharing duties with Henry Slaughter). Elvis immediately felt at ease with the young musician at that particularly fruitful session. When the much more experienced Cramer returned, Elvis asked for "the boy" to carry on playing.

Briggs played keyboards and clavinet with Elvis in the early seventies, first in the studio in 1972, and then in 1976 and 1977 our on tour. He also helped to arrange songs for Elvis' early Seventies Las Vegas performances.

Briggs played his last concert with Elvis in early 1977, when it became clear that Elvis was aware he was sleeping with previous girlfriend Linda Thompson—at one show, in a Freudian gesture, Elvis unplugged the pianist's instrument.

Briggs has played with a veritable who's who of country music, and worked with many more top musicians as a producer.

DAVID BRIGGS: "As far as I'm concerned, the best records that Elvis ever cut—I don't care what anybody thinks—are the ones that he did with Scotty and D. J. Everything after that was shit."

"BRINGIN' IT BACK"

Elvis recorded this country hit for Brenda Lee (written by Greg Gordon, who played clavinet on the session) on March 12, 1975 at RCA's Hollywood facility. It was first issued on *Today* that May, and came out as a single backed with "Pieces Of My Life" in October. It rose no higher than #65 on the *Billboard* Hot 100 as only 60,000 fans added it to their collection.

Later album releases are restricted to Seventies anthology *Walk A Mile In My Shoes*, with alternates on FTD releases *6363 Sunset* and *Today*.

A rare live version from 1974, on which Elvis sings bass while backing group Voice take the song away, came out on bootleg release *Desert Storm*.

"BRITCHES"

Elvis laid down this Sid Wayne / Sherman Edwards song for *Flaming Star* at Radio Recorders on August 8, 1960. It was beyond the pale for the movie—Elvis found it ridiculous and unbeliev-

able to sing while riding a horse—and was never released in Elvis' lifetime. It first came out on Vol. 3 of 1978 collection *Elvis: A Legendary Performer*, and later appeared on the *Double Features* issue for the movie.

BRONSON, CHARLES
(B. CHARLES DENNIS BUCHINSKI, 1921-2003)

A coalminer when young, Bronson was one of fifteen children born to Lithuanian parents in Pennsylvania, though he often played Latino roles. He started acting after serving in the Second World War.

Elvis worked with Bronson on *Kid Galahad* in late 1961, soon after Bronson had starred in *The Magnificent Seven*, which remained one of his best known roles, along with *The Great Escape* (1963), *The Dirty Dozen* (1967) and *Deathwish* (1974). Most reports state that there was on-set animosity between Bronson and Elvis, though not all entourage members recall frostiness between the actors. Bronson reputedly broke his hand trying to imitate Elvis' karate moves.

BROOKS, DUDLEY
(B. 1913)

This LA-born pianist joined Elvis' regular band in early 1957 for recording work on the soundtrack to Elvis' second film, *Loving You*. He played on many of Elvis' tracks at Radio Recorders in Los Angeles, and worked on later film soundtracks up to *Viva Las Vegas* in 1963. Brooks also co-wrote "Mama" and "We'll Be Together" for 1962 Elvis movie *Girls! Girls! Girls!*

Previously Brooks had worked with Charlie Christian, Bennie Goodman and Count Basie.

"BROWN EYED HANDSOME MAN"

Elvis was in on three versions of this Chuck Berry song with Carl Perkins and Jerry Lee Lewis during his immortal December 4, 1956 *Million Dollar Quartet* jam session. Chuck Berry had had a #7 R & B chart hit with the song earlier that year. Elvis was keen to record the song solo in 1967 but there were other songs on the agenda the next time he was in the studio.

Elvis reputedly ran through the song with other Chuck Berry hits in a 1972 or 1973 studio jam that has never seen light of day.

BROWN, JIM ED AND MAXINE

Accomplished country and western vocal singers Jim Ed (born 1924) and Maxine (born 1932) hit the big-time in 1954, before teaming up with baby sister Bonnie a year later as regulars at the Grand Ole Opry.

Elvis toured on the same bill as this brother-and-sister act in January 1955, on a slate organized and MC'd by Bob Neal—by many accounts, the Browns were by far the most popular act. Soon after, the Browns lent Elvis and the band a car after Bill Black totaled their usual ride. On August 14, 1955, Elvis went to Gladewater, Texas for Jim Ed and Maxine's parents' 25th anniversary party.

The Browns' 1959 song "The Three Bells" won them a Grammy nomination and was the first ever #1 on the pop, country, and rhythm 'n' blues charts. Jim Ed formed a successful duo with Helen Cornelius in the Seventies, and was still a Grand Ole Opry regular into the 2000s.

BROWN, JAMES
(1933-2006)

When the now Godfather of Soul played Memphis Coliseum in May 1966 he tried to get in touch with Elvis but every time he called Graceland he was informed that Elvis was sleeping. When they met a month later in LA at a Jackie Wilson concert, Brown said, "Man, Elvis, you sure do sleep a lot," causing Elvis to crack up with laughter. They remained good friends ever after.

In 1977, James Brown was one of the few industry heavyweights who came to Graceland for Elvis' funeral. He sat with the body on his own for a long time.

Originally from Barnwell, South Carolina, where he was born on May 3, 1933, as a youth Brown did time for petty crime and all sorts of odd jobs before he began singing with the Gospel Starlighters in 1952. After the group metamorphosed into the Famous Flames, Brown headed them up with a unique shouting soul/gospel style and a stage presence that generated a succession of hits through the Sixties: "Papa's Got a Brand New Bag," "I Got You (I Feel Good)," "It's a Man's, Man's, Man's World" and "Sex Machine." He also recorded songs that struck a strong chord with the black community ("Say It Loud—I'm Black and I'm Proud").

In the Seventies Brown used his wealth to buy radio stations, including one in Atlanta, Georgia where he had been employed as a shoe shine years earlier. He returned to the top of the charts in the Eighties with a Grammy-winning album "Living in America." Brown had later tangles with the law but has continued touring almost without cease. Brown is frequently cited as one of the most influential performers in the history of soul.

ELVIS SAID ABOUT JAMES BROWN: "They all copy him, but no one's got the soul of James Brown."

JAMES BROWN: "I wasn't just a fan, I was his brother . . .I love him and hope to see him in heaven. There'll never be another like that soul brother."

BROWN, TONY

Pianist Tony Brown, an actual son of a preacherman, was one of the Stamps in 1969 invited to see Elvis play Las Vegas on his return to live performing. Brown went backstage afterwards, where J. D. Sumner introduced him to Elvis.

Brown first started playing piano for Elvis in private as the keyboard player for Voice , the vocal group that Elvis put together in 1974. In 1975 he played on recording sessions, and then from 1976 to early 1977 was in the TCB Band, replacing Glen D. Hardin. Brown had previously played with country gospel group the Oak Ridge Boys. After Elvis, he toured with Emmylou Harris and went into producing. He worked his way up the music business ladder in Nashville and rose as high as President of MCA.

TONY BROWN: "Being on tour with Elvis is the one thing that defined who I am today."

BROWN, W. EARL
(B. 1928)

Composer, songwriter, musician and bandleader Walter Earl Brown conducted the orchestra that backed Elvis on his 1968 NBC TV Special. He was on hand to write the closing number for that show, Elvis' passionate finale "If I Can Dream,"

and also penned the hymn "Up Above My Head" that Elvis recorded for the show. Brown later worked on TV specials with Sonny & Cher, The Osmonds, Goldie Hawn and Steve Martin.

BUBBA HO-TEP

A 2002 movie adapted from a short story by Joe R. Lansdale, in which Elvis is still alive but is an old codger in a rest home in East Texas, after swapping lives with an Elvis impersonator years earlier. The franchise is set to be extended at time of writing with *Bubba Nosferatu* and possibly a third movie.

BUERGIN, MARGIT

A sixteen-year-old typist from Frankfurt who sought Elvis out soon after he arrived in Germany on Army service in 1958, grabbing his attention by asking a photographer she brought along to immortalize a kiss from Elvis. Dating ensued.

BULLOCK, BILL

RCA executive who played an integral part in negotiations with the Colonel to bring Elvis to RCA in November 1955. Bullock thereafter worked with Steve Sholes on directing Elvis' recordings and releases until the mid-Sixties.

"BULLFIGHTER WAS A LADY, THE"

A song Sid Tepper and Roy C. Bennett wrote for Elvis which he recorded for *Fun in Acapulco* at Radio Recorders on January 22, 1963.

The track has since appeared on the *Double Features* issue. Alternate takes have come out on FTD releases *Silver Screen Stereo* and the FTD *Fun in Acapulco* re-release.

BUNKLEY, BONNIE

A local Memphis girl who knocked on the gates of Graceland to ask Elvis to contribute to a benefit for her high school (Whitehaven) and ended up funding and some dates.

BURBANK '68—THE NBC TV COMEBACK SPECIAL

The first ever FTD release, from 1999, combining soundboard recordings and outtakes from Elvis' dressing room, NBC Studios and Western Recorders.

1. Danny Boy (instrumental)
2. Baby What You Want Me to Do (instrumental)
3. Love Me
4. Tiger Man
5. Dialogue
6. Lawdy, Miss Clawdy
7. One Night
8. Blue Christmas
9. Baby What You Want Me to Do
10. When My Blue Moon Turns to Gold Again
11. Blue Moon Of Kentucky
12. Dialogue
13. Heartbreak Hotel
14. Hound Dog
15. All Shook Up
16. Can't Help Falling In Love
17. Jailhouse Rock
18. Don't Be Cruel
19. Love Me Tender
20. Blue Suede Shoes
21. Trouble / Guitar Man (alternate take)
22. If I Can Dream (alternate vocal)
23. Let Yourself Go (instrumental)

BURBANK SESSIONS, THE (COMPLETE)

An unofficial soundboard release on the Audifon label on two LPs/three CDs of material from Elvis' 1968 NBC TV Special rehearsals.

TRACK LISTING:
VOL. 1
1. Dialogue
2. That's All Right
3. Heartbreak Hotel
4. Love Me
5. Baby, What You Want Me To Do
6. Dialogue
7. Blue Suede Shoes
8. Baby, What You Want Me To Do
9. Dialogue
10. Lawdy, Miss Clawdy
11. Are You Lonesome Tonight?
12. When My Blue Moon Turns To Gold Again
13. Blue Christmas
14. Tryin' To Get To You
15. One Night
16. Baby, What You Want Me To Do
17. Dialogue
18. One Night
19. Memories

VOL. 2
1. Dialogue
2. Heartbreak Hotel
3. Baby, What You Want Me To Do
4. Dialogue
5. That's All Right
6. Are You Lonesome Tonight?
7. Baby, What You Want Me To Do
8. Blue Suede Shoes
9. One Night
10. Love Me
11. Dialogue
12. Tryin' To Get To You
13. Lawdy, Miss Clawdy
14. Dialogue
15. Santa Claus Is Back In Town
16. Blue Christmas
17. Tiger Man
18. When My Blue Moon Turns To Gold Again
19. Memories

VOL. 3
1. Steve Binder Introduction / Dialogue
2. Heartbreak Hotel
3. One Night
4. Heartbreak Hotel
5. Hound Dog
6. All Shook Up
7. Can't Help Falling In Love
8. Jailhouse Rock
9. Don't Be Cruel
10. Blue Suede Shoes
11. Love Me Tender
12. Dialogue
13. Trouble
14. Dialogue
15. Trouble / Guitar Man
16. Dialogue
17. If I Can Dream

BUREAU OF NARCOTICS AND DANGEROUS DRUGS (BNDD)

See under POLICE BADGES

BURGESS, "SONNY"
(B. ALBERT BURGESS, 1931)

Arkansas-born Burgess has played rockabilly ever since "We Wanna Boogie," his first cut on Sun Records in 1956. According to Sam Phillips, if the audience for rockabilly hadn't fallen off in the Sixties, Burgess "could have been one of the greats." Elvis played on a bill with Sonny Burgess and his band "The Moonlighters" in Arkansas in late October 1955.

Elvis' early manager Bob Neal took on Burgess and his next band the Pacers in 1956.

Elvis' original guitarist Scotty Moore and backing group the Jordanaires played on Burgess's 1996 album, *Sonny Burgess*.

SONNY BURGESS: "Doing a show with Elvis was great . . . Besides being an outstanding singer, he was actually an ordinary, fun-loving guy who really loved to put on a show for his audience... You could just tell that Elvis Presley had the gift."

BURK, BILL E.

Burk covered the Elvis beat from the privileged vantage point of the *Memphis Press-Scimitar*, first reporting on Elvis in January 1955. Through their friendship, Burk obtained a real exclusive, the first interview with Elvis after he left the Army in 1960, on the train home to Memphis.

Burk founded and has edited the *Elvis World* magazine, which lays claim to be the longest running publication of its kind (since 1985). He is a prolific author of more than a dozen books on Elvis, including a noteworthy trilogy about Elvis' early years in which he lays bare many of the myths about Elvis' life before fame.

Book:
(OTHERS UNDER RELEVANT HEADINGS)
Elvis Through My Eyes, by Bill E. Burk, Burk Enterprises, 1996.

BURNETTE BROTHERS

It wasn't just Elvis and Bill Black who came out of the Lauderdale Courts project in Memphis to make music. Rockabilly pioneers Johnny and Dorsey Burnette also called the Courts home.

Johnny (1934-1964) and Dorsey (1932-1979) were two thirds of the Rock and Roll Trio, with guitarist Paul Burlison, that filled venues, cut records and came within a whisker of national fame, reaching the finals of "Ted Mack's Original Amateur Hour." The brothers later wrote hits for Ricky Nelson and embarked on solo careers. In the early Sixties Johnny followed the teen idol path with "Dreamin'" and "You're Sixteen," which was later covered by Ringo Starr.

Growing up in the same part of Memphis, Johnny clashed with Red West on the football field (reputedly coming off worse). Before performing, he had a promising career as an amateur boxer. In the Sixties, Johnny toured Australia (with singer Connie Francis) and the UK, something his more famous pal Elvis never managed.

Fast forward a generation and Johnny's son Rocky and Dorsey's son Billy both made rockabilly music. Billy Burnette also recorded a couple of Elvis tribute albums.

"BURNING LOVE"

Producer Felton Jarvis and various entourage pals had to persuade Elvis to try this upbeat number, written by Dennis Linde (and previously released by Arthur Alexander) at RCA's Hollywood Studio on March 28, 1972, at a time when Elvis was suffering the heartbreak of separation from Priscilla and choosing almost exclusively sad songs to record.

Jarvis's hunch paid off: on release in August 1972, with a guitar line overdubbed by songwriter Linde, the single shot to #2, backed with "It's a Matter of Time" on the B-side. Elvis' best-selling single in a couple of years was kept off out of top spot by Chuck Berry's one and only #1, "My Ding-A-Ling."

"Burning Love" had its first album outing on the *Aloha From Hawaii Via Satellite* release after the concert performance, though Elvis had been playing it live since he recorded it (as the *Elvis on Tour* documentary attests).

Just because it wasn't one of Elvis' personal favorites didn't stop "Burning Love" from becoming a latter-day Elvis classic. The studio version has since appeared on *Burning Love And Hits From His Movies Vol. 2, Double Dynamite, Elvis' Gold Records Vol. 5, Greatest Hits Vol. 1, The Top Ten Hits, Walk A Mile In My Shoes, Burning Love, Artist Of The Century, ELVIS 30 #1 Hits, Hitstory, Elvis By The Presleys, Elvis Live* and *The Essential Elvis Presley* to name a baker's dozen.

Platinum: A Life In Music, Burning Love ELVIS 30 #1 Hits Deluxe and FTD release *6363 Sunset* feature alternate takes from the original recording session.

Live, it's on *Elvis Aron Presley, The Alternate Aloha, The Live Greatest Hits, Live In Las Vegas, Elvis: Close Up* plus FTD offerings *Big Boss Man* and *Tucson '76*. A rehearsal from the *Elvis on Tour* period is on FTD release *On Tour—The Rehearsals*. Composer Dennis Linde sings the song as he wrote it on FTD release *Writing For The King*; Felton Jarvis's *Guitar Man* sessions update from 1980 is on FTD release *Too Much Monkey Business*.

BURNING LOVE

A 1999 BMG release of mainly live tracks recorded between 1971 and 1973, many of which would have graced a planned album with the working title *Standing Room Only*. That album was supplanted by the *Live at Madison Square Garden* album.

TRACK LISTING:
1. Burning Love
2. Never Been To Spain
3. You Gave Me A Mountain
4. I'm Leavin'
5. It's Only Love
6. Always On My Mind
7. It's Impossible
8. It's Over
9. Separate Ways
10. Fool
11. Hound Dog
12. Little Sister / Get Back
13. A Big Hunk O' Love
14. Where Do I Go From Here
15. For The Good Times
16. It's A Matter Of Time
17. An American Trilogy
18. The Impossible Dream

BURNING LOVE AND HITS FROM HIS MOVIES, VOL. 2

A collection of old movie songs not deemed good enough for re-release in the previous collection of movie material, *Elvis Sings Hits from His Movies Vol. 1*, harnessed to recent chart topping single "Burning Love" and released on Camden in November 1972. On initial release the album sold 700,000 copies, and charted at #22, the best to

date for a budget Elvis release. All in all, it stayed on the charts for 25 weeks.

TRACK LISTING:
1. Burning Love
2. Tender Feeling
3. Am I Ready
4. Tonight Is So Right For Love
5. Guadalajara
6. It's A Matter Of Time
7. No More
8. Santa Lucia
9. We'll Be Together
10. I Love Only One Girl

BURNS, GEORGE
(B.NATHAN BIRNBAUM, 1896-1996)

Elvis met George Burns on a trip to Las Vegas in July 1960, when he was photographed with the then (not quite) grand old man of comedy and Bobby Darin, who was opening Burns' show.

Burns made people laugh from the Twenties to the Nineties (until the late Fifties with wife Gracie Allen as comic duo Burns and Allen) on stage, on the radio in the movies, and when it was invented, on TV.

"The Comedian's Comedian" made a solo comeback in 1975 with an Oscar for his performance in *The Sunshine Boys* (1975). He also got to play God in three separate movies.

BURTON, JAMES
(B. 1939)

Burton was an ever-present member of the TCB band and played Fender Telecaster guitar on Elvis' later albums.

A native of Minden, Louisiana, where he was born on August 21, 1939, self-taught guitar legend James Burton served his apprenticeship at the Louisiana Hayride in the late Fifties and gained instant fame when he played the guitar lick on Dale Hawkins' legendary 1957 track "Suzie Q." Burton toured with Ricky Nelson and appeared on TV show "Ozzie and Harriet" from 1958 to 1965. His country-inspired "chicken picking'" lead guitar style, which he has described as a blend of Chet Atkins and Blues-style guitar, garnered him plenty of work as an in-demand West Coast session musician—over the years he played with the Everly Brothers, Sonny and Cher and the Beach Boys. Bob Dylan approached Burton to come on tour when he started playing more rock 'n' roll material in the mid-Sixties, but Burton had committed to TV show "Shindig." Years before he played with Elvis, Burton worked on demos put together by songwriter Don Robertson for Elvis to listen to before going into the studio. He also played the dobro, and released a single under the name Jimmy Dobro.

Elvis originally approached Burton to play on his 1968 NBC TV Special but Burton was booked with Frank Sinatra at the time.

In 1969, Elvis asked Burton to put together a band for his first Las Vegas residency at the International Hotel. After piecing together the future group, they got down to the business of learning songs, a hundred and fifty of them in six nights to be ready for Elvis.

Burton led Elvis' TCB band from its first Las Vegas performance at the International Hotel in 1969 to his last at Indianapolis in 1977, wowing the crowds with his solos after Elvis unleashed him with the words, "Play it, James." Burton continued to work as a session musician between Elvis concerts. In 1971 he recorded solo album *The Guitar Sounds of James Burton* using Nashville studio time booked for Elvis but cancelled owing to Elvis' eye problems.

In 1974, when Elvis met Eric Clapton (but in some tellings of the tale was unaware of quite how famous and accomplished the guitarist was), he humorously offered to hook him up with James Burton to maybe learn a thing or two.

In 1976, Burton came close to quitting with pianist Glen D. Hardin to tour with Emmylou Harris, but was persuaded to stay on by Tom Diskin.

Over the years, Burton has contributed his talents to music by Gram Parsons, John Denver, Buck Owens, Joni Mitchell and Elvis Costello among many others.

More recently, he has been a fixture at live Elvis anniversary concerts and on "Elvis—The Concert" tours.

Burton was inducted into the Rock and Roll Hall of Fame in 2001. He has used a Fender Telecaster since the age of fourteen, when he first started playing professionally. Elvis acknowledged Burton's surpassing skill in his humorous concert introductions, presenting Burton as Lightnin' Hopkins, Chuck Berry and other guitar greats.

More recently, he has been organizing his own international guitar festival in Shreveport, Louisiana. He was inducted into the Rock and Roll Hall of Fame in 2001, and is active in donating guitars to sick children to help them get better.

ELVIS SAID: "One of the funkiest chicken-pickin' son-of-a-guns you ever met in your life."

BUSH, GEORGE
(B. 1924)

In 1971, when US Ambassador to the United Nations, George I was the keynote speaker at the JCC luncheon, on the day that Elvis was honored with a Jaycee, one of the few awards he received during his life and the only one that he picked up publicly.

Bush served in World War II as a bomber pilot. He went on to serve as Director of the CIA and was elected President of the United States from 1989 to 1993.

BUSH, GEORGE W.
(B. 1946)

The two-term President of the United States visited Graceland with Japanese Prime Minister Junichiro Koizumi on June 30, 2006.

Previously it had been revealed by Laura Bush that as a child in the Fifties, the future President of the United States was sent to the principal's office at school after drawing sideburns on his face with charcoal and disrupting his music class with an Elvis impression.

BILL CLINTON IN 1992: "You know, Bush is always comparing me to Elvis in sort of unflattering ways. I don't think Bush would have liked Elvis very much, and that's just another thing that's wrong with him."

GEORGE W. BUSH: "He's obviously a major part of our music history. He had an international reputation."

BUTTREY, KENNY
(1945-2004)

Popular session drummer Kenny Buttrey, who played on many landmark Sixties and Seventies recordings including "All Along the Watchtower" and many Bob Dylan and Neil Young cuts, worked in the studio with Elvis at a May 1971

Nashville recording session after regular drummer Jerry Carrigan dropped out.

This wasn't his Elvis debut though: previously he played on Nashville recording sessions for *Harum Scarum* in 1965. Buttrey often worked with Elvis Nashville band regulars David Briggs and Charlie McCoy.

"By And By"

Elvis took on this upbeat Charles Tindley composition, originally titled "We'll Understand It Better By and By," at his May 26, 1966 *How Great Thou Art* session in Nashville. Pre-Elvis, the song was best known in a version sung by blues artist Blind Willie Johnson in 1930.

Elvis rocks the song on *How Great Thou Art* and later gospel compilations *Amazing Grace* and *Peace In The Valley*. Alternates may be found on FTD releases *Long Lonely Highway* and *So High*.

"By The Time I Get To Phoenix"

Glen Campbell was the first to have a hit with this song in 1968. It was written by Jimmy Webb and originally recorded by Johnny Rivers in 1966, since then many other artists have had their way with it, including Frank Sinatra, Isaac Hayes, Wanda Jackson and Nick Cave & The Bad Seeds. Elvis borrowed the song for a Glen Campbell take-off he did in concert in 1970.

BYERS, JOY
(B. 1937)

Prolific songwriter who wrote sixteen songs for Elvis, most of them for soundtracks. She sometimes co-wrote with producer husband William "Bob" Johnston (who later claimed that he wrote many of the tunes credited to his wife solo), and also penned a ballad Elvis liked very much, "It Hurts Me," with Charlie Daniels.

The Rebel, 1956.

CAGE, NICOLAS
(B. NICOLAS KIM COPPOLA, 1964)

The Hollywood actor—born into the Coppola family on January 7, 1964—played an Elvis fanatic in *Wild at Heart* (1990), and dressed up Elvis style in *Honeymoon in Vegas* (1992).

In 2002 he married Lisa Marie Presley. Their eventful marriage provided plentiful tabloid fare until their divorce less than two years later. Reputedly Cage broke the taboo of taking photos of the upstairs at Graceland, according to a web site that claims to show his pictures. Cage's one Oscar to date is for 1995 movie *Leaving Las Vegas*. Since leaving Lisa Marie, he married a former waitress named Alice Kim and had a son.

CALIFORNIA

- Anaheim
Elvis played the Anaheim Convention Center on April 23 and 24, 1973. Elvis performed here next on November 30, 1976 at the end of a tour.

- Big Bear
Elvis and Co. did location shooting for *Kissin' Cousins* at Big Bear in 1963.

- Fresno
Elvis appeared at the Selland Arena on April 25, 1973, and went back for more on May 12, 1974.

- Inglewood
Elvis performed two shows at the Forum on May 11, 1974.

- Long Beach
Elvis was at the Municipal Auditorium on June 7, 1956. He played the Arena for two nights, on November 14 and 15, 1972. On his visit on April 25, 1976, he was booked at the Arena once again.

- Los Angeles
Elvis' first LA show was at the Shrine Auditorium on June 8, 1956. He played two nights at the Pan Pacific Auditorium on October 28 and 29, 1957—the first caused such a scandal for Elvis' "lewd" dancing that he had to tone down his performance or risk arrest by the Los Angeles Vice Squad. No such problems on November 14, 1970, when his two shows at the Inglewood Forum set records for attendance and box office gross, eclipsing the previous record holders, the Rolling Stones.
See also separate entry for LOS ANGELES, HOMES AND HOTELS.

- Oakland
Elvis and his band played the Auditorium Arena on June 3, 1956. They performed at the Oakland Auditorium on October 27, 1957. The TCB Band and Elvis played the Coliseum on November 10, 1970, the first date on an 8-date national tour. He swung through town again on November 11, 1972.

- Pasadena
Elvis became a regular visitor to the Self-Realization Fellowship in Pasadena starting in 1965.

- Pacific Palisades
Elvis attended spiritual retreats with the Self-Realization Fellowship here in 1965.

- Sacramento
Elvis and Priscilla traveled up to Sacramento in the late Sixties to visit Priscilla's folks, Paul and Ann Beaulieu.

Candid photo of Elvis on his motorcycle in California in the 1970's

- San Bernardino
Elvis appeared at the Swing Auditorium on November 12 and 13, 1972. He played the venue again on May 10 and May 13, 1974 before going on to Tahoe for a two-week engagement.

- San Diego
Elvis played the Arena in San Diego on two nights, April 4 and 5, 1956. He was back on June 9, 1956, soon after his second appearance on the "Milton Berle Show." He returned to the International Sports Arena on November 15, 1970, and again on April 26, 1973 during a sweep through California. The next time he was in town, on April 24, 1976, Elvis performed at the Sports Arena.

- San Francisco
Elvis performed two shows at the Civic Auditorium on October 26, 1957. He went up to San Francisco for some R&R around the time he was shooting *Wild in the Country* in 1960. Elvis appeared with the TCB Band at the Cow Palace on November 13, 1970, and then on November 28 and 29, 1976.

CAMDEN RECORDS

A budget record label set up by RCA in 1969 that issued a number of Elvis albums through the mid-Seventies. The label was named after the record manufacturing plant location in Camden, New Jersey.

CAMPBELL, GLEN
(B. 1936)

Before he hit the big time Campbell was a session guitarist on Elvis' *Viva Las Vegas* soundtrack in 1963, on which he also sang back-up vocals. He recorded a number of demos from which Elvis chose his material in the mid-Sixties, up to and including 1967 movie *Stay Away, Joe*. As a session music he played on many tracks recorded in California, including songs by Frank Sinatra, The Righteous Brothers, The Monkees, Bobby Darin, The Mamas & The Papas; for a spell in the mid-Sixties he toured and recorded with The Beach Boys.

Campbell has since become much better known for his own country/pop hits: breakthrough 1967 single "Gentle On My Mind" and then "Wichita Lineman," "Galveston" and "Rhinestone Cowboy." He has also been a familiar face on TV, and acted opposite John Wayne in 1969 movie *True Grit* in a role for which Elvis had been in the running.

In 1970 Elvis began one of his shows with a quick take-off of Campbell's song, "By The Time I Get To Phoenix." Elvis took in Campbell's show at the Las Vegas Hilton in May 1972; Campbell returned the compliment. Elvis recorded Campbell hit "Gentle On My Mind" and also sang "Turn Around Look at Me" in concert.

CANADA

Elvis toured Canada in April 1957, though his date in Montreal fell victim to local concern at rowdy behavior, in a campaign spearheaded by a vocal Catholic lobby. Elvis first planned to perform north of the border in early 1956, before he became a household name, but the tour fell through when the promoters got cold feet.

- Ottawa
Elvis performed at the Ottawa Auditorium on April 3, 1957.

Elvis performing in Canada in 1957.

- Toronto
Elvis' first over-the-border show was at the Maple Leaf Gardens on April 2, 1957, in his glorious gold-leaf suit.

- Vancouver
Elvis performed at the Empire Stadium on August 31, 1957, though the show was stopped twice because of the crush of the 26,500-strong crowd by the stage.

Sixteen months after Elvis' death, commemorative LP *Elvis—A Canadian Tribute* was released on both sides of the border, making to #86 on the US LP charts and achieving gold record status.

Book:
Elvis in Canada, by Bill E. Burk, Propwash Publishing, 1996

"CANE AND A HIGH STARCHED COLLAR, A"

An accordion-heavy Sid Tepper / Roy C. Bennett effort that Elvis laid down at Radio Recorders on August 8, 1960 for *Flaming Star*. Accordionist Jimmie Haskell obliged on this and other soundtracks that year. The song was not deemed worthy of record issue until a version appeared on 1976 release *Elvis: A Legendary Performer Vol. 2*.

It has since appeared on the *Double Features* release for the movie, and *Elvis Sings Sid Tepper & Roy C. Bennett*.

"CAN'T HELP FALLING IN LOVE"

Elvis recorded this song for the *Blue Hawaii* movie soundtrack and LP on March 23, 1961 at Radio Recorders in LA, lavishing 29 takes on the tune before he was satisfied. Little did he know that this movie song, which he croons in the picture to a 78-year-old grandma, would be the show finale for so many hundreds of performances.

Released in late November 1961, in its fourteen weeks on the charts "Can't Help Falling In Love" made it to #2, paired with B-Side tune "Rock-A-Hula Baby," and soared past the million sales mark in the US. In the UK, it was #1 for four straight weeks.

The song is actually a traditional French 18th century tune called "Plaisir d'Amour" by Giovanni Martini, with words penned specially for the movie by George Weiss, Hugo Peretti, and Luigi Creatore. When Elvis was recording the song, he told the musicians that he would be thinking of a little girl called Priscilla who he had left behind in Germany.

Elvis chose "Can't Help Falling In Love" over "Such A Night," "What'd I Say" and Fifties finale "Hound Dog" as his closing number when he returned to live performing in August 1969. As well as providing a suitably romantic finale to his Seventies stage shows, the song remained for Elvis a personal declaration of love to his lady of the moment, and a slightly less personal declaration to thousands of smitten fans in the audience. At his final concerts, Elvis sang the song to girlfriend Ginger Alden, who was positioned on stage for just this moment..

Before its new lease of life in the Seventies, Elvis resuscitated the tune for his career-reviving NBC TV Special in 1968, featuring it in the show and on the tie-in LP.

Elvis' perennial closer, the song has featured on practically every live album of Elvis' since *From Memphis to Vegas/Elvis In Person*. During his lifetime, that included *Elvis As Recorded At Madison Square Garden*, *Aloha From Hawaii Via Satellite*, *Elvis Recorded Live On Stage In Memphis* and *Elvis in Concert*. Needless to say, he sings it in both of his Seventies film documentaries. Since then, it has come out on more releases than I'm willing to list here—he sang the song 750 times or more. Recent issues include *Elvis Aron Presley*, *That's The Way It Is—Special Edition*, *Live In Las Vegas*, *The Live Greatest Hits*, *Elvis: Close Up*, *Elvis at the Movies*, the 2007 *Viva Las Vegas* release, plus FTD releases *Elvis At The International*, *Writing For The King*, *All Shook Up*, *Polk Salad Annie*, *One Night In Vegas*, *The Impossible Dream*, *An American Trilogy*, *Summer Festival*, *Closing Night*, *Live In L.A.* *It's Midnight*, *Dragonheart*, *Big Boss Man*, *Dixieland Rocks*, *Dinner At Eight*, *Tucson '76* and *New Year's Eve*.

Alternates from the '68 Comeback Special have appeared on *Elvis NBC TV* reissues, *Memories: The '68 Comeback Special* and FTD rehearsals release *Burbank '68*.

The movie version of the song from the original studio session was released on the remixed and remastered 1997 *Blue Hawaii*. Alternate versions from that session have appeared on later albums including *Elvis Aron Presley*, the *Blue Hawaii* CD re-release, *Today Tomorrow & Forever*, and *Elvis: Close Up*. A pre-concert rehearsal lurks on FTD disc 6363 *Sunset*.

Since Elvis, the tune has been covered by performers as diverse as Bob Dylan, Julio Iglesias, Bono, UB40 and Pearl Jam.

CAPLAN, HARRY
(1908-1994)

Caplan produced two movies in a long career as an assistant director and production manager on films and TV shows, including one of Elvis' final Hollywood sorties, *Charro!* (1969).

CAREER

Elvis' career divides crudely into four phases: pre-Army rocker (1954-1958), post-Army movie star (1960-1967), Comeback kid/top Vegas act (1968-ca. 1972), and then a slow coda of decline. Simplistic as this may be, it does roughly describe the trajectory of his performing years.

Before he made it as a singer, Elvis' likely employment was industrial or blue collar. At his interview with the Tennessee State Employment Security Office after leaving school, Elvis said he wanted a job "dealing with people," and impressed the interviewer, despite his "rather flash dress and 'Playboy' appearance." Elvis initially sought a job as a machinist; a month later he was more specific and stated he wanted to operate "big lathes." He told the Employment Office that his priority was to help his dad work off his financial obligations. It was more or less at this time that Elvis recorded his first songs, out of his own pocket, at Memphis Recording Service.

After a month-long spell at M. B. Parker Company, he told the Employment Office that what he really wanted for was something that allowed him to "keep clean." He tried and failed to land jobs at Sears Roebuck, as a delivery boy, and at Kroger's grocery store. Elvis returned to Precision Tool for nine months—he had worked there during the summer as a 16-year-old—and then started driving a small delivery truck for Crown Electric, hoping to land a spot in as an apprentice electrician. His second self-paid recording session at Memphis Recording Service a year later was no more successful than the first. He tried to get into the music business as the singer with a band, only to be rebuffed by local gospel group the Songfellows, and then in May 1954 by Eddie Bond after an audition at the Hi-Hat Club.

In June 1954, Marion Keisker of Sun Records finally called Elvis back to see if he might be right for a tune Sam Phillips had that needed a singer. Elvis wasn't right, but this was his foot in the door. Phillips encouraged Elvis try out some songs with Sun musicians Scotty Moore and Bill Black. The oft retold story is that during a "rehearsal" at Sun Studio, Elvis spontaneously broke into Arthur "Big Boy" Crudup's "That's All Right," Sam Phillips rolled the tape and the rest, as they've been saying ever since, is rock 'n' roll history.

Elvis didn't give up his day job until his second single, "Good Rockin' Tonight." By this time he and the band had a regular slot on the Louisiana Hayride. Scotty and Bill baled out of the Starlite Wranglers and gave up their day jobs too.

Within six months, Elvis had made it to the top of the bill on a Hank Snow Jamboree Attractions show in Little Rock, Arkansas. Elvis and the "Blue Moon Boys" toured incessantly until the summer of 1955. By this time manager Bob Neal was being shadowed by Colonel Parker; before the year was out, Parker had taken full control of Elvis' career, was engineering a big-money move to RCA, and holding out the promise of national TV exposure and a movie career.

Things did not run smoothly at RCA to begin with. Elvis' first recording session was a disappointment all round. Until "Heartbreak Hotel" became a smash hit in March 1956, some at RCA were privately concerned that they had wasted a record amount of money on Elvis' contract.

Seasoned music business professionals advised Elvis to make hay while the sun shined. Nobody expected him to last more than a year or two, the average span of a "successful" recording artist.

Elvis was convinced that two-year stint in the Army would be the end of him as a recording star. There can be little doubt that Elvis saw acting as a safer long-term bet. Recast as a patriotic, parent-friendly version of his rebellious former self, in 1960 Elvis embarked on a schedule of as many as three pictures a year. Fans voted with their wallets: his more artistically-acclaimed post-

Army records sold far fewer copies than his movie soundtracks. The Colonel got the message and acted accordingly; Elvis soon became the highest-earning actor in Hollywood.

Elvis' outlet for artistic frustration in the Sixties was gospel. He never stopped singing gospel at home with his pals; in 1966 he took it into the studio to make *How Great Thou Art*. A new working relationship with producer Felton Jarvis helped to rekindle Elvis' interest in making music.

In 1968 Elvis resurrected his career with the NBC TV ("Comeback") Special, in which he showed the world that not only did he still "have it," he was at the very cutting edge. Elvis cemented his return with new material recorded at a new studio (American), and once more he was off and unstoppable.

When Elvis returned to live performing in Las Vegas in 1969, critics were lost for superlatives. *Rolling Stone* described his performance as "supernatural, his own resurrection." Regular projects including concert documentaries *Elvis: That's The Way It Is* (1970) and *Elvis on Tour* (1972) and the *Aloha from Hawaii* satellite broadcast kept boredom—Elvis' biggest enemy—at bay. After 1973, Elvis lacked the kind of challenge that would pull him out of his increasingly drug-centered behavior. A potential career turning point came and went in 1975, when Barbra Streisand asked Elvis to play the lead role in *A Star Is Born*. The Colonel's asking price was so high that Streisand's studio didn't even bother making a counter offer.

Right into his last year alive, given a reason like a new girlfriend to impress, Elvis was capable of rousing himself to perform at his best. When that was beyond him, his fans were so loving and indulgent that his best on any particular night was generally good enough.

Hid death in 1977 proved to be a blip in terms of earnings potential. Once the Colonel was divested of his overweening power and the Elvis Presley Estate returned to a sound financial footing, Elvis returned to the top of the entertainers' earnings league. The Colonel proved to be as correct about Elvis' death as he was about most business decisions: ultimately, it was business as usual.

For more information on Elvis' career, see Managers and Colonel Tom Parker.

ELVIS, IN 1956, when asked about girlfriends, said he was "engaged to only one—my career."

ELVIS SAID IN 1959: "Once you get a taste of show business, there's nothing like it."

ELVIS SAID IN 1962: "You're better off if what you're doing is doing okay, you're better off stickin' with it until time itself changes things."

PRISCILLA: "I look back now and realize that our love affair was dependent on how his career was going. During protracted periods of non creativity, his temper often flared."

RICHARD CORLISS: "As the pawn of Parker his manager, he was the last pop idol who did not control his own career."

Books:
Any good biography and . . .
Elvis Presley: The Rebel Years, by Lester Bangs, Schirmers 1987.
Elvis On The Road To Stardom 1955-1956, by Jim Black, WH Allen, 1988.
Elvis: The Early Years: Portrait of a Young Rebel, by Susan M. Doll, Signet/NAL, 1990.
Elvis: Rock 'n' Roll Legend, by Susan M. Doll, Publications International Ltd., 1994.
Elvis After Elvis: The Posthumous Career Of A Living Legend, by Gilbert B Rodman, Routledge, 1996.

"CARNY TOWN"

A Fred Wise / Randy Starr light rocker that Elvis recorded for the film *Roustabout* at a Radio Recorders booking on March 3, 1964. Repeat performances are limited to the *Double Features* release at the time of writing.

CARRIGAN, JERRY
(B. 1943)

Part of the legendary "Muscle Shoals Rhythm Section" so highly regarded in the music business that The Beatles took them along on their debut US tour, drummer Carrigan worked with colleagues Norbert Putnam and David Briggs in Nashville for many RCA artists. He played on Elvis' Nashville sessions in 1970 and 1971, and then on the Stax session in Memphis in 1973. Carrigan was much in demand on country hits coming out of Nashville in the Seventies, playing with all the top stars. He later toured with John Denver.

"CARRY ME BACK TO OLD VIRGINIA"

Elvis sang a line of the Virginia state song at a Las Vegas concert in April 1972. It has appeared only unofficially on bootlegs.

CARS

Cars have always been rock 'n' roll. The first ever rock 'n' roll song, "Rocket 88," was a paean to a souped-up Oldsmobile. Elvis was always into cars, from when he was a little kid walking along the street and daydreaming about one day owning a Cadillac. In his lifetime, Elvis is said to have purchased as many as 200 of that particular marque, along with hundreds of other cars for friends, family and even strangers who happened to be in the right place (a car dealership) at the right time (when Elvis was there).

Elvis took his driving test when he was sixteen, in his uncle Travis Smith's 1940 Buick. He seems to have been driving for quite a while by then: as early as 10 or 12, according to biographers who write that his parents allowed him time behind the wheel on local trips. The first car Elvis regularly drove was a 1941 (according to some a 1939 or a 1942) 12-cylinder green Lincoln Zephyr coupe, which his dad bought in the summer of 1951. The Zephyr had one smashed window covered over with a piece of cardboard, and often refused to start. In his last year of high school, pals who helped push the car to get it started would get a ride home for their trouble. Elvis won the Safe Driving Award at High School.

Elvis drove a Dodge pickup truck in his job for Crown Electric before he became a singer.

Either at the very end of 1954 or the very start of 1955, Elvis bought the first of many cars, a tan 1951 Lincoln Cosmopolitan. The car became his first band's official transport, with a roof rack for Bill Black's bass, and an *ad hoc* advertising slogan "Elvis Presley-Sun Records." Up until that time, the band had been racking up thousands of miles in Scotty Moore's 1954 Chevrolet Bel Air. The Lincoln was written off in March 1955, when Bill Black ploughed into the back of a hay truck in Arkansas. Elvis borrowed a car from Jim Ed and Maxine Brown for tour dates in Texas until he could find a new permanent ride: a pink and white 1954 Cadillac, which he later described as "the most beautiful car I've ever seen." That car went up in smoke, literally, on the night of June 5, 1955, at Fulton Arkansas, as Elvis and a girl he

had met at his evening show at Hope, Arkansas, were en route to Texarkana. Spookily, Gladys had a nightmare about this event the very night it happened. Scotty Moore went back to Memphis to pick up the car that Elvis had recently bought his folks, a Ford Crown Victoria, in Elvis' favored scheme of pink-and-white. Red West later said that this was the car Elvis enjoyed the most.

In July 1955, Elvis replaced the burnt out Cadillac with a brand-new 1955 Cadillac Fleetwood Sixty Special Sedan with a black top, and immediately had it repainted from blue to a shade of pink he had admired on a 1954 Studebaker Commander in a Memphis showroom. As ever, the car had a removable wooden roof rack to carry the band's instruments. That car suffered $1000 damage in early September when Scotty Moore had a head-on collision near Texarkana—an accident blackspot for Elvis' rides. This car also suffered regular damage from fans who etched their names into the paintwork (or, more considerately, daubed their phone numbers in lipstick).

With money now flowing in, Elvis picked up a yellow 1954 Cadillac Eldorado convertible a couple of days later. Sun Records principal Sam Phillips paid the insurance for the car. Elvis was so proud of his cars that he personally washed them between tour dates in late 1955, even though by this time he was earning upwards of $250 a night for performing.

By early 1956, Elvis was back in the pink and black Caddy and had also purchased a 1956 Plymouth station wagon for his parents. The Caddy's roof was painted white sometime earlier that year, before Elvis gave the car as a gift to his mother, though it was still occasionally pressed into service to ferry the band from show to show. Gladys didn't drive, but that wasn't the point: being able to buy his mother a Cadillac was two tons of proof that Elvis had made it. While hundreds of cars came and went, this car remained at Graceland, garaged, looked after and occasionally driven for the rest of Elvis' life. Along with a selection of Elvis' other vehicles, this car is on show at the automobile museum across Elvis Presley Boulevard from Graceland.

In 1956, as the national press scrabbled to find

out about this hot new singer, Elvis was regularly quizzed about his (extravagant) collection of four cars: three Cadillacs and a 1956 three-wheeler Messerschmitt mini-car which he used to scoot around Memphis. That year he seriously considered buying a Ford '32 Roadster, a hot rodders' favorite and a car he had always craved as a kid.

In June 1956, Elvis picked up a brand new convertible from Houston: an ivory-colored Cadillac Eldorado Biarritz. A year later he had the car customized with a new purple and white interior emblazoned with his initials, guitars on the floor mats, and body work modifications including rear fender skirts and a new purple paint job. This car is part of the collection at Graceland.

In mid-July Elvis exchanged his yellow 1954 Cadillac for a lavender 1956 Lincoln Premiere, which he kept for less than a month before upgrading to a 1956 Lincoln Continental Mark II, a $10,688 automobile. Daddy Vernon also got a pick-up truck for round-town errands, which Elvis also used to get around incognito.

The band took to riding between concerts in a 1957 black Cadillac limousine. This was probably the car that was vandalized by souvenir-hunting fans in Memphis in October 1956, when Elvis and girlfriend June Juanico dared to go to a local theater.

By late 1956, Elvis' fleet included two Harley-Davidson motorcycles, a 1956 Lincoln Continental, a 1956 Cadillac Eldorado, the 1950 1-ton Chevrolet Truck, and the bubble car. Driving the truck or a motorcycle with a girlfriend was one of the few opportunities Elvis had for privacy and some incognito time.

Before the year was out, Elvis had lavished $8,400 on a brand-new 1957 2-door hardtop Eldorado Seville. He also bought a tractor for work at Graceland, on which he posed for a photo before he moved in. By the summer of 1957, his fleet had grown to four Cadillacs including a limousine, a Lincoln Continental and a trio of sports cars.

In September 1957, Elvis made an appearance on local Memphis TV station WKNO to promote road safety and driver education—and kept pretty quiet about his burgeoning collection of speeding tickets.

Elvis leasing his 507 roadster.

Inside his 1969 Mercedes Limousine in 1971.

Elvis gave a 1956 Ford to girlfriend Anita Wood just before he left for his draft service in the Army in 1958.

On furlough from the army in 1958, Elvis bought a red Lincoln.

Out in Germany on Army service, Elvis had a black Mercedes sedan, a VW bug for his pals Red and Lamar to tootle around in, and a leased BMW 507 roadster (known locally as 'der Elviswagen')—a car so rare that only 252 were ever built. Elvis bought the car, shipped it back to the States, and later gave it to Ursula Andress. It was sold at auction in 1977 for $350,000. Elvis had previously bought a BMW Isetta bubble car, which he gave as a gift to Colonel Parker for Christmas 1957.

When Elvis was on base, he drove around in a jeep, which he maintained himself. Entourage members also recall a Mercedes 300 sedan.

Elvis tooled around Los Angeles in a maroon Cadillac convertible after he began working on films again in 1960. While working on *Flaming Star*, Elvis bought a black Rolls Royce Silver Cloud II.

Elvis' 1960 Lincoln Mark V limo went under the hammer at auction in early 2006 for over half a million dollars. The car had armor plating by specialist firm Hess and Eisenhardt, which made the limo John F. Kennedy was assassinated in. Elvis owned the car for 5 years.

Elvis bought a Cadillac Series 75 Fleetwood Limousine, which along with other vehicles from his fleet would be driven by entourage pals across the country to wherever Elvis might be working on his movies. This car was customized by George Barris in LA. Its gold respray was the least of the work; the car was tricked out with two phones, a bar, an entertainment unit and even an electric shoe buffer. In the Seventies, the car was donated to the Country Music Hall of Fame Museum.

Elvis' fleet going into 1962 consisted of a 1962 Mercury Comet station wagon, a 1962 Chrysler New Yorker station wagon, a 1960 Cadillac sedan, a 1960 Jeep, a 1960 Rolls Royce, a 1958 Harley-Davidson, his 1955 pink Cadillac 60, and that 1950 Chevy one-ton truck that he favored for getting round Memphis. He also picked up a Buick Riviera for the guys.

The Rolls lived in LA, along with a 1961 Cadillac limo. En route, Elvis sometimes picked up hitchhikers just to see the look on their face.

Elvis continued to update his fleet of Cadillacs every year during the Sixties and Seventies.

Billy Smith remembers Elvis buying a BMW in the early Sixties, which was one of the cars they drove back and forth between Memphis and L.A.

Elvis bought Priscilla a Corvair as a graduation present in 1963, after her family allowed her to move to Memphis and do her final year of High School there. Not long after, he gave Priscilla's car away to Alan Fortas.

For his film work, Elvis bought a Winnebago. Driving down from location work at Big Bear mountain near Los Angeles on *Kissin' Cousins*, the brakes gave out and Elvis had a tough time to scrub off speed using the gears and get back down the narrow, winding road.

Elvis owned a 1964 Rolls Royce Phantom V (of which only 793 were ever made). When The Beatles visited in 1965, Elvis and John Lennon compared notes on the car, which they both owned. He donated the car for a charity auction in 1968.

Elvis' 1965 car purchases included a 1966 Oldsmobile Tornado, and a go-kart that he loved to roar round the grounds of Graceland in. Before the year was out he had added a former Greyhound D'Elegance bus, which he sent off to be refurbished by George Barris before using it as his preferred mode of transport between Memphis and LA.

In 1966, he took delivery of a new Black Cadillac Eldorado convertible, and bought black and white Cadillac convertibles for Sonny West, Alan Fortas, Red West, Jerry Schilling, Larry Geller, Marty Lacker, Richard Davis and Joe Esposito (who got a maroon one). The next day, they all sat around Elvis' LA home and marveled that every last one of them had a Cadillac Eldorado convertible, the car they'd all dreamed of as kids.

Colonel Parker gave Elvis a 1967 black Lincoln Lehmann-Peterson limousine.

Elvis spent early 1967 buying more than three dozen pick-up trucks for himself, his relatives, his entourage and farm workers for use on the newly-acquired Circle G ranch. On one shopping spree Elvis spent $97,000 on pick-ups; not surprisingly, local truck dealers began to besiege the ranch. Elvis was so profligate that he bought extra vehicles just to be able to give them to workmen who were be fixing things up on the ranch. At the end of one such spree there was a pick-up truck too many; Elvis told Alan Fortas to give it away to one of the fans hanging around at the gates. When the guys got bored of racing their horses, they'd drag race their pick-up trucks, or attempt stunts on the tractor.

Elvis got into the habit of rewarding his pals and welcoming new guys who joined the team with a car. Sometimes he'd point out a car in a showroom and tell the lucky recipient that all they had to do was sort out the paperwork and it was theirs.

In April 1968, Vernon drove out Elvis' new black Lincoln Continental Mark II to LA, where he was working on *Live a Little, Love a Little*, a movie in which Elvis did most of the driving in the high-speed beach buggy opening scene.

Elvis bought a 1969 six-door Mercedes limousine in April 1970, which he wound up giving to Jimmy Velvet a few years later.

Elvis bought the first 1971 Stutz Blackhawk in LA in October 1970, reputedly paying $38,500 for the 490 h.p. vehicle. Competing stories circulate about its provenance: one is that the car Elvis bought had been pre-ordered for Frank Sinatra, but he persuaded Stutz company salesman Jules Meyers that it was better publicity for Elvis to have the car than Sinatra. An alternative story is that Elvis arranged for the dealer to drive the car out to his home so that he could test drive the one demonstrator—a prototype model—and then persuaded the reluctant dealer to sell him the car on the spot.

Entourage members told author Alanna Nash that the cars Elvis prized above all others were the ones that were his and his alone: in the Sixties, his Rolls Royce Phantom V; in the Seventies, his Stutz Blackhawk.

In December 1970, Elvis bought at least seven Mercedes Benzes: one for himself, one for Jerry Schilling, one for girlfriend Barbara Leigh, and one for Vernon who had been rebuking Elvis for his freewheeling spending. Just before Christmas he presented Mercedes Benz cars to Sonny West, Dr. Nick, and to former sheriff Bill Morris.

In late 1971 Elvis bought a second Stutz Blackhawk because the first was off the road following an accident—it took three years to repair the custom-made original. That year he also took possession of a white Stutz Bearcat, and bought a 1972 Cadillac station wagon for more sedate errands. One of Elvis' Stutzes played "Never On Sunday" when he hit the horn.

In the mid-Seventies, Elvis acquired a yellow De Tomaso Pantera Elvis. This car still has an unsightly collection of bullet holes fired by the King in ire and frustration.

Out in Palm Springs, Elvis bought a dune buggy from Liberace for scooting around in the desert. Of course, the guys needed their own dune buggies to keep him company.

In the summer of 1973, Marty Lacker remembers Elvis buying 29 cars and a motorcycle, all of which he gave away. Elvis' third Stutz Blackhawk was a 1973 model that he bought in the late summer of 1974. This is the car that is in the Graceland car museum. Soon afterwards, Elvis went on a spree, buying a Lincoln Continental Mark IV for Linda Thompson and for four entourage guys, and then went straight over the Cadillac dealership and bought five more cars to give away.

He received a white Rolls Royce from Priscilla as a gift in 1974, and in exchange gave her a Jaguar. That year he gave girlfriend Sheila Ryan a Corvette.

In 1975, Elvis spent $140,000 on fourteen Cadillacs to give to friends and a complete stranger who happened to be at the dealership while he was indulging his largesse. Dentist Lester Hofman also got a brand new Cadillac Seville that year.

By now, Elvis would give a car to new girl-friends after they'd been together a single day.

Elvis' next friends-and-family spree was in early 1976, when he spent $70,000 on Cadillacs and Lincolns for some of his friends on the Denver police force, a new car for Linda and one for Joe Esposito's girlfriend of the time, Shirley Dieu. He was unable to buy entourage pals Joe Esposito and Dave Hebler Maseratis, because there were none for sale in Memphis, so they had to make do with Cadillacs (though he had bought a quantity of Lincolns the day earlier, only to get his entourage pals to drive them all back when he found out that the showroom had-n't given him the bulk discount to which he was entitled). Elvis famously bought a car for a woman who just happened to be looking at a car at the Cadillac dealership. When the news made the rounds the next day, a radio announcer in Colorado said on air, "Elvis, if you're listening, I could use a car myself," and he too had his wish come true.

By this time, Elvis' fame for giving away Cadillacs was ripe for self-deprecating humor. At a show in Seattle in 1976, Elvis told the audience that if they all behaved, every one of them would get a Cadillac at the end of the show.

In 1976, Elvis bought himself a Ferrari to cheer himself up (also in the Graceland muse-um). It had the opposite effect; one day it conked out so he shot it. He had first tried out a Ferrari in 1960 but had not been sufficiently impressed to buy one.

He gave his last girlfriend Ginger Alden a Lincoln and a Triumph sports car, and even little Lisa Marie got in on the action, getting her own golf cart to tool around Graceland in. The last Cadillac Elvis owned was a 1977 Cadillac Seville.

Vernon requested all-white limousines for Elvis' funeral, which had to be driven in from many different states. Elvis' body was taken to Forest Hill Cemetery on August 18, 1977, in a 1977 Miller-Meteor Landau hearse.

The Elvis Presley Automobile Museum in Graceland Plaza was opened in 1989.

In 2005, the ESPN Hollywood show named Elvis as the #1 film driver of all time for his films *Speedway*, *Spinout* and *Viva Las Vegas* (the first of the movies in which he raised the profile of car racing).

See also GENEROSITY, GIFTS and entries for the dozens of people to whom Elvis gave cars. A number of web sites have impressively-docu-mented listings of Elvis' vehicles.

BILLY SMITH: "You didn't ever want Elvis to drive. He couldn't keep his mind on what he was doing. He'd leave the turn signal on half the time."

DVD:
   200 Cadillacs (2004)

CARSON, MARTHA
(B. IRENE AMBURGEY, 1921-2004)

Elvis played on a bill with the "Rockin' Queen of Happy Spirituals" Martha Carson at the Ellis Auditorium in Memphis on February 6, 1955. Carson's "Satisfied" had long been one of Elvis' favorites. He recorded the song at Sun but alas, the master went missing. Kentucky-born Carson was an early genre-bender, combining gospel, country and rockabilly during her Fifties career. She toured in the Forties with her husband James Carson, and then went solo. She signed with

RCA in the mid-Fifties and sang on the "Steve Allen Show."

CARTER, JIMMY
(B. 1924)

Elvis met the future president of the United States and his wife Rosalyn after he played Atlanta, Georgia in June 1973. Carter declared January 8, 1974 (Elvis' 39th birthday) "Elvis Presley Day" in Georgia, where he was governor at the time.

In his joke introduction to a 1976 show in Atlanta, Georgia, Elvis quipped that he was "Jimmy Carter's smarter brother"—Elvis indeed met the sometimes controversial Bill Carter in Memphis.

Soon after he was elected President in 1977, Carter sounded out Elvis about becoming an advisor on youth culture and music; Elvis had no chance to take up the position.

Elvis called President that year to put in a good word for his pal George Klein, who was going through legal troubles at the time. He made the call when he was in a less than incoher-ent moment; despite Carter calling back the fol-lowing day, the two did not speak again. Many years later, Carter pondered whether he might have been able to help save Elvis.

Genealogist John Anderson Brayton has claimed that Elvis and Carter were sixth cousins, once removed.

James Earl Carter Jr., born in Plains, Georgia on October, 1, 1924, was the 39th President of the United States from 1977-1981. Since his retirement from politics he has espoused many humanitarian causes and become a prolific author.

CARTER SISTERS

Elvis met June Carter (1929-2003) of the Carter Sisters on a Grand Ole Opry tour in 1955. June told Elvis to look her and husband Carl Smith up if he was ever in Nashville. When Elvis and Red West decided to take up her offer, they didn't let a little fact like nobody being home stop them. They broke in, fixed themselves some breakfast—in the process ruining some antique copper pans—and like the bears in Goldilocks, curled up asleep. Miraculously when Carl Smith walked in the following morning, he was happy to see them.

June Carter Cash wrote that the first she ever heard of Johnny Cash was when Elvis told her what a great singer he was and played her some records on a jukebox. June Carter married Johnny Cash, her third husband, in 1967.

Elvis and his band supported the Carter Sisters several times, until he worked his way up the bill and they supported him. Briefly they shared the same manager, Colonel Parker, before he became a one-client manager.

Elvis developed quite a crush on younger sister Anita (1933-1999). As a ruse to get close to her, at the end of a show Elvis feigned sickness and swooned into Anita's arms. The next time they played together, it was she who put on a fainting act. Red West says that despite having the hots for the other, they were too old-fashioned to do anything about it.

The Carter Sisters were the second generation of the singing Carter Family, from the late Twenties one of the first and most popular acts in pre-Second World War America. The original group of A. P. Carter and his wife Sara sang with cousin Maybelle (1909-1978). From the Fifties Maybelle toured with her daughters June and Anita as "Mother Maybelle and The Carter Sisters," and they were a regular act on the Grand Old Opry.

"CATCHIN' ON FAST"

Sixties beat for this Bill Giant / Bernie Baum / Florence Kaye *Kissin' Cousins* track that Elvis recorded without excessive conviction on September 30, 1963 at the RCA Nashville stu-dios. The *Double Features* issue brought it to pub-lic consideration again.

"CATTLE CALL, THE"

Elvis is said to have included this mid-Thirties Tex Owens number during his early shows in the mid-Fifties.

Rehearsal versions from the summer of 1970 and March 1972 have latterly appeared on offi-cial releases *Platinum, A Life In Music* and FTD release *One Night In Vegas* (in which Elvis attempts the yodel).

CASH, JOHNNY
(1932-2003)

"The Man in Black" was a musical innovator who did for country what Elvis did for rock 'n' roll, breaking it out to a much wider audience. Cash is one of just five performers to be inducted into both the Country and Rock and Roll Halls of Fame.

Cash knew all about Elvis early on; he was part of the crowd that heard the young singer at a pro-motional show for the Katz drugstore in Memphis in September 1954. Cash signed to Sun Records in 1955, originally as a rockabilly and rock 'n' roll artist.

For a few months in 1955, Johnny Cash and his band the Tennessee Two toured with Elvis through Texas, Mississippi and other points South. Cash later said: "I learned a lot about per-forming and projection from Elvis. I didn't have the charisma he had. I couldn't dance like he could. I wasn't as pretty as he was. But I learned a lot from him about stage presence and show business."

Cash told Tom Petty an anecdote about how Sam Phillips once loaded up Cash's car with Elvis records to take to Texas, where Cash was booked to tour, but instead Cash and his pals used the records for throwing practice off a cliff.

After Elvis left Sun for RCA at the end of 1955, Cash became Sun's top act. One of his early successes, "Get Rhythm," was a song he actually wrote for Elvis. Cash became the first Sun performer to bring out an LP in 1957 on the back of his country and crossover success "I Walk the Line."

Johnny Cash was born in Kingsland, Arkansas on February 26, 1932. After serving in the US Air Force (when he wrote "Folsom Prison Blues") he recorded for Sun records from 1955 to 1958, and then for Columbia. He occasionally dropped in and jammed with Elvis at Graceland, accord-ing to Elvis' pal Eddie Fadal.

In December 1956, Cash was at Sun Records when Elvis stopped by to jam with Carl Perkins and Jerry Lee Lewis, in what became known as the *Million Dollar Quartet* session. Some pundits believe that Cash did not stay much longer than the photo call before going off to do some Christmas shopping with his wife. Cash insists that he took part in the sing song. There are rumored to be a number of tracks on which Cash's voice is more prominent that have never been released; the doubts about his taking part may be explained by him singing in a much high-er register than usual.

In 1959, Cash did an impersonation of Elvis singing "Heartbreak Hotel" on TV show "Town Hall Party."

Cash performed for fifty years, wrote over a

thousand songs, sold over 50 million records, and was enormously influential on generations of musicians. He was awarded a National Medal of the Arts for artistic excellence in 2001.

In 2005 his life story was portrayed on the big screen in *Walk the Line*, starring Joaquin Phoenix.

Elvis was known to sing "I Walk The Line" and "Folsom Prison Blues" in concert to back up his comical claim to be Johnny Cash.

WILLIE NELSON: "Johnny Cash transcends all musical boundaries, and is one of the original outlaws."

JOHNNY CASH: "I loved that clean, simple combination of Scotty, Bill, and Elvis with his acoustic guitar."

JOHNNY CASH: "He was a kid when I worked with him. He was nineteen years old, and he loved cheeseburgers, girls, and his mother, not necessarily in that order (it was more like his mother, then girls, then cheeseburgers)."

Book:

Johnny Cash: The Autobiography, published by Harper, 1997.

DVD:

Elvis Presley and Johnny Cash Roadshow, 2006

The Million Dollar Quartet

In late 1956, Johnny Cash was at Sun Studio on the day that Elvis turned up to jam with Carl Perkins and Jerry Lewis, in a session that came to be known as the "Million-Dollar Quartet." Cash is the only one of the impromptu band members who is not on any of the material released 20 years and more after the event, though many people suspect that further tracks remain to be "rediscovered." Carl Perkins has said that Cash sang on several of the songs. Cash confirmed this: "I was farthest away from the mike and I was singing a lot higher than I usually did in order to stay in tune with Elvis, but I guarantee you I'm there." Different accounts, place Cash at the sessions from start to finish, only at the beginning, or only towards the end after Sam Phillips had alerted the press and wanted to add another of his talents to the mix. Cash is said at one stage to have used legal means to embargo release of the session.

CAUGHLEY, JAMES

Caughley became part of Elvis' gang in 1970, replacing Richard Davis as the guy in charge of Elvis' wardrobe. Caughley traveled with Elvis for a couple of years, including a November 1971 jaunt to Washington to visit girlfriend Joyce Bova. Caughley was known among Elvis' gang as "Hamburger James" because before he became a paid member of the group, he was allowed into Elvis' Memphis screenings on condition that he go out and get burgers when the cry went up, "Hamburger, James!" Entourage members later said that Caughley was drummed out of Elvis' employ after a beating for purloining some of Elvis' rings (and according to Marty Lacker, some of Elvis' "private" photos).

CBS

Before RCA bought out Elvis' recording contract from Sun in November 1955, Mitch Miller representing CBS inquired what it would cost to take things over from Sun. Elvis' then manager Bob

Everlasting Loyalty Card (1977).

Neal consulted with Sam Phillips at Sun, and came back with the figure of $18,000. Miller simply laughed the idea off.

Plans were announced in June 1977 for Elvis to do a one-hour TV special on CBS that fall, filmed as Elvis toured. The $750,000 fee was split 50/50 with the Colonel. Elvis became anxious about this deal as the shoot dates approached; he was past the point in his life where he was able to shift weight quickly for an upcoming challenge. CBS filmed Elvis in Omaha, Nebraska and Rapid City, South Dakota.

CBS aired *Elvis in Concert* in October 1977, two months after his death, documenting Elvis in his final ever tour.

"CHANGE OF HABIT"

Buddy Kaye and soundtrack king Ben Weisman wrote the title song for Elvis' last feature film. The band recorded the track at the Decca Universal Studios in Los Angeles on March 6, 1969; Elvis may have overdubbed his vocals later.

With no soundtrack album for Elvis' final movie, the song earned an initial release on *Let's Be Friends* in 1970, since when it has appeared on *Command Performances*, the *Double Features* issue for *Live a Little, Love a Little* et al, and *Elvis Movies*.

CHANGE OF HABIT

Elvis' final feature film was contracted as part of the deal with NBC for his 1968 TV special. Elvis started work on the movie in March 1969, weeks after rediscovering his mojo at American Studios in the session that spawned "In The Ghetto" and "Suspicious Minds."

The plot was a far cry from his travelogue 'n' bikini girl output: Elvis plays a socially-aware inner-city doctor called John Carpenter in a dramatized adaptation of Sister Mary Olivia Gibson's work with disabled children.

The movie was a Mary Tyler Moore vehicle before Elvis signed up.

Outside scenes were shot at the Mayfield Senior School in Pasadena, California.

Two songs didn't make it into the movie: "Let's Be Friends" and "Let's Forget About The Stars," though Elvis does perform a cameo of "Lawdy, Miss Clawdy" during the proceedings. "Rubberneckin'" was added to the movie for cross-promotional reasons.

On release in November 1969 the movie spent four weeks on the *Variety* Box Office Survey, rising as high as #17, significantly better than previous Elvis outings. It was not released in movie houses at all in the UK.

GEORGE KLEIN: "Elvis played a doctor and looked like a Greek god."

CREDITS:
Universal, Color.
Length: 93 minutes
Release date: November 10, 1969

Directed by: William A. Graham
Produced by: Joe Connelly (producer), Irving Paley (associate producer)
Written by: Eric Bercovici, John Joseph, James Lee, Richard Morris, S.S. Schweitzer
Music by: Billy Goldenberg
Cinematography by: Russell Metty
Film Editing by: Douglas Stewart
Art Direction by: Joe Alves
Set Decoration by: Ruby R. Levitt, John McCarthy Jr.
Costume Design by: Helen Colvig

CAST:
Elvis Presley	Dr. John Carpenter
Mary Tyler Moore	Sister Michelle Gallagher
Barbara McNair	Sister Irene Hawkins
Jane Elliot	Sister Barbara Bennett
Leora Dana	Mother Joseph

Edward Asner	Lt. Moretti
Robert Emhardt	The Banker
Regis Toomey	Father Gibbons
Doro Merande	Rose
Ruth McDevitt	Lily
Richard Carlson	Bishop Finley
Nefti Millet	Julio Hernandez
Laura Figueroa	Desiree
Lorena Kirk	Amanda
Virginia Vincent	Miss Parker
David Renard	Colom
Ji-Tu Cumbuka	Hawk
William Elliott	Robbie (as Bill Elliott)
Rodolfo Hoyos Jr.	Mr. Hernandez
Mario Aniov	1st Young Man
Ray Ballard	Ice Cream Clerk
Jim Beach	Father Witkowski
Timothy Carey	Ajax Market Manager
Rita Conde	Woman in Market
Steve Conte	Extra
Frank Corsentino	2nd Man
John Daheim	1st Underling
Robert De Anda	Teammate
Tony De Costa	Chino
Paul Factor	3rd Man
Linda Garay	Expectant Mother
Stella Garcia	Maria
Pepe Hern	Extra
Darlene Love	Backup singer
A Martinez	2nd Young Man
Troy Melton	2nd Underling
Lilith Miles	1st Stiletto Deb
Araceli Rey	Senora Gavilan
Ruben Rodriguez	Church Drummer
Stanley Schneider	Traffic Cop
Harry Swoger	Fat Man
Alex Tinne	Tony
Alex Val	Tomas
Roberto Vargas	Cuban Mainliner
Len Wayland	Police Sergeant
Caitlin Wyles	2nd Stiletto Deb

ADDITIONAL CREW:

Larry Germain	hair stylist
Bud Westmore	makeup artist
Phil Bowles	assistant director

Plot:

Elvis plays Dr. John Carpenter, an inner-city doctor working in a New York ghetto. Into his life come three future nuns from the Order of Little Sisters of Mary, who volunteer to help out at his clinic for two months before taking their vows.

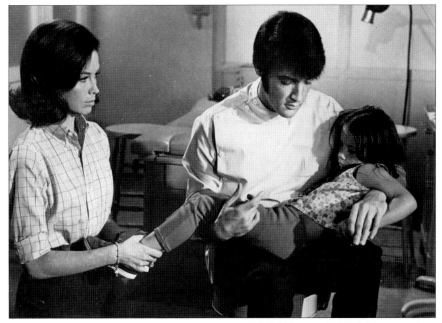

Elvis and Mary Tyler Moore in *Change of Habit*, 1969.

The conceit is that Dr. Carpenter has no idea that Michelle Gallagher (played by Mary Tyler Moore), Irene Hawkins (played by Barbara McNair) and Barbara Bennett (played by Jane Elliott) are novitiate nuns. If he knew, he wouldn't be so surprised that Sister Michelle studiously avoids his evident interest and charms.

The incognito nuns dress down in Sixties fashions and do everything they can to fit in; so much so that the local busybodies spread the word that they are prostitutes. The nuns help an autistic girl Amanda (played by Lorena Kirk) using therapy that might upset some today. Despite protests by local Catholics, the learner nuns stay on to organize a Saint's day carnival. At the carnival Sister Barbara challenges the local loan shark. When he physically attacks her, Dr. John steps in to save the day.

Mother Superior Joseph (played by Leora Dana) calls time on the novitiates. Before they return to the convent, Julio Hernandez (played by Nefti Millet), one of the tearaways that Michelle has been reaching out to, suffers a psychotic episode and attempts to rape her. Dr. John steps in to save the day.

Sister Barbara decides not to go into the convent because she feels that she can do more good on the outside. Sister Michelle is torn between serving her Lord and following her heart. She (and the audience) remain in doubt even in the finale, where Dr. John is singing at a folk mass. Her stark choice is expressed visually through juxtaposed images of Elvis and Jesus Christ.

In Elvis' last movie, no happy ending.

Songs: "Change Of Habit," "Rubberneckin'," "Have A Happy," "Let Us Pray"

CHARACTER TRAITS

At the risk of wasting words on the glaringly obvious, underneath all the trappings of fame, success, talent and charisma, Elvis was just a person. Like every human being he had his good points and his less good points. There is no single abiding truth about Elvis' character any more than there is about any one of us. We all change in our lives. The difference is that very few people live a life as full and as public as Elvis'.

This lengthy entry is an attempt to collate biographers' observations and the Elvis revealed in kaleidoscopic fashion in the many memoirs published about him, in order to illustrate the dif-

ferent aspects of his personality at various stages of his life.

One reason for Elvis' enduring appeal across countries, age groups and generations is undoubtedly that he appears as a conflicted mass of virtues, vices, loves and hates. Debilitatingly shy as an adolescent, Elvis became the world's best-known entertainer. A prankster supreme, he spent much of his adult life on an intense spiritual quest. Brought up in the Pentecostal church, Elvis was accused of doing the work of the devil. Famous for loving and leaving his women, he was unswervingly loyal to his mother. Imperious and commanding to those around him, Elvis had an overweening instinct to protect the people he loved. He was as sensitive to others as he could be egocentric. Publicly against the dangers of drugs, Elvis had a faith and a dependency on prescription medicines that ultimately cost him his life. Generous beyond compare, Elvis lived a life of wanton material consumption and luxury. A lightning rod for sexual desire, apart from circumscribed periods most notably at the start of his career and immediately after he was drafted into the Army, Elvis seemed to prefer companionship and longer-term relationships over serial promiscuity.

Every biographer concurs that the single greatest influence on Elvis' character was his mother Gladys. Their relationship was much closer than most mother/son bonds, and through his life Elvis adhered to many of her predilections and nostrums, though this diminished as the years went by. Devastating as her death was to him, it was not the first life-altering loss he suffered. Author Elaine Dundy speculates that as a surviving twin Elvis felt loss, guilt, and a sense of triumph as the survivor, and spent the rest of his life living this out: "Elvis might relate to friends and lovers with the intimate dependency of a twin looking for his other half, but he would always be the dominant one."

The biggest name in the performing arts was a model of humility. He knew that his star could wane just as quickly as it had waxed, that he could be "put out" like a light bulb. In an early interview he said how important it was to him that the "folks back home . . . think right of me. Just because I managed to do a little something, I don't want anyone back home to think I got the big head." His humility extended from word to deed. Already a national star, one day Elvis drove past an old man near Graceland who was in evident difficulty changing a tire; he circled round the block and changed it for him. For the first decade of his career, Elvis never stopped telling journalists how lucky he was. As he saw it, his side of the bargain with his fans was to strive to improve at what he did, as a singer and as an actor. Another aspect of this side of Elvis' character was a lifelong dedication to giving money to charitable causes and gifts to friends. Giving gifts was also a way that Elvis might say sorry to somebody; friends report he had an almost pathological inability to make a verbal apology.

A friend who knew him at school says that even as a kid, Elvis had a smile that said "I know something you don't." His first childhood sweetheart Eloise Bedford described young Elvis as "a loner." It wasn't until his mid-teens that his desire to make it as a singer was strong enough to overcome his innate shyness. One day Elvis took his guitar along to his cousin Bobbie's birthday party but only agreed to play if they turned the lights out. When relatives came round and Mamma Gladys asked him to get his guitar and play, he needed asking a number of times. Growing up, a battle played out in Elvis between the "morbidly shy" boy he was in the words of a school pal, and the young man who set out to shock by wearing the gaudiest, most flamboyant clothes and outfits he could afford.

The general consensus is that all his life, Elvis wanted to be noticed. Elaine Dundy writes, ." . . being unnoticed meant being powerless—a condition Elvis was unable to tolerate for any length of time."

Gladys brought up her only child to be scrupulously polite—good manners were a badge of pride and decency, especially among the poor. Grown-up and famous, Elvis' Southern Gentlemanly manners remained one of his hallmarks. Elvis would answer questions with a "Yes, ma'am" or "No, ma'am." His mother instilled into him the custom that it was impudent to call a stranger or somebody in a position of power or deserving of respect by their first name.

Elvis was brought up to respect authority. He expected his authority to be respected by his extended family and entourage. This is likely the reason why Elvis never seriously challenged the authority claimed and wielded by Colonel Parker. As immensely famous and powerful as he was in his private life, Elvis seemed to need a figure of authority in his life to whom he could defer and whose guidance he followed without question.

Elvis had the kind of charisma (the word derives from the Greek for "gift" or "divine favor") that would likely have taken him to the top of any life pursuit he attempted, though if he had remained a truck driver he might not have tapped into it quite so successfully. Millions of people were attracted to his public persona; in private, when he locked gaze with somebody, that person felt like they were the only person in the world. Jordanaire singer Neal Matthews sums up it: "When Elvis walked into a room, everybody there just knew his presence. He just had it." Bobby Wood, a top musician when he met Elvis at American Studio in 1969, recalls, "I knew when he was in the back parking lot. It was like that much charisma." Dave Hebler concurs: "He can walk into a room without saying a word and fill it with sunshine." The effect on the opposite sex was instant and devastating.

If charisma is anything, it's vital energy. Even as a kid, Elvis had so much energy that at times he bordered on the hyperactive. One of the things that appealed to the people in Elvis' orbit for most of his adult life was his happy-go-lucky nature, his declared desire to live life to the full, the way he took one day at a time and had what fun there was to be had. However, in at least one interview, he revealed a darker side of his nature and described moods where everything looked "dark and gloomy."

Elvis' anger was legendary; as his moods became increasingly dominated by the pharmaceutical drugs he took, it was often on a hair trigger. Elvis had an elephant's memory for slights, criticisms and rebukes. For example, in 1972 he strongly suspected that agreeing to do his first live show in New York City was a mistake because back in the Fifties the New York press had been so scathing about his TV and film debuts.

Elvis suffered from terrible backstage nerves backstage at the start of his career, and when he returned to live performing in the late Sixties. Afterwards he was so energized it took him a long time to come down.

Elvis was a perfectionist about his music until he ceased to have access to sufficiently good material. He cared passionately about becoming a respected actor until it became apparent that he simply was not going to get the roles. His long-term dedication to karate and other sports showed how much he cared about doing what he did well.

In mid-1957, a national sensation loved by teens and vilified by many parents, Elvis told *New York Herald-Tribune* columnist Joe Hyams, "I can't get it into my head that I'm property. People tell me you can't do this or that, but I don't listen to them. I do what I want. I can't change, and I won't change."

Elvis was very smart and had an inquiring mind, though until he went on his mid-Sixties reading binge he was embarrassed by his lack of formal education.

Elvis' attitude to women was full of paradox. Many childhood friends and family members have said that growing up Elvis preferred the company of women. As an adult, Elvis achieved emotional intimacy with and revealed his vulnerability and neediness to women, yet he expected his girlfriends to have no life outside his demands. Elvis wanted the women that stayed around in his life to be true to him. If one of his pals was getting too friendly with one of "Elvis' girls," he would make a semi-joking semi-serious remark that let everyone know exactly what the score was. Elvis' anachronistic attitudes to women—that they should stay in the home and bring up kids rather than have a career, and that women who had had children were a sexual turn-off—sooner or later became a contributing factor to the failure of his major relationships. Elvis preferred not to worry about upcoming problems but instead focus on the good things—either a Zen attitude or a very successful way of heading off other people's agendas or the complaints of women in his life. If Elvis had a favorite "type" of woman, it was beautiful and preferably malleable.

Elvis tended to act on instinct rather than reflection: his aptitude for making music, picking hits and choosing clothes proved that his instinct was a powerful weapon. His innate fashion sense served him well throughout his performing years, and became part of the ritual at Graceland in the Sixties, when he would make a dramatic, well-dressed entrance as he came down the stairs for dinner.

When Elvis was shipped off to the Army in 1958, for a while he slipped out of his very public persona and was much more himself. Girlfriend of the time Anita Wood rued the fact that he couldn't stay that way always; that was the way she liked him best.

In the immediate aftermath of Gladys's death, Elvis was so delirious with grief that he had to be prescribed tranquilizers and sleeping pills—a tan-

Candid photograph taken on the Graceland grounds in the 1960s.

gible occasion when prescription medicine made a positive difference in his life.

Despite his world-girdling fame, Elvis was not comfortable around outsiders, and would often belie this remnant of his youthful shyness by fidgeting, tapping his fingers or jiggling his leg.

Elvis had a tendency to dodge problems that were presented to him by people in life, complaining that he already had plenty on his plate or this was not a good time to deal with it.

Elvis had a deep spiritual yearning spawned by the perfectly valid question, "Why me?" After he met Larry Geller in 1964, for several years the overwhelming interest in his life was seeking some kind of meaning. During this time he delved into yoga, parapsychology, mysticism, numerology, spiritualism and metaphysics. The important people in Elvis' life—the Colonel, Vernon, Priscilla, the guys—thought that Elvis became "passive" rather than enlightened.

Elvis had a great memory—a true photographic memory according to some, capable of reciting an entire page of text after reading it once—at least until his consumption of prescription drugs started to unravel him in the Seventies. Elvis was a walking encyclopedia of songs; he would sometimes challenge people to try to name a song he couldn't sing; rarely if ever was he stumped. When Freddy Bienstock played him a song he had rejected nine months earlier after only eight bars, Elvis told him he didn't like it any more this second time round. Learning scripts was a cinch for him, and he would rarely need to gen up on set.

Elvis was well-known for quickly becoming bored in his professional and private life. He would become totally engrossed with a hobby for a short period, spending vast amounts of time and money, only to move on to some other consuming passion six months later. It happened in his music too: even when he was rescued from all those cookie-cutter movies by his renaissance in the 1968 NBC TV Special, and the touring he returned to in 1969, by 1973 his enthusiasm was palpably on the wane. According to drummer Ronnie Tutt, "I think the one thing if you knew anything about Elvis at all, I think a very insightful person, whether it be management or whoever, would have realized that Elvis does get bored easily. This was one reason why in his later career, he tended to tear through his old big hits—fans would feel shortchanged if they didn't hear them, but Elvis had run out of passion for them." For George Klein, the biggest lie about Elvis is that in his later years he suffered from loneliness and depres-

Signing autographs for admiring fans.

sion: "He was just bored . . . When he wasn't really active, he became bored." The way Steve Dunleavy puts it, "Cars, mansions, women, gadgets, friends—they were all toys to break up the monotony." In 1976, Elvis told several people close to him that not only was he bored, he was tired of being Elvis Presley. The converse of Elvis' abhorrence of boredom was that he would try extra hard when new people were around—new musicians, new friends.

Often overlooked by biographers, Elvis had a strong self-deprecating streak. At his first Las Vegas appearance in 1969, after so long off the stage, his introductory banter included references to himself as a "stone cold natural freak," and poked fun at his own abilities by declaring that he "was never a singer." Modesty and his ability to poke fun at himself on stage are enormously endearing traits in such a superstar.

Decades after he had become one of the most recognizable faces on the planet, when meeting a musician or songwriter for the first time Elvis would say "Hi, I'm Elvis Presley" and then fill in the other person on his past, as if everything he had done for years hadn't been front page news.

Even before he slid into the dependency on prescription drugs that hastened his demise, Elvis had an addictive personality. Elvis always wanted more of what he liked (or thought he liked).

From when he first started touring, Elvis got used to living life on the move. By the end of the Sixties he had homes in Memphis, LA and Palm Springs. Even if he had no work commitments, he would shuttle between these homes on a frequent but unpredictable basis, uprooting much of his entourage on a whim to keep him company.

Being the focal point of the entourage brought problems as well as advantages. Elvis wanted each individual in the group to focus on him, rather than on other members of the entourage, and he loathed it when intrigue and disharmony broke out within the group. Elvis was acutely aware of doing what he needed to do to bring people back into line and make sure that everyone knew who was boss, even if it took an angry outburst. To some in the entourage, Elvis was known as "Old Super Ears," less for his perfect pitch than for his uncanny ability to hear what other people were saying about him across a crowded room. Elvis held meetings with members of his entourage to discuss in fine detail plans for doing things outside the walls of Graceland, during which they would meticulously debate any changes to these plans.

According to girlfriend Barbara Leigh, Elvis was useless at keeping a secret. Cousin Billy Smith tells of how upset he was when he walked in on Elvis recounting a childhood secret of his to Priscilla, but then how Elvis made it up by entering into a pact that they would never reveal things about one another.

Elvis' nocturnal existence was partly the result of insomnia (and the medication he took for the condition), and partly a side-effect of his enormous fame, which meant that the normal, waking world was not a place he could venture out into. Girlfriend Linda Thompson says, "It was Elvis' world and we lived this kind of reversed life where we were awake all night and asleep all day." Elvis had his bedrooms blacked out against the light with heavy felt and aluminum foil. He also liked to keep his bedrooms cool: he kept the air conditioning on the whole time in his bedroom at Graceland to maintain a cool 60 degrees, and liked the lighting to be soft.

Many Elvis memoirs pinpoint 1968 and 1969 as his happiest time. He was newly married, he was the proud father of a new baby, the end of his crushing film commitments was in sight, his 1968 NBC TV Comeback special had been a triumph, he returned to making great, ground-breaking music at American Studios in Memphis, and he embarked on a wildly-successful return to live performing in Las Vegas.

According to Steve Binder, who worked with Elvis on the NBC TV Special, Elvis was well-read

Elvis, Priscilla and Lisa Marie.

and well-versed in the conspiracy theories surrounding the 1968 assassinations of Martin Luther King Jr. and Robert Kennedy.

Not surprisingly, a man who many women considered to be the most beautiful male in the world suffered from vanity. He retained this vanity until the end. In 1976, Sonny West said, "He believes that he has a face like King David."

Surrounded by paid courtiers and with fawning women hanging on his every word, Elvis was quite the raconteur. He told stories of his many adventures, embellishing the tales as he saw fit; he regaled private audiences with his philosophical and religious learnings and bible readings; and he told jokes or played pranks that would bring guaranteed hails of laughter from his personal gallery.

In 1972, Elvis jotted down the following phrases, under the title "Philosophy for a happy life": Someone to love. Something to look forward to. And something to do."

That year he had to get over the shock of his wife leaving him, and the humiliation that she had left him for another man, which he took as a major slight on his pride.

Elvis' behavior became increasingly erratic in the mid-Seventies, as he suffered problems related to drug abuse and physical ill-health. He would often fly into a temper and take out his aggression on inanimate objects: countless TV sets perished in a hail of bullets. His temper, according to Lamar Fike, was something he inherited from his mother: "Elvis' temper was her temper. Elvis would get mad and go bananas. His mother was the same way."

Elvis was aware that his personality and behavior were changing. Publicly on stage, and with friends in private, he mused aloud that he might be crazy. Jackie Kahane recalls him admitting that if he hadn't been famous, he would long since have been put away.

As the Seventies rolled on, Elvis was more and more self-destructive, and more and more insistent on trying out dubious "miracle" cures that only succeeded in heightening his still unacknowledged physical addiction to various different drugs. Paradoxically, his copious knowledge about all things medical made it easy for him to circumvent attempts by his regular medical practitioner Dr. Nichopoulos to curtail his reliance on prescription drugs. Dr. Nichopoulos has said that Elvis started "losing control" in late 1974 and early 1975.

On one tour in the summer of 1975, Elvis managed to harangue his audience, offend his female back-up singers so badly that they walked off stage, shoot up a TV set, hit his doctor with a ricocheting bullet, and throw two guitars and tens of thousands of dollars' worth of jewelry into the audience.

If Elvis trusted a person, that trust was total. Longtime entourage member Marty Lacker never saw Elvis read a contract, or even his own will.

In his final years, Elvis' mood swings alienated a number of his closest, long-term friends. Red West told writer Steve Dunleavy that he confronted Elvis about how his reliance on drugs was altering his character. Elvis' reaction was invariably anger, with accusations of disloyalty and a lack of respect for his ability to run his own life—the typical reaction of an addict. Many of the men closest to Elvis in his final years have spoken of how he seemed like a different person.

At this time, Elvis experienced delusional moments: reputedly at one stage in early 1976, he made plans with Red and Sonny West to take out all of Memphis's drug dealers. He reacted angrily to criticism, preferring to walk away than face friendly concern about his impulsive behavior.

Under the influence, Elvis seemed to lose interest in anything except for his possessions, regularly snubbing fellow-musicians who came to see him after shows. Sonny West said, "His ego is just out of control." In his last year, for the first time in his life Elvis was violent to a member of his entourage.

How far Elvis' mood could swing was summed up during two days of recording at Graceland in October 1976. On one night he was giving away clothes to some of the musicians who had come for the session, on the next night he burst into the recording studio with a submachine gun in hand as a prank—and then made his fleet of planes available to ferry the musicians home.

ELVIS SAID IN 1956: "I've been kind of nervous all my life. And now, going out on personal appearances all the time, I get so keyed up that I just can't relax."

ELVIS SAID IN 1962: "I'm proud of the way I was brought up to believe and to treat people, and to have respect for people."

ELVIS SAID IN 1965: "After all, I am one of the night people. The sun's down and the moon's pretty. It's time to ramble."

ELVIS SAID IN 1971: "When I do something there is no middle-of-the-road, it's all the way."

ELVIS SAID TO LARRY GELLER: "The world knows Elvis. They don't know me."

ELVIS SAID TO FELTON JARVIS IN 1976: "I'm just so tired of playing Elvis Presley."

D.J. FONTANA: "Elvis had this charisma about him. I don't think anybody could ever put their finger on what he did or how he did it. You could just sit and talk to him for a few minutes and he would mesmerize you. This is the way Elvis related to people."

MARTY LACKER: "The difference in Elvis and the image of Elvis was never greater than in the TV movies they've made about him. Nothing has been done that even comes close to capturing his personal power or the strength of his personality. He had a great deal of intensity, magnetism. That's the reason most of us stayed with him for so long."

JOE ESPOSITO: "Elvis was always in control, whatever he did."

LAMAR FIKE: "Elvis had a lot of personalities. Around us, he was a dominant badass. Around the public, he was 'Captain America, apple pie, and Mama.'"

RONNIE TUTT: "He's was one very impulsive type individual, and just the fact that anytime he would do something he would go all out. With him it's all out or nothing."

MACK GURLEY: "Elvis' love for people was his greatest quality. He tried to help everyone. He had to be way above the average person. He could have anything, and he shared it beautifully."

JACK CLEMENT: "Elvis was a very fun guy to be around. Everything with him was just kind of a party, more or less."

JOE GUERCIO: "He was real. There was nothing false about the man. He was just real."

BARBARA LEIGH: "I think that Elvis was really a very simple man by nature, but complex through his megastardom and fame. He was what he appeared to be—honest, kind, generous, loving, and forever the entertainer."

PRISCILLA: "During the lulls he wouldn't know what to do with himself. He was like a child. He would take pills or read or just eat—because he was bored."

LINDA THOMPSON: "Elvis was just unique, incredibly sensual and tender. He was funny and he was good. He was extreme in every aspect of his life."

LAMAR FIKE: "He couldn't keep a secret."

SHEILA RYAN: "The qualities that he had were almost not of this world, you know. They were, a lot of times, angelic . . . He was very much a little boy, had that little boy quality and I've often said, you know, before I met him, he had that smile and everyone interpreted that smile to be his sexy look. And it wasn't that at all. It wasn't a sexy look. It was his innocence, his vulnerability."

ELAINE DUNDY: "It was at the heart of his tragedy, his fatal flaw, that he was virtually . . . incapable of confronting his real enemies head on."

PRISCILLA: "Everyone . . . was aware of a change in his personality over the years he studied with Larry Geller. Elvis' vibrant personality was . . . passive and he was becoming more introverted."

MARION KEISKER: "Elvis was so innately ingenuous . . . I don't think he ever said a wrong thing into a microphone or camera his whole life."

LAMAR FIKE: "He was a person who got intimidated very easily by somebody with more intelligence or ability. As a result, a situation developed where he had to have people around him all the time. That's why he later assembled the entourage, the Memphis Mafia."

LINDA THOMPSON: "He was the most generous of men. He was the kindest, most sensitive, the funniest, most talented, most gorgeous and sexiest. He

Elvis speaking at Memphis charity event, 1961.

was all the wonderful things that only Elvis could be, and yet there were times when he was very, very difficult. His life was very difficult."

STEVE DUNLEAVY: "Presley is a man of immense sensitivity and intelligence. . . . Aware that people expect an entertainer of his stature to be something phenomenally different, he comes on with as much humility as time and circumstances allow. It is disarming."

DAVE HEBLER: "Everything Elvis does, everything that interests him, everything that he takes up, he grabs, strangles and beats it to death."

STEVE BINDER: "Elvis was scared to death of the Colonel's power. He felt ashamed. He was very, very submissive."

BILLY SMITH: "I think to some extent Elvis lost touch with the feelings of other people. He changed from humble to hard. Deep down, Elvis was a good person."

DAVE HEBLER: "He is like a ping-pong ball going down the hallway. You never know from one minute to the next whether he is going to point a gun at somebody, or he is going to kiss them, or what."

LARRY GELLER: "He had an innate energy that made him appear to be glowing from the inside."

LAMAR FIKE: "Elvis always kept his own world with him; he kept his own bubble."

ELISABETH STEFANIAK: "He had a way of making anyone feel they were the most important person in the world to him."

LARRY GELLER: "While he could mask his deepest private thoughts and bury the most painful memories, his emotions ran close to the surface."

PRISCILLA: "In the absence of any significant professional challenge, Elvis created his own real-life dramas."

MARION KEISKER: "My total image of Elvis was as a child . . . he was like a mirror in a way, whatever you're looking for, you are going to find in him."

LARRY GELLER: "Elvis was susceptible to certain pressures, largely because he tried desperately to please almost everyone."

JERRY SCHILLING: "Elvis was the most eclectic human being I've ever seen."

LARRY GELLER: "Any time Elvis made a gesture toward change, whether small or large and regardless of what it concerned, something inside him instinctively resisted."

PRISCILLA: "There was a big difference between the daytime Elvis and the nocturnal Elvis. When the sun went down another personality took over..."

JOE ESPOSITO: "Elvis was very insecure. He knew nothing about the Street. All he knew about was what he read in books."

LAMAR FIKE: "Elvis was the most insecure human being I've ever been around in my life... He was destiny's child, but he was never prepared to be what he was."

JIMMY VELVET: "Elvis was like a spoiled kid and he never really grew up."

SONNY WEST: "I really believe the only problem Elvis had was an addictive nature. You could see that sometimes in other parts of his life. If he had not had that addiction he would have been just fine."

LARRY GELLER: "He was a master at diverting attention from things he didn't want to deal with and creating whatever impression he desired."

Books:
    Any of the better Elvis biographies and memoirs, personal intuition and

Elvis: Images and Fancies, ed. Jac L. Tharpe, University Press of Mississippi, 1979.
The Inner Elvis: A Psychological Biography of Elvis Aaron Presley by Peter Whitmer, Hyperion Press, 1996.
Understanding Elvis: Southern Roots vs. Star Image, by Susan M. Doll, Routledge, 1998.

CHARITABLE WORKS

Growing up, Elvis had first hand experience of what it's like not to have enough money to make ends meet. Even before he was in a position to give money, according to childhood friend Buzzy Forbes Elvis played to the denizens of the Kennedy Veterans Hospital and the Glenview Home for Incurables, a year before he walked in to Sun.

As soon as did have money, he put his hand in his pocket and carried on doing so for the rest of his life. He gave time as well as money. Elvis visited sick children and corresponded with disabled fans who couldn't make it to his concerts; as a kid, he used to go with Gladys to the Poplar Street Mission to help the homeless.

Every Christmas Elvis made donations of $50,000 to $100,000 to 50 Memphis charities (*see* Sidebar). The vast majority of the donations he made were strictly on the condition of no publicity.

Once he was sufficiently well-known to be a big draw, Elvis played a number of charity concerts.

He played a set at a July 4, 1956 charity show in his hometown, at Russwood Park, for the Cynthia Milk Fund, at which he put up his diamond signature ring as a raffle prize.

Long after he became a national star, Elvis was happy to return to the Memphis events and venues where he first made his name. And if it was an

Elvis hands a check to Governor Bill Waller of Mississippi prior to his benefit performance at the Mississippi Coliseum to aid victims of tornadoes in the McComb area of South Mississippi, May 1975.

event for a good cause, so much the better. One of many such events was the E. H. Crump Memorial Football Game for which the proceeds went to the blind (the E.H. Crump company insured Elvis' automobiles). During his career, Elvis also sponsored many sports teams.

In the run-up to Christmas 1956, Elvis made a donation of toys to underprivileged children organized by the Marines. His goodbye show for the Louisiana Hayride that month raised money for the YMCA to build a swimming pool.

Elvis provided the initial funding for a youth center in his hometown of Tupelo by performing free at the Fairgrounds in September 1957 to an audience of 12,000. According to newspaper reports, Elvis turned down an offer of $10,000 to appear.

In April 1957, Elvis was at the first Coffee Day For Crippled Children fundraiser in Memphis. Two months later he was one of the main draws at Danny Thomas's Shower of Stars benefit at Russwood Park in Memphis.

In December 1957, Elvis showed up at a charity event held on the other side of the color bar when he went with George Klein to the charity Goodwill Revue at all-black radio station WDIA (known as "the Mother Station of the Negroes").

Elvis gave blood during his stint in Germany for the German Red Cross. His second Salk polio inoculation in 1959 was photographed for a March of Dimes publicity drive to combat infantile paralysis, as polio was originally known. He was also vaccinated in 1968 for a later publicity campaign.

During his Army days, Elvis perpetrated multiple acts of kindness, such as giving $2,500 to a fellow soldier whose parents had recently died in an accident so that he could afford to go home.

G. I. Blues previewed in a special screening to benefit the Hemophilia Foundation in late 1960, attended by Juliet Prowse, Ronald Reagan and Cesar Romero.

Elvis signed up to perform at the Memphis Charity Show on February 25, 1961, at the Ellis Auditorium, around the time that the Colonel was organizing Elvis' benefit concert on Hawaii for the USS Arizona. When he did these benefits, Elvis paid all of his own expenses. The $51,612 proceeds from the Memphis event was shared between thirty-eight local charities; $3,789 went to build the "Elvis Presley Youth Center" in Tupelo. A local paper proudly proclaimed: "Elvis Presley probably raised more money for charity in a day's work Saturday than any other entertainer in the history of showbiz."

Elvis' 1961 concert at Bloch Arena (Hawaii) raised $62,000 for the USS Arizona Memorial at Pearl Harbor.

In 1962, Memphis Mayor Loeb personally accepted a $50,000 donation to Memphis-based charities from Elvis on the set of It Happened at the World's Fair. The following year he donated $55,000 to local charities.

In early 1964, Elvis donated a yacht worth $55,000, the Potomac, which had formerly belonged to Franklin Delano Roosevelt, to St. Jude's Hospital, a children's' research clinic in Memphis after the initial intended recipient, the March of Dimes, turned down the gift.

Elvis received peer recognition from Bud Abbott, Barbara Stanwyck, Frank Sinatra and others on the set of Frankie and Johnny in 1965, in recognition of his $50,000 contribution (sometimes stated as $125,000) to the Motion Picture Relief Fund—the largest single donation ever made.

In 1966 Elvis donated his Dodge motor home to TEACH, a children's charity, after he had replaced it with a refurbished Greyhound bus. That Christmas he wrote checks for over $100,000 to local Memphis charities.

Memphis Mayor William Ingram and Tennessee Governor Buford Ellington declared September 29, 1967 "Elvis Presley Day" in honor of his ongoing charitable largesse.

Christmas came early for the Memphis Jewish Community Center Building Fund in early December 1967 when Elvis pledged a total of $10,500.

Elvis' 1964 Rolls Royce was auctioned off in July 1968 to raise $35,000 in funds for children's charity SHARE.

Elvis made a donation to the NAACP after recording "In The Ghetto" in 1969.

In 1970 Elvis made a donation of $7000 to the Los Angeles Police community relations program, the largest it had ever received.

Elvis made a $2000 donation to the Self-Realization Fellowship in 1971.

In the early Seventies, Elvis sent crime-fighting cop Buford Pusser a large anonymous donation after his home burned down in mysterious circumstances. Elvis attended his funeral after he died in shady circumstances in 1974.

In 1972 Elvis helped producer Felton Jarvis get and pay for a kidney transplant; this was just one of the many times that Elvis assisted friends in medical need.

In 1973 the audience at Elvis' Aloha from Hawaii TV special paid whatever they felt they could contribute to the local Kui Lee Cancer Fund, and in the end raised a total of $75,000, three times the initial estimate. Elvis started the

ball rolling with a $1,000 check, matched by RCA boss Rocco Laginestra.

Elvis donated the proceeds of a special show on Mother's Day at the Sahara Tahoe (Stateline) in May 1973 to the nearby Barton Memorial Hospital.

In early 1975, Elvis jumped at the Colonel's suggestion to organize a benefit show to raise money for victims of a tornado that ripped through McComb, Mississippi, which became the centerpiece of a tour through the South. Elvis personally handed over a check exceeding $100,000 to Mississippi Governor Bill Waller. That year, from his hospital bed Elvis donated $5,000 to the Jerry Lewis Telethon for the Muscular Dystrophy Association.

In December 1976, Elvis was made a member of the American Heart Association after setting up a collections booth at the Las Vegas Hilton during his shows.

Before his death, Elvis was keen to set up a charitable foundation that would fund a range of causes important to him.

Elvis' legacy of supporting deserving causes has been continued after his death. The Elvis Presley Estate helped to set up the Elvis Presley Memorial Trauma Center, which opened in 1983 at the Regional Medical Center in Memphis. The Trauma Center continues to be funded by the Elvis Estate and fans (through, among other things, subscription to the Tennessee Elvis license plate).

The Elvis Presley Charitable Foundation was set up by Elvis Presley Enterprises in 1984 (originally as the Elvis Presley Memorial Foundation) to uphold Elvis' tradition of giving; Lisa Marie Presley is the chairperson of the foundation. The EPCS sponsors a scholarship fund at the University of Memphis, and supports Presley Place, which much like Lauderdale Courts—the Federal housing project where the Presley family began to put poverty behind them they first moved Memphis in the late Forties—provides homeless families with everything they need to start putting their lives back on track.

Since his death, Elvis fan clubs around the world have followed their hero's lead and raised large sums of money for charity.

CHARITIES TO WHICH ELVIS DONATED

Abe Scharff YMCA
Alpine Guild
Arthritis Foundation
Ave Marie Guild Home for the Aged
Baptist Children's Home
Beale Street Elk's Club
Bethany Maternity Home
Boys Club of Palm Springs
Boys Club of Phoenix Arizona
Boys Town of Memphis
Braille Institute of America
Camp Courage
Commercial Appeal Fresh Air Fund
Convent of The Good Shepard
Crippled Children's Hospital
Cynthia Milk Fund
Duration Club Inc.
Elks Blues Bowl Committee
Elvis Presley Youth Center of Tupelo
Episcopal Home For Girls
Exchange Club
Family Service Of Memphis
Father Flanagan's Boys Town of Nebraska
Foundation for the Junior Blind
Fraternal Order of Police
Girls Club Of Memphis
Good Fellows
Goodwill Home for Children
Goodwill Industries
Happy Acres
Home for Incurables

Hospital for Crippled Adults
Howard Manor Christian Home
Jesse Mahan Center
Jewish Community Center
John Tracy Clinic
Junior League
Kennedy Hospital Christmas Fund
Kidney Foundation
King's Daughter's Trinity Circle
Le Bonheur Children's Hospital
Les Passes
Lions Club
Little City Of The Mid South
Los Angeles County Heart Association
Mary Galloway Home
Memphis Epilepsy Foundation
Memphis Heart Association
Memphis Hebrew Academy
Memphis Mothers Service
Memphis Press Scimitar Good Fellows
Memphis Shelby County Council For Retarded
    Children
Memphis Speech and Hearing Center
Memphis Union Mission
Mid South Cancer Research
Mile-O-Dimes Motion Picture Relief Fund
Memphis Speech and Hearing Center
Mothers YMCA Canteen
Muscular Dystrophy
Neighborhood House
Oncological Research Foundation
Orange Mound Day Nursery
Palm Springs Jaycees
Porter-Leath Children's Home
Salvation Army
Sarah Brown YMCA
Shelby United Neighbors
Sheltered Workshop
St. Gerald Hall
St. Joseph Indian School of Chamberlain South
    Dakota
St. Judes Children Research Hospital
St. Peters Orphanage
The Thalians of Beverly Hills California
United Cerebral Palsy
United Fund Of The Desert Communities
Variety Club of Memphis
West Tennessee Cancer Clinic
Whitehaven Jaycees Youth Service

Book:
The Best of Elvis: Recollections of a Great Humani-
tarian, by Cindy Hazen and Mike Freeman,
Memphis Explorations, 1992.

CHARLES, RAY
(1930-2004)

Before he started singing for a living, Elvis was a
Ray Charles fan; some of the first songs Elvis sang
professionally had been recent hits for the blind
singer born in Albany, Georgia, on September 23,
1930, who had his first success in 1951 with
"Baby, Let Me Hold Your Hand."

Charles was a music pioneer who mixed and
matched his genres—R & B, gospel and jazz—to
forge his own sound and pave the way for a new
generation of performers, heavily influencing what
became Soul. Charles scored a string of hits from
the mid-Fifties to the mid-Sixties, branching
into pop and country, and carried on performing,
making music and appearing on TV and in the
movies until a few months before his death in 2004.

Elvis recorded many Ray Charles songs over
the years: Charles originals "I Got A Woman"
and "What'd I Say," and songs Charles covered
including "Tryin' To Get To You," "You Don't
Know Me," "I Can't Stop Loving You," "I'm
Movin' On," "Your Cheatin' Heart," "Without
Love," "Blue Moon Of Kentucky" and the world's
most covered song, "Yesterday."

Elvis almost recorded "Leave My Woman

Alone" for the *Easy Come, Easy Go* soundtrack
but though the band laid down their track, Elvis
never added the vocals. Elvis is also reputed to
have covered "This Little Girl of Mine."

Charles won 13 Grammys including a lifetime
achievement award and was an inaugural inductee
into the Rock and Roll Hall of Fame.

"CHARRO!"

Written by Mac Davis and Billy Strange, Elvis
recorded this title song—indeed, the only song—
for the movie on October 10, 1968 at the Samuel
Goldwyn Studios. That day he worked with
drummer Carl O'Brian and arranger Hugo
Montenegro, who was fresh from working with
Ennio Morricone work on *The Good, The Bad and
The Ugly* soundtrack.

"Charro!" was released as the B-side to
"Memories" in February 1969, and of course has
its place on the 1990s *Double Features* series.
Other appearances over the years include LPs
Almost In Love, Elvis in Hollywood, and more
recently soundtrack compilations *Command
Performances, Elvis Movies* and *Elvis at the Movies*.

CHARRO!

Working titles for this script, written by movie
director Charles Marquis Warren—a veteran of
many a TV Western series—included *Jack Valentine,
Johnny Hang,* and *Come Hell or Come Sundown*.
Elvis began work on the Western in early July 1968,
just a week after he had completed taping his
NBC TV Special.

This is the only movie in which Elvis does not
sing during the action, though he did record a
title song (and one other track, "Let's Forget
About The Stars," which was not used).

Clint Eastwood turned down the lead role in
this pseudo-spaghetti Western before the project
came to Elvis. Elvis had plenty of cowboy actor
talent to work with, including regulars from
"Rawhide" and "Gunsmoke."

The movie script was originally much harder
hitting than the finished product. A number of
more violent scenes were left behind on the cutting room floor, as was a nude scene of actress Ina
Balin climbing out of a bath; a risqué opening
scene wasn't even filmed.

Location footage was shot at Apache Junction
and the Apacheland Movie Ranch, Arizona. The
movie was released nationwide in March 1969.
Many fans feel that if Elvis had done this kind of
movie towards the start of his film career, he
might have avoided the worst of his mid-Sixties
output, though critics were generally unimpressed—it was too late for Elvis to redeem his
feature film career.

CREDITS:
National General, Color
Length: 98 minutes
Release date: March 13, 1969

TAGLINES:
Elvis Presley as the one called CHARRO!
On his neck he wore the brand of a killer... On his
    hip he wore vengeance.
A different kind of role, a different kind of man.

Directed by: Charles Marquis Warren
Produced by: Charles Marquis Warren (producer),
    Harry Caplan (executive producer), George
    Templeton (associate producer)
Written by: Frederick Louis Fox (story), Charles
    Marquis Warren (screenplay)
Music by: Hugo Montenegro
Cinematography by: Ellsworth Fredericks
Film Editing by: Al Clark

ON HIS NECK HE WORE THE BRAND OF A KILLER.
ON HIS HIP HE WORE VENGEANCE.

A different kind of rôle...

A different kind of man.

NATIONAL GENERAL PICTURES

ELVIS PRESLEY *as the one called* CHARRO!

Casting by: Harvey Clermont
Art Direction by: James Sullivan
Set Decoration by: Charles Thompson

CAST:

Elvis Presley	Jess Wade
Ina Balin	Tracey Winters
Victor French	Vince Hackett
Barbara Werle	Mrs. Sara Ramsey
Solomon Sturges	Billy Roy Hackett
Lynn Kellogg	Marcie (saloon girl)
Paul Brinegar	Opie Keetch (barber)
Harry Landers	Heff (Hackett gang)
Tony Young	Mexican Lt. Rivera
James Almanzar	Sheriff Dan Ramsey
Charles H. Gray	Mody (Hackett gang)
John Pickard	Jerome Selby (general store)
Garry Walberg	Martin Tilford (hotel owner)
Duane Grey	Gabe (Hackett gang)
Rodd Redwing	Lige (Hackett gang)
Edward McKinley	Henry Carter (banker)
Robert Luster	Will Joslyn (livery stable)
James Sikking	Gunner (Hackett gang)
Jacqui Brandt	Bit part
Kathleen Darc	Bit part
Arnie Frank	Musician
Charlie Hodge	Mexican peon
Robert Karnes	Harvey (bartender)
Christa Lang	Christa
Megan Timothy	Bit part

ADDITIONAL CREW:

Gene Bartlett	makeup supervisor
William Reynolds	makeup supervisor
Jack Kirschner	post-production supervisor
Maurie M. Suess	unit production manager
George Templeton	assistant director
Roy Meadows	sound designer
John Mick	music editor
Robert Beck	special effects
George C. Thompson	special effects
Woodrow Ward	special effects
Steven Burnett	stunts
Ron Nix	stunts
Ron Stein	stunts
Charlsie Bryant	script supervisor
Robert Fuca	wardrobe
Roy Lindeberg	dialogue director

Plot:
Elvis plays Jess Wade, a former outlaw who,
riding through 1870s Mexico, runs into old gang

pals Vince Hackett (played by Victor French) and his psychopathic brother Billy Roy (played by Solomon Sturges). The brothers and their gang forcefully take him to their mountain hideout, where they have concealed the famous cannon used to secure Mexico's liberation from Spain, and which they want to auction off to the highest bidder.

Jess warns them that they will never get away with it. The gang has plans, though; Vince gave false information to the Mexican authorities and now they have Jess's face on Wanted posters for stealing the cannon. To make sure that he fits the description of the man suspected of the robbery (a gang member who suffered a neck wound in the raid and died soon after), Vince and Co. torture Jess with a branding iron.

Jess manages to escape and make it back over the border to the safety of Rio Seco, a town where his pal Sheriff Dan Ramsey (played by James Almanzar) is on his side. There he finds solace in the arms of Tracey Winters (played by Ina Balin), a dancer at the town saloon and formerly gang leader Vince's girl — another bone of contention between hero and villain.

Billy Roy rides into town and shoots the sheriff. Jess disarms him and throws him into jail. For his sins, Ramsey makes Jess a deputy.

As Jess warned the townspeople, Vince wastes no time in coming to rescue his brother. He gives Jess until sundown to free Billy Roy, but Jess says he will only turn him loose in exchange for the cannon, which rightfully belongs to Mexico.

The people of Rio Seco implore Jess to let Billy Roy go, fearful that the town will be destroyed by the cannon. Before they have a chance to mutiny, Jess rides Billy Roy out of town.

In the inevitable gunfight, the gang comes off worst, and Billy Roy is crushed by the runaway wagon carrying the gun. Jess arrests the defeated Vince and triumphantly hauls the cannon back into town. He hands back his deputy's badge to Sara (played by Barbara Werle), wife of the now perished Sheriff, and rides off into the sunset to return the cannon and prisoner Vince Hackett to Mexico.

Song: CHARRO!

CHAUFFEURS

Driving duties during Elvis' early touring years was shared by Elvis, band members Scotty Moore and Bill Black, and pals who kept him company like Gene Smith or Red West.

In the Seventies, Elvis had a chauffeur in LA called Gerald Peters, an Englishman who is said to have driven for Winston Churchill. Elvis dubbed him "Sir Gerald."

In Graceland, Elvis drove himself around, or one of the entourage guys did.

CHISCA HOTEL, MEMPHIS
(262 SOUTH MAIN)

Elvis performed with Sy Rose's Band on a Dewey Phillips-hosted evening here on March 9, 1956. It was from here, almost two years previously, that Dewey Phillips first played "That's All Right (Mama)," Elvis' debut single on Sun Records, on his WHBQ radio show. Before and after his rise to prominence, Elvis often dropped in at Dewey Phillips evenings at the hotel. On one such evening, in late March 1957, Elvis was involved in an altercation (across the road from the hotel) with Marine Private Hershel Nixon, who accused Elvis of drawing a gun and insulting his wife.

LEFT: Elvis with Ina Balin, his co-star in *Charro!*

"CHESAY"

Fred Karger, Ben Weisman and Sid Wayne collaborated on this knees-up that Elvis recorded at Radio Recorders for *Frankie and Johnny* on May 15, 1965, with Robert Corwin on accordion.

The song has since appeared on the *Double Features* release, and on the FTD *Frankie And Johnny* release (which also has alternates).

CHESNUT, JERRY
(B. 1931)

Elvis recorded several songs by this country songwriter: "Love Coming Down," "T-R-O-U-B-L-E" and "Woman Without Love," in addition to a couple of songs that Chesnut co-wrote with Billy Edd Wheeler ("Never Again" and "It's Midnight"), after Lamar Fike suggested him. Elvis was scheduled to record Chesnut song "The Wonders You Perform" at an ill-fated recording session at Stax in 1973—the song had previously been a hit for Tammy Wynette. Chesnut also wrote for Porter Wagoner and Dolly Parton, Jerry Lee Lewis, George Jones and Faron Young. He was named *Billboard* songwriter of the year in 1972.

JERRY CHESNUT: "I remember him as nothing amazing, nothing supernatural, never trying to impress anyone, just a simple, wonderful, sweet American kid that never really had a chance to grow up . . ."

CHILDHOOD

The shadow of Elvis' stillborn twin brother fell deeply over Elvis' childhood. Mother Gladys was very protective of her little boy. She wouldn't let him play out of her sight until he was older than most, and then she would go out and give other boys a piece of her mind (and her broom) if she found out they were giving Elvis a hard time. Elvis could hold his own in a scrap; kids then and now have to if they're not going to be teased mercilessly.

The first precocious indicator of Elvis' singing talent was at the Assembly of God Church where his Great Uncle Gains Mansell was a preacher. When Elvis was just a two-year-old tot (three or four in some versions of the story), during one service he wriggled free of his mother's grip to climb up with the choir and join in.

Biographer Peter Guralnick describes Elvis as "a solitary child who had constructed a world from his imagination."

Cousin Harold Loyd remembered Elvis as "real hyper. He would run and play so hard he just wear himself out." Though Elvis was high-spirited, it seems that Gladys taught him to respect limits. She brought him up as a church-going child who believed that all people are equal in the eyes of God.

When young Elvis got mad with his mom, he would cram his clothes into a bag and "run away" to Grandma Minnie Mae down the road.

When he was 10, Elvis' fondly-remembered fifth grade teacher Mrs. Oleta Grimes entered him into the talent show at the Children's Day of the annual Mississippi-Alabama Fair and Dairy Show, at the fairground in Tupelo. The daughter of Orville Bean and a neighbor of the Presleys, Mrs. Grimes had been much impressed with his singing at school morning prayer services. At the Fair, Elvis clambered up onto a chair and without accompaniment sang out Red Foley's "Old Shep," a sad ballad about a boy and his dog. Many years later, Elvis recalled winning fifth prize at the talent show, and also taking a beating from his mother for going on dangerous rides he wasn't supposed to.

Elvis was not a particularly popular boy at school in Tupelo, though he did earn a certain grudging renown for playing the guitar and singing. He had friends his own age from the Assembly of God church. After the family moved to Memphis in 1948, they moved into public authority housing and Elvis started spending time with older boys, playing guitar, singing and listening to music.

Though he usually stayed out of trouble, lively little Elvis did get into occasional scrapes. A kid he was wrestling broke a hip; he went swimming at the creek one day at a dangerous spot where his folks told him not to; he was caught trying to sneak into the Tupelo Fair with the son of the Fair's president, who gave them a round scolding but then let them in anyway. He made friends with Buzzy Forbes at the Lauderdale Courts project in Memphis after Forbes whacked him around the head with the comics he was holding, Elvis slapped him back, and then rather than beating each other up they smiled and became pals.

Elvis suffered bad acne as an adolescent—he later referred to it as "terminal acne"—which was visible in his very first press photographs. He was very much an outsider, not good enough at football and not enough of a fighter to be part of the in-crowd. When he started earning money from odd jobs, he could

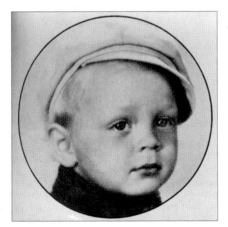

At two years old, this is the earliest known photo of Elvis.

Elvis Presley as a teenager.

indulge his penchant for flashy clothes to match the (then) unfashionably long hair he sported.

Elvis overcame his shyness when he was around musicians, finding a way to meet performers backstage and ask them questions. Jake Hess remembered him as "a bright-eyed boy . . . he just looked important even as a kid."

Elvis retained a childish side into adulthood. With his male friends, this emerged in pranks, coarse humor, and sophomoric behavior. With women he sometimes regressed into childish behavior, displaying a child's vulnerability and neediness. With Priscilla there were times when they play-acted, had pillow fights, even played hide and seek. Other girlfriends have talked about his enduring little-boy vulnerability.

ELVIS SAID: "I was an only child—a very protected and spoiled only child."

ELVIS SAID IN 1956: "We didn't have any money or nothing, but I always managed. We never had any luxuries but we never went hungry."

ELVIS SAID IN 1956: "My folks always made me behave whether I wanted to or not."

ELVIS SAID: "The very first thing I could remember in my life was sittin' on my mama's lap in church."

ELVIS SAID: "I was a nobody, a small town kid in the big city, without a dime in my pocket, not too good in class, kinda shy."

ELVIS SAID: ." . .I was brought up [by] my mother and father to believe and have respect for other people."

PETER GURALNICK: "Elvis grew up a loved and precious child."

SCOTTY MOORE: "He was just a typical coddled son . . . very shy—he was more comfortable just sitting there with a guitar than trying to talk to you."

LARRY GELLER: "Elvis was a big kid at heart."

CHILDREN

Elvis had a great rapport with kids. When little more than a kid himself, he was in charge with looking after his younger cousins when the family moved down to Pascagoula for a spell. At school, Elvis was more often than not friends with kids younger than him.

There's a story that in 1956 at Fox Studios he bumped into actress Maureen Stapleton, where both of them were doing a screen test. After he finished his, Elvis offered to look after her four-year old son, and took care of him until she was back.

With his serious girlfriends, he would fantasize about having kids; when she was alive, Gladys joined in too as they imagined the little Elvises and Dixies (or Elvis Jr. when he was with Anita Wood) who would one day be running around.

Elvis didn't become a father until the age of 32, long after the first press rumors that he had brought "love children" into the world (see below). When *Loving You* costar Dolores Hart went into a convent, a rumor did the rounds that she had gotten herself to a nunnery because she and Elvis had a child.

Kids featured prominently in many of Elvis' Sixties movies, sometimes (*It Happened at the World's Fair* and *Fun in Acapulco*) as smart-alek co-stars.

When Elvis had his first and only child with Priscilla, he was so enthusiastic that when he got back to Graceland he told anyone who would listen that he wanted 20 kids. Priscilla, just out of childbirth, waited for this, like all his enthusiasms, to blow over.

Elvis always became upset and angry if he saw news items about child abuse.

In 1975, when Elvis was hospitalized and being tended by girlfriend Linda Thompson, Elvis fantasized about having another child, this time a little boy. On one of these hospital stays, he persuaded the nursing staff to patch through the birth unit video feeds to his bedroom so that he and Linda could watch the newborns.

In 2007, German label Megaphon re-issued *Elvis for Babies*, a collection of Elvis instrumentals for tots.

PATERNITY SUITS AND CHILD CLAIMS

Rumors about Elvis making women pregnant go all the way back to his early teen years: it has been claimed that the family moved from Tupelo to Memphis because Elvis got a girl pregnant, skimpy as the evidence may be.

Elvis was landed with a high-profile paternity suit in the middle of a month-long Las Vegas tour in the summer of 1970. Patricia Ann Parker from Los Angeles claimed that Elvis impregnated her at his previous Las Vegas residency. While Elvis

Elvis, Priscilla and baby Lisa (October 1968).

made light of the claim from the stage, lawyer Ed Hookstratten hired a private eye called John O'Grady to turn up what he could about the woman. On October 19, 1970, Ms. Parker gave birth to a boy, whom she named Jason Peter Presley. A process server handed Elvis the papers for the suit in November 1970, while posing as a fan at Elvis' hotel when he was performing in LA. A year later, Elvis was cleared after a blood test proved that he was not the father. Elvis referred to the incident a few years later, in a rather befuddled speech during a concert at Las Vegas: "Turned out to be a complete conspiracy and hoax, man. There is just no way. I had a picture taken with that chick and that's all, and she got pregnant by the camera. You know what she did? She named the night . . .the night she named my wife was with me in L.A. Ain't no way I'm fooling around with her out there, are you kidding me?"

Since Elvis' death there has been a steady stream of people who have come forward with claims that they are Elvis' "love child." Two women have claimed to have had children called Deborah Presley after relationships with Elvis in 1954. A Germany nightclub singer called Margot Kuzma claimed that Elvis fathered a child who was born in late 1959.

A one-time country singer called Candy Jo Fuller claimed in 1978 to be Elvis' secret daughter, resulting from a liaison with her mother Terri Taylor in 1957.

In 1987, Tennessee woman called Lucy de Barbin published a book *Are You Lonesome Tonight?* in which she claimed that she had long been raising a child of Elvis' she had given birth to in secret in 1958, named Desiree Presley.

An Elvis child pretender, Elvis Presley Jr. (formerly called Philip Stanic) runs his own Elvis museum in Ohio.

In 2006, A man who claimed his name was Jason Presley was sent to the Utah state hospital for threatening judges who refused to investigate his claims that Elvis was murdered.

Book/DVD:
Elvis Presley Paternity Suit, by Bud Glass, Praytome Publishing, 2007.

ELVIS SAID: "I figure all any kid needs is hope and the feeling he or she belongs. If I could do or say anything that would give some kid that feeling, I would believe I had contributed something to the world."

A candid photograph from Red West's wedding (1961).

CHRISTMAS

Christmas was always important to Elvis. It became a big deal as soon as he started making money. For Christmas 1954, he spent every cent he made from his last pre-holiday Louisiana Hayride show on Christmas gifts, which the family opened at their Alabama Street home.

Elvis spent the Christmas of 1955 with the family at their new home on Getwell Street.

Christmas 1956 was at their Audubon Drive home, their first Christmas of true plenty.

Many Graceland traditions were established in 1957, the first Christmas the Presleys spent there. That year they had a revolving white nylon Christmas tree, put up red drapes, and Elvis installed a Santa sleigh and a train of eight reindeer put up in the garden out front, which are still a regular Christmas feature today, when over two million bulbs light up the property.

Billy Smith says, "In 1957 the first Christmas at Graceland was quite different from any other Christmas I had known before. It was like being in fairyland and Santa Claus was my first cousin." Elvis showed Santa-sized generosity, giving a newspaper seller a $100 bill to pay for a paper and then telling him to keep the change. That year, Elvis bought $2000 of fireworks, to be used for "War," a festive game he and friends repeated every year, in which two teams fired rockets at one another in the grounds of Graceland. However, Elvis' first Christmas at Graceland in 1957 was not quite the carefree joyousness it might have been—the draft lay mere months away.

Every year, the Colonel had a special card made up for Elvis to send out, sometimes portraying the Colonel too. The Colonel was expert in keeping himself and his client uppermost in the minds of the famous and powerful by sending out notes, cards and telegrams on any and every conceivable occasion.

Elvis spent Christmas 1958 at the Hotel Grunewald, Bad Nauheim, Germany with his father and pals. It was the same script in 1959, when Santa brought along Priscilla Beaulieu and plenty of soldiers from the base.

Elvis' first Christmas at home in Graceland without his mother was 1960, though he had the comfort of girlfriend Anita Wood.

It was a different story in 1961: with Vernon now living at Graceland with new wife Dee Stanley and her three kids, Elvis kept his distance and spent the festive season at the Sahara Hotel in Las Vegas.

The first Christmas Elvis spent with Priscilla on US soil was in 1962, when she came over on a "secret" visit; they threw a party for thirty pals. Elvis gave her a poodle, which she named Honey; Priscilla found a novelty cigarette box that played his tune "Surrender."

Christmas 1963 was a home affair with Priscilla and the family.

In the early to mid-sixties when he was spending a great deal of time in California working on movies, the household at Graceland gradually filled with excitement and anticipation as Elvis' return approached. Secretary Becky Hartley remembers: "There was just something magic about the holidays at Graceland, especially just before Christmas. You always knew Elvis was coming home. . . . There were lots of decorations and all that. The whole house would be lit up. It was homey and wonderful."

All the gang was at Graceland for Christmas 1964, with Elvis' extended family in attendance.

Elvis received a statue of Jesus from his entourage for his brand new meditation garden at Graceland in 1965.

On Christmas Eve, 1966, Elvis proposed to Priscilla and gave her a ring he had bought from Harry Levitch.

Elvis and Priscilla threw a Christmas Party at Graceland on Christmas Eve in 1967. In addition to the life-sized reindeer with the words "Merry Christmas to All, Elvis," he displayed a life-size Nativity scene and blue lights strung over eight trees.

Elvis spent his first Christmas as a daddy at home with his family in 1968.

For 1969, it was home at Graceland before starting in on rehearsals for his second Las Vegas engagement.

Christmas 1970 was a family affair at Graceland, after Elvis spent much of the month shuttling round the country for pleasure. He went that evening to the movies to see Robert Redford starring in *Little Fauss and Big Halsy*.

Christmas was shockingly early in 1971, arriving in May when Elvis went into a studio festooned with Christmas decorations to record material for *Elvis Sings The Wonderful World of Christmas*. He took the conceit the whole way by giving out gifts of gold bracelets with the legend "Elvis '71." Another family Christmas awaited at the traditional time of year; Priscilla and Lisa Marie flew in from LA and Elvis arrived at Graceland post haste from a tryst in Washington.

Elvis spent the next three Christmases at Graceland with Linda Thompson, though in 1974 it was a more muted affair as he was suffering the after-effects of an ulcer.

In 1975, as a treat Elvis took friends and family for a trip on the *Lisa Marie*. Elvis gave each passenger an item of jewelry he had bought from Lowell Hays, after the jeweler came around and laid out his wares on Elvis' bed for him to choose—Elvis spent around $60,000 on family, staff and his entourage.

New girlfriend Ginger Alden brightened up Elvis' Christmas in 1976, though for the first time in decades, Elvis went off on tour soon afterwards. The Christmas contingent that year was much reduced, just a few family members, Lisa Marie included, and a couple of entourage pals.

CHRISTMAS ALBUMS

Elvis' two original Christmas releases during his lifetime (*Elvis Christmas*, 1957 and *The Wonderful*

A holiday greeting from Elvis' home.

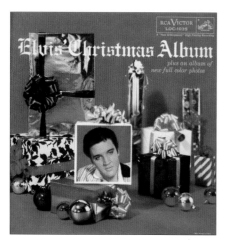

World of Christmas, 1971) have spawned many Christmas compilations. Together with the re-released version of that 1957 album, which it almost entirely replicated, 1970 album Elvis' Christmas Album has become Elvis' best-selling LP of all time. In 2006 BMG brought out Elvis Christmas, showcasing all of his festive songs plus four gospel tracks.

Book:
Christmas With Elvis, by Jim Curtin and Renata Ginter, Celebrity Press, 1999.

CHRISTMAS PEACE

A 2003 remastered BMG release of Christmas songs and gospel classics.

TRACK LISTING:
1. Blue Christmas
2. Here Comes Santa Claus (Right Down Santa Claus Lane)
3. White Christmas
4. Santa Bring My Baby Back (To Me)
5. I'll Be Home For Christmas
6. Santa Claus Is Back In Town
7. O Little Town Of Bethlehem
8. Christmas Message From Elvis / Silent Night
9. If Every Day Was Like Christmas
10. O Come, All Ye Faithful
11. The First Noel
12. On A Snowy Christmas Night
13. Winter Wonderland
14. The Wonderful World Of Christmas
15. It Won't Seem Like Christmas (Without You)
16. I'll Be Home On Christmas Day
17. If I Get Home On Christmas Day
18. Holly Leaves And Christmas Trees
19. Merry Christmas Baby
20. Silver Bells

DISC: 2
1. (There'll Be) Peace In The Valley (For Me)
2. I Believe
3. It Is No Secret (What God Can Do)
4. His Hand In Mine
5. In My Father's House
6. Known Only To Him
7. Mansion Over The Hilltop
8. Crying In The Chapel
9. How Great Thou Art
10. In The Garden
11. Where No One Stands Alone
12. Somebody Bigger Than You And I
13. Without Him
14. We Call On Him
15. Only Believe
16. Amazing Grace
17. An Evening Prayer
18. He Touched Me
19. He Is My Everything
20. If That Isn't Love

The 2-CD set was re-released in 2005 as Elvis: My Christmas #1

CHRISTMAS WITH ELVIS

Christmas came early in 1958—in September when RCA released a second EP of tracks from the previous year's Christmas album.

TRACK LISTING:
1. White Christmas
2. Here Comes Santa Claus
3. O Little Town Of Bethlehem
4. Silent Night

A 2005 2-CD box set of this name was released by BMG combining Elvis' Christmas Album and Elvis Sings The Wonderful World Of Christmas.

CHRISTOPHER, JOHNNY

Rhythm guitar player who featured on the tracks Elvis cut at Stax in late 1973 and later sessions, up to his March 1975 sessions in LA. Christopher co-authored Elvis songs "Always On My Mind" and "If You Talk In Your Sleep," and wrote "Mama Liked The Roses," which Elvis recorded in 1969.

CHURCH

Elvis' parents were regular attendees of the First Assembly of God Church, first in Tupelo (where they met) on Adams Street, then in Memphis, at 1084 E. McLemore. Elvis' uncles on his mothers' side preached in Tupelo.

The Church was an important community focus in the Presley's family life, especially when they fell on hard times in the late Thirties. Elvis' family would also travel to other churches that held all-day services to sing and have a good time.

The church tradition to which Elvis' family belonged has been disparagingly referred to by some as "Holy Rollers," for the enraptured congregants' shouts, speaking in tongues and violent body movements.

Elvis was baptized at the age of nine or ten in Tupelo. Rick Stanley says that Elvis attended Harrisburg Baptist Church in Tupelo when he was ten.

In his late teens, Elvis and his cousin Gene Smith became avid churchgoers because of the possibilities it offered to meet girls. Elvis regularly heard nationally-famous gospel quartet the Blackwood Brothers at his Memphis church.

When he was 19, Elvis, girlfriend Dixie and pals would go to hear the Rev W. Herbert Brewster at the "colored" Baptist Church on East

The First Assembly of God Church in Memphis, TN.

Trigg, in Memphis. Racial segregation was still on the statute books at this time.

In early interviews, Elvis said that the only reason why he had stopped regularly attending church was because he was on the road so much and often played shows on a Sunday.

Elvis would have attended Sunday services at the Army chapel in Germany but for the fact that his presence would have been a problem.

Elvis and girlfriend Anita Wood had to beat a hasty retreat from the First Assembly of God Church in Memphis at Easter 1960 because his presence created such a commotion.

In later life, when he embarked upon a more eclectic spiritual quest, Elvis began to believe that the church was wrong to operate on a basis of fear rather than love, and that in the wrong hands religion could be a dangerous weapon.

After Elvis died, fan and friend Janelle McComb raised money to build a chapel for fans to meditate near Elvis' birthplace in Tupelo, Mississippi.

ELVIS SAID: "I remember sometimes in church . . . it was often the preacher, who might not have had as good a voice, who was jumping around and getting them all worked up, who was the center of it all. It was like a bit of a show. And good."

ELVIS SAID TO LARRY GELLER IN 1964: " I always knew there was a real spiritual life, not the way the church dishes it out, you know, with hellfire and damnation and using fear."

T. G. SHEPPARD: "Maybe he was a minister of music."

ANNIE CLOYD PRESLEY: "It made me sad to know that Elvis' life was so miserable. I blame Vernon with a lot of it—and Tom Parker—but Elvis was a grown man. . . . Elvis had been raised in the Holiness Church. As far as I know, that's the only kind of church he ever went to. They taught a perfect life."

"CINDY, CINDY"

Elvis recorded this much-covered Thirties hit (originally titled "Get Along Home, Cindy," and covered by Ricky Nelson in the late Fifties) in an R'n'B version credited to Florence Kaye, Ben Weisman and Dolores Fuller in Nashville on June 4, 1970 for release on his Love Letters From Elvis album.

The song has since appeared on the Walk A Mile In My Shoes anthology.

Essential Elvis Vol. 4 features a different take from the same session; another version came out in 2000 on the That's The Way It Is box set.

CIRCLE G

In February 1967 Elvis bought this 163-acre ranch at Horn Lake, De Soto County, Mississippi, just 10 miles south of Graceland (Highway 301 where it meets Goodman Road) when it became clear that his new passion for horse riding was far bigger than Graceland could accommodate. He found the property himself—then a cattle ranch called Twinkletown Farm—one day when he and Priscilla were out on a motorcycle ride and he spotted a 50-foot high white cross by a small lake which he took as a sign that it was the place for him.

Elvis wound up paying owner and second-hand aircraft salesman Jack Adams $437,000, significantly over the market value, for a rather modest house on a road with some land. Marty Lacker says the price was $375,000, while the press reported that Elvis had paid over half a million dollars for the property. Vernon had conniptions when he heard of Elvis' intention and tried to get his son to back out of the deal. Elvis wouldn't, as he had made a "gentleman's agreement." They had to use Graceland as collateral to raise funds for the purchase.

Elvis at the Circle G Ranch, 1968, riding Domino.

Elvis named the place Circle G in homage to Graceland—and to the Circle Z ranch from his 1965 movie *Tickle Me*—though the name had to be officially changed to "Flying Circle G" because there was already a "Circle G" ranch in Texas.

After Elvis acquired the ranch, he briefly considered moving out of Graceland to a more modern home that he intended to build on the land he now owned in Mississippi. He got as far as asking Marty Lacker's brother-in-law Bernie Grenadier to draw up plans. He thought that he would give an acre to all of his guys so that they could build their own homes too, but within a couple of weeks he had changed his mind. Instead, he spent around $150,000 on trailers for all the entourage guys and their families. Circle G became Elvis' all-consuming passion and hobby as he set to work on converting it into a kind of cowboy-themed commune. He bought dozens of El Camino and Ranchero pick-up trucks for all the members of his entourage—Priscilla estimates he spent $100,000 on these alone—plus a Case tractor.

Initially, he retained the Santa Gertrudis cattle, and kept on Ralph Boucher to run things. From his own staff, Elvis chose Alan Fortas and Uncle Earl Pritchett to supervise affairs.

Elvis and Priscilla spent their real honeymoon here in May that year. Priscilla envisioned just herself and Elvis living there as happy newlyweds, sans entourage. Elvis had other ideas. He bought trailers for the guys in the entourage, lining up eight of them in a row, setting them up on concrete foundations and hooking up gas and electricity lines. It was more exciting for Elvis to live in a double-wide three-bedroom house trailer than the house, which he let cousin Billy Smith and his family use.

To begin with, the place was a cross between a commune and a dude ranch, with fun and communal living the order of the day. Elvis and the whole gang would spend up to two weeks at a time leading the frontier life. This idyll was short-lived. Fans set up a vigil outside the fence, but the property afforded far less privacy than Graceland. Elvis' spending ballooned out of control and the property was besieged by truck dealers hopeful of Elvis going on another dozen-truck spree. Things really began to unravel when entourage members and their wives began wanting to get back to their normal lives. By the summer, Elvis had returned to his usual Memphis pursuits of watching movies and hanging out with his pals at Graceland, and the ranch was put up for sale.

Equipment and farm paraphernalia was auctioned off on November 4, 1967, raising $108,000. By the end of the year, the ranch was out of Elvis' life, though it was not finally sold until May 1969, when the North Mississippi Gun Club acquired the property for $440,000—or so Elvis thought. In actual fact, the Gun Club, represented by Lou McClellan, defaulted and the deal was annulled (alternative versions of the story put the proceeds at $350,000, including an additional forty acre spread he had added to the property). The property was finally sold by the Presleys in 1973 to the Boyle Investment Company; because of extra building work in the meantime, Elvis actually made money on the property.

At the time of writing, plans were afoot to build a residential development on the land, following long-term plans to build a resort on the property.

PRISCILLA: "There was fun, laughter, and a lot of camaraderie."

RAY WALKER: "The happiest we ever saw Elvis was when he bought that ranch. He had some horses down there, and he was exercising, and he looked great, and he felt great."

"CITY BY NIGHT"

A Bill Giant / Bernie Baum / Florence Kaye song written for Elvis to record in Los Angeles in June 1966—the band laid down the instrumentals at Radio Recorders on June 28, Elvis overdubbed his vocals at the MGM Recording Stage two days later—destination the *Double Trouble* soundtrack—in the film, additional instruments were overdubbed.

The song has since appeared on the *Double Features* and FTD releases for the movie—the FTD one features an alternate take.

CKX

A U.S. entertainment company run by Robert Sillerman that acquired an 85% controlling stake in Elvis Presley Enterprises in 2005. The company subsequently acquired the company previously responsible for American Idol and hired Simon Fuller to assist in rebranding Elvis and his image.

The first two letters of the name "CFX" stand for "content is king."

The company has since expanded its "idol" portfolio by buying licensing rights to Muhammad Ali's name and image; it also represents David and Victoria Beckham, and owns a major movie talent agency.

Plans at the time of writing for the Elvis Estate include a themed casino deal with MGM Mirage and a plan to create a special Cirque du Soleil show to run permanently in Las Vegas, with worldwide shows spreading an "Elvis Experience" in the future. Plans have not yet been announced regarding redevelopment of real estate owned by the Elvis Presley Enterprises around Graceland, though it is expected that exhibition space will be expanded to display much more of the memorabilia owned by the Estate.

"CLAMBAKE"

The title song to a 1967 movie relies on a version of traditional "Shortnin' Bread" for its much repeated chorus. Elvis recorded the Ben Weisman / Sid Wayne tune and the rest of the soundtrack at RCA's Studio B in Nashville on February 22 and 23, 1967.

Later album releases include *Command Performances*, the *Double Feature* issue for the movie, *Elvis Movies* and *Elvis at the Movies*.

A reprise version featured on the *Double Features* release. More bluesy alternates have come out on FTD releases *Silver Screen Stereo* and of course, the FTD *Clambake* release. Winfield Scott's demo of an alternate song (with the same title) features on FTD release *Writing For The King*.

CLAMBAKE (LP)

This October 1967 release included a couple of songs that failed to make it into the movie, and an early taste of Elvis' musical resurgence in the form of "bonus" tracks "Guitar Man" and both sides of the recent single "Big Boss Man"/ "You Don't Know Me." Somebody's dissatisfaction with soundtrack material was evident in the fact that non-soundtrack material accounted for almost half of the tracks; this is Elvis' only soundtrack album that starts with a track that has nothing to do with the movie. It only sold 200,000 copies, even with a special blow-up wedding shot of Elvis and Priscilla, rising no higher than #40 in the charts during the 14 weeks it was in.

TRACK LISTING:
1. Guitar Man
2. Clambake
3. Who Needs Money
4. A House That Has Everything
5. Confidence
6. Hey, Hey, Hey
7. You Don't Know Me
8. The Girl I Never Loved
9. How Can You Lose What You Never Had
10. Big Boss Man
11. Singing Tree
12. Just Call Me Lonesome

The soundtrack songs reappeared in the Nineties on *Double Feature: Kissin' Cousins / Clambake*. In 2006 FTD brought out a 23-track collector's release of *Clambake* with extra tracks and plenty of alternate takes.

CLAMBAKE

Work on this movie was delayed two weeks because Elvis didn't want to leave his new ranch, Circle G, and then suffered concussion after a fall in his bathroom in LA. The Colonel was so furious with Elvis' delaying tactics that he took direct charge of Elvis' inner circle, one of the only times this happened in their long working relationship.

Elvis later referred to the film as his "Wedding Cake" movie, intimating that he only did it because he needed the money for his upcoming marriage with Priscilla.

Originally, the title of the movie was *Too Big For Texas*. Colonel Parker came up with the release title—actually a title he first proposed for the movie released as *Spinout*.

The plot uses a trading places device with a nod of the head to *Blue Hawaii*. The powerboat race finale was filmed at the Orange Bowl International Power Boat Regatta. Elvis was not involved in the externals shot for the movie in and around Miami, Florida.

One track, "How Can You Loose What You Never Had" didn't make it into the movie; seven did.

Flipper the dolphin makes a cameo in the movie.

The movie premiered on October 18, 1967 and went on public release on November 22, 1967.

On its first weekend, *Clambake* peaked at #15 on the Box Office Survey. It grossed $1.6 million, enough to earn out its meager budget.

A shot of Elvis in *Clambake*, 1957.

CREDITS:
United Artists, Color.
Length: 100 minutes
Release date: November 22, 1967

TAGLINE:
Barreling . . . biking . . . bikin-ing and belting out
  that wild Presley beat.

Directed by: Arthur H. Nadel
Produced by: Arthur Gardner, Arnold Laven, Jules
  V. Levy
Written by: Arthur Browne Jr.
Music by: Jeff Alexander
Cinematography by: William Margulies
Film Editing by: Tom Rolf
Casting by: Lynn Stalmaster
Art Direction by: Lloyd S. Papez
Set Decoration by: James Redd

CAST:

Elvis Presley	Scott Heyward / Tom Wilson
Shelley Fabares	Dianne Carter
Will Hutchins	Tom Wilson / Scott Heyward
Bill Bixby	James J. Jamison III
Gary Merrill	Sam Burton (owner of Burton Boat Co.)
James Gregory	Duster Heyward
Suzie Kaye	Sally
Harold Peary	Harold (doorman)
Sam Riddle	Announcer, Governor's Trophy Race
Angelique Pettyjohn	Gloria
Olga Kaya	Gigi
Jack Good	Mr. Hathaway (Shores Hotel manager)
Lee Krieger	Paul (bartender)
Amanda Harley	Ellie (Heyward's secretary)
Sue England	Cigarette girl
Marj Dusay	Waitress
Arlene Charles	Olive
Steve Cory	Bellhop
Melvin Allen	Crewman
Herb Barnett	Waiter
Corbin Bernsen	Boy at playground
Richard Davis	Bit part
Joe Esposito	Bit part
Teri Garr	Dancer
Charlie Hodge	Mr. Heyward's barber
Francis Humphrey Howard	Bit part
Jonathan Kramer	Dancer at Clambake party
Robert P. Lieb	Mr. Barasch
Dal McKennon	Bearded gas station attendant
Christopher Riordan	Beach boy
Lisa Slagle	Lisa
Red West	Ice cream vendor

ADDITIONAL CREW:

Claude Binyon Jr..	assistant director
Bob Warner	special effects
Alex Romero	choreographer

Plot:

One of the rare times in his on-screen life that Elvis plays a man of means . . .who really wishes he wasn't.

Wealthy Scott Heyward (Elvis) does not want to work for the family business, he wants to go traveling and tells father Duster (played by James Gregory) what he can do with the job.

When Scott gets to Miami Beach, he trades places with local waterski instructor Tom Wilson (played by Will Hutchins). It looks like a smart plan when his first client is Dianne Carter (played by Shelley Fabares), except that Dianne is a gold digger with her sights set on moneybags James Jamison (played by Bill Bixby), in town to compete in a powerboat race. Elvis/Scott tries to win her affections fair and square, without his money influencing her, while posing as impoverished waterski instructor Tom.

Scott runs into powerboat designer Sam Burton (played by Gary Merrill), who has made a boat so fast that it would win any race if it didn't break up at high speed. Scott suggests a special sealant he developed back when working for his father'. When Scott calls up to get the formula, father Duster knows where he is and hotfoots it out to Florida to find him.

Scott, Tom and a heir go-go girl helpers concoct the magic formula and apply it to the boat. Scott's father arrives and they reconcile. Scott is gung-ho to enter the race despite not properly testing the "GOOP" chemical formula. He just has time to karate chop some manners into James Jamison, protecting Dianne's honor in the process.

Scott triumphs in the race against all odds. Still pretending to be lowly Tom Wilson, he asks Dianne for her hand in marriage. She faints when she learns that he is not really Tom but wealthy Scott, in the happiest of endings she could have hoped for.

Songs:" Clambake," "Who Needs Money," "A House That Has Everything," "Confidence," "You Don't Know Me," "Hey Hey Hey," "The Girl I Never Loved"

"CLEAN UP YOUR OWN BACKYARD"

This bluesy single from the recent *Trouble with Girls* movie was released in mid-June 1969 with B-side "The Fair Is Moving On," to a distinct lack of public acclaim. Previous single "In The Ghetto" made #3, while this song peaked at #36, selling around 300,000 copies in its eight weeks on the charts– the single version had extra overdubbing not present in the soundtrack version. Elvis recorded the song, written by Mac Davis and Billy Strange, on October 23, 1968 at United Artist Recorders in LA.

"Clean Up Your Own Backyard" first saw album release on 1970 Camden LP *Almost In Love*. Later outings include *Elvis' Golden Records, Vol. 5*, *Command Performances* and *Elvis at the Movies*.

The non-overdubbed version came out on the Nineties *Double Features* soundtrack release for Elvis' late-period, soundtrack-free movies. A version of the track remixed by Felton Jarvis appeared in 1980 on the *Guitar Man* album, and subsequently on FTD release *Too Much Monkey Business*.

CLEMENT, JACK
(B. 1931)

A singer, songwriter and musician about town before becoming an engineer for Sam Phillips at Sun Studio, "Cowboy" Jack Clement was the man who switched on the tape in early 1956 for the legendary "Million Dollar Quartet" session, after he had gone in to the studio to record his new find, Jerry Lee Lewis.

Elvis knew Clement from bumping into him at Taylor's Restaurant, next door to Sun, and they played on the same bill at the Eagle's Nest in Memphis in 1954, where Clement led a Western swing band.

When asked about his reactions on first hearing Elvis in the summer of 1954, Clement was amazed by "the uninhibitedness of it all."

After Sun, Clement had an illustrious career as a producer of country, folk and rock music, working mainly out of Nashville. In the early Sixties, he worked with Elvis producer and sometime guitarist Chet Atkins. He was inducted into the Country Songwriters Hall of Fame in 1973. Clement returned to Sun Studio in the Eighties to engineer U2's album *Rattle & Hum*.

"CLIMB, THE"

A *Viva Las Vegas* track composed by Leiber & Stoller and sung by the Jubilee Four in the movie, though Elvis sang at the 1963 recording session with The Jordanaires (released in 2003 on the *Viva Las Vegas* FTD album).

CLINTON, BILL
(B. WILLIAM JEFFERSON BLYTHE IV, AUGUST 19, 1946)

The 42nd President of the United States (1993-2001) proudly proclaimed his liking for Elvis in his successful 1992 campaign for office. He played "Heartbreak Hotel" on sax on Arsenio Hall's prime time TV show, persuading many Southerners who would never have voted Democrat that he was worth their vote, and when the campaign was won he hired an Elvis tribute artist to perform at his inauguration.

Clinton's Secret Service code name was "Elvis."

In his re-election year, *The Economist* suggested that Clinton had modeled his political career on Elvis' own career trajectory. Greil Marcus agreed, publishing a book of articles written between 1992 and 2000 on the parallels of the lives of these two Southern boys.

Clinton has his own collection of Elvis memorabilia.

As well as leading the most powerful nation in the world for two terms, Clinton recently won two Grammy awards for spoken word albums (*Peter and the Wolf* and his biography *My Life*).

BILL CLINTON: "Elvis Presley was the first and the best. He is my favorite of all time."

GREIL MARCUS: "Elvis Presley won the 1992 election for Bill Clinton."

Book:
Double Trouble: Bill Clinton and Elvis Presley in a Land of No Alternatives, by Greil Marcus, Henry Holt and Co, 2000.

CLOSING NIGHT

A 2004 FTD release of the controversial closing night show(s) in Las Vegas from September 3, 1973 where Elvis badmouthed the Hilton management. After the midnight performance Elvis had his most serious bust-up with the Colonel and briefly fired him.

TRACK LISTING:
1. Also Sprach Zarathustra
2. See See Rider
3. I Got A Woman / Amen
4. Love Me
5. Steamroller Blues
6. You Gave Me A Mountain
7. Trouble
8. Long Tall Sally / Whole Lotta Shakin' Goin' On / Your Mama Don't Dance / Flip, Flop And Fly / Hound Dog
9. Love Me Tender
10. Fever
11. What Now My Love
12. Suspicious Minds / Bridge Over Troubled Water
13. Bridge Over Troubled Water
14. Suspicious Minds
15. Introductions
16. My Boy
17. I Can't Stop Loving You
18. An American Trilogy
19. A Big Hunk O'Love
20. The First Time Ever I Saw Your Face
21. Mystery Train / Tiger Man
22. How Great Thou Art
23. Help Me Make It Through The Night
24. Softly As I Leave You
25. Can't Help Falling In Love

CLOTHES

Mark Twain's saying that clothes make the man is more than passing true for Elvis. In his early life, wearing the flashest fashions he could find was one of the ways that he battled and beat his innate shyness, setting himself up for decades as a style leader and fashion icon.

As with Elvis' music, his life may be divided into broadly homogeneous periods: gaudy styles during his breakthrough period when he needed to get noticed; effortless Italian-tailored suits in the Memphis Mafia early Sixties; whatever his Hollywood wardrobe dressers gave him for the rest of the decade; the iconic leather look from his 1968 NBC TV Special; and then in the Seventies a succession of increasingly grandiloquent themed jumpsuit costumes, inspired initially by karate-wear and adopted to allow him freedom of movement on stage, later required to camouflage his increasing weight. Whether at home or in public, daughter Lisa Marie remembers that her daddy was always stylishly turned out.

As a kid growing up in straitened times, Elvis wore whatever he was given on the family hand-me-down vine. Generally it was overalls, often it was practical denim, though on special occasions Gladys would dress him up in colorful clothes, or in a checkered pants and white shirt outfit. In later life, Elvis wouldn't tolerate anyone around him wearing denim because it remained, for him, a uniform of poverty.

After the Presleys moved to Lauderdale Courts in Memphis, in his last couple of years at high school Elvis began sporting black satin pants with a pink stripe and loud shirts. He also liked to show off his ROTC uniform. At this time his eye for style was way ahead of his finances, and he was more often pressed up against the window of Lansky, the Memphis clothiers he patronized all his life, than actually going in to buy. One way he could get hold of fancy duds was when he went with Gladys to the Poplar Street Mission to help out; he could trawl through the donated clothes for dress pants and sports coats that he otherwise would not be able to afford.

In his last year at Humes High School, Elvis dressed trucker style, wearing a leather jacket and a red bandana around his neck, sometimes over brightly-colored pegged pants. He performed at the school concert in his last year wearing a red shirt.

Pink quickly became his hallmark color, a sure way to stand out against his contemporaries wearing in Levi's and T-shirts. Elvis stocked up on and around Beale Street, at the stores frequented by African-Americans, gradually building up a collection of sports coats on which he turned up the collars, loud shirts and dress slacks. Sunglasses day or night completed the look.

When Elvis was 19, the outfit he wore on his first date with girlfriend Dixie Locke was his favorite bolero jacket with a ruffled shirt and black pegged pants with a pink stripe. He wore this same outfit (with a pink shirt) to his unsuccessful audition for the Eddie Bond band in May 1954.

On Saturday nights Elvis sometimes hit the town in his own interpretation of a zoot suit, with loose black pants pulled in at the bottom.

For his High School Senior Prom, Elvis picked out a pink and black suit coat. Pink was his mom's favorite color, at least on a Cadillac, and that was good enough for Elvis to adopt it as his talisman.

Pink was also the dominant color when he turned up to try out with Scotty Moore at his apartment in the summer of 1954: pink slacks with a think black strip, a black shirt, and white shoes. Pink featured in his early performances too; if he wasn't wearing the pink slacks, it might be a pair of pink socks. Pink slacks and an orchid-hued shirt ensured that Elvis did not pass unnoticed in his 1954 pink-and-white Cadillac as he traveled between venues on tour in early 1955. RCA executive Chuck Crumpacker, scouting out Elvis before his label made a move, joked with the young singer that he didn't stand a chance of making it unless he started to dress just a little more flamboyantly.

By April 1956, Elvis was boasting to a reporter that he owned forty suits and twenty-seven pairs of shoes including one pair of blue-suede boots. He went motorcycling on his new Harley that year in the full Brandoesque get-up of black cap and black leather jacket—a look reprised for his 1968 NBC TV Special.

Once he was well on the way to national fame, new manager Colonel Parker persuaded Elvis of the benefits of dressing down. He dropped the gaudy pink in favor of understated but no less striking sharp-tailored blazers with velvet edging and thin stripes, invariably over black pants. Elvis showed up for rehearsals for his first national TV appearance (on "Stage Show") in a dark suit and black shirt. The first time Elvis appeared on *TV Guide* in September 1956 it was in a grey striped blazer and a white shirt, both from Lansky of Memphis. He wore black slacks and a patterned shirt to his first session at the Radio Recorders studio in Hollywood that year.

When the prodigal Elvis returned to Tupelo in September 1956 for a concert and a parade, he wore a blue shirt with rhinestone buttons his mama Gladys made for him. That year Elvis won the baffling accolade of the nation's "Worst Dressed Male TV star" for 1956, despite (because of?) the fact that he had been forced to wear a tux on "The Steve Allen Show."

Color was still in when he wanted to make an impression. Elvis wore a red shirt when he went out on his first date with long-term late Fifties girlfriend Anita Wood.

Elvis turned up to his recording session in June 1958, on furlough from the Army, in full uniform. In the service out in Germany, he wore regulation issue clothes, with the exception of dress uniforms which he had specially made. The night that Priscilla first came round to visit in 1959, he wore a red sweater and tan pants.

Elvis carried on wearing a dress uniform after his discharge from the Army out of choice, though he left behind his combat jacket and sergeant's stripes with Priscilla in Germany as a token of his love.

In 1960, Elvis continued with the more European-tailored look he had adopted when on furlough in Germany. The dark, Italian-cut suits, much like the ones favored by the "Rat Pack," and the dark glasses Elvis and his gang wore, led to a them being called the "Memphis Mafia," especially when they started toting suspicious-looking briefcases.

Elvis rolled in to Los Angeles to begin work on his first film after the Army, *G.I. Blues*, in a mohair suit, white ruffled shirt and a black ascot. The Memphis Mafia look was still in when Elvis arrived in Hawaii for his 1961 concert wearing a black suit, white ruffled shirt, dark tie and side-buckled black shoes. At this time, he favored Louis Roth creations. When Elvis and the gang turned up to shoot in the early Sixties, they were generally dressed in fancy suits, bright shirts and black boots. In Billy Smith's recollection, the phase of snappy

ABOVE LEFT: Elvis in his gold suit in the 1950's. ABOVE CENTER: Performing in Vegas 1971. ABOVE RIGHT: Elvis in the Peacock Suit in Philadelphia, June 1974. RIGHT: Elvis in the Gypsy Star Suit in Ashville, NC July, 1975. BOTTOM RIGHT: Elvis in his final concert in Indianapolis, June, 1977.

co-ordinated dressing ended not long after the Colonel joked that all dressed up in suits, the entourage looked like a bunch of old men.

For many years, Elvis was particularly fond of wearing a yachting cap—an item he sports in one of the most oft-reproduced photos of Elvis in his early teens.

Looking good was important. Girlfriend Sandy Ferra got a dressing down one day when she turned up at Elvis' LA home wearing slacks; he didn't speak to her for hours, then told her that he'd gone to the trouble of dressing up to meet her and he expected the same of her.

For $9,300, MGM fitted Elvis out for 1962 movie It Happened at the World's Fair with ten suits, two cashmere coats and fifty-five ties, all designed by the talented and expensive Sy Devore. Elvis knew all about Devore after Nancy Sinatra presented him with some dress shirts as a gift from Frank on his homecoming from the Army. Devore later revealed that Elvis was not a fan of underwear. Elvis purchased a good deal of clothing from Devore in LA; he also went to celebrity clothesier Jack Taylor.

Elvis was very fastidious about what he wore. He was unhappy filming a scene for Fun in Acapulco in which his character was outfitted in a short-sleeved shirt that wasn't tucked in to his trousers, because he would never do such a thing off-set. He kept hold of a Spanish-themed outfit after making the movie.

In his Sixties movies Elvis was dressed in all manner of fashions, from things he'd never wear like jeans (Kissin' Cousins) to women's clothing (Girl Happy) to very nice duds he was happy to take home afterwards. Perhaps surprisingly for a star who acted almost exclusively in musicals, with the exception of Frankie and Johnny Elvis was put in very few period pieces.

In his football playing days, Elvis fitted out his team with a uniform emblazoned with the team name "E.P. ENTP."

Priscilla says that Elvis favored clothes in black or white, and in bright hues such as red, blue, turquoise or emerald green—the colors he wanted her to wear too. Elvis made it a habit to dress up for dinner.

Elvis wore Italian dress boots that he bought from Hardy's shoes in Memphis. When they stopped manufacturing them, Elvis bought the pattern to that he could have them made bespoke.

When he went through a motorcycle phase in the mid-Sixties, Elvis took Marlon Brando as his role model and went the whole hog with black leather, cool glasses and that cap.

The day Elvis met The Beatles in 1965 he wore black slacks, a tight black bolero jerkin and a red shirt—an outfit he had been wearing to impress for a decade.

Around this time as he delved into spiritual matters he acquired a number of Indian-inspired fashions including kaftans.

Larry Geller says that Elvis' predilection for high-collared shirts grew out of illustrations of meditation masters he saw in David Andreas' book Through the Eyes of the Masters. Designer Bill Belew says that it was illustrations of eighteenth-century gentlemen that gave Elvis the idea, though many sources state that Elvis favored high collars because he believed his neck to be disproportionately long.

Elvis was already wearing Superfly-style fashions in 1966, when he recorded How Great Thou Art.

In 1967 cowboy style was definitely in. With his new Circle G ranch and dozens of horses, Elvis reported to RCA's Studio B facility in Nashville in full cowboy regalia including chaps to record songs for the Clambake soundtrack. Around about this time he had a special riding suit made up the same (natural) color as his hair.

On vacation in Hawaii, Elvis went local in a Hawaiian shirt, white cotton pants and the yachting cap he loved so much.

Elvis arrived to record at American Sound Studios in 1969 dressed in blue leathers and a white shirt.

Elvis did not wear t-shirts, and he only wore simple fruit-of-the-loom briefs. He generally refused to wear shorts on vacation because he considered his legs to be too skinny.

Immediately after his triumphant return to live performance in Las Vegas in the summer of 1969, Elvis changed into a sharp Bill Belew-designed high-collared "mod suit" with a bright scarf around his neck.

In the summer of 1970, Elvis rehearsed for his Vegas engagement in a succession of colorful patterned silk shirts over dark brown pinstriped bell-bottoms (as immortalized in That's The Way It Is).

In December 1970, Elvis turned up in Washington to meet the Deputy Director of the Federal Bureau of Narcotics and Dangerous Drugs John Finlator in a Bill Belew-designed purple suit with cloak, and a lion pendant recently bought from Sol Schwartz, his LA jeweler, plus his Tree of Life pendant engraved with the names of his entourage pals. This was the outfit he wore to see President Nixon,

LEFT: With Steve Allen, after the famous "Hound Dog" performance on The Steve Allen Show. ABOVE: Elvis on tour at the MGM.

accessorized with the outsized boxer's belt that the International Hotel in Las Vegas had given him for his champion performance.

When Elvis started needing prescription glasses in the early Seventies, he designed his own special take on the aviator style with his TCB logo and EP legend.

Elvis liked to sleep in custom-made white silk pajamas.

Dressed by Belew, in the Seventies Elvis was often to be seen in throwback dandified styles, with Edwardian collars, sweeping capes and paisley patterns. He favored cowboy boots offstage, and shiny leather boots onstage.

Elvis turned up at Stax Studio to record in July 1973 in a white suit with a black cape and a Superfly-style hat, the cape perhaps a way of concealing his extra poundage. When Elvis moved onto other styles he gave away his whole "Shaft" wardrobe to a black friend in Memphis.

In 1974 Elvis arrived at Dave Hebler's karate studio just outside Los Angeles in a black coat with red piping, wearing a turban.

In his final years, as his weight fluctuated, Elvis' clothes were regularly let out or tightened to accommodate his bulk. Off-duty, he favored stretch fabrics.

Hanging out at home or in Las Vegas, Elvis liked to lounge in a blue bathrobe.

In the spring of 1977, Elvis favored a black jumpsuit.

Elvis died in yellow and blue pajamas. He was laid to rest in a white casket in a white suit with a pale blue shirt and white tie.

ELVIS SAID IN 1956: "On the streets, out in public, I like real conservative clothes. But on stage I like 'em as flashy as you can get."

ELVIS SAID IN 1956: "They ask me why I wear the clothes I do. What can I say? I just like nice clothes, that's all. I like color and such. Is there something wrong with that?"

ELVIS SAID IN 1961: "I don't know that much about clothes."

GEORGE KLEIN: "He'd wear showbizzy-type stuff to school all the time."

JERRY SCHILLING: "There were no accidents in Elvis' look."

ANITA WOOD: "He never wore the same thing twice. You know, he'd just take them off and dump them."

PAMELA CLARKE KEOGH: "Elvis instinctively recognized the transformative power of clothing—and, indeed, his very life—to simultaneously draw attention to himself and set himself apart from others."

Book:
Elvis Fashion: From Memphis to Vegas, by Julie Mundy, Universe, 2003.

CLOVERS, THE

This popular black R 'n' B group inspired a young Elvis with their close harmonies on early Fifties hits "One Mint Julep," "Devil or Angel" and Leiber and Stoller's "Love Potion No. 9." For most of the Fifties, The Clovers were Atlantic Records' top act.

Elvis covered a number of Clovers hits, starting with a live performance of "Fool, Fool, Fool" in 1955 (not released until 1992 collection The King of Rock 'N' Roll). In the Sixties he laid down "Boss Nova Baby" for the Fun in Acapulco soundtrack, and the hard-edged "Down In The Alley" in 1966.

Elvis also recorded "Tell Me Why," written by Titus Turner who wrote regularly for the group. The Clovers, like Elvis, did well with English-language versions of Italian operetta tune "O Sole Mio," though The Clovers' "There's No Tomorrow" was roundly eclipsed by Elvis' "It's Now Or Never," the biggest-selling international single of his career.

COASTERS, THE

An R 'n' B band closely associated with songwriters Leiber & Stoller, who signed them to their own record label in the early Fifties, had a series of "novelty" successes with songs such as "Smokey Joe's Café," "Yakety Yak," "Charlie Brown" and "Poison Ivy."

Blending doo-wap, nascent rock 'n' roll and a good dollop of comedy, The Coasters had quite a winning formula in the late Fifties and early Sixties. After the Colonel ousted Leiber and Stoller as regular Elvis songwriters in 1960, the only Leiber & Stoller songs Elvis sang that decade were movie song covers of Coasters tunes "Little Egypt" and "Girls! Girls! Girls!." Coasters track "The Climb" also appeared in Viva Las Vegas, though it was sung by the Jubilee Four, not Elvis.

"C'MON EVERYBODY"

Elvis laid down this Joy Byers song—not to be confused with the 1958 Eddie Cochran tune of the same name—for the Viva Las Vegas movie and EP at Radio Recorders on July 9, 1963. In the movie, it serves as the backdrop for a joyous dance duet with Ann-Margret.

The song's first album release was on C'mon Everybody in 1971. Since then, it has appeared on the Double Features issue. Alternates are on FTD releases Silver Screen Stereo and Viva Las Vegas. Singer Bob Johnston's demo is on FTD release Writing For The King.

C'MON EVERYBODY

A July 1971 Camden label budget release of recycled movie tracks not previously released on vinyl. Sales ran out of steam after 100,000 copies and 11 weeks on the chart, when it registered a high of #70.

TRACK LISTING:
1. C'mon Everybody
2. Angel
3. Easy Come, Easy Go
4. A Whistling Tune
5. Follow That Dream
6. King Of The Whole Wide World
7. I'll Take Love
8. Today, Tomorrow And Forever
9. I'm Not The Marrying Kind
10. This Is Living

COHEN, NUDIE
(B. NUTYA KOTLYARENKO, 1902-1984)

A native of Kiev, Cohen was a failed actor who after literally working his way from the bottom up (sewing sequins onto strippers' G-strings in Times Square dives) found a niche in LA making Western suits for the most famous country stars of the Fifties, from Tex Williams to Porter Wagoner. When Hank Williams started buying from "Nudie of Hollywood," other stars at the Grand Ole Opry jumped on the bandwagon. Colonel Parker called on Nudie to make Elvis' $10,000 "solid gold suit" in 1957. Nudie later diversified into car customization, specializing in Cadillacs.

COLLECTIBLES

See MEMORABILIA AND MERCHANDISING.

COLLECTORS GOLD

A 1991 3-disc set of previously unreleased tracks and takes that divided Elvis' musical output into Hollywood, Nashville and Las Vegas. Highlights include the laughing version of "Are You Lonesome Tonight?" and a live version of "Rubberneckin'."

TRACK LISTING:
DISC 1   THE HOLLYWOOD ALBUM
1. G.I. Blues
2. Pocketful Of Rainbows
3. Big Boots
4. Black Star
5. Summer Kisses, Winter Tears
6. I Slipped, I Stumbled, I Fell
7. Lonely Man
8. What A Wonderful Life
9. A Whistling Tune
10. Beyond The Bend
11. One Broken Heart For Sale
12. You're The Boss
13. Roustabout
14. Girl Happy
15. So Close, Yet So Far
16. Stop, Look And Listen
17. Am I Ready
18. How Can You Lose What You Never Had

DISC 2   THE NASHVILLE ALBUM
1. Like A Baby
2. There's Always Me
3. I Want You With Me
4. Gently
5. Give Me The Right
6. I Met Her Today
7. Night Rider
8. Just Tell Her Jim Said Hello
9. Ask Me
10. Memphis Tennessee
11. Love Me Tonight
12. Witchcraft
13. Come What May
14. Love Letters
15. Goin' Home

DISC 3   LIVE IN LAS VEGAS 1969
1. Blue Suede Shoes
2. I Got A Woman
3. Heartbreak Hotel
4. Love Me Tender
5. Baby, What You Want Me To Do
6. Runaway
7. Surrender / Are You Lonesome Tonight?
8. Rubberneckin'
9. Memories
10. Introductions
11. Jailhouse Rock / Don't Be Cruel
12. Inherit The Wind

13. This Is The Story
14. Mystery Train / Tiger Man
15. Funny How Time Slips Away
16. Loving You / Reconsider Baby
17. What'd I Say

The name "Collectors Gold" was actually first used in 1982 as part of a UK-released box set of EPs (featuring alternate takes) titled *The EP Collection, Volume 2.*

COLLIE, BIFF
(1926-1992)

Biff Collie was a leading Houston DJ on WMPS who was so impressed with the Elvis show he saw at the Eagle's Nest in Memphis in November 1954 that he booked him for a $150 appearance at the Houston Hoedown he was arranging the following week. When he was in Houston, Elvis' date at the Palladium Club was extended for a further two nights "by popular demand."

Collie also invited Elvis and the Blue Moon Boys down after Christmas 1954 to play the Cook's Hoedown Club in Houston.

Collie was inducted into the Country DJ Hall of Fame in 1978.

COLORADO

- Aspen
Elvis, Priscilla, Lisa Marie and a select few entourage pals went on a ski vacation to Aspen in January 1969.

- Denver
Elvis played the Coliseum in Denver on April 8, 1956. He finished two tours at this venue in the early Seventies: on November 17, 1970 and on April 30, 1973. Elvis made a number of friends among the city's police force who helped out on security at his concerts. Elvis was at the McNichols Arena on April 23, 1976.

- Vail
Elvis flew to Denver, Colorado with seventeen friends and family for a 2-week vacation in Vail in January 1976. Though most of the group skied, Elvis' only taste of winter sports was snowmobiling. His nocturnal scootings provoked public complaints by then President Ford's daughter Susan, and unflattering coverage in the *National Enquirer.* Elvis briefly looked into buying a home in Vail.

"COLUMBUS STOCKADE BLUES"

A song Elvis knew from childhood, written by country pioneers Thomas Bardy and Jimmy Tarlton. No official recording exists, though Elvis sings a couple of lines as he launches into "Promised Land" on *Essential Elvis Vol. 5*, taken from a recording session at Stax Studios in 1973. At the time, Elvis told cousin Billy Smith that he first sang the song when he was just three years old.

"COME ALONG"

A swing-flavored track Elvis recorded at Radio Recorders on May 12, 1965 for the soundtrack of *Frankie and Johnny*, based on traditional tune reworked by David Hess, laid down at Radio Recorders. Since the original soundtrack release, the song has surfaced on the *Double Features* and FTD releases for the movie.

"COME WHAT MAY"

This track, written by Frank Tableporter, had been a hit for both Clyde McPhatter and Etta James before Elvis took it on in Nashville on May 28, 1966. Elvis had previously sung the song at Graceland with Jerry Lee Lewis (who recorded it for Sun, though the track was never released).

"Come What May (You Are Mine)"—to give it its full title—was selected as a rockier B-side for single release with "Love Letters" in June 1966.

Though never issued on an LP during Elvis' lifetime, it has since appeared on *From Nashville To Memphis* and *Tomorrow Is A Long Time.* Alternate versions have graced a number of later Elvis collections including *Collectors Gold, From Nashville To Memphis* and *Today Tomorrow & Forever* (complete with an Elvis gargle). FTD releases *Long Lonely Highway* and *So High* also feature alternates.

"COMEBACK SPECIAL" ON NBC, 1968

This hour-long TV show resurrected Elvis' career when he was perilously close to the end. Ever after the NBC TV Special has been more commonly known by its unofficial name, the "Comeback Special." For more information, *see* NBC TV SPECIAL.

COMEDY

Elvis had a well-exercised sense of humor was used to making people laugh, whether it was his entourage or a concert hall of fans. He had a quick wit, a way with words and he loved to tell or crack up over a joke. Once he got going it could take him a long time to quit.

It wasn't always that way. His relative outcast status as a teenager at school had him as the butt

A candid photo of Elvis at the Colorado Hotel in 1976.

of jokes for wearing weird clothes and sporting long hair.

Elvis often shared the bill with a comic turn or two in his busy touring schedule across the South as he established himself in the mid-Fifties. After he had conquered his initial stage fright Elvis became quite the funnyman with risqué banter and a knockabout routine with bassist Bill Black, who would mimic Elvis' wild moves, up to and including when Elvis slung his guitar round his neck.

One of the first things Colonel Parker did when he began managing Elvis' bookings was to try and stamp out this "unprofessional" behavior. If they had any run-ins at all in these first couple of years, it was over this. A year and a half into his career and poised to achieve national stardom, William Morris agent Harry Kalcheim felt the need to write to Parker and suggest that Elvis drop "the clowning."

During his first unsuccessful crack at breaking Las Vegas in April/May 1956, Elvis left his audience with pearls of cornball wisdom such as, "Don't go milking a cow on a rainy day. If there's lightning, you may be left holding the bag." He introduced "Blue Suede Shoes" as " 'Get Out Of The Stables, Grandma, You're Too Old To Be Horsing Around'." When bemused bandleader Freddy Martin tried to play along with the joke, Elvis suggested another made-up classic, "Take Back Your Golden Garter, My Leg Is Turnin' Green," and then "Darling, You Broke My Heart When You Went Away, But I'll Break Your Jaw When You Come Back." Performing that same song a month later, Elvis told his audience that they'd been playing the tune for 25 or 30 years, and described it as "not only sad, it's plum pitiful."

As well as a legendary appetite for pranks and horseplay, Elvis loved telling jokes and hearing them told. His entourage made the perfect traveling comedy environment. At times they would keep up a barrage of banter and repartee, sometimes including surreal wordplay as they riffed off one another. One example of this wordplay was when he referred to his favorite James Dean film as "Rebel Without A Pebble."

In the 70s, Elvis hired a number of comics as warm-up acts, many of them veterans of stage and TV. Comic turns included Sammy Shore, Nipsey Russell and Bob Melvin for a brief time, and then from late 1971 Jackie Kahane.

His return to touring allowed plenty of scope for joshing band members and fellow musicians. Occasionally this slipped into a pharmaceutically-fueled monologue that might get a little close to the bone for members of the audience or a musician singled out for teasing.

Elvis' on-stage shenanigans in Las Vegas at the end of his summer 1973 engagement led to a major bust-up with Colonel Parker, who accused him of unacceptable behavior after he horsed around on stage and then berated the Hilton management.

Elvis' concert introductions were a constant opportunity for comedy. Elvis enjoyed introducing himself and his band members as other singers or instrumentalists. Sometimes he was very inventive: he was known to run together his drummer and bass player's names to make "Tuttsheff" (a play on "tough shit"), or present Charlie Hodge as "Willie Booger" (slang for ghost or a mythical Bigfoot creature).

Later Elvis has provided an easy target for comics ever since his death. Dave Barry has quipped, "eventually everybody has to die, except Elvis." In one of his sketches, Bill Hicks suggests that Elvis didn't die from drugs but from shock at the bill he received from General Motors for giving away all those Cadillacs.

ELVIS SAID IN 1973 "I know we kid a lot and have fun and everything—but we really love to sing, play music and entertain people. As long as I can do that, I'll be a happy son of a bitch."

COMICS

Elvis was famously an avid comic book fan as a kid. His favorite character of all, Captain Marvel Jr.—who wore a cape and had a thunderbolt motif—is said to have inspired him to follow his dream and become a superhero in life (with his own cape and thunderbolt motif). It wasn't just Captain Marvel; Elvis collected and swapped Batman, the Lone Ranger, Superman, Tarzan and Hopalong Cassidy

Comics were by far and away the most popular form of literature when Elvis was growing up. Elvis carefully kept his comic books catalogued and in order, and would only lend them to friends or cousins who would give them back in good condition.

Since his death, Elvis has graced the pages of at least a dozen comic books. Many of these are graphic novel biographies; some, like 1991 series *Elvis Shrugged*, portray him as a fully-fledged superhero who saves the music industry from itself.

ELVIS IN COMICS—A SELECTION:

Elvis: The Swinging Kid, by Charles Hamblett, May Fair Books, 1962.
Elvis in "Tintin" magazine, Belgium, 1977.
Invasion of the Elvis Zombies, by Gary Panter, Arrebato Editorial, 1984.
Elvis for Beginners. A Writers and Readers Documentary Comic Book, by Jill Perlman and Wayne White, Unwin Paperbacks, 1996.
The King, by Rich Koslowski, Top Shelf Productions, 2005.

ELVIS SAID: "I was the hero of every comic book I ever read."

ELAINE DUNDY: "It was Captain Marvel, Jr., who helped mold Elvis' personality, humble and humorous, and who crystallized his desire to save the world and his family."

COMMAND PERFORMANCES: THE ESSENTIAL 60'S MASTERS II

A 1995 release showing that you can't get too much of a good thing, with 2 discs of songs from Elvis' Sixties soundtracks.

TRACK LISTING:
DISC: 1
1. G.I. Blues
2. Wooden Heart
3. Shoppin' Around
4. Doin' The Best I Can
5. Flaming Star
6. Wild In The Country
7. Lonely Man
8. Blue Hawaii
9. Rock-A-Hula Baby
10. Can't Help Falling In Love
11. Beach Boy Blues
12. Hawaiian Wedding Song
13. Follow That Dream (alternate take)
14. Angel
15. King Of The Whole Wide World
16. I Got Lucky
17. Girls! Girls! Girls!
18. Because Of Love
19. Return To Sender
20. One Broken Heart For Sale
21. I'm Falling In Love Tonight
22. They Remind Me Too Much Of You
23. Fun In Acapulco
24. Bossa Nova Baby
25. Marguerita
26. Mexico

27. Kissin' Cousins
28. One Boy, Two Little Girls
29. Once Is Enough
30. Viva Las Vegas
31. What'd I Say

DISC: 2
1. Roustabout
2. Poison Ivy League
3. Little Egypt
4. There's A Brand New Day On The Horizon
5. Girl Happy
6. Puppet On A String
7. Do The Clam
8. Harem Holiday
9. So Close, Yet So Far
10. Frankie And Johnny
11. Please Don't Stop Loving Me
12. Paradise, Hawaiian Style
13. This Is My Heaven
14. Spinout
15. All That I Am
16. I'll Be Back
17. Easy Come, Easy Go
18. Double Trouble
19. Long Legged Girl (With The Short Dress On)
20. Clambake
21. You Don't Know Me
22. Stay Away, Joe
23. Speedway
24. Your Time Hasn't Come Yet, Baby
25. Let Yourself Go
26. Almost In Love
27. A Little Less Conversation
28. Edge Of Reality
29. Charro!
30. Clean Up Your Own Back Yard
31. Change Of Habit

COMPLETE DRESSING ROOM SESSIONS

An unofficial 2000 release on the Memphis Sound label of Elvis rehearsing for the 1968 NBC TV Special

TRACK LISTING:
1. I Got A Woman
2. Blue Moon
3. Young Love
4. Oh Happy Day
5. Guitar Boogie (instrumental)
6. When It Rains, It Really Pours
7. Blue Christmas
8. Are You Lonesome Tonight?/That's My Desire
9. That's My Desire (continued)
10. That's When Your Heartaches Begin
11. That's When Your Heartaches Begin (continued)
12. Peter Gunn Theme / Baby What's Wrong
13. Love Me
14. When My Blue Moon Turns To Gold Again
15. Blue Christmas
16. Santa Claus Is Back In Town
17. Danny Boy (instrumental)
18. Baby What You Want Me Do (instrumental)
19. Love Me
20. Tiger Man
21. That's All Right, Mama
22. Peter Gunn Theme (instrumental)
23. Santa Claus Is Back In Town
24. Lawdy, Miss Clawdy
25. One Night
26. Blue Christmas
27. When My Blue Moon Turns To Gold Again
28. Blue Moon Of Kentucky
29. Dialogue
30. Baby What You Want Me Do
31. If I Can Dream (instrumental)
32. If I Can Dream (false start)
33. If I Can Dream

COMPLETE 50S MASTERS, THE

See THE KING OF ROCK AND ROLL: COMPLETE 50'S MASTERS

COMPLETE MILLION DOLLAR QUARTET, THE

A unique sound document as Elvis holds an impromptu jam with Carl Perkins, Jerry Lee Lewis and Johnny Cash at Sun Records in late 1956, re-released with additional material for the 50th anniversary in 2006, for the first time in order, and with improved sound quality.

TRACK LISTING:
1. Instrumental
2. Love Me Tender (instrumental)
3. Jingle Bells (Instrumental)
4. White Christmas (instrumental)
5. Reconsider Baby
6. Don't Be Cruel
7. Don't Be Cruel
8. Paralyzed
9. Don't Be Cruel
10. There's No Place Like Home
11. When The Saints Go Marchin' In
12. Softly And Tenderly
13. When God Dips His Love In My Heart
14. Just A Little Talk With Jesus
15. Jesus Walked That Lonesome Valley
16. I Shall Not Be Moved
17. Peace In The Valley
18. Down By The Riverside
19. I'm With A Crowd But So Alone
20. Farther Along
21. Blessed Jesus (Hold My Hand)
22. On The Jericho Road
23. I Just Can't Make It By Myself
24. Little Cabin On The Hill
25. Summertime Is Passed And Gone
26. I Hear A Sweet Voice Calling
27. Sweetheart You Done Me Wrong
28. Keeper Of The Key
29. Crazy Arms
30. Don't Forbid Me
31. Too Much Monkey Business
32. Brown Eyed Handsome Man
33. Out Of Sight, Out Of Mind
34. Brown Eyed Handsome Man
35. Don't Forbid Me
36. You Belong To My Heart
37. Is It So Strange
38. That's When Your Heartaches Begin
39. Brown Eyed Handsome Man
40. Rip It Up
41. I'm Gonna Bid My Blues Goodbye
42. Crazy Arms
43. That's My Desire
44. End Of The Road
45. Black Bottom Stomp
46. You're The Only Star In My Blue Heaven
47. Elvis Says Goodbye

COMPLETE ON TOUR SESSIONS, THE

A 3-volume bootleg collection of Elvis performances mainly from late March 1972 while preparing the Elvis On Tour concert documentary, a soundboard recording on Vicky Records, sometimes referred to as the "Gospel Disc."

TRACK LISTING:
VOL. 1
1. Johnny B. Goode
2. Separate Ways
3. You Gave Me A Mountain (w. false start)
4. I'll Remember You / Polk Salad Annie
5. Release Me
6. Proud Mary
7. Cattle Call / For The Good Times /

8. Somewhere Over The Rainbow
8. For The Good Times
9. Separate Ways
10. Always On My Mind
11. I Can't Stop Loving You
12. Funny How Time Slips Away
13. Burning Love
14. An American Trilogy
15. A Big Hunk O' Love
16. For The Good Times
17. See See Rider
18. El Paso / Dressing Room Conversation
19. It's Over
20. Film Title Revelation - Little Rock Concert Promoter Interview

VOL. 2
1. Sweet Sweet Spirit (partial) / I, John
2. Lead Me, Guide Me
3. Sweet Sweet Spirit
4. Nearer My God To Thee (w. reprise)
5. Lighthouse
6. George Klein Interview
7. Funny How Time Slips Away (multiple takes)
8. Proud Mary
9. Always On My Mind
10. Lighthouse (few lines) / I , John / I Need Your Lovin' Everyday
11. It's My Time To Praise The Lord
12. Time Has Made A Change / I Should Have Been Crucified
13. Elvis - Film Director Interview

VOL. 3
1. Don't Be Cruel (instrumental)
2. Love Me / All Shook Up
3. Heartbreak Hotel
4. Teddy Bear / Don't Be Cruel
5. Hound Dog
6. Lawdy, Miss Clawdy
7. Burning Love
8. For The Good Times (take 9)
9. See See Rider
10. Never Been To Spain / Help Me Make It Through The Night / The First Time Ever I Saw Your Face (partial)
11. For The Good Times (take 1)
12. For The Good Times (takes 3,5,6)
13. For The Good Times (take 7)
14. Vernon Presley Interview

COMPLETE SUN SESSIONS, THE

A 1987 RCA 2-LP set billed at the time as definitive, with master takes, multiple outtakes and liner notes from Peter Guralnick. Later CD issues have two songs fewer.

TRACK LISTING:
1. That's All Right (Mama)
2. Blue Moon Of Kentucky
3. Good Rockin' Tonight
4. I Don't Care If The Sun Don't Shine
5. Milkcow Blues Boogie
6. You're A Heartbreaker
7. Baby Let's Play House
8. I'm Left, You're Right, She's Gone
9. Mystery Train
10. I Forgot To Remember To Forget
11. I Love You Because
12. Blue Moon
13. Tomorrow Night
14. I'll Never Let You Go (Little Darlin')
15. Just Because
16. Tryin' To Get To You
17. Harbor Lights
18. I Love You Because
19. That's All Right (Mama)
20. Blue Moon Of Kentucky
21. I Don't Care If The Sun Don't Shine
22. I'm Left, You're Right, She's Gone
23. I'll Never Let You Go (Little Darlin')

24. When It Rains, It Really Pours
25. I Love You Because (multiple takes)
26. I'm Left, You're Right, She's Gone (multiple takes)

An updated and more complete import version with this title came out in 2006 with additional takes and interview material.

TRACK LISTING:
DISC 1:
1. ABC News Clip
2. That's All Right (Mama)
3. Blue Moon Of Kentucky
4. Good Rockin' Tonight
5. I Don't Care If The Sun Don't Shine
6. Milkcow Blues Boogie
7. You're A Heartbreaker
8. I Love You Because
9. Harbor Lights
10. Blue Moon
11. I'll Never Let You Go
12. Just Because
13. I Love You Because (Take 1)
14. I Love You Because (take 2)
15. That's All Right Mama (take 1, 3)
16. Blue Moon Of Kentucky (slow)
17. Tomorrow Night (no guitar solo)
18. Tomorrow Night (take 7)
19. Blue Moon (take 2)
20. Blue Moon (take 5)
21. I'm Left, You're Right, She's Gone (take 7)
22. I'm Left, You're Right, She's Gone (take 9)
23. I'm Left, You're Right, She's Gone (take 12)
24. I Love You Because (Whistling Intro.) (take 3)
25. Harbor Lights (take 3)
26. I'll Never Let You Go (alternate take)
27. I Don't Care If The Sun Don't Shine (takes 1-3)
28. I'll Never Stand In Your Way (demo)
29. It Wouldn't Be The Same Without You (demo)

DISC: 2
1. Interview
2. Baby Let's Play House
3. I'm Left, You're Right, She's Gone
4. I Forgot To Remember To Forget
5. Mystery Train
6. Tryin' To Get To You
7. When It Rains, It Really Pours
8. I'm Left, You're Right, She's Gone (slow)
9. I'm Left, You're Right, She's Gone (slow)(alternate take)
10. Fool, Fool, Fool (demo)
11. Shake, Rattle & Roll (demo)
12. Interview
13. That's All Right Mama (live)
14. Blue Moon Of Kentucky (live)
15. Tweedlee Dee (live)
16. That's All Right Mama (live)
17. Hearts Of Stone (live)
18. Money Honey (live)
19. I Don't Care If The Sun Don't Shine (live)
20. I Got A Woman (live)
21. Good Rockin' Tonight (live)
22. Baby Let's Play House (live)
23. Maybellene (live)
24. I'm Left, You're Right, She's Gone (live)
25. My Happiness
26. That's When Your Heartaches Begin

CONCERTS

Elvis set records with his vinyl output but it was live performing that put him on the map in 1954 and 1955, and live performing that was the focus of his musical passion throughout the Seventies. Elvis felt at home in the recording studio; he had a love affair with his fans on the road.

This entry contains general information on Elvis' live performing. For information on individual shows, look under entries for each State or for the venue itself. It should be noted that many of Elvis' early gigs were impromptu and poorly-documented; references in this encyclopedia refer to events at which it is certain Elvis played.

Elvis' first public engagement—the first of some 1,750 over a 23-year entertainment career—predated his debut Sun recording by some seventeen years when, according to his mother, as a two-year-old he wriggled free in church to join in with the choir. At school, Elvis did not shine academically, though by elementary school he was toting around a guitar and singing to anyone who would listen.

When he was in the fifth grade, he sang "Old Shep" at the Mississippi-Alabama Fair and Dairy Show, an event that attracted a crowd of up to 2,000 people. First prize went to a girl he knew called Shirley Jane Jones who sang "My Dreams Are Getting Better All the Time," though she later said that Elvis was bitterly disappointed that day because he only scraped fifth prize. Early Elvis biographers erroneously stated that Elvis won 2nd prize, worth $5 and a free ride on anything he wanted at the fair. For the record, Elvis left no trace at other talent contests he may have entered. He is said to have sung "Leaf On A Tree" as a goodbye song to his classmates at Milam.

Relatives have told interviewer that Gladys and Uncle Frank Smith would take Elvis to radio station WELO in Tupelo to sing on their amateur hour shows. Some people remember Elvis busking in Tupelo on Spring Street, though such recollections may be *post hoc*.

After the Presleys moved to Memphis, friends at the time recall Elvis regularly performing solo and with pals outside the Lauderdale Courts where they lived. According to Tupelo author Roy Turner, Elvis tried and failed at two more talent chows in town, held at the Lyric Theater.

Elvis' first adult performance came in his senior year at High School. He was act number 16 ("Guitarist . . . Elvis Prestly") at the Humes High School Annual Minstrel Show, held on April 9, 1953. Elvis later said: "I wasn't popular in school. I wasn't dating anybody . . . And then they entered me in this talent show, and I came out and did my "Till I Waltz Again with You," by Teresa Brewer . . . it was amazing how popular I became after that." Other versions have him singing "Keep Them Cold, Icy Fingers Off Of Me" and his faithful standby, "Old Shep." Of all the acts, Elvis was the one who was allowed the encore.

Before his first professional recording session, Elvis may have performed at the Silver Stallion night club in Memphis with Humes High School friends, based on the evidence of a plug in the Humes Yearbook.

Elvis' first live show as a professional is a matter of some dispute. Within a couple of weeks of laying down "That's All Right (Mama)" at Sun, Elvis and his bandsmen played a Saturday night slot at the Bon Air Club in Memphis, starting on July 17, 1954. Some biographers claim that Elvis first performed at the Overton Park Shell, in a bill put together by DJ Bob Neal, with hillbilly star Slim Whitman headlining, on July 30, 1954—Elvis himself said this in later years, but his memory was no more foolproof than anyone else's.

It has been claimed that in May 1953 Elvis hitched almost 300 miles south to Meridian, Mississippi, to compete in a talent show at the Jimmie Rodgers Festival, where he won second prize. Author Elaine Dundy speculates that this show is usually ignored by biographers because Elvis took against the town after they booed him off a year or two later for playing his new-fangled rock 'n' roll; other accounts have the date as a triumph for El, and most don't include it all.

An alternative claim for Elvis' first performance before a live audience was a gig before the

Moose Lodge at Columbia Mutual Towers, together with Ronnie Smith, just before Sun Records called Elvis in to rehearse with Scotty Moore and Bill Black. However, in July 1955, Elvis told an interviewer that he had never performed live before he cut his first record.

What is certain is that after "That's All Right (Mama)" came out, Elvis and the Blue Moon Boys landed a three-month weekend residency from the summer of 1954 at The Eagle's Nest in Memphis. Elvis' first performance at the venue may have been fronting the Scotty and Bill's band the Starlite Wranglers; Elvis chroniclers have also reported that in the summer of '54 Elvis sang with the Malcolm Yelvington Band.

With Sam Phillips, Scotty Moore and Bob Neal all actively seeking exposure for a hot young star on the up, it didn't take long for bigger, higher profile venues to show an interest. First up was the Overton Park Shell on a bill put together by Bill Neal. Before 1954 was out, Elvis had also performed at the Grand Ole Opry in Nashville and the Louisiana Hayride in Shreveport. With only two singles to his name, Elvis' main problem was material. As the months progressed, he and back-up band Scotty Moore and Bill Black expanded their repertoire with cover versions of popular hits; the fans went wild whatever he played, and the screaming was sometimes so loud that the music was effectively drowned out. Country singer Troy Deramus saw Elvis at the Louisiana Hayride: "He was wearing a pink-and-black suit and he moved like a snake inside his clothes. It drove the girls wild. While he was performing, he had to pull his pants up several times. They kept slipping down from all his squirming. He performed for quite a while, and every now and then he'd grin and the girls would scream more."

Life onstage with Elvis was a hostile place to be. Scotty Moore recalls, "It was bedlam onstage. The noise was so loud we couldn't hear him to play; we had to watch him . . . The audience would scream and we'd get bits and pieces, but for the most part we couldn't hear him."

Elvis toured incessantly through 1955, racking up more than 300 shows in the busiest year of his professional life, surviving car accidents, jealous boyfriends and overzealous female fans. He continued to keep up this hectic pace until the summer of 1956, by which time he had started to appear on national TV and was well on his way to becoming a coast-to-coast phenomenon. When Colonel Parker took over at the start of 1956, shrewdly he only booked Elvis into venues that he knew he could sell out. On the rare occasions that tickets shifted slowly in a new part of the country, Parker always came up with some smart gimmick to ensure that the venue was full to bursting.

With almost 500 shows and a number of full-blown fan riots under his belt, Elvis was ill-prepared for the lukewarm response he got from an older audience when he first played Las Vegas in the Spring of 1956. Despite his disappointment, he learned a thing or two about how to turn an audience around; he also realized that if he was to transcend his teen idol status to a wider audience, he needed to change his stage act, as the Colonel had been telling him for some time.

Elvis took off no more than a few days here and there in the two years after signing to Sun in July 1954. In July 1956 he finally took a month's vacation in Biloxi and Miami. He plunged right back into touring, though by this time the Colonel had started implementing his "leave 'em wanting more" policy and making sure that the tours were shorter. By the end of 1957 Colonel Parker had practically stopped booking Elvis for live shows.

Elvis effectively began a ten-year break from live concerts when he joined the Army in the Spring of 1958. The Colonel was adamant that Elvis should not take the soft option and join Special Services; singing for free was the last thing the Colonel wanted. Off base at his Bad

Nauheim home, Elvis often sat at the piano for long sing-song sessions with whoever was around, as his way of helping the time pass. On a couple of occasions he regaled fellow platoon members with an impromptu performance at the NCO Club. A cleaning lady in the room at one such performance was overcome by tears; Elvis consoled her with a kiss on the cheek.

Back from Germany, Elvis' movie commitments to no fewer than three Hollywood studios and to record label RCA meant that the Colonel had no interest in sending his boy out across the country. Elvis did no live performances in 1960 and just two concerts in early 1961: at a home-town charity benefit on "Elvis Presley Day" in Memphis, and in March that year to raise funds for a monument to the USS *Arizona* in Hawaii. This was Elvis' last live show until 1969, despite no lack of proposals. In late 1962, plans reached an advanced stage to send Elvis on a huge forty-three date tour, for which he would have been paid a cool $1 million, until RCA pulled the plug.

After almost a decade off the touring circuit, Elvis next felt the electricity of a live audience during recordings of his 1968 NBC TV Special. In July 1968—before the TV Special was aired—Elvis told an interviewer, "I miss the personal contact with audiences." In the days after the NBC Special aired in early December 1968, Tom Diskin announced that Elvis was considering a return to live concerts. The Colonel was already in advanced negotiations on a deal for Elvis to take a four-week engagement at the soon-to-opened International Hotel in Las Vegas, performing two shows a night, every night of the week.

Elvis spent much of the first half of 1969 putting together a stage show that conveyed the energy and intensity of his NBC TV Special. The basic structure of past hits and a smattering of new songs was to become a successful formula that Elvis replicated in over 1100 shows between 1969 and his death in 1977.

Elvis told his TCB band that what he wanted was for all his songs to be fresh, not imitations of how he had played them in the past. In the run-up to his International Hotel debut, Elvis and the band rehearsed at the RCA studio on Sunset Boulevard in LA. Elvis worked with Charlie Hodge between rehearsal sessions to whittle down the songs to a one-hour repertoire. Rehearsals shifted to Las Vegas a week before opening night, this time with backing vocalists. Final rehearsals took place in the concert hall with the thirty-piece International Hotel house orchestra conducted by Bobby Morris, who had helped with many of the arrangements.

The show was a huge triumph, though once again Elvis had to overcome a debilitating bout of nerves. His long overdue return to the live stage began with "Blue Suede Shoes," climaxed with showstopper "Can't Help Falling Love," and featured current hit "In The Ghetto." He told a journalist, "I've always wanted to perform on the stage again for the last nine years, and it's been building inside of me since 1965, until the strain became intolerable." Drummer Ronnie Tutt defines those first few shows as "incredibly electric, very, very high energy. . . . Not many performers evoke that kind of wild excitement and intensity." His boundless enthusiasm is apparent on live albums released at that time, in bootlegs and on recent FTD releases such as *Elvis At The International*.

The closing-night concert on Elvis' second month-long tenure at the International Hotel in the winter of 1970 is regarded by many one of the peak Elvis experiences, including an impromptu medley and a rare stage appearance by the Colonel. As ever, Elvis stuck by the Colonel's iron rule of never giving an encore; by now the

Elvis on stage in Canada in 1957

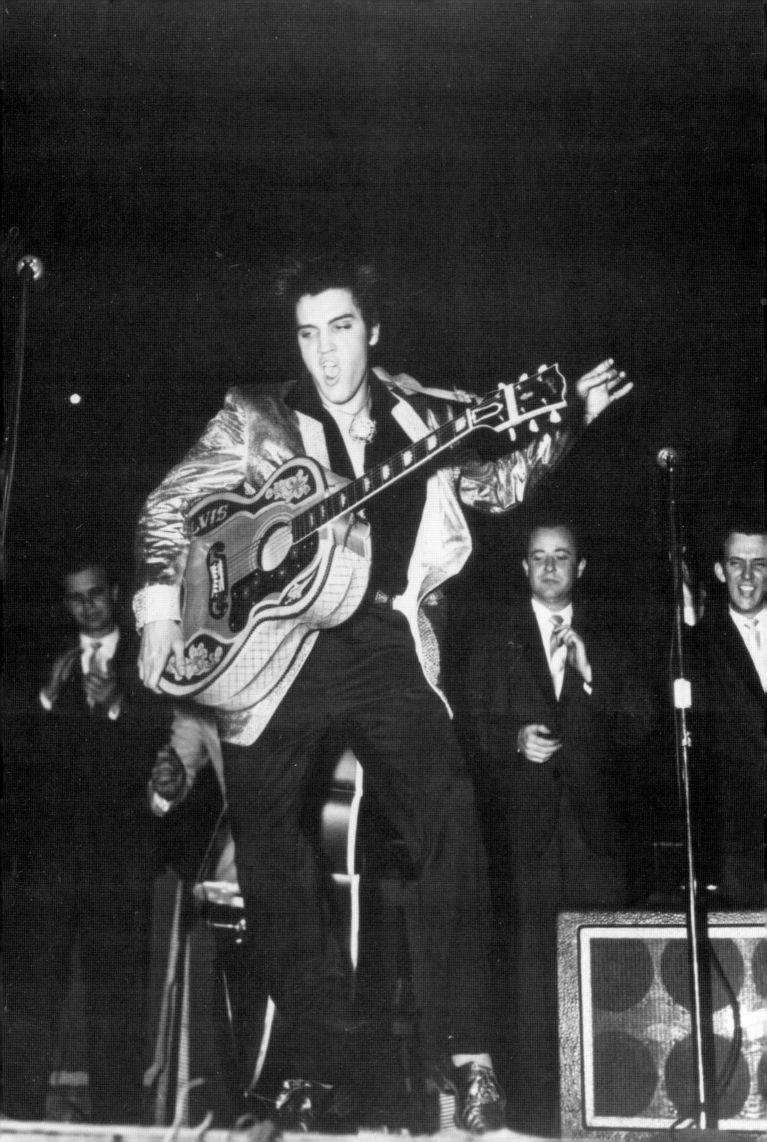

hotel management had impressed on Elvis the importance of keeping his show down to an hour so that the punters could be out at the gambling tables again—in the summer of 1969, if the fancy took him Elvis would overrun a long way on his midnight shows.

By early 1970, the Colonel was once more booking Elvis at venues outside Las Vegas. Elvis' three-night stint at the brand new Houston Astrodome was an unprecedented sell-out, attracting a quarter of a million people and underlining his renewed reputation as a king-sized attraction. The Colonel sent Elvis back out on the road in September 1970, on a six-date national tour. Every date sold out within a few hours of tickets being made available.

The general schedule for each show was an opening session by the Sweet Inspirations (or Voice between 1973 and 1975), then a comedian, and then the man himself.

In 1971 the Colonel upped Elvis' Las Vegas earnings from new hotel owners the Hiltons. Figures in hand, the Colonel pointed out that Elvis sold an average of 3,840 seats per day, compared with 3,000 for Tom Jones and 2,600 for Barbara Streisand.

In November 1971 the Colonel sent Elvis on a longer, 12-date tour, staring in Minneapolis and ending in Salt Lake City.

As Elvis returned to live performing, he followed a pattern of rehearsing new songs and then gradually discarding most of them before the first show in his Las Vegas residency. As the month progressed, more and more of the new material would be phased out. An hour long show did not provide a great deal of latitude to insert new material anyway. In 1972, the songs that made the cut were all songs of love lost after Priscilla told him she was leaving: "It's Over" and "It's Impossible" were two of the titles. That year Elvis also debuted a medley that would soon become one of his showstoppers: Mickey Newbury's "American Trilogy."

Many of these new songs found their way onto one of the six live albums RCA released in the early Seventies (RCA did not release any live Elvis albums at all until the 1968 NBC TV Special, and that was only live in the broadest sense of the term). Live albums got round Elvis' reticence to go into the studio, and also marked a fight back against the bootleggers, who had had a field day ever since Elvis started playing live again. Elvis' 1972 Madison Square Garden performance live album *Elvis As Recorded At Madison Square Garden* was brought out in double quick time precisely to head off the bootleg threat.

Backstage after a concert was either an exciting or a dangerous place to be for attractive women (depending on how much of an Elvis fan they were). Petula Clark recounted an occasion after a 1973 show when she went backstage with Karen Carpenter. One by one, Elvis' entourage left, until it was just Elvis making it very clear what his plans were for the rest of the night. Petula and Karen made their excuses and left.

By this time, when Elvis was touring he was leasing three planes to shift around 80 people, while trucks moved two complete stage set-ups to make sure that the next date was ready to roll.

Elvis' June 1972 concerts at Madison Square Garden reawakened insecurities in Elvis. Unusually for a live show, he, the band and the orchestra rehearsed for a few days, working out a slew of new tracks, very few of which were ultimately included in the show. Such was the demand for tickets to see Elvis that an unprecedented fourth show was added, making Elvis the only artist ever to sell out the Madison Square Garden four nights in a row. The shows grossed close to three quarters of a million dollars, a record for one of the most prestigious venues in the nation. The *New York Times*, so standoffish

about his talents in the past, hailed him as "A Prince From Another Planet."

Elvis went on a third tour in 1972 that started off in Lubbock, swung through the South West, took in California and ended on Hawaii.

Until Elvis' winter 1973 booking at the Las Vegas Hilton, his shows almost always went on regardless of his growing health problems. That year he suffered such a heavy bout of flu that he lost his voice and was forced to cancel a number of scheduled appearances. Nevertheless, 1973 became Elvis' banner year for live performing, as he gave a staggering 168 shows.

Crowds were as wild during Elvis' Seventies tours as they had been in the Fifties. In Sonny West's words, "They are ordinary honest men and housewives and stuff and yet when they get in that crowd when Elvis is up there, they become wild, wild animals."

Elvis' world-girdling *Aloha From Hawaii* concert broadcast live by satellite in early 1973, set up by the Colonel partly to placate Elvis' continuing desire to tour outside North America, only triggered more offers from Britain, Japan and Europe. The Colonel always found a way to put off the promoters and Elvis.

Elvis' summer season at the Las Vegas Hilton in 1973 began poorly and got worse as his intake of drugs hindered rather than helped his performance. One reviewer in the *Hollywood Reporter* was moved to write "It's Elvis at his most indifferent, uninterested, and unappealing . . .. His personality was lost in one of the most ill-prepared, unsteady, and most disheartening performances of his Las Vegas career . . .. It is a tragedy, disheartening and absolutely depressing to see Elvis in such diminishing stature." Fans also noticed that, out of character, Elvis was just going through the motions.

And yet Elvis was back on form by the time he returned to Las Vegas in the winter of 1974, and on a three-week tour of venues in the Southern states that March.

In 1974 Elvis went on three tours as well as fulfilling residencies at Las Vegas and Tahoe before the summer was over, in his June swing taking in many places in the deep south where he hadn't played for almost two decades. His fourth tour that year began badly, with Elvis looking out of sorts. Wherever he performed, reviewers noted his lack of energy and commitment. That year Elvis gave a staggering 156 concerts.

How well a concert came across—and how long Elvis and the band stayed on—depended a great deal on how enthusiastic the audience was. When a venue was really buzzing, Elvis might stay on for an extra 20 minutes or more.

In 1975, Elvis once again fitted in three tours before his summer 1975 residency in Las Vegas, starting in April 1975 with a sweep through the south and Florida, put together around a benefit concert for victims of a tornado in Mississippi. Performances from these dates were released in 1980 on the 8-disc box *Elvis Aron Presley*, as well as surfacing on many bootlegs. The FTD live selection *Southern Nights*, released in 2006, shows just how eclectic his song selection was during these tours.

By this time, there was an unmistakable slowdown in the pacing and energy of Elvis' performances. Once Elvis acquired his own planes, after each show a limo would take him directly from the venue and on to the next city, or sometimes back to Memphis.

By the end of his performing career, Elvis believed that he needed industrial quantities of drugs and pharmaceuticals to get on stage and through his tours. Dr. Nichopoulos administered a cocktail of drugs before he appeared to his fans, and after the show another medicine cabinet of drugs to calm him down.

In July 1975, an increasingly erratic Elvis came close to alienating his backing singers and band members. Back-up singers the Sweet Inspirations walked off in the middle of a show after they took exception to his on-stage teasing, and then Elvis flew into a rage with band members who reported late to the airport for their flight to their final destination on the tour (Asheville, North Carolina). Elvis took off in a huff, leaving them behind, but made peace by buying expensive pieces of jewelry for all the people he'd offended. At this concert his largesse included throwing a guitar and one of his rings into the audience.

Elvis' New Year's Eve '75 show in Pontiac, Michigan, earned the largest gross of any concert by a single performer up to that time. Elvis was particularly enthused at the huge turnout of 64,000 fans and told the audience it was the biggest live audience he had ever played.

According to Dick Grob, in his final years it was Elvis who wanted to go on tour after tour, rather than the Colonel. He was on the road practically every month in 1976 from March onwards, going on a total of nine tours as well as taking on long-term engagements at both the Sahara Tahoe and the Las Vegas Hilton. He toured incessantly partly to keep active, and partly because he needed the money for his latest and most expensive hobby, private airplanes.

During his last year alive, Elvis returned to many smaller venues where he had not performed since causing riots two decades earlier. He seemed little concerned with almost unanimously snide press comments about his weight, sloth and general disinterest.

Elvis reached a new low at his August 28, 1976 concert. He finally came out an hour and a half late, so out of sorts that he slurred his words and even forgot the lyrics to some of his most famous hits. Some fans were in tears by the end of the show.

The last time that Elvis attempted to play two shows in one day out on tour was in early September 1976, at Huntsville, Alabama.

Contrary to popular belief, Elvis could still defy his critics and put on a good show. His performances picked up soon after he met his last long-term girlfriend, Ginger Alden. Whenever she was in the audience (in Las Vegas in December, and during his New Year's performance) he found renewed vigor. However, his residency at Las Vegas in the run-up to Christmas included some below-par nights, including a threat to walk offstage because the microphones were too cheap.

The performance Elvis gave on New Year's Eve 1976 in Pittsburgh is considered by some to be among his finest—the last time was able to muster the energy of old, playing 28 songs in a two-hour show (officially released for the first time by FTD in 2003 with the title *Elvis New Year's Eve 1976*.)

That show attracted a record-breaking 62,500 concertgoers for an indoor event, and set a record for ticket income from a single performance of $850,000.

In 1977, Elvis' performances continued for the most part to be shaky. Perhaps because of this, he tended to tour smaller venues, often University concert halls rather than big-city stadiums. In Alexandria that March, he tellingly changed the lyrics of "Can't Help Falling In Love," his grand finale, to "Wise men know / When it's time to go . . ." By this time, as Peter Guralnick writes, for the entourage "the idea was simply to get Elvis out onstage and keep him upright for the hour he was scheduled to perform."

Some of his last live performances were released by FTD in 2002 on the *Spring Tours '77* album.

Elvis' last ever tour, his fifth in the first half of 1977, began in Springfield, Missouri on June 17. His final stage performance was at Indianapolis on June 26, 1977, where he put in a solid 80-minute show. At one date on the tour, he told the audience "In spite of what you may hear or you may have read, we're here, and we're healthy, and we're doing what we enjoy doing." CBS cameras had been shadowing Elvis on the road since May for ill-conceived live documentary *Elvis in*

Concert. Promoter Tom Hulett, who had been working with Elvis since the early Seventies, is quoted as saying that on the first date on that tour, it was like Elvis was saying "OK, here I am, I'm dying, fuck it."

Right at the very end of his life, Elvis was still hoping finally to go on a tour of Europe, and even had costume designer Bill Belew work up some ideas.

Elvis was an uncommon enough mortal for death to signal a hiatus rather than a permanent caesura to his live performing.

In 1995, a major concert event titled *Elvis— The Tribute* brought together artists ranging from Chet Atkins to Jerry Lee Lewis, Carl Perkins, Tony Bennett and Iggy Pop for a live show.

Following a mega-concert to celebrate the twentieth anniversary of Elvis' death in 1997, TCB band members have been performing around the world in *Elvis—The Concert*, with the King singing on a giant video screen projected above the band.

See also TOURS and STAGE ACT.

ELVIS SAID IN 1969: "I'm really glad to be back in front of a live audience. I don't think I've ever been more excited than I was tonight."

ELVIS SAID IN 1972: "You know, we do two shows a night for weeks, but we never let it get old. Every time is like we do it for the first time."

ELVIS SAID IN 1973: "A live concert to me is exciting because of all the electricity that is generated in the crowd and on the stage. It's my favorite part of the business—live concerts."

ELVIS SAID: "It's like a surge of electricity going through you. It's almost like making love, but it's even stronger than that . . . sometimes I think my heart is going to explode."

ELVIS SAID IN 1974: "There's not anybody on this stage . . . that wouldn't rather be here than anywhere else in the world."

TOM PERRYMAN: "Elvis could do it if there wasn't bet ten people [in the room]. He never realized what he had till later years."

RONNIE TUTT: "If the songs weren't up to a certain energy level, Elvis felt like it wasn't exciting enough. That's the way he liked it—exciting. If it was going too slow for him, he'd look around at me and catch my eye, and either move his leg or kind of move his arm, like ' Let's move it up a little bit,' or 'Crank it up'."

JOAN DEARY: "When people went to see him, they didn't care what he said; what mattered was the feeling he put into a song. They knew he put everything he had into every song he sang. He and the audience had a love affair."

DR. NICHOPOULOS: "He never seemed preoccupied with how many albums he made. He seldom or hardly ever read the newspaper about any of his shows. He was just concerned with the audience response. This is what turned him on and really pleased him."

CHER: "The first concert I attended was an Elvis concert when I was eleven. Even at that age he made me realize the tremendous effect a performer could have on an audience."

PAMELA CLARKE KEOGH: "Onstage, he was a better actor than he ever was in the movies."

Books:

Concert Tour souvenir albums were sold at Elvis shows in the Fifties (for individual tours) and the Seventies (one for each year). The tradition has been continued with the "Elvis the Tribute" and "Elvis in Concert" performances starting in the Nineties.

Hundreds of photo books of Elvis concerts are available from authors such as Joe Tunzi, Ger Rijff, Jim Curtin and Ed Bonja.

BMG'S 2006 RELEASE ELVIS LIVE IS A TASTER OF ELVIS ON STAGE, REMASTERED.

1. See See Rider
2. Johnny B. Goode
3. Mystery Train / Tiger Man
4. In The Ghetto
5. Suspicious Minds
6. The Wonder Of You
7. Polk Salad Annie
8. Walk A Mile In My Shoes
9. You've Lost That Lovin' Feelin'
10. I Just Can't Help Believin'
11. Bridge Over Troubled Water
12. You Gave Me A Mountain
13. An American Trilogy
14. Never Been To Spain
15. What Now My Love
16. Burning Love
17. My Way
18. Steamroller Blues
19. How Great Thou Art
20. Unchained Melody

CONCERTS WEST

A booking and promotions company set up by Tom Hulett, initially in Seattle, that worked with Colonel Parker from 1970, with Jerry Weintraub and the Management III company, to put on Elvis shows. The company is still going to this day as part of the AEG Group, and has put on shows for many top acts.

"CONFIDENCE"

A *Clambake* soundtrack song by Sid Tepper and Roy C. Bennett with a chorus not a million miles removed from show tune "High Hopes," recorded by the band in Nashville on February 22, 1967 and overdubbed by Elvis the day after (his rock bottom faith in the song apparent).

In the movie, the song is inserted into a medley of traditional songs ranging from "Here We Go Around The Mulberry Bush" to "Row, Row, Row Your Boat."

Since the soundtrack LP, the song has appeared on *Elvis Sings Hits from His Movies*, *Elvis Sings Sid Tepper & Roy C. Bennett*, the *Double Features* and FTD *Clambake* releases.

CONNECTICUT

- Hartford

Elvis played the Civic Center on July 28, 1976.

- New Haven

Elvis' 1975 tour took him to the Veterans Memorial Coliseum on July 16 and 17. He played there again on July 30, 1976.

CONNELLY, JOE
(1917-2003)

Producer of Elvis' final movie, *Change of Habit* (1969), who more frequently worked on TV shows variously as a producer, director and writer including on "Leave it to Beaver" and "The Munsters."

CONSPIRACY THEORIES

Unanswered questions about the circumstances of Elvis' death and what happened in the immediate aftermath have provided a mother lode of material for conspiracy theorists, generally revolving around a disbelief that he died at all. Those close to Elvis have always said without hesitancy (and often with palpable grief) that much as they were struck by disbelief when they first heard the news, he did indeed die that fateful day. Such denials have done little to dispel a growing body of articles, literature and movies that speculate on Elvis' continuing living and breathing presence on this Earth after August 17, 1977. There have also, over the years, been rumors of suicide and murder.

Academic writers studying the cult of Elvis have pointed out that a belief in transcendence of the boundaries of life are a staple in many religions.

See also the Sidebar ELVIS LIVES? under DEATH for details about Elvis' history as a member of the undead.

PATRICK LACY: "Part of the reason for so much misinformation about Elvis is fans' hunger for anything new or interesting or compelling about Elvis. This desire for information results in people writing books to satisfy that hunger."

Book:
Elvis Decoded—A Fan's Guide To Deciphering The Myths And Misinformation, by Patrick Lacy, AuthorHouse, 2006.

CONVERSATION

Elvis grew up in a close-knit family environment and lived his life surrounded by people. He loved to talk.

Brought up by a mother who valued old-time Southern manners, Elvis was courteous to a fault, answering questions with "Yes, sir" or "No ma'am" and meticulously addressing people by their last name. Members of his entourage, however, have said that in later years he cultivated the country boy image as a (wholly unnecessary) way to conquer the ladies.

Tell-all books on Elvis depict him cussing like a trooper—1999 unofficial CD *Finding the Way Home* has some choice language from his American Studio sessions—yet he abhorred swearing in women. Fans who have amassed bootlegs and a few of the FTD collectors' releases have had occasion to hear him in full flight.

Elvis had a knack of coming out with lines from the thousands of songs he knew that were pertinent to the situation. At emotional moments he might refer to his own hits or the titles and lyrics of songs he knew to convey how he felt.

One of the most famous faces on the planet, when he met new people Elvis would disarmingly present himself with the words, "Hi, I'm Elvis Presley."

On a trip to Las Vegas in 1962, Priscilla describes Elvis and Gene Smith communicating in a kind of made-up language of non-sequiturs.

With female intimates, Elvis sometimes resorted to the kind of baby-language he had used with Gladys. Priscilla writes that he said "sotties" for feet, called milk "butch," said "toophies" for teeth, "iddytream" for ice cream and "yuv" for love.

Even Elvis could resort to corny pick-up lines. More than one girlfriend has written in their memoirs that Elvis said "Where have you been all my life?"

Elvis had catchphrases he repeated at different periods in his life. After recording "Stranger In My Own Home Town" in 1969, he liked to repeat the line "you can't keep a good man down." In the mid-Seventies, in the midst of his wild and eccentric behavior, Elvis liked to say "everything in moderation."

Priscilla chose Elvis' oft-quoted proverb "Don't criticize what you don't understand, son. You never walked in that man's shoes" as the quotation to start her memoir *Elvis and Me*. Another favorite Elvis expression was, "If it ain't bleeding, it ain't hurting."

Every member of Elvis' entourage and every fan who was invited into his world says that the highpoints of being around Elvis were the rare times that they had one-on-one conversations with him, an experience invariably described as feeling like being the only person on the planet. If he had enough charisma to captivate tens of thousands of people in a concert hall . . .

Elvis' way of putting things off or not dealing with something he preferred to avoid was to say something would happen "when the time is right."

Elvis sometimes addressed people as "Chief"; in the Fifties, he used the greeting "Ace."

According to cousin Harold Loyd, if Elvis felt nervous he would start talking faster and faster.

The thing that frightened Elvis most before going before a live audience for the NBC TV Special in 1968 was the part of the show when he was scheduled simply to chat with the audience—a fear dispelled as soon as he came on stage with the humorous opening line, "Good night."

When lecturing people or seeking solace, Elvis liked to quote lines from his favorite spiritual passages, whether it be the Bible, *The Prophet*, the *Desiderata* or other books. If his interlocutor was less than enthusiastic, Elvis might quip, "When the pupil is ready, the teacher is willing."

Always a fan of comedy and laughter, Elvis was an accomplished mimic, happy to recite sidesplitting scenes from movies he liked, a Clouseau accent or Monty Python sketches.

Elvis habitually closed his concerts with the line, "Thank You, Thank You Very Much."

His last words alive were "Ok, I won't," in answer to Ginger Alden's advice not to fall asleep in the bathroom.

CD set: *Elvis: The Complete Word for Word—1955-77* (2006), 5 CDs of material, advertised as containing every known public Elvis interview.

BILLY SMITH: "Elvis had that kind of mumble and stutter way of talking."

GLEN D. HARDIN: "He was a very good listener. He loved to tell stories, he loved to hear stories, he just loved to hang out with the boys and have a real good time."

LARRY GELLER: "I've never met anyone in my life who spoke more eloquently without saying a word than Elvis."

LAMAR FIKE: "We'd find a saying we liked and bury it within six weeks."

PAUL SIMPSON: "A major difficulty facing anyone who writes about Elvis is his habit of telling people what he thought they wanted to hear."

Cooks
See FOOD and GRACELAND STAFF.

COSBY, BILL
(B.. WILLIAM H. COSBY, 1937)

Popular comic Bill Cosby stood in for Elvis in Las Vegas in August 1974, when he had to cancel his performance at the last minute through ill-health. The next night Cosby started the evening in the audience but slipped out as Elvis was launching into his infamous and aggressive drug-addled monologue. When Elvis noticed that Cosby had left the room, he launched into him too, suggesting that he blow the $10,000 fee he had just received up his nose.

Cosby's American dream-come-true story took him from crushing poverty in Philadelphia to the Navy to Temple University and then a career in stand-up in the early Sixties. He achieved national recognition on the Johnny Carson "Tonight Show" in 1963, effectively breaking through the color bar by establishing himself as the first popular mainstream African-American comedian. Perhaps best known for his no. 1-rated eponymously-named TV show that ran from 1984 to 1992, Cosby has been a familiar face on TV since the Sixties, when from 1965 to 1968 he played a lead role in the "I Spy" series. Since then he has collected Grammy awards for more than half a dozen comic records, and Emmys and Golden Globes for his TV and movie work.

COSMETICS

Elvis used Colgate toothpaste. His regular aftershave was either Aqua Velva or Brut, and he regularly used Neutrogena soap. A bottle of Hai Karate cologne from his bathroom is on display at Graceland.

When sunning himself at Graceland, he used Hawaiian Tropic; Patti Parry remembers him using "Man Tan" in Palm Springs to get bronzed for his *Aloha from Hawaii* special. He used Five Day Deodorant when he was performing in Las Vegas. Some writers have impugned Elvis' bathing habits in his later years, suggesting that he preferred to daub on cologne than take showers.

Elvis claimed that he didn't wear make up on stage until the very end of his life, when he was being filmed on tour by CBS for *Elvis in Concert*. Biographers disagree with him, noting that he wore mascara in his early years, just like his screen hero Tony Curtis—though Curtis didn't dare try out the blue eye shadow Elvis was seen sporting.

Elvis had his own makeup kit at home after he started working in Hollywood, and started using pancake makeup, eyeliner and mascara, before deciding to dye his eyebrows and eyelashes.

He shaved for many years with a Lektronic cordless razor.

In later years, Elvis wore a girdle to mask his weight.

Red West, Billy Smith and Anita Wood have all said that Elvis wore shoe lifts to make himself look taller, sometimes even putting them into his slippers around the house, though this has been disputed by other Elvis insiders.

COSMETIC SURGERY

In the fall of 1956, Elvis had plastic inserts made for his upper front teeth by a dentist in Beverly Hills. He did not get good value for his $150 investment, as they broke within a week, defeated by a meal at the State Cafe in Memphis. He reputedly had a nose job in 1957, though this has been strongly disputed. Freshly arrived in Hollywood, he also had some warts removed from his hands.

His Memphis dentist Lester Hofman put crowns on Elvis' teeth and undertook substantial dental work not long before he went off to the Army in 1958.

In 1959, Elvis embarked on a weekly herbal-based skin treatment he hoped would heal his acne scars, administered by a bogus doctor called Laurenz Johannes Griessel Landau.

Elvis had two crowns installed in February 1963.

In June 1975, against Dr. Nick's advice, Elvis booked himself in to the Mid-South Hospital for cosmetic surgery around his eyes, which was performed by Dr. Asghan Koleyni.

In his last year alive, tabloid newspapers ran stories that he had a full facelift and a nose job.

MARTY LACKER: "In the 70s, when he went to visit President Nixon, he had enough mascara for the Avon Lady."

BILLY SMITH on Elvis' 1975 procedure: "To me it ruined his eyes. He always had those sleepy, sexy eyes. And they took the droop out. The droop was part of his mystique."

COSTUMES AND DESIGNERS

Elvis was into theatrical clothes long before he strode a stage for money. At the very start of his career, the outfits he wore for his fans were simply the flamboyant clothes he bought from Lansky. With money, fame, new management, Hollywood and the challenges of age, he changed looks, designers and fashion.

Elvis played his first big show, at the Overton Park Shell in July 1954, in what would become his trademark pink suit, set off by a gray tie.

In his first few months as a performer, Elvis favored a high-lapelled white suit over a black shirt.

One of the most widely used publicity shots for Elvis immediately after he signed to Sun Records in 1954 portrayed the rising "Hillbilly" star in Western garb, the look favored by Scotty Moore and Bill Black in their previous Western Swing band, the Starlite Wranglers.

In his early touring days when it was just Elvis, Scotty and Bill on the road, the quality of their costumes sometimes suffered. Fellow performer Billie Jo Spears once took pity on Elvis' yellowing white shirt and faded black britches with a busted fly, and gave him a safety pin to fasten them better.

Elvis first played the Louisiana Hayride in a pink jacket, black shirt, red bow tie and two-tone black and white shoes. In early January 1955 he added crocodile-skin shoes and pink socks. His outfit for Lubbock around that time was an orange jacket, red pants and white buck shoes. The pink socks were on show for his January 15, 1955 Hayride performance, along with a rust-colored suit and a purple tie with black dots. This was reputedly the night that the Colonel first met Elvis.

For his February 5, 1955 regular Saturday date at the Louisiana Hayride, Elvis dared to wear pink pants and a pink tie, topped by a more sedate charcoal-colored jacket.

In late April that year Elvis played Seymour, Texas in a fire-engine red sports coat, white shirt and blue trousers. Elvis deliberately wore stage clothes a size or two too big so that when he shook, rattled and rolled he didn't rip the seams. These precautions were insufficient at a show in Belden, Mississippi, where Elvis went on stage with his trousers held together by a safety pin after he ripped them climbing into the building through a window in order to avoid being mobbed.

Elvis had to renounce his pink suit at a show in Jacksonville, Florida, in May 1955 when rioting fans ripped it off his body.

On a week-long tour of Texas in August 1955, Elvis performed in a colorblind-person's worst nightmare: a green jacket, pink shirt, red slacks and pink socks.

After meeting Bill Haley on a Hank Snow Tour in Oklahoma in October 1955, Elvis went back to the red jacket, which he wore for his performance captured on the never-released documentary *The Pied Piper of Cleveland: A Day in the Life of a Famous Disc Jockey.*

For his first appearance on national TV—on "Stage Show" in January 1956—Elvis wore a textured tweed jacket, black shirt and white tie—this was black and white TV, after all.

During 1956, Elvis' stage costumes included a plum-colored jacket and black trousers; a yellow and black striped sports coat; and an iridescent blue shirt with kimono collar, and black trousers.

For his July 1956 TV appearance on "The Steve Allen Show" Elvis belied his rebellious image by wearing a tuxedo for the first time in his life; Elvis was unhappy with the look, while fans protested at this taming of their wild idol.

Three days later, at Russwood Park in Memphis, he performed in black pants and a velvet blouson jacket, with red socks and a red tie.

At his September 1956 homecoming show in Tupelo, Elvis took the stage in a purple velveteen shirt his Ma had made (or was it a gift from Natalie Wood if you prefer this version of the story); some newspaper reports describe the color as bright blue). That month he made his first appearance on the "Ed Sullivan Show" wearing black pants, a patterned shirt and a plaid jacket.

For his third appearance on the "Ed Sullivan Show" in January 1957, Elvis sported a velvet shirt and a gold lamé vest.

In spring 1957, Elvis performed in a $2500 gold leaf suit commissioned by Colonel Parker from Brooklyn designer Nudie Cohen, a favorite with big-time country music artists and a legend in LA. Elvis was not completely enamored of the look, and soon substituted black pants for the gold ones—they tended to flake when he dropped to his knees in the act. He completed the effect with a pair of gold slippers that had rhinestones on the tassels. The Colonel let it be known that the "solid gold suit" cost $10,000. The photo on the cover of *Elvis Gold Records, Vol. 2* shows Elvis in all his gold-suited beauty. By the late summer of 1957, Elvis was performing all in black topped with the gold jacket. He wore the full suit just three times, though he performed in the jacket one more time, at his March 1961 benefit concert in Hawaii.

On film, Elvis was dressed by whoever was in charge of wardrobe at the studio *du jour*. On nine Paramount movies, it was eight-time Oscar winner Edith Head, who regarded Elvis as one of the easiest stars to dress as all it took was taking his innate style and adapting it to the particular movie.

Elvis was so fond of the flamenco outfit he wore in *Fun in Acapulco* that he kept it after filming, along with two black silk shirts—his favorite outfit when he first started buying clothes as a teenager was a bolero jacket. Over the years, Elvis ended up acquiring many a number of costumes he wore in movie roles (one fan favorite is his black leather motorcycle get-up from 1964 movie *Roustabout*). The Colonel's insistence on keeping a close eye on the budgets of Elvis' mid-Sixties movies is evident in his less-than-expensive outfits, not improved by an evident gain in Elvis' weight.

Marty Lacker told author Alanna Nash that he designed Elvis' wedding tuxedo, and made initial costume sketches for some of Elvis' movies.

The first time Elvis was dressed by costume designer Bill Belew was for the 1968 NBC TV Special. Belew designed Elvis' costumes from this moment on. For the Comeback Special, Belew came up with a white suit with a high Edwardian-style collar, and the tight black leather suit that for many is their favorite Elvis look. Elvis was instantly enthusiastic about both of these costumes, but refused to reprise his full 1957 gold suit look. In the end, he settled for a gold jacket over black tuxedo pants. The first time that Elvis wore a scarf as part of his costume—later a hallmark Elvis item—was as an accessory to his black leather outfit.

Bill Belew designed a karate-style "Cossack suit" with a dangling macramé belt for Elvis' return to live performing in the summer of 1969, at the International Hotel in Las Vegas. The original idea of reprising the leather suit from the TV special was impractical for two shows a night, every night for a month.

As a rule, Elvis preferred not to do costume changes because he didn't want to leave the stage and abandon his fans.

The first time Elvis played Vegas was the first time that he handed out scarves to his audience—a trick that killed two birds with one stone: first, he wiped off his perspiration, then he got to present a unique keepsake to an adoring fan.

Belew ushered in the start of Elvis' jumpsuit era at the start of the Seventies, when he designed a set of stage jumpsuits in black and in white for Elvis' second month-long engagement at the International Hotel in Las Vegas (January 1970), sewn from Italian gabardine and adorned with spangly beads. Initially Elvis tried out other types of costumes before deciding that the comfort factor of the jumpsuit and the full range of movement it

LEFT: Elvis wearing the infamous "Dragon suit," during a performance in South Bend, Indiana. RIGHT: Elvis playing a concert at the Spectrum in Philadelphia.

Sincerely
Elvis

allowed him on stage made it a winner, especially for his karate-style moves. Manuel (Manuel Cuevas) has also claimed paternity of Elvis' first jumpsuit. Marty Lacker says that Elvis already had a collection of jumpsuits in the Sixties that he used as leisurewear for cross-country road trips (Elvis in white, the entourage in black). Many of his performance jumpsuits were too delicate to be cleaned—reputedly Elvis freshened them up with a liberal dousing of Brut aftershave.

New for his third tour of duty in Vegas (and captured in concert movie *That's The Way It Is*) was a white bell-bottom jumpsuit with fringes, and a great increase in the number of red and blue scarves given out to audience members, ordered initially from IC Costumes in LA, and then from Mr. Guy in Las Vegas when he used up his stock. Joe Esposito recalls that the scarves were an update to an old idea of the Colonel's back in the Fifties, when Elvis threw out teddy bears while performing "Teddy Bear."

The first time that Elvis sported a cape on stage was at his final show of the summer in Las Vegas in September 1971. By his next Las Vegas tour of duty the cape had become a favorite for both Elvis and his fans.

Elvis' jumpsuits with their various embroidered designs cost around $1,500 each (ETAs are used to paying around $2,500 for replicas). His silk shirts set him back $125 a pop. Elvis' jumpsuit bill for his April 1972 tour exceeded $10,000.

Some of Elvis' costumes were worked up by Belew on the basis of an initial design concept from Elvis. These included the panther and peacock motifs, and the various patriotic American costumes he wore over the years. Elvis acknowledged his debt to Billy Eckstine for the high-collar look he pioneered (known as the "Mr. B. Collar").

Elvis stood resplendent in a gold cape on the stage at Madison Square Garden in New York, June 1972.

Elvis first wore his American Eagle jumpsuit and cape, designed by Bill Belew, at his January 1973 *Aloha From Hawaii* show. Elvis and Belew came up with the idea because Elvis wanted to wear a symbol that said 'America' to the worldwide audience; Belew recalled seeing a huge American eagle at the American Embassy in London and used that as his inspiration. The cape and belt—each worth $5,000 because of all the jewels and fine embroidery, making the whole outfit worth as much as $65,000—almost didn't make it into the show because the day before the live broadcast Elvis flung them into the audience at the end of a run-through. Belew and his team worked right through the night to manufacture replacements and fly them out to Honolulu in time. The same thing happened again: at the end of the show, Elvis flung both cape and belt into the audience. The heirs of the lucky recipient that night returned the cape to the Elvis Estate and it now features prominently at the end of the Graceland tour. Incidentally, the prototype cape that Belew made for Elvis was much longer and so heavy that when Elvis first wore it he toppled over backwards and couldn't get up.

Elvis temporarily ditched the cape in Las Vegas in the winter of 1974. It was briefly back by popular demand, though Elvis regarded it as a liability for his balance when fans grabbed at it.

In March 1974, Elvis made his entrance "like a streak of white lightning" according to one viewer, dressed in a white jumpsuit covered in jewels and nailheads. That summer, he performed in a two-piece leather costume rather than the regular jumpsuits.

When his weight began to spiral out of control, Elvis refused to allow anyone to measure him. Costume designer Bill Belew would have to guess how much to let out the jumpsuits by watching videos of recent performances. Elvis often complained on stage of how tight the (now

Now Elvis Now, International Hotel Vegas Poster..

$2,500) suits were, and how long it took him to get into them—especially if one of them split during his act, something that happened with increasing regularity as his girth increased.

Elvis personally asked Belew to make a design with two leopard heads meeting on one shoulder.

In 1976 Elvis' favorite show costume was his red white and blue bicentennial jumpsuit. For his tours in early 1977 Elvis could only fit into two costumes, his white Aztec jumpsuit and his blue and gold suit. By May that year, he was down to just the Aztec jumpsuit—the dark colors and a corset made him look a little less corpulent.

The costumes Elvis would have been wearing if he lived longer were already under development. Bill Belew was working on a jeweled cape with built-in lasers that Elvis could work by remote control.

A large number of Elvis' stage jumpsuits went on display at Graceland in 2007. That same year, costume-makers B&K Enterprises became the official licensee to recreate Elvis costumes for ETAs and fans.

ELVIS SAID IN LAS VEGAS, 1970: "If the songs don't go over, we can do a medley of costumes."

BILL BELEW: "You could be daring as a designer and put anything on Elvis and he could make it work."

Book:
Elvis: Photographing the King, by Sean Shaver, Timur Publishing, 1981.

Documentary:
Fit for a King, 2007.

ELVIS JUMPSUIT MOTIFS (*some of which were made in various colors*):

Ace of Spades
Adonis
Aloha Bald Headed Eagle
Amber/Gold Vine
American Eagle
Aztec
Bird
Blue Swirl
Braid
Burning Love
Chain suit
Chinese Dragon
Choker suit
Cisco Kid
Cluster
Colorful Flame
Concha
Conquistador
Double Porthole suit
Egyptian Pharaoh
Fireworks
Flame
Flower
Fringe suit
Gypsy
Herringbone
Inca Gold Leaf
Indian
Indian Feather
King of Spades
Lace suit
Lion
Mad Tiger
Matador
Mermaid
Metal Eye
Mexican Sundial
Multi-sequined suit

Nail Mirrored suit
Nail Studded suit
Orange Sunburst
Pale Blue Bird
Peacock
Phoenix
Prehistoric Bird
Rainbow
Rainfall
Saturn suit
Silver Bird
Sleek
Snake
Snowflake
Spanish Flower
Spectrum suit
Starburst
Sundial
Thin Green Leaf
Tiffany
Vine
V-Neck suit with puff sleeves
White Prehistoric Bird

"COTTON CANDY LAND"

Elvis recorded this Ruth Batchelor / Bob Roberts song for *It Happened at the World's Fair* at Radio Recorders in Hollywood on September 22, 1962. The film version is slightly shorter than the version that appeared on the soundtrack album.

In later years, RCA put the song on the *Elvis Sings For Children (And Grown Ups Too)* album—reissued more recently as *Elvis Sings For Kids*, the *Double Features* issue and the FTD release for the movie, which also contains alternates.

"COTTONFIELDS"

Elvis is said to have sung this 1941 Leadbelly (aka Huddie Ledbetter) tune at his very first concerts. He took on the song during filming for *That's The Way It Is* on July 15, 1970 (issued on the 2000 3-CD special edition). Much more deep-South barrelhouse than Beach Boys barber shop, Elvis' version had previously only appeared on bootleg.

"COULD I FALL IN LOVE"

Elvis laid down multiple versions of this Randy Starr composition as he self-harmonized for this *Double Trouble* soundtrack recording at Radio Recorders on June 28, 1966 (with further overdubs on June 30).

Since the soundtrack LP, "Could I Fall In Love" has appeared on the *Double Features* release (paired with *Spinout*). Alternates—including a harmony take—are on the FTD *Double Trouble* release.

COUNTRY MUSIC

Elvis made the transition from local Memphis phenomenon to regional success across the South by hitching his wagon to major touring packages on the Country circuit, first in shows organized by Bob Neal, then on the road with Hank Snow Attractions (in which Colonel Parker had more than a hand), playing on bills with many top country acts. These tours not only raised his profile, they underlined how different and dangerous Elvis was compared to anything else out there. In the fullness of time, Elvis' success helped to change the status of country music—or hillbilly music as it was still popularly known; the term Country music wasn't in vogue until the early Fifties. When he first began performing, however, wild young Elvis was just a little too out there for the nation's leading country shindig, the Nashville-based Grand Ole Opry. The Opry's loss was the Louisiana Hayride's gain; the Hayride was only too happy to snap him up on a long-term contract within months of his first Sun single.

After his less-than-successful performance at the Opry, Elvis confessed to Ernest Tubb that the kind of music he really wanted to play was country, but to make any money he was being advised to play this new-fangled style. Tubb advised him to make the money first, and then he could play whatever he wanted.

Modern-day country music developed out of traditional Southern hillbilly folk from the Southeast, blended with "cowboy"-style music from the Southwest, made popular by Hollywood singing cowboys such as Gene Autry and Tex Williams. Other variations on a Country theme with which Elvis grew up included honky tonk, bluegrass and Western swing—the genre that Elvis' original band members Scotty Moore and Bill Black were playing when they met in 1954.

Elvis' recipe for mixing up music styles to cook up a whole new genre blended together a pinch of hillbilly, a healthy dose of R&B and a smattering of special gospel sauce. All five of Elvis' singles for Sun Records had a country track on one side and an R&B rocker on the other. Greil Marcus notes that country music was familiarity and limitation for Elvis, and served as an antidote to the danger and excess of blues and rock 'n' roll. Elvis' first ever single, "That's All Right (Mama)," was backed with his unique rendition of Bill Monroe's bluegrass classic "Blue Moon Of Kentucky." When sound engineer Jack Clement first heard "That's All Right" on the radio, Elvis sounded to him like "a bluegrasser that was having fun without a banjo."

In November 1955, *Billboard* magazine's Annual Disc Jockey Poll hailed Elvis as the "Most Promising C&W Artist" of the year. When RCA signed Elvis from Sun at around this time, in-house publicity at the label billed it as "The Biggest C&W Record News of the Year!" As late as March 1956, *Billboard* was still describing Elvis as a "country warbler."

Though Elvis recorded for many, many years in Nashville, the epicenter of Country music, with top country session musicians backing him in the studio, he didn't record a full Country album until half-way through his second decade as an entertainer. *Elvis Country* grew out of a number of country tracks he laid down more or less spontaneously, as a means of putting off the material he was scheduled to record at a Nashville recording session in June 1970, along with a further few tracks laid down that September. As ever with Elvis, he serves up his music with a twist, in this case country shot through with gospel and blues.

"I've Got a Thing About You Baby," released as a single in early 1974, reached #4 in the Country charts, Elvis' highest placing in the category since 1958. In the mid-Seventies, Elvis' singles and albums regularly charted significantly higher on the Country charts than the overall *Billboard* chart. When Elvis died, "Way Down" was #1 on the Billboard Country singles chart. All in all, Elvis achieved 10 Country #1s between 1956 and 1981.

In his final years, Elvis was unquestionably singing more and more Country material. The second-last album RCA released in Elvis' lifetime, *Welcome to My World*, was a compilation of country cuts.

Elvis was inducted into the Country Music Hall of Fame in 1998, for his origins as a country singer and his long-lasting legacy in making country music a national rather than regional taste. His music had not always been so well-appreciated by the Country community. In the late Fifties, when rock and roll was sweeping everything before it, Country stalwarts thought that Elvis was going to be the death of the genre.

Elvis is one of very few artists to have been inducted into the Country the Rock and Roll Halls of Fame.

In 2005 a number of major country artists issued *A Country Tribute To Elvis*.

ELVIS' #1 COUNTRY HITS:

I Forgot To Remember To Forget, 1955
Heartbreak Hotel, 1956
I Want You, I Need You, I Love You, 1956
Don't Be Cruel, 1956
Hound Dog, 1956
All Shook Up, 1957
(Let Me Be Your) Teddy Bear, 1957
Jailhouse Rock, 1957
Moody Blue, 1976
Way Down, 1977
Guitar Man, 1981

ELVIS SAID IN 1970: "Country music was always a part of the influence on my type of music."

JERRY SCHILLING: "History has him as this good old country boy, but Elvis is about as country as Bono! He came from here, but he was not the boy next door, he was on the edge."

WAYLON JENNINGS: " If they'd got him a country band and let him loose, he'd have been happy."

COUNTRY MUSIC DISC JOCKEY CONVENTION

Elvis visited the 4th annual Country Music Disc Jockey Association convention in Nashville on the weekend of November 10 and 11, 1955, where he was named the most promising country male artist of the year. It was here that he first heard Mae Boren Axton's demo of "Heartbreak Hotel."

COUNTRY SIDE OF ELVIS, THE

A 2001 2-CD remastered Elvis country retrospective.

TRACK LISTING:
DISC 1:
1. It Wouldn't Be The Same Without You
2. Blue Moon Of Kentucky
3. I Love You Because
4. Just Because
5. I'm Left, You're Right, She's Gone
6. I Forgot To Remember To Forget
7. I'm Counting On You
8. How Do You Think I Feel
9. How's The World Treating You
10. Old Shep
11. Your Cheatin' Heart
12. (Now And Then There's) A Fool Such As I
13. There's Always Me
14. It's A Sin
15. Guitar Man
16. Just Call Me Lonesome
17. You Don't Know Me
18. After Loving You
19. Long Black Limousine
20. I'm Movin' On
21. I'll Hold You In My Heart (Till I Can Hold You In My Arms)
22. From A Jack To A King
23. Kentucky Rain
24. It Keeps Right On A-Hurtin'
25. If I'm A Fool (For Loving You)
26. Release Me
27. Funny How Time Slips Away

DISC 2:
1. Little Cabin On The Hill
2. There Goes My Everything
3. I Really Don't Want To Know
4. Tomorrow Never Comes
5. Faded Love
6. Make The World Go Away
7. Help Me Make It Through The Night
8. For The Good Times
9. Always On My Mind
10. You Gave Me A Mountain
11. I'm So Lonesome I Could Cry
12. Welcome To My World
13. Take Good Care Of Her
14. It's Midnight
15. You Asked Me To
16. Loving Arms
17. Talk About The Good Times
18. There's A Honky Tonk Angel
19. Fairytale
20. Green, Green, Grass Of Home
21. Susan When She Tried
22. T-R-O-U-B-L-E
23. She Thinks I Still Care
24. He'll Have To Go

CRAMER, FLOYD
(1933-1997)

Pianist Floyd Cramer joined Elvis, Scotty Moore and Bill Black on a tour of Texas in April 1955, and toured with them later that year through Arkansas.

One of the men who helped to create the "Nashville Sound," self-taught Cramer met Elvis at the Louisiana Hayride, where Cramer was a local and a regular. After Cramer moved to Nashville in 1955 he became a much-in-demand session musician for RCA. He was in on Elvis' first Nashville recording session for the label in January 1956, and returned for Elvis' June 1958 recording session. When Elvis went back into the studio in March 1960 after the Army, Cramer got a callback. He was a regular at Elvis' Nashville recording sessions right up to January 1968, sometimes featuring on organ.

A pioneer of the "slip note" style which involved a whole-tone slur up to a note from the one beneath, Cramer recorded with artists such as Pasty Cline, The Browns, Jim Reeves, Roy Orbison and the Everly Brothers. Cramer's recording career included the pickaxe sound effect in Jimmy Dean's offbeat hit "Big Bad John." Cramer emerged into the public eye in his own right when he scored a major instrumental hit in 1960 with "Last Date," which almost made it to #1.

He carried on playing through the Seventies and Eighties. In 1971 he made an album with former Elvis musicians Boots Randolph and Chet Atkins, titled *Chet, Floyd and Boots*.

CRAVENS, DON

Colonel Parker often hired this photographer to take pictures of Elvis in the early years.

Among others, he snapped Elvis with his gold disk for "Heartbreak Hotel," he went out to Germany in 1959 to document Elvis' life as a regular soldier for photos featured on the July 1959 LP *A Date With Elvis*.

Cravens shot Elvis again at the Beverly Wilshire Hotel in 1960 for *Life* magazine, and continued with his franchise of Elvis shots for future record releases and on set.

"CRAWFISH"

Elvis recorded this Fred Wise and Ben Weisman song at Radio Recorders on January 15, 1958 for

King Creole and its tie-in EP and LP. The screen version of the song has a much longer vocal contribution from singer Kitty White.

The track has since appeared on *Worldwide Gold Award Hits Vol. 2*, *The King Of Rock & Roll* and *King Creole* reissues. An unedited version came out on *Essential Elvis Vol. 3*.

CRAWFORD, JOAN
(B. LUCILLE FAY LE SUEUR, 1905-1977)

In 1959 Joan Crawford visited the Pepsi Cola plant—her then husband Alfred Steele was Chairman of the company—where Elvis' granddad Jessie Presley worked, and told him that his grandson was a fine boy.

A consummate movie star with a rags-to-riches background and a legendary tenacity for holding onto her fame, Joan Crawford won an Oscar for her role in 1945 movie *Mildred Pierce* and remained a Hollywood diva ever after. A year after she died, her daughter Christina famously published a scathing biography of her mother, *Mommie Dearest*.

Christina Crawford had a role in Elvis' 1961 movie *Wild in the Country*. According to Billy Smith, Elvis had an altercation with her after she objected to Joe Esposito lighting Elvis' cigar.

"CRAZY ARMS"

Elvis sings a few lines of this song, a million-selling hit for Ray Price in 1956 (written by Ralph Mooney and Charlie Seals), during his jam session with Jerry Lee Lewis and Carl Perkins on December 4, 1956, preserved for posterity in *The Complete Million Dollar Sessions*. Jerry Lee Lewis had just recorded the song for release on Sun; he gave it a full boogie woogie run-through after Elvis left the Sun building.

CREATORE, LUIGI
(B. 1920)

A producer and songwriter from Little Italy who for many years wrote with cousin Hugo Peretti, including Elvis songs "Can't Help Falling In Love," "Ku-U-U-I-Po" and "Wild In The Country"—plus "Froggy Went A'courtin'," which was never released in Elvis' lifetime.

During their careers, Creatore and Peretti produced Sarah Vaughan, LaVern Baker, Sam Cooke and The Isley Brothers, and were reputedly in the running to produce Elvis when he first moved to RCA in 1956.

CREEDENCE CLEARWATER REVIVAL

Elvis and Creedence Clearwater Revival swapped songs in the Seventies: Elvis did "Proud Mary," which became a live favorite, while CCR (a band with John and Tom Fogerty, Doug Clifford and Stu Cook, active between 1967 and 1972) covered Elvis' "My Baby Left Me."

CRIME

With the exception of an impressive collection of speeding tickets, Elvis strutted the stage many years before criminal derring-do was an asset for budding recording artists. Elvis' personal list of crimes and misdemeanors as a youth more or less started and finished with stealing eggs.

In 1959, when he was doing his military service in Germany, Elvis fell prey to the attentions of a man called Laurenz Johannes Griessel-Landau,

who claimed to offer a treatment that would prevent Elvis from getting wrinkles. The man insinuated himself into Elvis' entourage and then made advances to some of Elvis' male friends, and possibly to Elvis himself. When Griessel-Landau was shown the door, he threatened to publish compromising photographs he alleged to have of Elvis and his then underaged girlfriend Priscilla. Elvis contacted the FBI.

A distant cousin of Elvis' (cited in an interview by another cousin as Billy Mann) was found to be a little light-fingered with the petty cash in the late Fifties, and one of the new members of Elvis' entourage was fingered for thieving in 1960, after the Colonel came up with a plan to entrap him.

In the summer of 1970, Elvis was the victim of kidnap and assassination threats while he was contracted to perform at the International Hotel in Las Vegas. On August 26, 1970 the International Hotel security office received an anonymous tip off that Elvis was to be kidnapped that night. The following morning, a man visited Joe Esposito at his LA home and said that he would reveal the name of a man who intended to kill Elvis while he performed his last Saturday show of that Las Vegas tour in exchange if Esposito handed over $50,000. Behind the scenes, Elvis' lawyer Ed Hookstratten brought in PI John O'Grady to provide additional security, while Elvis flew in his personal cavalry of Ed Parker, Jerry Schilling and Red West as extra bodyguards. Elvis performed that night with a gun in each of his boots. The FBI was called in on this one too.

In 1973, a relatively new member of Elvis' entourage who Elvis befriended at one of his movie screenings and took on as a favor, was found to be forging Elvis' name on checks and purloining his rings, including one given to him by the Sahara Tahoe for setting a new attendance record. Elvis and some of the guys tried to haul the miscreant off a plane back to Memphis—Elvis reputedly ran onto the tarmac and stopped the plane, waving his Federal Bureau of Narcotics and Dangerous Drugs badge. They found the soon to be ex-entourage member in the lobby, took him back to the hotel in Las Vegas, gave him a good talking to and told him to make himself scarce.

An attempted swindle was headed off by the FBI involving one of Elvis' aircraft, a Lockheed JetStar that he purchased in 1975.

In one of his books, Larry Geller implies that Elvis never toured outside the US because unnamed organized crime interests dissuaded him from doing so, particularly after Elvis' worldwide satellite broadcast in 1973. It has also been alleged that organized crime had some leverage over Elvis and the Colonel because of his use of drugs.

Elvis felt that he was the victim of a con in the last year of his life, unwittingly furthered by pals Dr. Nichopoulos and Joe Esposito, who persuaded him to lend his name to a chain of racquetball courts. Elvis signed a document in which he was led to believe that he was contributing solely his name to the undertaking, before finding out that the document contained financial obligations.

Within two weeks of Elvis' death, a plot was thwarted to steal his body from the Forest Hills Cemetery and hold it for a $10 million ransom. Suspicions later surfaced that the plot was a ruse to persuade the local authorities to bend the rules and allow Elvis' body (and Gladys's too) to be buried at Graceland.

In her book, Graceland maid Nancy Rooks tells of several security violations at the house before and after Elvis' death, including a security guard who exposed himself indecently to children on the property and, after Elvis' death, an intruder who broke his way into the Jungle Room.

In the early Eighties, the FBI investigated the fraudulent sale of a Chevrolet Corvette Convertible that had been sold as previously belonging to Elvis.

Elvis' name crops up surprisingly often in modern-day crime reports, perhaps because misdeeds are far more likely to make the news than the

many acts of charity and kindness perpetrated habitually by Elvis fans and ETAs.

In recent years an Elvis impersonator helped to apprehend a felon who stole $300,000 worth of memorabilia from the Las Vegas Elvis-A-Rama museum, while another Elvis impersonator, Gary L. Randolph, sang Elvis songs to calm the felon, who was holding his girlfriend and young child hostage at gunpoint.

In 2005 a man was jailed for a $3.5 million online auction scam involving non-existent memorabilia, including, reputedly, a lock of Elvis' hair. Other people have been burned by online auctions.

Also in 2005, an employee of a council the UK was caught after embezzling close to $1 million which she spent on Elvis memorabilia and rare items.

In early 2006, an Australian woman was charged for stabbing her boyfriend after he played "Burning Love" over and over. She escaped a jail sentence when her convalescing boyfriend, a true Elvis romantic, pleaded for clemency and declared his undying love.

See also DEATH, FICTION, LAW SUITS and POLICE.

CROSBY, BING
(1903-1977, B. HARRY LILLIS CROSBY)

Bing Crosby fans are happy to argue that their man was as big a star and cultural phenomenon in the first half of the 20th century as Elvis was in the second. Crosby recorded many more songs than Elvis, spent almost twice as many weeks at number one (173 versus 80 according to a reputable web page comparison), and his total of 369 chart singles is more than twice Elvis' 149. Crosby also made twice as many movies as Elvis, and won 5 Oscars, one for acting (*Going My Way*, 1944) and four for songs. Crosby was also a driving force in major improvements to recording technology, investing his own money in the development of magnetic tape recording. Up until the late 1970s, Crosby was acknowledged as the world's biggest-selling solo recording artist—not bad for a man who took his nickname from comic book strip "Bingville Bugle."

Just as Elvis ushered in the era of rock and roll by drawing on music popular in the black community, Crosby made jazz a mainstream musical genre. They practically handed over the baton in 1954, bringing to an end two decades of unparalleled success for the crooner born in Tacoma, Washington on May 3, 1903. Crosby began his career with jazz trio the Rhythm Boys in the mid-Twenties before striking out solo in the early Thirties. Radio, records and movies followed in quick succession, including the famous series of *Road to . . .* films with Bob Hope. Crosby remained in the public eye through the Sixties and Seventies, notably as the host of a Christmas TV special.

Bing Crosby biographer Gary Giddins suggests that Elvis' rise to fame via recordings, then TV, then the movies, was a path forged originally by Bing Crosby, and then followed successfully by Frank Sinatra and Barbra Streisand. Colonel Parker had applied the same strategy to the talent he managed before Elvis.

Bing Crosby's interview in the *Hollywood Reporter* in 1956 was one of the first times that a top star acknowledged how big Elvis was going to be, and that he was here to stay. However, earlier that year he was quoted as saying that Elvis "will never contribute a damn thing to music."

Elvis recorded a number of Bing Crosby hits during his career, including "Blue Hawaii," "Blue Moon," "Silver Bells," "The Whiffenpoof Song," "Harbor Lights," "Sweet Leilani," "True Love," "Silent Night," and of course "White Christmas."

In 1962 Crosby was the first ever recipient of the Grammy lifetime award, which Elvis won in 1971. Crosby's son Gary acted with Elvis in the 1965 movie *Girl Happy*.

Crosby died two months after Elvis (on October 14) in 1977.

"Cross My Heart And Hope To Die"

Sid Wayne and Ben Weisman wrote this downbeat track for the *Girl Happy* soundtrack, which Elvis recorded in Hollywood at Radio Recorders on June 11, 1964. After an appearance on the *Double Features* soundtrack reissue, a number of alternates came out on FTD releases *Out In Hollywood* and *Girl Happy*.

Crown Electric

Elvis drove a delivery truck for this Memphis electrical contractor, located at 353 Poplar Ave., starting in April 1954, though his ambition was to use the job as a stepping stone to train as an electrician. He began to get experience wiring up houses when co-workers were off sick, but had second thoughts whether he was really cut out for the job. He carried on working for the company until mid-October 1954, several months after cutting his first record for Sun.

At Crown, he earned around $40 a week, which he dutifully handed over to his mom.

Company boss James Tipler and his wife Gladys went to see Elvis perform at the very start of his career, at the Eagle's Nest in Memphis, and again in 1970, when they took in one of Elvis' shows in Las Vegas.

Elvis' employee card when he worked at Crown Electric.

Crudup, Arthur "Big Boy"
(1905-1974)

Pioneering Delta blues singer and guitarist Arthur Crudup was born in Forest, Mississippi on August 24, 1905. He began his career as a blues singer after a musical upbringing in gospel. Crudup was briefly a member of the Harmonizing Four (a long-running group that Elvis sought out in the Sixties as a potential backing group) before launching out on a solo career. Crudup became a top R & B artist in the late Forties, recording for RCA's Bluebird label after he was discovered by a record executive singing on a Chicago street. Throughout his career Crudup had a series of wrangles over unpaid royalties. In the Sixties, when Crudup was sometimes referred to as the "Father of Rock 'n' Roll," he recorded for Fire Records and Delmark and later became a popular performer at festivals.

Crudup played an important *deus ex macchina* role in the Elvis story. Elvis was desperately trying to impress Sun Records chief Sam Phillips in July 1954 but was singularly failing with his repertoire of ballads until he spontaneously launched into Arthur Crudup's bone-jarring "That's All Right," a song Crudup had released without too much success in 1946. Sam Phillips pricked up his ears, recorded a few takes, and the rest.

Elvis later recorded Crudup compositions "My Baby Left Me" and "So Glad You're Mine" for RCA. In the early Sixties, he helped to finance Crudup's recording session at Fire Records.

"Crying In The Chapel"

Elvis recorded this Artie Glenn song early one Nashville morning on October 31, 1960, but put it on hold for release as a single for five long years because he was not satisfied with any of the takes he laid down with the Jordanaires. Previously, the song had been a hit for Darrell Glenn (Artie's son), Rex Allen, the Orioles, and the Statesmen—it had also been recorded by Elvis' former girlfriend Anita Wood. Later versions include one in the Nineties by Aaron Neville.

Elvis' sweet-voiced delivery finally saw the light of day in April 1965, after publishing issues had been sorted out with songwriter Artie Glenn, paired with B-side recording "I Believe In The Man In The Sky." This proved to be a perfect combination for the Easter market, meriting 13 weeks on the main *Billboard* chart and rising to #3 in the US (#1 in the UK). The single sold over a million copies in the US alone, and marked a much-needed return to record-selling form for Elvis—indeed, it was Elvis' only top five US hit in the six years to 1969.

The song had its first album release on the *How Great Thou Art* gospel LP in 1967. Since then it has featured on *Worldwide 50 Gold Award Hits Vol. 1*, *Elvis: A Legendary Performer Vol. 3*, *The Top Ten Hits*, the *Elvis' Gold Records Vol. 4* CD reissue, *Amazing Grace*, *Peace In The Valley*, *ELVIS 30 #1 HITS* (with extra, added banter on the deluxe edition), *Christmas Peace*, *Hitstory*, *Ultimate Gospel* and *Elvis Inspirational*.

The FTD *His Hand In Mine* release features the released version and first take from the original recording session. A live version from 1975 (in a medley with "Rip It Up") has featured on bootleg *Long Lost And Found Songs*.

"Crying Time"

Elvis sang this song while rehearsing in the studio for *That's The Way It Is* in 1970. Though never officially released, it appears on *From Hollywood to Vegas*, *Get Down And Get With It* and other bootlegs. Buck Owens wrote the song and made the first recording (with his Buckaroos) in 1964; Ray Charles had a top 5 hit with the song two years later.

Curtis, Tony
(b. Bernard Schwarz, 1925)

A hero to pre-fame Elvis, who saw Curtis in the movies when he worked as an usher in Memphis, and aspired one day to have his cool and success. Elvis later dyed his hair black, partly to match the dark locks and brooding looks of this leading man as he had seen him in 1952 movie *Son of Ali Baba*.

The two of them met on the Paramount lot many years later, though they never worked together. Curtis and Elvis were both top ten stars in the early Sixties—Elvis continued to be one of Hollywood's top earners for longer than his former idol.

Bronx-born Curtis got his first credited break in the movies in 1949 in *City Across the River*. He went on to star in *The Sweet Smell of Success* (1957) and highly-acclaimed Marilyn Monroe vehicle *Some Like It Hot* (1959), though his only Oscar nomination came opposite Sidney Poitier in *The Defiant Ones* (1958). He has remained a regular on screens large and small through to the 2000s, including a cult role opposite Roger Moore in Seventies TV detective series "The Persuaders." His daughter Jamie Lee Curtis (whose mother was *Psycho* star Janet Leigh) carried on the family film tradition.

Curtiz, Michael
(b. Manó Kertész Kaminer, 1888-1962)

Veteran director Curtiz directed Elvis in the Harold Robbins novel adaptation that was released as *King Creole* in 1958. Born in Hungary, Curtiz worked in Europe before moving to Hollywood in 1926. His 100+ movies include *The Adventures of Robin Hood* (1938), *Angels with Dirty Faces* (1938)—two of five movies he made that prolific year—*Casablanca* (1942), *Mildred Pierce* (1945) and *White Christmas* (1954). Curtiz also directed the original 1937 *Kid Galahad*—Elvis' remake was released in 1962.

Elvis was very much looking forward to working with a true Hollywood legend: no fewer than ten actors in Curtiz movies over the years received Oscar nominations. There is an anecdote that on the first day of shooting, Curtiz flew into one of his legendary tirades and asked where his "motherfucker" star had got to; Elvis, within earshot, walked over, said "You must be Mr. Curtiz" and politely introduced himself, an act of humility that ensured a successful working relationship. Though Elvis received no gongs, he long considered this to be his best celluloid performance.

D

"DAINTY LITTLE MOONBEAMS"

Recorded by Elvis at Radio Recorders on March 28, 1962 for *Girls! Girls! Girls!*, this song (variously attributed over the years to Leiber & Stoller, Charles O'Curran and just plain "unknown") did not receive official release until the 1993 *Double Features Girls! Girls! Girls!* reissue, though the one-minute ditty had already featured on several bootlegs by then.

DANCING

Elvis' arrival in the national consciousness in the mid-Fifties was as noteworthy for the way he moved as the way he sang and his appearance. A free-moving pelvis has always been perceived as a dangerous thing.

How Elvis got his moves has been explained in a number of different ways.

In interviews, Elvis said that his jittery, twitching dance style came about as a direct result of nerves the first time he performed before a large live audience at Overton Park Shell, a few weeks after cutting his first record for Sun. He was so nervous that his legs started jiggling, the crowd went wild, and when he went back out for an encore he wiggled some more. "The more I did, the wilder they went," and so his style was born. In another interview, he dated the origins of his loose-limbed style to his first rehearsals with Scotty Moore and Bill Black at Sun Studio, when he was so nervous that he started jigging and shaking on the spot. He explained: "The minute the music started, I wasn't me anymore. I couldn't have stopped moving around if I'd wanted to. Because all that motion was just as much a part of the music to me as the words I was singing." School pals remember Elvis starting to squirm and wiggle unconsciously as he accompanied himself on guitar, and laughing at the fact.

The wild reaction Elvis got the first couple of times he performed was a mystery to Elvis and the band, until they worked out it was his shaking leg. According to Scotty Moore, "The girls went crazy! . . . Elvis would just kinda roll up on the balls of his feet—kinda in a tense way—and with his arm playing rhythm and everything." It was almost as if, by unweighting and unbalancing himself on the balls of his feet, Elvis had no alternative but to quiver like a leaf in the wind. Early manager Bob Neal immediately advised Elvis to carry on doing whatever it was he was doing.

Various other claims have been made over the years: that he worked out his loose-limbed moves at Catholic Youth Organization dances; that he danced with plenty of girls at High School; that he drew inspiration from Beale Street blues singer Charlie Burse; that he got his moves from studying the inventor of the shimmy Gilda Gray; that he copied Wynonie Harris, Bo Diddley, Little Richard, Johnnie Ray or the most likely candidate, Statesman bass singer Jim "Big Chief" Wetherington. The truth about the origins of Elvis' dance style is much like the truth about the origins of his singing style. He blended what he knew to make something new; in other words, he didn't dance like nobody.

Elvis sometimes began his act in his early days by standing stock-still on stage. Bandman Scotty Moore came up and pretended to wind him up like a toy. Elvis picked up his guitar, started strumming and the crowd went wild. The noise from his audience was so loud that his band members couldn't hear what Elvis was singing but they coordinated with his movements.

Elvis' style was pilloried by detractors as a cross between a striptease and a malted milk machine, or a "lovesick outboard motor." According to band members Scotty Moore and Bill Black, the shaking, rattling and rolling was integral to how Elvis produced his unique sound. Elvis had no

qualms about telling interviewers that his style owed a lot to the religious quartets he enjoyed watching, especially when they did their more "rocking spirituals." What got the crowds of female fans was the way that he suddenly started shaking uncontrollably, as if he simply could not control his urges; the way that he surged towards their outstretched arms and looked like he was so much dangerous fun.

To many, the way Elvis moved was a scandal. Some of the most scathing criticism he suffered in his early years was leveled by critics who viewed his gyrations as simply obscene. Most of the time, Elvis did not rise to the bait. In August 1956, however, he patiently explained to a journalist, "I just get kinda in rhythm with the music, I jump around to it because I enjoy what I'm doing. I'm not trying to be vulgar. I'm not trying to sell any sex." Nevertheless, Elvis' unselfconscious early dance style was tamed by TV and by the Colonel's careful repositioning of his appeal

THIS PAGE: ELVIS PERFORMING IN THE 1950'S.

FACING PAGE: Elvis performing at a concert in 1956.

to a broader demographic during the breakout year of 1956. The "Ed Sullivan Show" famously only filmed Elvis performing from the waist up.

Elvis was instrumental in working out the steps for his classic dance sequence in *Jailhouse Rock*, along with choreographer Alex Romero.

In 1960, Elvis said that he never learned how to bop but he could do a slow dance. In private, he seemed to knew how to fast dance too; at home, he'd listen to music and happily dance around with girlfriends.

During his movie years, Elvis worked with choreographers such as Lance LeGuault more to map out his on-set movements than for his dance moves.

He ran through quite a number of dance styles over the years. Elvis did the twist in 1962 release *Girls! Girls! Girls!*; he did the twist again in *It Happened at the World's Fair*, as well as doing a waltz. In 1965 movie *Girl Happy* he tried and failed to persuade the world to "Do The Clam"; he had already struck out with "Do The Vega" in *Viva Las Vegas*, though in that film he also returned to some more successful choreography dancing with Ann-Margret to "C'mon Everybody."

When Elvis returned to live performing in the Seventies, there was a lot less leg-shaking and a whole lot more karate going on, in poses and as part of choreographic sequences. Former girlfriend June Juanico thought that this was a great way to camouflage the fact that though he had plenty of rhythm in his hands and feet, the body in-between was not such a great mover. In 1974, one surprised audience watched as Elvis and pals gave a lengthy karate demonstration on stage

As the years wore on, Elvis moved less. Fans didn't love him any the less if he was a little more static on stage.

ELVIS SAID: "My movements are all leg movements. I don't do nothing with my body."

ELVIS SAID: "Some people tap their feet, some people snap their fingers, and some people sway back and forth. I just sorta do 'em all together, I guess."

SONNY WEST, ON ELVIS CIRCA 1956: "Every time he moved, it seemed like a couple of hundred gals were getting it off."

ELAINE DUNDY: "Such wigglings and wrigglings had not been seen since the serpent caused man's expulsion from paradise."

"DANNY"

This Fred Wise and Ben Weisman song was very nearly the title song for Elvis' second Paramount feature, *King Creole*, before the movie name was changed from the novel's original title (*A Stone for Danny Fisher*). The song was excised from the picture, and then in 1960, retitled "Lonely Blue Boy," it became a huge international #1 for Conway Twitty.

Elvis' version, laid down at Radio Recorders on February 11, 1958, was first released posthumously on *Elvis: A Legendary Performer Vol. 3* in 1978. Since then it has appeared on the *King Of Rock & Roll* anthology, the 1997 RCA re-release of the *King Creole* soundtrack and *Essential Elvis Vol. 3*.

"DANNY BOY"

Elvis recorded this popular Irish ditty (written by Englishman Frederick Weatherly in 1910, to the tune "Londonderry Air") at Graceland on February 5, 1976 for release on the *From Elvis Presley Boulevard* album. More recently, the song has appeared on *Walk A Mile In My Shoes*, the CD reissue of *Moody Blue* and *Elvis Inspirational*.

A previous recording, made at home in Germany in 1959, saw release on 1984 album *A Golden Celebration* and FTD album *In A Private Moment*. Elvis had been heard singing at least as far back as 1958, on set while shooting *King Creole* (his character's name was Danny).

Alternate takes from the 1976 recording session at Graceland are included on *Platinum: A Life In Music* and popular FTD release *The Jungle Room Sessions*, as well as on a number of bootlegs.

An instrumental version is on NBC TV Special-related FTD album *Burbank '68*.

FTD live release *Tucson '76* features Elvis performing the song, though more often than not at Elvis concerts the song was sung live by Sherill Nielson in a medley with "Walk With Me."

DARBY, KEN
(B. KENNETH LORIN DARBY, 1909-1992)

Darby, a Hollywood composer, voice coach and orchestral arranger best known for his movie adaptations of Broadway musicals, worked with Elvis on his first movie *Love Me Tender*, for which he wrote all four songs ("Love Me Tender," "We're Gonna Move," "Let Me" and "Poor Boy," all of which were credited for publishing issues under the name of his wife, Vera Matson, with Elvis sharing the credits and royalties. The Ken Darby Singers provided back-up on the recordings—they previously featured on Bing Crosby's biggest-selling record, "White Christmas," a song that Elvis later covered.

Darby began his movie career as an orchestral arranger on *The Wizard of Oz* (1939). He won Oscars for his work on *The King and I* (1956), *Porgy and Bess* (1959) and *Camelot* (1967).

DARIN, BOBBY
(B. WALDEN ROBERT CASSOTTO, 1936-1973)

A great deal of mutual professional esteem linked Elvis and singer/actor Bobby Darin.

Born in the Bronx on May 14, 1936, Darin rose to fame around the same time as Elvis, appearing on "Stage Show" just two months after Elvis in 1956. He sang on a number of early song demos for Elvis before scoring his first chart-topping hits in 1958 with "Splish Splash" and the next year "Dream Lover," his Italian looks winning him many admirers in the teen idol stakes. His 1960 version of Bertolt Brecht/Kurt Weill song "Mack The Knife" earned him multiple Grammys, two millions sales and later became his trademark song. Darin's movie career avoided the cookie-cutter pitfalls of Elvis' and included an Oscar-nominated performance in *Captain Newman, M.D.* (1963).

Darin's was a chameleon career, in which, like Elvis, his music spanned multiple genres—from rock to folk to country to smooth standards and even, briefly, anti-establishment songs in the late Sixties; for much of the Sixties and the early Seventies he was a top Las Vegas draw. Elvis took in Bobby Darin's shows a number of times; Darin returned the compliment in Las Vegas in the Seventies (Elvis introduced him to the audience when he knew he was in the house).

Elvis recorded a number of songs Darin wrote and sang including "I'll Be There," "I Want You With Me" and "You're The Reason I'm Living." Both singers covered "Until It's Time For You To Go." Elvis also hired comic Nipsey Russell as the opener to live shows in 1971—Russell had worked with Darin in New York in the Sixties.

Darin was inducted into the Rock and Roll Hall of Fame in 1990. In 2004, Kevin Spacey starred as the erstwhile rock and roller in biopic *Beyond the Sea*.

BOBBY DARIN: "If you put Elvis Presley on one side of the street and all us Johnny-Come-Latelys on the other, the kids would be mobbing Elvis."

"DARK MOON"

Elvis sang and recorded this song at Graceland on a tape machine in 1966. It was found after his death and issued on *A Golden Celebration* (1984) and *Home Recordings* (1999) among others. Written by Ned. Miller, the song was originally a top five hit for Gale Storm in 1957.

DATE WITH ELVIS, A

Ten re-released tracks that RCA brought out on LP in late July 1959 to tide fans over until Elvis returned from Germany—the album art even featured a calendar with March 24, 1960 circled. In eight weeks on the *Billboard* LP chart, the album sold a disappointed 175,000 copies and peaked at #32. Half of the material came from Sun, with the other half almost entirely made up of movie soundtrack songs.

TRACK LISTING:
1. Blue Moon Of Kentucky
2. Young And Beautiful
3. (You're So Square) Baby I Don't Care
4. Milkcow Blues Boogie
5. Baby Let's Play House
6. Good Rockin' Tonight
7. Is It So Strange
8. We're Gonna Move
9. I Want To Be Free
10. I Forgot To Remember To Forget

"DATIN'"

Elvis overdubbed his vocal for this sparse Fred Wise / Randy Starr song on the *Paradise, Hawaiian Style* soundtrack at Radio Recorders on August 4, 1965 after the band laid down an instrumental on July 26—in the movie, it's a duet with Donna Butterworth.

After the original soundtrack release, the song has since appeared on the *Double Features* release (twinned with *Frankie and Johnny*). Early collectors' set *Elvis Aron Presley* features alternate takes; more alternates are on the FTD *Paradise, Hawaiian Style* soundtrack release from 2004.

DAVENPORT, JOHN

A pseudonym used by songwriter Otis Blackwell.

DAVIS, JIMMIE
(1899-2000)

A country singer and two-term Governor of Louisiana, "singing governor" Jimmie Davis is best known for writing the song "You Are My Sunshine." In 1944 he became governor of Louisiana after serving as Louisiana's chief of police. At the very end of his first term as governor, as a favor to staffer Bob Greer, in October 1948 Mr. Davis gave Elvis' future manager Tom Parker the honorary commission of Colonel. Davis continued to sing, though turned more to gospel than country, and was re-elected governor in 1960. He was inducted into the country hall of fame in 1972 and lived to the extremely ripe old age of 101.

DAVIS, (SCOTT) "MAC"
(B. 1942)

Singer, songwriter and actor Mac Davis saw Elvis at an early live show in Lubbock, Texas, when Elvis was still enough of an unknown to perform at a car dealership. Davis was born in Lubbock—Buddy Holly's home town—on January 21, 1942.

Davis returned to Elvis' world in February 1968 through arranger Billy Strange, Davis's sometime writing partner, who put forward their song "A Little Less Conversation" at a March 1968 recording session.

Elvis sang two Davis and Strange songs, "Memories" and "Nothingville," at the NBC TV Special in 1968.

When Elvis was recording at American Sound Studio in Memphis in early 1969, Davis came in personally to play Elvis his recent composition, "In The Ghetto." According to keyboard player Bobby Wood, "Elvis just shook his head when Mac got through with that song; Mac was shaking like a leaf."

Elvis also recorded Davis songs "Don't Cry, Daddy," "Clean Up Your Own Back Yard" and the title song to *Charro!* He was scheduled to record another of his songs, "Poor Man's Gold," during his 1969 American Sound Studio session, but never got round to laying down a vocal for the band track.

Davis also wrote songs for Kenny Rogers, Bobby Goldsboro, Glen Campbell and Nancy Sinatra, and scored a solo #1 hit in 1972 with "Baby Don't Get Hooked On Me."

Davis had his own TV variety show in the mid-seventies on NBC, and in 1974 was named "Entertainer of the Year" by the Academy of Country Music. He continued recording and acting through into the Eighties. Davis has a star on the Hollywood Walk of Fame. He was inducted into the Songwriters' Hall of Fame in 2006.

Davis presented 1987 Elvis documentary *Elvis, His Life And Times*, and 1993 tribute *America Comes to Graceland*.

Davis was inducted into the Songwriters Hall of Fame in 2006.

DAVIS, OSCAR
(1902-1975)

In 1954, Oscar Davis was helping Colonel Tom Parker organize shows for country singer Eddy Arnold. Davis had been a leading promoter in his own right, managing top country talent such as Hank Williams and Roy Acuff; he knew his way around the entertainment world so well that he had picked up the nickname "Baron of the Box Office."

Davis took in an early Elvis performance at the Eagle's Nest in late October 1954, and complimented him personally the following night when they met backstage at the Ellis Auditorium after an Eddy Arnold show, taking the opportunity to make discreet enquiries about Elvis' management situation. The oft-told story is that when Davis returned to meet Elvis and the band a week later, he walked in with Colonel Tom Parker, who by this time had muscled in on the project. The Colonel later talked down how impressed Davis said he had been by the effect Elvis had on the audience. Davis did better a couple of years later, signing up then unknown Sun artist Jerry Lee Lewis to a management contract; in early 1957 he attempted unsuccessfully to sign up Elvis' band members and backing singers.

DAVIS, RICHARD
(1930-2004)

A member of Elvis' entourage right through the Sixties, Elvis knew Richard Davis—"Broom" as he called him—from football games in Memphis. Davis became a pal and worked for Elvis as a wardrobe manager, valet, movie stand-in and

Sammy Davis Jr. in Elvis' dressing room during the filming of *That's The Way It Is, 1970*.

bodyguard. He traveled to the West Coast with Elvis in 1962 as his wardrobe man on 1962 movie *It Happened at the World's Fair*, and was Elvis' stand-in on more than twenty movies.

During his time in the entourage, Elvis gave Davis a white Cadillac convertible. Davis stopped working for Elvis in 1969, when the payroll was slimmed down and he didn't make the cut, though he traveled with Elvis again as wardrobe manager on his September 1970 six-date tour.

Davis was involved in an unfortunate incident in the summer of 1967 that led to the cancellation of a recording session RCA had set up for Elvis in LA, after Davis ran over and killed a gardener near Elvis' Bel Air home—the gardener had unexpectedly stepped out from a hedge.

Post-Elvis, Davis worked as a record company promotions manager, a casino host and a security guard.

RICHARD DAVIS: "We did everything together. When Elvis slept, we slept. When Elvis partied, we partied. When Elvis worked, we worked."

DAVIS, SAMMY JR.
(1925-1990)

Elvis met Sammy Davis Jr. on the *King Creole* set in 1958, and they both appeared on the show Frank Sinatra hosted to welcome Elvis back after his Army service in 1960—Davis sings "It's Nice To Go Trav'ling" with Elvis in the show. Elvis and Sammy Davis Jr. reciprocated with visits to one another's stage shows in the Sixties and Seventies; Elvis also reputedly gave Davis a valuable black sapphire ring.

Davis was a true all-round entertainer, an accomplished comedian, singer, dancer, musician and stage and screen actor, the son of dancers born in Harlem on December 8, 1925 who grew up on the road and made his stage debut when little more than a toddler (as "Silent Sam, the Dancing Midget").

In the late Fifties Davis was one of a growing number of African-American entertainers to break into mainstream white American entertainment—he refused to play before segregated audiences—and was one of very few who converted to Judaism. He appeared in 1960 movie *Ocean's Eleven* with fellow rat-packers Frank Sinatra, Dean Martin, Peter Lawford and Joey Bishop, the first of several Rat Pack movies. That year he received death threats for marrying (white) Swedish actress May Britt.

Davis's hits over the years include "Love Me Or Leave Me," "That Old Black Magic" and "The Candy Man" (from the 1971 screen adaptation of *Willie Wonka and the Chocolate Factory*). For many years he was a top Las Vegas attraction, and in the Seventies he hosted his own TV show.

SAMMY DAVIS, JR.: "There was something just bordering on rudeness about Elvis. He never actually did anything rude, but he always seemed as if he was just going to. On a scale of one to ten, I would rate him eleven."

MARTY LACKER: "Of all those guys out there. . . . who claimed to be one of Elvis' close buddies, only Sammy Davis Junior was really a friend."

DAY IN THE LIFE OF A FAMOUS DJ, A

See PIED PIPER OF CLEVELAND, THE: A DAY IN THE LIFE OF A FAMOUS DISC JOCKEY

DAY, JAMES CLAYTON
(1934-1999)

A steel guitar player who backed Elvis on tour in Texas in early 1955 and gigged with him on and off that year. Jimmy Day performed regularly with Ray Price's Cherokee Cowboys at that time. Over the years he backed many artists, including Jim Reeves, Hank Williams, Faron Young and Patsy Cline.

He was inducted into the Country Music Association Hall of Fame in 1999.

DE CORDOVA, FRED
(1910-2001)

Movie and TV director De Cordova worked with Elvis in 1965 on *Frankie and Johnny*, the last feature film he directed in a career that started with comedies and musicals in the 1940s. He was most successful on TV, for many years executive producing "The Tonight Show Starring Johnny Carson." He also directed future President of the United States Ronald Reagan in *Bedtime for Bonzo* (1951).

DEAN, JAMES
(B. JAMES BYRON DEAN, 1931-1955)

James Dean was an early favorite of Elvis', a star whose acting career he longed to emulate and a fellow focus of nascent youth culture in Fifties America. At the start of his career, Elvis was occasionally referred to as "the musical James Dean."

The archetypal teenage rebel, actor Dean lived fast and died young when he crashed his Porsche 550 Spyder in California on September 30, 1955. Elvis reputedly cried when he heard the news.

James Dean was born in Marion, Indiana on February 8, 1931. He grew up between this rural community and Los Angeles before starting out in acting. Broadway roles brought him his chance in Hollywood (at one stage he even tested stunts for the game show "Beat the Clock"). All-in-all, he only starred in three movies, though he had been appearing in TV shows since the early Fifties.

Dean is one of only half a dozen actors to receive an Oscar nomination for his first screen appearance; he is the only actor ever to be nominated twice for posthumous Oscars (in *East of Eden* and *Giant*).

Elvis was so admiring of Dean's performance in *Rebel Without a Cause* that he learned every one of his lines by heart.

In late 1955, as Colonel Parker was engineering Elvis' rise to national fame, he told William Morris agent Harry Kalcheim that Elvis would make excellent James Dean material on the silver screen. On the set of his first movie *Love Me Tender*, Elvis told producer David Weisbart that he would love to play Dean in the biopic he was planning; Weisbart later made a documentary rather than a feature.

When Elvis first went out to Hollywood in 1956, he befriended Nick Adams, who had been a close friend of Dean's. Also in 1956, the two teen idols featured in a one-off magazine, titled *Elvis and Jimmy*.

Like Elvis, in the Nineties Dean has featured on a popular US postage stamp.

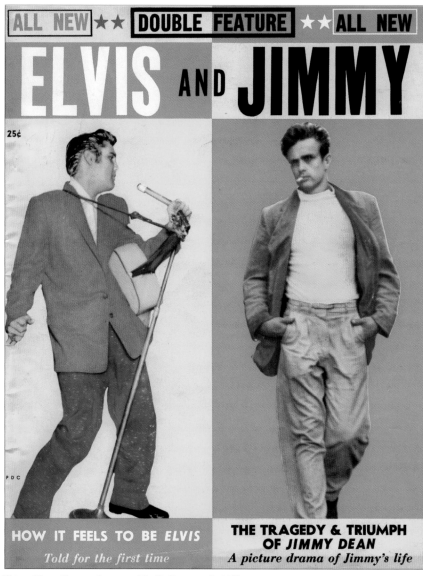

Elvis and James Dean on the cover of *Double Feature* in the 1960s.

ELVIS SAID: "I would never compare myself in any way to James Dean because James Dean was a genius in acting."

DEARY, JOAN

A New York-based RCA executive who worked with Elvis for several decades, initially in the Fifties in her role as secretary to RCA executive Steve Sholes, later in her capacity as an A&R executive with Harry Jenkins for Elvis' June 1972 concerts at Madison Square Garden in New York, and the *Aloha From Hawaii* album arrangements. In 1973 Deary worked on a project to put together a mainly live album for Elvis, with the working title *Fool*, before Felton Jarvis returned from ill-health and took over the project. When the Colonel sold Elvis' back catalog to the record label in 1973, Deary came up with the idea of the highly successful "Legendary Performer" series of records, starting with outtakes from Elvis recording sessions.

After Elvis' death, Deary combed through Elvis' collection of home recordings to find material worthy of release. In the Eighties she was responsible for compiling popular collectors' sets of previously unheard Elvis material and outtakes, notably *Elvis Aron Presley* and *A Golden Celebration* (for which she received a Grammy nomination).

Deary retired from RCA in 1987, by which time she had risen to the position of A&R Executive Director. For many years after, she was a popular speaker at Elvis fan club events. She died in 1999.

DEATH

There can be little doubt that Elvis' premature death—like the death of James Dean and Marilyn Monroe before him—has helped to cement his legend.

Elvis' death was one of those rare events that touched people so deeply that decades later they vividly recall where they were when they heard the news. Millions of people mourned his passing; hundreds of thousands of people spontaneously gathered at his home. As with so much in his life, Elvis' death changed social mores: it was the first time that the death of a performer and a celebrity made the top of the TV news and the main headlines.

More than most, Elvis lived his life with an awareness of death—one of the factors that prompted decades of spiritual questing. Elvis shared his mother's womb with a twin who was born dead. His mother's death, when he was 23, was a defining moment in his emotional life; ever after he felt a particular closeness to people in his entourage who, like himself, had lost a parent. Friends have also revealed that Elvis had quite a fascination with death, taking occasional trips to the Memphis morgue to indulge his curiosity or as a dare to people close to him, including entourage members and future wife Priscilla.

Elvis was highly aware that his mother died at the age of 42 (her stated rather than real age) as he passed that same landmark—the last birthday he was to celebrate. According to maid Nancy Rooks, Elvis often said that he wanted to die on the same day of the year as his Mama, August 14. A little more than a year before he died, a California newspaper wrote that when he performed "My Way the entire concert hall was gripped by an eerie silence, "like witnessing a chilling prophecy." During his December 1976 tour he wrote notes in which he expressed how much he was suffering.

Elvis' health had been in slow but relentless decline for three or four years before his heart finally gave out. He had been suffering from periods of depression and a niggling array of side-effects caused and exacerbated by the drugs he took to keep several medical conditions under control, as well as the more serious repercussions of his voluntary abuse of prescribed medicines.

And yet as Elvis approached his 42nd birthday in January 1977, he confided to Charlie Hodge and Larry Geller that he was looking forward to making major changes in his life. He planned to stop touring, and finally to get rid of the entourage that for so many years had acted as a membrane between Elvis and the world. His intentions reputedly included returning to serious acting, ditching the Colonel for Tom Hulett, perhaps marrying girlfriend Ginger Alden and having more children. . .

This optimism contrasts significantly with reports about Elvis' state of mind in the weeks before he died. Elvis told Felton Jarvis how tired he was of being Elvis Presley. He dropped hints that he wouldn't be around much longer. He refused to take his worsening health seriously and declined to have a full battery of medical tests. He began reminiscing more than ever, falling prey to flashbacks from his childhood and having strange dreams.

City of Memphis remembers Elvis, 1977.

THE CIRCUMSTANCES OF ELVIS' DEATH

After waking at 4 p.m. on August 15, 1977, Elvis watched TV on and off into the evening. Dr. Nichopoulos dropped off his usual medications, and found him to be in good health, if concerned that girlfriend Ginger Alden was not keen to accompany him on his upcoming tour, scheduled to begin in Portland the next day. Larry Geller visited and spent some time talking with Elvis. He remembers Elvis talking in a childlike voice, and saying "Angels fly because they take themselves so lightly."

Elvis and Ginger went our for a ride on one of Elvis' motorcycles, before Elvis developed a toothache and decided he needed to go see his dentist. Ricky Stanley brought in some food from the local Pizza Hut. Plans to see a movie at the local theater fell through, which put Elvis in a bad mood, compounding his usual anxiety before going off a tour. Elvis attended a 10:30 p.m. dentist's appointment with Dr. Hofman, and took along Ginger Alden to keep him company.

Dr. Nichopoulos received a call at 2 or 3 a.m., in which Elvis asked for a prescription for Dilaudid, a painkiller to help him with toothache after getting fillings. Though Elvis had Ricky Stanley pick up the prescription of six tablets of Dilaudid and fill it at the hospital, Dr. Nichopoulos says that Elvis didn't actually take the medication because a game of racquetball with Ginger, Billy and Jo Smith, which he played between 4 and 6 a.m. on August 16, took his mind off the pain. Afterwards, Elvis played the piano and sang for a while. When he and Ginger

retired upstairs, rather than go to sleep Elvis took a book off to the bathroom. Though he had already taken the sedative his doctor had left, he was unable to get to sleep, much as he knew he needed the rest before traveling. Ginger was already asleep when Elvis spoke with his doctor's nurse at 8 a.m., and arranged for more sedatives to be brought up - in Dr. Nick's recollection, one sedative and one placebo. Rick Stanley—one of half a dozen guys who usually took turns sleeping in the bedroom next to Elvis' to keep an eye on him if he got up in the night—was fast asleep downstairs, so Elvis' Aunt Delta Biggs went to the nurse's house to pick up the extra medication.

Overall, Elvis took three packets of sleeping pills prepared for him by his doctor that night: a mixture of anti-depressants, sleeping pills and placebos. Elvis told his Aunt Delta that he would see her when he woke up at 7 p.m.

Ginger awoke at 1:30 or 2 p.m. depending on accounts. When she saw that Elvis was not in bed, she went to look for him in his bathroom. She opened the door to find him face down on the floor. She later said, "I slapped him a few times, and it was like he breathed once when I turned his head. I raised one of his eyelids and his eye was just blood red, but I couldn't move him. I thought at first he might have hit his head, because he had fallen out of his black lounging chair and his face was buried in the carpet." Other accounts state that Elvis was discovered lying prone, in front of the toilet, with his pajama bottoms round his ankles; yet others state that he was in a pile of his own vomit, and that he had

been dead long enough to turn blue and for rigor mortis to set in.

Ginger called downstairs for help. Maid Nancy Rooks says that she was the first to race upstairs (other maids have made this claim too), soon followed by Al Strada, Joe Esposito and others. Joe Esposito placed a call to Memphis Fire Department Engine House No. 29 at 2.33 p.m, and Dr. Nichopoulos was paged to come to Graceland immediately. In some accounts, Charlie Hodge tried to give Elvis CPR. Paramedics Charles Crosby and Ulysses Jones arrived within minutes. Charles Crosby says that a woman—Vernon's nurse girlfriend Sandy Miller—was attempting mouth-to-mouth resuscitation on Elvis when they arrived. Ginger had been sent away; with Elvis were Vernon, Sandy, Joe Esposito, Al Strada, Charlie Hodge and later David Stanley, who told the paramedics that he thought Elvis had OD'd. By his account, David Stanley immediately began to clear away empty pill packets before the paramedics had finished trying to pump air into Elvis' lungs and revive him. The paramedics, assisted by people in the room, loaded Elvis onto a gurney and into an ambulance to take him to the hospital, accompanied by Joe Esposito, Al Strada and by some accounts Charlie Hodge. Dr. Nichopoulos arrived just as the ambulance was pulling out, and helped try to resuscitate him through heart massage, intubation and the insertion of an IV on the 15 mile trip to the Baptist Memorial Hospital. In the emergency room they carried on doing CPR until it was evident that there were no signs of life.

ABOVE: Friends and relatives file into the mausoleum to pay their last respects to Elvis Presley.
BELOW: The casket of Elvis Presley can be seen through the back window of the hearse, while thousands of fans watch from across the street.

that. By the time they were finally closed, as many as 25,000 people had filed past the coffin, but tens of thousands of people were turned away.

That evening family members and close friends held a vigil in the living room. The funeral was held in that same room on August 18 at 2 p.m.., followed by a brief service at the Forest Hill cemetery chapel).

Recriminations have continued into this millennium about Elvis' death, his body worn out at the age of 42. Accusations have fallen on Elvis' doctors, his entourage and the Colonel for failing to get Elvis to realize how imperiled his health had become. Almost to a person, people in Elvis' life have said that they tried to bring up the issue of his drug dependency but Elvis simply would not listen.

Elvis' personal physician, Dr. Nichopoulos, was cleared of over-prescribing drugs to Elvis in a jury trial brought by the Tennessee State Board of Medical Examiners in 1981.

Elvis' head of security at the time, Dick Grob wrote a 600-page book that provides a wealth of detail on the final stage of Elvis' life and the aftermath of his death.

PRESIDENT JIMMY CARTER, 1977: "Elvis Presley's death deprives our country of a part of itself. He was unique, irreplaceable. More than twenty years ago, he burst upon the scene with an impact that was unprecedented and will probably never be equaled. His music and his personality, fusing the styles of white country and black rhythm and blues, permanently changed the face of American popular culture. His following was immense. And he was a symbol to people the world over of the vitality, rebelliousness and good humor of this country."

FRANK SINATRA, 1977: "There have been many accolades uttered about Elvis' talent and performances through the years, all of which I agree with wholeheartedly. I shall miss him dearly as a friend. He was a warm, considerate and generous man."

COLONEL PARKER, 1977: "It's just like when he went in the army . . . This changes nothing."

GREIL MARCUS: "The enormity of his impact on culture, on millions of people, was never really clear when he was alive . . . When he died, the event was a kind of explosion."

OTIS BLACKWELL: "Some people you just figure are never going to die. Inside man, they'll always live. When they're gone, a certain piece goes and you just can't believe it."

CAUSE OF DEATH

After Elvis was officially pronounced dead, an autopsy was undertaken. At a press conference called before the autopsy was completed it was announced that the cause of death was cardiac arrhythmia, a condition that ranges in seriousness from minor palpitations to sudden, unexpected cardiac arrest. Sudden arrhythmia death syndrome, also known as SADS, is a cause of death of several hundred thousand people in the US every year, and is in effect a catch-all category for people whose death is brought on by a heart attack. In many cases, the condition is hereditary.

The autopsy results were never made public. At Vernon's instruction, they were delivered only to him. Dr. Nichopoulos, who was present at the procedure, recalls that they found hardening of one of Elvis' heart vessels, and an enlarged heart, along with hypertension.

To this day, medical experts continue to debate whether Elvis had a seizure, or his heart went into arrhythmia because he was straining on the toilet.

Two lab reports into Elvis' death indicated that he had as many as fourteen different sub-

Dr. Nick was given a ride back to Graceland in the same ambulance that had taken Elvis to hospital, so that the paramedics would be on hand in case they were needed when he broke the news to Vernon, who had a heart condition himself. Sam Thompson later recalled, "The whole place just filled, and people were crying and moaning. It was chaos." Maid Nancy Rooks says that before the doctor returned, she and Aunt Delta emptied Elvis' bathroom of all pills, bottles and syringes and threw them out in the trash (though some syringes escaped their sweep). They also remade Elvis' bed and changed the towels in the bathroom.

The above account is a composite from the kaleidoscopic recollections published over the years by practically every person who was at Graceland that day. Joe Esposito, the most senior member of Elvis' entourage, said that when Ginger Alden called down in panic saying that Elvis had fainted, Elvis' wardrobe man Al Strada was the first to be alerted. Esposito went racing upstairs, pulled up Elvis' pajama bottoms and called 911. Esposito did not give Elvis mouth-to-mouth, but attempted a heart massage. Vernon

came up, desperate. While they waited for the ambulance to arrive Lisa Marie ran into the room and Ginger bundled her back out. Billy Smith and others drove to the hospital as the doctors tried to revive Elvis. When it was clear that there was nothing to be done, Esposito called Priscilla and Colonel Parker, and arranged for a plane to pick up Priscilla from Los Angeles.

Elvis was officially recorded dead at 3:30 p.m. on Tuesday August 16, 1977. Up to 50,000 fans gathered outside Graceland after the public announcement of Elvis' death. The following morning, motorists driving to work in Memphis turned on their headlights as a sign of mourning. Overruling advice from security guards, at 3 p.m. Vernon threw open the music gates for two hours to let the crowd—quoted to be as large as 100,000 strong at one point—file past the open casket in Graceland's entrance hallway. Many mourners fainted from the emotion, some before they even got to the mansion door. Those that came round were given another chance to pay their respects. The gates were kept open for a further hour, and then an additional half hour after stances in his blood. Whether or not Elvis had subjected himself to similar pharmaceutical cocktails in the past, it has been suggested that this time the polypharmacy cocktail in his body irreversibly compromised his heart. An oft-quoted report by Bio-Science Laboratories states: "Of particular note is the combination of codeine, ethchlorvynol, and barbiturates detected in body fluids and tissue. The levels in the body fluids and tissues exceed some other known identifiable multiple drug overdose cases where codeine has been implicated." Physicians have gone on record to state that the level of codeine in Elvis' liver was around one third the amount usually found in fatal codeine overdose victims. The only drug trace found in Elvis' body that was close to fatal dosage was methaqualone (Quaalude).

However, the official coroner was of the opinion that none of the drugs in Elvis' system was present in sufficiently high quantities to contribute to his death. According to Dr. Jerry T. Francisco, the Shelby County Medical Examiner who was in charge of Elvis' autopsy: "Elvis Presley died in a matter of four short minutes of coronary arrhythmia, an irregular beating of the heart. Death occurred between 9 a.m. and 2 p.m. There's no way to be more precise than that. [The autopsy revealed] that there was severe cardiovascular disease present. He had a history of mild hypertension and some coronary artery disease. These two diseases may be responsible for cardiac arrhythmia, but the precise cause was not determined. Basically it was a natural death. The precise cause of death may never be discovered."

DR. NICHOPOULOS: "There's no way to know if things would have turned out differently if the regular procedure had been followed. There's certainly a possibility that if there'd been someone in the next room (as there should have been), then when Elvis had a cardiac arrhythmia and passed out they would have heard it. Whether they could have done anything or not, there's no way to know."

LAMAR FIKE: "I don't think Elvis ever thought he'd live long. I think he knew deep down in the back of his mind there was not much long life in that family."

JOE ESPOSITO: "The last couple of years were tough. it was tough for all of us because we know that was not the Elvis we knew! It was almost like he was sick and this other person took over—that was not him."

LAMAR FIKE: "If it hadn't been for Elvis' group, he would have died three years earlier... You never knew when the alarm was going to go off. But we literally kept that man alive."

PETER GURALNICK: ." . . All one has to do is look at Elvis' life, the accelerating dependence on medications available to him in almost unimaginable quantities, the willing enlistment of doctors who seemed never to give a thought to the dangers or likely consequences of what they were prescribing, and the incontrovertible evidence of the medical problems stemming primarily from the use of drugs that Elvis experienced over his last four years, to understand the causes of death."

JACKIE KAHANE: "Elvis committed suicide for want of another term. It saddened me to see such a big talent kill himself."

SUPERNATURAL EXPERIENCES

Many people in Elvis' life have told of strange experiences around the time of Elvis' death. Backup singer Larry Strickland dreamed of performing at a funeral to a faceless corpse just before Elvis died.

Racing over to Graceland when he first heard the news, the Elvis tape in George Klein's car broke right at the beginning of "Can't Help Falling In Love." Later that evening, when Klein and other pals gathered to watch the ten o'clock news about Elvis' death, all the TVs at Graceland spontaneously went out.

Immediately after Elvis' funeral at Graceland, as people were filing out of the house to ride to the chapel where he was to be buried, a large bough fell off a tree in the grounds with a loud crack. Billy Stanley recalls that Elvis had told him that after he died, there would be a sign to show that he was happy. However, funeral director Robert Kendall explains the event as being caused by a helicopter trying to get footage.

According to Larry Geller, the day before Elvis died, Vernon received a picture of a saintly figure with his face blanked out, just like the cover of the book Elvis was reading when he died.

Some people who have had near-death experiences and lived to tell the tale have said that they were greeted by Elvis himself as they crossed over to the other side—author Raymond A. Moody has written a book about the phenomenon called *Elvis After Life*.

SUICIDE? MURDER?

Some people, including Elvis-A-Rama museum owner Chris Davidson, believe that Elvis committed suicide because he was too unhappy to go on. The paramedics who first arrived on the scene were initially informed that the patient had overdosed. Albert Goldman claimed that Elvis attempted to kill himself in 1967, before he got married. Elvis' stepbrother David Stanley told the same author that he thought Elvis had taken his own life. He drew this conclusion from the empty pill envelopes and syringes scattered on the floor around Elvis' body in his bathroom, indicating that he had taken all of his medication at once, rather than in several doses during the night, as he usually did. However, this testimony conflicts with reports that girlfriend Ginger Alden was present as Elvis took his medication at the usual times during the night.

Cousin Billy Smith denies that Elvis would ever willingly have taken his life, because he believed that suicide was "a coward's way to go." Smith does not rule out that Elvis may have mistakenly overdosed. More than one of Elvis' cousins took their own lives; cousin Bobby Smith ingested rat poison; cousin Bobbi Mann took an overdose, and a couple of male cousins died young of alcohol-related illnesses.

It should also be borne in mind that Elvis is highly unlikely to have willingly subjected his daughter to the aftermath of his death—she was in the house at the time.

Vernon could not be dissuaded from his belief that his son was murdered; it has been conjectured over the years that the Mafia may have wanted to silence Elvis.

ELVIS' FIXATION WITH DEATH

Red West revealed that Elvis had quite an obsession with death. He attended as a friend of his, a Memphis policeman, was embalmed, and studied the whole process. Billy Smith remembers Elvis visiting the Memphis Funeral Home and asking morticians about their work following the death of cousin Junior Smith in 1961. Elvis would occasionally go out on trips to graveyards to see if any of his entourage got scared, and would also go down to the funeral home where his mother had been laid out, and in the middle of the night walk tour the embalmed bodies.

Elvis also had a fascination with birth. Dave Hebler tells of a time that Elvis took him to a Memphis maternity ward in the middle of the night and almost managed to persuade a woman to allow him to watch as she give birth.

ELVIS TOLD LARRY GELLER: "I'm not afraid of death. . . The soul's free. The soul is going back to God, going home again."

ELVIS LIVES?

Only Marilyn Monroe's death has eclipsed Elvis' in the entertainer conspiracy theory stakes, though in Elvis' case the fascination is far less about how he died than whether he even died at all. Certainly, in his movie career he was close to immortal: only the character Elvis played in his first feature film, *Love Me Tender*, ever dies, and even he comes back as a singing ghost.

In his last year alive, Elvis reputedly fantasized to cousin Billy Smith about taking on a new identity. It is this possibility that has fueled a popular vein of fiction, movies, internet chat room exchanges, sightings, aliases, alleged cameo Elvis appearances in movies (*Home Alone*, *Finding Graceland*), secret diaries, identity swaps and kidnappings, with the line between fictionalized accounts and hidden truths blurred at best. Donnie Sumner has also said that Elvis fantasized about just "disappearing" for a year or two.

Many fans' understandable reluctance to believe that their idol had died was bolstered by tabloid headlines that started in the first year after Elvis' death. For Elvis bibliographer Mary Hancock Hinds, the progenitor of the "Elvis is alive" strand of literature is author Gail Brewer-Giorgio, who wrote a novel about a singer obviously based on Elvis (called Orion in the book) who stages his own death. Brewer-Giorgio later claimed to have received phone calls and mail that she said was proof that Elvis was still alive, leading a decade later to publication of her book *Is Elvis Alive?*, which came with a tape allegedly of a conversation with a post-death Elvis. Brewer-Giorgio suggests that the reason Elvis' death was staged is because of his work as a secret federal agent for the US government. Photographs purporting to be of Elvis, including the mysterious appearance of an Elvis-like figure in a photo taken at Graceland after his death, and photos of Elvis soundalike Jimmy Ellis (who later performed under the name Orion) have been seen as signs that Elvis is still living and breathing on this earth.

A book titled *Is Elvis Alive?* first came out in 1981, written by Steven Chanzes who claimed that the body entombed at Graceland was that of an imposter.

Talk-show host Geraldo Rivera has long been delving into the Elvis may-be-alive issue, ever since hosting 1978 segment "The Elvis Cover Up" on ABC's 20/20 show. Psychics have been claiming contact with Elvis ever since.

Tabloids continue to report on Elvis sightings. For some reason, there is an Elvis sighting hotspot in Kalamazoo, Michigan, with a particular confluence around Burger King restaurants (despite the fact that in life, Elvis preferred Krystal burgers). "Elvis," living under one of his favorite aliases (*see* NAMES), has also been tracked down to Fort Worth, Texas.

Wright City, Missouri has had its very own "Elvis is Alive Museum" since 1990.

In 1992 a group of fans set up "the Presley Commission," modeled on the Warren Commission, to examine evidence surrounding Elvis' death. Their conclusion, published in 1995, was that Elvis deliberately faked his own death.

In 2001, Dr. Donald Hinton claimed that he had been treating Elvis for pain, and that he went by the name of "Jesse." The book predicted that all would be revealed in 2002.

In 2005, producer Dan Bliss auctioned off the iconic Hollywood Sign that overlooked tinseltown until 1978 on eBay to fund a documentary into Elvis' ongoing living and breathing presence on earth, entitled *The Truth About Elvis*. Filmmaker Adam Muskiewicz put up a $3 million reward for proof that Elvis is alive.

Elvis-is-alivers particularly want to know why Elvis' autopsy is embargoed by court until 2025, and why nobody ever claimed on his life insurance policy (whether or not he had an active policy is another question; the Elvis Estate has said that though Elvis had a medical for a Lloyds of London policy, he didn't actually take one out). Conspiracy theorists point to the fact that any heart condition Elvis had would surely have been picked up by one of his many eminent doctors.

Dr. Bill Beeny (not a medical doctor) claims that DNA tests from Elvis when alive and from the body in Elvis' casket do not match, a theory he expounds in his book *Elvis' DNA Proves He's Alive!*

People who filed past Elvis' coffin when it lay in state at Graceland had no doubt whatsoever that the man in the casket was Elvis.

The fact that efforts were made immediately after Elvis' death to "sanitize" the scene in order to protect his dignity and hide his drug dependency—all that investigators found were two syringes, and there were no pharmaceuticals in Elvis' bedroom or bathroom, not even common medications found in practically every household—and Vernon's insistence that the autopsy not be made public prove that there was a cover-up to preserve Elvis' privacy and dignity in death, but not necessarily that the circumstances of Elvis' death were suspicious, faked or misrepresented. Then again, truth can exceed the wildest of imaginings.

MARY HANCOCK HINDS: "Edgar Caycee, Nostradamus and Harry Houdini spent their lifetimes trying to prove what Elvis inadvertently demonstrated when he died — there is indeed life after death."

LARRY GELLER: "I'm not surprised that people want him alive, but Elvis Presley was laid to rest on August 18, 1977. He will live forever."

Books:

Coroner at Large, by Thomas Noguchi, Simon and Schuster, 1985.

Elvis After Life: Unusual Psychic Experiences Surrounding the Death of a Superstar, by Raymond A. Moody Junior, Peachtree Publishers, 1987.

Is Elvis Alive? The Most Incredible Elvis Presley Story Ever Told, by Gail Brewer-Giorgio, Tudor Publishing Company, 1988.

The Elvis Files: Was His Death Faked?, by Gail Brewer-Giorgio, Shapolsky publishers, 1990.

The Death of Elvis: What Really Happened?, by Charles C. Thompson II and James P. Cole, Delacorte Press, 199.1

The Elvis Sightings, Peter Eicher, Avon Books, 1993

Elvis: Murdered by the Mob, by John Parker, Arrow, 1994.

The King Is Dead: Tales of Elvis Post-Mortem, ed. by Paul L. Sammon, Delta, 1994.

The Elvis Conspiracy, by Dick Grob, Fox Reflections Publishers, 1995.

Elvis: Alive or Dead?, The Presley Commission, 1995.

Elvis Undercover: Is He Alive and Coming Back?, by Gail Brewer-Giorgio, Bright Books, 1999.

The Truth About Elvis Aron Presley: In His Own Words, by Dr. Donald Hinton, American Literary Press, 2001.

The Tupelo-Memphis Murders: A Psychological Study of Self-Destruction and Murder! Anon., Unquiet Grave Productions, 2004.

Elvis Decoded - A Fan's Guide To Deciphering The Myths And Misinformation, by Patrick Lacy, AuthorHouse, 2006.

The Resurrection of the King: The Most Compelling Elvis Is Alive Story Ever Told, by Bruce L. Kearns, BookSurge, 2007.

ELVIS' EPITAPH:

Elvis
Aaron
Presley

January 8, 1935
August 16, 1977

SON OF
Vernon Elvis Presley
AND
Gladys Love Presley

FATHER OF
Lisa Marie Presley

He was a precious gift from God
We cherished and loved dearly.

He had a God-given talent that he shared
With the world. And without a doubt,
He became most widely acclaimed;
Capturing the hearts of young and old alike.

He was admired not only as an entertainer,
But as the great humanitarian that he was;
For his generosity, and his kind feelings
For his fellow man.

He revolutionized the field of music and
Received its highest awards.

He became a living legend in his own time;
Earning the respect and love of millions.

God saw that he needed some rest and
Called him home to be with Him.

We miss you, Son and Daddy. I thank god
That He gave us you as our son.

By: Vernon Presley

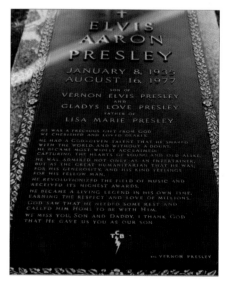

At the head of Elvis' tombstone, close friends installed an eternal flame with the following encomium:

TO ELVIS IN MEMORIAM

You gave yourself to each of us in
some manner. You were wrapped in
thoughtfulness and tied with love.
May this flame reflect our never
ending respect and love for you.
May it serve as a constant reminder
to each of us of your eternal presence.

Tommy Henley
Jerry Schilling
Letetia Henley
Dean Nichopoulos
Patsy Gambill
Dr. Geo. Nichopoulos
Al Strada
Janelle McComb
Felton Jarvis
Joe Esposito

Both of these inscriptions were drafted by Janelle McComb.

DECORATING

Elvis' philosophy for his living spaces, as indeed to some degree for his life, was to get things taken of in a flash. When it wasn't his woman of the time looking after the work, Elvis would hire a contractor and spend the minimum of time choosing what he wanted. He famously picked out the furnishings and furniture for the Jungle Room in a half hour. He also famously disliked antiques, as they reminded him of the second-hand furniture he'd grown up with.

See GRACELAND and Elvis' various homes for specifics.

"DELILAH"

Elvis never recorded this monster 1968 hit for Tom Jones but he did sing it while off-duty, and reputedly liked to use the song as material to warm up his voice. A line or two of the song appears in a couple of unofficial CDs including *Elvis Among Friends*; he may also have given it a blast in Lake Tahoe in 1976.

DEMETRIUS, CLAUDE
(1917-1988)

A songwriter who wrote for Louis Armstrong, Louis Jordan and B.B. King before being hired to write for Gladys Music in 1956. Over the next couple of years he provided a number of hits for Elvis (some co-written with Aaron Shroeder and others) including "I Was The One," "Mean Woman Blues," "Santa, Bring My Baby Back (To Me)" and gold record "Hard Headed Woman." He also wrote "Dixieland Rock."

DENNY, JAMES
(1911-1963)

A hard-nosed talent manager at the Grand Ole Opry when Elvis first played there in October 1954, variously credited with telling Elvis to go back to driving a truck and telling Sam Phillips that Elvis showed potential but was not right for the Opry. In 1956 Denny set up his own highly successful country promotions agency, and was later involved in Buddy Holly's early career.

Denny was voted into the Country Music Hall of Fame in 1966.

DESERT STORM

An unofficial 1996 2-disc release of the final concert from Elvis' 1974 Las Vegas summer season, remembered more for Elvis' meandering and off-the-cuff comments than his canoral performance, though he does some of the songs beautifully.

DeSHANNON, JACKIE
(B. SHARON MYERS, 1944)

Kentucky-born Jackie DeShannon started out as a rockabilly singer in the late Fifties before turning her hand to writing songs for Brenda Lee and others, and contributing to the growing influence of folk music on the Sixties musical scene. Among others, she wrote classic Sixties tunes "When You Walk In The Room," "Needles And Pins" and songs for Marianne Faithfull; she also supported The Beatles on their first US tour. Her greatest musical success, however, was a top-ten version of Burt Bacharach song "What The World Needs Now Is Love." She carried on writing hits into the Eighties (including Kim Carnes' "Bette Davis Eyes").

From the mid-Sixties, she would go and jam with Elvis at his LA home, and later took in his shows in Las Vegas. She is sometimes said to have dated Elvis, though in recent interviews she says she preferred friendship with him to romance.

"DETROIT CITY"

Elvis sang a few lines of this hit for Tom Jones (and also Bobby Bare and Dolly Parton) at a concert in Detroit in 1970. Fans can track this cameo down on unofficial release *Real Fun on Stage . . . And In The Studio* and others.

"(YOU'RE THE) DEVIL IN DISGUISE"

Elvis recorded this rocking Bill Giant / Bernie Baum / Florence Kaye composition at Studio B in Nashville on May 26, 1963, and quickly picked it to be his next single, paired with "Please Don't Drag That String Around." The lead track climbed to #3 in the US charts and sold almost 700,000 copies in 11 weeks. The song was even more of a success on the European market, spending multiple weeks at #1 in several markets. The song later came out on *Elvis Golden Records Vol. 4*, *For The Asking (The Lost Album)*, *From Nashville To Memphis* and hits packages *Worldwide 50 Gold Award Hits Vol. 1*, *The Top Ten Hits*, *Artist of the Century*, *ELVIS 30 #1 Hits*, *Hitstory* and *The Essential Elvis Presley*.

Alternate-seekers can find other versions on the *ELVIS 30 #1 Hits* deluxe edition and on FTD release *Long Lonely Highway*.

DEVORE, SY
(1908-1966)

Tailor to the stars Sy Devore moved from New York to Hollywood at the end of the Second World War and clothed the Rat Pack and Bob Hope, David Niven, John Wayne, Jerry Lewis and when he came out to spend time in Hollywood, Elvis, fitting him out with almost $10,000 of duds in 1962 for *It Happened at the World's Fair*.

See CLOTHES.

DIAMOND, NEIL
(B. 1941)

As Elvis was rediscovering his musical mojo at American Sound Studio in early 1969, one of the tracks he recorded was Neil Diamond's "And The Grass Won't Pay No Mind," the story goes in exchange for Diamond's agreement to forfeit his prior booking at American Sound Studio so that Elvis could take the time. Elvis also recorded Neil Diamond tune "Sweet Caroline" live in Las Vegas in 1970, for release on his *On Stage* album. When Diamond attended an Elvis show in Vegas, he introduced him from the stage as "a good friend."

Diamond is one of a select group of artists who has scored hits in three different decades, from the Sixties to the Eighties. Like many others, he started out as a songwriter closeted away in the Brill Building in New York, where among other tunes he wrote The Monkees' hit "I'm A Believer." His vast repertoire of songs include "Red, Red Wine," "Song Sung Blue," "You Don't Bring Me Flowers" (which he sang to great commercial success in a duet with Barbara Streisand in 1978), and "Love On The Rocks." He has also written soundtracks, acted in movies, and continued touring into the 2000s. He was inducted into the Songwriters' Hall of Fame in 1984, and received the Sammy Cahn Lifetime Achievement Award in 2000.

DIDDLEY, BO
(B. OTHA ELLAS BATES, 1928)

Elvis saw Mississippi-born Diddley perform at the Apollo Theater in New York in 1956, when he was in the Big Apple to appear on "Stage Show."

Known as "The Originator," Diddley's unique "freight train" beat and distorted guitar had an enormous influence on early rockers such as Buddy Holly and a later generation of English acts led by the Rolling Stones.

Diddley was raised in Chicago by his adoptive mother, Gussie McDaniel, and learned violin before he picked up a guitar.

Diddley had his first hits with Chess Records, "Bo Diddley" and "I'm a Man," in 1955. Though his record sales were never stratospheric in the US, he sold very well in the UK.

In later years Diddley complained that Elvis copied his wild on-stage moves, understandably bitter that his status as a rock pioneer did not translate into rock millions.

He was inducted into the Rock and Roll Hall of Fame in 1987.

BO DIDDLEY: "I'm the dude that Elvis Presley copied."

"DIDJA' EVER"

This Army-themed song, written by Sid Wayne and Sherman Edwards, was recorded for the *G.I. Blues* soundtrack at the RCA studios in Hollywood on April 27, 1960. It has only ever been released on soundtrack albums; the 1997 soundtrack re-release includes an alternate take.

"DIRTY, DIRTY FEELING"

A Leiber and Stoller rocker for Elvis to record in the early hours of April 4, 1960 in Nashville for the *Elvis Is Back!* album. The song was actually commissioned for 1958 movie *King Creole* but wasn't used at the time. "Dirty, Dirty Feeling" got a second screen chance when it was recycled for 1965 movie *Tickle Me*, including a new issue on the tie-in EP.

Later releases came on *Elvis Sings Leiber & Stoller*, the *Double Features* issue, *From Nashville To Memphis* and the FTD *Tickle Me* reissue. Alternate takes are on FTD releases *Fame And Fortune*, *Tickle Me* and *Elvis Is Back!*

DISCOGRAPHIES

Dozens of Elvis discographies have been published since the first informal pamphlet brought out in 1974 by future Elvis producer Ernst Jorgensen. No book is fully up-to-date for the simple reason that Elvis material continues to appear on a reliably regular basis (incredibly, up to a hundred new albums between official, unofficial, international and FTD releases each year).

Internet sites offer discographies with varying degrees of accuracy, often with information on take numbers, lyrics and more.

See also RECORD RELEASES.

Books:

Elvis Recording Sessions, by Ernst Jorgensen, Erik Rasmussen and Johnny Mikkelsen, JEE Productions, 1977.
Elvis: A Portrait in Music, by Paul Lichter, Jesse Books, 1983.
Elvis Sessions: The Recorded Music of Elvis Aron Presley, 1953-1977, I and II, by Joe Tunzi, J.A.T Productions, 1993 and 1996.
Solid Gold Elvis: The Complete Collectors Manual, by David Petrelle, Timewind Publishing, 1998.
Elvis Presley: A Life in Music: The Complete Recording Sessions, by Ernst Jorgensen, St Martin's Press, 1998.
Elvis For Everyone, by David Parker, published by Abstract Sounds Publishing, 2002.
Elvis Sessions III The Recorded Music Of Elvis Aron Presley, by Joseph A. Tunzi, J.A.T. Publishing, 2004.

DISKIN, TOM

For a man who was instrumental in managing Elvis' career from 1956 until his dying day, there is surprisingly little written about Colonel Tom Parker's "lieutenant" Tom Diskin. He was either hired by Parker in the early Fifties after the Colonel signed his singing sisters, who performed under the name "The Dickens Sisters," or Diskin hired Parker to work with him at Jamboree Productions but then somehow the Colonel took over the show. It has even been rumored that Diskin turned down the opportunity to manage Elvis outright.

For his forbearance, Diskin was a recipient (from the Colonel) of a portion of Elvis' music publishing companies when they were reconfigured in the early Seventies. On the proceeds, he bought a home next door to the Colonel's and made significant property investments. In her book on the Colonel, Alanna Nash describes Diskin as a long-suffering man who was subject to frequent humiliations.

Diskin accompanied Elvis on the Hank Snow Jamboree Tour in February 1955, the first tour organized by Elvis' new and soon-to-be exclusive manager Colonel Tom Parker, and chaperoned him as he did radio interviews.

In October 1955, while Elvis was on tour in Cleveland, Ohio, Diskin arranged for Elvis' parents Vernon and Gladys to sign a telegram which gave Colonel Tom Parker exclusive rights to negotiate a new recording contract for the singer. This move signaled the beginning of the end for Elvis' previous manager, Bob Neal.

Diskin was the Colonel's regular point man on early tours, flying with Elvis and his pal du jour (often Gene Smith at the time) as they shuttled between shows. He'd also attend recording sessions to liaise about song choices. In 1959 Diskin

prevailed on his boss to release "A Fool Such as I" rather than the other available candidates.

Later, when Elvis was churning out movies for three studios, Diskin was on hand as the Colonel's liaison. He continued to serve as the Colonel's representative at recording sessions.

Diskin went into business on his own after Elvis died. He outlived the Colonel by one year.

JOHN WILKINSON: "Tom Diskin could have taken over Elvis' career and things might have turned out a little different."

DIVORCE

Elvis and Priscilla legally separated in July 1972. Priscilla had been unhappy for some time about Elvis' serial infidelities, the last straw being compromising notes that she found at their Palm Springs home. Elvis' response—to encourage Priscilla to find more outside interests—eventually led her to become romantically involved with her karate teacher, Mike Stone.

Elvis initiated the divorce proceedings a month after the separation.

Priscilla initially agreed to a very modest settlement of $6,000 per month plus a $100,000 lump sum, arranged through Elvis' LA Lawyer Ed Hookstratten. In 1973, two months after the Colonel sold Elvis' back catalogue to RCA , Priscilla filed for an improved divorce settlement. She accepted a vastly improved package of a $2 million lump sum and monthly support exceeding $10,000, plus proceeds from the sale of their Los Angeles home and a small percentage of Elvis' music publishing income. Once their initial animosity had passed, both parties decided that for the benefit of Lisa Marie, they would conduct divorce proceedings as amicably as possible. When the divorce was finalized at the Santa Monica courthouse by Judge Laurence J. Rittenband on October 9, 1973, Elvis and Priscilla left arm in arm.

In 1974, when Elvis' stage ramblings were at their most loquacious, one night in Las Vegas he put the record straight that the divorce was because he was traveling too much, and that no other man or woman was involved. He also publicly revealed the value of the settlement.

LAWYER HARRY FAIN: "This man agreed to pay her this without any contest because he wanted to be generous and make her happy. I never met a man so unselfish."

BILLY SMITH: "Elvis changed a lot after he was married and after Lisa was born. But I think he changed the most after his divorce."

ANITA WOOD: "I had a little problem when Priscilla wanted to divorce Elvis because she should've known that there was going to be people in his life . . . they were gonna always be there."

DR. NICK: "He was partly responsible for the divorce. He encouraged Priscilla to get involved in other things and not sit around the house."

LAMAR FIKE: "His ego took a bruising when she left him, but he was responsible for that."

"DIXIELAND ROCK"

Elvis taped this Claude Demetrius / Fred Wise rocker for *King Creole* on January 16, 1958 at Radio Recorders. The version released on *King Creole* EP Vol. 2 was altered slightly for the soundtrack LP.

The song was reprised for 1971 album *Worldwide Gold Award Hits Vol. 2*, *The King Of Rock & Roll*, *King Creole* reissues, and 2006 album *Elvis Rock*.

DIXIELAND ROCKS

A 2001 FTD live release of Elvis performing in Murfreesboro, Tennessee, in May 1975.

TRACK LISTING:
1. Also Sprach Zarathustra
2. See See Rider
3. I Got A Woman / Amen
4. Love Me
5. If You Love Me (Let Me Know)
6. You Don't Have To Say You Love Me
7. All Shook Up
8. (Let Me Be Your) Teddy Bear/Don't Be Cruel
9. The Wonder Of You
10. Polk Salad Annie
11. Introductions / Johnny B. Goode / Long Live Rock'n'Roll
12. My Boy
13. T-R-O-U-B-L-E
14. I'll Remember You
15. Why Me Lord
16. Let Me Be There
17. An American Trilogy
18. Fairytale
19. Little Darlin'
20. Funny How Time Slips Away
21. Can't Help Falling In Love
22. Closing Vamp
23. Bridge Over Troubled Water
24. Love Me Tender

"DO NOT DISTURB"

A pared-down *Girl Happy* soundtrack tune written by Bill Giant, Bernie Baum and Florence Kaye that Elvis recorded on June 11, 1964 at Radio Recorders. After he'd lavished 36 takes on this song, Elvis had had enough and went home. It took him eight months to return to the studio. A selection of those many outtakes are on the 2003 FTD *Girl Happy* reissue, which (along with the Nineties *Double Features* release) has the final finished product.

"DO THE CLAM"

Elvis could never have suspected that ten years after cutting "That's All Right (Mama)" he would be making songs like this. Shipped by RCA in February 1965 to promote Elvis' upcoming movie *Girl Happy*, with "You'll Be Gone" on the B-side, the dance craze that never caught on failed as a single too, climbing no higher than #21 and selling around 350,000 copies despite two months in the *Billboard* Hot 100. Elvis recorded the Sid Wayne / Ben Weisman / Dolores Fuller track at Radio Recorders on June 12, 1964.

The Clam lives on through *Double Features* and FTD re issues for the movie, *Command Performances*, and *Elvis at the Movies*.

"DO THE VEGA"

Shades of "La Bamba" in this Bill Giant / Bernie Baum / Florence Kaye tune written for *Viva Las Vegas* but dropped from the movie and unreleased until *Singer Presents Elvis Singing Flaming Star and Others* in 1968, its sister album *Elvis Sings Flaming Star* and in the Nineties the *Double Features* CD covering *VLV*.

Elvis recorded the song at Radio Recorders on July 10, 1963. An alternate is on the 2003 FTD *Viva Las Vegas* release.

"DO YOU KNOW WHO I AM"

The world most certainly did know by the time Elvis recorded this Bobby Russell country ballad

at American Studio in the small hours of February 19, 1969.

The track first came out on the *From Memphis to Vegas* album, closely followed by *Back in Memphis*.

Since then, it has done duty on *From Nashville To Memphis* and *Suspicious Minds: The Memphis 1969 Anthology*.

FTD has brought out alternates on *The Memphis Sessions* and *Made in Memphis* (alternates also feature on bootlegs including *Real Fun On Stage . . . And In The Studio*).

DOCTORS

Elvis once told a journalist that if he had continued his studies past high school, he would have wanted to become a doctor. He owned and studied the Physicians Desk Reference at least from the early Sixties. Ultimately to his own detriment, Elvis could not be shaken from a strongly-held belief that medications existed for every ailment, and that if medications were prescribed or administered by a doctor, then there was simply no question of drug abuse. Over the years, many people have blamed Elvis' doctors for acquiescing to his toxic regime of drugs; however, in their defense, his physicians insist that because their patient was so willful and had so many potential sources to obtain prescription drugs, they believed that the lesser evil was to manage his intake of medications and where possible give him placebos.

Elvis' regular LA physician through the Sixties was a Dr. Gorsin.

Dr. Nichopoulos became Elvis' personal physician in Memphis from 1967, and treated him for the next ten years.

In Las Vegas, Elvis used a Doctor Thomas Newman before moving to Dr. Elias Ghanem, and for throat problems Dr. Sidney Boyer. Elvis saw a doctor in Palm Springs called George Kaplan.

Peter Guralnick writes that in early 1973 Elvis was being treated by as many as seven doctors in Las Vegas. That year Dr. Lawrence Wruble treated Elvis for his gastric problems, and eminent Memphis psychiatrists Dr. David Knott and Dr. Robert Fink, specialized in drug addiction, were called in to help with his prescription medicine dependency until Elvis banished them because he did not want psychiatrists involved.

In later years, Elvis had a series of compliant doctors and specialists he used in Memphis and elsewhere around the country (he could even send a plane to pick up supplies) to stock up on medications.

One doctor, Donald Hinton, has become a doyen of Elvis-is-alivers by claiming to treat Elvis to the present day.

See also HEALTH.

DENTISTS

Elvis was a great believer in oral hygiene, and regularly had work done on his teeth. When he met The Beatles, he was reputedly appalled at the condition their teeth were in. From the Fifties onwards, Elvis trusted his teeth to Memphis dentist Lester Hofman, who with his wife Sterling was an occasional visitor to Graceland. Hofman did dental work on Elvis his last night alive. In LA Elvis used a dentist called Max Shapiro, who also treated Elvis entourage members.

OPTICIANS

Elvis' optician, Dennis Roberts, calculated that he made almost 500 pairs of glasses for Elvis, the majority jewel-encrusted, many of which he distributed to members of his entourage. And that was just his Las Vegas optician. LA optician Hans Fiebig, who claims to have made the first pair of Elvis-style aviator sunglasses, made countless others embossed with "TCB" on one side and "EP" on the other, in chrome and in gold.

SONNY WEST: "Elvis had charm. He had ways of getting what he wanted. He 'bought' some doctors. He bought them Cadillacs and stuff to get what he wanted. It never seemed that obvious; he was always thanking them for what they did, but we all knew exactly what he was doing, and it wasn't always in his own best interests."

DOCUMENTARIES

People have been hungry for knowledge about Elvis for over half a century; documentary makers have always been eager to feed that need. Over the years, practically anyone who spent a block of time with Elvis and had access to a camera has made that footage available in one way or another (the families of Eddie Fadal and June Juanico in the Fifties; entourage pals handy with a home movie camera in the Sixties and Seventies). On top of this, a hard-working roster of Fifties TV clips, excerpts from Elvis' movies, Seventies concert moments and celebrity interviews provide the meat for the average Elvis documentary.

Elvis kicked things off himself with superlative concert movies *Elvis: That's The Way It Is* (1970) and *Elvis on Tour* (1972). *Elvis in Concert*, released posthumously in 1977, shows an Elvis most fans would rather remember to forget.

The earliest documentary footage of Elvis playing live (yet to be discovered) is a home movie shot in Texas in August 1955, released to mark the twentieth anniversary of Elvis' death. Fans have been waiting over fifty years to see the never officially-released documentary film *The Pied Piper of Cleveland: A Day in the Life of a Famous Disc Jockey*, shot in October that year to celebrate DJ Bill Randle.

A category apart is the biopic, based tightly or loosely on Elvis' life story (see Actors who have portrayed Elvis or Elvis-based characters).

Since the advent of the DVD, many documentaries have been released directly to market rather than being aired on TV. There are also many bootleg videos and DVDs in circulation among fans, either of taped Elvis specials or of film footage from unofficial sources. Increasingly, rare Elvis performances are appearing on DVDs brought out with meticulously-researched book packages.

A selection of Elvis documentaries (note: dates cited may differ from VHS or DVD release).

He Touched Their Lives (1980)—UK documentary about Elvis' effect on people's lives, presented by David Frost.
This Is Elvis (1981)—Archive footage, interviews and dramatizations; a later director's cut version followed.
Elvis Memories with Marge Thrasher (?)—Almost three hours of interviews collated by a local Memphis TV station.
Mondo Elvis (1984)—The farther side of Elvis fandom.
Elvis: Memories (1985)—Friends and families reminisce.
Elvis Presley's Graceland (1985)—The official guide, originally hosted by Priscilla, subsequently updated.
Elvis '56—In the Beginning (1987)—Elvis on TV and on stage the year he shot to fame.
Elvis: Story of a Legend (1987)—part of the A&E Biography documentary series.
Elvis, His Life and Times (1987)—Mac Davis and Lisa Hartman Black present Elvis' life.
Presley (1987)—Two-part BBC documentary narrated by Suzi Quatro.
Joe Esposito: My Home Movies of Elvis (1988)—Narrated by Esposito.
The Elvis Files (1990)—The matter of whether or not Elvis is alive, hosted by Bill Bixby, in two parts.
Elvis Memories (1991)—George Klein hosts.
Elvis: A Portrait by His Friends (1991)—Hosted by Marty Lacker.
Elvis: The Great Performances Vols. 1-3 (1992)—Narrated by George Klein and Bono, written by Peter Guralnick. Later versions narrated by Priscilla Presley.
Elvis, The Lost Performances (1992)—Previously unseen footage from *Elvis: That's the Way It Is* and *Elvis on Tour*.
Elvis in Hollywood (1993)—Focuses on Elvis' pre-Army movies.
Why Elvis? (1994)—Elvis' life through interviews.
The Elvis I Knew (1994)—Charlie Hodge remembers.
Private Presley (1994)—Elvis' Army years.
Elvis: The Complete Story (1996)—Elvis' life, with a focus on his movies.
Sun Days with Elvis (1996)—Focus on the Sun Years.
The Burger & the King: The Life & Cuisine of Elvis Presley (1996)—The Elvis story through food.
Elvis: Death of a Legend (1997)—Elvis' life story with a focus on his final period.
Elvis and the Presleytarians (1997)—A look at the cult of Elvis.
The Day Elvis Died (1997)—Elvis' life story
1st Ever Elvis (1997)—Home movie of an Elvis concert from August 1955 in Houston, TX.
Long Live The King—Country Salutes Elvis (1997)—VH1 anniversary tribute.
All The King's Men (1997 and later)—Vols. 1- 6. Memphis Mafia pals reminisce in great detail; includes previously unseen footage.
A Little Bit of Elvis (1998)—UK comedian Frank Skinner tracks down the true provenance of an Elvis shirt.
Famous Families: The Presleys (1998)—A Biography Channel production.
"E! True Hollywood Story": Elvis, the Hollywood Years (1998)
He Touched Me (1999)—A three-hour journey through Elvis' love of gospel.
Lost Elvis Home Movies (1999)—Eddie Fadal's daughter narrates footage from 1958.
Almost Elvis (2001)—A look at the world of Elvis impersonators.
Elvis: The Missing Years (2001)—Elvis in the Army, in Texas and in Germany.
Elvis: The Final Chapter (2001)—Elvis' last years.
Remembering Elvis (2001)—Elvis' life condensed into 48 minutes.
Elvis Presley's America (2001)—UK fan club experience in the US.
Rare Moments with the King (2001)—TV footage, press conferences and interviews
Welcome Home Elvis (2001) — Elvis' appearance on the Sinatra 1960 TV special.
Elvis & June: A Love Story (2002)—Carefree Elvis on vacation in 1956, including home movies.
Schmelvis (2002)—Exploring Elvis' Jewish roots.
The Definitive Elvis (2002)—Vast 8-DVD life story, subject to a lawsuit in the US.
Elvis Lives (2002)—Testimonials from musicians and entertainers about Elvis' continuing influence.
Classic Albums (2002)—The story of how Elvis made his first LP and burst onto the scene in 1956.
Early Elvis—From Country Boy to King of Rock'n'Roll (2002)—Hour-long doc. on Elvis' life.
Elvis: His Best Friend Remembers (2002)—Joe Esposito does the honors in this insider doc.
The Elvis Mob (2002)—The Memphis Mafia share their recollections.

Elvis Presley: His Early Performances (2002)—Elvis on stage and on TV.
Elvis: The Last 24 Hours (2003)—Elvis' final years, featuring the Jordanaires.
Elvis: The Journey (2003)—The Elvis story on a budget.
Elvis: King Of Entertainment (2003)—Elvis as performer, including rare early concert footage.
Elvis Presley: The Back Story (2003)—Two discs focusing predominantly on his army years.
Elvis—Birth of Rock 'N' Roll (2004)—Interviews and archive footage.
Elvis: Behind the Image Vols. 1 and 2 (2003/2005)—Interviews and previously unseen 8mm footage.
200 Cadillacs (2004)—Elvis' generosity explored.
Elvis—A 50th Anniversary Celebration (aka. *Elvis: 50 Years in Show Business*) (2004)—Musicians celebrate Elvis' influence fifty years on from "That's All Right (Mama)"
Elvis: 50 Years in Show Business (2004)—Musicians pay homage to Elvis
Return to Splendor (2004) — 8mm (soundless) fan footage of Elvis in concert, 1969 to 1975.
Elvis—The Echo Will Never Die (2004)—Life story presented by Casey Kasem.
Elvis by the Presleys (2005)—The DVD version of this EPE documentary with additional material.
Altered by Elvis (2006)—Fans and people who knew Elvis share how their lives were shaped by the man.
Elvis: The Memphis Flash (2006)—How it all started back in 1954.
Elvis Presley at the Seattle World's Fair (2006)—behind the scenes home movie shot by Albert Fisher.
Elvis, How Great Thou Art A Portrait of the Artist (2006)—adapted by Linda Ann McConnell from her book.
Elvis Presley Has Left The Building (2007)—How Elvis' death was covered thirty years earlier.
Elvis: Close As A Brother TV Special With George Klein (2007)—A friend reminisces.
Elvis—Up Close and Personal (2007)

Book:
Elvis—The Documentaries, by Joseph A. Tunzi, J.A.T. Productions, 2005

"DOES YOUR CHEWING GUM LOSE ITS FLAVOR (ON THE BEDPOST OVERNIGHT)?"

Improbably, Elvis sang a line from this 1959 Lonnie Donegan hit during a 1974 concert—it's on 2006 FTD release *I Found My Thrill*. The song hails all the way back to 1924, when Guy Lombardo had a hit with it as "Does Your Spearmint Lose Its Flavor . . ." The song was written by Billy Jones and Ernest Hare.

"DOG'S LIFE, A"

Sid Wayne and Ben Weisman came up with this song for *Paradise, Hawaiian Style*. Elvis was in good voice when he made the recording at Radio Recorders on July 27, 1965. Reissues are limited to the *Double Features* for the movie, issued together with *Frankie and Johnny*.
Alternate takes appeared on 1980 collectors set *Elvis Aron Presley*; several are on the FTD soundtrack release. In the movie, Elvis sings the song to a helicopter load of dogs, who join in with a yowling chorus.

"DOIN' THE BEST I CAN"

A Doc Pomus / Mort Shuman doo-wap song Elvis that Elvis laid down at the RCA Hollywood studios on April 27, 1960 for *G.I. Blues*. The song

came out on the soundtrack album and later on *Command Performances*, *Elvis Sings Mort Shuman & Doc Pomus*, the *G.I. Blues* 1997 CD release, and *Love Elvis*.
Alternates are on the *G.I. Blues* CD reissue, FTD release *Silver Screen Stereo* and 2003 release *Elvis: Close Up*.

DOLAN, KITTY

Elvis and Kitty met in the fall of 1957 in Las Vegas, where she was performing at the Tropicana. They were still good friends during his time serving in the Army. In 1959 she wrote an article in the *Movie Mirror* describing what it was like to be Elvis' girl, in which she suggested that her resemblance to a younger version of his mother certainly helped to kindle the attraction.

"DOMINICK"

If there is a nadir for Elvis' song output, this may well be it. Elvis disliked this Sid Wayne / Ben Weisman song Elvis so much when recording it in Nashville on October 1, 1967 for *Stay Away, Joe* (in which he sings the song to a bull) that he made producer Felton Jarvis swear it would never be released on record, not even after he died. He at least saw the funny side, and cracked up before he got to the end of the take . . .
Alas for Elvis' memory, the song appeared on the *Double Features* series in 1994, as well as on one or two unkind bootleg releases.

DOMINO, FATS
(B. ANTOINE DOMINO, 1928)

Elvis was performing Domino's classic "Blueberry Hill" in concert before he recorded it for the soundtrack album of his first movie for Paramount, *Loving You*. Elvis had always lionized the pianist and singer, the biggest selling African-American recording artist of the Fifties and—after Elvis—the best-selling rock 'n' roll singer of the decade.
Domino was born in New Orleans on February 26, 1928, and earned his musical chops playing boogie-woogie piano. He scored his first hit –co-written with bandleader Dave Bartholomew—in 1949 with "The Fat Man," considered by some to be the first ever rock 'n' roll record. Domino wrote practically all of his material, barring his biggest success, "Blueberry Hill."
Elvis and Fats met several times in Las Vegas in the Sixties when Elvis took in his shows. At a late Sixties press conference, Elvis declared that Domino was the real king of rock 'n' roll. Among Domino's many million-selling songs are "Ain't That A Shame" (a #1 hit for Pat Boone), "I'm Walkin' " and "My Blue Heaven."

SCOTTY MOORE: ". . . Anything like Fats Domino's stuff, real simple stuff with a beat behind it, well, [Elvis] couldn't get enough of that."

"DONCHA' THINK IT'S TIME"

Elvis cut this Clyde Otis / Willie Dixon track at Radio Recorders on February 1, 1958, during the extra time he was allowed to complete his film and recording commitments before going into the Army. It took two sessions (the first on January 23) and almost 50 takes before Elvis was happy, and even then the released track was spliced from three different takes. "Doncha' Think It's Time" was released as the B-side to "Wear My Ring

Around Your Neck," shipped by RCA in April, 1958, when it made it to #21 in the charts.
The first LP release, on *Elvis' Gold Records Vol. 2*, was an alternate splice. Later album releases include *Worldwide Gold Award Hits Vol. 2*, *Essential Elvis Vol. 3* and *The King Of Rock 'n' Roll*.
Alternates have appeared on *Essential Elvis Vol. 3* and *Today, Tomorrow & Forever*. Four takes and the original single master from that February session are on FTD release *50,000,000 Million Elvis Fans Can't Be Wrong*.

"DON'T"

Elvis first heard a demo of this Leiber / Stoller song in June 1957, choosing it over a ditty called "I'm A Hog For You" (later to be released by The Coasters). He taped it in a sweet-voiced style on September 6 at Radio Recorders. RCA released the song as a single in early January 1958, with "I Beg Of You" on the B-side. The Colonel was livid with Elvis for commissioning this song directly from the songwriters, without going through the usual publishing company channels.
"Don't" was in the charts for twenty weeks, for one of which it was #1, though it sold fewer than Elvis' previous single releases.
It featured on EP *A Touch of Gold* the following year, and later appeared on albums *Elvis' Gold Records Vol. 2*, *Worldwide 50 Gold Award Hits Vol. 1*, *The King Of Rock & Roll*, *Artist Of The Century*, *ELVIS 30 #1 Hits*, *Hitstory*, *Love Elvis* and many other hits packages. More recently, it was included on FTD release *50,000,000 Elvis Fans Can't Be Wrong*.
An Elvis rehearsal of the song in 1970 features on *Platinum: A Life In Music*.

"DON'T ASK ME WHY"

The B-Side to "Hard Headed Woman," released in June 1958, peaked at #28 in the charts (though it made #2 in the R&B charts), and stayed in the Top 100 for nine weeks overall. Written by Fred Wise and Ben Weisman, Elvis recorded the ballad at Radio Recorders on January 16, 1958.
Following release of *King Creole*, it came out on the soundtrack LP, and was then released on *A Touch of Gold* EP Vol. 3 weeks before Elvis returned to the States from his Army service in Germany.
It has since appeared on *Worldwide Gold Award Hits Vol. 2* and *The King Of Rock 'n' Roll*. A demo version of the track as sung by Jimmy Breedlove is on FTD release *Writing For The King*.

"DON'T BE CRUEL"

Elvis recorded this song—one of five Elvis songs in the Grammy Hall of Fame—at the RCA studios in New York City on July 2, 1956, insisting on 28 takes before he felt he'd done the song justice. Penned by Otis Blackwell, "Don't Be Cruel" proved to be a highly auspicious first song for new song publishers Hill & Range to bring to the Elvis party. Blackwell gave up 50% of the royalties and a co-writing credit to Elvis to ensure that the hottest new singer around covered it.
"Don't Be Cruel" was released as an A-side on one of the best-selling singles of all time, backed with "Hound Dog." After RCA shipped the disc on July 13, 1956, "Hound Dog" rose rapidly to number two in the charts, selling over a million copies before "Don't Be Cruel" overtook it and stole the #1 spot on the Billboard Top 100 chart, where it remained for seven weeks (as well as topping the country and R'n'B charts). Within six months, the record had sold almost 4 million copies.

Even after he recorded the song, Elvis was still such a fan that he saw Jackie Wilson sing it four times in Las Vegas. He says how great he thought Wilson's version was at *The Million Dollar Quartet* session later that year at Sun Records, and does a version of Elvis singing Jackie Wilson singing Elvis to prove it, along with two other attempts at the song. Elvis incorporated some of Wilson's vocal mannerisms into subsequent performances of the song, starting with his third appearance on the "Ed Sullivan Show" in January 1957 (on the notorious "from the waist up" night, reissued on record as part of the *This Is Elvis* tie-in release in the early Eighties). A performance from the "Ed Sullivan Show" featured on 2007 DVD release *Elvis #1 Hit Performances*; footage from the Tupelo homecoming show in 1956 recently appeared on DVD *Tupelo's Own Elvis Presley*).

"Don't Be Cruel" was the biggest selling of all Elvis' singles released in 1956, a year in which practically every one of his records broke industry records. By 1961, "Don't Be Cruel" had gone over the six million mark. Not surprisingly, the song was also put on EPs (*Elvis Presley* and *The Real Elvis*) and on his second album, *Elvis*.

Elvis' Fifties performances from the Mississippi-Alabama Fair and Dairy Show in September 1956 and the "Ed Sullivan Show" were released in 1984 album *A Golden Celebration*. A live version from his 1961 charity concert in Hawaii is on *Elvis Aron Presley*.

In 1968, Elvis sang the song with a horn section, big backing and flute for the NBC TV Special but it didn't make the cut for the show; this version later appeared on the 1991 *Elvis NBC TV Special* release, *Memories The '68 Comeback Special* and FTD issue *Burbank '68*.

The song is on practically every Elvis hits package ever released, including but not limited to *Elvis' Golden Records*, *Elvis: A Legendary Performer Vol. 1*, *Worldwide 50 Gold Award Hits Vol. 1*, *The King Of Rock & Roll*, *Elvis '56*, *Platinum: A Life in Music*, *Artist Of The Century*, *ELVIS 30 #1 Hits*, *Hitstory*, *Elvis Rock*, and *The Essential Elvis Presley* (2007 version).

Elvis sang the song in a medley with "Jailhouse Rock" at his inaugural Las Vegas engagement in August 1969, and by popular demand kept it in his repertoire through the Seventies, most often in tandem with "Teddy Bear." Live Seventies versions are to be found on *Elvis As Recorded At Madison Square Garden*, *Elvis Recorded Live On Stage In Memphis*, *Elvis Aron Presley*, *Collectors Gold*, *An Afternoon In The Garden*, *Live In Las Vegas*, *The Live Greatest Hits*, *Elvis: Close Up*, and the 2007 *Viva Las Vegas* (these last three w. "Jailhouse Rock").

More avid fans can turn to FTD releases *All Shook Up*, *Elvis At The International* (both with "Jailhouse Rock"), *Writing For The King*, *The Way It Was*, *An American Trilogy*, *Summer Festival*, *Live In L.A.*, *It's Midnight*, *Dragonheart*, *Dixieland Rocks*, *Dinner At Eight*, *Tucson '76*, *Unchained Melody*, *Spring Tours '77*.

Elvis was still singing the song to the end—CBS's cameras captured it on June 19 that year, in his last televised show on *Elvis in Concert*.

A backstage rehearsal from the *Elvis on Tour* documentary period has seen the light of day on *ELVIS 30 #1 Hits Deluxe Edition* and FTD release *6363 Sunset*.

"DON'T CRY, DADDY"

Written by Mac Davis and recorded at the landmark American Studio session on January 15, 1969, this song was released as a single in November 1969 with "Rubberneckin'" on the B-Side. Elvis strongly identified with the song's sentiments, as did at least 1.2 million other people who bought the record and sent it to #6 in the charts (where it stayed for a total of 13 weeks). Mac Davis's son inspired the song, uttering the

words to try and console his father, distraught at seeing images from the Vietnam war.

The track first came out on an album on *Worldwide 50 Gold Award Hits* (1970). It has since appeared on many others, including *Always On My Mind*, *From Nashville To Memphis*, *Suspicious Minds: The Memphis 1969 Anthology*, *Artist Of The Century*, the 2000 issue of *From Elvis in Memphis*, *Elvis 2nd to None*, *Hitstory* and *The Essential Elvis Presley*.

Elvis sang this song live in the first half of 1970, but dropped it at the beginning of his summer Las Vegas engagement. A February 1970 version came out on *Elvis Greatest Hits Vol. 1* in 1981. Other live releases from 1970 are on *That's The Way It Is—Special Edition*, *The Live Greatest Hits*, *Live In Las Vegas*, more recent reissues of *On Stage* and FTD releases *Polk Salad Annie* and *Writing For The King*.

When Elvis played the song live in concert, it was always a poignant moment—none more so than in 1997, when daughter Lisa Marie dueted with her father on video at the Memphis concert held to mark the twentieth anniversary of Elvis' passing.

In 2007, a 1970 live performance came out on disc two of DVD *Elvis #1 Hit Performances*.

"DON'T FORBID ME"

Elvis sang this Charles Singleton song while jamming in December 1956 at Sun Studio with pals Carl Perkins and Jerry Lee Lewis, in a session immortalized as *The Complete Million Dollar Sessions*. Elvis had a chance to record and release the song himself, but Pat Boone beat him to it and scored a million-selling number one hit. The 1956 singalong version, with "You Belong To My Heart," appeared on 2002 anthology *Today Tomorrow & Forever*.

"DON'T IT MAKE YOU WANNA GO HOME"

Not a song released officially during Elvis' lifetime, the Joe South track appears on bootlegs *The Brightest Star on Sunset Boulevard* and *There's Always Me*; a few lines of the song feature in Elvis' "Little Sister" medley recorded in 1970 and issued on the special edition release of *That's The Way It Is*.

"DON'T LEAVE ME NOW"

Elvis recorded this down tempo Aaron Schroeder / Ben Weisman composition at Radio Recorders on February 23, 1957 for release on his third album, *Loving You*. He recorded a second version of the track (the "movie version") for a scene in *Jailhouse Rock* that year—in actual fact, both versions featured in the movie. It was the second version, recorded at the MGM sound stage on May 9, 1957, that came out on the *Jailhouse Rock* EP. Both versions of the song have since appeared on anthology *The King Of Rock & Roll* and latter-day CD releases of *Loving You* and *Jailhouse Rock*.

Alternates have appeared on bootlegs, on *Essential Elvis Vol. 1*, the 1997 BMG release of *Jailhouse Rock*, FTD releases *Silver Screen Stereo* and *Flashback*, and on 2003 BMG release *Elvis: Close Up* (piano and movie versions).

"DON'T THINK TWICE, IT'S ALL RIGHT"

Elvis covered this 1963 Bob Dylan track (which Dylan brought out as the B-side to "Blowin' In The Wind" that year, and Peter, Paul and Mary also released) in a finger-pickin' country style at a proficuous May 1971 Nashville recording session—this particular track on May 16. The band

were having so much fun that they jammed for more than eleven minutes. A cut-down version came out initially on the 1973 *Fool* album. The long jam version appeared on bootlegs prior to official release on *Walk A Mile In My Shoes* in 1995, though an eight-minute version came out in 1979 on *Our Memories Of Elvis Vol. 2*.

"DON'T YOU KNOW I LOVE YOU"

Fats Domino's 1955 hit was a song to which Elvis sang along with pals at Eddie Fadal's house in 1958, recorded on a tape and bootlegged on *Forever Young, Forever Beautiful*.

DORSEY, JIMMY AND TOMMY
(JIMMY: 1904-1957, TOMMY: 1905-1956)

Big-band brothers Jimmy and Tommy led the California Ramblers in the Twenties, then the Dorsey Brothers Orchestra and, ultimately, "The Fabulous Dorseys," playing with many music greats and providing a springboard for many future stars, first and foremost Frank Sinatra. Jimmy played the alto sax and clarinet, while Tommy played the trumpet and trombone. Tommy was known as the most popular bandleader of the swing era.

The Dorsey Brothers were on RCA Victor, the record label Elvis signed to in late 1955. Within a couple of months, Elvis was enjoying his first national exposure on the Dorsey Brothers' TV showcase, "Stage Show."

After his second appearance on their Saturday night talent showcase, the Dorsey brothers took Elvis out on the town to the Roseland club.

DORSEY, THOMAS A.
(1899-1993)

Son of a preacher man, Dorsey began his career as a blues pianist in Chicago speakeasies, led a jazz band for Ma Rainey and composed hundreds of blues songs before he found the Lord.

Dorsey set himself up as a publisher of gospel music in 1932, and wrote among others spirituals "Take My Hand, Precious Lord" and "Peace In The Valley," both of which Elvis covered.

Dorsey was the first African-American to be inducted into the Nashville Songwriters Hall of Fame.

DOUBLE DYNAMITE

A two-LP anthology of previous Camden album Elvis tracks, brought out on Pickwick in December 1975.

TRACK LISTING:
1. Burning Love
2. I'll Be There (If Ever You Want Me)
3. Fools Fall In Love
4. Follow That Dream
5. You'll Never Walk Alone
6. Flaming Star
7. The Yellow Rose Of Texas / The Eyes Of Texas
8. Old Shep
9. Mama
10. Rubberneckin'
11. U.S. Male
12. Frankie And Johnny
13. If You Think I Don't Need You
14. Easy Come, Easy Go
15. Separate Ways
16. Peace In The Valley
17. Big Boss Man
18. It's A Matter Of Time

DOUBLE FEATURES

RCA reissued practically all of Elvis' film songs, remastered and with extra tracks, during the Nineties in this series. The first four CDs came out initially as a special set in January 1993; the rest followed through to 1995.

It Happened At The World's Fair / Fun In Acapulco
Kid Galahad / Girls! Girls! Girls!
Easy Come, Easy Go / Speedway
Flaming Star / Follow That Dream / Wild In The Country
Frankie And Johnny / Paradise Hawaiian Style
Harum Scarum / Girl Happy
Kissin' Cousins / Clambake / Stay Away, Joe
Live A Little, Love A Little / Trouble With Girls / Charro / Change Of Habit
Viva Las Vegas / Roustabout
Spinout / Double Trouble

"DOUBLE TROUBLE"

A Doc Pomus / Mort Shuman outing for the title track to this 1967 film, recorded by Elvis in June 1966 (he overdubbed his vocals on June 30, the day after the band laid down the instrumental track) at Radio Recorders. The song has since appeared on *Elvis In Hollywood, Elvis Sings Mort Shuman & Doc Pomus,* the *Double Features* release, *Command Performances* and 2006 BMG album *Elvis Movies*
Alternate takes are on the 2004 FTD soundtrack release.

DOUBLE TROUBLE (LP)

This soundtrack album was released in June 1967, with four bonus tracks in addition to eight songs from the movie. The album failed to sell more than 200,000 copies, and rose no higher than 47 in the charts.

TRACK LISTING:
1. Double Trouble
2. Baby, If You'll Give Me All Your Love
3. Could I Fall In Love
4. Long-Legged Girl (With The Short Dress On)
5. City By Night
6. Old Macdonald
7. I Love Only One Girl
8. There Is So Much World To See
9. It Won't Be Long
10. Never Ending
11. Blue River
12. What Now, What Next, Where To

FTD brought out a remastered version with many extras in 2004.

DOUBLE TROUBLE

Elvis reported to MGM in late June 1966 and was free to return to Memphis by early September. Originally titled *You're Killing Me,* the movie is a zany thriller set in England and Belgium without ever leaving the MGM lot—English character actors infused some authenticity, while the Wiere Brothers made their last ever movie as a trio of bumbling detectives.
Leading lady Annette Day was famously discovered by producer Judd Bernard in an antiques shop on Portobello Road in London. This was her debut movie and swansong all in one.
One song, "It Won't Be Long," was recorded but cut from the movie.
The ship set erected on the sound stage was so realistic that a number of extras had to be treated for seasickness.
Actor Norman Rossington has the unique distinction of working in Elvis and Beatles movies (*A Hard Day's Night*).

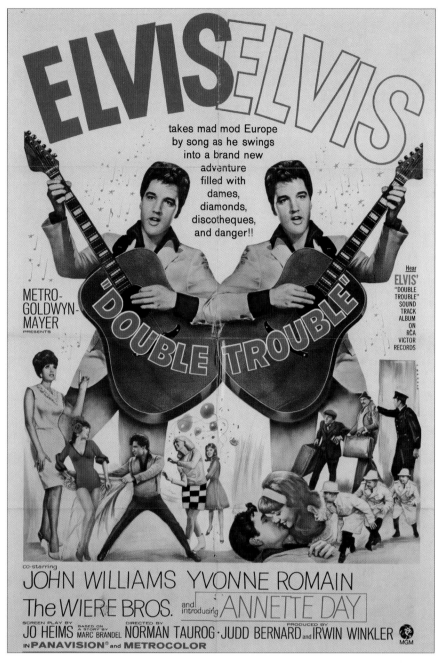

The movie opened a few weeks after *Easy Come, Easy Go,* which Elvis made for Paramount, and did similar, unspectacular business, ending up the year's 58th highest-grossing picture ($1.6 million) This was the movie in which Elvis had to sing "Old Macdonald"; as partial recompense, Elvis got to sing some worthwhile tunes, notably "Long Legged Girl (With The Short Dress On)" and a rare jazzy number, "City By Night"

BOOK PACKAGE: *Inside Double Trouble,* by Peter Verbruggen, Elvis Matters, 2007

ELVIS SAID: "I wasn't exactly a James Bond in this movie but then no one ever asked Sean Connery to sing a song while dodging bullets!"

CREDITS:
MGM, Color.
Length: 90 minutes
Release date: April 5, 1967

TAGLINES:
Elvis finds love, larceny and fun on the double.
Elvis with songs and adventures in mad mod Europe!

Directed by: Norman Taurog
Produced by: Judd Bernard and Irwin Winkler
Written by: Marc Brandell (novel), Jo Heims (screenplay)
Music by: Jeff Alexander
Cinematography by: Daniel L. Fapp
Film Editing by: John McSweeney Jr.
Art Direction by: George W. Davis, Merrill Pye
Set Decoration by: Henry Grace, Hugh Hunt
Costume Design by: Donfeld

CAST:
Elvis Presley	Guy Lambert
Annette Day	Jill Conway
John Williams	Gerald Waverly
Yvonne Romain	Claire Dunham
Chips Rafferty	Archie Brown
Norman Rossington	Arthur Babcock
Monte Landis	Georgie
Michael Murphy	Morley
Leon Askin	Inspector De Groote
John Alderson	Iceman
Stanley Adams	Capt. Roach
Maurice Marsac	Frenchman
Walter Burke	Mate
Helene Winston	Gerda
Harry Wiere	Detective
Herbert Wiere	Detective
Sylvester Wiere	Detective
Peter Balakoff	Policeman

Bob Bergy	Chicken Truck Driver
Hal Bokar	Masked Man
Barry Cole	Juggler
George Dee	Sleepy Man
Ted DeWayne	Acrobat
Luke Gerard	Peddler
Josh Harding	Seaman
Chester Hayes	Stilt walker
Rodney Hoeltzel	Juggler
Bob Homel	Moe
Mary Hughes	Watusi Dancer
Robert Isenberg	Pirate
Bob Johnson	Juggler
Murray Kamelhar	Policeman
Marilyn Keymer	Twin at London Night Club
Melody Keymer	Twin at London Night Club
George Klein	Bit part
Laurie Lambert	Child
Monique LeMaire	Flemish Clerk at Hotel Olympia
Frank Mitchell	Customs Officer
Jan Reddin	Night Club Dancer
Danny Rees	Juggler
Christopher Riordan	Young Englishman
Audrey Saunders	Acrobat
Ray Saunders	Acrobat
Ralph Smiley	Policeman
Bill Snyder	Acrobat
Jack Teagarden	Acrobat
Rick Teagarden	Acrobat
Sheryl Ullman	Patron

ADDITIONAL CREW:

Mary Keats	hair stylist
William Tuttle	makeup artist
Al Shenberg	unit production manager
Claude Binyon Jr.	assistant director
Van Allen James	sound editor
Franklin Milton	recording supervisor
J. McMillan Johnson	visual effects
Carroll L. Shepphird	visual effects
Carol Daniels	stunts
Patricia Casey	production assistant
Colonel Tom Parker	technical advisor
Alex Romero	choreographer

Plot:

Elvis plays Guy Lambert, an American rock singer on tour in London with his band the G-Men, where he is hotly contested by 17-year-old student Jill Conway (played by Annette Day) and sophisticate Claire Dunham (played by Yvonne Romain). Neither of these women turns out to be quite who they seem . . .

Jill's uncle Gerald (played by John Williams) scares Guy away with talk of marriage, and then makes sure that nothing untoward happens by sending Jill to boarding school in Belgium.

Guy looks forward to looking Jill up when his band plays Brussels, but then meets her on the Channel crossing, where each of them only just escapes an assassination attempt. Unbeknownst to Guy, smugglers Arthur Babcock (played by Norman Rossington) and Archie Brown (played by Chips Rafferty) have stashed diamonds in his luggage.

Guy sings at the Brussels nigh club, bumps into Claire again, offers a refuge to Jill who has run away from her school, dodges a bungled assassination attempt, and then in the nick of time finds out that Jill, who is hell-bent on seducing him, is not yet 18 — an important piece of information not just to ward off potential charges for underage sex, but because Jill is due to inherit a fortune on her upcoming birthday.

Jill goes with Guy to Antwerp for his next concert. All the while, the smugglers try to steal back Guy's suitcase. Jill makes the mistake of trusting a young man she meets; he has been hired by Uncle Gerald to kill her so that the Uncle gets the fortune. Guy arrives in the nick of time to karate the man to an accidental death. Guy enlists Claire's help to look after Jill, is arrested by three comic cops (played by the Wiere Brothers), and is charged with kidnapping Jill by wicked Uncle Gerald, now in situ.

In the nick of time (again) Guy escapes from the police station and rushes to Claire's place. It turns out that she too is in league with the wicked Uncle. Guy saves the heiress from asphyxiation, has the baddies arrested, and then Guy and Jill head off on what they think is a happy ending. Unfortunately the *SS Damocles* on which they set sail for England blows up and leaves them adrift on the English Channel, with a cache of jewels for company.

Songs: "Double Trouble," "Baby If You'll Give Me All Your Love," "Could I Fall In Love," "Long Legged Girl," "City By Night," "Old McDonald," "I Love Only One Girl," "There Is So Much World To See"

DOUGLAS, GORDON
(1907-1993)

In a career spanning six decades, Gordon Douglas directed Elvis in 1962 movie *Follow That Dream*. Douglas was the only director to direct both Elvis and Frank Sinatra. He cut his teeth on Thirties classics including *Our Gang* and many Hal Roach shorts and was still working into the late Seventies.

"DOWN BY THE RIVERSIDE"

Elvis' take on this traditional spiritual appears on *The Complete Million Dollar Sessions* from December 4, 1956, and on the soundtrack to *Frankie and Johnny* he sings it in a medley with "When The Saints Go Marchin' In" (recorded on a May 12, 1965 session at Radio Recorders, in an adaptation credited to songwriting team Bill Giant, Bernie Baum and Florence Kaye).

The *Million Dollar Quartet* version has since appeared on gospel anthology *Peace In The Valley*.

The movie medley has been reissued on *Elvis Sings Hits from His Movies Vol. 1*, the *Double Features* and FTD series of soundtracks, and also on the *Peace In The Valley* anthology.

"DOWN IN THE ALLEY"

Elvis' R&B version of Jesse Stone and The Clovers' 1953 hit appeared as a bonus track on his *Spinout* soundtrack album and on later compilations, as recorded in Nashville on May 25, 1966, with Charlie Hodge helping out on harmony.

Elvis' declaration that he was still alive and rocking during the low point of his soundtrack slough has since appeared on *Reconsider Baby*, *From Nashville To Memphis*, *Tomorrow Is A Long Time*, *Artist Of The Century*, *Elvis R 'n' B*, and the FTD *Spinout* reissue.

Alternate takes from that session are on the *From Nashville To Memphis* set and on FTD release *So High*. Live versions are on bootleg only—Elvis may in fact only have performed the song once in the Seventies.

DRAFT

Elvis registered for the Selective Service on January 19, 1953. On December 19, 1957 his draft letter was delivered personally to Graceland by Milton Bowers, Chairman of the local draft board.

In late 1957, as Elvis' draft drew near, the various US armed forces (with the exception of the Marines) competed to land this high-profile recruit. The Army offered a two-year posting with, most importantly, a deferment to allow Elvis to film *King Creole*; the Navy was prepared to set up a special "Elvis Presley company."

When the draft notice came in, Elvis told the press that serving was a "duty I've got to fill and I'm going to do it." Up until this time, rumors had been circulating that Elvis would take the easy option, join Special Services (as singer Eddie Fisher had done) and perform for the troops. Elvis genuinely did feel a patriotic duty to serve the American nation; he was also convinced that two years out of the public eye would kill of his career. As ever, the most significant influence was Colonel Parker, who was dead set against his boy playing for free, and did not want a public perception that Elvis was getting preferential treatment.

After his two-month deferment to complete *King Creole*, Elvis reported for duty on March 24, 1958 at 198 South Main Street, Memphis. He was assigned serial number 53 310 761 and put in charge of the group of 12 new recruits who traveled with him to Fort Chaffee, Arkansas. There he joined General Patton's Second Armored Division ("Hell on Wheels"), based at Fort Hood, Killeen, Texas.

DRAGONHEART

A 2003 FTD release of Elvis performing live at South Bend, Indiana, in October 1974 plus extras.

TRACK LISTING:
1. See See Rider
2. I Got A Woman / Amen
3. Love Me
4. Blue Suede Shoes
5. It's Midnight
6. Big Boss Man
7. Fever
8. Love Me Tender
9. Hound Dog
10. Heartbreak Hotel
11. If You Love Me (Let Me Know)
12. Bridge Over Troubled Water
13. Band introductions
14. Lawdy, Miss Clawdy 1:36
15. Band introductions
16. All Shook Up
17. Teddy Bear / Don't Be Cruel
18. Let Me Be There
19. It's Now Or Never
20. You Gave Me A Mountain
21. Johnny B. Goode
22. Hawaiian Wedding Song
23. Steamroller Blues
24. Can't Help Falling In Love
25. Closing vamp and announcements
26. Alright, Okay, You Win
27. Blue Christmas
28. Tryin' To Get To You

DRAKE, PETE
(B. RODDIS FRANKLINE "PETE" DRAKE 1932-1988)

A pedal steel guitarist, born in Atlanta, who recorded in Nashville with Elvis in the mid-Sixties, including five movie soundtracks and meatier fare "Big Boss Man" and "Guitar Man."

Drake began his career in the Drake Brothers band (brother Jack later became one of Ernest Tubb's Texas Troubadours). He became a popular session musician in Nashville, working with performers from Buddy Holly to The Everly Brothers and Elvis' fellow Sun artists Carl Perkins and Jerry Lee Lewis. Later he played on sessions for Joan Baez, Bob Dylan, George Harrison, Charlie Rich and Tammy Wynette among others. He had a hit in 1964 with his song "Talking Steel." In the Seventies he was a well-known country producer.

DREAMS

To many, Elvis' life is the American dream personified. He transcended humble origins to achieve his childhood ambition of becoming financially secure and earning a living as a performer— a dream shared by many millions in the age of American Idol. Nobody in his early years, least of all Elvis himself, could ever have imagined that he would still be one of the world's most recognizable celebrities half a century later.

As a child, Elvis' dream was simply to make enough money to look after his parents. This he had realized by the time he was twenty. Once he had tasted success as a singer, his dream was to make it in Hollywood and, ultimately, be considered a serious dramatic actor: mission accomplished on the first count, dream dashed by circumstance on the second.

By his twilight years, Elvis had been living the high life for so long that it was the only reality he knew. His impoverished upbringing was "like a dream," as he told friend Larry Geller, who for many years helped Elvis try and elucidate meaning from his dreams through various mystical books and texts.

Both of Elvis' parents had premonitionary dreams. When Elvis was just three, Vernon had such a vivid dream that the house was on fire that, still asleep, he went over to Elvis' crib, picked up his child and threw him to the floor, thinking that (in the dream) he was saving him by throwing him out of the window. Years later, Ma Gladys woke up with a start from a dream in which Elvis was imperiled by flames—this, on the very night that a car he was traveling in between shows caught fire. According to one story, young Elvis and both his parents awoke with the same nightmare about their home flooding. More usually, as a kid Elvis' nightmares were about being attacked.

When Elvis was doing his Army training, he had a vivid nightmare that all his fame and success suddenly vanished. He was convinced that this was a foretelling of his future.

In later years, Elvis told a number of friends about recurring nightmares in which he was on trial, but nobody (except his jewelers!) would defend him. The judge, dressed in white, carried a black medical bag, and the Colonel was the prosecuting attorney.

Nurse Marion Cocke recalls Elvis having a nightmare in late 1975 that he lost all his money, and soon after all his friends.

In one dream, Elvis was in the Holy Land, in a post-apocalyptic world, being driven round in a tank with Lisa Marie.

In 1975, a rather drug-addled Elvis told Linda Thompson of a dream in which his twin let him be born first and then suffocated.

Elvis dreamed of his last girlfriend, Ginger Alden, all in white, and soon afterwards proposed to her.

In his last months alive, Elvis experienced what he termed "prophetic" dreams. In one such dream Ginger turned into Gladys, then rode off into the sky on his favorite horse (once again as Ginger). His dreams of Gladys increased in frequency in 1977; he also began having recollections of long-forgotten childhood events. On at least one occasion Elvis dreamed he saw the face of God, manifested as a bright white light.

Peter Guralnick writes that his recurring dream in his final months was of abandonment, with all his money and friends disappearing.

After these nightmares, if his girlfriend was not staying with him, like a child Elvis might seek comfort and solace by climbing into bed with cousin Billy Smith and his wife Jo.

Decades after Elvis died, Tom Jones said that he had recurring dreams in which he tried to warn a young Elvis to avoid drugs because they would be fatal to him.

ELVIS SAID IN 1956: "I always felt that someday, somehow, something would happen to change everything for me, and I'd daydream about how it would be."

ELVIS SAID IN 1972: "When I was a boy I was the hero in comic books and movies. I grew up believing in that dream. Now I've lived it out. That's all a man can ask for."

GREIL MARCUS: "He took his dreams far more seriously than most ever dare, and he had the nerve to chase them down."

LAMAR FIKE: "Elvis had nightmares almost every night until he died. That's why he wouldn't sleep. And that's one reason he did so many pills."

"DRUMS OF THE ISLANDS"

Elvis recorded multiple versions of this traditional Polynesian song (with added slide guitar from Bernal Lewis) for the soundtrack of *Paradise, Hawaiian Style* in early August 1965, adding his overdubbed vocal to the band track on August 3 (the band did their bit on July 26) at Radio Recorders. He sings the song—arranged by and credited to Roy C. Bennett and Sid Tepper—twice in the movie.

The song has since appeared on *Elvis Chante Sid Tepper & Roy C. Bennett*, and on the standard *Double Features* and FTD releases. Alternate takes lurk on the 2004 FTD *Paradise, Hawaiian Style* release.

DRUGS

Elvis' unshakeable belief that for every ill there's a pill led to a dependency on pharmaceuticals that ultimately wore out his body by the age of 42. Friends, lovers and doctors tried unsuccessfully to warn him of his dependency. Elvis either didn't listen, told them that he had things under control, or advised them to mind their own business. His attitude was all the more paradoxical considering his opposition to street drugs and drug dependency. In 1970 he flew all the way to Washington to ask for a Bureau of Narcotics and Dangerous Drugs badge from President Nixon. Some years later he planned a personal crusade to kick Memphis's dealers off the streets.

Elvis referred to the pills he took as medication, not drugs. Many of the medicines to which he became addicted were freely prescribed in the Fifties and Sixties, when he first started taking them. The general consensus is that Elvis began taking amphetamines when he was doing his military service—the drug Benzedrine did not require a prescription in the US until a year after he went into the Army, and was regularly given out to soldiers to keep them alert in the field.

Out on the road in the Fifties, when a punishing schedule of a new town every day and multiple shows could stretch on for months, many musicians only managed by taking readily available solutions such as caffeine tablets No-Doz or over-the-counter remedies such as Benzedrine. Fellow Sun artist Barbara Pittman says, "Everybody was taking that stuff." Friends of Elvis' from Memphis have also claimed that he popped pills during his early touring years, and even had to have his stomach pumped once. His DJ Pal, Dewey Phillips, lost his job despite hosting Memphis's #1 show for the best part of a decade, partly because of his abuse of amphetamines and painkillers.

At home, Elvis' Ma Gladys put great faith in the ability of prescription diet pills to help her shift the weight she put on, and sort out her failing health. The pills she took in her last years alive may have hastened her demise. They were

also a potential source for Elvis: Lamar Fike has claimed that Elvis took Dexedrine and Desbutal from his mother, which she was taking to help cope with the "change of life."

In an interview on 1956 TV show "Hy Gardner Calling!" Elvis dodged a question about using marijuana. His sly smile was taken by some as an acknowledgement that an answer would be incriminating. Later that year there was at least one item of press speculation that the Mafia threatened to reveal Elvis had a "$100-a-day dope habit." However, such rumors are contradicted by assertions from entourage members in the late Fifties that they told girls who they brought to meet Elvis in Hollywood that they shouldn't even mention drugs, let alone do them.

When he was with Anita Wood, Elvis started experimenting with tanning pills.

A number of friends from the early Graceland days recall Elvis procuring "happy pills" from his dentist to alleviate pain after he had a lot of work done. Once he felt what these painkillers could do, he started taking them before his boisterous skating nights in Memphis. It has also been reported that the stimulant Dexedrine was consumed at Graceland in the early Sixties—yet another drug that wasn't strictly controlled until 1970.

Alanna Nash writes that Elvis took the edge off his Army training by using uppers and downers which he got from a Texas pal. She also says that he had long been used to purloining his mom's diet pills.

Elvis was so upset after his mother died—crying inconsolably, refusing to sleep and wandering around clutching her nightgown—that a doctor administered tranquillizers. Though Elvis had always had unusual sleeping patterns, this was the first time that he regularly took tranquilizers and sleeping pills.

In the Army, it wasn't uncommon for soldiers out on maneuvers to enhance their alertness by taking amphetamines like Dexedrine. According to Red West, this was the first time that Elvis regularly took pills. Soon after he met Priscilla he gave her some pills to help her with her schoolwork, which was suffering because she was spending so much time with Elvis; she stored them away in a little box of mementos she collected from Elvis when they first met.

After Elvis returned to the States, friends noticed a change in his character that they only later did they put down to the chemicals he was ingesting. He began to demonstrate mood swings, his temper was quicker to snap, and at times he behaved uncharacteristically violently. In 1960, while working on *Wild in the Country*, Elvis pulled a gun on some people in another car because he felt that they had offended him.

In their tell-all book about working for Elvis, bodyguards Red and Sonny West candidly admit that throughout the Sixties, Elvis and his entourage regularly took amphetamines and other pills. They started on Dexedrine and Dexamyl, and after a while moved on to Escotrol and Desbutal. To come down at the end of a day and finally get some sleep, they relied on Valium and stronger, addictive sedative-hypnotic tranquillizers like Placidyl (to which among others Justice Rehnquist was addicted for much of the Seventies).

Amphetamines, also known as speed, are a class of potentially addictive stimulants. Side effects are restlessness, insomnia, anxiety, aggressiveness, depression, and a host of physical problems. Because they prevent sleep, amphetamine abuse often leads to the use of other drugs in order to sleep. In later years, Elvis felt that he needed amphetamines to counteract the cocktail of heavy sleeping medications he took, thus embarking on a vicious cycle from which he was unable to break loose.

Amphetamines are widely used to treat attention deficit disorders, and sometimes for weight-loss purposes. Elvis and his pals took these drugs to fit even more fun into their already fun-packed days. There was no other way to keep going night after night and make it to a movie shoot the next day.

When Priscilla came to spend Christmas with Elvis in 1962, she found that he was taking Placidyl to get to sleep. Elvis gave her some to help her get over her jetlag and she was wiped out for two whole days.

Elvis is said to have first started taking downers—Seconal and "yellow jackets"—in the mid-Sixties, around about the time he worked on *Paradise, Hawaiian Style*. Sonny West told Steve Dunleavy that Elvis got concussion after falling in his bathroom because he was groggy from these downers.

Because of the variety of sleeping pills he took—according to Priscilla, as many as four Placidyls, Seconals, Quaaludes or Tuinals—Elvis started taking Dexedrine when he woke up to.

When Elvis was in the thick of his spiritual quest in 1965, he persuaded at least three members of his entourage (Alan Fortas, Red West and Sonny West) to try LSD, with the intention of watching what it did to them, and to see if the drug might work as inspiration to write a song. According to Larry Geller, it was Priscilla who was curious about trying the drug. When it came to experimenting with LSD, Elvis, Priscilla, Larry Geller and Jerry Schilling took the "trip" together; Sonny West was on call to make sure that things didn't get out of hand (In her memoir, Priscilla recalls that Lamar Fike, Jerry Schilling, Larry Geller, herself and Elvis took the LSD). Priscilla writes that it was such an extraordinary experience that they realized it was too dangerous to try again. However, by some accounts, Elvis, Priscilla and a friend sampled the drug again, this time feeling a euphoric sense of connection. They also ate pizza and watched sci-fi movie *The Time Machine*.

Elvis had some marijuana brownies made up and passed round his entourage that summer—he avoided smoking the drug because it hurt his throat. Priscilla says that they tried but didn't enjoy marijuana—it made them groggy and caused them to eat too much. John Lennon recalled that when The Beatles visited Elvis in 1965, Elvis refrained from smoking any of the "cigarettes that were offered around."

However, Larry Geller says that for a few days, Elvis smoked marijuana non-stop to see what it was like, before stopping so as not to harm his voice. Geller has also written that in the mid-Sixties Elvis' prescription cabinet contained amphetamines (for dieting), barbiturates (Seconal and Tuinal), and the painkiller narcotic Percodan.

From 1967, Elvis relied on "diet pills" to slim down for his later movies. According to Joyce Bova, he took Dexedrine to keep his weight down in the late Sixties and early Seventies.

Elvis dissuaded Priscilla from taking birth control pills before their marriage because, he said, they were still experimental and had side effects. Elvis' mood swings became increasingly frequent in the Seventies as his drug intake increased.

Marty Lacker recalls security man and former drug squad detective John O'Grady trying to persuade Elvis to spearhead a public anti-drugs campaign, and offering to help make contact with the deputy director of the Narcotics Bureau, John Finlator, who turned Elvis down on this initial approach.

In December 1970, Elvis met President Nixon, after writing him a letter in which he offered his services to help the government in its efforts to combat illegal drugs. Elvis was rewarded with the police badge he most craved, from the Federal Bureau of Narcotics and Dangerous Drugs (which, among other things, would make it much simpler to travel with his usual supply of medication, toted around by a member of his entourage in a make-up bag).

Bodyguards Red and Sonny West reveal in their book that Elvis significantly stepped up his pill intake in 1971, staying up for hours and hours and then going to bed for days. He began to take a lot of painkillers such as Percodan and Demerol. For the first time since he had resumed live performing, during his winter 1971 residency in Las Vegas the pills had an effect on his performance.

In early 1972, Elvis rationalized to girlfriend Joyce Bova that he took drugs because they helped him to get near the silence and stillness which he described as "the resting place of the soul." She observed that by the end of the year, he was more and more often relying on downers, the side effects of which included weight gain and even more pronounced mood swings. At the end of the year he swore off pills altogether for at least a couple of weeks as he got in shape for his *Aloha from Hawaii* performance.

Lamar Fike described Elvis' drug cocktail circa 1973 as Codeine (to which some biographers have said Elvis was allergic), Valium, Placidyl, Valmid and Butabarbital, all taken sequentially.

Members of Elvis' entourage in the Seventies have gone on record to say that the punishing pace and schedule of touring was simply untenable without resorting to chemical help. Elvis regularly had shots before he took to the stage: not narcotics, according to the man who administered them, Dr. George Nichopoulos, but B-12 shots and anti-allergy medication.

Drug abuse is generally credited for Elvis' rage in February 1973, after four men jumped on the stage during a show at the Las Vegas Hilton. Convinced that the men had been sent by Priscilla's new boyfriend, Mike Stone, he instructed members of his entourage to take out a contract on Stone. His anger passed before anything irredeemable was organized.

In May 1973, Vernon and the Colonel hired PI John O'Grady to try and staunch Elvis' supply of drugs, after his health began deteriorating significantly and he was forced to cancel a number of concerts. O'Grady identified three doctors and a dentist as Elvis' main sources. Vernon confronted Elvis—and quite possibly Priscilla did too—but Elvis could not be persuaded to go into a residential detox facility. Preventing the sources that O'Grady identified from supplying Elvis was only a temporary solution until Elvis found more compliant doctors to prescribe the medications he wanted. He could obtain prescriptions in the name of one of his entourage or somebody connected with them, and after 1975 could even send a plane to pick up supplies.

Later in 1973 Elvis was hospitalized in Memphis by Dr. Nichopoulos after he went on a so-called "acupuncture" cure of B-12 vitamins, Demerol, Cortisone and Xylocaine. This was the first of several times that Elvis was put on a detoxification regime. When Dr. Nick and Joe Esposito did a sweep of Elvis' bedroom, they confiscated three 1000-pill bottles of Dexedrine, Seconal and a sedative. Elvis somehow managed to persuade doctors to procure him drugs in hospital, while addiction specialists tried to get him to agree to go into a proper residential program (this, almost a decade before high-profile rehabilitation centers such as the Betty Ford Center). When he refused, they talked to him about his addictions and their potential consequences. For a while, he changed his behavior . . . At a subconscious level, there can be little doubt that Elvis was aware of his dependency. When recording "Good Time Charlie's Got The Blues" at the end of the year, he omitted the line "I take the pills to ease the pain, can't find the thing to ease my brain."

Elvis regularly took steroids from 1973 onwards to fight asthma (which he had suffered as a child), colitis and infections. These caused other medical problems, especially after the damage inflicted by the unorthodox "acupuncture" injections to which he submitted. Entourage members have said that Elvis inadvertently overdosed and had to be brought round, sometimes with Ritalin injections, at least twice in 1973. By this time, it was part of their duty to sweep Elvis' hotel rooms before leaving to ensure that no drug paraphernalia was left behind, which included taking the trash with them.

Sonny West says that if Elvis wanted to get a buzz, he would use Hycadan, a codeine-based cough medicine with narcotic effects if taken in large enough quantities. He might also take Emprin with codeine. There was one occasion in Palm Springs when Elvis and a female fan he had befriended at a Las Vegas show needed medical attention after overdosing on this drug, and the girl had to be taken to hospital. She reputedly suffered permanent damage from the incident.

Elvis is known to have tried cocaine—Dr. Nichopoulos summed up Elvis on cocaine as "sort of psychotic." One Memphis police captain says that they discovered a shipment of cocaine bound for Graceland and waited for Elvis to show up to collect it—which he never did. Larry Geller says that the only time Elvis used a street drug was liquid cocaine.

In his live performances between August and October 1974, Elvis' banter to the audience was peppered with drug-fuelled non-sequiturs. In his final Las Vegas show that year he vehemently denied the rumors of his drugs problems: "I hear rumors flying around—I got sick in the hospital. In this day and time you can't even get sick. You are strung out. By God I'll tell you something, I have never been strung out in my life, except on music. I got sick that one night, I had a hundred and two temperature, and they wouldn't let me perform, from three different sources I heard I was strung out on heroin. I swear to God, hotel employees, jacks, bellboys, freaks who carry that luggage up to your room, people, you know maids. And I was sick. But all across town, strung out. Don't you get offended ladies and gentlemen, I'm talking to someone else, if I find or hear an individual that has said that about me, I'm going to break their goddamn neck you son of a bitch, that is dangerous. . . . I will pull your goddamn tongue out by the roots."

Elvis was treated several times for breathing problems exacerbated by his use of opioid painkiller Demerol. Side-effects of this pethidine-based medicine include asthma, swelling of the breathing passages, dizziness and even unconsciousness. It can also compromise the digestive system.

When guys in the entourage shared their concerns with Vernon and Vernon broached the matter with Elvis, Elvis called in his entourage pals and told them in no uncertain terms that they had overstepped their mark. Sonny West recalls that Red West asked him why he couldn't just get along like he had in the past, during the good old days, to which Elvis replied "There are no more good old days." Like many substance abusers, Elvis displayed bizarre behavior. Billy Smith reported that there were times when they had to lure him into the bath, and when he was heavily sedated he could even become incontinent. And yet every time that Elvis' doctors tried to wean him off his addiction, he always found somebody in the entourage who would do his bidding and replenish his supply of prescription drugs. The Wests' threats to one of Elvis' stepbrothers and a member of a backing group only made a temporary difference.

The years before Elvis' death were not a straightforward decline. There were times when Elvis wanted to break out of the spiral of dependency, but then when he felt under stress, he fell back into bad habits. At Graceland, Dr. Nichopoulos could keep an eye on his medical intake and ensure that he lived a more healthy lifestyle. The problem was when Elvis was on tour—which he was often—and subject to great stresses. One entourage member recalls that Elvis even looked into owning his own pharmacy so that he would be less subject to the restrictions his doctor imposed.

Elvis' reliance on his "medications" grew slowly until he couldn't function without them. When

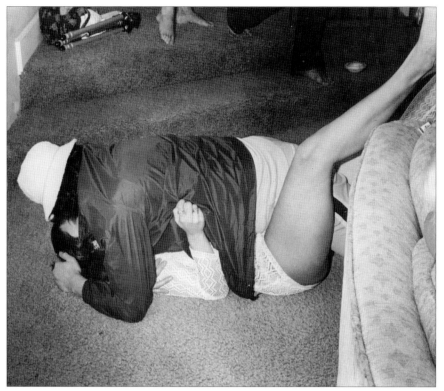
A photo of Elvis in Hawaii 1977.

he was on tour, Elvis was convinced that he needed a dizzying array of shots and concoctions to boost his energy and keep his voice in shape. According to Dr. Nichopoulos, Elvis' daily regimen was coffee, vitamins and an appetite suppressant (sometimes amphetamine-based) to start the day; he'd also take a decongestant and blood pressure medicine soon after waking up. Before going on stage, Elvis had a "voice shot"—a blend of herbs that Dr. Nick believed to have no medical value but Elvis insisted on. Elvis had a regular vitamin B-12 shot, and might ask for another decongestant before leaving for the venue. Just before he went on stage, somebody would administer eye drops—a mild local anesthetic—to help him with the bright lights and the reaction he suffered from dye running off his hair. After the show Elvis took blood pressure pills, and usually requested a sedative to bring him down, preferably Demerol. Dr. Nick gave Elvis placebo injections of saline solution, until Elvis became suspicious and ensured that his physician showed him the bottle first.

Friends and relatives who were aware that he was taking dangerous quantities of drugs also knew that he was in pain from a variety of health complaints, and that the pills were part of his strategy for handling the stresses of being responsible for the livelihood and wellbeing of so many people. When he was particularly run-down at the end of a tour, he might ask his doctor for a narcotic. In early 1975 Dr. Nick prescribed him Elavil, an antidepressant, to pull him out of a slump..

In Elvis' later years, arrangements were made to ensure that there was always somebody watching over him when he slept. This was after he almost overdosed by waking up and taking a heavy dose of prescription medicine on top of the dangerously large dose he had already ingested. After this, Dr. Nick persuaded Elvis to call him when he wanted more medication and the doctor would dispense on an ad hoc basis.

Sonny West recalls that Elvis took three "packets" of medicine a night to sleep. He also took large doses of Dilaudid, a highly potent and potentially addictive morphine-based analgesic generally prescribed to terminal cancer patients. Alanna Nash says that this became his "favorite narcotic."

At his worst, when he was so bloated and slow that he could hardly get through a concert, Elvis was battling the side-effects of his usual cocktail plus Donnatal, which he took to prevent spasms in the colon. Among the drug's side-effects are bloatedness, sweating, drowsiness, blurred vision and slurred speech.

In 1976, when in a delusional state, Elvis reputedly decided to round up local Memphis drug dealers and personally execute them. He illustrated his plan to Red West in his bedroom, surrounded by an arsenal of guns, rifles and semi-automatic weapons. He thought that he had the perfect cover because Graceland was full of musicians, with whom he was recording *From Elvis Presley Boulevard, Memphis, Tennessee*.

In 1976 for a spell Elvis found a doctor who prescribed him the anti-psychotic drug Sparine. When he took it, it would debilitate him completely.

It has been claimed that in 1977, Dr. Nick wrote out prescriptions to Elvis for 10,000 doses of amphetamines, barbiturates, painkillers, hormones, laxatives, decongestants, anti-histamines, narcotics, sleeping pills and tranquilizers, which Elvis was taking in six mega-doses per day.

Many years after Elvis' death, David Stanley claimed that there was a real possibility that Elvis committed suicide. On his last night alive, Elvis took his usual ration of drugs (Seconal, Placidyl, Valmid, Tuinal and Demerol, plus depressants and placebos), which he normally took in three separate doses over a space of time. Stanley says that when Elvis was found, he was surrounded by envelopes and syringes that indicated he had taken 33 pills and nine shots of Demerol. However, eminent physicians have pointed out that if Elvis had overdosed on sedatives, he would have gone into a coma rather than dying suddenly. The authorities found no evidence of this drug consumption following his death because members of the entourage cleaned up the scene before any outsiders arrived.

ELVIS TOLD LARRY GELLER: "The mind is stronger than these medications."

JOHNNY CASH: "Back in the '50s . . . in those days he was the last person on earth who needed dope.

He had such a high energy level that it seemed he never stopped—though maybe that's why they said he was on dope."

PRISCILLA: "He always assured me he didn't need pills, that he could never become dependent on them."

LARRY GELLER: "Elvis was imbued with an energy that was so potent, so dynamic he didn't need acid, and he knew it."

SONNY WEST: "By 1971, Elvis was a changed guy. He was no longer the shy, fun-loving kid from Memphis. No, he was just living for himself and all that damn junk he took. He was like a walking drugstore."

DR. NICHOPOULOS: "He was a person who thought that as far as medications and drugs went, there was something for everything."

BILLY SMITH: "Elvis wasn't bombed all the time. I'd say maybe 40% of the time in the Sixties. It got worse in the Seventies—probably 60% of the time. He always had pills in him, but he didn't get really bad until the last four years of his life. That's when you actually had to watch him."

LAMAR FIKE: "Elvis loved downers, and he loved getting totally fucked up. Downers will put weight on you pretty quick."

SONNY WEST: "Elvis didn't think he had that big a problem with drugs. He felt that he was in control, that he knew what he was doing, that he could quit when he wanted to . . . but it wasn't working."

MARTY LACKER: "Because he knew the PDR so well, Elvis new exactly what symptoms he needed to fake to get his pills."

BILLY SMITH: "With pills, Elvis said he wanted to get the same feeling that an alcoholic gets with booze, except not be totally out of control."

DR. NICHOPOULOS: "A lot of times when he'd get depressed, the narcotics would give him an 'up' feeling, as well as relieve his pain. He would always go back to something that made him feel good."

TOM JONES: "Elvis told me that he had tried taking different drugs just to keep sane."

RED WEST: "He takes pills to go to sleep. He takes pills to get up. He takes pills to go to the john, and he takes pills to stop him from going to the john. . . . He takes uppers and downers and very strong painkillers."

PETER GURALNICK: ". . . With his own encyclopedic knowledge of the PDR . . . he was able to manufacture the appropriate symptoms for virtually any kind of medication that might take his fancy."

CHARLIE HODGE: "Yes, Elvis took medications, but they were prescribed for him by Dr. Nick. And they were for very real conditions Elvis suffered from."

SONNY WEST: "He would go through periods where he would look after himself, and man, he would look like a Greek god. But then he would lapse back into popping the downers where the lapses got gradually closer and closer together. By the early Seventies, the only thing that would keep him straight was if he had a challenge. Then he would be the old Elvis again."

LARRY GELLER: "Sad to say, without medication Elvis wasn't as good, onstage or off, as he was when he had it."

BILLY SMITH: "There were two people who could have legally helped Elvis—Vernon and, after the wedding, Priscilla. And both of them turned their back."

DAVE HEBLER: "How do you protect a man from himself?"

CORONER THOMAS NOGUCHI: "The combination of prescription drugs he ingested in such quantities . . . caused the fatally irregular heartbeat in the first place."

DUETS

Apart from a limited number of lovey-dovey songs with leading ladies in the movies, the Colonel's insistence that Elvis got top billing ensured that Elvis' singing efforts were almost without exception solo. And yet Elvis had a great love of choral backing and vocal accompaniment. When he sang for his own edification, either at home (recorded in various home tapings) or at the exceptional *Million Dollar Quartet* session with Carl Perkins, Jerry Lee Lewis and Johnny Cash, he loved to twin with other voices.

In the Seventies, Elvis sometimes dueted live with backing vocal artists, especially the bass singers.

An import CD of Elvis duets was released in 2007, a year when he indulged in posthumous duets with Celine Dion ("If I Can Dream") and his daughter Lisa-Marie ("In The Ghetto").

ELVIS DUETS

"Crawfish" with Kitty White in *King Creole*

"Earth Boy" with Ginny and Elizabeth Tiu in *Girls! Girls! Girls!*

"Happy Ending" with Joan O'Brien in *It Happened at the World's Fair*

"How Would You Like To Be" with Vicki Tiu in *It Happened at the World's Fair*

"Husky Dusky Day" with Hope Lange in *Wild in the Country*

"I Will Be Home Again" with Charlie Hodge on *Elvis Is Back!*

"Love Me Tender / Witchcraft" with Frank Sinatra on the "Frank Sinatra Show"

"Mexico" with Larry Domasin in *Fun in Acapulco*

"Petunia the Gardener's Daughter" and "Look Out Broadway" with Eileen Wilson (mimed by Donna Douglas on screen) in *Frankie and Johnny*; Harry Morgan and Audrey Christie also take part in "Look Out Broadway"

"Queenie Wahine's Papaya" with Donna Butterworth in *Paradise, Hawaiian Style*

"Scratch My Back" with Marianna Hill in *Paradise, Hawaiian Style*

"Signs of the Zodiac" with Marlyn Mason in *The Trouble with Girls*

"Spring Fever" with Shelley Fabares in *Girl Happy*

"The First Time Ever I Saw Your Face" with Temple Riser

"The Lady Loves Me" and "Today, Tomorrow & Forever" and "You're The Boss" with Ann-Margret for *Viva Las Vegas*

"There Ain't Nothing like A Song" with Nancy Sinatra in *Speedway*

"Who Needs Money" with Ray Walker (mimed by Will Hutchins on screen) in *Clambake*

"Yoga Is As Yoga Does" with Elsa Lanchaster in *Easy Come, Easy Go*

DUKE OF PADUCAH
(B. BENJAMIN FRANCIS "WHITEY" FORD, 1901-1986)

In his first flush of touring, Elvis appeared on a number of bills with this hardworking hillbilly comedian who by this time was towards the end of his career. According to some sources, the Duke helped to persuade Vernon and Gladys that Elvis should sign up with the Colonel.

The Duke of Paducah was a popular comedy act from the mid-Thirties onwards. For three decades he was a regular on the Grand Ole Opry radio show, though he started out as a banjo player in popular Twenties combo Otto Gray & His Oklahoma Cowboys.

The Colonel was particularly partial to the Duke of Paducah's sideline as a purveyor of sausages, which he often gave away as gifts to important people.

The Duke of Paducah was inducted into the Country Music Hall of Fame the year he died.

DUNNE, PHILIP
(1908-1992)

A writer, director and producer for 20th Century Fox who directed Elvis in *Wild in the Country*. He was twice Oscar-nominated for his screenplays *David and Bathsheba* and *How Green Was My Valley*. Dunne was a co-founder of the Writer's Guild and a prominent activist during the "Hollywood Blacklist" period. His experience with Elvis was of "an excellent dramatic actor, a natural actor." Dunne wrote speeches for John F. Kennedy prior to his election to president.

DURDEN, TOMMY
(1920-1999)

A steel guitar player who wrote songs with Mae Boren Axton . . . most memorably, "Heartbreak Hotel," spawned by a newspaper photograph he saw of a suicide victim who left a note that read, "I walk a lonely street."

Decades later, Durden declared in an interview that the song paid his rent for over 20 years. He supplemented his income by playing steel guitar in back-up bands for Johnny Cash and Tex Ritter among others.

DVORIN, AL
(1923-2004)

Promoter Dvorin was an associate of Tom Diskin's and a friend of the Colonel's who worked to promote Elvis from 1956. Before joining the Colonel's staff, Dvorin had worked as a bandleader, booking agent and a talent agent in Chicago.

Dvorin is remembered as the concert announcer who told the audience "Elvis has left the building" in order to persuade people to vacate the premises after an Elvis show—though his paternity of the quote would seem to be apocryphal. Horace Logan, a Louisiana Hayride announcer, is credited by many as the originator of the phrase.

Dvorin promoted an Elvis tour through the Midwest, Canada and the East Coast in March and April 1957, along with promoter Lee Gordon, and also booked Elvis through the Northwest and Canada in August and September of that year. In November 1971, Dvorin once more took to the stage as an announcer, from then on concluding each of Elvis' shows with the famous line.

AL DVORIN: "He was a good man, a charitable man, the finest entertainer that ever lived."

ED BONJA: "Al did almost every job apart from performing on stage with Elvis itself! He was the booking agent, managed the tours, lighting guy, a bandleader and also helped set up everything."

DYLAN, BOB
(B. ROBERT ALLEN ZIMMERMAN, 1941)

Among the many musical inspirations in Bob Dylan's life, Elvis' rock 'n' roll was a wake-up call for a man who would become one of the most influential recording artists of the late Twentieth century.

Dylan—the only man to have more column inches in the 2006 edition of Encyclopedia of Popular Music than Elvis—was born in Duluth, Minnesota, on May 24, 1941. He moved to New York City in 1960, and after performing wherever he could find a stage in small clubs, was signed to Capitol Records in 1962 by legendary producer John Hammond. Much as he enjoyed Elvis' rock 'n' roll, Dylan's greatest hero was Woody Guthrie, who became more famous as the precursor to the Sixties folk revival movement than he ever was singing protest songs in the Thirties and Forties. In early interviews, Dylan spuriously claimed to have played piano on some of Elvis' early records.

Dylan wrote songs for many top performers. Elvis recorded Dylan compositions "Tomorrow Is A Long Time," released as a bonus track to the *Spinout* soundtrack album, and "Don't Think Twice, It's All Right," which came out on originally his 1973 album *Elvis (The Fool Album)*. Elvis also sang "Blowin' In The Wind" (sadly, only a home recording). Dylan returned the compliment, at one time or another covering half a dozen songs that Elvis sang including "A Fool Such As I," "Blue Moon," "Peace In The Valley" and "Tomorrow Night."

Elvis and Dylan worked with a number of the same musicians: Millie Kirkham, Bob Moore, Charlie McCoy, Kenneth Buttrey, Pete Drake, and Jerry Scheff. In the early Seventies, producer Bob Johnston attempted unsuccessfully to set up a joint recording session for Elvis and Dylan.

Dylan's own nasal singing style showed the world that a great singing voice was not a pre-requisite for recording fame. A significant influence on the new crop of singer/songwriters who began to find success in the Sixties, Dylan's songs became anthems for the protest movement, including classics such as "Blowin' In The Wind," "Like A Rolling Stone," "The Times They Are A-Changin'" and "Lay Lady Lay." He (reluctantly) became the voice of his generation, though some fans felt betrayed as he shifted gears from folk to rock, and later to country.

Dylan's first #1 didn't come until early Seventies hit "Knocking On Heaven's Door." He received a Lifetime Achievement Grammy in 1997, just one of many accolades he has accumulated in his long career. In 2000 he won an Oscar for best song, "Things Have Changed," from the movie *The Wonder Boys*. He has continued to record into the 2000s.

BOB DYLAN: "When I first heard Elvis' voice, I just knew that I wasn't going to work for anybody, and nobody was going to be my boss.."

BOB DYLAN: "The highlight of my career? That's easy, Elvis recording one of my songs."

BRUCE SPRINGSTEEN: "Bob freed the mind the way Elvis freed the body."

CHARLIE McCoy: "The difference between the two was that Bob usually left you to do your own thing while Elvis had a much clearer idea what he wanted."

EAGLE'S NEST, MEMPHIS

Elvis, Scotty Moore and Bill Black started what was to become a regular weekend attraction at this Memphis venue on Lamar Avenue on August 7, 1954, and played right through the fall, appearing at least a dozen times. The place was a top music venue, with Memphis DJ Sleepy-Eyed John Lepley's house band over the years including Jim Stewart (who later founded Stax Records) and Jack Clement (who went on to be a producer at Sun Records). The venue also had a swimming pool and served food at all hours.

Elvis' first gig as an interval act drew very few patrons—the venue was usually attended by an older crowd, and it took a little while for word to spread among Memphis teens.

Elvis' regular slot at the club attracted all manner of music business professionals. His November 17, 1954 show was attended by Biff Collie, a big DJ in Houston, who on the strength of Elvis' performance booked him for the Houston Hoedown he was arranging the following week, for a $150 fee—Elvis had started at the Eagle's Nest on just $10 a show.

Elvis made his final appearance at this venue, the first to give him a residency, on Friday, December 10, 1954.

"EARLY MORNING RAIN"

Elvis recorded this 1965 Gordon Lightfoot hit on March 15, 1971 in Nashville, for release on Elvis Now after he heard guitarist John Wilkinson playing the song at the Nashville studio; Wilkinson had played guitar on the original recording, and a number of times in later years he got Wilkinson to perform the song his concerts.

The tune was the last Elvis performed in Hawaii in 1973 during his trip for Aloha From Hawaii Via Satellite, early in the morning after the stadium had been cleared when recorded extra material for the delayed US broadcast. This version first came out on disc on Mahalo From Hawaii years later.

Elvis added the song to his live repertoire proper in 1974, and sang it regularly in his final years, right up to the Elvis in Concert documentary and album. Other live versions have appeared on concert bootlegs and on FTD albums It's Midnight, Tucson '76 and New Year's Eve.

The studio version has since appeared on Elvis Aron Presley Forever and Elvis in Nashville. An alternate from the Nashville studio session surfaced on 2007 FTD issue I Sing All Kinds.

"EARTH ANGEL"

A home recording made during Elvis' time in the Army exists of him singing this song, which had been a million-selling hit for The Penguins in 1954 and was written by Curtis Williams (though it is also credited to Jesse Belvin and, quite possibly Gaynel Hodge too). It was released posthumously on A Golden Celebration.

"EARTH BOY"

A Chinese-themed Sid Tepper / Roy C. Bennett Girls! Girls! Girls! soundtrack song, laid down in album and movie versions on March 28, 1962 at Radio Recorders, which Elvis sings with the Tiu sisters on film. Elvis' non-Chinese language version has since come out on the Double Features release for the movie, as well as on Elvis Chante Sid Tepper & Roy C. Bennett.

The movie version appeared on the 2007 FTD Girls! Girls! Girls! release.

EASTER SPECIAL

A 2001 FTD collection of alternate gospel tracks and rare material including a 1957 radio commercial in which Elvis supports the March of Dimes anti-polio campaign.

TRACK LISTING:
1. March Of Dimes
2. It Is No Secret
3. He Knows Just What I Need
4. Mansion Over The Hilltop
5. Joshua Fit The Battle
6. I'm Gonna Walk Dem Golden Stairs
7. Known Only To Him
8. Run On
9. Stand By Me
10. So High
11. Somebody Bigger Than You And I
12. We Call On Him
13. Saved
14. An Evening Prayer
15. Seeing Is Believing
16. There Is No God But God
17. He Is My Everything
18. Bosom Of Abraham
19. I Got A Feelin' In My Body
20. If That Isn't Love

"EASY COME, EASY GO"

Ben Weisman and Sid Wayne wrote the title song for this film, which Elvis laid down at Radio Recorders on September 28, 1966 (or, according to some sources, overdubbed at a later date). Actually, Weisman and Wayne originally submitted the song for previous movie Double Trouble, but when it didn't get picked for that they rewrote the words and tried again. The movie version differs from the version released on the soundtrack EP.

The song has since featured on budget albums C'mon Everybody, Double Dynamite, and more recently on Command Performances, the Double Features and FTD releases for the movie (the FTD release includes an alternate take) and Elvis Movies.

EASY COME, EASY GO (EP)

Elvis' last ever EP release, a six-track soundtrack disc released to coincide with the movie of the same name, has the dubious distinction of being his worst selling recording ever, persuading just 30,000 fans to part with their money.

TRACK LISTING:
1. Easy Come, Easy Go
2. The Love Machine
3. Yoga Is As Yoga Does
4. You Gotta Stop
5. Sing You Children
6. I'll Take Love

The songs were re-released in 1995 on a Double Feature album alongside the Speedway soundtrack.

TRACK LISTING:
1. Easy Come, Easy Go
2. The Love Machine
3. Yoga Is As Yoga Does
4. You Gotta Stop
5. Sing You Children
6. I'll Take Love
7. She's A Machine
8. The Love Machine (alternate take)
9. Sing You Children (alternate take)
10. She's A Machine (alternate take)
11. Suppose (Long version)

ABOVE: Rare cover of an Australian LP Easy Come, Easy Go
BELOW: Cover of the soundtrack from the movie Easy Come, Easy Go (1967).

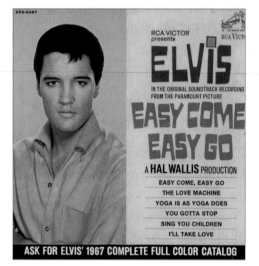

12. Speedway
13. There Ain't Nothing Like A Song
14. You're Time Hasn't Come Yet Baby
15. Who Are You (Who Am I)?
16. He's Your Uncle, Not Your Dad
17. Let Yourself Go
18. Five Sleepy Heads
19. Suppose
20. Your Groovy Self (Nancy Sinatra)

FTD released the tracks on the original EP plus extras in 2007.

EASY COME, EASY GO

Elvis reported to the studio for work at the end of September 1966, where he teamed up with Hollywood veterans Frank McHugh and Elsa Lanchester. Elvis' role as a Navy SEAL scuba diver required him to take diving lessons.

The movie went through a few working titles—A Girl in Every Port, Port of Call and Easy Does It—before producer Hal Wallis alighted on Easy Come, Easy Go. This was Elvis' final movie for Paramount; reputedly producer Hal Wallis took director John Rich aside and told him to "just put them through their paces" and get the thing done without spending too much money. The experience was enough for Rich to make this his final feature movie too.

Location work was at the Long Beach Naval Station.

Leading actress Dodie Marshall had already had played opposite Elvis in Spinout.

The movie opened in March 1967 to poor

reviews and worse box office, just scraping #50 on the year's Box Office Survey. At one stage, the studio reputedly considered not even releasing the picture. By year end, it had made close to $2 million in the States, and struggled into profit by the time international sales were added in.

When pal George Klein asked Elvis what this, his latest movie, was about, Elvis quipped, "Same story, different location."

CREDITS:
Paramount, Color
Length: 95 minutes
Release date: March 22, 1967

TAGLINES:
Scuba divin' . . . singin' . . . swingin' . . .
Skin-diving for treasure . . . adventure . . . and fun!

Directed by: John Rich
Produced by: Hal B. Wallis (producer), Joseph H. Hazen (executive producer), Paul Nathan (associate producer)
Written by: Allan Weiss and Anthony Lawrence
Music by: Joseph J. Lilley
Cinematography by: William Margulies
Film Editing by: Archie Marshek
Art Direction by: Hal Pereira, Walter Tyler
Set Decoration by: Robert Benton, Arthur Krams
Costume Design by: Edith Head

CAST:
Elvis Presley	Lt. Ted Jackson
Dodie Marshall	Jo Symington
Pat Priest	Dina Bishop
Pat Harrington Jr.	Judd Whitman
Skip Ward	Gil Carey
Sandy Kenyon	Lt. Marty Schwartz
Frank McHugh	Captain Jack
Ed Griffith	Navy Diver Cooper
Read Morgan	Ens. Tompkins
Mickey Elley	Ens. Whitehead
Elaine Beckett	Vicki
Shari Nims	Mary
Diki Lerner	Zoltan
Robert Isenberg	Artist
Elsa Lanchester	Madame Neherina
Tom Hatten	Lt.

ADDITIONAL CREW:
Nellie Manley	hair stylist
Wally Westmore	makeup supervisor
William W. Gray	unit production manager
Robert Goodstein	assistant director
John R. Carter	sound recorder
Charles Grenzbach	sound recorder
Paul K. Lerpae	special effects
Steven Burnett	stunts
Carol Daniels	stunts
Michael Dugan	underwater photographer
Farciot Edouart	process photographer
The Jordanaires	vocal accompaniment
Colonel Tom Parker.	technical advisor
David Winters	choreographer

Plot:
Elvis plays Navy frogman Lt. Ted Jackson who, while on maneuvers in the Pacific, comes across a treasure chest in the sunken wreck of the Port of Call. Unbeknownst to him, he is spotted by a couple on a boat nearby, Dina Bishop (played by Pat Priest, formerly of the Munsters) and boyfriend Gil Carey (played by Skip Ward).

Ted tries to get help from marine supply merchant Captain Jack (played by Frank McHugh), and then goes to see Jo Symington (played by Dodie Marshall), heir to the man who owned the Port of Call before it went down. Jo Symington's house is overrun by Sixties dropouts doing yoga, meditation and other beat pursuits. Ted finds himself in the middle of a yoga class given by Madame Neherina (played by Elsa Lanchester). Despite his ineptness, he makes an impression on heiress Jo, who confirms that the ship went down

with a treasure chest of gold coins along with a cargo of coffee, after Ted persuades her that his interest is purely academic, for the diving manual he is writing.

Teamed up with sidekick/pal Judd (played by Pat Harrington), Ted prepares to salvage the treasure. When Jo finds out, she is livid at his greed, but then agrees to take Captain Jack's place on the mission (Captain Jack turns out to be a landlubber, he was only a captain on a kids' TV show) on condition that they use some of the money they salvage to set up an arts center for her pals.

Alas, when they get to the dive site, Dina Bishop and Gil Carey are lying in wait. There's still time for more shenanigans before the matter is resolved. Back ashore, Captain Jack sides against Ted and his crew; Ted gets a little done at the "Easy Go-Go" club; Dina and Gil return to the site and dive before Ted , but Ted uses his superior diving skills to grab the chest. The bad guys can do nothing but look on from afar as Ted and Jo count up the coins—not gold, as expected, but $4,000 of copper. It's still enough to get work started on the art center project.

Songs: "Easy Come, Easy Go," "The Love Machine," "Yoga Is As Yoga Does," "You Gotta Stop," "Sing You Children," "I'll Take Love"

"(SUCH AN) EASY QUESTION"

Released as a single in late May 1965, with "It Feels So Right" on the B-side, Elvis actually recorded this Otis Blackwell / Winfield Scott easy-listening tune back on March 18, 1962 in Nashville. Both tracks were on the *Tickle Me* soundtrack, hence the single release, but they had previously appeared as album cuts respectively on *Pot Luck* (1962) and *Elvis Is Back!* (1960). The A-side peaked at #11, spent eight weeks in the charts and sold around half a million copies.

Later releases include *From Nashville To Memphis*, the *Double Features* and FTD issues for *Tickle Me*, *Hitstory* and *Elvis at the Movies*.

Alternates may be found on *Essential Elvis, Vol. 6* and FTD releases *Studio B: Nashville Outtakes* and *Pot Luck*.

"ECHOES OF LOVE"

Elvis recorded this Bob Roberts / Paddy McMains pop number to kick off his May 26, 1963 recording session for RCA in Nashville. The song was released the following year as a bonus track on the *Kissin' Cousins* soundtrack album.

The song did not make it onto the *Double Features* and FTD *Kissin' Cousins* reissues, but it is on *For The Asking (The Lost Album)* and the *From Nashville To Memphis* Sixties anthology.

Alternates have appeared on *Elvis: Close Up* and FTD album *Studio B: Nashville Outtakes*.

ECKSTINE, BILLY
(1914-1993)

Billy Eckstine was a popular African-American balladeer from the Forties onwards who scored a succession of smooth hits and is acknowledged as America's first black sex symbol. His bebop band in the Forties has to be one of the greatest line-ups of all time, featuring Charlie Parker, Dizzy Gillespie and Sarah Vaughn (and later including Dexter Gordon and Miles Davis among others).

One of Elvis' childhood musical heroes, Elvis sang part of Eckstine hit "I Apologize" at an early Sixties recording session, and is said to have auditioned with the song to Scotty Moore when he first started at Sun Records.

"ED SULLIVAN SHOW," THE

Elvis' three appearances on the "Ed Sullivan Show" in 1956 and early 1957 marked the watershed between being an up-and-coming hopeful and making top-tier status. Sullivan had been hosting a hugely popular Saturday night variety show since 1948, originally titled "Toast of the Town" before it was renamed "The Ed Sullivan Show" the year before Elvis' appearance. Quite simply, it was the biggest thing on TV and an arbiter of national taste. After Elvis did the "Ed Sullivan Show," the Colonel said no to all other TV offers until 1960.

Broadcast from CBS Studio 50 in NYC (later renamed *The Ed Sullivan Theater*, and more recently home to "The Late Show with David Letterman"), though Elvis was actually performing live from CBS Studios in Los Angeles, on September 9, 1956 over 80% of America's TV viewers (one in three of the entire population) watched Elvis perform " Don't Be Cruel," "Love Me Tender," "Ready Teddy," and a raunchy version of "Hound Dog." Show host Sullivan, occasionally lampooned as "the Great Stone Face," was actually replaced that night by actor Charles Laughton, as he was recuperating from a car accident.

For his second appearance on the show, Elvis performed "Don't Be Cruel," "Love Me," "Love Me Tender," and "Hound Dog" from the Maxine Elliott Theater on West 39th St in New York. The October 28 broadcast also attracted over 80% of all TV viewers.

Elvis' third appearance, from the same location on January 6, 1957, was the infamous performance when he was filmed from the waist up only, with the exception of his rendition of gospel classic "Peace in the Valley"—a stricture that Elvis found more humiliating the more he thought about it in later years. According to some TV historians, this expedient had been at the Colonel's suggestion.

At the end of the show, host Ed Sullivan strode forward to give Elvis a glowing testimonial: "This is a real decent, fine boy . . . We want to say that we've never had a pleasanter experience on our show with a big name than we've had with you."

Colonel Parker reputedly persuaded the Sullivan show to pay $15,000 per performance, three times the highest fee they had ever paid an artist, and a total of $50,000.

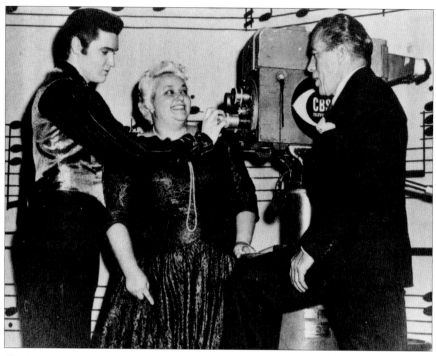
Elvis during rehearsal for the "Ed Sullivan Show"

Elvis' recordings from the Sullivan shows appeared on 1984 album *A Golden Celebration*.

Elvis Presley: The Ed Sullivan Shows, a DVD of all three of the Ed Sullivan shows on which Elvis appeared, was released in late 2006.

In 2007, an Australian TV show voted Elvis' appearance on the "Ed Sullivan Show" to be the fifth highest ranking "event which stopped the world."

ELVIS SAID IN 1970: "I first started in this business, I was a little, bitty guy with a shaky leg. So, Ed Sullivan saw me and said, 'Mmm, son of a bitch'. Anyway, they put me on TV and filmed me from the waist up."

PAMELA CLARKE KEOGH: "His appearance on 'Ed Sullivan' ripped 1950s in half, and America was never the same."

"EDGE OF REALITY"

The B-side to "If I Can Dream," released in November 1968, just before Elvis' NBC TV Special was aired, was written by Bill Giant / Bernie Baum / Florence Kaye and laid down at Western Recorders on March 7, 1968 for late Elvis movie *Live a Little, Love a Little*. Psychedelic Elvis failed to make it into the *Billboard* Hot 100 at all.

After its LP debut on *Almost In Love*, the track has been released on *Elvis' Gold Records Vol. 5*, *Command Performances* and the *Double Features* release for the movie. An alternate came out on FTD's 1999 album *Out in Hollywood*.

EDUCATION

Elvis' childhood and school days are well-documented by biographers, almost all of whom pass comment on Gladys's habit of walking her son to the school gates well into his teens. Though for most biographers this was a sign of maternal overprotectiveness, some suggest that it was a means to ensure that he did not cut class and stuck to his studies.

When he graduated from high school, Elvis was the pride of his family as the first to achieve this landmark. In later life, however, he was acutely aware of his lack of formal education. He made amends by reading avidly, particularly from the mid-Sixties onwards when he devoured spiritual and religious books supplied by his pal Larry Geller.

Elvis became an honorary member of Arkansas State College Tau Kappa Epsilon fraternity in the fall of 1960. He told the fraternity president that he would have liked to have gone to college himself. Some sources say that Elvis did try to enroll in UCLA evening classes but was turned down.

As part of his religious phase in the mid-Sixties, Elvis embarked on a program of self-improvement that including a great deal of reading not just for himself but for Priscilla and his entourage pals. At one point, he tried to institute a dictionary hour every day, in which all of the guys sat around learning new vocabulary.

Elvis returned to education in the early Seventies as the subject of a new wave of textbooks designed to appeal to the real interests of young people. By the late Seventies, the first academic university-level courses on Elvis were being taught. By the Nineties, entire Elvis conferences were delving into his impact on music, popular culture and society.

See also SCHOOLS.

ELVIS SAID IN 1958: "Right at the time, we didn't have enough money to go to college. I would have liked to have gone."

ELVIS SAID IN 1962: "I have my own way of learning . . . I learn from the people I work with. I learn from everyday life itself, being connected with a lot of different people."

ELVIS SAID IN 1962: There's not an intellectual son-of-a-gun walking the face of this earth that could make me believe a certain thing or something unless I really thought it."

LARRY GELLER: "Elvis was one of the brightest people I've known."

NORBERT PUTNAM: "He wasn't highly educated but he was a very quick study."

LARRY GELLER: "He wanted very desperately to be seen as an intelligent, thinking person."

EDWARDS, TIBBY

Elvis played on the same bill as Tibby Edwards on the Louisiana Hayride and on Hayride-promoted tours in 1955, and when in Shreveport spent time hanging out with the singer.

EDWARDS, TOMMY

WERE DJ Edwards, known as the "City Slicker turned Hillbilly," brought Elvis to Cleveland, Ohio to play the Hillbilly Jamboree in February 1955, and was one of the first DJs to take Elvis' beyond his home territory down South. Edwards brought Elvis to town three more times that year, and snapped a famous photograph of Elvis with Bill Haley.

"EL PASO"

Some sources say that Elvis occasionally slipped a line or two of this Marty Robbins country hit—the Grammy Country and Western song of the year for 1960—into Seventies concerts. Known recordings are from 1972 on unofficial CDs *Between Takes with Elvis* and *The Complete On Tour Sessions*; it's also on FTD release *Elvis On Tour—The Rehearsals*.

"EL TORO"

Giant, Baum and Kaye stepped up to the plate for this soundtrack tune in *Fun in Acapulco*, which Elvis recorded on January 23, 1963 at Radio Recorders.

Reissues over the years have been limited to the *Double Features* and FTD releases for the movie.

ELECTRIFYING!

A bootleg release on the Bilko label of Elvis rehearsing in the summer of 1970 before the start of his Las Vegas engagement.

TRACK LISTING:
1. That's All Right (Mama)
2. Twenty Days And Twenty Nights
3. Patch It Up
4. Love Me
5. Yesterday
6. Hey Jude
7. I Can't Stop Loving You
8. It's Your Baby, You Rock It
9. Ghost Riders In The Sky
10. Peter Gunn Theme
11. Hound Dog
12. Don't Cry, Daddy
13. Let It Be Me
14. Polk Salad Annie
15. The Lord's Prayer
16. My Country Tis Of Thee
17. Hava Nagila
18. My Baby Left Me
19. You Don't Have To Say You Love Me
20. Stranger In The Crowd
21. Blueberry Hill / Lawdy, Miss Clawdy
22. Heartbreak Hotel
23. One Night
24. It's Now Or Never

ELLIS AUDITORIUM, MEMPHIS

Elvis knew the Ellis Auditorium long before he ever played the venue from the times he had attended all-night gospel "singings" with his parents and with early girlfriend Dixie Locke (which Elvis continued to go to throughout he Fifties, as and when his own performing commitments allowed).

He first met his future backing band The Jordanaires at the venue after an Eddy Arnold concert in 1954.

Elvis was on the bill of a Bob Neal show at this venue on February 6, 1955, attended by an increasingly interested manager called Colonel Tom Parker.

Elvis performed two shows here on November 13, 1955, with Hank Thompson, Carl Smith, Charlene Arthur and fellow Sun artist Carl Perkins, as part of a "Western Swing Jamboree" celebrating KWEM DJ Texas Bill Strength, who was leaving Memphis for pastures anew.

Some sources cite Elvis as performing on December 19, 1955; he was most definitely at the venue, attending a charity show that featured wrestling bouts.

Elvis was back at the Ellis Auditorium on May 15, 1956, topping Bob Neal's Cotton Picking Jamboree with Hank Snow and The Jordanaires.

On his return from the Army, in 1960 Elvis went a couple of times to see the Holiday on Ice show here, once on a "Negroes" night.

Elvis' benefit concert here on February 25, 1961, was his penultimate show before a live audience until he filmed the NBC TV Special in 1968. He returned to the venue in 1970 to receive his Jaycee Award, and later that year went to the Gospel Quartet Convention.

ELLIS, JIMMY
(1945-1998)

Impersonating is one thing, building a career on the striking similarity of a singing voice and then getting trapped in that persona is quite another. This is what happened to Jimmy Ellis, known for a spell in the late Seventies and early Eighties first as "Friend," then as "Orion," as he recorded and performed in a voice uncannily reminiscent of Elvis.

Ellis had been singing since the mid-Sixties to mixed success, before in 1972 signing for Shelby Singleton, who by that had taken over the Sun Records name, and recording Elvis' first single "That's All Right (Mama)" and "Blue Moon Of Kentucky," with a question mark instead of the singer's name. The year after Elvis' death, Ellis was listed as "Friend" on an album of duets with Jerry Lee Lewis, leaving many people guessing who the mysterious singer was.

Ellis finally gained a name, "Orion," in 1979, borrowing the moniker of the singer fictionalized by author Gail Brewer-Giorgio, who had claimed she received a phone call from a mystery caller who sounded just like Elvis while she was writing a novel about a famous rock star called Orion. Under the name of Orion, Ellis released an album *Reborn*, on which he is pictured wearing a mask (though the original artwork of him rising from a coffin had to be withdrawn). Through the Eighties he scored some minor hits, particularly on the Country chart. Then, in 1983, Ellis cast the mask aside and attempted to forge a career in his own right.

He was killed during a robbery in 1998.

ELVIS (LP, 1956)

RCA shipped Elvis' second album in late October 1956, in good time for Christmas. All songs bar "So Glad You're Mine" were from Elvis' early September session at Radio Recorders. The album sold half a million copies on first release, entering the charts at #7 in its first week. It stayed in the charts for 32 weeks in total, of which five weeks at #1, and went on to sell more than 3 million copies.

TRACK LISTING:
1. Rip it Up
2. Love Me
3. When My Blue Moon Turns To Gold Again
4. Long Tall Sally
5. First In Line
6. Paralyzed
7. So Glad You're Mine
8. Old Shep
9. Ready Teddy
10. Anyplace Is Paradise
11. How's The World Treating You
12. How Do You Think I Feel

ELVIS (LP, 1968)

See NBC TV SPECIAL

ELVIS #1 HIT PERFORMANCES

A 2007 DVD of 15 Elvis performances spanning Fifties TV shows, movie scenes and Seventies shows. Outside the US, the DVD package, with additional material, was sold as *Elvis 30 #1 Hits DVD*.

US VERSION:
1. Heartbreak Hotel ("Stage Show")
2. Don't Be Cruel ("Ed Sullivan Show")
3. Hound Dog ("Milton Berle Show")
4. Love Me Tender ("Ed Sullivan Show")
5. All Shook Up (NBC TV Special)
6. Teddy Bear (Loving You)
7. Jailhouse Rock (Jailhouse Rock)
8. Stuck On You ("Frank Sinatra Show")
9. Are You Lonesome Tonight? (NBC TV Special)
10. Can't Help Falling In Love (Blue Hawaii)
11. Return To Sender (Girls! Girls! Girls!)
12. In The Ghetto (Elvis: That's The Way It Is)
13. Suspicious Minds (Elvis: That's The Way It Is)
14. The Wonder Of You (Elvis: That's The Way It Is)
15. Burning Love (Elvis: That's The Way It Is)

WORLDWIDE EXTRAS:
1. That's All Right (NBC TV Special)
2. Blue Suede Shoes (Paramount Screen Test)
3. I Want You, I Need You, I Love You ("Steve Allen Show")
4. Love Me ("Ed Sullivan Show")
5. Too Much ("Ed Sullivan Show")
6. Treat Me Nice (Jailhouse Rock)
7. Trouble (King Creole)
8. One Night (NBC TV Special)
9. A Big Hunk 'O Love (Aloha From Hawaii)
10. Wooden Heart (G.I. Blues)
11. Rock-A-Hula Baby (Blue Hawaii)
12. Bossa Nova Baby (Fun in Acapulco)
13. If I Can Dream (NBC TV Special)
14. Don't Cry Daddy (Elvis: That's The Way It Is)
15. An American Trilogy (Aloha From Hawaii)

ELVIS 30 #1 HITS

A 2002 RCA release to commemorate the 25th anniversary of Elvis' death, combining his US and UK #1 hits.

TRACK LISTING:
1. Heartbreak Hotel
2. Don't Be Cruel
3. Hound Dog
4. Love Me Tender
5. Too Much
6. All Shook Up
7. (Let Me Be Your) Teddy Bear
8. Jailhouse Rock

9. Don't
10. Hard Headed Woman
11. One Night
12. (Now And Then There's) A Fool Such As I
13. A Big Hunk O' Love
14. Stuck On You
15. It's Now Or Never
16. Are You Lonesome Tonight?
17. Wooden Heart
18. Surrender
19. (Marie's The Name) His Latest Flame
20. Can't Help Falling In Love
21. Good Luck Charm
22. She's Not You
23. Return To Sender
24. (You're The) Devil In Disguise
25. Crying In The Chapel
26. In The Ghetto
27. Suspicious Minds
28. The Wonder Of You
29. Burning Love
30. Way Down
31. A Little Less Conversation
    (JXL Radio Edit Remix)

ELVIS '56

A 1996 album with some previously unreleased takes of early songs.

TRACK LISTING:
1. Heartbreak Hotel
2. My Baby Left Me
3. Blue Suede Shoes
4. So Glad You're Mine
5. Tutti Frutti
6. One-Sided Love Affair
7. Love Me
8. Anyplace Is Paradise
9. Paralyzed
10. Ready Teddy
11. Too Much
12. Hound Dog
13. Anyway You Want Me (That's How I Will Be)
14. Don't Be Cruel
15. Lawdy, Miss Clawdy
16. Shake, Rattle And Roll (alternate take)
17. I Want You, I Need You, I Love You
18. Rip It Up
19. Heartbreak Hotel (alternate take)
20. I Got A Woman
21. I Was The One
22. Money Honey

A remastered version of album was re-released in 2003 with an alternate take of "Heartbreak Hotel."

ELVIS (THE FOOL ALBUM)
(LP, 1973)

Elvis' first album after his huge *Aloha From Hawaii* success contains recordings from the previous two years. Initially, the project had been under the direction of Joan Deary at RCA, who had envisioned another album of mainly live cuts —only one live track, "It's Impossible," made it onto vinyl.

The record-buying public was less than impressed with the revised (and renamed from "Fool" to "Elvis") offering. Released in July 1973, the album failed to sell more than 200,000 copies on release, and made it no higher than #52 in the charts. Thirteen weeks after appearing in the charts it dropped back off again, but like so many Elvis albums, it became a steady back catalogue seller.

TRACK LISTING:
1. Fool
2. Where Do I Go From Here?
3. Love Me, Love The Life I Lead
4. It's Still Here

5. It's Impossible
6. (That's What You Get) For Lovin' Me
7. Padre
8. I'll Take You Home Again, Kathleen
9. I Will Be True
10. Don't Think Twice, It's All Right

ELVIS: A LEGENDARY PERFORMER, VOLS. 1-4

RCA's first album release after acquiring the rights to Elvis' back catalogue in 1973, Volume 1 hit record stores in January 1974. Though rising no higher than #43 in the album charts, it sold steadily and ended up breaking through the ?æ million mark. The album opened up a whole new market, targeted at fans eager to snap up alternate versions, outtakes, extracts from interviews and more. RCA released a picture disc version in 1978.

TRACK LISTING:
VOL. 1 (1974)
1. That's All Right (Mama)
2. I Love You Because
3. Heartbreak Hotel
4. Excerpt from "Elvis Sails"
5. Don't Be Cruel
6. Love Me
7. Tryin' To Get To You
8. Love Me Tender
9. (There'll Be) Peace In The Valley (For Me)
10. Excerpt from "Elvis Sails"
11. A Fool Such As I
12. Tonight's All Right For Love
13. Are You Lonesome Tonight?
14. Can't Help Falling In Love

Volume 2, released in January 1976, combined classic Elvis cuts with previously unreleased material. It too sold steadily, notching up 750,000 sales but not exceeding #46 in the charts during its 17-week stay.

TRACK LISTING:
VOL. 2 (1976)
1. Harbor Lights
2. Interview (with DJ Jay Thompson, April 10, 1956, Wichita Falls)
3. I Want You, I Need You, I Love You
4. Blue Suede Shoes
5. Blue Christmas
6. Jailhouse Rock
7. It's Now Or Never
8. A Cane And A High Starched Collar
9. Presentation of awards to Elvis (Pearl Harbor Memorial, 1961)
10. Blue Hawaii
11. Such A Night
12. Baby, What You Want Me To Do
13. How Great Thou Art
14. If I Can Dream

Volume 3 was released in December 1978 with two previously unreleased tracks and some alternate takes, in standard and picture disc versions. The album stayed on the charts for 11 weeks and peaked at #113.

TRACK LISTING:
VOL. 3 (1978)
1. Hound Dog
2. Excerpts from TV Guide interview with Elvis and the Colonel
3. Danny
4. Fame And Fortune
5. Frankfort Special
6. Britches
7. Crying In The Chapel
8. Surrender
9. Guadalajara
10. It Hurts Me
11. Let Yourself Go
12. In The Ghetto
13. Let It Be Me

Volume 4 came out in November 1983 with two more novelties, including Ann-Margret duet "The Lady Loves Me," plus alternates.

TRACK LISTING:
VOL. 4 (1983)
1. When It Rains, It Really Pours
2. Tampa interviews by Ray and Norma Pillow
3. One Night (Of Sin)
4. I'm Beginning To Forget You
5. Mona Lisa
6. Plantation Rock
7. Swing Down, Sweet Chariot
8. The Lady Loves Me
9. Wooden Heart
10. That's All Right (Mama)
11. Are You Lonesome Tonight? (laughing version)
12. Reconsider Baby
13. I'll Remember You

Vols. 5 and up have been issued since 2005 with much previous unreleased material, on the unofficial Madison label.

ELVIS: ALOHA FROM HAWAII

See ALOHA FROM HAWAII

ELVIS AMONG FRIENDS

A 1996 release of material recorded at Graceland and in Lake Tahoe in 1976, on the Whitehaven label.

TRACK LISTING:
1. Bitter They Are, Harder They Fall
2. She Thinks I Still Care
3. The Last Farewell
4. Solitaire
5. Moody Blue
6. I'll Never Fall In Love Again
7. For The Heart
8. Hurt
9. Danny Boy
10. Never Again
11. Love Coming Down
12. Blue Eyes Crying In The Rain
13. Hurt (X-rated version)
14. Monologue / Delilah (excerpt)
15. Rip It Up (excerpt) / My Way
16. Burning Love
17. Why Me Lord
18. Elvis introduces Vernon
19. Early Morning Rain
20. Happy Birthday (Mandy)
21. Heartbreak Hotel
22. Ku-U-I-Po (excerpt) / Hawaiian Wedding Song
23. Can't Help Falling In Love

ELVIS ARON PRESLEY
(THE SILVER BOX)

A 1980 8-LP collectors' set of Elvis tracks, including a considerable amount of previously unreleased material, released to mark the 25th anniversary of Elvis signing for RCA. Material ranged from his first engagement in Las Vegas in 1956, to his May/June 1975 tour through Alabama, Texas, Louisiana, Mississippi and Tennessee. The premium price did nothing to prevent the box going platinum, and rising on release as high as #27 on the charts, where it enjoyed a 14-week stay.

TRACK LISTING:
AN EARLY LIVE PERFORMANCE
1. Heartbreak Hotel
2. Long Tall Sally
3. Blue Suede Shoes
4. Money Honey
5. Elvis monologue

AN EARLY BENEFIT PERFORMANCE
6. Introduction
7. Heartbreak Hotel
8. All Shook Up
9. (Now And Then There's) A Fool Such As I
10. I Got A Woman
11. Love Me
12. Introductions
13. Such A Night
14. Reconsider Baby
15. I Need Your Love Tonight
16. That's All Right (Mama)
17. Don't Be Cruel
18. One Night
19. Are You Lonesome Tonight?
20. It's Now Or Never
21. Swing Down, Sweet Chariot
22. Hound Dog

COLLECTORS GOLD FROM THE MOVIE YEARS
23. They Remind Me Too Much Of You
24. Tonight's All Right For Love
25. Follow That Dream
26. Wild In The Country
27. Datin'
28. Shoppin' Around
29. Can't Help Falling In Love
30. A Dog's Life
31. I'm Falling In Love Tonight
32. Thanks To The Rolling Sea

THE TV SPECIALS—ALOHA FROM HAWAII,
ELVIS IN CONCERT
33. Jailhouse Rock
34. Suspicious Minds
35. Lawdy, Miss Clawdy
36. Baby What You Want Me To Do
37. Blue Christmas
38. You Gave Me A Mountain
39. Welcome To My World
40. Tryin' To Get To You
41. I'll Remember You
42. My Way

THE LAS VEGAS YEARS
43. Polk Salad Annie
44. You've Lost That Lovin' Feelin'
45. Sweet Caroline
46. Kentucky Rain
47. Are You Lonesome Tonight?
    (Laughing version)
48. My Babe
49. In The Ghetto
50. American Trilogy
51. Little Sister / Get Back
52. Yesterday

LOST SINGLES
53. I'm Leavin'
54. The First Time Ever I Saw Your Face
55. Hi Heel Sneakers
56. Softly As I Leave You
57. Unchained Melody
58. Fool
59. Rags To Riches
60. It's Only Love
61. America The Beautiful

ELVIS AT THE PIANO
62. It's Still Here
63. I'll Take You Home Again, Kathleen
64. Beyond The Reef
65. I Will Be True

THE CONCERT YEARS
66. Also Sprach Zarathustra
    (2001 A Space Odyssey)
67. See See Rider
68. I Got A Woman / Amen
69. Love Me
70. If You Love Me (Let Me Know)
71. Love Me Tender
72. All Shook Up
73. Teddy Bear / Don't Be Cruel
74. Hound Dog
75. The Wonder Of You
76. Burning Love
77. Introductions
78. Johnny B. Goode

79. Hail, Hail Rock 'n' Roll
80. T-R-O-U-B-L-E
81. Why Me Lord
82. How Great Thou Art
83. Let Me Be There
84. An American Trilogy
85. Funny How Time Slips Away
86. Little Darlin'
87. Mystery Train / Tiger Man
88. Can't Help Falling In Love
89. Closing Vamp

ELVIS AS RECORDED AT MADISON SQUARE GARDEN

RCA rushed out this selection of songs from Elvis' June 1972 four-show engagement at Madison Square Garden in New York City in just eight days, in part to make a media event, in part to beat the bootleggers. To save time, the artwork was borrowed from previously-planned spin-off album from concert movie *Elvis On Tour*. The album, the first full-length commercial release of an Elvis concert, as recorded on June 10, 1972, sold half a million copies in two months. Though it peaked at #8 in the charts, it was on for 34 weeks, and ultimately achieved triple platinum status with cumulative sales of over three million copies.

TRACK LISTING:
1. Also Sprach Zarathustra
2. That's All Right (Mama)
3. Proud Mary
4. Never Been To Spain
5. You Don't Have To Say You Love Me
6. You've Lost That Lovin' Feelin'
7. Polk Salad Annie
8. Love Me
9. All Shook Up
10. Heartbreak Hotel
11. Medley: (Let Me Be Your) Teddy Bear /
    Don't Be Cruel
12. Love Me Tender
13. The Impossible Dream
14. Introductions by Elvis
15. Hound Dog
16. Suspicious Minds
17. For The Good Times
18. An American Trilogy
19. Funny How Time Slips Away
20. I Can't Stop Loving You
21. Can't Help Falling In Love
22. End Theme

Later, remastered releases have improved sound quality.

ELVIS AT THE INTERNATIONAL

A 2002 FTD release recorded soon after Elvis made an enthusiastic return to live performing in Las Vegas in the summer of '69.

TRACK LISTING:
1. Blue Suede Shoes
2. I Got A Woman
3. All Shook Up / Welcome
4. Love Me Tender
5. Jailhouse Rock / Don't Be Cruel
6. Heartbreak Hotel
7. Hound Dog
8. Memories
9. Mystery Train / Tiger Man
10. Monologue
11. Baby What You Want Me To Do?
12. Runaway
13. Reconsider Baby
14. Are You Lonesome Tonight?
15. Yesterday / Hey Jude
16. Introductions
17. In The Ghetto
18. Suspicious Minds
19. What'd I Say
20. Can't Help Falling In Love

ELVIS AT SUN

A 2004 BMG release commemorating the fiftieth anniversary of Elvis' first record, remastered and including an alternate take of "I Love You Because."

TRACK LISTING:
1. Harbor Lights
2. I Love You Because (alternate take 2)
3. That's All Right
4. Blue Moon Of Kentucky
5. Blue Moon
6. Tomorrow Night
7. I'll Never Let You Go (Little Darlin')
8. Just Because
9. Good Rockin' Tonight
10. I Don't Care If The Sun Don't Shine
11. Milkcow Blues Boogie
12. You're A Heartbreaker
13. I'm Left, You're Right, She's Gone
    (slow version)
14. I'm Left, You're Right, She's Gone
15. Baby Let's Play House
16. I Forgot To Remember To Forget
17. Mystery Train
18. Tryin' To Get To You
19. When It Rains, It Really Pours

ELVIS AT THE MOVIES

A 2007 BMG 2-CD set of remastered Elvis soundtrack songs.

TRACK LISTING:
CD 1:
1. Love Me Tender
2. (Let Me Be Your) Teddy Bear
3. Jailhouse Rock
4. Treat Me Nice
5. Hard Headed Woman
6. King Creole
7. G.I. Blues
8. Frankfort Special
9. Flaming Star
10. Lonely Man
11. Can't Help Falling In Love
12. Blue Hawaii
13. Rock-A-Hula Baby
14. Follow That Dream
15. King Of The Whole Wide World
16. Return To Sender
17. One Broken Heart For Sale
18. They Remind Me Too Much Of You
19. Bossa Nova Baby
20. Viva Las Vegas

CD 2:
1. What'd I Say
2. Kissin' Cousins
3. Little Egypt
4. Do The Clam
5. (Such An) Easy Question
6. I'm Yours
7. Shake That Tambourine
8. Frankie And Johnny
9. This Is My Heaven
10. All That I Am
11. I'll Be Back
12. Long Legged Girl (With The Short Dress On)
13. The Love Machine
14. Clambake
15. Let Yourself Go
16. Stay Away
17. A Little Less Conversation
18. Charro!
19. Clean Up Your Own Backyard
20. Rubbermeckin'

ELVIS BY REQUEST / FLAMING STAR (EP)

In April 1961 RCA put out this EP of the two songs Elvis liked best from the soundtrack of

Flaming Star, along with two big singles "Are You Lonesome Tonight?" and "It's Now Or Never," after a bootlegged version of the movie songs found its way onto radio stations. The EP, curiously pressed to play at 33 1/3 RPM, peaked at #14.

TRACK LISTING:
1. Flaming Star
2. Summer Kisses, Winter Tears
3. Are You Lonesome Tonight?
4. It's Now Or Never

ELVIS BY THE PRESLEYS

A 2005 documentary, DVD release with extra material, book and album presented and written "by the people closest to Elvis" (notably Priscilla, Lisa Marie and Patsy Presley, Priscilla's parents, Jerry Schilling and others).

The associated 2 CD release included home recordings and a previously unreleased take of "Jailhouse Rock."

TRACK LISTING:
DISC: 1
1. Tryin' To Get To You
2. Heartbreak Hotel
3. I Want You, I Need You, I Love You
4. I Got A Woman
5. Got A Lot O' Livin' To Do!
6. (There'll Be) Peace In The Valley (For Me)
7. Trouble
8. Hawaiian Wedding Song
9. Indescribably Blue
10. In The Ghetto
11. Suspicious Minds
12. I'll Hold You In My Heart (Till I Can Hold You In My Arms)
13. Bridge Over Troubled Water
14. You've Lost That Lovin' Feelin'
15. It's Over
16. Separate Ways
17. Always On My Mind
18. My Way
19. Burning Love
20. Welcome To My World
21. Steamroller Blues
22. I Got A Feelin' In My Body
23. If I Can Dream
24. A Little Less Conversation

DISC: 2
1. It Wouldn't Be The Same Without You
2. Jailhouse Rock
3. Anything That's Part Of You
4. You'll Be Gone
5. Too Much Monkey Business
6. Baby What You Want Me To Do
7. I'm So Lonesome I Could Cry
8. Blue Christmas

ELVIS' CHRISTMAS ALBUM

Such was the controversy surrounding Elvis in his early days that even something as anodyne as the Christmas album RCA released in mid-October 1957 with a sumptuous gatefold cover drew the wrath of "White Christmas" author Irving Berlin. Berlin wrote to radio stations up and down the country to tell them not to play the song because Elvis was such a rebel he profaned the spirit of the religious holiday. The album still made #1 (for a total of four weeks, with a brief hiatus while Bing Crosby's Christmas offering was at #1), and stayed in the charts for seven weeks. It sold over one and half million copies in reissues over the following decade. No other Elvis album sold more in the Fifties.

TRACK LISTING:
1. Santa Claus Is Back In Town
2. White Christmas
3. Here Comes Santa Claus
4. I'll Be Home For Christmas
5. Blue Christmas
6. Santa Bring My Baby Back (To Me)
7. O Little Town Of Bethlehem
8. Silent Night
9. Peace In The Valley
10. I Believe
11. Take My Hand, Precious Lord
12. It Is No Secret (What God Can Do)

The album was re-released in 1970 as *Elvis' Christmas Album* (minus the original gospel tracks but with the addition of "Mama Liked the Roses") on RCA's budget Camden label. Taken together, this album title ultimately became Elvis' best-selling LP of all, with over six million copies sold in the US alone (some sources put the figure above nine million).

TRACK LISTING:
1. Blue Christmas
2. Silent Night
3. White Christmas
4. Santa Claus Is Back In Town
5. I'll Be Home For Christmas
6. If Every Day Was Like Christmas
7. Here Comes Santa Claus (Right Down Santa Claus Lane)
8. O Little Town Of Bethlehem
9. Santa Bring My Baby Back (To Me)
10. Mama Liked The Roses

ELVIS CHRISTMAS

A 2006 BMG release of 19 Yule-themed tracks and 4 gospel songs.

TRACK LISTING:
1. Santa Claus Is Back In Town
2. White Christmas
3. Here Comes Santa Claus
4. I'll Be Home For Christmas
5. Blue Christmas
6. Santa Bring My Baby Back
7. O Little Town Of Bethlehem
8. Silent Night
9. Peace In The Valley
10. I Believe
11. Take My Hand, Precious Lord
12. It Is No Secret
13. O Come, All Ye Faithful
14. The First Noel
15. On A Snowy Christmas Night
16. Winter Wonderland
17. The Wonderful World Of Christmas
18. It Won't Seem Like Christmas
19. I'll Be Home On Christmas Day
20. If I Get Home On Christmas Day
21. Holly Leaves And Christmas Trees
22. Merry Christmas Baby
23. Silver Bells

ELVIS: CLOSE UP

Alternate takes of well-known songs on this multi-disc CD released by BMG in 2003 as a follow up to the well-regarded Today, Tomorrow & Forever box set, including 50s stereo masters, outtakes from early Sixties films, alternate takes and a Seventies live concert from San Antonio, Texas.

TRACK LISTING:
DISC: 1
1. (There'll Be) Peace In The Valley (For Me)
2. I Beg Of You
3. That's When Your Heartaches Begin
4. It's No Secret
5. Blueberry Hill
6. Have I Told You Lately That I Love You
7. Is It So Strange
8. Loving You (fast, take 5)

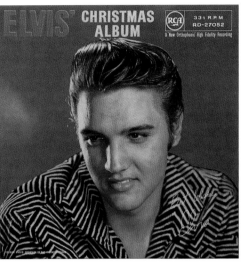

9. Loving You (fast, take 15)
10. Jailhouse Rock
11. Treat Me Nice (first movie version)
12. Young And Beautiful (record master)
13. Young And Beautiful (solo master)
14. Young And Beautiful (nightclub master)
15. I Want To Be Free (movie version)
16. I Want To Be Free (record master)
17. Treat Me Nice (second movie version)
18. Don't Leave Me Now (Elvis piano version)
19. Don't Leave Me Now (movie version)
20. (You're So Square) Baby I Don't Care

DISC: 2
1. G.I. Blues
2. Doin' The Best I Can
3. Wooden Heart
4. Pocketful Of Rainbows
5. Shoppin' Around
6. Frankfort Special
7. Big Boots (fast version)
8. Tonight's All Right For Love
9. Summer Kisses, Winter Tears
10. Flaming Star
11. Lonely Man (solo version)
12. In My Way
13. Forget Me Never
14. Wild In The Country
15. Lonely Man
16. I Slipped, I Stumbled, I Fell
17. Aloha Oe
18. Hawaiian Sunset
19. Ku-U-I-Po
20. No More
21. Slicin' Sand
22. Steppin' Out Of Line
23. Almost Always True
24. Moonlight Swim
25. Can't Help Falling In Love

DISC: 3
1. Make Me Know It
2. Soldier Boy
3. It Feels So Right
4. The Girl of My Best Friend
5. Surrender
6. Working on the Building
7. Starting Today
8. Kiss Me Quick
9. That's Someone You Never Forget
10. (Marie's The Name) His Latest Flame
11. I Met Her Today
12. Night Rider
13. Just Tell Her Jim Said Hello
14. Echoes of Love
15. Ask Me
16. Stand By Me
17. Somebody Bigger Than You and I
18. Without Him
19. Mine
20. Singing Tree
21. U.S. Male

DISC: 4
1. Also Sprach Zarathustra
2. See See Rider
3. Proud Mary
4. Never Been To Spain
5. You Gave Me A Mountain
6. Until It's Time For You To Go
7. Polk Salad Annie
8. Love Me
9. All Shook Up
10. (Let Me Be Your) Teddy Bear/Don't Be Cruel
11. Heartbreak Hotel
12. Hound Dog
13. How Great Thou Art
14. I Can't Stop Loving You
15. Love Me Tender
16. Suspicious Minds
17. Introductions
18. For the Good Times
19. Burning Love
20. An American Trilogy
21. Funny How Time Slips Away
22. Can't Help Falling In Love
23. Closing Vamp

ELVIS COUNTRY

This album, subtitled "I'm 10,000 Years Old" (with excerpts of the track of that name running through-out the album) grew almost spontaneously out of a particularly proficuous recording session at RCA's Nashville Studio B in 1970 which yielded enough country material for practically a whole album. When released in January 1971, Elvis' one and only "concept album" sold half a million copies, peaking at #12 in the *Billboard* LP charts, where it spent a total of 21 weeks—a reviewer in *Billboard* noted that the gospel chord progressions in many of the songs gave it a real Southern authenticity.

TRACK LISTING:
1. Snowbird
2. Tomorrow Never Comes
3. Little Cabin On The Hill
4. Whole Lotta Shakin' Goin' On
5. Funny How Time Slips Away
6. I Really Don't Want To Know
7. There Goes My Everything
8. It's Your Baby, You Rock It
9. The Fool
10. Faded Love
11. I Washed My Hands In Muddy Water
12. Make The World Go Away

A 2000 remastered release includes "It Ain't No Big Thing (But It's Growing)"; "A Hundred Years From Now"; "If I Were You"; "Got My Mojo Working" / "Keep Your Hands Off Of It"; "Where Did They Go, Lord"; and "I Was Born About Ten Thousand Years Ago."

In 2006 BMG released a new collection titled *Elvis Country*, one of six themed Elvis CDs.

TRACK LISTING:
1. For The Good Times
2. Take Good Care Of Her
3. She Wears My Ring
4. Always On My Mind
5. Snowbird
6. Green, Green Grass Of Home
7. Tomorrow Never Comes
8. A Hundred Years From Now
9. Kentucky Rain
10. Good Time Charlie's Got The Blues
11. It Ain't No Big Thing (But It's Growing)
12. Are You Sincere
13. Release Me
14. Funny How Time Slips Away
15. I'm So Lonesome I Could Cry
16. There's A Honky Tonk Angel (Who Will Take Me Back In)
17. If I'm A Fool (For Loving You)
18. Pieces Of My Life
19. Blue Eyes Crying In The Rain
20. I Can't Stop Loving You

ELVIS FOR EVERYONE (LP)

An alliterative title for an album that once again plundered Elvis' back catalogue of underused material. Released in August 1965 with a cash register on the cover (and originally planned under working titles *Today Only* and *Elvis' Anniversary Album*), *Elvis For Everyone* peaked at #10 in the LP charts, selling a quarter of a million copies as the public's appetite for Elvis offcuts continued to erode, though it did take 27 weeks to drop out of the charts again.

TRACK LISTING:
1. Your Cheatin' Heart
2. Summer Kisses, Winter Tears
3. Finders Keepers, Losers Weepers
4. In My Way
5. Tomorrow Night
6. Memphis Tennessee
7. For The Millionth And The Last Time
8. Forget Me Never
9. Sound Advice
10. Santa Lucia
11. I Met Her Today
12. When It Rains, It Really Pours

ELVIS' GOLD RECORDS
(VOLUMES 2, 4 AND 5)

A slightly different title for the second package of Elvis' early hits, released in November 1959 while he was away in Germany on Army service (volume one was named *Elvis' Golden Records*). Vol. 2 and ever after known by the memorable slug line "50,000,000 Elvis fans can't be wrong." The LP, adorned with Elvis in his gold laméÈ suit, is also sometimes known as *A Big Hunk O' Love*. A million purchasers bought this collection of ten hit singles, which peaked at #31 in the charts during its six week stay.

TRACK LISTING:
1. I Need Your Love Tonight
2. Don't
3. Wear My Ring Around Your Neck
4. My Wish Came True
5. I Got Stung
6. One Night
7. A Big Hunk O' Love
8. I Beg Of You
9. (Now And Then There's) A Fool Such As I
10. Doncha' Think It's Time

Later re-releases include "Santa Bring My Baby Back (To Me)," "King Creole," "Paralyzed" and "Party."

In 2007 FTD released a two-CD version of this album titled *50,000,000 Million Elvis Fans Can't Be Wrong*, with alternates of "Doncha' Think It's Time" and every recorded take of "A Big Hunk O' Love," "(Now And Then There's) A Fool Such as I," "Ain't That Loving You Baby," "I Need Your Love Tonight" and "I Got Stung."

Vol. 4 came out in January 1968. Though it initially sold only 350,000 copies and ran out of steam at #33 in the charts over a 22 week span. Elvis' final monaural LP sold in sufficient numbers to go gold.

TRACK LISTING:
1. Love Letters
2. Witchcraft
3. It Hurts Me
4. What'd I Say
5. Please Don't Drag That String Around
6. Indescribably Blue
7. (You're The) Devil In Disguise
8. Lonely Man
9. A Mess Of Blues
10. Ask Me
11. Ain't That Loving You Baby
12. Just Tell Her Jim Said Hello

Later CD versions include "Crying In The Chapel," "Return To Sender," "Rock-A-Hula Baby," "Bossa Nova," "Kissin' Cousins" and "Viva Las Vegas." The album was reissued with upgraded sound in 2007.

RCA brought out volume 5, covering Elvis' later years, in 1984. It did not make it into the charts.

TRACK LISTING:
1. Suspicious Minds
2. Kentucky Rain
3. In The Ghetto
4. Clean Up Your Own Back Yard
5. If I Can Dream
6. Burning Love
7. If You Talk In Your Sleep
8. For The Heart
9. Moody Blue
10. Way Down

Later CD versions include "Big Boss Man," "Guitar Man," "U.S. Male," "You Don't Have To Say You Love Me," "Edge Of Reality" and "Memories."

ELVIS' GOLDEN RECORDS
(VOLUMES 1 AND 3)

Shipped in March 1958, a few days before Elvis departed for his Army service, this LP of fourteen Elvis hits sold many millions of copies over the years. It rose to #3 on initial release, and stayed on the best-selling LP chart for forty weeks. The album returned to the charts for almost six months after Elvis' death.

TRACK LISTING:
1. Hound Dog
2. Loving You
3. All Shook Up
4. Heartbreak Hotel
5. Jailhouse Rock
6. Love Me
7. Too Much
8. Don't Be Cruel
9. That's When Your Heartaches Begin
10. (Let Me Be Your) Teddy Bear
11. Love Me Tender
12. Treat Me Nice
13. Any Way You Want Me (That's How I Will Be)
14. I Want You, I Need You, I Love You

The CD reissue adds "My Baby Left Me," "I Was The One," "That s All Right (Mama)," "Baby, Let s Play House," "Mystery Train" and "Blue Suede Shoes."

A second volume, confusingly named *Elvis' Golden Records Vol. 3*, hit record stores in August 1963. It sold 600,000 copies on initial release, made it as high as #3 on the charts (driven by smash hits "It's Now or Never" and "Are You Lonesome Tonight?," available on LP for the first time), and continued to sell well for years afterwards, even after it bowed out from the charts forty weeks later.

TRACK LISTING:
1. It's Now Or Never
2. Stuck On You
3. Fame And Fortune
4. I Gotta Know
5. Surrender
6. I Feel So Bad
7. Are You Lonesome Tonight?
8. (Marie's The Name) His Latest Flame
9. Little Sister
10. Good Luck Charm
11. Anything That's Part Of You
12. She's Not You

Later CD reissues add "Wooden Heart," "Wild In The Country," "Follow That Dream," "Can't Help Falling In Love" and "King Of The Whole Wide World."

"ELVIS HAS LEFT THE BUILDING"

A quote so famous that it has passed into modern parlance and taken on a post-Elvis life all its own.

Horace Logan uttered the words to try and calm a boisterous crowd at the end of Elvis' last ever performance at the Louisiana Hayride on December 15, 1956.

What he said was: "Please, young people... Elvis has left the building. He has gotten in his car and driven away . . . Please take your seats." Or, in the version Logan has in his autobiography, 'Ladies and gentlemen, please, Elvis has left the building. Now if you'll just return to your seats, we'll go on with the show." Or, in the version in Frank Page's book, "All right, er, Elvis has left the building. I've told you absolutely straight up to this point - you know that. He has left the building. He left the stage and went out the back with the policemen and he is now gone from the building."

Logan was in the unenviable position of trying to quieten down an audience more interested in trying to intercept Elvis outside the auditorium than watch any of the other acts lined up for the rest of that evening's Hayride show.

Al Dvorin wound up most of Elvis' Seventies concerts with the famous phrase, and has in the past been credited with first uttering the fateful words (as has Hayride announcer Frank Page). At some later Seventies concerts, backing singers from The Stamps sometimes delivered the fateful phrase that marked the end of an audience with the King.

A movie of the same name, starring Kim Basinger, was released in 2004.

The Shure Brothers Model 55S microphone over which Logan made his impassioned plea at the Louisiana Hayride was auctioned off in December 2005.

The Louisiana Hayride show at which the words were first spoken has come out on various Hayride compilations, including *The Louisiana Hayride Shows* from 1998 and *Good Rockin' Tonight* from 2000.

ELVIS IN CONCERT (CBS SPECIAL)

Using material from Elvis' final tour, CBS broadcast this TV special after Elvis' death—for many grieving fans, a controversial decision. The TV show featured material filmed in Omaha, Nebraska and Rapid City, South Dakota between June 19 and 21, 1977. Though evidently in poor physical condition, Elvis still puts on a show for his fans. At the end of the broadcast, Vernon thanked the fans for the condolences they sent to Graceland after Elvis' death.

The TV Special was directed by Rita Scott and Annett Wolf, who also conducted the fan interviews.

No official video of the TV broadcast ever came out; a DVD finally appeared to mark the 30th anniversary of the singer's death in 2007, though of course, unofficial versions, including extended and unedited footage, have been available as bootlegs for many years.

CREDITS:
CBS
Broadcast date: October 3, 1977 (repeated in 1978)

Songs: "Intro (Also Sprach Zarathustra)," "See See Rider," "That's All Right (Mama)," "Are You Lonesome Tonight?," "Teddy Bear"/"Don't Be Cruel," "You Gave Me A Mountain," "Jailhouse Rock," "How Great Thou Art," "I Really Don't Want To Know," "Hurt," "Hound Dog," "My Way," "Early Morning Rain," "Can't Help Falling In Love"

Directed by: Rita Scott, Annett Wolf
Produced by: Gary Smith (producer), Rita Scott (associate producer)
Written by: Annett Wolf

FEATURING:
Elvis Presley
James Burton
Charlie Hodge
Vernon Presley
Annett Wolf
Ginger Alden
Joe Esposito

ADDITIONAL CREW:
Gene Crowe	technical director
Tom Diskin	personnel coordinator
Mike Erwin	production assistant
Joe Esposito	coordinator
Wenda Fong	production assistant
Joe Guercio	musical director
Tom Hulett	tour director
Felton Jarvis	music coordinator
Pat Kellerher	transportation coordinator
Bill Knight	lighting director
Sheila Lauder	assistant to producers
Martin Murphy	engineer in charge
Doug Nelson	audio truck
George Parkhill	tour consultant
Phillip Seretti	sound re-recording mixer
Charlie Stone	stage production coordinator
Annett Wolf	second unit producer
Andy Zall	video tape editor

ELVIS IN CONCERT (LP)

Released in October 1977 to coincide with the screening of the TV special of the same name, the 2 disc album contains extra material not included in the broadcast. The release sold 1.5 million copies, peaking at #5 in the charts and remaining in the top 100 for seventeen weeks.

TRACK LISTING:
1. Elvis fan comments/Opening riff
2. Also Sprach Zarathustra
3. See See Rider
4. That's All Right (Mama)
5. Are You Lonesome Tonight?
6. (Let Me Be Your) Teddy Bear / Don't Be Cruel
7. Elvis fan comments
8. You Gave Me A Mountain
9. Jailhouse Rock
10. Elvis fan comments
11. How Great Thou Art
12. Elvis fan comments
13. I Really Don't Want To Know
14. Elvis introduces Vernon
15. Hurt
16. Hound Dog
17. My Way
18. Can't Help Falling In Love
19. Closing riff/Special message from Vernon
20. I Got A Woman / Amen
21. Elvis monologue
22. Love Me
23. If You Love Me (Let Me Know)
24. O Sole Mio (Sherill Nielsen) / It's Now Or Never
25. Tryin' To Get To You
26. Hawaiian Wedding Song
27. Fairytale
28. Little Sister
29. Early Morning Rain
30. What'd I Say
31. Johnny B. Goode
32. And I Love You So

ELVIS IN NASHVILLE

A 1988 RCA release of material Elvis recorded in Nashville in the Sixties and early Seventies.

TRACK LISTING:
1. I Got A Woman
2. A Big Hunk O' Love
3. Working On The Building
4. Judy
5. Anything That's Part Of You
6. Night Rider
7. Where No One Stands Alone
8. Just Call Me Lonesome
9. Guitar Man
10. Little Cabin On The Hill
11. It's Your Baby, You Rock It
12. Early Mornin' Rain
13. It's Still Here
14. I, John

ELVIS IN PERSON AT THE INTERNATIONAL HOTEL

The first two sides of 1969 double album *From Memphis to Vegas / From Vegas to Memphis* were issued under this title in November 1970. Like its sister album *Back in Memphis* (the other two sides), this LP sold around 100,000 copies each. The bulk of the material came from Elvis' midnight Las Vegas show on August 25, 1969; for many fans, Elvis at his absolute peak.

TRACK LISTING:
1. Blue Suede Shoes
2. Johnny B. Goode
3. All Shook Up
4. Are You Lonesome Tonight?
5. Hound Dog
6. I Can't Stop Loving You
7. My Babe
8. Mystery Train / Tiger Man
9. Words
10. In The Ghetto
11. Suspicious Minds
12. Can't Help Falling In Love

ELVIS INSPIRATIONAL

A 2006 BMG release of gospel and inspirational material.

TRACK LISTING:
1. If I Can Dream
2. Crying In The Chapel
3. Amazing Grace
4. Danny Boy
5. In The Ghetto
6. Mama Liked The Roses
7. An Evening Prayer
8. Put Your Hand In The Hand
9. You'll Never Walk Alone
10. How Great Thou Art
11. I'll Take You Home Again Kathleen
12. He Is My Everything
13. A Thing Called Love
14. And The Grass Won't Pay No Mind
15. If That Isn't Love
16. Help Me
17. Only Believe
18. Wonderful World
19. Bridge Over Troubled Water
20. The Impossible Dream

ELVIS IS BACK!

This LP was rushed out the door by RCA on April 8, 1960 so fast after Elvis' return to the States from Germany that the song titles on initial pressings were slapped on cover via printed stickers. Elvis was in great voice, singing a wider range of styles than ever before. Despite all that pent-up demand, the album only sold 300,000 copies on initial release, spending 56 weeks on the album chart and peaking at #2. Artistically-speaking, Ernst Jorgensen considers this "a triumph on every level." No fewer than six tracks from this album became million-selling singles in the US. However, because the album was significantly outsold by soundtrack releases later that year and the following year, for most of the rest of the decade Elvis' studio time was monopolized by soundtrack work.

TRACK LISTING:
1. Make Me Know It
2. Fever
3. The Girl of My Best Friend
4. I Will Be Home Again
5. Dirty, Dirty Feeling
6. Thrill Of Your Love
7. Soldier Boy
8. Such A Night
9. It Feels So Right
10. The Girl Next Door Went A' Walking
11. Like A Baby
12. Reconsider Baby

FTD brought out a 2-CD special of remixed outtakes and multiple alternates from these 1960 sessions (titled *Elvis Is Back!*) in 2005.

Publishers Elvis Unlimited brought out a book, DVD, record package under this title in 2007.

ELVIS MONTHLY

Official UK Elvis fan club magazine which lays claim to be the longest running Elvis fanzine in the world, run from 1959 until his death in 1972 by Albert Hand, Chairman of the Official Elvis Presley Fan Club of Great Britain and the Commonwealth. Hand was succeeded by Todd Slaughter, who like Hand is a prolific Elvis author.

Book:
Elvis: The Golden Anniversary Tribute: 50 Fabulous Years in Words and Pictures, 1935-1985, Pop Universal, 1984.

ELVIS MOVIES

In 2006 BMG brought out this film-themed anthology.

TRACK LISTING:
1. Love Me Tender
2. Loving You
3. Jailhouse Rock
4. King Creole
5. G.I. Blues
6. Flaming Star
7. Wild In The Country
8. Blue Hawaii
9. Follow That Dream
10. Girls! Girls! Girls!
11. Fun In Acapulco
12. Viva Las Vegas
13. Kissin' Cousins
14. Roustabout
15. Girl Happy
16. Frankie And Johnny
17. Spinout
18. Double Trouble
19. Easy Come, Easy Go
20. Clambake
21. Speedway
22. Stay Away, Joe
23. Charro!
24. Change Of Habit

ELVIS NOW

This LP, the core of which was made up of country songs recorded in Nashville in 1970 and 1971, sold around 400,000 copies after release in February 1972. It spent 19 weeks on the charts and reached #43.

TRACK LISTING:
1. Help Me Make It Through The Night
2. Miracle Of The Rosary
3. Hey Jude
4. Put Your Hand In The Hand
5. Until It's Time For You To Go
6. We Can Make The Morning
7. Early Morning Rain
8. Sylvia
9. Fools Rush In (Where Angels Fear To Tread)
10. I Was Born About Ten Thousand Years Ago

ELVIS ON TOUR (DOCUMENTARY)

This MGM documentary was filmed in April 1972, tracking Elvis as he did a 15-stop tour from Buffalo, New York to Albuquerque, New Mexico. Originally titled *Sold Out* and then *Standing Room Only*, the documentary included material from pre-tour rehearsal sessions in Los Angeles in late March that year, and additional inserts from Elvis' past.

Robert Abel and Pierre Adidge directed, wrote and produced the movie. The pair had also been behind Joe Cocker's 1970 concert film *Mad Dogs and Englishmen*.

The documentary includes segments of a 40-minute audio interview with Elvis in which he talks frankly about his musical background, his acting career and his life. The film also includes a tongue-in-cheek sequence of Elvis screen kisses, one after another—like the movies themselves, the background changes but the plot stays the same. The Colonel was reportedly not best pleased with this montage.

On release, the documentary spent two weeks on the *Variety* Box Office Survey, climbing as high as #13. It won a Golden Globe as a joint winner of the 1972 Best Documentary category, the only one of Elvis' films to achieve such a prestigious accolade. As well as excellent work by the writer/director team, the project featured a young editor by the name of Martin Scorsese. A multiple-view approach was used, making it possible to include archive footage and present as much Elvis as possible.

Unusually, no soundtrack album was released with this documentary. Initial plans to do so were shelved because of Elvis' high-profile Madison Square Garden live show and album release that summer.

Material that did not make it into the final cut has found its way onto a number of bootlegs, including *The Complete On Tour Sessions*, and more recently FTD releases *6363 Sunset* and *Elvis On Tour—The Rehearsals*.

CREDITS:
MGM, Color.
Length: 93 minutes
Release date: November 1, 1972

TAGLINE:
MGM presents a very different motion picture that captures all the excitement of ELVIS LIVE!

Songs: Johnny B. Goode, See See Rider, Polk Salad Annie, Separate Ways, Proud Mary, Never Been To Spain, Burning Love, Don't Be Cruel, Ready Teddy, That's All Right (Mama), Lead Me Guide Me, Bosom Of Abraham, Love Me Tender, Until It's Time For You To Go, Suspicious Minds, I John, Bridge Over Troubled Water, Funny How Time Slips Away, An American Trilogy, Mystery Train, I Got A Woman / Amen, A Big Hunk O' Love, You Gave Me A Mountain, Lawdy Miss Clawdy, Can't Help Falling In Love, Memories The Stamps: Lighthouse, Sweet Sweet Spirit.

Directed, produced and written by: Robert Abel, Pierre Adidge
Cinematography by: Michael A. Brown, David Myers
Film Editing by: Bert Lovitt, Martin Scorsese, Ken Zemke

FEATURING:
Elvis Presley
James Burton
Joe Esposito
Glen D. Hardin
Charlie Hodge
Jerry Scheff
The Stamps
J.D. Sumner
Ronnie Tutt
John Wilkinson
Jackie Kahane

ADDITIONAL CREW:
Wally Heider	sound
Yossi Eichenbaum	assistant editor
Joe Guercio	conductor
Col. Tom Parker	technical advisor
Jerry Schilling	assistant editor
Martin Scorsese	montage supervisor

ELVIS ON TOUR—THE REHEARSALS

In 2004, FTD released a long-awaited album of rehearsals prior to the concerts filmed for the documentary, recorded on March 30 and 31, 1972.

TRACK LISTING:
1. Proud Mary
2. Polk Salad Annie
3. See See Rider
4. A Big Hunk O'Love
5. Johnny B. Goode
6. Young And Beautiful
7. Love Me
8. Hound Dog
9. Lawdy, Miss Clawdy
10. For The Good Times
11. El Paso
12. Funny How Time Slips Away
13. Help Me Make It Through The Night
14. Release Me
15. Burning Love
16. Always On My Mind
17. The First Time Ever I Saw Your Face
18. Never Been To Spain
19. Separate Ways

ELVIS PRESLEY (EPs, LP)

In late March 1956, RCA launched a triple-barreled assault on America with three records bearing the sit-up-and-pay-attention title *Elvis Presley*:

An EP that made it to #24, selling 400,000 copies (then a record for this type of release).

TRACK LISTING:
1. Blue Suede Shoes
2. Tutti Frutti
3. I Got A Woman
4. Just Because

A double EP that sold 150,000 copies.

TRACK LISTING:
1. Blue Suede Shoes
2. I'm Counting On You
3. I'm Gonna Sit Right Down And Cry

Elvis on Tour, 1972 Golden Globe joint winner for Best Documentary Film.

The cover of Elvis' first US LP.

4. I'll Never Let You Go (Little Darlin')
5. I Got A Woman
6. One-Sided Love Affair
7. Tutti Frutti
8. Tryin' To Get To You

An LP combining seven tracks laid down at RCA plus five previously-unreleased Sun cuts, adorned with a photo taken by PoPsie at a 1955 Florida concert. *Elvis Presley* the album entered the charts at #11, rose rapidly to #1 and stayed there for ten weeks after displacing Harry Belafonte on May 5, 1956. The LP stayed at #1 for ten weeks. The disc stayed on the chart for four weeks shy of a full year—it sold 300,000 records on initial release—and was RCA's first ever pop album to earn more than $1 million. In November 1966, it became the first LP in history to rack up a million sales.

TRACK LISTING:
1. Blue Suede Shoes
2. I'm Counting On You
3. I Got A Woman
4. One-Sided Love Affair
5. I Love You Because
6. Just Because
7. Tutti Frutti
8. Tryin' To Get To You
9. I'm Gonna Sit Right Down And Cry (Over You)
10. I'll Never Let You Go (Little Darlin')
11. Blue Moon
12. Money Honey

A 50th anniversary remastered version of the album came out in 1985. In 2006, collector's label FTD released a remastered 2-CD deluxe set of the *Elvis Presley* LP, including early singles, multiple alternates and outtakes, and an early Elvis interview.

To keep the new star's name at the forefront of the record-buying public's consciousness, RCA shipped a second *Elvis Presley* EP on June 8, 1956, featuring two tracks from the album that weren't on the initial EP release. This release made it to #55 in the charts.

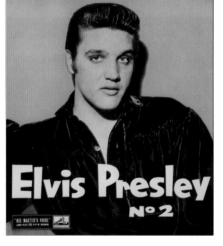

TRACK LISTING:
1. Shake, Rattle And Roll
2. I Love You Because
3. Lawdy, Miss Clawdy
4. Blue Moon

A number of promotional EP releases, all glorying in the name *Elvis Presley*, also came out in 1956, some to promote Elvis among DJs, others as part of a cross-selling promotion with RCA Victrola phonographs.

ELVIS PRESLEY BOULEVARD

See NAMES.

ELVIS PRESLEY ENTERPRISES (EPE)

The original Elvis Presley Enterprises was set up at the very start of Elvis' career by manager Bob Neal, initially in Memphis, to exploit what he hoped would be profitable merchandise opportunities. The company was rolled into Colonel Parker's operations after Elvis signed with him in 1955.

Elvis Presley Enterprises was re-established after Elvis' death to manage his Estate on behalf of the Elvis Presley Trust.

On Vernon's death in 1979, the Elvis Estate was worth as little as half a million dollars (and certainly no more than $5 million in any estimation). More pressingly, it was on the verge of bankruptcy: Parker had sold off Elvis' biggest money-earning rights to RCA in the early Seventies, and the cash flow situation was parlous. Having found Parker guilty of "self-dealing and overreaching," in 1981 control over Elvis' business interests was wrested from Parker and vested in EPE Inc. The Shelby County Probate Court named Priscilla and an accountant as executor and trustee on Lisa Marie Presley's behalf.

Kansas City businessman Jack Soden joined EPE in late 1981. His guidance is credited with saving the estate. He presided over the opening of Graceland to the public in the summer of 1982. EPE began a rigorous campaign to apply intellectual property laws to Elvis merchandise and licensing, fighting five major legal battles in the Eighties to reassert its control over the Elvis name. During this period, detractors referred to EPE as the "Darth Vader of the merchandising-licensing business."

EPE purchased the land over the road from Graceland, beginning renovations after existing tenants' leases expired in 1987 and purchasing more land in order to bring all Elvis-related operations around Graceland under its control.

After years of the Midas touch, EPE made a mis-step with an Elvis Presley themed restaurant on Beale Street, which it was forced to close down in 2003.

In February 2005, Elvis' sole surviving beneficiary, Lisa Marie sold an 85% stake in Elvis Presley Enterprises to Robert Sillerman's company CKX for $114 million. Lisa Marie commented, "We were doing good, but you can't stay the same. You either have to grow or go down." EPE has been making annual revenues of between $40 and $50 million in the 2000s.

EPE employs between 350 and 450 people in part-time and full-time jobs. As of 2006, Jack Soden remains CEO of the company, while Gary Hovey runs the LA office.

The name "Elvis Presley Enterprises" was used by Elvis for the touch football team he ran and played in when he was living in Los Angeles and Memphis in the early Sixties.

MARY HANCOCK HINDS: "The organization's aggressiveness and creativity in promoting and protecting Elvis is a significant factor in his staying power as a cultural fixture."

FROM THE EPE WEBSITE: "EPE's business extends far beyond the Graceland operation. It includes worldwide licensing of Elvis-related products and ventures, the development of Elvis-related music, film, video, television and stage productions, the ongoing development of EPE's Internet presence, the management of significant music publishing assets and more."

Books:
Elvis Inc.: The Fall and Rise of the Presley Empire, by Sean O'Neal, Prima Publishing, 1996.
Policing the Soul of Elvis, by David Wall, Pluto, 2000.

ELVIS PRESLEY MUSIC

Elvis' own music publishing company came into being as part of his record deal with song publishers Hill and Range, in November 1955, when he moved from Sun Records to RCA. A year later Elvis added "Gladys Music" to the mix, and registered with the American Society of Composers, Authors and Publishers as a means of having access to a wider choice of potential songs.

Elvis reputedly sold a portion of his stake in the company back to Hill and Range in the late Sixties to raise money.

Both companies were wound up when Hill and Range ceased trading in the early Seventies, to be replaced by Elvis Music and Whitehaven Music, which the Colonel set up to work with Freddy Bienstock.

ELVIS PRESLEY SPEAKS!

The first ever Elvis biography was written by *Memphis Press-Scimitar* reporter Bob Johnson. It sold out its initial print run almost immediately on publication in August 1956. However, the booklet spawned a law suit against Elvis by a young lady whose permission was not sought prior to publication of a photograph in which she featured.

In 1980 a clairvoyant claimed to have made contact with Elvis, and published the findings in a book of the same title (see Spirituality).

ELVIS PRESLEY YOUTH CENTER, EAST TUPELO

Elvis raised $10,000 for this project in a September 1957 concert at the Tupelo Fairgrounds, when he played to 12,000 people. His charity shows in 1961 and 1962 raised further funds for the project.

In February 1961, Elvis was much saddened when on a trip to show girlfriend Anita Wood and pal Joe Esposito where he grew up in Tupelo he discovered that not only had no work been done on the lot where the Youth Center was supposed to be built—land purchased from Orville Bean among others, just behind where Elvis was born—but even the sign announcing the project had fallen down.

The original plan to build an extensive Youth Center complex including a guitar-shaped swimming school was much scaled down. Elvis and Vernon apparently suspected that the funds they had raised had been diverted for other purposes.

ELVIS RAW—EARLY LIVE RECORDING

A 1997 release on the Peter Pan label of Elvis performing in Houston on March 19, 1955.

TRACK LISTING:
1. Interview With Bill Collie
2. Baby, Let's Play House
3. Blue Moon Of Kentucky
4. I Got A Woman
5. Good Rockin' Tonight
6. That's All Right
7. Interview With Scottie Moore

ELVIS RECORDED LIVE ON STAGE IN MEMPHIS

RCA captured Elvis' stage show at an extra date added to his March 1974 tour for this LP, after editing it down to album length. On release in July that year, it sold almost half a million copies and peaked at #33 in the charts (where it had a 13 week stay). The record contains Elvis' Grammy-winning track "How Great Thou Art."

TRACK LISTING:
1. See See Rider
2. I Got A Woman
3. Love Me
4. Tryin' To Get To You
5. Medley (Long Tall Sally / Whole Lotta Shakin' Goin' On / Your Mama Don't Dance / Flip, Flop and Fly / Jailhouse Rock / Hound Dog)
6. Why Me Lord
7. How Great Thou Art
8. Blueberry Hill / I Can't Stop Loving You
9. Help Me
10. An American Trilogy
11. Let Me Be There
12. My Baby Left Me
13. Lawdy, Miss Clawdy
14. Can't Help Falling In Love
15. Closing Vamp

FTD released a remixed version of the Mid-South Coliseum concert in 2004 with the same title but dispensing with the canned applause added to the album released thirty years previously.

TRACK LISTING:
1. Also Sprach Zarathustra
2. See See Rider
3. I Got A Woman / Amen
4. Love Me
5. Tryin' To Get To You
6. All Shook Up
7. Steamroller Blues
8. Teddy Bear / Don't Be Cruel
9. Love Me Tender
10. Medley: Long Tall Sally / Whole Lotta Shakin' Goin' On / Your Mama Don't Dance / Flip, Flop And Fly / Jailhouse Rock / Hound Dog
11. Fever
12. Polk Salad Annie
13. Why Me Lord
14. How Great Thou Art
15. Suspicious Minds
16. Introductions by Elvis
17. Blueberry Hill / I Can't Stop Loving You
18. Help Me
19. An American Trilogy
20. Let Me Be There
21. My Baby Left Me
22. Lawdy, Miss Clawdy
23. Funny How Time Slips Away
24. Can't Help Falling In Love

ELVIS SAILS

This EP, released in mid-November 1958, made it to #2 on the back of 60,000 sales. No music on this release, just 3 interviews based around edited highlights of the press conference and individual Q&As Elvis gave before leaving for his Army service in Germany (plus a 1959 calendar for fans to count off the days until his return).

Excerpts from the disc appeared on RCA's debut Elvis collectors' release, *Elvis: A Legendary Performer Vol. 1* in 1974.

ELVIS 2ND TO NONE

A 2003 BMG release following on from *ELVIS 30 #1 Hits*, including many more top ten tracks, recently-rediscovered and never-before-released tune "I'm A Roustabout," and a new remix.

TRACK LISTING:
1. That's All Right (Mama)
2. I Forgot To Remember To Forget
3. Blue Suede Shoes
4. I Want You, I Need You, I Love You
5. Love Me
6. Mean Woman Blues
7. Loving You
8. Treat Me Nice
9. Wear My Ring Around Your Neck
10. King Creole
11. Trouble
12. I Got Stung
13. I Need Your Love Tonight
14. A Mess Of Blues
15. I Feel So Bad
16. Little Sister
17. Rock-A-Hula Baby
18. Bossa Nova Baby
19. Viva Las Vegas
20. If I Can Dream
21. Memories
22. Don't Cry, Daddy
23. Kentucky Rain
24. You Don't Have To Say You Love Me
25. An American Trilogy
26. Always On My Mind
27. Promised Land
28. Moody Blue
29. I'm A Roustabout
30. Rubberneckin' (Paul Oakenfold remix)

ELVIS SINGS CHRISTMAS SONGS

An EP release to coincide with Elvis' first Christmas album in October 1957. Another #1, another half a million sales, and in the fullness of time another platinum seller.

TRACK LISTING:
1. Santa Bring My Baby Back
2. Blue Christmas
3. Santa Claus Is Back In Town
4. I'll Be Home For Christmas

ELVIS SINGS FLAMING STAR

Released in late March 1969 on RCA's budget label Camden, this compilation is in fact a re-release of *Singer Presents Elvis Singing Flaming Star and Others*, and has an identical track listing. The RCA version sold a total of half a million copies, but rose no higher than #96 in the charts during its 16-week stay.

TRACK LISTING:
1. Flaming Star
2. Wonderful World
3. Night Life
4. All I Needed Was The Rain
5. Too Much Monkey Business
6. The Yellow Rose Of Texas / The Eyes Of Texas
7. She's A Machine
8. Do The Vega
9. Tiger Man

ELVIS SINGS FOR CHILDREN (AND GROWN UPS TOO)

A 1978 release on RCA and other labels, first mooted by the Colonel in 1975, with previously releases songs plus "Big Boots." The album peaked at #130 on the *Billboard* main LP charts during an 11 week stay.

TRACK LISTING:
1. Teddy Bear
2. Wooden Heart
3. Five Sleepy Heads
4. Puppet On A String
5. Angel
6. Old MacDonald
7. How Would You Like To Be
8. Cotton Candy Land
9. Old Shep
10. Big Boots
11. Have A Happy

The album was re-released in 2002 as *Elvis Sings for Kids*.

ELVIS SINGS HITS FROM HIS MOVIES, VOL. 1

An album released in June 1972, presenting the cream of Elvis' not always memorable crop of movie songs. Initial sales topped out at 130,000 copies, and the album managed no better than a lowly #87 peak in the charts during its 15 week rise and fall.

TRACK LISTING:
1. Down By the Riverside / When The Saints Go Marchin' In
2. They Remind Me Too Much Of You
3. Confidence
4. Frankie And Johnny
5. Guitar Man
6. Long Legged Girl (With The Short Dress On)
7. You Don't Know Me
8. How Would You Like To Be
9. Big Boss Man
10. Old MacDonald

ELVIS SINGS LEIBER & STOLLER

Originally released in the UK in 1980, this album was reissued on CD in 1991 with bonus track "You're The Boss" (the duet version with Ann-Margaret)

TRACK LISTING:
1. Hound Dog
2. Love Me
3. Loving You
4. Hot Dog
5. I Want To Be Free
6. Jailhouse Rock
7. Treat Me Nice
8. (You're So Square) Baby I Don't Care
9. Santa Claus Is Back In Town
10. Don't
11. Trouble
12. King Creole
13. Steadfast, Loyal And True
14. Dirty, Dirty Feeling
15. Just Tell Her Jim Said Hello
16. Girls! Girls! Girls!
17. Bossa Nova Baby
18. You're The Boss
19. Little Egypt
20. Fools Fall In Love
21. Saved

ELVIS SINGS MORT SHUMAN & DOC POMUS

A 1985 UK release on RCA, re-released by the French arm of BMG in 2000 as *Elvis Chante Mort Shuman et Doc Pomus*, with additional alternate takes.

TRACK LISTING:
1. A Mess Of Blues
2. His Latest Flame
3. Little Sister
4. Surrender
5. Suspicion
6. Kiss Me Quick
7. Gonna Get Back Home Somehow
8. Night Rider
9. I Need Somebody To Lean On
10. Viva Las Vegas
11. Little Sister (alternate take)
12. Doin' The Best I Can
13. Double Trouble
14. Long Lonely Highway
15. Never Say Yes
16. What Every Woman Lives For
17. You'll Think Of Me
18. Doin' The Best I Can (alternate take)
19. His Latest Flame (alternate take)
20. Long Lonely Highway (alternate take)

ELVIS SINGS THE BLUES

Many fans wish he had spent more time doing just this . . . RCA released this themed compilation in 1983.

TRACK LISTING:
1. When It Rains, It Really Pours
2. New Orleans
3. It Feels So Right
4. A Mess Of Blues
5. Like A Baby
6. Reconsider Baby
7. I Feel So Bad
8. Give Me The Right
9. Beach Boy Blues
10. Big Boss Man
11. Stranger In My Own Home Town
12. Power Of My Love
13. My Babe
14. Got My Mojo Working
15. Steamroller Blues

ELVIS SINGS THE WONDERFUL WORLD OF CHRISTMAS

With Elvis' previous Christmas album, a 1970 reissue of his 1957 offering, having done such stellar business, the Colonel and RCA thought they were onto a winner with this new album, released in October 1971. It failed to chart, but it sold steadily that year and the next, racking up not far off half a million sales. Later reissues feature a bonus track. The album has since sold so steadily that as of 2006 it has triple platinum status.

TRACK LISTING:
1. O Come, All Ye Faithful
2. The First Noel
3. On A Snowy Christmas Night
4. Winter Wonderland
5. The Wonderful World Of Christmas
6. It Won't Seem Like Christmas (Without You)
7. I'll Be Home On Christmas Day
8. If I Get Home On Christmas Day
9. Holly Leaves And Christmas Trees
10. Merry Christmas Baby
11. Silver Bells

"ELVIS SUMMER FESTIVAL"

The Colonel's marketing title for Elvis' summer stints in Las Vegas, at the International (subsequently Las Vegas Hilton) Hotel, starting in 1970.

ELVIS: THAT'S THE WAY IT IS (DOCUMENTARY)

Recorded in the summer of 1970 in Las Vegas, for many fans this is the *non plus ultra* of Elvis in concert. The Colonel and MGM did a deal to make the movie in early 1970, after the Colonel pulled the plug on a previous deal for a country-wide closed-circuit pay-per-view concert with Filmways; he invoked a get-out clause in the $1.1 million contract after the *Los Angeles Times* ran an article on the event, in breach of the Colonel's stipulation that no advance press was permissible.

Director Denis Sanders set out to show how an Elvis concert was made from start to finish. He shot rehearsal footage at the MGM studio in Culver City (just one part of three weeks' rehearsal during which Elvis and the band worked on over sixty songs in total), rehearsals at the International Hotel, and then six shows at the International Hotel Convention Center between August 10 and 13, 1970. Material that didn't

make it into the hour-and-a-half-long movie has proven to be a treasure trove for Elvis fans over the years, with new material still being officially released for the first time well into the 2000s.

During filming, the Colonel quipped to Sanders that he wasn't looking for an Oscar-winning picture—Sanders had previously won Oscars for documentaries *Czechoslovakia* (1969) and *A Time Out of War* (1954). Veteran cinematographer Lucien Ballard had been winning awards for his work since 1935.

When Parker first saw the rough cut of *Elvis: That's The Way It Is*, he liked neither its fast-paced editing nor what he perceived as slurs on other performers and Elvis' film work.

Elvis first saw the documentary at a screening at MGM in December 1970. On initial release, *That's the Way It Is* made it to #22 on the Variety weekly box office takings list.

For the 2000/2001 "Special Edition," rehearsal footage was added, the fan interviews in the original were dropped (they had included the Chairman of the UK fan club and an Elvis convention in Luxembourg), and for audiophiles, the original sixteen-track masters were digitally remixed to 5.1 Dolby. A significant quantity of filmed material has remained unreleased outside of bootlegs.

BMG and FTD have continued to release more and more tracks from the extensive rehearsals in the 2000s (details below).

The 2007 two-disc DVD re-release commemorating the 30th anniversary of Elvis' death contains the original and the Special Edition.

CREDITS:
MGM, Color.
Length: 97 minutes (2001 version: 94 minutes + extras)
Release date: November 1, 1970

Songs (1970 version): Mystery Train / Tiger Man, Words, The Next Step Is Love, Polk Salad Annie, Cryin' Time, That's All Right (Mama), Little Sister, What 'd I Say, Stranger In The Crowd, How The Web Was Woven, I Just Can't Help Believin', You Don't Have To Say You Love Me, You Don't Have To Say You Love Me, Bridge Over Troubled Water, Words, You've Lost That Lovin' Feelin', Mary In The Morning, Polk Salad Annie, That's All Right (Mama), I've Lost You, Patch It Up, Love Me Tender, You've Lost That Lovin' Feelin', Sweet Caroline, I Just Can't Help Believin', Little Sister / Get Back, Bridge Over Troubled Water, Heartbreak Hotel, One Night, Blue Suede Shoes, All Shook Up, Polk Salad Annie, Suspicious Minds, Can't Help Falling In Love

The 2001 version does not feature "I Just Can't Help Believin' "Sweet Caroline" and "Bridge Over Troubled Water."

Directed by: Denis Sanders
Produced by: Dale Hutchinson (producer), Herbert F. Solow (producer), Rick Schmidlin (producer, special edition), George Feltenstein (executive producer, special edition), Roger Mayer (executive producer, special edition)
Cinematography by: Lucien Ballard
Film Editing by: Henry Berman, Michael Salomon (special edition)
Costume Design by: Bill Belew

FEATURING:
Elvis Presley
David Briggs
James Burton
Jerry Carrigan
Richard Davis
Joe Esposito
Joe Guercio
Glen D. Hardin
Charlie Hodge
Felton Jarvis

Elvis sneezes! (Candid shot from the 50s)

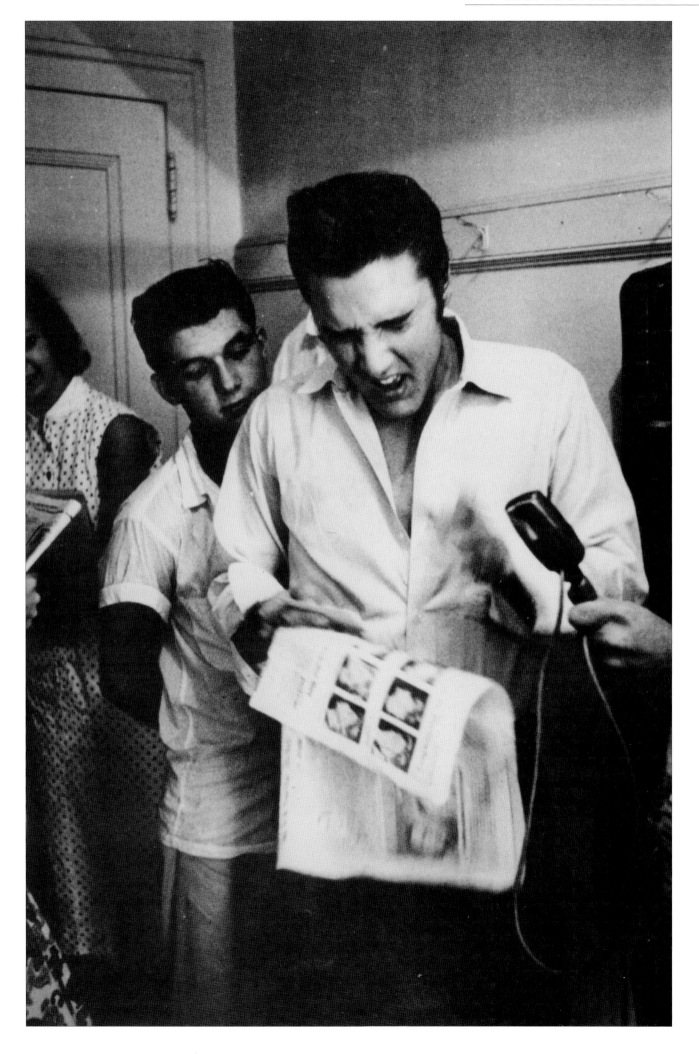

Millie Kirkham
Norbert Putnam
Jerry Scheff
Myrna Smith
Ronnie Tutt
Del 'Sonny' West
Red West
John Wilkinson
Charo
Xavier Cugat
Sammy Davis Jr.
Cary Grant
George Hamilton
Juliet Prowse

ADDITIONAL CREW:

Dale Hutchinson	unit production manager
John Wilson	assistant director
Robb Boyd	assistant music editor (2001 re-issue)
Lyle Burbridge	sound
Jim Fitzpatrick	sound re-recording mixer (2001 re-issue)
Larry Hadsell	sound
Greg Hedgepath	supervising sound editor (2001 re-issue)
Roy Prendergast	music editor (2001 re-issue)
Richard Davis	technical assistant
Tom Diskin	technical assistant
Joe Esposito	technical assistant
Lamar Fike	technical assistant
George Folsey Jr.	associate film editor
Felton Jarvis	technical assistant
Jim O'Brien	technical assistant
Romek Pachucki	technical assistant
Colonel Tom Parker	technical advisor
George Parkhill	coordinator for RCA records
Bill Porter	technical assistant
Michael Ripps	assistant editor
Sean Weber-Small	associate editor (special edition)
Del 'Sonny' West	technical assistant
Doug Byers	electrician

For album and CD releases, *see under That's The Way It Is*.

ELVIS—THE CONCERT

The former TCB band members who got back together to perform in Memphis on the twentieth anniversary of Elvis' death in 1997 have been touring the world with a video-projected Elvis ever since, at last realizing Elvis' dream of traveling the globe and taking his music to his international fans. The band plays its stuff as Elvis sings his heart out on a giant video screen. The Elvis footage comes from some of his finest filmed performances, including the 1968 NBC TV Special, *Elvis: That's The Way It Is* (1970), *Elvis on Tour* (1972) and *Elvis: Aloha from Hawaii, via Satellite* (1973).

The revolving Elvis—The Concert personnel roster is a veritable who's who of musicians and singers who worked with Elvis in the late Sixties and throughout the Seventies: Joe Guercio (musical director/conductor), The Sweet Inspirations (female backing vocals), former members of J.D. Sumner & the Stamps Quartet (male backing vocals), former members of The Imperials (male backing vocals), former members of Voice (male backing vocals), Millie Kirkham (soprano) and of course TCB Band members James Burton (lead guitar), Glen D. Hardin (piano), Jerry Scheff (bass guitar), and Ronnie Tutt (drums).

The event went into the Guinness Book of Records as the "first live tour headlined by a performer who is no longer living."

After a break, Elvis—The Concert returned to world touring in 2006.

A DVD of the 25th anniversary Elvis—The Concert performance in Memphis, titled *Elvis Lives*, was released in 2007, the year that another large Memphis extravaganza was held to com-

memorate the 30th anniversary of Elvis' passing. At this event, it was announced that Elvis—The Concert had played its last show.

RONNIE TUTT: "It's close enough to really be able to sense what it was like."

ELVIS THE CONCERT 1999 WORLD TOUR

A two-disc album of the Elvis vocals used in the original concert was released at the time, featuring a collection of Elvis' most impressive live performances of these songs.

TRACK LISTING:
DISC 1
1. Introduction: Also Sprach Zarathustra
2. See See Rider
3. Burning Love
4. Steamroller Blues
5. I Can't Stop Loving You
6. Johnny B. Goode
7. You Gave Me A Mountain
8. Polk Salad Annie
9. You've Lost That Lovin' Feelin'
10. Proud Mary
11. Never Been To Spain
12. Just Pretend
13. Make The World Go Away
14. In The Ghetto
15. How Great Thou Art
16. Bridge Over Troubled Water

DISC 2
1. Trouble / Guitar Man
2. Hound Dog
3. (Let Me Be Your) Teddy Bear / Don't Be Cruel
4. All Shook Up
5. Heartbreak Hotel
6. One Night
7. Love Me Tender
8. The Wonder Of You
9. Lawdy, Miss Clawdy
10. Funny How Time Slips Away
11. Suspicious Minds
12. I'll Remember You
13. A Big Hunk O' Love
14. My Way
15. An American Trilogy
16. Can't Help Falling In Love
17. Closing Vamp

ELVIS: THE FIRST LIVE RECORDINGS

A 1984 album of early Elvis performances from the Louisiana Hayride on the Music Works label.

TRACK LISTING:
1. Introduction with Elvis and Horace Logan
2. Baby, Let's Play House
3. Maybellene
4. Tweedlee Dee
5. That's All Right (Mama)
6. Recollections by Frank Page
7. Hound Dog

ELVIS: THE HILLBILLY CAT

A 1984 Music Works label release including live recordings of Elvis at the Louisiana Hayride.

TRACK LISTING:
1. Louisiana Hayride introduction
2. Elvis talks with Horace Logan
3. That's All Right (Mama)
4. Elvis talks with Horace Logan

5. Blue Moon Of Kentucky
6. Recollections by Frank Page
7. Good Rockin' Tonight
8. I Got A Woman

ELVIS VOL. 1

RCA shipped this EP in late October 1956 at the same time as his second album, Elvis. A million copies were sold (a first for an EP) before Christmas as fans drove "Love Me" up to #6 in the single charts, "When My Blue Moon Turns To Gold Again" to #27 and "Paralyzed" to #59, even though none of these tracks were actually released as singles.

TRACK LISTING:
1. Rip It Up
2. Love Me
3. When My Blue Moon Turns To Gold Again
4. Paralyzed

ELVIS VOL. 2

RCA waited only a month before releasing a second helping of tracks from Elvis' second album on EP, featuring "So Glad You're Mine" as the title track and "Old Shep," which made it to #47 on the singles charts.

TRACK LISTING:
1. So Glad You're Mine
2. Old Shep
3. Ready Teddy
4. Anyplace Is Paradise

ELVIS: WHAT HAPPENED?

The shock book by former entourage members Red and Sonny West, plus karate instructor and sometime bodyguard Dave Hebler, "as told" to *National Star* gossip columnist Steve Dunleavy, came out a year after they were fired by Vernon Presley.

The book was initially serialized in the UK in May 1977. Ballantine published "the bodyguard book" in the US at the beginning of August 1977, just two weeks before Elvis died.

Many fans have never forgiven these friends of Elvis' for their disloyalty in revealing the unsavory side of his life. Some fans believe that the book is full of bilious fabrications. Much of the information about Elvis' drug use and excess was revealed for the first time in this book.

According to the authors, their motivation for laying bare the bones of Elvis' life was finally to get him to face up to reality and do something about his destructive lifestyle before it was too late. It has been said that one of the reasons why they were fired in the first place is because Elvis flew into a rage after they challenged him about his addiction to prescription drugs.

Other entourage members have said that when Elvis heard that his former friends were writing a book about him, he was deeply concerned how it would be taken by his fans, and most importantly, what Lisa Marie would think years later.

Up until publication, Elvis hoped that either the guys would see sense, or the Colonel would do something to ensure that the book never saw the light of day. Elvis reputedly offered $50,000 to each former bodyguard if they pulled the plug on the book; there are also rumors that John O'Grady asked the Wests to "name their price" for abandoning the project, but as the book was intended as a wake-up call to Elvis, they were not interested

Elvis spoke to Red West while he was working on the book in an attempt to explain his side of the firing, and to dissuade West from going ahead with the exposé. At the end of a long phone call—taped by West—Elvis told his friend of more than twenty years: "You do whatever you have to do. I just want you and Pat to know I'm still here." West included the transcript of the conversation as an epilog to the book, though there have been claims that the printed version includes a number of omissions and, more scathingly, unfavorable additions. The recording has found its way onto bootlegs.

Though the book lifts the lid on the less salubrious goings-on in Elvis' life, it is unfailingly courteous to Elvis' mom Gladys, and praises Elvis' loyalty and generosity.

Larry Geller was surprised that the book ever saw the light of day because it was so libelous and full of lies. Entourage pals have offered conflicting opinions on whether or not Elvis ever read the book; Sonny West has said that Elvis saw the book in manuscript form before it was ever published. Billy Smith says that Elvis told him he would have the authors killed if the book harmed his career. Peter Guralnick writes that Elvis brushed off a preliminary approach from Frank Sinatra's entourage about helping to keep the book out of print.

Propelled by the proximity of its publication to Elvis' death, the book sold over three million copies.

Steve Dunleavy: "All three pray and hope that Presley will read the book and come to a realization that his life is leading him on a path to disaster."

Frontispiece of Book: "He will read and he will get hopping mad at us because he knows that every word is the truth and we will take a lie detector test to prove it. But just maybe, it will do some good."

Sonny West: "We wrote the book to put a challenge to Elvis.... No one had written anything that would wake him up and make him see what he was doing. We had kept our mouths shut for years. That was our loyalty to him, and our love for him. When we saw him going downhill we tried to stop him, and he didn't like it."

ELVISOLOGY

Elvisology—the study of Elvis—has a half-century heritage and shows no sign of being exhausted anytime soon. No area of Elvis' life, however tangential, has escaped the enquiries of authors or the searchlight of fan interest. There truly is Elvis for everyone: Elvis books, academic conferences, fan club meets where loyal fans of 50 years' standing debate the finer points of Elvis' life, documentaries, erudite and academic articles, completist collectors, internet chat rooms, 600,000 fans who visit Graceland every year, quiz books, memorabilia, anniversary events, and much more in store under the aegis of new Elvis rights owners CKX.

EMMONS, BOBBY
(B. 1943)

Bobby Emmons is a Memphis-born keyboards player who first worked with Elvis at his legendary American Studio sessions in early 1969.

At the start of the Sixties, he was part of the Bill Black Combo with Elvis' first bass player.

A studio musician at many top Memphis studios over the years, Emmons also played on Elvis' 1976 "Jungle Room sessions" in Graceland. He has written songs sung by performers ranging from B.J. Thomas to Waylon Jennings and Nora Jones.

"END OF THE ROAD"

Jerry Lee Lewis gave this composition of his—which he had just written and recorded as his first ever Sun single—a run-through on December 4, 1956, when Elvis was in the building for the jam

Cover of a British 1958 Elvis magazine.

that became the *Million Dollar Session*. Elvis is listening rather than singing.

ENGLAND

Elvis first mentioned going to England during his Army tour of duty in Germany in the late Fifties. The closest he got, on furlough, was Paris, where he was unavoidably detained by the entire chorus line of (English) Bluebelle girls.

Over the years, the Colonel fended off a number of requests to bring Elvis to England, including a $1 million offer from Screaming Lord Sutch, and a half-million-dollar contract for a week's performing at Earl's Court in London.

If Elvis wouldn't come to a venue near them, his English fans traveled in droves to see Elvis in Las Vegas in the Seventies. A party 250-strong at the Las Vegas Hilton in 1972 received Elvis' personal thanks during the show. In recognition, Elvis gave his tandem bicycle to the head of the UK fan club.

As in the US, in the UK Elvis holds many music sales records. He has scored more #1 hits than any other artist (21) and the most top 10 hits. Only Queen and The Beatles have spent more time on the album charts.

Over half of the visitors to Elvis' birthplace museum are reputedly from the UK.

Elvis came to England on film in 1966 in *Double Trouble* (shot entirely at MGM studios).

UK fan club Chairmen Arthur Hand and Todd Slaughter have been prolific Elvis authors. To this day, the fan club is the largest in the world with membership exceeding 20,000.

Mick Fleetwood: "I learned music listening to Elvis' records. His measurable effect on culture and music was even greater in England than in the States."

Books:

Elvis, UK: the Ultimate Guide to Elvis Presley's British Record Releases, 1956-1986, by John Townson, Gordon Minto and George Richardson, Blandford Press, 1987.

Elvis UK2: The Ultimate Guide to Elvis Presley's Record Releases 1986-2002, by John Townson and Gordon Minto, GP Electronics Ltd., 2002.

ENTERTAINER, THE

A 1978 bootleg of live recordings credited to the Louisiana Hayride, Eagle's Nest, Las Vegas and the Sahara Tahoe.

TRACK LISTING:
1. That's All Right, Mama
2. Blue Moon Of Kentucky
3. Tweedlee Dee
4. Flip, Flop And Fly
5. Good Rockin' Tonight
6. Baby Let's Play House
7. I Got A Woman
8. Blue Moon Of Kentucky
9. That's All Right
10. Polk Salad Annie
11. Kentucky Rain
12. I Got A Woman
13. Don't Cry, Daddy
14. It's Your Baby, You Rock It
15. Don't Think Twice It's All Right
16. Wooden Heart / Young And Beautiful
17. What Now My Love
18. Folsom Prison Blues / I Walk The Line
19. Return To Sender

ENTOURAGE

Elvis' entourage developed out of the twin needs of companionship and protection on the road during his itinerant touring days in 1954 and 1955. In one form or another, he lived with an elective extended family for the rest of his life.

When the concerts got too big for Elvis, Scotty and Bill alone to heave their stuff and look after themselves, Elvis called on members of his extended family and trusted pal Red West. It was some time before Elvis began paying the guys who kept him safe and delivered him on time to where he was playing next. By 1956, when he had Hollywood to look forward to, the guys who worked for Elvis were given job titles. Alan Fortas estimates that over the years as many as 50 different guys were in Elvis' gang, though at any one time the Memphis Mafia—a moniker the entourage picked up in the early Sixties for their Rat-Packer-style attire—waxed and waned between an average of four and eight members.

The money entourage members earned was not much more than the average blue-collar wage, but the fringe benefits took some beating: parties, girls, hanging out with the famous, every once in a while a great new car. In later years, Elvis' generosity and gift-giving extended to the wives and girlfriends of his inner circle. Members of the entourage suggest that Elvis was unmoved by their promptings that their salaries were low because he simply had no conception of what living cost. If Elvis did want to increase their salaries, he would find Vernon dead set against the idea.

The flip side of traveling with his own cohort meant that Elvis lived an insular life, within a protective bubble that curtailed spontaneity and hemmed in his horizons. Getting through the human shields to Elvis was a challenge even for the people he was working with. Director Philip Dunne, with whom Elvis worked in 1960, referred to the guys who stood between Elvis and the world as the "fart-catchers."

The demands of fame and more professional management under Colonel Parker led to an expansion in the entourage. In early 1956 Elvis stopped driving between shows with his band and started flying, accompanied by cousins Junior and Gene Smith, and by Red West, who had been Elvis' driver since early 1955. By the time Elvis arrived in New York for his second appearance on "The Ed Sullivan Show" in late October 1956, he was flying first class with Gene Smith, actor Nick Adams and Bitsy Mott, the Colonel's brother-in-law who for many years kept a weather eye on what Elvis was up to.

Elvis' entourage waxed and waned over the years, but for the most part it was a stable gang of guys consisting of cousins, school pals, musician friends from Sun, and in the pre-Priscilla years, a revolving coterie of young female fans lucky enough to be singled out and invited up to the house to hang out (Frances Forbes, Arlene Cogan and Barbara Glidewell among them). Many a pretty young fan figured that the best way to get to Elvis was to date one of his pals; erroneously, it turned out. If Elvis was interested in a girl, it was on an exclusive rather than a *droit de seigneur* basis.

In the early years, the entourage was much more democratic, in the sense that guys in the gang would say what they thought and not balk at standing up against Elvis. Elvis only pulled rank when he felt he need to.

Red West dates Elvis' change from being one of the guys to becoming a King-like figure overseeing his court around the time he filmed *Jailhouse Rock*. Afterwards, he behaved much more like Vince Everett, the character he played in the movie, expecting and demanding the people around him to light his cigars or fetch him a glass of water. Looking after Elvis' sense of emotional security was almost as important as making sure that he was physically secure.

Elvis soon mastered the art of keeping his court happy: it was a lot of fun to be part of his group, and for girls and boys, he always made sure there was some private time with each individual. Elvis made it abundantly clear to his guys that they were there for him, not to fraternize excessively among themselves. Some entourage members came and went pretty quickly: in 1957, Louis Harris and Tommy Young both followed a meteoric path into and out of the group.

By early 1958, Elvis' traveling companions were Cliff Gleaves, Lamar Fike, Alan Fortas, Gene Smith, Bitsy Mott, and sometimes George Klein. Colonel Parker insisted that the guys should go on the payroll, so that at least Elvis could partially write off the costs of paying for them.

The crew Elvis took to New Orleans for location work on *King Creole* included Alan Fortas, Gene Smith and Red West.

New members of the entourage could expect to be teased, ribbed and tested to see how they acted under pressure. Memphis Mafia initiation rites were more boisterous than sinister, and included being made to ride for hours on a rollercoaster at the Memphis Fairgrounds, or be an unwitting target in a punishing game of bumper cars. When cerebral hairdresser Larry Geller joined the gang he was drafted onto Elvis' team for a football match and was soon nursing a broken rib.

New members would have to adapt to a life of spending hours—sometimes days—just hanging around and waiting for something to happen. Then, when Elvis decided to do something or head off somewhere else, everybody would spring into action. Entourage members also got to live Elvis' night-for-day existence, and suffer the suspicions of Vernon and other family members, who never liked the fact that "the boys" hung around Graceland, eating them out of house and home, and then expecting to paid at the end of the month.

When very low after his mother's death, Elvis was reputedly disappointed with his Memphis pals because so few of them heeded his call to come and stay with him in Texas, where he was completing his Army training. He originally planned to hire a bus to bring them all down. In the end, the only Memphis regulars who came were Lamar Fike, Red West and cousin Junior Smith.

When Elvis was sent out to Germany in September 1958, he was by the familiar faces of Lamar Fike and Red West. He made some important new friends in the Army who became long-term members of the entourage: Joe Esposito, future foreman of the Memphis Mafia, and Charlie Hodge, a life-long friend and fellow-musician. While Elvis was away on maneuvers, entourage panels Lamar Fike and Road West went on trips across Europe.

Priscilla describes the start of her first visits with Elvis in Germany as always being uncertain, until she and the other people who had dropped by could gauge his mood. This was an art to which anyone invited into Elvis' inner circle quickly became attuned.

On Elvis' return from Germany and discharge from the Army, Graceland hosted new army pals Charlie Hodge and Joe Esposito, as well as Cliff Gleaves and Red West. Rex Mansfield, another Army pal who had agreed to join the gang, changed his mind at the last minute and went off to marry Elvis' secretary, Elisabeth Stefaniak.

When Elvis traveled from Memphis to LA in April 1960 to make his first post-Army movie, he took along Lamar Fike, Sonny West, cousin Gene Smith, Joe Esposito and Charlie Hodge. Red West and Cliff Gleaves were already in LA, pursuing their own careers in film.

In the early Sixties, Elvis and the guys unabashedly pursued an agenda of fun with a capital 'F', a lot of it sophomoric. The guys would mess about, tease one another, have water fights, set off firecrackers, fling ice cubes, play pranks on one another and generally act like big kids, often at swank hotels where they were staying and Elvis paid top dollar. When they camped out in Vegas between movies, Joe Esposito says, "It was a party like you wouldn't believe. Go to a different show every night, then pick up a bunch of women afterwards, go party the next night . . ."

While working on *Follow That Dream*, Elvis fired every single member of his entourage and then hired them all back before they had the chance to ship out.

By late 1961, Elvis' Hollywood escapades were conducted with Joe Esposito, Lamar Fike, Marty Lacker, Ray Sitton and Sonny West, who had a job on *Kid Galahad* as a stuntman. When Elvis flew to Hawaii in April 1962 to start filming *Girls! Girls! Girls!*, his travel companions were Joe Esposito, Alan Fortas, Ray Sitton, Gene Smith and Red West.

He took along Joe Esposito, Alan Fortas, Ray Sitton, Gene and Billy Smith, and recent additions Richard Davis and Jimmy Kingsley as extra security to Seattle for location work on *It Happened at the World's Fair*.

Arriving at a new hotel, Elvis' entourage sprang into action, unpacking his clothes, arranging his shoes (by color), setting up his sound system, turning on the TVs and getting things just the way Elvis liked them.

One of the few girls to be welcomed into the entourage was Patti Parry, who used to come to Elvis' LA home for parties and sometimes cut his hair. After she made the *faux pas* of answering then girlfriend Anita Wood's leading question about whether Elvis was dating anyone in LA, Elvis told her the entourage ground rules: first, deny everything; second, say nothing about anything she saw to anyone. Another rule, initially suggested by the Colonel and approved by Elvis, was no personal snapshots of Elvis.

After Priscilla moved in to Graceland, the girls who used to come up to the house to hang out with Elvis when he was in town were replaced by entourage members' wives and girlfriends. More and more of the guys began to marry, and the atmosphere around Graceland became less focused on the frenetic pursuit of fun. However, the party life continued out in LA, and later in Palm Springs—after Elvis' marriage, he used his Palm Springs home for parties, flying in female companions from Memphis, Las Vegas or further afield.

In early 1964 Elvis took a lengthy vacation in Las Vegas with Joe Esposito, Richard Davis, Alan Fortas, Jimmy Kingsley, Marty Lacker and Billy Smith.

A candid shot of Elvis with DJ, Scotty, and Bill.

As in any closed group, there was always jock-eying for position and status. Former entourage members have revealed that Elvis made it evident who his favorites were at any one time; conversely, entourage members would also be in his bad books and at risk of being fired (and most likely rehired). He would play people off against one another, and sometimes eavesdrop on conversations between the guys to catch them out later.

A number of simmering tensions overboiled in mid-1964, after hairdresser Larry Geller became a close friend of Elvis'. His escalating influence was resented by other members of the gang. That summer, Elvis fired Joe Esposito as group "fore-man" and appointed Marty Lacker in his stead. Esposito was out in the cold until the following year, but had been rehired by the time the Beatles made their house call on Elvis in LA in the sum-mer of 1965. Also there that night were Alan Fortas, Larry Geller, Red and Sonny West, Jerry Schilling, Billy Smith, Richard Davis, Mike Keaton, and Ray "Chief" Sitton.

The crew who flew out with Elvis to Hawaii for location work on *Paradise Hawaiian Style* in August 1965 consisted of Richard Davis, Larry Geller, Mike Keaton, Jerry Schilling, Billy Smith and Red and Sonny West. Larry Geller describes Elvis and his entourage descending on a film set as "a lot like a frat-house road show."

Senior entourage members Joe Esposito and Marty Lacker also acted as informal go-betweens for the Colonel—one of the reasons why Elvis fired Esposito in 1964 was because he suspected that Esposito was working more for the Colonel than for him. Usually, this informal arrangement worked well enough, though the Colonel would get angry if Elvis' habitual lateness started to look like a lack of professionalism. Things broke down in early 1967, when the Colonel was unable to get through to Elvis when Elvis was becoming later and later in starting work on his next feature, *Clambake*. In late February that year, the Colonel wrote Marty Lacker a stern letter informing him that this situation must not be allowed to occur again, or he would have to appoint an official person to fulfill the foreman's role. When Elvis finally flew to LA, he went with Larry Geller, Charlie Hodge, Marty Lacker, Ray Sitton, Billy Smith, Red West, and Gee Gee Gambill, who was married to Elvis' cousin Patsy.

The foreman's job included buying Christmas gifts on Elvis' behalf (after he made out a list). In the run-up to Christmas, some entourage members would start dropping hints to Elvis about what they wanted; the guys could also resort to telling a fellow entourage member about something they wanted, and then wait for that person to tell Elvis—it was not Elvis' habit to give gifts to people who requested them straight out.

During the years when Elvis was focusing on his spiritual seeking, he tried to include the guys in his discussions with Larry Geller, despite their evident skepticism (though a dozen guys signed a special Bible which they gave to Elvis for Christmas 1964). If Elvis was going to better himself, he wanted to share the experience and the benefits with the people in his life. The guys were as unenthusiastic as Priscilla; if anything, they felt that Elvis was changing for the worse, becoming more passive and supine, and less like the Elvis they knew. Grudging acceptance of Geller's influence turned to open hostility in late 1966 and early 1967. Geller described certain members of the gang as "trouble looking for a place to happen . . . one would hit a flash point and violence followed."

Elvis' purchase of the Circle G ranch in early 1967 marked the high water mark for the entourage as an extended family. The Graceland gang moved en masse into trailers and lived a communal life, before Elvis' Hollywood commitments interrupted the idyll. In fact, members of the entourage had already started drifting back to Memphis to be with their families, their stamina for a dude ranch existence no match for Elvis'.

When Elvis finally made it out to Hollywood, he sustained an injury that prevented him from starting work on *Clambake*. The Colonel flew into a rage, stormed into Elvis' home and put the entourage on notice. He told them that they were wearing Elvis down by taking their problems to him, and that in future they should go to Joe rather than Elvis. He also ordered that at least one entourage member should be with Elvis at all times, day and night. Larry Geller was made a persona non grata. After stamping his authority on Elvis' private living arrangements in a way he had not done before, the Colonel joined forces with Vernon to try and persuade Elvis to cut down on the number of people on the entourage payroll. Joe Esposito became sole foreman once more, while Marty Lacker was put in charge of "special projects," starting with Elvis' wedding. In entourage memoirs, many former members have said that the Colonel's intervention changed the nature of the group forever.

Elvis' May 1967 wedding to Priscilla Beaulieu was organized by the Colonel and created strong tensions in the group. Minutes before the ceremony, all of the entourage except best men Joe Esposito and Marty Lacker were told that there wasn't enough room for them to attend the ceremony proper—and this was already the reduced contingent who had been in LA with Elvis. They were invited to the reception afterwards but Red West was so offended that he didn't talk to Elvis for months; Larry Geller only found out about the

wedding in a supermarket tabloid. Entourage members have said in interviews that from this point, the group tended to be divided into top and bottom tier members.

Now that Elvis was a married man, the next time that he and his entourage traveled en masse from Memphis to LA for his upcoming movie (*Speedway*), the wives were invited along too. Elvis drove his Greyhound bus, leading a convoy of cars containing Joe Esposito, Billy Smith, Gee Gee Gambill, Jerry Schilling, Marty Lacker and all their wives, along with Charlie Hodge. They took their time over the trip, stopping off at sights along the way including the Grand Canyon. This was in many ways a swansong for the extended family Elvis had acquired over the last decade. Soon after, Jerry Schilling moved away to pursue his own career; Marty Lacker left Elvis in LA before the end of the filming on *Speedway* to return to the Circle G ranch where Alan Fortas had been left in charge.

When Elvis flew out to LA to shoot *Stay Away, Joe* in October 1967, he took along Joe Esposito, Gee Gee Gambill, Charlie Hodge, Billy Smith and Sonny West.

After Lisa Marie's birth on February 1, 1968, when he was in LA Elvis, Priscilla and the baby moved into a much smaller home that only had room for Charlie Hodge, Patsy, and Gee Gee Gambill.

On vacation in Hawaii in May 1968, Elvis, Priscilla and Lisa Marie's traveling companions were the Espositos, the Gambills and Charlie Hodge.

In Arizona to shoot the location scenes for *Charro!*, Elvis was with Joe Esposito, Alan Fortas, Gee Gee Gambill and Charlie Hodge, all of whom grew beards so that he felt less uncomfortable with the face furniture his character wore in the movie.

Chips Moman, with whom Elvis recorded at American Studio in Memphis in 1969, felt that Elvis was much more productive when his pals were kept out of the studio. When they were around, Elvis felt obligated to act up, perform and keep them amused. Elvis was also loathe to hear constructive criticism if any of his guys were around; on his own, however, he was all ears. During a jam on "Stranger In My Own Home Town," Elvis jokingly inserted made-up lyrics about going back to driving his truck again, followed by the ad lib "Old Joe, Charlie and Richard will starve to death / And Sonny will be in the Pen."

In May 1969, Elvis vacationed in Hawaii with Priscilla and Lisa Marie, plus the Espositos, the Fikes, the Gambills and Charlie Hodge.

When Elvis returned to live performing in Vegas in the summer of 1969, a new party season began for the entourage. Once more, there was a steady supply of attractive and available women. Musician Glen D. Hardin described the scene as a "silly boys' club. . . . Just one big party."

In 1970, the Colonel made another attempt to cut down the size of the entourage traveling with Elvis for his performance at the Texas Livestock Show, citing the need to maintain privacy. Elvis traveled to Houston with Vernon, Joe Esposito, Charlie Hodge, Gee Gee Gambill, Cliff Gleaves and Red and Sonny West.

With renewed acclaim, renewed self-confidence and a new source of income, Elvis' generosity reached new heights. Car dealers across Memphis and Los Angeles benefited as Elvis gave out cars to entourage members and friends who proved their loyalty. Elvis was not offended when entourage members sold the cars that he gave them; it was his way of giving them a bonus.

A reunion of sorts took place for all the wrong reasons in Las Vegas at the end of the summer in 1970, when Elvis called in old pals Red West and Jerry Schilling (and karate expert Ed Parker) to supplement his usual security detail and avert an assassination threat. As a token of his thanks, Elvis commissioned a dozen 14-karat gold name bracelets with the nickname of each of his pals engraved on the inside. Elvis also had the entourage guys' names engraved on a Tree of Life necklace.

When Elvis hit the road on tour in September 1970, he traveled with Joe Esposito (foreman), Richard Davis (wardrobe), Lamar Fike (lighting), Charlie Hodge (stage manager/assistant), and Dr. Nichopoulos serving as tour doctor. Former policeman Dick Grob joined the entourage to help with security; his police contacts came in handy for hiring extra security to work alongside regular bodyguards Red and Sonny West.

Elvis went with Jerry Schilling and Sonny West on his December 1970 jaunt to Washington to meet President Nixon and get himself a Federal Bureau of Narcotics and Dangerous Drugs badge for Christmas. He introduced the guys to the President and made sure that Nixon gave them White House mementos.

In May 1971, Elvis traveled to Las Vegas for R&R with Joe Esposito, Charlie Hodge, Red West, James Caughley and Mike Keaton. The first time that Elvis stayed at his new LA home on Monovale Drive was with Priscilla, Lisa Marie, Sonny and Judy West, and Charlie Hodge.

When Elvis flew to Washington in December 1971 for a tryst with Joyce Bova, he traveled (under the alias Jon Burrows) with Charlie Hodge, Sonny West and James Caughley.

By the early Seventies, some members of the entourage were earning close to $500 a week, and spending increasing amounts of time away from home and their families. However, Lamar Fike told author Alanna Nash that when he first went on to the payroll, he was earning $37.50 a week; not long before Elvis died, he was earning no more than $365 a week.

Not just Elvis' marriage but the marriages of several entourage members suffered. Joe Esposito, Jerry Schilling and Sonny West all divorced in the early Seventies. Elvis tried to save these marriages by giving his entourage members a bonus for a conjugal vacation on which to patch things up.

Elvis ruled over his entourage using a variety of strategies. If he thought things were getting out of hand, he might publicly berate one of the guys, in the knowledge that this rebuke would have an effect on them all. The ultimate punishment was being fired, though anybody who had been with Elvis for a while knew that after a cooling off period, the former entourage member was almost always offered back his job.

Elvis' November 1972 trip to perform in Hawaii turned into a one week business/pleasure trip, surrounded by his full-strength entourage of the time. As well as Lisa Marie, for the first time he traveled with girlfriend Linda Thompson. He also took out the three Stanley boys, James Caughley, Joe Esposito, Dick Grob, Gee Gee Gambill, Charlie Hodge, Dr. Nichopoulos and the Wests.

Elvis felt more under threat after the 1970 assassination scare. Increasingly reliant on drugs, he entered a period of unpredictable and delusional behavior. After Priscilla left him, he was convinced that her lover Mike Stone had hired some men to do him harm, and wanted to get Stone before Stone got him. Members of the entourage coped with these deeper, darker moments by waiting out his delusional moods. However, it was not easy for Elvis' most trusted aides to know when too much was too much and take a stand against his excess.

Soon after meeting Linda Thompson, Elvis added her brother Sam to his security detail. As the Stanley boys came of age, they too began to travel with Elvis and help him at Graceland. Their responsibilities included taking turns to sleep in the room next to Elvis', to make sure that nothing untoward happened during the night if he woke up. Older members of the entourage have since suggested that Elvis brought the Stanley boys into his inner circle because they were a useful conduit for getting hold of prescription drugs.

At Del Webb's Sahara Tahoe for seventeen days in May 1973, Elvis' entourage included the Wests, Jerry Schilling, Lamar Fike, Dick Grob, and karate

Elvis in Atlanta June 30, 1975.

champs Ed Parker and Dave Hebler. The next time he played Tahoe, he went with Joe Esposito, Sonny West, Charlie Hodge, Lamar Fike, Jerry Schilling, David and Ricky Stanley, and Al Strada, who had originally worked as a security guard at Elvis' LA home. For the next few years, these men accompanied him on his increasingly frequent tours around the States, for the most part with long-term girlfriend Linda Thompson.

Elvis took seventeen people with him to Vail, Colorado, for a winter vacation in January 1976. Tensions simmered over the two weeks. Much of the problem was that Elvis' mood swings were becoming increasingly extreme and unpredictable. On that vacation there were rows among entourage guys, and the atmosphere soured considerably. After the trip, Jerry Schilling handed in his notice.

In the final years, the highest paid member of the entourage was Joe Esposito, who was on a thousand dollars a week. All of the guys' salaries went through Vernon, and Vernon was notorious for hating to see money go out the door. By this time the gang reformed to go out on tour, but between engagements, when Elvis was in Memphis, they tended to return to their own lives.

When Elvis was home in 1976 and 1977, rather than spend time with the coterie of men and women he had surrounded himself with for two decades, he kept himself to himself. The exceptions were his girlfriend of the moment, and cousin Billy Smith and his wife Jo. Long-time entourage members who were still around, such as Red and Sonny West, more and more often found themselves at loggerheads with Elvis. Billy Smith remembers that Elvis, towards the end, preferred not to see old-timers Marty Lacker and Lamar Fike because they would sometimes challenge him about what he was doing to himself. Red and Sonny were fired by Vernon in July 1976, along with karate instructor Dave Hebler. Elvis then

fell out with Joe Esposito and his doctor of the previous ten years, George Nichopoulos, over a business venture to build a chain of racquetball courts across the country using the Presley name.

Unpopular as the tell-all book written by Red and Sonny West made them with fans, they claimed at the time that they were fired because they were the only guys in the entourage who had the courage to challenge Elvis about his drug abuse.

The last weeks he was alive, Elvis further reduced the number of people he had around him but still had time for Joe Esposito, George Klein, Jerry Schilling, Alan Fortas and Billy Smith. He spoke of his plans to live without an entourage, and told Larry Geller and Charlie Hodge that he'd had enough of "the Memphis Mafia scene."

Practically every one of Elvis' entourage members have written at length about their experiences with Elvis, in personal memoirs or in books about the Memphis Mafia. Many have collaborated with documentaries and guested at commemorative and fan events. Most of the Memphis-based members of Elvis' former entourage still stay in touch.

ELVIS SAID IN 1962: "They're pretty smart boys, and they've learned a lot just being around this industry, and traveling."

ELVIS SAID IN 1976: "There was friction created in the group. The vibes so bad, people were scared to move . . ."

JOE ESPOSITO: "We were like the secret service for Elvis."

LAMAR FIKE: "We were like a buffer zone around him."

JERRY SCHILLING: "Basically, the group was a reflection of Elvis."

PRISCILLA: "It was quite obvious that the boys picked up on Elvis' every mood."

PETER GURALNICK: "For all of his ability to sort of play the paterfamilias to this group of guys, to show a kind of confidence in terms of dealing with everyone else's problems, I think there was a lurking insecurity in all of his dealings that came out again and again."

JOE ESPOSITO, ABOUT WORKING WITH ELVIS, EARLY 70s: "It was like just one big happy family, working together and playing together."

BILLY SMITH: "You can't put that many guys together and have them get along 100% of the time. But we had what we called 'burning sessions'. We would slur one another pretty heavy."

DOTTY AYERS: "When we were around Elvis, everything was focused on him: how he felt, what he wanted to do, when he wanted to go to bed, when he wanted to get out, if he was in a good mood, if he was in a bad mood. Elvis was the total center of attention."

LARRY GELLER: "They surrounded and protected Elvis; they thought in terms of 'us' and 'them'. They seemed consumed by a mild case of bunker mentality."

JERRY SCHILLING: "Elvis didn't hire somebody because of their ability in a certain field . . . he hired people out of trust and friendship, and then it was up to you."

BILLY SMITH: "When we were with Elvis, the pressures of the outside world were taken away. We thought, 'Nothing can happen to him. If we're with him, we're safe.' .He had that kind of power over us."

Tony Brown: "It was an abusive relationship between Elvis and those guys, unhealthy, and only in hindsight can we see it. But you know, that happens with a lot of big celebrities: it's easy to feel invincible when you're totally surrounded with yes-men."

JERRY SCHILLING: "I always felt that as far as the management were concerned, the dumber you were the longer you lasted around Elvis."

LAMAR FIKE: "Elvis was a real gossipmonger. And he was two-faced, especially about other guys in the group. He put them down real bad. He put down the Colonel real bad, too."

LOWELL HAYS: "Elvis was shielded from the world. We treated him like a little god. We just did, you know."

PETER GURALNICK: "In the closed world in which they lived, the same stories were passed back and forth until they became common property, taking on the status of a larger myth whose literal origins were no longer relevant."

DAVID STANLEY: "There was a thing in Elvis' entourage that I call the 'loyalty factor'. You couldn't be around Elvis unless you are loyal."

ALAN FORTAS: "We felt his entourage was a sacred group, and that nobody in it would ever talk about his private life, especially to the press."

BILLY SMITH: "Vernon and Colonel tried to poison him about us. The guys were just a bunch of leeches, or hangers-on, in their opinion. And Elvis listened to all this bullshit from both sides, and at some time or another, he had to think that maybe that was true."

EPs

Though marginal today, in the Fifties EPs regularly outsold LPs, hence RCA's strategy of releasing Elvis material on multiple EPs in preference (or parallel) to LPs. EPs were so important that between 1957 and 1960 they had their own chart, on which Elvis EP *Loving You, Vol. 1* was the first ever #1. Some of Elvis' EP-released songs made it into the *Billboard* singles chart after being released as EPs.

The last Elvis EP release was attached to the movie *Easy Come, Easy Go*.

ELVIS EPS (WITH CATALOGUE NUMBERS):

1956
EPA 747	Elvis Presley
EPB 1254	Elvis Presley (double)
EPA 821	Heartbreak Hotel
EPA 830	Elvis Presley
EPA 940	The Real Elvis
EPA 965	Any Way You Want Me
EPA 992	Elvis Vol. 1
EPA 4006	Love Me Tender
EPA 993	Elvis Vol. 2

1957
EPA 994	Strictly Elvis
EPA 4054	Peace In The Valley
EPA 1 1515	Loving You
EPA 2 1515	Loving You
EPA 4041	Just For You
EPA 4108	Elvis Sings Christmas Songs
EPA 4114	Jailhouse Rock

1958
EPA 4319	King Creole Vol. 1
EPA 4321	King Creole Vol. 2
EPA 4340	Christmas With Elvis
EPA 4325	Elvis Sails

1959
| EPA 5088 | A Touch Of Gold Vol. 1 |
| EPA 5101 | A Touch Of Gold Vol. 2 |

1960
| EPA 5141 | A Touch Of Gold Vol. 3 |

1961
| LPC 128 | Elvis By Request / Flaming Star |

1962
| EPA 4368 | Follow That Dream |
| EPA 4371 | Kid Galahad |

1964
| EPA 4382 | Viva Las Vegas |

1965
| EPA 4383 | Tickle Me |

1967
| EPA 4387 | Easy Come, Easy Go |

In 1982, RCA released a collection of 11 EPs in a UK-only boxed set, including previously unreleased material, under the name *The EP Collection, Volume 2.*

GOLD AND PLATINUM EPS (16)

Elvis Presley (w. Blue Suede Shoes) - Gold
Heartbreak Hotel - Gold
Elvis Presley (w. Shake, Rattle & Roll) - Gold
The Real Elvis - Platinum
Elvis, Vol. 1 - Platinum x2
Love Me Tender - Platinum
Elvis, Vol. 2 - Gold
Peace in the Valley - Platinum
Loving You, Vol. 1 - Gold
Loving You, Vol. 2 - Platinum
Jailhouse Rock - Platinum x2
Elvis Sings Christmas Songs - Platinum
King Creole, Vol. 1 - Platinum
King Creole, Vol. 2 - Platinum
Follow That Dream - Platinum
Kid Galahad - Gold

EPSTEIN, BRIAN
(1934-1967)

One of very few pop music manager to rival the Colonel's fame in the Sixties, Epstein was with The Beatles when they visited Elvis in 1965. He spent much of the evening in a side room at Elvis' Bel Air home playing roulette with the Colonel.

Epstein offered to manage The Beatles the first time he saw them perform at The Cavern in their home town of Liverpool in 1961, and piloted them to worldwide success.

Rumors circulated in the press in early 1966 that the Beatles manager was considering adding Elvis to his roster of artists. After Epstein's premature death from an overdose of prescriptions drugs, The Beatles reputedly approached Colonel Parker to take over their management; the Colonel is said to have declined because Elvis would always be his #1 interest (or in another version of the story, the Colonel agreed but told the lads from Liverpool that Elvis would be his top priority).

ESPOSITO, JOANIE
(B. 1941)

Joanie Roberts was a dancer in Las Vegas when she met Joe Esposito in the early Sixties. She had married Joe by the time Priscilla came to live with Elvis, and became an important friend to her.

When Priscilla was preparing for her wedding, Joanie was her advisor and matron of honor.

Joanie and her two daughters Debbie and Cindy accompanied Priscilla when she traveled from Memphis to LA with three-week old Lisa Marie to join Elvis where he was working on *Live a Little, Love a Little.*

Priscilla's one true confidante according to Peter Guralnick, Priscilla counted on Joanie's help and discretion when she embarked on an affair with karate expert Mike Stone. Joanie's marriage to Joe broke up around the same time as Priscilla and Elvis'.

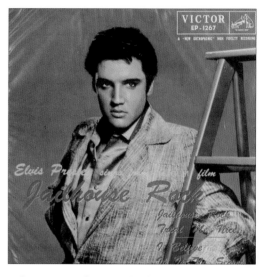

Joanie returned to Graceland to help out at Elvis' funeral. Priscilla sent Lisa Marie off to camp that summer with Joanie and Joe's kids.

ESPOSITO, JOE
(B. 1938)

Chicago-born accountant Joe Esposito became a regular member of Elvis' gang in Germany. Both of them were stationed at Ray Barracks, where Esposito was working as a finance clerk. Esposito met Elvis through Camp photographer, West Daniels, who asked Joe to come and make up the numbers at a weekend football match with Elvis. From that moment on, "Diamond Joe" Esposito, as Elvis called him because of the penchant he later developed for diamond jewelry (or "Espo" if he was in a rush, or sometimes "Lion," his karate name), became a key member of Elvis' entourage.

On Army leave in Paris, Elvis was particularly struck when after going out on the town, Esposito swept up all the receipts and told Elvis he could deduct them against income tax—something nobody in his entourage had done before.

Back in the States in 1960, Esposito was happy to go and work for Elvis. He quickly took on the unofficial role of "foreman," making sure that the gang did not get too far out of line. Vernon, who had taken over the running of Elvis' household finances, relied on Joe to keep on picking up receipts and keep a running total of outgoings.

Joe's first true taste of the Elvis experience was when he accompanied Elvis down to Miami Beach for the Frank Sinatra TV show welcoming Elvis home. During Elvis' hard-partying years in the early Sixties, Esposito was in the thick of the action. He walked his way onto at least eight Elvis movies, and is credited as a technical advisor on several more.

In the early Sixties, Joe Esposito lived in the garage apartment at Graceland when he was in Memphis.

Elvis fired Esposito in August 1964 after he found out that he was liaising with the Colonel behind his back. Biographers have written that Elvis considered Esposito's reports to the Colonel about his 'mental and emotional state' as a breach of all-important trust and loyalty. In her biography of the Colonel, Alanna Nash states that Esposito was Parker's "chief spy" in the entourage.

Esposito returned to the fold as "co-foreman" with Marty Lacker in March 1965, when Elvis was working on *Harum Scarum* in LA. In March 1967 the Colonel restored Esposito to the foreman's role after accusing Lacker of not doing enough to get Elvis to Hollywood to fulfill his contractual commitments. Joe and Marty Lacker were best men at Elvis' wedding to Priscilla two months later. By this time, Joe and Elvis knew each other so well that they would finish off one another's jokes.

Esposito and his wife Joanie vacationed with Elvis, Priscilla, Lisa Marie and others in the entourage when they went to Aspen and Hawaii in 1969. That year he also helped Elvis during preparations for his inaugural residency at the International Hotel in Las Vegas. Joe was the natural choice as road manager when Elvis returned to touring.

In addition to various gifts of cars over the years, for Christmas 1970 Elvis bought Joe a house in West LA.

Joe relocated to California on a full-time basis in the mid-Seventies, though he continued touring with Elvis. Elvis considered firing Joe in the summer of 1976 over a business venture that went sour. Elvis was happy to lend his name to a chain of racquetball courts, but then pulled out of the deal when he found out that he was expected to sink money into the venture too. They soon reconciled after this misunderstanding; Joe continued as Elvis' road manager right through to his final tour in the summer of 1977.

Joe was one of the first people into Elvis' bathroom when he was found there unconscious on August 16, 1977. Joe placed the call to the emergency services, and after Elvis was declared dead, took over the practicalities of arranging and coordinating Elvis' funeral. He was one of Elvis' pallbearers.

After Elvis, Joe worked as a tour manager for top artists such as Michael Jackson, John Denver, Wayne Newton and the Bee Gees.

As well as attending Elvis commemorative events, Esposito has appeared in a number of Elvis documentaries and served as a consultant on others. In 2002 he released his own DVD about his time with Elvis, *Elvis—His Best Friend Remembers*.

Books:

Good Rockin' Tonight: Twenty Years on the Road and on the Town With Elvis, by Joe Esposito and Elena Oumano, Simon and Shuster, 1994.

Elvis—Intimate and Rare: Memories and Photos from the Personal Collection of Joe Esposito, Elvis International Forum Books, 1997.

Remember Elvis, by Joe Esposito, published by TCB JOE publishing, 2006.

Elvis Straight Up, by Joe Esposito and Joe Russo, Steamroller Publishing, 2007.

ESSENTIAL ELVIS PRESLEY, THE

A 2007 BMG 2-CD release of remastered Elvis tracks.

TRACK LISTING:
DISC 1
1. That's All Right (Mama)
2. Baby, Let's Play House
3. Mystery Train
4. Heartbreak Hotel
5. I Was the One
6. Blue Suede Shoes
7. Hound Dog
8. Don't Be Cruel
9. Love Me Tender
10. All Shook Up
11. (There'll Be) Peace in the Valley (For Me)
12. Jailhouse Rock
13. Trouble
14. Fever
15. It's Now Or Never
16. Reconsider Baby
17. Are You Lonesome Tonight?
18. Little Sister
19. Follow That Dream
20. Can't Help Falling In Love
DISC 2:
1. Return to Sender
2. (You're The) Devil In Disguise
3. Bossa Nova Baby
4. Viva Las Vegas
5. Big Boss Man
6. A Little Less Conversation

7. If I Can Dream
8. Memories
9. In The Ghetto
10. Suspicious Minds
11. Don't Cry, Daddy
12. Kentucky Rain
13. Polk Salad Annie
14. Wonder Of You
15. I Just Can't Help Believin'
16. Burning Love
17. Always On My Mind
18. Steamroller Blues
19. Hurt
20. Moody Blue

ESSENTIAL ELVIS VOLS. 1-6

RCA brought out these themed Elvis albums from 1988 to 2000. Volumes include alternate takes, previously-unreleased material, top Elvis hits and between-takes banter. The series initially launched on the European market in late 1986.

TRACK LISTINGS (CD VERSIONS, INCLUDING EXTRAS):

VOL. 1—THE FIRST MOVIES (1988)
1. Love Me Tender
2. Let Me
3. Poor Boy
4. We're Gonna Move
5. Loving You
6. Party
7. Hot Dog
8. Teddy Bear
9. Loving You
10. Mean Woman Blues (alternate film version)
11. Got A Lot O' Livin' To Do
12. Loving You
13. Party
14. Lonesome Cowboy
15. Jailhouse Rock
16. Treat Me Nice
17. Young And Beautiful
18. Don't Leave Me Now
19. I Want To Be Free
20. (You're So Square) Baby I Don't Care
21. Jailhouse Rock
22. Got A Lot O' Livin' To Do
23. Loving You
24. Mean Woman Blues
25. Loving You
26. Treat Me Nice
27. Love Me Tender

VOL. 2—STEREO '57 (1989)
1. I Beg Of You
2. Is It So Strange
3. Have I Told You Lately That I Love You
4. It Is No Secret (What God Can Do)
5. Blueberry Hill
6. Mean Woman Blues
7. (There'll Be) Peace In The Valley
8. Have I Told You Lately That I Love You
9. Blueberry Hill
10. That's When Your Heartaches Begin
11. Is It So Strange
12. I Beg Of You
13. There'll Be Peace In The Valley
14. Have I Told You Lately That I Love You
15. I Beg Of You
16. I Believe
17. Tell Me Why
18. Got A Lot O' Livin' To Do
19. All Shook Up
20. Take My Hand, Precious Lord

VOL. 3—HITS LIKE NEVER BEFORE (1991)
1. King Creole
2. I Got Stung
3. (Now And Then There's) A Fool Such As I
4. Wear My Ring Around Your Neck
5. Your Cheatin' Heart
6. Ain't That Loving You Baby

7. Doncha' Think It's Time
8. I Need Your Love Tonight
9. Lover Doll (undubbed)
10. As Long As I Have You
11. Danny
12. King Creole
13. Crawfish (unedited)
14. A Big Hunk O' Love
15. Ain't That Loving You Baby
16. I Got Stung
17. Your Cheatin' Heart
18. Wear My Ring Around Your Neck
19. Steadfast, Loyal And True
20. I Need Your Love Tonight
21. Doncha' Think It's Time
22. I Got Stung
23. King Creole
24. As Long As I Have You

VOL. 4—A HUNDRED YEARS FROM NOW (1996)
1. I Didn't Make It On Playing Guitar
2. I Washed My Hands In Muddy Water (undubbed)
3. Little Cabin On The Hill
4. A Hundred Years From Now
5. I've Lost You
6. Got My Mojo Working / Keep Your Hands Off Of It (unedited)
7. You Don't Have To Say You Love Me
8. It Ain't No Big Thing (But It's Growing)
9. Cindy, Cindy
10. Faded Love (country version)
11. The Fool
12. Rags To Riches
13. Just Pretend
14. If I Were You
15. Faded Love
16. Where Did They Go Lord
17. It's Only Love
18. Until It's Time For You To Go
19. Patch It Up
20. Whole Lotta Shakin' Goin' On (unedited)
21. Bridge Over Troubled Water
22. The Lord's Prayer

VOL. 5— RHYTHM AND COUNTRY (1998)
1. I Got A Feelin' In My Body
2. Loving Arms
3. I've Got A Thing About You Baby
4. She Wears My Ring
5. You Asked Me To
6. There's A Honky Tonk Angel
7. Good Time Charlie's Got The Blues
8. Find Out What's Happening
9. For Ol' Times Sake
10. If You Don't Come Back
11. Promised Land
12. Thinking About You
13. Three Corn Patches
14. Girl Of Mine
15. Your Love's Been A Long Time Coming
16. Spanish Eyes
17. Talk About The Good Times
18. If That Isn't Love

VOL. 6—SUCH A NIGHT (2000)
1. Such A Night
2. Make Me Know It
3. Stuck On You
4. Fever
5. The Girl Of My Best Friend
6. Surrender
7. I Believe In The Man In The Sky
8. Give Me The Right
9. I'm Comin' Home
10. There's Always Me
11. Little Sister
12. I Met Her Today
13. Gonna Get Back Home Somehow
14. Night Rider
15. (Such An) Easy Question
16. Please Don't Drag That String Around
17. Memphis Tennessee
18. It Hurts Me

ESTATE, THE

Elvis was so generous in life that in death he left his heirs Vernon, Minnie Mae and Lisa Maria Presley only a tiny fraction of the money earned in his lifetime. Before he died, Vernon named Priscilla as executor to Elvis' Estate, with public accountant Joe Hanks and the Memphis National Bank of Commerce appointed co-executors. The year that Vernon died, 1979, Estate income amounted to $1.2 million (Graceland alone was costing around a half- million dollars per year in maintenance and taxes), of which the Colonel was due 50%. Most of this income was from licensing deals that the Colonel made after Elvis' death in a deal with Factors Etc. Inc., a company run by Harry Geissler, known at the time as "King of the Merchandisers." Very little money was coming in from Elvis' immense back catalogue because the Colonel had ill-advisedly sold it off to RCA in the early Seventies.

Attorney Blanchard E. Tual was appointed to investigate the propriety of the Colonel's management soon afterwards. His preliminary finding was that the terms of the Colonel's management contract was "beyond all reasonable bounds of industry standards" — which were between 15% and 25%. All earnings were paid to the executors rather than to Parker while the attorney conducted a second, more in-depth investigation. By this time, the Estate was on the brink of bankruptcy after the IRS made demands for almost $15 million in taxes on Graceland and royalties.

The case against the Colonel was settled out of Court. The Colonel was disqualified from any earnings for a five-year period. As part of the settlement, he was also enjoined to hand over his collection of Elvis audio recordings and visual images.

In the early Eighties, Elvis Presley Enterprises (EPE) set about putting the Elvis Estate back on a stable financial footing, under the guidance of businessman Jack Soden. At that time, many Elvis trademarks were unregistered and the vast majority of merchandise that spontaneously hit the market in the years after Elvis' death was unlicensed and unregulated. Slowly but surely, EPE wrested back control over Elvis' image and intellectual property, in the process forcing major changes in US copyright and trademark legislation. Fans were sometimes in the firing line. For example, Elvis fans who set up a memorial benefit

foundation in Elvis' name to raise funds for hospitals and healthcare were forced to shut down operations when the Estate told them that they would have to pay a fee to use the Elvis name.

The Estate's strategy included purchasing the properties on the opposite side of Elvis Presley Boulevard and bringing what had been unlicensed merchandising and memorabilia operations under Elvis Presley Enterprise control. In 1999, EPE purchased and redeveloped what became the "Elvis Presley's Heartbreak Hotel."

Priscilla ran the estate from Elvis' death. Her income was rumored to be between 2.5% and 5% of the Estate's earnings—which by the early 2000s was estimated at around $50 million per annum.

The Estate remains in Lisa Marie's name following the 2005 purchase of Elvis Presley Enterprises by businessman Robert Sillerman's CKX company.

LAMAR FIKE: "The estate does very, very well, 'cause it's a well-oiled machine."

Book:
Elvis: The Inventory of the Estate of Elvis Presley, edited by Richard Singer, Arjay Enterprises, 1996.

EVANS, MARILYN
(B. 1937)

A girlfriend of Elvis' in late 1956 after they met in Las Vegas, showgirl Marilyn was on Elvis' arm when he walked into Sun Studio in Memphis to say hi to old friends and ended up jamming for hours with fellow members of the world's most famous band that never was, the "Million Dollar Quartet."

"EVENING PRAYER, AN"

Elvis recorded a soulful version of this traditional hymn, a musical rendition of Psalm 19:12-13

credited to C.M. Battersby and Charles Gabriel (and a classic Mahalia Jackson track), on May 18, 1971 in Nashville. It first came out on the *He Touched Me* album, and later appeared on *He Walks Beside Me* and compilations *Amazing Grace, Peace In The Valley, Elvis: My Christmas #1, Christmas Peace, Elvis Inspirational* and the 2007 *Ultimate Gospel* release. Alternate versions are on FTD releases *Easter Special* and *I Sing All Kinds.*

"EVERYBODY COME ABOARD"

A Bill Giant / Bernie Baum / Florence Kaye soundtrack song for the finale of *Frankie and Johnny* that Elvis laid down in the wee hours at Radio Recorders in Hollywood on May 14, 1965.

The *Double Features* and FTD *Frankie And Johnny* releases are the only place to find the song since the original LP release—multiple alternates are on the FTD CD package.

"EVERYBODY LOVES SOMEBODY"

Elvis included a few lines of this song when Dean Martin was in the audience at a winter 1970 Las Vegas show. The occasion was immortalized on disc in *On Stage,* and on bootleg *True Love Travels on a Gravel Road.* Written by Irving Taylor and Ken Lane in 1948, the song had been a minor hit for Frank Sinatra before Dean Martin knocked The Beatles' "A Hard Day's Night" off the #1 spot in 1964 with it; he went on to use it as the theme song to his TV show.

"EYES OF TEXAS, THE"

Elvis recorded this song written by John Sinclair in a medley with "The Yellow Rose of Texas" for *Viva Las Vegas* on July 10, 1963, during a Radio Recorders session. It was subsequently released on early film compilation *Singer Presents Elvis Singing Flaming Star and Others.* The song later featured on *Double Dynamite,* and on the *Viva Las Vegas Double Features* and FTD releases.

Elvis sang a quick burst of the song sometimes when touring in Texas in the Seventies (it's on 2006 FTD release *Southern Nights*).

F

FABARES, SHELLEY
(B. MICHELE FABARES, 1944)

An actress with a career spanning five decades on screens great and small, Fabares worked with Elvis on three movies, *Girl Happy*, *Spinout* and *Clambake*. Her million-selling 1962 #1 hit "Johnny Angel" was knocked off top spot by Elvis' single "Good Luck Charm." Elvis is said to have pursued her mercilessly on set, all to no avail as she was in love with and faithful to future husband Lou Adler. However, in other tales she and he were as fond off-screen as they appeared on. Elvis later said Fabares was his favorite leading lady to work with.

Before working with Elvis, Fabares was best known for her TV work on "The Donna Reed Show." She has continued working through into the 2000s, and earned Emmy nominations for her work on "Coach."

FADAL, EDDIE

Eddie Fadal was working as a DJ in Waco, Texas when Elvis stopped by to promote a record in April 1956. They hit it off immediately, and Fadal traveled on tour with Elvis when he was passing through the state that year. When Fadal read in the papers that Elvis was being sent to Fort Hood for his basic Army training, he went to the base, tracked down Elvis and told him that he'd be welcome to come to his family home (located at 2807 Lasker) on weekends for home cooking. This Elvis did, driving 45 miles and bringing along girlfriend Anita Wood. Businessman Fadal built on a whole extra room to the house, decorated it in pink and black, put in a piano and gave Elvis a key. After Elvis' folks moved down to Killeen to be closer to their boy, they would all come round for meals, cooked up by Gladys and LaNelle Fadal.

Fadal taped some of the sing-songing that went on that summer—it came out on bootleg album *Forever Young, Forever Beautiful* the year after Elvis died. Some of these tracks made it onto official BMG release *The Home Recordings* many years later.

Eddie flew to Memphis for Gladys's funeral in August 1958, and stayed at Graceland for a month. Fadal remained friends with Elvis and his family for the duration, and went to see Elvis perform years later in Las Vegas. Fadal died in 1994.

His daughter Janice was for some time married to Elvis entourage member Lamar Fike.

Eddie's children Janice and Dana Fadal run the online Eddie Fadal Elvis Presley Museum.

Book:
Our Memories of Elvis, by Sean Shaver, Al Wertheimer and Eddie Fadal, Timur Publishing, 1984.

Video/DVD:
Lost Elvis Home Movies (1999)

"FADED LOVE"

A rock-propelled version of Bob Wills's 1950 country-and-western classic—written by Bob and John Wills—that Elvis recorded at Studio B in Nashville on June 7, 1970. An edited-down version was initially released on *Elvis Country*. The full version came out on Seventies compendium *Walk A Mile In My Shoes*, since when the song has been released on *The Country Side of Elvis*.

Two alternate takes appeared on *Essential Elvis Vol. 4* in 1996; Felton Jarvis also remixed the song in 1980 for his *Guitar Man* album (also on FTD release *Too Much Monkey Business*).

Elvis occasionally sang the song live in 1973—a version from this period is on FTD disc *Takin' Tahoe Tonight* as well as on bootlegs.

"FAIR IS MOVING ON, THE"

The B-side to "Clean Up Your Own Backyard," released in June 1969, was a song by British songwriting duo Guy Fletcher and Doug Flett that Elvis recorded at American Studio on February 21, 1969. It was released soon after on *From Memphis to Vegas / From Vegas to Memphis*, followed a year later by *Back in Memphis*. Since then, it has warranted release on *The Memphis Record*, *From Nashville To Memphis*, *Suspicious Minds: The Memphis 1969 Anthology* and the 2000 CD re-release of *From Elvis In Memphis*.

"FAIRYTALE"

Elvis recorded this country-style story of love lost by the Pointer Sisters, written by sisters Anita and Bonnie—among other achievements, the first all-women Afro-American group to play the Grand Ole Opry—at Sheila Ryan's suggestion on March 10, 1975 at the RCA Hollywood Studios.

It first came out as an album track on *Today*, followed in the fullness of time by a release on *The Country Side of Elvis* too.

An alternate studios takes was released in 1996 on *Great Country Songs*; another alternate from the studio that day is on the 2005 FTD release of *Today*.

A live version appeared immediately after Elvis' death on *Elvis in Concert*—Elvis sang the song live scores of times from 1975 on. Live versions are on bootlegs and FTD releases *New Year's Eve*, *Big Boss Man*, *Dixieland Rocks* and *Southern Nights*—Elvis often presented it as "the story of my life"; it's also on FTD concert discs *Unchained Melody* and *Spring Tours '77*.

FAME

Contrary to the received wisdom that Elvis owed his step up to national fame to Colonel Parker, many Elvis fans and scholars are convinced that he was going to be huge regardless of who managed him. There is little doubt, however, that Parker's shrewd and self-interested management of Elvis' career over the long term, including what later seemed like missteps—tying Elvis down to years of lucrative but increasingly banal and outdated movies; alienating songwriters who could provide decent material in favor of higher publishing royalties—ultimately led to Elvis' fame eclipsing that of any other single performer in the modern age.

It all started the night that DJ Dewey Phillips played Elvis' first single "That's All Right (Mama)" at Memphis radio station WHBQ. The station switchboard became jammed with callers who wanted to hear the song over and over again. Elvis went down to the station for an interview, and the boy who didn't sound like nobody became an instant Memphis celebrity. His fame spread out in concentric rings around the radio stations that played his music, consolidated by his high energy shows and word of mouth.

Music publisher Buddy Killen recalls, "Elvis would be nothing, totally unknown, and go into a city and perform, and he would become an instant star before he even left town. It was unreal."

In April 1956, when he had already appeared on national TV and signed with Paramount to make movies, Elvis demonstrated his down-to-earth realism about the fickleness of fame, telling a reporter it had all "happened so fast, I'm scared. You know, I could go out like a light, just like I came on."

By the end of that year, Elvismania had swept the nation and Elvis had earned enough money to buy all the cars and clothes he or his parents could want. He had moved his family to a house that a year earlier he could only have walked past and admired. And he had begun to acquire the entourage that would protect him from riots and violence, but also insulate him from having much if any experience of a normal life.

Elvis' wholehearted openness to and connection with his fans—a rarity then as it is now—was one way that he stayed in touch with his pre-fame life. He fervently believed that his side of the bargain with fame was to be there for his fans, without whom none of this would have happened.

There were times when Elvis felt uncomfortable with the distance between his private self and the public persona he was expected to adopt—something he mentioned at his 1972 press conference at Madison Square Garden, when he famously said, "The image is one thing, the human being is another, you know. It's very hard to live up to an image."

During Easter 1957 Elvis told Rev. Hamill of the Assembly of God church: "I have got more money than I can ever spend. I have thousands of fans out there, and I have a lot of people who call themselves my friends, but I am miserable. I'm doing what you taught me not to do, and I'm not doing the things you taught me to do."

When Gladys died in the summer of 1958, a grief-stricken Elvis told close friends that he wished he could turn his back on his public life once and for all, but felt bound to continue because too many people depended on him for their livelihoods.

Elvis never took it for granted that his fame was solid enough to survive two years out of the limelight when he was in the Army. But if he thought that out in Germany he would be able to lead a more normal life, he had another thing coming. Fellow-soldiers who had been serving for the previous two years might have been unaware that he was the hottest young performer the music industry had ever seen, but the local populace knew all about him. Just like when he was back home, Elvis regularly went to the gate to meet his fans and sign autographs. Just like back home, going out to a restaurant was a recipe for trouble. One day, on the way back to base after maneuvers, the soldiers Elvis was riding with decided to stop for sandwiches, ignoring Elvis' warning that he usually got into trouble it if was out in public. When they returned to their jeeps a few minutes later they were swamped by a crowd a hundred-strong who would not disperse until Elvis dispensed autographs.

Whatever fears he had that his career might not survive the Army were dispelled on his return to America. In 1960 Elvis starred in a huge TV Special with Frank Sinatra, scored three number one singles, released an album and made three movies.

Partly out of professional interest, partly out of curiosity at how they had dealt with fame, Elvis was fascinated by famous singing stars of the past such as Enrico Caruso.

Larry Geller describes Elvis' life as either "living in Memphis in seclusion or living in Beverly Hills in seclusion," with the only spontaneity and freedom on road trips between the two. It did not surprise Geller that Elvis fervently sought some kind of a meaning to his extraordinary life through an interest in spirituality and religion.

Other celebrities noted how much of his freedom Elvis had given up to fame. Muhammad Ali, who he met in 1973, later said, "I felt sorry for him because he didn't enjoy life the way he should. He stayed indoors all the time. I told him he should go out and see people." Entourage member Sonny West disagrees with this characterization of Elvis, claiming that he loved being recognized and enjoyed the thrill and buzz that he created wherever he went.

One of the reasons why Elvis lived a nocturnal life was that the day offered no cloak of anonymity. Larry Geller has stated that in many ways, Elvis' life was no more psychologically, socially or artistically challenging than that of a factory worker.

Fame brought dangers to those who shared Elvis' life. His bodyguards were prepared to take a bullet for their friend and employer. Priscilla writes in her memoir that she learned to "scout out the exits" when she was out in public with Elvis, in case things turned ugly.

Surrounded by a paid entourage and used to always getting his way in his personal sphere, Elvis seldom spent time with equals or with people who might contradict and challenge him. When somebody managed to break through and give Elvis constructive criticism, the result was often exceptional. Elvis' 1968 NBC TV Special and his memorable early 1969 recording sessions at American Studio happened because TV producer Steve Binder and record producer Chips Moman got Elvis on his own and challenged him to move in a new artistic direction.

Steve Binder once attempted to show Elvis that he could have a semblance of a normal life, taking him out of the studio onto Sunset Boulevard to prove it. Unfortunately, before long Elvis was stopping traffic.

Myrna Smith recalls Elvis sometimes going down from his hotel suite in Las Vegas and gambling on the tables like any other punter—as long as it was before or after his engagement. When he was on the bill, the place would be flooded with fans who mobbed him if he so much as set foot in the hotel lobby. Kathy Westmoreland says that Elvis did occasionally adopt a disguise so that he could go out into the world and do "normal" things.

Elvis' return to live performing cemented his position as a record-breaking attraction and a torchbearer for fame. His retreat into a chemically-altered world may have been his way of handling the attendant loneliness and isolation. However, he was also aware of how he had earned all the acclaim and wealth in his life. Among his possessions was a framed excerpt of a Theodore Roosevelt speech which states: "It is not the critic who counts; not the man who points out how the strong man stumbles, or where the doer of deeds could have done them better. The credit belongs to the man who is actually in the arena . . ."

Some of the "Elvis lives" conspiracy theories claim that Elvis finally had enough of fame and faked his own death to live a life incognito.

ELVIS SAID IN 1957: "I never expected to be anybody important. Maybe I'm not now, but whatever I am, whatever I will become will be what God has chosen for me."

ELVIS SAID IN 1962: "Once you get involved in this business and you're doing a public service, you're trying to entertain people, your life is not your own."

ELVIS SAID TO JOHN LENNON IN 1965: "We pay the price for fame with our nerves."

PAUL DOUGHER (SCHOOL PAL): "Naturally success changed Elvis, but not with me as far as our friendship went. It changed him as far as being unable to do the things he wanted to do at the time to wanted to do them. He couldn't get out and go like he wanted to."

JERRY SCHILLING: "People make movies and records and start acquiring this image, this star persona. Elvis had that in 1954. Nineteen years old and without a hit record."

COLONEL PARKER: "Elvis is a tremendous entertainer; certainly he would have made it without me, but I know that like all good things, too much can be harmful. I make sure Elvis isn't exploited and over-promoted."

JANELLE MCCOMB: "He burst onto the scene when everybody needed a sunrise. We'd come through depression and war. Everybody was ready to give vent to their emotions."

REX MANSFIELD: "In the spotlight he seemed to turn into another person."

JOHN LENNON: "He was a legend in his own lifetime, and it's never easy meeting a legend in his own lifetime."

ANN-MARGRET: "The thing that caused him the biggest problems was the enormous fame that engulfed him, because at heart Elvis was no saint or king but rather a kid."

PAT BOONE: "He was sort of imprisoned. I felt like he lived like Public Enemy #1 instead of the King of Rock 'n' Roll. It stunted his social and spiritual growth."

BILL MEDLEY: "He couldn't go out and if he did go out he literally had to take all of his people with him because something could or would happen."

ALLAN WEISS: "I remember something he said to me—'Do you know what I'd give to go out at one in the morning to get a hamburger? To go to the movies?' He was stifled by his fame. Crushed by it."

MARTIN AMIS: "Elvis was a talented hick destroyed by success."

RED WEST: "Elvis was like a prisoner. He couldn't get out and do things like other people.... Anybody who reaches his level and can handle it, congratulations, because I don't think anybody can do it."

PRISCILLA: "Elvis had been so young when he became a star that he was never able to handle the power and money that accompanied his fame... He never had the chance to be human, to grow up to be a mature adult, to experience the world outside his artificial cocoon."

PETER GURALNICK: "The kind of fame that Elvis experienced requires constant reinvention if one is to escape its snares—and, as more than one friend of Elvis remarked, his desire to escape was ambivalent at best; as much as he may at times have been tempted, he was not about to throw away the identity he had so assiduously created, he enjoyed being Elvis Presley."

SONNY WEST: "I knew that he would be remembered and loved for as long as his fans lived, but I didn't think about him getting new fans from the next generation like he has."

WOLFMAN JACK: "Two thousand years from now they'll still be hearing about Elvis Presley."

JOE ESPOSITO: "If he's up in heaven, he's saying, boy, look at all those crazy people out there still listening to me! Still writing books about me!"

Books:
Elvis: American Idol, by Susan M. Doll, Publications International, 2006

"FAME AND FORTUNE"

The title was a wish in vinyl after two years out of the studio owing to his Army service. Elvis laid down the Fred Wise / Ben Weisman composition on March 20, 1960 in Nashville for imminent release as the B-side of his first newly-recorded single in almost two years, with "Stuck On You" on the A-side. The last lines of the song laid down the challenge to his fans: "To know that you love me / Brings fame and fortune my way."

As a B-side the song peaked at #17. The track received an album release on *Elvis' Golden Records Vol. 3,* and later on *Worldwide Gold Award Hits Vol. 2, A Valentine Gift For You, The Great Performances, From Nashville To Memphis,* CD re-releases and the FTD classic album re-release of *Elvis Is Back!,* and *Hitstory.*

Elvis sang the song on his homecoming TV appearance on the "Frank Sinatra Show" in a taping less than a week after he laid the track down (released on *Platinum: A Life in Music*).

An early take from the original recording session has appeared on *Elvis: A Legendary Performer Vol. 3;* other takes were officially released on FTD albums *Fame and Fortune* and *Elvis Is Back!*

FAME AND FORTUNE

A 2002 FTD release focusing on Elvis' 1960 and 1961 Nashville output.

TRACK LISTING:
1. Make Me Know It
2. Soldier Boy
3. Stuck On You
4. Fame And Fortune
5. Like A Baby
6. It's Now Or Never
7. The Girl Of My Best Friend
8. Dirty, Dirty Feeling
9. Thrill Of Your Love
10. Such A Night
11. Girl Next Door Went A'Walkin'
12. Milky White Way
13. His Hand In Mine
14. He Knows Just What I Need
15. Surrender
16. In My Father's House
17. Joshua Fit The Battle
18. I'm Gonna Walk Dem Golden Stairs
19. Working On The Building
20. I'm Coming Home
21. Gently
22. In Your Arms
23. It's A Sin
24. Starting Today
25. Sentimental Me
26. Judy
27. Put The Blame On Me

FAMILY

The concept of family was central to Elvis' life. When he was growing up, the Presley family was particularly close-knit, even by the standards of the day. Biographer Elaine Dundy suggests that from a very early age, Elvis was used to looking after people. When his father was sent to jail, three-year-old Elvis did as much as any three-year-old could to be the little man of the house.

There was nothing that pleased Elvis more about his success than being able to provide financial security and luxury for his parents (whom he soon referred to, only partly in jest, as "his babies"). However, he was aware that his fame was a burden on them too. Not just was he away on the road for much of the time, but his parents, like him, had to relinquish much of their privacy.

A happy family portrait, 1968.

Over the years, Elvis became a one-man support system for countless relatives, many of whom lived at Graceland and were on the payroll in one capacity or another. The Graceland gates were staffed by Johnny and Travis Smith, Vester Presley and Harold Loyd; for many years, Patsy Presley worked as a secretary. The Smith boys—Billy, Bobby, Gene and Junior—all worked for Elvis at one time or other. At the end of his life, Billy Smith was one of the few people with whom Elvis wanted to spend time.

Some members of the family were less welcome than others: those who had looked down on this particular branch of the Presleys before it was anointed by fame, and those who ridiculed Elvis as a Mama's boy when he was growing up. When they came round to Graceland, Elvis knew it was for money. Nevertheless, cousins, uncles and distant relatives who found themselves in hardship knew that Elvis would help out.

As with so much in Elvis' life, his family relationships were anything but straightforward. Once he became famous, he acted as a parent to his parents. With Priscilla, he fulfilled the roles of both lover and pseudo-father, until she gave birth to Lisa Marie, when suddenly the idea of having sexual relations with her became almost taboo for him.

Beyond his blood relations, Elvis maintained an extended family of his entourage and their families too. At least one entourage member has said that some of Elvis' blood relations were resentful of them because they thought that they had a greater claim on the money Elvis paid them. Marty Lacker told Alanna Nash that no fewer than three members of Elvis' family had threatened to kill him at one time or another.

Elvis' largesse and generosity also extended to the families of significant women in his life. Many skeptical parents were won over by his enormous charm and let their precious girls spend time with him, despite his bad public reputation. Elvis' greatest challenge in this respect was to persuade Priscilla Beaulieu's family that his intentions were honorable. This he did, and soon their seventeen-year-old daughter was chastely living with relatives near Graceland, or so they thought. As a sign of his love for girlfriend Linda Thompson, Elvis bought her brother Sam a house and went to the maternity ward to visit Sam's wife when she gave birth to a baby girl in 1974.

Faith in the family was a fundamental reason why throughout his career Elvis entrusted his personal financial affairs to Vernon, a man without any formal training and at best possessing a limited understanding of business. Vernon was no match for the wily old Colonel, who reputedly referred to Elvis' family as "awful people."

Priscilla notes a propensity to worry in Elvis' family. If Elvis skipped calling home for a day, fear spread throughout the household that a catastrophe had befallen him. Elvis' family, certainly on his mother's side, had a history of short lives. A number of Elvis' uncles died untimely deaths, some of them from alcohol-related conditions.

Many members of Elvis extended family have written memoirs (see below and under individual name entries). There's even an Elvis "family store," called "The Kin of Rock and Roll," in Gettysburg, PA.

ELVIS' ANCESTRY

Elvis was a colorful palette of intermingled blood lines. With the caveat that no family tree for Elvis is 100% reliable for the simple reason that poor people and new migrants often leave little trace of their passage, genealogists have traced back the Presley lineage to Andrew Presley, a blacksmith who emigrated from Scotland to Anson County, North Carolina in 1745, and would have been Elvis' great-great-great-great-great grandfather. Alternative research has the family line deriving from German Johann Valentin Presler, who emigrated to the US in 1710. It has also been claimed that the Presley family originally hailed from Wales, Denmark or Albert Goldman's conclusion, Ireland.

Genealogists have also asserted that Elvis is directly if distantly related to famous figures including Abraham Lincoln, Jimmy Carter and Oprah Winfrey.

See under GLADYS PRESLEY and VERNON PRESLEY for information on Elvis' forebears.

ELVIS SAID IN 1956: "The happiest times I've ever had have been with my family."

ELVIS SAID TO PRISCILLA IN 1976: "I know I've done some stupid things, but the stupidest was not realizing what I had until I lost it."

ANITA WOOD: "It was a good close family. We had a lot of family gatherings at Graceland. They would all come there. And we would go to their house too."

BILLY SMITH: "After Gladys died, Elvis took her place. He became the dominant figure in the family. His daddy could try to talk to him, but nobody could tell him what to do."

PRISCILLA: "A genuine camaraderie was created at Graceland. We lived as one big family, eating, talking, arguing, joking, playing, and traveling together."

LARRY GELLER: "Elvis' family extended beyond his relatives to include all his employees, their wives or girlfriends, and their kids."

PETER GURALNICK: "He was surrounded by friends and relatives, all dependent on him, all looking to him for help, for guidance, for handouts—for something."

Books:
The Presley Saga: A Family History, by Richard Carlton Fulcher, Fulcher Publishing Company, 1978

One Flower While I Live: Elvis As I Remember Him, by the Reverend Nasval Lorene Presley Pritchett, Shelby House, 1987

Presley Family History, by Carol Johnson Hicks and Nancy Painter Thorn, 1993

Elvis: Precious Memories, by Donna Presley Early and Edie Hand, with Lynn Edge, The Best of Times, Inc., 1997

Precious Family Memories of Elvis, by Donna Presley Early, Edie Hand, Susie Pritchett, self-published, 1997 (photo book)

FANS

Few love affairs can have rivaled the one between Elvis and his fans. Love at first sight, first love, a lifelong bond, for millions of fans it was all this and more, a feeling undimmed either by Elvis' decline and death or by the passing years. A CNN poll in the 2000s revealed that 45% of all Americans consider themselves to be an Elvis fan.

Elvis felt the same way, and he let his fans know at every occasion. Karate instructor Ed Parker has written that Elvis' love affair with his fans even led to the break-up of his marriage to Priscilla.

From when he rose to fame in 1956 to when he died in 1977, wherever Elvis lived there was a 24-hour fan vigil outside his home. The incredible loyalty Elvis' fans demonstrated was mirrored by his enormous respect and gratitude towards them. Whenever he had the chance he talked with his fans, signed autographs, posed for pictures and made them feel special—he never forgot that the special life he led was all down to his fans.

ABOVE: Elvis at the Airport Roanoke in 1972.

FACING PAGE: Elvis at the Airport Roanoke in

Elvis was such a bolt from the blue when he started out that people remember where they were and what they were doing the first time they heard him on the radio. Live, the effect was scream-inducing, the original wall of sound. Once he overcame his early shyness, Elvis had a natural rapport with his fans. He didn't even need to sing for the concert hall to go wild. If he joked around, messed up the words, quit singing half way through a song, they only loved him more. Fellow-artist Wanda Jackson, who toured with Elvis in his first year as a performer, put it down to the fact that Elvis simply loved his audience: "He loved his fans more than anybody I've ever seen." Pre-Colonel, fans spread the word about this exciting new performer and fan clubs sprang up overnight when he played new venues.

Elvis was deeply grateful. In April 1956, Elvis told a reporter, "It makes me want to cry. How does all this happen to me?" His female fans—the vast majority of his constituency, at least in the beginning—were so raucous that Elvis' band members couldn't hear their own instruments and could only keep in time by synchronizing with Elvis' movements. Getting off the stage after a show sometimes required Elvis to outrun dozens and on occasion hundreds of girls. If they caught him they tore the clothes off his body to keep as souvenirs. After just such an episode, Elvis sprang to the defense of the riotous girls and told a journalist, "They don't mean any harm." Sometimes a girl would catch hold of him onstage—14-year-old Judy Hopper made it to Elvis' side at one of his September 1956 Tupelo Homecoming shows, and was rewarded with a backstage hug for the promise that she wouldn't repeat the exploit at the evening show.

Parents of Elvis fans deluged their local papers with complaints about Elvis' vulgarity and immorality. This only added to his appeal among their kids. It wasn't until Elvis did his patriotic duty and served two years in the Army (and was recording operetta-inspired songs like "It's Now or Never") that the older generation began to "get" Elvis. When Elvis played a two-week residency at the New Frontier Hotel in Las Vegas just as he was becoming a nationally-known figure, the older crowd was cool to say the least. *Variety* reviewed the occasion with the comment, "for teenagers he's a whiz; for the average Vegas spender, he's a fizz."

Elvis took his newfound high profile in his stride. When his car was vandalized at the Sun 'N' Sand Hotel in Biloxi on vacation, he merely moved to a different hotel. On the way back to Memphis from that trip he was mobbed by fans in Hattiesburg, Mississippi when he stopped for gas. Mobbing and vandalism were just two occupational hazards. The fifty girls who mobbed him after a show in Florida were described by fellow singer Faron Young as "rowdy as alligators"; Elvis needed a security escort to get out of the venue. Fans who couldn't get close to Elvis were content to take home the dust from the car he'd been driven in.

After Elvis moved his folks into a new home on Audubon Drive in Memphis, Colonel Parker advised changing their phone number on a regular basis to discourage nuisance callers.

Elvis' appeal to his female fans was not simply sexual: for many fans, he was a secret friend, a confidant, a focus for emotions they were otherwise unable to share, even an aspirational focus for a future life of fame and glamour. Though his initial fan base was overwhelmingly female, many men liked the rawness of his music and the idea of rebellion he embodied. Countless musicians who took up guitars and microphones in the Sixties and Seventies ascribe their desire to make a career out of rock 'n' roll to hearing Elvis for the first time.

Fans deluged Elvis with mail, grabbed whatever piece of him (or his cars) they could walk away with, and started giving him stuffed toys even before he released his first Teddy-related song in

late 1956, when an (untrue) rumor was printed that he was an avid collector. After the article came out, he became a collector by default.

In a rare public show of anger, Elvis defended his fans in the summer of 1956 to reporter Paul Wilder after a newspaper article accusing them of being "idiots": "Those kids that come here and pay their money to see this show come to have a good time . . . They're somebody's kids. They're somebody's decent kids, probably that was raised in a decent home."

Elvis was happy to put his mouth where his money was. Fan Jim Orwood told interviewers that one day when Elvis was signing autographs outside Graceland in 1956—he regularly went down to the gates to meet fans—Orwood asked Elvis if he would kiss his daughter Cheryl on the cheek. Elvis kissed the little girl, who had a large strawberry birthmark on her face. Ever after when she was teased, the little girl told her teasers that the mark was the spot where Elvis had kissed her.

Efforts were made to clean up Elvis' image as soon as the Colonel landed the TV slots and movie contracts that would turn Elvis into an A-lister. Fans got up a petition after Elvis was all gussied up in a tuxedo for the "Steve Allen Show"; they didn't want anybody messing with the rocker they knew and loved.

Some lucky fans were invited into Elvis' inner circle in the early years Barbara Glidewell, a Memphis girl who was injured at a charity show Elvis gave in town in 1956, was given Elvis' address backstage by Gladys and went round a number of times to hang out and listen to records with Elvis and friends at his Audubon Drive home, and later at Graceland too (despite teachers at school warning her that she would go to the devil).

Elvis and his management were well aware of how vital the more active fans were in lobbying DJs to play his latest releases and ensure that Elvis came out on top of popularity polls.

In January 1958, Elvis wrote to Colonel Parker to ask if RCA could release a recorded message to his fans. He explained to the Colonel: "I wanted to be able to thank them not only for buying my records and for their loyalty to me but also for the help they have given me in deciding the kind of songs to sing... I'm deeply grateful to them, and I want them to know it."

When Elvis rolled out of Memphis for his Army basic training, fans around the world went into mourning. On furlough at Graceland, Elvis came down to the gates in uniform to show off his insignia. Elvis was acutely aware that two years out of the limelight was a big risk to his career. As he sailed to Germany for his foreign posting, he said "I hope I'm not out of their minds. And I'll be looking forward to the time when I can come back and entertain again like I did."

Fans were instrumental in making this wish a reality. When Elvis went into the Army, fan club membership didn't go down, it doubled. Just before he sailed for Germany, Elvis told the media that he was getting upwards of 15,000 letters a week. When a new Elvis single came out, parties of fans bought up as many copies as they could to ensure that he stayed at the right end of the charts. In Florida, Mae Axton organized an Elvis event where almost 10,000 people came along just to hear Elvis records played in public.

Out in Germany, Elvis' pals Red West and Lamar Fike helped field the fan mail, passing on their Elvis signature copying skills to new secretary Elisabeth Stefaniak when she joined the team. The well-organized network of German Elvis fans around the base proved to be a logistical nightmare for Army command. When they went out on maneuvers, they had to make sure that Elvis parked his jeep somewhere concealed, or within the hour he'd be knee deep in onlookers.

As usual, Elvis sent a Christmas message to his fans back home in Memphis in 1959, thanking them for their concern and support but asking

them not to arrange a special homecoming for him at the end of his Army service.

Elvis personally thanked the heads of many fan clubs for all the work they did keeping his name in the news during his two year Army absence. Fan club president Naomia Stiers became a particular friend (Elvis called her "sweet lady").

Elvis by no means took it for granted that he could just pick up on his career where he had left off. After recording his first new singles in Nashville he told a reporter, "If I don't please the audience, the money don't mean nothing." RCA emblazoned his first single since his return with the legend that it was for his 50 million fans around the world, which since his time in the Army included many more men than before.

Elvis' train was mobbed by fans as it steamed through El Paso, Texas, en route to Hollywood where he was due to start work on *G.I. Blues*. He had to sneak out of the train in a siding before it pulled into Union Station in LA to give the waiting crowds the slip—a tactic he used on a number of occasions.

Fans saw Elvis' movie-making as a way to get close to the hero—the only way to do so as he practically stopped performing live in the Sixties. Ingenious fans tried to smuggle themselves into studios in the back of laundry trucks, or just plain breaking through security cordons on external shoots. The screams of enthusiastic fans watching Elvis shoot a scene for *Blue Hawaii* in 1960 made it into the movie (he's descending from a plane). His mere arrival on the island drew a crowd 3,000 strong. A tongue in cheek "Elvis Presley Underwater Fan Club" put on a performance to honor Elvis while he was in Florida in 1961 shooting *Follow That Dream*.

Elvis employed a team of secretaries to sort through the industrial amount of mail he received from all around the world, some from fans who wrote to him every single day. Fans sent gifts, sometimes expensive items of jewelry. Others sent him pornographic letters and photographs. Though secretaries sent out standard responses to the majority of Elvis' fan mail, he still signed a prodigious number of replies and Christmas cards. During the Sixties his office at Graceland dispatched newsletters to fan clubs about what he was up to and where he was going. Secretaries put fan photos into albums which were kept at Graceland—all except nude pictures that fans sent in, which were kept in a special drawer that was reportedly more often opened by guys in Elvis' entourage than by Elvis himself.

Fans continued to come up with enterprising ruses to meet their idol. One girl clambered up ten floors on fire escapes to get to his hotel balcony; another tried to gain entry to the floor Elvis had taken over at a Miami hotel by dressing up as a bell captain. When Elvis was showing The Beatles round his Bel Air home, they were aghast to discover a fan who had somehow managed to hide herself in his sauna.

Elvis continued his evening habit of walking down to the gates of Graceland. He'd let fans in, sign autographs, clown around, kiss the ladies and make their day. Elvis always had time for the less fortunate of his fans, the ill and the handicapped.

When Elvis and his entourage drove cross-country between Memphis and Los Angeles, motels where they holed up by day were often swamped by fans. It has been speculated that the Colonel kept tabs on their whereabouts through a member of the entourage, and then tipped off the local radio station. Within an hour, the fans were out in force.

In 1965, when Elvis was going through a period of soul-searching, he was conscious of the widening distance between himself and his fans. He stated in an interview, "I certainly haven't lost my respect for my fans. I withdraw not from my fans but from myself."

That year the Colonel came up with a singular solution to Elvis' reluctance to make personal appearances to promote his movies and soundtracks: he persuaded RCA to ship Elvis' gold Cadillac around the country as a stand-in for the publicity-shy star. If Elvis wouldn't go the fans, the fans were still happy to come to him. Whenever he arrived in LA or returned to Graceland, groups of fans still gave him an enthusiastic welcome.

Priscilla did not always regard the fans camped outside Graceland as a benefit. Sometimes when she went out and about, they would tail her. She writes in her memoir that she and Elvis almost immediately moved out of a new rented home in LA when they discovered that fans and reporters were gathering on a nearby hill to spy on them. She tells of one occasion when an overzealous female fan tailgated her dangerously close. When Priscilla got out to challenge her, the woman called her a whore; Priscilla says in her memoir that she laid her out and then went to get reinforcements from the house.

Fan club officers lived in hope of an invitation to Graceland. Almost to a woman, their most vivid recollection is how incredibly beautiful Elvis was. Elvis had a great memory for names and faces, and would surprise fans by remembering them years later, even if they had previously only met fleetingly.

The Colonel changed his promotional tack in the mid-Sixties, setting up a nationwide radio Mother's Day special. Elvis fans in the UK were actively campaigning to persuade their idol to quit the cookie-cutter movies, return to live performing, and at last tour outside the United States. By now somewhat reduced in number, a core group of Elvis fans could still be relied upon to go see his movies and buy his records.

Elvis' restored popularity following his December 1968 NBC TV Special led directly to his return to touring. He had long been missing the thrill of live performances, and the Colonel was happy to accept the lure of Las Vegas (for $100,000 a week). By June 1969 Elvis was back in front of his fans. Once more, at Graceland he would walk down to the gates in the evenings, chat with fans and sign autographs. Sometimes he would even sing—he told friends that this was his way of getting used to the crowds again, including a whole new crop of fans won over by the TV Special and his American Studio music output.

When Elvis went back on the road in the Seventies, fans had an ally in Colonel Parker, who clamped down on concert promoters handing out free tickets to local dignitaries so that as many tickets as possible were available for the fans.

Elvis' fans were famously loyal. Larry Geller recalls, "They all radiated a mixture of frenzied anticipation and pure love." In her memoir, Priscilla says that Elvis acutely felt the anticlimax of getting home in LA or Memphis to be a husband and father after weeks of adulation from his fans in Las Vegas. Even when Elvis was looking heavier and lacked the energy of his heyday, his fans could be counted on to react with the same adulation as ever.

Many of the fans at Elvis' Seventies concerts had been the screaming teenagers who saw him almost two decades earlier. Just because they were now mothers and in their thirties and forties didn't stop them from screaming and throwing their underwear on stage. When Dave Hebler began working security for Elvis, he was amazed that in a top-of-the-line venue like the International Hotel in Las Vegas, "respectable grown ladies" would wriggle out of their underwear, flash at Elvis and sling their lingerie onstage. He remembers once in Atlanta in 1973 fans tried to rush the stage, oblivious that there was a 10-foot drop between the seating and the stage. Despite the best efforts of police and security, a few ladies took the drop. Crowd mayhem also happened in Hampton Roads, where thirty policemen were swamped by a rampaging audience. The same happened in San Diego and in Springfield, Massachusetts. One of the duties of Elvis' body-

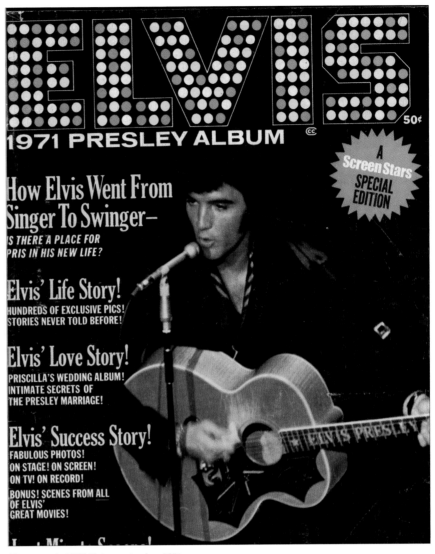

The cover of a 100% *Elvis* magazine from 1971.

guards was to pluck fainted fans from the floor before they were unwittingly crushed by others.

At concerts, fans still wanted a piece of Elvis. In later years, when he was sufficiently well-protected not to have to fear having his clothes ripped off, Elvis' hands would be covered in scratches from the nails of female fans eager to grab the scarves he dispensed. One woman at an Oklahoma City concert jumped off of a balcony in an attempt to get a scarf. Another woman was almost choked when two other women fought over a scarf wrapped around her neck—until Elvis saw what was going on and handed out more scarves. At some concerts in the mid-Seventies, in a genuine display of affection (and not just out of drug excess) Elvis even threw rings, capes and guitars out into the audience.

Gary Pepper, president of an Elvis fan club in Memphis, and a cerebral palsy sufferer, was bought a house by Elvis round the corner from Graceland, where Elvis sometimes went to get some quiet time away from Graceland. Elvis corresponded with a Swedish cerebral palsy sufferer called Karen, a fan whose condition was improved by his letters after carer Lena Canada suggested she write to him—the story is told in the movie *Touched by Love* (1980, also known as *To Elvis with Love*), and in a book.

By the mid-Seventies, Elvis' record releases were once again being purchased by a small but loyal group of core fans, though his concerts around the nation continued to be guaranteed sellouts.

Elvis still wanted to please his fans, though it was evident to all but his most uncritical devotees that his powers were on the wane. Despite negative reviews of a number of concerts that

year, Elvis' fans reacted with the same passion and acknowledgement as ever. One reporter wrote that the fans "were screaming for what he was, what he symbolizes, rather than what he is." On many nights, he still gave memorable performances and his voice was still in form. On one night, in the middle of a concert, he turned his back on the audience, stared at the band and reputedly mouthed words to the effect that the audience loved him whatever he did, even if he ignored them. This wasn't true of all fans; some came away from later concerts shocked at witnessing such a public demise.

In the last year of his life, after Elvis told Larry Geller that he never knew if a woman loved him for himself or for his fame, Geller replied that the one lasting love affair of Elvis' life was with his fans. Elvis had to agree. At the end of his concerts Elvis strode to each corner of the stage, got down on bended knee and thanked his audience; thanked them very much. He was still making grand gestures to his fans in his final year of performing. At Lake Tahoe, he arranged for a rose to be given to every member of the audience.

Tens of thousands of fans flocked spontaneously to Graceland when they heard news of Elvis' death. Every florist in Memphis had their entire stock bought up by fans. On the night before Elvis' funeral, the street outside Graceland became a parking lot, with people sleeping out in their cars. Local restaurants and well-wishers sent food to the house, some of which had to be ferried in by helicopter because it became impossible to open the main gates owing to the crush of despairing fans. The following day, Vernon decided to let Elvis' fans in to Graceland to see his son for the last time. The best

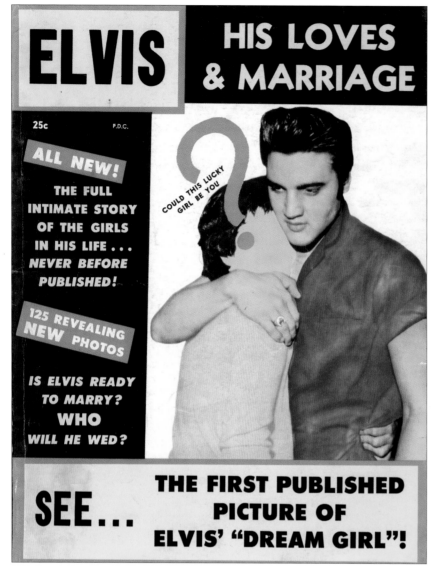

ELVIS

HIS LOVES & MARRIAGE

25c   P.D.C.

COULD THIS LUCKY GIRL BE YOU?

ALL NEW!
THE FULL INTIMATE STORY OF THE GIRLS IN HIS LIFE . . . NEVER BEFORE PUBLISHED!

125 REVEALING NEW PHOTOS

IS ELVIS READY TO MARRY? WHO WILL HE WED?

SEE... **THE FIRST PUBLISHED PICTURE OF ELVIS' "DREAM GIRL"!**

Highly collectible 1957 *Elvis* magazine.

estimate is that 20,000 people filed past Elvis' coffin in a few hours. It was too much for some; many passed out on the Graceland lawn, and one woman had a heart attack. Worse was to come in the night, when a car driven by an inebriated driver rammed into fans congregated outside, killing Alice Hovatar and Juanita Johnson and seriously injuring Tammy Baiter. The driver, Treatise Wheeler, was charged with second-degree murder once the police had rescued him from a crowd of appalled Elvis fans who wanted to mete out summary justice.

After Vernon's death in 1979, Priscilla took over the running of the Elvis Estate and began the long process of bringing all of his fan clubs under control. Opening up Graceland to visits in 1982 was a welcome development for the most fans, though for some their curiosity at seeing where the King lived was eclipsed by a feeling that his home was somehow being desecrated.

There are very few more inclusive and more international fellowships than the world's many Elvis fan clubs. Countless fervent Elvis fans had the chance to befriend their hero. As many as 500 privately-published fan-written books on Elvis have appeared over the years, many written by fan club presidents (Todd Slaughter, Sue Weigert et al). *Elvis and You: Your Guide to the Pleasures of Being an Elvis Fan,* published in 2000, has become something of a fan bible. Former chairperson of the UK Elvis Presley Fan Club Julie Mundy authored a highly acclaimed book on Elvis' clothes and costumes, *Elvis Fashion: From Memphis to Vegas,* in 2003. Fans continue to be a great source of information

to biographers and chroniclers researching the Elvis phenomenon.

Many Elvis fans have proclaimed themselves to be his "greatest." Thousands upon thousands of fans show their devotion by doing their all to mimic Elvis on stage. Steven Christopher has appeared on radio stations in a show called "Elvis on the Air," in which he challenges fans to test his knowledge of Elvis trivia. Self-styled "greatest fan" Paul MacLeod and his son Elvis Aron Presley MacLeod run an unofficial museum, called Graceland Too, showcasing a 40+ year collection of Elvis memorabilia.

The line between being a fan, a collector, an author and even an Elvis record and book publisher is beyond blurred. Collectors like Joseph Pirzada have brought out books, CDs and DVDs that feature rare Elvis performance material that has never been seen through official channels.

To this day, fans come together to commemorate Elvis during "Elvis Week," a series of events that has sprung up spontaneously to mark his passing, and to celebrate his life in the week around his birthday in January. For the thirtieth anniversary of his death in 2007, as many as 75,000 fans congregated in Memphis, on the night of August 15/16 filing through the grounds of Graceland to the Meditation Garden in a procession that lasted right through the night and into the morning.

ELVIS SAID IN 1956: "I just sing. I let the audience do the work."

ELVIS SAID: "The first time it happened, the first time that I appeared on stage it was a charity thing in Memphis, a place called the Shell. When I left the stage they were yelling and screaming and so forth and it scared me to death, man. I didn't know what I'd done, I went to the manager backstage, I said, 'What did I do? What did I do?' and he said, 'Well, whatever it is, go back and do it again.' So I went back out there and I did the same thing again. I really didn't know what the yelling was about. I didn't realize that my body was moving. It's a natural thing to me..."

ELVIS SAID IN 1956: "I just wish there was some way to go round to every one of 'em and really show that you appreciate their liking you and all."

ELVIS SAID IN 1956: "If it wasn't for getting mobbed, maybe clothes torn off... I would go right out in the middle of those people, but I hate to turn anybody down that wants autographs."

ELVIS SAID IN 1968, after girl fans scream for him: "Never ceases to amaze me baby, I tell ya."

ELVIS SAID IN A COMMUNICATION TO HIS FANS: "My thanks to you comes from right down here, right from the deep bottom of the happiest heart in this whole great big old world."

ELVIS SAID: "I want to entertain people. That's my whole life. To my last breath."

ELVIS SAID TO LARRY GELLER: "The fans, they know 'Elvis' but they don't know me."

ELVIS SAID TO JOHN WILKINSON: "If it wasn't for the fans, I'd be just another damn lounge singer."

COLONEL TOM PARKER: "The kids are the ones who made Elvis... without them he'd still be driving a truck."

PAMELA CLARKE KEOGH: "Unlike some celebrities who hide from the public's attention, Elvis believed he owed everything to his fans."

JOE ESPOSITO: "No matter what happened, Elvis always took time out for his fans."

PRISCILLA: "His audience was his true love."

JIMMY VELVET: "In the beginning on the road tours, the women, the girls, would want to come and see Elvis, but the boyfriends and husbands didn't want to; but they would go because they didn't want their girls to go alone. Well, they wound up being fans themselves when they saw the live shows, because Elvis was just darn good."

JOE ESPOSITO: "The President could have been waiting, he would sign autographs for his fans."

MINNIE PEARL: "He really literally was a prisoner because of the fans."

LOWELL HAYS: "He made so much money, and he had so much money, and he loved his fans and he loved the people he sang for so much, that he tried to give everything he made back to his fans."

RONNIE TUTT: "He wouldn't allow the seriousness of a paying crowd to keep him from getting tickled or getting crazy about something, he didn't care in that way."

JOAN DEARY: "A lot of fans know more about Elvis than the writers . . . You can't go out and mix with his fans unless you really know what you're talking about."

MARGARET THATCHER: "I love his music because he was my generation. But then again, Elvis is everyone's generation, and he always will be."

MARTY LACKER: "There were two sides to Elvis. The fans only saw one of them. He was a human being like the rest of us. He had problems, good fortune, faults and great attributes. Some fans tend to forget that or don't want to hear it but that is unfair to Elvis and his memory."

LARRY GELLER: "He needed the fans; he lived for their love."

DAVE MARSH: "There are people in places that count in the world, and people in places that don't. He is the son of the people who don't count, and their shining star. That's what makes him unique and what people still respond to."

GEORGE KLEIN: "If you're an Elvis fan, no explanation is necessary; If you're not an Elvis fan, no explanation is possible."

TODD SLAUGHTER: "You won't see our kind, decades from now. That is because music has changed, and with it what it means to be a fan."

Books:

Elvis Now—Ours Forever, edited by Bob Olmetti and Sue McCasland, self-published, 1977.

We Remember Elvis, by Wanda June Hill, Morgan Press, 1978 (revised edition BookSurge Pub., 2006).

Forever Elvis: The Memorial Tour to Memphis, by Todd Slaughter, World Publishing, 1980.

The Elvis Presley News Diary, by Bill and Moneen Johnson, Pyramid Media, 1981.

Elvis, This One's For You, by Arlene Cogan and Charles Goodman, Castle Books, 1985.

Dear Elvis: Graffiti from Graceland, by Daniel Wright and Mark Landon Smith, Mustang Publishing Co., 1996.

Elvis, You're Unforgettable: Memoirs from a Fan, by Frances Keenan, Axelrod Publishing, 1997.

Hurry Home, Elvis: Donna Lewis' Diaries, Vols. 1 and 2, Busted Burd Productions, 1996, 1997.

Letters to Elvis: Real Letters Written by His Faithful Fans, compiled by P. K. McLemore, 1997.

Elvis and You: Your Guide to the Pleasures of Being an Elvis Fan, by Laura Levin and John O'Hara, Perigee Trade, 2000.

Elvis: Behind The Image Vols. 1 and 2, with Sandi Miller, Bud Glass Productions 2005, 2006.

Documentary:
Altered by Elvis, 2006

FAN CLUBS

The original Elvis fan club was set up by Sun Records girl Friday Marion Keisker in the fall of 1954, weeks after Elvis cut his first ever single. When Bob Neal took over as Elvis' manager, the Elvis Presley Fan Club was run out of the WMPS radio station on Union Street in Memphis. Elvis Central moved to Box 417, Madison, Tennessee when the Colonel relieved Neal of his role as manager.

Kay Wheeler, later known as the "Queen of the Rock 'n' Bop," started the first national Elvis fan club, which she ran until the Colonel decided to roll her club into his own as a means of selling merchandise—Wheeler had been distributing photos free. Other fan clubs sprung up spontaneously: Sandra Cottrell founded the Elvis Presley Home Town Fan Club in Tupelo soon after he started performing; Valerie Harms set up a fan club in Texas which she claimed was the first; Gary Pepper also set up a club in Memphis. When Elvis played somewhere new, there was often a fan with a flair for organization who was happy to spread the word.

Parker's existing team was soon swamped by fan interest. Hiring a total of 21 employees to respond to letters, send out photos and bank the money fans sent it was only a temporary solution before Parker sub-contracted running of the club to merchandiser Hank Saperstein. By 1956, the official Elvis fan club address was Box 94, Hollywood, California.

There was no need for any impetus thereafter. Elvis fan clubs mushroomed around the country and soon around the globe, producing a plethora of magazines that have become highly sought after by Elvis memorabilia collectors. The Official Elvis Presley Fan Club of Great Britain, founded in 1956 by Jeannie Seward, claims the laurels as the oldest still-running fan club in the world, though one web source gives this accolade to French club La Voix d'Elvis, founded by Evelyne Bellemin. Fan clubs started up around the world, while umbrella organizations such as the International Elvis Presley Appreciation Society served to span international divides.

The Elvis publicity machine started cranking out product for fans who already had all his records. *Elvis Answers Back* was an early magazine in which Elvis shared his philosophy with his fans, complete with an interview on a gold-colored record, which came out in August 1956 attached to a special issue of *Teen Parade* magazine. The semi-scripted speech was titled "The Truth about Me" and cost 50 cents.

Fan clubs kept Elvis in the news during his Army years and offered a guaranteed outlet for record sales and box office income, even during Elvis' artistically lean years. As fans grew older, they shared their passion with their kids; many active fan club members nowadays were not even born before Elvis' death.

Since 1977, many fan clubs have made a point of continuing Elvis' generosity to charity. Each year a group of fan club presidents select one charity as a focus for club fundraising. In the late Seventies, fan clubs around the world banded together to set up the Elvis Presley International Memorial Foundation, to do good works in Elvis' name. The organization was shut down after the Elvis Estate began to charge licensing fees for use of the name.

Fan club leaders around the world have been a major force in publishing Elvis books and photos. Ger Rijff, who ran the Dutch Elvis Presley fan club for seven years, is one of the world's most prolific Elvis photo book authors. Fan clubs wholeheartedly embraced the internet, where they provide masses of information and serve as an instant conduit for Elvis news.

Fan club festivals continue around the world, not just in Memphis and Tupelo but also from Canada to Australia, marking the anniversaries of Elvis' birth and death, introducing Elvis to a new generation of fans, and raising money for charity. It has been estimated that in 2006, there were as many as 600 active Elvis fan clubs around the world, with an active membership exceeding half a million.

Fan clubs are renowned for their charitable works and imaginative ways of celebrating their hero. Dutch Club "It's Elvis Time" officially named a star "Elvis A. Presley" in 2007 (co-ordinates 06H22M;+62°   06'); the president of that club, Hubert Vindevogel, and Belgian fan club president Peter Haan were both awarded honorary citizenship of Shelby County in recognition of all the Dutch and Belgian visitors they had brought to Memphis over the years.

Books:
Elvis Presley, by Todd Slaughter, Mandabrook Ltd., 1977.

Elvis—For the Good Times, by Sue Weigart, self-published, 1978.

Tryin' To Get To You, by Valerie Harms, Atheneum, 1979 (republished by iUniverse, 2000).

Growing Up With The Memphis Flash, by Kay Wheeler and William A. Harbison, Tutti Frutti Productions, 1994.

FAN CLUB LIST IN THE 2000s

A somewhat incomplete list of fan clubs operating in the new millennium. Many fan clubs are very active on the internet—put the club name into your favorite search engine to find homepages and contact info—and are a great resource for the latest Elvis news, events and releases, as well as interviews with people who knew Elvis and music/DVD reviews.

The official Elvis site has a full list of approved fan clubs with contact information on its site in the fan relations section. The "Elvis and You" site at also features a comprehensive list of fan clubs and contact addresses.

UNITED STATES

2nd To None(	(TX)
A Billion Elvis Fans Can't Be Wrong	(AL)
Alabama Fans TCB For Elvis Club	(AL)
All Shook Up EPFC Of Harnett County(	NC)
All Shook Up	(MO)
All The King's Things	(CA)
Aloha Elvis Fan Club Of Northwest Florida	(FL)
Always Elvis	(NY)
Always Elvis Fan Club	(PA)
Always Loving You	(TX)
Always On My Mind TN/OH	(TN)
America's Legend	(SC)
America's Legend Elvis Presley Fan Club	(IN)
Assembly Of Elvis	(GA)
Because of Elvis Fan Club	(TX)
Blossomland For Elvis	(TN)
Blue Hawaiians for Elvis Fan Club	(CA)
Blue Moon Of Kentucky	(KY)
Bridgeport Texas And Surrounding Areas	(TX)
Burning Love Fan Club	(OK)
Burning Love For Elvis	(LA)
California Fans - All Shook Up	(CA)
California's Graceland	(TN)
Can't Get Enough Elvis	(GA)
Club Elvis	(IL)
Collector Fan Club	(CA)
Colorado Graceland Elvis Always Fan Club	(CO)
Crazy For Elvis	(IN)
Crazy For Elvis Fan Club	(NJ)
D & N's Elvis Presley Fan Club	(TX)
Don't Forget Elvis	(NC)
Echoes Of Our Love	(OH)
Electrifying Elvis Fan Club	(TN)
Elvis 44 1976	(NY)
Elvis 4-Ever King Fan Club	(SC)
Elvis Always Fan Club	(NC)
Elvis Always On My Mind	(OH)
Elvis Always On Our Mind	(MO)
Elvis Always On Our Minds	(LA)
Elvis Among The Stars	(TN)
Elvis And Friends	(PA)
Elvis Archives Fan Club	(WI)
Elvis Arkansas Style Fan Club	(AR)
Elvis Business Fan Club	(IL)
Elvis Chicago Style	(IL)
Elvis Circle Of Friends	(TN)
Elvis Club Of Albuquerque	(NM)
Elvis Connection	(WI)
Elvis Connections	(CA)
Elvis Country Fan Club	(TX)
Elvis Dixieland Fan Club	(FL)
Elvis Double Trouble Fan Club	(NJ)
Elvis Echoes of Love	(MI)
Elvis Express	(TN)
Elvis Extravaganza Fan Club	(OH)
Elvis Fan Club	(TX)
Elvis Fan Club Of Matthews - Mint Hill	(NC)
Elvis Fans From Hoosierland	(IN)
Elvis Fans In The Heartland	(IA)
Elvis Fans United	(NY)
Elvis Fantasy Fest Branch	(IN)
Elvis Fever Fan Club	(FL)
Elvis Fever Fan Club	(MD)
Elvis Flaming Starz	(NC)
Elvis For Everyone	(KS)
Elvis Forever	(WA)
Elvis Forever TCB Fan Club	(FL)
Elvis Forever Young	(MI)
Elvis Friends Are The Best Friendship Circle	(TX)
Elvis Friends Hollywood	(CA)
Elvis Friends International Fan Club	(OK)
Elvis Friendship Circle	(LA)
Elvis Guitar Man	(MD)
Elvis Happy Fan Club	(NJ)
Elvis Has Left The Building	(AZ)
Elvis He Touched Me	(GA)
Elvis Heart Of Gold Fan Club	(MO)
Elvis Hometown Fans Fan Club	(TN)
Elvis In My Heart	(IA)
Elvis In The Heart Of Dixie Fan Club of Alabama	(AL)
Elvis International	(NC)
Elvis Is In The Building Fan Club Of NJ	
Elvis Is Love	(FL)

Elvis signing autographs at Graceland in 1969

Elvis Just Pretend	(CO)	Of Alabama	(AL)	Friends Of Elvis	(NJ)
Elvis King Creole Fan Club Of Louisiana	(LA)	Elvis Presley's Love Me Tender Fan Club	(OH)	From Memphis to Philly	(PA)
Elvis Legend Forever	(TX)	Elvis Presley's Sweet Sweet Spirit Fan Club	(OH)	From The Heart Elvis Fan Club	(NC)
Elvis Little Sister Fan Club	(CA)	Elvis Radio Groupies	(IN)	Gate City Fan Club	(NC)
Elvis Lives On	(ID)	Elvis Rock 'N' Roll Fan Club Of St. Louis	(MO)	Gates Of Graceland Fan Club	(TN)
Elvis Lives On	(WA)	Elvis Rock-A-Hula Baby Fan Club	(HI)	Graceland Express	(TN)
Elvis Lives Forever Fan Club	(SC)	Elvis Rocks In Alabama	(AL)	Graceland's Rising Sun	(NH)
Elvis Love Exchange	(TX)	Elvis Second To None	(NC)	Greater New Orleans Elvis Fan Club	(LA)
Elvis Mafia	(VA)	Elvis Shake, Rattle And Roll Fan Club	(OH)	Happiness Is Elvis	(MN)
Elvis Memorial Fan Club of Hawaii	(HI)	Elvis Steamroller Blues Club	(IN)	Having Fun with Elvis	(TX)
Elvis Memories	(CA)	Elvis Still Rockin' Fan Club Of Georgia	(GA)	Heartbreak Hotel Elvis Fan Club	(TX)
Elvis Memories	(NJ)	Elvis TCB	(Southeast MI)	His Hand In Mine	(MO)
Elvis Memories Fan Club	(PA)	Elvis That's The Way It Is F.C. of Chicago	(IL)	Hunka Hunka Burning Love	(MO)
Elvis Memories Loop	(OH)	Elvis The King Fan Club	(FL)	I Believe	(IL)
Elvis Memphis Style	(MS)	Elvis The Legend Continues Fan Club	(TN)	I Love Elvis	(CA)
Elvis Network	(FL)	Elvis This One's For You Fan Club	(TX)	I Met Elvis Fan Club	(AR)
Elvis Now or Never	(NY)	Elvis Times	(OH)	I Was I Am Searching Elvis Fan Club	(TN)
Elvis Ol Friends	(GA)	Elvis Today	(IL)	If I Can Dream	(IL)
Elvis On Capitol Hill Fan Club	(CA)	Elvis Tribute Club	(OK)	If I Can Dream	(LA)
Elvis Presley Blazers	(AL)	Elvis Unlimited	(NJ)	If I Can Dream Elvis in Alabama Fan Club	(AL)
Elvis Presley Burning Love Fan Club	(IL)	Elvis World	(NJ)	If I Can Dream Elvis Fan Club	(AR)
Elvis Presley Continentals, Inc.	(FL)	Elvis Worldwide Fan Club	(MS)	If I Can Dream Elvis Fan Club	(OH)
Elvis Presley Fan Club At Lamb's Farm	(IL)	Elvis, AOTC Fan Club Of Alabama	(AL)	If I Can Dream Elvis Fan Club	(TX)
Elvis Presley Fan Club Of Capital District, Inc	(NY)	Elvis, Greatest Gospel Music Fan Club Of AR	(AR)	If I Can Dream Elvis Fan Club of Mass	(MA)
Elvis Presley Fan Club Of Florida	(FL)	Elvis, Treasure Coast, TCB Fan Club	(FL)	If I Can Dream F.C. of Washington State	(WA)
Elvis Presley Fan Club Of Mississippi	(AL)	Elvis, Tsalagi Usdi	(AL)	In Search Of Elvis	(CA)
Elvis Presley Fan Club Of Oklahoma	(OK)	Elvis: A Legend In His Time	(NC)	In The Spirit Of Elvis Presley	(CA)
Elvis Presley Fan Club Of Old Hickory/Hermitage		Elvis' Teddy Bears	(FL)	Indy True Blue Elvis Fan Club	(IN)
	(TN)	Elvis' Agents #1	(VA)	It's Only Love For Elvis Fan Club	(NY)
Elvis Presley Fan Club Of The Carolinas	(NC)	Elvis' Angels Fan Club	(LA)	Jailhouse Rock Confidential	(SC)
Elvis Presley Fan Club Of The Hudson Valley	(NY)	Elvis' Family Of Fans	(IA)	Jailhouse Rockers Of California	(CA)
Elvis Presley Fan Club Of The Upper Midwest	(MN)	Elvis' Family Of Friends	(MI)	Jailhouse Rockers Of Glendale	(CA)
Elvis Presley Fan Club Of West Pennsylvania	(PA)	Elvis' Hound Dog Fan Club	(KY)	Just Us And Elvis	(NC)
Elvis Presley Fan Club	(IL)	Elvis' Teddy Bears	(IL)	Kansas Fans For Elvis	(KS)
Elvis Presley Fans Of Alabama	(AL)	Elvisians from Another Planet	(CA)	Kentucky Rain Fan Club	(KY)
Elvis Presley Foundation	(VA)	EP Japan	(TN)	Kentucky Rain Keeps Pouring Down	(KY)
Elvis Presley Foundation Of New York	(NY)	Especially For Elvis	(NC)	King Creole Fan Club	(MD)
Elvis Presley Foundation Of NY	(NY)	Eternally Elvis TCB, Inc.	(FL)	King's Kids	(NY)
Elvis Presley Int'l F.C. Worldwide	(TN)	Expressly Elvis Fan Club Of Denver	(CO)	Laugh With Elvis Fan Club	(TX)
Elvis Presley Int'l Fan Club Of Philadelphia	(PA)	Fans of Elvis Fan Club Rhode Island	(RI)	Lawton's Elvis Friends	(OK)
Elvis Presley Loyalists Fan Club	(NJ)	Fifties Remember Elvis	(FL)	Little Presley Rascals	(FL)
Elvis Presley Memorial Society	(TN)	Fit for a King Fan Club	(GA)	Living The Dream	(OH)
Elvis Presley Memorial Society of Syracuse	(NY)	Flaming Star Over Texas	(TX)	Looking For Elvis Fan Club	(AL)
Elvis Presley Network (North)	(IL)	Follow That Dream Elvis Fans of Florida	(FL)	Love For Elvis Fan Club	(KY)
Elvis Presley Network/Fan Club	(CA)	For The Heart	(AL)	Loving Elvis	(KY)
Elvis Presley TCB Fan Club Of Chicago	(IL)	For The Love Of Elvis F.C. Of Northwest Indiana		Loving Elvis	(NY)
Elvis Presley TLC Fan Club	(CA)		(IN)	Loving Elvis Tenderly	(MN)
Elvis Presley's Charleston Friends	(WV)	For The Love Of Elvis	(IL)	Loving You Elvis Fan Club	(MS)
Elvis Presley's Good Luck Charms F.C.		Forever Elvis	(WI)	Loving You Elvis	(MD)
				Memories Of Elvis	(NJ)
				Memories Of Elvis - Waco	(TX)
				Memories Of Elvis Presley	(MO)
				Memories Of Elvis - Hattiesburg	(MS)
				Memphis Sideburns	(CA)
				Memphis Son	(NY)
				Memphis Teddy Bear Project	(TN)
				Mile High On Elvis - Denver	(CO)
				Music City Memories Of Elvis	(TN)
				My Wish Came True	(VA)
				Networking For Elvis	(IA)
				Neverending Elvis Presley Fan Club	(MT)
				New Elvis Fans	(KS)
				New Jersey Stage Association for Elvis	(NJ)
				North Jersey Knights For Elvis	(NJ)
				Oklahoma Fans For Elvis	(OK)
				Oklahoma's He Was The One	(OK)
				One And Only King Of Rock And Roll	(IL)
				One Nation Under Elvis Fan Club	(TX)
				Power Of My Love Fan Club	(GA)
				Presley Magic Fan Club	(NY)
				Pure Gold Elvis Presley Fan Club, Inc.	(FL)
				Quake, Rattle and Roll	(CA)
				Raised On Rock	(TX)
				Reflections of Elvis	(IN)
				Remembering Elvis with TLC in Alabama	(AL)
				Return to Sender	(VA)
				Rock-A-Hula Girls International	(CA)
				Rockin' With Elvis In The 50's	(AZ)
				Rubberneckin' For Elvis	(TN)
				See See Rider Fan Club	(FL)
				Share The Love Of Elvis	(NJ)
				Sharing The Memory	(VT)
				Simply Elvis	(OK)
				Sincerely Elvis Fan Club Of Michigan	(MI)
				Smokey Mountains Precious Memories	
				of Elvis Fan Club	(TN)
				Snorkeling Elvises	(FL)
				Society Of Admiration For Elvis	(TX)
				Steel Valley Remembers Elvis	(OH)

Candid shots from the 1950's of Elvis talking to fans.

Elvis greeting fans during his concert in Greensboro, North Carolina March 13, 1974.

Steel Valley Remembers Elvis	(OH)
Still Rockin' Elvis Fan Club	(GA)
Strictly Elvis Fan Club	(TN)
Stuck On Elvis Fan Club	(MO)
Suspicious Minds	(CA)
Sweet Sweet Spirit Of Elvis Fan Club	(TX)
Taking Care Of Elvis	(GA)
Taking Care Of Elvis Everyday	(PA)
Taking Care Of Elvis My Way	(TN)
Talk About The Good Times	(IL)
TCB	(TX)
TCB Elvis Presley Fan Club	(OH)
TCB Elvis Style	(LA)
TCB Elvis Style	(TX)
TCB EPFC	(VA)
TCB Fan Club	(IL)
TCB For Elvis	(MS)
TCB For Elvis Fan Club	(NC)
TCB in South Georgia	(GA)
TCB Of Alabama	(AL)
TCB 4 EAP Fan Club Of New York	(NY)
TCB 4 EAP Online Club Of Tennessee	(TN)
TCB-N-Tennessee	(TN)
TCEAPM With TLC Fan Club	(IL)
TCElvis 2001	(NY)
TCEM In Ohio With TLC	(OH)
TCM For Elvis	(IL)
TCP Memorial Benefit Committee	(IN)
Teddy Bear Fan Club	(PA)
Teddy Bear Project	(IL)
The Elvis Net	(WI)
The Elvis Presley Suite	(VT)
The Elvis Society	(MA)
The King's Connection	(NH)
The Memphis Connection	(TN)
The Presley Connection	(AL)
The Presleyites	(FL)
The Presley Nation Fan Club	(CA)
The Spirit Lives On	(OR)
The Sun Never Sets...On A Legend	(MO)
The Ultimate Elvis Presley Fan Club	(OH)
The Wonder of You Elvis Fan Club	(MD)
The Young and Beautiful Friends of Elvis Fan Club	(NJ)
Then, Now, And Forever Elvis Presley Fan Club	(MS)
Through Elvis' Eyes	(MS)
Till We Meet Again	(NJ)
Today, Tomorrow, And Forever Elvis F.C. Of Alabama	(AL)
Touched By Elvis	(GA)
Touched By Elvis Fan Club	(VA)
Tribute To Elvis Fan Club	(LA)
Tri-State Elvis Fan Club	(AL)
True Fans For Elvis Fan Club	(ME)
Trying To Get To You Elvis Fan Club Tadle	(TX)

Unforgettable Elvis Fan Club	(PA)
United States Association of Elvis Presley Fan Clubs	(FL)
Universally Elvis	(TN)
US Male Fan Club	(OH)
Vegetarians Who Like Elvis	(TN)
Viva Las Vegas	(NV)
Viva Las Vegas Memphis Fashion	(TN)
Walk A Mile In My Shoes	(WI)
Walk A Mile In My Shoes - An Elvis F.C.	(IL)
Walk A Mile In My Shoes Fan Club	(TN)
Way Down Burning Love Fan Club	(NE)
Ways We Remember Elvis	(NC)
We Got A Thing About Elvis	(CA)
We Remember Elvis Fan Club	(PA)
Welcome To Our Elvis World	(MD)
Wild In The Country Fan Club	(WA)
What Would Elvis Do	(MI)
Worldwide Elvis Presley Fan Club	(WA)
Worldwide Young Elvis Fans, Inc.	(AR)
Yoopers For Elvis	(MI)
Yours In Elvis Forever	(TN)

Rest of the World

Here are some of the clubs perpetuating Elvis' memory around the globe.

ARGENTINA
2001 Elvis Presley Fan Club Official de Argentina

AUSTRALIA
Elvis Australia
Elvis Information Network
Elvis Legends Social Club
Elvis Presley Fan Club (Newcastle/Hunter)
Elvis Presley Fan Club of Australasia
Elvis Presley Fan Club of Queensland
Elvis Presley Fan Club of Tasmania
Elvis Presley Fan Club of Victoria
Elvis Presley The Memories Of Elvis Fan Club
Elvis Wild in the Country
Gold Coast Elvis Fan Club
If I Can Dream Fan Club of Western Australia
OEPFC Western Australia
Sound Of Elvis Fan Club of South Australia
Southern Cross Silver Stars Elvis Fan Club
TCB EPFC Queensland

AUSTRIA
Austrian Elvis Presley Fan Club Of Modling
Elvis History World of the King
Elvis Presley Fan Club
Follow That Dream

BELGIUM
Elvis Matters
Elvis Memories
Elvis Presley Today Society
International Elvis Presley Fan Club

United Elvis Presley Society

BRAZIL
Brasil Elvis Presley Society
Elvis Alive Fan Club
Elvis Back
Elvis In Astrodome
Elvis Land Fan Club
Elvis on Tour in Brazil Fan Club
Elvis Presley Artist of the Century
Elvis Presley's Graceland
Elvis Presley's Kingdom
Elvis Today
Gang Elvis
Sao Paulo Elvis Presley Society

BLGARIA
Elvis Is Back, 2000

CANADA
Canadian Federation of Elvis Friends
Collingwood Rocks With Elvis
Elvis Capital of Canada Fan Club
Elvis in Canada
Elvis Keeps Rocking Fan Club
Elvis Lives Again
Elvis Lives Worldwide Fan Club
Elvis Presley Association of PEI
Elvis Til We Meet Again Fan Club
For the Love of Elvis
I'll Remember You Elvis Fan Club
King Creole Fan Club, QuéÈbec
King O' Mania
Loving You Elvis, OEPFC of British Columbia
Merritt B.C. Elvis Presley
Portuguese Elvis Presley Fan Club
Respectfully Elvis Fan Club
To Elvis With Love Fan Club

CHILE
Elvis Chile
Elvis in Chile
Elvis Para Siempre
Esto Es Elvis

CROATIA
Elvis Presley Fan Club Zagreb
Elvis Presley With Love Fan Club

CZECH REPUBLIC
Elvis Presley Fan Club Czech Republic

DENMARK
The Official Elvis Presley Fan Club of Denmark
Elvis Presley TLC Memorial Fan Club

FINLAND
The Official Elvis Presley Fan Club of Finland

FRANCE
Association Elvis Pour Toujours
Elvis It's Now and Forever
Elvis My Happiness
Elvis Presley Club of Italy in France
Elvis Presley Sun Dial Fan Club
La Voix D'Elvis Fan Club
Les Amis d'Elvis/Treat Me Nice
Love Me Tender Fan Club, Normandy

FRENCH POLYNESIA
IA Orana Elvis

GERMANY
Elvis Club Berlin
Elvis is Back - EPFC Goeppingen
Elvis Presley Fan Club Interessengemeinschaft
Elvis Presley Fan Club Munchen
Elvis Presley Gesellschaft
Elvis Presley Will Never Die Fan Club
Elvis' Sunrise Loop
My Little Friend Elvis Fan Club
Tiger Man - Federation of Munich Elvis Fans

GREECE
Elvis Forever Fan Club of Greece

HONG KONG
International Elvis Presley Fan Club

INDIA

INDONESIA
Elvis Fans Club

IRELAND
Elvis Is the King
Elvis Social Club
Inner Circle of Elvis and Friends
Irish Elvis Presley Fan Club
TCB Fan Club of Ireland

ISRAEL
Elvis Presley, 2nd to None
Elvis Presley Fan Club of Israel
The Star of Elvis Will Shine Forever in Israel
    Fan Club
You'll Never Walk Alone Fan Club of Israel

ITALY
Elvis Friends Fan Club Italia
Elvis Friends Fan Club Of Milan
Elvis Italian Collectors Club
Elvis Presley Fan Club of Italy
Elvis Presley Rock Fan Club
Elvis' Pen Friends
Grazie Elvis
International Elvis Presley Club of Italy
Old Shep - Elvis Presley Italian Fan Club

JAPAN
C'mon Elvis Fans in Japan Fan Club
Elvis Presley Fan Club (Tokyo)
Elvis Presley Society of Japan
Elvis World
Japanese Heart for Elvis

LUXEMBOURG
Elvis Presley Fan Club of Luxembourg

MACEDONIA
Elvis Presley Fan Club of Macedonia
King Mania EPFC

MALAYSIA
Elvis Presley Fan Club of Malaysia and Worldwide
Elvis Presley Today Tomorrow and Forever Fan
Club of Malaysia

MEXICO
Memories of Elvis Fan Club

NETHERLANDS
Elvis Artist of the Century
Elvis Music Promotion Fan Club
Elvisnews.com
It's Elvis Time - Official Dutch Fan Club
Legends of Rock and Roll

NEW ZEALAND
Elvis Presley Fan Club
Elvis the Reality
Memories of Elvis Fan Club

NIGERIA
Nigeria Chapter of Love for Elvis Fan Club

NORWAY
Flaming Star—The Official Elvis Presley
    Fan Club of Norway
Memphis Flash

PAKISTAN
Elvis Aaron Presley Fan Club

PERU
Forever Elvis Presley Fan Club

PHILIPPINES
Elvis Lucky 7 Fan Club
Elvis Presley Friendship Club

PORTUGAL
"Burning Star" Club Oficial de Fã„s de Elvis
Elvis 100% - Still Rockin'

ROMANIA
Elvis Presley Memories
From a Jack to a King

Candid photo from the 1950's.

King Presley
Love Me Tender Elvis Fan Club

RUSSIA
Official Russian Elvis Presley Fan Club

SINGAPORE
Elvis Lives!

SOUTH AFRICA
Elvis Presley Fan Club of Africa
Elvis Presley Love Me Tender Fan Club
Takin' Care of Business Official Elvis Presley Fan
Club of South Africa

SPAIN
Amigos de Elvis
Club de Fans d'Elvis Presley dels Paisos Catalans
Club Elvis
Elvis Presley Memories
Friends of Elvis Fan Club of Spain

SRI LANKA
Elvis Presley Fan Club

SWEDEN
Elvis Forever Uppsala
Tidskriften Elvis, OEPC of Sweden

SWITZERLAND
Elvis Show Fan Club
Suisse Romande EPFC
Suspicious Minds Fan Club
Swiss Elvis Team

TURKEY
Elvis Is In Istanbul Now
Elvis Turk
Immortal King Elvis

UKRAINE
Burning Love

UNITED KINGDOM
A-Team Elvis Presley Fan Club
Always and Forever Elvis - Petersborough
Bromsgrove Branch: Pledging Our Love
Capital Elvis—OEPFC London
Elvis 2001 Fan Club
Elvis A King Forever Fan Club UK
Elvis Aberdeen
Elvis Central
Elvis For Everyone - Norwich
Elvis For Everyone - UK
Elvis Forever International

Elvis Gospel Fan Club
Elvis In Essex Fan Club
Elvis In the Heart Of Kent
Elvis Is King
Elvis Now!
Elvis Presley Fan Club—Bedfordshire Branch
Elvis Presley Fan Club—Berkshire Branch
Elvis Presley Fan Club - Cambridgeshire Branch
Elvis Presley Fan Club - Cleveland Branch
Elvis Presley Fan Club - Derbyshire Branch
Elvis Presley Fan Club - Lancashire Branch
Elvis Presley Fan Club - Leicester Branch
Elvis Presley Fan Club - Middlesex and Herts
    Branch
Elvis Presley Fan Club - Norfolk Branch
Elvis Presley Fan Club—Northampton Branch
Elvis Presley Fan Club - Nottingham Branch
Elvis Presley Fan Club - Oxford Branch
Elvis Presley Film Society
Elvis Presley's Follow that Dream Fan Club
Elvis Remembered Fan Club
Elvis Social Club—Irish Branch of the OEPFC of
    Great Britain
Elvis Takes Fan Club
Elvis Today Tomorrow Forever
Elvisly Yours
Essential Elvis
Eternal Elvis
Exclusive Elvis Express
Flaming Star - England
Forever Elvis, Yorkshire
Friends Through Elvis - York
Gracelanders
Hertfordshire Elvis Presley Fan Club
House of Elvis
King Elvis International
Lincoln Elvis
Memories - England
Memphis King
Memphis Mafia Fan Club
Promised Land
Steadfast, Loyal, and True Elvis in Wolverhampton
Steadfast, Loyal and True Official OEPFC
Strictly Elvis U.K.
The Elvis Touch
The Official Elvis Presley Fan Club of Great Britain
    & The Commonwealth
This Is Elvis
Walk-A-Mile-In-My-Shoes Elvis Disabled Fan Club
West Midlands Elvis Presley Fan Club
Wonderful World of Elvis

VENEZUELA
Venezuela Elvis Fan Club

"FARTHER ALONG"

Elvis is at his dulcet best on this traditional spiritual on the 1956 *Million Dollar Sessions* and on the 1966 album *How Great Thou Art* (recorded by Elvis in Nashville on May 27 that year). The song is one of the extras added to the 2000 *That's The Way It Is* 3-CD box set, in the form of Elvis trying out his bass singing in rehearsals with the band. The 2000 gospel compilation *Peace In The Valley* presents all three versions for comparison. "Farther Along" was written by Reverend W. B. Stone in the late Thirties and was originally recorded by the Howell Carolina Hillbillies, the first in a long line of gospel groups (including The Stamps) that have covered the song.

The song can also be found on the various Million Dollar albums and on Nineties gospel compilation *Amazing Grace*.

FASHION

See CLOTHES, COSTUMES AND DESIGNERS

FATHER

Vernon Presley was Elvis' father but not his most influential father figure. When she was alive, Gladys was the dominant figure in the household. After Elvis took on Colonel Parker to manage him, the male figure of authority to whom Elvis deferred was the man to whom he paid 25% (and later 50%) of his earnings rather than his biological dad (though when the Colonel had a beef about something Elvis was doing or how he was acting, his usual first port of call was Vernon). Elvis would listen to his daddy, but as the breadwinner from an early age, Elvis had the final say. Moreover, Elvis was accustomed to being the uncontested authority in his private sphere, especially with his often much younger female partners.

In his book, *Elvis: What Happened?*, Red West suggests that Elvis enforced his own role as a father figure on those around him by ensuring that the guys in his entourage were not paid enough to become financially independent: "He likes to be a father figure, or a God figure."

Actor Arthur O'Connell played Elvis' character's father in two early Sixties movies, *Follow That Dream* and *Kissin' Cousins*.

ELVIS SAID IN 1957: "Colonel Parker is more or less like a daddy when I'm away from my own folks."

MARTY LACKER: "Elvis loved his father. The problem was Vernon, not Elvis. Early on, Vernon was basically jealous of Elvis. As the years went by, and the normal father-son roles reversed. Elvis became the provider."

FAULKNER, WILLIAM
(1897-1962)

Groundbreaking Nobel and Pulitzer prize-winning author Faulkner struck up a correspondence with Elvis after sending his condolences for Gladys's death. Faulkner's novels, based mainly in and around Mississippi, include *The Sound and the Fury* and *As I Lay Dying*; he also wrote screenplays (*The Big Sleep* for one).

FAVORITES
-*Actors:*
Elvis was a big James Dean and Marlon Brando fan. Aside from his method actor favorites, in interviews Elvis also said that he admired Richard

Vernon (CENTER) between Frank Sinatra and Elvis.

Widmark and Yul Brynner. Priscilla says that when they met, his acting idols in addition to Brando and Dean were Karl Malden and Rod Steiger. As a teenager, he liked the young Tony Curtis, who he saw at the movie house where he worked part-time as an usher. Twenties sex symbol Rudolph Valentino was also an actor with whom Elvis identified.

-*Actresses:*
Early in his career, Elvis told an interviewer that his favorite actresses were Eva Marie Saint and Kim Novak. Towards the end of his feature film career, he said that his favorite actress to work with was Shelley Fabares, though he had a thing about many of his leading ladies, Ann-Margret *in primis*.

-*Airline:*
"Presley Airlines"

-*Amusement ride:*
Zippin' Pippin at the Memphis Fairgrounds, when he wasn't on the dodgems.

-*Beverages:*
Mountain Valley water, Gatorade and Pepsi Cola.

-*Board games:*
Yahtzee (he generally won) and Monopoly.

-*Books:*
A voracious reader, in his later years Elvis traveled with a personal library which he transported in big trunks. Books that he would most often reach for included Gilbran's *The Prophet* and *Cheiro's Book of Numbers*. His copy of the PDR was very well thumbed, and he always had a bible to hand. He gave out dozens of copies of *The Impersonal Life* to friends. See Books Elvis read for more.

-*Comedians:*
Zany British humor particularly tickled Elvis' funny bone, notably Peter Sellers and Monty Python.

-*Colors:*
There's no doubt that pink was the color associated with Elvis in his breakthrough years. In a 1956 interview, he said that black was his favorite

color for clothes and white for cars. He later added blue—no fewer than 22 Elvis song titles include the word—and gold to his palette for costumes and home decoration.

-*Directors:*
After finishing work on *King Creole*, directed by Michael Curtiz, Elvis declared that at last he understood what a real director was. Norman Taurog was his favorite to work with, possibly because he was the least demanding.

-*Flower:*
Jasmine.

-*Food:*
Elvis was mighty partial to his mother's homemade apple pie. Fried pork chops were a firm favorite, often the meal he ate when he got back to Graceland after spending time in Hollywood. Of course, there were the legendary fried peanut butter and banana sandwiches, a non-delicacy that will eternally be associated with Elvis even though insiders swear that he ate them infrequently. For breakfast, industrial quantities of bacon singed to a crisp.

-*Gem stones:*
Black sapphires, diamonds.

-*Football team:*
Elvis looked out for the results of the Cleveland Browns (he was a great fan of runner Jim Brown's) and the LA Rams. He liked his own team, Elvis Presley Enterprises, which he ran and played on in the early Sixties. In 1974, he often attended games played by the Memphis Southmen (also known as the Memphis Grizzlies).

-*Gospel songs:*
Anything by the Blackwoods and The Statesman. Elvis very much liked Doris Akers' "Sweet Sweet Spirit," which J.D. Sumner and the Stamps sometimes sang during Elvis' Seventies shows. The song that is said to have meant most to him in his own repertoire was "How Great Thou Art."

-*Groups:*
In the mid-Fifties he declared a preference for the Platters. In 1959, Elvis said that Billy Vaughn and His Orchestra were mighty fine. When inter-

viewed by Peter Noone of Herman's Hermits in 1965, Elvis teasingly said that his favorite group after The Beatles was the Boston Pops, followed by the Boston Symphony. The Ink Spots were always a favorite, as were Ike and Tina Turner and the Righteous Brothers. See Musical influences for more.

-Hobbies:

Different hobbies at different times, all pursued with a passion.

-Movies:

See Movies, under Elvis' taste in movies.

-Movie Performances:

King Creole (1958)

-Peanut butter:

Skippy.

-Restaurant:

In his early years, before restaurants became out of bounds, Elvis frequently went to the Chenault Drive-in in Memphis. With a cook on hand 24-hours at day at Graceland, Elvis didn't often feel the need to go out.

-Singers (female):

In 1957, Elvis said that his female favorites were Patti Page and Kay Starr. In 1969 named Mahalia Jackson and the Ward Gospel Singers. He also liked classical soprano Kirsten Flagstad.

-Singers (male):

As a kid, Elvis liked hillbilly singers Mississippi Slim and Jimmie Rodgers. Fats Domino was a big favorite; Elvis would always take in his shows when he was in Vegas, where in 1956 he was also very taken by Jackie Wilson, then singing with Billy Ward and the Dominos. Elvis once said that his favorite singer was gospel artist Jake Hess, with whom he later worked on *How Great Thou Art*. In 1956, Elvis said that the greatest C&W singer he knew was Sonny James. Over the next couple of years he declared his appreciation for Bing Crosby, Perry Como, Frank Sinatra, Dean Martin, Tommy Sands, and the Four Lads.

When in the Army in the late Fifties, Elvis' favorite singer was Roy Orbison—he always asked what Orbison was doing musically when he called home.

In the early Sixties, Elvis liked listening to Andy Williams. Over the years Elvis professed his admiration for Pat Boone, Bobby Darin, Billy Eckstine Tom Jones, (and, courteously, just about any singer who he knew in the Las Vegas audience at one of his shows). In her memoir Priscilla lists Elvis' faves as Gary Puckett and the Union Gap. Marty Lacker recalls Brook Benton and Arthur Prysock among Elvis' favorites. See Heroes and Musical influences for more.

-Song:

When interviewers asked Elvis what his favorite songs was, Elvis generally mentioned his latest release. In May 1956, Elvis told Arkansas DJ Ray Green that his favorite song was his recent RCA track "I Was the One." Later that year his answer was "Don't Be Cruel." At a 1958 press conference he said that his favorite song was "Padre," by Toni Arden, and "You'll Never Walk Alone," both of which he later covered. By 1959, his answer to the inevitable "favorite song" question was "Don't." In 1961, he said his favorite of all so far was "It's Now Or Never," not so coincidentally his biggest ever seller. That was where the buck stopped—he still claimed this song as his favorite in 1972. In an interview, Charlie Hodge said that of his own output, Elvis' favorite albums were his gospel LPs.

-Store:

Lansky. See SHOPPING.

-Style of music:

In 1960, Elvis said his favorite was spiritual music, particularly the old colored spirituals. He sang gospel to warm up for recording sessions; he sang gospel to wind down in private after performing. He was drawn to ballads from an early age—every song he sang at Sun the first time he performed for Sam Phillips was a ballad. Not forgetting the blues, hillbilly, and after he helped to midwife it, rock 'n' roll . . . Elvis appreciated fine music regardless of genre. He looked up to operatic heroes of the past and was an avid consumer of the latest music trends throughout his life. The only type of music he expressed an antipathy for was jazz, though he sang one or two jazzy numbers himself.

FBI

Although the FBI never investigated Elvis for impropriety, files were kept on the singer throughout his career. Elvis' 663-page FBI file is available for consultation on the FBI web site. It documents riotous behavior at his concerts, complaints about the immorality of his music and his performances, attempts at extortion, and whether or not J. Edgar Hoover and Richard M. Nixon should have official meetings with the singer (the answers were no and yes). A significant proportion of the file refers to a fraud attempt regarding Elvis' airplanes perpetrated in 1976.

The first official complaint that the FBI received about Elvis went right to the top. In May 1956, J. Edgar Hoover was sent a letter by the editor of the local paper in LaCrosse, Wisconsin, in which he accused Elvis of indulging in "sexual gratification on stage."

The FBI began collecting news items on youth reaction to Elvis and on the potential for riots at his concerts. The bureau also began to accumulate material on extortion and assassination threats directed at Elvis. In 1959, the Bureau was informed about a blackmail attempt perpetrated by a German conman called Laurenz Johannes Griessel-Landau.

The Bureau was called in to advise when Elvis received an assassination threat in the summer of 1970.

Later that year, Elvis toured the FBI headquarters with six of his entourage and the former Sheriff of Shelby Country, Tennessee, Bill Morris. Elvis enjoyed the personal tour of exhibits at the Federal Building, featuring some of the grizzliest crimes in US history. However, he was disappointed not to meet one of his personal heroes, J. Edgar Hoover. In-house FBI correspondence reveals that the decision was taken in advance that "Presley's sincerity and good intentions notwithstanding, he is certainly not the type of individual whom the Director would wish to meet."

After Elvis' visit, FBI operative A. Jones wrote in his report, "Despite his rather bizarre personal appearance, Presley seemed a sincere, serious-minded individual who expressed concern over some of the problems confronting our country, particularly those involving young people." He went on to say: "Presley is of the opinion that The Beatles laid the groundwork for many of the problems we are having with young people by their filthy unkempt appearances, and suggestive music, while entertaining in this country during the early and middle Sixties. He advised that the Smothers Brothers, Jane Fonda and other persons in the entertainment industry of their ilk have a lot to answer for in the hereafter for how they have poisoned young minds by disparaging the United States in their public statements and unsavory activities."

Elvis offered to serve as an undercover agent if required, and for his efforts received a thank you note from J. Edgar Hoover (though rumors later circulated among Elvis-is-alivers that he did become a secret FBI operative), who declined to meet him.

In 1976, the FBI was brought in to investigate an attempt to defraud Elvis of a considerable amount of money in relation to leasing arrangements for his Lockheed Jetstar plane, part of an international white-collar crime ring.

Books:

Elvis-Top Secret: The Untold Story of Elvis Presley's Secret FBI Files, by Earl Greenwood and Kathleen Tracy, Signet, 1991

Video:

The Elvis Files, Sky Creative Media Group, 1998

FEATHERS, CHARLIE
(1932-1998)

Charlie Feathers was a rockabilly pioneer who recorded for several Memphis labels including Sun in the mid-Fifties without getting the national exposure other Memphis rockers achieved. He became a cult hero during the rockabilly revival in the Seventies and Eighties.

Feathers co-wrote Elvis' Sun hit "I Forgot To Remember To Forget." In later years, he claimed that he was instrumental in the production and arrangement of all of Elvis' early work at Sun.

FEARS

Elvis was one of the entertainment industry's most accomplished stage performers, capable of directing audience reaction through the entire range of human emotion, but before he went on, throughout his career he suffered (sometimes debilitating) stage fright.

Elvis described himself and fellow-band members Scotty Moore and Bill Black as "like a bunch of dead people, we were scared so bad" when they were waiting to go on for their first big live show at Overton Park Shell in the summer of 1954. His jangling nerves have been credited as the inspiration for his skittering, leg-twitching dance style.

According to some who lived within his orbit, beneath Elvis' kinglike demeanor lurked the unlikely character trait of insecurity. Secretary and onetime lover Elisabeth Stefaniak said that the first thing Elvis asked when he went to see her in hospital after she and Vernon were involved in a minor car accident, was whether there had been any funny business between them.

Elvis was terrified that his two years in the Army and out of the public eye would spell the end of his career.

Priscilla and other insiders have commented on a general sense of fear in the Presley family, a foreboding that something terrible might happen at any moment and destroy their good fortune.

In 1965, when the Beatles asked Elvis what did do avoid being scared by his squealing fans, Elvis told them that if they were really scared, they were in the wrong business.

Elvis was almost paralyzed by stage fright during taping of his 1968 NBC TV Special. So long had it been since he performed in front of a live audience that he asked for a clause in his contract that expressly excluded any live segment. He almost didn't go out at all to record the informal segment when he sits down and chats with the audience. Producer Steve Binder saved the day by telling him that even if he went out onto the stage, sat down, looked around and then walked off again, he had to go out and give it a try.

Elvis overcame major stage fright on his opening night at the International Hotel, Las Vegas in 1969, and at his *Aloha from Hawaii* concert in 1973. The day after his International Hotel debut he told the press he was a "little nervous for the first three songs, but then I thought, 'What the heck, get with it, man, or you might be out of a job tomorrow.' "

Larry Geller found a climate of suspicion among Elvis' friends and family regarding outsiders or anything outside their familiar world, whether it be people or ideas.

As a man very much in the public eye at a time when America suffered several high-profile assassinations, Elvis had reason to fear that he was a potential target. Red West confirms, "Elvis had a fear of someone shooting and killing him for no reason." He received death threats in every decade he was a performer, several times in Las Vegas.

Lamar Fike says that Elvis had a strong fear of snakes that manifested itself in shooting them at every opportunity.

Biographers have asserted that Elvis' relationship with Colonel Parker was based on an atavistic respect for and fear of figures in authority. Peter Guralnick puts forward another interpretation: that Elvis submitted so willingly to the Colonel's dominion over his career because he fervently believed Parker was his own personal good luck charm, and that without him it might all come to an end.

One reason why Elvis didn't ever separate from the Colonel's was his fear of confrontation. Elvis would go to great lengths to avoid facing up to situations he found unpleasant. A number of times Elvis reputedly asked members of his entourage to tell the Colonel he was fired, to which the Colonel replied that he'd believe it when he heard it from Elvis himself. It has been claimed that Elvis' fugue into pharmaceuticals was one of his ways of avoiding issues he found frightening or unpleasant.

In 1976, Elvis was very apprehensive about the contents of the book former bodyguards Red and Sonny West were writing. Larry Geller remembers Elvis in tears, mortified at what Lisa Marie and Vernon would think of him after the book came out. He worried less about his fans, who he suspected would not believe the former entourage members' claims.

ELVIS SAID IN 1972: "I've never gotten over what they call stage fright. I go through it every show."

LARRY GELLER: "Elvis harbored deep fears about saying certain things, because he didn't want to be wrong."

PRISCILLA: "He held in his fears and emotions until at times he would explode, tearing into anyone who happened to be around."

LARRY GELLER: "From Parker's point of view, the only good Elvis was a frightened Elvis."

PRISCILLA: "Elvis never showed any of his fears. He felt he had a responsibility to make everyone else feel secure."

"FEELINGS"

Elvis worked on a recording of this song at his final recording studio session at Graceland in late 1976 but never completed it. The song had been a big hit in the US a year earlier for Brazilian songwriter Morris Albert (who was later successfully sued for plagiarism by French songwriter Louis Gasté). Elvis' version has not been released to date.

FERRA, SANDY
(B. 1946)

Fourteen-year-old daughter of the man who owned the Crossbow club in LA, frequented by Elvis in 1960 when working on *G.I. Blues*. Elvis and Sandy hung out together in LA, and dated

for six years on and off; she danced in many of his movies over this period. Later, she married Memphis DJ Wink Martindale.

SANDY FERRA MARTINDALE: "We had a six year romance. It was great. He was the best kisser."

"FEVER"

Originally written by Otis Blackwell (under the pseudonym John Davenport) and Eddie Cooley in 1956, for Little Willie John, though best known through covers by Peggy Lee and a slew of skillful female vocalists, Elvis recorded a pared down version of this song in Nashville on April 3, 1960. It was initially released on *Elvis Is Back!*, since when it has appeared on later compilations such as *Pure Gold, A Valentine Gift For You, From Nashville To Memphis, Love Elvis*, and the 2007 *The Essential Elvis*.

Elvis added the song to his live repertoire in the summer of 1972 (a finger-snapping early live version features on 2005 FTD release *Summer Festival*) and sang it regularly right through to 1977. It's on *Aloha From Hawaii Via Satellite, The Alternate Aloha*, and on FTD live albums *Elvis Recorded Live On Stage In Memphis, I Found My Thrill, Closing Night, Live In L.A. It's Midnight, Dragonheart, Tucson '76, New Year's Eve* and *Spring Tours '77*

Alternate versions from the 1960 recording are on *Essential Elvis, Vol. 6*, and the FTD *Elvis Is Back!* release.

FICTION AND POETRY

Lovestruck fans have been writing poetry to Elvis ever since he started making teens scream. His starring role in novels and short stories didn't come until his remarkable afterlife. The trickle of Elvis fiction gradually became a flood from the late Seventies onwards, lending impetus to the nascent group of people who questioned whether or not Elvis really died at all.

According to the knowledgeable Bill E. Burk, Elvis fiction is far less popular with fans than with non-fans. That hasn't prevented a growing list of sci-fi, whodunit, short story and youth fiction writers and novelists from recasting Elvis on the printed page as an instantly-recognizable protagonist, theme or allegory, starting with Bernard Benson, who in late 1976 wrote and gave Elvis an allegory about his life titled *The Minstrel*.

Elvis continues to be a muse for poets, in many cases fans expressing their complex relationship to the object of their affections. A great many fans wrote poetry after Elvis' death—the Colonel too composed poems to his departed client some years later.

A POETRY AND FICTION SELECTION

Heartbreak Hotel, by Anne River Siddons, Simon & Schuster, 1976.
The Minstrel, by Bernard Benson, Putnam, 1977
Bill Adler's Love Letters to Elvis, by Bill Adler, Grosset and Dunlap, 1978.
Elvis, Come Back! by Sheila Jazzman, Western Elite Press, 1978.
Orion: The Living Superstar of Song, by Gail Brewer-Giorgio, Capricorn, 1979.
"Graceland Uber Alles," short story by Lester Bangs in *The Complete Elvis*, Delilah Books, 1982.
"Ike at the Mike," short story by Howard Waldrop.
Elvis: The Fotonovel, by Keith Baty and Robert Graham, Dell Publishing Company, 1983.

Stark Raving Elvis, by William McCranor Henderson, EP Dutton/Simon & Schuster, 1984.
The Elvis Murders: Will the Real Elvis Please Stand Up?, by Art Bourgeau, Burkley Publishing Group/Charter Mystery, 1985.
The Presley Arrangement, by Monte Nicholson, Vantage Press, 1987.
Ambient, by Jack Womack, Weidenfeld and Nicolson, 1987.
Elvis the King, by Boen Hallum, self-published, 1987.
Tender: A Novel, by Mark Childress, Harmony Books, 1990.
Comeback Tour: The Sky Belongs to the Stars, by Jack Yeovil, G. W. Books, 1991.
Graced Land, by Laura Kalpakian, Grove Weidenfeld, 1992.
Elvis Presley Calls His Mother After "The Ed Sullivan Show," by Samuel Charters, Coffee House Press, 1992.
Roses to Elvis, by Gail Brewer-Giorgio, Arctic Corp., 1992.
Heartbreak Hotel, by Cassie Miles, Harlequin Books, 1993.
Elvis Rising: Stories on the King, ed. by Kay Sloan and Constance Pierce, Avon Books, 1993.
Lonely Street, by Steve Brewer, Pocketbooks, 1994
Elvis in Aspic, Gorden DeMarco, West Coast Crime, 1994.
The King Is Dead: Tales of Elvis Post-Mortem, ed. by Paul L. Sammon, Delta, 1994 (short stories and non-fiction essays by Lou Reed, Greil Marcus, Roger Ebert, Martin Amis, and Janice and Neal Gregory).
Mondo Elvis: A Collection of Fiction and Poems About the King, ed. Lucinda Ebersole and Richard Peabody, St. Martin's Press, 1994.
Return to Sender: An Anthology of Poems for Elvis Presley, edited by Tony Charles and Gordon Wardman, Headlock Press, 1994.
That's All Right, Mama: The Unauthorized Life of Elvis' Twin, by Gerald Duff, Baskerville Publishers, 1995.
The Amazing Adventures of Space Elvis, by David S. Wall, published in Blipvert magazine, 1995.
The Strange Case of the Lost Elvis Diaries, by Barry Willis, Waynoka Press, 1995.
Return to Sender: The Secret Son of Elvis Presley, by Les and Sue Fox, West Highland Publishing Company, 1996.
The Groom Wore Blue Suede Shoes, by Jessica Travis, Silhouette Books, 1996.
Me, The Moon and Elvis Presley, by Christopher Hope, Macmillan, 1997.
Love Me Tender: The True Story of Marilyn and the King as Told by Karen Karma, Readhead Press, 1997.
Blue Christmas, by Sandra Hill, Linda Jones, Sharon Pisacreta and Amy Elizabeth Saunders.
Elvis over England, by Barry Hines, Michael Joseph Ltd., 1998.
Elvis Saves, by Bill Yancey, Xlibris Corporation, 1998.
The Elvis and Marilyn Affair, by Robert S. Levinson, Tor/Forge, 1999.
Another Song About the King, by Kathryn Stern, Random House, 2000.
Templars of the Christian Brotherhood, by David Paul and Geoffrey Todd, 1st Books, 2000.
Lamar's Rebellion, by James S. Gibons, Xlibris, 2000.
Elvis And Nixon, by Jonathan Lowy, Crown, 2001
Elvis and the Apocalypse, by Steve Werner, Xlibris, 2001.
All Shook Up: Collected Poems About Elvis, ed. Will Clemens, University of Arkansas Press, 2001.
Murder Boogies with Elvis, by Anne Carroll George, Morrow, 2001.
Elvis in the Morning, by William F. Buckley, Jr., Harcourt, 2001.
Elvis Live at Five, by John Paxson, Thomas Dunne, 2002.
Heartbreak Hotel, by Jeremy Reed, Orion Fiction, 2002.

Daniel Klein murder mysteries *Kill Me Tender, Blue Suede Clues, Viva Las Vengeance, Such Vicious Minds* (St. Martin's Minotaur, 2002-4).

Wings on a Guitar: August 16, 1977 - If Elvis Hadn't Died! by Glenda Ivey, Southern Charm, 2002.

Around Elvis, by Thorne Peters, Legend Enterprise, 2003.

Jesse, by Brian Devall, Aventine, 2003.

My Road Trip to the Pretty Girl Capital of the World, by Brian Yansky, Cricket, 2003.

Bubba Ho-Tep, short story and script by Joe R. Lansdale, Don Coscarelli, Night Shade Books, 2004.

The Return of the King: An Elvis Novel, by Michael Hodjera, iUniverse, 2004.

Chasing Elvis, by Glenn Marcel, Invisible College Press, 2004.

Graceland, by Chris Abani, Farrar, Straus and Giroux, 2004.

The Year the Music Changed: The Letters of Achsa Mceachern-Isaacs & Elvis Presley, by Diane Thomas, Toby Press, 2005.

Lips, by Byron Edwards, iUniverse, 2005.

Bright Light City: An Elvis Novel, by Michael Hodjera, iUniverse, 2006.

The Elvis Interviews, by Glen Bonham, Battlefield Publishing Inc., 2006.

Singing Elvis Badly, by Stephen Jones, AuthorHouse, 2007.

Elvis' Secret Legacy, by Cherry McKenzie, AuthorHouse, 2007.

What If ?: A Second Chance At Life For Elvis, by Roger Hannah, RK Hannah Publishing, 2007.

Eternal Flame, by Patricia Garber, Xlibris, 2007.

Faux Elvis, by Pat Cook, Outskirts Press, 2007.

Contract With The King, by Paul Pullens, AuthorHouse, 2007.

Chicken A La King, by Heidi Jacobsen, Lulu.com, 2007.

The Elvis Prophecy, by Allan Morrison, Lulu.com, 2007.

FIELDS, GEORGE

A multi-instrumentalist specialized in steel guitar, who played on Elvis' sessions for *Loving You* and *Blue Hawaii.*

50,000,000 ELVIS FANS CAN'T BE WRONG

See ELVIS' GOLD RECORDS, VOL. 2.

FIKE, LAMAR
(B. 1935)

Biographers generally state that Elvis met this 300-pound Texan some time in the latter half of 1956 at Sun Records, and immediately took a shine to him—though the tale of Fike meeting Elvis after crawling through the back window of Elvis' home at Audubon Drive in Memphis is more amusing, particularly considering that Fike is anything but svelte. Fike has said in interviews that they actually first met in 1954 via George Klein, and then met again through mutual friend Cliff Gleaves in 1956.

Fike was raised in Cleveland, Mississippi by a Jewish mother and a traveling salesman father.

When Fike read that Elvis had been hospitalized during filming of *Jailhouse Rock* he drove all the way from Texas to LA, where Elvis invited him to stay with the gang at the Beverly Wilshire Hotel. Fike moved in to Graceland for a spell that year, and claims to have been the first non-family entourage member to live on site.

Though Fike was briefly fired after getting into

a fight with Cliff Gleaves over a game of badminton in early 1958, he remained an entourage regular on and off for the rest of Elvis' life. He was the first of the gang to come down with Vernon, Gladys and grandma Minnie Mae to live with Elvis in Killeen, Texas, during his Army service. Fike had attempted to enlist to keep Elvis company—the only one of several Elvis pals to put this plan into action—but was turned down for his excess weight. Fike then accompanied Elvis to Germany.

In the entourage, Fike alternated between being a jester and the butt of jokes. He was always ready to mine a situation for laughs or send people up. Elvis variously called him "Buddha," "The Great Speckled Bird," and a succession of not-so-friendly weight-related names.

A story that Elvis never let Fike live down was when, in Paris, his friend fell for the chorus girls, only to find out as he was getting hot and heavy that this particular she was a he.

When Elvis returned to the States in 1960 and started in on his busy movie-making schedule, Fike's job was to organize transport.

Fike and Elvis parted company in mid-1962 after a row. Fike then spent a spell as a road manager for Brenda Lee. Elvis later helped land Fike a job working for his music publishers, Hill and Range, in Nashville. For many years Fike worked alongside Freddy Bienstock, pitching songs to Elvis for him to select for recording. Fike was the source of several songs that Elvis recorded at his American Studio sessions in 1969, including "Wearin' That Loved On Look" and "Inherit The Wind." In 1970, Fike brought Elvis several Shirl Milete compositions. That year, Fike returned to Elvis' employ as tour lighting manager. He worked with Elvis from then on, occasionally appearing on stage himself. The day Elvis died, Fike was in Portland, Oregon with the Colonel, making preparations for the first date on Elvis' upcoming tour. Fike was one of Elvis' pallbearers.

After Elvis, Fike went into music management, and worked with artists including Billie Jo Spears.

Fike was consulted by Albert Goldman for his disparaging biography of Elvis, published in 1981. He worked with David Stanley on (a previous) *Elvis Encyclopedia,* and was a prime source for Alanna Nash's books on the Memphis Mafia. At the time of writing, he had announced his memoir, *Fike: An Uncommon Journey,* for publication in 2007.

LAMAR FIKE: "Elvis didn't like being around other stars, but I loved it."

RED WEST: "He was a great guy who was just so funny without even trying, and he had a heart of gold, too."

MARTY LACKER: "Elvis liked him for a variety of reasons. One is that he needed somebody to pick on. Lamar is also brilliant."

Book:
Elvis Aaron Presley: Revelations from the Memphis Mafia, by Alanna Nash, with Billy Smith, Marty Lacker and Lamar Fike, HarperCollins, 1995.

"FIND OUT WHAT'S HAPPENING"

Elvis recorded this song, on July 22, 1973 at Stax. Written by Jerry Crutchfield and originally released by The Spindells in 1964—though it was a bigger hit for Bobby Bare in 1968—Elvis' version was released as an album track on *Raised On Rock.*

Vernon and the Colonel chose a version of this

song without overdubs for the second volume of *Our Memories of Elvis* in 1979.

Alternate takes have come out on *Essential Elvis Vol. 5* and 2006 FTD CD *Made in Memphis,* followed by a flood of outtakes on 2007 FTD CD *Raised On Rock.*

"FINDERS KEEPERS, LOSERS WEEPERS"

Elvis recorded this Dory and Ollie Jones tune on May 26, 1963 in Nashville. It was first released on the 1965 album *Elvis For Everyone.* Later album releases include *For The Asking* and *From Nashville To Memphis.* The first take from the Nashville session came out on 2000 FTD album *Long Lonely Highway.*

FINKEL, BOB

Hired by NBC boss Tom Sarnoff, the producer of Elvis' NBC TV Special was the man who brought creative minds Steve Binder and Bones Howe on board. While Finkel—made a member of the Snowmen's League by Colonel Parker—kept relations smooth, the team of Binder and Howe concocted a show that went far beyond the staid bounds of the deal that Parker thought that he had made for a Christmas show.

Finkel was one of very few people who succeeded in out-pranking the Colonel. During the making of the show Finkel and the Colonel exchanged photos of themselves in various military costumes. After taping of the show wrapped, Finkel had the giant red letters that spelled out "Elvis" set up in the Colonel's garden in Palm Springs for him to find when he next visited his vacation home.

FINLATOR, JOHN

The deputy director of the United States Bureau of Narcotics and Dangerous Drugs when Elvis rolled into Washington in late 1970 on a mission to obtain the law enforcement badge he cherished above all others: a federal agent in the fight against drugs. Elvis didn't take Finlator's polite no for an answer. He arranged an impromptu visit to President Nixon, Nixon called Finlator to the White House and Elvis got his badge.

In an article published in a 1973 book, Finlator revealed that there had already been contacts between his department and the entertainer before Elvis' trip to Washington.

FIRST ASSEMBLY OF GOD CHURCH

The Church in which Gladys grew up in East Tupelo. Part of the Pentecostal Church of God movement, the Assembly of God Church originated in Anderson, Indiana in 1916. The Church outlook was characterized by a strong belief in the existence of the Holy Spirit and its tangible healing power, and indicated the path to holiness through love. The Church also espoused a belief in speaking in tongues, the final judgment and a second coming. Church followers were expected to be moderate in everything they did, avoid going to the movies because it was a sin, and women were discouraged from wearing make-up or jewelry. Music was a fundamental part of worship; the Church was popular with working class people, and did not differentiate between black and white.

By the time Elvis was born, his parents attended church in a modest wooden building at 206 Adams Street, a couple of blocks away from where they were living. This was where Elvis, aged two, wriggled out of his mother's arms and tried to join in with the choir. When he was a little older, he was invited to sing with the congregation and his parents on merit, not just infant enthusiasm.

Several members of Gladys's family were ministers in this church, including Reverend Frank Smith, who helped to teach Elvis the rudiments of guitar. The congregation is now known as the East Heights Assembly of God Church.

When the Presleys moved to Memphis in 1948, they joined the congregation at the First Assembly church located at 1085 McLemore Ave.

Elvis was a regular churchgoer for several years after fame struck. In the Sixties he took against the idea of organized religion, though he continued to believe in parts of his First Assembly upbringing, notably the power to heal people through the laying on of hands, something which he himself attempted.

At the time of writing, the Assemblies of God movement has 2.6 million followers in the United States and over 50 million round the world.

CHERYL THURBER: "There was openness to the idea of music as part of the heart of the Christian experience and a way of openly and emotionally expressing those beliefs."

"FIRST IN LINE"

Elvis recorded this echo-heavy track by Aaron Schroeder & Ben Weisman on September 3, 1956 at Radio Recorders for imminent release on his second album, *Elvis*, and soon after on EP *Strictly Elvis*. It has since appeared on *The King Of Rock And Roll*.

"FIRST NOEL, THE"

Elvis recorded this seventeenth-century British carol on May 16, 1971 in a solemn hymn-like version released initially on *Elvis Sings The Wonderful World Of Christmas*. It has since featured on Yule-themed compilations *If Every Day Was Like Christmas*, *Blue Christmas*, *White Christmas*, *Christmas Peace*, and *Elvis Christmas*.

"FIRST TIME EVER I SAW YOUR FACE, THE"

Elvis may have first heard the song in the version recorded by Peter, Paul and Mary in the mid-Sixties; he likely also heard it in the Clint Eastwood movie *Play Misty For Me*. Early Seventies girlfriend Joyce Bova suggested that Elvis record the ballad originally written by Ewan MacColl for his wife Peggy Seeger in 1963.

Elvis' gave the song a studio run-through on March 15, 1971, initially in duets with backing singer Ginger Holladay and then Temple Riser, though in the end producer Felton Jarvis opted for a solo overdub vocal for release.

Elvis' version was first released as the B-side to "American Trilogy" in April 1972. That same year the song was a massive #1 hit for Roberta Flack, winning the "Song of the Year" Grammy (though she recorded the song three years earlier). Elvis' studio version has since appeared on *Elvis Aron Presley* and *Walk A Mile In My Shoes*.

Elvis added the song to his live repertoire in 1973. FTD release *Closing Night* features a live version of this song, while *Elvis On Tour—The Rehearsals* from 2004 contains a studio rehearsal from a year earlier. FTD's 2006 release *I Found My Thrill* includes an early 1974 performance dedicated to girlfriend Sheila Ryan. Other live versions are on FTD release *An American Trilogy*.

FIRSTS

Elvis carried on scoring firsts and setting records right through his career. This list is of "early firsts":

First recording session: June or July 1953
First single: "That's All Right (Mama)" / "Blue Moon Of Kentucky"(Sun 209), issued in mid-July 1954.
First radio airplay: July 7, 1954 on DJ Dewey Phillips' WHBQ show, right before a cat food commercial . . . though Fred Cook previously spun the disk for thirty seconds on WREC before taking it off because he hated it.
First interview: On Dewey Phillips' show that first night.
First time people heard Elvis . . . is etched indelibly into the minds of countless fans and music professionals, summed up succinctly by Sun engineer Jack Clement as, "Hey, I've been waiting for that!"
First official concert: Saturday, July 17, 1954, at the Bon Air in Memphis, with guitarist Scotty Moore and bass player Bill Black of the Starlite Wranglers (though Elvis later said his first show was at the Overton Park Shell on July 30).
First newspaper interview: with Edwin Howard in his *Memphis Press-Scimitar* column, titled "Overnight Sensation," July 27, 1954.
First *Billboard* record review: "That's All Right (Mama)," August 7, 1954. *Billboard* magazine editor Paul Ackerman wrote that Presley was "a potent new chanter who can sock over any tune for either the country or the R & B markets..." and concluding that he was "a strong new talent."
First time topping a bill: February 20, 1955, on a Hank Snow Jamboree Attractions show in Little Rock, Arkansas.
First fully-fledged riot: Jacksonville, Florida, May 13, 1955.
First magazine articles: June 1955, *Cowboy Song* (title: "Sun's Newest Star"); *Country Song Roundup*, September 1955, in which Elvis was referred to as a "folk music fireball."
First national chart single: "Baby Let's Play House" entered the *Cashbox* Country and Western chart on July 16, 1955.
First management contract with Colonel Parker: August 15, 1955.
First appearance on film: Elvis was filmed on stage with Bill Haley, Pat Boone, LaVern Baker, Roy Hamilton and others in Cleveland, Ohio, in October 1955, for a film about local DJ Bill Randle. *The Pied Piper of Cleveland: A Day in the Life of a Famous Disc-Jockey* was never released. An earlier home movie, shot by audience members at the Magnolia Gardens in Houston in August 1955 was released on video in 1997 as *1st Ever Elvis* and then a decade later on the "Ed Sullivan Show" DVD issue. Even earlier footage, from the Jimmie Rodgers Memorial Celebration on May 25, 1955, surfaced in 2006 on the *Memphis Recording Service* package, while a home movie from Lubbock, Texas, from earlier that spring, has also recently been found.
First appearance on national TV: "Stage Show," CBS, January 28, 1956.
First national US #1 hit: "I Forgot To Remember To Forget" made it to #1 on the *Billboard* Country & Western charts on February 25, 1956.
First home purchase: 1034 Audubon Drive, Memphis, March 12, 1956.
First album release: *Elvis Presley*, March 1956.
First gold record: Million-selling "Heartbreak Hotel," April 1956.
First *Billboard* pop US #1 hit: "Heartbreak Hotel," May 5, 1956.
First major national press article: "A Howling Hillbilly Success," *Life* magazine, April 30, 1956, closely followed by *Time* and *Newsweek*.
First biography: *Elvis Presley Speaks!* by Robert Johnson, 1956
First appearance on film: Wielding a ploughshare in *Love Me Tender*, released on November 21, 1956.

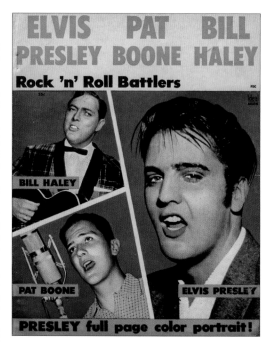

Elvis, Bill Haley, and Pat Boone in a rare magazine portrait, 1956.

"500 MILES"

Elvis tried out this Hedy West song, which had been a hit for Peter, Paul and Mary in 1962, at Graceland in 1966 with pals to a backing track ("Sing A Song With The Kingston Trio"). The resulting home recording saw the light of day on 2000 FTD release *In A Private Moment*.

"FIVE SLEEPY HEADS"

Based on a Johannes Brahms lullaby, Elvis recorded this song for the soundtrack of *Speedway*; it was cut from the movie but survived onto the soundtrack LP. Sid Tepper and Roy C. Bennett did the honors; Elvis laid down the track on June 20, 1967 at the MGM Studios. It was a perfect candidate for 1978 album *Elvis Sings For Children (And Grown Ups Too)*, re-released in 2002 as *Elvis Sings for Kids*, and also for *Elvis Chante Sid Tepper & Roy C. Bennett* and the *Speedway Double Features* release in the Nineties.

"FLAMING STAR"

Elvis recorded the title song for the movie of the same name on October 7, 1960 at Radio Recorders, along with a modified version for the end credits. The Sid Wayne / Sherman Edwards cowboy-themed tune made it onto the *Elvis By Request: Flaming Star* EP (where the song reached #14), and 1968 album *Singer Presents Elvis Singing Flaming Star and Others*. "Flaming Star" later appeared on 1975 release *Double Dynamite*. The end-credits version is on the 1995 *Double Features* release for the movie (the track also came out that year on *Command Performances*).

The original release has since appeared on *Elvis in Hollywood*, *Double Dynamite*, the *Double Features* release, and more recently *Hitstory*, *Elvis Movies* and *Elvis at the Movies*.

Both versions are on *Today, Tomorrow & Forever*, which, like the *Elvis: Close Up* collectors' set, offers a studio alternate.

The original release has since appeared on *Elvis in Hollywood, Double Dynamite*, the *Double Features* release, and more recently *Hitstory, Elvis Movies* and *Elvis at the Movies*.

Both versions are on *Today, Tomorrow & Forever*, which, like the *Elvis: Close Up* collectors' set, offers a studio alternate.

FLAMING STAR / WILD IN THE COUNTRY / FOLLOW THAT DREAM

A Double Features 1995 release.

TRACK LISTING:
1. Flaming Star
2. Summer Kisses, Winter Tears
3. Britches
4. A Cane And A High Starched Collar
5. Black Star
6. Summer Kisses, Winter Tears (movie version)
7. Flaming Star (end credits)
8. Wild In The Country
9. I Slipped, I Stumbled, I Fell
10. Lonely Man
11. In My Way
12. Forget Me Never
13. Lonely Man (Solo)
14. I Slipped, I Stumbled, I Fell (alternate master)
15. Follow That Dream
16. Angel
17. What A Wonderful Life
18. I'm Not The Marrying Kind
19. A Whistling Tune
20. Sound Advice

FLAMING STAR

The film rights for this dramatic Western had been kicking around Hollywood for a while, purchased originally in 1958 with Marlon Brando and Frank Sinatra cast as the brothers. Twentieth Century-Fox and Elvis agreed that playing the son of an Indian mother and white father, torn between two worlds on the Texas frontier, would be a good dramatic role for his return to filmmaking after a two year Army hiatus.

Working titles for this Western included *Flaming Lance* (the title of the original novel by Clair Huffaker), *Flaming Heart, Black Star* and *Black Heart*. The project was also known at an early stage under the title *Brothers of Flaming Lance*. The final title change (from *Black Star* to *Flaming Star*) cost the studio $5,000 because Elvis had to go back into the studio to lay down revised versions of the title song.

Elvis reported to Twentieth Century-Fox for preproduction on August 1, 1960. Once again, he was disappointed that songs gradually crept into the picture. He managed to get two of the four songs written into the script dropped, and a third, "Summer Kisses, Winter Tears," went the same way after the audience laughed during a test screening—the footage shot for the movie featured Elvis singing to the beat of an Indian drum. Nevertheless, the movie poster features Elvis strumming a guitar.

Location photography was at the Conejo Movie Ranch, Thousand Oaks, California, with externals shot in Utah.

Chief love interest Barbara Eden, later known for her starring role in late Sixties TV series "I Dream of Jeannie," got the part after Barbara Steele, the original actress signed up for the role, was deemed to have too strong a British accent.

The movie was released just one month after *G.I. Blues* after a Los Angeles premiere. It peaked at #12 on the *Variety* Box Office survey for the week. Sadly for Elvis' dramatic acting ambitions, the movie's relatively poor takings compared with his post-Army musicals cemented Colonel

Parker's conviction that the money was in light and fluffy rather than Oscar-worthy fare.

Many critics and fans consider the movie to be one of the finest Elvis ever made, along with *King Creole*. The scene in which he declares his love to Barbara Eden is certainly one of his most accomplished dramatic performances. Director Don Siegel was convinced that had he succeeded in keeping the songs out of the movie, it would have been a much bigger critical and commercial success (and might have changed the course of Elvis' subsequent film career).

In the absence of a soundtrack album (an EP came out later, though only in response to bootleggers), in 1968 songs from the movie and other orphan tracks were released on the album *Singer Presents Elvis Singing Flaming Star and Others*.

After the movie, Elvis was made a member of the Los Angeles Indian Tribal Council.

ELVIS SAID: "The part I have in Flaming Star is the least like myself."

CREDITS:
Twentieth Century-Fox, Color.
Length: 101 minutes
Release date: December 20, 1960

TAGLINE:
CHOOSE! . . . Between your white father and your Kiowa mother!

Directed by: Don Siegel
Produced by: David Weisbart
Written by: Clair Huffaker (novel), Clair Huffaker and Nunnally Johnson
Music by: Cyril J. Mockridge
Cinematography by: Charles G. Clarke
Film Editing by: Hugh S. Fowler
Art Direction by: Duncan Cramer, Walter M. Simonds
Set Decoration by: Gustav Berntsen, Walter M. Scott
Costume Design by: Adele Balkan

CAST::

Elvis Presley	Pacer Burton
Steve Forrest	Clint Burton
Barbara Eden	Roslyn Pierce
Dolores del Rio	Neddy Burton
John McIntire	Sam 'Pa' Burton
Rudolph Acosta	Buffalo Horn
Karl Swenson	Dred Pierce
Ford Rainey	Doc Phillips
Richard Jaeckel	Angus Pierce
Anne Benton	Dorothy Howard
L.Q. Jones	Tom Howard
Douglas Dick	Will Howard
Tom Reese	Jute
Marian Goldina	Ph'sha Knay
Bob Alder	Driver
Henry Amargo	Brave
Lon Ballantyne	Indian brave #1
Barbara Beaird	Dottie Phillips
Ray Beltram	Indian
Sharon Bercutt	Bird's Wing
Joe Brooks	Man #5 at Crossing
Monte Burkhart	Ben Ford
Larry Chance	Indian Chief
Virginia Christine	Mrs. Phillips
Tom Fadden	Man #1 at Crossing
Bob Folkerson	Posse man
Griswold Green	Man #2 at Crossing
William Herrin	Man #6 at Crossing
Pat Hogan	Indian brave #2
Foster Hood	Indian brave #3
Charles Horvath	Bit part
Ted Jacques	Hornsby

RIGHT: Poster for Elvis' sixth movie, *Flaming Star*, 1960.
BELOW: Another poster showing a different aspect of Elvis.

Richard Talmadge	second unit director
Warren B. Delaplain.	sound
E. Clayton Ward	sound
Eli Bo Jack Blackfeather	tunts
Charles Horvath	stunts
Loren Janes	stunts
Roy Jenson	stunts
Thomas A. Sweet	stunts
Richard Talmadge	stunt coordinator
Guy Way	stunts
Josephine Earl	dances stager
The Jordanaires	vocal accompaniment
Lionel Newman	conductor
Colonel Tom Parker	technical advisor
Edward B. Powell	orchestrator

Plot:

Elvis plays Pacer Burton, the son of a White father and Kiowa mother, in 1878 Texas. Pacer returns to the family ranch with half-brother Clint (played by Steve Forrest), where the family throws a surprise birthday party for Clint. Pacer sings, everybody has a good time, but then tragedy strikes when the Howard family, guests at the party, is massacred on their return to their ranch by a Kiowa Indian sortie.

Party guest Dred Pierce (Karl Swenson) the next day threatens the Burtons to make sure that they side with the white settlers against the Indians. Soon after, Kiowa chief Buffalo Horn (Rudolph Acosta) tries to enlist Pacer into his group of braves. When Pacer refuses, Buffalo Horn threatens the family's ranch.

Pacer and his Ma Neddy (played by Dolores del Rio) try to intercede with the Chief to save the family ranch and defuse the worsening situation. On the way home, they are attacked by Will Howard (played by Douglas Dick), out for revenge after his family was massacred by the Kiowas. Howard kills Pacer's friend Two Moons (Perry Lopez) and mortally wounds Pacer's mother. Pacer rides off to town to fetch the Doc (played by Ford Rainey), but the townspeople won't let him treat an "injun." Pacer kidnaps the doctor's daughter, the only way he can think of to get the townspeople to relent, but by the time he brings the Doc back to the ranch Neddy has wandered off into the hills to meet her "Flaming Star of Death." Pacer takes the body of his friend Two Moons back to the tribe, now getting ready for a new raid.

Angry with the Whites for not helping his dying mother, Pacer faces off with his brother Clint, and then rides into the hills to join his people. By the time he gets there, the Chief has been killed and brother Clint is gravely injured. Pacer bravely leads his brother back home, then, when he hears that their father has been killed, he turns to face the raiding Kiowa single-handedly. Mortally wounded, he returns to town to check that his brother Clint made it to safety, and then in the Indian way, heads out to the hills to seek his own "Flaming Star."

Songs: "Flaming Star," "A Cane And A High Starched Collar"

FLASHBACK

A premium 2004 FTD book of photos and text, plus an album of alternates and outtakes focusing on Elvis' music from 1956 to 1958.

TRACK LISTING:
1. Heartbreak Hotel
2. Money Honey
3. I'm Counting On You
4. I Was The One
5. Lawdy, Miss Clawdy
6. Shake, Rattle And Roll
7. I Want You, I Need You, I Love You
8. Rip It Up
9. Loving You (slow)
10. I Need Your Love Tonight
11. A Big Hunk O' Love
12. Ain't That Loving You Baby
13. A Fool Such As I
14. I Got Stung
15. That's When Your Heartaches Begin
16. It Is No Secret
17. Blueberry Hill
18. Have I Told You Lately That I Love You
19. Is It So Strange
20. Loving You (main title version)
21. Loving You (main title version 2)
22. Treat Me Nice (first version)
23. Young And Beautiful
24. I Want To Be Free
25. Don't Leave Me Now

"FLIP, FLOP AND FLY"

A two-for-one song which Elvis performed on his first ever national TV appearance on the Dorsey brothers' "Stage Show" on January 28, 1956, after starting off with another Big Joe Turner hit "Shake, Rattle and Roll." The song was written by Joe Turner and Jesse Stone (credited as Charles Calhoun; Turner published the song in the name of his wife, Lou Willie Turner), and was originally a hit in 1955. The "Stage Show" performance was given a record release on on *A Golden Celebration* and *Platinum: A Life in Music*. A version with extra overdubbed drumming featured in 1981 on the *This Is Elvis* release.

Elvis reprised the song for hits medleys in the mid-Seventies. Live versions have appeared on *Elvis Recorded Live On Stage In Memphis* (and its FTD sibling, recorded on March 20, 1974), and on FTD live releases *I Found My Thrill* and *Closing Night*, as well many bootlegs from 1973/1974.

FLORIDA

- Daytona Beach

Elvis' first live show in Florida was at the Peabody Auditorium on May 7, 1955, on a Hank Snow Attractions tour. He returned for two shows on July 30, 1955, and a further two shows on the evening of August 9, 1956.

- Fort Myers

Elvis played the City Auditorium on May 9, 1955, and was a late addition to the bill at the New City Auditorium on July 25, 1955 on a Grand Ole Opry tour headlined by comic Andy Griffith.

- Hollywood

Elvis kicked off his first tour of 1977 on February 12 at the Sportatorium.

- Jacksonville

Elvis played the Gator Bowl on May 12 and 13, 1955, and the new baseball stadium on two nights in late July 1955 (28th and 29th). One of those nights at the Gator Bowl Elvis made the mistake of quipping that he'd see the girls in the audience backstage. Unbeknownst to him, somebody had left a gate slightly open. In the resulting melee, Elvis had his clothes ripped off his body in an all-girl riot, and only escaped worse by taking refuge on top of the showers. He returned to play the new baseball stadium on February 23 and 24, 1956 (going on with the second show after he collapsed from exhaustion). He played the Florida Theater on August 10 and 11, 1956.

Almost sixteen years later Elvis returned to the Veterans Memorial Coliseum for two shows on April 16, 1972. He played the same venue on April 25, 1975. On September 1, 1976 he did a show at the Coliseum, where he also played on May 30, 1977.

- Lakeland

Elvis appeared that the Polk Theater on August 6, 1956. Next time round, on April 27 and 28, 1975, he sold out the Civic Center Arena, which he also played on September 4, 1976.

- Miami

Elvis played three shows at the Olympic Theater on August 3 and 4, 1956. He spent a week in town in March 1960, recording with Frank Sinatra for the *Welcome Home Elvis* TV show.

- Miami Beach

Elvis played two shows at the Miami Beach Convention Center on September 12, 1970.

- Ocala

Elvis played the Southeastern Pavilion on May 10, 1955.

- Orlando

Elvis' appearance on May 11, 1955 was at the Auditorium, followed on July 26 and 27 by two shows at the Municipal Auditorium. He was back for two more shows on August 8, 1956. Twenty-one years later Elvis took the stage at the Sports Stadium on February 15, 1977.

- Pensacola

Elvis played three shows at the City Auditorium on February 26, 1956.

- St. Petersburg

Elvis played three shows at the Florida Theater on August 7, 1956. His next performance in town was at the Bayfront Center on September 3, 1976. His last show there was at the same venue on February 14, 1977.

- Sarasota

Elvis managed to fit in four shows at the Florida Theater on February 21, 1956.

- Tampa

Elvis did a show at the Fort Homer Hesterly Armory on May 8, 1955, followed by two shows on July 31, 1955, and then three shows on February 19, 1956. He was back for more at the same venue on August 5, 1956.

He returned fourteen years later to the Curtis Hixon Convention Center on September 13, 1970, where he was back for repeat performances on April 26, 1975 and September 2, 1976.

- West Palm Beach

Elvis played three shows at the Palms Theater on February 20, 1956. He next played the Auditorium on February 13, 1977.

"FLOWERS ON THE WALL"

Elvis sang a few lines of this Statler Brothers song during a recording session in February 1966. Though never released officially, it appears on an unofficial album of alternative takes from the movie soundtrack *Spin-in . . . Spinout.*

FOLEY, RED
(B. CLYDE JULIAN "RED" FOLEY, 1910-1968)

During a long and illustrious career, Red Foley was a leading light in country music. He scored 38 top 10 hits on his own and achieved plenty more success with the Andrews Sisters and Kitty Wells. Born in Blue Lick, Kentucky, on June 17, 1910, Red Foley began performing with the Cumberland Ridge Runners before striking out on his own. He was a regular at the Grand Ole Opry from 1946, and is credited with helping to make it a nationally-known music platform. Foley's best known hits are "Chattanoogie Shoe Shine Boy" and "Tennessee Saturday Night" (a song Elvis is reputed to have sung during an early show). The first country singer to record in Nashville, the first country singer to have his own network radio show, and from 1954 to 1960 host of the Ozark Jubilee TV show, Foley publicly welon his own. He was a regular at the Grand Ole Opry from 1946, and is credited with helping to make it a nationally-known music platform. Foley's best known hits are "Chattanoogie Shoe Shine Boy" and "Tennessee Saturday Night" (a song Elvis is reputed to have sung during an early show). The first country singer to record in Nashville, the first country singer to have his own network radio show, and from 1954 to 1960 host of the Ozark Jubilee TV show, Foley publicly welcomed the effect Elvis had on music, shaking up country music with the new genre of rock 'n' roll.

Elvis recorded a number of songs made popular by this country gospel artist, including "Just A Closer Walk With Thee," "I Believe," "It Is No Secret," "Just Call Me Lonesome," "Mansion Over the Hilltop," "Shake A Hand," "Old Shep" and "(There'll Be) Peace In The Valley (For Me)," which Foley made the first ever million selling gospel song. As a kid, "Old Shep" was Elvis' party piece.

Foley was inducted into the Country Music Hall of Fame in 1967, and warrants his own star on the Hollywood Walk of Fame.

FOLK MUSIC

RCA incongruously described Elvis as a "folk singer" on his early albums, still unsure what to call his new style of music..

In the Sixties the folk revival made soundtrack Elvis sound decidedly behind the times. Elvis may have been recording second-rate songs but he was listening to Peter, Paul and Mary, Bob Dylan, Gordon Lightfoot, James Taylor and the rest of the folk pack. When Elvis finally got the chance to wriggle out from the constraints of soundtrack songs and could choose his own material at the end of the Sixties, he recorded quite a number of his favorites. He even hired mixed male/female quartet the Nashville Edition in 1971 to try and get some of those folk harmonies onto his own records. After *Elvis Country*, he briefly considered doing an *Elvis Folk* concept album.

"FOLLOW THAT DREAM"

The up-tempo title track for the movie of the same name was written by Fred Wise and Ben Weisman. Elvis recorded this and the other soundtrack songs at Studio B in Nashville on July 2, 1961.

The song originally came out on the soundtrack EP, since when it has appeared on *C'mon Everybody*, *Elvis in Hollywood*, *Double Dynamite*, later CD reissues of *Elvis' Golden Records Vol. 3*, the *Double Features* release for the movie, *Hitstory*, *Elvis Movies*, *Elvis at the Movies* and *The Essential Elvis Presley* (2007 release)

Alternate takes have been released over the years on *Elvis Aron Presley*, *Command Performances*, *Today Tomorrow & Forever* and the FTD release for this movie.

FOLLOW THAT DREAM (EP)

Released to coincide with the movie in May 1962, this soundtrack EP managed a respectable half million sales, though it rose no higher than #15 in the EP charts.

TRACK LISTING:
1. Follow That Dream
2. Angel
3. What A Wonderful Life
4. I'm Not The Marrying Kind

The tracks were included on Double Features issue *Flaming Star / Follow That Dream / Wild In The Country* in the Nineties; FTD brought out an album of alternates and outtakes in 2004.

Elvis with Ann Helm from *Follow That Dream*, 1962.

FOLLOW THAT DREAM

This Mirisch Brothers light comedy was originally titled *Pioneer, Go Home*, after the 1957 Richard Powell novel on which it was based. The title was changed reputedly because the songwriters found it impossible to find a rhyme for "pioneer." Other title contenders that came and went were *Here Come the Kwimpers*, *It's a Beautiful Life* and *What a Wonderful Life*. Author Powell was less than happy that Elvis was going to play the lead, but in the end thought he did a good job.

Location shooting at several Florida locations (Crystal River, Tampa, Inverness, Ocala, Inverness, Yankeetown and Bird Creek.) took place in late July and early August 1961, during a heatwave that sent temperatures well above 100.

Love interest Anne Helm was chosen over Tuesday Weld and Connie Stevens.

Scriptwriter Herman Raucher was fired after he came up with dialogue that the studio didn't think fitted the characters. His version became a play the following year.

The movie wrapped on August 28, 1961. One movie song, "A Whistling Tune," was cut from the movie and rerecorded for Elvis' next picture, *Kid Galahad*.

The movie premiered in Ocala, Florida, on April 11, 1962. On release it went straight onto the National Box Office Survey at #5.

Years later, Tom Petty said in an interview that the shooting of this movie near his home was what prompted him to become a singer.

ERIC BRAUN: "Presley's portrayal of guileless innocence has never been bettered."

CREDITS:
The Mirisch Corporation / United Artists, Color.
Length: 109 minutes
Release date: May 23, 1962

TAGLINE:
Want a Lift? Elvis Presley's Funniest . . . Happiest . . . Dreamiest . . . Motion Picture!

Directed by: Gordon Douglas
Executive producer: Walter Mirisch
Producer: David Weisbart
Written by: Richard Powell (novel Pioneer, Go Home!), Charles Lederer, Herman Raucher (play Pioneer, Go Home!)
Music by: Hans J. Salter

Cinematography by: Leo Tover
Film Editing by: William B. Murphy
Art Direction by: Mal Bert
Set Decoration by: Fred M. MacLean

CAST:
Elvis Presley	Toby Kwimper
Arthur O'Connell	Pop Kwimper
Anne Helm	Holly Jones
Joanna Moore	Alicia Claypoole
Jack Kruschen	Carmine
Simon Oakland	Nick
Roland Winters	Judge
Alan Hewitt	H. Arthur King
Howard McNear	George
Frank DeKova	Jack
Herbert Rudley	Mr. Endicott
Gavin Koon	Eddy Bascombe
Robin Koon	Teddy Bascombe
Robert Carricart	Al
John Duke	Blackie
Harry Holcombe	Governor
Pam Ogles	Adriane Pennington
Red West	Bank guard

ADDITIONAL CREW:
Madine Danks	hair stylist
Dan Striepeke	makeup artist
Herbert E. Mendelson	production manager
Allen K. Wood	production supervisor
Bert Chervin	assistant director
Tom Coleman	property master
Buddy Myers	sound
Charles G. Schelling	sound effects editor
Jack Solomon	sound
Robert Tracy	music editor
Ruth Hancock	wardrobe
Sid Mintz	wardrobe
Colonel Tom Parker	technical advisor
Dolores Rubin	script supervisor

Plot:

off before the Governor officially opens the highway, but Pop Kwimper (Arthur O'Connell) declares that he's homesteading.

With such good fishing, the family makes money selling fishing tackle. They take out a loan from the local bank to build a dock in a comic scene where the bank employees think that they're being held up. The word spreads and more people pull up trailers. The burgeoning community is further swelled by mobsters Nick and Carmine (played by Jack Kruschen and Simon Oakland), who set up a gambling operation in the knowledge that the new community isn't yet under any jurisdiction.

Toby, newly elected sheriff, sets a curfew. The hoods send their henchmen to teach Toby a lesson, but they're no match for his karate antics. When mobsters Nick and Carmine bring in reinforcements, they suffer the same fate, and their plan to blow up the Kwimper's home backfires when Holly naïOvely takes the bomb to Nick's trailer just before it explodes.

Next, the Kwimpers have to deal with a new threat. Vampish social worker Alicia (Joanna Moore) sashays in and tries to seduce Toby—who furiously recites his times tables to keep his red-blooded passion in check. When her plan fails, she takes out a court order to remove the kids. Toby and his father win their day in court and persuade the Judge (Roland Winters) to reunite the family. Back home, Toby snuggles up to girl next door Holly Jones for a happy ending.

Songs: "What A Wonderful Life," "I'm Not The Marrying Kind," "Sound Advice," "On Top Of Old Smokey," "Follow That Dream", "Angel"

FOLLOW THAT DREAM LABEL

See FTD

"FOLSOM PRISON BLUES"

Elvis sang this Johnny Cash staple together with "I Walk The Line" at live shows in Las Vegas and Lake Tahoe in 1969 and 1970. Elvis' version has never been released officially, though it's on a number of bootlegs, including The Entertainer.

Cash was inspired to write the song—his second ever single for Sun in 1956—after watching the movie *Inside the Walls of Folsom Prison* during his Army service in Germany. The song won Cash a Grammy for Best Country and Western Male Vocal in 1969.

FONTANA, D. J.

(B. DOMINIC JOSEPH FONTANA, 1931)

Drummer D. J. Fontana first played drums with Elvis when the singer was still an almost complete unknown, doing his first show at the Louisiana Hayride in October 1954. Fontana later said he retained the job because he knew how to keep his drumming to the background. He was talking literally as well as figuratively; that first night his kit was set up offstage and out of sight, the norm on the country circuit where a drum accompaniment was still frowned upon. As so often, other versions of the story have been told, for example Bill Morris, who claimed he put Fontana up for the job after he improvised on drums for Elvis on tour in Texas in early 1955.

Not in doubt is that D.J. drummed with Elvis for the next 15 years, up to and beyond the 1968 Comeback Special. All in all, Fontana played on 460 RCA cuts with Elvis, recorded at almost fifty different sessions, and appeared with Elvis on TV shows and in five movies.

Fontana was not the first drummer to play on an Elvis record. That honor went to Jimmie Lott,

who wielded the sticks on "I'm Left, You're Right, She's Gone" in February 1955, followed by Johnny Bernero on the July 1955 Sun session that yielded "Mystery Train."

Fontana was born in Shreveport, Louisiana, on March 15, 1931. He began playing drums for country singer and future Hayride promoter T. Tommy Cutrer, and then spent a spell providing the boom-boom for girls at strip joints. Fontana was hired as a staff drummer at the Louisiana Hayride in 1953. He played with Elvis and the Blue Moon Boys during their regular Saturday evening residency from then on, and started going out on tour with Elvis in the summer of 1955. Fontana said that he adapted his drumming style on tour to synchronize with Elvis' gyrations—a technique he perfected during his strip club years—because it added extra impetus to Elvis' movements, and because drumming on the beats of Elvis' thrusts was the only way to stay in time with the deafening noise coming up from the squealing audience.

Though he had been playing with Elvis live for some time, Fontana only officially joined the band in late 1955 and first recorded with Elvis in January 1956, after Elvis had signed to RCA. Either side of 1960, Fontana was often flanked in the studio by a second drummer, usually Buddy Harman or Hal Blaine. Fontana worked regularly with Elvis in the studio through the Sixties, as well as branching out to drum for a roll call of great music performers, from Ace Cannon to Gene Vincent, Porter Wagoner, Paul McCartney and Dolly Parton.

The last time that Fontana played live with Elvis and original guitarist Scotty Moore was in the intimate interlude on Elvis' 1968 NBC TV Special.

In 1983 Fontana wrote his memoir, *D. J. Fontana Remembers Elvis.* In 1988 he teamed up with Scotty Moore for *All the Kings Men,* an album that won the Nashville Music Award for Independent Album of the Year.

To this day, Fontana is still recording. In 2005 his personal website advertised his services as a drummer and producer for anyone interested in recording in Nashville.

D.J. FONTANA: "Elvis was one of those guys that had a lot of nervous energy. A super hyper guy—super hyper, always jumping around or doing something."

LEVON HELM: "Elvis and Scotty and Bill were making good music, but it wasn't rock 'n' roll until D.J. put the backbeat into it."

Book:
D. J. Fontana Remembers Elvis by D.J. Fontana, Curtis Wood Publications , 1981.

FOOD

Elvis' King-sized taste in food is legendary. Many people who couldn't name more than a couple of Elvis songs know that he was a sucker for deep-fried peanut butter and banana sandwiches (though Lisa-Marie has said that she never saw him eat even one). Less clichéEd but more veritéE is Elvis' love of the simple, Southern cooking he grew up with—the way his Ma and grandma made it, including black-eyed peas, red-eye gravy and heavy coconut cakes.

By all accounts, as a child Elvis was a poor eater—the classic start for people who develop eating disorders in later life. Delicacies were not an option on the Presley family table. In the lean years, Vernon supplemented their diet by hunting birds, rabbits, sometimes even squirrels.

Billy Smith remembers that as a kid Elvis always carried his own knife and fork and refused to eat with any other implements. As an adult, when he

drank from a cup, he set his mouth very close to the handle because he thought it was likely to already have had a mouth on that part.

During his senior year at Humes High School, Elvis' standard lunch was two ice cream sandwiches. Elvis' favorite candy as a kid was Babe Ruth and PayDay bars.

When Elvis first started performing in and around Memphis, he and his bandmates subsisted on bologna sandwiches. As they struck out to neighboring States, he filled up on standard Fifties teen fare of cheeseburgers and milkshakes (the more the merrier), and those peanut butter and banana sandwiches if he could get them, preferably with a little added bacon goodness.

When he was working in the studio, Elvis sent out for Krystal burgers and fries. This was often the first thing he did when he arrived; alternately, it was an excellent way to engineer a break if he was not in the mood to make music. He even sent out for Krsystals when he was in hospital in the Seventies and was supposed to be on a liquid-only diet.

In his first ever magazine interview, Elvis' girlfriend Dixie Locke claims that Elvis could put away "eight deluxe cheeseburgers, 2 bacon, lettuce, tomato sandwiches, and topped it off with three chocolate milk shakes." Lamar Fike remembers Elvis particularly liked a meal of purple-hull peas, sliced tomatoes, bacon and mashed potatoes; he also says that there was a period of two years in which Elvis practically subsisted on crispy bacon, mashed potatoes, sauerkraut and gravy, all mixed up with sliced tomatoes.

In 1956, Elvis told an interviewer that he was a big Jello fan. He also chewed gum: over the years, Spearmint, Double Mint and Juicy Fruit were his favorite flavors.

In 1957, the MGM commissary put crispy bacon, mash and gravy on the menu specially for Elvis while he was shooting *Jailhouse Rock.* A journalist who interviewed him in his dressing room at the time recorded his meal as mashed potatoes, gravy, nine slices of bacon, a quart of milk, a glass of tomato juice, lettuce, six slices of bread and four pats of butter. Restaurant critic Gael Greene recalls that after having sex with Elvis sometime that year, he ordered a fried egg sandwich.

Dinners were a big deal at Graceland. Elvis rarely ate alone. He sat at the head of the table in the dining room, just inside the front door, where food was served on a Wedgwood Buckingham set. In the Sixties Elvis and Priscilla would dress for dinner. Outside the main meal, Elvis and his entourage could rely on a round-the-clock team of cooks always ready to rustle something up.

Before Elvis left for his Army service, Mamma Gladys cooked Elvis' favorite dish of pork chops, mashed potatoes and gravy for her son and a bunch of his pals, and finished off the meal with her own homemade apple pie.

Wieners and sauerkraut was another dish Elvis liked, filling up during his Army (cultural?) training before heading out to Germany. Once he was out in the wilds of West Germany, he preferred his grandma's home cooking to the local food. In Joe Esposito's words, "He wasn't much of a wiener schnitzel guy."

Elvis had Arlen Cogan ship out boxes of Reese's peanut butter cups to Germany when he was away on Army service. Elvis remained an inveterate candy-bar eater throughout his life.

The first time Priscilla met Elvis in 1959, he impressed her by wolfing down five huge bacon and mustard sandwiches, preferably on rye toast.

Before the end of his time in Germany, Elvis went through a fad phase with yoghurt; as was his wont, indulging in the food to excess. He went back onto the yoghurt in the late Sixties, at a time when for many he looked his most lean and handsome.

When Priscilla moved to Graceland, she oversaw preparation of his favorite breakfast. After

Unissued prototype "Wheaties" box

glugging down lashings of hot coffee, Elvis' extremely late breakfast consisted of Spanish omelet, home fries and two pounds of bacon crisped to blackness. Alternatively, Elvis might go for pork sausage wrapped in fried biscuits.

In the mid-Sixties, one of Elvis' entourage members turned Elvis on to the pleasures of chicken soup.

In the big-eating Seventies, breakfast was the meal Elvis consumed in the late afternoon before going on stage, stocking up on scrambled eggs, toast and extra crispy bacon. Back at Graceland his cooks knew to make him a huge (and tempting) spread of eggs, a pound of King Cotton bacon, plenty of biscuits, maybe some cereal, and for variety's sake a side of sausage and toast. At breakfast time he drank orange juice and coffee (served with half & half and as a concession to diet, Sweet 'n' Low). If he ordered pancakes, he'd go with apple sauce rather than maple syrup.

After Priscilla moved into Graceland, she attempted to instill some order into the kitchen by arranging a single menu for each mealtime, rather than letting anyone who was around put in their menu request with one of the cooks—there was always someone on duty, 24 hours a day. Generally, the Graceland kitchen was stocked at all times with the kinds of foods that Elvis might want. Aunt Delta (Briggs) was spending around $500 a week on food in the late Sixties, enough to keep Elvis and his pals in hotdogs and eskimo pies. Between meals, Elvis and friends could help themselves to the array of snacks he had on hand in the basement den, between the pool room and the TV viewing room.

Elvis' favorites were generally fried and served with lashings of buttery sauce or red-eye gravy (made from pork fat). He once ate meatloaf every night for dinner for six months (eight months or a year by some accounts). Another Elvis favorite was Southern dish buttermilk and corn pone.

He disliked fish so much that he wouldn't allow it to be cooked at all in the house, though when he was finally persuaded to taste salmon, he became a convert.

Exotic cuisines didn't appeal, though Joe Esposito occasionally pitched in with some Italian home cooking.

Soon after their marriage, Priscilla attempted to make one of Elvis' favorites, lasagna, and invited the entourage round. It was a disaster as she forgot to boil the pasta before putting it in the oven. When Elvis saw how upset she looked, he manfully ate up the food on his plate, and everybody else followed suit.

Whether it was fried chicken, well-done steak—when ordering a meal on the road, Elvis always specified well-done—or meatloaf at home with all the trimmings, the portions had to be King-sized. Vegetables that couldn't be fried in animal fat of some description did not make it onto the dinner table, though Elvis' Ma served up okra to Elvis and friends in 1957.

Billy Smith recalls that during a particularly lean time when they were growing up, the family had to eat turnip greens for a week and Elvis swore he'd never touch them again. Smith also mentions that the families would scavenge fruit and vegetables from the local fruit stand.

Riding the range at the Circle G ranch, friends remember Elvis carrying round entire packs of hot dog and hamburger buns and eating his way through them. Not surprisingly, when he finally turned up to start work on his next movie, *Clambake*, he was significantly overweight.

It has been claimed that Elvis would consume up to 94,000 calories of food in a day when he was on a binge. According to Ed Parker and other friends, his junk food jags were comfort eating pure and simple.

Elvis won the dubious accolade for the #1 greatest rock and roll excess in music magazine "Blender," for flying himself and some police pals to Denver in 1976 to satisfy a craving for peanut butter, jelly and bacon baguettes, known as "Fool's Gold," meant to feed eight but suitable for a single Elvis. When the gang arrived in Denver on the *Lisa Marie*, 22 of these sandwiches were waiting for them in a hangar, served by the proprietor of the Colorado Gold Mine company restaurant himself. The snack ended up costing $3,387 (multiply by 4 for 2005 prices). In Elvis' defense, he came up with the plan as a means of avoiding a recording session that RCA had set up in his own home.

Other famed Elvis binges include five banana split ice cream sundaes for breakfast before a concert in Baltimore, and according to Albert Goldman, $100 of popsicles in one night. When he was comfort eating, it was nothing for Elvis to polish off a whole cake at a time. For a slightly healthier snack, he might make it a fruit pie or two.

Banana pudding was always on hand at Graceland for those middle-of-the-night cravings. He had a real sweet tooth, and loved to eat homemade cakes and pies, particularly banana cream, chocolate or egg custard. (In *Double Trouble*, Elvis' character claims to take 418 lumps of sugar in his tea!). Elvis loved bananas even as a kid. What all these recipes have in common is plenty of sugar, which was the way his Mamma made desserts. It wasn't all calorific stuff, though: in summer Elvis kept a supply of chopped up watermelon and cantaloupe in his bedroom fridge.

When out in Palm Springs, Elvis ate a lot of pan-fried hamburgers and mashed potato, or grilled steaks.

There have been rumors that at the end of his life, Elvis had special glasses made with a built-in mirror so that he could eat lying down while watching TV.

Dr. Nichopoulos says that it was much harder to try and limit Elvis' food consumption at Graceland, where the cooks wanted to "mother him," than it was out on the road. Entourage members remember that at one stage when he was particularly in thrall to prescription drugs, he subsisted on yoghurt and fresh fruit.

His digestive problems in later life weren't just caused by what he ate but when he ate. He often wolfed down a big meal of cheeseburgers and fried potatoes just before turning in. A few months before he died, Elvis almost choked on a cheeseburger as he dropped off. Despite putting on significant amounts of weight, Elvis' bloated appearance was predominantly due to sluggish digestion and the side effects of the many medicines he was taking.

On his last night alive, a member of Elvis' entourage ordered in pizzas.

DRINK

Elvis loved drinking Pepsi Cola. His soda fountain down in the basement at Graceland dispensed Pepsi as well as his other favorites, Mountain Valley mineral water and Nesbitts Orange Soda.

On his personal jet, Elvis used to sip Gatorade and diet Dr. Pepper. Water and Gatorade kept him going on stage too.

Childhood memories of the effect booze had on family members—stories abound of violent episodes by Presley and Smith relatives under the influence—put Elvis off alcohol, though he would partake of alcoholic beverages to celebrate special occasions such as toasting in the New Year. He told William McDaniel that he made an exception to this general rule in Las Vegas, because "if you don't drink out there they think there's something wrong with you." In the name of art Elvis got drunk a couple of times when making *Wild in the Country*, once for a scene with Tuesday Weld. Elvis drank vodka now and then after co-star Hope Lange turned him on to it.

Billy Smith remembers him a couple of years later going on an occasional drinking binge in Las Vegas, usually vodka and tonics.

When The Beatles visited him in LA in 1965, Elvis offered whisky and seven-up but only touched the seven-up himself. Elvis downed Bloody Marys when he went to see Barbra Streisand in Las Vegas, before his first engagement there. In 1974, Elvis reputedly decided to find out what it was like to be drunk and spent three or four days drinking non-stop.

ELVIS DIETS

With a naturally fast metabolism in his younger years, Elvis could dispatch prodigious quantities of his favorite Southern-style dishes. Eating at this pace was more than his body could take in later years.

To reduce his weight for a film or a concert tour, Elvis tried a succession of diets, some at the extreme end of faddishness, others involving "magic pills." He went on single food diets, liquid diets and fasts. One health food diet required food to be shipped from an LA health food store. Even if he was already on a diet, if he read about some new miracle way to lose weight, he'd want to try that out instead. He tried eating just no-calorie Jell-O all day—it has been claimed that he was on this diet the day he died.

In the Sixties a masseuse warned Elvis that his poor diet would cause him digestive problems if he didn't make a change. Elvis rationalized his King-sized consumption by telling people that he needed to replenish his energy and keep the show on the road. Larry Geller tried to turn Elvis on to health foods in the mid-Sixties, after taking him to see nutritionist Wilma Minor in LA; in the Seventies Dr. Nichopoulos made concerted attempts to get Elvis to eat properly and lose weight through exercise.

There were times when Elvis tried to reform his eating habits, but he seldom managed more than a few days before asking one of the Graceland cooks to make him a burger or bring him some ice cream.

ELVIS-LICENSED FOODS

Elvis Presley Enterprises has been licensing an increasing number of food and drink-related Elvis products. Memphis-based coffee firm Ugly Mug Coffee has produced a range of special blends including "Love Me Tender." Reese's brought out a special banana-flavored Elvis version of its peanut butter cup in 2007.

Graceland Cellars sell a number of Elvis-themed wines, ranging from The King Cabernet Sauvignon to Jail House Red Merlot, Blue Suede Chardonnay and seasonal tipple Blue Christmas.

PEANUT BUTTER AND BANANA SANDWICHES

The secret to Elvis' peanut butter and banana sandwiches, as remembered by friend Arlene Cogan, is to mash up the banana with the peanut butter. Maid Mary Jenkins says that it's essential to toast the bread first, before frying up the concoction in plenty of foaming hot butter.

A later variation on the calorie-rich sandwich theme was "Fools' Gold," an amalgam of peanut butter (a full jar), strawberry jam (another full jar) and crispy bacon (1 lb) on a baguette. Friends and relatives all concur that Elvis ate these monsters only once in a while.

BILLY SMITH "Maybe food was love in that house."

NANCY ROOKS: "He loved to eat, especially in the later years."

PRISCILLA: "Cooking for Elvis was easy: I'd just take whatever we were having and burn it."

DAVID ADLER: "Food, his first love, was the love that destroyed him."

JERRY SCHILLING: "He ate out of depression."

LARRY GELLER: "Elvis' daily diet was a textbook example of how not to eat."

Books:

A veritable cottage industry has grown up around Elvis' culinary habits, including but not limited to:

Presley Family Cookbook , by Vester Presley and Nancy Rooks, Wimmer Cookbooks, 1980

Are You Hungry Tonight, by Brenda Butler, Grammercy, 1992.

The Life and Cuisine of Elvis Presley, by David Adler, Three Rivers Press, 1993 (later adapted into a documentary)

Fit For A King: The Elvis Presley Cookbook, by Elizabeth McKeon, Ralph Gevirtz and Julie Bandy, with recipes from Alvena Roy, who cooked for Elvis at Graceland, Gramercy, 1998

The Presley Family & Friends Cookbook: A Cookbook and Memory Book from Those Who Knew Elvis Best, by Edie Hand, Darcy Bonfils, Ken Beck, Jim Clark, Donna Presley Early, Cumberland House Publishing, 1998 (republished as *All Cooked Up: Recipes and Memories from Elvis' Friends and Family* in 2005)

Eating The Elvis Presley Way, by David Adler, Blake Publishing, 2002

Graceland's Table: Recipes and Meal Memories Fit for the King of Rock and Roll, by Ellen Rolfes, Rutledge Hill Press, 2005

"FOOL"

Elvis' reproachful rendition of this 1969 Wayne Newton song (written by Carl Sigman and James Last) was recorded at RCA's Hollywood Studio on March 28, 1972. The track was first released as the B-side to 1973 single "Steamroller Blues," when it reached #17 on the *Billboard* chart.

A few months later it came out as the first track on *Elvis (The Fool Album)*. It has since appeared on compilations including *Elvis Aron Presley*, *Walk A Mile In My Shoes*, *Burning Love* and *The Country Side Of Elvis*.

An alternate take—take #1—came out on 2001 FTD album *6363 Sunset*.

At least eight Elvis songs contain the word "fool" in the title, not quite rivaling the word "blue" for frequency.

"FOOL, THE"

Two recordings exist by Elvis of this 1956 Sanford Clark hit (written by Lee Hazlewood but credited to his wife Naomi Ford), one a home taped version made in Germany in 1959, which many years later found its way onto *A Golden Celebration* after appearing on bootlegs, and a country blues version laid down in Nashville on June 4, 1970 for release on *Elvis Country* the following year. Since then, the song has appeared on Seventies anthology *Walk A Mile In My Shoes*

The first take from the Nashville session came out on posthumous album *Essential Elvis Vol. 4*. *Today, Tomorrow & Forever* features the 1959 home recording in an alternate take.

"FOOL, FOOL, FOOL"

When one just isn't enough . . . Originally an R&B hit, written by Nugetre (an acronym for Ertegun, of Atlantic records fame) for the Clovers and later Kay Starr—a singer Elvis counted among his favorites—Elvis performed this song at the KDAV radio station in Lubbock, Texas, in January (some say February) 1955, to promote his concerts at the Fair Park venue. It can be heard on *The King Of Rock & Roll* anthology, *Sunrise* and—a demo acetate—the 2006 release of *The Complete Sun Sessions*.

A live Louisiana Hayride performance from January 1955 recently surfaced on *Memphis Recording Service Vol. 2*.

"(NOW AND THEN THERE'S) FOOL SUCH AS I, A"

When finally released as a single with "I Need Your Love Tonight" by RCA in mid-March 1959, this Bill Trader-penned track climbed as high as #2 in the charts, shifting over a million copies and staying on the charts for almost four months. Previous recordings by Hank Snow, and later The Robins, hadn't even come close.

Elvis recorded "(Now And Then There's) A Fool Such As I" in Nashville on June 10, 1958 as a duet with Jordanaire Ray Walker, while on two weeks' furlough from his Army training.

The track first had an album release on *Elvis' Gold Records Vol. 2*. The song has since graced many compilations including *Worldwide 50 Gold Award Hits Vol. 1 Elvis: A Legendary Performer, Vol. 1*, *The King Of Rock 'n' Roll*, *Great Country Songs*, *Artist Of The Century*, *The Country Side of Elvis*, *ELVIS 30#1 Hits*, *Hitstory*, *Love, Elvis*, . An alternate from the original recording session appeared on *Essential Elvis Vol. 3*. Nine takes are on FTD release *50,000,000 Million Elvis Fans Can't Be Wrong*.

Live versions released on record include *Elvis Aron Presley* (a rare performance from 1961) and the *That's The Way It Is*—Special Edition (as performed in 1969).

"FOOLS FALL IN LOVE"

The B-side to "Indescribably Blue," released in January 1967, Elvis recorded this Leiber and Stoller song on May 28, 1966, in Nashville. The tune was originally recorded by The Drifters back in 1957, when it did significantly better in the charts than the #102 Elvis' version managed. "Fools Fall In Love" first came out on an album in 1971, on budget release *I Got Lucky*. It has since been released on *Double Dynamite*, *From Nashville to Memphis*, *Elvis Sings Leiber & Stoller* and *Tomorrow Is A Long Time*. An alternate appeared on FTD release *Long Lonely Highway* in 2000.

"FOOL'S HALL OF FAME"

When Elvis performed this Sun records track by Rudi Richardson in Seattle in 1957 he told the audience it would be his next single. He intended to record it at his September 1957 session but work on his Christmas album took priority. This is one of the songs that may one day be rediscovered in a forgotten vault—D.J. Fontana said in an interview decades later that they did try it out in the studio.

Erstwhile fellow Sun artists Johnny Cash and Roy Orbison also recorded the song at Sun, and also failed to see it released for many years.

Memphis football game, 1960's.

"FOOLS RUSH IN (WHERE ANGELS FEAR TO TREAD)"

Elvis' version of this classic song was more inspired by Ricky Nelson than Frank Sinatra, Glenn Miller or Etta James, all of whom took it on, when he recorded it in Nashville on May 18, 1971 for release on the album Elvis Now. Curiously, guitarist James Burton played on both Elvis and Ricky Nelson's versions.

Elvis' take on the song has only been re-released since then on alternate form, on *Today, Tomorrow & Forever* and FTD release *I Sing All Kinds*. A slower, home recorded version of the tune—written by Rube Bloom and Johnny Mercer in 1940—features on *In A Private Moment*, as taped in 1966.

FOOTBALL

Football was Elvis' sport. He played in after-school games between white and black boys until his parents grounded him when one boy was admitted to the hospital where Gladys worked at the time. Elvis was in the High School squad for the Tigers at Humes. but though he could potentially have made the team as a guard, he was hounded out by Coach Boyce, who would not tolerate his long hair. Up until the time when fame kept him on the road, Elvis played regularly with pals and local kids at Guthrie Park in Memphis. In 1956 Elvis told an interviewer that the position he played was end. Out on tour, Elvis assiduously read and studied football magazines and was extremely knowledgeable about players and teams.

Elvis and his Army pals used to play a game on weekends near Elvis' off-base home in Bad Nauheim during his tour of duty in the late Fifties. The biggest problem was that they sometimes had to stop to let shepherds drive their flocks over the field mid-game . . . and resume on a suddenly slippery surface.

Elvis' dedication to the game was rewarded on his 25th birthday when his pals handed him a trophy for "Most Valuable Player, Bad Nauheim Sunday Afternoon Football Association. 1959."

Though it was touch football Elvis played, he broke a finger in October 1960 during a game at

Graceland. In the early Sixties when he was living in LA and making movies, Elvis set up his own team, Elvis Presley Enterprises, and played football with a group of guys including fellow musicians Pat Boone and Ricky Nelson (though Pat Boone's wife often came and dragged him off the field), actors Gary Lockwood, Bob Conrad, Kent McCord and Lee Majors, and the occasional pro player, at De Neve Park (314 N. Beverly Glen, Bel Air). Elvis was generally on the winning side. Red and Sonny West claim that they played as many as four or five games in a row if they had taken some amphetamines. Afterwards, there would be painkillers on hand for their aches and pains.

The studios urged Elvis to wear a helmet after he sustained a bad cut near his eye during an impromptu game while he was doing soundstage work on It Happened at the World's Fair.

When he was in Memphis, Elvis played regular touch football at Whitehaven High School, not far from Graceland (4851 Elvis Presley Boulevard)—he played end. He also sponsored a local youth team.

Even as a 27 year-old, Elvis declared that he would love to play football at the highest level. He was a great fan of Cleveland Browns runner Jim Brown, whom he met a couple of times. A number of other football stars visited Elvis on set over the years.

Elvis can be seen playing football with a huge smile on his face in his last two movies, The Trouble With Girls and Change of Habit.

He was an enthusiastic ever-present fan when the Memphis Southmen were an active football franchise in 1974. The last time he played a game was on his final vacation in Hawaii in March 1977. He was still attending local Tennessee football games in the last weeks of his life.

JERRY SCHILLING: "I wouldn't call Elvis a natural football player, but what he didn't have he far exceeded with determination."

"(THAT'S WHAT YOU GET) FOR LOVIN' ME"

Elvis laid down this tongue-in-cheek track in Nashville on March 15, 1971. Written by Canadian singer/songwriter Gordon Lightfoot, Elvis knew the tune from the version recorded in 1964 by Peter, Paul and Mary. It was released on Elvis (The Fool Album) and Nineties collection Walk A Mile In My Shoes. Alternate versions are on Today, Tomorrow & Forever and FTD release I Sing All Kinds.

FOR LP FANS ONLY

This album of ten previously released Elvis cuts appeared in the still-relatively new LP format in February 1959. The record sold 200,000 copies and peaked at #19 during eight weeks on the charts.

TRACK LISTING:
1. That's All Right (Mama)
2. Lawdy, Miss Clawdy
3. Mystery Train
4. Playing For Keeps
5. Poor Boy
6. My Baby Left Me
7. I Was The One
8. Shake, Rattle And Roll
9. I'm Left, You're Right, She's Gone
10. You're A Heartbreaker

The CD reissue also includes "Money Honey," "Tryin' To Get To You" and "Blue Suede Shoes."

"FOR OL' TIMES SAKE"

A weepie that Elvis recorded at Stax Studios on July 23, 1973 that had been a hit earlier that year for Tony Joe White (who also wrote "Polk Salad Annie"). The song came out as the B-side to "Raised On Rock," released as a single in late 1973. Album releases include Raised On Rock and Walk A Mile In My Shoes. An alternate take was released in 1998 on Essential Elvis, Vol. 5; many more are on the 2007 FTD Raised On Rock reissue.

FOR THE ASKING (THE LOST ALBUM)

A 1991 collection of studio cuts that Elvis recorded in Nashville in May 1963 and early 1964. RCA originally planned to release this material as an album before soundtrack commitments took precedence. Instead, the tracks were distributed over the following years as B-sides and "bonus tracks" on soundtrack albums.

TRACK LISTING:
1. (It's A) Long Lonely Highway
2. Western Union
3. Witchcraft
4. Love Me Tonight
5. What Now, What Next, Where To
6. Please Don't Drag That String Around
7. Blue River
8. Never Ending
9. (You're The) Devil In Disguise
10. Finders Keepers , Losers Weepers
11. Echoes Of Love
12. Slowly But Surely
13. It Hurts Me
14. Memphis Tennessee
15. Ask Me

"FOR THE GOOD TIMES"

Elvis recorded this Kris Kristofferson hit on March 27, 1972 at RCA's Hollywood studio, though it wasn't released until a few months before Elvis' death on the Welcome to My World album (since when it has featured on Walk A Mile In My Shoes, Burning Love, The Country Side Of Elvis and the 2006 release of Elvis Country). Alternate takes from the session have appeared on Platinum: A Life In Music and 6363 Sunset.

Elvis sang a couple of lines of the song offstage during his 1972 Elvis on Tour documentary. Composed by Kris Kristofferson but first recorded by Bill Nash (then Kristofferson, then Ray Price), Elvis covered the song at his June 1972 Madison Square Garden concert, released as Elvis as Recorded at Madison Square Garden. An Afternoon In The Garden showcases another performance from the venue.

More recently-issued versions of this song include a pared-down rehearsal version on 2004 FTD release Elvis On Tour—The Rehearsals and an alternate take from the original recording session on 2005 album Love, Elvis. Further live versions may be found on Elvis: Close Up and FTD releases Summer Festival (from 1972) and Southern Nights (from 1975).

"FOR THE HEART"

A Dennis Linde song Elvis recorded at Graceland on February 25, 1976, released as the B-side of "Hurt" a month later. Linde added his own bass line to the song in a later overdub. The song had previously been released by Teresa Brewer.

In his lifetime, Elvis' version featured on From Elvis Presley Boulevard, Memphis. It has since appeared on compilations Our Memories Of Elvis Vol. 2, Elvis' Golden Records Vol. 5, Walk A Mile In

My Shoes, Artist Of The Century, and CD releases of Moody Blue.

Alternate-take seekers are in luck on Platinum: A Life In Music, Today Tomorrow & Forever, The Jungle Room Sessions and Made in Memphis.

"FOR THE MILLIONTH AND THE LAST TIME"

Elvis recorded this latin-flavored Roy C. Bennett/Sid Tepper song in Nashville on October 15, 1961. The song didn't see the light of day until 1965 album Elvis For Everyone.

It has since been reissued on Elvis Chante Sid Tepper & Roy C. Bennett and From Nashville To Memphis.

Alternates are on FTD releases Studio B: Nashville Outtakes and Pot Luck.

FORD, SUSAN

The daughter of then President Ford was staying in Vail, Colorado when Elvis and his gang were vacationing there in early 1976. Elvis declined an invitation to a party held in her honor. Some days later, Ford lent her voice to complaints about the noise Elvis and his pals made on their nocturnal snowmobile rides.

FOREIGN LANGUAGES

Elvis' early-Sixties movie heyday saw him assay a number of foreign tongues. He sang in Hawaiian and Spanish on several soundtrack songs. He made the occasional foray into Italian, notably "Santa Lucia" on the Viva Las Vegas soundtrack. He sings in German on "Wooden Heart," and he even attempts some Chinese in Girls! Girls! Girls!

Elvis' best-selling single of all time was an English-language version of Neapolitan classic "O Sole Mio."

Though he did not speak foreign languages, Elvis got a real kick out of speaking with his cousin Gene Smith in a made-up language.

ELVIS SAID IN 1958: "Me record an Italian song? I don't know if I could cut the mustard."

FOREVER YOUNG, FOREVER BEAUTIFUL

A bootleg release on Memphis Flash records released in 1978 of Elvis singing with pals at Eddie Fadal's house in Waco, Texas, in 1958.

TRACK LISTING:
1. I Understand
2. Happy Happy Birthday Baby
3. I Can't Help It (If I'm Still In Love With You)
4. Who's Sorry Now?
5. Happy Happy Birthday Baby (6 times)
6. Tumbling Tumbleweeds
7. Baby Don't Ya Know
8. Tomorrow Night
9. Little Darlin'
10. Just A Closer Walk With Thee

"FORGET ME NEVER"

A Fred Wise / Ben Weisman ditty that Elvis recorded at Radio Recorders on November 7, 1960 for Wild in the Country before the title was changed from Forget Me Never and the song became surplus to requirements. It was initially released on 1965 album *Elvis For Everyone*.

It has since appeared on *Separate Ways* and the *Flaming Star / Wild in the Country / Follow That Dream Double Feature* release. An alternate take is on 2003 collection *Elvis: Close Up*.

FORTAS, ALAN

Elvis met the powerfully-built All-Memphis football player—related to Supreme Court judge Abe Fortas—through pal George Klein in July 1957, and quickly added him to the entourage, initially as a bodyguard. Fortas was invited to join Elvis in Germany during his Army service, but changed his mind when he heard from Red West that life out there was a bore.

Elvis' nickname for Fortas was "Hog Ears."

Alan Fortas married Jo in 1964. As a gift, Elvis gave him the red Corvair he had bought for Priscilla a year earlier.

Fortas came and went from the entourage, but when he could, Elvis liked to have him as part of his crew, especially out in Los Angeles. Among his duties were transport logistics and wrangling Scatter the chimp.

Marty Lacker says that Alan Fortas took a number of overdoses because of the pressure he felt as he was being contested by his wife and Elvis.

In 1967, Elvis put Fortas in charge of his new Circle G ranch when he had to go to LA to film *Clambake*.

Fortas played percussion on a guitar back in Elvis' 1968 NBC TV special.

Over the years, Fortas received Elvis' 1960 Lincoln Mark V limousine, and later other vehicles including a white Cadillac convertible.

Fortas headed off on his own (or was fired) in 1969 but later remained on friendly terms with Elvis. Fortas spent a spell trying to break into acting in Hollywood, and then, back in Memphis, managed TJ's nightclub.

He was still seeing Elvis at the end.

Fortas was one of several of Elvis' pals to feature on screen in 1988 movie *Heartbreak Hotel*. He worked with Alanna Nash on his first Elvis Book, published in 1987, *My Friend Elvis*.

Billy Smith: "Alan fit like a glove. He just won everybody's heart. And if he didn't win it, he'd con your heart."

Book:
Elvis—From Memphis To Hollywood, Memories from My 12 Years with Elvis Presley by Alan Fortas w. Alanna Nash, Popular Culture Ink, 1992.

FORSHER, TRUDE
(1920-2000)

Austrian-born Trude Forsher worked as a personal secretary to Colonel Parker (and sometimes for Elvis) from 1956 to 1962. She met the Colonel through her cousins, the Aberbachs of Hill & Range, and was in the thick of the action as Elvis began his movie career. After Elvis, she worked as a TV producer.

Book:
The 'Love Me Tender' Years Diary, by Trude Forsher, ed. James Forsher, Book Surge, 2006

"FORT LAUDERDALE CHAMBER OF COMMERCE"

An unlikely title for this melodic Sid Tepper / Roy C. Bennett soundtrack song on *Girl Happy*,

which Elvis recorded on June 11, 1964 at Radio Recorders in Hollywood. The song has since appeared on the usual suspects: *Elvis Chante Sid Tepper & Roy C. Bennett*, and the *Double Features* and FTD movie reissues.

"FOUNTAIN OF LOVE"

Elvis laid down this latin-themed Bill Giant / Jeff Lewis tune on March 18, 1962 at Radio Recorders for the *Pot Luck* album. The original release has since seen the light of day on the *From Nashville To Memphis* anthology. Alternate takes have appeared on FTD albums *Studio B: Nashville Outtakes* and *Pot Luck*.

FOUR LADS

Elvis professed admiration for this close-harmony Canadian vocal group founded by James Arnold, Bernard Toorish, Connie Codarini and Frank Busseri. They came to prominence backing Johnnie Ray on his big 1951 hit "Cry," and had many hits of their own through the mid-Fifties, including "Moments To Remember" and "Standing On The Corner."

"FRANKFORT SPECIAL"

A Sid Wayne / Sherman Edwards composition with echoes of "Mystery Train" that Elvis recorded for *G.I. Blues* on May 6, 1960 at Radio Recorders. The film version included an overdubbed horn section.

More recently, the song came out on *Elvis at the Movies*.

Elvis: A Legendary Performer Vol. 3 features an alternate version that Elvis recorded on April 27. Additional alternates are available on the 1997 BMG *G.I. Blues* release, *Elvis: Close Up* and FTD album *Silver Screen Stereo*.

"FRANKIE AND JOHNNY"

Elvis recorded his action-packed version of this jazz standard on May 14, 1965 at Radio Recorders. Released as a single with B-side track "Please Don't Stop Loving Me" to drum up publicity for the movie, it made it to #25 in the charts and sold close to 400,000 copies over its eight weeks in the Hot 100.

This "murder ballad" is so old that nobody can say exactly where and when it was first sung, nor what the original title was (over the years it has been recorded as "Frankie and Albert" and "He Done Me Wrong," the title under which Hughie Cannon registered his copyright). It originated in the 1800s either in New Orleans or St. Louis, Missouri. The version Elvis sang was reworked by Alex Gottlieb, Fred Karger and Ben Weisman for the movie.

It has since appeared on albums including *Elvis Sings Hits From His Movies Vol. 1*, *Double Dynamite*, *Elvis in Hollywood*, the *Double Features* soundtrack re-release, *Command Performances*, *Hitstory*, *Elvis Movies*, the FTD soundtrack re-release and *Elvis at the Movies*.

Alternate takes of the song have appeared on FTD releases *Out in Hollywood* and *Frankie and Johnny* (which also features the movie version that Elvis recorded).

It has been claimed that Elvis sang this song to fellow pupils at Milam Junior High School.

FRANKIE AND JOHNNY (LP)

The soundtrack LP rose no higher than #20 in the charts on release in March 1966, selling fewer than 300,000 copies during its 19-week stay..

TRACK LISTING:
SIDE 1:
1. Frankie And Johnny
2. Come Along
3. Petunia The Gardener's Daughter
4. Chesay
5. What Every Woman Lives For
6. Look Out Broadway
SIDE 2:
1. Beginner's Luck
2. Down By The Riverside / When The Saints Go Marchin' In
3. Shout It Out
4. Hard Luck
5. Please Don't Stop Loving Me
6. Everybody Come Aboard

In 1994, the soundtrack was released as *Double Feature: Frankie & Johnny—Paradise Hawaiian Style*

TRACK LISTING:
1. Frankie And Johnny
2. Come Along
3. Petunia The Gardener's Daughter
4. Chesay
5. What Every Woman Lives For
6. Look Out Broadway
7. I've Got Beginner's Luck
8. Down By The Riverside / When The Saints Go Marchin' In
9. Shout It Out
10. Hard Luck
11. Please Don't Stop Loving Me
12. Everybody Come Aboard
13. Paradise, Hawaiian Style
14. Queenie Wahine's Papaya
15. Scratch My Back
16. Drums Of The Islands
17. Datin'
18. A Dog's Life
19. House Of Sand
20. Stop Where You Are
21. This Is My Heaven
22. Sand Castles

FTD brought out an album of *Frankie and Johnny* outtakes and alternates in 2003.

FRANKIE AND JOHNNY

Elvis' rare outing in a costume drama was at least the third celluloid version that drew inspiration from a song that itself has been reworked countless times.

The movie closely follows the 1936 movie of the same name, starring Helen Morgan and Chester Morris, which itself borrowed from 1930 movie *Her Man*. Of course, no Elvis character since his first movie was allowed to die, so the ending was rewritten with added happiness.

Elvis began preproduction on this movie on May 11, 1965. It has been said that he came up with the idea for the movie because he liked the song.

During filming, Elvis developed a strong rapport with leading lady Donna Douglas, best known for her tomboy vamp character Elly May Clampett in Sixties TV comedy "The Beverly Hillbillies." They talked for hours about religion and books and even meditated together..

Despite being a United Artists production, the movie was actually shot at MGM studios. The finished product premiered on March 31, 1966 at Baton Rouge, Louisiana, in a screening attended by all three leading ladies but no Elvis.

On general release, the movie peaked at #48

on the *Variety* National Box Office Survey, despite having a relatively high budget compared with recent Elvis vehicles.

The woman kills man topic has continued to inspire filmmakers. Michele Pfeiffer and Al Pacino starred in a 1991 version of the story.

CREDITS:
United Artists, Color.
Length: 87 minutes
Release date: June 24, 1966

TAGLINE:
Elvis is Johnny!
Elvis turns the land of the blues red hot with 12 great songs!

Directed by: Frederick de Cordova
Produced by: Alex Gottlieb(associate producer), Edward Small
Written by: Nat Perrin (story), Alex Gottlieb (screenplay)
Music by: Fred Karger
Cinematography by: Jacques Marquette
Casting by: Harvey Clermont
Art Direction by: Walter M. Simonds
Set Decoration by: Morris Hoffman
Costume Design by: Gwen Wakeling

CAST:
Elvis Presley	Johnny
Donna Douglas	Frankie
Harry Morgan	Cully
Sue Ane Langdon	Mitzi
Nancy Kovack	Nellie Bly
Audrey Christie	Peg
Robert Strauss	Blackie
Anthony Eisley	Clint Braden
Joyce Jameson	Abigail
William 'Billy' Benedict	Sleeping bum
Judy Chapman	Earl Barton dancer
Henry Corden	Gypsy
Jerome Cowan	Joe Wilbur
George Klein	Bit part
Jack Littlefield	Croupier
Dee Jay Mattis	Earl Barton dancer
James Millhollin	Costume shop proprietor
Cliff Norton	Eddie
Eddie Quillan	Cashier
Richard Reeves	Man on street
Naomi Stevens	Princess Zolita
Wilda Taylor	Earl Barton dancer
Larri Thomas	Earl Barton dancer
Howard Wendell	Man at table
Robert Williams	Blackjack dealer
Dave Willock	Pete
Dick Winslow	Orchestra leader

ADDITIONAL CREW
Dan Greenway	makeup artist
Joan St. Oegger	hair stylist
Harold E. Knox	production supervisor
Herbert S. Greene	assistant director
Max Frankel	property master
Alfred R. Bird	sound effects editor
Edna Bullock	music editor
Al Overton	sound
Clem Portman	sound re-recorder
Charles E. Dolan	special effects
Earl Barton	choreographer and musical staging
Wesley Jeffries	wardrobe coordinator
Fred Karger	conductor
Grant Whytock	supervising editor

Plot:

Elvis plays Johnny, a man torn between his love for Frankie (played by Donna Douglas) and his penchant for gambling. Frankie gets the upper hand when Johnny vows to reforms his profligate ways. Things are looking good for the couple as they sing for a living on a Mississippi gambling showboat the *Mississippi Queen*, run by Clint Braden (played by Anthony Eisley).

One day, gypsy fortune-teller Princess Zolita (played by Naomi Stevens) tells Johnny that a redhead soon to appear in his life will bring him luck at the gambling table. Jealousy ensues when the redhead turns out to be Nellie Bly (played by Nancy Kovack), ex-girlfriend of boat owner Clint Bladen, newly returned from New York. She wastes no time in using Johnny to make Braden jealous enough to marry her.

Frankie mistakes Johnny's interest in Nellie as carnal (it's merely venal). Johnny's sidekick Cully (played by Henry Morgan) writes a song about Frankie and Johnny that promises to make their fortune and becomes the star turn in their act, only they don't have the money to make it to New York and the big time. Frankie, meanwhile, mistakes Johnny's interest in Nellie as carnal (it's merely venal).

With Nellie at his side, Johnny wins a fortune, loses a fortune, and then wins a fortune again, unaware that in fact this last time it is Frankie who is with him, at a masked ball.. Jealous Bladen has a fight with Johnny, which he loses. Frankie, unimpressed with his return to gambling, throws all of Johnny's his winnings out of the window, and it looks like it's all over for our hero.

Bladen's bodyguard Blackie (played by Robert Strauss) has the bright idea of bumping Johnny off by substituting a real bullet for the blank Frankie fires at him during their stage performance of the song. Live on stage, Frankie shoots, Johnny falls, and he'd be stone dead if it wasn't for the good luck charm bearing a cricket that Frankie had given him, which fortuitously deflects the real bullet away from his heart.

The happy ending has Frankie realizing that she loves Johnny just the way he is, and Nelly understanding finally persuading that her future lies with Clint Braden to propose and make an honest woman of her.

Songs: "Come Along," "Petunia The Gardener's Daughter", "Chesay," "What Every Woman Lives For," "Frankie And Johnny," "Look Out Broadway," "Beginner's Luck," "Down By The Riverside"/"When The Saints Go Marchin' In," "Shout It Out," "Hard Luck," "Please Don't Stop Loving Me," "Everybody Come Aboard"

"FRANK SINATRA SHOW"

Elvis recorded this show at the Fontainebleau Hotel in Miami, on March 26, 1960, less than a month after returning to America following his honorable discharge from the Army. Billed as a "Timex Special," the TV show is also sometimes referred to as *Welcome Home Elvis*, *Frank Sinatra's Welcome Home Party for Elvis Presley* or *It's Nice To Go Traveling*. In the show, which aired on ABC on May 12, 1960, Elvis performed "Stuck On You" and "Fame And Fortune," the two new tracks on his latest single, and sang duets with Sinatra, one on "Witchcraft," one on "Love Me Tender." Not for the first time on TV, Elvis wore a tuxedo (see "The Steve Allen Show") Elvis also contributed to "It's Nice To Go Trav'ling," a song featuring fellow guests Nancy Sinatra, Joey Bishop and Sammy Davis Jr.

Though some critics have written that the performances lack a little spontaneity, the two men reputedly had a lot of fun in rehearsals.

For his appearance, his first on TV in over three years, Colonel Parker landed Elvis an outlandishly large fee of $125,000. The show garnered a 41.5% audience share (65% according to Ernst Jorgensen). The Colonel left nothing to chance, stacking the audience with Elvis fans who were needlessly instructed to go wild when Elvis came out.

Elvis' recordings of "Stuck On You" and "Fame And Fortune" from the show were released on 1997 compilation *Platinum: A Life In Music*. The "Witchcraft" / "Love Me Tender" duet is on *From Nashville To Memphis*.

DVDs:
Welcome Home Elvis (2001—J.A.T. productions)
"Frank Sinatra Show": *Welcome Home Elvis* (2003—Quantum Leap productions)

Elvis arriving for the Sinatra TV special, 1960.

FRAZIER, DALLAS
(B. 1939)

Country singer/songwriter Frazier Dallas started out in the music business touring with Ferlin Husky while still very young. He released his first single the same year as Elvis. By the Sixties he was working in Nashville as a songwriter for Brenda Lee, Willie Nelson, Charley Pride, Jack Green and Connie Smith, as well as scoring hits for himself ("Elvira") and a new generation of country artists.

Elvis sang Frazier songs "There Goes My Everything," "Wearin' That Loved On Look," "True Love Travels On A Gravel Road" and "Where Did They Go, Lord."

FRIENDS

Elvis grew up in an extended family and was used to having countless cousins around; Billy Smith remembers that Vernon and Gladys had very few friends before and after Elvis struck fame. Until his last couple of years at high school, biographers frame him as more or less a loner at school; he had a few friends, often younger than himself, and was not part of the popular groups or cliques. Elvis later told interviewers that he became instantly popular when people realized that he had a talent with a guitar. Post-fame, Elvis never needed to spend another moment alone. He rarely ever did.

From the time that Elvis became a national star, he had his own entourage support system, later nicknamed the Memphis Mafia, with whom he traveled, had fun, played pranks, hatched plans, raised hell and generally had a good time. Dozens of people considered themselves to be Elvis' best friend. Elvis had the ability of the truly charismatic to make people feel that they were supremely important in the time they spent together. The fact that the majority of these friends were on his payroll undoubtedly colored the quality and equality of these friendships. Elvis was very much top dog, the uncontested focus of all attentions in his peer group. The only time Elvis ever deferred judgment was in the presence of someone in a position of authority (usually Colonel Parker).

If people who knew Elvis from his schooldays were surprised to hear him on the radio, they were amazed that there was little change in their friendship after he became a national star. People Elvis hadn't seen in years who dropped by to Graceland found a man who was happy to see them, listened attentively to what they'd been up to, invited them to come round more often, and in some cases helped them out financially.

Long before Elvis became popular with an entourage of guys and before he began performing, he found it easy to befriend girls. By the time he was headlining across the South, girls were lining up outside his home, hoping to be picked out to join in the fun. Many were.

During his first year touring, Elvis shared his life with fellow band members Scotty Moore, Bill Black and later D.J. Fontana—years that he would later reminisce about as great times.

Elvis gathered an entourage around him more out of a need for security than friendship, at least initially. He surrounded himself with favored cousins and guys he knew from playing football who were happy to come along for the ride, pals having fun together. As Red West says, "He was just one of the boys. He would often share the driving on long gigs. We had shared everything, even our women." When they went onto the payroll, there was a subtle shift in the terms of their friendship, not least because of Elvis' ability to hire or fire. Elvis gradually expanded the entourage with guys he met through trusted old friends like George Klein, while other guys were added to the gang if they showed character. For instance, a 17-year-old called Will McDaniel, who worked at the Rollerdrome skating rink in Memphis, had the temerity to knock Elvis down during a high-spirited skating game. Rather than getting the beating he fully expected, Elvis told Red West to give McDaniel the "Graceland phone number."

In the main, though, Elvis did not take kindly to being challenged by any of his friends, and made it clear when he felt that he wasn't the cen-

Elvis and Frank Sinatra during rehearsal for the Sinatra TV Show.

ter of attention. When Barbara Glidewell, one of the girls who spent time hanging round Graceland, brought a date along to the Memphis Fairground one night, Elvis had the guy take the rollercoaster for forty minutes straight, until he got sick.

When Elvis first went out to Hollywood, he began hanging out with young and edgy actors like Nick Adams and Natalie Wood, but soon preferred to spend time with his own entourage.

During his time away from Memphis in the Army Elvis made a whole new set of friends. Afterwards, he invited Joe Esposito, Charlie Hodge and Richard Davis to become paid members of his entourage.

Several old high school pals, including George Klein and Paul Dougher, turned down Elvis' requests for them to join the payroll and work for him. They each told him that they preferred their friendship to remain straight-up friendship.

Loyalty was paramount for Elvis. He was firm friends with high school pals Red West and George Klein for practically his whole life. Elvis took it very badly when West and his cousin Sonny wrote their no-holds-barred book in 1976 (after Elvis had fired them).

In the early Sixties, when he was spending considerable time in Hollywood, Elvis' new friends were almost exclusively girlfriends. Biographers have advanced a number of reasons why Elvis preferred to stay out of the Hollywood buddy system: he liked being first among unequals in his entourage; he suffered a sense of inferiority

about his Southern roots; or he felt that he could not trust strangers because invariably they wanted something out of him, they were interested in "Elvis the image" rather than "Elvis the man."

Every evening Graceland would fill with people. Before Elvis came down, he had someone tell him who was around. If a name was mentioned of somebody who he wasn't keen on, Elvis might not come down all evening.

With the exception of Charlie Hodge (a musician before he met Elvis) and Red West (who wrote some songs for him) Elvis did not spend a lot of time with musicians, despite regularly going out to see fellow singers perform in Los Angeles and Las Vegas. Seventies band members have said that the Colonel actively discouraged people on the payroll from socializing with Elvis outside of rehearsals, and that the entourage over-zealously shielded Elvis from outsiders who got in touch.

One exception was Tom Jones, with whom Elvis struck up a firm friendship. Priscilla told Jones that Elvis was thrilled to spend time with somebody who was on his musical wavelength.

When a music industry or actor friend did stop by to visit, Elvis invariably had somebody from the entourage sit in. Entourage members recall that Elvis never made the first move with somebody else, and even contemporaries who came into his life were not allowed to become a regular presence, either by the entourage, or by Elvis.

When he was performing in the Seventies, Elvis readily made friends with people who dropped by to say hello backstage after a show.

Sometimes he would chat for hours. Many people later commented on how interested a listener Elvis was—not the first character trait one expects to find in a superstar.

In Palm Springs, Elvis often hung out with working men who would come up to play basketball up at his house. He also made many friends among police officers in the towns where he lived.

Despite their differences and initially acrimonious divorce proceedings, Elvis and Priscilla made a conscious effort to put antipathy behind them and remain good friends for Lisa Marie's sake.

Elvis still had plenty of acquaintances among famous performers and screen stars who were happy to come and see him in Las Vegas and say hello backstage afterwards. One night in February 1973 he namechecked Ann-Margret, George Hamilton, Ernest Borgnine, Dane Clark, Mama Cass and Buzz Aldrin. Another night, it was Petula Clark, Guy Marks, Phyllis McGuire and Liza Minnelli.

From the period when Elvis' life became increasingly ruled by drugs—the general consensus is that this occurred in 1973/1974—he was less interested in hanging out with guys from the entourage and meeting new people. Concern at his appearance was part of the problem; revealing his darker side was another; letting people get close enough to voice their concern at his abuse of prescription drugs was perhaps the strongest underlying motive.

He became more and more of a misanthrope in his final years, barely tolerating other musicians around, and no longer seeing many long-established friends. His entourage slowly unraveled. Elvis fired Red and Sonny West, and fell out with Dr. Nichopoulos and Joe Esposito over a business deal that went sour.

By 1977, Elvis was disillusioned with all but a select few friends. In June that year, while Graceland was full of people packing up for Elvis' forthcoming tour, Vernon sounded off about how disappointed Elvis was that only Billy Stanley, Charlie Hodge and Larry Geller were really there for him. In his final months, Elvis felt most comfortable spending time with cousin Billy Smith.

ELVIS SAID IN 1959: "I've made a lot of friends in the Army among the men that I would have never made before."

ELVIS SAID IN 1962: "It's important to surround yourself with people who can give you a little happiness."

ELVIS TOLD LARRY GELLER HIS MOTHER'S WISDOM ON FRIENDS: "Don't forget where you came from. When you're on top, everyone will love you, everyone will want something, but if you slip, they'll all be gone."

PRISCILLA: "Once you bonded with him . . . there was no going back."

RONNIE TUTT: "He was a team player though he was very much an individual, but he felt very strongly about people he surrounded himself with."

DICK GROB: "Elvis was special, he was a friend who never asked for anything except your loyalty, but he gave completely of himself. He was a friend for life."

LAMAR FIKE: "Elvis looked for oddballs. Some people might theorize that he picked guys like that to make sure they'd be faithful to him. I don't think he had any rhyme or reason for it. But he did like underdogs..."

LARRY GELLER: "He was gracious and gave you his full attention, whether you were the President or his gardener."

BILLY SMITH: "Most show people made Elvis uncomfortable. He thought they were judging him."

PRISCILLA: "Elvis expected total loyalty from his friends. If he was betrayed, he would just cut that person out of his life."

PATTI PARRY: "Elvis was basically a 19-year-old truck driver and he was still shy but with his friends he could really relax."

MYRNA SMITH: "He was kind of a recluse in many respects, a loner to some degree, but he liked people."

BILLY SMITH: "Elvis wanted friends who were in touch with that Southern world that he came from... He wanted this little group that talk the same way he did and ate the same kind of food. He also had a tough time being alone."

LINDA THOMPSON: "You have to remember that Elvis was completely isolated from the world. He surrounded himself with about thirteen men and me. He was closed off to other people—other stimuli."

STEVE DUNLEAVY: "Presley never just likes someone; he loves them and will give to the point of suffocation. He never just dislikes someone; he has the rare ability to hate with an awe-inspiring passion."

LARRY GELLER: "Once Elvis befriended you, he might see your flaws, but he worked around them. He found the good in each person and turned a blind eye to everything else."

RED WEST: "The Colonel treated all of Elvis' friends hot and cold, hot and cold. He was friendly, but he always kept his distance."

BILLY SMITH: "I never knew if he cared as much about the guys as we cared about him."

"FROGGY WENT A'COURTIN'"

Elvis rehearsed this Hugo Peretti / Luigi Creatore / Jimmie Rodgers track in July 1970. Though it went unreleased during his lifetime, it came out on *Walk A Mile In My Shoes* in 1995.

"FROM A JACK TO A KING"

Elvis laid down this track—a favorite of both Vernon's and Priscilla's, written by Ned Miller in 1957—on January 21, 1969. It wasn't on the list of songs he was planning to record that session but Elvis gave it a whirl after his Daddy dropped by to see him at American Studio. Elvis' version was originally released on the album *From Memphis To Vegas* and soon after on sister-album *Back in Memphis*.

More recently, it has appeared on compilations *From Nashville To Memphis*, *Great Country Songs*, *Suspicious Minds: The Memphis 1969 Anthology* and *The Country Side of Elvis*.

The first three takes from the studio are on 2001 FTD release *The Memphis Sessions*.

FROM ELVIS IN MEMPHIS

The first album to come out of Elvis' Memphis recording session at American Sound officially marked Elvis' return to form. *Rolling Stone* magazine found the album to be "flatly and unequivocally the equal of anything he has ever done." Many fans agree. On release in May 1969, half a million of them bought copies, keeping it in the charts for 24 weeks and propelling it to #13. It has been a strong seller ever since.

TRACK LISTING:
1. Wearin' That Loved On Look
2. Only The Strong Survive
3. I'll Hold You In My Heart (Till I Can Hold You In My Arms)
4. Long Black Limousine
5. It Keeps Right On A-Hurtin'
6. I'm Movin' On
7. Power Of My Love
8. Gentle On My Mind
9. After Loving You
10. True Love Travels On A Gravel Road

11. Any Day Now
12. In The Ghetto

A remastered version was released in 2000 with bonus tracks The Fair Is Moving On, Suspicious Minds, You'll Think Of Me, Don't Cry Daddy, Kentucky Rain and Mama Liked The Roses.

FROM ELVIS PRESLEY BOULEVARD, MEMPHIS, TENNESSEE

Recorded at Graceland in February 1976 after Elvis showed no inclination to go back into a recording studio, this April 1976 release made #1 on the country charts but failed to rouse the general public beyond #41 in the main *Billboard* charts, though it did stay in the charts for seventeen weeks. Still, it scored a gold record.

TRACK LISTING:
1. Hurt
2. Never Again
3. Blue Eyes Crying In The Rain
4. Danny Boy
5. The Last Farewell
6. For The Heart
7. Bitter They Are, Harder They Fall
8. Solitaire
9. Love Coming Down
10. I'll Never Fall In Love Again

FROM HOLLYWOOD TO VEGAS

An unofficial 1974 release.

TRACK LISTING:
1. Loving You
2. Husky Dusky Day
3. On Top Of Old Smokey
4. Dainty Little Moonbeams
5. Girls! Girls! Girls! / Aura Lee
6. Signs Of The Zodiac
7. Folsom Prison Blues
8. I Walk The Line
9. Oh Happy Day
10. I Ain't About To Sing
11. I Need Your Lovin' Everyday
12. I Got A Woman / Amen
13. Crying Time
14. Lovely Mamie
15. Long Tall Sally
16. Flip Flop And Fly
17. My Boy
18. Hound Dog
19. All Right Baby
20. The Complete Aloha Press Interview

FROM MEMPHIS TO VEGAS / FROM VEGAS TO MEMPHIS

Elvis' first double album showcased more new material recorded at American Studio in early 1969 and his first live performances at the International Hotel in Las Vegas with the new TCB Band. Initially released together in October 1969, this collector's set sold 300,000 copies and rose to #12 in the charts during its 24-week stay. In 1970 the albums were re-released individually as *Elvis In Person at the International Hotel* (live) and *Back in Memphis* (studio).

TRACK LISTING:
  (From Memphis To Vegas)
SIDE 1
  Blue Suede Shoes
  Johnny B Goode
  All Shook Up
  Are You Lonesome Tonight?
  Hound Dog
  I Can't Stop Loving You
  My Babe

SIDE 2

Mystery Train / Tiger Man
Words
In The Ghetto
Suspicious Minds
Can't Help Falling In Love
(From Vegas To Memphis)

SIDE 3

Inherit The Wind
This Is The Story
Stranger In My Own Home Town
Little Bit Of Green
And The Grass Won't Pay No Mind

SIDE 4

Do You Know Who I Am?
From A Jack To A King
The Fair Is Moving On
You'll Think Of Me
Without Love (There Is Nothing)

FROM NASHVILLE TO MEMPHIS: THE ESSENTIAL 60S MASTERS

A 1993 5-disc boxed set of 130 remastered studio recordings from Elvis' most prolific decade, including a number of previously unreleased versions.

TRACK LISTING:

DISC: 1

1. Make Me Know It
2. Soldier Boy
3. Stuck On You
4. Fame And Fortune
5. A Mess Of Blues
6. It Feels So Right
7. Fever
8. Like A Baby
9. It's Now Or Never
10. The Girl Of My Best Friend
11. Dirty, Dirty Feeling
12. Thrill Of Your Love
13. I Gotta Know
14. Such A Night
15. Are You Lonesome Tonight?
16. Girl Next Door Went A'Walking
17. I Will Be Home Again
18. Reconsider Baby
19. Surrender
20. I'm Comin' Home
21. Gently
22. In Your Arms
23. Give Me The Right
24. I Feel So Bad
25. It's A Sin
26. I Want You With Me
27. There's Always Me

DISC: 2

1. Starting Today
2. Sentimental Me
3. Judy
4. Put The Blame On Me
5. Kiss Me Quick
6. That's Someone You Never Forget
7. I'm Yours
8. His Latest Flame
9. Little Sister
10. For The Millionth And The Last Time
11. Good Luck Charm
12. Anything That's Part Of You
13. I Met Her Today
14. Night Rider
15. Something Blue
16. Gonna Get Back Home Somehow
17. (Such An) Easy Question
18. Fountain Of Love
19. Just For Old Time Sake
20. You'll Be Gone
21. I Feel That I've Known You Forever
22. Just Tell Her Jim Said Hello
23. Suspicion

24. She's Not You
25. Echoes Of Love
26. Please Don't Drag That String Around
27. (You're The) Devil In Disguise
28. Never Ending
29. What Now, What Next, Where To
30. Witchcraft
31. Finders Keepers, Losers Weepers
32. Love Me Tonight

DISC: 3

1. (It's A) Long Lonely Highway
2. Western Union
3. Slowly But Surely
4. Blue River
5. Memphis Tennessee
6. Ask Me
7. It Hurts Me
8. Down In The Alley
9. Tomorrow Is A Long Time
10. Love Letters
11. Beyond The Reef (original undubbed master)
12. Come What May (alternate take)
13. Fools Fall In Love
14. Indescribably Blue
15. I'll Remember You (original unedited master)
16. If Every Day Was Like Christmas
17. Suppose (Master)
18. Guitar Man / What'd I Say (original unedited master)
19. Big Boss Man
20. Mine
21. Just Call Me Lonesome
22. Hi-Heel Sneakers (original unedited master)
23. You Don't Know Me
24. Singing Tree
25. Too Much Monkey Business
26. U.S. Male

DISC: 4

1. Long Black Limousine
2. This Is The Story
3. Wearin' That Loved On Look
4. You'll Think Of Me
5. A Little Bit Of Green
6. Gentle On My Mind
7. I'm Movin' On
8. Don't Cry, Daddy
9. Inherit The Wind
10. Mama Liked The Roses
11. My Little Friend
12. In The Ghetto
13. Rubberneckin'
14. From A Jack To A King
15. Hey Jude
16. Without Love (There Is Nothing)
17. I'll Hold You In My Heart (Till I Can Hold You In My Arms)
18. I'll Be There (If Ever You Want Me)
19. Suspicious Minds
20. True Love Travels On A Gravel Road
21. Stranger In My Own Home Town
22. And The Grass Won't Pay No Mind
23. Power Of My Love

DISC: 5

1. After Loving You
2. Do You Know Who I Am
3. Kentucky Rain
4. Only The Strong Survive
5. It Keeps Right On A-Hurtin'
6. Any Day Now
7. If I'm A Fool (For Loving You)
8. The Fair Is Moving On
9. Who Am I?
10. It's My Way / This Time / I Can't Stop Loving You (jam)
11. In The Ghetto (alternate take)
12. Suspicious Minds (alternate take)
13. Kentucky Rain (alternate take)
14. Big Boss Man (alternate take)
15. Down In The Alley (alternate take)
16. Memphis Tennessee (alternate take from 1963 session)
17. I'm Yours (alternate take undubbed)
18. His Latest Flame (alternate take)

19. That's Someone You Never Forget (alternate take)
20. Surrender (alternate take)
21. It's Now Or Never (original undubbed master)
22. Love Me Tender / Witchcraft (From 'The Frank Sinatra Timex Special')

FTD (FOLLOW THAT DREAM LABEL)

In 1999 RCA/BMG announced a specialist Elvis collectors' label "to complement the commercial and artistic level of RCA's retail release schedule by issuing repertoire that is considered of interest to serious Elvis fans and collectors."

The label has launched a large quantity of limited-edition releases spanning home recordings, outtakes, remastered hits, movie soundtracks and soundboard recordings of live concerts, many with accompanying books. FTD remastered classic albums offer a selection of alternate takes and improved sound quality. Soundtrack albums include photos and reprints of cinema lobby cards. FTD is hoping to release live albums from every major Elvis tour and Las Vegas/Lake Tahoe season. Much of the previously-unreleased material on FTD has been tracked down by producers Ernst Jorgensen and Roger Semon from collectors, and most has been remixed by Kevan Budd.

Ernst Jorgensen: "We're not really limited in the Follow That Dream thing because we're not selling a lot and we don't need to sell a lot."

FTD Releases

1999:
Burbank '68 (live jam session from NBC TV Special)
Out In Hollywood (studio outtakes)
In A Private Moment (home recordings, Germany and LA)

2000:
The Jungle Room Sessions (Jungle Room outtakes)
Long Lonely Highway (studio outtakes)
Tucson '76 (live, June 1, 1976)
Too Much Monkey Business (Eighties remixes by Felton Jarvis and Chip Young revisited)
One Night in Vegas (live, August 10, 1970)

2001:
6363 Sunset (studio, 1972 and 1975)
Easter Special (gospel outtakes and alternates)
Dixieland Rocks (live, May 6, 1975)
The Way It Was (live/studio outtakes and book)
The Memphis Sessions (studio outtakes remixed by Dennis Ferrante)
Silver Screen Stereo (studio outtakes)
It's Midnight (live, Las Vegas, August 24, 1974)

2002
Fame and Fortune (studio outtakes, early Sixties)
Spring Tours '77 (live)
The Nashville Marathon (studio outtakes, June/September 1970)
Dinner at Eight (live, Las Vegas December 13, 1975)
Elvis at the International (live, August 23, 1969)

2003:
New Year's Eve 1976 (live, Pittsburgh December 31, 1976)
Studio B: Nashville Outtakes (studio outtakes, 1961 to 1964)
Fun in Acapulco (movie soundtrack)
It Happened at the World's Fair (movie soundtrack)
Girl Happy (movie soundtrack)
Dragonheart (live, South Bend, Indiana October 1, 1974)
Takin' Tahoe Tonight (live, May 13, 1973)

Viva Las Vegas (movie soundtrack)

Harum Scarum (movie soundtrack)

Frankie and Johnny (movie soundtrack)

So High (outtakes from Nashville, 1966 to 1968)
    2004:

The Impossible Dream (live, Las Vegas, January 1971)

Elvis Recorded Live on Stage in Memphis

Spinout (movie soundtrack)

Flashback (studio outtakes and book)

Paradise, Hawaiian Style (studio outtakes)

Polk Salad Annie (live rehearsals and show, Las Vegas, 1970)

Double Trouble (movie soundtrack)

Closing Night (live, Las Vegas, September 3, 1973)

Follow That Dream (movie soundtrack)

Kid Galahad (movie soundtrack)

Elvis On Tour—The Rehearsals (studio outtakes, March 1972)
    2005:

Elvis Is Back! (studio outtakes)

Big Boss Man (live, Las Vegas, March 1975)

Rockin' Across Texas (live, Fifties, with book)

Elvis Today (studio outtakes)

Tickle Me (movie soundtrack)

All Shook Up (live, Las Vegas, August 26, 1969)

Summer Festival (live, Las Vegas, August 11, 1972)
    2006:

Loving You (movie soundtrack)

Southern Nights (live, Spring 1975)

Something for Everybody (studio outtakes)

Made in Memphis (studio outtakes and home recordings from 1969, 1973 and 1976)

Clambake (movie soundtrack)

I Found My Thrill (live, Las Vegas, January 27, 1974)

Elvis Presley (studio outtakes)

Let Yourself Go (live, NBC Special material, 1968)

Writing for the King (400 page book, CDs of Elvis live, songwriter tunes)
    2007:

Unchained Melody (live, Charlotte, February 1977)

An American Trilogy (live, Las Vegas, February 1972)

50 Million Elvis Fans Can't Be Wrong (remixed classic album, outtakes)

Live in LA (live, May 1974, plus book)

I Sing All Kinds (studio outtakes, Nashville 1971)

Easy Come, Easy Go (remixed soundtrack EP, outtakes)

Raised On Rock (album re-release with outtakes)

Girls! Girls! Girls! (movie soundtrack)

Pot Luck With Elvis (remixed classic album, with outtakes)

FULCHINO, ANNE

RCA's publicity director in New York had been hankering after an artist like Elvis to promote. The first time she met him she was impressed by how single-minded he was and yet how willing to learn. She was less impressed with the old handshake-buzzer trick he played. She masterminded his publicity from when he signed with RCA through the Sixties.

ANNE FULCHINO: "He wanted it, and he had the talent."

FULLER, DOLORES
(B. 1923)

Dolores Fuller co-wrote a dozen songs for seven different Elvis movies in the Sixties. An ex-model, for a portion of the Fifties she starred in several of Ed Wood's B-movies, as well as being his lover.

After writing for Elvis, Fuller wrote for singers including Peggy Lee and Nat King Cole. She ran her own record company, Dee records, in the Sixties. In the 1994 movie on Ed Wood she was portrayed by Sarah Jessica Parker. She is sometimes credited as "Dee Fuller" on her compositions.

"FUN IN ACAPULCO"

Ben Weisman and Sid Wayne wrote the title track for the movie and soundtrack LP of the same name. Elvis recorded the song at Radio Recorders on January 23, 1963.

The song was included on BMG's 2006 themed release *Elvis Movies*, and has also featured on *Elvis in Hollywood*, *Command Performances*, and the *Double Feature* and FTD soundtrack re-releases.

FUN IN ACAPULCO (LP)

This soundtrack album very nearly didn't see the light, as the Colonel and RCA wrangled about whether it should have a gatefold sleeve and how much it should cost. In the end it came out with two bonus tracks in November 1963, to coincide with the movie release, climbing to a very respectable #3 position in the charts, despite the worrying trend of selling 200,000 copies fewer than the *Girls! Girls! Girls!* from a year earlier.

TRACK LISTING:
1.   Fun In Acapulco
2.   Vino, Dinero Y Amor
3.   Mexico
4.   El Toro
5.   Marguerita
6.   The Bullfighter Was A Lady
7.   (There's) No Room To Rhumba In A Sports Car
8.   I Think I'm Gonna Like It Here
9.   Bossa Nova Baby
10. You Can't Say No In Acapulco
11. Guadalajara
12. Love Me Tonight
13. Slowly But Surely

Like many of Elvis' Sixties song-light soundtrack albums, this one was re-released in the Nineties in the *Double Feature* series, in this case paired with *It Happened At The World's Fair*. It has also had the boxed set/alternate take/extra track treatment on an FTD 2003 release.

FUN IN ACAPULCO

Hal Wallis and writer Allan Weiss began plotting Elvis' next goodtime sunny location movie while Elvis was working on *Girls! Girls! Girls!*, much of which was shot in Hawaii. Alternative titles considered and rejected were the unimaginative *Holiday In Acapulco* and *Vacation In Acapulco*.

Principal photography began in late January 1963, all in Hollywood. Location material was added later, without Elvis having to set foot over the border. The most persuasive reason given by biographers for Elvis not making the relatively easy journey to Mexico was that he was persona non grata in the country after riots set off by comments he had allegedly made about Mexican women. Paradoxically, Paramount printed up passports as a publicity gimmick, and used them in the movie posters.

There are shades of Elvis' real-life manager Colonel Parker in the character of his fearless 8-year-old manager, played by Larry Domasin (who, years before Parker, had the temerity to take 50% of Elvis' earnings).

One of the divers is future Kiss frontman Gene Simmons.

The film went on nationwide release at the end of November 1963. It spent three weeks in the *Variety* National Box Office Survey, peaking at #5, though by the end of the year it was only the 33rd highest-grossing film. On its initial run the movie failed to make back its $3 million cost but with international sales factored in, like every other Elvis feature, it made money.

CREDITS:
Paramount, Color.
Length: 97 minutes
Release date: November 27, 1963

TAGLINES:
Come With Elvis to Fabulous Acapulco!
Elvis never had it like this!
Go with Elvis to Acapulco, the one place, the fun place . . .

Produced by: Hal B. Wallis
Directed by: Richard Thorpe
Writing credits: Allan Weiss
Executive producer: Joseph H. Hazen
Associate producer: Paul Nathan
Music by: Joseph J. Lilley, Pepe Guízar
Cinematography by: Daniel L. Fapp
Film Editing by: Stanley E. Johnson
Art Direction by: Hal Pereira, Walter Tyler
Set Decoration by: Robert Benton, Sam Comer
Costume Design by: Edith Head

CAST:

Elvis Presley	Mike Windgren
Ursula Andress	Marguerita Dauphin
Elsa Cardenas	Dolores Gomez
Paul Lukas	Maximillian Dauphin
Larry Domasin	Raoul Almeido
Alejandro Rey	Moreno
Robert Carricart	Jose Garcia
Teri Hope	Janie Harkins
Robert Alderette	Taxi Driver
Marco Antonio	Bullfighter
Salvador Baguez	Mr. Perez, La Perla Manager
Loren Brown	1st Diver
Edward Colmans	Mr. Delgado, Ambassador Club Manager
Mike De Anda	Guard at La Perla
Robert De Anda	Bellboy
Luis De Urban	M.C. at the Hilton
Don Diamond	Waiter
Elly Enriquez	2nd Diver
Charles Evans	Mr Harkins
Stella Garcia	Señorita at Torito's
Martin Garralaga	Tropicana Hotel Manager
Teri Garr	Extra

Elvis with Ursula Andress in *Fun in Acapulco*.

A shot from the 1963 film *Fun in Acapulco*.

Alex Giannini	Bartender
Genaro Gomez	Bullfighter
Stuart Gray	3rd Diver
Ralph Hanalei	5th Diver
Bob Harvey	Waiter
Tom Hernández	Photographer
Roberto Iglesias	Maitre D'/Waiter
John Indrisano	Hotel Guest
Carmelo Manto	Bullfighter
Howard McNear	Dr. John Stevers
Alberto Monte	Bullfighter
Alberto Morin	Mr. Ramírez, Hilton Manager
Francisco Ortega	Desk Clerk
Adele Palacios	Secretary
Rachel Parra	Castanet Player
Linda Rand	Girl
David Renard	Photographer
Linda Rivera	Señorita at the Telegraph Desk
Gene Simmons	Diver
Darlene Tompkins	Miss Stevers
Mary Treen	Mrs Stevers
Ronald Veto	4th Diver
Red West	Poolside Guest

ADDITIONAL CREW:

Nellie Manley	hair stylist
Wally Westmore	makeup supervisor
Michael D. Moore	assistant director
Charles Grenzbach	sound recorder
Hugo Grenzbach	sound recorder
Paul K. Lerpae	special photographic effects
Kim Kahana	stunts
Farciot Edouart	process photographer
The Four Amigos	vocal accompaniment
The Jordanaires	vocal accompaniment
Warren Low	supervising editor
Richard Mueller	color consultant
Charles O'Curran	musical number staging
Colonel Tom Parker	technical advisor
Irmin Roberts	.second unit photographer

Plot:

Elvis plays Mike Windgren, a former trapeze artist (with a dark secret) who takes a job as a sailor on a boat in Acapulco. He loses this much-needed job when the yacht-owner's daughter Janine (Teri Hope) tattles on him after he spurns her advances.

Big-talking shoeshine boy Raoul Almeido (played by Larry Domasin) hears Mike sing one day and improbably offers to manage his singing career. The kid has cousins everywhere, and lands Mike a job at the Acapulco Hilton, conveniently managed by one such cousin (Alberto Morin). Between one number and another Mike makes quite an impression on female bullfighter Dolores Gomez (played by Elsa Cardenas). He meets love interest number two, Marguerita (Ursula Andress), while standing in for regular lifeguard Moreno (played by Alejandro Rey).

Moreno is also a high-diving champion and a jealous guy. He plots his new rival's downfall after learning of Mike's fatal flaw, a fear of heights that cost his brother's life at the circus. Moreno's plan, to make Mike look bad by challenging him to do the famous Acapulco high dive, looks like it has every chance of success. First, Moreno engineers a fight with Mike. He feigns being unable to perform his usual nightly high dive and waits for Mike to show himself up in front of everyone.

Instead, much to everyone except Moreno's eternal benefit, Mike scales the 136-foot high La Perla cliff, glances down at Marguerita and launches out into a perfect 10 dive. There's nothing left to do but live happily ever after.

Songs: "Fun In Acapulco," "Vino, Dinero Y Amor," "I Think I'm Gonna Like It Here," "Mexico," "El Toro," "Marguerita," "The Bullfighter Was A Lady", "(There's) No Room To Rhumba In A Sports Car," "Bossa Nova Baby," "You Can't Say No In Acapulco," "Guadalajara"

FUNERAL

Elvis' funeral took place two days after he died, at 2 p.m. on Thursday August 18, 1977, in the living room at Graceland. His body had been prepared at the Memphis Funeral Home, where funeral director Robert Kendall laid Elvis to rest in an $8,000 coffin identical to the one his mother was buried in, flow in from Oklahoma. Pal Larry Geller went to the funeral home to do Elvis' hair for the last time.

Elvis' body was brought back to Graceland at midday on August 17 to lay in state. For two days 150 Shelby County deputies and Air National Guard military sentries lined the driveway as an honor guard.

Friends and family came to pay their respects, say their last goodbyes and see Elvis for the final time. James Brown spent a long time sitting next to the coffin. The men in charge of Elvis' security —Dick Grob and Sam Thompson—kept a vigil over Elvis' body at night because there were rumors that there might be an attempt to steal the body.

On August 17, Vernon had the gates of Graceland thrown open to allow fans to see their hero for the last time. Flowers and cards lined the driveway, as people waited patiently for hours to file past the casket, placed just inside the front door. Many people were unable to get in, despite the initial viewing window of two hours being extended by an hour and a half.

On August 18, more people attended the funeral service at Graceland than there was room to sit in the living room; many stood in the dining room area, including Colonel Parker, who arrived for the funeral dressed in a Hawaiian shirt and steadfastly avoided approaching the coffin.

The ceremony was scheduled to last half an hour but went on for much longer.

The religious part of the ceremony was officiated by Reverend C. W. Bradley from the nearby Wooddale Church of Christ, who emphasized Elvis' love of family, determination and decency: "Perhaps because of his rapid rise to fame and fortune he was thrown into temptations that some never experience. Elvis would not want anyone to think that he had no flaws or faults. But now

ABOVE: Crowd of mourners line up to pay their last respects.

BELOW: Elvis' funeral procession.

that he's gone, I find it more helpful to remember his good qualities, and I hope you do too."

Friend and evangelist Rex Humbard delivered a sermon. Jackie Kahane gave a eulogy, and Elvis' favorite hymns were sung by many of the singers who had backed him on stage over the years, including J. D. Sumner and the Stamps, the Statesmen, James Blackwood and Kathy Westmoreland. Most of the people who attended the funeral were too upset to remember much about it. Indeed, ever since Elvis' death, many of them had been in a state shock, disbelief and debilitating grief ever since they heard the news.

SONGS AT ELVIS' FUNERAL

James Blackwood and Kathy Westmoreland: "How Great Thou Art."
Jake Hess "Known Only to Him"
Kathy Westmoreland "My Heavenly Father Watches Over Me."
J. D. Sumner and the Stamps: Medley including "His Hand in Mine" and "Sweet, Sweet Spirit."

The 900lb copper casket required more than a dozen pallbearers, including Joe Esposito, Dr. George Nichopoulos, Felton Jarvis, Jerry Schilling, George Klein, Lamar Fike, Billy Smith, Charlie Hodge and Gene Smith. Colonel Parker was asked to help carry the casket but he declined. As they brought Elvis out of Graceland, a large bough broke off from one of the trees in the grounds.

Fans surged towards the hearse and long line of seventeen white limousines, part of a 50-car motorcade taking Elvis' casket and the mourners to Forest Hill cemetery, preceded by police motorcycles, and followed by a bus full of Elvis' band members. A distraught fan threw herself at the hood of the hearse. People in Memphis that day remember that the city was numb with grief. An armada of vans—by some accounts as many as a hundred—was required to ferry the flowers to the cemetery. Vernon later gave instructions for the flowers to be given away to fans.

Many celebrities had been expected to attend the 5-minute service at the Forest Hill cemetery chapel. Only Ann-Margret, James Brown, and George Hamilton made it to the funeral, though

newspapers speculated that those who were coming included Burt Reynolds, John Wayne, Farrah Fawcett and Sammy Davis Jr. At the end of the ceremony, Vernon cried out repeatedly, "Daddy will be with you soon."

Elvis was buried in a white linen suit (purchased by Vernon a couple of weeks earlier, and never worn by Elvis in life), a light blue shirt and dark blue tie. He wore a TCB ring and a metal bracelet that Lisa Marie wanted him to have. Elvis was interred next to his mother at Forest Hill Cemetery, (located at 1661 Elvis Presley Boulevard). Both of their bodies were later moved to the Meditation Garden in Graceland.

Before he died, Elvis did not leave specific requests for his funeral beyond the fact that he didn't want people wearing black. He is also said to have told people he did not want to be buried, hence the original arrangement for his casket to be put into a mausoleum above ground.

Elvis' body, and Gladys's too, was transferred to the Meditation Garden at Graceland on October 2, 1977 and buried in two of four graves that Vernon ordered to be dug—the other two were for himself and for Grandma Minnie Mae when their time came.

It was calculated that as many as a million people visited Elvis' grave at Forest Hills Cemetery, causing congestion and problems for the cemetery. Security was a major issue, especially after the police uncovered a plot to raid Elvis' mausoleum. Before Vernon was able to transfer the bodies of his wife and child to Graceland, he needed to get his neighbors' approval and lobby local councilors to rezone the property. He had to abandon his initial plan to build a mausoleum at Graceland when he was quoted figures of up to $1 million. A very short, private service was held for the reinterrment.

In 2002, reports surfaced that the Presley family set up a fake attempt to steal Elvis' body from the cemetery to hasten approval from the local County administration, which had already turned down Vernon's original application. The men arrested for plotting to steal Elvis' body were never brought to court.

Ghoulishly, it has been reported that Elvis' brain and major organs were stored at Baptist Memorial Hospital after the autopsy—a report many fans would like to believe untrue. At the time of writing, Elvis' original burial place at

Forest Hill Cemetery was still empty, though there have been reports that it is for sale.

JOAN DEARY: "I couldn't tell you one word that was said at those services—not one word. I wasn't thinking or listening. I was just staring at that coffin in total disbelief."

Book:
The King Is Dead, by Robert Holton and Lisa Burrell, Katco Literary Group, 1998 (a book by the funeral home director).

"FUNNY HOW TIME SLIPS AWAY"

Elvis chose this Willie Nelson song as a new tune for his return to live performing in Las Vegas in August 1969. Live versions from Elvis' first Las Vegas season in the summer of 1969 have appeared on *Collectors Gold* and *Today, Tomorrow & Forever*. Elvis sang the song live hundreds of times, right until his last year on the road, even occasionally trying it out as an alternative show-closer to "Can't Help Falling In Love."

Elvis made a studio cut of "Funny How Time Slips Away" on June 7, 1970 for album release on *Elvis Country*. This version has since appeared on *Platinum: A Life in Music, Walk A Mile In My Shoes, Great Country Songs, The Country Side Of Elvis* and the 2006 *Elvis Country* themed release,

He sang it live on *Elvis as Recorded at Madison Square Garden* (and *An Afternoon in the Garden*), and as part of the *Elvis on Tour* documentary in 1972 (a rehearsal version later came out on FTD album *Elvis On Tour—The Rehearsals*).

Later live performances may be found on bootlegs plus official albums *Elvis Aron Presley, Elvis: Close Up*, the FTD version of *Elvis Recorded Live On Stage in Memphis, Takin' Tahoe Tonight!, Live in L.A., Dixieland Rocks, Tucson '76* and *New Year's Eve*.

G

GAMBILL, MARVIN "GEE GEE"
(1944-2005)

Husband of Elvis's double first cousin Patsy Presley, who went to work with Elvis as a driver and then wardrobe man in the mid-Sixties, and was a core part of the crew for many years. Marvin and Patsy spent a lot of time with newlywed Elvis and Priscilla in the late Sixties, and traveled regularly with the Presleys through the early Seventies.

GAMBLING

Gambling may not have been one of Elvis' vices, but the effects of Colonel Parker's gambling habit arguably conditioned the last phase of his working life as much as any other factor.

Elvis played games for money as a way of passing the time. He played blackjack with the Colonel and Walter Matthau in New Orleans, where he was shooting *King Creole*. In 1960 he reputedly lost $10,000 playing craps in Las Vegas. Chastened by the experience, he thereafter gambled using "house" money; it made no difference whether he won or lost, but his presence was guaranteed to attract others to the tables. Red West remembers a time that another guy bet on the exact same throws as Elvis, and made so much money that he wanted to give some of his winnings to Elvis. Elvis refused.

On set in the Sixties, the entourage guys would while away the hours playing poker or hearts. When they played blackjack at Elvis' home, Elvis was always banker.

Gambling was illegal in Florida when Elvis was there to film *Follow That Dream* in 1961, so all of the gambling paraphernalia used in the film had to be smuggled in.

Elvis had a roulette table built into a coffee table that he owned in Los Angeles in the mid-Sixties.

Elvis played a gambler in *Frankie and Johnny* (1966).

The Colonel's penchant for roulette became a matter of press speculation after Elvis signed up for month-long residencies in Las Vegas from 1969. Some commentators believe that the reason why Elvis kept going back to Las Vegas twice a year for six years was because having racked up huge debts, the Colonel was keen to stay in the good graces of casino management. Elvis was gilt-edged collateral. Estimates of the Colonel's losses run from $1 million per year to around $40 million over six years. The Colonel was reportedly capable of losing a million dollars at a single session.

Rumors in the Seventies that the Colonel was considering selling up Elvis' management contract were supposedly linked to his need to pay off gambling debts.

Elvis occasionally had a flutter before or after his Las Vegas residencies. According to the Lamar Fike, when the entourage was in Vegas, they regularly gambled away their pay checks.

PRISCILLA: "Elvis wasn't a serious player—it didn't matter if he won or lost. He played for the fun of it."

ALANNA NASH: "Gambling fed the obsessive twins—Wisdom and Folly—of Parker's personality, which made him by turns calculating and reckless, self-protective and self-destructive."

GARDNER, "BROTHER" DAVE
(1926-1983)

Popular Southern comic and singer who played the Ellis Auditorium in Memphis in 1960, and then after the show went with Elvis and his entourage for some late-night skating at the Rollerdrome. Gardner was on the bill for Elvis' February 1961 charity show in Memphis. He was at the height of his fame at that time, with TV appearances and best-selling comedy records to his name. His career went into a slow decline from 1962, when he was arrested for the possession of marijuana.

GARLAND, HANK "SUGARFOOT"
(B. WALTER GARLAND, 1930-2004)

In 1957 this accomplished guitarist—one of the most highly-rated session musicians of his day, inventor of "hillbilly jazz" and a much in-demand Nashville session musician—was hired to replace original band member Scotty Moore when he quit over a contractual dispute.

Born in Cowpens, South Carolina on November 11, 1930, Garland was a regular on the Grand Ole Opry by the age of fifteen. By nineteen, he had a million-selling record, "Sugarfoot Rag," under his belt. As part of the famed Nashville "A-team," Garland played on hits by Red Foley, the Louvin Brothers, Jerry Lee Lewis, Roy Orbison, Webb Pierce, Charlie Rich, Pasty Cline and many more. Known principally as a country artist, Garland was also a virtuoso jazz guitarist who jammed with many jazz greats in New York during the Fifties and early Sixties.

Garland played on Elvis' Nashville sessions either side of his time in the Army, sometimes guesting on bass too. Garland had cameos on a couple of Elvis' post-Army movies after he came back from the war. After shooting *Blue Hawaii*, Elvis gave Garland the ukulele he used in the movie. Garland last worked with Elvis on the soundtrack session for *Follow That Dream* in July 1961. He would doubtless have remained a member of Elvis' band for much longer if his career hadn't come to an end in September 1961 when a car accident left him in a coma for many months. After a long convalesce, he returned to playing but never regained his earlier renown.

A biopic on Garland, *Crazy*, came out in 2006.

ELVIS SAID: "Hank is one of the finest guitar players in all of the country."

GARR, TERI
(B. 1949)

The first time this Oscar-nominated actress appeared on a movie screen was as an uncredited extra dancing in Elvis' 1963 movie *Fun in Acapulco*. She worked as an extra/dancer on six (by some accounts as many as nine) Elvis movies before carving out a very successful and long-lasting acting career.

Post-Elvis she guested in "Star Trek" and landed a role in Monkees movie *Head*. Her career took off in the Seventies with performances in *Young Frankenstein*, *Close Encounters of the Third Kind*, and an Oscar-nominated appearance opposite Dustin Hoffman in *Tootsie*. Garr is still a regular in the movies and on TV, though she has been fighting multiple sclerosis since 1999.

GATLIN, LARRY
(B. 1948)

Gatlin grew up listening to gospel music in his home town of Seminole, Texas. He started performing when he joined sometime Elvis back-up group The Imperials, before getting a break as a songwriter through Dottie West. Gatlin's debut album came out in 1973, the year that Elvis recorded his song "Help Me." In 1976 Elvis recorded another Gatlin composition, "Bitter They Are, Harder They Fall."

Gatlin had his greatest success with his brothers in The Gatlin Brothers, scoring a string of country pop hits in the late Seventies through the Eighties.

GELLER, LARRY
(B. 1939)

Hairdresser Larry Geller first cut Elvis' hair at his LA home in May 1964 after Alan Fortas called up the Jay Sebring salon, looking for somebody to replace Elvis' previous hairdresser, Sal Orefice. Elvis was impressed by Geller's haircut. He was deeply moved by their four-hour talk about deep and meaningful topics. Elvis told Geller his life story and confessed in tears that he was desperately seeking some kind of meaning to his life.

Geller was hired on the spot as the latest member of Elvis' entourage. He became Elvis' main confederate during a concerted three-year period of inquiry into religion, spiritualism, metaphysics and mysticism, sharing his books and his knowledge with Elvis. Skeptical members of the entourage disparaging referred to him as Elvis' "guru" or the "swami."

Geller was born on August 8, 1939. He first met Elvis when he was in LA to play a show in 1957, when he strode right up to him in the stage-area car park and said hi. Around that time Geller began working as a hairdresser, though his real ambition was to break into acting.

Geller went back to Graceland with Elvis, bringing along his wife Stevie and their kids. Over the next few years he was a regular visitor. Though Elvis enjoyed the intellectual stimulation of his company, other members of the entourage saw him as an annoyance and a threat.

Just before Christmas 1964, Geller was arrested at Graceland on suspicion of trafficking marijuana, as part of a federal inquiry into drugs and prostitution in Hollywood involving his former salon boss Jay Sebring. Geller was taken downtown for questioning, kept in a cell overnight, and then driven back to Graceland early the following morning, after Elvis placed a call to the Mayor of Memphis.

In 1965, Geller was with Elvis on a road trip to LA, crossing the Arizona desert, when Elvis spotted a cloud formation that he took as a sign of mystic revelation. In his memoir, Geller reports that this was at the exact same spot where years earlier Geller had had a similar experience.

According to Marty Lacker, it was Larry Geller who planted the seed in Elvis' mind of becoming a kind of "New Age evangelist." By 1967, the Colonel was blaming Geller for Elvis' increasing reluctance to continue with his hamster-wheel professional life churning out low-budget Hollywood movies. Colonel Parker succeeded in banishing Geller after Elvis had a fall in his bathroom and suffered concussion before reporting for work on *Clambake*. While Elvis convalesced, the Colonel told him that he believed Geller had hypnotized him using some kind of mind-control technique.

Geller was no longer permitted to spend any time alone with Elvis, not even when he was cutting his hair.

Not long before Geller and Elvis parted company, Geller's house in LA was burgled. In his memoir, Geller says that the burglary—in which only select items were taken such as Elvis' astrological and numerological charts—took place the one and only time that he and his family spent a day at the Colonel's home in Palm Springs.

Though Elvis had told Geller at the start of 1967 that he wanted him to be one of his best men at his upcoming wedding, by the time Elvis was married in May Geller wasn't even invited to the ceremony—he read about the wedding in a tabloid paper.

Over the next few years, Geller ran a bookshop in LA, opened an alternative school, and continued his spiritual studies. In the summer of 1972 (1973 by some accounts), Geller saw Elvis perform in Las Vegas and brought along a copy of a one-off journal he had published called *New Age Voice*. Elvis is said to have carried that pamphlet around with him for quite some time, and on at least one occasion regaled his audience with excerpts from the metaphysical treatise. Elvis named the backing group he put together in the summer of 1973 "Voice" after the publication.

In 1974, Geller married his second wife, Celest. According to Geller, that year Elvis commissioned him to write the screenplay for the karate movie he was planning to make.

Geller returned to Elvis' entourage full-time after a major shake-up of personnel in the summer of 1976. Geller toured with Elvis in August and September that year, sometimes acting as his unofficial personal healer. Elvis gave Geller a Lincoln Mark V in June 1977—by no means his first automotive gift. Geller was with Elvis on his final vacation, to Hawaii, in 1977.

In early August 1977, Geller had such a strong premonition that Elvis was going to die that he called Graceland in the middle of the night to check that everything was OK.

Geller has written a number of books about Elvis, worked on Elvis-related movie projects and often attended Elvis-related events ever since. In his memoir *If I Can Dream: Elvis' Own Story*, he writes in the introduction that the book is an attempt to realize a project that was close to Elvis' heart at the end of his life: to write a book and explain to the world the man behind the Elvis image.

ELVIS SAID TO PRISCILLA: "Larry knows more about the spiritual world than all the preachers and Catholic priests and religious fanatics put together."

LARRY GELLER: "From the very beginning, the basis of my relationship with Elvis was our pursuit of life's spiritual aspects."

PRISCILLA: "We were all threatened by Elvis' involvement with Larry. It was keeping him from us."

MARTY LACKER: "The more time Geller spent with Elvis, the more Elvis got involved with these religions. And the more involved in God, the more obsessed he became."

Books:

If I Can Dream: Elvis' Own Story, by Larry Geller and Joel Spector with Patricia Romanowski, Simon and Schuster, 1989.

Elvis' Search For God, by Larry Geller and Jess Stearn, Greenleaf Publications, 1998 (a revised version of 1980 book *The Truth About Elvis*.

Leaves of Elvis' Garden, by Larry Geller, Bell Rock Publishing, 2006.

GELLER, URI
(B. 1946)

Paranormalist Uri Geller reputedly performed his signature spoon-bending for Elvis backstage in Las Vegas in the Seventies. In 2006, Geller was part of a three-person consortium that bid for Elvis' former Memphis home at 1034 Audubon Drive on eBay in 2006, only to be pipped at the last by music producer Mike Curb. Geller had been planning to turn the house into a museum of the paranormal; he later sought legal recourse over the sale.

GENEROSITY

Generosity is one of Elvis' lifelong character traits. He was giving things away almost before he had anything to give away, making gifts of his scant toys to pals for their birthdays at elementary school. Elvis' generosity was idealistic and individual. He gave generously to charities because he felt it was important to help those less fortunate than himself. He paid every cent of tax for which he was liable because he felt it was important to pay his dues. He gave gifts to the people around him because he loved to see the look on the recipient's face, though of course, he was aware of the power that such gift-giving brought him in inter-personal relationship.

As soon as he had catered to the material needs of himself and his family, Elvis started giving back. He played a charity show at Memphis's Russwood Park on July 4, 1956, the first of many he gave during his career.

Pals from High School and family members in financial difficulty knew that they could count on Elvis. He would, however, get very angry if he felt that people were taking advantage of his generosity Three girls who visited Elvis at Graceland with local football star Billy Fletcher went home with some teddy bears without asking. When Elvis realized, he asked for them to be returned. Fletcher and one contrite girl came back. Elvis thanked her, and then said she could take a couple of bears away with her, the point of principle made.

Elvis' generosity stemmed in part from his Christian upbringing. Kathy Westmoreland wrote in her memoir that Elvis believed in giving a tithe of his income to good works. She details his sending limousines out in Memphis to help old people get around. There are countless untold stories of Elvis' Christian charity (a definition of true charity is not seeking recompense or renown for such acts). If Elvis saw someone in need near Graceland, he might well stop and help out. Nick Adams was once with Elvis when they drove past a homeless man. By the time Elvis had circled back to give him some money, he was gone. Despite looking round side streets and stores, there was no trace of the vagrant. By the time they got back to Graceland, Elvis was in tears at thoughts of the man's hard life. Eddie Fadal once witnessed Elvis place five hundred-dollar bills into a blind man's begging cup in downtown Memphis.

In the Army, Elvis bought every soldier in his outfit an extra set of fatigues so that they would always have a clean uniform for inspection—a major hardship for the average soldier if their two standard issue uniforms were dirty. He also paid for TVs to be put in all the dayrooms on base.

Over the years, Elvis helped out a number of fellow-musicians in financial straits. Elvis is said to have given money to pay back tax for Roy Brown, who originally wrote and sang Elvis' early hit "Good Rockin' Tonight." He has been credited with funding recording sessions for Arthur Crudup in the Sixties, after years when the blues singer was unable to land a recording contract. In 1974, Elvis gave a $1000 to help R 'n' B great Ivory Joe Hunter, who was seriously ill. In 1975 Elvis sent money to help pay for Jackie Wilson's hospital bills after he suffered a stroke.

Spontaneous acts of generosity include sending a $1000 check to police officer James Bullock who lost a leg while on duty, after Elvis heard about the incident on the radio.

Elvis' generosity was not limited to the less-well off. When The Beatles came to visit in 1965, he sent each of them home with a complete set of his records.

Dentist Lester Hofman received several cars from Elvis, and on one occasion that he and his wife admired an organ at Graceland, Elvis had it packed up and delivered to his dentist's home.

In 1970, en route to Washington with pal Jerry Schilling, Elvis (who never carried money) got Schilling to hand over all the cash he had on him to give to a returning Vietnam vet he met on the plane.

A few days before taking the stage for his *Aloha From Hawaii* concert in January 1973, Elvis gave away his ruby-encrusted belt, part of his American Eagle jumpsuit/cape combo, to Jack Lord's wife. The replacement that was feverishly made overnight only lasted a couple of days; Elvis flung it into the crowd at the end of his worldvision gig.

Memphis jeweler and friend Lowell Hays Jr. has said that Elvis was always buying gifts for friends and fans, at least a piece of jewelry every day. Hays was a recipient of Elvis' most frequent act of generosity, giving the gift of a brand new car: in Hays's case a new Lincoln Continental Mark IV and a Mark V.

After his summer 1974 engagement in Las Vegas, Elvis bought himself a new car plus a further twelve for friends, family and staff. Before the year was out, he bought a home for pal entourage member Jerry Schilling, just one of the houses he purchased for friends.

In 1974, Elvis visited a sick young fan who had written to him from Monroe, Louisiana, and gave the boy a garnet cross as a gift. At a concert in the same location, he gave a little girl in the audience his Diamond Medallion Cross necklace because she reminded him of his daughter (the scene is featured in the 1979 TV movie *Elvis*; Rhonda Boler, who received the cross, sold it at auction in 1989).

Elvis bought a house in Memphis for long-term girlfriend Linda Thompson in the spring of 1975.

Though much of his generosity was simply for the pleasure of giving, Elvis knew how to buy his way (back into) people's affections. In 1975, after almost his entire female backing group walked off stage in anger at his teasing, Elvis spent $85,000 (though some estimates put the figure at three times this amount) on jewelry from Lowell Hays to re-establish some peace and harmony. Before the month was out, Elvis had bought a jet for the Colonel (which the Colonel sent back on the grounds that he couldn't afford to run it) and distributed 14 Cadillacs to friends, including one to a complete stranger called Mennie Person who happened to be peering into the window of the Madison Cadillac dealership in Memphis, where Elvis regularly bought his cars from lucky salesman Howard Massey, just as Elvis was on his spree. Around this time he also loaned his physician Dr. Nick $200,000 to build a new house, interest free.

Elvis purchased a top-of-the-line wheelchair for a Memphis woman he read about in the newspaper one day, which he delivered himself. That day he was in such a generous mood that he gave his car to the woman's daughter after she admired it, and found a job for the daughter's boyfriend.

Later in 1975, Elvis bought a Pontiac Grand Prix and jewelry for nurse Marion Cocke, who had looked after him during his recent stays at the Baptist Memorial Hospital in Memphis. Also in 1975, at one concert in Asheville, North Carolina, Elvis famously threw one of his rings into the crowd.

Elvis gave long-serving maid Mary Jenkins as many as seven cars over the fourteen years she worked for him, and bought her a house when she retired.

One of Elvis' trademark outbursts of generosity in early 1976—buying cars for people who had helped him out, friends and family—made it onto the local news in Denver, where Elvis was vacationing at the time. When local radio presenter Don Kinney quipped that he'd like a car too, Elvis sent him round a Cadillac Seville. Elvis reputedly gave away as many as 200 cars in his lifetime.

In 1976, Elvis gave J. D. Sumner money to buy a new tour bus for his group the Stamps. In October that year, after Elvis' wayward behavior led to the cancellation of a recording session at Graceland, Elvis tried to make things up to Sumner by sending him back to Nashville in his own white limousine, and then told him to keep the car.

The day after his last birthday, Elvis had a fancy store in Palm Springs open after hours for girlfriend Ginger Alden and various entourage wives and girlfriends to go on a spree, on his dollar—by no means the first time he had done this.

Less than two weeks before his death, Elvis gave his wedding ring from his marriage to Priscilla to step-brother David Stanley, in the hope that it would help save his marriage with his wife Angie. The ring has since been sold at auction multiple times.

Marty Lacker estimates that Elvis gave away perhaps a hundred cars and pickup trucks to friends, and was giving away over $100,000 to charities in Memphis every Christmas.

BARBARA LEIGH: "Elvis was the most generous person I've ever met both with his money and himself. He loved giving gifts and watching people's faces when they got them."

FARON YOUNG: "You never told that fucker you liked something or he'd hand it to you."

SHEILA RYAN: "The biggest joy that he had was in giving."

LARRY GELLER: "Elvis' generosity often drove Vernon to distraction."

LAMAR FIKE: "I think Elvis didn't like to see any kind of injustice, but if it didn't directly affect him, he was a little bit indifferent . . . He cared more about helping individuals than helping masses of people or a cause."

SAM THOMPSON: "Elvis was tuned into all the people around him, his friends that needed things; but he wanted to be the one who initiated it."

LAMAR FIKE: "The elaborate gift giving was also a Band-Aid for the abuse he heaped on you the rest of the time. That was the blessing and the curse of Elvis."

DVD:
200 Cadillacs, by Image Entertainment

"GENTLE ON MY MIND"

Elvis was in strong voice on this multi-Grammy-winning song by John Hartford that he recorded on in the early hours of January 15, 1969 at American Studio. He redid the his vocal a few days later, immediately after nailing "In The Ghetto."

Hartford was inspired to write the song after watching the movie *Dr. Zhivago*. He had a hit with it in 1967, before Glen Campbell won a Grammy the following year for his version of the tune. Campbell later picked it as the theme tune to his TV variety show "The Glen Campbell Goodtime Hour," which ran for four seasons from 1969. Aretha Franklin was one of many other artists to cover this popular song (including along with Frank Sinatra, Andy Williams, Patti Page and Dean Martin) before Elvis' version appeared on *From Elvis In Memphis*. It has since graced later Elvis country compilations including *Welcome To My World* and , *From Nashville to Memphis*, *Great Country Songs* and *Suspicious Minds: The Memphis 1969 Anthology.*.

"GENTLY"

This Murray Wisell / Edward Lisbona love song was recorded by Elvis in Nashville in on March 12, 1961 as a cut for the *Somebody For Everybody* album. It has since been released on Sixties anthology *From Nashville to Memphis*.

Alternate takes came out in 1991 on *Collectors Gold* and on FTD releases *Fame And Fortune* and *Something For Everybody* (2002 and 2006 respectively).

GENTRY, BOBBIE
(B. ROBERTA STREETER, 1944)

Born in Chickasaw Country, Mississippi, where she grew up poor, after a spell as a showgirl in Las Vegas, Bobbie Gentry studied at the LA Conservatory of Music and then signed to Capitol records. In 1967, her first single included three-million seller "Ode To Billie Joe," which won no fewer than four Grammys that year. Gentry wrote most of her own songs and was a talented producer. In the late Sixties she staged her own Las Vegas act. She presented her own TV series briefly on either side of the Atlantic in the early Seventies. In 1978 she retired from show business.

Gentry was reportedly in the running for a role in Elvis' late movie *The Trouble with Girls*. She saw Elvis perform in Las Vegas and hung out backstage after the show.

Elvis recorded Gentry's composition "Let It Be," and also "Gentle On My Mind," which Gentry had sung in a duet with Glen Campbell in 1968. Elvis also sang a few lines of Gentry's "Ode To Billie Joe" in the studio in 1967. Gentry returned the favor in the 2000s, when her version of "In The Ghetto" featured on the *Country sings Elvis* tribute album.

GEORGIA

- Atlanta

Elvis played the Sports Arena on December 2, 1955 and the Fox Theater on March 14 and 15, 1956, sharing the venue with screenings of Tony Curtis in *The Square Jungle*. Elvis was at the Paramount Theater on June 22-24, 1956, the first show he did with The Jordanaires as his backing singers.

Elvis played the Omni, Atlanta, four times on his June/July 1973 US tour, adding June 21 and July 3 to the original June 29 and 30 shows due to popular demand. The next time Elvis was in town was for three nights, from April 30 to May 2, 1975. He performed at the Omni from June 4 to June 6, 1976, and fitted in another show that year on December 30.

- Augusta

Elvis performed at the Bell Municipal Auditorium on March 20, 1956 and June 27, 1956.

- Macon

Elvis wowed the Coliseum here on April 15, 1972. He kicked off his 1975 touring schedule here on April 24, 1975, and also performed here on August 31, 1976. He was next in town on June 1, 1977.

- Savannah

Elvis appeared at the Sports Arena on June 25, 1956. He did a show at the Civic Center on February 17, 1977.

- Waycross

Elvis played The City Auditorium on February 22, 1956.

GERMANY

Elvis first set foot in West Germany for his Army service at Bremerhaven on October 1, 1958, to a rapturous welcome from fifteen hundred fans and massed ranks of newsmen. When he arrived at his final destination, Friedberg, he was put in the Ray Kaserne barracks, home to 1st Battalion, 32nd Armor Regiment, 3rd Armored Division.

A week later Elvis was living offbase with his father, grandmother and Memphis pals Red West and Lamar Fike at the Hilberts Park Hotel in Bad Nauheim. They moved to more luxurious quarters

BELOW: Elvis at an Army press conference in Germany.

FACING PAGE: A candid of Elvis in Germany.

at the Hotel Grunewald resort hotel in Bad Nauheim before the end of October 1958. Elvis rented out the second floor (his room, Room 10, is still available for rent), and paid for a kitchen to be installed. Before long, Elvis and his gang's hi-jinks led to them being given their marching orders by the manager, Herr Schmidt, after Elvis and Red caused a small fire during a shaving-cream fight.

With Elvis making quite a splash in West Germany, an East German newspaper ran an article accusing Elvis of being a vital weapon in the US atomic war effort. Nevertheless, Elvis and his pals got on well with the locals, roughhousing and having firework fights with the boys, and establishing (sometimes very) friendly relations with the girls.

After spending time with his unit on maneuvers in Grafenwöhr, Elvis and his family moved into a five-bedroom house at 14 Goethestrasse, which they rented from Frau Pieper for $800 per month (significantly over the market rate). Frau Pieper carried on living on the premises, and often had heated battles with Grandma Minnie Mae, who was not happy with her meddlesome presence. Most evenings, Elvis would meet with fans and sign autographs.

In early March, 1959 Elvis and his Memphis pals traveled to Munich to see actress Vera Tschechowa, who he had met during a photo session for the March of Dimes. He also traveled to Frankfurt and Stuttgart.

Elvis' fans in Germany referred to Elvis as their "rock and roll matador."

Memories of Elvis' time in Germany remain alive: Bad Nauheim was one of many places around the globe that organized events to commemorate the thirtieth anniversary of Elvis' passing in 2007.

See also ARMY.

ELVIS WROTE: "The German people are very nice and friendly but there is no place like the good ole U.S."

RED WEST: "All of us, particularly Elvis, liked the Germans. They weren't Southerners, but they were kind of straight people who were very honest and looked you right in the face when they talked to you."

Books:
Private Presley, ed. Diego Cortez, FEY Verlags GmbH, 1978.
Private Presley: Elvis in Germany—the Missing Years, by Andreas Shroer,, Oskar Hentschell, Michael Knorr and W.A. Harbinson, Boxtree Press, 1993.

DVD:
Elvis in Germany

"GET A JOB"

Elvis sang this Silhouettes song for fun, with a tape recorder running, which is how it come it wound up many years later on unofficial release *The Long Lost Home Recordings*. It had been a #1 hit when it came out in 1958.

"GET BACK"

Elvis made this 1969 Beatles hit his own by rolling it into a medley with "Little Sister" in his live shows during the early Seventies; it became something of a regular for him in 1972. He sang the Lennon & McCartney tune—the only Beatles song released with the name of another a

non-Beatle credited artist, in this case pianist Billy Preston—in rehearsals for the concert documentary *Elvis That's The Way It Is*; the song was on the documentary but not released on album disc until BMG's 3-disc CD special in 2000, which features two versions.

Elvis' version recorded on August 13, 1970 was first released in 1980 collector's set *Elvis Aron Presley*. Later live Elvis performances have Since then it has appeared on *Burning Love, Live in Las Vegas*, and FTD releases *Summer Festival* and *An American Trilogy*.

GET DOWN AND GET WITH IT

A 1998 Fort Baxter bootleg of Elvis rehearsing for Las Vegas in the summer of 1970.

TRACK LISTING:
1. Stagger Lee
2. Got My Mojo Working
3. I've Lost You
4. Stranger In The Crowd
5. The Next Step Is Love
6. You Don't Have To Say You Love Me
7. Sweet Caroline
8. Yesterday
9. Hey Jude
10. I Can't Stop Loving You
11. It's Your Baby, You Rock It
12. Crying Time
13. Ghost Riders In The Sky
14. Runaway
15. It's Now Or Never
16. Peter Gunn Theme
17. Love Me
18. One Night
19. Alla' En El Rancho Grande
20. That's All Right
21. Twenty Days And Twenty Nights
22. Patch It Up
23. Cotton Fields
24. Sylvia
25. Stranger In The Crowd
26. How The Web Was Woven
27. I'll Take You Home Again, Kathleen

GHANEM, ELIAS DR.
(1939-2001)

Dr. Elias Ghanem was Elvis' regular doctor in Las Vegas from 1972 onwards. Born in Haifa, Israel to Lebanese parents, Ghanem emigrated to the US in 1963. He moved to Las Vegas in 1971 after qualifying as a doctor at Duke University. Over the years, he became known as "the physician to the stars," treating Liberace, Ann-Margret, Michael Jackson, Bill Cosby and others famous patients. He also developed a reputation in Las Vegas for treating patients without health cover.

Elvis stayed with the doctor twice in the fall of 1974 to cure his intestinal problems. The doctor put him on a liquid food diet and sedation. Ghanem and regular Memphis doctor Dr. Nichopoulos advised Elvis to cancel his summer 1975 engagement as he continued to suffer from breathing difficulties, fatigue and depression. Elvis visited Dr. Ghanem again in the summer of 1976, between tours.

Dr. Ghanem was Elvis' traveling tour doctor in the summer of 1976, after the singer fell out with Dr. Nick. Over the years Elvis gave the flamboyant doctor a Mercedes and a Stutz.

Like Dr. Nichopoulos, Dr. Ghanem has told biographers that he tried his best to pass off placebos to Elvis to keep his drug intake under control. He once threatened to sue ABC TV for implicating him in the procurement of drugs to Elvis.

Colonel Parker, who lived in Las Vegas during the last years of his life, continued to see Dr. Ghanem.

"GHOST RIDERS IN THE SKY"

Elvis was in on an instrumental version of this Stan Jones song during rehearsals for the July 1970 concert documentary *Elvis That's The Way It Is*. It was first released officially over thirty years later on FTD album *The Way It Was*, after circulating for some time on bootlegs.

"G.I. BLUES"

The title track of the movie, written by Sid Tepper and Roy C. Bennett, was recorded on April 27, 1960, at RCA's Hollywood studios, for initial release on the movie soundtrack album. Rereleases may be found on *Elvis in Hollywood, This Is Elvis, Command Performances, Elvis Movies*, and recently released on *Elvis at the Movies*.

Alternate takes have appeared on *Collectors Gold, Elvis Chante Sid Tepper & Roy C. Bennett*, a UK collection of EPs, *Today, Tomorrow & Forever* and *Elvis: Close Up*.

G.I. BLUES (LP)

Elvis was said to be disappointed with the quality of the material he was supplied for the soundtrack, after his favored songwriters Leiber and Stoller pulled out of the running. The public had no such problems, making it his best-selling LP to date—and the highest entry of any Elvis LP, rocketing to #6 in its first week—when it came out in October 1960. The LP sold 700,000 copies and took the coveted #1 spot in the charts—nothing could shift it for 10 weeks. The album remained in the chart for a total of 111 weeks, and went on to sell more than 3.5 million discs.

TRACK LISTING:
1. Tonight Is So Right For Love
2. What's She Really Like
3. Frankfort Special
4. Wooden Heart
5. G. I. BG.I. Blues
6. Pocketful Of Rainbows
7. Shoppin' Around
8. Big Boots
9. Didja' Ever
10. Blue Suede Shoes
11. Doin' The Best I Can

"Tonight's All Right For Love" was released in Europe instead of the opening track due to copyright issues. The track has since been included on CD reissues.

Alternate takes of several G.I. Blues songs came out in 1982 on UK-only boxed set *The EP Collection, Volume 2*.

An expanded 1997 version of the album contained many alternative takes and movie versions ("Big Boots," "Shoppin' Around," "Frankfort Special," "Pocketful Of Rainbows," "Didja' Ever," "Big Boots," "What's She Really Like" and "Doin' The Best I Can").

G.I. BLUES

Producer Hal Wallis flew out to Germany in the summer of 1959, when Elvis still had eight months of his Army service to go, to meet his star and do some location work on Elvis' first movie in two years, at the time known under working title *Christmas in Berlin*. Wallis shot some footage near Frankfurt in a picturesque town called Idstein, though none of this material was used in the end.

At one stage of pre-production, the film's title might have been changed to *Dog Face*, a track

Elvis as Tulsa McLean in *G.I. Blues* (1960).

The rollicking story of America's lovin' G.I.s!
Swing out and sound off with Elvis in the red, white
and blue star-bright show of the year.

Directed by: Norman Taurog
Produced by: Hal B. Wallis
Associate producer: Paul Nathan
Written by: Edmund Beloin, Henry Garson
Music by: Joseph J. Lilley
Cinematography by: Loyal Griggs
Art Direction by: Hal Pereira, Walter Tyler
Set Decoration by: Sam Comer, Ray Moyer
Costume Design by: Edith Head

CAST:

Elvis Presley	Tulsa McLean
Juliet Prowse	Lili
Robert Ivers	Cookie
James Douglas	Rick
Letícia Román	Tina
Sigrid Maier	Marla
Arch Johnson	Sgt. McGraw
Mickey Knox	Jeeter
John Hudson	Capt. Hobart
Ken Becker	Mac
Jeremy Slate	Turk
Beach Dickerson	Warren
Trent Dolan	Mickey
Carl Crow	Walt
Fred Essler	Papa Mueller
Ron Starr	Harvey
Erika Peters	Trudy
Ludwig Stössel	Puppet show owner
The Jordanaires	Themselves
Edit Angold	Marla's landlady Mrs. Hagermann
Robert Allison Baker III	Puppeteer
Robert Boon	German guitarist
Harper Carter	1st MP
Edward Coch	Bandleader
Walter Conrad	Chaplain
Liz Dubrock	Brunette
Britta Ekman	Britta (the redhead)
Edward Faulkner	Red
Bess Flowers	Customer at the Café Europa
D.J. Fontana	Musician
Marianne Gaba	Bargirl
Marilyn Gladstone	Blonde
Joe Gray	Soldier
Willy Kaufman	Café manager
Fred Kruger	Herr Klugmann
Karen Mann	Waitress
Tip McClure	2nd MP
Hannerl Melcher	Girl singer
Torben Meyer	Head waiter
Harold Miller	Customer at the Café Europa
Scotty Moore	Musician
Elisha Mott	Sergeant
Judith Rawlins	Fritzie
Gene Roth	Businessman #1
Donald G. Sahlin	Puppeteer
Michael Sargent	3rd MP
Edson Stroll	Sgt. 'Dynamite' Bixby
Sally Todd	Bargirl
Blaine Turner	Bartender
Dick Winslow	Orchestra leader
F. Alton Wood	Puppeteer
Roy Wright	Businessman #2
Trude Wyler	Bit part

ADDITIONAL CREW:

Nellie Manley	hair stylist
Wally Westmore	makeup supervisor
Michael D. Moore	second unit director
Charles Grenzbach	sound recorder
Harold Lewis	sound recorder
John P. Fulton	special photographic effects
Joe Gray	stunts
Farciot Edouart	process photographer
Joseph J. Lilley	conductor
Warren Low	editorial supervisor
Jack Mintz	dialogue coach
Richard Mueller	color consultant
Charles O'Curran	.choreographer

that Leiber and Stoller had written for the project. Another rejected title, *Café Europa*, was used in a number of European markets..

Elvis rolled into LA by rail with a pack of buddies on two railway cars hired by the Colonel to start pre-production in late April 1960. Principal photography was completed by June 24, 1960. At a late stage, Elvis' character name was changed from Tulsa McCauley to Tulsa McLean. In the romantic comedy McLean (like Elvis) has Cherokee blood.

Owing to local labor laws, three sets of twins had to be hired to play the one baby in the movie.

The movie was the first of nine directed by Norman Taurog. Taurog reputedly put his daughter Priscilla—just one year younger than the girl Elvis had left behind in Germany—into the movie as an uncredited extra in the puppet show audience.

The movie had a sneak preview in Dallas on August 18, 1960. Elvis attended a screening with co-star Juliet Prowse and gossip columnist Hedda Hopper on September 12, 1960. On national release in the last week of November 1960, it rocketed up to the #2 spot on the *Variety* National Box Office Survey, and ended the year as the fourteenth biggest box office grossing movie, generating $4.3 million. Elvis told the press that he made this movie "because it was one way I had to show all the guys with whom I served in the Army how much I respected them." Critics were divided, for the most part not overly enthused by the unsophisticated plot, though Elvis won plaudits for his acting.

G.I. Blues was nominated for two musical-related awards in 1961: best soundtrack album Grammy, and WGA best-written musical.

CREDITS:
Paramount, Color.
Length: 104 minutes
Release date: November 23, 1960

TAGLINES:
Elvis as the gay, singing sensation . . . oast of the world's girls . . . envy of every man in the army!

G.I. Blues (1960).

Elvis with Juliet Prowse (right), G.I. Blues.

Elvis and "friend," G.I. Blues.

Colonel Tom Parker	technical advisor
David S. Parkhurst.	technical advisor (military)
Bob Baker	puppeteer
Godfrey A. Godar..	second unit assistant camera
George Pink	second unit assistant camera

Plot:

Elvis plays G.I. Tulsa McLean, stationed in Germany with pals Cookie (Robert Ivers) and Rick (played by James Douglas). They while away their time performing in a rock band called "The Three Blazes," saving the money they make to open a nightclub when they get back to the US. Their dream looks like coming true when they get a chance to play the big Armed Forces Show.

Everything is thrown into jeopardy when all their money winds up on a bet that a fellow platoon member, Dynamite, can spend a night with cabaret dancer Lili (played by Juliet Prowse), renowned at the base for never dating a G.I.

Dynamite is transferred to another base before he can try his hand. Tulsa has to take his place. Lili takes Tulsa out to see the sights of Frankfurt, only for Tulsa to really fall for her. He gets cold feet about going through with the bet and pulls out.

Fate intervenes the following evening when Tulsa agrees to babysit for an army pal and his fiancée. Clueless about looking after a baby, Tulsa calls Lili for help. She invites him over to her place, where they look after the baby all night long, thereby winning the bet.

Lili flies into a rage with Tulsa when she finds out that he used her to win a bet. Tulsa's commanding officer is so shocked by his conduct that he promises to transfer Tulsa away from the base before he has a chance to sing at the show.

Fortunately for all concerned, Lili learns that Tulsa really was selflessly babysitting for his pals to allow them to go off and marry. Tulsa and Lili agree to get hitched and then sing us out at the big Armed Forces Show.

Songs: "What's She Really Like," "G.I. Blues," "Doin' The Best I Can," "Blue Suede Shoes (on a jukebox)," "Frankfort Special," "Shoppin' Around," "Tonight Is So Right For Love," "Wooden Heart," "Pocketful Of Rainbows," "Big Boots," "Didja' Ever"

Box set:

Book/DVD *Inside GI Blues,* by Megan M. Murphy and Henryk Matraszek, 2006

GIANT, BAUM AND KAYE

The prolific Hill & Range songwriting team of Bill Giant, Bernie Baum and Florence Kaye landed songs in many of Elvis' Sixties movies, including some memorable tunes such as "(You're The) Devil In Disguise." In one feverish two-year period the combo came up with 22 soundtrack songs. All in all, Bill Giant wrote 42 songs for Elvis, of which all but one with Baum and Kaye—he wrote the other, "Fountain Of Love," with Jeff Lewis.

GIFTS

Elvis' gift-giving was legendary. Nobody important to him went empty-handed. Elvis referred to gifts as "happies." According to many recipients over the years, the reason Elvis gave gifts so lavishly and so often was because he loved seeing the look on their face.

Intended or otherwise, gifts also reinforced the power-balance in his relationships, served as rewards and reinforced all-important loyalty. Elvis sometimes used gifts as a way of saying sorry.

For a spell in the Seventies, Elvis traveled with his own personal jeweler, Lowell Hays, so that he could have a ready supply for when he felt the urge to give a gift.

Not everybody accepted: early girlfriend June Juanico, adhering to Southern custom, eschewed the many gifts Elvis offered because she understood that a gentleman who gives gifts would want something in return. She later said, "Think of all the Cadillacs I passed up!"

In 1956, Elvis gave the maid who looked after the family at Audubon Drive a car when he found out that she had to walk a mile from her home to get to the nearest bus stop.

Faron Young once told Elvis that he liked the look of one of his Harleys. Elvis threw him the keys and told him to take it.

Elaine Dundy suggests that Elvis' gifts were in essence in exchange for trust. She recounts an incident during his first Christmas at Graceland in 1957, when Elvis gave six members of staff a $1,000 bill bonus (and handed out $100 bills to his younger cousins). He actually gave the high-denomination notes to his entourage members after taking them one-by-one into his bedroom and leaving them alone for a few moments with several $1,000 bills lying around, as a test of their trustworthiness. All but one passed the test, and that person was never "made to feel welcome at Graceland again." Incidentally, the same cousin is the likely culprit who took the photo of Elvis in his casket for *National Enquirer.*

It wasn't all big-ticket items, either. Elvis made a point of greeting his co-stars with lavish bunches of flowers. He gave *King Creole* co-star Jan Shepard a stuffed tiger at her birthday party in 1958.

Girlfriend Anita Wood received many gifts from her beau, from a diamond ring to a car and no end of toys and jewelry.

When Priscilla first visited Memphis for Christmas 1962, he gave her a poodle puppy, which she named Honey. When she came to live there permanently the following year, Elvis gave her a Corvair for her to get to and from school. One of the first things he did was go out and buy her a $1,500 wardrobe of clothes, all of which he picked himself. Elvis was still buying her gifts a decade later after their divorce.

After Elvis discovered *The Impersonal Life,* a book written anonymously in 1917, he gave copies to the people who mattered to him, often copies in which he had scribbled his own annotations and a personal dedication.

When filming on *Frankie and Johnny* finished in May 1965, Elvis gave cast and crew members a watch designed by jeweler Harry Levitch, depicting a cross and a Jewish star. That year he bought a Cadillac for Marty Lacker and gave Lamar Fike enough money to buy himself a large house.

Elvis' birthday gift to the Colonel in 1965 was an electric golf cart. Over the years Elvis also gave him a bubble car, a boat and an airplane.

While working on *Spinout,* Elvis gave his brand new Sony video camera to director Norman Taurog, even though the technology was so advanced that it took weeks for entourage members to find a replacement.

Elvis gave *Speedway* co-star Nancy Sinatra a car with the name of the movie on one door, and their names on the other.

For Christmas 1967, Elvis gave the Colonel a $595 gold Accutron watch, plus a watch to the Colonel's lieutenant Tom Diskin.

Elvis handed out $100 and $200 gift vouchers from Goldsmith's Department store for Christmas 1968.

In January 1969, Elvis was so pleased to be working at American Studio at the same time as Roy Hamilton, one of his musical heroes, that he gave him a song, "Angelica," that he had intended to record himself.

Elvis went on a major spree in the run-up to Christmas 1970. After buying a small arsenal of guns for himself and friends, he bought a house for Joe Esposito and his wife in LA, and purchased three Mercedes cars, one for himself, one

Elvis with June Juanico whom he briefly dated in the 1950's.

for Jerry Schilling, and one for girlfriend Barbara Leigh. At this time he gave his girlfriends guns to make sure that they would be safe.

In December 1970 Elvis gave pal Dick Grob a new Cadillac as a wedding gift, and allowed him to use his Palm Springs home for his wedding party. Vernon challenged Elvis about his excessive spending that year.

Elvis presented Priscilla's brother Don with a brand new Mustang when he came for a visit to Graceland in the late Sixties (they also welcomed him home at McGuire Air Force base when he finished his tour of duty in Vietnam in 1971).

In early 1971, Elvis gave a Mathey-Tissot watch engraved by jeweler Harry Levitch to all nine of his fellow Jaycees award winners.

Larry Geller says that over the years, Elvis gave him many watches, many items of his clothing, a Cadillac, a motorcycle, a mobile home, a pick up truck, a horse and more.

The first that time Dave Hebler went to Elvis' LA home, he drove away in a new Mercedes 280 SL to which Elvis had handed him the keys. Because the car was nominally Charlie Hodge's, another Mercedes—a 450 SL—was purchased to replace it.

The first Christmas that Elvis spent with Linda Thompson he gave her a mink coat plus a fox suede coat. Red and Sonny West suggest that over their four-year relationship Elvis bought her more than 1/4 million-worth of jewelry. Elvis also bought a house in Memphis for her brother in the summer of 1973.

Elvis' generosity reached its zenith in the mid-Seventies, when he started buying cars by the dozen to give to friends, members of staff and even passing strangers, all for the pleasure of watching their face light up the instant he gave them the gift.

He pushed a car on karate pal Ed Parker, despite his protestations that he already had three. Then he bought Parker's wife a $12,000 mink coat.

Red and Sonny West estimate that Elvis gave J.D. Sumner around $100,000-worth of jewelry in gifts. They also remember a time when he took his gift-giving to new heights by handing out rings to members of an audience and the band at a show in Greensboro, North Carolina in 1975. On that tour, Elvis threw his customized Gibson guitar out into the audience.

Within weeks of meeting new girlfriend Ginger Alden in late 1976, Elvis had given her a Lincoln Continental, a Triumph TR6, as many as five fur coats, and extended his largesse to the rest of her family (fur coasts and jewelry, as well as improvements to the family home).

All of these gifts were above and beyond the lifestyle that Elvis lavished on the people around him.

For many fans, just being around Elvis was a gift in itself

See also Cars, Charitable works, Generosity and Jewelry

GIFTS ELVIS RECEIVED

What to get a man who from the age of twenty could buy anything his heart desired?

For Christmas 1964, Marty Lacker bought a Bible and a dozen of Elvis' pals signed a branch of the tree of life on the first page. Elvis didn't react quite as planned: he refused to accept the gift until Larry Geller added his name to the dedication.

The entourage spent $500 on a Jesus statue for Christmas 1965, which was installed in the new Meditation Garden.

Many of the gifts that fans sent Elvis for Christmas were donated to local children's hospitals.

The International Hotel in Las Vegas acknowledged Elvis' great success by giving him an all-expenses-paid vacation for himself and eight others on Hawaii; they also gave him a $10,000 gold belt fashioned like a boxing championship winners' belt, with the words "World's Championship/Attendance Record/Las Vegas Nevada/International Hotel" spelled out in diamonds.

Elvis was presented with a limited edition Rolex "King Midas" watch and a Stetson hat after his 1970 performances at the Annual Texas Livestock Show in Houston.

See also CHRISTMAS.

ELVIS SAID TO RED WEST IN 1975: "What do you think I give you guys all these gifts for? It's to make up for the hell I put you through, for the work you guys do."

FELTON JARVIS: "Elvis told me he gave things to people sometimes to show them that it was no big deal. That their life would be just the same after they got it as it was before."

SAM THOMPSON: "He absolutely despised people who fawned and hinted and put him in a posture where he felt like he had to give gifts because they wanted them or asked for them."

"GIRL HAPPY"

Doc Pomus and Norman Meade wrote the catchy title track for the movie of the same name. Elvis recorded the song on June 10, 1964 at Radio Recorders. Curiously, it was speeded up prior to release on the album soundtrack. The tune has since appeared on *Elvis in Hollywood*, the Double Features issue for the movie, *Command Performances*, and more recently *Elvis Movies*.

A different take appeared on 1991 album *Collectors Gold*; the original tempo version and several others came out on 2003 FTD release *Girl Happy*. The tune more recently appeared on 2006 BMG album *Elvis Movies*.

GIRL HAPPY (LP)

The 1965 soundtrack LP added lackluster sound production to an unexceptional collection of songs and failed to rise past #8 on its initial release (though the LP stayed in the charts for 31

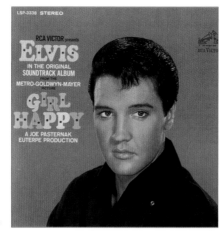

Cover of the soundtrack album Girl Happy (1965).

weeks). Elvis' voice was slightly speeded up on some of the tracks; the final track was a bonus not in the movie.

TRACK LISTING:
1. Girl Happy
2. Spring Fever
3. Fort Lauderdale Chamber Of Commerce
4. Startin' Tonight
5. Wolf Call
6. Do Not Disturb
7. Cross My Heart And Hope To Die
8. The Meanest Girl In Town
9. Do The Clam
10. Puppet On A String
11. I've Got To Find My Baby
12. You'll Be Gone

The soundtrack got the *Double Trouble* treatment in 1993 with *Harum Scarum*. FTD brought out a remixed soundtrack with outtakes and alternates in 2003.

GIRL HAPPY

Elvis began work on this MGM production on June 22, 1964. By the end of July the movie had wrapped.

Before the final title was chosen, the producers toyed with *The Only Way to Love* and *Girl Crazy*. This was the first of three times that Elvis worked with Shelley Fabares, who he later said was his favorite co-star.

As well as Elvis' eleven songs, Shelley Fabares and Nita Talbot sang "Read All About It."

One of the actors in the movie was Jackie Coogan, star of Chaplin's 1924 classic *The Kid*. Future "Grizzly Adams" protagonist Dan Haggerty also had a bit part.

Location work took place in Fort Lauderdale, where producer Joe Pasternak had set previous spring break movie *Where The Boys Are* with early Elvis co-star Dolores Hart.

Sadly for choreographer David Winters, the world never did take up 'The Clam', the dance he invented for Elvis in the movie.

The movie premiered on April 7, 1965, and finished the year as the 25th highest-grossing movie in the US, earning a little over $3 million.

CREDITS:
MGM, Color.
Length: 96 minutes
Release date: April 14, 1965

TAGLINES:
Over his head in LOVE, GIRLS, SONGS and LAUGHS!
Elvis jumps with the campus crowd to make the beach 'ball' bounce!

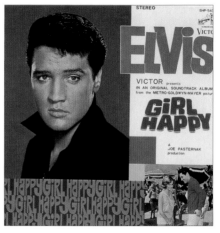

A Japanese LP of Girl Happy.

Directed by: Boris Sagal
Produced by: Joe Pasternak
Written by: Harvey Bullock, R.S. Allen
Music by: George Stoll
Cinematography by: Philip H. Lathrop
Film Editing by: Rita Roland
Art Direction by: George W. Davis, Addison Hehr
Set Decoration by: Henry Grace, Hugh Hunt

CAST:

Elvis Presley	Rusty Wells
Shelley Fabares	Valerie Frank
Harold J. Stone	Big Frank
Gary Crosby	Andy
Joby Baker	Wilbur
Jimmy Hawkins	Doc
Nita Talbot	Sunny Daze
Mary Ann Mobley	Deena Shepherd
Fabrizio Mioni	Romano Orlada
Jackie Coogan	Sgt. Benson
Peter Brooks	Brentwood von Durgenfeld
John Fiedler	Mr. Penchill
Chris Noel	Betsy
Lyn Edgington	Laurie
Gail Gilmore	Nancy
Pamela Curran	Bobbie
Rusty Allen	Linda
Beverly Adams	Girl #2
George Cisar	Bartender at the Kit Kat Club
Theresa Cooper	Girl
Nancy Czar	Blonde on the beach
Stasa Damascus	Girl #3
Jim Dawson	Muscle man
Mike De Anda	Bartender at the Sandbar Club
Darren Dublin	Driver
Tommy Farrell	Louie
Ted Fish	\Garbageman
Milton Frome	Police captain
Teri Garr	Extra
Norman Grabowski	"Wolf Call" O'Brien
Dan Haggerty	Charlie
Alan Hanley	1st Waiter at 77 Club
Hank Jones	Boy
Ralph Lee	Officer Jones
Kent McCord	Extra
Julie Payne	Girl #1
Richard Reeves	Officer Wilkins
Olan Soule	2nd Waiter at 77 Club
Red West	Extra in Kit Kat Club

ADDITIONAL CREW:

Sydney Guilaroff	hair stylist
William Tuttle	makeup supervisor
Lindsley Parsons Jr.	assistant production manager
Jack Aldworth	assistant director
Franklin Milton	recording supervisor
Bob Herron	stunts
Colonel Tom Parker...	technical advisor
David Winters	choreographer

and winds up in jail. Rusty decides to spring her by digging a tunnel. By the time he finishes breaking his way into jail, she has been bailed out by Big Frank, now in town and furious with Rusty for letting his little girl get into so much trouble.

Fortunately for the happy ending, Big Frank sees the error of his ways and realizes that a man prepared to put himself into all kinds of danger for his girl would make good marriageable material after all.

Songs: "Girl Happy," "Spring Fever," "Fort Lauderdale Chamber Of Commerce," "Startin' Tonight," "Wolf Call," "Do Not Disturb," "Cross My Heart And Hope To Die," "The Meanest Girl In Town," "Do The Clam," "Puppet On A String," "I've Got To Find My Baby"

The film poster for *Girl Happy*, starring Elvis and Shelley Fabares.

BELOW: Elvis as Rusty Wells in *Girl Happy* (1965).

Plot:

Elvis plays Rusty Wells, a singer with a band that have been packing the punters in at a Chicago nightclub owned by Big Frank (Harold J. Stone). Rusty is itching to get away from the Windy City for some Florida sun, but Big Frank doesn't want to let his golden goose go.

Rusty finally persuades Big Frank to send him and his combo (played by Gary Crosby, Joby Baker and Jimmy Hawkins) to Fort Lauderdale to keep a watchful eye on his college-age daughter Valerie (Shelley Fabares), as she heads off on spring break with a couple of girlfriends. They join her at the Seadrift Motel.

Valerie seems intent only on curling up with her books, so Rusty and friends look for work. They land a concert and Rusty meets the beautiful Deena (played by Mary Ann Mobley). At the club, Rusty rescues Valerie from the heavy attentions of her date, Brentwood Von Durgenfeld (played by Peter Brooks)—the first in a series of comic capers in which Valerie gets deeper and deeper into trouble.

Each time Rusty saves her, he falls more and more in love. Valerie is not immune to Rusty's charms, but then she finds out that Rusty has been hired by her father to look after. She gets drunk, starts an improvised striptease,

GIRL HAPPY AT THE WORLD'S FAIR

A 1997 bootleg release on the Bilko label.

TRACK LISTING
1. Girl Happy
2. Beyond The Bend
3. Take Me To The Fair
4. Cotton Candy Land
5. Puppet On a String
6. How Would You Like To Be
7. Cross My Heart And Hope To Die
8. One Broken Heart For Sale
9. The Meanest Girl In Town
10. Relax
11. I'm Falling In Love Tonight
12. Do Not Disturb
13. Spring Fever
14. They Remind Me Too Much Of You
15. Happy Ending
16. You'll Be Gone

"GIRL I NEVER LOVED, THE"

Elvis recorded this Randy Starr ballad for *Clambake* on February 21, 1967 at RCA's studios

in Hollywood. The version in the movie featured overdubbed strings. The song later came out on the *Double Feature* re-release paired with *Kissin' Cousins*. Alternate takes are on the 2006 FTD *Clambake* issue.

"GIRL NEXT DOOR WENT A WALKIN'"

Elvis recorded this *Elvis Is Back!* album track—a.k.a. "The Girl Next Door"—in in the early morning of April 4, 1960 in Nashville. The song had been written and originally released the previous year by Elvis' fellow Humes High School graduate Thomas Wayne (with Bill Rice) on Scotty Moore's Fernwood label.

The track has since appeared on Sixties anthology *From Nashville to Memphis*.

Outtakes have appeared on 2002 FTD album *Fame And Fortune* and 2005 FTD release *Elvis Is Back!*, as well as on bootleg *There's Always Me*.

"GIRL OF MINE"

Elvis laid down this Les Reed and Barry Mason song at Stax Studios in on July 24, 1973. The song was first released on the *Raised On Rock* album later that year. A version without overdubs came out in 1979 on *Our Memories of Elvis*, while an alternate appeared on 1998 BMG release *Essential Elvis, Vol. 5—Rhythm and Country*. Further alternates are available on the 2007 FTD *Raised On Rock* release.

"GIRL OF MY BEST FRIEND, THE"

Elvis recorded this Beverly Ross / Sam Bobrick (real name Bunny Lewis) song on just after midnight on April 43, 1960 at the RCA studios in Nashville. It was released soon after on *Elvis Is Back!* in the US, and then rushed out as a single in Europe when copyright problems over the melody to "It's Now Or Never" forced a delay in release on the other side of the Atlantic. Elvis soundalike Ral Donner released the song as a single and made it to the *Billboard* Hot 100 top twenty in 1961.

As well as appearing on a number of Elvis compilations *From Nashville to Memphis* and *over the yearsArtist of the Century*, alternate takes are to be found on *Essential Elvis Vol. 6* and *Elvis: Close Up*. A slightly slower version was released in 2002 on FTD album *Fame And Fortune*; FTD released multiple alternate takes from the original recording session on 2005 2-CD set *Elvis Is Back!*

GIRLFRIENDS

This section necessarily covers "girlfriends" in the broadest sense of the term, from women Elvis kissed to long-term lovers to women whose liaisons with the king were more in the mind than in the flesh.

Elvis metamorphosed from a shy and unpopular outsider at High School to a man whose sex appeal held millions in thrall.

Elvis loved women and women loved him back. Over the years, Elvis developed preferences and established his rules. One was that no member of his entourage could move in on a girl he was interested in; nor would he ever show interest in a girl who had been with a member of his entourage.

Romantically inclined, Elvis told several girlfriends before Priscilla—and some after her—that he was serious about marriage, but he made it very

Movie Life, April 1958—"Are You Elvis' Mystery Girl?"

clear to them that the less they bothered him about his fidelity, the better it would be for all concerned. Many friends have commented that Elvis hated to spend the night alone; a woman to share the night was in many ways a necessity for him.

Entourage members have stated that for Elvis, potential girlfriends were divided into "foxes" and "dogs." In later years, girlfriends were referred to as "lifers" and "queens for a day."

Long as it is, this entry is by no means exhaustive; it should be considered more as a 'greatest hits' than a definitive anthology. Beyond its scope—and under the radar—are dozens and dozens of adoring fans who were plucked from the gates of Graceland or picked from a Las Vegas audience to spend some private time with the King. Many of Elvis' putative girlfriends were actually the imaginings of gossip columnists or film studio press departments. It should also be noted that since Elvis' passing, a number of women come forward to "admit" a romantic liaison with the King. He is not around to dispute their claims.

Biographers tend to agree that Elvis' first girlfriends were all the way back in elementary school. In fourth grade he was infatuated with Caroline Ballard, daughter of the pastor at the First Assembly of God Church in East Tupelo. Eloise Bedford has told biographers that she was Elvis' first childhood sweetheart, from as early as second or third grade.

When he was 13, Elvis wanted to get married to Magdalen Morgan, another girl he met at his favored youth pick-up joint, the First Assembly of God church.

Elvis wasted no time in singing his way into the affections of Betty McMahan and then Billie Wardlaw after his family moved to Lauderdale Courts in Memphis in 1948. When Billie tried to curb Elvis' interest by telling him that she couldn't come out because she had nothing to wear, Elvis took her round a pair of jeans. At High School, Elvis dated Jonell Johnson. Six months before he became an object of desire for as many screaming teenage girls as could pack into a concert hall, Elvis began going steady with 14-year-old Dixie Locke, a sophomore at South Side High in Memphis. Having a little lady back home whom he intended to marry was not a sufficient counterweight to ignore the mass hysteria that broke out at his earliest shows. Whether or not the first screams were from girls paid to yell— apparently a practice at the time—it soon got real. Elvis took very little time to realize that he could

pick the prettiest girl of the bunch after the show and take off with her for some fun afterwards. One such girlfriend, Shirley Delgado, whisked out of the crowd by Elvis after a Louisiana Hayride show and presented by Elvis to his band with the words "Look what I found!," became a regular pal when Elvis was away from home.

During his time with Dixie, Elvis maintained self-control when he was home in Memphis, though according to some sources, he had a dalliance with a young lady called Patty Philpot.

For a while, his gentlemanly upbringing kept him from moving in on other men's girls. Plenty of men already wanted to punch out his lights because of the hypnotic effect he had on their girls. Fellow musician and future Sun soundman Jack Clement states that at an early show he was worried about going on stage to announce Elvis because he didn't want to give him too much time to schmooze his girlfriend (and future wife).

According to Red West, when Elvis relaxed his initial Southern gentleman morals, he went on a real spree: "Once he discovered how easy he could get girls, we were routing them through his bedrooms two and sometimes three a day." Questioned by an interviewer at that time about what he did with the girls who threw themselves at him, Elvis was only half-joking when he said, "I take them."

On his regular jaunts to Shreveport to play the Louisiana Hayride, Elvis saw a lot of Carolyn Bradshaw.

In May 1955, a pack of girls chased Elvis across a football field in Mobile, Alabama. That same month he famously set off a riot at a performance in Jacksonville with his throw-away comment, "Girls, I'll see you backstage." On that occasion, Elvis was lucky to get away without his clothes and shoes.

In June 1955, Elvis invited fan June Juanico backstage. She had only gone along to his show because a friend saw him the previous night and described him as "the most gorgeous man ever." They met up again in 1956 in Memphis. That year she accompanied him on tour, and he went on vacation to her home town, Biloxi. The Colonel organized damage-limitation when rumors spread that Elvis was engaged to marry Juanico.

Elvis' perceived availability was an important part of his appeal. In an interview made specially for fans and distributed in a fan-oriented magazine, Elvis denied that he had ever been with a girl for more than three weeks. The line he spun to interviewers was that the rare times he was in Memphis he dated different girls but there was no special lady in his life.

During those early years on tour, Elvis shared the bill with plenty of attractive young women. He had a fling with the future Queen of Rockabilly Wanda Jackson during tours they shared in 1955 and 1956, but was too shy to make a move on his favorite Carter sister, Anita.

As well the girlfriends for whom biographers can provide names, Elvis enjoyed a steady flow of pretty young fans, many in their early teens, who came to the gates of his Memphis home, first at Audubon Drive, then at Graceland. According to Alan Fortas, "Elvis was attracted to the younger girls . . . because he felt they were more pure than a woman of an older age." Fan and friend Frances Forbes was once such girl. She was invited up to the house when she was fourteen: "Fourteen was a magical age with Elvis; it really was." Some of these girls remained regular visitors for years, others weren't invited back. Women who were part of Elvis' inner circle were expected not to have boyfriends—better still, not to have had any boyfriends at all. Fellow Sun-artist Barbara Pittman remembers, "Elvis was like a kid in a candy store trying to make up for all those lost years when he couldn't get a girl."

In 1956, Elvis spent time with Barbara Hearn in Memphis. Andrea June Stephens was the lucky winner of a "Win a date with Elvis" competition

in early 1956, which she had to share with reporters at a late-night diner. Elvis was also was more than just friendly with Kay Wheeler, founder of his first national fan club.

When Hollywood called, he had a fling with one of the world's most eligible young women, actress Natalie Wood. That year there were rumors in the gossip columns that Elvis had a romance with heiress Judy Spreckels, though she described herself as "like a sister."

In November 1956, Elvis livened up his stay in Las Vegas by dating dancer Dottie Harmony, who was invited to Memphis to spend Christmas with him. He also stepped out with Sandy Preston and Kathy Gabriel on that busy Las Vegas trip.

On the famous day when the "Million Dollar Quartet" spontaneously formed at Sun Studio, Elvis was chaperoned by Marilyn Evans, another Vegas conquest.

Yvonne Lime was a visitor over Easter 1957, after she met Elvis on the set of *Loving You*. Elvis' movies proved to be an excellent dating agency, stocked with beauty queens, dancers, starlets and pretty girls only too happy to come to a party. Elvis is said to have had a fling with Joan Bradshaw, who he also met on *Loving You*. He dated actress Anne Neyland after meeting her on the set of *Jailhouse Rock*, and also spent time with Venetia Stevenson in 1957 and starlet Sharon Wiley.

Movie company press departments actively encouraged off-screen romance gossip to initiate word-of-mouth buzz about films in production. Elvis was reputedly infatuated with Judy Tyler, his co-star in *Jailhouse Rock*. Other Hollywood ladies linked to Elvis in his pre-Army days include Dolores Hart and Rita Moreno (they saw Dean Martin perform together in 1957). Mamie Van Doren has said that she and Elvis went out on a date and necked after he took in her show in Las Vegas in the Fifties.

Elvis began seeing Memphis beauty queen, DJ and singer Anita Wood in the summer of 1957. On their first date he took her back to Graceland and then up to his bedroom, where they kissed. Anita was Elvis' love for the next five years, until she was supplanted by Priscilla.

In October 1957, Elvis befriended female wrestler Penny Banner after she was on a bill at the Ellis Auditorium in Memphis, and then asked her back to Graceland, perhaps to learn some moves.

That same month he enlivened a ten-day vacation in Las Vegas by dating exotically-monikered burlesque dancer Tempest Storm, going against his usual predilection in only dating younger women. Elvis also dated singer Kitty Dolan sometime in late 1957. Restaurant critic Gael Greene wrote about a night of passion and egg sandwiches with Elvis. Fan Arlene Cogan said that she had an on-and-off relationship with Elvis for a number of years starting in 1957.

In January 1958, Sophia Loren spotted Elvis at the Paramount Studio commissary, went over, and declaring to photographer Bob Willoughby (who immortalized the moment) "I love him" proceeded to muss up his hair and give him a kiss. That year Elvis also dated a girl called Melinda, one of the few females who could give as good as they got in the roller skating battles that Elvis organized.

Sonny West describes Elvis circa 1958 as "good-looking as hell, but he seemed to take all the girls falling all over him as a bit of a joke. It hadn't gone to his head."

Red West says that around the time Elvis went into the Army he really played the field.

Elvis met enterprising German model Margit Buergin within a few days of his arrival in Germany. She turned up at the hotel where he and his family was staying with a photographer in tow to take a picture of him kissing her. Buergin was just one of many local girls with whom Elvis pursued international relations. One girl took Elvis home to her

Priscilla in Germany with Elvis during his time in the Army.

Elvis with girlfriend Linda Thompson at the Kang Rhee Institute in Memphis, Tennessee.

Elvis with one time fiancé Ginger Alden.

parents' place for the night—something that would never happen back home. Secretary Elisabeth Stefaniak remembers "at least a couple of girls each week, more on weekends." Stefaniak was in a position to know: the 19 year-old stepdaughter of a US sergeant, hired by Elvis to look after his fan mail in Germany, kept Elvis company on nights when he had no other female companionship.

Janie Wilbanks, who met Elvis at Memphis train station as he was en route to his foreign posting, came out to stay with him in early 1959.

In the interests of international relations, Elvis had a fling with nightclub dancer Angelika Zehetbauer. His name was also linked, among others, with Heli Priemel and Siegrid Schutz.

Elvis traveled to Munich in March 1959 to see an experimental theatre production featuring actress Vera Tschechowa, who he had met during a March of Dimes photo shoot. Though they only saw each other three times, the press made much of their relationship. Every night he was in Munich Elvis made a beeline to the Moulin Rouge strip club. One night, Elvis didn't even make it back to the hotel. When he returned to

Munich on furlough in June 1959, he saw a Moulin Rouge dancer whose act culminated in her wearing nothing but an Elvis Presley record.

In Paris in 1959, Elvis and friends invited the entire Lido chorus line of Bluebelle girls back to their hotel suite. The girls were so late to work the following evening, that the first show had to be delayed. One girl, Jane Clarke, caught up with Elvis four years later at the Tropicana Hotel in Las Vegas.

After returning to the US from Germany in 1960, Elvis dated Bonnie Bunkley, a 19-year-old Memphis girl who knocked on the gates of Graceland to ask Elvis to help fund her school.

Entourage members who were there recall Elvis cutting loose when he hit Hollywood; one said that he had enough women for four men. On *G.I. Blues*, he reputedly dated co-star Juliet Prowse, who at that time was very publicly engaged to Frank Sinatra. On that movie Elvis was surrounded by an Austrian beauty queen and a recent Playboy playmate of the month. In 1960, Elvis met young Sandy Ferra, daughter of the man who owned the Crossbow club, and hung out with her. Carol Connors, singer with The Teddy Bears, says that they dated for nine months after Elvis said he wanted to meet her. Singer and actress Connie Stevens dated Elvis for a year or so in the early Sixties. Elvis had a fling with *Wild in the Country* co-star Tuesday Weld, and apparently got serious enough about wardrobe girl Nancy Sharp to go and meet her parents in Missouri; hers is the female voice that can be heard in some of Elvis' 1960 home recordings.

Elvis hooked up with co-star Anne Helm during the 1961 shooting of *Follow That Dream*. He also became involved with Joan Blackman, with whom he worked on *Blue Hawaii* and *Kid Galahad*; they originally met in Hollywood before his two years in the Army. *Blue Hawaii* was a busy time for Elvis, if it is true that he also dated Pamela Austin, with whom he later worked on *Kissin' Cousins*.

On *It Happened at the World's Fair*, Elvis' eye reputedly fell on actress Yvonne Craig, later to play Batgirl in the Sixties TV series—she returned to act opposite him in later movie *Kissin' Cousins*. He was also reputedly seeing actress Sharon Hugueny that year, and while in Seattle dated local girl Sue Wouters. In early 1963, Priscilla Beaulieu became a live-in girlfriend after Elvis persuaded her parents to send her to Memphis for her final year of High School, winning them over with the promise that his intentions were serious and honorable. Within a couple of weeks, Priscilla had moved out of Vernon's house and moved in to Graceland. One entourage member says that Elvis started straying within a few months of Priscilla's arrival.

Marty Lacker says that Elvis' parties in Los Angeles weren't really parties: they would sit around watching TV with up to 150 girls plucked from the front gate, all of whom would be trying to catch Elvis' eye. At the end of the night (by which time it was often morning), Elvis would retire to his room with a girl or few.

Elvis weaved his Memphis magic on love interest Ursula Andress, with whom he worked on *Fun in Acapulco*, or so the story goes. Contrasting tales have him so intimidated that he wouldn't take his shirt off in front of her.

Priscilla protested at Elvis' Casanova reputation when the press went into a frenzy at his off-screen romance with *Viva Las Vegas* co-star Ann-Margret. Many of the guys in Elvis' entourage have said that of all Elvis' women, she was the one best suited to him, the one with whom he had the most fun. By the end of the year, he was faced with a straight choice between one and the other. Ann-Margret may have been more of a soulmate, but she fell short on Elvis' conviction that a wife should stay at home and not pursue a career. According to Marty Lacker, "he cared a lot about Ann-Margret, but because of pressure, marrying Priscilla was the decision he made."

Elvis reputedly had a fling with Phyllis McGuire in 1964—at that time a favorite of mob boss Sam Giancana—and she watched him perform at the Hilton Hotel in Las Vegas in 1969; one source says they had a blazing row at that time.

Press office hype notwithstanding, Elvis was happy to be just friends with his co-stars. Deep and meaningful conversations were the order of the day with Donna Douglas on the set of *Frankie and Johnny*. Former Miss Mississippi/Miss America Mary Ann Mobley worked with Elvis on *Girl Happy* and *Harum Scarum* and found him to be the "perfect gentleman" (though there were rumors that not all of Elvis' behavior was gentlemanly).

Elvis made three movies with Shelley Fabares, cited by biographers as one of his favorite co-stars and by some as a girlfriend. Elvis reputedly dated *Spinout* co-star Deborah Walley (who only wanted to marry him in the movie).

Fans continued all the while to congregate outside his LA home in the hope of being invited in to spend the evening with Elvis. The reality was much more likely to be a night of passion with one of the entourage guys than with their hero.

Elvis finished his movie career as he had started it, with rumors of on-set romance. Elvis and co-star Nancy Sinatra were seen holding hands on the set of *Speedway*. Billy Stanley thought that they looked like sweethearts; Nancy admitted to no more than a kiss. Elvis is also said to have had an affair with actress Susan Henning, with whom he worked on *Live a Little, Love A Little* (and who featured in a scene cut from the final version of the *NBC TV Special* the following year).

After their marriage in 1967, Elvis was not prepared to give up his dalliances altogether, though with Priscilla spending a lot more time with him and the arrival of Lisa Marie the following February, his opportunities diminished. Their rented home in Palm Springs still provided a bolt-hole for the guys to invite some female friends for a little no-strings-attached play.

Las Vegas changed everything. Once more, Elvis had the pick of 2000 screaming fans every night. Even between singing engagements, Elvis enjoyed the easy delights of Sin City; gossip columnist Rona Barrett spotted him in Las Vegas with a girl on each arm in October 1969. Barbra Streisand's boyfriend Jon Peters has claimed that Elvis had a Las Vegas liaison with her too.

In 1969, Elvis started an affair with Capitol Hill staffer Joyce Bova that lasted a couple of years. In 1970 he became involved with Barbara Leigh, after she had come backstage at one of his Las Vegas

Confidential magazine cover featuring a story about Elvis autographing girl's breasts, 1957.

concerts with MGM head James Aubrey. Elvis slipped a tiny pencil and scrap of paper under the table for her to write down her number.

In Las Vegas and later on tour, dozens of beauties vied with each other to catch Elvis' eye during a performance, in the hope that they might meet him backstage and more. If Elvis spotted a woman who had the combination of beauty and innocence he admired, he'd send one of his guys to go and invite her backstage after the show. After they got over their inevitable shock at meeting their hero, Elvis won them over through his politeness and interest in what they had to say. Entourage members were sufficiently well-schooled in their principal's tastes to keep an eye out for likely candidates and invite them backstage.

Girlfriends Barbra Leigh and Joyce Bova rallied in the spring of 1971 to keep Elvis company when he was hospitalized in Nashville with eye problems: Leigh visited him in hospital, then Joyce Bova accompanied him back to Memphis after he was discharged. That year Elvis is also said to have dated a woman called Vicki Peters.

At the end of 1971, Priscilla told Elvis she was leaving him. Elvis took solace by spending a lot of time on tour, where there was as much no-strings attached female company as he might want. Back in Memphis, he started dating blondes after years of brunettes, and had a fling with a Las Vegas dancer called Sandra Zancan. In 1972, he started seeing beauty queen Linda Thompson, with whom he would be involved for many years, and found time for young actress Cybill Shepherd too.

Linda Thompson had the field to herself for as long as any of Elvis' women, as his inseparable partner in Memphis and on tour. By the summer of 1974, however, Elvis had a new girlfriend called Sheila Ryan, who attended most of his shows in Las Vegas, while Linda Thompson stayed home at Graceland. He was also dating an LA-based model called Mindi Miller in Los Angeles, who went with him on tour once.

From the early Seventies, Elvis had an occasional fling with his backing singer, soprano Kathy Westmoreland. In his final year, Kathy Westmoreland sometimes stayed the night with Elvis if nobody else was around.

Peggy Lipton wrote in her autobiography that she was intimate with Elvis around this time. Lamar Fike told Alanna Nash that Elvis stopped seeing Lipton when it became clear that she was wanted to get him involved with Scientology.

Elvis also had an affair with Annie Hall Smith, who at the time was married to his step-brother Billy Stanley. The marriage did not survive; Billy and Elvis' friendship did.

In 1974, Elvis ran into old friend Janice Pennington, and asked her round for dinner. She told him she couldn't because she was engaged. When he asked if there were any more like her at home, she put him in touch with her younger sister Ann, who dated Elvis for the best part of a year.

In 1975 Elvis went on tour with Miss Georgia, Diana Goodman.

Also in 1975, Elvis made new friends at the Memphis Memorial Stadium. The first time that hostess Melissa Blackwood came round to Graceland, he gave her a car. Overwhelmed, she fled. She was replaced by another Memphis Southmen hostess, Joe Cathy Brownlee (who, breaking his usual rule, had previously gone out with Charlie Hodge). Elvis whisked her out to Palm Springs and showered her with jewelry.

According to maid Nancy Rooks, Elvis had a fling with a Maggie, an African-American woman who worked as a secretary for Vernon.

The last serious girlfriend in Elvis' life was Ginger Alden, a 19-year-old beauty queen who he met through pal George Klein in late 1976. Linda Thompson moved out and Ginger Alden moved in, after Alden went on tour with him. Elvis discussed marriage and babies with her, though entourage members have declared that by the summer his interest in her had cooled significantly.

By April 1977, Elvis had found a new occasional love interest. He took twenty year-old bank teller Alicia Kerwin off to Las Vegas on the *Lisa Marie* with cousin Billy Smith and his wife Jo. Alicia received the almost obligatory gift of a car.

All these loves later, in his last year alive Elvis confided to pal Larry Geller that he could never be sure if women loved him for who he was, or because he was "Elvis Presley."

ELVIS SAID IN 1956: "I never was a lady killer in high school. I had my share of dates, but that's all."

ELVIS SAID (IN A LETTER SENT OUT TO FANS IN 1956): "Just being near girls makes me kinda nervous and tingley all over, like getting shocked, but I like it!"

ELVIS SAID IN 1961: "It's kind of funny. You go out with a girl a couple times and it's a big romance."

ELVIS SAID IN 1962: "The older you get, the more you look for other things other than just dating a different girl every night. You'd like a little more companionship . . ."

JOHNNY CASH: "He had so many girls after him that whenever he was working with us, there were always plenty left over. We had a lot of fun."

RED WEST: "Elvis cared about all the women he was with—whoever he was with at the time, he loved."

ANNE HELM: " In those days we were very promiscuous, and of course he was having a lot of affairs, but we really adored one another, I mean, I really loved him. I just sensed that his life was very compartmentalized."

LINDA THOMPSON: "Considering the fact that he had so many women at his disposal, he did quite well. He showed a lot of restraint even though the press might not indicate that he did."

PAMELA CLARKE KEOGH: "Elvis wooed women with a dizzying combination of charm, truculence, Southern good manners, underlying sexual tension, and just enough little boy neediness..."

MYRNA SMITH: "Some of Elvis' many romances ran concurrently. . . . But the girls wouldn't mind because they would be in different hotel rooms—sometimes different floors of the same hotel."

DAVID STANLEY: "Elvis always had women. That was just his life. I mean when he married Priscilla he had women; after Priscilla he had women. But toward the end of his life, when he began to get on medication, I'm sure these women were frustrated, because he really just got to where he couldn't do anything."

SONNY WEST: "We had girls coming out of our ears. It's not very hard when you say you work for Elvis. God, the offers I got from women were incredible."

LARRY GELLER: "With a few significant exceptions, women who stuck with Elvis took orders, never talked back and didn't mind being treated like slaves."

"GIRLS! GIRLS! GIRLS!"

Elvis recorded the fast-paced title track (with a Boots Randolph sax solo) for the movie of the same name in on March 27, 1962 at Radio Recorders. Another song with the same title, written by Blackwell and Scott, had been rejected and the Leiber/Stoller composition, recorded by The Coasters in 1960, was drafted in at a late stage for the movie and accompanying album.. The movie finale version came out on the 1993 *Girls! Girls! Girls! Double Feature* release. In 2006 the song featured on BMG release *Elvis Movies*; previous sorties for the song include albums *Elvis in Hollywood*, *Elvis Sings Leiber & Stoller*, and *Command Performances*,..

GIRLS! GIRLS! GIRLS! (LP)

Shipped a couple of weeks before the movie went on nationwide release in November 1962, the LP peaked at #3 in the charts, selling considerably less than the soundtrack for Blue Hawaii earlier in the year but still lasting for 32 weeks on the charts.

TRACK LISTING:
1. Girls! Girls! Girls!
2. I Don't Wanna Be Tied
3. Where Do You Come From
4. I Don't Want To
5. We'll Be Together
6. A Boy Like Me, A Girl Like You
7. Earth Boy
8. Return To Sender
9. Because Of Love
10. Thanks To The Rolling Sea
11. Song Of The Shrimp
12. The Walls Have Ears
13. We're Coming In Loaded

The movie soundtrack plus extras was re-released as *Double Features Kid Galahad / Girls! Girls! Girls!* in 1993.

TRACK LISTING:
1. King Of The Whole Wide World
2. This Is Living
3. Riding The Rainbow
4. Home Is Where The Heart Is
5. I Got Lucky
6. A Whistling Tune
7. Girls! Girls! Girls!
8. I Don't Wanna Be Tied
9. Where Do You Come From
10. I Don't Want To
11. We'll Be Together
12. A Boy Like Me, A Girl Like You
13. Earth Boy
14. Return To Sender
15. Because Of Love
16. Thanks To The Rolling Sea
17. Song Of The Shrimp
18. The Walls Have Ears
19. We're Coming In Loaded
20. Mama
21. Plantation Rock
22. Dainty Little Moonbeams
23. Girls! Girls! Girls! (End title version)

FTD brought out a remastered version of the album plus the usual collection of outtakes in 2007.

GIRLS! GIRLS! GIRLS!

Elvis reported to Paramount to begin work on this movie on March 26, 1962. Production moved to Hawaii on April 7 for location shooting. The movie wrapped on June 8, 1962.

Working titles included *A Girl in Every Port*, *Gumbo Ya-Ya*, *Jambalaya* and *Welcome Aboard* before the movie's location was shifted to Hawaii to capitalize on the huge success of 1961 Paramount movie *Blue Hawaii*. Elvis was mobbed by 7,500 adoring fans when he arrived at the Hawaiian Village Hotel.

Elvis felt distinctively uneasy with the movie's contrived plot and some of the song material. Though "Return To Sender" was a cast-iron hit, he also had to take on songs like "Song Of The Shrimp." As well as the fourteen tracks in the movie, Elvis recorded two more that did not feature ("Plantation Rock" and "Mama").

It wasn't just Elvis who didn't believe in the material. The story goes that writer Edward Anhalt was persuaded to work on this movie after producer Hal Wallis gave him the job to write the script for *Becket*.

Alexander T. Didio	Crewman on tuna boat
Pamela Duncan	Cigarette girl
Richard H. Fairservice	Skipper of tuna boat
Gavin Gordon	Mr. Peabody (hat shop manager)
June Jocelyn	Woman in hat shop
Robert M. Kupihea	Busboy
Lance LeGault	Bass player at nightclub
Anna Wai Hong Lin....	Hostess
Rolf MacAlister	Laurel's father
Ann McCrea	Mrs. Arthur Morgan
Jack Nitzsche	Piano player - lounge band
Nestor Paiva	Arthur Morgan
Linda Rand	Village woman
Edward Sheehan	Man on dock
Mary Treen	Mrs. Figgot (hat customer)
Wilfred Watanabe	Crewman on tuna boat
Red West	Bongo-playing crewman on tuna boat
Stanley White	Crewman on tuna boat
Masako Yoshimoto	Fluffy girl

Elvis as Ross Carpenter in *Girls! Girls! Girls!* (1962).

Elvis' main love interest in the movie, Stella Stevens, had two years earlier won a Golden Globe for Most Promising Newcomer and featured as a Playboy Playmate of the month.

Girls! Girls! Girls! premiered in Honolulu on October 31, 1962. It garnered a nomination for a Golden Globe in the best Musical category, and won Elvis 2nd place in the Laurel Awards for top male musical performance.

The movie opened in late November 1962, rising immediately to #6 on *Variety's* Box Office Survey, but barely breaking into profit despite grossing over $2.5 million in the US alone before the year was out. In the fullness of time, it more than made back the extra money lavished on the location.

CREDITS:
Paramount, Color.
Length: 106 minutes
Release date: November 21, 1962

TAGLINE:
The Swingin'-est Elvis! + Girls + Songs. Who could ask for anything more?

Directed by: Norman Taurog
Produced by: Hal B. Wallis
Written by: Allan Weiss (story), Edward Anhalt and Allan Weiss (screenplay)
Associate producer: Paul Nathan
Music by: Joseph J. Lilley
Cinematography by: Loyal Griggs
Film Editing by: Stanley Johnson
Art Direction by: Hal Pereira, Walter Tyler
Set Decoration by: Sam Comer, Frank R. McKelvy
Costume Design by: Edith Head

CAST:
Elvis Presley	Ross Carpenter
Stella Stevens	Robin Gantner
Jeremy Slate	Wesley Johnson
Laurel Goodwin	Laurel Dodge
Benson Fong	Kin Yung
Robert Strauss	Sam (owner of the Pirate's Den)
Guy Lee	Chen Yung
Frank Puglia	Papa Stavros
Lily Valenty	Mama Stavros
Beulah Quo	Madam Yung
Ginny Tiu	Mai Ling
Elizabeth Tiu	Tai Ling
Alexander Tiu	Mai Ling's brother
Frank Atienza	Guest
Barbara Beall	Leona Stavros
Betty Beall	Linda Stavros
Kenneth Becker	Mack (drunk at Pirate's Den)
Marjorie Bennett	Mrs. Dicks (hat customer)
Hal Blaine	Drummer - lounge band
Richard Collier	Hotel clerk

Elvis, in center, in dancing scene from *Girls! Girls! Girls!*

ADDITIONAL CREW:

Nellie Manley	hair styles supervisor
Wally Westmore	makeup supervisor
Michael D. Moore	assistant director
Charles Grenzbach	sound recorder
Harold Lewis	sound recorder
Farciot Edouart	process photography
The Jordanaires	vocal accompaniment
Joseph J. Lilley	conductor
Warren Low	supervising editor
Jack Mintz	dialogue coach
Richard Mueller	color consultant
Charles O'Curran	musical number staging
Colonel Tom Parker	technical advisor
Irmin Roberts	photographer: second unit

Plot:

Elvis is salty seafarer Ross Carpenter, a man who takes people out for fishing charter trips on the *West Wind*. Though Carpenter used to own the boat, he had to sell it to Papa Stavros (played by Frank Puglia). Kindhearted Stavros is allowing Ross to live on the boat between tours, on the understanding that as soon as Ross has the money, he'll buy it back.

Everything changes when Mama Stavros falls ill. Papa Stavros suddenly needs to liquidize all their assets, the "West Wind" included. Ross has to come up with the money to buy the boat immediately or risk losing it.

He seeks solace with girlfriend Robin Gartner (played by Stella Stevens), sings a little at her club, the Pirate's Den, and then lands a date with Laurel Dodge (played by Laurel Goodwin) after helping her out of a tight spot with a drunken beau. They go sailing and, despite trying to fight it, feel the unmistakable tug of love.

Papa Stavros meanwhile has sold Ross's former boat to yacht broker Wesley Johnson (played by Jeremy Slate). Johnson substantially ups the price he wants from Ross to $10,000. Despite Ross's best efforts to make the extra money by singing at the club and taking people out on fishing trips, it's just too much. Then he slugs the yacht broker and it's all over.

Unbeknownst to Ross, Laurel enlists her wealthy father's help to buy the boat. When Ross finds out, he accuses her of trying to buy his affections. He goes into hiding with the Chinese family he knows at Paradise Cove. Laurel tracks him down with the help of Wesley the broker. Though still angry, Ross valiantly boards the boat with his pal Chen (played by Guy Lee) to save Laurel from the yacht broker's unwanted attentions.

Ross realizes that he has let pride blind him. He tells Laurel that the boat is no longer the most important thing in his life; she is. Cue a singing, dancing finale to a reprise of title track "Girls! Girls! Girls!"

Songs: "Girls! Girls! Girls!," I "Don't Wanna Be Tied," "We'll Be Together", "A Boy Like Me, A Girl Like You," "Earth Boy," "Return To Sender," "Because Of Love," Thanks To The Rolling Sea," "Song Of The Shrimp," "The Walls Have Ears," "We're Comin' In Loaded," "Dainty Little Moonbeams," "Girls! Girls! Girls!" (reprise)
The Amigos: "Mama;"
Stella Stevens: "Never Let Me Go", "The Nearness Of You", "Baby, Baby, Baby" (actually sung by Gilda Maiken).

"GIVE ME THE RIGHT"

A bluesy love song composed by Fred Wise and Norman Blagman that Elvis recorded in on March 12, 1961 at the RCA studios in Nashville for the *Something For Everybody* LP.

It has since appeared on *Elvis Sings The Blues, A Valentine Gift For You,* and *From Nashville to Memphis.*.

Collectors Gold features the first take from the studio session. Additional alternates are on

Essential Elvis, Vol.ume 6 and the 2006 FTD version of *Something For Everybody.*

GLEASON, JACKIE
(B. HERBERT JOHN GLEASON, 1916-1987)

Brooklyn native Gleason was a major figure in early TV, an all-round entertainer who at various times was a comedian, variety show host, dramatic actor and "mood music" composer. "The Great One"—as Orson Welles dubbed him—also had quite a reputation for a hard-drinking, hard-playing lifestyle. Gleason became a household name in 1950 as a presenter of the "Cavalcade of Stars" variety show and "The Jackie Gleason Show."

Despite his conviction that Elvis would just be a flash in the pan, Jackie Gleason was the man who gave the singer his first break on national television when he booked him to appear on "Stage Show," hosted by Tommy and Jimmy Dorsey on CBS. Gleason's sketch show "The Honeymooners" was on immediately after "Stage Show" and benefited from the surge of young viewers Elvis' performance attracted.

Gleason appeared regularly on TV until the early Seventies. As a dramatic actor, he was nominated for a Best Supporting Actor Oscar in *The Hustler* opposite Paul Newman.

GLEAVES, CLIFF
(1930-2002)

Cliff Gleaves, a DJ, sometime Sun Records singer and general good-time Charlie, moved in with Elvis and his family to their Memphis home on Audubon Drive in November 1956 to help out Elvis and his folks after Red West went into the Marines. As a member of Elvis' inner circle over the next few years, Gleaves was with Elvis at Sun Studio for the impromptu *Million Dollar Quartet* jam; he was with Elvis as he went out to Hollywood, and he was with Elvis when he drove back to Memphis to spend his first ever night at Graceland in 1957. Gleaves continued to travel extensively with Elvis until he went off on his army service, even landing a one-line speaking part in Elvis movie *King Creole.*

Gleaves suffered slight burns at Graceland during a fireworks battle Elvis arranged in the grounds during the Christmas 1957 festivities. He traveled out to Killeen, Texas to join Elvis during his Army training in 1958. He then went to Bad Nauheim, Germany, after Red West had enough of the staid life out in Germany.

Back in the States, Gleaves set out to forge his own path in Hollywood. He went with Elvis to LA for the shooting of *G.I. Blues,* but was fired after misbehaving on set, prompting Vernon to send a telegram to Colonel Parker stating "Mr. Cliff Gleaves is no longer connected with us in any way, and we are in no way responsible for his doings."

Over the years, Gleaves returned to Graceland a number of times. He was part of the gang who cheered Elvis on when he returned to performing in Las Vegas in 1969 and then started touring again, with his record-breaking 1970 show in Houston.

"GO EAST, YOUNG MAN"

Elvis took Giant, Baum and Kaye's advice and went to Nashville to record this *Harum Scarum* soundtrack song in on February 26, 1965. Since its initial release on the soundtrack LP, the song has only resurfaced on the *Double Features* and FTD releases for the movie.

"GOD CALLS ME HOME"

Elvis slipped a few of lines of this gospel song—written by Odis Moore—into his midnight show

Elvis in Houston, Texas, February 20, 1970.

in Las Vegas on December 11, 1975., Aat the time of writing, it was available only on bootleg releases include *Long Lost And Found Songs.*

"GOIN' HOME"

This country-flavored Joy Byers tune was a late bonus addition to the Speedway soundtrack album, which Elvis recorded in Nashville in on January 15, 1968. Elvis was in such good humor that it took thirty takes before he was sufficiently straight-faced to get a master done. At one stage, defeated by giggles, he joked, "I just don't know what I can do to improve on this . . . except go home!"

The song has since popped up on the *Double Features* release (paired with *Kissin' Cousins*), and *Tomorrow Is A Long Time.*

Alternate takes have come out on *Collectors Gold* and FTD release *So High.*

GOLDEN CELEBRATION, A

A well-respected 1984 6-LP set released to mark the 50th anniversary of Elvis' birth, put together for RCA by Gregg Geller and comprising early live material, TV shows, previously unreleased recordings and alternate takes that has had a long shelf-life. It was re-released in 1998 as a 4-CD collection.

TRACK LISTING (CD VERSION):
DISC: 1 THE SUN SESSIONS
1. Harbor Lights
2. That's All Right (alternate takes)
3. Blue Moon Of Kentucky (alternate take)
4. I Don't Care If The Sun Don't Shine (alternate take)

5. I'm Left, You're Right, She's Gone
   (slow version)
6. I'll Never Let You Go (Little Darlin')
   (alternate take)
7. When It Rains, It Really Pours
   (alternate take)

THE DORSEY BROTHERS STAGE SHOW
8. Shake, Rattle And Roll / Flip, Flop And Fly
9. I Got A Woman
10. Baby, Let's Play House
11. Tutti Frutti
12. Blue Suede Shoes
13. Heartbreak Hotel
14. Tutti Frutti
15. I Was The One
16. Blue Suede Shoes
17. Heartbreak Hotel
18. Money Honey
19. Heartbreak Hotel

DISC: 2 THE MILTON BERLE SHOW
1. Introductions
2. Heartbreak Hotel
3. Blue Suede Shoes
4. Dialogue
5. Blue Suede Shoes
6. Hound Dog
7. Dialogue with Milton Berle
8. Dialogue
9. I Want You, I Need You, I Love You

THE STEVE ALLEN SHOW
10. Dialogue with Steve Allen
11. I Want You, I Need You, I Love You
12. Dialogue with Steve Allen
13. Hound Dog

THE MISSISSIPPI/ALABAMA FAIR
AND DAIRY SHOW
14. Heartbreak Hotel
15. Long Tall Sally
16. Introductions and presentation
17. I Was The One
18. I Want You, I Need You, I Love You
19. Dialogue
20. I Got A Woman
21. Don't Be Cruel
22. Ready Teddy
23. Love Me Tender
24. Hound Dog
25. Interviews w. Vernon and Gladys Presley,
    Nick Adams, a fan and Elvis

DISC: 3
1. Love Me Tender
2. I Was The One
3. I Got A Woman
4. Announcement
5. Don't Be Cruel
6. Blue Suede Shoes
7. Announcement
8. Baby, Let's Play House
9. Hound Dog
10. Announcement

THE ED SULLIVAN SHOW
11. Don't Be Cruel
12. Monologue
13. Love Me Tender
14. Ready Teddy
15. Hound Dog
16. Don't Be Cruel
17. Ed Sullivan
18. Love Me Tender
19. Ed Sullivan presents Elvis
20. Love Me
21. Hound Dog
22. Elvis' closing remarks
23. Introduction
24. Hound Dog
25. Love Me Tender
26. Heartbreak Hotel
27. Don't Be Cruel
28. Too Much
29. Monologue
30. When My Blue Moon Turns To Gold Again
31. Ed Sullivan monologue
32. (There'll Be) Peace In The Valley

DISC: 4 ELVIS AT HOME
1. Danny Boy
2. Soldier Boy
3. The Fool
4. Earth Angel
5. I Asked The Lord (He's Only A Prayer Away)

COLLECTORS' TREASURES
6. Excerpt from an interview for TV Guide
7. My Heart Cries For You
8. Dark Moon
9. Write To Me From Naples
10. Suppose

BURBANK, JUNE 27, 1968
11. Blue Suede Shoes
12. Tiger Man
13. That's All Right
14. Lawdy, Miss Clawdy
15. Baby What You Want Me To Do
    (alternate take)
16. Monologue
17. Love Me
18. Are You Lonesome Tonight?
19. Baby What You Want Me To Do
    (alternate take)
20. Monologue
21. Blue Christmas
22. Monologue
23. One Night
24. Tryin' To Get To You

"GOLDEN COINS"

Elvis laid down this *Harum Scarum* song by Bill Giant / Bernie Baum / Florence Kaye in Nashville on , February 26, 1965. Alternates are on the FTD release for the movie, and the song naturally featured on the Nineties *Double Feature* re-release.

GOLDEN GATE QUARTET

A black gospel group from Virginia with a heritage dating back to the 1934, leading exponents of the so-called "Jubilee" style that combined jazz and blues rhythms with barbershop harmonies. Led by Willie Johnson, they achieved nationwide renown in the Thirties and Forties. Gladys was a fan of the Golden Gate Quartet. Elvis heard them perform live a couple of times. The first time was in Paris in 1959; after the show, Elvis spent the rest of the night singing with them. Elvis' first gospel album from 1960, *His Hand in Mine*, features a number of songs popularized by the Golden Gate Quartet. In the mid-Sixties, Elvis worked with a couple of members of the group, at that time singing with The Jubilee Four, on movie soundtracks for *Viva Las Vegas* and *Girl Happy*.

GOLDENBERG, BILLY
(B. 1936)

The man who produced and arranged Elvis' musical numbers on the 1968 NBC TV Special, called in late in the day to replace Billy Strange. Goldenberg had previously worked as an accompanist to Barbara Streisand on her live shows. In 1969 Elvis hired Goldenberg as his arranger for his final feature film, *Change of Habit*.

Goldenberg later went on to score hundreds of TV show and movies, including Steven Spielberg's first major movie, *Duel* (1971).

GOLDMAN, ALBERT
(1927-1994)

Author of a splenetic 1981 biography that painted Elvis in a very bad light. Goldman's biography on John Lennon was a similarly galvanizing lightning rod for fan hatred, though Lenny Bruce

faired better in Goldman's life. Goldman was also a professor of English.

Books:
Elvis, McGraw-Hill/Avon, 1981
Elvis: The Last 24 Hours, St. Martin's Press, 1991

"GONNA GET BACK HOME SOMEHOW"

Elvis recorded this amped-up Doc Pomus / Mort Shuman track in on March 18, 1962 at RCA's Nashville studios for release on the *Pot Luck* album.

The song has since appeared on *Elvis Sings Mort Shuman & Doc Pomus* and *From Nashville to Memphis*.

Rougher early oOuttakes and alternates have appeared are to be found on *Essential Elvis Vol. 6*, *Today, Tomorrow & Forever* and 2003 FTD releases *Studio B: Nashville Outtakes* and *Pot Luck*.

"GOOD LUCK CHARM"

This #1 single, released at the end of February 1962 with B-side "Anything That's Part of You," was Elvis' first chart-topping hit in a year, though it sold fewer copies than previous single "Can't Help Falling In Love." It stayed at #1 for two weeks (five in the UK). Elvis recorded the easygoing Aaron Schroeder / Wally Gold song in on October 15, 1961 in Nashville. After its first album release on *Elvis' Golden Records Vol. 3*, it has featured on many compilations, including recent sets *Worldwide 50 Gold Award Hits Vol. 1*, *The Top Ten Hits*, *From Nashville to Memphis*, *Artist Of The Century*, *ELV1S 30 #1 Hits* and *Hitstory*.

The initial take and two others from the recording session were released on 2006 FTD album *Something For Everybody*; Robert Moseley's demo is on FTD release *Writing for the King.*.

"GOOD ROCKIN' TONIGHT"

This Roy Brown rocker was chosen by Sam Phillips to be the A-side of Elvis' second single, after the new boy recorded it (most likely) on September 10, 1954 at Sun and for released later that month, backed with "I Don't Care If The Sun Don't Shine." Elvis' version followed Roy Brown's original in 1947, and Wynonie Harris's higher-tempo and more successful recording a year later. Brown is said to have taken his inspiration for this song from wartime radio announce-

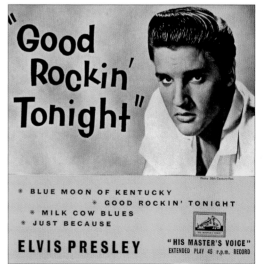

RCA Victor Special Products Black Label vinyl issue EP (USA, 1988).

ment "Good evening America, there's good news tonight."

During Elvis' early days on the road, "Good Rockin' Tonight"this song was a great real crowd favoritepleaser. Live versions are available on Louisiana Hayride compilations and a plethora of bootlegs.

An alternate mix of the Sun original version of the song came on out early on 1959 Elvis album *A Date With Elvis*, and also graced RCA EPs *Good Rockin' Tonight* and *A Touch of Gold Vol. 1*..

The studio original may be found is not surprisingly on every Sun compilation including *The Sun Sessions*, *The Complete Sun Sessions* (the 2006 version of this title also contains a live version), *Sunrise* and *Elvis at Sun*. It;s also on *The King Of Rock And Roll* anthology and compilations *Platinum: A Life in Music* and *Artist Of The Century*, as well as on independent release *Memphis Reocrding Service Vol.1* (studio) and *Vol. 2* (live). Louisiana Hayride compilations and a plethora of bootlegs. most Live versions are available on More recently, The track was the opener on BMG's 2006 release *Elvis R'n'B*.

GOOD ROCKIN' TONIGHT

A 2-CD documentary-style presentation of Elvis recorded chronologically at the Louisiana Hayride from 1954 to 1956, issued in 2000, reissued as *Playing With Fire*.

TRACK LISTING:
DISC 1:
1. That's All Right
2. Blue Moon Of Kentucky
3. Hearts of Stone
4. That's All Right
5. Tweedlee Dee
6. Money Honey
7. Blue Moon Of Kentucky
8. I Don't Care If the Sun Don't Shine
9. That's All Right
DISC 2:
1. Good Rockin' Tonight
2. I Got a Woman
3. Tweed lee Dee
4. I'm Left, You're Right, She's Gone
5. Baby Let's Play House
6. Maybellene
7. That's All Right
8. I Was the One
9. Love Me Tender
10. Hound Dog
11. Elvis Has Left the Building

"GOOD TIME CHARLIE'S GOT THE BLUES"

Elvis recorded Danny O'Keefe's only hit (he took it to #9 in 1972) at Stax Studios on December 13, 1973. It was released on his *Good Times* album. Elvis sang the song live in concert in the summer of 1974, though at the time of writing it has only appeared on bootlegs. An alternate take from the studio came out in 1998 on *Essential Elvis, Volume 5*. The song featured on Nineties anthology *Walk A Mile In My Shoes* , 2000 re-released album *Promised Land* and on 2006 BMG release *Elvis Country*.

GOOD TIMES

This March 1974 album of material recorded at Stax the previous year did much better in the country charts on release (peaking at #5) than it did in the general charts (barely scraping to #90), on the back of 200,000 sales.

TRACK LISTING:
1. Take Good Care Of Her
2. Loving Arms
3. I Got A Feelin' In My Body
4. If That Isn't Love
5. She Wears My Ring
6. I've Got A Thing About You Baby
7. My Boy
8. Spanish Eyes
9. Talk About The Good Times
10. Good Time Charlie's Got The Blues

GOODWILL REVUE (WDIA)

In December 1957 (1956 by some accounts), Elvis went to this Memphis charity event organized by the black American radio station WDIA, and watched featured artists Ray Charles, BB King, Rufus Thomas, Bonita Cole, The Moon glows, Bobby Bland, Brook Benton and more. When Elvis stepped out from behind the curtain, he was hailed by the audience as a hero (and mobbed by the female contingent).

GORDON, LEE
(1923-1963)

Promoter who worked with Al Dvorin putting together tours for Elvis, notably a tour of California in the fall of 1957. Gordon tried to persuade Colonel Parker to let him book Elvis on a tour of Australia—he had previously taken many American rockers down under. His vain hope was that scheduling some shows in Hawaii, halfway to Australia, might turn the Colonel round to his way of thinking.

GORDY, EMORY JR.

Elvis worked with Nashville bass player Gordy in March 1972 as a session musician, and then took him to Las Vegas and on tour in 1973 when regular bassist Jerry Scheff was unavailable for personal reasons. Gordy played in more than a hundred shows with Elvis.

He is a Grammy award-winning player, producer and arranger who has also worked with Emmylou Harris and his wife Patty Loveless among many, many others.

GOSPEL

It's no exaggeration to say that Elvis grew up on musical diet in which gospel was the staple. Biographers invariably hark back to toddler Elvis climbing up on stage to sing with the local church choir when he was barely two years old. Elvis sang gospel for his own pleasure for the rest of his life. Until he became too famous to attend, he regularly went to see gospel performed in Memphis, and he managed to attend the National Quartet Convention in Memphis for many years after he became worldwide famous. The only Grammys he won during his career were for his gospel albums, which have been long and steady sellers and fan favorites.

Elvis' mother's favorite group were the Blackwood Brothers, who played regularly at their local church, the First Assembly of God in Memphis. The Presleys and later teenaged Elvis regularly attended all-night gospel singing sessions at the Ellis Auditorium in Memphis. Elvis liked the more flamboyant Statesmen, with bass singer Jim "Big Chief" Wetherington and lead singer Jake Hess, who combined aspects of black gospel traditions with the Southern gospel Elvis grew up with.

Before Elvis persuaded Sun Records principal Sam Phillips to sign him to the label, he tried and failed to join Gospel group the Songfellows.

The emotional charge that Elvis habitually put into his songs came straight out of gospel. When he became a top performer, Elvis made a point of working with practically every one of his boyhood heroes. Indeed, all of his backing groups over the years had a gospel background.

Elvis played on the same bill as two of the gospel quartets he loved as a teenager, The Statesmen and the Blackwood Brothers, at a July 4 show in De Leon, Texas, in 1955 put on by promoter W. D. Nowlin, along with local singer Slim Willet and the Farren Twins. That night, Elvis is said to have only performed Gospel songs.

When left to his own devices, Elvis favored singing gospel. The vast majority of the material he sang with his "Million Dollar Quartet" pals Jerry Lee Lewis and Carl Perkins at Sun Records in late 1956 was gospel.

The first that the record-buying public knew of Elvis' great love for gospel was when he sang "Peace In The Valley" on the "Ed Sullivan Show" in January 1957. Though it has been speculated that Elvis included the song in his set to sanitize his rebel rocker image, the next week he was in the studio recording this and other songs for a gospel-themed EP.

Elvis went to an all-night gospel session at the Ellis Auditorium in March 1957, and sang gospel at Sam Phillips' place with girlfriend Yvonne Lime in April that year. He walked out of an MGM soundtrack recording session in LA when the line producer tried to curtail a gospel jam session with the Jordanaires—Elvis' regular way of loosening up and getting into the mood for a night's recording.

Elvis cut his very first Gospel album, *His Hand in Mine*, in late 1960, soon after returning from two years in the Army. The album meant an enormous amount to Elvis. It was a tribute to the music his mother loved, and to the groups he grew up admiring such as the Blackwood Brothers and the Statesmen, along with the Golden Gate Quartet, who he had seen perform the year before in Paris.

When it became too onerous to go out to gospel singings in public, Elvis sang gospel at home with the more musically-minded members of his entourage such as Charlie Hodge and Red West; sometimes he would invite the Blackwoods round to sing. In the Seventies, he put together his own trio, Voice, with whom he could sing his favorite gospel songs whenever he wanted.

After years of recording below-par movie soundtrack material with which he had little connection, in 1966 Elvis paved the way for his 1968 NBC TV Special/American Studio renaissance by laying down a selection of Gospel-based songs that he had been working on with Red West and Charlie Hodge, for his album *How Great Thou Art*.

Elvis' love of gospel shines through in many of the tracks he recorded in Memphis at Chips Moman's American Studio in early 1969. He sang some gospel on-screen in his final feature film, *Change of Habit* (1969).

When Elvis returned to the stage, he brought praise of the Lord to Sin City, almost always including a gospel interlude to the show.

Elvis attended the Gospel Quartet Convention at the Ellis Auditorium in Memphis for two nights running in October 1970. On the second night he sang as part of an impromptu quartet with James Blackwood, J. D. Sumner and Hovie Lister of The Statesmen. Whenever he could, Elvis would sneak in to the Quartet Convention after the acts had already started singing, so that he wouldn't steal the limelight.

Elvis recorded his third and final gospel album, *He Touched Me*, in Nashville in 1971. This time he added more contemporary rock arrangements to songs he had grown up with, and included compositions written by contemporary composers.

Sometimes after doing two shows in Las Vegas,

he'd sing gospel with pals in his hotel suite until daylight to wind down.

There is no doubt that many people have started listening to gospel through Elvis' love of the music. He was inducted into the Gospel Music Hall of Fame in 2001.

One of the highlights of the 2007 commemoration of Elvis' death was a gospel concert on the Graceland lawn, at which The Imperials, The Sweet Inspirations and The Stamps performed.

ELVIS SAID IN 1957 "I know practically every religious song that's ever been written."

ELVIS SAID IN 1972: "It more or less puts your mind to rest. At least it does mine, since I was two."

ELVIS SAID: "Since I was two years old, all I knew was gospel music. That music became such a part of my life it was as natural as dancing. A way to escape from my problems, and my way of release."

ELVIS SAID: "Gospel music is the purest thing there is on this earth."

JAMES BLACKWOOD: "Elvis had a great feel for gospel music."

DVD:
He Touched Me, Vols. 1-2 (2005 and later reissues)

"GOT A LOT O' LIVIN' TO DO"

Elvis laid down several versions of this Aaron Schroeder / Ben Weisman track for the *Loving You* soundtrack at Radio Recorders in on January 12, 1957. The song came out on the *Loving You* LP and the second EP from the film in the summer of 1957. All in all, three versions of the song were used in the movie—Elvis laid down opening and finale versions a week after the album version at the Paramount Sound Stage. The mMovie versions did not officially began to appear on until the first volume of *Essential Elvis* in the Eighties.

The song has appeared come out on several Elvis compilations over the years including *Worldwide Gold Award Hits Vol. 2*, *The Great Performances*, and *Essential Elvis Vols. 1* and *2*, *The King Of Rock And Roll*, *Artist of the Century*, *Elvis By The Presleys*, and *Elvis Rock*. .

The movie finale version was released on the 1997 anniversary *Loving You* release. The master is on *Today, Tomorrow & Forever*. In 2006, FTD released a fully-restored version of the track on its 2-CD *Loving You* issue, which also features the opening and finale versionsplus two alternates. BMG included the song on its 2006 themed release *Elvis Rock*.

"GOT MY MOJO WORKING"

Recorded during a jam by Elvis at Studio B, Nashville in on June 5, 1970 in a high tempo medley with Priscilla Bowman's "Keep Your Hands Off Of It," this song has been an R 'n' B standard since Muddy Waters' hit from 1957—though generally credited with writing the song, Waters merely covered it a year after it was written by Preston Foster and was first recorded by Ann Cole.

Elvis' take on the song, a studio session jam that was so much fun he ends it with a chuckle. A pared down version of the recording, first saw public release on 1971 album *Love Letters from Elvis*, before repeat issues on *Elvis Sings The Blues* and the *Walk A Mile In My Shoes* anthology. The unedited jam was released in 1996 on *Essential Elvis Vol. 4*. The song was included on the 2000 re-release of *Elvis Country*, and has appeared on multiple bootlegs over the years.

GRACELAND
(3764 ELVIS PRESLEY BOULEVARD)

Vernon and Gladys Presley found Graceland, an 18-room Tennessee limestone building, during their house hunting mission in early 1957, after Elvis gave them a $100,000 budget and told them to go hunting for a nice farmhouse. Their first home, at Audubon Drive, offered insufficient distance between the family and the fans, and the genteel neighbors were getting restless.

Located on Highway 51 South in the area of Whitehaven and set on just under 14 acres of land, at that time Graceland was a good few miles beyond Memphis's urban sprawl. By the late Sixties, Memphis had expanded to claim the land around Graceland, anchoring Elvis' home in suburbia.

The house was named after the great-aunt of the couple who originally built the house, Dr. Thomas and Ruth Brown Moore, in 1939, to a design by architects Furbringer and Ehrman. The property had been in Mrs. Moore's family since it was turned into a cattle farm by S. E. Toof, a Memphis newspaper owner in the 1860s. The "Grace" of the property's name was Mr. Toof's daughter.

One look at the semi-abandoned property was all it took for Elvis to hand a $1000 deposit to realtor Virginia Grant. The property, bought from Mrs. Ruth Brown Moore (daughter), had fallen into disrepair and was being used by local kids to have parties. Prior to that, the nearby church had sometimes held services on the site. The main competitor for the purchase of the property was the Memphis YMCA.

After selling their home on Audubon Drive and putting down a further $10,000 in cash, the

Presleys took out a 25-year mortgage to meet the $102,500 asking price. The purchase was filed in late March 1957. Elvis hired Sam Phillips' decorator, a man called George Golden, to redesign the interior in his trademark futuristic style and bold colors. Gladys gave her input on the color scheme for the living room and oversaw purchasing of the soft furnishings. Elvis ordered the famous guitar-motif iron gates from the Veterans Ornamental Ironworks in Phoenix, Arizona, for which he paid $1,752. The gates were set into the 8-foot-high wall of Alabama fieldstone that is now covered in fan graffiti. A kidney-shaped pool was installed by the Paddock of California company, at a cost of over $8,000. Elvis had a basement den installed, complete with an ice cream bar and a movie projector. All in, Elvis spent as much on the renovation and furnishings as he paid for the building.

Elvis' folks moved in on June 16, 1957, when Elvis was still in LA finishing work on *Jailhouse Rock*. He spent his first night in his new home on June 26. Cousins, aunts and uncles moved onto the property to keep his folks company while Elvis was away and to help out with the upkeep of the mansion. Select entourage members also moved in while Elvis was in residence.

Graceland afforded Elvis and his family greater privacy but it still had fans on a 24-hour vigil outside the gates when he was in residence. One of the most striking things about the home for two decades of the world's most famous entertainer is its relatively modest size in this, the age of the McMansion. Graceland was even smaller when Elvis bought it; as well as extra living space that he added later in the grounds, in the Sixties Elvis walled in the patio for a den, with a high round

Christmas in Graceland, 1957 with the family.

A candid of Elvis at home in Graceland, 1960.

table around which Elvis and his pals would congregate, before the area was refurbished into what is now known as "the Jungle Room."

Sadly, Elvis was only to spend one Christmas at his lifelong home with both parents. Gladys's death in August 1958, while Elvis was in Texas completing his Army training, laid a pall of sadness on what until then had been a happy home. After Gladys' burial, Elvis spent over a week hiding away in his bedroom. While he was living in Germany on his Army service, he dreaded returning to Graceland because he would find it empty with his mother gone.

In 1960, work began on converting the property's four-car garage into a two-bedroom apartment for Vernon, his new love (and soon to be wife) Dee Stanley and her three children. The house was particularly busy after Elvis' return to the States, and he seemed keen to make up for lost party time. Often there were two or three dozen people milling around the house. Elvis' girlfriend Anita Wood recalls, "There were never many times when you were alone. There were people everywhere—all over the house. You could not call it your house—everyone was there, all the time, in every room...."

Vernon signed a quitclaim making Elvis sole owner of Graceland in the summer of 1960. Elvis insisted upon this to ensure that Dee Stanley wasn't marrying his daddy for money. He was still mad at her for tinkering with some of the soft furnishings his mother had chosen when they first moved in. Vernon and Dee Stanley soon moved out to a house round the corner, which Elvis could access directly from the grounds. Vernon still came to Graceland every day to work in his office, set up in an outhouse at the end of the carport, next to the old smokehouse.

Major renovations were timed to coincide with Elvis' trip to Honolulu to film *Blue Hawaii* in the spring of 1961. For his $5,000 outlay Elvis had the living room, dining room, kitchen and main bedroom remodeled; he fitted mirrors in the stairways and added gold-colored carpets and padded walls to his private dressing room.

In July 1962, Elvis took steps to ensure that his haven would survive urban expansion when he bought the land on the opposite side of Highway 51. Previously owned by the Graceland Christian

Church, this land is now the Graceland visitor center.

In the Sixties it became a tradition for Elvis to host a big July 4th fireworks party, which usually degenerated into a (generally) good-natured brawl for E and his pals, a summer version of the fireworks war they waged at New Year's.

Elvis was always happy to get back home to Graceland after his enforced stays in California. A cavalcade of cars would come driving through the gate, horns blaring, and sometimes make a few triumphant circuits of the driveway before finally pulling up at the front door.

When Priscilla Beaulieu came over from Germany to visit for Christmas 1962, Elvis made sure that he was with her the first time she saw Graceland.

In 1963 Vernon supervised some minor renovations including the planting of new trees in the grounds, new porches front and back, a lick of paint around the house, and tamper-proof window screens. Whenever they redecorated, Elvis always wanted new furniture. When he grew up they had always had old stuff, so it had to be new—antiques did not qualify. Superannuated furniture wasn't thrown out, it was stored in the attic. The Presley family sometimes heard noises in the attic, and assumed that it might be a sign that Gladys's spirit inhabited the place. If interviewers ever asked Elvis whether he had plans to move out of Graceland, he always gave a definitive negative: as far as he was concerned, it was the one place that reminded him most of his mother.

In 1965, Elvis commissioned a Meditation Garden, after he had started attending the Self-Realization Fellowship in LA. The garden—complete with marble statues, stained glass inserts, a fountain and variable underwater lighting—cost $21,000.

An extension was built off the pool patio in early 1966 to house Elvis' new slot-car racing set. His slot-car craze didn't last long, but the room, decorated in green and white, made a perfect location for Elvis and Priscilla's Memphis wedding reception, which they held on May 29, 1967. Afterwards, the area was converted into the Trophy Room, housing Elvis' gold records and some of his costumes—with a few additional exhibits, this is how the room is laid out today. Before it was converted into this room, this part of the grounds had contained a walkway to the music room, two large trees, and Elvis' barbecue pit. Before moving them to the Trophy Room, Elvis' gold records had adorned the walls in the basement den.

Around this time, the patio at the back of the house was closed in and paneled to provide another den. This area later became the Jungle Room.

Elvis' Graceland bedroom was redecorated in 1966 by Bernie Grenadier and has retained almost the same décor ever since. Behind large black padded double doors, the bedroom was done up in a red and black Spanish motif design on the walls and a dark green Naugahyde ceiling with two built-in TV screens. A double row of recessed neon tubes circled the wall just below ceiling height. Elvis had had an office and a refrigerator up there for some time before this remodeling. When the bathroom was later remodeled with a large circular shower and black bathroom fittings, his barber's chair was moved to the bathroom off the trophy room.

Elvis' outsize bed—8 foot by 8 foot—had fold-out armrests built into the headboard so that he would be comfortable reading or watching TV.

Early 1967 saw major work on the barn behind Graceland, as it was adapted to make stabling for the many horses Elvis bought for himself, his family and friends. Elvis referred to the barn thereafter as "The House of the Rising Sun," a pun on the name of his favorite palomino horse. He also had an area behind the house turned into a riding ring. Expansion of the riding ring led to the removal of a couple of small outbuildings, and

threatened to take over most of the property before Elvis found and purchased a ranch nearby, which he renamed the Circle G (the G was for Graceland). Elvis spent a lot of time at the ranch at the beginning of 1967, but by the summer he had lost interest. The wholesale changes to Graceland's landscape included knocking down a small wooden cottage where Travis Smith, Elvis' uncle who worked at the gates, lived with his family. Elvis hired a bulldozer and personally demolished the place, after setting fire to it first for good measure.

After she moved in to Graceland in 1967, Aunt Delta Briggs became the effective head of the household. She made sure that everything was shipshape, and often took on shopping duties.

The anti-theft window screens installed in 1963 were upgraded with ironwork in 1967. Toward the end of the year Elvis and Priscilla hired an architect to design a nursery for the second floor, as well as undertake a little remodeling around the house.

By the time Elvis brought his wife and child home to Graceland on February 5, 1968, the former back corner bedroom was decorated in a yellow and white color scheme and turned into a nursery, though for some time baby Lisa Marie slept in a bassinet in her parents' room.

The circular drive at Graceland was ideal for go-kart races. Naturally, Elvis held the record. When Elvis purchased a set of golf carts, races could cover practically every inch of the property's 14 acres.

In the summer of 1969 Elvis arranged with the next-door Graceland Christian Church for an easement to the church driveway so that he could drive in and out of Graceland unmolested. In exchange, Elvis paid to repave the Church driveway. When Elvis' body was brought back to Graceland to lie in state before his funeral, this was the direction the hearse took.

Elvis spent much of that year living at his other homes or vacationing, returning to Graceland only for the holiday season and brief spells. Over the years he spent practically every Christmas, July 4th and birthdays at Graceland.

In early 1970 Elvis had some work done in the basement, carving out a small apartment for Charlie Hodge, refurbishing the bar and installing new cabinets in the recreation room.

Apart from Charlie Hodge, guests would either sleep in one of the house's five bedrooms, or stay at the Howard Johnson Motel nearby.

Graceland security was beefed up in early 1971 with the addition of a four-monitor surveillance system with cameras at the gates and in a number of rooms around the house. When Elvis didn't feel up to dealing with people face to face, he would watch what was going on instead. Billy Smith remembers that Elvis stopped regularly going down to the gates to talk with fans in 1971.

Graceland changed address when Highway 51 was renamed Elvis Presley Boulevard following a vote by the Memphis City Council in 1972.

Graceland underwent its last major renovation during Elvis' lifetime in 1974, when Linda Thompson did the supervising. The blue, white and gold dining room and living room had a makeover with red dining room chairs and red living room furniture, plus the addition of chandeliers and paneling. This was when the "Jungle Room" came into existence, complete with a waterfall and green shag pile carpet on the floor, walls and ceiling. Known by Elvis and his pals simply as "the den," this décor reminded Elvis of happy times spent in Hawaii, plus he had the fun of his daddy's reaction when he saw it in the house—Vernon had told Elvis that he'd seen this furniture in a store and it was the ugliest furniture he'd lain ever eyes on. Elvis loved the waterfall but only turned it on for special occasions as it tended to splash. When the Jungle Room was built, eating habits changed too as a small breakfast nook table that used to close off the kitchen on that side of the house,

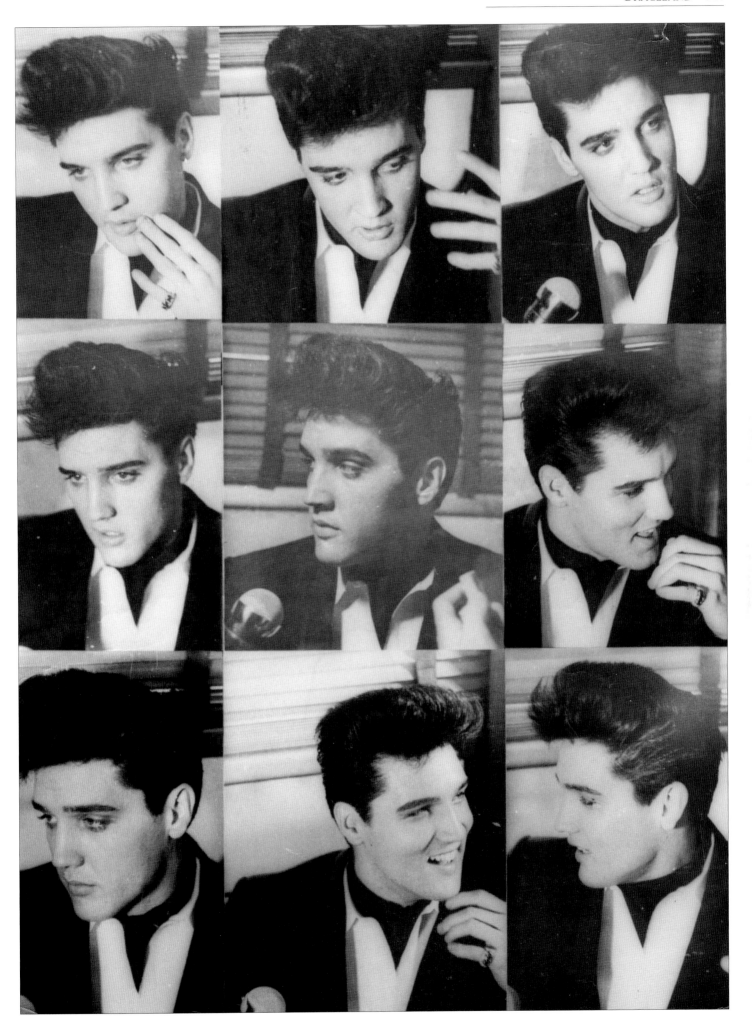

Shots from a Graceland press conference in 1960.

Elvis at the gates of Graceland.

where Elvis and pals often ate, was removed to make a step-through passageway. The basement pool room was redesigned by William Eubanks, using 350 yards of draped cotton and a Tiffany lampshade; while the TV room took on its zappy yellow and blue color scheme.

That year, Graceland featured on the cover of Elvis' live album, *Elvis Recorded Live On Stage In Memphis*.

In the fall of 1974, Elvis' cousin Billy Smith and his family came to live in a $20,000 3-bedroom trailer which Elvis bought and had parked in the Graceland grounds. Vestiges of the family's impoverished roots still remained in the form of a working henhouse—hardly a usual megastar possession.

A new outhouse was built in 1975 for Elvis' personal racquetball court, complete with piano lounge, pinball tables, gym equipment and lavish changing room facilities upstairs.

The Jungle Room was converted into a temporary recording studio for a session in February 1976 that provided material for Elvis' next album, *From Elvis Presley Boulevard, Memphis, Tennessee*. For a while, Elvis toyed with the idea of keeping the room as a recording studio—he'd always wanted to have one at home. The room resumed its previous function, and once again little Lisa Marie could curl up and take naps on the big armchair by the waterfall.

By the summer of 1976, Elvis used Graceland as a place to hole up and stay out of view not just from the public but from family and friends, with the exception of a few intimates such as Billy Smith. The house briefly became more animated after Elvis got together with new girlfriend Ginger Alden in late 1976, but in 1977 he was once again asking close pals to call before they came to visit.

Legions of fans who for years had wanted nothing more than to walk through the gates of Graceland had their wish come through under the worst possible circumstances on August 17, 1977, when Vernon opened the gates to allow them into the house to pay their final respects to their hero. Elvis' body was laid to rest in the meditation garden in October that year, alongside his mother, after being moved from his initial burial place down Elvis Presley Boulevard at Forest Hill Cemetery.

Immediately after Elvis' death, Aunt Delta had the lock changed on the door at the top of the stairs leading to Elvis' private quarters. Very few people have been up to Elvis' floor since, though photos purporting to show the upstairs rooms have appeared on the internet and in the book *Elvis, Linda and Me,*

The rhythms of life at Graceland carried on relatively unchanged even without Elvis—over the years, the household had functioned for long periods while he was away in Hollywood or on tour, and in his will, had Elvis made provisions for his surviving relatives to live on at Graceland. Staff who worked at Graceland after Elvis' death have mentioned strange goings-on such as doors slamming and lights flickering without any human intervention.

Following Vernon's death in 1979, with rising solvency problems for the Estate and running costs of around $500,000 per year, the Mayor of Memphis drafted a multi-million dollar plan to buy Graceland for the city.

Priscilla Presley opened Graceland to the public on May 4, 1982. Prior to this, the house's décor was restored to how Priscilla had decorated Graceland before Linda Thompson's modifications. In a public statement, Priscilla said, "Elvis was very proud of his home, and any time guests would come in he was more than willing to show them through the house. I think he'd be very pleased to know that the house is shown in this way.... If there is to be a Graceland at all, this is the way we have to do it." That first year, admission cost $5. Many curious fans came to see the King's palace; some Elvis enthusiasts were appalled at what they saw as a desecration of his home.

The kitchen was left off the tour until Aunt Delta Biggs passed away in 1993. In 2006, there were reports that a secret room in Graceland, off the tour, houses many Elvis artifacts. What is not a secret is that the Elvis Estate has a vast amount of Elvis memorabilia in storage, destined in future for exhibition.

Graceland Plaza, on the other side of Elvis Presley Boulevard, was redeveloped by Elvis Presley Enterprises in the late Eighties and purchased outright in 1993.

Every Christmas the kitchen comes back to life when Priscilla, Lisa Marie and relatives congregate at the house for a holiday party.

Elvis, his father, mother and grandmother are all buried in the meditation garden.

GRACELAND FACTS

Graceland is located at 3764 Elvis Presley Blvd (the numbering is rarely given as 3734), and lies 9 miles south of downtown Memphis.

Around 600,000 people visit Graceland every year, making it the second most-visited residence in the United States of America after the White House.

Every year, the Graceland candlelit vigil held on the day Elvis died in August attracts up to 40,000 people, and up to 75,000 on landmark anniversaries. The ceremony started as an impromptu gathering on August 15, 1979, when members of the Elvis Country Fan Club entered the gates at Graceland and held a vigil. Before fans are allowed up to Graceland to pay their respects and leave flowers and cards, friends of Elvis' have a little time in the Meditation Garden. In 2007, fans lined up right through the night to file past Elvis' grave and pay their respects.

Priscilla fronted a guided tour of the mansion in 1985 in a one-hour video titled *Elvis Presley's Graceland*. Audio guides to Graceland have been narrated by Lance LeGault and by Lisa Marie.

In the summer of 2004, Sirius radio launched its all-Elvis satellite radio channel, broadcasting from a newly-built studio at the Graceland visi-

tor's center. As well as playing from an extensive back catalogue of Elvis cuts, DJs sometimes invite Graceland visitors to share their Elvis thoughts.

Gracelandcam is a web window onto Elvis' former home. It's on the official elvis.com site at.

Graceland offers visitors a number of tours, culminating in the $68 (early 2007 price) VIP tour that includes the mansion, the Sincerely Elvis museum, the Automobile Museum, his twin jets and a temporary exhibit (at the time of writing "Elvis After Dark"), preferential access and a keepsake memento.

The Graceland Platinum tour costs $30 and includes the Sincerely Elvis museum, Elvis Presley Automobile museum, Elvis' twin jets and the temporary exhibition.

A standard mansion tour costs $25. Parking costs $5.

Lisa Marie retained ownership of Graceland after the recent deal with Robert Sillerman and his company CKX.

Graceland was placed on the National Register of Historic Places in 1991. The property was designated a National Historical Landmark in 2006.

GRACELAND STAFF IN ELVIS' DAY

A small army of maids, cooks, gardeners, electricians, yardmen and security operatives worked at Graceland after the Presleys moved to the property in 1957.

Initially, the Presley family had Alberta Holman (whom Elvis called "Alberto VO5," or just plain Oh-Five) working and cooking for them. She was assisted over the years by Pauline Nicholson, Mary Jenkins, Lottie Tyson, Daisy, and Nancy Rooks. Staff worked shifts to ensure that there was daytime and nighttime coverage of household needs. They also got to partake in the fun too, and were invited along to some of the nights when Elvis hired out the Memphis Fairgrounds.

In 1962, Elvis had three guards working 8-hour shifts on the gate, and two maids in the house.

Alvena Roy started cooking at Graceland in 1963, before moving out to cook for Elvis in LA (where Elvis had originally hired Jimmy and Lillian Jackson to work as butler and cook in his rented accommodation; in later years, Elvis had a maid called Henrietta in Los Angeles, and a couple called Bernard and Rene Sinclair who were hired in 1968 to work as butler and cook at Hillcrest Drive).

Elvis bought her a house when she retired. Hattie worked at Graceland, keeping Priscilla and Grandma Minnie Mae company when Elvis was away.

Mary Jenkins cooked for Elvis at Graceland from 1963 to 1977, usually on the morning shift. Elvis nicknamed her "Maywee" and bought her multiple cars and a house over the years. She also had a role in 1981 Elvis docudrama *This Is Elvis*—as herself.

Pauline Nicholson worked for Elvis from 1963, and featured in the *This Is Elvis* biopic. Ernestine Williams also worked as a maid for a while.

Nancy Rooks worked for Elvis from 1967 to 1977, after getting the job through the local Memphis Employment Office, first as a housekeeper, then as a cook. She stayed on after 1977 to look after Elvis' surviving relatives at Graceland. She too has written multiple books, and appeared in *This Is Elvis*.

Henrietta Gibson was Lisa Marie's nanny when she stayed at Graceland.

George Coleman was the electrician at Graceland from when the Presleys first moved in.

Maggie Smith was taken on as a maid in 1974, and immediately received a car.

Albert Clark Jr. was a handyman at Graceland for over a decade.

Uncle Earl Pritchett (married to Vernon's sister Nasval Presley), was the head groundskeeper / yard man while Uncle Vester Presley and other relatives worked the gate for many years, helped by a succession of assistants including, George Lewis, Sterling Pepper, Billy Swan and Fred Stoll.

People who worked at Graceland for any length of time invariably spent time chatting with Elvis—sometimes even singing with him—and had occasion to experience his humanity and generosity.

Books

(Books in addition to the many guidebooks, photo-books and cookery books published over the years):

The Maid, the Man and the Fans: Elvis is the Man, by Nancy Rooks, Vantage Press, 1984

Memories Beyond Graceland Gates, by Mary Jenkins, West Coast book Publishers, 1989

Graceland: The Living Legacy of Elvis Presley, by Chet Flippo, Collins Publishers, 1993

Graceland: Going Home With Elvis, by Karal Ann Marling, Harvard University Press, 1996

Over the Fence: A Neighbor's Memoirs of Elvis, by Sara Erwin, self-published, 1997

Inside Graceland: Elvis' Maid Remembers by Nancy B. Rooks and Jim Cox, published by Xlibris, 2005

Elvis: The Personal Archives, Jeff Scott, Channel Photographics, 2005 (photographs of Elvis' possessions at Graceland)

Graceland: An Interactive Pop-Up Tour, by Chuck Murphy, Quirk Books, 2006

FREDDY BIENSTOCK: "He was very proud of Graceland without putting on any airs about it."

PRISCILLA: "It wasn't a home, but rather an open house, available to the guys and their dates—all with Elvis' approval, of course."

LINDA THOMPSON: "Life was interesting at Graceland. There were times when it was like living a fairytale, you know, and Elvis truly was Prince Charming."

DR. NICHOPOULOS: "When Elvis was at Graceland, everyone waited on him hand and foot. Everyone knew how to please him.... Graceland was his security blanket. He had made memories of his mother there. He certainly got into less trouble medically when he was there than he did other places."

LARRY GELLER: "From the front Graceland appeared to be a small-scale model of a grand mansion. If you removed the four white columns and the front portico, it would resemble the average large shuttered stone house found in any upper-class suburb."

PRISCILLA: "He turned Graceland into a private playground for us all. He had gun-shooting contests and also 'screaming thrill rides' when he packed several people into his custom-built golf cart and raced around the grounds at top speed."

MARY HANCOCK HINDS: "When Elvis died, Graceland was the financial savior of his estate."

LISA MARIE: "Graceland is like a time capsule. Nothing has changed, nothing's been touched."

GRAHAM, WILLIAM (BILL)
(B. 1933)

Graham worked for 50 years career as a director, mainly on TV. In 1969 he directed Elvis in his final film, *Change of Habit* (1969). In 1993 he helmed TV movie *Elvis and the Colonel: The Untold Story*.

GRAMMY AWARDS

The three Grammys Elvis won in his lifetime for all for his gospel music, out of the fourteen nom-inations he garnered during his lifetime.

In 1995, "Heartbreak Hotel" was inducted into the Grammy Hall of Fame, followed in 1998 by "Hound Dog" and "That's All Right (Mama)," "Suspicious Minds" in 1999, "Don't Be Cruel" in 2002 and "Are You Lonesome Tonight?" in 2007.

See also AWARDS.

GRAND OLE OPRY

More than any other institution, the Grand Ole Opry has defined country music. This haven for old time, then hillbilly, and finally country and western music, broadcast live on WSM Radio from Nashville, Tennessee, is the United States' longest running radio show, going out on the air ever since November 28, 1925 in an uninterrupt-ed sequence spanning over 4000 shows, after its first broadcast (under the name "WSM Barn Dance" by founder George Dewey Hay.

When Elvis was young, his family listened to the Grand Ole Opry on the radio every Saturday night (according to at least one biographer, their radio was hooked up to the battery of one of the family's old cars).

Elvis must have felt that he had made it when he landed a slot on the venerable show less than three months after cutting his first record. He rented a tuxedo for what turned out to be his one and only performance at the Grand Ole Opry. On October 2, 1954, at the Ryman Auditorium he sang "Blue Moon Of Kentucky" during the Hank Snow portion of the show. Opry management advised him not to do "That's All Right (Mama)" because that was asking just too much from the regular audience. His unique take on the blue-grass song he did perform was challenging enough. Some commentators write that Elvis was downright unpopular; others describe the audi-ence as polite if unenthusiastic. He got no encore.

Nevertheless, he did enough to earn himself a repeat booking on the last Sunday in November, 1954, on a line-up featuring Kitty Wells and Jimmy and Johnny, with whom he shared the bill the first time. Elvis was forced to cancel as he didn't have enough time to get from Houston to Nashville.

There is a story (denied strenuously by people who knew the man) that Grand Ole Opry direc-tor Jim Denny was unimpressed with Elvis and told him he should go back to truck driving. Elvis was said to have been so devastated by this rejec-tion that he abandoned his stage costume at a gas station on the drive home to Memphis.

Years later, the Colonel brought Denny to see Elvis on the set of *Jailhouse Rock*; he told the star that he had always believed in him. Elvis was reportedly unimpressed.

Though Elvis didn't play the Opry again, he did tour under the Opry umbrella. He made joint top-billing in February 1955 with the Duke of Paducah and country legends Mother Maybelle and her daughters, the Carter Sisters, on the "WSM Grand Ole Opry" tour of Arkansas, arranged by Jamboree Attractions. Elvis was a late addition to a Grand Ole Opry seven-day tour of Florida in late July 1955, headlined by comedi-an Andy Griffith. He then toured Ohio and Missouri with Opry stalwarts Roy Acuff and Kitty Wells in late October 1955.

After far eclipsing any star of the Grand Old Opry Elvis did not return until the end of 1957, when he went to an evening with Gordon Stoker of the Jordanaires. He briefly appeared on stage to greet the crowd, but spent the rest of the time backstage (wearing another tuxedo).

The Opry continued at the Ryman Auditorium until 1974, when it moved to the purpose-built Opry Auditorium. It continues to be broadcast, though now on TV.

Elvis said in 1970: "The Grand Ole Opry was the first thing I ever heard, probably."

GRANDPARENTS AND GREAT GRANDPARENTS

See FAMILY, GLADYS PRESLEY and VERNON PRESLEY

GRANT, CURRIE
(b. 1932)

A member of the US Air Force whom Elvis met in Wiesbaden, where he coordinated a variety show for Air Force families at the Eagle Club. Currie and his wife Carole (who was singer Tony Bennett's sister) took Priscilla round to meet Elvis where he was staying in Bad Nauheim, Germany. At the time, Currie was posted with Air Force Intelligence, where he worked as a clerk.

Currie collaborated with author Suzanne Finstad on her less than flattering 1997 book on Priscilla, *Child Bride*, which claims that Priscilla approached Currie about meeting Elvis with the purposeful intention of entrapping the singer and was sexually promiscuous. Priscilla Presley suc-cessfully brought a lawsuit against Currie for alle-gations he made.

GREAT COUNTRY SONGS

A 1996 album featuring a number of alternate takes and a posthumous remix of "Guitar Man," re-released in 2003.

TRACK LISTING:
1. I Forgot To Remember To Forget
2. Blue Moon Of Kentucky
3. When My Blue Moon Turns To Gold Again
4. Old Shep
5. Your Cheatin' Heart (alternate take)
6. (Now And Then There's) A Fool Such As I
7. Just Call Me Lonesome (alternate take)
8. There Goes My Everything (alternate take)
9. Kentucky Rain
10. From A Jack To A King
11. I'll Hold You In My Heart (Till I Can Hold You In My Arms)
12. I Really Don't Want To Know
13. It Keeps Right On A-Hurtin'
14. Green, Green Grass Of Home (alternate take)
15. Fairytale (alternate take)
16. Gentle On My Mind
17. Make The World Go Away
18. You Asked Me To
19. Funny How Time Slips Away
20. Help Me Make It Through The Night (alternate take)
21. Susan When She Tried
22. He'll Have To Go
23. Always On My Mind
24. Guitar Man (1980 remix)

GREAT PERFORMANCES, THE

The last Elvis Presley album to be released on vinyl (alongside CD) in 1990, re-released with a variety of track listings over the years.

TRACK LISTING:
1. My Happiness
2. That's All Right
3. Shake, Rattle & Roll / Flip Flop & Fly

4.   Heartbreak Hotel
5.   Blue Suede Shoes
6.   Ready Teddy
7.   Don't Be Cruel
8.   (Let Me Be Your) Teddy Bear
9.   Got a Lot O' Livin' to Do!
10. Jailhouse Rock
11. Treat Me Nice
12. King Creole
13. Trouble
14. Fame And Fortune
15. Return To Sender
16. Always On My Mind
17. American Trilogy
18. If I Can Dream
19. Unchained Melody
20. Memories

GREAT PERFORMANCES, THE

A well-regarded 3-part video montage of Elvis' career through the years, originally released in 1992, narrated by George Klein and in later editions Priscilla Presley.

GREATEST HITS VOL. 1

A 1981 gold-selling release of live concert recordings, some of tracks never previously released in live versions.

TRACK LISTING:
1.   The Wonder Of You
2.   A Big Hunk O' Love
3.   There Goes My Everything
4.   Suspicious Minds
5.   What'd I Say
6.   Don't Cry, Daddy
7.   Steamroller Blues
8.   The Sound Of Your Cry (unedited)
9.   Burning Love
10. You'll Never Walk Alone

GREETINGS FROM GERMANY

A bootlegged CD of home recordings from 1959, when Elvis was in the Services in Germany, issued in 1998.

TRACK LISTING:
1.   At The Hop (Piano Solo)
2.   I'll Take You Home Again Kathleen (slow version)
3.   Apron Strings
4.   It's Been So Long Darling
5.   Earth Angel (Intro)
6.   There's No Tomorrow
7.   I'll Take You Home Again Kathleen (slow version)
8.   Que Sera / Hound Dog
9.   I Asked The Lord
10. I'll Take You Home Again Kathleen (fast version)
11. Apron Strings
12. Number Eight (On The Jukebox)
13. At The Hop (2 Lines Only)
14. Que Sera/ Hound Dog
15. Piano solo
16. Send Me Some Lovin'
17. Soldier Boy
18. Earth Angel
19. Danny Boy
20. The Fool
21. I'm Beginning To Forget You
22. I Asked The Lord
23. Mona Lisa
24. I'm Beginning To Forget You
25. I Can't Help It (If I'm Still In Love With You)
26. Every Effort Has Been Made...

GREEN, IRVING
(1916-2006)

Record executive who founded Mercury Records in 1944, a pioneering label that hired R'n'B and hillbilly acts ignored by the mainstream record industry of the day. Among few regrets in a long and varied life, Green admitted to making a mistake when he turned down Colonel Parker's offer of Elvis' contract, publishing rights included, for $35,000 before he moved from Sun to RCA.

"GREEN GREEN GRASS OF HOME"

Though Elvis didn't record this hit until March 10, 1975, when he first heard Tom Jones sing it in 1966 (for whom it was UK Christmas #1 that year) he liked it so much that he kept calling up DJ pal George Klein to play it on his radio show. Red West says that he first alerted Elvis to the Claude "Curly" Putnam Jr. composition when he heard it on Jerry Lee Lewis' first country album. Porter Wagoner also covered the song before Jones. The song was reputedly inspired by the a scene from Marilyn Monroe movie *The Asphalt Jungle*.

After Elvis finally recorded his mid-tempo version of the song, it came out as the closing track on the *Today* album. It has more recently appeared on *Walk A Mile In My Shoes*, *The Country Side of Elvis* and the 2006 *Elvis Country* release.

A version of the song without overdubs was on *Our Memories of Elvis, Vol. 2*

The *Great Country Songs* album features an alternate take of this song (as do FTD releases *6363 Sunset* and *Today*). Somewhat surprisingly, Elvis performed the song live only a limited number of times in 1975. Officially-released live versions include *Live in Las Vegas* and FTD album *Big Boss Man*.

GRENADIER, ANNE AND BERNIE

Bernie built an extension at Graceland to house Elvis' newly-bought slot-car racing set, in what later became known as the Trophy Room, and designed the waterfall for the den (later the Jungle Room). He also redecorated Elvis' bedroom at Graceland and designed the Meditation Garden. Bernie was married to Anne, Marty Lacker's sister. Vernon is said to have had a blazing row with Bernie over the cost of the Meditation Garden.

GREYHOUND BUS

For many years in the Sixties, Elvis and pals used a Greyhound bus that the Colonel hired to travel to recording sessions in Nashville and sometimes longer journeys, though Elvis also had the option of using his Dodge Motor Home.

Elvis bought his own (second-hand) double-decker Greyhound bus in 1965. Customized by George Barris, the bus was equipped with a stereo, TV and eight-track tape.

He took it for its maiden trip in February 1966, for a weekend away in LA, even though Barris had not completely finished the job, though it was ready by the time he drove home to Memphis after shooting *Spinout* in April 1966. The bus became Elvis' main mode of transport between Memphis and LA, followed by a flotilla of cars. More often than not, Elvis would do the driving. Usually it would take four or five days to make the trip, driving by night and holing up by day in motels.

GRIESSEL-LANDAU, LAURENZ JOHANNES

A self-proclaimed doctor whose skin treatment Elvis began using in late 1959. Griessel-Landau was shown the door after he made sexual advances to members of Elvis' entourage and possibly to Elvis himself—he had been giving him massages as part of the treatment. In her autobiography, Priscilla describes him as a "half-made German masseur." When Elvis discontinued his treatment, the "doctor" threatened to reveal to the press what he knew about Elvis and an under-age girl.

Just after Christmas 1959, Elvis reported the whole incident to the Army Provost Marshal, and the FBI was called in. Griessel-Landau received a small payment to cease and desist and get on a plane to England, but then returned demanding more money. This was the point at which Elvis reported he was being blackmailed.

GRIFFITH, ANDY
(B. 1926)

Hillbilly comic and actor Andy Griffith headlined a bill on a seven-day tour of Florida on which Elvis featured as a late addition, "by popular demand," in the last week of July 1955. Griffith also appeared with Elvis on "The Steve Allen Show" in a comedy sketch in July 1956.

Griffith went on to star as Sheriff Andy Taylor in the popular *Andy Griffith Show* in the Sixties, and then as evergreen detective *Matlock* two decades later. Griffith was also in Elia Kazan's 1957 movie *A Face in the Crowd*, about a country comedian starts in Memphis before turning his entertainment talents to politics.

GRIMES, OLETA

Elvis' fifth grade teacher at the East Tupelo Consolidated School, a near neighbor in Tupelo and daughter of Orville Bean, Oleta entered Elvis into his first talent competition, at the Children's Day of the annual Mississippi-Alabama Fair and Dairy Show. Elvis visited her in later years.

GROB, DICK

Elvis met this Palm Springs police weapons training expert in 1967, on duty outside Elvis' rented house to keep the peace. Elvis brought out some lemonade to the squad car and that was the start of a 10-year friendship.

When Elvis returned to live performing in 1969, he asked Grob—who had also served as an Air Force fighter pilot—to join his staff as a bodyguard. and to use his police background to liaise with local police departments wherever Elvis was scheduled to perform. Colonel Parker liked to hire extra security for events from local police ranks, and Grob was an ideal man to help arrange things.

Elvis was happy to lend his Palm Springs home to Grob for his wedding reception in December 1970, and make him a wedding gift of a nice new Cadillac.

One of Grob's duties was to shepherd Lisa Marie between Memphis and Los Angeles.

Grob took over as a joint head of security after Elvis dispensed with the services of Red and Sonny West in the summer of 1976.

Grob says that one of the things he is proudest of is that he was able to ensure that he was on the scene immediately after Elvis' death, which meant that there were no press leaks regarding the autopsy or photos of Elvis in the morgue.

After Elvis, Grob began training other people in the techniques he used to provide security.

Book:
The Elvis Conspiracy, by Dick Grob, Fox Reflections Publishers, 1995.

"GUADALAJARA"

Elvis laid down the an improved vocal for this song on February 27, 1963, a month after the instrumental original track was recorded at Radio Recorders session on January 23. Written by Pepe Guízar—known as the Musical Painter of Mexico—in 1937, the song has been a mariachi standard ever since. Elvis' version came out on the *Fun in Acapulco* soundtrack, and later on *Burning Love and Hits from His Movies, Vol. 2*, and on the *Double Feature* and FTD soundtrack rereleases..

A different studio take from the session was included on *Elvis: A Legendary Performer Vol. 3*. Further alternates are on the FTD version of the soundtrack album.

Elvis occasionally trotted the song out live in his final years.

GUERCIO, JOE

Director of the orchestra at the International Hotel in Las Vegas, Joe Guercio worked with Elvis from the summer of 1970 onwards, at the time that the concert movie *That's The Way It Is* was being filmed.

The working arrangement went so smoothly that the Colonel asked hotel management if Guercio could travel with Elvis on the road. This he did, conducting a twenty-something piece band for Elvis right through to 1977. In most cases, he had a free hand to develop orchestral arrangements for Elvis' songs.

It was Guercio who developed Elvis' dramatic entrance to the sound of Richard Strauss's *Also Sprach Zarathustra*. One version of the story is that Guercio's wife planted the seed in his mind after hearing the song in the movie *2001: A Space Odyssey* and commented, "You'd think Elvis was about to enter!"

Elvis often ribbed Guercio and his band during his introductions. He sailed a little close to the wind at a 1976 gig in Philadelphia when he criticized the bands' low-cost outfits and called them the "fantastic Joe Guercio Cheapies."

Guercio conducted at Elvis' funeral. During his career he has worked with Patti Paige, Barbra Streisand, Diana Ross and Diahann Carroll. In recent years, Guercio has toured with Elvis—The Concert.

JOE GUERCIO: "He started a whole 'nother thing."

JOE GUERCIO: "Following Elvis is kind of like following a marble—you never know where it's going to go."

"GUITAR MAN"

Elvis recorded this track with songwriter Jerry Reed as his own personal guitar man at Nashville on September 10, 1967. Reed's version may have only made it to #53 on the Billboard Country chart earlier that year but it got sufficient airplay for , Elvis to heard it, and he put in a call to lay down the track himself. When Elvis went into the studio to record it, Reed was hired at the last minute as he was the only musician who could produce the sound that Elvis wanted.

A song that became indelibly-associated with Elvis' latter-day career resurgence had an inauspicious start when a planned single release was shelved owing to a publishing dispute. The more countrified version Elvis first recorded made it onto the *Clambake* soundtrack album. Released as a single in early January 1968, it climbed to #43 on the charts, with "Hi-Heel Sneakers" on the B-side. Only 300,000 copies were sold; Elvis' fanbase was not yet ready to believe that he still had it in him to rock.

The original studio recording has not surprisingly graced many a later compilation. It's on *Elvis Sings Hits from His Movies Vol. 1*, *Elvis in Nashville*, CD versions of *Elvis' Gold Records Vol. 5*, *Artist Of The Century*, *Tomorrow Is A Long Time* and *The Country Side of Elvis*.

On June 29 and 30, 1968, Elvis made multiple recordings of the song—rewritten to serve as a kind of autobiographical template—to bookend the 1968 NBC TV Special. "Guitar Man" was used in an opening medley with "Trouble," and in the closing medley right before his bravado finale "If I Can Dream," and has pride of place on the tie-in album release (titled, simply, *Elvis*).

Alternates abound of this track.

The song has not surprisingly graced many a later compilation. An unedited master version appeared on *From Nashville To Memphis* from the Nashville recording, including a snatch of "What'd I Say" as Elvis rocks out. *Platinum: A Life In Music* showcases yet another version. Fans of the track will find no fewer than six versions (rehearsals and recordings) on 1998 album *Memories: The Comeback Special*. An early rehearsal first take came out in 2002 on *Today, Tomorrow & Forever*.

The song is also on the FTD label's debut release, *Burbank '68*. FTD showcases furthers takes on 2002 release *Long Lonely Highway*, 2003 release *So High* and several rehearsal versions from a week before the main TV Special recording session on *Let Yourself Go*. Naturally, it's on the many bootlegs of TV Special rehearsals and outtakes.

Surprisingly, Elvis did not perform this natural-born crowd-pleaser of a song when he returned to live performing the following year.

Felton Jarvis released a remixed version of the song as a single in 1980 from his *Guitar Man* album project; that single , when it made it to the top of the *Billboard* Country chart, and earned a reissue on 1996 album *Great Country Songs* and FTD re-release *Too Much Monkey Business*.

GUITAR MAN

A 1980 RCA album release of Elvis tunes remixed by Felton Jarvis and Chips Moman, with new musical backing tracks (some featuring the original songwriters). Five of Elvis' vocal tracks were previously unreleased alternates. The LP reached #49 on the *Billboard* album chart.

TRACK LISTING:
1. Guitar Man
2. After Loving You
3. Too Much Monkey Business
4. Just Call Me Lonesome
5. Loving Arms
6. You Asked Me To
7. Clean Up Your Own Backyard
8. She Thinks I Still Care
9. Faded Love
10. I'm Movin' On

GUITARS

The story of how Elvis got his first guitar has been recounted so many times that it has shape-shifted in the process. The most accredited version is as told by one Forrest Bobo, the salesman at the Booth Hardware Store (on 114 W. Main Street) who sold Elvis the guitar. He says that Gladys bought the guitar to divert her 11-year-old boy from the .22 rifle he had his heart set on. Bobo later said, "He just cried and cried, he was so disappointed." In a letter mounted in the store, Bobo states that Elvis had earned the money himself from running errands, though

Elvis the "Guitar Man" and friends.

most biographers state that Gladys handed over the $7.75 plus 2% sales tax for the instrument.

Other versions of the story have Elvis' first guitar as a 9th, 10th, 11th or even 12th birthday present, in some tellings bought by Vernon, and in lieu of a bicycle rather than a rifle. It has also been claimed that the instrument came from a department store rather than the Tupelo Hardware Store, and cost $12.

Before this full-sized instrument, as a kid Elvis likely had a pasteboard toy guitar that he pretended to play while he sang. Neighbors in Tupelo have also mentioned Elvis trading a toy for a home-made guitar constructed out of discarded lard cans, or improvising a guitar out of a broom and pretending to play it.

Elvis took his guitar to school in the 6th and 7th grades, on the lookout for a chance to sing and play. In the 8th grade after some toughs stole his guitar and cut the strings, other kids clubbed together to buy him some replacement strings. Elvis picked up guitar-playing tips from obliging uncles (Reverend Frank Smith is often named), Uncle Hubert Tipton (according to Billy Smith), and, after the family moved to Memphis, from older boys at Lauderdale Courts. He also did some book-learning. Elvis' enthusiasm for the instrument had to overcome his daddy's reported admonition, "I haven't met a guitarist who was worth a damn."

At the time he got his callback to Sun in the summer of 1954, Elvis is likely to have still been playing this original guitar. Talking later about his first live performance, Elvis said that he took his guitar out with him "to sort of keep me company . . . it was the best friend I ever had." However, it has been reported that in times when he had no money, Elvis had pawned it for cash until his next payday.

There are conflicting stories about when Elvis bought a better instrument once the money started coming in. Scotty Moore says that Elvis traded in his old guitar for a Martin 000-18 and then a 1942 Martin D-18 which he bought for $175 from the O.K. Houck Piano Company, a Memphis music store on Union Avenue.

The store proprietor, Bob Johnson, apparently gave Elvis $8 for his old guitar, and threw it out there and then, even though, according to Elvis in an interview he gave soon after, "it still played pretty good." Johnson wouldn't have thrown out a perfectly serviceable second-hand Martin. Elvis customized his new guitar(s) with his name written diagonally across the guitar body in metal letters just below the strings.

He favored a flat-top rather than an arch-top design, because it was easier to spin the instrument round on stage and beat out percussion on the back, as he did on many of his Sun and early RCA tracks. On stage, Elvis hit his guitar hard and was always breaking strings, remembers Scotty Moore.

Elvis traded up to the Martin D-28 in July 1955, a $500 instrument (though the one he bought may have been second hand). Once again, he applied his name with stick-on letters. Not only did the instrument produce a better sound, it had a leather cover which protected the guitar from his belt buckle during performances. Around the same time, bandsmen Scotty Moore exchanged his Gibson ES 295 for a Gibson L5 at the O. K. Houck Piano Company.

Elvis moved onto a Gibson J200 N in October 1956. He was famous enough not to have to buy his own guitars any more—Scotty Moore was sponsored by Gibson, as was session guitarist Tiny Timbrell. Elvis acquired a replacement model in 1960 on his return from the Army when there was insufficient time to refurbish his original. According to Scotty Moore, this instrument was Elvis' favorite. Elvis played this guitar in concert on and off right through to the end of his life (he uses it in his 1968 NBC TV Special).

Elvis nevertheless played a wide selection of other acoustic and electric guitars in his movies and on stage in the latter part of his career. Among these are a Bigson Dove Jumbo that he used on stage during the 70s. Elvis he owned a 1968 Southern Jumbo (or SJ) which he played at home more than on stage. He played out his last final concerts on a Martin D-28, the guitar he used on his last ever concert at Indianapolis in June 1977.

In 1966 Elvis bought a twelve-string guitar to add to his collection. He undoubtedly favored acoustic guitars over electric, though during his 1968 NBC TV Special he plays an electric guitar borrowed from Scotty Moore and a Hagstrom V-2 owned by Al Casey. Scotty Moore's Gibson Super 400 that Elvis played on his Comeback Special was on display at the Memphis branch of the Hard Rock CaféÈ on Beale Street at the time of writing. Elvis sports Fender electric guitars in several of his movies, though he doesn't actually play them. In Easy Come, Easy Go he mimes a lead guitar riff on what eagle-eyed fans have identified as a Fender bass.

Elvis began learning bass guitar in the mid-Sixties, getting some personal pointers from Paul McCartney when they met in 1965. He had picked up a bass many years earlier, on "Baby I Don't Care" from the Jailhouse Rock soundtrack back in 1957, when regular bassist Bill Black had an argument with his new electric Fender Bass. Elvis bought a bass guitar from Bel Air Camera in LA in 1971.

In 1970 Elvis performed with a 1956 J200 and a 1964 Gretsch Country Gentleman electric guitar (model 6122). He strummed a variety of Gibson guitars in the Seventies, hand-engraved and customized with karate emblems and his name inlaid in pearl.

Elvis' later guitars had to survive the rigors of being tossed to Charlie Hodge, who caught them (most of the time). A couple of guitars wound up in the audience when Elvis hurled them away in disgust. In some shows, he played a Martin E-76 Bicentennial Commemorative.

Disparaging comment has unfairly been passed over the years about Elvis' guitar-playing skills beyond beating the back for rhythm on his early Sun cuts. He did know his way around the fretboard. He plays on the Million Dollar Quartet, on some of the material in the 1968 NBC TV Special, in Elvis: That's The Way It Is, and in many early takes of songs he recorded, where he played rhythm guitar to illustrate what he wanted. Almost always, he played an acoustic instrument.

In 1996 Gibson produced a limited edition of the Elvis Presley Signature SJ-200 acoustic guitar modeled on the one Elvis played when he returned to the stage in Las Vegas in 1969.

When Elvis was decorating his new home Graceland, he had a guitar design on the front gates, and was photographed soon after they were installed wearing shoes emblazoned with guitar designs.

ELVIS GUITARS

Tupelo Hardware Store Guitar (until 1954)
Martin 000-18 (1954)
1942 Martin D-18 (1954/55)
1955 Martin D-28 (1955/56)
1956 Gibson J200 (1956/71)
1958 Isana Black Pearl guitar (1958/60)
1960 Gibson J200 (1960/68)
1968 Hagstrom Viking II (1968)
1963 Gibson (1968)
1964 Gretsch Country Gentleman (1970)
1969 Gibson Ebony Dove (1971/75)
1968 Gibson Ebony J200 (1974/75)
1970s Gibson Dove Custom (1975/76)
1974 Guild F50 (1976)
1970s Martin D35 (1976/77)
1970s Martin D28 (1977)

ELVIS SAID IN 1955: "See, I'm just singin', I'm not . . . I play the guitar but they don't record it."

ELVIS SAID IN 1956: "I can plunk on it pretty good, and follow a tune if I'm really pressed to do it. But I've never won any prizes and I never will."

ELVIS SAID ON STAGE IN 1969: "Contrary to a lot of beliefs, I can play a little bit."

FOREST BOBO, TO ASSUAGE A DISAPPOINTED YOUNG ELVIS: "If you play that, you might be famous someday."

JOHNNY CASH: "I never heard that guitar on any of his records after Sun, but just him and that guitar alone, that was enough for me."

D.J. FONTANA: "He played pretty good blues guitar."

"GUITAR MAN"

Elvis recorded this track with songwriter Jerry Reed as his own personal guitar man at Nashville on September 10, 1967. Reed's version may have only made it to #53 on the Billboard Country chart earlier that year but it got airplay, Elvis heard it, and he put in a call to lay down the track himself. When Elvis went into the studio to record it, Reed was hired at the last minute as he was the only musician who could produce the sound Elvis wanted.

A song that became indelibly-associated with Elvis' latter-day career resurgence had an inauspicious start when a planned single release was shelved owing to a publishing dispute. The more countrified version Elvis first recorded made it onto the Clambake soundtrack album. Released as a single in early January 1968, it climbed to #43 on the charts, with "Hi-Heel Sneakers" on the B-side. Only 300,000 copies were sold; Elvis' fan-base was not yet ready to believe that he still had it in him to rock.

On June 29 and 30, 1968, Elvis made multiple recordings of the song—rewritten to serve as a kind of autobiographical template—to bookend the 1968 NBC TV Special. "Guitar Man" was used in an opening medley with "Trouble," and in the closing medley right before his bravado finale "If I Can Dream."

The song has not surprisingly graced many a later compilation. An unedited master version appeared on From Nashville To Memphis from the Nashville recording, including a snatch of "What'd I Say" as Elvis rocks out. Platinum: A Life In Music showcases yet another version. Fans of the track will find no fewer than six versions (rehearsals and recordings) on 1998 album Memories: The Comeback Special. An early rehearsal first take came out in 2002 on Today, Tomorrow & Forever.

The song is also on the FTD label's debut release, Burbank '68. FTD showcases furthers takes on 2002 release Long Lonely Highway, 2003 release So High and several rehearsal versions from a week before the main TV Special recording session on Let Yourself Go. Naturally, it's on the many bootlegs of TV Special rehearsals and outtakes.

Surprisingly, Elvis did not perform this natural-born crowd-pleaser of a song when he returned to live performing the following year. Felton Jarvis released a remixed version of the song as a single in 1980, when it made it to the top of the Billboard Country chart.

GUITAR MAN

A 1980 RCA album release of Elvis tunes remixed by Felton Jarvis and Chips Moman, with new musical backing tracks (some featuring the original songwriters). Five of Elvis' vocal tracks were previously unreleased alternates. The LP reached #49 on the Billboard album chart.

GUNS

Elvis' acquisitive passion for cars was rivaled only by his passion for guns, though he started collecting guns earlier.

Famously, when he went home with his first ever guitar as an 11-year-old he was upset because what he'd really wanted was a rifle.

Elvis passed out of R.O.T.C. with a civil war musket.

Elvis was given a Winchester shotgun for skeet shooting by Eddie Bellman, a friend in Biloxi in the summer of 1956. Billy Smith remembers Elvis owning a .22 at this time.

Elvis' appreciation of the power of the gun was underlined by an incident in Memphis in 1957, when he silenced a Marine who had been giving him a hard time by holding a replica gun he'd brought back from Hollywood to the man's head and ordering him to stand to attention—an incident for which Elvis later wrote an apology.

In his early years, Elvis kept a Colt .45 Automatic at Graceland for protection.

In the Army, Elvis achieved pistol sharpshooter level and won a marksman's medal with a carbine. Of less use in later life was his tank weapon proficiency.

Driving to San Francisco in 1960, Red West remembers Elvis pointing a derringer at a carful of guys who gave Elvis and pals the finger. Later that year, working on Western *Flaming Star* in 1960 Elvis learned a selection of pistol tricks from Indian-born stuntman Rodd Redwing.

Elvis regularly carried a gun during the Sixties, and gave Priscilla a derringer to secret on her person for her own security.

Elvis was officially allowed to carry a pistol from 1964 onwards, after he was appointed a Shelby County Deputy Sheriff. His burgeoning collection of police badges made it legal for himself—and later many members of his entourage—to carry arms.

He kept a stock of air guns at Graceland for target practice. At one stage the smokehouse by Vernon's office was converted into a shooting gallery.

Elvis' renown for blasting away at inanimate objects dates back at least as far as his first night's performance in Las Vegas in 1969, after which he shot out a TV showing a Western.

When Elvis began to receive assassination and kidnap threats, he got into the habit of taking to the stage armed. On August 29, 1970, after Joe Esposito received a threat that somebody was planning to kill him during the show, Elvis performed with a pistol in each boot. He made sure bodyguards Red and Sonny West were equipped with two guns each, in case the first misfired.

That year saw the start of a major buying spree. As well as a Colt Cobra and Beretta pistols that he commissioned his LA jewelers to decorate with gold, he spent $20,000 on guns at Kerr's Sporting Goods in LA (32 hand guns, a shotgun and a rifle, including two gold-plated pieces), as he armed himself, his friends and even some customers who happened to be in the store at the time, including Paul Newman. Elvis repeated the gun-buying exercise in Las Vegas.

Elvis went to Sonny West's wedding accessorized with no fewer than five guns about his person.

Dee Stanley recalls that Elvis never went anywhere without at least two guns.

Elvis on the porch at Graceland.

Elvis added Palm Springs policeman and weapons expert Dick Grob to his entourage to look after security and no doubt help with his burgeoning weapons cache. As a little extra Christmas present for 1970, Elvis stocked up on more guns and supplies from Taylor's Gun Shop in Memphis. He took no fewer than five of these guns to Sonny West's wedding between Christmas and the New Year: one under each arm, one front and back in his belt, and a sneaky four-shot Derringer in one of his boots. He carried on buying into 1971, adding some Smith & Wessons and then filling his gun cabinet at his Palm Springs home.

At a 1971 recording session, Elvis demonstrated how karate could be used to disarm an assailant, during which a gun went flying across the recording studio. This was the last time that the Imperials worked with Elvis.

When Elvis was given a tour of the FBI headquarters in Washington, he snuck a .25 automatic into the building (likely his pearl-handled silver .25 automatic, one of his favorites), ignoring official requests for everybody in the party to disarm. Apparently the weapon clattered onto the bathroom floor in full view of two FBI agents; Elvis calmly reholstered it and carried on as if nothing had happened.

Before 1971 was out, Elvis added up a Colt Python, half a dozen others guns and two more derringers to his collection.

In 1973, Elvis took delivery of two gold-plated Werther revolvers, one of which he gave to Jack Lord. He had already given a commemorative pistol to President Richard Nixon in 1970.

Elvis was not afraid to use his guns. Reputedly he shot at a car in Beverley Hills after the driver made a rude gesture. He once almost hit girlfriend Linda Thompson when he took a pot shot at a bull's eye on a promotional image of himself in his Las Vegas suite (or a light switch in some versions of the story). The bullet went through the wall and into a bathroom where it narrowly missed Thompson's knee and exited though a mirrored door. The gun he used was a .22 Savage, reputedly his favorite revolver.

During his winter 1974 Las Vegas tour Elvis shot up a number of TVs (once because he wanted to lower the volume to talk on the phone) and a chandelier. Elvis would take out TV sets if singers he didn't like came on. Mel Tormée and Robert Goulet, who he thought were "all technique and no emotion," were favorites for target practice. Invariably, this behavior would elicit hoots of laughter from members of his entourage. Goulet was Elvis' favorite target, perhaps because he had been friends with former girlfriend Anita Wood years earlier while Elvis was in Germany on his Army service. He was also known to throw things at the TV if Jim Nabors was on.

In 1975 at least one TV bit the dust on tour in Asheville, North Carolina. Elvis' Beretta went off one day while he was waving it around and the ricocheting (but slowed) bullet struck personal physician Dr. Nichopoulos close to the heart. The Doc was shaken but unhurt (some accounts

Candid photo of Elvis in the 1950's.

have the bullet ricocheting out of the TV and zipping past Vernon before glancing into Dr. Nick). Other inanimate objects that fell foul of Elvis' gunplay include at least one toilet at Graceland.

Target practice was a favorite way for Elvis to perk himself up on a slow day. Various gunplay escapades included shooting up a poolful of balloons, and shooting out lightbulbs. He once emptied one—possibly two—guns into his Ferrari when it wouldn't start. Despite the protests of his travel companions, Elvis sometimes even fiddled with guns when flying (on his own jets).

Elvis was capable of pulling a gun in moments of anger. It has been alleged that he put a gun to the head of entourage member Lamar Fike and waved a loaded gun at Jerry Schilling on vacation in Vail, Colorado. Other incidents include pulling a gun on Red West, until West told him that the next time he did it, he had better be prepared to use it.

He is also said to have put a gun to singer Jimmy Dean's head after Dean joked that Elvis had kept him waiting for over an hour.

In October 1976, Elvis effectively ended a recording session at Graceland by bursting into the Jungle Room brandishing a Thompson machine gun. The only casualty was the record RCA was planning to bring out.

Elvis took out his anger on his bedroom window in Graceland in late spring 1977.

As a rule, Elvis kept his guns loaded, except for the first barrel, as a safety precaution in case the gun fell and went off accidentally. Sonny West later explained that the empty chamber meant that if Elvis fired a gun in a fit of rage, he had the chance to stop what he was doing before he killed somebody.

On days when he wasn't packing a pistol, Elvis could always walk around with a cane he owned that had a dagger built into it.

Elvis' gun collection at his death is said to have numbered a very appropriate 38 pieces, including an M-16, a Thompson submachine gun, an M-16 assault rifle, a sawn-off shot gun and the James Bond favorite, a Walther PPK.

A 9mm Smith & Wesson pistol owned by Elvis was stolen from the museum opposite Graceland in 2007 but recovered on site.

RED WEST: "He would buy an armory if he had the chance. He is kinky about guns."

GURALNICK, PETER
(B. 1943)

The "definitive" Elvis biographer—with the humility to preface the first volume of his biography as *his* story of Elvis, not *the* story of Elvis—has been writing about music in magazines like *Rolling Stone* and *Living Blues* since the Sixties, and first wrote about Elvis in 1967.

Guralnick spent eleven years researching his two-volume biography, interviewing hundreds of people along the way. *Last Train to Memphis* covers Elvis' life up to 1958, *Careless Love* the following two decades. Guralnick co-wrote (with Ernst Jorgensen) *Elvis Day by Day*, and has contributed text to recent Elvis BMG/RCA releases. He has written biographies on Sam Cooke and Robert Johnson, works on soul music and the blues, short stories and novels.

PETER GURALNICK: "I wanted to rescue Elvis Presley from the dreary bondage of myth, from the oppressive aftershock of cultural significance."

Books:
Last Train To Memphis, by Peter Guralnick, Little, Brown and Company, 1994.
Careless Love, The Unmaking Of Elvis Presley by Peter Guralnick, Little, Brown and Company, 1999.

"HAIL, HAIL ROCK 'N' ROLL"

Elvis sang this Chuck Berry song (actually a line from Berry song "School Days") in concert regularly from a number of times in 1975 and 1976, though he occasionally performed it in the early Seventies. Elvis' performances of the song have been released officially on *Elvis Aron Presley* and FTD issues *Dixieland Rocks*, *New Year's Eve* and *Big Boss Man*.

HAIR

Elvis' trademark quiff, sideburns and pompadour are remain a statement and a signifier half a century and more after he first applied three types of grease to manufacture the perfect DA.

Elvis' natural hair color was a sandy light brown that bordered on blond. As he grew up it darkened from the light blond visible in his early childhood photos. Ma Gladys always made sure that young Elvis was well-turned out to go to school, including properly brushed hair when many of his contemporaries went uncombed.

In his junior year at high school, Elvis did his best to grow sideburns and started to groom his hair using Rose Oil hair tonic and Vaseline. His long hairstyle with hair parted on one side and quiffed forwards was not unique among kids his age, though the common style was still the crew-cut. It had the desired effect of making him stand out from his contemporaries, and less-desired repercussions like teasing and being thrown out of the school football team. In a 1972 press conference, Elvis recalled that boys would lay in wait to jump him because of his long hair. At school, Elvis was derided as "Miss Elvis" and "squirrel."

For his high school graduation, Elvis ventured out in a less-than-successful semi-perm.

One of the reasons that biographers ascribe to Elvis quitting his job at Precision Tool in 1954 was continual teasing over the length of his hair (though according to George Klein, Elvis left because he was actually too young for the position).

Elvis began dying his hair black before he ever cut a record. Many friends and family members recall that Elvis dyed his hair because he wanted to mimic the look of his screen idol, Tony Curtis. Cousin Billy Smith remembers that it was Gladys who suggested he give it a try, to bring out the blue of his eyes. Elvis' initial attempt, using boot polish, was less than successful. He soon perfected his look. Within two years, Elvis' hairstyle was being copied across America, not just by men but by loyal female fans.

Elvis did not consistently dye his hair until some time after he became nationally famous. The reshot ending for *Love Me Tender* has him with black hair, while in the rest of the movie his hair is its natural color. Elvis' trademark quiff gave way to a (very convincing) buzz-cut wig for the prisons scenes in 1957 movie *Jailhouse Rock*, a movie for which he reputedly refused to shave off his sideburns. However, he did shave them off for his next movie, *King Creole*.

Those sideburns . . . Elvis' sideburns fascinated America in the mid-Fifties. Interviewers invariably asked him why he grew them (he had always "admired" them), and how old he was when they first sprouted (17). In 1956, more than 5,000 fans answered a quiz to win hairs taken from Elvis' sideburns

Sideburns were synonymous with rebellion and edginess, though they had first been in fashion a century earlier, sported by Union General Ambrose Burnside.

By 1957, Elvis conceded that he was now stuck with the 'burns as a trademark feature. Fascination with his facial hair only began to wane when the press switched its focus to how he would react to having his hair cut for the Army— a matter of such importance that Republican

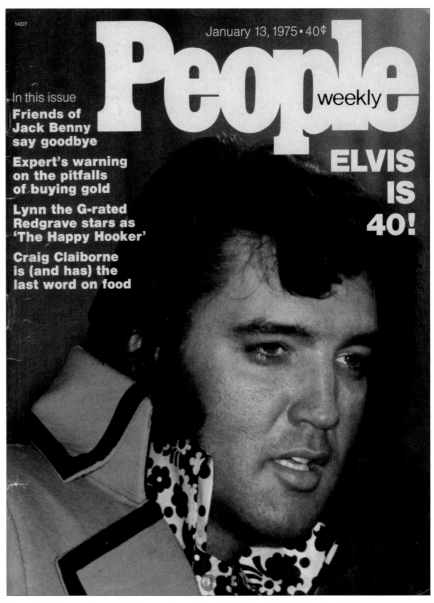

The only *People* magazine cover Elvis appeared on during his lifetime, 1975, with the iconic sideburns.

Senator Clifford Case made a ruling that Elvis would indeed receive a standard Army haircut on enlistment.

His follicles had a rest during his Army days; photographs taken at a press conference soon after his return to America in March 1960 show his hair his natural color. He survived without his trademark sideburns too. Sergeant Ira Jones remembers Elvis replying to a compliment that he looked better without them by saying, "I feel better too, but they're worth a million bucks apiece."

Elvis was still fielding questions about plans for his hairstyle on his return to the States in 1960. With the exception of allowing his hair to return to its natural color around the time that he filmed *Follow That Dream* in 1961, dramatic black was back. When Priscilla moved in with him in 1963, he got her to dye her already dark hair the same blue black color he favored.

He wore an unconvincing blond wig to play his own twin in *Kissin' Cousins* (1964). Even with his more common black coloring, Elvis' hair in movies was not always immediately recognizable as hair: *Time* magazine described his hairstyle in 1966 movie *Spinout* as "like a swatch of hot buttered yak wool."

When Elvis lived the ranch life at the Circle G in 1967, he let his hair go *au naturel*. Elvis grew back the sideburns around this time and kept them; they're visible even with the beard he grew for one of his last movies, cowboy movie *Charro!*

Elvis owned a barber's chair that he used for haircuts at Graceland. One of the maids was instructed to sweep up all of the cuttings to ensure that nobody tried to sell them. Despite these precautions, (purported) strands of Elvis' hair exchange hands for far more than their weight in gold on eBay.

In 1970, on a visit to the FBI headquarters, Elvis explained that his long hair and gaudy clothes were merely the tools of the trade.

In his later years, Elvis had to use dye his hair to cover up white in his eyebrows and hair. Having his hair dyed was a chore that Elvis sometimes attended to in the middle of the night when he couldn't sleep, roping in girlfriends or members of his entourage.

By 1977, his sideburns were almost completely white and his hair was beginning to look like Vernon's. The physical stresses of his last few months took its toll on his hair too, with the first signs of thinning according to Larry Geller.

Thirty years after his death, a survey in the UK voted Elvis' hairstyle the most iconic of all time, ahead of Marilyn Monroe's locks.

HAIRDRESSERS

In the Fifties, Elvis went to Jim's Barbers in downtown Memphis (on Beale and Main). After he started spending time in Los Angeles, Elvis has his hair cut by Sal Orefice, occasionally Patti Parry (Patti Gerson after she married) and then Larry Geller, who became a close friend. On set, a succession of stylists teased Elvis' hair; Paramount hairdresser Nellie Manley worked with him on no fewer than nine movies. At a pinch, Red West would pick up the scissors.

In Las Vegas in the early Sixties, Elvis used Sahara Hotel hairdresser Armond.

Larry Geller took over from 1964 to 1967, and then again from the mid-Seventies.

After Geller, Elvis had his hair cut by Homer "Gill" Gilleland in Memphis—he had cut Elvis' hair in the Fifties—and occasionally cut his hair on tour. Rick Ayers sometimes cut his hair too. Carrie White occasionally trimmed Elvis at home in LA. Charlie Hodge added hair trimming and dyeing duties to his other tasks for much of the Seventies.

ELVIS SAID IN 1958: "My hair is my trademark."

ELVIS SAID: "When I was old enough to grow side-burns, I grew them; I got criticized a lot for them and kicked off the football team."

RED WEST ON THE YOUNG ELVIS: "I have never known any other human to take more time over his hair. He would spend hours on it, smoothing, mussing it up and combing it and combing it again."

LARRY GELLER: "He believed that black hair gave him a stronger appearance and brought out his eyes."

HALEY, BILL
(B. WILLIAM JOHN CLIFTON HALEY, 1925-1981)

When Elvis first started out, Haley was the only rock 'n' roll artist to have hit the top of the charts. Needless to say, he was one of Elvis' early role models.

Billy Haley is generally credited with raising the curtain on the age of rock 'n' roll, or at the very least, being the first white musician to play the nascent genre. As early as 1951, Haley and his then band, the Saddlemen, covered "Rocket 88," the Jackie Brenston and his Delta Cats' tune deemed by most rock historians to be the first proper rock 'n' roll song.

Haley's 1953 "Crazy Man Crazy" was the first rock 'n' roll single to make it into the American charts, while "Shake, Rattle and Roll," Haley's cover of the Big Joe Turner song, was the first rock 'n' roll single to sell a million copies.

Bill Haley & His Comets recorded their hall-mark hit "Rock Around The Clock" in 1954. The song became a runaway success in 1955, after it featured in the credits of James Dean's teen rebel movie *Blackboard Jungle*. "Rock Around The Clock" topped the charts for two whole months and is estimated to have sold over 25 million copies in total.

Haley was born in Highland Park, Michigan, on July 6, 1925. An unlikely vanguard hero to a movement known for its wildness and rebellion, Haley was born blind in one eye, was always self-conscious about his appearance, and was the wrong side of thirty by the time he became nationally famous.

He began his music career in the mid-Forties with the Downhomers. He formed his own country band which went through a few name and personnel changes before they started playing R 'n' B with a hint of country, three years before Elvis graduated from High School. The band changed their name to the Comets as they became more popular among teens.

Elvis played on the same bill as Haley a few times in 1955. After they shared a stage in Oklahoma in October 1955, Elvis adopted a kiss curl for his next performances. The two featured on the same bill in Cleveland, Ohio toured with Hank Snow Attractions that year. Elvis often traveled with Haley between shows. Elvis boosted his early limited repertoire with Haley's signature tune, "Rock Around The Clock" late that year.

In October 1958, Elvis saw Haley perform in Frankfurt and Stuttgart during his military service in Germany. By this time, Presley was the undisputed king of rock 'n' roll but Haley was its no. 1 world ambassador, touring successfully and repeatedly across Europe.

Elvis went on to cover a number of songs that Haley had covered before him, including "Shake, Rattle And Roll" and "Rip It Up." Haley continued to perform through the Sixties, in part to pay off his tax liabilities to the government.

HAMILTON, GEORGE
(B. 1939)

This Memphis-born actor was a friend of the Colonel's in the early Sixties as he settled into his position as a perma-tanned leading man. Elvis knew his older brother William from high school.

Hamilton played Hank Williams in *Your Cheatin' Heart* (1964), a role that was initially mooted for Elvis. In June 1964, Hamilton and then girlfriend Lynda Bird Johnson visited Elvis on the set of *Girl Happy*. Hamilton was a regular visitor to Elvis' Vegas shows in the Seventies, and was one of very few celebrities to attend Elvis' funeral.

Hamilton's highest profile roles include *All The Fine Young Cannibals* (opposite Natalie Wood, 1960), *Love at First Bite* (1979), *The Godfather, Part III* (1990), and in 2006 an appearance on TV show "Dancing with the Stars."

HAMILTON, ROY
(1929-1969)

A virtuoso singer with a mellifluous voice who blended gospel and pop, Hamilton was one of Elvis' early musical heroes. Hamilton was born in Leesburg, Georgia on April 16, 1929. Classically trained, Hamilton had a solid grounding in gospel and in boxing before he won a talent contest at the Apollo Theater as an 18-year-old. His first hit, "You'll Never Walk Alone" at the end of 1953, was the first in a string of R'n'B chart-toppers through the mid-Fifties, but between 1956 and 1958 exhaustion forced him out of the business. He continued to make records throughout the Sixties.

In January 1969, Elvis took half a day off recording at American Studio to spend time with Hamilton, who was also working there at the time. Elvis was so thrilled that he gave Hamilton one of the songs he was intending to record himself, "Angelica." Hamilton died of a stroke just a few months later.

According to some sources, Elvis had met Hamilton many years, earlier, backstage at concert in Cleveland, Ohio for a (never-released) film production about DJ Bill Randle.

Elvis sang a number of songs Hamilton brought to prominence, including both sides of Hamilton's first single ("You'll Never Walk Alone" and "I'm Gonna Sit Right Down And Cry)," and big ballads "Unchained Melody," "Hurt," "Without A Song," "I Believe," "Pledging My Love" and "You Can Have Her."

"HANDS OFF"

Elvis was captured singing a version of this R & B hit, written and first recorded by Priscilla Bowman and Jay McShann in 1955, on a 1960 home recording not officially released until 1999 disc *The Home Recordings*.

HANK SNOW ENTERPRISES AND JAMBOREE ATTRACTIONS

Colonel Parker and Hank Snow became partners in this music promotions company in the early Fifties. When Colonel Parker took over Elvis' management from Bob Neal, it was, at least as far as Hank Snow thought, through their joint company. The Colonel ultimately had other plans.

One of the first things that Colonel Tom Parker did for Elvis when they met was land him the excellent exposure of touring on the Hank Snow Jamboree in February and May 1955, through the Southern states and as far afield as Florida. Elvis won large numbers of new fans from the people who came to see Hank Snow, Faron Young, Mother Maybelle and the Carter Sisters, Onie Wheeler, Jimmie Rodgers Snow and others.

HAPPINESS

The title of the first song Elvis ever recorded, "My Happiness," was less than prophetic about his own life.

Elvis may have brought happiness to millions of people around the globe, but for much of his adult life, happiness was an elusive commodity. Fame, wealth, success, good looks, love and adulation were not enough to sustain his happiness for forty-two years.

A number of factors conspired against Elvis' long-term happiness. Almost universally, biographers agree that the loss of his mother just two years after his rise to the top was a watershed event that had a lifelong influence. The lack of freedom he suffered as the flip side of his compact with fame squeezed much of the spontaneity out of his life. When he wasn't working, boredom lay in ambush. Privately, Elvis had to deal with the paradox of almost total dominance and responsibility in his own personal realm, in contrast to minimal actual power over the direction of his career (with the exception of his early years and perhaps his resurgence in 1968-1970).

Being Elvis the public persona was something he undoubtedly enjoyed; it also had its costs. His reliance on drugs in his later years became a symptom, cause and effect of his lack of happiness.

D.J. FONTANA: "I don't think Elvis was the happiest man in the world."

MARTY LACKER: "Elvis wanted to be happy. He just didn't know how to do it."

BILLY SMITH: "When he got unhappy, he liked to go buy cars."

PRISCILLA: "Elvis was a giving soul who touched and gave happiness to millions all over the world and continues to be respected and loved by his peers."

"HAPPY BIRTHDAY"

Like most members of humanity who lived in the Twentieth century, Elvis sang this song—written by schoolteacher sisters Patty and Mildred Hill in 1893 and believe it or not in copyright until 2030—at appropriate moments, sometimes on stage to band members or to a special lady in the audience. There's a version on *Collectors Gold*, and many more on live bootlegs from 1969 to May 1977.

"HAPPY ENDING"

Elvis recorded this Ben Weisman / Sid Wayne song for a rare duet (at least in the movie version with Joan O'Brian) at Radio Recorders on August 30, 1962, foras the finale of *It Happened at the World's Fair*. The song later appeared on 1978 album *Mahalo From Elvis*, and on the later *Double Feature* and FTD soundtrack reissues.

Alternate takes galore are on the FTD version of the soundtrack, issued in 2004.

"HAPPY, HAPPY BIRTHDAY BABY"

A recording of Elvis singing this 1957 #5 hit for the Tune Weavers surfaced on a home recording made by Eddie Fadal, with whom Elvis stayed during his Army training in Texas in 1958, on bootleg release *Forever Young, Forever Beautiful*. Fadal says Elvis loved listening to this song so much that he wore out seven copies of the record. The song was written by Gilbert Lopez and Margo Sylvia.

"HARBOR LIGHTS"

Elvis crooned his way through this ballad during his first professional recording session at Sun Studio on July 5, 1954. Sam Phillips put the song on hold as he waited for the new boy to come up with something a little different for his first release—Elvis' version was too similar to the half-dozen or so recordings made by artists including Sammy Kaye and Bing Crosby, since Jimmy Kennedy and Hugh Williams (a pseudonym for Will Grosz) penned the song in the late Thirties.

Elvis' version "Harbor Lights" was not released until the very end of his life, when in 1976 RCA included it on retrospective compilation *Elvis: A Legendary Performer Vol. 2*. It has since featured on anthologies *A Golden Celebration* and *The King Of Rock And Roll*, plus many Sun compilations including *The Complete Sun Sessions* and *Elvis at Sun*. It's also to be found on *Memphis Recording Service Vol. 2*.

An alternate take is on *Sunrise* and , *Today, Tomorrow & Forever* and the 2006 issue of *The Complete Sun Sessions*.

"HARD HEADED WOMAN"

This bluesy #11 single, written by Claude Demetrius, came out on June 10, 1958, a little before *King Creole* hit the screens. B-Side "Don't Ask Me Why" rose no higher than 28 on the charts. Though some sources state that Elvis' A-side was kept off the top of the charts by the Tune Weavers' "Purple People Eater," as a two-week chart-topper it has been included in later commemorative reissues of Elvis' 21 US #1 hits. Both were

Elvis recorded "Hard Headed Woman"—not to be confused with the Cat Stevens song of the same name—at at Radio Recorders in on January that 15 that year, at during Elvis' his final recording session before being the drafted into the Army. This was the last Elvis record to be released on the home market in 78 rpm format, his last in the *Billboard* Top 100 before the start of the *Hot 100*, and his Elvis' first to qualify for RIAA gold record certification—a category officially established earlier that year.

The song appeared on the *King Creole* soundtrack album, 1959 EP *A Touch of Gold Vol. 1*, and has since featured on many hits collections including *Worldwide 50 Gold Award Hits Vol. 1*, *The Top Ten Hits*, most ,*The King Of Rock And Roll* anthology, the 1997 *King Creole* album re-release, recently *Artist of the Century*, *ELVIS 30 #1 Hits*, *Hitstory*, themed album *Elvis Rock* and *Elvis at the Movies*.

"HARD KNOCKS"

Elvis recorded this Joy Byers (hard) rocker for *Roustabout* at Radio Recorders in on March 2, 1964. It has appeared on the original, *Double Feature* and FTD versions of the *Roustabout* album, and popped up on a bootleg of home recordings, *The Long Lost Home Recordings*.

"HARD LUCK"

A Ben Weisman / Sid Wayne harmonica-driven blues track that Elvis recorded for the *Frankie and Johnny* soundtrack in in the early hours of May 14, 1965 at Radio Recorders in Hollywood, with vocals re-recorded a week later at the Goldwyn Studios. As well as the original soundtrack LP, tThe song is naturally has come out on the later *Double Feature* and FTD versions of the album. In the movie, Elvis is accompanied on harmonica by a shoe-shine boy who has just picked up some of his winnings.

HARDIN, GLEN D.
(B. 1939)

Pianist Hardin replaced Larry Muhoberac in Elvis' TCB Band in January 1970, and played live and in the studio until early 1976. During that time he helped to arrange some of the songs Elvis covered, including "Bridge Over Troubled Water."

Born in Collingsworth County, Texas, on April 18, 1939, Hardin first saw Elvis at a 1955 show in Lubbock, Texas. Hardin began playing for a living after leaving the US Navy in the early Sixties. He toured with Buddy Holly's band The Crickets after the singer's death, and then appeared on the TV show "Shindig" alongside TCB guitarist James Burton. Burton actually got in touch with Hardin when he was first putting together the band, but Hardin said no the first time round.

Over the years he worked with artists from Bing Crosby to Linda Ronstadt, John Denver, Johnny Rivers, Waylon Jennings and Roy Orbison. In 1976 he began touring with Emmylou Harris, and decided that that was where his future lay as Elvis went into his final decline.

Hardin is one of the TCB musicians who have toured with Elvis—The Concert. He is also an accomplished songwriter, having composed a 1965 #1 hit, "Count Me In"

"HAREM HOLIDAY"

A title track contender for *Harum Scarum* (and indeed, the title used for the used as the movie title in some international markets) written by Peter Andreoli, Vince Poncia Jr. and Jimmie Crane, Elvis recorded this song in on February 26, 1965 at the RCA studios in Nashville; he had to return to redo his vocals on March 9. "Harem Holiday"It appeared on the movie soundtrack LP, and followed years later by the *Double Features* reissue and *Command Performances*. Two alternate takes are on the 2003 FTD soundtrack re-release.

HARMAN, MURREY "BUDDY"
(B. 1928)

Drummer Buddy Harman played back-up drums and percussion at Elvis' May 1958 recording session in Nashville. He continued to drum and provide percussion on Elvis' post-Army sessions in 1960, and gigged with Elvis on the few occasions he played live in the early Sixties (including his Memphis Charity Show in 1961). Harman worked

on recording sessions with Elvis on and off until 1970, including at least nine movie soundtracks.

Born in Nashville, Tennessee, Harman began as a jazz drummer before he became the first ever house drummer at the Grand Ole Opry and helped to create the "Nashville Sound." Drummers being much-looked-down-upon in country music at that time, Harman earned extra money by working in strip clubs (as did longtime Elvis drummer D.J. Fontana. Over the years, Harman laid down the beat for trademark songs by Patsy Cline, Marty Robbins, the Everly Brothers, Johnny Cash, Tammy Wynette and Roy Orbison... He is sometimes credited as the drummer who has played on the most recordings (over 18,000 according to one source).

HARMONIZING FOUR

An African-American jubilee-style close-harmony vocal group led by Joseph "Gospel Joe" Williams. Founded in Richmond Virginia in the late Twenties, the group came to prominence backing Sister Rosetta Tharpe. Elvis loved to listen to the band, particularly accomplished bass singer Jimmy Jones, who unlike most bass singers often took the lead. Elvis sounded out the Harmonizing Four to back him for his Sixties gospel album *How Great Thou Art* but they were unavailable. He covered Harmonizing Four songs "Somebody Bigger Than You And I" and "Only Believe."

HARMONY, DOROTHY "DOTTIE"

Elvis dated this Las Vegas showgirl in 1956, inviting her to join him in Memphis over Christmas and taking her Christmas shopping at the Lamar Airways Center in town. Before she returned to Las Vegas, she accompanied with Elvis to his preliminary draft medical in Memphis.

HARRIS, WYNONIE
(1915-1969)

Elvis was a big fan of the self-proclaimed "Mr Blues," a pioneering R 'n' B artist from Omaha, Nebraska, who was at his most popular in the late Forties and early Fifties, when his hits included "Good Rockin' Tonight," the song Elvis recorded for his second single at Sun.

An accomplished drummer and dancer in his youth, Harris developed quite a reputation for hard living and highly-risquéÈ lyrics, with a string of hits including "Wynonie's Blues," "All She Wants To Do Is Rock," "I Like My Baby's Pudding," "Good Morning Judge" and "Lovin' Machine." The huge success of white rockabilly gradually spelled the end of his success, though there is a strong argument that Harris was the man who truly started rock 'n' roll by adding a gospel-inspired backbeat to Roy Brown's original "Good Rockin' Tonight."

Harris said that "Don't Be Cruel" was his favorite Elvis cut.

HENRY GLOVER: "When you saw Elvis, you were seeing a mild version of Wynonie."

HARRISON, GEORGE
(1943-2001)

Beatle George Harrison, known as the "quiet Beatle," told of the "rock 'n' roll epiphany" he experienced as a young teenager when he heard "Heartbreak Hotel" wafting out of a house as he was riding by on his bicycle.

Born in Liverpool on February 25, 1943, the lead guitarist for The Beatles originally joined their precursor group, The Quarrymen, when he was just fifteen. After he became interested in Eastern religion in the mid-Sixties, it remained an important factor in his life. Harrison met Elvis with the rest of The Beatles in 1965. Harrison was one of the first entertainers to organize a charity relief concert (his concert for Bangladesh in 1971). He worked as a film producer in the Eighties, helping to found the company that backed Monty Python's movie *The Life of Brian*. Also in the Eighties, he returned to recording with supergroup The Traveling Wilburys.

Elvis recorded George Harrison's composition "Something."

GEORGE HARRISON, AFTER SEEING ELVIS BACKSTAGE, 1972: "He was immaculate. He seemed to be eight foot tall and his tan was perfect. I felt like a grubby little slug and he looked like Lord Shiva."

HART, DOLORES
(B. 1938, DOLORES HICKS)

Elvis worked with Dolores Hart on his first two Paramount movies, *Loving You* (her movie debut) and *King Creole*. Elvis described her as "the nicest girl I've ever met." In an interview published in the early Nineties, Hart extolled Elvis' virtues as a friend, and confirmed they were never romantically involved.

Nicknamed "Whistling Britches" by Elvis, Hart was a top female star for five years, acting opposite Anthony Quinn, Robert Wagner and Montgomery Clift. She was signed up by Hal Wallis after he was tipped off about a this talented and untutored young actress who was in a school production of *Saint Joan*.

In 1963 Hart turned her back on a successful Hollywood career to enter a convent, where she rose to become a Reverend Mother. She has remained a voting member of the Academy of Motion Arts and Sciences, alongside her role as Prioress at the Benedictine Regina Laudis Abbey in Bethlehem, Connecticut.

Dolores Hart with Elvis in *Love Me Tender* (1956).

DOLORES HART SAID IN 1959: "Elvis is a young man with an enormous capacity of love... but I don't think he has found his happiness. I think he is terribly lonely."

HARUM SCARUM (LP)

Elvis' regular players couldn't be hired for the soundtrack sessions in Nashville owing to short notice, so Elvis was backed by Charlie McCoy on guitar, Henry Strzelecki on bass, Kenny Buttrey on drums, Rufus Long on flute and Ralph Strobel on oboe. The soundtrack songs plus two bonus tracks were released to coincide with the movie in late 1965. *Harum Scarum* sold 300,000 copies, making it to #8 during its 23-week stay on the charts.

TRACK LISTING:
1. Harem Holiday
2. My Desert Serenade
3. Go East, Young Man
4. Mirage
5. Kismet
6. Shake That Tambourine
7. Hey, Little Girl
8. Golden Coins
9. So Close, Yet So Far (From Paradise)
10. Animal Instinct
11. Wisdom Of The Ages

In 1993, as part of the original 4CD *Double Feature* release, RCA brought out *Harum Scarum* with *Girl Happy*.

TRACK LISTING:
1. Harem Holiday
2. My Desert Serenade
3. Go East, Young Man
4. Mirage
5. Kismet
6. Shake That Tambourine
7. Hey, Little Girl
8. Golden Coins
9. So Close, Yet So Far
10. Animal Instinct
11. Wisdom Of The Ages
12. Girl Happy
13. Spring Fever
14. Fort Lauderdale Chamber Of Commerce
15. Startin' Tonight
16. Wolf Call
17. Do Not Disturb
18. Cross My Heart And Hope To Die
19. The Meanest Girl In Town
20. Do The Clam
21. Puppet On A String
22. I've Got To Find My Baby

FTD brought out a remastered version of *Harum Scarum* with 14 extra tracks in 2003.

HARUM SCARUM

In the ongoing quest to find new backdrops for Elvis' Sixties movie output, he went East in this MGM movie. Elvis did all the work he needed without having to leave LA, and in just one month, starting March 15, 1965—long enough to churn through working titles *In My Harum*, *Harum Holiday* and *Harem Scarum*. The movie was released in some international markets as *Harem Holiday*.

Initially, Elvis was excited to play such a Valentinoesque role. Priscilla recounts in her memoir that Elvis returned home in full costume and make-up before his enthusiasm for the project inevitably waned.

Even Colonel Parker found this picture to be one step too far. He suggested trying to fix the

plot's unintended ridiculousness by adding a talking camel narrator (it worked for Bob Hope and Bing Crosby in *Road to Morocco*), so that people would laugh with rather than at the movie. Studio publicity owned up to the movie's spoofiness in its advertising.

To keep costs down, "King of the Quickies" producer Sam Katzman recycled scenery form Cecil B. DeMille's 1925 colossus *King Of Kings*; costumes were borrowed from *Kismet* (1944). Even Elvis' dagger had a movie pedigree (from 1939 picture *Lady of the Tropics*). Reputedly as the film looked like it was going to go over budget, Katzman simply ripped four pages out of the script.

After the movie wrapped, Elvis gave director Gene Nelson an autographed picture inscribed, "Someday we'll do it right."

Iverson Ranch near Los Angeles stood in for the Arabian desert.

Songs "Wisdom Of The Ages" and "Animal Instinct" didn't make it into the movie but survived on the soundtrack album.

None of the above seemed to have harmed the movie's initial box office receipts. Opening in time for Thanksgiving 1965, it claimed eleventh place on the *Variety* Box Office Survey, and ended the year at #40 spot among top movie grossers, generating $2 million in the US alone.

CREDITS:
MGM, Color.
Length: 95 minutes
Release date: November 24, 1965

TAGLINES:
1001 Swingin' Nights as Elvis brings the Big Beat to Baghdad in a riotous rockin' rollin' adventure spoof!!!
The golden age of romance and song!

Directed by: Gene Nelson
Written by: Gerald Drayson Adams
Produced by: Sam Katzman
Music by: Fred Karger
Cinematography by: Fred Jackman Jr.
Film Editing by: Ben Lewis
Art Direction by: H. McClure Capps, George W. Davis
Set Decoration by: Henry Grace, Don Greenwood Jr.
Costume Design by: Beau Vanden Ecker, Gene Ostler, Margo Weintz

Elvis in *Harum Scarum*, 1965.

CAST:

Elvis Presley	Johnny Tyronne
Mary Ann Mobley	Princess Shalimar
Fran Jeffries	Aishah
Michael Ansara	Prince Dragna
Jay Novello	Zacha
Phillip Reed	King Toranshah
Theodore Marcuse	Sinan
Billy Barty	Baba
Dirk Harvey	Makar
Jack Constanzo	Julna
Larry Chance	Capt. Herat
Barbara Werle	Leilah
Brenda Benet	Emerald
Gail Gilmore	Sapphire
Wilda Taylor	Amethyst
Vicki Malkin	Sari
Ryck Rydon	Mustapha
Richard Reeves	Bedouin
Joey Russo	Yussef
Red West	Assassin
Carolyn Carter	'Sands of the Desert' heroine
Suzanne Covington	Naja
Judy Durell	Cashier
Robert La Mont	President of Babalstan
Ralph Lee	Noble
Hugh Sanders	U.S. Ambassador
Maja Stewart	Princess

ADDITIONAL CREW:

Sydney Guilaroff	hair stylist
William Tuttle	makeup artist
Don L. Cash	makeup artist
Bobby Stone	unit production manager
Lindsley Parsons Jr.	assistant production manager: MGM
Eddie Saeta	assistant director
Franklin Milton	recording supervisor
Chuck Hicks	stunts
Glenn Randall Jr.	stunts
Paul Stader	stunts
Earl Barton	choreographer
The Jordanaires	vocal background singers
Fred Karger	conductor and music supervisor
Colonel Tom Parker	technical advisor

Plot:

Elvis plays Johnny Tyronne, a Hollywood matinee idol traveling through the Near East to promote *Sands of the Desert*, his latest movie. So impressive is he on screen with a sword and karate that he is invited to the secret kingdom of Lunarkand by the King's brother, Prince Dragna (played by Michael Anzara) for an audience with his royal sibling King Toranshah (played by Phillip Reed).

Johnny is kidnapped by a gang of ne'er do wells after spending an evening with the evil Aishah (Fran Jeffries); the gang of assassins want Johnny to him to work for them. To soften him up, Johnny is tempted by a harem of lovelies and then threatened by a mean fellow with a whip. Johnny bribes local thief Zacha (played by Jay Novello) to help him escape. He jumps over the palace walls but finds himself in the private apartments of Princess Shalimar (played by Mary Ann Mobley).

Shalimar takes pity on Johnny and agrees to help him escape. She rustles up some Arabian horses but then Johnny tells her that he was kidnapped as part of a plot to assassinate an important guy. Princess Shalimar realizes that her father the King is in mortal danger and rushes off to warn him.

Johnny is recaptured by the band of assassins. This time they threaten to kill everybody who helped him escape if he doesn't do as he's told. Johnny is taken prisoner once more after Princess Shalimar recognizes him at the feast celebrations. He manages to escape again, aided by his Arabian carnival pals. Johnny catches up with the Princess just as she is setting the King straight about where Johnny's real allegiances lie. They work out that the man behind the plot is the King's evil brother, Prince Dragna, who has been swayed by the offer of riches by an oil company keen to drill in their desert land.

It looks like it's too late when the King is deposed, then Johnny saves the day by vanquishing the chief of the assassins Sinan (Theodore Marcuse). The king reappears and beats his evil brother in a duel. Johnny's reward is the chance to marry the beautiful Princess Shalimar and sing about it all in Las Vegas in a show with his "harem of dancing jewels."

Songs: "Harem Holiday," "My Desert Serenade," "Go East Young Man," "Mirage," "Kismet," "Shake That Tambourine," "Hey Little Girl," "Golden Coins," "So Close Yet So Far "

"HAVA NAGILA"

Elvis sang this traditional Jewish song, but not for release . . . a version during rehearsals in the summer of 1970 only made it onto bootleg releases including *Electrifying!* and *The Cream of Culver City*.

"HAVE A HAPPY"

The last soundtrack song Elvis ever had to record (perhaps to a heavy sigh of relief) was this Ben Weisman, Buddy Kaye and Dolores Fuller tune for *Change of Habit* in on March 6, 1969 at Decca Recording Studios in Los Angeles. In the absence of a soundtrack album, it was first released on the *Let's Be Friends* budget LP in 1970 (re-released on CD in 2006). It has since appeared on *Elvis Sings for Children and Grownups Too!* (re-released as *Elvis Sings for Kids* in 2002) and the *Double Features* issue *Live A Little, Love A Little / Charro! / The Trouble With Girls / Change of Habit*.

"HAVE I TOLD YOU LATELY THAT I LOVE YOU"

Elvis recorded this much-traveled Scott Wiseman song in on January 19, 1957 at Radio Recorders for release as an album track on *Loving You*, and soon after, EP *Just For You*.

The tune was inspired by Wiseman's wife, Lulubell, when she visited him in hospital one day in 1944 and uttered the words he used for the song title. Before Elvis, it had been a hit for many performers including Gene Autry, Bing Crosby and Tex Ritter.

Elvis' version has since appeared on *The King Of Rock And Roll*, BMG and FTD *Loving You* reissues,

Four alternate takes from the recording session were released in 1989 on *Essential Elvis Vol. 2*; the master came out on the *Elvis:Close Up* collection, and an alternate found its way onto FTD release *Flashback*.

HAVING FUN WITH ELVIS ON STAGE

Released on the Boxcar label, belonging to the Colonel but manufactured by RCA's Custom Record division, this August 1974 album consists of excerpts of onstage banter from Elvis' shows after he started touring again in 1969, with the music (except for one or two false starts) rigorously stripped out to make "A Talking Album Only."

The Colonel initially sold these records at concerts. When RCA released the album in October 1974, it sold 130,000 copies, enough to creep into the charts and peak at #130.

Boxcar brought out four further volumes of *Having Fun on Stage with Elvis* onstage banter in the Nineties and Noughties. Other talk-oriented bootlegs have carried the baton too.

HAWAII

Hawaii was one of Elvis' favorite destinations for work or play. He gave high profile concerts on the island, he made three movies there and when he went on vacation, the first place he thought of was Hawaii.

Elvis' first performances in Hawaii were reputedly the result of Colonel Parker losing a bet over dice with promoter Lee Gordon. Elvis made the four-day trip to Honolulu on the USS *Matsonia* on

Elvis as Johnny Tyronne in *Harum Scarum*, 1965

ABOVE: Elvis on vacation in Hawaii, ca 1968.
LEFT: Elvis on his last vacation in Hawaii in 1977.

RIGHT: A CANDID OF ELVIS IN HAWAII IN THE 1950'S.

November 5, 1957, returning to LA eight days later on the USS *Lurline*. These were his final live performances before he was drafted into the Army.

While Elvis was away in Germany on Army duty, the Colonel suggested to Paramount producer Hal Wallis that Elvis might do very well in a Hawaii-themed picture. Wallis agreed, and put him in three (*Blue Hawaii*, *Girls! Girls! Girls!* and *Paradise, Hawaii Style*), requiring the not-so-hardship of location work on the islands. The Colonel was right that Elvis and Hawaii were a lucrative combination; he was wide of the mark, however, in his belief that Hawaiian music was set to be the next big thing after rock 'n' roll.

Elvis was as popular in Hawaii as he was on the mainland. In Spring 1962, he had to fight his way through a crowd of almost 10,000 screaming fans to get to his hotel, in the process losing his sailor's cap, diamond ring and jewel-encrusted tie clip.

Elvis, Priscilla, 3-month old Lisa Marie and a small entourage went to Hawaii on vacation for two weeks in May 1968, and then again in May 1969. Elvis returned in October 1969 on a trip paid for by the International Hotel as a reward for his sell-out engagement in Las Vegas that summer, traveling with Priscilla, Lisa Marie, Vernon and Dee, the Espositos, the Gambills and the Schillings.

Elvis topped up his tan in May 1972 prior to his Madison Square Garden shows with a trip to Hawaii on a ten-day vacation with his dad, his step-mother and a few of his pals.

After his triumphant *Aloha From Hawaii* concert in 1973, Elvis' visits to the island became more sporadic. He preferred to go to Palm Springs if he was seeking the sun, or to other vacation spots, such as Colorado. Then, in March 1977, he took his girlfriend Ginger Alden, her family and enough friends to make it a party of 38 for a vacation to Hawaii, staying first at the Hilton Rainbow Tower before heading off to rented beach houses at Kailua (Kaapauni Drive). The vacation was cut short a week or so later when Elvis sustained damage to his eye from sand.

To commemorate Elvis, a statute was unveiled outside the Honolulu International Center Arena (which has since changed name to the Neal Blaisdell Center) to mark the thirtieth anniversary of his passing.

CONCERTS

- Honolulu

Elvis performed before two full houses at the Honolulu Stadium on November 10, 1957. He played the Bloch Arena on March 26, 1961, in a specially-arranged benefit concert to raise funds for a memorial to the sailors who died on the USS *Arizona*—the event that prompted the US to enter the Second World War—supported by the Jordanaires and his Nashville studio band of the time. Recordings of the show appeared on 1980 collector's set release *Elvis Aron Presley*.

Elvis performed at the Honolulu International Center on November 17 and 18, 1972, ending an 8-date tour that month (footage is on 2006 DVD *Blue Hawaii '72*).

Elvis returned in January 1973 to make broadcast history in the world's first live satellite global broadcast, once again at the International Convention Center. His first performance on January 13, a "dress rehearsal" known later as *The Alternate Aloha*, was recorded in case anything untoward happened during the following night's show. The next evening Elvis' show was beamed around the world by satellite (with the exception of North America) in *Aloha From Hawaii via Satellite*.

- Pearl Harbor

Elvis played the Schofield Barracks on November 11, 1957, aptly performing for military families in his last concert before doing his own military service.

See also HOTELS.

CHARLIE HODGE: "Elvis used to say the people of Hawaii were among the friendliest he ever met."

MAYOR MUFI HANNEMANN: "Elvis remains an idol and a hero to so many of us. Hawaii considers him an adopted son."

Books:

Elvis In Hawaii, by Jerry Hopkins, Bess Press Inc., 2002 (also)

"HAWAIIAN SUNSET"

Regular movie songwriters Sid Tepper and Roy C. Bennett wrote this soundtrack song for Blue Hawaii, the first song that Elvis recorded at the soundtrack session for the movie on March 21, 1961 at Radio Recorders in Los Angeles.

Later outings for the song include Blue Hawaii reissues and an alternate released An alternate take came out on Elvis: Close Up in 2003. Bootleg album Plantation Rock contains features a version Elvis sang in rehearsals for his Aloha from Hawaii concert.

"HAWAIIAN WEDDING SONG"

This Blue Hawaii movie song is a traditional Hawaiian tune with English words, adapted by Charles King, Al Hoffman and Dick Manning. Elvis recorded his version at Radio Recorders on March 22, 1961 for the movie finale and accompanying soundtrack LP. The song had recently been a million-selling hit for Andy Williams, and had also been a hit for Bing Crosby ten years earlier. It has since been tracklisted on Elvis albums Command Performances, Elvis By The Presleys and Love Elvis, An alternate take—the first—from Elvis' original session came out in 2001 on FTD release Silver Screen Stereo.

Elvis serenaded new bride Priscilla with the song as he carried her over the threshold of their Palm Springs house in May 1967.

He reprised the song in Hawaii in 1973 as an add-on to his Aloha From Hawaii Via Satellite performance, re-recorded the song in the early hours of January 15, 1973, immediately after his globe-encircling satellite broadcast from Hawaii, to be inserted into the US version of Aloha From Hawaii Via Satellite (the recording didn't make it onto the soundtrack but wasn't released until 1978 on posthumous albumon ly Mahalo from Elvis). A version also exists from his dress rehearsals, which came out on the album The Alternate Aloha. In actual fact, he had tried it out half a dozen times before that live in the early Seventies.

Further live versions performed in 1974 and 1975 have appeared over the years on bootlegs and, on official releases Live in Las Vegas and on FTD issues It's Midnight, Dragonheart, Big Boss Man and Southern Nights. He sang it in 1976 and 1977 too; tThe song also features on Elvis' last concert album recorded for release in his lifetime, Elvis in Concert.

HAWKINS, HOYT

Baritone singer Hoyt Hawkins of the Jordanaires sang with Elvis from 1956 to 1970. He played piano and organ on Elvis' earliest gospel recordings, released as the Peace In The Valley EP, and Elvis' first Christmas album, and contributed tambourine to other recordings. In the late Sixties he sometimes lent a hand on piano and organ at studio sessions.

HAYS, LOWELL JR.

Owner of a jewelers at 454 South Perkins, in Memphis, which remained in the family until early 2006, Lowell Hays Jr. was Elvis' "official jeweler" from late 1970 onwards. Common friend Dr. George Nichopoulos originally took Lowell Hays to meet Elvis in the late Sixties, one evening when Elvis was getting in some shooting target practice outside Vernon's office, wearing a mink coat with a hood to keep off the rain. Elvis did his Christmas shopping in 1970 at the Memphian Theater between movies, sneaking into the bathrooms with the jeweler to pick out his purchases.

Hays designed Elvis' TCB ring and the TLC necklaces that Elvis gave out to his favorite boys and girls. Estimates of what Elvis spent on purchases from Hays over the years run as high as $1 million.

Elvis sometimes invited Lowell Hays Jr. and his wife on tour with him, a briefcase of jewelry at the ready for those must-give moments. At one concert, Hays became an improvised bodyguard and intercepted a man who had jumped on stage to attack Elvis. On another tour, Elvis bought practically Hays's entire cache of jewelry as peace offerings for female backing singers after he offended them on stage.

Hays made an engagement ring which Elvis presented to girlfriend Ginger Alden on January 26, 1977. He took the stone from Elvis' personal TCB ring because there was no time to find an identical stone, as Elvis wanted to do.

On retiring from his store, Hays intended to continue selling replicas of Elvis jewelry at.

"HE"

Never released during Elvis' life, this home recording of a Jack Richards and Richard Mullen gospel song, sung by the McGuire Sisters in the mid-Fifties, features on In A Private Moment many years after it was taped some time in 1960.

"HE IS MY EVERYTHING"

Elvis recorded this spiritual for the his He Touched Me album at RCA's Nashville studios in on June 9, 1971, three years after this Dallas Frazier modern gospel track was first laid down by Charlie Walker. It has since appeared on Elvis inspirational compilations He Walks Beside Me, including Amazing Grace, Peace In The Valley, Elvis: My Christmas #1, Christmas Peace and Elvis Inspirational. An alternate version from the original recording session came out in 2001 on FTD release Easter Special.

"HE KNOWS JUST WHAT I NEED"

In On October 30, 1960, Elvis recorded this 1955 Mosie Lister spiritual in Nashville for release on his first gospel album, His Hand In Mine. The song was one of many he sang for his own edification while away on his Army service in Germany.

"He Knows Just What I Need" is on Elvis gospel collections Amazing Grace and Peace In The Valley. Alternate takes feature on several FTD releases, including Easter Special, His Hand in Mine (half a dozen outtakes) and Fame and Fortune.

"HE TOUCHED ME"

The title track (and most the bulk of the other material) on Elvis' Grammy-winning 1972 album He Touched Me was recorded in RCA's Studio B in Nashville in May 1971—this song on May 18. The song"He Touched Me" was penned by Bill Gaither, a member of the Gospel Music Association Hall of Fame. It was released as a single with "Bosom Of Abraham" in February 1972, selling around 50,000 copies, and then on the album of the same name three months later. Ten thousand copies of the single had to be recalled because it was erroneously manufactured to be played at 33 1/3 rather than 45 RPM.

The track has since featured on compilations Amazing Grace, Peace in the Valley, Christmas Peace and Ultimate Gospel among others. Platinum: A Life In Music features an alternate take.

HE TOUCHED ME (LP)

This Grammy-winning gospel album came out in April 1972. Though initially selling fewer than 200,000 copies and failing to chart any higher than #79, it remained a strong back-catalog seller for many years.

TRACK LISTING:
1. He Touched Me
2. I've Got Confidence
3. Amazing Grace
4. Seeing Is Believing
5. He Is My Everything
6. Bosom Of Abraham
7. An Evening Prayer
8. Lead Me, Guide Me
9. There Is No God But God
10. A Thing Called Love
11. I, John
12. Reach Out To Jesus

He Touched Me is also the title of a two-volume DVD documentary of Elvis' gospel, narrated by Sander Vanocur, shown on TV, released on video in 1999 and re-released several times since then.

HE WALKS BESIDE ME

A gospel/inspirational album released by RCA the year after Elvis died, including two previously unreleased takes. It peaked at #113 in the Billboard general album chart, and made it into the top ten on the Country chart.

TRACK LISTING:
1. He Is My Everything
2. Miracle Of The Rosary
3. Where Did They Go Lord?
4. Somebody Bigger Than You And I
5. An Evening Prayer
6. The Impossible Dream
7. If I Can Dream
8. Padre
9. Known Only To Him
10. Who Am I?
11. How Great Thou Art

"HE'LL HAVE TO GO"

An album track on Elvis' final album, Moody Blue, written by Joe and Audrey Allison and first sung by Billy Brown in 1959 (Jim Reeves took it to #2 that same year). Elvis probably couldn't have chosen a more poignant title for the final song he ever completed at a studio session, at Graceland on the night of October 30, 1976. A rough mixn alternate came out on 2000 FTD release The Jungle Room Sessions. The tune has also appeared on anthology Walk A Mile In My Shoes on and country compilations Great Country Songs and The Country Side of Elvis.

"HE'S YOUR UNCLE, NOT YOUR DAD"

A hotchpotch of a soundtrack song by Sid Wayne and Ben Weisman, written for Speedway and recorded by Elvis in on June 21, 1967 at MGM's studios in Culver City—at least, the instrumental track was. By this time, Elvis was had long since taken to overdubbing his vocals. Since the sound-track LP, the song has only come out on the *Double Feature* release, and presumably on the later FTD release.

HEALTH

To wear out a body by the age of forty-two takes some doing. Elvis succeeded through high living and abuse of prescription drugs that stemmed—paradoxically—from a strongly-held belief that whatever ailed him, modern medicine had a pharmaceutical cure.

Considering the fast-paced life he led for all of his adult years, Elvis remained in reasonably good health until his mid-thirties. His increased drug intake coincided with (but was not wholly moti-vated by) a welter of niggling health problems for which he needed medication.

Elvis' final years were more a succession of ups and downs than a straight-line decline. When he was in good spirits, Elvis could still be kingly on stage even in his final year alive. When he was down, his life was ruled by the pharmaceuticals he took to get him through the day, until unwant-ed side effects or excessive prescription drug con-sumption forced him into hospital. Dr. Nichopoulos has always maintained that he tried to get Elvis to make changes to his life, to reduce the stress that prompted him to seek chemical assistance, all to little effect.

As a child, there were times when Elvis' family didn't have money to buy medicines and had to resort to folk remedies. Elvis suffered a serious bout of tonsillitis when he was a kid. Years later, Vernon told a reporter that he and Gladys prayed to God to save their child. Young Elvis often caught colds, and suffered from bad bouts of asthma—so bad that neighbors recall him rubbing his back against trees to try and scratch the asthmatic itch.

When he began touring in 1954, Elvis began a lifestyle where healthy living was the least of his priorities. Food and sleep were optionals, to be grabbed where and when possible. A young and healthy Elvis survived for many months on a pun-ishing schedule before finally collapsing with exhaustion in early 1956 after a concert in Jacksonville. Despite the doctor's advice to slow down, Elvis was back on stage the following day.

In 1956, as part of a March of Dimes health campaign, Elvis was inoculated with the newly-developed Salk anti-polio vaccine.

In June 1957, Elvis was admitted to the Cedars of Lebanon Hospital in LA during the filming of *Jailhouse Rock* to remove a capped tooth after he aspirated it filming the dance sequence. Characteristically, he sent a letter of thanks to the staff: "I want you to know how very much I appreciate your very wonderful treatment while I was there. When I went in I was all shook up but I left loving you."

Elvis had his draft pre-induction physical at the Kennedy Veterans Hospital in Memphis, where Captain Leonard Glick gave him a clean bill of health.

During his time in Germany, Elvis hurt a knee when thrown from a jeep, and was ordered to take three days' rest. He spent six days in hospital in Frankfurt in early June for tonsillitis and a high fever. He returned to the 97th General Hospital, Frankfurt, in October with the same complaint after going off on maneuvers and sleeping out on frozen ground. Priscilla writes in her memoir that on one occasion when he was taken to hospital for tonsillitis it was to get out of such maneuvers; in hospital, she watched him use a lighter to ensure that the thermometer registered a high tempera-ture. Billy Smith has a different recollection: that one of the times Elvis was in hospital in Germany for tonsillitis was because of carbon monoxide poi-soning after Elvis and others rigged up a home-made heater for their jeep out on maneuvers.

Elvis gave blood for the German Red Cross—his blood type was "O"—and had a second Salk polio inoculation in 1959 as part of the March of Dimes campaign.

Back from the Army, Elvis was in the wars. He damaged a hand doing karate workouts on the set of *G.I. Blues* but had to go through with the love scene anyway. He broke a finger in 1960 playing (heavy) touch football at Graceland. His worst health problems in the early Sixties were the result of boisterous scrapes and bruises, mostly his own doing from overenthusiastic football, karate, firework wars and nights out power-skating or at the Memphis Fairgrounds. He had to have stitch-es in a cut above his eye after a fight scene went wrong in *Roustabout* (1964).

By the mid-Sixties, friends noted that Elvis' enthusiasm for what he did for a living was on the wane. For the first time, he missed recording ses-sions by calling in sick with a cold, only to make good a couple of days later with overdubs. Priscilla recalls in her memoir that he was prescribed anti-depressants after he began to spend days on end in his room. In recent years, it has been speculated that Elvis suffered from bipolar disorder.

Jerry Schilling recalls in his memoir that in 1964, Elvis occasionally used an oxygen mask.

Some of Elvis' health-related absences from Hollywood were because he just didn't feel like going in to work. On *Harum Scarum*, he offered to call in sick to help under-pressure director Gene Nelson (and allow him extra time for script rewrites). Elvis admitted to Nelson, "I can get sick in such a hurry you'd be surprised."

Elvis suffered various minor horse riding-relat-ed ailments on his ranch in 1967, not least saddle soreness, the first ailment for which long-term physician Doctor Nichopoulos treated him. He also dislocated cartilage in his chest when Red West rode past and knocked him over.

He sustained minor concussion when he tripped over a TV cord in the bathroom at his rented LA rented home that spring, delaying the start of filming on *Clambake*. Not only did this cost two weeks of expensive thumb-twiddling for the studio, it brought the Colonel rushing in to sort out what he perceived as the bad influences in Elvis life. Larry Geller, ousted from the entourage soon after, suspects that Elvis was kept under seda-tion, possibly given narcotic drugs, and that his increased reliance on medication may be traced back to the aftermath of this incident.

Elvis had to miss a night or two of his record-ing session at American in Memphis in early 1969 due to laryngitis.

When Elvis paid an impromptu house call on President Nixon at the White House in late 1970, he had an allergic reaction to penicillin he was taking for an eye infection, and/or from excess consumption of chocolate, which appar-ently brought him out in a rash.

Elvis began to suffer from repeated and nig-gling health problems from 1971. His winter engagements at the International Hotel in the early Seventies were increasingly blighted by bouts of flu. Never wanting to disappoint his fans, Elvis played on. Some of his Las Vegas shows in the winter of 1971 were reduced to just half an hour to preserve his voice.

Elvis was hospitalized in March 1971 after just one day of a recording session in Nashville, when Dr. Nick and consultant ophthalmologist Dr. David Meyer recommended he should go to the Baptist Hospital to treat his iritis and secondary glaucoma. For weeks, Elvis recounted how he had to have a cortisone injection right into the eye-ball, without anesthetic. He went for follow-up treatment at the Memphis Eye and Ear Hospital.

Elvis had to cancel some shows in Las Vegas in the summer of 1971 due to throat problems. ENT specialist Dr. Sidney Boyer helped him back to sufficient health to complete the engagement, and received a brand new Lincoln Continental for his trouble.

Candid photo of Elvis with a broken finger in the 1960's.

That summer, the Colonel, Vernon and Priscilla all told Elvis that he needed to take better care of himself. Rather than alter his lifestyle, Elvis developed a superstitious reliance on various shots and concoctions before and after going on stage, including regular B-12 shots from personal physician Dr. Nichopoulos, in the belief that the vitamin would boost his energy levels.

Elvis had an ankle support fitted at the Baptist Memorial Hospital in Memphis in the summer of 1972. There were times that year when he was seeing doctors as frequently as five times a day—an addiction to medicine as much as to the "helpers" medicine prescribed.

He suffered recurring flu and bouts of laryngitis throughout his winter 1973 tenure at the Las Vegas Hilton. When not slowed by a virus, reviewers described Elvis as listless and disaffected. Against doctors' advice, the show went on, though as a concession Elvis performed once rather than twice nightly. One evening, he substituted the words "I wish I was in the Doctor's office" for "I wish I was in Dixie" during "An American Trilogy." He did miss a few nights of this engagement—up until then, a rarity for Elvis. On another night, , he took a break mid-show when he completely lost his voice due to congestion. Ministrations from Dr. Boyer allowed him to return to the stage. After this event, Elvis saw Dr. Boyer on a regular basis to clear congestion from his throat before he per-formed in Las Vegas, alongside his new regular Las Vegas general doctor, Elias Ghanem.

During his May 1973 engagement at Stateline, Nevada, ill-health once again caused Elvis to cancel shows, though at least one entourage member suspects that Elvis feigned illness because he did not want to perform. By this time, the Colonel and Vernon were sufficiently alarmed by his reliance on prescription medicine to hire private investigator John O' Grady to try and find out where Elvis was getting his supplies from. Whatever channels they succeeded in shut-ting down, Elvis found other ways to obtain the medicines he wanted.

Elvis' erratic behavior prompted by heavy pre-scription drug intake short-circuited Elvis' recording session at Stax in the summer of 1973. Soon afterwards, he checked in to Baptist Hospital in Memphis. On this and other stays in hospital, Dr. Nichopoulos strove to keep Elvis' addiction to prescription drugs off his medical charts so that they did not leak out into the public domain.

Elvis fractured a finger on his left hand doing karate practice in September 1973, not long after finishing up at the Las Vegas Hilton for the summer.

Eye problems caused by auditorium lighting and hair dye running caused Elvis pain when he was on stage, and caused recurring conjunctivitis. He continued to suffer eye problems and deteriorating general health in the fall of 1973. As he shuttled between Palm Springs, Memphis and LA, he consulted a growing team of doctors about his various ailments, some of which were exacerbated by a diet regime prescribed to Elvis by one of his California doctors, involving shots of Novocaine, Demerol, cortisone and B-12. This "treatment" left Elvis bloated, addicted to Demerol and prey to breathing difficulties. Dr. Nichopoulos persuaded Elvis to go into hospital to undergo detoxification, substituting Demerol with Methadone. After this ordeal, Elvis spent two and a half months recuperating at home, on a reduced drug regime administered by Dr. Nick. Even then, Elvis was capable of getting "extras" through entourage members or household staff.

To cap of a bad health year, Elvis had to have surgery for an ingrown toenail on Christmas Eve. Nineteen seventy-four began with ongoing foot problems and multiple visits to the dentist. Elvis also suffered a throat ailment, going to see his long-term West Coast ENT specialist Dr. Kantor in LA in February 1974, before embarking on a three-week sweep through Southern states on his first tour in five months.

That year he had a liver biopsy, which he described to a bemused audience in Las Vegas during one of his more colorful monologues. His adrenal glands had sustained damage by this time, and required ongoing treatment with cortisone.

After a grueling touring schedule, in October 1974 Elvis checked in with Las Vegas doctor Elias Ghanem. The doctor, who had a special wing of his house for celebrity patients, diagnosed Elvis with a non-penetrating ulcer crater and recommended bed rest and a liquid diet—the doctor referred to this cure as his "sleep diet." Elvis returned for a second dose of this treatment six weeks later, accompanied by Linda Thompson and Charlie Hodge. In the meantime, after Elvis experienced breathing difficulties, Doctor Nichopoulos sent a nurse to look after him at Graceland, and then decided to hospitalize him for two weeks at Baptist Memorial.

Over the Christmas holidays, the Colonel took the decision to call the Las Vegas Hilton and cancel Elvis' winter 1975 engagement, partly because of his medical condition, partly because he had been getting reports from members of the entourage that Elvis had been behaving unreasonably and erratically.

Elvis had a genetic weakness, known as a ganglionic fold, where the colon is weaker than usual. His bowel problems were initially caused by this problem, and then were exacerbated by his regimen of drugs. In 1975 Dr. Nichopoulos tried but failed to find somebody to give Elvis a partial colostomy to resolve the problem.

Not surprisingly, Elvis grew despondent about his bloated appearance and his continued bouts of poor health. His throat was a constant weak spot, with a build up of catarrh that threatened his voice. A big believer in injections, Elvis persuaded Dr. Nick to administer decongestants by injection because he thought that shots worked better. Dr. Nichopoulos later said, "It was difficult trying to get away from giving him shots all the time." In later years, part of Elvis' pre-concert warm-up was a shot of something to make sure that he didn't suffer from "desert throat," a particular problem in Vegas.

Elvis was rushed to hospital with breathing difficulties on the night of January 29, 1975. Public statements described his hospitalization as caused by "liver problems"; though these may have been present, once again his breathing difficulties were likely prescription-medicine related—the Wests describe a number of times when Elvis went into breathing spasms after taking medication. Linda Thompson stayed with him in hospital once more; to while away the two weeks' bed rest, they watched the newborn babies in the nursery ward via closed circuit television.

Lamar Fike says that in some of his most addled moments, Elvis engaged in self-mutilation, picking away at a wound until it got infected as an excuse to obtain more medication.

Once again that summer, Elvis' regular slot at the Las Vegas Hilton was cut short because he was in no physical condition to perform. He got through his opening show by sitting down for most of it. The engagement was called off after three days, officially because of a "fatigue state." The Colonel refused to go out and cancel the show on the last evening at the last minute because the audience was already seated in the auditorium; he suggested Elvis get Vernon to do it—knowing that this would make Elvis go on. The last thing Elvis ever wanted to do was disappoint his fans, even if performing took an immediate physical toll. His glaucoma played up under the lights, and his high blood pressure meant that when he came off stage he immediately had to lie down with cold packs on his eyes for an hour. He also started suffering from arthritis in the neck and upper back.

Back in Memphis, Elvis checked in to the Baptist Memorial Hospital for another two weeks—he told a concerned Priscilla that he was just getting some rest. During his stay, tests were carried out on his chronic intestinal ailments, high cholesterol, and depression. When he returned home, Dr. Nick's nurse Tish Henley alternated with two nurses from hospital, Marion Cocke and Kathy Seamon, to make sure that Elvis had 24-hour home care. Dr. Nick told Elvis that the nurse was a precaution not so much for him but for his father and grandmother, who had also been ill. Even after he had recuperated and returned to touring, Elvis retained Cocke's services as a night nurse.

Out on tour in 1976, Elvis' lack of energy was evident to his band members. Ronnie Tutt ruefully recalls, "There were nights he was so tired or so down I felt like I had to physically hit the drums much, much harder than I had before."

When private investigator John O'Grady, who had worked with Elvis for the best part of a decade, saw him perform at the Sahara Tahoe in the spring of 1976 he was shocked at the bad shape he was in: "He was fat. He had locomotive attacks where he couldn't walk . . . I really thought he was going to die."

Albert Goldman writes that Elvis was forced to wear diapers in his later years, as a result of incontinence caused by his prescription drug abuse. This has been disputed by Dr. Nichopoulos, who says that the only time Elvis had "accidents" was when he was self-medicating and too sedated to get out of bed. This stopped when Dr. Nichopoulos took control over Elvis' medication, administering and dispensing throughout the day.

A side-effect of the ACTH cortisone Elvis took to help his adrenal glands was puffiness and general fluid in the body. In later life Elvis suffered from Type 2 diabetes, triggered by his steroid intake. He had to take regular medicine for this in addition to medication for mild hypertension and glaucoma.

Elvis performed in Las Vegas in December that year despite having damaged his ankle in a fall. The *Memphis Press-Scimitar*'s review of his final evening included the prophetic sentence, "One walks away wondering how much longer it can be before the end comes." By now, Elvis had to contend with serious liver problems—the organ was

three times normal size and not functioning properly—as well as his long-term digestive disorder that was exacerbated by his drug consumption.

Nevertheless, in the fall of 1976, Elvis told Red West that his health was in excellent shape, and that he had recently had a head-to-toe physical for an insurance policy with Lloyds of London. According to George Klein, "I don't think Elvis really knew how sick he was. I don't think anybody knew. We knew he wasn't in the greatest of health, but we had no earthly idea that he was as sick as he was." Larry Geller, on the other hand, believes that Elvis knew how serious his condition was. He checked into the Baptist Hospital for a few days' observation in early 1977, but refused to undergo any invasive testing, according to Geller because he sensed that he was near the end and wanted to go.

Elvis began 1977 in good spirits with new girlfriend Ginger Alden. Friends noticed greater vim and energy when she was around, though he was despondent when she refused to accompany him on tour.

Elvis' health improved in March 1977 when he took Ginger Alden and some pals to Hawaii, though he was forced to cut short this final vacation when sand damaged his eye. As soon as he went back out on tour, he was back on his punishing pharmaceutical regimen. He had to reschedule a number of shows in the spring of 1977 due to ill-health.

When it came, Elvis' death—officially from coronary arrhythmia—came as a shock and a surprise. Several Elvis insiders later said that they thought Elvis was suffering from terminal cancer. Larry Geller claims that Elvis' death spared him the agony of leukemia, which he didn't know he had. This diagnosis would explain his fatigue, pain and bruising. Kathy Westmoreland has said that Elvis told her in his last year that he had been diagnosed with bone cancer (she has also said that he suffered this for many years, and that though it had metastasized, it did not kill him). In *Elvis: His Life from A-Z*, Fred Worth and Steve Tamarius write that Dr. Nichopoulos told several of Elvis' close friends that he had suffered already three heart attacks before the final fatal cardiac arrest; Kathy Westmoreland has said that Elvis had a congenital heart condition (one lobe of his heart was twice normal size) and in addition to his other health conditions, he suffered from seizures that gave the appearance of being drunk.

After his death, an employee at the hospital where Elvis was taken for his autopsy described his arteries as those of an 80 year-old man: "His body was just worn out."

ELVIS AS THERAPY

Elvis' music and his readiness to send personal messages and visit fans suffering from health problems was of great succor to many. A Mental Health Institute in Davenport, Iowa, played his early recordings for therapeutic purposes, and reported that his music helped patients "get back in step with the world."

Elvis' correspondence with a Swedish cerebral palsy sufferer called Karen was turned into a book and a movie, *Touched by Love*. Many more fans were touched by Elvis' kindness and attentiveness.

HEALING HANDS

Elvis combined a belief in the power of medication with a belief in the power of healing energy through meditation. He was convinced that he inherited from his mother the ability to heal by laying on hands, Elvis demonstrated these powers on various members of his entourage, who have said that whatever Elvis did, it made a difference. In 1974, Elvis went to the home of a waiter who served him in his suite at the Las Vegas Hilton to lay hands on his wife, who was suffering from cancer. It was this man, Mario, who was fired by Hilton management for breaking hotel rules regarding staff fraternization with VIP guests, and whom Elvis defended on stage in his tirade against the Hilton management that so upset the Colonel.

Elvis was far less successful in healing himself, though his body's ability to withstand the onslaught of prescription medicines for so long may have been as much as he could have hoped for.

ELVIS SAID IN APRIL 1977: "The spirit is willing, but the flesh is weak."

LAMAR FIKE: "Elvis was in the hospital five times in the last seven years. It was always for detox, but it was under the guise of other things."

GEORGE KLEIN: "Elvis, when he'd be feeling sick, he'd have to go out and perform in front of fifteen thousand people... He went on the stage many times sick as a dog, with a bad cold or the flu or a sore throat. He hated to disappoint his fans."

DR. NICHOPOULOS: "I think Elvis was like so many people who have alcohol or drug problems. I think that most of these people have the ability to rationalize and feel like they have control of the situation, that they can start and stop it whenever they want to. Therefore, they don't feel like they are addicted."

Books:

I Called Him Babe: Elvis Presley's Nurse Remembers, by Marian J. Cocke, Memphis State University Press, 1979.

Health and Happiness Elvis Style: Building a better planet through Elvisness, by Kristi Weldon, BookSurge Publishing, 2007.

HEARN, BARBARA
(B. 1937)

A girlfriend of Elvis' from back home in Memphis in 1956, whom he had known since his school days. Hearn traveled with Elvis and Nick Adams in September 1956 to Tupelo, where Elvis appeared at the Mississippi-Alabama Fair and Dairy Show. She is said to have made him the gold lame' vest he wore on his final "Ed Sullivan Show" appearance.

"HEART OF ROME"

B-side ballad to "I'm Leavin'," released in June 1971, featuring geographically-incorrect pseudo-Mexican horns. The single failed to find enough buyers to make it into the charts. Elvis recorded the song in Nashville on June 6, 1970. The original album release on *Love Letters from Elvis* was stripped of the overdubs. The song was wWritten by Geoff Stephens, Alan Blaikley and Ken Howard, Elvis' version of the song has since appeared on the *Walk A Mile In My Shoes* anthology .

An alternate first take came out on 2002 FTD album *The Nashville Marathon*; a bawdy rehearsal version of the song is on bootleg *The Brightest Star on Sunset Boulevard.*

"HEARTBREAK HOTEL"

Written by Mae Boren Axton and Tommy Durden, Elvis' first single for RCA was famously inspired by an article about a man who killed himself after leaving a suicide note with the chill-ing words "I walk a lonely street." Durden or Axton (the more commonly cited) spotted the piece in a Miami newspaper, titled "Do You Know This Man?" The duo's regular songwriting partner Glenn Reeves was much less taken by the premise and went out to buy some provisions. By the time he returned half an hour later, Axton and Durden had finished the song.

Axton was so sure that the song was a winner that she presented it to Elvis' then manager, Bob Neal, as Elvis' "first million-seller." When Axton played Elvis the demo in Nashville, at the annual Disc Jockey Convention, Elvis agreed. Axton clinched the deal with the sweetener of a songwriting credit (and a third of writers' royalties) if he picked the song as his first release for new label RCA. She was not bluffing when she told Elvis this would be worth enough money to take his folks for a vacation by the ocean—which Elvis saw for the first time from the hotel where Axton put him up in Jacksonville earlier in 1955. When the money came through, Elvis took his parents for that ocean-view trip, and invited Axton and her kids along too.

The first time Elvis performed the song is likely to have been in Swifton, Arkansas, in December 1955, when he announced it as his first hit. "Heartbreak Hotel" was the second song he recorded (after "I Got A Woman") at his first ever RCA session in Nashville on January 10, 1956. Apart from some typical Elvis vocal mannerisms, his rendition is said not to differ greatly from the Glenn Reeves' demo.

RCA's attempt to replicate Sam Phillips' famed Sun echo effect by using the stairwell as an echo chamber was less than successful. According to biographer Donald Clarke, "The sound quality of that first session was not good . . . It was a disgraceful recording for 1956 but a good song for Presley." Sam Phillips went so far as to describe the result as a "morbid mess," while Steve Sholes' bosses at RCA suggested recording the whole thing over again.

RCA started shipping the "Heartbreak Hotel" single on January 27, 1956, with "I Was The One" on the B-side. *Billboard* described the single as "a strong blues item wrapped up in his usual powerful style and a great beat." It didn't appear in the charts until March 3, and then began a slow but steady climb to #1, where it stayed for eight weeks (seventeen weeks at #1 in the country chart). "Heartbreak Hotel" also made it to #5 on the R 'n' B chart, and was the title track for an EP released in April 1956.

Sales picked up after Elvis' performance of the song on CBS's "Stage Show," on February 11, 1956. When Elvis first played the song on his regular Louisiana Hayride slot on February 25, 1956, the crowd went wilder than it had done for any Elvis song before

The single sold a million copies within two months of release. The next time Elvis was in Nashville to record a new single for RCA, he was presented with a gold record, in a moment preserved for posterity by photographer Don Cravens. Though it was already #1, Elvis' first smash hit was introduced as "Heartbreak Motel" by an ill-informed hometown announcer at the Ellis Auditorium in Memphis in May 1956 (in the Seventies, Elvis once spoofed his own song title as "Holiday Inn").

Elvis performed what was to become the biggest-selling single of 1956 on the "Milton Berle Show" and the "Ed Sullivan Show."

"Heartbreak Hotel" has a rightful place on just about every Elvis compilation ever released—a selection includes *Elvis' Golden Records Vol. 1, Worldwide 50 Gold Award Hits Vol. 1, The Top Ten Hits, Elvis: A Legendary Performer Vol. 1, This Is Elvis, The Great Performances, The King Of Rock And Roll, Elvis '56, Artist Of The Century, ELVIS 30 #1 Hits, Hitstory, Elvis By The Presleys, Elvis Rock,* and *The Essential Elvis Presley.*

The song has been a live favorite since the first

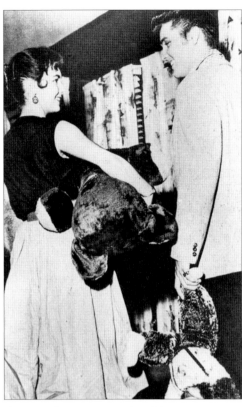

Elvis with Barbara Hearn in Memphis, 1950's.

time that Elvis sang it before a live audience. The cornocupia of live "Heartbreak Hotels" starts in Feburary 1956 and run right through to 1977. As well as various independent Hayride releases, early period live performances may be found on *A Golden Celebration* (which has six pre-Army live performances, including TV recordings from "Stage Show," "The Milton Berle Show" and "The Ed Sullivan Show," and from Elvis' homecoming at The Mississippi/Alabama Fair And Dairy Show, which more recently came out on independent release *Memphis Recording Service*), *The King Of Rock 'n' Roll, Elvis Aron Presley* (a 1956 Las Vegas performance and his 1961 Hawaii benefit show),, *Live In Las Vegas* and *Today Tomorrow & Forever.* The "Stage Show" performance was recently issued on the *Elvis #1 Hit Performances* DVD.

Elvis' NBC Special period is amply-represented with a variety of versions on *Memories: The '68 Comeback Special, Tiger Man,* the original *Elvis NBC TV Special* release, its later deluxe reissue, and FTD release *Burbank '68*—the song kicked off his oldies medley in the TV show.

Elvis played the song consistently in live shows from 1969 to 1973, and reasonably regularly thereafter. Live performances are immortalized on *Viva Las Vegas* (the 2007 release), *Collectors Gold, Live In Las Vegas* (multiple version), *The Live Greatest Hits,* the *That's The Way It Is* and *Elvis on Tour* documentaries (and various associated album releases for the former), *Walk A Mile In My Shoes, Elvis:Close Up, An Afternoon In The Garden, Elvis As Recorded At Madison Square Garden* and on FTD issues *Elvis At The International, Writing For The King, All Shook Up, The Way It Was, Summer Festival, Dragonheart, Southern Nights* and *Spring Tours '77.*

Alternate takes from the original recording session have found their way onto *Platinum: A Life In Music, Elvis '56* and FTD issues *Flashback* and *Elvis Presley.* The Glenn Reeves demo was re-exhumed for 2006 FTD release *Writing for the King.* An Elvis rehearsal of the song from 1972 has surfaced on *ELVIS 30 #1 Hits* (2 CD Edition), after a sneak preview for collectors a year earlier on FTD release *Elvis 6363 Sunset.*

Covers of the song started to come out within

months of its initial release, including a parody version by Stan Freberg and a cover by vocal group The Cadets. Other notable covers are by John Cale, a Willie Nelson / Leon Russell duet, Lynyrd Skynrd and Guns' N' Roses. In 1984, mockumentary band Spinal Tap assayed a barbershop version of this song at Elvis' Graceland grave.

In 1995, the song was elected into the Grammy Hall of Fame.

A special CD single was released to commemorate the fortieth anniversary of this seminal track in 1996, with two versions of the song plus two versions of "I Was The One."

To mark its fiftieth anniversary, in January 2006 BMG released "Heartbreak Hotel," a 3-track CD single that reclaimed the #1 spot in the Billboard chart 50 years on. Commemorative reissues are likely to continue well into the 21st century. off the medley on Elvis' 1968 NBC TV, and 1970 documentary Elvis: That's The Way It Is. "Heartbreak Hotel" was an obligatory part of his Seventies live performances. Alternate takes from the original recording session have found their way onto Platinum: A Life In Music, Elvis '56 and FTD issues Flashback and Elvis Presley among others. The Glenn Reeves demo saw the light of day on 2006 FTD release Writing for the King. Covers of the song started to come out within months of the song's initial release, including a parody version by Stan Freberg and a cover by vocal group The Cadets. Other notable covers are by John Cale, a Willie Nelson / Leon Russell duet, Lynyrd Skynrd and Guns' N' Roses. In 1984, mockumentary band Spinal Tap assayed a barbershop version of this song at Elvis' Graceland grave.

In 1995, the song was elected into the Grammy Hall of Fame.

A special CD single was released to commemorate the fortieth anniversary of this seminal track in 1996, with two versions of the song plus two versions of "I Was The One."

To mark its fiftieth anniversary, in January 2006 BMG released "Heartbreak Hotel," a 3-track CD single that reclaimed the #1 spot in the Billboard chart 50 years on.s

"Heartbreak Hotel" is on just about every Elvis compilation ever released. Over fifty versions of the track have made it onto disc over the years, including the big-band version.

JOHN PEEL: "It might sound pretty safe now but in the context of what was happening in the 1950s, hearing Heartbreak Hotel was as shocking as if someone was dancing naked in your living room."

HEARTBREAK HOTEL

RCA released the Heartbreak Hotel EP in late April 1956. Evidently the public was too busy buying the single to bother with the EP. Only "Money Honey" made it into the charts, never climbing above #76, as the title track peaked in the pop charts.

TRACK LISTING:
1. Heartbreak Hotel
2. I Was The One
3. Money Honey
4. I Forgot To Remember To Forget

HEARTBREAK HOTEL, MEMPHIS

Directly across from Graceland on Elvis Presley Boulevard in Memphis, this 128-room "boutique hotel" has long been a favorite with Elvis fans. Nowhere else in the world offers 24-hour Elvis videos. At the time of writing, Elvis Presley Enterprises were considering plans to redevelop the site.

"HEARTS OF STONE"

Written by Rudy Jackson, recorded initially by The Jewels in 1954 but more successfully released by The Charms, Elvis performed this song at live shows in late 1954 and 1955. Elvis' version appeared on 1999 album Sunrise; it is also on 2006 import issue The Complete Sun Sessions, several and on many Louisiana Hayride compilations and Memphis Recording Service Vol. 2.

HEBLER, DAVE
(B. 1937)

Dave Hebler is a karate instructor who worked with Ed Parker in the Seventies, and took part in a public demonstration with Elvis and others at the Tennessee Karate Institute in September 1974. He first met Elvis through Parker in 1972, when Elvis visited his karate school in LA. Both Elvis and Hebler were going through divorce proceedings at the time, and hit it off immediately. Elvis hired Hebler to help with security. Elvis gave Hebler a Mercedes sports car soon after they met, and a Lincoln Continental Mark IV Coupe in the summer of 1975.

Hebler remained on Elvis' payroll until July 1976, when he was dismissed with long-time entourage members Red and Sonny West. Hebler had been involved in some heavy-handed bodyguarding that had resulted in several law suits being brought against Elvis.

Elvis later told Red West that Hebler had been a negative influence within the entourage, describing him as "undermining and sneaky." Hebler joined the West cousins in writing the best-selling book Elvis: What Happened?

More recently, Hebler was involved in a minor controversy after auctioning off a shirt he had claimed Elvis wore in Tupelo in 1956. The purchaser, UK TV personality Frank Sinner, paid £28,000 for the item, and evidently decided to recoup his investment by making a TV show about the history of the shirt, during which discovered that the item was not genuine. When Hebler met with Skinner, he claimed that Elvis had duped him about the origins of the shirt.

In late 2005, the Kenpo Karate Grandmaster helped to launch a program promoting self-defense for women.

"HELP ME"

Elvis recorded this country-tinged flavored spiritual in on December 12, 1973 at Stax Studios in Memphis, for initial release as the B-side to "If You Talk in Your Sleep" in May 1974. Written by Larry Gatlin, the song was first a hit for Kris Kristofferson a year before Elvis' version made it to #6 on the Billboard country chart.

Elvis added the song to his live repertoire throughout 1974, and continued to sing it, to a lesser extent, during his final years.

A live version appears on Elvis Recorded Live On Stage In Memphis.;T the studio version first made its LP debut appeared on 1975 album on Promised Land, since when it has appeared on Amazing Grace, Ultimate Gospel and Elvis Inspirational.. Both versions are on 2000 compilation Peace in the Valley.

A track Elvis sang in concert from 1974 to 1977, fFurther live versions may found on Live in Las Vegas and on FTD albums I Found My Thrill, Live in LA, Southern Nights, Tucson '76 and Spring Tours '77.

"HELP ME MAKE IT THROUGH THE NIGHT"

Elvis gave this Kris Kristofferson country ballad the works in RCA's Nashville studio in on May 17, 1971. A Grammy winner for Kristofferson and for Sammi Smith, Elvis' version of the song

was released as track one on the Elvis Now album in 1972 (and later appeared on Welcome to My World). Posthumous album appearances include The Country Side of Elvis.

Rejected studio takes have featured on 1996 album Great Country Songs and 2007 FTD release I Sing All Kinds. A studio rehearsal prior to the Elvis On Tour documentary was released on 2004 FTD album Elvis On Tour—The Rehearsals. Elvis sang the song in concert every now and then through the Seventies: (official releases include are to be found on FTD discs Takin' Tahoe Tonight, Closing Night, Southern Nights, Dinner At Eight, and Tucson '76).

HENDRICKSON, ALTON

A hard-working studio guitarist with a jazz background who played on several of Elvis' LA soundtrack recording sessions between 1962 and 1965. Hendrickson's work features on records as diverse as The Monkees and "Moon River."

HENLEY, LETETIA "TISH"

A nurse who worked for Dr. Nichopoulos, Henley moved in to live in a trailer behind Graceland so that she could give Elvis better round-the-clock care in the Seventies. She sometimes also traveled with Elvis on tour. Tish's name appears on the eternal flame in the Meditation Garden at Graceland where Elvis is buried, along with the name of her husband Tommy, a former Deputy Sheriff who sometimes helped with security at Graceland.

HENSLEY, TOMMY

A bass player who sang with Voice, Hensley was on hand for the Elvis recording session held at his Palm Springs home in September 1973, which yielded a couple of tracks for the Raised on Rock album.

"HERE COMES SANTA CLAUS (RIGHT DOWN SANTA CLAUS LANE)"

Elvis recorded this 1947 Gene Autry tune at a Radio Recorders session in on September 6,1957. The track came out on Elvis' first festive album, Elvis' Christmas Album, and soon after on the Christmas with Elvis EP. In recent years the song has been re-released on been re-released on updated versions of Elvis' Christmas Album,albums If Every Day Was Like Christmas, The King Of Rock And Roll, Christmas Peace and Elvis Christmas.

HEROES

In addition to childhood comic books heroes, musical influences and favorite actors that Elvis adopted as a model for his own career ambitions, once he became a performer Elvis' admiration turned to the few entertainers who had made as big a splash as he.

One such hero was Rudolph Valentino, the ultimate male sex symbol of the Twenties. Elvis enjoyed the prospect of making 1965 movie Harum Scarum because one of Valentino's most famous roles had been his 1921 silent movie The Sheik. Elvis was a great fan of world-famous Italian tenor Enrico Caruso (1873-1921); he collected Caruso recordings and watched his biopic, The Great Caruso, many times. Not quite coincidentally, when Walter Matthau sarcastically introduces Elvis' character before his performance of "Trouble" in King Creole, he nicknames him "Caruso, the busboy."

Elvis had a great deal of admiration for that original showman of bling, Liberace.

Elvis with Liberace during their 1956 meeting.

His lifelong love of gospel explains the number of gospel quartet singers whom Elvis considered to be heroes, from J.D. Sumner to Jake Hess and "Big Chief" Witherspoon. Elvis worked with the majority of these men over the course of his career.

Over the years, in interviews Elvis was lavish in his praise of a great number of fellow singers. Among his contemporaries, Elvis thought so highly of Roy Orbison that he didn't cover anything that Orbison recorded. When Elvis did record material originally sung by his pre-fame favorites, he always did his utmost to improve on the original. If he failed to achieve this in the studio, his instinct was to put the song aside and move on to something else.

Outside the world of entertainment, Elvis' heroes included Generals MacArthur and Patton. When he found out that World War II General Omar Bradley, who had fought with Patton, was a near neighbor in Bel Air, Elvis went round to make his acquaintance, and visited with him a number of times. He also cited J. Edgar Hoover as a personal hero.

A lengthy list of latter-day musicians have cited Elvis as a hero. The raw energy of his early rock 'n' roll was the spark that ignited many a rock career in the Sixties, Seventies and beyond. Elvis was—and remains—a hero to millions of his fans.

ELVIS SAID: "I admire anybody that's good, regardless of what kind of singer they are."

LINDA THOMPSON: "Probably the most valuable lesson that I derived from my time with Elvis is that there are no real heroes in life.... we are all subject to human fallibility. It wasn't fair to Elvis to put him up on a pedestal and not expect him to be human."

DAVID BOWIE: "Elvis was a major hero of mine. I was probably stupid enough to believe that having the same birthday as him actually meant something."

EDDIE MURPHY: "That's my idol, Elvis Presley. If you went to my house, you'd see pictures all over of Elvis. He's just the greatest entertainer that ever lived. And I think it's because he had such presence. When Elvis walked into a room, Elvis Presley was in the fucking room."

CHUCK D OF PUBLIC ENEMY: "Elvis was a hero to most / But he never meant shit to me, you see / Straight-up racist that sucker was, simple and plain / Motherfuck him and John Wayne."

HESS, DAVID
(B. 1936)

A New-York born singer and songwriter who first recorded "All Shook Up" (under the pseudonym David Hill), and laid down a number of demos for Elvis at Shalimar, where he worked at the beginning of his career, up to and including a demo of "It's Now Or Never" in 1960. Elvis sang several Hess compositions (once again, credited to David Hill), including "I Got Stung," "Come Along" and "Sand Castles." Hess's own singing career peaked with "Two Brothers" and a version of Cliff Richard hit "Living Doll" in 1959. He went on to become a record industry executive and actor in horror movies.

HESS, JAKE
(B. WILLIAM JESSE HESS, 1927-2003)

Elvis worked with one of his singing idols and his gospel group the Imperials in 1966, on his gospel album How Great Thou Art, and later recordings and live shows into the early Seventies.

Jake Hess was born in Alabama on December 24, 1927, into a family of twelve children that made ends meet by singing as a choir. Jake made his family debut aged just five. He began singing professionally as a 16-year-old with the John Daniel Quartet. In 1948, he became the lead singer of the Statesmen Quartet, one of Elvis' favorites during his youth. Many Elvis biographers (and gospel singer James Blackwood) have identified Hess's style a major influence on the young Elvis. In later years, Hess recalled Elvis, aged just 9 or 10, coming along to Statesmen concerts in Tupelo and asking for advice on how to get into the music business.

Hess beat Elvis to the Grammy for Best Sacred Performance in 1968 for "Beautiful Isle Of Somewhere," when Elvis' version of "You'll Never Walk Alone" was nominated. Hess won a total of four Grammys during his career.

Hess sang "Known Only To Him" at Elvis' funeral in 1977, twenty-four years after he had done the same for Hank Williams. Hess was inducted into the Gospel Music Hall of Fame in 1982. In later years, he was a regular on Bill Gaither's Homecoming Friends.

JAKE HESS: "Elvis was one of those individuals, when he sang a song, he just seemed to live every word of it. There's other people that have a voice that may be greater than Presley's but he had that certain something that everybody searches for all during their lifetime."

HESTON, CHARLTON
(B. JOHN CHARLES CARTER, 1924)

Elvis first met Charlton Heston on the Paramount lot when Heston was shooting Ben-Hur (for which he won an Academy Award).

Elvis announced Heston's presence to the audience at one of his Las Vegas concerts in 1973, and told an anecdote about how on a rainy day he had turned to Heston and said, "Moses, make it stop raining." Sonny West remembers that particular show as one of Elvis' best.

Heston is best known for his colossal roles in Ben Hur, The Ten Commandments (1956), and as the hero of Planet of the Apes (1968). Latterly, Heston was president of the National Rifle Association.

"HEY BO DIDDLEY"

Elvis referenced Bo Diddley's signature song in concert during the Seventies while Ronnie Tutt went wild on the drums. It appears on bootleg recording A Hot Winter Night in Dallas.

"HEY, HEY, HEY"

Joy Byers wrote this up-tempo number for Elvis to record in on February 22 and 23, 1967 at RCA's Nashville studios as part of the Clambake soundtrack session. The song has since taken a bow on the Double Feature and FTD soundtrack re-releases; the latter features the inevitable alternates takes are on the 2006 FTD Clambake release.

"HEY JUDE"

Elvis gave this Lennon/McCartney classic a whirl at American Studio in Memphis in on January 21, 1969. He only did a couple of takes, with the intention of returning to it at a later date. When it came out in 1968, The Beatles single was became their longest-lasting #1 in the US, both in track length (over seven minutes) and in staying power (nine weeks) and track length (over seven minutes).

Elvis failed to quite nail the vocals during his three hour recording session, which is why his version took several years to make it onto vinyl despite the below-par vocals on Elvis' version, the song was released a few years later on Elvis Now, followed at a distance of decades by From Nashville to Memphis.and Suspicious Minds: The Memphis 1969 Anthology.

A splice of two takes from the original session came out the 2000s on FTD disc The Memphis Sessions.

Elvis sang the song live in 1969 and 1970 in Las Vegas in with a Beatles medley with song "Yesterday"—it's on Elvis Aron Presley, Elvis Live in Las Vegas, the 2007 Viva Las Vegas release, and on FTD releases issues Elvis at the International, All Shook Up, Too Much Monkey Business (see Guitar Man) and Writing for the King, as well quite a large number of as the inevitable concert bootlegs.

"HEY, LITTLE GIRL"

More up-tempo Joy Byers fare that Elvis recorded in Nashville, in the early hours of February 26, 1965, for Harum Scarum. Apart from the Double Feature release for the movie in the Nineties, it has come out on the FTD reissue, along with outtakes. Outtakes are also on FTD releases Out In Hollywood and Harum Scarum.

"HI-HEEL SNEAKERS"

Elvis recorded the bluesy B-side to "Guitar Man" in on September 11, 1967 at Studio B in Nashville, for release in January 1968. The song wasn't on the Hill & Range playlist, but guitarist Chip Young suggested they give giving it a try. Elvis and the studio band had such a good time when they laid down the track that the master came in twice as long as required a standard single release, and so they had to cut it down to under three minutes. for the single—Tthe unedited version was first officially released on From Nashville To Memphis.

Originally a hit for Tommy Tucker in 1964 (credited under his real name, Robert Higginbotham), Elvis' exuberant interpretation failed and was overlooked for an album release until after Elvis' death. It made its vinyl 33 debut when it came out on Elvis Aron Presley in 1980, since then it has featured on Reconsider Baby, Tomorrow Is A Long Time and Elvis R 'n' B.

FTD's 2003 album So High features an alternate outtake. The song has attracted an illustrious list of cover artists, including Jerry Lee Lewis, Stevie Wonder, JoséÈ Feliciano, Ike and Tina Turner, Sammy Davis Jr., Rahsaan Roland Kirk and Paul McCartney among others.

"HIDE THOU ME"

Elvis is in fine gospel voice to a piano accompaniment in on a home recording of this 1880 Lowry / Francis Crosby hymn, recorded in 1966 and released many years later on the Peace in the Valley anthology, Today, Tomorrow & Forever and In A Private Moment.

"HIGH NOON (DO NOT FORSAKE ME OH MY DARLIN')"

Elvis slipped in a line from Tex Ritter's theme tune to the Oscar-winning Western during his September 1967 recording of "Guitar Man" (much later released on Platinum: A Life In Music).

HILTON HOTEL, LAS VEGAS

See INTERNATIONAL HOTEL, and NEVADA.

HILL & RANGE

The premier country music publishing company played a key role in the sale of Elvis' recording contract with Sun Records to RCA in 1955, and was the main conduit of songs for Elvis for decades after.

Founded in LA in 1943 by the Aberbach Brothers, the company's first act was Spade Cooley and His Western Swing Band, which scored a country chart #1 with "Shame on You." They soon snapped up Bob Wills and a host of top country talent, including Ernest Tubb, Eddy Arnold and Hank Snow, all of whom Colonel Parker at one time managed before Elvis' talents were known outside the Presley household.

Hill & Range executive Grelun Landon entered into discussions with Elvis' manager Bob Neal about publishing a folio of Elvis songs in May 1955. Colonel Tom Parker put the kibosh on the deal as soon as he got wind of it, but used the contact to try and persuade company manager Julian Aberbach to help back a buyout of Elvis' contract from Sun Records . . . though a competing version of the story has Julian tipping off the Colonel about a hot new singer called Elvis.

Company lawyer Ben Starr was present in Memphis on November 21, 1955 for the signing of Elvis' new recording contract for RCA. Hill and Range contributed $1,000 (or $2,500 as Julian Aberbach recalled in 2002) as an advance on a 50-50 song publishing partnership with Elvis, through the newly-formed Elvis Music company. By some accounts, the publishing company actually put up half of the money for the RCA buyout of Elvis' Sun contract. As part of the overall deal, Hill & Range also purchased the publishing rights to almost all of Elvis' Sun songs registered to Sam Phillips' Hi-Lo Music company, reputedly for an additional $15,000. Elvis and the Colonel were to receive a third of songwriting royalties on future recordings.

The first song that Hill and Range provided Elvis was "Don't Be Cruel," which Elvis recorded in early July 1956. Company representative Freddy Bienstock became the liaison with Elvis, playing Elvis demos to choose from prior to going into the studio. Hill and Range commissioned songwriters to write for Elvis, offered Elvis songs for which they already had the rights, or negotiated with songwriters to give up a third of their mechanical royalties (to Elvis and Hill & Range) in the hope that extra sales would make the songwriters money in the end. When Elvis established himself as the world's most profitable entertainer, Hill & Range were able to persuade top songwriters to produce material for him, even under these unfavorable conditions.

From *Loving You* onwards, Hill and Range was involved in the pre-selection of soundtrack material for Elvis to pick for his movies. When the company received the script, it commissioned competing teams of songwriters, most of whom were based in New York, to write the songs, get approval from the movie production company, and then submit them to RCA who would pass them on to Elvis for his final selection.

After Elvis' return from the Army, the songs Hill & Range commissioned were increasingly dictated by the strict requirements of movie soundtracks to fit specific scenes or titles. Effectively, Elvis had a much reduced pool of songs to choose from. Such demand for material (up to 50 tracks a year) inevitably led to lower quality. More established writing teams balked at forfeiting their royalties on songs that weren't necessarily even going to be released. To supply all the movie song demand, Hill & Range sometimes hired songwriters to add lyrics to traditional (out of copyright) tunes, or write English-language versions of popular European hits.

By 1967, in his rare non-soundtrack studio sessions Elvis began recording material he had found himself, or old R'n'B songs he had always liked. Hill & Range were forced to compromise with a songwriter when Elvis recorded "Guitar Man," a song whose rights Jerry Reed refused to hand over to an Elvis publishing company. For a while, the freshest, most passionate recording Elvis had made in years looked like it wasn't going to come out at all.

Hill and Range's stranglehold on the songs Elvis recorded was definitely broken in 1969, when Elvis reported for duty at Chips Moman's American Studio in Memphis and laid down an amazing 26 tracks. Elvis finally put his foot down and overruled the song publishing company representatives who wanted to keep him away from recording material to which they had not secured the rights—material that included "Suspicious Minds" and "In The Ghetto." Elvis got his way that time, but when he returned to American the following month, it was on the understanding that all the material he sang had already been cleared. Chips Moman was so annoyed by the hassles that he was put off working with Elvis again.

By 1971, Elvis was more or less uninterested in the songs that Hill & Range were offering. Hill & Range seemed to be unable or unwilling to cut deals on the folk-based material Elvis wanted to record at that time.

At the firm's peak in the early seventies, it was the world's number one independent music publishing company. However, after Julian suffered a heart attack in 1973, his brother Jean sold the company to Warner Chapell, though they astutely retained 50% of Elvis' catalogue. Elvis continued to work with former Hill and Range representative Freddy Bienstock, who by that time was well on his way to building his own song publishing empire.

BILLY SMITH: "Hill and Range was great in the beginning. But they became stagnant in later years. Colonel just got too greedy."

DON ROBERTSON: "I got the impression that they tried to prevent him from even seeing material unless they had already made a deal for it. I don't know how much he was even aware of that."

HILLBILLY CAT LIVE, THE

A bootleg release on Spring Fever Record Club of two Elvis concerts on the same day on August 24, 1970 in Las Vegas plus extras.

TRACK LISTING:
1. That's All Right
2. I Got A Woman
3. Tiger Man / Dialogue
4. Love Me Tender
5. I've Lost You
6. I Just Can't Help Believin'
7. You've Lost That Lovin' Feelin'
8. Polk Salad Annie
9. Introductions
10. Johnny B. Goode
11. Introductions cont'd.
12. The Wonder Of You
13. Heartbreak Hotel
14. One Night
15. All Shook Up (part)
16. Blue Suede Shoes / Whole Lotta Shakin' Goin' On
17. Hound Dog
18. Bridge Over Troubled Water
19. Suspicious Minds
20. Release Me
21. Can't Help Falling In Love
22. I Got A Woman / Ave Maria (part)
23. Polk Salad Annie
24. Heartbreak Hotel
25. One Night
26. Hound Dog
27. When The Snow Is On The Roses

HINTON, EDDIE
(1944-1995)

This Muscle Shoals blues guitarist recorded with Elvis in Nashville in 1970, when regular lead guitarist James Burton was unavailable. He played on "Snowbird," "Rags to Riches," "Where Did They Go Lord" and "Whole Lotta Shakin'."

During his career, Hinton worked with Aretha Franklin, Wilson Pickett, The Staple Singers, Boz Scaggs, Otis Redding and reggae legend Toots Hibbert. Hinton also recorded a number of albums of his own material.

"HIS HAND IN MINE"

Elvis laid down this Mosie Lister song at a Nashville recording session in on October 30, 1960 as the title track for his first gospel album. The song had been a hit for The Statesmen the year before Elvis cut his first single at Sun.

RCA re-released "His Hand In Mine" as a single in time for Easter 1969, paired with "How Great Thou Art." Despite critical acclaim for Elvis' gospel talents, the single only sold 25,000 copies. Since then, the song has been a staple on Elvis gospel compilations—it's on *Amazing Grace*, *Peace in the Valley* and *Ultimate Gospel*. It also appeared on yultide release *Christmas Peace*..

Fans of the track can find alternate takes on *Platinum: A Life In Music*, FTD release *Fame and Fortune*, and no fewer than five different takes on the FTD *His Hand in Mine* issue. A tape reputedly is also rumored to be in collectors' hands exists of Elvis singing the song in Germany in 1959.

HIS HAND IN MINE (LP)

Elvis' first gospel LP was released in November 1960, rising to #13 in the charts during its 20-week journey. Elvis' visceral love of gospel allowed him to record practically the entire album in a single all-night session. The album has been a steady seller ever since, and achieved Platinum status.

TRACK LISTING:
1. His Hand In Mine
2. I'm Gonna Walk Dem Golden Stairs
3. In My Father's House
4. Milky White Way
5. Known Only To Him
6. I Believe In The Man In The Sky
7. Joshua Fit The Battle
8. Jesus Knows Just What I Need
9. Swing Down, Sweet Chariot
10. Mansion Over The Hilltop
11. If We Never Meet Again
12. Working On The Building

Extra tracks filled out later versions (It Is No Secret, You'll Never Walk Alone and Who Am I).

FTD brought out a 2CD collectors' edition in 2006 with many, many alternate takes.

"(MARIE'S THE NAME)
HIS LATEST FLAME"

Elvis recorded this Doc Pomus / Mort Shuman pop song in at a rocking Nashville session in the early hours of on June 26, 1961. A few months earlier the song had been recorded by Del Shannon, for whom it was originally written as a follow-up to his smash hit "Runaway."

In the studio, Elvis and his Nashville band had such fun with the song that they did extra runthroughs even after they had finally decided on achieved a version they liked, and decided on a master cut.

A little over a month later, the song was in the stores as the A-Side of a single, paired with "Little Sister" on the B-Side. The song spent almost three months in the charts, peaking at #4; it made it all the way to #1 in the UK.

Album releases include *Elvis' Golden Records Vol. 3*, *Worldwide Gold Award Hits Vol. 2*, *This Is Elvis*, , *Elvis Sings Mort Shuman & Doc Pomus*, *From Nashville to Memphis*, *Artist of the Century*, *ELVIS 30 #1 Hits* and *Hitstory*.

Alternate versions have appeared on *The EP Collection Vol. 2*, *Elvis Sings Mort Shuman & Doc Pomus*, *From Nashville To Memphis*, *ELVIS 30 #1 Hits* (2 CD version), *Elvis: Close Up*, and FTD releases *Studio B: Nashville Outtakes* (a rehearsal) and *Something For Everybody* (the best part of a dozen await fans of the song). Songwriter Mort Shuman's demo is on FTD release *Writing for Elvis*.

Hit Making Team

In 2005, Elvis' backing group the Sweet Inspirations and a number of brass musicians who recorded and played with Elvis in the latter part of his career hit the recording studios for an album written by John Krondes. Names associated with the project at various times included The Jordanaires, D.J. Fontana, Millie Kirkham, Bobby Ogdin, the American Studio band and Ronnie Tutt, with Joe Esposito acting as Chairman. The planned CD, *If I Can Dream*, billed as the first new Elvis music in almost thirty years, had not been released at the time of writing.

Hitstory

A 2006 4-disc Elvis boxed set combining *Elvis 30 #1 Hits* and *Elvis 2nd To None*, plus a bonus disc (another two discs in markets outside the US).

Track listing:
1. Heartbreak Hotel
2. Don't Be Cruel
3. Hound Dog
4. Love Me Tender
5. Too Much
6. All Shook Up
7. (Let Me Be Your) Teddy Bear
8. Jailhouse Rock
9. Don't
10. Hard Headed Woman
11. One Night
12. (Now And Then There's) A Fool Such As I
13. A Big Hunk O'Love
14. Stuck On You
15. It's Now Or Never
16. Are You Lonesome Tonight?
17. Wooden Heart
18. Surrender
19. (Marie's The Name) His Latest Flame
20. Can't Help Falling In Love
21. Good Luck Charm
22. She's Not You
23. Return To Sender
24. (You're The) Devil In Disguise
25. Crying In The Chapel
26. In The Ghetto
27. Suspicious Minds
28. The Wonder Of You
29. Burning Love
30. Way Down
31. A Little Less Conversation
32. That's All Right
33. I Forgot To Remember To Forget
34. Blue Suede Shoes
35. I Want You, I Need You, I Love You
36. Love Me
37. Mean Woman Blues
38. Loving You
39. Treat Me Nice
40. Wear My Ring Around Your Neck
41. King Creole
42. Trouble
43. I Got Stung
44. I Need Your Love Tonight
45. A Mess Of Blues
46. I Feel So Bad
47. Little Sister
48. Rock-A-Hula Baby
49. Bossa Nova Baby
50. Viva Las Vegas
51. If I Can Dream
52. Memories
53. Don't Cry, Daddy
54. Kentucky Rain
55. You Don't Have To Say You Love Me
56. An American Trilogy
57. Always On My Mind
58. Promised Land
59. Moody Blue
60. I'm A Roustabout
61. Rubberneckin' (Paul Oakenfold remix)
62. I Beg Of You
63. My Wish Came True
64. Ain't That Lovin You Baby
65. Fame And Fortune
66. I Gotta Know
67. Flaming Star
68. Follow That Dream
69. One Broken Heart For Sale
70. Kissin' Cousins
71. Such A Night
72. Ask Me
73. (Such An) Easy Question
74. I'm Yours
75. Puppet On A String
76. Love Letters
77. Separate Ways
78. Steamroller Blues
79. If You Talk In Your Sleep
80. My Boy

Ho, Don

(1930-2007)A Hawaiian performer of exotically-mixed lineage, Don Ho was a big act in the second half of the Sixties. Elvis' song "I'll Remember You" was initially released by Ho. A photo taken during one of Elvis' Las Vegas shows appears to depict Ho and Elvis kissing, after Ho asked Elvis for a kiss on the cheek and then turned his face away at the last moment. Ho's highest-placing single was "Tiny Bubbles"; in the Seventies he made a number of TV appearances. He continues performing to this day.

Hobbies

Ultimately, Elvis really only had one hobby: keeping boredom at bay, generally through the pursuit of fun. A young man with huge disposable income, an ever-present coterie of entourage pals and plenty of leisure time, Elvis tried no end of pastimes over the years. Karate, slot-car racing, watching TV, hiring out local movie theaters, roller-skating, taking in concerts when in Las Vegas, fairground hi-jinx, horse riding, reading, seeking the meaning of life, girls . . . whatever hobby he lent himself to, Elvis approached it with passion and gusto.

In a 1956 interview, Elvis stated his hobbies as motorcycle riding and waterskiing. Riding a motorcycle was something he did for the rest of his life—he went for a ride the day before he died. Collecting and driving cars also qualified as one of his life-long hobbies.

With more money in his pocket than he could possibly spend on just himself, in his pre-Army years Elvis treated his wide circle of friends to

A candid photos of Elvis water-skiing in Biloxi, Mississippi in 1956.

nights at the Memphis Fairgrounds, the skating rink, or local movie theaters that he hired out for all-night screenings.

Every home Elvis owned had a den, a room designed for partying. The first house he rented in Los Angeles housed a collection of pinball machines and a pool table. Elvis and co. played a lot of pool whether they were in Memphis or LA, usually 8-ball or Rotation. Graceland had a den plus a whole basement given over to leisure pursuits. When these palled, there were always pranks and practical jokes, which for Elvis and his entourage were practically a vocation. Logistics permitting, Elvis would sometimes go out to listen to other singers and bands in LA, Memphis and Las Vegas.

It was in the Army that Elvis started practicing karate, his most enduring hobby. He actively practiced martial arts for close to two decades.

Elvis' lifelong passion for football continued far beyond school. He set up his own team to play on, sponsored local youth teams in Memphis, and for a spell in the early Sixties was an expert on professional teams and players through assiduous viewing of games (he had films sent out specially to him)

Elvis lines up a shot (1956).

and a subscription to all the football magazines.

In the mid-Sixties, Elvis turned increasingly to a spiritual quest. Through Larry Geller, he became involved with the Self-Realization Fellowship and practiced yoga and meditation. His reading tastes changed accordingly. For the next couple of years, Elvis seemed happier curled up with a book than indulging his more customary fun-time escapades.

Elvis started 1966 with a big thing for slot-car racing, after Priscilla gave him a huge set for Christmas. He learned scuba diving for his role as a Navy Seal in *Easy Come, Easy Go*, but didn't take it up with the gusto he reserved for his favorite pastimes, even though he spent thousands of dollars on scuba diving gear.

By the beginning of 1967, horse riding had become such a consuming passion that Elvis bought himself a ranch, the Circle G, and spent like he had never spent before.

Before the year was out, he had returned to the tried-and-tested pursuits of hiring out the Memphian Theater to screen movies, renting out the Memphis Fairgrounds, or for a change going to the Whitehaven Plaza for night-time bowling parties. By day, he found time to indulge a new hobby of target shooting, for which he bought rifles, targets and all the paraphernalia.

Elvis had less of a need for time-consuming pursuits from 1968, when he threw his energy and enthusiasm back into his music and performing. Singing was not only a profession, it was also something Elvis loved to do in his spare time. After performing in Las Vegas or taking in another singer's show, Elvis might meet up and spend the rest of the night singing (with Tom Jones, Andy Williams, Bobbie Gentry and others). Just as singing gospel was Elvis' way of warming up for a recording session, singing gospel was how he cooled down again after a high-octane stage performance.

In 1970, Elvis' new hobby became security. To avert repeated kidnap and assassination threats, Elvis purchased himself and his entourage a whole arsenal of guns, and actively pursued friendships with policemen around the country (he had always been a friend of local Memphis law enforcement officers).

Elvis spent time at the local police firing range, and at night would drive around with a police scanner so that he could go to crime scenes and see the Memphis police at work first hand. Around this time he became the most exclusive of collectors: a collector of legally-valid police badges.

Racquetball became one of Elvis' passions in the Seventies, after Dr. Nichopoulos suggested he play as a way to improve his fitness.

In 1974, Elvis threw himself heart and soul into his karate. He backed the foundation of a karate institute in Memphis, held demonstrations and made plans to produce his own karate film.

He took up most expensive hobby of all in 1975: aircraft. At one stage he owned five of these high-maintenance toys. Not surprisingly, this hobby sent his finances into a tailspin.

In his final year alive, increasingly dogged by ill-health, Elvis became something of a recluse at Graceland. According to Dr. Nichopoulos, he spent his time at home meditating, reading or watching TV.

ELVIS SAID IN 1956: "I wouldn't call girls a hobby. It's a pastime."

HODGE, CHARLIE
(1934-2006)

Elvis met this singer and rhythm guitarist as they traveled across the States en route to their Army posting in Germany in September 1958. Elvis requested to share a cabin with Hodge on the ship to Germany, rather than bunk with the sergeants

he had been put in with. They spent the four days of the boat ride to Bremerhaven singing and talking, and struck up a friendship that lasted until the end of Elvis' life. Hodge, however, recalls meeting Elvis some years earlier, backstage after one of Hodge's performances with his gospel band, The Foggy River Boys, in Memphis.

Hodge was born in Decatur, Alabama, on December 14, 1934. He went to a local music school and began performing as a singer in a gospel quartet with Bill Gaither. Hodge's group, The Foggy River Boys, landed a regular slot on Red Foley's Ozark Jubilee TV show, backing singers such as Gene Autry and Roy Rogers. Diminutive (5' 3") Charlie famously sang standing on an upturned Coke crate.

Back in the US, Elvis and Charlie recorded a duet of "I Will Be Home Again," one of the songs they sang on the ship out to Germany, for *Elvis Is Back!*

Elvis took Hodge with him to Hollywood for *G.I. Blues*, his first movie after Army service. Hodge went onto Elvis' payroll as a member of the entourage, contributing not just his companionship and musical talents but also his sense of humor. Of the many names Elvis called Charlie over the years, the more respectful included "Slewfoot," "Waterhead" and "Sir Charles."

Hodge featured as a backing singer on a number of Elvis tracks, many of which he had sung harmonies on with Elvis in private. Hodge and Elvis shared a musical upbringing in gospel. Out in Hollywood, Hodge appeared in Elvis movies *Clambake, Stay Away Joe* and *Charro!*

In 1961, Hodge took some time out from Elvis to work with country singer Jimmy Wakely.

In 1966, he moved in to Elvis' LA home in Bel Air while Elvis worked on *Spinout*.

Hodge played piano on several Elvis recordings including "Beach Shack," recorded in 1966, and "Suppose" recorded in 1967. During this period, Hodge's and Red West's opinions were so important to Elvis' recording decisions that Freddy Bienstock of Hill & Range referred to the two of them as the "Imperial Council."

Hodge played rhythm guitar and contributed backing vocals on a portion of Elvis' 1968 NBC TV special. He featured in all of Elvis' documentaries and TV broadcast concerts, from *Elvis: That's The Way It Is* through *Elvis on Tour* and *Aloha from Hawaii* to *Elvis in Concert*. After Elvis' death, he appeared as himself in several Elvis biopics and documentaries, starting with 1979 TV movie *Elvis*.

In 1969, Charlie helped Elvis plan and rehearse material for his first month-long residency in Las Vegas at the International Hotel. When Elvis returned to touring, Hodge was appointed stage manager and #1 assistant. Onstage, Charlie sang harmony, brought him water, caught the guitars he flung, gave Elvis prompts when he needed them, and was his official scarf-replenisher after Elvis adopted the gesture into his stage act. Hodge also sometimes dueted with Elvis on stage.

In early 1970, Elvis had work done on two rooms in the Graceland basement to make an apartment for him.

Hodge played acoustic guitar on the songs Elvis laid down for RCA at a recording session in Palm Springs in the fall of 1973. Unlike many long-term members of Elvis' entourage, Hodge remained close to Elvis until the very end. He appeared on stage with Elvis in his last concerts, and was one of very few people Elvis was willing to spend time with in his final months alive.

Hodge went with Larry Geller to the funeral home to do Elvis' hair for the final time, and was a pallbearer at Elvis' funeral. He carried on living at Graceland for a few months after Elvis' death, until Vernon asked him if he was happy continuing to look after security for Elvis' grave, or preferred to do his own thing—though some versions of the story have Charlie given little choice in whether to stay or leave.

After Elvis, Charlie married Jennifer. He performed in Elvis tribute shows and toured the world keeping Elvis' memory alive. He died of lung cancer in 2006. He was honored at the 2007 Rock and Roll Hall of Fame induction ceremony.

CHARLIE HODGE: "I was the only trained musician of the guys and I guess Elvis needed someone he liked who was also a musician."

SONNY WEST: "He idolized Elvis and his life was totally connected to Elvis. Our lives revolved around Elvis, but Charlie existed for Elvis."

Book:
Me'n'Elvis, by Charlie Hodge and Charles Goodman, Castle Books, 1988.

Video:
The Elvis I Knew, 1994

HOLIDAY ON ICE

Elvis saw this show a couple of times in Germany when he was away on his Army service, and then went to see it a week after his return to Memphis at the Ellis Auditorium.

HOLLY, BUDDY
(B. CHARLES HARDIN HOLLEY, 1936 -1959)

The story goes that Holly put together his first band after seeing Elvis play his hometown, Lubbock, Texas early in 1955. Within two months, Holly was opening the bill on Elvis' return to town. That's not quite the whole story.

Holly was born in Lubbock, Texas on September 7, 1936. By the age of 15, he was writing and performing "western and bop" songs with pal Bob Montgomery as "Buddy and Bob," and already beginning to incorporate R 'n' B elements into his compositions. It was with this new material and an expanded band that Holly supported Elvis a second time (or perhaps a third time, if Holly as sometimes reported played during Elvis' June 1955 Lubbock shows) in October 1955, an occasion when Elvis is said to have told Holly that he would help get him a place on the Louisiana Hayride. According to Cricket Jerry Allison, Holly taught Elvis "Money Honey" in early 1955.

After a brief and unsuccessful contract with Decca, Holly's first hit was "That'll Be The Day" in early 1957, the title coming from the line John Wayne repeats through 1956 western *The Searchers*. The song was credited to The Crickets to circumvent contractual problems with his previous label.

Buddy Holly and The Crickets became an instant success. Holly toured the UK in 1958, one of several rock acts to cross the pond. His performances became a major inspiration for the Sixties invasion of British rock and roll artists, from The Beatles to the Rolling Stones.

Holly's career was cut short on February 3, 1959, less than two years after his first hit, when he was killed in a plane crash with fellow rockers Ritchie Valens and J. P. "The Big Bopper" Richardson—"the day the music died" for Don McLean in his 1971 song "American Pie." Elvis sent a telegram when he learned of the tragedy.

In two short years Holly became a headline rock 'n' roll act, toured extensively, and earned a reputation as a significant innovator. Aside from his unique vocal style, Holly was one of the first (white) rock 'n' rollers to rely on his own songwriting skills, the first to standardize the singer,

ABOVE: Candid photo of Elvis in 1960's.

RIGHT: Hollywood Elvis in Hollywood 1956.

lead and rhythm guitar, bass and drummer line-up, and he pioneered the use of double-tracked vocals and studio overdubs. Holly was one of the original ten inductees into the Rock and Roll Hall of Fame in 1986.

BUDDY HOLLY: "Without Elvis, none of us could have made it."

Book:
Elvis & Buddy: Linked Lives, by Alan Mann, Music Mentor 2002.

"HOLLY LEAVES AND CHRISTMAS TREES"

Red West wrote this festive song with Glen Spreen for Elvis to record at RCA's Nashville facilities in on May 15, 1971 for his upcoming festive release *Elvis Sings The Wonderful World of Christmas*. A fresh take was released on The tune has since appeared on *If Every Day Was Like Christmas* in 1994 (plus an alterante take), on appeared more recently. The tune has followed by *Christmas Peace* and *Elvis Christmas*. FTD release *I Sing All Kinds* offers more alternate fare.

HOLLYWOOD

Elvis had a love/hate relationship with tinsel-town. Hollywood loved Elvis for his solid gold box office; Elvis was ultimately ambivalent.

Fifties girlfriend Anita Wood recalls that Elvis couldn't wait to get back to Memphis once his shooting commitments were over.

He spent a great deal of time in the Sixties making movies, living in a variety of homes in Bel Air, dating a string of leading ladies and comely dancers, establishing a court away from home, making mayhem on set and recording at a range of studios, but he did not become part of the Hollywood celebrity scene.

In 1965, ready to return to Memphis after filming yet another movie (one of 31 feature films he made in all), Elvis confided in Larry Geller that he had no desire to head back to Hollywood, though with Priscilla by that time living in Graceland, Elvis' Hollywood escapes allowed him the freedom to live an unattached life.

See also Movies, individual studio names and film titles.

Elvis' star on the Hollywood Walk of Fame was located at 6777 Hollywood Boulevard, between Ray Charles and Vivien Leigh (or Highland Ave. and McCadden). Due to subsidence, an additional star was added for Elvis behind the Four Ladies of Hollywood gazebo at La Brea.

ELVIS SAID IN 1969: "I wasn't ready for that town and they weren't ready for me."

ELVIS SAID TO LARRY GELLER: "The whole place seems like a damn movie set, and everyone's actin' and kissin' your butt. That's why when I finish a movie, I hit it. I get my butt back to Memphis."

HAL WALLIS: "A Presley picture is the only sure thing in Hollywood."

BILLY SMITH: "When Elvis first went out to Hollywood, he was green as a gourd."

ARLENE COGAN: "Elvis hated Hollywood; he hated it with a passion."

ALANNA NASH: "An argument can be made that whatever Parker's intent, Hollywood helped keep Elvis a big star and in the money during a period when his record career might have languished, especially in the protest-and-psychedelic era."

Book:
Elvis Presley in Hollywood: Celluloid Sell Out, by Gerry McLafferty, Trans-Atlantic Publications, 1990.

"Home Is Where The Heart Is"

A pared-down Sherman Edwards/Hal David ballad for the *Kid Galahad* soundtrack and EP, recorded by Elvis at Radio Recorders in on October 26, 1961, his second bout of studio time that month. The song first came out on LP in 1971, on *I Got Lucky*. Since then, it has been *Double Featured* and come out (in an An alternate movie version) featured take on 2001 FTD release *Silver Screen Stereo*.

Home Movies

Elvis had a movie camera in the Sixties that he and members of his entourage used frequently. Footage from this camera and home movies shot from the Fifties onwards by Eddie Bellman, Eddie Fadal, Joe Esposito and others have all appeared on documentaries over the years, in addition to large numbers of fan-made home movies, some of which have only publicly been released for the first time in the 2000s.

Elvis also had an early video camera that he used to shoot private bedroom material.

Home Recordings

Elvis grew up in a household where singing was a common form of entertainment. After his elevation to fame, he didn't need a crowd to sit down at the piano and have a sing-song.

The most complete and famous recording of Elvis singing for pure personal pleasure took place not at home but at Sun Studio, on what became known as the Million Dollar Quartet session. Other such gems unearthed over the years may feature less accomplished singing companions than Carl Perkins and Jerry Lee Lewis, but they offer plenty of spontaneity and good-humored fun.

When Elvis was in Germany, he recorded songs with pal Charlie Hodge on a rudimentary tape recorder, none of which passed muster for official RCA release at the time. Many of the songs that Elvis sang at pal Eddie Fadal's house in Texas in 1958, in Germany in 1959, at his LA home in the early Sixties, at Graceland in 1966 and at Sam Thompson's home in the Seventies, first made it to public ears on bootleg discs. RCA began putting out versions of these songs considerably later, eking out one or two on collectors' releases prior to opening up the vaults for 1999 albums *The Home Recordings* and *In A Private Moment*.

For the literal-minded, Elvis did make some professional-quality home recordings in the Seventies, when RCA despaired of getting him back into the studio. He laid down a few tracks at his Palm Spring home, and recorded much of his final album at Graceland. RCA first offered to set Elvis up with a recording studio at Graceland just before he set off for his Army service in 1958, but had a change of heart when executives realized that if they extended this privilege to one of their artists, they'd be flooded with requests for similar perks.

Home Recordings, The

This 1999 BMG album, mainly from the mid-Sixties, is Elvis singing for the pleasure of singing, mainly at a piano accompanied by Red West and/or Charlie Hodge.

TRACK LISTING:
1. When The Saints Go Marchin' In
2. I Understand Just How You Feel
3. I Asked The Lord
4. I'm Beginning To Forget You
5. Mona Lisa
6. Hands Off
7. Make Believe
8. If I Loved You
9. What Now My Love
10. Tumblin' Tumbleweeds
11. San Antonio Rose
12. Tennessee Waltz
13. Show Me Thy Ways, O Lord
14. After Loving You
15. I've Been Blue
16. Mary Lou Brown
17. It's No Fun Being Lonely
18. Suppose
19. Indescribably Blue
20. Write To Me From Naples
21. My Heart Cries For You
22. Dark Moon

Homes

Born into poverty, Elvis lived his first 18 years at more than a dozen different addresses. Practically the first thing Elvis did after signing his big-money contract for RCA was put a down payment on a home for his family. A year later, he upgraded to Graceland, the place he called home for the rest of his life.

After the shuttling of his 1950s touring days, Elvis became used to a life on the move. In the Sixties, he divided his time between Memphis and LA, with occasional weekend jaunts to Las Vegas at the beginning of the decade and Palm Springs at the end. Even when he had no commitments, for a period from 1969 he shuttled between his various homes and the places he liked to vacation, often spending no more than a few days before moving on to the next.

Elvis grew up with a large and proximate extended family around him. During portions of his childhood, his parents lived with cousins, in-laws and a variety of Presleys and Smiths. Once installed at Graceland, Elvis provided a home for many of his relatives over the years, including Grandma Minnie Mae, Uncle Travis, Aunt Lore and their kids Billy and Bobby, Aunt Delta, and at various times, members of the entourage.

For detailed information on Elvis' homes, see under the entries for Memphis, Tupelo, Los Angeles, Palm Springs, Texas, Germany, Circle G, and of course Graceland.

ELVIS' HOMES

No other aspect of Elvis' life—apart from girl-friends—is riddled with more inconsistencies than where he lived (and when exactly he lived at these locations) during his early days. What follows is a best-guess list of Elvis' homes.

TUPELO, MISSISSIPPI
306 Old Saltillo Road,
510½ Maple Street,
Reese Street
904 Kelly Street
(Pascagoula, Mississippi—cabin at unknown location)
Berry Street
North Commerce Street
Mulberry Alley
1010 North Green Street.

MEMPHIS, TENNESSEE
370 Washington Street
572 Poplar Avenue
185 Winchester Avenue (Lauderdale Courts)
698 Saffarans Street
462 Alabama Avenue
2414 Lamar Avenue
1414 Getwell Street
1034 Audubon Drive,
3764 Bellevue Avenue (now Elvis Presley Boulevard)

A 17- year-old Elvis in the 11th grade in Lauderdale Courts.

LOS ANGELES, CALIFORNIA
525 Perugia Way, Bel Air
10539 Bellagio Road, Bel Air
10550 Rocca Place, Bel Air
1174 Hillcrest Road
144 Monovale Drive, Holmby Hills

PALM SPRINGS
1350 Ladera Circle
285 Via Lola, Camino del Norte
845 Chino Canyon Rd.

OTHERS:
605 Oak Hill Drive, Killeen, Texas
14 Goethestrasse, Bad Nauheim, Germany.
Circle G Ranch, off Rt. 301 in Horn Lake, DeSoto County, nr. Walls, Mississippi

Honeymoon

On their honeymoon, Elvis and Priscilla flew to their home in Palm Springs on Frank Sinatra's Learjet "Christina." They stayed there from May 1 to May 4, 1967, then returned to Memphis and headed off to the Circle G ranch, where they spent a few weeks in freshly-wedded bliss.

Hooton, Arthur

An old pal of Elvis' who was part of his early entourage, unfortunately nicknamed "Arthritis" and "Arturo Van Hooten" by Elvis. Among other travels, Hooten was with Elvis on his summer 1956 vacation to Biloxi, Mississippi, and accompanied Elvis to Chicago in March 1957 for his first ever show in the city.

Hoover, J(ohn) Edgar
(1895-1972)

Director of the FBI for 48 years, Hoover was responsible for turning the bureau into a major crime busting outfit and, during World War II, counter espionage organization, including the surveillance of suspected Communists in the US.

Hoover was born in Washington, D.C. Before the age of 30, he was running the Bureau of Investigation, the precursor to the FBI. He remained one of America's most powerful figures until his death, according to some sources through his power to intimidate successive presidents. Over his tenure, he expanded the FBI's independence and increased its number of staff by a factor of ten.

In 1970, when touring the FBI headquarters in Washington, Elvis declared that Hoover was "the greatest living American" who had done more for his country than any other. Elvis was very keen to meet the FBI boss on that trip, a feeling not shared by Hoover, who instructed underlings to deny Elvis a meeting on his two trips to Washington in late 1970.

Elvis told the agent who showed him round FBI headquarters that he would be happy to serve the bureau in any capacity he could. Hoover subsequently wrote Elvis a thank-you note, assuring him that he would "keep in mind your offer to be of assistance."

MARTY LACKER: "I really think he wanted to meet Hoover to get an FBI badge."

HOPKINS, JERRY

A former Rolling Stone journalist and contributing editor, Jerry Hopkins wrote the multi-million selling Elvis: A Biography in 1971, one of the few major biographies to appear during the singer's lifetime. Hopkins has extended his portfolio of Elvis books over the years, and written biographies of rock icons Jim Morrison (who is said to have suggested that he should write the Elvis biography in the first place), Jimi Hendrix and David Bowie.

Books:
Elvis: A Biography, Simon & Schuster, 1971.
Elvis: The Final Years, St. Martin's Press, 1980.
Elvis in Hawaii, Bess Press, 2002.
Aloha Elvis, by Jerry Hopkins, Bess Press 2007.
Elvis: A Biography (revised edition), Plexus Publishing, 2007.

HORSES AND RIDING

Elvis became an accomplished rider when he was trained for his 1960 cowboy movie *Flaming Star*, though his first screen appearance on horseback was in *Love Me Tender*. In 1960, while learning to ride his horse for *Flaming Star*, his mount bolted all the way back to his stall but Elvis managed to hang on.

He developed a serious interest in riding towards the end of 1966 when he bought a horse called Domino for Priscilla. When he rode the animal himself, he decided he wanted a horse of his own. Elvis being Elvis, one thing led to another and before long he had purchased a wardrobe of riding clothes and equipment from the Ben Howell and Son Saddlery in Whitehaven, a pair of his'n'hers bay horses (Jerry Schilling found Elvis' $3,500 horse, "Rising Sun" for him), a horse for Priscilla's pal Sandy Kawelo to keep her company, and then he embarked on a horse-buying spree that ended with the purchase of an almost half-million dollar ranch, much to Vernon's despair.

Rising Sun was Elvis' name choice; the show-trained animal had been known by the name Midget's Vandy by his previous owner. Elvis bought a horse for his father, which was called Midnight Sun. He acquired a black Tennessee Walker called Traveler (known at his new home as Bear). Over the next few months he added a horse called Keno for Red West (later rechristened "Big Red"), and a whole string of others

A scene from *Charro!* (1969).

including Bear, Beauty, Buckshot, El Poco, Flaming Star, Golden Sun, Lady, Mare Ingram, Scout, Sheba, Star Trek, Sundown, Thundercloud and Traveler.

Elvis' new-found love of horse riding wrought major changes in his life. Rather than sleeping by day and being active by night, he rode by day and did what most other people do at night. To begin with, Elvis was actively looking after the horses when they were stabled at Graceland, helping to clean up the barn and buying more equipment for this new hobby.

To the delight of his fans, Elvis would sometimes show off his riding skills in the grounds at Graceland. In early February 1967, Elvis spent $5,000 on a saddle-horse, and paid for alterations to the land around Graceland to create a larger riding area. It soon became clear that Elvis needed far more space than Graceland allowed for this new hobby. He acquired a ranch in Mississippi, which he renamed Circle G, and added more people to the Presley payroll, notably groom Mike McGregor.

Elvis had lost interest in the ranch by the end of that summer, though he didn't sell up until 1969. He transferred the horses back to Graceland, where they were stabled in the barn (known as "House of the Rising Sun"). Elvis, friends and family continued to ride in the fields that once lay behind Graceland. When Lisa Marie was old enough, he bought her a pony too. By this time, Priscilla had moved out and taken Domino with her to California.

Rising Sun lived at Graceland until 1993, where he is buried in the back paddock. Descendents of Elvis' horses live on at Graceland.

PRISCILLA: "The happiest I ever saw him was when he developed a passion for horses."

HOSPITALS

See HEALTH.

"HOT DOG"

Elvis laid down this Leiber and Stoller song in on January 17 or 18, 1957 for the movie *Loving You*, at the Paramount Scoring Stage. It The song made it onto was released on the *Loving You* EP and LP, a year after the tune it was first recorded by R & B artist Young Jessie. In Elvis' lifetime the song appeared also on *Worldwide Gold Award Hits Vol. 2*. It has since appeared on *Elvis Sings Leiber & Stoller*, *Essential Elvis Vol. 1*, *The King Of Rock And Roll*, and on the FTD release *Loving You*.

HOT WINTER NIGHT IN DALLAS, A

A bootleg of Elvis' show on December 28, 1976, released in 1998 on the Fort Baxter label.

TRACK LISTING:
1. Also Sprach Zarathustra
2. See See Rider
3. I Got A Woman / Amen
4. Love Me

5.   Fairytale
6.   You Gave Me A Mountain
7.   Jailhouse Rock
8.   It's Now Or Never / O Sole Mio
9.   Tryin' To Get To You
10.   Blue Suede Shoes
11.   My Way
12.   Polk Salad Annie
13.   Band introductions
14.   Early Morning Rain
15.   What'd I Say
16.   Johnny B. Goode
17.   Ronnie Tutt Drum Solo
18.   Jerry Scheff Bass Solo
19.   Tony Brown Piano Solo
20.   David Briggs Piano Solo
21.   Love Letters
22.   School Days
23.   Hurt
24.   Unchained Melody
25.   Can't Help Falling In Love
26.   Closing Vamp

HOTELS WHERE ELVIS STAYED

A comprehensive list of hotels where Elvis stayed is beyond the scope of this encyclopedia, considering the many hundreds of towns he played during his lifetime. During his early touring days, Elvis and the band would sleep where they could. Fame opened the doors of the nation's top hotels, though the boisterous behavior of Elvis and his entourage sometimes soured the welcome.

Elvis' hotel arrangements became simpler in the Seventies. After the Hilton chain took over the International Hotel in Las Vegas, when Elvis traveled across the country where possible he would stay in Hilton hotels or inns. If not, he was happy with anywhere modern such as a Holiday Inn (a company part-owned by Sam Phillips) or other chain motels. When Elvis was on tour, he would invariably black out his bedroom window with foil to keep out the daylight if he was at the hotel for sleep; otherwise, he hired rooms in hotels to have somewhere to hang out before a show.

Elvis and his entourage were not always the most popular of guests. Horsing around, they might set a fire (once, to smoke Elvis out of his bedroom), or have a water battles that started with pistols and ended up with buckets. In later years, TVs and chandeliers were at risk from projectiles.

Fan web sites are a good source of information on which of these hotels still have an "Elvis suite" that they rent out. Where no hotel is listed, if it was in the Seventies, it's reasonably certain that Elvis lodged at a local Hilton.

- Albuquerque
Elvis and his entourage regularly made an over-day stop at the Holiday Inn or the Western Skies Motel when driving between Memphis and LA in the Sixties.

- Atlanta
Elvis stayed at the Souffers, Hyatt Regency and the Atlanta Hotels during his Seventies dates.

- Big Bear
Elvis and co. stayed at the Cedar Lake Lodge while shooting *Kissin' Cousins* in 1963.

- Biloxi
On vacation with pals in the summer of 1956, Elvis stayed at the Sea 'N' Sand Hotel, and later at the Gulf Hills Dude Ranch.

- Bloomington
Elvis took rooms at the Registry Hotel when he passed through town in 1976.

- Buffalo
Elvis stayed at the Statler Hotel in the Fifties and Seventies.

- Chicago
Elvis took a night-long pit stop at the O'Hare Inn near the airport before taking a flight to LA in March 1960. He stayed at the Marriott in 1970, en route between Memphis and LA, and at the Arlington Hilton when performing in town in 1977.

- Cincinnati
Elvis stayed at the Netherland Hilton in 1976 and 1977.

- Columbus, Ohio
Elvis stayed at the Ramada Inn and Stouffer's Dayton Plaza Hotel in the Seventies.

- Crystal River
Elvis stayed at the Port Paradise Hotel for location shooting on *Follow That Dream*.

- Dallas
In 1970 and 1971, Elvis and entourage pals stayed at the Royal Coach Motor Hotel.

- Detroit
In 1957, where else would Elvis stay but at the Cadillac Sheraton?

- Des Moines
Elvis stayed at the Downtown Ramada Inn in 1974, and at the Holiday Inn for his final trip in 1977.

- Duluth
Elvis stayed at the Radisson when he played town in 1976 and 1977.

- Eugene
Elvis stayed at the Valley River Inn during his November 1976 shows.

- Evansville
Elvis took rooms at the Evansville Executive Inn in 1976.

- Germany
On arrival in Germany for his Army service, Elvis and his entourage stayed in several hotels before renting a private house. His entourage stayed at the Ritters Park Hotel (Bad Homburg) before they all moved into Hilberts Park Hotel (Bad Nauheim) and then the Hotel Grunewald (also Bad Nauheim). On a side trip to Munich, Elvis and friends stayed at the Hotel Edelweiss.

-Hawaii
On his first trip in 1957, Elvis stayed at the Hawaiian Village Hotel on Oahu (in room 14A). He returned in 1961 for his USS Arizona memorial benefit concert, and stayed there again in April 1962 to film *Girls! Girls! Girls!*. He returned to this hotel for his performances in Honolulu in mid-November 1972.

On a May 1969 vacation, Elvis and his immediate family plus select members of the entourage stayed at the Ilikai Hotel (where he stayed in 1965 when shooting *Paradise, Hawaiian Style*) and one weekend at the Coco Palms Hotel, where he shot much of *Blue Hawaii*. This hotel (Elvis stayed in cottage #56) was damaged in a 1992 hurricane; it is scheduled to reopen in 2008.

By the time Elvis was on the island to do his *Aloha From Hawaii* concert in January 1973, favorite haunt the Hawaiian Village had become the Hilton Hawaiian Village. Elvis stayed at the Rainbow Tower in March 1977, moving on to Kailua for the remainder of his vacation.

- Houston
In 1970, when in town to perform at the Annual Texas Livestock Show, Elvis and his entourage stayed at the Astroworld Hotel.

Elvis and Priscilla on vacation in Kauai, an island off of Hawaii, at the Coco Palms Resort.

- Jacksonville
When Elvis performed in this Florida town in the Seventies, he stayed at The Hilton Towers (in room 1010).

Lake Tahoe/Stateline
Elvis spent a night at Del Webb's Sahara Tahoe in January 1962. When playing the venue in the Seventies, not surprisingly he stayed on-site at the Sahara Tahoe (since renamed the Horizon Casino Resort).

- Las Vegas
The first couple of times Elvis stayed in Las Vegas he roomed at the New Frontier Hotel; his vacation in 1956 was more successful than his singing engagement there. In 1957, he vacationed at the Sahara Hotel, which became his regular haunt; he spent Christmas 1961 at the hotel. In June 1962, Elvis whisked Priscilla Beaulieu off to the Sahara for 12 days when she was on a visit from Germany. Elvis combined business with pleasure in 1963, when *Viva Las Vegas* location shooting took place at his regular Vegas hotel, the Sahara, where he stayed in the Presidential Suite—democratically, other Vegas hotels were used for location work.

In May 1967, Elvis, Priscilla, friends and family stayed at the Aladdin Hotel to celebrate their wedding. Elvis stayed there on weekend jaunts that year, and returned for a longer spell with his pals after completing work on *Stay Away, Joe* in December 1967. The property has since become Planet Hollywood, Las Vegas.

From the summer of 1969 when he began performing live again, Elvis worked, rested and played at the International Hotel (later the Las Vegas Hilton), staying in the Imperial Suite on the 30th floor, where the bedroom was themed in green. On his first engagement, he had to make do with a suite on the 29th floor. Elvis' enormous suite has since been split into three luxury apartments.

- Los Angeles
For his March 1956 screen test at Paramount, Elvis stayed on the 11th floor of the Hollywood Knickerbocker Hotel at 1714 Ivar Ave (since converted into apartments). He returned to the hotel in August 1956, for the start of shooting on his first movie, *Love Me Tender*. Elvis' band continued to stay at the Knickerbocker after Elvis

moved on to the Beverly Wilshire (9500 Wilshire Blvd), Colonel Parker's favored LA location. From April 1957, Elvis rented out the penthouse apartment and four-bedroomed presidential suite, which he packed with pals Gene and Junior Smith, George Klein, Arthur Hooton and Bitsy Mott. The Beverly Wilshire was Elvis' regular LA haunt until his hi-jinks became just a little too boisterous, and Elvis moved to a rented house in Bel Air in September 1960 with his gang. Now known as the Regent Beverly Wilshire, the hotel continues to be a regular port of call for A-list stars. The suite Elvis regularly stayed in goes for $3,500 per night (2005 price).

- *Louisville*
Elvis stayed at the Seal Bark Hotel in the Fifties.

- *Memphis*
He may not have stayed there for longer than lunch, but on February 25, 1961 the Hotel Claridge hosted a special lunch hosted by Tennessee governor Buford Ellington and Memphis Mayor Henry Loeb to celebrate "Elvis Presley Day."

During renovations at Graceland in 1974, Elvis stayed at the Howard Johnson motel just down the street, which was also the regular destination for Graceland guest overflow. Many years earlier, Elvis had gone to the Peabody Hotel for his high school prom. As a youth he frequented the Chisca Hotel (272 South Main) home to WHBQ. He stayed at the Rivermont Hotel in January 1971, before going to pick up his Jaycees award.

- *Miami*
Elvis and his entourage stayed at the Fontainebleau Hotel in March 1960, when he was in town to record his appearance on the Frank Sinatra TV show.

- *Mobile*
Elvis stayed at the Bama Motel and then at the Admiral Semmes Hotel in the Fifties and again in 1970, though the last time he was not impressed by how run down the place had become.

- *Napa*
While doing location work on *Wild in the Country*, Elvis and the film crew stayed at the Casa Bellevue Motel.

- *Nashville*
Elvis stayed at the Andrew Jackson Hotel, where Tom Parker had first started operating in Nashville a decade earlier, in the fall of 1955. It was at this hotel that Elvis first heard a demo of "Heartbreak Hotel," played to him by Mae Boren Axton.

In the early Sixties, Elvis favored the Anchor Hotel after his late night recording sessions. In 1966 Elvis stayed at the Albert Pike Motel between sessions; in 1968, he stayed at the Jack Spencer Motor Hotel.

When recording in 1971, Elvis holed up at the Quality Court Motel between sessions.

- *New Orleans*
Elvis and his entourage stayed on the tenth floor of the Roosevelt Hotel (subsequently renamed the Fairmount Hotel) in February 1958 during location shooting for *King Creole*.

- *New York*
Elvis and Colonel Parker stayed at the Hotel Victoria on 51st St on November 30, 1955, and at the Warwick Hotel on W52nd St. on January 25, 1956 (Elvis had room 527), before his first TV appearance on the CBS "Stage Show." Elvis used to this hotel throughout 1956, the year that his TV appearances brought him national acclaim.

In June 1972, Elvis hired out the entire top floor of the New York Hilton for himself and his entourage when he played Madison Square Garden.

- *Oklahoma City*
Elvis chose the Biltmore in 1956.

- *Ottawa*
Elvis overnighted at the Beacon Arms Apartment Hotel when he was in town in 1957.

- *Palm Beach*
When Elvis played town in 1977, he stayed at the Hilton.

- *Paris*
In 1959, Elvis and pals stayed at the Prince de Galles hotel at 33 Avenue George V, with a view over the Champs-ElyséÈes.

- *Philadelphia*
Elvis used the Bellevue-Stratford and Hilton hotels for his Seventies shows.

- *Phoenix*
Elvis stayed at the Phoenix Skyrider Hotel in 1961. He took a suite of rooms at the Superstition Inn near Phoenix in July 1968, during location filming for *Charro!* (1969). He stayed at the Townhouse Hotel when he played shows here in the Seventies.

- *Portland, Oregon*
When he first played town in 1957, Elvis stayed at the Multnomah Hotel. In the early Seventies, he stayed at the Benson Hotel and in 1976 at the Sheraton Hotel.

- *Roanoke*
Elvis stayed at the Hotel Roanoke in 1955.

- *San Francisco*
Elvis briefly stayed at the Del Webb Town House in April 1973, when he was here to see one of Ed Parker's karate championships.

- *Seattle*
Elvis and his gang settled into the 14th floor of the Doric New Washington in September 1962 to shoot *It Happened at the World's Fair*. On tour in the Seventies, he was at the Fairmount Olympic.

- *Shreveport*
Elvis stayed at the Captain Shreve Hotel for his first and last performances at the Louisiana Hayride; during his early days he sometimes plumped for more budget-conscious alternatives such as the Al-Ida Motel and the Shirley Temple Courts.

- *St. Louis*
Over the years, Elvis stayed at the Hotel Chase, the Chase Park Plaza and the Bel Air Hilton.

- *Sweetwater, Texas*
In 1955, Elvis and the band stayed at the Palomino Motel.

- *Toledo*
Elvis stayed at the Commodore Perry in 1956, and at the Sheraton-Westmore in 1977.

- *Topeka*
Elvis was at the Hotel Dansan in 1956.

- *Tulsa*
Elvis stayed at the Fairmont Mayo in 1972 and 1974.

- *Vancouver*
Elvis stayed in room 1226 at the Georgia Hotel in 1957.

- *Washington D.C.*
When Elvis flew in to Washington DC in December 1970, he stayed in rooms 505/506/507 at the Washington Hotel. He was there in November 1971 to visit his girlfriend Joyce Bova.

- *Wichita*
Elvis was at the Lassen Hotel in 1956.

"HOUND DOG"

In 2004, *Rolling Stone* magazine ranked "Hound Dog" at no. 19 in the top 500 Songs of All Time. Back in 1956, for legions of people round the world, it was the song that delivered them their first irresistible dose of Elvis.

In May 1956, between his own performances in Las Vegas, Elvis sat in on a rocked-up Freddie Bell and the Bellboys' version of a Willie Mae "Big Mama" Thornton song, which had been an R & B smash for her in 1953. Elvis almost immediately incorporated the song into his own live act, using the Freddie Bell and the Bellboys version as his template, right down to the jokey line about the rabbit, though he naturally knew the Big Mama Thornton version, a growling blues song that had been penned by New York white guys Leiber and Stoller. Producer Johnny Otis also had a credit on the original release; in later years, Mama Thornton claimed that her input was so essential to the finished article that she should have had a credit too.

Before Elvis even got near a recording studio, his "Hound Dog" was the talk of the nation: his June 5, 1956 TV performance on the "Milton Berle Show" set off a hue and cry from concerned citizens and appalled critics. The next time that Elvis performed it on TV—for The Steve Allen Show" on July 1—he was tamed by a tuxedo and humiliated by being made to sing the song to a real live hound dog (a basset by the name of "Sherlock," no less).

The next day Elvis finally laid the track down on acetate at the RCA studios in New York. He wasn't satisfied until he had wrung out 31 takes of the song.

In the weeks between laying down the track and release, hardly an interview went by without Elvis being asked when the song was going to come out because the fans were going crazy waiting. Colonel Parker joked with RCA executives that "Hound Dog" was going to be such a huge hit that the company would have to change its symbol from the "Victor Dog" to the "Hound Dog."

When "Hound Dog" was shipped by RCA in mid-July 1956, as the B-side to "Don't Be Cruel,"

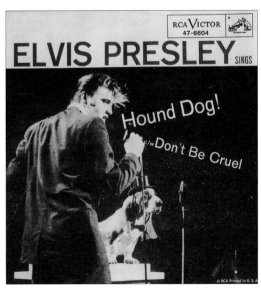

Elvis Presley's remake of Big Mama Thornton's "Hound Dog" was released as a single in 1956.

it lived up to all the hype. The track shot up to number two in the charts, and was kept off the top only by the A-side song. All in all, the two-sider shifted 4 million (some sources say 6 million) copies in 1956 alone. In compensation for its eclipse by "Don't Be Cruel" on the main charts, "Hound Dog" made it to #1 on the R & B and country charts. The song also came out on EPs *Elvis Presley* and *The Real Elvis* in 1956.

Elvis instantly added "Hound Dog" to his repertoire, and it immediately became the rousing finale to his live shows. He played out his final show at the Louisiana Hayride with "Hound Dog" in December 1956, and he sang it every opportunity that came up on TV that year.

Live recordings from the original year of the Hound Dog have appeared on a number of Hayride recordings, *A Golden Celebration* (1956 TV performances, plus his Homecoming Show in Tupelo), *This Is Elvis* (1956 TV shows), *Today Tomorrow & Forever*, and *Elvis Aron Presley* (his 1961 US Arizona Memorial performance and a live performance from 1975). The scandal of Elvis' performance on the "Milton Berle Show" was reissued on 2007 DVD *Elvis #1 Hit Performances*.

Elvis performed a high-energy version of the song for his "oldies" medley on the famed NBC TV Special in 1968. A recording from this landmark event appeared on the tie-in LP release *Elvis* (the original NBC TV Special album), while others from the period have since appeared on *Memories: The '68 Comeback Special* and inaugural FTD release *Burbank '68*.

Elvis introduced "Hound Dog" as his "special song" on his return to the live stage in Las Vegas in August 1969, recorded for posterity on *From Memphis To Vegas*. Not surprisingly, he reprised the song for the vast majority of his live performances. During Elvis' life, live versions adorned *Elvis in Person*, *Elvis As Recorded At Madison Square Garden* (followed at a distance by *An Afternoon In The Garden*), *Aloha from Hawaii Via Satellite*, *Elvis Recorded Live On Stage in Memphis* and *Elvis in Concert*.

Posthumous (and more recent) releases of early Las Vegas performances are to be found on *Viva Las Vegas* (2CD version), *Live In Las Vegas* (multiple performances), *Burning Love, Elvis: Close Up* and *The Live Greatest Hits*.

Though the song didn't make it into either of Elvis' early Seventies documentaries, rehearsal versions of the song are on later album releases *That's The Way It Is - Special Edition* and FTD's *The Way It Was*. For the second movie, in the 2000s FTD released a run-through on *Elvis On Tour—The Rehearsals* collection.

The song is amply covered on FTD live releases *Elvis at the International*, *Writing For The King*, *All Shook Up*, *Polk Salad Annie*, *The Impossible Dream*, *An American Trilogy*, *Summer Festival*, *Takin' Tahoe Tonight*, *Closing Night*, *Live In L.A.*, *It's Midnight*, *I Found My Thrill*, *Dragonheart*, *Big Boss Man*, *Tucson '76*, *New Year's Eve*, *Spring Tours '77* and *Unchained Melody*.

To mix things up a little bit, Elvis often eased his way into the high octane intro by telling a soft-voiced story before blasting the audience with the high-volume opening line. He also sometimes played around with the words, at various times turning the dog into an aardvark, warthog or some other critter.

The original studio version is a must on practically every Elvis "best of" compilation, right the way back to 1958 release *Elvis' Golden Records*. Later outings include *Worldwide 50 Gold Award Hits, Vol. 1*, *Elvis: A Legendary Performer, Vol. 3*, *Elvis Sings Leiber & Stoller*, *The Top 10 Hits*, *The King Of Rock And Roll*, *Elvis '56*, *Platinum: A Life in Music*, *Artist Of The Century*, *ELVIS 30 #1 Hits*, *Hitstory*, *Elvis Rock* and *The Essential Elvis Presley*.

A home recording in which Elvis exchanges the lyrics with "Que Sera" came out on 1998 bootleg *Greetings From Germany*.

The track has pride of place on practically every Elvis "best of" compilations.

In 2004, *Rolling Stone* magazine placed the song at no. 19 in the top 500 Songs of All Time. Elvis watched Freddie Bell and the Bellboys perform a rocked-up version of this Willie Mae "Big Mama" Thornton hit from 1953 (when it stayed at the top of the R & B charts for seven weeks) a number of times when he was in Las Vegas in May 1956, though he no doubt knew the original too. Elvis almost immediately incorporated the song into his own live act, using the Freddie Bell and the Bellboys version as his template, including their jokey line about the rabbit. Thornton's growling blues version had been written by New York white guys Leiber and Stoller (producer Johnny Otis had a credit on the original), though in later years Mama Thornton claimed that it was her input that made the song.

The original pressing of the song by Big Mama Thornton may have had an influence on Sam Phillips's decision to sell off Elvis' management contract. Sun artist Rufus Thomas's answer record "Bear Cat" was the label's biggest hit to date when it came out in 1953, but it was so closely patterned on the original that Phillips had to pay songwriters Leiber and Stoller a substantial sum of money after losing a lawsuit. It has been suggested that Phillips needed to realize some cash to pay off his debt, and Elvis' contract was his biggest asset. Songwriters Jerry Leiber & Mike Stoller went on to supply Elvis with a slew of hits.

The song also came out on EP *The Real Elvis* in 1956. Album releases during Elvis' lifetime include *Elvis' Golden Records* and *Elvis Recorded Live On Stage In Memphis*. He performed a high-energy version of the song in one of his medleys on the famed NBC TV Special in 1968. He introduced it as his "special song" on his return to the live stage in Las Vegas in August 1969, recorded for posterity on *From Memphis To Vegas*. Not surprisingly, he reprised the song for the vast majority of his live performances—at least 50 different versions of Elvis doing "Hound Dog" have been released over the years, not to mention dozens and dozens of performances on bootleg.

In concert in the Seventies, Elvis often eased his way into the raucous intro by telling a sweet little soft-voiced story before kapowing the audience with the opening line. To liven up his umpteenth performance of the song, he was not averse to playing around with the words and turning the dog into an aardvark, warthog or some other critter.

ELVIS SAID IN 1956: "It's a beautiful song. Has great lyrics—four lines."

"HOUSE OF SAND"

This Bill Giant / Bernie Baum / Florence Kaye soundtrack tune for *Paradise, Hawaiian Style* was recorded at Radio Recorders, with the band laying down the instrumentals on July 27 in late July, 1965 and, with Elvis laying down movie and record version the vocals at a subsequent session in early on August 4 for movie and record versions.

The song has since appeared on the *Double Feature* and FTD releases for the movie; the latter includes an alternate takeAlternate fans can find a different take on the 2004 FTD release covering the movie.

"HOUSE THAT HAS EVERYTHING, A"

Elvis recorded this Sid Tepper / Roy C. Bennett track for *Clambake* on February 21, 1967 in Nashville.

Later appearances are on *Elvis Sings Sid Tepper & Roy C. Bennett* and the *Double Features* release (with *Kissin' Cousins* and *Stay Away, Joe*).

Alternate takes are on the FTD *Clambake* release from 2006.

HOUSTON, CISSY
(B. EMILY DRINKARD, 1932)

One of the Sweet Inspirations, the all-female backing group that performed with Elvis from 1969 onwards, though in more recent times best known for being the mother of singer Whitney.

Houston grew up in New Jersey as part of a family that sang gospel—she began performing at the age of five. She was signed to Atlantic in the Sixties, where she sang backing for many great soul and R & B acts, including Aretha Franklin and other Atlantic and Muscle Shoals performers.

Houston only sang with Elvis for s short while before embarking on a solo career at the start of the Seventies (she sang the original of "Midnight Train to Georgia"). She continued performing into her fifties and beyond.

"HOW CAN YOU LOSE WHAT YOU NEVER HAD"

Elvis recorded this Ben Weisman / Sid Wayne song in on February 21, 1967 at RCA's Nashville studio for the *Clambake* soundtrack. Though it didn't make it into the film, it was included on the soundtrack LP, and in the fullness of time on the *Double Feature* release for the movie, paried with *Kissin' Cousins*. An alternate version appeared on *Collectors Gold*; FTD's 2006 version of *Clambake* offers the original and further alternates.

"HOW DO YOU THINK I FEEL"

Elvis recorded this Wayne Walker / Webb Pierce-composed song in on September 1, 1956 at Radio Recorders in Los Angeles. It had been a hit for both Red Sovine and Jimmie Rodgers Snow in 1954. Elvis' version was released as an album cut on the Elvis LP and on the Strictly Elvis EP. He'd had a stab at recording it back in his Sun days, but neither he nor Sam Phillips had been happy with the result.

The song has since appeared on n recent years, the song was reissued onl *The King Of Rock And Roll* and *The Country Side of Elvis*.

A Sun rehearsal featuring Scotty and D.J. Fontana features on bootleg *Unsurpassed Masters* and on independent release *Memphis Recording Service Vol. 2*.

"HOW GREAT THOU ART"

Elvis first recorded this song as the title track of his second gospel album in at RCA's Nashville Studios on May 25, 1966. It was later released as the B-side on a single with "His Hand in Mine" in March 1969, in time for Easter that year, when it failed to chart.

The swelling spiritual was first released in the English language by George Beverly Shea in 1955, though the song's roots go back to the Old Continent and the previous century. It was originally a 19th century Swedish hymn written by Carl Boberg, which was translated into German, Russian and finally into English by Stuart Hine in the late Forties. Before Elvis, the Blackwood Brothers and The Statesmen had covered the song.

Elvis is said to have performed the song as far back as 1956 with the Blackwoods. In the lead-up to his 1966 recording, he had been singing it so often at Graceland with Charlie Hodge that Ernst Jorgensen speculates this was "the most in-depth rehearsals he had ever undertaken! In the studio, Elvis slowed down the pace for added dramatic effect. One by one, he recorded each of the four quartet roles, becoming so deeply involved that by the end of recording, he almost fainted. Jerry Schilling later said it was "as if his inner being was leaving his body."

By the end of 1970, "How Great Thou Art" had become one of the high points of Elvis' live act. In 1974 it won him a Grammy for "Best Inspirational Performance" for his rendition on the *Elvis Recorded Live On Stage in Memphis* LP, the one most often reproduced on gospel compilations. Even in his final concerts when his energy was ebbing, Elvis gave his all on this one.

Since lending itself as the title track for his 1966 gospel album, the original studio cut has appeared on *Elvis: A Legendary Performer, Vol. 2*, *He Walks Beside Me*, *Amazing Grace*, *Peace in the Valley*, *Ultimate Gospel*, *Christmas Peace*, and *Elvis Inspirational* among others.

An alternate take from the 1966 studio session may be heard on *Platinum: A Life In Music*. An early live performance of this song, from Las Vegas in 1971, came out on 2004 FTD album *The Impossible Dream*.

Elvis sings regularly sang the song right up to the end; it made the cut for his the song during one of his final concerts, recorded for the *Elvis in Concert* documentary and album.

Other live versions have appeared on *Elvis Aron Presley*, *Amazing Grace*, *Peace in the Valley*, *Live in Las Vegas and*, *Elvis: Close Up* and *Elvis Live*. More live versions are to be found , and on FTD live albums *Closing Night*, *It's Midnight* and *Dinner at Eight* and *Unchained Melody*.

HOW GREAT THOU ART

A gospel album recorded at an energy-charged Nashville recording session in 1966, that Elvis was particularly proud of in later years.. Many commentators regard this album as Elvis' statement of intent to make the music he wanted, after years of lackluster material.

According to Larry Geller, Elvis was more closely involved in choosing the material for this album than any other. To get the atmosphere right in the studio, Elvis had the lights turned down low and candles lit.

As well as his usual Nashville studio musicians, Elvis was joined for the first time by gospel vocal group The Imperials, fortifying the sound produced by The Jordanaires. The LP sold 200,000 copies on its initial release in February 1967, spending a total of 29 weeks on the *Billboard* album charts and peaking at #18, despite no single being released for extra promotional punch. The album sold consistently ever afterwards to multiple platinum status. Perhaps more important to Elvis, it won him the first Grammy award of his long career, the 1967 "Best Sacred Performance" award. The album also picked up an award for Best Engineered Album of 1967, trumping Sergeant Pepper.

When Elvis left Nashville the mix he approved had his voice even further back than usual, to favor the gospel harmonies he loved. He reportedly became livid with rage when he heard the pre-release album and found that his voice had been brought up in the mix.

TRACK LISTING:
1. How Great Thou Art
2. In The Garden
3. Somebody Bigger Than You And I
4. Farther Along
5. Stand By Me
6. Without Him
7. So High
8. Where Could I Go But To The Lord
9. By And By
10. If The Lord Wasn't Walking By My Side
11. Run On
12. Where No One Stands Alone
13. Crying In The Chapel

Later releases of the album also featured "Peace In The Valley."

"HOW THE WEB WAS WOVEN"

Elvis laid down this crescendo of a ballad in on June 5, 1970 during a Nashville recording session, a year after Jackie Lomax released the Clive Westlake / David Most composition. The version in Elvis' concert documentary *Elvis: That's The Way It Is* and accompanying LP features Elvis at the piano. The song has since appeared on *Walk A Mile In My Shoes*, *That's The Way It Is—Special Edition* and multiple bootlegs before aAn official alternate from the Nashville studio session did not appear surfaced on until 2002 FTD album *The Nashville Marathon*.

"HOW WOULD YOU LIKE TO BE"

Elvis recorded this playful ditty, written by new (to him) songwriters Ben Raleigh and Mark Barkan, on September 22, 1962 at Radio Recorders for *It Happened at the World's Fair* and the tie-in LP; in the movie, he sings it with Vicki Tiu. In November 1966, the song came out as the B-side to "If Every Day Was Like Christmas."

The track appeared on 1972 album *Elvis Sings Hits from His Movies*, and was a shoe-in for the 1978 Pickwick release *Elvis Sings For Children* (re-released in 2002 as *Elvis Sings for Kids*). The *Double Feature* release for the movie wouldn't have been complete without it; an alternate take is on the FTD *It Happened at the World's Fair* release from 2003.

"HOW'S THE WORLD TREATING YOU"

Elvis laid down a minimalist version of this 1953 Eddy Arnold hit in Nashville in on September 1, 1956. The track saw public release on the *Elvis* album that same year. The song was written by Boudleaux Bryant and Chet Atkins, who was producing Elvis on that particular recording session. It later appeared on 1957 EP *Strictly Elvis*. More recently it's been seen on the album *The King Of Rock And Roll* and *The Country Side of Elvis*.

HOWE, BONES
(B. DAYTON HOWE, 1933)

Howe worked on Elvis' 1968 NBC Comeback Special show, assisting director Steve Binder and producing the new songs Elvis that recorded for the show.

Howe and Elvis had actually met a decade earlier, when Elvis first worked at the Radio Recorders studio in LA; at that time, Howe was working an assistant engineer to Thorne Nogar. During his career, Howe produced records for artists ranging from Jerry Lee Lewis to 5th Dimension and Tom Waits, and won a Grammy for his work. He went on to work as a high-level record executive and movie music coordinator.

HULETT, TOM

Promoter Tom Hulett managed Concerts West, the company that staged Elvis' concerts during the 1970s, as well as working with other big event stars like Jimi Hendrix and Led Zeppelin.

In 1976, as Elvis' health and ability to perform went into decline, Elvis sought solace from Hulett after the Colonel criticized one of his performances. Hulett told him, "You are the biggest entertainer there is, and everybody loves you," all that Elvis needed to carry on touring, despite the scathing reviews.

Larry Geller says that just before he died, Elvis was planning finally to cut loose from Colonel Parker and install Hulett as his manager.

TOM HULETT (on the first time he ever saw Elvis): "When he walked onstage, the place exploded, and he exploded, and it was one of the greatest nights of show business I've ever seen in my life."

HUMBARD, REX
(B. 1919-2007)

One of the first ever TV evangelists through his Cathedral of Tomorrow church, Humbard delivered a sermon at Elvis' funeral in August 1977. Humbard was one of the first preachers to turn to the new medium of TV in 1949, and his shows earned him a worldwide following.

Elvis had met him in 1975 (and dedicated a performance of "How Great Thou Art" to him in Las Vegas at the end of that year). The following December, Elvis confided in the pastor that he felt that his life lacked all meaning. Humbard is said to have been a secret visitor to Graceland during the last years of Elvis' life.

HUMES HIGH SCHOOL

After the Presleys moved from Tupelo to Memphis, Elvis was enrolled in eighth or ninth grade (depending on who's telling the story) at the Humes High School (as Elvis Aaron, with two As), located at 659 N. Manassas Street. A number of fellow pupils at the school, like Elvis, had moved to Memphis from poorer rural areas, along with the children of blue-collar workers in good jobs.

According to Vernon, on his first day Elvis was so upset by the move to this 1,600 pupil school that he ran back home, "bug eyed" with nerves. That year, one classmate recalls parents contributing to a fund to help the Presley family out; Elvis was coming to school with holes in his shoes.

In his first year at school, Elvis achieved an A in language, Bs in spelling, history and physical education, and a C in music, arithmetic and science. When music teacher Elsie Marmann told him that he couldn't sing, Elvis brought his guitar in, sang to the class and got her to admit that her assertion was a matter of taste, not of substance. His report card gradually settled down to a C average.

In his junior year, starting in 1951, Elvis began to show the self-confidence that would conquer his shyness. He started to grow his hair long and slick it back, and he began to wear more flamboyant clothes. He'd also sometimes play the role of class clown. That year he tried, and failed, to join the school football team, only managing a few weeks in the squad.

Elvis went to his senior prom with Regis Wilson Vaughn, whom he was dating at the time.

Elvis performed in public with a guitar at the school's annual Minstrel Show, in April 1953, in front of 1600 people. Every year Principal

Thomas C. Brindley used the variety concert to raise money for pupils who didn't have money for extra-curricular school activities. Pals of Elvis' were surprised he managed to overcome his shyness, prop one leg up on a chair on stage and perform.

During his final year at Humes, Elvis got into trouble for frequently falling asleep. Biographers do not concur on the level of Elvis' commitment to school in his later years. Some Elvisologists highlight his lack of interest in academic subjects; others point to the school yearbook which shows him as an active participant in all kinds of extra-curricular activities, not just ROTC (Reserve Officer Training Corps.) but the Biology, English, Speech and History clubs. Elvis' graduation from high school—with a good conduct certificate, despite the occasional paddling—was a proud first for his immediate family. He graduated on June 3, 1953, as part of Class 202.

After he had left Humes, he returned to the following year's Minstrel Show with girlfriend Dixie Locke.

Elvis remained (almost) lifelong friends with a number of pals from Humes, notably George Klein and Red West. At his Seventies shows, Elvis was happy to invite former Humes classmates backstage to reminisce about the old days if he or Red West found out that they were in the audience.

On January 13, 1956, Elvis returned to his high school for an impromptu ten-minute performance on Father's Night, before attending the Humes and South Side High School graduation ceremony at Ellis Auditorium on May 30, 1956.

He took pals along to visit his senior-class homeroom teacher Mildred Scrivener (who had predicted Elvis would make it big) in September 1956, and donated $900 for the school to buy new uniforms for its ROTC officer training program. Today, the school is known as Humes Junior High School. As of 2006, there was a campaign to rename the establishment the Elvis A. Presley Junior High School.

MARY SANDERS-ANDERSON (CLASSMATE): "We all knew that he was different, very, very, different . . . We later found out just how different he was."

MARTY LACKER: "He was basically a loner. He had a couple of friends he hung around with but that was it."

Book:
Early Elvis: The Humes Years by Bill E. Burk, Red Oak Press, 1990.

HUMOR

Elvis always had time for jokes, pranks and comedy turns. His propensity to crack jokes on stage was something that Colonel Parker tried to drum out of him when he first took over management duties. Apart from the occasional witty riposte in his dealings with the press (when asked what kind of woman he thought he'd marry, Elvis answered, "A blonde, or a brunette, or a redhead, or a technicolor"), Elvis kept his humor confined to his private life, often in the form of pranks with his entourage pals, who could always be counted upon to laugh at his jokes. When Elvis returned to live performing in the Seventies, his stage banter provided him with a new outlet for his sense of humor—often to the Colonel's displeasure.

At the outset of his career Elvis mocked the authorities in Jacksonville, Florida, after they threatened him with jail if he indulged in his "obscene movement." Up on stage, Elvis simply waggled his finger during his performance; the audience went just as wild as if he'd unleashed his most free-hipped gyrations.

On one of his "Ed Sullivan Show" appearances, Elvis presented the song he was about to sing as one of the saddest songs he'd ever heard, with beautiful lyrics, and then burst into a raucous opening of "Hound Dog." He liked this joke so much that he used variations of it throughout his performing career.

Elvis had a quick wit in social situations. When he met Tony Curtis on the Paramount lot, Curtis told Elvis to call him by his first name, rather than the formal "Mr. Curtis" Elvis was using. When asked what he should call Elvis, without batting an eyelid Elvis replied: "Mr Presley."

Elvis was capable of cracking up for half an hour at a time, and was known for his incredibly infectious laugh. If he was seized by a laughing fit during recording, nothing serious would happen in the studio for quite a while. A practical joke or a funny moment in a movie (Monty Python or Peter Sellers) could have the same effect, reducing Elvis to a giggling wreck.

Offstage, Elvis enjoyed partaking in surreal, rapid-fire free-association repartee, and talking in funny voices that wouldn't have been out of place in a Peter Sellers comedy.

Steve Dunleavy writes that the only thing that kept Elvis going back to Hollywood for his interminable film commitments in the Sixties was the chance to indulge in horseplay on set.

Elvis got a kick out of recording songs with racy lyrics camouflaged as humor—something that applied to many of the R & B originals he covered in his early days. In the studio and during rehearsals he would often mess around substituting words to make those present crack up—one of the reasons why outtakes and the FTD series of releases are so popular with serious fans. The rehearsals featured in the revised cut of Elvis: That's The Way It Is show just how much clowning around was involved when Elvis was on form. He'd also happily swap lyrics round on his songs to rib members of the band—in 1970, two lines of "Are You Lonesome Tonight?" were transformed into "do you gaze at your bald head and wish you had hair," at the expense of a follicly-challenged backing singer, resulting in Elvis cracking up for the rest of the song (the famous "laughing version").

Elvis jokingly referred to his first million-selling smash hit as "heartburn motel." In 1956, he told his Las Vegas audience, "I'd like to stand out here and shake, rattle and roll for ya all night, but we're booked in Alcatraz tomorrow night, we got a long drive ahead of us . . ."

In the depths of his Sixties soundtrack recording session hell, when he found all kinds of excuses to avoid turning up to work with the band and instead made solitary overdubs at a later date, sometimes Elvis was reduced to helpless laughter at the inanity of the material he was expected to cover. FTD releases of soundtracks from this period have Elvis in fits of giggles.

The guys with whom Elvis surrounded himself were as much up for pranks and jokes as he was. They waged mock wars using anything and everything that came to hand, from water to shaving cream to Roman candles. Lamar Fike was often the joker in the pack, quick with the side-splitting observation. His weight also made him the butt of jokes, and an obvious candidate for taking pratfalls that sent the other guys into convulsions of laughter.

Elvis' midnight concerts in Las Vegas often found him ad-libbing risquéè and humorous lines to his best-known songs, and cracking up as a result. A favorite target was the song "Blueberry Hill," which over the years he twisted into a number of side-splitting alternatives (spliced together into a virtual medley on 2006 FTD release I Found My Thrill).

Elvis regularly introduced his Las Vegas shows with a joke line, deliberately announcing the venue as a rival Vegas hotel, and himself as some other singer. He'd also take in comic acts in Las Vegas—he apparently liked Joan Rivers's humor and saw her perform.

Elvis was quick to riff off comments from the floor. When a fan called out a request to sing "Just Pretend," quick as a flash Elvis replied, "Honey, I've been pretending for sixteen years."

There was humor backstage too, especially at the end-of-engagement parties Elvis held for his band members and entourage. One such moment, when Jackie Kahane and Felton Jarvis mercilessly mock Elvis, appeared on CD in 2003. Titled Reading of the Diary, the pre-prepared sketch shows that Elvis was more than capable of taking an extended joke at his own expense.

ODE TO A ROBIN

A favorite Elvis ditty (he recites it on 2006 FTD album Made in Memphis, though it had already appeared on bootlegs such as A Private Moment with the King):

As I awoke this morning, when all sweet things are born,
A robin perched upon my sill to greet the coming dawn
He sang his song so sweetly, and paused for a moment's lull.
I gently raised the window, and crushed his fucking skull.

HUMOROUS BOOKS ON ELVIS:

The Two Kings: Jesus & Elvis, by A.J. Jacobs, Bantam, 1994
Where's Elvis? Documented Sightings Through the Ages, by Daniel Klein and Hans Teensma, Viking Penguin, 1997
The Gospel of Elvis: The New Testament, by Bob Laughlin, Writers Club Press, 2001
Life Lessons From Elvis, by Anthony Rubino, Thomas Nelson, 2006

PRISCILLA: "Elvis' sense of humor was contagious. He laughed about things that often wouldn't make sense to anyone else, yet anyone around him would usually end up laughing too."

JOHN LENNON, ON THE TIME THEY MET IN 1965: "It was Elvis' sense of humor that stuck in my mind. He liked to laugh and make others laugh too."

SONNY WEST: "I wish we had a full-length documentary on the way we all carried on... It would be a heck of a comedy."

LAMAR FIKE: "His humor was so unusual, and so hip and inside, that few people caught it."

KATHY WESTMORELAND: "He just had a special knack for finding humor in everything most of the time."

LARRY GELLER: "Elvis was one of the funniest people I ever met. . . . his wry sense of humor and funny way of looking at things had us cracking up most of the time."

PAMELA CLARKE KEOGH: "Life around Elvis was very fast and funny; the humor was sort of like Monty Python, very inside."

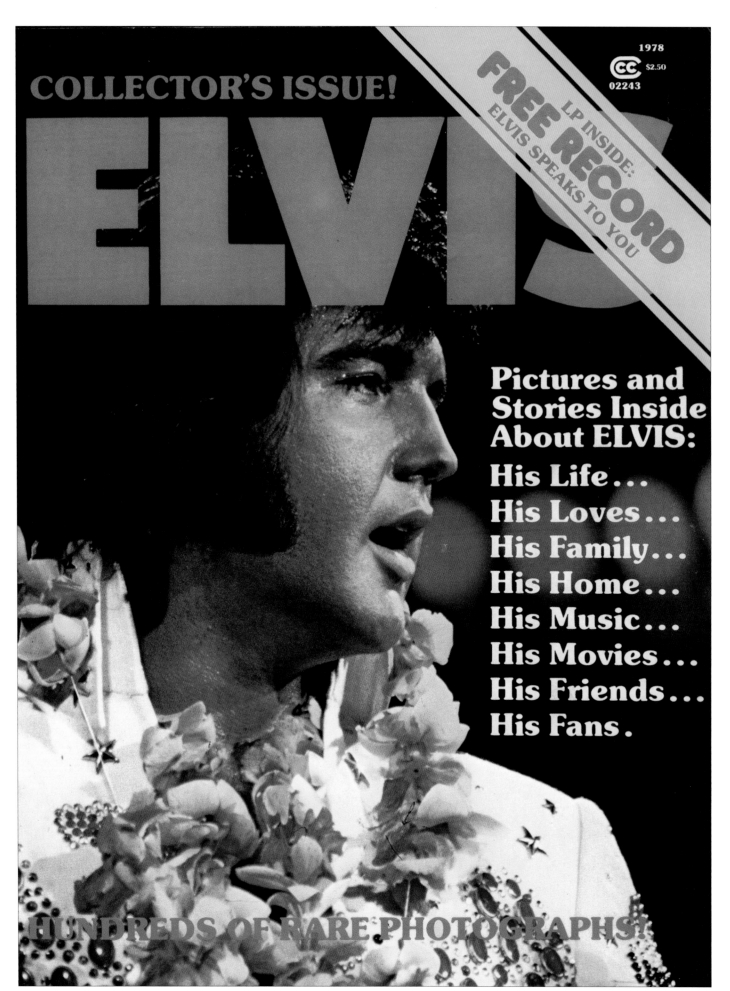

COLLECTOR'S ISSUE!

ELVIS

1978
$2.50
02243

LP INSIDE:
FREE RECORD
ELVIS SPEAKS TO YOU

Pictures and
Stories Inside
About ELVIS:

His Life…
His Loves…
His Family…
His Home…
His Music…
His Movies…
His Friends…
His Fans.

HUNDREDS OF RARE PHOTOGRAPHS!

1977 U.S. Tribute magazine.

HUMPERDINCK, ENGELBERT
(B. ARNOLD GEORGE DORSEY, 1936)

This British-born crooner who borrowed his name from a 19th-century German composer performed in the late Fifties under the name Gerry Dorsey. Humperdinck sat in on various Elvis shows in Las Vegas, including one at the Hilton in 1976 when he shared a table with Roy Orbison. When Elvis presented the singers from the stage, he dubbed them "some of the finest singers in the world."

After her divorce, Priscilla and her sister went to an Engelbert Humperdinck concert in Miami, where the crooner reputedly propositioned his friend and rival's ex.

Elvis performed a number of songs that were hits for Humperdinck, including "Release Me" and "There Goes My Everything."

ENGELBERT HUMPERDINCK: "I learned about humility, charm and how to work an audience from watching Elvis in concert. If you're going to steal—and every performer does it from someone at some time—then steal from the best, which Elvis was."

"HUNDRED YEARS FROM NOW, A"

Elvis recorded this Lester Flatt / Earl Scruggs song in Nashville on June 4, 1970, strumming on guitar himself. Never released during his lifetime, it first came out on *Walk A Mile In My Shoes*. Another take appeared on *Essential Elvis Vol. 4*. That playful take plus one other from the session appeared on 2002 FTD release *The Nashville Marathon*. The song also featured on BMG's 2006 release *Elvis Country* (having appeared on the CD reissue of the original *Elvis Country* too).

HUNT, DR. WILLIAM ROBERT

The sixty-eight year-old obstetrician who attended Gladys Presley in her home on January 8, 1935, when Elvis Aron and his stillborn twin brother Jesse Garon came into the world. The local doctor was called in by the midwife, Edna Robertson (in some accounts Edna Martin), after she ran into difficulties.

HUNTER, IVORY JOE
(1914-1974)

Veteran R & B pianist, singer and songwriter Ivory Joe, born in Kirbyville, Texas, had a solid reputation among early rock cognoscenti before his first crossover hit "Since I Met You Baby" in 1956, his only top-40 hit which peaked at #12. Though long-lasting personal fame eluded him, Joe was a prolific songsmith, by some accounts penning as many as 7,000 songs, and ran his own record labels too. In later years, he dabbled in country, and continued recording well into the Sixties.

One of Elvis' personal favorites was Hunter's 1950 hit "I Almost Lost My Mind," which he came close to recording himself in 1956.

Elvis met Hunter at Graceland in the summer of 1957, when pal George Klein brought him over. Elvis promised to record one of his latest tracks, "My Wish Came True," which he did soon after. Around this time, Elvis also recorded Hunter compositions "Ain't That Loving You Baby" and "I Need You So."

At a 1971 recording session Elvis unwound from his contracted output of Christmas and gospel numbers with Hunter hits "I Will Be True," "It's Still Here" and "I'll Take You Home Again Kathleen."

When Elvis heard that Hunter was seriously ill in the summer of 1974, he sent $1,000 to help with the hospital bills. In the accompanying letter, Elvis wrote: "Joe is a great talent and has been an inspiration to many artists that have come along. It hurts me deeply to hear of his condition."

"HURT"

Elvis sang from the heart when he launched into this 1954 Roy Hamilton R&B hit (written by Jimmie Crane and Al Jacobs) at a Graceland recording session in on early February 5, sliding into February 6, 1976. During the recording session, on one take, Elvis added an impromtpu ripe selection of cuss words (a version that saw the light of day years later on 1996 bootleg *Elvis Among Friends*).

The song was released as a single in March 1976, paired with "For the Heart" on the B-side. The record initially failed to sell more than 250,000 copies; indeed, it only just crept into the top thirty, peaking at #28. Album appearances followed on *From Elvis Presley*

Boulevard, Memphis Tennessee and a live version on *Elvis in Concert* (album and broadcast documentary).

Ernst Jorgensen writes that the (straight version of the) song was "probably the most convincing recording of Elvis' twilight career." He which is why he, included an alternate version take of the song on *Platinum: A Life In Music*. Further Graceland session alternates are on *Today, Tomorrow & Forever* and FTD's *The Jungle Room Sessions*.

Posthumous LP releases of the master run from *Always On My Mind* to *Walk A Mile In My Shoes*, CD releases of *Moody Blue*, and the 2007 *The Essential Elvis Presley* issue.

Elvis sang the song live on a regular basis from March 1975 through to his final performances. Live versions recordings are available on on may be found FTD releases *Tucson '76 and*, *New Year's Eve* and *Unchained Melody*.

An alternative take from the Graceland session is on *Today, Tomorrow & Forever* and FTD's *The Jungle Room Sessions*.

"HUSKY DUSKY DAY"

A traditional song that Elvis sang *a capella* on the movie soundstage with Hope Lange for *Wild in the Country* in 1960. Though never officially released, it has appeared on several bootlegs, including such as *From Hollywood To Vegas*, *Eternal Elvis* and *Real Fun On Stage . . . And In The Studio*.

"HY GARDNER CALLING!"

Elvis was interviewed on this WRCA-TV phone-themed television show from the Warwick Hotel immediately after his July 1, 1956 performance on "The Steve Allen Show." Some commentators have taken as an admission of guilt Elvis' decision not to venture a response to the question whether he used marijuana to get into his on-stage frenzy. Sharing the show that night was an Egyptian dancer, a veteran bandleader, and the anonymous author of a book called *I Was A Dope Addict*.

"I Apologize"

No full version of Elvis singing this song, a top-ten hit for Billy Eckstine in 1951, has ever been released officially, though Elvis does assay a brief excerpt in the run up to a take of "Beyond The Bend," released on *Collectors Gold*, from during a recording session in on September 22, 1962. Originally written by Al Hoffman, Al Goodhart and Ed Nelson, in 1931 the song became an early hit for Bing Crosby. Rumors have surfaced that Elvis laid down this track on a lost recording at Sun. He still remembered enough of the song at a 1974 Tahoe show to sing a line or two at a 1974 Tahoe show.

"I Asked The Lord (He's Only A Prayer Away)"

Elvis made a home recording of this Johnny Lange / Jimmy Duncan gospel song during his time in Germany in the service with the Army. Posthumously, RCA released a version of the tune on 4-disc collection *A Golden Celebration*. Alternate home recordings have since appeared on *The Home Recordings* and the 2000 *Peace in the Valley* compilation.

"I Beg Of You"

At a Radio Recorders session in February 1957, Elvis strove through several unsuccessful blocks of studio time before he laid down the version cracking of "I Beg Of You" on February 23. That master that first saw release the light of day in January 1958 as the B-side to "Don't."

"I Beg Of You" rose to #8 in the charts, came within a whisker of #1 on the country charts, and helped make the disc a platinum-seller. In short order, the song came out on EP *A Touch of Gold, Vol. 1* and on LP *Elvis' Gold Records Vol. 2*. Since then, it has come out on *Worldwide 50 Gold Award Hits Vol. 1*, re-releases of *Loving You*, *The King Of Rock And Roll* and *Hitstory*.

Several of the many and particularly varied alternate takes of this Rosemarie McCoy and Kelly Owens composition have come out appeared over the years on *Essential Elvis Vol. 2*, *The King Of Rock And Roll*, *Today, Tomorrow & Forever*, *Elvis: Close Up*, and BMG and FTD's 2000s *Loving You* releases.

"I Believe"

Elvis packed plenty in the of emotion into to this song when he recorded it at Radio Recorders in on January 12, 1957. Written by Ervin Drake, Irvin Graham, Jimmy Shirl and Al Stillman, the song was originally a hit for Jane Froman in 1953 on the back of her TV show. Elvis favorite Roy Hamilton also covered the songtune, though the biggest-selling version was by Frankie Laine, for whom it set a record for the most weeks at #1 in the UK.

Elvis' version was released on the *Peace In The Valley* EP and *Elvis' Christmas Album* the year he recorded it. It was revived for 1971 budget album *You'll Never Walk Alone*, before more recently appearing on compilations *Essential Elvis Vol. 2*, *Amazing Grace*, *The King Of Rock And Roll*, *Peace in the valley*, *Christmas Peace* and, *Elvis Christmas* and the reissued *You'll Never Walk Alone*. Alternates are, at the time of writing, confined to bootlegs (i.e. *Just A Closer Walk With Thee*).

"I Believe In The Man In The Sky"

Originally released on Elvis' 1960 gospel album *His Hand in Mine* and, recorded at RCA's Nashville studios in on October 30 that year, this track was the B-side to "Crying In The Chapel," which sold very strongly on release as a single for Easter 1965. Written by Richard Howard, the song had previously been a success for The Statesmen. RCA featured the song on *Worldwide Gold Award Hits, Vol. 2*; BMG has brought out the originally-released recording on several recent compilations, from *Amazing Grace* to, *Peace in the Valley* and *Ultimate Gospel*.

The first take from Elvis' October 1960 recording session is on *Essential Elvis, Vol. 6* and on FTD's *His Hand in Mine* 2-CD release from 2006, which also features other outtakes. Bootleg *Just A Closer Walk With Thee* offers several alternates.

"I Can Help"

Elvis gave this Billy Swan #1 hit from 1974 an upbeat treatment at the RCA studios in Hollywood on March 11, 1975 for release on the album *Today*. After the session, producer Felton Jarvis gave Swan (an Elvis fan) a memento from the session—a pair of socks Elvis had worn.

The track has since come out on *Walk A Mile In My Shoes*. An unremixed version of the song, just the way it was recorded on the single take Elvis laid down, was included on *Our Memories of Elvis, Vol. 2* and 2005 FTD release *Today*.

"I Can't Help It (If I'm Still In Love With You)"

Elvis sang this Hank Williams hit for pleasure many times, at least twice within the range of home recording equipment microphones—it was his and Anita Wood's special song. As well as at Eddie Fadal's place in Texas in 1958, he recorded a version while in Germany in 1959, released for the first time officially many years later on *Platinum: A Life In Music*.

"I Can't Stop Loving You"

A country #1 for Don Gibson in 1958 and the biggest-selling tune of 1962 as sung by Ray Charles, "I Can't Stop Loving You" became an instant Elvis showstopper when he returned to the stage in Las Vegas in 1969—that initial big-band version complete with perfectly-timed screaming fan is on *From Memphis To Vegas* (aka *Elvis In Person at the International Hotel*). He continued to sing the song with regularity right through to the summer of 1974. He also dusted it off after a two-year hiatus for his last ever concert in June 1977.

Elvis actually first got to grips with the song at an American Studio jam session in February 1969, in a jam session for producer Chips Moman before he worked it up for the stage.

Elvis relied on "I Can't Stop Loving You" before closing number "Can't Help Falling In Love" at his June 1972 New York Madison Square shows, as released on the live album. An alternate performance from the venue appeared in 1977 on *Welcome to My World* (and in 1997 on *An Afternoon in the Garden*). Elvis also included this big number on his *Aloha From Hawaii* set in 1973, and when he played his home town in 1974 (*Elvis Recorded Live On Stage in Memphis*, when he gave it the medley treatment with "Blueberry Hill").

Live versions of the song abound on dozens of bootlegs. Alternate Various official concert recordings have appeared on CD reissues of *On Stage*, *Live in Las Vegas*, *Elvis: Close Up*, the 2006 issue of *Elvis Country*, and FTD releases *All Shook Up*, *Polk Salad Annie*, *The Way It Was*, *One Night in Vegas*, *Takin' Tahoe Tonight*, *Closing Night*, *I Found My Thrill*, *Live in LA* and *Southern Nights*.

Elvis rehearsing the song in 1970 is on the recent collectors' issues of *Elvis: That's The Way It Is*. The version from the initial recording session, paired with "This Time," is finally saw the light of day on in the Nineties on anthology *From Nashville to Memphis*, and later that decade on the 1999 BMG album *Suspicious Minds: The Memphis 1969 Anthology*.

"I Couldn't Live Without You"

Elvis' personal back-up band members of Voice attempt gave this song—written by pianist Per Erik ("Pete") Hallin—a whirl at Elvis shows, in the summer of 1974. It is available ,on bootleg only.

Icon

Elvis has transcended the status of iconic performer to become an icon of fame itself.

Through sound judgment, shrewd management and just plain old good fortune, the multiple times that Elvis and his handlers remade his image over the course of his career kept him at the top of the field for his lifetime and beyond. Ever since, the Elvis template has been followed assiduously by many an entertainer since, most successfully perhaps by at the head of the pack Madonna.

In fact, the iconic Elvis is a succession of Elvis from different times in his career: Elvis as rebel, Elvis as rocker, Elvis as American dream come true, patriotic soldier, matinee idol, crooner, legend revivified, Las Vegas entertainer, victim of excess, then after his death—long after his death—his elevation to a more general and homogeneous cultural icon, shorthand for success and excess, marking his posthumous career as the world's biggest money-making dead celebrity.

For fans, Elvis has been an iconic beacon in their lives since the first time they heard or saw him, not just as a figure to look up to, but as a man with whom they felt (and feel) they share much in common. For his early detractors, he was the devil in disguise; for record and movie studio executives, a success so huge that for decades the hunt was on for the 'new Elvis'; for punk rockers, a fat holdover from the past worthy of derision; for new generations of young people, the guy whose songs they've heard on Disney cartoons.

Elvis' metamorphosis into an iconic figure may have felt more like fossilization as it started to move ahead in the Seventies. People who knew him agree that when Elvis was making new music and faced a new challenge, he was happy. By the time he performed his globe-girdling live show *Aloha From Hawaii*, his ever-loving fans were more interested in the old hits than anything new he brought to the table.

See also Academic Studies.

Dr. Garry Enders: "Elvis Presley is the supreme socio-cultural icon in the history of pop culture."

Leonard Bernstein: "Elvis is the greatest cultural force in the twentieth century. He introduced the beat to everything, music, language, clothes, it's a whole new social revolution - the Sixties comes from it."

Elvis at a press conference in Las Vegas (1969).

Greil Marcus: "Elvis Presley is a supreme figure in American life, one whose presence, no matter how banal and predictable, brooks no real comparisons."

Norbert Putnam: "I always felt that he was responsible for every detail, every nuance, of his image."

Pauline Kael: "The mixture in Elvis—part artist, part exhibitionist, part good ol' boy, part romantic kid, part unknown—could have fused only in pop culture, and it didn't fuse for long."

Marc Bolan: "He was the greatest living pop idol in the whole of the world."

Pamela Clarke Keogh: "In life, Elvis was a legend. In death, he became that thing he feared most, a myth."

Robert Plant: "He was so, so cool."

Books:

Elvis: A Tribute to His Life, by Susan M. Doll, Publications International Ltd, 1989.

Elvis: Man and Myth, by Sara Parker Danielsen, Bison Books, 1990.

"I Didn't Make It On Playing Guitar"

A jam Elvis improvised to warm up at his June 6, 1970 recording session in Nashville, not released officially until 1996 album A Hundred Years From Now (also known as Volume 4 of Essential Elvis).

"I Don't Care If the Sun Don't Shine"

Elvis gave this song a rockabilly treatment at Sun Studio on September 10, 1954, for release on the B-side of his second single, "Good Rockin' Tonight." After his contract was bought out by and transferred to RCA, his new label reissued the single and put the song on EP Any Way You Want Me (from which the song charted at #74), and later the A Date With Elvis album. Posthumously it has appeared on Sun compilations.

Mack David originally wrote the song for Walt Disney animated movie Cinderella, though the song did not make it to the final cut of the picture. In the early Fifties, it was a hit for Patti Page and Dean Martin among others.

The master and an alterante came out on the 1987 Sun anthology The Complete Sun Sessions (the 2006 version of this title ups the number of alternates to three and also features a live version). Sun Sessions featured an alternate mix, A Golden Celebration went with an alternate too, and Sunrise featured the master and an alternate. The original recording has since appeared on The King Of Rock And Roll and Elvis at Sun.

Live performances from 1955 may be heard on Sunrise, several various Louisiana Hayride albums, Memphis Recording Service Vol. 2 (Vol 1. features a studio version), and many bootlegs.

"I Don't Wanna Be Tied"

Giant, Baum and Kaye penned this Girls! Girls! Girls! tune for Elvis to record for the soundtrack and accompanying album at Radio Recorders on March 28, 1962. The song was originally known by the title "Twist Me Loose." It's on the soundtrack album and Double Features release from the Nineties. Bootleg Elvis Rocks and the Girls Roll has an alternate take to the spliced version that was originally released; official alternates were first issued on the 2007 FTD Girls! Girls! Girls! release.

"I Don't Want To"

A Janice Torre/Fred Spielman song that Elvis recorded in sweet-voiced style for Girls! Girls! Girls! at Radio Recorders in at the start of the soundtrack session on March 26, 1962. The song was cut from the movie but appeared on the soundtrack album and later the Double Features issue for the movie. More recently, it has appeared on the FTD soundtrack re-release

"I Feel So Bad"

Elvis recorded this 1954 Chuck Willis R & B hit in Nashville in on March 12, 1961. It was released as an A-side (on Elvis' insistence) over B-side track "Wild In The Country," the title song from his upcoming movie, in early May 1961. Fans bought the song in sufficient numbers to warrant #5 in the charts during a nine-week stay, selling over 600,000 copies. The song had its first album outing on Elvis' Golden Records Vol. 3. "I Feel So Bad" has since appeared on compilations including Worldwide Gold Award Hits, Vol. 1, Elvis Sings The Blues, Reconsider Baby, From Nashville to Memphis, Elvis 2nd to None, Hitstory and Elvis R 'n' B.

The first take from the Nashville session came out on Platinum: A Life In Music and 2006 FTD release Something For Everybody.

"I Feel That I've Known You Forever"

In Nashville on March 19, 1962 Elvis recorded this Doc Pomus / Alan Jeffreys ballad, for release soon after on the Pot Luck album. The song did double duty three years later when it found its way into the Tickle Me soundtrack and EP in 1965.

Later official outings are for the original release are limited to From Nashville to Memphis.

Alternate takes have appeared on FTD discs Long Lonely Highway, Studio B: Nashville Outtakes, Tickle Me and Pot Luck.

"I Forgot To Remember To Forget"

Elvis' fifth and final single on Sun Records (Sun 223) was released with "Mystery Train" in August 1955 and immediately entered regional charts in Florida, Tennessee and Texas. Two months later the song was on the Billboard national country music, jukebox and radio play charts; by the end of February it had become Elvis' first national #1 hit, after 24 weeks on the Country & Western charts. Boosted by an immediate re-release on his new label RCA at the end of 1955, the song totaled forty weeks on the country chart, a feat never bettered on any Billboard chart by any Elvis single.

Elvis recorded the Stan Kesler/Charlie Feathers composition on July 11, 1955. The song became was something of a Sun standard, recorded over the years by co-credited writer Charlie Feathers, Toni Arden, Johnny Cash and Jerry Lee Lewis.

RCA continued its one-track assault on the nation by bringing out "I Forgot To Remember To Forget" on EP Heartbreak Hotel in 1956 and on LP A Date With Elvis in 1959. The song has since appeared on The Sun Sessions, both of The Complete Sun Sessions releases, The King Of Rock And Roll, Great Country Songs, Sunrise, The Country Side of Elvis, Elvis at Sun, Elvis 2nd to None and Hitstory. It's also on independent release Memphis Recording Studio Vol. 2.

I Found My Thrill

A 2006 FTD concert release from Las Vegas, January 27, 1974 plus bonus tracks from later dates and a virtual "Blueberry Hill" medley.

Track listing:
1. Also Sprach Zarathustra
2. See See Rider
3. I Got A Woman / Amen
4. Love Me
5. Let Me Be There
6. You've Lost That Lovin' Feelin'
7. Sweet Caroline
8. Love Me Tender
9. Long Tall Sally / Whole Lotta Shakin' Goin' On / Your Mamma Don't Dance / Flip, Flop And Fly / Jailhouse Rock / Hound Dog
10. Fever
11. Polk Salad Annie
12. Spanish Eyes
13. Suspicious Minds
14. Introductions
15. I Can't Stop Loving You
16. Help Me
17. An American Trilogy
18. Let Me Be There
19. Can't Help Falling In Love / Closing Vamp
20. My Baby Left Me
21. Tryin' To Get To You
22. The First Time Ever I Saw Your Face
23. I Found My Thrill (Medley)

"I Got A Feelin' In My Body"

Elvis was at Stax on December 10, 1973 to record this funky Dennis Linde spiritual. The song came out on Good Times in 1974, with Dennis Linde's overdubbed guitar playing on the original release. Posthumously the song has come out on Our Memories of Elvis, Vol. 2, Walk A Mile In My Shoes, the 2000 reissue of Promised Land, Peace in the Valley and Elvis by the Presleys.

Essential Elvis, Vol. 5, Today, Tomorrow & Forever and FTD release Easter Special all feature alternate takes.

"I Got A Woman"

Elvis adopted this Ray Charles song into his live act in early 1955 while the original was still storming up the charts, and was still . Elvis continued to performing it "I Got A Woman" on his final tours more than two decades later.

Ray Charles combined the sacred with the profane when he put his unambiguously earthy lyrics to the music of gospel hymn "My Jesus Is All I Need." Charles's single rose to #2 on the Billboard R & B charts in early 1955.

This was the song that Elvis chose to launch commence his first ever recording session for RCA, in Nashville on January 10, 1955. Released as a single in late August 1956 with "I'm Counting On You" on the B-side, despite coming immediately after "Blue Suede Shoes" the song failed to chart—perhaps Charles's hit was still too fresh in people's minds to shell out for the Elvis variation. In some markets, including the UK, the song was released as "I Got A Sweetie." Undaunted, RCA put the track onto multiple EP releases in 1956 and included it on his first album, Elvis Presley.

"I Got A Woman" was one of three songs Elvis first performed on national TV, on CBS's "Stage Show" on January 28, 1956 (the recording is on A Golden Celebration, along with a live version from later that year recorded at the Mississippi-Alabama Fair and Dairy Show).

Earlier live performances are on a variety of albums from Elvis' Louisiana Hayride days, and on

Elvis '56, the 2006 version of *The Complete Sun Sessions*, and on independent *Memphis Recording Service* releases, which include Elvis at a March 1955 Houston show, plus footage of Elvis at the Mississippi-Alabama Fair and Dairy Show..

Elvis Aron Presley features a version from Hawaii in 1961 and on tour in 1975.

Elvis reprised "I've Got A Woman" for pleasure at recording sessions (Nashville, June 1970, later released on *Elvis in Nashville*), and in rehearsals for the tour covered on by documentary *Elvis: That's The Way It Is*.(versions from this period have come out on later albums *That's The Way It Is Special Edition* and FTD release *The Way It Was*). His 1972 performance in Hampton Roads, Virginia, features on the *Elvis on Tour* documentary.

He .Elvis consistently sang the song in medleys during his Seventies shows, sometimes taking the tune back to its religious roots in combination with "Amen." Two A brace of early live versions from his return to performing are on *Live in Las Vegas*, while others are on *Collectors Gold* and the 2007 release of *Viva Las Vegas*. He was still singing it live in his final months; a late version is on documentary/album *Elvis in Concert*.

The song featured on 1974 live album *Elvis Recorded Live on Stage in Memphis*, and is to be found on dozens and dozens of bootlegs and official FTD live releases from the Seventies, including FTD fare *Elvis At The International, Writing For The King, All Shook Up, Polk Salad Annie, Summer Festival, Closing Night, Takin' Tahoe Tonight, I Found My Thrill, Live In L.A, It's Midnight, Dragonheart, Big Boss Man, Dixieland Rocks, Dinner At Eight, Tucson '76*, and *New Year's Eve*. Bootlegs include the song in combination with "Ave Maria," and with "You Don't Know Me."

The original recording has since come out on *Pure Gold, The King Of Rock And Roll, Elvis By The Presleys* and *Elvis R 'n' B* among others.

Alternate takes from the original RCA session are on *Platinum: A Life in Music*, a collection that also features the Elvis singing the song at a raucous back-stage jam version rehearsals before the NBC TV Special in 1968—the song didn't make the cut for the finished show. This version has featured on many bootlegs and is also on FTD release *Let Yourself Go*.

Further alternates from are 1956 are on *Today, Tomorrow & Forever* (one from the studio session, one which also which showcases a raucous high-energy live version of "I've Got A Woman" from Ellis Auditorium, Memphis, in early 1956), and on the 2006 FTD issue of *Elvis Presley*.

If there's one song Elvis may have recorded at Sun on tapes that disappeared, this is likely to be it.

"I GOT LUCKY"

Fuller, Weisman and Wise combined their talents on this *Kid Galahad* soundtrack song for the movie and accompanying EP, recorded by Elvis in on October 27, 1961 at Radio Recorders.

The song has since resurfaced on the *Double Feature* release covering the movie, *Command Performances*, and the FTD *Kid Galahad* release.

An alternate master came out on 2001 FTD release *Silver Screen Stereo*, though like the vast majority of everything Elvis ever recorded, bootlegs of alternates have long been supplying demand among fans.

I GOT LUCKY

A collection of previously unreleased movie songs filled out this Camden budget LP, released in October 1971. Like companion issue *C'mon Everybody* from three months earlier, the album struggled to find 100,000 takers, and consequently did no better than #104 in the charts.

TRACK LISTING:
1. I Got Lucky
2. What A Wonderful Life
3. I Need Somebody To Lean On
4. Yoga Is As Yoga Does
5. Riding The Rainbow
6. Fools Fall In Love
7. The Love Machine
8. Home Is Where The Heart Is
9. You Gotta Stop
10. If You Think I Don't Need You

"I GOT STUNG"

The B-Side to "One Night," released in October 1958, was recorded with Elvis on furlough from the Army in the early hours of June 11 in Nashville that year. It was the last song he officially recorded for 21 months. On release, it made it to #8 in the charts in the US, and #1 in the UK. Writing credits: Aaron Schroeder and David Hill.

"I Got Stung" initially appeared in LP form on *Elvis' Gold Records, Vol. 2*. Since then, it has featured on hits collections including *Worldwide 50 Gold Award Hits, Vol. 1, The Top Ten Hits, Essential Elvis Vol. 3, The King Of Rock And Roll, Elvis 2nd to None, Hitstory* and *Elvis Rock*.

Multiple alternate takes have come out on *Essential Elvis Vol. 3, Today Tomorrow & Forever, Flashback* and *50,000,000 Million Elvis Fans Can't Be Wrong* (all 24 takes!).

"I GOTTA KNOW"

The B-side to "Are You Lonesome Tonight?" made it to #20 on the charts after release in early November 1960. Elvis recorded the Paul Evans / Matt Williams in the early hours of April 4 that year, at RCA's Studio B in Nashville, not long after Cliff Richard in the UK. The track had earned an album run out on *Elvis' Golden Records Vol. 3*. It has subsequently appeared on *Worldwide 50 Gold Award Hits, Vol. 1, From Nashville to Memphis* and *Hitstory*.

The first take from the recording session came out on An alternate take is on 2005 FTD release *Elvis Is Back!*

"I HEAR A SWEET VOICE CALLING"

This Bill Monroe spiritual was one of many Elvis and friends sang at the December 1956 *Million Dollar Quartet* session, though they only sang a couple of lines before moving on. The song is on the *Million Dollar Quartet* release, *The Complete Million Dollar Quartet*, and on the *Peace in the Valley* gospel collection, as well as on bootlegs.

"I, JOHN"

Elvis recorded this William Johnson/George McFadden/Ted Brooks gospel song in Nashville on June 9, 1971, for release on his third and last gospel album, *He Touched Me*. It has since appeared on *Elvis in Nashville* and *Ultimate Gospel* as well as on the *Amazing Grace* and *Peace in the Valley* gospel compilations (both of which also include a rehearsal version of the song from the *Elvis on Tour* documentary in 1972).

A snatch of this mesmeric William Gaither spiritual that surfaced on a tape of home recordings made in 1966 at Graceland is on FTD release *In a Private Moment*. A half-a-dozen live version performances of the song in Las Vegas between 1969 and 1972 have thus far have only appeared on bootlegs.

"I JUST CAN'T HELP BELIEVIN' "

Elvis sang this Cynthia Weil / Barry Mann song, a big hit for B.J. Thomas in 1970, in Las Vegas. His on August 13, 1970, during performance his a Las Vegas engagement was filmed for *Elvis: That's The Way It Is*—the track opens the original soundtrack album.

More recent album releases include *Walk A Mile In My Shoes , Artist Of The Century*, the 2000 collectors' set *That's The Way It Is, Greatest Hits Live, Love Elvis, Elvis Live* and, *The Essential Elvis Presley* and the 2007 *Viva Las Vegas* release..

Officially-released alternate versions are on *The Live Greatest Hits, Live in Las Vegas* and FTD albums *One Night in Vegas* and *Writing for the King*, in addition to the standard complement of bootlegs.

Rehearsals prior to the 1970 engagement, featured on the *Elvis: That's The Way It Is* documentary, came out on 2001 FTD release *The Way It Was*.

The song was cut from the 2001 DVD reissue of the documentary.

"I JUST CAN'T MAKE IT BY MYSELF"

Elvis got by with a little help from his friends on this Herbert Brewster spiritual during his famous December 1956 jam session at Sun, released officially many years later on *The Million Dollar Quartet*, the *Complete Million Dollar Quartet* and the *Peace In The Valley* gospel compilation.

"I LOVE ONLY ONE GIRL"

A Sid Tepper / Roy C. Bennett potboiler from the soundtrack of *Double Trouble*, recorded by Elvis at Radio Recorders in on June 29, 1966. After the soundtrack album, the song was recycled on 1972 budget issue *Burning Love and Hits from His Movies*. Since the movie's *Double Feature* treatment in the Nineties, tThe 2004 FTD revised *Double Trouble* release re-issued the track plus includes an alternate (first) take.

"I LOVE YOU BECAUSE"

The first song that Elvis ever recorded professionally, at Sun Studio on July 5, 1954, was a 1949 #4 country chart hit for composer Leon Payne, a prolific blind singer/songwriter from Texas who played with Bob Wills before forming his own band and becoming a Louisiana Hayride regular.

"I Love You Because" had been comprehensively covered—by Ernest Tubb, Gene Autry, Clyde Moody, Eddie Fisher and Patti Page—before Elvis gave it a try. During a break after the fifth unsuccessful take, Elvis, Scotty and Bill began goofing around with another song, "That's All Right (Mama)" and Elvis found his groove.

Sam Phillips passed over Elvis' initial efforts on this song in favor of "That's All Right (Mama)" for the inaugural Elvis single on Sun. After RCA acquired ownership of all Elvis' Sun recordings, Elvis' new label included the song on his first EP and LP, both titled *Elvis Presley*, and then paired it with B-side track "Tryin' To Get To You" for release with half-a dozen other singles together at the end of August 1956.

As Elvis' first commercially-recorded song, "I Love You Because" is a fixture on Elvis Sun compilations,and of course it was included on Fifties anthology *The King Of Rock And Roll*. In the 2000s it has appeared on *The Country Side of Elvis*.

This was one of the first songs for which RCA started to mine the potential of an alternate take and was first released on the 1974 compilation *Elvis: A Legendary Performer Vol. 1*, and another on *The Sun Sessions* from 1976. All five takes from the session came out on the 1987 and 2006 pressings of *The Complete Sun Sessions*. Alternates have also been issued piecemeal on *Sunrise* and *Elvis at Sun*. Leon Payne's original features as a bonus track on 2002 Charly release *Elvis Presley At The Louisiana Hayride*; *Memphis Recording Service Vol. 2* also tracklists the song in a remixed version..

"I Met Her Today"

Elvis recorded this Don Robertson / Hal Blair cut at Studio B, Nashville, in in the small hours of October 16, 1961. The track didn't appear on vinyl until 1965 album *Elvis For Everyone*. In 1972, it was re-issued on budget LP release *Separate Ways*.

Aside from appearing on the big Sixties box set *From Nashville to Memphis*, the song was included as a bonus on later CD issues of *Pot Luck*.

Aalternates of "I Met Her Today" have been officially been released on since 1991 compilation *Collectors Gold* andon *Essential Elvis Vol. 6* and *Elvis: Close Up*. A more countrified take studio version is on 2003 FTD release *Studio B: Nashville Outtakes*; and further outtakes are on FTD release *Pot Luck*.

"I Miss You"

Elvis recorded this soft-toned ballad, written by Donnie Sumner, at his Palm Springs home in on September 23, 1973 to fill out his quota of material for the *Raised On Rock* album, which came out later that year. Sumner provided backing on the track, along with the other members of Elvis' personal backing group, Voice.

The track was subsequently released on the *Always On My Mind* LP.

An alternate version—take one—came out on *Today, Tomorrow & Forever* in 2002. Further Half a dozen alternates are on the 2007 FTD *Raised On Rock* release.

"I Need Somebody To Lean On"

Elvis sails mighty close to cool jazz on this Doc Pomus / Mort Shuman track, which he laid down at Radio Recorders in on July 10, 1963 for the *Viva Las Vegas* movie soundtrack and EP. The tune only came out on an LP in 1971, on (*I Got Lucky*)., and yYears later it was released on *A Valentine Gift For You* and the *Double Feature* release for the movie.

Only one alternate take has officially been released, on UK issue *Elvis Sings Mort Shuman & Doc Pomus* and FTD albums *Out in Hollywood* and *Viva Las Vegas*.

"I Need You So"

Elvis recorded this piano-heavy Ivory Joe Hunter tune in on February 23, 1957 at Radio Recorders, for issue on the *Just For You* EP and *Loving You* LP later that same year. It's rare outings since then are limited to *The King Of Rock And Roll* and *Loving You* reissues.

Hunter's original, which made it to #2 on the *Billboard* R & B chart in 1950, is a bonus track on 2002 Charly release *Elvis Presley At The Louisiana Hayride*. There is speculation that Elvis also laid down this track at Sun, but no such recording has yet surfaced.

"I Need Your Love Tonight"

Elvis recorded this Sid Wayne / Bix Reichner rocker on furlough from the Army in on June 10, 1958. When it came out as the B-side to "(Now and Then There's) A Fool Such As I" in mid-March 1959, the tune climbed to #4 in its own right, the first time that both sides of an Elvis single had made it into the top five since "Hound Dog" / "Don't Be Cruel." An album release followed on *Elvis' Gold Records Vol. 2*.

The UK-released single was an alternate take. *Elvis Aron Presley* features the song in a live performance from Hawaii in 1961. The original recording later saw release on the albums *Worldwide Gold Award Hits, Vol. 2*, *The Top Ten Hits*, *This Is Elvis*, *The King Of Rock And Roll*, *Elvis 2nd to None*, FTD album *Flashback*, *Hitstory* and *Elvis Rock*.

Alternates are on *Essential Elvis Vol. 3* (three two of them), *Platinum: A Life In Music* and *Today, Tomorrow & Forever*, while 2007 FTD release *50,000,000 Million Elvis Fans Can't Be Wrong* has all eighteen takes from the original recording session.

A home recordings is listed on bootleg release *The Long Lost Home Recordings*.

"I Need Your Lovin' Everyday"

Elvis sang this song, written by Don Gardner and Bobby Robinson, in concert in the early Seventiessummer of 1971. It's on bootlegs including *From Hollywood to Vegas*, *Sold Out*, *The Complete On Tour Sessions*, *Live and Unleashed*, *Twenty Days And Twenty Nights*.

"I Really Don't Want To Know"

Elvis gave this Howard Barnes and Don Robertson song the full treatment when he recorded it in Nashville on June 7, 1970. A #2 country hit for Eddy Arnold in 1954, and later, in 1961, a more up-tempo hit for Solomon Burke, Elvis' version was released as a single in early December 1970, with "There Goes My Everything" on the B-side, as a taster to the forthcoming *Elvis Country* album. Elvis' version spent nine weeks on the *Billboard* Hot 100, reaching #21 (#9 on the country chart, his first top ten success in this department since 1958) and selling a respectable 700,000 copies on initial release in the US.

The song came out on *Elvis Country*, *Worldwide Gold Award Hits Vol. 2*, *Welcome To My World*, *Walk A Mile In My Shoes*, *Great Country Songs*, *The Country Side of Elvis* and a plethora of concert bootlegs.

Elvis reprised the song in his final concerts (it's on the *Elvis in Concert* documentary and album). The song also features on FTD album *Unchained Melody*. There is no sign of a rumored recording from the beginning of Elvis' Sun career, though it is rumored that this is one of the songs that Elvis tried out when he first auditioned with Scotty Moore and Bill Black.

DON ROBERTSON: "I was really proud of the way Elvis did my song... He did it in a different way than it had been done before, kind of bluesy, a bit like a rock waltz with a lot of feeling."

"I Shall Be Released"

Elvis sang a couple of verses of this Bob Dylan song towards the end of his May 20, 1971 session in Nashville to loosen up and have some fun. The result didn't appear until 1995 album *Walk A Mile In My Shoes*.

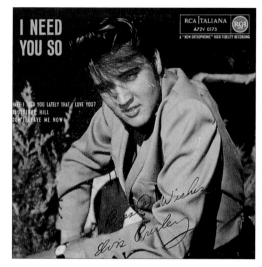

Cover from Italian LP of *I Need You So*.

"I Shall Not Be Moved"

Elvis and special friends sang this traditional spiritual during the Million Dollar quartet session at Sun in December 1956. In the version Elvis sang, the traditional gospel song was credited to John Benton. As well as the Million Dollar quartet releases, the song appeared on 3-CD gospel compilation *Peace in the Valley*.

I Sing All Kinds

A 2007 FTD release of outtakes from Elvis' early 1971 Nashville sessions.

TRACK LISTING:
1. Bosom Of Abraham
2. I've Got Confidence
3. An Evening Prayer
4. (That's What You Get) For Lovin' Me
5. Early Morning Rain
6. Fools Rush In
7. Help Me Make It Through The Night
8. It's Still Here
9. I Will Be True
10. Until It's Time for You To Go
11. It's Only Love
12. I'm Leavin'
13. Love Me, Love the Life I Lead
14. Padre
15. Seeing Is Believing
16. A Thing Called Love
17. Put Your Hand In The Hand
18. Johnny B. Goode (part)
19. I'll Be Home On Christmas Day
20. Holly Leaves And Christmas Trees
21. If I Get Home On Christmas Day
22. It Won't Seem Like Christmas
23. I'll Be Home On Christmas Day

"I Slipped, I Stumbled, I Fell"

When Elvis recorded this *Wild in the Country* soundtrack song by Fred Wise and Ben Weisman at Radio Recorders on November 8, 1960, the plan was originally to release two versions, sung in different keys, as an A-side and B-side. In the end the higher-key version came won out as an album track on *Something For Everybody* in 1961; the lower key version had to wait until *Collectors Gold* in 1991.

During Elvis' lifetime, the track came out on *Separate Ways*.

Alternate takes have since appeared on half a dozen bootlegs plus official releases the *Double Features* release (*Flaming Star/Wild In The Country / Follow That Dream*(which also sports the master)) and *Elvis: Close Up*.

"I THINK I'M GONNA LIKE IT HERE"

Don Robertson and Hal Blair penned this laid-back travelogue song for the *Fun in Acapulco* soundtrack, which Elvis committed to tape in on January 22, 1963 at Radio Recorders. The song next appeared on the Nineties *Double Feature* series of soundtrack re-releases.

Different takes were used in the film and on the album. The alternate master came out in 2001 on FTD album *Silver Screen Stereo*. Six additional takes from the studio session are on the FTD *Fun in Acapulco* release.

"I UNDERSTAND (JUST HOW YOU FEEL)"

In the summer of 1958, Elvis sang this song with pals at Eddie Fadal's house in Waco, Texas. The song appeared on the bootleg *Forever Young, Forever Beautiful* before an official release in 1999 on *The Home Recordings*. Pat Best wrote the song; the Four Tunes had a Rhythm & Blues chart hit with the song in 1954.

"I WALK THE LINE"

Elvis smuggled this archetypical hallmark Johnny Cash song into his August 1970 shows in Las Vegas, Lake Tahoe and Detroit. The song is on bootlegs including *From Hollywood To Vegas*, *The Entertainer*, *Long Lost And Found Songs* and the aptlysmartly-named *The Man In White*. For Cash, the ode to marital fidelity in the face of overwhelming temptation was a career-making #2 country hit when Sun Records released it in 1956 on.

The song provided the title for the 2005 Cash biopic *I Walk The Line*, twenty-five years after it was used as the title for a John Frankenheimer movie starring Gregory Peck and Tuesday Weld.

"I WANT TO BE FREE"

Leiber and Stoller wrote this track specially for Elvis movie *Jailhouse Rock*. He recorded the song—the breakout hit for his Vince Everett character in the movie—on May 3, 1957, after an unsuccessful attempt on April 30, 1957 at Radio Recorders. A different version from the one used in the movie came out on the *Jailhouse Rock* EP and 1959 album *A Date with Elvis*.

The song features on LPs *Worldwide Gold Award Hits Vol. 2*, *Elvis Sings Leiber & Stoller* and *Essential Elvis Vol. 1*.

The movie version was not officially released until *The King Of Rock 'N' Roll* box set in 1992 (alongside the originally released version). Both versions are on 1997 release *Jailhouse Rock* and 2003 release *Elvis: Close Up*. *Today, Tomorrow & Forever* features a splice of different alternates. FTD release *Flashback* offers a binaural version of the master take.

"I WANT YOU, I NEED YOU, I LOVE YOU"

This was the only song that Elvis, Scotty, Bill and D.J.—joined in the studio by pianist Marvin Hughes and his then trio of backing singers—managed to recorded in Nashville on April 14, 1956 after the flight that brought them in was so harrowing that they weren't in the mood to record any more. In the end RCA had to splice together two takes of this Maurice Mysels/Ira Kosloff ballad for the A-side of Elvis' second sin-

gle for RCA. When it shipped in early May 1956, with Arthur Crudup number "My Baby Left Me" on the B-side, it peaked at #3 in the charts—until the last minute, RCA executives were unsure which song to release as the A-side. Sales came in around the 1.3 million mark, boosted by its Country chart placement at #1..

The song first appeared in EP form on *The Real Elvis*, and in album form on *Elvis' Golden Records Vol. 1*.

Live performances on TV "Milton Berle Show," the "Steve Allen Show," and at the Mississippi-Alabama Fair and Dairy Show, all in 1956, are on *A Golden Celebration*. The "Steve Allen Show" performance recently came out on the *Elvis #1 Hit Performances* DVD.

Later re-releases were on *Worldwide 50 Gold Award Hits Vol. 1*, *The Top Ten Hits*, *Elvis '56*, *Elvis 2nd to None*, *Hitstory*, *Elvis By The Presleys* and *Love Elvis*.

Studio alternates have been released on *Elvis: A Legendary Performer Vol. 2* (with a lyrics flub), *The King Of Rock And Roll* (which includes the standard track for comparison), *Platinum: A Life In Music*, *Today Tomorrow and Forever*, and *Flashback*. For the completist, 2006 FTD release *Elvis Presley* offers nine different takes.

"I WANT YOU WITH ME"

A Woody Harris rocker written for Bobby Darin that Elvis recorded for *Something For Everybody* at the Nashville studio on March 12, 1961. The song has since appeared on the Sixties collection *From Nashville to Memphis*. The first take from the session is released on *Collectors Gold* and the FTD issue *Something For Everybody* (2006).

"I WAS BORN ABOUT TEN THOUSAND YEARS AGO"

Elvis' life certainly contained enough incident for a 10,000 year span. He first considered recording this traditional gospel song (known variously as "The Bragging Song" and "The Great Historical Bum") in 1967, and for a while it was in the running for inclusion on the song list of his winter 1970 Las Vegas engagement. He finally got round to recording a pop gospel adaptation of the song on June 4, 1970 in a single jam-style take. Credited to Elvis Presley, the song was used in itty bits on *Elvis Country*. Two years later, the it song was released sent out into the world in its entirety, on the 1972 album *Elvis Now*. The song has since appeared on *Walk A Mile In My Shoes* and the 2000 album *Elvis Country* reissue.

"I WAS THE ONE"

This ballad of love lost, written by Aaron Schroeder, Claude Demetrius, Hal Blair and Bill Peppers, was chosen for the B-side of "Heartbreak Hotel," Elvis' first single for his new label RCA. Recorded on January 11, 1956 in Nashville with a three-part doo-wap backing, the song rose to #23 in the general charts and became a country chart #1. Elvis later said he was proud of his vocal performance on this song. "I Was The One" first appeared in album form on *For LP Fans Only*. In Elvis' lifetime, it also came out on *Worldwide Gold Award Hits Vol. 1*, and has since appeared on *A Valentine Gift For You* and on the CD issue of *Elvis' Golden Records Vol. 1* among others.

He performed the song on "Stage Show" in early 1956 and live that year (*A Golden Celebration* features the TV performance and the song as performed at the Mississippi-Alabama Fair and

Dairy Show). A live version from May 1956 is on 2002 box set *Today, Tomorrow & Forever*. He also included the tune at his final Hayride performance (on various Louisiana Hayride collections) in late 1956.

Elvis reprised the song during rehearsals for 1970 documentary *That's The Way It Is* (first officially released on *Platinum: A Life In Music* in 1997), and gave it a whirl during the taping (issued years later on *Walk A Mile In My Shoes* and on the 2000 *That's the Way It Is* release). An alternate studio version of the song appeared in 1996 on the anniversary "Heartbreak Hotel" CD single; previously unreleased alternates have featured on 2004 FTD release *Flashback* and 2006 FTD issue *Elvis Presley* (no fewer than six).

The original studio recording has more recently featured on *Elvis '56* and *The Essential Elvis Presley*.

The song came out as a posthumous single in 1983, with "Wear My Ring Around Your Neck" on the B-side

"I WASHED MY HANDS IN MUDDY WATER"

Elvis laid down a rocked-up jam version of this Joe Babcock country song in on June 7, 1970 at the RCA studios in Nashville. The recording was shortened for release on *Elvis Country* Songwriter Babcock was working as a back-up singer for Elvis at this time (and had already worked with him in 1963). The song had previously been recorded by Stonewall Jackson, Charlie Rich and Johnny Rivers. A full version of "I Washed My Hands In Muddy Water" appeared in 1995 on *Walk A Mile In My Shoes*.

Platinum: A Life In Music features a version from rehearsals for *That's The Way It Is*, as does the 2000 *That's The Way It Is - Sspecial Eedition* release. *Essential Elvis Vol. 4* includes an undubbed version.

"I WILL BE HOME AGAIN"

Soon Within a month of the after Elvis returning home again after the Armywish implicit in the title came true, Elvis April 1960 in he cut this Bennie Benjamin / Raymond Leveen / Lou Singer composition in Nashville at the end of a very long session that had begun the night before (on April 3, 1960) and yielded for the *Elvis Is Back!* album. Elvis decidd to do the song, in a duet with new pal Charlie Hodge, who had interested Elvis in the . Hodge introduced Elvis to the work of the Golden Gate Quartet, for whom this was a standard.

The song was not featured on posthumous albums with the exception of *From Nashville to Memphis*, the song has not featured on posthumous albums.

"I WILL BE TRUE"

A poignant Elvis sings to his own piano accompaniment on this recording of an Ivory Joe Hunter track laid down at RCA's Nashville studios in on May 19, 1971, which wasn't for released until on *Elvis (The Fool Album)*. Other albums on which the studio recording has appeared include *Elvis Aron Presley* and *Walk A Mile In My Shoes*.

An earlier home recording from 1959 features on *Platinum: A Life In Music* (as part of the Bad Nauheim medley), on FTD release *In A Private Moment* and on a number of bootlegs of songs he recorded during his stay in Germany. An alternate from the Nashville recording session is on FTD release *I Sing All Kinds*.

"I Wonder, I Wonder, I Wonder"

Elvis sang this Daryl Hutchinson composition—a hit for Louis Armstrong back in 1947 and later the Four Aces—at home in 1960. It was first officially released in 1999 on early FTD release *In A Private Moment*.

"If Every Day Was Like Christmas"

A Red West composition, recorded by Elvis in Nashville in on June 10, 1966 after West laid down a guide vocal track. The song came out as a single in good time for Christmas that year, with "How Would You Like To Be" on the B-side. Though the song failed to chart and sold fewer than 200,000 copies on initial release, it was a steady seller in later years. In Elvis' lifetime, the song appeared on the 1970 *Elvis' Christmas Album*. An undubbed version of the song appeared on *Memories Of Christmas* in 1982.

The song More recently, the song lent its title to a 1994 album, and has since appeared on *From Nashville to Memphis* and festive compilation *Christmas Peace*.

If Every Day Was Like Christmas

RCA released this Christmas compilation album in 1994 including some alternate takes

TRACK LISTING:
1. If Every Day Was Like Christmas
2. Blue Christmas
3. Here Comes Santa Claus (Right Down Santa Claus Lane)
4. White Christmas
5. Santa Bring My Baby Back (To Me)
6. I'll Be Home For Christmas
7. O Little Town Of Bethlehem
8. Santa Claus Is Back In Town
9. It Won't Seem Like Christmas (Without You)
10. If I Get Home On Christmas Day
11. Holly Leaves And Christmas Trees
12. Merry Christmas Baby
13. Silver Bells
14. I'll Be Home On Christmas Day (alternate take)
15. On A Snowy Christmas Night
16. Winter Wonderland
17. The Wonderful World Of Christmas
18. O Come, All Ye Faithful
19. The First Noel
20. It Won't Seem Like Christmas (Without You) (alternate take)
21. Silver Bells (alternate)
22. Holly Leaves And Christmas Trees (alternate take)
23. I'll Be Home On Christmas Day
24. Christmas Message From Elvis
25. Silent Night

"If I Can Dream"

"If I Can Dream" was written overnight by W. Earl Brown as the anthemic finale to Elvis' 1968 NBC TV Special, a last-minute substitute for the Christmassy number the Colonel had originally wanted. The song was a message of hope and all-out commitment for America as a nation and Elvis as a performer. Elvis always infused his songs with emotion. On June 23, 1968, at Western Recorders he poured so much energy and feeling into his vocal that by the end of the fifth take he passed out from exhaustion. Steve Binder remembers him "writhing on the cement floor in an almost fetal

position." Afterwards, Elvis was entranced as he listened to the track over and over. The following evening he returned to the studio with Scotty Moore and D.J. Fontana to play the song to them repeatedly. The performance was unrepeatable; when they filmed the show six days later, he lip synched to the backing track.

Initially released as a single in early November 1968 with "Edge Of Reality" on the B-side, "If I Can Dream" sold slowly until the NBC TV Special was broadcast in early December. Sales of 800,000 propelled it to #12 during a 13-week run in the charts, Elvis' best in close to four years (since "I'm Yours").

The version of the song broadcast on the show differs slightly from the one released on the accompanying album.

"If I Can Dream" has been on many albums since its first vinyl appearance on the tie-in album, titled *Elvis* on release. It has been on , including: *Worldwide 50 Gold Award Hits Vol. 1*, *Elvis: A Legendary Performer, Vol. 2*, *Elvis' Gold Records Vol. 5*, *The Great Performances*, *Artist Of The Century*, *Elvis 2nd to None*, *Elvis By The Presleys*, *Love Elvis*, *Elvis Inspirational* and *The Essential Elvis Presley*.

Alternate takes have come out on *He Walks Beside Me*, *Platinum: A Life In Music*, *Memories: The '68 Comeback Special*, and FTD releases *Burbank '68—The NBC TV Comeback Special* and *Let Yourself Go*, as well as on many bootlegs.

In the wake of 9/11, the "If I Can Dream" video and song were reissued on a special four-track CD, *America The Beautiful*, in aid of the Red Cross Liberty Disaster Relief Fund.

In 2007, as part of the "Idol Gives Back" charity special, Celine Dion joined Elvis in a technologically-spliced duet of the song. The live studio audience saw ETA Ryan Pelton perform; the TV audience saw Dion singing with Elvis cut from the NBC TV Special and extracted from the background. That same year, Elvis' show-closer was released on DVD *Elvis #1 Hit Performances*.

ELVIS SAID: "This was too good, I just couldn't turn it down."

ERNST JORGENSEN: "Elvis sang as if he were pleading for his very life."

"If I Get Home On Christmas Day"

A Tony Macaulay track that a vibrato-heavy Elvis laid down in on May 15, 1971 at Studio B in Nashville for *Elvis Sings The Wonderful World of Christmas*. The track has since appeared on Elvis Christmas anthologies *If Every Day Was Like Christmas*, *Christmas Peace* and *Elvis Christmas*. Alternate fans should look to FTD release *I Sing All Kinds*.

"If I Loved You"

Elvis sang this Rodgers and Hammerstein classic at home in 1966, in a recording unearthed at Graceland thirty years later. The tune first appeared officially on *The Home Recordings* and FTD release *In A Private Moment*.

"If I Were You"

Elvis recorded this song by Gerald Nelson at on a June 8, 1970 studio session in Nashville, for subsequent release on *Love Letters From Elvis*. It's also on the 2000 version of *Elvis Country*. One alternate has been officially released, on 1996 issue *Essential Elvis Vol. 4*.

"If I'm A Fool (For Loving You)"

A Stan Kesler tune that Elvis recorded at American Studio in the wee hours of February 21, 1969, after Vernon visited the studio. Vernon liked "If I'm A Fool" as sung by Bobby Wood, who was playing piano at the session. After introducing the two of them, Elvis just went ahead and covered the song. They wrapped that night before getting the perfect take; in consequence, the song was relegated to release on 1970 budget album *Let's Be Friends*.

"If I'm A Fool (For Loving You)" has since cropped up on *Suspicious Minds: The Memphis 1969 Anthology*, *The Country Side of Elvis* and the 2006 version of *Elvis Country*.

An alternate take came out in 2001 on the FTD *Memphis Sessions* album.

"If I Loved You"

Elvis sang this Rodgers and Hammerstein classic at home in 1966, in a recording unearthed at Graceland thirty years later. The tune first appeared officially on *The Home Recordings* and FTD release *In A Private Moment*.

"If That Isn't Love"

A modern gospel composition written by Dottie Rambo that Elvis recorded at Stax Studios on December 16, 1973, released on *Good Times* the following year. Later album appearances include *Amazing Grace*, *Peace In The Valley*, the 2000 re-release of *Promised Land*, *Christmas Peace* (*Elvis: My Christmas #1*) and, *Elvis Inspirational*.,

Alternate takes are on *Essential Elvis, Vol. 5* and FTD disc *Easter Special*.

"If The Lord Wasn't Walking By My Side"

A rousing gospel tune composed by Henry Slaughter (who played organ on the session) that Elvis recorded at the RCA studios in Nashville on May 28, 1966 for the album *How Great Thou Art*. The song has since featured on gospel compilations *Amazing Grace*, *Peace In The Valley* and *Ultimate Gospel*.

Alternates are on *Today, Tomorrow & Forever* and the FTD release *So High*.

"If We Never Meet Again"

Elvis laid down this melancholy Albert Brumley composition in on October 30, 1960 at RCA's Nashville facilities for the *His Hand In Mine* gospel album. The song is on the usual gospel compilations—*Amazing Grace*, *Peace In The Valley* and *Ultimate Gospel*.

The first take from the recording session came out for the first time officially on the FTD *His Hand In Mine* re-issue.

"If You Don't Come Back"

Elvis laid down this sparse yet funky Leiber and Stoller track—a hit for The Drifters a decade earlier—at Stax Studios in Memphis in on July 21, 1973. It first came out on the *Raised On Rock* in late 1973.

FTD included an alternate take on 2006 release *Made in Memphis*; *Essential Elvis. Vol. 5* from 1998 has another alternate, and while the 2007 FTD release of *Raised On Rock* features several more.

Elvis, 1956.

"If You Love Me (Let Me Know)"

Elvis first added this Olivia Newton John country song—written by former Shadows guitarist John Rostill, who was also Newton John's manager during the early part of her career—to his tour repertoire in 1974, the same year that she had a #5 hit with it in the US. Elvis sang "If You Love Me" hundreds of times over the years. A version recorded live on April 25, 1977 made it onto Elvis' final album, *Moody Blue*.

A pPerformances of the song from June that Elvis' last ever tour year wasere filmed and recorded by the CBS crew working on *Elvis in Concert*, and released as on an album soon after his death in 1977. Another concert from the same period appeared on the *Elvis Aron Presley* box set. Many late-era bootlegs feature the song, along with official. Official albums with alternate live performances include FTD releases *It's Midnight*, *Dragonheart*, *Big Boss Man*, *Dixieland Rocks*, *Tucson '76* and *Spring Tours 77*.

"If You Talk In Your Sleep"

Elvis laid down this track, written by Red West and Johnny Christopher, at Stax Studios, Memphis on December 11, 1973. On release in May 1974 (with "Help Me" on the B-side) it made it to #17 in the *Billboard* Top 100 chart, principally on the back of radio airplay, though it was not a stellar seller. At a live show that year, Elvis announced to the audience that the song's full title was "If You Talk In Your Sleep, Don't Mention My Name, And If You Walk In Your Sleep, Forget Where You Came."

Albums featuring the song include *Promised Land*, *Elvis' Gold Records Vol. 5*, *Walk A Mile In My Shoes* and *Hitstory*. An alternate from the Stax recording session is on *Today, Tomorrow & Forever*.

Live recordings have officially been released on *Live in Las Vegas* and FTD disc *It's Midnight*. FTD release *Too Muck Monkey Business* features a remixed versions of the song.

"If You Think I Don't Need You"

Red West and Joe Cooper wrote this Sixties-flavored R&B tune for Elvis to record in on July 9, 1963 at Radio Recorders for the Viva Las Vegas soundtrack and EP.

It's on albums *I Got Lucky*, *Double Dynamite* and the *Double Features* release for *Viva Las Vegas*,

Alternate takes are included with the original on the FTD *Viva Las Vegas* release from 2003.

"I'll Be Back"

Elvis gave this blues-lite soundtrack tune by Sid Wayne and Ben Weisman a run through at Radio Recorders in on February 17, 1966 for the *Spinout* soundtrack. The song came out on the accompanying LP, and almost three decades later on the *Double Feature* release for the movie, followed in short order by *Command Performances*. More recently, it , since when it has reappeared on *Elvis at the Movies*. The FTD *Spinout* release offers the original but no alternates.

Illinois

- Carbondale

Elvis' show at Southern Illinois University Arena was on October 27, 1976.

- Champaign

Elvis performed at the University of Illinois Assembly Hall on October 22, 1976.

- Chicago

Elvis played his first ever show in town at the International Amphitheatre on March 28, 1957, one of the few occasions he wore his full gold-leaf suit. He was back in Chi-town to play the Chicago Stadium on June 16 and 17, 1972. He started his 7th tour of 1976 with two dates at the Chicago Stadium , October 14 and 15. Elvis last played the venue on May 1 and 2, 1977.

"I'll Be Home For Christmas"

This Kim Gannon/Walter Kent/Buck Ram composition from 1943 had been a million-seller for Bing Crosby before it was picked for the *Elvis' Christmas Album*, which Elvis laid down at Radio Recorders in Los Angeles oin September 7, 1957. The song came out on EP on *Elvis Sings Christmas Songs* at the same time as the LP.

A decade later the song was lined up to be the closing track on Elvis' 1968 NBC TV Special, the last of the original Christmas-themed songs to survive the format change of the show. At the last minute it was supplanted by "If I Can Dream."

"I'll Be Home For Christmas" is on the usual selection of latter-day Christmas albums, from *Memories Of Christmas* to *If Every Day Was Like Christmas*, *Blue Christmas*, *Christmas Peace* and *Elvis Christmas*,.

An alternate take is on *Platinum: A Life In Music*.

"I'll Be Home On Christmas Day"

Elvis recorded this blues-tinged Michael Jarrett festive song in on May 16, 1971 at Studio B for his new Christmas album *Elvis Sings The Wonderful World of Christmas*. An unsuccessful attempt to improve on what they had the following month only came out on 1982 release *Memories of Christmas*.

The originally-released song is on Christmas compilations *Christmas Peace* and *Elvis Christmas*.

Alternates are on *If Every Day Was Like Christmas*, *Platinum: A Life in Music*, *Today Tomorrow & Forever* and FTD release *I Sing All Kinds*.

"I'll Be There (If Ever You Want Me)"

Elvis recorded this Bobby Darin tune on January 23, 1969 at American Studio, at the session he sang "Suspicious Minds." Though Darin recorded the song in 1960, it won greater popular acclaim in s most popular a version was by British songsters Gerry and The Pacemakers in 1964.

Elvis' version first appeared on 1970 album *Let's Be Friends*. Later it was included on *Double Dynamite*, *From Nashville to Memphis* and *Suspicious Minds: The Memphis 1969 Anthology*.

The 1980 *Guitar Man* remix came out in 2000 on FTD release *Too Much Monkey Business*.

"I'll Hold You In My Heart (Till I Can Hold You In My Arms)"

Elvis recorded this hit for Eddy Arnold in 1947 (and Eddie Fisher in from 1951) at American Studio, Memphis on January 23, 1969. Commentators have pointed out thatfrom his effortlessly elaborate phrasing it wass evidence that Elvis had sung the popular love song plenty of times before at home. Written by Eddy Arnold, Hal Horton and Tommy Dilbeck, Elvis' version of the song was first released on *From Elvis In Memphis* later in 1969. It has subsequently come out on *From Nashville to Memphis*, *Great Country Songs*, *Suspicious Minds: The Memphis 1969*

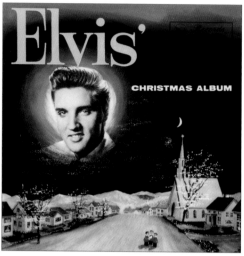

RCA Victor Black "Dynagroove" Label Christmas Album (New Zealand).

Anthology, *The Country Side of Elvis* and *Elvis By The Presleys*.

A four-and-a-half minute version take of the song is on *Artist Of The Century*. FTD's *Too Much Monkey Business* features a 1980 Felton Jarvis remix of the song.

"I'll Never Fall In Love Again"

Not Burt Bacharach's but Lonnie Donegan and Jimmie Currie's version was recorded by Elvis at Graceland on the morning of February 5, 1976. A million-selling hit for Tom Jones in 1969, the song as sung by Elvis appeared on 1976 album *From Elvis Presley Boulevard, Memphis, Tennessee*, and more recently the CD reissue of *Moody Blue*. A pre-overdub version is on *Our Memories of Elvis* and a number of bootlegs.

An alternate take is on FTD CD *The Jungle Room Sessions*.

"I'll Never Know"

Elvis sang this poignant Fred Karger, Sid Wayne and Ben Weisman ballad at his June 5, 1970 Nashville recording session. It was released on *Love Letters From Elvis* the following year. The song is on the 2000 Special Edition *That's The Way It Is* release. An outtake is on 2002 FTD release *The Nashville Marathon*.

"I'll Never Let You Go (Little Darlin')"

This track was the A-side on one of seven singles released by RCA at the end of August 1956, with B-side "I'm Gonna Sit Right Down and Cry You." Elvis recorded this Jimmy Wakely song (written for Gene Autry in 1943) at Sun Studio on September 10, 1954, and may have run through the song on his first professional recording session that July. RCA took over ownership of the song when it acquired Elvis' contract in late 1955. As RCA released everything they had in their possession to ride the wave of Elvismania, "I'll Never Let You Go" was pressed into service on the *Elvis Presley* EP and LP.

The song has since featured on *The Sun Sessions*, *The King Of Rock And Roll*, *Elvis At Sun* and *The Complete Sun Sessions* (the 2006 version of which is an alternate take). Further alternates have appeared on *A Golden Celebration* and *Sunrise*. The Jimmy Wakely original is on *Elvis Presley At The Louisiana Hayride*.

JIMMY WAKELY: "Fifteen years ago I wrote a song called 'I'll Never Let You Go (Little Darlin')' and nothing happened. Presley put it into one of his albums and so far I've gotten $4,300 in royalties."

"I'LL NEVER STAND IN YOUR WAY"

The second time that Elvis paid to record a demo at the Memphis Recording Studio was on January 4, 1954. He sang this recent Joni James hit, providing his own accompaniment on guitar, and then tried out "It Wouldn't Be The Same Without You." The track did not see release until 1997, when it was issued on *Platinum: A Life In Music*, followed swiftly by an appearance on *Sunrise*, and later the 2006 version of *The Complete Sun Session*. The song was written by Fred Rose and Walter "Hy" Heath.

"I'LL REMEMBER YOU"

Elvis recorded this by Hawaiian performer Kui Lee in Nashville on June 12, 1966, after Red West and Charlie Hodge laid down a tracking vocal while Elvis stayed away from the studio. Elvis first heard the song in a version sung by Don Ho; he connected with its poignancy and the song became one of his most-often performed concert staples in the Seventies. That Nashville recording was initially released as a bonus track on the *Spinout* soundtrack LP (in 1999, it came out on *Tomorrow Is A Long Time*). An alternate take from the 1966 studio session is on FTD disc *So High*. In the Nineties, the unedited master came out on the *From Nashville to Memphis* box set and on *Platinum: A Life In Music*.

Seventies live recordings have been released from his Madison Square Garden engagement in June 1972 (not the show recorded for the live album, and not until *Elvis: A Legendary Performer Vol. 4* in 1983). The song was on the playlist for the *Aloha From Hawaii Via Satellite* concert and album, and is on quite a number of live bootlegs from the Seventies. Live performances have additionally been released on *The Alternate Aloha* and *Elvis Aron Presley*, and on FTD albums *An American Trilogy*, *Big Boss Man*, *Dixieland Rocks* and *Southern Nights*.

"I'LL TAKE LOVE"

Elvis recorded this horn-heavy song by Dolores Fuller and Mark Barkan for *Easy Come, Easy Go* in on September 28, 1966, after the band had laid down the instrumental track at Radio Recorders—Elvis might have done his vocals at the Paramount Studio Recording Stage. The song was in the movie and initially released on EP.

The song made its album debut on *C'mon Everybody* in 1971. It has since appeared on the *Double Trouble Feature* release for the movie, and on the FTD re-release for the movie, which also includes alternate takes.

"I'LL TAKE YOU HOME AGAIN KATHLEEN"

Home recordings of Elvis getting his vocal chords around this song as he whiled away the hours in Germany in 1959 include a fast and slow version which appeared on bootlegs before an official release as part of the "Bad Nauheim Medley" on *Platinum: A Life In Music* in 1997. Elvis finally recorded (a decidedly slow) version of the song at Studio B in Nashville on May 19, 1971, though that didn't see release until *Elvis (The Fool Album)* two years later.

The Kathleen in question was the wife of Illinois schoolteacher Thomas Westendorf, who wrote the piece in 1875, on a day when he must have forgotten that her name was Jeanie.

The version of the song on the *Elvis Aron Presley* and *Walk A Mile In My Shoes* collectors' box sets are without overdubs. Both fast and slow home recordings are on 1999 BMG disc *In A Private Moment*.

More recently, the studio version appeared on 2006 BMG release *Elvis Inspirational*.

"I'M A ROUSTABOUT"

An Otis Blackwell/Winfield Scott R & B composition that Hal Wallis rejected for the 1964 Paramount movie because of its insubordinate lyrics, after Elvis committed the track to tape at Radio Recorders on March 3, 1964. . The song vanished for four decades, was rediscovered and then was was released as a curio in 2003 on the album *Elvis 2nd To None*. It's also on *Hitstory*.

"I'M BEGINNING TO FORGET YOU"

Elvis sang this Willie Phelps song—a hit for Jim Reeves in 1959—during his stay in Germany. A home recording first appeared officially on 1983 album *Elvis: A Legendary Performer Vol. 4*. Since then, an a capella version came out on the 1997 release *Platinum: A Life In Music*. The home recording is also on *In A Private Moment* and *The Home Recordings*.

"I'M COMIN' HOME"

Elvis put down his version of this Carl Mann track—written by Charlie Rich and originally produced by Sam Phillips—in on March 12, 1961 during a Nashville recording session, for release on the *Something For Everybody* album. The track was included many years later on the *From Nashville to Memphis* anthology.

Alternate takes have come out on *Essential Elvis Vol. 6*, *Platinum: A Life In Music* and FTD releases *Fame And Fortune* and *Something For Everybody*. The Carl Mann original is on 2002 release *Elvis Presley At The Louisiana Hayride*.

"I'M COUNTING ON YOU"

Elvis recorded this Don Robertson ballad at his first ever session for new label RCA, in on January 11, 1956, for release on his double-EP and LP titled Elvis Presley. The song was subsequently picked as the B-side to "I Got A Woman" in late August 1956.

Posthumous releases include *The King Of Rock And Roll*, *The Country Side of Elvis* and FTD release *Flashback*. An alternate take features on *Platinum: A Life In Music*. Half a dozen alternates appeared on 2006 FTD release *Elvis Presley*.

"I'M FALLING IN LOVE TONIGHT"

A Don Robertson ballad that Elvis taped at Radio Recorders in on September 22, 1962 for *It Happened at the World's Fair*.

The song was included on Nineties soundtrack anthology *Command Performances* a year or two after reappearing on the *Double Features* re-release for the movie.

Alternate takes first appeared in 1980 on *Elvis Aron Presley*. The 2003 FTD *It Happened at the World's Fair* release for the movie has even more alternates and outtakes.

"I'M GONNA BID MY BLUES GOODBYE"

A Hank Snow song covered briefly by Elvis during the *Million Dollar Quartet* jam, on the usual selection of MDQ issues.

"I'M GONNA SIT RIGHT DOWN AND CRY (OVER YOU)"

Elvis recorded this Joe Thomas / Howard Biggs composition in New York on January 31, 1956.

RCA packaged it as the B-side to " I'll Never Let You Go," which shipped in late August 1956, and released it on double EP and LP *Elvis Presley* that same year.

The tune has since come out on Fifties anthology *The King Of Rock And Roll*. There are long-standing rumors that Elvis also performed this song at the Louisiana Hayride in 1954.

"I'M GONNA WALK DEM GOLDEN STAIRS"

A spiritual in an arrangement credited to Cully Holt, formerly of The Jordanaires, that Elvis recorded in Nashville on the last day of October 1960 for the *His Hand In Mine* gospel album, reserving the adaptation credit for himself..

The song is has since been issued on gospel anthologies *Amazing Grace* and *Peace In The Valley*.

Alternates are abound on FTD albums *Fame And Fortune*, *Easter Special* and the FTD version of *His Hand In Mine*.

"I'M LEAVIN'"

Elvis recorded this poignant song in Nashville on May 20, 1971. Elvis The singer and RCA were so pleased with his the performance on the Michael Jarrett / Sonny Charles tune that they brought it out almost immediately as a single, with "Heart Of Rome" on the B-side. Though a favorite of Elvis' (and later many fans), the single did not catch fire. It, and only made it to #36 in the main *Billboard* chart, though it did make climb to it to #2 on the Easy Listening chart.

Elvis sang the song regularly in concert up until the end of 1974, so it's on many bootlegs and a number of official releases (FTD's *Southern Nights*, *It's Midnight, Southern Nights* and *Takin' Tahoe Tonight*, as well as on BMG release *Live in Las Vegas*).

The studio version has since appeared on *Elvis Aron Presley*, *Walk A Mile In My Shoes*, *Artist Of The Century* and *Burning Love*. A studio alternate is on FTD release *I Sing All Kinds*.

"I'M LEAVING IT UP TO YOU"

Elvis sang this Don Harris / Dewey Terry song from 1957 at a few live shows in the Seventies. Bootlegs only for this one (*Leavin' It Up To You*, *Sold Out*, *If I Loved You . . .*).

"I'M LEFT, YOU'RE RIGHT, SHE'S GONE"

Written by Sun staff steel guitarist Stan Kesler and Bill Taylor, reputedly having drawn their inspiration from a Campbell's soup commercial, Elvis recorded what was to become the rockabilly B-side to his fourth Sun single (with "Baby, Let's Play House") some time in early March of 1955, for before being rushed out the door release on April 10, 1955 as Sun 217. Incidentally, when the song was initially registered, the title was "I'm Right, You're Left, She's Gone." A slower version of the song, recorded at the same time, didn't see official release until 1984 collection *A Golden Celebration*.

The song was reissued as a single by RCA as soon as they had bought out Elvis' contract with Sun. The song subsequently appeared on EP *Any Way You Want Me*. In later years it came out on *For LP Fans Only* *The Sun Sessions* and *The Country Side of Elvis*.

The slow version and multiple alternates came out on *The Complete Sun Sessions*, with even more outtakes on the LP issue and the 2006 re-issue. Alternates may also be found on *Sunrise* and Fifties anthology *The King Of Rock 'n' Roll*. Both fast and slow versions (sometimes called titled as "My Baby's Gone") are on 2004 BMG release *Elvis at Sun*, and on 2006 independent release *Memphis Recording Service Vol. 2.*

Elvis sang the song live at many early Fifties shows. Live recordings are available on *Sunrise*, the 2006 *Complete Sun Sessions*, and many of the Louisiana Hayride retrospectives and *Memphis Recording Service Vol. 2.*.

"I'M MOVIN' ON"

Elvis provided his personal take on Hank Snow's huge 1950 hit in in an early morning session on January 15, 1969 at American Studio in Memphis. Elvis' version of this updated country classic was released on *From Elvis In Memphis* that same year. Later album outings include *The Memphis Record*, *From Nashville to Memphis* and *The Country Side of Elvis*. *Guitar Man* features a remixed version and with a new instrumental track.

An alternate mix came out in 1999 on *Suspicious Minds: The Memphis 1969 Anthology*. A remixed version from the *Guitar Man* sessions is on FTD release *Too Much Monkey Business*. FTD release *The Memphis Sessions* showcases further alternates/outtakes.

"I'M NOT THE MARRYING KIND"

Certainly true in on early July 2, 1961 when Elvis recorded this Mack David/Sherman Edwards tune in Nashville for *Follow That Dream* and the accompanying soundtrack EP. The song was first released on an album a decade later, on the *C'mon Everybody* LP., and then Iin the Nineties it came out on the *Double Feature* release for the movie, and in the 2000s it was on the FTD movie reissue.

"I'M SO LONESOME I COULD CRY"

Elvis told the entire world during the *Aloha From Hawaii Via Satellite* show that this was "probably the saddest song I ever heard," and proceeded to back up his claim with a live demonstration. Hank Williams took his own composition to #1 in 1949. The melancholy lyrics have appealed to dozens of performers since, among whom B. J. Thomas sold a million copies of his cover in 1966; sometime Elvis player Charlie McCoy took the song on in 1972.

Elvis sang "I'm So Lonesome I Could Cry" within range of a microphone at Sam Thompson's house in November 1973 (on FTD 2000s release *Made in Memphis* and bootlegs).

In addition to the *Aloha From Hawaii* album release, 1973 live Elvis recordings of "I'm So Lonesome I Could Cry" have appeared on *The Alternate Aloha*, *Welcome to My World*, *Walk A Mile In My Shoes*, *The Country Side of Elvis*, *Elvis By The Presleys* and the 2006 album titled *Elvis Country*.

"I'M WITH A CROWD BUT OH SO ALONE"

This Ernest Tubb/Carl Story song was one of many Elvis and pals joked around with this one during their *Million Dollar Quartet* jam session in late on December 4, 1956.

"I'M YOURS"

Elvis recorded this Don Robertson ballad at Studio B, Nashville on June 26, 1961. It was initially put out on the *Pot Luck* album, though it had been considered and passed over for the *Blue Hawaii* soundtrack before that.

In the summer of 1965, it was recycled on the *Tickle Me* soundtrack and chosen as a single to promote the movie, faced with B-side track "(It's A) Long Lonely Highway" (which had also appeared before, on the *Kissin' Cousins* album). The song notched up half a million sales, and made it to #11 in the *Billboard* Hot 100 (#1 on the easy listening chart).

The song has also appeared on 2007 release *Elvis at the Movies*.

Half a dozen alternates have been released: on *From Nashville To Memphis*, *Today Tomorrow & Forever*, and on FTD albums *Long Lonely Highway*, *Studio B: Nashville Outtakes* and *Pot Luck*. The FTD *Tickle Me* album release features the undubbed single and LP masters.

IMPERIALS, THE

Gospel quartet The Imperials were founded in 1963 by Jake Hess, a Southern gospel legend and one of Elvis' early singing heroes from his time as lead singer with the Statesmen. When Elvis' first choice, the Harmonizing Four, pulled out of a recording session booked for Nashville in May 1966, Jake Hess and the Imperials, as they were originally known, stepped into the breach, much to Elvis' delight, after secretary Mary Lynch suggested them as the ideal group for his forthcoming gospel album, *How Great Thou Art*. A characteristic of the group was their clean-living attitude to life, which was written into their contracts.

Elvis engaged a revised Imperials line-up—ill-health had forced Jake Hess to leave in the interim and Armond Morales had taken over as leader—as backing for his inaugural Las Vegas concerts in the summer of 1969, alongside new female backing group the Sweet Inspirations. Elvis frequently sang with the group offstage too, winding down after shows by singing a little gospel.

The Imperials were unable to accompany Elvis when he embarked on his first tour in twelve years in September 1970, soon after the Las Vegas season filmed for concert documentary *Elvis: That's The Way It Is* (in which they feature), but they were back for his 8-date tour that November. They continued to work with Elvis until his November 1971 tour, when they were replaced by J.D. Sumner and his new group, the Stamps. Their final recording session with Elvis was the gospel album *He Touched Me*, in Nashville, the early summer of 1971. Reasons adduced for why they ceased working with Elvis range from a financial despite with the Colonel to shock at Elvis' gun-waving shenanigans.

The Imperials backed singer Jimmy Dean for a spell, and then returned squarely to their gospel roots. Since the Seventies, over two dozen singers have joined and left the group, in the process building up a heritage of four Grammys, seventeen Doves, and a place in the Gospel Music Hall of Fame.

See Backing groups for The Imperials line-ups during their Elvis years.

TERRY BLACKWOOD: "The Imperials never met a kinder man, a more generous man, who cared about people, and he made us feel so welcome, every time we were with him."

IMPERSONAL LIFE, THE

Elvis was given this book by Larry Geller in 1964 soon after they met, and it quickly became one of Elvis' lifelong favorites. First published in 1914 as an anonymous work, author Joseph Brenner's narrative stance directly addresses the reader from the divinity within. The book's thesis is that God as the creative spirit dwells within us all, though only true seekers have access to this godhead through meditation and stripping away the falsities of the personality and chatter of the mind. The God presence is expressed by the "little voice" in us all.

Elvis bought dozens and dozens of copies of this book over the years. He re-read the book constantly, underlining significant passages and then handing copies over to people who were important in his life.

CHAPTER HEADINGS

I AM
Be Still—and KNOW—I AM God
I, Life, God
Consciousness, Intelligence, Will
The Key
Thinking and Creating
The Word
My Idea
The Garden of Eden
Good and Evil
Use
Soul Mates
Authority
Mediums and Mediators
Masters
The Christ and Love
Finding Me
Union

"I AM the Innermost, the Spirit, the animating Cause of your being, of all life, of all living things, both visible and invisible. There is nothing dead, for I, the Impersonal ONE, AM all that there is. I AM Infinite and wholly unconfined; the Universe is My Body, all the Intelligence there is emanates from My Mind, all the Love there is flows from My Heart, all the Power there is, is but My Will in action."

Book:
Impersonal Life: The Little Book in Which Elvis Found the Light: Graceland Edition, by W. Laviolette, DeVorss & Co., 2001.

IMPERSONATORS

ETAs (Elvis Tribute Artists), as impersonators prefer to be known, are the tangible evidence that Elvis is still alive and still wowing the world from on stage.

In the early years, the singers who began impersonating Elvis practically as soon as his new sound started to earn him a following were known as rivals rather than impersonators—a distinction that has everything to do with chronology and little to do with substance. A student called Carl "Cheesie" Nelson mimicked Elvis from the stage before a Texarkana performance as early as December 1954, and continued to do so through 1955, once filling in for Elvis who was delayed because of a car crash.

More accomplished rivals carved out careers of their own as early rockers; a few soundalikes found a niche replicating Elvis' voice, either on demos or under their own name: Ral Donner covered Elvis songs in the Fifties and Sixties, and made a tribute album with members of Elvis' original band after Elvis died (Elvis also covered one of Donner's songs, "The Girl Of My Best Friend," in 1960); Ronnie McDowell has voiced Elvis on TV movies. It should also not be forgotten that many top music stars of the Sixties, Seventies and Eighties started out impersonating Elvis in the privacy of their bedrooms.

Impersonators were out in force as early as 1956, as part of the parade welcoming Elvis home to Tupelo before his September shows.

27. I'll Take You Home Again Kathleen (Slow)
28. There's No Tomorrow
29. Number Eight (On The Jukebox)

IN DREAMS OF YESTERDAY

A Czech fan club release on Memory records of Elvis' June 28, 1974, 8:30 pm show in Milwaukee, Wisconsin.

TRACK LISTING:
1. See See Rider
2. I Got A Woman / Amen
3. Turn Around, Look At Me
4. Love Me
5. Tryin' To Get To You
6. All Shook Up
7. Love Me Tender
8. Hound Dog
9. Fever
10. Polk Salad Annie
11. Why Me Lord
12. Suspicious Minds
13. Band Introduction
14. I Can't Stop Loving You
15. Help Me
16. Bridge Over Troubled Water
17. Let Me Be There
18. Funny How Time Slips Away
19. Big Boss Man
20 Steamroller Blues
21. Can't Help Falling In Love

"IN MY FATHER'S HOUSE (ARE MANY MANSIONS)"

The Blackwood Brothers hit was an easy pick for Elvis to include on his first gospel album, *His Hand In Mine*. Written by Aileene Hanks, Elvis recorded the track in Nashville in the wee hours of October 31, 1960.

The song is on Elvis' gospel compilations *Amazing Grace*, *Peace In The Valley*, and later this millennium also on *Christmas Peace* (aka *Elvis: My Christmas #1*).

Seven alternates and outtakes are on the FTD version of *His Hand in Mine*; one of these is also on *Fame And Fortune*.

"IN MY WAY"

Elvis recorded this romantic Fred Wise / Ben Weisman quickie for *Wild In The Country* at Radio Recorders on November 7, 1960. In the absence of a soundtrack album, the track was first released five years later, on *Elvis For Everyone*. In the Seventies, it appeared on budget album *Separate Ways*. In the Nineties, it was re-released on the *Flaming Star / Wild In The Country / Follow That Dream* Double Feature issue.

The first two takes from the studio session are on *Silver Screen Stereo* and *Elvis: Close Up* respectively.

"IN THE GARDEN"

A popular gospel song since the early 1900s, Elvis recorded this melodious tune (written by Charles Austin Miles) for *How Great Thou Art* at RCA's Studio B in Nashville, on May 27, 1966. It was one of the hymns sung at Gladys's funeral.

The song has since appeared on gospel/ Christian compilations *Amazing Grace*, *Peace In The Valley* and *Christmas Peace*.

"IN THE GHETTO"

Elvis was initially in two minds about whether or not to record this protest song written by Mac Davis; he was convinced it had the potential to be a "smash," as he told writer Mac Davis when he played him the song at American Studio, but he had never sung a message song before (outside of gospel). Elvis prevailed over initial reservations from George Klein and American Studio boss Chips Moman, who wanted Roy Hamilton to do the song (though according to Lamar Fike the tune was originally earmarked for football star Rosey Grier). He also had to stand up to a reticent Colonel Parker, who believed this was the wrong kind of material for his boy. Reputedly, the song had previously been rejected by Righteous Brother Bill Medley and Sammy Davis Jr. before Elvis heard the demo.

Elvis recorded this hugely important song at American Studio in twenty-three takes on January 20, 1969, in one of Memphis's very own black ghettos, less than three miles from the Lorraine Motel where Martin Luther King Jr. had been assassinated nine months earlier. During the mixing process, Elvis was initially unconvinced about adding female vocals, but then agreed that they were good for the song. Prior to release, RCA dropped the song's subtitle—its original title was "In The Ghetto (The Vicious Circle)"; it was this vicious circle that Mac Davis wanted to convey when he first sat down to write the song.

Released in April 1969 with "Any Day Now" on the B-side, the first single to come out from his watershed American Studio sessions signaled Elvis' return to chart-topping form. The single sold 1.2 million copies, and climbed as high as #3 on the *Billboard* Hot 100 (#2 in the UK). A month later the track appeared on the album *From Elvis In Memphis*, the first of many album appearances that over the years have included *Worldwide Gold Award Hits Vol. 1, Pure Gold, The Top Ten Hits, Elvis: A Legendary Performer Vol. 3, Elvis' Gold Records Vol. 5, From Nashville to Memphis, Artist Of The Century, ELVIS 30 #1 Hits, Elvis By The Presleys, Hitstory, Elvis Inspirational* and *The Essential Elvis Presley*.

For the first couple of years after Elvis returned to the stage, "In The Ghetto" was an emotive live favorite. It was on the playlist for his Las Vegas International Hotel debut in August 1969 and on the live album from the engagement, *From Memphis To Vegas / Elvis In Person* (reprised on *Greatest Hits Live*, the re-released issue of *On Stage*, and *Elvis Live* among others; the earliest version so far released, from August 21, came out in 2007 on the *Viva Las Vegas* 2 CD release).

Other live versions released officially—in addition to the inevitable bootlegs—include *Elvis Aron Presley*, the 3-CD release of *That's The Way It Is*, *Live in Las Vegas*, *The Live Greatest Hits*, *Elvis: Close Up*, and FTD releases *Elvis At The International, Writing For The King, All Shook Up* and *Polk Salad Annie*.

Alternate cuts from the American studio session have surfaced on *From Nashville To Memphis, Platinum: A Life In Music, Suspicious Minds: The Memphis 1969 Anthology, The Memphis Sessions* and *Today, Tomorrow & Forever*. A very early run-through of the song featured on 2006 FTD release *Made in Memphis*. The song also underwent Felton Jarvis's Eighties remix treatment, in a version that didn't come out until 2000 FTD album *Too Much Monkey Business*. Elvis' vocal solo denuded of instrumentation plus an alternate take were bonus tracks on the deluxe 2-CD edition of *ELVIS 30 #1*.

The song has since been covered by artists ranging from Dolly Parton to Candi Staton, Nick Cave & The Bad Seeds, Bobbie Gentry, Mica Paris and Eric Cartman of "South Park" fame. Lisa Marie's voice was mixed in with Elvis' for a 2007 version of the song and an accompanying video, released to raise funds to help the homeless in New Orleans and quickly a #1 download in countries across the world.

WAYNE JACKSON: "We were actually in the ghetto, and here was Elvis singing a pertinent song about the South and the social climate of the day."

"IN YOUR ARMS"

Elvis recorded this playful Aaron Schroeder/ Wally Gold rocker for the *Something For Everybody* album at RCA's Studio B in Nashville on March 12, 1961.

The song has since come out on *From Nashville to Memphis*. The first take from the recording session is on FTD releases *Fame And Fortune* and *Something For Everybody*. A home recording appeared on bootleg *The Long Lost Home Recordings*.

INCOME

See MONEY

"INDESCRIBABLY BLUE"

Elvis recorded this ballad in Nashville on June 10, 1966. It was written by Darrell Glenn, and suggested to Elvis by Lamar Fike. On release as a single in January 1967, with B-side "Fools Fall in Love," it peaked at #33 in the charts, selling 300,000 copies. First album release was on *Elvis' Gold Records Vol. 4*. The first take came out in the 2000's on *Today, Tomorrow & Forever*.

A home-recorded version from earlier in 1966 officially surfaced for the first time in 1999 on *The Home Recordings*.

INDIANA

- *Bloomington*
The Indiana University Assembly Hall hosted Elvis on June 27, 1974. In 1976, Elvis started an 11-day tour at the Athletic Center on May 27.

- *Evansville*
Elvis played the Roberts Municipal Coliseum on June 13, 1972. By the time he next played there (on October 24, 1976) it had been renamed the Roberts Stadium.

- *Fort Wayne*
Elvis performed at the Memorial Coliseum on

Performing for the last time in Indianapolis June 26, 1977.

March 30, 1957, and then again on June 12, 1972. He returned to give another show on October 25, 1976.

- Indianapolis

On December 4, 1955, Elvis embarked on a four-day residency with Hank Snow at the Lyric Theater.

He played the Fair Grounds Coliseum on tour on April 12, 1972, and the Expo Convention Center on October 5, 1974. Elvis gave the last performance of his lifetime at the Market Square Arena on June 26, 1977.

- South Bend

Elvis and the band played the University of Notre Dame's Athletic and Convention Center on September 30 and October 1, 1974 (released by FTD in 2003 as *Dragonheart*). They returned for more on October 20, 1976.

- Terre Haute

Elvis performed at the Hulman Civic Center on July 9, 1975.

"INHERIT THE WIND"

Rock, soul, country and gospel all jostle on this Eddie Rabbitt song that Elvis recorded at American Studio on January 16, 1969. for release later that year on the *From Vegas to Memphis* album. It has since appeared on *The Memphis Record*, *From Nashville to Memphis* and *Suspicious Minds: The Memphis 1969 Anthology*.

A live version that Elvis performed in August 1969 in Las Vegas came out in 1991 on *Collectors Gold*.

INK SPOTS

While he was growing up, Elvis loved listening to the vocal harmonies of this black quartet, founded in Indianapolis in the mid-Thirties and regular chart-toppers through to the early Fifties. In 1953, when teenaged Elvis plucked up the courage to go to the Memphis Recording Service and pay to record two songs, one of them was Ink Spots number "That's When Your Heartaches Begin."

The Ink Spots were an important precursor to the doo-wap strand of early rock 'n' roll. Their best known hits were "If I Didn't Care," "Do I Worry" and "Into Each Life Some Rain Must Fall."

Over the years, Elvis sang Ink Spots spirituals "It Is No Secret (What God Can Do")," "Somebody Bigger Than You And I," and lead singer Bill Kenny's hit from 1952 "There Is No God But God."

INTERNET

Elvis' virtual home is, of course, EPE's . Fan-club run websites such as the Elvis Information Network are excellent sources for Elvis news and all things Elvis, with its comprehensive database ranging from lyrics to news, an encyclopedia, fan events and a lively members' forum.

Elvis fan clubs and fan sites form a network of globe-encircling communities, with new sites going live every month. Elvis chat rooms are invariably lively and filled with incredibly knowledgeable (and sometimes opinionated) members, including many people who knew Elvis.

Discologists are particularly well-served with sites that list every Elvis song, every album that songs have appeared on, alternate takes, sound quality, songs Elvis didn't record but could have/would have, studio recording sessions databases and similar information. Sites that take advantage of user-generated

Performing for the last time in Indianapolis June 26, 1977.

content such as online booksellers and music stores are also chock-full of fan input about the King.

Acclaimed fan sites include (but are by no means limited to) Elvis Unlimited and all of them provide links to further virtual Elvis destinations to explore.

Elvis even has his own search engine at , while offers a comprehensive rundown on Elvis' recordings.

At the time of writing, a search for "Elvis Presley" on Google returned 2.5 million results.

A number of Usenet newsgroups/Google groups are Elvis themed, and many of the musicians with whom Elvis worked over the year have set up their own fascinating websites.

Elvis has recently acquired a presence on MySpace (thekingelvis), and his own YouTube channel (), in addition to the enormous amount

of material that fans have posted to this and other video sites.

A NOTE ON THE LACK OF INTERNET REFERENCES IN THE BODY OF THIS ENCYCLOPEDIA

Here today, here tomorrow but not necessarily here for the length of time that this old-fangled book remains in print, we have refrained from listing website address under individual entries. Anyone armed with a little patience and rudimentary search engine skills can find thousands and thousands of Elvis sites and in-depth information on practically anything even remotely Elvis-related.

INTERNATIONAL HOTEL, LAS VEGAS

As a direct result of Elvis' career-resurrecting NBC TV Special, which was broadcast in December 1968, the Colonel started negotiating with interested parties for Elvis' return to live performing. The biggest offer that came his way was from a venue that hadn't even been built yet, the 30-story International Hotel in Las Vegas, which at the time was planned to be the world's largest hotel with 1,512 rooms.

The initial approach to the Colonel was from Bill Miller just two weeks after the "Comeback Special" aired. Elvis was hired to perform on a one-month contract by owner Kirk Kerkorian in December 1968, for $100,000 a week over a four-week engagement. Signed in April 1969 (two months after a publicity photo of the signing at the hotel building site), the contract included complimentary suites at the brand new hotel for both Elvis and the Colonel, plus provisions for a concert documentary and an option for a repeat engagement.

In the run up to his first live performance in many years, Elvis set to work at Graceland with Charlie Hodge on structuring the show. In a pattern that was to be repeated for the remainder of his live performing days, Elvis picked, worked up and prepared a large number of new songs, some of which he played in his early shows, but very few of which he actually persevered with until the end of the run.

Barbra Streisand was the first act to play the newly-opened 2,000-seat Showroom, a week before Elvis' opening gig on July 31, 1969. To make sure that he played in front of a friendly crowd, Elvis flew out two planeloads of pals from Memphis, though George Klein remembers that he asked his pals to come and see him on the second night, after he'd got the nerves out of the way. The audience for that first night included celebrity pals Paul Anka, Fats Domino, Ann-Margret, Wayne Newton, Phil Ochs, Dick Clark, Carol Channing, Pat Boone and Cary Grant, and familiar faces such as Sam Phillips.

Elvis overcame a king sized bout of nerves before he made it onto the stage, after opening acts by the Sweet Inspirations and comedian Sammy Shore. Elvis ripped into "Blue Suede Shoes" and immediately hit his stride, earning almost unanimous rave revues for his performance. True to form, the Colonel tweaked the contract to extract more money for his client and himself at the earliest opportunity which, as it turned out, was on the hotel coffee shop tablecloth immediately after Elvis' triumphant opening night.

For the better part of a month, Elvis kept up the same level of success for a grueling two shows a night, one at 8:15 p.m., the other at midnight. "The stage was his living room," recalls Eddie Fadal, "it gave him the biggest thrill to see them excited, especially in Las Vegas." Felton Jarvis, who recorded Elvis' performances between August 21 and 26 for live album From Memphis To Vegas, later said "He was like a wild man, he was all over the stage . . . he almost hurt himself."

Elvis' month long engagement sold more than 100,000 tickets and grossed in excess of $1.5 million. Ticket sales were only part of the story: when Elvis was in town, the hotel's income from all operations doubled, while the maitre d' could suddenly expect no end of tips from fans who wanted the better seats. In appreciation, Hotel Vice President Alex Shoofey gave Elvis and eight friends an all expenses paid trip to Hawaii.

Elvis' second residency in January 1970 brought a few changes to the personnel (Glen D. Hardin on piano, Bob Lanning on drums, and Ann Williams replacing Cissy Houston in the Sweet Inspirations). Elvis made the show less of a retrospective by introducing new material by artists he admired, some of which—"Proud Mary," "Polk Salad Annie," "Walk a Mile in My

Shoes" and "Sweet Caroline"—soon became live show favorites. He also tried to keep the show down to an hour by reining in his banter; the hotel preferred to have guests back in the casino sooner rather than later. This second run, starting on January 26, 1970, was the first time that Elvis performed on stage in jumpsuits. Towards the end of the month-long engagement he incorporated a further few tracks so that there would be sufficient material for upcoming live album, On Stage. The hotel once again benefited enormously from his residency, filling its rooms during what would otherwise have been the low season.

For Elvis' third engagement in the summer of 1970, he worked with orchestra director Joe Guercio, and had the members of his original band back; Kathy Westmoreland replaced Millie Kirkham, the first time she sang with Elvis.

The hotel was taken over by the Hilton group in mid-1971, though for some time to come Elvis continued to announce his arrival on stage as at the International. The Colonel was happy for Elvis to continue his twice-yearly residency with the new management, and did not invoke the get-out clause Elvis had in his contract.

Footage of Elvis' suite at the hotel circa 2004 appeared in The TCB Gang—The Way It Was DVD, released in 2006.

ELVIS SAID AFTER HIS FIRST SHOW IN 1969: "This has been one of the most exciting nights of my life."

RED WEST: "It was the challenge he needed, and he really went at it."

INTERNATIONAL POPULARITY

Elvis' fame spread round the globe faster than any performer before him, riding the wave of new-fangled television in addition to his presence on vinyl, radio, press and film. Wherever Elvis' records arrived, he struck a resonant chord with young people at a time when nations across the world were beginning to enjoy prosperity after the destruction and hardships of the Second World War. He was as popular with fans on the far side of the globe as on the far side of the United States, with homegrown fan clubs springing up wherever his records were released.

For fans in the UK, Australia, Japan, Thailand, even the Soviet Union—where Elvis fans, known as "stilyagi," listened to bootlegged albums sold on used X-ray platters from hospitals; the first official Elvis release in the former Eastern block was not until Pure Gold in 1975—Elvis was considered to be as much "theirs" as he was "ours." Elvis was equally influential on the development of music and youth culture outside the States as in it, and was just as strong a seller in many markets outside North America: for example, he notched up more #1 hits in the UK than he did in the US.

To make up for the international tours Elvis never made, fans had to be content with Elvis' frequent movies, which, according to Colonel Parker's right-hand man Tom Diskin, "reach his fans in the remotest corners of the world, something it would take the best part of his life to do in concert appearances."

INTERNATIONAL TRAVEL

An entire entry on a topic that can be wrapped up in two words: Elvis didn't. And it was one of the few regrets in his life.

The underlying reason why, with half the world clamoring to see him, Elvis never performed outside North America only became clear after Colonel Parker died and it was revealed that

he had originally entered the US as an illegal alien. The Colonel minimized the risk of being unmasked by immigration officers by avoiding travel outside the US, and did everything in his power to keep Elvis within US borders.

The only shows that Elvis played outside of the States were in Canada in 1957. That same year the Colonel turned down serious tour offers from South America and Australia, the latter arranged by persistent Australian promoter Lee Gordon, who was involved in Elvis' first tour to Hawaii.

As early as 1956, Elvis told hometown paper the Memphis Press Scimitar that he wanted to go to England.

Elvis told the press conference before he left for Germany in 1958 that he had had to put plans for a European tour on ice. Out in Germany, he gave hints that he would have performed given the chance, even behind the iron curtain "if certain people think I should."

It's impossible to known just how many lucrative offers the Colonel turned down from outside the States, with the exception of offers made publicly at press conferences. Early in his career, the Colonel employed a variety of stratagies to talk Elvis out of following the trail blazed by a growing number of Fifties rock 'n' roll artists, who toured extensively in the UK and continental Europe. The Colonel argued that Elvis couldn't just show up in Europe without a comprehensive, properly planned schedule, otherwise millions of fans might be disappointed.

News items appeared in 1959 claiming that Elvis was booked to do a six-day tour of Australia after he finished his service in the Army.

In 1961, Elvis batted a reporter's question about a European tour directly to the Colonel. Deadpan, the Colonel replied, "We're waiting for a good offer."

For most of the Sixties, Elvis' itinerant rovings between Memphis, Los Angeles, Las Vegas, Hawaii and later Palm Springs amply satisfied his wanderlust. With Elvis eschewing live performance for his movie career, the Colonel had a ready-made excuse to turn down international offers. Even private travel was out of the question; the Colonel pointed out that having waited so long, fans would be upset if Elvis visited their country but didn't perform.

Elvis and Priscilla had plans to travel after they married in 1967—plans they abandoned when they found out soon afterwards that Priscilla was pregnant.

Among the many offers for Elvis to perform that flooded in after his NBC TV Special in 1968, some were from European promoters. Elvis publicly announced that he was keen to do a European tour, just as soon as he got this "feel back" for live shows. Immediately after Elvis' triumphant return to live performing at the International Hotel in Las Vegas in the summer of 1969, a ££1 million offer was publicly made for Elvis to perform just two shows at Wembley Stadium in London. There and then, the Colonel told the man, "just put down the deposit." Tom Jones's manager also tried to entice Elvis with a $1m offer in the Sixties.

In 1969, the Colonel once again talked Elvis out of going on vacation to Europe. In his memoir, Larry Geller suggests that the Colonel enlisted two men who claimed that they were RCA employees to persuade Elvis that it would be far better to go to Europe once all of the plans had been put in place. Whenever the question popped up at a press conference, Elvis continued to tell the press that he was expecting to go on an international tour in 1970, then 1971, then 1972.

When Elvis finally cornered the Colonel about arranging an international tour, the Colonel came up with the idea of the worldwide satellite broadcast which became known as Aloha From Hawaii.

Entourage members Joe Esposito and Jerry Schilling traveled to Europe in 1973, around the time that Elvis and the Colonel had a bust up that briefly interrupted their long-standing business relationship. After the success of *Aloha*—in some parts of the world up to 90% of households watched—Elvis was even more keen to take off around the world. The Colonel continued to sideline proposals, including a lucrative set of engagements in Australia.

In 1975, the Colonel not only turned down a firm tour offer from the UK, he said no to $5 million and then $10 million offered by the Khashoggis to play a date at the Pyramids in Egypt—Elvis was mustard keen, but by now the Colonel more than had the measure of how to dampen his ardor. The Colonel also declined $1 million per night offers from Australia, Germany and Japan, in addition to a number of multi-million dollar offers from South American businessmen, this time claiming that ticket prices would be too high for his fans in Europe, that there would be problems for Elvis to carry all his medications across international borders, or that it would be impossible to guarantee the levels of security Elvis required. Sonny West concurs that it was the "guns and the pills" that made it impossible for Elvis to tour outside the US.

Elvis was still trying to get the Colonel to arrange a world tour in his last months alive, this time a tour of Europe with a side-trip to Japan. A few months before Elvis' death, the Colonel reputedly contacted Led Zeppelin manager Peter Grant to make preliminary enquiries about promoting an Elvis European tour.

Many years later, the Colonel claimed that Elvis never played in Europe because he didn't want to perform at outdoor venues, which was all that he was offered. The Colonel's second wife, Loanne, has said that Parker had a passport and so would have been free to travel.

ELVIS SAID IN GERMANY IN 1958: "Maybe someday I can come back, when my Army tour is up, as an entertainer, and then I'll have more time and maybe I'll have an opportunity to kind of make myself at home over here. Arriverderci! No, that's Italian, isn't it?"

CHARLIE HODGE: "He wanted to tour Europe badly and especially wanted to perform in Germany and France as he had such happy memories of being in both countries. He wanted to repay the people for their hospitality and of course his fans in other countries. . . . We never really knew why the Colonel said no to them. . . . It used to annoy the hell out of Elvis. He got very angry about it more than one time."

LARRY GELLER: "Elvis longed to see the rest of the world."

DUKE BARDWELL: "To deny him that was the last nail in the coffin. He didn't have anything to look forward to, and so he just went deeper and deeper into the things that let him hide."

ALANNA NASH: "It wasn't that Parker couldn't leave the country. Through the years, he accumulated many influential friends in all ranks of government... who could have solved this problem with a single phone call. The truth of the matter was that Parker didn't want to leave the country."

LAMAR FIKE: "The last great frontier for him was the world outside the United States and Canada. But the Colonel would always talk him out of it."

IOWA

- Ames
Elvis performed at the James W. Hilton Coliseum on May 28, 1976.

- Des Moines
Elvis played the Veterans Memorial Auditorium on May 22, 1956. He next performed at the venue on June 20, 1974. The last time he performed there was on his final ever tour, on June 23, 1977.

- Sioux City
Elvis and his original band were at the Municipal Auditorium on May 23, 1956.

IRS

The US tax authorities examined Elvis' 1955-1960 tax returns, but ultimately only quibbled about excessive movie income listed as expenses rather than earnings. Elvis was keen to pay all the money he owed in taxes, as a patriotic gesture to the nation. Lamar Fike says that the Colonel recommended Elvis to submit his books to the IRS periodically for them to check that he had paid every penny in tax, which at the time had a 90% top rate.

The IRS hit Elvis' estate with multi-million dollar demands for back taxes after his death, almost pushing the Estate into bankruptcy. In his 1968 movie, Elvis' character is shadowed by tax inspector Nancy Sinatra.

COLONEL PARKER: "I consider it my solemn duty to put Elvis in the 90% tax bracket."

"IS IT SO STRANGE"

A Faron Young tune covered by Elvis on the *Just For You* EP, released in late summer 1957 and recorded on January 19, 1957 at Radio Recorders. Six weeks earlier weeks Elvis had tried out the song with pals at Sun Records in what was to become *The Million Dollar Quartet*. The first time that the tune as crooned by Elvis came out on an album was *A Date With Elvis*. Subsequent album releases include *Separate Ways*, *The King Of Rock And Roll*, the 1997 re-release of *Loving You* and the FTD *Loving You* release

Alternate takes have appeared on *Essential Elvis Vol. 2*, *Today Tomorrow & Forever*, *Elvis: Close Up* and FTD release *Flashback*.

"ISLAND OF LOVE"

A Sid Tepper / Roy C. Bennett soundtrack song about the island of Kauai for *Blue Hawaii* that Elvis recorded on March 22, 1961 at Radio Recorders in Los Angeles. A female backing track was added to the movie version. The song has since appeared on the *Blue Hawaii* re-issue in 1997.

One alternate came out in 2001 on FTD release *Silver Screen Stereo*; many more outtakes had previously appeared on bootleg.

"IT AIN'T NO BIG THING (BUT IT'S GROWING)"

Elvis sang this Charlie Louvin country hit in Nashville on June 6, 1970 for the simple reason that he felt like it, not because it was one of the tracks put forward by his song pluggers. Written by Neal Merritt, Shorty Hall and Alice Joy Merritt, the song first came out on his *Love Letters From Elvis* album. Subsequent album releases include *Walk A Mile In My Shoes*, *Elvis Country* (the 2000 and 2006 issues) and the *Blue Suede Shoes Collection*.

Essential Elvis Vol. 4 features an alternate take, as does FTD release *The Nashville Marathon*.

"IT FEELS SO RIGHT"

Elvis recorded this sassy Fred Wise/Ben Weisman number on March 20, 1960 in Nashville. The song was rushed into production for the *Elvis Is Back!*

album and sent out the door double quick to waiting fans hungry for new Elvis music after his two year Army hiatus. Five years later, in May 1965, the song was recycled for the soundtrack of *Tickle Me* and as the B-side to promotional single "(Such An) Easy Question." With waning record sales the norm by this time, the song only made it to #55 in the charts.

Alongside a limited number of posthumous album releases (*Elvis Sings The Blues*, *A Valentine Gift For You* and *From Nashville to Memphis*), several alternate takes have appeared, on *Platinum: A Life In Music*, *Elvis: Close Up*, and FTD releases *Long Lonely Highway*, *Tickle Me* and *Elvis Is Back!* (which has four).

IT HAPPENED AT THE WORLD'S FAIR (LP)

The soundtrack album to this MGM movie, released in April 1963, carried a premium price but mustered a scant twenty minutes of music. It made it to #4 in the charts and stayed on the Billboard Top LP chart for seventeen weeks, though all-told it only sold half what some of his previous soundtrack offerings had done.

TRACK LISTING:
1. Beyond The Bend
2. Relax
3. Take Me To The Fair
4. They Remind Me Too Much Of You
5. One Broken Heart For Sale (movie version)
6. I'm Falling In Love Tonight
7. Cotton Candy Land
8. A World Of Our Own
9. How Would You Like To Be?
10. Happy Ending

The LP was re-released in 1993 as part of the Double Feature series, paired with *Fun in Acapulco*.

TRACK LISTING:
1. Beyond The Bend
2. Relax
3. Take Me To The Fair
4. They Remind Me Too Much Of You
5. One Broken Heart For Sale (movie version)
6. I'm Falling In Love Tonight
7. Cotton Candy Land
8. A World Of Our Own
9. How Would You Like To Be
10. Happy Ending
11. One Broken Heart For Sale
12. Fun In Acapulco
13. Vino, Dinero Y Amor
14. Mexico
15. El Toro
16. Marguerita
17. The Bullfighter Was A Lady
18. (There's) No Room To Rhumba In A Sports Car
19. I Think I'm Gonna Like It Here
20. Bossa Nova Baby
21. You Can't Say No In Acapulco
22. Guadalajara

The 2003 FTD release contains the usual mixture of remastered originals and alternate versions.

IT HAPPENED AT THE WORLD'S FAIR

Elvis' first picture for MGM in a new four-movie deal was this film located in Seattle, shot during the Seattle Century 21 Expo, for which city landmarks the Space Needle and monorail were built.

Elvis reported for preproduction work in late August 1962 and settled right in to Clark Gable's old dressing room at the studio. Working titles discarded along the way included *Take Me to the*

Fair, Mister Will You Marry Me? and *Take Me Out to the Fair.*

On location, keeping Elvis safe from the vast crowds attending the fair—all in all, 10 million people—required a 100-strong security detail of Elvis' black-suited entourage, a large number of off-duty police officers and plain-clothes detectives from Pinkerton.

Multiple Oscar-winning director of photography Joseph Ruttenberg worked on the movie, rising to the challenge of capturing practically every single ride at the futuristic fare.

Kurt Russell made his movie debut as a shin-kicking 11-year-old in the movie.

Little Vicky Tiu landed the part after her sister Virginia had to turn down the role for a prior commitment. Vicky grew up to become first lady of Hawaii, as the wife of governor Ben Cayetano. Elvis was released from the movie in early November.

When the movie went on nationwide release a week after its April 3, 1963 LA premiere, it failed to make the top fifty grossers of the year. Still, $2.25 million by the start of 1964 was a tidy profit.

Soundtrack songs "One Broken Heart For Sale" and "They Remind Me Too Much Of You" were chosen for the tie-in single.

CREDITS:
MGM, Color.
Length: 105 minutes
Release date: April 10, 1963

TAGLINE
Swinging higher than the space needle with the gals and the songs at the famous World's Fair!

Directed by: Norman Taurog
Produced by: Ted Richmond
Written by: Si Rose, Seaman Jacobs
Music by: Leith Stevens
Cinematography by: Joseph Ruttenberg
Film Editing by: Fredric Steinkamp
Art Direction by: Preston Ames, George W. Davis
Set Decoration by: Henry Grace, Hugh Hunt

CAST:
Elvis Presley	Mike Edwards
Joan O'Brien	Diane Warren
Gary Lockwood	Danny Burke
Vicky Tiu	Sue-Lin
H.M. Wynant	Vince Bradley
Edith Atwater	Miss Steuben
Guy Raymond	Barney Thatcher
Dorothy Green	Miss Ettinger
Kam Tong	Uncle Walter Ling
Yvonne Craig	Dorothy Johnson
Herbert Bress	Craps Shooter
Don Brodie	Dice Player
George Cisar	Craps Shooter
Max Cutler	Cab Driver
John Daheim	Rough Poker Player
Jacqueline deWit	Emma Johnson
Evelyn Dutton	Rita
Joe Esposito	Carnival Man
John Francis	Guard
Sandra Giles	Lily
Paul Gorss	Poker Player
Tom Greenway	Lt. Staffer
John Hart	Bit part
Linda Humble	Redhead on monorail
John Indrisano	Poker Player
Sid Kane	Dice Player
Pete Kellett	Policeman
Jong Ook Kim	Chinese Attendant
Paula Lane	Waitress
Bill Lee	Mello Man singer
Kathryn MacGuinness	Second Attendant
Mike Mahoney	Airport Guard
Troy Melton	Poker Player
George Milan	Craps Shooter
Joe Quinn	Craps Shooter
Thurl Ravenscroft	Mello Man singer
Hal Riddle	Dice Player
Kurt Russell	Boy who kicks Elvis
J. Lewis Smith	Mechanic
Max Smith	Mello Man singer
Olan Soule	Henry Johnson
Erna Tanler	Concessionaire
Russell Thorson	Sheriff Garland
David Tyrell	Guard
Charles Victor	Craps Shooter
Patrick Waltz	NASA Recruiting Officer
Red West	Fred
Robert Williams	Mr. Farr
Wilson Wood	Mechanic

ADDITIONAL CREW:
Sydney Guilaroff	hair stylist
William Tuttle	makeup artist
Al Jennings	assistant director
Franklin Milton	recording supervisor
Jack Baker	musical number staging
Colonel Tom Parker.	technical advisor
Robert Fuca	set costumer

Elvis with Joan O'Brien in *It Happened at the World's Fair,* 1963.

Plot:

Elvis plays pilot Mike Edwards, who with partner Danny Burke (played by Gary Lockwood) is a not very successful crop duster. Their plane (affectionately named Bessie) is impounded because of unpaid bills resulting from Danny's gambling habits. They decide to hitchhike to the World's Fair in Seattle to make some money, and are picked up by Chinese farmer Uncle Walter Ling (Kam Tong) and little Sue-Lin (played by Vicky Tiu, in her debut and final movie role).

Mike looks after Sue-Lin and takes her round the fair while Uncle Walter attends to business. Danny tries to raise the money they need to get their plane back by playing a little poker. Mike is a little too indulgent on what he lets Sue-Lin eat. When she feels poorly, he takes her to Fair nurse, Diane Warren (played by Joan O'Brien). Mike feigns a sore eye just to get to see the nurse again. Diane is not fooled; Mike tries again, this time paying a little boy (Kurt Russell) to kick him in the shins so that he has a real injury. Nurse Diane agrees to tend to Mike only because her matron insists; this is all Mike needs to finagle her to the Space Needle restaurant for some food.

The course of love does not run smooth. The little boy gives the ruse away when he asks Mike if he'd like another kick. Sue-Lin informs Mike

that her uncle has not returned. Mike takes her back to the trailer where he's staying, at Century 21 Estates. The little girl decides to play Cupid and tells Diane over the phone that she has a fever. When Diane comes over, she and Mike kiss and make up. Danny returns too, with a money-making scheme to fly some cargo to Canada and then get their plane out of hock.

Before they have a chance to bed the little girl down at a pal's place, child welfare officer Miss Ettinger (Dorothy Green) knocks on the door and drags the tot away. Mike goes to the Welfare Office, only to learn that Sue-Lin has managed to escape. He races to the Fair, where he suspects she'll be.

Finally ready to fly the cargo, Danny's pal Vince (H.M. Wynant) says the kid can't come along as he doesn't want the police to get suspicious. Diane turns up, protesting her innocence at calling out child welfare. Mike discovers that the cargo is illegal furs. Vince takes Diane and Sue-Lin hostage but is disarmed by the little girl. Mike metes out fisticuff justice and then turns the ne'er do well over to the police. Uncle Walter reappears just in time, leaving Mike and Diane to declare their love and, in a metatextual moment, sing us out with "Happy Ending."

Songs: "Beyond The Bend," "Relax," "Take Me To The Fair," "They Remind Me Too Much Of You," "One Broken Heart For Sale," "I'm Falling In Love Tonight," "Cotton Candy Land," "A World Of Our Own," "How Would You Like To Be," Happy Ending".

"IT HURTS ME"

A favorite ballad of Elvis' for many years after he recorded it on January 12, 1964 at Studio B, this song had its first airing by Jerry Jackson the previous year. Elvis' emotion-charged cover of the track, penned by Joy Byers and Charles E. Daniels, was first released as the B-side to 1964 single "Kissin' Cousins"; such a strong B-side that the song made it up to #29 in the charts in its own right. "It Hurts Me" first saw album release on Elvis' Gold Records Vol. 4. Later album releases for the song include Worldwide Gold Award Hits Vol. 2, For The Asking (The Lost Album), From Nashville to Memphis, Artist Of The Century and Love, Elvis.

Elvis reprised the power ballad for the "Nothingville" road medley section on his NBC TV Special, recorded in June 1968; the track was one of many that had to be cut from the broadcast version of the Comeback Special due to time constraints. This recording came out on Elvis: A Legendary Performer Vol. 3, the 1991 release of NBC TV Special, and Memories: The '68 Comeback Special. A splice of two takes from pre-show rehearsals appeared on 2006 FTD album Let Yourself Go.

The first take from that original Nashville session came out in 2000 on Essential Elvis, Vol. 6. For no apparent reason, the single released originally on the Italian market came out senza vocal backing track and orchestration.

Sadly not recorded for posterity was the version with special lyrics that Elvis sang to the Colonel for his birthday on June 26, while they were working on the NBC Special, in which Elvis felt sufficiently on top of his game to lampoon the Colonel with the line "Is it too much to ask for one lousy tired ol' Christmas song?"

"IT IS NO SECRET (WHAT GOD CAN DO)"

Elvis recorded this sober hymn on January 19, 1957 at Radio Recorders for his Peace In The Valley EP. At the end of year, it came out as the closing track on Elvis' Christmas Album. Stuart Hamblen composed the song in 1950, a year after he gave up drinking and dedicated his life to the Lord. After losing his radio show for refusing to play a commercial for alcohol, in 1952 Hamblen ran for President of the United States for the Prohibition Party. Prior to Elvis, the song had been covered by a number of artists, including Red Foley and the Andrews Sisters.

Gospel compilations and festive albums including You'll Never Walk Alone the reissue of His Hand In Mine, Amazing Grace, Peace In The Valley, Christmas Peace and Elvis Christmas all feature the song, as does Fifties anthology The King Of Rock And Roll.

Alternate takes have appeared on Essential Elvis Vol. 2 (the first three of the session), bootleg Just A Closer Walk With Thee, Elvis: Close Up and FTD releases Easter Special and Flashback.

"IT KEEPS RIGHT ON A-HURTIN'"

A 1962 top-3 hit for Johnny Tillotson about the enduring nature of grief, sung by Elvis with a tip of his hat to his country origins on February 20, 1969 at American Studio. The track came out on the first available album, From Elvis In Memphis.

The song has subsequently appeared on From Nashville to Memphis, Great Country Songs and The Country Side of Elvis.

An alternate take came out in 1999 on Suspicious Minds: The Memphis 1969 Anthology.

"IT WON'T BE LONG"

A Sid Wayne / Ben Weisman song that Elvis recorded for Double Trouble in on June 29,1966, without too much enthusiasm, that ended up on the cutting room floor but made it onto the soundtrack album. As well as resurfacing on the Double Feature Double Trouble release in the Nineties, alternate takes are on the FTD version of the soundtrack album.

"IT WON'T SEEM LIKE CHRISTMAS (WITHOUT YOU)"

Elvis recorded this J. A. Balthrop composition on May 15, 1971 in Nashville, when he laid down the bulk of material for his Elvis Sings The Wonderful World Of Christmas album. The song has since graced Christmas Peace and Elvis Christmas.

Alternate versions have come out on If Every Day Was Like Christmas and FTD release I Sing All Kinds.

"IT WOULDN'T BE THE SAME WITHOUT YOU"

Elvis sang this song at his second ever recording session at Sun Records on January 4, 1954, once again a trip he paid for that was more about getting noticed than what he actually put down on acetate. The country song had been a hit for Al Rogers and his Rocky Mountain Boys in 1950, though it was penned by Jimmy Wakely and Fred Rose some years earlier. This Elvis demo was finally released in 1999 on Sunrise, since when it has come out on The Country Side of Elvis, Elvis by the Presleys and the 2006 release of The Complete Sun Sessions.

"ITO EATS"

A distinct banana-boat influence in this Sid Tepper / Roy C. Bennett effort for the Blue Hawaii movie and album soundtrack, which Elvis laid down at Radio Recorders on March 22, 1961. Alternates have come out solely on Blue Hawaii bootlegs.

"IT'S A MATTER OF TIME"

B-side to "Burning Love," a big hit for Elvis in the summer of 1972, Elvis recorded this Clive Westlake song on March 29, 1972 at the RCA studios in Hollywood. The tune may have made it to #36 in the charts under its own steam but it didn't warrant a full-priced US album release: it came out in 1972 on Burning Love and Hits from His Movies and in 1975 on Pickwick album Double Dynamite. Posthumous album releases include Walk A Mile In My Shoes, 1999 BMG CD Burning Love, and bootleg Long Lost And Found Songs. An alternate take appeared on 2001 FTD album 6363 Sunset.

"IT'S A SIN"

A sweet-and-high-voiced cut composed by Fred Rose and Zeb Turner that was Eddy Arnold's breakthrough hit in 1947. Elvis recorded the song in Nashville on March 12, 1961 for release on the Something For Everybody album. The track has appeared posthumously on From Nashville to Memphis and The Country Side of Elvis. Alternate takes from the recording session are on FTD releases Fame And Fortune and Something For Everybody.

Eddy Arnold's version is on Elvis Hayride album Elvis Presley At The Louisiana Hayride. Over the years, the song has also been covered by country stars including Red Foley, Don Gibson, Marty Robbins and Willie Nelson.

"IT'S A SIN TO TELL A LIE"

Though never recorded for release, Elvis sings this Fats Waller song (written by Billy Mayhew) in a 1966 home recording that came out on 1999 FTD album In A Private Moment.

"IT'S A WONDERFUL WORLD"

Sid Tepper and Roy C. Bennett wrote this feelgood soundtrack song for Roustabout, which Elvis recorded at Radio Recorders on March 2, 1964. The song may have originally been titled "I Never Had It So Good." Some sources state that this song was in contention for a Best Song Oscar nomination. It has latterly appeared on the Roustabout Double Feature issue.

"IT'S BEEN SO LONG DARLING"

Elvis sang this Ernest Tubb hit for fun while living in Germany. A version appears on Platinum, A Life In Music as part of the "Bad Nauheim Medley." It's also on bootlegs and FTD release In A Private Moment.

"IT'S CARNIVAL TIME"

Ben Weisman and Sid Wayne wrote this carnival barker's song for the Roustabout soundtrack. Elvis recorded it at Radio Recorders on March 3, 1964. Later album releases are restricted to Roustabout re-issue disks.

"IT'S DIFFERENT NOW"

At Stax Studios on July 21, 1973 Elvis recorded this Clive Westlake song, previously a big hit for Cilla Black in 1970. The track remained unreleased until it appeared on Walk A Mile In My Shoes in 1996. An unedited rehearsal appeared in 2007 on FTD release Raised On Rock.

"IT'S EASY FOR YOU"

This Tim Rice/Andrew Lloyd Webber ballad was one of the last songs Elvis recorded for release, at the Jungle Room session on October 29, 1976. The song of love lost came out on Moody Blue in 1977. A remixed first take from the session is on FTD release The Jungle Room Sessions.

"IT'S IMPOSSIBLE"

This big, Vegas ballad credited to Sid Wayne and Armando Manzanero was part of Elvis' live repertoire in 1971 and early 1972. His performance on February 16, 1972 was recorded for inclusion on Elvis (The Fool Album) the following year. The song was originally a Spanish-language hit for Vikki Carr, titled "Somos Novios," before Perry Como took the English-language version to the top 10 in 1970.

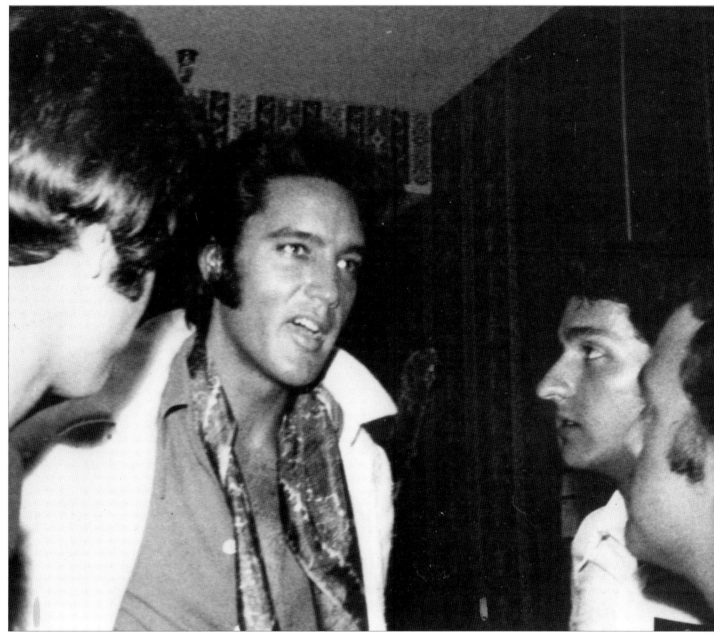

Elvis with French fans in his dressing room, Las Vegas.

Elvis' version later came out on albums *Pure Gold*, *Walk A Mile In My Shoes*, *Burning Love*, *Live in Las Vegas*, *Love Elvis* and the inevitable bootlegs. It's also on FTD release *An American Trilogy*.

"IT'S MIDNIGHT"

Elvis recorded this track—written by Billy Edd Wheeler and Jerry Chesnut—at Stax Studios on December 10, 1973, for release as the B-side ballad to Chuck Berry rocker "Promised Land" in late September 1974. The song appeared on the *Promised Land* LP soon after. Later album releases in the US: *Our Memories Of Elvis*, *Always On My Mind*, *Walk A Mile In My Shoes* and *The Country Side of Elvis*. The track made it to #9 on the *Billboard* country chart when released as a single. Elvis sang the melancholy song live from the summer of 1974. Versions are on *Live in Las Vegas*, FTD releases *It's Midnight*, *Dragonheart*, *Big Boss Man*, and *Southern Nights*, and of course plentiful bootlegs.

Studio alternates have appeared on *Platinum: A Life In Music* and *Made in Memphis*.

IT'S MIDNIGHT

A 2001 FTD live release of Elvis performing in Las Vegas, ca. August 1974.

TRACK LISTING:
1. See See Rider
2. I Got A Women / Amen
3. Love Me
4. If You Love Me Let Me Know
5. It's Midnight
6. Big Boss Man
7. Fever
8. Love Me Tender
9. All Shook Up
10. The Wonder Of You
11. I'm Leavin'
12. Softly As I Leave You
13. Spanish Eyes
14. Hound Dog
15. You Gave A Mountain
16. Polk Salad Annie
17. Introductions
18. If You Talk In Your Sleep
19. Why Me Lord?
20. Teddy Bear / Don't Be Cruel
21. How Great Thou Art
22. Let Me Be There
23. Early Morning Rain
24. Hawaiian Wedding Song
25. Can't Help Falling In Love

"IT'S MY WAY"/ "THIS TIME" / "I CAN'T STOP LOVING YOU"

Elvis kicked off his second set of sessions at American Studio in Memphis on February 17, 1969, with this jam medley, after he heard it was a tradition to sing "This Time," a song Chips Moman had helped to write years earlier. Never released in Elvis' lifetime, the recording made it onto 1993 compilation *From Nashville to Memphis*, and at the end of the decade *Suspicious Minds: The Memphis 1969 Anthology*.

"IT'S NICE TO GO TRAVELING"

Elvis chipped in for the finale of this song, with Frank Sinatra, Joey Bishop, Sammy Davis Jr. and Nancy Sinatra, at the start of the "Frank Sinatra

Show" welcoming him back to US TV after his Army service. The song was written by Sammy Cahn and Jimmy Van Heusen.

"It's No Fun Being Lonely"

A Red West composition that Elvis sang among friends in 1966, released decades later on *Home Recordings*.

"It's Now Or Never"

Elvis personally commissioned a new English-language version and arrangement of "O Sole Mio" from Freddy Bienstock of Hill & Range while he was still in Germany with the Army. Elvis knew the song from his childhood, from a well-worn Enrico Caruso 78rpm disc his mother often played.

Within a month of returning to the States, Elvis recorded the Aaron Schroeder / Wally Gold adaptation in Nashville on April 3, 1960. Despite the vocal challenge, he nailed a perfect upbeat version of the song in just five takes, hitting the power finale with an accomplished tenor's ease, despite the concerns he expressed to the session engineer.

A hit in the US for Tony Martin a decade earlier under the title "There's No Tomorrow" (and later covered by the Clovers), for Elvis the song was a statement of musical intent, a signal that he was much more than just a flash in the pan rock'n'roller.

When he heard the pre-release acetate, Elvis was so annoyed with RCA's remix that he refused to let the label issue it until they put it back the way he had left it. "It's Now Or Never" came out in July 1960 with "A Mess Of Blues" on the B-side. It zoomed up to #1 in the US (for five weeks, out of twenty in the top 100) and the UK (for nine weeks, though it wasn't released until five months later owing to copyright problems), selling many millions of copies on each market. The song was nominated *Billboard* vocal single of the year for 1960.

"O Sole Mio" is a classic Neapolitan love song written by Giovanni Capurro and Eduardo di Capua in 1898. Ever since, it has been a staple for tenors, including revered twentieth-century greats Enrico Caruso and Mario Lanza, both of whom Elvis admired—Lanza died around the time that Elvis commissioned his new version.

During his lifetime, Elvis liked to test people out by asking them what his best-selling single was. Nobody ever guessed it was this. The single is estimated to have sold as many as 30 million copies, making it arguably the best selling single of all time . . . an argument fans of many other performers are happy to have.

After its stellar performance as a single, the tune came out on EP *Elvis By Request* and had its first LP release on *Elvis' Golden Records Vol. 3*. Since then it has featured on many Elvis hits collections, including *Worldwide Gold Award Hits Vols. 1, Elvis: A Legendary Performer Vol. 2, The Top Ten Hits, From Nashville To Memphis, Platinum: A Life in Music, Artist Of The Century, ELVIS 30 #1 Hits, Love Elvis, Hitstory,* and *The Essential Elvis Presley*.

Elvis sang the song live the year after he recorded it at the USS *Arizona* benefit concert (a performance released on the *Elvis Aron Presley* box set). He often performed it during his Seventies shows, particularly towards the end of his after 1974 life, in later years combining it with "O Sole Mio," which he either sang himself or got Sherill Nielsen to perform: one such performance is on the *Elvis in Concert* LP and documentary.

In addition to many bootlegs, live versions have been officially released on *Live in Las Vegas* and FTD CDs *The Impossible Dream, Spring Tours '77, Southern Nights* and *Dragonheart*. Elvis sang the song in Italian (at least, backing singer Sherill Nielson did) and the English versions back to back at shows issued by FTD under the titles *New Year's Eve* and *Unchained Melody*.

A rehearsal version from 1970 is on the *That's The Way It Is* special edition release and assorted bootlegs.

All of the alternate takes from the original Nashville studio session have been released, variously on the 2-CD issue of *ELVIS 30 #1 Hits* and FTD releases *Long Lonely Highway, Fame And Fortune,* and *Elvis Is Back!*, which includes several of them. The undubbed master features on *From Nashville To Memphis*.

Elvis practicing the previous English-language version, "There's No Tomorrow," while still in Germany came out on *In A Private Moment*.

ELVIS SAID: "It wasn't rock 'n' roll but it had a beat behind it. I thought it turned out pretty good."

"It's Only Love"

Recorded at RCA's Studio B facility in Nashville on May 20, 1971, this song was put out as a single in September 1971 with "The Sound of Your Cry" on the B-side. In six weeks on the *Billboard* Hot 100 it failed to break into the top fifty (by one place), and sold under 150,000 copies on initial release in the US.

B. J. Thomas first recorded the song in 1969. It was written by Mark James (with Steve Tyrell); James was also responsible for Elvis hits "Always On My Mind" and "Suspicious Minds." "It's Only Love" did not receive an album release until 1980 collectors' box *Elvis Aron Presley*. In the Nineties it came out on *Walk A Mile In My Shoes* and *Burning Love*. Alternates are featured on *Essential Elvis Vol. 4* and FTD release *I Sing All Kinds*.

"It's Over"

A song of love dissolved that Elvis incorporated into his stage act in 1971, a few months before Priscilla told him it was indeed over. A recording of Elvis singing the Jimmie Rodgers song (not to be confused either with the country-singing Jimmie Rodgers Elvis grew up listening to, or with the Roy Orbison song of the same name) was made in Las Vegas in February that year. He was still singing it in January 1973 for *Aloha From Hawaii Via Satellite*, though he performed it live only a few times after that. The Aloha release is also on *Walk A Mile In My Shoes* and *Elvis By The Presleys*.

Other live recordings are on *The Alternate Aloha, Burning Love, Live In Las Vegas,* and FTD releases *Summer Festival* and *An American Trilogy*. It also crops up on *Elvis On Tour* and other bootlegs.

"It's Still Here"

It was just Elvis and a piano on this Ivory Joe Hunter weepie in Studio B, Nashville, on May 19, 1971. The song came out on *Elvis (The Fool Album)* in 1973. "It's Still Here" has since made a cameo on *Elvis Aron Presley* and *Elvis in Nashville*.

Walk A Mile In My Shoes features a version without even the minimal overdubbed bass of the original album release. An alternate has since appeared on FTD release *I Sing All Kinds*.

"It's Your Baby, You Rock It"

A Shirl Milete / Nora Fowler country song with a gospel backing that Elvis recorded in Nashville on June 5, 1970, for release on *Elvis Country* the following year.

In addition to bootlegged alternates from the session (including there's a jam version of the song on 1978 bootleg *The Entertainer*), "It's Your Baby, You Rock It" has since appeared on *Elvis in Nashville* and *Walk A Mile In My Shoes*. FTD disk *The Nashville Marathon* includes an alternate take from the session.

"I've Been Blue"

A snippet of a song written by Red West that Elvis sang at home in 1966. The track first came out on 1999 release *The Home Recordings*.

"I've Got A Thing About You, Baby"

Elvis recorded this Tony Joe White song at Stax Studios in Memphis on July 22, 1973 for release as a single in January 1974 with "Take Good Care Of Her" on the B-Side. Though it didn't score any higher than #39 on the general *Billboard* chart during its twelve-week arc, the song made it to #4 on the country chart, selling around half a million copies in the process. "I've Got A Thing About You, Baby" got its album release on *Good Times*, followed through the years with appearances on *This Is Elvis, Walk A Mile In My Shoes* and *Platinum: A Life in Music*

An alternate take has come out on *Essential Elvis Vol. 5*.

"I've Got Confidence"

Elvis gave Andraé Crouch's soul gospel tune an infusion of rock when he recorded it in Nashville on May 18, 1971 for release on *He Touched Me*. The track has since been re-released on gospel compilations *Amazing Grace* and *Peace In The Valley*. An alternate is on FTD release *I Sing All Kinds*.

"I've Got To Find My Baby"

Joy Byers wrote this song for the *Girl Happy* soundtrack, which Elvis recorded in in mid-the early hours of June 12, 1964 at Radio Recorders in Hollywood. The song has since come out on the *Double Features* and FTD *Girl Happy* re-releases.

"I've Lost You"

A single released in July 1970 with "The Next Step Is Love" on the B-side that Elvis recorded on June 4, 1970 in Nashville. Written by Ken Howard and Alan Blaikley, this power ballad had previously been recorded in the UK by Southern Comfort. On release, Elvis' single sold a steady half a million copies, but failed to climb any higher than #32 in the charts. First album release was a live version on *That's The Way It Is*, from August 1970. He sang the song in concert that year and that year alone.

The song later came out on *Worldwide Gold Award Hits Vol. 2, Always On My Mind, Walk A Mile In My Shoes, Artist Of The Century* and *Greatest Hits Live*.

Essential Elvis Vol. 4 and *The Nashville Marathon* feature alternate takes from the studio session. A rehearsal prior to the *That's The Way It Is* performance came out on 2001 FTD issue *The Way It Was*.

Alternative live recordings may be found on the *That's The Way It Is* special edition, *The Live Greatest Hits* and FTD release *One Night In Vegas*.

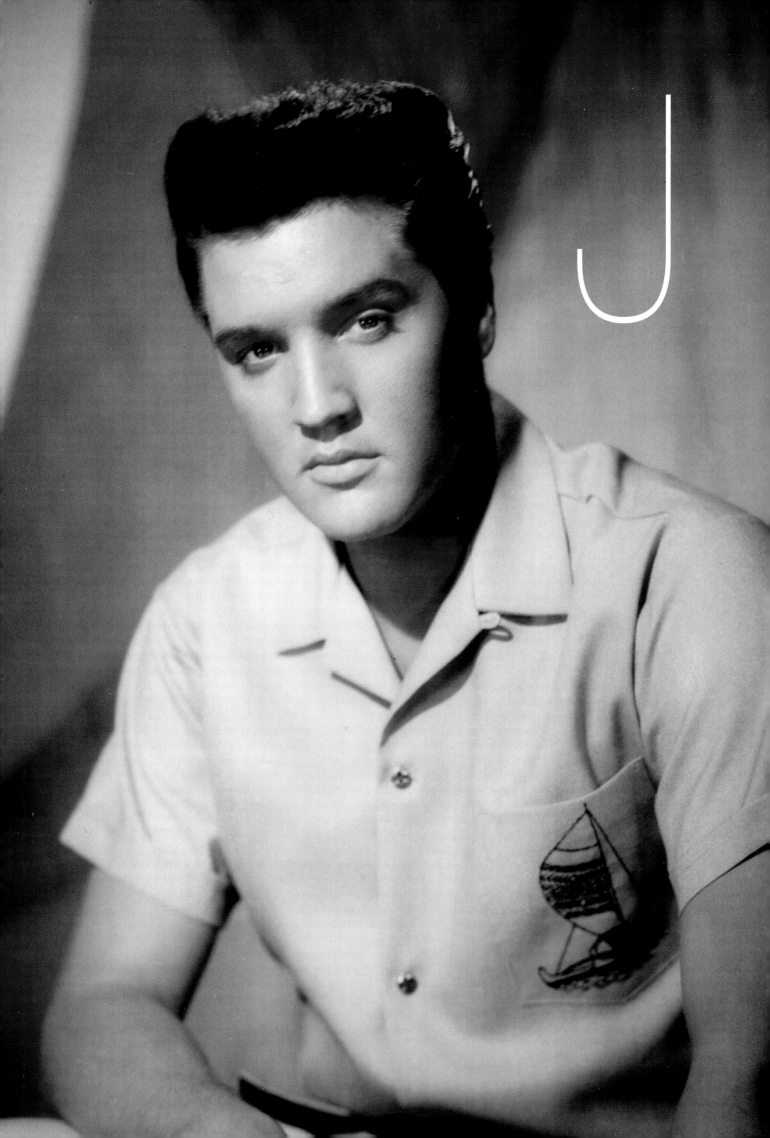

JACKSON, MAHALIA
(1911-1972)

Elvis met the "true queen of spiritual singers" (Little Richard's words) on the set of *Change of Habit*, his last narrative picture, in 1969. Remembered for her blues-influenced gospel style in songs such as "Amazing Grace," "Move On Up A Little Higher," "Didn't It Rain," "How I Got Over" and "Peace In The Valley," Jackson was the leading light of gospel for almost half a century, during which time she sang for two presidents and performed just before Martin Luther King Jr. came to the stage to make his "I Have a Dream" speech in Washington in 1963, spurred by her calling out "Tell them about the dream!" In the late Fifties and Sixties she made some forays into jazz and R&B, and hosted a radio show on CBS that was the first to broadcast black gospel nationwide. She won a Lifetime Achievement Grammy the year she died.

JACKSON, MICHAEL
(B. 1958)

If anybody has had a life as conditioned by the dictates and strictures of fame as Elvis, that person is Michael Jackson. Jackson has lived in the public eye since the age of five, when he started singing with family group the Jackson 5, and had his first hit single on Motown aged eleven with "I Want You Back." As an adult he mastered the art of musical (and physical) transformation to stay at the top of the industry for two decades, winning the title "the King of Pop" for smash hits like "Beat It" "Billy Jean" and "Thriller." *Thriller* has sold more than 100 million copies worldwide, more than an every other LP in history.

Jackson was married to Lisa Marie for 18 months from May 1994, after a secret ceremony in the Dominican Republic. They divorced amicably in 1996. In later interviews, Lisa Marie has said that she thought Jackson may have used the marriage as a public relations exercise at a difficult time for him, following his first brush with the law over inappropriate behavior with minors.

For a spell, Jackson owned the rights to a number of Elvis songs through his publishing company, which also owned the rights to much of The Beatles back catalogue.

JACKSON, WANDA
(B. 1937)

Seventeen year-old Jackson played on the same bill as Elvis Presley in late July 1955, and then again in 1956. Born on October 20, 1937, Jackson had been performing since her early teens, landing a slot on local Oklahoma radio before being talent-spotted by country singer Hank Thompson. Elvis was instrumental in encouraging the young singer/guitarist to shift from country gospel to rockabilly, to the "country with a beat" that he was singing. From then on, she blazed the trail for later female rockers and earned the title the "Queen of Rockabilly." Up until the early Seventies, she followed the original Sun records formula that was so successful for Elvis, putting out a country side and a rockabilly side on her singles.

Elvis and Wanda's relationship added the romantic to the musical, within the strictures of their heavy touring schedules, and the presence of Wanda's dad Tom, who was her constant chaperone.

In 1960 Jackson recorded "Let's Have A Party," a track Elvis almost covered for his 1957 film *Loving You*. In the Sixties, Jackson had hits in Japan and Germany, and then in later years turned to country and gospel, twice making it to the nomination stage for a Grammy.

After a decades-long layoff, Jackson recently returned to the recording studios, among other things making an Elvis tribute album released in early 2006, *I Remember Elvis*.

WANDA JACKSON: "He broke into my train of thought and made me realize I could stretch myself."

JACKSON, WAYNE
(b. 1944)

A trumpet player who played on Elvis' Memphis recording sessions at American Studio (1969) and Stax (1973), for many years Jackson was a member of the Mar-Keys on the Stax label. As part of the "Memphis Horns," Wayne worked on over 300 #1s for the likes of Aretha Franklin, Otis Redding, Neil Diamond, the Doobie Brothers, Joe Cocker and U2. He became a friend of Elvis' and saw him many of the nights he opened in Las Vegas in the Seventies.

"JAILHOUSE ROCK"

When he laid down this track at Radio Recorders on April 30, 1957, with the exception of his plangent NBC TV Special performance eleven years later Elvis pushed his voice further than on anything he ever recorded.

D.J. Fontana and Scotty Moore were the creative input behind what is one of the most instantly recognizable intros to any rock song ever recorded. Some music critics have noted shades of the intro to Glenn Miller's "The Anvil Chorus" in the opening, though the Forties swing hit is itself an update of an aria from Verdi opera *ll Trovatore*.

This future Leiber & Stoller classic was released as a single in late September, rustling up some publicity for the movie release. The song spent 27 weeks on the *Billboard* Top 100—seven of those at #1—and sold over 2 million copies in its first flush, helped by its parallel #1 placements on the R & B and Country charts. In the UK, "Jailhouse Rock" was the first single ever to enter the charts at #1.

B-side song "Treat Me Nice" registered a respectable #27 in the charts—though Elvis expected "Treat Me Nice" to outsell the A-Side.

Soon afterwards, the song came out as the title track on an EP. The song first saw LP release on *Elvis' Golden Records*. Later album releases include *Elvis: A Legendary Performer Vol. 2*, *Worldwide Gold Award Hits Vol. 1*, *Pure Gold*, *Elvis: A Legendary Performer Vol. 2*, *This Is Elvis*, *Essential Elvis Vol. 1*, *The Great Performances*, *Elvis Sings Leiber & Stoller*, *The King Of Rock And Roll*, *Platinum: A Life in Music*, *Artist Of The Century*, *ELVIS 30 #1 Hits*, *Hitstory*, *Elvis Rock*, *Elvis Movies*, *The Essential Elvis Presley* and *Elvis at the Movies*.

The song was a shoe-in for Elvis to include in his NBC TV "Comeback" Special in 1968, raising a big hand of applause when he broke into the song during the arena segment of the show. As well as the album released when the show aired, recordings from the NBC TV Special have appeared on *Elvis Aron Presley*, *Memories: The '68 Comeback Special*, and FTD release *Burbank '68* as well as the inevitable string of bootlegs.

When Elvis returned to live performing in Las Vegas in the summer of 1969, he paired the hit with "Don't Be Cruel" in a medley. Many live performances of "Jailhouse Rock" followed in his live oldies medleys, particularly in 1971, 1973, 1974, 1976 and 1977. Live performances from Las Vegas circa 1969 are on *Collectors' Gold*, *Live In Las Vegas*, *The Live Greatest Hits*, and on FTD releases *Elvis At The International*, *All Shook Up*, *Tucson '76* and *Writing for the King*.

Live performances from 1974 are on *Recorded Live On Stage In Memphis* and FTD release *I Found My Thrill*. FTD releases *Tucson '76* and *New Year's*

Elvis sings *Jailhouse Rock*.

Eve feature live performances from 1976. Official live releases from Elvis' final year are on the album from CBS documentary *Elvis In Concert* and FTD discs *Spring Tours '77* and *Unchained Melody*.

The master version of the song is on *Elvis: Close Up*, while the movie version is on 1997 BMG release *Jailhouse Rock* and sundry bootlegs.

Alternate takes from the original Radio Recorders session surfaced on 1988 release *Essential Elvis Vol. 1*; FTD's 2001 release *Silver Screen Stereo* features a faster take recorded just before the master. The never-before-released first take came out on the second CD in 2005 package *Elvis by the Presleys*.

JAILHOUSE ROCK (EP)

Released at the end of October, this EP of five songs from the movie soundtrack sold a million and comfortably made #1, despite stiff opposition for a competing Elvis EP of Christmas songs.

TRACK LISTING:
1. Jailhouse Rock
2. Young And Beautiful
3. I Want To Be Free
4. Don't Leave Me Now
5. Baby I Don't Care

JAILHOUSE ROCK (CD)

Forty years after the movie's initial release, BMG issued a soundtrack album with extra tracks.

TRACK LISTING:
1. Jailhouse Rock
2. Treat Me Nice
3. I Want To Be Free
4. Don't Leave Me Now
5. Young And Beautiful
6. (You're So Square) Baby I Don't Care
7. Jailhouse Rock (movie version)
8. Treat Me Nice (movie version)
9. I Want To Be Free (movie version)
10. Young And Beautiful (movie version)
11. Don't Leave Me Now (alternate master)
12. Love Me Tender
13. Poor Boy
14. Let Me
15. We're Gonna Move
16. Love Me Tender (end title version)
17. Let Me
18. We're Gonna Move
19. Poor Boy
20. Love Me Tender

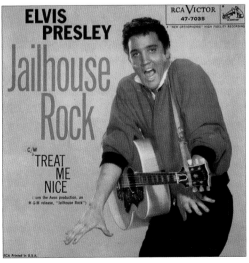

Elvis' "Jailhouse Rock" was a number one hit single in the U.S. for seven weeks.

ABOVE: Elvis in the bar scene from *Jailhouse Rock*, 1957.

RIGHT: Elvis as Vince Everett with Mickey Shaughnessy (Hunk Houghton).

JAILHOUSE ROCK

Elvis' first movie for MGM was the last time that he was given the challenge of playing an anti-hero. Hard is it may be to conceive of now, the movie caused no end of scandal: the idea of a convict as the hero of a celluloid tale was a million miles from usual Hollywood icon fare; in the picture, Elvis killed a man; he swore on screen (the now innocuous 'Hell'); and in one scene he and co-star Judy Tyler both lie on a bed.

The story incorporated a version of Elvis' real life backstory, and defiantly played up the bad boy part of his reputation. Fans around the world loved it, despite the savaging the movie received at the hands of most critics.

MGM initially intended the movie to be called The *Hard Way* and then *Jailhouse Kid* before alighting on the final title—though the project the studio initially discussed with Colonel Parker when they signed Elvis was known as *The Rock*. The name of Elvis' character, Vince Everett, also wavered through various last name alternatives (Matthews, Delwyn, Jackwood, Ledway, Edwards and Edmunds) before firming up as Everett.

Elvis was given the dressing room MGM had previously assigned to Clark Gable when he reported for principal photography on May 13, 1957.

Top talent was brought on board. Screenplay writer Nedrick Young had an Academy Award for *The Defiant Ones*, Leiber and Stoller were supplying songs, and three-time Oscar nominee Pandro Berman served as producer—a man whose five decades of experience included bringing together Fred Astaire and Ginger Rogers, and launching the careers of half a dozen top Hollywood stars.

The first scene filmed on set was the "Jailhouse Rock" sequence. Elvis gave a great deal of input when choreographer Alex Romero realized that the moves he had originally planned just weren't working out. Elvis demonstrated how he danced to some of his songs, and the choreographer worked out a whole new plan for the production number. The "Jailhouse Rock" scene is one of very few from vintage Hollywood that has remained as powerful and effective today as it was when it was made, rather than looking like a period piece. Many modern-day music critics cite the sequence as the blueprint and inspiration for the music video genre. Gene Kelly, in the studio to watch some of the shooting, certainly knew it was

a winner and applauded Elvis after a run-through.

Life imitated art when Elvis aspirated a dental cap sliding down a pole during that dance scene. Removal of the cap required a surgeon probing very close to Elvis' vocal chords—in the movie, Elvis' character's career is imperiled by an injury to his vocal chords. During filming, Elvis engaged in some real-life heroics, helping to carry co-star Jennifer Holden to safety after a fire in her dressing room.

Elvis managed to get band members Scotty Moore, Bill Black and D.J. Fontana bit parts in the movie; songwriter Mike Stoller also cameos as a piano player.

Elvis first saw the movie at a special screening with his folks in Memphis ten days before its October 17, 1957 premiere, also in Memphis, which was attended by actress Anne Neyland. In later years he preferred not to screen the movie because it reminded him of the tragic death of leading lady Judy Tyler soon after the movie wrapped.

Jailhouse Rock came in as the third highest box office draw the week it was released, and ended up the fourteenth highest-grossing movie of the year, earning a total of around $4 million.

The movie was re-released in March 1960 to coincide with Elvis' discharge from the Army.

The picture has the unusual distinction of winning multiple awards more than three decades after it was released. Leiber and Stoller received an ASCAP award in 1991 for the song "Jailhouse Rock"; in 2004 the movie was put on the

National Film Registry by the National Film Preservation Board.

The seminal "Jailhouse Rock" sequence has become visual shorthand for early, edgy rock 'n' roll not just in nostalgia film clips, but in modern stage shows such as Gwen Stefani's 2007 tour.

Book:
Inside Jailhouse Rock, edited by Ger Rijff, Tutti Frutti, 1994

DVD:
Jailhouse Rock Deluxe Edition (2007)

CREDITS:
MGM, Black and white
Length: 96 minutes
Release date: November 8, 1957

TAGLINE:
Elvis in Action as Never Before!
His First Big Dramatic Singing Role—Elvis Presley
at his Greatest

Directed by: Richard Thorpe
Produced by: Pandro S. Berman
Written by: Nedrick Young (story), Guy Trosper

Music by: Jeff Alexander
Cinematography by: Robert J. Bronner
Film Editing by: Ralph E. Winters
Art Direction by: Randall Duell, William A. Horning
Set Decoration by: F. Keogh Gleason, Henry Grace

CAST:
Elvis Presley	Vince Everett
Judy Tyler	Peggy Van Alden
Mickey Shaughnessy	Hunk Houghton
Vaughn Taylor	Mr. Shores (narrator)
Jennifer Holden	Sherry Wilson
Dean Jones	Teddy Talbot
Anne Neyland	Laury Jackson
Dorothy Abbott	Woman in restaurant

Peter Adams	Jack Lease
François André	Waiter
Robert Bice	Bardeman (TV studio manager)
Bill Black	Bass player
Don Burnett	Mickey Alba
George Cisar	Jake (bartender)
Fred Coby	Jerry (bartender)
John Daheim	Tough guy in bar
John Dennis	Mail clerk #1
Francis De Sales	Surgeon
Elaine DuPont	
Joan Dupuis	Girl in record shop
Bess Flowers	Van Alden party guest
D.J. Fontana	Drummer
William Forrest	Head of studio
Jo Gilbert	Bit part
Bill Hale	Guard
Percy Helton	Sam Brewster
Jack Herrin	Bit part
Bill Hickman	Guard who whips Vince
Harry Hines	Hotel clerk
Bob Hopkins	Announcer
John Indrisano	Convict
Walter Johnson	Shorty (bartender)
Donald Kerr	Studio photographer
Frank Kreig	Drunk
S. John Launer	Judge
Alyn Lockwood	Bit part
John Logan	Bit part
Tom Mayton	Mail clerk #2
Joe McGuinn	Studio gateman
Tom McKee	TV director
Carl Milletaire	Mr. Drummond
Frank Mills	Shooting gallery proprietor
Orv Mohler	Bit part
Scotty Moore	Guitar player
Tracey Morgan	Girl in booth
Gloria Pall	Striptease artist
Charles Postal	Bit part
Robin Raymond	Dotty
Grandon Rhodes ..	Professor August Van Alden
Dick Rich	Prison guard
Hugh Sanders	Prison warden

Elizabeth Slifer	Cleaning lady
K.L. Smith	Worker
Mike Stoller	Piano player
Glenn Strange	Matt (convict)
Bob Stratton	Orderly
William Tannen	Record distributor
Arthur Tovey	Bit part
Paula Trent	Bit part
Katherine Warren	Mrs. Van Alden
Steve Warren	Assistant director
Dan White	Paymaster
Russ Whitney	Man
Linda Williams	Girl in bathing suit
Matt Winston	Bit part
Wilson Wood	Recording engineer
Jack Younger	Bit part

ADDITIONAL CREW:
Kathryn Hereford	associate producer
William Tuttle	makeup artist
Hank Moonjean	assistant director
Robert E. Relyea	assistant director
A. Arnold Gillespie	special effects
Joe Gray	stunts
Loren Janes	stunts
Jeff Alexander	music supervisor
Colonel Tom Parker.	technical advisor
Elvis Presley	choreographer: Jailhouse Rock sequence
Alex Romero	choreographer

Plot:
Elvis begins the rags to riches tale of Vince Everett as a truck driver kicking back after a hard week's work with a drink at a local bar. He winds up in a fight over a local lady's honor, in the process killing his assailant. He is sent to jail for manslaughter, the sentence one to ten years..

In the penitentiary he meets Hunk Houghton (played by Mick Shaughnessy), a country singer who has the run of the jail. Hunk lets Vince play his guitar and sees that the boy has real promise, but he keeps this opinion to himself. When a TV talent show broadcasts from the jail, Vince's per-

Elvis in San Francisco publicizing *Jailhouse Rock*, 1957.

formance of "I Want To Be Free" is a big hit. Hunk keeps Vince in the dark about his success by hiding the fan mail because he wants Vince to sign a 50/50 management contract. Vince signs on the dotted line. Before he is released, Vince is caught up in a prison riot, for which he receives a lashing as punishment.

Back on the outside after serving 14 months, Vince teams up with A&R woman Peggy Van Alden (played by Judy Tyler). Peggy quits her amoral boss and sets up record company Laurel Records with Vince. The ensuing success brings out the worst in Vince, leaving Peggy bitterly disappointed. After Hunk is freed from jail, Vince agrees to help get him a slot playing on a TV show, but the singer is now way out of date.

Vince triumphs with the "Jailhouse Rock" scene, which brings him fame, a million-dollar movie contract, and a slew of easy women, as poor spurned Peggy looks on. Adding financial indignity to romantic disappointment, Vince agrees to sell the record company without consulting Peggy. A resentful Hunk gives Vince the just desserts he has been seeking for so long. Hunk's punch to the throat not only knocks Vince out, it puts his ability to sing in jeopardy.

After a successful operation, Vince realizes how lucky he is, what great friends he has, recovers his singing voice and prepares to live happily ever after.

Songs: "Young And Beautiful," "I Want To Be Free," "Don't Leave Me Now," "Treat Me Nice," "Jailhouse Rock," "(You're So Square) Baby I Don't Care"

Mickey Shaughnessy: "One More Day"

"JAMBALAYA (ON THE BAYOU)"

Elvis often sang a verse or two of this track in concert in the mid-Seventies. A recording of the whole song features on bootleg live CD *A Profile*, and on 2006 FTD release *Southern Nights* from a show in Louisiana in the spring of 1975. The song was written and originally recorded by Hank Williams in 1952, for whom it was a #1 hit, and has been covered by dozens of artists including Jerry Lee Lewis, Hank Williams Jr., The Carpenters, Hoyt Axton and Waylon Jennings.

JAMES, MARK
(B. FRANCIS RODNEY ZAMBON, 1940)

Classically-trained songwriter Mark James started out in the music business with his own group, Francis Zambon and the Naturals, in the Fifties. He had more success a decade later as a house writer for American Studio. James had previously released "Suspicious Minds" and "Moody Blue" with his own band, the Mark James Trio, before Elvis covered them. James also wrote Elvis hits "Always On My Mind," "It's Only Love" and "Raised On Rock."

James played "Suspicious Minds"—written after his divorce—to Elvis at the New Year's Party on December 31, 1969 at T.J.'s in Memphis. Other James compositions were sung by B.J. Thomas and Mac Davis.

JAPAN

Elvis was always big in Japan. If he had ever toured internationally, Japan would have been high on his list.

In 1963, Elvis considered doing an English-language version of Kyu Sakamoto's hit "Sukiyaki" —the only Japanese language song ever to top the Billboard Charts—but the idea was scrapped when the original did so well in its own right.

In 1966, a Japanese company approached the Colonel with a view to making an Elvis movie. The Colonel put them off by telling them that his client was fully booked for the next three years.

At his 1972 press conference before playing Madison Square Garden, Elvis said that Japan was one of the places he wanted to go on tour.

As many as a couple of thousand Japanese fans flew to Hawaii to watch Elvis perform during his *Aloha from Hawaii* concert, and sat in on the previous day's dress rehearsal (later released as *The Alternate Aloha*).

The best known of the many Japanese Elvis fans is former Japanese prime minister Koizumi, who visited Graceland in the summer of 2006 with George W. Bush.

JARVIS, FELTON
(B. CHARLES FELTON JARVIS, 1934-1981)

Born in Fulton County, Georgia, on November 16, 1934, Felton Jarvis was Elvis' record producer in the studio and on tour from 1966 until Elvis' death and a close friend.

Jarvis first saw Elvis perform when he was on a bill with Hank Snow in Norfolk, Virginia, in 1955, where he was serving in the US Marines. Out of the service, Jarvis tired to emulate Elvis' success by fronting his own band, but did not find success. One of his early songs was a tribute song to the king, titled "Don't Knock Elvis."

Jarvis moved over to the other side of the mixing desk and worked with an artist called Marvin Benefield, whose name he changed to Vince Everett (the name of Elvis' character in *Jailhouse Rock*), producing Elvis-like records for fun. He soon moved on to a job as a producer with ABC Records, where he worked with Fats Domino, Lloyd Price, Tommy Roe and Gladys Knight among others. Chet Atkins hired him to work for RCA out of Nashville in 1965. The following year, Jarvis was assigned to Elvis—a real thrill for him—partly on the recommendation of his pal

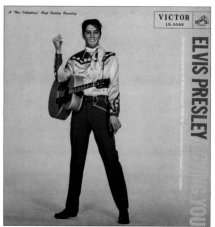

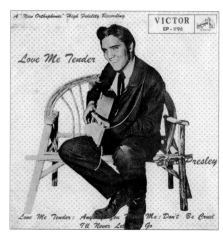

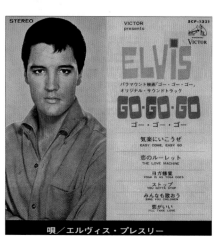

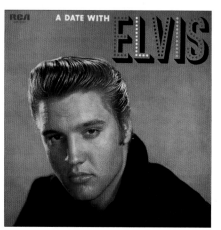

ELVIS IN JAPAN:

TOP LEFT: This Japanese version is a extremely rare album.

CENTER: The Japanese version of *Loving You* is the rarest Elvis Album in existence.

RIGHT: Very rare EP (Japan) *Love Me Tender.*

BOTTOM LEFT: Japanese EP *Elvis go-Go-Go.*

LEFT: A Japanese version of *A Date with Elvis.*

Jim Malloy, the studio engineer who would record Elvis' Nashville sessions until 1970, and who had first met Elvis soon after he joined RCA. By all accounts, Atkins was relieved to be able to hand over Elvis' production to a man who was better suited to working Elvis' out-of-kilter hours.

Jarvis first produced an Elvis recording session in 1966—Elvis' first in Nashville for two and half years. Elvis and Felton hit it off immediately. They came from a similar musical background: both grew up on gospel, and then when they came of age enthusiastically embraced the first wave of rock 'n' roll. Material from this session was used for Elvis' highly acclaimed gospel album *How Great Thou Art*.

Elvis enjoyed Jarvis's offbeat sense of humor—he used to keep a pet boa constrictor in his office; Jarvis also had something of a reputation as a ladies' man, something that Elvis could relate to. They clicked musically too; when Elvis said he wanted a big sound for his new gospel album, Jarvis helped him get it. Most of all, Jarvis was just the kind of cheerleader in the studio that Elvis needed after years of being left to his own devices. Jarvis would also play an important part in helping Elvis get back to more inspiring and suitable material. In the meantime, Jarvis set to work remixing and overdubbing Elvis' soundtrack recordings, which began to improve in quality after a steady decline.

In a 1967 interview, Jarvis said "I love him like a brother." He remarked that Elvis was a joy to work with, adding: "He's so down to earth and real and sincere about anything and everything."

In 1968, Jarvis was relegated to a background position when Billy Strange took over production duties and Elvis worked with Bones Howe on the career-saving NBC TV Special. Before the year was out, however, Jarvis was back behind the controls, trying to breathe some life into the masters Elvis had laid down for his final MGM feature film, *The Trouble with Girls*.

Jarvis's was one of the encouraging voices that prompted Elvis to seek out a new direction and record at American Studio in Memphis. Songs such as "In The Ghetto" and "Suspicious Minds" came out of those early 1969 sessions. This was not all good news for Jarvis; his position as Elvis' regular producer was briefly threatened by the success of his work with American supremo Chips Moman. Jarvis's name was supplanted by Moman's on the credit for the first single released from the session, "In The Ghetto," until the Colonel resolved the situation by removing both names from the *Billboard* chart credit.

Jarvis continued to produce other artists for RCA, including Floyd Cramer, Jim Ed Brown and Nat Tuckey. Until the summer of 1969—just three days after the end of his honeymoon with his new wife, Chet Atkins' secretary Mary Lynch—Jarvis began working solely with Elvis and accompanied him to Las Vegas for his debut at the International Hotel.

In June 1970, he left RCA's employ altogether and was hired directly by Elvis. From this time on, Jarvis produced all of Elvis' recordings. Elvis' enthusiasm was evident, as he launched into the most productive recording session of his entire career. The thirty to forty masters (as many as forty according to some sources) Jarvis put in the can over a five night session not only were enough for two planned albums, there were leftovers for the upcoming *That's The Way It Is* soundtrack LP and material that would be doled out as singles and album cuts over the next two years. Jarvis gave Elvis encouragement in the studio when he needed it, and the rest of the time let Elvis follow his creative instincts as he worked with the band through to the finished song.

Once Elvis left the building, Jarvis had to hire three engineers (Bergen White, Cam Mullins and Don Tweedy) to help him get through the tracks.

Jarvis joined Elvis in Las Vegas, and hit the road when he began touring further afield. Back in the studio a year later, Jarvis came close to repeating this fruitful experience, getting 30 masters out of Elvis in a week long session at Studio B.

Ill health kept Jarvis off Elvis' two week tour at the Sahara Tahoe in 1971, the first time he hadn't been at the mixing desk since Elvis had returned to touring. Despite requiring dialysis, Jarvis managed to helm Elvis' recording sessions in 1972. That year Elvis helped Jarvis out with the kidney transplant he needed, practically as well as financially; the record producer had been on a list for a transplant for a long time, but when Elvis made a call on Jarvis's behalf, a kidney match was found within a week.

Jarvis was back at the controls at Stax in 1973, but from now on Elvis' studio time was a matter of diminishing returns. The July Stax sessions produced barely enough material for one album. RCA blamed Jarvis and wanted him fired; Elvis refused point blank. At the next Stax session, with more engineers on the job and Jarvis sourcing some new songs from Bob Beckham, things went much more smoothly.

From this point on, the problem was less how much Elvis would record than getting him into a studio at all. Finally, the mountain came to Mohammed and RCA set up a mobile studio at Graceland in 1976. The pickings were slim in terms of quantity (and to some minds, quality). Either side of these sessions, Jarvis had to confine himself to recording Elvis on tour to fulfill his commitment to the record label. Jarvis continued to tour with Elvis until not long before Elvis died, when he pulled out because he no longer wanted to spend so much time away from his wife and home.

It was Jarvis who told the Nashville musicians gathered in August 1977 to fly off on tour with Elvis that the tour was off because of an "act of God." He then flew the tour plane on to Memphis to see what help he could be in the aftermath of Elvis' death. Felton Jarvis was a pall-bearer at the funeral.

After Elvis, Jarvis produced for Carl Perkins and Elvis-soundalike Ronnie McDowell.

In 1980, Jarvis renewed his working relationship with Chips Moman to remix the material Elvis had laid down at American Studio in 1969, adding new instrumentals but retaining Elvis' vocals in a ground-breaking use of overdubs and sampling, which has long since become the norm in the industry. Jarvis died in January 1981, before the resulting *Guitar Man* album had completed its run in the charts.

Just two weeks before he died, Jarvis recorded a tape about his experiences of working with Elvis, later released as limited-release LP *Felton Jarvis Talks About Elvis* (since reissued on bootlegs).

FELTON JARVIS: "He is a great person. . . . I don't think anyone will ever equal Elvis as a performer."

BILLY SMITH: "Recording with Felton energized Elvis quite a bit."

PETER GURALNICK: "They had a relationship based on shared enthusiasms and mutual respect, and Elvis liked to say of his producer that he was the only man he knew who could get along with anyone."

JENKINS, HARRY

An RCA vice president who took over from Bill Bullock to work with the Colonel and Elvis in 1965. Jenkins was the label's representative at many Elvis recording sessions thereafter, including the American Studio session that produced "Suspicious Minds" and "In The Ghetto." On

that occasion his input was vital to overcome entrenched positions over song publishing that threatened to derail the entire project. When Jenkins sided with studio owner Chips Moman over the Colonel, he saved the day.

JENNINGS, WAYLON
(1937-2002)

Inducted into the Country Music Hall of Fame, Jennings started out as a bass player for Buddy Holly's band The Crickets . . . famously giving up his seat on the doomed flight on which Holly perished to fellow-performer the Big Bopper. Afterwards, Jennings formed his own rockabilly band, and then worked as a DJ and record producer before landing a recording contract as a country singer in the mid-Sixties.

Jennings became a major star in his own right in the Seventies, with a form of country that combined honky tonk with a harder rock edge. A maverick within the C&W world, Jennings notched up sixteen #1 Country singles, and was a member of country supergroups The Outlaws (with Willie Nelson) and The Highwaymen. Outside music, he provided the narration to TV series "The Dukes of Hazzard."

Elvis recorded one Waylon Jennings song, "You Asked Me To," and considered others over the years.

"JESUS WALKED THAT LONESOME VALLEY"

Elvis and friends included this traditional gospel song in their December 4, 1956 jam session at Sun Studio, Elvis and Jerry Lee Lewis swapping the lead. More recently, the song came out on gospel anthology *Peace In The Valley*. The 2006 version of the *Million Dollar Quarter* prolongs the pleasure with an extra verse.

JEWELRY

There can be little doubt that Elvis was several jewelers' best friend. As soon his newfound wealth had satisfied the Presley family's immediate needs of a home and more cars than they could possibly drive, Elvis began what would become a lifelong habit of buying, wearing and giving away jewelry.

In truth, he began his jewelry collection almost as soon as royalty checks started rolling in, purchasing some baubles to go with the clothes he bought from Lansky of Beale Street.

He bought a horseshoe diamond ring while he was still working his way through the regional concert circuit. In March 1956, he added an initialed signature ring in 14 carat gold set in white diamonds which cost him $185. For a long time he wore a star sapphire that was given to him by admirer (some say girlfriend) Judy Spreckels.

In spring 1957, Elvis briefly toured in a $2,500 gold-leaf suit and gold colored slippers with rhinestones, until he decided that this was too much even for his flamboyant tastes. He continued to buy jewelry for himself and for friends and family ever after, at one stage in the Seventies (according to jeweler Lowell Hays Jr.) not letting a day go by without buying at least one item.

Elvis had special watches made in 1965 by Harry Levitch, which he gave to the cast and crew he worked with on *Frankie and Johnny*. Every thirty seconds the black dial on each watch alternately revealed a cross and a Star of David.

For his 1967 wedding, Elvis sported diamond and sapphire cufflinks and a platinum watch studded with the same gems. Jeweler Harry Levitch made the ring Elvis presented to Priscilla when he asked her to marry him, and also his wedding band.

Elvis began stocking up on TCB rings and charms in 1970, for himself and for his most trusted entourage members. Elvis' official jeweler from 1970, Memphis man Lowell Hays Jr., has said that he designed Elvis' trademark TCB (taking care of business) rings and TLC (tender loving care) necklaces, though there is some evidence that Elvis had been wearing TCB jewelry since at least 1966.

In further recognition of the loyalty of his entourage pals, and in a flush of emotion after surviving an assassination threat in Las Vegas, Elvis bought a dozen tube bracelets—each one had the entourage member's name engraved on the front, and on the back something witty from Elvis, usually a nickname—and four ladies chain/pendant sets from Beverly Hills jewelers Sol Schwartz and Lee Ableser. Elvis also had a tree of life necklace made for himself engraved with the names of all his entourage pals at that time.

In September 1970, the International Hotel gave Elvis an oversized boxer-style gold belt declaring him to be the World Attendance Record Champ. Elvis wore this belt with pride in public many times. The hotel management also gave him a ram's head necklace after a later month in residence.

Elvis' love of jewels extended to what for most people are ordinary items. He had hundreds of pairs of glasses made either with his initials or the TCB symbol, most out of 14 karat gold, some encrusted with sapphires or diamonds. He was also quite a watch collector, among others owning a Patek and an Omega digital watch, one of the earliest digital timepieces.

By the early Seventies, Elvis was buying his jewelry in bulk. As well as repeat purchases of TCB and TLC items, in March 1971 Elvis placed an order for 25 watches from Harry Levitch in Memphis.

In the run-up to Christmas 1971, Elvis bought a $1000 dollar watch, a $500 ring and a $1,200 chain from Memphis jeweler Lowell Hays. In 1972, he spent $3,456 on a diamond and ruby ring for himself at Lowell Hay's store.

In 1973, Linda Thompson designed a white gold pendant necklace in the shape of a cross, inlaid with diamonds and both of their birthstones, with a symbolic gold wedding band and two hearts.

On stage in Las Vegas in 1974, Elvis claimed that he had nineteen tapes on his fingers to keep all his rings on, and even then every once in a while one of them would bounce off during a particularly energetic karate move. Many of his costumes were studded with crystals and semi-precious stones, as well as Swarovski crystals.

Elvis designed a TCB ring with Lowell Hays in 1975, something that said "ELVIS" in 78 diamonds and gold and black jade—with a central 11.5 carat diamond, the biggest he ever bought—made from yellow gold and with black onyx. A few days later, after a bust-up with members of his band, Elvis said he was sorry by spending $137,616 on reconciliatory jewelry. At one concert that year, Elvis reached into Hays' case for a ring which he gave to a woman in the audience who was holding a red rose. The crowd went wild and Elvis gave away as many as fifteen more rings during the show. Thereafter, many fans asked Elvis for his ring during shows. He was also known to give away pieces of jewelry to ailing fans—one boy was given a garnet cross.

In 1975, Elvis bought jewelry as Christmas presents for all his loved ones and close friends.

Elvis' "lucky stones" were dark sapphires, black pearls and black diamonds, one of which a pal sourced for him in 1976, after he'd been looking for fourteen years. As well as diamonds, Elvis

had a predilection for colored stones such as sapphires, rubies and emeralds.

JEWELERS

Harry Levitch
Lowell Hays
Schwartz and Ableser

LOWELL HAYS, JR.: "I remember when Elvis gave me my necklace. It was kind of like being knighted."

JIMMIE RODGERS MEMORIAL CELEBRATION

Elvis was invited to Meridian, Mississippi to perform at one of five venues during the Jimmie Rodgers Memorial Celebration on May 25, 1955, in remembrance of the "the man who started it all," "it" being Country and Western. Over ten thousand people flocked to an afternoon barbecue that day, and more than 60,000 saw the midday parade of all the performers the following day, when Elvis performed at the Junior College Stadium. Notables in attendance included Jimmie Davis (Louisiana's former "singing governor"), Tennessee governor Frank Clement, Dizzy Dean, Slim Whitman, Webb Pierce, Faron Young and Red Foley.

Claims have been made that in 1953 Elvis hitchhiked with his guitar to the festival the first year it was run to try his luck in a talent contest.

Footage from this performance is on the *Memphis Recording Service Vol. 2* DVD.

"JINGLE BELLS"

Home Recordings features Elvis starting in on this Christmas classic before he moves onto "I Asked The Lord." Initially titled "The One-Horse Open Sleigh," "Jingle Bells" was written in the 1850s by J. S Pierpoint. The song was among those covered by Elvis and pals as The Million Dollar Quartet (an instrumental version is on the 2006 version of *The Million Dollar Quartet*). Bootleg *Rockin' With Elvis April Fools Day* also features a snatch of the song in an instrumental version from 1975.

JOBS

With many mouths to feed on a limited income, for families like the Presleys it was a case of all hands on deck. In Tupelo, Elvis made some money (or was sometimes paid in food) helping to run deliveries for a local grocery store. After the family moved to Memphis, Elvis mowed lawns for better-off neighbors, and then in the fall of 1950, when he was in 10th grade, got a job as an usher at the Loew's State Theater at 152 S. Main St, Memphis, earning $12.50 a week for a shift from 5 p.m. to 10 p.m. He lost the job after punching a fellow-usher who ratted on him for getting free tastes from the girl who sold popcorn and candy bars. In Memphis he also had a paper route.

In the summer of 1951, Elvis got a job in a factory belonging to the Precision Tool company, where for $27 a week he worked a spindle drill press operator on the rocket shell manufacturing line. He got the job on the recommendation of his Uncle Travis Smith, who also worked there.

Some biographers state that Elvis returned to work at the Loew's State in April 1952, until he was fired for fighting with another usher.

To qualify for a job at the Upholsterers Specialties Company in the summer of 1952, Elvis added an extra year to his age to take himself up to 18. In the month that he worked there, he earned $109. In September 1952 year he found work at the MARL Metal Products furniture manufacturers, where he worked on furniture assembly.

The summer after graduating from high school, Elvis took a month-long job as an assembler at the M. B. Parker Company. Soon after, he told the Tennessee Employment Office that he was looking for a line of work in which he could "keep clean," and then faced the reality of going back to work at Precision Tool as a sander, shelf assembler and drill operator. He worked there for nine months, at $1.55 per hour.

Most likely in April 1954, Elvis found a job as a truck driver for Crown Electric delivering supplies to construction sites for $1 an hour (a little more by some accounts). Even before he got the job, he had been sporting a red bandanna round his neck, a style popular with truckers at the time. By all accounts he loved driving the truck around town—sometimes past the Memphis Recording Service. The job consisted of loading and unloading electrical equipment and sweeping floors, before, he hoped, earning an apprenticeship as an electrician. Elvis retained this job until October 1954, three months after Sun released his first single and his career as a performer took up all his time. For years afterwards, Elvis kept a truck as part of his fleet of vehicles so that he could drive round town incognito.

In 1962, Elvis revealed to a reporter that he had always fancied the idea of becoming a doctor. If he had had the money to go to college, that's what he would have done. He kept up a lifelong interest in medicine, in later years using his extensive knowledge of the Physician's Desk Reference to persuade doctors to prescribe him the medications he wanted.

In the Seventies, when Elvis' interest in law enforcement went beyond collecting police badges and he started hanging out with cops and sometimes going out on patrol in his own version of a squad car, Elvis said that if he hadn't been a singer, he would probably have become a policeman. Certainly, a number of kids he grew up with followed this career route.

Later in the Seventies, when his passion for karate was at its zenith, Elvis told a number of martial arts professionals that if he hadn't been an entertainer, he would likely have gravitated to this field to make a living.

Fame and wealth did little to dampen Elvis' dedication to hard work—provided that the work in hand was something he wanted to do. Few performers have been as upfront as Elvis about the debt he felt he owed his fans. When he returned to touring after his years entrapped in Hollywood B-movie land, Elvis put himself through schedules so grueling that it took more than plain human strength to get through them. Even if he was not in great form, Elvis always wanted to give his fans a good show. Dr. Nichopoulos has said that in his final years, when Elvis was losing strength and subject to periods of despondency, this incessant touring was a defense.

JOHN, ELTON HERCULES
(B. REGINALD KENNETH DWIGHT, 1947)

Elton John was born on March 25, 1947, and grew up in Pinner, just outside London, attending a the Royal Academy of Music as a child. He chose his stage name by combining the names of two of the guys in his first ever band, Long John Baldry and Elton Dean.

Elvis wearing the Tree-of-Life Medallion given to him by Marty Laker, Charlie Hodge, and other Memphis Mafia members in 1967 on his 32nd birthday.

Elton John saw Elvis perform in Maryland in June 1976, and later said that Elvis "already seemed like a corpse." This concert visit thrilled Lisa Marie, who was a great fan and played Elton John's records at Graceland. Soon after, John is said to have offered to write a song for Elvis.

Working with lyricist Bernie Taupin, Elton John's hits include early Seventies anthems "Crocodile Rock," "Rocket Man," "Saturday Night's Alright," and a cover of "Lucy In The Sky With Diamonds," taken from five consecutive #1 US chart albums. His song "Candle In The Wind" became the world's best-selling single after its re-release to commemorate the life of Princess Diana.

In 1992, Elton John beat Elvis' record for the most consecutive years of Top 40 *Billboard* singles chart hits, with an uninterrupted run since his 1970 debut single, "Your Song."

More recently, John penned a song about Elvis' hometown, "Porch Swing In Tupelo."

"JOHNNY B. GOODE"

Elvis covered Chuck Berry's rocker during his debut Las Vegas engagement. His 1000 watt performance on in August 24, 1969—a 1000 watt performance on in August 24, 1969—a 1000 watt performance was released on *From Memphis To Vegas*. Elvis' version is just one of hundreds of covers of this seminal rock 'n' roll song.

Elvis sang the song live hundreds of times over the next eight years, and was known to break into exuberant jams during lulls at studio sessions—one such moment came out on 2007 FTD release *I Sing All Kinds*. A 1972 version of Elvis performing the song featured for the closing credits of Elvis documentary *Elvis On Tour* (a full version of this studio recording was not released until 2004 FTD album *Elvis On Tour—The Rehearsals*). The song was also part of the line-up in *Aloha From Hawaii Via Satellite* in 1973, appearing in both the broadcast and on the album..

When Chuck Berry originally brought out the song in 1958—as a boy, he lived on Goode Street in St. Louis—it was a top ten hit on the *Billboard* Hot 100 chart. This and a Beethoven string quartet were the only two songs sent out on the 1977 Voyager space mission to represent human achievement.

Elvis' original August 24, 1969 live recording has since appeared on *Platinum: A Life In Music*, *Elvis In Las Vegas* and *Elvis Live*.

Other live versions have appeared on bootlegs and on albums *Elvis In Concert, Elvis Aron Presley* and the *That's The Way It Is Special Edition* release. Further versions are on FTD discs *The Impossible Dream, Dragonheart, Dixieland Rocks* and *New Year's Eve*..

JOHNSON, BOB

In December 1954, Sam Phillips alerted this *Memphis Press-Scimitar* journalist that he should get down to the Sun recording studios post-haste as Elvis had dropped by to say hi and was jamming with pals and Sun artists Carl Perkins, Jerry Lee Lewis and Johnny Cash. That day was ever after known as the "Million Dollar Quartet" session after Johnson's felicitous choice of words in the next day's paper. In 1956, Johnson wrote the first Elvis biography ever published.

JOHNSON, LYNDA BIRD
(B. 1944)

Daughter of then President Johnson, LBJ visited Elvis on set on *Girl Happy* in 1964, with her then boyfriend George Hamilton.

JOHNSON, LYNDON BAINES
(1908-1973)

After Elvis played two high-profile charitable benefits in the spring of 1961, Colonel Parker wrote to the then Vice-President Johnson offering their services to the nation, "in any capacity, whether it is to use our talents or help load the trucks." Johnson sent Elvis and the Colonel his thanks for all the money they contributed to the memorial for the sunken USS Arizona.

The Colonel had become friends with the future president of the United States when he was a Texas Senator in 1959, when he brought Eddy Arnold to play at Johnson's ranch, gratis. Soon after, the Colonel enrolled him into his Snowmen's League.

Texan born LBJ took over as the 36th President of the United States in 1963 after John F. Kennedy was assassinated, and remained in office until 1969. Some sources state that LBJ visited Elvis on the set of *Spinout* in 1966.

JONES, TOM
(B. THOMAS JONES WOODWARD, 1940)

Ten years after Elvis had concert halls of women swooning at his songs, Welsh singer Jones was repeating the feat. Elvis first met the singer in 1965, while he was on his first ever tour of the States. Jones visited with Elvis on the set of his movie *Paradise Hawaiian Style*. Jones was flabbergasted that Elvis not only knew all the songs on his debut album, he started singing them back to the boy from Pontypridd. In Jones's words, "I was really dumbfounded. I was thrilled that he even knew who I was. Our friendship started right then."

Elvis was a huge fan of Jones' "Green Green Grass of Home," a big hit in 1966. In a strange case of déjà vu, when he first heard Jones sing, Elvis was convinced that he was black.

Elvis and Priscilla watched Tom Jones perform at the Flamingo in Las Vegas in April 1968. Elvis later admitted to his pal that he had come along to study the Welshman's performance as a precursor to returning to the stage himself. Elvis came away convinced that it was worth trying his hand in front of a live audience again—some commentators have noted a hint of Jones' act in Elvis' comeback concert moves.

Jones spent time with Elvis and friends on vacation in Hawaii in 1968, when according to Jones, with a pair of guitars, they "sat down like two kids . . . whey they first meet and want to play together.."

After some of his own shows at the International Hotel in Las Vegas in the summer of 1969, Elvis and Tom Jones sometimes met up and sang the night away in Elvis' hotel suite. The following year, Tom Jones covered Jerry Reed's Elvis themed song, "Tupelo Mississippi Flash."

In the early Seventies, there were rumors that Elvis and Jones would star in a movie together.

In the summer of 1973, Elvis tried to find a new backing group to help out his pal Jones, but ended up taking the group on himself when it transpired that Jones had just signed up The Blossoms and couldn't back out of the contract. "Voice," as Elvis named the group, became his own personal off-stage singing companions for the next couple of years. Elvis went to Jones' show at Caesar's Palace, and was called up on stage to take a bow. Singer Sherill Nielsen suspects that Elvis got a secret kick out of walking on stage during the Welshman's show and getting a greater reaction out of the female fans than the man on the bill. Jones returned the favor, often attending Elvis' shows in the summer of 1974. Backstage, the pals continued to meet up and sing for pleasure.

Born in South Wales on June 7, 1940, Jones' breakthrough single in 1965, "It's Not Unusual," came after a couple of years knocking on the door

of success, initially performing as Tommy Scott in a Welsh beat combo called The Senators. Legions of underwear-throwing female fans made him a big hit in Vegas, and he hosted his own TV show either side of 1970. His career has had its lulls but he's another entertainer with durability built in to his DNA.

Elvis recorded a number of songs sung by the powerful baritone Jones, including his big hits "Green, Green Grass Of Home," "Without Love" and "I'll Never Fall In Love Again." Both singers covered "Any Day Now," "Proud Mary," "Yesterday," "Hey Jude," "You've Lost That Lovin' Feelin' ," "The Impossible Dream" and "Polk Salad Annie" among others.

Tom Jones featured prominently in 2004 Elvis documentary *Elvis—A 50th Anniversary Celebration*.

ELVIS SAID ON STAGE IN 1969: "He's one of the most fantastic performers I've ever seen."

TOM JONES: "Elvis was an icon. For him to tell me he liked my voice meant a lot."

TOM JONES: "I learned from Elvis to move while I was on stage.... I thought, 'I want to go out there and do what I feel is natural for me'. It worked. Yeah, I really got the whole idea from watching Elvis."

JAMES BURTON: "Whenever I worked with Tom Jones, all we did was talk about Elvis!"

JORDANAIRES, THE

Elvis first met The Jordanaires after they backed country singer Eddy Arnold at the Ellis Auditorium in Memphis in late November 1954, when Bob Neal took them backstage. The Jordanaires had just sung "Peace In The Valley"—a track that Elvis would later cover. Though still an unknown, the Elvis blurted out that one day he would love to have The Jordanaires sing on his records.

That day arrived remarkably soon. Jordanaire Gordon Stoker plus Ben and Brock Speer sang back up vocals at Elvis' first ever recording session for his new label, RCA, in Nashville on January 11, 1956, contributing to "I Got A Woman," "Money Honey" and "Heartbreak Hotel." The full Jordanaires group took over from the Speers after Elvis and Stoker agreed that the backing vocals weren't quite up to snuff without that full quartet sound.

The Jordanaires first appeared on stage with Elvis in Atlanta, Georgia in June 1956. They backed him on the "Milton Berle Show" on June 5, 1956, and then went on to do "The Steve Allen Show" and the "Ed Sullivan Show" soon after. Elvis' first recording session with the full quartet was in New York City the day after the "Steve Allen Show," when he recorded "Hound Dog" and "Don't Be Cruel" amongst other songs. That year The Jordanaires achieved considerable renown in their own right, taking first place on the Arthur Godfrey Talent Show (for which Elvis had failed the audition a year before).

The Jordanaires recorded with Elvis again in Los Angeles in September 1956, after the Colonel took them on under the same terms as Elvis' band: $200 per week when on tour, and $100 a week when not. With an initial line-up of Gordon Stoker, Neal Matthews, Hoyt Hawkins and Hugh Jarrett, The Jordanaires were Elvis' regular backing group from 1956 to 1970, working on most of his recording sessions and many of his movies—they appear on screen in several movies too, including *Loving You* (the closing number), *King Creole* and *G.I. Blues*. Ray Walker took over as bass singer from Hugh Jarrett in 1958. Joe Babcock briefly replaced Hoyt Hawkins at the

Kenny Rogers with Priscilla.

May 1963 Nashville recording sessions (and teamed up with Elvis again in 1970, as part of backing group The Nashville Edition).

The Jordanaires name was older than the group that backed Elvis all those years. The original Jordanaires began in Springfield, Missouri in 1948, with a line-up of Bob Hubbard, Bill Matthews, Monty Matthews and Culley Holt that performed regularly on the Grand Ole Opry, and sang back up to country stars Red Foley, Hank Snow and Jimmy Wakely. In the mid-Fifties, some of that original line-up started the Foggy River Boys (which at one stage featured a young Charlie Hodge).

When not working with Elvis, The Jordanaires lent their suave voices to others, including Elvis' supposed rival Ricky Nelson.

Jordanaires Gordon Stoker (lead), Hoyt Hawkins (baritone), Neal Matthews (tenor) and Ray Walker (bass) returned to back Elvis on the road in 1970, after regular backing singers of the time The Imperials were unable to go out on tour. Though Elvis was keen to continue working with the Jordanaires, the group had too many commitments in Nashville to take up his invitation. Apart from some overdubs in 1971, that was the last time Elvis worked with these gospel greats.

Before, during, and after Elvis, The Jordanaires worked with many of the artists who came to Nashville to record, including Patsy Cline, Jim Reeves, Jerry Lee Lewis, Pat Boone, Carol Channing, Johnny Cash, Jimmy Buffett, Kenny Rogers, Tammy Wynette, Dolly Parton and (literally) thousands more. They are also known in music circles for inventing the Nashville number system of chord annotation, which continues to be used to this day.

After Elvis' death, The Jordanaires released tribute album *The Jordanaires Sing Elvis' Gospel*

Favorites. The latest Jordanaires line up has continued to fly the flag for Elvis into the 2000s.

During its sixty year heritage , the group has won accolades for singing on more top ten hits than any other group—at one time, eight out of the top ten chart singles had The Jordanaires on backing vocals. The Group has been inducted into the Gospel, Rockabilly, Country and Vocal Group Halls of Fame.

Elvis said: "Let's face it, if it hadn't been for you guys, there might not have been a me."

JORGENSEN, ERNST

Growing up in Denmark, Ernst Jorgensen became hooked on Elvis in the Sixties, particularly by the question of why one Elvis album would have great music and the next be best forgotten. He amassed information on Elvis as a hobby and with a couple of pals released discographies and booklets for Elvis fans. Jorgensen went to work for record company BMG in Denmark (BMG took over RCA in 1986), where he started working with Roger Semon on producing European Elvis releases. The two of them were then taken on to reorder the Elvis Presley catalogue, a job that involved listening to every minute of tape Elvis ever recorded for his record company. Since making his statement of intent with a 1991 3-disc collection of previously unheard alternates and takes in *Collectors Gold*, Jorgensen and Semon have tirelessly ordered, catalogued and tracked down rare Elvis material. In the Nineties, he masterminded the box sets of Elvis' Fifties, Sixties and Seventies recordings. He has continued his work with boxed sets, new themed albums to introduce Elvis to a younger audience, and for collectors, the FTD series of releases.

Jorgensen has shared his knowledge in his books *Elvis Presley: A Life in Music* and *Elvis Day By Day*.

ERNST JORGENSEN: "Early on, my friends and I found out that we actually knew more about Elvis' recordings than most people did. Then it took on its own life. This helped create an inner drive to keep going to find out more because I already knew more than most."

ERNST JORGENSEN: "I think my greatest challenge . . . was to get Elvis re-established as a significant and important artist and not just a stupid joke in The National Enquirer because there was a tendency in the media to treat him like that. I think fifteen years later that has been achieved."

"JOSHUA FIT THE BATTLE"

Elvis recorded this 1850s African-American spiritual, first sung by slaves in the pre-Civil War days, on October 30, 1960 in Nashville for the *His Hand In Mine* album. It was also released in February 1966 as a single with B-side "Known Only to Him"; neither side made it into the charts.

The song has since appeared on *Amazing Grace, Peace In The Valley* and *Ultimate Gospel*.

Alternate takes are on FTD releases *Easter Special, Fame and Fortune*, and particularly *His Hand In Mine*. Bootleg *Just A Closer Walk With Thee* offers another interpretation.

JUANICO, JUNE

Elvis had more than a brief fling with this Biloxi beauty in 1955 and 1956.

Juanico met Elvis after a friend took her along to see him perform at the Keesler Air Force Base—the second night in a row for the friend. Elvis spotted Juanico in the crowd and later asked her to show him around Biloxi. When she told him that there was nothing to see, he shot back, "Well, show me nothing."

June flew out to Houston with Elvis to pick up a new 1956 ivory Cadillac Eldorado Biarritz convertible, and then spent the rest of the week staying in Memphis. In the summer of 1956, Elvis decided to spend his first proper vacation since becoming a performer in Biloxi, with June the main reason why.

Rumors soon appeared in the press that wedding bells were in the air for the new music sensation and the local beauty. On the Colonel's advice, Elvis went onto a local radio station to deny the engagement rumors, and then went back to spend some quality vacation time with his folks and June's mother and step-father, Eddie Bellman, some of it deep sea fishing. Bellman's home movies of the this time form the centerpiece of 2002 documentary *Elvis & June: A Love Story*.

June later admitted that Elvis did propose to her that summer, with the caveat that she would have to wait a few years—Elvis had solemnly promised to the Colonel that he "wouldn't do anything stupid" to wreck his career. Speculation continued as June, or "Widdle Bitty" as he addressed her in a loving telegram, accompanied Elvis to play shows in Miami after his summer layoff. June paid Elvis a return visit in Memphis in October 1956.

In March 1957, when Elvis' train home from LA to Memphis passed through New Orleans, Elvis met up with June again and asked her to keep him company back in Memphis. June told him that the reason she had to say no was because she was engaged. She was married in Biloxi in June that year—Elvis did not attend.

Juanico and Elvis met again in 1962, and she later saw Elvis during his first residency at the International Hotel in Las Vegas, in 1969.

JUNE JUANICO: "I had the feeling that Elvis was probably the most handsome, perfect, flawless creature that I had ever laid my eyes on."

Book:
Elvis In the Twilight of Memory, June Juanico, published by Arcade, 1997.

Documentary:
Elvis & June: A Love Story (2002)

"JUDY"

Elvis recorded this gentle Teddy Redell rocker in on March 12, 1961 in Nashville, for release on *Something For Everybody*. The track did double duty as the B-side to "There's Always Me" in August 1967. "Judy" made it to #78 on the charts, twenty-two places lower than the A-side track.

The tune has since reappeared on albums *Elvis in Nashville* and *From Nashville to Memphis*.

Alternate versions and takes have appeared on *The EP Collection Vol. 2*, and on FTD releases *Fame And Fortune* and *Something For Everybody*.

JUNGLE ROOM SESSIONS, THE

A 2000 FTD release of outtakes and alternates from Elvis' February and October 1976 Graceland recording sessions.

TRACK LISTING:
1. Bitter They Are, Harder They Fall
2. She Thinks I Still Care
3. The Last Farewell
4. Solitaire
5. I'll Never Fall In Love Again
6. Moody Blue
7. For The Heart
8. Hurt
9. Danny Boy
10. Never Again
11. Love Coming Down
12. Blue Eyes Crying In The Rain
13. It's Easy For You
14. Way Down
15. Pledging My Love (un-edited master)
16. He'll Have To Go (rough-mix master)
17. Fire Down Below (instrumental incl. America The Beautiful)

"JUST A CLOSER WALK WITH THEE"

Elvis is said to have first performed this Sister Rosetta Tharpe spiritual—a hit for Red Foley in 1950—at a July 4, 1955 gospel-only concert he gave in De Leon, Texas. When he sang the song again at Eddie Fadal's house in Texas, circa 1958, Fadal had the tape rolling, hence Elvis can be heard singing the song on bootlegs *Forever Young, Forever Beautiful* and *Just A Closer Walk With Thee*.

JUST A CLOSER WALK WITH THEE

A 2000 CD issued by the Czech Elvis Presley Fan Club on the Memory Label, featuring alternate takes and rare gospel material.

TRACK LISTING:
1. I Believe (alternate take)
2. Peace In The Valley (multiple alternate takes)
3. Take My Hand Precious Lord (alternate take)
4. It Is No Secret What God Can Do (multiple alternate takes)
5. Just A Closer Walk With Thee
6. I Asked The Lord (Long Version)
7. Milky White Way (multiple alternate takes)
8. His Hand In Mine (two alternate takes)
9. I Believe In The Man In The Sky (multiple alternate takes)
10. He Knows Just What I Need (multiple alternate takes)
11. Mansion Over The Hilltop (alternate take)
12. In My Fathers House (multiple alternate takes)
13. Joshua Fit The Battle (alternate take)
14. Swing Down, Sweet Chariot (alternate take)
15. I'm Gonna Walk Dem Golden Stairs (Take 1)
16. If We Never Meet Again (Take 1)
17. Known Only To Him (alternate take)
18. Crying In The Chapel (first three takes)
19. Working On The Building (first two takes)
20. Excerpt From "Elvis Answers Back"

"JUST A LITTLE BIT"

Elvis recorded this restrained rocker—initially a hit for Tiny Topsy in 1959, written by John Thornton, Piney Brown, Ralph Bass and Earl Washington—in a single take at Stax Studios on July 22, 1973. It appeared on *Raised On Rock*, and in the Nineties on *Walk A Mile In My Shoes*.

"JUST A LITTLE TALK WITH JESUS"

One of the many gospel songs that Elvis and Jerry Lee Lewis traded harmonies on at Sun Studio in December 1956, in what became *The Million Dollar Quartet* session. The song was written by prolific gospel composer Clevant Derricks and was a standard for several decades after the Rangers Quartet had a hit with it in 1939.

"JUST BECAUSE"

The A-side to one of the seven singles released simultaneously by RCA in late August 1956, eclipsed in chart performance by B-side "Blue Moon." Elvis recorded the song on or around September 10, 1954, while still at Sun, and sang it live that fall. Originally written by Bob and Joe Shelton and Sid Robin in 1933, Elvis' version didn't come out until his first RCA EP and LP in the spring of 1956 (both titled *Elvis Presley*). The rockabilly tune was recycled on *A Date With Elvis* to tide over his fans while he was away on Army duty in 1959. It has since appeared on *The Sun Sessions*, *The Complete Sun Sessions*, *The King Of Rock And Roll*, *Sunrise*, *The Country Side of Elvis* and *Elvis at Sun*.

"JUST CALL ME LONESOME"

Elvis recorded this 1954 country hit for Eddy Arnold and Red Foley (and written by Rex Griffin) on September 10, 1967 at the RCA Studios in Nashville for the *Clambake* soundtrack.

It has since appeared on *Elvis in Nashville*, *From Nashville to Memphis*, *Tomorrow Is A Long Time* and *The Country Side of Elvis*.

Alternate takes have been released on *Great Country Songs* and FTD issue *So High*.

A remixed version of the song from 1980 appeared on *Guitar Man* and then in 2000 on FTD album *Too Much Monkey Business*.

"JUST FOR OLD TIME SAKE"

A *Pot Luck* ballad by Sid Tepper and Roy C. Bennett that Elvis recorded on March 18, 1962 in Nashville. The track was included on anthology box set *From Nashville to Memphis*. Alternates have come out on FTD releases *Long Lonely Highway*, *Studio B: Nashville Outtakes* and *Pot Luck*.

JUST FOR YOU

An EP released in late August 1957, featuring the final songs from the Loving You LP that had not previous been released as EPs, plus "Is It So Strange." The EP peaked at #2 on the EP charts.

TRACK LISTING:
1. I Need You So
2. Have I Told You Lately That I Love You
3. Blueberry Hill
4. Is It So Strange

"JUST LET ME MAKE BELIEVE"

Elvis' is reputedly one of the backing voices on this Sixties singalong home recording that was put up for auction by former security consultant Dick Grob three decades later. Written by Ronald Blackwell and covered by Roy Orbison in the late Sixties, the song has appeared on Elvis bootlegs including *From The Bottom Of My Heart, Vol. 2*.

"JUST PRETEND"

A Doug Flett/Guy Fletcher ballad perfect for Elvis' powerful delivery, recorded on June 6, 1970 while the *That's The Way It Is* crew was on hand. Elvis sang the song live in 1970 and then again in 1975. *Live In Las Vegas*, *That's The Way It Is - Special Edition* all feature live performances from 1970; a 1975 performance is also on *Live In Las Vegas* and a selection of bootlegs.

FTD release *The Way It Was* offers a version of Elvis rehearsing the song in 1970. The original recording reappeared on Seventies anthology *Walk A Mile In My Shoes*. An alternate take from the studio session is on *Essential Elvis Vol. 4*.

"JUST TELL HER JIM SAID HELLO"

The breezy B-Side to "She's Not You"—featuring Elvis breaking into a falsetto—made it to #55 during its five-week spell on the charts on release in July 1962. Elvis recorded the Leiber/Stoller tune on March 19 that year in Nashville. The track was not released on album until 1968 compilation *Elvis' Gold Records Vol. 4*, since when it has made a cameo on *Worldwide Gold Award Hits Vol. 2*, *Elvis Sings Leiber & Stoller* and *From Nashville to Memphis*.

Alternate takes have appeared on *Collectors Gold* and *Elvis: Close Up*, and on FTD releases *Long Lonely Highway*, *Studio B: Nashville Outtakes* and *Pot Luck*.

K

KAHANE, JACKIE
(1921-2001)

Canadian-born stand-up comedian Kahane began opening for Elvis at his concerts in November 1971. He had previously worked as a warm-up man for Wayne Newton. In 1961 he was named one of the outstanding comics of the year by Time magazine; a decade later he was a regular on Johnny Carson's "The Tonight Show." Kahane warmed up Elvis' overwrought audiences until Elvis' death; he was hand-selected by Colonel Parker because his act got laughs without resorting to "dirty" jokes.

Kahane can be seen doing his stuff on 1972 documentary *Elvis on Tour*.

Kahane wrote and delivered the eulogy at Elvis' funeral"Barry Adelman helped him put the eulogy together, and the Colonel asked him to do the job.

After Elvis, Kahane did warm-up for Tina Turner and Dionne Warwick among others, and started his own production company.

JACKIE KAHANE: "It was a great ride."

KALCHEIM, HARRY

William Morris agent Kalcheim was alerted by Colonel Tom Parker about Elvis in early 1955, and agreed that the singer's voice was "very special." Colonel Parker's contact with Kalcheim was a vital part of his strategy to wrest control over Elvis' management from Bob Neal.

Kalcheim arranged for Elvis to go to New York and audition for the "Arthur Godfrey Talent Scouts" TV show on March 23, 1955, six months before Parker officially became Elvis' manager. As Colonel Parker was engineering Elvis' transfer from Sun Records to RCA, Kalcheim suggested that Elvis could feature in a Hollywood short movie. The Colonel disagreed and told the agent that he was better suited for James Dean style movies. The Colonel turned out not to be bluffing when he wrote, "Believe me, if you ever follow one of my hunches, follow up on this one and you won't go wrong."

As soon as the Colonel wrapped up Elvis' new recording contract with RCA, Kalcheim approached NBC TV about a slot for Elvis, whom he described as a new version of teen idol Johnnie Ray. After Kalcheim arranged Elvis' screen test for Paramount producer Hal Wallis in March, 1956, he unsuccessfully tried to get Elvis a 15-minute radio series.

The Colonel ignored Kalcheim's advice for Elvis to tour the Northeast to increase his national profile, preferring to pursue the relatively new medium of TV. The Colonel (or Bill Randle) used other contacts to get Elvis his first TV appearance on "Stage Show." The outcry over Elvis' "scandalous" performance on the "Milton Berle Show" prompted Kalcheim to suggest that the singer tone down his act. The Colonel took this advice to heart as he engineered his boy's repositioning from rebel rocker to popular mainstream attraction.

KANSAS

- Abilene
Elvis played the Expo Center on October 9, 1974, the final date on his fourth tour that year.

- Topeka
Elvis played the Municipal Auditorium on May 21, 1956.

- Wichita
Elvis performed two shows at the Forum on May 18, 1956. He played the Henry Levitt Arena on June 19, 1972. When he next played town it was at the Wichita State University venue on October 7, 1974 and again on December 27, 1976.

KANTER, HAL
(B. 1918)

Sometime director and long-time writer Hal Kanter was hired by Paramount producer Hal Wallis to write and direct Elvis' first movie for the studio, *Loving You*. This was Kanter's directorial debut, after years of writing scripts and material for Bob Hope, (Dean) Martin & (Jerry) Lewis and TV variety star George Gobel. As research, Kanter shadowed Elvis for a while in late 1956, spending time with him in Memphis and on his farewell performance at the Louisiana Hayride.

In 1961, Kanter wrote the screenplay for Elvis blockbuster *Blue Hawaii*, for which he received an American Musical nomination from the Writers' Guild of America.

Kanter later found success in TV, executive producing Seventies hit "All in the Family" and racking up six Emmy nominations. More recently, he has written the scripts for the Academy Awards ceremony. His 1998 biography, *So Far, So Funny*, contains a chapter about his time working and being with Elvis.

KARATE

Elvis' interest in karate goes back to a magazine article he read while doing his Army service in Germany. The article was about former marine Hank Slomanksi, who was said to have taken on 150 adversaries in a day and beat every one. Elvis signed up for lessons three times a week in the Shotokan style with expert German instructor Jü‚rgen Seydal. That year he traveled to Paris with Seydal to attend a karate demonstration by Master Tetsuji Murakami.

In early 1960, Elvis attended a demonstration of a new street-fighting karate technique developed by instructor Ed Parker in Los Angeles. In July that year he received his first-degree black belt certificate after a five-hour test that included taking on two assailants at once. Elvis proudly carried the certificate with him in his wallet at all times, though detractors have claimed that Elvis was actually given the certificate in Chito-Ryu on an honorary basis by instructor Hank Slomanksi, who was in Memphis giving a demonstration.

Studying karate, Elvis built on his personal interest in fighting (learned on the streets of Tupelo and Memphis, and used in self-defense to protect himself from angry and antagonistic boyfriends). Fight scenes, often with pal Red West, became a staple of his movies, both on screen and off. Karate was involved in one form or another in *G.I. Blues*, *Wild in the Country*, *Blue Hawaii*, *Follow That Dream*, *Kid Galahad*, *Kissin' Cousins*, *Roustabout* and *Harum Scarum*, in which he paralyzes a big cat with a single blow. He's still dispatching villains with well-aimed chops in 1967 release *Double Trouble*.

When Elvis first started out as a karateka, very few people in the States "much less Hollywood" knew anything about the martial arts. A decade before Bruce Lee made his movies, Elvis introduced many people to the martial art through demonstrations.

Fellow actors and crew on Elvis' movies would have seen him killing time between scenes breaking bricks and boards. In Red West's recollection, after filming *Blue Hawaii* in 1961, they left broken boards all over the beach. When working on *Girls! Girls! Girls!*, Elvis practiced karate in the hotel, perfecting his technique at board-breaking until Paramount executive Hal Wallis got him to stop because he was beginning to delay the movie. A bruised hand that Elvis sustained working out karate moves during the shooting of *G.I Blues* did not delay shooting, and is visible in some of the publicity shots for the movie and associated LP.

Elvis received his honorary second-degree black belt in the Chito-Ryu style of karate in October 1963. He kept this certificate card in his wallet from then until the day he died.

Elvis and Priscilla attended Ed Parker's karate championship in Honolulu during their vacation in May 1968. A karate-based dance scene was originally filmed for his NBC TV Special before being cut from the final show.

Karate was unquestionably Elvis' favored way of staying in shape. When he returned to performing in Las Vegas in 1969, karate-type moves began to feature in his stage act, including punches, kicks and low-stance moves. Elvis took in another Ed Parker demonstration in Las Vegas during his summer 1969 residency in town.

Not just Elvis' entourage but his band members were also initiated into the martial arts. Drummer Ronnie Tutt was keen to do karate lessons with Elvis because it gave him an insight into how Elvis was likely to move onstage.

Elvis began studying Tae Kwon Do ("the way of the foot and the fist")with Korean Master Kang Rhee in March 1971, soon after being awarded a fourth-degree black belt, and continued with him for the next few years. Elvis flew him in for lessons when he performed in Las Vegas, and helped him out financially to set up his own karate institute. Kang Rhee gave Elvis his karate name "Tiger."

One recording session in Nashville in May 1971 was abandoned after Elvis' overenthusiastic demonstration of how to disarm a gunman with a karate kick ended up damaging Chip Young's handmade guitar.

Elvis received his fifth-dan black belt in Kenpo Karate in February 1972, around the time that he found out that Priscilla, now separated, was seeing karate champ Mike Stone. She ascribes the self-confidence she needed to tell Elvis that she wanted to leave as one of the positive effects of studying the martial arts. This would have been scant consolation for Elvis, who encouraged her to study karate in the first place.

At a 1972 karate demonstration in LA, Ed Parker paired Elvis with Dave Hebler for sparring. Hebler recalls that Elvis wasn't as proficient at karate as his ranking indicated, but then Hebler was a leading exponent of the art.

Elvis proudly displayed an International Kenpo Karate Association emblem on the guitar he used in the *Aloha From Hawaii* broadcast, offering free publicity for the discipline on the world's most viewed TV show ever.

Elvis made sixth-degree black belt in Kenpo Karate in April 1973. Soon afterwards, Elvis had a falling out with teacher Ed Parker, when he went to San Francisco with his girlfriend Linda Thompson and a big entourage only to find that without asking him, the California Karate Championships had been using his name and likeness. This specifically contravened a clause prohibiting Elvis from doing any personal publicity in the thirty days leading up to a lengthy booking in Tahoe. Elvis turned round and left immediately. The next day, Kang Rhee awarded Elvis a seventh-degree belt in his own specialty, Pasaryu, once again more on the strength of his famous pupil's dedication and sincerity than his competition achievements.

One night after a show in Las Vegas, Elvis accidentally broke a young woman's ankle while showing off karate moves in his suite. Though Elvis paid for all of Beverly Albrecq's treatment and physiotherapy, she later brought a lawsuit

Elvis practicing Karate at the Kang Rhee Institute in Memphis, TN.

against him. Sometimes Elvis got hurt too: he broke a finger on his left hand while working out with instructor Kang Rhee in Las Vegas in September 1973.

Other people in Elvis' circle were on the receiving end of Elvis' karate showboating. Step-brother Ricky Stanley was sometimes an unwilling participant in an exhibition that Elvis gave using sharp knives, which he twirled around his relative, leaving him unscathed but not unshaken. When bassist Duke Bardwell first joined the TCB band, Elvis unexpectedly whirled round and threw a punch that stopped so close to Bardwell's face that one of Elvis' rings was touching his skin.

Elvis' passion for karate reached its zenith in 1974, when he helped found the Tennessee Karate Institute in Memphis (at 1372 Overton). He put Red West and his cousin Bobbi Mann (later Bobbi Wren) in charge, and hired Bill "Superfoot" Wallace, a karate champion known for his Kumite skills, as chief instructor. Elvis took lessons from Wallace, and paid for him to have specialist acupuncture treatment for a long-term injury. That year Elvis also helped fund the US Karate Team on a tour of Europe.

Elvis put on a karate exhibition with his karate pals Ed Parker, Bill Wallace, Dave Hebler and Red West at the Tennessee Karate Institute in September 1974. He also announced his intention to make a karate movie (see Sidebar). At this time, Ed Parker elevated Elvis to eighth-degree black belt level ("Master of the Art"). Elvis claimed that every day before taking to the stage in Las Vegas he and some of his entourage had a two-hour karate session. He also told his Las Vegas audience that he had been practicing karate every day of his life for sixteen years.

Elvis' stage act, which had long incorporated various stylized karate moves, featured a full half-hour karate demonstration with Red West one night in August 1974 at the Hilton in Las Vegas. This may have been more a result of him getting carried away because of the prescription medicine he was taking than an up-front decision. The band played "If You Talk In Your Sleep" while Elvis went through an involved karate routine. Half-way through, Elvis broke into giggles and told the audience, "I'm just laughing my career away."

Around this time, Elvis gave karate certificates to all the band members and entourage guys who had been studying with him. According to Linda Thompson, Elvis' passion for karate was one of the few things that kept him going in his later years.

Elvis was the founder member of the TCB Martial Art Organization, designed to promote the sport of karate, for which he wrote a credo based on body conditioning, mental condition and meditation. Elvis believed very strongly in the code of ethics and discipline that underpins the martial arts, which dovetailed with his own spiritual studies. He described karate as "helping a person help himself."

Elvis more or less ceased doing karate when his health deteriorated in 1975, though while his entourage pals did the workouts, Elvis sat in during the initial meditation sessions.

Elvis said: "It's something that's really helped me in discipline, mind control, body control, self-confidence and all round . . . I've never had to use it to hurt anybody and I hope I never would have to."

ED PARKER: "Elvis was a damn good black belt by any standards. He had a lot of guts and pain didn't bother him. If he got hit while we were working out he took it like a man . . . He was tough and had a lot of courage."

JOE ESPOSITO: "It gave him a lot of confidence."

KANG RHEE: "He was perfectionist."

PRISCILLA: "Among our group, Elvis wasn't known for his precision in karate."

DAVE HEBLER: "You had the idea if Elvis had really dedicated himself to the art, he could be good. But he only played at it. He never really worked hard at it and drove himself."

ELVIS' KARATE MOVIE(S)

In 1974, Elvis was very keen to produce and bankroll a karate movie. Before abandoning the idea, he toyed with the idea of a feature film and a karate documentary. For his putative karate spy thriller *The New Gladiators* (according to some sources, sometimes referred to by working title "Billy Easter" or "The Ten Fingers of Memphis"), Elvis commissioned a script and had forty minutes of material filmed in Memphis. The documentary was to be based on Ed Parker's competition feats.

In November 1974, with Jerry Schilling in charge as executive producer, plans moved forward with shooting of karate competitions in Europe and California. Schilling set up an office in LA, and hired editor Bert Lovitt to make a demo reel in order to raise some financing. Larry Geller says that Elvis hired him to write a script, worked up from the idea of the history of martial arts from the time of Genesis onwards. Elvis was not going to star in this documentary, but produce and narrate it. Actor, producer and writer Rick Husky"who Elvis had met years earlier when he was inducted into the Tau Kappa Epsilon fraternity at Arkansas State was involved in the other karate-themed project. Husky wrote a 30-page treatment about a CIA agent who runs a karate school and battles against drug dealers. According to one source, in the closing scene Elvis practiced moves that signified the Lord's Prayer in Indian sign language, while a vast number of people mirrored his moves.

Against the Colonel's wishes, Elvis sunk over $100,000 in the project. By Christmas that year, Elvis had pulled the plug on the movie, even though the team had only just started screening material to putative investors. Ed Parker recalls that the project came to naught because the Colonel believed that Elvis in a karate film was too much of a stretch for his fans.

A bootleg video of 20 minutes of footage appeared in the late Nineties.

Books:
Elvis' Karate Legacy, by Carman, Wayne, Legacy Entertainment Inc., 1998

KARGER, FRED
(1916-1979)

Marilyn Monroe's one-time voice coach and lover worked as music director/conductor on three of Elvis' mid-Sixties movies: *Kissin' Cousins*, *Frankie and Johnny* and *Harum Scarum*. As well as taking care of orchestral arrangements, Karger was credited with co-writing several soundtrack songs. The son of early MGM producer and director Maxwell Karger, Fred was twice married to Ronald Reagan's first wife Jane Wyman. He worked on many movie productions over the years, including *From Here To Eternity*, *Pal Joey*, *Bye Bye Birdie*, *Your Cheatin' Heart* and *Gidget*. The trivia footnote to Mr. Karger's life is that he died 16 years to the day after Marilyn Monroe.

KARLSON, PHIL
(1908-1985)

A renowned director of early Fifties film noir, Karlson cut his teeth on Abbott and Costello shorts and directed unknown starlet Marilyn Monroe in her first proper film role, in *Ladies of the Chorus* (1948).

In 1961, Karlson directed Elvis in *Kid Galahad*. Later that decade he made two Dean Martin movies, followed by his biggest commercial success, *Walking Tall* (1973).

KATZ DRUGSTORE, MEMPHIS

Elvis was booked to perform at the opening of a drug store at the brand new Airways Shopping Center (2256 Lamar Ave.), advertised as the "World's Largest Super Drug Store." In the publicity Elvis was billed as "the newest Memphis hit in the recording business," despite the fact that he was just two months into his recording career. On September 9, 1954 throngs of teenagers including Johnny Cash turned up to hear Elvis, introduced by former Humes High school classmate George Klein. That day Elvis performed from the back of a flatbed truck.

KATZMAN, SAM
(1901-1973)

Katzman's career as producer mirrored the foibles of Hollywood genre popularity, from Westerns to sci-fi, from hippie and biker movies to Elvis Presley musicals, of which he produced three. His greatest asset for his studio employers was his ability to bring in movies on time and on budget. Not for nothing was he known as "King of the Quickies." On *Kissin' Cousins* he hired Gene Nelson as director, musician, scriptwriter and choreographer. On *Harum Scarum*, there is a story that when a film supply company quoted more than he thought reasonable for hiring some chickens, he went out to a farm supplier and bought a dozen live birds.

As well as the two Elvis movies he worked on, Katzman has a credit on a staggering 250 productions. A decade before Elvis he produced *Rock Around The Clock* (1956). Katzman's other claim to popular culture fame is coining the term "beatnik" one day when he misheard somebody actually saying "beat, Nick."

KEATON, MIKE

Elvis hired Mike to take the step up to paid entourage member in September 1964, when he was rearranging the personnel. Keaton, who Elvis knew from the First Assembly of God church (and who had a wife called Gladys), worked on and off with Elvis into the Seventies.

"KEEP YOUR HANDS OFF OF IT"

Elvis broke into this song during a June 5, 1970 jam of "Got My Mojo Working" in the RCA studios, Nashville. It had originally been a hit for Billy Hughes and His Pecos Pals when Elvis was a lad of nine, and was a song that he played and sang with pals at Lauderdale Courts before he signed for Sun.

Elvis' version (with added overdubs) came out the following year on *Love Letters From Elvis*.

Later album releases include *Walk A Mile In My Shoes* and the 2000 version of *Elvis Country*.

The full unedited jam was released in 1996 on *Essential Elvis Vol. 4*.

"KEEPER OF THE KEY"

Another spiritual song in the *Million Dollar Quartet* roster, as Elvis and pals work out which key the song is in. Carl Perkins sings the melody, with Elvis on impromptu backing vocals. The track was written by Beverly Stewart, Harlan Howard, Kenny Devine and Lance Guynes, and had recently been released by Wynn Stewart.

KEISKER, MARION
(1917-1989)

Sam Phillips' assistant at Sun Records was the first person in the music business to spot Elvis' talent. Her favorable impression of the boy who had stopped into the Memphis Recording Service to cut some acetates on his own dollar, the kid with the unique voice, led her a year later to remind Sam Phillips and Scotty Moore at the coffee shop next to the studio about "the boy with the sideburns" who was a good ballad singer and might be the right voice for a song Phillips had picked up recently. He wasn't, but Sam put Elvis in touch with Scotty Moore to work something up, and that something turned out to be "That's All Right (Mama)."

Keisker had worked at WREC, a radio station located in the basement of the Peabody Hotel, since she was barely a teenager. Over the years, she hosted music shows, news broadcasts and talk radio, as well as writing and producing programs for the station. In 1950, a divorcee with a child, she threw in her lot with WREC engineer Sam Phillips and helped him realize his ambition of setting up his own studio, the Memphis Recording Service. With Sam, she turned the two-room space on Union Ave. into a working studio, and then wore various hats once the business was up and running. Often described as Sam Phillip's secretary, she was also a sometime engineer, office manager and general front desk friendly face. Biographers invariably note that Keisker threw herself into the undertaking of making the Memphis Recording Service into a viable business out of love for Sam Phillips. Decades later, she told an interviewer, "I was totally enamored of Sam. All I wanted was for Sam to do whatever would make him happy." Finding Elvis certainly achieved that.

In July 1953, when Elvis walked into the studio and put down his $4 to record a ten-inch acetate, Keisker most likely flipped the switch on the master tape to make a copy of the boy's untutored singing because she wanted her boss Sam to hear it; most likely, because in a competing version of the Elvis creation myth, Sam Phillips was in the building, rather than at the next-door caféÈ, which often served as impromptu office space for the two-person business.

When Phillips did eventually call Elvis in to see what he had to offer and the boy conjured up his first single, Keisker may have been the one who landed it radio airplay for the first time. According to Bill Burk she personally took the finished acetate to WREC, where DJ Fred Cook gave the song its first public spin.

Red West has said that years later when Elvis read that it was Sam Phillips alone who "discovered" him, he would tell anyone within earshot that it was Marion Keisker who put two and two together and suggested to Sam that that young Elvis might just be the white boy who could sing with a black sound that Phillips had been looking for.

Sam Phillips described Marion Keisker as "the only subscriber to the New Yorker in Memphis." Elvis saw other qualities in her too, and would stop by at Sun to say hello and chat before and after he became Sun's big-name artist. Keisker was as much a fan as any other; she told Peter Guralnick that when she was in an audience watching Elvis perform in 1955 "something she rarely had time for" she was shocked and surprised to find that she was screaming along with the other female fans in the crowd.

Phillips used the money from selling Elvis' contract to shore up the radio station he had launched in Memphis. Keisker returned to the airwaves in time to announce that RCA was the label that had signed Sun's star. Keisker continued to work at Sun until 1957, when she fell out with Phillips and joined the Air Force as a commissioned officer.

Elvis ran into Marion Keisker at the enlisted men's club in Freiburg, Germany, during a press conference to mark the end of his Army service in Germany; she was covering the event for the Armed Forces Television Network. When Elvis spotted Captain MacInness (her married name), he said he didn't know "whether to kiss you or salute," to which she replied "In that order." After the event, Elvis put in a good word for her when she was chastised for excessive fraternization by her superiors.

Elvis was so overjoyed to run into Keisker again at the Jaycees award ceremony in January 1971 that he invited her to join his tableful of pals.

ELVIS SAID: "It if wasn't for that lady, I would never have got a start . . . she was the one who had faith, she was the one who pushed me."

MARION KEISKER: "It was a busy Saturday afternoon. The office was full of people wanting to make personal records. He came in, said he wanted to make a record. I told him he'd have to wait and he said OK. He sat down. While he was waiting, we had a conversation. He said he was a singer. I said, 'What kind of singer are you?' He said, 'I sing all kinds.' I said, 'Who do you sound like?' He said, 'I don't sound like nobody.' "

MARION KEISKER, IN A 1954 PRESS INTERVIEW: "This boy has something that seems to appeal to everybody."

MARION KEISKER: "Whatever you were looking for, you were going to find in him. It was not in him to lie or say anything malicious. He had all the intricacy of the very simple."

KENNEDY, AARON

Elvis owes his middle name to Vernon's best friend in Tupelo, who according to some sources was living at Vernon's father's house when Elvis and twin brother Jesse came into the world in January 1935.

Vernon signed over the deed to the house he owned for a year on Berry Street, Tupelo, on July 18, 1946, after Vernon fell behind with the $30 monthly payments.

KENNEDY, JERRY

Guitarist Kennedy began working as a session musician with Elvis in Nashville in late 1961, after Hank Garland sustained serious injuries in a car accident. Kennedy was one of four guitar players (with Scotty Moore, Grady Martin and Harold Bradley) to work on Elvis' May 26/27, 1963 recording session in Nashville. Kennedy had a long association with Mercury records, over the years acting as a scout and producer before going into management.

KENTUCKY

- *Lexington*
Elvis played through the flu at the YMCA Arena on March 21, 1956.

- *Louisville*
Elvis played the Rialto Theater with Hank Snow on December 8, 1955, in a private show for Philip Morris company employees. He appeared at the Jefferson County Armory on November 25, 1956.

Elvis and the TCB band played the Freedom Hall at the State Fair and Expo Center on November 7, 1971. They performed a show at the Fair and Expo Center's Freedom Hall on June 26, 1974. Elvis played the Freedom Hall at the start of his 5th tour of 1976 (July 23), and was back on May 21, 1977.

"KENTUCKY RAIN"

An American Studio contemporary country recording from February 19, 1969, released as a single in January 1970 with "My Little Friend" on the B-side. This Eddie Rabbitt / Dick Heard composition, the fourth single from Elvis' Memphis recording sessions, sold 600,000 copies on initial release but failed to scale the heights of previous singles, peaking at #16 in the charts. Nevertheless, "Kentucky Rain" became Elvis' 50th gold record, and stayed on the chart for nine weeks.

The song has since appeared on *Worldwide Gold Award Hits Vol. 1*, *Pure Gold*, *Elvis' Gold Records Vol. 5*, *From Nashville to Memphis*, *Great Country Songs*, the re-released version of *On Stage*, the 2000 re-release of *From Elvis In Memphis*, *The Country Side of Elvis*, *Elvis 2nd to None*, *History*, the 2006 version of *Elvis Country* and *The Essential Elvis Presley*.

In early 1970 Elvis incorporated "Kentucky Rain" into his stage act. Live versions have come out on *Elvis Aron Presley*, *The Live Greatest Hits*, *Live In Las Vegas* and on FTD releases *Polk Salad Annie* and *Writing for the King*, in addition to the inevitable bootlegs.

Alternate takes from the American Studio session have since appeared on the *From Nashville To Memphis* box set, *Suspicious Minds: The Memphis 1969 Anthology* and on 2001 FTD release *The Memphis Sessions*. The track was also remixed by Jarvis for *Guitar Man* in 1980 (but not released for two decades, until FTD CD *Too Much Monkey Business*).

KERKORIAN, KIRK
(b. 1917)

A renowned builder of mega-hotels, outdoing himself three times to build the then-largest hotels in the world in Las Vegas, Kerkorian made his first fortune with the Trans International Airlines company, and since the Sixties has been one of the richest men in the US. He commissioned the International Hotel, which lured Elvis back to live performing in 1969. In the early Seventies, Kerkorian took over the then-ailing MGM studios.

In 2006, Kerkorian was still in the Forbes 400 with an estimated worth in excess of $9 billion, and was said to own half of the hotel rooms on the Las Vegas Strip.

KESLER, STAN

Stan Kesler played steel guitar on Sun Records hillbilly releases. In early February 1955, he took the melody of a commercial for Campbell's Soup as his inspiration for Elvis' fourth single, "I'm Left, You're Right, She's Gone." Other Kesler compositions that Elvis sang are: "I Forgot To Remember To Forget," "If I'm A Fool For Loving You," "Playing For Keeps" and "Thrill Of Your Love." Kesler worked as an engineer at Sun Studio in the Fifties, Sixties and Seventies. In the latter part of the Sixties, Kesler pieced together the house band that became the mainstay of American Studio's incredible string of hits.

KESSEL, BARNEY
(1923-2004)

This accomplished jazz guitarist from Muskogee, Oklahoma was called in for session work in March 1962 for the *Girls! Girls! Girls!* soundtrack. He was invited back for Elvis' LA soundtrack recording sessions up to *Paradise, Hawaiian Style* in 1966. Over the years Kessel worked with Artie Shaw, Oscar Peterson and Ben Webster, and did session work for contemporary acts including the Beach Boys. He also released some solo albums.

KID GALAHAD (EP)

Released to coincide with the opening of the movie, this six-song soundtrack EP only just made it to #30 in the charts, selling a total of 400,000 copies on initial release (it did better in the UK, ultimately becoming Elvis' highest-selling EP release). The EP versions of the song were shortened from the masters Elvis recorded in October 1961.

TRACK LISTING:
1. King Of The Whole Wide World
2. This Is Living
3. Riding The Rainbow
4. Home Is Where The Heart Is
5. I Got Lucky
6. A Whistling Tune

An album version was released as *Double Features Kid Galahad / Girls! Girls! Girls!* in 1993.

TRACK LISTING:
1. King Of The Whole Wide World
2. This Is Living
3. Riding The Rainbow
4. Home Is Where The Heart Is
5. I Got Lucky
6. A Whistling Tune
7. Girls! Girls! Girls!
8. I Don't Wanna Be Tied
9. Where Do You Come From?
10. I Don't Want To
11. We'll Be Together
12. A Boy Like Me, A Girl Like You
13. Earth Boy
14. Return To Sender
15. Because Of Love
16. Thanks To The Rolling Sea
17. Song Of The Shrimp
18. The Walls Have Ears
19. We're Coming In Loaded
20. Mama
21. Plantation Rock
22. Dainty Little Moonbeams
23. Girls! Girls! Girls! (End Title Version)

The soundtrack got the FTD alternates and outtake treatment in 2004.

KID GALAHAD

In late October 1961, Elvis began work on this musical drama, a remake of a 1937 classic starring Edward G. Robinson, Bette Davis and Humphrey Bogart. The original had been directed by Michael Curtiz (who two decades later directed Elvis in *King Creole*).

Elvis was tutored in the arts of pugilism by former world welterweight champ Mushy Callahan. To add further authenticity, reigning welterweight champ Orlando de la Fuente also had a role in the movie.

Location shooting began at Hidden Lodge, Idyllwild, California in early November 1961, before a California snowstorm sent the crew scurrying back to Hollywood the actors were relieved that they no longer had to shiver in the summer clothes required for the story.

Elvis as Walter Gulick in *Kid Galahad* (1962).

Relative newcomer Charles Bronson plays Elvis' coach in the movie. Elvis and tough guy Bronson got on famously badly. Future Oscar-winner Gig Young raised the acting level as Elvis' boxing manager but could do little to breathe life into the rather lifeless plot development.

Elvis finished work on the picture in time to head for Las Vegas that Christmas.

The song "Love Is For Lovers" was recorded but cut from the movie.

The movie opened at #9 on the *Variety* Box Office chart at the end of August 1962, and ended up grossing a little under $2 million, making it the 37th highest-grossing movie of the year. The fact that earnings from this more serious and dramatic movie were considerably lower than *Blue Hawaii* was the final proof if proof was needed for the Colonel and Hollywood executives that Elvis should be plugged exclusively into bikini/travelogue pictures, his fate for the next 18 films starting with *Girls! Girls! Girls!*, in which Elvis' character was nicknamed "Sir Galahad."

CREDITS:
The Mirisch Corporation / United Artists, Color.
Length: 95 minutes
Release date: August 11, 1962

TAGLINE:
Presley packs the screen's biggest wallop . . . with the gals . . . with the gloves . . . with the guitar!

Directed by: Phil Karlson
Produced by: David Weisbart
Written by: Francis Wallace (story), William Fay
Music by: Jeff Alexander
Cinematography by: Burnett Guffey
Film Editing by: Stuart Gilmore
Casting by: Lynn Stalmaster
Art Direction by: Cary Odell
Set Decoration by: Edward G. Boyle

CAST:
Elvis Presley — Walter Gulick, aka Kid Galahad
Gig Young — Willy Grogan
Lola Albright — Dolly Fletcher
Joan Blackman — Rose Grogan
Charles Bronson — Lew Nyack
David Lewis — Otto Danzig

Robert Emhardt — Maynard the cook
Liam Redmond — Father Higgins
Judson Pratt — Howie Zimmerman (Joie Shakes' trainer)
Ned Glass — Max Lieberman
George Mitchell — Harry Sperling, store owner
Roy Roberts — Jerry Bathgate, promoter
Michael Dante — Joie Shakes
Richard Devon — Marvin (Danzig's hood)
Jeff Morris — Ralphie (Danzig's hood)
Chris Alcaide — Danzig's Hood #3
Edward Asner — Assistant DA Frank Gerson
Mushy Callahan — Romero fight referee
Orlando De La Fuente — Ramon 'Sugarboy' Romero
Nick Dimitri — Boxer
Joe Esposito — Bit part
Frank Gerstle — Romero's manager
Joe Gray — Trainer
Harold 'Tommy' Hart — Bailey fight referee
Kip King — Round card carrier, Romero / Galahad fight
Mike Lally — Ringside fan
Jimmy Lennon Sr. — Fight announcer
George J. Lewis — Romero's trainer
Ralph Moody — Peter J. Prohosko, garage owner
Gil Perkins — Freddie
James Rawley — Doctor
Bert Remsen — Max, policeman
Jeffrey Sayre — Bevis

Elvis on the set of *Kid Galahad* (1962).

Charles Sherlock	Bailey's handler
Al Silvani	Training camp spectator
Paul Sorenson	Joe, security guard
Sara Taft	Father Higgins' Housekeeper
Hal Taggart	Fight crowd extra
Sailor Vincent	Cornerman
Ralph Volkie	Venue steward
Del 'Sonny' West	Bit part
Harry Wilson	Bailey fight spectator
Bill Zuckert	O'Grady, Finance repo man

ADDITIONAL CREW:

Alice Monte	hair stylist
Lynn Reynolds	makeup artist
Robert Relyea	unit manager
Allen Wood	production supervisor
Jerome Siegel	assistant director
Frank Agnone	property master
Lambert Day	sound
Del Harris	sound effects editor
Robert Tracy	music editor
Milt Rice	special effects
Joe Gray	stunts
Marshall M. Borden	assistant editor
Charlsie Bryant	script supervisor
Eugene Busch	dialogue coach
Irene Caine	wardrobe
Mushy Callahan	boxing advisor
Ben Henrikson	wardrobe
Colonel Tom Parker	technical advisor
Jack Spicer	best boy

Plot:

Elvis plays Walter Gulick, a soldier who returns from the army keen to find a job in his hometown of Cream Valley, in the Catskills. Opportunity knocks at a boxer's training camp run by Willy Grogan (played by Gig Young), a once-respected boxing promoter who has slipped into bad company and a gambling habit.

Walter is hired as a sparring partner for Joie Shakes (played by Michael Dante) for $5 per round. His hope is to earn enough money to open his own garage. He starts learning the ropes with trainer Lew Nyack (Charles Bronson). After taking a pasting, Walter KOs the champ and suddenly he's in training, with the name Kid Galahad and a whole fake history. Meanwhile, Willy's sister Rose (Joan Blackman) has fallen in love with the young boxer. The boxing manager's sister has good reason to worry when she learns that Walter is booked to fight in a televised bout but he has hardly had enough time to train properly. Walter is beaten to within an inch of his life, but then once again recovers to floor his opponent.

Willy blows up when he realizes that there's some funny business going on between Walter and his sister. Unchastened, Walter wants to fight one more bout; if he can defeat lethal fighter Kid Sugarboy, he'll have the money he needs to quit and open up that garage.

Local hood Otto Danzig has other ideas. When he is unable to corrupt Walter's trainer Lew, he gets his thugs to break the trainer's hands. Walter shows up and knocks their lights out. Willy thwarts Danzig's evil plan to get one of his guys to pretend to look after Walter in the ring and then cut him if he's doing too well.

Walter aces his big bout, preparing the way for the film's happy ending. Willy wins back his own girl, and then gives his personal blessing to Walter and sis Rose to get married.

Songs: "King Of The Whole Wide World," "This Is Living," "Riding The Rainbow," "Home Is Where The Heart Is," "I Got Lucky," "A Whistling Tune"

KING, B.B.
(B. RILEY B. KING, 1925)

Born in Itta Bena, Mississippi ten years before Elvis, "Blues Boy" King got his nickname while working as a DJ at WDIA in Memphis, having shortened the moniker from the original mouthful "Beale Street Blues Boy." King's virtuoso blues guitar with his trademark bent notes and powerful voice had been gracing clubs and studios for many years before he achieved mainstream success in the late Sixties, after a new generation of accomplished white blues guitarists including Eric Clapton publicly stated their debt to the King of the Blues.

In a career spanning more than sixty years, King and his guitar Lucille have placed more than 70 R&B chart singles. His best-known songs include "The Thrill Is Gone" and "Every Day I Have The Blues."

In his memoirs, King says that he and Elvis knew each other from the blues clubs on Beale Street in the early Fifties. King had already recorded for Sam Phillips at Sun before Elvis got his chance, though a contractual wrangle with RPM Records led to him leaving. Elvis shared the stage with King at the WDIA Goodwill Review of 1956. After Elvis put in a good word for King with hotel management in Las Vegas, in the Seventies King sometimes played the lounge while Elvis played the showroom.

B.B. King has continued performing well into the 2000s, and runs a successful chain of blues clubs. King was inducted into the Blues Foundation Hall of Fame in 1984, and received a Lifetime Achievement Grammy Award in 1997. He was awarded the Presidential Medal of Freedom in 2006.

B.B. KING: "I remember Elvis as a young man hanging round Sun Studios. Even then, I knew this kid had a tremendous talent."

B.B. KING: "Elvis, he was unique. And he loved the blues, it was a pity he didn't do more."

"KING CREOLE"

Another Leiber and Stoller classic that Elvis recorded on January 23, 1958 at Radio Recorders, after the session a week earlier had not produced a master for release. The chosen master was initially released on the soundtrack EP, and then soon after on the soundtrack LP.

Later album releases include *Worldwide Gold Award Hits Vol. 2, Elvis Sings Leiber & Stoller, The Great Performances*, the Nineties re-release of *Elvis' Gold Records Vol. 2, Elvis 2nd to None, Hitstory, Elvis Movies, Elvis Rock* and *Elvis at the Movies*.

Multiple alternate takes are available on 1990 LP *Essential Elvis Vol. 3.* and the 1997 re-released soundtrack album. One of these alternates also featured on *The King of Rock 'n' Roll* box set, after being a staple on bootlegs.

KING CREOLE, VOLS. 1 & 2 (EPs)

Rather than releasing an LP from a soundtrack that Elvis personally believed was simply not strong enough, RCA released two EPs to mark the movie release"one at the start of July, the other at the end. Commercially the plan was a winner as both topped the EP chart, selling around half a million copies each. The first volume stayed on the charts for 29 weeks, the longest of any Elvis EP.

TRACK LISTING:
VOL. 1
1. King Creole
2. New Orleans
3. As Long As I Have You
4. Lover Doll

VOL. 2
1. Trouble
2. Young Dreams

3. Crawfish
4. Dixieland Rock

KING CREOLE (LP)

Riding the publicity generated by Elvis' posting to Germany, in mid-September 1958 RCA released a full long-player from the movie, which apart from "Steadfast, Loyal And True" was all material previously released on EPs. The LP just missed out on the #1 spot, selling 250,000 copies over 15 weeks on the chart.

TRACK LISTING:
1. King Creole
2. As Long As I Have You
3. Hard Headed Woman
4. Trouble
5. Dixieland Rock
6. Don't Ask Me Why
7. Lover Doll
8. Crawfish
9. Young Dreams
10. Steadfast, Loyal And True
11. New Orleans

RCA re-released the album in 1997 with movie versions of the songs and alternate takes ("King Creole," "As Long As I Have You," "Danny," "Lover Doll," "Steadfast Loyal And True," and "King Creole").

KING CREOLE

Elvis' name was first mooted for the starring role in this movie in January 1957, under the working title *Sing, You Sinners.*

Elvis reported for preproduction on January 13, 1958, making use of a two-month deferral period before he went into the Army.

Producer Hal Wallis had initially purchased the movie rights to Harold Robbins' novel *A Stone for Danny Fisher* with either Ben Gazzara or James Dean in mind, depending on source. A stage version of the story had already been a success off-Broadway.

For Elvis, the lead character's profession was changed from a boxer to a singer, and the location shifted from New York to New Orleans. The decision to change the working title to *King Creole* was based as much on the fact that the Leiber/Stoller soundtrack song was the strongest of the tunes recorded for the movie as any other criterion.

Paramount put Elvis in the dressing room recently vacated by Anna Magnani.

Portions of the movie were filmed on location in New Orleans. Elvis' songs blend a Dixieland feel with his customary rock. Locations included the French Quarter and Lake Pontchartrain.

Good-girl love interest Dolores Hart had also featured opposite Elvis in *Loving You.* Bad-girl love interest Carolyn Jones later played Morticia in *The Addams Family*; she had previously played small roles in Marilyn Monroe vehicle *The Seven Year Itch* and James Dean movie *East of Eden.*

When Elvis saw an early finished copy of the movie, he was pleased that at last he had had a real chance to do some acting he told director Michael Curtiz as much when they finished production. As ever, more and more songs were added to the mix as production unfolded. A number of critics who had previously panned Elvis' acting abilities gave him rave reviews. Elvis ever after cited *King Creole* as the best of his screen performances.

As well as Elvis' 11 songs, Liliane Montevecchi delivered "Banana." "Danny," which at an early stage was earmarked as the title track, was cut from the movie and soundtrack releases.

The movie went on nationwide release on July 2, 1958, with Elvis out on military service. Though it reached #5 on the *Variety* National

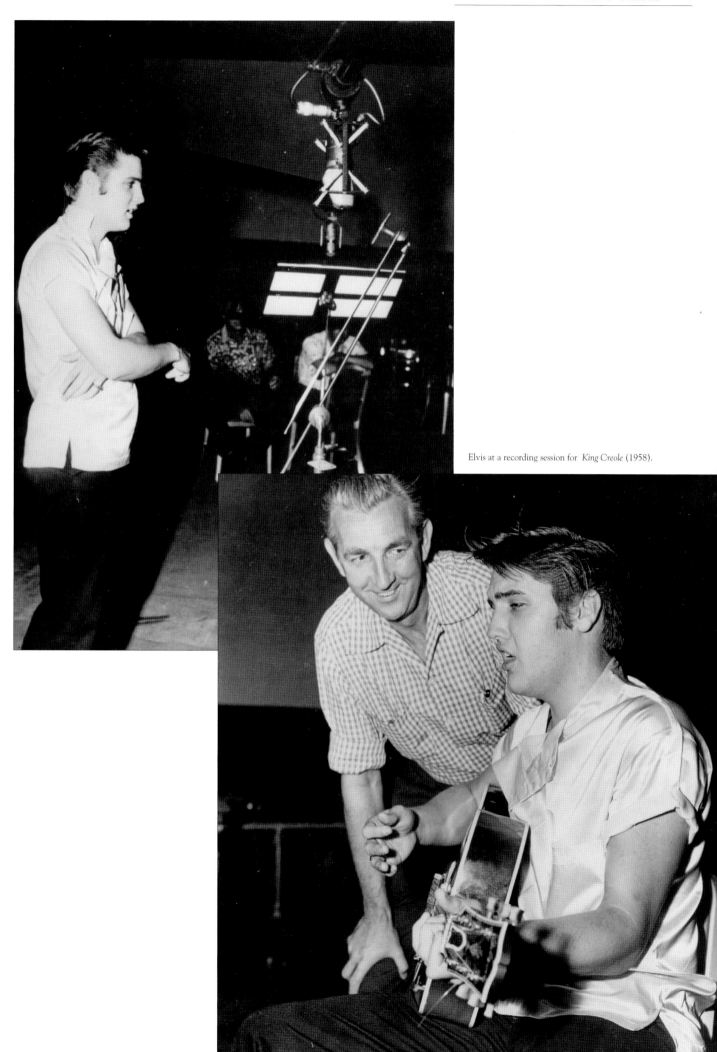

Elvis at a recording session for *King Creole* (1958).

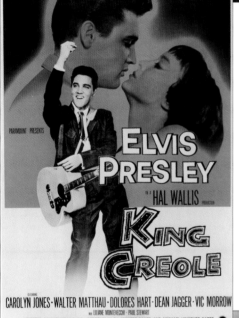

ABOVE: Elvis as Danny Fisher, with Walter Matthau as Maxie Fields in *King Creole*, 1958.

BELOW: Elvis with Vic Morrow as Shark in *King Creole*.

Box Office chart, the movie started the trend for Elvis' more critically-acclaimed and purely dramatic roles doing less well at the box office than his frothier fare.

HOWARD THOMPSON in the *New York Times*: "Elvis Presley can act."

ERIC BRAUN: "Elvis was never more sensitive or dynamic."

Book:
 Inside King Creole, by Ger Rijff, Jean-Paul Commandeur and Glen Johnson, Tutti Frutti, 1999

CREDITS:
Paramount, Black and White
Length: 116 minutes
Release date: July 2, 1958

TAGLINE:
Back on screen for the first time in a year!

Directed by: Michael Curtiz
Produced by: Hal B. Wallis
Associate producer: Paul Nathan
Written by: Harold Robbins
    (novel *A Stone for Danny Fisher*),
    Herbert Baker and Michael V. Gazzo
Music by: Walter Scharf
Cinematography by: Russell Harlan
Art Direction by: J. McMillan Johnson, Hal Pereira
Set Decoration by: Sam Comer, Frank R. McKelvy
Costume Design by: Edith Head

CAST:

Elvis Presley	Danny Fisher
Carolyn Jones	Ronnie
Walter Matthau	Maxie Fields
Dolores Hart	Nellie
Dean Jagger	Mr. Fisher
Liliane Montevecchi	Forty Nina
Vic Morrow	Shark
Paul Stewart	Charlie LeGrand
Jan Shepard	Mimi Fisher
Brian Hutton	Sal
Jack Grinnage	Dummy
Dick Winslow	Eddie Burton
Raymond Bailey	Mr. Evans
Val Avery	Ralph
Hazel Boyne	Woman who asks for water
Sam Buffington	Dr. Michael Cabot
Candy Candido	Doorman at the King Creole night club
Lilyan Chauvin	Catherine
Charles Evans	Mr. Furst, Drug store manager
Franklyn Farnum	Bit part
Barbara Gayle	Sales girl
Ned Glass	Hotel desk clerk
Cliff Gleaves	Bit part
Rita Green	Hat check girl
Helene Hatch	Mrs. Pearson
Kay Haydn	Girl
Trustin Howard	Master of Ceremonies at the King Creole
John Indrisano	Collector
Jackie Joseph	Sales girl
Alexander Lockwood	Dr. Patrick
Walter Merrill	Mr. McIntyre
Jacqueline Park	Sales girl
Ziva Rodann	Entertainer
Ric Roman	Eddie
Tony Russel	Chico, Bartender at the Blue Shade night club
Susanne Sidney	Sales girl
Blanche Thomas	Woman
Nina Vaughn	Bit part
Kitty White	Street vendor
Fred Winston	Shark's brother

ADDITIONAL CREW:

Nellie Manley	hair stylist
Wally Westmore	makeup supervisor
Michael Moore	assistant director
Charles Grenzbach	sound recorder
Harold Lewis	sound recorder
John C. Hammell	music editor
John P. Fulton	special photographic effects
Farciot Edouart	process photographer
Warren Low	supervising editor
Charles O'Curran	musical number staging
Colonel Tom Parker	technical advisor
Norman Stuart	dialogue coach

Plot:

Elvis is Danny Fisher, a troubled teenager with an attitude. He's doing badly at school not just because he needs to earn money by odd-jobbing in French Quarter bars, but because he has an unemployed and unsympathetic father (played by Dean Jagger).

As in *Jailhouse Rock,* Elvis' character gets in trouble through his gallant efforts to protect a woman (in this case alcoholic gangster's moll Ronnie, played by Carolyn Jones). First, he's kicked out of school, then he's waylaid by a gang, but he fights back so spiritedly that that they ask him to join. Singing "Lover Doll" to distract the victims while his new-found pals rob a store and then a diner, Danny manages to get a date with sympathetic waitress Nellie (played by Dolores Hart).

Danny gets his break as a real singer, then Charlie LeGrand (Paul Stewart) offers him a regular gig at his night club, the King Creole. Family troubles only delay his acceptance. When he takes to the stage, he is a big hit. Local gangster Maxie Fields (played by Walter Matthau) attempts to coerce Danny into coming to sing at his competing club, but Danny resists. Ronnie warns Danny that Maxie is not a man to be crossed, and advises him to clear out of town. Danny stays, his dad takes a beating, and then gangster Maxie Fields steps in to pay for the operation Danny's father now needs, even though it was he who ordered the beating.

Danny gives Maxie Field a pasting, then Maxie Fields has his boys beat Danny to within an inch of his life. Ronnie nurses Danny back to health; Danny requites her love, despite being engaged to the mild-mannered Nellie. When gangster Maxie catches up with them, he dispatches Ronnie to a lingering death in Danny's arms, but rather than killing Danny too, winds up killing himself. Danny finishes with a number at the nightclub, chastened and ready for the customary happy ending of wedding bells.

Songs: "Crawfish," "Steadfast Loyal And True," "Lover Doll," "Trouble," "Dixieland Rock," "Young Dreams," "New Orleans," "Hard Headed Woman," "King Creole," "Don't Ask Me Why," "As Long As I Have You"

KING, MARTIN LUTHER
(1929-1968)

The Baptist minister and 1964 Nobel Peace Prize winner famous for his civil rights activism was assassinated on the balcony of his room at the Lorraine Motel, Memphis on April 4, 1968. Elvis was shocked by the event, and appalled that it could have happened in his home town.

Over the years, Elvis was known to declaim Martin Luther King's famous "I Have a Dream" speech, which King pronounced at the Lincoln Memorial in 1963. Elvis greatly admired the Reverend, and came close to meeting him in 1966. Elvis' *Live a Little, Love a Little* co-star Celeste Yarnall has said that Elvis broke down crying in her arms when Martin Luther King Jr.'s funeral was shown on TV.

KING OF ROCK AND ROLL, THE
—THE ESSENTIAL 50s MASTERS

A 5-disc set of Elvis tracks, issued initially in 1992, chronologically ordering Elvis output from his rock 'n' roll heyday. The premium-priced collector's box leavened with extras was so eagerly awaited by Elvis fans that it went platinum.

TRACK LISTING:

DISC 1:
1. My Happiness
2. That's All Right
3. I Love You Because
4. Harbor Lights
5. Blue Moon Of Kentucky
6. Blue Moon
7. Tomorrow Night
8. I'll Never Let You Go (Little Darlin')
9. I Don't Care If The Sun Don't Shine
10. Just Because
11. Good Rockin' Tonight
12. Milkcow Blues Boogie
13. You're A Heartbreaker
14. Baby Let's Play House
15. I'm Left, You're Right, She's Gone
16. Mystery Train
17. I Forgot To Remember To Forget
18. Tryin' To Get To You
19. When It Rains, It Really Pours
20. I Got A Woman
21. Heartbreak Hotel
22. Money Honey
23. I'm Counting On You
24. I Was The One
25. Blue Suede Shoes
26. My Baby Left Me
27. One-Sided Love Affair
28. So Glad You're Mine
29. I'm Gonna Sit Right Down And Cry (Over You)
30. Tutti Frutti

DISC 2:
1. Lawdy, Miss Clawdy
2. Shake, Rattle And Roll
3. I Want You, I Need You, I Love You
4. Hound Dog
5. Don't Be Cruel
6. Any Way You Want Me (That's How I Will Be)
7. We're Gonna Move
8. Love Me Tender
9. Poor Boy
10. Let Me
11. Playing For Keeps
12. Love Me
13. Paralyzed
14. How Do You Think I Feel
15. How's The World Treating You
16. When My Blue Moon Turns To Gold Again
17. Long Tall Sally
18. Old Shep
19. Too Much
20. Anyplace Is Paradise
21. Ready Teddy
22. First In Line
23. Rip It Up
24. I Believe
25. Tell Me Why
26. Got A Lot O' Livin' To Do!
27. All Shook Up
28. Mean Woman Blues
29. (There'll Be) Peace In The Valley (For Me)

DISC 3:
1. That's When Your Heartaches Begin
2. Take My Hand, Precious Lord
3. It Is No Secret (What God Can Do)
4. Blueberry Hill

5. Have I Told You Lately That I Love You
6. Is It So Strange
7. Party
8. Lonesome Cowboy
9. Hot Dog
10. One Night Of Sin
11. (Let Me Be Your) Teddy Bear
12. Don't Leave Me Now
13. I Beg Of You
14. One Night
15. True Love
16. I Need You So
17. Loving You
18. When It Rains, It Really Pours
19. Jailhouse Rock
20. Young And Beautiful
21. I Want To Be Free
22. (You're So Square) Baby I Don't Care
23. Don't Leave Me Now
24. Blue Christmas
25. White Christmas
26. Here Comes Santa Claus (Right Down Santa Claus Lane)
27. Silent Night
28. O Little Town Of Bethlehem
29. Santa Bring My Baby Back (To Me)
30. Santa Claus Is Back In Town
31. I'll Be Home For Christmas

DISC 4:
1. Treat Me Nice
2. My Wish Came True
3. Don't
4. Danny
5. Hard Headed Woman
6. Trouble
7. New Orleans
8. Crawfish
9. Dixieland Rock
10. Lover Doll
11. Don't Ask Me Why
12. As Long As I Have You
13. King Creole
14. Young Dreams
15. Steadfast, Loyal And True
16. Doncha' Think It's Time
17. Your Cheatin' Heart
18. Wear My Ring Around Your Neck
19. I Need Your Love Tonight
20. A Big Hunk O' Love
21. Ain't That Loving You Baby
22. (Now And Then There's) A Fool Such As I
23. I Got Stung
24. Interview With Elvis (Aug. 22, 1958)

DISC 5:
1. That's When Your Heartaches Begin
2. Fool, Fool, Fool
3. Tweedlee Dee
4. Maybellene
5. Shake, Rattle And Roll
6. Blue Moon Of Kentucky
7. Blue Moon
8. I'm Left, You're Right, She's Gone
9. Reconsider Baby
10. Lawdy, Miss Clawdy
11. Shake, Rattle And Roll
12. I Want You, I Need You, I Love You
13. Heartbreak Hotel
14. Long Tall Sally
15. Blue Suede Shoes
16. Money Honey
17. We're Gonna Move
18. Old Shep
19. I Beg Of You
20. Loving You (slow version)
21. Loving You (fast version)
22. Young And Beautiful
23. I Want To Be Free
24. King Creole
25. As Long As I Have You
26. Ain't That Loving You Baby (fast version)

"KING OF THE WHOLE WIDE WORLD"

A rare raunchy sax on an Elvis tune in this Ruth Batchelor / Bob Roberts rocker that Elvis put down at Radio Recorders for the Kid Galahad soundtrack and EP on October 27, 1961. It took Elvis over thirty takes before he got to where he wanted to go. The song featured over the opening credits in the movie.

Album releases began with *C'mon Everybody*, before reissues on *Command Performances*, the *Double Features* release for the movie, CD reissues of *Elvis' Golden Records Vol. 3.* and *Elvis at the Movies*.

Bootlegs of the song's many alternates and out-takes were in circulation for a long time before one with light-spirited banter was officially released on *Today, Tomorrow And Forever*, and later on FTD albums *Out In Hollywood* and *Kid Galahad*.

KINGSLEY, JIMMY

A member of Elvis' entourage from 1960 for a few years, who stayed on in LA to become a stunt man. He died in 1989.

KIRKHAM, MILLIE

Elvis was so impressed with this soprano singer's voice when he heard her on Ferlin Husky song "Gone" that he asked RCA executive Steve Sholes to call her in to work on "Blue Christmas" in 1957. Kirkham worked with Elvis on and off for the next eighteen years. She was in good voice on the *His Hand In Mine* gospel album recorded in 1960, and continued to hit the high notes for the rest of the Sixties. She joined him on stage in the summer of 1970, after he returned to live performing at the International Hotel; she appears in the concert documentary *Elvis: That's The Way It Is*.

Kathy Westmoreland took over soprano duties for the rest of the Seventies. Kirkham made a brief return in 1975, singing on tracks for Elvis' *Today* album and nearly going out as an emergency replacement back-up singer when Elvis' regulars walked out later that year.

"KISMET"

Elvis recorded this Sid Tepper / Roy C. Bennett ballad for *Harum Scarum* on February 25, 1965 in Nashville. The first two takes from the session are extras on the 2003 FTD updated movie soundtrack release.

"KISS ME QUICK"

Elvis recorded this Doc Pomus / Mort Shuman composition on June 25, 1961 in Nashville. The song was first released as the opening track on the *Pot Luck* album a year or so later. When it came out as a single in April 1964 with "Suspicion" on the B-side, it failed to make it any higher than #34. The attenuating factors that both tracks had already appeared on the *Pot Luck* album, and that the B-side was already riding high in the charts, but in a version sung by Terry Stafford did not make up for the fact that it was the worst selling single Elvis had ever released on RCA, and this at a time when The Beatles were taking the States by storm.

The song later appeared on *Elvis Sings Mort Shuman & Doc Pomus* and *From Nashville to Memphis*.

Two alternate takes came out in 2003, on *Elvis: Close Up* and FTD album *Studio B: Nashville Outtakes*; a further alternate is on the FTD *Pot Luck* release.

"KISSIN' COUSINS"

Elvis recorded this Fred Wise / Randy Starr composition in October 1963, to be released as a single in February 1964, with "It Hurts Me" on the B-Side. It sold around 750,000 copies on initial release, and made it up to #12 on the *Billboard* charts during its nine-week arc. It ultimately went gold.

After the soundtrack album, the song has appeared on *Worldwide Gold Award Hits Vol. 1*, the *Double Features* soundtrack release, the *Elvis' Gold Records Vol. 4* CD reissue, *Command Performances*, *Hitstory*, *Elvis Movies* and *Elvis at the Movies*.

"KISSIN' COUSINS NO. 2"

This Giant / Baum / Kaye track wasn't used as the title song but made it onto the movie soundtrack album (with Elvis' voice doubled up, one for each character) and the closing credits. It was recorded in September 1963 in Nashville, though Elvis dubbed his vocals on October 10 or 11 in LA.

It has since appeared on the 1993 *Double Features* soundtrack release. An alternate take appeared on 2001 FTD album *Silver Screen Stereo* (the Hillbilly overdub).

KISSIN' COUSINS (LP)

This soundtrack album was released soon after the movie in spring 1964, with two studio songs in addition to the soundtrack material. It stayed on the charts for over six months, peaking at #6 and selling around 300,000 copies.

TRACK LISTING:
1. Kissin' Cousins (#2)
2. Smokey Mountain Boy
3. There's Gold In The Mountains
4. One Boy, Two Little Girls
5. Catchin' On Fast
6. Tender Feeling
7. Anyone (Could Fall in Love With You)
8. Barefoot Ballad
9. Once Is Enough
10. Kissin' Cousins
11. Echoes Of Love
12. (It's A) Long Lonely Highway

This soundtrack received the *Double Feature* reissue treatment with *Clambake* and *Stay Away, Joe* in 1993.

TRACK LISTING:
1. Kissin' Cousins (#2)
2. Smoky Mountain Boy
3. There's Gold In The Mountains
4. One Boy, Two Little Girls
5. Catchin' On Fast
6. Tender Feeling
7. Anyone (Could Fall In Love With You)
8. Barefoot Ballad
9. Once Is Enough
10. Kissin' Cousins
11. Clambake
12. Who Needs Money
13. A House That Has Everything
14. Confidence
15. Hey, Hey, Hey
16. You Don't Know Me
17. The Girl I Never Loved

18. How Can You Lose What You Never Had
19. Clambake (reprise)
20. Stay Away, Joe
21. Dominick
22. All I Needed Was The Rain
23. Goin' Home
24. Stay Away

KISSIN' COUSINS

Elvis arrived in LA for preproduction on the MGM lot in early October 1963 for his first true low-budget quickie that took only 17 days to shoot, despite the fact that every scene had to be shot twice: Elvis played one role opposite stand-in Lance LeGault, then they switched wigs and did the scene the other way round final editing was not quite tight enough to prevent a glimpse or two of the stand-in's face. Elvis later said that if he'd know what a pain in the ass the shooting would have been, he might have turned the movie down.

Location shooting was at Big Bear mountain, near Los Angeles.

After the relatively high budget of previous movie *Viva Las Vegas*, the Colonel kept the budget on a tight reign. With Sam Katzman installed as producer, the whole project came in at $1.3 million, of which the majority went to the star. Katzman and director Gene Nelson had just completed teen flick *Hootenanny Hoot*, featuring among others Johnny Cash.

Breaking from standard Elvis practice, the songs in this movie were selected by Gene Nelson and Fred Karger. The soundtrack was unusually recorded in Nashville, with Elvis doing overdubs on the MGM soundstage. Director Gene Nelson played congas on the soundtrack. One song, "Anyone (Could Fall In Love With You)," was cut.

The head of the 13-strong Kittyhawk tribe of girls was played by Ronald Reagan's daughter, Maureen. The rather strong supporting cast included Emmy winner Glenda Farrell, and Oscar, Tony and Emmy winner Jack Albertson.

Bizarrely, the film title featured in Elvis' second ever movie, 1957 picture *Loving You*, in on-screen newspaper headline "That's Kissin', Cousins."

The movie premiered on March 6, 1964 in Phoenix and went on national release soon after. It opened at #11 on the National Box Office Survey. *Kissin' Cousins* wound up the 26th highest-grossing movie of the year, closing in on $3 million.

Publicity included free candy kisses for cinemagoers. Colonel Parker later toyed with the idea of making a TV series from the movie's premise.

Screenwriters Gene Nelson and Gerald Drayson Adams were nominated for the WGA best American musical award.

CREDITS:
MGM, Color.
Length: 96 minutes
Release date: March 6, 1964

TAGLINES:
Elvis has a blond-haired twin the gals swoon over
Elvis feudin', Elvis lovin', Elvis swingin' . . . as he joins his mountain kinfolk for a hey, hey, hayride to good ol' mountain music!

Directed by: Gene Nelson
Produced by: Sam Katzman
Written by: Gerald Drayson Adams, Gene Nelson
Cinematography by: Ellis W. Carter
Film Editing by: Ben Lewis
Art Direction by: George W. Davis, Eddie Imazu
Set Decoration by: Budd Friend. Henry Grace, Wayne Hartunian

CAST:
Elvis Presley	Josh Morgan / Jodie Tatum
Arthur O'Connell	Pappy Tatum
Glenda Farrell	Ma Tatum
Jack Albertson	Capt. Robert Jason Salbo
Pamela Austin	Selena Tatum
Cynthia Pepper	Cpl. Midge Riley
Yvonne Craig	Azalea Tatum
Donald Woods	Gen. Alvin Donford
Tommy Farrell	M. Sgt. William George Bailey
Beverly Powers	Trudy
Hortense Petra	Dixie Cate
Robert Stone	General's aide
Robert Carson	Gen. Sam Kruger
Joe Esposito	Mike
Gail Ganley	Hillbilly dancer
Teri Garr	Extra
Wayne Hartunian	Hillbilly dancer
Lonni Lees	Minnie
Lance LeGault	Elvis' double
Kent McCord	Extra
Maureen Reagan	Lorraine (leader of the Kittyhawks)
Joan Staley	Jonesy
W.J. Vincent	Hairy Willie

ADDITIONAL CREW:
Sydney Guilaroff	hair stylist
William Tuttle	makeup artist
Eli Dunn	assistant director
Franklin Milton	sound
Van Allen James	sound editor
Lance LeGault	stunts
Harold Belfer	choreographer
Fred Karger	musical director
Colonel Tom Parker.	technical advisor

Plot:

Elvis is Lt. Josh Morgan, a Tennessee pilot dispatched by the US Air Force to persuade the moonshine-making Tatum family to give up their land on Big Smokey Mountain so that the nation can build a much-needed missile base (the story was drafted not long after the Cuban missile crisis).

Josh and his platoon receive a hostile reception, only to find out that they are taking fire from two pretty girls, Selena (Pamela Austin) and Azalea Tatum (Yvonne Craig), who jump on Josh

Elvis as Josh Morgan and Elvis as Jodie Tatum in *Kissin' Cousins* (1964).

when they learn he's a distant cousin. Walking proof of kin arrives in the form of Jodie Tatum, the girls' brother, played by none other than Elvis in a blond wig.

The platoon is invited back to the Tatums for a bumper meal of possum tails and worse. Josh Morgan's commanding officer Captain Salbo (played by Jack Albertson) falls ill; the family still refuses to sign away its property. The Kittyhawks a tribe of man-starved wild girls need to be fended off by the Tatum family, much to the disappointment of the platoon soldiers. Meanwhile, Jodie becomes sweet on army stenographer Midge Riley (played by Cynthia Pepper).

Josh has an idea that the best way to a girl's heart is new clothes. He gets the Army to buy the

Tatum girls some new duds but while they're in town they let slip that the Air Force wants to build a missile base. Ma Tatum (played by Glenda Farrell) is not happy when the girls return from town and model their new bikinis.

Meanwhile, back in Washington, General Donford (Donald Woods) is enraged to see the supposedly secret missile base plastered all over the newspapers and decides to sort the mess out himself. The Kittyhawks kidnap the platoon men one by one, but are then enlisted by Captain Salbo to prevent the General from reaching the Tatum's place. Ma Tatum calls on the Air Force men to help track down Pa Tatum (Arthur O'Connell) who has failed to return from a hunting trip. Josh saves the day, occasioning a great deal of partying back at the ranch, fueled by general high spirits and "Mountain Maidens' Breath" moonshine.

When the furious General finally arrives, he is placated by Ma's home cooking and moonshine. Pappy agrees to rent half the mountain to the nation, on condition that no government official or tax officer is allowed onto the Tatum side of the mountain. Cue declarations of marrying intent all round (Josh picks Azalea), more celebration and the prospect of everybody living happily ever after.

Songs: "Kissin' Cousins," "Smokey Mountain Boy," "One Boy Two Little Girls," "Catchin' On Fast," "Tender Feeling," "Barefoot Ballad," "Once Is Enough"

KLEIN, GEORGE
(b. 1935)

Elvis met George Klein at Humes High School the year he moved to Memphis from Tupelo. Before High School was over, Klein had become president of Elvis' class, school yearbook editor and all-round overachiever. He became a DJ after apprenticing to Dewey Phillips, and quickly made a name for himself in and around Memphis.

A friend of Elvis' for the duration, the well-connected Klein introduced a number of guys to Elvis who joined his inner circle, and over the years more than one important female companion.

Known to Elvis as "D.J." (and later to his radio fans as G.K.), Klein traveled with Elvis to New York in 1956, accompanied him to the WDIA Goodwill Revue back in Memphis, and from 1957 until Elvis left for the Army, was part of Elvis' paid entourage. Elvis is said to have paid for a nose job. After Elvis' return from Germany, Klein pursued his media career and remained close friends with Elvis, often visiting with him at Graceland.

In the Sixties, Klein became director of WHBQ in Memphis and through his own TV show, "Talent Party," was a major local figure in Memphis. He got to know large numbers of musicians through his work, and was something of a conduit for Elvis to meet people in the music industry. In 1966 Klein vacationed in LA while Elvis was working on his latest movie, *Double Trouble* (in which Klein landed a bit part), and introduced Elvis both to James Brown and Jackie Wilson. Klein also had a bit part in *Frankie and Johnny*. Elvis' Christmas gift to his pal that year was a yellow Cadillac convertible; the year before it had been an initialed gold wristwatch.

George Klein was one of very few of Elvis' friends to be invited to Elvis' wedding in May 1967. Klein reciprocated at his own wedding to longtime girlfriend Barbara Little in Las Vegas on December 5, 1970, where Elvis was best man. Elvis flew out his family out for the occasion and gave Klein use of his suite at the International Hotel.

Klein takes credit for introducing Elvis to then Miss Tennessee Linda Thompson in July 1972 . . . though the lady in question remembers otherwise. Four years later Klein tried to make lightning strike twice when he brought round then current Miss Tennessee, Terry Alden, and her younger sisters Rosemary and Ginger. Elvis eschewed Miss Tennessee for younger sister Ginger, herself the reigning Miss Mid-South Fair / Miss Traffic Safety.

Elvis placed a call to the President of the United States, Jimmy Carter, in June 1977 to try and intercede on Klein's behalf in a federal case against him for mail fraud, of which he was later found guilty.

George Klein was a pallbearer at Elvis' funeral. Since Elvis' death, Klein has been a regular at Elvis commemorative events. Klein has appeared in an Elvis-themed movies *Heartbreak Hotel* and *Finding Graceland*, and featured in a number of Elvis documentaries. He continues to be a philanthropist and fundraiser for good causes.

In recent years, Klein has worked as a host at the Horseshoe Casino in town. He has also been known to take celebrity guests such as Tom Jones round Graceland, and hosts a weekly syndicated Elvis radio show, *George Klein's Original Elvis Hour,* which is also on Sirius radio.

At the time of writing, Klein was working on his Elvis book *Elvis Presley: The Family Album.*

JERRY SCHILLING: "There are no barriers to the love for GK in this city."

KNECHTEL, LARRY
(B. 1940)

This versatile musician played bass on Elvis' soundtrack session for *Live a Little, Love a Little* in 1968, and bass and keyboards on the Arena segment of Elvis' NBC TV Special later that same year.

Knechtel got his break with Duane Eddy, and later worked with the Beach Boys and Simon & Garfunkel (his is the piano on "Like A Bridge Over Troubled Water"). In the Seventies he played with Bread, and then continued to be much in demand as a session musician.

"KNOWN ONLY TO HIM"

Elvis explored the upper reaches of his vocal range when he laid down this song"a favorite not just for Elvis but for many gospel groups, written by Stuart Hamblen in the early Fifties"on October 30, 1960 at Studio B in Nashville, for his second gospel album *His Hand In Mine.* He's also reputed to have sung the song at his gospel only show in De Leon, Texas on July 4, 1955.

In 1966 the song came out as the B-side to "Joshua Fit the Battle," but failed to chart.

Friend and colleague Jake Hess sang this song at Elvis' funeral eleven years later.

Posthumous releases include *He Walks Beside Me,* gospel anthologies *Amazing Grace* and *Peace In The Valley,* and *Christmas Peace.*

Alternate takes from the original recording session are on FTD releases *Easter Special* and *His Hand In Mine.*

KOIZUMI, JUNICHIRO
(B. 1942)

The Prime Minister of Japan from 2001 to 2006 is Elvis' most high-profile fan in Asia. He shares a birthday with Elvis, has released a popular CD of his favorite Elvis songs, and in front of the cameras dueted with Tom Cruise on "I Want You, I Need You, I Love You."

At the end of Koizumi's 2006 State trip to the US, he and President Bush flew to Memphis for an official visit to Graceland, eating fried peanut butter and banana sandwiches on Air Force One on the way. Koizumi was given a personal tour of Elvis' home by Priscilla and Lisa Marie, and broke into "Love Me Tender" in the Jungle Room.

JUNICHIRO KOIZUMI, on visiting Graceland: "It's like a dream . . .. There's Elvis song: To Dream Impossible (he sings). My dream came true . . .. Thank you very much for treating me nice . . .."

JUNICHIRO KOIZUMI'S FAVORITES:

I Want You, I Need You, I Love You; Wear My Ring Around Your Neck; I Was The One; Any Way You Want Me; Have I Told You Lately That I Love You; That's When Your Heartaches Begin; Don't; (Now And Then There's) A Fool Such As I; It's Now Or Never; Are You Lonesome Tonight?; No More; Can't Help Falling In Love; The Wonder Of You; Bridge Over Troubled Water; You Don't Have To Say You Love Me; The First Time Ever I Saw Your Face; Amazing Grace; An American Trilogy; The Impossible Dream; Separate Ways; You Gave Me A Mountain; My Boy; An Evening Prayer; If I Can Dream; Hawaiian Wedding Song.

KRISTOFFERSON, KRIS
(B. KRISTOFFER KRISTOFFERSON, 1936)

Born in Brownsville, Texas on June 22, 1936, Kristofferson followed his Air Force General father into the services (as an Army helicopter pilot) after studying at Oxford on a Rhodes Scholarship. It was in England that he began his singing career under the name Kris Carson.

Five years after joining the Army he abandoned the certainty of a Captain's wage to try his hand as a songwriter in Nashville. It took several years of struggle before his song "Me And Bobby McGee" had chart success with Roger Miller. By the time Janis Joplin's posthumous release of that same tune went to #1 on the *Billboard* Top 100 in 1971, Kristofferson was a popular Country artist in his own right, with songs like "Help Me Make It Through The Night" and "For The Good Times," both of which Elvis covered (along with "Why Me Lord").

Kristofferson's film career took off in the early Seventies, peaking with *Alice Doesn't Live Here Anymore* and *A Star Is Born,* a movie in which the lead role had originally been offered to Elvis. Kristofferson's film career continued strongly through to the Eighties.

"KU-U-I-PO"

A laid-back Hugo Peretti/Luigi Creatore/George Weiss composition that Elvis sang in *Blue Hawaii,* recorded at Radio Recorders in Hollywood on March 21, 1961 and released on the soundtrack LP.

Elvis made an after-show recording of the song"whose title translates as "Hawaiian sweetheart" on Honolulu following the January 1973 satellite broadcast performance, for inclusion in the US version of the "live" broadcast.

This recording wasn't released until 1978, on *Mahalo From Elvis.* It has since appeared on later releases of the *Aloha From Hawaii Via Satellite* album, *The Alternate Aloha* and bootlegs.

Alternate takes from the '61 studio session came out on *Elvis: Close Up.*

LACKER, MARTY
(B. 1937)

Lacker's family moved to Memphis in 1952 from New York. Lacker knew Elvis from Humes High School but had no idea that he was a musician, let alone a future star. He was amazed when he heard Dewey Phillips play Elvis on the airwaves for the first time in July 1954, and announce that "That's All Right (Mama)" was by a boy from Humes called Elvis Presley. Lacker saw Elvis perform for the first time a couple of months later, when he was the entertainment for the inauguration of the brand new Katz Drugstore in Memphis.

Lacker hadn't seen Elvis for a couple of years when George Klein asked him to come up with him to Graceland one evening in 1957. Elvis was as friendly as he had been before he became famous, and told Marty he could come back any time he wanted by Marty's accounts, that wound up being most nights that Elvis was in town.

Marty Lacker was working in radio in 1961 before Elvis put him on the payroll. The first movie he traveled for was *Kid Galahad* in late 1961. Lacker had to think long and hard before he went along, because unlike most of the Memphis Mafia, he had a wife and a child. In July 1962 Lacker ceased working for Elvis to take a job at Memphis radio station WHBQ; he later ran a radio station in Knoxville.

Lacker rejoined the gang and was promoted to "foreman" after Elvis fired Joe Esposito in the summer of 1964. He has said that his job title was "Chief Personal Aide" from 1961-1968, though in 1967 the Colonel demoted him to running "Special Projects." In 1964, Marty, his wife Patsy and their children Sheri, Angie and Marc lived in a converted garage at Graceland. They moved out in 1966.

Initially, the Colonel had so much faith in Lacker that he referred to him as "Colonel, Jr." Elvis referred to him as "Moon," in reference to his bald spot. When the Colonel become concerned at Elvis' increasing reluctance to fulfill his soundtrack recording obligations, he encouraged Lacker to make sure that he allowed plenty of time to ensure that Elvis traveled from Memphis when he needed to. The Colonel's expectation was that Lacker called every day, as Joe Esposito had done. Lacker has stated in interviews that he felt that his loyalty lay more with Elvis than with the Colonel.

The situation changed in March 1967, when it took a concerted struggle to get Elvis even to go to LA, let alone report to the studios to start work on *Clambake*. After Elvis had an accident and suffered concussion, the Colonel took charge of the situation, insisted on Elvis shaping up, and reinstated Joe Esposito as sole foreman.

Lacker was one of two best men at Elvis' wedding to Priscilla in May 1967. Later that year he left the Elvis payroll and started a record company in Memphis (where he helped to promote Rita Coolidge's early career). He moved on to work at American Studio, and was one of the guys who was most insistent on Elvis doing a session there in January 1969. Lacker later ran a music publishing company, and tried to get Elvis more interesting material. In 1973, Lacker suggested to Elvis that he fulfill his latest RCA recording commitments at the Stax studio in Memphis, where he was then working, not far from Graceland on MacLemore Ave. Lacker continued to travel with Elvis on and off until midway through 1976.

Books:
Elvis: Portrait of a Friend, by Marty Lacker, Patsy Lacker, and Leslie S. Smith, Wimmer Brother Books, 1979
Elvis Aaron Presley: Revelations from the Memphis Mafia, by Alanna Nash, with Billy Smith, Marty Lacker and Lamar Fike, HarperCollins, 1995

"LADY LOVES ME, THE"

Elvis recorded this feisty Sid Tepper / Roy C. Bennett duet with Ann-Margret at Radio Recorders on July 11, 1963 for *Viva Las Vegas*. The song was originally a frontrunner to be the title track for the movie before the picture's title changed.

Owing to the Colonel's concerns about Elvis sharing billing, "The Lady Loves Me" was kept off the soundtrack EP and for many years was only available on bootlegs. The contrary duet finally saw official release in 1983, on *Elvis: A Legendary Performer, Vol. 4*. It has since been included on the *Double Features* issue for *Viva Las Vegas*. Alternate takes are on FTD issues *Silver Screen Stereo* and *Viva Las Vegas*.

"LADY MADONNA"

Though never released during Elvis' lifetime, he gave this Lennon / McCartney song a run-through on May 17, 1971 at Studio B in Nashville. His version was not released until Nineties box set *Walk A Mile In My Shoes*. An instrumental version has appeared on bootlegs.

LANDON, GRELUN
(1923-2004)

In the Fifties, Grelun Landon was a representative of song publisher Hill & Range, with responsibility for many Grand Ole Opry stars. In May 1955, Landon was one of the first music industry executives to see unknown phenomenon Elvis Presley perform, at the Jimmie Rodgers Memorial Celebration. He immediately alerted his bosses, the Aberbach brothers, and began negotiations about putting together a song folio, combining sheet music and promotional photos. Landon was with Elvis when he was in New York for his TV debut in early 1956.

Landon moved on to RCA, where he served as head of publicity, West Coast, for a long spell. In 1973, Landon supervised Elvis' Palm Springs recording session. He co-authored *The Encyclopedia of Folk, Country and Western Music* in 1969, and served on the Grammy selection committee for many years.

LANGE, HOPE
(1931-2003)

This Oscar-nominated actress (for *Peyton Place* in 1957) began her stage career at the tender age of 12 on Broadway. She made her movie debut with Marilyn Monroe in *Bus Stop* (1956), and starred opposite Elvis in the 1961 release *Wild in the Country*, a film for which she rewrote and improved her own lines, to director Philip Dunne's admiration. Lange won two Emmys for her role on TV series "The Ghost and Mrs. Muir" in the late Sixties, and continued acting through the Seventies.

LANNING, BOB

Drummer who replaced Ronnie Tutt in the TCB Band for Elvis' winter 1970 residency at the International Hotel in Las Vegas, recorded and released as the album *On Stage*.

LANSBURY, ANGELA
(B. 1925)

British-born Angela Lansbury has had a long and illustrious career. Two out of her first three film appearances, *Gaslight* (1944) and *The Picture of Dorian Gray* (1945), earned her best supporting actress Oscar nominations. Since then she has delighted all ages with performances ranging from 1971 children's classic *Bedknobs and Broomsticks* to her long-running TV role in "Murder, She Wrote" (1984-1996).

In 1961, thirty-five year old Angela Lansbury played twenty-five year old Elvis' mother in *Blue Hawaii*.

For years afterwards, every Mother's Day Lansbury received a card from Elvis (though she believed the Colonel sent them).

LANSKY BROTHERS' MEN'S SHOP (LANSKY)

When Elvis first became interested in fancy clothes, this clothes store at 126 Beale Street was his mecca.

Elvis used to window-gaze on breaks from his first job as an usher at the Loew's State Theater. When manager Bernard Lansky invited him in to look around, Elvis told him he'd rather not: "I don't have no money, but when I get rich, I'll buy you out." Lansky said he'd prefer it if Elvis bought from him, rather than buy him out.

Lansky was founded in 1946 by brothers Bernand and Guy. The store branched out from selling Army surplus to cater to the clothing needs of a predominantly black Beale Street clientele, including many artists who recorded for Sun in the early years. The store had a reputation among flashy dressers from far and wide; pimps and gamblers would buy big hats and zoot suits before Elvis made the store his own.

Elvis began buying clothes from Lansky before fame was anything more than a dream. He bought his pink and black high school prom coat from here. He purchased his flamboyant stage wear and sports jackets here, and true to his word, he became the store's number one customer. In the Sixties, when he was in town Elvis would happily make daily trips to Lansky to see what was in. When Elvis was into the Superfly look in the early Seventies, Lansky was the place he went.

In 1957, Elvis gave Bernard Lansky his little Messerschmitt car, in exchange for a couple of hours with free run of the store to pick out anything he wanted. The following year, Lansky spent a great deal of time at Graceland under saddened circumstances, helping out around the place and ensuring that everyone had the clothes they needed for Gladys's funeral. Lansky also provided the suit in which Elvis was buried.

The store has since moved from its original location and is now at 149 Union Ave., at the Peabody Hotel, where among other items it sells the designs that made it "clothier to the King," plus new Elvis-inspired items.

BERNARD LANSKY: "He was a dynamite young man; not only was he a good customer, but he was a PR man for us all over the country.... We started doing a fantastic business."

BERNARD LANSKY: "I put his first suit on him, and I put his last suit on him. It was a white suit that I had made for him."

LANZA, MARIO

(B. ALFREDO ARNOLD COCOZZA, 1921-1959)

Elvis told a number of people over the years that his greatest influence as a singer was this Italian-American opera tenor and movie star.

In some ways, Elvis' career mirrored Lanza's: both spent time working as a truck driver, both

Movie still of Elvis with Hope Lange from *Wild in the Country*, 1961.

were signed to RCA, both were drafted into the armed forces, both had successful movie careers, and both struggled with weight problems.

Elvis starred in two movies with Lanza's niece, Dolores Hart. Elvis is said to have met Lanza in Los Angeles in a meeting set up by Steve Sholes, and later stayed in touch by phone.

Lanza was the first recording artist to sell 2.5 million copies of an album, and was described by opera legend Maria Callas as having the greatest tenor voice of the day; Arturo Toscanini called Lanza's "the greatest voice of the twentieth century."

Elvis recorded a number of songs Lanza had sung, including English-language versions of "O Sole Mio" ("It's Now or Never") and "Torna a Surriento" ("Surrender"), as well as "Danny Boy," "You'll Never Walk Alone" and "Santa Lucia."

ELVIS SAID IN 1972: "I had records by Mario Lanza when I was seventeen, eighteen years old, I would listen to the Metropolitan Opera. I just loved music. Music period."

CHARLIE HODGE: "He loved Mario Lanza's voice. In fact he could sing as high as Mario Lanza."

LANCHESTER, ELSA
(1902-1986)

Elvis played opposite this seasoned Hollywood professional in *Easy Come, Easy Go*, including a yoga-themed duet.

The British-born actress, dancer, and all-round thespian scaled greater heights during her very long career, including Oscar nominations for her supporting roles in *Come to the Stable* (1949) and *Witness for the Prosecution* (1957). She is best remembered for her eponymous role in *Bride of Frankenstein* (1935).

Her husband, actor Charles Laughton, stood in for host Ed Sullivan the first time that Elvis was on the "Ed Sullivan Show" in September 1956. Lanchester later summed up her film career as "large parts in lousy pictures and small parts in big pictures."

LAS VEGAS

No matter that Elvis wasn't born here and never had a house here, he is indelibly associated with Las Vegas, an adopted son whose "Viva Las Vegas" song has become the city's theme tune. And all from inauspicious beginnings.

Though nothing came of it, William Morris talent agent Harry Kalcheim tried to land Elvis a Las Vegas gig for Colonel Parker in February 1956. Elvis first visited the town on April 6, 1956, on a day's break to the New Frontier Hotel, where Colonel Parker was negotiating Elvis' contract for a two-week booking in the 1,000 capacity Venus Room. Elvis played the venue between April 23 and May 6, 1956, backed by Freddy Martin and his Orchestra, and suffered his first setback as a performer. The older, more staid crowd didn't know what to make of him; a *Newsweek* article described Elvis as "somewhat like a jug of corn liquor at a champagne party." Still, Elvis and his band had time to check out other acts and see what the competition had to offer. (Private recordings of the closing night came out on 1980 album *Elvis Aron Presley*).

Elvis returned to Vegas for pleasure in November 1956, staying for a week at the New Frontier Hotel. In October 1957, he took a ten day vacation, this time at the Sahara Hotel.

In 1960, Elvis took time off from filming *G.I. Blues* to spend a couple of weekends in Las Vegas with his pals. Las Vegas became a popular stop-off for Elvis and his entourage en route between Memphis and LA, a trip they drove on a regular basis in the early Sixties. Elvis would also sometimes fly in to town from Memphis for the weekend with a few entourage pals.

Elvis spent plenty of time in Vegas in the fall of 1961 and early 1962 when he wasn't working on movies, often preferring the lure of the desert to his Graceland home.

When Priscilla Beaulieu came to the States for a secret visit in 1962, Las Vegas was where Elvis spirited her away.

Viva Las Vegas (1964) was shot at Elvis' favorite hotel, the Sahara, and at other locations in and around town, including Lake Mead Marina.

In January 1964, Elvis and the guys took a long vacation in Vegas, most evenings going out to see performers including Fats Domino, Della Reese, Don Rickles, Tony Martin and the Clara Ward Singers.

Elvis, Priscilla, the Colonel, Elvis' family and select members of his entourage secretly arrived in Vegas on May 1, 1967 for Elvis and Priscilla's wedding at the Aladdin Hotel. There was something rather Vegas about the whole thing, with its restricted guest list and seeming spur-of-the-moment preparations, considering that this was a top entertainer officializing an 8-year relationship.

While filming *Speedway* in the summer of 1967, Elvis alternated taking weekend trips to Las Vegas and Palm Springs. Elvis and Priscilla spent a few days in town in August 1967. Elvis and the members of his entourage who went with him to LA to keep him company while he filmed *Stay Away, Joe*, recuperated for a week in Vegas in early December, before heading home to Memphis that Christmas.

After Elvis' resounding success on his 1968 NBC TV Special, broadcast in the run-up to Christmas 1968, the Colonel began fielding offers to play Las Vegas. The International Hotel, owned by Kirk Kerkorian and at that time still under constructions, won the contest, offering $100,000 per week (though Elvis had to pay for his band and backup singers). Elvis was originally asked to be the opening act in the two thousand seat concert hall, but the Colonel wisely waited for another performer to iron out any initial gremlins at the venue.

The show Elvis played on July 31, 1969 was the first of 837 performances, all sold out, at the International Hotel / Las Vegas Hilton, with a new band put together specially for the occasion. His season broke all the records, selling over 101,000 tickets for $1.5 million in box office receipts.

Elvis was back the following January, usually the lowest of the low season in town' to show that where other stars had failed, he could not only pack people in, he could bring them to town in the first place. Before he even stepped out on stage, the cash tills began spinning as Elvis merchandise flew off stands and more importantly, hotel rooms and casinos filled up.

The International Hotel soon became a home from home. After his shows, Elvis would entertain friends and celebrity concertgoers in his 5000 sq. ft. suite, for which he had given his own input on the decoration.

For the first few engagements, Priscilla and the wives of entourage members would come down and spend the weekends in Las Vegas, as well as the opening and closing nights. As their marriage began to founder, Elvis whittled this down until a little before he split from Priscilla, the wives were only there for the opening night. The rest of the nights were party time for the boys.

In early 1971, Elvis was in Las Vegas during an earthquake, an experience he described as "the weirdest feeling I ever had in my life."

Elvis sometimes stayed in Vegas after his own run had ended, to take in shows by pals Ann-Margret or Tom Jones, or just to enjoy the hospi-tality of the International Hotel (after 1971, renamed Las Vegas Hilton).

Vegas may have lured Elvis back to live performing, but within a couple of years it had turned him into what drummer Ronnie Tutt referred to as something of a caged lion. By 1973, Elvis is said to have had enough; before his final show that summer he said that he wanted to quit. Biographers agree that this was not something the Colonel could countenance: the Colonel's king-sized gambling habits required Elvis to act as a kind of singing collateral, ensuring that his debts would never actually be called in.

Elvis continued to play Las Vegas through to his final Christmas, by which time he was perfectly happy to tell the audience that he hated the town.

Vegas has kept up its love affair with Elvis. As well as the Hilton and its "Elvis Suite," Las Vegas has boasted Elvis museums, Elvis-A-Rama and Elvis, Elvis, Elvis, and offers quickie weddings at half a dozen "Elvis chapels."

To mark the 30th anniversary of Elvis' death ABC News produced a two hour TV show focusing on Elvis' influence on Las Vegas (and vice versa).

See also Las Vegas Hilton, International Hotel and Nevada for more information on concerts.

A DISCONSOLATE ELVIS ON STAGE IN LATE 1976, TO THE AUDIENCE: "I hate Las Vegas."

PETER GURALNICK ON ELVIS' SIXTIES VACATIONS IN VEGAS: "He loved Las Vegas for one reason above all: Time was meaningless here, there was no clock, there were no obligations."

MARTY LACKER: "Elvis was the first act in Vegas history to make a hotel a profit on the show."

LAMAR FIKE: "Nobody goes to Vegas and plays four weeks any more — they do five days, tops."

BONO: "I think the Vegas period is underrated. I find it the most emotional. By that point Elvis was clearly not in control of his own life, and there is this incredible pathos."

LAS VEGAS HILTON

Elvis put this hotel on the map (3000 Paradise Road) with his twice-yearly, month-long residencies starting in the summer of 1969, and continued to do so after it was purchased by the expanding Hilton chain in 1971. Immediately after Elvis' first engagement for his new bosses, days after playing at Lake Tahoe for more money"the Colonel pressed Hotel management to increase Elvis' income. A new, improved contract was signed in the spring of 1972, offering Elvis a stepped fee rising to $150,000 per week for his month long residencies. Colonel Parker managed to add an extra $50,000 annual consideration for his own work as a consultant to the Hilton chain, a fee that he continued to draw for the rest of his life.

Elvis' winter 1973 booking was bedeviled by ill-health, forcing the cancellation of quite a few shows. He had to postpone his winter 1975 residency until March, when his final night turned into a gala performance to mark the opening of the hotel's huge new extension, attended for the first time by Conrad Hilton.

All told, Elvis made 837 performances at the Hilton and its forerunner the International Hotel, where he was watched by 2.5 million paying customers. The year after his death, a bronze statue of Elvis was unveiled at an Elvis convention, "Always Elvis," organized by the Colonel and attended by Priscilla and many members of the former Memphis Mafia.

The Imperial Suite, Elvis' home from away home on the 30th floor, is now known as the Elvis Suite.

Elvis performing in Las Vegas, 1970.

ELVIS SAID IN 1974: "I never liked the way this show-room is decorated. It's difficult for a performer to work this room because of its width."

LAST DAY ALIVE

See DEATH

LARRY GELLER: "During those last months Elvis was besieged by crippling physical illness, substance addiction, the threat of exposure, the fear that he would be forced to face a questioning public, an overwhelming sense of having failed to protect his father, and especially his daughter, from the glare of negative, damaging publicity he had so deftly eluded until then. The mistakes of his past, the pressure of his present, and the uncertainty of the future crushed him."

"LAST FAREWELL, THE"

Elvis sang this song, composed by Roger Whittaker with words by a radio competition winner called Ron Webster, on February 2, 1976 at his Graceland recording session for release on *From Elvis Presley Boulevard, Memphis, Tennessee*. The orchestral arrangement was overdubbed at a later date.

An alternate take is on FTD release *The Jungle Room Sessions*.

LATENESS

Stars and royalty have the prerogative to be late; Elvis made use of this prerogative in his private life but not so much in his professional dealings. In his early years, Colonel Parker instilled in Elvis that punctuality was the best way of being taken seriously by major players in the entertainment industry. Once he was a star, Elvis continued to follow this advice . . . most of the time. In the Fifties, Red West remembers getting dressed down by the Colonel because Elvis refused to leave one town for the next day's show because he was having such a good time with a girl he had met backstage.

Outside work commitments, it was Elvis who decided what happened and when. Entourage members recall long periods of inactivity at Graceland, waiting around for something, anything"to happen, and then there being a sudden flurry of activity. Elvis was habitually late to screenings at the Memphian Theater that he arranged himself. In the Seventies, the flurry of activity might be Elvis deciding on the spur of the moment that that he wanted to fly out to one of his other homes, in which case the guys had minimal time to throw clothes into a suitcase and get to the airport.

For much of the Sixties, there was simply no question of being late to work for filming, where even minimal delays cost the production many thousands of dollars. Towards the middle of the decade, as Elvis became increasingly reluctant to head to Hollywood for yet another forgettable picture, the Colonel relied on entourage foremen Joe Esposito and Marty Lacker to get Elvis to work on time. By 1967, it was a struggle to persuade Elvis even to leave Memphis for Los Angeles; that spring he put off his departure for weeks, and when he arrived he had a domestic accident that further delayed shooting on *Clambake* and resulted in the Colonel berating Elvis and his pals.

On his return to performing in Las Vegas, Elvis' main problem with lateness was one his fans were happy to have: his shows consistently overran. Hotel management was keen for the audience to be back in the casino as quickly as possible; Elvis sometimes just wanted to keep on going beyond his 50-minute limit.

In the studio, it was a different story. Elvis could not be rushed. He arrived when he arrived, usually in the evening, ready to work through the night, and he took his own sweet time warming up, either singing gospel or jamming, until he felt like starting in on the song list.

By the mid-Seventies, Elvis was less than eager to step into the studio at all. A number of musicians who worked with him enjoyed the work but ultimately couldn't cope with the fact that Elvis might turn up many hours late to a recording session, or not show up at all. The situation did not improve when RCA finally realized that the only way to get Elvis to record was to take a mobile studio to Graceland. Elvis could be late even in his own home.

Towards the very end of his life, health problems and physical ailments and the difficulties of getting ready to perform sometimes caused Elvis to be late on stage.

PRISCILLA SAID: "Except when he was working, he had a cavalier attitude toward time."

LAUGHTON, CHARLES
(1899-1962)

British-born actor Charles Laughton starred in such vintage Hollywood classics as *Mutiny on the Bounty* and *The Hunchback of Notre Dame*. He would have starred in *I, Claudius* if co-star Merle Oberon had not been seriously injured in a car crash during filming. It was a car crash that placed Laughton center stage as a stand-in host for Ed Sullivan on "The Ed Sullivan Show" the first time that Elvis appeared on this TV showcase in September 1956.

LAURENCE, DOUGLAS

Laurence produced no fewer than three Elvis movies, all released in 1968: *Speedway*, *Stay Away, Joe* and *Live a Little, Love a Little*, almost half of all the movies he produced in his career. When not working in the movies, he also helped to arrange entertainment for major Las Vegas hotels.

"LAWDY, MISS CLAWDY"

Elvis recorded his version of this 1952 Lloyd Price R&B #1 (the original featuring Fats Domino on the piano; Shorty Long tickled the ivories for Elvis) on February 3, 1956 at the RCA studios in New York. It was first released on the EP Elvis Presley a few months later, and then a few months after that came out as the B-side to "Shake, Rattle and Roll," the only track out of seven singles that RCA released simultaneously that had not been on Elvis' first album. With so much Elvis on offer, it's less than surprising that this knock out combination failed to chart.

The song's first LP release wasn't until *For LP Fans Only* in 1959. The track has since appeared on *Artist Of The Century*, *Elvis '56* and *Elvis R 'n' B*.

"Lawdy, Miss Clawdy" kicks off a medley of old hits in the 1968 NBC TV Special that ends in a tale about the scandal that accompanied Elvis' early career, and was released on the accompany album *Elvis* (NBC TV Special). Elvis is practically stripping his gears with the power he puts into the song in this version, from the second show on

June 27; he also sang it at the earlier show, and in the studio during rehearsals, versions that have been a favorite with bootleggers over the decades. Alternate NBC TV Special versions from rehearsals and the various tapings are on *Elvis Aron Presley*, *A Golden Celebration*, *Tiger Man*, *Memories: The '68 Comeback Special*, and FTD disc *Burbank '68*.

Alternate takes from the original session have come out on *The King Of Rock 'N' Roll*, *Platinum: A Life In Music* and FTD releases *Flashback* and *Elvis Presley*, the latter of which features the entire evolution of the song in the studio through all 12 takes, with Elvis remarkably consistent throughout.

Before Elvis returned to live performing, the song made a cameo as the character he plays in his final feature movie, *Change of Habit* (1969), hums it to a piano accompaniment.

The song was a regular pick during many of Elvis' Seventies shows, particularly in 1971 and 1974; in February 1970, he combined the song in a medley with "Blueberry Hill."

A particularly bluesy studio version from 1972 was released in 2004 on FTD album *Elvis On Tour"The Rehearsals*; a live version from his concert at Hampton Roads features in the documentary.

A 1972 live performance is on *An American Trilogy* ; a 1974 live version is on *Elvis Recorded Live On Stage In Memphis*; another later that year is on FTD release *Dragonheart*. A live version from 1976 is on *Spring Tours '77*.

In *A Private Moment* features a home-recorded version from 1960.

LAW SUITS

Elvis weathered his share of legal proceedings during his career; in his final years he was embroiled in half a dozen cases.

He appeared at a traffic court in Memphis on March 1, 1956, testifying against a woman charged for reckless driving who drove into the back of his Eldorado in a garage.

In June 1956, Elvis had his photograph taken in a Main Street cafe in Memphis with his head on the shoulder of a young woman named Robbie Moore. When the photo appeared in instant Elvis bio *Elvis Presley Speaks!* she threatened to sue him for an invasion of privacy. The legal action was settled out of court for $5,500.

Before the year was out, a number of Elvis' neighbors at Audubon Drive unsuccessfully tried to have a public nuisance judgment served against Elvis.

In late March 1957, Elvis appeared in court for pulling a gun on US Marine Private Hershel Nixon. On March 25, Elvis met with Judge Boushe and had the case dismissed, after sending a six-page handwritten apology by telegram to the plaintiff.

A dancer who worked under the name Little Egypt sued Elvis' music publishing company, Paramount and RCA for singing the song of that title without her permission in 1964 movie *Roustabout*. The case was thrown out of court, she did not get the $2.5 million she was seeking, and she probably did not pass go.

Beverly Albrecq, a young woman whose ankle was accidentally broken by Elvis during a karate demonstration in his suite after a Las Vegas show in the summer of 1973, sued Elvis two years later. The action was settled for $5,000. Up to the time of the law suit, Elvis had been paying the woman's medical and rehabilitation expenses.

Kiajo Peter Pajarinen sued Elvis' bodyguard Red West and two others for assault in September 1973. The charges were finally dismissed some time after Elvis' death.

Elvis was hit with another lawsuit, this time for over $6 million, by property developer Edward L. Ashley, this time after an incident at the Sahara Tahoe Hotel when Ashley attempted to gain entry to Elvis' suite after shorting out the lighting on Elvis' floor. Elvis' bodyguards "strongly" dissuaded him from his intention. The suit failed but step-brother David Stanley believes that Elvis settled out of court for around one tenth of that figure, because Red West had hit the plaintiff after he had been handcuffed and immobilized.

By 1976, Elvis and his entourage were involved in half a dozen law suits, including legal actions regarding one of his planes and an ill-advised scheme to open a chain of racquetball courts bearing his name. That year, Elvis told Red West that worries over all these lawsuits contributed to his decision to fire West, his cousin Sonny and karate master Dave Hebler that year, as lawyers and his father had been advising for some time.

After Elvis' death, Elvis Presley Enterprises was so forceful and proactive in wresting back control over the Elvis name, image and likeness that it set new precedents in copyright legislation on celebrity legacies. EPE was instrumental in getting the Personal Rights Protection Act of 1984 (known as "The Elvis Law") onto the statue books in Tennessee and later nationwide.

See also POLICE

LAWYERS

For such a wealthy and influential man, Elvis retained surprisingly few legal advisors during his career. The simple reason was that all of his business arrangements went through Colonel Parker and his organization. If and when Elvis needed a lawyer, Parker sorted things out.

Elvis' regular Memphis attorneys were Charles Davies and Drayton Beecher Smith II.

In the Fifties, Elvis used Evans, Petree and Cobb to buy Graceland.

In the Sixties, when Elvis bought the Circle G ranch he used Charles Davis.

In the Seventies, California lawyer Ed Hookstratten oversaw behind the scenes work on paternity suits, worked out the terms for Elvis' original divorce settlement from Priscilla, and helped to defend against law suits caused by over-exuberant bodyguarding. He was first called in to work for Elvis after entourage member Richard Davis accidentally ran over and killed a gardener in Beverly Hills.

Attorney Harry M. Fain defended Elvis in the paternity suit brought by Patricia Parker in 1970, and arranged his divorce settlement with Priscilla in 1973.

Lawyer Ronald Dwyer won a case for Elvis against the four men who jumped on stage in Las Vegas in February 1973 and later claimed $4 million in damages for how they were treated.

JOE HAZAN: "If Elvis had a lawyer on his own, there would have been no Parker. No lawyer would have permitted Parker to take over a client like he did."

"LEAD ME, GUIDE ME"

This track, released on Elvis' 1972 gospel album He Touched Me, was recorded in Nashville on May 17, 1971. The song was written and originally recorded by Doris Akers in 1954.

Subsequent releases of the studio version include Ultimate Gospel, Amazing Grace and Peace In the Valley"the latter two gospel anthologies also feature Elvis singing the song with backing group The Stamps backstage during filming of 1972 documentary Elvis on Tour.

"LEAVE MY WOMAN ALONE"

The instrumentals and backing tracks were laid down for this Easy Come, Easy Go soundtrack piece, but Elvis failed to record the vocals. The song was written and originally recorded by Ray Charles in the mid-Fifties. It is on the 2007 FTD soundtrack re-release.

LEE, BRENDA
(B. BRENDA MAE TARPLEY, 1944)

Elvis met the diminutive singer, known as "Little Miss Dynamite," in 1960, on the set of his movie Wild in the Country. She was briefly in the running for a role in his next picture, Blue Hawaii.

In the Sixties, sometime entourage member Lamar Fike was road manager to Ms. Lee. That decade, she was the fourth biggest charting act with her style of country pop, which was at its peak of popularity in the early part of the decade. Lee began as a child performer in the mid-Fifties, and went through a rockabilly phase before her first hits in 1960.

One of Elvis' later hallmark songs, "Always On My Mind," was originally a hit for Brenda Lee. He introduced her to the audience at one of his Las Vegas shows in the early Seventies.

LEE, KUI
(B. KUIOKALANI LEE, 1932-1966)

Chinese-born Lee lived in Hawaii from the age of five, where he became a leading poet and singer. Lee wrote "I'll Remember You," a track covered by Elvis in 1966 after its original recording by Don Ho. The song was one of Elvis' show regulars for years afterwards. Elvis sang the song during his groundbreaking satellite performance, Aloha From Hawaii, in 1973, and heartily agreed to journalist Eddie Sherman's suggestion to make the concert a benefit for the Kui Lee Cancer Fund, for which $75,000 was raised.

LEECH, MIKE

Bass player, percussionist and arranger at Chips Moman's American Studio who worked with Elvis in 1969, playing bass and doing the arrangements on tracks including "Suspicious Minds." Leech occasionally played bass at other Elvis sessions up to March 1975. During his career, he worked with a wide range of musicians, from Neil Diamond to Johnny Cash, Bobby Womack, B.J. Thomas, Joe Tex and Dionne Warwick.

LED ZEPPELIN

A star-struck Robert Plant and John Paul Jones met Elvis in Las Vegas in 1973, after Elvis expressed a desire to meet these guys who were selling "tickets quicker than me." When John Paul Jones admired Elvis' $5,000 watch, Elvis immediately proposed a swap for his $10 Mickey Mouse watch.

Zeppelin saw Elvis in concert a few times as Elvis' guest at Las Vegas, the first time talking for hours after the show, and caught him in LA too in 1974.

ROBERT PLANT: "He knew that he was locked in this self-parody."

LEGAULT, LANCE
(B. WILLIAM LANCE LE GAULT, 1935)

Elvis' stunt double in a number of movies, before beginning a long acting career starting with Girls! Girls! Girls! that continues to the present day. A choreographer and musician by training, the day Elvis met him (while filming Wild in the Country) LeGault mentioned that he'd be playing bass that night at a gig, and then was shocked to see Elvis show up. Thereafter Elvis often took ladies he was dating to LeGault's show.

LeGault sings "Return to Sender" in Girls! Girls! Girls! the movie with Elvis. In a Kissin' Cousins blooper, LeGault's face is actually visible in one scene instead of Elvis'. He was particularly active in Viva Las Vegas, doing the choreography and doubling for Elvis in his 20-foot fall off a diving board.

LeGault helped Elvis with moves in front of the camera for a number of films, and worked with him on choreography during rehearsals for his 1968 NBC Special. He appears in the informal section of the TV show, shaking a tambourine.

After Elvis, LeGault continued acting, appearing among other roles as Colonel Decker in the "A Team" and Colonel Green in "Magnum, P.I.." LeGault's sonorous voice provides the narration on the Graceland audiotour.

LEGION OF DECENCY

Founded in 1933 as the Catholic Legion of Decency, this organization was a self-appointed guardian of morality and values in a battle to protect audiences from "vile and unwholesome moving pictures." For several decades, the organization had considerable influence in Hollywood. Elvis movies were an easy target for criticism and a degree of public scandal, though the organization reserved its biggest campaigns for films that pushed back sexual barriers or showed what, for the day, was extreme violence.

LEIBER AND STOLLER
JERRY LEIBER: B. APRIL 25, 1933, BALTIMORE
MIKE STOLLER: B. MARCH 13, 1933, LONG ISLAND

Leiber and Stoller were one of the best-known songwriting teams to come out of the Brill Building in New York, where many of the hits of the Fifties and Sixties were penned prior to the Sixties singer/songwriter revolution.

The duo were coming into their prime when they teamed up with Elvis for his early film work. They had already written material for R&B artists including Jimmy Witherspoon, Floyd Dixon and Big Mama Thornton ("Hound Dog," which Elvis covered in 1956), but their best-selling work was still ahead of them. Before they met, Stoller heard that Elvis had taken their song "Hound Dog" to the top of the charts when songwriting partner Leiber greeted him on the dock in New York after his rescue from the Andrea Doria liner, which went down in 1956.

Elvis first met the songwriters in LA, at the Radio Recorders studio in April 1957, when he was recording four of their tracks for Jailhouse Rock. They got on so well that the songwriters acted as co-producers for the rest of the session. Leiber and Stoller were hired as producers by RCA for Elvis' next studio session (the tracks for his first Christmas album plus a couple of Leiber and Stoller singles). They were soon back to work with Elvis on the soundtrack to King Creole in their new role as staff producers. Tom Diskin confirmed in writing to RCA in early 1958 that Elvis "is able to work out ideas with them, and has confidence working with them."

Stoller and Elvis became friends as well as colleagues while working on *Jailhouse Rock* (in which Stoller made a cameo as Vince Everett's piano player). The Colonel knew a threat when he saw one. One day when he stopped by Elvis' hotel and found them playing pool together, the Colonel took Elvis aside and the next thing Stoller knew, Elvis was telling him that he should leave because the Colonel was upset. It wasn't the pool but the fact that the songwriters offered their composition "Don't" directly to Elvis that was the bone of contention.

Elvis had been so pleased with how he worked with Leiber that he wanted to cancel his final recording session before he was drafted when he heard that Leiber couldn't make it because he was laid up in hospital with pneumonia.

Leiber and Stoller submitted two songs for Elvis' first movie on his return from the Army, "Dog Face" and "Tulsa's Blues." Neither of these songs made it into the picture as relations unraveled with the Colonel. The Colonel insisted on contractual conditions that were far more stringent than Leiber and Stoller would agree. The Colonel also criticized Leiber for suggesting a future movie project involving Elia Kazan directly to Elvis. For the Colonel, this was the final straw. Elvis' desire to have the duo at the *G.I. Blues* recording sessions counted for little.

Apart from a few tracks that Elvis recorded in the spring of 1962, songs that had already been sung by other singers, that was it for Leiber & Stoller and Elvis. They have the distinction of being the first major figures in Elvis' professional life to refuse to work with Elvis because of the direction the Colonel was taking his career, though Freddy Bienstock ventured that they stopped writing for Elvis because they didn't want to keep on having to go out to California.

All in all, Elvis recorded 23 Leiber and Stoller compositions, including two on 1973 album *Raised On Rock*.

As well as the material they wrote for Elvis, Leiber and Stoller's early rock 'n' roll classics include "Poison Ivy," "Yakey Yak," "Riot In Cell Block #9," "Stand By Me," "Spanish Harlem," "Love Potion #9" and "On Broadway," sung by a roll-call of ground-breaking rock and roll and early soul artists from the Fifties onwards. After Elvis, they found success writing for The Coasters and The Drifters. At various times, they also ran their own record labels.

In 1972, Elvis invited Leiber and his family to watch him perform his first ever show in New York City, at Madison Square Garden. The next day, Elvis called Leiber to ask why he didn't like the show. Elvis had spotted him among the 40,000-strong audience, leaving early to beat the crowds!

The next year, Elvis put two Leiber and Stoller songs on his album *Raised on Rock*.

Leiber and Stoller have been inducted into practically every Hall of Fame for which they are eligible.

See ELVIS SINGS LEIBER & STOLLER.

ELVIS' LEIBER & STOLLER COLLECTION

Hound Dog
Love Me
Hot Dog
Loving You
Jailhouse Rock
Treat Me Nice
I Want To Be Free
Baby I Don't Care
Santa Claus Is Back In Town
Don't
Trouble
King Creole
Steadfast, Loyal And True
Dirty, Dirty Feeling

Just Tell Her Jim Said Hello
She's Not You (co-written by Doc Pomus)
Girls! Girls! Girls!
Bossa Nova Baby
You're The Boss
Little Egypt
Fools Fall In Love
Saved
If You Don't Come Back
Three Corn Patches

MIKE STOLLER: "We thought we were the only white kids who knew anything about the blues but he knew all kinds of stuff."

JERRY LEIBER: "We thought he was like an idiot savant, but he listened a lot. He knew all of our records.... And he was a workhorse in the studio, he didn't pull any diva numbers."

JERRY LEIBER: "Our respect for him grew over time. Our disdain was the disdain we felt for white people."

LEIGH, BARBARA
(b. 1946)

Elvis had an affair with actress, model and original Vampirella Barbara Leigh from 1970 to 1972, as her career was beginning to take off. During this period, she was also involved with Steve McQueen and MGM executive James Aubrey, making it a trio of influential married men. Leigh met Elvis in Las Vegas after one of his performances in August 1970, when she was accompanying Aubry. As Joe Esposito notes, "they just connected."

For Christmas 1970, Santa Elvis gave Leigh a Mercedes. Though she sometimes traveled with Elvis on tour, they managed to keep their affair secret. Red West says that though Leigh helped to nurse Elvis through a serious bout of glaucoma, Elvis dropped her when he found out, belatedly, that she had previously been married and even had a kid, both turn-offs in his book.

After they split up, Elvis kept in touch through Joe Esposito, with whom she has remained friends.

BARBARA LEIGH: "Elvis was beautiful, the most beautiful man I'd ever seen."

BARBARA LEIGH: "We tried spending as much time together as we could manage, but it wasn't easy with his career, his marriage, his other women and my work schedule. Life was always a challenge with the King."

Book:
The King, McQueen and the Love Machine, by Barbara Leigh, Xlibris, 2002.

LENNON, JOHN
(1940-1980)

The accepted wisdom is that The Beatles were Elvis' biggest rival. In truth, the driving force of the band, John Lennon, had no qualms telling people how important Elvis' music had been in his life.

Born in Liverpool on October 9, 1940, when 15 year-old Lennon heard Elvis singing "Heartbreak Hotel" on the radio, "it was the end for me." He later said that the Elvis song persuaded him that what he wanted to do with his life was be a musician.

Lennon's pre-Beatles outfit The Quarrymen were known to cover "Hound Dog" and "Blue Suede Shoes" at their early gigs.

The one time that Elvis and John Lennon met was in 1965, during The Beatles' second US tour,

Elvis in the 1950's with his stuffed dog Nipper (the RCA Victor mascot) which he used as a stage prop when singing Leiber & Stoller's song "Hound Dog."

when they visited him in LA. They spent the evening comparing experiences, singing songs and, it seems, getting on well, though many references to the meeting refer to it as frosty occasion, in the spirit of fomenting a rivalry between Elvis and the new kids on the block. When the Beatles finally left, at 2 a.m., John recalled: "It was Elvis' sense of humor that stuck in my mind. He liked to laugh and make others laugh too. Which was why I put on a Peter Sellers voice again as we walked out of the door and said, "Tanks for ze music, Elvis"and long live ze King!""

During a separation from Yoko Ono in the Seventies, John Lennon briefly moved to the Beverly Wilshire Hotel in LA principally, the story goes, because that was where Elvis had stayed.

Also in the Seventies, Lennon sought advice from Elvis on how to cope with the US Immigration Department's attempts to deport him because for a previous marijuana possession conviction in the UK. Lennon followed Elvis' advice and made a public statement against drugs. Lennon wore an Elvis pin during his appearance at the Grammy Awards in 1975.

JOHN LENNON: "It was Elvis who really got me buying records. . . . When I heard "Heartbreak Hotel," I thought 'this is it' and I started to grow sideboards and all that year."

JOHN LENNON: "There's only one person in the United States that we really wanted to meet - not that I'm sure he wanted to meet us—and that was Elvis. It is difficult to describe how we felt about him. We just idolized the guy so much."

LEPLEY, SLEEPY-EYED JOHN

Elvis got one of his first breaks playing a regular slot at the Eagle's Nest club in Memphis, run by top local DJ Sleepy-Eyed John Lepley. Sleepy-Eyed John initially made disparaging comments about this new-fangled music when he played Elvis' first single on his WHHM show ("Blue Moon Of Kentucky" rather than "That's All Right (Mama)." According to Peter Guralnick, Vernon had to be restrained physically from defending his son's honor. Sleepy-Eyed John gave Elvis his first booking, as an act during the intermissions for his Western Swing shows at the Eagle's Nest. Many biographers state that Lepley made discreet enquiries about managing Elvis but was rebuffed by Scotty Moore, who had already filled the position.

"LET IT BE ME"

In 1970 Elvis sang this power ballad live in Las Vegas (originally a French song titled "Je t'appartiens" written by Pierre Delanoe and Gilbert Bécaud, and sung by Bécaud in 1955), with English-language lyrics written by Mann Curtis. The song was first a hit in the States for the Everly Brothers in 1960.

A recording came out that year on live album *On Stage*. A version from an earlier show during that same Vegas February run came out on *Elvis: A Legendary Performer Vol. 3*. The song has since appeared on bootlegs, *Walk A Mile In My Shoes*, *Live in Las Vegas*, *Love Elvis* and FTD release *Polk Salad Annie*.

"LET ME"

Elvis recorded this song on September 4, 1956 at Radio Recorders for his debut movie *Love Me Tender*. It came out on the soundtrack EP, not a tough choice as there were only four songs in the movie, before appearing on stopgap Army years LP *A Date With Elvis* in 1959. Elvis gets a credit on this song, alongside Vera Matson (a pseudonym used by composer Ken Darby).

"Let Me" subsequently came out on *Worldwide Gold Award Hits Vol. 2*, *Essential Elvis Vol. 1*, *The King Of Rock And Roll*, and *Jailhouse Rock* (which includes an alternate take of Elvis singing solo).

"LET ME BE THERE"

Elvis rocked out with this song on March 20, 1974 in his home town, for release on *Recorded Live On Stage In Memphis* and later *Moody Blue*. A million-selling Grammy winner for Olivia Newton John in 1973 (written by John Rostill), Elvis regularly performed the pop country song through much of 1974 and 1975.

Alternate officially released live performances are on *Elvis Aron Presley* and FTD albums *I Found My Thrill*, *Dragonheart*, *It's Midnight*, *Big Boss Man* and *Dixieland Rocks* plus a number of bootlegs.

"(LET ME BE YOUR) TEDDY BEAR"

See "TEDDY BEAR"

"LET US PRAY"

Elvis recorded this Buddy Kaye / Ben Weisman pop gospel tune for *Change of Habit* twice: a film version on March 5, 1969 at the Decca Recording Studios in LA, and the redubbed version released two years later on *You'll Never Walk Alone* at a session in Nashville some time that September.

In the Nineties the song appeared on the *Double Features* release for Elvis' final four movies. It has also appeared on gospel anthology *Peace In The Valley*.

The alternate master came out on 2000s box set *Today, Tomorrow & Forever*.

"LET YOURSELF GO"

Elvis initially recorded this bluesy Joy Byers song at MGM Studios in Culver City on June 21, 1967 for *Speedway*. It was released as the B-side to May 1968 single "Your Time Hasn't Come Yet, Baby" to promote the movie. Later, it came out on the movie soundtrack LP. Subsequent releases for this version are limited to the *Double Features* re-issue of the *Speedway* soundtrack and *Command Performances*.

A rocked-up version featured as part of Elvis' June 1968 recording session for the upcoming NBC TV Special; the song was slated to be part of the road medley section began with "Nothingville" but was cut from the broadcast version along with the "bordello scene" it accompanied. This recording came out in 1978 on *Elvis: A Legendary Performer Vol. 3*, and in the Nineties on the *Elvis NBC TV Special* re-release and *Memories: The '68 Comeback Special*. It has since appeared on *Elvis at the Movies*.

An instrumental version is on FTD release *Burbank '68*. A spliced version combining multiple takes from 1968 is on 2006 FTD issue *Let Yourself Go*.

LET YOURSELF GO

A 2006 FTD CD of previously unreleased outtakes from rehearsals and the recording of Elvis' 1968 NBC TV Special.

TRACK LISTING:
1. Trouble / Guitar Man (opening takes)
2. Nothingville
3. Let Yourself Go (Parts 1-3)
4. Guitar Man (escape section 1, fast takes)
5. Guitar Man (after karate section)
6. Little Egypt
7. Trouble / Guitar Man (after karate section)
8. Big Boss Man
9. It Hurts Me (parts 1 and 2)
10. Guitar Man (escape section 1)
11. Sometimes I Feel Like A Motherless Child / Where Could I Go But To The Lord (gospel part 1)
12. Up Above My Head / I Found That Light (gospel part 2)
13. Saved (gospel part 3)
14. If I Can Dream
15. Memories (alternate)
16. I Got A Woman
17. Blue Moon / Young Love / Oh, Happy Day
18. When It Rains, It Really Pours
19. Blue Christmas
20. Are You Lonesome Tonight? / That's My Desire
21. That's When Your Heartaches Begin
22. Peter Gunn Theme
23. Love Me
24. When My Blue Moon Turns To Gold Again
25. Blue Christmas / Santa Claus Is Back In Town

"LET'S BE FRIENDS"

Elvis recorded this undemanding Chris Arnold / Geoffrey Morrow / David Martin ballad at the Decca Studios in Hollywood on March 5, 1969, with a view to the song appearing in his final feature *Change of Habit*. The song was subsequently dropped from the soundtrack and selected as the title track to a budget LP released the following year. The only other official release has been on the *Double Feature* release for *Change of Habit*.

LET'S BE FRIENDS

A budget LP released in April 1970 on the Camden label, featuring the title tracks from two movies that didn't warrant a soundtrack release, plus unreleased movie songs that wound up on the cutting room floor and a couple of orphaned tracks from American Studio. The album initially sold around 400,000 copies, but failed to chart higher than 104 because of the relatively low takings the cut-price album generated. In the fullness of time it went platinum.

TRACK LISTING:
1. Stay Away, Joe
2. If I'm A Fool (For Loving You)
3. Let's Be Friends
4. Let's Forget About The Stars
5. Mama
6. I'll Be There (If Ever You Want Me)
7. Almost
8. Change Of Habit
9. Have A Happy

BMG released a CD version of the album in 2006.

"LET'S FORGET ABOUT THE STARS"

The instrumentals for this A.L. Owens country song were laid down in mid-October 1968 at the Samuel Goldwyn Studios in LA, originally for the movie *Charro*. Elvis added vocals at a later overdub session. After it was cut from the picture the track featured on soundtrack grab-bag album *Let's Be Friends* in 1970. The song is also on the 1995 *Double Features* album featuring songs from the movie.

LEVITCH, HARRY

A Memphis jeweler and philanthropist who, among other charitable deeds, helped kids through high school including Elvis' pal Red West.

Within days of signing for RCA in November 1956, Elvis walked into Harry Levitch's Elvis store at 159 Union Avenue to get his jewelry started. He added to it when he had the chance, including in 1960 a horseshoe diamond ring, and in 1962 a fourteen-karat diamond-encrusted tie pin.

Levitch designed a religious-themed watch combing a cross and a Star of David which Elvis gave out as gifts to the cast and crew on *Frankie and Johnny* in 1965. For his Christmas gifts that year, Elvis ordered more gold watches from Levitch, including one initialed "EP" and one initialed "GK" (for George Klein). Elvis also bought diamonds rings, bracelets, pendants and a butterfly pin as presents that Christmas.

In February 1966, Elvis picked up matching horseshoe designs on a white-gold man's ring and a woman's pin, plus a Valentine's charm.

Levitch made the ring that Elvis presented to Priscilla on Christmas Eve 1966 when he asked her to marry him. Levitch made a one-off platinum wedding band for Elvis in 1967, decorated with eight baguette-cut diamonds surrounded by a border of 16 full-cut diamonds, eight being Elvis' lucky number. Levitch also supplied Priscilla's three-carat diamond ring, which he and his wife Frances personally delivered to Las Vegas for the wedding (at which Levitch was one of the select few to attend the actual ceremony).

LEWIS, JERRY LEE
(B. 1935)

Jerry Lee Lewis took a more roundabout route to Sun Records than Elvis, not making it until two years after Elvis first recorded. Lewis had been turned down plenty of times in Nashville before engineer Jack Clement "discovered" him for Sun while Sam Phillips was on a rare vacation and hired him as a session piano player.

Lewis was born poor in Ferriday, Louisiana on September 29, 1935. He developed his style very young, mixing and matching the Southern Pentecostal gospel and boogie-woogie he heard growing up. His mother enrolled him into bible college, where Lewis was promptly expelled for singing gospel songs in a rock 'n' roll style.

Known for having the best piano left-hand in the

music business, Elvis once said that if could play the piano like Jerry Lee he'd quit singing. Lewis was initially billed as Jerry Lee Lewis and his Pumping Piano. After he began recording at Sun, in 1957 he hit the big time with "Whole Lotta' Shakin' Goin' On" and then "Great Balls of Fire." Sam Phillips believed that Lewis was going be the next Elvis for him; Lewis recorded at Sun for the next seven years.

Jerry Lee "the Killer" Lewis was the original bad boy of rock 'n' roll. Lewis was wild in his stage act, kicking his piano stool across the stage and playing the piano with his feet and other body parts. He reputedly once set fire to his piano at the end of his act to make sure that nobody, not even Chuck Berry, could follow him.

To his own detriment, Lewis's wildness extended into his personal life. He effectively sabotaged his hugely promising career by taking in matrimony for his third wife Myra Gale Brown, who was his 13 year-old cousin (actually, a second cousin once removed).

Elvis and Jerry Lee Lewis spent a memorable evening jamming together with fellow Sun artists Carl Perkins (and perhaps Johnny Cash) at what was later dubbed the "Million Dollar Quartet" session. Lewis was playing piano at a Carl Perkins recording for Sun when Elvis showed up and stayed on to jam. Lewis was the last man to leave that day; the final tracks on the *Million Dollar Quartet* releases are just Lewis and the piano. Lewis's first single on Sun, "Crazy Arms," featured during this session. At the time, Elvis told journalist Bob Johnson, "I think he has a great future ahead of him."

The widely-held view that Elvis and Jerry didn't get on is disputed by many people who spent time at Graceland in the Fifties, who remember Jerry Lee Lewis coming round to play piano and jam with Elvis.

Elvis impressed Priscilla in Germany the first night they met by doing a Jerry Lee Lewis impression at the piano, bashing the keys so hard that a glass of water almost toppled off the instrument.

After the scandal broke about Jerry Lee Lewis' marriage in 1958, Lewis' records were banned from the radio and he could only play live in small locales. He had a spell of success in Europe in the mid-Sixties. Chart success finally returned for Lewis at the end of that decade; he notched up a string of country hits, though he continued to sing rock 'n' roll during his live performances.

Drugs and alcohol were more likely to bring Lewis news exposure in the Seventies. In 1976, he accidentally shot his bassist Butch Owens (who lived to tell the tale). In November that year, Lewis was arrested outside Graceland, making a ruckus, waving a gun and saying that Elvis had invited him in. His message was "You just tell him the Killer's here." Elvis watched the scene on Graceland's closed circuit camera system, and gave orders that the gates should not be opened.

Jerry Lee Lewis' topsy-turvy life made him an obvious contender for a biopic (1989 movie *Great Balls of Fire*). Three years earlier Lewis was one of the first rock stars to be inducted into the Rock and Roll Hall of Fame.

Over the years, Elvis sang Lewis's signature composition "Whole Lotta Shakin' Goin' On" and covered a great number of songs that Lewis also covered (including "I Forgot To Remember To Forget," "What'd I Say," "Green Green Grass Of Home," "Hi-Heel Sneakers" and more).

Lewis namechecked Elvis in early songs "Lewis Boogie" and "It Won't Happen To Me." In the early Seventies, Lewis released some duets with a mystery singer whose voice sounded a great deal like Elvis', but belonged to Jimmy Ellis. Lewis also took part in a major 1995 Elvis tribute concert.

LIBERACE
(B. WLADZIU VALENTINO LIBERACE, 1919-1987)

Elvis met the flamboyant entertainer, known as "Lee" to his friends, in Las Vegas in May 1956,

and made sure he took in his show when he spent a week in Sin City in November 1956. Reputedly Liberace suggested to Elvis that he should add more flamboyant costumes to his act. Soon after, Elvis began performing in that "solid gold" suit. The overblown performing costumes that Elvis wore in the early Seventies had more than a hint of the Liberace about them.

A number of well-known photos of the pair were snapped at that 1956 meeting, after the performers swapped jackets and instruments. Elvis brought home Liberace's autograph for his mother.

Liberace dropped by backstage after one of Elvis' Vegas shows in the Seventies. Elvis held Liberace in high esteem as an entertainer, and often had a seat reserved in case Liberace could make it. Elvis felt a particular bond with the entertainer because they were both born alongside a stillborn twin.

Liberace's 50-year entertainment career began as a classically-trained child prodigy pianist. He switched to popular music in 1940, but it wasn't until the Fifties that he became America's most recognizable easy-listening singer and pianist. For a few years in the early Fifties he hosted his own TV show and had some success in Hollywood; in the Seventies he became a Las Vegas fixture.

LICHTER, PAUL

An Elvis collector, memorabilia trader and a prolific author of Elvis books. Lichter founded the Elvis Unique Record Club in 1970 and published an Elvis fanzine, *Memphis Flash*, for over a decade. He lays claim to being the world's most widely-read Elvis author, with 20 million copies sold of his sixteen books.

"LIFE"

Elvis recorded this existential Shirl Milete song during his bumper June 1970 Nashville sessions (this track was laid down on June 6). When it appeared for public purchase almost a year later it was as a single, accompanied by spiritual "Only Believe" on the B-side. Despite the proximity of its April release to Easter, the record sold no more than 275,000 copies, peaking at #53 on the *Billboard* Hot 100 during the five weeks it remained on the charts.

"Life" saw its first album release on *Love Letters From Elvis*. Since then, it has appeared on the *Walk A Mile In My Shoes* and *Peace In The Valley* anthologies.

Alternate takes have come out on *Today, Tomorrow & Forever* and FTD release *The Nashville Marathon*.

LIFE MAGAZINE

In its April 30, 1956 issue, *Life* magazine covered Elvis' rise to nationwide fame in an article entitled "Howling Hillbilly Success," the first national magazine to take note of the Elvis phenomenon in its pages, and the first of its many Elvis articles.

For his return to the States after his Army service in 1960, *Life* was keen to feature Elvis on its famous front cover. The offer was withdrawn after the Colonel asked for a $25,000 fee, rather than the more usual remuneration of priceless publicity.

Books:
Elvis: A Celebration in Pictures, by the Editors of Life Magazine, 2002.
Remembering Elvis 30 Year Later, by the Editors of Life magazine, 2007.

Special Collector's Edition autographed for Paul Lichter.

"LIGHTHOUSE"

Elvis sang this modern gospel track, written and first performed by The Original Hinsons, in March 1972 during rehearsals in a medley with gospel song "I, John." It's on bootleg disk *The Complete On Tour Sessions*. In the *Elvis on Tour* documentary, backing group The Stamps perform the song.

LIGHTFOOT, GORDON
(b. 1938)

In the early Seventies, Elvis recorded two songs by this Canadian folk songwriter, "Early Morning Rain" and "For Lovin' Me," which had been big hits in the mid-Sixties. Lightfoot himself had some significant success in the early Seventies with songs such as "If You Could Read My Mind" and "Sundown."

"LIKE A BABY"

Elvis sang this sax-driven R&B Jesse Stone song at a Nashville recording session on April 3, 1960, for release on the *Elvis Is Back!* LP. The song had been a hit for Vikki Nelson and Toni Arden before Elvis, and for James Brown after. "Like A Baby" has since been released on *Elvis Sings The Blues*, *From Nashville to Memphis* and *Artist Of The Century*.

A take with a false start came out on the *Collectors Gold* release; additional alternates are on 2002 FTD release *Fame And Fortune* and 2005 FTD release *Elvis Is Back!*, which features Elvis on acoustic guitar and a selection of outtakes.

LIME, YVONNE
(B. 1938, LATER YVONNE FEDDERSON)

In April 1957, this Hollywood starlet visited Elvis in Memphis, where she was proudly shown round Elvis' new home Graceland, and spent an evening at Sam Phillips' place which concluded in impromptu gospel singing and an early breakfast.

At Graceland in April, 1957 with Yvonne Lime, his girlfriend at the time.

Lime and Elvis met on the set of *Loving You*, in which she had an uncredited role. She worked as an actress through the Fifties and Sixties, and was a regular in "Father Knows Best" on TV. After retiring from the screen she dedicated her time to charity as a founder member of International Orphans Inc., the forerunner to child abuse prevention charity Childhelp USA.

LINDE, DENNIS
(1943-2006)

Texas-born Linde composed three songs that Elvis sang in the Seventies: "Burning Love," "For The Heart" and "I Got A Feelin' In My Body," providing guitar overdubs for his own songs during Elvis' recordings. He also provided overdubbed guitar parts for Elvis' Stax sessions in 1973, and played some additional bass for Elvis' 1976 Graceland recordings.

During his long career, Linde wrote songs for Garth Brooks, the Dixie Chicks and Eddie Raven. He was BMI songwriter of the year in 1994 and elected to the Nashville Songwriter Hall of Fame in 2001.

LIPTON, PEGGY
(B. 1946)

This Long Island-born model and actress had a dalliance with Elvis in the early Seventies, while she was in her highest-profile acting role as Julie Barnes in "The Mod Squad" (for which she won a Golden Globe). She also had a reputation for high-profile boyfriends during her "rapaciously romantic period," including Paul McCartney, Sammy Davis, Jr. and Keith Moon. In 1974 she married Quincy Jones. In the early Nineties she resumed her acting career in "Twin Peaks," and has continued to work ever since.

PEGGY LIPTON: "He was a rock and roll hermit who surrounded himself with people who adjusted their lives to his reality. To meet him you had to enter his bubble."

LISA MARIE AIRPLANE

Elvis bought a decommissioned Corvair 880 from Delta in early 1975. After extensive modification, the plane that he renamed the *Lisa Marie* became his personal jet from late fall that year.

See AIRPLANES.

"LISTEN TO THE BELLS"

Elvis sang a few lines of this The Statesman song as he was warming up for a take of "It's Only Love" in the studio in May 1971. It appears on *The Essential Elvis* collection Vol. 4.

"LITTLE BIT OF GREEN, A"

Elvis recorded this ballad of lost love, written by the team of Chris Arnold / Geoffrey Morrow / David Martin, on January 14, 1969 at American Studio in Memphis. It first came out on *From Memphis to Vegas / Back in Memphis*. More recently, it has appeared on *From Nashville to Memphis* and *Suspicious Minds: The Memphis 1969 Anthology*.

"LITTLE CABIN ON THE HILL"

Elvis sang this country classic, first recorded by Bill Monroe's Bluegrass Boys in 1947 (co-written by Lester Flatt), during the *Million Dollar Quartet* jam session, mimicking Monroe's delivery in the original. The recording from late 1956 can be found on the various *Million Dollar Quartet* issues.

Elvis next laid down the track on June 4, 1970 at the Nashville session that provided most of the material for the *Elvis Country* album. The 1970 version has since featured on *Elvis in Nashville*, *Walk A Mile In My Shoes* and *The Country Side of Elvis*. The first take from 1970 appeared on *Essential Elvis Vol. 4* in 1996.

"LITTLE DARLIN' "

A concert staple for Elvis from early 1975, a playful live version from Elvis' 1977 Saginaw, Michigan concert came out on Elvis' last album *Moody Blue*.

Alternate live performances of the Ink Spot-inspired tune (written by Maurice Williams, originally released in 1956 by The Gladiolas, and also a million-seller for The Diamonds), have appeared on *Elvis Aron Presley* and FTD live albums *Big Boss Man*, *Dixieland Rocks*, *Southern Nights* and *Spring Tours '77*.

A tape recording of Elvis singing along to the Diamonds at Eddie Fadal's home in Texas in 1958 came out on bootleg *Forever Young, Forever Beautiful*.

"LITTLE EGYPT"

Elvis recorded this Leiber and Stoller song (a 1961 hit for The Coasters) for the *Roustabout* soundtrack on March 2, 1964 in Hollywood studio Radio Recorders, a cut above his usual soundtrack standards.

He reprised the song as part of the "Nothingville" road medley for the NBC TV Special, recorded in Los Angeles in June 1968, performed in the studio in front of the TV cameras and issued on the *NBC TV Special* album.

The original Little Egypt was an exotic dancer named Ashea Wabe who caused quite a stir at the 1893 Chicago World's Fair. A movie of the same name was made by Universal in 1951, directed by Frederick De Cordova, who was later to direct Elvis in *Frankie and Johnny*.

The *Roustabout* version has since come out on *Elvis Sings Leiber & Stoller*, the *Double Trouble* series release for the movie, *Command Performances* and *Elvis at the Movies*.

Latter-day releases from the 1968 recording session are on *Memories: The '68 Comeback Special* and the multi-disc re-release of the *NBC TV Special*.

An alternate take from the 1964 session is on FTD release *Out in Hollywood*; an alternate from 1968 is on FTD disc *Let Yourself Go*.

"LITTLE LESS CONVERSATION, A"

Elvis got funky after far too long with this song put together in five minutes by Mac Davis and Billy Strange at a Hollywood Coffee Shop. Elvis laid down the track on March 7, 1968 at Western Recorders studio. When it came out as a single, it passed under the radar of all but Elvis' most hardened fans, the ones who were still buying after years of unengaging material. On initial release in September 1968 with "Almost in Love" on the B-side, "A Little Less Conversation" climbed no higher than #69 and mustered just about 100,000 sales.

The track featured in the film *Live A Little, Love A Little* but wasn't released on LP until 1973 budget album *Almost In Love*. It next appeared in 1995, when two versions appeared on the *Double Feature* re-release and one on *Command Performances*, followed more recently by *The Essential Elvis Presley* and *Elvis at the Movies*.

The public may not have recognized a winner first time round but the song turned out to have staying power. A revised recording from June 1968 intended for the NBC TV Special that was cut at the last minute rose like a phoenix in the new millennium when, remixed by JXL, it swept to #1 in the UK and many other international territories"a version that has since appeared on *Elvis by the Presleys*, *ELVIS 30 #1 Hits*, *Hitstory* and *The Essential Elvis Presley* (2007).

Alternate takes from the original recording session have appeared on *Almost In Love* and the *Double Features* album for *Live a Little, Love a Little*. The discarded NBC version came out on *Memories: The '68 Comeback Special*.

LITTLE RICHARD
(B. RICHARD WAYNE PENNIMAN, 1932)

To some, Little Richard is "The Real King of Rock and Roll," though he himself is quoted to have said "Elvis may have been the king of rock-'n'roll, but I am the queen." Among his other titles is the "Architect of Rock 'n' Roll."

Little Richard was born in Macon, Georgia on December 5, 1932. He grew up on a diet of down South gospel and started playing boogie-woogie and jump blues in the early Fifties. Before long, he had developed his own extravagant idiosyncratic type of R 'n' B, one of the strands of nascent rock 'n' roll. His first big hit "Tutti Frutti," was a song that like Elvis' "That's All Right (Mama)" was something that he knocked up while messing around during a studio break.

Little Richard had a string of hits in 1956 and 1957, and quickly earned credits in four early rock movies.

As Elvis rose to national prominence in 1956, he covered a number of Little Richard songs to fill out his repertoire. Little Richard already had done well with the songs he chose: "Tutti Frutti," "Long Tall Sally" (both of which Little Richard co-wrote) and "Ready Teddy" and "Rip It Up." By the time Richard racked up hits with "Slippin' And Slidin'," "Good Golly, Miss Molly" and "The Girl Can't Help It," Elvis was big enough to have his own stable of songwriters.

In 1957, Little Richard gave up rock and rolling ways to become a Pentecostal minister (after reputedly taking the launch of the Soviet Sputnik as a sign to mend his wanton ways). Few performers had come close to matching Little Richard's onstage explosiveness or his unapologetic camp.

Little Richard confined himself to gospel for a few years, and then in the early Sixties returned to rock 'n' roll, taking his show round Europe with then unknown local openings acts The Beatles, and later The Rolling Stones. He also signed up a guitarist called Maurice James, better known by his performing moniker, Jimi Hendrix (who, incidentally, saw Elvis perform in Seattle in 1957).

In later years, Little Richard has continued to perform gospel and rock 'n' roll, and be his larger-than-life self. He was one of the first performers to be inducted into the Rock and Roll Hall of Fame when it was established. He won an honorary Lifetime Achievement Grammy Award in 1993. As an ordained minister, Little Richard has also performed one or two celebrity weddings (ask for references from Cyndi Lauper, Bruce Willis and Demi Moore, and Bruce Springsteen).

"LITTLE SISTER"

Elvis recorded this Doc Pomus / Mort Shuman track in Nashville on June 26, 1961 for almost immediate single release as the B-side of "(Marie's the Name) His Latest Flame." Elvis picked up the song after Bobby Darin had turned it down. As soon as Elvis and the Nashville band recorded it, engineer Bill Porter said "We've got a classic" (words which can be heard on 2003 FTD release *Studio B: Nashville Outtakes*). Alternate takes from the session are on *Elvis Sings Mort Shuman & Doc Pomus*, *Essential Elvis Vol. 6*, and half a dozen on 2006 FTD release *Something For Everybody*.

"Little Sister" made it to #5 in the charts on initial release, selling around 700,000 units during its three months in the charts. It did even better in the UK, claiming #1 for four straight weeks. The track made its first album appearance on *Elvis' Golden Records Vol. 3*. Other albums on which the song appears include *The Top Ten Hits*, *Worldwide Gold Award Hits Vol. 1*, *From Nashville to Memphis*, *Artist Of The Century*, *Elvis 2nd to None*, *Hitstory* and *The Essential Elvis Presley*.

Elvis often sang the live in the Seventies, particularly in 1972 and 1977. For his live shows in 1970 Elvis worked the song up in a medley with "Get Back," to be found on *Elvis Aron Presley*, various bootlegs and FTD release *Summer Festival*. A rehearsal of the song was included in the *That's The Way It Is* documentary. Other live release are on *Elvis in Concert*, the *That's The Way It Is* Special Edition, *Burning Love*, *Live in Las Vegas*, and FTD releases *An American Trilogy*, *New Year's Eve*, *Spring Tours '77* and *Unchained Melody*.

LIVE A LITTLE, LOVE A LITTLE / CHARRO! / THE TROUBLE WITH GIRLS / CHANGE OF HABIT (DOUBLE FEATURE)

To wind up Elvis' Double Feature series, in 1995 RCA released a double double-feature of songs from Elvis' last four features plus extras.

TRACK LISTING:
1. Almost In Love
2. A Little Less Conversation
3. Wonderful World
4. Edge Of Reality
5. A Little Less Conversation (album version)
6. Charro!
7. Let's Forget About The Stars
8. Clean Up Your Own Backyard
9. Swing Down, Sweet Chariot
10. Signs Of The Zodiac (w. Marlyn Mason)
11. Almost
12. The Whiffenpoof Song
13. Violet
14. NYU
15. Clean Up Your Own Backyard (undubbed version)
16. Almost (undubbed version)
17. Have A Happy
18. Let's Be Friends
19. Change Of Habit
20. Let Us Pray
21. Rubberneckin'

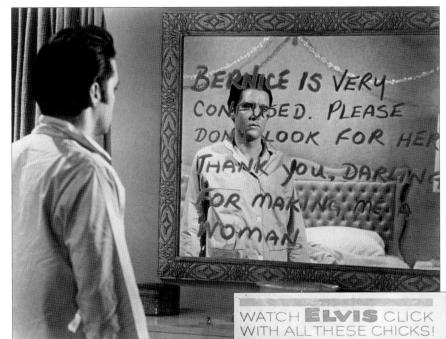

Elvis as Greg Nolan in *Live A Little, Love A Little* (1968).

LIVE A LITTLE, LOVE A LITTLE

This 1968 comic caper was based on Dan Greenburg's novel *Kiss My Firm But Pliant Lips*, which was also one of the working titles for the movie (along with *Bumblebee Oh Bumblebee* and *Born Rich*).

Elvis reported for preproduction in early March 1968. All was done and dusted by May 1.

The movie departed from the standard Elvis formula by tipping its hat to the hippy happenings of the Sixties, including a psychedelic scene in which Elvis' character is drugged.

Scenes were shot in and around Hollywood, including the *Hollywood Citizen-News* offices, along the Malibu coast, at Marineland and at the Los Angeles Music Center.

The movie features Dick Sargent, the actor who replaced Dick York to become "Darrin #2" in TV show "Bewitched" (and had a bit part in Elvis' first movie, *Love Me Tender*). Twenties crooner Rudy Vallee also appeared in the movie, as did Vernon, Joe Esposito and Red West, all of whom had bit parts.

The song that didn't make the cut was "Let's Live A Little," originally title track material. The remainder of the four-song soundtrack showed signs of Elvis' imminent resurgence.

On nationwide release in October 1968, the movie did poor business. It didn't even warrant release on some markets such as the UK. This was also director Norman Taurog's last ever movie.

CREDITS:
MGM, Color.
Length: 94 minutes
Release date: October 23, 1968

TAGLINES:
Watch Elvis click with all these chicks!
Elvis shoots the works from dawn to darkroom as a pinup photographer who doesn't want to get pinned down.

Directed by: Norman Taurog
Produced by: Douglas Laurence
Written by: Dan Greenburg (novel), Michael A. Hoey (screenplay)
Music by: Billy Strange
Cinematography by: Fred J. Koenekamp
Film Editing by: John McSweeney Jr.
Art Direction by: Preston Ames, George Davis
Set Decoration by: Henry Grace, Don Greenwood Jr.

CAST:

Elvis Presley	Greg Nolan
Michele Carey	Bernice / Betty / Suzie / Alice
Don Porter	Mike Lansdown
Rudy Vallee	Louis Penlow
Dick Sargent	Harry Baby
Sterling Holloway	Milkman
Celeste Yarnall	Ellen
Eddie Hodges	Woodrow (delivery boy)
Joan Shawlee	Robbie's mother
Mary Grover	Miss Selfridge
Emily Banks	Advertising company receptionist
Michael Keller	Art director
Merri Ashley	Secretary #1
Phyllis Davis	Secretary #2
Ursula Menzel	Perfume model
Susan Shute	Model #1
Edie Baskin	Model #2
Gabrielle	Model #3
Ginny Kaneen	Model #4
Susan Henning	Sally the Mermaid
Morgan Windbeil	Motorcycle cop #1
Benjie Bancroft	Motorcycle cop #2
Lonnie Burr	Cool dude #2
Russ Bender	Editor

Larry Billman	Dream sequence dancer
Thordis Brandt	Blonde
Ann Doran	Landlady
Veronica Ericson	Woman #2
Joe Esposito	Workman at newspaper
John Hegner	Robbie Pussycat
Bruce Hoy	Dancer
Marcia Mae Jones	Woman #1
Britt Lomond	Cool dude #3
Brooke Mills	Model in lobby
James Oliver	Cool dude #1
Vernon Presley	Model
Hal Riddle	Man in elevator
Bartlett Robinson	Doctor
Myrna Ross	Female companion
Paul Sorenson	Workman
Hiroko Watanabe	Masseuse
Red West	Newspaper vendor
John Wheeler	Workman
Heidi Winston	Model

ADDITIONAL CREW:

Mary Keats	hair stylist
William Tuttle	makeup coordinator
Lindsley Parsons Jr.	unit production manager
Al Shenberg	assistant director
Franklin Milton	recording supervisor
Carol Daniels	stunts
Jack Baker	choreographer, "A Little Less Conversation"
Michael A. Hoey	assistant to producer
Jack Regas	choreographer, Dream Sequence

Plot:

Elvis is Greg Nolan, a photographer with a sideline in singing. Life is sweet until the day he meets wacky Bernice (played by Michele Carey) on the beach. Bernice responds to his reticence to make love to her immediately by getting her Great Dane run him into the ocean.

By the time the dog lets him out, Greg has pneumonia. Bernice, an artist who changes her name practically as often as her clothes, nurses him back to health at her home, which is populated by a torrent of guests and visitors, one of whom, Harry Baby (played by Dick Sargent), claims to be Bernice's deceased husband.

Greg is unceremoniously dumped from his job for disappearing without a word. Meanwhile, unbeknownst to Greg, Bernice moves all of his stuff from his apartment and terminates his rental agreement.

Ready by now to question his own sanity, Greg goes out to get a new job. Two jobs, in fact, for competing companies in the same building: an advertising agency run by Louis Penlow (played by Rudy Vallee), and girlie magazine *Classic Cat* run by the roguish Mike Lansdown (played by Don Porter). Slapstick ensues as Greg becomes a quick-change artist to meet the contrasting dress codes at each workplace.

Bernice finds Greg a beautiful new apartment that is way too expensive for him. At a dinner party, Greg throws a punch at Harry. At another party held by boss Mike Lansdown, Greg gets lucky with a girl called Ellen (played by Celeste Yarnall) only to take her home and find Bernice there, acting bizarrely. Later, when Bernice shares a bed with Greg, she builds a wooden partition down the middle.

Greg returns to the beach house to find Bernice after she has run off again, leaving behind a message that she is "very confused" after their time in bed. There's more fisticuffs with the ineffectual Harry, and then a bookend of a finale as the Great Dane chase Bernice into the ocean and there's a happy ending kiss. Albert the dog gets the closing shot.

Songs: "Wonderful World," "Edge Of Reality," "A Little Less Conversation," "Almost In Love"

LIVE GREATEST HITS, THE

A 2001 BMG International album of Elvis concert classics from between 1969 and 1973.

TRACK LISTING:
1. Blue Suede Shoes
2. Heartbreak Hotel
3. Jailhouse Rock / Don't Be Cruel
4. Are You Lonesome Tonight?
5. One Night
6. I've Lost You
7. I Just Can't Help Believin'
8. In The Ghetto
9. Don't Cry, Daddy
10. Kentucky Rain
11. The Wonder Of You
12. Polk Salad Annie
13. Suspicious Minds
14. All Shook Up
15. Hound Dog
16. You Don't Have To Say You Love Me
17. Until It's Time For You To Go
18. Burning Love
19. An American Trilogy
20. A Big Hunk O' Love
21. Can't Help Falling In Love

LIVE IN L.A.

A 2007 FTD soundboard recording of Elvis playing LA in 1974, accompanied by a book.

TRACK LISTING:
1. Also Sprach Zarathustra
2. See See Rider
3. I Got A Woman / Amen
4. Love Me
5. Tryin' To Get To You
6. All Shook Up
7. Teddy Bear / Don't Be Cruel
8. Love Me Tender
9. Steamroller Blues
10. Hound Dog
11. Fever
12. Polk Salad Annie
13. Why Me Lord
14. Suspicious Minds
15. Introductions
16. I Can't Stop Loving You
17. Help Me
18. An American Trilogy
19. Let Me Be There
20. Funny How Time Slips Away
21. Big Boss Man
22. Can't Help Falling In Love
23. You Can Have Her

LIVE IN LAS VEGAS

A 4-CD box set released in 2001 of Elvis doing what he does best in the town he played most, from highly-acclaimed 1969 and 1970 performances to rare material from 1974 / 1975 and his first ever Las Vegas engagement in 1956.

TRACK LISTING:
Disc: 1
1. Blue Suede Shoes
2. I Got A Woman
3. All Shook Up
4. Elvis greets the audience
5. Love Me Tender
6. Jailhouse Rock / Don't Be Cruel
7. Heartbreak Hotel
8. Hound Dog
9. I Can't Stop Loving You
10. Johnny B. Goode
11. Baby What You Want Me To Do
12. Runaway
13. Are You Lonesome Tonight?
14. Yesterday / Hey Jude
15. Introductions
16. In The Ghetto
17. Suspicious Minds
18. What'd I Say
19. Can't Help Falling In Love
20. Elvis talks about his career

DISC: 2
1. That's All Right (Mama)
2. I Got A Woman
3. Hound Dog
4. Love Me Tender
5. There Goes My Everything
6. Just Pretend
7. I Just Can't Help Believin'
8. Something
9. Men with broken hearts
10. Walk A Mile In My Shoes
11. You've Lost That Lovin' Feelin'
12. Polk Salad Annie
13. One Night
14. Don't Be Cruel
15. Love Me
16. Instrumental Vamp
17. Heartbreak Hotel
18. Introductions
19. Bridge Over Troubled Water
20. Suspicious Minds
21. Can't Help Falling In Love
22. When The Snow Is On The Roses

DISC: 3
1. See See Rider
2. Release Me
3. Sweet Caroline
4. The Wonder Of You
5. Polk Salad Annie
6. Proud Mary
7. Walk A Mile In My Shoes
8. In The Ghetto
9. Let It Be Me
10. Don't Cry, Daddy
11. Kentucky Rain
12. Long Tall Sally
13. I Can't Stop Loving You
14. Suspicious Minds
15. Never Been To Spain
16. You Gave Me A Mountain
17. It's Impossible
18. It's Over
19. Hound Dog
20. Little Sister / Get Back
21. A Big Hunk O' Love
22. The Impossible Dream
23. An American Trilogy

DISC: 4
1. Heartbreak Hotel
2. Long Tall Sally
3. Blue Suede Shoes
4. Money Honey
5. Promised Land
6. It's Midnight
7. If You Talk In Your Sleep
8. I'm Leavin'
9. Why Me Lord
10. Help Me
11. Softly As I Leave You
12. My Baby Left Me
13. It's Now Or Never
14. Hawaiian Wedding Song
15. Tryin' To Get To You
16. Green, Green Grass Of Home
17. You're The Reason I'm Living
18. Big Boss Man
19. Burning Love
20. My Boy
21. And I Love You So
22. Just Pretend
23. How Great Thou Art
24. America The Beautiful

ABOVE: Elvis on stage in Los Angeles in the 1950s.
BELOW: Elvis in his "I Got Lucky Suit" at the L.A. Forum, November 1970.

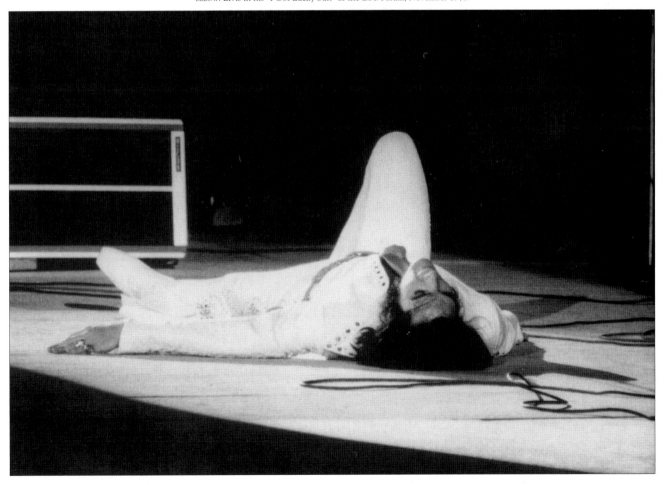

Elvis, with Gary Lockwood, right in *It Happened at The World's Fair*.

LIVE IN LAS VEGAS '73

A soundboard recording bootleg released on STEN in 1993.

TRACK LISTING:
1. That's All Right
2. I Got A Woman
3. Love Me
4. Mystery Train
5. Sweet Caroline
6. You've Lost That Lovin' Feelin'
7. Polk Salad Annie
8. Something
9. Johnny B. Goode
10. Don't Be Cruel
11. Heartbreak Hotel
12. Blue Suede Shoes
13. Little Sister / Get Back
14. It's Now Or Never
15. Hound Dog
16. The Impossible Dream
17. Yesterday / Hey Jude
18. In The Ghetto
19. Suspicious Minds
20. What'd I Say
21. Can't Help Falling In Love
22. It's Over
23. A Big Hunk O' Love
24. It's Impossible.

LOCKE, DIXIE
(B. 1940)

Dixie Locke was a 14-year-old sophomore at South Side High School in Memphis when she caught sight of Elvis at a First Assembly of God church function in January 1954. The first time they spoke was when they deliberately on purpose bumped into one another at the Rainbow Rollerdrome. That evening Elvis turned up wearing a bolero jacket, and got to drive her home in his 1941 Lincoln. The very next day Elvis took her out to the movies; within two weeks he had brought her home to meet mom and dad.

Elvis and Dixie stayed together for the six months still to elapse before Elvis cut his first record, and then for the year that he toured incessantly round small venues across the South. In the spring and summer of 1954, they went to the movies several times a week and took in various music events, including DJ Bob Neal's *High Noon Round-Up* at the WMPS Studio, where the Blackwood Brothers often sang. They sometimes went to Riverside Park, where he would play his guitar and sing.

Dixie was away on a family holiday in the summer of 1954, on the fateful days when Dewey Phillips first started spinning Elvis' debut disc. On her way back to Memphis from Florida, Dixie heard Elvis' version of "Blue Moon Of Kentucky" on the car radio. Much as she wanted, she couldn't go and see his earliest performances because she was too young to gain admittance.

When Elvis was in Memphis, he was with Dixie, but they were rare times as he was almost always out on the road. On May 6, 1955, he ducked out of his tour with Hank Snow's All Star Jamboree to return to Memphis for Dixie's junior prom at South Side High, together with his cousin Gene Smith and Bessie Wolverton, a good friend of Dixie's.

By the time they had been together for eighteen months, Elvis was spending up to four weeks at a time out of Memphis. Dixie wound up seeing more of Elvis' folks than she did Elvis. Inevitably, she found a new sweetheart who was more suitable marriage material than the roving Elvis. Dixie didn't have the heart to tell Elvis, but felt that she could tell Gladys that it was over. Elvis took it very hard; he had been convinced that one day they would be married.

On May 29, 1956, Elvis took Dixie out for a ride on his motorcycle after her high school graduation dress rehearsal. In early 1957, he dropped by to say hello not long after her wedding. It has been reported that, Dixie, long since Mrs. Emmons, told her mother that if Elvis had come back and said that he'd made a mistake, she'd have been prepared to think again.

Dixie rushed to Elvis' side in August 1958 when he asked her to come to Graceland after his mother's funeral. They talked about the past and cried together.

ELVIS SAID: "She was kind of small with long, dark hair that came down to her shoulders and the biggest smile I've ever seen anywhere. She was always laughing, always enjoying herself... We were a big thing. I gave her my high school ring . . . For two years we had a ball."

DIXIE LOCKE: "I thought he was the most gorgeous thing I'd ever seen. He was a very shy person, but when he started singing he put so much into putting the music across that he kind of lost himself."

LOCKWOOD, GARY
(B. JOHN GARY YUSOLFSKY, 1937)

A versatile screen and TV actor who in Elvis' early Sixties movies played Elvis' antagonist in *Wild in the Country* and pal in *It Happened at the World's Fair*. He was part of Elvis' LA cohort of football pals during this period. Later in the decade, Lockwood a role in the first ever episode of Star Trek, and in groundbreaking sci-fi movie *2001: A Space Odyssey*.

LOGAN, HORACE
(1916-2002)

Horace Lee "Hoss" Logan was the founder and program director of the Louisiana Hayride starting in 1948. A major figure in the careers of many tyro performers who got their break on the Hayride, Logan is most famous for desperately pleading with the young crowd at the Hirsch Youth Building in Shreveport to sit down as "Elvis has left the building" on December 15, 1956, when Elvis returned to give his farewell Hayride show. After Elvis walked off stage, the crowd had started to leave too, despite another dozen acts waiting in the wings for their turn on the show.

Logan began as a radio announcer in 1932 after winning a contest for the job. He joined KWKH after the war as program director, and soon established the station's "Louisiana Hayride" show as an upstart rival to the Grand Ole Opry.

Various tales have circulated as to how Elvis landed this first big break on his climb to fame. Logan was first alerted to this new performing phenomenon within a couple of weeks of the release of Elvis' debut single, either by Billy Walker or Slim Whitman who saw what Elvis did to the crowd at the Overton Park Shell in the summer of 1954. Sam Phillips and Scotty Moore likely landed the high-profile weekly engagement through one or other of the promoters who was arranging Elvis' shows across the South.

Logan left the Hayride in 1957 and went on to work in radio across the country. He spent much of the Sixties producing the "Big D Jamboree" in Dallas.

MERLE KILGORE: "When he gave you an introduction, you thought the president of the United States was coming on."

Book:
Elvis, Hank, and Me: Making Musical History on the Louisiana Hayride, by Horace Logan and Bill Sloan, St. Martin's Press, 1998.

LONDIN, LARRIE
(1943-1992)

A highly-respected Nashville session drummer. Chet Atkins said he was the greatest drummer in the world" drafted in to tour with Elvis in early 1976 and then again on Elvis' final three concert dates after regular sticksman Ronnie Tutt pulled out. At Londin's first session for Elvis, an overdub for his 1970 Christmas album, Londin was so emotional to play for his idol that he broke down in tears.

Londin started out as a house drummer at Motown. During his career Londin played with a great many renowned musicians, including Hank Snow, the Everly Brothers, Neil Young, Chet Atkins, B.B. King and Dolly Parton and Al Green..

LONELINESS

Elvis was used to having people around growing up, and he made it his business to have people around him at all times as an adult"hardly difficult for a man with immense charisma and huge financial reserves.

At several times in his life, he revealed feelings of loneliness. In a 1956 interview, Elvis said that sometimes he liked just going off to be on his own, in the peace and quiet, to think. In the early years, he would get into his old truck and ride around, wearing a motorcycle helmet to make sure that nobody recognized him. By the end of 1957, the incessant touring and travel had revealed to Elvis the price of fame: "I sometimes get lonely as hell. A lot of times I feel miserable, don't know which way to turn. Even though I'm surrounded with people, I get lonely and stare at the wall."

At Graceland, Elvis had no need to fear being alone; the house was thronged with people day and night. If none of his friends or family were around, he could talk and sometimes sing with the staff; and there were always the fans at the gate.

George Klein and other friends have said that rather than lonely, Elvis just got plain bored. Red West remembers that during his month-long residences in Las Vegas during the Seventies, Elvis was a virtual prisoner in his hotel suite, because if he showed his face in public he would simply be mobbed. According to West, "There's only one way that can go; the way it did."

ELVIS SAID: "People think I'm lonely, but I love that lonesome feelin'."

ELVIS SAID TO LARRY GELLER IN 1964: "I swear to God no one knows how lonely I get. And how empty I really feel."

ELVIS WROTE IN 1976: "I don't know who I can talk to anymore. Nor to turn to. I only have myself and the Lord. Help me Lord to know the right thing."

ELVIS SAID AT A SHOW IN 1977: " 'Are You Lonesome Tonight?' And I am, and I was . . ."

DOLORES HART: "Elvis is a very lonely man."

ANNE NEYLAND, 1957: "I think he's at a stage now where he's just given up trying to make himself a little more normal life. He's one of those people who cannot be alone. He feels he has to surround himself with close friends as a sort of protection against loneliness because you can be very lonely in a mob of strangers."

RED WEST, 1976: "It's kind of sad. All that money, all the homes and all the comfort, and yet Elvis doesn't know if he has a friend in the world. He doesn't know if the people who hang around him are there because of the money or because of him."

PETER GURALNICK: "He constructed a shell to hide his aloneness, and it hardened on his back. I know of no sadder story."

SONNY WEST: ." . . He could appear to be the loneliest person in the middle of a large crowd. At times, there was a feeling that he gave off that appeared to be very vulnerable."

RICK STANLEY: "He hated to be alone."

"LONELY MAN"

Elvis recorded this song in an orchestrated and a pared-down version at Radio Recorders on November 7, 1960 for Wild in the Country. The Bennie Benjamin / Sol Marcus track was cut from the movie but resurfaced a few months later as the B-side to "Surrender" in February 1961. "Lonely Man" reached #32 in the charts.

The song has since appeared on LPs Elvis' Gold Records Vol. 4, Worldwide Gold Award Hits Vol. 2, Command Performances and Elvis at the Movies. The Elvis-and-guitar solo version first appeared in 1991 on Collectors Gold. Both versions are on the Double Features release from 1995.

The first take from the original session is on Today, Tomorrow & Forever and Elvis: Close Up, which also features another alternate, as does FTD release Out in Hollywood.

"LONESOME COWBOY"

Elvis laid down this melodramatic Sid Tepper / Roy Bennett track, the first of many Elvis would record by this prolific duo"on January 15, 1957 at Radio Recorders for the movie Loving You. It was released on volume two of the Loving You EP and on the soundtrack LP in the summer of 1957.

Later releases are on Worldwide Gold Award Hits Vol. 2, Essential Elvis Vol. 1, The King Of Rock And Roll and the FTD Loving You soundtrack release.

"LONG BLACK LIMOUSINE"

This soulful tune, written by Vern Stovall and Bobby George, was the first track that Elvis laid down at his soon-to-be-legendary American Studio sessions in Memphis, on January 13, 1969. The song had been recorded by Glen Campbell and Gordon Terry in the early Sixties; a year before Elvis sang it with unbridled passion, Jody Miller took it into the lower reaches of the country charts.

"Long Black Limousine" was initially released on From Elvis In Memphis, since when it has featured on From Nashville to Memphis, Suspicious Minds: The Memphis 1969 Anthology and The Country Side of Elvis.

Two alternate takes appeared on 2001 FTD disk The Memphis Sessions. A version with revised instrumentation came out on FTD release Too Much Monkey Business.

"LONG LEGGED GIRL (WITH THE SHORT DRESS ON)"

Elvis recorded this half-length song, the heaviest rock song he had done in many years, for the Double Trouble soundtrack at Radio Recorders on June 29, 1966. In April 1967, the J. Leslie McFarland / Winfield Scott collaboration was released as a single to publicize the movie release. It failed to climb any higher than #63 in the charts, selling 200,000 copies on initial release. The B-side was "That's Someone You Never Forget."

The song was released on the Double Trouble soundtrack LP, then on Almost In Love, Elvis Sings Hits from His Movies, Command Performances and Elvis at the Movies. Alternates have appeared in recent years on Today, Tomorrow & Forever (the alternate master) and the 2004 FTD Double Trouble release.

"LONG LIVE ROCK AND ROLL (SCHOOL DAYS)"

Elvis occasionally sang this Chuck Berry classic on tour from the Spring of 1975. A version was released posthumously on Elvis Aron Presley in 1980. A late 1975 performance from Las Vegas has appeared on bootleg releases including Unsurpassed Masters; FTD release Dixieland Rocks features the song in a medley with "Johnny B.

Goode" from May 1975, while a mid-1976 performance is on FTD release Tucson '76. The song had been a #3 Billboard Hot 100 hit for Berry back in 1957 under the title "School Days."

"(IT'S A) LONG LONELY HIGHWAY"

Elvis recorded this Doc Pomus / Mort Shuman song on May 27, 1963 in Nashville. It was first released as the B-side to August 1965 single "I'm Yours," though in actual fact an alternate from the Tickle Me movie, in which Elvis sings the song, was released by mistake.

The song was first released on LP as a bonus song on the Kissin' Cousins soundtrack. It has later appeared on For The Asking (The Lost Album) and From Nashville to Memphis.

The LP master is on the 2005 FTD Tickle Me release; the single master reappeared on the FTD issue Long Lonely Highway. Both versions came out in 1985 on Elvis Sings Mort Shuman & Doc Pomus.

LONG LONELY HIGHWAY

A 2000 FTD CD of never previously released alternates.

TRACK LISTING:
1. It's Now Or Never
2. A Mess Of Blues
3. It Feels So Right
4. I'm Yours
5. Anything That's Part of You
6. Just For Old Time Sake
7. You'll Be Gone
8. I Feel That I've Known You Forever
9. Just Tell Her Jim Said Hello
10. She's Not You
11. Devil In Disguise
12. Never Ending
13. Finders Keepers, Losers Weepers
14. (It's A) Long Lonely Highway
15. Slowly But Surely
16. By And By
17. Fools Fall In Love
18. Come What May
19. Guitar Man
20. Singing Tree
21. Too Much Monkey Business
22. Stay Away (slow version)

LONG LOST AND FOUND SONGS

A 1992 live bootleg from various Seventies concerts, issued on the Vault Recorders label.

TRACK LISTING:
1. Just Pretend
2. It's A Matter Of Time
3. Tiger Man
4. Down In The Alley
5. Such A Night
6. Loving You
7. Crying In The Chapel
8. Roses Are Red / I'll Be There (If Ever You Want Me)
9. You're The Reason I'm Living
10. Crying Time
11. San Antonio Rose
12. Where No One Stand Alone
13. When God Calls Me Home
14. Bathroom chat
15. Blue Suede Shoes
16. Young And Beautiful
17. Are You Lonesome Tonight?
18. If You Love MeIf You Love Me (Let Me Know)
19. Folsom Prison Blues / I Walk The Line

20. Amen
21. I Got A Woman
22. You Don't Know Me / I Got A Woman
23. Raised On Rock
24. Memphis Tennessee
25. Bridge Over Troubled Water
26. The First Time Ever I Saw Your Face

LONG LOST HOME RECORDINGS, THE

An unofficial 2002 release on the Memory Records label of Elvis singing for fun.

TRACK LISTING:
1. As Long As I Have You
2. Wild In The Country
3. Do Not Disturb
4. Hard Knocks
5. In Your Arms
6. I Really Don't Want To Know
7. I Need Your Love Tonight
8. Get A Job
9. How Great Thou Art
10. Fame And Fortune
11. Steamroller Blues
12. Tonight
13. Mystery Train
14. That's When Your Heartaches Begin
15. Pocketful Of Rainbows
16. Shoppin' Around
17. Love Me
18. Moonlight Swim
19. Doing The Best I Can
20. Have I Told You Lately That I Love You
21. We Call On Him
22. The Walls Have Ears
23. They Remind Me Too Much Of You
24. Tutti Frutti
25. Separate Ways
26. Spanish Eyes
27. Johnny B. Goode
28. It's Over
29. Moonlight Swim

LONG, SHORTY

The oxymoronically-named pianist was hired for Elvis' January/February and July 1956 New York recording sessions, tinkling the ivories on some of Elvis' best-known songs such as "Don't Be Cruel," "Hound Dog," "Tutti Frutti" and "Blue Suede Shoes."

"LONG TALL SALLY"

Elvis sang this frenetic Little Richard shouter, written by Richard and credited to Enotris Johnson, Richard Penniman and Robert "Bumps" Blackwell, during his first, ill-fated engagement in Las Vegas in early May 1956. Undaunted at its lack of success, he reprised the song at Ellis Auditorium on May 15, 1956, introducing it as "recorded by a friend of mine called Little Richard. I never met him, but here's his song." A live recording from this 1956 date has appeared on *Elvis Aron Presley*, *The King Of Rock 'n' Roll*, *Live in Las Vegas* (with some geographic liberty) and *Today, Tomorrow & Forever*. A live version from Tupelo in September that year is on *A Golden Celebration*.

Elvis finally recorded the song at Radio Recorders on September 2, 1956. It first came out on his second LP *Elvis*, and on the *Strictly Elvis* EP.

For Little Richard, the song was his second million-seller, reaching the top 10 of the general *Billboard* chart in early 1956 (soon followed by the almost inevitable Pat Boone cover). The song has since been covered by hundreds of artists,

including Paul McCartney who performed it when he auditioned for John Lennon's first band The Quarrymen.

"Long Tall Sally" was perfect material when Elvis wanted to pick up the pace of his live shows in the Seventies. Versions are on *Live in Las Vegas* and FTD albums *Polk Salad Annie* and *Closing Night*.

Elvis paired the song in a medley with "Whole Lotta Shakin' Goin' On" for his 1973 *Aloha From Hawaii Via Satellite* concert.

By the time he performed in his hometown in 1974 (*Elvis Recorded Live On Stage In Memphis*), the medley took in most of his early career, including "Your Mama Don't Dance," "Flip, Flop And Fly," "Jailhouse Rock" and "Hound Dog." FTD album *I Found My Thrill* features an alternate early 1974 "Long Tall Sally" medley.

"LOOK OUT, BROADWAY"

Elvis is in cabaret mode in this duet with Eileen Wilson (who provided the singing voice for Donna Douglas on screen in *Frankie and Johnny*). The track was written by Fred Wise and Randy Starr and recorded on May 14, 1965 at Radio Recorders.

Aside from resurfacing on the *Double Features* issue of the movie in the Nineties, alternate takes are on the FTD *Frankie and Johnny* release from 2003.

LORD, JACK
(B. JOHN JOSEPH PATRICK RYAN, 1920-1988)

Elvis invited Jack Lord and his wife Marie to his *Aloha From Hawaii* concert in January 1973. The star of Hawaii Five-0 from 1968 to 1980 received Elvis' compliments on stage when Elvis said Lord was "his favorite actor in the world." Elvis gave Lord a gold-plated Werther revolver, and Marie a diamond (or emerald) ring . . . plus the jewel-encrusted belt he was intending to wear during the performance, causing a panic in the costume department. The Lords gave Elvis an antique six-string banjo. They remained in contact until the end of Elvis' life, and sent to see him perform in Las Vegas half a dozen times, in their honor, Elvis once led the band in a snatch of the Hawaii Five-0 theme.

Lord was trained at the Actors' Studio, and was also an accomplished painter. One of his early breaks was as a CIA agent in James Bond movie *Dr. No*, one of Elvis' favorites.

"LORD'S PRAYER, THE"

Elvis tackled the Lord's Prayer in what the sleeve notes refer to as an "informal performance" during rehearsals for *That's The Way It Is* in the summer of 1970, and returned to it again on May 16, 1971 during a Nashville session. The sung version of the prayer"best known in its Mahalia Jackson version"was released posthumously on *Essential Elvis Vol. 4*, *Peace In The Valley* and bootlegs, especially of times he quoted lines during shows.

LOS ANGELES

Elvis spent more time in Los Angeles than any other city except Memphis.

His first sojourns in the city of the stars were in hotels, until in 1960 his antics became too much for management at the Beverly Wilshire.

Elvis rented a variety of homes in LA, mainly in the Bel Air community in Beverly Hills. Though he was required to spend long periods in

town to fulfill his movie commitments, he often went away for weekends. Las Vegas was his favorite destination, though from the mid-Sixties he also spent plenty of weekend in Palm Springs, where he rented and later purchased a home (and where the Colonel had a place too). In the early Sixties, Elvis and pals sometimes went out on the town to see singers like Sammy Davis Jr. and Bobby Darin at venues including the Crossbow Club, the Moulin Rouge, the Cloister, the Coconut Grove and the Ambassador.

Elvis only bought his first home in LA in 1967. In 1970, he placed a down payment on a new, larger house.

In the early Seventies, Elvis may have spent almost as much time based in LA as in Memphis, though he unfailingly returned to his hometown for Christmas and his birthday every year.

Elvis played no more than half a dozen shows in LA. (*See* CALIFORNIA)

See also LIVE IN L.A.

LOS ANGELES HOMES

The first private house Elvis stayed in was at 525 Perugia Way, in Bel Air, Beverly Hills, which he rented in 1960 for $1,400 from a man called Ali Khan. Elvis used this house, once owned by the Shah of Iran and designed by Frank Lloyd Wright, periodically from September 1960 to 1965, apart from a spell in late 1961 when he rented a large Spanish-style house at 10539 Bellagio Road with a bowling alley in the basement, near the Bel Air Hotel, in Beverly Hills. As well as a den, the house acquired a sauna after Colonel Parker gave it to Elvis as a gift. In 1966, Elvis moved to a new location in Bel Air, 10550 Rocca Place, rented from landlady Mrs. Reginald Owen. Elvis had the ranch-style house redecorated to accommodate himself, Priscilla, Marty Lacker and Charlie Hodge.

Priscilla found the first LA house Elvis owned in November 1967, a home at 1174 Hillcrest Road, on the Trousdale Estate in Beverly Hills, which they purchased for around $400,000. The four-bed-room home was smaller than Elvis' previous LA residences, and better suited to a new, toned-down life style with baby Lisa Marie. Originally, Elvis had wanted to buy the house next door, but that was snapped up by Danny Thomas. The Presleys put the house on the market in 1971 for $550,000, but kept hold of it after trading up in 1970 to a new home at 144 Monovale Drive, Holmby Hills for $339,000. This house offered greater privacy and a sufficient number of bedrooms to have members of the entourage to stay. Priscilla oversaw significant renovations on the house through most of the first half of 1971, with the intention that Elvis would have all of the amenities, a den, a theater, a pool room and an office, that he had been heading off to their Palm Springs home for. The first time Elvis stayed there for any length of time was in October 1971. In early 1972, Elvis was back at the unsold Hillcrest property, with Priscilla, now separated, staying at the Monovale Drive home. The Hillcrest home was finally sold in August 1973, for $450,000. After the sale of that property, Elvis stayed at the Monovale property during his visits to LA. Elvis sold this house in June 1975 to Telly Savalas for $625,000.

LOUISIANA

- Alexandria

Elvis performed at Jimmie Thompson's Arena on March 11, 1955. Fast-forward 22 years to his next shows, at the Rapides Parish Coliseum on March 29 and 30, 1977.

Elvis performs at the Louisiana Hayride (1956).

- Bastrop

Elvis concluded his second Jamboree Attractions tour at South Side Elementary School on February 24, 1955.

- Baton Rouge

Elvis wowed the High School on a reduced version of the Hank Snow All Star Jamboree on May 2, 1955 (though some sources state he was in Jennings that night). He was definitely at the Plaquemine Casino Club on July 1, 1955, on his way to his usual Saturday Hayride performance. Elvis failed to make it to town for the premiere of his 1966 movie *Frankie and Johnny*. He was next in Baton Rouge on June 17 and 18, when he performed at the Louisiana State University Assembly Center; he returned on July 2, 1976. He was due to play the venue again on March 31, 1977, but had to cancel the date at the last minute due to fatigue. That show was rescheduled for May 31.

- Lake Charles

Elvis did a show at the Civic Center on May 4, 1975.

- Monroe

Elvis played the West Monroe High School Auditorium on February 18, 1955, the last date of that particular Hank Snow Jamboree Tour. Almost two decades later he filled the Civic Center (March 4, 1974), the Memorial Coliseum at Auburn University the following night, and then the Civic Center on March 7 and 8. This Elvis hotspot got more on May 3, 1975.

- New Orleans

The first venue that Elvis played in New Orleans was the Jesuit High School, where he was on the bill with Ann Raye on February 4, 1955. He played the Municipal Auditorium on May 1, 1955, as a "Special Added Attraction" to Hank Snow's All Star Jamboree. He performed at the Pontchartrain Beach Amusement Park on September 1, 1955, in front of 20,000 people attending the "Hillbilly Jamboree" and the "Miss Hillbilly Dumplin' " competition.

Elvis spent some vacation time in New Orleans in 1956 with girlfriend June Juanico, visiting the city sights and the Pontchartrain Beach Amusement Park. After a performance at the Municipal Auditorium on August 12, 1956, Elvis was awarded the key to the city. New Orleans experienced a near-riot in February 1958 after the mayor announced an "Elvis Presley Day" to celebrate the King and his entourage coming to town for location work on *King Creole*.

- Shreveport

Elvis' first big break was a regular Saturday night slot at the Louisiana Hayride in Shreveport, where he held a residency from November 1954. Over the next year and a half, he performed at the Municipal Auditorium more than forty times. That first month in Shreveport, Elvis and the boys added an appearance at the Lake Cliff Club (where they received a frosty reception from the fans of regular Friday night act Hoot and Curley). In December 1956, Elvis played the Louisiana Fairgrounds one last time, as part of the deal to annul his regular weekly contact.

On June 7, 1975, Elvis returned to play the Hirsch Coliseum. He last played this venue on July 1, 1976.

LOUISIANA HAYRIDE

Municipal Auditorium, Shreveport, Louisiana.

The first major venue to offer Elvis the chance to perform to a much wider audience (almost four thousand in the auditorium, and many more over the airwaves) was this weekly three-hour show syndicated on radio stations across much of the South and West. After Elvis' first night at the Hayride, three months after releasing his debut single, he signed an "apprenticeship contract" for a weekly Saturday night slot, which he filled most weekends until he became a national attraction.

Founded by Horace "Hoss" Logan (and named after a book by Harnett Kane), the Louisiana Hayride was a premier country music show broadcast from Shreveport between 1948 until 1960, running the Grand Ole Opry close in popularity. It was known for taking a chance on up-and-coming talent. Before Elvis, the Louisiana Hayride scouted among others Hank Williams, Kitty Wells, Jim Reeves, Slim Whitman, and Hank Snow; not for nothing was it known as "The Cradle to the Stars." In its heyday, the three-hour show was broadcast across a network of regional "hayride stations," led by sponsor station KWKH, whose signal covered much of the Mid-South. The Hayride could be heard in up to 28 states.

After playing the Eagle's Nest in Memphis on October 15, 1954, Sam Phillips drove Elvis and the band to Shreveport, seven hours from Memphis. On Saturday October 16, 1954, Elvis took to the stage and quickly went through his two-song repertoire. That first night Elvis performed on a bill headlined by Tibby Edwards and Merle Kilgore. Because he was a relative unknown, Elvis was announced by Frank Page rather than top MC Horace Logan. Page introduced the young man as "only 19 years old; he has a new distinctive style. Elvis Presley! Would you give him a nice hand?" The audience turned out to be so bemused by Elvis' new sound and wild antics that, in the words of one commentator, they "just sat on their hands when he finished." Later that evening Elvis returned for a repeat set. This time he followed the advice fellow musicians had given him backstage: he started a little more subdued and picked up as he went on. This time the crowd went wild; some members of the audience spontaneously rushed the stage. Merle Kilgore looked on as "Elvis just destroyed 'em on that next performance."

How exactly Elvis landed this significant break has been told different ways by different people at different times. Horace Logan first heard about Elvis from musicians Slim Whitman and Billy Walker, who had watched Elvis get a bigger reaction than their established acts that summer in Memphis. Sam Phillips is said to have arranged Elvis' debut slot on the Louisiana Hayride through Pappy Covington (who later promoted Elvis on early 1955 tours of Arkansas and Texas). Phillips also sent Elvis' one-and-only record to DJ T. Tommy Cutrer, who had a country show on KCIJ.

Elvis did well enough to warrant a return on Saturday November 6, 1954. This time, he

Elvis at the Louisiana Hayride (1955).

expanded his repertoire with covers of "Sittin' On Top of the World," The Clovers' hit " Fool, Fool, Fool" and Roy Hamilton's "I'm Gonna Sit Right Down And Cry." Elvis was accompanied by his parents Vernon and Gladys, there to see their boy and to sign a contract that would have Elvis performing at the Hayride every Saturday night for a whole year and earning the grand sum of $18 per show (Scotty Moore and Bill Black were on $12 each).

The weekly Hayride show was where Elvis developed his stage act. Announcer Frank Page watched as Elvis "developed his wiggle, his snarl and his mumble." Promoter Tillman Franks recalled that it took Elvis only a month to land the coveted spot as the closing act. The ripples Elvis was making reached as far as *Billboard* magazine in December, 1954, which gave "the youngster with the hillbilly blues beat" a write-up as "the hottest piece of merchandise on the . . . Louisiana Hayride at the moment." By Christmas 1954, Elvis had added current hits by Otis Williams and the Charms ("Hearts Of Stone") and Joe Turner ("Shake, Rattle And Roll") to his set.

In September 1955, manager Bob Neal renegotiated Elvis' Hayride contract, bumping up his fee to $200 per night (with a $400 penalty built in for every Saturday show missed, an increasingly common event as Elvis' star was on the ascendant). By the end of that month, Elvis was top of the bill. When Colonel Parker took over Elvis' bookings, it took all of his wiles to extricate Elvis from this deal for more lucrative dates elsewhere. The Colonel didn't manage until April 1956, when the Hayride accepted a $10,000 cashier's check to buy out the remaining six months of the contract (twice what it was actually worth).

Elvis did his final regular Saturday night show on March 31, 1956. The Hayride's forsaken young audience had one last chance to see their hero at the end of the year that saw him crowned as the biggest star in popular music. Elvis returned to Shreveport on December 15, 1956, with director/scriptwriter Hal Kanter in tow doing research for his upcoming film *Loving You*, to play the Hirsch Youth Center at the Louisiana Fairgrounds. This was the night that announcer Horace Logan placated the overexcited young crowd by pronouncing his oft-repeated phrase, "Elvis has left the building."

HAYRIDE ALBUMS

Many bootlegs of Elvis performing at the Hayride have come out over the years, including two released on the Music Works label in 1984 (*Elvis: The First Live Recordings* and *Elvis: The Hillbilly Cat*), *The Louisiana Hayride Shows* on the Goldies label in 1998, and *Good Rockin' Tonight* on Music Mill from 2000. More recent releases include *Elvis Presley at the Louisiana Hayride* (2003) and in 2006 a combined book and 2-disc CD set titled *Elvis at the Hayride*.

The *Memphis Recording Service* book/DVD package includes audio of Elvis and the band's first performance at the Hayride on October 16, 1954.

FRANK PAGE, HAYRIDE ANNOUNCER: "The Hayride was the hottest thing in country music from about 1947 to 1957. In those 10 years we formed more stars and found more talent than probably any other show . . . even the Grand Ole Opry."

SLIM WHITMAN: "It was popular from Louisiana to Texas, Arizona and even California. You could sell fifty thousand records off the stage of the Louisiana Hayride."

LOUVIN BROTHERS

In the Forties and Fifties, Charlie (b. 1927) and Ira (1924"1965) were a popular gospel and country duo known for their close harmonies. Elvis shared the bill with them in 1955 at venues in Arkansas and Virginia. He later recorded "It Ain't No Big Thing (But It's Growing)" in 1970, a hit for Charlie Louvin two years previously.

LOVE

Throughout his adult life, Elvis was a figurehead of love for millions of adoring female fans. He also inspired fierce love and loyalty in the guys who were part of his entourage.

Elvis grew up cocooned in maternal love that most biographers describe as smothering. Gladys, whose middle name was Love, in homage to a friend of her mother's, loved Elvis more than anything in her life, and Elvis loved her right back. The case has been made that Gladys was the love of Elvis' life.

After the age of puberty, Elvis was a serial romantic who fell deeply in love with a good many of the great many girlfriends in his life: Dixie Locke, June Juanico, Anita Wood, Priscilla, Ann-Margret, Linda Thompson and quite a few ladies in-between. When Elvis was in love it was total, though like in many other things, his attention span was not always that long.

He remained a romantic until his the very end of his life. Within weeks of meeting Ginger Alden, his last major girlfriend, he was talking about marriage and making babies. Every woman he fell in love with, he hoped would be his soul mate. The hard knocks of life set him back but never dissuaded him from his quest.

Being Elvis' #1 girl required sacrifices. When Elvis sailed to Germany, a reporter asked if he would get married if he met the right girl out in Germany. Elvis replied, "The way I look at it, if you find someone you're in love with and she's in love with you, she will understand about my career, and she will . . . she wouldn't want to do anything to hurt it." Dixie Locke, June Juanico and Anita Wood all had to abide by this precept.

According to Ann-Margret, for a number of Elvis insiders, the woman who came closest to being his true soul mate, one of the real tragedies of fame for Elvis was that he rarely felt he could trust his instincts in love: so many women were drawn to him because they wanted things from him, whether it be material gifts or a chance to raise their own profile. An exception to this rule was daughter Lisa Marie, for whom Elvis' paternal love and indulgence was king-sized and legendary.

The one place that Elvis could trust the loving feeling was on stage: he once described performing in front of an adoring crowd as a "completed circle of love."

ELVIS IN A 1959 LOVE LETTER: "True love holds its laurels through the ages no matter how loud the clamor of denial."

ELVIS SCRIBBLED IN A BOOK: "When you're not in love, you're not alive."

ELVIS SAID AFTER HIS DIVORCE: "You can love someone and be wrong for them."

LINDA THOMPSON: "Elvis had a great capacity for love, which I think is commendable."

PAMELA CLARKE KEOGH: "Like few men, he chased love, both giving and receiving; believing in its power like he believed in God."

LARRY GELLER: "He was an honest man who sincerely cared about those he loved and about those who loved him."

BILLY SMITH: "Elvis was somewhat fickle. He'd be madly in love for a little while, and then somebody else would come along, and he'd think, 'Here's someone who understands me a little more.' "

LISA MARIE: "I had unconditional love."

Book:
Caught in a Trap: Elvis Presley's Tragic Lifelong Search for Love, by Rick Stanley and Paul Harold, Word Publishing, 1992.

"LOVE COMING DOWN"

Elvis recorded this track, written by Jerry Chesnut, on February 6, 1976 at Graceland for his *From Elvis Presley Boulevard, Memphis, Tennessee* album. The song has since come out on *Walk A Mile In My Shoes* and the 2000 reissue of the *Moody Blue* album.

FTD releases *The Jungle Room Sessions* and *Made in Memphis* feature alternates.

LOVE, ELVIS

A 2005 BMG love-themed compilation, all songs previously released except for an alternate take of "For The Good Times."

TRACK LISTING:
1. Are You Lonesome Tonight?
2. Can't Help Falling In Love
3. Always On My Mind
4. It's Now Or Never
5. Love Me Tender
6. I Want You, I Need You, I Love You
7. Don't
8. (Now And Then There's) A Fool Such As I
9. Any Way You Want Me (That's How I Will Be)
10. Surrender
11. Hawaiian Wedding Song
12. Doin' The Best I Can
13. Fever
14. It Hurts Me
15. I Just Can't Help Believin'
16. The Wonder Of You
17. Let It Be Me
18. It's Impossible
19. For The Good Times
20. There Goes My Everything
21. And I Love You So
22. You Don't Have To Say You Love Me
23. Unchained Melody
24. If I Can Dream

"LOVE IS A MANY SPLENDORED THING"

Elvis used to sing this song, written by Sammy Fain and Paul Francis Webster and a #1 hit for The Four Aces in 1955 (and the Oscar winning song that year) at home with Charlie Hodge and Red West singing harmony. No recording has surfaced by Elvis.

"LOVE IS FOR LOVERS"

Elvis is said to have recorded this song, written by Ruth Batchelor and Sharon Silbert, for the movie *Kid Galahad* in October 1961. The song was cut from the movie and never seen again.

"LOVE LETTERS"

Recorded on May 26, 1966 in Nashville, "Love Letters" was rushed out the door the next month as a single with B-side "Come What May." The ballad was originally written by Edward Heyman and Victor Young for the 1945 movie of the same name, and was a top 5 hit for Ketty Lester in 1962.

Elvis' version sold 400,000 copies, but failed to chart any higher than #19 in seven weeks. It first appeared on an album as part of *Elvis' Gold Records Vol. 4* (followed at a distance by *A Valentine Gift For You, From Nashville to Memphis, Tomorrow Is A Long Time* and *Hitstory*).

Elvis recorded a more countrified version of the song in Nashville on June 7, 1970, when session pianist David Briggs said that he wanted to put in a better performance than he did the first time around. This version was released as the title track to the *Love Letters From Elvis* album in 1971.

Collectors Gold presents an alternate version from the original recording session, as does *Today Tomorrow & Forever*, and FTD releases *The Nashville Marathon* and *So High*. The 2000 *That's The Way It Is* Special Edition features a version from 1970.

"Love Letters" sung at later Seventies shows are on FTD releases *Tucson '76, New Year's Eve* and *Unchained Melody*.

LOVE LETTERS FROM ELVIS

RCA's first 1971 Elvis album release eschewed newly-recorded material from Nashville for unreleased tracks recorded a year earlier. The album (provisionally titled Festival), sold a bare minimum 300,000 copies, and peaked at #33 in the charts.

TRACK LISTING:
1. Love Letters
2. When I'm Over You
3. If I Were You
4. Got My Mojo Working / Keep Your Hands Off Of It
5. Heart Of Rome
6. Only Believe
7. This Is Our Dance
8. Cindy, Cindy
9. I'll Never Know
10. It Ain't No Big Thing (But It's Growing)
11. Life

"LOVE MACHINE, THE"

An easy-going *Easy Come, Easy Go* soundtrack song composed by Gerald Nelson, Fred Burch and Chuck Taylor. The band recorded instrumentals at Radio Recorders on September 29, 1966; Elvis added vocals later. In 1971, the track made it onto budget movie collection LP *I Got Lucky*. Alternate takes have come out on the *Double Features* soundtrack release, on *Today, Tomorrow & Forever* and on the FTD soundtrack re-release

"LOVE ME"

Elvis recorded the track with a full complement of emotion-charged mannerisms at Radio Recorders on September 1, 1956. Though not released as a single, the Leiber and Stoller tune made it to #6 on the singles chart in late 1956 by virtue of its release on the *Elvis Vol. 1* EP. Elvis sang the song on the "Ed Sullivan Show" the same month he recorded it (released 25 years later on *A Golden Celebration*).

The song had previously been a hit for Willie and Ruth in 1954, though songwriters Leiber and

Stoller claimed that they had deliberately set out to write a stinker as a send-up of sappy Country songs. Though Jimmie Rodgers Snow also did well with the number, the songwriters admitted to Elvis that he did it best.

"Love Me" appeared on Elvis' second album, *Elvis*, before warranting a reissue on *Elvis' Golden Records*. Years later it appeared on anthologies *Worldwide Gold Award Hits Vol. 2, Elvis Sings Leiber & Stoller, The King Of Rock And Roll, Elvis '56, Artist Of The Century, Elvis 2nd to None* and *Hitstory*.

Elvis reprised the tune for his NBC TV Special in 1968, but like many other songs time did not allow for inclusion in the finished show. Rehearsals and performance versions have inevitably found their way onto later albums: *Elvis: A Legendary Performer Vol. 1, A Golden Celebration, Memories: The '68 Comeback Special, Tiger Man*, plus FTD releases *Burbank '68"The NBC TV Comeback Special* and *Let Yourself Go*.

A 1970 version of the song came out on the 3-disc latter-day release of *That's The Way It Is* Special Edition; a rehearsal of "Love Me" from the period is on FTD release *The Way It Was*.

Few songs were more likely to feature in an Elvis live show during the Seventies: it was the cue for giving out scarves and collecting kisses. It's on many dozens of bootlegs, and on official releases including *Elvis Aron Presley, Elvis As Recorded At Madison Square Garden, An Afternoon In The Garden, Aloha From Hawaii, The Alternate Aloha, Elvis Recorded Live On Stage In Memphis, Elvis In Concert, Live in Las Vegas* and *Elvis: Close Up*.

Then there are the FTD releases: *The Impossible Dream, Writing For The King, An American Trilogy, Elvis on Tour"The Rehearsals, Summer Festival, I Found My Thrill, Live in L.A., Closing Night, It's Midnight, Dragonheart, Big Boss Man, Dixieland Rocks, Dinner At Eight, Tucson '76, New Year's Eve* and *Unchained Melody*.

"LOVE ME, LOVE THE LIFE I LEAD"

Elvis recorded this song by the team of Roger Greenaway and Tony Macaulay in Nashville on May 21, 1971, at a time when it was quite the message to Priscilla. Elvis was initially unimpressed with the results of this, the last track he recorded at the end of an eight-night studio booking. "Love Me, Love The Life I Lead" was retrieved for the *Elvis (The Fool Album)* in 1973. An alternate appeared in 2007 on FTD release *I Sing All Kinds*.

"LOVE ME TENDER"

Elvis recorded the song for the soundtrack of his first movie, then titled *The Reno Brothers*, on August 24, 1956 (the single version). He laid down the movie end-title version on October 1, 1956; both versions were recorded at the Fox Studios soundstage in Hollywood.

Movie voice arranger Ken Darby adapted the song from Civil War-era balled "Aura Lee," originally written by W. Fosdick and George Poulton and put to music in the 1860s. Owing to publishing issues, Darby used his wife's name Vera Matson for the credit, shared with a certain Elvis Presley.

Before the track was issued as a single in October 1956, (paired with "Any Way You Want Me" on the B-side), it had had national exposure on the "Ed Sullivan Show." RCA received over a million pre-orders, enough to make "Love Me Tender" the first record ever to go gold before even being in stores. The clamor was one reason why the movie title was changed in extremis to match the song title. On release, "Love Me Tender" notched up four weeks at #1.

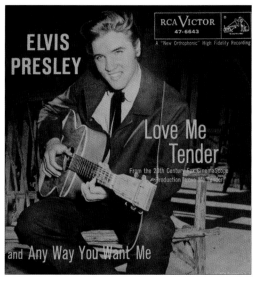

Elvis Presley's 1956 single, "Love Me Tender."

The song spawned its own EP timed to coincide with the movie release. It first came out in LP format on *Elvis' Golden Records*, since when it has graced many a hits package and anthology, including *Worldwide Gold Award Hits Vol. 1, Elvis: A Legendary Performer Vol. 1, Pure Gold, This Is Elvis, The King Of Rock And Roll, Platinum: A Life in Music, Artist Of The Century, ELVIS 30 #1 Hits, Love Elvis, Hitstory, Elvis Movies, The Essential Elvis Presley* and *Elvis at the Movies*.

Elvis sang the song on all of his appearances on the "Ed Sullivan Show" that fall and early 1957 (many years later released on *A Golden Celebration*, which also features a fall 1956 performance from the Mississippi-Alabama Fair and Dairy Show and Elvis' farewell Louisiana Hayride appearance in December 1956).

He sang the song on the "Frank Sinatra Show" to mark his homecoming in 1960"or rather Elvis sang one line and Frank Sinatra took over from there, while Elvis sang Sinatra classic "Witchcraft" (released in 1993 on collector's edition *From Nashville to Memphis*).

For his 1968 NBC TV Special, Elvis switched lyrics, ad-libbing the jocular slip "You have made my life a wreck," knowing full well that new wife Priscilla was in the audience. Versions sung for the show are to be found on the original tie-in album, *Memories: The '68 Comeback Special* and FTD disk *Burbank '68*.

Back before a live audience, in his stage act, "Love Me Tender" became the cue for Elvis to tour the front row of the audience and kiss as many pretty girls as time would allow. To many female fans, even to Priscilla before she met Elvis, the song was an invocation they couldn't resist. He sang the song almost religiously at his shows ever after, though in his last year it became something of a rarity.

Early Las Vegas performances are on *Collectors Gold* and *Live In Las Vegas*, and on FTD releases *Elvis At The International, Writing For The King, All Shook Up, Polk Salad Annie, One Night In Vegas* and *The Impossible Dream*.

Performances of "Love Me Tender" feature in both of Elvis' early Seventies documentaries (*That's The Way It Is* and *Elvis on Tour*). He sang it at Madison Square Garden (*Elvis As Recorded At Madison Square Garden, An Afternoon In The Garden*); other live versions from 1972 are on *Elvis: Close-Up* and FTD release *Summer Festival*.

On the final night of his summer 1973 Vegas engagement Elvis regaled the Hilton Hotel audience with an X-rated version. The song featured during Elvis' 1974 Memphis show, but was not included on the accompanying album (though it is on the FTD release of *Elvis Recorded Live On Stage in Memphis*). Other live performances are on

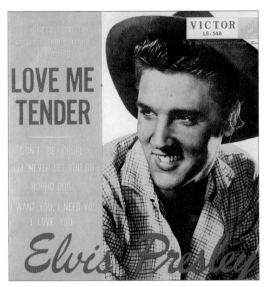

Elvis Presley's "Love Me Tender." rare 10" LP (Japan).

the *Elvis Aron Presley* box set and on FTD issues *Closing Night, I Found My Thrill, It's Midnight, Live in L.A., Dragonheart,* and *Dixieland Rocks.*

The end-title version from the movie first came out officially in 1986 on *Essential Elvis Vol. 1,* followed a decade later by anniversary *Jailhouse Rock* album releases.

An instrumental version from late 1956 appeared a full half-century later on *The Complete Million Dollar Quartet.*

In 1978 Linda Ronstadt's cover of the song was unofficially mixed into a duet with Elvis.

LOVE ME TENDER (EP)

Shipped by RCA in late November 1956, the EP all four songs from the movie, including gospel-tinged "We're Gonna Move" and "Poor Boy." The EP sold in excess of 600,000 copies and stayed in the charts for 11 weeks, peaking at #9.

TRACK LISTING:
1. Love Me Tender
2. Let Me
3. Poor Boy
4. We're Gonna Move

LOVE ME TENDER

An album name for at least five releases since Elvis' death, most produced outside the United States.

LOVE ME TENDER

Elvis' first day at work on a film set was at the Twentieth Century-Fox lot on August 20, 1956, on what was initially known as *The Reno Brothers,* a movie set in the immediate aftermath of the Civil War. Elvis had recently signed a multi-picture deal with Paramount but the Colonel shrewdly incorporated a clause allowing him to work with other studios. Principal photography began two days later, and soundtrack work two days after that. The movie wrapped on October 8, 1956, though not before a less melancholy ending was filmed.

According to Hal Kanter, Elvis' role in the movie was expanded from one that had just a few lines. The part had already been turned down by Jeffrey Hunter and Robert Wagner by the time it came Elvis' way. Another movie about the Reno brothers, *Rage at Dawn,* had been released just a

Elvis, with Richard Egan and Debra Paget in *Love Me Tender* (1956).

year earlier, starring Randolph Scott and with Denver Pyle playing the Elvis role.

Elvis got cold feet about doing the picture at all when he read the script and saw that his character died at the end. Girlfriend June Juanico recalls persuading him by saying that she tended to remember the characters who had a tragic fate far longer than those who live happily ever after. *Love Me Tender* turned out to be the only Elvis movie in which he did not get top billing, and in which he played an out-and-out anti-hero (as opposed to a good guy with redeemable character flaws).

Elvis developed an enormous crush on Debra Paget, but this was before he developed the habit of off-screen entanglements with his leading ladies. Paget, at that time, was seeing Howard Hughes.

Songs were added to the movie after Elvis joined the project. Right from the start of Elvis' movie career, the Colonel planned to promote the movie through the songs and vice versa. According to June Juanico, Elvis was initially led to believe that he wouldn't be singing the title song on screen at all, but rather in the background. In the end, four songs featured in the movie, all written by vocal arranger Ken Darby. Elvis received *pro forma* co-writing credits and publishing royalties.

Location shots were at the Twentieth Century-Fox Ranch in Malibu Creek State Park, and in the San Fernando Valley.

In the ending shot originally, Ma Reno rings the bell for her three remaining sons to come in for dinner. A new ending was shot for the movie while Elvis was in New York City (for his second appearance on "The Ed Sullivan Show"), in which Elvis' character features as a ghostly presence singing the title song.

Elvis attended a private preview at the Loew's State Theater in Memphis on November 20, 1956, accompanied by his parents and June Juanico.

The movie premiered at the Times Square Paramount in New York City on November 15, 1956. As many as 1,500 Elvis fans began lining up for tickets the night before, stretching as far as Grand Central Station, rumor has it that the

Colonel organized this stunt, which was as highly visible as the 50-foot tall Elvis cut-out looking down from the theater awning. Twentieth Century-Fox is said to have distributed more prints of this movie than any other movie in its history.

In its first week, the movie made $540,000, beaten only by (posthumous) James Dean / Elizabeth Taylor blockbuster *Giant.* It finished the year as the 23rd highest grossing movie.

The press was united in its scathing reviews of Elvis' performance, at the height of the moralistic outcry over the effect the young man from Memphis was having on the nation's youth.

ELVIS SAID IN LATE 1956: "It was an old, old picture, storywise, and I shouldn't have been in it from the beginning."

Book:

Elvis in Hollywood: Photographs from the Making of Love Me Tender, by Steve Pond, New American Library/A Plume Book, 1990.

CREDITS:

Twentieth Century-Fox, Black and White.
Length: 89 minutes
Release date: November 21, 1956

TAGLINES:

Hear Elvis sing
It's Mr. Rock 'n' Roll... in the story he was born to play!
You'll Love Him Tender in the Story He Was Born to Play!

Directed by: Robert D. Webb
Produced by: David Weisbart
Written by: Maurice Geraghty (story), Robert Buckner
Music by: Lionel Newman
Cinematography by: Leo Tover
Film Editing by: Hugh S. Fowler
Art Direction by: Maurice Ransford, Lyle R. Wheeler
Set Decoration by: Fay Babcock, Walter M. Scott
Costume Design by: Mary Wills

CAST:

Richard Egan	Vance Reno
Debra Paget	Cathy Reno
Elvis Presley	Clint Reno
Robert Middleton	Mr. Siringo
William Campbell	Brett Reno
Neville Brand	Mike Gavin
Mildred Dunnock	Martha Reno
Bruce Bennett	Major Kincaid
James Drury	Ray Reno
Russ Conway	Ed Galt
Ken Clark	Mr. Kelso
Barry Coe	Mr. Davis
Paul E. Burns	Jethro
Heinie Conklin	Train passenger
Steve Darrell	Train conductor
Joe Di Reda	Soldier
Tom Greenway	Paymaster
Frank Griffin	Bit part
L.Q. Jones	Pardee Fleming
Jay Jostyn	Major Harris
Frank Mills	Train passenger
Edward Mundy	Auctioneer
Bob Rose	Station agent
Dick Sargent	Confederate soldier
Jerry Sheldon	Train conductor
James Stone	Storekeeper

ADDITIONAL CREW:

Ben Nye	makeup artist
Helen Turpin	hair stylist
Stanley Hough	assistant director
Alfred Bruzlin	sound
Harry M. Leonard	sound
Ray Kellogg	special photographic effects
Martha Crawford	stunt double for Debra Paget
John Epper	stunts
Ken Darby	vocal supervisor
Charles LeMaire	executive wardrobe designer
Colonel Tom Parker	technical advisor
Edward B. Powell	orchestrator
Sam Benson	wardrobe
Frank J. Calabria	additional cameraman: New York

Plot:

Elvis plays Clint Reno, the youngest of three brothers at the time of the Civil War. Posing as Union soldiers, Clint's brothers and fellow confederates steal $12,250 from a Federal Army train. They head home, unaware that years ago they were reported killed, and that since then Clint has married Cathy (played by Debra Paget), formerly brother Vance's girlfriend.

On his return, Vance (played by Richard Egan) accepts this state of affairs and resolves to

ABOVE: Elvis in *Love Me Tender* (1956).

RIGHT: Mildred Dunnock as Martha Reno.

FACING PAGE: Elvis as Clint Reno.

seek pastures anew. Before he can put his plan in action, Major Kincaid (played by Bruce Bennett) and a Pinkerton detective arrive with a warrant for the brothers' arrest. Clint gets platoon pal Mike Gavin (played by Neville Brand) to spring the brothers from the county jail. Vance decides that the best course of action is to return the stolen money, against the wishes of his partners in crime. He takes the money back to his former girlfriend Cathy, who has been having second thoughts about being with Vince.

Jealous Clint teams up with Vance's former Platoon Sergeant to track down his brother. Tragically, Clint shoots Vance on his way to return the money. Clint then tries to protect his wounded brother, but ends up being shot by Mike Gavin and dying in Cathy's arms, in his last breath optimistically claiming, "Everything's gonna be all right."

Songs: "Love Me Tender," "We're Gonna Move," "Let Me," "Poor Boy"

"LOVE ME TONIGHT"

Don Robertson wrote this track for Elvis. It was recorded at Studio B, Nashville on May 26, 1963, and then released as a bonus extra on the Fun in Acapulco soundtrack album.

The song has since come out on *For The Asking* and *From Nashville to Memphis*.

An alternate take appeared on *Collectors Gold*; FTD release *Studio B: Nashville Outtakes* includes a slower-tempo version of the song.

"LOVE SONG OF THE YEAR"

Chris Christian wrote this song, which Elvis recorded at Stax in Memphis on December 12, 1973. It came out on 1975 album *Promised Land*.

"LOVELY MAMIE"

Elvis recorded this snatch of song to his own guitar accompaniment (borrowing the tune of

"Alouette") for 1968 movie *Stay Away Joe* while on set. It appeared on Seventies bootleg *From Hollywood To Vegas*.

"LOVER DOLL"

A slow-paced Sid Wayne / Abner Silver song for the *King Creole* soundtrack, recorded by Elvis on January 16, 1958 at Radio Recorders. The version released on EP *King Creole Vol. 1* is without the Jordanaires, though their overdub made it onto the soundtrack LP.

In later decades, "Lover Doll" has appeared on *Worldwide Gold Award Hits Vol. 2* and *The King Of Rock And Roll*. The undubbed version resurfaced on 1991 album *Essential Elvis Vol. 3* and the 1997 reissue of *King Creole*.

LOVERS

See GIRLFRIENDS.

"LOVING ARMS"

Elvis recorded this rueful Tom Jans ballad at Stax on December 13, 1973. It was first released on the *Good Times* album. Later releases are on *Walk A Mile In My Shoes*, the 2000 reissue of *Promised Land*, and on *The Country Side of Elvis*.

An alternate take came out on *Essential Elvis, Vol. 5*. The track was also re-engineered for the 1980 *Guitar Man* album (and the *Too Much Monkey Business* FTD re-release), from which it was a 1981 single release.

"LOVING YOU"

It took Elvis several days of recording to come up with a version of this downbeat Leiber/Stoller song that satisfied RCA boss Steve Sholes. At the first time of asking, Elvis felt uncomfortable on the vast, impersonal soundstage at Paramount. Ten days later (at Radio Recorders on February 24, 1957) the band struggled with a series of mistakes on multiple takes of main, end title and "farm" versions of the song.

Shipped by RCA in mid-June 1957 as the B-Side to "Teddy Bear," the track made #20 in the charts. Boosted by the vastly successful A-side, "Loving You" remained on the charts for close to six months on a record that sold well over a million copies. It appeared soon after on the *Loving You* EP and LP, and subsequent reissues on *Elvis' Golden Records*, *Worldwide Gold Award Hits, Vol. 1* and *Pure Gold*.

When Elvis returned to the stage in 1969, he delivered "Loving You" in a live medley with "Reconsider Baby""immortalized on 1991 release *Collectors Gold*.

Recordings from the original soundstage session were posthumously released on *Essential Elvis Vol. 1* and *The King Of Rock 'N' Roll* (main title and movie versions).

Entire albums of alternates have come out over the years. *Essential Elvis Vol. 1* started the ball rolling, before multiple alternates came out on *The King Of Rock 'n' Roll*, *Today Tomorrow & Forever* and *Elvis: Close Up*. FTD issue *Flashback* featured another version, and then in 2006 an entire FTD CD on the *Loving You* re-release was filled with takes of the song.

FTD also brought out a 1959 home recording on *In A Private Moment*.

LOVING YOU (EP)

Two four-track EPs, the first a sneak preview of the upcoming album of the same name released in June 1957, which made it to #1 on the EP chart and earned gold record status. Two weeks after the Loving You album release, RCA unleashed the second EP, driven by "Mean Woman Blues" to #4 on the EP chart.

TRACK LISTING:
VOL. 1
1. Loving You
2. Party
3. (Let Me Be Your) Teddy Bear
4. True Love
VOL. 2
1. Lonesome Cowboy
2. Hot Dog
3. Mean Woman Blues
4. Got A Lot O' Livin' To Do

LOVING YOU (LP)

Elvis' third album featured all the tracks from the movie on side one plus a selection of songs from early 1957 RCA sessions. Released in July that year, the album shot to #1 in just two weeks despite competition from two *Loving You* EPs that covered the same territory. It claimed top spot for 10 out of the 29 weeks it was in the charts.

TRACK LISTING:
1. Mean Woman Blues
2. (Let Me Be Your) Teddy Bear
3. Loving You
4. Got A Lot O' Livin' To Do
5. Lonesome Cowboy
6. Hot Dog
7. Party
8. Blueberry Hill
9. True Love
10. Don't Leave Me Now
11. Have I Told You Lately That I Love You
12. I Need You So

An anniversary re-release in 1997 added alternates and extras "Tell Me Why," "Is It So Strange," "One Night Of Sin," "When It Rains, It Really Pours," "I Beg Of You," "Party," "Loving You" up-tempo version, and "Got A Lot O' Livin' To Do" finale version.

BMG issued a remastered version of the album in 2005.

LOVING YOU (CD ON FTD)

Release of the original album tracks plus all the takes from one of the recording sessions, all remastered.

TRACK LIST:
DISC: 1
1. Mean Woman Blues
2. (Let Me Be Your) Teddy Bear
3. Loving You
4. Got A Lot O' Livin' To Do
5. Lonesome Cowboy
6. Hot Dog
7. Party
8. Blueberry Hill
9. True Love
10. Don't Leave Me Now
11. Have I Told You Lately That I Love You?
12. I Need You So
13. One Night
14. I Beg Of You
15. All Shook Up
16. That's When Your Heartaches Begin
17. Tell Me Why
18. Is It So Strange
19. When It Rains, It Really Pours
20. One Night (Of Sin)
21. I Beg Of You (alternate master)
22. Loving You (end version)
23. Party (alternate master)
24. Loving You (main version)
25. Loving You (farm version)
26. Got A Lot O' Livin' To Do (finale)
27. Mean Woman Blues (version #2)
28. Loving You (main version #2)
29. Loving You (farm version #3)
30. Blueberry Hill (acetate)
31. Got A Lot O' Livin' To Do (main version, acetate)
DISC: 2
1-50: Loving You (mono and stereo takes)

LOVING YOU

Elvis' movie debut for his main studio, Paramount, was crafted around his own meteoric rise to fame. In so doing, it addressed his complaint about the first and only picture he had filmed so far, *Love Me Tender*, in which he felt that the character he played was too far from his own personality and experience.

Writer / director Hal Kanter spent time with Elvis in Memphis, saw what he did to the crowd at his Hayride farewell, and used this research to good effect in this movie version of Mary Agnes Thompson's short story, "A Call for Mitch Miller," which had originally appeared in *Good Housekeeping* magazine.

Before it received its release title, the movie was known variously as *Lonesome Cowboy*, *Something for the Girls*, and *Running Wild*, the title Ed Sullivan kindly plugged the last time that Elvis was a guest on his show.

Development of the story moved forwards hand and hand with song selection, a practice that from *Loving You* was adopted for the rest of Elvis' movie career. It also set the template for a regular feature of Elvis movie plotting: two women fighting over him to set up a romantic denouement.

Before Elvis reported for work on January 21, 1957, the film title had been changed to match the Leiber and Stoller song "Loving You." Outdoor scenes were shot at the Jessup Ranch, north of Hollywood. Elvis was released from his studio commitments on March 8, 1957.

People who knew Elvis concur that the portrait of Deke Rivers is very much a snapshot of Elvis circa late 1956. Deke Rivers is a young singer who, like Elvis, occasionally has problems with men jealous about his effect on women; like Elvis, he has a wily manager, the first in half-a-dozen Elvis movies where his manager is hard-nosed and not always above-board. Making the conceit even more realistic, Elvis' regular band members had bit parts in the picture. The script even gave Elvis the chance to reply to the vilification he had been suffering in real life. At one point, a pained Deke/Elvis says: "They make it sound like folks ought to be ashamed just listening to me sing!"

Gladys and Vernon and some friends from Memphis were in town during shooting. Director Kanter used them as extras during the scene where Elvis performs the movie's title track and "Got A Lot O' Livin' To Do." Gladys and Vernon can be seen happily clapping along. Famously, after his mother died the following year, Elvis could never bring himself to watch the movie. Kanter also screen tested Gladys and Vernon with Elvis. According to Kanter, Elvis had the negative destroyed because his mother hated how sallow and heavy she looked.

Two Leiber and Stoller songs initially lined up for the movie""Live It Up" and "Without You," wound up surplus to requirements.

Though the movie premiered at the Strand Theater in Memphis on July 9, Elvis skipped the event, preferring to watch the movie at a private screening with his folks and girlfriend Anita Wood.

The picture opened nationwide in the last week of July 1957, and reached the #7 spot on *Variety* magazine's Box Office Survey. The movie had a second run while Elvis was away in Germany in the Army.

HAL KANTER: "It has been said by critics, and by reviewers, and historians, and trivia buffs who go in for that sort of thing, that Loving You was probably a more realistic view of the Elvis persona, his life and his style, than any film that he made after that."

Book:
Inside Loving You, by Ger Rijff and Chris Giles, Running Wild Productions, 2003.

CREDITS:
Paramount pictures, Color
Length: 101 minutes
Release date: July 30, 1957

TAGLINE:
Back on the screen . . . For the first time in a year!

Directed by: Hal Kanter
Produced by: Hal B. Wallis
Executive producer: Paul Nathan
Written by: Mary Agnes Thompson (story),
    Herbert Baker, Hal Kanter
Music by: Walter Scharf
Cinematography by: Charles Lang
Film Editing by: Howard A. Smith
Art Direction by: Albert Nozaki, Hal Pereira
Set Decoration by: Sam Comer, Ray Moyer
Costume Design by: Edith Head

CAST:

Elvis Presley	Jimmy Tompkins (Deke Rivers)
Lizabeth Scott	Glenda Markle
Wendell Corey	Walter (Tex) Warner
Dolores Hart	Susan Jessup
James Gleason	Carl Meade
Ralph Dumke	Jim Tallman
Paul Smith	Skeeter
Kenneth Becker	Wayne
Jana Lund	Daisy Bricker
Grace Hayle	Mrs. Gunderson
Hugh Jarrett	Bit part
Heather Ames	Rowdy fan at concert
Kathie Anderson	Sis Jessup
Bill Black	Eddie (bass player)
Madge Blake	Hired agitator
Joan Bradshaw	Bit part
Timothy Butler	Buzz Jessup
Melinda Byron	Bit part
Drew Cahill	Bunk
Gwen Caldwell	Leola
David Cameron	Mr. Castle
Florine Carlan	Autograph seeker #1
Leo Castillo	Teenager
Sydney Chatton	Ed Grew
Harry Cheshire	Mayor
Les Clark	Bit part
Hal K. Dawson	Police lieutenant
Beach Dickerson	Glenn
Carole Dunne	Teenager
Elaine DuPont	Teenager
Sue England	Sorority Girl
Myrna Fahey	Autograph seeker #3
D.J. Fontana	Drummer
William Forrest	Mr. Jessup
Joseph Forte	Editor
Joe Gray	Extra
Donna Jo Gribble	Teenager
Michael Hadge	Teenager
Chuck Hamilton	Extra at fair
Helene Hatch	Bit part
James W. Horan	Barney
Jerry Hunter	Teenager
Kenner G. Kemp	Stage director
Nancy Kilgas	Autograph seeker #2
Jack Latham	TV announcer
Yvonne Lime	Sally
Brenda Lomas	Bit part
Audrey Lowell	Bit part
Gail Lund	Candy
Mike Mahoney	Messenger
Carla Merey	Bit part
Michael A. Monahan	Teenager
Scotty Moore	Guitar player
William H. O'Brien	Crowd extra
Steve Pendleton	Mr. O'Shea
Gladys Presley	Audience member at Grand Theater
Vernon Presley	Audience member at GrandTheater
Joy Reynolds	Bit part
Vernon Rich	Harry Taylor
Linda Rivera	Bit part
Cecile Rogers	Sorority girl
Dick Ryan	Mack (stage doorman)
Jeffrey Sayre	Photographer
Karen Scott	Waitress at Buckhorn Tavern
Almira Sessions	Bit part

Wendell Corey, Elvis, Dolores Hart, and Lizabeth Scott in *Loving You* (1957).

Trude Severen	Twin audience member at GrandTheater
Maida Severen	Twin audience member at GrandTheater
Steffi Sidney	Bit part
Joy Stoner	Bit part
Julius Tannen	Frank (Buckhorn Tavern manager)
Jeanette Taylor	Teenager
Irene Tedrow	Mrs. Jessup
Heather Tuscany	Teenager
Dave White	Pitchman
Buck Young	Assistant director
Skip Young	Teddy

ADDITIONAL CREW:

Wally Westmore	makeup artist
James A. Rosenberger	assistant director
Howard Beals	sound editor
John P. Fulton	special effects
Joe Gray	stunts
Farciot Edouart	process photographer

Elvis and Jimmy Tompkins/Deke Rivers) and Lizabeth Scott as Glenda Markle in a scene from *Loving You*.

Candid shot of Elvis during the filming of *Loving You* (1957).

Bernie Lowe	lyricist
Karl Mann	lyricist
Richard Mueller	color timer
Charles O'Curran	choreographer

Plot:

Elvis plays Deke Rivers, a Texas truck driver who's delivering beer to a political rally where he winds up singing a rock song to great acclaim. The girls go wild and on the spot he's hired by publicist Glenda Markle (played by Lizabeth Scott), a well-connected manho was once married to bandleader Tex Warner (played by Wendell Corey), with whom she fixeager ws Tompkins up.

Deke seems to be less interested in the money and the renown than in young singer Susan (Dolores Hart). Once Deke stars touring with the band, his notoriety spreads, boosted by Glenda's wily publicity stunts. Unbeknownst to Deke, Glenda arranges for him to go solo, effectively firing the rest of the band and Susan, spurred by the ulterior motive that Glenda now has a better chance to win Deke's affections for herself. Deke, meanwhile, reveals that he isn't Deke at all, he's an orphan called Jimmy Tompkins.

Glenda almost succeeds before Deke becomes aware of her duplicity, and learns that she was formerly married to Tex, who still carries a torch for her. With a make-or-break TV show hanging in the balance, Glenda chases after Deke, releases him from the contract he has signed to her. In the finale, Deke makes it to the TV studio just in time to take over the world (and bring back together Glenda and Tex, the two people who made him such a success).

Songs: "Got A Lot O' Livin' To Do," "(Let's Have A) Party," "(Let Me Be Your) Teddy Bear," "Hot Dog," "Lonesome Cowboy," "Mean Woman Blues," "Loving You"
Dolores Hart: "Dancing On A Dare," "Detour," "The Yellow Rose."

LOYD, HAROLD
(b. 1931)

One of Elvis' cousins who for a spell as a teenager lived with Elvis and his family in Tupelo after his mother died (Gladys' sister Rhetha Smith) and his father remarried.

In later years, Loyd was one of many family members who lived at Graceland under professional auspices. In 1961, he was hired for three weeks to work security at the Graceland gatehouse. He worked the job for 31 years, in the Seventies joined by his son Robert.

After Elvis' death, Loyd made a tribute record, "A Prayer for Elvis." In 2007, his son Roger brought out a memoir titled *Growing Up in the Shadow of a King.*

HAROLD LOYD: "Elvis' mother was a great woman, she was like a mother to me."

Book:
The Graceland Gates by Harold Loyd and George Baugh, Modern Age Enterprises, 1978 (republished as *(Elvis Presley's Graceland Gates,* 1987).

M

MacArthur, Douglas
(1880-1964)

US General and Medal of Honor winner famous for leading the US campaign in Asia during the Second World War, one of three major wars in which he fought.

Elvis was fond of MacArthur's 1951 "Farewell Address" to Congress (which starts, "I stand on this rostrum with a sense of deep humility and great pride. . . .). More than fond, Elvis knew it by heart and was happy to recite it at length if circumstance warranted. Elvis would sometimes use General MacArthur's famous line "I Shall Return" as he was taking his leave, or adapt the speech ending to "I bid you a fond, affectionate, fucking farewell."

"MacArthur Park"

Elvis never recorded this 7-minute hit officially, but he interjected a few lines in June 1968 while recording his NBC TV Special, later available on bootleg release *The Burbank Sessions* and FTD official album issues. Elvis said that if Richard Harris hadn't got there first, he would happily have recorded the song, which had been written in 1967 by Jimmy Webb.

Made in Memphis

A 2006 FTD release of outtakes from Elvis' recording sessions in his home town (at American Studio, Stax, and Graceland, plus home recordings taped by Sam Thompson, including Elvis' favorite scurrilous poem).

TRACK LISTING:
1. In The Ghetto
2. You'll Think Of Me
3. Do You Know Who I Am
4. If You Don't Come Back
5. Three Corn Patches
6. Find Out What's Happening
7. It's Midnight
8. Thinking About You
9. You Asked Me To
10. Solitaire
11. She Thinks I Still Care
12. Moody Blue
13. Bitter They Are, Harder They Fall
14. Love Coming Down
15. For The Heart
16. Baby What You Want Me To Do
17. I'm So Lonesome I Could Cry
18. Spanish Eyes
19. See See Rider
20. That's All Right (Mama)

Mafia

Elvis had his Memphis Mafia, so-named for the dark Italian-style suits he and his entourage took to wearing after his return from the Army in 1960.

According to some authors, Elvis had run-ins with the real Cosa Nostra. May Mann writes that the Mafia made an attempt to muscle in on Elvis' money-making potential early in his career, but was thwarted by Colonel Parker's insistence on not giving up a cent. Rumors circulated that the Mafia threatened to expose Elvis for using drugs in his early years.

Other authors have alluded to later contact between Parker and the Mafia, notably with regard to Elvis' deal to become a regular act in Las Vegas, where a significant amount of Mafia business was transacted. It has been speculated that the only way for Parker to settle his debts to the mob was to hand over a proportion of Elvis' earnings.

An FBI report in 1973 alleged that Elvis had been receiving cocaine from Mafia contacts in Las Vegas.

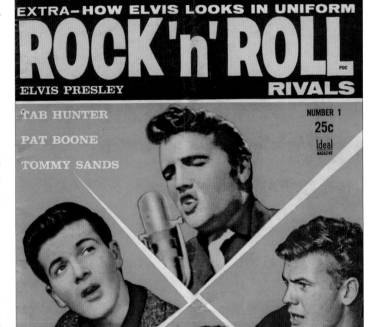

ABOVE: Rare 1957 Rock 'n' Roll magazine cover.

RIGHT: The rarest of all 1980's Elvis magazines.

In 1993, author John Parker claimed that Elvis was bumped off because of dangers to the Mafia if he testified in a major fraud case.

Book:
Elvis: The Secret Files, by John Parker, Anaya Publishers Ltd, 1993.

Magazines

As Elvis emerged into the bright lights of publicity, photograph-filled fan magazines became the first publicly-available literature on Elvis. In those early years, Elvis had to share billing with fellow teen heart-throbs Pat Boone, Tommy Sands and Tab Hunter.

Ever after, Elvis became a magazine and press staple in heavyweight news titles, movie magazines, music papers and, increasingly towards the end of his life, tabloid fare.

Elvis' death provoked a flurry of souvenir magazines from well-known titles such as *Photoplay*, along with commemorative issues from dozens of smaller publishers. Music magazines *Rolling Stone* and *Crawdaddy* published some outstanding articles on the importance of being Elvis: *Rolling Stone* dedicated half of its pages to Elvis in its September 1977 issue.

Commemorative magazines and special issues continue to appear at every major Elvis anniversary, feeding the flourishing trade in Elvis memorabilia.

Entire magazine series have documented Elvis' life and works. The *Elvis Yearbook* ran from 1960 to 1977; *Modern Screen* ran an Elvis Life Story series in five issues from 1979 to 1980.

Many fan clubs have run long-established magazines, though in recent times much of this material has migrated to the online world.

Magazine companies continue to bring out special collectors' magazines undaunted by the decades since Elvis' demise. This included, in 2007, DeAgostini publication *Elvis The Official Collector's Edition*.

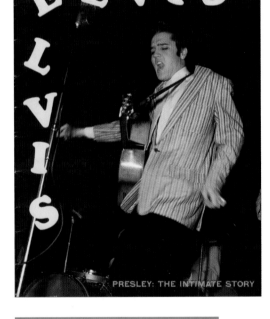

A SELECTION OF ELVIS FAN MAGAZINES OVER THE YEARS

Essential Elvis
Elvis Monthly
Elvis International
Elvis The Magazine
Elvis The Record
Elvis The Man And His Music
Elvis Today
Elvis Unlimited
Elvis World
Elvisly Yours
Flaming Star
It's Elvis Time
The Elvis Magazine
The Official British Fan Club magazine

See also FIRSTS and PRESS

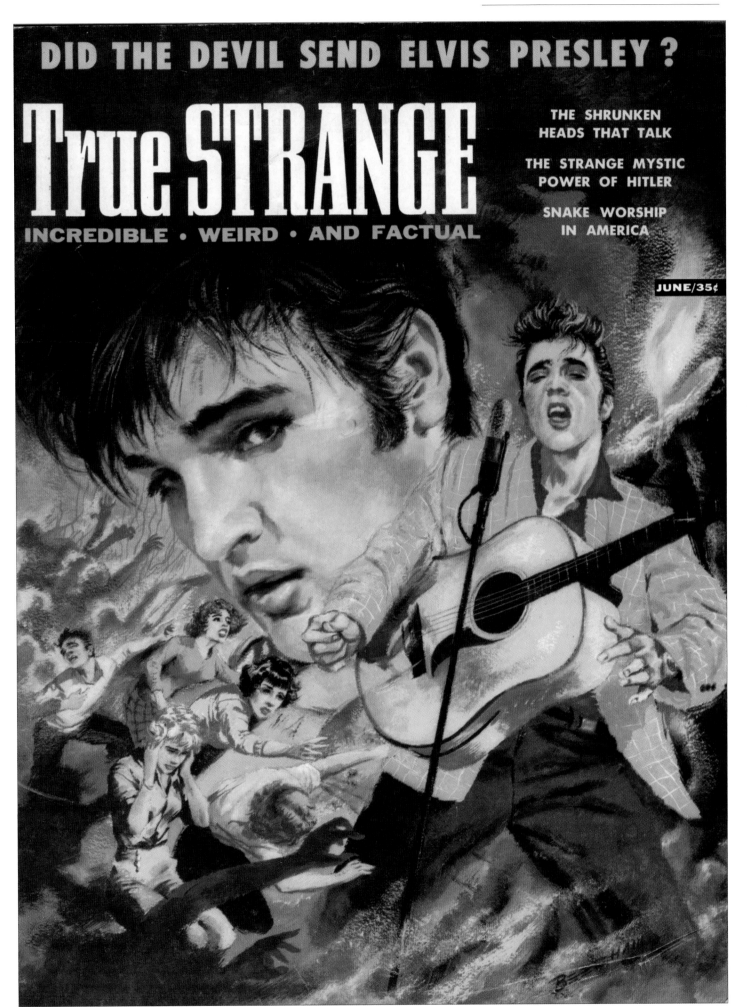

A highly collectible 1950's magazine.

MAHALO FROM ELVIS

A 1978 album on the Pickwick label featuring the songs that Elvis recorded for the US broadcast of his 1973 *Aloha Via Satellite* concert, plus mainly Hawaiian-themed movie songs. The album failed to chart

TRACK LISTING:
1. Blue Hawaii
2. Early Morning Rain
3. Hawaiian Wedding Song
4. Ku-U-I-Po
5. No More
6. Relax
7. Baby, If You'll Give Me All Your Love
8. One Broken Heart For Sale
9. So Close, Yet So Far (From Paradise)
10. Happy Ending

MAINE

- Augusta
Elvis' one and only performance in the state of Maine was at the Civic Center on May 24, 1977.

"MAKE BELIEVE"

This Oscar Hammerstein/Jerome Kern tune from Twenties musical *Showboat* was sung by Elvis within range of a home tape some time in late 1960, and released on 1999 album *The Home Recordings*.

"MAKE ME KNOW IT"

This Otis Blackwell track was the first song that Elvis cut after his return from the Army, at his first recording session in almost two years, held at the RCA studios in Nashville on March 20, 1960.

The song was released as an album track on *Elvis Is Back!* In the Nineties, it was the opening track on Sixties anthology *From Nashville to Memphis*.

Alternates have appeared in the 2000s on *Essential Elvis Vol. 6*, *Today Tomorrow & Forever*, *Elvis: Close Up*, plus FTD releases *Fame And Fortune* and *Elvis Is Back!* (half a dozen alternates and outtakes).

"MAKE THE WORLD GO AWAY"

Elvis laid down this Hank Cochran song—a hit for Ray Price in 1963 and Eddy Arnold in 1965—on June 7, 1970 in Nashville for the *Elvis Country* album.

The song has since appeared on *Walk A Mile In My Shoes*, *Great Country Songs* and *The Country Side of Elvis*.

An alternate take from the recording session came out on 1977 compilation *Welcome To My World*.

Elvis sang the song long live a few times in the early Seventies. One version is on the *That's The Way It Is* special edition release, another on FTD disc *The Impossible Dream*.

"MAMA"

Charles O'Curran and Dudley Brooks whipped up this sentimental tune for *Girls! Girls! Girls!* Elvis recorded the song on March 28, 1962 at Radio Recorders, though it didn't see release until the *Let's Be Friends* album in 1970, followed later that decade on Pickwick release *Double Dynamite* and

then the 1993 *Girls! Girls! Girls! Double Feature* album. The version of the song that made it into the movie was sung by The Amigos.

Alternates appeared on and the FTD *Girls! Girls! Girls!* release.

"MAMA LIKED THE ROSES"

Elvis is said to have cried the first time that he heard the demo of this Johnny Christopher song. He recorded it at American Studio on January 16, 1969. It was released as the B-side to "The Wonder of You" in April 1970, and soon after appeared on the 1970 reissue of *Elvis' Christmas Album*.

Subsequent releases include *The Memphis Record*, *Suspicious Minds: The Memphis 1969 Anthology*, *From Nashville to Memphis*, the 2000 reissue of *From Elvis In Memphis* and *Elvis Inspirational*.

MANAGEMENT III

A concert promotion company run by talent agent/manager Jerry Weintraub, who founded the company in 1965, who worked on putting on Elvis shows with Tom Hulett of Concerts West (responsible for rock extravaganzas including Hendrix and Led Zeppelin), and Dallas entrepreneur Terry Bassett.

Management III first became involved with Elvis concerts on a September 1970 tour arranged with Colonel Parker and RCA, starting in St. Louis, Missouri. The Colonel soon found cause to complain about how they went about their business, and in early 1972 set up a concert promotion company with RCA to help coordinate tour arrangements. RCA brought Management III back on board to play a greater role organizing Elvis' tours from early 1974.

MANAGERS

When Sam Phillips unleashed Elvis' first single on an unsuspecting world, nobody had any idea how fast Elvis' stock was set to rise. Elvis would roll into a small town as an unknown and leave as a star. It soon became apparent that the boy needed management beyond Phillips making calls to DJ pals of his, though this worked well enough in the first few months: a call to Shreveport DJ Tommy Cutrer helped to land Elvis' first high-profile regular engagement, on the Louisiana Hayride. Scotty Moore lent a hand co-ordinating Elvis and the band's bookings, while promoters such as Cutrer assisted with bookings in territories farther across the mid-South

Moore threw in the towel when it became evident that managing Elvis was more than just a side line.

Memphis DJ and promoter Bob Neal took over officially six months after Elvis recorded his first single, and looked after Elvis' affairs for most of 1955. Neal initially involved the Colonel because he wanted to book Elvis on Hank Snow tours. By the summer of 1955, the Colonel had persuaded Neal that his superior contacts with record labels, film studios and talent agencies were better suited for the next stage in Elvis' career, the transfer to a major record label.

Colonel Parker nominally took over managing Elvis' affairs when Elvis and Vernon signed a contract naming him as Elvis' "special adviser" on August 15, 1955. A tussle ensued between the Colonel, busy working behind the scenes with his Hollywood and New York contacts, and Neal, who continued to manage Elvis' tour bookings right up to November 1955. The Colonel succeeded in masterminding RCA's buyout of Elvis' Sun Records contract in mid-November 1955. Neal resigned as Elvis' road manager in early 1956.

From then on in, it was Colonel Tom Parker all the way. Briefly, in 1973, Elvis and Parker fell out. There was speculation inside and outside the entourage that Elvis might take on new management with either Jerry Weintraub or Tom Hulett of Management III, but the moment passed, not least because the Colonel presented Vernon with a $2 million severance claim.

JOAN DEARY: "In the very beginning the Colonel was like a lightning rod.... The Colonel brought him to the attention of the whole country, the whole world as a matter of fact.... Later on, I think that Elvis could have done a great deal more creatively under different management or direction."

MARTY LACKER: "There were a hundred managers and there who could have handled Elvis' career a whole lot better."

MANN, BILLY

Cousin Mann has the dubious distinction of being the family member persuaded by *National Enquirer* to take a photograph of Elvis in his coffin at Graceland. In the Fifties, he was a sometime member of Elvis' entourage, until he was told his presence was no longer wanted (allegedly after he had stolen some cash from Graceland).

MANN, BOBBIE

Elvis' cousin (daughter of Gladys's older sister Lillian), whose married name was Wren, in 1974 became a partner of Elvis' in opening the Tennessee Karate Institute.

MANN, MAY

A columnist and author who drew upon her years as an entertainment reporter and interviews with Elvis and the Colonel to write Elvis books in the Seventies and early Eighties.

Books:
Elvis and the Colonel, by May Mann, Drake Publishers, 1975 (reissued in 1977 by Pocket Books as *The Private Elvis*)
Elvis Why Don't They Leave You Alone? by May Mann, Signet, 1982

MANSELL, GAINS

Elvis' mother's uncle became a preacher at the Assembly of God Church close to the Presley home in 1937.

MANSFIELD, REX
(B. DONALD MANSFIELD)

One of Elvis' best buddies during his military service, after they met during their induction into the Army and traveled by bus trip from Memphis to Fort Chaffee in March 1958. They became firm friends after Mansfield took over Elvis' guard duty when Anita Wood came to visit in Texas, and refused the $20 Elvis offered because he would have done the same "for any other GI whose girl was waiting to see him." Elvis invited Rex back to Graceland during leave before they were both posted out to Germany.

Their friendship continued through their time in Germany, where Mansfield became Elvis' first regular karate sparring partner. "Rexadus," as Elvis called him, was a regular visitor to Elvis' Bad Nauheim home, and traveled with Elvis to Paris. When they were discharged from the Army, Elvis asked him to come and be part of his paid entourage. What Elvis did not know was that ever since Elvis had met Priscilla in Germany, Mansfield and Elvis' then secretary Elisabeth Stefaniak had been falling in love. Rex declined the job and three months later married Stefaniak in Florida.

Books:
Elvis the Soldier, by Rex and Elisabeth Mansfield, Collectors Service GmbH, 1983 (including recording of AFN Elvis interview).
Sergeant Presley - Our Untold Story Of Elvis' Missing Years, by Rex and Elisabeth Mansfield, ECW Press, 2002.

"MANSION OVER THE HILLTOP"

Elvis recorded this spiritual on October 30, 1960 at Studio B in Nashville for release on his first gospel album, *His Hand in Mine.* Written by Ira Stamphill, the song first came to public notice in a recording by Red Foley in 1953. It's also on anthologies *Amazing Grace, Peace In The Valley* and *Christmas Peace.*

FTD releases *Easter Special* and *His Hand In Mine* feature alternate takes.

MARCUS, GREIL
(B. 1945)

Journalist, author, rock critic and cultural commentator who has written extensively about Elvis and his place in modern American culture, placing him in a musicological, sociological and political context. Marcus's essay on Elvis, published in his 1975 book *Mystery Train,* was one of the first to anchor Elvis firmly in mainstream cultural studies.

Books:
Mystery Train, by Greil Marcus, E. P. Dutton, 1975
Dead Elvis, by Greil Marcus, Doubleday, 1991
Double Trouble: Bill Clinton and Elvis Presley in a Land of No Alternatives, by Greil Marcus, published by Henry Holt and Co, 2000.

"MARGUERITA"

Elvis recorded this Mexicanized Don Robertson song for the soundtrack of *Fun in Acapulco* at Radio Recorders on January 22, 1963.

Following its release on the soundtrack LP, it has come out on the *Double Features* issue for this movie and *Command Performances.* An alternate take appeared in 2003 on the FTD version of *Fun in Acapulco.*

MARRIAGE

Elvis' first marriage was the lovestruck yearning of a wishful thirteen-year-old, when he added his name and that of "Magdline"—Magdalen Morgan, a girl whom he met at the First Assembly of God church—on the blank lines of his parents' own marriage certificate.

For a man who loomed large in the fantasies of so many young women, marriage was more than an occupation no-no. The Colonel laid down the law soon after he took over managing Elvis: marriage would wreck his career.

In early interviews, Elvis would inevitably be asked if he was ever going to settle down, or what type of girl he expected to marry. Elvis denied that he had any special girl, claiming that he never dated anybody for longer than three weeks. His first serious girlfriend, Dixie Locke, knew otherwise, as did June Juanico, whom Elvis dated in 1956; she says they talked of marriage at the same time as Elvis was vigorously denying any such plans in public.

During his Army time in Germany, Elvis wrote letters to girlfriend Anita Wood expressing his desire to marry her. He had had to quash rumors of a secret marriage to her even before he left for Germany.

The one exception to Elvis' strenuous marriage denials was Priscilla Beaulieu, or more specifically, her parents Ann and Paul. They only consented to their daughter visiting and then staying with Elvis in America after Elvis persuaded them that his intentions were serious and honorable.

As Lamar Fike puts it, "the markers were called" in late 1966, three and a half years after Priscilla moved to Memphis, and after she had passed her 21st birthday. According to Sonny West, after Priscilla's father talked to the Colonel about Elvis making good on his promise, the Colonel told Elvis that he had to either marry Priscilla or call it off. In her memoir, Priscilla characterizes the situation as being Elvis' decision and his alone. The Colonel, who had recently stepped in to take personal control over Elvis' private life and entourage, set up the whole thing, for once using his skills to avoid any publicity rather than create as much brouhaha as possible. He organized the wedding with Las Vegas pal Milton Prell, in the process offending several key members of Elvis' entourage who were not invited to the "intimate" wedding ceremony.

After the ceremony and a minimal honeymoon, the newlyweds returned to Memphis and a communal existence on the Circle G ranch, which Elvis had recently purchased.

Apart from a brief hiatus immediately after his one marriage and after the birth of Lisa Marie the following February, it did not take long for rumors to appear in the press that the marriage was not going well. Elvis was spotted in Las Vegas with admiring female fans around him, and he carried on living his itinerant lifestyle between his various homes, often without his wife and young daughter in tow. For the gossip-mongers, events that may have been completely innocent, such as Priscilla coming to see Elvis perform at Houston in early 1970, were construed as attempts to salvage their failing matrimony. Elvis and Priscilla separated in early 1972.

Elvis and Linda Thompson, who were together from mid-1972 until less than a year before his death, are known to have discussed marriage. His final flame, young beauty queen Ginger Alden, has said that not only did Elvis discuss marriage with her, their wedding plans were at an advanced stage. Elvis proposed to the her in late January 1977, two months after they met, at a time when marriage was so much on his mind that he held a wedding ceremony in Palm Springs for his LA dentist Max Shapiro, at which Larry Geller officiated. Geller has said that Elvis asked him to do the same for he and Ginger, either in late summer that year, or in other accounts on Christmas Day, in a Greek Orthodox Church. Contrasting with this view is the opinion of a number of Elvis' friends, who suggest that Elvis was never serious about marrying Ginger.

Such is Elvis' known married life. Since Elvis became a sex symbol in the mid-Fifties, any number of women has claimed that they secretly married Elvis; the one thing they have in common is that in every such instance the marriage license turns out to have been mislaid or unwittingly destroyed.

See also WEDDING.

ELVIS QUIPPED ON STAGE IN 1956: "Why buy a cow when you can get milk under the fence?"

ELVIS SAID IN 1956: "Even after I get married, I'll have to keep working. You can't starve to death just because you're married."

Elvis and Priscilla in Germany.

ELVIS SAID IN 1961: "When I fall deeply in love it will happen. I'll decide on the spur of the moment, but it won't be an elopement... but a church wedding."

ELVIS SAID ABOUT HIS WEDDING: "It was in there over and done so quick I didn't realize I was married."

PRISCILLA: "He felt guilty and confused about his natural reaction to female advances and I believe that this was his greatest fear when it came to marriage."

LAMAR FIKE: "Elvis proposed to a lot of girls in the early years, but I think he thought that was what he was supposed to do."

MARTY LACKER: "By rights Elvis shouldn't have married; he really didn't want to be married. He wanted to have a child — he wanted a son — but he didn't really want everything else that went along with it."

LAMAR FIKE: "Life at Graceland never really changed that much after the marriage. Elvis just went out beyond the boundaries of Graceland more because he still wanted to roar."

BILLY SMITH: "Elvis expected us to be married to him. He didn't want you to put anybody before him. My wife's greatest struggle was with Elvis. She thought she was in a battle with him over me. And she was."

MARL METAL PRODUCTS

For a couple of months, Elvis worked a full shift at this furniture manufacturing company (208 Georgia Avenue) after school, earning a dollar an hour. He quit the job after it became apparent that he was too tired at classes during his final year at High School.

MARTIN, BECKY

A pal of Elvis' from their Tupelo school days at East Tupelo Consolidated School, she remained a friend after he hit the big time, and saw him occasionally through the Seventies. Her "Elvis room" became a tour destination for Elvis fans.

MARTIN, DEAN
(B. DINO PAUL CROCETTI, 1917-1995)

When Elvis was finally given a chance to audition for Sam Phillips at Sun Records, he tried out quite a number of Dean Martin songs. In a 1956 interview, Elvis declared that Martin was one of his favorite singers.

Martin tried and failed to entice Elvis onto his television show in October 1956. The Colonel turned up his nose at an offer of $30,000, and then in mid-1957 raised his price to $75,000, which frightened Martin off for good.

Elvis went to a birthday party for Dean Martin on the Paramount lot in June 1960, where Elvis and Shirley MacLaine helped Deano cut the cake.

Born in Ohio on June 7, 1917 to an immigrant barber, Martin worked in a factory, as a boxer and then as a croupier before launching a singing career under the name Dean Martini. He did not taste major success until he teamed up with comedian Jerry Lewis, one night when a comedy act quit the show that he and Lewis were on and they decided to go on stage together. Between 1949 and 1956, Martin and Lewis were the most popular comic duo in the nation. After dissolving their partnership, Martin continued his long and varied career as a singer, movie actor, TV show presenter and high profile Rat Pack celebrity.

Elvis and Martin both covered "I Don't Care If The Sun Don't Shine" and "Gentle On My Mind."

Elvis sang a few lines of Martin song "Everybody Loves Somebody" when Deano was in the audience for one of his Las Vegas shows in 1970, and launched into "That's Amore" for a similar reason in 1975.

SAM PHILLIPS: "That little bit of mischievousness that he had in his soul when he cut up a little bit—[Elvis] loved Dean Martin's singing."

PAUL SIMPSON: "Arguably, Dean Martin influenced almost every ballad Elvis ever recorded."

NORBERT PUTNAM: "In the 1970s, towards the end, he almost started sounding like Dean Martin."

MARTIN, GRADY
(1929-2001)

Session guitarist from a Tennessee country background hired for Elvis' Pot Luck session in Nashville in 1962, where he adding his vibes playing to the mix. He recorded several other times with Elvis in Nashville on soundtrack scores and RCA sessions on and off up to 1967. Much in demand in Nashville in the Fifties and Sixties, where among others he played for Hank Williams, Buddy Holly, Marty Robbins, Brenda Lee and Roy Orbison, Martin later toured with Jerry Reed and then Willy Nelson. Martin first played guitar on an Elvis song in 1956: a cover of "Tryin' To Get To You" recorded by Johnny Carroll.

MARTINDALE, WINK
(B. WINSTON MARTINDALE, 1934)

A local Memphis DJ while still at college and later a TV show host on whose "Top Ten Dance Party" show Elvis appeared in 1956, Martindale first met Elvis when he came in for an interview on Dewey Phillips' show on WHBQ after his debut single "That's All Right (Mama)" received its initial airplay.

Martindale scored his own record hit in 1959 with spoken-voice release "Deck Of Cards," a surprise million-seller.

Martindale visited Elvis on set while he was shooting his first movie after the Army, G.I. Blues.

In the Sixties, Martindale began hosting game shows on national TV. All in all, he presented nineteen different formats, including "Gambit," "Tic Tac Dough," "The Last Word" and "Trivial Pursuit." In 2006, he earned a star on the Hollywood Walk of Fame.

In the Seventies, Martindale married former Elvis girlfriend Sandy Ferra. He narrated a radio special on Elvis in 1971, and a tribute show after Elvis' death in 1977.

MARX, GROUCHO
(B. JULIUS HENRY MARX 1890-1977)

Elvis and the cigar-wielding comic genius from the Marx Brothers never met but their paths crossed in the media more than once. In the late Fifties, as TV host of "You Bet Your Life," during an interview with the head of the Elvis Presley Fan Club Marx failed to mention Elvis Presley even once, and then quipped that he seldom mentioned Elvis' name at all unless he stubbed his toe.

Marx died on August 19, 1977, just three days after Elvis, and suffered the fate of his passing being almost ignored as the nation grieved for Elvis.

"MARY IN THE MORNING"

Elvis recorded this Johnny Cymbal / Michael Rashkow track—a 1967 hit for Al Martino—on June 5, 1970 at Studio B in Nashville. He performed the song live in 1970, while being filmed for That's The Way It Is. The studio recording was chosen for the original That's The Way It

soundtrack release; this and a live performance from 1970 were on the 2000 That's The Way It Is—Special Edition collection. Elvis and the band rehearsing the song later came out on FTD release The Way It Was.

The song also featured on the Walk A Mile In My Shoes anthology.

Alternates from the original studio session have appeared on FTD release The Nashville Marathon.

"MARY LOU BROWN"

A Red West composition sung by Elvis and friends at Graceland in 1966, released years later on The Home Recordings.

MARYLAND

- Baltimore

Elvis played the Civic Center on November 9, 1971. He next returned on May 29, 1977, when he left the stage for half an hour mid-show because he felt too sick to continue. When he returned, to rapturous applause, he quipped "When ya gotta go, ya gotta go."

- College Park

Elvis kicked off his fall 1974 tour at the University of Maryland Cole Fieldhouse on September 28, 1974.

- Landover

Elvis did a show at the Capital Center Arena on June 27, 1976. He next played the venue on May 22, 1977.

MASON, MARLYN
(B. 1940)

In her long career, this actress starred opposite Elvis in The Trouble with Girls (1969) and performed a rare duet with him; while working together, Elvis called her "Cap" because she was wearing one when they first met. Mason has worked predominantly in TV, including popular favorites "Dr. Kildare," "Bonanza," the original "Perry Mason," "The Man from U.N.C.L.E.," "Hogan's Heroes" and "Marcus Welby M.D.."

MASSACHUSETTS

- Boston

Elvis and the TCB band played the Boston Garden on November 10, 1971.

- Springfield

Elvis made one fan ecstatically happy when he played the Civic Center on July 14, 1975 by hefting his guitar into the audience. Elvis next played the venue on July 29, 1976.

MATA, SRI DAYA
(B. FAYE WRIGHT, 1914)

Born in Utah on January 31, 1914, Faye Wright met yogi Paramahansa Yogananda in 1931, persuaded her parents to let her join his ashram, and went on to become the Mother of the Self-Realization Fellowship in 1955. Elvis met her (as Sri Daya Mata) in 1965, when he first started visiting the organization's headquarters in Pasadena. For a couple of years, she was an important presence in his life as a spiritual advisor and a rare outsider in whom he could confide. After a two-year hiatus from 1967, Elvis got back in touch in the late Sixties and into the early Seventies. Towards the end of the time that she knew him, she found him to be "not at peace."

DAYA MATA: "I urged him to take time for himself and his spiritual well-being, but he was very much pulled toward his following, he wished to please them, they gave him love."

PRISCILLA: "She was an attractive woman who looked remarkably like Gladys Presley, and he was captivated by her serenity and spiritual presence. She epitomized everything he was striving to be."

MATSON, VERA

A composer who wrote a number of songs for Elvis' first film, Love Me Tender, including the title track based on the melody from Civil War song "Aura Lee" . . . except she didn't, it was her husband, composer and vocal arranger Ken Darby, who crafted the songs and used his wife's maiden name for the credit and royalties.

MATTHAU, WALTER
(B. WALTER JOHN MATTHOW, 1920-2000)

Oscar-winner Matthau worked with Elvis on King Creole (1958), three years into his own cinematic career. It took several years more for Matthau to make top billing in a string of movies with Jack Lemmon in the Sixties. Matthau won a Best Supporting Oscar for The Fortune Cookie (1966), and to great acclaim reprised a role he had played on Broadway in the screen version of The Odd Couple (1968). Towards the end of his career he cornered the market in Grumpy Old Men.

WALTER MATTHAU: "I was amazed at how beautiful this kid was and how talented he was and how kind."

MATTHEWS, NEAL JR.
(1929-2000)

Nashville-born singer Neal Matthews backed Elvis from 1956 to 1970 as the second tenor in the Jordanaires. He was also an instrumentalist who stepped in on guitar and bass at Elvis recording sessions either side of 1960. It was Matthews who developed the Nashville chord numbering system, which had an enormous effect on the music industry.

Book:
Elvis: A Golden Tribute, by Neal Matthews, 1985

MATTINSON, BERNIE

A drummer who played on a Elvis' Paramount soundtrack sessions recorded in LA, from King Creole through Blue Hawaii to Roustabout.

"MAYBELLENE"

A live version of Elvis singing this Chuck Berry song was recorded at the Louisiana Hayride on August 20, 1955 but wasn't released until Elvis: The First Live Recordings in 1984. It has since featured on other releases including The King Of Rock And Roll, Louisiana Hayride compilations and a 2006 import update of The Complete Sun Sessions,

though as yet there is no sign of a rumored version that Elvis is said to have laid down at his first label.

Berry's first hit is a reworked version of Bob Wills' Thirties country hit "Ida Red," retitled using the name of a cow Berry remembered from a childhood nursery rhyme. The tale of cars and girls was a crossover smash, making it to #5 in the Billboard Top 100 in 1955. DJ Alan Freed received a credit reputedly in exchange for spinning the record, as did DJ Russo Frato. In 2004, Rolling Stone magazine rated the song #18 in its 500 greatest songs of all time.

MCCARTNEY, PAUL
(B. JAMES PAUL MCCARTNEY, 1942)

Born in Liverpool on June 18, 1942, McCartney teamed up with John Lennon in his first band, skiffle combo The Quarrymen, when he was just fifteen. Together the duo penned the vast majority of songs that made The Beatles the most famous band in the world during the Sixties. Elvis covered Lennon / McCartney compositions ("Yesterday," "Hey Jude," "Lady Madonna" and "Get Back") in later years.

In 1965, McCartney met Elvis with the rest of The Beatles in Los Angeles. He gave Elvis some tips on playing bass—Elvis tried out Paul McCartney's bass line from "I Feel Fine"—and they swapped stories on what it was like to have their own "–mania." When asked his impressions of the evening with Elvis, Paul McCartney replied "Odd." Later, he asked one of the entourage members if Elvis might ever be interested in recording one of his songs.

After the Beatles split, McCartney fashioned a successful solo career. He later recorded with Elvis' regular Fifties drummer D.J. Fontana, and bought the original stand-up bass that Bill Black played in Elvis' early touring years.

In 1990, McCartney contributed his version of "It's Now Or Never" to NME's Elvis tribute album The Last Temptation of Elvis.

McCartney is now Sir Paul McCartney, after receiving a knighthood in 1997. He was inducted into the Rock and Roll Hall of Fame (as a solo performer) in 1999.

PAUL MCCARTNEY: "When we were kids growing up in Liverpool, all we ever wanted was to be Elvis Presley."

MCCOMB, JANELLE
(1921-2005)

A family friend of the Presleys from Tupelo, Janelle was instrumental in establishing monuments to Elvis in his birthplace. She collaborated on the Tupelo Youth Center that Elvis helped to fund; she worked to raise funds for a chapel near Elvis' birthplace in Tupelo, after she asked him what he might like done in his honor and he replied "a chapel so my fans would have a place to meditate," and she helped to set up the Elvis Birthplace museum.

In 1971, Elvis asked Janelle to write a poem for Lisa Marie—McComb wrote "The Priceless Gift." In 1976, he commissioned a poem for Vernon. After Elvis died, Vernon commissioned her to write the inscription for Elvis' tomb.

MCCOY, CHARLIE
(B. 1941)

Session guitarist, bassist and harmonica player (billed as "the fastest harp in the West") who started playing on Elvis movie soundtracks in the

mid-Sixties, making his debut on the Harum Scarum album and working on seven movies all told, as well as many sessions for RCA, including the material for gospel album How Great Thou Art—it may have been his presence at that session that persuaded Elvis to try his first Dylan song, "Tomorrow Is A Long Time." At a pinch, McCoy could also pick up a trumpet, as he did on Speedway.

Born in Oak Hill, West Virginia on March 28, 1941, McCoy established himself as a much-in-demand Nashville session musician in the Sixties. He was called in by Felton Jarvis in 1970 to work on Elvis' recordings there; he last recorded with Elvis in 1971.

Among others, McCoy recorded with Roy Orbison, Bob Dylan, Paul Simon and Joan Baez. He also had a successful solo career, winning a Grammy for Best Country instrumental performance in 1973 for his album The Real McCoy.

CHARLIE MCCOY: "I thought, 'Gee, it's a shame. This is the greatest recording artist in the world and he's got this bad material to work with. Obviously, either, number one, he doesn't have a choice, or number two, he's just so easy-going that he doesn't want to create any flak.' "

MCDOWELL, RONNIE
(B. 1950)

McDowell hit the big time with his multi-million selling 1977 tribute song to Elvis, "The King Is Gone," which made it to #13 on the Billboard Hot 100. Thereafter, he provided Elvis' singing voice for several made-for-TV Elvis biopics. In the Eighties, McDowell made a name for himself with a number of top 10 Country hits. In later years, he has toured with Elvis' original band members and backing singers The Jordanaires.

MCLEAN, DON
(B. 1945)

Elvis recorded McLean ballad "And I Love You So" in 1975. The New Rochelle-born folk artist cut his teeth in the music business working with Pete Seeger in the Sixties before scoring a huge hit in 1971 with "American Pie," a song that eulogized rock 'n' roll pioneer Buddy Holly (and which contains a reference to Elvis as "The King").

MCLEMORE, ED

Promoter Ed McLemore owned the Dallas Sportatorium, which hosted popular Saturday night hillbilly music show the Big D Jamboree, which was broadcast live on KRLD radio in the Fifties. Elvis' appearances on the show, starting from April 1955, helped to spread his fame through Texas. The Dallas Sportatorium was best known for the wrestling bouts it staged; performers from Hank Williams to Carl Perkins and Johnny Cash got to play from a stage built over the ring.

MCPHATTER, CLYDE
(1932-1972)

Born in Durham, North Carolina on November 15, 1932, McPhatter formed his first group, a gospel group, when he was just thirteen. He joined Billy Ward & The Dominos as lead singer in 1950, in time to deliver some of the first recognizable rock 'n' roll songs as the genre emerged out of R&B. McPhatter left to form his own group, The Drifters, in 1953, and was one of the first artists signed by Ahmet Ertegun at his new label Atlantic.

Elvis was a big fan of McPhatter's and covered "Money Honey" and "Such A Night" (1954 hits for McPhatter with the Drifters), "Come What May" and "Without Love." McPhatter and Elvis both covered "White Christmas." After finishing his draft in 1955, McPhatter became a major influence on nascent soul music. He was posthumously inducted into the Rock and Roll Hall of Fame in 1987.

ELVIS SAID TO SAM PHILLIPS: "If I had a voice like that man, I'd never want for another thing."

"MEAN WOMAN BLUES"

Elvis recorded this song, written by Claude Demetrius, for his first Paramount movie *Loving You* on January 13, 1957 at Radio Recorders. Until late in the day, the song was in the running to be the movie finale, before it was replaced by "Got A Lot O' Livin' To Do." It was first released on the *Loving You* EP (Vol. 2) and soundtrack album, since when it has appeared on *Worldwide Gold Award Hits Vol. 2*, *Elvis Aron Presley*, *Essential Elvis Vol.. 2*, *The King Of Rock And Roll*, *Elvis 2nd to None*, *Hitstory* and *Elvis Rock*.

The film version (recorded nine days after the record version) came out on *This Is Elvis* and 1988 album *Essential Elvis Vol. 1*.

The song was later covered by illustrious fellow Sun alumni Jerry Lee Lewis and Roy Orbison, who scored a top ten hit with it in 1963.

A recently-rediscovered version from the original tape appeared on the 2006 FTD issue *Loving You*.

"MEANEST GIRL IN TOWN, THE"

Joy Byers wrote this frenetic tune for Bill Haley and the Comets, who recorded it for release in 1964 under the title "Yeah, She's Evil." Elvis recorded the song for the *Girl Happy* soundtrack at Radio Recorders on June 10, 1964. It later came out on the *Double Feature* issue for the movie, and may be found on movie-related bootlegs. Alternate takes have appeared on FTD releases *Out In Hollywood* and *Girl Happy*.

MEASUREMENTS

Elvis was 6 feet tall, give or take a fraction of an inch. On his driver's license, his height is stated at 6' even, and that's the measurement he volunteered to interviewers in the Fifties. He was measured at 5' 11¼" on induction into the Army in 1958. At a concert in 1974 he said that he was 6' 1 ½"; some biographers have stated his height as 6' ½." It has been claimed that Elvis wore lifts in his shoes to add an inch or two to his height, though that would seem unnecessary as he already wore 2"-heeled boots to perform on stage. In movies where the height of Elvis' character is visible on a driving license or a Wanted poster, it's given as 6' 2."

In his youth and in his 1968-1970 prime, Elvis had a 32" waist, 31" inseam, and 42" chest measurement (40" in his younger days). His neck measurement for most of his life was 15½"; at his death, Elvis wore a 16½" collar and 35" sleeves.

He wore size 12 shoes (11D-sized boots in the Army).

Elvis' regular adult weight was 180 pounds, though he fluctuated from a little below to considerably above that mark.

MEDITATION

Elvis discovered meditation in the mid-Sixties through Larry Geller. He quickly discovered its benefits, and on a wave of enthusiasm asked Larry Geller and Marty Lacker to commission a meditation garden at Graceland so that he or anybody visiting the house could enjoy a place to spend some quiet time or have a private conversation. Lacker's brother-in-law Bernie Grenadier was drafted in to do the work, in an area previously used to grow vines. Before 1965 was out, the garden was ready, including a statue of Jesus modeled after a statue at the Lake Shrine of the Self-Realization Fellowship in California, where Elvis had been going to meditate. Unlike the Beatles, whose involvement in transcendental meditation was very public in the late Sixties, Elvis kept his interest in the practice under wraps.

Elvis meditated for half an hour before heading to the recording studio in Nashville in 1966 to record tracks for gospel album *How Great Thou Art*. In the Seventies, he added a period of meditation to the beginning of karate sessions with members of his entourage. Even if he wasn't fit enough to do karate, he would do the meditation.

Elvis and his nearest and dearest are buried at the Graceland Meditation Garden, the last place that people visit on the tour of his home.

Elvis said to Larry Geller: "Meditation is better than any drug I know. I can relax, I can breathe deeper, I'm calmer."

MELLO MEN, THE

This backing group stood in for The Jordanaires to record tunes for *It Happened at the World's Fair* in September 1962. They appear on film during "One Broken Heart For Sale," which along with "They Remind Me Too Much Of You" was released as a single. They also worked with Elvis on several other LA-based soundtrack sessions.

The Mello Men were a long-running vocal group originally founded by bass singer Thurl Ravenscroft in 1947. The group continued to back top singers right through to the Seventies. They also had a very profitable sideline in voicing cartoon characters for well-known Disney movies.

MEMOIRS

The odds are good that nobody who walked this earth has occasioned the writing of more memoirs than Elvis. Books have appeared from Elvis' wife, myriad girlfriends, practically every last one of his entourage pals, a fair proportion of band members, family members, many of the Graceland staff, and dozens of in-for-the-long-haul fans, in addition to the memoirs of other celebrities that feature a chapter or a passage on Elvis. Read enough of them—as a surprisingly large number of fans have—and you get a composite view of who Elvis was, what he got up to, and how he affected so many people's lives, though the genre is not without examples of authorial self-aggrandizement, rose-tinted recall and not-so-hidden agendas.

MEMORABILIA

With a huge and loyal fan-base for over half a century, it's little wonder that there's such a thriving market for anything Elvis, from items he owned to the sweat-soaked scarves he gave away, original fan literature and a range of merchandise so vast that Elvis is as much a trailblazer in the merchandising industry as he was in the music industry.

Early manager Bob Neal had the foresight to found Elvis Presley Enterprises, the entity that, in various guises, has managed all things Elvis, right at the very start of Elvis' career. Before long, the company was marketing an array of items from statues to dolls, clothing, charm bracelets and more. When the Colonel took over, things stepped up in all directions, as he made a deal with an external merchandiser and brought to market trading cards, plates, candy, cosmetics, calendars and a full gamut of tschochkes.

In 1956, as well as the torrent of vinyl released by RCA, fans could collect a set of 66 bubble gum cards, each with an Elvis photo and an interview question.

By 1957, the Colonel had as many as 60 different items on sale, including lipstick in Hound Dog orange, Heartbreak Hotel pink and Tutti Frutti red. Elvis came up with his own ideas too, suggesting "Teddy Bear" candy to cash in on his #1 hit "(Let Me Be Your) Teddy Bear." Fans could also buy the "Elvis Presley Game," a board game aimed squarely at his female admirers. Another early novelty item was an RCA "Victrola phonogram" emblazoned with a picture of Elvis and sold by the RCA company—a much updated model compared to the wind-up Victrola Elvis' parents owned in his youth.

Many items of memorabilia did not start out as products. Elvis was scrupulously diligent in signing autographs for fans and allowing them to take away things to do with him, from the shreds of clothing ripped from his body in his fan-wild Fifties heyday to boards he smashed during karate demonstrations.

A consummate consumer, in his lifetime Elvis churned through an impressive quantity of clothes, cars, jewelry and other objects, many of which he happily gave away to anybody who so much as admired them. An increasing number of these gifts have been appearing at auction, in many cases sold off by the heirs of the people to whom Elvis presented them. Elvis police badges and guns have come onto the market, as have items of clothing and personal notes previously housed at non-EPE museum collections that have closed down.

Countless actors, musicians and back-stage staff who worked with Elvis have rued the fact that they did not retain items that he gave them, or hold on to Elvis cast-offs that today might be worth a small fortune. Photographer Ed Bonja recalls the Colonel asking him to dispose of a dozen jumpsuits Elvis no longer wanted in the Seventies; if he hadn't sent them back to Vernon he would be sitting on a tinsel-mine.

The Colonel often handed out Elvis calendars as mementoes—he was known to do so in lieu of tips at restaurants. He could not have suspected that years later these and indeed any of the publicity material from Elvis' concerts exchange hands for hundreds of dollars.

Elvis fans around the world have their "Elvis rooms" to fill with Elvis memorabilia. Round the world the most avid memorabilia aficionados have put their Elvis collections on display, sometimes in custom-built Elvis museums, including major Australian collector Greg Page; Jim Curtin, who spent years buying and selling Elvis memorabilia before auctioning off his 50,000-item collection for a reputed $1.5 million in early 2006; Jimmy Velvet, who had such a large collection that he ran a museum opposite Graceland; and UK-based Sid Shaw, who has managed the Elvisly Yours business since the late Seventies.

Fans cherish first-issue records, especially from Elvis' Sun days, and all kinds of rare and limited-edition releases. Other collectors seek out anything that Elvis touched, from handkerchiefs and scarves to Elvis X-rays, blood, urine or saliva purportedly smuggled out from the hospitals he frequented in his twilight years. Offcuts of Elvis hair are commonly available online. EBay has carried old prescription medicine, a cupful of water from which Elvis supposedly drank, and a vial of sand that Elvis is said to have trampled while filming *Blue Hawaii*. Products have included "Elvis Sweat," "Love Me Tender Dog Chunks" and Elvis Jell-O molds, in among the more traditional novelty Elvis toys, figurines, commemorative cards, books, ornaments, lamps, throws, teddy bears and sundry other items bearing Elvis' likeness.

Fan letters have long been a staple of the memorabilia market, though understandably very few were personally drafted by the man himself—responding to the thousands of items of fan mail he received every week at the height of his fame would be impossible for any human being. When he first started out, he did scribble his own thank yous to fans. By 1956, when he had become a national sensation, a team of nine secretaries in Nashville did nothing but respond to his fan mail. Later, entourage members became well-versed in the art of signing for Elvis. The memorabilia market is one where *caveat emptor* applies, particularly to printed items that can be relatively easily reproduced

The biggest-ticket items of memorabilia are ultimately Elvis homes. His first owned home in Memphis controversially exchanged hands for $1 million in 2006. In early 2007 a property advertised as Vernon and Elvis' mid-Seventies hideaway, an hour from Memphis, was put up for auction in excess of $3 million.

Official EPE outlet offers no fewer than 21 different categories of Elvis goods, from "Accessories" to "Toys and Plush."

AUCTIONS

At the time of writing, EBay had a dedicated Elvis section that on any random day presents as many as 20,000 Elvis items of memorabilia for sale. It should be noted that seasoned collectors require more than just a simple accompanying letter to trust the provenance of high-ticket Elvis items.

Major Elvis auctions were held in 1994, 1995, 1996, 1997 and 1999 (many items from Graceland included), for which copious catalogs were printed.

Original Elvis paraphernalia fetches prices at the very top end of the memorabilia market. Original Sun singles change hands for multiple thousands of dollars (though not the copies that were reissued in 1973). A genuine certified Elvis guitar pick is worth close to $1,000, as is a genuine signed photo. Original albums and even first editions of well-regarded books realize significant sums. A copy of the first ever Elvis biography *Elvis Presley Speaks!* went for $1,300 in 1999. A love letter that Elvis sent to his girlfriend Anita Wood in 1958 from Germany raised over $20,000 at auction. The major 1999 Elvis auction generated $8,000 for Elvis' 6th grade report card, $3,500 for a 1955 show contract, $65,000 for Elvis' first RCA contract, $250,000 for Elvis' 1956 Lincoln Continental Mark II, and $70,000 for a jumpsuit that Elvis wore in concert in 1971. Receipts and handwritten notes exchanged hands for several hundreds of dollars. One of Elvis' guitars, a Gibson J200, sold for $55,000 in 2002. An old Elvis credit card fetched around $70,000. A 1960 Cadillac Coupe DeVille belonging to Elvis sold for around $40,000 in 2006. A belt Elvis wore on stage in Hawaii in 1972 raised $66,000 in 2006. An unused ticket to a 1956 Elvis concert fetched over $1,500 in 2006. A paper cup Elvis reputedly drank from on stage was sold for $200 in early 2007. Elvis' wedding ring, which he gave away not long before his death in 1977, was put up for auction in December 2006 and fetched $135,000. A signed copy of "Cheiro's Book of Numbers" fetched $4,000 in 2007. A guitar that

1950's ad for an Elvis doll.

Elvis used in *Follow That Dream* and *Kid Galahad* raised $68,000 in 2007; a gold-plated revolver fetched close to $30,000 in 2007.

Books:

The Elvis Catalog: Memorabilia, Icons, and Collectables Celebrating the King of Rock 'n' Roll, by Lee Cotten, Doubleday, 1987.

Elvis Collectables, by Rosalind Cranor, Overmountain Press, 1994.

All the King's Things: The Ultimate Elvis Memorabilia Book, by Bill Yenne and Ming Louie, Bluewood Books, 1994.

Everything Elvis, by Pauline Bartel, Taylor Publishing Company, 1995.

Presleyana: The Elvis Presley Record Price Guide, Vols. I-VI, by Jerry Osborne, O'Sullivan Woodside and Co., 1980-2007.

Elvis: Memories and Memorabilia, by Richard Buskin, Salamander Books, 1995.

Elvis! An Illustrated Guide to New and Vintage Collectables, by Steve Templeton, Courage Books, 1996.

Official Price Guide to Elvis Presley Records and Memorabilia, by Jerry Osborne, House of Collectibles/Ballantine Publishing Group, 1998.

Elvis Presley Memorabilia: An Unauthorized Collector's Guide, by Sean O'Neal, Schiffer, 2001.

Memorabilia boxes:

Elvis Box, Chronicle Books, 2001

The Elvis Treasures, by Robert Gordon, Villard, 2002 (book, CD and facsimiles sourced from Graceland)

"MEMORIES"

One of the stand-out songs that Elvis recorded for his 1968 NBC TV Special, on June 23, 1968 at Western Recorders in Hollywood. Elvis was so enamored of the Mac Davis / Billy Strange ballad that it became the only song to merit a full runthrough alongside monumental finale "If I Can Dream"—though the version released on record is longer than the "live" version from the show.

When the song came out as a single in late February 1969 with "Charro!" on the B-side it only sold around 300,000 copies, peaking at #35 in the charts.

"Memories" has made up for its initial quiet showing with long-lasting popularity: the original recording has since appeared on *This Is Elvis* (serving as the closing theme, as it did for the *Elvis on Tour* documentary), *Elvis' Gold Records Vol. 5*, *The Great Performances*, *Elvis 2nd to None*, *Hitstory* and *The Essential Elvis Presley*.

The song was a live favorite for Elvis the first summer that he returned to performing in 1969.

Live versions from Las Vegas appeared on bootlegs before coming out in 1991 on *Collectors Gold*. Another version from that summer 1969 engagement appeared on FTD release *Elvis at the International*.

His live performances for the Comeback Special have appeared on *Memories: The '68 Comeback Special* and *Tiger Man*. The stereo master version is on *Today Tomorrow & Forever*; an alternate take from the 1968 TV rehearsals featured on 2006 FTD album *Let Yourself Go*.

MEMORIES OF CHRISTMAS

A 1982 RCA gold-selling LP that includes some previously unreleased versions of tracks.

TRACK LISTING:
1. O Come, All Ye Faithful
2. Silver Bells
3. I'll Be Home On Christmas Day
4. Blue Christmas
5. Santa Claus Is Back in Town
6. Merry Christmas Baby (full version)
7. If Every Day Was Like Christmas (undubbed)
8. Christmas Message From Elvis
9. Silent Night

MEMORIES: THE '68 COMEBACK SPECIAL

A long-awaited 2-CD release of the NBC TV Special with additional material from Elvis in rehearsal and Elvis performing the first of his two sit-down shows at his landmark 1968 TV appearance.

TRACK LISTING:
Disc: 1
1. Trouble / Guitar Man
2. Heartbreak Hotel
3. Hound Dog
4. All Shook Up
5. Can't Help Falling In Love
6. Jailhouse Rock
7. Don't Be Cruel
8. Blue Suede Shoes
9. Love Me Tender
10. Baby What You Want Me To Do
11. Trouble / Guitar Man
12. Gospel Medley: (Sometimes I Feel Like A Motherless Child / Where Could I Go But To The Lord / Up Above My Head / Saved)
13. Memories
14. A Little Less Conversation
15. Road Medley: (Nothingville / Big Boss Man / Let Yourself Go / It Hurts Me / Guitar Man / Little Egypt / Trouble)
16. If I Can Dream

Disc: 2
1. When It Rains, It Really Pours
2. Lawdy, Miss Clawdy
3. Baby What You Want Me To Do
4. That's All Right
5. Heartbreak Hotel
6. Love Me
7. Baby What You Want Me To Do
8. Blue Suede Shoes
9. Baby What You Want Me To Do
10. Lawdy, Miss Clawdy
11. Are You Lonesome Tonight?
12. When My Blue Moon Turns To Gold Again
13. Blue Christmas
14. Tryin' To Get To You
15. One Night
16. Baby What You Want Me To Do
17. One Night
18. Memories
19. If I Can Dream

MEMPHIAN THEATER
(LOCATED AT 51 SOUTH COOPER)

For many years, after the final show of the day Elvis rented out this moviehouse to hold all-night movie sessions for himself and friends, sometimes as often as several nights a week.

In 1981, the world premiere of *This Is Elvis* took place at the venue.

In 1985 the Theater was converted into the Playhouse on the Square. During Elvis Week, tours are available for Elvis fans visiting Memphis.

MEMPHIS

Elvis was thirteen when his family moved from Tupelo, Mississippi to a boarding house on 370 Washington Street, Memphis. In 1948, Memphis was a city of 300,000 people that was attracting large numbers of the post-war poor. Living in close proximity to other new migrants at the Memphis Housing Authority's Lauderdale Courts broadened Elvis' musical horizons by placing him firmly in a city that, for its size, has had a disproportionately large influence on the development of popular music.

Local success and then international fame did not diminish Elvis' love for his adopted home town. He later purchased houses in Los Angeles and Palm Springs, but even when he was spending long periods of time in Hollywood making movies, Graceland was always the place he came home to. He continued to patronize the Rainbow Rollerdrome, the Memphis Fairgrounds and the Memphian Theater, the places he had enjoyed as a young unknown, hiring them out for himself and his friends.

On his return to Memphis in 1960 after two years in the Army, when asked what he missed most about the city, Elvis blurted out, "Everything!."

Memphis Mayor Henry Loeb and Tennessee governor Buford Ellington officially declared February 25, 1961 "Elvis Presley Day" in acknowledgement of Elvis' contribution to his home town on the day that he gave two charity show concerts to benefit a total of 26 local charities. Elvis consistently supported needy members of the local community from the first year that he became a big earner. A week later, Elvis told the Tennessee legislature in Nashville that he would never give up his home in Memphis.

As well as Elvis' regular Memphis pastimes of hiring out the roller-skating rink or movie house, in the mid-Sixties he started going to the Robert E. Lee Raceway in Whitehaven to watch car racing.

Proud as Elvis was of his Southern roots and Memphis heritage, he was mortified that Martin Luther King was assassinated in his home town.

January 8, 1974 was declared "Elvis Presley Day" by the city and county Mayor of Memphis, who marched down Elvis Presley Boulevard to Graceland.

Memphis today is synonymous with Elvis. In 1997, *The Economist* estimated that Elvis was responsible for the bulk of the city's annual tourist revenues of around $2 billion, in an industry employing 37,000 people.

On its web site, EPE estimates that Graceland visitors contribute $150 million to the Memphis economy.

MEMPHIS—A BRIEF HISTORY

Situated in Shelby County, Memphis is the largest city in Tennessee, with a population approaching 700,000. Memphis was originally founded on the west bank of the Mississippi River by Andrew Jackson in 1819, though there had been a fort on the site of this major crossing since 1797. Jackson named the new city after the old capital of Ancient Egypt, located just south of Cairo, also on the west bank of that country's major river. The city became a major staging point for Union troops during the Civil War after the confederates were defeated, and then evolved into a significant trading waystation thanks to its river access and railroad. It remains a major center of industry and a transportation hub, in part thanks to its status as the headquarters of Federal Express.

The "Home of the Blues" and the "Birthplace of Rock 'n' Roll," Memphis has been a breeding ground of new musical trends for over a century. By the end of the Sixties, Memphis was the premier location in the US for recording, built on the reputations of Sun, Stax and American Studio and many smaller outfits. A staggering one out of every four inductees to the Rock 'n' Roll Hall of Fame is from Memphis and environs.

MEMPHIS HOMES

-Alabama St.

In 1953, the family rented an apartment for $50 a month in a Victorian building at #462 Alabama St., opposite their previous apartment in Lauderdale Courts. This was where they were living as Elvis' career first began to take off. They moved out in late 1954 to an apartment on Lamar Avenue. The two-story apartment building was later demolished for a major road.

-Audubon Drive

Elvis put down a $500 deposit on the first house his family had ever owned, a seven-room home on 1034 Audubon Drive in an upmarket suburb of Eastern Memphis. Elvis and his parents completed the purchase of the new-built $29,500 four-bedroom property from the Welsh Plywood Corporation on March 12, 1956—though according to some sources, the house had been built a few years previously.

For their money, the Presleys had their first taste of relative luxury: a one-floor ranch-style dwelling with its own car port in a part of town where their neighbors were more likely to be country club members than recipients of federal benefits.

Elvis' parents supervised the move while he was touring the South. It wasn't until early May that Elvis had a chance to spend a few days in his new home, in his pink-themed bedroom. In the interim, the patio at the back of the house had been covered over, converted into a den and furnished with an almost full-sized pool table (there wasn't space for anything larger), and his growing collection of gold records hung on the wall. Soon after moving in, work began on a 50-foot granite swimming pool, the biggest private pool in town, which was ready in time for the summer.

It took less than a year for the Presleys to realize that the level of interest Elvis generated was incompatible with living in such an accessible location. A *Life* magazine feature showed girl fans leaning up against the house, their ears glued to the outside of Elvis' bedroom wall. Fans took blades of grass from the lawn as mementos. Putting a fence up made little difference.

The Presleys used the $55,000 they received for the Audubon Drive home to trade up to Graceland, much to the relief of the neighbors, whose genteel lives had been all shook up by the never-ending pilgrimage of Elvis fans.

In 2006, Uri Geller made an attempt to by the house at an eBay auction, with the intention of turning it into a museum of the paranormal. He failed to foresee that the purchase would become embroiled in legal actions after the previous own-

Elvis at his house on Audubon Drive, 1956.

Elvis, 17-years-old, at Lauderdale Courts.

housing was approved, they moved to the Lauderdale Courts. Billy Smith, however, reckons that Elvis did not live here; Smith's family did. A few years later, Elvis frequented the Poplar Tunes record store at 308. Elvis' Poplar Ave. home has since been demolished.

-Saffarans Street
On January 7, 1953 the Presley family left public housing and moved into a house opposite Elvis' high school, at 698 Saffarans Street. They moved to Alabama Avenue in April 1953. Once again, this house is long gone. Some biographers state that the family lived at 398 Cypress Street during this period.

-Washington Street
The family's first place of residence in Memphis after they moved to town in November 1948 was a boarding house at #370 Washington Street, for which they paid $11 a week. The property has since been demolished.

For a chronological listing, see HOMES.
For concerts in Memphis, see TENNESSEE.

ELVIS SAID AT CHRISTMAS 1959: "Seeing the city of Memphis, my family, friends, and fans, will be the most welcome sight in the world to me."

ELVIS SAID IN 1969: "It all started right here in Memphis for me, man."

ELVIS SAID IN CONCERT AT A MEMPHIS SHOW IN 1974: "It's always been said that a person cannot return to their hometowns, but you have disproven that theory completely."

CHIPS MOMAN: "Most everybody in Memphis kind of took Elvis for granted — didn't pay any attention to how big a star he really was. Remember, he was a home-town boy. He's bigger now in Memphis than he ever was in his best days when he was alive."

RICK STANLEY: "He wasn't only the King of Rock and Roll. He was also the King of Memphis."

Book:
Memphis Elvis-Style, by Cindy Hazen and Mike Freeman, John F. Blair Publisher, 1997.

Video/DVD:
Elvis Presley's Memphis (2001)

MEMPHIS CHARITY SHOW

Elvis rehearsed for his 1961 charity show at Graceland with longtime band members Scotty Moore and D. J. Fontana, the Jordanaires and a selection of his favorite Nashville session musicians.

The Charity Show at the Ellis Auditorium was in fact two shows, on what State Governor and Memphis Mayor officially named "Elvis Presley Day." On February 25, 1961 more than ten thousand people paid a total of over $50,000 to watch Elvis perform, after being introduced by comedian George Jessel. Elvis concluded the evening off with an after-party at Graceland.

MEMPHIS FAIRGROUNDS

A poor kid, Elvis used to sneak in to the fairground if he didn't have the admission fee. That problem went away; his thrill-seeking remained as a lifelong Elvis pleasure.

In September 1956, Elvis took new Hollywood pal Nick Adams to the Memphis Fairgrounds several nights running, on one occasion clambering

---

ers sold the property to music producer Mike Curb, who at the time of writing was planning to donate the house to Rhodes College for their school of music history.

-Getwell Street
The Presley family moved to 1414 Getwell in late September or early October 1955, paying $85 a month in rent. Though hardly highbrow, it was a definite step up the ladder for them. This was where Elvis was living when he finally signed his big deal with RCA. The last premises that the Presleys rented before buying has since become a mall.

-Graceland
The Presley family purchased their long-term home in late March 1957 for $102,500. Set in its own grounds, at that time the 3764 Bellevue Blvd. home was several miles outside Memphis.
See GRACELAND.

-Lamar Avenue
Elvis moved his family to a rented brick home at #2414 some time in May 1955. They stayed there for around six months before trading up to larger premises on Getwell Street. The building has since been converted into a day care facility for children.

-Lauderdale Courts
Not long after moving to Memphis, the Presleys made a successful application for public housing and were assigned a two-bedroom first-floor apartment (# 328) at 185 Winchester Ave. in the 499-apartment Memphis Housing Authority's Lauderdale Courts development. When they moved in to their new home in September 1949, they paid $35 a month in rent (later raised to $43 a month). Elvis' bedroom was the larger of the two, with a view out onto Third Street.

Now on the National Register of Historic Places, the development was built in the late Thirties as part of the Franklin D. Roosevelt Works Progress Administration program. The specific purpose of this type of housing was to provide a stepping stone for new migrants to town, allowing them to find work, establish themselves and then move on. The apartments had indoor plumbing and fitted kitchens—a definite step up for the Presleys.

Elvis spent his adolescence here, hanging out with pals such as Paul Dougher, Buzzy Forbes and Farley Guy and getting into and out of teenage scrapes. Friends recall him sneaking off to the basement laundry room to practice guitar. He also hung around on the fringes of some of the older kids who were into music.

As the Presley's financial situation improved, they ran foul of the public housing income threshold. After some to-ing and fro-ing, the Presleys received their final eviction notice on November 17, 1952, and had to vacate the property by February 28, 1952. From here, they moved to an apartment on Saffarans Street.

The whole development was earmarked for redevelopment in the Nineties, until Elvis fans helped to persuade the local authorities to refurbish the site. Lauderdale Courts went upmarket and is now known as "Uptown Square." The former Presley apartment, complete with period furnishings and modern amenities, is available for overnight rent for under $250 (2007 prices).

-Poplar Ave.
It is generally believed that Elvis' family moved to a rooming house at 572 Poplar Ave in Memphis in May 1949, in a poor part of town where they shared this large house with a number of other families (at least three other families used the same bathroom), paying $35 per month for the privilege. When their application for public

Elvis at the Memphis fairgrounds in the 1960s.

up on stage to take a bow with tenor Dennis Day. Elvis' girlfriends could expect many of their dates to involve several dozen friends at the fairgrounds.

Before long, Elvis was drawing more of a crowd than the fairground attractions and it became simpler just to hire out the whole fairgrounds from owner Malcolm "Wimpy" Adams after hours: $2,000 bought freedom of this children's paradise until dawn. There were times when Elvis rented the Fairgrounds for his pals and extended family three or four nights a week, picking up the tab even for what his guests ate and drank.

Elvis especially liked the dodgems, which he turned into a boisterous exercise in team combat. Split into two teams, Elvis and friends fought a war of attrition by whiplash. He loved the Zippin' Pippin rollercoaster too. A fearless rider, he'd go round and round and round and round until his guests felt queasy and headed for terra firma. Elvis once enlisted Will McDaniel ("Bardahl" as Elvis nicknamed him) in a $50 bet with the man who ran the rollercoaster ride. Elvis won the money when Bardahl rode the ride more daringly than the Coaster manager would try.

Elvis rented out the Memphis Fairgrounds (by then known as Libertyland) about a week before he died for nine-year old Lisa Marie, girlfriend Ginger Alden's niece, and a duck line of kids belonging to friends and family. For the first time in years, Elvis rode all of his favorite rides again.

When Libertyland shuttered in 2005, Elvis' favorite ride, Zippin' Pippin, was purchased by the Carolina Crossroads development in Roanoke, NC.

MEMPHIS FLASH HITS LAS VEGAS, THE

A bootleg CD of live songs and sometimes wayward banter released with Kay Wheeler's book *Growing Up With The Memphis Flash*.

TRACK LISTING:
1. Elvis talks with sound engineer Bill Porter
2. Good Time Charlie's Got The Blues
3. It's Midnight
4. Introducing Richard Egan
5. Big Boss Man
6. Let Me Be There
7. Introducing Neil Diamond
8. Holy Holy (one line only)
9. Heartbreak Hotel
10. You're The Reason I'm Living
11. Along Came Jones (one line only)
12. Elvis fools around with intro to Hound Dog
13. Hound Dog / Are You Sincere
14. Fever (long version)
15. I'll Fight . . .
16. "Strung-out" dialogue
17. Lawdy, Miss Clawdy

MEMPHIS GRIZZLIES

In 1974, Elvis got into the habit of taking a busload of pals to watch the Memphis Southmen—better known as the Memphis Grizzlies—at the Memphis Memorial Stadium, during the two years that they had the franchise in the World Football League. Elvis usually sat in the press box to watch the matches. After the football franchise was revoked, the Grizzlies name passed on to the local basketball team.

MEMPHIS MAFIA

The moniker for Elvis' entourage was first coined by a press columnist—James Bacon is a likely candidate—or by a surprised bystander who watched Elvis and a 10-man black-suited retinue exit a limousine in Las Vegas in 1960. On his return from Europe, Elvis and his pals took to appearing in public dressed in Italian-tailored suits and toting briefcases, in homage to European style and perhaps to Frank Sinatra's Rat Pack.

Elvis didn't like the name according to Alan Fortas, but the guys liked the sound of it.

The entourage varied in number from just a few at the beginning and end of Elvis' professional life to as many as thirteen. All of the guys did jobs for Elvis; they also shared in the fun, laughed at his jokes, kept him entertained, played pranks, served as bodyguards, acted as a buffer zone, sang with him and generally kept him company, in exchange for a relatively modest salary.

Memphis mafia memoirs and "as told to" books have shone light into many previously hidden corners of Elvis' private and professional life.

See ENTOURAGE and entries for individual members.

EDDIE FADAL: "The Memphis Mafia isolated him. They were afraid someone else would encroach on their territory, so they tried to keep everybody else out. It was a tough ring around Elvis, and I don't think Elvis realized that."

JERRY SCHEFF: "During the last years, these people in the so-called Memphis Mafia got into this Howard Hughes thing, where they could pick and choose who could see him."

Books:
Revelations Of The Memphis Mafia by Alanna Nash, HarperCollins, 1995, reissued as *Elvis and the Memphis Mafia*, HarperCollins, 2005.
Personal memoirs by the majority of Elvis' close associates.

Documentaries:
The Elvis Mob
All The King's Men Vols. 1-6

MEMPHIS PRESS-SCIMITAR

The local newspaper may have influenced young Elvis' decision to chance his arm with Sam Phillips, when the paper ran an article on Phillips' latest discovery, The Prisonaires, a convict quartet serving time at the Tennessee State Penitentiary.

Immediately after his first single in July 1954, Sun Records producer Marion Keisker accompanied Elvis to the local newspaper for an interview with journalist Edwin Howard. The paper has covered all things Elvis ever since.

MEMPHIS RECORDING SERVICE

Radio engineer Sam Phillips realized a boyhood dream when he converted a former Auto Repair Shop at 706 Union Avenue, Memphis into his very own recording studio in 1950, ably assisted by secretary/girl Friday Marion Keisker, having taken out a loan from a colleague at the WREC radio station.

The entrepreneurial Phillips advertised the Memphis Recording Services under the slogan "We Record Anything, Anywhere, Anytime," from $4 vanity acetates like the ones an unknown called Elvis Presley recorded in the summer of 1953 to audio recordings of weddings, funerals and beauty pageants. It all helped to fund his true interest: building up a roster of R & B artists, initially for other record labels such as Chess of Chicago, and then under his own Sun Records label.

Paying out of his own pocket—or loaned the money by pal Ed Leek in one story—Elvis laid down a two-sided acetate of "My Happiness" and

"That's When Your Heartaches Begin," reputedly for his mother's birthday though that was still the best part of a year away. Elvis' most meticulous biographers have failed to pin down the exact date that this event occurred; Billy Smith recalls that it was June 13, 1953, though the date has also been stated as June 5; more recently, the book *Memphis Recording Service* has asserted that the fateful date was August 22. Elvis was likely thrilled and intimidated to step into the studio where B.B. King, Bobby Bland, Willie Nixon and Howling Wolf had been making their music.

In January 1954 (most sources cite the fourth of the month; the book *Memphis Recording Service* states that it was January 6) Elvis returned to record two country tracks for another vanity disc: "I'll Never Stand In Your Way" and "It Wouldn't Be The Same Without You" (in some biographies, the second track is stated as "Casual Love Affair"). These novice forays into recording did not lead to immediate success, but they served the purpose of marking Elvis' card with Sam Phillips and his assistant Marion Keisker.

Elvis made a habit of dropping by to say hi, a tactic that paid off on June 26, 1954 when Keisker suggested to Phillips that they call in "the boy with the sideburns" to audition. Keisker and/or Phillips got Elvis to run through "Without You," a ballad sourced from Nashville publisher Red Wortham, and then Scotty Moore and Bill Black took Elvis off to put him through his paces.

Elvis' history dwells not at all on how many other doors the young hopeful knocked on at that time. He was definitely turned down by at least two bands for which he auditioned, while B. B. King's manager Robert Henry almost certainly rejected Elvis before he received his Sun callback.

Elvis recorded all of his early singles here until he signed for RCA in late 1955.

SAM PHILLIPS: "I opened the Memphis Recording Service with the intention of recording singers and musicians from Memphis and the locality who I felt had something that people should be able to hear."

MARION KEISKER: "With many difficulties we got the place and we raised the money, and between us we did everything—we laid all the tile, we painted the acoustic boards, I put in the bathroom, Sam put in the control room."

MEMPHIS RECORDING SERVICE

A two-volume book/DVD/DVD-Audio package *Elvis Presley - Memphis Recording Service*, written by Joseph Pirzada and John Michael Heath, includes interviews, live recordings and a reproduction single, published by Memphis Recording Services Ltd., 2005/2006. Volume one features Elvis' first ever Louisiana Hayride show, from October 16, 1954.

Pirzada prides himself on achieving the best possible sound quality, and claims to have tapped sources that official channels have not.

The company followed this up with a volume on Elvis' Tupelo homecoming concert

TRACK LISTING:
VOL. 1
1. My Happiness
2. That's When Your Heartaches Begin
3. That's All Right
4. Blue Moon Of Kentucky
5. Good Rockin' Tonight
6. I Don't Care If The Sun Don't Shine
7. Lucky Strike (advert while Scotty and Bill tune up)
8. That's All Right (Mama) (live)
9. Blue Moon Of Kentucky (live)
10. Milkcow Blues Boogie
11. You're A Heartbreaker

VOL. 2
1955 STUDIO
1. Baby Let's Play House
2. I'm Left, You're Right, She's Gone
3. I Forgot To Remember To Forget
4. Mystery Train
5. Tryin' To Get To You
6. When It Rains It Really Pours
7. How Do You Think I Feel?
1955—JANUARY 6, LUBBOCK TEXAS
8. Fool, Fool, Fool
9. Shake, Rattle, And Roll
INTERVIEWS
10. Mae Axton interviews Elvis
11. KSIJ Radio commercial
12. Bob Neal interview Elvis, Scotty and Bill
1955 LIVE RECORDINGS
LOUISIANA HAYRIDE—JANUARY 15TH
13. Hayride begins jingle
14. Hearts Of Stone
15. That's All Right (Mama)
16 . Tweedlee Dee
LOUISIANA HAYRIDE—JANUARY 22ND
17. Money Honey
18. Blue Moon Of Kentucky
19. I Don't Care If The Sun Don't Shine
20. That's All Right (Mama)
EAGLE'S HALL, HOUSTON TEXAS—MARCH 19
21. Good Rockin' Tonight
22. Baby Let's Play House
23. Intro / Blue Moon Of Kentucky
24. Intro / I Got A Woman
25. Intro / That's All Right (Mama)
LOUISIANA HAYRIDE—APRIL 30TH
26. Tweedlee Dee
LOUISIANA HAYRIDE—JULY 16TH
27. I'm Left, You're Right, She's Gone
LOUISIANA HAYRIDE—AUGUST 20TH
28. Baby Let's Play House
29. Maybellene
30. That's All Right (Mama)
31. Hayride ends jingle
1954 STUDIO
32. I'll Never Stand In Your Way
33. It Wouldn't Be The Same Without You
34. Harbor Lights
35. I Love You Because
36. Blue Moon
37. Tomorrow Night
38. I'll Never Let You Go (Little Darlin')
39. Just Because
40. I'm Left, You're Right, She's Gone (slow version)

The UK-based label has continued to issue early Elvis material in book/DVD-audio packages. In 2007, it brought out releases on Elvis' 1956 homecoming concerts in Tupelo (*see under* TUPELO *for tracklisting*), and *New York RCA Studio 1: The Complete Sessions*, from his July 1956 recording session in New York

TRACKLIST:
1. Blue Suede Shoes
2. My Baby Left Me
3. One-Sided Love Affair
4. So Glad You're Mine
5. I'm Gonna Sit Right Down And Cry (Over You)
6. Tutti Frutti
7. Lawdy, Miss Clawdy
8. Shake, Rattle and Roll
9. Hound Dog
10. Don't Be Cruel
11. Any Way You Want Me
12. Lawdy Miss Clawdy (12 takes)
13. Shake, Rattle and Roll (12 takes)
14. My Baby Left Me (Arthur 'Big Boy' Crudup)
15. Hound Dog (Freddie Bell & the Bell Boys)
16. So Glad You're Mine (Arthur 'Big Boy' Crudup)

MEMPHIS SESSIONS, THE

An eagerly-awaited 2001 FTD release of outtakes from Elvis' January 1969 American Studio sessions, as they recorded and without later overdubs.

TRACK LISTING:
1. After Loving You
2. Stranger In My Own Home Town
3. In The Ghetto
4. Suspicious Minds
5. Any Day Now
6. Only The Strong Survive
7. Wearin' That Loved On Look
8. Do You Know Who I Am
9. And The Grass Won't Pay No Mind (undubbed master)
10. You'll Think Of Me
11. Power Of My Love
12. This Is The Story
13. True Love Travels On A Gravel Road
14. Long Black Limousine
15. Kentucky Rain
16. Without Love (There Is Nothing)
17. Hey Jude (splice)
18. If I'm A Fool (For Loving You)
19. From A Jack To A King
20. I'm Movin' On

MEMPHIS STATE UNIVERSITY

Elvis was booked to play at the College as part of a Student Government Association blood drive in early November 1954 (most likely on November 8). In later years, Elvis returned to play racquetball.

"MEMPHIS TENNESSEE"

Elvis laid down a pop-flavored version of the 1959 Chuck Berry standard on May 27, 1963 at RCA's Nashville Studios. The recording was originally slated for release as the B-side to "Bossa Nova Baby" in October 1963 but Elvis wasn't satisfied with the results and decided to re-record.

The new version, from a session at Studio B, Nashville on January 12, 1964, suffered more delays when Elvis decided that he wanted the song to come out at the right time. That right time came and went in 1964: as RCA was preparing to release the song as a single, Lonnie Mack had a hit with an instrumental version, and then Johnny Rivers recorded his own version (reputedly after hearing Elvis' unreleased acetate at Graceland) which went to #2, titled simply "Memphis."

Elvis' own "Memphis Tennessee" finally came out on album *Elvis For Everyone*, and subsequently on *From Elvis Presley Boulevard Memphis Tennessee, For The Asking, From Nashville To Memphis* and *Artist Of The Century*.

The original studio recording—known as the "Jungle Version"—first appeared on *Collectors Gold* in 1991; an alternate take from that session featured on *From Nashville To Memphis*.

Essential Elvis Vol. 6 and FTD release *Studio B: Nashville Outtakes* contain alternate takes from the 1964 session. Elvis very occasionally performed the song live in the Seventies.

MEN

A number of Elvis commentators have stated that Elvis felt most comfortable in the company of women. Growing up at school, he was ostracized by his peers for dressing unconventionally and not excelling at sport.

Fame changed everything. Elvis' early days on the road were three guys just having a great time, though his spellbinding effect on women disgruntled many a boyfriend and led to threats and episodes of violence. When the Elvis character died in his first movie *Love Me Tender*, in some theaters the men cheered while their girlfriends wept.

A higher profile required more security, marking the start of Elvis' paid entourage. This soon evolved into a traveling court, a bubble around a man who, it seems, never completely lost his early shyness about meeting new people. In his relationships with other guys, Elvis was almost always the first among non-equals.

ELVIS SAID IN 1962: "I like a man who's pretty much the same all the time, is pretty straight. He's himself to a certain extent."

BOB NEAL: "He was always unhappy about the reaction from the boys because he very much wanted to be one of the boys . . . but the boys reacted very violently in many areas because, I suppose, of the way the girls acted."

"MEN WITH BROKEN HEARTS"

A live recording of Elvis reciting an extract from this 1950 Hank Williams poem put to music during an August 1970 show in Las Vegas was released in the Nineties on *Walk A Mile In My Shoes* and later on *Live in Las Vegas*. Billy Eckstine and Perry Como also covered the song, Perry Como the same year as Elvis.

The poem was one that Elvis often quoted:

"You never stood in that man's shoes, or ever saw things through his eyes; or stood and watched with helpless hands, while the heart inside you dies. So help your brother along the way, no matter where he starts. For the same God that made you made them too, these men with broken hearts."

MERCHANDISE

Elvis has been a merchandising king for as long as the world has known his name. Even before there were any items bearing his likeness, fans made their own merchandise by ripping off his clothes and treasuring the shreds, or jealously collecting the dust from the car he traveled in.

Colonel Parker was a music industry trailblazer for groundbreaking merchandising deals before he took over Elvis' management contract. Parker scaled up the Elvis merchandising carried out by Bob Neal's original cottage industry operation by contracting out to LA-based merchandiser Hank Saperstein and his Special Projects company in mid-1956, to add to his stable of The Lone Ranger among others.

RCA and the film studios took care of the vast majority of Elvis merchandising in the Sixties, though there remained plenty of scope for bootleggers and DIY manufacturers in what at that time was a largely unpoliced industry. In 1974, the Colonel brought merchandising back in-house through a company he set up for the purpose, Boxcar. In 1976, unauthorized supplier Factors Etc., Inc. was so successful in selling Elvis-related products that the Colonel decided to make the company an official merchandiser, in exchange for a 25% cut of profits.

The foundation of Elvis Presley Enterprises Inc. in the early Eighties stamped some order onto the market through a number of landmark legal cases. EPE has been actively seeking merchandising opportunities through partnership deals in recent years. In 2006, EPE authorized companies to produce fabrics with Elvis images for the industry, a line of clothing, Elvis debit and credit cards, bicycles, house keys, trading cards and an Elvis commemorative revolver, in addition to the games, knick-knacks, plush toys, figurines, trivia games and other items already on sale. Additions in 2007

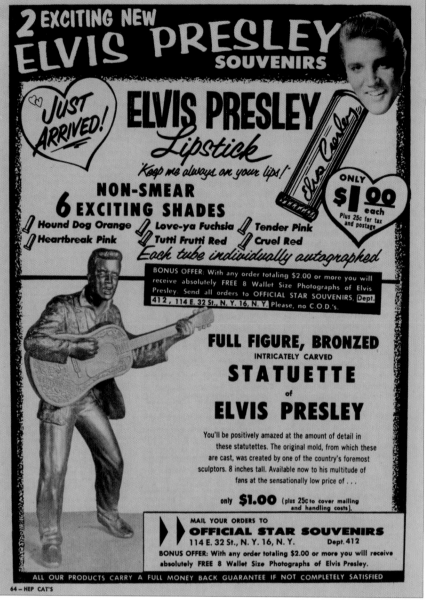

1950's ad for Elvis Presley Lipstick.

included a line of Elvis shoes and an Elvis debit card Anachronistic articles abound, including a Swarovski Elvis cell phone, disposable cameras that snap photos of the subject together with Elvis, and an "animatronic" Elvis head; it is ever the collectors' hope that today's merchandise becomes tomorrow's memorabilia.

The commercial development across Elvis Presley Boulevard from Graceland is an object lesson to any merchandiser about how to segment and multiply the merchandising opportunities for a celebrity-likeness brand. When James Brown passed away in late 2006, his family looked to the example of the Elvis Presley Estate. As of 2006, more than 200 official licensees are authorized to use the Elvis name on their products.

See also MEMORABILIA and ELVIS PRESLEY ENTERPRISES.

PRISCILLA said of 1956: "Elvis was everywhere, on bubblegum cards and Bermuda shorts, on diaries and wallets and pictures that glowed in the dark."

JERRY HOPKINS: "Never in the history of entertainment had another personality been so completely and relentlessly merchandised as Elvis."

"MERRY CHRISTMAS BABY"

Blues meets Santa in this uninhibited jam at Nashville's Studio B on May 15, 1971, during

which Elvis had such a great time that he is heard exhorting band mate Norbert Putnam to get with it. Originally a top ten blues hit for Johnny Moore's Three Blazers back in 1949, various other performers including Chuck Berry had taken it on before Elvis.

Released in a truncated version as a single in November 1971 with "O Come, All Ye Faithful" on the flip side, Elvis' version of this Lou Baxter / Johnny Moore composition failed to chart, selling fewer than 100,000 copies over two Christmas seasons; sales can't have been helped by the fact that the song had already come out on the LP *Elvis Sings the Wonderful World of Christmas*.

The almost 8-minute long unedited master—minus the overdubbed James Burton guitar solo—was released on 1982 album *Memories Of Christmas*.

Latter-day releases include *This Is Elvis* (short version), *If Every Day Was Like Christmas*, *Reconsider Baby* (longer version), *Walk A Mile In My Shoes*, *Artist Of The Century*, *Christmas Peace* and *Elvis Christmas*.

"MESS OF BLUES, A"

Ever since the B-Side to "It's Now Or Never," released in July 1960, rose to #32 in the charts under its own steam, it has been popular with bluesophile Elvis fans. He recorded the Doc Pomus / Mort Shuman song on March 20, 1960, in his first session after returning from his Army service at the RCA studios in Nashville.

The track made its LP debut on *Elvis' Golden Records Vol. 4*. Subsequent album releases are *Worldwide Gold Award Hits Vol. 1*, *Elvis Sings Mort Shuman & Doc Pomus*, *Elvis Sings The Blues*, *From Nashville to Memphis*, CD reissues of *Elvis Is Back!*, *Artist Of The Century*, *Elvis 2nd to None*, *Hitstory* and *Elvis R 'n' B*.

The first take from the 1960 session was released in 1997 on *Platinum: A Life In Music*; remixed alternates of this take have since appeared on FTD releases *Long Lonely Highway* and *Elvis Is Back!* (which includes multiple alternates).

METAPHYSICS

For much of his life, Elvis was convinced that the nature of his birth, specifically the death of his twin brother Jesse Garon, was a sign that he was pre-ordained for a special existence. Elvis spent decades studying spirituality and investigating the esoteric, though by his final years he acknowledged that many things lay beyond his ken.

Elvis dedicated himself to the study of metaphysics after he met Larry Geller, known by the entourage as "Elvis' guru." He delved into Eastern religions, tried yoga, meditated, read widely about spirituality, tried his hand at faith healing, concocted sermons for his captive audience of friends and girlfriends, worked out a personal theory of reincarnation, decided that his fame and success was for a higher purpose, and was reputedly convinced that he witnessed alien visitations to Earth, one of which, in Bel Air in 1966, was corroborated by Sonny West.

In pursuing these avenues of enquiry, Elvis was building on elements that had been part of his upbringing.

Once again according to Larry Geller, Gladys healed Elvis as a child through the laying on of hands and prayer. Geller himself saw Elvis heal a man who had suffered a heart attack; Elvis is also said to have healed Jerry Schilling after a motorcycle accident. In Priscilla's memoir, she says that a touch of Elvis' hands would dissipate the most powerful headache.

Though Elvis' (belief in this) talent was not publicized, in the Seventies it wasn't uncommon at shows for fans to bring along sick children in the hope that Elvis would touch and heal them.

ELVIS SAID IN 1962: "I look at myself strictly as a human being who is, like I said, has been very lucky, but whose life . . . I have blood running through my veins . . . and can be snuffed out in just a matter of seconds, and not as anything supernatural or better than any other human being."

ELVIS SAID: "There are no coincidences . . . There's more to this than meets the eye."

ELVIS SANG IN 1968: "As long as a man has the strength to dream, he can redeem his soul and fly."

RED WEST: "There's a lot of strange things to Elvis, a lot of strange things. That's why I don't believe he is any ordinary human."

LARRY GELLER: "Despite his faith in the power of fate and destiny, he believed that we're impelled by certain qualities and influences to make our own choices in life."

JOE ESPOSITO: "He was always gullible when it came to those things. He was always trying to figure out why he was the one chosen—he was into all these things that you couldn't solve. He liked to show his intelligence by trying to find the answers that no one else knew."

Elvis on tour for MGM.

MEXICO

Elvis and cousin Gene Smith took a brief trip down Mexico way in 1956 according to Billy Smith.

Elvis was all set to travel to Mexico for *Fun in Acapulco* until the Colonel advised against it, citing an incident south of the border a couple of years earlier when Elvis had been falsely quoted as saying he would rather "kiss three Negresses . . . than one Mexican girl." This malicious rumor sparked off a campaign to keep Elvis' music off the airwaves in the capital, and followed a rumor that Elvis had popped up in Mexico to get married.

A showing of *G.I. Blues* in 1960 caused such a riot in Mexico City that the government banned Elvis movies altogether. This was not an isolated occurrence: previous Elvis movies had been interrupted by teenagers vandalizing movie houses. The authorities had been less than keen about the prospect of Elvis attending a rock 'n' roll festival in 1957, to which he had been invited.

Book:

Refried Elvis: The Rise of the Mexican Counterculture, by Eric Zolov, University of Calif. Press, 1999.

"MEXICO"

A Latin-lite Sid Tepper / Roy C. Bennett song that Elvis recorded at Radio Recorders on January 22, 1963 for the *Fun in Acapulco* soundtrack, with a vocal contribution from Larry Domasin in the movie.

In addition to the later *Double Feature* release for the movie, "Mexico" has also appeared on *Command Performances*.

Alternates are on *Today Tomorrow & Forever* and FTD releases *Out In Hollywood* and *Fun in Acapulco*.

MGM

Elvis may have signed his first film contract with Paramount and released his first movie through Twentieth Century-Fox, but he wound up making more movies for MGM than any other studio, starting with 1957 hit *Jailhouse Rock*.

Colonel Parker struck a four-picture deal with MGM in January 1961, snaring Elvis a $400,000 per movie fee plus a further $100,000 in expenses and musical fees, and a 50% share of profits above $500,000. MGM producers saw no reason to meddle with the winning Elvis bikini / travelogue formula that had done so well at the box office for Paramount and Twentieth Century-Fox, so over the next four years Elvis made *It Happened at the World's Fair*, *Viva Las Vegas*, *Kissin' Cousins*, and *Girl Happy* for the studio.

The Colonel negotiated a new deal with the studio in January 1965, this time for a cool $1 million for the first picture (*Harum Scarum*) and $750,000 for the following two (*Spinout* and *Double Trouble*).

Only *Harum Scarum* was actually in the can before MGM extended the deal for a further four movies (*Speedway*, *Stay Away*, *Live a Little, Love a Little* and *The Trouble with Girls*), fixing Elvis' take at $850,000 per movie plus 50% of profits. The studio may not have been so generous—this was at the very top end of the Hollywood pay scale—if they had known that Elvis' later movies were heading for an unstoppable slide.

By the early 1970s, MGM's fortunes were closely associated with Kirk Kerkorian, founder of the International Hotel in Las Vegas. Once Elvis signed for Kerkorian's hotel, MGM was the natural choice to shoot a concert movie at Kerkorian's flagship Las Vegas property, earning Elvis a further half million dollars.

MOVIES ELVIS MADE WITH MGM

Jailhouse Rock (1957)
It Happened at the World's Fair (1963)
Kissin' Cousins (1964)
Viva Las Vegas (1964)
Girl Happy (1965)
Harum Scarum (1965)
Spinout (1966)
Double Trouble (1967)
Stay Away Joe (1968)
Speedway (1968)
Live a Little, Love a Little (1968)
The Trouble with Girls (1969)
That's the Way It Is (documentary 1970)
Elvis on Tour (documentary 1972)

MICHIGAN

- Ann Arbor

Elvis sang at the Crisler Arena on April 24, 1977.

- Detroit

Elvis first came to the Detroit Fox Theater on May 25, 1956. He played the Olympia Stadium on March 31, 1957. Fifteen years later, he was back at the Olympia on April 6, 1972. He had to pull up short after only half an hour onstage at the Olympia Stadium on September 29, 1974, due to illness, but played the venue a second time on October 4, 1974. Elvis last performed at the venue on April 22, 1977.

- Kalamazoo

Elvis came to the Wings Stadium on October 21, 1976. He played here again on April 26, 1977.

- Pontiac

Elvis performed a one-off New Year's Eve show at the Silverdome on December 31, 1975, which at the time set a record for the largest ticket takings by any performer on a single night. Elvis landed the gig after the Rolling Stones pulled out.

- Saginaw

The Civic Center hosted Elvis on April 25, 1977, and called him back for an extra show at the end of that tour on May 3, 1977.

"MICKEY MOUSE CLUB MARCH, THE"

All in the name of pranking and fun, Elvis came out on stage in Las Vegas on April 1, 1975 wearing mouse ears and launched into the Mouse's theme song. He repeated the escapade in Atlanta the next month and at Tahoe the following May, though some sources claim that he first pulled the trick in 1972. The Vegas version made it onto bootleg release *Rockin' With Elvis April Fools Day*. A few bars of the song are on 2006 FTD release *Southern Nights*.

MILAM JUNIOR HIGH SCHOOL

Elvis started sixth grade at this Tupelo school in September 1946, where he was taught by a Mrs. Quay Web Camp and later Virginia Plumb. After a non-descript academic start, Elvis began to excel at spelling, physical education and, not surprisingly, music. He suffered a great deal of teasing for his poverty; he came (literally) from the wrong side of the tracks in East Tupelo, and came to school in the poor-man's uniform of overalls. By seventh grade, he was regularly bringing his guitar to school to play during recess and lunch. He sometimes played and sang in front of the class, despite the protestations of some of the kids.

By the eighth grade he had earned some popularity, and may have been elected to the student council. When some bullies cut his guitar strings, classmates clubbed together to buy him a replacement set of strings. He did not finish eighth grade as the Presley family moved to Memphis that year.

When Elvis returned to Tupelo to play his "homecoming" concert at the Mississippi-Alabama Fair and Dairy Show in 1956 he invited along his Milam classmates.

Located at the intersection of North Gloster Street and Jefferson Street (address 720 Jefferson Street), the school is now known as Milam Elementary.

MRS. CAMP: "Elvis was always one of my main characters in homeroom and chapel programs. He would talk, sing, and play anything you wanted him to."

"MILKCOW BLUES BOOGIE"

On a rare break from touring, Elvis recorded this track for his third single at Sun Studio in November or early December 1954, depending upon the Elvis chronicler, together with B-side song "You're A Heartbreaker." The single was released by Sun just after Christmas and sold well locally. Elvis' version starts off sounding much like James "Kokomo" Arnold's original 1934 version (titled "Milk Cow Blues") before surging ahead into a rocked-up rendition. Before Elvis, the song had been covered by Robert Johnson and then Bob Wills, from whose version Elvis borrowed an extra verse.

Elvis' "Milkcow Blues Boogie" first appeared on an album when RCA put it out on *A Date With Elvis* in 1959. It later came out on *The Sun Sessions*, *The King Of Rock And Roll*, *The Complete Sun Sessions*, *Sunrise* and *Elvis at Sun*.

"MILKY WHITE WAY"

On October 30, 1960 in Nashville Elvis arranged and adapted this traditional gospel track for the *His Hand in Mine* album. In February 1966, it was chosen for the A-side of a single—with "Swing Down, Sweet Chariot"—that failed to chart. Elvis knew the song from a 1948 version by the Trumpeteers.

Later album appearances are on gospel anthologies *Amazing Grace*, *Peace In The Valley* and *Ultimate Gospel*. An alternate take came out on *Platinum: A Life In Music* in 1997. Multiple alternates are to be had on the FTD *Fame And Fortune* and *His Hand in Mine* releases.

MILLION DOLLAR QUARTET

On December 4, 1956, Elvis and girlfriend of the month Marilyn Evans dropped in to Sun Studio to say hi just as Carl Perkins was finishing up a recording session. When Elvis began jamming with Perkins and session piano-player Jerry Lee Lewis, Sam Phillips astutely left the tape rolling (though Jack Clements recalls that he was recording Jerry Lee Lewis before the jam session began and therefore lays claim to this opportunistic stroke of genius).

While the boys were singing their hearts out, Phillips got *Memphis Press-Scimitar* journalist Bob Johnson to hotfoot it over with a photographer to immortalize this fortuitous moment. Johnson came up with the memorable "Million Dollar" moniker in his piece the next day, in which he wrote that the "quartet could sell a million." In his article, Johnson says that Elvis kicked it all off with "Blueberry Hill" and from that moment on "the joint was really rocking." He later summed up the atmosphere as "an old-fashioned barrel-house session with barbershop harmonies."

Over the next two or perhaps even three hours the singers tackled out a medley of their favorite gospel, rock 'n' roll and country songs. Many fans and pundits consider this spontaneous jam session be the holy grail of Elvis material, a pure and spontaneous outpouring of music for the fun of it.

As well as the headline singers, Perkins' band of Clayton Perkins, Jay Perkins and drummer W. S. Holland also featured, while Charles Underwood played rhythm guitar on some of the earlier songs in the session (Elvis almost recorded one of Underwood's songs the following year). There has been debate whether or not Johnny Cash actually sang during any of the session—at least, the portion that was recorded—or was merely around for the photo call; Cash maintained in his autobiography that his voice is indeed in the mix.

The first Million Dollar Quartet release was a bootleg from 1980 featuring seventeen tracks, before an official version came out in the UK on the Charly label the following year. An expanded

bootleg appeared in 1987, followed once again by an official Charly release, and then at long last an official release in the US.

Sun catalogue owner Shelby Singleton had wanted to bring out some of the material in 1977 before a court injunction from the surviving "quartet" members stopped him. An even longer—and chronologically accurate—release appeared in 2006 under the name *The Complete Million Dollar Quartet*. Fans hope that the material released so far is only a portion of the reputed two and a half hours recorded on that December day, and that more gems await discovery. There is documentary evidence that the impromptu jam included the songs "Blueberry Hill" and "Isle Of Golden Dreams" among others, neither of which have seen release so far; more likely, the tape did not run for the whole session, or has not survived the passage of time.

In 1986, original Million Dollar Quartetists Johnny Cash, Jerry Lee Lewis and Carl Perkins were joined by Roy Orbison at Sun Studio to record a flashback album, *Class of '55*.

The Million Dollar Quartet album outsells any other disc at modern-day Sun Studio.

THE MILLION DOLLAR QUARTET ALBUM (1990)

TRACK LISTING:
1. You Belong To My Heart
2. When God Dips His Love In My Heart
3. Just A Little Talk With Jesus
4. Jesus Walked That Lonesome Valley
5. I Shall Not Be Moved
6. Peace In The Valley
7. Down By The Riverside
8. I'm With A Crowd But So Alone
9. Farther Along
10. Blessed Jesus (Hold My Hand)
11. As We Travel Along On The Jericho Road
12. I Just Can't Make It By Myself
13. Little Cabin Home On The Hill
14. Summertime Is Past And Gone
15. I Hear A Sweet Voice Calling
16. Sweetheart You Done Me Wrong
17. Keeper Of The Key
18. Crazy Arms
19. Don't Forbid Me
20. Too Much Monkey Business
21. Brown Eyed Handsome Man
22. Out Of Sight, Out Of Mind
23. Brown Eyed Handsome Man
24. Don't Be Cruel
25. Don't Be Cruel
26. Paralyzed
27. Don't Be Cruel
28. There's No Place Like Home
29. When The Saints Go Marchin' In
30. Softly And Tenderly
31. Is It So Strange
32. That's When Your Heartaches Begin
33. Brown Eyed Handsome Man
34. Rip It Up
35. I'm Gonna Bid My Blues Goodbye
36. Crazy Arms
37. That's My Desire
38. At The End Of The Road
39. Black Bottom Stomp
40. You're The Only Star In My Blue Heaven
41. Elvis farewell

An extended version, *The Complete Million Dollar Quartet*, was released in 2006 to mark the 50th anniversary of this unique jam session.

WHO SINGS LEAD ON WHAT

"You Belong To My Heart": Elvis Presley
"When God Dips His Love In My Heart": Elvis Presley, Jerry Lee Lewis

"Just A Little Talk With Jesus": Elvis Presley, Jerry Lee Lewis

"Jesus Walked That Lonesome Valley": Elvis Presley, Jerry Lee Lewis

"I Shall Not Be Moved": Elvis Presley, Jerry Lee Lewis

"Peace In The Valley": Elvis Presley

"Down By The Riverside": Elvis Presley, Jerry Lee Lewis

"I'm With A Crowd But So Alone": Elvis Presley

"Farther Along": All

"Blessed Jesus (Hold My Hand)": Elvis Presley, Jerry Lee Lewis

"As We Travel Along On The Jericho Road": Elvis Presley, Jerry Lee Lewis

"I Just Can't Make It By Myself": Elvis Presley, Jerry Lee Lewis

"Little Cabin Home On The Hill": Elvis Presley

"Summertime Is Passed And Gone": Elvis Presley, Carl Perkins

"I Hear A Sweet Voice Calling": All

"Sweetheart You Done Me Wrong": All

"Keeper Of The Key": Carl Perkins

"Crazy Arms": Jerry Lee Lewis

"Don't Forbid Me": Elvis Presley

"Brown Eyed Handsome Man": Elvis Presley, Jerry Lee Lewis

"Out Of Sight, Out Of Mind": Elvis Presley

"Brown Eyed Handsome Man": Elvis Presley, Jerry Lee Lewis

"Don't Be Cruel": Elvis Presley

"Don't Be Cruel": Elvis Presley

"Paralyzed": Elvis Presley

"Don't Be Cruel": Elvis Presley

"There's No Place Like Home": Elvis Presley

"When The Saints Go Marchin' In": Elvis Presley, Jerry Lee Lewis

"Softly And Tenderly": Elvis Presley, Jerry Lee Lewis

"Is It So Strange": Elvis Presley

"That's When Your Heartaches Begin": Elvis Presley

"Brown Eyed Handsome Man": Elvis Presley

"Rip It Up": Elvis Presley

"I'm Gonna Bid My Blues Goodbye": Elvis Presley

"Crazy Arms": Jerry Lee Lewis

"That's My Desire": Jerry Lee Lewis

"At The End Of The Road": Jerry Lee Lewis

"Black Bottom Stomp": Jerry Lee Lewis (instrumental)

"You're The Only Star In My Blue Heaven": Jerry Lee Lewis

ELVIS SAID: "I hate to get started in these jam sessions, I'm always the last one to leave. Always."

SAM PHILLIPS: "That was just something that happened, you know, one of those off-the-wall things that could only occur at Sun records... It was like everything I had worked to build was there in that one little room."

MILSAP, RONNIE
(B. 1944)

Born blind in Robbinsville, North Carolina on January 16, 1944, Milsap was a child prodigy in violin before learning to play a slew of other instruments.

He released his first single aged 20, and began touring in the mid-Sixties as part of J.J. Cale's band.

Elvis hired Milsap several years running to provide entertainment at his New Years' bashes in the late Sixties and early Seventies. In January 1969, Milsap played piano and sang backing vocals for Elvis during his American Studio session in Memphis.

After moving to Nashville in the early Seventies, Milsap scored a string of country hits, more than any other singer except Conway Twitty. He has won six Grammys.

Elvis on the Milton Berle show with Debra Paget.

"MILTON BERLE SHOW"

Elvis performed on the "Milton Berle Show" broadcast from the USS Hancock, San Diego, on April 3, 1956. He was paid $3,000 for the appearance, and $5,000 for his June 5 appearance from the NBC studio in Los Angeles.

On his first show, Elvis performed "Heartbreak Hotel" and "Blue Suede Shoes" twice, either side of a comedy sketch in which Berle played Elvis' long-lost twin, Melvin Presley, and claimed to have taught "Elvin" everything he knew. Other guests on that show included Esther Williams.

On his second outing, Elvis performed "I Want You, I Need You, I Love You" and "Hound Dog" in an infamous TV moment that scandalized the self-appointed upholders of the nation's morality. Elvis' appearance on the show won him a national audience of enthralled teenagers, and heralded the true start of a critical backlash in the press. The New York papers competed to be the most scathing about Elvis' performance, demeanor, singing talents and dance moves; as many as 800,000 letters of complaint were sent in to the network (the number varying wildly in different accounts). Fans loved it as much as the morally-strict hated it; for many Elvis fans, Elvis' performance of "Hound Dog" is as good as it got on his Fifties TV appearances.

On this second show, Elvis was involved in a skit with actress Debra Paget (labeled as "out of Elvis' league" by Berle in the sketch, a prophesy that proved to be true enough in real life). The episode also featured comedian Arnold Stang, Sheena Queen of the Jungle star Irish McCalla, and child singer Barry Gordon.

Recordings of Elvis on the "Milton Berle Show" came out on 1984 album A Golden Celebration. Video of the shows has yet to be released officially on DVD, though a number of "grey" Elvis DVDs include footage from the show.

NEW YORK JOURNAL REVIEW

"The sight of the young Mr Presley caterwauling his unintelligible lyrics in an inadequate voice, during a display of primitive physical movement is difficult to describe in terms suitable to a family newspaper. It has caused the most heated reaction."

Book:
Shock, Rattle and Roll; Elvis Photographed During "The Milton Berle Show," by Ger Rijff, Trevor Cajiao, Michael Ochs and Jean Paul Commandeur, Sterling Pub. Co., 1998.

"MINE"

Elvis recorded this Sid Tepper / Roy C. Bennett song in Nashville on September 10, 1967, for insertion into the *Speedway* soundtrack. The song had previously been submitted and rejected for *Paradise, Hawaiian Style.*

"Mine" was left off the *Double Feature* soundtrack reissue, but is on later anthology *From Nashville to Memphis.* Alternates have surfaced on *Elvis: Close Up* and FTD release *So High.*

MINNESOTA

- *Duluth*
Elvis played a concert in Bob Dylan's home town (at the Duluth Arena) on October 16, 1976; he returned on April 29, 1977.

- *Minneapolis*
Elvis played the Metropolitan Sports Center on November 5, 1971 at the start of a 12-date tour. He was next in town on October 17, 1976 at the same venue.

- *St. Paul*
Elvis and his band played two shows at the Auditorium on May 13, 1956. On October 2 and 3, 1974, he performed at the Civic Center with the TCB band. His final performance at the venue was on April 30, 1977.

"MIRACLE OF THE ROSARY"

Elvis recorded this track on May 15, 1971, at a Nashville session arranged to produce material for a new Christmas album; he was back in the studio to add a harmony overdub four days later. This song didn't make the cut for the Christmas album, but it appeared on 1972 album *Elvis Now.*

Originally written and recorded by Lee Denson in 1960, Elvis picked this song to record first at the session because he knew Denson from way back at Lauderdale Courts in Memphis.

The song has since come out on *He Walks Beside Me* and gospel anthologies *Amazing Grace, Peace In The Valley* and *Ultimate Gospel* (the 2004 issue, not the 2007 re-release). *Platinum: A Life In Music* features the first take from the studio session.

"MIRAGE"

This Bill Giant / Bernie Baum / Florence Kaye song for *Harum Scarum* was laid down in Nashville on February 26, 1965, with Elvis adding his vocals on March 9. The song has since appeared on the *Double Features* reissue for the movie.

MIRISCH BROTHERS

In 1960, the Mirisch Brothers (Walter, Harold and Marvin) teamed up with United Artists to make a lucrative deal with the Colonel for two movies. *Follow That Dream* and *Kid Galahad* were the result. The producers decided not to take up an option for two future productions.

Elvis' Mirisch movies did not deviate too far from his usual celluloid output, despite the company's reputation for high-quality movies by creative directors of the caliber of Billy Wilder and John Sturges. In and around the period Elvis was on board, the Mirisch Brothers company produced some memorable pictures including *Some Like It Hot* (1959), *The Magnificent Seven* (1960), *The Apartment* (1960), *West Side Story* (1961) and later Elvis favorite, the original *The Pink Panther*.

Walter Mirisch, the driving force behind the company, was President of the Academy of Motion Picture Arts and Sciences for five years in the Seventies.

MISSISSIPPI

- Amory
Elvis played the National Guard Armory on a bill with Johnny Cash and Carl Perkins on either December 12, 1955, though it may have been a day later.

- Belden
Elvis' appearance at the High School Gym on June 15, 1955 required gymnastics for him even to get into the building—he had to crawl in through a window at the back of the building to avoid being mobbed.

- Big Creek
Elvis played the Big Creek High School Gym on March 28, 1955.

- Biloxi
Elvis and his band played to a sellout crowd at the brand new air-conditioned Slavonian Lodge club on June 26, 1955. The next two nights he performed at the Airman's Club at Keesler Air Base on a tour arranged by Mississippi promoter Frank "Yankie" Barhanovich. Elvis retuned to the Biloxi Community House on November 6, 1955, followed by two more nights at the Keesler Air Force Base on November 7 and 8.

In the summer of 1956, when Elvis took his first proper vacation in almost two years of pell-mell touring, he chose Biloxi to be near girlfriend June Juanico. Elvis took his folks and entourage members Red West, Gene and Junior Smith and Arthur Hooton along for the ride.

- Booneville
The Junior College Auditorium hosted Elvis on January 17, 1955, in an event sponsored by the Kiwanis Club. Before going on stage Elvis was interviewed by local DJ Lynn McDowell on WBIP. He returned to play the Von Theater on January 3, 1956.

- Bruce
Elvis played two nights at the Bruce High School Gym on June 14, 1955 on a bill with Onie Wheeler and the Miller Sisters. Elvis was paid $450, one quarter of the take.

- Charleston
Elvis played the High School, as did Johnny Cash and David Houston, on January 2, 1956.

- Clarksdale
Elvis performed at the City Auditorium on January 12, 1955, on the first night of a two-week tour with Jim Ed and Maxine Brown. Elvis next played the venue on March 12, 1955; he passed through once more on September 8, 1955 on a five-day tour with Johnny Cash.

- Corinth
On January 18, 1955, Elvis played the Alcorn County Courthouse at a concert sponsored by the Jaycees and promoted by Buddy Bain. He was back on April 7, 1955, billed as "Country Music Star Elvis Presley."

- Grenada
Elvis was booked at the American Legion Hut on April 20, 1955.

- Houlka
Elvis likely played a venue in this town on September 27, 1955.

- Horn Lake
In February 1967, Elvis paid $437,000 for 160-acre Twinkletown Farm, just a short drive from Graceland. He changed the name to Circle G Ranch and made it the base for his newly-acquired stable of horses and an experiment in communal living. He was here with Priscilla for their honeymoon that May, but had lost interest by the end of the year.

- Houston
Elvis likely played the Armory on October 25, 1955.

- Jackson
At the Mississippi State Fair Coliseum, Elvis played a benefit concert for the tornado victims at nearby McComb on May 5, 1975 that raised over $100,000. He returned to play the State Fair Coliseum on June 8 and June 9, 1975, and the Mississippi State Fair Civic Center on September 5, 1976.

- McComb
Elvis played the High School Auditorium in this town on September 9, 1955.

- Meridian
When Elvis performed at the American Legion Hall during the third annual Jimmie Rodgers Memorial Celebration on May 25, 1955 he was called back for an almost endless succession of encores. The following day he played the Junior College Stadium, and may have continued performing with local musicians Carl Fitzgerald and Leon Baughn at the Hamasa Temple Ballroom after hours. It has also been speculated that Elvis competed at a talent show during the first Memorial Celebration two years previously.

- Randolph
Elvis' date on February 1,1955 at the High School was on a bill with local favorite Bud Deckelmen. He played a follow-up show on January 6, 1956.

- Ripley
Elvis played the High School Gym here on February 7, 1955.

- Tocopola
Elvis performed at the High School on March 29, 1955.

- Tupelo
Elvis' first professional performance at his birthplace town was at the Fairgrounds on August 1, 1955 when he was touring with Webb Pierce, Red Sovine, Wanda Jackson, Bud Deckelman, Charlie Feathers and the Miller Sisters. That day, he played before a crowd of 3,000 (half of the town's population). He returned a national star to play two triumphal shows at the 49th Mississippi-Alabama Fair and Dairy Show on September 26, 1956, back where a decade earlier he had competed in a children's talent competition aged ten (on October 3, 1945), wearing glasses to correct a lazy eye and standing on a chair to reach the microphone. This time, he gave a show for a total of 20,000 screaming fans, at one point during the evening show having to stop and ask everybody to quieten down and stop shoving towards the stage. One newspaper chronicled the occasion: "The native-son rock and roll idol arrived amid wailing sirens in a white Lincoln Continental and turned an already gaudy fair into shrieking pandemonium . . ." Elvis' 1956 performance—on a day that was proclaimed Elvis Presley Day across the state—was released in 1984 on *A Golden Celebration* among others. A DVD of Elvis performing six songs came out in 2007 as *Tupelo's Own Elvis Presley*. Other acts at the Fair (on the following days) included Ernest Tubb, the Blackwood Brothers, the Statesmen, the Oak Ridge Quartet and Eddy Bond.

Almost exactly a year later, on September 27, 1957, Elvis played a benefit show for the Elvis Presley Youth Center at the Fairgrounds before a crowd over 12,000-strong.

MISSISSIPPI SLIM

See AUSBORN, CARVEL LEE.

MISSOURI

- Cape Giradeau
Elvis played a show at the Cape Arena Building on July 20, 1955, the first of two nights with Wanda Jackson and Bud Deckelman.

- Gobler
Elvis played the B&B Club on April 8, 1955.

- Kansas City
Elvis and the band had run for it after 20 minutes on stage when the crowd rioted at the Municipal Auditorium Arena on May 24, 1956. DJ Fontana wound up in the orchestra pit, and the drums and bass were wrecked. A more sedate audience awaited when Elvis played the same venue on November 15, 1971. He gave two shows there on June 29, 1974. His April 21, 1976 appearance was at the Kemper Arena, which was also on his last ever tour—Elvis passed through on June 18, 1977.

- Poplar Bluff
Elvis played the Armory on March 9, 1955.

- St. Louis
Elvis played the Missouri Theater on a tour with Grand Ole Opry stars from October 21 to 23, 1955. He failed to appear for his slot on the first show on the final day, justifying himself with the excuse that he'd lost his wallet. He was back at the Kiel Auditorium on January 1, 1956 on a Grand Ole Opry bill with Hank Snow and Webb Pierce. Elvis headlined the same venue on March 29, 1957. Elvis and the TCB band played the Kiel Auditorium on September 10, 1970, June 28, 1973, and March 22, 1976.

- *Sikeston*

Elvis performed at the National Guard Armory on January 21, 1955 and again on September 7, 1955, taking the opportunity to stay with great-uncle Floyd Presley.

- *Springfield*

Elvis and his band played the Shrine Mosque on May 17, 1956. His next performance in town was on June 17, 1977, when he started a tour at the Hammons Center, Southwest Missouri State University.

MITCHUM, ROBERT
(1917-1997)

In 1957, Robert Mitchum tried to enlist Elvis to play his son in *Thunder Road* (1958). Elvis may have been keen but Colonel Parker would not have his boy playing a moonshiner.

Born in Bridgeport, Connecticut on August 6, 1917, Mitchum was a hard man who played hard men. A latecomer to acting after a checkered youth including boxing bouts and time on a chain gang, by the late Forties Mitchum was established as a leading star of noir and westerns. His bad boy image was only reinforced when he was imprisoned in 1949 for possessing marijuana. Mitchum remained synonymous with cool for decades, topping a 1968 poll of teenagers as the coolest male. During a long career, he acted in close to 150 movies, though he only achieved one Oscar nomination for his work in *The Story of G.I. Joe* (1945).

MOBLEY, MARY ANN
(B. 1939)

This Biloxi-born former Miss America (1959) co-starred with Elvis in *Girl Happy* and *Harum Scarum*, both of which came out in 1965, the year that Mobley won a Golden Globe for Most Promising Newcomer alongside fellow-recipient Mia Farrow.

Elvis later said that she was one of his favorite co-stars. Born on February 17, 1939, Mobley went on to feature in many iconic TV series including "Perry Mason," "Mission Impossible," "The Man From U.N.C.L.E." and "The Virginian." She was the original TV Batgirl, though she was soon replaced by another Elvis movie veteran, Yvonne Craig. Mobley has continued to be seen on TV into the 2000s, as well as acting as a trustee for charities including the March of Dimes and the Crohn's and Colitis Foundation.

MOMAN, CHIPS
(B. LINCOLN WAYNE MOMAN, 1936)

Best known as a record producer, Moman is also a guitarist and a songwriter, known as "Chips" for his skills around the gambling table. As a four-teen-year old Moman hitchhiked from Georgia to Memphis and started playing guitar for with Johnny and Dorsey Burnett before touring with Gene Vincent.

In his early twenties he helped to co-found the Stax McLemore Avenue studio (originally under the "Satellite" name), where many R 'n' B and early soul greats recorded. He wrote career-defining songs for Aretha Franklin ("Do Right Woman"), Waylon Jennings ("Luckenbach, Texas") and B.J. Thomas among others, and for Stax and American produced artists including Booker T. and the MGs, Bobby Womack, Carla Thomas, The Box Tops, Wilson Pickett and Dusty Springfield.

Moman set up American Studio after he was ousted from Stax in 1964. He proceeded to recruit what for many years was one of the finest house bands in the business, building the studio into a thriving business that recorded many of Atlantic Records' greatest hits while developing its own sound and pioneering the use of horns.

Moman was very much his own man with his own way of doing things. Rather than use huge high-quality speaker stacks in the studio, he preferred tiny car speakers to listen to the music he was recording because that was how the record-buyers would be hearing the songs. He had strong views on how things should be recorded and wasn't afraid of telling people what he thought—a breath of fresh air for Elvis when he recorded at American Studio in 1969. The resulting sessions were among the most productive of Elvis' entire career in terms of quantity and quality, yielding classic cuts such as "In The Ghetto," "Suspicious Minds" and "Kentucky Rain."

Interference from song publishers Hill & Range, unhappy with Moman slipping Elvis songs for which they had not already secured publishing deals, and from the Colonel who weighed in for the same reason, almost derailed the entire output. In the end, Moman stared down the various tiers of Elvis' management to pick the tracks for the first album of songs recorded at American, *From Elvis In Memphis*. Most of the tunes he picked were songs on which Moman controlled the publishing rights—a major exception from standard Elvis management working practice. Though he won the battle, Moman became so incensed with the attritional haggling that after Elvis' second session at American, he never wanted to work with him again.

In the Seventies, Moman moved to Atlanta, then Nashville, then West Point Georgia, in every location opening and running successful recording studios.

CHIPS MOMAN, about Elvis, 1969: "One of the hardest working artists I have ever been associated with."

CHIPS MOMAN: "When it was just him and me, one-on-one, he was just one of the easiest people to work with."

MARTY LACKER: "Chips was the owner and founder of American, and he was also the chief engineer, cook and bottle washer. He wrote songs and played occasional guitar on the sessions. Everybody respected him."

"MONA LISA"

A version of Elvis singing this Jay Livingston / Ray Evans composition originally penned for the movie *Captain Carey, USA* (a huge hit for Nat King Cole in 1950) was taped in April 1959 while Elvis on military service in Germany. Years later it came out on *Elvis: A Legendary Performer Vol. 4, The Home Recordings* and bootlegs.

MONEY

Elvis grew up in poverty to live an adult life of immense wealth. At the start of his singing career, the Presleys briefly transited through middle-class affluence but from then on it was high-spending all the way. Elvis' attitude was that since he was making money, he should be spending money. This included giving the IRS its full take and handing out a not insignificant portion of his earnings to charities and deserving causes. Over the course of his entertainment career, he is estimated to have grossed $200 million. And yet when Elvis died in 1977, his estate was in real danger of bankruptcy.

Elvis was a child of the working poor. Straitened circumstances caused the Presleys to move many times in and around Tupelo, Mississippi, and sometimes further afield as they followed Vernon in his quest for work. Houses and cars were bought and repossessed as the family failed to keep up payments. Great-aunt Christine Roberts Presley told one interviewer that Elvis' folks were as "poor as Job's Turkey." Graceland archives are full of deeds and receipts detailing Vernon's need to borrow money to make ends meet.

Biographers disagree about whether Elvis experienced hunger in the late Thirties but are unanimous in describing a life of hardship. When Vernon was sentenced to three years' jail for altering a check, the family were kicked out of their home and for a while moved in with relatives and survived on handouts. Out of jail, Vernon was sometimes unable to work because of a bad back. Even when he and Gladys were both working, their earnings remained low: in 1947, the year before they moved to Memphis, according to the family income tax return they earned a total of $1913.29 from Vernon's job as a salesman and Gladys's employment as a seamstress. After the move to Memphis in 1948, at high school Elvis sometimes didn't have money for lunch. The parents of wealthier classmates contributed funds to anonymous pupils in need of extras; Elvis was one of the beneficiaries.

Work was easier to come by in Memphis, and the family's public housing was a help. The family was eventually forced to move from their Lauderdale Courts accommodation because both of Elvis' parents were in work, and by this time Elvis was contributing to the Presley coffers through odd jobs. He still felt the stigma of being poor. When he went out with a school pal Mack Gurley, he'd ask to be dropped off a few blocks away from his home, where the houses were fancier, and walk the rest of the way.

Elvis filed his first income tax return for the 1953 financial year, declaring income of $916.33 from jobs at M. B. Parker (where, according to Lamar Fike, Elvis was working when he made his first vanity acetate at the Memphis Recording Service) and Precision Tool. He stated his occupation as a "semi-skilled" worker.

When Elvis made his performing debut, it was for the less-than-princely sum of $10 per show. Touring incessantly through 1954 to promote his first two singles, Elvis' earnings started to add up to considerably more than the family was used to. He and his band members earned $50 for his first few Memphis shows. His first appearance on the popular Louisiana Hayride netted him $125. For most of his first year touring, Elvis, Scotty and Bill were making $50 each per booking. After playing the Paladiam Club in Houston in November, 1954, along with the money that he sent home he dispatched a famous telegram:

HI BABIES, HERE'S THE MONEY TO PAY THE BILLS. DON'T TELL NO ONE HOW MUCH I SENT I WILL SEND MORE NEXT WEEK. THERE IS A CARD IN THE MAIL. LOVE ELVIS.

The first tour arranged by Colonel Tom Parker, on the Hank Snow Tour in February 1955, was a step up the earnings ladder as Elvis made $850 for four dates. At this stage, Elvis was pocketing half of the overall take, with the other half going to the band. Through 1955, Elvis and co. were grossing at least $1,000 a month, though out of this they had to pay expenses for transport, accommodation and booking fees. The last month that the pot was split among the band was September 1955, when they shared gross income of $3,300. From October, the Colonel introduced a new deal for Scotty Moore and Bill Black: a flat rate of $200 per week on the road performing, and a $100 per week retainer otherwise. By this stage Colonel Tom Parker was in charge of bookings, and was passing on to Elvis $250 for venues where he had a following, and $175 for shows where he was a relative unknown.

RCA's buyout of Elvis' contract with Sun Records on November 21, 1955 brought Elvis and his family the first foretaste of wealth. RCA paid an outlandish sum (for the industry) of $35,000, of which Elvis received $5,000 on signature from RCA and $1,000 from song publisher Hill and Range, minus the Colonel's 25% commission. Not surprisingly, Elvis went off on a spending spree, splashing out $600 at Ed's Camera Shop, $61.29 at the Wells Clothing Store, $39.04 at the Harry Levitch jewelry store, and $50 at the Lansky Brothers' clothes shop on Beale Street. Elvis' performance fees rose as an immediate result of his transfer to RCA, but they were still in the low hundreds of dollars. Elvis' 1955 tax return put his total income at $25,240.15, fully 25 times more than he had been making as a factory worker and truck driver two years previously.

Nineteen fifty-six brought the step up to TV and the movies. Elvis banked $1,250 per appearance for his debut TV bookings on CBS's "Stage Show," though the value in terms of national exposure was much, much higher. He now had enough to buy a house for himself and his parents, just as he had promised as a kid. Elvis was very proud of their new Audubon Drive home; as he later did at Graceland, he took great pleasure in showing old friends round and pointing out all the items he had bought for himself and for his Ma.

By March 1956, Elvis was making around $1,000 a day for three shows. He bought a $185 EP initial ring in March 1956 from NY jeweler Benny Kaplan, and for his mother the ultimate symbol of feminine luxury, a mink coat that she would have little reason ever to wear.

A 2-week tour earned Elvis $21,679.04 for 23 shows in April 1956, a month in which he made one and half times net what he had grossed during the entire previous year. He pocketed around $10,000 for a weeklong tour in June 1956 and a $5,000 fee for his appearance on "The Steve Allen Show." By the end of August, Colonel Parker was charging $500 a performance or $2,000 for Elvis performances. Elvis continued to school himself in the ways of profligacy, managing to burn through $750 with pals Jean and Junior Smith at the Long Beach amusement park in Los Angeles before the start of filming on *Love Me Tender*.

Elvis landed a $5,000 guarantee plus 60% of gate receipts for his Tupelo Homecoming performance in September 1956—all of which he immediately gave back to the town to build a youth center.

The Colonel's uprated contract with RCA generated a fresh $135,000 advance and a guaranteed $1,000 per week over the next five years. Elvis' now nationwide star status ensured a fee of almost $18,000 when he played to 26,500 people at the Cotton Bowl in Dallas, Texas, in October 1956.

Though Elvis was pulling in enough money to buy whatever he wanted (a house, car after car after car, all mod cons for his folks), Vernon's life-long experience of poverty prompted him to badger Elvis against excess. For the next twenty years, Vernon would try to act as a brake on Elvis' spending. Harold Loyd remembers Vernon berating Elvis even for buying too many guitar picks.

By the end of 1956, *Variety* proclaimed that Elvis had already earned a million dollars. His tax return for the year was not quite so hyperbolic: $282,349.66. He exceeded this figure within the first five months of 1957 as his movie earnings and record royalties began to rival his income from live performances.

Before the year of 1957 was out, Colonel Parker persuaded Paramount producer Hal Wallis to up Elvis fee for his second picture to $100,000 from the contractually-agreed $20,000 dollars. While Elvis was in Germany on Army service, Colonel Parker bumped the figure up another notch to $175,000 at Paramount, and $200,000 per picture plus profit share at Twentieth Century-Fox. Elvis' earnings for 1958 topped a million dollars before

tax, including his regular Army pay, which rose from $78 to $122.30 a month after he was promoted to Specialist 4th Class.

For his return to the States, Colonel Parker negotiated for Elvis an unheard-of $125,000 fee for a single guest TV appearance on Frank Sinatra's show. By now, Joe Esposito was helping to exert at least some control on the paperwork involved in Elvis' spendthrift ways. Colonel Parker also tried to curb the hemorrhage of expenses: he hired a bus to take Elvis and his pals back to Memphis from Miami after the "Frank Sinatra Show," rather than the private railroad car they took on the way out.

In 1960, Elvis placed Vernon in charge of his personal finances, set him up in his own Graceland annex office and hired a secretary to bank the earnings and settle the bills. Biographers and commentators almost invariably note that this arrangement proved to be a significant handicap: Vernon's untutored comprehension of accounting and investment strategies resulted in Elvis' large earnings never being properly invested—it seems that the only scheme Vernon ever alighted upon in the Seventies, a mining operation, wound up losing $2.5 million. Another downside was that Vernon's were the only eyes to check Elvis' side of his dealings with the Colonel, and the Colonel, who could face down the most hardened Hollywood executive, was never going to be intimidated by Vernon.

The Colonel continued to renegotiate existing contracts for improved fees and play one commissioning party off against another. Elvis' take from Paramount jumped to $175,000 per picture and then $200,000, plus he signed a new contract with MGM at $400,000 per picture, plus expenses, plus half of the profits.

Elvis declared income of almost $1.7 million for 1961, over half from movie deals. In 1962, he earned almost exactly the same amount. In late 1963, the Colonel bested himself with a one-picture deal with United Artists worth three quarters of a million dollars plus a 50% share of profits. Elvis' tax declaration for 1963 stated his income at $1.8 million, two-thirds from movies; that year Elvis paid Uncle Sam $800,000 in tax. He broke through $2 million in 1964, of which three-quarters was from movies.

The cover of Elvis' 1965 LP, *Elvis for Everyone*, featured a reckoning of all the income earned by each of his twenty-two albums to date.

When the Colonel made his final bump of Elvis' movie fees to the magical $1 million figure, his client had been one of the top ten Hollywood money-making film stars since 1961, but by this time his box office exploits had already peaked. In 1966, Elvis earned over $3 million, all but $650,000 of which was from movies. *Clambake* (1967) was the last time that Elvis commanded a seven-figure fee, just at the moment that Elvis discovered his first ultra-expensive hobby: horses. Between late 1966 and the summer of 1967, Elvis bought dozens of horses, a 160-acre ranch to ride them on, dozens and dozens of pick-up trucks, farm machinery, mobile trailers for his pals to sleep in, and all the trappings of a life of the range. Elvis' spending was so prodigious that he single-handedly drove up the market for horses in Northern Mississippi as horse breeders scrambled to charge up to ten times the regular price for their steeds. During the time Elvis owned the Circle G ranch, his outgoings rose to $60,000 per month, without even considering capital investments. In her memoir, Priscilla estimates that the ranch escapade ended up costing almost $1 million. Alanna Nash suggests that when he acquired the Circle G ranch, Elvis was spending addictively. In desperation, Vernon is said to have asked the Colonel to get Elvis back to work as quickly as possible on his next Hollywood picture.

Elvis declared a little over $3.5 million in income to the IRS for 1967, over three-quarters from movies. In 1968 he made up the movie

shortfall with income from his NBC TV appearance to stay at $3.5 million. Elvis' first long-term engagement in Las Vegas in 1969 was contracted at $100,000 per week. After his triumphant first night, the Colonel famously parlayed this up to a cool $1 million on the coffee shop tablecloth for a total of eight weeks per year, though Elvis' portion of this figure was minus show expenses and the Colonel's increasing cut. Elvis declared earnings of $2,350,000 for 1969, of which just over $1 million was generated by movies. From this point on, he began earning from his two month-long engagements at the International Hotel in Las Vegas what he had been making in Hollywood.

When Elvis headed back out onto the road his headline earnings rose even higher. Yet out of the $600,000 Elvis grossed in the first two months of 1970, he only took home around $175,000 after expenses of over $130,000, commission to the Colonel and to the William Morris Agency, and sizeable bonuses for his entourage and band. As his spending increased, his need to be earning on tour increased in consequence. In late 1970, Vernon and Priscilla confronted Elvis about his king-sized purchases of guns, cars and jewelry. Elvis' reaction was, for one of the rare times in his life, to storm out of Graceland and disappear. This was the time that he traveled to Washington and finagled an audience with President Nixon, though despite his wealth, or rather because of it, the practicalities of the trip were extremely complex for the simple reason that like true royalty, Elvis did not carry cash.

Elvis' 1970 gross earnings exceeded the $4 million mark for the first time, though he paid a whopping $1.7 million in income tax. He grossed almost $4 million again in 1971, of which almost two-thirds from shows; a portion of this income was subject to the Colonel's new 50/50 split.

Elvis' 1972 tours, generally lasting around 10 days each, earned him a cool half a million dollars after expenses and the Colonel's 1/3 slice. Elvis also made over $250,000 after expenses for his month-long Las Vegas residency. All in all, he declared earnings of almost $6 million that year, over $4 million from shows.

The next year began with a million-dollar deal for the ground-breaking *Aloha from Hawaii* satellite broadcast, which would come in handy for the divorce settlement with Priscilla later in 1973. The Colonel realized an additional $5 million that year by selling the rights to Elvis' entire back catalogue to RCA, at the same time securing a revised 7-year contract extension with the record company. After Elvis' death, this deal was cited as proof that the Colonel was not acting in the best interests of his client. Taking all of the side-deals and extra into account, the Colonel made $6.2 million, against Elvis' $4.65 million before tax.

With all this additional income and incrementally higher performing fees, for 1973 Elvis declared earnings of over $8 million to the IRS, generated almost evenly by the publishing rights deal and his live shows.

In three weeks of touring in March 1974, Elvis grossed over $2 million ($800,000 after Colonel's commission and expenses), thanks to his contracted 65% take of gross gate receipts. He grossed a further $2 million from an 18-date tour in June 1974. That year Elvis and the Colonel split over $4 million from tours plus a further $750.000 from his Vegas and Tahoe engagements, and a further $750,000 in RCA royalties. Elvis closed the year with earnings of over $7 million, and yet still managed to spend $700,000 more than he banked.

Elvis' two-week long spring 1975 tours were worth around $?æ million each. After his third tour of 1975, Elvis went on his biggest spree yet, buying a Gulfstream jet for the Colonel (which he turned down as an unnecessary extravagance), almost $100,000 in jewelry for the backing singers he had offended, and no fewer than fourteen Cadillacs which he snapped up in one go, one of which he gave to a complete stranger.

Rare exclusive outtake photo from Elvis' 1958 film King Creole. This was Elvis' favorite movie role and today is considered his finest Hollywood performance.

Then there was his own fleet of airplanes. After he started with his first plane in early 1975, he quickly put together a fleet of five planes; though he eventually reduced the fleet to two, he sustained enormous costs.

Money continued to roll in with abundant ease—Elvis' New Year's Eve 1975 concert was worth $300,000 after expenses but before the Colonel, yet Elvis found himself in a cash-flow crisis. In December 1975, he was forced to take out a two-year $350,000 loan from his bank, the National Bank of Commerce, to cover his payroll expenses, putting up Graceland as collateral. That Christmas Eve, Elvis awoke from a nightmare in which he lost all his money and discovered that he was friendless as well as penniless.

Elvis toured incessantly in 1976, grossing around $1 million for each 2-week of his swings. He had signed an agreement to split touring proceeds 50/50 with the Colonel at the start of the year; in deference to Elvis' ongoing cash-flow problems, they continued with their previous 2/3 to 1/3 split after expenses. The 50/50 arrangement finally went into effect mid-way through 1977, by which time Elvis was grossing more than $2 million from each two-week tour.

When well-meaning friends suggested that Elvis take a break from touring and tend to his health, Elvis replied that he had around forty people working for him, and that he was responsible for their living. The Colonel too, with his penchant for gambling, also required significant financial throughput. When he died, Elvis' banked assets were around $5 million dollars—less than a year's earnings. His estate was valued at $7.6 million before tax.

For many years, Elvis was the single largest taxpayer (from income) in the United States. Some have said that this was a failing of the Colonel's: the Colonel's aversion to using tax shelters may have been because, as a secret illegal immigrant, he did not want government official snooping into his affairs. Whether or not that was the case, Elvis publicly declared that paying his fair share of tax was his patriotic duty.

Elvis' unstinting generosity was a smaller contributory factor to his need to keep touring and earning to the end. Secretary Becky Hartley remembers processing many loans that Elvis made that he wrote off immediately. She has also expressed surprise that some of the beneficiaries have since talked ill of Elvis since his death.

Paradoxically, all through the Seventies the Colonel turned down multi-million dollar offers for international tours, any of which would, at a stroke, have solved both Elvis' cash flow problems. Fearing that he might face difficulties as an illegal immigrant, the Colonel had no intention of leaving the US, and he was never keen on sending Elvis abroad with other managers such as Tom Hulett or Jerry Weintraub, with whom he worked on US concert promotions.

After Vernon's death in 1979, for the first time external lawyers began to examine the Estate's finances. A full investigation was launched when the exceptional size of the Colonel's commissions was discovered. At this point, legal recourse was sought, not by Priscilla and her co-executors, but by the judge who was originally appointed to allow the Colonel to continue representing the Estate's interests on Priscilla's behalf, as he had done for Vernon.

Court-appointed attorney Blanchard E. Tual conducted the investigation. He was surprised to discover that not only had nobody in Elvis' organization checked the statements the Colonel submitted, but the Colonel had succeeded in removing all industry-standard audit clauses from his dealings with RCA and the William Morris Agency. The smoking gun was the 1973 sale of Elvis' back catalogue to RCA, a deal on which, through a complex system of calculations and rights payments, the Colonel actually made more money than his client.

If in life Elvis was a money-making machine, ever since his Estate began promoting his name and likeness as a brand he has become a top global earner. According to Forbes magazine, in 2004 Elvis was the most profitable "dead celebrity" franchise, worth around $45 million. Elvis was temporarily relegated to second position in 2005 when a portion of Kurt Cobain's estate was sold off, taking his earnings for that year above Elvis'. In the hands of management company CKX, the Elvis brand can be expected to increase in value.

Elvis' image appeared in 2007 on fake British bank notes.

THE VALUE OF MONEY

For perspective, here are median (most common) annual male incomes in the US*:

1950: $2,570
1955: $3,358
1960: $4,080
1965: $5,023
1970: $6,670
1975: $8,853
1980: $12,530
1985: $16,311
1990: $20,293
1995: $22,562
2000: $28,343

*US census data.

ELVIS SAID IN 1962: "I like to entertain people. The money or the financial end of it is not the greatest aspect as far as I'm concerned. It can't be, because if it was it would show."

ELVIS SAID IN 1965: "I guess if you are poor you always think bigger and want more than those who have everything."

ELVIS SAID IN 1976: "In doing business and things of that nature, I don't . . . I don't do that."

ELVIS SAID (PARAPHRASING THOMAS CARLYLE): "Adversity is sometimes hard upon a man; but for one man who can stand prosperity, there are a hundred that will stand adversity."

ELVIS SCRIBBLED IN THE MARGINS OF A BOOK: "Wealth certainly does not bring happiness."

COLONEL PARKER: "As long as Elvis can write a check for something he wants, he doesn't care how much money is in the bank."

LARRY GELLER: "Despite Elvis' dramatic, occasionally blustery style and hair-trigger temper, he actually felt entitled to or deserving of very little."

ANNIE CLOYD PRESLEY: "Vernon loved a dollar better than anybody. Vernon loved money, and I blame him for a lot of it. Gladys never got high and mighty, and Elvis never got high and mighty, but Vernon did."

BILLY SMITH: "Money, or rather the control of money, was power in that camp. Even for Elvis. Sometimes he would go out and spend a lot of money just to aggravate Vernon."

ALBERT GOLDMAN: "If he had sheltered his income from the taxman and invested it intelligently, Elvis Presley could have been as wealthy as Bob Hope."

PRISCILLA: "Unfortunately, Vernon and Elvis were leery of business matters requiring financial advice. Vernon operated on pure instinct, refusing any suggestion of tax breaks, which he found too complicated to consider."

LARRY GELLER: "As far as Vernon was concerned, Elvis threw away money and didn't know the value of a dollar. In a sense, that is literally true. Except for the cost of cars and jewelry, two things he seemed to be buying all the time, Elvis had no idea what things cost and couldn't care less."

"MONEY HONEY"

Clyde McPhatter and the Drifters took "Money Honey" to #1 on the R 'n' B charts for 11 weeks in 1953. Elvis sang the song at his first recording session for new label RCA in Nashville, on January 10, 1956, in homage to one of his favorite singers, in a version that owes much to the McPhatter original.

Elvis had added the song to his repertoire within six months of his first single and been playing it live since at least January 1955. He felt comfortable enough with the song to take it on at one of his first ever televised appearances, "Stage Show" (released years later on A Golden Celebration).

The song first came out on Elvis' first ever LP, Elvis Presley, in March 1956, followed closely by inclusion on EP Heartbreak Hotel. "Money Honey" made it to #76 in the charts on the strength of this EP release, but failed to chart when it was released as a single by RCA in late August 1956, with "One-Sided Love Affair." Since its album debut, the song has appeared on The Complete Sun Sessions, Elvis '56, and the CD reissue of For LP Fans Only.

Live performances from 1955 have appeared on Sunrise and Hayride compilations; a live performance from Las Vegas in 1956 is on Elvis Aron Presley, The King Of Rock 'n' Roll, Live in Las Vegas, and Today Tomorrow & Forever.

Almost 15 years later, Elvis rehearsed this tune prior to his summer 1970 Las Vegas engagement, filmed for That's The Way It Is (and released on 1997 album Platinum: A Life In Music). FTD releases with alternate takes: Flashback and Elvis Presley.

MONOLOGUE, THE

A bootleg LP release of Elvis from a show during his opening Las Vegas run in 1969 plus extras.

TRACK LISTING:
1. Elvis monologue about his career
2. Jailhouse Rock / Don't Be Cruel
3. Memories
4. Lawdy, Miss Clawdy
5. Until It's Time For You To Go
6. Oh Happy Day
7. Sweet Inspiration
8. More
9. Hey Jude
10. What Now My Love
11. Are You Lonesome Tonight? (laughing version)
12. I, John
13. Baby What You Want Me To Do
14. I'm Leavin'
15. What'd I Say

MONROE, BILL
(1911-1996)

Born in Rosine, Kentucky on September 13, 1911, Monroe was a songwriter, mandolin player and bandleader who started out playing with his brothers before founding his own band, The Kentuckians. When he landed a regular spot at the Grand Ole Opry in 1939, he changed the band's name to "The Bluegrass Boys" and invented a style all his own. For many years he was an Opry fixture, developing a reputation as a talent-spotter for many up-and-coming country artists.

Himself the originator of a genre—the term "bluegrass" came from his band, "The Blue Grass Boys" of Kentucky—Monroe is, like Elvis, one of a handful of performer to have been inducted into three musical halls of fame: Country Music, Bluegrass and Rock 'n' Roll.

Monroe was heard around Nashville complaining at the travesty Elvis made of his song "Blue Moon Of Kentucky," released as the B-side to Elvis' first ever single "That's All Right (Mama)." Monroe later explained, "What kinda bothered me, you know, was changing it from my way of singing, the bluegrass style, to another style. That's the only thing. I didn't know how it was going to work out."

After Elvis met the bluegrass singer when they both performed at the Grand Old Opry in October 1954, a polite if not contrite Elvis apologized for the new style, and Monroe wished him luck with it. "Later," said Monroe, "I got to where I liked it. It sold real good." Monroe's version was re-released not long afterwards, and in later years he revisited the song in a much more Elvis-like version.

Elvis recorded Monroe classic "Little Cabin On The Hill" in 1970, a song that he had taken on at his 1956 *Million Dollar Quartet* singalong, in addition to Monroe tunes "I Hear A Sweet Voice Calling" and "Sweetheart You Done Me Wrong."

MONROE, MARILYN
(B. NORMA JEAN MORTENSEN, 1926-1962)

Marilyn and Elvis are the world's most famous couple who never met.

Born into hardship on June 1, 1926, Marilyn defied the odds to become the leading sex symbol of her day, starring in films such as *The Asphalt Jungle* (1950), *All About Eve*, (1950), *How to Marry a Millionaire* (1953), *Bus Stop* (1956), *The Prince and the Showgirl* (1957), *Some Like It Hot* (1959) and *The Misfits* (1961). Her three husbands included baseball legend Joe DiMaggio and famed playwright Arthur Miller.

The fame of these two icons of Twentieth Century entertainment and sex appeal has endured far longer than their mortal lifespan. Not surprisingly, they have plenty in common. They both had mothers called Gladys. They both possessed beauty that captivated the imagination of millions of fans, and had a special power over the camera. They both incarnated the American dream, rising from poverty to fame and fortune before dying in tragic and somewhat mysterious circumstances. They both started to dye their hair at the start of their careers. They were both big enough stars to help bring about changes to the way that their industries operated. They both had difficulties being taken seriously as proper dramatic actors. They both made memorable performances at Madison Square Garden. They both died in August. Actions were taken after Marilyn and Elvis' deaths to cover up the unflattering circumstances of their passing. Both of them have incredibly loyal fan communities. Like Marilyn Monroe, Elvis' status as the biggest sex symbol of his day complicated the business of sex: living up to their partners' expectations was quite a burden.

Enticing as the story may seem, claims by Byron Raphael that Elvis and Marilyn met some time in 1956 and were passionate lovers have been discounted for a number of reasons, not least that Raphael's claimed role as part of Elvis' entourage has not been corroborated by the guys who were there at the time. The idea of such an affair has exercised more than one novelist over the years. Elvis and Marilyn have enjoyed a more tangible union in art, academia, and as male and female archetypes of glamour, fame and a tragic demise.

One of Marilyn's former boyfriends, Fred Karger, was musical director on several of Elvis' movies. A decade apart, Elvis and Marilyn worked with some of the same Hollywood studio hairdressers and make-up artists.

In one of Marilyn's last movies, *Let's Make Love* (1960), she sings a song ("Specialization") with lyrics that reference Elvis.

MONTGOMERY, ELIZABETH
(1933-1995)

Though Elvis never worked with the actress who still graces small screens around the world in *Bewitched*, in 1961 he worked with her husband, actor Gig Young, on *Kid Galahad*. One day when she came on set, Elvis asked Gig if he would take Elvis' brand new Rolls Royce in exchange for Montgomery. In the spirit of the moment, Gig asked if the car was used or not . . . or said he'd that he'd think about it as the car was a newer model depending on who tells the story. According to some sources, Montgomery visited Elvis at Graceland a couple of times afterwards, strictly on a friendship basis.

Montgomery first received recognition with an Emmy nomination (the first of nine) for her role as a bad girl in TV show "The Untouchables" in 1959, before going on to play the world's favorite suburban witch for almost a decade.

MONTY PYTHON

Elvis was a monster Python fan, capable of reciting Python episodes by heart with the best of them. When recuperating from a serious bout of ill-health in early 1975, he cheered himself up by watching reruns of his favorites. He saw in the new year of 1976 with a marathon Monty Python-watching session on his plan and at Graceland. Elvis saw *Monty Python and the Holy Grail* many times, and taught girlfriend Linda Thompson whole chunks of dialogue so that they could recite them and fall about laughing. One of his favorites was the "Nudge Nudge" sketch—he sometimes called people "Squire" in homage; Elvis is also known to have occasionally injected Python references into his live shows.

MICHAEL PALIN: "When I read much later on that, in the declining years of his life, Elvis himself watched *Monty Python and the Holy Grail*, that just blew my mind because Elvis more than anybody changed my whole perception of pop music with 'Heartbreak Hotel' . . ."

"MOODY BLUE"

Elvis recorded this country-flavored Mark James song at Graceland on February 4, 1976. It was released as a single in late November 1976, with "She Thinks I Still Care" on the B-side. James had originally released the song in 1974, to no great success. Elvis' version made it to #1 on the country chart, and #31 on the general chart, where it stayed for 13 weeks.

The song lent its title to Elvis' final album of new material in 1977. Later album appearances are on *This Is Elvis, Elvis' Gold Records Vol. 5, Walk A Mile In My Shoes, Platinum: A Life in Music, Elvis 2nd to None, Hitstory,* and *The Essential Elvis Presley.*

Alternates on FTD's 2000 release *The Jungle Room Sessions* include a "blue" version; other alternates are on FTD disk *Made in Memphis.* Rare live versions are on FTD release *Unchained Melody.*

MOODY BLUE

The last album released while Elvis was alive—in blue vinyl no less—in July 1977 brought together cuts recorded at the Jungle Room sessions and a second side of live tracks recorded by Felton Jarvis on the road during Elvis' early 1977 tours. Boosted by a wave of sentiment after Elvis' death the month after the album's release, it sold over two million copies and spent 31 weeks on the Top

LPs chart, peaking at #3, and taking the #1 spot on the country album chart.

TRACK LISTING:
1. Unchained Melody
2. If You Love Me (Let Me Know)
3. Little Darlin'
4. He'll Have to Go
5. Let Me Be There
6. Way Down
7. Pledging My Love
8. Moody Blue
9. She Thinks I Still Care
10. It's Easy For You

A remastered 2000 release included extra tracks ("Hurt," "Never Again," "Blue Eyes Crying In The Rain," "Danny Boy," "The Last Farewell," "For The Heart," "Bitter They Are Harder They Fall," "Solitaire," "Love Coming Down" and "I'll Never Fall In Love Again") but lacks "Let Me Be There."

"MOONLIGHT SONATA"

Elvis was enough of an all-round musician and a good enough piano player to play classical music for his own delectation. A recording of Elvis playing Beethoven's Moonlight Sonata and singing along with the piano chords at Graceland in 1966 surfaced many years later on *A Private Moment*—for some time, Elvis dabbled with the idea of having lyrics written for the melody. He also worked with 1968 NBC TV Special arranger Billy Goldenberg on the piece during rehearsals for the show—bootleg recordings only thus far.

"MOONLIGHT SWIM"

Elvis recorded this *Blue Hawaii* track written by Sylvia Dee and Ben Weisman on March 22, 1961 at a Radio Recorders session. Four decades after release on the soundtrack album, an edited alternate take came out on *Elvis: Close Up.* Two taped versions feature on bootleg *The Long Lost Home Recordings.*

MOORE, BOB
(B. 1932)

This Nashville-born bass player started playing at the Grand Ole Opry at just 15. Over his long career he played with singers ranging from Frank Sinatra to Roy Orbison, Bob Dylan, Connie Francis, Sister Rosetta Tharpe and Simon & Garfunkel (his is the bass on "Bridge Over Troubled Water"). All told, he is said to have worked on over 17,000 recording sessions. He had a big hit himself with instrumental track "Mexico" in 1961.

Moore began working with Elvis at his 1958 Nashville sessions, after being called into the studio only because the studio engineers were unable to find his bass, which they wanted to use for the session. Elvis had him play a few tracks, liked what he heard and called him back when he returned to recording in 1960. Moore actually knew the Colonel before he knew Elvis, from the Colonel's days managing Eddy Arnold.

Moore was an Elvis regular throughout the Sixties, right up until Elvis put together the TCB band for Las Vegas; he was on stage with Elvis the few times Elvis performed live during this period. When Moore couldn't make it owing to other commitments, he was replaced by players including Henry Strzelecki.

In 1994 *Life* magazine named Moore the top "Country Bassist" of all time.

MOORE, MARY TYLER
(B. 1936)

A popular Emmy-winning actress on TV from her work on "The Dick Van Dyke Show," a year before she embarked on her own eponymous TV show in the Seventies Mary Tyler Moore played a nun opposite Elvis in his last feature movie, *Change of Habit* (1969). Moore had gotten her first break in 1955 as the Hotpoint Elf during a commercial on the "Ozzie and Harriet Show." After seven seasons of her top-rated newsroom comedy show, Mary Tyler Moore starred in a number of films including *Ordinary People* (1980), for which she won an Oscar. Her production company MTM has been responsible for a slew of popular TV shows including *Rhoda* and *Hill Street Blues*. She has continued acting into the 2000s.

MOORE, MICHAEL D.
(B. 1914)

Director of *Paradise Hawaiian Style*, after working as assistant director to Norman Taurog on half a dozen Elvis pictures during the Sixties; he first worked with Elvis as assistant director on *King Creole*.

MOORE, SCOTTY
(B. WINFIELD SCOTT "SCOTTY" MOORE III, 1931)

Born in Gadsden, Tennessee on December 27, 1931, Scotty Moore began playing guitar professionally in 1952, after serving for four years in the United States Navy.

As lead guitar in Elvis' original band, Moore is credited with an enormous influence on the early development of rock 'n' roll. His mishmash of country and blues riffs played through a particular type of amplifier did for guitars what Elvis was doing for vocal delivery, synthesizing different traditions to forge a new sound.

Scotty was playing guitar for honky-tonk Memphis outfit Doug Poindexter and the Starlite Wranglers when he first walked into Sam Phillips' Sun Records label, a month or two before Elvis got his call back, to recorded Starlite Wranglers single "My Kind of Carryin' On" (Sun 202).

When Sam Phillips decided to give the boy with the sideburns a tryout, he suggested that Scotty run the rule over the him—Scotty also served as a talent scout for the fledgling record label, as well as holding down a steady job at his brother's company, University Park Dry Cleaners, and occasionally finding work as a session guitarist When Scotty called up Elvis and asked if he wanted an audition, Elvis was at the movies; Gladys hauled him out of the movie house to call Scotty back.

The following day, July 4, 1954, Elvis went to Scotty's Belz Ave. apartment, and did his best to impress Scotty Moore and fellow Starlite Wrangler, bass player Bill Black. Elvis didn't do enough to land a contract there and then, but later on Scotty and Sam Phillips decided that it was worth giving Elvis an audition in the studio. The very next evening, Scotty Moore and Bill Black accompanied Elvis as he ran through his favorite ballads. Sam Phillips was unimpressed, until, just messing around, Elvis belted out the opening lines to Arthur "Big Boy" Crudup's blues hit "That's All Right (Mama)" and Scotty and Bill joined in. Sam Phillips told them to do whatever they had just done again, this time with the microphone on.

This was the eureka moment in Elvis' career. The next two days found the trio back at Sun Studio, running through options for the B-Side before finally alighting on a heavy backbeat version of "Blue Moon Of Kentucky." During those

Elvis and Scotty Moore performing a concert during the 1950's.

early recording sessions, Phillips directed Moore to play with a little more attack than he usually did, rather than Moore's natural predilection for Chet Atkins-style picking. Years later, Phillips remembered telling Moore, "We don't want none of that soft bullshit. We want some biting bullshit!"

On July 12, 1954 Scotty Moore officially became Elvis' manager and booking agent, signing a contract for a 10% commission with Elvis' parents (see Sidebar). As well has his interest as a manager, Scotty was also set to receive 25% of earnings from the group, as did Bill Black, while Elvis took 50% of the pot.

It was at the Starlite Wranglers regular booking at the Bon Air club in Memphis that Elvis had his first chance to perform, singing the two songs from his single on Saturday, July 17 during a pause between Starlite Wrangler sets.

It did not take long for Moore to realize that Elvis needed far more managing than an inexperienced part-timer could offer. He contacted DJ Bob Neal to help organize shows across Tennessee, Mississippi and Arkansas, and then freed Elvis from their contract so that he would sign with the much-better connected Neal. Then, in mid-December 1954, Scotty Moore unwittingly helped to make an initial contact with Colonel Tom Parker organization by getting in touch with his associate Tom Diskin at Jamboree Attractions and asking if they might be interested in setting up bookings for Elvis. A month later, Scotty received a stock reply that there was little call for "hillbilly entertainers" in and around Chicago.

Scotty Moore and Bill Black toured extensively with Elvis in those early years, billed initially as the "Blue Moon Boys." They added D. J. Fontana on drums, and recorded at Sun and later RCA. Until Elvis began to be nationally-known, by all accounts it was three guys (plus an occasional friend or cousin of Elvis') out on the road, having a good time. The bonhomie began to dispel as Elvis began flying between shows while the band drove.

Elvis felt uncomfortable with the musicians provided by Twentieth Century Fox for his first movie, *Love Me Tender*, and made sure that for subsequent movies he had his own band in the studio. Starting with *Loving You*, Scotty was joined on guitar by "Tiny" Timbrell. Elvis also managed to land on-screen time for his band members in his next movie projects.

In September 1957, Scotty and Bill Black handed in their resignation. The catalyst for the break-up of Elvis' original band was a disagreement about recording time for instrumentals that the band members wanted to release on their own. The underlying reason was growing discord about money; the band members had been on the same flat fee since the days when Elvis had been merely a regional draw, while in the meantime Elvis' earnings had gone through the roof. Elvis tried to get Scotty back, but then when Scotty told the *Memphis Press-Scimitar* that Elvis had reneged on a promise to pay his band members more because he was earning more, Elvis wrote a letter to Scotty, declaring "If you had come to me, we would have worked things out. But you went to the papers and tired to make me look bad . . . All I can say to you is 'good luck'." In the end, a $50 a week pay rise was enough to entice Scotty and D.J. Fontana back.

With Elvis away on military service from 1958, Moore released a single with the Scotty Moore Trio, and then produced a hit song, "Tragedy," for Thomas Wayne (full name Thomas Wayne Perkins, brother of Johnny Cash's guitarist) on his own label, Fernwood. When Elvis returned to the US, he recorded Thomas Wayne song (whose rights were owned by Scotty's label) "Girl Next Door Went A Walking."

Scotty went back into the studio with Elvis in Nashville as he began to cut tracks again after his Army hiatus. He continued to work on recording sessions for Elvis, though after 1958 guitar great Hank Garland was on hand to lead the way. Garland's serious car accident in late 1961 put Scotty back in charge, this time with Jerry Kennedy providing additional fretwork assistance.

From 1960 to 1964, Moore worked as a production manager for Sam Phillips back in Memphis. In 1964, he moved to Nashville to set up Music City Recorders, according to some sources with backing from Elvis. He continued to play guitar on Elvis' recording sessions through the Sixties, up to and including June 1968, when Elvis flew him out to LA for the NBC TV Special. Teamed up with original drummer D.J. Fontana, Scotty Moore wound up his performing career with Elvis just the way it had started, a small band playing on a small stage.

After the show was taped, Elvis talked with Scotty about a European tour that never happened. When Elvis was putting together a new live band, Moore was one of the people who simply had too much happening professionally to drop everything and be at Elvis' beck and call. Scotty never saw Elvis again after 1968.

In the Seventies, Moore worked as a successful studio producer and engineer, and ran a tape-duplication business. He worked in TV in the late Seventies and early Eighties, engineering for singers including Ringo Star and Tracy Nelson. He performed in 1992 at the Ellis Auditorium in Memphis with many former Elvis regulars in the "Good Rockin' Tonight" show. He has been honored by the world's greatest guitarists, and has continued to perform live into his Seventies.

Scotty Moore was inducted into the Rock and Roll Hall of Fame in 2000, during the fiftieth annual induction dinner, presented aptly by Mike Leiber and Jerry Stoller.

PERSONAL MANAGEMENT CONTRACT ENTERED INTO BETWEEN W. S. MOORE III AND ELVIS PRESLEY

WHEREAS, W. S. Moore, III, is a bandleader and a booking agent, and Elvis Presley, a minor, aged 19 years, is a singer of reputation and renown, and possesses bright promises of large success, it is the desire of both parties to enter into this personal management contract for the best interests of both parties.

This contract he is joined in and approved of by the Father and Mother of Elvis Presley, Vernon Presley and Mrs. Vernon Presley.

IT IS AGREED that W. S. Moore, III, will take over the complete management of the professional affairs of the said Elvis Presley, book him professionally for all appearances that can be secured for him, and to promote him, generally, in his professional endeavors. The said W. S. Moore, III, is to receive, as his compensation for his services, ten (10%) percent of all earnings from engagements, appearances and bookings made by him for Elvis Presley.

IT IS UNDERSTOOD AND AGREED that this is an exclusive contract and the said Elvis Presley agrees not to sign any other contract pertaining to his professional work nor make any appearances at any time for any other person or manager or booking agent, for a period of one (1) year.

Now, we, Vernon Presley and Mrs Vernon Presley, father and mother of Elvis Presley, join in this contract for and in his behalf, confirm and approve of its terms and his execution of same and our signatures are affixed thereto.

The said W. S. Moore, III, agrees to give his best efforts to the promotion and success of the said Elvis Presley professionally.

SIGNED AND EXECUTED on this 12th day of July 1954.

[Signed by Scotty Moore, Elvis Presley, Vernon Presley and Gladys Presley]

SCOTTY'S GUITARS

When Scotty met Elvis, he was playing a semi-acoustic Gibson ES 295 jazz guitar. He upgraded to a Gibson L5 CES (cutaway electric Spanish) around the time he recorded "Mystery Train" with Elvis. This was the guitar he used on practically all of Elvis' Sun recordings. Scotty was playing a Super 400 CES from *Jailhouse Rock* onwards (Elvis wields it on the 1968 NBC TV Special; at the time of writing this guitar was on display at the Memphis Hard Rock Café).

An important factor in Scotty Moore's unique sound on the latter Sun sides was his EchoSonic amps.

SCOTTY'S ELVIS TRIBUTE ALBUMS

In 1964, Moore released an album of instrumentals from Elvis tracks on which he had played. Brought out on Epic, *The Guitar That Changed The World* did not have much of an impact on the charts.

Scotty Moore's 1997 tribute album *All The King's Men* featured an impressive line-up of guitar greats paying homage to Elvis.

Book:
That's Alright, Elvis: The Untold Story of Elvis' First Guitarist and Manager, by Scotty Moore and James Dickerson, Diane Pub. Co, 1997.

SCOTTY MOORE: "When we did 'That's All Right (Mama)', Sam said, 'What are y'all doing?' We said, 'We don't know.' ... But when we heard a playback, we knew we had some kind of rhythm, a little different rhythm, but none of us knew what to call it, so we didn't call it anything at that time."

KEITH RICHARDS: "When I heard 'Heartbreak Hotel', I knew what I wanted to do in life. It was as plain as day. All I wanted to do in the world was to be able to play and sound like that. Everyone else wanted to be Elvis. I wanted to be Scotty."

ELTON JOHN: "It was Scotty Moore's guitar riff when he was doing 'The Steve Allen Show' that got me into rock music."

EDDIE BOND: "I think the sound was discovered accidentally. Scotty and Bill were playing real country. Scotty was a country guitar picker, but he loved Chet Atkins . . . he couldn't play Chet Atkins very good, but he played what he did know like Chet Atkins would have if Chet Atkins didn't know how to play . . . It came out like something new."

MORAN, MIKE

RCA staff engineer brought in from New York to ensure that Elvis' recording sessions were more productive, starting with the December 1973 session at Stax in Memphis. Moran worked with Elvis right through to his final studio recordings in the Jungle Room at Graceland in late 1976.

"MORE"

Elvis dabbled with a few lines of this Oscar-winning song (originally titled "Ti guarderòÙ nel cuore") from 1963 Italian movie *Mondo Cane* in concert on his return to Vegas. Written by Riz Ortolani and Nino Oliviero (with English words by Norman Newell), the song is on bootlegs including *The Monologue* and *To Know Him is to Love Him*.

MORGAN, MAGDALEN

A contender for Elvis' first girlfriend, when he was 13 Elvis penned her name and his onto his parents' marriage certificate, and the date September 11, 1948. When asked about their relationship years later, Magdalen said "It was just a very sweet relationship. At that time, if you just held hands, it was very serious. And we did hold hands a lot."

MORRIS, BILL

The Sheriff of Shelby County was a long-term friend of Elvis' from his Tupelo days. Morris appointed Elvis as a Special Deputy Sheriff in 1964. In 1970, Morris arranged for Elvis and a couple of entourage pals to be taken on a tour to the National Sheriffs' Conference Building in Washington, and was with Elvis when he toured the Federal Building. As a token of his respect, Elvis gave Morris a Mercedes Benz for Christmas that year. It was Morris who nominated Elvis for the Jaycees Outstanding Young Men of the Year Award, an honor that Elvis was particularly proud to receive in early 1971.

MOSCHEO, JOE
(b. 1937)

A singer (pianist and songwriter) with the Imperials, who backed Elvis from 1966 to 1971. Moscheo has taken part in Elvis tribute concerts, and produced a documentary and written a book about Elvis and gospel.

Book:
The Gospel Side of Elvis, by Joe Moscheo, Faithwords, 2007

"MOST BEAUTIFUL GIRL IN THE WORLD, THE"

Elvis slipped in a line or two of this huge 1973 hit for Charlie Rich during his January 27, 1974 concert, released for bootleg posterity on *Real Fun On Stage . . . And In The Studio* and on 2006 FTD issue *I Found My Thrill*. Elvis broke into the song in a mock serenade of comic Marty Allen. At the time he promised the audience he would learn the song—written by Billy Sherrill, Rory Bourke and Norro Wilson—and perform it all the way through.

MOTHER

So close was Elvis to his mother Gladys that the vast majority of Elvis biographers cite this as the single most important bond in his life. Cousin Harold Loyd confirms, "She was so protective of him. If Elvis just whimpered, she would run to him."

After the stillbirth of Elvis' twin, Gladys knew that she was unable to have another child. All her mothering went on Elvis. As a kid, he was sometimes teased for being a mama's boy: she walked him to school far longer than most kids, and she wouldn't allow him to go out and play rough games.

As a grown man, for Elvis the very concept of motherhood had an aura of sanctity. Many biographers have commented that he was sexually turned off women who were mothers; he dropped one girlfriend soon after finding out she had a child, and authors speculate that Elvis did not have sexual relations with Priscilla after she became pregnant with Lisa Marie; in her memoir, Priscilla counters that this was their most sexually active time, though after Lisa Marie was born, Elvis was less interested.

In Elvis' personal hierarchy, about the worst insult a man could make was "son of a bitch." Sonny West remembers Elvis launching a pool cue at a woman who once called Elvis this at his LA home.

Elvis had his own mother's day special show on radio one year in the Sixties; he also did a mother's day charity benefit in Tahoe in 1973,

WHEN ELVIS WAS A KID, HE FAMOUSLY TOLD HIS MOM, "When I grow up, Mama, I'm going to take care of you."

LARRY GELLER: "Elvis was a mama's boy, and he sought women he could respect the same way he had respected his mother, women who possessed his mother's values."

MOTORCYCLES

Elvis acquired a Harley-Davidson in the first flush of wealth in early 1956. He bought a new Harley KH in November 1956, which he used to take Natalie Wood for a spin around town later that year; Nick Adams followed up on the old Harley.

Elvis traded up for a newer model in 1958, and carried on with Harleys until Jerry Schilling bought a Triumph 650 in 1965. Elvis liked the bike so much that he bought one for himself and a dozen for his entourage. He also had to buy a trailer after complaints from his Beverly Hills neighbors: "El's Angels" drove the bikes out of the exclusive Bel Air enclave on the trailer before heading for the Hollywood Hills; they'd also enjoy freaking people out by revealing Elvis' identity.

A new 1966 Harley-Davidson Electric Glide joined the Elvis collection in October 1965; he bought a Honda Dream 350 for Priscilla.

In later years, Elvis particularly liked riding police-style Harleys. He went three-wheeled in 1975, when he invested in some chopper-style trikes specials that summer. He managed to get a speeding ticket on one over-exuberant ride.

A consignment of new Harleys led to the cancellation of Elvis' October 1976 recording session at Graceland; he was far more interested in trying out the bikes than in making music.

Riding a motorbike was as incognito as Elvis could hope to be, though tearing down Elvis Presley Boulevard at 110 miles per hour he would hardly go unnoticed.

Elvis remained an enthusiastic rider right up to the end of his life. On his last day alive, Elvis went for a burn with girlfriend Ginger Alden, accompanied by Billy and Jo Smith.

Elvis rode a modest scooter with Ann-Margret in *Viva Las Vegas*. He rode a Honda 350 Superhawk in 1964 movie *Roustabout*. He was back on a bike again for *Stay Away Joe* (1968).

The legend of Elvis' Harley made the news at the turn of the millennium in an insistent urban legend, usually about a farmer who buys an old Harley only to discover that it was a gift from Priscilla to Elvis, and is therefore worth hundreds of thousands of dollars.

In 2007, a Harley-Davidson dealership opened for business at the Graceland visitor center, and a limited edition signature Elvis Harley Davidson replica (of a 1957 KH) was announced.

WILLIAM WRIGHT: "I think he knew more about motorcycles than he knew about people."

A photograph by Alfred Werteimer, entitled "Elvis Motorcycle".

MOTOR HOMES

Elvis and his folks lived in a Stylemaster Mobile Home briefly during his basic training at Fort Hood, Texas.

In early 1962, Elvis bought an air-conditioned Dodge House Car which he had refurbished in Florida by Jimmy Sanders, complete with a double bed, kitchen and two additional bunks, to use as his main mode of transport between Memphis and Hollywood rather than the Greyhound buses that the Colonel had been hiring. After he had had it customized by George Barris, Elvis drove then 17-year-old Priscilla, freshly-arrived from Germany, to Vegas for a 12-day trip.

The Motor home saw plenty of action as Elvis shuttled back and forth between Memphis and LA (trailed by the guys in a Chrysler station wagon), until Elvis upgraded to a decommissioned Greyhound bus in late 1965, which once again he had refurbished by Barris, but he was still using the Dodge in early 1966 to drive to Los Angeles to shoot *Spinout*. In the fall of 1966 the Colonel donated the Dodge to the TEACH charity for children.

When he owned the Circle G ranch, Elvis, the entourage and their families lived in a series of double-wide house trailers. Elvis bought a gargantuan trailer for cousin Billy Smith in 1974, so that he could live on the grounds of Graceland with his family.

MOTT, BITSY
(B. ELISHA MATTHEW MOTT, 1918-2001)

A short-stop and half-decent hitter for the Philadelphia Phillies in 1945, Colonel Parker's brother-in-law. Bitsy Mott was enlisted into working as Elvis' road manager and security advisor after the Colonel took over Elvis' contract in 1955. Mott was a fixture around Elvis in the pre-Army years and immediately after Elvis' return, though once Elvis surrounded himself with a much larger entourage, Mott retreated to more of a background role, though he carried on working with Elvis on and off up to 1970.

Mott had bit parts in two Elvis movies: he played a sergeant in *G.I. Blues* and a state trooper in *Wild in the Country*.

When Mott saw Elvis perform in 1976 he was shocked at how bad a state he was in. The diminutive Mott (called "Bitsy" for his size) spent his twilight years entertaining children as a birthday party clown.

"MOVE ON UP A LITTLE HIGHER"

Elvis sang this Mahalia Jackson belter when in the mood. This song was the hit that made Jackson a household name from 1948. No Elvis recording has been released.

MOVIES

Elvis loved the movies. The call of Hollywood in 1956 was, as he explained to reporters, a dream come true. With great humility and a desire to learn the acting trade, Elvis embarked on a film career that spanned 33 movies (31 feature films, more than Marilyn Monroe in her entire career) but gradually had to face the reality that he was never going to be taken seriously as a dramatic actor; the cold financial reality of the studio bottom line and the Colonel's voracious deal-making put paid to his ambitions. On the other side of the balance, Elvis' movies were enormously successful at the box office, at one stage making him the highest-paid actor in Hollywood, and they were the only way that his international fans—and, during the Sixties, his home fans too—could see him and watch him perform.

Though Elvis' first movie, *Love Me Tender*, was one that he instantly regretted doing—he had trouble identifying with the character he played, it wasn't the greatest picture and he was disappointed that despite assurances to the contrary he was made to sing—the rest of his pre-Army movies gave him a chance to develop as an actor. Yes, he was typecast into playing impoverished young men who discover a talent for singing, but the roles gradually expanded after *Loving You*, allowing him to play an anti-hero in *Jailhouse Rock* and then his personal favorite, the critically-acclaimed *King Creole*.

Everything changed after the Army. The Colonel's cross-promotional strategy of using songs to promote the movies and the movies to promote soundtrack and single releases fenced Elvis into musicals. The death knell to Elvis' ambitions came with the relatively poor box office performance of his more dramatically accomplished (and more critically-successful) pictures from the early Sixties, *Flaming Star*, *Wild in the Country* and *Follow That Dream*. Quick-buck projects took precedence over heavy-hitter directors (George Cukor, George Stevens, Sidney Lumet and Nicholas Ray) who at one stage or another expressed an interest in working with Elvis. Elia Kazan tried several times to get Elvis on board for movies projects but the Colonel consistently demurred. Even as Elvis' feature film career was drawing to a close, John Schlesinger and Roman Polanski were interested in working with Elvis. By this time, Hollywood had got what it wanted out of him: all told, Elvis' movies grossed over $200 million.

As a young teen, Elvis and friends would sneak off to see movies though it was against the precepts of the First Assembly of God church, to which his parents belonged. According to at least one source, Elvis didn't see his first movie until Vernon took him when he was thirteen—on condition that Elvis didn't tell Gladys. Other sources state that by this time Elvis was already a seasoned moviegoer, a matinee veteran of "Flash Gordon," cowboy heroes Gene Autry, Roy Rogers and Tex Ritter, and *The Wizard of Oz*.

One of Elvis' first ever jobs was as an usher at the Loew's State Theater in Memphis when he was fifteen.

Elvis successfully screen-tested for producer Hal Wallis at Paramount Studios on March 26, 1956, by performing two scenes from *The Rainmaker*, a romance starring Burt Lancaster and Katharine Hepburn that was in preproduction at the time. According to then girlfriend June Juanico, "Elvis was tickled to death when he knew he was going to Hollywood. This was his dream."

All kinds of rumors circulated in the gossip columns about the projects and co-stars Elvis would be lined up with; there were even suggestions that he might be teamed up with comedian Jerry Lewis, who had recently split from Dean Martin.

Colonel Parker's contract with Paramount shrewdly reserved the right for Elvis to do one film per year for another studio. This explains how Elvis made his screen debut in Twentieth Century-Fox production *Love Me Tender*. In what quickly became an inescapable precedent for all of his movies, when Elvis was presented the proj-

ect he was contracted to act, not sing. He was asked to do the title song, and before he knew it, a couple of other songs.

When Elvis got cold feet about doing the movie—his ambition was to follow in the dramatic footsteps of his favorites Marlon Brando and James Dean, not burst into song at the least excuse—Colonel Parker told him that they could either do it his way and make money, or do it Elvis' way and not make money. No guesses who won. The Colonel's insistence on long studio contracts ensured financial security but constrained Elvis' level of choice over what movies he did; like Hollywood stars of old, Elvis became beholden to the cash-driven desires of his producers rather than his own artistic priorities. The irony is that Elvis effectively relinquished his chance to achieve artistic self-fulfillment at precisely the moment that top stars were breaking loose from the shackles of the all-powerful studios.

Love Me Tender was the only one of Elvis' movies to premiere in New York City. After a mixed audience response, the studios preferred to open subsequent Elvis movies in his fan heartlands. Elvis' first words on film were "Vance! Brett!," as he called out to his on-screen brothers, though in fact his first on-screen utterance was a "Whoa!" to his horse His first screen kiss had to wait for Jana Lund in his second movie, *Loving You*. From this movie onwards, many of Elvis' screen vehicles reflected his rags-to-riches story and his prominence as a musical figurehead. Other features from Elvis' real life also made it into his movie characters' lives, including his status as a twin, his Cherokee blood and in several movies an overreaching manager, not to mention his interest in cars and girls, and empathy with kids.

If Elvis had been hoping to build on the varied characters he had played before going into the Army, he was disappointed that the first movie was made-to-measure to cash in on his status as America's most famous soldier. In a pattern that would be repeated until he lost his enthusiasm for making movies altogether, Elvis went into the G.I. Blues project keen but came out of it distressed at how many sub-par songs had been shoehorned into the story. He told Priscilla at the time that the movie was "a joke."

Between March 1960, when Elvis was discharged from the Army, and the end of the year, Elvis worked on no fewer than three movies. During this time he did no touring, so apart from a charity concert or two, Elvis' fans had to go out and buy movie tickets to see him. This they dutifully did, seeing the movies over and over until they memorized the dialogue. Elvis kept up this pace through the early Sixties: in 1962, his three movies made it into the top 50 grossers, led by *Blue Hawaii* which finished a very respectable fourteenth (the others were, in order or popularity, *Girls! Girls! Girls!* and *Kid Galahad*).

Blue Hawaii marked a watershed in the quality of Elvis' output. Vastly more successful than Elvis' more dramatic pictures *Flaming Star*, *Wild in the Country* and *Kid Galahad*, the studios took notice that Elvis' simple, formulaic fare was a much better box office bet, while the spin-off album from *Blue Hawaii* monopolized the #1 spot for twenty weeks to become the best-selling LP of his lifetime. From this point on, Elvis' movies combined glamorous locations, dancing girls in bikinis and Elvis bursting into song.

Nineteen sixty-two proved to be the box office nadir of Elvis' career: he was officially named the Top Box Office Draw of the year in May 1962. In 1963, partly because he was cranking out so many movies, Elvis was still the seventh highest grossing box office star in the States, and dropped only one place the following year. Though his movies were ranking in the 40s and 50s by 1966, he spent five years as one of the top ten grossing movie stars in the business.

Blue Hawaii's success was eclipsed by *Viva Las Vegas*, which, spurred on by sizzling on-screen

chemistry with co-star Ann-Margret, proved to be Elvis' biggest grossing film of all at $5.5 million in the US on initial release. *Viva Las Vegas* was the last of Elvis' movie to maintain A-list production values including a big-name director. Because *Viva Las Vegas* was over budget and cut into the Colonel's profit-sharing plans, he persuaded the studios to keep a tighter rein on spending. The age of the Elvis quickie was born: *Kissin' Cousins* was shot in just 17 days, while in *Roustabout* Elvis was riding around on a little Honda rather than a proper Harley.

Elvis flew into a rage when Paramount producer Hal Wallis implied in a 1964 interview that the studio could only make "quality" movies because it also made less worthy commercially-successful pictures like the Presley movies. In 1964 and 1965, Elvis worked on seven quickie movies, some of which like *Tickle Me* didn't even warrant their own soundtrack but merely repackaged album cuts.

Many of the cast and crew on Elvis' movies worked with him multiple times. Elvis worked with former leading ladies Barbara Stanwyck, Elsa Lanchester, Glenda Farrell, Joan Blondell and Una Merkel. He also worked with veteran characters actors Arthur O'Connell, Carl Betz, Frank McHugh, and even Twenties crooner Rudy Vallee, who was still well-enough known when filming *Live a Little, Love a Little* for elderly ladies to push past Elvis to get his autograph. There were also plenty of aspiring young actresses and dancers who turned up in one, two or three Elvis productions—Teri Garr set the record with half-a-dozen; the lucky ones got to become extras in Elvis' LA party lifestyle too.

In the mid-Sixties, UK fan magazine *Elvis Monthly* dismissed Elvis' movies as "puppet shows for not overbright children." The Colonel's criteria for picking movies for his client had nothing to do with script quality but upfront payment and at least a 25% cut of the take. When director Gene Nelson sent the Colonel the *Kissin' Cousins* script for suggestions, the only comment the Colonel made was that reading the script would cost $25,000 extra. With the exception of *Roustabout*, for which screenwriter Allan Weiss interviewed the Colonel, he was uninterested in reading any of the scripts that the studios prepared for his client—though there is some evidence that the Colonel had some hands on influence on the development of some of Elvis' later scripts. Elvis detected the Colonel's hand in the disparaging spoof yoga scene inserted into *Easy Come, Easy Go*. What the Colonel cared about was that a film like *Kissin' Cousin* came in at a budget of $650,000, while he and Elvis shared $750,000 before even starting on soundtrack sales and music publishing royalties.

Elvis had no illusions about the low quality fare he was making, but there were compensations beyond the six and seven-figure earnings. He got to clown around on set with his pals, find a new leading lady or dancer with whom to liaise, and enjoy a bachelor life on the West Coast after Priscilla moved in to Graceland.

Much as he enjoyed joking around between takes, practicing karate, having a game of touch football or playing elaborate pranks—or in the mid-Sixties, reading his books on spirituality in his trailer or talking with fellow actors about metaphysics—Elvis was invariably professional when it came to putting in the hours. He was never a prima donna; Red West doesn't recall him ever throwing a tantrum. Larry Geller says that Elvis took making movies as a job, and was professional about how he went about it. In their book *Elvis: What Happened*, Red and Sonny West say that after G.I. Blues, Elvis was habitually on amphetamines during filming. The proof, they claim, is that he talks much faster in the movies he made after he went into the Army than he did in the antebellum pictures. Red West also says that Elvis hated doing the later movies: "The money was all that mattered. They didn't give a damn about the person that had to bear the burden of being in them: Elvis."

According to entourage members, Elvis got up the courage to challenge the Colonel about the quality of his movies after doing *Girl Happy*, but was fobbed off by the Colonel's nostrum that as long as Elvis' films were making money, they shouldn't risk a change. George Klein says that Elvis' pals also questioned the Colonel about why Elvis couldn't do better-quality movies, or at least better songs.

In a career otherwise replete with firsts and records, Elvis was never really given a chance to fulfill his acting ambitions and the promise of his early celluloid roles. Over the years, a number of more dramatic roles were proposed for the Colonel's consideration (see SIDEBAR: MOVIES ELVIS CONSIDERED OR WANTED). The Colonel's stock answer was that it all depended on coming up with the money, but then he requested a stratospheric fee and a share of the profits that were far beyond the industry norm, even for a leading man. The great disappointment of Elvis' movie career is the list of magnificent movies for which he was at one stage in the running. And yet Elvis continued to be one of Hollywood's best-paid actors until the end of 1966.

According to Joe Esposito, the toughest times for Elvis were when he received the script and saw that it was another throwaway picture. Elvis also hated having to sit around all day with a grin on his face for the publicity photos, many of which show Elvis in a state of high forbearance.

While shooting *Easy Come, Easy Go*, Elvis had a rare set-to with director John Rich, after Rich ordered Elvis' entourage off set for causing Elvis to laugh during a shot. Elvis explained to the director that the only reason he was doing these movies was because they were fun; the minute they stopped being fun, he'd stop doing them—and he still did eight more after this.

By 1967, the Colonel could no longer ignore Elvis' disaffection with what he termed his "bikini travelogue" pictures. For the first time, the Colonel began soliciting movie studios where he still had deals in place for "good rugged stories." The last four pictures that Elvis made were more grown-up. By his final feature, *Change of Habit*, the storywriters were even dabbling with social issues, in what may well have been conceived as a movie version of "In The Ghetto." The problem was that the audience for Elvis' pictures had already dwindled perilously close to breakeven. The rich vein of profits mined for so long—Elvis ground out 28 movies in 8 years—petered out before the end of the decade. The Colonel's solution to Elvis' waning popularity was to head to the small screen and the NBC TV Special, which immediately led to the offer to return to live performing at the International Hotel in Las Vegas (and an opportunity for Elvis publicly to exorcize his movie demons by joking about them).

Though Elvis never made another feature film, he never actively retired from the movie business. In 1972, at his Madison Square press conference Elvis hinted that he and the Colonel were looking for the right movie project. Even in 1976, Elvis was still on the lookout for a chance, finally, to show what he could do as an actor.

Two concert documentary films appeared during Elvis' lifetime: *Elvis: That's the Way it Is* (1970) and *Elvis on Tour* (1972); the latter was the only Elvis movie to win a high profile award, a Golden Globe. There has also been a persistent rumor that Parker paid for one or two of Elvis' winter 1970 Las Vegas concerts to be filmed—when Elvis was at his absolute performing peak—as a demo for MGM.

For some Elvis fans, the lack of dramatic kudos in Elvis' celluloid career is far less important than how he looked (a little puffy and paunchy at times, but in top shape again from June 1968 onwards when he recorded the NBC TV Special).

The thirtieth anniversary of Elvis' death has brought a smorgasbord of Elvis movie re-releases on DVD, many with extras.

ELVIS' MOTION PICTURES

Love Me Tender (1956)
Loving You (1957)
Jailhouse Rock (1957)
King Creole (1958)
G.I. Blues (1960)
Flaming Star (1960)
Wild in the Country (1961)
Blue Hawaii (1961)
Follow That Dream (1962)
Kid Galahad (1962)
Girls! Girls! Girls! (1962)
It Happened at the World's Fair (1963)
Fun in Acapulco (1963)
Kissin' Cousins (1964)
Viva Las Vegas (1964)
Roustabout (1964)
Girl Happy (1965)
Tickle Me (1965)
Harum Scarum (1965)
Frankie and Johnny (1966)
Paradise, Hawaiian Style (1966)
Spinout (1966)
Easy Come, Easy Go (1967)
Double Trouble (1967)
Clambake (1967)
Stay Away, Joe (1968)
Speedway (1968)
Live a Little, Love a Little (1968)
Charro! (1969)
The Trouble With Girls (1969)
Change of Habit (1969)

ELVIS SAID IN 1967 to George Klein about his latest film: "Same story, different location."

ELVIS SAID TO MARLYN MASON IN 1968: "I'd like to make one good film before I leave, I know this town's laughing at me."

ELVIS SAID IN 1969: "I did Loving You, loving her, loving as many as I could get my hands on at the time."

ELVIS SAID IN 1972: "It was a job. That's how I treated it. But I cared so much I became physically ill. I didn't have final approval on the script, which means that I couldn't tell you 'This is not good for me.' I don't think anyone was consciously trying to harm me. It was just that Hollywood's image of me was wrong and I knew it and I couldn't say anything about it."

COLONEL PARKER, 1960, about Elvis' movies: "They'll never win any Academy Awards. All they're good for is to make money."

PAULINE KAEL: "He starred in thirty-one movies, which ranged from mediocre to putrid, and just about in that orde.r"

VERNON: "He never had script approval or control over the songs in his pictures or over anything else."

BILLY SMITH: "The problem for Elvis was that even the worst pictures made damn good money."

PAMELA CLARKE KEOGH: "Elvis wasn't really making movies. They were more like episodic television shows shot in Panavision accompanied by fabulous lobby posters."

BEN WEISMAN: "Some people today mock his movies . . . Elvis' movies were fun. They were healthy. And his movies always made money."

MILLIE PERKINS, ACTRESS: "He never used his star power—never. Maybe he should have."

EDWARD ANHALT, SCREENWRITER: "All you had to do was find out how many songs he wanted, and write the dialogue in between the songs."

GENE NELSON: "The typical Elvis movie was 10 or 11 musical numbers, frivolous, and sex-oriented in a very nice, mild way. Pretty girls were mandatory, lots of them."

LARRY GELLER: "Elvis loved films, and he studied them carefully."

LAMAR FIKE: "By the time Elvis figured out he was being screwed around, it was too late. He signed too many contracts."

Books:

Elvis in Hollywood, by Paul Lichter, Simon and Schuster, 1975 with tie-in CD of the same name.

The Films and Career of Elvis Presley, by Steven and Boris Zmijewsky, 1976

Reel Elvis! The Ultimate Trivia Guide to the King's Movies, by Pauline C. Bartel, Taylor Publishing Company, 1994

Elvis Presley—Hollywood Years, by Ben Weisman ,1992

Elvis! Elvis! Elvis! The King and His Movies, by Peter Guttmacher, Metro Books/Friedman /Fairfax, 1997

The Elvis Film Encyclopedia, by Eric Braun, Overlook Press, 1997

Elvis Presley: Silver Screen Icon: A Collection of Movie Posters, by Steve Templeton, Overmountain, 2002

Elvis Cinema And Popular Culture, by Douglas Brode, McFarland and Co., 2006

DVDs:

Elvis at the Movies (2002)

9-disc Box set: *Elvis: the Ultimate Film Collection - Graceland Edition* (2006)

8-disc Box set: *30th Anniversary Collection / Lights! Action! Elvis!—King Creole, G.I. Blues, Blue Hawaii, Roustabout, Girls! Girls! Girls!, Fun in Acapulco, Paradise Hawaiian Style, Easy Come Easy Go* (2007)

4-disc Box set: *The Elvis Presley MGM Movie Legends Collection—Clambake, Frankie and Johnny, Follow That Dream, Kid Galahad* (2007)

6-disc Box set: *Elvis: The Hollywood Collection—Charro!, Girl Happy, Kissin' Cousins, Live a Little, Love a Little, Stay Away Joe, Tickle Me* (2007)

MOVIES ELVIS CONSIDERED OR WANTED

There may be no sure thing in Hollywood except for an Elvis picture, but one sure thing is that movie projects are often touted around many actors, directors and producers before getting made, if they get made at all. Below is a collection of movie roles in connection with which Elvis' name was associated:

- *The Girl Can't Help It* (1956). Elvis was given a chance to feature alongside fellow rock 'n' roller Gene Vincent and Eddie Cochran, but the Colonel did not want Elvis to be one of many, so he asked for more money than the producers were prepared to pay.
- *The Way to the Gold* (1957) originally had Elvis cast in the role of the prospector played by Jeffrey Hunter; the Colonel asked for more than Twentieth Century-Fox was willing to pay.
- *The James Dean Story* (1957). Before the production became a documentary, Elvis was high on the list of actors to play one of his own favorites.
- *The Love Maniac* was a 1957 Twentieth Century-Fox project that was to have paired up Elvis and Jayne Mansfield.
- *The Defiant Ones* (1958). Elvis was reputedly keen to play the role of John 'Joker' Jackson that went to Tony Curtis; the prospect of playing another convict after *Jailhouse Rock* is unlikely to have thrilled the Colonel.
- *Cat on a Hot Tin Roof* (1958). Elvis was reportedly offered the role of Brick, played to great effect

Elvis with Hal Wallis signing his first film contract

by Paul Newman opposite Elizabeth Taylor.

- *Thunder Road*, a 1958 movie written by and starring Robert Mitchum about a veteran returning from the Korean War. Mitchum personally asked Elvis' to play his son. Colonel Tom Parker was dead set against the idea of Elvis in a family of moonshiners; he relied on his usual tactic of asking for an unfeasibly high fee and percentage of profit.

- *Gidget* (1959). Producer Joe Pasternak, who later worked with Elvis on *Girl Happy* (1965), was reputedly keen to cast Elvis as a surfer in this original beach movie.

- *The Fugitive Kind* (1959) was a movie version of Tennessee Williams' play "Orpheus Descending," directed by Sidney Lumet and starring Marlon Brando and Anna Magnani. Williams originally wanted Elvis in the lead role. Quentin Tarantino has also said that he thought Elvis would have been perfect in this movie.

- *West Side Story* (1961), a film Elvis greatly admired, could have been an Elvis vehicle if director Robert Wise had got his way and nabbed Elvis to play the role of Tony (or Bernardo depending on sources). The producers originally wanted top singers to play gang members.

- *Sweet Bird of Youth* (1962) was another dramatic role that Elvis was approached about, but the Colonel considered too bleak. Paul Newman stood in. Another Oscar-rated movie declined.

- *Gay Purr-ee*, a 1962 animated feature for which Elvis was offered a quarter of a million dollars for two days' voiceover and singing work. Colonel Parker said no, partly on the strength of opposition from Paramount.

- *Too Late Blues* (1962) was originally offered to Elvis before Bobby Darin took the lead.

- *A Walk On The Wild Side* (1962) was put forward in 1960 by Jerry Leiber, with Elia Kazan as director with the promise of the script being crafted around Elvis, but the Colonel ruled it out on the principle that he was in charge, not Leiber.

- *Bye Bye Birdie* (1963), about a rock 'n' roll idol not unlike Elvis, was to have featured a couple of Elvis songs before the Colonel declined. The role went to Dick Gautier instead. If the Colonel had said yes, Elvis might have met *Viva Las Vegas* co-star Ann-Margret a little sooner.

- *Your Cheatin' Heart* (1964). A Hank Williams biopic, for which Elvis was reputedly in the running in 1961 before either Colonel Parker decided that it would not be enough of a money-spinner or Williams' widow Audrey ruled Elvis out because she didn't want her husband's life to be eclipsed by Elvis' star billing. The movie was made three years later with Parker protégé George Hamilton.

- *The Fastest Guitar Alive* (1967), directed by Michael D. Moore, who worked on many films with Elvis as an assistant director, was originally conceived with Elvis in the starring role as a guitar-toting Confederate. Elvis' loss was Roy Orbison's gain.

- *Midnight Cowboy* (1969). George Klein remembers Elvis being in with a shot for the role that won Jon Voight an Oscar nomination and director John Schlesinger the statuette in 1969. The Colonel was horrified at the idea of his boy playing a male prostitute, even though by this time the Colonel had started actively soliciting for meatier roles. Elvis was not known for his tolerance of homosexuality either.

- *True Grit* (1969). Elvis was briefly considered for the role of the Texas Ranger opposite John Wayne until as ever the Colonel's demands (for top billing, in a Duke picture) proved to be insurmountable. Glen Campbell got the role.

- *The Godfather* (1972). Elvis reputedly wanted the Tom Hagen role (played in the movie by Robert Duvall) in the original godfather flick but was not even considered for an audition.

- *A Star is Born* (1976). After Barbra Streisand saw Elvis perform in Las Vegas in early 1975, she went backstage with boyfriend Jon Peters to offer Elvis the male lead in her remake of this classic Hollywood tale of hope, talent, ambition and decline, already a three-time box office success in

decades gone by. Elvis was initially mustard keen, until the Colonel demanded such a huge deal (reputedly a million dollars plus half of the profits) that nothing came of it. It has also been suggested that Elvis might not have been too happy at the idea of playing a washed-up singer.

PROJECTS ELVIS CONSIDERED PRODUCING

There was talk of Elvis being involved in a Kui Lee biopic project around the time of his *Aloha From Hawaii* concert in 1973.

Elvis embarked on two karate movie projects in the Seventies: *The New Gladiators* was the working title for a karate documentary that Elvis bankrolled in 1974. *Billy Easter* was a movie project Elvis was still considering in his last years, about an undercover agent who uses his karate skills to defeat drug dealers.

Elvis spoke with Paul Newman in the Seventies about potentially working together, though nothing came of it.

Elvis was reputedly interested in producing a biopic about his favorite numerologist, Cheiro, taking the lead role himself.

MOVIES AND TV SHOWS IN WHICH ELVIS SONGS AND ELVIS-LIKE CHARACTERS HAVE FEATURED:

The list is by no means complete:

MOVIES:
3000 Miles to Graceland (2001)
A Face in the Crowd (1957)
A Life Less Ordinary (1997)
Alien Autopsy (2006)
Backbeat (1994)
Big Fish (2003)
Black Hawk Down (2001)
Blow Dry (2001)
Book of Love (1990)
Bruce Almighty (2003)
Bubba Ho-Tep (2002)
C.R.A.Z.Y. (2005)
Cast Away (2000)
Christmas with the Kranks (2004)
Clay Pigeons (1998)
Cocktail (1988)
Cool Cats—25 Years of Rock 'n' Roll Style (1983)
Coyote Ugly (2000)
Dave (1993)
Dear America: Letters Home from Vietnam (1987)
Desert Hearts (1985)
Diner (1982)
Eat the Peach (1986)
Eddie Presley (1992)
Elvis Is Alive! I Swear I Saw Him Eating Ding Dongs Outside the Piggly Wiggly's (1998)
Elvis Has Left the Building (2004)
Elvis Took a Bullit (2001)
Elvis Meets Nixon (1997)
Fanny and Elvis (1999)
Finding Graceland (1998)
Fools Rush In (1997)
Frequency (2000)
Gorod Zero (1988)
Grease (1978)
Great Balls of Fire! (1989)
Gypsy Magic (1997)
Happy Feet (2006)
Heart of Dixie (1989)
Heartbreak Hotel (1988)
Heaven Help Us (1985)
Hollywood Rocks the Movies: The Early Years 1955-1970 (2000)
Honeymoon in Vegas (1992)
Hounddog (2007)
I'll Be Home for Christmas (1998)

Intolerable Cruelty (2003)
Inventing the Abbotts (1997)
It's Only Make Believe (1989)
Jeff Buckley: Fall in Light (1999)
Jerry Maguire (1996)
Joe Versus the Volcano (1990)
Leningrad Cowboys Go America (1989)
Leroy & Stitch (2006)
Lethal Weapon (1987)
Liberty Heights (1999)
Lilo & Stitch (2002)
Living Legend: The King of Rock and Roll (1980)
Look Who's Talking Now (1993)
Look Who's Talking Too (1990)
Looney Tunes: Back in Action (2003)
Men in Black (1997)
Mischief (1985)
Miracle on 34th Street (1994)
My Fellow Americans (1996)
Mystery Train (1989)
Naomi & Wynonna: Love Can Build a Bridge (1995)
New York Minute (2004)
Ocean's Eleven (2001)
October Sky (1999)
Pleasantville (1998)
Practical Magic (1998)
Pulp Fiction (1994)
Romance & Cigarettes (2005)
Ricky Nelson: Original Teen Idol (1999)
Scorpio Rising (1964)
Sgt. Bilko (1996)
Shark Tale (2004)
She-Devil (1989)
Sorted (2000)
Speechless (1994)
The Client (1994)
The Dark Half (1993)
The Headhunter
The In-Laws (2003)
The Long Kiss Goodnight (1996)
The Man in the Moon (1991)
The Night We Called It a Day (2003)
The Odd Couple II (1998)
The Princess Diaries 2: Royal Engagement (2004)
The Rookie (2002)
The Skeleton Key (2005)
The Tall Guy (1989)
The Thing Called Love (1993)
The Woman Who Loved Elvis (1993)
Things We Did Last Summer (1977)
This Is Spinal Tap (1984)
Tin Men (1987)
Top Secret (1984)
Touched by Love (1980)
Walk the Line (2005)
Wild at Heart (1990)
William Eggleston in the Real World (2005)

TV SHOWS:
"ALF"—Suspicious Minds (1989)
"CMT Crossroads"—Melissa Etheridge & Dolly Parton (2003)
"Crossing Jordan"—Miracles and Wonders (2002)
"Designing Women"—various (1986-1993)
"Eerie, Indiana" (1991)
"Ed"—Mixed Signals (2001)
"Entourage"—Oh, Mandy (2005)
"ER" –If Not Now (2006)
"Father Ted"—Competition Time (1995)
"Freddy's Nightmares"—Heartbreak Hotel (1989)
"Friends"—The One in Vegas: Part 1 (1999)
"Full House"—Mad Money (1988)
"Give My Head Peace"—various (2001-)
"Johnny Bago"—Spotting Elvis (1993)
"Johnny Bravo"—various (1997-2004)
"L.A. Law"—Pygmalion (1987)
"Las Vegas" (2005, 2006)
"Lipstick on Your Collar" (1993)
"Quantum Leap"—Memphis Melody (1993) (in which Red West's son, John Boyd, plays his father)
"Sledge Hammer!"—All Shook Up (1986)
"Sliders"—The King is Back (1995)

"The Adventures of Mark and Brian"—various (1991)

"Best of the Worst" (1991)

"The Charmings"—A Charming Halloween (1987)

"The Lone Gunmen" (2001)

"The Simpsons"—The Tell-Tale Head (Bart Simpson's blackboard scrawl, 1990), Viva Ned Flanders (1999)

"The Last Precinct"—Pilot (1986)

"The Twilight Zone"—The Once and Future King (1986)

"WKRP In Cincinnati"—Long Live the King (1992)

See also DOCUMENTARIES and ACTORS WHO HAVE PORTRAYED ELVIS OR ELVIS-BASED CHARACTERS FOR ELVIS-THEMED PRODUCTIONS.

ELVIS' TASTE IN MOVIES

From boyhood, Elvis escaped to the movies whenever he had the chance. He was at the Suzore No. 2 Theater (279 N. Main) watching *The Best Years of Our Lives* on the night that his first record was first played on the radio, and had to be hauled out to go down for an interview with WHBQ DJ Dewey Phillips. He was a big Tony Curtis fan during his days working as an usher at a Memphis movie house. He loved method actors Marlon Brando and James Dean; he could recite whole chunks of dialogue from *Rebel Without A Cause* as he was on the cusp of breaking into the movies himself, having on some accounts seen the movie 44 times. Another Dean favorite of Elvis' was *Giant*. Elvis could also reel off dialogue from Brando pictures *The Wild One* and *On the Waterfront*, both of which he studied to help his own acting. The Internet Movie Data Base (IMDB) lists Elvis' favorite films as *Rebel Without a Cause* (1955), *A Streetcar Named Desire* (1951) and *Dirty Harry* (1971).

Playing up to a dozen shows a week when he first started touring didn't dampen Elvis' enthusiasm for the movies. When he could, he would go and catch one of the latest flicks. In 1956 he told an interviewer that of the year's films, he had particularly enjoyed *Picnic*, *Helen of Troy* and *The Man with the Golden Arm*. In the Fifties, Elvis loved listening to Mario Lanza's voice in *The Student Prince*.

One of the first extravagances Elvis allowed himself when he began earning significant money was to buy a projector, as well as a camera and a lighting rig, though he mainly used it to screen cartoons to pals at his Audubon Drive home. Later, the excitement of having his own projector at Graceland (and later one at his LA home) paled against the pleasures of taking over the Memphian Theater after-hours—or the Malco—where he would be joined by friends and family and view all of the latest releases back-to-back. When he was ready, he'd shout out "Roll 'em!." In later years Elvis hired out the General Cinema in Whitehaven or the Crosstown Theater. He was still hiring out movie theaters the last week he was alive (the General Cinema, where he saw *The Spy Who Loved Me*). Elvis' favorite seat was plumb in the middle.

Before heading off to Germany, Elvis took in *No Time for Sergeants* at a Waco movie house.

Elvis was a big fan of *West Side Story* when it came out in 1961. He saw a screening at the Memphian Theater, and then had the projectionist replay his favorite scene, the "Cool" song and dance, over and over again. He also loved *To Kill a Mockingbird* and *Lawrence of Arabia* (and thought the former should have beaten the latter to the 1962 Oscar). Another favorite was the first in the James Bond franchise, *Dr. No*.

Going out to the movies supplanted his rougher pursuits such as roller-skating and riding the Fairgrounds after Priscilla came to live with

him in 1963. That year he watched *The Nutty Professor* three times, as well as releases including *Village of the Damned* and *Harold Lloyd's World of Comedy*. One of his favorites that year was *A Gathering of Eagles*, an air force adventure starring Rock Hudson.

According to Priscilla, Elvis' favorite film of all time was *The Way of All Flesh* (1940), a tale of a family surviving great hardship. She says that he identified so strongly with the movie that at one stage he considered becoming involved in a remake. Other favorites of his in the years immediately after Priscilla joined him at Graceland were *Les Miserables*, *Wuthering Heights*, *It's a Wonderful Life*, *Miracle on 34th Street*, *Mr. Skeffington*, and *Letter from an Unknown Woman*.

Elvis screened Peter Sellers' comedy *Dr. Strangelove* five times in quick succession after it came out in 1964. Marty Lacker estimates that Elvis watched this movie as many as 50 times. Other popular favorites at this time were the spate of biblical epics, *The Great Escape* and the Hitchcock's horror flick, *Marnie*. Elvis watched a lot of horror movies, and took particular pleasure in other people's fright.

In 1965, Elvis enjoyed old favorites like *Dr. Strangelove*, and *Dr. No*, along with the latest James Bond flick *Thunderball* and other major releases from that year.

In the spring of 1966, he caught up on his movies with pals by hiring out the Crosstown Theater (at 400 North Cleveland), where among other titles he took in *The Magnificent Seven*, *The Ten Commandments*, *A Fine Madness* and *Plague of the Zombies*. One of his favorites from 1966 was Peter Sellers' *After the Fox*. Towards the end of the year he also saw Ann-Margret's latest, *Stagecoach*.

In 1967, Elvis watched the original *Casino Royale* and kept up with Peter Sellers' *A Shot in the Dark* and old favorite *After the Fox*. In 1968, he saw *The Thomas Crown Affair* and *Hang 'Em High* at the Memphian Theater, once again dividing his private screenings between this venue and the Crosstown Theater. He absolutely loved Sellers' *The Party*.

In January 1970, Elvis first saw George C. Scott in *Patton*, a movie that so enthralled him that he learned the opening speech by heart. Elvis had a 16mm projector set up in his new Palm Springs home in 1970 so that he could stay up to date with recent releases when he was out in the desert.

Around this time, Elvis continued to block-book the Memphian and sometimes the Crosstown during his increasingly rare stays in Memphis—the lure of LA, Palm Springs, and side trips with his buddies all competed for his attention. On all but a very few occasions, he was happy for friends, family, acquaintances and employees tag along.

1971 movies Elvis watched included *Shaft*, *The Hunting Party*, *Dirty Harry* and *Straw Dogs*. After his break-up with Priscilla in early 1972, Elvis took to only inviting close friends to his almost nightly screenings.

One of Elvis' all-time favorites was gritty 1972 Blaxploitation flick *Across 110th Street*. Elvis saw the movie so many times that he knew the dialogue off by heart, as he proved to pals in January 1976 when he reeled the whole movie off from start to finish. He also liked *Superfly*.

Elvis owned one of the first video set-ups, and in his final years was particularly fond of watching Mel Brooks' *Blazing Saddles*, Peter Sellers movies, and episodes of zany Brit comedy *Monty Python's Flying Circus* at home.

In January 1974, Elvis hired a screening room at MGM to see *The Exorcist*. That year Elvis' leisure time tended to be taken up more with karate than movie-going.

He saw *Monty Python and the Holy Grail* five times in a row when it came out in 1975.

On the night he died, Elvis planned to watch *MacArthur* for the umpteenth time.

"MR. SONGMAN"

Elvis recorded this Donnie Sumner choral country song in Nashville on December 12, 1973. It was first released on *Promised Land*, Elvis' fourth to last album, before in 1975 coming out as the B-side to "T-R-O-U-B-L-E." The song has since merited a posthumous release on *Walk A Mile In My Shoes*

MUHOBERAC, LARRY

Pianist who played on Elvis movie soundtrack sessions in the mid-Sixties starting with *Frankie and Johnny*; he had previously appeared live with Elvis in 1961, billed as Larry Owens, at Elvis' Memphis charity shows.

James Burton drafted Muhoberac into the original TCB Band for Elvis' first Las Vegas residency at the International Hotel in 1969. Muhoberac was replaced by Glen D. Hardin from 1970. Perhaps Muhoberac's longest-lasting legacy was to suggest Elvis' longtime drummer Ronnie Tutt to Burton.

During his career, Muhoberac played with artists including Ray Charles, Neil Diamond, Al Martino and Tina Turner.

MUNICH

Elvis visited Munich on leave in early March 1959, the lure being an actress called Vera Tschechowa who he had met during a March of Dimes photo shoot. With pals Red West and Lamar Fike, Elvis saw the actress in a German-language play, made multiple trips to strip club Moulin Rouge, visited the film studios at Mü̱nchen-Geiselgasteig, and went for a boat ride on Lake Starnberg.

Elvis passed through Munich for a couple of days again in early June 1959, en route to Paris.

See also GERMANY.

Book:
The Ultimate Elvis in Munich Book, by Andreas Roth, self-published, 2004.

MURPHY, GEORGE
(1902-1992)

US Senator with whom Elvis struck up a friendship on a plane to Washington in December 1970, and who became part of Elvis' impromptu plan to become a federal agent in order to help preserve America from decadence and communism.

Murphy could empathize with what it was like for an entertainer to want to serve his country. After decades dancing and acting in Hollywood, Murphy went into politics, first as the President of the Screen Actors' Guild, and then from 1964 in the US Senate, spiritually paving the way for fellow-actor and politico Ronald Reagan (whose father Murphy played in 1943 picture *This is the Army*).

MUSCLE SHOALS

This small Alabama town, self-proclaimed "Hit Recording Capital of the World," is renowned for providing many of the musicians behind the hits of the Sixties and Seventies, at a small recording studio that attracted the likes of Aretha Franklin, Wilson Pickett, the Rolling Stones, Millie Jackson, Bob Dylan, Otis Redding, Rod Stewart, Paul Anka, the Staples Singers, Jimmy Cliff and as they say in the business, many, many more.

Elvis was backed at various times by "Muscle Shoals Rhythm Section" players (aka "Swampers") Jerry Carrigan, Norbert Putnam and David Briggs.

The Muscle Shoals Sound Studios closed down in 2005, but the original FAME studio (3614 Jackson Highway) is on the National Register of Historic Places.

MUSEUMS

Graceland is the Elvis museum par excellence, its facilities set for expansion by EPE now that it is run by CKX. However, other Elvis museums continue to show some of the vast amounts of Elvis memorabilia in circulation, many of them labors of love by fans.

For many years, Jimmy Velvet ran an Elvis Presley Museum over the road from Graceland, just one of several that he has curated.

The Elvis-A-Rama museum in Las Vegas closed in 2006 when it was purchased by EPE, in preparation for a new official Las Vegas Elvis attraction. After the sale, former Elvis-A-Rama proprietor Chris Davidson was considering opening an Elvis-themed museum in Hawaii.

The Elvis Presley Museum in Pigeon Forge, Tennessee, claims to house the world's largest collection of Elvis memorabilia.

Graceland Too in Holly Springs, Mississippi is a tribute to Elvis handmade by Paul McLeod and his son Elvis Aaron Presley McLeod.

The Dreamland Presley Museum in St. Mary's, Ohio, opened in 2006.

The Fadal family have opened an online Elvis Presley Museum.

Little Graceland is a fan museum in Los Fresnos, Texas.

Informal Elvis museums displaying Elvis memorabilia exist around the world in bars and cafés owned by Elvis fans.

In late 2006, there were newspaper reports of an Elvis museum being planned for London.

MUSIC

Elvis' influence on the recording industry, on popular music and on fame itself has yet to be rivaled. As Peter Guralnick writes, Elvis was "someone whose ambition it was to encompass every strand of the American musical tradition." Elvis' synthesis of those many strands—gospel, hillbilly, R 'n' B, ballads, and later easy-listening, folk and opera—made him a trailblazer whose appeal spans the generations.

Over half a century later, it's easy to overlook quite how revolutionary Elvis was when he first started making music. Though by no means the first rock 'n' roller to hit the airwaves, the sound of his early Sun Records releases was so unique that pals of Elvis' were shocked to hear his name announced after the track was played; a significant proportion of listeners, and radio DJs too, thought that there was so much "race" in the young man's voice that he had to be black.

With hindsight, Elvis might look inevitable. He wasn't, regardless of the many books about how Sam Phillips was on the lookout for somebody like Elvis. Elvis took his share of knock backs before a fortuitous set of circumstances set him on his way as a recording artist. Even more fortuitous was how Elvis and his band got their fresh, raw sound. It took Elvis messing around with a song he wasn't meant to be recording, the peculiar acoustics of the Memphis Recording

Service, Scotty Moore's idiosyncratic guitar and a total lack of a drummer. Or, as Elvis succinctly told Louisiana Hayride announcer Frank Page when he asked how Elvis and his band came up with their new sound, "To be honest, we just stumbled upon it."

A clue to how different Elvis' music was comes from the shifting monikers used to pigeonhole it. Before it was referred to as rock 'n' roll—more accurately, rockabilly—Elvis and the Blue Moon Boys' sound was referred to as "Boppin' Hillbilly," "Western Bop" and even "Catbilly."

Critics' opinions differ wildly on the moment when Elvis ceased to be an innovator and driver of new music. Absolute purists claim that Elvis put his best work behind him when he began using a drummer, that is, before he had released three singles. John Lennon famously commented that Elvis died when he went into the Army (an assertion repeated by Eddie Tenpole on punk song "The Great Rock 'n' Roll Swindle"). More generous commentators such as Ernst Jorgensen look to 1960 album *Elvis Is Back!* as a great artistic triumph. The majority of critics acknowledge that the Elvis of 1968, during the NBC Comeback special and soon after at his American Studio recording sessions, was back on the cutting edge. However, the beginning of this Elvis renaissance was already apparent in 1967, when Elvis worked with Jerry Reed to record his song "Guitar Man," combining country with R'n'B to forge a whole new fiery sound. In gospel, Elvis' favorite genre of all, he remained an innovator right through to the Seventies.

For Elvis, music was all about feel. Scores of musicians with whom he worked say that nobody could pour more emotion into a song. The joy of making music shines through in Sun single "Mystery Train," in which Elvis simply can't hold back a whistle-like yelp and a chuckle. Greil Marcus describes Elvis' early music as "emotionally complex music that can return something new each time you listen to it." Ernst Jorgensen qualifies it as full of "natural swing and underplayed charm," though after he moved to RCA, this was replaced by "energy and toughness."

Elvis' musical creativity was almost exclusively reserved for the studio or the stage. He never learned to read music and he only ever had a rudimentary command of the guitar, but his perfect ear allied to an unerring instinct for a hit were enough to make him an international star. With the minor exception of contributions to a few tracks written by pals Red West and Charlie Hodge, Elvis' lack of songwriting skills may seem an anomaly today, but it was the norm back in the day when Elvis started out.

Though Elvis was eclectic in his tastes, he was not a musical omnivore. In the late Fifties he admitted that he didn't understand either opera or jazz. However, his record collection contained some jazz and many operatic recordings by his favorite Mario Lanza. He was an avid consumer of music, buying the latest records in the dozens and playing records in his den and bedroom. The bulk of his collection was made up of gospel acts. Elvis had a rule at Graceland too: that nobody ever put on one of his own recordings.

As a mature artist, what Elvis did so well was to allow his instinct to guide him across genres, adding rock to gospel, blues to country or any combination of the above to make a song sound the way that he heard it in his head. Most of his standout tracks pull off this trick.

Many fans rue the fact that in the Seventies Elvis did not take up any of the offers to work together that came in from performers such as Elton John, David Bowie, Bruce Springsteen and Bob Dylan.

ELVIS SAID IN 1956: "I've never had any music lessons . . . I've always enjoyed music of any kind."

ELVIS SAID IN 1956: "[Music] ties me up. It makes me forget everything else except the beat and the sound. It tells me more than anything else I've ever known, how good, how great it is just to be alive."

ELVIS SAID IN 1956: "I've never copied anybody, and I've also never heard any style like mine. I just originated it accidentally, more or less."

ELVIS SAID IN 1960: "I work strictly on instinct and impulse. I don't read music . . . I choose songs with the public in mind. I try to visualize it as though I'm buying the record myself. Would I like it?"

ELVIS SAID IN 1970: "It's a combination of country music, gospel, and rhythm and blues, all combined . . . . As a child I was influenced by all of that."

ELVIS JOKED: "I don't know anything about music. In my line you don't have to."

GREIL MARCUS: "His music was the most liberating event of our era because it taught us new possibilities of feeling and perception, new modes of action and appearance, and because it reminded us not only of his greatness, but of our own potential."

RONNIE TUTT: "Elvis was never trained in music. He was just a natural musician. He just played by feel, and if it felt right and did the right thing to him, then he liked it."

BOBBY WOOD: "The thing I guess that sticks in my mind about Elvis was you couldn't fool him about feel. I mean this guy knew soul and he knew feel."

JOAN DEARY: "Elvis had great vocal range, and he continued working to expand his range and develop his voice. His music repertoire was unbelievable."

HUEY LEWIS: "A lot has been written and said about why he was so great, but I think the best way to appreciate his greatness is just to go back and play some of the old records . . . Time has a way of being very unkind to old records, but Elvis' keep getting better and better."

ERNST JORGENSEN: "When Elvis died, it was as if all perspective on his musical career was somehow lost."

CHARLIE HODGE: "I think Elvis would have loved to have been an opera singer."

PETER GURALNICK: "You don't have to like Elvis Presley—but it's impossible, if you listen to his music, not to recognize both his achievement and his originality."

PAUL GAMBACCINI: "His music has become a kind of popular classic music."

JERRY SCHEFF: "He loved to sing for people, he loved to knock people out."

Books:

Elvis Presley: A Study in Music, by Robert Matthew-Walker, Midas Books, 1979 (a revised version appeared as *Heartbreak Hotel: the Life and Music of Elvis Presley* in 1988)

Aspects of Elvis: Tryin' to Get to You, by Alan Clayson and Spencer Leigh, Sidgwick & Jackson, 1994

Talking Elvis: In-Depth Interviews with Musicians, Songwriters and Friends, by Trevor Cajiao, Tutti Frutti Productions, 1998

Elvis Presley: A Life in Music: The Complete Recording Sessions, by Ernst Jorgensen, St Martin's Press, 1998

MUSICAL INFLUENCES

Elvis was factually correct if a little disingenuous when in 1953, the first time he walked into a recording studio, he told Marion Keisker of Sun Records, 'I don't sound like nobody.' Elvis sound-

Elvis in the Imperial Suite, Las Vegas, 1971.

ed like a young man with a remarkable voice who had soaked up music like a sponge.

Elvis' earliest singing experience was as a toddler at the First Assembly of God church in East Tupelo, where two of his uncles preached. Family members recall him clambering onto the dais to join in hymn singing when he was just two. Going to church and hearing gospel was a regular part of life for the Presley clan; between school prayers and singing in church, the first songs Elvis learned were hymns.

Elvis' family had a radio and listened to hillbilly music on the Grand Old Opry radio show. They heard the Carter Family, Jimmie Rodgers, Hank Williams, Roy Acuff, Ernest Tubb and Bob Wills, along with gospel favorites like the Blackwood Brothers and the Statesmen—Elvis particularly liked charismatic bass singer "Big Chief" Wetherington. Afro-American spirituals were also a major influence on Elvis' formative music years, including work by pop-gospel pioneer Sister Rosetta Tharpe. Throughout his career, Elvis drew backing singers from the gospel harmony groups he admired before hitting the big time.

In Tupelo, Uncle Jimmy Smith took Elvis and other kids to the WELO Jamboree, a weekly talent show broadcast from the Tupelo courthouse. Local guitar hero Mississippi Slim, aka Carvel Lee Ausborn, encouraged Elvis to sing and learn the guitar; the first working musician he had occasion to meet, Mississippi Slim offered Elvis tangible evidence of what the music profession could do for a man.

As early as the fifth grade, Elvis was taking his guitar to school and providing accompaniment during assembly time in the morning, when at school they sang hymns and patriotic wartime songs.

According to some but by no means all biographers, pre-fame Elvis jammed with other guys at the Lauderdale Courts project where he lived in Memphis, including Bill Black, whose mother and brother lived there. Some sources claims that teenaged Elvis headed to clubs in West Memphis to listen to Willie Mitchell at Danny's, or go the Plantation Inn where the music was a blend of black blues and white hillbilly.

Rhythm and blues—until 1948 known as "race" music—had been popular with black audiences for some time before it was picked up by white teenagers as the Fifties wore on. The beginnings of a sea change in youth culture was noted by *Billboard* magazine in early 1954, mere months before Elvis' first single, in an article titled "Teenagers Going for 'Music with a Beat' ."

Black artists Roy Hamilton, Clyde McPhatter and The Drifters, and LaVern Baker all exerted a strong influence on Elvis' tastes and vocal style at the start of his career, as did R 'n' B vocal groups The Clovers and Billy Ward and the Dominoes, whose lead singer was Jackie Wilson. His musical heroes also included early Sun artists Bobby Bland and Little Junior Parker.

Elvis was always upfront about his debt to African-American singers. In a 1956 interview, he said: "The colored folks been singing it and playing it just like I'm doin' now, man, for more years than I know. They played it like that in the shanties and in their juke joints, and nobody paid it no mind 'til I goosed it up. I got it from them. Down in Tupelo, Mississippi, I used to hear old Arthur Crudup bang his box the way I do now, and I said if I ever got to the place where I could feel all old Arthur felt, I'd be a music man like nobody ever saw."

And yet when he first started out, Elvis considered himself to be a country singer. Alongside gospel and R 'n' B, Hillbilly was the other major genre that influenced Elvis. All of his early singles on Sun had one country side, though Elvis' version was usually so different from the original as to be almost unrecognizable.

Four months after recording his first single,

Elvis confessed to Ernest Tubb—one of his country influences, along with Hank Snow, Red Foley, Eddy Arnold and Roy Acuff—that what he really wanted was to be a country singer. A record store owner, radio presenter and prominent Opry performer in his own right, Tubb advised Elvis to keep on doing whatever he was doing if it was bringing him success. Practically a mantra for Colonel Parker, Elvis took this advice to heart. Eight years later Elvis told a reporter that much as he was interested in trying out new things musically, it seemed foolish to rock the boat: "If I can entertain people with things I'm doing, well, I'd be a fool to tamper with it."

Elvis' predilection for close vocal harmonies —he fought many battles with record company executives who wanted to bring Elvis' voice forward and hide the harmonies—came from listening to gospel and vocal groups like the Ink Spots.

Within two years of starting out in the business, Elvis was being hailed as the most exciting new act of the last ten years. A North Carolina news-sheet described his style as a combination of Johnnie Ray and Frankie Laine. In May 1956, Elvis told the *Memphis Press-Scimitar* that his musical heroes were "Crosby, Como, Sinatra, all the big ones. They had to be good to get there. I've always been partial to Dean Martin."

According to D.J. Fontana, Elvis listened to singers with "big voices" like Enrico Caruso and Mario Lanza, — with whom Elvis shared a prodigious three octave range—and closer to home, Sam Cooke and Dean Martin. Elvis was an avid music consumer as well as a consummate music maker. In the early Sixties, he saw plenty of musical acts in LA and Las Vegas including Fats Domino, Jackie Wilson, Della Reese, and the Clara Ward Singers. Of course, being Elvis he had to arrive as the house lights went down and leave before the end of the last song.

Elvis always listened to gospel. In the midSixties he spent a lot of time listening to Jimmy Jones, the bass vocalist for the Harmonizing Four. At a time when his own music output was stagnating, Elvis kept up with the new folk movement, particularly Peter, Paul and Mary. From the British invasion, he listened to the Dave Clark Five. Larry Geller remembers that Elvis thought Jagger was a joke, and that he danced like a "crazed chicken on LSD." Also according to Geller, Elvis liked Bob Dylan's songs but was not too enamored of his delivery.

Ascertaining Elvis' influences is often a matter of looking at who previously recorded the songs he chose for himself. During his long career, he recorded many of the songs he knew and loved growing up. At Sun Records he'd just go ahead and record them; at RCA, he had to run them by song publishers Hill & Range, though he might just launch into them with the band as a recording session drew to a close.

See also: HEROES and FAVORITES

ELVIS SAID: "I really can't say what I like or that I was influenced by any one particular thing. I've been associated with rock & roll but I had records by Mario Lanza, the Metropolitan Opera . . ."

PETER GURALNICK: "He sucked up influences like litmus paper."

CHARLIE HODGE: "He would be Billy Eckstine, he would be Bill Kenny of the Ink Spots, he would be Hank Snow—all these people became Elvis Presley by the time he started touring. He had all these people inside of him."

MUSICIANS WITH WHOM ELVIS WORKED

. . .are scattered liberally throughout this book.

Elvis worked with many of the greatest instrumentalists and vocalists of his day. When the call came, most musicians leapt at the chance to work with Elvis. Even musicians for whom working with Elvis seemed in prospect like just another session have since talked about the man's extraordinary charisma, humility, musicianship and diligence.

Elvis immediately created a good working rapport by introducing himself to new musicians. His opening gambit of "Hi, I'm Elvis Presley" was a leveling statement if ever there was one from the world's most iconic recording artist. Elvis also did his homework, engaging relative newcomers and young players in genuinely interested talk about their recent work.

ELVIS SAID: "For my recording sessions I work with ear musicians, not sheet musicians. They're great. You just hum or whistle or sing a tune for them twice and then they get to work, and inside a minute or two the joint is jumping."

MUSICIANS INFLUENCED BY ELVIS

This already prodigiously-long book would need a government weight warning on the front if it listed all of the musicians Elvis has influenced. A case can be made that anybody who has recorded a pop song since Elvis first laid down an acetate at Sun Records has been influenced to some degree.

Countless rock and roll singers who grew up in the Fifties and Sixties were inspired by seeing one of Elvis' early concerts or hearing an early Elvis hit. Musicians from Buddy Holly to John Lennon (who told Elvis in person that before him, there was no-one) to Bob Dylan to David Gilmour to Al Green to Cher to Mick Fleetwood to Elton John to Isaac Hayes to Bruce Springsteen have gone on record about the illumination in their lives of first hearing Elvis.

Guitar greats Eric Clapton and Jimmy Page have both cited Scotty Moore's guitar on 1955 hit "Baby Let's Play House" as what got them hooked on guitar.

The eureka moment of discovering Elvis was not always to do with his Fifties rock 'n' roll releases, either. Harry Nilsson cited the soundtrack to *Frankie and Johnny*, in which Elvis combines Dixieland music with a "Sixties sensibility," as a major influence on his own later work.

Both John Lennon and Bob Dylan went into a deep depression for weeks when they heard that Elvis had died.

In the late Seventies, when many punk musicians reviled Elvis as part of the antiquated establishment, The Smiths put a picture of young Elvis on one of their early singles.

Beastie Boy Mike D said Elvis was a major influence on the band because "He was the first person to sport B-boy gold."

The first record Billie Joe Armstrong of Green Day ever bought was Elvis Presley's *The Sun Sessions*.

The most successful rock band of the past twenty years, U2, have made Elvis tribute songs and included Elvis in the 2007 video parade of twentieth century icons in the video to their song `Window In The Skies."

JOHNNY CASH: "Every show I did with him, I never missed the chance to stand in the wings and watch. We all did. He was that charismatic."

WAYLON JENNINGS: "His records just stirred something in me. Then, and for the rest of my life, there was nobody like him."

Elvis with George Hamilton

GORDON STOKER OF THE JORDANAIRES: "Elvis inspired guys to pick up a guitar and start singing. He inspired me to stay in the business. He made me want to sing more, and sing better, and try to do a good job at everything I did."

JOHN LENNON (TO ELVIS): "Before there was you there was no one."

BOB DYLAN: "When I first heard Elvis' voice I just knew that I wasn't going to work for anybody; and nobody was going to be my boss... Hearing him for the first time was like busting out of jail."

JIM MORRISON: "Elvis is the best ever, the most original. He started the ball rolling for us all. He deserves the recognition."

ROGER DALTRY: "I had always wanted to be like Elvis, to be a Rock 'n' Roll star, but I couldn't sing so I joined a mod band instead."

BRIAN SETZER: "I don't think there is a musician today that hasn't been affected by Elvis' music. His definitive years - 1954-57 - can only be described as rock's cornerstone. He was the original cool."

ISAAC HAYES: "Elvis was a giant and influenced everyone in the business."

AL GREEN: "Elvis had an influence on everybody with his musical approach. He broke the ice for all of us."

MICK JAGGER: "No-one, but no-one, is his equal, or ever will be. He was, and is supreme."

ROD STEWART: "Elvis was the king. No doubt about it. People like myself, Mick Jagger and all the others only followed in his footsteps."

ELTON JOHN: "If it hadn't been for Elvis, I don't know where popular music would be. He was the one that started it all off, and he was definitely the start of it for me."

KEITH RICHARDS: "Before Elvis, everything was in black and white. Then came Elvis. Zoom, glorious Technicolor."

CLIFF RICHARD: "I owe Elvis my career and the entire music business owes him its lifeline."

PHIL SPECTOR: "You have no idea how great he is, really you don't. You have no comprehension - it's absolutely impossible. I can't tell you why he's so great, but he is. He's sensational."

K. D. LANG: "He had total love in his eyes when he performed. He was the total androgynous beauty. I would practice Elvis in front of the mirror when I was twelve or thirteen years old."

MADONNA: "Without Elvis, you're nothing."

MUSICAL INSTRUMENTS

Elvis played proficient rhythm guitar and a pretty mean piano, but so accomplished was his voice as a maker of music that he never learned to play any instrument beyond what sufficed for his own accompaniment. According to Jack Clement, "Elvis could have been a hell of a musician... But he just never bothered to learn more chords. He didn't need to, really. He was having a ball—really enjoying it."

In his early years, Elvis would sometimes mess around on drums too—he is reputed to have made a cameo on the skins with Onie Wheeler in January 1955. He definitely picked up and played bass on 1957 number "Baby I Don't Care." The first time he played the piano live in concert was in the mid-Seventies.

D.J. Fontana: "He was a quick learner, so he could play any instrument - fairly decent."

MUSICALS

See THEATER PRODUCTIONS

"MY BABE"

Elvis sang this 1955 "Little Walter" Jacobs hit, written by Willie Dixon and Charles Stone, in blues overdrive at his August 1969 Las Vegas shows (after a set of jokey false starts). The song—actually a secular version of Sister Rosetta Tharpe's "This Train"—was initially released on *From Memphis To Vegas* and soon after on *Elvis In Person at the International* Hotel. It also appeared on 1983 album *Elvis Sings The Blues*. A version recorded during the following night's show appeared on *Elvis Aron Presley* in 1980. Another live performance from this Vegas engagement came out on *Today, Tomorrow & Forever*. After 1969, Elvis only sang this song a few times more live in 1971 and 1972.

"MY BABY LEFT ME"

This thumping rockabilly Crudup tune bears more than a passing similarity to Elvis' first ever single "That's All Right (Mama)." As the B-side to Elvis' second single for RCA, it perpetuated the winning Sun formula of a blues side paired with a ballad, in this case A-side "I Want You, I Need You, I Love You." Recorded at RCA's New York studios on January 30, 1956, the single shipped on May 4, 1956, and sold a total of 1.3 million discs. It came out on EP *The Real Elvis* a few months later, but did not make its album debut until 1959 release *For LP Fans Only*. Later album releases include *Worldwide Gold Award Hits Vol. 2*, *This Is Elvis*, *Reconsider Baby*, *The King Of Rock And Roll*, the CD issue of *Elvis' Golden Records Vol. 1*, *Elvis '56*, *Artist Of The Century* and *Elvis R 'n' B*.

A 1970 rehearsal of the song in preparation for *That's The Way It Is* has made it onto later releases associated with the documentary.

Elvis reprised the song half a dozen times in concert in 1974. Live versions from this period are on *Elvis Recorded Live On Stage in Memphis* and *Live in Las Vegas*. In 2006 FTD released another live version from 1974 on *I Found My Thrill*.

"MY BOY"

Elvis first performed this Richard Harris tearjerker in Las Vegas in the summer of 1973. Originally written in French by Jean Claude Francois and Jean-Pierre Boutayre as "Parce que je t'aime mon enfant," the song had been anglicized by Bill Martin and Phil Coulter and brought to an English-speaking public by the Irish actor in 1971.

Elvis recorded the song at Stax on December 12, 1973. In the US, the track first appeared on the *Good Times* album. RCA subsequently released the song as a single in the US in January 1975, backed with "Thinkin' About You." It just made it to #20 in the charts, selling a little under 200,000 copies, but it became a big hit in the UK.

The song subsequently appeared on the following albums: *Always On My Mind*, *Our Memories of Elvis* (no overdubbing), *Walk A Mile In My Shoes*, the 2000 re-issue of *Promised Land* and *Hitstory*.

Live versions have appeared on *Live in Las Vegas* and FTD disks *Big Boss Man* and *Dixieland Rocks*. Elvis singing the song live before he laid it down at Stax can be found on numerous bootlegs (three versions are on *Take These Chains From My Heart*) and on 2004 FTD release *Closing Night*.

"MY COUNTRY, 'TIS OF THEE"

The melody of the British national anthem, with patriotic American words penned by Samuel F. Smith in the 1830s, served as an unofficial national anthem for the US for many years that century. Elvis gave it a whirl in July 1970 during rehearsals for *Elvis: That's The Way It Is*. It has only appeared on unofficial releases including *Electrifying*.

"MY DESERT SERENADE"

Stanley Gelber wrote this *Harum Scarum* soundtrack song, delivered to tape professionally by Elvis on February 25, 1965 in Nashville. Aside from a reissue on the *Double Features* release for *Harum Scarum*, the only other official releases of this song are an alternate take on *Today, Tomorrow & Forever* and a selection of outtakes on the FTD release for the film.

"MY HAPPINESS"

Elvis chose to record this popular ballad at his first ever recording session, for which he paid $3.98 (Ernst Jorgensen puts the going rate at $8.25 for a two-sided acetate) in the summer of 1953 at Sam Phillips' Memphis Recording Service Studio. Elvis told Studio assistant Marion Keisker that he was recording the song for his mother. His voice on the recording was hopeful rather than forceful. Elvis had apparently serenaded more than one girlfriend with the tune before plucking up the courage to walk into Phillips' premises at 706 Union Ave.

The song was only released four decades later on *The Great Performances*, since when it has appeared on *The King Of Rock 'N' Roll*, *Sunrise*, *The Complete Sun Sessions* and independent release *Memphis Recording Service*.

Composed 20 years before Elvis recorded it by Betty Peterson and Borney Bergantine, "My Happiness" had been *Billboard*'s "Record of the Year" in 1948 for The Steeles. It was later covered by the Pied Pipers and Ella Fitzgerald.

"MY HEART CRIES FOR YOU"

In 1966, Elvis sang this early Fifties hit for Dinah Shore and later Guy Mitchell, written by Percy Faith and Carl Sigman. The home recording was released after Elvis' death on *A Golden Celebration* and *The Home Recordings*.

"MY LITTLE FRIEND"

Elvis recorded this song, composed by Shirl Milete, at American Studio on January 16, 1969. It was released as the-B-side to "Kentucky Rain" in January 1970, and soon after on the LP *Almost In Love*.

Since then, the track has appeared on *From Nashville to Memphis* and *Suspicious Minds: The Memphis 1969 Anthology*.

"MY WAY"

Elvis' first recording of this classic remembrance past track on June 10, 1971 in Nashville was never released in his lifetime—indeed, it didn't see the light of day until 1995 anthology *Walk A Mile In My Shoes*. The first Elvis version of this

Lost Elvis photo from Loving You

song to be released was the one from his *Aloha From Hawaii Via Satellite* repertoire, though he began singing the song live during his summer 1972 season in Las Vegas.

Indelibly associated with Frank Sinatra, the track actually first came out in France as a love song called "Comme d'Habitude," written by Claude François, Jacques Revaux and Gilles Thibaut. Sinatra recorded the song in 1969 after asking Paul Anka if he had any good new material — Anka had just the thing, an English version of a song he had heard on TV on a trip to France. Sinatra's version sold a million copies in the States; it stayed on the UK charts for more than two years. Singers from David Bowie to Sid Vicious have also covered the tune (Bowie actually wrote the first English version, titled "Even A Fool Learns To Love"; the Vicious version is typically sardonic).

"My Way" was an obvious choice for Elvis' first posthumous single, with "America The Beautiful" on the B-side. On release, it made it to #22 on the Hot 100 and went on to sell over a million copies.

Alternate live versions on official releases include *The Alternate Aloha*, *Elvis in Concert*, *This Is Elvis*, *Elvis Aron Presley*, *Platinum: A Life In Music*, *Elvis By The Presleys* and *Elvis Live*; it's also on FTD concert issues *Summer Festival*, *New Year's Eve*, *Unchained Melody* and *Spring Tours '77*.

▬▬▬▬▬▬▬▬▬▬▬▬▬▬▬

ELVIS SAID IN 1970: "That's a very good song, ladies and gentlemen, but I wouldn't want it associated with my own personal life."

▬▬▬▬▬▬▬▬▬▬▬▬▬▬▬

"MY WISH CAME TRUE"

The B-side to "A Big Hunk of Love," shipped on June 23, 1959, reached #12 and sold over a million copies. Elvis laid down his mannered adaptation of this Ivory Joe Hunter song, complete with exuberant choral backing, almost two years earlier: the released version is from Radio Recorders on September 6, 1957, though he tried to improve that performance on February 1, 1958 just before shipping out for the draft. Some sources state that Elvis attempted a gargantuan eighty takes of this song before settling for a master.

The track made its album debut on *Elvis' Gold Records Vol. 2*. Later appearances include *Worldwide Gold Award Hits Vol. 2*, *The King Of Rock And Roll* and *Hitstory*.

"MY WOMAN, MY WOMAN, MY WIFE"

Elvis sang this 1970 Marty Robbins Grammy-award winning song during a 1976 concert in San Diego.

"MYSTERY TRAIN"

One of Elvis' most emblematic songs, Elvis laid down the B-side to his fifth and final single on Sun Records (Sun 223) paired with "I Forgot to Remember to Forget" on July 11, 1955. After the track was re-released by RCA in November that year, it rose to #11 on the *Billboard* country chart as Elvis dawned on America.

The track had previously come out in 1953 on Sun Records, sung by Herman (Little Junior) Parker and his band the Blue Flames; Parker shared the songwriting credit with Sam Phillips. The day Elvis recorded the song at Sun, drummer Johnny Bernero provided the percussion.

The pared-down and essential song is a development of the shuffling train-rhythm songs popular in early blues (Lonnie Johnson), hillbilly (the Carter Family and Bill Monroe) and then rock 'n' roll (Bo Diddley).

Elvis' joyous Sun rendition of "Mystery Train" reappeared on October 1956 EP *Any Way You Want Me* and 1959 album *For LP Fans Only*. It has since graced anthologies *The Sun Sessions*, *The Complete Sun Sessions*, *The King Of Rock 'N' Roll*, *Platinum: A Life in Music*, *Sunrise*, the CD issue of *Elvis' Golden Records Vol. 1*, *Artist Of The Century*, *Elvis at Sun*, *Elvis R 'n' B* and *The Essential Elvis Presley*.

On Elvis' post-Hollywood return to the stage he often sang this song live as it lent itself well to a medley of early hits. The first time he tried this, on his return to Las Vegas in 1969, he paired an R 'n' B version of the song with "Tiger Man" (released on *From Memphis To Vegas/Elvis in Person* and more recently on *Elvis Live*). Another night's show was selected for inclusion on *Collectors Gold*, while FTD releases *Elvis at the International* and *All Shook Up* feature alternates from the same Las Vegas run.

Elvis used the "Mystery Train" / "Tiger Man" medley as a warm-up jam for his June 1970 recording session in Memphis Nashville (released in 2002 on FTD disc *The Nashville Marathon*). Live versions from the Vegas season that year are on *That's The Way It Is - Special Edition* and FTD release *The Way It Was*. The song also features in his other Seventies concert documentary, *Elvis on Tour*.

Later concert performances of "Mystery Train" medleys are on *Elvis Aron Presley* and on FTD discs *One Night In Vegas*, *The Impossible Dream*, *Closing Night*, *Dinner At Eight* and *Spring Tours '77*.

Bizarrely, the song was used during the War in Iraq as a soundtrack to an amateur video of Iraqi contractors shooting at civilians. More felicitously, in 2006 the song was covered by Bruce Springsteen as part of his Seeger Sessions release and tour.

MYSTICISM

It is hardly surprising that with millions of people worshipping him, Elvis spent years trying to work out why he of all the young guitar-toting hopefuls in the world was picked for such anomalous and enduring fame.

To answer this question, in the mid-Sixties Elvis turned his energies and attentions to a spiritual quest that took him through yoga, Eastern religions and mysticism. Elvis came to the conclusion that there was some kind of special purpose to his life, a reason why all of this had happened to him, and that was to use his powers for good. That he had such powers was constantly reinforced whenever he was on stage and in more intimate situations when he had an almost mesmeric hold on people—countless people have reported that Elvis' charisma was so great that they could sense his presence before he even entered the room.

At one time or another, Elvis subscribed to a number of esoteric and mystic beliefs. He sometimes talked about his own particular version of

reincarnation that could be described as "only the strong survive": powerful people have the power to return.

Elvis believed that he had the power to heal through the laying on of hands, transferring the pain away through his own fingers. When one of the guys in his entourage was in pain, he would put his hands on the area that hurt and tell them that he was drawing out the pain. His belief in his powers was strengthened by his pals invariably reporting that they felt better afterwards; they would not want to disappoint him. An entourage member recounted an episode when Elvis tried to prove his special powers by stopping the car in the desert near Palm Springs and focusing hard on the single tiny cloud in the sky to try and get it to disappear. Ten minutes later, the guys in the entourage said that they'd seen it change shape.

Priscilla writes that Elvis explained the stars were propelled through the universe by energy. During his Sixties inquiring stage he would see strange sights in mundane things: angels in the water pumped out by sprinklers or faces in the textured paint on a ceiling. She believes he made this stuff up to keep boredom at bay at a time in his life when his work brought him no satisfaction.

Red West recalls a time that Elvis ordered his caravan to stop in the desert where Highway 66 approaches the Grand Canyon and told everyone to look up at the sky. Red West saw "a giant cloud formation above . . . this cloud formation is formed in the shape of two very definite likenesses of two heads. One was Elvis Presley and one was Joseph Stalin." In Larry Geller's telling of this same anecdote, there was one cloud, it looked like Joseph Stalin, and the event took place hours after Elvis had asked Geller why he had received no sign that his spiritual and religious inquiry was leading somewhere. As the cloud formation of Stalin turned into a representation of Jesus Christ, Elvis ecstatically interpreted the moment as a sign that he had been filled with divine love, and that he had just been granted a revelation of Christ and the Anti-Christ.

A number of friends and relatives have written that Elvis believed in mind-reading, and often performed demonstrations with members of entourage of his skills. Larry Geller puts this down to Elvis' great perception and intuition, plus that fact that he lived in close proximity to these people for many years.

To friends, Elvis passed on his belief that if you willed for something strongly enough, you could make it happen—the thesis that underlies many a modern self-help book. He is said to have proved this theory to Kathy Westmoreland by making a cloud in the shape of a poodle disperse. Elvis told pianist Tony Brown, "No one can deny you of what you're meant to have if you want it bad enough."

▬▬▬▬▬▬▬▬▬▬▬▬▬▬▬

RED WEST: "I have seen some strange things happen with that man, and I just can't think they are all coincidence."

DAVE HEBLER: "I have seen him manipulate crowds like he was Hitler. It was weird, man."

LARRY GELLER: "I've read that Elvis studied Buddhism, practiced bending spoons, held séances through which he contacted his mother, and believed that after his death he would return in the spirit and the body of someone else. None of the statements is true."

▬▬▬▬▬▬▬▬▬▬▬▬▬▬▬

NADEL, ARTHUR
(1921-1990)

Elvis' director on *Clambake* (1967) only directed one other movie, though he directed frequently for TV from the late Fifties to the late Seventies. At the *Clambake* wrap party, Elvis' entourage gave Nadel a friendly pie in the face—he was practically the only person on set who had not been "pied" during shooting.

NAMES

Elvis is one of the rare few who has reached the apogee of fame: being known by his first name only.

His exotic and memorable moniker was his father's doing. Vernon recycled his middle name for his son's first name. Though hardly common, there were one or two other Elvises in Lee County, Mississippi, from where the Presleys hailed; according to census data, the name "Elvis" has been in the top 1000 US names for over a century. For all that, the way Vernon pronounced his son's name was more like "Evis"—he never pronounced the "l" (one source claims that in actual fact, the doctor who first filed the baby's name wrote it down as "Evis Aaron").

Elvis' middle name was also picked by Vernon, as a tip of the hat to his best friend Aaron Kennedy, though on his son's birth certificate Vernon spelled it with one 'a' only. In adulthood, Elvis preferred the more standard biblical spelling "Aaron," which in fact was how his birth was recorded in official state records. According to Marty Lacker, Elvis made a conscious decision to use the conventional spelling in 1966. The Elvis Presley Estate prefers the standard spelling (and the one that Vernon chose for Elvis' tombstone): Aaron.

Stillborn twin brother Jesse Garon was named after grandfather Jesse; as per local tradition, his middle name rhymed with his brother's.

The etymology of the name "Elvis" is said to derive from *alviss*, the old Norse word for "all wise." An alternate origin hails from Wales, as the anglicized form of Elwys. Incidentally, Wales also includes an area called Preseli, the western-most district in the province, which was the source of the stones used to build the prehistoric Stonehenge monument in England. Also in the running in the Elvis etymology stakes is a 6th-century Irish saint called Ailbhis. Some sources state that the name came over to America with immigrants from England and Scotland, where it was originally spelled "Helwiss" or "Helwys."

The origins of the name Presley have been variously ascribed to a variation of "Priestly," a "dweller by the Priest's wood," or alternately to an anglicized version of the German family name Pressler.

An inveterate seeker of meaning in everything around him, Elvis was acutely aware that his name is an anagram of "lives," though in the Fifties his detractors focused on the anagram "evils." During his spiritual phase, Elvis would say that "El" was a short form of "Elohim," God of the Ancient Hebrews, while "Vis" was an Indian word for strength.

The first time that Dewey Phillips spun an Elvis disc on the airwaves in July 1954, the DJ twisted the unfamiliar name into what sounded like "Elton Preston." The first time that Scotty Moore heard Elvis' name, he thought it sounded like "a name out of science fiction"; Elvis' other original band member, Bill Burk, heard the name and asked a pal, "What's an Elvis?" During his early performances, Elvis suffered all kinds of name indignities. At one time or another he was introduced as Elvin, Elvis Pressley, Ellis Presley, Alvis Presly or Elvis Prestley, the mistakes cropping up even on advertising bills for shows he was headlining. Elvis was still chuckling over this two decades later: he presented himself at a June 1974 concert in Texas as "Alvis Paisley."

On his penultimate "Stage Show" TV appearance (St. Patrick's Day 1956), as an Irish-themed shenanigan our man was billed as "Elvis O'Presley." Also in 1956, Prince Rainier III of Monaco, newly married to Grace Kelly, told the press that the one name they would not be giving to their first-born was "Elvis."

In the Army, Elvis' commanding officer addressed him curtly as "Presley."

In 1965, Elvis told a reporter that he would name any daughter of his "Gladys."

Elvis signed his checks "E. A. Presley." To those close to him, Elvis was simply "E," "El" or sometimes "Boss." Maids at Graceland called him "Mr. Elvis." Elvis' karate name, given to him by Kang Rhee, was "Tiger" or "Master Tiger."

Elvis gave nicknames to all of the important people in his life: friends, family, girlfriends and colleagues (see under individual entries).

Elvis used a number of aliases when he wished to travel incognito. Elvis and family traveled as the Carpenters when they went on vacation to Hawaii in May 1969—Dr. John Carpenter was the name of the character Elvis had played in the movie he had just completed, *Change of Habit*, and an alias he used a number of times.

When Elvis went to Washington in December 1970 to meet President Richard Nixon, Elvis stayed at a hotel under the name Jon Burrows. Sometimes he used the name Colonel Jon Burrows. Elvis gave out this name as a code name for close friends, so that they could get through by phone or send mail without it being submerged in the torrent of fan mail. A strand of Elvis-is-alivers believe that after feigning death, Elvis carried on his life under this assumed name.

Elvis developed an elaborate system of code names that allowed certain people to call him at Graceland without raising suspicion. Ursula Andress called and asked for "Alan"; Ann-Margret asked for "Bunny" or "Thumper."

During Elvis' hospital stay, medical tests were filed under the alias "Aaron Sivle" to ensure patient privacy.

The Colonel often referred to Elvis as "my attraction" or "my boy." Elvis and everybody else in his orbit called Parker "Colonel" rather "the Colonel." The Colonel announced himself as "Colonel Snow" to Vernon when he called him at Graceland.

For the record, the plural of Elvis is "Elvi."

Fans beware: research has shown that "Elvis" is one of the world's most popular (and therefore most easy-to-guess) computer passwords.

ELVIS MOVIE CHARACTER NAMES

Clint Reno (*Love Me Tender*)
Jimmy Tompkins / Deke Rivers (*Loving You*)
Vince Everett (*Jailhouse Rock*)
Danny Fisher (*King Creole*)
Tulsa McLean (*G.I. Blues*)
Pacer Burton (*Flaming Star*)
Glenn Tyler (*Wild in the Country*)
Chad Gates (*Blue Hawaii*)
Toby Kwimper (*Follow That Dream*)
Walter Gulick, aka Kid Galahad (*Kid Galahad*)
Ross Carpenter (*Girls! Girls! Girls!*)
Mike Edwards (*It Happened at the World's Fair*)
Mike Windgren (*Fun in Acapulco*)
Josh Morgan / Jodie Tatum (*Kissin' Cousins*)
Lucky Jackson (*Viva Las Vegas*)
Charlie Rogers (*Roustabout*)
Rusty Wells (*Girl Happy*)
Lonnie Beale (*Tickle Me*)
Johnny Tyronne (*Harum Scarum*)
Johnny (*Frankie and Johnny*)
Rick Richards (*Paradise, Hawaiian Style*)
Mike McCoy (*Spinout*)
Ted Jackson (*Easy Come, Easy Go*)
Guy Lambert (*Double Trouble*)
Scott Heyward / Tom Wilson (*Clambake*)

Joe Lightcloud (*Stay Away, Joe*)
Steve Grayson (*Speedway*)
Greg Nolan (*Live a Little, Love a Little*)
Jess Wade (*Charro!*)
Walter Hale (*The Trouble with Girls*)
Dr. John Carpenter (*Change of Habit*)

ROADS NAMED AFTER ELVIS

A ten-mile stretch of US Highway 51 South was renamed Elvis Presley Boulevard on January 19, 1972. Until the town started hanging the road signs on wires over intersections, there was a spate of souvenir-hunting thefts of "Elvis Presley Boulevard" road signs. At its northern end, the road is still Bellevue Boulevard, the name it had when Elvis purchased Graceland. Memphis also boasts Elvis Presley Plaza, just south of the downtown area.

The Elvis Aron Presley Memorial Highway is part of Highway 78 connecting Tupelo, Mississippi with Memphis, Tennessee. The 104-mile stretch of road was renamed in December 1977.

The street where Elvis was born in Tupelo was renamed Elvis Presley Drive on the second anniversary of his passing; this entire area of town was renamed Elvis Presley Heights at the same time.

There's an Elvis Presley Ave. in Shreveport, Louisiana.

The Mid-South Coliseum in Memphis was almost named the Elvis Presley Coliseum when it was built in the late Sixties.

Elvis' name graces streets as far off as Italy, where in 2007 the town of Parma named a street Via Elvis Presley.

PAUL SIMON: "His name was about the weirdest I'd heard. I thought for sure he was a black guy. My grandmother thought he was Jewish, she thought he was called Alvin."

NASH, ALANNA

Journalist and author of an as-told-to memoir of four of Elvis' closest friends, and a biography of Colonel Tom Parker.

Books:
Elvis, From Memphis to Hollywood, by Alan Fortas with Alanna Nash, Popular Culture Ink, 1992.
Elvis Aaron Presley: Revelations from the Memphis Mafia, by Alanna Nash, with Billy Smith, Marty Lacker and Lamar Fike, HarperCollins, 1995.
The Colonel, published by Simon & Schuster, 2003.

NASHVILLE

The capital of Tennessee, two hundred miles northeast of Memphis, was for most of Elvis' career a home from home for recording. In the century after its foundation, Nashville was known as the "Athens of the South" for its seats of learning and cultural opportunities. From the Nineteen Twenties, the popularity of the Grand Ole Opry brought the town a new reputation as Music City. Elvis recorded more than 200 songs at RCA's Nashville facilities between 1956 and 1971.

Elvis' first session for new label RCA was at 1525 McGavock Street on January 10 and 11, 1956, in a building owned by the Methodist TV, Radio and Film Commission. Elvis' initial experiences were not unalloyed joy. He had pointedly not been a success when he played the Grand Ole Opry in Nashville 1954, and he was not too satisfied with the results of his two 1956 recording sessions at the facility.

FOLK SONGS AND COUNTRY

JULY
Twenty-Five Cents

BLUE SUEDE SHOES

YES I KNOW WHY

HEARTBREAK HOTEL

I DON'T BELIEVE YOU'VE MET MY BABY

WHY BABY WHY

I WAS THE ONE

IF YOU DO DEAR

I WANT TO BE LOVED

ELVIS PRESLEY

THE LIFE AND LOVES OF ELVIS PRESLEY
INSIDE PHOTO STORY! WEBB PIERCE — REAL HOME BODY
WHAT MAKES HANK SNOW TICK ● A FARMYARD VISIT WITH EDDY ARNOLD

CHARLIE WALKER
Voice Of Texas

HOMER AND JETHRO
Story In A Nutshell

LEE SUTTON
Country Crusader

YOU & ME

SO DOGGONE LONESOME

WHAT AM I WORTH

IF YOU WERE MINE

I'VE CHANGED

HOW FAR IS HEAVEN

I'M MOVIN' IN

I'VE GOT FIVE DOLLARS AND IT'S SATURDAY NIGHT

Folk and Country Songs, 1956 magazine cover.

In consequence, he chose to do most of his Fifties sessions at Radio Recorders in Hollywood. He did not return to Nashville until the session he snuck in before departing for Germany on Army service in June 1958, for the first time using a mainly Nashville-based group of players to record a slew of up-tempo numbers. By this time, RCA had moved its operations a few hundred yards down the road to the new state-of-the-art Studio B at 30 Music Square West / Demonbreun Street.

To keep his long-anticipated first recording session after the Army in March 1960 a secret, local studio musicians were that told they would be working with Jim Reeves. Later that year, Elvis returned to Nashville to cut his first gospel album, *His Hand in Mine*.

Nashville was the obvious place for RCA to send Elvis to record studio material for the label and fit in any soundtrack work that couldn't be completed in Los Angeles. Elvis worked consistently in Nashville, his sound influenced by Nashville's matchless "A Team" of session musicians, who formed the core of Elvis' studio band through the Sixties and beyond.

Elvis once again abandoned Nashville after a particularly unproductive two-day session in early 1968. With his NBC TV Special, American Studio sessions and return to live performing to keep him busy, he did not return until June 1970, when he entered the most country-flavored period of his recording career. Elvis continued to record prodigious numbers of tracks in Nashville until his last ever completed session in town, in June 1971, when he laid down material for his final gospel album, *He Touched Me*.

After this date, RCA found it so hard to get Elvis into a studio at all that they were forced to rely on live recordings, and even then had to be content with what they could eke out of him in his home town, either at Stax studios or in his own den at Graceland.

In its twenty years of operation before closing down in 1977, RCA's Studio B generated so many chart-toppers that it earned the nickname "The Home of a Thousand Hits." The premises later became home to the Country Music Hall of Fame and Museum, and was returned to its original décor in the mid-Nineties. Since 2002, the studio has been used by students on the Mike Curb College of Entertainment and Music Business program. Tours of the studio are arranged through the Country Music Hall of Fame and Museum, which has since moved its main collection to a new location.

RCA's original Nashville recording facility on McGavock Street, where Elvis recorded "Heartbreak Hotel," was purchased by car dealer Lee Beaman in 1999. In early 2006, he tore the building down and made Joni Mitchell's lyric a reality by putting up a parking lot.

NASHVILLE MARATHON, THE

A 2002 FTD release of alternate and outtake Elvis in a mainly country mood from June 1970.

TRACK LISTING:
1. Mystery Train / Tiger Man (informal jam)
2. Twenty Days And Twenty Nights
3. I've Lost You
4. The Sound Of Your Cry
5. Bridge Over Troubled Water
6. How The Web Was Woven
7. The Next Step Is Love
8. I'll Never Know
9. Life
10. Love Letters
11. Heart Of Rome
12. Mary In The Morning
13. Sylvia
14. It's Your Baby, You Rock It
15. It Ain't No Big Thing
16. A Hundred Years From Now
17. Tomorrow Never Comes
18. Snowbird
19. Rags To Riches
20. Where Did They Go, Lord

National Academy of Recording Arts and Sciences (NARAS)

See AWARDS

NATIONAL GENERAL PICTURES

Elvis signed to do a picture for this studio in the fall of 1967. The one-picture deal ended up producing *Charro!* (1969), and added $850,000 in earnings to Elvis and the Colonel's pile.

NBC

In 1965, NBC's West Coast Vice President Tom Sarnoff initiated contact with the Colonel about the possibility of Elvis doing a film for TV. At this time, NBC was a sister-company to RCA, under the management of General Electric.

The Colonel floated the idea of an Elvis TV Christmas Special to Sarnoff in October 1967. As negotiations proceeded, the Colonel managed to insert a feature film into the deal as well. The final contract was worth $1.1 million plus a 50% share of profits on the movie—what turned out to be Elvis' last feature film, *Change of Habit* (1969), which NBC co-produced with Universal Studios.

As pre-production work began on the TV Special, the show's production team, led by Bob Finkel, persuaded Elvis to use the show as a look back over his whole career and remind the world just who he was; they also persuaded the Colonel to drop his cherished idea of an anodyne Christmas-themed show. This was one of very few occasions that the Colonel was outmaneuvered in business. Finkel and director Steve Binder's tenacity proved to be instrumental in resurrecting Elvis' career. The show, titled simply *Elvis* when first broadcast, stands as a document of Elvis in peak condition.

In 1973, NBC paid a million dollars for the right to create history by showcasing Elvis in the first ever world-girding "live" satellite broadcast, *Aloha from Hawaii via Satellite*. Perhaps the Colonel got his own back this time by ensuring that "live" only pertained to parts of the world that were not the United States.

NBC TV SPECIAL (AKA THE "COMEBACK SPECIAL" OR THE "'68 SPECIAL")

Colonel Parker's plan to pull Elvis' career out of a potentially fatal tailspin was to put him back on TV after an eight-year gap. The Colonel talked with NBC about a Christmas Special, modeled loosely on a Christmas radio show he had arranged for 1967, including a Christmas greeting from Elvis and new songs that they could sell over the festive season.

Bob Finkel was appointed show producer in March 1968. He immediately put his imprimatur on the project, suggesting to Elvis that he use the show to remind the world what he could really do. Elvis was immediately enthusiastic.

Finkel brought in director Steve Binder and his partner Bones Howe. While Elvis took a vacation in Hawaii, writers Chris Bearde and Allan Blye put together a structure in which Elvis looked back over his life in song, only to wind up back where he started . . . and go out on a Christmas song. The writers are said to have based the structure on Belgian playwright Maurice Maeterlinck's play *L'Oiseau Bleu* (*The Blue Bird*), a coming-of-age story in which a brother and sister travel far and wide in search of the blue bird of happiness only to discover it finally when they return home, having defeated the spirit of darkness.

With the assassinations of Martin Luther King and Robert Kennedy all too fresh in everyone's mind, at a late stage in the proceedings Binder asked vocal arranger Earl Brown to write a number to close the Special that conveyed Elvis' reaction to such dark times. Earl Brown filled the brief overnight with "If I Can Dream." Elvis was so impressed with this finale that for once he rode roughshod over the Colonel's objections.

Billy Goldenberg was hired as musical director on the show after Elvis' original choice—Billy Strange, with whom he had worked on his most recent film—was fired for not delivering an arrangement in time. Parker was not at all happy that this occurred; Strange had written "A Little Less Conversation," the planned single release for Elvis' upcoming film, and the song had originally been slated to serve as the linking music between the different segments. Elvis too was ambivalent about a new man coming in, especially when he heard that Goldenberg wanted to change his sound and bring a whole orchestra into the picture. Elvis only agreed to give it a try on condition that if he didn't like what they did in the studio, they'd make wholesale changes.

Elvis spent days rehearsing for the show in LA, practicing every single segment and pre-recording material. He was fully involved in making changes to the script and the running order; many songs had to be sacrificed for time and through-line considerations. At one stage, Elvis was so enthused with working on the show that he had a bed brought in to his dressing room so that he wouldn't have to waste time by going home. As rehearsals progressed, Steve Binder had the idea of inserting a segment that revealed the relaxed Elvis he saw during informal jam sessions. Parker vetoed the idea of taking cameras backstage documentary style, but then Elvis suggested calling in his original band members Scotty Moore and D.J. Fontana to replicate the feeling. Originally, the plan was to use just ten minutes of the jam session. In the end, the whole thing was shown right the way through.

At the Western Recorders studio sessions, Elvis threw himself body and soul into his work, particularly the new songs written for the show. Much of this material appeared on the associated album and was used during recording of the show as backing tracks to which Elvis sang live. Elvis also rehearsed in the dressing room for the live segment with original band members Scotty and D.J., a moment taped by Joe Esposito (from which tracks have appeared on *Platinum: A Life In Music*, a great many bootlegs and recent FTD releases *Burbank '68* and *Let Yourself Go*).

Recording of the show proper in Studio 4 at NBC Color City (3000 W. Alameda Ave. in Burbank) began on June 27 with two hour-long performances of the "informal" or "sit down" section with Scotty Moore and D. J. Fontana, according to many commentators the world's first ever unplugged session.

Before going out in front of a live audience for the first time in seven years Elvis suffered a total crisis of nerves. Steve Binder and Joe Esposito feared that at the last minute Elvis was going to pull out altogether. The answer to Elvis' question "What if they don't like me?" was the answer to whether or not he still had a career. Elvis went out, won over the audience with his wit and humility, and performed with an intensity that he matched but never bettered in any of his subsequent live shows. He sweated so profusely that

Madison Square Garden promotional paper.

his leather suit had to be reshaped before the next evening's taping, for the "stand-up" section when he sang solo on a boxing-ring of a stage. On a final, extra day he re-recorded portions of the medley and the section in which, dressed in a white suit, he delivers the finale "If I Can Dream." Far more material was shot and recorded than was used in the finished show, even after sponsor Singer insisted on cutting the bordello scene (later released on the *One Night With You* and Special Deluxe edition video/DVD). Also cut from the show were fired-up renditions of "Tiger Man" and "Tryin' To Get To You."

The opening credits for the show, SINGER presents ELVIS, aired on the evening of December 3, 1968. Broadcast on a Tuesday night more than three weeks before Christmas Day—anything but a prime festive line-up slot—the show was the highest-rated TV program of the entire Christmas season, pulling in 42% of America's viewing public on the night and beating anything that NBC screened all year. The majority of TV critics may not have been convinced that the 33 year-old rocker was worthy of resurrection, but the show has ever after been known as the "Comeback Special" because it put Elvis squarely back at the top of the entertainment business. The show was repeated the following summer, with "Tiger Man" in place of the final token Christmas hold-out, "Blue Christmas."

The original album release became Elvis' first gold album since 1963, spending 32 weeks on the top LPs chart and peaking at #8. An unofficial bootleg of soundboard recordings from the rehearsals and recordings came out in the Eighties as *The (Complete) Burbank Sessions*. In 1998, BMG released two remastered albums of *Elvis*, as the show and accompanying album were originally titled, including significant amounts of previously unreleased material: the two-disc

Memories: The '68 Comeback Special, and *Tiger Man*, an album of Elvis' second sit-down show, issued for the first time in its entirety. Collectors' label FTD have released a great deal of previously (officially) unavailable versions of Elvis' work in preparation for these shows, including the first ever release on the label in 1999, *Burbank '68*, and then in 2006 *Let Yourself Go*, featuring previously unreleased outtakes from Elvis' June 20-24 rehearsal sessions and studio time.

The cut gospel medley featuring "Sometimes I Feel Like A Motherless Child" (sung by backing singers The Blossoms, not Elvis), "Where Could I Go (But To The Lord)", "Up Above My Head" and "Saved" has appeared on *Memories: The '68 Comeback Special*, gospel anthology *Peace In The Valley* and FTD release *Let Yourself Go.*.

Many video and DVD versions of the show have appeared over the years, including the 1985 release of the first sit-down show as *One Night With You* and more recently the 2004 3-DVD release *Elvis: '68 Comeback Special Deluxe Edition*, containing all available video footage, including all four of the shows performed in Burbank for the broadcast.

ELVIS SAID AT THE PRESS CONFERENCE: "I'm doing a television special now because we figure the time is right and today's music is right. Also, I thought I ought to do this special before I get too old."

ELVIS SAID AT THE START OF PRE-PRODUCTION: "I want everyone to know what I can really do."

ELVIS SAID DURING REHEARSALS: "I'm never going to sing another song I don't believe in. I'm never going to make another picture I don't believe in."

ELVIS SAID DURING THE SHOW: "It's been a long time, baby . . ."

ELVIS SAID AFTERWARDS: "I was petrified . . . as soon as I got hold of the mike, my hands were shaking."

PETER GURALNICK: "It was definitely not cool in 1968 to like Elvis."

PRISCILLA: "For two straight months he worked harder than on all his movies combined. It was the most important event in his life."

ADRIAN WOOTTON: "This is MTV twenty years before MTV."

SCOTTY MOORE: "We had a ball getting ready for the show. Looking at it now, it's obvious Elvis had a good time, too. We weren't trying to pick up any music awards or anything—just went out and had fun, and that's the way it came off."

T. G. SHEPPARD: "That was the jump-start for Elvis' career again—that special. I was amazed by how great he looked and how he still had that magnetism."

GREIL MARCUS: "It was the finest music of his life. If ever there was music that bleeds, this was it."

CREDITS:
NBC, Color.
Length: 76 minutes
Broadcast date: December 3, 1968

Directed by: Steve Binder
Produced by: Steve Binder, Bob Finkel (executive producer), Thomas Foulkes (associate producer), Bones Howe (producer), Norman Morrill (co-producer)
Written by: Chris Bearde, Allan Blye
Cinematography by: Jerry Smith
Film Editing by: Wayne Kenworthy, Armond Poitras
Art Direction by: Eugene McAvoy

Set Decoration by: Glen Huling, Jerry Masterson
Costume Design by: Bill Belew

CAST:

Elvis Presley	Himself
D.J. Fontana	Himself (drummer)
Scotty Moore	Himself (guitarist)
Buddy Arett	Himself
Barbara Burgess	Girl with 'Big Boss Man'
Alan Fortas	Himself
Susan Henning	Blonde Girl
Charlie Hodge	Himself (guitarist)
Fanita James	Herself (The Blossoms)
Jean King	Herself (The Blossoms)
Lance LeGault	Himself
Tanya Lemani	Belly Dancer
Darlene Love	Herself (The Blossoms)
Christopher Riordan	Dancer

ADDITIONAL CREW:

Claude Thompson	makeup artist
John Freschi	lighting director
William Cole	sound
Earl Brown	vocal arranger
Mike Deasy	musician
Jack Elliot	additional music arranger
Tom Foulkes	associate director
Billy Goldenberg	musical director
Yonko Inone	assistant to choreographer
Eddie James	assistant to choreographer
Ann McClelland	production assistant
Karl Messerschmidt	technical director
Patricia Rickey	production assistant
Jaime Rogers	choreographer
Claude Thompson	choreographer
Tom Diskin	unit production manager
Joe Esposito	unit production manager
Lamar Fike	unit production manager
Gene Marcione	unit manager

NBC TV Special—'68 Comeback (Original release title, simply Elvis)

The original vinyl release came out in late November 1968, two weeks before the show aired. It stayed on the Billboard Top 100 LP chart for 32 weeks, and achieved #8 at its highest. The tracks were recorded at Western Recorders and NBC's Burbank studios, and included excerpts of dialogue from the taped show.

TRACK LISTING:

1. Trouble / Guitar Man
2. Lawdy, Miss Clawdy / Baby, What You Want Me to Do
3. Heartbreak Hotel / Hound Dog / All Shook Up / Can't Help Falling In Love / Jailhouse Rock / Love Me Tender
4. Where Could I Go But to the Lord / Up Above My Head / Saved
5. Blue Christmas
6. One Night
7. Memories
8. Nothingville / Big Boss Man / Guitar Man / Little Egypt / Trouble / Guitar Man
9. If I Can Dream

The 1991 release, titled Elvis NBC TV Special, added the following tracks not released on the original:

"Don't Be Cruel," "Blue Suede Shoes," "Baby What You Want Me To Do" (reprise), "That's All Right (Mama)," "Tiger Man," "Tryin' To Get To You," "Let Yourself Go" and "It Hurts Me."

Neal, Bob
(1917-1983)

Bob Neal was responsible for managing the early part of Elvis' career, for 13 months promoting his shows across a broad swathe of the South before Colonel Parker stepped in and made the deals that brought Elvis national acclaim. Billy Smith considers Bob Neal the manager who really set Elvis on his way.

Bob Neal was a big name around Memphis, a DJ and a radio producer of music and drama shows on local station WMPS. He began in radio after coming to America from the Congo, where his parents had worked as missionaries, and became an announcer and DJ after moving to Memphis in 1942.

Neal was best known for his country show the "Bob Neal Farm Program," which he hosted from 1948. He began promoting shows in and around Memphis on the back of the popularity of this show, many of which young Elvis attended. By the time Elvis walked into Sun Studio, Neal was helming two regular daily shows on the radio, running a record shop and had recently started a management agency. Neal had the contract for music shows at the Ellis Auditorium in Memphis, as well as summer shows at the Shell in Overton Park. He also had a sideline in joke telling, which he sometimes indulged in as a warm-up for Elvis and his original band in the early days.

The same month that Sam Phillips first recorded Elvis at Sun records, he persuaded Neal to add Elvis to the bill of his "Hillbilly Hoedown" at Overton Park Shell in Memphis in the summer of 1954. Elvis' first manager Scotty Moore was happy to get some assistance from Neal with management. Neal had the contacts, and his radio shows were heard not just in Tennessee but in parts of Mississippi and Arkansas.

One of the first things that Neal did was to help Elvis out with money to buy a bigger car to travel between venues. Neal was instrumental in Elvis obtaining his first regular region-wide exposure at the Louisiana Hayride. It was Neal who invited Oscar Davis, an associate of Colonel Tom Parker, to the Eagle's Nest in Memphis to see Elvis in late November 1954. A month later, Elvis officially took on Bob Neal as his booking manager, The management contract made the local Memphis Press-Scimitar newspaper, in an item dated December 29, 1954, the day Elvis released his third single "Milkcow Blues Boogie" / "You're a Heartbreaker."

Neal's management contract officially commenced on January 1, 1955, a month when Elvis played multiple shows practically every day in Texas, Mississippi, Arkansas and Louisiana. Neal took a modest 10% of receipts; another 10% of the take was set aside for promotion. Elvis got half of the remainder; the band split the rest. Neal draw on a network of promoters to spread Elvis' renown, calling on Biff Collie in Houston, Bill Mack at Fort Worth, and Mae Axton in Jacksonville, Florida.

Elvis did what he could to help Neal out too. In early February 1955, he and his band played Messick High School and Messick Junior High to help Bob's son, Sonny, in his campaign to be elected to the student council.

On Sunday February 6, 1955, between Elvis' two shows at the Ellis Auditorium, Bob Neal brought together all of the men who were nurturing the young star's career. At Palumbo's Restaurant that day were Bob Neal, Sam Phillips of Sun Records, Colonel Tom Parker and his associate Tom Diskin. In the spring of 1955 Neal pressed Colonel Parker for a repeat booking on a Hank Snow tour. He also explored other avenues to take Elvis national, contacting TV show "Arthur Godfrey's Talent Scouts" on the recommendation of Cleveland Ohio DJ Bill Randle. Almost concurrently, Colonel Parker was asked by a William Morris agent to set up an audition at the same show. Parker agreed to pay for Elvis' trip to New York on condition that he represented Elvis on any bookings that might come out of the audition. Neal agreed to the Colonel's condition but the audition did not go well.

On March 15, 1955, Elvis signed a revised one-year agreement with Bob Neal, under which Neal earned a revised 15% commission. This contract was still in force eight months later when Colonel Parker completely took over Elvis' management.

Neal continued to send Elvis off on extensive tours, branching into new parts of Texas and New Mexico. In spring and early summer 1955, Elvis toured Chuck Lee, Gene Kay, and Dub Dickerson, and then with Ferlin Huskey, the Carlisles and Martha Carson. In late May 1955, Neal received a letter from the Colonel in which he said that if Neal wanted, he would be happy to "carry the ball," though he was already in negotiations with entertainment industry contacts. By early June, major recording companies such as MGM Records were beginning to make firm inquiries about buying out Elvis' contract from Sun Records. While Elvis was touring Texas in mid-June 1955, Neal traveled to the Colonel's base in Madison, Tennessee, where they hashed out an agreement: Neal would remain Elvis' manager in name but the Colonel would do all of Elvis' bookings and continue to seek a major label. Neal tried to convince Elvis that his future lay elsewhere rather than with Sun Records—much what Sun principal Sam Phillips was thinking as he considered the prospect, for the first time, of making a significant sum from one of his acts.

In September 1955, Neal negotiated a major pay rise for Elvis in a new one-year deal with the Louisiana Hayride, which took effect from November 11, 1955. Soon afterwards, with Colonel Tom expressing his strong disapproval at this deal, Neal extinguished their partnership and at least briefly, seemed keen to take over fully once again. By this time, however, the Colonel was close to completing the deal that would take Elvis from Sun to RCA. When Neal learned that Colonel Tom had told Sam Phillips that he was buying out Elvis' recording contract, Neal tried to intervene but it was too late. Neal was present at Sun Studio on November 21, 1955, when Sam Phillips handed over Elvis' recording contract to RCA executives. Neal continued to provide personal management services to Elvis for another four months, as he was contracted to do. Songwriter Mae Axton considers Neal was honorable throughout, and gracefully bowed out of the picture because he knew he had taken Elvis as far as he could go. In later interviews, Neal has said that he made a personal choice to continue with his life as it was, staying close to his family and his many music business interests in Memphis.

Days before Elvis' first RCA single "Heartbreak Hotel" came out, Neal told Colonel Parker that he could no longer accompany Elvis as road manager on his February 1956 tour because of his radio show commitments, bringing to an end his time as Elvis' manager.

Elvis remained on good terms with his former manager, or "Bobert" as he sometimes called him. In March 1956, Elvis was at Bob Neal's record shop signing autographs. On May 15, 1956, Elvis headlined the Bob Neal Cotton Pickin' Jamboree, part of the 22nd annual Cotton Carnival in Memphis.

Neal used some of the money from the Elvis deal to go into business with Sam Phillips and establish the Stars Incorporated agency. He went on to manage a number of Sun alumni, including Johnny Cash, Jerry Lee Lewis, Carl Perkins and Roy Orbison.

More than a decade later, Neal was a guest of Elvis' at his opening Las Vegas International Hotel show.

Bob Neal: "I was thinking one day and asked Elvis had he got a manager. He said 'No' and well I said I've never been a manager but let's try it. So I was his manager for about a year and a half."

On stage in Vegas 1973

"Nearer My God To Thee"

Elvis sang this traditional hymn in a medley with "Turn Your Eyes Upon Jesus" during rehearsals for *Elvis on Tour* on March 31, 1972. Though never released during his lifetime, it appears on gospel anthologies *Amazing Grace* and *Peace In The Valley*, plus bootlegs.

Nebraska

- Lincoln

Elvis played the University of Nebraska Coliseum on May 19, 1956. He was at the Pershing Municipal Auditorium on June 20, 1977, on his last ever tour.

- Omaha

Elvis and his band played the Civic Auditorium on May 20, 1956. The Auditorium Arena was the venue for shows on June 30 and July 1, 1974, and then again on April 22, 1976. His show here on June 19, 1977 was recorded by CBS for its TV special.

Nelson, Gene
(b. Leander Eugene Berg, 1920-1996)

An accomplished actor and dancer, after he hung up his dancing shoes Nelson directed Elvis movies *Kissin' Cousins* (1964) and *Harum Scarum* (1965). As a teenager, Elvis had seen Nelson when he was in Memphis promoting a movie.

On *Kissin' Cousins*, the multi-talented director played congas, rewrote the script and assisted with choreography.

Nelson won a "Most Promising Newcomer" Golden Globe for his acting in 1951. Highlights of his directing career include top-rated Sixties and Seventies TV series "Star Trek," "I Dream of Jeannie," "Gunsmoke," "Ironside," "The Streets of San Francisco" and "Starsky and Hutch."

Nelson, Ricky
(b. Eric Hilliard Nelson, 1940-1985)

The only singer to come remotely close to rivaling Elvis' record sales in the late Fifties and early Sixties, Nelson was the man for whom Life Magazine coined the term "teen idol." He started out on the family radio show "The Adventures of Ozzie & Harriet" before graduating to TV with his folks in "Here Come The Nelsons" as a twelve year-old. Nelson began singing as the wind-up to the TV show, and added a considerable air of respectability to rock 'n' roll—he was a clean-cut kid America had watched grow up.

Ricky's 1957 TV performance of Fats Domino hit "I'm Walkin'"—which he initially recorded because his girlfriend had said how much she liked Elvis' singing—helped to shift a million records in the following week. Nelson sang songs written by rockabilly pioneers Johnny and Dorsey Burnette, and was supported by a band of top musicians including Elvis' future guitarist James Burton and his then backing singers The Jordanaires.

The press rubbed their hands at the prospect of a rivalry which did not exist in real life. Nelson came along to the party Elvis threw after he played Los Angeles in November 1957.

Nelson's recording career remained strong until the British invasion struck in 1964. He continued in his parents' sitcom until the mid-Sixties and had a successful run in other TV projects and in the movies.

Nelson and his wife Kris saw Elvis perform in Las Vegas in August 1970. By this time, Rick Nelson as he preferred to be known, had put together his country rock outfit, the Stone Canyon Band.

After his death in a plane crash in 1985, Nelson was inducted into the Rock 'n' Roll and the Rockabilly Halls of Fame.

Nelson, Willie
(b. 1933)

Born in Fort Worth on April 30, 1933, Nelson took his time to make it to the top, working as a DJ and an unsuccessful singer in the Fifties before penning hit songs for others such as Patsy Cline, Faron Young and Billy Walker in the Sixties. His first big hit was "The Red Headed Stranger" in the mid-Seventies, when as part of the Outlaw Movement (outlawed from Nashville), he concocted an amalgam of different styles with a honky-tonk overtone and became a big crossover success. Nelson continued to score major hits through the Eighties and embarked on a screen career.

Elvis included Nelson's "Funny How Time Slips Away" in his opening sets in Las Vegas and sang it right through the Seventies. The last song that Elvis ever sang, at Graceland, was "Blue Eyes Crying in the Rain," an old Roy Acuff number that had been a huge hit for Nelson in 1975. Nelson's Eighties version of "Always On My Mind" was a bigger hit than Elvis'. Nelson also had some success covering "Heartbreak Hotel," and was part of the celebrity songster line-up on tribute album *A Country Tribute to Elvis*.

A founder member of country supergroup The Highwaymen, Nelson was inducted into the Country Music Hall of Fame in 1993. His outlaw attitude resulted in trouble with the IRS in the Eighties, and drugs woes after substances were found on his tour bus in the 2000s. Nelson is also known for founding Farm Aid, a festival that raises money to help impoverished farmers.

Nevada

- Las Vegas

Elvis' career as a bastion of the Las Vegas entertainment industry got off to an inauspicious start at the end of April 1956 when he began a residency at the Venus Room in the New Frontier Hotel, on a bill with Freddie Martin and His Orchestra. At precisely the moment that Elvis was scoring his first national pop chart #1 single with "Heartbreak Hotel" and his first album #1 with *Elvis Presley*, the older audience at the hotel was less than impressed and Elvis received a frosty reception on opening night. He managed to turn things round but the residency was not a success; by some accounts it was cut short from a month to two weeks. Recordings of Elvis during this engagement first appeared officially on *Elvis Aron Presley* in 1980. Elvis did not forget the slight and stayed away for the next thirteen years. Then, in 1969, he put together an impressive new band for the start of a month-long residency at the International Hotel beginning on July 31, 1969, the first of many, many shows that he cranked out at the rate of two per night. After opening acts the Sweet

Inspirations and comedian Sammy Shore, and after an almighty case of stage fright, Elvis slipped onto the stage and began his act with "Blue Suede Shoes." From start to finish the invited audience was on its feet. Elvis was in tip top form and received almost unanimous rave revues in the press. That very evening the Colonel met with International Hotel President Alex Shoofey to renegotiate Elvis' recently inked contract. Performances from this opening engagement were recorded for release on live album *From Memphis to Vegas*, which came out just a few months later (and was re-released the following year as *Elvis In Person at the International Hotel*). FTD brought out a recording of his August 23, 1969 midnight show in 2002, titled *Elvis At The International*, considered by some fans to be among Elvis' finest ever performances. Recent CDs from Elvis' initial burst of 57 shows at the International Hilton include 2001 release *Live in Las Vegas*, FTD's 2005 release *All Shook Up*, which features the famous "laughing version" of "Are You Lonesome Tonight?" that for years was only available on bootlegs, and BMG's 2007 release *Viva Las Vegas*.

For his second month-long engagement the following winter, Elvis revamped the song list and introduced a new look: the jumpsuit. He paraded several of these Bill Belew-designed garments, which allowed him to move more freely around stage and parade his karate-inspired moves. Once again, Elvis kicked off his tenure with a celebrity invite-only show. The Sweet Inspirations and Sammy Shore warmed up the already-enthusiastic crowd for another triumphant month. Some fans consider his final midnight performance of the engagement, on February 23, 1970, to be one of the pinnacles of his career. This show went on until three in the morning and included an interlude of Elvis on the piano performing a "Lawdy, Miss Clawdy"/ "Blueberry Hill" medley. Recordings from earlier in the engagement were issued that year as the album *On Stage* (and in 2004 came out as *Polk Salad Annie* on FTD).

For his third booking at the International, hotel musical director Joe Guercio led the orchestra for what the Colonel marketed as the "Elvis Summer Festival."

Elvis was back for a month from late January 1971 at the International Hotel, with the focus shifted towards ballads and inspirationals, and a rocking "Mystery Train" / "Tiger Man" medley—FTD's 2004 release *The Impossible Dream* offers a show from January 28, 1971.

By the summer of 1971, reviewers had begun to detect that Elvis' enthusiasm was beginning to wane. From this moment onwards, the International had passed into the hands of the Hilton Group and been renamed the Las Vegas Hilton.

At the start of 1972, the new additions Elvis made to his repertoire were maudlin, reflecting his state of mind after Priscilla had announced she was leaving. He played the hotel from August 4 through to Labor Day in 1972, enjoying visits from new girlfriends Linda Thompson and Cybill Shepherd. One show and some extra songs from this period was released in 2005 by FTD as *Summer Festival*.

Elvis' eighth engagement began on January 26, 1973. This residency was interrupted by cancelled shows as Elvis suffered from flu.

In the summer of 1973, though he rehearsed a lot of new material, after a more muted than usual audience reaction to his opening night on August 6, the "Elvis Summer Festival" returned to tried and tested crowd-pleasers. After the final show Elvis had his biggest ever row with Colonel Parker, who remonstrated against Elvis' entrance on lighting man Lamar Fike's back with a toy monkey round his neck, and a performance of "What Now My Love" on a bed. The last straw for the Colonel

Elvis performing at the New Frontier Hotel in Vegas 1956.

was Elvis' criticism of hotel management for threatening to fire a waiter called Mario who worked there (though by some accounts, Elvis took this step are the Colonel refused to intercede on his behalf). Elvis' swipes at management included altering the lyrics to "Love Me Tender" to "Adios you Muttha, Bye Bye Poppa too, To hell with the Hilton Hotel, And screw the showroom too." This concert was released officially on FTD under the title *Closing Night* in 2004.

Once again, Elvis rehearsed a great deal of new material before taking the stage at the Las Vegas Hilton Showroom in January 1974, though by now he was contracted for two rather than four weeks. The only songs that made the cut for the duration of the engagement were Larry Gatlin's "Help Me," Kris Kristofferson's "Why Me Lord," and Olivia Newton-John's hit "Let Me Be There." Elvis performed despite ongoing tooth and foot ailments. Shows from this engagement were released in 2006 on FTD album *I Found My Thrill*.

The summer of 1974 saw Elvis return to form in a revamped Las Vegas show featuring new songs and many more blues numbers that the *Hollywood Reporter* reviewed as the best show in three years: "[Elvis] looks great, is singing better than he has in years, and was so comfortable with his show—almost all new songs—the packed Hilton showroom gave him several standing ovations." Nevertheless, the new-look show was nowhere to be seen from the second night on, when the by now old 2001 theme and medleys returned. By the end of the run, Elvis was indulging in his famous and sometimes addled monologues, some of which have appeared on bootlegs such as *Desert Storm*.

The Colonel called off Elvis' planned January 1975 residency at the Las Vegas Hilton a month in advance, as Elvis was suffering from an ulcer compounded by general melancholia at turning forty. The engagement was rescheduled to run from mid-March. As usual, in rehearsals Elvis tried out new material, very little of which made it into the actual show, which this time ran from March 18, with the gala "invitation only" show held on the final night. In 2005, FTD brought out a concert from this period, titled *Big Boss Man*.

Ill-health got the better of Elvis again during his two-week summer engagement, beginning on August 18. In his opening show he spent most of the concert sitting down. In one show, he sang a song lying down. On August 21, the Hilton issued a press release saying that Elvis had been advised to cancel by his medical team. Elvis made up the dates from December 2, though on doctors' orders he reduced his nightly performances from two to one. The Hilton sold out every night, and enjoyed double the usual occupancy. FTD issued a December 1975 concert, *Dinner At Eight*, in 2002.

Elvis' final stint at the Hilton was in the run-up to Christmas 1976, in what was billed as a "Pre-Holiday Jubilee." Elvis began his residency on December 2, doing his best to fight fatigue but occasionally fluffing his lines. He ended in a sour mood with off-color comments: on December 12 he told his audience what members of his entourage had known for a long time, "I hate Las Vegas."

- Reno
Elvis took a day trip to Reno in November 1968, on a break from filming *The Trouble with Girls*. The first date he ever played in town was on November 24, 1976 at the Centennial Coliseum.

- Stateline (Lake Tahoe)
Elvis played the High Sierra Room at the Sahara Tahoe in Stateline, Nevada for two weeks in late July and early August 1971, earning $300,000. He returned for seventeen dates in May 1973, but had to call an early halt to the tour through illness and excess prescription drug use (FTD 2003 release *Takin' Tahoe Tonight* features a show from this run).. His May 1974 residency went more smoothly, though he did have to can-

cel two shows because of flu. Elvis made up the missed dates from 1973 with four nights (and eight shows) running from October 11, 1974. He later played an 11-day engagement at the High Sierra Theater from April 30 to May 9, 1976.

"NEVER AGAIN"

A Billy Edd Wheeler / Jerry Chesnut ballad that Elvis selected to record at his February 6, 1976 Graceland session . The song featured on the album *From Elvis Presley Boulevard, Memphis, Tennessee*. Later appearances are on *Our Memories of Elvis Vol. 1* (without overdubs) and the 2000 re-release of *Moody Blue*. An alternate came out on FTD release *The Jungle Room Sessions*.

"NEVER BEEN TO SPAIN"

In 1972, Elvis often sang this rousing tune in concert. The song was written by Hoyt Axton, son of Mae who scribed "Heartbreak Hotel," and had been a top 5 hit for Three Dog Night the year before.

The first Elvis version to come out on record was on 1972 disc *Elvis as Recorded at Madison Square Garden*, following his show there on June 10. A studio rehearsal prior to the shows filmed for 1972 documentary *Elvis On Tour* came out in 2004 on FTD release *Elvis On Tour—The Rehearsals*. Other live versions are on *Walk A Mile In My Shoes*, *An Afternoon In The Garden*, *Burning Love, Live In Las Vegas*, *Elvis: Close Up* and *Elvis Live*. It's also on FTD releases *Summer Festival*, *Writing for the King*, *An American Trilogy* and *Summer Festival*.

"NEVER ENDING"

Elvis recorded this Buddy Kaye / Phil Springer composition on May 26, 1963. It was released as the B-side to "Such A Night" in mid-July 1964 but failed to chart. It first appeared on an LP in 1967, as a bonus song to the *Double Trouble* soundtrack album, since when it has been reissued on *For The Asking (The Lost Album)* and *From Nashville to Memphis*.

The first take from the Nashville session came out on FTD album *Long Lonely Highway*.

"NEVER SAY YES"

. . . to another movie . . . Actually, this Doc Pomus / Mort Shuman soundtrack tune for *Spinout*, recorded by Elvis at Radio Recorders on February 17, 1966 was better than the average. Later releases are on *Elvis Sings Mort Shuman & Doc Pomus* and the *Double Feature* release for the movie.

Alternate takes may be found on *Today Tomorrow & Forever*, and the FTD *Spinout* re-issue.

NEW MEXICO

- Albuquerque
Elvis and his original band played the Armory on April 12, 1956. He played the last concert on his April 1972 nationwide tour here at the Tingley Coliseum on April 19.

- Carlsbad
Elvis played the Sports Arena on February 11, 1955, and the Legion Hut the following day.

- Hobbs
Elvis sang at the American Legion Hall here on April 27, 1955.

- Roswell
Elvis played a date at the North Junior High School Auditorium on Valentines Day, 1955, his first participation on the Hank Snow Jamboree tour.

"NEW ORLEANS"

Elvis laid down this Sid Tepper / Roy C. Bennett composition—songwriter Bennett's personal favorite of the many that the team wrote for Elvis —at Radio Recorders on January 5, 1958 for *King Creole* and release on the soundtrack EP (Vol. 1) and LP.

"New Orleans" is to be found on *Worldwide Gold Award Hits Vol. 2*, *Elvis Sings The Blues*, *The King Of Rock And Roll*, and *Platinum: A Life in Music*.

NEW YEAR'S EVE

A 2003 FTD 2-CD release of Elvis' December 31, 1976 New Year's concert at Pittsburgh, previously available on bootleg only.

TRACK LISTING:
DISC 1:
1. Also Sprach Zarathustra
2. See See Rider
3. I Got A Woman / Amen
4. Big Boss Man
5. Love Me
6. Fairytale
7. You Gave Me A Mountain
8. Jailhouse Rock
9. O Sole Mio / It's Now Or Never
10. My Way
11. Funny How Time Slips Away
12. Auld Lang Syne
13. Introductions
14. Blue Suede Shoes
15. Tryin' To Get To You
16. Polk Salad Annie
DISC 2:
1. Band introductions
2. Early Morning Rain
3. What'd I Say
4. Johnny B. Goode
5. Solos
6. Love Letters
7. School Days
8. Fever
9. Hurt
10. Hound Dog
11. Are You Lonesome Tonight?
12. Reconsider Baby
13. Little Sister
14. Unchained Melody
15. Rags To Riches
16. Can't Help Falling In Love
17. Closing Vamp

NEW YEAR'S EVE

After he made it big, Elvis organized his own New Year's entertainment with the exception of three years when he was the entertainment himself: in 1955 at the Louisiana Hayride, and in 1975 and 1976 at Pontiac and Pittsburgh respectively.

Elvis threw two parties at new home Graceland in the late Fifties before he was shipped off to Germany for his Army service. For the new year of 1959 and 1960 he held parties at his home in Bad Nauheim. He saw in 1961 at Graceland. The following year he was in Las Vegas, the only time that he deliberately stayed away from Memphis, where Vernon had just remarried.

For the last day of 1962 and 1963, Elvis hired the Manhattan Club in Memphis, where Rufus Thomas was the star turn. Elvis hired out the Memphian Theater to celebrate the incoming new year of 1965. He held parties once again at the Manhattan Club to see in 1966 and 1967, though he didn't actually show for the second party, where Willie Mitchell provided the sounds.

To ring in 1968, the year he became a father, Elvis threw a party at the Thunderbird Lounge at 750 Adams. Music was provided by Flash and the Board of Directors, the Bar Kays, Vaneese Starks and Billy Lee Riley.

For 1969 it was the same venue and a similar roster of musicians: The Short Cuts, Flash and the Board of Directors, Billy Lee Riley and B. J. Thomas.

The action moved to new club T.J.'s, where Alan Fortas was working, to see in 1970. Music that night was from house singer Ronnie Milsap, Flash and the Board of Directors, Vaneese Starks and Mark James.

T.J.'s was once again the venue to ring in 1971 with a similar band line-up.

Priscilla told Elvis she was leaving him at the end of 1971. Whatever he originally had planned, Elvis downscaled to a small Graceland gathering.

Elvis started 1973 with three days' solid movie viewing at the Memphian Theater. The following year's festivities were scotched by health problems. The start of 1975 saw Elvis in somber mood at Graceland as his fortieth birthday loomed.

For the first time in two decades, on December 31, 1975 Elvis had a working New Year with a concert at Pontiac, Michigan that grossed over $800,000. Elvis flew back home to Memphis and spent the rest of the New Year's celebration with Linda Thompson, Lisa Marie and selected pals watching Monty Python.

Elvis' last New Year's Eve alive was spent entertaining thousands at the Civic Center Arena in Pittsburgh, Pennsylvania.

NEW YORK

- Binghampton
Elvis came to the Broome County Veterans Memorial Arena on May 26 and 27, 1977.

- Buffalo
Elvis' first concert in New York State was at the Memorial Auditorium on April 1, 1957. He returned at the start of his 1972 tour on April 5. He began a tour on June 25, 1976 at the Memorial Auditorium.

- New York City
Elvis' first trip to New York City was to audition for the "Arthur Godfrey Talent Scouts" radio and TV show on March 23, 1955. He flew from Memphis with band members Scotty Moore and Bill Black for a 2:30 p.m. slot at 501 Madison Avenue. They did not get a call back.

He was back in town the following year for a far higher profile TV show. His second performance on "The Ed Sullivan Show" was shot at the Maxine Elliott Theater on West 39th St. He recorded some of his most iconic songs including "Blue Suede Shoes" and "Don't Be Cruel" in New York City in January and July 1956, and shot a revised ending for Love Me Tender in late October 1956 at the Junco Studio on E 69th St.

Elvis passed through the Brooklyn Army Terminal in September 1958, en route from Fort Hood to his Army posting in Germany.

He didn't play his first concert in the Big Apple until his Madison Square Garden exploit in 1972—he hadn't bothered coming to town for the shooting of his final feature, Change of Habit, which was set in Manhattan. Ever since he had

received a hail of deprecation from the New York press in the Fifties, Elvis had considered New York to be hostile territory for this particular Southern boy. The intense nerves he suffered before going on stage at Madison Square Garden spurred him to great heights. He garnered some of the finest reviews of his career for the four shows he gave between June 9 and 11, before 80,000 people including John Lennon, George Harrison, David Bowie, Bob Dylan and Art Garfunkel. His June 10 evening performance was recorded and released in record time on the album Elvis as Recorded at Madison Square Garden. The afternoon show was released on An Afternoon In The Garden in 1997.

ELVIS SAID TO A HOMETOWN AUDIENCE IN 1956: "You know, those people in New York are not gonna change me none. I'm gonna show you what the real Elvis is like tonight."

- Niagara Falls
Elvis played an afternoon and an evening show at the International Convention Center on June 24, 1974. He performed there twice more on July 13, 1975.

- Rochester
Elvis appeared at the Community War Memorial Auditorium on July 26, 1976, and on May 25, 1977.

- Syracuse
Elvis played the Onondaga War Memorial Auditorium on July 25 and 27, 1976.

- Uniondale
Elvis played the Nassau County Veterans Memorial Coliseum, within easy reach of New York City, on June 22, 23 and 24, 1973. He played two more shows there on July 19, 1975.

NEWTON, WAYNE
(B. 1942)

The once and future kings of Las Vegas have a number of things in common beyond being the highest-paid performers on the Strip in their time.

Born in Norfolk, Virginia on April 3, 1972, like Elvis Newton has Cherokee blood. Like Elvis, he has long been an exponent of the martial arts. Newton came to national prominence via TV, performing a dozen times on the Jackie Gleason Show—Gleason also gave Elvis his first break on national TV, on "Stage Show" in 1956.

Newton's "Danke Shoen" was a hit in 1963 but his career really began to take off in the Seventies. In the Eighties he took over Elvis' mantle in Las Vegas, winning the Entertainer of the Year award multiple times. His earnings were so vast that he could afford to buy a stake in the Aladdin Hotel (where Elvis and Priscilla were married in 1967) and became involved in breeding Arabian stallions, a pursuit of the truly rich. Newton has performed so many times in Vegas that the city has a Wayne Newton Day, and renamed the road running into town from McCarran Airport Wayne Newton Boulevard. In the Eighties, the National Enquirer ran an article reporting that Elvis' spirit visited and spoke with Newton.

Newton was invited to Elvis' inaugural Vegas performance at the International Hotel in 1969. In later years, Elvis occasionally joshed his audience by introducing himself as Wayne Newton.

Elvis recorded Newton's 1969 hit "Fool" in 1972. Years later, Newton wrote "The Letter," a song inspired by a desperate note Elvis reputedly wrote during his final tour of duty in Las Vegas.

Newton made a cameo in 2004 movie Elvis Has Left The Building.

NEWTON-JOHN, OLIVIA
(B. 1948)

Elvis added two Olivia Newton-John songs to his live show repertoire in the mid-Seventies: "If You Love Me (Let Me Know)" and the Grammy-award winning song "Let Me Be There." Both artists covered a songs including "My Boy" and "It's Midnight."

Born in Cambridge, England on September 26, 1948 but raised in Melbourne, Australia, Newton-John was one of the best-selling female singers of the Seventies and the early Eighties, taking an iconic role in Grease (1978) opposite John Travolta and monopolizing the #1 spot for ten weeks in 1981 with "Let's Get Physical." She began her long climb to fame with a spell in all-female group (and movie) Toomorrow, put together by the same team that brought the world The Monkees, and then became a regular on Cliff Richard's TV shows and concert performances in the early Seventies.

Newton-John took part in the tribute project A Country Tribute to Elvis. She has continued recording and touring, and is a successful businesswoman in a number of fields.

"NEXT STEP IS LOVE, THE"

A country crackle in his voice for this Paul Evans / Paul Parnes track that Elvis recorded in Nashville on June 7, 1970, initially for release as the B-side to "I've Lost You."

A rehearsal of the song features in the That's The Way It Is documentary—a version that came out years later on FTD Release The Way It Was. A live performance from the stage of the International Hotel made its way onto That's The Way It Is Special Edition and FTD release One Night in Vegas.

The studio release later appeared on Worldwide Gold Award Hits Vol. 2 and Walk A Mile In My Shoes. Alternate takes from the original Nashville session are on Today Tomorrow & Forever and FTD release Nashville Marathon.

NEYLAND, ANNE

The actress who played Laury Jackson in Jailhouse Rock went out on at least one date with Elvis during filming, and visited him during his brief hospitalization at the Cedars of Lebanon in LA. Her first ever role was as a dancer in Singin' in the Rain (1952). She also had roles in Hidden Fear and Ocean's Eleven.

NICHOLS, CARL AND WILLY

Friends of Vernon and Gladys Presley, Carl Nichols worked as a contractor on improvements to Graceland after the Presleys purchased it (incurring a picket of Graceland because he was non-union). The couple accompanied Vernon and Gladys to LA to see Elvis shoot his second movie, and wound up as extras in Loving You. Vernon took the Nichols along to see Elvis during filming of Flaming Star in 1960.

NICHOPOULOS, DEAN
(B. 1955)

Dr. Nick's son was a friend of Elvis' and a regular racquetball opponent from the mid-Seventies. Dean was part of a large group of friends and family that Elvis treated to a winter vacation in Vail in 1976, and for a spell from 1975 was on the payroll helping with costumes and security.

NICHOPOULOS, GEORGE CONSTANTINE "DR. NICK"
(B. 1927)

Elvis first called out Dr. Nichopoulos in February 1967, on the recommendation of Barbara Little, girlfriend and future wife of George Klein's who worked at Dr. Nichopoulos's medical practice. "Dr. Nick," as he became known, paid a call on Elvis at his ranch, the Circle G. There was immediate friendship and complicity between the two, perhaps because of the nature of Elvis' ailment: saddle sores from Elvis' latest hobby, horseback riding. The doctor prescribed some ointment, they talked, and Dr. Nick obliged Elvis by telling Colonel Parker that his patient was not fit to travel to LA to start work on his next movie, *Clambake*. Marty Lacker, however, has said that Dr. Nick first treated Elvis in 1966 for a heavy cold.

Born in Ridgway, Pennsylvania, and qualified as a doctor at Vanderbilt Medical School in 1959, Dr. Nick has become a controversial figure since Elvis' death. As Elvis' personal physician, he was responsible for writing out prescriptions for tens of thousands of pills. He had the unenviable task of trying to combat Elvis' predilection for self-medication, which he did through placebos and replacement medicines. He also tried to close down Elvis' alternate supply lines, persuading members of the entourage and later his pilots to let him know when Elvis was trying to get a consignment of new meds delivered. Despite these good intentions, many fans have felt that Elvis' personal physicians was irresponsible in not standing up to his famous patient—though when he did, Elvis briefly fired him—and was ultimately part of the problem rather than the solution.

Dr. Nick began traveling with Elvis on tour in 1970. Out on the road, Dr. Nick administered the bewildering array of shots and pills that Elvis was sure he needed to perform. He was on hand when Elvis began to have health crises, and was the one who invariably persuaded Elvis to go into hospital to be weaned off drug dependencies.

As a way of making sure that Elvis didn't suffer the weight gains that were both a symptom and a cause of his encroaching health problems, Dr. Nick got Elvis to take up racquetball. After Elvis came out of hospital in early 1974, Dr. Nick put Elvis on a regime where he didn't self-medicate but instead received medicines either from Dr. Nick or from nurse Tish Henley.

From 1974, Dr. Nick was on call as a kind of live-in medical and general counselor. After he had done his normal day's work, Dr. Nick called in to see Elvis after he woke up and sometimes stayed for a few hours. These regular visits were vital if Elvis was to be kept fit and interested, and therefore away from places like Las Vegas where he could easily fall back into prescription drug-abuse. For a spell, Dr. Nick made sure that he was present whenever Elvis visited another physician or dentist, to prevent him from talking them into writing additional prescriptions. He even contacted the makers of Dilaudid to order a batch of specially-made pills that looked identical to the real thing but were placebos.

In July 1975, Elvis flew into a rage at his doctor for cutting down on his medication (Dr. Nichopoulos took away a boxful of medications Elvis had obtained from a dentist out on tour, and refused to give them back). Elvis was particularly resentful because this exchange took place in front of members of his entourage. Not long after this, a gun that Elvis was playing with accidentally went off and the ricocheting bullet bounced off Dr. Nick's chest. Thankfully, it caused him no harm. Soon after, Elvis lent his doctor a $200,000 interest-free sum to build himself a new home. This and a further loan in 1977 further complicated the relationship between the doctor and his famous patient.

Dr. Nick says that he never charged Elvis for house calls because he considered himself to be a friend. He only billed Elvis while away on tour, for the amount he would have earned if he had stayed at home working at his practice. Over the years, Elvis gave Dr. Nick many pieces of jewelry and watches.

The doctor flew out to see Elvis on vacation in Vail, Colorado, in early 1976, bringing his family along for the ride. That year Elvis fell out with Dr. Nick over a business venture to launch a nation-wide chain of racquetball clubs. On Elvis' next tour, he took along Las Vegas doctor Dr. Ghanem instead of Dr. Nick.

Dr. Nick was restored to his habitual role when the Colonel called him in to get Elvis back into shape after tour reviews were scathing about his physical condition. Dr. Nichopoulos agreed, on condition that Elvis apologized—one of the very few times that Elvis ever said he was sorry.

Nichopoulos rushed to Graceland on August 16, 1977 when Elvis was discovered laying face down in his bathroom by girlfriend Ginger Alden. He arrived just in time to ride in the ambulance as Elvis was taken to Baptist Hospital—though as with much surrounding Elvis' death, this version of events has been disputed. Dr. Nick returned to Graceland to break the news to Vernon, worried that it might give him a heart attack.

Dr. Nick was a pallbearer at Elvis' funeral. Not long afterwards, Nichopoulos believes that an assassination attempt was made on his life when a friend sitting next to him at a football game was shot in the shoulder.

Alanna Nash calculates that Dr. Nick pre-scribed close to 20,000 pills in the last three years of Elvis' life. The Tennessee Board of Medical Examiners, which in 1980 acquitted Dr. Nick for overprescribing drugs not just to Elvis but to Jerry Lee Lewis and a number of other patients, stated that he prescribed 5,300 pills and doses of medicine to Elvis in 1977 (the figure is 10,000 in some accounts). Before he was cleared of acting unethically—many members of Elvis' entourage testified on Dr. Nick's behalf—his license was suspended for three months.

In recent years, Dr. Nichopoulos has appeared in Elvis documentaries *Elvis: His Life and Times* and *The Burger & The King*. His medical license was revoked permanently in 1995, after he was accused once again of over-prescribing. Briefly, he worked as tour manager for Jerry Lee Lewis. His collection of Elvis artifacts was a touring exhibit in recent years, titled "Memories of Elvis." His most recent job has been assessing disability insurance claims by FedEx employees.

DR. NICHOPOULOS: "He liked to talk about medicines and the PDR, and what kind of symptoms do you get with this and what you have—I was amazed at how much he had educated himself."

DR. NICHOPOULOS: "Elvis would call other physicians to get extra drugs, so I had to get full co-operation from everyone around him on trying to limit those extras he was getting."

PETER GURALNICK: "I think if you were looking for an indictment, it would not be of Doctor Nick, who's been used as a scapegoat for the whole thing, but it would be of an approach to medicine that permeates our society."

LAMAR FIKE: "How many doctors do you know who 'borrow' six-figure amounts from their patients?"

BILLY SMITH: "He really was trying to help him, I think. But Elvis outsmarted him."

MARTY LACKER: "Dr. Nick truly cared about Elvis but he got caught up in a lifestyle that he shouldn't have and it made him do things he shouldn't. He's a good man and people have been too harsh on him."

NICKNAMES

Marion Keisker used the mnemonic "Timothy Sideburns" on the first vanity acetate that Elvis paid to record at the Memphis Recording Service in the summer of 1953. To make herself understood around Sun before he joined the artists' roster, she referred to him as "the kid with the sideburns."

Elvis no doubt liked this better than "Elvy," which he was called as a kid when he wasn't being accused of being a Mama's Boy.

As the world struggled to pigeonhole what kind of music Elvis was actually making, he was originally known as the "hillbilly cat"—hillbilly at the time meant "country and western" rather than hick. In the early days, Tom Diskin referred to Elvis as "The Cat" when talking with Colonel Parker, who soon adopted the nickname "my boy" for Elvis, or "son" directly to his face. In Hong Kong, Elvis later became known as "King Cat."

In January 1955, DJ Frank Page introduced Elvis to the Louisiana Hayride audience at Shreveport as the "Memphis Flash." In September that year, he was billed as "The FireBall Star of Records and the Famous Louisiana Hayride" at a Jamboree event in New Orleans. In late 1955 and early 1956, promotional material referred to Elvis as "the King of Western Bop," while his mesmeric effect on female fans brought him the accolade "King of Swoon." The "King" moniker stuck once people settled on rock 'n' roll as the name for Elvis' new-fangled music; *Variety* referred to him as "the King of Rock 'n' Roll" in October 1956; columnist May Mann has also claimed credit for crowing him the King—a nickname Elvis did his best to disavow.

Elvis also picked up a string of other nick-names, including "Mr. Teenager," "Sir Swivel Hips," "Wiggle Hips," "The Country Cat," and the "Hillbilly Bopper."

He picked up his least-favorite sobriquet "Elvis the Pelvis" during his early days touring in Texas. In a rare outburst to the press—usually, Elvis was unfailingly polite—he fumed, "I don't like to be called Elvis the Pelvis. I mean, it's one of the most childish expressions I've ever heard coming from an adult. Elvis the pelvis. My pelvis has nothing to do with what I do."

In 1956, promotional material referred to Elvis as "Mr. Dynamite." He was advertised as the "Folk Music Fireball" in Mississippi in early 1956, and as "Country Music's Mr. Rhythm" in Florida. For his first Las Vegas booking at the New Frontier Hotel, Colonel Parker came up with the slug line "America's Only Atomic Powered Singer." In 1960, *Time* magazine described Elvis as "the boy with the coin in the groin."

If brevity is the hallmark of familiarity, those close to Elvis could not improve on nicknames "E," "El" or E.P. Among his entourage he might also be known as "Big E," "Big El" or "The Chief." Some sources state that Elvis used "Alan" as an incognito code name.

Elvis referred to himself in a love note to Anita Wood as "The Thing," though in later years he more commonly referred to himself as "Crazy," which he had inscribed on the underside of a bracelet he wore.

Jokingly, Elvis might introduce himself to people (including Priscilla, the first time they met) as "Elvis Pretzel," a name reputedly coined by Humphrey Bogart.

Elvis was a black-belt coiner of nicknames. Anyone who was anyone in his life had one, two or more Elvis-given cognomens. Gladys, to Elvis, was "Satnin'," a name he also applied to Priscilla and to his most special girlfriends. Priscilla called Elvis "Fire Eyes" because of his temper.

Even Colonel had his named rearranged: on stage in 1969, Elvis called him "Colonel Sanders,"

"Beginnings-Elvis Style" LP (USA) from the "Memphis Flash."

rather than his more usual mocking moniker, "Admiral."

See also NAMES . . .

NIELSEN, SHAUN (SHERILL)

Born in Montgomery, Alabama, Nielsen began singing in church only just a little older than Elvis was.

As an adult tenor, Sherill Nielsen first sang with Elvis as part of The Imperials on 1966 album *How Great Thou Art*.

Elvis contacted Nielsen in 1973 and asked him to come out to Las Vegas with some pals, where he intended to introduce them to Tom Jones, who he knew was looking for a new backing group. When that didn't work out, Elvis took on the new group (named Voice by Elvis). Sherill left Voice following a disagreement in March 1974, but returned to sing on tour with Elvis from May that year.

Elvis rated his talents very highly, publicly introducing Nielsen during one concert as "the greatest tenor in gospel music." All in all, Nielsen performed with Elvis more than five hundred times, dueting with Elvis on "Softly As I Leave You" and "Spanish Eyes," and singing "O Sole Mio" as the lead-in to Elvis' "It's Now Or Never." On nights when Elvis was out of sorts, Nielsen sometimes "doubled" Elvis on high notes.

Nielsen stayed with Elvis 'til the end—his rendition of "O Sole Mio" featured in 1977 live album *Elvis in Concert*.

Nielsen has sung with three different groups that have been inducted into the Gospel Music Hall of Fame: The Speer Family, The Imperials and The Statesmen.

"NIGHT LIFE"

Elvis recorded this Bill Giant / Bertie Baum / Florence Kaye track at Radio Recorders on July 9, 1963, with the idea of it being used in *Viva Las Vegas*. After the song was cut from the movie it languished in the RCA vaults until the *Singer Presents Elvis Singing Flaming Star and Others* album in 1968 (re-released the following year as *Elvis Sings Flaming Star*). The tune later appeared on the *Double Features* and FTD releases for *Viva Las Vegas*.

An alternate take has seen the light of day on FTD discs *Out In Hollywood* and *Viva Las Vegas*.

"NIGHT RIDER"

Elvis laid down this fast-paced Doc Pomus / Mort Shuman tune in the early morning of October 16, 1961 at Studio B in Nashville. The cut came out the following year on the *Pot Luck* album, and returned to vinyl as part of the recycled *Tickle Me* soundtrack EP in the mid-Sixties. The original recording later graced *Elvis in Nashville* and *From Nashville to Memphis*.

Alternate takes abound (Elvis had another stab at the song on March 18, 1962) on *Collectors Gold*, *Elvis Sings Mort Shuman & Doc Pomus*, *Essential Elvis Vol. 6*, *Elvis: Close Up* and FTD releases *Studio B: Nashville Outtakes*, *Tickle Me* and *Pot Luck*.

NIXON, HERSHEL

In March 1957, this US Marines Private initiated a law suit against Elvis over an incident outside the Chisca Hotel in Memphis, during which Elvis allegedly threatened him with a gun and insulted his wife. The matter was set-

tled out of court; Elvis wrote Nixon a lengthy apology (addressed to "Herschel") and explained that the Marine called out to him just as he was showing some pals a Hollywood prop pistol.

NIXON, RICHARD MILHOUS
(1913-1994)

Richard Nixon was born at Yorba Linda, California, on January 9, 1913. He was a two-term President of the United States (the country's 37th president) from 1969 until he was forced to resign as a result of the Watergate scandal. In his life he overcame a poor upbringing and political reverses to make it to the top, until hubris brought him down.

In December 1970, Elvis handwrote a letter to Nixon on American Airlines stationery expressing his admiration and his desire to be of service to the nation, specifically by becoming a federal narcotics agent. After touching down in Washington Elvis dropped his letter at the White House gates at 6:30 a.m. on December 21, 1970, and then went on a fruitless trip to the BNDD headquarters to try and secure a badge directly. Later that morning, Nixon's office put a call through to Elvis asking him to be at the Old Executive Office Building in 45 minutes. There he was met by Egil "Bud" Krogh, responsible for managing Nixon's drugs policy.

Elvis picked up his pals Jerry Schilling and Sonny West and hotfooted it over to meet the President. By all accounts, these very different men hit it off. During their half-hour meeting just before lunchtime, Elvis presented Nixon with a commemorative World War II Colt .45 pistol—Elvis had a turquoise-handled example himself, monogrammed with his initials—and showed the President his police badges and photos of Lisa Marie. President Nixon gave instructions for Elvis to be given the badge he had come to Washington to get. Elvis brought in entourage pals Jerry Schilling and Sonny West, to whom Nixon gave cufflinks and broaches bearing presidential seals. Before being ushered out of the Oval Office, Elvis gave the Prez a little hug.

Elvis' express wish for his meeting with Nixon to remain secret (though there are claims that it was Nixon who suggested secrecy) survived for little more than a year before the *Washington Post* broke the story.

In 1975, ex-president Nixon called Elvis in hospital to wish him better, returning Elvis' solicitous call to Nixon when he had been ill earlier that year.

As with most everything Elvis did, the meeting has become an unwitting merchandising opportunity: the National Archives sells a range of paraphernalia bearing photos of the former President and the King.

NIXON SAID TO ELVIS: "You dress kind of strange."

ELVIS REPLIED TO NIXON: "Well, Mr. President, you got your show, and I got mine."

NIXON DESCRIBED ELVIS AS: "a sincere and decent man, with flamboyance covering up his shyness."

Books:
The Day Elvis Met Nixon, by Bud Krogh, Pejama Press, 1994.
Elvis Presley, Richard Nixon, and the American Dream, by Connie Kirchberg and Marc Hendrickx, McFarland & Company, 1999.

TV movie:
Elvis Meets Nixon, (1997)

Elvis with President Richard Milhous Nixon at the White House, December 21, 1970. The most requested photograph from the National Archives—more than any other photo or document—including the Bill of Rights and the Constitution.

ELVIS' LETTER.

Dear Mr. President.

First, I would like to introduce myself. I am Elvis Presley and admire you and have great respect for your office. I talked to Vice President Agnew in Palm Springs three weeks ago and expressed my concern for our country. The drug culture, the hippie elements, the SDS, Black Panthers, etc. do NOT consider me as their enemy or as they call it The Establishment. I call it America and I love it. Sir, I can and will be of any service that I can to help The Country out. I have no concern or Motives other than helping the country out.

So I wish not to be given a title or an appointed position. I can and will do more good if I were made a Federal Agent at Large and I will help out by doing it my way through my communications with people of all ages. First and foremost, I am an entertainer, but all I need is the Federal credentials. I am on this plane with Senator George Murphy and we have been discussing the problems that our country is faced with.

Sir, I am staying at the Washington Hotel, Room 505-506-507. I have two men who work with me by the name of Jerry Schilling and Sonny West. I am registered under the name of Jon Burrows. I will be here for as long as it takes to get the credentials of a Federal Agent. I have done an in-depth study of drug abuse and Communist brainwashing techniques and I am right in the middle of the whole thing where I can and will do the most good.

I am Glad to help just so long as it is kept very Private. You can have your staff or whomever call me anytime today, tonight, or tomorrow. I was nominated this coming year one of America's Ten Most Outstanding Young Men. That will be in January 18 in my home town of Memphis, Tennessee. I am sending you the short autobiography about myself so you can better understand this approach. I would love to meet you just to say hello if you're not too busy.

Respectfully,
Elvis Presley

P. S. I believe that you, Sir, were one of the Top Ten Outstanding Men of America also.

I have a personal gift for you which I would like to present to you and you can accept it or I will keep it for you until you can take it.

"NO MORE"

Elvis recorded this latin-flavored Don Robertson / Hal Blair English-language update of 19th century Spanish song "La Paloma" on March 21, 1961 at Radio Recorders for the Blue Hawaii soundtrack. The Burning Love and Hits from His Movies album featured the song in the Seventies.

Elvis laid down a live version of the track on January 14, 1973, immediately after recording his Aloha From Hawaii Via Satellite performance, though it was only released in 1978 on the Mahalo From Elvis album. This recording has since appeared on the reissued version of Aloha From Hawaii Via Satellite; an alternate from that night is on Today Tomorrow & Forever.

Alternate takes from the 1961 session have appeared on the 1997 Blue Hawaii reissue CD and on Elvis: Close Up.

"(THERE'S) NO ROOM TO RHUMBA IN A SPORTS CAR"

It remains unknown whether songwriters Fred Wise and Dick Manning conducted actual research for this song, which Elvis recorded on January 23, 1963 for Fun in Acapulco at Radio Recorders. The song later came out on the Double Feature release for the film.

NORRIS, CHUCK
(B. CARLOS RAY NORRIS, 1940)

Norris was born to Irish and Cherokee parents and grew up in Ryan, Oklahoma. After studying Tae Kwon Do while stationed in Korea in the late Fifties, Chuck Norris became a top US karate champion: from 1968 until his retirement in 1974, he held the Professional Full-Contact World Middleweight Karate title.

Norris ran a martial arts institute in Los Angeles where among others he taught Steve McQueen and the Osmonds. Elvis sent Priscilla to study karate there under Mike Stone, for whom Priscilla left Elvis in 1972. Norris focused on acting after his karate schools folded. He had his first big break in Return of the Dragon (1973), and then played Colonel James Braddock in the Missing In Action trilogy in the Eighties. In the Nineties he was the lead in CBS series Walker, Texas Ranger.

NORTH CAROLINA

- Asheville
Elvis played the City Auditorium on May 17, 1955. He returned on September 16, 1955. Elvis and his band played three nights at the Civic Center (July 22-24) to round off his summer 1975 tour, and in holiday mood threw rings and a guitar into the audience.

- Burlington
On February 15, 1956 Elvis played the Walter Williams High School Auditorium. The booth at the Brightwood Inn restaurant nearby where he ate a hamburger is decorated in tribute to Elvis.

- Charlotte
Elvis played the Carolina Theater on February 10, 1956, attracting 6,000 people to four shows and sending a thousand more away disappointed. He performed at the Coliseum on June 26, 1956.

He appeared with the TCB band at the Coliseum on April 13, 1972, where he returned for two shows on March 9, 1974. He also played two shows there on March 20, 1976. Elvis closed out his February 1977 tour with shows at the Coliseum on February 20 and 21, 1977—at one of these shows, his girlfriend's sister, Terry Alden, played classical pieces on the piano. A soundboard recording of the February 20 concert was released in 2007 by FTD, titled Unchained Melody.

- Fayetteville
The Cumberland Country Memorial Auditorium hosted Elvis from August 3 to 5, 1976 at the end of a tour.

- Greensboro
Elvis squeezed in four shows on February 6, 1956 at the National Theater. He played the Coliseum here on April 14, 1972 (filmed for Elvis

Elvis on stage in Greensboro, North Carolina April 14, 1972.

on *Tour*) and again on March 13, 1974. On July 21, 1975 he played the Veterans Memorial Coliseum. He was at the Coliseum on June 30, 1976, and began one of his last tours here on April 21, 1977.

- High Point

Elvis played four shows at the Center Theater on February 7, 1956.

New Bern

Elvis first played the Shrine Auditorium on May 14, 1955, and then returned on a tour with the Hank Snow Jamboree on September 13, 1955.

- Raleigh

Elvis' last show on his May 1955 Hank Snow All Star Jamboree tour was at the Memorial Auditorium on May 19, 1955. He returned to the same venue on September 21, 1955, and played four shows at the Ambassador Theater on February 8, 1956.

- Thomasville

Elvis played the High School Auditorium in this town on September 17, 1955.

- Wilson

Elvis played the Fleming Stadium on September 14, 1955. He played the Charles L. Coon High School on February 14, 1956, once again adding an extra late-night show due to public demand.

- Winston-Salem

Elvis appeared at the Carolina Theater on February 16, 1956.

"NOTHINGVILLE"

A Billy Strange / Mac Davis tune that was the first song Elvis recorded for the NBC TV Special on June 20, 1968 at Western Recorders, as the opener for the "road medley" segment. The track was included in the show and featured on the accompanying release. The song has since been released on *Memories: The '68 Comeback Special*. Alternate takes have appeared on FTD release *Let Yourself Go*.

"NUMBER EIGHT (ON THE JUKEBOX)"

A ballad that Elvis sang at home in Germany 1959, released officially many years later on *In A Private Moment* after being available on bootleg only. Little did Elvis know that when he became interested in numerology, this would be "his" number.

NUMBERS AND NUMEROLOGY

During the Sixties, when he embarked in earnest on his spiritual quest to find meaning in his life, Elvis developed a fascination with numbers and numerology that he retained for the rest of his days. He always traveled with a copy of *Cheiro's Book of Numbers*, and read many other numerology tomes over the years including Corinne Heline's *The Sacred Science of Numbers*.

Elvis studied the Kabbalah with pal Larry Geller in the mid-Sixties and drew up number charts for the important people in his life. According to the Kabbalah, every character in the Hebrew alphabet has a corresponding number which reveals hidden truths about things and persons. Numerology traces its roots back to Pythagoras and his conviction that everything corresponds to a number. In many Asian countries, a belief in auspicious and inauspicious numbers colors people's actions. In the West, plenty of people still feel foreboding at the arrival of Friday, 13th.

Elvis understood himself to be an "8" person, somebody who "hides their feelings in life but do what they please." Both Gladys and Priscilla were "7"s, supposedly temperamentally drawn to the mystical, though Priscilla showed scant sign of accompanying Elvis on his spiritual and mystical quest. Colonel Parker was also an "8" as his birth day was 26 (which, added together, makes "8").

Elvis reputedly added the additional "a" to his middle name "Aaron" because it was more auspicious in numerological terms.

Elvis found practical as well as spiritual uses for his interest. He sometimes looked up a person's birth date and then used the resulting number as a guide to what kind of gemstone to buy as a gift.

SOME ELVIS NUMBERS:

Jailhouse Rock prison number: 6239 and 9240.
Racecar # in *Viva Las Vegas*: 7
Airplane call signs: Convair Jet: N880EP, Jet Commander N777EP
Social Security # (issued in September 1950): 409 - 52 - 2002
Selective service #: 40 86 35 16
US Army draft #: 53 310 761
Sheriff #: 6
Union membership (American Guild of Variety Artists): 165890
Phone numbers (1970): Memphis: 398 4427, 398 4882, 398 9722. Los Angeles: 278 3496, 278 5935, 274-8498. Palm Springs: 325-3241
Bank account # (National Bank of Commerce, Memphis): 011-143875
Tennessee driver's license: 2571459

FROM "CHEIRO'S BOOK OF NUMBERS" ABOUT NUMBER EIGHTS: "These people are invariably much misunderstood in their lives, and perhaps for this reason they feel intensely lonely at heart — and they generally play some important role on life's stage, but usually one which is fatalistic or as the instrument of fate for others."

LARRY GELLER: "On the most basic level, he was a perfect 8, someone concerned with the material and the spiritual, intense, ambitious, lonely and misunderstood."

LARRY GELLER: "The science of numbers, letters, symbols and cycles appealed to him, because it imposed a system on the universe.... There was no such thing as coincidence; nothing happened at random."

Elvis wearing his Memphis Indian Suit onstage in Las Vegas, December 1976.

"O COME, ALL YE FAITHFUL"

Traditional Yule cheer in this harmony-filled version that Elvis recorded at Studio B on May 16, 1971 for release as the B-side to a bluesy "Merry Christmas Babe," in good time for the festive period. Album runouts include *Elvis Sings The Wonderful World of Christmas*, *If Every Day Was Like Christmas*, *Blue Christmas*

Christmas Peace and *Elvis Christmas*. An alternate take from the session came out in 1982 on *Memories Of Christmas*.

"O LITTLE TOWN OF BETHLEHEM"

A shoe-in for Elvis Christmas albums *Elvis' Christmas Album* in 1957, laid down at Radio Recorders on September 7, 1957. The lyrics were originally written as a travel poem in 1868 by Boston pastor Phillips Brooks and set to music the following year by his church organist Lewis Redner.

The song came out on festive EP *Christmas With Elvis* in 1958. Latter-day releases include *If Every Day Was Like Christmas*, *The King Of Rock And Roll*, *Christmas Peace* and *Elvis Christmas*.

O'CONNELL, ARTHUR
(1908-1981)

After a small role in Orson Welles' *Citizen Kane*, Arthur O'Connell enjoyed a long and successful career as a character actor, winning two Oscar nominations and playing opposite Elvis in early Sixties movies *Follow That Dream* and *Kissin' Cousins*.

O'CURRAN, CHARLIE
(1913-1984)

Musical director O'Curran worked with Elvis on Paramount productions from *Loving You* to *Fun in Acapulco*, doing double duty as a choreographer and sometime songwriter ("Mama," "We'll Be Together" and "Dainty Little Moonbeams"). O'Curran was married to singer Patti Page, one of Elvis' favorite female vocalists.

ODETS, CLIFFORD
(1906-1963)

One of America's top playwrights from the Thirties onwards and a charter member of the Group Theater—responsible for developing what later became known as method acting—Odets crossed Elvis' path by writing the screenplay for *Wild in the Country*.

"ODE TO BILLIE JOE"

Elvis sang a few lines of this 1967 Bobbie Gentry multi-Grammy winning hit at a Nashville September 1967 recording session, just before launching into "Hi-Heel Sneakers." It was released many years later on *From Nashville to Memphis*.

O'GRADY, JOHN

This former Head of the Hollywood Narcotics Detail was hired as a private investigator on Elvis' behalf in the summer of 1970 to find out about a woman who had filed a paternity suit against Elvis. He was kept on to provide added security in Las Vegas to counter a threat to assassinate Elvis while he performed. Elvis asked O'Grady to help fix up a meeting with his contacts in Washington as part of his quest to get a Federal Bureau of Narcotics and Dangerous Drugs badge.

O'Grady drew on his narcotics training in 1973, when lawyer Ed Hookstratten, retained by the Colonel and Vernon, hired him to find out who was supplying Elvis with his secret supply of prescription drugs.

In Elvis' off-the-wall monologue at the end of his summer 1974 Las Vegas engagement, he introduced O'Grady from the stage and recommended his book. Off-stage, Elvis referred to the P.I. as "Reverend" because he was not a man for cussing.

O'Grady was so shocked at how bad Elvis looked when he saw him perform at Stateline, Nevada, in May 1976 that he enlisted the help of Ed Hookstratten to try and get Elvis into a drug rehabilitation program. That summer, O'Grady acted as a go-between in an attempt to persuade former entourage members Red and Sonny West and Dave Hebler to drop the book they were planning to publish.

Book:
The Life and Times of Hollywood's Number One Private Eye, by John O'Grady and Nolan Davis, published by J. P. Tarcher, Inc, 1974.

OHIO

- Cincinnati
Elvis performed at the Cincinnati Gardens on November 11, 1971. He played there next on June 27, 1973. He was at the Riverfront Coliseum on March 21, 1976, and played there again on June 25, 1977, the second to last time he took to the stage.

- Cleveland
Elvis' first live show outside the South was at the Circle Theater on February 26, 1955. The occasion was a Hillbilly Jamboree event hosted by local DJ Tommy Edwards; on this trip, Elvis and the band met well-known DJ Bill Randall, who would be of great help later on. Elvis returned to play the Circle Theater on October 19, 1955 as an added attraction to a Grand Ole Opry bill featuring Roy Acuff and Kitty Wells. The following day Elvis played an afternoon show at the Brooklyn High School Auditorium and an evening show at St Michaels Hall. The earlier of these shows was filmed for a never-released short film about DJ Bill Randle, titled *The Pied Piper of Cleveland: A Day in the Life of a Famous Disc Jockey*. Elvis returned to play the Arena on November 23, 1956.

Elvis was next in town at the Cleveland Public Hall Auditorium on November 6, 1971. On June 21, 1974, he performed at the Convention Center Public Hall.

- Columbus
Elvis played two shows at the Veterans Memorial Auditorium on May 26, 1956. He performed at the St. John Arena on June 25, 1974.

- Dayton
Elvis performed in the University of Dayton Fieldhouse on May 27, 1956. He appeared at the University of Dayton Arena on April 7, 1972, and came back for two shows on October 6, 1974. He played the University of Ohio on October 26, 1976.

- Richfield
Elvis was at the Coliseum on July 10 and July 18, 1975, and again on October 23, 1976.

- Toledo
Elvis played two shows at the Sports Arena on November 22, 1956. He had long since downsized to one show per day when he returned to perform at the University of Toledo Centennial Hall on April 23, 1977.

- Troy
Elvis appeared at the Hobart Arena on November 24, 1956.

"OH HAPPY DAY"

Elvis initially considered incorporating this traditional spiritual into his 1968 NBC TV Special.

The year after Elvis' TV Special a version by the Edwin Hawkins Singers became the first ever cross-over hymn, making it into the top #5 in the *Billboard* charts and winning a Grammy in 1970.

The hymn was originally written by Philip Doddridge and published in 1755; a new refrain was added by Edward Francis Rimbault a century later.

The song made it into at least one of Elvis' summer 1970 shows in Las Vegas, but not onto the original *That's The Way It Is* album release—fortunately remedied on the 2000 3-CD boxed set, which features Elvis singing his heart out during a stage rehearsal (also released on the *Peace In The Valley* gospel compilation) held on August 7, 1970. An Elvis rehearsal from 1968 came out in 2006 on FTD release *Let Yourself Go*.

OKLAHOMA

- Altus
Elvis was in Altus for a show on June 24, 1955.

- Guymon
Elvis played the High School Auditorium on June 1, 1955.

- Lawton
Elvis played the McMahon Memorial Auditorium and the Southern Club on June 23, 1955, on a bill with Leon Payne and Chuck Lee.

- Oklahoma City
Elvis shared a bill with Bill Haley at the Municipal Auditorium on October 16, 1955, and headlined at the same venue on April 19, 1956. When he played the State Fair Grounds with his TCB Band on November 16, 1970, Governor Dewey Barlett named Elvis an "honorary Okie." Elvis returned to town, playing the Myriad Center Arena on July 2, 1973. Elvis began his third tour of 1975 at the Myriad Convention Center Arena on July 8, 1975. He played the venue for the last time on May 28, 1976, and then gave shows on two nights at the University of Oklahoma Lloyd Noble Center on March 25 and 26, 1977.

- Tulsa
Elvis played the Fairgrounds Pavilion on April 18, 1956. The TCB band backed him next time round, when he was on the bill at the Civic Assembly Center on June 20, 1972. He began a three-week Southern swing at the Mabee Special Events Center (the Oral Roberts University) with two shows on March 1 and 2, 1974. The last time he played this venue was on July 4, 1976.

"OH HOW I LOVE JESUS"

Elvis sang this traditional hymn at Graceland. A recording from 1966 features on *Platinum: A Life In Music*, *A Private Moment* and on *Peace In The Valley—The Complete Gospel Recordings*.

"OLD MACDONALD"

Elvis was spared having to make the animal sounds when he recorded this jazzed-up children's favorite on June 29, 1966 at the MGM Sound Stage for the *Double Trouble* soundtrack. Randy Starr took the songwriting credit. The song has since appeared on the movie soundtrack reissues and on *Elvis Sings Hits from His Movies*, *Elvis Sings For Children (And Grown Ups Too)*,

Elvis in the "White Tie Suit," Oklahoma City, November 16, 1970.

Elvis Sings for Kids . . . Elvis singing for his supper was not alone: Frank Sinatra had scored a top 30 chart hit with the song in 1960.

"OLD SHEP"

The first song that Elvis performed publicly as a ten-year-old at a talent contest at the Mississippi-Alabama Fair and Dairy Show appeared on his second album and was released on EP *Elvis Vol. 2* in 1956, when it was good for #47 in the charts.

"Old Shep" was written in 1933 by Red Foley (with some help from Willis Arthur) about his boyhood pet, a German Shepherd called Hoover. As a youngster, Elvis sang the lachrymose ditty so often that his school pals and teachers grew sick of it. Teacher Mrs. Grimes remembered it differently: "He had such feeling . . . that the little boys and girls cried when he sang this song."

Elvis laid down the track on September 2, 1956 at Radio Recorders, and played his own piano accompaniment. This was right in the middle of the public hue and cry about his wild rock 'n' rolling ways.

More recently, "Old Shep" has raised its head on *Double Dynamite, Separate Ways, Elvis Sings For Children (And Grown Ups Too), Great Country Songs, The Country Side of Elvis* and *Elvis Sings for Kids.*

An alternate take previously only available on bootlegs was chosen for *The King Of Rock 'N' Roll* anthology. Reputedly an alternate take appeared on a limited number of the original 1956 *Elvis* LPs.

"ON A SNOWY CHRISTMAS NIGHT"

Elvis laid down this seasonal track written by Stanley Gelber on May 16, 1971 at Studio B in Nashville, for his *Elvis Sings The Wonderful World Of Christmas* album later that year. It's since been on Yuletide releases *If Every Day Was Like Christmas, Christmas Peace* and *Elvis Christmas.*

"ON THE JERICHO ROAD"

See "AS WE TRAVEL ALONG THE JERICHO ROAD"

"ON TOP OF OLD SMOKEY"

There's a brief snatch of Elvis singing this song in his 1962 movie *Follow That Dream.* The 10-second snatch of sound had only appeared on bootlegs until in 2004 FTD included it on its re-issue of the movie soundtrack. Elvis also launched into the song at the start of one of his December 1973 Stax recording sessions.

"ONCE IS ENOUGH"

A Sid Tepper and Roy C. Bennett sax-fired rocker that Elvis recorded on September 29, 1963 in Nashville for *Kissin' Cousins.* The song has since come out on the *Double Features* release and on *Command Performances.*

"ONE BOY, TWO LITTLE GIRLS"

One of five Bill Giant / Bernie Baum / Florence Kaye tunes that Elvis recorded in the fall of 1963 for the Kissin' Cousins soundtrack at the same session as in the above entry. Later releases as per "Once Is Enough"

"ONE BROKEN HEART FOR SALE"

This mid-tempo pop single, shipped in January 1963 with "They Remind Me Too Much of You" on the B-side, has the dubious distinction of being Elvis' first RCA release to fail to make the top five or even the top ten: it peaked and slid from #11 during its 9-week chart tour of duty, though still managed to go gold.

Elvis recorded this Otis Blackwell / Winfield Scott composition at Radio Recorders on September 22, 1962 for *It Happened at the World's Fair.* The version released on the single was edited down to not much longer than a minute and a half. The track has since come out on anthologies *Worldwide Gold Award Hits Vol. 1, Mahalo From Elvis, Command Performances, Hitstory* and *Elvis at the Movies.*

The movie version of the song first appeared in 1991 on *Collectors Gold,* since when it has also been on the *Double Features* release. Studio alternates are on the FTD *It Happened at the World's Fair* release.

"ONE NIGHT (OF SIN)"

Laid down at Radio Recorders on February 23, 1957, this raunchy track shipped on October 21, 1958 with "I Got Stung" on the B-side. Originally an R & B hit for Smiley Lewis in 1956, Elvis' single peaked at #4 and spent 17 weeks in the chart; in the UK it claimed #1 for 3 weeks. In the US, the single sold 1.5 million copies to become his most successful seller since "Jailhouse Rock."

"One Night" obtained its initial album release on *Elvis' Gold Records Vol. 2* and appeared on EP *A Touch of Gold Vol. 2.* It has since been included on *Worldwide Gold Award Hits Vol. 2, Elvis: A Legendary Performer Vol. 4, The King Of Rock And Roll, Artist Of The Century, ELVIS 30 #1 Hits* and *Hitstory.*

The first time that Elvis recorded this song (on January 18, 1957) was with its original title, "One Night of Sin." The less-than-oblique reference to an orgy was considered too risquéÈ by RCA, which arranged for a lyric substitution and a re-recording. Elvis' unexpurgated version wasn't publicly released until the Eighties on *Elvis: A Legendary Performer Vol. 4.* It has since appeared on *Reconsider Baby, The King Of Rock And Roll* and the 1997 reissue (and later FTD release) of *Loving You.*

Even after toning down the lyrics, RCA decided that the song was better held in reserve for a future single release than hidden away as an album track on *Loving You,* as originally intended.

A live version from Elvis' 1961 Pearl Harbor charity concert was released on *Elvis Aron Presley.*

Elvis sang a snatch of this song—written by Dave Bartholomew and Pearl King—in one his medleys on the NBC Comeback special. The song featured on the original album release. Other recordings from rehearsals and live tapings have since appeared on *A Golden Celebration, Memories: The '68 Comeback Special, Tiger Man* and FTD release *Burbank '68.*

Elvis performed this song during his August 1970 shows covered on *That's The Way It Is,* and continued to sing it with some regularity live until the end of 1972. The song was restored to his stage act from late 1975. Live versions are available on *Walk A Mile In My Shoes, That's The Way It Is - Special Edition, Live In Las Vegas,* and *The Live Greatest Hits,* and also on FTD issues *The Way It Was, An American Trilogy* and *Summer Festival.*

ONE NIGHT IN VEGAS

An FTD album of an Elvis show from August 10, 1970 in Las Vegas, with additional material from pre-show rehearsals.

TRACK LISTING:
1. That's All Right
2. Mystery Train / Tiger Man
3. I Can't Stop Loving You
4. Love Me Tender
5. The Next Step Is Love
6. Words
7. I Just Can't Help Believin'
8. Something
9. Sweet Caroline
10. You've Lost That Lovin' Feeling
11. You Don't Have To Say You Love Me
12. Polk Salad Annie
13. I've Lost You
14. Bridge Over Troubled Water
15. Patch It Up
16. Can't Help Falling In Love
17. Words
18. Cattle Call / Yodel
19. Twenty Days And Twenty Nights
20. You Don't Have To Say You Love Me

"ONE-SIDED LOVE AFFAIR"

A boogie-woogie B-Side to the single "Money Honey," recorded by Elvis on January 30, 1956 at RCA's New York studios and released by the label in late August 1956, by which time the Bill Campbell song had already appeared on Elvis' first album and double EP. The track later filled out the *A Date With Elvis* album. More recently it has appeared on *The King Of Rock And Roll* and *Elvis '56.*

"ONE TRACK HEART"

Elvis recorded this pop soundtrack tune for *Roustabout,* written by the Bill Giant / Bernie Baum / Florence Kaye team, on March 3, 1964 at Radio Recorders. As well as coming out on the soundtrack album, the song has shown up on the *Double Feature* release for the movie.

"ONLY BELIEVE"

Written by Paul Rader and originally sung by the Harmonizing Four in 1957, Elvis' bluesy interpretation of this gospel song was first released on non-gospel album *Love Letters From Elvis,* after Elvis recorded it in Nashville on June 8, 1970.

"All things are possible / If you'll only believe" —belief alone was insufficient to help propel the song into the top 50 as the B-side of a single with "Life" soon after Easter 1971.

Subsequent album releases are *Amazing Grace, Peace In The Valley, Christmas Peace* and *Elvis Inspirational.* A live version from 1971 is on bootleg *All Things Are Possible* and FTD release *The Impossible Dream.*

"ONLY THE STRONG SURVIVE"

This poignant R&B song, written by Kenny Gamble, Leon Huff and Jerry Butler, had only just been released by Jerry Butler when Elvis laid it down at American Studio on February 19, 1969. Butler's #4 *Billboard* Hot 100 chart success scotched any chance of a single release for Elvis' essentially similar version.

"Only The Strong Survive" first saw public release on *From Elvis In Memphis* a few months after Elvis recorded the track. It has since come out on *From Nashville to Memphis, Artist Of The Century* and *Suspicious Minds: The Memphis 1969 Anthology.*

An alternate is on FTD release *The Memphis Sessions;* a remixed version appeared on FTD release *Too Much Monkey Business.*

"ONLY YOU"

Elvis performed The Platter's weepie "Only You" at the Louisiana Hayride in December 1955 and some dates in early 1956, though he did not record it for release. This #5 hit from 1955 was written by Ande Rand and Buck Ram.

ON STAGE

The bulk of this album, released in June 1970, was recorded live at the International Hotel between February 17 and 19, 1970, along with a couple of tracks from Elvis' first engagement in Las Vegas the previous August, and recent single "The Wonder of You." Officially titled *On Stage—February 1970*, the album sold half a million copies and was good for #13 in the charts.

TRACK LISTING:
1. See See Rider
2. Release Me
3. Sweet Caroline
4. Runaway
5. The Wonder Of You
6. Polk Salad Annie
7. Yesterday
8. Proud Mary
9. Walk A Mile In My Shoes
10. Let It Be Me

A CD reissue included In The Ghetto, Don't Cry Daddy, Kentucky Rain, I Can't Stop Loving You, Suspicious Minds and Long Tall Sally.

In 2004, FTD released *Polk Salad Annie*, a concert from the same period featuring many of the same tracks plus rehearsals of new material that Elvis performed for the *On Stage* album.

ORBISON, ROY KELTON
(1936–1988)

Elvis held Roy Orbison in very high regard, publicly stating that Orbison had "the most perfect voice" and referring to him as "the greatest singer in the world" during one of his Vegas concerts. Orbison's respect for Elvis is evident: he went to Elvis shows from 1954 to 1976; his first band, the Wink Westerners, played "That's All Right (Mama)" at their own early shows; and Orbison's original recording of "Ooby Dooby" on the Jew-EL label featured early Elvis hit "Trying' To Get To You" on the B-side. The first time that Elvis and Orbison met was in 1955, when Elvis and Johnny Cash were guests on local Odessa, Texas TV station KOSA-TV, on which Orbison had his own show. Orbison took in many of Elvis' shows as he conquered Texas that year.

Born in Vernon, Texas on April 23, 1936, "The Big O" started playing at the age of thirteen. He landed a contract with Sam Phillips at Sun Records in 1956 and scored his first success with "Ooby Dooby"—a track that was offered to Elvis before Orbison recut it for Sun. Though initially popular with rockabilly fans, Orbison's career stalled after he made a move to RCA. It took off again after he joined Monument Records, on the recommendation of Chet Atkins. "Only The Lonely" put him at the top of the charts and was the first of several singles to sell a million—and another song reputedly offered to Elvis. Other memorable Orbison hits from this time were "Crying" and "Pretty Woman"—a song that Elvis loved.

Orbison headlined a tour in Europe with the not-quite-famous Beatles in 1963 (making him the only artist to play on the same bill as Elvis and the Beatles).

Orbison returned to prominence in the 1980s, winning a Grammy with Emmylou Harris for

Candid Elvis autographing a photograph, 1968.

"That Lovin' You Feelin' Again." His song "In Dreams" featured in David Lynch movie *Blue Velvet*, and soon after Orbison teamed up with Bob Dylan and George Harrison in the band the Traveling Wilburys,

Long revered as a master songwriter, Orbison's three-octave range was the envy of many a fellow-singer. As a mark of respect, Elvis never covered any of Orbison's self-penned compositions; the closest he came was interjecting a line of "Running Scared" into a take while recording "Tomorrow Never Comes" in Nashville, in June 1970.

Two years after Elvis' death, Orbison recorded Elvis tribute song "Hound Dog Man."

Orbison won a second Grammy for another duet—with k.d. lang^in 1987, the year that he was inducted into the Rock and Roll Hall of Fame.

OREGON

- Eugene

Elvis played the University of Oregon McArthur Court on November 25 and 27, 1976.

- Portland

Elvis played a date at the Multnomah Stadium on September 2, 1957. He returned on November 11, 1970 to the Memorial Coliseum, where he also performed on April 27, 1973. He was at the Portland Memorial Coliseum on November 26, 1976.

ORIGINAL ELVIS PRESLEY COLLECTION, THE

A 1996 BMG Netherlands anthology of 50 Elvis CDs with an accompanying booklet and certificate of authenticity, collating all of the album releases during Elvis' lifetime (most of the film soundtracks in the *Double Feature* Nineties reissue format).

ALBUMS FEATURED:
Elvis Presley
Elvis
Loving You
Elvis' Christmas Album
Elvis' Golden Records
King Creole
For LP Fans Only
A Date With Elvis
50,000,000 Elvis Fans Can't Be Wrong
Elvis Is Back!
Double Features: Flaming Star / Follow That Dream / Wild In The Country
G.I. Blues
His Hand In Mine
Something For Everybody
Blue Hawaii
Pot Luck With Elvis
Double Features: Kid Galahad / Girls! Girls! Girls!
Double Features: It Happened At The World's Fair / Fun In Acapulco
Elvis' Golden Records Vol. 3
Double Features: Kissin' Cousins / Clambake / Stay Away, Joe
Double Features: Viva Las Vegas / Roustabout
Double Features: Harum Scarum / Girl Happy
Elvis For Everyone

Double Features: Frankie & Johnny / Paradise, Hawaiian Style
Double Features: Spinout / Double Trouble
Double Features: Easy Come, Easy Go / Speedway
How Great Thou Art
Elvis' Golden Records Vol. 4
Double Features: Live A Little, Love A Little / The Trouble with Girls / Charro! / Change Of Habit
NBC TV Special
From Elvis In Memphis
In Person
Back In Memphis
On Stage
That's The Way It Is
Elvis Country
Love Letters From Elvis
Elvis Sings The Wonderful World Of Christmas
Elvis Now
He Touched Me
Elvis As Recorded At Madison Square Garden
Aloha From Hawaii Via Satellite
Elvis (Fool Album)
Raised On Rock
Good Times
Recorded Live On Stage In Memphis
Promised Land
Today
From Elvis Presley Boulevard, Memphis, Tennessee
Moody Blue

At the time of writing, plans were in place to reissue a 30-album set under the same name to mark the 30th anniversary of Elvis' passing.

OSBORNE, JERRY

Former DJ and prolific Elvis author with many Elvis books and magazines to his name, including a line of catalogs with prices for original Elvis records and collectibles. A syndicated columnist, Osborne has been consulted by Elvis Presley Enterprises.

OUR MEMORIES OF ELVIS

RCA released this two-volume tribute to Elvis in 1979, with Vernon and the Colonel pictured on the cover. All of the tracks are shorn of the over-dubs added for original release.

TRACK LISTING:
Vol. 1
1. Are You Sincere
2. It's Midnight
3. My Boy
4. Girl Of Mine
5. Take Good Care Of Her
6. I'll Never Fall In Love Again
7. Your Love's Been A Long Time Coming
8. Spanish Eyes
9. Never Again
10. She Thinks I Still Care
11. Solitaire

VOL. 2:
1. I Got A Feelin' In My Body
2. Green, Green Grass Of Home
3. For The Heart
4. She Wears My Ring
5. I Can Help
6. Way Down
7. There's A Honky Tonk Angel (Who Will Take Me Back In)
8. Find Out What's Happening
9. Thinking About You
10. Don't Think Twice It's All Right

OUT IN HOLLYWOOD

A 1999 FTD album of soundtrack outtakes and alternates.

TRACK LISTING:
1. Mexico
2. Cross My Heart And Hope To Die
3. Wild In The Country
4. Adam And Evil
5. Lonely Man
6. Thanks To The Rolling Sea
7. Where Do You Come From
8. King Of The Whole Wide World
9. Little Egypt
10. Wonderful World
11. This Is My Heaven
12. Spinout
13. All That I Am
14. We'll Be Together
15. Frankie And Johnny
16. I Need Somebody To Lean On
17. The Meanest Girl In Town
18. Night Life
19. Puppet On A String
20. Hey, Little Girl
21. Edge Of Reality
22. Baby I Don't Care

"OUT OF SIGHT, OUT OF MIND"

Elvis gave this song a whirl during *The Million Dollar Quartet* session at Sun Records in December 1956. Written by Ivory Joe Hunter and Clyde Otis, the song had been a top thirty hit for The Five Keys earlier that year. The song may be found on all *Million Dollar Quartet* releases.

"OVER THE RAINBOW"

The best song of the 20th century according to the American Record Industry, written by Harold Arlen and Yip Harburg for Judy Garland in *The Wizard of Oz*. Elvis assayed the song during rehearsals in 1972. It has only come out on bootlegs such as *Backstage with Elvis* and *The Complete On Tour Sessions*.

OVERTON PARK SHELL, MEMPHIS

Elvis played one of his very first concerts with heroes Slim Whitman and Billy Walker at this Memphis outdoor venue on July 30, 1954, in a park just a few blocks from Sun Records, watched by his parents, record producer Sam Phillips and girlfriend Dixie Locke. "Ellis Presley," as he was erroneously billed, played his entire repertoire of two songs from recently-released single, "That's All Right (Mama)" and "Blue Moon Of Kentucky." Legend has it that he was so nervous that during his performance his leg began to shake and tremble, driving the crowd wild. This was purportedly the moment when the hallmark move of Elvis idol Jim "Big Chief" Wetherington became Elvis'. Elvis was so popular he went back on stage to perform an encore of "Blue Moon Of Kentucky"

On August 5, 1955, Elvis was one of the headliners before a 4,000-strong audience for Bob Neal's 8th annual Country Music Jamboree, on a bill with Webb Pierce, Sonny James and Johnny Cash. He was back as a spectator on June 1, 1956 to watch Sun artists Johnny Cash, Carl Perkins, Roy Orbison and Warren Smith.

Built in 1936, at the time of writing the landmark was undergoing renovation.

OWENS, A. L "DOODLE"
(B. Arthur Leo Owens)

Elvis sang a number of songs written by this country singer/songwriter: "Let's Forget About The Stars," (with Dallas Frazier) "True Love Travels On A Gravel Road," "Wearin' That Loved On Look" and "Where Did They Go, Lord" and (with A. Solberg) "Singing Tree."

Owens was inducted into the Nashville Songwriters Hall of Fame in 1999.

OWENS, LARRY

See LARRY MUHOBERAC

P

PACHUCKI, AL

A Nashville-based RCA studio engineer who worked on Elvis sessions from *How Great Thou Art* in 1966 through to the Stax sessions in the summer of 1973.

"PADRE"

One of Elvis' favorite songs (as told to an interviewer in 1958), released on the 1973 album *Elvis (The Fool Album)*, after he recorded the melodramatic track in Nashville on May 15, 1971. The original was a French song, titled "Padre Don José . . .," by Jacques LaRue and Alain Romans. The version Elvis knew and loved was a million-seller sung by Toni Arden in 1958, with English lyrics by Paul Webster. Marty Robbins had a top 5 country hit the year before Elvis recorded the song. Since its original album release, the song has appeared on *He Walks Beside Me*. An alternate is on FTD release *I Sing All Kinds*.

PAGE, PATTI
(B. CLARA ANN FOWLER, 1927)

No female singer outsold Patti Page in the Fifties. Her 1950 "Tennessee Waltz" is the only single in history to top the pop, country and R&B charts at the same time, and for many decades was the biggest selling-single by any female singer; Page is also remembered for novelty hits like "Doggie In The Window." Born in Muskogee, Oklahoma on November 8, 1927, Page took her stage name from early sponsor Page Milk.

In 1957, Elvis stated that Page was one of his favorite female vocalists—though in a recent interview Page has said that in reality, she was the favorite of Elvis' mother, Gladys. By the time Elvis made his statement, Page had helmed her own TV show and was working in the movies. She continued to chart into the mid-Sixties.

The first song that Elvis ever recorded professionally, "I Love You Because," had been a hit for Patti Page. She also covered "I Don't Care If the Sun Don't Shine," "Love Letters" and "Gentle On My Mind" before Elvis got to them. He is also known to have sung "Tennessee Waltz" for his own edification at home.

Elvis met Page in Las Vegas in 1956, when he took his mother to see one of Page's shows. They met up later on the sets of several movies on which her husband Charles O'Curran worked as a choreographer. Page even had a cameo as an extra in *Blue Hawaii*.

PAGET, DEBRA
(B. DEBRALEE GRIFFIN, 1933)

Before co-starring with Elvis in his first movie, *Love Me Tender*, Debra Paget had already appeared with him on the small screen in a skit on "The Milton Berle Show," during which host Berle warned Elvis that she was out of his league. And so it proved to be.

Born in Denver on August 19, 1933, by the age of sixteen Paget was headhunted by 20th Century-Fox to play a string of exotic roles. Paget had been acting since she was fourteen (in *Cry of the City*, 1948), and went on to star in around 20 movies (including *The Ten Commandments*) before retiring from the screen to marry a Chinese-American millionaire in 1964.

Paget helped Elvis learn his lines for the movie. They went out on the town and visited Paget's family home, but Elvis' crush was unrequited. At this time, Paget was linked in the gossip papers with Howard Hughes. In a 1997 interview, Paget said that Elvis asked her to marry him . . . but she declined because her parents would never allow her to wed a rock 'n' roll singer. Members of Elvis' entourage have confirmed that Elvis' infatuation continued for some time; at least one Memphis Mafioso has remarked on how similar Priscilla looked to Paget.

DEBRA PAGET: "Before I met him, I figured he must be some sort of moron."

JOE ESPOSITO: "He was flipped over Debra . . . He carried a torch for her all during the making of that movie and even after it. But it never happened."

PALM SPRINGS

Elvis started visiting Palm Springs in the mid-Sixties as a guest of the Colonel's. He became a more frequent visitor when the Colonel rented a home for him in 1966. Elvis honeymooned at this desert resort with Priscilla at the 1350 Ladera Circle property. He, Priscilla and Lisa Marie spent Easter 1968 at another rented house at 285 Via Lola. He holed up there for a week in Palm Springs in July 1968 after pouring his heart and soul into his 1968 NBC TV Special, and recuperated in September following the wrap on *Charro!*

From 1969, Palm Springs became Elvis' favored weekend destination. In 1970, he and Priscilla finally got down to house hunting for a place to buy. By this time he was flying out to Palm Springs from Memphis, as well as driving out on weekends from Los Angeles.

Elvis and Priscilla spent their fourth wedding anniversary at their Palm Springs home in May 1971. More often, Elvis used Palm Springs as a bolt-hole where he could live a bachelor lifestyle with his pals. Palm Springs was also the one place where he could expect not to be bothered in any way.

After the separation from Priscilla in 1972, Elvis continued to go to Palm Springs, first with new girlfriend Linda Thompson, then from the summer of 1974 with Sheila Ryan. Elvis shuttled between Palm Springs, Memphis, LA and sometimes Denver in the mid-Seventies; the trips become even more frequent after he acquired his own fleet of planes.

PALM SPRINGS HOMES

In 1966, Elvis rented a large home at 1350 Ladera Circle in the Las Palmas district. It was Colonel Parker who found the house and settled the annual $21,000 rental bill. In 1967, Elvis took his new bride Priscilla to the home for a two-day honeymoon after getting hitched in Vegas. Soon after it was built in the early Sixties, the property appeared on the cover of Look magazine as "The House of Tomorrow," with modernist features such as a 64-foot built-in curved sofa and centralized vacuuming. Now known as the "Elvis Honeymoon Hideaway," tours of this property were available at the time of writing.

In 1968, the Presleys stayed at a new rental property in Camino del Norte while looking for a place to buy. They purchased their own place at 845 Chino Canyon Rd. in April 1970 for close to $100,000. Elvis and Priscilla spent a significant amount of time in this five-bedroomed 5040 sq. foot house in the Little Tuscany neighborhood. The Presleys added a swimming pool to the property, and then a basketball court. The predominant color scheme was red and black. Work began on a new master bedroom with a view over the valley before Elvis and Priscilla split up. In 1973, Elvis recorded some material here for his album *Raised on Rock*.

The Elvis Estate sold the house in 1979. The last time that the property changed hands was for $1.25 million in September 2003. For a period, it was turned into a tourist attraction, where for $1,000 tourists could sleep in Elvis' bedroom. The venture ran into legal troubles soon after, and the house was put back on the market in 2005 for twice its 2003 asking price.

JERRY SCHILLING: "Elvis loved his home in Palm Springs. It was where he went to relax after a tour. People didn't bother him in Palm Springs."

LARRY GELLER: "He loved the desert, the air, how he felt when he was there. He always found the people very friendly. No one hassled him."

"PARADISE, HAWAIIAN STYLE"

Giant, Baum and Kaye wrote this title song for the movie of the same name. Elvis obliged at Radio Recorders in early August 1965, laying down his vocal track after the band recorded instrumentals on July 27. The film version of the song—initially titled *Hawaii, USA*—featured additional overdubs compared with the version released on the soundtrack album.

Elvis used a few words from this song as the intro to his *Aloha From Hawaii via Satellite* broadcast in 1973.

Alternate takes from 1965 may be found on the FTD soundtrack release.

The song has since been reissued on *Command Performances* in addition to the *Double Features* and FTD *Paradise, Hawaiian Style* soundtrack re-releases.

PARADISE, HAWAIIAN STYLE (LP)

This soundtrack LP, released in June 1966, spent 19 weeks in the charts but ran out of steam at #15. It continued Elvis' diminishing sales curve, undercutting previous soundtrack album *Frankie and Johnny*, which itself sold fewer than 300,000 copies.

TRACK LISTING:
1.   Paradise, Hawaiian Style
2.   Queenie Wahine's Papaya
3.   Scratch My Back
4.   Drums Of The Islands
5.   Datin'
6.   A Dog's Life
7.   House Of Sand
8.   Stop Where You Are
9.   This Is My Heaven
10.   Sand Castles

The Nineties *Double Features* soundtrack re-release was paired with *Frankie and Johnny*.

FTD brought out an album of outtakes and alternates from the movie in 2004.

PARADISE-HAWAIIAN STYLE

If it ain't broke, don't fix it had been the Colonel's movie-making mantra for close to a decade, but this reworking of Elvis' previous Hawaiian escapades came perilously close to breakdown.

Working titles for this tropical musical comedy were *Hawaiian Paradise*, *Song of Hawaii*, *Polynesian Paradise* and *Hula Heaven*. Elvis turned up a week late for shooting in early August 1965, overweight and underwhelmed.

Petula Clark turned down the love interest role before it was given to Suzanna Leigh. To add an authentic native touch, dance sequences were choreographed by a man from the Polynesian Cultural Center in Laie, on the island of Oahu. The first scene was shot at Hanuma Bay; other locations included the Hanalei Plantation Resort on Kauai, the Maui Sheraton Hotel, and the Kona Coast.

Perhaps more interesting to Elvis than the filming itself was meeting The Beatles and Tom Jones (separately) before he wrapped on set on the last day of September, 1965.

One song, "Sand Castles," didn't make it into the movie but stayed on the soundtrack album. Child actress and Golden Globe nominee Donna Butterworth had a rare solo in an Elvis picture, with "Bill Bailey, Won't You Please Come Home."

A lack of social awareness by producer Hal Wallis resulted in fights between Tongans and Samoans over the use of a Samoan war boat crewed by Tongans.

Paradise, Hawaiian Style premiered in Memphis on June 9, 1966, and opened nationally on July 6, 1966. The movie still managed to turn a profit, taking $2.5 million before the end of the calendar year, making it the 40th highest-grossing picture of the year.

CREDITS:
Paramount, Color.
Length: 91 minutes
Release date: July 6, 1966

TAGLINES:
All Elvis breaks loose in the Swinging Swaying Luau-ing South Seas!

Directed by: Michael Moore
Produced by: Joseph H. Hazen (executive producer), Paul Nathan (associate producer), Hal B. Wallis (producer)
Written by: Allan Weiss (story), Anthony Lawrence and Allan Weiss (screenplay)
Cinematography by: W. Wallace Kelley
Film Editing by: Warren Low
Art Direction by: Hal Pereira, Walter H. Tyler
Set Decoration by: Robert R. Benton, Sam Comer, Ray Moyer
Costume Design by: Edith Head

CAST:
Elvis Presley	Rick Richards
Suzanna Leigh	Judy Hudson (Friday)
James Shigeta	Danny Kohana
Donna Butterworth	Jan Kohana
Marianna Hill	Lani Kaimana
Irene Tsu	Pua
Linda Wong	Lehua Kawena
Julie Parrish	Joanna
Jan Shepard	Betty Kohana
John Doucette	Donald Belden
Philip Ahn	Moki Kaimana
Mary Treen	Mrs. Belden
Steve Brodie	Bit part
Fred Carson	Guard
Don Collier	Andy Lowell
Chanin Hale	Job applicant
Sandy Kawelo	Dancer
Deanna Lund	Bit part
Doris Packer	Mrs. Barrington
Grady Sutton	Mr. Cubberson
Gigi Verone	Peggy Holdren
Red West	Rusty, Rick's antagonist
Edy Williams	Brunette

ADDITIONAL CREW:
Nellie Manley	hair stylist
Wally Westmore	makeup artist
Robert Goodstein	production manager
James A. Rosenberger	assistant director
Adam John Backauskas	props
John Carter	sound director
Charles Grenzbach	sound director
Romaine Birkmeyer	special effects
Fred Carson	stunts
Kim Kahana	stunts

Elvis as Rick Richards in Paradise- Hawaiian Style (1966).

Hubie Kerns	stunts
Gene LeBell	stunts
Farciot Edouart	process photographer
Joseph J. Lilley	conductor
Warren Low	editorial supervisor
Colonel Tom Parker	technical advisor
Jack Regas	choreographer
Jack Saper	assistant to producer
Nelson Tyler	helicopter photographer

Plot:
Elvis is Rick Richards, an airline pilot who comes home to Hawaii to set up a charter plane and helicopter company after losing his previous job (for a change) over a woman (for a change).

Rick fails to persuade old friend Danny Kohana (played by James Shigeta) to join the venture. Undeterred, Rick goes through his little black book of former girlfriends to drum up some business. Sheraton Hotel hostess Lehua Kawena (played by Linda Wong) obliges with plenty of customer referrals, and Danny decides to join the fledgling business, named Danrick Airways. A string of comic capers with admiring females brings further business and all looks set fair.

It takes all of Rick's helicoptering skills to avert a disaster while flying pedigree dogs out to a wealthy dog fancier. Collateral damage occurs to the pride of FAA representative Donald Belden (played by John Doucette), who Rick inadvertently runs into a ditch. Complaints from Belden (whose wife suffered a bad back in the accident) and the dog owner result in Rick's pilot's license being temporarily revoked.

When Rick takes Danny's little daughter Jan (played by Donna Butterworth) on a jaunt to a distant beach she hides the ignition key in the sand and they are forced to stay overnight. Enraged, Danny quits the partnership and storms off with his little girl, only to disappear mysteriously.

Permanently risking his pilot's license, Rick and pretty airline secretary Judy Hudson (played by English-born actress Suzanna Leigh) head off on a search and rescue mission. Rick finds his erstwhile partner with a broken leg after an emergency landing.

There is one last chance to save their licenses now, at a Polynesian festival where Belden is the guest of honor. Rick successfully argues his case, and Belden agrees a stay of execution on Danrick Airways after Rick's heroics. The happy ending is incomplete before Judy reveals that the wedding

ring she wears is just a precaution. Rick sings us out with "Drums of the Islands."

Songs: "Paradise Hawaiian Style," "Queenie Wahine's Papaya," "Scratch My Back," "Drums Of The Islands", "A Dog's Life," "Datin'," "House Of Sand," "Stop Where You Are," This Is My Heaven."

"PARALYZED"

Elvis recorded this Otis Blackwell composition on September 2, 1956 at Radio Recorders, for release on his second album, *Elvis*, later that year. The song also came out on the first volume of the *Elvis* EP, making it to #59 in the charts by this route.

Elvis threw "Paralyzed" into the mix during the December 1956 *Million Dollar Quartet* jam with Carl Perkins and Jerry Lee Lewis, this time a little slowed down.

The original studio version has since been released on *Worldwide Gold Award Hits Vol. 2*, *The King Of Rock And Roll*, *Elvis '56*, and the CD re-release of *Elvis' Gold Records*. RCA released the single posthumously in 1983.

PARAMOUNT STUDIOS

Keen to tie down America's hottest young singing star, Paramount offered Elvis a seven-picture deal on the strength of his March 1956 screen test, starting at $15,000 for the first picture and rising to $100,000 by the seventh. The Colonel inserted a clause that allowed Elvis to make a movie for another studio every year. By the time the studio had a property for Elvis, the Colonel had persuaded Hal Wallis to raise Elvis' fee with a $50,000 bonus for *Loving You* and twice that for *King Creole*. Paramount premiered their first Elvis movie at their flagship theater, at the Paramount Building on Broadway in New York City.

The Colonel renegotiated Elvis' Paramount deal in October 1958, bumping his fee to $175,000 per picture. He did it again in early 1961, uprating the contract to a five-movie deal starting at $175,000 per movie for the first three pictures (*Blue Hawaii*, *Girls! Girls! Girls!* and *Fun in Acapulco*), and then $200,000 for *Roustabout* and *Paradise—Hawaiian Style*. Elvis was already earning far more at the studios where he was making his non-Paramount pictures.

Elvis' final Paramount agreement, signed in April 1966, resulted in a hike to $500,000 per picture for Elvis and the Colonel, plus 20% of profits. The contract contained a clause requiring one movie in which Elvis didn't have to sing at all, but by now Elvis was disillusioned about making movies, especially at Paramount, which had long since consigned Elvis to their quick-and-cheap production line. His final effort, *Easy Come, Easy Go*, yielded his worst selling soundtrack album to date.

Now owned by Viacom, Paramount Pictures is the oldest operating studio in Hollywood. In days gone by the studio of Valentino and Bing Crosby, Elvis signed to Paramount Pictures just as it began to go into decline.

MOVIES ELVIS MADE WITH PARAMOUNT:

Loving You (1956)
King Creole (1958)
G.I. Blues (1960)
Blue Hawaii (1961)
Girls! Girls! Girls! (1962)
Fun in Acapulco (1963)
Roustabout (1964)
Paradise, Hawaiian Style (1966)
Easy Come, Easy Go (1967)

PARENTS

Vernon Presley and Gladys Love Smith, for whom Elvis effectively became a surrogate parent as soon as he became the family's biggest earner, even referring to his progenitors as "his babies." He looked after them for the rest of his life and beyond.

See also VERNON PRESLEY, GLADYS PRESLEY

PARIS

Elvis hired a whole private train carriage with pals Lamar Fike, Charlie Hodge and Rex Mansfield in June 1959 to travel from Munich to Paris for a two-week vacation. They took a top-floor suite at the Prince de Galles hotel, booked by Hill & Range boss Jean Aberbach, with a view over the Champs-Élysées. Despite assurances to the contrary, the one time that Elvis ventured out by day, he was mobbed at a café by hundreds of fans. Thereafter, he declined all invitations to see the sights.

Elvis' preferred sightseeing was Paris by Night: nightclubs the Carousel, Moulin Rouge, Folies Bergères, the Lido (where, flouting the Colonel's orders not to sing for free, one night Elvis reputedly sang "Willow Weep For Me"), and then late-night club Le Bantu, by which time Elvis and his pals would be surrounded by Bluebelle girls picked up at the Lido. The boys had such a good time that they cancelled their return train trip to stay a day longer, and got back to base just in time following a trans-national limousine ride.

Elvis returned to Paris on leave in January 1960 with entourage pals plus German karate teacher Jü,rgen Seydel. On the five-day trip, Elvis went to five karate classes given by Japanese master Tetsuji Murakami. He also took in a show by Gospel group the Golden Gate Quartet.

ELVIS SAID IN 1960: "It's a gay town. I mean, if you like nightlife and everything."

Book:

Elvis à Paris, by Jean-Marie Pouzenc, La Revue Elvis My Happiness, 1999.

PARKER, ED
(B. EDMUND KEALOHA PARKER, 1931-1990)

Elvis met Hawaiian-born Kenpo Karate Senior Grandmaster Ed Parker in 1960, after he saw a demonstration, the first of many Parker karate demonstrations that Elvis took in over the years.

Parker was brought up a Mormon and graduated from Brigham Young University.

Elvis studied karate with "The Father of American Karate" (or just plain "Mr. Karate") in Los Angeles in the Sixties. Elvis was the most famous of Parker's celebrity students, who included Nick Adams and Natalie Wood. Parker was responsible for introducing Bruce Lee to American audiences at one of his International Karate Championships, and worked in Hollywood training stuntmen and acting himself in karate-themed movies. He also appeared in a couple of the original Pink Panther movies.

In 1969, Parker presented Elvis with a business proposition to publicize American Kenpo, a discipline that Parker himself had developed.

Elvis flew Parker in to Las Vegas in August 1970, after he received a death threat. From this time, Parker sometimes provided additional security for Elvis backstage and onstage. Parker later recommended karate pal Dave Hebler to help with Elvis' security. Parker worked on and off with Elvis right up until his last concerts, and was with Elvis in his home state when Elvis was on vacation in Hawaii in March 1977. Over the years, Parker also gave demonstrations at the Tennessee Karate Institute, a martial arts studio that Elvis helped to set up.

Elvis briefly fell out with Parker in 1973, after he became angry with Parker for using Elvis' name in advertising for the California State Karate Championships without Elvis' say-so. By the following year they had made up sufficiently for Elvis to involve Parker in his plans to produce a karate movie.

Parker allowed his celebrity students, including Elvis and Priscilla, to wear black uniforms during lessons. Normally only instructors of American Kenpo could wear black *gi*.

Elvis gave Parker a Cadillac (despite Parker's strenuous protestations), and some of his personal initialized jewelry—EP worked equally well for the karate champ. Elvis nicknamed Parker "Kahuna"; according to Parker's Elvis biography, Elvis sometimes called him "my second daddy."

Books:

Inside Elvis, by Edmund K. Parker, Rampart House, 1978

PARKER, MARIE

Like many in the Elvis story, the Colonel's wife was from humble origins. Maria Mott, as she was born, met and married pre-Colonel Parker in 1935 at a carnival where they both worked. At that time Mrs. Ross, she already had two divorces behind her and two kids, one of whom she had given up for adoption. The other child, Bobby, suffered from multiple sclerosis, and died around the same time as Elvis.

Tales conflict about when they married, but it seems that it was soon after they met. Together, the family eked out an existence working carnivals for a little while longer before the Colonel got his job as a dogcatcher in Tampa and then parlayed his wife into music management.

Once the Elvis money began to flow in, the Colonel's biggest indulgence was to buy his wife nice things (in industrial quantities, according to some). Marie Parker became good friends with Mother Maybelle Carter. Colonel Parker jokingly referred to his wife as "Miz' Rie." Lisa Marie's name was chosen partly for Marie Parker. Elvis dedicated a live performance of "Are You Lonesome Tonight?" to Mrs. Parker at a 1969 Las Vegas show.

Marie Parker began to suffer from early senility in the early Seventies. She died in 1986.

ANNE FULCHINO: "They were two of a kind, and nothing was ever going to change them."

ALANNA NASH: "He let Marie all but rule him."

PARKER, PATRICIA ANN

In 1970, a woman claimed that Elvis fathered her son after a tryst in Las Vegas. When her boy was born, she named him Jason Peter Presley. Her legal claim for child support was served on Elvis while he was performing on stage at Inglewood in 1970. Elvis countersued. Blood analysis and a lie-detector test proved Elvis right and the waitress dropped her suit.

PARKER, THOMAS ANDREW, COLONEL
(B. ANDREAS "DRIES" CORNELIS VAN KUIJK, 1909-1997)

There is no more controversial figure in the Elvis story than Colonel. Many Elvis fans are convinced that the Colonel's management regime stopped Elvis from fully expressing himself as a musician and as an actor, and may unwittingly have hastened his premature demise. The Colonel has his fans too. It is historical fact that he masterminded the most successful career of any performer in the history of entertainment. Elvis Presley Enterprises is unfailingly courteous about the Colonel and appreciative of his contribution to Elvis' career, success and longevity. Within Elvis' inner circle, Joe Esposito says, "The stories of the Colonel taking advantage of Elvis, they're not true . . . Overall, the two of them were a team." Red West was always impressed by the hard bargains the Colonel drove, and respected the fact that the Colonel's word was sacrosanct. Documentary director Constant Meijers described the Colonel as, "A nobody who needed a somebody to be anybody." Biographer Alanna Nash sums him up thus: "A master illusionist in business and in the business of life, Tom Parker made things appear and disappear at will, and created something very great out of nothing . . . including himself."

Elvis' loyalty to his manager was always stronger than his dissatisfaction with the low-grade movies and soundtracks he was making through the Sixties: he felt that he had given his word to Parker, and he felt that he owed him his huge success. Parker's loyalty to Elvis was simpler: Elvis was his sole client and his entire livelihood.

Until 1981, the Colonel claimed to be a native of Huntington, West Virginia. In among the many colorful stories about his carnival past, he asserted that he had been orphaned young, as a kid worked for his uncle (proprietor of the Great Parker Pony Circus), then after running food concessions and even working briefly as a side-show palmreader, he began managing and promoting circuses. He was forced to drop this fabrication in 1981, when Albert Goldman's biography revealed that in actual fact Parker was born Andreas Cornelis van Kujik in Breda, Noord-Brabant, in the Netherlands, on June 26, 1909.

In reality, the Colonel was fortunate not to be unmasked a number of times before 1981. The Colonel's elder brother Ad visited him in the States in 1961 and wrote an article about the trip in *Rosita* magazine, which had helped to finance the trip. An Elvis fan club magazine published the truth about his origins in 1967. In 1977, immediately after Elvis' death, Dutch journalist Dick Vellenga received an anonymous tip-off about the Colonel's Dutch origins; his informant also said that before fleeing Holland, the Colonel had murdered a greengrocer's wife, Anna van den Enden—a thesis that Alanna Nash puts forward in her 2000s biography.

Parker's need to keep his origins a secret influenced some of the decisions that shaped Elvis' career. It is hard to come up with a more compelling reason for why the Colonel prevented an international star like Elvis from touring outside North America. Another of the Colonel's little secrets, his unrestrained gambling, may have been the prime motive for Elvis working so hard and so long in Las Vegas, rather than pursuing projects that might have kept boredom at bay.

Elvis and the Colonel shared a number of defining character traits. Like Elvis, the Colonel had sufficient charisma to bring people under his sway. Like Elvis, he loved a prank. Like Elvis, he was remarkably talented in his chosen field of endeavor. Like Elvis, he had a legendary temper. Like Elvis, he didn't drink—he told Joe Esposito that his whole personality changed and he became dangerously aggressive. Like Elvis, he surrounded himself with an entourage (though unlike Elvis, many of his protégés were more like surrogate sons, while the Colonel played the severe father). Like Elvis, the Colonel was a sleepwalker. Like Elvis, he considered loyalty paramount in the people around him—Tampa printer Clyde Rinaldi who advanced Parker a small loan in the Depression years, was richly rewarded decades later with the contract to print all of Elvis' merchandise. Like Elvis, the Colonel had an addictive streak—for the Colonel, it was gambling. Unlike Elvis, he was a habitual early riser. Unlike Elvis, he loved meeting new people if only to prove to them and himself that his were the sharper wits. Unlike Elvis, Parker's personal musical taste was for Lawrence Welk and his ilk (Joan Deary says that he was tone deaf).

Parker's early year

Colonel Thomas Andrew Parker was Andreas Cornelis van Kujik, born in Holland at the Van Gend en Loos building, on Veermarktstraat 66, in the town of Breda. The "van" in the family name hints at a noble lineage but by the time of his grandparents, the family was one of itinerant vendors, and his father was worked as a livery man. "Dries" was the seventh of eleven children his parents had, two of whom died as infants.

As a boy, Dries worked as a barker at carnivals in his hometown. He displayed many of the attributes that would be so useful to him in later years: telling stories, pulling pranks and showing a nose for making business out of nothing. Working part-time at a circus, he learned to perform tricks on horseback. One day his father gave

Elvis and Colonel Tom Parker at the wrap party for the film *Fun in Acapulco* (1963).

him a beating for putting on a show in front of his brothers and sisters and told him that he would never amount to anything; Biographer Alanna Nash traces the Colonel's lifelong delight in humiliating others to this formative event. Dries first tried to run away from home when he was 11. He left school early to work a variety of jobs. When he moved to Rotterdam as a 15-year-old, he worked on the boats in the port town. He first talked about sailing from Holland to America to make his fortune when he was 17. As an 18 year-old he emigrated illegally into the States, possibly after jumping ship from the vessel on which he was employed. He stayed in Hoboken, then traveled with a Chautauqua educative tent show. Briefly, he returned to Holland, before returning to America for good at age twenty.

Parker's entente with animals put him in good stead to work in carnival outfits. One of the jobs Parker is said to have had in the carnival was as part of an elephant act where he lay down in front of the pachyderms (he retained a lifelong fascination with elephants and elephant figurines).

After enlisting in the US Army (he is said to have taken the name Tom Parker from the captain who interviewed him when he joined) with the name Parker, he spent two years with the 64th Regiment of the Coast Guard Artillery at Fort Shafter in Honolulu. He then re-enlisted at Fort Barrancas, Pensacola, Florida. In later years, the Colonel would tell people that he served in the Navy and the Marines.

In actual fact, during his second period in the force he went AWOL and was listed as a deserter —a fact that the Colonel managed to keep under wraps when he was investigated by the courts in the early Eighties in connection with mismanaging Elvis' finances. Alanna Nash tracked down the records of his punishment—solitary confinement—from which he emerged with a psychosis that led to a couple of months in a mental hospital. He was subsequently discharged form the Army for a "constitutional psychopathic state," or an honorable discharge due to illness according to other sources.

Thomas Parker went to work with a pony show outfit in Tampa, Florida, and then worked a variety of jobs including food concessions and gaming carnivals. He began to build up his network of contacts, cultivating associations with men in authority and men of influence that would later serve as the foundation for his success.

Over the years, biographers have cited a number of inventive Colonel scams from this period. He sold hot dogs in a bun with mini-franks at each end and just coleslaw in the middle; another version of the scam is that he sent customers off with no meat in the bun at all, then when they came back to complain he pointed to a frank in the dirt near the stall which he had put there himself. One tale Elvis loved was how the Colonel would hand people their change but retain a quarter which he had stuck to the inside of a ring on one of his fingers. Other purported escapades include earning a living as a Santa Claus, and even selling Bibles to the widows of deceased men (a trick used by Ryan O'Neal in the 1973 movie *Paper Moon*). *See* SIDE-BAR: A COLORFUL PAST

While working as an animal officer for the Tampa Humane Society (initially as a dogcatcher in some sources), Parker came up with the novel idea of canine funerals, for which he sold

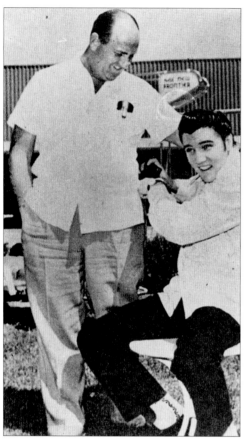

Elvis and Colonel Parker in the 1950's.

and supplied all the paraphernalia including headstones.

Parker's talent management career

Parker's earliest experience organizing and managing events was at Tampa Humane Society benefits. The first major singer that the Colonel took on was Gene Austin, though as with so much in the Colonel's backstory, the line between truth and fiction is blurred. One of the first of the crooners, Austin's career had stalled since his song "My Blue Heaven" had become the highest-selling single of all time—supplanted in the early Forties by Bing Crosby's "White Christmas."

During the war years, the Colonel obtained a deferral because he had a dependent (his step-son), though he remained "available for military service." He continued to move into promotions, booking shows for Roy Acuff and comic Minnie Pearl at the local National Guard Armory, when he came up with the bright idea of selling tickets through a coupon promotion at local grocery stores. Acuff declined the Colonel's advances for a permanent management deal, but he did suggest that Parker could do something for up-and-coming country musician, Eddy Arnold. Parker also started to manage some bookings for Ernest Tubb, one of several Grand Ole Opry artists for whom he worked as an advance man. He was not averse to trying a comic turn himself at some of the smaller tent shows he helped organize.

In 1945, Parker put pen to paper on a deal for 25% of Arnold's earnings as his manager. In a prelude to what he would do for Elvis, the Colonel dedicated all of his energies to bringing his client national fame, covering thousands of miles to arrange tours and promote dates. At Arnold's shows, the Colonel and his family worked the aisles selling merchandise—something he would also do for Elvis.

Parker impressed Arnold with his inventiveness and his ability to drum up interest wherever he went—often through press articles written by free-lancer "Tom Parker." Arnold climbed to the top of the Country tree, racking up five #1 hits in 1948; one of his singles from this period spent a whole

year at #1. Parker set up a product sponsorship tie-in for his client with the Purina company, one of the first ever money-making schemes set up by a manager for a performer. In a dry run for Elvis, Parker landed Arnold a recording contract with RCA, and then persuaded him to leave the Grand Old Opry for television, Las Vegas and motion pictures. By this time Parker no longer needed to use the free telephones at the Grand Ole Opry's Ryman Auditorium. Parker also developed working relationships with song publishers Hill & Range and the William Morris Agency, both of whom would be instrumental in the rise of Elvis.

Parker's managerial zeal included taking his wife and an assistant to stay for long periods with the Arnolds in Madison. Parker eventually bought his own home in the town, which became his center of operations.

Parker became a colonel in 1948, when Louisiana Governor and erstwhile country singer Jimmie Davis elevated Mr. Parker to the honorary rank of colonel. Long before receiving this honorific, Parker had been asking people to refer to him as "the Gov," though one member of Elvis' entourage has said that during his Army service back in the Thirties, Parker used to book hotel rooms as a "Colonel" because officers got preferential treatment.

Parker set up his office with assistant Tom Diskin, whom had he met in Chicago, and secretary Jim O'Brien. Both of these men remained with the Colonel for the duration. Arnold became less and less happy with the Colonel. Not long after finding out that Parker had started working with Hank Snow (the Colonel had already helped out country yodeler Slim Whitman in the late Forties), in August 1953 Arnold fired Parker. The Colonel forced Arnold to settle their working relationship through a $50,000 buyout, even though they had a gentleman's agreement rather than a contract—a tactic he employed to good effect years later with Elvis: the one time that Elvis got up the guts to fire him, the Colonel countered with a huge settlement claim that frightened the Presleys into submission. With Arnold, the Colonel also managed to hold on to the right to organize concerts in specific markets, while at the same time taking over responsibility for all of Hank Snow's bookings, TV, film and recording contracts. Parker used Snow—a singer Gladys liked very much—as an important bargaining chip to persuade Elvis to sign with him. Parker and Snow established "Hank Snow Enterprises and Jamboree Attractions," a successful promotions outfit for leading country and hill-billy stars, until young people started wanting to listen to a newfangled type of music that as yet had no name.

The rise of Elvis

It almost goes without saying that conflicting stories circulate about how Elvis and Colonel Tom Parker first crossed paths. A strong candidate for alerting the Colonel to this new phenomenon was sometime associate Oscar Davis, who took in an Elvis show in late November 1954 while in Memphis arranging a booking for Eddy Arnold at the Ellis Auditorium. Other people have claimed credit over the years, not least Hank Snow, DJ Uncle Dudley (aka Ernest Hackworth) and Gabe Tucker, who later worked for the Colonel. In the book *Memphis Recording Service*, it is asserted that Tom Diskin (and therefore the Colonel) was already aware of Elvis as early as late October 1954.

Immediately before becoming involved with Elvis, Colonel Tom Parker and Tom Diskin had been managing Tommy Sands, a singer who, though two years Elvis' junior, was already a relative veteran, having began his recording career as a thirteen year old. Whoever it was who first mentioned Elvis' name to Parker, there can be no doubt that the Colonel was actively looking for an artist who sang the new music.

The general consensus among Elvistorians is that Colonel Tom Parker and assistant Tom Diskin first saw Elvis perform at the Louisiana Hayride on Saturday January 15, 1955. Ernst Jorgensen puts this fateful meeting a few days earlier, at a well-received show Elvis gave in New Boston, Texas; D. J. Fontana concurs that the Colonel took in a number of Elvis in the Texarkana region without announcing his presence before the Hayride date. After the Hayride appearance, the Colonel told Elvis' then manager Bob Neal that he would be happy to use his superior contracts to get Elvis onto higher prestige tours, starting with the Hank Snow tours of which he was a joint proprietor.

The battle over Elvis' fate was joined in earnest on February 6, 1955, at the Palumbo Restaurant in Memphis. Though the meeting was convened by Bob Neal, the Colonel took over and told Sam Phillips that Elvis' career would best be served by moving to a bigger label than Sun.

The first show that the Colonel booked for Elvis was either the Fair Park Coliseum in Lubbock, Texas, on February 13, 1955, or according to the majority of biographers, a four-day booking on the Hank Snow Tour starting at Roswell, New Mexico that month, billed as "Elvis and his Bop Band" below Hank Snow, hill-billy comic the Duke of Paducah, Charlene Arthur, and Jimmie Rodgers Snow.

The Colonel told promoter A. V. "Bam" Bamford that Elvis was "a great artist, but will need lots of buildup before he's a good investment." Parker was already hard at work on doing just that. By early March, piqued by the Colonel's solicitations, William Morris agent Harry Kalcheim was suggesting an audition for Elvis with the "Arthur Godfrey Talent Scouts." Elvis' official manager Bob Neal had already made some headway with the New York TV show before the Colonel muscled in, offering to pay Elvis' traveling expenses on condition that any monies earned through subsequent bookings would go through the Colonel's organization. Meanwhile, the Colonel was warning associate Tom Diskin that they had to be very careful that they, rather than Bob Neal, reaped the benefits of their contacts.

Parker was also at work on finding Elvis a "proper" national record label. Eventual winners RCA were just one of the labels in contention. Through Nashville producer Owen Bradley, the Colonel informed Paul Cohen of Decca that Sun was prepared to sell up Elvis' recording contract, but Cohen balked at the $8,000 fee Bob Neal initially quoted. According to some sources, Sam Phillips offered Bradley a direct opportunity to buy out Elvis' contract. Spurred on by reports of Elvis stealing shows headlined by established stars, Cohen called Neal again, only to learn that the price had now gone up to $20,000.

The Colonel accompanied Elvis on his early May 1955 tour of Florida. After Elvis barely escaped from a riot that claimed his clothes and shoes in Jacksonville, claimed Parker no longer had any doubts that the boy was headed for extraordinary things. On May 26, 1955, in a letter to Bob Neal, the Colonel euphemistically wrote: "If ever you wish to tie in with me closely and let me carry the ball, I will be happy to sit down with both of you and try to work it out." After the Colonel mooted a possible booking in Las Vegas, which was outside the compass of Neal's orbit, on June 17, 1955, Neal agreed to allow the Colonel to handle all of Elvis' bookings, provided that Neal remained Elvis' manager in name. By now, Steve Sholes at RCA Records was considering making a firm bid for Elvis' contract. Mercury Records boss Irvin Green reputedly turned down Elvis when the Colonel offered Elvis and publishing rights for $35,000; Columbia Records boss Mitch Miller was initially interested but pulled out long before it got to that figure (though according to some reports, Columbia Records came back in at a late stage with an offer of $40,000 that the Colonel turned down).

By the end of July, Colonel Parker was sending out Elvis publicity that failed to mention Sun Records at all. Parker discussed with Diskin, Hank Snow and Bob Neal the possibility of buying Elvis out of his contract with Sun Records for $10,000, in exchange for a 2% share of Elvis' royalties from record sales (Elvis was only on 3% at Sun, as opposed to industry standard 5%). Parker effectively took over representation of Elvis, through Hank Snow Attractions, on July 24, 1955, though Bob Neal continued as Elvis' official manager until the end of the year, and was officially contracted to manage Elvis until March 1956.

Parker took it upon himself to teach Elvis about the responsibilities of being a performer. When promoter Ed Lyon complained that Elvis' unprofessional conduct had ruined a show in Batesville, Arkansas, Colonel Tom sent a $50 refund, and then berated Elvis' manager Bob Neal. The Colonel also wrote to Vernon Presley, telling him that he had had a great deal lined up that had fallen through because it was impossible to find Bob Neal in time.

On August 15, 1955, the Colonel achieved the next small step in wresting complete control over Elvis from Neal. Elvis signed a new contract that made Colonel Tom Parker his "special adviser" responsible for practically all management issues (see SIDEBAR). Rather than surrendering, however, Bob Neal started to fight back. In mid-September, Neal negotiated a year-long extension to Elvis' Saturday night Louisiana Hayride deal for a much improved fee, and then pulled out of his partnership with the Colonel. The Colonel forwarded a copy of this parting correspondence to Elvis; seeming to accept defeat with good grace, Parker told Elvis that he hoped they would work together sometime in the future. In the meantime, he continued to line up a big label buyer for Elvis' contract with Sun.

On October 20, 1955, Elvis' parents signed a telegram contract prepared by Tom Diskin which gave the Colonel "sole and exclusive" rights to represent their son in all recording contract negotiations. Alanna Nash suggests that Parker turned up with two contracts the day Elvis signed, one for management by Hank Snow Jamboree Attractions (for Elvis' parents, Hank Snow was a guarantee), the other for management exclusively by Colonel Tom A. Parker, and later pulled a switcheroo.

Four days later, the Colonel telegrammed Sam Phillips to ask him his final price for selling Elvis' contract to an assured buyer. Meanwhile, he attempted to conclude an agreement with Steve Sholes and Bill Bullock of RCA, who refused to go above $25,000. On October 29, Colonel Parker traveled to Memphis to agree terms with Sam Phillips of a non-refundable $5,000 down payment as an option on a $35,000 buyout of Elvis' Sun recording contract. Parker was also in contact with Harry Kalcheim at William Morris about launching Elvis' movie career, which he described as "something like the James Dean situation."

RCA kept Colonel Parker fretting until the final day of the option he had taken out with Sam Phillips. On November 15, 1955 the Colonel airmailed Phillips the $5,000 down payment out of his own funds. The deal shrewdly included an RCA purchase of Elvis' back catalogue from Sun; when Johnny Cash moved to Columbia three years later, his new releases were undermined by Phillips' canny Sun reissues. The Colonel also made sure that like Bing Crosby, Elvis would have a slice of the publishing rights for the songs he sang.

On November 21, 1955, Elvis' contract was officially transferred to RCA records. The

The Colonel and Elvis during the filming of *Clambake*, 1967.

Colonel picked up an immediate $1,500 commission on the advance Elvis received from RCA and song publishers Hill and Range, and could expect a healthy cut from Elvis' 5% royalty. The $40,000 that RCA forked out was the highest figure that any record company had paid for a singer.

Elvis sent the Colonel a telegram overflowing with gratitude:

Dear Colonel, Words can never tell you how my folks and I appreciate what you did for me. I've always known and now my folks are assured that you are the best, most wonderful person I could ever hope to work with. Believe me when I say I will stick with you through thick and thin and do everything I can to uphold your faith in me. Again, I say thanks and I love you like a father. Elvis Presley.

Elvis did indeed stay with the Colonel through thick and thin, though his assertion that his folks were overjoyed was not wholly true. His mother Gladys had taken a visceral dislike to the Colonel, but succumbed after the Colonel went on a mother's charm offensive and persuaded her that getting Elvis into bigger venues would ensure that he was better protected from the kind of riotous behavior she so feared. However, she was displeased when the Colonel set about creating what he thought was the right image for Elvis' family as god-fearing, hard-working country stock, which included an active role for herself and Vernon. According to Marty Lacker, "Gladys was a pretty good judge of people, and if she didn't like you, you had a problem. She didn't like Colonel Parker." Elvis, who generally avoided going against his mother's will, was conflicted by his mother's instant dislike for the Colonel but had pressed on in the belief that the Colonel was his best hope for stardom.

Parker claimed all of his business expenses from Elvis over and above a 25% commission on all revenues. Elvis later bragged that the Colonel's industry-standards busting fee was a badge of honor.

With Elvis' recording future assured, the Colonel switched his focus to getting his handsome young star movie exposure through William Morris agent Harry Kalcheim. The Colonel traveled with Elvis as he became a huge concert draw after his appearance on CBS's "Stage Show," by this time selling out three or four shows a day at each venue. Parker told an associate, "I'm using the old circus style promotion and it's paying off. No gimmicks and giveaways. Just plain old advertising. It's coming, it's here, and now it's gone." This frenetic pace took a heavy toll on Elvis: he collapsed in Jacksonville after one show, diagnosed with exhaustion.

In March 1956, the Colonel put into practice the final element of his strategy to wrest complete control over Elvis: he wound up his business association with Hank Snow and his promotions company. Snow was livid, fully believing that he was as much in charge of Elvis' contract as the Colonel. The courts decided otherwise when Snow initiated legal proceedings against the Colonel.

On the day that Elvis reported to Paramount Studios for his screen test, he signed an agreement with the Colonel appointing him as his "sole and exclusive Adviser, Personal Representative, and Manager in any and all fields of public and private entertainment." Paramount immediately signed Elvis to a seven-picture deal, though the Colonel managed to retain the right for Elvis to make one movie per year with another studio. Right from the start, Elvis' film deals included perks for the Colonel such as office space and seconded staff. Ensconced in Hollywood, the Colonel did everything within his power to act as a filter between Elvis and studio executives, whom to some degree he viewed as potential rivals. Though nominally staying out of the realm of musical creativity, the Colonel clamped down on any music professional who he believed was getting too close to Elvis; through song publishers Hill & Range, who were involved in the deal to buy out Elvis' contract from Sun, the Colonel later wielded a degree of indirect control over the material submitted to Elvis.

As Elvis became nationally known through his TV appearances, the Colonel refused anything but star billing. From May 1956, almost all of Elvis' shows were just Elvis and the band. One of the Colonel's favorite early tricks was to turn down bookings, claiming that Elvis was fully booked, only to let it be known that he might be able to shuffle things around if a premium was paid. The Colonel thus doubled Elvis' official rate at a stroke.

While Elvis was taking his first vacation in two years of incessant touring, in the summer of 1956 the Colonel delivered a slot on the influential "Ed Sullivan Show" and wrapped up a merchandising deal with Hank Saperstein for a $35,000 advance against 45% of licensing fees and royalties. He also masterminded a campaign to fight back against the self-appointed guardians of public morality (who were becoming increasingly vociferous as Elvis took rock and roll into mainstream white youth culture), and impressed on Elvis that however much in love he might be with a particular young lady—Elvis spent his vacation in Biloxi with girlfriend June Juanico—he would undo all of their hard work if his female fanbase began to believe that he was taken.

Aside from occasional minor signs of rebellion—during the soundtrack sessions for *Loving You*, Elvis snubbed the Colonel by refusing to record "Castles In The Sand," a song written by Colonel employees Trude Forscher and Byron Raphael—Elvis was recognizant and grateful.

Consolidating Elvis

By now, the Colonel was trying to impose his particular theory on supply and demand, reigning in his client to avoid overexposure, which he told RCA executive Steve Sholes was "like sunburn." In the summer of 1956, the Colonel criticized RCA for releasing every track on Elvis' first album on a set of six singles. He Colonel obtained a written assurance from the label that in future they would not release singles without his prior written consent. On October 18, 1956 Elvis signed a new, improved contract with the label, the first of many improved deals that the Colonel hammered out over the years, in the process browbeating a generation of RCA record executives.

After bumping up Elvis' fee with a $50,000 bonus for his first Paramount film, rather than the contractually-agreed figure of $15,000, in February 1957, the Colonel arranged for Elvis to make a film at MGM. Upping the ante on Paramount considerably, the Colonel obtained a $250,000 fee for his client plus 50% of net profits. At the time, the Colonel claimed this was the biggest deal ever made in Hollywood.

Parker lost no opportunity to profit from side deals from the start. Starting with Elvis' first film, *Love Me Tender*, the Colonel received a "Technical Advisor" credit: this perk included an office and staff on loan from the studio, plus as much as an additional $25,000 for his services. Parker received this credit on twenty of Elvis' movies.

Elvis' relationship with the Colonel is magnificently expressed in a photo taken backstage before his second appearance on "The Ed Sullivan Show" in October 1956. While show host Sullivan is explaining something to a smiling Colonel Parker, Elvis, putting the finishing touches to his hair, has his eyes focused firmly and anxiously on the Colonel.

At the same time, the Colonel's huckster side was on display at the wrap party of *Loving You*, where he personally gave away Elvis promotional material to the people who had been working with Elvis for months. In 1957, his promotional initiatives to keep Elvis in the news included hiring elephants emblazoned with Elvis Presley's name; he also announced the formation of an "Elvis Presley Midget Fan Club." However, he turned down all offers from TV: Bill Bullock suggested Elvis as a presenter for the "Galaxy of Stars" TV special in June 1957 but the Colonel wasn't interested.

The Colonel persuaded Paramount to quintuple the previously agreed fee for his next movie, to $100,000. He set to work on RCA with a barrage of side-deals that the record company was in no position to refuse: at the Colonel's request, RCA agreed to pay Elvis (and therefore the Colonel) for all photographs used on future albums, starting with $10,000 for the 1957 Christmas album and $6,000 for the Christmas EP.

The Colonel also began his outwardly-inexplicable lifelong battle against lucrative offers for Elvis to tour outside the States. The one time he wavered was in 1957, when he agreed (or lost a bet over dice according to some versions of the story) to let Australian-born promoter Lee Gordon book Elvis for a performance in Hawaii. In later years, the Colonel fended off countless multi-million dollar offers to tour outside the US; he also turned down invitations for Elvis to sing for President Nixon at the White House, and a show at Carnegie Hall in New York City.

The Colonel continued to be vigilant against anybody wielding "undue influence" on his sole charge. After one 1957 recording session, the Colonel upbraided songwriters (and at that particular session producers) Leiber and Stoller for offering songs directly to Elvis without going through publishers Hill & Range. He underlined his dominance of Elvis' business relations by sending the songwriting duo a blank page for them to sign for their *King Creole* soundtrack contract, informing them that he would fill in the details later.

In January 1958, the Colonel tipped off LA DJs about exactly when Elvis was coming to town to start shooting *King Creole*, so that when he arrived crowds lined the streets where he passed. This was a trick that in one form or another the Colonel favored to produce a media-worthy event.

With Elvis' Army service looming, Elvis feared for his very career. The Colonel seemed far more concerned that Elvis should not be inveigled into performing for free. Rightly as it turned out, the Colonel calculated that doing his Army service like any patriotic American would bring Elvis mainstream acceptance and broaden his appeal beyond his initial rock 'n' roll fan base. This ruled out the soft option of singing as part of Special Services. Ernst Jorgensen describes the Colonel's "New Elvis" as: "a red-blooded American boy, a creature wholesome enough to walk right into the hearts of grown-up fans." The Colonel also reminded Elvis that marriage was off the agenda for long-term sweetheart Anita Wood.

Colonel Parker's strict rationing of Elvis' recording time was unpopular with RCA executives, who in 1958 were concerned that they had far too little material to release while Elvis was away on Army service. When Elvis returned to the recording studio for RCA after a long layoff in June 1958, it was with a substantially new band that produced a whole lot more instrumental power. Elvis was impressed; Colonel Parker thought that the improved band provided needless competition for his boy.

One of the rare occasions that Elvis displayed anger towards the Colonel was after his mother's death, when the Colonel came to Graceland and started giving out orders, as sometimes he had done before. The Colonel told Elvis to clear everybody out of the place as Gladys's casket lay in the white room; Elvis refused.

Parker tried to make up for diminishing revenue streams during Elvis' Army absence by coming up with a product advertising contract. His attempts through William Morris Agency yielded no takers at the $100,000 fee the Colonel set, though Revlon was interested in using Elvis to endorse their Top Brass hairdressing product. The Colonel managed to negotiate a royalty payment for at least 100,000 copies of an EP of Elvis' press conference before embarking for Germany from RCA; *Elvis Sails!* sold 60,000 copies only.

In October 1958, Parker renegotiated Elvis' deal with Paramount to $175,000 for his first post-Army film (*G.I. Blues*), and an option for three more movies on a rising scale, against 7½% of gross receipts. Parker also improved the terms of Elvis' deal with 20th Century-Fox to $200,000, an option for another picture, and a 50/50 profit split with the studio after costs.

At Elvis' behest, in 1959 the Colonel tried to shorten his Army service by persuading top brass that Elvis was more useful back in the States, helping with recruitment. The stratagem, which included sending photographer Don Cravens out to Germany, was less than successful.

The Sixties

What Parker arranged for Elvis' return was a slot on the Frank Sinatra TV show, in exchange for a record guest appearance fee. That still left time before Elvis set foot on US soil to renegotiate Elvis' contract with RCA, upping his royalty by a full percentage point over the previous 5%, and also granting the Colonel approval on all promotion and publicity.

With Elvis back, Parker's promotion machinery swung into top gear. Everywhere Elvis went, fan clubs were warned in advance and the press was on hand to record the adulation. The railway club car that the Colonel hired to take him, Elvis, Elvis' entourage and the Colonel's staff from Memphis to LA to begin work on *G.I. Blues* stopped at stations along the way for Elvis to sign autographs and appear before his adoring fans. Parker turned Elvis' time on set into a sequence of publicity opportunities with fan club members and even visiting royalty. He also definitively removed his biggest potential rival from the picture, after Jerry Leiber committed the unpardonable crime of talking directly to Hill & Range about a possible future movie project for Elvis.

In November 1960, Parker landed Elvis an even more lucrative film deal with United Artists and the Mirisch Brothers company: a cool half a million dollars plus a 50% share of profits for two movies, *Follow That Dream* and *Kid Galahad*.

Between deals, Parker enjoyed dressing up as Father Christmas on the set of *Wild in the Country* in the run-up to Christmas 1960. On the set of *Kid Galahad* he had fun with members of Elvis' entourage, hypnotizing Sonny West and getting him to insult the director. Sometimes the Colonel hypnotized the entire entourage and made them pretend to be dogs, with the grand finale of setting them all on one member of the crew—generally Lamar Fike. On the set of *Paradise—Hawaiian Style* Parker persuaded Billy Smith to act like a monkey and Charlie Hodge to mimic a dog. Larry Geller speculates that Elvis' gang played along with this "suggestive" hypnotism for fun; they knew that it was in their best interests to go along with it. Steve Binder, producer of Elvis' NBC TV Special, years later said that he believed the Colonel had "the magic power . . . Before Elvis did anything, the Colonel would take him quietly into a room and use his amateur hypnotism talent on him. Elvis was very insecure. But fifteen minutes later, he would come out oozing confidence, convinced that he was the greatest performer who ever walked on the stage." In her biography of the Colonel, Alanna Nash concurs that Parker hypnotized Elvis before he went out to perform in 1968, his first live show in seven years.

Parker's longest-running prank of all was his bogus club, the Snowmen's League of America, which it reputedly cost nothing to join but thousands to leave. Parker handed out club memberships in this self-declared secret society to his confederates and to important figure who he thought might be useful to him at some time.

In late 1960 and early 1961, Colonel Parker uprated Elvis' movie contract with Paramount and struck a four-picture deal with MGM. He made it a trifecta of contract renegotiations by rejigging Elvis' RCA contract for significantly higher income, 25% of which was for Parker himself. By this point, the Colonel was making close to $120,000 annually from RCA alone.

Elvis and Colonel Tom Parker in 1960.

Elvis and the Colonel, 1960.

The oft-repeated criticism that Parker relegated artistic concerns below monetary considerations fails to take into account the Colonel's keen perception of how the market responded to Elvis "product." After his return from the Army, Elvis' musically-accomplished album *Elvis Is Back!* sold barely a third as many copies as the *G.I. Blues* soundtrack, while the more dramatic *Flaming Star* was a much smaller box office draw than blockbuster hit *Blue Hawaii*.

Parker received a family visit in the Spring of 1961 when his brother Ad came to stay. The Colonel presented him to many colleagues as his brother, but nobody drew the conclusion that if his brother was Dutch, then the Colonel was probably Dutch too. Remarkably there was no publicity about the visit in the States, considering that the whole trip had been sponsored, paid for and featured in Dutch magazine *Rosita*.

In 1961, a Hollywood gossip column reported that Bob Hope was so intrigued with the Colonel, whom he had met at an MGM party, that he wanted to make a film of his life. Colonel Parker's reaction? "No money, no deal."

Parker rang in the new year of 1962 with yet another new contract between Elvis and RCA. As well as boosting guaranteed earnings from the record label, the contract for the first time provided for a 50/50 split between Elvis and the Colonel for "side deals" (excluding royalties).

Parker continued to turn down all offers apart from movies; by now the Colonel had consolidated his system of using the movie soundtracks to fulfill Elvis' RCA recording commitments.

Before 1962 was out, the Colonel had beaten his headline figure record in a one-picture deal with Allied Artists: $750,000 income on a budget capped at $1.5 million, and half of any profits above that. The resulting film, *Tickle Me*, cut costs even further by re-using songs from previous Elvis albums.

Parker emerged from his studio office space in 1963 to hire MGM producer Sam Katzman, aka "King of the Quickies," to work on *Viva Las Vegas* and staunch the budget overrun—important so as not to dent the profit-share he had negotiated. Collateral damage that the Colonel might have appreciated was downscaling the prominence of co-star Ann-Margret, who came far closer to a co-lead than any other actor in an Elvis film before or after.

In late 1963, the Colonel reassured Paramount producer Hal Wallis that Elvis was not getting too plump and jowly to play starring roles in the movies. The Colonel began 1964 by buying Franklin D. Roosevelt's former yacht, the *Potomac*, for $55,000, with the intention of Elvis donating it to the March of Dimes at just about exactly the time that the Beatles' were making their first tour of the US. The March of Dimes spoiled the photo opportunity by declining the gift, which needed a lot of work to be made seaworthy again. Instead, Elvis donated the

boat to Danny Thomas for St. Jude's Hospital in Memphis. In time for the press ceremony, the Colonel had the boat repainted on just the side facing the dock where the press pack gathered.

Elvis' 1964 movie *Roustabout* offered the Colonel a chance to get involved at the script level. He added his knowledge of carnival and circus life, and lobbied for carnival workers to be painted in a positive light—services for which he earned $25,000 above his agreed income. Previously, the Colonel's involvement in the storyline of Elvis' movies had been more through Parkeresque characters—hard-nosed manager types—in movies such as *Loving You*, *Jailhouse Rock* and *Fun in Acapulco*.

The Colonel ended the year with not one but two new movie contracts: a two-picture deal with United Artists, and a three-picture deal with MGM in which, for the first time, the Colonel broke through the magical $1 million mark (which the studio doled out in weekly installments), plus 40% of profits.

Now that record sales were undeniably flagging, the Colonel focused on record promotion for the first time in years with "Crying In The Chapel," an April 1965 single that briefly reversed Elvis' chart decline. Promotion of the single included sponsorship of a nationally-broadcast Mother's Day radio show featuring inspirational Elvis songs.

By 1965, the Colonel had long since dropped the pretence of shielding his client from overexposure. That year saw three movie releases, seven singles, three albums and an EP. Aptly, the sign on the door of the Colonel's office at MGM read "Elvis Exploitations." At no time did the Colonel have wider control over every aspect of Elvis' career than in this period, from the movies he made to the songs he released. Little wonder that it coincided with Elvis' escape into spirituality and a quest to find some meaning in life.

The Colonel continued to justify his complete control over Elvis' career with more contract negotiations. Six months of negotiation with Paramount in 1966 raised Elvis' fee to $500,000 per picture. The Colonel had also inserted a clause that Paramount was liable to pay an additional $25,000 if Elvis wore any of his own clothes or jewelry in a movie.

Next up for renegotiation was Elvis' longstanding record contract with RCA. Though Elvis' record sales were on a steady downward trend, the Colonel bumped up Elvis' annual advance by 50% and obtained a bonus without relinquishing any future royalties.

Rumors surfaced in 1966 that the Colonel might be ready to relinquish his position as Elvis' manager. According to gossip columnist Dorothy Manners, Beatles manager Brian Epstein was considering a buy-out of the Colonel's contract with Elvis. Meanwhile, the Colonel signed a new four-picture deal with MGM, and persuaded the William Morris Agency to loan him a house in Palm Springs for himself and to host Elvis on weekends off from filming. Elvis and the Colonel spent Thanksgiving at the Colonel's Palm Springs freebie house that year.

In the summer of 1966, the Colonel negotiated a further $100,000 payment from RCA, split 50/50 with Elvis, to release songs on the new eight-track format. RCA were still willing to pay what the Colonel asked, even though Elvis' singles were no longer making it into the top ten; his Christmas 1966 release, "If Every Day Was Like Christmas" failed to make it even into the top 100.

Elvis and the Colonel's business arrangements slid closer to a partnership in a new representation contract that came into force on January 1, 1967: the Colonel continued to receive a 25% commission on Elvis' salary from movies and standard record company advances, but henceforth was officially entitled to 50% of any other earnings: profits, royalties above basic payments, and all special side deals.

Relations between mentor and protégé became strained in February 1967, with Elvis' marriage looming—entourage members have speculated that the Colonel advised Elvis to marry Priscilla at long last—and after Elvis began to dedicate his time and energies to buying horses and fixing up the newly-purchased Circle G ranch just outside Memphis. The Colonel became increasingly frustrated at being unable to get in touch with Elvis for weeks at a time. Worse, Elvis showed no sign of going to LA to start work on his next movie project, *Clambake*. When Elvis suffered concussion in a bathroom fall in 1967, further delaying the start of principal photography, the Colonel burst into Elvis' private life. He berated the entire entourage and threatened them *en bloc* with being fired. His rage was directed particularly at Larry Geller (whom the Colonel believed had been putting ideas into Elvis' head that had made him less reliable), and at Marty Lacker (whom he demoted from his "co-foreman" post). The Colonel gave Elvis an ultimatum: either obey me completely or lose everything, including your home and your fans. The Colonel banished all talk of spirituality or religion, made it clear to Larry Geller that he was no longer welcome, and let the rest of the entourage know that they were not to bring their problems to Elvis "as if he was some kind of Jesus Christ figure."

At around this time, the Colonel turned the wheel another notch in his favor in a revised recording contract with RCA, which he extended all the way to 1980. Elvis actually took a cut in his guaranteed advance royalties to $200,000 per year (down from the $300,000 he was contracted to receive until 1970). The new contract also gave Parker the incentive to find new "merchandising opportunities" on which he could earn 50%.

Parker's newfound status overseeing not just Elvis' career but his private life too reached its apogee at Elvis and Priscilla's May 1967 wedding. The Colonel decided where the event was held, masterminded the press-dodging arrival, and ruled on which members of the entourage were allowed into the ceremony. Larry Geller read about the wedding in a paper; a few weeks earlier Elvis had told Geller he wanted him to be his best man.

With all of Elvis' major deals in place, the Colonel dedicated himself to side-deals for 1967 and came up with an extra $60,000 payment from RCA for the *Clambake* soundtrack LP and a plan to revive Elvis' 1957 Christmas album through a nationwide radio show promotion. He went into damage limitation mode in July 1967, canceling a planned recording session after one of Elvis' bodyguards, Richard Davis, was involved in a car accident fatality. Fearing adverse publicity, the Colonel sent Elvis and Priscilla away from Los Angeles to Las Vegas.

The Colonel netted Elvis an $850,000 fee plus the by-now-customary 50% of profits with National General Pictures for *Charro!*, the last feature movie deal that he would make. The days of multiple ongoing deals with Hollywood studios were over, and the Colonel decided that the time had come to go back to TV. In January 1968, a $1 million deal was announced with NBC to make a Christmas TV Special (Parker had been holding out for this figure) and a future movie. Wittingly or otherwise, the Colonel had set in motion Elvis' career resurrection. Fancy footwork by producers Steve Binder and Bones Howe shifted the brief for the show away from a saccharine seasonal show to a celebration of Elvis' entire musical career, as for once the Colonel was outmaneuvered. He held on fiercely to at least one Christmas tune in the show, and had to content himself with wresting back publishing rights to the recordings for release by RCA at a later date. Producers Steve Binder and Bones Howe tried until the bitter end to obtain even a small percentage of revenue from a future vinyl release, but the Colonel wouldn't budge. Instead, he assured them that they'd enjoy "a million-dollar experience."

For once, Elvis was free to follow his creativity, flanked by professionals whose goal was to make something memorable, not make the most possible money. Elvis rediscovered all of the passion and grit that had been leeched out of him over the previous decade. The Colonel kept on pressing for at least one Christmas number in the package—so often that in a reworded version of "It Hurts Me" that Elvis sang for the Colonel's birthday, he altered the lyrics to tease him about the "one lousy Christmas song." When the Colonel saw a rough cut of the show without the Christmas number, he threatened to pull the plug on the whole project. The crisis was averted when NBC reinstated "Blue Christmas."

After recording the special that June, the Colonel proved that he had lost none of his nous by extracting *ex gratia* payments from RCA for single and album releases in 1968 beyond the number contractually agreed, $50,000 for running his side of the promotion operation, and money for 250,000 Colonel-supplied promotional photographs. By the Seventies, the Colonel was hiring photographers to take live shots of Elvis and deciding which pictures to send RCA for album art. The Colonel also banked a $35,000 advance on royalties for a Singer-sponsored special LP of old Elvis material (originally released as *Singer Presents Elvis Singing Flaming Star*), and then had RCA bring out its own version a few months later.

So emphatically did Elvis prove he was still a supreme showman that immediately after the NBC TV Special was broadcast, the Colonel was locked in negotiations with the William Morris Agency about Elvis playing for two or four weeks in Las Vegas for $300,000 or $500,000, figures not dissimilar to what he had been earning over a similar time scale on his movies. The interested party, the then-under-construction International Hotel, insisted on Elvis performing two shows per night rather than the Colonel's initial offer of two shows per night on Fridays and Saturdays only.

Once the deal was struck, the Colonel went to town on publicity, buying up practically all of the billboards in Las Vegas and on the road from California. For the first and most certainly not the last time, he plastered the International Hotel with Elvis banners, pictures and merchandise, funded by a $100,000 payment from RCA to cover his promotional costs. Elvis overcame debilitating nerves yet again and triumphed. After his hugely successful opening performance, the Colonel appeared backstage and for one of the few times anyone can remember, embraced his boy with real emotion. Parker struck while the iron was hot to renegotiate Elvis' contract. That very night he famously drew up a revised contract on the tablecloth at the hotel coffee shop with International president Alex Shoofey. Elvis' salary was bumped up to $125,000 per week, in exchange for an option to keep Elvis coming back to the International Hotel twice a year until 1974, plus a further $50,000 upfront bonus, taking the deal past the magical $1 million mark. The hotel management had reason to be happy with the deal, as for once the Colonel had failed to build a riser into Elvis' fee.

The Colonel berated Elvis towards the end of that first engagement for going back to sexually-charged banter with his audience—a tendency he had worked hard to eradicate from Elvis' stage act in his early years. The Colonel next slipped in a side-deal with RCA for an additional $20,000 payment to release material from Elvis' first run at the International Hotel in Las Vegas, and then made a further deal to release four Elvis albums on RCA's new budget label Camden.

The Seventies

In Las Vegas, the Colonel was already planning further live engagements before Elvis had finished his opening spell at the International Hotel, accepting an offer for Elvis to appear at the Houston Astrodome in February 1970. He was also spotted by reporters taking advantage of the close proximity of roulette tables while in Las Vegas.

Colonel Parker's tight rein on costs shifted from movie budgets to touring expenses, band members included. Many of the musicians Elvis initially contacted, including members of his original band, were unable to become part of the TCB band because of the terms on offer; some of the initial TCB band players could not stay on because the Colonel was not prepared to guarantee them the future income they needed to give up their other earnings.

In early 1970, the Colonel put together a $1.1 million deal for a pay-per-view event to be broadcast in movie houses across the country, at the time claiming that this was the highest fee ever secured for a performer at a single event. Before planning was too far advanced, the Colonel cancelled the event on the grounds that it was leaked to the press without authorization by the promoter. He immediately set up a substitute project, a concert film shot at the International Hotel, with hotel owner and MGM's new chief Kirk Kerkorian.

In the summer of 1970, the Colonel went on a publicity offensive, the "Elvis Presley Summer Festival," a title he adopted for Elvis' subsequent August appearances in Las Vegas.

In September 1970, the Colonel put Elvis back out on the road for the first time in thirteen years, starting with a six-date national tour. Parker's special wrinkle was to spread the risk by running the tour as a joint venture with RCA for one concert, and with Management III for four of the dates, in exchange for a guaranteed $240,000 up front. The Colonel needn't have worried, demand was so high that concerts sold out almost immediately. Less than a month later, the Colonel arranged an eight-day tour with promoters Concerts West, this time for a $1 million upfront payment against 65% of gate receipts. The Colonel made it a condition of the deal that the money was delivered within 24-hours. Jerry Weintraub passed this stiff test with minutes to spare.

Not for the first time, in December 1970 the Colonel complained to Elvis about not being able to get in touch with him. He had some consolation, though, from extending his $100,000 annual personal consulting fee with RCA to 1975.

When Elvis returned to the road in the Seventies, the Colonel went back to his itinerant role, advance planning and working out logistics as he had in the Fifties. He would fly into a venue ahead of a show to make sure that all the tickets were sold, and if not invent imaginative ways to shift any stubborn final tickets. At Tahoe, he ensured that Elvis broke the venue's attendance records by doubling the number of seats at the dinner tables. He would add more dates only after he had sold out earlier shows. Shrewdly, he hired extra security from local police forces.

To his credit, the Colonel had more or less insulated Elvis against falling sales after his brief post-NBC and American Studio resurgence. Volume 2 of 4-LP anthology *Elvis Worldwide Gold Award Hits* sold a paltry 50,000 copies, but Elvis' contract called for a non-refundable $350,000 advance. RCA attempted to counter with a flurry of "extras," in 1971 releasing 3 budget albums in addition to Elvis' contractual requirements. Rumors circulated once more that the Colonel might be ready to sell his interest in Elvis. The Colonel's assistant Tom Diskin vehemently denied any discussions with Tom Jones's manager Gordon Mills.

Elvis' November 1971 tour was the first for which the Colonel and Elvis adopted a new 2/3—1/3 split.

The Colonel made sure that he was paid by promoters and venues upfront, in cash, while at the same time squeezing expenses as tight as he could: no free food and drink was available for band members backstage, and they could expect to be fined if they were late to the tour bus.

The Colonel opened a new avenue for earnings in early 1972 when his All Star Shows company entered into an agreement with Management III and the newly-formed RCA Record Tours company to promote Elvis' upcoming tours. The Colonel used this set-up for Elvis' second and last MGM concert documentary, *Elvis on Tour*, which was recorded that Spring.

Looking after number one also meant looking after number two. As part of the improved contract he negotiated for Elvis with the Las Vegas Hilton, the Colonel added a $50,000 annual "consulting" fee, which he is said to have continued to draw for the rest of his life.

In September 1972, the Colonel inked a deal guaranteeing $4 million income for Elvis and himself from RCA Record Tours, which put up the money as an advance against gate receipts. The Colonel also pulled in an additional $250,000 in professional services fees for his own All Star Shows company.

Immediately after Elvis' *Aloha From Hawaii* live performance, in mawkish mood the Colonel wrote Elvis a letter: "I always know that when I do my part, you always do yours in your own way and in your own feeling in how to do it best . . . You above all make all of it work by being the leader and the talent. Without your dedication to your following it couldn't have been done." At the press conference before the event, less than truthfully the Colonel told the press that there would be no pictures of his own family because he didn't "get the kind of money Mr. Presley gets."

Parker strongly advised Elvis to take a sabbatical on recording in early 1973, less out of concern for Elvis' worsening health than because he working out a new song publishing arrangement after long-term associates Hill & Range had shut up shop.

Parker's next deal was the one that years later would be held up in court as damning evidence that he had not acted in his client's best interests. In exchange for a one-off $5.4 million payment in early 1973, the Colonel signed away Elvis' entire back catalogue to RCA. Elvis and the Colonel split this payment 50/50, as per a new understanding that covered all of Elvis' recording income. By the time the consultancy contracts and promotions side deals were factored in, the Colonel actually earned more than 50% of the $10.5 million total. In the Colonel's defense, it was Elvis' need for cash to pay his divorce settlement with Priscilla that prompted the deal in the first place; the Colonel managed to bump up RCA's initial offer by 75%.

Long-standing tensions finally came to a head between Elvis and the Colonel in the summer of 1973. On the final night of Elvis' Las Vegas Hilton summer residency, Elvis criticized the hotel management for firing a chef with whom he had become friendly. After the show, the Colonel confronted Elvis about his unprofessional conduct. For the first time that anyone could remember, they had a public, stand-up row, after which Elvis plucked up the courage to fire the Colonel. The Colonel informed Elvis he quit anyway, and that he would be sending a final bill for his services. Elvis' rage withered when faced by the $2 million claim (up to $10 million in some accounts) that the Colonel sent. Within two weeks, much to the Colonel's (and Vernon's) relief, the whole thing was patched up; the Colonel made a concession that until Elvis' finances were back on track, he would take a lower percentage. Entourage members have since claimed that Elvis wanted to fire the Colonel many times but never had the guts to do it personally. The furthest he would go is ask one of the entourage guys to call the Colonel and tell him his services were no longer required, only for the Colonel to say something along the lines of "tell him to tell me himself." Marty Lacker told Alanna Nash of a rumor that Elvis was involved in a hit-and-run accident while driving his truck for Crown Electric before he became famous that was hushed up, suggesting that the Colonel might have used this knowledge as a weapon to keep Elvis in thrall. The Colonel also advised Elvis not to discuss business with members of the entourage, yet another way to head off any potential interference.

In the fall of 1973, the Colonel turned his attentions to RCA. He called a halt to further recording for the upcoming album *Raised On Rock* and suggested that Felton Jarvis should be taken off the project. The Colonel then forced RCA to delay the release of *Elvis: A Legendary Performer*, their first Elvis back catalogue project, when he found out the label were planning to issue it at the same time as *Raised On Rock*.

Meanwhile, the Colonel set up a new company, Boxcar, to handle Elvis merchandising. Elvis had a 15% stake in the new company, against the Colonel's 40%; the remainder of the stock was distributed to Colonel stalwarts Tom Diskin, Freddy Bienstock and George Parkhill, an RCA executive who was seconded to the Colonel's office. The company's name is said to have been inspired by gambling parlance for double sixes in the game of craps. Though initially set up for merchandise distribution, the Colonel immediately turned Boxcar into a private record label with *Having Fun with Elvis On Stage*, a spoken-word album of excerpts from Elvis' onstage monologues. Being the Colonel, he persuaded RCA to cough up a $100,000 advance on royalties and a promise to distribute the album worldwide. In the background, the Colonel had quietly started taking on new artists, including Elvis' backing singer Kathy Westmoreland, as well as running his own merchandising operations at Elvis shows to counter the large number of bootleggers who were selling unauthorized Elvisware.

In March 1974, the Colonel appeared on stage with Elvis in Houston, after Vernon led him out on a donkey. The significance of this symbology continues to baffle Elvis fans.

In late 1974, the Colonel cancelled Elvis' upcoming Las Vegas residency. Elvis was suffering the effects of an ulcer, and mentally was very low as he approached his 40th birthday. A couple of days after Elvis' birthday, the Colonel flew into town with concert promoter Tom Hulett to persuade Elvis to do a benefit concert for the victims of a tornado that had ripped through McComb, Mississippi.

For a final time, in 1975 the Colonel successfully dissuaded Elvis from doing a project that he wanted to do, after Barbra Streisand asked him to play the role eventually played by Kris Kristofferson in her upcoming movie, *A Star Is Born*. Beside his doubts about Streisand's boyfriend's directorial abilities and his unease at Elvis have to share top billing, the Colonel's salary demands of $1 million plus half of all profits was far more than any studio would be prepared to pay. After the event, the Colonel asserted that it was Elvis who suggested asking for more than the production company could accept, though this does not chime with the enthusiasm recalled by many members of Elvis' entourage.

The Colonel took another turn on stage on the last night of Elvis' early 1975 tour of duty in Las Vegas, appearing as Santa Claus. Not long afterwards he turned down a gift from Elvis of a Gulfstream jet, saying that he didn't need it and couldn't afford it.

In August 1975, the Colonel had to handle another crisis as poor health jeopardized Elvis' Las Vegas Hilton summer season. When Elvis told the Colonel on his third night that wanted to cancel, the Colonel told him to go on with the performances as there was insufficient time to cancel, but then arranged for the rest of the engagement to be called off.

That year Parker opposed RCA's intention to release singles that had previously been issued on Elvis' most recent album of new material: he argued that it was neither fair to fans nor worthwhile for RCA to expect people to pay for songs that they already owned. RCA suggested the idea in the first place because the label had nothing new to release, and by now Elvis was avoiding recording studios.

The Colonel finally became a full 50/50 partner in Elvis' principal money-making activity at the time, touring, in a seven-year deal signed in January 1976. As he later explained to the legal authorities, he did not put the arrangement into effect immediately, as Elvis was suffering severe cash flow problems—exacerbated by his spending on airplanes (for himself) and cars (as gifts).

In July 1976, the Colonel confronted Elvis about how badly he had let his health deteriorate, and berated him for the falling quality of his show performances. According to second wife Loanne Parker, the Colonel was incredibly distraught one day near the end when Elvis couldn't be woken for a meeting they had arranged. This may be the same incident that Larry Geller recounts, when the Colonel came to see Elvis in his hotel room in Louisville as Dr. Nichopoulos was trying to revive the singer by dunking his head in a bucket of ice water. The Colonel reputedly took one look, demanded that he be made presentable to go on stage that evening, and then hobbled out on his cane.

Press rumors appeared once more in April 1977 that the Colonel was reluctantly preparing to sell his management contract with Elvis, as the only way to pay off his gambling debts—he reputedly lost $1.4 million in one night at the end of Elvis' December 1976 tour. These articles also speculated the relationship between manager and client had irremediably broken down. Both allegations were roundly denied by the Colonel. Some Elvis insiders have stated that Elvis was seriously thinking about taking on new management, with promoter Tom Hulett the most likely candidate. Dr. Nichopoulos remembers that Elvis preferred to avoid dealing with the Colonel at all during the last few months of his life.

Larry Geller accuses Parker of willful abnegation of his duty by not doing whatever it took to prevent publication of the West/Hebler book *Elvis: What Happened?*, which was a source of great anxiety and unhappiness for Elvis.

After Elvis

Biographers attribute varying levels of callousness to the Colonel after Elvis died. Greil Marcus quotes him responding to a journalist's question about what he would be doing next, with "Why, I'll just go right on managing him!" Alanna Nash has him down saying, "Elvis isn't dead. Just his body is gone"; other quotes attributed to the Colonel include, "It don't mean a damn thing, it's just like when he was in the Army."

At Elvis' funeral, the Colonel refused to go near the casket, and was thought by many to be inappropriately dressed in a floral shirt.

Before even traveling to Graceland, the Colonel flew to New York to talk with RCA about getting Elvis product out. He also held meetings with merchandisers, legal and illegal, to ensure that as much of the upcoming bonanza as possible contributed to the cause. In actual fact, the Colonel was overstepping his authority: Elvis' heir, Vernon Presley, had not yet given him permission to act on his behalf, though at the first available opportunity—the day of Elvis' funeral—the Colonel presented Vernon with papers to sign.

A year after Elvis died, the Colonel began to talk of Elvis as a son.

The Colonel's hold on Elvis' legacy only began to unravel when an astute judge ordered an investigation into how he had conducted his management of the Estate. Two investigations were undertaken by court-appointed attorney Blanchard E. Tual, in which he found evidence of fraud. Tual described Parker's sale of Elvis' back catalogue to RCA in 1973 as "the worst decision ever made in the history of rock 'n' roll." Parker had also made novice mistakes, such as failing to register Elvis with BMI for songwriter performance royalties. In 1981, four years after Elvis' death, the court ordered that no further payments should be made to the Colonel, and despite protestations from the Elvis Presley Estate, proceedings were launched against the Colonel and RCA for collusion,.

The Colonel fought not only to protect his name, he countersued in an effort to become a co-beneficiary of the Estate, alongside Lisa Marie. During hearings, he asserted that as a Stateless person, he could not be sued under US law—an assertion that was thrown out of court, and ignored the fact that having served in the US Army, the Colonel would have been entitled to US citizenship anyway.

. In 1983, the Presley Estate won a court action against the Colonel. The matter was settled out of court after the Colonel sold some Presley masters to RCA in exchange for a $2 million payoff; RCA also released over $1 million in royalties, backdated a decade. In reports to the Court, Attorney Blanchard E. Tual's findings about Colonel Parker's management were that: " From the documentation there can be no shadow of doubt per adventure that the Colonel did not respect his fiduciary role with Elvis Presley and the several agreements he entered into with RCA and others . . . could not—ever—have been in Elvis' best interests. In particular, the "buy-out" with its collateral agreement cannot be viewed other than with the gravest doubt as to the Colonel's probity."

After Elvis' death, Parker said that he first began to realize what damage Elvis was doing to himself in 1974. When he broached the subject with Elvis, the singer told him to mind his own business. However, members of the entourage believe that as along as Elvis performed on stage, the Colonel turned a blind eye.

On the tenth anniversary of Elvis' death, Parker appeared on Ted Koppel's *Nightline* show and stated his version of the fact.

The first book to accurately document Tom Parker's early life, written by Dutch journalist Dirk Vellenga and Mick Farren, was published in 1988.

EPE made peace with the Colonel in the late Eighties, after which he was invited to Elvis commemorative events. In the late Eighties, the Colonel talked of opening an Elvis museum in his hometown of Madison. The Colonel was invited back to Graceland, and agreed to sell the rest of his collection, a full 35 tons of archives and memorabilia, in exchange for a $2 million dollar payment..

Parker continued to work as an entertainment consultant to the Hilton Group until his death, though his perks gradually dwindled over the years. After first wife Marie died, his former secretary Loanne Miller moved in with him. They married in 1990.

Parker celebrated his 80th birthday at a lavish dinner held at the Las Vegas Hilton. He lived out his final years in a suburban setting, with his much younger wife looking after him, and a daily trip to the casino to play the slot machines. An author who interviewed him in the Nineties discovered that the Colonel maintained a secret Elvis shrine in his home.

To mark the Colonel's 85th birthday, Elvis Presley Enterprises issued 32-page pamphlet *Elvis and Colonel Tom Parker: The Partnership Behind the Legend*, detailing the Colonel's importance to Elvis' career, and including poems that the Colonel wrote about his client.

On January 21, 1997 the Colonel died in Las Vegas of a stroke. He was 87. Of the estimated $100 million that the Colonel earned over his twenty-year association with Elvis, at his death he left an estate worth $1 million.

PARKER'S COLORFUL PAST

Bearing in mind that some of the tales that the Colonel spun about his past were designed to conceal his illegal immigrant roots, his anecdotes about a show pony school and dancing chickens (encouraged so to do by the hotplate they were

Elvis and the Colonel in Tucson.

on) may or may not have been true. Other potentially apocryphal stories include his boast of painting sparrows yellow and selling them as canaries.

In the early Fifties, the Colonel was associated with the sale of Hadacol, a cure-all elixir that made millions for its inventor, a former senator called LeBlanc. The elixir in part owed its popularity to a high alcohol content, a boon especially in the largely dry South.

The Colonel's hypnotic powers have been corroborated by Sonny West, who recalls getting down on all fours with other entourage members after being mesmerized into believing that they were dogs. Billy Smith later confirmed that the Colonel had primed them to take their cue from a certain gesture he made. Actor Bill Bixby also said that he and the Colonel worked out a special code for a similar trick that the Colonel pulled on one movie set.

Among the more outlandish stories about Parker is that he made money by taking bets on how much spicy mustard and pepper he could swallow —almost infinite amounts, it turned out. To tease Hal Wallis, who, annoyed by Parker's constant haggling, asked him to "see the big picture," Parker had a huge photo of himself emblazoned with the legend "the big picture" hung in Wallis's office while he was out.

ELVIS' FIRST CONTRACT
with the Colonel, signed by Elvis, Vernon, Tom Parker and Tom Diskin.

AGREEMENT
SPECIAL AGREEMENT between ELVIS PRESLEY, known as artist, his guardians, Mr and/or Mrs Presley, and his manager, MR BOB NEAL, of Memphis, Tennessee, hereinafter referred to as the Party of the First Part, and COL. THOMAS A. PARKER and/or HANK SNOW ATTRACTIONS of Madison, Tennessee, hereinafter known as the Party of the Second Part, this date, August 15, 1955.

COL. PARKER is to act as special adviser to ELVIS PRESLEY and BOB NEAL for the period of one year and two one-year options for the sum of two thousand five hundred dollars ($2500.00) per year, payable in five payments of five hundred dollars ($500.00) each, to negotiate and assist in any way possible the build-up of ELVIS PRESLEY as an artist. Col Parker will be reimbursed for any out-of-pocket expenses for traveling, promotion, advertising as approved by ELVIS PRESLEY and his manager.

As a special concession to Col. Parker, ELVIS PRESLEY is to play 100 personal appearances within one year for the special sum of $200.00 (two hundred dollars) including his musicians.

In the event that negotiations come to a complete standstill and ELVIS PRESLEY and his manager and associates decide to freelance, it is understood that Col. Parker will be reimbursed for the time and expenses involved in trying to negotiate the Association of these parties and that he will have first call on a number of cities, as follows, at the special rate of one hundred seventy-five dollars ($175.00) per day for the first appearance and two hundred fifty dollars ($250.00) for the second appearance and three hundred fifty dollars ($350.00) for the third appearance: San Antonio, El Paso, Phoenix, Tucson, Albuquerque, Oklahoma City, Denver, Wichita Falls, Wichita, New Orleans, Mobile, Jacksonville, Pensacola, Tampa, Miami, Orlando, Charleston, Greenville, Spartanburg, Asheville, Knoxville, Roanoke, Richmond, Norfolk, Washington D. C., Philadelphia, Newark, New York, Pittsburgh, Chicago, Omaha, Milwaukee, Minneapolis, St Paul, Des Moines, Los Angeles, Amarillo, Lubbock, Houston, Galveston, Corpus Christi, Las Vegas, Reno, Cleveland, Dayton, Akron, and Columbus.

Col. Parker is to negotiate all renewals on existing contracts.

GAMBLING

Biographers cite the Colonel's gambling habit as a prime motive for why Elvis played Las Vegas twice a year, every year from 1969 until his death. Some people believe that the Colonel had already run up significant debts in Las Vegas before he committed his client to playing the town in lieu of those debts.

Biographers state that the Colonel was capable of gambling for 12 or 14 hours at a stretch, only ever on games of chance such as roulette, craps, or the Wheel of Fortune.

Biographers have speculated that it was almost as if the Colonel saw these games of chance as the ultimate challenge to his hypnotic powers, which were so effective over mortals. When the Colonel gambled, he gambled alone at the table. He loved to have a crowd of onlookers, especially when he was winning. His roulette tactic of covering as many numbers as possible may have brought more frequent wins, but it also led to higher losses when his luck gave out.

Parker would say "let's go down to the office" when he wanted to hit the tables in Vegas.

It was Julian Aberbach's view that the Colonel gambled away all of his money in a wanton act of self-destruction. By the time of Elvis' death, the Colonel reputedly owed the Las Vegas Hilton $30 million. Alanna Nash intimates that as a consequence of his gambling debts, the Colonel's management of Elvis' affairs was conditioned by mafia interests that were only too happy to have Elvis drawing punters to Sin City.

The Colonel severely reprimanded family members and associates if he found out that they had started gambling.

JEAN ABERBACH: "I think the reason for his gambling and going to Vegas was primarily to look like a big shot."

GORDON STOKER: "The thing people don't know is, [Elvis] was working to pay the Colonel's gambling debts. They forced him to work."

THE COLONEL'S CHARACTER TRAITS

The Colonel never lost his showman instincts, and over the years was photographed with his star client in a bewildering variety of costumes and get-ups—often with Elvis simply in his civvies.

The Colonel's penchant for showmanship included one Hollywood meeting where he made his pitch using a crystal ball as a prop, uttering the numbers he wanted as he pretended to read the future. At the end of one grueling set of negotiations with MGM, much to Elvis' amusement the Colonel threatened to kill the deal at the last minute unless the studio threw in the cheap glass ashtray on the meeting table.

Parker seemed to have an insatiable appetite for proving that he was top dog. Reputedly the Colonel conducted a meeting with 20th Century-Fox bosses for the first time (at an office they had loaned him at the studios) after having them ushered into the bathroom, where he was sitting on the toilet.

Parker referred to his employees as "the Colonel's Army." The complete loyalty he expected from all members of staff included frowning on liaisons outside the office—marriage of an associate was deemed to be a threat. There have also been reports that he bullied and humiliated his own staff; however, some of his employees remained with him for many decades.

Parker had a vindictive streak. He took great pleasure in blocking the careers of people whom he considered had crossed him or acted against his interests.

According to his second wife Loanne, Parker had a prodigious memory: he recalled everything, without having to write things down.

Parker suffered multiple heart attacks from a relatively early age. He had his first heart attack in the early Fifties, not long after Eddy Arnold fired him. He had another mild heart attack soon after he took over Elvis' contract. According to Alanna Nash, the Colonel tried unsuccessfully to offload Elvis' contract at this time to make provisions for his wife in case before it was too late. Nash also ventures that the Colonel sometimes used his weak heart as a weapon to coerce Elvis.

Even after living in the United States for thirty years, the Colonel couldn't pronounce his "r's" and still had a hint of an accent, particularly when he became angry.

The Colonel walked with a cane, partly because he had a bad back, partly because he liked the look of it, partly because he got sympathy for it, and partly because he could use it to threaten people.

Parker had little apparent interest in sexual conquest; there is anecdotal evidence that he hated being touched, even casually, and especially by a woman.

Jerry Weintraub, who worked with the Colonel in the Seventies, says that Parker was a spiritual man who prayed to Buddha.

Parker's lifelong infatuation with Western lore may be one reason why Elvis wound up in so many Western movies. Parker himself wore a Stetson and chose a covered wagon for his company logo.

According to Larry Geller, Elvis and the Colonel generally had a 5-minute courtesy phone call every week. As a rule, they rarely met. Elvis was not happy when he felt that the Colonel was interfering in his private life, or even worse, interfering in his music, which he sometimes did by siding with RCA in disputes about whether Elvis' voice should be brought forward in the final mix. Priscilla says in her memoir that Elvis suffered sleepless nights of impotent rage because he did not have the courage to stand up to the Colonel.

Parker was a past master at roping people into his network of contacts. He assiduously sent cards, greetings and thank you notes for birthdays, anniversaries and show openings, never missing an occasion to shore up and strengthen his network. His ultimate achievement in this field was his exclusive yet bogus club, the Snowmen's League of America

Parker reputedly showered compulsively, as often as three times a day, and then emerged in a cloud of 4711 cologne.

KERNELS OF THE COLONEL'S BUSINESS PHILOSOPHY

Parker had two rules of business: nothing is free, and see the money before you close a deal.

"Always keep them on their toes."

"Always look to improve your position."

"If you can't operate from a position of strength, do not operate."

"You don't have to be nice to people on the way up if you're not coming down."

"Overexposure is like a sunburn. It can hurt."

"The Colonel is the boss."

"The stars come and go, but a manager can work until he dies."

"Human nature says that people want most what they cannot have."

"Always leave them wanting more."

"It's better to be feared than liked."

"If someone else should ride on our back then we should get a better saddle."

"I make 'em stay 'til they see things my way."

ELVIS SAID IN 1956: " I don't think... I don't know for sure... I don't think I'd have ever been very big if it wasn't for him. He's a very smart man."

ELVIS SAID IN 1957: "Colonel Parker is more or less like a daddy when I'm away from my own folks . . . he doesn't meddle in my affairs... and never butts into recording sessions."

ELVIS SAID IN 1965: "I always place the greatest trust in Colonel Parker. He is the man who has done most for me and I am convinced that if he says for me to do something, that's the best thing in my interest."

ELVIS SAID IN 1970, ONSTAGE AT THE INTERNATIONAL HOTEL: "He's not only my manager, but I love him very much."

ELVIS SAID: "We more or less picked each other. It was like this: the Colonel said . . . 'If you want me as your manager, I will do the best I can.' And I told him, 'If you want to manage me, I'll work for you.' It was a deal like that."

COLONEL PARKER SAID IN 1993: "I sleep very good at night. And Elvis and I were friends."

COLONEL PARKER SAID IN 1993: "I never looked on him as a son, but he was the success I always wanted."

CHET ATKINS: "Whatever he cost Elvis, he was worth it, because Elvis would have lost that luster in no time if it hadn't been for the Colonel."

PETER GURALNICK: "Elvis was the Colonel's dream, the perfect vehicle for all the Colonel's elaborately worked out and ingenious promotional schemes.... The Colonel 'slept, ate and breathed Elvis'."

ALANNA NASH: "Parker's most important place in music history may be as the man who almost single-handedly took the carnival tradition first to rock and roll, and then to modern mass entertainment, creating the blueprint for the powerful style of management and merchandising that the music business operates by today."

FREDDY BIENSTOCK: "The Colonel was very sharp. The schemes he would dream up . . . Like booking Elvis into a very small theatre or movie house and in keeping the box office closed until he could photograph the lines of people waiting to get in. He was full of those ideas."

JUNE JUANICO: "I really didn't care for Parker that much. You could smell the Colonel around the block, you know—with his cigar. I thought the Colonel was a manipulative shyster of a man."

PRISCILLA: "Colonel Parker's theory was: 'If you want to see Elvis Presley, you buy a ticket.' . . . He stuck to that policy to the day Elvis died."

RED WEST: "It was just as if Tom Parker and Elvis Presley were born and destined to meet.... With Elvis and him it was like a joint and socket who had been looking for each other."

BILL RANDLE: "Parker didn't want anything known about anybody who had done anything with Presley in the beginning because that meant the Parker myth couldn't be created. Parker is himself, like Presley, partially a myth."

BUZZY FORBES: "You hear an awful lot about, 'If it wasn't for Colonel Tom Parker, Elvis wouldn't have become such a big star.' I don't think Elvis could have hid his candle under a bed, he would have made it with or without Parker."

HAL WALLIS: "He is a shrewd, clever businessmen and a supersalesman."

MARTY LACKER: "He was good in the early years but he wouldn't change with the times. He treated Elvis like a carnival show."

GEORGE KLEIN: "I think 90% of what the Colonel did for Elvis was good, 10% was wrong."

MAE AXTON: "Elvis loved the Colonel, and he trusted him implicitly."

HAL KANTER: "Colonel Parker was a man who had Elvis' best interests at heart. But he had Tom Parker's best interest even closer to heart than he did Elvis."

BILLY SMITH: "In the Sixties, Colonel influenced him a whole lot more than people ever knew. A lot of what Elvis said, it was the Colonel's dictate."

JIMMY VELVET: "The Colonel wasn't around a lot. He was always one or two steps ahead, doing what he did; but, from what I could see, the Colonel was really great for Elvis. The Colonel could make anything happen—just had a way about him, he had a magic."

STEVE BINDER: "The Colonel used to sit at a meeting with those cold steel-blue eyes staring at me like he was trying to get a subliminal message into my brain. I'd stare back, knowing that there was nothing he could do. Yet he did convince me that there is such a thing as mind control. That strange hypnotic way he had of exercising total control and power over Elvis. That kind of hold is totally unexplained in terms of either of deals or loyalties between people."

BILLY GOLDENBERG: "He always reminded me of the characters that Sydney Greenstreet or Burl Ives or Orson Welles played... it was like he was playing a game of some sort, putting on the whole world."

MARTY LACKER: "Parker's a hustler and a con artist, and he's out for Parker."

HORACE LOGAN: "Parker takes credit for everything. He takes credit for discovering Elvis. He takes credit for molding Elvis. He takes credit for building Elvis' career. The son of a bitch ought to be hung up by his balls. He practically destroyed one of the greatest talents that ever lived."

SONNY WEST TOLD STEVE DUNLEAVY: "Without Colonel Tom there would never be an Elvis Presley."

LOANNA PARKER: "His focus was what can I do to better present Elvis. What can I do to better protect Elvis when it comes to contracts and business affairs."

MARTY LACKER: "I think Elvis, to a point, cared about the Colonel because of the early days . . . . Elvis basically was concerned with one thing other than his entertaining: he just wanted to have enough money to do whatever he wanted to do, whenever he wanted to do it."

JERRY SCHILLING: "As different as they might appear, they had the same kind of egos. And neither ever wanted to display vulnerability—to the other or anyone else."

ALANNA NASH: "Elvis made fun of the Colonel to the guys, yet he remained subservient to his face."

CHARLIE HODGE: "He wasn't the ogre many people make him out to be."

LARRY GELLER: "Elvis gradually lost respect for the Colonel because he felt he was being used. He didn't feel the Colonel really cared for him as a human being. Elvis respected the Colonel for how he launched his career, but he felt it was mishandled later on."

RED WEST: "I have heard all the stories about Colonel Tom, but I know one thing: once he gave his word and his handshake, he would have rather lost an arm then go back on it."

ALANNA NASH: "The tale of Colonel Thomas Andrew Parker, né Andreas Cornelis van Kuijk, is, beneath the veil of secrecy, a tragedy, and very nearly the stuff of Shakespeare."

FREDDY BIENSTOCK: "Colonel Parker was like Elvis' security blanket and Elvis knew that he could never have had that amount of success without Colonel Parker."

SONNY WEST: "I think he was the best manager ever."

LARRY GELLER: "Parker's world lacked a moral center."

JERRY LEIBER: "He worshipped him as a maker and savior . . . despised him because he was never able to take control of his own life."

PRISCILLA: "From the old school, the Colonel was considered a coldhearted businessman, but in truth he had stayed faithful and loyal to Elvis, even when his career began to slip."

LARRY GELLER: "Ultimately, Parker's power over Elvis was as strong as it was because Elvis gave it to him."

LAMAR FIKE: "The Colonel just never got it that Elvis needed a creative challenge. In those final years it was a case of 'if only...' "

DR. BEECHER SMITH III: "There were villainous elements, but... [he] was instrumental in establishing many of the things the Estate benefits from today. His greatest sin was not being savvy about the state of the industry during the last five or ten years of Elvis' life."

Books:

At various times during his life, the Colonel claimed to be working on his memoir, *How Much Does It Cost If It's Free?* He told writer Hal Kanter that the best thing about the book was that he planned to sell advertising space on the front and back covers. Parker reputedly turned down a $100,000 advance, claiming that he stood to make much more from these advertising sales.

Elvis and the Colonel, by May Mann, Drake, 1975
Elvis and the Colonel, by Dirk Vellenga and Mick Farren, Delacorte Press, 1988
My Boy Elvis: The Colonel Tom Parker Story, by Sean O'Neal, Barricade Books, 1998
Colonel Tom Parker, by James L. Dickerson, 1st Cooper, 2001
The Colonel, by Alanna Nash, published by Simon & Schuster, 2003.

Documentary:
Looking for Colonel Parker, by Constant Meijers, 1999

PARRY, PATTI
(B. 1943)

British-born Patti Parry—Elvis called her Patricia—is known as the only female member of the Memphis mafia. She met Elvis when she was 17, and hung around with the gang when they were in Los Angeles, occasionally cutting his hair. She went on to work as a Beverly Hills hairdresser, but would travel to be with Elvis in Las Vegas and Palm Springs. She also flew out to Hawaii to do Elvis' hair for the *Aloha from Hawaii* concert.

PATTI PARRY: "I was his Little Sister. I was a very lucky girl."

PARTON, DOLLY
(B. 1946)

Country Ma'am Parton grew up in a family that, like Elvis', was part of the Church of God community.

Elvis was all set to record her 1974 hit "I Will Always Love You" until Parton balked at giving up half the publishing—a wise move considering that Whitney Houston's 1993 cover of the song generated many millions in royalties for Parton. She had also turned down an initial approach for Elvis to cover "Coat Of Many Colors."

In 2006, Parton featured in an advert promoting tourism in Tennessee with Elvis Presley, as borrowed from a *Clambake* scene.

Parton has won seven Grammys and been nominated for Academy Awards during a career that began when she was a child performer. She wrote hit songs for others before sculpting out a career for herself as one of RCA's top country artists. She has scored more than 50 top ten country hits and sold in excess of 100 million records. She has been inducted into both the Country and the Songwriters' Halls of Fame.

DOLLY PARTON: "Riding in a convertible with Elvis? What more could a girl ask for?"

"(LET'S HAVE A) PARTY"

Elvis recorded album and movie versions of this song by Jessie Mae Robinson for *Loving You* at Radio Recorders on January 22, 1957. It was released on the EP that came out just before the movie, and then on the LP of the same name. "Party" came out with "Got A Lot O' Livin' To Do" in late 1957 in the UK, where it made it to #2 in the charts. Original and alternate version of the song are on *Essential Elvis Vol. 1* and on *The King Of Rock And Roll*. A remastered version is available on *Elvis Rock*, while several alternate takes are on the FTD version of *Loving You*.

PASTERNAK, JOE
(1901-1991)

This Hungarian-born producer worked on three Oscar Best Picture-nominated movies in the Thirties and Forties. He worked with Elvis favorite Mario Lanza in the Fifties, and produced two Elvis films for MGM in the Sixties: *Girl Happy* (1965) and *Spinout* (1966). Pasternak once quipped, "Never make an audience think. It always worked for me."

"PATCH IT UP"

This song was released as the B-side to "You Don't Have To Say You Love Me" in October 1970, a single that flashed in and out of the charts in just three weeks and climbed no higher than #90. Elvis recorded the energetic Eddie Rabbitt / Rory Bourke tune in Nashville on June 8 that year, when *That's The Way It Is* was being filmed—a live version went onto the concert movie soundtrack and later onto the 2000 *That's The Way It Is—Special Edition* release The studio version appeared soon after its single release on *Worldwide Gold Award Hits Vol. 2*, and later on *Walk A Mile In My Shoes.*

Other live versions may be found on 2007 release *Viva Las Vegas* and on FTD release *One Night In Vegas.*

An alternate take from the studio session came out on *Essential Elvis Vol. 4* in 1996.

"PEACE IN THE VALLEY"

Elvis sang this gospel number on his third "Ed Sullivan Show" appearance, on January 6, 1957. It has been reported that the network specifically asked Elvis to include the song in his set to sanitize his image; alternately, Elvis insisted on performing the song because his mother Gladys liked it so much. Whichever version of the story is true, Elvis' TV performance of this spiritual is incongruously book-ended by wild female squeals and screams. He had actually limbered up with the song a month earlier, when he sang a truncated version with Carl Perkins on guitar and Jerry Lee Lewis providing harmony during the *Million Dollar Quartet* session.

Exactly a week after appearing on the "Ed Sullivan Show," Elvis breezed into Radio Recorders to lay down the song for RCA. He nailed it almost immediately and signed off saying, "I can sing this song all day."

"Peace In The Valley" was initially released on an EP of the same name; though not actually released as a single, the song earned a #39 placement on the *Billboard* Top 100.

Thomas A. Dorsey wrote "(There'll Be) Peace In the Valley (For Me)" for the Queen of Gospel, Mahalia Jackson, to record in 1939; Red Foley had a top ten Country hit with the song in 1951. Gospel composer Herbert Brewster was so impressed with Elvis' version of the song that he dubbed it "one of the best gospel recordings I've ever heard."

The track went onto *Elvis' Christmas Album* in 1957, and later *You'll Never Walk Alone, Elvis: A Legendary Performer Vol. 1, Double Dynamite, The King Of Rock And Roll, Amazing Grace, Christmas Peace, Ultimate Gospel, Elvis By The Presleys , Elvis Christmas* and in remastered form *The Essential Elvis Presley* .

Alternative studio recordings can be enjoyed on *A Golden Celebration, Essential Elvis Vol. 2, Platinum: A Life In Music,* the *Peace In The Valley* anthology from 2002, *Today Tomorrow & Forever,* and *Elvis: Close Up.*

PEACE IN THE VALLEY (EP)

RCA released a 4-track EP in good time for Easter 1957. The EP sold over 400,000 copies, an outlandish amount for a gospel record, and for decades a record for this format.

TRACK LISTING:
1. (There'll Be) Peace In The Valley (For Me)
2. It Is No Secret
3. I Believe
4. Take My Hand, Precious Lord

PEACE IN THE VALLEY—THE COMPLETE GOSPEL RECORDINGS

A 3-CD BMG compilation released in 2000, marketed as containing all of the gospel Elvis recorded.

TRACK LISTING:
DISC 1:
1. His Hand In Mine
2. I'm Gonna Walk Dem Golden Stairs
3. In My Father's House
4. Milky White Way
5. Known Only To Him
6. I Believe In The Man In The Sky
7. Joshua Fit The Battle
8. He Knows Just What I Need
9. Swing Down, Sweet Chariot
10. Mansion Over The Hilltop
11. If We Never Meet Again
12. Working On The Building
13. Crying In The Chapel
14. How Great Thou Art
15. In The Garden
16. Somebody Bigger Than You And I
17. Farther Along
18. Stand By Me
19. Without Him
20. So High
21. Where Could I Go But To The Lord
22. By And By
23. If The Lord Wasn't Walking By My Side
24. Run On
25. Where No One Stands Alone
26. We Call On Him
27. You'll Never Walk Alone
28. Who Am I
29. Life

DISC 2:
1. Only Believe
2. He Touched Me
3. I've Got Confidence
4. Amazing Grace
5. Seeing Is Believing
6. He Is My Everything
7. Bosom Of Abraham
8. An Evening Prayer
9. Lead Me, Guide Me
10. There Is No God But God
11. A Thing Called Love
12. I, John
13. Reach Out To Jesus
14. Miracle Of The Rosary
15. Put Your Hand In The Hand
16. I Got A Feelin' In My Body
17. Help Me
18. If That Isn't Love
19. Help Me (live, 1974)
20. Why Me, Lord (live, 1974)
21. How Great Thou Art (live, 1974)
22. Farther Along
23. Oh Happy Day
24. I, John
25. Bosom Of Abraham
26. You Better Run
27. Lead Me, Guide Me
28. Turn Your Eyes Upon Jesus / Nearer My God To Thee

DISC 3:
1. When The Saints Go Marchin' In
2. Just A Little Talk With Jesus
3. Jesus Walked That Lonesome Valley
4. I Shall Not Be Moved
5. Peace In The Valley
6. Down By The Riverside
7. Farther Along
8. Blessed Jesus (Hold My Hand)
9. On The Jericho Road
10. I Just Can't Make It By Myself
11. I Hear A Sweet Voice Calling
12. When The Saints Go Marchin' In
13. Softly And Tenderly
14. Peace In The Valley
15. It Is No Secret (What God Can Do)
16. I Believe
17. Take My Hand Precious Lord
18. I Asked The Lord
19. He
20. Oh How I Love Jesus
21. Show Me Thy Ways, O Lord
22. Hide Thou Me
23. Down By The Riverside / When The Saints Go Marchin' In
24. Sing You Children
25. Swing Down, Sweet Chariot
26. Let Us Pray
27. '68 Gospel Medley: Sometimes I Feel Like A Motherless Child / Where Could I Go But To The Lord / Up Above My Head / Saved
28. The Lord's Prayer
29. How Great Thou Art (live, 1977)
30. Peace In The Valley ("Ed Sullivan Show," 1957)

PEARL, MINNIE
(B. SARAH OPHELIA COLLEY, 1912-1996)

Minnie Pearl was a comic fixture at the Grand Ole Opry for over 50 years. Colonel Parker handled bookings for Pearl in the days before he took on Elvis, and asked her to be on the bill with Elvis when he performed his 1961 Hawaiian benefit show.

Born in Centerville, Tennessee, on October 25, 1912, Pearl worked as a dance teacher before taking to the stage in the persona of a small-town girl. She made her debut at the Opry in 1940 and never looked back, for many years featuring regularly on popular TV show "Hee Haw." She was inducted into the Country Music Hall of Fame in 1975.

PENNSYLVANIA

- Philadelphia

Elvis played four shows at the Sports Arena on April 5 and 6, 1957, to the usual wall of screaming fans. He suffered the indignity of being pelted by eggs during the last show by some rowdy students; when a hurled tomato actually broke his

guitar strap, Elvis stopped and threatened to take the guy on, right there on stage.

Things went better the next time round at the Spectrum on November 8, 1971. He was back at the Spectrum for two shows on June 23, 1974, and then on June 28, 1976. The last time he played the venue was on May 28, 1977.

- Pittsburgh

Elvis played the Civic Center Arena on June 25 and 26, 1973. He played a New Year's Eve show there on December 31, 1976 (released by FTD as *New Year's Eve*).

PEPPER, GARY
(1932-1980)

Gary Pepper founded and ran the Elvis Tankers fan club, named after Elvis' Army battalion, from 1959 to 1963. A cerebral palsy sufferer, Pepper became a friend of Elvis' and was often invited to Elvis' Graceland soirees. For a spell, Pepper's father Sterling worked the gates at Graceland; Elvis paid a regularly $400 monthly stipend to help out Pepper and his family, and is said by some sources to have bought them a house nearby. In the early Sixties, Pepper brought out his own fanzine, wrote for British fan club magazine *Elvis Monthly*, and developed quite a network of contacts and fans himself.

PERKINS, CARL
(1932-1998)

Recalled as a talented rockabilly pioneer deserving of greater success than he ultimately achieved, Perkins stood on the cusp of Elvis-sized fame when ill-fortunate struck. Born in Tiptonville, Tennessee, on April 9, 1932, Perkins grew up in a family of poor sharecroppers and was taught guitar by black neighbors. His first musical outfit—the Perkins Brothers Band—played local honky-tonks in and around Jackson, Tennessee, and developed their own amalgam of R 'n' B and country, fuelled by the songs that Carl wrote.

Perkins later spoke of seeing Elvis play a school gym at Bethel Springs, Tennessee, in September 1954. After the show, he asked Elvis if he should approach Sun Records, which he did the following month. Other versions of the story cite Perkins' decision to contact Sam Phillips as coming after he heard Elvis' first single, "That's All Right (Mama)," on the radio.

Sun Records principal Sam Phillips signed Perkins before the year was out and released his first single, "Movie Magg," on one of his second-string labels. Phillips positioned Perkins more as a hillbilly act than anything else, until he sold Elvis' contract to RCA and was looking for the next big thing in rockabilly, a man he already had on the Sun roster. Perkins and Elvis shared the bill at a few early shows—Johnny Cash recalls a night in December 1955 when Perkins succeeded for the first and only time in upstaging Elvis.

In early, 1956 Perkins' "Blue Suede Shoes" became the first single ever to make it to the top of the pop, R 'n' B and country charts simultaneously, and was Sun Records' first million-selling single. The song did so well that until Elvis' "Heartbreak Hotel" finally picked up after a slow start, Chet Atkins feared that RCA had signed the wrong Sun artist.

Perkins' "Blue Suede Shoes" was at #2 and still climbing when on March 21, 1956 when the singer was involved in a serious car accident in Delaware as he drove to New York for his big break on the nationally-broadcast "The Perry Como Show," which would have pitted him directly against Elvis who was appearing for the last time on the Dorsey Brothers' variety vehicle, "Stage Show." Elvis sang

"Blue Suede Shoes" on March 24, 1956, while Perkins was in the hospital convalescing.

Though Perkins' version outsold Elvis', it has remained indelibly associated with the more famous performer. Colonel Parker sent flowers to Perkins and his brothers, and Elvis' band stopped in to see Perkins en route from New York to Memphis; Elvis couldn't make it as he was in LA for his screen test, but he sent a telegram offering to do anything he could, and wishing him and his brothers a speedy recovery

Before Elvis usurped his title, Carl Perkins was briefly billed as the King of Rock 'n' Roll. Many later performers have said how strongly they were influenced by Perkins' songwriting (he wrote for Johnny Cash and Patsy Cline among others; The Beatles recorded five Perkins songs, more than any other songwriter outside the band), and by his original rockabilly guitar licks.

Elvis dropped in on Perkins during a recording session at Sun in December 1956, and then stayed to jam with him and new Sun signing Jerry Lee Lewis, in a session that came to be known as "The Million Dollar Quartet." Perkins played guitar, harmonized on many of the tracks and took lead vocals on "Keeper Of the Key."

Sadly, Perkins' career never recovered the loss of momentum caused by that car smash. He continued recording strong rockabilly material for Sun without ever replicating the success of "Blue Suede Shoes." He changed record labels a couple of times, but only received recognition in the Sixties as an inspiration to the new generation of British groups, starting with The Beatles.

Perkins was on the bill at Elvis' July 5, 1976 concert in Memphis. By this time, he was a fixture in Johnny Cash's touring band. After Elvis' death, Perkins was one of many artists to release a tribute song ("The Whole World Misses You").

Carl Perkins was inducted into the Rock 'n' Roll Hall of Fame in 1987.

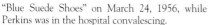

CARL PERKINS: "He never really died and never will. . . . He cut a path through the world! He's gonna be history, man."

LEFT: Elvis at the Philadelphia Hilton (6.23.74).   ABOVE: Elvis performing at the Philly Spectrum (5. 28. 77).

PERRYMAN, TOM

Promoter Tom Perryman enthusiastically played Elvis' earliest singles on his KSIJ-AM radio show "The Hillbilly Hit Parade" and was one of the first to book Elvis outside the Memphis area, sending him to many venues in North-East Texas starting with the Mint Club in Gladewater. In late January 1955, Perryman took Elvis on a sweep through East Texas oil country. He organized another Texas tour in August 1955, with Jim Ed and Maxine Brown, on which Hayride drummer D. J. Fontana played throughout.

TOM PERRYMAN: "When Elvis was performing, everyone had the same basic reaction. It was almost spontaneous. It reminded me of... going to these 'Holy Roller' Brush Arbor meetings: seeing these people get religion."

"PETER GUNN THEME"

Elvis is known to have strummed this Henry Mancini tune in the late Sixties and early Seventies. Microphones captured the moment. It's on a number of bootlegs including *The Complete Dressing Room Sessions*, and on 2000 official release *That's The Way It Is—Special Edition* and 2006 FTD album *Let Yourself Go*.

PETER, PAUL AND MARY

Elvis was an avid fan of this New York-based folk group. Peter Yarrow (b. 1938) , Noel "Paul" Stookey (b. 1937) and Mary Travers (b. 1936) were "manufactured" by music impresario extraordinaire Albert Grossman in the early Sixties. They were soon spearheading the folk revival and blazing a trail for more overtly political artists like Bob Dylan. "PP&M" quickly built up a strong enough following to survive the British invasion from 1964.

Elvis loved the group's close harmonies and enjoyed singing their songs with pals at Graceland in the Sixties. In the Seventies, he covered some of the same material, including "Don't Think Twice, It's All Right," "The First Time Ever I Saw Your Face" and "(That's What You Get) For Lovin' Me."

Peter, Paul and Mary are best known for "Where Have All The Flowers Gone," Grammy-winning "If I Had A Hammer," "Puff (The Magic Dragon)," "Blowin' In The Wind" and "Leaving On A Jet Plane."

The Group has continued recording on Warner ever since they began in 1960. They were inducted into the Vocal Group Hall of Fame in 1999.

PETERS, GERALD

A limousine driver Elvis hired in LA in 1970, affectionately nicknamed "Sir Gerald" by Elvis. Peters sometimes drove to Las Vegas to work for Elvis when he was in town. The chauffeur claimed a driving pedigree that went all the way back to driving Winston Churchill.

PETERSON, CASSANDRA
(B. 1949)

When she was seventeen, the actress who went on to play Elvira met Elvis while she was dancing and he was playing in Las Vegas. She has said that Elvis did not have sex with her after she said she was a virgin—all she got was a goodbye kiss. Elvis advised her to get out of Las Vegas before she became one of the city's jaded career showgirls.

PETS

Elvis loved his pets. In boyhood, he looked after pets including two small dogs that he named Woodlawn and Muffy Dee. He also had a dog

ABOVE: Elvis on horseback at Graceland in the late 1950's.

LEFT: Lisa Marie with Snoopy and Brutus.

called Tex, who like "Old Shep" had to be put down. In the Fifties, soon after he started making money, he bought a pet dog called Boy.

Once ensconced at Graceland, he bought many dogs for himself, and later as gifts for important women in his life: Sweat Pea for Gladys (a little before moving to Graceland), toy poodle Little Bit for Anita Wood, a poodle called Honey for Priscilla, and Foxhugh (a Maltese) for Linda Thompson.

Out in Germany, Elvis kept a poodle called Champagne who was given to him by a fan.

By the end of 1960 Elvis' pet collection at Graceland included a monkey, spider monkeys, peacocks, mynah birds, chickens, pigs, poodles and a Great Pyrenees dog called Muffin. Elvis and Priscilla had a collie called Baba (or Babbie) at Graceland in the mid-Sixties (said to have made an appearance in his movie *Paradis—Hawaiian Style*, though also reputedly capable of growling at any man other than Elvis). At Graceland in later years he kept a pair of poodles called Hugo and Samson, and a basset hound, which he called Sherlock.

Elvis' Great Dane Brutus—one of a pair—may or may not have featured in his movie *Live a Little, Love a Little* depending on the source. The other Great Dane, Snoopy, certainly did not get a shot at stardom.

Elvis had a chow called Get Lo in the Seventies, who outlived his master by a year.

His largest pets, horses, lived on the premises from 1967 onwards.

Aunt Delta brought along her poodle Stuff along when she came to live at Graceland. Elvis later made her a gift of a Pomeranian, Edmond.

Elvis acquired his first monkey, a spider monkey called Jayhew, back in 1956, to liven up the porch at Audubon Drive. In 1961, he acquired a high-spirited chimp called Scatter, whose successor in the late Sixties was a monkey called J Hug. Another monkey, Bambi, was given to Elvis by fans in the mid-Sixties.

With the exception of a cat called Puff that Lisa brought with her from Los Angeles, Elvis was not so hospitable to felines, though the strays who sometimes turned up in the grounds would be found new homes. He did reputedly have a cat before he moved into Graceland, named Wendell after *Loving You* co-star Wendell Corey.

See also ANIMALS

"PETUNIA, THE GARDENER'S DAUGHTER"

A big band sound for this Sid Tepper / Roy C. Bennett *Frankie and Johnny* soundtrack tune that Elvis recorded at Radio Recorders on May 14, 1965, in an on-screen duet with Donna Douglas. The song reappeared on the *Double Feature* album in the Nineties.

PHILLIPS, DEWEY "DADDY-O" (1926-1968)

In Memphis in the early Fifties, if you wanted to know what was on the cutting edge of music, Dewey Phillips was the man to listen to on radio

station WHBQ. Phillips hosted "Red, Hot and Blue," a hugely popular and eclectic Memphis radio show that attracted music lovers across the color divide, years before segregation came to an end. He was also a pioneering figure in the history of DJing, and is generally credited as the first of the fast-talking and zany DJs that have thronged the airwaves ever since.

In 1950, Dewey and Sam Phillips (no relation) founded "The Phillips Label," which only brought out one single by Joe Hill Louis before folding; their friendship, however, remained strong enough for Dewey to describe Sam as like a brother to him.

In early July 1954—the accredited date is either July 7 or 8—when Sam Phillips brought Dewey Elvis' freshly-recorded acetate of "That's All Right (Mama)," the DJ couldn't wait to play it on his radio show, broadcast from a studio at the Hotel Chisca in downtown Memphis. With Elvis' parents Vernon and Gladys listening in from home, and Elvis unaccountably at the movies, the radio station switchboards were besieged as soon as he played the track. Dewey played the song repeatedly, between 6 and 15 times in a row depending on accounts, and declared that it was "gonna be a hit." Such was the clamor that Dewey called the Presley home to try and get Elvis to come down. Elvis' folks yanked him out of the movie house, sent him downtown, and Elvis had his first interview as a recording star on the very first night one of his songs was played on air. At the end of the interview, Elvis asked Phillips when he was going to actually start doing the interview. Phillips told him he'd just done it, and Elvis is said to have broken into a cold sweat.

Phillips may have been the first DJ to play an Elvis song on the radio all the way through, but history records that he was not the first to put needle to vinyl on air. That accolade goes to Fred Cook at rival station WREC, who put the record on and then took it off almost immediately.

Elvis was a nationally-known star when in March 1956 he returned to the Chisckasaw Ballroom at the Chisca Hotel to perform with Sy Rose and his band on a Dewey Phillips "Red Hot and Blue Dance Session" bill. Until it caused too much of a ruckus, Elvis regularly showed up at the venue for fun between tours.

Elvis paid for Dewey Phillips to join him in NYC in the run-up to his second appearance on "The Ed Sullivan Show" in October 1956.

Elvis was one of the first guests to appear on Phillips' new TV slot, "Phillips' Pop Shop," on the last day of 1956, a couple of months after Elvis brought round Natalie Wood to meet his DJ pal.

Elvis' relationship with his former mentor began to falter when the DJ visited during the filming of *Jailhouse Rock*. The worse for alcohol, Phillips offended Yul Brynner by calling him "a short little mother," and then, after returning to Memphis, aired a pre-release copy of "Teddy Bear" after Elvis had asked him not to. They made up, but Phillips continued to get into trouble, losing his DJ job at WHBQ in July 1958 after one too many drink and drugs-fuelled incidents. Phillips stayed in radio, over the next decade working at a variety of smaller stations.

Elvis attended Dewey Phillips' funeral in Memphis in October 1968.

ELVIS SAID IN 1968: "We were very good friends, and I have always appreciated everything he did for me in helping me in my career in the early days."

Book:
Dewey and Elvis—The Life and Times of a Rock 'n' Roll Deejay, by Louis Cantor, University of Illinois Press, 2005.

PHILLIPS, SAM
(B. SAMUEL CORNELIUS PHILLIPS, 1923-2003)

WREC radio engineer Sam Phillips opened the Memphis Recording Service in January 1950 at 706 Union Ave. with assistant Marion Keisker. For Phillips, the Memphis Recording Service was a dream come true, his own business where he could be immersed in sound (to his mind, "God's best creation"). Converting this dream into a commercially-viable reality took hard work for the fledgling company: to make ends meet, Phillips recorded conventions, weddings, kids' choir auditions and even funerals, while operating an open door policy for whatever talented musicians might walk in off the street. Not for nothing was the Memphis Recording Service's slogan "We Record Anything, Anywhere, Anytime."

Phillips' plan to compete against the successful and established music coming out of nearby Nashville was to focus on "Negro artists of the South who [want] to make a record [and have] no place to go." It took a couple of false starts before he alighted on Sun Records as his vehicle for fame. Previously, he set up the Phillips Records label in 1950 with DJ friend Dewey Phillips, but that folded after just one release, Joe Hill Louis single "Boogie In The Park" / "Gotta Let You Go." Before going solo with Sun Records in March 1952, Phillips had a contract to record master tapes which he subsequently leased to major labels such as Chess in Chicago and RPM Modern in LA. It was under such an arrangement that Phillips recorded what many people consider to be the first ever rock 'n' roll record, Jackie Brenston's "Rocket 88."

Within its first year, Sun recorded B.B. King, Joe Hill Lewis, Rufus Thomas and Howlin' Wolf, then Junior Parker and country acts such as Doug Poindexter and his Starlite Wranglers.

Phillips had to overcome major hurdles to keep the business afloat, not least the logistics of making records that might come back unsold, doing his own publicity, maintaining a complex web of contacts for local, regional and national distribution (he later calculated that he drove over 60,000 miles a year to promote his artists with radio stations and distributors) and paying out royalties (though he squeezed this down to 3% rather than the industry standard 5%, and often managed to retain publishing rights on songs that went through his hands). When it looked like his long-cherished dream of running his own studio was going to go belly up, he reputedly drank heavily, and for a spell was taken to a mental hospital where is he said to have received electric shock treatment. Then, when the label finally had its first hit single—Rufus Thomas's "Bearcat"—it became embroiled in a court action for libel that threatened to bankrupt the firm.

Sam Phillips was born on January 5, 1923 in the rural Alabama farming community of Florence. The youngest child of eight, his first taste of music was as the captain of the Coffee High School Band. He was unable to study law at university because he had to help support the family, working a number of jobs including one at a funeral parlor. He got his start in the music business as a radio engineer and an announcer in Alabama and Nashville before in 1945 moving to Memphis with his wife, Rebecca, and two young sons Knox and Jerry. In Memphis he was hired by WREC, where as well as looking after sound he also filled a DJ slot under the radio name "Pardner." Opening his own recording studio had been his lifelong ambition, but he did not quit the day job as a DJ at WREC until two years after opening the Memphis Recording Service.

Sam Phillips' search for new talent took him into unexpected places: in 1953, he discovered The Prisonaires quartet at the Canton Tennessee State penitentiary. Phillips paid for them to record (under armed guard) at Sun Studio. Elvis biographers have speculated that press coverage of this unusual recording session in the Memphis Press-Scimitar prompted Elvis to try his hand at the Memphis Recording Service and pay for a vanity recording of a two-sided acetate: "My Happiness" and Ink Spots favorite "That's When Your Heartaches Begin," which Elvis crooned to his own guitar accompaniment. Ever after, there has been speculation as to whether Phillips was at the Studio the first time that Elvis walked in; he may have been in the café next door, or he may have come back towards the end of Elvis' tremulous first time in front of a studio mike.

Elvis returned six months later, this time to record country songs "I'll Never Stand in Your Way "and "It Wouldn't Be The Same Without You," once again on his own dime, and once again, with no end product bar the acetate he drove home with afterwards.

Phillips finally had Elvis called into the studio in late June or early July 1954 to try out on "Without You," a song he had acquired for which he needed a singer. Phillips was not impressed with the result, though it gave him a chance to hear Elvis sing his way through practically every ballad he knew. After sending Elvis off to work up some tunes with Starlite Wranglers' guitarist Scotty Moore and bass player Bill Black, Elvis returned to the studio, and once more failed to excite Phillips, until the "boy with the sideburns" unexpectedly broke into an idiosyncratic version of Arthur "Big Boy" Crudup's "That's All Right." Phillips made them do it again just like they'd done it goofing around, recorded it on the spot and released it as Elvis' first single.

Sam Phillips played the acetate to DJ Dewey Phillips, who promised to spin it on his evening radio show. Phillips also persuaded DJ pal (and Elvis' future manager) Bob Neal to add Elvis to the "Hillbilly Hoedown" he was organizing at Overton Park Shell a couple of weeks later, featuring Louisiana Hayride regulars Slim Whitman and Billy Walker. Phillips paid for advertising to help raise his young charge's profile on the bill, precociously describing Elvis as a "new Memphis Star." He also worked all his contacts to get Elvis a booking at the Grand Ole Opry, in Nashville, which he finally managed on October 2, 1954.

Phillips was instrumental in developing the unique impact of Elvis' first three-piece band, diverting Elvis towards more high-tempo tracks than the ballads he naturally favored, and advising Scotty Moore to toughen up his guitar-playing. All of Phillips' Sun recordings benefited from his experience as a radio engineer and his use of what Bob Neal called an "electronic-slap-back type sound" created through a tiny delay in the re-recording process, which Phillips achieved by relaying the recording to a second machine and then bouncing it back to the master machine.

Phillips has said that he knew Elvis was bound for success after a polished performance at the Louisiana Hayride in mid-October 1954, when the singer showed that he could "stand on his own." By this time, it was clear that managing Elvis' burgeoning career needed more than part-time guidance. After initially putting guitarist Scotty Moore in charge of managing Elvis' bookings, Phillips passed the baton on to Bob Neal.

Within six months of Elvis' first professional recording session at Sun Studio, Sam Phillips was acknowledged in a Memphis Press-Scimitar article for finding "A white man's voice singing Negro rhythms with a rural flavor."

By early 1955, Colonel Parker had been alerted to this hot new talent. Without waiting for any official representation rights, the Colonel began gauging interest among major record labels to buy out Elvis' recording contract from Phillips. On February 6, 1955, Sam Phillips met with Colonel Tom Parker at the Palumbo restaurant, opposite the Ellis Auditorium where Elvis was playing, and heard for the first time from the Colonel that Elvis needed a "proper" record label if he was to progress. The Colonel was already in talks with RCA, with whom he had worked in the past. Prompted by the Colonel's soundings, other major record labels, starting with MGM and Decca, began to contact Sam Phillips to see if Elvis' contract was up for sale. There have been rumors that during this period, Phillips actively tried to sell Elvis' recording contract himself to Dot Records in LA, but owner Randy Wood balked at the $7,500 asking price. Phillips received a telegram from the Colonel on October 24, after Parker had persuaded Elvis' parents to sign a contract giving him exclusive management rights over the performer, in which he asked Phillips to name his price for the contract buyout. On October 29, Phillips told the Colonel that he wanted a $5,000 non-refundable down payment by November 15, as an advance on a $35,000 buy out fee.

All the time that Elvis' fate was being monetized and haggled over, the boy himself just wanted to stay with Sun. According to fellow Sun-artist Barbara Pittman, Elvis was concerned that after going to RCA Victor he'd have a couple of hits and then vanish like so many other performers. Sun engineer Jack Clement has said, "Sam sold him to get the money," which he used to settle debts—some incurred by the court settlement for plagiarism regarding Rufus Thomas's "Bearcat," and the remainder to fund another of his long-held ambitions, his very own radio station, "all-girl" WHER, in downtown Memphis. Phillips also found the money useful to develop his burgeoning roster of rockabilly stars such as Carl Perkins (who, with "Blue Suede Shoes," scored Sun's biggest hit to date just two months after Elvis left the label), Jerry Lee Lewis, Johnny Cash, Roy Orbison, Billy Lee Riley and Sonny Burgess. Phillips has gone on record to say that he did not want to sell Elvis' contract at all, and only quoted a figure of $35,000 because he thought it was so high it would frighten off Colonel Parker.

There were no hard feelings between Elvis and Sam. When he was in Memphis, Elvis sometimes dropped into Sun Studio—most famously in December 1956 for the impromptu jam released decades later as The Million Dollar Quartet. Elvis also would stop in at Phillip's house, sometimes with pal Dewey Phillips for a game of pool. In 1957, Elvis he paid a courtesy visit to Phillips, and went home with the latest records Sun had released. Elvis gave a joint press conference with Philips in February 1961 in Memphis about his upcoming charity benefit show. After this, the two men rarely met.

Phillips' career at Sun nominally continued for a further decade, though by 1963 his interest had waned considerably, and Sun came perilously close to folding. He was never interested in expanding his operation into a huge national player, as he much preferred being involved in every aspect of the business. That year, he founded a new label, Phillips International, which also had some success, but gradually he spent less time working on his labels and more on other interests, bringing in his brothers and later his sons to help run the show.

Phillips sold the Sun label to record producer Shelby Singleton in 1969. That year, Elvis invited Phillips to the gala opening night of his return to live performing at the International Hotel in Las Vegas. Phillips had reservations about the orchestral backing for the "boy with the sideburns" he had recorded with just two other bandsmen fifteen years earlier, but became a complete convert after watching what Elvis could do on stage.

Phillips ended up a very wealthy man not from his record business dealings but from a shrewd early investment in a start-up Memphis hotel chain called Holiday Inn. In the late Sixties, he stated a label called Holiday Inn Records (with hotel chain founder Kemmons Wilson) that among others recorded Charlie Feathers, Buck Griffin and "Ironing Board" Sam Moore. In the Seventies, Phillips focuses on running a chain of radio stations, including WLVS, which he named for his biggest discovery of all.

Sam Phillips was inducted into the Rock and Roll Hall of Fame in its inaugural year, 1986.

SAM PHILLIPS: "If I could find a white man who had the Negro sound and feel, I could make a million dollars."

SAM PHILLIPS: "My primary intention was to do something different, and to give an opportunity to talent that never had the opportunity or probably never would have."

SAM PHILLIPS: "Elvis Presley always liked to come back to see us when he could. He was a genuine sort of person, very keen but somewhat lacking in confidence. Elvis was very bright, and he loved music. He comprehended all kinds of music. He was very easy to work with."

SAM PHILLIPS: "I have one real gift and that gift is to look another person in the eye and be able to tell if he has anything to contribute, and if he does, I have the additional gift to free him from whatever is restraining him."

SAM PHILLIPS: "I've been told so many times that I was an inspiration to people who went into the business, who felt, 'If he can do it, we've got a chance,' and I have to say that makes me feel better than anything in the world. It's the greatest thing."

BOB NEAL: "Sam Phillips is credited with discovering a different sound but he had been a radio engineer prior to that time and I know we had done some things on radio programs in Memphis on commercials where we used the electronic-slap-back-type-sound and everything. Sam more or less was the first one that really capitalized on that sound on his recordings."

JACK CLEMENT: "Elvis was always loyal to Sam, always called him 'Mr. Phillips'."

DICK CLARK: "Sam was a one of a kind. He discovered so much talent in a short length of time."

TODD MORGAN (EPE): "One can't help but wonder how different Elvis' life and career would have been, or how the world of music and pop culture would have been different, had Sam not been there, at that moment."

JERRY SCHILLING: "My friend was Elvis Presley and my hero was Sam Phillips. Sam had the eye and the vision of knowing what American music and black music, blues and R&B was all about . . . Sam was the godfather of the whole thing."

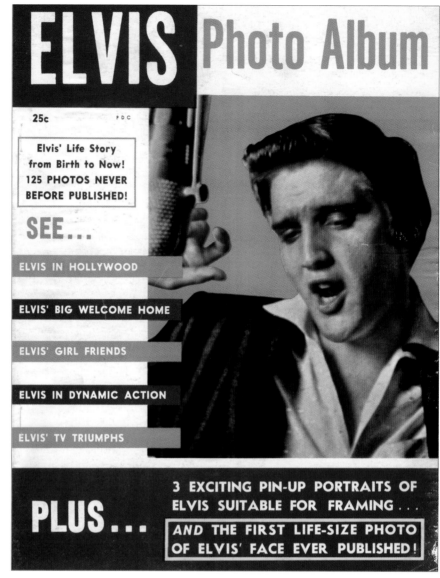
Cover of a 1950s exclusively Elvis magazine.

PHILIP MORRIS COMPANY

Elvis played two shows exclusively for the tobacco company's employees in late 1955, one in Virginia and one in Kentucky.

PHOTOGRAPHERS AND PHOTOGRAPHY

Elvis' striking looks played a significant part in his success. From his earliest concerts, the band made extra money by selling photos of Elvis for 50 cents. Demand for Elvis photos has never waned. The biggest-selling books on Elvis are photo books. Photo-book authors Joe Tunzi, Ger Rijff and Paul Lichter have all authored 20 or more books so far, and do not appear to have finished yet.

This booming industry came into being after Elvis' death. In life, Elvis photos were much more likely to be found in film and gossip magazines than between book covers—or in marketing material distributed to fans and fan clubs.

Elvis' first publicity photographs were snapped by Memphis photographer William Speer in 1954, who also took some brooding Elvis shots in the summer of 1955.

The most iconic photographs of a young Elvis were taken by Al Wertheimer, who in 1956 uniquely had unfettered access to Elvis onstage and off for several months.

Colonel Parker's nose for side deals included taking over responsibility for supplying photographs to RCA, usually keeping a close eye on costs to maximize his return. The movie companies were responsible for their own publicity stills—according to Joe Esposito, sitting for hours with a fixed smile on his face was one of the things Elvis hated most about his time in Hollywood.

An incalculable number of candid Elvis snaps are in the hands of fans who took them at live shows, airports, as close as they could get to film shoots, and in Europe when Elvis was off on R 'n' R in Paris and Munich. Other major sources for the new, never-before-seen photos are family members and members of the entourage, though in theory only Joe Esposito and Priscilla were exempt from the blanket ban on taking photographs of off-duty Elvis.

Surprisingly, through the Seventies the Colonel only employed one official photographer, Tom Diskin's nephew Ed Bonja.

Elvis was a keen photographer too. One of his earliest purchases with his earnings was a camera, and when he arrived in LA in March 1956 for his first screen test, Elvis wore a camera draped around his neck. He played a photographer in 1968 movie *Live a Little, Love a Little*, and is also said to have enjoyed "bedroom photography" over the years.

SOME ELVIS PHOTOGRAPHERS:

Keith Alverson
Ed Bonja
Ed Braslaff
Don Cravens
Robert Dye
David Hecht
Bob Heis
George Hill
Marvin Israel
Jay Leviton
Sandi Miller
Judy Palmer
PoPsie
John Reggero
Jim Reid
Ken Ross
Sean Shaver
William Speer
Guy Sterling
Laurens van Houten
Al Wertheimer
Ernest Withers

WILLIAM SPEER: "He came off that dead film like dynamite. Either you've got it or you haven't."

A CONCISE PHOTO-BOOK SELECTION
(more great books are out there)

Elvis in Hollywood, by Paul Lichter, Simon and Schuster, 1975
The Elvis Presley Scrapbook, by James Robert Parish, Ballantine Books, 1975
Elvis Presley: An Illustrated Biography, by W. A. Harbinson, Joseph, 1975

My Life with Elvis, by Becky Yancy, St. Martin's Press, 1977

The Boy Who Dared to Rock: The Definitive Elvis, by Paul Lichter, Dolphin Books / Doubleday, 1978

Elvis '56: In the Beginning, by Alfred Wertheimer and Gregory Martinelli, Macmillan, 1979

The Life of Elvis Presley. With Intimate Memories of Charlie Hodge, Dick Grob and Billy Smith, by Sean Shaver and Hal Noland, Time Publishing Inc, 1979

Fond Memories of Elvis: 1954-1977, Twenty-Three Years of Photos, Vols. I and II, by Jim Reid, 1980/1981

Long Lonely Highway: A 1950's Elvis Scrapbook, by Ger Rijff, Pierian Press, 1985

Elvis, All My Best, by Paul Lichter, Jesse Books, 1989

Elvis '69 - The Return, by Joseph A. Tunzi, J.A.T. Productions, 1991

Elvis Fire in the Sun, by Ger Rijff, Atomium Books, 1991

The Elvis Album, by Millie Ridge, Gallery Books, 1991

Elvis: Golden Ride on the Mystery Train, Vols. 1 - 3, Jim Hannaford Publications, 1986-1994

The Unseen Elvis: Candids of the King from the Collection of Jim Curtin, by Jim Curtin, Little Brown, 1992

Private Presley: Elvis in Germany —the Missing Years, by Andreas Shroer, Oskar Hentschell, Michael Knorr and W.A. Harbinson, Boxtree Press, 1993

Elvis and the Stars: From the Collection of Jim Curtin, Morgin Press, 1993

Elvis: King of Rock 'n' Roll, by Susan M. Doll, Publications International, 1994

Elvis: His Life in Pictures, by Todd Morgan and Laura Kath, Artabras Publishers/Abbeville Publishing Group, 1997

The Official Elvis Presley Fan Club Commemorative Album, 1935-1977, by Julie Mundy, Virgin Books, 1997

Elvis Immortal: A Celebration of the King, by Carl Waldman, Jim Donovan and Paul Lichter, Legends Press, 1997

Elvis: The Concert Years, 1969-1977, by Stein Erik Skar and Paul Grunland, 1997

Photographs and Memories, by Joe Tunzi, J.A.T. Productions, 1998

Elvis on Stage, by Keith Alverson, Elvis Unlimited Productions, 2000

Millennium Elvis: As Good as It Gets / Larger Than Life, by Paul Lichter, 2000

Caught in a Trap, by Arjan Deelen, Laurens van Houten, 2002

Elvis: A Celebration, by Mike Evans, DK, 2002

Elvis at 21, New York to Memphis, by Alfred Wertheimer, Insight, 2006

Elvis & The Birth Of Rock: The Photographs Of Lew Allen, Genesis Publications, 2007

PIANO

Elvis picked up a guitar before he plinked out a tune on the piano but he apparently considered himself more proficient on the ivories than with a guitar. Early girlfriend Dixie Locke remembers that Elvis could pick up the melody line to any song he heard on the radio after it came over the airwaves a couple of times. With no instrument at home while he was growing up, Elvis learned how to play more or less by osmosis where and when he found a piano—a situation that became much more common after he started singing professionally.

Elvis played piano on at least one take of early Sun single "Tryin' To Get To You." He tinkled the ivories on a number of tracks on his second album, *Elvis*, sharing the work with Jordanaire Gordon Stoker at the Radio Recorders sessions. He played piano on "Lawdy, Miss Clawdy," on "Old Shep," on "Wear My Ring Around Your Neck" and on *Jailhouse Rock* soundtrack song "Don't Leave Me Now."

He spent some time on the piano stool at Sun during the *Million Dollar Quartet* session before handing off to piano whiz Jerry Lee Lewis. He is also said to have played piano on the first take of "Peace In The Valley" in 1957.

Elvis hired a piano when he was out in Germany, and often sang and played his way through potential new material with pal and fellow draftee Charlie Hodge or anyone else who was around.

Elvis played piano during the recording session for his *How Great Thou Art* album in 1966, during which he played on at least one take of "Beyond The Reef."

In 1968, Elvis relaxed between rehearsals for his NBC TV Special by practicing Beethoven's "Moonlight Sonata" backstage (one of a number of classical tracks he picked up).

At the start of the following year, he played at American Studio on "After Loving You" and "I'll Hold You In My Heart." In his final movie, *Change of Habit*, he plays an instrumental version of "Lawdy, Miss Clawdy."

At one of his May 1971 recording sessions in Nashville, Elvis felt comfortable enough with Ivory Joe Hunter songs "It's Still Here," "I Will Be True" and classic "I'll Take You Home Again Kathleen" to provide his own piano accompaniment. That year he also played "How The Web Was Woven" on stage.

At many Seventies concerts, fans loved the emotionally-charged moment when Elvis would belt out a song to his own solo piano accompaniment (in a style that Ernst Jorgensen describes as "staccato"). Piano-accompanied Elvis concert favorites included "Unchained Melody," the inspirational "You'll Never Walk Alone" and sometimes "Blueberry Hill."

ELVIS' PIANOS

Elvis bought his first piano, an upright, in September 1955. Elvis had an organ in the first home he owned, at Audubon Drive in Memphis, which he bought for his mother.

In 1957, he purchased his first grand piano for $795, a used white 1940 Knabe for Graceland (which had previously been used at Ellis Auditorium, and has changed hands for a thousand times its purchase price since then, most recently at auction in 2007).

In 1961, Elvis went on a major spending spree at Jack Marshall Pianos and Organs in Memphis, purchasing a Schimmel piano and organ and an Allan organette for Graceland.

Elvis bought a Baldwin grand piano for Graceland for Christmas 1967 (though some reports state that it was a gift from Priscilla in 1969), which replaced the old Knabe.

Elvis chose a Sterling Clark for his Palm Springs home in 1973. In 1974 he exchanged his Baldwin for a Story and Clark, which is still at Graceland to this day, covered in gold leaf.

A special "Elvis signature edition" Baldwin upright piano has been on sale since 2005.

ELVIS SAID IN 1956: "I don't play it exactly the way you're supposed to. I just hit whatever keys look good to me. It's a lot of fun, and sometimes I'll play along while I'm singing."

EDDIE FADAL: "Elvis loved putting on a record and playing the piano along with the record and changing the style of the singer to the way he would do it. He did that hours upon hours."

GLEN D. HARDIN (laughing): "I thought he was about the worst piano player I ever heard!"

"PIECES OF MY LIFE"

Elvis laid down this track of melancholy reminiscence on March 12, 1975, at the RCA studios in Hollywood. The track was first released on the *Today* album, and featured as the B-side to single "Bringin' it Back" later that year. It was written by Troy Seals in 1974, and first recorded by Charlie Rich. Elvis listened to the finished track over and over when he cut it—the last song he would ever record in a studio environment.

The song was picked for inclusion on posthumous albums *Always On My Mind*, *Walk A Mile In My Shoes* and the 2006 BMG release *Elvis Country*. Alternates have appeared on *Today Tomorrow And Forever* and on the 2005 FTD version of *Today*.

PIERCE, WEBB
(B. WEBB MICHAEL PIERCE, 1921-1991)

This Louisiana Hayride and Grand Old Opry star was a top honky tonk country performer, scoring thirteen Billboard chart #1s in the 1950s. His biggest hit came in 1953, with the classic drinking song "There Stands The Glass."

Born in West Monroe, LA, on August 8, 1921, Pierce got his big break at the Louisiana Hayride, where his band included future Elvis pianist Floyd Cramer and future Elvis promoter Tillman Franks. Pierce moved on to the Opry in 1952 as a replacement for Hank Williams.

Elvis toured with Webb Pierce on a number of occasion when he was just starting out, including at the Jimmie Rodgers Memorial Celebration. The flamboyant Pierce was one of many established performers who discovered to their cost that it was simply not possible to follow Elvis.

Elvis covered Pierce composition "How Do You Think I Feel" in his first year with RCA.

Pierce was inducted into the Country Music Hall of Fame in 2001.

WEBB PIERCE, CA. 1955: "That boy could put us all out of business"

PIED PIPER OF CLEVELAND, THE: A DAY IN THE LIFE OF A FAMOUS DISC JOCKEY

This short film profiling Cleveland DJ Bill Randle was shot on October 20, 1955 during a specially-staged concert at the Brooklyn High School in Cleveland, Ohio. The bill that day was a snapshot of early rock 'n' roll, featuring Bill Haley, Pat Boone, The Four Lads and Priscilla Wright, plus relative unknown Elvis Presley who sang from his Sun repertoire of "That's All Right (Mama)," "Blue Moon Of Kentucky," "Good Rockin' Tonight," "Mystery Train" and "I Forgot to Remember to Forget." Some commentators suggest that also on the bill were LaVern Baker, Roy Hamilton and Johnnie Ray.

For reasons best understood by legal minds, the movie was not released at the time and has never been released since, though some sources state that it was shown once in Cleveland. One compelling reason why the film was cast into limbo may have been that the William Morris Agency allegedly sought "proper payment" of at least $50,000 for Elvis' appearance in the movie.

The uncertainty about whether a copy of the film survives is compounded by a mystery about who might own it. Originally made by Universal, in 1991 film producer Ray Santilli (best known for his involvement in the Roswell alien autopsy footage) is said to have paid Bill Randle $1.9 million for rights to the film, and then sold them on to Polygram for $2.2 million. If there is a holy grail for Elvis fans, then this footage—variously described as either 48 minutes or 20 minutes—is it.

PAT BOONE: "Elvis was shy until he got on stage and then he just exploded."

CREDITS:
Studio: Universal
Directed by: Arthur Cohen
Produced by: Bill Randle
Cinematography by: Jack Barnett

CAST:
Franny Beecher
Pat Boone
Johnny Grande
Bill Haley
Rudy Pompilli
Elvis Presley
Bill Randle
Al Rex
Billy Williamson

PLANT, ROBERT
(B. 1948)

Elvis became pals with the Led Zeppelin front man in the Seventies, after inviting the band to see him perform at Las Vegas. Plant later visited Elvis at Graceland, where they sang Elvis songs including "Love Me." The autograph Elvis gave Plant read, "To Robert, a true friend. Treat me like a fool, Elvis Presley."

Led Zeppelin were one of the world's most successful rock bands from 1968 to 1980, spurred by Plant's wailing vocals and Jimmy Page's soaring riffs.

"PLANTATION ROCK"

A Giant / Baum / Kaye soundtrack effort that Elvis recorded on March 28, 1962 at Radio Recorders for *Girls! Girls! Girls!*, which escaped release until 1983 on *Elvis: A Legendary Performer Vol. 4*, though that version was an alternate splice corrected on the film's *Double Features* album in 1993.

An alternate appeared on the 2007 FTD *Girls! Girls! Girls!* release.

PLATINUM: A LIFE IN MUSIC

A 1997 4-disc box set released to commemorate the 20th anniversary of Elvis' death, featuring a significant number of alternate takes, home recordings of Elvis singing and more.

TRACK LISTING:
DISC 1:
1. I'll Never Stand In Your Way
2. That's All Right (alternate takes)
3. Blue Moon (alternate take)
4. Good Rockin' Tonight
5. Mystery Train
6. I Got A Woman (alternate take)
7. Heartbreak Hotel (alternate take)
8. I'm Counting On You (alternate take)
9. Shake, Rattle and Roll / Flip, Flop & Fly
10. Lawdy, Miss Clawdy (alternate take)
11. I Want You, I Need You, I Love You (alternate take)
12. Hound Dog
13. Don't Be Cruel
14. Rip It Up (alternate take)
15. Love Me Tender
16. When The Saints Go Marchin' In (home recording)
17. All Shook Up
18. (There'll Be) Peace In The Valley (For Me) (alternate take)
19. Blueberry Hill
20. (Let Me Be Your) Teddy Bear
21. Jailhouse Rock
22. New Orleans
23. I Need Your Love Tonight (alternate take)
24. A Big Hunk O' Love (alternate take)
25. Bad Nauheim medley: (I'll Take You Home Again Kathleen, I Will Be True, It's Been So Long Darling, Apron Strings, There's No Tomorrow)

DISC 2:
1. Stuck On You
2. Fame And Fortune
3. It's Now Or Never
4. It Feels So Right (alternate take)
5. A Mess Of Blues (alternate take)
6. Are You Lonesome Tonight?
7. Reconsider Baby
8. Tonight Is So Right For Love (alternate take)
9. His Hand In Mine (alternate take)
10. Milky White Way (alternate take)
11. I'm Comin' Home (alternate take)
12. I Feel So Bad (alternate take)
13. Can't Help Falling In Love
14. Something Blue (alternate take)
15. Return To Sender
16. Bossa Nova Baby (alternate take)
17. How Great Thou Art (alternate take)
18. Guitar Man (alternate take)
19. You'll Never Walk Alone (alternate take)
20. Oh How I Love Jesus
21. Tennessee Waltz
22. Blowin' In The Wind
23. I Can't Help It (If I'm Still In Love With You)
24. I'm Beginning To Forget You (solo)
25. After Loving You

DISC 3:
1. I Got A Woman
2. Tiger Man
3. When My Blue Moon Turns To Gold Again
4. Tryin' To Get To You
5. If I Can Dream (alternate take)
6. In The Ghetto (alternate take)
7. Suspicious Minds (alternate take)
8. Power Of My Love (alternate take)
9. Baby, What You Want Me To Do
10. Words
11. Johnny B. Goode
12. Release Me
13. See See Rider
14. The Wonder Of You
15. The Sound Of Your Cry (alternate take)
16. You Don't Have To Say You Love Me
17. Funny How Time Slips Away
18. I Wash My Hands In Muddy Water
19. I Was The One
20. Cattle Call
21. Baby, Let's Play House
22. Don't
23. Money Honey
24. What'd I Say
25. Bridge Over Troubled Water

DISC 4:
1. Miracle Of The Rosary (alternate take)
2. He Touched Me (alternate take)
3. Bosom Of Abraham (alternate take)
4. I'll Be Home On Christmas Day (alternate take)
5. For The Good Times (alternate take)
6. Burning Love (alternate take)
7. Separate Ways (alternate take)
8. Always On My Mind (alternate take)
9. An American Trilogy
10. Take Good Care Of Her (alternate take)
11. I've Got A Thing About You Baby
12. Are You Sincere (alternate take)
13. It's Midnight (alternate take)
14. Promised Land (alternate take)
15. Steamroller Blues
16. And I Love You So (alternate take)
17. T-R-O-U-B-L-E
18. Danny Boy (alternate take)
19. Moody Blue
20. Hurt (alternate take)
21. For The Heart (alternate take)
22. Pledging My Love (alternate take)
23. Way Down (alternate take)
24. My Way
25. Jaycees Speech (excerpt)

PLATINUM: A LIFE IN MUSIC

Since its publication by St. Martin's Press in 1998, this book by Ernst Jorgensen (with a foreword by Peter Guralnick) has been the standard work of reference on Elvis' music and recordings.

PLATTERS, THE

When early interviewers asked Elvis inflammatory questions about rock 'n' roll, he cited Platters songs such as "The Magic Touch," "The Great Pretender" and "My Prayer" as evidence of the great music coming out of the new genre.

Found in 1953, the Platters started out as a doo wap group before manager Buck Ram penned a string of hits for the them. The Platters were an early crossover success, migrating from the R & B to the pop charts thanks to the smooth vocals of lead tenor Tony Williams. The Platters were the first rock 'n' roll group to achieve a top-10 album.

Elvis sang Platters hit "Only You" during early performances at the Louisiana Hayride. The Platters later returned the favor by covering "Love Me Tender."

The Platters also hits with covers of classics "Smoke Gets In your Eyes" and "Harbor Lights" (a song that Elvis recorded during his first proper session at Sun).

The Platters were inducted into the Rock 'n' Roll Hall of Fame in 1990, and were initial inductees when the Vocal Group Hall of Fame was founded in 1998.

"PLAYING FOR KEEPS"

This song, written by Stan Kesler, was recorded on September 1, 1956 at Radio Recorders for release as the B-Side to "Too Much," which RCA brought out in January 1957. It climbed to #34 in the charts, and subsequently appeared on *For LP Fans Only*. It is also to be found on *Worldwide Gold Award Hits Vol. 1*, *A Valentine Gift For You* and *The King Of Rock And Roll*.

"PLEASE DON'T DRAG THAT STRING AROUND"

Elvis recorded this sax-heavy Otis Blackwell / Winfield Scott tune on May 26, 1963 at Studio B in Nashville for almost immediate release as the B-side to "(You're The) Devil in Disguise" The track had its first album release on *Elvis' Gold Records Vol. 4*.

It was included on the second volume of *Worldwide Gold Award Hits*, and appears on *For The Asking (The Lost Album)*. A remastered version is available on *From Nashville to Memphis*. Alternate takes are on *Essential Elvis, Vol. 6* and FTD release *Studio B: Nashville Outtakes*.

"PLEASE DON'T STOP LOVING ME"

Elvis recorded this Joy Byers song, (said by David Neale to be a reworking of Gigliola Cinquetti's 1964 Eurovision song contest winner "Non ho l'eta per amarti") on May 13, 1965 at Radio Recorders, as a soundtrack item for *Frankie and Johnny*. When released as the B-side to "Frankie And Johnny" in March 1966, the song made it to #45 in the charts in its own right.

It is, of course, included in the *Double Feature* soundtrack repackage, and on compilation albums *Command Performances* and *Today, Tomorrow & Forever* (an alternate take).

Elvis in concert 1974 wearing the rare and beautiful Tiger Jumpsuit

"PLEDGING MY LOVE"

Elvis recorded his final B-side at Graceland on October 29, 1976 for release in June 1977 with "Way Down" and as an album track on *Moody Blue*. Written by Ferdinand Washington and Don Robey, the song had been a #1 R & B hit for Johnny Ace in 1955 (not long after he played a game of fatal Russian Roulette), and had also been covered by Elvis favorite Roy Hamilton.

The song has since appeared on *Walk A Mile In My Shoes* and *Elvis R 'n' B*.

An alternate version featured on *Platinum: A Life In Music*; FTD issue *The Jungle Room Sessions* features a 5-minute version.

"POCKETFUL OF RAINBOWS"

On May 6, 1960 Elvis recorded this Fred Wise / Ben Weisman song at Radio Recorders for *G.I. Blues*—in the movie, Juliet Prowse lip synchs along to a few lines. An April 28, 1960 recording of the song at RCA's Hollywood studios failed to yield a workable version (though it did appear years later on UK release *The EP Collection, Vol. 2*).

Alternate versions have surfaced on *Collectors Gold*, the 1997 *G.I. Blues* reissue, *Today Tomorrow & Forever* and *Elvis: Close Up*.

"POISON IVY LEAGUE"

A class-conscious soundtrack tune from *Roustabout*, written by Giant / Baum / Kaye and recorded at Radio Recorders, Los Angeles on March 2, 1964. It appeared on the soundtrack LP and later on the *Double Feature* re-release. It is also available on *Command Performances*.

POLICE

Elvis had genuine respect for the authority and standing of police officers, and for what he saw as the spontaneous excitement of their working life. Before he became a singer, Elvis considered a job in the police force; many of the kids he grew up with in Tupelo and at the Lauderdale Courts pursued just such a career.

At the very outset of his career, Elvis' most frequent experience with policemen was when they issued him with speeding tickets, though the boys in blue quickly became a fixture at Elvis concerts to protect him from over-enthusiastic fans and their disgruntled boyfriends. In the Seventies, Elvis made many friends from within the police community, contributed liberally to police benevolent funds, was himself a deputy in many counties across the States, had a badge collection that rivaled the most well-traveled cop, and owned a full range of police paraphernalia. In consequence, he benefited from a tendency for the police to overlook misdemeanors such as vehicle infractions; he and his entourage were legally permitted to carry guns; and the Colonel's savvy policy of hiring off-duty cops as additional security for Elvis shows allowed greater latitude in handling problems out of the glare of publicity.

Within a short time of becoming a performer, credible death threats ensured that Elvis was frequently shadowed by a Memphis police department detail. In the Fifties, Captain Woodward was assigned to looking after Elvis. Whenever Elvis drove out of Graceland, the police were alerted and usually a patrol car would shadow Elvis' cavalcade to ward off any danger.

Within the first year of his performing career, Elvis played five shows in a benefit for the Beaumont, Texas police department, organized by promoter Ed McLemore.

In September 1956, as part of the moral backlash against Elvis, the San Diego police chief threatened to throw the singer in jail for disorderly conduct if he came back to town and performed the way he had done that spring. Elvis was also given official police "no wiggle" warnings in Kentucky (November 1956) and in Los Angeles (October 1957).

Elvis was charged with assault and battery and disorderly conduct in October 1956 after gas station attendant Ed Hopper told Elvis to clear off his forecourt when he was mobbed by fans. Hopper emerged from the experience with a black eye, and, along with fellow gas station attendant Aubrey Brown, a $25 fine; charges against Elvis were dropped when it was proven that Hopper hit Elvis first. Elvis later interceded to try and get Hopper his job back.

Elvis was on the right side of the blue line in November 1956, when he agreed to put in an appearance at a new driver education program in Memphis, the "Beginner Driving Range."

In August 1958, the Memphis Highway Patrol tried to cheer Elvis up as he mourned the passing of his mother by taking him up on helicopter rides over town.

When Elvis returned home to Graceland after two years in the Army, the last leg of the journey from the train station at Memphis was in the squad car driven by his pal Captain (and later Inspector) Fred Woodward, who had been helping out Elvis with personal security.

Elvis was made an honorary Shelby Country deputy sheriff in 1964.

Elvis hired a special police guard to protect Priscilla and new-born Lisa Marie at the Baptist Hospital after she was born on February 1, 1968.

In 1970, Elvis donated $7,000 to the LAPD community relations program, on condition that the donation remained anonymous. Chief Davis gave Elvis a gold commissioner's badge. That year Shelby County Sheriff Roy Nixon (later Memphis's mayor) made Elvis a Chief Special Deputy, with his own standard-issue police paraphernalia, rather than just an honorary deputy—a rank to which the entire Memphis Mafia was elevated at that time. Elvis made a flying visit to Memphis Police headquarters in the early hours of Christmas Day "to say hello" to members of the force serving the public on the public holiday.

On tour in 1970, Elvis befriended two off-duty cops who had been hired to protect him. When he invited detectives Ron Pietrafeso and Jerry Kennedy to come and watch him perform in Las Vegas, he hinted that that they might get him another police badge to add to his collection. By this time, he had former drug squad officer John O'Grady working for his security operation; later in the decade, former police officer Dick Grob ran Elvis' security, acting as a personal bodyguard and liaising with police departments in municipalities where Elvis was scheduled to perform.

Elvis made many friends within the Memphis force, starting with Bill Morris, a friend of Vernon's from back in the Tupelo days. Elvis regularly invited officers Fred Fredrick and Robert Ferguson along to film screenings at the Memphian Theater. According to entourage members, Elvis could listen for hours to policemen talking about the calls they had gone out on.

Elvis signed himself and his entourage members up to the National Sheriffs Association during his December 1970 visit to Washington.

Elvis' fascination with the police became his main hobby in the early Seventies. He sometimes went down to practice at the police firing range, and rode around in patrol cars with serving officers. In early 1971, Elvis had his Mercedes customized with a police radio and blue lights, and bought himself shoulder holsters, chemical weapons and handcuffs. One of his nighttime pursuits was to cruise around town with a police scanner, and then show up at crime scenes to watch the action as it unfolded. The West cousins told Steve Dunleavy that Elvis would also sometimes pull over an unsuspecting motorist, gun drawn, flash his police badge and rebuke them for poor driving.

Out on tour in the Seventies, Elvis flashed his official narcotics badge to local officers and let it be known that he would like one of the local badges too. It was his friendship with high-ranking Memphis policemen rather than the narcotics badge that allowed him some vital slack later on. When the Memphis police discovered a consignment of cocaine bound for Graceland, they waited (in vain) for somebody to pick it up from a nearby hotel, rather than raid Graceland as they might normally have done.

Elvis obtained a police uniform in 1976—a captain's uniform no less—from Denver police pals Jerry Kennedy and Ron Pietrafeso. When on a whim Elvis decided to go on vacation to Vail, Colorado, they helped him find accommodation. By way of thanks, Elvis bought Lincolns and Cadillacs for them and for police doctor Dr. Gerald Starkey (who, according to Peter Guralnick, shocked Elvis by refusing to prescribe him some Dilaudid). A month later Elvis was back in Denver for the funeral of Eugene Kennedy, whom he had met on the force. He brought along J.D. Sumner and the Stamps to sing at the funeral. When Elvis got back to Graceland for the recording session he was supposed to be doing, he appeared in his Denver police captain's uniform. Elvis fell out with these pals after they talked to him about his increasing impulsiveness and erratic behavior. According to Red and Sonny West, two undercover narcotics officers tried to persuade Elvis that he needed professional help at a residential facility to tackle his drug addiction.

Elvis made the rank of captain in the Memphis Police Reserve force in early 1976. He put his new status to use when he happened across a car wreck in March 1976: he stopped, flashed his badge and helped the accident victims. That year, he hatched an ill-advised (and thankfully never implemented) plan to round up drug dealers in Memphis and eliminate them. He had already been out on drug busts with friends of his in the Memphis narcotics department, wearing a ski-mask to remain incognito. Elvis boasted to entourage members that he had been in the thick of action in Denver on a drug bust, using his karate to immobilize one of the bad guys—though Dick Grob, who had been with Elvis that evening, did not corroborate the story.

Elvis swore pal Larry Geller in as a police commissioner in 1977, convinced that he had the authority to do so.

Elvis retained the desire to play the hero during the last few months of his life. On his final tour, he got out of his limo at a gas station at one in the morning to break up a fight between two youths and a gas station attendant. The shock of seeing Elvis instantly defused the situation and the people involved took photographs instead of trading blows.

Many local police officers volunteered without pay to help with security for Elvis' funeral, guarding Graceland and then saluting the hearse as it was escorted by motorcycle police officers to the cemetery.

JO CATHY BROWNLEE: ." . . He always had the secret desire to be some kind of law enforcement officer. He admired the hell out of the police here in Memphis—it was like he would just love to change places with them."

Book:
Elvis in the Beat of the Night, by Bob Ferguson, Phillips Memphis, 2007

POLICE BADGES

Elvis began collecting police badges when he was still regularly getting pulled over for speeding. He was made an honorary captain of the Louisiana State Highway Patrol in 1956.

For Elvis, every badge told a story, and was the result of his perseverance in persuading the right people to give him what he wanted. There was a practical reason for these badges, too: they enabled him and his entourage to legally carry guns as they traveled.

In 1964, Elvis was appointed a "Special Deputy Sheriff" of Shelby Country, a promotion from "Honorary Chief Deputy Sheriff." He told Sheriff Bill Morris of his long-term interest in law enforcement, and claimed that he had applied to be a Memphis cop just before his music career took off.

Elvis was given a gold deputy's badge by Houston Sheriff Buster Kern in 1970 (the Colonel got one too). He was made an honorary deputy sheriff in Shelby Country (Memphis) that September by Sheriff Roy Nixon, and then in October got an official deputy sheriff badge, which allowed him to carry a pistol and make arrests. For his birthday that year, members of Elvis' entourage had the badge gold plated and encrusted with diamonds and rubies.

The badge that Elvis coveted most of all was a Federal Bureau of Narcotics and Dangerous Drugs badge. The story goes that Elvis decided he had to have one after meeting Hollywood voice-over artist Paul Frees, who showed him the badge he had been given for his undercover work. In late 1970, for the only time in all his years as a celebrity, Elvis slipped out of Graceland and went off without telling anybody where he was going. After picking up an entourage member or two and some money, he went to Washington to see if he could get that badge. He was not put off by his failure to meet BNDD Director John Ingersoll, or by his unsuccessful meeting with Deputy Director John Finlator (during which Elvis offered a $5000 donation, in return for which he was only offered an honorary badge, not the official one he wanted). Elvis' speculative letter drafted on American Airlines notepaper, however, procured an unscheduled audience with President Richard Nixon, and Nixon made sure that his patriotic young guest did not go away without his BNDD Special Assistant badge. Elvis believed that this badge gave him the authority to carry guns and whatever pharmaceuticals he wanted anywhere in the country.

A photo taken on December 28, 1970, after Sonny West's wedding, immortalizes Elvis, Vernon, entourage members and sheriff friends, all proudly displaying their badges.

Among his collection of badges, Elvis received one from Tupelo Sheriff Bill Mitchell. He continued to pick up badges—official rather than honorary wherever possible—in as many Counties as he could on his tours, and never left Memphis without taking along his collection.

BILLY SMITH: "He eventually had hundreds of them suckers."

MUG SHOTS

A pair of Elvis mug shots from 1970 exist that were originally taken either by the Memphis or Denver Police Departments for one of Elvis' police badges, though it has been suggested that they were taken in Washington for his BNDD badge. British artist Russell Young has turned these photos into silkscreen prints.

SPEEDING TICKETS

Zipping state to state on a madcap touring schedule in his early years, Elvis had more than one scrape with traffic cops. He once told a journalist about an incident just before Christmas 1954, when he was pulled over on his way home from Shreveport with fellow band members Scotty Moore and Bill Black. The officer decided, in true Christmas spirit, to let them off with a warning, much to Elvis' relief as the money he had in his pocket was intended for Christmas shopping rather than paying a speeding fine.

Elvis was pulled over near Shreveport in early April 1955 for speeding at 80 mph in his brand new Cadillac for which he posted $25 bond before his arraignment appearance on April 5.

Elvis collected two speeding tickets in Memphis in March 1956, on March 2 and on March 8, which required a court appearance. He added to his collection in Hattiesburg, Mississippi on July 29, 1956, en route to see girlfriend June Juanico in Biloxi. In Fort Worth, Elvis was nabbed for speeding in July 1958.

In late 1965, Elvis was stopped for speeding at 4 a.m. near Graceland, on the way home from a late-night screening session at the Memphian Theater. Entourage members have told of Elvis driving at over 100 m.p.h. down his home road.

LAMAR FIKE: "We'd get so damn many tickets that Elvis put a pool of money together just to pay them."

POLITICS

Elvis was too smart to alienate half his fans by publicly pledging allegiance to one of America's political parties, though his later views on hippies and illegal drugs put him more towards the right-hand side of the political spectrum. Elvis aides have confirmed that very early on, Colonel Parker impressed on Elvis that there was no upside to making his political views known.

When he first began mesmerizing audiences across the world, in the Soviet Union the press held Elvis up as what was wrong with youth in America.

As a publicity stunt prior to the premiere of Elvis' first film Love Me Tender, in late October 1956 Colonel Parker had "Elvis for President" buttons handed out during the unveiling of a 40-foot high Elvis cutout outside the Times Square Paramount Theater in New York City.

In the run-up to the 1956 election, Elvis declared that he was going to vote for the Democrat candidate, Adlai Stevenson—the only time that he declared a partisan affiliation. However, according to other Elvis intimates, Elvis was naturally a conservative.

Elvis worked with Clifford Odets and Philip Dunne, two well-known left-wing Hollywood luminaries, on Wild in the Country in 1960.

Elvis may not have agreed with all of his politics, but he considered President Kennedy to be a good man.

In the late Sixties, Elvis made some political statements through his choice of music, starting with the socially-engaged finale to his NBC TV Special, "If I Can Dream." He went one step further in early 1969, when he recorded "In The Ghetto."

Elvis reportedly enjoyed teasing entourage member Jerry Schilling for his left-leaning views.

In 1970, Elvis met President Richard Nixon and offered his services to the nation as a Federal Agent to fight against "drug abuse and Communist brainwashing techniques," which he claimed to have been studying for a decade.

Rumors briefly circulated in the early Seventies that the Republican party considered Elvis to be potential vice-president material.

Death has done little to stifle Elvis' electability. A 1992 book by "The Committee to Elect the King" launched a campaign for Elvis to win the presidency that year. Elvis Presley has been on the ballot paper too: in a local city election in Calumet, Minnesota, Elvis was a little off the pace with only one vote in November 2005.

Elvis has also featured in the lives of Presidents Jimmy Carter, Bill Clinton, and Bushes I and II. In life, he believed that the president should always be supported, regardless of his political affiliation.

Presidential contender for 2008 Mitt Romney used Elvis song "A Little Less Conversation" as part of his nomination campaign.

ELVIS SAID IN 1971: "I believe that entertainers should entertain and make people happy and not try to impose his personal philosophy on anyone through songs, television or through the guise of comedy."

ELVIS SAID IN 1972: "I don't have any other aspirations in politics or anything of that nature."

SONNY WEST: "Elvis was very private about his political views, but was passionate about them in private with those of us and friends that he could trust."

LARRY GELLER: "He had no interest in politics, which is interesting considering how pro-America he was."

MARTY LACKER: "He liked the president no matter what party they were in."

PHIL OCHS: "If there's any hope for America, it lies in a revolution, and if there's any hope for a revolution in America, it lies in getting Elvis Presley to become Che Guevara."

LAMAR FIKE: "I think he would have been happy being the President and absolute despotic monarch of the United States."

"POLK SALAD ANNIE"

Elvis included this 1969 Tony Joe White song in some of his earliest Las Vegas performances but it didn't become a concert staple until 1970. The first version to come out on record, from a February 18, 1970 performance, was released on On Stage. Though not released as a single in the US, it was a major worldwide hit as a 45. Additional versions from 1970 have appeared on Elvis Aron Presley, Live in Las Vegas, The Live Greatest Hits, Elvis Live and That's The Way It Is—Special Edition. Both of Elvis' Seventies documentaries feature the song, and it is on dozens and dozens of bootlegs, as you might expect of a crowd-pleaser that he performed live close to 500 times. Elvis always seemed to get a kick out of the spoken lead-in and the funky exchange of nonsense syllables with the Sweet Inspirations towards the end.

Other live versions released in his lifetime are on Elvis As Recorded At Madison Square Garden and Elvis Recorded Live On Stage In Memphis.

The song has been anthologized on various compilation albums such as Walk A Mile In My Shoes, Artist Of The Century, Today Tomorrow & Forever, Elvis: Close Up, and The Essential Elvis Presley.

Live recordings released posthumously are included in An Afternoon In The Garden and FTD releases The Way It Was, Dinner At Eight, Tucson '76, It's Midnight , Dixieland Rocks, Spring Tours '77, New Year's Eve, The Impossible Dream, Elvis On Tour—The Rehearsals, Polk Salad Annie, Summer Festival, I Found My Thrill, Southern Nights, An American Trilogy, Live In LA, Writing For The King and One Night In Vegas.

POLK SALAD ANNIE

A 2004 FTD album of Elvis live in Las Vegas during his second season, mainly from the February 15, 1970 midnight show.

TRACK LISTING:
1. I Got A Woman (incomplete)
2. Long Tall Sally
3. Don't Cry, Daddy
4. Hound Dog
5. Love Me Tender
6. Kentucky Rain
7. Let It Be Me
8. I Can't Stop Loving You
9. Walk A Mile In My Shoes
10. In The Ghetto
11. Sweet Caroline
12. Polk Salad Annie
13. Introductions
14. Suspicious Minds
15. Can't Help Falling In Love
16. Release Me (Feb. 19)
17. See See Rider (Feb. 17)
18. Proud Mary (Feb. 19)
19. The Wonder Of You (Feb. 18)
20. Release Me (rehearsal)
21. See See Rider (rehearsal)
22. The Wonder Of You (rehearsal)

POMUS, DOC
(B. JEROME SOLON FELDER, 1925-1991)

Doc Pomus and Mort Shuman were an accomplished songwriting team who signed up with Hill & Range while Elvis was in the Army in the late Fifties, and churned out hits together for nine years.

When Elvis stepped back into the recording studio for the first time in 1960, he recorded "A Mess Of Blues," the first of 18 tracks that Doc Pomus wrote for him (fifteen with Mort Shuman).

Childhood polio did not stop Brooklyn-born Pomus from a successful decade as a blues singer in the Forties and early Fifties. In the mid-Fifties, he teamed up with his longtime pianist Mort Shuman to become the lyricist in one of the top songwriting duos of the day. Pomus and Shuman wrote hit songs for Bobby Darin, Dusty Springfield, Ray Charles, the Beach Boys, Ben. E. King, The Drifters, Bob Dylan, Led Zeppelin, Bruce Springsteen and as they used to say in the record ads, many, many more.

Elvis songs written by the duo include "A Mess of Blues," "Little Sister," "Surrender," "Viva Las Vegas" and "(Marie's The Name) His Latest Flame." Catchy motifs from their songs have reappeared in many pop hits ever since—Abba are said to have borrowed a lick or two.

Pomus was inducted into the Songwriters Hall of Fame the year after his death.

See ELVIS SINGS MORT SHUMAN & DOC POMUS

Book:
Lonely Avenue, by Alex Halberstadt, Da Capo Press, 2007

"POOR BOY"

Elvis recorded this Vera Matson / Elvis Presley-credited song at Radio Recorders on August 24, 1956 for release on the *Love Me Tender* EP in November that year, and later, on the album *For LP Fans Only*. The song was actually written by vocal arranger Ken Darby, who inserted this and other songs into the film. It achieved a singles chart placing at #35 on the back of its EP release.

"Poor Boy" has since appeared on compilation album *Worldwide Gold Award Hits Vol. 2*, and has come out posthumously on *Essential Elvis Vol. 1* and on the *King Of Rock And Roll* box set. The 1997 *Jailhouse Rock* CD contains two versions.

"POOR MAN'S GOLD"

Elvis never completed his recording of this Mac Davis song because as he they were laying it down at American Studio in 1969 he was distracted by a passing siren and dissolved into laughter. The band later finished up their work on the tune but Elvis did not. The result did not officially see the light of day until the 1999 American Studio compilation *Suspicious Minds: The Memphis 1969 Anthology*, though it had already come out on bootleg before then.

POPSIE (WILLIAM S. RANDOLPH)
(1920-1978)

Famous celebrity photographer William "PoPsie" Randolph was hired by Colonel Tom Parker to immortalize Elvis several times in his breakthrough year, starting with his RCA contract signature in December 1955, and including the July 1956 shoot at RCA's New York recording studio which provided material for the cover of Elvis' debut LP Elvis Presley.

PORTER, BILL

RCA's studio engineer, with whom Elvis started working in Nashville in 1960 after his discharge from the Army. Porter was an instrumental contributor to developing the "Nashville sound." He worked on hundreds and hundreds of hits, including 11 number ones. In addition to Elvis, Porter also worked with Roy Orbison and the Everly Brothers.

Porter later opened his own studio in Las Vegas, and worked as Elvis' sound man when the King started performing regularly at the International Hotel. He carried on in this capacity right through to Elvis' last Las Vegas engagement, and regularly accompanied Elvis and the TCB band out on the road.

Porter was the first audio engineer to be inducted into the Audio Hall of Fame.

"PORTRAIT OF MY LOVE"

Elvis was recorded singing this 1961 Steve Lawrence top ten hit (written by Cyril Ornadel and David West, and later performed by Frank Sinatra, Nat "King" Cole and Perry Como) backstage at Las Vegas in 1973, and quite possibly a year or so earlier. The song is on bootleg discs *Special Delivery From Elvis Presley* and *Suzie Q*.

POT LUCK WITH ELVIS (LP)

Mainly recorded in Nashville at two very fruitful sessions in mid-March 1962, *Pot Luck* is an honest title for an LP that combined this material with soundtrack songs from *Follow That Dream* and a cast-off from *Blue Hawaii*. RCA shipped the album in early June 1962. On initial release it sold around 300,000 copies, enough to take it to #4 in the charts, where it enjoyed a 31-week parabola.

TRACK LISTING:
1. Kiss Me Quick
2. Just For Old Time Sake
3. Gonna Get Back Home Somehow
4. (Such an) Easy Question
5. Steppin' Out Of Line
6. I'm Yours
7. Something Blue
8. Suspicion
9. I Feel That I've Known You Forever
10. Night Rider
11. Fountain Of Love
12. That's Someone You Never Forget

Later CD versions include "I Met Her Today," "She's Not You," "You'll Be Gone," "For The Millionth And The Last Time" and "Just Tell Her Jim Said Hello."

FTD brought out a remixed version of the album with many outtakes in 2007.

"POWER OF MY LOVE"

Elvis considered recording this song in 1966 but laid down this Giant / Baum / Kaye blues number at American Studio on February 18, 1969. It first came out on *From Elvis In Memphis* that same year.

The song has since appeared on *The Memphis Record*, *Elvis Sings The Blues* and the *From Nashville to Memphis* anthology. Alternate takes are on *Platinum: A Life In Music*, the *Suspicious Minds* 2-CD release from 1999 and FTD release *The Memphis Sessions*.

PRANKS

Elvis was famed for his boyish pranks and japes. He spent his adult life indulging a talent (or vice, if you were on the receiving end) that was already well-developed in Elvis the kid. He was almost fired from his first proper job, as an usher at the Loew's State Theater, one day when he ran down the aisle and for a joke shouted "Fire"! After the movie hall was evacuated, Elvis appeased the manager by telling him that he genuinely thought that there was a fire upstairs.

On his first tour of the RCA building in New York, Elvis shook hands with the people who would be instrumental in promoting his future success with a joke electric buzzer hidden in his hand. This was after Colonel Parker had been trying for the best part of a year to impress on Elvis that his zany humor made him look unprofessional.

When recording "All Shook Up," Elvis kept poking back-up singer Gordon Stoker to try and make him mess up. Stoker made it almost the whole way through, only to come in slightly early on the final "yeah, yeah." Elvis livened up the proceedings in the recording studio not just by playing tricks on people but by improvising risqué lyrics. When recording "There's Always Me" in 1961, with a wink Elvis changed the lyric to "When the evening shadows fall and you're wondering who to ball . . . There's always me."

For his first Christmas at Graceland, Elvis divided up his friends and family into two teams ranged along either side of the big tree in the middle of the pasture, and then had a fireworks battle, the first of the bi-annual firework wars that he held at New Year's and on July 4th. Wearing helmets, leather jackets and gloves, two teams of guys blasted roman candles at one another until they ran out, which could be hours later. Stray Roman Candles sometimes blasted into the house and started small fires. On one occasion, the fire department was called in to put out a blaze that had smoldered through an air conditioning unit. Plenty of guys in the entourage bore scars from these pitched battles.

On one fireworks battle night, Vernon unwittingly picked up and put into his mouth some brightly-colored explosive pellets that Elvis had put into a bowl and left in the Graceland kitchen. When Vernon bit down on them, they went off, much to everybody (except Vernon's) mirth. Elvis was also known to fling firecrackers into rooms at Graceland as a joke.

Fire was involved in a trick that Elvis sometimes pulled to impress the already swooning girls invited up to his suite: he would spell out his name on a glass coffee table in lighter fluid and then set fire to it.

In Germany, water pistol battles were the order of the day. When they got bored of this, Elvis and his reduced entourage moved on to pillow fights and shaving-foam fights. One such battle resulted in Elvis being thrown out of the hotel he and his family had been staying in up to that point, when entourage members decided to smoke Elvis out of his room.

A prime consideration for Elvis when inviting a new guy into his entourage was whether they could make him laugh and take a joke. Water pistol fights would degenerate into guys flinging whole buckets of water at one another. While working on *Clambake*, Charlie Hodge's shirt was soaked, and then when it was hung out to dry Elvis kept coming back to douse it with water so that it never dried. Firecracker fights were so common that Charlie Hodge remembers movie director Arthur Nadel turning up for work one day with a German war helmet for protection.

Less extreme but equally amusing tomfoolery included shifting all of the furniture from a hotel room and then calling room service. By the time the bellboy had sent the manager up, Elvis and the gang had put all of the furniture back in place.

Colonel Parker's supreme accomplishment in the art of the practical joke may have been one of the reasons why Elvis showed him such reverence. Alan Fortas characterized the Colonel as "somewhere between a practical joker and a con artist." Elaine Dundy claims that many of the practical jokes that the Colonel played on Elvis were designed to keep him in his place, citing the fact that he kept a model of the jail used in *Jailhouse Rock* on his desk to remind Elvis that he knew the family's dirty secret: that Vernon had done time in jail. Colonel Parker drew on his carny experience to stage elaborate acts of hypnotism on film sets (in which entourage members eagerly participated); perhaps his greatest prank—his most practical joke of all—was his bogus organization, the Snowmen's League of America, to which he recruited the great and the good.

Anita Wood remembers a time when they primed her to say the worst possible word—she was so innocent she had no idea what it meant—while riding around in a car. The whole carful of men cracked up so badly that they had to pull over.

The entourage tried to give as good as they got. On *G.I. Blues*, Elvis' pals repeatedly rapped on Elvis' dressing room door as he was entertaining co-star Juliet Prowse, warning Elvis that Frank Sinatra (who Prowse was seeing at the time) was on the way. They did this several times, and then on the day that Sinatra really did arrive Elvis didn't believe them.

Elvis' pet chimp, Scatter, was a fleet-footed prank machine who liked to get drunk and indulge in the kind of upfront lewd behavior two-legged primates can only dream of. What he lacked in subtlety, his master more than made up for. Elvis had a large two-way mirror built into the ladies changing room by his pool in LA when he was living on Bellagio Road. He was prepared to get covered in earth to crawl in to indulge in a little illicit viewing. He had a similar mirror built

into the closet of one of the bedrooms at an LA house. Whenever a couple went into that room, people would cram into the closet to watch. Elvis sometimes took his girlfriends in too for a view.

Billy Smith was on the receiving end of an unwitting prank when Elvis decided to stop him flying back to Memphis—Elvis had fired everybody in a fit of pique but then had one of his usual changes of heart—by calling the airport and having Smith arrested on the pretext that his cousin had run off with some of Elvis' possessions.

The prime venue for japes was undoubtedly the film set, particularly as the quality and the expectations of Elvis' movies waned. Guys in the entourage would initiate pranks on set to cheer Elvis up; at a certain point, the only thing that kept Elvis on set was the prospect of larking around. The joke apotheosis was *Clambake*, where they engaged in water fights, firecracker battles and pie-throwing contests (though not all at once).

Richard Davis remembers Elvis throwing camera flash bulbs into his swimming pool and using them for gun target practice because of the exciting pops they made when hit (he had tired of blasting away at model ships). Davis once hid in the rafters on a movie soundstage to bombard his fellow Memphis Mafiosi with water-filled balloons, and doused Elvis as he walked out of his trailer in full make-up.

On *The Trouble With Girls*, Elvis and Marlyn Mason would rile the director by furtively inhaling helium before a take and then acting with silly high voices. Even as he did this, with typical Southern politesse Elvis addressed the director as "Mr. Tewksbury."

After Elvis' Las Vegas musical director Joe Guercio compared working with the King to following a marble rolling down concrete steps because he chopped and changed his stage show so often, the next day Guercio found his dressing room and his costumes stuffed with marbles, and a sign on the mirror saying "Follow the marble, E. P.."

It became customary for Elvis and his pals to finish his Las Vegas month-long residencies with a huge water fight.

Elvis once persuaded a group of non-American fans who pulled up outside Graceland that notwithstanding the fact that he was the spitting image of Elvis, he was not in fact Elvis.

For Christmas 1971, Elvis gave friends and family McDonald's gift certificates and got a kick out of the look on their faces—before giving out the real gifts. Elvis sometimes built a prank into his legendary gift-giving. In June 1977, he had Billy Stanley drive up in a rusted old jalopy and, apologizing to Larry Geller, presented Geller with this gift, with the excuse that he hadn't been able to find a new Lincoln Continental Mark V anywhere in Memphis. Ricky Stanley then pulled up in a brand new Lincoln, as Elvis and Billy cracked up with laughter.

Arguably the most elaborate and outrageous of all of Elvis' pranks was plotted with bodyguards Sonny and Red West, and the complicity of some security guards at the Hilton Hotel in 1972. The target of the prank was J.D. Sumner and his gospel group the Stamps. According to the Wests in their book, they set up an elaborate "assassination attempt" on Elvis, complete with blank bullets, in which two security guards were "killed," J.D. Sumner threw himself across Elvis to protect him, and Donnie Sumner was knocked out by a blank bullet.

One night after performing at the Hilton in Las Vegas, Elvis and pals painted one (in some tellings several) of the old-fashioned figures on the wall that Elvis referred to as "fat funky angels" black. At the following night's concert, Elvis told his audience about this act of derring-do (one of these performances was released by FTD in 2001 as *It's Midnight*). At following shows, Elvis joked with the audience that his artistic talents rivaled Michelangelo's.

Once in Las Vegas, walking through the back-

stage area at the Hilton, Elvis and a few entourage pals veered off from their standard route and trooped across the lounge stage where Righteous Brother Bill Medley was singing "You've Lost That Lovin' Feelin'." Elvis nonchalantly said hi, to the amusement and amazement of the audience. It was so much fun that Elvis did it again the following evening, this time with a 10-man retinue.

In the mid-Seventies, Elvis took girlfriend Sheila Ryan out in his Pantera sports car. On the Interstate he accelerated up to 130 mph and then asked her to reach over to take the wheel as he leaned over to do something.

During his last year touring, when his singing powers and stamina were not always up to his high standards, Elvis livened up proceedings by flinging cups of water at members of the band.

PRECISION TOOL

Soon after moving the family to Memphis in 1948, Vernon joined brothers-in-law Travis and Johnny Smith and his own brother Vester at munitions maker the Precision Tool Company, located at 1132 Kansas Street, South Memphis.

In 1951, when he was 16, Elvis worked a summer job at the factory as a spindle drill press operator, which he lost when it was discovered that he was too young for the post.

By some accounts, Elvis returned there as a sander and drill operator in September 1953, after graduating from high school, along with his cousin Gene Smith. By this time he had already financed his first recording session at the Memphis Recording Service.

Elvis with his cousin, Gene Smith in the early 1950's.

PRELL, MILTON

A pal of the Colonel's, a hotel owner in Las Vegas (the Sahara, and later the Aladdin) who on the Colonel's behalf arranged Elvis and Priscilla's wedding in 1967. Rumors abounded a couple of years later that he was also in involved in the deal to bring Elvis to perform in Las Vegas—according to authors Albert Goldman and Alanna Nash, doing the mob a favor in the process.

PRESIDENTS

Elvis was nationally-known under the administrations of six presidents, from Dwight Eisenhower to Jimmy Carter. He met Presidents Nixon, Carter (when he was still governor) and Bush Sr. (then US ambassador to the United Nations). In a thesis espoused by Greil Marcus, Elvis served as a model and a talisman for fellow Southerner Bill Clinton.

It has been claimed that Elvis—or more likely the Colonel—turned down invitations to five presidential inaugurations. When, Nixon's head of entertainment called the Colonel to ask Elvis to perform for the President, the Colonel asked for a cut-price $25,000 fee, which was still $25,000 more than the White House ever paid a performer.

President George Bush Jr. visited Graceland with Japanese Prime Minister Koizumi in 2006.

RONALD REAGAN: "He epitomized America, and for that we shall be eternally grateful. There will never be anyone else like him. Let's all rejoice in his music."

PRESLEY, ANNIE CLOYD

Elvis' cousin by marriage, after she wed Sales Presley, a cousin of Vernon's.

PRESLEY, DEE STANLEY
(STEPMOTHER)

See STANLEY, DEE

PRESLEY, GLADYS LOVE SMITH
(MOTHER)
(1912-1958)

There is no doubt among fans, friends and biographers that the greatest formative influence in Elvis' life was his mother Gladys. Their relationship was close to symbiotic, until fame took Elvis out of the maternal orbit. The loss of his mother just four years into his career was the biggest shock that Elvis endured in his life.

Gladys Love Smith was born to cotton farming parents Robert Lee Smith and Doll Mansell on April 25, 1912 in Pontotoc County, Mississippi, one of eight (some sources say nine) children. Her surviving siblings were John, Clettes, Travis, Lillian, Levalle, Rhetha and Tracy. The family was looked down on by many because of their poverty and need of charity. They were also, among other things, moonshiners.

Growing up, Gladys's large family moved every couple of years, always hoping to find greener pastures in the countryside around Tupelo. Biographer Elaine Dundy describes Gladys as a chubby, sweet, naturally indolent little girl, a combination of shy and headstrong. As a girl, she loved dancing and music in general. Friends remember young Gladys as a life-and-soul kind of girl, though she also had darker, anxiety-filled moments.

Elvis' parents, Gladys and Vernon Presley.

Gladys dated quite a number of boys, some of whom wanted to marry her, before meeting Vernon.

Gladys's father Bob died when she was 19, plunging the family into penury. Her mother Doll a long-term invalid, Gladys worked as a seamstress. The children scattered to live with various relatives, and Gladys became very much involved in the First Assembly of God church, where uncle Gains Mansell was a preacher.

Gladys met Vernon through the First Assembly Church after she moved to a house in East Tupelo near the Orville S. Bean dairy farm, where Vernon's family was living. After a two-month romance they eloped to be married, undaunted by the fact that Vernon—four years Gladys's junior—was a year shy of eighteen, and therefore below marriageable age. The couple borrowed three dollars, traveled the short distance to Pontotoc County and were married on Saturday, June 17, 1933. At the time, Gladys was working at the Tupelo Garment Center as a sewing machine operator, for which she earned two dollars a day. When she was pregnant, she was moved from the sewing section to the ironing section where she had to stay on her feet all day.

On January 8, 1935, Gladys gave birth to twin boys at the Old Saltillo Road house in East Tupelo. Dr. William R. Hunt delivered the first of the boys, Jesse Garon, at 4 a.m., stillborn. Gladys suffered hemorrhaging after giving birth to Elvis and his dead twin, and she spent more than three weeks in hospital convalescing afterwards. Her colleagues at the Garment Center raised $30 for baby things that the young family couldn't afford. Relatives remember that Gladys suffered from "bad nerves" after the birth of the twins. She was particularly twitchy and anxious, and sometimes had trouble sleeping.

Gladys's mother Doll died the same year that Elvis was born. Both of her parents were buried in unmarked graves at Spring Hill.

Things took a turn for the worse in June 1938, when Vernon was incarcerated for forging a check. Gladys went to stay with relatives, and had to take a five-hour bus ride with her three-year old boy to the Mississippi State Penitentiary to see her husband. Vernon was released after eight months of his three-year sentence, partly on the strength of a petition that Gladys got up for him. The fall that his Daddy was away, Elvis went out with Gladys to pick cotton and supplement her earnings from her job at the Mid-South Laundry. It was memories of times like this that prompted Elvis, as a boy, to tell his mother that when he

grew up he would make sure that she never had to worry about putting food on the table.

Elvis spent the bulk of his childhood living in East Tupelo, apart from periods when the family followed Vernon in his travels to find work. When Elvis was seven, when Vernon was away working, Gladys had a miscarriage and had to be admitted to hospital.

Gladys is universally described as a protective mother. Cousin Harold Loyd remembers that Gladys would give kids a beating if she thought that they were messing with her boy. Elvis would get a taste of this medicine if he willfully disobeyed her and ran off to play rough sports, from which she banned him—it would be Gladys rather than Vernon who did the disciplining.

Gladys was working as a seamstress at the time

Vernon, Elvis and Gladys in their hometown of Tupelo, Mississippi.

Elvis with Betty McMahon in Lauderdale Courts.

that she bought Elvis his first guitar for his eleventh birthday. Famously, she walked Elvis to school well into his teens, not because she didn't want to let him out of her sight—Elvis was already sloping off to hear music by this time—but because she wanted to make sure that he got to school and studied so that his lot would be better than that of his parents. Billy Smith recalls that without Elvis knowing, Gladys sometimes shadowed him back home again at the end of the day, to ensure that he stayed safe. However, childhood friends of Elvis' remember him walking with a gang of kids to school in East Tupelo; pals at Lauderdale Courts in Memphis also recall walking to school with Elvis after the Presleys moved to town in 1948.

Gladys, Vernon and Elvis lived in two different boarding houses in Memphis before applying for public housing. The home service advisor for the Memphis Housing Authority, a Miss Jane Richardson, looked favorably on their application, reporting that Mrs Presley and her son Elvis seemed "very nice and deserving." Three months later, the family moved into a publicly-owned apartment at Lauderdale Courts, the grandest living quarters they had ever called their own.

In Memphis, Gladys went to work as a seamstress at Fashion Curtains and took a second job at Britling's Cafeteria, before in November 1951 landing a job as a nursing assistant at St. Joseph's Hospital, close to Lauderdale Courts. When the hospital offered her a proper nursing course, Gladys had to decline as she did not have the requisite elementary level of schooling. Unfortunately, the extra income she was earning pushed the family over the public housing qualifying threshold, though Vernon's protestations that the family were still trying to pay off old debts led to their rental agreement being extended at a higher rent.

According to many biographies, Elvis walked off the street and into the Memphis Recording Service studio to cut his first record in 1953 for his mother's birthday. Heart-warming as the story may be, its veracity is suspect as Gladys's birthday was the best part of a year away. In a March 1956 radio interview Elvis confirmed that he cut the record for his mother, but not specifically for her birthday. Billy Smith's impression is that Elvis intended the disc to be a Christmas present but he couldn't keep it a secret.

A year later, Gladys and Vernon were tuned in to Dewey Phillips' show on WHBQ when he first played Elvis' unreleased single, "That's All Right (Mama)." Listeners were so fired up about this new sound that the DJ called the Presley home

and asked for Elvis to come down; Gladys and Vernon pulled Elvis out of the movie house and dispatched him to the Hotel Chisca for his first ever interview.

In early 1956, Elvis presented his mom—who never learned to drive—with his pink and white Cadillac. This car stayed in the family and is on display at Graceland. Elvis had been buying things for his mother ever since the money first started coming in, to make good on his childhood promise. One of his earliest gifts was an electric mixer; the following day he bought a second mixer, his reasoning being that with one at either end of the kitchen, his mother wouldn't have to walk too far.

Tales abound concerning Gladys's almost extra-sensory bond with her son. When Elvis' Cadillac caught fire at Fulton, Arkansas, on June 5, 1955, as he was driving between venues, Gladys woke with a start, certain that something bad had happened. She had premonitions on nights when there were riots at his shows, and knew about the tooth cap that he aspirated while filming *Jailhouse Rock* before she was told Red West has said that Elvis inherited some of his Ma's supernatural sensitivities.

After Elvis' initial flush of fame, Gladys made friends among the Memphis performing community. She spent time with Elvis' then manager Bob Neal's wife, Helen, and with country singers Slim and Mary Rhodes. When they moved into their new home on Audubon Drive, Gladys helped to oversee the decoration and furniture-buying. Coming from poverty, Gladys put her old furniture into storage; it moved with her, destined for the attic, when the Presleys upgraded to Graceland—Elvis too shared this pack-rat mentality.

Gladys occasionally traveled to see her son perform. She was at one of his shows in Biloxi, Mississippi, in late June 1955, and drove to Arkansas to see him that September. At one show where a large group of girls swarmed towards her boy, Gladys is said to have waded in and pulled them off. After the full-blown riot at Jacksonville, Florida, Gladys preferred not to be a witness to the dangers her son so willingly endured.

Gladys instinctively took against Colonel Parker, though she was always polite and civil to his face. For one of the few times while she was alive, Elvis went against Gladys's gut feelings and threw in his lot with the man who promised to make him a millionaire. Gladys was even less pleased when the Colonel decided that she and Vernon needed to have their image massaged into that of simple, god-fearing country folk.

With Elvis almost permanently on the road,

they only saw each other rarely. Happy as she may have been for his success and the material improvements in her life, the price that Gladys paid was hardly seeing the son who had been the single focus in her life. She worried constantly about what might be happening to her little boy, and was concerned by the swelling postbox from irate parents who criticized Elvis for the effect he was having on their own little darlings. When a preacher in Florida denounced him as "a new low in spiritual degeneracy," Elvis had to call his mother to calm her down.

In November 1956, Elvis set up song publishing company "Gladys Music" and registered it with the American Society of Composers, Authors and Publishers. Gladys received a direct stipend from the firm that bore her name.

Gladys was concerned that Elvis was living so fast that he would wear himself out before he was thirty. Lamar Fike remembers Elvis and Gladys worrying so much about one another that they'd get into huge fights: she was anxious that something would happen to him on the road, while he grew increasingly worried about her drinking.

In her final years, Gladys reportedly told friends she wished that her family "could just go back to being poor again." Rather than having Elvis at their Audubon Drive home, Gladys and Vernon had an incessant flow of fans which only increased the rare times that Elvis was home. When they moved to Graceland the fans were kept on the other side of the fence, but if anything it was even more of a gilded cage for Gladys: no mink coat or fancy chicken coop could make up for the loss of sharing the life of her only child.

Gladys was hospitalized briefly at the end of January 1957, and had to delay a trip with Vernon to join Elvis in Hollywood where he was working on *Loving You*, his first movie for Paramount. She preferred not to have the operation recommended to remedy her bloating and gallstones and instead traveled out to Hollywood with their pals Carl and Willy Nichols. Gladys and Vernon appear as extras in a scene of the film where Elvis performs "Loving You" and "Got A Lot O' Livin' To Do," Gladys happily clapping along. After her death, Elvis was reportedly unable to bring himself to screen the movie.

Moving into Graceland gave Gladys a temporary lift as she looked after the refurbishment. She soon became despondent at how cut off they were, and how little she saw of Elvis. By most accounts, she turned to drink. Gladys had always liked a beer (Billy Smith remembers her favorite tipple as "Schlitz Tall Boys"). Her weakness for alcohol is cited by many as the underlying cause of the gradual decline in her health, with at least one biographer stating that at Graceland she started favoring vodka.

When Elvis was away, Gladys superstitiously refused to touch anything in his room until he came back. She was scared of him flying, so Elvis chose to travel by land. He explained to her that nothing was going to happen to him because he was surrounded by an entourage. Elvis continued to seek her advice, though invariably she told him to look for the answer in the bible. When Elvis was home, Gladys was always accommodating and welcoming to his girlfriends, with whom she shared the pangs of his absence, and fantasticated about future grandchildren.

For Gladys's first and only Christmas at Graceland, she cooked for her extended family and enjoyed the company of her son before he went off to *King Creole* and his impending draft.

Gladys tended to keep a low profile when the house was filled with Elvis' pals—more than one biographer says because she was incapacitated by drink or for the diet pills she took. Family members recall her watching the comings and goings from the kitchen, always with a cheery word for the people traipsing through. Some biographers recollect Gladys being worn down by the constant

Elvis with his parents in 1956.

flow of people, and by the telephones ringing at all hours. Going out incognito also became a problem, as Gladys too would be mobbed in the streets.

Her health continued to deteriorate in 1958, not least because she was extremely concerned about what would happen to Elvis in the Army. Girlfriend of the time Anita Wood recently told an interviewer, "She did not see another happy day from the day they received that notice." Gladys suffered from lassitude, bloating and depression, and was treated for gallstones by Dr. Evans, her physician, though he was not informed of her drinking. In her memoir, Priscilla says that when Gladys was ill, Elvis would sometimes sleep in her bed. Many decades later, Vernon's second wife, Dee Stanley, claimed in a *National Enquirer* article that Elvis had incestuous relations with his mother.

Elvis was unable to call his Mother for two weeks after he was sent to Fort Hood in Texas for his Army training. When he finally did place a call, from pal Eddie Fadal's home in nearby Waco, they spent an hour crying on the phone.

In June 1958, Elvis was very keen on Gladys and Vernon moving out to Texas to be closer to him during his army training. The 400-mile drive was a hardship for her, but after moving from the trailer Elvis had initially hired and parked near the base into a three-bedroom home in Killeen, she cooked for Elvis when she felt strong enough, or left it to Grandma Minnie Mae when she didn't. They made plans for Gladys to come out with the rest of the family to Germany, though at first she was not at all keen on him being posted out of the country. They planned to tour Europe together when Elvis was on leave.

Gladys continued to downplay her failing health (much as Elvis would do in later life). She lost her appetite, suffered bouts of depression, and generally felt poorly—all symptoms of the hepatitis that would hasten her end. She was also on medication commonly prescribed to women going through menopause.

On August 8, 1958 Elvis persuaded her to seek proper medical care in Memphis to see her regular physician, Dr. Charles Clarke. The following day, Gladys was admitted to the Methodist Hospital for a liver condition. It took Elvis three days to get emergency leave but as soon as he could he flew to Memphis to be by her side. The day before she died, the doctors told her that her condition was improving. Gladys had one of her premonitions that she would never see Graceland again. Elvis also had a premonition on the night she died, when at Graceland he became highly agitated and was convinced that something was wrong.

At 3:15 A.M. on August 14, 1958, Gladys died in her hospital bed with Vernon by her side. Officially, the cause of death (like Elvis 19 years later) was a heart attack, though by this time Gladys's liver was highly compromised by advanced hepatitis. She was 46 (though Elvis, who died at 42, believed that she was 42; on her wedding certificate, she had taken four years off her age).

Elvis entered a period of severe and inconsolable grief. Billy Smith recalled Elvis at the hospital crying out, "She's all we ever lived for. She was always my best girl." Gladys's body was taken to Graceland the following day and laid out in her favorite baby-blue dress within a glass-topped casket placed in the music room. Elvis had to be led away because he would not stop touching her and talking with her in the "baby talk" language they used; witnesses remember him trying to get her to wake up and talk to him.

Elvis' original plan—to have the funeral at Graceland—was changed because in Colonel Parker's estimation it would have been impossible to guarantee security, though the fans who had spontaneously congregated outside Graceland were hardly rowdy. The funeral was held at 3:30 p.m. on August 15, 1958, at the Memphis Funeral Home, and was officiated by the Reverend James E. Hamill. As the coffin was carried out of Graceland, Elvis broke down and cried, "Everything I have is gone—everything I've ever worked for. I got all this for her and now she's gone. I don't want any of it now."

For the funeral, Elvis flew in Gladys's favorite band, The Blackwood Brothers, to sing her favorite song "Precious Memories," plus "Rock of Ages," "I Am Redeemed, "Take My Hand, Precious Lord" and "In The Garden." By the time the service was over, close to 3,000 people thronged the church.

Gladys Love Smith Presley was buried at the Forest Hill Cemetery. Elvis broke down again at the graveside and cried out: "I lived my whole life for you." James Blackwood remembers Elvis giving her a last kiss, and in tears saying, "Mother, I would give every dime I have and even dig ditches just to have you back." It has been reported that Elvis was so consumed with grief that he tried bodily to stop the coffin being lowered into the ground, and then attempted to jump into the grave with Gladys, though not all of those present have recalled this desperate gesture. Gladys's grave was adorned with a cross and stone angels. Elvis sent fresh flowers every week until his own

death 19 years later. Within two weeks of his mother's death, Elvis had received more than 100,000 cards and letters of condolence, 200 bouquets of flowers and 500 telegrams. When he returned to Texas, he ordered his mother's room to be left exactly as it had been when she was alive. Billy Smith says that Elvis felt a good deal of guilt about all the worry he put his mother through, and sometimes expressed a belief that she had worried herself to death on his account.

Gladys's remains were moved to Graceland at the same time as Elvis' in October 1977. The inscription on Gladys's monument at Graceland reads "She was the sunshine of our home." The original wording from 1958 was the much more somber: "Not mine but thy will be done."

Not long after Gladys' death, Elvis had to leave a Connie Francis concert because he was so upset when she sang the song "Mama." In 1960, Elvis visited his mother's grave the day after Vernon married his new love, Dee Stanley. The gospel album he recorded soon after his return from Germany, *His Hand in Mine*, was in part a testament to his mother and the music she loved. By 1962, he acknowledged that her death had helped him mature: "I think that things like that—as tragic as they are—tend to make you a little better human being . . . You learn more about yourself.

In the mid-Sixties, Elvis added a Jewish star to Gladys's tomb. Around this time, he told a journalist that whenever he was in Memphis, he made weekly visits to the cemetery. In 1966, Elvis said that he would never leave Graceland because of his mother's presence, which he still felt in and around the house Other members of the family have said that they believed Gladys's spirit inhabited the house and watched over them. Red West recollects that long after she died, Elvis still referred to his mom in the present tense, as if she was still alive.

Two weeks after Lisa Marie was born, Elvis and Priscilla visited Gladys's grave with flowers and a card from all three of them.

A few months before Elvis died, as he was returning to Graceland by car he caught sight of a fan at the gates, Ellen Marie Foster, whom he

NOT MINE
BUT THY WILL BE DONE

The original grave of Gladys Presley.

Elvis, with Vernon and Gladys, at the first home he bought on Audubon Drive in 1956.

thought was a reincarnation of his mother. He invited her in, and later gave her a ring that he had given to his mother a couple of years before she died. The ring is now at Graceland. Several of Elvis' important girlfriends had a look in their eyes that reminded Elvis of his mother.

Elvis' pet name for his Ma was "Satnin' "—a term variously explained as meaning a tasty morsel of fat, or satin; in later years, he called her "Baby Girl." Gladys is said to have spoken to him with the baby words that her boy had used in his infancy.

GLADYS' FAMILY TREE

Elvis' great-great-great-grandparents on his mother's side, William Mansell (1795-1842) and his wife, lived in Mississippi. His wife was a full-blooded Cherokee called Morning Dove White (1800-1835). Mansell's father Richard had fought in the Revolution. From his name, Mansell, it can be deduced that the family originated from the Le Mans area in France. Genealogists have traced thee family line through Scotland and Northern Ireland before traveling across the Atlantic.

Before marrying his wife, William Mansell twice fought against the Indians and Andrew Jackson. The Mansells settled in Alabama. Their son John Mansell (1828-1880), was great-great grandfather to Elvis; he begat more than a dozen children with his wife Elizabeth Gilmore (b.1830), though he also took additional common-law wives. His son White Mansell (b. 1849) married Martha Tackett (1853-1887), a Jewish girl. Their daughter Octavia Lavenia (known as "Doll" for her frailty, 1876-1935), married her younger cousin Robert Lee (Bob) Smith (1880-1931), and gave birth to Gladys and many other children.

It should be noted that this, and Vernon's family tree, are best-guess genealogical estimates, drawing heavily on the research carried out by Elaine Dundy.

BILLY SMITH: "So many of the relatives—I'd say 10 or so—died pretty young, especially on the Smith side of the family."

GLADYS SAID TO ELVIS: "No matter what people say about you, son, you know who you are and that's all that matters."

GLADYS SAID: "My boy wouldn't do anything bad, no such thing. He is a good boy, a boy who has never forgotten his church upbringing and he hasn't changed one bit."

ELVIS SAID: "My mama raised me right."

ELVIS SAID AT HIS MOTHER'S FUNERAL: "Goodbye, darling, goodbye. I love you so much. You know how much I lived my whole life just for you."

ELVIS SAID IN 1958: "It wasn't only like losing a mother, it was like losing a friend, a companion, someone to talk to, I could wake her up any hour of the night if I was worried or troubled about something, well, she'd get up and try to help me."

ELVIS SAID IN 1964: "When I'm home back at Graceland, I know she's there. I can feel it."

ELVIS SAID: "The bottom dropped out of my life the day my mother died. I thought that I had nothing left. In a way I was right."

BILLY SMITH: "Aunt Gladys is the biggest key to Elvis."

PRISCILLA: "It was Gladys who kept Elvis aware of the difference between right and wrong, of the evils of temptation, and of the danger of life in the fast lane."

FAYE HARRIS (TUPELO NEIGHBOR): "Gladys thought Elvis was the greatest thing that ever happened and she treated him that way."

LAMAR FIKE: "She had only a third-grade education. But God-durn, she was smart as a whip."

ELAINE DUNDY: "The evidence indicates that Elvis was trained, rehearsed, and coached by Gladys—all her frustrated desires mixing with her dramatic flair—as thoroughly and as seriously as any other potential professional singer is coached."

BARBARA PITTMAN: "Gladys thought Parker was just the biggest crook that ever lived. She couldn't stand him. Parker was always coming in, trying to order her around, telling her how to dress, how to act in front of people, and the image that he was creating for her . . . just infuriated her."

ANNIE PRESLEY: "Gladys was proud and happy about Elvis' success at first, but after they moved to Graceland she was always saying how much she wished she was . . . poor again."

AUNT LILLIAN SMITH: "After Elvis became famous, Gladys was never happy another day. Only when he'd come back, the little he could, to be with her in Memphis, then she'd be all right for a spell. But the further along he got, the more she worried."

LAMAR FIKE: "I think Elvis' fame killed her. No doubt in my mind. If it didn't kill her, it sure as heck hastened her death."

GEORGE KLEIN: "There wasn't any discussion when Gladys told Elvis to do something. He did it."

ARLENE COGAN: "It wasn't Elvis' fame that scared Gladys. She was proud of Elvis and what he had accomplished. Gladys would look out the windows at Graceland, at the mobs of people waiting for a glimpse of Elvis, and she'd tell me she was afraid they would hurt him."

AUNT LILLIAN SMITH: "After Gladys died, he changed completely. He didn't seem like Elvis ever again."

RED WEST: "You could see the love almost tumble out of her whenever she talked of Elvis. Elvis was the same way to her."

GEORGE KLEIN: "The stories about his love for Gladys are not exaggerated. When she died, he was in mourning for a long time —extreme mourning, physically crying all the time. He was completely destroyed."

LARRY GELLER: "If Elvis was 'obsessed' with Gladys, it was with her life and their love for each other, what she taught him, things she had warned him about, and the irony of her having died when she did."

BILLY SMITH: "Aunt Gladys was a good person. I actually remember her as an outgoing and fun loving person. . . She was always laughing and carrying on. But those photos of her later on make her look sad because she was sick."

IMELDA MARCOS: "He was ahead of his time because he had such deep feelings. He had the privilege of deep feelings because he was deeply loved by his mother, Gladys. He was able to appreciate profound beauty in sounds. And he started a musical revolution. They say all revolutions start from love."

STEVE DUNLEAVY: "Elvis' devotion to his mother, and her devotion to him constitute perhaps one of the truly great love stories of our time."

PRISCILLA: "Elvis believed that his mother had eventually given up on life."

LARRY GELLER: "He held to the Christian belief that he would be reunited with his mother in death."

Book:
Elvis and Gladys, by Elaine Dundy, published by Macmillan, 1985.

PRESLEY, JESSE GARON (TWIN)

Jesse Garon was delivered stillborn at 4 a.m. on January 8, 1935, just before his twin brother Elvis Aron. Jesse was buried the next day in a cardboard box in an unmarked grave at Priceville Cemetery, not far from Tupelo—the family was too poor to afford a proper casket. Billy Smith suggests that the family deliberately misled people about where Jesse was buried, and that he was at another cemetery nearby.

Some authors state that the actual place where Jesse Garon is buried remains unknown. In later years, Elvis is said to have tried and failed to track down his buried twin. Vernon made two trips to Tupelo the month after Elvis died in an attempt to locate Jesse Garon's grave. Vernon's wish was to "reunite" the family at the time that he moved Elvis' and Gladys's bodies to the Graceland meditation garden. A memorial plaque was erected instead, on which the baby's name is spelled "Jessie."

Both Elvis' mom and dad had a history of twins in their families. An oft-told story about Elvis' birth is that though his mother was sure she was pregnant with twins, the midwife didn't realize until after the dead twin, Jesse Garon, came out. Grandma Minnie Mae blamed the death of Elvis' twin on the doctor for not realizing in time that Gladys was carrying two babies.

Gladys is said to have told Elvis as a child that his twin lived on in him, giving him extra strength. Throughout his childhood, Elvis often went to visit his twin's grave in Tupelo. Elvis told Larry Geller that growing up he often heard a voice in his head that he assumed was his dead brother talking to him; Geller replied that this little voice was the voice of living intelligence that lies within us all.

Though Elvis always assumed that Jesse was an identical twin, this was never medically verified.

Elvis biographer Elaine Dundy considers the death of Elvis' twin brother to be the single most important aspect of Elvis' youth, and one of the reasons why Elvis was convinced that he would grow up to live a special life. Clinical psychologist Peter Whitmer writes in his book *The Inner Elvis* that being a "twinless twin" strongly conditioned Elvis' life: death does not break the phenomenon of twin bonding. Elvis' dislike of ever being alone could be interpreted as a legacy of sharing his mother's womb with Jesse Garon.

Elvis felt great affinity with twins that he met in life.

On one of his first TV appearances, show host Milton Berle concocted a skit in which he purported to play Elvis' long-lost twin brother. Twin themes abound in Elvis' movies. Elvis appeared as twins in *Kissin' Cousins,* in a blond wig to differentiate between the two. Twin motifs crop up in other movies: twins are in an audience scene during *Loving You;* Elvis' character is in a sea of twin babies at the end of *G.I. Blues;* his on-screen family adopts twins in *Follow That Dream;* and twin girls are seen dancing in *Double Trouble.*

ELVIS SAID: "They say when one twin dies, and the other grows up with all the qualities of the other."

LARRY GELLER: "Elvis believed that there was great meaning to Jesse's life and death."

PAMELA CLARKE KEOGH REPORTS ELVIS SAYING,: "From the moment I realized I was a twin, I had a feeling my brother would have lived if it hadn't been for me. I was plagued by the thought that I may have hurt him in some way, or wrapped my arms or legs around him so he couldn't breathe when we were in our mom's womb together."

Book:
The Inner Elvis: A Psychological Biography of Elvis Aaron Presley by Peter O. Whitmer, published by Hyperion Books, 1996.

PRESLEY, JESSIE (J.D.) (GRANDFATHER)
(1896-1973)

Elvis' grandfather on his father's side had a reputation as a hard-drinking, hard-fighting, mean-spirited lady's man. One biographer tracked down evidence that he had four wives at one time. Like the line of Presley men that came after him, Jessie D. McClowell Presley was remarkably good looking.

J.D. Presley married Minnie Mae Hood when he was 17 and she was 25, in Fulton, Mississippi. He later got a job at Orville Bean's dairy farm. It was here that his son Vernon was working when Elvis was born.

By all accounts, J.D. was a tough guy to have as a father. Vernon's mother Minnie Mae later declared that all five of their kids married young because they could not wait to escape from under the same roof. Famously, Jessie refused to bail out Vernon when he got in trouble with the law for forging a check, though he was perfectly happy to do exactly that for son-in-law Travis Smith, who was also implicated in the misdeed. Not surprisingly, Vernon never saw eye to eye with his father after this.

In early 1936, Jessie's brother Noah (Elvis' great-uncle) was elected mayor of East Tupelo.

In 1947, Jessie filed for divorce from his wife, Elvis' grandmother, Minnie Mae, claiming that she had deserted him. It seems, however, that by this time he had left the family home for Kentucky, where he found a job as a night watchman at the Pepsi bottling plant in town.

Jessie went to watch his grandson perform when he played a show in Louisville in November 1956. Elvis is said by some biographers to have given his grandfather a Ford Fairlane and a TV. Two years later, Jessie Presley made an ill-fated attempt to become the second famous singing Presley, releasing a record under the title *The Roots Of Elvis*.

When Elvis returned to play Louisville in November 1971, he introduced his grandfather on stage.

Jessie died in March 1973; Elvis did not attend the funeral.

PRESLEY, LISA MARIE
(B. 1968)

In July 1967, when Elvis told the world that his new wife Priscilla was expecting a baby, he declared, "This is the greatest thing that has ever happened to me."

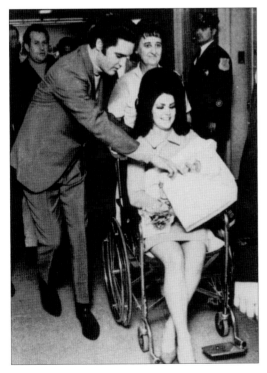

Elvis and Priscilla with Lisa Marie on the day of her birth (12.5.68) leaving the hospital.

ABOVE: Priscilla's father, Lisa-Marie, Elvis, Priscilla and Vernon, (1968).

RIGHT: Elvis and baby Lisa Marie.

BELOW RIGHT: Elvis with Lisa Marie.

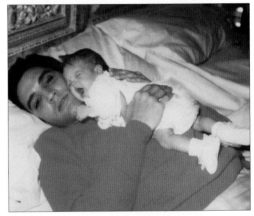

Lisa Marie was conceived in a trailer at the Circle G Ranch according to the calculations of entourage members, or on Elvis and Priscilla's wedding night in the estimation of most biographers. After a nine-hour labor, at 5:01 pm on February 1, 1968 Lisa Marie was delivered into the world at the Baptist Hospital, Memphis, with a headful of dark hair . Elvis was so nervous beforehand that he had the entourage rehearse the trip from Graceland to the hospital, complete with a dummy convoy to throw off the press. When the moment came, everybody was so tense that Jerry Schilling initially took Priscilla to the dummy hospital. Elvis and Priscilla had resolved to call the baby John Barron if it had been a boy. The "Marie" part of their daughter's name is said to be in homage to Colonel Parker's wife, though Anita Wood recalls that when they looked ahead to having children, the name they wanted for their girl was Alisa Maria—Wood's middle name was Marie. Elvis' pet names for his little girl were Yisa, Buttonhead and Injun.

Lisa Marie's first birthday was celebrated at Aspen, Colorado, on a winter vacation. She spent her second birthday with her mom at the International Hotel, watching her daddy do his stuff on stage at the dinnertime show. During her earliest years, Elvis was often on the road, while Priscilla was, as she puts it in her memoir, "torn between the two of them" and unable to really cater to her little girl's needs.

Elvis was an extremely indulgent father. If there was any disciplining to do, that was generally Priscilla's job. Elvis tried to make up for not being at home by bringing his little girl all kinds of gifts.

Lisa Marie celebrated her fourth birthday with her daddy in Palm Springs. Lisa was of an age to remember when she saw him on stage at Long Beach, California, in November 1972. She was with Elvis at Graceland for her fifth birthday, and then a few months later saw him perform in Anaheim.

The summer after her parents split up, Lisa Marie spent a substantial amount of time with her daddy in Memphis. Among other diversions, he took her along to his Stax recording session that July. With Priscilla living in LA, Lisa Marie had the run of Graceland; getting her way was simply a matter of threatening the maids and nannies that she would get them fired.

Between the ages e of four and nine, Lisa Marie spent summers and Christmases with Elvis and his girlfriend Linda Thompson (who remembers Elvis as an uncommonly affectionate and loving parent, if perhaps not as strict as he could have been). Wild child Lisa Marie enjoyed being in a household where her dad might wake her up in the middle of the night and get her to stand on the table and sing. Lisa Marie had as playful a streak as her father: she loved sneaking up and tickling him. It was child heaven to have your own blue golf cart, and a big round bed with a built in TV, radio and mirror. When she was a little older, she graduated to making prank calls to random numbers. Priscilla attempted to be a counterweight by keeping her on a stricter regime in LA.

Elvis was in Los Angeles in February 1974 to tend to Lisa Marie when she had her tonsils out. He arranged for her to meet Michael Jackson in

Elvis with his family, ca 1973.

PRISCILLA, ON THE DAY LISA-MARIE WAS BORN: "The man in my hospital room that day was the man I loved, and will always love . . . He didn't have to act the part of Elvis Presley, superstar. He was just a man, my husband."

BECKY HARTLEY: "Elvis was all smiles after Lisa Marie was born. He was just very excited."

JOE ESPOSITO: "Elvis spoiled her, he would buy her anything she wanted."

DAVID BRIGGS: "Elvis loved and worshipped Lisa Marie. . . . He was as protective as any dad. From what I saw, she was the most important thing in his life."

LINDA THOMPSON: "Elvis gave her, I think, the one thing that is vital for a parent to give a child, and that is unequivocal love."

PRISCILLA: "She's very strong-willed."

PRISCILLA: "She never really felt the divorce. We were still loving even after the divorce because we liked each other."

PRISCILLA: "Her daddy handed everything over to her on the proverbial silver platter, which created conflict when she'd come home and have to deal with reality. We had a running debate on how she was to be raised."

May 1974, when the Jackson 5 were the next act to play the Del Webb Sahara Tahoe at Stateline, Nevada, after him. That same year she got to meet her heart-throb of the time, David Cassidy, after Elvis sent a limousine to pick him up.

Lisa Marie was at Elvis' impressive New Year's Eve 1977 show in Pittsburgh, after spending Christmas with him at Graceland. Larry Geller remembers that she would sit and wait outside her daddy's bedroom door every day until he finally woke up. Not long before he died, Lisa Maria told her daddy, "I don't want you to die." Elvis told her not to worry.

Lisa Marie was on an extended Graceland visit on August 16, 1977. In one account of the pandemonium surrounding his death, she ran into the bedroom while members of the entourage were attempting to revive her daddy, only to be led out by Ginger Alden. A maid has stated that Lisa Marie stayed in her room with cousin Laura while all the commotion occurred. When Lisa Marie was told that her daddy had been taken to hospital, she vented her feelings by tearing round the grounds on her golfcart. She later called Linda Thompson to tell her that her daddy had died. Her mother Priscilla advised her to stay out of the way with Grandma Minnie Mae.

Lisa Marie continued to visit relatives at Graceland after her daddy died, though often she slept at Patsy Presley's house.

Elvis' daughter's life has been tabloid fare since a young age. She told radio man Howard Stern that she lost her virginity (to a drug dealer) when she was 15. Much of her schooling was in boarding schools, including one where she was expelled for possession of drugs. Before the end of her formal education, she studied at a Church of Scientology establishment.

At the age of 20, she married musician and fellow-Scientologist Danny Keough. On May 29, 1989 she gave birth to Danielle Riley, who has since started a career as a model. She gave birth to son Benjamin Storm born on October 21, 1992. She divorced her first husband in 1994.

Lisa Marie legally came into her inheritance on her 25th birthday.

She married Michael Jackson in the Dominican Republic in 1994, not long after meeting him again (and without warning her mother about what she was planning). The union lasted until 1996.

Her marriage to Nicolas Cage in 2002 famously lasted just 108 days, though they had been together for two years before that. Unmarried,

they remain friends, as does Lisa Marie and first husband Danny Keough.

Lisa Marie told an interviewer that her whirlwind marriages are the result of her attraction to artists, to people who are "shaking it up" and are "different." In that same interview, she also said that she was proud to declare herself completely insane (as Elvis had no qualms about doing on stage in the early Seventies).

In January 2006, Lisa Marie married her musical director, Michael Lockwood, whom she met through first husband Danny Keough (another member of her band). The wedding was a traditional Japanese ceremony, in Kyoto, Japan, at which her first husband and children were respectively best man, bridesmaid and groomsman.

Lisa Marie surprised many doubters by bringing out two accomplished albums as a singer: *To Whom It May Concern* (2003) made it to #5 on the *Billboard* chart, followed up in 2005 by *Now What*, which made it to #9. Both albums were platinum sellers.

She has said that her personal favorites among Elvis' songs are "the darker, sadder songs" from the Seventies: "Mary In The Morning," "In The Ghetto," "Just Pretend" and "Solitaire." She has also expressed a preference for his Fifties black and white movies.

Lisa Marie's reputed spending of between $5 and $7 million per year in the mid-2000s is said by some to have hastened the sale of a significant stake in Elvis Presley Enterprises to businessman Robert Sillerman.

LISA MARIE: "I remember him as my dad but he was a very exciting dad."

LISA MARIE: "Anything my father did for me or gave me was done out of love. I'm sure I had moments when I was a snot. But my mom was there to smack me back to the other side."

LISA MARIE: "I had anything but a happy childhood. Two words: lonely and deep. I was very lonely and way too deep for someone so young."

LISA MARIE: "I'm pretty unsolicited, unedited, no-holds barred in my speech patterns and my behavior."

LISA MARIE: "I have never met a man who could cope with me, who I am, the Presley name. Which is why I married someone even more famous than myself."

PRESLEY, MINNIE MAE
(GRANDMOTHER)
(1893-1980)

Born Minnie Mae Hood in Fulton, MS on June 17, 1893, Elvis' grandma grew up at a time when the kids had to help out with running the household and making ends meet. As a girl, Minnie Mae earned extra money for the family by going out to cook for people who were incapacitated. Years later, Gladys learned her cooking skills from her mother-in-law.

Minnie Mae Hood married J.D. Presley in 1913. They had five children: Vernon, Gladys (Earline), Vester, Nasval ("Nash," later an ordained minister) and Delta Mae.

Grandma Minnie Mae moved in with Elvis and his parents in 1947, after her husband left her, though it was J.D. Presley who filed for divorce.

Thereafter "Dodger," as she was affectionately known by Elvis—after an incident when, during a childhood temper tantrum, he hurled a baseball at her which she dodged—was part of Elvis' household, another maternal figure (if he needed one) who called him "son."

Minnie Mae moved into Graceland with the Presleys in 1957. She had a blue-painted room upstairs, before moving to the downstairs bedroom (originally where Vernon and Gladys slept when they first moved into the house). She had her own TV, and en suite bathroom, and her own piano too—she was a good musician, capable of playing a number of instruments. Many of the stuffed toys that fans sent Elvis wound up in Grandma's room.

Minnie Mae traveled with Vernon and Gladys to be with Elvis in Killeen, Texas, while he was there on Army training. She went out to Germany when he was posted there later in 1958—her first time out of the country and first time on a plane. In the absence of Gladys, Minnie Mae ran the household, doing the cooking and supervising the cleaning. Elvis' spirited grandma had a running battle with the Presleys' German landlady; she is said to have once laid her out for bothering her while she was rustling up some food.

Back at Graceland, with a staff to take over the household duties, Grandma Minnie Mae spent more time in her room, indulging her passion for snuff.

Words of grandmotherly advice included reminding an extremely nervous Elvis as Priscilla went into hospital to give birth to their child that it was Priscilla, not him, having the baby.

Minnie Mae habitually wore immaculate dresses with built-in aprons. She wore dark glasses at all times and she was light phobic. Aged seventy-eight, Minnie Mae and Elvis' Aunt Delta Biggs—both ladies who liked a tipple—went with Dr. George Nichopoulos to one of Elvis' Las Vegas shows in the summer of 1970, the first time that she ever saw him perform live on stage.

Minnie Mae outlived both her son Vernon and grandson Elvis. She resided at Graceland until her death in May 1980, towards the end wheelchair-bound and very frail. She dyed her hair black until her dying day. Aunt Delta moved into Grandma's room after she died. Minnie Mae is buried in the Graceland meditation garden.

MINNIE MAE, IN RESPONSE TO SOMEBODY TELLING HER THAT HER GRANDSON SANG LIKE A BLACK MAN: "Fiddlesticks! My boy sings better."

PRISCILLA: "She helped raise Elvis as if he were her own son, somewhat spoiling him as grandmothers do."

ANITA WOOD: "She was a very country, down to earth woman."

DOTTY AYERS: "Elvis loved Grandma Presley just like he did Gladys. He would kiss on her and hug her. She would slap him when he would get carried away, jumping around and playing tricks on her and everything. She would just slap the devil out of him."

NANCY ROOK: "[She was] the stabilizing force, the feminine touch, that had kept Graceland going."

PRESLEY, NOAH (GREAT-UNCLE)

Elvis' great-uncle Noah—the son of Rosella Presley—was elected mayor of East Tupelo a year after Elvis was born. Noah Presley worked for many years as a store owner and a school bus driver. He is remembered as a positive influence on the community.

PRESLEY, PATSY

Elvis' double first cousin is the daughter of Vester Presley and Clettes Smith. The cousins saw plenty of one another growing up, and for a spell lived in the same house as kids.

Patsy worked as Elvis' secretary from 1963. Her husband, Gee Gee Gambill, joined the entourage. Priscilla became good friends with Patsy after she moved out to Graceland in 1963. Elvis bought Patsy a horse when he went cowboy crazy in early 1967, so that she could ride with Priscilla. Patsy was at Elvis and Priscilla's wedding. When Priscilla first suspected that she might be pregnant, Patsy was the one she called for advice. Patsy, husband Gee Gee Gambill and their child spent time with the Presleys in LA in the early Seventies, staying in a small cottage on their Hillcrest Drive property.

After Lisa Marie was born, she spent a lot of time with Patsy's kids. In the period following Elvis' death, when Lisa Marie came to Memphis she often stayed with Patsy's family.

Patsy Presley remarried to Mr. Geranen. She contributed to 2005 documentary and book *Elvis by the Presleys*.

PRESLEY, PRISCILLA BEAULIEU
(B. PRISCILLA ANN WAGNER, MAY 24, 1945)

Fourteen-year-old Priscilla Beaulieu was five thousand miles from home when she was unexpectedly summoned to meet the world's most famous performer, in what turned out to be the start of a nine-year courtship, three-year marriage and lifetime association with Elvis.

Priscilla's father, navy pilot James Wagner, was killed in a plane crash not long after she was born in Brooklyn. Her mother married Priscilla's stepfather Paul Beaulieu when she was three; they decided not to tell the girl that he wasn't her biological father until she happened upon a photo in her early teens, by which time Priscilla was an eldest child with two siblings (another two babies were to come later for her parents), and had lived in five or six locations due to her step-father's military postings. Before moving to Wiesbaden in Germany, Priscilla lived in Austin, where she was her Junior High Queen at the Del Valley Junior High School

Priscilla met Elvis at his Bad Nauheim home on September 13, 1959, after Currie Grant, a friend of Elvis' who worked in Army Special Services, spotted her at the Eagle Club (frequented by servicemen and their families), asked if she wanted to meet Elvis and brought her round. Early Elvis entourage member Cliff Gleaves has also claimed his role as matchmaker. Staying with Currie Grant at the time, Gleaves has said that they bumped into Priscilla at a swimming pool, described her to Elvis, and brought her over after Elvis expressed an interest in seeing her for himself.

Priscilla showed up in a blue and white sailor dress, her hair in ringlets. In her autobiography she remembers, "I thought I looked cute, but being only fourteen, I didn't think I'd make any kind of impression on Elvis." That night, Elvis serenaded her with "Rags to Riches," "Are You Lonesome Tonight," "End of the Rainbow," "I Asked the Lord," "The End"—quite a concert. Priscilla remembers that the more silent and nervous she became, the more Elvis tried to impress her. She was chaperoned back home at the end of the evening, though more scandalistic accounts of the evening have Elvis and Priscilla going up to his bedroom that first night. Later, Elvis reportedly raved to pal Charlie Hodge "Did you see the structure of her face? It's like almost everything I've ever looked for in a woman." Many commentators have noted the similarity in looks between the young Priscilla and Debra Paget, Elvis' co-star in his first movie *Love Me Tender*, for whom he had an unrequited passion.

Priscilla returned a week later, this time accompanying Elvis up to his room after he promised he'd treat her "like a sister." She says that their first kiss, a goodbye kiss, was at the end of that evening. Priscilla started going to Elvis' place every evening, and gained a reputation at the local Army school as "Elvis' girl." The late nights caused her grades to suffer—she altered a 'D' to a 'B' on a report card so that her folks wouldn't use her worsening grades to curtail her nocturnal visits.

In her memoir, Priscilla writes that one night a friend of Elvis'—a man whom she nicknames Kurt—attempted to molest her. Though never named, it has been speculated that it was somebody who knew her before she met Elvis, or a soldier at the local barracks.

For Christmas 1959, Elvis gave Priscilla a gold watch and a pearl and diamond ring. "Cilla," as he immediately nicknamed her, gave Elvis a set of bongo drums. To her initial horror and later satisfaction, she found out that Elvis had a stack of bongos down in the basement, but kept hers out in full view. During their time together in Germany, Priscilla was not under any illusion that Elvis was a one-woman man: she saw letters from Elvis' girl back home, Anita Wood, and witnessed incidents at Elvis' place that revealed intimacy with other women in his orbit.

Before Elvis left Europe, he told her that he loved her and would not forget her. Priscilla was the one person who rode in the car with Elvis to the airport for his flight back home. After he left, her parents warned Priscilla (and fervently hoped) that the relationship was unlikely to continue after Elvis had gone.

According to Charlie Hodge, Elvis did not touch Priscilla until the day they were married. Billy Smith is of the opinion that Elvis and Priscilla first had sex in Germany. Priscilla writes that Elvis repeatedly cooled things down sexually, putting off intercourse until "the time was right."

After Elvis was back in the public eye, Priscilla appeared in *Life* magazine, described as the "Girl He Left Behind," snapped at the Rhine-Main air base waving Elvis goodbye. Priscilla soon discovered what it was like to have a mailbag filled with letters from people she didn't know, some of them unfriendly, others a little too friendly. Back in America, Elvis raved to friends about her beauty, particularly her eyes, which he said were the most beautiful he had ever seen, while reciting his usual script in public: that there was no special woman in his life.

Three weeks after leaving Germany, Elvis called Priscilla, dashing her parents' hope that it had been a flash in the pan. From then on, they exchanged letters (on Elvis' advice, she addressed her letters to aide Joe Esposito, on pink paper so that they stood out from the rest of the mail). According to some Memphis mafia memoirs, Elvis arranged for Priscilla to come over secretly for Christmas 1960 and stay with Vernon and Dee Stanley, though Priscilla makes no mention of this in her own memoir, and most biographers place Elvis in Anita Wood's arms at this time.

They renewed their acquaintance in June 1962, when, now aged 17, Priscilla flew out to LA to spend two weeks with Elvis. Her parents agreed to let her travel on condition that she stay with a married couple, the Barrises, whom Elvis knew. During her two-week visit she spent one night with Elvis and his gang at the house he was renting in Beverly Hills, before driving in his motor home to Las Vegas for a 12-day visit, leaving just enough time for Elvis, Priscilla and the gang to get back to LA before a tearful goodbye. Priscilla's first taste of living with Elvis was a foretaste of how he would manage her life: he picked out new clothes for her, advised her how she should wear her hair, and got her to use more make up. To keep up with Elvis' high-paced lifestyle, Priscilla also took the pills that Elvis and his entourage used—a regime she had already noted in Germany. All the while, Priscilla's parents believed that she was staying in LA because of the daily postcards they received, all written in advance and mailed with an LA postmark.

Elvis continued to work on Priscilla's parents to let their little girl live in Memphis. Elvis told Captain Beaulieu that he loved his step-daughter, that he would respect her, put her through school and then marry her, and that she would stay with his father and his new wife round the corner, not with him at Graceland.

A little before Christmas in 1962, Priscilla arrived in New York (traveling under the name Priscilla Fisher so that she would pass under the press radar), where she was met by Vernon Presley and his wife, Dee Stanley who accompanied her to Memphis. After spending a couple of days adjusting to the time difference—not helped by the excessively strong sleeping pills Elvis gave her on arrival—she was given the tour of where he grew up, and then fitted right in to the usual activities of movies, roller-skating and Graceland socializing. Priscilla spent New Year's Eve watching fireworks at Graceland and then going to the Manhattan Club with a couple of hundred of Elvis' friends and family. Elvis tried but failed to extend her three-week stay. She returned to Graceland for keeps in March 1963, this time chaperoned by her step-father. He agreed that she could stay in Memphis as long as she lived with Vernon and Dee, and complete her senior high school year at the Immaculate Conception High School. Becky Hartley, Graceland secretary at the time, remembers Priscilla as "beautiful and sweet and shy." Members of the entourage were impressed by her sophistication, maturity and easy manner. Sonny West described her as "every bit as mature as all of us guys put together."

Living at Graceland

Elvis joined Priscilla at Graceland as soon as he had completed filming *Fun in Acapulco*. He bought her a red Corvair (and later a lavender Chevy sports coupé) so that she could drive herself to and from school. When the local newspapermen began asking questions about Priscilla, Elvis said that she was preceding the rest of her family, and that their families had become firm friends in Germany. After this initial interest, rumors about Elvis' live-in underage girlfriend stayed out of print; Jerry Lee Lewis's career was ruined once his marriage to a 13-year old cousin became public knowledge.

Elvis bought Priscilla an entire new wardrobe, spending four hours with her shopping in downtown Memphis and picking out most of the clothes himself. She completed her studies in May that year at Immaculate Conception High School. However, Priscilla confessed in her memoir that with all those late nights, she only managed to get her high school diploma by copying answers from a fellow student, in exchange for inviting her up to Graceland. Elvis was not at her graduation; he waited outside in the limousine, so as not to cause a commotion, but by the time Priscilla walked out of the school with her diploma, Elvis was surrounded by a group of nuns asking for his autograph.

With Priscilla at Graceland, Elvis spent less time in boisterous pursuits and more time holding screenings at the Memphian Theater. Her arrival also marked an end to the hordes of people who just hung around Graceland, sometimes filling every downstairs room.

In her memoir, Priscilla describes the reality of living at last with Elvis at Graceland as exchanging one set of restrictions for another. She wasn't allowed to bring friends back to the house because outsiders were not welcome. She had to ask Vernon for an allowance, and Vernon was never best pleased at handing out money. While Elvis was away for long spells in Hollywood, she busied herself around the home, making sure that things were right for when he came home; when he was in residence, she tried to manage the kitchen, pamper him and live up to his image of the perfect woman. Priscilla's way of dealing with insecurity and gnawing suspicion that Elvis was playing the field was meticulously to study everything that Elvis wanted in a woman, and try to make herself into that woman.

Priscilla took dancing, modeling and drama classes at the Patricia Stevens Finishing and Career School. Elvis is said to have told Larry Geller that he was trying to give Priscilla what he had been unable to give his mother: a chance to educate herself. And yet when Priscilla went out and earned a little money modeling for a nearby store Elvis told her to give it up.

Elvis kept delaying Priscilla's planned trip to Hollywood while he was making *Viva Las Vegas*. He tried to placate her suspicions that he was romancing leading lady Ann-Margret by assuring her that he could never be interested in a woman who put her career above all else—one of his strongly-held traditional Southern beliefs. When Priscilla pressed him about rumors she read in the gossip magazines, he said that there was something going on with Ann-Margret, but it was between the director and his co-star. According to Jo Smith, Priscilla turned to studying her rival's movies to try to be more like her and win Elvis back.

In November 1963, Priscilla finally traveled to Hollywood to be with Elvis while he was working on *Kissin' Cousins*. After Ann-Margret admitted to the British press that there was indeed something going on between her and Elvis, Colonel Parker stepped in and ordered that Priscilla be packed off back to Memphis before the media picked up on her.

In her memoir, Priscilla details how difficult it was to live through her late teens and early twenties in the shadow of a larger-than-life personality. There is no question that one of the attractions of a much younger woman was that Elvis found it easier to mold and remake her in his own image. Priscilla portrays her life at this time as ". . .Elvis' doll, his own living doll, to fashion as he pleased." When she emerged into public, Elvis and Priscilla looked strikingly alike, with similar hairdos and similar coloring. Priscilla's preferred solution to Elvis' infidelities was to travel with him as often as he allowed. If she challenged him directly, he utilized attack as his best form of defense.

Larry Geller has described Elvis and Priscilla's relationship in the mid-Sixties as like "a perpetual junior-high-school date." Lamar Fike recalls that in the mid-Sixties, Priscilla began to seek the same kind of behavior from the entourage wives that Elvis expected from his entourage guys.

Rumors about an impending marriage were sufficiently loud in the summer of 1966 for Vernon to issue a denial. Despite Priscilla's increasingly frequent presence on Elvis' LA trips, he still found plenty of opportunity to enjoy close relationships with his leading ladies or starlets on his movies. He brushed off a love note that she found, and when she insisted, he threatened to send her home to her parents, once telling her pack her clothes before relenting at the last minute.

Elvis bought a horse for Priscilla as a gift a little before Christmas 1966, starting off what became Elvis' most expensive and consuming hobby to date. That Christmas Eve, Elvis gave her a much smaller but more meaningful gift: a three-and-a-half karat diamond ring (encircled by smaller diamonds that could be worn separately) and his proposal of marriage.

Elvis insiders have intimated that Elvis' decision to marry Priscilla was down to pressure from her parents, to what one has referred to as "markers being called in." Five earlier, Elvis had persuaded Priscilla's parents that his intentions were honorable. As 1966 drew to a close, Priscilla's parents reputedly ran out of patience. According to at least one member of the entourage, Elvis managed to postpone the wedding to Priscilla beyond the original date. Billy Smith says that Elvis married Priscilla because she made it clear she would be prepared to "tell her story" if he failed to follow through. Elvis reputedly told Marty Lacker that he faced a lawsuit if he didn't marry her.

Priscilla flew out to LA in March 1967 to be with Elvis after he injured himself in a fall at his Bel Air home. On May 1, 1967, Elvis and Priscilla married in Las Vegas. Friends remember Elvis as calm and cool before the ceremony; Priscilla, to many, seemed terrified. After the wedding, Priscilla set out to live up to Elvis' expectations of what a wife should be, including learning how to cook the food he liked. Out at the Circle G ranch on their "honeymoon" with all of the entourage and their families on the range, Priscilla kept house in the huge trailer they temporarily called home.

Elvis presented Priscilla a ruby and sapphire charm for her 24th birthday that year. Priscilla found out that she was pregnant in the second week of June 1967, just before accompanying Elvis to LA for his next film project, *Speedway*. Though there can be no doubt that the couple wanted to have children, they would not have planned a pregnancy during their first few days as man and wife. Priscilla's hopes that marriage would mean spending more time together—rather than Elvis spending weeks and weeks away in Los Angeles—were only partially realized. In October 1967, Priscilla flew out to join Elvis in Sedona, Arizona, with other entourage wives and girlfriends, where he was working on *Stay Away, Joe*.

RIGHT: Elvis and Priscilla during their wedding ceremony in 1967. BELOW: At the Aladdin Hotel in Vegas after the ceremony.

For Christmas 1967, Priscilla bought the father of her unborn child a $1500 watch. When Priscilla was seven months pregnant, out of the blue Elvis surprised her by asking for a trial separation. Priscilla did not move out, and Elvis never mentioned the subject again. She carried on doing ballet, horse-riding and taking part in vigorous activities right up until the eighth month. In her memoirs, Priscilla writes that she was so insecure during her pregnancy because Elvis had made remarks about pregnant women "letting themselves go" that she dieted rigorously and at full term weighed no more than her usual weight.

Priscilla gave birth to Lisa Marie Presley on February 1, 1968, at the Baptist Hospital, Memphis. The time of the birth was registered at 5:01 p.m. A month or so after the baby was born, the family moved to LA, where Elvis reported to work for *Live a Little, Love a Little*, and then preparations for his NBC Special TV, before which Elvis, Priscilla and select pals from the entourage flew to Hawaii for a two-week vacation. Gossip columnist Rona Barrett suggested that Elvis and Priscilla split up in July 1968. In LA, Priscilla got back into shape after her pregnancy and resumed her dance classes. She performed for the first time, singing and dancing at LA colleges; the attention and validation she received from the dance instructor led to a brief affair.

Elvis took his family on multiple vacations in 1969, first to Aspen, then to Hawaii, along with the ubiquitous entourage pals and their wives. That summer, buoyed by the success of his Comeback Special, he returned to performing in Las Vegas: this was the first time that Priscilla ever saw him do a show, almost ten years after meeting him. Elvis gave Priscilla a black fox coat for Christmas 1969; Priscilla gave Elvis a shirts, slacks and a velvet suit made by costume designer Bill Belew.

Elvis resumed dissuading Priscilla and the other wives from coming out to LA where he was working on films. Priscilla's suspicions of infidelities were confirmed on a trip to the Las Vegas suite, where she found that her clothes had been moved (in Las Vegas, the entourage would clear out all of her clothes from the closet and then rehang them in the same order, it seems not quite well enough); later, she also stumbled over lewd letters in Palm Springs. Elvis' winning strategy of brazening it out was so successful that she admits to feeling guilty for making accusations.

A Presley family portrait in 1971.

Surprisingly, when Joe Esposito told Elvis that he knew Priscilla had been visiting the home of her male modern dance teacher, Elvis told him to keep his nose out of his wife's business. Billy Smith has said that she also "got pretty involved with somebody in the entertainment field."

In January 1970, the family traveled with Elvis to Las Vegas, where he was due to start his second month-long engagement at the International Hotel. After this trip, Priscilla put in an appearance at the start and sometimes the end of Elvis' month-long Vegas residencies but stayed away the rest of the time. That spring, they finally bought their own home in Palm Springs, and spent a considerable amount of time there that year, though thereafter Elvis tended to use it as a hideaway for bachelor pursuits. Elvis nevertheless threw a surprise 25th birthday party for Priscilla in Memphis that May 24.

Elvis' return to live performing, renewed success and adulation spelled the beginning of the end for their relationship. He stayed away for increasingly long periods of time, and when he was back home, he suffered from boredom at the comparatively lackluster life he was used to on the road. When Priscilla was at his closing night performances in Vegas, she recalls scanning the beauties in front row seats to see if Elvis was directing his gaze at any one of them. People close to Elvis had already noted that he was increasingly relying on prescription medicines in 1970. It may not be a coincidence that Elvis and Priscilla's relationship began to deteriorate around this time.

Priscilla suffered a fright just before Christmas 1970, when Elvis ran out of Graceland and disappeared into thin air, insensed that his wife and father had ganged up to confront him about excessive spending. A day later Elvis told Sonny West to let Priscilla know that he was safe and sound, but not where he was—in Washington, attempting to finagle a Bureau of Narcotics and Dangerous Drugs badge to add to his collection, and meeting President Richard Nixon in the process.

For Christmas 1970, Priscilla gave Elvis the black bell-bottomed suit which Elvis wore to Sonny West's wedding three days later. Priscilla spent much of 1971 supervising the decoration at the new home they had bought in Los Angeles. Priscilla took up karate with Ed Parker in the spring of 1971, and continued learning with Elvis' new Tae Kwon Do teacher Kang Rhee. More rumors about an estrangement between Elvis and Priscilla made it into print in the fall of 1971. By

the end of 1971, their marriage was, as Priscilla describes it in her memoir, a part-time affair; she would send Elvis polaroids of Lisa's growth and latest antics. Red West said in his book that there were times when Priscilla wouldn't see Elvis for up to seven weeks at a time.

Though they spent Christmas together in Memphis, members of the entourage recall a frostiness between Priscilla and Elvis. On December 30, Priscilla took Lisa Marie back with her to Los Angeles. Elvis told his friends and family that Priscilla had decided to leave him as she did not love him anymore.

Post Elvis

Priscilla was at a front row table for the start and finish of Elvis' winter 1972 engagement at the Las Vegas Hilton. It was here that she told him she was romantically involved with another man, Mike Stone, her latest karate instructor, whom she had first met backstage when Stone had provided security for a record executive who came to a show. Entourage members had more than an inkling that something was afoot but nobody had dared to tell Elvis: Lisa Marie had reputedly mentioned to a member of the entourage that she had seen her mom and Stone "wrestling" in a sleeping bag; Sonny West said in his book that he caught sight of Priscilla and Stone sharing a shower when he walked into the LA house unannounced. In her memoir, Priscilla writes that when Elvis found out that she was having an affair, he "forced himself on her" in his hotel room in Las Vegas, telling her that this was how a real man made love to his woman. In Priscilla's accounts, this was before she told him that she was leaving; in the majority of other biographies, this incident occurred after she told Elvis that she was involved with Stone.

The legal separation came through on July 26, 1972. Elvis gave Priscilla half-ownership of the two Los Angeles properties they owned at the time. In the settlement—it was actually Elvis who filed for the divorce to protect Priscilla and Lisa Marie from the press—Priscilla was awarded a $100,000 lump sum and $1,500 per month in alimony and child support. Priscilla sued for an improved settlement in May 1973, in a case that was settled by October. In exchange for joint custody of Lisa Marie, Priscilla was now entitled to $10,000 per month in alimony and child support, a 1/2 million payment, half the value of the LA home that had been recently sold, and a royalty on revenues from Elvis' song publishing companies. Ex-husband and ex-wife left the courthouse

hand-in-hand.

After an initial period of melancholy and recrimination, Elvis' relationship with Priscilla found a more stable form. When together after the divorce, Elvis and Priscilla seemed to be genuinely affectionate to one another. Elvis confided to Billy Smith two years after the separation that he still loved Priscilla. Larry Geller has written that Elvis never really got over the humiliation of Priscilla leaving him—nobody left him, it was always he who tired of people in his life—and he was particularly susceptible to the shame of her cuckolding him.

Priscilla still came to Elvis' Las Vegas shows. On the closing night of his summer 1974 Hilton residency, she was the target of some pointed onstage comments, including the revelation that the divorce settlement was worth a total of $2 million, and that they were still on good terms because they were still giving each other expensive gifts. They remained friends; Elvis is said to have sometimes put a new girlfriend on the phone to Priscilla for rapid instruction in what Elvis liked and needed. Towards the end of his life, Elvis told Larry Geller that it had taken him a long time to realize that Priscilla was much more like a sister than a soulmate. According to Priscilla, they were at the stage where they could laugh at their shortcomings, and in her memoir she hints that the future may even have augured a reconciliation.

Priscilla returned to Graceland on the *Lisa Marie* early on the morning after Elvis died, with various other friends but not Ed Parker and former girlfriend Linda Thompson, whom she did not want to board.

Not long after Elvis' funeral, Vernon named Priscilla as an executor of Elvis' estate. Two years later Vernon died, and Priscilla took over control of the Elvis Estate. Under Priscilla's guidance the Estate escaped bankruptcy and was returned to financial stability. Some members of Elvis' family and entourage have been critical of how forcefully she took over, but nobody denies that she was instrumental in helping to make the Estate not just a commercial success but a pioneering example of how to manage an entertainer's legacy. In recent interviews, Priscilla has said that she thinks Elvis' demise was in some way brought about by him losing sight of his purpose in his life, and that he was "a victim of his own career."

Priscilla shared her personal life with actor Michael Edwards from 1978 to 1985. Edwards put Priscilla in touch with Scientology (though it has also been said that she joined the organization on the recommendation of John Travolta). Edwards later wrote a less-than-flattering book about Priscilla. A scurrilous picture is also painted of her in a 1997 book by Suzanne Finstad, *Child Bride: The Untold Story of Priscilla Beaulieu Presley*, in which she claims that Priscilla was a sex-crazed young girl, that the couple made love on their second date, and that her relationship with Elvis was a well-planned campaign for a life of wealth and fame.

From 1986 to 2006 Priscilla lived with Brazilian writer and director Marco Garibaldi (born in 1955), with whom she had a son, Navarone Garibaldi, who was born on March 1, 1987.

In her professional life, after leaving Elvis she became a partner in an LA boutique called Biss and Beau, which was a favorite haunt of many A-list actresses. She had begun designing when she was still Elvis, making up outfits that she would wear to the opening and closing shows in Las Vegas.

Her first TV appearance was as a co-host of TV series "Those Amazing Animals" opposite Burgess Meredith and Jim Stafford. She began her acting career opposite Tony Orlando in a 1983 episode of "The Fall Guy," before landing a high-profile role for five years as Jenna Wade in TV soap "Dallas." She was also a regular in the *Naked Gun* movie franchise in the late Eighties and early Nineties. Before she appeared on screen she reputedly turned down a role as an original "Charlie's Angels." In the late Nineties, she appeared in ABC TV show "Spin City."

Priscilla launched a range of fragrances in 1988 with names such as Moments, Experiences, Roses and More, and more recently has branched out with a line of linens. At the time of writing, she was lining up to co-produce a remake of one of Elvis' favorite movies, Peter Sellers' *The Party*. She previously executive produced 1998 movie *Finding Graceland*. In 1998, as Lisa Marie became increasingly active in running the Elvis Presley Trust and Elvis Presley Enterprises, Priscilla moved to an advisory role.

In Elvis biopics, she has been played by Season Hubley (1979) and Antonia Bernath (2005).

Priscilla Presley is also involved in the Dream Foundation, which was set up to make wishes come true for terminally ill people.

Elvis' pet names for Priscilla were Cilla, Little One, "Satnin' " and "Nungen" (meaning "young one").

ELVIS SAID TO PRISCILLA the first time he set eyes on her: "Well, what have we here?"

ELVIS SAID: "Of all the women in my life, she definitely has the most beautiful face. Her features are classic."

ELVIS SAID ON STAGE IN 1974: "Boy, she is a beautiful chick. I'll tell you for sure. Boy, I knows 'em when I picks 'em."

PRISCILLA SAID: "The first six months I spent with him were filled with tenderness and affection."

PRISCILLA SAID: "I was a young girl but he was so lonely during that time in Germany—he was so far away from home in strange surroundings, and mourning the death of his mother, and I think he connected with me. He could talk to me about what he was feeling. And he knew I wasn't going to tell anyone. For some reason, I felt very protective of him."

PRISCILLA SAID: "I had everything that Elvis had been looking for in a woman: youth and innocence, total devotion, and no problems of my own. And I was hard to get."

PRISCILLA SAID: "While my classmates were deciding which colleges to apply to, I was deciding which gun to wear with what sequined dress."

PRISCILLA SAID: "The more we were together the more I came to resemble him in every way. His tastes, his insecurities, his hang-ups—all became mine."

PRISCILLA SAID: "I wanted to create a home. I wanted to have children. I wanted him to be a husband. It was never going to be that way . . . He had created a lifestyle that was really very necessary for him because he couldn't get around without fanfare."

PRISCILLA SAID: "As a person, he was wonderful. He really was a great person. He was full of life. He had a great sense of humor. Very talented, of course, but very caring to his parents. There was a very endearing quality about Elvis."

PRISCILLA SAID: "I don't have an addictive personality and living with someone who has an addictive personality was very, very difficult and very hard to watch."

PRISCILLA SAID: "He taught me everything: how to dress, how to walk, how to apply makeup and wear my hair, how to behave, how to return love—his way. Over the years he became my father, husband, and very nearly God."

PRISCILLA: "It's a challenge to speak about him in that people want to know so much about him and it's never enough. And you question, how much is

Priscilla was a regular in the *Naked Gun* movie franchise.

enough, how much to give . . . There's a line that one has to say that's it, I have to give him the respect that he always wanted as far as his privacy."

BILLY SMITH: "In the beginning, Priscilla was like every other woman —Elvis thought she was pretty, and her coloring was a lot like his mother's. And he realized she look like Debra Paget."

PAMELA CLARKE KEOGH: "No matter how you looked at it, hers was an impossible task."

CHARLIE HODGE: "Elvis loved her, he told me that many times. And while he may not have wanted to get married when he did she was the love of his life."

LARRY GELLER: "Despite the wide disparity in their ages, Priscilla gave Elvis stability."

BILLY SMITH: "Elvis was too good a teacher because real quick-like, Priscilla grew to be just like him."

LAMAR FIKE: "I'll give you Elvis' relationship with her in a nutshell: You create a statue. And then you get tired of looking at it."

RED WEST: "Deep down, I believe that Priscilla was only one of two he ever really did love in his whole life."

SONNY WEST: "Priscilla could have anything she wanted, but the thing she wanted most was Elvis. In the last couple of years she was with him, he was away from her 85% of the time."

LARRY GELLER: "Her leaving him was, after Gladys' death, probably the toughest single blow in his life."

DR. NICHOPOULOS: "Elvis had a very good relationship with Priscilla after their divorce. He continued to do things for her and she continued to accommodate his wishes as far as Lisa Marie was concerned."

TONY BROWN: "I honestly believe that when Priscilla left him, he just gave up. A lot of us thought that."

Books:
Elvis and Me, by Priscilla Presley with Sandra Harmon, published by Berkley, 1986 (a TV movie of the same name was made in 1988).
Priscilla, Elvis, and Me, by Michael Edwards, St. Martin's Press, 1988.
Priscilla and Elvis: The Priscilla Presley Story, by Caroline Latham, New American Library, 1985.

Child Bride: The Untold Story of Priscilla Beaulieu
  Presley, by Suzanne Finstad, Harmony Books,
  1997.

PRESLEY, SALES

Vernon's cousin, with whom Elvis' parents lived
when they moved to Pascagoula, MI during the
war years to work in a munitions factory. Married
to Annie Presley.

PRESLEY, VERNON ELVIS (FATHER)
(1916-1979)

Biographers tend to characterize Vernon as a third
party in his own family, an outsider looking in on
the uncommonly strong bond between his wife
and his child. After Gladys's death, Vernon's role
in charge of Elvis' finances, and more importantly
the mismatch of his abilities compared with the
wily Colonel's, is credited by many as a reason why
Elvis remained in the Colonel's thrall for the duration. Interviews conducted by biographers reveal a
man whose fear of returning to poverty resulted in
avarice; he is lambasted by some as lazy and keen
to take advantage of the good fortune that came
to him through his son; whatever his character
traits, no biographer disputes Elvis' love for and
trust in his father. With his good looks, Vernon
always had an eye for the ladies. Relatives have
said that he also had a liking for the bottle, and his
work-shy attitudes are said to have made it hard if
not impossible for his small family to pull themselves out of the widespread poverty of Elvis'
youth. At least one biographer ascribes Elvis'
desire—from a tender age—to look after his
mother and to work his way to success as a reaction to character traits in his father.

Early years

Vernon Elvis Presley was born in Fulton,
Mississippi on April 10, 1916, and grew up in the
poorest white area of Tupelo. Vernon left school
early but showed little propensity to work.
Vernon's dad, J.D. Presley, was the type to always
criticize his son, though Vernon is said to have
been his mother Minnie Mae's favorite. J.D. kicked
Vernon out of the family home when he was fifteen and sent him to work on a farm in Mississippi.
Vernon served a brief apprenticeship in carpentry,
at which he showed skill but not application. For a
spell, Vernon worked as a truck driver.

Vernon and Gladys eloped to be on June 17,
1933, mere months after meeting at the local First
Assembly of God church, notwithstanding the fact
that Vernon, at 17, was below the legal age limit
for matrimony. Soon afterwards, Vernon took out a
loan of $180 from Orville Bean, the dairy farmer
for whom he and other Presleys worked, to build a
house. Aided by his father and brothers, he put up
a shotgun shack next to his parents' place on the
Old Saltillo Road in East Tupelo. Vernon repaid
the loan as rent, though keeping up with payments
was not easy for a man who seemed unfortunately
talented at losing jobs. When Elvis was born in
1935, Vernon was happy to be a pappy but desperately sad over the dead twin boy.

Vernon was in trouble with the law in late
1937, when he and two other men—brother-in-
law Travis Smith and Lether Gable—were arrested and incarcerated at Lee County Jail for "uttering a forged instrument." They were charged of
altering a check for four dollars received from
Orville Bean for a pig (to either $14 or $40
depending on who's telling the story), because
they thought that they should have been paid
much more for the animal. J.D. Presley stood bail
for his son-in-law but refused to do so for Vernon,
presumably to teach him a lesson.

On May 25, 1938, Vernon and Travis were sentenced to three years at the Mississippi State

ABOVE: Elvis with Gladys and Vernon in 1956.

Penitentiary at Parchman. Vernon began his
prison term on June 1. Without his earnings coming in, Gladys and Elvis had to give up their house
and move in with relatives in East Tupelo. Three
year-old Elvis regularly accompanied Gladys once
every couple of weeks to see Vernon in jail, taking
public transport to "Parchman Farm" a hundred
miles south. Vernon was released from jail on
February 6, 1939, after a petition from the citizens
of the county and a letter from Mr. Orville Bean,
whose check Vernon was convicted of forging.
Vernon's jail time was concealed from the press
throughout Elvis' lifetime, and only became public knowledge after Elvis' death. In life, Elvis only
told the story to his physician, Dr. Nick: in the
version Elvis told, Vernon was imprisoned after
stealing food from a grocery store to feed the family, which had gone hungry for a day or two—this
may have been the version that Elvis was told by
his parents. According to some sources, while in
jail Vernon was bull whipped.

After his early release, Vernon may briefly have
worked for the Leake and Godlett Lumber Co.
before he found work with the Federal Works
Project Agency (WPA), a New Deal agency that
assigned him to a Lee County Sanitation Project
where he worked as a carpenter and later a cement
finisher. Under this New Deal program, he earned
$30.10 for a 140 hour working month. Within three
months, his pay had risen to $52 per month as a
skilled carpenter. However, the family's financial
troubles continued when a local bank repossessed a
car after Vernon defaulted on a loan—it took him
until June 1943 to pay back the money still owing.
In 1940, Vernon replaced the sequestered car with a
1930 Chevrolet truck, and then the following year
bought a 1932 Chevrolet coupe. The WPA placement ended after 18 months, in November 1940.

Spared a call-up after the United States entered
the Second World War because of his family obli-

gations, Vernon next found employment at the
S&W Construction Company, 50 miles away in
Sardis, Mississippi, but he quit in early 1942. That
year he helped to build a prisoner of war camp in
Como, Mississippi. For his next job he had to trav-
el 300 miles to the Ozark Triangular Division
Camp of the J. A. Jones Construction Co., before
finding work nearer home at the Ferguson Oman
Gulf Ordnance plant in Aberdeen, Mississippi,
where he earned a dollar an hour as a carpenter.
His next job, as a carpenter for the Dunn
Construction Company in Millington, Tennessee,
paid $1.25 an hour, and lasted for two months.
After a brief spell in early 1943 working at the
Pepsi Cola Bottling Company in Tupelo, Vernon
took his family to the Mississippi Gulf Coast to
work at the Moss Point Shipyard, not far from
Pascagoula, joining family members Sales and
Annie Presley (though some biographers state that
Vernon took the family to Pascagoula in 1940). He
quit after just one month and took the family back
to Tupelo (or stuck it out for nine months according to some). Back in Memphis, Vernon returned
to the Dunn Construction Company, and then ran
deliveries for the L. P. McCarty and Sons grocery
store. His 1943 tax declaration stated total income
of $1232.88, a significant improvement on the
poverty of Elvis' earliest years.

In August 1945, Vernon bought a new house,
once again from Orville Bean. The four-room
dwelling cost $2,000, for which Vernon put down
his $200 savings. By July 1946, Vernon had fallen
behind with payments, and decided to sign the
house over to his best friend, Aaron Kennedy.
The Presleys found new accommodation in
Tupelo proper, first on Commerce Street, and
then on Mulberry Alley, a block or two from
Tupelo's poor black neighborhood, and very
much on the wrong side of the tracks. In 1945,
Vernon became a deacon at the First Assembly of

God Church. A year or two later, he was accused of using his work truck to run moonshine and trade in articles of dubious provenance. He was fired from his job delivering for vegetable wholesaler L. G. McCarty, and in some accounts was advised by the authorities to leave town.

Memphis

In November 1948, the family packed up and left for a new life in Memphis, Tennessee. Elvis later said, "Dad packed all our belongings in boxes and put them on top and in the trunk of a 1939 Plymouth. We left Tupelo overnight. We were broke, man, broke." Vernon got a job at the Precision Tool Company in South Memphis, and the family found accommodation at a rooming house on 370 Washington Street. Vernon moved to a new job nearer home at the United Paint Company. In June 1949, the family applied for public housing. Three months later they were accepted into the Memphis Housing Authority's Lauderdale Courts development. A bad back prevented Vernon from working full-time, so though the family was living in a better environment than ever before, money remained tight. Gladys was, for a spell, the family's main breadwinner, while Elvis completed High School and started earning money as well.

Relatives remember that Vernon was not one for demonstrative shows of affection, but like his son was a joker and "full of life." He had a good singing voice, as did Gladys, and the whole family would join in for a sing-song. By most accounts, Gladys was the force in the household. According to Lamar Fike, Vernon was "scared to death" of Gladys, not just for a tongue-lashing but because she was capable of violence. Vernon could be just as aggressive to her when he drank. Years later, Billy Smith told of a time at Graceland when Elvis found out that Vernon had hit Gladys, and threatened to kill him if he ever laid a hand on her again.

When Elvis first started out in the music business, he was below the age of majority. His parents had to put their signatures to his management contract with Scotty Moore and his residence at the Louisiana Hayride. Elvis' earnings went straight back to Gladys and Vernon, who from the earliest days had the job of keeping track of Elvis' finances. It is Marty Lacker's opinion that Elvis' financial problems in the later years of his life and the lack of investments during his long career may directly be ascribed to the fact that Vernon knew so little about money, and indeed only had a third-grade education. The only major investment Vernon made, in a mining operation during the Seventies, resulted in a $2.5 million loss.

By May 1955, Elvis had bought his folks a brand new pink-and-white Ford Crown Victoria and made sufficient money for the family to move out of their apartment into a single-family home on 2414 Lamar Street. Before the end of the year the Presleys had moved up another rung on the property ladder, to an $85-a-month rental at 1414 Getwell Street, Memphis.

In the battle to manage Elvis' rise to national fame, the Colonel courted Vernon assiduously and necessarily, as Gladys had a visceral dislike of him. Vernon signed a contract with the Colonel in August 1955, but then in September 1955, Vernon put his signature to a revised one-year contract with the Louisiana Hayride arranged by Neal, promising Elvis $200 a show.

By the time the Colonel engineered the transfer of Elvis' recording contract from Sun to RCA, Elvis had become the family's sole provider. He celebrated by buying his parents a brand-new 1956 Plymouth station wagon, gave his mom his Cadillac, and then bought the family their first ever home, a $29,500 property on Audubon Drive. In the summer of 1956, Elvis invited his folks to join him on vacation in Biloxi on their first seaside vacation.

In September 1956, the senior Presleys took a drive down memory lane to Tupelo with Elvis,

ABOVE: Vernon with gun, ca 1960's.

RIGHT: Vernon with second wife, Dee Stanley.

girlfriend Barbara Hearn and pal Nick Adams, where Elvis performed at the Mississippi-Alabama Fair and Dairy Show. The previous time they had seen him perform at the venue was when, aged 10, he had sung unaccompanied at a talent competition. In early 1957, Elvis' folks came out to Hollywood to watch the shooting of their son's first picture for Paramount, *Loving You*, and took part as extras. On their return to Memphis, Vernon and Gladys set about finding a new home where they would no longer be besieged by fans, as they were at Audubon Drive. In March 1957, they called Elvis in Hollywood to tell him about Graceland. Elvis' folks moved into the house two months later, while Elvis was out in Hollywood filming *Jailhouse Rock*.

Biographers note that by this time the father/son relationship had been almost completely transposed, with Elvis the breadwinner and his parents the dependents; Elvis sometimes even referred to them as his "babies." Vernon and Elvis found a *modus vivendi*. Red West remembers an episode during those early Graceland days when Elvis was sparring with West and Vernon came over. Vernon asked for the gloves. Elvis and Vernon circled for a while, neither of them attempting a blow, until Elvis slipped off his gloves and they hugged.

Vernon had a little more responsibility when Elvis was drafted into the Army. After Elvis completed his basic training at Fort Hood, Elvis brought his folks down to live with him offbase, first in a mobile home, then in Killeen. Elvis was temporarily separated from his parents when he sent them back to Memphis in early August 1958 for Gladys to get hospital treatment. A bed was set up for Vernon to stay with her; Vernon was at her bedside when she died deep in the night a few days later.

When it was time for Elvis to be shipped out to Germany, Vernon followed with his mother Minnie Mae and Elvis' pals Red West and Lamar Fike, taking a room at the Ritters Park Hotel in Bad Homburg. The whole gang moved to the more upmarket Hotel Grunewald a few weeks later at Bad Nauheim, a twenty-minute drive from the base. Out in Germany, Vernon purchased a tape recorder on which he recorded many candid moments of Elvis and pals horsing around and singing songs. For Christmas 1958, Vernon gave Elvis an electric guitar.

Vernon and Elvis' secretary Elisabeth Stefaniak were involved in a car accident on a German Autobahn in late March 1958. Briefly, rumors circulated that not only was Elvis involved in the crash, but had been killed. Elvis' initial concern was apparently that his father might have been up

to no good with Stefaniak, who was part of Elvis' German harem.

Soon afterwards, Vernon did start having an affair with a soldier's wife, Dee Stanley. The lady left her husband and took their three kids back to the States in June 1959. Vernon followed, either out of his own volition or because Elvis was furious with him for taking up with another woman less than a year after Gladys died. Vernon was ostracized not just by Elvis but by other members of the family; some biographers suggest that he had been serially unfaithful in his marriage too. Back in the States, Vernon took the opportunity to represent the Presley family at Colonel Parker's fiftieth birthday party in Madison. When Vernon returned from Germany for good at the end of Elvis' military service, it was with Dee Stanley in tow. They married in July 1960 in Hunstville Alabama—Elvis did not attend. For a spell, Vernon and Dee stayed in Panama City after Elvis banned them from using "Mom's room" and told them that they should live in the apartment out back (later Vernon's office). Vernon moved out of Graceland with his new wife and stepchildren at the end of 1961, into a home round the corner at 3650 Hermitage Drive. Whatever temporary frostiness there may have been between father and son had dissipated by spring 1962, when Vernon and Dee joined Elvis in Hawaii where he was filming *Girls! Girls! Girls!* Vernon was also on set in November 1962 for *It Happened at the World's Fair.*

Vernon and Dee flew to New York to pick up Priscilla Beaulieu and bring her back to Memphis for Christmas 1962. Her parents had been reassured that their little girl would be staying at Vernon's place round the corner from Graceland. By April 1963, Priscilla moved to Memphis permanently. Though putatively residing with Vernon, she was actually living with Elvis at Graceland.

In late 1964, Vernon and his new family moved to a new-built Tudor-style home at 1266 Dolan Drive, on a plot of land that had originally been part of the Graceland grounds, accessible via a gate at the back of the property. Many evenings, Elvis would stroll over to spend time with Vernon, watch some TV, and hang out. The family vacation for 1965 was accompanying Elvis and his gang to Hawaii for location shooting on *Paradise—Hawaiian Style.*

Vernon continued to look after Elvis' finances and run Graceland, hiring his pal Carl Nichols to undertake some renovations on the property. In practically everything he did, Vernon displayed the attitudes of a man who had lived a life of poverty: he hated to see money wasted, and was dogged by the fear that all of the wealth from which he benefited might one day simply disappear. Elvis' cousin Harold Loyd colorfully described Vernon as the type of man who was "so tight they could squeeze a nickel 'til the buffalo falls off." As a matter of principle, Vernon turned down Elvis' sporadic requests to raise the modest salary paid to his entourage members, arguing that they enjoyed so many perks and extras that they were already amply rewarded. When Elvis embarked on his truly expensive hobbies—in 1967, the Circle G ranch; in the Seventies, car buying sprees and airplane acquisitions—Vernon had conniptions. Vernon tried and failed to talk Elvis out of the ranch purchase, and then watched in despair as Elvis went on a huge spending spree, buying dozens of horses, pick-up trucks, horse trailers, riding gear, tractors, trailers for the guys to live in and more.

Soon after Elvis' Las Vegas wedding, Vernon and Dee visited Elvis in LA, while he was working on *Spinout.* Elvis granted his father power of attorney in February 1968, five days after daughter Lisa Marie was born. That Spring, Vernon joined Elvis in LA, and was given a bit part in Elvis movie *Live a Little, Love a Little.* Vernon dressed up as Santa Claus for Lisa Marie's first Christmas in 1968.

Vernon once again became concerned about Elvis' spending in the latter part of 1970, when Elvis splurged $20,000 on firearms, bought several cars for friends, and purchased a house for Joe Esposito. Elvis' solution was to buy his father a Mercedes. Vernon countered by enlisting Priscilla's help to confront Elvis about his spending. Rather than address the issue, Elvis slipped out of Graceland and headed off incognito to Washington, initially intending to see girlfriend Joyce Bova, but managing to meet President Nixon.

During the years when Elvis was accumulating police badges, Vernon was named an honorary captain.

Money worries led Vernon to support the Colonel in the infamous deal he struck with RCA in 1973 to sell off Elvis' entire back catalogue. In the summer of 1973, Vernon played an instrumental role in the one explicit and up-front row between Elvis and the Colonel. When Elvis fired the Colonel, the Colonel sent Vernon a settlement claim so huge that Vernon counseled healing the rift.

In 1974, Vernon separated from Dee Stanley. He and Sandy Miller (a nurse from Denver whom he had been seeing ever since he had brought her to Memphis to look after him following a heart

Elvis with his father Vernon, ca 1977.

scare) moved into a new house that he bought at 1293 Old Hickory Road. They later moved back to the Dolan property which Dee had initially been awarded in the divorce settlement.

Entourage members have described Vernon's propensity to play the field whenever he could, taking full advantage of the times that he joined Elvis on tour in the Seventies. Entourage memoirs state that there was little love lost between Vernon and Elvis' paid companions, as he suspected that they were all out to exploit his son.

Vernon suffered a heart attack in January 1975. He was taken to the Baptist Memorial Hospital, where he was put in a room near his son, who had been hospitalized to recover from breathing problems induced by the prescription medicine he was taking.

In the summer of 1976, Vernon called Red West, Sonny West and Dave Hebler, and told them that owing to financial constraints, their employment with Elvis was being terminated with a single week's notice. For Red and Sonny, this was an unceremonious end to over two decades living and working with Elvis, and led to them writing the first book that raised the curtain on Elvis' rather singular lifestyle.

Elvis and his Las Vegas doctor Elias Ghanem rushed Vernon to the hospital after one of Elvis' performances at Las Vegas in December 1976 for another suspected heart attack, though it was mild enough for him to be up and about the following day.

Vernon occasionally made an on-stage cameo appearance at Elvis' shows. He appeared the last time that Elvis ever played before a paying crowd, in Indianapolis in June 1977.

Vernon was one of many people who tried unsuccessfully to persuade Elvis to go to hospital during the final weeks of his life. Cousin Billy Smith has accused Vernon of not doing enough to tackle Elvis' addiction to prescription drugs.

After Elvis

As the executor and trustee to Elvis' will, following Elvis' death in August 1977 Vernon threw open Graceland to tens of thousands of grieving fans, allowing them to say their goodbyes in the belief that this is what his son would have wanted. Vernon confided to several people that Elvis did not die of "natural" causes but was murdered.

Vernon moved back to Graceland in 1978 to be near his mother and sister, preferring the remodeled annex to the main building.

It has been written that the only interview Vernon gave in his lifetime was in the January

1978 issue of *Good Housekeeping.* However, he was present at Elvis' 1972 Madison Square Garden press conference, and earlier that year he was interviewed by the filmmakers of the *Elvis on Tour* documentary—a seven-minute excerpt has appeared on bootleg disc *The Complete On Tour Sessions.*

Vernon had another heart attack on October 26, 1978. Back at Graceland after a period of hospitalization, he was too weak to walk and began relying on a wheelchair. His heart finally gave out at Graceland on June 26, 1979 (incidentally, the Colonel's birthday). Friends noted that his health went downhill rapidly after Elvis died. A service was held for Vernon in the front room at Graceland, and then he was buried in the meditation garden.

In 2007, Vernon posthumously released his first ever record, "Don't Close Your Door," which he recorded to tape in 1973 on the King Productions label.

VERNON'S FAMILY TREE

The Presley line has been traced back as far as Andrew Presley Jr., a Scottish-born solider who fought in the Revolutionary War, though a competing family tree has this ancestor as Andreas, hailing originally from Germany. His children, with wife Elizabeth, include Dunnan Presley Sr., father of Dunnan Presley Jr., who with Martha Jane Wesson (1861-1900) were the parents of Rossella Wesson Presley (1862-1924). Rosella did not let being unmarried prevent her giving birth to close to a dozen children, including J.D. Presley, who married Minnie Mae Hood and sired Vernon.

VERNON SAID: "Poor we were, I'll never deny that. But trash we weren't."

VERNON SAID TO LARRY GELLER ON THE DAY OF ELVIS' FUNERAL: "I guess Elvis found what he was always searchin' for. Now he's at peace, and he's with God, where his heart was all along."

ELVIS SAID: "My father was a common laborer, he didn't have no trade, just like I didn't have."

ELVIS SAID IN 1960: "He's all I got left in the world. I'll never go against him or stand in his way."

ELVIS SAID IN 1960: "He stood by me all these years and sacrificed things he wanted so I could have clothes and lunch money and go to school."

ELVIS SAID ON STAGE IN 1974: "He's a bigger man than I am, boy."

MARTY LACKER: "Vernon loved Elvis... but the only thing really that Vernon was concerned about was whether he was going to be poor again—whether Vernon was going to be poor. That clouded some of his thinking."

BILLY SMITH: "Elvis got his flashiness from Vernon, both in his behavior and the way he dressed."

LARRY GELLER: "Vernon was never a take-charge person."

MARTY LACKER: "Vernon would just strut around like he was king of the hill when Elvis wasn't at home."

LAMAR FIKE: "In Vernon, I saw a man who was bewildered by everything. Deep down, I think he was a good person."

PRESLEY, VESTER
(1914-1997)

Vernon's brother, born on September 11, 1914, came to live with the Presleys at Graceland after they moved in and was one of the trusted family relatives who worked at the gates, though he was initially employed as a groundskeeper. Vester is one of several uncles credited with teaching Elvis his first guitar chords. Vester's marriage to Gladys's sister Clettes cemented the closeness between the families. They had a daughter, Patsy Presley.

Before his death in 1997, Vester was the first and generally only Presley that fans could expect to see when they visited Graceland. He played himself in the 1981 Elvis biopic *This Is Elvis*, and appeared in the mid-Eighties Elvis documentary *Elvis: Memories*.

Books:

A *Presley Speaks*, by Vester Presley and Deda Bonura, published by The Wimmer Brothers, 1978.

The Presley Family Cookbook, by Vester Presley and Nancy Rooks, Wimmer Cookbooks, 1980.

PRESS

Elvis has been selling newspapers and magazines as long as he's been selling records.

His first newspaper interview was with Edwin Howard in the *Memphis Press-Scimitar* in late July 1954, chaperoned by Sun employee Marion Keisker. Apart from small articles in local papers announcing upcoming concerts, when Elvis started touring he looked after his own advance promotion through radio interviews with DJs (some of whom were promoters of the events he played; many of these early interviews later found their way onto vinyl). However, by early 1955 the *Memphis Press-Scimitar* was proudly trumpeting Elvis' arrival with a feature titled "Suddenly Singing Elvis Presley Zooms Into Recording Stardom."

Outside of trade papers, almost all press coverage of Elvis' breakthrough was scandalistic and fear-mongering about his effect on morals in general and young girls in particular. As PRs around the world are aware, any news is good news. The scathing criticisms ultimately helped to spread Elvis' renown and increase curiosity among young people. In 1956, when Elvis made it into the national press, the New York papers ran less than complimentary items, while Ed Sullivan notoriously claimed that he'd rather broadcast a test pattern than present Elvis Presley on his show . . . until Elvis' skyrocketing popularity forced him to recant.

Elvis told an early interviewer that he did his best to avoid reading his bad press. In the many interviews he gave as he rose to the top, Elvis was unfailingly gracious to journalists who challenged him about the most pernicious rumors, and was usually magnanimous enough to say that he had no ill-will to newspaper critics because he knew they were just doing their jobs. Elvis reached his limit when a Florida newspaper piece described him as a "no-talent performer riding the crest of a wave of mass hysteria": he retorted that the writer was an idiot who "just hates to admit that he's too old to have any more fun." Even at that interview, Elvis still expressed his appreciation and admiration for what journalists did, admitting that without the journalists, nobody in the entertainment business would amount to very much.

Gradually articles began to appear when it became impossible to ignore Elvis' enormous money-making success, and then mainstream newspapers such as the *New York Times* began praising his distinctive voice. *Newsweek* magazine wrote its first feature on Elvis in mid-May, 1956. However, the majority of the coverage about Elvis saw journalists competing to denounce him, his singing and the effect he had on his audience as a scandal or worse.

Local Memphis press coverage was naturally extensive from the day that Elvis began to create a stir, and continues to this media-infused day. Memphis reporters such as Bill E. Burk, who has covered Elvis since the Fifties, have also published fascinating investigative books on Elvis' early life based on meticulous, primary research

Not all early national press coverage was anti-Elvis. Influential LA columnist Louella Parsons wrote a piece titled "Elvis Doesn't Have Any Wickedness In His Heart." Highbrow publications including *The New Yorker*, the *Sunday Times*, *The New Republic* and *Harper's* tried to investigate what lay beyond the hype in serious articles on what the Elvis phenomenon represented.

In his early years, Elvis kept a scrapbook of press cuttings, (sometimes referred to as "the Green Scrapbook"). In one interview, he said that he only kept the favorable stuff; in another, he said that he had started collecting the criticisms, because he wanted to study them and better himself.

The Colonel's initial strategy when he started managing Elvis was maximum exposure in the minimum time, through the medium of TV rather than the press. By the end of 1956, he had switched to a "leave 'em wanting more" approach, which included paring back press access to movie launches and major concert tours.

When Elvis reported for duty to the Army in 1958, press access priorities were limited to stage-managed set pieces such as when he reported for the draft and traveled to and from Germany. The one exception was in the immediate aftermath of his mother's death in August 1958. Larry Geller has written in his memoir that this intrusion into Elvis' life—which, he claims, was masterminded by Colonel Parker—persuaded Elvis to keep his distance from the press in future.

The Colonel was able to exert a far greater control over what details emerged about Elvis' colorful private life than would be imaginable today. Hundreds of people might troop through Graceland or one of Elvis' LA homes over the course of an evening yet not a word made it into the press about drugs or sexual shenanigans. Priscilla moved into Graceland soon after supposedly going to live with Vernon and Dee Stanley, but the presence of an underage girlfriend was kept out of the gossip pages. Entourage members abided by strict rules: don't show press to Elvis, don't criticize his shows, don't

New York Press Conference.

Press Conference, Bismark Hotel, Chicage, March 1957.

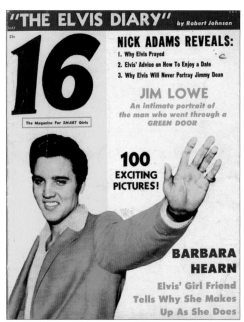

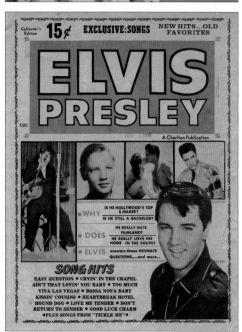

TOP TO BOTTOM: Elvis on the cover of *16 Magazine* in May 1957; The cartoons of Elvis make this 1958 magazine highly collectible; Extremely rare 1965 *Elvis* magazine.

talk to the media and never discuss his personal life.

Rather than conceding interviews, for most of the Sixties, the Colonel relied on the movie studios and RCA to keep Elvis' name in the news. Pictures of Elvis were worth more than Elvis' taped words, and there were always fan club circuits to circulate messages from Elvis that bypassed the national press.

Colonel Parker arranged press conferences to keep Elvis in the public eye before and after his time in the Army, press conferences for his high-profile charity work (though his regular giving continued anonymously), one judiciously timed to coincide with the arrival of The Beatles in the States, one immediately after his wedding to Priscilla in 1967, and press conferences to mark major Elvis events such as the 1968 NBC Special, Elvis signing to play Las Vegas in 1969, and in 1972 a press conference before going on stage at Madison Square Garden—an occasion when Elvis was particularly self-assured and candid about his life and his relationship with his fans.

In the mid-Sixties, *Time* magazine called the Colonel and offered to put Elvis on the cover. The Colonel asked for $25,000, at a time when stars were usually happy for the enormous national exposure alone. When *Time* demurred, the Colonel told them point blank, "We don't need you," despite the fact that an epitaphic quality had crept into mainstream press articles about Elvis before his 1968 NBC TV Special.

One of the few times when Elvis did read his reviews was after his triumphant return to live performing in Las Vegas in the summer of '69. Joe Esposito went out to get all the papers so that Elvis and the gang could revel in the triumph. Elvis was so full of confidence that at one August 1969 show in Las Vegas he conducted an onstage mock interview with a cricket that had somehow got into the Showroom..

Elvis' increasing drug use and more erratic behavior in the Seventies made it imperative to prevent leaks. It became part of the entourage's job to sweep Elvis' hotel rooms before checkout to make sure that no evidence or paraphernalia was left behind.

To protect Priscilla from invasive press attention around the time of their divorce, it was Elvis who filed the action and Elvis' whose address was on the legal document.

By 1973, stories were beginning to appear in the gossip pages that not all was right in Elvis' private life. The following year, Elvis took a swipe at what he called "those movie magazines" and the falsehoods they wrote about him during an onstage rant at the Las Vegas Hilton Hotel.

Entourage members continued to shield Elvis from unfavorable reviews. A 1973 review of one Elvis performance in Las Vegas described him as "the Colonel's mechanized doll." An August 1976 concert was described by journalist Bob Claypool as a "depressingly incoherent, amateurish mess served up by a bloated, stumbling and mumbling figure."

The *National Enquirer* did not wait for Elvis' death to run lurid front page headlines about Elvis: "Elvis at 40—Paunchy, Depressed and Living in Fear."

Press rumors in early 1977 abounded that Elvis had become too paranoid to record, and that the Colonel was threatening to cancel his tours if he didn't fulfill his recording commitments. The *National Enquirer* gleefully ran a story about "Elvis' Bizarre Behavior" a few months before his death. Nevertheless, the first major revelations about Elvis' wayward behavior did not appear in the press until just a few months before his death, in the run-up to publication of Red and Sonny West and Dave Hebler's book *Elvis: What Happened?*

After Elvis died, the *National Enquirer* printed a photograph of Elvis in his casket, taken by a cousin of Elvis' (said to be Billy Mann, recruited by a *National Enquirer* photographer at a local bar, in exchange for anywhere between $10,000 and $30,000 depending on accounts), despite a strict

ban on cameras at the funeral. That issue of the tabloid sold 6.7 million copies, the highest number of any *National Enquirer* issue.

When Elvis died, Elvis Specials appeared in the widest imaginable variety of newspapers and magazines around the world.

In 1980, Neal and Janice Gregory published a book examining media reaction to Elvis' death.

ELVIS SAID IN 1956: "I guess no matter how hard you try to be fair and good with people, there's always those few who are gonna make up stories no matter what you do."

ELVIS SAID (ABOUT PRESS CONFERENCES) IN 1960: "I get a big thrill out of 'em . . . because you have all these different people there with different questions and they're poppin' 'em to you like a district attorney. And you're sitting there like you were on trial for something."

ELVIS SAID IN 1976: "I find out more stuff about myself in the paper than anywhere else."

ALANNA NASH: "By not allowing Elvis to be seen or heard in interviews, Parker made him into the object of nearly limitless romantic fantasy, from a pious innocent who loved his mom and his Lord to a wiggling, greasy god of sex."

ERNST JORGENSEN: "The almost universal gloating and tabloid derision that erupted after his death was in many ways a tragic reversal of the bright image of hope and promise with which Elvis had started out his career."

MARY HANCOCK HINDS: "The mainstream media's love affair with celebrity was born the day Elvis died."

Books:

The Elvis Presley Story, edited by James Gregory, Hillman Books, 1960 (early articles anthology).

When Elvis Died: Media Overload & the Origins of the Elvis Cult by Neal and Janice Gregory, Communications Press, 1980.

Elvis: A 30-Year Chronicle: Columns, Articles, Stories and Features Exactly As Originally Reported 1954-1983, by Bill E. Burk, Osborne Enterprises, 1985.

Elvis In Private, by Peter Haining, St. Martin's Press, 1987.

The Elvis Presley Scrapbooks, 1955-1965, edited by Peter Haining, Robert Hale, 1991 (mainly UK).

PRICE, RAY
(B. 1926)

Country singer Price became a household name at the Grand Ole Opry in the early Fifties, later acquiring his own band, the Cherokee Cowboys. By the middle of the decade he had become so recognizable with hits such as "Crazy Arms" (a song that Jerry Lee Lewis took on during the *Million Dollar Quartet* jam session) that a certain kind of 4/4 beat was named after him. Elvis is said to have toured on the same bill as Price in his early years. Songs they both covered include "Release Me," "Make The World Go Away," "She Wears My Ring," "Help Me" and "For The Good Times."

Price was elected to the Country Music Hall of Fame in 1996.

PRISONAIRES, THE

Sam Phillips discovered this close-harmony Afro-American quartet at the Tennessee State Penitentiary, and paid for them to be transported to his new Sun label studios in June 1953 to record their first hit, "Just Walkin' In The Rain" (later a #2 hit for Johnnie Ray in 1956).

Biographers concur that an article in a Memphis paper about The Prisonaires first alerted young Elvis to Sun Records and Sam Phillips. The Prisonaires did not have another hit after this, though they became a favorite of the then Tennessee governor and were sometimes let out to play at official State functions.

Elvis visited lead singer Johnny Bragg at Tennessee State Prison in March 1961, en route back to Memphis from Nashville, where he had just been honored by the Tennessee State Legislature. Lead Tenor Bragg (who later recorded solo) was joined by tenor John Drue, baritone William Stewart, tenor Ed Thurman and bass Marcell Sanders. It has been rumored that Elvis was once backed by the group at an early Nashville appearance.

PROFILE, THE KING ON STAGE, A, VOLS. 1 AND 2

A bootleg box set on Fort Baxter, released in 1995 and 1996, of Elvis concerts ca. 1973-1975 plus backstage rehearsals.

VOL. 1

TRACK LISTING:
1. Also Sprach Zarathustra
2. See See Rider
3. I Got A Woman / Amen
4. Love Me
5. Steamroller Blues
6. You Gave Me A Mountain
7. Trouble
8. Blue Suede Shoes
9. Rock Medley
10. Love Me Tender
11. Fever
12. What Now My Love
13. Suspicious Minds
14. Band introductions
15. My Boy
16. Release Me
17. American Trilogy
18. Mystery Train / Tiger Man
19. Help Me Make It Through The Night
20. How Great Thou Art
21. Can't Help Falling In Love
22. Closing Vamp

DISC 2
23. Stagger Lee
24. Got My Mojo Working
25. Spanish Folksong
26. Cotton Fields
27. See See Rider
28. When My Blue Moon Turns To Gold Again
29. Blue Christmas
30. I Got A Woman
31. Love Me
32. Tryin' To Get To You
33. All Shook Up
34. Love Me Tender
35. Hound Dog
36. Fever
37. Polk Salad Annie
38. Why Me, Lord
39. Suspicious Minds
40. Band introductions
41. I Can't Stop Loving You
42. Help Me
43. Bridge Over Troubled Water
44. Let Me Be There
45. Johnny B. Goode
46. Can't Help Falling In Love

DISC 3
47. Jambalaya
48. Love Me
49. If You Love Me (Let Me Know)
50. Love Me Tender
51. All Shook Up
52. Teddy Bear / Don't Be Cruel
53. The Wonder Of You
54. Polk Salad Annie
55. Band introductions
56. Johnny B. Goode

57. Steamroller Blues
58. T-R-O-U-B-L-E
59. I'll Remember You
60. Why Me, Lord
61. Let Me Be There
62. American Trilogy
63. Hound Dog
64. Funny How Time Slips Away
65. Little Darlin'
66. Can't Help Falling In Love

DISC 4
67. If You Love Me (Let Me Know)
68. You Gave Me A Mountain
69. Tryin' To Get To You
70. It's Now Or Never (incl. Blue Hawaii excerpt)
71. Little Sister
72. Teddy Bear / Don't Be Cruel
73. Help Me
74. My Way
75. Polk Salad Annie
76. Hurt
77. Blueberry Hill
78. Danny Boy (sung by Sherill Nielsen)
79. Walk With Me (sung by Sherill Nielsen)
80. Unchained Melody
81. Little Darlin'
82. Can't Help Falling In Love

VOL. 2

TRACK LISTING:
1. See See Rider
2. I Got A Woman / Amen
3. Love Me
4. Tryin' To Get To You
5. All Shook Up
6. Love Me Tender
7. You Don't Have To Say You Love Me
8. Hound Dog
9. Fever
10. Polk Salad Annie
11. Why Me, Lord
12. Suspicious Minds
13. Band introductions
14. I Can't Stop Loving You
15. Help Me
16. Bridge Over Troubled Water
17. Let Me Be There
18. The Wonder Of You
19. Big Boss Man
20. The First Time Ever I Saw Your Face
21. American Trilogy
22. It's Now Or Never
23. Can't Help Falling In Love
24. Closing Vamp

DISC 2
25. See See Rider
26. Dialogue
27. I Got A Woman / Amen
28. Love Me
29. If You Love Me (Let Me Know)
30. It's Midnight
31. Big Boss Man
32. Fever
33. Dialogue / Love Me Tender
34. Hound Dog
35. Band introductions
36. Blue Christmas
37. All Shook Up
38. Teddy Bear / Don't Be Cruel
39. Tryin' To Get To You
40. Killing Me Softly (by Voice)
41. When It's My Time (by the Stamps Quartet)
42. Heartbreak Hotel
43. Let Me Be There
44. How Great Thou Art
45. Hawaiian Wedding Song
46. Blue Suede Shoes
47. Dialogue
48. Can't Help Falling In Love
49. Closing Vamp

DISC 3
50. See See Rider
51. I Got A Woman / Amen
52. Love Me
53. If You Love Me (Let Me Know)
54. It's Midnight
55. Big Boss Man

56. Fever
57. Love Me Tender
58. Hound Dog
59. Band introductions
60. Lawdy, Miss Clawdy
61. Band introductions
62. All Shook Up
63. Teddy Bear / Don't Be Cruel
64. Heartbreak Hotel
65. Why Me, Lord
66. Promised Land
67. You Gave Me A Mountain
68. Let Me Be There
69. Hawaiian Wedding Song
70. Can't Help Falling In Love
71. Closing Vamp

DISC 4
72. Also Sprach Zarathustra
73. See See Rider
74. I Got A Woman / Amen
75. Love Me
76. If You Love Me (Let Me Know)
77. And I Love You So
78. Big Boss Man
79. It's Midnight
80. Promised Land
81. Green, Green Grass Of Home
82. Fairytale
83. Band introductions
84. My Boy
85. I'll Remember You
86. Let Me Be There
87. Teddy Bear / Don't Be Cruel
88. Hound Dog
89. You're The Reason I'm Living
90. Can't Help Falling In Love
91. Closing Vamp

"PROMISED LAND"

"Aw, get on it . . ." says Elvis and this 1964 Chuck Berry rocker became part of Elvis' discography after he recorded the song at Stax Studio ten days before Christmas in 1973. On release in September 1974, paired with "It's Midnight" on the B-side, the single reached #14 in the charts, though it sold fewer than a third of a million copies during its 13-week arc. The song fared better in the UK, reaching #9.

Berry is said to have written the song about crossing the States while in jail for "transporting a girl across state lines for immoral purposes."

Elvis sang the song in concert between the summers of 1974 and 1975.

"Promised Land" appears on 1981 RCA album *This Is Elvis* and on the *Walk A Mile In My Shoes* anthology. It is also to be found on *Artist Of The Century*, *Elvis 2nd to None* and *Hitstory*.

Live versions are included on *Live In Las Vegas*, and on FTD albums *Big Boss Man* and *Southern Nights*.

Alternate takes have appeared on *Platinum: A Life In Music*, *Essential Elvis Vol. 5* and *Today Tomorrow & Forever*.

PROMISED LAND (LP)

This album, released in January 1975, was the third album of material from Elvis' 1973 recording sessions at Stax in Memphis. The album sold around 300,000 copies on initial release, good enough for #47 in the charts, a better performance than the other two Stax albums.

TRACK LISTING:
1. Promised Land
2. There's A Honky Tonk Angel (Who Will Take Me Back In)
3. Help Me
4. Mr. Songman
5. Love Song Of The Year
6. It's Midnight

7.   Your Love's Been A Long Time Coming
8.   If You Talk In Your Sleep
9.   Thinking About You
10. You Asked Me To

A remastered version initially released in 2000 included bonus tracks "Loving Arms," "I Got A Feelin' In My Body", "If That Isn't Love," "She Wears My Ring", "My Boy," "Spanish Eyes," "Talk About The Good Times" and "Good Time Charlie's Got The Blues."

"PROUD MARY"

Elvis added this Creedence Clearwater Revival hit (written by John Fogerty) to his repertoire in January 1970 for his second month-long residency at the International Hotel in Las Vegas. A recording from his February 16 performance was released on Elvis' On Stage album. Though seemingly made for Elvis' voice, this live performance falls a little short of the original, which, the same year Elvis recorded, just missed #1 spot on the Billboard Hot 100 charts.

Elvis sang the song regularly in concert until the summer of 1972 (and reprised it a few times in 1974). The song featured in 1972 documentary Elvis on Tour. Live versions of the song are available on: Elvis As Recorded At Madison Square Garden, Walk A Mile In My Shoes, An Afternoon In The Garden, Live In Las Vegas, Elvis: Close Up and 2007 release Viva Las Vegas, in addition to FTD releases Polk Salad Annie, An American Trilogy, Elvis On Tour—The Rehearsals and Summer Festival.

PROWSE, JULIET
(1936-1996)

Born in India to South African parents, Prowse trained as a dancer from a very young age. She was spotted by a casting agent dancing at a club in Paris, and landed a role in the 1960 movie Can-Can, opposite Frank Sinatra, to whom she later became engaged. Prowse was elevated to national celebrity status when Soviet Premier Khrushchev denounced a rehearsal for Can-Can as immoral.

Prowse's biggest role was opposite Elvis in his 1960 movie G.I. Blues. Rumors of off-screen romance between Elvis and his leading lady were a regular feature of Elvis' movies; if it took place on this movie, the girl in question would have been dating Frank and Elvis at the same time.

Prowse was in the running for Elvis' next Paramount movie, Blue Hawaii, but failed to agree terms. No terms were necessary for her cameo in the audience at Elvis' 1970 show, captured on camera for the documentary Elvis: That's The Way It Is.

Known for having the world's most beautiful legs, Prowse continued to work in television and on the stage. In 1976 she earned the distinction of being the first ever guest star on "The Muppet Show."

PUBLISHING DEALS

Long-term income in the music industry is generated by royalties from publishing rather than the boom-and-bust income from hits. One of the first things that the Colonel did for Elvis was ensure him a slice of song publishing income through special ad hoc song publishing companies set up in partnership with song publishers Hill and Range. Though financially a savvy move, the Colonel's insistence on Elvis only singing material for which he could acquire rights, rather than material that was just plain good and right for him, later became an artistic liability.

Elvis named his original companies Elvis Music publishing and Gladys Music publishing. Gladys drew money directly from Gladys Music;

Vernon received a percentage from Elvis Music Inc., and later from Whitehaven Music. Hill & Range actually ran the companies and distributed their earnings.

Many songs that Elvis might have wanted to sing were off-limits because no sympathetic publishing deal could be arranged. This wasn't a problem in his first flush of fame, when he was the hottest singer on the planet. By the Sixties, many established songwriters were unwilling to forsake up to a third of their royalties just to have Elvis sing one of their songs. One way that Elvis circumvented the problem was to pick songs that were already in the public domain, either traditional songs or gospel tracks, on which Elvis' name sometimes appears as arranger and/or adaptor, both of which entitled him to additional royalties. Elvis is also credited on some of his Fifties hits as a songwriter (and on a handful of later songs penned by entourage members), though the song publishing royalty was strictly applied by the Colonel to all of his Fifties and Sixties material.

In the late Sixties, Elvis' music publishing empire expanded through a stake in American Music, which opened up new possibilities. However, by the Seventies life was harder for the people trying to ensure Elvis' significant song publishing income as he became more inclined to record songs he suggested directly in the recording studio, for which no deal had been cut in advance; negotiating with a songwriter after the track was in the can was a weak negotiating position.

The Colonel revamped Elvis' song publishing companies in 1973, taking over after partner and song supplier Hill and Range quit the business. Peculiarly, the Colonel had a 40% stake in Whitehaven Music, against Elvis' 15%, with the remainder distributed among men who worked for the Colonel. In later years, Elvis set up Aaron Music and Mr. Songman Music.

See also SONGS.

SONGS ON WHICH ELVIS HAS A CREDIT
ADAPTION

"Amazing Grace"
"America, The Beautiful"
"By And By"
"I Was Born About 10,000 Years Ago"
"I'll Take You Home Again Kathleen"
"I'm Gonna Walk Dem Golden Stairs"
"O Little Town Of Bethlehem"

ARRANGEMENT
"Santa Lucia"
"So High"
"Stand By Me"
"Swing Down, Sweet Chariot"

ADAPTATION AND ARRANGEMENT
"Aloha Oe"
"Farther Along"
"Joshua Fit The Battle"
"Milky White Way"
"O Come All Ye Faithful"
"Run On"
"The First Noël"

CO-WRITER
"All Shook Up"
"Don't Be Cruel"
"Let Me"
"Love Me Tender"
"Paralyzed"
"Poor Boy"
"That's Someone You Never Forget"
"We're Gonna Move"
"You'll Be Gone"

"PUPPET ON A STRING"

Elvis recorded this down-tempo Sid Tepper and Roy C. Bennett tune on June 20, 1964 at Radio

Recorders for Girl Happy. The song was reprised for release as the B-side to "Wooden Heart" in October 1965, when it racked up a respectable half million sales, climbing as high as #14 in the charts during a 10-week stay. Elvis' "Puppet on a String" is not to be confused with Sandie Shaw's 1967 UK hit of the same name.

After an initial LP appearance on the movie soundtrack, it later featured on Worldwide Gold Award Hits Vol. 2, and was a natural choice for 1978 LP Elvis Sings For Children (And Grown Ups Too), later reissued as Elvis Sings for Kids. It resurfaced on the Double Feature series in combination with Harum Scarum, and made the cut for Command Performances and more recent Elvis issues, ELVIS 30 #1 HITS, ELVIS 2nd to None and Hitstory.

Alternate takes have appeared on Out In Hollywood and Today Tomorrow & Forever.

PURE GOLD

Ten surefire hits came out on this mid-price album first issued by RCA in March 1975. It was not eligible for the charts, despite selling over half a million copies on original release (and ultimately more than 2.5 million).

TRACK LISTING:
1.   Kentucky Rain
2.   Fever
3.   It's Impossible (live)
4.   Jailhouse Rock
5.   Don't Be Cruel
6.   I Got A Woman
7.   All Shook Up
8.   Loving You
9.   In The Ghetto
10. Love Me Tender

"PUT THE BLAME ON ME"

On March 12, 1961 Elvis recorded this Kay Twomey / Fred Wise / Norman Blagman song for the Something For Everybody album at Studio B in Nashville. It was one of a handful of songs on the Tickle Me EP released four years later. "Put The Blame On Me" was anthologized on From Nashville to Memphis.

The first two takes from the Radio Recorders session have appeared on FTD releases Fame and Fortune, Tickle Me and Something For Everybody.

"PUT YOUR HAND IN THE HAND"

Elvis recorded this Gene MacLellan pop gospel track—a hit for Ocean in 1971, first released by Beth Moore, and later a Grammy winning performance for soul artist Shirley Caesar—on June 8, 1971 at RCA's Nashville studios for initial release on Elvis Now. It was later incorporated into religious-themed compilations Amazing Grace, Peace In The Valley—The Complete Gospel Recordings and more recently Elvis Inspirational. The first take from the session appeared on FTD issue I Sing All Kinds.

PUTNAM, NORBERT

By his own calculations, Muscle Shoals musician Putnam has worked on over 10,000 recordings with a rollcall of the greatest recording artists. He has worked as a producer, a music publisher and has his own record label based in Memphis. Putnam played bass for Elvis in the studio a number of times in the Seventies, the last time at Graceland in early 1976 when he filled in for Jerry Scheff. He first started playing in the mid-Fifties in a band that played Elvis and Carl Perkins covers.

Q

QUATRO, SUZI
(B. 1950)

Rocker Suzi had always been an Elvis fan but when the call came from the Man to come and say hi at Graceland she felt too shy, and later cited this as the biggest regret of her life.

Quatro came to prominence on the wave of glam rock that was initially popular in the UK and Australia, including a cover of "All Shook Up." In the US, she was perhaps best known for her role in Seventies TV series "Happy Days."

Quatro, who has described herself as Elvis' #1 fan, has recorded Elvis tribute song "Singing With Angels" (with James Burton) and covered a number of classic Elvis tracks. She has featured prominently in well-regarded Elvis documentaries, including *Elvis: 50 Years in Show Business*, and hosted a BBC radio show commemorating the thirtieth anniversary of Elvis' death in 2007.

Suzi Quatro: "I first saw him in September 1956, on "The Ed Sullivan Show," singing "Don't Be Cruel," and honest to God, I had my first sexual thrill!"

"QUE SERA"

Never officially released, Elvis sang this 1956 Best Oscar Song winner during his Army service posting in Germany. The home recording appears on bootleg release *Greetings From Germany*, in a mash of a version with lyrics borrowed from "Hound Dog."

"QUEEN WAHINE'S PAPAYA"

Not a metaphor for a female body part but a Giant/Baum/Kaye song for *Paradise—Hawaiian Style* that Elvis sang faster and faster and faster when he recorded his vocal dub on August 4, 1966. The band laid down the instrumental at Radio Recorders on June 27, 1965. The released version was a splice of two takes. In the movie, Elvis duets with Donna Butterworth.

The song has since appeared on the Nineties *Double Features* release. One alternate take has come out, on the 2004 FTD *Paradise, Hawaiian Style* release.

Every public declaration Elvis made has been transcribed, published and pored over; it seems that nobody who spent any time with Elvis has evaded the clutches of posterity. Quotes are sprinkled liberally throughout this encyclopedia to reflect the multiplicity of views concerning who Elvis was and how he affected people. A selection follows:

A note on quotes:

The word perfect recollections of conversations that occurred many years earlier so commonly found in memoirs and interviews occur solely in the realm of biography, not real life.

ELVIS SAID ABOUT HIS MUSIC IN 1956: "It's a healthy thing. You don't have to be doped up to do it."

ELVIS SAID IN 1956: "I don't even smoke or drink, and I started singing as a gospel singer and come from a Christian home."

ELVIS SAID IN June 1956: "I can't believe that music could cause anybody to do anything wrong. And what I'm doing is nothing but music."

ELVIS SAID IN AUGUST 1958, AFTER HIS MOTHER'S DEATH: "There are too many people that depend on me, I'm in too far to get out."

ELVIS SAID: "Values are like fingerprints. Nobody's are the same, but you leave 'em all over everything you do."

ELVIS SAID: "I don't know anything about music. In my line you don't have to."

ELVIS SAID: "Truth is like the sun. You can shut it out for a time, but it ain't goin' away."

PETER GURALNICK ON ELVIS' ACHIEVEMENT: "The proclamation of emotions long suppressed, the embrace of a vulnerability culturally denied, the unabashed striving for freedom."

BONO: Elvis changed everything—musically, sexually, politically . . . He was a Fifties-style icon who was what the Sixties were capable of, and then suddenly not. In the Seventies, he turned celebrity into a blood sport, but interestingly, the more he fell to Earth, the more godlike he became to his fans."

PHIL SPECTOR: "You have no idea how great he is, really you don't. You have no comprehension—it's absolutely impossible. I can't tell you why he's so great, but he is. He's sensational."

TONY BROWN: "He really was . . . basically just a good Southern guy who happened to be really handsome and really could rock the world . . . He was just a regular guy in my opinion who grew up being a superstar."

Books—Elvis speaks:
Elvis in His Own Words, compiled by Mick Farren and Pearce Marchbank, Omnibus Press, 1977.
The World According to Elvis: Quotes from the King, by Jeff Rovin, HarperCollins, 1992.
The Quotable King, edited by Elizabeth McKeon and Linda Everett, Cumberland House, 1997.
Elvis Word For Word, by Jerry Osborne, published by Osborne Enterprises, 1999.

Books—Quotes on Elvis:
Elvis! The Last Word: The 328 Best (and Worst) Things Anyone Ever Said About 'the King', edited by Sandra Choron and Bob Oskam, Citadel Press, 1991.
Before Elvis, There Was Nothing, edited by Patrick Higgins, Carroll & Graff Publishers, 1994.

Books—A selection about Elvis presented as interviews with friends and family :

Elvis in Quotes, Elvisly Yours, 1987.
Elvis Up Close: In the Words of Those Who Knew Him Best, by Rose Clayton and Dick Heard, Turner Publishing, Inc., 1994 (republished as *Elvis By Those Who Knew Him Best* in 2003).
Elvis Aaron Presley: Revelations from the Memphis Mafia, by Alanna Nash, with Billy Smith, Marty Lacker and Lamar Fike, HarperCollins, 1995.
Remember Elvis, by Joe Esposito, TCB Joe Publishing, 2006.

R

RABBITT, EDDIE
(B. EDWARD THOMAS RABBITT, 1944-1998)

A Brooklyn-born country artist who before embarking on his own successful career wrote a number of successful songs for others. Elvis recorded Rabbitt compositions "Inherit The Wind," "Patch It Up" and "Kentucky Rain." Rabbitt had a string of major hits from the mid-Seventies to the late Eighties, spanning 16 #1 country singles and a number of pop crossover hits, including "Every Which Way But Loose" and "I Love A Rainy Night."

RACE

The shift in perception of Elvis' influence and position in race relations is a barometer of the times. When Elvis first took to a stage, self-proclaimed upholders of the prevailing morality reproached him for sounding black, for daring to sing "race" music, as R & B had been known until the late Forties; by 1989, he was denigrated by Chuck D. of Public Enemy as a racist.

Criticisms that Elvis "stole black music" or more simply was a Southern racist overlook the fact that in deed, Elvis was an integrationist. Years before Rosa Parks refused to give up her bus seat to a white man and the American Civil Rights Movement began to overturn centuries of institutionalized racism, Elvis was sneaking off to black churches to listen to gospel, and by many accounts, heading down to Beale Street to go to black blues clubs. Elvis' tastes in music were untrammeled by the color bar; like many young white Americans ever since, he aspired to the kind of styles worn by African-Americans.

No shortage of articles have appeared over the years vilifying Elvis' appropriation of black culture. While many African American authors have extolled the way that Elvis brought different races together in his lifetime and was a positive force in breaking down the pernicious barriers of segregation. Singers Bo Diddley and Ray Charles have said that Elvis stole his act from African American performers; for B.B. King, the very term "rock and roll" was a way of drawing a line under black rhythm and blues. Yet pioneering artists Rufus Thomas, Little Richard and Jackie Wilson have all acknowledged Elvis' importance in helping black artists reach America's mainstream white audience.

Greil Marcus points out that the line between white and black in music heritage is sometimes so fine as to be invisible. Elvis has been upbraided for taking Big Mama Thornton's hit "Hound Dog" and making it his own, yet the song was actually written by Jewish songwriting duo Leiber and Stoller. In interviews, Elvis scrupulously acknowledged the origins of the music that swept him to fame, listing the African-American artists he liked and listened to whenever a journalist asked him about his own favorites—hardly the behavior of a man keen on passing off somebody else's music as his own. In a piece published before a general 1956 show in Mississippi, a local paper ascribed Elvis' "unique voice quality" to his "childhood surroundings in which country music and Negro blues were everyday music to him." Elvis sang the kind of music he liked, in the pre-singer/songwriter age when it was the norm for singers to cover material written by others.

When he was growing up, Elvis and his family spent a spell living a block or two away from the poor black quarter in Tupelo. When he was twelve or thirteen, Elvis worked for a black-owned grocery store, helping out with deliveries to make some extra money.

In the late Forties and early Fifties, if a young music fan like Elvis wanted to hear gospel, blues or jazz, they went to a black church, club or bar. When Elvis walked into Sun Records in 1953 to record his first, self-paid disc, he was walking into a record label whose roster was almost entirely made up of black artists, and was run by a man who, famously, was looking for a white man who could sing black. Elvis was ostracized by members of his family for his liking of R & B: Billy Smith told author Alanna Nash, "My family thought, 'Goddurn, why don't you just go down there on Beale Street and live with 'em?'"

When Elvis' records first received airplay on local radio stations in Memphis, many listeners were sure he was black. On air, DJ Dewey Phillips deliberately asked Elvis what High School he had attended to tip people off that he was white—schools were still segregated at that time. Sam Phillips ran into difficulties getting some of Elvis' earliest records played by some white-owned stations because they sounded too "Race." Elvis' early nickname the "Hillbilly Cat" was a way of flagging that even though he "sang black," Elvis was actually white.

Before Elvis, the limited number of white singers who covered R & B songs usually toned down the words. At Sun, Elvis' take was often to borrow a verse from here and a verse from there and build his own tune—he did this with country and bluegrass or R & B. However, by the time Elvis moved to RCA, the racier lyrics were bowdlerized.

Although Elvis is best known for popularizing "black" music among whites, black fans came to see his shows too. A concert at Greensboro, NC, in February 1956 recorded that 249 "colored" people attended out of the total audience of 2900. Elvis' mesmeric effect on female fans knew no skin-color boundaries.

Black community newspaper *Memphis World* reported in June 1956 that Elvis broke the local segregation laws by attending the Fairgrounds Memphis amusement park on "colored night." He also attended an ice show at Ellis Auditorium reserved "for negroes," and invited the entire orchestra and skating company to visit him at Graceland.

As Elvis rose to fame, the supremacist White Citizens Council issued angry communiqués about Elvis' incorporation of black song and dance into his act and the Ku Klux Klan announced a committee to "do away with this cannibalistic, negro-loving rock and roller." A number of Nashville music executives made protestations to the *Billboard* chart that they should not be listing Elvis' music on the Country charts at all because it was "colored music."

Elvis once again broke through the race barrier in December 1956, when he went to the WDIA Goodwill Review, a twice yearly charity event held by Memphis's black radio station. Elvis' brief curtain call was greeted by rapturous applause and was covered in the local black press. Elvis was back the following year to see the show and chat with musicians backstage.

In the summer of 1957, Elvis had to contend with accusations of derogatory comments about black people. Elvis gave an exclusive interview to a *Jet* magazine reporter to put right a slanderous statement that had been attributed to him after a show in Boston ("The only thing black people can do for me is shine my shoes and buy my music"). Elvis told the reporter, "People who know me know I wouldn't have said that." Researchers have shown that Elvis cannot have made the remark in Boston as claimed, as he did not play the town until 1971.

The closing number for Elvis' 1968 NBC TV Special, "If I Can Dream," was inspired by his sorrow at the assassination of Martin Luther King Jr.

in his hometown just three months earlier. Steve Binder, who produced the show, characterized Elvis as "a guy who was not prejudiced, who was raised in the heart of prejudice, but who was really above all that."

After Elvis began touring again in 1970 after his triumphant return to the stage in Las Vegas, the first venue he was invited to play was Houston. When one of the event organizers suggested that Elvis come without the "black girls"–backing singers the Sweet Inspirations—Elvis said that if they weren't coming, he wouldn't be coming either.

Elvis' colorblindness extended to his Vegas show-opening skit of introducing himself as other performers. Over the years, he introduced himself as Bill Cosby, Little Richard and Flip Wilson among others.

Though Elvis did occasionally display prejudice against African-Americans in private as a hangover from his upbringing, in his deeds and the people he admired, it was clear that he in no way felt color to be important.

ELVIS' RACIAL ORIGINS

Elvis' own lineage reveals him to be a one-man melting pot. Genealogists tend to ascribe his bloodline to a blend of Scottish/Irish and French, with a bit of Cherokee and Jewish mixed in (there have been claims that he had gypsy blood too). Throw in Germanic and/or Welsh, according to some biographers, and you have Everyman Elvis.

ELVIS AS AN AMERICAN-INDIAN IN MOVIES

The character played by Elvis in *G.I. Blues*, like Elvis, had Cherokee blood. He also played American Indian characters in *Flaming Star* and *Stay Away, Joe.*

The concept of a half-Indian/half-white character who is ostracized because of his race in *Flaming Star* (generally regarded as one of his finest dramatic performances) led to the movie being banned in South Africa.

REPORTER LOUIE ROBINSON IN *JET* MAGAZINE, 1957: "To Elvis, people are people, regardless of race, color, or creed."

PETER GURALNICK: "[Sam Phillips] thought he sensed in Elvis a kindred spirit, someone who shared with him a secret, almost subversive attraction not just to black music but to black culture, and to an inchoate striving, and a belief in the equality of man."

SAM PHILLIPS: "[Elvis] tried not to show it, but he felt so inferior. He reminded me of a black person in that way."

CONGRESSMAN EMMANUEL CELLER, 1957: "Rock and Roll has its place and has given great opportunity to talent, especially among the colored people, but the music of Elvis Presley and his animal gyrations violate all that I know to be in good taste."

BILLY SMITH: "Elvis was Southern, and so he joked sometimes. But Elvis had all kinds of people working for him—black, white, Jews, Italians, Mexicans, Greeks . . . Elvis always looked at the person, not what race he or she was."

BONO: "The Beatles, the Rolling Stones, Creedence Clearwater Revival were all introduced to the blues through Elvis. He was already doing what the civil-rights movement was demanding: breaking down barriers."

JOE PERRY, AEROSMITH GUITARIST: "Probably the most important thing he did was bring black music to white ears . . . You can't say enough about what he contributed. He laid the groundwork for breaking out, and the rest is history."

Elvis as Pacer Burton in Flaming Star, *1960.*

CHET ATKINS: "He was white, but he sang black. It wasn't socially acceptable for white kids to buy black records at the time. Elvis filled a void."

LITTLE RICHARD: "He was an integrator. Elvis was a blessing. They wouldn't let black music through. He opened the door for black music."

RUFUS THOMAS: "It wasn't Elvis who denied black musicians credit, that was white society and white culture."

BILLY SMITH: "Basically, Elvis liked blacks. He liked black music, of course, but he also liked black artists in the business. And black sports heroes."

JACKIE WILSON: "A lot of people have accused Elvis of stealing the black man's music, when in fact, almost every black solo entertainer copied his stage mannerisms from Elvis."

CHUCK D: "Elvis never meant shit to me, but still he was legit. He was a talent. He never meant shit to me because he used a long line of black cats, like Little Richard and Chuck Berry, that, to me, had more talent than he did."

Book:
Race, Rock, and Elvis (Music in American Life), by Michael T. Bertrand, University of Illinois Press, 2000.

RACQUETBALL

Elvis' interest in racquetball began in the Seventies when his main physician, Dr. Nichopoulos, suggested that they play together as a way to keep his weight down and stay healthy. Elvis played at the Jewish Community Center, at Memphis State University and at the YMCA before having his own court built in an outhouse at Graceland in 1975. Elvis last played racquetball just hours before he died.

RACQUETBALL BUSINESS VENTURE

In early 1976, Elvis went into a partnership with Dr. Nichopoulos, Joe Esposito and property developer T. Michael McMahon to develop a nation-wide racquetball club franchise under the "Presley Center Courts" brand. Elvis entered the deal believing that all he would be contributing was his name. In exchange, he would be helping out pals Joe Esposito and Dr. Nick, and retain a 25% stake in the venture. He was furious when he found out that he was expected to fund the venture too. He told Red West that the project ballooned to $1.3 million, which would have required him to mortgage Graceland. Elvis pulled out of the deal before the year was out. The whole experience put a serious dent in his previously rock solid relationships with Esposito and Nichopoulos. Michael McMahon took Elvis to court for breach of contract a year later. Elvis settled out of court, reputedly by extending the property developer a $50,000 loan.

ELVIS SAID: "What started out just as a friendship and favor and everything just turned into a $1,300,000 project."

RADIO

The centrality of radio to the music industry when Elvis was growing up is hard to comprehend in the age of MTV and MP3s. The radio was one way that Elvis listened to R'n'B and the kind of music his folks would not have had at home; all he had to do was tune in to Memphis station WDIA.

Radio was also the way that most people first heard Elvis. Popular regional radio DJs had the power to make a newcomer's career. Elvis conquered his initial fans at shows organized by popular radio DJs across the Mid-South, and picked local DJ Bob Neal as his first proper manager. Before he had made half a dozen live appearances, Elvis and his band played on West Memphis radio station KWEM.

Chart positions were based partly on airplay (hence the power of DJs and, later in the Fifties, the payola scandal that rocked the industry).

According to consolidated Elvis legend, the first DJ to play an Elvis record on air was Dewey Phillips. Such was the reaction from his listeners that he played the song over and over, and on the spot invited the unknown young singer down to the radio station for an impromptu interview. True Elvis aficionados know that it was actually Fred Cook on WREC who first broadcast Elvis over the airwaves, after Marion Keisker brought him a copy of the freshly-cut disk. Cook took Elvis' version of "Blue Moon Of Kentucky" off the record deck after just thirty seconds, declaring it to be "the worst piece of shit I've ever heard." Other contenders for that first spin were DJs Uncle Richard (WMPS) and Sleepy-Eyed John Lepley (WHHM), both of whom were given advance copies of Elvis' inaugural single.

There is, it should be noted, a possibility that Elvis' first radio broadcast actually predated the summer of 1954 by nine years. His talent show act at the Mississippi-Alabama Fair and Dairy Show may well have received coverage on local Tupelo radio station WELO. It has also been claimed that juvenile Elvis had a turn on the WELO Black and White Jamboree show, hosted by Mississippi Slim.

In late February 1955, en route to Cleveland Ohio for their first show outside the South, Elvis and band members Scotty Moore and Bill Black stopped off at radio stations to introduce themselves and try and drum up some air time promotion. This was the regular process by which they enticed new fans in new territories.

By the time he had become a national star, in late 1956 Elvis put in a performance at the WDIA Goodwill Review, a charitable event staged by all-black radio station WDIA in

Memphis, known as "The Mother Station of the Negroes," though segregation was still in place in the US and strictly-speaking he was barred from singing. Curiously, at one stage WDIA had a policy not to play music by white artist Elvis.

A number of DJs willfully lost their jobs by defying radio station bans on playing Elvis records. A San Francisco DJ called Bruce Vanderhoof played "Love Me Tender" more than a dozen times in a row to make his point.

In 1971, Jerry Hopkins put together a 12-hour radio show called "The Elvis Presley Story," narrated by Wink Martindale. Elvis marveled to friends that anybody would want to spend 12 hours talking about him.

Elvis' strong radio presence lives on undiminished by his death. Since 1988, DJ Jay Gordon has been hosting a weekly Elvis slot called "Elvis Only" on stations across the US and Canada.

Elvis is the first recording artist to have his very own exclusive channel. Broadcast daily from Graceland, Elvis Radio features a roster of DJs with strong Elvis connections and people knew him personally. Regular slots include "The Elvis Radio Vaults," "Elvis Soundtrack Songs," "Elvis IQ," and "Celebrity Hotline with George Klein." In the summer of 2004, Sirius announced that it was launching an All Elvis radio station on Satellite Radio.

Book:
Elvis: A Radio History from 1954 to 1955, by Aaron Webster, Republic of Texas 2002.

RADIO RECORDERS
(7000 SANTA MONICA BOULEVARD, CORNER OF ORANGE DRIVE)

In September 1956, Elvis recorded material for his second RCA album at this independent studio in Hollywood, after an itinerant nine months during which RCA had him recording in half a dozen studios.

Elvis immediately got on well with chief engineer Thorne "Thorny" Nogar, assisted among others by Jim Malloy and Bones Howe. Elvis tended to use the Annex building at (1032 N. Sycamore Ave.), known as "Studio B."

RCA failed to persuade Elvis to record in Nashville for any longer than a brief period, and once his Hollywood career began, it made sense to organize his recording commitments for the label around his film schedule. In January 1957, Elvis returned to Radio Recorders to lay down "Don't Be Cruel," "All Shook Up," "I Believe," "Peace In The Valley" and "Take My Hand, Precious Lord." In April 1957, he recorded soundtrack material for *Jailhouse Rock* in advance of shooting. It was at the studio that Elvis first met songwriters Leiber and Stoller, who had penned "Hound Dog" and "Love Me." In late summer, during the middle of a heatwave, Elvis somehow managed to get into the mood to cut tracks for his first Christmas album, plus some new singles material including "Treat Me Nice."

Elvis laid down tracks for Paramount movie *King Creole* in January and early February 1958 with a vastly expanded band including a full brass section of Ray Siegel, Mahlon Clark, John Ed Buckner, Justin Gordon, Elmer Schneider and Warren Smith, plus additional back-up singer Kitty White. Various Jordanaires also mucked in on percussion duties. RCA was mustard keen to get Elvis to record plenty of material to eke out while he was away on military service. Alas for the label, Elvis was not in the mood, especially when he found out that owing to behind the scenes wrangles, Leiber and Stoller would not be working with him in the studio as producers. Elvis took 48 takes to nail B-side track "Doncha' Think It's Time," his love affair with Radio Recorders seemingly on the wane.

Elvis began work on the *G.I. Blues* soundtrack at RCA's Hollywood studio in 1960, but soon transferred to Radio Recorders because he felt much more comfortable in the more intimate studio environs. A couple of months later he recorded the soundtrack to *Flaming Star*. Before the year was out he was working on yet another soundtrack, this time *Wild in the Country*.

In the last week of March 1961 Elvis, his Nashville based studio group and LA session players laid down fifteen tracks in three very fruitful days, destined mainly for the *Blue Hawaii* soundtrack.

Elvis recorded the soundtrack to *Kid Galahad* here in late October 1961, and began work on *Girls! Girls! Girls!* in late March 1962. *It Happened at the World's Fair* followed in September 1962, and *Fun in Acapulco* in January 1963. Six months later Elvis laid down the soundtrack for *Viva Las Vegas*, by this time working with a vast cohort of musicians that included a brass section, organist and additional percussionist, as well as his usual complement of backing singers. This session was the first where Elvis resorted to separate overdubs for his vocal track.

Elvis broke a long string of soundtrack recordings in 1963 when the Colonel persuaded him to record the songs for *Kissin' Cousins* at RCA's facilities in Nashville and then do additional vocal work at the MGM soundstage.

He was back in March 1964, however, to do soundtrack recordings for *Roustabout*, and then in June for *Girl Happy*. On that occasion he racked up 36 takes on "Do Not Disturb" and still was not satisfied with the song's quality. A year later, he was back at Radio Recorders making music for *Frankie and Johnny* with his regular Nashville musicians plus a couple of additions.

Elvis began 1966 working on the soundtrack to *Spinout* with his Nashville players. In late June 1966 he returned to work on the soundtrack to *Double Trouble*, though he finished off the job on the MGM soundstage. What had changed in the interim was meeting new producer Felton Jarvis, with whom he had an enormously productive recording session in Nashville. For his next movie soundtrack, *Easy Come, Easy Go*, Elvis started right on the Paramount soundstage, ending his long association with the Los Angeles studio.

RADIO RECORDERS HISTORY

For many years LA's largest independent facility, Radio Recorders attracted a succession of top music stars signed with record labels that did not have their own West Coast recording facilities, including the likes of Jimmie Rodgers, Louis Armstrong and Sam Cooke among others. The studio also recorded the first stereo album in the US (a 1957 Louis Armstrong recording), and was a technology pioneer in many respects.

Originally founded in 1933, the company's name derived from its main business at the time, recording radio shows and advertising slots for major radio stars of the day. In the late Forties, Radio Recorders moved to their premises on Santa Monica Blvd., which had originally been built by the Victor Talking Machine Company in the late Twenties.

In 1960, the company merged with Universal Recorders and, as Radio Universal Recorders, advertised itself as the largest recording studio in the U.S. It was taken over by the EMC Corporation in 1963. By the mid-Sixties, the facility had changed its name to "The Annex."

Despite the studio changing hands a number of times since Elvis' day, not only is it still a recording facility, the recording space previously known as Studio B has been renamed Studio E in honor of Elvis. Since 1986, the facility has been run by Paul Schwartz under the name Studio 56.

See also RECORDING SESSIONS.

ERNST JORGENSEN: "Elvis took an instant liking to Thorne [Nogar], finding in him someone whose judgment he could trust, someone who could actually help in the studi.. . .."

"RAGS TO RICHES"

Recorded at Studio B, Nashville, on September 22, 1970, Elvis released this 1953 #1 Tony Bennett number—written by Richard Adler and Jerry Ross, and previously an R&B hit for Billy Ward and the Dominoes—as a single in February 1971 with "Where Did They Go, Lord" on the B-side. The single sold around 400,000 copies, but failed to rise any higher than #33 in the charts.

The song has been included on collectors' albums *Elvis Aron Presley (The Silver Box)*, *Walk A Mile In My Shoes* and *That's The Way It Is—Special Edition*. *Essential Elvis Vol. 4* offered an alternate take, with another alternate on 2002 release *The Nashville Marathon*.

Elvis rarely if ever sang this song live, an exception being his New Year's Eve 1976 concert in Pittsburgh, available on the FTD album *New Year's Eve*. Rumors have also circulated that Elvis covered the song during his Sun years.

RAINMAKER, THE

Elvis was handed the script of this 1956 Burt Lancaster and Katharine Hepburn movie for his Hollywood screen test. There was some speculation that he was being considered for the starring role in this movie, through pre-production was already well underway by the time William Morris agent Harry Kalcheim sent Elvis the script. This did not prevent Elvis from telling an interviewer in April 1956 that he would be making his motion picture debut in this movie—most likely not in the Lancaster role but in a secondary role. *The Rainmaker* started shooting in June 1956, and garnered two Academy award nominations.

"RAINY NIGHT IN GEORGIA"

Elvis sings the title of this Tony Joe White song in a limousine with pals in 1972 documentary *Elvis on Tour*. The song had been a big hit for Brook Benton in 1970, and was later covered by a slew of great vocalists including Ray Charles and Randy Crawford. Reputedly Elvis was due to record this song during his aborted 1977 recording session in Nashville.

"RAISED ON ROCK"

Elvis was preaching to the converted with this Mark James song which he laid down at Stax Studio on July 23, 1973. It appeared as a single soon after, shipping at the end of September with "For Ol' Times Sake" on the B-side Despite the promising combination of Elvis and Stax, the single peaked at #41 in the charts; it sold 250,000 copies over its nine-week chart run.

The song served as title track to an album released a few months later. It was anthologized in *Walk A Mile In My Shoes*; Mark James' version of the song appeared on FTD release *Writing For The King*; a rough mix is the 2007 FTD *Raised On Rock* release.

TOP: A still photo from Elvis' screen test for *The Rainmaker*. Had Elvis taken the role, it would have been his first ever film role. BOTTOPM: Elvis screen testing opposite Frank Faylen.

RAISED ON ROCK

This LP—subtitled "For Ol' Times Sake"—hit the stores in October 1973, after RCA managed to cobble together enough material in two recording sessions over the summer by adding a couple of tracks recorded at Elvis' home in Palm Springs. Record executives were surprised when this one sold fewer than 200,000 copies, never rising above #50 in the charts in 13 weeks.

TRACK LISTING:
1. Raised On Rock
2. Are You Sincere
3. Find Out What's Happening
4. I Miss You
5. Girl Of Mine
6. For Ol' Times Sake
7. If You Don't Come Back
8 Just A Little Bit
9. Sweet Angeline
10. Three Corn Patches

FTD released a 2-disc version in 2007 featuring remastered originals and outtakes.

RANDLE, BILL
(B. WILLIAM MCKINLEY RANDLE JR. 1923-2004)

Time Magazine named Bill Randle America's Top DJ in the mid-1950s. Randle was one of the first music professionals outside Elvis' home territory to spot his talent and take a chance on actively promoting the young hopeful.

Born in Detroit, Michigan on March 14, 1923, Randle initially worked as a jazz concert promoter before becoming a disk jockey and landing a slot at Cincinnati station WERE, where he got into trouble with radio station managers for playing records by black artists. By the mid-Fifties he had a syndicated Saturday morning show on CBS out of New York. He started playing Elvis record "Good Rockin' Tonight" in Cleveland rather than New York because he thought it would go down better outside the Big Apple.

Randle was the first DJ outside the South to book Elvis on tours. He brought Elvis to Ohio several times in 1955, including one occasion that October when he invited Elvis to perform on a bill that was being filmed as part of a documentary about his life, *The Pied Piper of Cleveland: A Day in the Life of a Famous Disc Jockey*. If it had ever been released, the documentary would have been Elvis' first appearance on film.

For a spell, Randle was a frontrunner to take over Elvis' management contract before Colonel Parker won the day. Randle entered negotiations with song publishers Hill & Range about signing Elvis to a management deal while Colonel Parker was wrapping up his own deal with the music publishing company.

With a proven track record of promoting newcomers through extensive airplay on his radio shows, Randle's contacts were instrumental in fixing up Elvis' first TV appearance—on Jimmy and Tommy Dorsey's "Stage Show"—in early 1956, though most biographers credit Colonel Parker with fixing this up. Randle is said to have persuaded producer Jackie Gleason to cut an extravagant six-slot deal (for a newcomer) in exchange for an under-the-table publishing kickback. Randle's almost prescient introduction of Elvis on the show—on which Elvis was hailed as "Randle's latest discovery"—recorded the moment as "television history" in the making.

Randle had previously tried to get Elvis a slot on the "Arthur Godfrey Talent Scouts," and was still within Elvis' orbit in April 1956 when he played his first engagement in Las Vegas.

In the late Fifties, Randle helped to establish the careers of Bobby Darin and Sam Cooke.

After his career in radio, Randle became a lawyer and a university lecturer, though he kept in his hand at his first love, radio, hosting a show up to his death.

PETER GURALNICK: "Bill Randle was a legend in radio at that time."

TONY BENNETT: "I would not be where I am today if it were not for Bill Randle."

RANDOLPH, BOOTS
(B. HOMER LOUIS RANDOLPH III, 1927-2007)

Born in Paducah, Kentucky on June 3, 1927, Boots Randolph was a saxophonist who first played in the studio with Elvis on an all-night recording session in Nashville in early April 1960 and returned for sessions up to September 1967, helping out on claves or percussion as required. He played on a total of eight Elvis soundtrack albums, and claims to e the only sax player to solo with Elvis. He also performed live with Elvis at his 1961 Hawaii charity show.

Randolph became a regular player with RCA's Chet Atkins in the Fifties, and also played sax at sessions for Owen Bradley. He played with Roy Orbison on "Pretty Woman," and is the man who played the crazy sax on "Yakety Sax," better known as the theme to *The Benny Hill Show*. He also has credits on records by a whole range of artists, from Buddy Holly to Johnny Cash. In the Seventies, Randolph opened his own club in Nashville.

RAT PACK

See SAMMY DAVIS JR., DEAN MARTIN and FRANK SINATRA.

RAY, JOHNNIE
(B. JOHN ALVIN RAY, 1927-1990)

For modern music historians, Ray is the missing link between Frank Sinatra and Elvis Presley as the magnet for screaming female fans. Born in Dallas, Oregon on January 19, 1927, Ray became one of the original teen idols with his single "Cry," backed by the Four Lads, which spent three months at the top of the charts in 1951; B-Side cut "Little White Cloud That Cried" made it to #2.

Born with American-Indian ancestry in his bloodline, Ray overcame almost complete deafness to become a pop star. His music owed much to the Rhythm & Blues artists that young Elvis listened to before striking out into showbiz—when they first heard him on the radio, many people thought that Ray, like Elvis a few years later, was black. Ray's peculiarly plaintive singing delivery earned him the epithet the "Nabob of Sob" and the "the Prince of Wail."

On his rise to prominence Elvis was sometimes compared with this singer, whose energy-charged stage performances included smashing up instruments and rolling around on the floor. DJ Bill Randle described Elvis as a little like Johnnie Ray when he introduced him to a national TV audience for the first time, on "Stage Show," in early 1956; a South Carolina newspaper wrote that Elvis was like "Johnnie Ray with a little of Frankie Laine thrown in."

The teenaged girls who went crazy for Ray when he performed were unaware that offstage his preference was for men. Television, the movies (*There's No Business Like Show Business*) and foreign tours followed, until Ray's career went into terminal decline after a court case for indecency in Australia in the late Fifties.

Elvis met Ray on his first performing engagement in Las Vegas, in May 1956. Elvis saw Ray again in Las Vegas in late 1962. As well as "Cry," Ray's hits included "All Of Me," "Such A Night" and "Flip, Flop and Fly," the last two of which Elvis also covered.

Ray made something of a comeback in the early Seventies. He died of alcohol-related problems in 1990.

RCA (RADIO CORPORATION OF AMERICA) / RCA VICTOR

Parker worked hard to convince Country A&R chief Steve Sholes that the buzz he was getting from his field agents was all true. Parker did not let a little thing like Sam Phillips' disinterest in selling his star artist's contract get in the way; when Phillips informed Parker in early 1955 that he was not interested, the Colonel tried to interest Sholes in another of his artists, Tommy Sands. This was many months before Parker had any official role in Elvis' management.

By early 1955, a number of major record companies had been alerted to the commotion the new singer was causing. In May 1955, Elvis' stock at RCA began to rise vertiginously as the label scrambled to sign its first newfangled rock 'n' roll act. Sholes—who knew Parker from his dealings on behalf of Eddy Arnold and Hank Snow—heard encouraging reports about the rising young star through RCA's East Tennessee, Virginia and Carolinas representative Brad McCuen and Country & Western promotions chief Chick Crumpacker, who took in Elvis' show Meridian, Mississippi (which they attended to watch new RCA signing Jimmie Rodgers Snow) and Richmond, Virginia. Crumpacker later said: "What really got the listeners was his energy . . . the effect was galvanic." He sent all four of Elvis' singles to his boss Steve Sholes.

RCA's interest redoubled as Colonel Tom Parker schemed to extricate Elvis from his contract with Sun Records. Some biographers have written that before Parker entered into his management contract with Elvis, in July 1955, RCA made Parker a $12,000 payment for "settlement and delivery of Presley to RCA," or, alternatively, a $5,000 bonus for Presley and a further $20,000 advance payable on future record royalties. The package included a guarantee that Elvis would appear on network television within 60 days of signing on—among other interests in the nascent TV industry, RCA was a sponsor of the "Milton Berle Show."

By late October, when Colonel Parker had informed Sam Phillips that he was going to buy out Elvis' Sun records contract, RCA singles manager Bill Bullock and Steve Sholes told the Colonel that the company was not prepared to go beyond $25,000. The Colonel prevailed, but not before RCA tested the Colonel's mettle, only agreeing to the deal Colonel Parker had brokered with Sam Phillips for $35,000 plus back royalties that Sun owed Elvis, on the last day of the option, November 15, 1955.

All the while, the Colonel had been negotiating with other major labels: Ahmet Ertegun's Atlantic Records offered a maximum of $25,000, while Columbia went up as high as $40,000. RCA officially announced their success at a contract signing ceremony at the Sun Studio on November 21, 1955. Elvis' new contract was for a minimum of eight tracks per year; it included single-year options for a further two years in exchange for a 5% royalty. The $35,000 Sun contract purchase price was to be paid back from half of Elvis' royalty, while the singer also received a $5,000 non-refundable bonus. Other sources have put the final figure as high as $50,000, which would explain why Columbia were frozen out of the dealings at a late stage. To give an idea of the scale of this deal, Atlantic had just bought the contract of proven recording star Ray Charles for $2,500.

ELVIS' GOLD CAR ON TOUR
FOR RCA VICTOR RECORDS

A rare RCA promotional postcard featuring "Elvis' Gold Car."

The Colonel shrewdly involved song publishers Hill & Range in the deal, thereby avoiding having to put up too much of his own money to wrest Elvis away from the record label that discovered him.

Ten days later, Elvis and Colonel Parker were in New York meeting RCA president Larry Kanaga. Publicity director Anne Fulchino set up a photo shoot of the label's newest signing with top executives, Eddy Arnold, and shots that would appear on Elvis' first album.

RCA ISSUED THE FOLLOWING INTERNAL PRESS RELEASE SOON AFTER SIGNING ELVIS.

BIGGEST C & W RECORD NEWS OF THE YEAR!

In <u>Elvis Presley</u> we've acquired the most dynamic and sought-after new artist in country music today, one who's topped the "most promising" category in every trade and consumer poll held during 1955!

Promotion is being spearheaded with disc jockey records to the entire Pop and C&W "A" lists, and initial coverage of more than 4,000 destinations!

. . .

The tunes: I FORGOT TO REMEMBER TO FORGET and MYSTERY TRAIN. The number: 20/47-6357. The name: <u>ELVIS PRESLEY</u>, one that will be your guarantee of sensational plus-sales in the months to come!

RCA's first move was to re-release Elvis' final single on Sun, "I Forgot To Remember To Forget" b/w "Mystery Train." The big label's strong promotion campaign on Country & Western record stations sent the single right back up to number one in the new year. Within a month of the official signing ceremony, RCA had re-released every one of Elvis' Sun singles.

Elvis chose the ballads "I'm Counting On You" and "I Was The One" for his first RCA recording session in Nashville in January, out of the ten songs that RCA executive Steve Sholes had sent him. The recording session produced a much fuller sound than on Elvis' Sun recordings, as Elvis was backed by accomplished musicians Chet Atkins, Floyd Cramer and a backing trio featuring Jordanaire Gordon Stoker and two Speer brothers, even though RCA was keen to replicate the pared-back, echo-laden freshness that Sam Phillips had so effortlessly achieved at Sun.

That first recording session generated significant concern within the company. Anxiety about the quality of Elvis' first songs was compounded by single "Heartbreak Hotel" selling very slowly to begin with: it took more than four weeks to make it into the charts. With Carl Perkins' new single "Blue Suede Shoes" racing up the charts, executives wondered whether they had signed the wrong Sun artist. Steve Sholes reacted by bringing forward plans for an Elvis LP and an EP, though Elvis was so locked in to a busy touring schedule that it was hard to find time for him to go into a studio. Doubts began to dissipate after Elvis got his first national exposure on CBS's "Stage Show" and the waves Elvis had been making regionally began to ripple across the nation.

In his first year with the label, RCA shipped everything it could to try and make back its investment and cash in on Elvis' rising popularity as quickly as possible, just in case his meteoric rise was going to be followed by a rapid fall. The label shipped three Elvis records on March 23, 1956: an EP entitled *Elvis Presley* with his version of "Blue Suede Shoes"; double EP *Elvis Presley* with eight tracks, all taken from Elvis' first LP, and that first self-titled LP. The bulk of the material had come with Elvis from Sun when RCA signed him up.

Elvis' Nashville recording session in April 1956 yielded just one song, "I Want You, I Need You, I Love You," as he struggled to adapt to his new home, new musicians and a new recording environment.

After all of the scandal whipped up by Elvis' pelvis-powered appearance on the "Milton Berle Show" in mid-1956, RCA's vice president personally reassured Colonel Parker that the negative press would not be a problem.

Elvis' next block of studio time for RCA was at the company's New York studios, where on July 2, 1956 he recorded "Hound Dog," "Don't Be Cruel" and "Any Way You Want Me." Steve Sholes was hardly a hands-on studio producer, and Elvis' working relationship with Chet Atkins, brought in to produce his first RCA session, was not one that he wanted to pursue, so for the first time Elvis was completely in control of the recording session and was able to insist on doing as many takes as he needed to make the songs sound just the way he wanted: in the case of "Hound Dog," 31 takes.

At the end of August 1956, RCA contemporaneously issued seven Elvis singles in an unprecedented sales barrage. Six of the singles featured the twelve tracks on Elvis' first album, while the seventh, "Shake, Rattle And Roll"/ "Lawdy, Miss Clawdy," had previously been issued on EP. All told, these singles sold 1.6 million copies; only one of them, "Blue Moon," actually reached the charts.

Looking to the long term, the Colonel was not pleased with such massive exposure and let the label know. He also fought a rearguard action against RCA's desire to surround Elvis with much more lush and complex instrumental recordings. The Colonel believed that Elvis fans wanted to hear Elvis; Elvis, on the other hand, was a big fan of vocal harmonies and in later years sometimes insisted on RCA remixing a track before release because his voice had been brought forward in the mix at the expense of the backing singers.

SONG SELECTION

In theory, Elvis had the right of approval over which songs RCA released, though often he followed the Colonel's advice. Many biographers have insisted on Elvis' control over this aspect of his career. The truth is a little more complex: for the bulk of his career the material from which Elvis could choose was channeled to him through song company Hill & Range. The vast majority of soundtrack material consisted of songs written to strict criteria for specific film scenes. During periods when RCA had very little Elvis product available, they put out what they had, even if that meant using songs that Elvis had, for one reason or another, decided he did not want to include on his upcoming releases. Elvis' endgame-defying comeback in the late Sixties was driven to a large extent by his striking out to new song sources at American Studio in Memphis, but by the early Seventies RCA had resorted to recycling masters that Elvis had previously nixed—the 1972 *Love Letters* album being a case in point.

Colonel Parker uprated Elvis' contract with RCA in September 1956, obtaining an advance of $135,000 plus weekly $1,000 payments. A highly appreciative Elvis sent a happy anniversary letter to RCA President General David Sarnoff in October that year.

Four months elapsed between early September 1956 and January 1957 without RCA succeeding in getting Elvis back into the recording studio. At Radio Recorders in Hollywood, Elvis laid down material for a single and a gospel EP before recording *Loving You* soundtrack material. The harrowing experience of trying to reconcile film producer Hal Wallis' and RCA's divergent opinions about which were the best takes and cuts persuaded the Colonel to try and keep RCA executives out of movie soundtrack recordings.

In January 1957, RCA exercised its option to extend Elvis' contract a further five years to October 15, 1966. Reacting to RCA's previous Elvis binge—when the record label released every Elvis song they had as a single—Colonel Parker told Steve Sholes that he did not want more than four Elvis singles released in any one year. To make his point, a single that had been lined up for release in the first half of 1957, "One Night" backed with "I Beg Of You," was put on hold indefinitely while Elvis worked on tracks for *Jailhouse Rock*.

In September 1957, RCA hired songwriters Leiber and Stoller to work for the label as independent producers, not just with Elvis (as they had done on *Jailhouse Rock*) but with other talent too.

Colonel Parker put the kibosh on a suggestion by Bill Bullock that Elvis make a classical album in 1958. The record label was further disappointed when, during his final sessions at Radio Recorders before heading off for his military service, Elvis produced very few finished tracks beyond his requirement for the *King Creole* soundtrack. Worse, because Elvis had final say on what cuts could be released, he embargoed some of the material because he wasn't satisfied with the finished

The 1960 album, *Elvis is Back!*, was Elvis Presley's first album release after being honorably discharged from the Army.

performance: "Your Cheatin' Heart," for instance, did not see the light of day until 1965.

RCA tempted Elvis to return to Nashville for the first time in two years on furlough from the Army in June 1958. All five of the tracks he recorded at that session, including "I Need Your Love Tonight" and "A Big Hunk O' Love," wound up on singles as the record company eked out the twelve songs they had in the can over the next two years; Elvis remained uncooperative when it came to allowing tracks he considered "unfinished" to be released. Also in 1958 (or 1959, depending on accounts), RCA purged a significant portion of the outtakes they had purchased from Sun Records when they bought out Elvis' contract, to make way for new material. For many latter-day fans of early Elvis, this was an unforgivable move, though it should be remembered that Sam Phillips regularly re-used tape at Sun, so RCA may not have destroyed a large amount of material.

Steve Sholes tried and failed to persuade Colonel Parker to get Elvis to record some new material while he was out on his military service in Germany. Parker told Sholes that it would simply have to ration its Elvis releases to one every twenty weeks. Parker also turned down Bill Bullock's offer to fly Elvis and several friends to Nashville for a three-day recording session. Desperate for new material, RCA even suggested that Elvis simply sing karaoke-style into a tape machine and they would add the instrumentals back in the States. The Colonel held firm.

In 1960, the Colonel renegotiated Elvis' RCA contract in time for his homecoming from the Army. As well as improved royalties and approval on all publicity material, new clauses meant that Elvis' movie recordings would count towards his required annual output of two LPs and eight singles, and all fees to musicians and other musical personnel were now excluded from Elvis' (and therefore the Colonel's) royalties. This new deal effectively cut RCA out of the process of material selection, as Hill & Range were in charge of providing songs for three movies a year. Elvis (and the Colonel) still had the power to decide which of the songs presented to them they wanted to record, but the potential pool of material was much reduced as by this time leading songwriters were reluctant to submit to the harsh royalty terms the Colonel imposed.

So important was Elvis' return to the States that RCA dubbed his March 4, 1960 homecoming "E Day." RCA welcomed Elvis back with a gift of a top of the range TV/radio as a reward for breaking the 50 million record sales barrier. Within two weeks, RCA ensconced Elvis in their Nashville recording studios, and then cranked up

their pressing plants to full volume to manufacture a million copies of new single "Stuck On You" for release on March 23. Two weeks later, Elvis recorded a further twelve songs in Nashville, and RCA started pressing the critically-acclaimed *Elvis Is Back!* LP. Later that year, in addition to film-related releases, the label released Elvis' first gospel album, *His Hand in Mine*, underlining Elvis' newfound mainstream appeal after doing his duty and serving in the Army.

The Colonel kicked off 1961 by further improving the terms of Elvis' RCA deal with a guaranteed $400,000 annual payment against royalties (up from $300,000). In his first five years with RCA, Elvis had sold a staggering 75 million records and the label was not about to let him go. The deal included guaranteed royalties of 5% on a million sales for Elvis' singles, regardless of how many copies they actually sold.

RCA executive Bill Bullock continued to try to persuade Elvis to have a recording studio built at Graceland, paid for by the record company, as an attempt to circumvent Elvis' reluctance to record in Nashville. RCA retracted the offer whey they realized that if they built a studio for Elvis, many of their top artists would want one too. Instead, RCA gave Elvis a selection of early Sixties hi-tech.

The Colonel continued to have his say in what Elvis tracks RCA released. He told Bill Bullock that he wanted to see "Wild In The Country" backed with a second song from the movie. In the end, the label went with Elvis' suggestion to release "I Feel So Bad" on the single, as the A-Side rather than the B-Side.

Colonel Parker continued to fine-tune Elvis' RCA contract, raising the amount Elvis earned as a guaranteed advance on royalties. He also set the precedent for a 50/50 split between Elvis and himself on "side projects" (which included free office space for the Colonel at RCA's LA headquarters), and then added an additional ex-gratia annual $100,000 payment (later reduced to $75,000), and an additional one percent royalty for the Colonel and Elvis to split down the line.

In early 1962, Colonel Parker laid down the law to RCA that Elvis and Elvis alone would select what recorded material appeared on his albums. The Colonel also told Bill Bullock that it was up to the Colonel whether or not he would allow RCA to release the soundtracks to Elvis' movies on the label.

In 1963, executive Anne Fulchino visited Elvis on set in Hollywood to see if she could persuade him to record material not strictly associated with his movies. Elvis agreed that he would like to do other songs, but the Colonel got wind of the proposal and headed it off. RCA top brass then circulated a memo instructing everybody to "always be friendly with the Colonel."

Before the end of 1963, RCA extended its option on Elvis' contract to tie him down until the end of 1971. January 1964 proved to be Elvis' last RCA-only recording session for almost two and a half years. Before returning to the studio to record gospel album *How Great Thou Art* in May 1966, Elvis worked exclusively on soundtrack songs. The material that RCA accumulated through 1963 and January 1964, originally intended for album release, was put to one side to clear the way for planned soundtrack releases. Parceled out as B-sides and bonus tracks over the following years, these tracks were finally released together in 1990 as *For The Asking (The Lost Album)*.

The label next acceded to the Colonel's demands for a rejig of his contract in late 1965. Under the revised terms, as well as extending the deal a year to 1972, Elvis' non-refundable annual advance on royalties was raised to $300,000 per year. Royalties remained at 7% on domestic sales and 6% on foreign, rather than the standard rate of 5%. The Colonel also added a $175,000 bonus to the package, and raised his own annual "photographs and consulting" fee to $30,000.

In early 1966, RCA took up their option to extend Elvis' contract to the end of December 1974. The Colonel took this as a cue to renegotiate the whole deal, ultimately extending it all the way through to 1980. Though the annual nonrefundable advance remained unchanged at $300,000, the Colonel agreed to a lower rate of $200,000 in future—a sign that Elvis' worth to RCA had peaked. Elvis received a further $100,000 advance in 1966 for the licensing of his music on brand new music format eight-track.

On January 8, 1966 RCA sent Elvis a birthday telegram thanking him for his "understanding and cooperation" in making 1965 the biggest year so far for their partnership. That year Bill Bullock was replaced by Harry Jenkins as RCA's liaison with the Colonel. RCA tried a new tack, releasing two gospel singles at the same time from the *His Hand in Mine* album, (A-sides "Joshua Fit The Battle" and "Milky White Way"), in an attempt to build on the success of "Crying In The Chapel," Elvis' most successful single in some time, which had been released the previous Easter. RCA had also wanted Elvis to lay down some new pop material at this time, but the singer was more focused on his spiritual songs, even failing to record a Christmas single, on which the Colonel and RCA executives had hoped to turn around Elvis' diminishing singles sales.

A year later, the Colonel negotiated an additional $60,000 payment for the *Clambake* soundtrack album and promotion for Elvis' 1957 Christmas album. In July 1967, RCA set up a rare non-soundtrack recording session for Elvis at their Studio A facility on Sunset Boulevard in LA. By this time they had practically no new unreleased material left for singles, not even songs that Elvis had recorded but initially embargoed for release. The Colonel decided to postpone this session after Elvis associate Richard Davis was involved in a car accident in which a gardener was killed near Elvis' home; the session was eventually rescheduled for early September in Nashville.

RCA paid out additional monies in 1968 for Elvis releases above and beyond his annual contractual obligation of four singles and two albums, notably the LP associated with the 1968 NBC TV Special. Elvis and the Colonel shared $20,000 for this privilege; the Colonel also pocketed a $50,000 payment to his company for promotions. In March 1969, RCA brought out *Elvis Sings Flaming Star* on its fledgling Camden label, a budget offshoot for which it was the first release.

Early in 1969, RCA executive Harry Jenkins proved to be a vital ally for Elvis at American Studio when a row developed over publishing rights that threatened to derail any of the songs that Elvis recorded apart from the Hill and Range-sourced tracks he was contracted to record. If Jenkins had not sided with Elvis, Elvis' career-resurrecting songs "In The Ghetto" or "Suspicious Minds" may never have seen the light of day.

RCA sent Felton Jarvis to record Elvis live in Las Vegas in August 1969 and February 1970, each of which yielded a full album of material old and new, and a rich vein of live performances and recorded rehearsals that made it onto bootleg albums in the Seventies and Eighties (and onto official collectors' releases in the Nineties and Noughties).

RCA paid an additional $20,000 in late 1969 for the live singles ("Suspicious Minds" and "Don't Cry, Daddy") and the *From Vegas to Memphis/From Memphis to Vegas* album that came out of Elvis' summer residency at the International Hotel in Las Vegas.

In December 1969, RCA made a deal to release three Elvis albums in 1970 and a further album in 1971 on its Camden label, in exchange for a $300,000 advance on royalties. This led to the paradoxical situation that fans were presented with bottom-of-the-barrel soundtrack scrapings and a Christmas re-release at the same time as some of the most passionate and challenging work that Elvis ever recorded (during his American Studio sessions), soon to be further compounded by a the four-LP *Worldwide Gold Award Hits* package. As it had done a decade and a half earlier, the record label was keen to maximize its revenues from Elvis after his resurgence. This time round, Parker had no qualms about potential overexposure.

Colonel Parker uprated Elvis' RCA deal in March 1971, with three albums slated for release on the Camden label in 1972 in exchange for an advance of close to $200,000, split 50/50 between them. The big earner at this time was a second *Gold Award Hits* LP, for which the advance payment exceeded half a million dollars.

RCA took full advantage of Elvis' renewed productivity under producer Felton Jarvis. In 1970 and 1971, Elvis managed bumper recording sessions in Nashville, laying down thirty or so tracks each time. With judicious handling, this was enough for three albums and singles for the foreseeable future. However, a multi-day session scheduled for March 1971 had to be cancelled after just one day due to Elvis' ill health, in a foretaste of the problems RCA would encounter from this point on.

Rather than firing off all of this new material at once—much of which showcased Elvis at his heartfelt and committed best—RCA continued to mine Elvis' back catalogue of hits, near misses and movie songs that were beyond the pale even for the pictures for which they had been written.

In early 1972, at the Colonel's promptings, RCA set up RCA Record Tours to help coordinate Elvis' nationwide live appearances, as the label was gearing up for a new Elvis live album. The record label originally recorded material for the album in Las Vegas, but in the end switched the project to Elvis' Madison Square Garden performances in June that year. In late 1972, RCA scraped the bottom of Elvis' admittedly deep barrel with an album that rehashed stale movie songs along with recent hit single "Burning Love."

RCA was a major player in negotiations for the unprecedented *Aloha from Hawaii* worldwide live satellite broadcast of an Elvis concert in early 1973. The company produced the tour through its RCA Record Tours arm and released the LP simultaneously worldwide. RCA remained the sole sponsor of Elvis' concerts up and down the country through to the end of 1973, having coughed up a $4 million advance on gate receipts.

In early 1973, RCA put pen to paper to a significantly different Elvis deal when it purchased his entire back catalogue for a one-off $5.4 million payment. The deal raised a large sum from songs that had already been released and re-released countless times at a time when Elvis needed the money to pay for his divorce settlement; it also covered all the outtakes and unreleased material, a veritable gold mine for future use. The brainchild of executive Mel Ilberman, the deal covered everything recorded up to the date of signature (March 1, 1973). At the same time Elvis signed a new seven-year deal with RCA for two albums and four singles per year, for a guaranteed half a million dollars annually against royalties. However, after tax Elvis wound up being paid just $2 million for all of his recordings to date. The Colonel failed to keep Elvis' royalty rate at the same high levels as in the past, and as a Memphis court showed in the early Eighties, when all side deals were taken into account, the Colonel actually banked more money from the deal than the client on whose behalf he was supposedly acting.

One immediate effect of the deal was that RCA became more demanding. The company laid out its roadmap for the year: 24 new masters for a pop album, two singles and a gospel album. Elvis was not in any fit state to produce such a large amount of material when he reported to Stax Studios in

the summer of 1973, managing less than half what the record company wanted. By this time he was physically and mentally debilitated by his excessive intake of prescription drugs.

RCA flexed its new-found muscle over Elvis' back catalogue, releasing *Elvis: A Legendary Performer*, Volume 1 in early 1974. As well as classic Elvis hits, the album contained Sun outtakes, interviews, and tracks that had failed to make the cut from Elvis' '68 Comeback Special. The first of a long series for RCA, the Elvis record went gold, selling more than Elvis' next three new studio albums combined, and proving not just that the Colonel had made a big error in selling off his client's most valuable asset, but that Elvis continued to suffer the repercussions of poor song selection. Back-catalogue albums could also be counted on to sell long-term, something that was no longer true of new Elvis releases.

In the summer of 1974, the Colonel resorted to persuading RCA to manufacture a spoken word album of Elvis' onstage banter, for release under the Colonel's own Boxcar label.

RCA continued to have a tough time getting anything new out of Elvis. His March 1975 recording session in LA, the first in fifteen months, produced a bare minimum of material for a new album. Elvis became embroiled in a row with the record company over retaining the services of producer Felton Jarvis: RCA wanted him replaced, Elvis didn't. Elvis won.

RCA bowed to Elvis' evasive tactics by sending a mobile studio to Graceland in late January 1976. After an initial delay, producer Felton Jarvis put twelve new tracks in the can by the end of the first week. A later session at Graceland, however, yielded just a couple of tracks before Elvis' wild behavior scuppered the session.

RCA's last new material from Elvis was recorded on the road by Felton Jarvis during his 1977 tours. On his last ever live performance in Indianapolis, RCA awarded Elvis a special presentation plaque to commemorate their two billionth pressing at their local plant, which happened to be of forthcoming Elvis album *Moody Blue*.

Elvis' death triggered a record buying frenzy among Elvis' fans. Even after stepping up production at all its plants, RCA failed to satisfy worldwide demand for Elvis discs.

RCA was implicated in lawsuits fought and won against Colonel Parker by the Elvis Estate in the early Eighties, for colluding with the Colonel and effectively defrauding their biggest star. By the time of his death, Elvis was estimated to have sold more than half a billion records for the label.

In the years immediately after Elvis' death, RCA issued greatest hits packages and box sets, gradually making available a greater spread of Elvis material, much of it previously unreleased. Joan Deary remained in charge of Elvis releases until her retirement in 1987, after which A&R director Gregg Geller took over the running of Elvis' catalog. Ernst Jorgensen and Roger Semon took over in the late Eighties and set about cataloguing and reissuing the vast wealth of Elvis material that languished in the RCA vaults. Under their impetus, the label released the landmark "Masters" series Elvis' covering Fifties, Sixties, and Seventies recordings, followed in the late Nineties by box sets.

In recent years, the label has reissued improved versions of all of Elvis' catalogue and extra material on themed releases. Since 1999, RCA/BMG has broadly adopted a twin approach to selling Elvis: hit packages and theme-led collections, alongside special collector issues on the *ad hoc* FTD (Follow That Dream) label, which for the first time has officially brought out material that for decades had been left to bootleggers, with the benefit of modern studio technology and remastering techniques. A significant amount of this material, particularly the live shows, have been bought back from collectors.

To commemorate the 50th anniversary of

Elvis' first recording session for RCA, in early 2006 all of Elvis' 21 US #1 hits were reissued as CD singles in a special boxed set.

See also RECORD SALES, RECORDING SESSIONS.

JOAN DEARY: "RCA paid Elvis' recording costs. But compared to other artists of his caliber who went into the studio and recorded for us, his costs were very cheap. He could go into the studio, work all night, and in three sessions you might get six or seven hit songs. With most artists you were lucky if you got one hit."

RCA CORPORATE HISTORY

RCA was initially founded in 1919 by General Electric as its radio arm, manufacturing radio sets. After acquiring the Victor Talking Machine Company in 1929 (and changing its name to RCA Victor), it began to make phonographs too. The company also developed interests in a nationwide network of radio stations through the National Broadcasting Company (NBC).

Just before the Second World War, the company became a pioneering manufacture of TV sets. In the late Forties, RCA brought 45 rpm records to the market. Other RCA-designed formats, such as the 8-track cartridge, were less successful.

In the Seventies, RCA diversified heavily and became a conglomerate before ultimately overstretching itself. The company was sold back to GE in the mid-Eighties, and then GE sold RCA/Ariola records to German partner Bertelsmann to form BMG. BMG merged with Sony Music Entertainment in August 2004 to become Sony BMG; a portion of the company's heritage was acquired by the Thomson company.

RCA RECORDING SESSIONS

Elvis began his RCA recording career on January 10, 1956 at the label's Nashville studios (1525 McGavock Street), with guitarist Chet Atkins and pianist Floyd Cramer augmenting his regular band. He returned the following day for some work with Jordanaires singer Gordon Stoker plus Ben and Brock Speer on backing vocals. After the session, RCA executives were dubious; they had more ballads in the can than they had bargained for, and apart from "Heartbreak Hotel," which they suspected was going to be huge, the sound mix on the other songs was a little muddy. With producer Steve Sholes taking a back seat in production and Chet Atkins not quite hitting it off with Elvis, it was a tough transition for a man who, up until then, had been under the firm stewardship of Sam Phillips in the studio.

Elvis laid down six tracks including "Blue Suede Shoes" at RCA's New York studio (155 E. 24th Street) on January 30 and 31, 1956, with his regular band plus pianist Shorty Long. He added "Shake, Rattle And Roll" and "Lawdy, Miss Clawdy" on February 3, 1956.

In April 1956, Elvis and his band flew to Nashville to record "I Want You, I Need You, I Love You" among others. That July he laid down "Hound Dog," "Don't Be Cruel" and "Any Way You Want Me" at RCA's New York studios while in town for the "Steve Allen Show."

From this point on, Elvis' recording sessions for RCA were more or less restricted to rare outings at Radio Recorders as movie soundtrack session took precedence. He managed one in early September 1956, one in January and February 1957, one in September 1957, and one in February

1958 before heading off to the Army. Two years after his last less than successful attempt, Elvis returned to Nashville (this time "Studio B") in June 1958 on furlough from the Army to record five future single tracks with D. J. Fontana, the Jordanaires, Hank Garland, Chet Atkins, Bob Moore, Buddy Harman and Floyd Cramer. Biographers write that Elvis was impressed by the added punch of the extra band members, and realized how much more he could achieve if he looked beyond his original band.

Elvis was rushed straight back into Studio B in March 1960 to record new single "Stuck On You" and "Fame And Fortune." After the all-night session he told a reporter that "it all came natural again." He returned to Nashville two weeks later, in one marathon all-night session laying down 12 tracks including "It's Now Or Never" and "Are You Lonesome Tonight" with the full complement of Nashville musicians Elvis had worked with before, plus saxophonist Boots Randolph.

Elvis worked on the G.I. Blues soundtrack at RCA's 6363 Sunset Boulevard facility in late April, 1960, but once again the experience persuaded him to return to his preferred West Coast studios, Radio Recorders, for his other soundtrack commitments.

He was back in Nashville in the fall of 1960 to record His Hand in Mine and his upcoming single "Surrender" for RCA, and then again in March 1961 for a marathon all-night session in which he laid down twelve tracks, all of which showcased the more pop-inflected style Elvis had been developing; the bulk of these songs wound up on his next RCA album, Something For Everybody.

Elvis was back at Studio B in late June 1961 to record new singles and material for his 1962 album Pot Luck, and then again in early July 1961 to lay down to tracks for his next movie, Follow That Dream. In October Elvis squeezed out five more tracks at Studio B, including new single "Good Luck Charm"/"Anything That's Part Of You." Elvis completed the material for 1962 album Pot Luck at Studio B over two days in March 1962.

RCA did not have Elvis to themselves again until May 1963, when he cut fourteen tracks at Studio B. Though he went into the studio with the intention of recording an album, these tracks ended up being released piecemeal as singles (starting with "(You're The) Devil in Disguise") and extras on soundtrack albums. After more soundtrack album recording sessions at Radio Recorders in Hollywood, Elvis next went to Studio B in Nashville to lay down the songs for Kissin' Cousins in September 1963.

In January 1964, Elvis rode his Harley from Graceland to Studio B to record tracks including "Memphis Tennessee" and "It Hurts Me." He returned in February 1965 for the Harum Scarum soundtrack session, but did not make it back to the Nashville studios to record specifically for RCA until May 1966. After years of going through the motions, Elvis found renewed vigor with new producer Felton Jarvis, and in four all-night recording sessions laid down enough material for new gospel album How Great Thou Art and plenty of new singles. Some commentators date Elvis' slow return to form in the late Sixties to this moment. He next dubbed vocals for a few more tracks after a session he missed due to illness in June 1966 in Nashville.

Soundtrack work on Clambake was hastily shifted from LA to Studio B in February 1967 when the Colonel realized that Elvis would simply not be torn away from the Circle G ranch he had just bought near Graceland.

An August 1967 recording session in LA was postponed to September and shifted to Nashville. Elvis worked on "Guitar Man," "Big Boss Man" and "You'll Never Walk Alone" (FTD release So High showcases alternates from this period). Three weeks later Elvis was back laying down tracks for his next movie, Stay Away, Joe—in complete contrast to his previous visit he was so upset at the lack of quality of the songs he was expected to sing that he made producer Felton Jarvis promise that one of them, "Dominick," would never see the light of day on vinyl. Elvis recorded some additional soundtrack material plus "U.S. Male" in Nashville in mid-January 1968.

RCA was not directly involved in any of Elvis' "Comeback" recordings for the NBC TV Special, despite issuing a tie-in LP. When Elvis was next in the studio recording tracks for his label, it was under the guidance of Chips Moman at American Studio in early 1969. RCA undertook the first of its live Elvis recordings during his opening Las Vegas residency that summer (for From Memphis To Vegas), and again in February 1970 (for the On Stage album).

In June 1970, after years of preferring recording facilities in LA and, latterly, the American Studio in Memphis, Elvis spent five days at Studio B, recording a whopping 35 masters with a new studio band put together by producer Felton Jarvis, who had just gone full time to produce Elvis' recording sessions and engineer his live performances. By this time, technology had advanced to allow 16-track recording. Material from these sessions fed years of album releases, providing the backbone for Elvis Country and Love Letters From Elvis, as well as material for the upcoming MGM documentary Elvis: That's The Way It Is. FTD release The Nashville Marathon from 2002 features many alternates and outtakes from this session. Elvis was back in Nashville for a two-day recording session after his six-date tour in September 1970.

Elvis next traveled to Nashville in March 1971, where he focused on recording more folk-based material, including Peter, Paul and Mary songs such as "The First Time Ever I Saw Your Face." However, Elvis only managed one full day of recording before he pulled out with eye problems, and was hospitalized for a few days. He returned to Nashville in mid-May to complete the session, in a week laying down thirty masters: gospel tracks, future pop releases, a few off-the-cuff jam sessions and material for a new Christmas album. To get Elvis in the Christmas mood, producer Felton Jarvis had a Christmas tree set up in the studio. Elvis returned to complete his contractually required tracks for RCA in June at a further three nights' recording.

RCA recorded Elvis' Las Vegas shows in February 1972 for a putative live album that was shelved in favor of his Madison Square Garden show. Only a few of these recordings were released in Elvis' lifetime; the majority didn't come out until Nineties anthology Walk A Mile In My Shoes. In late March 1972, Elvis laid down some tracks for future RCA singles and rehearsed for his upcoming tour at the company's Hollywood studio. RCA recorded Elvis' performances at Madison Square Garden in New York City in 1972, and to defeat the bootleggers released the live album a mere 8 days after Elvis finished his final NYC gig.

The next live date that RCA recorded was Elvis' Aloha From Hawaii performance in January 1973. RCA attempted to remedy Elvis' reluctance to go into the studio by persuading him to record close to home in July 1973, at the famous Stax Studio, with some of the musicians from American Studio in 1969, plus James Burton and Ronnie Tutt from the touring band. Elvis proved to be less than reliable, missing the first night's session altogether and bailing out to Los Angeles before the roster of songs had been recorded. Bobby Wood, who played at both session, remembers that the atmosphere was simply too diluted because there were so many people in the studio. That September, RCA tried another tack: they dispatched a mobile recording studio to Elvis' Palm Springs home to record voice tracks for the instrumentals producer Felton Jarvis had laid down at Stax.

Elvis was coaxed back to Stax in December 1973, with a backing group almost a dozen strong, including new addition Voice. Felton Jarvis managed to complete eighteen masters for RCA, including "I Got A Feelin' In My Body" and "If You Talk In Your Sleep," though by this time, Elvis was recording his songs more or less identically to how they sounded on the demos.

RCA sent out a mobile recording studio for the last show on Elvis' March 1974 tour in Memphis, aptly titled Elvis Recorded Live On Stage in Memphis. The company failed to get Elvis into a recording session at all that year, despite increased contractual commitments following the company's buyout of his back catalogue

In March 1975, Elvis reported for duty at RCA's 6363 Sunset Boulevard studio for a three-day session, right before his rescheduled winter Las Vegas engagement. He laid down just enough material for the album Today. (FTD put together an album of outtakes and alternates of Elvis' 1972 and 1975 LA recordings on 6363 Sunset).

Elvis' next album, From Elvis Presley Boulevard, Memphis, Tennessee and some future singles were recorded at Graceland in February 1976, when it became clear that Elvis the mountain would have to go to Mohammed. Elvis' next RCA session, in October that year, was also held in an improvised studio set up in the Jungle Room, but on the second night Elvis disappeared not long after coming down because a consignment of new Harleys had arrived. The session was abandoned when he returned to the Jungle Room wielding a submachine gun as a prank. Elvis later apologized, and used his planes to ferry the musicians back to Nashville and LA. The last song he ever recorded in a studio environment (apart from live recordings) was "He'll Have To Go," which was released on Moody Blue.

Elvis was booked for studio time in January 1977, at the Creative Workshop studio in Nashville. After a by now customary delay, Elvis arrived in Nashville where his stage band, plus guitarist Chip Young and percussionist Randy Cullers, were ready and waiting, but he didn't ever make it to the studio, his excuse being that he had a sore throat.

RCA's final attempt to coax some new material out of Elvis was to send Felton Jarvis out on tour in the Spring of 1977. Jarvis diligently recorded Elvis at work, trying and more often than not failing to get him to sing new songs; Elvis preferred to please his fans, and his fans tended to prefer that he play the songs they knew and loved. Nevertheless, enough material was found to complete the Moody Blue album.

See also BAND.

"REACH OUT TO JESUS"

Elvis' version of this smooth Ralph Carmichael spiritual was recorded in Nashville at a June 8, 1971 session for release on He Touched Me. The song appears on gospel compilations Amazing Grace, Peace In The Valley and Ultimate Gospel.

"READY TEDDY"

On September 3, 1956 Elvis laid down this Robert Blackwell/John Marascalco song at Radio Recorders, around the same time that it was an R&B chart #1 for Little Richard. Elvis' version was released on his second LP, Elvis, and on 1956 EP Elvis Vol. 2.

The same month he recorded it, he sang it live on the "Ed Sullivan Show" and at the Mississippi-Alabama Fair and Dairy Show (both performances were released years' later on A Golden Celebration). The song was also included on The

ELVIS AND THE PRESS.

Great Performances, The King Of Rock And Roll and on *Elvis '56*. It also featured in the 1972 documentary *Elvis on Tour*.

REAL ELVIS, THE

An EP shipped by RCA in mid-August 1956, featuring latest singles "Don't Be Cruel" and "Hound Dog." The EP sold 400,000 copies.

TRACK LISTING:
1. Don't Be Cruel
2. I Want You, I Need You, I Love You
3. Hound Dog
4. My Baby Left Me

REAL FUN ON STAGE . . . AND IN THE STUDIO

An unofficial release of Elvis monologues, instrumentals, one-liners, alternate takes and rare studio material.

TRACK LISTING:
1. Having fun with Elvis on stage #1
2. Old McDonald
3. Ghost Riders In The Sky

4. Peter Gunn Theme
5. Running Scared
6. Having fun with Elvis on stage #2
7. How The Web Was Woven
8. I'll Take You Home Again Kathleen
9. Cattle Call
10. Having fun with Elvis on stage #3
11. The Eyes Of Texas Are Upon You
12. Speedway
13. With A Song In My Heart
14. How Do You Think I Feel
15. Huh-huh-huh
16. Having fun with Elvis on stage #4
17. I Didn't Make It On Playing Guitar
18. Yellow Rose Of Texas
19. Don't Be Cruel
20. Young Love
21. Happy Day
22. Guitar Boogie
23. Peter Gunn Theme
24. Danny Boy
25. That's My Desire
26. If I Can Dream
27. Having fun with Elvis on stage #5
28. Guadalajara
29. Charlie Pride Song #1
30. Charlie Pride Song #2
31. The Most Beautiful Girl In The World
32. Detroit City

33. That's Amore
34. Young Love #2
35. When The Swallows Come Back To Capistrano
36. Poor Man's Gold
37. Do You Know Who I Am (alternate takes)
38. Backstage with Elvis, San Antonio, TX
39. Husky Dusky Day
40. On Top Of Old Smokey
41. Old McDonald

"RECONSIDER BABY"

Elvis sang this classic blues hit, written and first recorded by Lowell Fulson in 1953, during his impromptu *Million Dollar Quartet* jam in late 1956. He recorded a version for release on *Elvis Is Back!* on April 4, 1960 in Nashville—the first Elvis song with a sax solo (from Boots Randolph). Elvis and co. laid down the song at 7 in the morning, at the end of a twelve-hour session.

A live performance from Elvis' first engagement at the International Hotel in Las Vegas, recorded in August 1969, came out on *Collectors Gold* in 1991; another, even more spontaneous live version came out on 2002 FTD release *Elvis*

At The International. Other live versions can be heard on *An Afternoon In The Garden* and on FTD releases *New Year's Eve* and *Unchained Melody*—Elvis occasionally surprised the more blues-loving of his fans by performing the song live in 1972, 1976 and 1977.

The song crops up on a series of collector albums: *The King Of Rock 'n' Roll, Elvis Sings The Blues, Reconsider Baby, From Nashville to Memphis, Walk A Mile In My Shoes, Platinum: A Life in Music, Artist Of The Century, Elvis R 'n' B* and *The Essential Elvis Presley.*

Alternates from the original April 1960 recording session have appeared on 2005 FTD release *Elvis Is Back!* His 1961 Hawaii charity performance is on *Elvis Aron Presley. Elvis: A Legendary Performer Vol. 4* features a performance from Madison Square Garden in June 1972.

RECONSIDER BABY

A 1985 RCA release with a fan attracting complement of alternate takes and mixes.

TRACK LISTING:
1. Reconsider Baby
2. Tomorrow Night
3. So Glad You're Mine
4. One Night (Of Sin)
5. When It Rains, It Really Pours
6. My Baby Left Me
7. Ain't That Loving You Baby (alternate take)
8. I Feel So Bad
9. Down In The Alley
10. Hi Heel Sneakers
11. Stranger In My Own Hometown (without overdubs)
12. Merry Christmas Baby (long edit)

RECORD COLLECTION

A musical omnivore, Elvis was an eclectic and enthusiastic record collector. At his death, he left behind a record collection two thousand items strong. Elvis started acquiring records as soon as he had the money; fame and fortune later allowed him to send out a member of his entourage to block buy the entire chart. The largest part of his collection—which spanned all genres, including jazz (Duke Ellington, Herb Alpert), the one genre that he publicly said he "didn't get"—was dedicated to gospel, mainly Southern white vocal groups such as The Blackwoods, The Statesmen, the Speer Family and the Brock Brothers. He also had a number of religious records, including several by the Mormon Tabernacle Choir.

Elvis' early collection focused on R&B, including favorites Johnny Ace, Faye Adams, LaVern Baker, Ray Charles, Joe Turner, Little Walter and Ivory Joe Hunter. He kept tabs on the emergence of soul through the likes of Clyde McPhatter, Ben E. King, Sam Cooke, Etta James, James Brown and Smokey Robinson.

Naturally, Elvis had a peerless collection of discs by Sun artists, from R&B pioneers like Bobby Bland Rufus Thomas to Johnny Cash and Jerry Lee Lewis. He also had a fine collection of B.B. King LPs.

Elvis' collection of opera was spearheaded by his favorite Mario Lanza. For classics, he favored offerings from the Boston and Chicago Symphony Orchestras. He owned plenty of Christmas favorites, starting with an early copy of *Jingle Bells* by Bing Crosby and the Andrews Sisters, and not surprisingly owned records by singing stars like Frank Sinatra, Dean Martin, Harry Belafonte and Tony Bennett. His collection of female vocalists included Brenda Lee, Connie Francis, Aretha Franklin, Pasty Cline, Patti Page, and later Gloria Gaynor.

Just starting out, Elvis often listened to ballads by artists ranging from Bing Crosby to the Ink Spots, the Platters and Pat Boone. In later years, he bought discs by the men who might have been considered rivals to his crown as a sex symbol: Bobby Darin, Cliff Richard, Tom Jones and Engelbert Humperdinck to name just a few. While his own musical output flagged in the mid-Sixties, he listened to the folk movement, particular LPs from Peter, Paul and Mary, and *Odetta Sings Dylan.*

His collection also contained plenty of "easy listening" material (Acker Bilk, Max Bygraves), and after Lisa Marie was born, a number of David Cassidy LPs.

His Country collection was more up-to-date than others, with records from Eddy Arnold, Jim Reeves, Ray Price, Bobbie Gentry and Rita Coolidge, in addition to albums by many of the artists whose material he covered in later years.

He also kept up with what was happening in early Seventies rock, with discs by Mott the Hoople, Free and the Allman Brothers; his interest in the genre did, however, wane as the Seventies progressed.

For those lighter moments, he might put on a comedy album, Charles Boyer's spoken songs of love, sing-a-long LPs by the Kingston Trio, or rousing speeches including an LP recorded b General Owen Bradley.

Elvis had a jukebox at Graceland from which music could be relayed around the house. One thing that he did not religiously collect was his own records; it has been noted that his own Elvis collection was incomplete.

SCOTTY MOORE: "Even when he couldn't afford them, he was buying them. And he was always playing them. He played those records to death. He bought all kinds: pop, gospel, blues."

RECORD CONTRACTS

See RCA, COLONEL TOM PARKER.

RECORD RELEASES

The *Elvis Encyclopedia* presents information about US original releases during Elvis' lifetime, and significant US releases since. With as many as 100 official and unofficial Elvis releases in any given year, it is beyond the scope of this project to cover all of Elvis' releases, or any but the most significant international issues. However, many excellent discographical works exist on paper and online. Website has more information about recording sessions than any but the most completist fan could wish for.

In this work, to find out about Elvis albums, EPs and singles, look under general category entries and individual titles. In the main, we have not covered special single releases such as the "Gold Standard" series, Elvis samples on multiple-artist releases like *Perfect for Parties,* spoken-word material from interviews, special DJ releases, and cross promotions including other acts on RCA.

Elvis' RCA records did not have an official release date but rather a shipping date: with millions of clamoring fans, the label's priority was, for decades, simply to get the disks into sales outlets.

When he was with Sun, Elvis only managed five single releases; he was far too busy touring and building up a following to spend more than a minimum of time in the studio. After he signed for RCA, Elvis releases came fast and furious: as well as his first single "Heartbreak Hotel," RCA re-released all five of his Sun singles, and then began a barrage of EPs, double EPs and an album

in order to recoup the huge outlay paid to sign him. In August 1956, the label released every single track on Elvis' first album on a set of six singles. By 1957, in a bid to prevent overexposure, the Colonel had imposed strict control over what records RCA could release and when.

Once Elvis had embarked on his movie career, RCA's release schedule was in the main dictated by soundtrack material and film commitments. When Elvis returned to live performing in 1969, the label was relieved to be able to add live recordings to their Elvis catalogue, particularly as the Seventies wore on and Elvis became increasingly reluctant to go into a studio.

Following the Colonel's landmark 1973 deal to sell Elvis' back catalogue, the label began to package the treasure trove of Elvis' earlier recordings, setting a precedent for the marketing of Elvis' music ever since. Post-1977, Elvis releases have covered all possible market segments, from the nostalgia market to educating new fans to anthology box sets, to hardcore fan-led official versions of material from live performances and studio sessions that had previously only been available on bootleg.

In the 2000s, RCA has focused on enticing new fans to Elvis' music, while in parallel launching regular releases on special collectors' label Follow That Dream (FTD). These releases scrupulously feature alternate takes, rehearsal material, previously-unavailable live shows and home recordings from every period in Elvis' career. This policy has diminished but not extinguished the procession of "unofficial" releases available to Elvis fans. A relatively recent phenomenon, triggered by the 50-year copyright rule in certain countries, is for rare early Elvis material to be released by independent (but not bootleg) labels such as *Memphis Recording Service.*

See also DISCOGRAPHIES, SUN RECORDS, RCA, FTD, RECORD SALES.

RECORD SALES

It is commonly believed that Elvis made a total of 665 recordings—this figure excludes bootlegs, alternate versions, song snippets and originally unreleased material, which makes the number of songs that Elvis released since 1954 substantially higher than this figure. Elvis is credited with 114 Top 40 US hits (and 138 entries on the *Billboard* Hot 100/Top 100 chart)

More than half a century after he first captivated music fans, Elvis retains an impressive number of record sales records. Though there is some dispute (at time of writing) whether Elvis or Madonna has the greatest number of Billboard 100 top 10 hits, Elvis racked up the best-selling singles of the Fifties ("Hound Dog / Don't Be Cruel" and the Sixties ("It's Now Or Never"). "Don't Be Cruel," "Teddy Bear" and "Jailhouse Rock" were such smash hits that they hit number one on the pop, country and R'n'B charts,

Scratch the surface of Elvis' official record selling prowess, though, and it becomes clear that few sciences are less exact than chartology (see Sidebar). Elvis fans happily boast that he has sold more records than any other recording artist, bar none; Beatles fans contest that claim with vigor.

Elvis is estimated to have sold over 1 billion records worldwide (of which around 40% outside the US) since his first release in 1954. Some sources qualify this figure as a "singles equivalent," obtained by multiplying album sales figures. Men in the know, such as Ernst Jorgensen, believe that Elvis probably has sold around 1 billion records, based on the fact that his worldwide sales are as much as twice as high as US-only sales.

RCA have never released official sales totals for Elvis' output, yet the company have long billed Elvis as the "Biggest Record Seller of All

Time": in 1997, the label announced that his worldwide sales figure was up to 1.4 billion records worldwide. Other estimates of Elvis' overall selling power are much lower.

According to the RIAA, by the summer of 2006 Elvis had sold 118.5 million albums, second to The Beatles on 169 million; meanwhile, a 2004 music industry estimate of album sales puts Elvis' worldwide total at over 300 million (and his singles sales tot up to a further quarter of a billion). Not in doubt in this panorama of shifting sands is that Elvis has racked up 150 singles and albums that have had made it to gold sale record, and the only other recording artists to have 24 multi-platinum hits are The Beatles (and there were four of them).

In the mid-2000s, according to the RIAA, Garth Brooks overtook Elvis as the biggest-selling solo artist of all time. It should be noted, however, that modern record sales accounting is far more precise than it was back in the day. The exact sales figures for Elvis pressings in the Fifties, when he ruled the charts supreme, will never be known, as RCA is said to have lost much of this information. Further, there are claims that the company never released the true figures of the huge number of Elvis records sold in the aftermath of his death, when every single one of the label's record manufacturing plants were churning out Elvis discs.

Other reasons why Elvis is not as far out in front in record sales tallies as he is in the icon stakes are: chart calculation methods have changed over the years in ways that penalize artists whose careers began further in the past; totals are rounded up or down to RIAA record award thresholds, which is unfavorable to an artist like Elvis who released so much; records for which no certifiable sales figures exist are estimated conservatively; and releases under licensing arrangements with other labels are not included.

Elvis' first single, "That's All Right (Mama)" "Blue Moon Of Kentucky" sold so swiftly in and around Memphis that DJs across the South up and took notice. Though the reputed total of 20,000 copies may not have made a ripple nationally, it was a vast number for a local unknown. Singles two and three sold decently but not as rapidly as the first, though Elvis and his band were almost permanently on tour, playing venues and promoting their tracks on radio stations across the Mid-South.

In August 1955, Colonel Tom Parker told Hill and Range—the song publishing company he was trying to bring on board to help fund the buyout of Elvis' contract with Sun Records—that to date Elvis had sold over 100,000 records.

Elvis first decided on singing breakthrough single "Heartbreak Hotel" ten days before he signed to RCA. Despite a slow start, that first RCA single gained sufficient momentum to break through the million sales barrier in the US within two

months of release and, for the first time, put Elvis at the top of the pop pile. Everything he did turned to gold: his first LP hit #1 and stayed there for ten weeks to become RCA's first ever million-dollar pop release. His follow-up single to "Heartbreak Hotel," "I Want You, I Need You, I Love You," stacked up the highest number of pre-orders yet seen. From "Heartbreak Hotel" in 1956 to "Return To Sender" in 1962, every one of Elvis' singles made it into the top ten—a total of 29 consecutive releases.

In Elvis' first year with the label, RCA sold either 10 or 12.5 million singles depending on source, and close to 3 million albums. Put another way, Elvis was single-handedly responsible for more than half of the label's entire revenues from singles in 1956. "Don't Be Cruel" / "Hound Dog" alone shifted over three million discs. In the summer of 1956, so many Elvis singles were in the charts that it resembled an Elvis top 10. Elvis was responsible for the top selling singles of 1956 ("Don't Be Cruel" / "Hound Dog") and 1957 ("All Shook Up"), and had one single or another at #1 on the Billboard charts for almost half of 1956. After Elvis performed upcoming single "Love Me Tender" on the "Ed Sullivan Show" in the fall of 1956, RCA received a record-breaking one million advance orders (at a time when the US population was half what was by 2007).

All four of Elvis' 1957 singles sold more than two million copies. Both of the albums and all three of the EPs released that year went to #1. The *Loving You* album rocketed to top spot in just two weeks from release, the fastest of any Elvis album before or since.

Despite spending most of the year in the Army and out of the public eye, Elvis' 1958 singles effortlessly sold a million copies, his EPs half a million, and the *King Creole* album sold well but fell just short of the top spot. Such was pent-up fan demand for anything Elvis that even a spoken-word release of Elvis' press conference before setting sail for Germany (packaged as *Elvis Sails*) found 100,000 takers.

By the time Elvis was ready to return to the US after his military service in early 1960, *Billboard* reported that with eighteen million singles to his name, he had outsold every other recording artist in history—all within four years of joining a major label. Other public estimates at the time put the total at closer to forty-five million copies sold, consisting of a staggering 25 individual million-selling single titles and a brace of million-selling albums.

Elvis' fears that his career would not survive two years out of the limelight were unfounded: his first four singles after his return from the Army all went to #1, though his first album, *Elvis is Back!* failed to hit #1. As far as the Colonel was concerned, this hiccup provided justification for his strategy to throw his client lock, stock and barrel into movie-related recordings: *G.I. Blues* stayed in the charts for a staggering 111 weeks,

ELVIS AROUND THE WORLD

CLOCKWISE FROM TOP: Iceland, Brazil, Chile, Argentina, France, and Cuba (Elvis's only release in Cuba). Most of these albums are super rare.

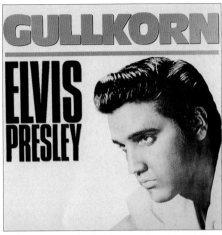

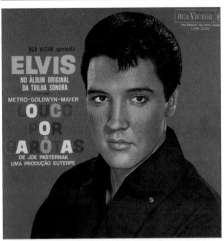

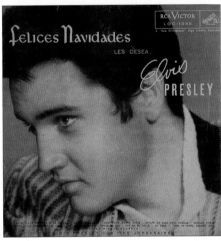

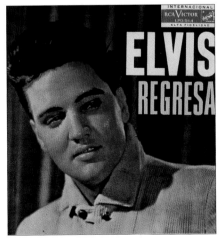

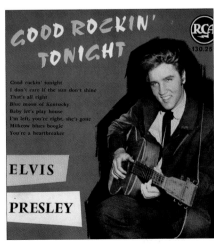

the longest of any Elvis album; *Blue Hawaii* was an even stronger seller, shifting over 2 million copies in its first year and retaining the #1 spot for five straight months. So huge were its sales that no Elvis album outsold it during his lifetime.

On February 25, 1961, "Elvis Presley Day" in Memphis, RCA presented Elvis with a diamond-studded watch to mark his achievement of selling over 75 million records. RCA offered Elvis guaranteed royalties on a million sales for his singles regardless of how many copies they actually sold, in exchange for retaining the right to release singles from Elvis' albums after their release (rather than before, as the Colonel had previously stipulated).

By 1962, Elvis had settled down to a formula of three movie-related soundtrack releases per year. "Good Luck Charm," released in February 1962, proved to be Elvis' last #1 single until "Suspicious Minds" in 1969. "One Broken Heart For Sale," released in early 1963, was the first Elvis single since he joined RCA that failed to make the top ten. The drop-off in his overall sales numbers was an industry-wide phenomenon. Elvis nevertheless broke through the worldwide sales threshold of 100 million records in April 1963.

With his studio albums significantly underselling his soundtrack albums, in 1963 RCA opted to put out another greatest hits package (*Elvis Golden Records Vol. 3*) rather than the new material he had recorded in Nashville earlier that year; these tracks were parceled out as "bonuses" to bulk up later soundtrack releases. Ernst Jorgensen suggests that the policy of bundling Elvis' hit singles on the "golden" series of albums and not putting high profile singles onto his studio albums such as *Something For Everybody* and *Pot Luck* seriously diminished the appeal of these albums, and skewed the label's policy even further towards plucking singles from movie soundtracks.

Elvis released his worst selling single since signing to RCA in April 1964: "Kiss Me Quick"/ "Suspicion" sold just 200,000 records, in part because the B-side song had recently ridden high in the charts in a version sung by Terry Stafford.

The *Roustabout* soundtrack album brought about a return to chart-topping popularity for Elvis in late 1964, selling 450,000 copies and claiming the #1 spot for a week in January 1965. However, the album had to contend with emerging music trends: the week before *Roustabout*, The Beach Boys held the number one spot; the week after, it was The Beatles. *Roustabout* was Elvis' last taste of the top of the LP charts until *Aloha from Hawaii* in 1973.

The next soundtrack album, *Girl Happy*, resumed the downwards trend, but then in April 1965 Elvis returned to the top ten in the singles chart with "Crying In The Chapel," a gospel tune that he had recorded five years earlier. Tapping a different demographic, the song sold over 2 million copies in the US and abroad. Elvis' 1965 US record sales were a little more than half the quantity he achieved in 1960, but he remained a huge asset to RCA, especially when international sales were taken into account. The soundtrack to *Harum Scarum* still scraped into the top ten albums . . . just, and RCA was happy to concede an improved contract in the fall of that year.

By the mid-Sixties, with the exception of seasonal releases Elvis' single sales had more or less flat-lined at around 400,000 copies per issue. RCA tackled the problem through leveraging quantity rather than quality, bringing out more singles to maintain the bottom line. This tactic was harder to achieve with albums, as soundtrack sales continued to decline and fans showed increasing reluctance to spend money on previously-released tracks that were recycled on offerings such as *Elvis For Everyone* (which failed to shift even 300,000 copies). His record sales bottomed out in early 1967 with the *Easy Come, Easy Go* soundtrack EP, which only just scraped 30,000 buyers.

It wasn't until February 1968 release "U.S. Male" that an Elvis single reached the top thirty again, though he had already served notice that he was returning to his rocking roots with previous release "Guitar Man" (both tracks written by Jerry Reed). All the other Elvis singles released in 1968 sank almost without trace. In the months before the 1968 NBC TV Special aired, three potentially strong singles including "A Little Less Conversation" and "You'll Never Walk Alone" failed to make it any higher than #69 in the charts, while the *Speedway* album tanked at #82 in the album charts. Strong material like "Guitar Man," "Big Boss Man" et all failed to persuade fans to part with their money, and Elvis was teetering on the brink of consignment to the nostalgia circuit.

Then came the 1968 NBC TV Special, not for nothing known as "The Comeback Special." Elvis' climb back to the top of the singles chart began with a #12 placement for the show finale "If I Can Dream." The spin-off album, titled simply *Elvis*, sold an almost identical half a million copies on original release to his 1956 LP of the same name.

The first single released from the American Studio sessions in early 1969, "In The Ghetto," re-established Elvis as a chart-topper with sales well over the million mark. "Suspicious Minds" did even better in the second half of the year, conquering the #1 spot for the first time in over seven years. It was also his last ever #1 single.

Elvis was presented with five golden records

LISTING OF ELVIS RECORDINGS

DATE COMMISSIONED	STUDIO	LOCATION
Summer of 1953 (best guess August 22)	Self-paid recording session, Memphis Recording Service	Memphis, Tennessee
January 4, 1954	Self-paid recording session, Memphis Recording Service	Memphis, Tennessee
July 5 - 6, 1954	Sun Studio	Memphis, Tennessee
August 19, 1954	Sun Studio	Memphis, Tennessee
September, 1954	Sun Studio	Memphis, Tennessee
October 16, 1954	"The Louisiana Hayride", Live	Shreveport, Louisiana
November/December, 1954	Sun Studio	Memphis, Tennessee
January 6, 1955	Fair Park, Live	Lubbock, Texas
January/February 1955	"The Louisiana Hayride", Live	Shreveport, Louisiana
February, 1955	Sun Studio	Memphis, Tennessee
March, 1955	Sun Studio	Memphis, Tennessee
March 19, 1955	Eagles Hall, Live	Houston, Texas
April 30, 1955	Radio station	Gladewater, Texas
April/July 1955	"The Louisiana Hayride", Live	Shreveport, Louisiana
July 11, 1955	Sun Studio	Memphis, Tennessee
August 20, 1955	"The Louisiana Hayride", Live	Shreveport, Louisiana
November, 1955	Sun Studio	Memphis, Tennessee
January 10-11, 1956	RCA Studios	Nashville, Tennessee
January 30 – February 3, 1956	RCA Studios	New York, New York
January - March, 1956	CBS "Stage Show", CBS studios	New York, New York
April 3, 1956	NBC "The Milton Berle Show", USS Hancock	San Diego, California
April 14, 1956	RCA Studios	Nashville, Tennessee
May 6, 1956	New Frontier Hotel	Las Vegas, Nevada
June 5, 1956	NBC "The Milton Berle Show", NBC Studios	Los Angeles, California
July 1, 1956	NBC "Steve Allen Show", The Hudson Theater	New York, New York
July 2, 1956	RCA Studios	New York, New York
August 24; September 4-5; October 1,1956	20th Century-Fox Studios	Los Angeles, California
September 1-3, 1956	RCA (at Radio Recorders)	Hollywood, California,
September 9, 1956	CBS "Ed Sullivan Show"	Los Angeles, California
September 26, 1956	Mississippi-Alabama Fair and Dairy Show, Live	Tupelo, Mississippi
October 28, 1956	CBS "Ed Sullivan Show"	New York, New York
December 4, 1956	Sun Studio jam (Million Dollar Quartet)	Memphis, Tennessee
January 6, 1957	CBS "Ed Sullivan Show"	New York, New York
January 12-13, 1957	RCA (at Radio Recorders)	Hollywood, California,
January – February, 1957	Paramount Studios (at Radio Recorders)	Hollywood, California
January 19, 1957	RCA (at Radio Recorders)	Hollywood, California,
February 23-24, 1957	RCA (at Radio Recorders)	Hollywood, California,
April 30; May 3, 1957	MGM (at Radio Recorders)	Los Angeles, California
May 9, 1957	MGM Studios	Los Angeles, California
September 5-7, 1957	RCA (at Radio Recorders)	Hollywood, California,
January 15/16 and 23; February, 11 1958	Paramount Studios, Radio Recorders	Los Angeles, California
February 1, 1958	RCA (at Radio Recorders)	Hollywood, California,
June 10, 1958	RCA Studio B	Nashville, Tennessee
1959	Home recordings	Bad Nauheim, Germany
March 20, 1960	RCA Studio B	Nashville, Tennessee
March 26, 1960	The Frank Sinatra Show, The Fontainebleau Hotel	Miami, Florida
April 3, 1960	RCA Studio B	Nashville, Tennessee
April 27 – 28, 1960	Paramount (at RCA Studios)	Los Angeles, California
May 6, 1960	Paramount (at Radio Recorders)	Hollywood, California
August 8; October 7, 1960	20th Century-Fox (at Radio Recorders)	Hollywood, California
October 30, 1960	RCA Studio B	Nashville, Tennessee
November 7-8, 1960	20th Century-Fox (at Radio Recorders)	Hollywood, California
Fall 1960	Home recordings	Los Angeles, California
March 12, 1961	RCA Studio B	Nashville, Tennessee
March 21-23, 1961	Paramount (at Radio Recorders)	Hollywood, California
March 25, 1961	Bloch Arena, Live	Pearl Harbor, Hawaii
June 25, 1961	RCA Studio B	Nashville, Tennessee
July 2, 1961	United Artists/Mirisch Bros. (at RCA Studio B)	Nashville, Tennessee
October 15, 1961	RCA Studio B	Nashville, Tennessee
October 26-27, 1961	United Artists/Mirisch Bros. (at Radio Recorders)	Hollywood, California
March 18-19, 1962	RCA Studio B	Nashville, Tennessee
March 26-28, 1962	Paramount (at Radio Recorders)	Hollywood, California
August 30; September 22, 1962	MGM (at Radio Recorders)	Hollywood, California
January 22-23, 1963	Paramount (at Radio Recorders)	Hollywood, California
May 26-27, 1963	RCA Studio B	Nashville, Tennessee
July 9-11; August 30, 1963	MGM (at Radio Recorders)	Hollywood, California

after the last of three shows in Houston in early 1970, for singles "In The Ghetto," "Suspicious Minds" and "Don't Cry, Daddy," and for albums *From Elvis in Memphis* and *From Memphis to Vegas / From Vegas to Memphis*.

Elvis' 1970 albums *Elvis Country* and documentary tie-in *That's The Way It Is* both made it into the top twenty. The singles released from these albums, in the main, were more conservative choices, ballads with complex arrangements, that failed to scale the upper echelons of the charts.

Elvis' best-selling album of all time is, surprisingly, the 1970 version of 1957 release, *Elvis' Christmas Album*, which steadily sold its way past six million copies in the US alone. The first year of his last decade was a bumper time for Elvis: once

more a hot property after his highly-acclaimed comebacks on TV, in Las Vegas and on the road, RCA released no fewer than eight Elvis albums.

After this renaissance, Elvis' record sales went into a gentle decline from which, apart from a fillip or two in 1972 and 1973, they would not recover. As in the past, RCA reacted by ramping up the number of releases, bringing out no fewer than three budget albums and another volume in the *Worldwide Gold Award Hits* series. Elvis' end-of-year Christmas fare sank without a trace, even with bluesy crossover single "Merry Christmas Baby."

Where studio albums were failing, live albums succeeded. Elvis was back in the top ten with instant live album *Elvis as Recorded at Madison Square Garden*, which became his Elvis' bestselling

LP in almost a decade by going gold within two months. The next single, "Burning Love," came within a whisker of making #1, and sold a million copies in under a month in the summer of 1972.

February 1973 release *Aloha from Hawaii via Satellite* was Elvis' first #1 album (strictly-speaking, a double-album) since the *Roustabout* soundtrack in 1965. Later studio albums resumed the downwards trend: 1973 album *Raised On Rock* sold just a couple of hundred thousand copies, at a time when repackaged hits collections in the *Elvis: A Legendary Performer* series—the first LP to combine old favorites with previously unheard versions—sold almost four times as well.

Once again, a live album came to RCA's rescue: *Elvis Recorded Live On Stage in Memphis*, released in the summer of 1974, went on to sell close to half a million copies on initial release. The next Elvis single to put in a decent performance was "Promised Land," released in September 1974, though that only climbed to #14 after heavy investment to ensure airplay.

Novelty album release *Having Fun with Elvis On Stage*, a collection of Elvis' concert banter which RCA put out in late 1974, sold almost as well as his most recent studio albums—a sign that Elvis' fan base could always be counted on to buy his latest releases, but barring a major media event or public exposure, the market for new Elvis material was limited at best.

The last single that RCA released during Elvis' lifetime, "Way Down," and the last album (*Moody Blue* released in July 1977), charted respectively at #18 and #3, boosted by the swell of emotion triggered by Elvis' premature death.

Immediately after his death, it was reported that RCA shipped as many as 20 million records in a single week, though according to Ernst Jorgensen, official sales figures for this period were not retained and have failed to appear in official RIAA tallies.

Significant anniversaries of his death have provided a marketing opportunity to bring out Elvis hits packages and previously unavailable material, starting with "The Elvis Medley" (an amalgam of "Jailhouse Rock," "Teddy Bear," "Hound Dog," "Don't Be Cruel," "Burning Love" and "Suspicious Minds") released as a single in 1982.

The passing decades have done little to diminish Elvis' ability to sell records. The *ELVIS 30 #1 Hits* album of remastered songs released in 2002 took just three weeks to exceed sales of a million copies and went straight to #1. By early 2006, it had earned quadruple platinum status.

RECORD RECORDS

In late 2005, news reports announced that Madonna had tied with Elvis for the most Billboard 100 top 10 hits, after "Hung Up" became her 36th hit over a 21 and a half year career. Elvis fans points out that if both sides of Elvis' early double-A-side hits are taken into account, Elvis' tally rises to 38. Also in late 2005, Mariah Carey tied Elvis' record of 17 #1 singles on the Billboard Hot 100. Out in front, The Beatles have 20 #1s (21 including "Long And Winding Road," as stated in some sources).

When it comes to top 40 singles, Elvis' figure of 114 is almost twice as many as his nearest rival, Elton John. Elvis also has totaled the highest number of weeks (80) at the #1 spot.

During his career Elvis placed 149 songs in the Billboard Top 100: 18 singles and 10 albums went to #1. No other artist can rival this.

Elvis also has the distinction of more RIAA-certified multi-platinum (over 2 million sales) albums than any other recording artist, and a record number of platinum sales certificates (over 70).

See also GOLD AND PLATINUM AWARDS under SINGLES, EPS AND ALBUMS.

DATE COMMISSIONED	STUDIO	LOCATION
September 29-30, 1963	MGM at Studio B	Nashville, California
October 10, 1963	MGM Studios	Los Angeles, California
January 12, 1964	RCA Studio B	Nashville, Tennessee
March 2-3; April 29; May 14, 1964	Paramount (at Radio Recorders)	Hollywood, California
June 10-12; June 15, 1964	MGM (at Radio Recorders)	Hollywood, California
February 24-26, 1965	MGM (at RCA Studio B)	Nashville, Tennessee
May 12-14, 1965	United Artists (at Radio Recorders)	Hollywood, California
July 26-27; August 2-4, 1965	Paramount (at Radio Recorders)	Hollywood, California
February 16-17, 1966	MGM (at Radio Recorders)	Hollywood, California
February 1966 / early 1967	Home Recordings	Los Angeles, California
May 25-28, 1966	RCA Studio B	Nashville, Tennessee
June 10-12, 1966	RCA Studio B	Nashville, Tennessee
June 28-30, 1966	MGM (at Radio Recorders and MGM Studios)	Hollywood, California
September 28-29, 1966	Paramount Studio	Los Angeles, California
February 21-23, 1967	RCA Studio B	Nashville, Tennessee
March 20, 1967	RCA Studio B	Nashville, Tennessee
June 20-21, 1967	MGM Studios	Los Angeles, California
September 10-11, 1967	RCA Studio B	Nashville, Tennessee
October 1, 1967	MGM (at RCA Studio B)	Nashville, Tennessee
January 15-16, 1968	MGM (at RCA Studio B)	Nashville, Tennessee
March 7, 1968	MGM (at Western Recorders)	Hollywood, California
June 20-23, 1968	NBC "Comeback Special" (at Western Recorders)	Hollywood, California
June 24-25, 1968	NBC "Comeback Special" (dressing room rehearsals)	Burbank, California
June 27, 1968	NBC "Comeback Special" live segment at NBC Studios	Burbank, California
June 29, 1968	NBC "Comeback Special" arena segment at NBC Studios	Burbank, California
October 15, 1968	National General (at Samuel Goldwyn Studio)	Los Angeles, California
October 23, 1968	MGM (at United Artist Recorders)	Los Angeles, California
January 13-16; January 20-23, 1969	American Studio	Memphis, Tennessee
February 17-22, 1969	American Studio	Memphis, Tennessee
March 5-6, 1969	Universal (at Decca Universal Studio)	Los Angeles, California
August 21-26, 1969	International Hotel, Live	Las Vegas, Nevada
February 15-19, 1970	International Hotel, Live	Las Vegas, Nevada
February 18, 1970	International Hotel, rehearsals	Las Vegas, Nevada
June 4-8, 1970	RCA Studio B	Nashville, Tennessee
July 15; July 29, 1970	MGM rehearsals (at MGM Soundstage)	Los Angeles, California
July 24, 1970	MGM rehearsals (at RCA Studios)	Los Angeles, California
August 4; August 7, 1970	MGM rehearsals (at the International Hotel)	Las Vegas, Nevada
August 10-13, 1970	MGM/RCA (at the International Hotel, live)	Las Vegas, Nevada
September 22, 1970	RCA Studio B	Nashville, Tennessee
March 15, 1971	RCA Studio B	Nashville, Tennessee
May 15-21, 1971	RCA Studio B	Nashville, Tennessee
June 8-10, 1971	RCA Studio B	Nashville, Tennessee
February 14-17, 1972	RCA (Hilton Hotel, live)	Las Vegas, Nevada
March 27-29, 1972	RCA Studio B	Los Angeles, California
March 30-31, 1972	MGM (at RCA Studio C)	Los Angeles, California
April 5, 1972	MGM (Memorial Auditorium, live)	Buffalo, New York
April 9-18, 1972	MGM/RCA, Live shows	Hampton Roads, Virginia
		Richmond, Virginia
		Greensboro, N. Carolina
		San Antonio, Texas
June 10, 1972	RCA (Madison Square Garden, live)	New York, New York
January 12; January 14, 1973	RCA (Honolulu International Center Arena, live)	Honolulu, Hawaii
July 20-25, 1973	Stax Studios	Memphis, Tennessee
September 22-23, 1973	RCA (at Elvis's home)	Palm Springs, California
November 1973	Home recordings at the Thompson Home	Memphis, Tennessee
December 10-16, 1973	Stax Studios	Memphis, Tennessee
March 20, 1974	RCA (Mid-South Coliseum, live)	Memphis, Tennessee
August 16, 1974	RCA Studios (rehearsals)	Los Angeles, California
March 10-12, 1975	RCA Studio C	Los Angeles, California
May 6-June 9, 1975	Live concert recordings	Various locations
December 13, 1975	Hilton Hotel, Live	Las Vegas, Nevada
February 2-8, 1976	RCA (at Graceland)	Memphis, Tennessee
October 29-30, 1976	RCA (at Graceland)	Memphis, Tennessee
March-May, 1977	RCA (live concert recordings)	Various locations
June 19 and 21, 1977	CBS (live recordings)	Omaha, Nebraska
		Rapid City, SouthDakota

NOTE: This list includes early known unofficial recordings but does not include soundboard or audience recordings from the many hundreds of shows Elvis performed in the Seventies.

MOST US #1 HITS:

Bing Crosby: 38
The Beatles: 20
Elvis: 18

ELVIS' BEST-SELLERS

SINGLE:
"It's Now Or Never"

ALBUM:
Blue Hawaii, outsold posthumously by the 1970 version of *Elvis' Christmas Album*

ELVIS IN THE UK

As of late 2005, Elvis remained the most successful recording artist in the UK charts, having racked up the most chart time of any band or artist. In the 2000s he has extended his lead with three reissued singles taking #1 spot in 2005 alone. At the time of writing, Elvis had more #1 hits in the UK, 21, than any other, having sold as many as 25 million discs (though estimates start at around 20 million) and achieved 77 top ten singles. He also has established the record for the most consecutive weeks in the UK chart (144 weeks from 1960 to 1963). Elvis' total of more than 2,500 weeks in the UK singles and album charts is unsurpassed by any other entertainment act. *The King*, a UK 2 CD release that came out in the week of the 30th anniversary of Elvis' death, went into the charts at #1.

CHARTOLOGY

Obvious as it may seem, it should be borne in mind that chart position and record sales are not the same thing, and the way that these criteria is calculated has changed many times over the years. When Elvis started out, chart positions were partly determined by airplay, which in turn depended to some extent on how far record companies were willing to plug a particular record. Overall sales charts (the *Billboard* Hot 100) and charts for specific genres have changed their methods of calculation over the years, making comparisons between different recording artists in different periods problematic. Changes in record buying patterns as new formats have appeared (singles, EPs, LPs, cassettes, 8-track, CDs, digital formats) and the advent of different music-purchasing habits (the primacy of albums over singles from the Eighties, digital downloads) leave plenty of latitude for music fans to champion their particular favorite as record holder.

For example, the relative importance of different release formats has varied over the years. By the late Fifties, overall singles sales had peaked and began to decline slowly. LPs accounted for a greater proportion of sales in the Sixties, while EPs gradually faded out of the mass market.

Further complicating matters, *Billboard* singles charts were calculated on the sales and airplay of both sides of each 7" up until 1968. Singles could chart for either of their sides, depending on sales, and the final standing also included radio airplay and jukebox placements. Chart positions have also been rated on the dollar value of sales, hence Elvis' album releases on RCA's "budget" label Camden charted much lower than their sales numbers warranted, while many Elvis releases on mail order,

magazine- or TV-related labels have not figured at all, despite achieving significant sales.

Even more complicated is the fact that RIAA totals only include gold or above rated albums, so the many Elvis albums released in the States that failed to garner overall sales of 500,000 contribute nothing at all to Elvis' official sales total. This is not the case for bands like The Beatles, which released far fewer albums (all of which were big sellers).

Gold record awards were introduced in 1958 for sales of half a million records—Elvis earned his first for "Hard Headed Woman." Platinum records were introduced for sales of one million records in the year before Elvis' death. Records that sell 10 million copies have been eligible for diamond awards since 1999.

For information on Elvis' Gold and Platinum releases, look under ALBUMS, EPS and SINGLES.

D.J. FONTANA: "Elvis didn't want anything complicated, and that's why he sold records, I think. You could understand what he was doing."

ERNST JORGENSEN: "Elvis' music was developed in the 'singles' era, where the others launched their careers when albums had become the main product."

RECORDING SESSIONS

For much of his career, Elvis was at his most relaxed self when he was making music in the studio. The degree of relaxation he displayed sometimes exasperated RCA executives in the early years; he had to be allowed the time to say hi to everyone and loosen up by running through old favorites and gospel classics with his backing singers before even being remotely ready to start in on the recording agenda. Until the years when he was consigned to churning out banal soundtrack songs, once he got going, his perfectionist side took over and he would attempt take after take until he and the massed musicians came up with a version that matched how he heard the song in his head. If he failed to produce a take that worked, he had the contractual right to prohibit RCA from releasing the track—a right that he exercised regularly in the Fifties, but ever less as the Sixties progressed.

In contradiction to the widely held belief that Elvis had control over the production side of his musical career, Marty Lacker has said that it was the Colonel who had final approval on the mix before RCA started printing out records. Elvis became aware of this and would hit the roof if there had been changes to the finished song compared with the acetates he had taken home from the actual sessions.

Elvis' first ever recording was the vanity acetate that he laid down at the Memphis Recording Service on his own dollar in the summer of 1953. Though most biographies portray this as a portentous moment when a shy young man made a bold attempt to find his calling, in actual fact recording songs and even messages on disc was a popular pastime in the early Fifties—even department stores had special recording booths.

It took a few attempts for Elvis to come up with something that impressed Sun Records principal Sam Phillips. That record, "That's All Right (Mama)," was pure right place, right time happenstance, as Elvis and bass player Bill Black began messing around during a break from "proper" recording. Scotty joined in, Sam told them to hold it while he started the tape, and what started out as an impromptu cover became Elvis' first single.

From very early on, Elvis relied on his musical instincts about what sounded right to him, though it took Sam Phillips' intuition to steer Elvis towards the kind of material that would make the young singer's name, rather than the

old-fashioned ballads to which Elvis naturally gravitated. In 1954 and 1955, Elvis spent so much time on the road that only rarely did he make it into Sun Studio to record—all in all, he managed eight brief sessions. A touch of echo was a hallmark of the Elvis sound from his Sun Studio years onwards; savvy engineers knew to add it in after he moved to RCA.

After Elvis switched to RCA, his nominal producer, Steve Sholes, proved to be hands-off in the studio, and the man Sholes brought in to help Elvis, Chet Atkins, failed to get the best out of Elvis. The resulting freedom Elvis enjoyed in the studio as his own producer allowed him to explore his creativity and innovate until the quality of his material started to wane.

After Sun, Elvis became very particular about where he would record and when. If he didn't feel the vibe was right, the session tended to be unproductive. After the intimate settings of Sun Studio, he felt uncomfortable working on the vast, impersonal soundstages that were the norm in Hollywood. Every studio had its own particular sound, and there can be no doubt that Elvis produced his most successful and innovative work in the more quirky and more focused environments of Sun Studio, American Studio and Radio Recorders.

With very few exceptions—notably the recording sessions prior to his 1968 NBC TV "Comeback" Special—Elvis preferred to record his songs straight through. Most of Elvis' recording sessions were all night affairs, starting in the early evening and running through the night for as long as the sound was right. Ernst Jorgensen has said that Elvis' perfectionism had "less to do with faultlessness than it did with emotional satisfaction." He would keep making new takes until he was satisfied with his own vocal performance. For the title track of *Loving You*, the 32nd take was the one, and that was on the third or fourth recording session when they'd tried to nail it. In 1958, Elvis and the band racked up 48 takes on "Doncha' Think It's Time"; even on 1964 soundtrack song "Do Not Disturb," Elvis struggled through 36 takes and threatened to "beat the hell out of it if it takes 94 years of hard labor. I'll come back after the picture and record it for hours!" During recordings, if he wanted to hear a song played back to assess his performance, Elvis would tap the top of his head; if he thought it was no good, he'd make a throat cutting gesture.

In later years, Elvis got out of this habit. For many of his later soundtrack sessions, he added his vocal as an overdub after the band had laid down the instrumental, and in his final years, if he went into the studio at all, it would be to run through the tracks as rapidly as possible.

Much as RCA executives might have been unhappy that Elvis could take an entire session to produce one or two tracks, he was by far and away the label's greatest asset and was allowed his foibles. At one Fifties session an executive tried to curtail Elvis' usual warm-up of singing gospel with The Jordanaires; when Elvis found out, he railed and walked out. In the Sixties, Elvis added new wrinkles to the saga of getting recorded material done: he might suddenly discover that he had a cold and postpone the session, feel an irrepressible urge to eat hamburgers (which in turn might lead to sending out for enough to feed everyone in the studio a couple of times over), or he might head off to shoot some pool and then record some more afterwards.

When Elvis returned to the studio after his stint in the Army, Chet Atkins helmed his first studio sessions, with a highly accomplished studio band that Elvis was more at ease asking for opinions and input. While he was in Germany, RCA had struck a deal with the unions to record all material released by the company at its own Studios, initially ruling out Elvis' usual West Coast haunt, Radio Recorders. In later years, to circumvent strict union rules on hours of work and breaks, Elvis' engineers occasionally resorted to filing made-up times on the log sheets.

Elvis' first post-Army session, in March 1960, was attended by his entire management team and much of RCA's top brass. This was the first time that Elvis was recorded using a three-track process—stereo was first used in 1958. With so much pent-up musical energy, Elvis laid down a record (for him) six finished tracks in a single session. Two weeks later during an all-night session he powered through a dozen tracks including two of his biggest-ever hits, "It's Now Or Never" and "Are You Lonesome Tonight?."

From this point on, how happy and comfortable Elvis felt about the material he was recording could generally be gauged by his productivity. On October 30, 1960, in a marathon session for his first gospel album, *His Hand In Mine*, Elvis laid down thirteen completed tracks, including future smash hit singles "Surrender" and "Crying In The Chapel."

In 1960 and 1961, Elvis recorded more than 100 studio tracks for his contracted RCA albums, gospel LP and soundtrack commitments. In 2002 FTD released 27 songs from this period on *Fame And Fortune*.

By June 1964, the paucity of the material he was being presented by Hill & Range, almost all of which was for movie soundtracks, led Elvis to stay out of recording studios for eight months. Soon after, he began avoiding recording sessions if he could, preferring his studio band to record their instrumentals and overdubbing his vocals at a later date. During the "cookie-cutter movie" period, Elvis sometimes didn't bother with the sham of selecting the multiple songs that Hill & Range submitted for each movie slot—he only got to choose from this already pared down pool. At their direst, Elvis refused to let tracks be committed to vinyl, though it was beyond his contractual reach to keep songs out of the movies themselves.

Elvis finally rediscovered the creative joy and energy of working in the studio when he recorded gospel album *How Great Thou Art* in 1966. Once again, Elvis and his musician pals stayed on in the studio after most of the musicians had gone home, having fun and laying down tracks they'd known and loved all their lives. After this session, Elvis sent a thank-you note to Felton Jarvis—the first time that they worked together.

Elvis habitually turned up late for recording sessions or postponed soundtrack sessions. However, once he arrived, he was the consummate professional. Unusually, he cancelled an RCA studio session in August 1967 owing to unforeseen circumstances—one of Elvis' entourage ran over and killed a pedestrian in one of Elvis' cars, and the Colonel spirited Elvis away to Las Vegas to head off any scandal. That session, postponed and shifted to Nashville, saw Elvis attacking new material with renewed vigor alongside singer/songwriter/guitarist Jerry Reed.

One of the ways that Elvis got round the strictures of the limited material Hill & Range supplied was to begin his recording sessions by warming up with an oldie or two. If Elvis and the musicians worked the song up to a completed version, it was hard for the powers that be to refuse using it at a future date. This was after studio musicians were warned not to pitch any material to Elvis for which rights had not already been cleared.

In early 1968, Elvis complained to RCA that they had altered the mix on "Guitar Man" prior to its release as a single—as ever, Elvis his voice more tightly blended with the band, rather than out on its own. He also held out for mono recordings of a couple of the songs from his NBC TV Special because he preferred the punch that would otherwise be lost through stereo separation.

Tellingly, when Elvis was most engaged with his material, he was capable of living normal daylight hours rather than his habitual nocturnal existence. In the run-up to taping of his NBC TV Special in 1968, he reported for rehearsals at 9 a.m. sharp. At the session where he laid down showstopper "If I Can Dream," he ended up exhausted on the floor—something that happened at his *How Great Thou Art* sessions in 1966.

Elvis' friends and producer Felton Jarvis suggested that he arrange his first post-NBC Special session at Chips Moman's American Studio in Memphis, the first time he had recorded in hometown since his Sun days. The change of venue and studio band had the desired effect, and for the first time in a long time, the session was helmed by a producer with very definite ideas and the self-belief to impose his aural vision on superstar Elvis. Technology had moved on too; at American, the singer's voice was recorded afterwards, on one of eight tracks, though when the band did their work Elvis got to lay down a scratch vocal. After the recording, Chips Moman set to work on laying down additional vocal tracks and horn inserts, though behind-the-scenes management wrangles almost sidelined the whole productive session.

Elvis' restored enthusiasm continued through 1970 and a marathon session in Nashville that generated three dozen tracks (minimal takes for each song yielded up to eight tracks per night); part of this process was filmed upcoming concert movie *Elvis: That's The Way It Is.*

Soon enough, Elvis' recording sessions once more become a duty rather than pleasure. The increasing options technology offered to put things right in post-production meant that Elvis generally spent much less time working on songs in the studio; he would do two or three takes and then move on, rather than take time with the band to work up complex, original arrangements of the songs he covered.

At the second of his Stax sessions in 1973, Elvis did lavish time on each track, assisted by a pared-down band and almost a dozen backing singers—on the nights when he was in a good mood. In a bad mood, he'd do no more than two or three takes for each song. By the end of the seventh night, Elvis was having such a good time he didn't want to leave. The results of theses sessions were released on albums *Good Times* and *Promised Land.*

Through the Seventies, RCA got round Elvis' general reluctance to go into the studio by recording live albums and re-issuing back catalogue material. With the exception of the LA recording session that yielded enough material for Elvis album *Today*, RCA simply could not get him into the studio. By 1976, it was clear that the mountain had to go to Mohammed. RCA bit the bullet and sent a mobile recording studio to Graceland, parked it outside the Jungle Room and let Elvis do his thing at home.

By this time, the label was happy if Elvis recorded anything at all, let alone applied the high standards on which he had built his career. His last ever recording session came to a dramatic end when Elvis and entourage pals burst into the Jungle Room dressed as gangsters and brandishing guns as a Halloween stunt. Elvis' last ever recording session generated no tracks at all. In January 1977, he traveled to Nashville for a session arranged at the Buzz Carson Creative Workshop, but turned around and left without setting foot in the studio.

See also RCA, RADIO RECORDERS, NASHVILLE

A NOTE ABOUT RECORDING DATES

Dates under song entries in this book refer to the session. Owing to uncertainties about the accuracy of studio log files, this information does not always reflect whether that track was recorded past midnight and therefore the following day.

FTD

Specialist label FTD offers releases that give fans an opportunity to eavesdrop on how Elvis worked in the studio. Multiple versions and outtakes of songs, including Elvis' banter with the band, provide a concrete illustration of Elvis' creative process and the way that he developed a song from rehearsal through to master. Before the FTD label was set up in 1999, such material was only available on bootleg.

ELVIS SAID IN 1956: "I have to warm up. I have to get the feeling of what I'm doing."

ELVIS SAID IN 1960: "I think it would be a bad mistake if I had somebody else telling me what to record and how to record it, because I work strictly on instinct and impulse . . . I choose songs with the public in mind. I try to visualize it as though I'm buying the record myself."

PETER GURALNICK: "Time meant nothing to him in the studio. If he felt like singing spirituals, he would sing spirituals to his heart's content . . . If the feeling wasn't there, you waited until it got there, you didn't try to define it too precisely before it showed up—and if something else happened to show up while you're waiting, well, then, you took advantage of that."

ERNST JORGENSEN: "Elvis was chasing something he heard in his head; if he couldn't get it down on tape he'd just abandon the song and keep RCA from releasing it . . ."

D.J. FONTANA: "He liked to record late at night, but he wouldn't push himself. If he wasn't in the right mood, he'd stall or sing gospel or talk. Sometimes he'd just say, 'I ain't singing good. Let's go home. The hell with it.' We'd all come back the next night and everything would go great."

NEAL MATHEWS: "Elvis was more relaxed in the studio than any place."

ALFRED WERTHEIMER: "Often the only way the musicians knew how well they were playing was by his mood and movements. Rapidly changing movements meant uncertainty. A glint in the eyes meant good. A flashing smile said great."

FELTON JARVIS, 1967: "He likes the relaxed atmosphere and the informal feeling and let's try a lot of different things . . . He plays guitar and he plays bass and piano. He's a pretty talented guy."

GORDON STOKER: "Elvis knew what he was doing and knew how he worked best. His schedule and style may have been unorthodox, but apparently Elvis thought everyone understood."

BEN WEISMAN: "When he came into the studio, he was always prepared, very prepared. He was a perfectionist. He was totally in control of everything except the engineering."

FELTON JARVIS: "Elvis had to sing a song the way he felt like singing it at the moment he was recording it.... Sometimes he'd get down to business very quickly; other times he just wanted to sit around playing gospel and singing for hours. When he actually started working, though, he was fast and efficient. Elvis didn't make many mistakes."

Book:
Elvis Presley, A Life In Music, by Ernst Jorgensen, published by St. Martin's Griffin, 1998.

REED, JERRY
(B. JERRY HUBBARD, 1937)

Country singer, guitarist and songwriter Jerry Reed was regularly recording with Chet Atkins in Nashville when Atkins' secretary Mary Lynch called him in to help Elvis on a version of Reed's recent hit "Guitar Man." Elvis had heard the song on the radio and slipped it into a recording session, but none of the highly accomplished guitar players on hand could reproduce Reed's unique sound. Reed (who had developed his own special guitar tuning) hotfooted it over from a fishing trip, not even bothering to change clothes before pitching up in at the studio. The session, in September 1967, saw Elvis finally get his mojo working again.

Elvis recorded Reed's song "U.S. Male," with Reed on guitar, a few months later in January 1968. Reed returned the compliment with his own Elvis tribute song "Tupelo Mississippi Flash," his first to chart in the top twenty. In the Seventies, Reed used the song to title a whole album, in which he also covered "Blue Moon Of Kentucky." Elvis later covered Reed compositions "Talk About The Good Times" and "A Thing Called Love."

Born in Atlanta, GA on March 20, 1937, Reed started out as a rockabilly performer before moving into Country. His first taste of success was when Gene Vincent covered his composition "Crazy Legs" in 1958. After moving to Nashville, Reed worked as a songwriter and session player for the best part of the Sixties, until he scored his first hit with "Guitar Man." His biggest hit came with "When You're Hot, You're Hot" in 1971; he landed his own TV show in the early Seventies after appearing as a regular guest on Glen Campbell's show. Later in the Seventies, Reed turned his talents to acting, working with Burt Reynolds in a slew of movies including the *Smokey and the Bandit* series. More recently, he has appeared opposite Adam Sandler.

Reed teamed up with Felton Jarvis in 1980 to lay down new instrumental tracks for remixes of Elvis' American Studio recordings, released on the album *Guitar Man*. He has continued paying tributes to Elvis ever since, singing "Elvis Has Left The Building" in 1998.

REEVES, JIM
(B. JAMES TRAVIS REEVES, 1923-1964)

One of the most popular Nashville country singers of the Fifties and Sixties, "Gentleman Jim" only went into the singing businesses after his baseball playing career with the St. Louis Cardinals was cut short by injury. He scored his first hit with "Mexican Joe" in 1953.

Born in Galloway, Panola County, Texas on August 20, 1923, Reeves met an untimely end while still in his prime in an airplane accident in 1964. His fans still wanted more, and he continued to score #1 hits in the US and abroad until 1969. A leading light of the more pop-oriented "Nashville sound," Reeves developed a style that owed as much to crooners as his Country predecessors that ensured a chart presence all the way into the Eighties.

On his way up, Elvis appeared on Louisiana Hayride bills with the already-established Reeves. After the event, Reeves sardonically remarked that Elvis used the same musicians and microphone but sold better.

Elvis covered many songs that his fellow RCA artist had made his own—Reeves was the label's up-and-coming hope for 1955—including "He'll Have To Go," "I'm Beginning To Forget You" and "Welcome To My World."

Reeves was inducted into the Country Hall of Fame in 1967.

REFERENCE BOOKS ON ELVIS

Elvis reference books range from pocket-sized trivia pamphlets to monster encyclopedic tomes.

Dedicated Elvis fans know that every book on Elvis qualifies as a reference book. The most outlandish conspiracy theory and wildest unsubstantiated rumor add to the overall Elvis myth and mystique, contributing to the kaleidoscopic picture of a man—flesh and blood he was—who has had such a lasting effect on popular culture and such a huge resonance on millions of individuals around the world.

Elvis Encyclopedias have been around in one guise or another since at least the mid-Sixties.

For decades, the most widely used single resource for Elvis information was *Elvis—His Life From A to Z*, by Fred L. Worth and Steve D. Tamerius, published by Contemporary Books in 1988. This itself was an expanded version of 1981 publication *All About Elvis*.

Biographies abound, yet the two-volume work by Peter Guralnick, *Last Train to Memphis* and *Careless Love*, is generally considered to stand head and shoulders above anything else. Much as Guralnick has tried to brush off the epithet "definitive," his works have set the standard by which all others are judged.

For Elvis' body of music, no man has more first-hand experience than Ernst Jorgensen, who began collating Elvis discographies for fun as a fan and has ended up managing Elvis' legacy for RCA/BMG for more than a decade, together with Roger Semon. His 1998 book, *Elvis Presley: A Life in Music*, is regarded as the definitive resource for fans.

Guralnick and Jorgensen teamed up to write *Elvis Day by Day* (Ballantine, 1999), a chronology of Elvis' life and work that draws directly from the Elvis Presley Enterprise archives.

For the vast literature that has grown up around Elvis, *Infinite Elvis: An Annotated Bibliography*, by Mary Hancock Hinds, published by A Capella Books, 2001, offers a guided tour of many hundreds of books.

Many fans have also written incredibly passionate and informative reference works on the object of their allegiance, and of course, the internet hosts dozens of sites packed with Elvis information.

Consult the bibliography and specific entries for additional information.

A SELECTION OF OTHER POPULAR REFERENCE BOOKS:

The Complete Elvis, edited by Martin Torgoff, G. P. Putnam and Sons/Delilah Books, 1982.

E is for Elvis: An A-to-Z Illustrated Guide to the King of Rock 'n' Roll, by Caroline Latham and Jeannie Sakol, NAL Books, 1990.

Best of Elvis, by Susan M. Doll, Publications International, 1996.

All Shook Up - Elvis Day By Day, 1954 -1977, by Lee Cotten, Popular Culture Ink, 1998.

Elvis, the Early Years: A 2001 Fact Odyssey, by Jim Curtin and Renata Ginter, Celebrity Press, 1999.

Elvis and You: Your Guide to the Pleasures of Being an Elvis Fan, by Laura Levin and John O'Hara, Perigee Trade, 2000.

The Rough Guide to Elvis, by Paul Simpson, Rough Guides, 2002, revised in 2004.

REHEARSALS

For the majority of his career, rehearsing was a studio pursuit for Elvis, though he did listen to and pick out demos prior to a session, and often tried out tunes he liked with pals at home (a proportion of which have made it onto publicly-released home recordings albums).

At the start of his career, Elvis played so regularly that had little time or need for rehearsal. He barely found a gap to get back to Sun Studio to record, let alone rehearse.

He had a prodigious natural ability to learn a song after just one listening, and would then try it out in different ways until he came up with the one that he thought worked best.

His Sixties sabbatical from live performing generated a calamitous attack of nerves when he finally geared up for his NBC TV Special. He worked up a new repertoire for his first Las Vegas engagement in 1969 with Charlie Hodge, and then with the newly-formed TCB band. The band spent weeks learning his entire back catalogue when they realized that on stage Elvis might decide to sing practically anything from his repertoire without prior warning.

That first Vegas engagement established a pattern in which Elvis and the band learned and rehearsed a lot of new material before each run began, only to drop the new tunes within a couple of days because Elvis felt that audience reacted less favorably to the new songs than to the hits they knew and loved.

The atmosphere of an Elvis rehearsal was captured by the cameras for *Elvis: That's The Way It Is* and *Elvis on Tour*. Elvis rehearsed for his *Aloha from Hawaii* show with a full concert run-through the night before. Elvis rehearsing in the studio (and the many outtakes he went through before coming up with a finished version of his songs, arguably a vital part of his rehearsal process) features prominently on many FTD releases and on bootlegs that focus on material leading up to his major concerts.

"RELAX"

A sultry Sid Tepper/Roy C. Bennett song with a tip of the hat to "Fever," which Elvis recorded on August 30, 1962 at Radio Recorders for *It Happened at the World's Fair*. The song later appeared on the *Mahalo From Elvis* LP, and on the *Double Features* release for the movie, twinned with *Fun in Acapulco*.

Jazzy alternate takes grace the FTD version of the *It Happened at the World's Fair* soundtrack, released in 2003.

"RELEASE ME"

Elvis injected some rock into this much-covered country classic when he sang it in Las Vegas on February 18, 1970. The performance was recorded by RCA for live album *On Stage*.

Songwriter Eddie Miller first recorded the song in 1953 (Miller wrote the track with a little help from his friends Robert Yount and James Pebworth, who also goes by the names Dub Williams and Robert Harris; some sources also cite William McCall), under its original title "Won't Someone Please Release Me." The song was reputedly inspired by Miller overhearing a woman ask the question of her husband, from whom she wanted a divorce. The following year, Jimmy Heap took the song higher up the charts, in a process repeated by Kitty Wells, Ray Price and Esther Phillips, all of whom had measures of success with the song in the Fifties and early Sixties. Engelbert Humperdinck had a top-five pop chart hit with the song in 1967, when it was the most played jukebox song of the year.

Elvis sang the song live sporadically through the Seventies, and included it on the playlist for his last ever concert.

Elvis albums featuring the song include *Welcome to My World*, and compilations *Platinum: A Life in Music*, *Live in Las Vegas*, *The Country Side of Elvis* and *Elvis Country* (the 2006 version).

"Release Me" is on FTD concert releases *The Impossible Dream*, *Polk Salad Annie*, *Takin' Tahoe Tonight!*, *Southern Nights* and *Unchained Melody*, in addition to numerous bootlegs.

Rehearsal versions have been included on FTD releases *Polk Salad Annie* and *Elvis On Tour—The Rehearsals*.

Elvis in the 50s.

RELIGION

Elvis grew up in the First Assembly of God church and lived his life believing in God. As an adult, his spiritual search led him to explore other religions and philosophies, and largely abjure organized religion.

Gladys read Elvis stories from the Bible during his formative years, when attending Church was a major part of his family's life; a number of his uncles were ordained priests in the church, and at one stage Vernon was a deacon.. Gospel and hymns, the first music to which Elvis was exposed as a tot, became a lifelong love.

On his rise to national fame, Elvis was viewed by some as a threat to the morals of a nation. Preachers competed in issuing dire warnings to their congregations, some openly declaring that Elvis was the work of the devil. In the words of gospel vocalist James Blackwood, "In the very beginning there were some in the church world that did not accept Elvis because of some of his body movements. But many of his fans were devout church people, and they loved Elvis as well as the rock 'n' roll fans. Elvis had such a wide appeal."

Months before his first record came out, in May 1954 Elvis and then girlfriend Dixie Locke went along to an Oral Roberts Crusade meeting. After Elvis found fame, the evangelist is said to have approached Colonel Parker about Elvis appearing on his TV programming.

One of the first things that Colonel Parker did for his new client as he groomed him for Hollywood was to highlight Elvis' poor, church-respecting background. In actual fact, for the First Assembly of God church to which the Presleys had gone, the very act of watching a movie was considered a sin.

In January 1957, Elvis sang gospel song "Peace In The Valley" on the "Ed Sullivan Show" and revealed his religious side to the nation. He continued to sing religious songs for work and pleasure for the rest of his days.

In 1958, when mourning his mother, Elvis told former girlfriend Dixie Locke that he envied fellow musician Jimmie Rodgers Snow, who had turned his back on the entertainment business to become a minister. Childhood friend Becky Martin has said that Elvis once told her that he wished he could have become a preacher and used his life in good deeds.

Elvis was thrilled to cut his first gospel album, *His Hand in Mine*, in 1960 on his return from the Army. A genre that Elvis strongly associated with his mother, he had always played gospel to get into the mood at recording sessions; in later years, he would sing gospel through the night to wind down after a live show. As well as the dozens of gospel tracks Elvis sang in his career, he recorded some specifically Catholic songs such as the "Lord's Prayer" and "Miracle Of The Rosary."

In 1964, on the cusp of his thirtieth birthday, his career seemingly on a downswing and new English bands exciting young America as he had a decade earlier, Elvis embarked on a spiritual quest to find answers to life's big questions and the to question that always loomed in his mind, the imponderable why me? He found a confederate in hairdresser Larry Geller, who gave Elvis an accelerated course in spiritual learning and offered him a friendship based on this shared interest. Geller writes in his memoir that he and Elvis were following "the Socratic injunction, to know thyself, and so find personal fulfillment."

Elvis began holding impromptu bible readings in his Los Angeles home to assembled friends and fans. On bus trips between Memphis and LA, Elvis engaged in long philosophical and religious discussions with Geller in the hope that some of his skeptical entourage might become interested.

Elvis explained to Larry Geller that he had turned his back on the teachings of the church in which he was raised because the "hellfire and brimstone" approach instilled a fear—rather than a love—of God. However, in his studies of world religions and esoteric practices such as the Kabbalah, he did so with reference to his own religious roots; for example, by using the Kabbalah to uncover hidden meanings in the Old Testament.

By March 1965, after a year of intense reading and mulling, Elvis was dismayed that he still had not what he considered to be an "experience of God." Soon afterwards, he believed that he saw the faces of Stalin and Jesus in a high bank of cloud over the desert. He was so shaken by this experience that for a brief moment, he considered quitting the music and movie business and joining a monastery—a threat that the Colonel took seriously enough to keep a close eye on Larry Geller's influence and, two years down the line, effectively bar him from Elvis' inner circle.

As part of his religious inquiry, Elvis became involved with the Self-Realization Fellowship in 1965. He started wearing a Jewish chai symbol ("chai" is the Hebrew word for "life" or "living"), and had a Star of David added to Gladys's gravestone. It is not certain whether he adopted these symbols because he knew that his great-grandmother on his mother's side, Martha Tackett, was Jewish. Larry Geller says in his memoir that Gladys revealed this secret about their lineage to Elvis but told him to keep it secret from Vernon. Geller also says that Elvis believed his Jewish ancestry was "something precious and sacred," and that he even toyed with the idea of studying Hebrew at one time so that he could read Jewish religious books in the original.

That year he commissioned Memphis jeweler Harry Levitch to design a watch that featured a cross, a star of David and the "chai" symbol, which he gave out as a gift to co-workers on United Artists picture *Frankie and Johnny*. When asked why he was combining all these symbols, Elvis reputedly replied, "I don't want to miss out on heaven due to a technicality."

Incidentally, Jewish neighbors of young Elvis' in Memphis, Alf and Jeannette Fruchter, told a biographer that Elvis would come round on the Sabbath to help the family with the things that they were not allowed to do that day.

Elvis' period of intense religious introspection suffered a hiatus in early 1967, when the Colonel banished Geller from Elvis' inner circle and, together with Priscilla, just before their wedding, persuaded Elvis to make a bonfire of his books. Elvis nevertheless remained a religious man (and continued to buy, read, annotate and give way religious and spiritual texts). Girlfriend Barbara Leigh, who had an affair with Elvis from 1970 to 1972, said that Elvis would pray if he thought it would help in any given situation.

Elvis consciously wanted to use his talents and influence for good. Sri Daya Mata of the Self-Realization Fellowship says that when he returned to live performing, "he wanted to be a great spiritual influence" on the people who came to see him and help them have a closer relationship with God.

Some friends remember Elvis' religious zeal as more highfalutin' than sincere. Pal Charlie Hodge recalls Elvis standing on a table at his Palm Springs home and recounting tales of Jesus from the Bible to women who were flown in to party: "He was real serious, but he would get the stories all wrong."

Steve Dunleavy writes that although Elvis made significant donations to Catholic (and Jewish) charities, he believed that Catholicism was "a dangerous branch of Christianity." According to Red and Sonny West, Elvis sometimes had disparaging things to say about Catholics and Jews. Red West said, "Deep down Elvis is very prejudiced and he made no secret about it." Elvis did have a number of Jewish friends among his coterie: George Klein, Alan Fortas, Marty Lacker and Larry Geller.

A number of religious organizations tried to use Elvis' religious voracity to their own ends. Scientology, for example, was keen to get Elvis involved, but when he read their literature—and even visited their headquarters—he felt that they were too much like the church he grew up in. Entourage members have said that he believed that the church of Scientology practiced mind-control, and that he walked out because he thought they were only interested in him for his money. The Scientology movement had to wait until after Elvis' death to add a Presley to their roster: first Priscilla, and then Lisa Marie, who in interviews has credited Scientology with keeping her on the right side of insanity. Claims have more recently surfaced that Elvis had a copy of the *Book of Mormon* in his room when he died. Donny Osmond has said that in the Seventies, Elvis used to talk to his mother about the text; Elvis' long-term karate teacher Ed Parker was brought up in the Mormon faith.

When TV evangelist Rex Humbard and his wife Maude Aimee visited Elvis backstage in late 1976—during the show, Elvis dedicated "How Great Thou Art" to the couple—Elvis asked if the Lord Jesus was going to return soon. Humbard said he thought he would. Humbard later said, "I could see he was reaching back to the past—that spirituality, that feeling that he had years and years before that had been planted in his heart." At their meeting, Elvis reputedly dissolved into tears when Maude Aimee told him, "If you fully dedicated your life to God you could lead millions of people into the kingdom of the Lord." Some biographers have written that Elvis "recommitted his life to Jesus Christ" at this time. In Larry Geller's recollections, Elvis believed that Jesus was "the flower of humanity," a man of compassion and suffering.

Stepbrother Rick Stanley has said that Elvis was in a particularly religious mood the day before he died. As well as recommending his stepbrother to listen to people who talked to them about Jesus, Elvis prayed for his sins.

Elvis' funeral in 1977 was a religious affair, officiated by Reverend C. W. Bradley of the Wooddale Church of Christ. Rex Humbard gave a sermon.

See also SPIRITUALITY and MYSTICISM

ELVIS AND THE BIBLE

Elvis took to heart his mother's advice, that the answer to any problem could be found by consulting the good book. He knew the Bible inside out and quoted it at apposite moments.

Las Vegas showgirl Dottie Harmony, who stayed with the Presleys in late 1956, remembered spending evenings reading the Bible. Awestruck fans, girlfriends and entourage members received Elvis Bible readings in the Sixties and Seventies. Reputedly Elvis' favorite passage was St. Paul's paean to the power of love, Corinthians 13; other sources state that it was Corinthians 10:13 ("No temptation has seized you except what is common to man. And God is faithful; he will not let you be tempted beyond what you can bear. But when you are tempted, he will also provide a way out so that you can stand up under it.") Larry Geller says that Elvis' favorite was the Book of John.

One of Elvis' most of-cited quotes from the Bible was ,"And ye shall know the truth, and the truth shall set you free." It was this phrase that Elvis' entourage friends inscribed in a Bible that they gave him for Christmas 1964.

Elvis played a religious yet troubled man in *Flaming Star*. During the movie, he twice quotes from the bible (Matthew 27:46 and Genesis 7:10).

ELVIS—THE RELIGION?

From the very start, to many fans Elvis became an idol of quasi-religious adulation. This adulation ranged from a belief that Elvis was imbued with super-human qualities (heroes and idols often are), was immune to death (the Elvis is alive believers), and that "relics"—items that Elvis owned or touched—were and are worth large amounts of money or personal risk (the Elvis memorabilia market). To this day, many fans have an Elvis room or some kind of shrine in their homes, a treatment reserved for deities in other cultures. As years have passed since his death, commentators suggest that Elvis has started acquiring the characteristics of a modern-day deity; Elvis churches have been established, if in most cases with humorous intent, aside from the Elvis-dressed priests who perform weddings in Las Vegas and beyond.

Elvis was well-aware of the power he had: he described his fanbase to Larry Geller as his "ministry," as God's way of getting a message across through the universal language of music.

In life, Elvis was treated by his intimates as a minor divinity. More than one commentator has likened the entourage that Elvis gathered around him to a priesthood. In death, people who were associated with Elvis and well-known figures in the Elvis universe continue to spread the word.

Some commentators have claimed that Elvis identified with Jesus Christ, or at the very least struggled with the possibility that he might actually be Jesus. This assertion contradicts his public declarations that he was not "the King," a title that he loathed and believed applied only to Jesus Christ.

Larry Geller writes that Elvis believed that an element of Christ dwells in us all, and that "he truly felt that he was chosen to be here now as a modern-day savior, a Christ," in the sense of his power and potential as a force for good. The link between Elvis and Christ was made explicit on film by William Graham, who directed Elvis' final feature film Change of Habit, in the very final scene when Elvis' face is intercut with images of Jesus.

In his final days alive, Elvis was particularly interested in finding out more about the Turin Shroud, which for decades has been held up as a proof that Jesus Christ did exist. It has been claimed that the book Elvis was reading when he died was Ian Wilson's book, The Shroud of Turin.

Marty Lacker remembers an occasion in Los Angeles when Elvis woke up, looked out of the window and saw a bird with the head of Jesus.

A whole strand of Elvis literature has grown up around Elvis' purported religious credentials. Cinda Godfrey wrote a book claiming that Elvis was the Messiah. John Strausbaugh defines the nascent religion of Elvis as "Elvism." Gregory Reece's thesis is that Elvis is a perfect messiah for the consumer age, "just the kind of god we need these days because he cannot be taken too seriously."

ELVIS SAID IN 1956: "I belong to the First Assembly of God Church and have gone to church since I could walk."

ELVIS SAID IN 1956: "I believe in God, I believe in Him with all my heart. I believe all good things come from God. That includes all the good things that have come to me and to my folks... Being religious means that you love God and are real grateful for all He's given, and want to work for Him. I feel deep in my heart that I'm doing all this."

ELVIS SAID IN 1956: "I don't believe I'd sing the way I do if God hadn't wanted me to."

ELVIS SAID IN 1956: "My Bible tells me that what he sows he will also reap, and if I'm sowing evil and wickedness it will catch up with me."

ELVIS SAID IN 1957: "God created everybody equal and I would never say that I didn't like anybody."

ELVIS SAID: "I am not the King. Jesus Christ is the King. I'm just an entertainer."

ELVIS SAID: "I ain't no saint, but I've tried never to do anything that would hurt my family or offend God."

ELVIS SAID TO LARRY GELLER: "I always knew there was truth to my religion. Somehow I never lost faith in God, despite those old preachers tryin' to make people feel guilty for things they never done. I always knew that deep inside me there were answers that went beyond their rigid old closed minds."

ELVIS SAID TO LARRY GELLER: "If we went back into everyone's family tree, if we went back one hundred, five hundred years, a thousand years, if we could go that, I'll bet we'd find that everybody living today has some Jewish blood and that we all come from the same place."

ELVIS SAID TO LARRY GELLER: " I have the power of heaven or hell in me, and that's what I've got to learn to balance... I've got to learn how to conquer that hell."

ELVIS WROTE: "God loves you, but he loves you best when you sing."

ELVIS SAID IN 1976: "What profiteth a man if he gains the world and loses his own soul?"

GREIL MARCUS: "Hillbilly Calvinism was also at the root of his self-respect and his pride: the act of his ambition."

LARRY GELLER: "He remained a Christian his whole life, but not a Christian to the exclusion of anything else. He was open to other beliefs and teachings, and even then he realized that no one has all the answers."

J.D. SUMNER: "Besides Jesus Christ, there's no greater man [than Elvis] that ever lived."

RICK STANLEY: "He was a true believer who made his own rules so that his beliefs could blend with the way he lived his life."

GEORGE HARRISON: "Christ said, 'Put your house in order', and Elvis said 'clean up your own backyard', so if everybody tries to fix themselves up rather than trying to fix everybody else up there won't be a problem."

LITTLE RICHARD: "Elvis was God-given, there's no other explanation. A Messiah comes around every few thousand years, and Elvis was it this time."

BRUCE SPRINGSTEEN: "Elvis is my religion. But for him, I'd be selling encyclopedias right now."

RAY WALKER: "He was one of the best-read people I have ever met on the subject of religion."

NANCY ROOKS: "He truly believed in an afterlife."

Books:

God's Works Through Elvis, by Rev Martin R. Long, Exposition Press, 1979.
Elvis People: The Cult of the King, by Ted Harrison, HarperCollins, 1993.
The Gospel of Elvis: Containing the Testament and Apocrypha Including All the Greater Themes of the King, by Solomon Church, The Summit Publishing Group, 1995.
E: Reflections On The Birth Of Elvis Faith, by Johan Strausbaugh, Blast Books, 1995.
Elvis' Search for God, by Jess Stearn, Larry Geller, Greenleaf Publications, 1998.
The Elvis-Jesus Mystery: The Shocking Scriptural and Scientific Evidence That Elvis Presley Could Be The Messiah Anticipated Throughout History, by Cinda Godfrey, Revelation Pub, 1999.
The Ways of Elvis: Lessons from His Life, by John Dawson, Tapestry Press, 2002.
Schmelvis: In Search of Elvis Presley's Jewish Roots, by Max Wallace and Jonathan Goldstein, ECW Press, 2002.
The Tao of Elvis, by David Rosen, Harvest Books, 2002.
Prayers of Elvis, by Madeleine Wilson, Shalom Publishing, 2002.
Elvis Religion: The Cult of the King, by Gregory L. Reece, I. B. Tauris, 2006.

RESERVE OFFICER TRAINING CORPS (ROTC)

Elvis enrolled in ROTC in his 10th grade. He achieved an overall grade C for his first term and grade B for his second, scoring an A in English and an F in typing.

RESTAURANTS AND BARS ELVIS FREQUENTED

Not surprisingly for a man whose favorite cuisine was down-home home-cooking, had cooks on call 24-hours a day, could expect to be mobbed if he showed his face in public, and had no particular liking for alcoholic beverages, going out to bars and restaurants was not high on Elvis' agenda; that said, one former entourage member came up with the novel view that Elvis seldom ate out because he had terrible table manners.

The exception to this rule was in his first flush of performing. Constant touring in 1954 and 1955 made Elvis an expert on diners across the Mid-South and Texas. Back home in Memphis he had plenty of money to go out to his favorite haunts, if he wanted to forsake Mama Gladys' home cooking, but then she so looked forwards to him coming home.

In his family's Tupelo days, Elvis is said to have gone to Johnnie's Drive-in, though a family too poor to have enough food for the table was not likely to have made a habit of eating out.

In his pre-fame days, Elvis and pals often patronized K's Drive-In. When recording at Sun, like many performers and the Sun staff Elvis regularly stopped in at Taylor's Restaurant next door (since converted into the Sun Studio café). He also ate at the State Café.

When in New York for his first TV slot on "Stage Show," Elvis and the Colonel dined at the Hickory House Restaurant.

Driving through Dallas in 1956, Elvis stopped in at the Midway Café

On his first date with Anita Wood, Elvis, his date and several pals ate hamburgers at Chenault's Drive-in (1402 Bellevue Boulevard South, later Elvis Presley Drive), a restaurant he often patronized when in town because he could rely on the owners cordoning off a special area so that Elvis and friends could hang out unmolested. The 24-hour restaurant has since closed down.

Elvis often ate at the Coffee Cup in West Memphis, until he and fellow Army recruits were hounded out of the place when they stopped there on their way to induction in 1958. Not even in backwoods Germany during his military service could Elvis expect to just stop into a bar without hundreds of fans magically appearing in the time it took to polish off a frankfurter.

Other Memphis haunts where Elvis ate before and after the draft include the Terrace Room (a favorite before heading to the Rainbow Rollerdrome for all-night skate sessions), the Great Western Steakhouse on 1298 Madison, the Ranch House Restaurant, and Earl's Hot Biscuits.

He ate at Memphis's self-proclaimed oldest restaurant, the Arcade Diner (540 S. Main St.), which still boasts the "Elvis booth," and would of course regularly order Krystal burgers for takeout.

Elvis reputedly liked to eat at the Bill Williams Chicken House restaurants, specializing in "Fried Chicken, Savage Style."

In the Sixties, Elvis occasionally went Italian at Coletta's on 1063 South Parkway, from where he and Priscilla sometimes ordered take-out pizza. At 4101 on what is now Elvis Presley Boulevard, he sometimes ate at the Gridiron Restaurant—the owners say that he occasionally wore a disguise to ensure privacy. Another local haunt was the Piccadilly Cafeteria.

The Four Flames restaurant, at 1085 Poplar, hosted a banquet for Elvis in 1971 to celebrate the Jaycees award. This too has since closed. On rare occasions Elvis might sneak out with girlfriend Linda Thompson in the Seventies for a taste of forbidden fruit at McDonald's. The far simpler option was to send out one of the entourage guys to pick up burgers or pizza.

In Los Angeles, Elvis occasionally went to the Luau restaurant in Beverly Hills, which had a private room. He is also said to have dropped in to the Formosa Café during filming of *Kid Galahad*. In the early Sixties, he frequented the club run by Sandy Ferra's father, The Red Velvet, where Tony Ferra always reserved a couple of booths for Elvis and his crew in case they turned up. He sometimes patronized nightclubs on Sunset Strip in the Sixties to see music acts, and sometimes snuck in after the lights had gone down to watch other performers on his trips for business or pleasure to Las Vegas.

ELVIS-THEMED RESTAURANTS

The Elvis Estate attempted to launch a series of Elvis-themed restaurants with a flagship property in Memphis the early 2000s, but the venture ran into serious cash flow problems.

Until 2006, Anna's Steakhouse in Memphis was a popular Elvis-themed haunt, owned and run by Anna Hamilton, who attended the same Humes High, as had Elvis. Her collection of memorabilia has since moved to the Superior Restaurant, at 159 Beale Street.

Ever since he purchased control of the Elvis Estate, fans have speculated Bob Sillerman is planning to launch a worldwide chain of Elvis-themed restaurants. By the time you read this, there may be one open near you.

Hard Rock Cafés in many locations prominently display Elvis memorabilia.

"RETURN TO SENDER"

One of the prime exceptions to the generally-accepted rule that Elvis' movie songs were of low quality, this catchy number, written by Otis Blackwell and Winfield Scott, first came out as a single backed with "Where Do You Come From" in October 1962, trailing the release of the movie Girls! Girls! Girls! Elvis recorded the track on March 27 that year at Radio Recorders. Though it just failed to make #1, it sold over a million copies; in the UK it was #1 for three weeks. One estimate is that the song has racked up 14 million sales in the US to the present day.

"Return To Sender" came out on the soundtrack LP, and later on *Worldwide Gold Award Hits Vol. 1*, *The Great Performances*, the *Double Features Girls! Girls! Girls!* re-release, *Command Performances*, and more recently on the *Elvis' Gold Records Vol. 4* CD reissue, *Platinum: A Life in Music*, *Artist Of The Century*, *ELVIS 30 #1 Hits*, *Hitstory*, *The Essential Elvis Presley* and *Elvis at the Movies*.

For some time after the song came out, fans sent letters to Elvis at nonexistent addresses just to get the envelope back stamped "return to sender, address unknown."

Elvis with Kang Rhee at the Vegas Imperial Suite.

RHEE, KANG

Elvis began studying Tae Kwon Do with this karate instructor in Memphis from 1970, after he was recommended by Elvis' long term teacher Ed Parker. As well as hiring Rhee to teach himself, Priscilla and several entourage guys, according to Rhee Elvis also ran his karate choreography moves by the karate master before putting them into action on stage in Las Vegas.

Rhee was invited along to Elvis' Stax recording session in the summer of 1973. According to an engineer there that day, Rhee was the only one among the entourage and RCA executives who had the courage to express his true opinion and tell Elvis that he didn't like a track they were listening back to.

Elvis is said to have given "Master Rhee" $50,000 to set up his own school, the Kang Rhee Institute of Self Defense, and of course, at least one Cadillac.

Rhee has featured in Elvis documentaries *Elvis: Memories* and *200 Cadillacs*.

KANG RHEE: " . . .He has a mental and physical very high standard as a martial artist: spiritual and mental is much more strength. Stronger than any other person I can think of."

RHODE ISLAND

- Providence

Elvis and the TCB Band performed at the Civic Center Auditorium on June 22, 1974. They did two shows on June 26, 1976, and a further show on May 23, 1977.

RHYTHM & BLUES

Before the Nineties, R&B was an expression coined by Jerry Wexler in 1949 (or in alternate histories, invented directly by *Billboard* Magazine) to describe an emerging amalgam of blues with gospel in which the beat was much more upfront than in the past. The term was also adopted as a catchall for black music that was neither jazz nor gospel, as a replacement to the distinctly downbeat moniker 'race records', which until that time *Billboard* had used to label its charts of African-American music.

Initiated by artists like Wynonie Harris and Muddy Waters (and characterized by syncopation and blues-derived chords), rhythm and blues swept away the boogie woogie and jump blues that had in turn supplanted bebop jazz and later hard bop.

R & B was the cutting edge of music in the early Fifties before the term rock 'n' roll was coined. Some music historians assert that rock 'n' roll was the white version of R&B, though this theory does not fit with the generally acknowl-

Elvis in his signature Aztec Indian jumpsuit in Providence, Rhode Island, June 22, 1975.

edged fact that the first recognizable rock 'n' roll record was "Rocket 88," by Ike Turner's band Jackie Brenston and his Delta Cats—a track that initially appeared on the R & B charts.

During his formative years, Elvis was an avid fan of top R&B singers Ray Charles and Wynonie Harris. When he met songwriters Leiber and Stoller on the set of *Jailhouse Rock*, Elvis surprised the erudite New Yorkers with his vast knowledge of even the most obscure R&B acts.

Over his career, Elvis covered more than fifty R & B hits (if the definition is stretched to include songs that originated in the Thirties but were covered by R & B artists). This number eclipses Pat Boone, who has been a target of accusations that he built his career on the backs of blacks.

Since its origins, the term R & B has mutated several times. In the Sixties, a crop of hard-edged British bands reformulated R&B. In the Seventies, it became a blanket term for soul and funk; by the mid-Eighties, it was beginning to be adopted to cover hip hop and modern African-American pop.

ONE OF BMG'S THEMED RELEASES FOR 2006 WAS *ELVIS R 'N' B*.

TRACK LISTING:
1. Good Rockin' Tonight
2. That's All Right, Mama
3. Baby, Let's Play House
4. Lawdy, Miss Clawdy
5. My Baby Left Me
6. So Glad You're Mine
7. I Got A Woman
8. Shake, Rattle And Roll
9. When It Rains, It Really Pours
10. Tryin' To Get To You
11. Mystery Train
12. Trouble
13. Big Boss Man
14. Reconsider Baby
15. I Feel So Bad
16. Hi Heel Sneakers
17. Down In The Alley
18. A Mess Of Blues
19. Stranger In My Own Home Town
20. Pledging My Love

ELVIS' #1 R&B HITS:

Don't Be Cruel / Hound Dog, 1956
All Shook Up, 1957
(Let Me Be Your) Teddy Bear, 1957
Jailhouse Rock, 1957

RUFUS THOMAS: "Elvis did far more for the resurgence of rhythm and blues, which white people called rock 'n' roll, than anyone else has ever done."

RICH, CHARLIE
(1932-1995)

Born in Colt, Arkansas on December 14, 1932, Charlie Rich moved to Memphis after getting out of the US Air Force and spent some time working as a session musician and songwriter for Sam Phillips at Sun, contributing to hits by Sun roster artists including Jerry Lee Lewis and Johnny Cash. Prior to entering the service, he had his own group, the Velvetones, fronted by his wife-to-be, Margaret Ann. Rich's first hit was "Lonely Weekends" on Phillips International in 1960.

Elvis recorded Rich composition "I'm Comin'

Home" and previous Rich hits "Big Boss Man," "I Washed My Hands In Muddy Water" and "Pieces Of My Life." He would have added "Sittin' And Thinkin' " to the list if publishing wrangles had not stood in the way.

Rich brought out records in five separate decades and had his greatest success in the early Seventies with "Behind Closed Doors" and "The Most Beautiful Girl," which topped the country and pop charts and won a Grammy; Elvis ad-libbed a snatch of this latter song during one of his own Seventies shows. Rich's final album was produced by Peter Guralnick. The "Silver Fox," as he was known, also appeared in two movies in the Eighties.

RICH, JOHN
(B. 1925)

This director, best known for TV hits "The Dick Van Dyke Show," "Gunsmoke," "The Andy Griffith Show" and "All in the Family," worked with Elvis on *Roustabout* (1964) and *Easy Come, Easy Go* (1967), which was his final feature film. Rich worked in TV well into his seventies, and garnered three Emmys during his long career.

RICHARD, CLIFF
(B. HARRY RODGER WEBB, 1940)

The UK's answer to Elvis in the Fifties and a poster-boy for longevity in the entertainment business, Richard was born in India. Growing up in the UK, he knew he wanted to be a rock star the instant that he first heard "Heartbreak Hotel" on the radio of a parked car.

After establishing himself as a top-selling rock 'n' roller in 1958 with his debut hit "Move It," backed by the Shadows—a band that found plenty of success in the Sixties in its own right—Richard embarked on a successful movie career before gradually moving to the middle of the market as The Beatles usurped his youth appeal. He has continued to record into the 2000s in the UK, but has scored only a few top 10 hits in the US. The only solo artist to have had more #1 singles than Richard in the UK is Elvis.

Elvis recorded a number of songs that Richard had previously released, including "I Gotta Know" and "Wonderful World." Richard has covered many Elvis numbers during his career.

In a 1969 press conference, Elvis recalled meeting Cliff Richard, though the time that Richard knocked on Elvis' door in Germany to say hello, nobody was home. Richard has since said that he declined an opportunity to meet Elvis a year before his death because he heard that Elvis was not in great shape and did not want to be disappointed when he met his hero.

CLIFF RICHARD: "No one was ever going to be like Elvis and no one has been and that's how it should be."

"RIDING THE RAINBOW"

Elvis recorded this up-tempo Ben Weisman / Fred Wise song for the *Kid Galahad* movie and EP on October 26, 1961 at Radio Recorders, without excessively evident enthusiasm.

The song was included on the *I Got Lucky* album in the Seventies, and reissued in 1993 as part of the Double Feature series with *Girls! Girls! Girls!* A more laid back first-take version featured on 2001 FTD release *Silver Screen Stereo*.

RIGHTEOUS BROTHERS

Bobby Hatfield (1940-2003) and Bill Medley (born 1940), the unrelated Righteous Brothers, were among Elvis' favorite vocalists. Elvis covered Righteous Brothers songs "Unchained Melody" and "You've Lost That Lovin' Feelin'," both hits for the group in its banner year, 1965. Elvis knew about the group from their days on TV show "Shindig," when he would get members of his entourage to phone in requests direct to the leading exponents of "blue-eyed soul."

Medley and Hatfield formed the group in 1963. Before coming under the tutelage of Phil Spector, they were a more standard R&B outfit. They had a string of hits in 1965 and 1966, when they returned to self-production, retaining Spector's hallmark "wall of sound." Medley went solo in 1968; Hatfield soldiered on as a Righteous Brother with Jimmy Walker for a few more years.

Bill Medley became friends with Elvis when they met during Elvis' NBC TV Special recording sessions. Before he returned to live performing himself, Elvis interrupted a Righteous Brothers performance in Las Vegas by standing up in the audience and—as a prank—breaking into song. Backstage, they talked about music, their influences, and the fact that they both sounded black. In future years, they often met up in Las Vegas, where Medley regularly performed at the Hilton lounge.

After Elvis' death, Medley recorded the song "Old Friend" as a tribute to his pal. The Righteous Brothers reformed in later years, and continued to perform right up to Hatfield's death.

ELVIS SAID ON STAGE IN 1975: "They've had some of the best records since Fats Domino."

RIJFF, GER

A former President of the Dutch Elvis Presley fan club who has compiled approaching two dozen books of Elvis photographs, published through his own companies.

RILEY, BILLY LEE
(B. 1933)

Riley was one of the rockabilly artists Sam Phillips launched after Elvis left the Sun label at the end of 1955. Ultimately, Riley earned more of a living from backing Jerry Lee Lewis, Carl Perkins et al on guitar, bass, drums and harmonica than in his own right as a solo performer, despite memorable tunes such as "Flying Saucer Rock And Roll" and "Red Hot" (released as Billy Riley and His Little Green Men).

Riley provided the music at Elvis' 1968 and 1969 New Year's parties in Memphis, and continued to record his blues-influenced output—he had grown up in cotton-picking territory around Pocahontas, Arkansas—for a variety of labels, some of which he founded and helped run.

Riley had recently released "I've Got A Thing About You Baby" when Elvis recorded it in 1973.

Riley was inducted into the Rockabilly Hall of Fame in 1996, and has been a popular performer since the post-punk rockabilly revival.

RIOTS

If Elvis' early detractors were to be believed, the mere curl of his lip or swivel of his hip were sufficient to turn young people into wild, slavering animals. They may have had a point. Many of Elvis' shows in his initial years of touring had to be kept short and sweet and were only completed thanks to police intervention to keep the lid on riotous behavior. The scandal was that rather than testosterone-fuelled young men threatening to tear the place down, it was hormone-charged young women.

Elvismania showed its violent side at Jacksonville, Florida, on May 13, 1955 when hundreds of girls broke through security and trapped Elvis in his dressing room, where they proceeded to shred his clothes from his body. Elvis was partly to blame, when he said off-handedly to the 14,000-strong audience, "Girls, I'll see you backstage." He had to be rescued from the top of a shower cubicle, and only just managed to hold on to his pants. The police shoved Elvis through a window to safety in a police vehicle. Some Elvis chroniclers state that a similar fate befell Elvis the next time he played Jacksonville that July.

Red West remembers a small club outside Lubbock in the early days where a pitched battle broke out between the guys in the crowd, half of whom loved Elvis, half of whom loathed him. The man at the center of the heated debate just kept on singing. Meanwhile, the girls in the audience saw their chance and stormed the stage, threatening to overwhelm Elvis until Red West spirited him to a waiting car.

The floor collapsed because so many people crammed into a high school gym to see Elvis in Bono, Arkansas in September 1955.

DJ Bill Randle hosted a show in Cleveland, Ohio in October 1955 at which Elvis smashed up his guitar, unleashing mass hysteria among the audience. Randle later said, "We needed police to get him out of the hall."

In Kansas City on May 24, 1956, the band lost half of their instruments and drummer D.J. Fontana was pulled off the stage into the orchestra pit. A concert in Canada ended with fans rushing over to the stage and practically turning it over as they looked for Elvis. In Portland, Oregon, a concert was abandoned in September 1957 due to rioting fans.

The FBI kept tabs on these riots in its files but took no action.

Elvis had the power to start a riot even when he wasn't on the bill. At a Johnny Horton show he attended in Temple, Texas, during his Army days, Horton announced that Elvis was backstage and the audience rushed the band.

Elvis set off a series of riots in Mexico City following false rumors that he had slandered Mexican women, though it may have been a case of local teenagers using Elvis movie showings as an excuse for vandalism. Even the East German authorities blamed Elvismania for rioting youths who almost killed a border guard in Berlin in 1958.

Something as seemingly innocuous as Elvis' first movie appearance in Love Me Tender almost set off a riot at the New York premiere, when fans turned rowdy after they found out that Elvis was not going to be in attendance. Once more, the FBI was notified. Projection of that film was interrupted by hecklers in Minneapolis.

Fans had fewer changes to mob their idol in the Sixties. Film shoots provided a chance to try and break through security or nab Elvis as he arrived at the airport, as was the case in Hawaii when he flew in to shoot Girls! Girls! Girls! in 1962 and was relieved of all his jewelry. His security might have know this would happen; it was the same story when he arrived on the island in 1961 to do his charity show for the USS Arizona monument. Invariably, Elvis forgave his fans the more boisterous forms their adulation took.

Elvis was still capable of whipping up a riot in the Seventies when he hit the road again. In 1972 at Macon, Georgia fans rushed the stage at his afternoon show in the surge to grab scarves—a problem that entourage members had to watch out for, lest fans became trampled underfoot. This was a particularly big problem if children were brought to the show, or wheelchair-bound fans who could not get out of the way.

Near-riots occurred at Elvis' Tahoe shows when crowds were worried that they weren't going to be admitted to the venue because the management had overbooked.

In February 1977, Elvis was almost caught by a mob of fans as he made his limousine getaway from a show at St. Petersburg, Florida. A month later he prompted a near-riot when he cancelled a show at Baton Rouge with the band and backing singers were already out on the stage.

A last riot for Elvis almost took place at 6 p.m. on August 17, 1977, when at 6. p.m. the police announced that the viewing of Elvis' body was over and they needed to close the music gates to Graceland.

ELVIS SAID IN 1957: "A crowd of people can hurt you and not even realize they're doing it."

ELVIS TOLD SONNY WEST: "When they stop attacking me, I'm dead."

"RIP IT UP"

Another hit for Little Richard in 1956 written by Robert Blackwell and John Marascalco, another cover for Elvis later that same year. Robert "Bumps" Blackwell originally wrote "Rip It Up" as a country track. At John Marascalco's suggestion he reworked it for Little Richard, whose version became a million-selling R&B #1, and also climbed to #17 on the Hot 100 chart.

Bill Haley had already covered the song by the time Elvis committed his version to tape at Radio Recorders on September 3, 1956. Elvis' version was initially released on the EP Elvis, Vol. 1 and his second LP Elvis. He also added the song to the mix at his impromptu Million Dollar Quartet jam at Sun Studio late in 1956.

"Rip It Up" has come out on Worldwide Gold Award Hits Vol. 2, I Was The One, The King Of Rock And Roll, Elvis '56 and Elvis Rock.

A version laid down four takes before the master was released in 1997 on Platinum: A Life In Music. Another outtake is on Today Tomorrow & Forever, while four early takes feature on 2004 FTD release Flashback. Very occasionally, Elvis included this song in his Seventies live sets, though at the time of writing such versions have only seen the light of day on bootlegs (such as Elvis Among Friends).

RIVALS

Elvis has no rivals in terms of success, fan dedication, cultural impact and longevity. During all phases of his career—the rebellious rockin' Fifties, his Hollywood Sixties, and then after his 1968 NBC "Comeback" Special his Vegas touring years—Elvis broke records and stood head and shoulders above the competition, as a moneymaker if not necessarily an innovator. It is a phenomenal achievement that three decades after he made his last record, he remains so popular and such an iconic figure.

In terms of zeitgeist, Elvis' greatest rivals were, before him, Bing Crosby and Frank Sinatra, and in the Sixties, the Beatles and Bob Dylan.

As soon as Elvis achieved national fame, he was quickly elevated into a category of his own. Apart from rare exceptions, the many excellent black artists rocking and rolling before Elvis did not have access to the same kind of market as Elvis because in the Fifties the music business was still largely segregated. Sam Phillips midwifed a slew of rockabilly acts at Sun that for one reason or another failed to emulate Elvis' long-term success: Carl Perkins looked to be following a similar trajectory before suffering a bad car accident;

Jerry Lee Lewis self-destructed by marrying his 13-year-old cousin a year after he hit the big time; much of the rest of Phillips' roster had to wait for the Eighties rockabilly revival to receive national acclaim, and that was more likely to be in European nations than their own home country. Other white rockers such as Bill Haley could not compete with Elvis' sex appeal and charisma.

In 1956, the year that Elvis became a national phenomenon on his new record label RCA and began his thirteen year association with Hollywood, his biggest rival for the teenaged record-buying public was Pat Boone. The press attempted to whip up antagonism between the two but Elvis scotched all rumors, declaring, "Pat's one of the nicest guys I ever met."

Once it was apparent that Elvis had eclipsed all of his potential rivals, the question in the music press turned to was going to be the "new Elvis" or the "next Elvis." A slew of singers appeared in Elvis' wake who either copied his vocal mannerisms or the echo-heavy style of his early recordings at Sun. Gene Vincent sounded so much like Elvis that Elvis' band members initially thought that he had snuck off to make a record without them. Eddie Cochran made a name for himself as an early leather-clad rock 'n' roller.

Tommy Sands's star waxed and waned more quickly than Elvis', though seventeen year-old Ricky Nelson became a big rock 'n' roll record shifter for a six-year spell from 1957, with a ready-made launch platform on the family TV show "The Adventures of Ozzy and Harriet." That year, youth-focused magazines desperate for some kind of rivalry for Elvis looked as far afield as calypso crossover king Harry Belafonte.

Bobby Darin and Bobby Vee also had successful spells in the rock 'n' roll limelight, and Buddy Holly was just getting into top gear when his life was tragically cut short, along with fellow rockers Ritchie Valens and The Big Bopper.

Another so-called rival who was nothing of the sort was late-Fifties heartthrob Fabian (who had a hit with the song "Hound Dog Man"). Bobby Rydell was a major teen idol in the early Sixties, though by this time Elvis had broadened his audience considerably beyond the youth market. Jackie Wilson earned the epithet "the Black Elvis."

Women were eligible for Elvis rivalry too. Various singers were billed as "the female Elvis" in the Fifties, from Janis Martin to Wanda Jackson—Martin was promoted by RCA in 1957 with debut single "My Boy Elvis" to make the link crystal clear. Elvis' Sixties co-star Ann-Margret was also dubbed "the female Elvis."

The Colonel actively repositioned Elvis for long-term success during his spell away in the Army. Throughout the Sixties, Elvis' success was not threatened by his musical rivals for the simple reason that he had his own loyal fanbase who would go and see whatever movie he was in and buy the accompanying soundtrack. This explains the apparent anomaly that during Elvis' lifetime, his best-selling album was the soundtrack to Blue Hawaii.

The Beatles replaced Elvis as the focus of youthful exuberance in the mid-Sixties, followed by harder edged groups like the Rolling Stones and a wave of folk revival singer-songwriters. New singers like Tom Jones and Engelbert Humperdinck muscled in on Elvis' sex symbol territory later in the decade, but no matter how the press might have tried to set up rivalries, Elvis' reaction was to meet and befriend these newcomers. In public, he was unfailingly magnanimous. By the time artists like Jimi Hendrix, The Doors and Pink Floyd were pushing back the boundaries of heavy rock, Elvis was an unrivaled institution.

WORLDWIDE ELVIS

Elvis' failure to perform outside North America meant that there was ample space for home-grown talent to challenge Elvis for the rock 'n' roll crown. The UK had Tommy Steele and then Cliff Richard, who has managed to keep a successful music career going since the Fifties. Perhaps it is a testament to the power of Elvis' appeal that the French and Italian "answers to Elvis," respectively Johnny Hallyday (who did some direct translations of Elvis hits such as "A l'hôtel des coeurs brisés") and Little Tony are still going strong today, as are many other "national Elvises" around the world including Sweden's Little Gerhard (whom Elvis met in Frankfurt in 1958). Meanwhile, the Communist bloc had their very own "Red Elvis," a native of Colorado called Dean Reed who for a spell was more popular than Elvis in South America, and in the Sixties was adopted by the Eastern bloc as their very own rock idol, complete with fan clubs and a movie career.

ELVIS SAID IN 1956: "I was the first one to come out with it . . . But those people that are using the style, I don't blame 'em. I'd probably jump on the bandwagon too."

ELVIS SAID IN 1972: "I think there's room for everybody. I hate to criticize another performer."

PRISCILLA: "One of Elvis' outstanding attributes was his conviction that there was room for anyone with a talent in the entertainment field."

RIVERS, JOHNNY
(B. JOHN RAMISTELLA, 1942)

Musician who hit the top of the charts in the mid-Sixties with "Poor Side Of Town" and "Secret Agent Man," and had long been a friend of Elvis TCB guitarist James Burton. Rivers successfully covered many R&B tracks before starting his own record company and working as a producer.

For a while, Johnny Rivers became persona non grata at Graceland after he laid down a version of "Memphis" not long after Elvis played him a demo of the song and told him it would be his next record.

In the summer of 1972, Rivers went to see Elvis perform in Las Vegas with their friend in common, Larry Geller.

ROBBINS, MARTY
(1925-1982)

Born in Glendale, Arizona on September 26, 1925, versatile successful country singer Robbins was one of the first major stars that Elvis met, when they appeared on the same bill at the Grand Ole Opry in the fall of 1954. Before the year was out, Robbins had covered Elvis' first single "That's All Right (Mama)" in a country style—he also did country versions of Chuck Berry and Little Richard rockers, with added fiddle. Robbins and up and coming later Elvis shared the bill on a June 1955 tour of the South.

Robbins scored his first big hit in January 1953 with "I'll Go On Alone," and soon became a Grand Ole Opry fixture.

Elvis added Robbins song "You Gave Me a Mountain" to his live repertoire in 1972. He also covered "My Woman, My Woman, My Wife" and "El Paso" live in concert in the Seventies.

Robbins was inducted into the Nashville Songwriters Hall of Fame in 1975 and the Country Music Hall of Fame in 1982, two months before he died of a heart attack.

ROBERTS, BOB

Roberts composed half a dozen soundtrack songs for Elvis, "Echoes Of Love" with Paddy McMains,

and the rest with Ruth Batchelor, as well as writing some classic show tracks such as "Into Each Life Some Rain Must Fall," which he co-wrote with Eddie Fisher.

ROBERTS, HOWARD
(1929-1992)

Accomplished LA-based session guitarist Roberts played on Elvis' *Flaming Star* soundtrack sessions in 1960, *Paradise, Hawaiian Style* in 1965 and *Change of Habit* in 1969. Roberts scored minor success with his solo jazz work and played guitar on a number of seminal Sixties TV theme tunes including "The Twilight Zone" and "I Dream of Jeannie." In later years he became a well-respected guitar teacher and founded the Guitar Institute of Technology.

ROBERTSON, DON
(B. 1922)

Born in Beijing, China on December 5, 1922, Robertson wrote many of Elvis' finest ballads.

The first Robertson composition that Elvis recorded was "I'm Counting On You," at his inaugural RCA session in 1956. An established songwriter with many country hits to his name, Robertson was initially disappointed when his publishing company told him that the song had been given to an unknown.

After moving to LA in the early Fifties, Robertson penned "I Really Don't Want To Know" for Eddy Arnold, through song publishers Hill & Range. Robertson was also a performer in his own right, scoring a million-selling hit in 1956 with "The Happy Whistler." He is known for inventing a unique piano style—"Nashville Piano" or the "slip-note" style—which was favored by early Elvis pianist Floyd Cramer.

Robertson was one of the few regular songwriters to meet Elvis, after the singer invited him to Radio Recorders in 1961. After this, they became friends. Robertson played piano and organ on the soundtrack to *It Happened at the World's Fair* in 1962.

All in all, Elvis sang 14 songs written or co-written by Robertson: "Anything That's Part Of You," " I Really Don't Want To Know," "I'm Counting On You," "I'm Falling In Love Tonight," "Love Me Tonight," "Marguerita," "Starting Today," "There's Always Me" And "They Remind Me Too Much Of You." He Also Composed "I Met Her Today," "I Think I'm Gonna Like It Here," "I'm Yours," "No More," and "What Now, What Next, Where To" with Hal Blair. When not working for Elvis, he found time to write 1964 #1 hit "Ringo" for Lorne Greene.

Robertson was inducted into the Nashville Songwriter's Hall of Fame in 1972.

In 2003 Robertson released a CD of the demos he submitted to Elvis, *Songs For Elvis . . . And Then I Wrote*.

ROCK 'N' ROLL

Elvis did not invent rock 'n' roll, but he was the face of the revolution that swept through mainstream America and much of the rest of the world. By the time Elvis started making music professionally, Bill Haley had already charted with "Crazy Man Crazy." Elvis was still playing high school gyms when Haley scored the first ever #1 rock single, "Rock Around The Clock," in 1955.

The consensus among aficionados is that the first true rock 'n' roll song was "Rocket 88," a

paean to an Oldsmobile thrown together Jackie Brenston and his Delta Cats (the band was in reality Ike Turner's) en route to Memphis to record at Sam Phillip's Memphis Recording Service studios in 1951. Claims can be staked farther back by a large number of R & B pioneers: early Elvis single "Good Rockin' Tonight" was written and first performed by Roy Brown as far back as 1947, and had been a huge hit for R & B innovator Wynonie Harris. Elvis' early hits also included work by another major rock 'n' roll antecedent, Big Joe Turner.

Multiple sources credit Cleveland DJ Alan Freed with coining the term "rock and roll" in 1951 after playing Bill Haley's "Rock This Joint" or Wild Bill Moore's "We're Gonna Rock, We're Gonna Roll." Incidentally, Freed himself was for a while referred to as the King of Rock 'n' Roll, though his credentials were later tarnished by a payola scandal. Initially, the term referred to Rhythm & Blues played by white musicians, to differentiate it from Rhythm & Blues itself. Since then, the definition has evolved to reflect Elvis' innovation of combining Rhythm & Blues (itself spawned by a combination of blues and gospel, plus a pinch of jazz) with Country & Western. Elvis' innovation at Sun is explicit within the confines of one song, early single "Milkcow Blues Boogie," which he starts off down-tempo and then breaks into a version that's "real, real gone." In its very earliest forms, rock was propelled by either the piano or saxophone rather than a lead guitar. In Elvis' case, for his first Sun recordings the beat came from the singer and musicians, without a drummer at all.

Lost in the mists of slang etymology, the term rock and roll originated in the black community as a euphemism for vigorous sex . . . or as an early 20th century term to describe the swaying and moving of black Pentecostal worshippers in church. The word "rock" appeared initially in gospel song titles from the Twenties onwards. A 1922 song by Trixie Smith is titled "My Man Rocks Me (With One Steady Roll)."

When he first opened for business, Sam Phillips recorded almost exclusively black R&B artists who did not get airplay on white stations because the music was known as Rhythm & Blues, itself a recently-coined term for what had been known up until the end of the Forties as "race music."

As soon as the term rock 'n' roll became popular, it started spawning its own sub-genres. Rockabilly combined rock with country-inflected hillbilly, opening up whole new markets for what had originally been a black sound –this was, to many people's mind, the genius of Sam Phillips at Sun Records. The common denominator to rockabilly music was a strong backbeat, a three-chord progression and a captivating melody.

For much of its history, Rock 'n' Roll has been synonymous with edginess and danger. The genre's beginnings sparked off a brand new development: youth culture. American adolescents defined themselves through a form of music that their parents did not like and did not understand—the first time this had happened—spearheaded by a host of new performers including black rock 'n' roll innovators such as Little Richard and Bo Diddley. The perceived perils of rock 'n' roll went beyond riots and screaming girls to the lifestyle of many early rock 'n' roll stars and their run-ins with the law: Chuck Berry went to jail for soliciting a 14-year-old waitress, Jerry Lee Lewis married his 13-year-old cousin, and drugs and/or alcohol and/or casual sex were often to be found in places where touring rock 'n' rollers went.

Opinion-column writers, men of faith and politicians queued up to criticize this new music. The New York *Daily News* proposed a midnight curfew for anyone under the age of 21. In its early days, rock 'n' roll in general and Elvis in particular stood accused of planting "dirty feelings" in the minds of pure young women.

By mid-1956, rock 'n' roll had sufficient traction to propel Elvis' "Heartbreak Hotel" and Carl Perkins' "Blue Suede Shoes" to the top of the national *Billboard* charts, opening the floodgates for a rising tide of rockers. Elvis' Sun formula of releasing singles with a rock 'n' roll song on one side and a ballad on the other continued at RCA right up to the early Sixties, when Elvis branched out into more vocally-demanding songs and, not long after, became mired down in increasingly anodyne soundtrack fare. All this time, he acknowledged that rock 'n' roll was what he did best.

Elvis was already gravitating back to rock-flavored songs before his 1968 NBC TV "Comeback" Special, as new producer Felton Jarvis' helped to steer Elvis back to his rock 'n' roll roots with sessions that yielded "Guitar Man," "Big Boss Man" and "Hi-Heel Sneakers"; for more than half a decade, Elvis' rocking had been confined to all-too-rare soundtrack songs such as "Long Legged Girl."

By this time, rock 'n' roll was simply known as rock, and was more generally associated with the new wave of British artists who "invaded" North America from the mid-Sixties onwards, before splintering into a kaleidoscope of rock sub-genres.

In his Seventies touring years, Elvis fans got their rock fix through nostalgic Fifties medleys rather than new material, though Elvis did record some country rock in the early Seventies among his more maudlin quota of ballads. One of the enduring appeals of bootleg records and collectors' issues is the opportunity to hear Elvis rocking out during studio jams that, for the most part, remained unreleased during his lifetime.

Half a century of rock 'n' roll has failed to displace Elvis from his place at the apogee of rock 'n' roll: a 2007 ABC poll confirmed Elvis as the #1 rock 'n' roll star of all time.

ORIGINAL INDUCTEES TO THE ROCK AND ROLL HALL OF FAME, 1986.

PERFORMERS:
Chuck Berry
James Brown
Ray Charles
Sam Cooke
Fats Domino
The Everly Brothers
Buddy Holly
Jerry Lee Lewis
Elvis Presley

LITTLE RICHARD EARLY INFLUENCES:
Robert Johnson
Jimmie Rodgers
Jimmy Yancey

LIFETIME ACHIEVEMENT AWARD
(NON-PERFORMER):
John Hammond

NON-PERFORMERS:
Alan Freed
Sam Phillips

BMG released Elvis *Rock in 2006*, one of six themed albums of remastered hits.

TRACK LISTING:
1. Don't Be Cruel
2. Hound Dog
3. Blue Suede Shoes
4. Tutti Frutti
5. Heartbreak Hotel
6. Jailhouse Rock
7. I Got Stung
8. A Big Hunk O' Love

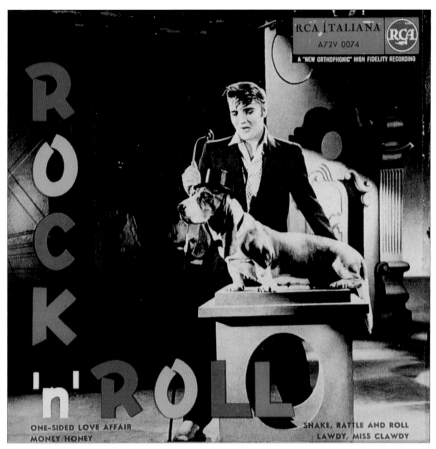

RCA Italiana release, "Rock'n'Roll".

9. Wear My Ring Around Your Neck
10. Hard Headed Woman
11. King Creole
12. I Need Your Love Tonight
13. Too Much
14. All Shook Up
15. Long Tall Sally
16. Rip It Up
17. Got A Lot O' Livin' To Do!
18. Party
19. Mean Woman Blues
20. Dixieland Rock

ELVIS SAID IN THE EARLY DAYS: "I ain't got no definition of rock 'n' roll, I just feel it very strongly."

ELVIS SAID IN 1956: "I enjoy rock and roll . . . As long as it lasts, as long as it sells, I'll continue doing it, as long as that's what the people want. And if they change, if it dies out, I'll try to do something else, and if that doesn't work, I'll just say, well I had my day."

ELVIS SAID IN 1958: "Rock and roll has been around for many years. It used to be called rhythm & blues . . . I personally don't think it will ever die completely out, because they're gonna have to get something mighty good to take its place as far as the young people are concerned."

ELVIS SAID IN 1968: "Rock and Roll is basically gospel, or Rhythm & Blues. It sprang from that, people have been adding to it."

FRANK SINATRA: "Rock and roll is the most brutal, ugly, and degenerate, vicious form of expression. Sly, lewd, in plain fact dirty. A rancid smelling aphrodisiac—and the martial music of every sideburned delinquent on the face of the earth."

GREIL MARCUS: "Rock 'n' roll is the simple demand for peace of mind and a good time."

BILL MEDLEY: "If it wasn't for Elvis, rock and roll could have become a fad."

BONO: "In Elvis, you have the blueprint for rock 'n' roll: The highness — the gospel highs. The mud — the Delta mud, the blues. Sexual liberation. Controversy. Changing the way people feel about the world. It's all there with Elvis."

BOB DYLAN: "He is the deity supreme of rock and roll religion as it exists in today's form. Hearing him for the first time was like busting out of jail. I thank God for Elvis Presley."

PAMELA CLARKE KEOGH: "Rock and roll and Elvis' music in particular unhinged women."

BRIAN SETZER: "His definitive years, 1954-57, can only be described as rock's cornerstone. He was the original cool."

TIM RICE: "If he didn't create rock 'n' roll, he defined it."

JERRY SCHEFF: "He had a great voice, and wanted to be known for that voice. He wanted to sing songs that showed off the virtuosity of his voice. Rock 'n' roll songs didn't do that, and he didn't want to do them. Anytime anybody does a medley of some songs, you know that they don't want to do these songs."

"ROCK-A-HULA BABY"

A fusion offering on the B-side to "Can't Help Falling In Love" from the *Blue Hawaii* soundtrack, which Elvis laid down at Radio Recorders on March 23, 1961 for release that November. Written by Fred Wise, Ben Weisman and Dolores Fuller, the song made it to #23 on the singles chart in its own right and featured on the *Blue Hawaii* LP. It did even better in the UK, warranting a full month at #1.

"Rock-A-Hula Baby" has since appeared on anthologies *Worldwide Gold Award Hits Vol. 1*, *Command Performances*, the *Elvis' Gold Records Vol. 4* CD reissue, *Elvis 2nd to None*, *Hitstory* and *Elvis at the Movies*.

An additional take appeared as a bonus track on the 1997 *Blue Hawaii* album reissue.

"ROCK AROUND THE CLOCK"

Elvis sang Bill Haley's seminal rock hit at shows in late 1955, including a Louisiana Hayride radio broadcast from Gladewater, Texas. The song was one of many that RCA offered to Elvis to record in 1956: he declined. Elvis' live performance has yet—at the time of writing—made it onto an official release.

Written by Max Freedman and Jimmy De Knight, Bill Haley's 1954 release became the first ever rock 'n' roll *Billboard* Top 100 #1 single only when it was released for a second time, after it featured in 1955 teen flick *Blackboard Jungle*.

ROCKABILLY

Rockabilly was born when the defining characteristics of rock 'n' roll and hillbilly (country) were thrown together in the mid-Fifties, with a pinch of bluegrass for good measure. Sam Phillips was instrumental in developing the characteristic sound of a slapped bass and plenty of echo on the vocals, though Leonard Chess was doing something similar in Chicago.

DJ Dewey Phillips, an early Elvis fan, is credited with coining the term by on air when he said "they're rockin' country music, they're rockabillys." In other chronicles, the term was first used by Bill Flagg, who recorded his hit song "Go Cat Go" in 1956..

Many rockabilly historians credit Elvis with inventing the genre: his first ever professional Sun recording session yielded seminal rockabilly hit "That's All Right (Mama)." However, Bill Haley was performing recognizably rockabilly material as far back as 1952.

After Elvis moved to RCA and was slowly but inevitably repackaged to appeal to a more mainstream audience, Sam Phillips carried on launching new rockabilly artists who played in the pared-down rockabilly style. Carl Perkins looked to be a flagbearer of the movement until his career was checked by a car accident. Jerry Lee Lewis possessed the necessary wildness and raw energy until he was derailed by scandal, and Buddy Holly's vocal acrobatics took the genre in a new direction before he was killed in a plane crash.

Sun's roster included rockabilly artists Sonny Burgess, Billy Lee Riley, Charlie Feathers, Warren Smith and Wanda Jackson among others. A roll call of rockabilly greats encompasses much of the early music made by Johnny Cash, Johnny Burnette, Eddie Cochran, Gene Vincent, Roy Orbison and Ricky Nelson, and many other less-well known rockers of the Fifties.

Many overlooked rockabilly artists had a second shot at fame in the late Seventies and early Eighties, when the genre came into post-punk fashion and a new crop of artists led the so-called "rockabilly revival." The most commercially-successful of these bands were The Stray Cats, who were followed by a host of "psychobilly" bands. For many original exponents of the genre, the rockabilly revival opened up a chance to tour in Europe and be appreciated for their pioneering and innovative role in the development of modern music.

CARL PERKINS: "The music we did in the early Fifties, what they call 'rockabilly', was basically country music. I think the very bottom line of rockabilly music was country boys influenced with country music and then Southern black spirituals—maybe not altogether the black spirituals, but that rhythm—that FEEL—that black music had."

PETER GURALNICK: "Rockabilly is the purest of all rock 'n' roll genres."

GREIL MARCUS: "Rockabilly fixed the crucial image of rock 'n' roll: the sexy, half-crazed fool standing on stage singing his guts out."

ROCKEFELLER, NELSON ALDRICH
(1908-1979)

Elvis, Vernon and Vernon's new family met Nelson Rockefeller in June 1967, when he was visiting the MGM lot to record a patriotic talk album. At the time the future Vice-President of the United States was serving his third of four terms as Governor of New York State.

ROCKIN' WITH ELVIS APRIL FOOLS DAY

A 1995 bootleg release on the Claudia label of Elvis' April 1, 1975 dinnertime and midnight shows in Las Vegas. A second volume came out titled *On A April's Fool Day, Vol. 2*.

TRACK LISTING:
VOL. 1
1. See See Rider
2. Dialogue
3. I Got A Woman / Amen
4. Dialogue
5. Love Me
6. If You Love Melf You Love Me (Let Me Know)
7. And I Love You So
8. Big Boss Man
9. The Wonder Of You
10. Burning Love
11. Band introductions
12. Elvis introduces singer Roy Clark and the owner of the Las Vegas Hilton
13. My Boy
14. I'll Remember You
15. Let Me Be There
16. Elvis introduces actor Hugh O'Brian
17. How Great Thou Art
18. Hound Dog
19. Fairytale
20. Can't Help Falling In Love
21. Closing Vamp

VOL. 2
1. Also Sprach Zarathustra
2. See See Rider
3. I Got A Woman / Amen
4. Love Me
5. If You Love Melf You Love Me (Let Me Know)
6. And I Love You So
7. Big Boss Man
8. It's Midnight
9. Burning Love
10. Introduction by Elvis
11. What'd I Say
12. Drum solo
13. Bass solo
14. Piano solo
15. Electric piano solo
16. School Days
17. Introduction of Colonel Parker / Jingle Bells (instrumental)
18. You Do Something To Me (one line)
19. You Don't Have To Say You Love Me
20. The Wonder Of You
21. Let Me Be There
22. American Trilogy / Help Me Make It Through The Night
23. Mickey Mouse March
24. Little Darlin'
25. Don't Be Cruel
26. Steamroller Blues
27. Can't Help Falling In Love
28. Closing Vamp

RODGERS, JIMMIE

(B. JAMES CHARLES RODGERS, 1897-1933)

As a favorite of Mama Gladys's, Elvis heard Rodgers's trademark yodel often when growing up.

Country music's first superstar, known variously as "The Singing Brakeman" and "The Mississippi Blue Yodeler," Rodgers was born in Meridian, Mississippi on September 8, 1897. He won a talent contest as a twelve-year-old and ran away to sing before his father hauled him back to work on the railways with him. The tuberculosis that finally killed him forced Rodgers to quit work on the railways in his twenties. During a six-year music career, Rodgers pioneered a fusion style that blended hillbilly with blues and jazz influences to became the first nationally-famous country music star.

His most famous songs, released on RCA Victor, included "Waiting For A Train," "Jimmie The Kid," "Jimmie's Mean Mama Blues" and "Train Whistle Blues."

Though Elvis wasn't born before the so-called "Father of Country Music" died, in May 1955 he played at the third annual Jimmie Rodgers Memorial Celebration in his hometown of Meridian, Mississippi. Elvis' hillbilly material went down a storm but his new fangled rock 'n' roll left the audience cold.

Rodgers was one of the initial three inductees into the Country Music Hall of Fame when it was established in 1961. He earned a place at the Rock and Roll Hall of Fame in 1986 as a founding father of the genre.

GREIL MARCUS: "Elvis followed Rodgers' musical strategy and began the story all over again."

"ROSES ARE RED (MY LOVE)"

Elvis sang this 1962 Bobby Vinton million-seller (written by Al Bryon and Paul Evans) in concert a few times. It appears on bootleg recordings such as *Long Lost Songs* and *Ultra Rare Trax*.

"ROUSTABOUT"

Elvis recorded the film title track—a composition by the songwriting team of Bill Giant, Bernie Baum and Florence Kaye—on April 29, 1964 at Radio Recorders, for the movie and release on the album of the same name. Additional instrumentation featured on the movie version.

The song has since appeared on *Command Performances* and on *Elvis Movies*.

A straight-through version (as opposed to the overdubbed vocals on the version released originally) appeared in 1991 on *Collectors Gold*. An alternate take is included on *Today Tomorrow & Forever*. A special promotional copy of the song was distributed to theaters for the film release.

A competing composition for the title slot in the movie, written by Otis Blackwell and Winfield Scott, was recorded, discarded and then rediscovered and released as "I'm A Roustabout" in the 2000s on *Elvis 2nd to None*.

ROUSTABOUT (LP)

Elvis' best-selling soundtrack LP for a couple of years hit the stores in October 1964, despite the fact that prior to release RCA had insufficient faith in the material to release a single, and a replacement title track was rerecorded at the last minute. The album sold 450,000 copies and, at

Barbara Stanwyck, Elvis and Joan Freeman in *Roustabout*, 1964.

ROUSTABOUT

Paramount producer Hal Wallis briefly flirted with the idea of putting Elvis in a ski-based movie before plumping for this tale of circus folk.

Colonel Parker contributed his inside knowledge of carnival and circus life to the creative process, in a movie that cast a much-maligned group of people in a favorable light. Lifelong amusement arcade fan Elvis told the press that it was a dream come true to play a carnival character.

The working title for the movie was *Right This Way Folks*—for a change, only one working title even though the project took three years to go from inception to completion.

Elvis arrived for pre-production work on February 26, 1964. Location shooting was at the Hidden Valley Ranch, at Thousand Oaks, not far from LA, from early March 1964, and at various other city locations over the following six weeks. To recreate a big tent, three soundstages were combined on the Paramount lot, the first time this was ever attempted.

Hollywood royalty embellished the cast in the form of Barbara Stanwyck (in a role that was originally offered to Mae West).

Elvis sustained stitches over one eye after he persuaded director John Rich to allow him to do his own stunt work in a fight scene. Rich added a band-aid for the following scenes to cover over the stitches. Elvis later had a row with the director when he refused to allow Elvis to use the Jordanaires to back him for one of the songs. Rich's reasoning was that it would beggar believability to have back-up singing in a movie scene

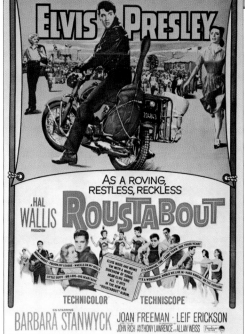

last for an Elvis album, claimed the number 1 spot on the LP chart, albeit for just one week.

TRACK LISTING:
1. Roustabout
2. Little Egypt
3. Poison Ivy League
4. Hard Knocks
5. It's A Wonderful World
6. Big Love, Big Heartache
7. One Track Heart
8. It's Carnival Time
9. Carny Town
10. There's A Brand New Day On The Horizon
11. Wheels On My Heels

The Nineties *Double Features* album version is doubled up by songs from *Viva Las Vegas*.

Elvis as Charlie Rogers in *Roustabout*.

Publicity shot for *Roustabout* (1964).

where Elvis sings while riding a motorbike. Rich asked Elvis where he intended to place the backing singers in the shot; Elvis replied, "Same damn place as the band!"

Then unknown Raquel Welch landed her first speaking line in this movie. *Jaws* villain Richard Kiel also featured as the strong man, just one of the collection of uncommonly-configured people more usually seen in carnival sideshows than in Hollywood movies. Vertically-challenged Billy Barty is in the movie; he went on to a bigger role in later Elvis movie *Harum Scarum*.

Roustabout managed to conquer the #8 spot on the *Variety* Box Office Survey on release in November 1964, grossing a total of $3 million in its first year after release and making it to #28 on the 1965 box office list. The movie was nominated for a WGA best-written American musical award. Many fans feel that this is one of Elvis' better Sixties movies.

Elvis' motorcycle antics on the "Wall of Death" carnival ride spawned 1986 film *Eat the Peach*, about two Irish lads inspired by Elvis' feat of derring-do.

Book/DVD:

Inside Roustabout, by Megan Murphy, Elvis Unlimited, 2006.

CREDITS:
Paramount, Color.
Length: 101 minutes
Release date: November 11, 1964

TAGLINE:
Elvis Presley as a Roving, Restless, Recklesss, ROUSTABOUT

Directed by: John Rich
Produced by: Hal B. Wallis
Written by: Allan Weiss (story and screenplay), Anthony Lawrence (screenplay)
Executive producer: Joseph H. Hazen
Associate producer: Paul Nathan
Music by: Joseph J. Lilley
Director of photography: Lucien Ballard
Art Direction by: Hal Pereira, Walter Tyler
Set Decoration by: Robert Benton, Sam Comer
Costume Design by: Edith Head

CAST:

Elvis Presley	Charlie Rogers
Barbara Stanwyck	Maggie Morgan
Joan Freeman	Cathy Lean
Leif Erickson	Joe Lean
Sue Ane Langdon	Fortune teller Madame Mijanou
Pat Buttram	Harry Carver
Joan Staley	Marge
Dabbs Greer	Arthur Nielsen
Steve Brodie	Fred the Pitcher
Norman Grabowski	Sam
Jack Albertson	Lou
Jane Dulo	Hazel
Joel Fluellen	Cody Marsh
Wilda Taylor	Little Egypt
Beverly Adams	Cora
Billy Barty	Billy the midget
Kenneth Becker	Gregg
Lynn Borden	College student
Owen Bush	Man
Steve Condit	Boy with balloons
Roger Creed	Deputy
Richard DiPaolo	Farmer #1
Connie Ducharme	Bit part
Mercedes G. Ford	Dancer
Joseph Forte	Concessionaire
Carey Foster	Bit part
Linda Foster	College student
Jimmy Gaines	Boy
Maugene H. Gannon	Harry Carver's secretary
Teri Garr	Carny dancer
Joy Harmon	College Girl
Chester Hayes	Clown
Barbara Hemingway	Fat lady
Marianna Hill	Viola
Teri Hope	College student
Jerry James	Stage manager
Howard Joslin	Candy concessionaire
Ray Kellogg	Motorcycle concessionaire
Kenner G. Kemp	Carnivalgoer
Richard Kiel	Strongman
Lance LeGault	Carnival barker for Little Egypt number
Theodore Lehmann	Farmer #2
Arthur Levy	Carny motorcycle rider
Buddy Lewis	Barker
Diane Libby	Sexy girl
Mike Mahoney	Deputy
Max Manning	Juggler
Eddie Marr	Barker
Bob Matthews	Barker
Kent McCord	Bit part
Lester Miller	B.J. Lewis, fire eater
Dean Moray	Boy with balloons
Linda Rand	College student
Toby Reed	Dick
Christopher Riordan	Carnival worker
Dianne Simpson	Elephant girl
K.L. Smith	Sheriff
Bert Stevens	Carnivalgoer
Katie Sweet	Little girl
John Turk	Volcano man
Jesse Wayne	Bit part
Raquel Welch	College girl at Mother's Tea House
Red West	Carnival worker
Jack Whalen	Barker
Glenn R. Wilder	Craig

ADDITIONAL CREW:

Nellie Manley	hair stylist
Wally Westmore	makeup supervisor
Michael Moore	assistant director
John Carter	sound recorder
Charles Grenzbach	sound recorder
Paul K. Lerpae	special photographic effects
Lance LeGault	stunts
May Boss	stunts
Charles Thomas	stunt driver
Earl Barton	musical number staging
Farciot Edouart	process photographer
The Jordanaires	vocal accompaniment
Joseph J. Lilley	conductor
Warren Low	supervising editor
Richard Mueller	color consultant
Colonel Tom Parker	technical advisor

Plot:

Elvis is Charlie Rogers, a boy with a quick temper and a dream to succeed as a singer. Roughing up the customers at Mother's Tea House is not company policy, so he loses his job and gets carted off to jail (though in an early version of the script, the character's initial problem was being drummed out of the Army for cowardice). Charlie is bailed out of jail by Marge (Joan Staley), a waitress who is sweet on him. Once sprung, he gets on his trusty Honda motorbike and rides off to Phoenix to make his fortune. Before he can get there, he has an accident with Maggie Morgan (Barbara Stanwyck), Cathy Lean (Joan Freeman) and fractious driver Joe Lean (Leif Erikson). Maggie offers Charlie a job as a roustabout for her carnival while he waits for spare parts to arrive.

After passing up (then unknown) extra Raquel Welch in an earlier scene, Charlie falls for Joe's daughter, Cathy Lean. She is slow to respond to his advances, and fortune teller Madame Mijanou (played by Sue Ane Langdon) competes for his affections.

Despite Joe's misgivings, Cathy finally relents when Charlie's singing revives the ailing carnival's fortunes. Predatory rival carnival owner Harry Carver (played by Pat Buttram) is happy to take Charlie on, but Charlie does the right thing and stays loyal.

Charlie's temper gets the better of him and he slugs a carnival customer. The customer seeks revenge by claiming that carny folk stole his wallet (which he actually lost). Carnival owner Joe is arrested. Charlie finds the wallet but rather than springing Joe from jail, decides to bide his time, and in the process take a daredevil motorbike ride on the Wall of Death.

When Joe finds out that Charlie has left him in jail, he knocks Charlie down (a rarity for an Elvis character) and gives him his marching orders. Charlie has no compunction as he starts singing for the rival carnival, a move that looks like it will sound the death knell for his old pals.

Cathy pleads with Charlie to come back to the carnival. Before he gets the girl, saves the carnival with the money he has earned from the rival outfit and ensures that they all live happily ever after, Charlie is laid out once again by Joe (still a rarity for an Elvis character).

Songs: "Roustabout," "Poison Ivy League," "Wheels On My Heels," "It's A Wonderful World," "It's Carnival Time," "Carny Town," "One Track Heart," "Hard Knocks," "Little Egypt," "Big Love Big Heartache," "There's A Brand New Day On The Horizon"

ROYALTY

The King of Rock 'n' Roll had a number of royal visits on the set of G.I. Blues in 1960: three Scandinavian princesses (Astrid of Norway, Margaretha of Sweden and Margretha of Denmark), and then King Bumibhol Adulyadej and Queen Sirikit of Thailand.

Elvis was approached about performing before Queen Elizabeth II of England at the 1961 Royal Command Variety Performance in London. Needless to say, the Colonel erected insurmountable barriers to the appearance, as he did with every other engagement offered to his client outside North America.

DAVE HEBLER ONCE DESCRIBED ELVIS: "like isolated royalty . . . Despite his humble beginnings, he hasn't had contact with the outside world for many years."

RUBIN, MICHAEL "MYER"

A bass player who recorded with Elvis in 1960 for the *Flaming Star* and *Wild In The Country* soundtracks, having also worked with Elvis in 1956 on an ill-fated recording session for *Love Me Tender*. Some sources also credit him for work on the *Jailhouse Rock* soundtrack.

"RUBBERNECKIN'"

Credited to Dory Jones and Bunny Warren (but actually written by Ben Weisman), this unmistakably Sixties track was recorded on January 20, 1969 during Elvis' mammoth American Studio sessions. It featured in Elvis' new stage act at Las Vegas that summer, and initially came out as the B-side to "Don't Cry, Daddy" in November that year, as well as finding a berth in Elvis' final feature film, *Change of Habit*.

The song has since appeared on *Almost in Love* and *Double Dynamite*, and on the final *Double Feature* release of Elvis soundtrack songs in the mid-Nineties. A remastered version is on *From Nashville to Memphis* and *Suspicious Minds: The Memphis 1969 Anthology*.

A Vegas performance from August 26, 1969 appeared on *Collectors Gold* in 1991 (and more recently on FTD release *All Shook Up*).

Like "A Little Less Conversation," this track rose again in a dance-mix resurgence which went all the way to #1 on the *Billboard* singles chart, courtesy of a 2003 Paul Oakenfold remix. Versions of the remix have appeared on *Elvis 2nd To None* and *Hitstory*, multiple remixes came out on German album *Rubberneckin'* and on the remixed single re-release.

The song's most recent cameo is on 2007 release *Elvis at the Movies*.

"Run On"

Elvis provided the arrangement for this traditional hymn, recorded in Nashville on May 5, 1966 for the gospel album *How Great Thou Art*, and one that Elvis knew from the Golden Gate Quartet version.

Elvis' "Run On" has since graced religious-themed anthologies including *Amazing Grace*, *Peace In The Valley* and *Ultimate Gospel*. It was also selected for the *Artist Of The Century* anthology. Alternate takes of the song appear on FTD releases *Easter Special* and *So High*.

"Runaway"

This monster #1 for Del Shannon in 1961, written by Max Crook and Del Shannon, was one of the tracks that Elvis added to his concert repertoire when he first returned to the stage in Las Vegas in 1969.

A recording from Las Vegas on August 25, 1969 that year came out on the 1970 *On Stage* album. The same performance has since been released on *Live in Las Vegas* and the 2007 *Viva Las Vegas* issue.

Collectors Gold, a 1991 release, featured another live performance from the same Las Vegas engagement (more recently on FTD release *All Shook Up*). Further performances are to be found on the *Today Tomorrow & Forever* anthology and on FTD release *Elvis at the International*.

"Running Scared"

Elvis sang a line of this 1961 Roy Orbison #1 hit before launching into "Tomorrow Never Comes" at his June 1970 Nashville recording session. Captured on tape, it was officially first on the *Walk A Mile In My Shoes* box set. Elvis occasionally sang a line or two of the song live (versions on bootlegs), and reportedly attempted the song at his final Graceland recording session.

Russell, Jane
(B. 1921 ERNESTINE JANE RUSSELL)

One of Hollywood's leading ladies in the Forties and Fifties shared a stage with Elvis at a Danny

Thomas fundraising event for St. Jude's Children's Hospital in 1957.

Russell got her movie break in Howard Hughes' *The Outlaw* (1943) after he had spotted her working as a receptionist for his dentist. She is probably best remembered opposite blonde bombshell Marilyn Monroe in *Gentlemen Prefer Blondes* (1953). Alongside her movie career, Russell has worked tirelessly for the World Adoption International Fund, which has placed over 50,000 children with new families.

Russell, Kurt
(B. 1951)

This actor, who played Elvis in John Carpenter's 1979 TV biopic, had personal memories to draw upon: his first ever movie appearance was as the tyke who kicked Elvis in the shins during *It Happened at the World's Fair*.

Russell turned to acting after an injury curtailed a promising career in baseball. His best-known movies include *Escape from New York* (1981), *The Thing* (1982), *Silkwood* (1983), *Backdraft* (1991), and more recently *Poseidon* (2006). He also donned an Elvis jumpsuit in 2003 heist movie *3000 Miles to Graceland*, and provided the voice of Elvis in *Forrest Gump* (1994).

Russell, Nipsey
(B. JULIUS "NIPSEY" RUSSELL, 1918-2005)

In 1971, Nipsey Russell opened for Elvis at the Sahara Tahoe, on a two-week engagement.

Variously dubbed "The Poet Laureate of Television," "The Poet Laureate of Comedy" and "Harlem's Son of Fun," the versatile Nipsey Russell trained as a dancer, led a successful career as a comedian on many popular variety shows in the Sixties, in the Seventies reinvented himself as a game show panelist, and kept up a stage career too. Russell is perhaps best remembered on the silver screen for his role as the Tin Man in *The Wiz*, a 1978 remake of *The Wizard of Oz*.

Russwood Park, Memphis

Elvis played a hometown show in Memphis on July 4, 1956 to benefit local charities, organized by the Cynthia Milk Fund. He attended the venue at other fundraising events, and performed again at Danny Thomas's Shower of Stars fundraiser for St. Jude's Hospital on June 28, 1957.

Ryan, Sheila
(B. 1954)

October 1973 *Playboy* cover girl Sheila Ryan met Elvis in Las Vegas after Joe Esposito spotted her in

Kurt Russell as Elvis.

the audience. Backstage after the show, to break the ice, Elvis playfully threw a grape at her that hit her right between the eyes (don't try this at home, unless you're Elvis). Ryan told an interviewer that when Elvis emerged from his dressing room, their eyes met and she knew, instantly, that they would be spending a lot of time together.

From the summer of 1974, Elvis flew her out to join him on tour, setting her up to compete for his affections with live-in girlfriend Linda Thompson.

Ryan was with Elvis during his March 1975 recording session in LA; he was looking at her as he recorded "And I Love You So." By the summer of that year, she was unwilling to go off on tour with Elvis and do the "mothering" that she says Elvis sought from his girlfriends once the initial flash of romance had passed. She met actor James Caan around this time and they married in January 1976, though the marriage only lasted a year.

She has appeared in Elvis documentaries *Elvis: The Final Chapter* and *The Definitive Elvis: Elvis and Priscilla*. In 2006, Ryan auctioned a bottle of Elvis' prescription medicine on EBay.

SHEILA RYAN: "I was very young, very naïve, very Mid-Western, a blank canvas."

SAGAL, BORIS
(1917-1981)

Killed tragically after filming a helicopter scene, this Russian-born director worked with Elvis in *Girl Happy* (1965). He directed most frequently on TV, though he also helmed *The Omega Man* (1971).

SAHARA HOTEL, TAHOE

See NEVADA

SAINTE- MARIE, BUFFY
(B. BEVERLY SAINTE-MARIE, 1941)

In 1971, Elvis recorded "Until It's Time For You To Go," written by this Canadian Cree Indian folk singer. During her career, Sainte- Marie sang country, rock and politically-motivated protest songs and ballads. For many years she was a TV regular on "Sesame Street." She later won an Oscar for writing the title song for the movie *An Officer and a Gentleman*.

"SAN ANTONIO ROSE"

Elvis never officially recorded this 1938 Bob Wills song, but a home recording made at Graceland in 1966 made it out into the world on *Home Recordings*.

Former Elvis pianist Floyd Cramer had a top 10 hit with an instrumental version of the song in 1961.

Elvis very occasionally sang the song live: bootleg *Long Lost And Found Songs* of his September 1, 1970 performance features the track.

"SAND CASTLES"

A last-minute addition to the August 2, 1965 *Paradise, Hawaiian Style* recording session at Radio Recorders that made it onto the soundtrack album but not into the motion picture release. The song is by Herb Goldberg and David Hess, and may originally have been titled "Sands Of Time." The 2004 FTD release covering the movie features alternate takes of Elvis' overdubbed vocals.

SANDS, TOMMY
(B. THOMAS ADRIAN SANDS, 1937)

Before Colonel Tom Parker signed Elvis, Tommy Sands was his great hope for breaking into the emerging teen market.

Sands was born in Chicago on August 27, 1937. The Colonel had him under management from the age of 13, by which time he was already a veteran performer on Louisiana Hayride radio station KWKH.

Sands played on the same bill as Elvis at a January 1, 1955 show promoted by Biff Collie in Houston, Texas. He has been quoted as saying that it was he who alerted the Colonel to the huge impact Elvis was having.

In February 1955, when it looked like it was going to be hard for the Colonel to prise Elvis away from Sun Records, Tom Diskin tried to deflect RCA's growing interest in Elvis onto Tommy Sands; A&R head Stephen Sholes was having none of it.

After the Colonel became Elvis' exclusive

Magazine cover from the 1950s featuring Elvis, Tommy Sands and Harry Belafonte.

manager, he helped Sands land a role in 1957 TV drama *The Singing Idol*, a feature that was more than loosely based on the relationship between the Colonel and Elvis (though the Colonel figure comes across as something of a psychopath). On the back of the this drama, Sands' song "Teen-Age Crush" made it to number two in the charts.

He reprised the young-singer-made-good role on the silver screen in 1958 movie *Sing Boy, Sing*, which also featured Elvis' pal Nick Adams and early mentor DJ Bill Randle.

Thereafter, Sands appeared regularly on TV variety shows, continued to score hits until 1963 and acted in film until 1967. He was married to Nancy Sinatra for five years in the early Sixties, and later appeared in a number of episodes of TV classic "Hawaii Five-O" among others.

SANFORD, BILLY
(B. 1940)

A Nashville guitarist who was drafted in to play at Elvis' February 1976 Graceland recording session. Sanford has played with artists ranging from Kenny Rodgers to Roy Orbison and Tammy Wynette.

"SANTA BRING MY BABY BACK (TO ME)"

"Teddy Bear" in Christmas guise in this Aaron Schroeder/Claude Demetrius composition that Elvis recorded on September 7, 1957 at Radio Recorders for release on *Elvis' Christmas Album* later that year (and the 1970 re-release). The song also came out on 1957 EP release *Elvis Sings Christmas Songs*, and later on *The King Of Rock And Roll*, latter-day releases of *Elvis' Gold Records Vol. 2*, and on seasonal anthologies *If Every Day Was Like Christmas*, *Christmas Peace* and *Elvis Christmas*.

"SANTA CLAUS IS BACK IN TOWN"

Leiber and Stoller frantically put together this bluesy track under the working title "Christmas Blues" at the Radio Recorders studio for Elvis to sing on September 7, 1957, to join the rest of his first Yule LP, *Elvis' Christmas Album* (reissued in 1970 and many times since).

This particular Santa rode back into town in 1965, a full two months before Christmas as the A-side to a single paired with "Blue Christmas" (another Elvis track that made its debut on that 1957 album). Though it failed to make the top

100, this seasonal disk sold long enough and steady enough to earn almost platinum status.

"Santa Claus Is Back in Town" has since appeared on *Elvis Sings Leiber & Stoller*, *The King Of Rock And Roll*, *Artist Of The Century* and on Christmas-themed releases *Memories Of Christmas*, *If Every Day Was Like Christmas Christmas Peace* and *Elvis Christmas*.

Alternate takes of the song can be found on *Tiger Man*, *That's The Way It Is—Special Edition* and on FTD release *Let Yourself Go* (a rehearsal version for Elvis' NBC TV Special that was dropped before broadcast).

"SANTA LUCIA"

Elvis recorded this traditional nineteenth-century Neapolitan number—a favorite with tenors since before the days of Caruso—at Radio Recorders on July 10, 1963 for Viva Las Vegas. Though it made it into the movie, the song did not appear on the tie-in EP.

A year later, it came out on the *Elvis For Everyone* LP. It has since graced *Burning Love and Hits from His Movies*, the *Double Features Viva Las Vegas* re-release, and, more recently the FTD *Viva Las Vegas* soundtrack issue.

SAPERSTEIN, HANK

Colonel Parker sold merchandiser Saperstein the first exclusive rights to Elvis merchandising in 1956, marking the start of a long and profitable association with a man who had made his name promoting tie-ins that included Lassie-related products and giveaway toys in cereal boxes. Saperstein had dozens of Elvis products out within the first year of their association.

SARNOFF, TOM
(B. 1927)

Tom Sarnoff was Vice President of NBC's West Coast division in 1967 when Colonel Parker began negotiating a deal for Elvis to do a show on their network—putatively, Elvis' first appearance on the small screen since 1960. Sarnoff had initially approached the Colonel a couple of years earlier.

A $1 million deal with the Colonel for the TV Special plus a later movie for the studio was not sufficient for the Colonel to agree to Sarnoff's suggestion that Elvis appear on another NBC show during shooting of his own Special; for that, he was required to pay a further $250,000.

In later years, Sarnoff was Chairman of the National Academy of Television Arts and Sciences.

"SATISFIED"

Elvis is said to have recorded this much-covered 1952 Martha Carson hit at Sun Studios on September 10, 1954, on a tape that has since gone missing. Ever since there have been rumors that an acetate exists in collector's hands.

SAVALAS, TELLY
(B. ARISTOTELIS SAVALAS, 1921-1994)

In 1975, when he was at the height of his popularity as shaven-headed detective Kojak, Telly Savalas bought Elvis' former Monovale Drive home in LA.

Savalas' other roles include arch-villain Ernst Blofeld opposite George Lazenby (as James Bond) in *On Her Majesty's Secret Service*.

Elvis and Savalas became friends in 1961 when Elvis was working on *Kid Galahad*. Savalas came to many of Elvis' shows in the Seventies, usually getting a call-out from stage.

"SAVED"

Elvis recorded this Leiber and Stoller gospel romp at Western Recorders on June 22, 1968 for the spiritual medley on his NBC TV Special. It had originally been recorded by LaVern Baker in 1960, for whom it won a Grammy.

Elvis had previously considered using the song on the *Easy Come, Easy Go* soundtrack. "Saved" formed part of the broadcast medley, and was included on the tie-in LP, titled simply *Elvis*.

In later years, the song appeared on the *Elvis Sings Leiber & Stoller* LP.

Alternates are on *Memories: The '68 Comeback Special*, gospel anthology *Peace in the Valley* and FTD albums *Let Yourself Go* and *Easter Special*.

SCANDAL

Elvis polarized from the very start. The public outlet he gave his young fans, especially female fans, for expressing their passions and sexual desire, broke age-old taboos and inflamed self-styled upholders of decency.

Compounding news reports of unruly behavior and rioting as he played bigger and bigger venues, within a few months of his stage debut, Elvis was involved in a public scandal when a girl exposed herself to him at the Cotton Club dance hall in Lubbock after one of his shows, and a photograph of the event wound up in the local press.

Complaints by clergy and moralistic members of the community that had been confined to the local press moved on to a bigger stage when Elvis started appearing on national television. The day after his June 5, 1956 performance on the "Milton Berle Show," *Daily News* critic Ben Gross lamented "popular music has reached its lowest depths in the 'grunt and groan' antics of one Elvis Presley." Reverend Robert Gray told *Life* magazine that he regarded the new singer as "a new low in spiritual degeneracy"; Reverend Charles Graff defined Elvis the "whirling dervish of sex." Briefly, producer Hal Wallis had second thoughts about contracting Elvis to Paramount Studios, and the "Steve Allen Show," which had already booked Elvis, came close to canceling his appearance.

As if there wasn't enough scandal around Elvis' rocketing rise, press organizations were not beyond manufacturing unflattering stories. Elvis was once accosted in his dressing room by a beauty who had arrived backstage, only for a photographer to burst in and try and snap the moment. Rumors were circulated that Elvis had once shot his mother, the antecedents of later inventions in which Elvis was falsely accused of denigrating African-Americans, Mexicans and military personnel.

Reviled and vilified more prominently than any gangster rap or death metal group in the 2000s, after his appearance on the "Milton Berle Show," Elvis made a slew of quotes exculpating his music, as the Colonel masterminded a PR campaign to let the world know all about Elvis' religious upbringing.

Elvis' appearance on "The Steve Allen Show" saw him much toned down, dressed in a tuxedo and singing "Hound Dog" to a bemused basset hound. For his fans, this was the real scandal: an angry deputation gathered outside the NY recording studio where Elvis was laying down his latest tracks for RCA, holding up placards that called for the return of "The Real Elvis." Their protest

had been preceded by irate housewives from Syracuse, NY, who petitioned Steve Allen not to allow Elvis onto his show at all.

His sanitized performance on that show did little to appease his critics. Herb Rau wrote in the *Miami* News, "Elvis can't sing, can't play the guitar and can't dance. He has two thousand idiots per show . . ."; influential Hollywood gossip columnist Hedda Hopper labeled Elvis "the most obscene, vulgar influence on young America today."

Elvis' early detractors were no match for the enormous acclaim (and spending power) of his fans. It took mere months for top TV variety host Ed Sullivan to eat his words about never having the likes of Elvis on his show, a perfect platform for Elvis to cement his national appeal and, for the first time, show the country his love of gospel.

Riots at live shows continued. In late 1957, Colonel Parker was officially warned by the Los Angeles Vice Squad not to allow Elvis to wiggle and bump on his second night's performance in Los Angeles or the performer would be sent to jail. The threat came after Elvis' first night's act included him feigning sex on stage . . . with stuffed dog Nipper. The LAPD turned up the following evening with a film camera to dissuade these antics; as Elvis recounted during his NBC TV Special, for the entire show the only thing he wiggled was his little finger. Similar tactics, dubbed by the press as a "no-wiggle restriction," had been enforced by Kentucky police in November 1956.

Elvis' first movie after returning from the Army, *G.I. Blues*, fell foul of the Legion of Decency, which termed it "highly objectionable in its theme and treatment"—the Legion later objected to some of the dance sequences in *Viva Las Vegas*. However, the Elvis that returned from the Army was an All-American boy who had served his country with honor, paid his fair share of taxes, and raised vast sums of money for charitable causes.

By the early Seventies, Elvis had come almost full-circle. In early 1971 he received a Jaycee award as one of the "Ten Outstanding Young Men of the Year"; he was held up as a shining example of an upstanding citizen and a living symbol of the American Dream. Weeks earlier Elvis had sent a letter to the Deputy Director of the Bureau of Narcotics and Dangerous Drugs in which he expressed his opinion that "motion pictures and rock music are directly responsible for much of the confusion in this country," offering his services to combat this and the twin menace of drugs and Communism.

After his Army service, with the exception of movie studio-placed items in gossip columns linking Elvis with his co-star of the day, Elvis' management was singularly successful at keeping scandal at bay. Until the final year of his life and the publication of the tell-all book *Elvis: What Happened?* by former bodyguards, the Colonel, Elvis' entourage and various media handlers kept a lid on his prescription drug excesses, sexual peccadilloes and wild behavior, though the press did get wind of the excessive zeal demonstrated by Elvis' bodyguards in the Seventies.

ELVIS SAID IN 1956: "If I did think I was bad for people, I would go back to driving a truck, and I really mean this."

ELVIS SAID IN 1956: "I guess the more popular you are, the more criticism you get."

ELVIS SAID: "There ain't nothing bad about it. I would never do it if I thought it was bad. There is nothing planned in this. It's just music and singing, that's all."

ELVIS SAID IN 1956: "Regardless of who you are or what you do, there's gonna be people that don't like you. There were people that didn't like Jesus Christ. They killed him and Jesus Christ was a perfect man."

SCATTER (THE CHIMP)

One of Elvis' more demanding entourage members, Scatter joined the gang in 1961 and remained a regular companion for several years, until he committed one too many misdemeanors and was sent back home to Graceland. Depending on his mood, Scatter would either let people hold him like a baby, act like an out-of-control sophomore, or (the reason for his name) scatter his shit around the room.

Elvis bought Scatter from Memphis TV entertainer Bill Killebrew, after Alan Fortas saw the chimp on TV. Elvis paid a couple of hundred dollars for him, and then bought him a wardrobe of suits and ties. The chimp had already been trained to wear clothes, drink whisky, and make inappropriate sexual advances to anyone in a skirt, something that became a regular party trick at Elvis' LA place in the pre-Priscilla years. When drunk, the chimp had no qualms about engaging in public masturbation.

Elvis enjoyed walking around with Scatter on his shoulder, and took him out to Hollywood, where from Kid Galahad onwards he was a constant source of amusement, described by one biographer as "a walking id" for Elvis and the gang.

Scatter got into all kinds of trouble. Alan Fortas would dress him up in a chauffeur's cap, drive Elvis' Rolls Royce with the chimp on his lap, and duck out of sight when another car went by so that the oncoming driver thought the chimp was driving the Roller. A pal of the entourage's, a former stripper called Brandy Marlow, once simulated sex with the chimp during a party. As a prank, Scatter was reputedly once let loose in a bedroom where Alan Fortas was making love to a girlfriend and tried to join in.

Scatter finally overstepped the mark when he climbed into Sam Goldwyn's office at MGM (or in other tellings, gatecrashed a party next door to Elvis' LA home and scared the guests senseless). Elvis sent Scatter back to Memphis, where he lived in a cage and pined for his former life. He came to an untimely end some time later, reputedly poisoned in revenge by a maid whom he bit; other sources pin his demise on alcohol-related liver problems.

SCHEFF, JERRY

Much in-demand session bass guitarist Jerry Scheff recorded with Johnny Mathis, Neil Diamond, Pat Boone, Sammy Davis Jr., Dionne Warwick, Nancy Sinatra, Linda Rondstadt and Barbra Streisand before he began working with Elvis in the TCB Band in 1969. Scheff was the band's bass player for the duration, with the exception of a two-year hiatus between 1973 and April 1975, when he took a sabbatical (and was replaced by Emory Gordy Jr. and Duke Bardwell).

San Francisco-born Scheff graduated to the bass via the tuba. He played with guitarist James Burton on TV show "Shindig" in the early Sixties, and had a background in jazz and the blues, though most of his session work for West Coast pop and rock.

Scheff first played on an Elvis session in 1966, when he was called in to overdub some basslines for the Double Trouble soundtrack. He also stepped in on trumpet at the Easy Come, Easy Go session later that year.

When Scheff was invited to audition for Elvis and his new touring band, he didn't think that he wanted the job at all. He changed his mind when he found the audition to be a thoroughly enjoyable blues run out.

Within a year of joining Elvis' stage band, Scheff worked with The Doors on their L.A. Woman soundtrack, and may have switched bands permanently if Jim Morrison hadn't died soon after.

Scheff would have joined the ranks of Elvis songwriters if Elvis had laid down a vocal to his composition "There's A Fire Down Below," for which the band recorded an instrumental track at Elvis final, aborted recording session at Graceland in October 1976 (released in 2000 on FTD album The Jungle Room Sessions); Shakin' Stevens covered the song on his 2007 album.

After Elvis, Scheff toured in the band of high-profile acts including Bob Dylan, Bette Midler, John Denver, and Elvis Costello. He has also toured as part of the Elvis—The Concert project.

SCHILLING, JERRY
(B. 1942)

Jerry Schilling met Elvis in Memphis when as a 12-year-old he played football with a group of older boys including Elvis at Guthrie Park. Schilling was a good enough player for the seven-year age difference not to matter; besides, Elvis was not yet famous and sometimes had trouble making up numbers on the football field.

Born on February 6, 1942, Schilling grew up with his grandparents after his mother died when in his infancy. He trained to be a history teacher and played football for Arkansas State University. Then, in 1964, he played touch football with Elvis again. After the game, Elvis' asked him to come along to LA where he was due to start work on his latest film, Tickle Me. Schilling threw in his career plans and went to work for his friend.

Within the entourage, Elvis dubbed him "Milk," a reference to his healthy lifestyle, though his initial moniker was "Mr. Bodybuilder." In later years, Elvis called him "Cougar."

Schilling ended up being part of Elvis' gang on and off until 1976, though his employment was almost terminated soon after it began. Elvis became highly suspicious of the new boy when he found Schilling and Priscilla chatting in the kitchen late one night; he was unaware of the unspoken rule, that no entourage member should be seen to be overly-friendly with Elvis' girl. In his early years, Schilling's main role was as a bodyguard.

The youngest member of the long-term entourage, Schilling was an outspoken member of the group for his left-leaning political views. Red West has described Schilling as the most independently-minded of Elvis' long-term entourage members. If Elvis started cussing him out, Schilling would more than likely just walk out of the room.

In March 1967, two months before Elvis and Priscilla got hitched, Schilling married girlfriend Sandy Kawelo in Las Vegas. They had met in the summer of 1965, when she was a dancer Elvis film Paradise, Hawaiian Style. Elvis

was unable to attend as he was still recuperating from concussion he had sustained in a fall in his bathroom. Schilling didn't attend Elvis' wedding either: he was one of Elvis' close friends whom the Colonel barred from the wedding ceremony. This slight may have had something to do with Jerry Schilling deciding soon after to head off on his own and train as a film editor in Los Angeles.

Schilling was a stand-in for Elvis on Stay Away, Joe, and had an uncredited role as the Deputy Sheriff in 1969 movie The Trouble With Girls.

Schilling flew to Las Vegas at Elvis' request in August 1970, to help protect him against a criminal assassination threat at the International Hotel. It was Schilling whom Elvis called in December 1970, after he had stormed out of Graceland because Priscilla and Vernon were giving him a hard time about his overspending. Elvis flew to meet Schilling in LA, having previously flown to Washington to find solace with girlfriend Joyce Bova. Schilling then returned to Washington with Elvis to get the law enforcement badge his boss coveted above all others: a Federal Bureau of Narcotics and Dangerous Drugs badge.

From this time on, Schilling's main role was to look after Elvis' public relations.

Schilling worked as assistant editor with the producer and director of 1972 documentary Elvis on Tour. Schilling's first marriage broke up in early 1973. His relationship with a new girlfriend foundered after Elvis slept with her. For a while, Schilling took a room at Elvis' LA home.

Elvis put Schilling in charge of his karate movie project in late 1974. Around this time, Elvis bought Schilling a house in Hollywood Hills (where he was still living at the time of writing). Elvis is said to have told Schilling, "I know . . . your mother died when you were a year old, and you never had a home, and I wanted to be the one to give it to you."

In the mid-Seventies, Schilling moved in with Elvis back-up singer Myrna Smith. Soon after, they married. He has since remarried, to Cindy.

Schilling left Elvis' employ in early 1976, after a series of disagreements within the entourage. Apparently he told Elvis at the time that he valued friendship over "the job." Red West claims that Elvis pulled a gun on Schilling not long before he quit.

Schilling was one of the pallbearers at Elvis' funeral. After Elvis, he worked in the film and music business, road managing for Billy Joel and the Beach Boys among others. He briefly managed Lisa Marie when she was in her late teens. Schilling remained on friendly terms with Colonel Parker's after Elvis' death, and was a speaker at his funeral. He has acted in a number of feature films, including 1988 movie Heartbreak Hotel, and appeared in several Elvis documentaries over the years, including a central role in Elvis By The Presleys.

In 2007, Schilling was the star attraction on "The Elvis Cruise," which traveled around the Caribbean.

Book:
Me And A Guy Named Elvis by Jerry Schilling and Chuck Crisafulli, Gotham Books, 2006

SCHOOLS

Elvis started first grade at the East Tupelo Consolidated School, five minutes' walk from his home on Lake Street, in the fall of 1941. The school was later renamed after its driving force for many years, Superintendent Lawhon. Elvis attended the school until 1946. Elvis generally stayed out of trouble and was of average ability as far as schoolwork was concerned, though even at that young age he loved to sing. School pal Odell Clark remembers, "If he could get one person to listen to him, he would sing their ear off."

After his family moved into Tupelo, Elvis started junior high at Milam High in Tupelo. In eighth grade, he transferred to Humes High School in Memphis, after his family made the move to the big city. Some biographies state that Elvis' first school in Memphis was, briefly, the Christine School on Third Street, though this is disputed. Schools were still racially segregated at this time.

Elvis received his high-school diploma on June 3, 1953, a day that filled his parents with pride—he was the first person in his immediate family to achieve this level of education. Elvis proudly displayed the certificate in his trophy room and showed it to friends.

Though Elvis' public persona in the Fifties was that of a young hellraiser, despite his flamboyant attire during his later school years, he seems to have been a diligent student whose prime intention was to adhere to his parents' wishes and better himself through education—he could always have left school at sixteen and started working, as many of his friends did. Some of his contemporaries remember him as a teacher's pet; the school yearbook for his graduation ventured no prophecy about his future: rather, with Elvis Presley leaving, it mentioned that a new position had opened for teacher's pet.

Only in his final year did Elvis cut some classes; rather than rebelliousness, the biggest threat to his studies was tiredness from the job he held down. Years later, Elvis admitted to Larry Geller that he was surprised he got his diploma because he spent more time daydreaming about being a star like Tony Curtis or Marlon Brando than doing his schoolwork.

Elvis sometimes joked about the fact that he managed to fail music one year at high school. His favorite class in his last year was wood shop.

See also Education, Milam Junior High School and Humes High School.

"SCHOOL DAYS"

*See "*HAIL, HAIL ROCK 'N' ROLL."

Elvis at his high school graduation picnic in 1953.

SCHROEDER, AARON
(B. 1926)

Brooklyn-born composer and producer Schroeder co-wrote sixteen Elvis songs in the early part of his career with a wide selection of co-writers (most frequently Wally Gold) through song publisher Hill & Range. In the early Sixties, Schroeder branched out and began his own publishing company and the Musicor label, which launched the career of Gene Pitney.

SCHWARTZ AND ABLESER JEWELERS
(247 North Beverly Dr., Beverly Hills, CA)

Elvis ordered his first ever TCB pendants for his entourage in the fall of 1970 from this Beverly Hills jeweler, spending $90 each on the 14-karat charms. For good measure he also picked up two diamond rings, ten TCB symbols on chains, and an extra TCB ring. From this time on, Elvis regularly bought TCB jewelry from the store. For Christmas 1970, Elvis spent upwards of $20,000 there.

The Ableser name is still in jewelry retail, out of a store in Encino, CA.

SCOTLAND

Elvis' family line has been traced back to Scot Andrew Presley. Elvis was unaware of any such lineage, and only visited Scotland because the plane carrying him back from his Army service to the US touched down to refuel at Prestwick in early 1960. Elvis is believed to have disembarked and spent an hour and a half at the airport, his only time on British soil.

One strand in the Presley genealogical trail leads back to the parish of Lonmay, in Northeastern Scotland. Andrew Presley, the tenth son of another Andrew Presley and Elspeth Leg, is said to be the forbear who emigrated to the United States in 1745 (though other bearers of the Presley name in Aberdeenshire dispute this).

A special black, baby blue, gold and pink tartan, known as Presley of Lonmay, was created to mark the 30th anniversary of Elvis' passing in 2007.

Book:

The Presley Prophecy, by Allan Morrison, Lulu.com, 2007—a novelized story about Elvis' Scottish ancestor.

SCOTT, WINFIELD

Scott composed half-a-dozen songs for Elvis, including "Long Legged Girl (With The Short Dress On)," "Return To Sender" and "Please Don't Drag That String Around." He worked most often with Otis Blackwell, and was also responsible for a number of LaVern Baker hits, including "Tweedlee Dee," one of the first songs that Elvis performed live.

"SCRATCH MY BACK"

Elvis laid down this Bill Giant / Bernie Baum / Florence Kaye song for the soundtrack of *Paradise, Hawaiian Style* on July 26, 1965 at Radio Recorders. In the movie, he sings it as a duet with Marianna Hill. The song has since appeared on the *Double Features* series in the Nineties, and on an FTD reissue in the 2000s which included an alternate take.

SCREEN TEST

As he was making the step up to national fame, Elvis traveled to Los Angeles for a Paramount Studios screen test between March 26 and 28, 1956. For the test, Elvis performed two scenes opposite Frank Faylen from the Studio's upcoming production The Rainmaker, watched by Hal Wallis and director Frank Tashlin. Wallis instructed Elvis to act like himself rather than attempt to act "like John Barrymore." Elvis was so nervous that he stuttered his way through the scenes. His acting performance may have been untutored, but the massed ranks in the studio saw that when he performed in playback to his own hit, "Blue Suede Shoes" (using a prop guitar) he lit up the screen.

On the strength of this color screen test, Elvis was offered a movie contract with an option for a further six pictures, earning $15,000 for the first film, and a fee rising to $100,000 for the seventh.

Despite being the first studio to sign Elvis to a contract, Paramount was the second studio to release an Elvis movie. Twentieth Century-Fox was the first to unleash Elvis in the theaters with its movie *Love Me Tender*.

Elvis' screen test has since featured in the *Elvis in Hollywood* documentary. His performance of "Blue Suede Shoes" was in the *Great Performances* documentary, and in the 2007 international DVD release *Elvis 30 #1 Hits DVD*.

It has also been claimed that Elvis also ran through a scene with Cynthia Baxter because Hal Wallis wanted to see how he fared opposite a woman. If this took place, it was either at the original screen test, or a week or so later on a return trip to Hollywood. Shelley Winters wrote in her memoir that Elvis screen tested with Natalie Wood for the film version of Broadway musical *Girls of Summer*.

ELVIS SAID IN 1956: "I took a straight acting test. And actually, I wouldn't care too much about singing in the movies."

HAL WALLIS: "After a few minutes I knew he was a natural in the way Sinatra was. And with just as much personality."

HAL KANTER: "I was absolutely astonished at how adroit the man was in handling the scene, and the animal magnetism of the man just jumped off the screen."

SECRETARIES

Over the years, Elvis employed a string of secretaries to look after his affairs. They included Elisabeth Stefaniak in Germany, Pat Boyd (who left to marry Red West), double cousin Patsy Presley, Becky Hartley (married name Yancy, with Elvis from 1962 to 1975), Bonya McGarrity, Paulette Shafer (whose father Paul supplied Elvis with movies for his theater nights), and Jeanne LeMay.

After Vernon moved out of Graceland in the early Sixties, the secretary worked in the annex, sitting behind an old army-issue desk.

Book:

My Life with Elvis: The Fond Memories of a Fan Who Became Elvis' Private Secretary, by Becky Yancey and Cliff Linedecker, St Martin's Press, 1977.

SEDAKA, NEIL
(B. 1939)

Elvis recorded Sedaka song "Solitaire" in 1976. A classically-trained pianist, Brooklyn-born Sedaka was a teen-market star in the late Fifties with hits such as "Oh! Carol," for Elvis' label RCA Victor, as well as penning a string of hits for other artists, starting with Connie Francis's "Stupid Cupid" in 1958.

Sedaka's compositions have been hits for a slew of artists running from ABBA to Andy Williams. He pursued a successful solo career of his own until 1963, and then staged a career revival in the Seventies with 1975 #1 hit "Laughter In The Rain."

"SEE SEE RIDER"

Elvis added this traditional song to his repertoire in Las Vegas in February 1970. When he reprised the song for his January/February 1972 Las Vegas engagement, it was as a high-octane opener, a position it retained throughout the remainder of his performing career. The first vinyl release of Elvis singing the song came out on his 1970 On Stage live album.

"See See Rider," or "C. C. Rider" as it is sometimes known, already had a seasoned history before Big Bill Broonzy had a hit with it in 1920, and "Mother of the Blues" Ma Rainey made a successful recording in 1925. Since then, it has been covered by a who's-who of blues artists, rhythm and blues performers and rockers ranging from Ray Charles to Chuck Willis, LaVern Baker, the Animals and Mitch Ryder. Debate continues to this day on the meaning of the title, specifically whether it refers to a "country circuit preacher," a guitar, a prostitute or a slang term whose meaning has not survived the onrush of time.

Elvis performances of the song were caught on camera for his *Elvis on Tour* documentary, his *Aloha from Hawaii Via Satellite* show, and the late-period *Elvis in Concert* documentary.

As Elvis' standard opener immediately after he made his entrance to the strains of the 2001 theme "Also Sprach Zarathustra," the song has been on a multitude of Elvis live albums and compilations since its *On Stage* debut, including *Aloha From Hawaii Via Satellite, Elvis Recorded Live On Stage In Memphis, Elvis In Concert, Elvis Aron Presley, The Alternate Aloha, Walk A Mile In My Shoes, Platinum: A Life In Music, Live In Las Vegas, Today Tomorrow & Forever, Elvis: Close Up, Elvis Live*, and the 2007 version of *Viva Las Vegas*.

FTD releases featuring the song include *Polk Salad Annie, An American Trilogy, Summer Festival, Takin' Tahoe Tonight, Closing Night, I Found My Thrill, Elvis Recorded Live On Stage In Memphis, Live In LA, It's Midnight, Dragonheart, Big Boss Man, Dixieland Rocks, Dinner At Eight, Tucson '76* and *New Year's Eve*, not to mention hundreds and hundreds of concerts bootlegs.

Rehearsal versions are on FTD releases *Polk Salad Annie, 6363 Sunset, On Tour—The Rehearsals* and *Made in Memphis*. Elvis sang an excerpt from the song to just his own acoustic guitar at Sam Thompson's house in 1973 (on bootlegs such as *A Private Moment with the King*).

"SEEING IS BELIEVING"

Elvis laid down this Red West / Glen Spreen revival song on May 19, 1971 in Nashville. It was first released on his gospel album *He Touched Me* the following year. The song is included on gospel compilations *Amazing Grace* and *Peace In The Valley*. Alternate takes appear on FTD releases *Easter Special* and *I Sing All Kinds*.

SELF-REALIZATION FELLOWSHIP

Elvis became interested in this organization, founded in Boston in 1920 by Paramahansa Yogananda, in early 1965, soon after his 30th birthday, at a time when he was increasingly disaffected with the Hollywood gravy train, and in the company of Larry Geller had begun actively seeking a spiritual meaning to his life.

The Fellowship is based on Yogananda's teachings—based on the kriya yoga and meditation traditions practiced by his own guru in the Himalayas—which espouse the pursuit of "attaining a personal experience of God" through an ecumenical blend of Eastern and Western religious traditions.

Aside from the undoubted spiritual benefits he obtained, when Elvis was studying kriya yoga at the Fellowship he had the rare experience of being just another seeker. Still, being Elvis, he asked the head of the organization for some accelerated insight, without doing the required practice. For a while in the mid-Sixties, Elvis made frequent trips to the organization's Mount Washington headquarters; he created his meditation garden at Graceland to try and replicate the atmosphere at his own home.

Though Elvis turned his attention away from matters of the spirit in the late Sixties after the Colonel stepped in to steer him away from this "dangerous" path he was taking, he did maintain contact with the organization, and resumed his visits to Fellowship leader Sri Daya Mata when he returned to live performing.

Elvis' involvement with the group was never popular with Priscilla or the guys in the entourage. When news leaked out in 1971 of Elvis' links with the Fellowship, gossip columnist Rona Barrett suggested that what she qualified as Elvis' bizarre behavior was a direct result; she even claimed that the Yogananda had told Daya Mata "that Elvis was the next savior."

By the 2000s, the organization ran meditation centers in more than sixty different countries

SELLERS, PETER
(B. RICHARD HENRY SELLERS, 1925-1980)

Elvis' funny bone was particularly tickled by Peter Sellers' absurd and zany brand of humor. Dr. Strangelove was one of Elvis' lifelong favorite movies. He screened everything the British comic made, and he loved the Clouseau character in the Pink Panther franchise. Elvis enjoyed mimicking many of Sellers' comic voices, and of course the karate episodes from the Clouseau movies were right up his street.

Sellers was born in Southsea, England, on September 8, 1925. He rose to fame in Britain as part of the surreal Fifties radio production *The Goon Show*, recorded comic music albums with future Beatles producer George Martin, and achieved international stardom with his 1964 appearance in Stanley Kubrick's movie *Dr. Strangelove*. A year before he died, Sellers received his second Oscar nomination for his bittersweet performance in *Being There*.

SEMON, ROGER

A British-born record executive who since the mid-Eighties has worked with Ernest Jorgensen to put together Elvis releases. After being hired by RCA in America, it became Semon's job to root out lost Elvis material, reorder the Elvis catalogue, assemble reissues, and, in recent years manage the FTD collectors' series of Elvis releases as an associate producer.

A childhood Elvis fan since first hearing "It's Now Or Never," Semon initially joined RCA in 1973 as a salesman for London. In the Eighties, he worked in marketing. He initially began compiling Elvis releases for the UK, before teaming up with Jorgenson to restore Elvis' work and revive Elvis' reputation through Sony/BMG.

"SEND ME SOME LOVIN'"

A home recording of Elvis singing this 1956 Leo Price hit—written by John Marascalco and Leo Price, and later covered by Little Richard, Sam Cooke and John Lennon—as he whiled away the hours during his Army service in Germany, is on the bootleg release *Greetings From Germany*.

"SENTIMENTAL ME"

During a Nashville recording session on March 12, 1961, Elvis laid down this sweet-voiced million-selling Ames Brothers hit from 1950 (written by Jimmy Cassin and Jim Morehead) for his album *Something For Everybody*. It was included on the budget *Separate Ways* LP, and then on *Double Dynamite*, before being anthologized on *From Nashville to Memphis* in the Nineties. An alternate take appears on FTD issue *Fame And Fortune*.

"SEPARATE WAYS"

Red West (with Richard Mainegra) wrote this song for Elvis while he was in the midst of his separation from Priscilla in early 1972. He recorded the song at the RCA studios in Hollywood on March 27, 1972. By the time it came out as a single with "Always on My Mind" on the B-side, Elvis was already going steady with new girlfriend Linda Thompson. The track made it to #20 on the *Billboard* Hot 100 following its release in November 1972, and went on to sell half a million copies in the US alone.

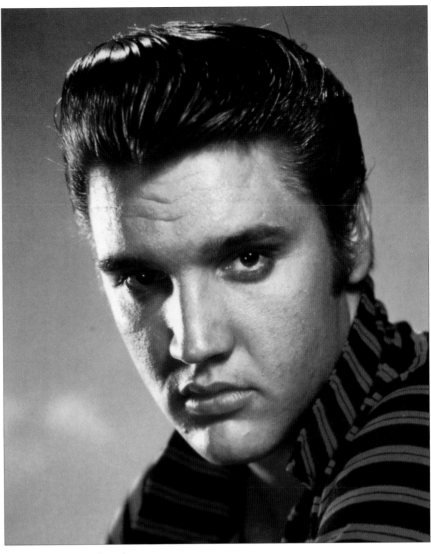

Studio portrait 1956, Hollywood.

"Separate Ways" became the title track to a budget album a month after its initial release as a single. It subsequently came out on *Double Dynamite*, and then posthumously on *Always On My Mind*, *Walk A Mile In My Shoes*, *Burning Love*, *Elvis By The Presleys* and *Hitstory*.

A different take appeared on *Platinum: A Life In Music* in 1997, and a rehearsal version for the *Elvis On Tour* documentary (in which it also features) came out on 2004 FTD release *Elvis On Tour—The Rehearsals*.

SEPARATE WAYS (LP)

Shipped in December 1972 and issued on RCA's budget label Camden, this album showcased a selection of Elvis ballads and movie tracks, including Elvis' latest single. If ever there was an album that was a barometer of Elvis' mood at the time, this was it. The album sold 300,000 on initial release, good for #46 in the charts during an 18-week stay.

TRACK LISTING:
1. Separate Ways
2. Sentimental Me
3. In My Way
4. I Met Her Today
5. What Now, What Next, Where To
6. Always On My Mind
7. I Slipped, I Stumbled, I Fell
8. Is It So Strange
9. Forget Me Never
10. Old Shep

SEX APPEAL

Elvis' effect on women in his audience was instant and overpowering from the first time he took to a stage with band members Scotty Moore and Bill Black. After that first appearance, he claimed that he had no idea what he had done to warrant this phenomenon, but he managed to replicate it on a nightly basis and use it as the foundation for his enormous and lasting popularity with his female fans. Practically overnight, the shy high school boy with a hit-and-miss history with girls turned into a magnet for female sexual desire.

Comparable to Twenties heart-throb Valentino in the legitimized outlet that Elvis provided for female sexual desire at a time of repressed sexual mores, Camille Paglia has called Elvis a "revolutionary sexual persona." The classical and somewhat androgynous beauty of his features, his unashamedly sexual gyrations on stage, and his exhortations to rock, rock, rock meant one thing to a whole generation of young women: he was sex unleashed.

Decades before academics began investigating and codifying Elvis' sex appeal, bemused fellow artists struggled to understand the unprecedented mass hysteria among his fans. Country singer Porter Wagoner, who shared the bill with Elvis on an early tour, asked a girl in the audience who was in the midst of sexual transport just how Elvis affected her. "Oh my God," she gushed. "All over. Just all over me." Promoter and songwriter Mae Axton asked a delirious girl at an Elvis gig she had helped promote what was so special about this new kid. Her response: "He's just a great big, beautiful hunk of forbidden fruit."

admirers notwithstanding his traditional Southern abhorrence of homosexuality. Gender studies authors have noted that some lesbians consider their identification with Elvis as an indicator of their sexual orientation.

ELVIS SAID IN THE MID-FIFTIES: "I'm not trying to be sexy. I didn't have no idea of trying to sell sex. It's just my way of expressing how I feel when I move around."

RAQUEL WELCH: "When I was 13, I saw him [Elvis] perform live and I suddenly understood what sex is all about. I was screaming at the top of my lungs."

PRISCILLA: "He was the sexual idol of millions and could choose whomever he wanted, whenever he wanted. I quickly learned, for my own survival, not to ask too many questions."

DOLLY PARTON: "He was the sexiest thing I'd ever seen in my life."

RICHARD CORLISS: "There was something feminine about Elvis. His mouth formed the pout of a sullen schoolgirl; his hair was swathed in more chemicals than a starlet's; his hips churned like a hooker's in heat. Presley was manly too, in a street-punk way. For him, the electric guitar was less an instrument than a symbolic weapon — an ax or a machine gun aimed at the complacent pop culture of the Fifties."

SEX LIFE

For a man who had untold numbers of attractive women at his beck and call, it is not surprising that Elvis was a promiscuous man. Some of the people who knew him as he was elevated to the pantheon of sex god likened him to a kid let loose in a candy store.

A never-ending flow of pretty young fans was invited to spend time with Elvis in Memphis (first at Audubon Drive, then at Graceland). Madly in love, they were overjoyed when he hugged and canoodled; to a woman, (those who have talked) have said what a great kisser he was. During these early days, Elvis seems to have been interested in typical Fifties high-school sexual pursuits, which by modern lights would be considered almost innocent—either that or the girls are too modest to admit what would have been outrageously precocious behavior for barely post-pubescent girls in the Fifties.

Later Elvis girlfriends who have revealed details of the sexual side of their relationships confirm that Elvis was more interested in petting and canoodling than penetrative sex. In later years, his libido was diminished by medical conditions and his prescription drug intake.

Writer Elaine Dundy speculates that sexual promiscuity may have been in Elvis' genes—his great-great grandfather on his mother's side populated much of the local county. Elvis' father and grandfather were both handsome men who were popular with the ladies. Larry Geller qualifies Elvis' promiscuity as occurring only at certain well-defined periods of his life. Geller says that when adoring women were invited to party with Elvis and his pals, it was strictly old school, even during the more sexually liberated Sixties.

Even at times during the early years when Elvis let himself go and indulged in the steady flow of willing women ushered into his room by members of his entourage, what tales have filtered out indicate that the intimacy and playfulness of spending a night with another human being—admittedly pretty and female—was as important to Elvis as the sex.

Geller's testimony does not apply to Elvis' wild early touring days, nor to the late Sixties and early Seventies, when Elvis returned to performing and his entourage routinely invited the most beautiful women in the audience to come and

Elvis' protestations that he wasn't selling sex were moot: the entertainment business was doing the selling. Within six months of his debut record, the potential financial implications of Elvis' sex appeal was raising eyebrows among recording industry executives. As early as January 1955, Colonel Tom Parker's lieutenant Tom Diskin presciently wrote that Elvis "is absolutely going to be one of the biggest things in the business in a very short time" because "he gets the girls excited the way Frank Sinatra used to do it. And he's as good-looking as all heck." One of the earliest articles about Elvis in the local Memphis press ran under the headline, "He's Sex!"

It wasn't just that Elvis had a way with girls; he mesmerized them into a kind of mass hysteria that had never before been seen on such a scale. From his earliest concerts, female fans were more vocally enthusiastic than male fans. In January 1955, hundreds of teenage girls mobbed Elvis and demanded autographs when he played the City Auditorium at San Angelo, Texas, even though he was still enough of an unknown to be billed in publicity material as "Alvis Presley."

By May 1955, the hysteria was ready to explode. After a May 1955 show in Jacksonville, Florida, Elvis had to be rescued from a baying horde of fifty girls who had managed to rip most of his clothes off. Mae Axton, who helped to get Elvis out of trouble that May night, recalls: "They wanted to grab him, tear him apart, but they knew they could never really have him. And that just made them want him more." Once the story made it into the papers, grabbing a piece of Elvis became a nationwide female sport. From that moment on, Elvis required a police escort in addition to his burly buddies.

When Elvis landed his first movie contract with Paramount, producer Hal Wallis explicitly thought that Elvis would become the new Rudolph Valentino.

In his bad-boy heyday, when he was on stage Elvis had to dodge apartment keys that girls hurled at him in the vain hope of enticing him home afterwards. Other fans scrawled their phone numbers on his car windows in lipstick, or swept the dust from his car as a keepsake. Young women up and down the country plastered their rooms with posters of Elvis and fantasized of him as their dream man in the Fifties, Sixties, Seventies and beyond.

So great is Elvis' sex appeal that it has transcended his life (many women still think he's #1); it has even transferred to Elvis impersonators, many of whom enjoy the reflected sex appeal that their Elvis tributes bring them. A 2007 poll by UK broadcaster Channel 4 saw Elvis take second spot in the top ten greatest sex symbols, behind Angelina Jolie but three places above the next highest-placed male (Brad Pitt).

Though there were extended periods in his life when Elvis took full advantage of his matchless sexual appeal, when asked about his status as a sex symbol he invariably feigned shyness. According to Larry Geller, Elvis knew that this was a genie he had to keep in the bottle.

It should be remembered that Elvis' sexual charge exploded in much chaster times. Even in the Sixties, known now as a decade of free love, on-screen Elvis didn't even share a bed with one of his co-stars until one of his final feature films, *Live a Little, Love a Little*.

Elvis' androgynous appeal was not lost on the gay community. He had plenty of homosexual spend some private time with Elvis backstage after the show.

Marty Lacker divides Elvis' attitude to sexual conquest into pre- and post-Army periods: before being drafted, Elvis looked sexually dangerous but wasn't; when he came out, he may have had a new all-American boy next-door image but "he was basically a predator." However, just before he was drafted in 1958, Elvis most certainly played the field. Around this time, he reputedly told exotic dancer Tempest Storm, "I'm as horny as a billy goat in a pepper patch" and raced her to bed.

Mid-Fifties girlfriend Wanda Jackson recalled, "There were things you could and couldn't do, and my daddy made sure I never crossed that line." Early flame June Juanico said: "Elvis was a wonderful kisser. How do you describe soft lips, slightly parted, not too much, but just perfect? And he sometimes opened his mouth about three inches—sucked off part of my nose." Photographer Al Wertheimer snapped Elvis in oscular action in 1956—one of his most famous photos adorns 2005 BMG album *Love, Elvis*.

In her memoir, Juanico states that Elvis did not want sexual intercourse with her because he wanted to marry her.

Countering this view of relatively anodyne high-school sexual appetites, Red West remembers a day in the mid-Fifties when he and Elvis picked up two girls and took them back to Red's mom's apartment. Elvis was so vigorous in his love-making that he snapped a board under the bed. According to one of his traveling companions in Paris in 1959, Elvis had his way with 22 out of the 24 Bluebelle girls working at the Lido during his visit.

Right through to the Sixties, if Elvis was serious about a woman, he wanted to save sexual intercourse for marriage. Elvis told German girlfriend Elisabeth Stefaniak that he didn't have full intercourse with girls he saw "on a regular basis" because he couldn't risk them becoming pregnant. This did not preclude a full range of other nocturnal activities. In a letter Elvis sent to pal Alan Fortas in Germany, he described his time with a new girlfriend out there as "Grind City."

In her memoir, Priscilla Presley writes that Elvis wanted to save "full" sex until their wedding night because, he told her, intercourse was "a very sacred thing" for him. They did find plenty of other ways of indulge sexual intimacy, none of which were "perverted or in any way harmful" Priscilla specifies in her memoir. Before he left Germany and Priscilla, he turned down her urgings to consummate their rapport; unauthorized biographers have controversially claimed that Elvis and Priscilla had sexual intercourse soon after meeting, and that before they married (eight years later), Priscilla had an abortion.

Anita Wood, with whom Elvis was going steady before he left for Germany, revealed that Elvis "had a fetish about tiny feet." Barbara Leigh said that Elvis liked to see his ladies in small white lace panties which let wisps of pubic hair out—a penchant that diligent biographers have traced back to a glimpse of white panties that Elvis was afforded when, as a kid, he was wrestled with a girl. Some entourage members have suggested that in his later years, Elvis enjoyed getting women to wrestle in their panties; he allegedly involved Priscilla in these games, and is said to have photographed and videoed some of these erotic bouts. In his Elvis biography, Peter Guralnick writes that Joe Esposito returned this material to Priscilla after Elvis' funeral. Elvis made sure that he was not part of the footage—indeed, entourage members have reported that almost had a phobia about anyone seeing him naked.

It would seem that Elvis' preference for very young women was prompted by his traditional Southern idea of purity. Elvis reputedly told Alan Fortas, "I'll never break a virgin. There are too many whores around." Lamar Fike remembers

Elvis quipping, "Fourteen to sixteen [years old] will you get you twenty [years in jail]," but that didn't stop him picking out many younger fans to come up and spend some private time with him.

Entourage members have reported that Elvis' sexual tastes included watching. Billy Smith says that Elvis got into pornography in the mid-60s, including some rather extreme Scandinavian hardcore. Though Larry Geller disputes the veracity of such claims, a number of biographies state that Elvis had two-way mirrors installed in the pool house changing room and in a bedroom at one of his Los Angeles homes. It has also been claimed that when the opportunity arose, Elvis spurned the chance to engage in group sex. Reputedly on an occasion when two of his pals were in bed with a woman, Elvis refused the woman's invitation to join in because he had no desire to be involved in a sex act with other men.

When Elvis was most earnestly pursuing a spiritual path in the mid-Sixties, he went through a period of sexual abstinence. At the time, he told Priscilla, "We have to control our desires so they don't control us. If we can control sex, then we can master all other desires."

Priscilla writes in her memoir that she and Elvis finally consummated their relationship on their wedding night in May 1967. Priscilla almost immediately became pregnant. As soon as she gave birth to Lisa Marie, she found herself on the wrong side of Elvis' demarcation line that excluded mothers from his sexual purview.

In 1968, while taping his NBC TV Special, according to Alanna Nash, Elvis got so worked up during his performance that he had a "sexual emission" while he was on stage.

Girlfriend Joyce Bova has confirmed Elvis' belief that mothers shouldn't have sex once they have given birth. Elvis felt that there was something morally wrong about sleeping with a woman who had had a child; it was against his own personal code knowingly to have sex with a married woman. When he found out that a woman he was seeing in the Seventies had become a mother at a young age, he dropped her.

Girlfriend Barbara Leigh has said that Elvis never let her see him naked. She describes him as the best kisser of any man she's known, and also that he was not sex-crazed. As well as liking the lights out, Elvis never urinated at a stall in a public bathroom, he always took a booth.

Cassandra Peterson said that she and Elvis did not sleep together because Elvis' entourage never left the two of them alone.

By the early Seventies, Elvis' drug intake was sometimes sufficient to make him less than fully capable. Seventies girlfriend Peggy Lipton was disparaging about Elvis' sexual prowess in her memoir, likening him more to a teenage boy than to a man.

In Las Vegas, Lamar Fike says that Elvis continued to enjoy watching girls wrestling for his sexual edification, and confirms the story that first appeared in the Wests' book that Elvis had a girlfriend waiting for him in one hotel room while he went to another to watch this show. Billy Smith says that Elvis liked to be masturbated and then ejaculate into the girl's hair. In her memoir, Cybill Shepherd takes credit for introducing Elvis to cunnilingus.

Step-brother Rick Stanley has said that for Elvis, defeating loneliness by having a bed-time companion was more important than the sex. Many of Elvis' girlfriends have reported that Elvis was interested in just being together, perhaps singing, reading and generally horsing around. Singer Kathy Westmoreland shared Elvis' bed for many nights before having sex. Sheila Ryan told one interviewer, "Sex was never important to him, you should think it was, but it really wasn't. Of course we did have sex, but the cuddling and kissing was far more important to Elvis . . . Real romance as I was hoping for, never really took place."

Many of Elvis' girlfriends in the Seventies have described the trajectory of their relationship as a stage of getting-to-know you petting, a little sex on the side, and then a transformation of their role into a kind of mothering figure to look after his emotional and physical needs.

Elvis referred to his penis as "little Elvis," which may be interpreted as a derisory reference to what is rumored to have been a less-than-average length. Whether or not that's true, "Little Elvis" has made it into the vast slang canon of euphemisms for the male organ. Early drummer Joe Morris recalls seeing Elvis wadding toilet paper into the front of his pants before a show because it drove the girls wild. TV host Ed Sullivan reputedly believed that Elvis packed something into his pants so that when he shook his leg, it looked like he was shaking another part of his anatomy too. However, a man involved in one of Elvis' early TV appearances publicly commented on how well-endowed Elvis seemed.

Albert Goldman wrote that Elvis enjoyed romping in bed with teenage girls, who were instructed to wear white panties. He also claimed that Elvis complained that sexual intercourse was painful for him because he was uncircumcised.

What is not in doubt is that Elvis' generosity to his friends extended to the sexual arena. He tried to find an older girl to "initiate" Billy Smith when he was fifteen, and is said to have hired a prostitute for Lamar Fike because he thought that Fike wasn't getting enough action for himself. He was also generous with his good kissing, enthusiastically locking lips with scores of women in his audience at his Seventies shows.

Sonny West described Elvis' tastes in women as petite and feminine: "He is not a boob man, he is an ass and leg man." Women with big feet were a real turn-off. West has also said that Elvis would sometimes hire two prostitutes and pay them to "make it with each other." Then, if he had a girl in his own room, he'd go back and finish off with her.

Larry Geller's recollections are diametrically opposed: he says that Elvis would turn around and walk out of a room if he caught some of his entourage pals watching pornography. Elvis became even more concerned about performance anxiety as his regime of prescription drugs comprised his bodily functions. It has been suggested that Elvis rationalized his likely impotence with his final long-term girlfriend Ginger Alden by planning out an old-fashioned courtship in which sexual intercourse stayed off the menu until marriage.

Rick Stanley told a magazine in 1989, "When Elvis wanted a girl, someone would go find him one. We called it trolling. Elvis would look around and say, 'It's time to go trolling,' and we knew what that meant. Somebody had to go downstairs and select four or five girls for him to look over. I introduced him to a lot of girls, and members of the entourage introduced him to some. It was usually me, because I knew his taste — tall, clean girls." Once they were up in his suite, Elvis would engage in small talk, often about numerology or astrology, and work out which one he wanted. Then the girl would be told that Elvis was likely to have a meal in bed, that he always wore pajamas, and that he liked his female companies to be freshly-showered. They might also be told that Elvis loved back and shoulder massages.

JUNE JUANICO: Elvis was a very sensitive person, very tender—sensitive on the inside. On the outside, he was macho."

LINDA THOMPSON: "He was not nearly as promiscuous as people might assert. There were a lot of women friends that Elvis had, even when he was with me, and they truly were just friends."

BARBARA LEIGH: "He wasn't into sex that much but more into religion, teaching and sharing his thoughts with anyone who wanted to listen. He loved being the teacher, sharing his knowledge of his favorite books with his pupils."

LAMAR FIKE: "Elvis was the King of Kink... He pushed the edge of the envelope all the time because he could get away with it. He was continually testing the limits of acceptable behavior."

ANN PENNINGTON: "He really did like more than anything just to cuddle and kiss; the other just wasn't very important."

SHEILA RYAN: "I've read bits and pieces about his sexual behavior, and how perverse and bizarre it was, and it really wasn't. It was innocent. . . . Adolescent innocence was what it was all about."

Priscilla: "Being in the fast lane, he was exposed to every pleasure available in life. Ordinary thrills sometimes were not enough, especially when he was under the influence of powerful drugs."

CYBILL SHEPHERD: "He was a wonderful lover, very sexy."

MYRNA SMITH: "Most of his relationships weren't sexual. Elvis just liked pretty women, and your spending the night in his room didn't necessarily mean it was sexual."

LARRY GELLER: "He didn't need to be worshipped or made love to by just anyone. Elvis wanted something rarer and more precious: to be loved."

HOMOSEXUALITY

By all accounts, Elvis had an old-fashioned Southern abhorrence of homosexuality, but his hold on the sexual fantasies of a generation went beyond his female constituency long before gay admirers heard the lyric in "Jailhouse Rock" about one jailbird complementing another's cuteness.

In the Fifties, rumors circulated that Elvis' friendship with Nick Adams was more than just a friendship.

In 1959, bogus doctor Laurenz Johannes Griessel Landau reputedly made sexual advances to Elvis in Germany.

A scene in Fun in Acapulco had to be reshot several times because Elvis kept squirming around. In the end, he told the director the reason why: one of the six guys who held him aloft kept grabbing at his balls. The offending actor was ejected from the scene. During subsequent Hollywood fight scenes, Elvis asked entourage pals who were working as extras to make sure that none of the actors could get close enough to make a grab.

Larry Geller suspects that in the mid-Sixties the Colonel hired a man to proposition him up in order to test whether he was homosexual (and therefore a danger to Elvis).

Author David Bret suggests that the Colonel used a secret knowledge of Elvis' homosexuality to keep him under control.

Actor Jonathan Rhys-Meyers, who portrayed Elvis in 2005, caused a furor among Elvis fans when he suggested that Elvis must have been gay because of his mother fixation and his penchant for "spangly gold."

RED WEST: "Elvis don't like fags, man."

BILLY SMITH: "I hate to say it, but Elvis was prejudiced about homosexuals."

SEYDEL, JÜRGEN
(B. 1917)

The "father of German karate" was Elvis' first karate teacher, starting in late 1959. Seydel accompanied Elvis on a trip to Paris in January 1960, where they went to five lessons with shotokan style master Tetsuji Murakami.

"SHAKE A HAND"

Elvis was in fine voice when he recorded a gospel-inflected version of this 1953 Faye Adams R&B classic in the early hours of March 12, 1975, many years after RCA first suggested it to him, at the label's Hollywood studio. The song—written by Joe Morris—came out on his Today album; it had previously been a hit for Elvis favorites LaVern Baker and Jackie Wilson. In later years, "Shake A Hand" has appeared on RCA's Seventies anthology Walk A Mile In My Shoes. Alternates were released many years later on FTD albums 6363 Sunset and Today. Elvis briefly included the song in his live repertoire in 1975.

"SHAKE, RATTLE AND ROLL"

Elvis added this Big Joe Turner 1954 R&B hit (almost immediately covered by Bill Haley) to his repertoire soon after he began performing. One such early renditions was broadcast over the KDAV radio station in Lubbock, Texas, in January or February 1955, to promote his concerts at the Fair Park venue. The song, written by Charles Calhoun—aka Jesse Stone—provided Elvis with his opener for his first TV appearance, on the Dorsey brothers' "Stage Show" in January 1956. By February 3 that year, the track was in the can for RCA—the one and only time that Elvis and his original band did their own backing vocals for RCA, following Elvis' session at the label's New York studios.

RCA released the song as a single in late August 1956, with "Lawdy, Miss Clawdy" on the B-side, though its first appearance on vinyl was on the second Elvis Presley EP issued that June. The single was lost in the fray as RCA issued practically every Elvis track they had at that time in the same barrage of 45s.

Elvis' energetic rendition of the song made its album debut on For LP Fans Only. Later album releases include the This Is Elvis album and Elvis R 'n' B.

Alternate takes from the original session came out in 1996 on Elvis '56, in 1997 and in 2004 on FTD release Flashback. Alternates from the original session also feature on Sunrise and Today Tomorrow & Forever. Three versions of the song are to be found on The King Of Rock 'n' Roll, including that 1955 Lubbock radio recording (which also graces independent release Memphis Recording Service Vol. 2). The version Elvis performed on Stage Show on January 28, 1956 appeared on A Golden Celebration, The Great Performances and Platinum: A Life In Music. Elvis' TV performances on "Stage Show" and "The Milton Berle Show" featured an ending that blended in to sister-track "Flip, Flop and Fly," a medley that Elvis reprised a few times on stage in 1973 and 1974 (one such example is FTD release Takin' Tahoe Tonight).

A demo version from Sun came out in 1987 on The Complete Sun Sessions. All 12 takes of the song appeared together on 2006 FTD album Elvis Presley, including a version with the more risqué lyrics that neither Elvis (nor Bill Haley before him) dared to include on their recordings.

"SHAKE THAT TAMBOURINE"

Elvis laid down this Bill Giant, Bernie Baum and Florence Kaye song on February 24, 1965 for Harum Scarum. The man doing the shaking is Jordanaire Hoyt Hawkins, all the way through the 28 takes Elvis lavished on this slight song (many of which were resuscitated in the 2000s on the FTD Harum Scarum release). The song has also resurfaced on the Nineties Double Features issue for the movie, and in 2007 on Elvis at the Movies.

SHAVER, SEAN
(B. 1943)

A freelance photographer who documented Elvis throughout his career, accumulating as many as 80,000 pictures from 1967 to Elvis' end. Shaver's photographs and the many books in which he has been involved have long been fan favorites.

Books:
The Life of Elvis Presley. With Intimate Memories of Charlie Hodge, Dick Grob and Billy Smith, by Sean Shaver and Hal Noland, Time Publishing Inc, 1979.
The Elvis Book, Vols. 1—4, Sean Shaver, Timur Publishing, 1980—1991.
Our Memories of Elvis, by Sean Shaver, Al Wertheimer and Eddie Fadal, Timur Publishing, 1984.
Elvis In Focus, by Sean Shaver, Timur Publishing, 1992.

SHEPARD, JAN

Elvis' co-star on King Creole who played his sister (and seven years later had a small part on Paradise, Hawaiian Style). Elvis surprised her by turning up to her birthday party in early 1958, giving her gifts of a stuffed tiger and a movie camera that she promptly used to film Elvis. Shepard had a flourishing career in Sixties TV, taking in major Westerns such as "Bonanza," "Gunsmoke," "The High Chaparral" and "The Virginian."

SHEPHERD, CYBILL
(B. CYBILL LYNNE SHEPHERD, 1950)

Elvis met Memphis beauty queen Cybill Shepherd in July 1972, and dated for a short while. Shepherd visited Elvis during his Las Vegas Hilton engagement that year (though one entourage member has said that they first had a fling in 1966).

Born on February 18, 1950 in Memphis, Shepherd had modeled since winning the 1966 Miss Teenage Memphis parade. She made her acting debut after director Peter Bogdanovich spotted her on the cover of a magazine at a supermarket checkout, made her acquaintance and cast her as the lead in The Last Picture Show (1971). After a couple of flops, Shepherd had a role in Martin Scorsese's landmark movie Taxi Driver (1976), but by the early Eighties had left Hollywood altogether. She returned to TV as a comedienne with Bruce Willis in "Moonlighting" in the late Eighties, and then landed her own sit-com, "Cybill," in the mid-Nineties. She has also carved out something of a career as a jazz singer.

Book:
Cybill Disobedience: How I Survived Beauty Pageants, Elvis, Sex, Bruce Willis, Lies, Marriage, Motherhood, Hollywood, and the Irrepressible Urge to Say What I Think, by Cybill Shepherd and Aimee Lee Ball, HarperCollins, 2000.

SHEPPARD, T. G.
(B. WILLIAM BROWDER, 1944)

T. G. Sheppard was a pal of Elvis' from the early Sixties, after they met at the skating rink Elvis regularly hired in Memphis. At this time, he was making pop tunes under the name Brian Stacy, and was an opening act for The Beach Boys.

Later that decade, Sheppard worked for RCA, acting as a liaison between Elvis and the record company, and helping to promote Elvis records.

Elvis invited Sheppard to fly with him on the *Lisa Marie* to his New Year's Eve concert in Pontiac on December 31, 1975.

In the Seventies, Sheppard had success in his own right as a country pop singer, starting with a #1 in 1975 ("Devil In A Bottle"). Sheppard scored a succession of 15 top ten hits through to 1982.

"SHE THINKS I STILL CARE"

B-side to "Moody Blue," a single released in late 1976, around the time that Elvis' long-term relationship with Linda Thompson finally unraveled, and a track on Elvis' last album, *Moody Blue*. Written by Dickey Lee—whom Elvis knew from Memphis and his days at Sun—the song had originally been a hit for George Jones in 1962. Elvis recorded his version on February 2, 1976 at Graceland.

The song later featured on *Our Memories of Elvis* (without overdubs), *Guitar Man* (with remixed instrumentation) and on anthology album *The Country Side of Elvis*. An alternate take was selected for anthology disk *Walk A Mile In My Shoes*. Other alternate versions are included on *Today Tomorrow & Forever*, and on FTD releases *The Jungle Room Sessions*, *Made In Memphis* and *Too Much Monkey Business* (again, a remixed version).

"SHE WEARS MY RING"

Elvis recorded this *Good Times* album track at Stax studios on December 16, 1973. He had been singing the song at home for years—at least since 1960, when he made a home recording released decades later on *In A Private Moment*. The song is a version of turn-of-the-20th-century Spanish-language song "La Golondrina," with English words by Boudleaux and Felice Bryant. Elvis' recorded version has enjoyed posthumous re-release (stripped of overdubs) on *Our Memories of Elvis*, on the 2000 expanded reissue of *Promised Land*, and on the 2006 *Elvis Country* release.

An alternate take came out on *Essential Elvis Vol. 5*.

"SHE'S A MACHINE"

The instrumentals for this *Easy Come, Easy Go* soundtrack song, written by Joy Byers, were laid down at Radio Recorders on September 29, 1966, though Elvis likely added his vocals at a later date. The track didn't come out on vinyl until 1968 soundtrack round-up *Singer Presents Elvis Singing Flaming Star and Others* (re-issued the following year as *Elvis Sings Flaming Star*).

The movie version (with added harmonica) first appeared on the *Easy Come, Easy Go Double Features* issue. Elvis disliked the song sufficiently for it to be left out of the picture and off the soundtrack EP. Some of his attempts to whip it into shape are on the 2007 FTD *Easy Come, Easy Go* soundtrack re-release.

"SHE'S NOT YOU"

Elvis recorded this mellifluous Doc Pomus / Jerry Leiber / Mike Stoller ballad at a fruitful session in Nashville on March 19, 1962, for release in July that year as a single accompanied by "Just Tell Her Jim Said Hello" on the B-side. The record sold 800,000 copies during its ten-week Hot 100 tenure, making it to #5 at its peak; it made it to #2 on the R & B chart, and did even better in the UK, holding the #1 spot for almost a month.

The following year "She's Not You" was included on *Elvis' Golden Records Vol. 3*. It has since appeared on the first volume of *Worldwide Gold Award Hits*, *Top Ten Hits*, *From Nashville to Memphis* and *Artist Of The Century* . Alternate takes are available on *ELVIS 30 #1 Hits* (and therefore also on *Hitstory*), as well as on FTD releases *Long Lonely Highway* and *Pot Luck*.

SHOLES, STEVE
(1911-1968)

A major executive with RCA, Sholes worked his way up through the company after joining as a messenger boy in 1929—a job he took to help fund his way through Rutgers University. Born in Washington, D.C. on February 12, 1911 and a musician himself, Sholes landed a full-time post for the company after graduating, and rose to the position of Country and R&B division chief in 1945.

From his post in Nashville, Sholes recruited big names to the label including Chet Atkins, Eddy Arnold, The Browns, Hank Snow, Jim Reeves and, in 1955, Elvis Presley. Sholes and fellow RCA executive Coleman Tily traveled to Memphis on November 21, 1955 to sign the contract that sealed Elvis' future (and his past Sun masters) for RCA.

According to RCA colleague Joan Deary, Sholes's belief in Elvis was instrumental in the label signing the budding star. Sholes had to overcome stiff opposition from other RCA executives, and put his own job on the line by making a deal that was the biggest for any pop artist in music business history.

Sholes was nominally producer when Elvis reported to his first RCA recording session in January 1956. The results of that session sent shockwaves through RCA's New York head offices. Apart from "Heartbreak Hotel," RCA top brass scorned the lack of clarity in the recorded material; somebody even suggested that Sholes should have signed Elvis' Sun stablemate Carl Perkins instead. In following studio sessions, Chet Atkins took over the producers' role, though he and Elvis didn't hit it off. Increasingly, Elvis was left in charge of executive decisions in the studio.

By the time Elvis' appeal spread nationwide following his TV appearances, the company knew that Sholes had called it right. However, though Sholes remained Elvis' official A&R (artist and repertoire) man, the Colonel's plan to put Elvis in the movies minimized his influence on the direction Elvis' musical career took.

In 1957, Sholes was instrumental in pushing for RCA to build a recording studio in Nashville (on Seventeenth Avenue South), and in so doing made a major contribution to what would come to be known as the "Nashville Sound." Sholes oversaw an Elvis session there in June 1958, just before the label's biggest star shipped out to Germany, and carried on nominally helming sessions after Elvis' return. Elvis' success was partially responsible for Sholes's continuing promotions up to the post of RCA West Coast manager in 1961.

Sholes continued to produce Elvis' RCA sessions through the Sixties, working with Chet Atkins again, right up until 1966, when Elvis first

started working with Felton Jarvis. Sholes was increasingly unhappy with the diminishing quality of the songs Elvis was forced to churn out for his back-to-back movie commitments, but the Colonel held all the cards

Sholes was inducted into the Country Music Hall of Fame in 1967. At the time of his death, he was RCA's VP for all pop A&R, working out of New York.

SHOPPING

Elvis' dress rehearsal for future fame took the form of window shopping outside Memphis clothiers Lanskys on Beale Street, a favorite Memphis purveyor of fine and flamboyant garments. As soon as Elvis had a little disposable income from his first full-time jobs, he began to purchase the outfits popular with musicians and smart-dressing black men about town, forsaking his previous clothing haunt, the National Shirt Shop.

Once Elvis began making big money in early 1956, his shopping *modus operandi* was see, like and buy. Friend Ronnie Smith described the first house Elvis bought, at Audubon Drive in Memphis, as looking like "a furniture store, 'cos everything he liked he'd buy, and if he liked it real well he'd buy two of 'em."

When fame made incognito shopping impossible, Elvis had Memphis department stores open up for him at midnight for Christmas shopping. In later years, he would have his favorite jewelers make house calls to Graceland. He was also a welcome regular at all manner of car dealerships around Memphis.

The first time that Priscilla came out to visit in the early Sixties, Elvis spent two hours in a Las Vegas boutique with her, personally picking out elegant outfits for her to try. He bought the garments if he liked how they looked on her, and was not overly interested in what she thought of them. Soon after she came to live with him at Graceland, they went on a four-hour after-hours shopping extravaganza at Laclede's on Union Avenue, which Priscilla described in her memoir as "a personalized lesson in the Elvis Presley Fashion Course."

In 1967, when he acquired the Circle G ranch, Elvis would spend time in the basement at Sears buying up power tools and the like.

ELVIS SHOPPED AT . . .

Charlie's Record Shop, a record store on North Main Street, was one of Elvis' favorite haunts as a teenager, where he would go to buy blues and R&B records. He persuaded the store owner to put his first acetate recording from the Memphis Recording Service Studios onto his store jukebox. Elvis stocked upon records before going into the Army at Pop Tunes and Home of the Blues.

Elvis and his mother bought the initial furnishings for Graceland at Goldsmith's Department Store (4545 Poplar Avenue). Elvis would sometimes go down to the store after hours with friends and tell them to get what they wanted. Elvis, family and friends would also frequent other department stores such as Lowenstein's and Sears.

In 1963, Elvis stocked up on books at the Readin' & Ritin' Shop on Highway 51 South.

Elvis bought the furniture for the Jungle Room at Donald's Furniture Store; the wall and ceiling carpet came from Elvis' regular carpeting suppliers, Duck's Carpets.

Elvis' Las Vegas girlfriends could look forward to a host of new outfits from Suzie Creamcheese.

See also CARS and JEWELRY.

"Shoppin' Around"

Elvis recorded this Sid Tepper / Roy C. Bennett / Aaron Schroeder rocker at Radio Recorders in Hollywood on May 6, 1960 for the soundtrack of *G.I. Blues*. First time around, the song had been released by Rusty Draper in 1958. Elvis' version has since appeared on *Command Performances* and the 1997 *G.I. Blues* deluxe reissue.

Alternate takes, some from an earlier session at RCA's own Hollywood studios on April 27, started to filter out on 1980 collectors' set *Elvis Aron Presley*, followed by *Elvis Chante Sid Tepper & Roy C. Bennett*, the deluxe 1997 version of *G.I. Blues*, *Elvis: Close Up* and FTD release *Silver Screen Stereo*.

Shore, Sammy
(b. 1930)

Comedian who was one of the opening acts for Elvis at his first Las Vegas residency in the summer of 1969 at the International Hotel. Shore opened for Elvis up until the summer of 1971, when comedian Nipsey Russell took over the job.

Sammy Shore founded The Comedy Store on the Sunset Strip in LA in 1972, which he ran with his wife Mitzi. To this day, Shore proudly refers to himself as "The Man Who Made Elvis Laugh." His son Pauly has followed him into the laughs business.

"Shout It Out"

Bill Giant, Bernie Baum and Florence Kaye came up with this soundtrack manifesto for Elvis, who duly committed it to tape for the Frankie and Johnny soundtrack at Radio Recorders on May 13, 1965. After appearing on the soundtrack album, the song came out on the Double Feature issue for the movie in the Nineties, and on the FTD reissue in the 2000s (in the latter case, with a few alternate takes).

"Show Me Thy Ways (Oh Lord)"

Elvis sang this hymn, written by Hazel Shade, at Graceland in the mid-Sixties. A home recording has come out on *The Home Recordings* and the *Peace In The Valley* anthology.

Shower Of Stars Benefit

On June 28, 1957, Elvis put in an appearance at this event, held by Danny Thomas to benefit St. Jude's Hospital. For the occasion, Elvis shared the stage with singers Ferlin Huskey and Roberta Sherwood, plus Hollywood stars Jane Russell, Susan Hayward and Lou Costello.

Shuman, Mort
(1936-1991)

With songwriting partner Doc Pomus, Shuman was one of the most talented denizens of the "Brill Building" in New York, and wrote many of Elvis' Sixties songs. Classically-trained Shuman generally wrote the music for their pieces, which were recorded by a host of artists and sold over 100 million copies in all. In the Sixties, the duo moved to the UK. After 1965, Shuman traveled on to France, where he wrote for Johnny Hallyday, worked with Jacques Brel and became a popular recording artist in his own right.

Ernst Jorgensen defines Shuman's formula for hits as "chorus, break, and gimmick."

Aside from penning fifteen tracks for Elvis, the Pomus / Shuman team also penned rock classics such as "Save The Last Dance For Me," "Teenager In Love" and "Sweets For My Sweet."

After a three-year Shuman layoff, Elvis recorded a Mort Shuman solo effort, "You'll Think Of Me" during his American Studio session in 1969.

Mort Shuman was inducted into the Songwriters Hall of Fame the year after his death.

See Elvis Sings Mort Shuman & Doc Pomus

Sidney, George
(1916-2002)

The scion of a New York theater family, Sidney began his career as a child actor before cutting his directorial teeth on the *Our Gang* comedies in the late Thirties and going on to become one of MGM's top directors of musicals. As well as directing Elvis in *Viva Las Vegas* (1964), Sidney also directed *The Three Musketeers* (1948) and *Annie Get Your Gun* (1950).

Sidney's previous movie before working with Elvis on *Viva Las Vegas* involved directing Ann-Margret in *Bye Bye Birdie*.

Siegel, Don
(1912-1991)

Director of *Flaming Star*, one of Elvis' most dramatically-accomplished movies, who went on to direct (and mentor) Clint Eastwood in his career-cementing role in *Dirty Harry* (1971). Immediately prior to working with Elvis, Siegel directed a film called *Hound-Dog Man*. Other well-known Siegel titles include the original *Invasion of the Body Snatchers* from 1956, and John Wayne's swansong feature, *The Shootist* (1976).

Don Siegel: "Elvis surprised me with his sensitivity."

Siegel, Ray

Bassist and tuba player who played on the recording sessions for *King Creole* at Radio Recorders in Santa Monica. After Elvis' return from the army, Siegel was a regular at L.A.-based soundtrack sessions right up to *Paradise, Hawaiian Style* in 1966.

"Signs Of The Zodiac"

A duet penned by Buddy Kaye and Ben Weisman for *The Trouble With Girls* movie that Elvis recorded at United Artist Recorders on October 23, 1968 with co-star Marlyn Mason. Elvis was practically on auto-pilot, mere weeks before the triumphal broadcast of the 1968 NBC TV Special. The song did not warrant an official record release until its *Double Features* outing in 1995, though it had appeared on a number of bootlegs before then.

Sightings

See Death

"Silent Night"

Elvis sings this song on *Elvis' Christmas Album*, as recorded at Radio Recorders on September 6,

1957 and released in time for the festive season that year.

The German-language original, "Stille Nacht," began as a poem written in the early 1800s by Austrian priest Josef Mohr. It was set to music by Franz Gruber, according to legend after the priest discovered that the church organ had stopped working just before Christmas.

Bing Crosby's English-language version was the best-selling song of the Forties, eclipsed during his career only by "White Christmas." "Silent Night" has become one of the world's oft-covered songs.

Elvis' version came out on the *Christmas With Elvis* EP in 1958, and has since done duty on later versions of *Elvis' Christmas Album*, and on compilations *Memories Of Christmas*, *Blue Christmas*, *The King Of Rock And Roll*, *If Every Day Was Like Christmas*, *Christmas Peace* and *Elvis Christmas*.

Sillerman, Robert F.X.
(b. 1949)

New-York born businessman who bought Elvis Presley Enterprises in February 2005 through his company CKX, paying $114.2 million for an 85% stake in the business: $50 million in cash, $26 million in stock, $25 million to pay off EPE debt, and $6.5 million to Priscilla Presley. In exchange, CKX obtained a 90-year lease on Graceland, rights to the Elvis name, image, likeness and trademark, publishing rights to 650 songs, and royalty rights to Elvis' post-1973 songs and to 24 Elvis movies. Lisa Marie Presley retained a 15% stake in Elvis Presley Enterprises; Priscilla has become a company director and consultant to CKX.

Prior to CKX, Sillerman built up a radio empire and then the country's largest live concert promotions enterprise, SFX Entertainment, which he sold respectively for $2.1 billion and $4.4 billion. He is also a theater impresario who has invested in Mel Brooks' productions *The Producers* and *Young Frankenstein*.

Bob Sillerman: "I don't think you can own something that's as big as Elvis Presley. I think I feel a sense of stewardship. But not ownership."

"Silver Bells"

Elvis covered this 1951 hit for Bing Crosby and Carol Richards—written by Ray Evans and Jay Livingston—during a Nashville recording session on May 15, 1971, for release on *Elvis Sings The Wonderful World of Christmas* that year.

The song has been anthologized on Christmas-themed albums *Memories Of Christmas*, *Blue Christmas*, *Christmas Peace* and *Elvis Christmas*. An alternate version came out on *If Every Day Was Like Christmas*.

Silver Screen Stereo

An FTD release from 2001 of soundtrack outtakes and alternates.

Track listing:
1. Loving You
2. Jailhouse Rock
3. Don't Leave Me Now
4. Tonight Is So Right For Love
5. Frankfort Special
6. Doin' The Best I Can
7. Shoppin' Around
8. Summer Kisses, Winter Tears
9. In My Way

10. Hawaiian Wedding Song
11. Island Of Love
12. Angel
13. I Got Lucky (alternate master)
14. Home Is Where The Heart Is
15. Riding The Rainbow
16. The Bullfighter Was A Lady
      (alternate master)
17. I Think I'm Gonna Like It Here (alternate
      master)
18. Viva Las Vegas
19. The Lady Loves Me
20. You're The Boss
21. Today, Tomorrow And Forever
22. C'mon Everybody
23. Kissin' Cousins (hillbilly version)
24. There's So Much World To See (alternate
      master)
25. Clambake (w. reprise)
26. Almost

SILVERS, PHIL
(1911-1985)

Comedian Phil Silvers saw Elvis perform the first time the tyro singer played Las Vegas, in April 1956. Silvers' wildly successful Fifties character Sgt. Bilko in *The Phil Silvers Show* (which began its run titled "You'll Never Get Rich") was knocked off top spot in the June 1956 viewing figure tally by Elvis' appearance on "The Milton Berle Show."

Silvers started out in Vaudeville before graduating to the movies in the early Forties. He won multiple Emmys and Tonys during his long career.

SIMON AND GARFUNKEL

Paul Simon and Art Garfunkel (both born in Queens, New York, in 1941) were a top vocal duo from 1964 to 1970, when Garfunkel left to pursue a solo career, , though they did occasionally tour together after that. Paul Simon, who wrote all their material, went on to have the more successful and eclectic future as a solo performer.

Simon and Garfunkel began as a vocal duo in the late Fifties, under the name Tom & Jerry, but did not score a hit until they adopted a more folk-based sound and scaled the top of the charts with "Sound Of Silence." Their song "Mrs. Robinson" graced emblematic late-Sixties Dustin Hoffman movie *The Graduate*.

Elvis recorded "Like A Bridge Over Troubled Water," a big hit from their last album as a duo, in 1970.

Simon went on to return the compliment by titling his 1986 album of South-African inspired music *Graceland*. He has hailed Elvis as one of his early style idols and performing heroes.

SINATRA, FRANK
(B. FRANCIS ALBERT SINATRA, 1915-1998)

Elvis told an interviewer in 1956 that he liked Frank Sinatra as a singer, mere months before Sinatra came out with a withering rebuke of rock 'n' roll. Before very publicly burying their differences in 1960, in private Sinatra reputedly viewed Elvis as "a loser." Whether or not he truly believed this, from a professional point of view Elvis proved to be the death knell to Sinatra's lingering status as a heart throb, though he continued to sing, act and helm TV shows for a further thirty-five years.

Born in Hoboken, New Jersey, on December 12, 1915, Sinatra rose to fame singing with the Tommy Dorsey band in the early Forties, after a spell with local vocal group the Hoboken Four.

Elvis and Frank Sinatra during the filming of *The Welcome Home Elvis* TV Show.

When he went solo in 1942, Sinatra was one of America's first teen idols. Into his second decade as a popular crooner, Sinatra won an Oscar for *From Here To Eternity* just as Elvis was stepping through the door at Sun Studio.

Sinatra successfully overcame the inevitable changes in music trends and tastes to become a much-loved, long-lived entertainer, with a sideline as the high-living leader of the Rat Pack. He married four times, including a six-year marriage to Ava Gardner, and had three children from his first marriage (to childhood sweetheart Nancy Barbato). Such was his standing in the entertainment industry for half-a-century that he garnered a slew of nicknames, the best-known being "The Voice," "Ol' Blue Eyes," and "The Chairman of the Board."

In 1960, Colonel Parker selected Frank Sinatra's TV show for Elvis' return to the US media after two years away serving in the Army. Elvis and his gang holed up in Miami for a week to work on the show. Elvis taped the show on March 26, 1960, though it didn't air for six weeks. The highlight of the show was a duet in which two Twentieth-century icons swapped harmonies and traded songs: Elvis sang "Witchcraft," while Frank did "Love Me Tender." Referring to their trademark moves, Sinatra quipped, "We work in the same way, only in different areas." He also introduced his daughter Nancy to Elvis on stage.

Sinatra was one of a number of Hollywood luminaries to thank Elvis personally for his $50,000 contribution to the Motion Picture Relief Fund in 1965.

In 1967, Sinatra lent Elvis his jet to whisk him and Priscilla to Las Vegas for their still-secret wedding.

In 1969, Elvis took Sinatra's mantle as the biggest draw in Las Vegas. There were no hard feelings: Elvis attended at a party in Las Vegas thrown by Frank for his daughter Nancy, after her August 29, 1969 performance at the International Hotel, where she had the unenviable task of following Elvis. Elvis put back the start of his winter 1974 Las Vegas residence by a day so as not to clash with Frank Sinatra's "comeback" performance at Caesar's Palace.

Sinatra gave Elvis a call in August 1975 when he heard that he was ill and in hospital. They remained in touch by phone; Elvis sought Sinatra's advice about the upcoming publication of his bodyguards' tell-all exposé. Some biographers have ventured that Frank offered to involve some of his more colorful acquaintances and make the problem go away.

FRANK SINATRA IN THE LATE FIFTIES: "His kind of music is deplorable, a rancid smelling aphrodisiac . . . sung, played and written for the most part by cretinous goons. It fosters almost totally negative and destructive reactions in young people." (to which Elvis responded: "I admire the man. He has a right to say what he wants to say . . . but I think he shouldn't have said it.")

FRANK SINATRA IN THE LATE SEVENTIES: "There have been many accolades uttered about Elvis' talent and performances through the years, all of which I agree with wholeheartedly. I shall miss him dearly as a friend. He was a warm, considerate and generous man."

SINATRA, NANCY
(B. 1940)

Frank Sinatra's first child from his marriage to Nancy Barbato, Nancy Jr. appeared on Elvis' homecoming TV show in 1960. She had been at the party thrown by the Army on Elvis' return from his military service in Germany, just before his official discharge, a few weeks earlier.

Born on June 8, 1940, Nancy Sinatra grew up in full view of the public gaze. For her fourth birthday, father Frank had a hit with a song "Nancy With The Laughing Face." After studying the performing arts for more than a decade, Nancy finally took her bow as a performer on TV during Frank's Welcome Home Elvis Special in 1960. Between 1960 and 1965, she was married to one-time teen idol Tommy Sands.

Nancy Sinatra's singing career peaked with her 1966 hit "These Boots Are Made For Walkin'," written and arranged by Lee Hazlewood. She went on to sing early Bond theme "You Only Live Twice," and was a bee-hived, mini-skirted Sixties style leader. She had a successful run as an actress on the silver screen and TV, culminating opposite Elvis in Speedway, released in 1968. On set, Nancy reportedly told Elvis that he was one of the two men she most respected in the world—the other being her father, Frank. During shooting, Nancy and Elvis were spotted holding hands. Rumors about a liaison between the two were not new: back in 1960, press reporters in Germany had goaded Priscilla into revealing more about her relationship with Elvis by telling her that Elvis and Nancy were sweethearts. Later, Priscilla and Nancy became friends; Sinatra threw a baby shower before little Lisa Marie was born.

When Nancy starred opposite Elvis, she was fresh from screen success in early biker flick The Wild Angels with Peter Fonda, which gave her enough clout for the unique honor of scoring a solo song ("Your Groovy Self") on an Elvis soundtrack release, as well as her duet with him ("There Ain't Nothing like A Song"). Another duet she sang, "Something Stupid" with Pop Frank, was also a big success for her.

Elvis, the Colonel and the entire entourage watched Nancy Sinatra performing at the International Hotel in Las Vegas the day after Elvis finished his first run there in the summer of 1969—Elvis, as was his custom, snuck in after the house lights were turned down.

After taking time out to raise her family, in the 2000s Nancy returned to singing with a high profile collaborative album. She appeared on-screen in an episode of TV show "My First Time" in 2006. She continues to perform live. She has also appeared in Elvis-themed documentary footage, including This Is Elvis.

SING BOY, SING

A 1958 movie starring Tommy Sands that was unofficially known as "The Elvis Presley Story" for its similarities with Elvis' rise to fame and his relationship with svengali Colonel Parker. The project originated as a Kraft Music Hall drama on TV, titled The Singing Idol. It was adapted for the big screen, despite reputed interference from Colonel Parker, who did not want 20th Century-Fox to portray him and his star in a disparaging light. Some Elvis commentators have suggested that in actual fact the Colonel actively wanted the film to be made, in part because he had previously represented Tommy Sands and wanted the former teen idol to get the role.

The movie was produced and directed by Henry Ephron and scripted by Paul Monash (who wrote the original TV drama) and Claude Binyon.

Elvis saw the movie with his then girlfriend Anita Wood and a number of pals just before he left Memphis for his Army tour of duty in Germany. Friends have reported that the movie shook Elvis up a great deal, because it struck him as a loss of innocence.

"SING YOU CHILDREN"

New (to Elvis) writing team Gerald Nelson and Fred Burch chipped in with this soundtrack song for Easy Come, Easy Go and the accompanying EP. Elvis recorded the song at Paramount Studios on September 28, 1966. It later featured on the You'll Never Walk Alone LP, and appeared again as part of the Peace In The Valley compilation. In addition to the original version, an alternate take was included on the Double Features soundtrack re-release in the 1990s, and on the 2007 FTD soundtrack re-release.

SINGER SEWING MACHINE COMPANY

As sole sponsors of Elvis' 1968 NBC Special TV appearance, Singer had final approval over the content of the show, and rights for a tie-in Elvis album of re-releases. Not in itself a problem, except that when they agreed to come on board, the Colonel was convinced that he was seeking a sponsor for a Christmas-themed show, not a reaffirmation of Elvis' position on the cutting edge of contemporary music. Company chief Alfred DiScipio was sufficiently forward-looking to accept the new autobiographical format, though the company drew the line at the bordello scene in the planned TV show, and had it dropped from the broadcast version of the show.

SINGER PRESENTS ELVIS SINGING FLAMING STAR AND OTHERS

As part of its sponsorship of Elvis' NBC TV Special, in November 1968 the venerable sewing machine manufacturers brought out this hotch-potch of past soundtrack releases plus a preview of "Tiger Man" from the as yet unbroadcast TV show. The album was sold exclusively through the company's stores over a three month period. RCA re-released the compilation on its new Camden label as Elvis Sings Flaming Star in March 1969.

TRACK LISTING:
1. Flaming Star
2. Wonderful World
3. Night Life
4. All I Needed Was The Rain
5. Too Much Monkey Business
6. The Yellow Rose Of Texas / The Eyes Of Texas
7. She's A Machine
8. Do The Vega
9. Tiger Man

"SINGING TREE"

Elvis recorded this A.L. "Doodle" Owens / A. Solberg tune on September 11, 1967 in Nashville to flesh out the Clambake movie soundtrack and LP; he provided his own harmonies while he was at it.

The song is to be found among the selections for From Nashville to Memphis, the Double Features release for Clambake, and 1999 album Tomorrow Is A Long Time. Alternates have surfaced on Elvis: Close Up and FTD releases Long Lonely Highway and So High.

SINGLES

Elvis' record companies—Sun in 1954/1955, RCA thereafter—issued the following singles during his lifetime.

See individual titles in this encyclopedia for release dates, chart positioning and other information. Information about singles that RCA reissued as part of their "Gold Standard Series" for collectors, and special promotional versions for music professionals, may be found in the many excellent Elvis discographies available.

LIST OF SINGLES (WITH CATALOG NUMBERS):

1954		
Sun 209	That's All Right / Blue Moon Of Kentucky	
Sun 210	Good Rockin' Tonight / I Don't Care If The Sun Don't Shine	
1955		
Sun 215	Milkcow Blues Boogie / You're A Heartbreaker	
Sun 217	Baby Let's Play House / I'm Left, You're Right, She's Gone	
Sun 223	I Forgot To Remember To Forget / Mystery Train	
1956		
20 / 47-6420	Heartbreak Hotel / I Was The One	
20 / 47-6540	I Want You, I Need You, I Love You / My Baby Left Me	
20 / 47-6604	Don't Be Cruel / Hound Dog	
20 / 47-6636	Blue Suede Shoes / Tutti Frutti	
20 / 47-6637	I Got A Woman / I'm Counting On You	
20 / 47-6638	I'll Never Let You Go / I'm Gonna Sit Right Down And Cry	
20 / 47-6639	I Love You Because / Tryin' To Get To You	
20 / 47-6640	Just Because / Blue Moon	
20 / 47-6641	Money Honey / One-Sided Love Affair	
20 / 47-6642	Shake, Rattle And Roll / Lawdy, Miss Clawdy	
20 / 47-6643	Love Me Tender / Any Way You Want Me	

Elvis with Nancy Sinatra.

1957

20 / 47-6800	Too Much / Playing For Keeps
20 / 47-6870	All Shook Up / That's When Your Heartaches Begin
20 / 47-7000	(Let Me Be Your) Teddy Bear / Loving You
20 / 47-7035	Jailhouse Rock / Treat Me Nice

1958

20 / 47-7150	Don't / I Beg Of You
20 / 47-7240	Wear My Ring Around Your Neck / Doncha' Think It's Time
20 / 47-7280	Hard Headed Woman / Don't Ask Me Why
47-7410	One Night / I Got Stung

1959

47.7506	(Now And Then There's) A Fool Such As I / I Need Your Love Tonight
47-7600	A Big Hunk O' Love / My Wish Came True

1960

47 / 61-7740	Stuck On You / Fame And Fortune
47 / 61-7777	It's Now Or Never / A Mess Of Blues
47 / 61-7810	Are You Lonesome Tonight? / I Gotta Know

1961

47 / 61-7850	Surrender / Lonely Man
47 / 61-7880	I Feel So Bad / Wild In The Country
47 / 61-7908	(Marie's The Name) His Latest Flame / Little Sister
47 / 61-7968	Can't Help Falling In Love / Rock-A-Hula Baby

1962

47 / 61-7992	Good Luck Charm / Anything That's Part Of You
47-8041	She's Not You / Just Tell Her Jim Said Hello
47-8100	Return To Sender / Where Do You Come From

1963

47-8134	One Broken Heart For Sale / They Remind Me Too Much Of You
47-8188	(You're The) Devil In Disguise / Please Don't Drag That String Around
47-8243	Bossa Nova Baby / Witchcraft

1964

47-8307	Kissin' Cousins / It Hurts Me
447-0639	Kiss Me Quick / Suspicion
47-8360	What'd I Say / Viva Las Vegas
47-4800	Such A Night / Never Ending
47-8440	Ask Me / Ain't That Loving You Baby
447-0720	Blue Christmas / Wooden Heart

1965

47-8500	Do The Clam / You'll Be Gone
447-0643	Crying In The Chapel / I Believe In The Man In The Sky
47-8585	(Such An) Easy Question / It Feels So Right
47-8657	I'm Yours / Long Lonely Highway
447-0650	Puppet On A String / Wooden Heart
447-0647	Santa Claus Is Back In Town / Blue Christmas
47-8740	Tell Me Why / Blue River

1966

447-0651	Joshua Fit The Battle / Known Only To Him
447-0652	Milky White Way / Swing Down, Sweet Chariot

47-8780	Frankie And Johnny / Please Don't Stop Loving Me
47-8870	Love Letters / Come What May
47-8941	Spinout / All That I Am
47-8950	If Every Day Was Like Christmas / How Would You Like To Be

1967

47-9056	Indescribably Blue / Fools Fall In Love
47-9115	Long Legged Girl / That's Someone You Never Forget
47-9287	There's Always Me / Judy
47-9115	Big Boss Man / You Don't Know Me

1968

47-9425	Guitar Man / Hi Heel Sneakers
47-9465	U.S. Male / Stay Away
47-9600	You'll Never Walk Alone / We Call On Him
47-9547	Your Time Hasn't Come Yet, Baby / Let Yourself Go
47-9610	A Little Less Conversation / Almost In Love
47-9670	If I Can Dream / Edge Of Reality

1969

47-9731	Memories / Charro!
74-0130	His Hand In Mine / How Great Thou Art
47-9741	In The Ghetto / Any Day Now
47-9747	Clean Up Your Own Back Yard / The Fair's Moving On
47-9764	Suspicious Minds / You'll Think Of Me
47-9768	Don't Cry, Daddy / Rubberneckin'

1970

47-9791	Kentucky Rain / My Little Friend
47-9835	The Wonder Of You / Mama Liked The Roses
47-9873	I've Lost You / The Next Step Is Love
47-9916	You Don't Have To Say You Love Me / Patch It Up
47-9960	I Really Don't Want To Know / There Goes My Everything

1971

47-9980	Rags To Riches / Where Did They Go, Lord
47-9985	Life / Only Believe
47-9998	I'm Leavin' / Heart Of Rome
48-1017	It's Only Love / The Sound Of Your Cry
74-0572	Merry Christmas Baby / O Come All Ye Faithful

1972

74-0619	Until It's Time For You To Go / We Can Make The Morning
74-0651	He Touched Me / Bosom Of Abraham
74-0672	An American Trilogy / The First Time Ever I Saw Your Face
74-0769	Burning Love / It's A Matter Of Time
74-0815	Separate Ways / Always On My Mind

1973

74-0910	Steamroller Blues / Fool
APBO 0088	Raised On Rock / For Ol' Times Sake

1974

APBO 0196	I've Got A Thing About You Baby / Take Good Care Of Her
APBO 0280	If You Talk In Your Sleep / Help Me
PB 10191	Promised Land / It's Midnight

1975

PB 10191	My Boy / Thinking About You
PB 10278	T-R-O-U-B-L-E / Mr. Songman
PB 10401	Bringin' It Back / Pieces Of My Life

1976

PB 10601	Hurt / For The Heart
PB 10857	Moody Blue / She Thinks I Still Care

1977

PB 10998	Way Down / Pledging My Love
PB 11165	My Way / America The Beautiful

1978

PB 11212	Unchained Melody / Softly As I Leave You

NOTES

From 1965 release "Kiss Me Quick," RCA regularly released singles as "Gold Standard Series" issues.

Many boxed sets of Elvis singles have come out since his death. In 2005, Sony issued a limited edition of all of Elvis' 18 UK #1 singles at the rate of one per week, including a bonus track, on CD and vinyl. They repeated the feat with 18 non-#1 singles in 2007.

In early 2006, Sony issued a limited edition box set of Elvis' 20 #1 US singles, each reissued on CD with B-sides.

GOLD AND PLATINUM SINGLES (53)

Heartbreak Hotel / I Was The One—Platinum X2

Blue Suede Shoes / Tutti Frutti—Gold

I Want You, I Need You, I Love You / My Baby Left Me—Platinum

Hound Dog / Don't Be Cruel—Platinum X4

Love Me Tender / Any Way You Want Me—Platinum X3

Too Much / Playing For Keeps—Platinum

All Shook Up / That's When Your Heartaches Begin—Platinum X2

(Let Me Be Your) Teddy Bear / Loving You—Platinum X2

Jailhouse Rock / Treat Me Nice—Platinum X2

Don't / I Beg Of You—Platinum

Wear My Ring Around Your Neck / Doncha' Think It's Time—Platinum

Hard Headed Woman / Don't Ask Me Why—Platinum

I Got Stung / One Night—Platinum

(Now And Then There's) A Fool Such As I / I Need Your Love Tonight—Platinum

A Big Hunk O' Love / My Wish Came True—Gold

Stuck On You / Fame And Fortune—Platinum

It's Now Or Never / A Mess Of Blues—Platinum

Are You Lonesome Tonight? / I Gotta Know—Platinum X2

Surrender / Lonely Man—Platinum

I Feel So Bad / Wild In The Country—Gold

(Marie's The Name) His Latest Flame / Little Sister—Gold

Can't Help Falling In Love / Rock-A-Hula Baby—Platinum

Good Luck Charm / Anything That's Part Of You—Platinum

She's Not You / Just Tell Her Jim Said Hello—Gold

Return To Sender / Where Do You Come From—Platinum

One Broken Heart For Sale / They Remind Me Too Much Of You—Gold

(You're The) Devil In Disguise / Please Don't Drag That String Around—Gold

Bossa Nova Baby / Witchcraft—Gold

Kissin' Cousins / It Hurts Me—Gold

What'd I Say / Viva Las Vegas—Gold

Ain't That Loving You, Baby / Ask Me—Gold

Crying In The Chapel / I Believe In The Man In The Sky—Platinum

I'm Yours / Long Lonely Highway—Gold
Puppet On A String / Wooden Heart—Gold
Blue Christmas / Santa Claus Is Back In Town—
   Platinum
Tell Me Why / Blue River—Gold
Frankie And Johnny / Please Don't Stop Loving
   Me—Gold
If I Can Dream / Edge Of Reality—Gold
In The Ghetto / Any Day Now—Platinum
Clean Up Your Own Back Yard / The Fair Is
   Moving On—Gold
Suspicious Minds / You'll Think Of Me—
   Platinum
Don't Cry, Daddy / Rubberneckin'—Platinum
Kentucky Rain / My Little Friend—Gold
The Wonder Of You / Mama Liked The Roses—
   Gold
I've Lost You / The Next Step Is Love—Gold
You Don't Have To Say You Love Me / Patch It
   Up—Gold
I Really Don't Want To Know / There Goes My
   Everything—Gold
Burning Love / It's A Matter Of Time—Platinum
Separate Ways / Always On My Mind—Gold
Way Down / Pledging My Love—Platinum

Posthumous releases:
   My Way / America The Beautiful—Gold
   That's All Right—Gold
   Good Rockin' Tonight—Gold

"Sittin' On Top Of The World"

Within six months of cutting his first record at
Sun, upstart performer Elvis covered this blues
standard in live shows. Written by Walter
Vinson, the song had been a big hit for Bob Wills
in 1935 and for Ray Charles in 1949.

Sitton, Ray "Chief"

A new addition to Elvis' entourage in 1961,
Sitton was part of the gang that went to Florida
while Elvis was working on Follow That Dream.
Sitton, an imposing presence, had caught Elvis'
attention among the fans who gathered regularly
at the Graceland gates. Sitton traveled with Elvis
on and off up to the time of the Circle G ranch,
and was with him when Elvis met the Beatles in
Los Angeles in 1965.
   According to some long-term entourage members, Ray Sitton was let go because he sometimes
drank and borrowed Elvis' cars to go cruising
without first asking permission.

6363 Sunset

A 2001 release from FTD of songs that Elvis
recorded at RCA's Sunset Blvd. studio in 1972
and 1975, including material from rehearsals
prior to the *Elvis on Tour* documentary.

Track listing:
1. Always On My Mind
2. Burning Love
3. For The Good Times
4. Where Do I Go From Here
5. Fool
6. It's A Matter Of Time
7. See See Rider
8. Until It's Time For You To Go
9. A Big Hunk O' Love
10. All Shook Up
11. Heartbreak Hotel
12. Teddy Bear / Don't Be Cruel
13. Can't Help Falling In Love
14. Green, Green Grass Of Home
15. Susan When She Tried
16. And I Love You So
17. Bringin' It Back
18. T-R-O-U-B-L-E

"Sixteen Tons"

Elvis performed Tennessee Ernie Ford's mining
song at the Louisiana Hayride in December 1955,
and is said to have sung the song for his own edification at Graceland in the Sixties. The song was
originally written by Merle Travis in 1947,
though it was not until Ford's 1955 recording that
it became a #1 hit—before Elvis' "Love Me
Tender," it held the record for being the fastest-
ever million seller.

Skating

One of Elvis' favorite ways to spend a night from
his pre-fame days until well into the Sixties was
to hire out the Rainbow Rollerdrome (at 2881
Lamar Ave, Memphis) and take 100 pals along
for a whole night of skating shenanigans. The
high points of these sorties were rough games
such as "Knock Down," where two teams lined up
at either end of the rink and then skated full pelt
into one another. The goal was to knock the
opposition to the floor; the team with the most
players left standing was the winner. Entourage
members have reported that Elvis had a trick of
cuffing opponents around the head as he skated
past.
   Another favorite game was "Crack the Whip,"
where one person revolved as a central anchor
with chains of skaters spinning off them.
Centrifugal force eventually propelled the skaters
on the arms of the whip to such speeds that they
had to let go. Girls played "Crack the Whip," but
not "Knock Down."
   Various pads were available to cushion the
inevitable blows during this sustained bout of
wheeled war, though it seems that the customary
practice for surviving these boisterous nights was
to take painkillers beforehand.

Elvis said: "If you're man enough to get out there,
then you better be man enough to take the licks."

Slaughter, Todd
(b. 1945)

Long-time Official Elvis Presley Fan Club of
Great Britain president who has written and
compiled multiple books on Elvis, edited the *Elvis
Monthly* magazine, founded an Elvis museum in
the UK, contributed forewords and liner notes to
Elvis books and reissues, and more recently hosted an Elvis hour on UK satellite radio.

Sleep

Sleep was a battlefield for Elvis throughout his life.
As a child, he had sleeping problems; as an adult,
he had fully-fledged sleeping disorders which
strongly conditioned his mood and behavior.
   During their early Tupelo days, the Presley
family only had one bed, so Elvis was used to
sleeping in the same bed as his parents. Family
members recall that Elvis displayed uncommon
sleep patterns even as a baby: left to his own
devices, he would sleep until late into the day.
   Growing up, Elvis often suffered nightmares.
Right through childhood and all the way up until
his late teens, there were nights when Elvis sleepwalked. In one incident, while a teenager he

walked out of the family home fast asleep dressed
only in his underwear—a girl he knew called out
to him and he woke up, mortified. Somnambulism
was a family trait on both sides of his family, and
Gladys had her own insomnia troubles during
Elvis' infancy, and had to resort to medication to
get a good night's sleep.
   Elvis' sleeping problems worsened with the
irregular life of a traveling performer. When he
first started out, he toured incessantly, playing a
nightly show (or two) and then driving through
the small hours to the next venue. During those
frenetic early days, Elvis got by with three or four
hours' sleep per night. Like many people in the
music business, he relied on freely-available over-
the-counter drugs to get over his sleep deficit. In
an early interview, he liquidated a question about
his sleeping habits with the quip: "Sleep? What's
that?"
   Elvis always wanted to have someone to sleep
in his room—a girlfriend or an entourage member—to counter his nightmares, and the harm
that he might do himself while still asleep.
Reportedly, he would thrash around and throw
things if he was having a nightmare about a fight.
If Elvis was having a nightmare, Billy Smith
recalls that it wasn't just a question of shaking
him awake, because he might well lash out.
   Sleeping in the same bedroom as his parents
had been an insurance policy against his sleep-
walking as a kid. He was still occasionally sleep-
walking during those early touring days. Later on,
members of his entourage got into the habit of
locking balcony doors when he was staying in
hotels to make sure he didn't sleepwalk into the
void—Elvis almost sleepwalked out of an 11th
floor window of the Beverly Wilshire hotel while
in LA making *Loving You*.
   Away from Graceland, more often than not his
hotel was besieged by boisterous fans who would
wake him up. Writer and director Hal Kanter,
who accompanied Elvis to Shreveport in 1956,
looked on in surprise as a bleary-eyed Elvis leaned
out of his hotel room and pleaded with his fans to
quieten down and let him get some shuteye.
   With a permanent houseful of friends and family, Elvis could order his whole life around his
inability to sleep. The nocturnal lifestyle Elvis
led, however, was a major trial for Memphis
friends who held down regular jobs. More than
one was fired for falling asleep at work; Elvis
invariably stepped in and helped out by putting
the guy on the Graceland payroll for a while.
   Elvis' shift to a diurnal existence in the Army
did little to quell his insomnia. On the contrary,
he had to wake up at 5 a.m. every morning in
order to make it back onto base from his home
nearby. At this time, the Army condoned the
use of amphetamines to keep soldiers alert on
maneuvers; many biographers have stated that
this was the time when Elvis began to rely regularly on drugs. One of the first gifts that Elvis
gave Priscilla were pills to help her cope with
early school starts after spending late nights
with him.
   In 1962, Elvis told an interviewer that he only
slept four hours per night. Entourage members
have talked of competitions among the gang to
see who could pop pills and stay up the longest.
   When traveling between Memphis and LA,
Elvis and his gang usually drove by night and
slept by day. Sometimes their sleep was curtailed
by fans congregating outside their motel—more
than one entourage member suspects that the
Colonel tipped off local fans as a knee-jerk
exploitation of publicity opportunities.
   Elvis would be forced out of his natural rhythm
when he was shooting his movies, some of which
required early (morning) starts. The only other
times when he could be enticed back into the
more common circadian rhythms was when he
was involved in outdoor hobbies: when he had
his ranch, the Circle G; when he was on vacation
in Hawaii; and when he went on winter vacation

to Vail, where the fun was to be had by day, on a snowmobile.

Elvis was basically nocturnal. At home in Memphis, Elvis generally started his day around 3 or 4 p.m.. The pharmaceutical help he needed to fall asleep in the first place meant that it took a couple of hours before he was really alert. The hours after midnight were when Elvis would leave Graceland to go and see movies, hire the local fairgrounds, or go skating. Elvis' Graceland bedroom always had the heavy drapes closed. When he began touring again in the Seventies, one of the first things to be done was to black out Elvis' hotel bedroom.

Insomnia was one of the first things that Dr. Nichopoulos treated Elvis for when he began seeing him in 1967. According to Dr. Nick, Elvis was incapable of sleeping for any longer than three hours at a stretch without waking up and needing more pills.

In the Seventies, Elvis found sleep increasingly hard to come by, even with the adjuvant of prescription drugs. On nights when Elvis simply couldn't get to sleep, if he didn't have a girlfriend with him (and sometimes even if he did) he'd call up one of the guys to keep him company and talk until he drifted off. During bouts of insomnia, in Las Vegas and at Graceland Elvis might wander around and climb into bed with one of his entourage guys and his wife to talk.

In the Seventies, on the recommendation of mutual doctor Dr. Nichopoulos, Sam Phillips gave Elvis tapes of ocean sounds to play when he wanted to sleep, especially when out on tour.

In the early Seventies, Elvis told an interviewer that it took him four or five hours to wind down from the high energy levels of a show. As a result, he and his gang became completely nocturnal, sleeping all day and staying up all night. Doing matinee shows was a very great stretch for Elvis' circadian rhythms.

In his later years, when he required significant quantities of sleeping pills, there was always somebody in the room with him in case he started choking—Linda Thompson intervened several times to save him. After she left, it would generally be one of the Stanley boys, or perhaps a female companion, who looked out for him.

In his final years, the sedatives Elvis took to get to sleep had not had time to flush from his system when he made his entry onto the stage for his concerts. Fortunately, he knew the material so well that he rarely stumbled before he got into the full swing, boosted by the energy of his loving audiences.

ELVIS SAID IN 1956: "They say you learn how to relax when you get older. I hope they're right."

ELVIS SAID IN 1965: "The sun's down and the moon's pretty. It's time to ramble!"

ELVIS SAID: "The world is more alive at night. It's like God ain't lookin' . . ."

LAMAR FIKE: "He fought insomnia until he died — a combination of nightmares and his day-for-night schedule."

JOE ESPOSITO: "He liked to go to bed when the sun came up. We were vampires."

"SLICIN' SAND"

Elvis recorded this up-tempo Sid Tepper / Roy C. Bennett song for the *Blue Hawaii* soundtrack on March 21, 1961 at a Radio Recorders session.

Alternate versions are on the 1997 release of the soundtrack, *Elvis Chante Sid Tepper & Roy C. Bennett* and *Elvis: Close Up*.

SLIPPIN' 'N' SLIDIN' WITH ELVIS

A 2003 Czech Elvis fan club release on the Memory Records label of Elvis' midnight show in Lake Tahoe on April 30, 1976, plus rare live extras.

TRACK LISTING:
1. Also Sprach Zarathustra
2. C. C. Rider
3. I Got A Woman / Amen
4. Love Me
5. If You Love Me (Let Me Know)
6. You Gave Me A Mountain
7. All Shook Up
8. Teddy Bear / Don't Be Cruel
9. Tryin' To Get To You
10. Steamroller Blues
11. My Way
12. Band introductions
13. Early Morning Rain
14. What'd I Say
15. Johnny B. Goode
16. Drums solo
17. Bass solo
18. Piano solo
19. Lady Madonna (instrumental)
20. Love Letters
21. School Days (Hail Hail Rock'n'Roll)
22. Hurt (version 1)
23. Hurt (version 2)
24. Hound Dog
25. Jailhouse Rock
26. An American Trilogy
27. Can't Help Falling In Love
28. Such A Night (version 1)
29. Loving You
30. Until Then
31. Young And Beautiful
32. What Now My Love (spoken)
33. You Can Have Her
34. Such A Night (version 2)

SLOT-CAR RACING

This was Elvis' #1 passion going into 1966. Priscilla bought him a set for Christmas in 1965, but before January was out Elvis had upgraded to the best racing system he could find, the "Highspeed Raceway Road America," which set him back almost $5,000. And that was before he commissioned an ad hoc extension to Graceland specially to house the set. Elvis and the guys became so heated about the races that sessions sometimes ended in fisticuffs. Elvis' passion for the pursuit inevitably waned before long, but the extension survived and was converted into the Trophy Room.

"SLOWLY BUT SURELY"

Ben Weisman and Sid Wayne wrote this song, which Elvis recorded on May 27, 1963 in Nashville. It first appeared as a bonus track on the *Fun in Acapulco* LP, before being recycled in 1965 movie (and EP) *Tickle Me*.

It has since graced *For The Asking (The Lost Album)*, and *From Nashville to Memphis*. An alternate version has come out on FTD releases *Long Lonely Highway* and *Tickle Me*, which also features a remastered version of the original.

SMALL, EDWARD
(1891-1977)

In a fifty-year career as a producer from silent film to TV serials, in 1965 Small produced Elvis' movie *Frankie and Johnny*.

SMITH, BILLY
(B. 1943)

Billy's family and Elvis' family lived together in Memphis when they first moved to town in 1949. A younger cousin by seven years, Billy looked up to Elvis long before he became famous.

When Elvis bought Graceland, Billy's father Travis was installed as head gatekeeper. Billy, Travis and mother Lorene lived in a cottage (that Elvis bulldozed to make more room for horse riding in the late Sixties). They moved out of Graceland in 1960, after Elvis' return from Army service.

In 1960, Billy Smith went on to Elvis' payroll. He later admitted that the transition from family member to entourage guy whose job was to take orders was so hard for him to swallow that Elvis nicknamed him "Mighty Mouth."

In 1961, aged nineteen, Elvis' cousin went on the road with the gang to Florida, where his famous cousin was shooting *Follow That Dream*. Elvis also took Smith along to LA to do odd jobs, look after wardrobe and keep things running smoothly.

Billy Smith married his sweetheart Jo Norris in 1962. He took time out from Elvis to be with his wife, though he did occasionally heed his cousin's call and travel with him. Smith made it onto film, doubling for Annette Day in a scene on *Double Trouble* (1967). In 1968, he left the payroll to look after his ailing father, Travis, who was suffering from cirrhosis.

Billy Smith went back to work for Elvis briefly in 1970. He returned again in late 1974, as the entourage was going through major changes, after Elvis promised him that he would not have to travel and leave his family. That September, Elvis bought Billy a double-wide three-bedroom trailer so that he could live on the grounds at Graceland. Elvis and Billy became particularly close in the latter years of Elvis' life; when Elvis was in hospital, Billy often stayed with him. Elvis knew that Billy was with him for all the right reasons.

In June 1976, Billy Smith was practically the only person Elvis wanted to see when home at Graceland between tours.

Billy and his wife Jo traveled with Elvis and new girlfriend Ginger Alden to Las Vegas and LA in early February 1977. In Elvis' final months alive, he floated the idea of making Billy his foreman to replace Joe Esposito.

Smith was one of the last people to see Elvis alive: they played racquetball in the early hours of the morning that Elvis died, August 16, 1977.

Billy Smith moved away from Graceland after Elvis' death—Vernon insisted that the trailer stay at Graceland. Smith worked for a spell as a Graceland Tour Guide Supervisor, and edited Elvis magazine *Elvis the Record*. His reminiscences, in Alanna Nash's book *Revelations from the Memphis Mafia*, provide a powerful insight into what it was like to live alongside his famous cousin.

Book:

Elvis Aaron Presley: Revelations from the Memphis Mafia, by Alanna Nash, with Billy Smith, Marty Lacker and Lamar Fike, HarperCollins, 1995.

BILLY SMITH: "Elvis used to tell everybody how close we were. He'd tell people, 'I actually raised him.' " . . . I always followed Elvis around like a little puppy dog. I was totally captivated by him."

BILLY SMITH: "Elvis was a way of life for me, Jo, and our two sons."

BILLY SMITH: "There is never a day that goes by that I don't think of him and something that he's said. It either brings a smile or a tear. And, which ever it is, I'm thankful!"

ALANNA NASH: "If ever Elvis Presley had a best friend, it was Billy [Smith]"

LARRY GELLER: "During those last months, Billy was Elvis' anchor, a link with the past, someone who understood what Elvis used to be, what Elvis longed to believe he still was."

SMITH, BOB
(B. ROBERT LEE SMITH, DIED 1932)

Gladys's father and Elvis' maternal grandfather, from photographs it is evident that Elvis inherited the shape of his eyes. According to many Elvis genealogists, Smith's wife Octavia "Doll" Mansell was his cousin.

SMITH, BOBBY
(1941-1968)

Billy Smith's older brother was part of Elvis' gang in the early years. According to Billy, his brother was "turned" by Elvis' success. He spent a spell in a mental institution after joining the National Guard, and then misused his association with Elvis to start passing off checks that he signed in lieu of Elvis, before graduating on to cars that he claimed were for Elvis but which he kept until he was found out. He killed himself by taking rat poison in 1968.

SMITH, FRANK W.

One of Elvis' uncles on his mother's side, Smith was a pastor at the First Assembly of God church in Tupelo who took Elvis and other local kids to the Saturday afternoon WELO Jamboree talent show, broadcast from the Tupelo courthouse. Smith encouraged Elvis to learn how to play the guitar, and may have been the man who taught him "Old Shep," the song young Elvis performed at a talent contest when he was 10.

SMITH, GENE

Elvis' younger cousin was a friend and childhood playmate when they were growing up and through their teenage years, nicknamed "Smiff" by Elvis. The cousins worked together when Elvis was at Precision Tool, and went off on double dates.

Gene Smith's mother was Gladys's sister Levalle, who married Edward Smith. Many memoirs describe Gene Smith as a man who gladly played the fool, and invented his own mock language in which he would babble away.

When Elvis first hit the road, Gene was part of the original Memphis entourage, helping out backstage while Red West assisted with driving and security. Gene was with Elvis when he traveled to San Diego for his first appearance on the "Milton Berle Show," and was part of the gang for Elvis' initial stays in Hollywood—columnist Louella Parsons described him as "a character straight out of a book."

Smith returned to the fold after Elvis completed his Army service in Germany. He was with Elvis at Graceland (sometimes with his wife Louise, who was there the day that Priscilla arrived), and out on the road where he looked after Elvis' kit and wardrobe. Soon after, Gene was put in charge of Elvis' fleet of cars. Red West remembers Smith putting on fake tan to go driving up and down Sunset Strip when Elvis and his pals first hit LA after his Army years.

Elvis and Gene had a falling out in 1962 over the fate of some jewelry, but they made up afterwards. Gene remained an occasional member of the gang until the late Sixties.

Smith worked as a truck driver in later years. He died in Memphis in 1999.

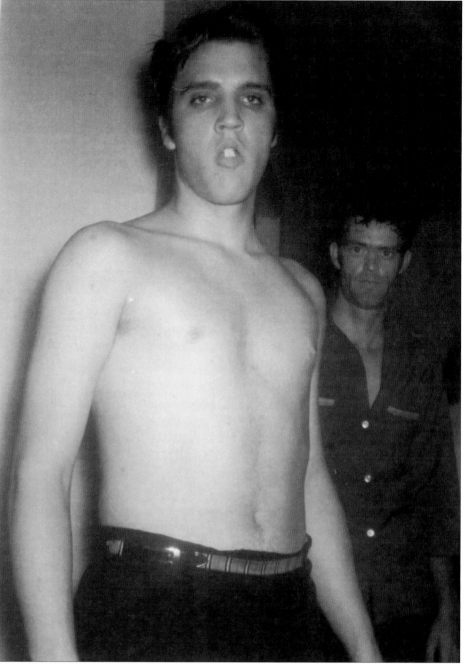

Elvis in Jacksonville with his first cousin, Junior Smith, a member of the "Memphis Mafia."

MARTY LACKER: "Gene was crazy, but he made Elvis laugh . . . In high school, Gene was the closest thing Elvis had to a brother."

Book:
Elvis' Man Friday by Gene Smith, Light Of Day Publishing , 1992.

SMITH, GLADYS LOVE

See PRESLEY, GLADYS

SMITH, JOHNNY

Elvis' uncle on his mother's side helped Elvis learn the rudiments of the guitar he received on his 11th birthday. After fame came along, Johnny was one of the family members employed to guard the Graceland gates. Johnny Smith died in July 1968 of kidney failure, aged 46.

SMITH, "JUNIOR"
(B. CARROLL SMITH, 1932-1961)

Travis's son Junior was a cousin of Elvis' whom he took along sometimes when he first went on tour. Travis was not long back from Korea, where he had been drafted and sent to fight. By mid-1957, Elvis was loath to take Junior along as part of his entourage because of the crazy things he would get up to, especially when he drank.

Junior Smith died in Billy Smith's bed in early 1961 from alcohol poisoning, though the death was reported as a heart attack. Much as he wanted to, Elvis was unable to attend the funeral as he was due in Hollywood to reshoot the ending of *Wild in the Country*.

SMITH, LILLIAN

Gladys's elder sister was a very religious lady who upbraided Elvis in the mid-Sixties for seeking other religious truths beyond the church in which he had been raised. Lillian married Charlie Mann, and was mother to Bobbie and Billy.

SMITH, MYRNA

One of the Sweet Inspirations, and still carrying the baton for Elvis in tribute concerts, Smith provided backing vocals for Elvis for most of the Seventies, including studio sessions in Elvis' final years. In 1975, Elvis gave her a Cadillac Eldorado in recognition of her loyalty: she was the only one of the backing group not to walk off during a concert at Norfolk, Virginia, after he made cutting remarks about them on stage. Myrna Smith became romantically involved with and later married Elvis' long-time entourage member, Jerry Schilling. She went on find some success as a songwriter.

Smith is on stage and on screen in all of Elvis' Seventies shows from *That's The Way It Is* to *Elvis in Concert*, and has featured in a number of Elvis documentaries, including 2004 release *200 Cadillacs*.

Myrna Smith: "We didn't realize before we worked with Elvis that he was so great. The first night we sang with him, when he opened in Vegas, I thought it was just a one-time occurrence. . . . And then the next night came —'Yeah!'"

SMITH, TRACY

Elvis' uncle on his mother's side, whom Elvis supported when he needed extra help. Tracy was mentally slow after suffering a high fever as a child. He died in 1966, just shy of his fiftieth birthday.

SMITH, TRAVIS

Elvis' uncle on his mother's side, married to Lorraine and the father of Billy and Bobby, his family moved into a house Elvis had built for them at Graceland almost as soon as Elvis and his folks moved in. Years earlier, the whole family had accompanied Elvis' parents as they upped sticks from Tupelo and moved to Memphis.

Travis was one of the first gatekeepers at Graceland—he had initially been hired to man the gates at Elvis' Audubon Drive property before they moved to Graceland—and was the man that fans first befriended to try and get in to see the king. Travis died in August 1973.

SMOKING

Elvis liked to smoke thin cigars—cigarillos. Tiparillos were his favorite. He occasionally smoked a cigarette (reputedly Tareytons) but very rarely did he light up in public. He said in 1962 that he didn't even know how to inhale. In later years, Elvis sometimes smoked Hav-A-Tampa cigars and Roi-Tan blunts. A shopping list from Graceland lists El Producto Diamond Tips and El Producto Altas.

According to entourage recollections, the cigars Elvis smoked were Hav-a-Tampa Jewels, Rum Crooks, and Villiger Kiels (also a favorite), which a member of the entourage would light when he picked one up.

Elvis smokes thin cigarillos in late movie *The Trouble with Girls*.

"SMOKEY MOUNTAIN BOY"

A Lenore Rosenblatt / Victor Millrose song for the soundtrack of *Kissin' Cousins*, laid down in Nashville on September 30, 1963, for which Elvis overdubbed vocals on October 10 at the MGM

Candid photo of Elvis with cigarillo in 1972.

Studios. One of very few Elvis tracks to feature a banjo, the song resurfaced on the Nineties *Double Features* soundtrack reissue

"SMORGASBORD"

Sid Tepper and Roy C. Bennett wrote this song for Elvis to record in February 1966 for the *Spinout* soundtrack. The song later received the *Double Features* treatment with *Double Trouble*. Alternates have appeared on bootlegs and on the FTD *Spinout* release.

SNEER

Elvis' lopsided lip-curling bad-boy sneer, which almost invariably morphed into a puppyish smile, was a trademark part of his stage act for the first ten years of his career. Adopted by countless singers to denote their hard rocking credentials, in his later performing years Elvis took pleasure in mocking the affectation.

SNOW, HANK
(B. CLARENCE EUGENE SNOW, 1914-1999)

"Hank, the Singing Ranger" was a top country and western attraction in the early 1950s, and a regular at the Grand Ole Opry for 46 years. To this day, his 1950 hit "I'm Movin' On" holds the record for the highest number of consecutive weeks at number one: 21 (Elvis covered the track in 1969).

Born in Brooklyn, Nova Scotia, Canada on May 9, 1914, Snow ran away to sea aged just 12. He started his singing career in Halifax, modeling himself on Jimmie Rodgers, and became known as the Yodeling Ranger. Snow's status as a Grand Ole Opry regular from 1950 provided the springboard for US success after a decade on Canada's airwaves. From his debut hit "I'm Movin' On"

through to 1955, Snow notched up two dozen top-10 hits, branching out into other musical styles and earning himself a worldwide following.

Just as Elvis was taking his first steps in the music business in Memphis, Colonel Tom Parker signed a management contract with Snow that included setting up a joint talent and booking agency with the singer.

Snow first became aware of Elvis in 1954, during Elvis' not wholly-successful appearance at the Grand Ole Opry, when he featured on the Snow section of the show. Some sources claim that Hank Snow introduced Elvis to Colonel Tom Parker directly, while others claim that the Colonel first became aware of the young singer through their joint business venture. Others still have stated that it was Hank Snow, not the Colonel, who first contacted RCA with a view to engineering a buyout of Elvis' Sun contract.

Whatever the origins of the relationship, Elvis was one of the acts that Parker booked onto the Hank Snow Jamboree Tour in February 1955 (advertised as "Elvis and his Bop Band"). Elvis returned as a "Special Added Attraction" on the May 1955 Jamboree Tour, on a bill that featured Faron Young, the Willburn Brothers, Mother Maybelle and the Carter Sisters, Jimmie Rodgers Snow and Onie Wheeler. On this tour, Faron Young recalled that in Orlando, Florida the audience started to chant Elvis' name for an encore just as Hank Snow walked out on stage. Snow had disregarded Young's advice about letting Elvis go on last—even at this early stage in his career, nobody could follow Elvis. The announcer came back on stage to placate the crowd for the headline star, but when he mentioned that Elvis was backstage signing autographs, half the crowd vanished.

Snow's partnership with Colonel Tom Parker in Hank Snow Attractions saw him playing an integral part in negotiations with Elvis' then manager Bob Neal to buy out Elvis' Sun Records contract and switch to a major label. One of the sweeteners in this negotiation, at least for Bob Neal, was a possible slot for Elvis on a weekly television show that Snow was hoping to start. At a personal level, Snow won over Gladys Presley's reticence about Elvis throwing in his lot with Colonel Parker, for whom she had developed an instant dislike.

Neal booked Elvis on a number of Hank Snow Jamboree Attractions tours in 1955. By the time Elvis was sharing the stage with the country's most popular rocker, Bill Haley, in Oklahoma, Elvis was receiving higher billing them Hank Snow.

Hank Snow accompanied business partner Colonel Parker to Memphis in November 1955 to witness the signing of Elvis' Sun Records contract buyout by RCA. Two weeks later, Elvis featured as an "extra added attraction" on a Hank Snow tour of Indiana, on a bill with the Carter Family and country comedian Rod Brasfield.

Elvis continued touring with Snow, notably as part of a Grand Ole Opry package to usher in the new year in 1956. He played his last tour as a supporting act to Hank Snow in mid-January 1956, on a six-day sweep through Texas.

In mid-March 1956, Colonel Parker informed Hank Snow that he was winding up their business partnership beyond booking dates for Snow himself. Some biographers have stated that the Colonel formally bought out Snow's stake in their partnership; if he did, it was for a sum of money that reflected Elvis' value as a hopeful newcomer, not the future king of rock and roll.

For the next five years, Snow sought legal redress for his role in the 13-month negotiations to wrest control of Elvis' career from Sun Records and Elvis' previous manager, Bob Neal. He was unsuccessful in his intent.

Snow had a major hit in 1962 with "I've Been Everywhere," and another, "Hello Love," in 1974. He continued to play the Opry into the Nineties; during his long career, he sold over 70 million records.

Elvis tipped his hat to this man who mentored him to national fame by covering not just his signature song, but a number of country classics that Snow sang, including "(Now And Then There's) A Fool Such as I."

Hank Snow was inducted into the Nashville Songwriters International Hall of Fame in 1978 and the Country Music Hall of Fame in 1979.

SNOW, JIMMIE RODGERS
(B. 1936)

Elvis became friends with Hank Snow's son when they toured together on his father's jamborees in 1955. Elvis invited Snow to stay at Graceland in early 1958. Elvis offered to bring him out to Hollywood and get him a part in King Creole, but Snow declined: he had already decided that the next step for him in life was to become a pastor, not a film star. After he took the cloth, Jimmie Rodgers Snow preached against the dangers of rock 'n' roll.

In later years, Snow hosted the Grand Ole Gospel Time slot at the Grand Ole Opry. For many years, he has preached his mission at a church in Nashville. It is said that Kris Kristofferson was inspired to write "Why Me Lord" (which Elvis later covered) after a mass given by Snow.

Elvis covered two Jimmie Rodgers Snow hits, "Love Me" and "How Do You Think I Feel," in 1956—Snow had originally released them on the RCA label in 1954.

JIMMIE RODGERS SNOW: "I remember how cool he was . . . He was the change that was coming to America."

"SNOWBIRD"

On September 22, 1970, Elvis recorded this Gene MacLellan song during the Nashville sessions that produced the bulk of material for his Elvis Country LP. That same year, the song had been a hit for Anne Murray; a year later, Chet Atkins won a Grammy with an instrumental version.

Elvis performed the song live in 1971 (a version may be found on 2004 FTD release The Impossible Dream).

Elvis' original recording has since been included on Walk A Mile In My Shoes and on the 2006 Elvis Country update. Alternative takes are on Today Tomorrow & Forever and on FTD album The Nashville Marathon (a slightly faster first take).

SNOWMEN'S LEAGUE OF AMERICA

Colonel Parker established this tongue-in-cheek club—a parody of the "Showman's League of America"—as a homage to his ability to "snow" people out of their money before melting away. The club slogan was "Let it snow, let it snow, let it snow."

Membership of the club was by invitation only by the High Potentate, who happened to be Colonel Parker. Parker went so far as to create joke merchandise for his members, such as "Essence of Mosquito Manure" cologne. Club members received club literature, but true to form, the main portion of the Snowmen's Report on Advanced Techniques was as blank as the driven snow, because, as it is explained within, "wordiness has been avoided."

As with so much to do with the Colonel, claims about the club may or may not be wholly accurate. What is certain is that the Colonel was happy to bestow the "honor" of membership on influential and important figures from the upper echelons of the entertainment business and politics. Early members included Paramount producers Hal Wallis and Joe Hazan; it has variously been reported that top performers Milton Berle, Bing Crosby, Bob Hope and Frank Sinatra were all made members by the Colonel, along with US president Lyndon Baines Johnson. Membership was free, but getting out reputedly cost $1,000 (or $10,000 depending on accounts).

The only one of Elvis' entourage invited by the Colonel to join the club was Larry Geller, as a backhanded acknowledgement of Geller's influence over Elvis in the mid-Sixties.

Parker gleefully referred to himself as "The Snowman"; he sometimes announced himself on the phone as "Colonel Snow" when he called Graceland.

SNOWMOBILING

Elvis went snowmobiling in Aspen, Colorado in January 1969, and loved it so much that he bought three Jetstars in Memphis, with special treads so that they could be ridden round the grounds at Graceland.

His nocturnal snowmobiling exploits in Vail in January 1976 led to complaints from other vacationers, including 18-year-old Susan Ford, daughter of then President Gerald Ford.

"SO CLOSE, YET SO FAR (FROM PARADISE)"

This Joy Byers composition is a firm fan favorite that Elvis recorded on February 25, 1965 at Studio B in Nashville for the Harum Scarum soundtrack. It later cropped up on Mahalo From Elvis, and then was paired with Girl Happy on the Double Feature release in the Nineties; it was also

included on the Command Performances anthology. Alternate takes of the song are on Collectors Gold, the FTD release for Harum Scarum, and the inevitable selection of bootlegs.

"SO GLAD YOU'RE MINE"

This Arthur Crudup song from 1946 came out on Elvis' second album, Elvis and EP Elvis, Vol. 2, after Elvis recorded a rock meets boogie-woogie version on January 30, 1956 at the RCA Studios in New York City.

The song has since graced Reconsider Baby, The King Of Rock And Roll and the Elvis '56 commemorative album from 1996. It also made the cut on 2006 themed album Elvis R 'n' B. It's also on 2007 independent Memphis Recording Service release New York RCA Studio 1: The Complete Sessions.

The Arthur Crudup original featured on 2002 Charly label issue Elvis Presley At The Louisiana Hayride / The Original Roots of Elvis Presley

"SO HIGH"

Elvis recorded this joyous traditional gospel number—originally popularized by the Golden Gate Quartet—in the early hours of May 27, 1966 during his Nashville session for religious album How Great Thou Art. Buddy Harman provided the upfront drums and cymbals.

Elvis' rendition has since appeared on anthologies Amazing Grace, Peace In The Valley and Ultimate Gospel. Alternates of this and of the other tracks on that album came out in 2003 on the So High FTD release. Another alternate take is on FTD issue Easter Special.

SO HIGH

A 2003 FTD release of remixes and alternates from Elvis' 1966-68 sessions in Nashville, at a time when he was beginning to get his mojo back.

TRACK LISTING:
1. Run On
2. Stand By Me
3. Down In The Alley
4. Tomorrow Is A Long Time
5. Love Letters
6. So High
7. By And By
8. Somebody Bigger Than You And I
9. Without Him
10. If The Lord Wasn't Walking By My Side
11. Come What May
12. I'll Remember You
13. Guitar Man
14. Mine
15. Singing Tree
16. Just Call Me Lonesome
17. Hi-Heel Sneakers
18. You Don't Know Me
19. We Call On Him
20. You'll Never Walk Alone
21. Jam (Muleskinner Blues)
22. Stay Away
23. U.S. Male
24. Too Much Monkey Business
25. Goin' Home

"SOFTLY AND TENDERLY"

Elvis wrapped his vocal chords around this traditional gospel song with pals Carl Perkins and Jerry Lee Lewis during the Million Dollar Quartet sing-along at Sun Studio on December 4, 1956. As well as featuring on the various recordings to come out of that session, it has appeared on gospel anthology *Peace in the Valley*.

"SOFTLY AS I LEAVE YOU"

For many fans at Elvis' later concerts, "Softly As I Leave You" was a poignant tune sung by a man who sensed that the end was drawing near. Antonio De Vita and Giorgio Calabrese original-ly wrote the song for Italian songstress Mina, titled "Piano" (which in Italian means "softly"). The English-language version, written by Hal Shaper, was recorded by Charles Boyer and later Frank Sinatra before Elvis adopted the song in concert at the end of his summer 1973 Las Vegas engagement, when he introduced it as one of the prettiest songs he'd ever heard.

In 1975, Elvis sang this ballad in a duet with backing singer Sherrill Nielsen, speaking the words while the tenor sang. A recording of the song from a live performance in Las Vegas that December was issued as a posthumously-issued B-side to "Unchained Melody." A rehearsal from the summer of 1974 came out on the *Walk A Mile In My Shoes* anthology.

Live versions from the Las Vegas years are on *Elvis Aron Presley*, *Live In Las Vegas*, and on FTD releases *Closing Night*, *It's Midnight* and *Dinner At Eight*, as well as on a plethora of bootlegs.

"SOLDIER BOY"

Elvis recorded this doo-wap *Elvis Is Back!* album track, written by David Jones and Theodore Williams Jr. (and previously a 1955 hit for the Four Fellows), fresh back from the Army at his March 20, 1960 Nashville session.

In the Nineties, the song resurfaced on Elvis' *From Nashville to Memphis* Sixties anthology.

A 1959 home recording from Germany saw the light of day on 1984 album *A Golden Celebration*. Alternate takes from the 1960 studio session are on *Essential Elvis Vol. 6*, *Elvis: Close Up* and on FTD album *Fame And Fortune*; FTD release *Elvis Is Back!* features half-a-dozen takes of the song.

According to *Elvis: His Life From A to Z*, this was Elvis and Anita Wood's "special song."

"SOLITAIRE"

Elvis laid down this grandiloquent Neil Sedaka ballad (lyrics by Phil Cody) in a recording session at Graceland on February 3, 1976, for subsequent release on *From Elvis Presley Boulevard, Memphis Tennessee*. Back in 1972, in had been the title track for Neil Sedaka's album, though it did not achieve hit status until Andy Williams released it a year later.

Elvis' version of the song was released as the B-side to posthumous single "Are You Sincere" in 1979.

In later decades, the song has featured on com-memorative albums *Our Memories of Elvis*, *Always On My Mind*, and on the 2000 *Moody Blue* re-release.

FTD have issued alternates on *Jungle Room Sessions* and *Made in Memphis*.

"SOMEBODY BIGGER THAN YOU AND I"

Elvis recorded his basso profundo version of this 1951 Ink Spots hit for his *How Great Thou Art* album in Nashville on May 27, 1966. The track, written by Johnny Lange, Walter Heath and Joseph Burke, had previously been covered by Elvis favorites Jimmy Jones, and by the Harmonizing Four.

Elvis' version has since appeared on religious-themed albums *He Walks Beside Me*, *Amazing Grace*, *Peace In The Valley* and *Christmas Peace*.

Alternate takes can be heard on *Elvis: Close Up* and FTD releases *Easter Special* and *So High*.

"SOMETHING"

Elvis covered this million-selling 1969 Beatles song—the only one of the group's singles to be written by George Harrison—live in concert from 1970 to 1975 a couple of dozen times. Frank Sinatra also liked to sing the song, which he said was "the greatest love song ever written." Indeed, it's sufficiently popular among singers to have become the second-most covered of all Beatles songs.

Elvis added the song to his live repertoire for his summer 1970 Las Vegas engagement, though it didn't see public release until the *Walk A Mile In My Shoes* anthology in 1995 (rehearsals prior to the engagement appeared on the 2000 *That's The Way It Is* special edition and on FTD release *The Way It Was*).

Elvis also included the song as part of his January 1973 *Aloha From Hawaii Via Satellite* per-formance (it's on both the official album and *The Alternate Aloha*).

Live versions from 1970 are also on *Live in Las Vegas* and on FTD releases *One Night In Vegas* and *Writing For The King*. *The Impossible Dream* fea-tures a 1971 performance.

"SOMETHING BLUE"

A Paul Evans / Al Byron ballad that Elvis record-ed in Nashville on March 18, 1962 at the start of the session for the *Pot Luck* album. Since then, it has appeared on the *From Nashville to Memphis* anthology.

Platinum: A Life In Music features a different take; 2003 FTD release *Studio B: Nashville Outtakes* has a further two, with more on the FTD *Pot Luck* issue.

SOMETHING FOR EVERYBODY

This LP shifted 300,000 copies and stayed at #1 for three weeks after its release in June 1961, racking up a total of 25 weeks in the Hot LP chart. Almost the whole album was recorded in Nashville in March 1961.

TRACK LISTING:
1. There's Always Me
2. Give Me The Right
3. It's A Sin
4. Sentimental Me
5. Starting Today
6. Gently
7. I'm Coming Home
8. In Your Arms
9. Put The Blame On Me
10. Judy
11. I Want You With Me
12. I Slipped, I Stumbled, I Fell

In 2006 FTD released a collector's edition of this album with outtakes and alternates, plus non-soundtrack singles recorded at the time ("I Feel So Bad," "Little Sister," "His Latest Flame," "Good Luck Charm" and "Anything That's Part Of You").

"SONG OF THE SHRIMP"

Considered by many to mark the nadir of Elvis' soundtrack material, this *Girls! Girls! Girls!* song was on Elvis' list of tracks to record in Nashville on March 27, 1962. Written by soundtrack stal-warts Roy C. Bennett and Sid Tepper, to Elvis' credit he sings the Banana Boat Song-inspired tune with the unwavering application of a profes-sional.

The "Song Of The Shrimp" rode again on the *Double Features* release for the movie, and on the *Elvis Chante Sid Tepper & Roy C. Bennett* album, which also features the songwriters' demo.

SONGFELLOWS

This young gospel group, helmed by Cecil Blackwood and associated with the Blackwood Brothers Quartet, turned Elvis down in the spring of 1954 when he auditioned to join them. Elvis later said that he was told he "couldn't sing"; other members of the group at the time remem-bered that the problem wasn't that he couldn't sing, it was that he "couldn't sing harmony." After the tragic death of members of the Blackwood Quartet a year afterwards, Elvis was asked to join the Songfellows, but by this time he had already started making his own music at Sun and was more interested in seeing how far that would go.

SONGS

Gospel, rock, ballads, country, pop, rockabilly, old standards, hymns, blues, Neapolitan classics and weepies . . . Elvis really did sing all kinds. From an impressively early age, Elvis had a natural ability to assimilate song. He once boasted to his Sergeant, Ira Jones, that he knew just about every song written; Jones tried him out and found that he couldn't name a song that Elvis didn't know. Though not musically-trained, Elvis had some exceptional qualities as a musician: he could sing a new song word- and note-perfect after listening just a few times to the demo.

Estimates of the number of songs that Elvis recorded during his twenty-three year career veer from the six hundreds to eight hundred and thir-ty, though one persistently-quoted figure is 744. This encyclopedia has entries for over 850 songs that Elvis sang, recorded, jammed on, or ad-libbed a line or two of in concert.

Estimates vary so widely on the number of songs that Elvis sang depending on whether or not they include songs that were never completed, alternate takes, lines of songs recorded in concert for official release, snatches of song Elvis ad-libbed on stage captured by bootleggers or soundboard recordings, home recordings never intended for release, studio jams, and rehearsal material that has not featured on an official album. If all these songs are added into the equation, the total number of songs that Elvis sang within the range of a microphone exceeds 1,200, and that's before even counting the vast library of songs that Elvis is rumored to have recorded but have failed to appear in the public domain (*see* SIDEBAR below).

At Sun, many of the songs Elvis sang were tunes to which Sam Phillips had publishing rights that had already been sung by other Sun artists—on some of these songs, Phillips had a lucrative song-writing credit. Elvis took these songs as templates and then reworked them until they sounded whol-ly his own, as if he was the first to sing them.

Elvis' early songs became so popular so quickly that within six months of his first single release, country stars Smiley Maxedon and then Marty Robbins both had a crack at "That's All Right (Mama)."

Elvis' sixth sense for a hit song in the early part of his career made him a recording-industry Midas. For his first RCA sessions, Steve Sholes sent Elvis demo tracks to pick from. The track that proved to be his mainstream breakthrough, "Heartbreak Hotel," was one that Elvis had decided to do before he even put pen to paper for RCA.

As part of the deal that took Elvis from Sun to RCA, publishers Hill & Range supplied Elvis with demos of prospective material alongside material that RCA had pre-selected. Elvis discarded most of this material out of hand, though he did record songs that went on to be major hits. Hill & Range gradually took over the task of finding suitable material for Elvis, drawing on songwriters from the famous Brill Building in New York, the crucible where hundreds of hits were forged in the days before singers were expected to write their own material. If Hill & Range's demos didn't fire Elvis up, RCA always had some covers he could fall back on, or Elvis would suggest some of his own favorites. In the halcyon Elvis year of 1956, RCA evidently feared that their most expensive ever new recording artist would be a flash in the pan, and put out every track he had already released on the Sun label to maximize their returns.

For Elvis' first Paramount movie, *Loving You*, Hill & Range commissioned top songwriting team Leiber and Stoller to write specifically for Elvis. Many of these early movie songs were recorded in multiple versions so that they could be used several times during the course of the movie.

In his early years, top-tier songwriters were happy to write a practically-guaranteed Elvis smash hit even though Hill & Range required them to relinquish a third of their writing royalties from record sales (but not airplay) to the Colonel and Elvis. Otis Blackwell, who penned many of Elvis' early hits, gave up half of his royalties, in the knowledge that it would be worth it in the end. However, over the course of his entire career, most of Elvis' recorded output consists of covers of songs that had already been popularized by other artists.

The type of song that Elvis sang changed after his return from the Army. From 1960, the Colonel had lined him up for as many as three movies a year, each of which required up to a dozen soundtrack songs. With the exception of his *Elvis is Back!* album recorded immediately after his return, practically all of his songs were written for specific slots in a movie, often in a rush, and inevitably the quality began to suffer. The fall in quality was, for a long time, masked by the fact that Elvis' loyal fans could be relied upon to buy whatever records their idol put out. He still scored huge hits, though: "It's Now Or Never" was a major departure from his rock 'n' roll beginnings that outsold any single he released before or afterwards.

The way it worked was that Freddy Bienstock of song publishers Hill & Range sent the movie script to different teams of songwriters, who then competed to write the best song for each title/slot in the movie (originally selected by the director). Elvis then had final say on these songs, though often this came down to picking the best of a bad lot.

For songwriters, the gamble of giving up some percentage points to Elvis was worth it even on movie soundtrack albums: if one of their songs was released as a single, their earnings would be substantially higher. Some of the soundtrack songs have stood the test of time; many are forgotten by all but the most idiosyncratic Elvis fans. Producers were happy as long as there was one song they considered strong enough for the airplay that would drive fans to buy tickets. The Colonel was happy because he was indulging his mantra of cross-selling: using the songs to sell the movie, and using the movie to sell soundtrack albums.

Not surprisingly, Elvis gradually became disillusioned with the material he was being given as

the decade wore on. By the mid-Sixties, he often made excuses not to attend soundtrack recording sessions at all, preferring to overdub his vocals on his own at a later date. In the book *Elvis: What Happened?*, Red West says that sometimes Elvis delegated film song selection to him. Some sources have stated that Elvis wound up simply signing off the director's recommendations.

Elvis continued to have last call over which of his recordings would be released as a single, his intuition still as good with less-promising material as it had been with his stellar songs of the Fifties. This held true until the mid-Sixties, when he was all but carried away on a river of flotsam and jetsam that many of his long-term fans were no longer prepared to buy. Gordon Stoker remembers Elvis in the studio, physically trying to get as much distance between himself and the microphone as possible: "The material was so bad that he felt like he couldn't sing it."

During this fallow period, Elvis' passion for song turned inwards to become a private pursuit. He would sing the songs he liked at home with Charlie Hodge, Red West and anyone who was around, from gospel to the latest hits he heard on the radio. It was his studio session for 1966 gospel album *How Great Thou Art* that rekindled Elvis' passion for the songs he loved; it was not until the breath of fresh air that was his 1968 NBC TV Special that Elvis decided that enough was enough, that he would only sing songs he believed in.

He took this philosophy into his groundbreaking American Studio sessions in early 1969, where he romped through a whole new catalogue of songs, despite the disapproval of Hill & Range and the Colonel's management team. According to Marty Lacker, when Elvis expressed his desire to cut songs for which no publishing deal was already in place, the Colonel instructed his man Tom Diskin to leave the session at American Studio. If this is true, this was the only time after Elvis' Sun days that this extra layer of control wasn't in place.

From around the time of his 1968 Comeback, the new material that Elvis favored was something of a barometer of his state of mind (despite his strenuous on-stage protestations to the contrary). In the early Seventies, during his separation from Priscilla, Elvis had a predilection for songs of heartbreak.

When he returned to live performing, before his Las Vegas engagements Elvis rehearsed plenty of new songs, only to drop the vast majority of the new material because his fans reacted best to the hits they knew and loved. During his live performances in the Seventies, at one time or another at least 75 new tracks made it onto his repertoire, not including his one-liners and song interjections, but very few of them remained long-term.

With his classic hits, when performing live in later years Elvis kept things fresh by changing the arrangements, altering the way he sang them, cracking up halfway through, interjecting a change mid-flow in order to see if he could catch out his band members.

For almost the entire first decade of Elvis' career, it was an exception rather than the rule for singers to write their own material. Elvis' only true forays into songwriting were with pal Red West, though his name is credited on many more songs either for publishing reasons, or because the songs were traditional and not registered to any songwriter. Because he did not write his own material, in theory he was free to pick and choose songs by some of the finest songwriting talent of the day. He was insistent on obtaining the rights to sing songs that he heard and really liked, at least during the early part of his career, and then again from a little before his Comeback Special. The zenith of this freedom came when he recorded at Chips Moman's American Studio in Memphis in 1969, a move that spawned memorable later Elvis classics such as "In The Ghetto" and "Suspicious Minds."

In the Seventies, Elvis became increasingly likely to record songs he came up with (for which no publishing deal was in place) than the material proposed by his song publishers. His once prodigious memory for songs became dimmed by his excess intake of prescription drugs, leading to the less than ideal situation of having to sing new songs from a crib sheet, or sometimes live being prompted by somebody under the plexiglass stage.

When Elvis' song publishing arrangements changed in 1973, a wider circle of sources opened up for new material, including producer Felton Jarvis and Elvis' pet backing group Voice. Elvis picked out the demos he liked, publishing deals were made, but by this time he no longer had the drive to make take after take until he came up with his own, highly unique interpretation. In 1975, Elvis sang his way through an entire recording session in LA that did not include a single song on one of his special publishing deals.

In 2004, *Rolling Stone* magazine published a list of the 500 Greatest Songs of All Time. Elvis had eleven songs on the list, the highest, at #19, being "Hound Dog." Bob Dylan's "Like A Rolling Stone" was #1. In a 2007 *Rolling Stone* survey, "That's All Right (Mama)" came top out of the "Forty Greatest Songs That Changed The World."

Six Elvis songs had been inducted into the Grammy Hall of Fame by 2007: "Hound Dog," "Heartbreak Hotel," "That's All Right (Mama)," "Suspicious Minds," "Don't Be Cruel" and "Are You Lonesome Tonight."

ELVIS SAID IN 1971 (quoting a 1929 Vincent Youmans song he knew through Roy Hamilton): "Without a song the day would never end. Without a song a man ain't got a friend. Without a song the road would never bend. Without a song . . .' So I keep singing a song..."

ELVIS SAID IN 1972: "Every song is like we do it for the first time and that's one of the secrets."

ELVIS SAID IN 1972: "It's hard to find the material nowadays . . . it's very difficult to find any good hard rock songs. If I could find them I would do them."

ELVIS SAID IN 1974: "I must have recorded four hundred songs that start out with 'Wellllllllll . . . .' So it's easy to do the wrong one . . . the same's true with women, ya know."

SCOTTY MOORE: "He had rhythm in his voice. He could hear a song and he knew what he could do with a song. And nobody else could do it."

D.J. FONTANA: "Elvis had such a keen ear. He could listen to a song once or twice, and he knew it. But he had his own ideas. He was picking the songs, all these big monster hits, and he was always right. So after a while what could we tell him? We couldn't tell him what to record; we'd have been crazy. He had the reins."

GORDON STOKER: "He put his heart into every song... Every word of every song meant something to him and I think that's the reason his music has continued to live on."

JOE ESPOSITO: "When Elvis sang, he sang with his heart and his body."

BILLY SMITH: "He always tried his best, even with the worst song."

NORBERT PUTNAM: "A great song is a wonderful thing, but Al Green and Elvis could sing the phone book, and I would love it. With Presley, you could give him a very trite lyric, and he could inject such emotion and power that would give you goose bumps. It's not the lyrics. It's the artist's emotion, the timbre of the voice."

ERNST JORGENSEN: "As long as Elvis felt he had something to add to a song he had no compunction about challenging an existing version—that was how he'd got his start, after all."

ELAINE DUNDY: "What Elvis conveyed to millions was the ecstatic experience of singing itself."

DON ROBERTSON: "It was to tough to come up with really great songs to fit all those movie script situations. And it was kind of sad to me to see Elvis involved in less than top quality, first-rate things. However, all of our staff writers were just spitting out songs to fit specific situations and to help move those movie plots along."

BILL PORTER: "It was Elvis' choice, but he didn't have the initial picking. They led him to hear what they wanted him to hear. If he didn't like it, he'd say 'No, I don't want to do it.' "

JOAN DEARY: "Those soundtrack songs drove me up a wall. They just seemed to get worse and worse. It was to Elvis' credit that he was even able to perform those songs—I mean, 'Queenie Wahine's Papaya'! Gimme a break."

J.D. SUMNER: "He had the ability to squeeze every drop of emotion out of every word in every line of a song."

HORACE LOGAN: ." . . But those lousy, stinking horrible, terrible songs Elvis did in those movies! And those movies! My God, a lesser talent would have been destroyed by that crap!"

FREDDY BIENSTOCK: "Once we started on the MGM contract, with four pictures a year, it was like a factory... I would mark those scenes where a song could be done without being absolutely ridiculous, and then I would give those scripts to seven or eight songwriting teams. I'd wind up with four or five songs for each spot, and then I would take them to Elvis and he would choose which one to do. But there was no way to have better music, because from the moment one picture was finished, we would have to get started on the next one."

STEVE BINDER SAID IN 1968: "There's no limit to where he can go if he has the material."

CHIPS MOMAN: "Elvis had a good ear for music, and if he didn't think he could do a song he'd toss it out."

MARTY LACKER: "Hill & Range and Parker deserve much of the blame for the crap he recorded in the mid-Sixties."

BOBBY WOOD: "You can tell the songs Elvis really liked. Like any artist, he sang the heck out of 'em."

Books:

The Essential Elvis: The Life and Legacy of the King as Revealed through 112 of His Most Significant Songs, by Samuel Roy and Tom Aspell, Rutledge Hill Press, 1998.

Elvis The #1 Hits: The Secret History of the Classics, by Patrick Humphries, Ebury, 2002.

Roots Of Elvis, by David Neale, published by iUniverse, 2003 (associated with an updated website).

Untold Gold: The Stories Behind Elvis' #1 Hits, by Ace Collins, Chicago Review Press, 2005.

Writing for the King, by Ken Sharp, published by FTD, 2006.

50 ESSENTIAL ELVIS SONGS—

SOURCE: *The Rough Guide to Elvis,* by Paul Simpson, 2002

My Happiness
That's All Right (Mama)
Blue Moon Of Kentucky
Good Rockin' Tonight
Baby Let's Play House
Mystery Train
Tryin' To Get To You
Heartbreak Hotel
Money Honey
My Baby Left Me

Lawdy, Miss Clawdy
Shake, Rattle And Roll
Hound Dog
Don't Be Cruel
Love Me
All Shook Up
One Night
Jailhouse Rock
Trouble
It's Now Or Never
Are You Lonesome Tonight?
Reconsider Baby
Can't Help Falling In Love
(Marie's The Name) His Latest Flame
Little Sister
Return To Sender
It Hurts Me
How Great Thou Art
Tomorrow Is A Long Time
I'll Remember You
Guitar Man
If I Can Dream
Love Me Tender
Long Black Limousine
In The Ghetto
Suspicious Minds
Stranger In My Own Hometown
Any Day Now
Polk Salad Annie
I Really Don't Want To Know
I Just Can't Help Believin'
Merry Christmas Baby
I'm Leavin'
American Trilogy
Burning Love
Always On My Mind
Good Time Charlie's Got The Blues
Promised Land
Way Down
Unchained Melody

FAVORITE ELVIS SONGS as voted by Elvis fans in Holland for a 2007 Elvis release

Suspicious Minds
Always On My Mind
In The Ghetto
Are You Lonesome Tonight?
American Trilogy
Can't Help Falling In Love
Jailhouse Rock
Love Me Tender
My Boy
It's Now Or Never
My Way
I Just Can't Help Believin'
Wooden Heart
Blue Suede Shoes
(You're The) Devil In Disguise
If I Can Dream
The Wonder Of You
Burning Love
Don't Cry, Daddy
Crying In The Chapel
Return To Sender
One Night
You've Lost That Lovin' Feeling
How Great Thou Art (live 1974)
Don't Be Cruel
Bridge Over Troubled Water
You Gave Me A Mountain
(Let Me Be Your) Teddy Bear
Memories
Just Pretend
(Marie's The Name) His Latest Flame
A Little Less Conversation
Heartbreak Hotel
Guitar Man
(Now And Then There's) A Fool Such As I
Polk Salad Annie
Kiss Me Quick
Viva Las Vegas

You Don't Have To Say You Love Me
That's All Right (Mama)
Loving You
I'll Remember You
Don't
All Shook Up
Suspicion
Kentucky Rain
Such A Night
Hound Dog
I Can't Stop Loving You
Are You Lonesome Tonight? (Laughing version)

SONGS ELVIS IS REPUTED TO HAVE SUNG

For decades, fans have avidly speculated about hundreds of songs that Elvis may or may not have recorded (for Sun, RCA or during the recording of movie studio soundtracks) or sung live (to fill out his repertoire in the early days, or as one-offs at concerts in the Seventies) without ever leaving a public trace.

Many "missing" Elvis songs from his Sun years are in actual fact songs sung by other artists at the label, where it was common practice to recycle material. Some likely candidates come from a 1955 Hill & Range folio of songs that featured four Elvis songs and a further eleven tracks by other artists—if Elvis did record any of these songs, the tapes were not passed on to RCA when the label bought out his contract at the end of 1955. That said, it is known that many of Elvis' early castoffs were destroyed by RCA when they reorganized their storage facilities in the late Fifties.

Other hopefuls consist of songs that Elvis and the band played as they warmed up before getting down to serious business, played their way through without the tape running, or else the tape was running but was later reused.

Further likely candidates include songs that Elvis sang in the first eighteen months of his career as he toured incessantly and fleshed out his sparse repertoire with popular hits of the day. Some potential missing Elvis songs are tracks that feature on studio session notes for which no tapes correspond. Particularly for movie soundtrack songs, confusion has arisen over competing songs for certain slots, some of which exist in demo form but were not recorded, or else were recorded under different track titles (or performed by Elvis' co-stars, or by other artists to be used as background music in the movie).

In Elvis' later years, a number of instrumental tracks were laid down, some with guide vocals, for which Elvis either did not ever record a vocal, or did not record a satisfactory part. Further confusion exists over songs people assume to be by Elvis but are not, such as the duets Jerry Lee Lewis released in the Seventies with Elvis soundalike Jimmy "Orion" Ellis, various rocking efforts by performers who significantly tipped their hat to Elvis (from Gene Vincent to Freddie Mercury), and even song titles published in press reviews of Elvis concerts where the reporter misheard or misconstrued the song name. Then there are the many, many one-liners and excerpts that Elvis enjoyed slipping in to his Seventies shows: bootleggers have profitably staked out this territory on unofficial releases such as *Live and Unleashed* (later released as *We Have Not Rehearsed Them*).

In addition to songs which have specific entries in this Encyclopedia—the criterion is that they have come out on official or unofficial records—there follows a selection of songs that fans hope might—just might—one day become publicly available:

"A Shoulder To Cry On"
"All I Really Want To Do"
"Always Late (With Your Kisses)"

"Bad Moon Rising"
"Birds Fly High"
"Bivouac"
"Blue Guitar"
"Blue Monday"
"Bo Diddley"
"Book Of Happiness"
"Born To Lose"
"Bourbon Street"
"Breakin' The Rules"
"Breathless"
"Candy Kisses"
"Carolyn"
"Casual Love Affair "
"Chain Gang"
"Chautauqua"
"Come Out, Come Out"
"Cool Water"
"Country Bumpkin"
"Cryin' "
"Crying Heart Blues"
"Daddy, Don't You Walk So Fast"
"Dark As A Dungeon"
"Delta Lady"
"Diana"
"Don't Let The Sunshine Fool You"
"Ecstasy"
"Fabulous"
"Fire Down Below"
"Give Me More, More, More (Of Your Kisses)"
"Good Looking Woman"
"Gone"
"Guilty"
"Hawaiian Sunrise"
"Holy Holy"
"Hooked On A Feeling"
"House Of The Rising Sun"
"I Almost Lost My Mind"
"I Can See Clearly Now"
"I Don't Hurt Anymore"
"I Hear You Knocking"
"I Played The Fool"
"I Saw The Light"
"If Not For You"
"It Ain't Me Babe"
"It'll Be Me"
"Jelly Roll King"
"Joy"
"Juanita"
"Keep Them Cold, Icy Fingers Off Of Me"
"Leave My Woman Alone"
"Let's Live A Little"
"Like A Rolling Stone"
"Little Girl"
"Little Mama"
"Lonely Avenue"
"Lonely Teardrops"
"Long Journey"
"Love Bug Itch"
"Love Gone"
"Love Will Keep Us Together"
"Loving Her Was Easier"
"Loving You, Baby"
"Me And Bobby McGee"
"Memory Revival"
"Mexican Joe"
"Muskrat Ramble"
"My Garden Of Prayer"
"My Love For You"
"Night Train To Memphis"
"Nine Pound Hammer"
"No Lonesome Tune"
"No Particular Place To Go"
"Now Is The Hour"
"Oh, Lonesome Me"
"Okie Boogie"
"On Wisconsin"
"One Too Many Mornings"
"Onward To Victory"
"Pink Cadillac"
"Play A Simple Melody"
"Playing With Fire"
"Potpourri"
"Precious Memories"

"Puppy Love"
"Rag Mop"
"Ready For Love"
"Remembering"
"Return To Me"
"Rock Of Ages"
"Rockin' Little Sally"
"She Belongs To Me"
"Since I Met You Baby"
"Snow Don't Fall"
"Stormy Monday Blues"
"Sunshine"
"Talkin' 'Bout Your Birthday Cake"
"Teardrops"
"Tears On My Pillow"
"Tennessee Dancin' Doll"
"Tennessee Partner"
"Tennessee Saturday Night"
"That's The Stuff You Gotta Watch"
"The Best Thing"
"The Big Hurt"
"The Great Pretender"
"The Old Wooden Church"
"This Little Girl Of Mine"
"Three Good Reasons"
"Tiger By The Tail"
"Too Late To Worry, Too Blue To Cry"
"Twenty Flight Rock"
"Twist Me Loose" (see "I Don't Wanna Be Tied")
"Wabash Cannonball"
"Walking Down The Line"
"We Both Went Our Ways"
"We Had It All"
"We Shall Overcome"
"We're Gonna Live It Up"
"Wheel Of Fortune"
"Whistling Blues"
"Without You"
"Woman Shy"
"Yeah, Yeah, Yeah"
"You Can't Blame A Guy For Trying"
"You Are My Sunshine"
"You Do Something To Me"
"You Turned The Tables On Me"
"Your Life Has Just Begun"
"Your Song"

In the 2000s, songwriter Paul Terry King sold what he claimed were two songs that he wrote with Elvis in 1973, "Just Like Rolling Up Hill" and "If I'd Only Bought Her Roses."

Books:
Off and Back on the Mystery Track, by Edwin Meijers, All Shook Up! Productions, 1995
Fred Worth and Steve Tamerius's book *Elvis: His Life from A to Z* is a good resource for the backstory to these songs; fan websites on the net are also rife with speculation about tracks that Elvis may or may not have covered.

SONGWRITERS

In an active recording career that spanned twenty-three years, Elvis worked on material written and composed by hundreds of songwriters, from literal unknowns (a vast category of "traditional" songs) to the best of the Brill Building crop, and on through many top songsmiths of the Sixties and Seventies.

For many fans, the reason why Elvis' output went stale during the Sixties—up to his 1968 Comeback Special—may directly be ascribed to the methods the Colonel used to distance Elvis from the process of commissioning songs. Though the Colonel undoubtedly did this for commercial reasons, in order to ensure that Elvis earned extra by taking a slice of songwriters' royalties, it also enabled him to exert a strong degree of control over his client who, nominally at least, was free to pick and choose his own material. The Colonel also maintained control by ensuring that all new mate-

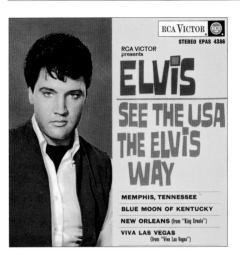

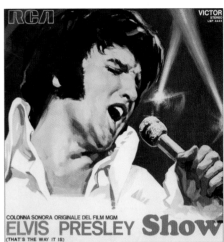

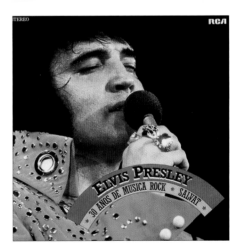

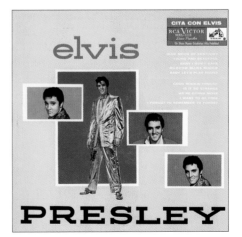

AN ELVIS POTPOURRI
TOP TO BOTTOM: Rare New Zealand EP, Italian release, and two from Mexico.

rial was channeled through song publishers Hill & Range, and in the Sixties, by locking Elvis into a carousel of mediocre movie soundtrack songs that monopolized his studio time and prevented him from doing anything else. From a purely financial point of view, the Colonel chose the right strategy: record sales after Elvis' return from the Army were much stronger for soundtrack songs than for Elvis' more critically-acclaimed RCA albums.

At Sun, Elvis drew most of his material from Sam Phillips' abundant in-house talent, which didn't require expensive publishing deals. After Elvis moved to RCA, song publishers Hill & Range took over the task of procuring material, relying on top songwriting teams from New York such as Leiber & Stoller, Aaron Schroeder, Ben Weisman and Claude Demetrius (all of whom wrote with a revolving roster of partners), and of course Otis Blackwell.

The strictures of the Colonel's policy—that Elvis would retain a third of royalties on the songs he sang—gradually had an effect on which songwriters were prepared to submit material. With the exception of Elvis' biggest single hits, songwriters could expect to make around $2,500 for a soundtrack song. When the Colonel found out that Leiber & Stoller had dared to suggest a project directly to Elvis, he made sure that they would never have the opportunity again by making it clear to Elvis that he would not tolerate this, thereby putting paid to an extremely proficuous partnership.

In the Sixties, the vast majority of songs Elvis sang were written in a rush to precise script specifications. The quality tended to be higher for his RCA cuts. In 1961, Elvis included a couple of Don Robertson cuts on *Something For Everybody*.

Inevitably, quality suffered as the quantity of songs commissioned from songwriters increased —in 1961, Elvis recorded almost fifty songs. The songwriters were going flat out: prolific soundtrack duo Sid Tepper and Roy C. Bennett once penned five movie songs in a single afternoon. Elvis' hardest-working songwriter of all, Ben Weisman, has a credit on 57 Elvis tracks, the vast majority used in films.

On some movie soundtrack sessions a songwriter was kept on hand for last minute compositions, though as a rule Elvis did not meet his songwriters. For *It Happened at the World's Fair*, Ben Weisman did the honors on a hasty finale, while Don Robertson was not only present, he played piano on the recordings of his own pieces.

It wasn't unusual for as many as three hundred demos to be submitted initially for a movie. This number was whittled down to enough material to fit on an LP or sometimes EP. If a songwriter's work didn't make it into the picture, they more or less wrote off their time, though there was a slim chance that a rejected song might be reconsidered for a later film.

In 1964, Elvis only recorded three non-soundtrack songs. When he was unleashed on a diamond like "It Hurts Me," he threw himself into the recording with enormous emotional charge. On the rare occasions that Elvis had studio time to record directly for RCA during this period, if he didn't like what was available, he relied on old favorites or took solace in laying down tracks for a gospel album.

New songwriting talent was instrumental to Elvis' reinvigorated output at the end of the decade, before and after his 1968 NBC TV Special, including the likes of Mac Davis, A.L. Owens, Neil Diamond and writers to whom Elvis was introduced by American Studio principal Chips Moman.

In the early Seventies, Elvis recorded songs by Kris Kristofferson, Buffy Sainte-Marie, Bob Dylan and Gordon Lightfoot among others. However, plenty of tunes that songwriters wrote with Elvis in mind slipped through the cracks: in the Sixties, Paul McCartney asked a member of Elvis' entourage if he thought there was any chance Elvis would sing one of his songs; in the Seventies,

David Bowie is said to have written "Golden Years" in the hope that Elvis would sing it; Elton John offered to write songs for Elvis, and Bruce Springsteen sent material to Elvis' management.

Also in the early Seventies, Freddy Bienstock was bringing new English songwriters to Elvis' attention through his UK company Carlin Music, while former entourage members such as Lamar Fike, who had gone into the music business, also brought in new material.

By the mid-Seventies, Elvis was spending some of his increasingly rare studio time helping out songwriting pals—not just Red West but also members of his backing group Voice—while lamenting the changes in the music industry that had turned independent songwriters into something of dying breed. When Elvis started out, singers sang and songwriters wrote songs. By the early Sixties, the onus had started shifting to singer-songwriters, led by Bob Dylan, The Beatles and the folk revival movement.

Over the course of his career, Elvis obtained writer and co-writer credits on 33 songs, including some of his major early successes including "Let Me," "Love Me Tender," "Poor Boy" and "We're Gonna Move."

ELVIS SAID IN 1972: "I'll take songs from anywhere or from anybody if they're good . . . It could be just completely an unknown person or just anybody that writes a song, if they can get it to me. If it's good, I'll do it."

DON ROBERTSON: "When Elvis sang one of my songs, I never had the feeling that he was throwing them away like artists do . . ."

Book:
Writing for the King, by Ken Sharp, FTD, 2006, is the most complete resource with over 100 songwriter interviews and 2 CDs of previously unreleased live Elvis circa 1969 to 1972, plus songs sung by the original songwriters.

LIST OF ELVIS SONGWRITERS

Richard Adler, Doris Akers, Peter Andreoli, Paul Anka, Chris Arnold, Eddy Arnold, Kokomo Arnold, Willis Arthur, Chet Atkins, Hoyt Axton, Mae Boren Axton, Joe Babcock, Burt Bacharach, Thomas Baker-Knight, Mark Barkan, Howard Barnes, Dave Bartholomew, Ralph Bass, Ruth Batchelor, C.M. Battersby, Tim Baty, Bernie Baum, Lou Baxter, Gilbert Bécaud, Bennie Benjamin, Roy C. Bennett, John Benton, Borney Bergantine, Irving Berlin, Felix Bernard, Chuck Berry, Howard Biggs, Otis Blackwell, Robert "Bumps" Blackwell, Norman Blagman, Alan Blaikley, Hal Blair, Rube Bloom, Sam Bobrick, Johnny Bond, Rick Bonfa, Rory Bourke, Lillian Bowles, Dudley Brooks, Phillips Brooks, Ted Brooks, Piney Brown, W. Earl Brown, Albert Brumley, Boudleaux Bryant, Felice Bryant, Fred Burch, Joseph Burke, Jerry Butler, Joy Byers, Al Byron, Giorgio Calabrese, Bill Campbell, Ralph Carmichael, Bert Carroll, Jimmy Cassin, Ray Charles, Sonny Charles, Lincoln Chase, Jerry Chesnut, Chris Christian, Johnny Christopher, James B. Coats, Hank Cochran, Phil Cody, William Cook, Eddie Cooley, Joe Cooper, Sam Coslow, Phil Coulter, Jimmie Crane, Luigi Creatore, Max Crook, Francis Crosby, Andraé Crouch, Arthur "Big Boy" Crudup, Jerry Crutchfield, Jimmie Currie, Johnny Cymbal, Charles Daniels, Ken Darby (Vera Matson), Bobby Darin, Joe Darion, Hal David, Mack David, Mac Davis, Ernesto De Curtis, Gian Battista De Curtis, Antonio De Vita, Sylvia Dee, Louis DeJesus, Pierre Delanoe, Clevant Derricks, Kenny Devine, Neil Diamond, Tommy Dilbeck, Luther Dixon, Willie Dixon, Lonnie Donegan, Pino Donnagio, Rev. Thomas A. Dorsey,

Ervin Drake, Jimmy Duncan, Tommy Durden, Bob Dylan, Sherman Edwards, William Robert "Billy The Kid" Emerson, Paul Evans, Ray Evans, Charlie Feathers, Sid Feller, Fred Fisher, Lester Flatt, Guy Fletcher, Doug Flett, John Fogerty, Red Foley, Nora Fowler, Claude FrançÁois, Dallas Frazier, Albert Frisch, Dolores "Dee" Fuller, Lowell Fulson, Charles Gabriel, Kenny Gamble, Kim Gannon, Larry Gatlin, Stanley Gelber, Bobbie Gentry, Bobby George, Bill Giant, Barry Gibb, Maurice Gibb, Robin Gibb, Don Gibson, Ray Gilbert, Geoffrey Giuliano, Mel Glazer, Artie Glenn, Darrell Glenn, George Goehring, Walter Gold, Herb Goldberg, Charles Goodman, Al Goodheart, Alex Gottlieb, Greg Gordon, Irvin Graham, Roger Greenaway, Barry Greenfield, Rex Griffin, Will Grosz, Franz Gruber, Pepe Guizar, Arthur Gunter, Lance Guynes, Roy Hall, Shorty Hall, Stuart Hamblen, Oscar Hammerstein, Lou Handman, Aileene Hanks, Woody Harris, Lorenz Hart, John Hartford, John Hathcock, Billy Hayes, Lee Hazlewood, Walter Heath, Dick Heard, Sonny Hendrix, David Hess, Edward Heyman, Robert Higginbotham, Billy Hill, Bob Hilliard, Stuart Hine, Joel Hirschhorn, Charlie Hodge, Al Hoffman, Cully Holt, Hal Horton, Harlan Howard, Ken Howard, Richard Howard, W. O. Hoyle, Jerry Reed Hubbard, Leon Huff, Ivory Joe Hunter, Daryl Hutchinson, Al Jacobs, Mark James, Tom Jans, Michael Jarrett, Alan Jeffreys, Waylon Jennings, Enotris Johnson, Jay Johnson, William Johnson, William Johnston, David Jones, Dory Jones, Ollie Jones, Alice Joy, Bert Kaempfert, Martin Kalmanoff, Fred Karger, Al Kasha, Buddy Kaye, Florence Kaye, Jimmy Kennedy, Bill Kenny, Arthur Kent, Walter Kent, Stan Kesler, Walter Kent, Charles King, Pearl King, Pee Wee King, Baker Knight, Ira Kosloff, Kris Kristofferson, Dorothy LaBostrie, Johnny Lange, Johnny Lantz, Augustin Lara, Jacques Larue, James Last, Dickey Lee, Kui Lee, Mylon LeFevre, Jerry Leiber, Mitch Leigh, John Lennon, Raymond Leveen, Al Lewis, Jeff Lewis, Gordon Lightfoot, Joseph Lilley, Dennis Linde, Edward Lisbona, Mosie Lister, Jay Livingston, Jerry Livingston, Jack Lloyd, Kenny Loggins, Joe Hill Louis, Bernie Lowe, Robert Lowry, Tony Macaulay, Ewan MacColl, Gene MacLellan, Richard Mainegra, Barry Mann, Kal Mann, Dick Manning, Armando Manzanero, John Marascalco, Sol Marcus, Barry Mason, Bill Martin, David Martin, Layng Martine Jr., Percy Mayfield, Paul McCartney, Rosemarie McCoy, George McFadden, J. Leslie McFarland, Don McLean, Paddy McMains, Norman Meade, Johnny Mercer, Neal Merritt, Jim Messina, Donald Meyer, Charles Austin Miles, Shirl Milete, Eddie Miller, Ned Miller, Victor Millrose, Domenico Modugno, Josef Mohr, Chips Moman, Russell Moody, Johnny Moore, Jim Morehead, Joe Morris, Lee Morris, Geoffrey Morrow, David Most, Maurice Mysels, Simon Napier-Bell, Ed Nelson, Gerald Nelson, Willie Nelson, Mickey Newbury, Alex North, Charles O'Curran, A.L. "Doodle" Owens, Buck Owens, Cliff Owens, Kelly Owens, Clyde Otis, Vito Pallavicini, Junior Parker, Paul Parnes, Leon Payne, Richard Penniman (Little Richard), Bill Peppers, Hugo Peretti, Betty Peterson, Sam Phillips, Jack Pittman, Anita Pointer, Bonnie Pointer, Doc Pomus, Vince Poncia Jr., Elvis Presley, Lloyd Price, Claude Putnam, Eddie Rabbitt, Paul Rader, Ralph Rainger, Ben Raleigh, Buck Ram, Dottie Rambo, Jay Ramsey, Michael Rashkow, William Raskin, Teddy Redell, Lewis Redner, Bix Reichner, Les Reed, Don Reid, Jacques Revaux, Bill Rice, Denny Rice, Tim Rice, Charlie Rich, Marty Robbins, Bob Roberts, Don Robertson, Don Robey, Lee Robin, Sid Robin, Jessie Mae Robinson, Jimmie Rodgers, Richard Rodgers, Alan Romans, Fred Rose, Leon Rose, Vincent Rose, Lee Rosenberg, Lenore Rosenblatt, Beverly Ross, Jerry Ross, John Rostill, Bobby Russell, Buffy Sainte-Marie, Jack Sallee, Stephen Schlacks, Winfield Scott, Aaron Schroeder, Earl Scruggs, Troy Seals, Neil Sedaka, Del Shannon, Hal Shaper, Billy Joe Shaver, Bob Shelton, Joe Shelton, Jimmy Shirl, Mort Shuman, Carl Sigman, Abner Silver, Paul Simon, Lou Singer, Charlie Singleton, Margie Singleton, Henry Slaughter, Danny Small, Al Smith, Richard Smith, Hank Snow, Eddie Snyder, A. Solberg, Joe South, Phil Spector, Fred Spielman, Glen Spreen, Phil Springer, Ira

Stamphill, Randy Starr, Geoff Stephens, Leith Stevens, Beverly Stewart, Larry Stock, Mike Stoller, Jesse Stone, Carl Story, Vern Stovall, Billy Strange, Richard Strauss, Al Stillman, Gene Sullivan, Donnie Sumner, Billy Swan, Frank Tableporter, Bill Taylor, Chuck Taylor, James Taylor, Sid Tepper, Gilles Thibaut, Joe Thomas, Wayne Carson Thompson, John Thornton, Johnny Tillotson, Charles Tobias, Fred Tobias, Janice Torre, Bill Trader, Ernest Tubb, Roy Turk, Big Joe Turner, Lou Willie Turner, Titus Turner, Zeb Turner, Kay Twomey, Steve Tyrell, John Francis Wade, Jimmy Wakely, Wayne Walker, Ed Warren, Earl Washington, Ferdinand Washington, Cindy Walker, Wayne P. Walker, Wiley Walker, Mayme Watts, Sid Wayne, Thomas Wayne, Frederick Weatherly, Jimmy Webb, Andrew Lloyd Webber, Paul Webster, Ron Webster, Cynthia Weil, Bernard Weinman, Benjamin Weisman, George Weiss, Red West, Thomas Westendorf, Clive Westlake, Billy Edd Wheeler, Tony Joe White, Roger Whittaker, Vicki Wickham, Dave "Curly" Williams, Hank Williams, Hugh Williams, Matt Williams, Maurice Williams, Paul Williams, Theodore Williams Jr., Victor Williams, Chuck Willis, Bob Wills, John Wills, Ray Winkler, Fred Wise, Scott Wiseman, Murray Wisell, Sid Wyche, Faron Young, Victor Young, Hy Zaret

"Sound Advice"

Elvis recorded this Bill Giant / Bernie Baum / Florence Kaye song on July 2, 1961 during a Nashville session for his upcoming movie *Follow That Dream*, but did not want to see it issued on the soundtrack EP. It came out on 1965 album *Elvis For Everyone*. Ray Walker provided the whistling intro in the movie version. The song resurfaced on the *Double Features* soundtrack release in the Nineties.

"Sound Of Your Cry, The"

Elvis laid down this Bill Giant / Bernie Baum / Florence Kaye track on June 4, 1970 in Nashville. It was chosen to be the B-side on September 1971 single release "It's Only Love."

An unedited version came out on 1981 compilation *Greatest Hits Vol. 1*. The original recording has since featured on *Walk A Mile In My Shoes*. *Platinum: A Life In Music* features an alternative take; 2002 FTD release *The Nashville Marathon* has a 5-minute version.

Soundtracks

Like 'em or loathe 'em, Elvis spent much more of his studio time recording songs for movie companies than directly for his record label. This is all the more paradoxical considering that for his first few years in Hollywood, Elvis wanted nothing more than to act in serious, dramatic movies, rather than break out into improbable song at unlikely moments. Alas, the market reality of the Colonel's clever cross-promotion strategies made this impossible in any of his 31 feature films.

And yet many of Elvis' biggest hits, including "Love Me Tender," "Jailhouse Rock" and "Can't Help Falling In Love," were movie songs. The *Blue Hawaii* LP remained the world's best-selling movie soundtrack for sixteen years, until *Saturday Night Fever* in 1977. Since then its sales have only been eclipsed by a handful of other soundtrack albums, all of which (with the exception of Prince's *Purple Rain*) are multi-artist efforts.

From his movie debut until the late Sixties, the Elvis songs in every movie were a vital part of the marketing effort. The Colonel's successful strategy was to leverage the songs to promote the movie, and then use the movie to persuade people to buy soundtrack records. Soundtrack EPs and then albums came out for movies well into the twilight of Elvis' feature film career. Even after Elvis stopped making feature films, songs that had failed to make the cut on soundtrack LPs wound up on one or other of the budget and mid-price albums that RCA released in the early Seventies.

Elvis had a sincere dislike for recording on the huge soundstages commonly in use in Hollywood when he arrived in 1956. He complained to Paramount during the making of his first movie for the studio, *Loving You*, in early 1957. When Elvis failed to produce acceptable versions of the tracks he was laying down, Paramount producer Hal Wallis realized that it was better for all concerned if Elvis was allowed to work at the Radio Recorders studio in Santa Monica, where he felt comfortable.

After his return from military service in 1960, Elvis started to record some of his soundtracks at RCA's Studio B in Nashville, though he continued to record the vast majority of his movie songs at Radio Recorders in Los Angeles, with a studio band of L.A.-based players. On movies like *Girls! Girls! Girls!* which featured over a dozen songs, the studio musical director (in this case Charles O'Curran) rehearsed the band on the numbers before Elvis set foot in the studio—a far cry from Elvis' customary working practice of working up arrangements directly with the band.

By 1964, after churning out three films a year since his return from the Army, Elvis was heartily disillusioned with the sausage-factory soundtrack process. When Colonel Parker offered him the opportunity to make his next film, *Tickle Me*, by recycling old songs from albums, Elvis was more than happy to agree, even though it meant using songs that were leftovers at best.

Elvis stayed out of the studio altogether for eight months—a very long time for him—prior to going to Nashville's Studio B to record the soundtrack to *Harum Scarum* in 1965. His disinterest in the material translated into the inordinate number of takes he required for some of the songs.

By 1966, Elvis no longer felt comfortable at Radio Recorders and preferred to lay down his musical numbers directly on the MGM or Paramount lots—a decision that no doubt pleased the Colonel because it kept down costs. *Clambake* would have been recorded on the United Artists soundstage, if Elvis had not been too preoccupied with his new ranch to fly to LA. Instead, he laid down most of the tracks in Nashville, and finished up in LA. For 1968 movie *Speedway*, Elvis sent Freddy Bienstock back to work to find some new material because he didn't like the selections from which he was expected to choose.

Though not strictly a soundtrack, Elvis recorded the title track for *Charro!* at the Samuel Goldwyn Studios soundstage in October 1968. That same month he began laying down the songs for *The Trouble with Girls* at United Artists Recorders. He recorded the soundtrack for his last Hollywood film, *Change of Habit*, in March 1969 at the Decca Universal Studio.

Much as critics have tended to write off Elvis' soundtrack songs as, at best, anodyne fare (and at worst the reason why Elvis stopped making rock 'n' roll and Blues), many fans enjoy the movie songs because they take them back to a certain time and place in their lives. Even the most thrown-together Elvis soundtrack usually contains one or two hidden gems.

RCA began to package orphaned soundtrack songs on budget albums from the late Sixties onwards. A TV-merchandised album, *Elvis in Hollywood*, came out in 1975 with the title tracks from most of Elvis' movies.

Soundtrack recording sessions and offcuts have long provided profitable pickings for bootleggers because of the relative ease of obtaining outtakes and alternates from sources other than RCA. In 1980, bootleggers showed a sense of humor with the release of a 37-song collection of Elvis' worst soundtrack songs, titled *Elvis' Greatest Shit*.

In the Nineties, BMG reissued almost all of Elvis' soundtrack material on the *Double Features* series. *Command Performances: The Essential 60's Masters II*, a 1995 2-disc release, provided a movie-oriented counterweight to the first volume of the Sixties anthology series *From Nashville To Memphis: The Essential 60's Masters*. In the mid-2000s, BMG released soundtrack-themed collections *Elvis Movies* and *Elvis at the Movies*.

Since 1999, Collectors' label FTD has been working its way through a program of soundtrack re-releases, featuring remixed tracks and a plethora of alternate takes. The specialist label has also released soundtrack anthologies *Out in Hollywood* and *Silver Screen Stereo*.

ROY C. BENNETT: "It has always been a disappointment to me as a songwriter that some fans regarded his movie songs as mediocre or just plain bad. . . . These songs were written for specific spots in the movies and the topics were therefore limited to particular situations and locales."

ERNST JORGENSEN: "There are good songs on almost every soundtrack album but there are also bad songs on most of the soundtrack albums as well. The strongest Sixties soundtrack is Blue Hawaii, there's nothing that even comes close."

"South Of The Border"

Elvis threw in a couple of lines from this 1939 Gene Autry song as he was recording "You'll Be Gone" in the studio in March 1962. The bootleggers got it on *There's Always Me* and *Unsurpassed Masters Box 2*.

South Carolina

- Charleston

Elvis and his band played two shows at the County Hall on March 18, 1956, immediately after appearing on CBS's "Stage Show." After he headlined at College Park on June 28, 1956, Elvis playfully nibbled at a female reporter's hand, an act that became the headline item in press coverage of the show.

- Columbia

The Township Auditorium hosted Elvis on March 19, 1956. He next played town on February 18, 1977, when he was at the Carolina Coliseum.

- Spartanburg

Elvis squeezed in four shows at the Carolina Theater on February 9, 1956.

South Dakota

- Rapid City

Elvis was the first act ever to play the Rushmore Plaza Civic Center on one of his last ever tours. Portions of his June 21, 1977 show appeared in CBS TV concert documentary *Elvis in Concert*.

- Sioux Falls

Elvis did a show at the Arena on October 18, 1976. He played the venue again on June 22, 1977.

Southern Nights

A 2006 FTD live release of Elvis on tour from April to June 1975.

TRACK LISTING:
1.   That's All Right

2. It's Now Or Never
3. Help Me
4. Steamroller Blues
5. Heartbreak Hotel
6. Release Me
7. Polk Salad Annie
8. I'll Remember You
9. Little Darlin'
10. Bridge Over Troubled Water
11. Tryin' To Get To You
12. You Gave Me A Mountain
13. Help Me Make It Through The Night
14. Fairytale
15. Jambalaya
16. Big Boss Man
17. It's Midnight
18. Promised Land
19. Trouble
20. T-R-O-U-B-L-E
21. Hawaiian Wedding Song
22. Blue Suede Shoes
23. For The Good Times
24. I Can't Stop Loving You
25. I'm Leavin'

"SPANISH EYES"

Elvis recorded this 1965 Freddy Quinn release (written originally as an instrumental piece by Bert Kaempfert, before Charles Singleton and Eddie Snyder added words; Al Martino took it to #15 on the Hot 100 in 1966) at Stax on December 16, 1973, for release on the *Good Times* album. Home recordings of the song made earlier that year by Sam Thompson have appeared on bootlegs such as *Elvis, Live & Unplugged* and on FTD release *Made In Memphis*.

Alternative takes from the Stax session have appeared on *Our Memories of Elvis* and later compilations such as *Essential Elvis, Vol. 5*. The song also featured on the 2000 reissue of the *Promised Land* LP.

Elvis regularly performed the song live in 1974: it's to be found on FTD albums and *It's Midnight* and *I Found My Thrill*, in which he duets with Sherill Nielsen.

SPECIAL DELIVERY FROM ELVIS PRESLEY

A 1979 bootleg release of Elvis during rehearsals for his Winter 1972 engagement at the Las Vegas Hilton.

TRACK LISTING:
1. Love Me Tender
2. Love Me Tender
3. In My Dreams
4. Spring Fever
5. Portrait Of My Love
6. Hawaiian Wedding Song
7. King Creole
8. Faded Love
9. Wild In The Country
10. Can't Help Falling In Love
11. When The Snow Is On The Roses
12. Trouble / Guitar Man / Little Egypt
13. Tomorrow Never Comes
14. Separate Ways
15. Next Step Is Love
16. That's All Right
17. Words
18. Rags To Riches
19. The Sound Of Your Cry
20. (Let's Have A) Party

There as also an Australian EP released with this same name.

SPECTOR, PHIL
(B. 1940)

Bronx-born Spector is one of very few non-performing music industry figures to have achieved international public renown. His carefully-constructed Wall of Sound productions—which Spector himself defined as "Wagnerian"—ushered in a new age of musical possibility in the Sixties as he built up layered constructions unlike anything that had been attempted previously in the pop world.

Spector began his music career in the late Fifties with one-hit wonder group the Teddy Bears, helping to write their single big hit, "To Know Him Is To Love Him." After this, Spector became apprenticed to songwriters Leiber & Stoller. He helped to keep the wolf from the door by, among other things, producing demos for Elvis. Spector then set up on his own, working out his hallmarked sound with girl group the Ronettes, and then developing it with the Righteous Brothers among others.

Spector later worked with the Beatles, as a group, and singly with John Lennon and George Harrison.

Spector has a credit on Righteous Brothers' hit "You've Lost That Lovin' Feelin'," which Elvis sang live in the Seventies.

In the 2000s, he returned to the public eye when he was accused of murder.

SPEEDING TICKETS

See POLICE

"SPEEDWAY"

Elvis recorded the opening track for the film of the same name soon after the band laid down their instrumentals on June 20, 1967 at MGM Studios. The song was written by Mel Glazer and Stephen Schlacks.

After release on the soundtrack LP, "Speedway" was double-featured with *Easy Come, Easy Go* in the Nineties, and anthologized on *Command Performances* and *Elvis Movies*.

SPEEDWAY (LP)

The soundtrack album was released in May 1968. As well as six songs from the movie, the LP featured two tracks that had wound up on the cutting room floor, plus a further three "bonus" songs. It barely made a dent on the charts, running out of oomph at #82 before slipping back into oblivion after 13 weeks.

TRACK LISTING:
1. Speedway
2. There Ain't Nothing Like A Song
3. Your Time Hasn't Come Yet, Baby
4. Who Are You?
5. He's Your Uncle Not Your Dad
6. Let Yourself Go
7. Your Groovy Self
8. Five Sleepy Heads
9. Western Union
10. Mine
11. Goin' Home
12. Suppose

These tracks were re-issued in 1993 on a *Double Features* album with *Easy Come, Easy Go* (with the exception of "Mine," "Western Union" and "Goin' Home").

SPEEDWAY

Elvis began pre-production on this movie on June

19, 1967, six weeks after he married Priscilla, and started work by going into MGM's studios to put the songs down. By this time, Elvis had whittled down the time it took to churn out a movie to a couple of months: principal photography was complete by August 18.

This particular Elvis-as-driver tale was initially offered to Sonny and Cher. Petula Clark turned down the role taken by Nancy Sinatra, the second time she declined an Elvis movie. Director Norman Taurog, who was almost blind by this time, found a role for one of his granddaughters, Victoria Paige Meyerink.

Discarded titles included long-time favorite *Pot Luck*, as well as *Guitar City* and *So I'll Go Quietly*.

Externals were shot at the Low's Motor Speedway in Concord, North Carolina, and at the Riverside International Raceway in California. Elvis' participation was not required, but many leading race drivers of the day made cameos, and the film provided plenty of work for Hollywood's finest stunt drivers.

"Western Union," "Five Sleepy Heads" and "Suppose," all cut from the movie, magically reappeared in versions aired in Asia. Nancy Sinatra got to sing "Your Groovy Self" solo—a first for another artist in an Elvis movie—as well as her duet with Elvis.

The film premiered in Charlotte, North Carolina, in June 1968, and motored into profit with $3 million in takings, though it did not rise any higher than #40 on *Variety*'s annual Box Office Survey.

Speedway was actually released after the next movie that Elvis shot, *Stay Away, Joe*.

CREDITS:
MGM, Color.
Length: 94 minutes
Release date: June 12, 1968

TAGLINES:
Smooth, fast and in high gear!

Directed by: Norman Taurog
Produced by: Douglas Laurence
Written by: Phillip Shuken
Music by: Jeff Alexander
Cinematography by: Joseph Ruttenberg
Film Editing by: Richard Farrell
Art Direction by: Leroy Coleman, George W. Davis
Set Decoration by: Henry Grace, Don Greenwood Jr.

CAST:

Elvis Presley	Steve Grayson
Nancy Sinatra	Susan Jacks
Bill Bixby	Kenny Donford
Gale Gordon	R.W. Hepworth
William Schallert	Abel Esterlake
Victoria Paige Meyerink	Ellie Esterlake
Ross Hagen	Paul Dado
Carl Ballantine	Birdie Kebner
Poncie Ponce	Juan Medala
Harry Hickox	The Cook
Christopher West	Billie Jo
Beverly Powers	Mary Ann (Miss Beverly Hills)
Richard Petty	Himself
Buddy Baker	Himself
Cale Yarborough	Himself
Dick Hutcherson	Himself
Tiny Lund	Himself
G.C. Spencer	Himself
Roy Mayne	Himself
Harper Carter	Ted Simmons
Bob Harris	Lloyd Meadows
Michele Newman	Debbie
Courtney Brown	Carrie
Dana Brown	Billie
Patti Jean Keith	Annie
Carl Reindel	Mike
Gari Hardy	Dumb blonde
Charlotte Stewart	Lori

rather than paying his client's taxes.

The solution they come up with is to get a business management company to send them IRS tax expert Susan Jacks (played by Nancy Sinatra) to tag along and make sure that the government gets every penny to which it is entitled.

Steve and Susan start off badly but they arrive at a working arrangement through a series of songs and dances. Their entente breaks down when new business manager R. W. Hepworth (played by Gale Gordon) decides to limit Steve to a $100 living allowance; Kenny gets only half that.

Steve tries and fails to charm Susan into making the allowance more reasonable with a bouquet of roses, which she swiftly uses to put out a stovetop fire. Bad news follows: the items they

LEFT: Elvis as Steve Grayson in *Speedway*.

BELOW: With Nancy Sinatra and Bill Bixby.

Sandy Reed	Race announcer
Ralph Adano	Dado's crew
Dee Carroll	Secretary
Arlene Charles	1st Guitarist's girlfriend
George Cisar	Portly bald man
Sharon Garrett	Go-Go dancer
Karen Hamilton	Willa
Barbro Hedströ^m	2nd Waitress
Morgan Hill	2nd Assistant
Charlie Hodge	Guitarist
Robert James	Dado's crew
Marilyn Jones	3rd Guitarist's girlfriend
William Keene	Taxpayer
S. John Launer	Mayor Fiergol
Cassandra Lawton	2nd Guitarist's girlfriend
Gary Littlejohn	Dado's crew
Tom McCauley	Dado's crew
John McDonnell	Lori's bridegroom
Jamie Michaels	5th Waitress
Sally Mills	1st Waitress
Burt Mustin	Coffee shop janitor
Kathy Nelson	4th Waitress
Ward Ramsey	Dado's crew
Hal Riddle	1st Assistant
Rita Rogers	Bit part
Dianne Stanley	3rd Waitress
Robert Stevenson	Mr. Tillman
Claude Stroud	Drunk
Sheryl Ullman	6th Waitress

ADDITIONAL CREW:

Sydney Guilaroff	hair stylist
William Tuttle	makeup artist
Rex Bailey	unit production manager
Lindsley Parsons Jr.	assistant production manager
Dale Hutchinson	assistant director
Franklin Milton	recording supervisor
Carroll L. Shepphird	special effects
Bud Ekins	stunts
Max Balchowsky	stunts
Carol Daniels	stunts
Bob Herron	stunts
Carey Loftin	stunts
Michael A. Hoey	dialogue coach
Bill Shaw	gaffer

Plot:

Elvis is Steve Grayson, a champion stock-car driver who races a Dodge Charger. Steve and his manager / best friend Kenny Donford (played by Bill Bixby) lead a life of ease, winning races, living high on the hog, and distributing some of their winnings to deserving causes; they give one car to a widower with four children.

Steve's world is thrown into chaos when the IRS demands $145,000 in back taxes, a figure that is as unpalatable as it is unpayable since Kenny has been splurging money to the horses

have given away to people in need are also set to be repossessed. Worse still, Kenny gambles away all of the rest of their money.

Steve's charms finally win Susan over. She persuades her boss to let him keep his car, which he was going to have to sell, so now he can race his way out of trouble.

There are still some obstacles to surmount before the happy ending is achieved. Steve's performance in the "Charlotte 600" is imperiled by a stowaway mechanic and then a terrible crash, but he still manages to come in third, winning enough prize money to keep the IRS off his back and win the girl.

Songs: "Speedway," "Let Yourself Go," "Your Time Hasn't Come Yet Baby," "He's Your Uncle Not Your Dad", "Who Are You," "There Ain't Nothing Like A Song"

SPEER, BEN AND BROCK

These two members of the singing Speer Family, a Southern gospel group going strong since the Twenties, were called in with Gordon Stoker to provide a fuller vocal sound for Elvis on his first RCA recordings sessions. They were relieved of their duties when Stoker brought along the rest of the Jordanaires to sing, giving Elvis the full four-part harmonies he wanted.

Ben and Brock were both later inducted into the Gospel Music Hall of Fame, as was the entire family Group in 1998.

SPELLING, AARON
(1923—2006)

The man who came to be known as the world's most prolific TV producer was an unknown writer in 1958 when he traveled with his wife, actress Carolyn Jones, to New Orleans where she and Elvis were doing location work on *King Creole*.

Among Spelling's many huge hit series, with producing partner Leonard Goldberg, are "The Mod Squad," "The Love Boat," "Melrose Place," "Fantasy Island," "Charlie's Angels," "Starsky and Hutch" and "Dynasty."

SPIN-IN . . . SPINOUT

A bootleg on The Real McCoy label of outtakes and alternates from movie soundtrack recording sessions.

TRACK LISTING:
1. Spinout (Take 2)
2. Adam And Evil (Takes 1, 2)
3. Smorgasbord (Take 1)
4. Adam And Evil (Take 6)
5. Am I Ready (Takes 3, 4)
6. Adam And Evil (Take 9)
7. Never Say Yes (Takes 1, 2)
8. Adam And Evil (Take 10)
9. All That I Am (Takes 1, 2)
10. Adam And Evil (Take 11)
11. Stop, Look And Listen (Takes 1, 2, 3)
12. Adam And Evil (Take 12)
13. Beach Shack (Takes 1, 2, 3)
14. Adam And Evil (Take 13)
15. Am I Ready (Takes 5, 6)
16. Adam And Evil (Take 14)
17. Smorgasbord (Take 4)
18. Adam And Evil (Take 15)
19. All That I Am (Take 6)
20. Adam And Evil (Takes 17, 18)
21. Adam And Evil (Take 16)

"SPINOUT"

Elvis recorded the Sid Wayne, Ben Weisman and Dee Fuller track on February 17, 1966 at Radio Recorders in Hollywood. Released in mid-September, a month before the movie, with "All That I Am" on the B-side, the single spent seven weeks on the Hot 100 and reached a high of #40.

It has since appeared on *Elvis in Hollywood*, the *Double Features* re-release for the movie, *Command Performances* and *Elvis Movies*. An alternate take is available on the FTD reissue of the soundtrack album, while another features on FTD soundtrack anthology *Out In Hollywood*.

SPINOUT (LP)

Released in October 1966 to coincide with the movie, this soundtrack album included three non-soundtrack bonus songs from Elvis' exuberant Nashville recording session with new producer Felton Jarvis. The album outsold Elvis' recent soundtrack releases, but nevertheless failed to climb any higher than #18 on the charts during its 32-week stay.

TRACK LISTING:
1. Stop, Look And Listen
2. Adam And Evil

3. All That I Am
4. Never Say Yes
5. Am I Ready
6. Beach Shack
7. Spinout
8. Smorgasboard
9. I'll Be Back
10. Tomorrow Is A Long Time
11. Down In The Alley
12. I'll Remember You

The *Double Features* version, released in 1994, was paired with *Double Trouble*.

TRACK LISTING:
1. Stop, Look And Listen
2. Adam And Evil
3. All That I Am
4. Never Say Yes
5. Am I Ready
6. Beach Shack
7. Spinout
8. Smorgasbord
9. I'll Be Back
10. Double Trouble
11. Baby If You'll Give Me All Your Love
12. Could I Fall In Love
13. Long Legged Girl (With The Short Dress On)
14. City By Night
15. Old MacDonald
16. I Love Only One Girl
17. There's So Much World To See
18. It Won't Be Long

FTD released a remixed version of the original soundtrack LP with additional alternates and outtakes in 2004.

SPINOUT

This movie went through a number of working titles, including *Raceway, Never Say No, Never Say Yes, Jim Dandy, After Midnight, Always at Midnight, Never at Midnight* and even *Clambake* (which was later recycled for another film) before acquiring its final moniker. In its earliest drafts the Elvis character wasn't even a racecar driver, until MGM weighed in, convinced that Elvis movies worked best if they featured cars. So as not to confuse international fans with racing terminology, the movie wound up being titled *California Holiday* for the UK market.

Elvis began work on the movie on February 11, 1966. During shooting, some Elvis fans managed to break through the security cordon at a racetrack and were almost run over during high-speed filming.

All shooting was either at the MGM lot or nearby locations, including Dodger Stadium and the Ascot Motor Car Racing Ground. Elvis was free to go home after principal photography finished on April 8.

MGM's publicity department went overboard for *Spinout*, producing and distributing thousands of press kits to mark Elvis' 10th anniversary in the movie biz. Theaters also ran a tie-in essay writing contest on "The Perfect American Male" (see plot description below).

The casting directors raided newly-defunct TV family drama "The Donna Reed Show" for three of *Spinout*'s main characters: Shelley Fabares, Carl Betz and Jimmy Hawkins.

On release in November 1966 (after a mid-October preview showing in Memphis), *Spinout* went on to become the 57th highest grossing feature of the year.

CREDITS:
MGM, Color.
Length: 90 minutes
Release date: November 23, 1966

TAGLINES:
Elvis sings nine great new toe-tapping tunes!
It's Elvis with his foot on the gas and no brakes on the fun!!!
. . . singing! . . . chasing! . . . racing! . . . romancing! . . . swinging!
Directed by: Norman Taurog
Produced by: Joe Pasternak (producer), Hank Moonjean (associate producer)
Written by: Theodore J. Flicker and George Kirgo
Music by: George Stoll
Cinematography by: Daniel L. Fapp
Film Editing by: Rita Roland
Art Direction by: Edward Carfagno, George W. Davis
Set Decoration by: Henry Grace, Hugh Hunt

CAST:

Elvis Presley	Mike McCoy
Shelley Fabares	Cynthia Foxhugh
Diane McBain	Diana St. Clair
Dodie Marshall	Susan
Deborah Walley	Les
Jack Mullaney	Curly
Will Hutchins	Lt. Tracy Richards
Warren Berlinger	Philip Short
Jimmy Hawkins	Larry
Carl Betz	Howard Foxhugh
Cecil Kellaway	Bernard Ranley
Una Merkel	Violet Ranley
Frederick Worlock	Blodgett
Dave Barry	Harry
Inge Jaklyn	Brunette beauty
Thordis Brandt	Bit part
Victoria Carroll	Award-winning beauty
Arlene Charles	Bit part
Nancy Czar	Platinum beauty
Phyllis Davis	Bit part
Judy Durell	Girl
Joe Esposito	Shorty's pit crew
Gay Gordon	Bit part
Josh Harding	Bit part
Inga Jacklin	Brunette beauty
Jay Jasin	Race announcer
Jeanmarie	Bit part
Fredda Lee	Bit part
Deanna Lund	Redhead beauty
James McHale	Shorty Bloomquist
Joanne Medley	Blond beauty
Christopher Riordan	Party guest
Sheryl Ullman	Bit part
Red West	Shorty's pit crew
Rita Wilson	Bit part
Virginia Wood	Blond beauty #2

ADDITIONAL CREW:

Sydney Guilaroff	hair stylist
William Tuttle	makeup artist
Al Shenberg	unit production manager
Claude Binyon Jr.	assistant director
Franklin Milton	recording supervisor
J. McMillan Johnson	special visual effects
Carroll L. Shepphird	special visual effects
Jerry Brutsche	stunt driver
Bob Harris	stunt driver
Carey Loftin	stunts
Jack Baker	musical number staging
Michael Hoey	dialogue supervisor
Colonel Tom Parker	technical advisor
Robert Van Eps	music associate
Mike Deasy	musician
James V. King	camera operator

Plot:

Elvis is back in the driver's seat as he plays Mike McCoy, a singer and part-time race driver who is confronted with three lovely ladies—a writer, a drummer and a rich daddy's girl—all of whom are desperate to marry him, while he manfully strives to preserve his status as a confirmed bachelor.

Mike's 427 Cobra is run off the road in an impromptu race with a mystery young woman, who roars off leaving him in a ditch. He raises money to get the car repaired for an upcoming race in Santa Fe by performing at a local club

Elvis as Mike McCoy in *Spinout*, 1966.

with his band. Afterwards, Mike turns down an offer to play a gig for a wealthy man's daughter because the band is already committed to a tour and he is a man of principle.

When Elvis and his band, including pretty female drummer Les (played by Deborah Walley) camp out for the night, Mike intercepts a mystery blonde who has been following him. It's writer Diana St. Clair (played by Diane McBain), who fesses up that she's doing research for a novel, *The Perfect American Male*. If she picks him, she promises she'll marry him. When Les overhears this, she lets slip that she too is secretly in love with Mike.

The band finds out that their tour has been cancelled because of Mike's refusal to sing for the rich man's daughter. However, the tour will be back on if they take the whopping fee on offer and do the deed. This turns out to be even less of a hardship for Mike when he finds out that the man involved is millionaire race car designer Howard Foxhugh (played by Carl Betz).

Imagine everybody's surprise when they discover that the mystery lady who ran Mike off the road at the start of the film and the daughter whose party they are playing is one and the same, Cynthia Foxhugh (Shelley Fabares). After singing a song, Mike gives her a piece of his mind. She responds by telling him that she wants to marry him, much to the chagrin of her father's secretary Philip Short (played by Warren Berlinger), who is predictably in love with her.

Mike relinquishes a chance to race Foxhugh's fancy car after the millionaire disparages his qualities as a future son-in-law. Foxhugh then gets local police officer Tracy Richard (played by Will Hutchins) to chase Mike and his band members off their campsite. They simply move into the next-door house, after persuading the residents to go off on a second honeymoon.

A party ensues as Mike's band members try to distract his thoughts of marriage by filling the house with pretty girls. The entire cast of the movie converges on the party. Writer Diane shifts her marriage designs to Foxhugh senior. Drummer Les spots her chance and finally dances with Mike, only to field a declaration of love by police officer Tracy Richard.

Mike barely has time to hotfoot it over to the race. Despite his car breaking down en route, he races anyway in a disqualified racer's ride. After winning the race and the fabulous prize money put up by Foxhugh, Mike personally marries off all of the girls who were after him to their respective beaus and ends the movie singing his single and happy heart out.

Songs: "Spinout," "Stop Look And Listen," "Adam And Evil,"" All That I Am," Never Say Yes," "Am I Ready," "Beach Shack", "Smorgasbord," "I'll Be Back "

SPIRITUALITY

Elvis' upbringing was rooted in religion and spirituality. As a boy, his family's social world revolved around the First Assembly of God church. As a grown man, he never stopped seeking a spiritual purpose and meaning in his extraordinary life.

Along the way, Elvis suffered his share of metaphysical crises. In 1958, he told the pastor at the First Assembly of God church in Memphis that he was miserable despite his fame and fortune, because the way he was living his life went completely against the morality of his religious upbringing. Soon after his mother's death that year, he toyed with the idea of following his friend Jimmie Rodgers Snow and forsaking rock 'n' roll for the cloth. The thing that held him back was the responsibility he felt towards the many family and friends whose livelihood depended on his continuing career.

In the mid-Sixties, as his hopes of being taken seriously as a dramatic actor receded and new British groups were usurping his place at the top of the charts, Elvis turned inwards and embarked on a concerted spiritual quest. When new hairdresser Larry Geller came round to give him a trim in April 1964, Elvis bared his soul and found a fellow-seeker of meaning in life. For a while, Elvis jokingly referred to Geller as his "guru"—a term wielded more as an insult by the rest of Elvis' entourage—and reputedly began viewing himself as a "divine messenger." For the next few years, Elvis would tell anyone who cared to listen that this spiritual quest was the most important thing in his life.

Soon after they met, Larry Geller gave Elvis a book, *The Impersonal Life*, that had a huge impact on him. The central tenet of the book is the recommendation to try and move towards the "Christ Consciousness" in the self (the "I am") by quieting the mind and listening and learning with the heart. Elvis gave away many dozens of copies of this book, often with his own handwritten annotations scrawled in the margins. In one book, *Through the Eyes of the Masters: Meditations and Portraits*, Elvis noted down, "God loves you but he loves you best when you sing."

During this period, Elvis embarked on a study of world religions, including Buddhism and Judaism, and subscribed to a belief in theosophy: that every religion contains parts of the divine truth, and that there is a universal brotherhood between all men. It helped that he saw a resemblance to his mother in pictures of Russian-born Madame Helena Blavatsky, who founded the theosophical society in New York in 1875. He also pursued his interest in numerology, which forms an integral part of theosophy.

One day in March 1965, Elvis stopped his motorhome in the desert in awe at a cloud formation in which he could see the face of Joseph Stalin, which then mutated into the face of Jesus. Before they arrived in California, the vehicle caught fire. The spiritual revelation Elvis had in the desert en route from Memphis to Los Angeles in early 1965 was, according to Larry Geller, "one of the most significant experiences of his personal life," one that stayed with Elvis for many years as his first personal experience of the divine. Around this time, Elvis experimented with psychedelics such as LSD and marijuana, believed by some to be a path to altered consciousness.

That same month Elvis found an organization that he would be part of for the rest of his life: the Self-Realization Fellowship, which espouses beliefs drawn from the millennial traditions of yoga and meditation in India. The central tenet of these teachings, once again, is that God resides in us all.

Elvis' increasing fascination with metaphysical questions was reflected in the Easter 1965 release of two gospel recordings originally recorded five years earlier. He may have taken it as a sign from above that this new single outsold any single he had released in years. The next album that Elvis made was the Grammy-winning gospel disc *How Great Thou Art*.

Elvis' interest in meditation, which he developed through his visits to the Self-Realization Fellowship, inspired the Meditation Garden at Graceland, which he had installed close to the swimming pool in late 1965. Meditation was, for Elvis, a way of restoring calm and, more importantly, stilling the noise in order to hear the tiny voice of reason he believed we all have inside, but which is usually drowned out by the bustle of our busy minds.

According to Geller, not just the fun-loving entourage members but Colonel Parker felt threatened by Elvis' "religious kick." Not long after Elvis began mentioning that he might want to give it all up and take time off, the Colonel seized his chance to oust Geller from Elvis' inner circle. In quick succession, Elvis burned his cache of spiritual books, and finally married long-term girlfriend Priscilla. The symbolic bonfire of his spiritual readings did little to extinguish his interest. Throughout the rest of his life, he continued to acquire (and continued to give away to people he cared about) copies of the books he found to be enlightening and important. These books included Ram Dass's *Be Here Now*, and Kahlil Gibran's *The Prophet*, which he had read and appreciated since the mid-Fifties, when then girlfriend June Juanico first gave him a copy; Elvis could and did recite whole passages of these books from memory.

Elvis kept up his readings in the Seventies, after his divorce from Priscilla. Despite their skepticism, he made a point of including those around him—members of his entourage and his step-brothers—in the habit of reading and inquiring about life's big issues.

In the Seventies, karate became an important conduit for Elvis' spirituality. One of the reasons why Elvis was so keen to produce a karate film was to convey values that he considered to be intrinsic to karate and universal to mankind, in a movie where good triumphs over evil.

Elvis suffered a moment of deep spiritual crisis after his closing Las Vegas show in December 1976. Backstage, in tears, he confessed to TV evangelist Rex Humbard that his life lacked meaning. Around about this time, Elvis increasingly took refuge in prayer, seeking the God within.

Since his death, Elvis has become a spiritual touchstone for many. Authors have compared his life to Jesus, viewed him as a sacrificial victim to the modern media, painted him as a lay leader of men and morals, analyzed his position as the figurehead of a nascent religion, and written self-help books based on lessons drawn from his life and beliefs.

See also METAPHYSICS, MYSTICISM, NUMBERS AND NUMEROLOGY, and RELIGION.

ELVIS SAID TO LARRY GELLER: "All I want is to know the truth, to know and experience God. I'm a searcher, that's what I'm all about."

ELVIS SAID TO LARRY GELLER: "I've always felt an unseen hand on my shoulder, guiding my life. There had to be a reason why I was plucked out of millions and millions of lives to be Elvis."

Priscilla: "The spiritual side of Elvis was a dominant part of his nature."

DAVE MARSH: "Unless you understand that Elvis Presley was more than anything a spiritual leader of our generation, there's really no way to assess his importance, much less the meaning of his music."

BARBARA LEIGH: "Elvis' spiritualism is well known by anyone who ever spent any time with him. You couldn't help but see that in him. He was an old soul."

TONY BROWN: "I think he was on a different plane than we were. I think he was . . . a higher plane."

T. G. SHEPPARD: "I think Elvis often thought he was a prophet... Everything in his life was connected to spirituality, numerology, colors."

MYRNA SMITH: "Elvis loved to talk to you and delve into your spirituality."

LARRY GELLER: "In his heart Elvis desperately wanted to live up to his ideal of a moral person."

SRI DAYA MATA: "Here was someone who had everything the world could offer . . . it didn't satisfy him. There was still an emptiness, and the only way to fill it was to turn within."

MARTY LACKER: "Elvis felt he was put on earth for a specific purpose. He didn't know what the purpose was, unless he had a lot of pills in him."

LAMAR FIKE: "Elvis was only human even if many want to sanctify him to a higher level. On an emotional level he was no different to you or I... He had feelings, strong feelings, and he was searching for what eludes so many of us, inner fulfillment and inner peace."

DAVID S. WALL: "In death, he has acquired spiritual significance which displays all the signs of turning into a religion."

Books:
Elvis Presley Speaks, by Hans Holzer, New English Library, 1980.
Herrre's Elvis: Broadcasting from the Stars, by Margoz Blua, Blua Creations, 1981.
Elvis Aaron Presley: His Growth and Development as a Soul Spirit Within the Universe, by Paula Farmer, Prime Books, 1996.

SPORTS

Elvis regularly played softball and touch football as a kid, but he wasn't one of the boys that everybody wanted on their team. Elvis loved playing football through high school and beyond. He attended spring practice in his later High School years, and though he was talented, he wasn't big enough to make the first team. He ended up quitting because he had to get a job (or because the Coach disapproved of how long he wore his hair, depending on story versions). Pal Paul Dougher, from his teen days, believes that had Elvis put his mind to it, he could have become a good football player, though Elvis himself admitted that he was too slight to make it against the beefier players. He continued to play touch football until well into his thirties, at one stage organizing his own team in Los Angeles and Memphis.

After the Presley family moved to Memphis, Elvis and the kids he knew at Lauderdale Courts played a lot of corkball—a homespun version of baseball, using a broom handle and a piece of cork with tape around it.

In an early press interview, Elvis stated that he also liked waterskiing and boxing.

He ran off some of his Christmas excess in 1956 by playing touch football with pals including Red West in Memphis. Badminton was briefly popular with Elvis and his entourage on the expansive lawns around Graceland.

Another sport that Elvis enjoyed was roller-skating. He frequently hired out the Rainbow Rollerdrome in Memphis, including after Christmas 1957; he went to the venue every night for a week before he had to leave for his Army service in early 1958; he was back again in 1960, after his return from Germany, happy to clown around on skates with his pals.

While in Germany, Elvis and his pals regularly held touch football games on Sundays. During his German stay, he started learning karate, a discipline that he studied assiduously up to a few years before he died.

On July 3, 1960, Elvis went boating with pals on McKellar Lake, Riverside Park, Memphis—the day that his father married Dee Stanley.

Elvis spent two weeks learning how to ride a horse in August 1960, as he prepared for his role in cowboy movie *Flaming Star*. He later became a keen rider. Before the decade was out, he had bought and sold dozens of horses and his very own ranch.

According to Red West, Elvis seldom if ever used the swimming pools at his various homes.

Elvis had a basketball court at his home in Palm Springs, and often organized night-time games against local guys.

In the mid-Seventies, encouraged by Dr. Nick, Elvis took up racquetball, sometimes playing several nights (early mornings) a week.

SPRECKELS, JUDY
(B. 1932)

The press had a field day with the friendship between Elvis and sugar family heiress Judy Spreckels that bloomed after he went to Hollywood in early 1956. For the next year or two, she was a regular part of his entourage; she remained in touch with him until his death.

Spreckels went to see him perform at his first, not wholly successful Las Vegas booking in April 1956.

The four blackstar sapphire ring that Ms. Spreckels gave Elvis was recycled many years later into the engagement ring that Elvis presented to Priscilla. Spreckels was part of the crowd that waved Elvis off to the Army two years later, not long after traveling to Graceland to help console him after Gladys's untimely death.

Elvis afforded her a namecheck on stage in Las Vegas in 1974.

In later years, Spreckels made a name as a writer and publisher, and as a horse breeder.

JUDY SPRECKELS: "We loved each other . . . But it was just a really terrific friendship."

"SPRING FEVER"

Elvis lavished a couple of dozen takes on this laid-back Bill Giant / Bernie Baum / Florence Kaye tune for *Girl Happy* at Radio Recorders on June 11, 1964, in a duet with co-star Shelley Fabares.

After appearing on the soundtrack album, the track was later reissued in the *Double Feature*

Elvis with Judy Spreckels in Las Vegas, 1956.

series with *Harum Scarum*. Multiple alternate takes of the song came out on the FTD *Girl Happy* release, after being available only on bootleg.

SPRING TOURS '77

An FTD release from 2002 showcasing Elvis during some of his final performances.

TRACK LISTING:
1. That's All Right (Mama)
2. Are You Lonesome Tonight?
3. Blue Christmas
4. Tryin' To Get To You
5. Lawdy, Miss Clawdy
6. Fever
7. Heartbreak Hotel
8. If You Love Me (Let Me Know)
9. It's Now Or Never
10. Little Sister
11. (Let Me Be Your) Teddy Bear / Don't Be Cruel
12. Help Me
13. Blue Suede Shoes
14. Hound Dog
15. Jailhouse Rock
16. Polk Salad Annie
17. Bridge Over Troubled Water
18. Big Boss Man
19. Fairytale
20. Mystery Train / Tiger Man
21. Unchained Melody
22. Little Darlin'
23. My Way

SPRINGFIELD, DUSTY
(B. MARY O'BRIEN, 1939-1999)

Springfield's Dusty in Memphis LP, recorded at American Studio in Memphis, came out on the very same day that Elvis first walked through the door of American Studio to begin his recording session. Springfield's LP, featuring "Son Of A Preacher Man," confirmed her Sixties status as a top blue-eyed soul singer, despite originally hailing from leafy Hampstead in London, England.

Springfield began her career with a vocal trio before fronting family act The Springfields in the early Sixties. She pursued a solo career after traveling to Nashville to record, gaining a following with early hit "I Only Want To Be With You." She remained popular through to the early Seventies, and then had a resurgence in the late Eighties singing with the Pet Shop Boys.

Elvis later covered Springfield classic "You Don't Have To Say You Love Me," a song he often took on live.

SPRINGSTEEN, BRUCE
(B. 1949)

After playing a gig in Memphis in 1974, "the Boss"—incidentally, the inscription that Elvis had on a desktop nameholder at his Graceland press conference after returning from the Army in 1960—jumped the wall at Graceland to go and meet the King. His intention to visit Elvis that night was thwarted by the Graceland security guards, who were unimpressed with his spiel about what a big rock star he was.

Born in Freehold, New Jersey on September 23, 1949, it took singer/songwriter Springsteen ten years of playing small clubs before in 1975 he broke through to a national audience with his third album, *The Wild, the Innocent & the E Street Shuffle* and was hailed as the future of rock 'n' roll. Springsteen's biggest selling-album, *Born in the USA*, came in 1984, though he has remained a top recording artist and performer ever since.

In interviews, Springsteen has cited seeing Elvis' performance on the "Ed Sullivan Show" as his inspiration for becoming a musician. Springsteen sported an Elvis Fan Club badge on his guitar strap in the cover photo of 1975 album *Born To Run* (from a long-defunct NYC-based fan club called the King's Court).

During his long and politically-committed career spanning rock and folk, Springsteen has won Grammys and an Academy Award, and has the remarkable distinction of writing an anti-war protest song, "Born In The U.S.A.," that was adopted by his political opponents (Ronald Reagan) for their campaign. Springsteen has covered a number of Elvis songs during his career, including "Follow That Dream," "Mystery Train" and "Viva Las Vegas"; he has also penned his own Elvis tribute song, "Johnny Bye Bye."

BRUCE SPRINGSTEEN: "Anybody who sees Elvis Presley and doesn't want to be like Elvis Presley has got to have something wrong with him."

BRUCE SPRINGSTEEN: "There have been a lotta tough guys. There have been pretenders. And there have been contenders. But there is only one king . . . He wrote the book."

BRUCE SPRINGSTEEN: "It was like he came along and whispered some dream in everybody's ear, and somehow we all dreamed it."

STAGE ACT

The shy kid who dressed funny at school turned out to be an instant on-stage natural. He surprised his classmates and teachers on April 9, 1953 when he took part in the Humes annual minstrel show and won cascades of applause and approval—a vast improvement on his stage debut when, aged 10, he took to the stage at the Mississippi-Alabama Fair and Dairy Show, wearing glasses, and climbed up onto a chair to sing "Old Shep."

Elvis famously told reporters that his leg-jiggling, hip-shaking way of moving was simply an unpremeditated response to stage nerves. As a tyro performer, Elvis apparently believed that the incredible reaction he elicited from his audiences was because they were naturally enthusiastic people, rather than anything to do with what he was doing on stage.

In interviews that he gave after he had risen to national prominence, Elvis patiently explained that the way he moved was triggered by the infectious beat and the effect the music had on him, and was not an intended provocation of a sexual nature. Whatever its genesis, from his earliest shows the way he moved on stage drove his audi-

ence wild and provided a template for future rock performers. On stage, he looked like he was having the best time of anybody in the place. At crescendo points in a song, Elvis seemed unable to contain his raw energy, and like a wild animal he suddenly marauded towards the audience to mesmeric effect.

At his earliest shows, original band members Scotty Moore and Bill Black were very much part of the visual act. While Moore played the straight man of the trio, Bill Black mimicked Elvis' moves and clowned around with his bass. To make sure that they got an encore when they played on multi-performer bills, after leaving the stage Elvis would stick his head and shoulders out of the curtain and shake electrically (a trick mimicked to good effect by the ever-willing Black).

Almost as soon as Elvis was out of the blocks, it was clear that nobody could follow him. Several big name acts found to their detriment that the audience simply screamed for Elvis or melted away after he left the stage.

By the spring of 1955, Elvis was supremely confident in his abilities and was using his time on stage to crack jokes and flirt shamelessly with the prettier girls.

On tour in May 1955, RCA representatives who had come along to an Elvis show to check on the label's latest hot signing, Jimmie Rodgers Snow, went back to their boss talking only of Elvis, whose on-stage shenanigans that night included getting rid of his chewing gum by spitting it out into the audience.

Elvis developed a number of expedients for raising the audience's temperature to boiling point. Sometimes he started a show like a big floppy doll, until Scotty Moore wound him up like a clockwork toy and off he went. At other concerts he stood behind the mike without moving a muscle, that trademark sneer imprinted on his face, until the girls screamed so loud that he finally sprang into action, seemingly powered by their raucous energy. Martha Carson, who toured with Elvis that year, says that she taught Elvis his much-used move of plunging down onto one knee and pulling down the microphone stand at an angle.

Many recordings from early Elvis shows are practically obliterated by a wall of fan screeching so loud that Elvis' band members couldn't hear their own instruments. The only way they could keep time was by synchronizing with Elvis' movements. According to Scotty Moore, "We were probably the only band in the world that were literally directed by an ass." For drummer D.J. Fontana, his previous experience playing drums for strip shows was excellent training.

Elvis soon felt sufficiently comfortable on stage to joke around with the crowd and tell off-color jokes, though after he became involved, Colonel Tom Parker expunged this behavior from his act. Not only did the Colonel consider it unprofessional, it sometimes riled other acts on the bill such as the Duke of Paducah, who made his living from comedy. In the Colonel's view, Elvis should "go on the stage as a singer, stay on the stage as a singer, and come off like a singer." The Colonel's remonstrations and efforts by manager Bob Neal were not enough to prevent a school principal from canceling an Elvis show half an hour in, after he told a risqué joke that involved "milking."

Elvismania wasn't just a danger to the morality of young people, Elvis' physical safety was sometimes threatened by rampaging female fans who would go to any lengths to get hold of him or, failing that, take home a shred of his clothing as a souvenir.

Immediately after Elvis signed to RCA records in late 1955, Colonel Parker was told by his assistant Tom Diskin that Elvis' performances were improving, but he could still pace the act better. External critics were less harsh. In January 1956, DJ Don Davis described Elvis as "six foot of spring

steel who really knows how to sell a song."

Friends and early entourage members have revealed that despite the adoring crowds, Elvis always felt insecure before taking the stage before a live audience. Even after two years of performing before delirious crowds, Elvis used to wonder, "Are they gonna like me, or are they gonna throw rocks at me?" Around this time, Elvis confided in an interviewer that he tried to dissipate the tension before a show by walking around, swallowing and clenching his fists.

Even after Elvis had signed to a major label, he continued to pepper his stage act with jokes and comic patter—perhaps one reason why his April 1956 shows before an older crowd in Las Vegas fell flat. A William Morris Agent told Colonel Parker that it would be best to drop the skits, though he was amazed at the unique reaction Elvis' singing provoked: "One has to see this to understand and appreciate what he does to an audience." Reviewing an Elvis concert at Winston-Salem, a local paper described the singer as "the remarkable young man with the long hair, the pearly teeth, the stylish slouch, the incredible conceit."

By 1956, partly out of showmanship, partly out of prudence, Elvis was escorted onstage by two armed guards. The danger came not just from the potentially rowdy female fans who made up the bulk of his audience, but from a growing outcry about the delinquency and vulgar behavior rock 'n' roll stood accused of promoting. In May 1956, a newspaper editor in LaCrosse, Wisconsin, contacted the head of the FBI to complain that Elvis' act consisted of "sexual self-gratification on stage." Far-right political groups threatened to stop Elvis in his tracks, and there were also plenty of boyfriends ready to sock Elvis for the mesmerizing effect he had had on their girlfriends.

Lighting at Elvis' early shows was exclusively color, with no white lights. As a rule, Presley did not perform an encore: it kept 'em wanting more, and more importantly it gave him a sporting chance of getting out of the venue without being mobbed or worse.

After an August 1956 show in Jacksonville, Florida—a town where an Elvis performance had triggered a riot a year earlier—Judge Marion Gooding warned the singer to tone down his act or face arrest. By this time, Elvis' TV appearances had turned him into a national lightning rod for moralistic opprobrium. Judge Gooding was not swayed by Elvis' assertion that his mother approved of everything he did on stage, and told him know that there was an arrest warrant waiting for him if he performed any of his trademark pelvic gyrations. Elvis faced similar police threats at other venues during the Fifties, most famously in Los Angeles in October 1957, when he was subject to a "no wiggle" ban.

Where logistics permitted, Elvis' handlers were instructed to whisk him out of harm's way via a trapdoor in the stage and rush him to a waiting vehicle—this was the escape route that Elvis took at the end of his return-of-the-prodigal-son concert in Tupelo in 1956.

The screaming and fan hysteria continued long after Elvis' film career took off and the Colonel scaled back his concert commitments. A paper in Detroit reviewed a concert in March 1957 with the words "the trouble with going to see Elvis Presley is that you're liable to get killed."

The Colonel's new strategy for his sole client after two years away in the Army was to reposition him as a mainstream box office draw. Apart from his appearance on the "Frank Sinatra Show"—which Peter Guralnick describes as "a modified Elvis, who suggests motion without precipitating it," Elvis only made two live performances up to until 1968, both for charity shows.

On stage in Vegas 1969.

Elvis' ground-breaking 1968 NBC TV Special only came about because the Colonel needed to find a way to revive Elvis' wilting career, after almost a decade of confining his appearances to before movie studio cameras. Fortunately, Elvis overruled the Colonel's wishes for a run-of-the-mill festive Christmas special and used the TV time to show the world that he was still a top performer, not just in major staged numbers but in what was arguably the first ever "live and unplugged" session, recreating the atmosphere of his early road shows. Success was by no means an inevitable outcome. At a late stage, Elvis almost pulled out from taping the informal segment of the show because of a bout of debilitating nerves.

Concert promoters quickly lined up to put Elvis back in front of his fans. The Colonel had no hesitation in signing Elvis up to a deal for a month-long residency at the brand new International Hotel in Las Vegas, for which Elvis put together a new band and worked out a new act with entourage member Charlie Hodge. Once again overcoming a very strong bout of nerves, Elvis quickly slipped into easy banter with the audience, ad libbing and veering off into territory described by the Colonel as "off color." Bill Browder (aka T. G. Sheppard), who was there, says: "He really was different when he came back to stage work. He was full of piss and vinegar. He had the eye of the tiger. Man, he went out there and just grabbed people by the neck... He was phenomenal."

For his second residency in Las Vegas, Elvis brought in new songs, new costumes—an array of once-piece jumpsuits allowing freer movement—and a new way of moving based on karate moves. Reviewing the concert for *Life* magazine, Albert Goldman noted that the show featured a number of static poses, which he describes not particularly flatteringly as "Elvis . . . the Discus Hurler, Elvis as Sagittarius, Elvis as the Dying Gaul."

By his third month-long tour of duty Elvis was back to full stage confidence, chatting and bantering with the audience, cracking jokes, and for the first time showering the audience with scarves, which he was soon ordering by the hundred. The handing out of the scarves became a ritual that required Elvis first to use them to mop his brow, then bless them with a kiss, and only then were they ready to be thrown out to the forest of clamoring arms in the audience. Elvis was also unfailingly generous in donating kisses to the prettier ladies in the audience.

Incredibly, the first time that Elvis actually heard his performance as he was giving it was in 1970, when new promotions company Management III hired onstage monitors—during every one of his shows until then Elvis had had to put up with notoriously unreliable in-house PA systems.

At least in the years immediately after his return to live performing, Elvis' stage shows were relatively impromptu events. Elvis, the band, the backup singers and the orchestra had rehearsed long enough and often enough to be able to sing whatever Elvis felt like singing. He wasn't afraid to halt a song and start again if he thought there was something wrong, often throwing in a self-deprecating comment. He would also sometimes challenge his band members by starting into a song that nobody expected. If the mood took him, he would change the running order, extend a song or mess around with the words . . . As guitarist James Burton said, "We had great eye contact on stage, and we watched him a lot. I never took my eyes off him because you never knew what was gonna happen next."

In 1971, orchestra leader Joe Guercio and Elvis developed a high-impact entrance, using an adaptation of *Also Sprach Zarathustra* by Richard Strauss—a tune widely known at the time for its use in Stanley Kubrick movie *2001: A Space Odyssey*—as he strode out onto a darkened stage.

Also in 1971, Elvis developed the dramatic sweeping gesture with his arms wide, sporting his cape of choice, at the end of his show. He also used this move to great effect on songs during the act. According to Peter Guralnick, "His costumes, his jewelry, and the poses that he struck only added to the sense of iconography increasingly attendant upon his performance, consciously contributing to the impression that he was somehow larger than life."

Dramatic entrances were very much Elvis' forte. Space permitting, this included a ceremonial drive round the venue with members of the entourage and sometimes Vernon too. Back on the road for the first time in over a decade, for Elvis' Houston concerts in early 1970, Elvis made his entrance to the rodeo arena in an open jeep.

Elvis kept up a running joke at the start of his shows of introducing himself as someone else. He variously told his audience of fans that he was Johnny Cash, Wayne Newton, Pat Boone, Sammy Davis Jr., Bill Cosby, Little Richard, Frankie Avalon, Tom Jones, and even the NBC peacock.

Elvis' early 1972 Las Vegas concerts featured much less talk between songs. This was not so much because he was listening to the Colonel, but because he was not in a talkative mood with Priscilla so recently gone from his side.

From 1972, Elvis launched into his live repertoire with "See See Rider," a track that remained his opener until the end. Only on very rare occasions did he open with anything else, for example "That's All Right (Mama)" or "Big Boss Man."

On stage in his Vegas years, Elvis was an inveterate water sipper in his battle to alleviate "Vegas throat." Entourage members have intimated that Elvis was also a master at developing instant "Vegas Throat" if he wanted to shirk the rest of an engagement.

Elvis' reliance on prescription drugs began to take their toll on his energy levels a few years after he resumed his live stage career. He was convinced that he required an elaborate cocktail of pharmaceuticals to put in a decent performance for his fans. Under the influence, he was capable of some rather bizarre behavior. At a Houston concert in March 1974, during Elvis' performance of "Let Me Be There," Vernon led the Colonel on stage riding a miniature donkey. At one show, Elvis only stayed out for only 22 minutes (in Lamar Fike's recollection), and for one of the few times in his career was booed by his audience. Fike has said that as early as the summer of 1971, Elvis was slurring and messing around on stage so much that people walked out.

Elvis' presentations of the band to the audience was often a moment for light comedy. Elvis expressed his gratitude and horsed around while the band played an instrumental version of "Comin' Home, Baby" (a song written by Bob Dorough and Ben Tucker and a 1962 hit for Mel Tormé), or sometimes "Green Onions" (Booker T and the MG's million-selling instrumental from 1962).

The unfurling of the Stars and Stripes as part of "American Trilogy" performance became one of the signature moments of Elvis' performances in 1974. For his summer 1974 Las Vegas engagement, Elvis laid down a statement of intent with a revamped show—no 2001 theme tune for his entry, no medley of old hits, plenty of new material and plenty of blues—but as in the past, by the second night he returned to his tried-and-tested Vegas formula out of concern that the audience was less responsive than usual. On one evening's show, Elvis and Red West put on a full karate demonstration—the Colonel, when he heard, was less than pleased. Between late August and his final show in Las Vegas that September, fired by his intake of prescription medicine, Elvis seemed more interested in delivering monologues than singing. He concluded that month-long res-

idence with a rambling monologue that featured off-color comments about his relationship with Priscilla (who happened to be there for the occasion), a strong denial of rumors about his drug taking, violent threats against whoever was spreading such rumors, and far too much information about recent medical procedures he had sustained. Naturally, this speech has made it out onto bootlegs such as *Desert Storm*.

By 1975, Elvis' whole stage show was slowing down. Jerry Scheff, who returned to play bass after a sabbatical, found that the tempo of the show was very different to how it had been a couple of years earlier. Elvis was unable to shift his excess weight before he hit Vegas, so he had to eschew many of his usual karate moves. There was still plenty of fun to be had: the last night in Las Vegas at the start of the year culminated in a huge on-stage water fight, and then Lamar Fike and the Colonel coming on stage dressed as Santa. Elvis also had a long-term running gag with lighting man Lamar Fike where he would ask for a light on him and Fike would flat out refuse.

For a while in 1975, perhaps to compensate for his lower energy levels, Elvis began a new practice of sending a champagne bucket out into the audience for song requests. His honesty and humanity won the audience over every time, even when he admitted that he'd ripped his trousers. It also helped that practically every show he did, Elvis told the audience that they were fabulous, the best he had ever had. What the fans didn't see was that before each performance, Elvis clasped his hands together in front of his forehead and prayed for energy.

Red West tells of one concert in North Carolina in 1975 when Elvis showered an unresponsive audience (and the band, with whom he had argued the previous night) with $30,000 worth of jewelry. In Springfield, Mass., that year, Elvis flung his guitar into the audience, announcing that "whoever gets the guitar can keep the damned thing, I don't need it anymore." Fans at Asheville, North Carolina, not only walked away with another guitar that Elvis hurled into the audience, one of them also went home with a ring worth $6,500. By this time, Elvis had long been wearing band aids over his rings on stage so that adoring fans wouldn't pull the rings from his fingers.

By 1976, Elvis was allowing solos to his band members. There were times in 1976 and 1977 when Elvis fluffed the words to some of his songs, and sometimes looked disinterested. He could be seen on stage checking lyrics, even to some of his standards, and is said to have used a prompter below the stage. His voice was always strong on the gospel numbers; according to J.D. Sumner, around this time Elvis flirted with the idea of putting together all-gospel shows.

Elvis was back to his energy-filled self at his New Year's Eve 1976 concert, impressing a sell-out crowd and new girlfriend Ginger Alden with a two-hour show. At one point he was rolling around on stage as he belted out "Hurt," and he went through a full repertoire of karate moves.

In early 1977, Elvis persuaded his girlfriend's sister, Terry Arden, to come up on stage during a concert and play some classical pieces on the piano.

Elvis' final tour performances in 1977 included moments that even his most ardent fans found hard to handle. In Baltimore, Elvis wandered off-stage for half-an-hour mid-way through the show. He got no ovation at the end, a real rarity. Deliberately or otherwise, he also sometimes fluffed his scarf giveaways. It was his practice to hand on-stage assistant, back-up singer and water carrier Charlie Hodge his rings before making his way to the front of the stage to give some lucky ladies a sweat-drenched scarf. On at least one occasion, he handed Charlie the scarf and proceeded to throw his diamond ring into the crowd.

Ever since his return to the stage in 1969, Elvis' had been closing his shows with "Can't Help Falling In Love"; he sang the song to his girlfriend if she was in the audience (or on stage, as Ginger Alden was during his final shows), or else to the prettiest woman in the audience, as a cue that she could have some private Elvis time backstage after the show. Often during his Vegas tenure the number he sang before this closing song was something that he threw in on the spur of the moment.

Such was the unconditional love of his fans that even when Elvis tripped over the lyrics or messed up (as he did on "Are You Lonesome Tonight?" in one of his last concerts, filmed for *Elvis in Concert*), all it took was some self-deprecating laughter for Elvis to turn things around and for the crowd to appreciate that they had witnessed an extra-special personalized performance. Right up to the end, his ability to connect with his audience remained undiminished; some fans believe that in his final concerts his humility, fallibility and evident physical frailty are an important part of his performing heritage.

Elvis left the stage after his customary "Thank you, thank you very much." If he was on tour rather in Las Vegas, he was whisked straight into a limousine and away, in as much of a trance as his most fervent fans, while announcer Al Dvorin told the crowd "Elvis has left the building."

ELVIS SAID IN 1956: "When I sang hymns back home with Mom and Pop, I stood still and I looked like you feel when you sing a hymn. When I sing this rock 'n' roll, my eyes won't stay open and my legs won't stand still. I don't care what they say, it ain't nasty."

ELVIS SAID IN 1956: "If I just stood out there and sang and never moved a muscle, the people would say well my goodness, I can stay home and listen to his records."

ELVIS DESCRIBING THE 1968 NBC TV experience: "Frightening. Scary. But fabulous. I will do more live shows."

ELVIS SAID IN 1972: "Funny thing happened to me about a year ago. It was an intermission and the lights were still on and I looked out and saw the crowd of people and I got weak in the knees. You know, all of a sudden it just scared me to death 'cause I'm used to going out when the lights are down, so I've never gotten over what they call stage fright. I go through it every show . . .
Before I go on stage I'm pretty much thinking about the show. I never get completely comfortable with it at any given time and I don't let the people with me get too comfortable with it. I remind them that it's a new crowd out there, they haven't seen us before so it's gotta be like the first time we go on."

ELVIS CHARACTERIZED HIS STAGE ACT IN 1974 as: "Entertain you, sing a lot of songs, walk around and sweat, give some scarves away, kiss some people, whatever."

ELVIS SAID IN 1976: "Singing, being onstage, making people happy—that's my life's blood. That's my moment of glory."

ELVIS TOLD KATHY WESTMORELAND: "I want to die onstage."

WANDA JACKSON: "He was just the greatest showman—a showman deluxe."

PETER GURALNICK: "His energy was fierce; his sense of competitive fire seemed to overwhelm the shy, deferential kid within; every minute he was onstage was like an incendiary explosion."

D.J. FONTANA: "On stage he could feel the audience out in about five or ten minutes. He knew the songs they wanted to hear for some reason, and he could work that crowd to his benefit. He was really good."

LARRY GELLER: "A playful sneer, a flirtatious glance, a shrug, a bump—each little gesture was tested, incorporated, expanded, refined, until by early 1958 . . . his mastery of his style was complete."

KATHY WESTMORELAND: "I have yet to witness any other entertainer with so great a gift."

SHERILL NIELSEN: "Elvis was very good at knowing how to pace his show... If you do too many slow songs you're gonna put 'em to sleep; too fast, you'll wear them out."

JOHN WILKINSON ON ELVIS' FIRST NIGHT IN LAS VEGAS: "The whole night was filled with electricity. It was like grabbing an electrical wire. I don't think we ever played better than those few opening nights of his triumphant return."

MYRNA SMITH: "When he'd walk onstage.... it was like a roar of electricity, you know, and you just plugged into it and became a part of it while you were out there. I've never seen that with any other performer, and I've worked with some big names."

MUSICAL DIRECTOR JOE GUERCIO: "Charisma makes a star. Elvis was a happening. He could walk across the stage and not even have to open his mouth."

TOM JONES: "He always seemed to be nervous about actually going onstage completely sober."

RENEE GRANT-WILLIAMS (VOICE COACH): "He had very strong legs, which he used as the basis for his support. He literally pushed into the floor using that karate-type crouch. He kept his entire upper body very loose so that it could resonate. And the way he cocked his head over the microphone really allowed the sound to vibrate freely."

BOBBY OGDIN: "Even on his final tour, Elvis Presley's shows created the strongest audience electricity of anybody I've ever worked with. When Elvis walked on stage it was like an explosion of response and screaming and flashbulbs and everything."

LARRY GELLER: "Elvis lived to perform."

GREIL MARCUS: "A real glow passes back and forth between Elvis and his audience, as he shares a bit of what it means to transcend the world of weakness, failure, worry, age and fear..."

"STAGE SHOW"

Colonel Tom Parker generally gets the plaudits for landing Elvis his first national TV appearance on this CBS Saturday night variety show—produced by Jackie Gleason and hosted by Jimmy and Tommy Dorsey—through agent Steve Yates sometime in mid-December 1955. However, DJ Bill Randle has claimed that he made the initial contact. Randle most certainly introduced Elvis on the first of the six "Stage Shows" on which he appeared, and Bob Neal was still (at least nominally) Elvis' manager at the time that the initial booking was made.

Elvis and Colonel Parker flew into New York three days before the show. When Elvis' band arrived, they rehearsed at the Nola Studios, at that time located between 51st and 52nd Streets. The show was actually recorded at the CBS Studios on Broadway between 53rd and 54th Streets. The half-hour show went out before Gleason's sketch show, *The Honeymooners*.

Elvis made his first appearance on the show that aired at 8 p.m. on January 28, 1956, after an act of xylophone-playing choirgirls. In a moment of high prescience, Cleveland DJ Bill Randle announced to the studio audience "We like at this time to introduce to you a young fellow, who like many performers, Johnnie Ray among them, come out of nowhere to be overnight very big stars. This young fellow we met for the first time while making a short movie. We think tonight that he's going to make television history for you.

We'd like you to meet him now — Elvis Presley. And here he is!"

Elvis performed a medley of Big Joe Turner hits, "Shake, Rattle And Roll" followed by "Flip, Flop And Fly," before concluding with "I Got A Woman," a song that producer Jackie Gleason suggested at the last minute. The headline act that night was Sarah Vaughan.

The "Stage Show" management immediately took up its option for a further two Elvis appearances to add to the four they had already contracted. They had to wait until March, though, owing to Elvis' ongoing Saturday night performing commitments at the Louisiana Hayride.

Elvis' second appearance on the show, the following Saturday (February 4, 1956), showcased "Tutti Frutti" and "Baby Let's Play House." After the show, the Dorsey brothers took Elvis out on the town to the Roseland nightclub. Elvis' fellow guests that night included comedian Joe E. Brown, and chimps Tippy and Cobina.

On his third appearance, (February 11, 1956), Elvis previewed "Heartbreak Hotel" and "Blue Suede Shoes," the songs that would bring him nationwide fame. By this time, Elvis' performances had helped the "Stage Show" to eclipse the slot champion, the "Perry Como Show," in the ratings. The special guest that night was Ella Fitzgerald; Jackie Gleason did the comic turn.

His fourth TV performance, on February 18, 1956, included Little Richard's "Tutti Frutti" and "I Was The One," the B-side to his latest single. The show went out slightly later, at 8:30 p.m., and featured George De Witt and an acrobatics troupe.

Elvis and his band returned to New York for rehearsals at the Nola Studio on March 17, 1956, for an evening appearance on the show. Elvis reprised "Heartbreak Hotel" and "Blue Suede Shoes." Fellow guests included British-born comedian Henny Youngman and child prodigy organist Glenn Derringer.

After watching the show, agent Harry Kalcheim advised Elvis to start his next (and last) "Stage Show" appearance with "Blue Suede Shoes." Instead, Elvis chose to perform The Drifters' "Money Honey" on his March 24, 1956 appearance, in a show with guests Glenn Derringer and Jack E. Lonard.

Elvis' fee of $1,250 per show was of little consequence compared to the enormous value of the nationwide exposure he garnered. For the extra two show option, his fee rose to $1,500.

Recordings of Elvis' performance on the show, in front of a live audience, were released in 1984 on the album *A Golden Celebration*. A bootleg of all six shows (*Elvis—The Dorsey Shows*) came out in 1993. One of his performances of "Heartbreak Hotel" is on 2007 DVD *Elvis #1 Hit Performances*.

REPORTER BOB JOHNSON: "Presley puts intensity into his songs. Over-emotional? Yes. But he projects. He 'sells'. Elvis has arrived... But you can't throw that much into something without it telling. It'll wear him out. It will exhaust him emotionally and physically. He's 20 now. If he's wise, he'll slow down a little and live another 20 years."

ERNST JORGENSEN: "The nation got its first look at Elvis Presley: an awkward, wild, almost bizarre young man, who made faces straight out of a silent movie farce while shaking his legs in a manner that had more to do with Saturday-night Southern Baptist revivals than prime-time TV."

"STAGGER LEE"

Elvis sang a raunchy snatch of this Lloyd Price song (based on a much-covered traditional blues murder ballad) in July 1970 rehearsals before his Las Vegas

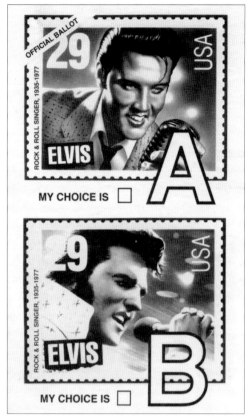

The ballot for the Elvis Stamp (1993).

residency, snaffled and released on bootleg album *Get Down And Get With It* and the *Profile* series. It first came out officially on the extended 2000 *That's The Way It Is* collectors' edition.

STAMPS

Elvis was the first performer to feature on a US commemorative postage stamp, launching the Legends of American Music series on a 29 cent stamp issued on January 8, 1993. Brought out to mark the 58th anniversary of his birth, the stamp was chosen in a public poll between a "young Elvis" or an "old Elvis": the Fifties version, designed by Mark Stutzman, won the battle of the dueling Elvii.

No other commemorative stamp has sold more copies in the US (over 500 million). After its release, the stamp spawned a whole sub-segment of Elvis memorabilia, despite the certainty that it will not have much more than sentimental value for a long time to come: an estimated 124 million of these stamps were still in the hands of their owners as of 2006.

This philatelic honor came a full fifteen years after Elvis' first appearance on a stamp, issued in Grenada.

Elvis commemorative stamps have been issued in around 50 countries (a number necessarily imprecise as more and more Elvis commemorative stamps appear). The island of St. Vincent has been the most prolific issuer of Elvis stamps so far, run close by the Central African Republic, Madagascar and Guyana. Many of these stamps are designed by specialists Jean-Louis and Paul Puvilland.

Books:
Elvis on Stamps: A Pictorial Reference, by R. G. King and Floyd Kidd, Smokey Mountain Publishing Co., 1997.
Elvis in the Post, by Josephine Woodward, TCB Publishing, 1997.

STAMPS, THE

Bass singer J.D. Sumner's new group toured with Elvis in November 1971 for the first time. They remained Elvis' male backing vocals and studio group until Elvis' final concert. They joined him in the studio in March 1972 at RCA's Studio C in Los Angeles, and featured on the concert documentary *Elvis On Tour* filmed that year. For a time, they were supplanted by Elvis' in-house vocal group, Voice, but they were regularly with Elvis when he performed live, at many concerts providing a half-hour opening set. The Stamps backed Elvis during the *Aloha from Hawaii via Satellite* broadcast in 1973, and featured on *Elvis in Concert* in 1977.

The Stamps personnel during Elvis' time included J.D. Sumner, Ed Enoch, Bill Baize, Tony Brown, Donnie Sumner, Richard Sterban, Ed Wideman, Dave Rowland, Ed Hill and Larry Strickland. Buck Buckles participated in overdubs at Elvis' final RCA recording session and was on the road with Elvis in 1977.

On one occasion in 1976, when the Stamps had a prior concert commitment that clashed with a recording session at Graceland, Elvis flew them back from North Carolina, and then solved the problem of how they were going to get home to Nashville by giving them his limousine—for keeps, claiming that he was getting a new one.

The Stamps Quartet franchise had been around since Frank Stamps founded the group in 1924. Billed as the longest-running gospel quartet of all time, the group was the first white gospel outfit to record for a major label. J.D. Sumner purchased the group name in 1962, with James Blackwood.

The record on Elvis' bedroom record player when he died was a J.D. Sumner & The Stamps acetate. The Stamps sang at Elvis' funeral, not long after singer Larry Strickland had a dream that he would be singing at a funeral.

The Stamps, like backing group The Jordanaires, released a tribute to Elvis after his death, *Elvis' Favorite Gospel Songs*, and later *Memories of Our Friend Elvis*. J. D. Sumner disbanded the group in 1980, but they reformed in the early Nineties and have been popular guests ever since at Elvis tribute events in the US and internationally. The Group is still going strong under the tutelage of lead singer Ed Enoch, and has been a member of the Gospel Music Hall of Fame since 1997.

Book:
Where Is Elvis? by Ed Hill and Don Hill, Cross Roads Books, 1979.

"STAND BY ME"

Elvis is in fine voice for his version of this Sister Rosetta Tharpe gospel song, which he recorded on May 26, 1966 during his Nashville sessions for the *How Great Thou Art* album. The song was written by famed gospel composer Charles Tindley, though Elvis has a credit on the release.

This was a song that Elvis enjoyed singing at home; one version was taped during his Army service in Germany.

It is included on the *Amazing Grace* and *Peace In The Valley* gospel anthologies. Alternate takes of the song can be found on *Elvis: Close Up* and FTD releases *Easter Special* and *So High*.

Two bootleg albums of outtakes from the Nashville gospel session have taken this song for their title.

STANLEY, BILLY
(B. WILLIAM JOB STANLEY, JR. 1953)

Elvis' stepbrother Billy was seven years old and the eldest of three brothers when his mother married Vernon Presley in 1960. Elvis immediately

won the little boys' hearts by quipping to his father that he had always wanted a little brother, and now in one fell swoop he had three. The huge piles of toys the kids woke up to the following morning cemented the deal.

The kids spent as much time at Graceland as they could. For all the gifts and presents he gave them, having Elvis as a step-brother was like being related to Santa Claus.

Billy joined Elvis' entourage in the early Seventies, and picked up the Elvis nickname "Charles Manson."

Billy's first marriage, to Annie Hall Smith, foundered after she and Elvis had an affair. The marriage didn't last but Billy remained within Elvis' orbit until the end of his famous step-brother's life.

Books:
Elvis, We Love You Tender, written with mother and brothers, Delacorte Press, 1980.
Elvis, My Brother by Billy Stanley and George Erikson, St. Martin's Press, 1989.

STANLEY, DAVID EDWARD
(B. 1956)

David was four when his mother Dee married Vernon Presley. All grown up, he worked with Elvis from 1972, initially helping with his touring wardrobe, then working as a bodyguard and earning the Elvis epithet "Head Hunter."

Sonny West writes that in the early Seventies, when Elvis saw himself as a crusader against street drugs, he enlisted David and his brothers to help stamp out drug use at their Memphis school.

In 1990, David Stanley came forward to suggest that Elvis may have committed suicide. After battling drug dependency, David Stanley became a businessman and motivational speaker.

Stanley wrote, produced and directed 2007 Elvis-themed motion picture *The HeadHunter*, based on his own life story as a teenaged bodyguard to Elvis.

Books:
Life With Elvis, by David E Stanley and David Wimbish, Fleming H. Revell Company, 1986
The Elvis Encyclopedia, David E. Stanley, General Publishing Group, 1994
Raised on Rock—Growing Up At Graceland, by David E. Stanley and Mark Bego, Mainstream Publishing Projects, 1996

DVD:
From the Shadows of the King to Solutionary Dynamics, David Stanley, 2003

STANLEY, DAVADA "DEE," NEÉ ELLIOT
(B. 1925)

Dee Presley—she retained the Presley last name after her divorce from Vernon—was born in Clarksville, Tennessee. She contacted Elvis after he moved to Germany and asked him if he would like to come round for a meal some time; she had long been a fan, and seen him perform live. Lamar Fike remembers that rather than going himself, Elvis sent Vernon along to have a coffee with her.

Dee Stanley had been married for ten years and had three children when she met Vernon. Biographers have stated that she was already in the process of separating from her husband—a former bodyguard to General Patton—when she met Vernon; alternately, the story runs that Vernon initially befriended Dee and her husband, Master Sergeant Bill Stanley, and went out drinking with them on a regular basis before initiating an affair with Dee. Peter Guralnick writes that

Bill Stanley even tried to enlist Vernon's help in trying to save his marriage, after he began to suspect that she was cheating on him.

Elvis was highly displeased that his father began seeing another woman so soon after Gladys had died. Stanley left Germany for America in June 1959, with Vernon ostensibly in hot pursuit. During that trip Vernon introduced Dee to his father Jessie, living in Louisville at the time, and showed her round Graceland. When Vernon returned to Germany, Dee was by his side. Marty Lacker says that Dee's former husband Bill Stanley received a handsome payoff for signing divorce papers.

Vernon and Dee were married in Huntsville, Alabama on July 3, 1960. Elvis perfunctorily told the press: "She seems pretty nice. I only had one mother and that's it. There'll never be another. As long as she understands that, we won't have any trouble." Before Vernon and Dee got hitched, Elvis made sure that all his property and assets were transferred out of Vernon's name, as he had his suspicions that she might be a gold digger. Elvis did not attend the wedding.

Dee and Elvis set up a *modus vivendi* that was basically for her to stay out of sight, though he had plenty of time for her kids. This arrangement foundered when Elvis returned to Graceland in late 1960 after filming *Wild in the Country* to find that Dee had changed some drapes in his absence—drapes that Gladys had chosen. He flew into a rage and accused her of trying to replace his mother. Not long afterwards, Vernon, Dee and her kids moved out of Graceland to a property round the corner.

When Priscilla arrived, she became friends with Dee, her kids and Vernon. Dee would keep Priscilla company and take her out around town during the long stretches when Elvis was away in Hollywood making movies.

Stanley brought her kids along with husband Vernon in 1967 to meet then New York governor Nelson Rockefeller in Los Angeles, where Elvis was shooting *Speedway*.

Stanley went away on vacation with Linda Thompson (destination Puerto Rico) in November 1974 for a week. Dee separated from Vernon in late 1974, after she found out that he had been having an affair with Denver nurse Sandy Miller.

She secured a divorce settlement from Vernon in late 1977 that included the house where she was still living. Vernon then bought the house on Dolan Drive back from her.

According to Priscilla Presley, Elvis never got on with Stanley, and would get up and leave the room if she walked in. He did, however, make an effort to be civil to her on special occasions.

Dee Stanley later incurred the wrath of many Elvis fans by making claims in the *National Enquirer* and on TV that, among other things, Elvis was gay and had incestuous relations with his mother.
Books:
Dee Presley and her sons Billy, Ricky and David worked with journalist Martin Torgoff on their book *Elvis, We Love You Tender*, published in 1980 by Delacorte Press. She also worked with Caroline Latham on her unauthorized biography of Priscilla, *Priscilla and Elvis*.
The Elvis Family Photo Album, by Dee Presley, Jimmy Velvet Publishing, 1998

STANLEY, RICK
(B. RICHARD EARL STANLEY, 1954)

The middle Stanley boy was six when his mother married Vernon. Rick became part of Elvis' entourage in 1971 after he quit school, followed soon after by his brothers, and over the objections of his mother Dee Stanley, who wanted her sons to go to college.

Elvis with David Stanley in 1975 on the *Lisa Marie*. The plane was named for his daughter.

Rick helped out with wardrobe on tour. According to *Elvis A-Z*, Elvis nicknamed him "Reckless Rick." He was arrested during the years he worked for Elvis for trying to fill a forged prescription for Demerol, one of the drugs to which Elvis was addicted. Stanley was with Elvis the last night he was alive.

Soon after Elvis died, Rick studied to become a preacher and ever after has served as an ordained Baptist minister.

RICK STANLEY: "I try to tell people that Elvis was a chapter of my life; he's not the book. What's more important to me are my wife and children and my ministry."•

Books:
Elvis, We Love You Tender, written with mother and brothers, Delacorte Press, 1980.
The Touch Of Two Kings: Growing Up At Graceland by Rick Stanley and Michael K. Haynes, 1986.
Caught in a Trap: Elvis Presley's Tragic Lifelong Search for Love, by Rick Stanley and Paul Harold, Word Publishing, 1992.

STANWYCK, BARBARA
(B. RUBY CATHERINE STEVENS, 1907-1990)

In a film career spanning fifty-nine years on screens great and small, "the best actress who never won an Oscar" had to be content with four Academy Award nominations for classics including *Double Indemnity* (1944) and great public acclaim for her roles in popular TV dramas "The Big Valley" in the Sixties and "The Thorn Birds" in the Eighties. The highest-paid woman in America by the end of the Second World War, Stanwyck finally received an honorary Academy Award in 1982, to add to her three Emmys and a Golden Globe.

In 1964, Barbara Stanwyck worked with Elvis in *Roustabout*, in a role originally offered to Mae West. Elvis loved working with such Hollywood royalty; he enjoyed chatting with her on set, after overcoming a rocky start when he arrived late and thought (wrongly) that she had complained. Stanwyck only made one more movie after *Roustabout*.

In 1965, Stanwyck and other screen stars attended a ceremony to acknowledge Elvis' $50,000 charitable donation to the Motion Picture Relief Fund in 1965.

BARBARA STANWYCK: "Elvis is that rare exception, a young star who is also a gentleman."

STARLITE WRANGLERS

Scotty Moore and Bill Black were in this established Memphis hillbilly band, splendiferously named Doug Poindexter's Starlite Wranglers, when they first recorded at Sun Studio for Sam Phillips. The tracks they laid down—"Now She Cares No More For Me" and Scotty Moore composition "My Kind Of Carryin' On"—were released as a single around the time that Elvis was first called in to Sun. In the summer of 1954, Phillips suggested the two musicians give a local unknown called Elvis Presley a try-out, see what they could work out, and then come down to the studio and do some recordings.

Elvis first took to the stage backed by Scotty and Bill during the interval at a Starlite Wranglers show at the Bon Air club ten days after his first recording session, as far as anyone knows. The rest of the band—lead singer and guitarist Doug Poindexter plus Tommy Seals on steel guitar, Millard Yow on fiddle, and Clyde Rush on guitar—were not best pleased about this new development, and by the end of the summer the group had all but disbanded.

Though Poindexter fronted his band with a typical nasal sound to his delivery, his one and only Sun single offered a foretaste of the rockabilly sound that his electric guitarist and bass player would develop with Elvis. A few sources name Poindexter as an uncredited presence on Elvis' early recordings; others suggest that Elvis may have briefly even fronted the band.

STARR, KAY
(B. KATHERINE STARKS, 1922)

When Elvis went for his first professional recording session at Sun Studio, he opted to cover Kay Starr hit "Harbor Lights." Three years later, Elvis told an interviewer that Starr was among his favorite female singers, though by then her string of hits, which began in the late Forties with "You Were Only Foolin' " and continued through the Fifties with "Wheel Of Fortune" (which stayed at #1 for ten weeks in 1952) was drawing to a close.

Born in Dougherty, Oklahoma on July 21, 1922 to an Iroquois Indian father, Starr initially made a name for herself as a Western Swing and jazz singer before crossing over to new-fangled rock. She was still performing into the Nineties.

STARR, RANDY
(B. WARREN NADEL, 1930)

This New-York born singer had some modest success in 1957 with "After School," but scored more long-lasting income writing film tunes for eight Elvis movies: four tunes solo ("Could I Fall In Love," "The Girl I Never Loved," "Old MacDonald" and "Who Needs Money"), plus half a dozen with Fred Wise ("Adam And Evil," "Carny Town," "Datin'," "Kissin' Cousins" and "Look Out, Broadway"; they also adapted "Yellow Rose Of Texas" and "The Eyes Of Texas"); he also wrote "Almost In Love" with Rick Bonfa.

"STARTIN' TONIGHT"

Elvis recorded this college-break *Girl Happy* song by Lenore Rosenblatt and Victor Williams at Radio Recorders on June 12, 1964. The song was in the movie, on the LP and on the *Double Feature* and FTD soundtrack re-releases.

"STARTING TODAY"

A sweet-voiced Don Robertson ballad that Elvis recorded in Nashville on March 13, 1961 as an album cut on *Something For Everybody*.

Alternates have appeared on *Elvis: Close Up* and on FTD releases *Fame And Fortune* and *Something For Everybody.*

STATESMEN

Elvis listened to plenty of songs by the Statesmen—they were Vernon's favorite gospel group—during his formative years. Founded in 1948 in Atlanta, Georgia by pianist Hovie Lister, the group included Mosie Lister, who wrote many of the gospels songs Elvis covered on his gospel albums, and Elvis favorites Jake Hess and Jim "Big Chief" Wetherington, plus in the original line-up Bobby Strickland, Bervin Kendricks and Gordon Hill.

From the early Fifties, the Statesmen and the Blackwood Brothers often joined forces and sang together. In 1952, the Statesmen starred in their own syndicated TV show.

Like Elvis, the Statesmen were signed to RCA Victor. Elvis covered a number of gospel tunes that had been hits for the Statesmen on his gospel albums, particularly on his *How Great Thou Art* LP; in July 1955, Elvis was thrilled to play on the same bill as his heroes.

The Statesmen came to sing at Elvis' funeral in 1977.

STAX STUDIO

With Elvis increasingly reluctant to travel to Nashville or LA for studio sessions, he tried a couple of recording session at Stax Records in Memphis in July and December 1973. The July session was close to a disaster. The studio was ill-equipped for the many musicians and backing singers Elvis had invited along. Worse, Elvis was very much out of sorts, arriving so late on the first evening that nothing was recorded at all. On the second evening he was slowed and slurred by prescription drugs. After putting up a Christmas tree to set the mood for the Yule-flavored tracks he was scheduled to record, Elvis took down the tree with a karate kick, alienated the rhythm section (who didn't come back), managed to put down a few songs and then checked into the Baptist Hospital in Memphis.

The tracks Elvis did manage to record came out on *Raised on Rock*. Three songs ("Good, Bad, But Beautiful," "The Wonders You Perform" and "Color My Rainbow") were recorded by the band without Elvis ever laying down a vocal—he had already stormed out after discovering that his favorite microphone had gone missing. Outtakes from this session saw the light of day in 2006 on FTD release *Made in Memphis*; the Elvis-free instrumental tracks came out in 2007 on the FTD *Raised on Rock* reissue.

When Elvis returned to Stax in December, it was with Linda Thompson and Lisa Marie in tow. A much more downbeat and successful session ensued, after RCA brought in uprated equipment and a platoon of engineers. Elvis laid down the best part of two albums' worth of songs, for *Good Times* and *Promised Land*, in what turned out to be the last highly productive studio recording session of his career.

STAX HISTORY

Founded originally as Satellite Records by former musician Jim Stewart and his sister Estelle Axton, Stax Records (STewart and AXton) operated out of a premises on East McLemore and College in Memphis from 1959 to 1976, on the site of the former Capitol Theater, not far from the church in East Trigg where young Elvis sometimes went to listen to black gospel singing.

In its heyday, the studio defined a Southern soul sound through artists such as Rufus and Carla Thomas, the Mar-Keys, Booker T., Sam and Dave, Wilson Pickett and Otis Redding (on their Volt subsidiary), and become known as "Soulsville, USA." The label went into decline in the late Sixties following the death of top artist Otis Redding, and a catastrophic deal with Atlantic that saw the end of a long-standing distribution agreement and resulted in the label losing its entire back catalogue. A new spate of hit records in the early Seventies, spearheaded by Isaac Hayes (who said 'hi' to Elvis when he was recording at Stax in 1973), was not enough to stave off bankruptcy a few years later.

Stax Studio at 926 E. McLemore Avenue, built on the site of the original studio, is now a museum. The original building was demolished in 1989.

STAX TRAX

A 1989 unofficial release on the Bilko label of rare, undubbed material from Elvis' recording sessions at Stax.

TRACK LISTING:
1. If You Talk In Your Sleep (alternate take)
2. Mr. Songman (alternate take)
3. Promised Land (undubbed version)
4. Love Song Of The Year (undubbed version)
5. Help Me (undubbed version)
6. Sweet Sweet Spirit (rehearsal)
7. Your Love's Been A Long Time Coming (undubbed version)
8. Thinkin' About You (undubbed version)
9. You Asked Me To (undubbed version)
10. It's Midnight (undubbed version)
11. There's A Honky Tonk Angel (undubbed version)

"STAY AWAY"

The opening song for the movie Stay Away, Joe is a variation on the traditional English folk song "Greensleeves," a tune that Elvis had always liked. Elvis recorded this up-tempo Sid Tepper / Roy C. Bennett version of the song on January 16, 1968 in Nashville. It was released immediately as the B-side to "U.S. Male" in February 1968, rising to #67 and staying on the charts for five weeks.

The song has since featured on the Double Features issue with *Kissin' Cousins* and *Clambake*, and on *Tomorrow Is A Long Time*. Alternate takes have been included on the 1973 *Almost In Love* re-release, *Today Tomorrow & Forever*, and *Elvis at the Movies*. Further alternates are on FTD releases *Long Lonely Highway* (a slower version) and *So High*.

"STAY AWAY, JOE"

Elvis recorded the title song for this movie, composed and worded by Ben Weisman and Sid Wayne—and owing a heavy debt to traditional Southern song "Pick A Bale"—at a Studio B session in Nashville starting on October 1, 1967. With no soundtrack release, the song didn't come out until 1970 budget movie album *Let's Be Friends*. A non-overdubbed version was wrongly released first time round on the *Almost In Love* album that same year, and then deleted from later releases of that LP.

The *Stay Away, Joe* songs later got the Double Features treatment with *Kissin' Cousins* and *Clambake*. "Stay Away, Joe" also features on *Command Performances* and *Elvis Movies*.

STAY AWAY, JOE

Elvis began shooting this Western comedy—based on a bestselling novel by Dan Cushman which had already been a successful Broadway play—on location in Sedona, Arizona (much of it on the Bradshaw Ranch) on October 9, 1967. Some scenes were also shot at Cottonwood. Elvis' new wife Priscilla was, exceptionally, allowed along, as were the wives of other entourage members. Elvis threw a goodbye lunch for the crew on November 27, 1967 before leaving Los Angeles.

The movie's rejected working titles were *Bumblebee* and *Born Rich*.

Stay Away, Joe vies for the prize of containing the most fights and the most female conquests of any Elvis vehicle. It also features another movie low for Elvis: the song "Dominick," which he croons to a bull (a song he made producer Felton

Jarvis promise to refuse ever to release on vinyl).

One song didn't make the cut: "Goin' Home."

As many as 140 American Indian extras were hired for the party scenes. Elvis played opposite seasoned Hollywood professionals Burgess Meredith (fresh from playing The Penguin in the Sixties TV version of "Batman"), Joan Blondell, Thomas Gomez and Katy Jurado.

When the film opened it peaked at #65 in the *Variety* Box Office Survey; it failed to gross more than $1.5 million.

This was the first Elvis movie to go out into the world without so much as an accompanying soundtrack EP or LP release.

CREDITS:
MGM, Color.
Length: 102 minutes
Release date: March 8, 1968

TAGLINES:
Elvis is kissin' cousins again, and also friends, and friends of friends, and even some perfect strangers!
He's playing Indian—but he doesn't say "How," he says "When"!
Elvis goes West . . . and the West goes wild!"

Directed by: Peter Tewksbury
Produced by: Douglas Laurence (producer), Michael A. Hoey (associate producer)
Written by: Dan Cushman (novel), Michael A. Hoey and Burt Kennedy (screenplay)
Music by: Jack Marshall
Cinematography by: Fred J. Koenekamp
Film Editing by: George W. Brooks
Art Direction by: Carl Anderson, George W. Davis
Set Decoration by: Henry Grace, Don Greenwood Jr.

CAST:
Elvis Presley	Joe Lightcloud
Burgess Meredith	Charlie Lightcloud
Joan Blondell	Glenda Callahan
Katy Jurado	Annie Lightcloud (Joe's stepmother)
Thomas Gomez	Grandpa
Henry Jones	Hy Slager (Bank president)
L.Q. Jones	Bronc Hoverty
Quentin Dean	Mamie Callahan (Glenda's daughter)
Anne Seymour	Mrs. Hawkins
Douglas Henderson	Congressman Morrissey
Angus Duncan	Lorne Hawkins
Mike Lane	Frank Hawk
Susan Trustman	Mary Lightcloud
Warren Vanders	Hike Bowers (stockman)
Buck Kartalian	Bull Shortgun
Maurishka	Connie Shortgun
Caitlin Wyles	Marlene Standing Rattle
Marya Christen	Bille-Jo Hump
Del 'Sonny' West	Jackson He-Crow
Jennifer Peak	Little Deer
Brett Parker	Deputy Sheriff Hank Matson
Michael Keller	Orville Witt
David Cadiente	Other Indian
Joe Esposito	Workman
Harry Harvey	Judge Nibley
Robert P. Lieb	Announcer at rodeo
Dick Wilson	Car salesman

ADDITIONAL CREW:
Sydney Guilaroff	hair stylist
William Tuttle	makeup artist
William R. Finnegan	unit production manager
Lindsley Parsons Jr.	assistant production manager
Dale Hutchinson	assistant director
Franklin Milton	recording supervisor
Carol Daniels	stunts
Archie Fire Lame Deer	stunt double
Ron Stein	stunts
Thomas A. Sweet	stunts

Elvis with Katy Jurabo in 1968's *Stay Away Joe*.

Plot:

Elvis plays ex-rodeo rider Joe Lightcloud, a home-coming hellraiser who persuades Congressman Morrissey (played by Douglas Henderson) to set him up with some cattle and a bull as part of a US government Indian management scheme. He intends to farm with his father Charlie (played by Burgess Meredith).

At a wild party to celebrate, Joe gets into a fight with rowdy pal Frank Hawk (played by Michael Lane) because he wants his girl. Meanwhile, the cows break loose, Joe's stepmother Annie (played by Katie Jurado, who put on weight specially for the part) makes a sit down protest in a bathtub in the front room, and the prize bull winds up as dinner.

Joe, who can con a man almost as successfully as he can sweet-talk a woman, visits old flame Glenda Callaghan (played by Joan Blondell), now a storeowner. He makes a play for her pretty daughter Mamie (played by Quentin Dean). Glenda chases him out, but he returns with a ruse to get her out of the way so that he can romance her girl in peace. For much of the rest of the movie, Glenda is in hot pursuit of Joe and Mamie with a loaded shotgun.

After Joe is forced to sell his remaining cattle to try and buy a new bull, Congressman Morrissey threatens the family with a jail term for selling off government property. Joe manages to solve the problem with a new bull, Dominick—to whom he is forced to sing at one point—only to find out that he has bought a rodeo bull, not a stud.

Resolution appears on the horizon when Joe has the bright idea of raking in money by challenging people to ride the feisty bull. When the Congressman arrives to take him to jail, Joe persuades him that he has enough money to buy many more head of cattle than he is accused of selling. Glenda catches up with Joe to force him to marry her little girl, until Joe persuades her and the priest Glenda has brought along that all they have done is kiss.

The obligatory wedding finale is between Joe's sister Mary (played by Susan Trustman) and her high-class beau Lorne Hawkins (played by Angus Duncan). By this time, the happy ending for boisterous Joe could only be an all-out fight with some of his buddies that literally brings the house down.

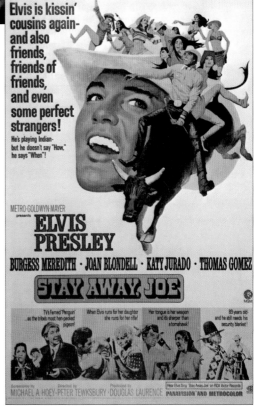

Songs: "Stay Away," "Stay Away Joe", "Lovely Mamie", "Dominick", "All I Needed Was The Rain"

"STEADFAST, LOYAL AND TRUE"

Elvis recorded two versions of this Jerry Leiber / Mike Stoller ditty for *King Creole*: the movie version on January 16, 1958 at Radio Recorders, and a version for the LP with overdubs from the Jordanaires (in Nashville, on June 19) at the Paramount Soundstage on February 11, 1958.

The song has resurfaced on *Elvis Sings Leiber & Stoller* and was included on *The King Of Rock And Roll* anthology. The undubbed movie version master first appeared on *Essential Elvis, Vol. 3* in 1991, since when it has been tracklisted on the 1997 re-release of *King Creole* and *Today*

Tomorrow & Forever.

"STEAMROLLER BLUES"

A live blues track issued as a single in March 1973 (from Elvis' January 14, 1973 *Aloha From Hawaii* performance) coupled with "Fool" on the B-side, designed to whip up interest in the delayed U.S. showing of Elvis' satellite broadcast from earlier in the year. The disc sold around 400,000 copies on first release, climbing to #17 in the charts during its 12-week stay.

Elvis first added the James Taylor track to his repertoire in Las Vegas in the summer of 1972, though he had been keen on it since he heard Taylor's original on his album *Sweet Baby James*. The song was a live staple for Elvis through 1973 and was one he sometimes pulled out at later shows.

The song is well-represented on live Elvis albums from the Seventies: it's on *Greatest Hits Vol. 1* and *The Alternate Aloha* (both from the pre-Aloha rehearsal), *Elvis Sings The Blues, Walk A Mile In My Shoes, Elvis By The Presleys, Hitstory, Elvis Live* and *The Essential Elvis Presley* (from 2007). The version Elvis sang live in Memphis in March 1974 came out on *Platinum: A Life In Music* in 1997 and on the 2004 FTD release *Elvis Recorded Live On Stage in Memphis*. Further live recordings are to be found on FTD releases *Takin' Tahoe Tonight, Closing Night, Live In LA, Dragonheart* and *Southern Nights*, in addition to the inevitable bootlegs.

A rehearsal for *The Steve Allen Show*, 1956. (LEFT TO RIGHT: Andy Griffith, Imogene Coca, Steve Allen and Elvis.)

STEFANIAK, ELISABETH
(B. 1939)

Elvis met this 19 year-old stepdaughter of US Army sergeant Raymond McCormick one evening at the Tower Theater in Grafenwö^hr, after she asked him for an autograph. Elvis asked her to sit next to him for the movie, and soon after they began dating. Elvis spent Thanksgiving of 1958 with Stefaniak and her family. Soon afterwards, Elvis asked her parents if bilingual Stefaniak could come and work as his secretary. Elvis and Stefaniak were friends and more—she would spend the nights with him if he didn't have any other special lady—until he started seeing Priscilla. According to Stefaniak, Grandma Presley picked up on the attraction between Elisabeth and Elvis' friend, Sergeant Rex Mansfield, and because she did not like the way that Elvis had started ignoring Elisabeth since meeting Priscilla, Minnie Mae told them to go for it.

Stefaniak followed Elvis back to America to continue as his secretary after Elvis' two-year stint in the Army came to an end. Elvis gave her a yellow Lincoln to use, but she didn't have too much opportunity. Not long after arriving in Memphis, Stefaniak left for Florida, where her stepfather was stationed. While she was there she telegraphed Elvis the news that she was going to marry Rex Mansfield that June. Though Elvis was invited to the wedding, he did not attend. Nor, indeed, did he ever see her again.

Books:

Elvis the Soldier, by Rex and Elisabeth Mansfield, Collectors Service GmbH, 1983 (including recording of AFN Elvis interview).

Sergeant Presley—Our Untold Story Of Elvis' Missing Years, by Rex and Elisabeth Mansfield, ECW Press, 2002

"STEPPIN' OUT OF LINE"

Elvis recorded this hi-tempo, sax-fired Fred Wise

/ Ben Weisman / Dolores Fuller song for the *Blue Hawaii* soundtrack at Radio Recorders on March 22, 1961, but it was dropped from the movie before it hit the screens. However, it found release on the *Pot Luck* album that very same month in 1961.

The movie version and additional takes finally came out on the 1997 movie soundtrack re-release, after more than three decades available only on bootleg. A further alternate is on *Elvis: Close Up.*

"STEVE ALLEN SHOW," THE

On July 1, 1956 Elvis appeared on the second-ever episode of NBC's "The Steve Allen Show," a Sunday night variety showcase broadcast from the Hudson Theater in New York City.

Sprucing up his rebel image, Elvis wore a tuxedo, and took part in a comic interlude, "Range Round-up," with Andy Griffith, Imogene Coca and Steve Allen. Elvis' character was called "Tumbleweed" Presley, in a foreshadowing of the string of Westerns he'd wind up doing on the big screen.

Elvis' set started with his latest single "I Want You, I Need You, I Love You," followed by "Hound Dog," which he sang to a real live basset hound in a skit that many—including Elvis—found demeaning. Eagle-eyed fans have pointed out that Elvis subconsciously wipes his hands on his jacket in a gesture of disgust.

Elvis earned $5,000 and a great deal of scandal-abating exposure for his night's work. His presence on the show brought NBC its best performance in that Sunday evening prime time slot for two years. However, for years afterwards, Elvis viewed the experience as a public humiliation. Sam Phillips called Elvis immediately after the show aired to ask him what had happened to the Elvis he knew.

Recordings of Elvis' performance came out in 1984 on the album *A Golden Celebration*. Video of Elvis' performance was limited to a Japanese bootleg until 2007 DVD release *Elvis #1 Hit Performances* (the 2-DVD version).

STEVENS, CONNIE
(B. CONCETTA ROSALIE ANN INGOLIA, 1938)

In 1961, Elvis dated actress/singer Connie Stevens—born in Brooklyn on April 9, 1938 to jazz musician parents. Stevens's singing career spanned the late Fifties and Sixties. She rose to national prominence with her role in TV series "Hawaiian Eye" from 1959 to 1962, after a slew of film roles beginning with *Dragstrip Riot* in 1958. In the late Sixties, Stevens married singer Eddie Fisher. She continues to act to this day. She has also launched a line of cosmetics, and is a well-known philanthropist.

STEVENSON, VENETIA
(B. 1938)

Elvis dated this London-born actress briefly in 1957, the year that she began her four-year acting career, and soon after she had left actor Russ Tamblyn. She later married Everly brother Don.

STOKER, GORDON
(B. 1924)

As a member of The Jordanaires, Gordon Stoker sang back-up with Elvis for fifteen years from 1956. He made a cameo on the piano at Elvis' original studio recording of "Hound Dog" because pianist Shorty Long was late to the session, and pinch-hit on the ivories on several other early Elvis recording sessions for RCA, including Elvis' first gospel session at Radio Recorders in January 1957, and his early 1960s sessions. Stoker even picked up an accordion on "For The Millionth And The Last Time."

Born on August 3, 1924 in Gleason, Tennessee into a family of musicians, Stoker went to Nashville as a piano-playing twelve-year-old. He joined the Jordanaires as their pianist in 1950, and started singing as a tenor in 1953.

Stoker first sang with Elvis at his original RCA session in January 1956, with Speer brothers Ben and Brock. Later that year, Stoker brought along the rest of his group. The Jordanaires remained Elvis' favored backing band for a decade and a half, until Stoker and friends reluctantly had to decline Elvis' invitation to come back out on the road with him because they already had prior commitments.

Stoker has since said that he rued the fact he was unable to carry on working with Elvis, because if he had continued to be surrounded by the people he had always worked with, he might not have gone into the physical decline that culminated in his premature death.

STOLLER, MIKE

See LEIBER AND STOLLER

STONE, JESSE
(B. CHARLES E. CALHOUN, 1901-1999)

Stone wrote many memorable early rhythm 'n' blues songs, generating material for Big Joe Turner, The Drifters, The Clovers, Ray Charles and Roy Hamilton—practically a who's who of Elvis' favorite R 'n' B artists when he first entered the music industry.

Born into a family of traveling players in Atchinson, Kansas on November 16, 1901, Stone ran his own jazz band in the Twenties, and became a fixture at the Apollo Theater in Harlem. He was one of the first artists signed to the new Atlantic Records label, over the years working as a producer, arranger and talent-spotter, as well as writing songs. It was Stone who penned the first-ever cross-over rock 'n' roll #1, "Shake, Rattle And Roll." Reputedly, in his bid to buy out Elvis' contract from Sun Records, Atlantic principal Ahmet Ertegun lined up Stone as Elvis' future producer.

Elvis recorded Stone compositions "Shake, Rattle And Roll," "Flip, Flop And Fly," "Money Honey," "Like A Baby" and "Down In The Alley."

STONE, MIKE

Born in Hawaii, Mike "the Man of" Stone was a washin-ryu style karate blackbelt who taught Priscilla Presley karate in the early Seventies in LA. He became a top exponent of full-contact karate after beginning his fight career in 1963, following a three-year stint in the US Army. Stone was the first grand champion at Ed Parker's 1964 world tournament; over an 18-month period he was undefeated in 89 black belt bouts (though there are claims he lost one bout in this time), and became US karate's first "superstar."

Elvis and Priscilla first met Stone when he competed in and won at a karate tournament in Hawaii in May 1968, where they were on vacation. Stone dropped in backstage after one of Elvis' Las Vegas concerts in 1971; at the time, he was serving as a bodyguard for record producer Phil Spector. Elvis introduced Stone to audience that night as a two-year Grand International Champion. By this time, Stone was more involved in promoting, as public interest in the martial arts boomed; he was also working as a bodyguard for musicians and, reputedly, underworld figures.

Elvis got on well with Stone and suggested that he give lessons to Priscilla (an alternative story is that Stone was recommended by Chuck Norris, who had owned a chain of karate schools; in her memoir, Priscilla says that this took place in 1972, and that after sitting in on a lesson with Stone, she decided to go to Chuck Norris's classes to avoid the 45-minute drive from Beverly Hills to Orange County).

Stone became romantically involved with Priscilla in the period before or immediately after she separated from Elvis, depending on accounts. He was still married at the time to Fran, with whom he had two children, Lorie and Shelley. Stories also differ about how Elvis found out about the affair: it has been claimed that little Lisa Marie told him that she had seen Stone and her mom "wrestling" in a sleeping bag on a camping trip; that Sonny West caught them in a shower together; and that a Los Angeles maid tipped off members of the entourage that Stone had been spending rather a lot of time at the house.

Elvis' Southern male pride was perhaps more wounded by his wife sleeping with another man than her wanting to leave him. Such was Elvis' instant loathing for the man that members of the entourage made sure that no television within earshot played "The Streets of San Francisco," because the lead character, played by Karl Malden, was called Lt. Mike Stone.

In 1973, after four fans mobbed Elvis on stage in Las Vegas, Elvis resolved that he wanted Stone killed because he was convinced that Stone had sent the men to harm him. Bodyguards Sonny and Red West stalled for long enough for Elvis to see sense and call off the plan, though not before Red had found out that a hit would cost $10,000. According to Jerry Schilling in his memoir, Elvis' anger was compounded by his suspicion that Stone had persuaded Priscilla to stop sending Lisa Marie to spend time with him at Graceland.

Priscilla and Stone broke up in 1975. He has since worked in the film industry and lectured. For the last twenty years he has lived in the Philippines. At the time of writing, he was working on a documentary about his life.

"STOP, LOOK AND LISTEN"

Elvis recorded this 1964 Rick Nelson hit at Radio Recorders on February 16, 1966 for the soundtrack of *Spinout* and the accompanying LP. The song, written by Joy Byers, later appeared in the movie's *Double Features* release.

Alternate takes are to be found on *Collectors Gold* and the FTD *Spinout* re-issue of 2004.

"STOP WHERE YOU ARE"

One of six Bill Giant / Bernie Baum/ Florence Kaye compositions for the Paradise, Hawaiian Style soundtrack that Elvis' studio band laid down at Radio Recorders on July 27, 1965. Elvis contributed his vocal overdubs on August 3.

The song has since come out on a Nineties *Double Features* release (paired with *Frankie & Johnny*) and the FTD movie reissue, which also features an alternate take.

STORM, TEMPEST
(B. ANNIE BLANCHE BANKS, 1928)

The flame-haired "Queen of Burlesque" stepped out (and stayed in) with Elvis in 1957, while he was spending some vacation time in Las Vegas.

They caught up again at one of Elvis' 1970 Las Vegas shows.

Born in Georgia, Storm ran away from childhood abuse to become a Hollywood film star but found much more durable success in burlesque. At one stage, she reputedly insured her 44D "moneymakers" for a million dollars.

In her memoir, she claims to have had liaisons with rich and powerful men from JFK to Sammy Davis Jr. and Engelbert Humperdinck. She was still performing well into her Seventies.

Book:
Tempest Storm: The Lady Is a Vamp, by Tempest Storm and Bill Boyd, Peachtree Pub., 1987.

STRADA, AL

After being hired as a security guard to look after Priscilla and Lisa Marie in LA in 1972, Strada became a regular member of Elvis' entourage, first with responsibility for security, then looking after Elvis' wardrobe on the road. Strada was at Graceland on the day that Elvis died, making preparations to pack up clothes and costumes for the upcoming tour. He was the first of the guys to go upstairs and try and resuscitate Elvis when Ginger Alden discovered him dead and called down in panic.

Strada is one of very few long-term entourage members who has kept his Elvis memories completely to himself.

STRANGE, BILLY
(B. WILLIAM E. STRANGE, 1930)

All-round West Coast musician Billy Strange first worked with Elvis playing guitar on soundtrack recording sessions starting in 1962 with *It Happened at the World's Fair*. He got the callback to play on *Viva Las Vegas* and *Roustabout* too. Strange later graduated to producing Elvis soundtrack sessions, and got a music director credit on Elvis movies *Live a Little, Love a Little* and *The Trouble with Girls*.

Strange did just about every job in the music industry, from singer to much-in-demand session guitarist, songwriter, conductor, arranger and music publisher. He was responsible for famous arrangements including Nancy Sinatra's "These Boots Are Made For Walking," and the Sinatra father/daughter duet "Something Stupid." He also released his own instrumental recordings of film and TV theme tunes that launched a hybrid musical style that came to be known as "lounge-abilly," and worked with West-Coast artists including the Beach Boys, Jan and Dean and The Monkees in the studio and sometimes out on tour.

Elvis asked producer Steve Binder to hire Billy Strange as musical director for his 1968 NBC TV Special, though before the show went into production he was replaced by Billy Goldenberg.

Over the years, Strange co-wrote Elvis hits "Clean Up Your Own Back Yard," "A Little Less Conversation," "Nothingville," "Memories" and "Charro!."

In the Seventies, Strange opened up his own song publishing company in Nashville.

"STRANGER IN MY OWN HOME TOWN"

Originally a blues hit for "Poet of the Blues" Percy Mayfield, Elvis recorded a horn-driven R&B version of the song at American Studios on February 17, 1969. Elvis' version first came out on the album *From Vegas to Memphis* (*Back in Memphis*).

It has since appeared on *The Memphis Record*, *Elvis Sings The Blues*, *From Nashville to Memphis*, *Suspicious Minds: The Memphis 1969 Anthology*, *Artist Of The Century* and *Elvis R 'n' B*.

A version recorded during rehearsals for *That's The Way It Is* in the summer of 1970 was included on 1995 anthology release *Walk A Mile In My Shoes*; in 2001, FTD included another version (without the overdubbed strings) on *The Memphis Sessions* album, which had previously appeared on

1985 album *Reconsider Baby*.

A full unexpurgated jam rehearsal version with additional (personal) over-18 lyrics has appeared on bootleg *Brightest Star on Sunset Boulevard*.

"STRANGER IN THE CROWD"

Winfield Scott wrote this song for Elvis to record on June 5, 1970, at a Nashville session filmed as part of the *That's The Way It Is* documentary. The song made it onto the documentary tie-in LP. Elvis played the song live at least once during that Las Vegas season. It also appears on *Walk A Mile In My Shoes*.

An alternative take as well as the original release is included in the *That's The Way It Is* Special Edition. Along with the other songs that Elvis rehearsed at this Nashville session, "Stranger In The Crowd" has long been a favorite target for bootleggers.

STREISAND, BARBRA
(B. BARBARA JOAN STREISAND, 1942)

Actress, singer and all-round performer, the woman Leonard Maltin dubbed the Queen of Show Business was born in Brooklyn, New York on April 24, 1942. Streisand came to prominence as a theater actress in *Funny Girl* (1964) on Broadway, after a successful few years with a nightclub act and a couple of albums for Columbia to her name. She soon fronted her own TV specials for CBS (winning five Emmys), and recorded many, many best-selling albums. Her first film role was reprising her stage part in *Funny Girl* (1968), an encore that won her an Oscar. By the end of the Seventies, Streisand was the best-selling female singer of all time in the US, outsold only by Elvis and The Beatles.

Barbra Streisand was the first singer to perform at the newly-built International Hotel in Las Vegas in July 1969, taking a four-week residency before Elvis kicked off at the end of the month. Elvis and his new TCB stage band took a break from their own rehearsals to attend Barbra's closing night show. George Klein recounts that when Elvis and his entourage went backstage, Barbra started making disparaging remarks about his flashy attire. Elvis let one slight pass, another one too, but at the third he let her have it with both barrels: he told her she had a big conk and that she was the ugliest star in Hollywood. The end of the anecdote is that she started laughing and from then on they were the best of friends. Priscilla recalls the initial meeting as starting off badly when Elvis questioned what Streisand had ever seen in Elliot Gould—her husband until 1971.

Streisand has won countless Grammy awards as well her two Oscars. Her first #1 was the theme tune to a film in which she starred, *The Way We Were*; her second number one was "Evergreen," from *A Star Is Born*. She is the only artist to have #1 albums on the *Billboard* charts in the Sixties, Seventies, Eighties and Nineties, and has produced and directed a number of award-winning movies.

In March 1975, Streisand offered Elvis a role in her forthcoming movie, a remake of *A Star Is Born*, after watching Elvis perform in Vegas (Elvis introduced her to the audience during the concert). Though Elvis was initially interested in returning to the screen in this project, in the end their respective management teams were unable to agree terms and Elvis' interest waned. An alternative recollection of what happened from a number of entourage guys is that Elvis changed his mind about doing the movie (in some tellings, he realized that that he could never get back into

shape for the role) and put the Colonel up to naming an unacceptable price. For many fans and some biographers, the Colonel's insistence on an outlandish fee and top billing scuppered Elvis' last chance to break out of his downward spiral.

STRICKLAND, LARRY

A member of Elvis' back-up gang from 1974 through the Stamps, Strickland worked on Elvis' later albums, including *From Elvis Presley Boulevard, Memphis, Tennessee*, recorded at Graceland in early 1976. Elvis sometimes dueted on stage with the bass singer as part of his stage act.

LARRY STRICKLAND: "He was a frustrated bass singer and he loved that low part."

STRICTLY ELVIS

An EP shipped in late January 1957 featuring more material from Elvis' second album. The EP sold 200,000 copies.

TRACK LISTING:
1. Long Tall Sally
2. First In Line
3. How Do You Think I Feel
4. How's The World Treating You

STRZELECKI, HENRY

Alabama-born bass-player Strzelecki was a popular Nashville session musician who worked frequently with Hank Garland and Chet Atkins. In his early career he played in a family group, and wrote novelty hit "Long Tall Texan." He worked with Elvis on the *Harum Scarum* soundtrack, and later filled in on the *How Great Thou Art* sessions in 1966.

As well as playing with a great many artists who have recorded in Nashville (Bob Dylan and Waylon Jennings to name just two), Strzelecki has also had a successful career in song publishing and production.

"STUCK ON YOU"

Marking Elvis' comeback after two years out serving the nation, RCA printed over a million copies of this single and rushed it from the studio to the pressing plant and out to stores in late March 1960 with B-side track "Fame And Fortune." Advance orders exceeded a staggering 1.25 million. Three weeks later the single had claimed the #1 spot on the *Billboard* charts; it stayed at #1 for four weeks, and remained in the charts for a total of 16 weeks, boosted by Elvis' performance of the song on the "Frank Sinatra Show" (a version released many years later on *Platinum: A Life in Music*; a video of this performance came out on 2007 DVD release *Elvis #1 Hit Performances*).

The song was written by Aaron Schroeder and J. Leslie McFarland, who undoubtedly drew inspiration from Elvis' huge 1957 hit "All Shook Up." Elvis recorded the song at the RCA studios in Nashville on March 21, fresh back from Germany. As a single, it was Elvis' first true stereo release.

The song's first album release did not come until 1963 issue *Elvis' Golden Records Vol. 3*.

The track has since appeared on *Worldwide Gold Award Hits Vols. 1*, *Top Ten Hits*, and in remastered form on *From Nashville to Memphis*, *Artist Of The Century*, *ELVIS 30 #1 Hits* and *Hitstory*. Alternate takes are available on *Essential Elvis Vol. 6*, *ELVIS 30 #1 Hits Deluxe Edition*, and FTD releases *Fame And Fortune* and *Elvis Is Back!*

STUDIO B: NASHVILLE OUTTAKES

A 2003 FTD release of alternate Elvis takes recorded in Nashville between 1961 and 1964.

TRACK LISTING:
1. Kiss Me Quick
2. That's Someone You Never Forget
3. I'm Yours
4. (Marie's The Name) His Latest Flame (rehearsal)
5. Little Sister
6. For The Millionth And The Last Time
7. Anything That's Part Of You
8. I Met Her Today
9. Something Blue
10. Gonna Get Back Home Somehow
11. (Such An) Easy Question
12. Fountain Of Love
13. Just For Old Time Sake
14. Night Rider
15. You'll Be Gone
16. I Feel That I've Known You Forever
17. Just Tell Her Jim Said Hello
18. Echoes Of Love
19. Please Don't Drag That String Around
20. Love Me Tonight
21. Western Union
22. Memphis Tennessee
23. Ask Me

SUCCESS

Elvis' success stands transcendent; his very name is shorthand for iconic status and worldwide fame. When he died, it was as if the air was sucked out the lungs of millions of people around the world. Carl Perkins did not court controversy when he said, "We've lost the most popular man that ever walked on this planet since Christ himself was here."

As Elvis' career accelerated into top gear, Elvis told reporters that success was like "a dream to me." He humbly acknowledged that success would only last for as long as he could "continue to please the public." He told another interviewer, "half the time I don't know from one day to the next where I'm going, 'cos I have so much on my mind and I'm tryin' to keep up with everything, and trying to keep a level head."

In the early days, Elvis defined success as being able to provide for his mother, move her to a nice house, and buy her lots of things. He soon learned to appreciate and share the trappings of success with the wider circle of family and friends that he gathered around himself. He was always scrupulously grateful to his fans, not just signing autographs (and sometimes risking life and limb), but in the Fifties and early Sixties inviting countless adoring female fans into his life.

The nature of and reason for Elvis' success—the question of why he, Elvis Presley, had been plucked from what would otherwise have been an unremarked-upon blue-collar existence—was something that exercised him greatly in the Sixties, prompting him to embark on a concerted spiritual quest.

People sometimes forget how hard Elvis worked hard to remain a success. When he went off to his two-year posting in Germany, he fully expected to come back to nothing. Instead, he came back more popular than ever as a mainstream music and film entertainer. When that vein of success was close to being mined out, in 1968 he defied oblivion with his NBC TV Special, known ever after as the "Comeback Special," showing his old fans that he still had the fire and passion of his rocking youth, while at the same time conquering a whole new generation of fans. He continued the comeback in the summer of 1969 with his triumphal show at the newly-built International Hotel in Las Vegas, where after his opening night many critics who had been ready to write him off lauded his commanding performance. Elvis played over a thousand shows during the final phase of his career, often battling ill-health to give his fans what they came to see: an outstanding performance by an outstanding performer.

Even thirty years after his death, Elvis continues to push back the barriers of what constitutes success. He regularly tops the list of highest-earning dead celebrities, and his home is the second-most visited residence in the United States (after the White House). The challenge for the keepers of the Elvis flame is to maintain his profile high with upcoming generations of music fans.

See also AMBITION, CAREER, FAME, ICON.

ELVIS SAID IN 1956: "When my first record came out it was a little eerie. . . . I thought people would laugh."

ELVIS SAID IN 1956: "I hope I won't change. I hope I'll never be like some of the people I've seen, who forget that they never could have been successful or happy at all without God's help."

ELVIS SAID IN 1958: "I happened to come along at a time in the music business where there was no trend . . . I mean the people were looking for something different and I was lucky."

BILLY SMITH: "Elvis was doing fairly good from '54 to '55. But when the Colonel came along, bang! Instant success!"

ED PARKER: "He gives things to people without even knowing who they are, and with no thought of ever seeing them again. That's what he does. He just likes to share his success. It's as simple as that."

LARRY GELLER: "Success for Elvis meant never worrying about money or anything else. That's what he'd hired the best professionals to do, and he fully believed that they'd do what was best for him without his having to ask."

"SUCH A NIGHT"

This single, released on July 14, 1964 with "Never Ending" on the B-side, was taken from four-year old LP *Elvis Is Back!* and recorded by Elvis in the early hours of April 4, 1960 in Nashville as part of the material he recorded for his homecoming album.

The decision to re-release the track as a single four years later came after Conway Twitty released a version of the song that did well in the charts. Elvis' version sold 300,000 copies, which was insufficient to propel it any higher than #16.

Written by Lincoln Chase, the song was first sung by Clyde McPhatter and the Drifters in 1953. Johnnie Ray's cover the following year was considered so scandalous that it was banned from the radio in the US; over the Atlantic, it made it to #1.

Elvis made a home recording of the number in 1959, the year he was stationed in Germany. He rarely played the song live in the Seventies, despite briefly considering it as a closing number when rehearsing for his 1969 Las Vegas live return.

The original release is to be found on compilation albums such as *From Nashville to Memphis*, *Artist Of The Century* and *Hitstory*.

Alternates have been coming out since *Elvis: A Legendary Performer Vol. 2* in 1976, and include *Elvis Aron Presley* (a live performance from Hawaii in 1961), *That's The Way It Is—Special Edition*, and *Essential Elvis Vol. 6—Such A Night*. FTD release *Fame And Fortune* features another alternate, while the 2005 remastered and remixed FTD version of *Elvis Is Back!* offers a smorgasbord of alternates, including one in which Elvis fluffs the start.

SUCH A NIGHT

An Australian EP released by RCA in 1975.

TRACK LISTING:
1.   Such A Night
2.   It Feels So Right
3.   Like A Baby
4.   Make Me Know It

SUICIDE

Claims have been made over the years that Elvis died by his own hand. Stepbrother David Stanley said as much in 1990 in an interview, though his opinion was not shared by the doctors and coroner involved in the aftermath of Elvis' death.

Nevertheless, very few people dispute that Elvis' abuse of drugs significantly weakened his system, and his physical deterioration was a significant source of unhappiness in his life.

See DEATh (SIDEBAR: SUICIDE? MURDER?)

DAVE HEBLER, 1976: "It is absolute insanity that a human being would want to commit slow suicide, which I feel he is doing with the drugs."

SULLIVAN, ED
(B. EDWARD VINCENT SULLIVAN, 1902-1974)

Ed Sullivan switched from newspapers to TV when CBS hired him for a weekly variety show in the Thirties. Though he lacked the performing background of his rivals, Sullivan built a reputation for picking and promoting exciting new acts and performers. He was the first US TV presenter to host The Beatles, in a show that, at that time, was the most watched show ever on American TV. Such was his influence that he managed to get prominent entertainers such as The Rolling Stones to tone down their lyrics (they renamed the song "Let's Spend The Night Together" to "Let's Spend Some Time Together"). He also provided the first national platform for comics Woody Allen, Richard Pryor and Rowan and Martin among the thousands of acts who debuted on his variety show.

Born in Manhattan, New York on September 28, 1902, Sullivan started out as a newspaper reporter before becoming a columnist and then migrating to the radio. Before the second world war, he turned his hand to writing and acting in the movies with *Mr. Broadway* and others. In 1948, his Sunday night TV show "Toast of the Town" made this unprepossessing man an unlikely household name in the increasing number of US homes that had a new-fangled TV set. Renamed "The Ed Sullivan Show" in 1955, Sullivan continued to present his variety showcase on the nation's screens until 1971. He also made cameos in a number of movies, including 1963 Elvis-themed flick *Bye Bye Birdie*, and kept up his newspaper column and radio presence for

the best part of half a century. Sullivan was also notorious for getting his revenge on people he believed had crossed him, many of whom, perhaps not coincidentally, were rivals for the nation's televisual affections.

Ed Sullivan initially made a public declaration that he would not invite rabble-rouser Elvis onto his show in 1956. The huge audiences Elvis was pulling in on rival TV variety shows persuaded him to change his mind.

FRED ALLEN: "Ed Sullivan will stay on the air as long as other people have talent."

SUMMER FESTIVAL

A 2005 FTD release of Elvis' performances from his August 11, 1972 dinner show in Las Vegas plus extras.

TRACK LISTING:
1.   Also Sprach Zarathustra
2.   See See Rider
3.   I Got A Woman
4.   Until It's Time For You To Go
5.   You Don't Have To Say You Love Me
6.   You've Lost That Lovin' Feelin'
7.   Polk Salad Annie
8.   What Now My Love
9.   Fever
10. Love Me
11. Blue Suede Shoes
12. One Night
13. All Shook Up
14. Teddy Bear / Don't Be Cruel
15. Heartbreak Hotel
16. Hound Dog
17. Love Me Tender
18. Suspicious Minds
19. Introductions
20. My Way
21. An American Trilogy
22. Can't Help Falling In Love / Instrumental closing
23. Little Sister / Get Back (August 11)
24. It's Over   (August 11)
25. Proud Mary (August 12)
26. Never Been To Spain (August 12)
27. For The Good Times (August 12)
28. A Big Hunk O'Love (August 12,)
29. Tiger Man (August 12)

"SUMMER KISSES, WINTER TEARS"

Elvis recorded this Fred Wise / Ben Weisman / Jack Lloyd song in a sweet-voiced style at Radio Recorders on August 8, 1960 for Flaming Star. The song wound up being cut from the picture when the audience unexpectedly burst into laughter at a pre-release screening.

"Summer Kisses, Winter Tears" first appeared on 1961 EP *Elvis By Request—Flaming Star*, before finding a berth on the *Elvis For Everyone* album in 1965.

The *Collectors Gold* release from 1991 featured an alternate take, as did *Elvis: Close Up* and FTD release *Silver Screen Stereo*. A slightly different version appears alongside the standard on the Nineties *Double Features* release for *Flaming Star* (this is the movie version, in which Elvis is accompanied by an Indian chief on a drum).

"SUMMERTIME"

Elvis made a personal request for this song at his New Year's party for 1968, and danced to the tune with seven months' pregnant Priscilla.

"SUMMERTIME IS PASSED AND GONE"

Elvis and friends sing a line from this Bill Monroe and The Bluegrass Boys hit from 1946 during his *Million Dollar Quartet* jam session at Sun Studios on December 4, 1956. It's on the usual *MDQ* releases.

SUMNER, DONNIE
(B. 1942)

A second-cousin of J. D. Sumner's (J. D. adopted Donnie's sister), Donnie Sumner joined the Stamps gospel quartet in 1965 as a singer, arranger and songwriter, and won Grammy nominations for his compositions. He met Elvis around this time, with J.D. Sumner.

Sumner sang with Elvis as part of the Stamps from 1971 to 1973, including work on *Elvis on Tour* and *Aloha from Hawaii*.

Sumner left the Stamps in 1973 but swiftly returned to work with Elvis when the singer hired him as part of his own personal gospel quartet, Voice.

Sumner played piano on the few tracks that Elvis recorded in Palm Springs in the fall of 1973—released on the *Raised on Rock* LP—including his own compositions "Mr. Songman" and "I Miss You."

Sumner continued to perform with Elvis and sing with him at home until late 1976. Soon after Elvis' death, he become a full-time minister.

SUMNER, J. D.
(B. JOHN DANIEL SUMNER, 1924-1998)

A member of one of Elvis' favorite gospel groups, the Blackwood Brothers, since 1954, bass singer J. D. Sumner was also a founder member of the National Quartet Convention and the Gospel Music Association. One Elvis biographer has written that for young Elvis, J. D. Sumner was "Elvis' Elvis." When Elvis was no more than 14, he regularly went to see the Blackwood Brothers perform and befriended the group backstage. J. D. Sumner recalls, "I used to let him in the back door for our shows for nothing; and the first thing I knew, he let me in the back door of his concerts for nothing."

Born on November 19, 1924 in Florida, as a four year-old J.D. Sumner knew that he wanted to grow up to be a bass singer like his hero, Frank Stamps. He joined the Sunshine Boys, then moved on to the Blackwood Brothers. He quit the Blackwood Brothers in 1965 after buying the rights to the Stamps Quartet name.

Elvis invited J.D. Sumner and his group the Stamps to tour with him in November 1971 as a replacement for the Imperials. From that moment on, the group toured with Elvis and recorded backing vocals in the studio, starting with Elvis' March 1972 RCA session that yielded hits such as "Always On My Mind," "Burning Love" and "Separate Ways." The group was captured on film in concert movies *Elvis on Tour*, *Aloha from Hawaii* and *Elvis in Concert*. Sumner and the Stamps took over from Voice on tour with Elvis from late 1975, and continued to sing with Elvis until the end.

Over the years, Elvis lavished a number of gifts on Sumner, including money for a tour bus, a limousine, expensive jewelry and a selection of Elvis' old early Seventies outfits—Sumner apparently referred to his left hand as "Elvis Presley's hand" because of all the rings Elvis had given him.

Sumner and his group the Stamps sang hymns at Elvis' funeral. He also recorded tribute song "Elvis Has Left The Building," and two albums of Elvis gospel favorites.

Sumner once held the world record for the lowest recorded note, a "double low C," on his song "Blessed Assurance." Elvis regularly introduced Sumner on stage as the "lowest bass singer in the world," and let him prove it on live songs such as "Help Me" and "Why Me Lord."

Sumner sang with the Masters V from 1980, after disbanding the Stamps.

CHARLIE HODGE: "J.D. Sumner was just as bad as Elvis, he loved a good practical joke especially if it wasn't on him."

Book:
Elvis: His Love for Gospel Music and J.D. Sumner, by J. D. Sumner and Bob Terrell, WCI Publishing, 1991.

SUN RECORDS

Sam Phillips' record label, which grew out of his Memphis Recording Service, was a driving force behind the R&B and rock 'n' roll revolution that swept through popular music in the US in the early Fifties. Soon after founding the Memphis Recording Service (motto: "We Record Anything, Anywhere, Anytime"), Phillips started a record label with top local DJ Dewey Phillips (no relation), with the intention of signing unknown African-American blues performers. Their first release, Joe Hill Louis single "Gotta Let You Go," turned out to be their last. Phillips continued to record on behalf of established labels, including in 1951 what is generally regarded as the first ever rock 'n' roll recording, Jackie Brenston and his Delta Cat's "Rocket 88" (though in actuality, the band belonged to Ike Turner, and the new sound they achieved was less Phillips' intervention than the fact that the guitarist's amp was damaged en route to the studio because it fell from the car roof).

In February 1952, Sam Phillips launched his own Sun Records label with Jackie Boy and Little Walter's "Blue In My Condition" and "Sellin' My Whiskey." Actually recorded by Walter Horton and Jack Kelly, the songs had previously been turned down by Chess, for whom Phillips regularly recorded. However, Phillips got cold feet before distributing this record. According to the book *Memphis Recording Service*, Sun's first actual release was saxophone player Johnny London's song "Drivin' Slow"

Sun Records' first hit was Rufus Thomas's "Bearcat," an "answer record" to "Hound Dog" that Phillips was so quick to bring out that Thomas's response followed Big Mama Thornton's original into the R&B charts within two weeks, making it to #3. Alas for Sam Phillips, this huge success threw the nascent record label into serious jeopardy: Phillips lost a plagiarism case brought on behalf of Big Mama Thornton, and he was forced to pay such a large amount in damages that he thought he may have to close down. Phillips worked his way back by recording local Memphis greats Howlin' Wolf , B. B. King, "Little Junior" Parker and the Blue Flames, and Ike Turner, as well as extending into the white hillbilly market.

Elvis came into the picture against this backdrop, though his path to a contract with Sun was hardly smooth. The young singer paid for a couple of recording sessions out of his own pocket before catching Phillips' ear sufficiently to earn an audition. In June 1954, Phillips invited Elvis in to the studio to try out "Without You," a song written by an inmate of the state penitentiary. As Marion Keisker later said, "We got Elvis to come in and try, but he couldn't do the song to satisfy Sam. That might have been the end of it, but something stirred Sam's interest."

Keisker was the one who had initially taken the boy's money, set up the mike and cut the disk when he had come in to record his first vanity acetates almost a year earlier. Many biographers feel that if she hadn't kept a copy of the disc herself to play to Sam later (months passed before she got the chance), Elvis simply wouldn't have had a chance to record at Sun, and may not have had a career in the music industry at all. Phillips was most likely out at a wedding the first time that Elvis stopped by, making the money he needed to keep the studio afloat.

After he finished his regular job on Monday, July 5th 1954, Elvis joined Scotty Moore and Bill Black for a rehearsal session at Sun during which Elvis sang his way through his favorite ballads. Once again, Sam Phillips was less than impressed . . . until, during a break, Elvis broke into an idiosyncratic rendition of Arthur "Big Boy" Crudup's "That's All Right (Mama)." Sam Phillips' instincts told him to record a few takes of this impromptu session, and he decided that this could well be an A-side for Elvis' first single. The improvised tune was propelled by Elvis' rhythmic delivery, Bill Black's slapped bass and Scotty Moore trying to play guitar as Sam advised, as dirty as he could. On the spot, Sam Phillips achieved what he later defined that as "a spontaneous rhythm thing."

Phillips suspected that they were onto something, the "something different" he had been looking for ever since he opened the doors to the Memphis Recording Service four years earlier. Scotty Moore recalls that when he heard those first songs played back, his reaction was, "Good God! They'll run us out of town when they hear this!" Elvis' reaction? He is said to have cried when he saw his name on that first record, Sun 209.

The day when Elvis cut his first disk has been named the most significant moment in music history in the UK by readers of *Mojo* magazine.

The same line-up returned over the next couple of days, trying out various possible B-Sides before finally settling on "Blue Moon Of Kentucky," which before Elvisification was known as a bluegrass classic by Bill Monroe.

Elvis formally signed to Sun Records on July 26, 1954. He was contracted for a minimum of eight tracks over the following two years, with an option for Sun Records to renew for a further two years. Elvis' royalty rate was 3% of the wholesale price.

Elvis recorded the two tracks for his second single, "Good Rockin' Tonight" and "I Don't Care If The Sun Don't Shine," on September 11, 1954 (Sun 210), though according to some accounts he booked the studio time two weeks later. Sam Phillips was so sure that he was onto something that between Elvis' first and second singles, Sun Records put out no other material and merely focused on getting Elvis' first record out to as wide an audience as possible.

Released in late September, Elvis' follow-up single repeated Sam Phillips' template of one blues-based track and one up-tempo rendition of a country song. It sold very respectably, but wasn't as successful as his first release.

Elvis was so busy touring for the rest of the year that it wasn't until early- (or mid-) December that he returned to the studio to record "Milkcow Blues Boogie" and "You're A Heartbreaker," for Sun release #215, issued on December 28, 1954.

The new year began as the previous one had ended, with a busy schedule of live shows keeping Elvis out of the studio. In the first week of February 1955—debate continues about the exact dates—Elvis, Scotty and Bill laid down the A-side to the follow-up single, "Baby Let's Play House," and recorded a version of Ray Charles' tune "I Got A Woman." They also made an unsuccessful stab at "Tryin' To Get To You." B-side track "I'm Left, You're Right, She's Gone" was written specially for the occasion by

Five of Elvis' singles, released by Sun Records.

Sun steel guitarist Stan Kesler; in early March Elvis recorded slow and up-tempo versions, on which Memphis teenage drummer Jimmie Lott added the first drum part on any Elvis record.

In late March 1955, the Colonel insisted to Elvis' official manager Bob Neal that the performer's contract with Sun was hindering his career because of poor distribution outside Sun's home territory. The Colonel brokered an agreement with Bob Neal that it was best for all parties if Elvis' bookings were handled by the Colonel's larger, better-connected organization. This was the first phase in the Colonel's strategy of prising Elvis away from Sun Records and signing him to a nationally-prominent label. Elvis was dead set against the idea at first, but behind the scenes Parker engineered a deal with RCA that yielded up-front monies to buy out Elvis' contract with Sun at a favorable fee, including promises of national exposure that Sun could never offer. For Sam Phillips and Sun, the lure of such unprecedented money for a relatively unknown artist would mean financial security after years of uncertainty. Elvis' very success had been proving

to be a problem, because of the back royalties owed to their budding star.

Engineer Jack Clement has said that the acoustics of the studio changed depending on how sales were going: it sounded different if the place was stacked with returned and unsold records. Stacks of returns were a fact of life, as record companies like Sun massively and optimistically printed discs in the hope that their releases would be a hit.

During a two-week break from touring in early July 1955, Elvis laid down three new tracks at the studio: "I Forgot To Remember To Forget," written for him once again by Stan Kesler, "Mystery Train," sung originally by Little Junior Parker and produced by studio owner Sam Phillips the first time round in 1953, and "Tryin' To Get To You," previously a hit for R&B combo the Eagles.

The Colonel's masterstroke came in October 1955, when he persuaded Elvis' parents Vernon and Gladys to authorize him and his business partner Hank Snow to make a new record deal for Elvis with a new label.

Elvis' last ever recording session at Sun

Records was on October 30, 1955, when he sang "When It Rains, It Really Pours" as a potential B-side for "Tryin' To Get To You." The session ended abruptly without a viable version of the song, and it was not until February 1957 that Elvis put down a satisfactory version of the song for release by RCA.

The official signing of Elvis' new contract with RCA and the transfer of his previous recordings took place at Sun Studio on November 21, 1955, at a meeting attended by Sam Phillips, Steve Sholes, Coleman Tily, Colonel Tom Parker, Tom Diskin, Hank Snow, a lawyer for song publisher Hill & Range, Bob Neal, and Elvis and his parents Vernon and Gladys. Not everything Elvis had recorded with Sun made the journey; Phillips had previously recorded over some of Elvis' earlier tapes. An unspecified number of the demos, alternate masters and tapes that were transferred to RCA were unfortunately discarded in the late Fifties as RCA weeded out old material from its vaults, though many fans continue to hope that this goldmine of early Elvis material may one day be rediscovered.

Though Elvis would willingly have stayed at Sun, performer Barbara Pittman is sure that his career would have tailed off if he hadn't made a move to a major label. At the time, Sun proprietor Sam Phillips was very keen on buying his way into radio stations, and discovering the next hot artist to follow Elvis.

Post Elvis, Sam Phillips continued to record new acts, finding and discovering future greats including Johnny Cash, Carl Perkins, Roy Orbison and Jerry Lee Lewis, plus a long list of rockabilly notables through the rest of the Fifties.

Elvis dropped in to his old stomping ground on December 4, 1956, while Carl Perkins was doing a recording session. When Elvis started jamming with Perkins and pianist Jerry Lee Lewis, recently signed to Sun, Sam Phillips left the tape running. Johnny Cash was the fourth member of the "Million Dollar Quartet," as it was named by local journalist Bob Johnson.

Sam's brother Judd, who had helped with promotion and sales since Sun was founded, left to set up his own label in 1958. The studio moved to a new, larger premises at 639 Madison Avenue in 1959; not long afterwards, Phillips set up a studio in Nashville. Sun continued to turn out records in the Sixties but lost its reputation as an innovator as Phillips pursued other avenues of interest. The label's last release, by a group called Load of Mischief, came in 1968. The following year, Phillips sold the label and all of its recordings to Shelby Singleton.

In 1970, at a press conference Elvis declared that his early Sun records now sounded "funny" to him: "They got a lot of echo on 'em, man."

The original building at 706 Union Ave. was converted back into a studio in 1987, and to this day functions as a recording studio. Many major recording artists have made the pilgrimage to Sun's single, open-plan recording studio, including U2, Def Leppard, John Fogerty, Dennis Quaid and Bonnie Raitt. Sun Studio has been a National Historic Landmark tourist attraction since 2003, and is one of Memphis's top tourist destinations.

Elvis' Sun output has been collected and released at regular intervals since his death, each time with more material, generally with the sound improved in modern-technology enhanced mixes (*The Sun Sessions*, *Sunrise*, *Elvis at Sun* and more). Fans can look forward to more Sun-branded Elvis merchandise following a 2006 deal between Sun and EPE.

SAM PHILLIPS: "Everything had to be a stinger, and it had to have great rhythm."

JACK CLEMENT: "Sun was just a place that was a lot more experimental than most. I think that is the main thing that made it happen. It was just the only place them weirdoes could go."

STAN KESLER: "At Sun you always felt at home. Sam had a way of making everybody feel like a king when he walked in the door."

BOB NEAL: "I think Sam always wanted to be the whole ball of wax, which possibly was the reason that Sun Records did not expand, and later on folded."

BOB DYLAN: "On Sun Records the artists were singing for their lives and sounded like they were coming from the most mysterious place on the planet."

GREIL MARCUS: "The music Sun produced was ominous, funny, kicking up rhythm and bursting with exuberance, determination, and urgency, full of self-conscious novelty and experiment."

WAYNE JACKSON: "Sun Studios is probably the most important place in the world for rock'n'roll... you can certainly feel that something very important happened in that room."

Books:

Elvis, The Sun Years: The Story of Elvis Presley in the Fifties, by Howard A. DeWitt, Popular Culture Ink, 1991

Good Rockin' Tonight: Sun Records and the Birth of Rock 'N' Roll, by Colin Escott and Martin Hawkins, St. Martin's 1991

Early Elvis: The Sun Years, by Bill E. Burk, Propwash Publishing, 1997

SUN SESSIONS, THE

The US version of this British release (marketed originally as *The Sun Collection*) came out as an album in March 1976. It climbed no higher than #76 in the charts on the back of 300,000 sales, but became a strong long-term seller for RCA.

TRACK LISTING:
1. That's All Right (Mama)
2. Blue Moon Of Kentucky
3. I Don't Care If The Sun Don't Shine
4. Good Rockin' Tonight
5. Milkcow Blues Boogie
6. You're A Heartbreaker
7. I'm Left, You're Right, She's Gone
8. Baby Let's Play House
9. Mystery Train
10. I Forgot To Remember To Forget
11. I'll Never Let You Go (Little Darlin')
12. I Love You Because
13. Tryin' To Get To You
14. Blue Moon
15. Just Because
16. I Love You Because (alternate)

The album has been reissued many times with alternate takes and extra songs.

SUNRISE

A 1999 2-CD release of live and studio material featuring alternate takes from Elvis' early years. The first disc is mainly of master takes, while the second offers alternates, outtakes and banter, and also features a cameo from Carl Perkins.

TRACK LISTING:
DISC 1:
1. That's All Right (Mama)
2. Blue Moon Of Kentucky
3. Good Rockin' Tonight
4. I Don't Care If The Sun Don't Shine
5. Milkcow Blues Boogie
6. You're A Heartbreaker
7. Baby Let's Play House
8. I'm Left, You're Right, She's Gone
9. I Forgot To Remember To Forget
10. Mystery Train
11. I Love You Because
12. Harbor Lights
13. Blue Moon
14. Tomorrow Night
15. I'll Never Let You Go (Little Darlin')
16. Just Because
17. I'm Left, You're Right, She's Gone
18. Tryin' To Get To You
19. When It Rains, It Really Pours
DISC 2:
20. My Happiness
21. That's When Your Heartaches Begin
22. I'll Never Stand In Your Way
23. It Wouldn't Be The Same Without You
24. I Love You Because
25. That's All Right (Mama)
26. Blue Moon Of Kentucky
27. Blue Moon
28. I'll Never Let You Go (Little Darlin')

29. I Don't Care If The Sun Don't Shine
30. I'm Left, You're Right, She's Gone
31. Fool, Fool, Fool
32. Shake, Rattle & Roll
33. I'm Left, You're Right, She's Gone
34. That's All Right (Mama)
35. Money Honey
36. Tweedlee Dee
37. I Don't Care If The Sun Don't Shine
38. Hearts Of Stone

SUPERSTITION

Elvis had no qualms admitting that he was superstitious at a 1961 press conference, though he would not elaborate beyond broken mirrors. Gladys was certainly a very superstitious person.

See also MYSTICISM

"SUPPOSE"

Elvis originally recorded this ballad at home with Charlie Hodge in 1966 (released years later on *Home Recordings*) and was so enamored of the song that he got Felton to gather together a band in Nashville on March 20, 1967 to overdub instrumentation. The result of this session, however, did not see release until the Nineties anthology *From Nashville to Memphis*. Elvis tried again, laying down two versions in the early hours of June 21, 1967, with the intention of including the Sylvia Dee / George Goehring composition in *Speedway*. After it was cut from the picture, one version was included on the soundtrack album as a bonus track, while the other, longer version had to wait for the movie's *Double Features* release in the Nineties.

An undubbed version from 1966 came out years later on *A Golden Celebration*.

Elvis author Paul Simpson speculates that this piano-led Elvis song may have offered John Lennon a template for "Imagine."

"SURRENDER"

An up-tempo anglicized version of Neapolitan classic "Torna a Surriento," with words by Doc Pomus and Mort Shuman, that Elvis recorded in Nashville on October 30, 1960, at a session otherwise monopolized by gospel tracks for the *His Hand In Mine* album. Elvis evidently couldn't resist measuring himself up against his hero Mario Lanza, one of many artists who had recorded the Italian original, written by Ernesto and Gian Battista De Curtis and first released in 1902.

Elvis' "Surrender" fronted a single in early February 1961 with B-side "Lonely Man," a track recorded for (but dropped from) upcoming film *Wild in the Country*. Though the single sold 750,000 copies rather than the million of "Are You Lonesome Tonight?," it still easily made it to #1 during its 12 weeks in the charts. It did even better in the UK, claiming the top spot for five whole weeks.

The first album release for this song came on *Elvis' Golden Records Vol. 3*. It has subsequently appeared on *Worldwide Gold Award Hits Vol. 1*, *Elvis: A Legendary Performer Vol. 3*, *From Nashville To Memphis*, *Artist Of The Century*, *ELVIS 30 #1*, *Love Elvis* and *Hitstory*.

Alternate versions are on *Elvis Sings Mort Shuman & Doc Pomus*, *From Nashville To Memphis*, *Essential Elvis, Vol. 6*, *ELVIS 30 #1 Hits Deluxe 2 CD Edition* and *Elvis: Close Up*. FTD release *Fame And Fortune* features an alternate, while the 2006 FTD reworking of 1960 album *His Hand In Mine* includes five alternate takes of the song plus the official version.

A rare live version from 1969 that segues into "Are You Lonesome Tonight?" came out on 1991 anthology *Collectors Gold*.

"SUSAN WHEN SHE TRIED"

Elvis recorded this country-pickin' track at the RCA Hollywood studios on March 11, 1975 for release on the album *Today*. Don Reid's song first came out a year previously, sung by the Statler Brothers.

"Susan When She Tried" is included on *Walk A Mile In My Shoes*, *Great Country Songs* and, in remastered format, on *The Country Side of Elvis*. The FTD releases 6363 *Sunset* has an alternate version; the FTD release of *Today* sports several.

"SUZIE-Q"

This Dale Hawkins hit from 1957—on which Elvis' Seventies guitarist James Burton played the catchy riff—was never released by Elvis officially, though a recording of Elvis singing a few lines of the song surfaced on a bootleg recording of a show he performed in Norfolk, Virginia, in July 1975 (the album takes its name from the song).

The song has also been covered by Creedence Clearwater Revival and José Feliciano among others. Burton is known to have broken into the song at a 1970 recording session, in the hope that Elvis might pick up on it.

SUZIE Q

A bootleg release of a live Elvis show from 1975 on the Astra label.

TRACK LISTING:
1. True Love Travels On A Gravel Road
2. Portrait Of My Love
3. You Don't Have To Say You Love Me
4. Any Day Now
5. My Way
6. You Don't Know Me
7. Faded Love
8. Good Time Charlie's Got The Blues
9. Turn Around Look At Me
10. When My Blue Moon Turns To Gold Again
11. You Can Have Her, I Don't Want Her
12. Blue Christmas
13. Suzie Q
14. Blueberry Hill

"SUSPICION"

Elvis recorded this Doc Pomus / Mort Shuman ballad with a restrained rocking chorus on March 19, 1962 at Studio B in Nashville, for initial release on the *Pot Luck* album. The song came out later as the B-side to the ill-fated "Kiss Me Quick" single, released in April 1964, to fight off a cover version by competing singer Terry Stafford . . . unsuccessfully, it turned out: Elvis' version failed to chart while Stafford's cover made it to #3.

The song has since featured on *From Nashville to Memphis*. It also appears on *Elvis Sings Mort Shuman & Doc Pomus*, the later French version of which, *Elvis Chante Mort Shuman & Doc Pomus*, contains an alternate of the song and the songwriters' demo. An alternate is also included on *Essential Elvis, Vol. 6*, and on FTD release *Pot Luck*.

"SUSPICIOUS MINDS"

Producer Chips Moman proposed this song to Elvis on the last night of his initial session bookings at American Studio, on January 23, 1969. Songwriter Mark James (real name Francis Rodney Zambon) had tried and failed to record a viable version of the song at the Studio not long before Elvis' session. Encouraged by his pals, who recognized its hit potential, Elvis nailed the song in just four takes, the last song in a string of great tunes admirably performed. Briefly, it looked like this masterful performance would never see the light of day as studio owner Chips Moman refused to succumb to the Colonel's standard, disadvantageous (for Moman) music publishing deal.

Shipped in late August 1969 with B-side "You'll Think Of Me," the song turned out to be Elvis' first #1 single since "Good Luck Charm" in 1962, and was the final #1 single release of his career.

Felton Jarvis adapted the American single release candidate by adding a horn section coda after a false ending, which was how Elvis had been performing the song in Las Vegas during his return to live performing at the International Hotel. Some critics have claimed that Jarvis altered the original less for music reasons than to put his own imprimatur on a track that had been produced by Moman and his studio band (who had also recorded the song with songwriter Mark James). The "Suspicious Minds" that RCA originally released was put together from three takes, and at 4'22" clocked in as Elvis' longest #1 hit. "Suspicious Minds" sold 1,250,000 copies on initial release.

The song's first album release was a seven-minute plus live version on *From Memphis To Vegas/Elvis In Person at the International Hotel*.

Until mid-way through 1974, "Suspicious Minds" was a staple in Elvis' live shows; only very occasionally did he give it a run-out afterwards. The song featured in his documentaries *Elvis: That's The Way It Is* and *Elvis on Tour*. He also sang the song during the *Aloha From Hawaii* satellite broadcast (reprised in 1981 TV movie *This Is Elvis* and the tie-in album release).

The studio release has appeared on myriad collections, including *Elvis' Gold Records Vol. 5*, *Worldwide 50 Gold Award Hits Vol. 1*, *From Nashville To Memphis*, the 2000 re-release of *From Elvis In Memphis*, the CD reissue of *On Stage*, *Artist Of The Century*, *ELVIS 30#1 Hits*, *Hitstory*, *Elvis By The Presleys*, and *The Essential Elvis Presley*.

Alternate takes from the original session have appeared on *From Nashville To Memphis*, *Platinum: A Life In Music*, *Suspicious Minds: The Memphis 1969 Anthology*, *ELVIS 30#1 Hits* and FTD release *The Memphis Sessions*. Pre-show rehearsals may be found on FTD release *The Memphis Sessions* and bootlegs such as *The Brightest Star on Sunset Boulevard*.

Live versions have come out on *Elvis As Recorded At Madison Square Garden*, *Aloha From Hawaii Via Satellite*, *Elvis Aron Presley*, *Greatest Hits Vol. 1*, *The Alternate Aloha*, *An Afternoon In The Garden*, *Walk A Mile In My Shoes*, *That's The Way It Is—Special Edition*, *Live In Las Vegas* (multiple versions), *The Live Greatest Hits*, *Elvis: Close Up* and *Elvis Live*.

Further live versions may be found on FTD releases *Elvis At The International*, *Writing For The King*, *All Shook Up*, *Polk Salad Annie*, *The Impossible Dream*, *An American Trilogy*, *Summer Festival*, *I Found My Thrill*, *Takin' Tahoe Tonight*, *Closing Night*, *Elvis Recorded Live On Stage In Memphis* and *Live In L.A.* On FTD release *Elvis At The International*, Elvis plays around with multiple false fade-out endings; FTD release *Closing Night* features a surreal version of the song, with the band playing "Suspicious Minds" while Elvis sings the lyrics from "Bridge Over Troubled Water."

In 1999, the song was inducted into the Grammy Hall of Fame. It was voted #91 on the Rolling Stone magazine list of the 500 greatest songs. For many Elvis fans, it's their personal #1— it topped a 2007 BBC poll of Elvis favorites. "Suspicious Minds" has been much covered, notably by Waylon Jennings and Jessi Colter, Dee Dee Warwick, Candi Staton and the Fine Young Cannibals.

SUSPICIOUS MINDS: THE MEMPHIS 1969 ANTHOLOGY

All the hits and more from the American Studio session on this 1999 BMG release, including previously unpublished material and alternate takes.

TRACK LISTING:
DISC 1
1. Wearin' That Loved On Look
2. Only The Strong Survive
3. I'll Hold You In My Heart
4. Long Black Limousine
5. It Keeps Right On A-Hurtin'
6. I'm Movin' On
7. Power Of My Love
8. Gentle On My Mind
9. After Loving You
10. True Love Travels On A Gravel Road
11. Any Day Now
12. In The Ghetto
13. Mama Liked The Roses
14. Suspicious Minds
15. You'll Think Of Me
16. Don't Cry, Daddy
17. The Fair Is Moving On
18. Kentucky Rain
19. Stranger In My Own Home Town
20. Without Love (There Is Nothing)

DISC 2
1. It's My Way / This Time / I Can't Stop Loving You
2. After Loving You (alternate take)
3. Without Love (alternate take)
4. I'm Movin' On (alternate mix & vocal)
5. From A Jack To A King
6. It Keeps Right On A-Hurtin' (alternate take)
7. True Love Travels On A Gravel Road (alternate take)
8. Power Of My Love (alternate take)
9. You'll Think Of Me (alternate take)
10. If I'm A Fool (For Loving You)
11. Do You Know Who I Am
12. A Little Bit Of Green
13. And The Grass Won't Pay No Mind
14. This Is The Story
15. I'll Be There (If Ever You Want Me)
16. Hey Jude
17. Rubberneckin'
18. Poor Man's Gold (incomplete)
19. Inherit The Wind
20. My Little Friend
21. Who Am I?
22. Kentucky Rain (alternate take)
23. Suspicious Minds (alternate take)
24. In The Ghetto (alternate take)

SWAN, BILLY
(B. 1942)

Singer/songwriter Billy Swan, born at Cape Girardeau, Missouri on May 12, 1942, grew up listening to country music and rockabilly. His first impact on the music business was his composition "Lover Please," which Clyde McPhatter took to the top ten in 1962 (and was worth a Grammy for Kris Kristofferson and Rita Coolidge thirteen years later). After moving to Memphis, he began writing for the Bill Black Combo, and in 1963 took a job as a gate guard at Graceland, before becoming a janitor (a job he passed on to colleague Kris Kristofferson) at Columbia studios. At Columbia, he worked his way up to become a producer.

Elvis recorded Swan's trademark song "I Can Help" in 1975.

In 2000, Swan recorded an album at Sun, *Like Elvis Used to Do*, on which he took on some classic Elvis tracks.

In recent years, Swan has been touring with former Elvis guitarist James Burton.

SWAYZE, PATRICK
(B. 1952)

The Hollywood leading man told reporters in 2005 that four psychics have told him that Elvis watches over him as a guardian angel. Elvis was apparently not watching in the late Eighties, when Swayze auditioned for but failed to land the part of Elvis in TV movie *Elvis and Me*.

Swayze , who would have become a professional dancer if he had not sustained a knee injury, is best known for his performances in *Dirty Dancing*, *Ghost* and *City of Joy*.

"SWEET ANGELINE"

Written by Chris Arnold, David Martin and Geoffrey Morrow, Elvis laid down the vocal for this song—initially recorded at Stax Studio on July 25, 1973—at his Palm Springs home on September 22, 1973 for the *Raised On Rock* album. The raw instrumental came out on the FTD *Raised on Rock* reissue in 2007.

"SWEET CAROLINE"

Elvis sang this 1969 Neil Diamond love song live in Las Vegas from his winter 1970 engagement, and kept it in his concert line up through 1971 (he brought it back in 1974, and very occasionally afterwards).

The breakthrough song for Diamond sold a million copies and made it into the top 5.

Of Elvis' versions, a performance from February 16, 1970 came out on the *On Stage* album. A rehearsal from the summer of 1970 featured in the original documentary *That's The Way It Is* (but not the 2001 DVD reissue), and was issued on vinyl in 1980 on *Elvis Aron Presley*.

Alternate live versions are on *Live In Las Vegas* and *That's The Way It Is—Special Edition*. The song may also be found on FTD issues *Polk Salad Annie*, *One Night In Vegas*, *The Way It Was*, *The Impossible Dream* and *I Found My Thrill*. It's also on various bootlegs of Elvis rehearsal sessions from 1970.

"SWEET INSPIRATION"

A Grammy-nominated hit for the Sweet Inspirations in 1968 (written by Wallace Pennington and Lindon Oldham), Elvis' backing group often sang this song during show warm-ups. Elvis sang a version of this song a couple of times during his summer 1970 Las Vegas engagement (on August 20 and September 1), and quite possibly during his 1969 season too. It has appeared on a number of bootleg LPs including *The Monologue* and *A Dinner Date With Elvis*.

SWEET INSPIRATIONS

Founded in 1963 and initially known simply as "the Group," this long-time Atlantic Records backing band made up of Cissy Houston, Doris Troy and Dee Dee Warwick, sang backup on some of the standout tracks of the Sixties for artists including Aretha Franklin, Dionne Warwick, The Drifters, Wilson Pickett, Gene Pitney and Van Morrison.

By 1968, renamed the Sweet Inspirations, Cissy Houston, Sylvia Shemwell, Myrna Smith, and Estelle Brown began to bring out albums in their own right. Whitney Houston's mother Cissy was a member of the group until she was replaced by Ann Williams in 1970.

"The Sweets" worked with Elvis from 1969 in Las Vegas right through until the end. He hired them sight unseen after hearing a recording of their signature song, "Sweet Inspiration." In the Seventies, the Sweet Inspirations regularly opened for Elvis. They may be seen on concert documentary movies *Elvis: That's The Way It Is*, *Elvis on Tour*, *Aloha from Hawaii* and *Elvis in Concert*.

Elvis had a bust up with the band in July 1975 in Greensboro, NC, when in an out-of-sorts moment he told them they smelled like catfish, prompting two of the Inspirationsno Kathy Westmoreland, about whom Elvis had been making lewd remarks to the audience. To make up, Elvis bought jewelry for almost everyone in the band.

The group did not perform for over a decade, and then reformed in the mid-Nineties, adding Portia Griffin to the line-up. Myrna Smith, Estelle Brown and Portia Griffin are still very much on the Elvis circuit, performing with Elvis tribute artists and recording as part of the Hit Making Team initiative. They brought out a tribute album in 2007.

ELVIS SAID IN 1969: "They help me get a feeling and get to my soul."

MYRNA SMITH: "He added our group because he wanted the spice of soul, but he didn't want it to be overbearing."

CD:
Sweet Inspirations Sing Elvis (2007)

"SWEET LEILANI"

Elvis sang this song—an Academy Award song of the year for Bing Crosby from his 1937 movie *Waikiki Wedding*, written by Harry Owens—at Graceland in 1960 with friends. Like many other Elvis private croonings, it has since found its way out into the world, in this case on *In A Private Moment*.

"SWEET SWEET SPIRIT"

A classic gospel song that Elvis loved, sung at many of his shows (and at his funeral) by J.D. Sumner and the Stamps. No official recording of Elvis singing this song has been released, though he does sing a couple of bars during a rehearsal at Stax in 1973, on unofficial disc *Stax Trax*.

"SWEETHEART YOU DONE ME WRONG"

One of the many songs in the repertoire of Elvis and friends at the Sun Records jam session on December 4, 1956, preserved for posterity by Sam Phillips as *The Million Dollar Quartet*. The song was originally a hit for Bill Monroe in 1947.

"SWING DOWN, SWEET CHARIOT"

Elvis recorded a jazzy version of this traditional hymn in the early hours of October 31, 1960 at Studio B in Nashville for his gospel album *His Hand in Mine*. It was selected for later release as a B-side to the "Milky White Way," which shipped in mid-February 1966 but failed to chart. This version has since appeared on gospel anthologies *Amazing Grace*, *Peace In The Valley* and *Ultimate Gospel*.

Elvis recorded a second version of the song for the soundtrack to *The Trouble With Girls* on October 23, 1968. This was not released until 1983 issue *Elvis: A Legendary Performer Vol. 4*; it has since appeared on the *Double Features* issue for the movie and, more recently, the *Peace In The Valley* anthology.

Multiple studio alternate takes from 1960 are included in the FTD reissue of *His Hand In Mine* and *Today Tomorrow & Forever*.

A unique live performance of the track from Elvis' Hawaii benefit performance in 1961 was issued on the *Elvis Aron Presley* anthology.

T

TACKETT, MARTHA
(1853-1887)

Elvis' mother's great-grandmother on the maternal side (daughter to Abner Tackett and Nancy Burdine), said by some biographers to be Jewish. As the Jewish faith is matrilineal, this would make Elvis Jewish too, though Elvis' cousin Billy Smith disputes this.

"TAKE GOOD CARE OF HER"

Elvis recorded this song at Stax Studios in the early hours of July 22, 1973 for release as the B-side to "I've Got A Thing About You Baby" in January 1974, not long after Johnny Mathis's version had made it into the *Billboard* Hot 100.

A hit first time round for Adam Wade in 1961, written by Ed Warren and Arthur Kent, the song made its Elvis album debut on *Good Times*. It is anthologized on *Our Memories of Elvis* (without overdubs) and *Walk A Mile In My Shoes*. The song is included as a country favorite on *The Country Side of Elvis* and on the 2006 version of *Elvis Country*.

Alternate takes have come out on *Platinum: A Life In Music* and *Today, Tomorrow & Forever*.

"TAKE ME TO THE FAIR"

This jaunty song was originally planned as the title track for *It Happened at the World's Fair* before the movie title was changed. Written by Sid Tepper and Roy C. Bennett, Elvis recorded the song at Radio Recorders on August 30, 1962, the first track he laid down that session. The song came out originally on the soundtrack album, and in the fullness of time on the *Double Features* release for the movie.

A pair of alternates was released on the FTD soundtrack release.

"TAKE MY HAND, PRECIOUS LORD"

First released on the *Peace In The Valley* EP and then *Elvis' Christmas Album*, Elvis recorded this Thomas Dorsey spiritual (written after his wife and baby daughter had died, and in Dorsey's own estimation the greatest song he ever wrote) at Radio Recorders on January 13, 1957. Elvis certainly knew the song from the Golden Gate Quartet version that his mom liked—it was also Martin Luther King, Jr.'s favorite gospel song.

Elvis' version of this gospel classic reappeared on the *You'll Never Walk Alone* LP, and is on *Essential Elvis, Vol. 2* and The *King Of Rock And Roll*. It also has pride of place on gospel anthologies *Amazing Grace*, *Peace In The Valley*, *Ultimate Gospel* and *Elvis Christmas*. An alternate is on unofficial Czech release *Just A Closer Walk With Thee*.

"TAKE THESE CHAINS FROM MY HEART"

Elvis sang this posthumous 1953 Hank Williams hit at his August 28, 1973 Las Vegas show, and delivered a line or two in concert on other occasions. Written by Fred Rose and Hy Manning, Elvis' version made it out for public consumption on bootleg album *Take These Chains From My Heart*.

TAKE THESE CHAINS FROM MY HEART

A bootleg album on the EPL label of an Elvis concert in Las Vegas.

TRACK LISTING:
1. Also Sprach Zarathustra
2. See See Rider
3. I Got A Woman / Amen / I Got A Woman
4. Love Me
5. Steamroller Blues
6. You Gave Me A Mountain
7. Trouble
8. Blue Suede Shoes
9. Long Tall Sally / Whole Lotta Shakin' Goin' On / Your Mama Don't Dance / Flip, Flop And Fly / Jailhouse Rock / Hound Dog
10. Love Me Tender
11. Fever
12. Bridge Over Troubled Water
13. Suspicious Minds
14. Introductions
15. My Boy
16. Take These Chains From My Heart
17. My Boy
18. Release Me
19. My Boy
20. I Can't Stop Loving You
21. American Trilogy
22. Heartbreak Hotel
23. Mystery Train / Tiger Man
24. The First Time Ever I Saw Your Face
25. How Great Thou Art
26. Johnny B. Goode

TAKIN' TAHOE TONIGHT

A 2003 FTD release focused mainly on Elvis' Mothers' Day show on May 13, 1973.

TRACK LISTING:
1. Also Sprach Zarathustra
2. See See Rider
3. I Got A Woman / Amen
4. Help Me Make It Through The Night
5. Steamroller Blues
6. You Gave Me A Mountain
7. Love Me
8. Blue Suede Shoes
9. Long Tall Sally / Whole Lotta Shakin' Goin' On / Your Mama Don't Dance / Shake, Rattle And Roll
10. My Way
11. Hound Dog
12. What Now My Love
13. Suspicious Minds
14. Band introductions
15. I'll Remember You
16. I Can't Stop Loving You
17. Bridge Over Troubled Water
18. Funny How Time Slips Away
19. It's Over
20. Release Me
21. Faded Love
22. Can't Help Falling In Love
23. I'm Leavin' (earlier show)
24. A Big Hunk O' Love (earlier show)

"TALK ABOUT THE GOOD TIMES"

Gospel meets country on Elvis' upbeat version of this Jerry Reed song, recorded at Stax Studio in Memphis on December 14, 1973 and first released on the *Good Times* album.

The track has since appeared on *Walk A Mile In My Shoes*, the 2000 reissue of *Promised Land* and *The Country Side of Elvis*. An alternate version is on *Essential Elvis Vol. 5*.

TAMBLYN, RUSS
(B. 1934)

Elvis and pal Nick Adams visited the dancer/actor at his home in Topanga Canyon when in LA filming *Jailhouse Rock*, to practice some dance moves for the movie. Though he has played in scores of movies since his movie debut aged just 13, written scripts and acted as his daughter's manager, Tamblyn is indelibly remembered as Riff in *West Side Story*. His sole Oscar nomination came for his role in *Peyton Place*.

TARANTINO, QUENTIN
(B. 1963)

The nouveau splatter director had an Elvis moment four years before directing his first feature *Reservoir Dogs*, when he was an extra in a 1988 episode of "Golden Girls": his character was dressed as an Elvis impersonator—a role he reprised on the same TV series two years later.. In 1992, he landed an acting role in Elvis-themed movie *Eddie Presley*. A decade later, he rued the fact that Elvis wasn't alive as he'd have liked to cast him in *Kill Bill*. Tarantino certainly has form in resurrecting Hollywood actors' careers

TAUROG, NORMAN
(1899-1981)

Norman Taurog has the distinction of directing more Elvis movies than any other director. He helmed Elvis' first movie after finishing his Army service, aptly titled *G.I. Blues*, one of over 140 features he made during a long Hollywood career that he began as a child actor.

Born in Chicago, IL on February 23, 1899, Taurog began directing comedy films as a callow twenty-year old. By the age of 32, he was the youngest-ever recipient of an Academy Director's Award (for 1931 movie *Skippy*). Other notable Taurog vehicles include Oscar-nominated *Boys Town* and *The Adventures of Tom Sawyer* (both 1938).

In the Fifties and Sixties, Taurog specialized in music-based comedies, working with the likes of Jerry Lewis and Dean Martin before picking up

Director Norman Taurog on the set *G.I. Blues* with Elvis.

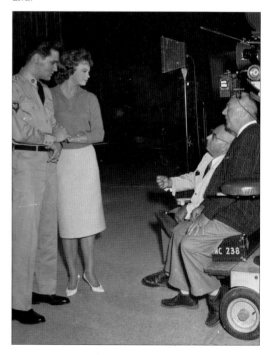

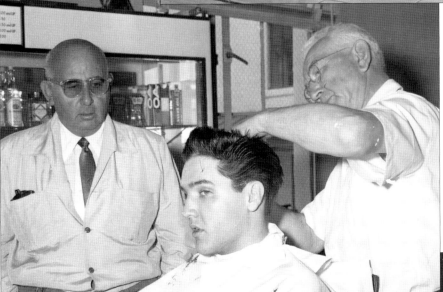

Elvis with director Norman Taurog on
the set G.I. *Blues* the first of nine movies
he was to direct him in.

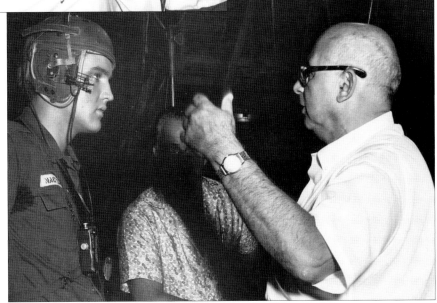

with Elvis. *G.I. Blues* was the first of nine Elvis movies Taurog worked on during the Sixties at multiple studios, making him Elvis' #1 director (and a favorite with the entourage for his indulgence of their high-spirited behavior on set). Taurog switched studios to MGM to make *It Happened at the World's Fair*. By the time he wrapped his final Elvis movie, *Live a Little, Love a Little* in 1968 Taurog had all but succumbed to blindness, after years of failing sight.

Taurog's other Elvis movies were *Blue Hawaii*, *Girls! Girls! Girls!*, *Tickle Me*, *Spinout*, *Double Trouble* and *Speedway*.

NORMAN TAUROG: "I was proud of the job we did if not of some of the material, but I don't think Elvis ever reached his peak as an actor. I always wanted to direct him as a cold-blooded killer."

TAYLOR, JAMES
(B. 1948)

Elvis had been listening to folk artist James Taylor long before he started playing Taylor composition "Steamroller Blues" live in concert.

Born in Boston on March 12, 1948, Taylor was a reflective singer/songwriter who carried the Sixties folk revival movement into the Seventies with hits including "Sweet Baby James," "Carolina On My Mind," and "You've Got A Friend" (written by Carole King). For a spell, Taylor was married to singer Carly Simon. Taylor has continued to tour ever since. He was inducted into the Rock 'n' Roll and Songwriters Halls of Fame in 2000, since when he has made something of a chart comeback.

TCB

"Taking Care of Business" became a mantra for Elvis and his gang in the last decade of his life, and provided the name for his stage band in his latter years.

The expression originated in Sixties African-American slang: Aretha Franklin ad libbed the term "TCB" in her 1967 version of Otis Redding's song "Respect" (R-E-S-P-E-C-T / Find out what it means to me / R-E-S-P-E-C-T / Take care, TCB). TCB was also the name of a 1968 live Motown TV Special showcasing the label's top acts that year.

It has been claimed that Elvis was already using the term as early as 1966, on a set of 14-Karat gold pendants featuring a zigzag lightning bolt design that he and Priscilla came up with, and which he had made up by the Schwartz and Ableser Jewelry in LA while filming *Spinout*. The majority view, however, is that Elvis commissioned his jeweler to make the first batch of ID bracelets in 1970: one for Elvis and six for entourage guys. Taking Care of Business was what Elvis expected his entourage members to do; TLC—Tender Loving Care—was the corollary for the important women in his life.

Before 1970 was at an end, Elvis had the TCB logo lightning bolt emblazoned on the frames of his prescription glasses, and had TCB rings made and given out to a wider circle of people. When he started assembling his own mini-fleet of airplanes, the TCB logo was emblazoned on the tail-fin. The TCB symbol features prominently in the games room at Graceland. Elvis had a TCB ring on his hand when he lay in state in his coffin, though this was slipped off before the casket was closed.

For Elvis, taking care of business really meant telling one of his crew to get something done. This hands-off approach was evident in how he left the Colonel in complete control of his business deal-

ings (he never even read the contracts), and put Vernon in control of his personal finances.

DESIGN ORIGINS

A variety of origins have been ascribed to Elvis' choice of the lightning bolt symbol, apart from the motif conveying the concept of Taking Care of Business "in a flash."

It may have been an unconscious reference to the Captain Marvel Jr. character he loved as a kid. Other explanations regarding the genesis of the symbol include Elvis and Priscilla flying through a major storm and then coming up with the idea of a lightning bolt; a statue in the Graceland Meditation Garden surviving a lightning strike; or something that Elvis adopted from the West Coast mafia, for which it was a symbol, because he liked the idea of their dangerousness. A more simple explanation might be that the lightning bolt was the insignia of Elvis' tank battalion.

The lightning bolt symbol has more recently been associated with Harry Potter, in the form of the birthmark on his forehead indicating his special powers. It was used at one time by David Bowie in his Ziggy Stardust phase, though the roots of the symbol can be traced all the way back to the attributes of gods in many of the world's ancient religions. For the gods, lightning bolts were a weapon, a sign of creativity and a symbol of power. For the Navajo, the lightning bolt symbolized salvation and divine goodness. Lightning bolts were wielded by Viking god Thor and Greek god Zeus. In several world religions, they signify fear or sudden enlightenment.

MARTY LACKER: "Elvis just flat out didn't want to bother with business—period."

TCB BAND, THE

Put together in 1969 for Elvis' first long-term Las Vegas engagement at the International Hotel, in one shape or another this band played with Elvis until his untimely death in 1977.

The band worked on their own album the year after Elvis died (a 1978 LP, *The TCB Band*, which was never released), and from 1998 on, has performed in touring show "Elvis—The Concert."

Band leader, guitarist James Burton, was instrumental in assembling the band after Elvis called him in early 1969. Burton and rhythm guitarist John Wilkinson never missed a show from the beginning. Other core members of the band include drummer Ronnie Tutt, bassist Jerry Scheff, and pianists Glen D. Hardin and David Briggs. On stage, the band worked with Elvis' multifarious backing singers, and an orchestra led by musical director Joe Guercio (who has described the TCB band as "the best").

In 2007, the TCB band launched an official website.

See also BAND

"(LET ME BE YOUR) TEDDY BEAR"

Shipped in mid-June 1957, one of Elvis' best known hits was, unsurprisingly, a million-seller and a long-term number one when issued as a single with fellow movie soundtrack song "Loving You" on the B-Side. Elvis recorded this Kal Mann / Bernie Lowe number at Radio Recorders on January 24, 1957 (though some sources state he recorded it ten days earlier). The song spent seven out of its 24 weeks in the *Billboard* Top 100

charts at #1, and also scaled the heights of the Country and R'n'B charts before it was through.

First time around, on the Colonel's advice, when he sang the song live Elvis flung cute little cuddly teddy bears into the audience—not that the crowd needed any incitement to act as out of control as real live bears. Graceland was soon filled with hundreds of teddy bears sent in by fans who wanted nothing more than to let Elvis be their Teddy Bear.

In short order, the song was released on volume one of the *Loving You* EP and the soundtrack LP, and later on anthologies *Elvis' Golden Records Vol. 1*, *Worldwide 50 Gold Award Hits Vol. 1*, *Elvis Sings for Children and Grown-Ups Too*, *This Is Elvis*, *Essential Elvis Vol. 1*, *The Great Performances*, *The King Of Rock And Roll*, *Platinum: A Life in Music*, *Artist Of The Century*, *Elvis Sings for Kids*, *ELVIS 30 #1 Hits* (the two CD edition includes a rehearsal from 1972, which is also on FTD release 6363 *Sunset*), *Hitstory* and *Elvis at the Movies*.

In the Seventies, Elvis often sang the song in a live medley with "Don't Be Cruel." It became a standard at practically every one of his shows from 1974 onwards, though he was already singing it regularly from 1972. A plethora of live versions are therefore available, starting with official RCA albums *Elvis As Recorded At Madison Square Garden*, *Elvis In Concert*, *Elvis Aron Presley*, *An Afternoon In The Garden* and *Elvis: Close Up*.

FTD release *Loving You* has a remastered version of the studio original, and live versions are on *Writing For The King*, *An American Trilogy*, *Summer Festival*, *Elvis Recorded Live On Stage in Memphis*, *Live In LA*, *It's Midnight*, *Dragonheart*, *Dixieland Rocks*, *Dinner At Eight*, *Tucson '76*, *Spring Tours '77* and *Unchained Melody*.

TEDESCO, TOMMY
(1930-1997)

This much-in-demand West Coast session guitarist, dubbed "The Most Recorded Guitarist in History" played in the studio with Elvis on many soundtrack albums in Los Angeles, from *Girl Happy* in 1964 through to *Charro* in 1968, and was part of the band for the NBC TV "Comeback" Special.

Over a career spanning thousands of recordings, Tedesco played with practically all of the greats; his guitar-playing is also on many of the most familiar TV themes of the Sixties and Seventies.

TELEPHONE

When he first started touring, Elvis spent a lot of time calling friends and family back home in Memphis. Every night he spent away from home he would always call Gladys to let her know he was okay—otherwise she wouldn't sleep for worrying.

Once he became famous, Elvis had to continually have his phone number changed. As soon as his number became public knowledge (which, invariably, it did, as Elvis would happily give it out to girls he met), the thing would ring off its cradle. The ringing phone would jangle Mama Gladys's nerves   and the telephone company soon started to make a fuss about changing the number on such a regular basis.

At Graceland, Elvis had a gold-plated phone in his bedroom. He had green and red phones throughout the house: the red phones were an intercom system. He was one of the first people in the world to have a phone installed in his car, and of course he had phones installed on his planes.

Elvis hated talking on the phone, according to Lamar Fike, and always got entourage mem-

Elvis press conference at Madison Square Garden, 1972.

bers to place calls on his behalf. Incoming calls were fielded by other people though, to avoid suspicion, Elvis instructed certain female callers to use code names for whom they wanted to speak to. In his final years, if Elvis felt lonesome at night, he would call people up to talk through the small hours. One of the problems of making calls to people he didn't usually call was that they might believe he was a crank making a call—when Elvis rang John Wilkinson to ask him if he'd like to join his band, Wilkinson slammed the phone down, thinking it was a friend of his pulling a prank.

Elvis' home number in Memphis was still being changed every now and then in the Seventies

See NUMBERS

"TELL ME WHY"

Suggested by Elvis for his first recording session of 1957 (he recorded it at Radio Recorders on January 12 that year), this spiritual did not see release as a single until the run-up to Christmas 1965, when it managed #33 in the charts (with B-side track "Blue River"), achieving overall sales of 400,000 and ultimately going gold.

The song wasn't released for so long because of fears that it was too similar to traditional spiritual "Just A Closer Walk With Thee"—a track which, incidentally, Elvis was known to have sung if not recorded—and might have triggered a lawsuit.

Before Elvis, many stars including Sister Rosetta Tharpe and Red Foley had done well with the Titus Turner song. Elvis' version has since been reissued on *Worldwide 50 Gold Award Hits Vol. 2, A Valentine Gift for You, Essential Elvis Vol. 2* and *The King Of Rock And Roll*. Remastered versions are on the 1997 reissue of *Loving You* and the 2006 FTD *Loving You* release.

"TENDER FEELING"

Elvis added overdubs of his vocals to this Bill Giant, Bernie Baum and Florence Kaye adaptation of traditional ditty "Shenandoah" for the movie *Kissin' Cousins* on either October 10 or 11, 1963 in Nashville, after the instrumental tracks were laid down on September 29. It originally came out on the movie soundtrack, followed by *Burning Love and Hits from His Movies* and subsequently the *Double Features* reissue.

TENNESSEE

- Covington
Elvis played the Ruffin Theater as part of a Grand Ole Opry-style show promoted by theater owner / songwriter Jack Sallee on March 16, 1955.

- Johnson City
Elvis began his first tour of 1976 with three nights at the Freedom Hall Civic Center from March 17 to 19. He played the same venue on February 19, 1977.

- Kingsport
Elvis played the Civic Auditorium on September 22, 1955.

- Knoxville
Elvis first played Knoxville on April 8, 1972, when he did two shows at the University's Stokely Athletic Center. He was back there for two shows on March 15, 1974, in a warm-up for

his Mid-South Coliseum show in Memphis the following day. He played there again at the start of his fourth tour of 1977, on May 20, 1977.

- Madison
Elvis never played here; Colonel Parker ran his business from his home here on Gallatin Road.

- Memphis
Elvis' first ever shows were at the Bon Air, the Eagle's Nest and at Overton Park Shell. Other Memphis venues where he performed in the first two years of his career include Katz Drug Store, Memphis State University, Ellis Auditorium and Russwood Park (see individual entries for dates at all these venues). In his first month or two as a performer he may have played Bellevue Park and the Kennedy Hospital (on August 29).

Elvis was a seasoned professional by the time he returned to play two shows on February 25, 1961 at the Ellis Auditorium as part of the Memphis Charity Show.

Thirteen years elapsed before his next hometown performance, at the Mid-South Coliseum on March 16 and 17, 1974. The shows sold out almost immediately, so the Colonel put on an extra date to close the tour on March 20, and invited RCA to record the event for a future live album (*Elvis Recorded Live On Stage in Memphis*). Almost 50,000 fans attended the four shows on March 16 and 17.

Elvis closed out his May/June 1975 tour at the Mid-South Coliseum on June 10, 1975 (recordings later appeared on *Elvis Aron Presley*), and then a year later finished up another tour at the venue on July 5, 1976.

Death has not prevented Elvis from posthumous stage appearances in Memphis. He has celebrated his own major anniversaries on video while band members play live in "Elvis—The Concert" at the Fed Ex Forum.

- Murfreesboro
Elvis performed at the Middle Tennessee State University Athletic Center on March 14, 1974, and went back for more on March 19. Demand was so great that he played there three times on his spring 1975 tour (April 29 and May 6 and 7). In 2001, FTD released a live album from these last two dates, titled *Dixieland Rocks*.

- Nashville
Considering that he recorded so much in this town, apart from his sole appearance at the Grand Ole Opry on October 2, 1954 (and later that same evening on the WSM "Midnight Jamboree" radio show live from Ernest Tubb's record store), Elvis only played Nashville one more time: the Municipal Auditorium on July 1, 1973. There are also rumors that Elvis appeared at a charity event in Nashville at some stage during his early years.

- Paris
Elvis and the band headlined a mainly country bill at the City Auditorium in town on March 7, 1955.

TENNESSEE KARATE INSTITUTE

See KARATE

"TENNESSEE WALTZ"

Elvis' take on this country classic, written by Redd Stewart / Pee Wee King and a #1 record-breaking hit for Patti Page in 1950, is preserved in this 1966 home recording, which featured on *Platinum: A Life In Music* and *The Home Recordings*.

TEPPER, SID
(B. 1918)

With writing partner Roy C. Bennett, Sid Tepper provided the bulk of the songs for Elvis' early Sixties movies *G.I. Blues* and *Blue Hawaii*—five for each. The first song that they wrote for him was "Lonesome Cowboy," for *Loving You* in 1957. Only five of the 42 songs that the duo wrote for Elvis were not for a movie: the first that Elvis recorded outside of a soundtrack was "For The Millionth And The Last Time" in October 1961. These two prolific songwriters never met Elvis.

Tepper and Bennett were already well-established before they began writing for Elvis. They wrote more than three hundred songs together, including fifteen hits for Cliff Richard, including his biggest seller "The Young Ones."

In 2001, a French Elvis fan club teamed up with BMG France to bring out an album of Tepper / Bennett songs, *Elvis Chante Sid Tepper & Roy C. Bennett*. Lisa Marie honored the duo in 2002 for their contribution to Elvis' output.

TEWKSBURY, PETER
(B. HENRY PETER TEWKSBURY 1923-2003)

Tewkesbury made a name for himself in TV directing popular Emmy-nominated Fifties shows like "Father Knows Best" before moving on to the movies, one of which was Elvis' 1968 release *Stay Away, Joe*. After retiring from Hollywood, Tewksbury moved to Vermont, where he was known to locals less for his Hollywood glamour than for his job on the cheese counter at the local co-op.

TEXAS

- Abilene
Elvis played the Fair Park Auditorium on February 15, 1955, as he embarked set off on a Hank Snow Jamboree tour. He is likely to have returned on May 30, 1955, for the first date on a tour organized by Bob Neal. He played the Fair Park Auditorium again with Johnny Cash et al on October 11, 1955. He performed at the Taylor County Coliseum on March 27, 1977.

- Alpine
On February 10, 1955, Elvis appeared at the High School in a benefit for the Future Farmers of America.

- Amarillo
On June 2, 1955, Elvis played the City Auditorium. He was at the Municipal Auditorium on October 13, 1955, and then again on April 13, 1956. He performed at the Civic Center Auditorium on June 19, 1974 (released on 2005 FTD CD *Rockin' Across Texas*).

- Andrews
Sources disagree as to whether Elvis played Andrews on June 7 or 9, 1955.

- Austin
Elvis and his band played Dessau Hall on March 17, 1955, the Sportcenter on August 25, 1955, the Skyline Club on the evening of October 6, 1955, and the Coliseum on January 18, 1956. The next time Elvis was in town was over twenty years later, when he performed at the Municipal Auditorium on March 28, 1977.

- Beaumont
Elvis played five benefit shows for the local police at the City Auditorium on June 20 and 21, 1955. He returned on his last ever tour with Hank Snow (also his last ever shows as a support act) on January 17, 1956.

Elvis in concert in Johnson City, Tennessee March 17, 1976 wearing his Blue Phoenix jumpsuit.

- Big Spring

As part of the TNT Records tour, Elvis played the City Auditorium here on April 26, 1955.

- Breckenridge

On April 13, 1955, Elvis played the High School. According to the local paper, young women "swooned" every time he was on stage. He performed at the American Legion Hall on June 10, 1955.

- Brownwood

An impressive third show on the same day in a different Texas town for Elvis on July 4, 1955, at the Memorial Hall. Elvis returned on October 10, 1955 on a bill with Johnny Cash and others.

- Bryan

Elvis played a date in town on August 23, 1955.

- Carthage

Elvis was on the bill with fellow Louisiana Hayride performers to mark the opening of the Carthage Milling Company's new facility at an afternoon show on November 12, 1955.

- Cherry Spring

Elvis started a 7-day tour with Johnny Cash, Wanda Jackson and Porter Wagoner at the Cherry Springs Dance Hall on October 9, 1955.

- College Station

Elvis began a four-day Hayride tour at the G. Rolle White Coliseum here on October 3, 1955.

- Conroe

On August 24, 1955, Elvis played a show at the Davy Crocket High School Football Stadium, on a stage improvised out of two flatbed trucks parked side by side. Elvis didn't let the fact that he tripped over on the stairs up to the stage stop him from delivering a trademark performance.

- Corpus Christi

Elvis played the Hoedown Club on July 4, 1955, and the Memorial Coliseum on April 16, 1956—a show that resulted in rock 'n' roll being banned from the venue, though apparently the offending performer that night was not Elvis.

- Dallas

Elvis topped a bill featuring country performer Sonny James, Hayride favorite Hank Locklin and others at the Big D Jamboree on April 16, 1955, in an event promoted by Ed McLemore at the Sportatorium, for which he earned $225 per night. Elvis returned to the event on May 28 and 29, June 18 and July 23, 1955. On September 3, 1955, Elvis played a late show at the Round-Up Club. He performed at the Dallas Cotton Bowl on October 11, 1956, traveling to the stage in an open convertible before entertaining his biggest crowd to date: 32,000 people. During his Army training at Fort Hood, Elvis sometimes headed off to Dallas for some big-city R&R with Anita Wood and Eddie Fadal.

Elvis spent a couple of days on a jaunt to Dallas with two pals from the entourage in January 1969, and made a number of brief trips there in 1970 and 1971 with various entourage pals in tow.

He played the Memorial Auditorium on Saturday November 13, 1971, and the Convention Center's Memorial Auditorium on June 6, 1975. He played a show at the Memorial Auditorium on December 28, 1976 (bootlegged on A Hot Winter Night in Dallas).

- De Kalb

Elvis chronicler Peter Guralnick mentions an unconfirmed gig at the High School in De Kalb on March 4, 1955.

- De Leon

On July 4, 1955 Elvis performed at Hodges Park.

- El Paso

Elvis and his band played a date at the Coliseum on April 11, 1956. The next time he hit the Coliseum was with the TCB band on November 10, 1972. For his June 2, 1976 appearance, he was booked in to the Civic Center Coliseum.

- Fort Worth

Elvis was at the North Side Coliseum for an afternoon show on May 29, 1955, before his evening show at the Sportatorium in Dallas. He played the same Fort Worth venue on January 20, 1956, and gave two shows there on April 20, 1956. Next up was the Tarrant County Convention Center with the TCB band on June 18, 1972. Elvis began a June 1974 tour at the Tarrant County Convention Center with two shows on June 15 and 16, 1974. He played the same venue on June 3, 1976 and July 3, 1976 (Rockin' Across Texas, a 2005 FTD CD release, features this concert). In the Nineties, a journalist claimed to have tracked Elvis down to Fort Worth, where he was allegedly living under the assumed name Jon Burrows.

- Gainesville

Elvis played a poorly-attended concert off his beaten track in Owl Park on April 14, 1955.

- Galveston

Elvis played the Municipal Auditorium on January 16, 1956.

- Gaston

On an early swing through East Texas, Elvis played the High School in this town on January 28, 1955.

- Gilmer

The Rural Electric Administration Building was where Elvis played on January 26, 1955; he was at the Junior High School Gym on September 26, 1955.

- Gladewater

Elvis likely first played the Mint Club, Gladewater in mid-November 1954 to a very sparse audience, in a show promoted by DJ Tom Perryman, who was one of the first DJs to help launch Elvis outside his home territory. Perryman continued to book him at the venue through mid-December 1954, championing Elvis on his radio shows and sending him out on tour across North-East Texas. Elvis was back in Gladewater playing the High School on a Louisiana Hayride-sponsored bill on April 30, 1955. He performed at the Baseball Park on August 10, 1955, and then a few days later made a private visit to town to celebrate the 25th anniversary of Jim Ed and Maxine Brown's parents. Elvis returned to perform at the Gladewater High School on November 19, 1955, in another show that was broadcast over the radio, and was a sell-out full house.

- Gonzales

Elvis played the Baseball Park on August 26, 1955.

- Greenville

Elvis played the City Auditorium on October 5, 1955.

- Hawkins

Elvis played the Humble Oil Company Camp recreation hall on January 24, 1955.

- Henderson

Elvis played a date at the Rodeo Arena on August 9, 1955

- Houston

Elvis played regularly in Houston during his early touring days, thanks in no small part to strong support from local DJ Biff Collie. Collie organized a date at the Paladium Club on November 26 and 27, 1954, one of the first times he played outside Memphis. In quick succession, Elvis rocked town at the Eagle's Hall and Cook's Hoedown Club on December 28, 1954, as the top act on a Hayride bill promoted once again by Collie as a "Yule Tide Jamboree." Elvis played the Grand Prize Jamboree at Eagle's Hall on March 19, 1955, on a bill where, despite being the top act, Elvis' last name was misspelled "Pressley," and the crowd was warmed up by Hoot Bigson and Tommy Sands. Recordings were made of this performance, released on the Peter Pan label in 1997 as Elvis Raw (and a decade later included on the Memphis Recording Service package). Elvis was back on April 2 for a show so oversold that 2,000 people failed to get into the venue, when the Louisiana Hayride-sponsored entertainment was broadcast from the City Auditorium with a bill that included Slim Whitman, Hoot and Curley, Tibby Edwards and Floyd Cramer.

On April 24, 1955, Elvis performed twice: in the afternoon at Magnolia Gardens, and in the evening at Cook's Hoedown Club. Elvis was back at Magnolia Gardens and Cook's Hoedown on May 22, 1955, and then at Magnolia Gardens again on June 19, 1955; he played both venues once again on August 7, 1955. He needed the extra capacity of Municipal Auditorium as a national draw on April 21, 1956. He played two shows at the Coliseum on October 13, 1956.

Fourteen years elapsed before Elvis returned to town—Houston was the first place that he played outside Las Vegas after returning to performing. He appeared between February 27 and March 1, 1970, at the Houston Livestock Show and Rodeo (at the Astrodome), for a $150,000 fee, and was the first performer to play the then new venue. Elvis' performances ensured record crowds for the annual event that year: more than 250,000 people watched him perform.

Elvis and the TCB band appeared at the Hofheinz Pavilion on November 12, 1971. They played the Astrodome twice on March 3, 1974, and spent two nights (June 4 and 5, 1975) at the Hofheinz Pavilion. Elvis played The Summit on August 28, 1976, in a concert delayed for an hour and a half because he was feeling out of sorts.

- Kilgore

Elvis swung through here on August 12, 1955, at Driller Park.

- Killeen

No public performances but basic army training for Elvis in April 1958 at Fort Hood, where he was stationed at the start of his army service. After basic training, Elvis moved off-base, staying first in a three-bedroom mobile home, before renting a 2000 sq. ft. house on 605 Oak Hill Drive (some sources say 906) from Judge Chester Crawford, for an inflated $1500 a month. The modest location where Elvis lived with his family and select Memphis pals soon turned into a mini-Graceland, besieged by local fans, Army families and a steady stream of Memphis friends whom Elvis invited down to visit. The property was most recently up for sale in 2006.

- Longview

Elvis played the Reo Palm Isle Club on January 27, 1955, March 31, 1955, August 11, 1955, and again on November 18, 1955.

- Lubbock

Although there is some dispute about the exact date, on or around January 6, 1955, Elvis played Fair Park at Lubbock, sharing a bill with Jimmy and Johnny, and Billy Walker (recordings surfaced on the Memphis Recording Service package in 2006). He played Lubbock again on February 13, on a bill that featured a young Buddy Holly, who at the time was part of country and western duo Buddy and Bob.

Elvis was back in town at the Cotton Club on April 29 that year. He played two shows in Lubbock on June 3, 1955: at the Johnson-Connelly Pontiac Showroom, and at the Fair Park Coliseum. On October 15, 1955, he played both the Fair Park Auditorium and the Cotton Club. His April 10, 1956 performance at the Fair Park Auditorium was so popular that an extra show had to be added later that evening.

Lubbock welcomed Elvis and the TCB band to the Municipal Coliseum on November 8, 1972. He last played the venue on May 31, 1976.

- Midland

Elvis appeared at the High School Auditorium on Friday January 7, 1955, on a bill with a selection of Louisiana Hayride performers, and returned to town on May 31, 1955. He played there again on October 12, 1955, on tour with Johnny Cash and Wanda Jackson.

- Mount Pleasant

Elvis played the American Legion Hall in late August 1955 (either 21 or 28 depending on sources).

- New Boston

Elvis played the High School Gym on January 11, 1955, in a show hosted by DJ "Uncle Dudley" (aka Ernest Hackworth).

- Odessa

Elvis performed at the Senior High School Field House on February 16, 1955, his two shows sponsored by the Voting Home Owners Club. Roy Orbison was among the 4,000-strong crowd who caught the show—he later said that he thought Elvis' "energy was incredible." Elvis returned to the town on April 1, 1955, for a date at the Ector County Auditorium, where the band was augmented by Hayride pianist Floyd Cramer; that night as many as 2,000 fans were turned away. Elvis returned to the High School Field House on May 31, 1955, and again on October 14, 1955. His one Seventies appearance was once again at the Ector County Coliseum, on May 30, 1976.

- Paris

Elvis and his band headlined a bill at the City Auditorium on March 7, 1955, with Betty Amos, Onie Wheeler and Jimmy Work. He played the Boys Club Gymnasium on October 4, 1955.

- Port Arthur

Elvis' first performance after signing for RCA was at the Woodrow Wilson High School on November 25, 1955.

- San Angelo

Elvis played the City Auditorium on January 5, 1955, topping the bill ahead of Hayride favorites Billy Walker, Jimmy and Johnny, and Peach Seed Jones. He was back on February 17, this time as part of a Hank Snow Jamboree Tour.

- San Antonio

Elvis played the Municipal Auditorium on January 15, 1956 on a Hank Snow tour, and then returned on April 15, 1956 on a tour organized by A. V. Bamford. He also put in an appearance at the Bexar Country Coliseum on October 14, 1956.

Elvis played the Convention Center Arena on April 18, 1972, in a show that was filmed for documentary *Elvis on Tour* (audio recordings were released on 2003 box set *Elvis: Close Up*). He next played the Convention Center on October 8, 1974, and then kicked of a tour in the summer of 1976 with a show at the Convention Center Arena on August 27.

- San Marcos

Elvis played an afternoon show at the Southwest Texas State University on October 6, 1955.

- Seymour

Elvis squeezed in a second show on the night of April 25, 1955, after performing in Wichita Falls, an hour's drive away. Elvis fans had to wait a long time to catch him at the High School; en route he ran out of gas.

- Stamford

Elvis did a show at the High School on April 15, 1955, and came back for more at the Roundup Hall High School Gym on June 17, 1955.

- Stephenville

Elvis' second show of the day, after De Leon, to celebrate July 4, 1955, was at the Recreation Hall.

- Sweetwater

Elvis played the Auditorium in Sweetwater on June 8, 1955.

- Tyler

On January 25, 1955, Elvis performed at the Mayfair Building. He played town again on a date in May, and returned on August 8, 1955, on the first date of a Tom Perryman tour.

- Vernon

Elvis played a date in Vernon on June 22, 1955.

- Waco

Elvis was with the Louisiana Hayride show when it played the Heart O' Texas Arena on April 23, 1955. The line-up of Elvis, Slim Whitman, Jim Reeves, Jim Ed and Maxine Brown and Jimmy C. Newman drew one of the biggest crowds ever to attend the venue, in excess of 5,000. The following year, Elvis topped the bill at the same venue on April 17 and on October 12.

- Wichita Falls

On April 25, 1955, Elvis played the M-B Corral on a tour organized by San Antonio-based TNT Records. He appeared at Spudder Park on August 22, 1955 with fellow Hayride artists Johnny Horton and Betty Amos. He filled the Memorial Auditorium on January 19, 1956, and returned to the same venue on one of his final A. V. Bamford promotions appearances, on April 9, 1956.

SCOTTY MOORE: "I thought we never would get out of Texas. In fact, think we could still be in Texas."

Book:
Elvis In Texas, by Lori Torrance, Stanley Oberst, Republic of Texas Press, 2002

Book + CD
Rockin' Across Texas, by Torrance and Oberst, published by FTD, 2005 with 2 CDs of Seventies live material.

"THANKS TO THE ROLLING SEA"

A drum-heavy Ruth Batchelor / Bob Roberts ditty that Elvis recorded for *Girls! Girls! Girls!* in Nashville on March 26, 1962.

The song has since appeared on the *Double Features* movie soundtrack reissue.

An alternative *a capella*-style take was released on 1980 collection *Elvis Aron Presley*. Another alternate is on FTD release *Out In Hollywood*, and on the FTD *Girls! Girls! Girls!* release.

"THAT'S ALL RIGHT (MAMA)"

Elvis' first single, claimed by many music aficionados to mark the beginning of the rock 'n' roll era, was the result of a happy confluence of factors on July 5, 1954, the day that Elvis finally got his chance to record some tracks at Sun Records. Elvis started out with some ballads, which did not make much of an impression on principal Sam Phillips. Then, during a break, he launched into an idiosyncratic version of Arthur "Big Boy" Crudup's hit "That's All Right" to his own guitar accompaniment. Bill Black joined in with a slapped bass line, guitarist Scotty Moore picked up the beat, and Sam Phillips peeked out from the recording booth to ask them what they were doing. Whatever it was, he wanted them to do it again, this time with the microphones on. Half a dozen takes later and he had a music 101 moment in the can.

Such is the generally-told story of Elvis' rock 'n' roll birth. In a 1957 interview, Elvis contradicted this version by claiming that Phillips called him in specifically to record something, anything by Crudup. Crudup had actually had two shots at the song Elvis chose in the summer of 1954: once in 1949, and once in 1946, when the title and chorus were "I Don't Know It."

Elvis recorded B-side track "Blue Moon Of Kentucky" the following day. His first single was rushed out as Sun Records #209 by the middle of the month (the most likely date is July 19, 1954). Though only released locally, sales extended as far as New Orleans and clocked up a very respectable 7,000 units (some accounts put initial sales at as high as 20,000).

The song was so popular among Memphis youth that the line Elvis hums in the song became a greeting among initiates. Fellow musicians were quick to pick up on the phenomenon: before the year was out, Marty Robins had released a version that made it into the top ten on the *Billboard* country chart.

"That's All Right (Mama)" was one of very few Sun recordings that RCA decided not to reissue after signing Elvis. The original studio recording (to which Elvis' new label added extra reverb) didn't come out on an album until *For LP Fans Only* and EP *A Touch of Gold Vol. 2*, both of which were released in 1959 to tide his fans over while he was in the Army. In later years, the track has appeared on *Elvis: A Legendary Performer Vol. 1*, *The Sun Sessions*, *This Is Elvis* (another remix), *The Great Performances*, *The Complete Sun Sessions*, *The King Of Rock And Roll*, *Sunrise*, the CD issue of *Elvis' Golden Records Vol. 1*, *Artist Of The Century*, *Elvis 2nd to None*, *Elvis at Sun*, *Hitstory*, *Elvis R 'n' B*, and *The Essential Elvis Presley* (2007 version).

Alternative takes from the original recording session have appeared on *A Golden Celebration*, *The Complete Sun Sessions* (the 2006 version also includes live performances), *Platinum: A Life In Music* (the first three takes), and *Sunrise*. In 2005, a reproduction of the original Sun Mother Master, stripped of the additional echo added on the RCA remix, was made available as part of the *Memphis Recording Service* package, which also features a live performance of the song from Elvis' first ever Louisiana Hayride engagement. A number of Hayride recordings have been released on discs including *The Hillbilly Cat*, *Good Rockin' Tonight / Playing With Fire* and *Elvis At The Louisiana Hayride*. An early live version surfaced on 1999 release *Sunrise*. Elvis also sang the song live at his 1961 Hawaii benefit appearance, released many years later on *Elvis Aron Presley*.

In the run-up to his NBC TV Special, Elvis worked up his first hit with an urgency he hadn't mustered in years, but in the end it didn't make it into the final broadcast. Elvis' June 27, 1968 performance of the song has since made it out on *Elvis: A Legendary Performer Vol. 4*, *A Golden Celebration*, 1991 Comeback Special reissue album *Elvis NBC TV Special, Memories: The "68 Comeback Special*, and *Tiger Man*.

Back on stage in the Seventies, Elvis incorporated "That's All Right" into his act on a regular basis, though after 1972 he sang it more sparingly; on very rare occasions, he even began his set with the song that had launched his career. A rehearsal and performance of "That's All Right" featured in concert documentary *Elvis: That's The Way It Is* but not the associated LP release—two live versions from that summer period in 1970 later came out on *That's The Way It Is—Special Edition*. A bluesy rehearsal from that time only circulated on bootleg until FTD brought out *The Way It Was* in 2001. The original recording also features in documentary *Elvis on Tour*.

Live versions of the song from Seventies performances feature on *Elvis As Recorded At Madison Square Garden, Elvis In Concert, An Afternoon In The Garden, Live In Las Vegas* and FTD releases *One Night In Vegas, The Impossible Dream, Southern Nights* and *Spring Tours '77*.

A commemorative fiftieth-anniversary CD single including an alternate take of the song came out in 2004; TV Guide also released a commemorative mini-CD that year with a previously unreleased live version of the song.

In 2006, FTD released a home-recorded version of Elvis singing the song in 1973 (on *Made in Memphis*), which had previously only been available on bootleg.

Elvis' "That's All Right (Mama)" was elevated to the Grammy Hall of Fame in 1998. In 2007, a *Rolling Stone* survey anointed it as the "the greatest song that changed the world."

SCOTTY MOORE after recorded the song: "It's good, but what is it?"

"THAT'S AMORE"

Elvis paid homage to Dean Martin by incorporating a line from his 1953 million-selling hit during a March 1975 Las Vegas show at which Deano was present. A bootleg recording of the song is on *Rockin' Against The Roarin' Falls*.

There have been rumors that Elvis included the song in his early repertoire, when he was a regular at the Eagle's Nest in Memphis in 1954. "That's Amore," written by Jack Brooks and Harry Warren, first appeared in Dean Martin / Jerry Lewis comedy *The Caddy*.

"THAT'S MY DESIRE"

Elvis and friends tackled this former Louis Armstrong and Frankie Laine hit (Jerry Lee Lewis putting in a virtuoso piano and singing performance) during the *Million Dollar Quartet* session. Though not singing, Elvis is listening

A decade later, Elvis segued into the song after "Are You Lonesome Tonight?" during backstage rehearsals for the NBC TV Special. This version was restricted to bootlegs until 2000s FTD release *Let Yourself Go*.

"THAT'S SOMEONE YOU NEVER FORGET"

Elvis wrote this song correction, Elvis came up with the title and pal Red West wrote the song, with some lyrical input from El., for him to record in Nashville on June 25, 1961. As well as appearing on the Pot Luck album in 1962, it came out as the B-side to April 1967 single "Long Legged Girl (With the Short Dress On)," when it charted at #92.

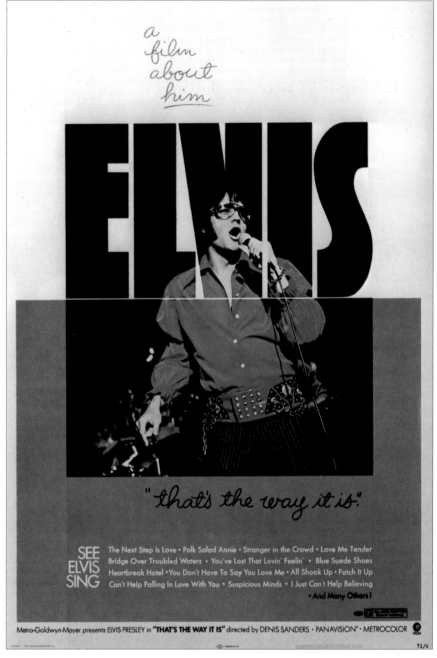

SEE ELVIS SING   The Next Step Is Love • Polk Salad Annie • Stranger in the Crowd • Love Me Tender Bridge Over Troubled Waters • You've Lost That Lovin' Feelin' • Blue Suede Shoes Heartbreak Hotel •You Don't Have To Say You Love Me • All Shook Up • Patch It Up Can't Help Falling In Love With You • Suspicious Minds • I Just Can't Help Believing • And Many Others !

Metro-Goldwyn-Mayer presents ELVIS PRESLEY in "THAT'S THE WAY IT IS" directed by DENIS SANDERS • PANAVISION® • METROCOLOR

It has since been included on the *From Nashville To Memphis* and *Artist Of The Century* compilations. *From Nashville To Memphis* also features an alternative take; further alternates have seen release on *Elvis: Close Up* and FTD albums *Studio B: Nashville Outtakes* and *Pot Luck*.

THAT'S THE WAY IT IS (LP)

Released in November 1970 as a tie-in to the *Elvis: That's the Way It Is* documentary, this album combined four full songs from the documentary with a further eight tracks from Elvis' June 1970 Nashville recording session. The album racked up over half-a-million in sales, and peaked at #21 in the charts during its 23-week stay.

TRACK LISTING:
1. I Just Can't Help Believin'
2. Twenty Days And Twenty Nights
3. How The Web Was Woven
4. Patch It Up
5. Mary In The Morning
6. You Don't Have To Say You Love Me
7. You've Lost That Lovin' Feelin'
8. I've Lost You
9. Just Pretend
10. Stranger In The Crowd
11. The Next Step Is Love
12. Bridge Over Troubled Water

THAT'S THE WAY IT IS— SPECIAL EDITION

A 3-disc box Special Edition was released in 2000 with a great deal of new live and rehearsal material—for many collectors, one of the finest testaments to Elvis as a live performer as he entered the third act of his career.

TRACK LISTING:
DISC:1
1. I Just Can't Help Believin'
2. Twenty Days And Twenty Nights
3. How The Web Was Woven
4. Patch It Up
5. Mary In The Morning
6. You Don't Have To Say You Love Me
7. You've Lost That Lovin' Feelin'
8. I've Lost You
9. Just Pretend
10. Stranger In the Crowd
11. The Next Step Is Love
12. Bridge Over Troubled Water
13. Love Letters
14. When I'm Over You
15. Something
16. I'll Never Know
17. Sylvia
18. Cindy, Cindy
19. Rags To Riches

A still from the 1970 documentary, *That's the Way It Is*.

A candid photo of Elvis during rehearsal for *That's the Way It Is* (1970).

DISC: 2
1. That's All Right (Mama)
2. Mystery Train / Tiger Man
3. Hound Dog
4. Love Me Tender
5. Just Pretend
6. Walk A Mile In My Shoes
7. There Goes My Everything
8. Words
9. Sweet Caroline
10. You've Lost That Lovin' Feelin'
11. Polk Salad Annie
12. Heartbreak Hotel
13. One Night
14. Blue Suede Shoes
15. All Shook Up
16. Little Sister / Get Back
17. I Was The One
18. Love Me
19. Are You Lonesome Tonight?
20. Bridge Over Troubled Water
21. Suspicious Minds
22. Can't Help Falling In Love

DISC: 3
1. I Got A Woman
2. I Can't Stop Loving You
3. Twenty Days And Twenty Nights
4. The Next Step Is Love
5. You Don't Have To Say You Love Me
6. Stranger In The Crowd
7. Make The World Go Away
8. Don't Cry, Daddy
9. In The Ghetto
10. Peter Gunn Theme (instrumental)
11. That's All Right (Mama)
12. Cottonfields
13. Yesterday
14. I Can't Stop Loving You
15. Such A Night

16. It's Now Or Never
17. (Now And Then There's) A Fool Such As I
18. Little Sister / Get Back
19. I Washed My Hands In Muddy Water
20. Johnny B. Goode
21. Mary In The Morning
22. The Wonder Of You
23. Santa Claus Is Back In Town
24. Farther Along
25. Oh Happy Day

See also WAY IT WAS, THE (an FTD book/CD release)

"THAT'S WHEN YOUR HEARTACHES BEGIN"

This was the second track that Elvis laid down at his first ever recording session, when he paid $4 to make a vanity acetate at the Memphis Recording Service Studios in the summer of 1953, along with "My Happiness." Elvis knew the song as performed by the Ink Spots, for whom it had been a hit in 1951. The track was actually first recorded back in the late Thirties by Shep Fields (and his Rippling Rhythm Orchestra). The writing credit is William Raskin, Billy Hill and Fred Fisher.

Elvis sang the song during his jam with former Sun Studio pals Carl Perkins and Jerry Lee Lewis in December 1956, in what came to be known as the *Million Dollar Quartet*.

He re-recorded the slow-dance ballad at Radio Recorders on January 13, 1957 for release as the B-Side to smash hit single "All Shook Up"; it made it to #58 in the charts in its own right. The song scored its first album release on *Elvis' Golden Records Vol. 1*. Since then, it has appeared on

Worldwide 50 Gold Award Hits Vol. 1.

As well as the 1957 recording, Fifties anthology *The King Of Rock 'n' Roll* featured Elvis' tremulous 1953 recording. More recently, this piece of history has appeared on *Sunrise*, and on the 2006 version of *The Complete Sun Sessions*. It has also come out on Joseph Pirzada's independent release *Memphis Recording Service*.

Alternate takes from the 1957 studio session came out many years later on *Essential Elvis Vol. 2*, *Elvis: Close Up* and FTD releases *Flashback* and *Loving You*. A version that Elvis rehearsed for the NBC TV Special but ultimately discarded appeared in the 2000s on FTD release *Let Yourself Go*, after circulating for many years on bootlegs.

THEATER PRODUCTIONS
(DRAMAS, MUSICALS, BALLET AND DANCE)

In life, Elvis bestrode the stage as a musician, not as an actor, though not for want of offers. Tennessee Williams wanted Elvis to play the lead role in his play "Orpheus Descending," which was first staged in 1957, but the Colonel did not approve of this particular career path.

In death, Elvis characters have appeared around the globe in plays, musicals and even ballets. With the recent popularity of pop-led musicals, Elvis' back catalogue has been heftily plundered in recent years, with a spate of Elvis-inspired musicals hitting the boards, including *Hunk a Hunk a Burnin' Love*, *All Shook Up*, and *This Is Elvis*.

A PARTIAL LIST OF PRODUCTIONS:

DRAMAS
Operation Elvis, by C. P. Taylor (1978)

The King and Me, by Hanif Kureishi (1983)
Toronto, Mississippi, by Joan MacLeod (1989)
It's Now or Never!, by Miles Tredinnick (1991)
Elvis and Juliet, by Fred Willard (1994)
Garon Presley: Taking Care of Business in a Flash
   (1995)
Elvis Monologues, Lavonne Mueller (1998)
Martha, Josie and the Chinese Elvis (2006)
Elvis People (2007)
The Elvis Test (2007)

MUSICALS
Elvis Lives, with Larry Seth (1977)
The King—The Musical (1977)
Elvis: On Stage, produced by Jack Good (1979)
Elvis, An American Musical (1981)
Are You Lonesome Tonight, by Alan Bleasdale (1985)
*Elvis: An American Musical / Elvis: A Musical
   Celebration*, by Robin Rabinowitz (1988/1989)
Elvis Mania, with Johnny Seaton (1984)
Armageddon: The Musical, by Robert Rankin (1990)
The Elvis Cantata, by Paul Dolden (1995)
Miracle in Memphis, by Malcolm Lowe (1996)
All Shook Up, by Joe DiPietro (2005)
Hunka Hunka Burnin' Love, conceived by Will
   Friedwald, Jay Leonhart and Jack Lewin (2006)
This Is Elvis: Viva Las Vegas, producer Bill
   Kenwright (2006)
Million Dollar Quartet, by Escott and Mutrux (2006)
Walking in Memphis, by Shaky Russell (2006)
Elvis: The Ultimate Performance Concert (2006)
Elvis at the Movies (2007)

BALLET/DANCE
Concerto For Elvis, written by Ben Weisman, chore-
   ography by Ann Marie de Angelo (1988)
The King Is Dead, by Stephen Petronio (1995)
Blue Suede Shoes, by Dennis Nahat (1996)
The King, by Peter Schaufuss (1999)

"THERE AIN'T NOTHING LIKE A SONG"

This holdover song from *Spinout*, written by Joy Byers and Bob Johnston, made it onto the *Speedway* soundtrack. Elvis recorded it at the MGM Studios on June 20, 1967, with Nancy Sinatra adding overdubbed vocals. Since then its only later appearance has come on the *Double Features* reissue for the movie from the Nineties.

"THERE GOES MY EVERYTHING"

Elvis recorded this 1966 Jack Greene (and later Engelbert Humperdinck) hit, written by Dallas Frazier, (for whom it won a CMA Song of the Year award), on June 8, 1970 in Nashville. Elvis' version of the country ballad first came out as the B-side to "I Really Don't Want to Know" in December 1970, on a rare all-country single. Soon after, it made its LP debut on *Elvis Country*.

Since then it has appeared on anthologies *Worldwide Gold Award Hits Vol. 2*, *Walk A Mile In My Shoes*, *Country Side of Elvis* and *Love Elvis*. An alternate take from the original session appeared on the *Great Country Songs* album.

Elvis sang the song live in concert a few times in 1970 and 1971. Live versions have been preserved for posterity on *Greatest Hits Vol. 1*, *That's The Way It Is—Special Edition*, *Live In Las Vegas* and FTD release *The Impossible Dream*.

"THERE IS NO GOD BUT GOD"

Elvis laid down this jaunty 1952 hit for Ink Spots lead singer (and song composer) Bill Kenny on June 9, 1971 in Nashville, for release on his gospel album *He Touched Me*.

It has since been included on Elvis religious medley albums *Amazing Grace* and *Peace In The Valley*.

An alternate take came out recently on FTD release *Easter Special*.

"THERE'S A BRAND NEW DAY ON THE HORIZON"

An uplifting end-of-soundtrack song for *Roustabout* that Joy Byers wrote to a tune based loosely on "John Brown's Body." Elvis recorded film and vinyl versions of the song at Radio Recorders on March 3, 1964.

The song has since come out on the *Double Features* treatment for the movie, and on the *Command Performances* anthology.

"THERE'S A HONKY TONK ANGEL (WHO WILL TAKE ME BACK IN)"

Elvis recorded this Troy Seals & Denny Rice country ballad on December 15, 1973—it was a #1 country chart hit for Conway Twitty that year—at Stax Studio for release on the album *Promised Land*.

It later appeared on the commemorative *Our Memories of Elvis* issued in the year of Elvis' death, and then came out as a posthumous single in 1979 (when it reached #6 in the country chart). It's also on *The Country Side of Elvis*, and the 2006 themed *Elvis Country* issue.

An alternative take is on *Essential Elvis, Volume 5—Rhythm And Country*.

"THERE'S ALWAYS ME"

Recorded on March 12, 1961 at Studio B in Nashville and originally released on Elvis' 1961 *Something for Everybody* album, this Don Robertson ballad became a single in the summer of 1967, with "Judy" on the B-side, to make up for a lack of newly-recorded material for release. Although it sold slightly better than the previous single, it failed to chart any higher than #56, and only managed to survive in the top 100 for six weeks.

During a playful moment in the studio, Elvis altered the lyrics to "When the evening shadows fall / And you're wondering who to ball   "

The song is included on *From Nashville to Memphis* and on *The Country Side of Elvis*.

Alternative-take fans should look to *Collectors Gold*, *Essential Elvis Vol. 6.*, *Today Tomorrow & Forever* and FTD's 2006 *Something for Everybody* release.

THERE'S ALWAYS ME

A 1995 unofficial release on Bilko of studio outtakes, mainly from the Sixties, collecting four volumes (8 discs) of high sound-quality lesser-known Elvis.

"THERE'S GOLD IN THE MOUNTAINS"

A Bill Giant / Bernie Baum / Florence Kaye paean to mountain girls in this *Kissin' Cousins* soundtrack song that the band recorded on September 29, 1963 in Nashville. Elvis added his vocal overdubs on October 10 at the MGM soundstage. Apart from the soundtrack LP, the only other official release is on the *Double Features* series.

"THERE'S NO PLACE LIKE HOME"

A universally-known song, based on an aria by Sir Henry Bishop—with a little help from John Howard Payne—to which Elvis and pals gave a rockabilly treatment during the *Million Dollar Quartet* jam session on December 4, 1956, the last time that Elvis recorded (albeit informally) at Sun Studio.

"THERE'S NO TOMORROW"

During his time in the Army in Germany in 1959, Elvis sang this English adaptation of "O Sole Mio," written by Al Hoffman, Leo Corday and Leon Carr, and a #2 hit for Tony Martin in 1950.

Elvis' version surfaced years later as part of the so-called "Bad Nauheim Medley" of tracks on *Platinum: A Life In Music*. When he returned home after serving his country, he recorded the song in a version written specially for him as "It's Now Or Never."

"There's No Tomorrow" is also on 1999 FTD release *In A Private Moment*.

"THERE'S SO MUCH WORLD TO SEE"

Sid Tepper and Ben Weisman unusually teamed up for this *Double Trouble* soundtrack song, recorded on June 28, 1966 at Radio Recorders. Alternates have appeared in the 2000s on FTD releases *Silver Screen Stereo* and the specialist label's reissue for *Double Trouble*.

"THEY REMIND ME TOO MUCH OF YOU"

Elvis recorded this smooth Don Robertson ballad on September 22, 1962 at Radio Recorders for upcoming movie *It Happened at the World's Fair*. The song was very nearly ditched because of similarities to "Chapel In The Moonlight," until Robertson, who was at the session, made an alteration and saved the day.

In early 1963, it was released as the B-side to "One Broken Heart For Sale," but failed to rise any higher than #53 in the charts. It came out on the *It Happened at the World's Fair* soundtrack soon afterwards.

"They Remind Me Too Much of You" has since graced *Worldwide Gold Award Hits Vol. 2*, *Elvis Sings Hits from His Movies*, *Command Performances* and *Elvis at the Movies*.

An alternate take, the first that Elvis attempted at the recording session, appeared on 1980 collectors' set *Elvis Aron Presley*. A further alternate is on *Today Tomorrow & Forever*; several more feature on the 2003 FTD soundtrack release.

"THING CALLED LOVE, A"

Elvis explored the bass reaches of his range on this playful Jerry Reed song in Nashville on May 19, 1971, three years after its initial release by Jimmy Dean. Elvis' version scored an initial album release on *He Touched Me*, though that same year, 1972, Johnny Cash brought out a single version that ran out of steam just before reaching #1 on the country chart.

Elvis' version has since appeared on *Amazing Grace*, *Peace In The Valley* and *Elvis Inspirational*.

A rehearsal take is offered on *Today Tomorrow & Forever*; the first take from the Nashville session is on FTD label release *I Sing All Kinds*.

"THINKING ABOUT YOU"

This country ballad, written by Tim Baty and recorded at Stax Studios on December 12, 1973, came out as the B-side to single "My Boy" in January 1975, when it also appeared on the *Promised Land* album.

The song was a selection on the commemorative *Our Memories of Elvis* (in a version without overdubs). It later appeared on the *Walk A Mile In My Shoes* anthology. Alternative versions are to be found on *Essential Elvis, Vol. 5* and on FTD release *Made in Memphis*.

THIS IS ELVIS

A 101-minute 1981 docudrama including a good deal of then recently-found footage, directed by Malcolm Leo and Andrew Solt, released with an accompanying album from RCA. The Warner Brothers movie, on which Colonel Parker served once again as a technical adviser, included a quantity of filmed interviews and press conferences with Elvis, sanctioned by Graceland. The $5 million biopic premiered at the Memphian Theater in Memphis. The version that came out on video was expanded to 144 minutes and included home movies shot by Priscilla and early co-star Dolores Hart. The production did not appear on DVD until 2007.

THIS IS ELVIS (DOUBLE LP)

A 1981 RCA album tie-in to the docudrama, featuring a remixed version of "That's All Right (Mama)," interviews and several other alternates. The album failed to make it into the LP chart top 100.

TRACK LISTING:
1. (Marie's The Name) His Latest Flame
2. Moody Blue
3. That's All Right (Mama)
4. Shake, Rattle And Roll / Flip, Flop And Fly
5. Heartbreak Hotel
6. Hound Dog
7. Hy Gardner interview (excerpt)
8. My Baby Left Me
9. Merry Christmas Baby
10. Mean Woman Blues (movie version)
11. Don't Be Cruel
12. Teddy Bear
13. Jailhouse Rock
14. Army swearing in
15. G. I. BG.I. Blues
16. Departure for Germany press conference
17. Home from Germany interview
18. Too Much Monkey Business (alternate take)
19. Love Me Tender
20. I've Got A Thing About You Baby
21. I Need Your Love Tonight
22. Blue Suede Shoes
23. Viva Las Vegas
24. Suspicious Minds
25. Jaycees award to Elvis excerpt
26. Promised Land
27. Madison Square Garden press conference excerpt
28. Always On My Mind
29. Are You Lonesome Tonight?
30. My Way
31. An American Trilogy
32. Memories

"THIS IS LIVING"

Elvis laid down this Ben Weisman / Fred Wise ditty for *Kid Galahad* on October 27, 1961 at Radio Recorders, though he let The Jordanaires take half the song before joining in. The track came out initially on the *Kid Galahad* EP, before turning up on albums *C'mon Everybody* and the *Double Features* soundtrack re-release in the Nineties.

"THIS IS MY HEAVEN"

Elvis laid down the vocal for this Bill Giant / Bernie Baum / Florence Kaye tune, written to close out *Paradise, Hawaiian Style*, on August 2, 1965, once the band had recorded instrumentals on July 27 at Radio Recorders.

After coming out on the soundtrack LP, in the Nineties it was double-featured with *Frankie and Johnny*, and came out on *Command Performances*. More recently it has showed up on *Elvis at the Movies*.

Outtakes are available on *Today, Tomorrow And Forever* and on FTD releases *Out In Hollywood* and *Paradise, Hawaiian Style*.

"THIS IS OUR DANCE"

A Les Reed / Geoff Stephens slow-dance composition that Elvis recorded in Nashville on June 6, 1970. It was first released on *Love Letters From Elvis*.

"THIS IS THE STORY"

A Chris Arnold / Geoffrey Morrow / David Martin composition that Elvis recorded at American Studio on January 13, 1969. The song came out on *From Memphis To Vegas* (and *Back in Memphis*).

A remastered version is included on *From Nashville to Memphis*. The song also features on *Suspicious Minds: The Memphis 1969 Anthology*. Alternates from the American recording session were released officially in 2001 on FTD album *The Memphis Sessions*.

A live version, part of Elvis' initial season at Las Vegas (taken from his August 26, 1969 performance), was released in 1991 on *Collectors Gold* and in 2005 on FTD live album *All Shook Up*.

"THIS TIME"

Elvis sang this song, originally written by Webb Pierce and Wayne Walker, at Chips Moman's studio in Memphis (American Studio) on February 17, 1969, finishing it off with a verse of "I Can't Stop Loving You." The song was not released until the nineties, when it came out as an extra on the *From Nashville to Memphis* Sixties anthology album. It has since appeared on *Suspicious Minds: The Memphis 1969 Anthology*.

"THIS TRAIN"

Elvis sang a verse of this traditional gospel song during a Lake Tahoe show in July 24, 1971 to illustrate how similar it was to his own 1955 recording, "My Babe."

THOMAS, DANNY
(B. MUZYAD YAHKOOB, 1914-1991)

Comedian, actor and philanthropist Danny Thomas founded the St. Jude Children's Research Hospital in Memphis Tennessee, through fundraising benefits that, among others, attracted Elvis Presley.

Thomas is best remembered for his starring role in ABC TV 1950s family comedy "Make Room for Daddy" (later renamed "The Danny Thomas Show"), which all told ran for 11 seasons. He went on to produce popular Sixties TV staples "The Andy Griffith Show" and "The Dick Van Dyke Show."

In 1964, Elvis donated Franklin D. Roosevelt's former yacht the *Potomac* to the Hospital through Thomas.

THOMAS, RUFUS
(1917-2001)

Thomas began his career as a comedian in the Thirties, before taking up a central position on the Memphis music scene as a DJ on black station WDIA, where he was instrumental in promoting rising stars such as B.B. King, Junior Parker, Ike Turner and Bobby Bland.

Thomas's own singing career provided the first national hit for the nascent Sun Records label in 1953, with answer record "Bearcat." Thomas had plenty of occasion to meet Elvis when he dropped round to WDIA Goodwill events in the mid-Fifties, effectively flouting the color bar. They also met in the Sixties, when Elvis sometimes hired Thomas for his Memphis parties.

Thomas went on to record at Stax Records, where his daughter Carla was also a star—his best-selling record of this time was "Walking The Dog." Thomas's recording career continued into the early Seventies. Since them he has put in a cameo on film in *Mystery Train* (1989) and continued to broadcast on WDIA.

THOMPSON, LINDA DIANE
(B. 1950)

Beauty queen Linda Thompson first met Elvis through RCA employee Bill Browder (whom Elvis befriended in the early Sixties after meeting him at the skating rink he often hired; Browder later went to work with RCA, and later still, recorded under the name T.G. Sheppard). Thompson was perfectly willing to pass up the opportunity to meet Elvis until her friend Jeannie LeMay—at the time Miss Rhode Island—answered yes on her behalf. Elvis' pal George Klein has also been credited with introducing the couple that July 1972 at one of Elvis' Memphian Theater movie evenings.

Elvis was mightily impressed and called Thompson in the middle of the night to tell her how much he'd enjoyed meeting her. He had to hold his horses, though, as Linda went off as planned on a family vacation until the end of the month. Thompson then accompanied Elvis to Las Vegas, where she remained by his side for most of his summer 1972 residency. From that time on, wherever Elvis went, Linda went too. Thompson later said that Elvis broke his monogamy record and stayed faithful to her for the entire first year they were an item—she claims that there was not a minute of those first 365 days that they did not spend together.

Born on May 23, 1950 in Memphis, before meeting Elvis, Thompson had accumulated a slew of beauty queen titles, including Miss Liberty Bowl, Miss Memphis State (her major was in English), and the 1972 Miss Tennessee USA pageant title. Elvis' pet names for her were "Ariadne" and sometimes "Mommy." She called him "Bunting," "Baby Bunting" or "Buttons."

After Elvis met Linda, he dropped his harem of girlfriends, the one-night girls and longer-term companions like Barbara Leigh and Joyce Bova. Entourage members unanimously agree that in

Elvis and Linda Thompson at the Memphis Gospel Show.

Linda, Elvis found a soul mate, a Southern belle with a zany sense of humor that matched his own. On one occasion when they were on the way to the movies at the Memphian Theater, Linda told some fans that they were mistaken, the man they thought was Elvis was in reality a guy called Charlie who was impersonating Elvis, to their own enormous mirth.

Linda was religious too, and took some convincing to move in with Elvis. She put her imprimatur on Graceland in 1974, when she supervised a major refurbishment that included new additions such as the "Jungle Room," and a new red theme for the dining room. By this time, Elvis had resumed normal girlfriend service and was seeing former Playboy model Sheila Ryan. For the rest of their time together, Linda had to share her man with this new flame and the many women whom Elvis inevitably met on the road.

Thompson nurtured Elvis through the bad times as his health worsened and, physically, he became increasingly compromised by his prescription drug addictions. In November 1973, Linda moved into Memphis Baptist Memorial Hospital for two weeks to be with Elvis. She is credited in many biographies of saving Elvis' life several times: in January 1975, she awoke to find Elvis having difficulty breathing and had him rushed to hospital. Once again, she stayed with him at the Baptist Memorial Hospital in Memphis, where they spent the day watching infants in the maternity ward on a closed-circuit TV system. Dr. Nichopoulos has said that he liaised closely with Linda in an attempt to keep Elvis out of the kinds of situations that were bad for him, and, conversely, encourage him to take up a healthy lifestyle.

By the end of 1975, it was clear to Linda that her role in Elvis' life was more as a caring, motherly figure than as #1 girlfriend. In November that year, once again she stayed with him in hospital and nursed him back to health afterwards.

Whether or not she took it as a hint that it was time for her to start thinking of moving out of Memphis, in April 1975 Elvis bought Linda a house near Graceland (at 1254 Old Hickory). That year, Elvis also rented her an apartment in LA, on Holman Avenue; she moved to a bigger apartment soon afterwards. Elvis also bought a house for her parents, where they lived until 1978, when Vester Presley and family moved in; Elvis is said to have showered her with jewelry during their relationship. Linda was keen to spend more time in LA as she tried to kick start a career in the movies. In July 1976, she accompanied Elvis to Las Vegas to visit Dr. Ghanem, after which Elvis stayed with her in LA (by this time, he had sold his Los Angeles home).

Linda joined Elvis at the beginning of his November 1976 tour, only for Elvis to suggest a few days later that she might prefer heading back to Memphis, ostensibly to clear the way for new girlfriend Ginger Alden. When Linda got wind of this she left for good; she later said that she had been trying to "wean herself off him" for eight months by this time, so great was her fear of what lay in store for Elvis. Even after Linda left, she kept in touch by phone during his final months alive.

Around the time that she left Elvis, Linda became involved with Elvis' pianist David Briggs, a relationship that continued for several years.

In August 1977, Lisa Marie called Linda Thompson to tell her that her daddy had died— Lisa Marie had been just four when they first met, and they have stayed in touch ever since. Thompson returned to Graceland for Elvis' funeral. Braving looks of disapproval, Linda wore a lavender-colored dress, in acknowledgement of Elvis' express desire for people not to wear black at his funeral.

By 1979, Linda was working as an actress, including roles on TV shows "Hee Haw," "Law & Order," "Beverly Hills 90210," "Fantasy Island," "CHiPs" and more.

In 1981, actress Stephanie Zimbalist played Linda in made-for-TV movie, *Elvis and the Beauty Queen*. Thompson appeared that year in made-for-TV movie *This Is Elvis* (and has since featured in a number of Elvis documentaries).

Also in 1981, Thompson married 1976 Olympics decathlon gold medalist / actor Bruce Jenner, with whom she had two sons before divorcing in 1983. In 1991, she married composer and record producer David Foster, and started penning lyrics to his songs, including the theme songs to movies *Pretty Woman* and *The Bodyguard*, for which she won an Oscar nomination. When they were together, Elvis had been highly impressed by her poetry and had tried, unsuccessfully, to get her to contribute her poems for lyrics.

She separated from husband David Foster in 2005, after taking part in a reality show called "The Princes of Malibu" about their sons.

Book:
Elvis, Linda & Me: Unseen Pictures & Untold Stories from Graceland, by Jeanne LeMay Dumas, AuthorHouse, 2006.

GIFTS

Elvis bought Linda a mink coat for their first Christmas together, in addition to the usual complement of cars. He gave her a White Maltese in 1973, named Foxhugh. He also had his jeweler make a waist chain with letters that spelled "My love, my life," which was then welded around Linda's waist.

Linda designed a cross necklace (now on display in Graceland) for Elvis to wear on stage, with two hearts, both of their birthstones, and diamonds set in gold.

LINDA THOMPSON SAID: "We just hit it off immediately because we grew up in Memphis, we had the same religious beliefs, the same love for our family, devotion to mother and father. We had the same sense of loyalty, we enjoyed the same cuisine because we were both Southerners."

LINDA THOMPSON SAID: "Life with Elvis wasn't all Camelot. There was a lot of heartache, and he exhibited a lot of self-destructive behavior."

LINDA THOMPSON: "We were very much a part of each other. There were times when he was the father and I was the daughter, times when I was the mummy and he was the baby... We kind of just geared off each other and understood the moods and became what the other needed for the moment."

LINDA THOMPSON SAID: "It was very difficult for me because Elvis was my first major love. It was hard for me to know that if I was not with him, someone else would be. Women were so readily available to him."

LINDA THOMPSON SAID: "There were a number of things that led to the dissolution of our relationship. The primary one was just watching Elvis slowly self-destruct. It got too painful for me. I tried so many things—so many ways to get him to take better care of himself—to stop using so much prescription medication. Nothing seemed to work."

LINDA THOMPSON said: "I had to go. For my own sanity I had to go. It was time."

JOE ESPOSITO: "Linda is one of those people who's always up Linda was great for Elvis."

BECKY HARTLEY: "When Elvis was going with Linda Thompson, they seemed to be happy. She seemed real good for him."

PETER GURALNICK: "It was a great romance but a great burden, too, and far from her world enlarging, she discovered like others before her, it actually shrank."

LAMAR FIKE: "I think Elvis came closer to being in love with Linda than anybody. He cared for Linda a lot."

LOWELL HAYS: "I think he really loved Linda, but he just couldn't bring himself to marry her. When he broke up with her it was downhill from then on."

MARTY LACKER: "She spent four years basically taking care of Elvis... She was like a mother, a sister, a wife, a lover and a nurse."

CHARLIE HODGE: "I believe that if Linda had been there that morning he might not have died. . . . . She didn't take sleeping pills, and would've gone over and... moved him over on his back, and he might possibly be alive today."

THOMPSON, SAM

In the summer of 1976, after Elvis fired Red and Sonny West from running his security, Linda Thompson's brother Sam quit his job with the Memphis Sheriff Department and his law school studies to work security on tour with Elvis. Thompson was heavily involved in Elvis' security arrangements from then on, including accompanying Lisa Marie between her parents' houses. Elvis had already helped Sam and his wife Louise buy their house by then, as a favor to Linda.

Thompson and fellow security man Dick Grob stayed with Elvis' body all night on the day before his funeral in August 1977.

Sam made home recordings of "I'm So Lonesome I Could Cry," "Spanish Eyes," "See See Rider" and "That's All Right (Mama)," along with some Elvis and Linda duets, in November 1973. These songs appeared on bootlegs over the years (recently on the album *Hound Dog*) before receiving official release on the FTD label album *Made In Memphis* in 2006; a taster was included on *Elvis By The Presleys* a year earlier.

Sam Thompson later became a General Session judge in Shelby Country (Memphis).

Book:
Elvis on Tour: The Last Year, by Sam Thompson, Still Book Publishing Company, 1992.

THORNTON, BIG MAMA
(B. WILLIE MAE THORNTON, 1926-1984)

Blues-singer Big Mama had a big voice and, for most of her life, a stage presence large enough to justify her performing name. Her smash 1953 hit "Hound Dog," backed by Johnny Otis and his band, stayed at #1 on the *Billboard* R&B chart for almost two months. Three years later, Elvis' "Hound Dog" obliterated her impressive sales record. In later years, Thornton was quoted complaining that Elvis had ripped off her song, though the evidence is that she didn't actually write it—duo Leiber & Stoller have the credit. Nevertheless, she claimed that the song was only a success the first time round because of the changes that she added when recording it. Regardless of the veracity of her claim, she has reason to feel aggrieved: all that she earned from the biggest hit of her working life was $500.

Born on December 11, 1926 in Montgomery, Alabama, Thornton learned her craft singing gospel, before working her way onto the popular music circuit through the Harlem Review in the Forties. Though she never made it as high in the charts after "Hound Dog," she continued to sing, play the harmonica and hit the drums, and was a major draw at music festivals in the Sixties and Seventies. She was an inspiration to a new generation of women blues singers, including Janis Joplin.

Big Mama Thornton was inducted into the Blues Foundation Hall of Fame in 1984, the year that she died in a Los Angeles boarding house.

have featured on *A Golden Celebration*, the 1991 release of *Elvis NBC TV Special* and *Tiger Man*.

A 1970 jam version came out on FTD release *Nashville Marathon*. A 1975 jam version made it onto *Walk A Mile In My Shoes*. For those who are looking, the song lurks on countless bootleg issues, most often twinned with "Mystery Train."

Tantalizing for Fifties Elvis fans is the prospect that he may have recorded the song back in his Sun days. Elvis said as much at a number of early live shows, when he stated that "Tiger Man" was the second song he ever recorded at the studio.

TIGER MAN

A 1998 BMG CD of previously unreleased Elvis singing his heart out at the second of his informal tapings for the 1968 NBC TV Special (the June 27, 1968 8 p.m. show)

TRACK LISTING:
1. Heartbreak Hotel
2. Baby What You Want Me To Do
3. Introductions
4. That's All Right (Mama)
5. Are You Lonesome Tonight?
6. Baby What You Want Me To Do
7. Blue Suede Shoes
8. One Night
9. Love Me
10. Tryin' To Get To You
11. Lawdy, Miss Clawdy
12. Santa Claus Is Back In Town
13. Blue Christmas
14. Tiger Man
15. When My Blue Moon Turns To Gold Again
16. Memories

"'TILL I WALTZ AGAIN WITH YOU"

This Teresa Brewer song—a #1 hit for her in 1953—showed Elvis what singing could do for his popularity when he performed it at the Humes High School Annual Minstrel Show in 1953, his final year at school. Some sources state that he sang it at the High School Christmas show a year earlier.

Incidentally, Elvis recorded the Teresa Brewer song "For The Heart" in 1976, and took her Vegas shows in the Seventies.

TILLOTSON, JOHNNY
(B. 1939)

Tillotson was in Mae Boren Axton's Florida High School class when she was helping to promote Elvis in 1955, and had a chance to interview Elvis for the school paper. His long-lasting singing career began in Nashville in the late Fifties, though it wasn't until 1960 that he achieved his first big hit, a #2 song "Poetry In Motion," which he recorded with Elvis session stalwarts Floyd Cramer and Boots Randolph.

Elvis covered Tillotson composition "It Keeps Right On A-Hurtin'" in 1969. Tillotson had hits with "I'm So Lonesome I Could Cry," "Pledging My Love" and "Funny How Time Slips Away," all of which Elvis covered. Unlike Elvis, Tillotson toured far and wide around the globe (and continued to do so well into the 2000s).

TIMBRELL, HILMER J. "TINY"
(1917-1992)

Canadian-born guitarist Timbrell first started working with Elvis on the Paramount lot, recording songs for *Loving You* in early 1957. He contin-

ued to play on film soundtracks for a decade, up until *Speedway* in mid-1967.

During his long career, Timbrell also appeared on film a number of times invariably in the role of a guitarist. Timbrell is known among music business aficionados for helping to convert music to the Nashville numbering system popular with musicians like Scotty Moore; he was also the West Coast representative for the Gibson company. Much as Timbrell would have liked to have Elvis endorse the company's guitars (which Elvis was playing), the Colonel would not hear of it. Scotty Moore was happy to endorse his products.

TIME

Time magazine wrote its first feature on Elvis in mid-May, 1956. The reviewer of Elvis' debut RCA single, "Heartbreak Hotel," described the new singer's voice as "a high, unpleasant quaver reminiscent of Johnnie Ray at his fiercest, and a rich basso that might be smooth if it were not for his spasmodic delivery." Undaunted, Elvis became the world's most famous entertainer, and in the fullness of time, topped the magazine's "Man of the 20th Century" poll.

"TIME HAS MADE A CHANGE IN ME"

Elvis sang this song in concert in March 1972. Written by Oren Parris and Harkins Freye, the song was a hit on Sun Records for Jimmy DeBerry way back in 1953, and was also covered by the Oak Ridge Boys. Elvis' version is on bootleg *The Complete On Tour Sessions*.

TIMELINE

Of the many Elvis chronology books in circulation, at the time of writing the most generally esteemed is *Elvis Day by Day*, by Peter Guralnick and Ernst Jorgensen.

Book:
Elvis Day by Day, by Peter Guralnick and Ernst Jorgensen, Ballantine books, 1999.

"TIPTOE THRU THE TULIPS"

Elvis slipped in a line or two from this song—a 2-million selling stage tune from just before the Depression, revived by Tiny Tim in 1968—during filming of his 1968 NBC TV Special in June that year. Owners of bootleg *The Burbank Sessions* and the Special Deluxe DVD have the pleasure of listening to it.

TODAY

This 1975 album of material (full title: *Elvis Today*) came out in May, barely two months after Elvis laid down the tracks at RCA's Studio C in Los Angeles, at what turned out to be Elvis' last ever studio recording session. RCA was more in a hurry to get the album out the door than fans were to buy it: the disk sold fewer than 400,000 copies, and placed no higher than #57 on the charts during its 13 week arc. It did make it to #4 on the country charts.

TRACK LISTING:
1. T-R-O-U-B-L-E
2. And I Love You So

3. Susan When She Tried
4. Woman Without Love
5. Shake A Hand
6. Pieces Of My Life
7. Fairytale
8. I Can Help
9. Bringin' It Back
10. Green, Green Grass Of Home

In 2005, FTD re-released the album with remastered tracks from the LP, plus the tracks before they were overdubbed (and bassist Duke Bardwell's lines were replaced), and additional alternate takes.

"TODAY, TOMORROW AND FOREVER"

Elvis sang this Bill Giant / Bernie Baum / Florence Kaye weepie—which borrowed its melody from Franz Liszt's tune "Liebestraume"—in *Viva Las Vegas* as a duet with Ann-Margret. He also recorded a solo version of the song at the July 11, 1963 Radio Recorders session. Elvis is at the piano in the movie as he delivers the tune.

The evidence is that Colonel Parker intervened to prevent the duet from coming out on vinyl. The Elvis-only version was first released on the movie tie-in EP, and later made its LP debut on budget release *C'mon Everybody*. It has since seen the light of day on the Nineties *Double Features* issue for *Viva Las Vegas*.

Alternates from the solo version have appeared on FTD releases *Silver Screen Stereo* and *Viva Las Vegas*.

The touching lovers' duet (ending in a wistful sigh) is on the 2002 compilation that takes its name from the song; an alternate take of the duet may be found on that FTD *Viva Las Vegas* release.

TODAY, TOMORROW & FOREVER

A 4-disc boxed set of previously unreleased tracks and alternates of Elvis in the studio (and live) spanning his entire career, released in 2002 to mark the twenty-fifth anniversary of his death.

TRACK LISTING:
Disc 1
1. Harbor Lights
2. I Got A Woman
3. Shake, Rattle And Roll
4. I Want You, I Need You, I Love You
5. Heartbreak Hotel (live '56)
6. Long Tall Sally (live '56)
7. I Was The One (live '56)
8. Money Honey (live '56)
9. I Got A Woman (live '56)
10. Blue Suede Shoes (live '56)
11. Hound Dog (live '56)
12. Rip It Up
13. Don't Forbid Me / You Belong To My Heart
14. I Beg Of You
15. (There'll Be) Peace In The Valley (For Me)
16. Is It So Strange
17. Got A Lot O' Livin' To Do (movie master)
18. Loving You (farm version)
19. Treat Me Nice
20. Young And Beautiful
21. I Want To Be Free
22. Steadfast, Loyal And True (undubbed master)
23. Doncha' Think It's Time
24. I Need Your Love Tonight
25. I Got Stung
26. The Fool

DISC 2
1. Make Me Know It
2. Are You Lonesome Tonight?

3. G.I. Blues
4. Pocketful Of Rainbows
5. Flaming Star (main and end title versions)
6. Swing Down, Sweet Chariot
7. Lonely Man (solo)
8. There's Always Me
9. Can't Help Falling In Love
10. I'm Yours
11. Follow That Dream
12. Anything That's Part Of You
13. King Of The Whole Wide World
14. Gonna Get Back Home Somehow
15. A Boy Like Me, A Girl Like You
16. They Remind Me Too Much Of You
17. Mexico
18. Witchcraft
19. Today, Tomorrow And Forever (duet)
20. Ask Me
21. Roustabout
22. Puppet On A String
23. My Desert Serenade
24. Please Don't Stop Loving Me
25. This Is My Heaven
26. Never Say Yes
27. Hide Thou Me

Disc 3
1. Love Letters
2. If The Lord Wasn't Walking By My Side
3. Come What May
4. Indescribably Blue
5. Long Legged Girl (With A Short Dress On) (alternate master)
6. The Love Machine
7. You Don't Know Me (movie version)
8. Big Boss Man
9. We Call On Him
10. Stay Away
11. U.S. Male
12. Wonderful World
13. Guitar Man (opening version)
14. Where Could I Go But To The Lord
15. Memories
16. Almost
17. In The Ghetto
18. True Love Travels On A Gravel Road
19. Let Us Pray (alternate master)
20. Baby What You Want Me To Do (live '69)
21. Funny How Time Slips Away (live '69)
22. Runaway (live '69)
23. My Babe (live '69)
24. What'd I Say (live '69)

Disc 4
1. See See Rider (live '70)
2. Polk Salad Annie (live '70)
3. Walk A Mile In My Shoes (live '70)
4. The Next Step Is Love
5. Life
6. Snowbird
7. (That's What You Get) For Lovin' Me
8. Until It's Time For You To Go
9. Fools Rush In
10. A Thing Called Love (rehearsal)
11. I'll Be Home On Christmas Day
12. Where Do I Go From Here?
13. No More
14. Take Good Care Of Her
15. I Miss You
16. I Got A Feelin' In My Body
17. If You Talk In Your Sleep
18. Promised Land
19. Your Love's Been A Long Time Coming
20. Pieces Of My Life
21. For The Heart
22. She Thinks I Still Care
23. Hurt

"Tomorrow Is A Long Time"

Elvis recorded this bluesy, pared-down Bob Dylan song in Nashville at the end of his May 25, 1966 session. By the time he got round to doing the song as a warm-down from a successful night's

work recording tracks for his gospel album *How Great Thou Art*, it was light outside.

The song initially featured as a bonus track on his *Spinout* soundtrack album. Dylan himself didn't make a cut of the track until 1971. Elvis knew it as sung by Odetta, and by folk duo Ian And Sylvia, who first recorded it in 1963.

Elvis doing Dylan later came out on *A Valentine Gift For You*, *From Nashville to Memphis*, *Tomorrow Is A Long Time*, *Artist Of The Century* and the FTD *Spinout* re-release.

The six-minute jam version from the Nashville session was released in 2003 on FTD disc *So High*, after decades as a bootleg favorite.

Tomorrow Is A Long Time

A 1999 BMG release of Elvis songs recorded between mid-1966 and January 1968. This is another of Elvis' "Lost Albums" of songs that could never be released together when he recorded them because of his crushing soundtrack commitments. Many critics consider this period the genesis of the Elvis comeback in his NBC TV Special.

Track listing:
1. Too Much Monkey Business
2. Guitar Man
3. Tomorrow Is A Long Time
4. U.S. Male
5. Big Boss Man
6. Love Letters
7. Indescribably Blue
8. Fools Fall In Love
9. Hi-Heel Sneakers
10. Down In The Alley
11. Come What May (You Are Mine)
12. Mine
13. Just Call Me Lonesome
14. You Don't Know Me
15. Stay Away
16. Singing Tree
17. Goin' Home
18. I'll Remember You

"Tomorrow Never Comes"

Elvis laid down this Ernest Tubb / Johnny Bond track in Nashville on June 7, 1970, for initial release on his *Elvis Country* LP. Tubb originally had a hit with the song in 1949, after which it was covered by many other artists, including Slim Whitman and B.J. Thomas.

Elvis' version has since come out on *The Country Side of Elvis* and the 2006 *Elvis Country*.

Walk A Mile In My Shoes features a version with a false start; FTD released an alternate take in 2002 on *The Nashville Marathon*.

The Ernest Tubb original is on *Elvis Presley At The Louisiana Hayride / The Original Roots Of Elvis Presley*.

"Tomorrow Night"

Elvis recorded this Blue-moonesque track, written by Sam Coslow and Will Grosz and previously a hit for both Lonnie Johnson and LaVern Baker, at Sun Studio on September 10, 1954, though it didn't see release for over a decade, when it came out on *Elvis for Everyone* with a whole new set of instrumentation, including a rare (for an Elvis record) harmonica solo.

Elvis was well-practiced with this one before Sam Phillips ever called him in: he regularly serenaded girlfriend of the time, Dixie Locke, with the song.

Elvis improvised a bass line to the LaVern Baker recording of "Tomorrow Night" in the summer of 1958, with then girlfriend Anita Wood, at Eddie Fadal's home. The recording escaped into the world on bootleg *Forever Young, Forever Beautiful*.

The original Sun version has since seen the light of day on *Reconsider Baby*, *The Complete Sun Sessions* (the 2006 reissue has a further take), *The King of Rock 'n' Roll*, *Sunrise* and *Elvis at Sun*.

Lonnie Johnson's 1948 version is on *Elvis Presley At The Louisiana Hayride / The Original Roots Of Elvis Presley*.

"Tonight Carmen"

Elvis dropped in a line of this Marty Robbins song before reprising "A Hundred Years From Now" during a June 1970 Nashville recording session. The moment wasn't released officially for many years, until it appeared on *Essential Elvis Vol. 4*.

"Tonight Is So Right For Love"

This *G.I. Blues* soundtrack song, written by Sid Wayne and Abner Silver, was recorded by Elvis in the early hours of April 28, 1960 at the RCA studios in Hollywood.

The song was left off the soundtrack LP release in Europe because of copyright wrangles (owing to the tune's similarity to Jacques Offenbach's "Barcarolle"). It was substituted by the similar "Tonight's All Right For Love."

Later album appearances include *Burning Love and Hits from His Movies* and several remixed *G.I. Blues* soundtrack re-releases. Alternate takes have appeared on the 1988 *G.I. Blues* re-release, *Platinum: A Life In Music* and FTD release *Silver Screen Stereo*.

"Tonight's All Right For Love"

A last-minute composition for the G.I. Blues soundtrack (credited to Wayne and Silver, plus Joseph Lilley), based on the Strauss melody "Geshicten auf dem Wienerwald." Briefly, the songwriters considered titling the song "Vienna Woods Rock 'n' Roll." Elvis recorded the song at his May 6, 1960 Radio Recorders session.

This track did not see release in the US until 1974, when it appeared on the first volume of *Elvis: A Legendary Performer*. Since then it has been included on *G.I. Blues* soundtrack re-releases.

Alternates have come out on 1980 box set *Elvis Aron Presley*, and this millennium on *Elvis: Close Up*.

"Tonite Tonite"

Elvis tried out this Mello Kings original at home. The recording found its way onto *The Long Lost home Recordings* (listed as "Tonight" on the track listing).

"Too Much"

This single, released in early January 1957, spent a month at #2 in the charts paired with B-side "Playing for Keeps." The song racked up a total of 17 weeks on the *Billboard* top 100, and went on to sell two million copies. It was only kept from the top spot by Pat Boone's huge hit "Don't Forbid Me." Elvis recorded the Lee Rosenberg / Bernard Weinman track at Radio Recorders on September 2, 1956.

Hep Cat's Review featuring Elvis.

Elvis sang the song on his third "Ed Sullivan Show" appearance in January 1957. The audio was released many years later on *A Golden Celebration*; the performance is on the *Elvis 30 #1 Hits DVD*.

The song made its album debut on Elvis' *Golden Records*. It was included on Elvis' *A Touch of Gold* EP, and a decade later on *Worldwide 50 Gold Award Hits Vol. 1*. Posthumous compilations that feature the song include *The King Of Rock And Roll*, *Elvis '56*, *ELVIS 30 #1 Hits*, *Hitstory* and *Elvis Rock*.

"Too Much Monkey Business"

The first Elvis version of this 1956 Chuck Berry rocker to be released was on *Singer Presents Elvis Singing Flaming Star and Others* in late 1968 (released a few months later as *Elvis Sings Flaming Star*), after he laid down the track in Nashville on January 15, 1968. He had covered the song twelve years earlier during the Sun Studio jam that became the *Million Dollar Quartet* session, but wasn't released in the US officially until 1990.

The 1968 version has come out on *From Nashville to Memphis* and *Tomorrow Is A Long Time*. This version received new instrumentation in Felton Jarvis's 1980 project *Guitar Man* (and, later in the FTD version of this album, which borrowed the song's name for its title, *Too Much Monkey Business*).

Alternates began with 1981 release *This Is Elvis*, and have continued through FTD releases *Long Lonely Highway* and *So High*. An alternate also spiced up the *Elvis By The Presleys* release.

Too Much Monkey Business

A 2000 FTD release of Elvis remixes and Elvis tracks with new instrumentation, as overseen by Felton Jarvis and Chips Moman for the 1980 *Guitar Man* album project at the Young'Un Studio in Nashville.

TRACK LISTING:
1. Burning Love
2. I'll Be There (If Ever You Want Me)
3. Guitar Man
4. After Loving You
5. Too Much Monkey Business
6. Just Call Me Lonesome
7. Loving Arms
8. You Asked Me To
9. Clean Up Your Own Backyard
10. She Thinks I Still Care
11. Faded Love
12. I'm Movin' On
13. I'll Hold You In My Heart (Till I Can Hold You In My Arms)
14. In The Ghetto
15. Long Black Limousine
16. Only The Strong Survive
17. Hey Jude
18. Kentucky Rain
19. If You Talk In Your Sleep
20. Blue Suede Shoes

Touch Of Gold, A

Volume one of this EP was released in mid-April 1959, as a reissue of recent gold hits plus "Good Rockin' Tonight" from Elvis' Sun days, to keep Elvis fans ticking over in the run-up to his return from Germany. The EP sold a steady 130,000 copies but failed to make the charts.

All three of these EPs followed the formula of three RCA hits plus one Sun hit, with a gradually increasing number of gold lamé Elvii on the front. Volume two did only slightly better business

when it came out in September 1959. Volume three, released in late February 1960, sold a paltry 50,000 but scraped to #17 in the charts on the back of Elvis' impending homecoming.

TRACK LISTING:
VOL. 1
1. Hard Headed Woman
2. Good Rockin' Tonight
3. Don't
4. I Beg Of You
VOL 2
1. Wear My Ring Around Your Neck
2. Treat Me Nice
3. One Night
4. That's All Right (Mama)
VOL 3
1. All Shook Up
2. Don't Ask Me Why
3. Too Much
4. Blue Moon Of Kentucky

Alternate takes of two songs on Vol. 2 were released in 1982 on UK release *The EP Collection, Volume 2*.

Tours

Elvis hit the road immediately after "That's All Right (Mama)" first lit up the airwaves, heralding the start of a frenetic two years of touring during which he racked up 100,000 miles in his first year alone. Elvis' schedule was enough to have worn down an Olympic athlete: he'd play a show or two until late, party and eat, drive through the night to the next venue, sleep a few hours, soundcheck in the afternoon, grab a burger or three, then knock the socks off another audience in another town and maybe another state.

Apart from a couple of forays into Florida, Elvis' early tours focused on the mid-South and Texas, areas where he could count on advance publicity via radio stations that played his music, such as the Louisiana Hayride network, or areas where he was promoted by far-sighted local DJs. Elvis' regular residence at the Louisiana Hayride did a great deal to build up a regional fanbase and spread the word across the South. The results were enough for record company A&R men to sit up and take notice of the effect that Elvis had on audiences. Even as his popularity spread through 1955, certain areas remained out of bounds: New York was considered hostile territory to a boy from the South; Elvis did not play any dates on the West Coast until the summer of 1956, by which time he had already performed on national TV and had a Hollywood movie contract.

Soon after he started making movies, the Colonel began ratcheting back Elvis' touring commitments. There was more money to be made from the movies by this time than from even the biggest concert venues. The Colonel's restricted-exposure strategy was in full effect by the time that Elvis returned to America after his Army service in Germany: Elvis made just two live concert appearances from his return to US soil up until 1968. Plans for a 43-date tour in 1962 fell through when RCA balked at the $1 million advance the Colonel requested; a similar plan bit the dust for a similar reason in 1966. Instead of Elvis, the Colonel sent out Elvis' Cadillacs on tour, to publicize his movies. According to Paul McCartney, this provided inspiration for The Beatles' *Sergeant Pepper's Lonely Hearts Club* album, which the band recorded with the idea of letting the album tour instead of the band.

The Colonel warmed to the idea of his boy going back out on the road only when it became obvious that there was little more to be mined from the vein of cheap but lucrative movies he had been churning out for the best part of the decade. The NBC TV Special showed the world that Elvis still had it in him to dazzle a live audience, even though the Colonel had initially con-

ceived it as a Christmas-themed showcase.

Such was the success of the Comeback Special, as it became known, that the offers came pouring in for Elvis to perform live. After a couple of hugely successful seasons in Las Vegas, the Colonel sent Elvis back out on the road, first to Houston, then on proper mini-tours. The routine—it did not take long for it to become a routine—was for Elvis and his entourage to fly into town, go to sleep, get up the following afternoon, do the evening show and then fly on to the next town; Colonel Parker flew ahead to set up hotels (Elvis and he would have a whole floor each), hire up to sixty local police officers to look after security, organize limos including decoys, and work out all of the routes in advance. At one stage, Elvis' seventies tours involved up to 100 people who traveled with him on three separate airplanes.

As Tour Manager, Joe Esposito walked Elvis onto the stage and guided him round any obstacles. At the end of a show, Elvis was blinded from looking into the spotlights for so long; it was Joe's job to lead him off to the waiting limousine that whisked him out of the building.

According to Dr. Nichopoulos, Elvis' health went into decline in 1974 partly as a result of his grueling tour schedule—his most hectic since the fifties, with two nightly bookings at Lake Tahoe as well as his usual Las Vegas engagements, plus plenty of time on the road playing other venues. The Colonel would not accept that Elvis' health was no longer up to this grueling schedule for up to ten or twelve days at a time. Neither would Elvis: almost to prove that he still had it in him, in 1975 he embarked on a touring schedule as demanding as anything he had attempted in decades: 29 shows in Las Vegas, followed by 50+ dates across the South and North East.

In the last year of his life, Elvis tried his best to ignore his ill-health and toured almost as incessantly as in his first year. Biographers have suggested a variety of reasons why he was so keen to be on the road: awareness that he had needed to keep making money as fast as he was spending it; a desire to please his fans; an addiction to the buzz of performing; a ruse to keep new girlfriend Ginger Alden by his side; a way of escaping the close control on his intake of prescription drugs to which he was subjected at home in Graceland; or perhaps more simply, to show people that he was still Elvis.

In 1977, Elvis was out on the road for ten days of every month. With less physical energy to draw on, he tended to start off slowly, but as was the case throughout his life when faced with a challenge, he worked his way up to the pace. Even though he only toured until June, in 1977, the year of his death, no other touring act in America earned as much as Elvis from ticket sales, even including dates he had to cancel due to ill-health. This is even more remarkable considering that by this time, he was often performing at smaller venues.

Elvis has toured extensively since his death. In 1978, the Colonel arranged an event at the Las Vegas Hilton called "Always Elvis," attended by Vernon, at which a statue of Elvis by sculptor Carl Romanelli was unveiled. The Colonel promoted the event and charged $15 for a day ticket. Manager Jerry Weintraub later toured this multimedia show round the country.

From 1997, video footage of Elvis at his peak, accompanied by live music played by members of the TCB band, has traveled the world to entertain fans—something that Elvis was unable to do during his mortal existence.

See also Concerts; for individual dates, look under the relevant State.

ELVIS SAID IN 1956: "I've been to a lot of places, but I haven't seen any of 'em really."

ELVIS SAID IN 1969: "I want to do more live shows, and I want to tour again very much."

FELTON JARVIS: "Elvis didn't have nothing but the road."

Books:

Did Elvis Sing In Your Hometown?, by Lee Cotton, High Sierra Books, 1995 and 1997.

The King on the Road: Elvis on Tour, 1954-1977, by Robert Gordon, St Martin's Press, 1996.

Elvis: The Concert Years, 1969-1977, by Stein Erik Skar and Paul Grunland, 1997.

Elvis on Tour: The Last Year, by Sam Thompson, Still Book Publishing Company, 1992.

Elvis, Standing Room Only, 1970-1975, by Joe Tunzi, J.A.T. Productions, 1994.

Elvis '57: The Final Fifties Tours, by Alan Hanson, iUniverse, 2007.

TRAINS

Though Elvis generally preferred cars and later planes to trains, if he wasn't driving he rode trains to get to his commitments from the mid-Fifties up until soon after his return from the Army.

Elvis took a train to and from New York City in early 1957 for his third appearance on "The Ed Sullivan Show." When on furlough in Europe, he hired a private carriage to travel to Munich and to Paris.

Elvis took a train from New York to Memphis after his discharge from the Army in 1960. He hired a carriage to travel to Miami for the "Frank Sinatra Show," and took another from Memphis to Los Angeles to report for duty on his first movie back, *G.I. Blues*. The Colonel loved the opportunity for publicity that the train offered, and made sure to phone ahead to stationmasters to tell them that Elvis would be passing through but NOT TO TELL THE PRESS. The resulting crush of fans at every station en route made these Sixties journeys slow, triumphant processions. Very often, the only way for Elvis to actually get off the train once he reached his destination was to have it stop a little way outside the final station and make a dash to a waiting car.

TRAMMEL, SONNY

Sonny Trammel was a steel guitarist with the Louisiana Hayride band who in January 1955 joined Elvis on his busy touring schedule. Trammel also played with Webb Pierce, Jim Reeves and Johnny Horton.

TRAVEL

Few presidents seeking re-election cover as much ground as Elvis did on his tours and travels—over 100,000 miles during his first year, most of that covered on poor roads in old jalopies. As a performer, he quickly made up for never having spent a night away from home before he cut his first record for Sun.

In the Sixties, Elvis regularly traversed the Southern states as he traveled between Memphis and various movie factories in Los Angeles, usually traveling in a convey involving a bus and various entourage guys in cars.

In the Seventies, Elvis tended to travel by plane. In the early part of the decade, he tended to travel from venue to venue; by the end of his life, he preferred to commute direct to the venue from Graceland and return home afterwards.

Elvis' plans for international travel were consistently thwarted by Colonel Parker, who one way or another always succeeding in persuading Elvis not to make trips outside North America. It is a paradox that the world's most famous performer of the last fifty years never performed to a paying audience outside North America.

Since 1977, Elvis has spawned his very travel industry. People flock to Memphis not just to see Graceland (600,000 people a year visit Elvis' for-

Rare RCA Sampler LP from RCA Italiana. Featuring Elvis, Lena Horne, Sophia Loren and Harry Belafonts.

mer home, a number that Elvis Estate owners CKX expects to rise through the million mark) and Sun Studio, but also the sites where Elvis spent his youth and adult life.

Tupelo is a tourist destination almost solely because of its most famous son. Elvis tourism has also generated millions of visitor dollars in other locations closely associated with his life, from Las Vegas and Los Angeles to Hawaii and Palm Springs, not to mention venues where he performed, hotels and restaurants he frequented along the way, locations where his movies were shot, sites in Germany with which he was associated during his Army posting, studios where he laid down tracks or recorded TV shows, Elvis museums and waxworks, places that hold Elvis festivals and more.

In 2007, Elvis' travel appeal was extended to a series of EPE-licensed cruises to popular vacation destinations.

See also Airplanes, Cars, Trains, International travel and entries for specific locations.

Books:

Elvis Presley Boulevard: From Sea to Shining Sea, Almost, by Mark Winegardner, Atlantic Monthly Press, 1988.

Roadside Elvis—The Complete State-By-State Travel Guide for Elvis Presley Fans, by Jack Barth, Contemporary Books, 1991 (republished as *Travels with Elvis*, Gramercy, 1999).

Placing Elvis: A Tour Guide to the Kingdom, by Sharon Colette Urquhart and Werner Riefling, Paper Chase, 1993.

The Elvis Atlas: A Journey Through Elvis Presley's America, by Michael Gray and Roger Osborne, Henry Holt & Co., 1996.

Memphis Elvis-Style, by Cindy Hazen and Mike Freeman, John F. Blair Publisher, 1997.

The Field Guide to Elvis Shrines, by Bill Yenne, Last Gasp, 2004.

Follow Me to Tennessee, by Andrew Hearn and Andrew Snelgrove, Essential Elvis, 2007.

"TREAT ME NICE"

The B-side to the "Jailhouse Rock" single, released in late September 1957, this Leiber and Stoller song was the tune that Elvis was keenest to take on at a Radio Recorders session convened to provide material for Elvis' first Christmas album on September 9, 1957; he had already recorded what would turn out to be the movie version of the song at the same venue on May 3. While "Jailhouse Rock" looked down from the top of the charts, the B-side managed a respectable #27 in its own right, and even spent one week at #1 on the Country chart.

After its shelf life as a single, "Treat Me Nice" made it onto the EP *A Touch of Gold* and LPs *Elvis' Golden Records Vol. 1*, *Worldwide 50 Gold Award Hits Vol. 1*, *The Great Performances*, *Elvis Sings Leiber & Stoller*, *The King of Rock And Roll*, the 1997 *Jailhouse Rock* CD (which also featured the movie version; the record and movie version initially came out together on 1988 disc *Essential Elvis, Vol. 1*; the movie version has since appeared on FTD release *Flashback*). More recently, the record version has come out on *Artist Of The Century*, *Elvis 2nd to None*, *Hitstory* and *Elvis at the Movies*.

Alternate versions of both the movie and record cut are on *Elvis: Close Up*; *Today Tomorrow & Forever* features a sole outtake.

The *Elvis 30 #1 Hits DVD* features footage of Elvis performing the song in *Jailhouse Rock*.

TRIBUTES AND TRIBUTE SONGS

Elvis novelty records, answer records, rip-offs, retreads and honest-to-goodness tributes began to appear almost as soon as Sun brought out single #209 in the summer of 1954: by the end of the year, Marty Robbins had covered Elvis' version of "That's All Right (Mama)" and young hopefuls were beginning to mimic Elvis' unique style.

Ever since, countless rock 'n' roll artists have paid their implicit debt to Elvis with a tribute song. After all, he forged the template for rock 'n' roll success.

Death turned the tribute trickle into a flood. Between August 1977 and January 1, 1978, no fewer than 200 Elvis tribute songs were recorded. The first was laid down within two days of his death, appropriately enough at Scotty Moore's studio in Nashville, where Ronnie McDowell and Lee Morgan recorded their hit song "The King Is Gone."

Former Elvis musicians and backing singers have been at the leading edge of the huge number of musicians to have paid tribute to Elvis through music. Scotty Moore was an Elvis tribute veteran, having released a tribute album of Elvis instrumentals, *The Guitar That Changed The World*, in the mid-Sixties. Bill Black's Combo also issued popular instrumentals of early Elvis hits. Original bandsmen Scotty Moore and D.J. Fontana played with a stellar cast of guest musicians influenced by Elvis in the *All The King's Men* project (with Keith Richards, Ron Wood, Jeff Beck, Cheap Trick and the Band). Gospel quartet The Stamps recorded two Elvis tribute albums after his death: *Elvis' Favorite Gospel Songs* and *Memories of Our Friend Elvis*. The Jordanaires have also brought out Elvis tributes, including *The Jordanaires Sing Elvis' Gospel Favorites* and *Christmas To Elvis From The Jordanaires*. More recently, Voice have got in on the act with *Remembering Elvis at Christmas* and *Voice sings Elvis' Favorite Gospel Songs*, as have the Sweet Inspirations with *Sweet Inspirations Sing Elvis*.

On-stage tributes have been enormously popular since video technology allowed a truly king-sized Elvis to rise virtually from the grave. Ultimate live tribute Elvis—The Concert has backed the giant video Elvis since the 1997 20th anniversary commemorative show in Memphis, and (posthumously) given Elvis' band and a simulacre of their leader the opportunity to tour the world. Many other artists have made public performance tributes to the man that started it all. *Elvis—The Tribute* was a 1995 concert staged by Chet Atkins, Jerry Lee Lewis, Carl Perkins, Tony Bennett and Iggy Pop.

In truth, tributes take place on a nightly basis all around the globe. Elvis impersonators are by their very nature Elvis Tribute Artists, though some—such as psychobilly band Elvis Hitler—have a distinctly idiosyncratic approach to their métier. One of the world's largest Elvis events, held every year in Baltimore, is the weekend-long "Night of 100 Elvises", to benefit the Johns Hopkins Children's Center. The Elvis Presley Estate officially sanctioned its first ever ETA contest to coincide with the 2007 anniversary celebrations.

Recorded tributes abound. Erstwhile Sun companions Johnny Cash, Jerry Lee Lewis, Carl Perkins and Roy Orbison teamed up for tribute song "We Remember The King" on their 1986 *Class of '55* album. In 2005, *A Country Tribute to Elvis* united Glen Campbell, Billie Jo Spears, Don McLean, Willie Nelson, Olivia Newton-John and more. *It's Now Or Never—The Tribute To Elvis* is a compilation featuring Carl Perkins, Michael Bolton, Michael Hutchence and more. *Honeymoon In Vegas* is an Elvis-themed soundtrack album featuring Billy Joel and John Mellencamp. *The Last Temptation of Elvis* is a compilation featuring Paul McCartney, Bruce Springsteen, Robert Plant, The Cramps, The Jesus And Mary Chain, Hall & Oates and more.

Perhaps not surprisingly for a man who made his name mixing up musical genres, musicians have lined up to interpret Elvis songs in a completely different style. *All Shook Up* is a reggae album of Elvis songs by various artists released in November 2005. Genre-mashing tribute group Dread Zeppelin have been blending Elvis with

reggae since 1989. Barry Manilow recently brought out covers of classic Fifties hits including "Are You Lonesome Tonight?" and "Unchained Melody." In 2007, Shawn Camp and Billy Burnette (son of Dorsey Burnette) squared a certain circle by forming *The Bluegrass Elvises* and taking Elvis right back to his hillbilly roots.

Elvis novelty records have been coming thick and fast since the mid-Fifties, many of them by Elvis apologists and enamored fans. *Elvis Mania* and *To Elvis With Love* are a pair of 1995 CDs of this ilk.

A SAMPLING OF ELVIS TRIBUTE SONGS, ALBUMS, NOVELTY SONGS AND NAMECHECKS

Acoustic Coffee House: *Tribute To Elvis*
Al Anderson: "It Came From The South"
Alabama: "Changes Comin' On"
Alan Charing: "Wake Up Elvis"
Alannah Myles: "Black Velvet"
Albert King: *Blues For Elvis*
Albert King: *King Does the King's Things*
Alden Sawyer: "Halfway To Elvis"
Alex Chilton: "I Wish I Could Meet Elvis"
Alice Cooper: "Disgraceland"
Alton Yi: "Idol"
Angelmaye North: "Presley The King (Cadillac Man)"
Ann-Margret: "Bye Bye Birdie"
Aztec Two-Step: "Scotty Moore, Bill Black And Elvis"
Bela Fleck & The Flecktones: "Life Without Elvis"
Bellamy Brothers: "Elvis, Marilyn And James Dean"
Belle & Sebastian: "A Century Of Elvis"
Beth Peterson: *For Elvis The World Cries*
Betty Hamar: "Precious Memories Of Elvis"
Betty Riley: "The Saga Of Elvis Presley"
Big Audio Dynamite: "Harrow Road"
Big Head Todd: "Elvis"
Big Head Todd: "Midnight Radio Elvis"
Big Ross: *Elvis Presley's Golden Hits*
Bill Hurley: *Angel To Memphis: A Tribute To Elvis*
Bill Medley: "Old Friend"
Bill Parsons: "All American Boy"
Bill Parsons: "I'm Hangin' Up My Rifle"
Billie Jo Spears: *I'm So Lonesome I Could Cry*
Billy & Eddie: "The King Is Coming Back"
Billy Adams & The Rock-A-Teers: "Return Of The All American Boy"
Billy Boyle: "My Baby's Crazy 'Bout Elvis"
Billy Burnette: "The Colonel And The King"
Billy Burnette: "Welcome Home Elvis"
Billy Crain: "A Tribute To Elvis"
Billy Joe Ward: "Tribute To A King"
Billy Joel: "Elvis Presley Blvd."
Billy Ray Cyrus: "Hey Elvis!"
Billy Ray Cyrus: "Redneck Heaven"
Billy Swan: "Memphis Rocks"
Billy Swan: *Like Elvis Used To Do*
Billy Walker: "I Saw Elvis At Wal-Mart"
Bitch Funky Sex Machine: "Elvis, Satan & Jimmy Page"
Bob Dylan: "Summer Days"
Bob Dylan: "Went To See A Gypsy"
Bob Haley: "Lisa Daddy Loves You"
Bob Lowery: "Dashboard Elvis"
Bobby Bare: "I'm Hanging Up My Rifle"
Bobby Freeman: "Elvis Goodbye"
Bongo Poets: "Hypertext Elvis"
Boxcar Willie: "The Day Elvis Died"
Brenda Joyce: "To Elvis"
Bruce Springsteen: "Johnny Bye Bye"
Bucky Dee James and the Nashville Explosion: *The Hits of Elvis Presley*
Bryan Adams: "Hey Elvis"
Burger Ink: "Elvism"
Buzz Jefferson: "A Lonely Christmas Without Elvis Presley"
Carl Perkins: "The Elvis Presley Express"
Carl Perkins: "The Whole World Misses You"
Carmella Rosella: "Oh! It Was Elvis"
Carnival Art: "Little Elvis"

Cee Cee Chapman: "What Would Elvis Do?"
Charlie Sexton: "Graceland"
Chicago: "Bigger Than Elvis"
Chris Marshon: "God Called Elvis Home"
Chris Smith: "The King Of Rock 'N' Roll Song"
Chubby Checker: "The Class"
Chuck Prophet: "Apology"
Cindy Lee Berryhill: "Elvis Of Maryville"
Clive Gregson: "Don't Step In My Blue Suede Shoes"
Confederate Railroad: "Elvis & Andy"
Confederate Railroad: "Queen Of Memphis"
Cowboy Junkies: "Blue Moon Revisited"
Crack The Sky: "Elvis Was My Daddy"
Cybelvis Monroe: "Champagne Dreams"
Cyndi Lauper: "White Man's Melody"
Dale Magee: "Long Live The King"
Dan Bern: "Graceland"
Dance Hall Crashers: "Elvis And Me"
Danny Mirror: "I Remember Elvis Presley"
Danny Roberts: "Memphis Cowboy"
Dave Howell & The M&M Band: "It Takes Pride"
David Byrne: "Finite=Alright"
David Lee: "Journey To Graceland"
David Price: "Love Him Tender, Sweet Jesus"
D.C Ryder: "Tupelo 1935"
Deke Rivers & The Hansen Brothers: "If It Wasn't For Elvis"
Denis Leary: "Elvis And I"
Denzil: "Bastard Son Of Elvis"
Didjits: "Elvis' Corvette"
Dire Straits: "Calling Elvis"
Dodie Stevens: "Yes, I'm Lonesome Tonight"
Don Hart: "Presley On Her Mind"
Don McLean: "American Pie"
Donna Visone: "Elvis Magic"
Dorothy Carlson and Ray Jones: "Salute To Elvis"
Doug Anthony All Stars: "Dead Elvis"
Doug Demarche: "Lisa"
Douglas Roy: "Disco To The King"
Dread Zeppelin: *Un-Led-Ed*
Dread Zeppelin: *The First No-Elvis*
Duran Duran: "Hallucinating Elvis"
'Echo' Chambers: "Elvis, Say That You're Mine"
Eddie Karr: "Elvis"
Eighteen Visions: "That Ain't Elvis Playing Piano"
El Vez (The Mexican Elvis): Various
Elton John: "Porch Swing In Tupelo"
Elliott Murphy: "On Elvis Presley's Birthday"
Elvis Angel: "Elvis, Mama & Lisa Marie"
Elvis Costello: "The Delivery Man"
Emmylou Harris: "Boy From Tupelo"
Erik Sitbon: "Tupelo Boy"
Evangeline: "Elvis Of The Night"
Fabian: "Hound Dog Man"
Faith Hill: "Bringing Out The Elvis"
Felton Jarvis: "Don't Knock Elvis"
Figures On A Beach: "Elvis' House"
Flies On Fire: "Baptize Me Over Elvis Presley's Grave"
Flying Circus: "Me And Elvis"
Frank Zappa: "Elvis Has Left The Building"
Frankie Allen: "Just A Country Boy"
Fred Eaglesmith: "105"
Fred Eaglesmith: "Alcohol & Pills"
Fred Eaglesmith: "Mighty Big Car"
Gary Lewis & The Playboys: "I Saw Elvis Presley Last Night"
Gene Summers: "Goodbye Priscilla (Bye Bye Baby Blue)"
Genee Harris: "Bye Bye Elvis"
Gene Vincent: "Story Of The Rockers"
Generation X: "King Rocker"
George Hamilton IV: "If You Don't Know"
George Jones: "The King Is Gone (And So Are You)"
Gillian Welch: "Elvis Presley Blues"
Glen Campbell: "Hound Dog Man"
Gods Child: "Female Elvis"
Gothik: "Elvis Christ"
Gram Parsons: "Return Of The Grievous Angel"
Greg Brown: "Jesus And Elvis"
Hal Ketchum: "Small Town Saturday Night"
Hamell On Trial: "Big As Life"
Harold Loyd: "A Prayer For Elvis"
Heather Eatman: "Too Tired To Be Elvis"
Homer And Jethro: "Houn' Dog"

Hudson Brothers: "Hollywood Situation"
Human Radio: "Me & Elvis"
I Am: "Elvis"
Intensive Care: "Elvis Presley Heart"
Jack Brand: "Elvis, We're Sorry We Fenced You In"
Jackie Kahane: "Requiem For Elvis"
Jana Thompson: "Merry Christmas From Lisa Marie"
Janis Martin: "My Boy Elvis"
Jaybee: "Elvis In The Army"
J.D. Sumner: "Elvis Has Left The Building"
Jean Sampson: "The Troubadour From Memphis"
Jenny Nicholas: "Elvis"
Jerry Kennedy: *Jerry Kennedy's Dancing Guitars Rock the Hits of the King*
Jerry Reed: "Elvis Has Left the Building"
Jerry Reed: "Tupelo, Mississippi Flash"
Jerry Reed: *Tupelo Mississippi Flash*
Jesse King: "Elvis In Heaven"
Jim Camilli: "A Tribute To The King Of Rock & Roll"
Jim Ford: "The Story Of Elvis Presley"
Jim Matthews: "We'll Have A Blue Christmas"
Jim Van Hollebeke: "The Legend Lives"
Jimmy Ellis: "I'm Not Trying To Be Like Elvis"
Jimmy Ellis—Various, including *By Request—Ellis Sings Elvis*
Jimmy Buffett: "Elvis Imitators"
Jimmy Buffett: "Elvis Presley Blues"
Jimmy Brown: *The King*
Jimmy Frey: "Elvis Forever"
Jimmy Lafave: "Elvis Loved His Mama"
Jimmy Webb: "Elvis And Me"
Jimmy Woodall: "Uncle Sam's Call"
Jo Ann Perry: "Yes, I'm Lonesome Tonight"
John Fogerty: "Big Train From Memphis"
John Gorka: "That's Why"
John Hiatt: "Riding With The King"
John Hiatt: "Tennessee Plates"
John Trudell: "Baby Boom Che"
Johnny Devlin (The New Zealand Elvis)—*Various*
Johnny Farago: "The King Is Gone"
Johnny Farago: *Pour Les Amateurs d'Elvis*
Johnny Murrell: "Elvis In Heaven"
Johnny Rusk: *A Tribute to Elvis*
Johnny Wakelin: "Tennessee Hero"
Joni Mitchell: "The Windfall (Everything For Nothing)"
Julie Lang: "Elvis"
June Carter Cash: "I Used To Be Somebody"
Kaleidoscope: "Angels' Song: Dear Elvis Presley"
Kate Bush: "King Of The Mountain"
Kathy Westmoreland: "My Father Watches Over Me"
Kathy Westmoreland: "You Were The Music"
Keith Bradford: "Somewhere Elvis Is Smiling"
King Junior: *A Tribute To The King*
Kirsty Maccoll: "There's A Guy Works Down The Chip Shop Swears He's Elvis"
Kyf Brewer: "Turning Into Elvis"
Lalo Guerrero: "Elvis Perez"
LaVern Baker: "Hey Memphis"
Lee Tully with Milt Moss: "Around The World With Elwood Pretzel"
Leon Everette: *Goodbye King Of Rock 'N' Roll*
Leon Russell: "Elvis & Marilyn"
Lind Espen: "It's A Damn Shame About You"
Lisa Marie Presley: "Lights Out"
Lisa Marie Presley: "Nobody Noticed It"
Little Lambsie Penn: "I Want Elvis For Christmas"
Little River Band: "Home On A Monday"
Little Tony: *Tony canta Elvis*
Live Gold: "To Elvis, With Love"
Living Colour: "Elvis Is Dead"
Liz Phair: "Elvis, Be True"
Lou Monte: "Elvis Presley For President"
Loudon Wainwright III: "Happy Birthday Elvis"
Louie Fontaine: "Elvis Is The King"
Louise Hoffsten: "Bringing Out The Elvis"
Major Bill Smith: "Requiem For Elvis"
Marillion: "King"
Mark Cohen: "Walking In Memphis"
Matrimony: "Elvis Superstar"
Mecca Normal: "Who Shot Elvis?"
Merle Haggard: "From Graceland To The Promised Land"

Merle Haggard: *From Graceland To The Promised Land*
Michael Daugherty: "Dead Elvis"
Michele Cody: "Merry Christmas Elvis"
Mo Klein and the Sergeants: "Alright Private"
Moist: "Picture Elvis"
Mojo Nixon: "619-239-King"
Mojo Nixon: "Elvis Is Everywhere"
Mojo Nixon & Skid Roper: "Bo Day Shus"
Mott The Hoople: "All The Way From Memphis"
Neil Young: "He Was The King"
Neil Young: "My My. Hey Hey (Out Of The Blue)"
Neil Young: "Old King"
Nick Cave & the Bad Seeds: "Tupelo"
Nik Turner: "Bones Of Elvis"
Odds: "Wendy Under The Stars"
O.M.D.: "Bloc Bloc Bloc"
Original Fetish: "I'm Glad Elvis Is Dead"
Otis Blackwell: *These Are My Songs*
Otto Bash: "The Elvis Blues"
Passengers (U2): "Elvis Ate America"
Pat Boone: *Pat Boone Sings Guess Who?*
Patricia Emanuele & Chris Martino: "The Best Of My Life"
Pat Minter: "Let's Let Elvis Get Some Sleep"
Patsy Sexton: *Elvis On My Mind*
Patty Loveless: "I Try To Think About Elvis"
Paul Dragon: *Golden Memories*
Paul Mousavi: "Where's Elvis?"
Paul Porter: "The King Ain't Dead"
Paul Randal: "I'm Lonesome For You"
Paul Simon: "Graceland"
Paul Simon: *Graceland*
Paul White: "Elvis, Christmas Won't Be The Same Without You"
Per Granberg: *Rockabye, Rollabye*
Peter De Bree and The Wanderers: "Hey! Mr. Presley"
Phil Ochs: *Gunfight at Carnegie Hall*
Phil Lynott: "King's Call"
Pinkart & Bowden: "Elvis Was A Narc"
P.Q Rock & Roll: "All About Elvis"
Prefab Sprout: "Moondog"
Prince (Not) Prince: "Face Down"
Public Enemy: "Fight The Power"
Ral Donner: "The Day The Beat Stopped"
Ral Donner: *The Day The Beat Stopped*
Randel Porter & Mark Hancock: "Elvis Presley For President"
Ray Herndon: "My Dog Thinks I'm Elvis"
Ray Jennings: "Graceland Tour"
Ray Stevens: "I Saw Elvis In A UFO"
Ray Stevens: "Mama's In The Sky With Elvis"
Red Elvises: "Elvis And Bears"
Red Sovine: "The King's Last Concert"
Reed Harper and The Three Notes: "Oh Elvis"
R.E.M.: "Man In The Moon"
Rev. Billy C. Wirtz: "What Would Elvis Do?"
Rhino: "Bugs & Friends Sing Elvis"
Richard Thompson: "From Galway To Graceland"
Rick Ardesano: "Angel From Heaven"
Rick Dees: "He Ate Too Many Jelly Donuts"
Rick Dees & His Cast Of Idiots: "I Wanna Be Elvis"
Rita Bevis: "The Ballad Of Elvis Presley"
Ringo: "Goodbye Elvis"
Robbie Robertson: "American Roulette"
Robbie Williams: "Advertising Space"
Robert Cunningham: "Long Live The King"
Robert Mitchum: "What Is This Generation Coming To?"
Robyn Hitchcock: "Queen Elvis"
Ron McKee: "Elvis, We Miss You Tonight"
Ronnie Kaye: "The King Is Dead"
Ronnie McDowell: "The King Is Gone"
Ronnie McDowell: "Tupelo's Too Far"
Ronnie McDowell: *Elvis, A Tribute To The King*
Ronnie McDowell and the Jordanaires: "I Just Wanted You To Know"
Roy Hall: "You Ruined My Blue Suede Shoes"
Roy Orbison: "Hound Dog Man"
Roy Williams: "I Remember Elvis"
Shaun Nielsen: *The Songs I Sang For Elvis*
Sheryl Crow: "Maybe Angels"
Shiloh: "God Brought The Curtain Down"
Skip Jackson: "The Greatest Star Of Them All"
Sleepy C: "Elvis Beats"

Slo Leak: "Elvis Slept Here"
Sonny Burgess: "Bigger Than Elvis"
Sonny Cole: "I Dreamed I Was Elvis"
Sonny Cole: *I Dreamed I Was Elvis*
Soulshaker: "Hot For Elvis"
Space: "A Liddle Biddy Help From Elvis"
Spitfire: "This Ain't Vegas And You Ain't Elvis"
Stan Freberg: "Heartbreak Hotel"
Stark Raving Chandler: "Elvis"
Steve Goodman: *Elvis Imitator*
Steve Schickel: "Leave My Sideburns Be"
Studio 99: *Ladies And Gentlemen Elvis Has Not Left The Building*
Subway to Sally: "Elvis Lives"
Supergarage: "Elvis"
Susan Rose: "Elvis Is Just Away"
Suzi Quatro: "Singing With Angels"
Swing Cats: *Special Tribute To Elvis*
Terry Stafford: *Suspicion*
Terry Taylor: "Pretend I'm Elvis (For Just One Night)"
Terry Turner: "A Dedication To The King"
The 101 Strings: *101 Strings Play a Tribute to Elvis Presley*
The Bobolinks: "(I Wanna Be) Elvis Presley's Sergeant"
The Beach Boys: "Do You Remember?"
The Bush Band: "Too Many Kings"
The Cramps: "A Date With Elvis"
The Earls Of Suave: "Yabba Dabba Do"
The Eurythmics: "Angel"
The Fabulous Mclevertys: "Don't Blame It On Elvis"
The Greats: "Marching Elvis"
The Hansen Brothers: "My Friend Elvis"
The Holly Twins: "I Want Elvis For Christmas"
The Johnnys: "Elvisly Yours"
The Kids: "Elvis And Me"
The KLF: "Elvis On The Radio, Steel Guitar In My Soul"
The Problems: "The Gift Of Elvis"
The Red Elvises: "Ballad Of Elvis And Priscilla"
The Residents: "Elvis And His Boss"
The Residents: *The King & Eye*
The Rock Odyssey: "A Tribute To Elvis"
The Serious Brothers: "It's Another Joyful Elvis Presley Christmas"
The Sophisticates: "When Elvis Marches Home Again"
The Strangemen: "Elvis Inside Of Me"
The Stray Cats: "Elvis On Velvet"
The Superstar: "All American Boy"
The Swirling Eddies: "Outdoor Elvis"
The Teardrops: "Goodnight Elvis"
The Threeteens: "Dear 53310761"
The Thunderbird Singers: *The King's Music*
The Tractors: "The Elvis Thing"
The Unknown: "I Have Returned"
The Valentines: "The Sock"
The Who: "Real Good Looking Boy"
The Wildhearts: "Velvet Presley"
T.I.D.E.: "Elvis Don't Come Back From The Grave"
Tim Rice / Andrew Lloyd Webber: "King Of My Heart"
Tink Grimmett: "A Tribute To Elvis"
Tiny Tim: "I Saw Mr. Presley Tiptoeing Thru The Tulips"
Tom Holbrook: "Oh Yes, He's Gone"
Tom Petty: "Free Fallen"
Tom Waits: "Burma Shave"
Tommy Duren: "Elvis"
Tony Copeland: "The Passing Of A King"
Tosca(Opera): "Chocolate Elvis"
Trisha Yearwood: "Wrong Side Of Memphis"
U2: "A Room At The Heartbreak Hotel"
U2: "Elvis Presley & America"
Uncle Bonzai: "Only Elvis"
Van Morrison: "In The Days Before Rock & Roll"
Various artists: *A Tribute To Elvis Presley, The Boy Who Would Be King*
Various artists: *Elvis Connection*
Various artists: *International Elvis Impersonators Convention*
Various artists: *Night Of 100 Elvises*
Various artists: *To Elvis: Love Still Burning*
Vester Presley: "A Message To Elvis Fans And My Friends"
Vicki Knight: "To Elvis In Heaven"

Vince Everett: *Elvis On My Mind—The Legend Lives On*
Virginia Lowe: "I'm In Love With Elvis Presley"
Wall Of Voodoo: "Elvis Bought Dora A Cadillac"
Wally Fowler: "A New Star In Heaven"
Wally Fowler: *Wally Fowler Sings a Tribute to the King*
Wanda Jackson: *I Remember Elvis*
Warren Zevon: "Jesus Mentioned"
Warren Zevon: "Porcelain Monkey"
Was (Not) Was (w. Leonard Cohen): "Elvis' Rolls Royce"
Wayne Newton: "The (Elvis) Letter"
Werner Muller: *Werner Muller Plays Elvis Presley's Greatest Hits*
Willie "Loco" Alexander: "Abel And Elvis"
(With Love From) Audrey: "Dear Elvis"
Wynonna Judd: "Just Like New"
Wynonna Judd: "Sometimes I Feel Like Elvis"
Zoe And The Alexander Band: *Swingin' With Elvis*
Zombie Ghost Train: "Buried Next To The King"

Books:
Discography of Elvis Tribute and Novelty Records 1956-1981, by Howard F. Banney, Pierian Press, 1987.
Elvis—His Life From A to Z,∏ by Fred L. Worth and Steve D. Tamerius, Contemporary Books, 1988.

TRIVIA

Where the trivia begins and the serious reference ends depends on how great an Elvis fan you are. Few human lives have been as picked apart and put back together as that of one Elvis Aron Presley. Elvis fans have an unslakable thirst for "new" facts, and for books that challenge their knowledge of the man. When it came out in 1988, *Elvis—His Life From A to Z,* by Fred L. Worth and Steve D. Tamerius claimed to contain every known fact about Elvis, and is a resource that many Elvis fans have used ever since to answer Elvis questions and respond to the kind of queries raised in the books listed below. With heavyweight biographies and musical chronicles of Elvis' life coming out since, not to mention a continuing flood of memoirs, there are an awful lot of Elvis fans in this world who know prodigious amounts of information about Elvis. This book may well swell the number of well-informed fans.

Books:
Elvis Special 1982, by Todd Slaughter, Albert Hand, 1982.
On the Throne With the King: The Ultimate Elvis Bathroom Book, by Chuck Oliver, Dowling, 1999.
The Ultimate Elvis Quiz Book: What Do You Know About the King of Rock & Roll?, by W. Kent Moore and David Logan Scott, Rutledge Hill Press, 1999.

"TROUBLE"

Elvis recorded this Leiber and Stoller rocker at Radio Recorders on January 15, 1958 for *King Creole.* The song initially came out on the movie soundtrack EP and LP. It has since appeared on *Worldwide Gold Award Hits Vol. 2, Elvis Sings Leiber & Stoller, The Great Performances, The King Of Rock 'n' Roll, Artist Of The Century, Elvis 2nd to None, Elvis By The Presleys, Hitstory, Elvis R 'n' B* and the 2007 *The Essential Elvis Presley* release.

This was a song that Elvis evidently took great pleasure reprising for his 1968 NBC Comeback Special, when, in a medley with "Guitar Man," it provided the narrative backbone to the June 1968 show. The song was track one on the tie-in LP *Elvis,* and has since featured on a plethora of Comeback Special bootlegs and FTD releases.

Multiple alternates are on *Memories The '68 Comeback Special* and FTD releases *Burbank '68* and *Let Yourself Go.* Elvis performing the medley came out on the 2007 international DVD release *Elvis #1 Hit Performances.*

He occasionally dusted off the song in concert in the Seventies. A down-tempo version of the song from his summer 1973 Las Vegas residence is on FTD release *Closing Night.* A rare 1975 performance is on FTD release *Southern Nights.* A demo version from when Elvis first heard the track was included on FTD release *Writing for the King.*

"T-R-O-U-B-L-E"

Elvis recorded this piano-propelled Jerry Chesnut rocker in Nashville on March 12, 1975. A month later it was in record stores as a single with "Mr. Songman" on the B-side. The single failed to rise any higher than #35 in the charts, with sales of around 200,000 copies (though it made it to #11 in the country chart). The tune was soon pressed into service as the opening cut for late album *Today.* It has since appeared on *Platinum: A Life in Music, Walk A Mile In My Shoes* and *The Country Side of Elvis.*

This song was one of very few recordings from Elvis' later years to earn a permanent slot in his stage show, at least for the rest of the year that he recorded it. Live versions are reproduced on collector's set *Elvis Aron Presley* and, more latterly, on FTD releases *Dixieland Rocks* and *Southern Nights.*

Alternate takes from the 1975 recording session have cropped up on FTD releases *6363 Sunset* and the 2005 release of *Today.* The song as sung by Jerry Chesnut came out on FTD release *Writing for the King.*

TROUBLE WITH GIRLS, THE

Elvis' final MGM feature (and penultimate movie) had a 10-year gestation period: it was originally conceived as a movie vehicle for Glenn Ford and previous Elvis leading-lady Hope Lange. Elvis was first mooted for the lead role as far back as 1961.

At this late stage in his career, Elvis is given more latitude than usual to act. Unusually for an Elvis flick, not only is E. not in every scene, the movie tends towards being more of an ensemble piece than a star vehicle. It's also the only murder mystery of his career.

The original title *Chautauqua* was dropped after Colonel Parker's objections that such an unfamiliar name would hinder marketing efforts. The Colonel actually toured with one such traveling show when he first came to the US in the Twenties, though they actually originated several decades earlier as religiously-uplifting self-improvement and lecture tours, working out of Chautauqua, New York—hence the name. The movie's full and somewhat misleading title was changed to *The Trouble with Girls (And How to Get Into It).*

Elvis began work on the movie in late October 1968—his second with director Peter Tewksbury in a year—and was free to head home a week before Christmas.

In the movie, Elvis plays a role that is much more Colonel than Elvis, supported by an accomplished cast of actors including Vincent Price, John Carradine and Sheree North. *The Trouble with Girls* also featured cameos by future "Brady Bunch" baby Susan Olsen, and baseball star Duke Snider.

The movie features many people other than Elvis doing the singing; by this time in his career, there was little market for a tie-in soundtrack release, though the gospel songs and "Clean Up

Your Own Backyard" are among the stronger of Elvis' film fare, and for a change, actually fit the movie context rather than being simply fitted in as song-and-dance interludes.

The picture opened in early September 1969. By this time, neither movie studios nor the Colonel were keen on releasing figures about how much profit Elvis movies were making.

CREDITS:
MGM, Color.
Length: 97 minutes
Release date: September 3, 1969

TAGLINES:
This is Elvis '69- his new look.
A musical movie that takes Elvis across the country . . . into trouble! trouble! trouble!
Elvis knows The Trouble With Girls And How To Get Into It.

Directed by: Peter Tewksbury
Produced by: Lester Welch (producer), Wilson McCarthy (associate producer)
Written by: Mauri Grashin (story), Day Keene (novel) and Dwight Babcock (novel); Arnold Peyser (screenplay) and Lois Peyser (screenplay)
Music by: Billy Strange
Cinematography by: Jacques Marquette
Film Editing by: George W. Brooks
Art Direction by: Edward Carfagno, George W. Davis
Set Decoration by: Henry Grace, Jack Mills, Robert R. Benton
Costume Design by: Bill Thomas

CAST:

Elvis Presley	Walter Hale
Marlyn Mason	Charlene
Nicole Jaffe	Betty Smith
Sheree North	Nita Bix
Edward Andrews	Johnny
John Carradine	Mr. Drewcolt
Anissa Jones	Carol Bix
Vincent Price	Mr. Morality
Joyce Van Patten	Maude
Pepe Brown	Willy
Dabney Coleman	Harrison "Harry" Wilby
Bill Zuckert	Mayor Gilchrist
Pitt Herbert	Mr. Perper
Anthony "Scooter"	Teague Clarence
Med Flory	Constable
Robert Nichols	Smith
Helene Winston	Olga Prchlik
Kevin O'Neal	Yale
Frank Welker	Rutgers
John Rubinstein	Princeton
Chuck Briles	Amherst
Patsy Garrett	Mrs. Gilchrist
Linda Sue Risk	Lily-Jeanne Gilchrist, Auditioning singer
Charles P. Thompson	Cabbie
Leonard Rumery	First farmhand
William M. Paris	Second farmhand
Kathleen Rainey	Third farmhand
Hal James Pederson	Soda jerk
Mike Wagner	James "Chowderhead"
Brett Parker	Iceman
Duke Snider	The Cranker
Pacific Palisades High School Madrigals Singing Ensemble	
Joe Esposito	Gambler
William H. O'Brien	Extra in hotel lobby
Susan Olsen	Auditioning singer
Jerry Schilling	Deputy Sheriff

ADDITIONAL CREW:

Mary Keats	hair stylist
William Tuttle	makeup artist
Robert Vreeland	unit production manager
Lindsley Parsons Jr.	assistant production manager
John Clark Bowman	assistant director
Franklin Milton	recording supervisor
Jonathan Lucas	choreographer

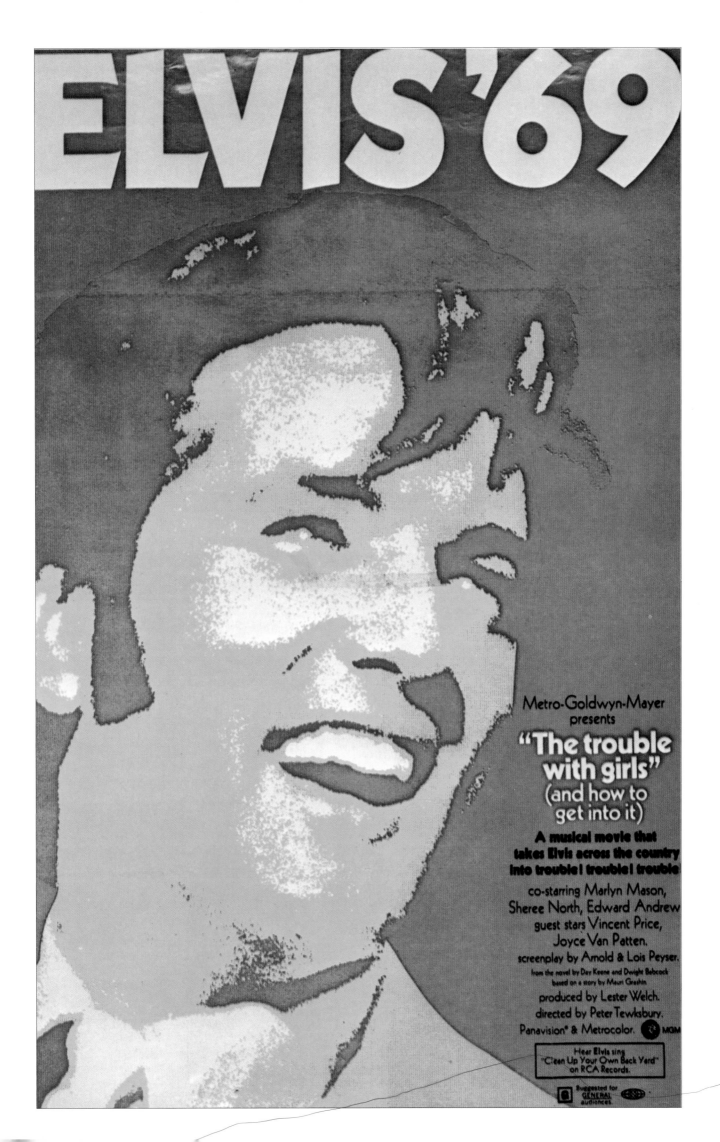

Plot:

Elvis plays white-suited Walter Hale, the singing manager of a 1920s Chautauqua-style traveling tent show that has come to Radford Center, Iowa to entertain and amuse the townsfolk.

Trouble rears its head when Elvis' love interest and all-round entertainer Charlene (played by Marlyn Mason) wants to unionize the show, while there's an unseemly battle among local women for their kids to get pride of place in the show parade.

Nita Bix (played by Sheree North) is romantically involved with local pharmacist Harrison Wilby (played by Dabney Coleman), until his body turns up in the midst of one of the acts. A Chautauqua performer with a sideline in card-sharping is arrested on suspicion of his murder, but then Walter finds out that the finger of guilt really points at Nita.

To restore the show's dwindling audiences, Walter puts on a show which he bills as the moment when the real murderer will be unmasked. After a slapstick delay or two for comic effect, Nita comes on stage and confesses that it was she who killed Wilby, in an act of self defense. She will be tried in court but can have some expectation of leniency.

Charlene is so furious at these goings-on that she refuses to stay with Walter, despite her evident love for him. The happy ending is only ensured after Walter gets the police to round Charlene up and put her on the train that he's riding out of town.

Songs: "Swing Down Sweet Chariot," "The Whiffenpoof Song," "Violet," "Clean Up Your Own Backyard," "Signs Of The Zodiac," "Almost"

"TRUE LOVE"

Elvis recorded a melodic version of this Cole Porter song at Radio Recorders on February 23, 1957, when it was still fresh in people's minds as sung by Bing Crosby and Grace Kelly in *High Society*. It initially appeared on the soundtrack EP and LP of Elvis' movie *Loving You*; it has since come out on the 1997 and 2005 BMG soundtrack reissues, and on the FTD release for the movie. It's also on *The King Of Rock And Roll* anthology, and has long been a prime candidate for Elvis love song compilations

"TRUE LOVE TRAVELS ON A GRAVEL ROAD"

Recorded at American Studio on February 17, 1969, Elvis originally released this A.L. Owens / Dallas Frazier country song on *From Elvis in Memphis*. Duane Dee had already had the song out in late 1968, though his version failed to make it into the top 50 of the *Billboard* country chart.

Elvis' version has since appeared on *The Memphis Record* and the *From Nashville To Memphis* anthology.

The original and an alternate are on *Suspicious Minds: The Memphis 1969 Anthology*. Further alternates may be found on *Today Tomorrow And Forever* and FTD release *The Memphis Sessions*. Rare live versions have appeared on bootleg only.

TRUE LOVE TRAVELS ON A GRAVEL ROAD

This 1995 unofficial album on the Laurel and Cupido labels features tracks from Elvis' January and February 1970 Las Vegas shows.

TRACK LISTING:
1. All Shook Up
2. I Got A Woman
3. Long Tall Sally
4. Elvis talks
5. Don't Cry, Daddy
6. Monologue / Everybody Loves Somebody
7. Hound Dog
8. Love Me Tender
9. Kentucky Rain
10. Let It Be Me
11. I Can't Stop Loving You
12. See See Rider
13. True Love Travels On A Gravel Road
14. Sweet Caroline
15. Polk Salad Annie
16. Band introductions
17. Kentucky Rain
18. Suspicious Minds
19. Can't Help Falling In Love

"TRYIN' TO GET TO YOU"

Elvis recorded this Margie Singleton / Rosemarie McCoy track at Sun Records on July 11, 1955, after abortive attempts earlier that month. Sam Phillips' original plan was to issue the song (on which Johnny Bernero played drums) as Elvis' sixth Sun single, with Billy "the Kid" Emerson's blues song "When It Rains, It Really Pours" on the flip side, but Elvis moved to RCA before this could happen. R&B group the Eagles had previously brought out the song in 1954.

RCA acquired the unreleased master as part of its buyout of Elvis' Sun contract (and reputedly lost an earlier, incomplete take that Elvis ran through at Sun on February 5, 1955). Elvis' new label released the track as the B-side to "I Love You Because," one of seven singles shipped simultaneously in late August 1956, and in short order added it to Elvis' first album *Elvis Presley* and multiple EPs of the same name. Since then, it has graced *The Sun Sessions*, *The Complete Sun Sessions*, the CD version of *For LP Fans Only*, *The King Of Rock And Roll*, *Sunrise*, *Artist Of The Century*, *Elvis at Sun*, *Elvis By The Presleys*, *Hitstory* (European edition), and *Elvis R 'n' B*. It's also on the 2000s FTD reissue of Elvis' first LP, *Elvis Presley*.

"Tryin' To Get To You" was a strong candidate for Elvis' live medley on the NBC TV Special. He taped it at two shows on June 27, 1968, but it was ultimately dropped for the broadcast show owing to time constraints. These performances have since filtered out on *Elvis: A Legendary Performer Vol. 1*, *Elvis Aron Presley*, *A Golden Celebration*, the 1991 *Elvis NBC TV Special* album re-release, *Platinum: A Life In Music*, *Memories: The '68 Comeback Special* and *Tiger Man*.

The song was restored to Elvis' live repertoire from 1974 at shows he played in Memphis (*Elvis Recorded Live On Stage In Memphis*, the original and 2000s FTD release) and Los Angeles (FTD release *Live In LA*). Further live version are on *Live In Las Vegas*, and on FTD issues *I Found My Thrill*, *Dragonheart*, *Southern Nights*, *Dinner At Eight*, *New Year's Eve*, *Spring Tours '77* and *Unchained Melody*. Elvis was still "Tryin' To Get To You" on his last ever tour in June 1977 (recorded for posterity on the *Elvis on Concert* documentary and tie-in album).

TSCHECHOWA, VERA
(B. 1940)

Elvis met this 18 year-old actress in January 1958 on a photo shoot for the March of Dimes in Germany. When he had three days leave that March, he went to Munich where he bought all the seats to an experimental play she was in. He

saw her every day of that trip; he also made a couple of visits to the Moulin Rouge strip club (once with Vera), a visit to a local film studio, and a trip to Lake Starnberg.

Tschechowa, the great-niece of Russian author Anton Chekhov, went on to have a long and successful acting career. More recently she has distinguished herself as a documentary director.

TUBB, ERNEST DALE
(1914-1984)

Elvis met Tubb, the "Texas Troubadour" on October 2, 1954, immediately after playing the Grand Ole Opry for the first and last time. Like many Opry guests before him, Elvis went to the Ernest Tubb Record Shop at 720 Commerce Street in Nashville to play a slot on the live Midnight Jamboree radio show. That night, the well-established country singer counseled the tyro performer to carry on doing whatever was bringing him so much success, after Elvis complained that he would much rather be singing some ballads than this new-fangled rock 'n' roll.

Tubb was born in Crips, Texas, on February 9, 1914. Over a career spanning five decades, Tubb (known as E.T. to friends) was a honky-tonk singer, songwriter, electric guitar pioneer, and an actor. He built on his first record, "The Passing Of Jimmy Rodgers," to become the highest-profile country star of the day, with hits "I'm Walking The Floor Over You," "Waltz Across Texas" and "Rainbow At Midnight." For close to forty years, Tubb was a Grand Ole Opry headline act. During the war years, the Colonel got a foothold in the music business by helping to promote Tubb. Always mindful of the encouragement he had been given by the wife of his idol, Jimmie Rodgers, Tubb took great pleasure in giving young singers a break: he helped Elvis, he helped the Everly Brothers, and he helped many others too.

Elvis later covered Tubb composition "Tomorrow Never Comes." They both covered "Blue Christmas," "The Yellow Rose Of Texas" and "I Love You Because."

Tubb was inducted into the Country Music Hall of Fame in 1965 and the Nashville Songwriters Hall of Fame in 1970. Tubb continued performing through many years of ill-health, almost right up to his death.

TUCSON '76

A 2000 FTD live concert release from the year before Elvis died.

TRACK LISTING:
1. See See Rider
2. I Got A Woman
3. Amen
4. Love Me
5. If You Love Me (Let Me Know)
6. You Gave Me A Mountain
7. All Shook Up
8. Teddy Bear
9. Don't Be Cruel
10. And I Love You So
11. Jailhouse Rock
12. Help Me
13. Fever
14. Polk Salad Annie
15. Early Morning Rain
16. What'd I Say
17. Love Letters
18. Long Live Rock And Roll
19. Hurt
20. Burning Love
21. Help Me Make It Through The Night
22. Danny Boy
23. Hound Dog

24.   Funny How Time Slips Away
25.   Can't Help Falling In Love

"TUMBLIN' TUMBLEWEEDS"

Elvis sang this 1934 Sons Of The Pioneers track (written by group leader Bob Nolan) at home in Graceland in 1966. A tape of the occasion has come out on *The Home Recordings*; Elvis also sang the song eight years earlier at Eddie Fadal's home in Waco (bootlegged on *Forever Young, Forever Beautiful*).

TUNZI, JOSEPH A.

One of the world's most prolific Elvis authors, with more than twenty books to his name, specializing in photo books about specific events and tours through his own publishing operation, J.A.T. Productions. Many of Tunzi's books feature exclusive interviews and recordings. He has also published a number of DVD titles, including the *Elvis Presley Hot Shots And Cool Clips* series.

TUPELO, MISSISSIPPI

Elvis' hometown was East Tupelo, Lee County, where his parents' families lived, and where Elvis was born in a shotgun shack on January 8, 1935.

The name Tupelo derives either from the Chickasaw word for lodging place or gum tree (before the civil war, the town was known as Gum Pond). Founded in 1859, the town grew substantially after the arrival of the railroad. Nowadays, the Tupelo population is around 35,000 people. Around the time that Vernon and Gladys met, Tupelo was a town of around 6,000 people, most of whom worked on farms or for one of the thriving local textiles companies.

When Elvis was 15 months old, a tornado ripped through the area, killing 235 people. Little Elvis sat out the disaster in his paternal grandparents' house, which survived unscathed; the church opposite, however, was razed to the ground. Another tornado swept through on January 7, 1946, forcing Elvis and his mom to take refuge in a storm cellar.

Life in Tupelo was tough when Elvis was growing up. Most families had no electricity and outdoor toilets. Much of the populace had to draw their own water from just three wells—a job that often fell to kids like Elvis. At Junior High School, Elvis was one of the poorest kids in his class; photos of the time show him as the only child wearing the poor man's uniform of overalls.

The year that East Tupelo merged with Tupelo, 1948, was the year that the Presleys left Tupelo for Memphis. Not only did the bigger city offer greater job opportunities for Vernon, it was a place where nobody knew that he had spent time in jail. It has also been speculated that Vernon left town because he had been caught running moonshine on the side during his delivery job, and had been advised to clear out of Tupelo altogether.

Twelve years after moving away, in 1956 Elvis returned triumphantly to Tupelo at an event billed as his homecoming. After an Elvis-themed parade of forty floats, the prodigal son was driven down Main Street, where the stores were adorned with Elvis-themed displays. At the packed Fairgrounds, Elvis was lauded by then Governor, J. P. Coleman, and presented with a guitar-shaped (and guitar-sized) key to the city. That day, Elvis gave two shows at the Mississippi-Alabama State Fair and Dairy Show, not a mile from where he had grown up. Video of Elvis performing at one of the two shows turned up on a DVD titled *Tupelo's*

Own Elvis Presley, released by the Memphis Recording Service in 2007.

Elvis not only put Tupelo on the map, in the words of the local paper circa 1957 he was referred to as "the best ambassador any town could have." Elvis returned that year to play a benefit concert for the Elvis Presley Youth Center, the last time that he ever made a public appearance in town. Elvis' relationship with the powers that be soured when he found out that despite donating tens of thousands of dollars to set up a youth center in his name, no work had been done on the project for years. He continued to return to town on a regular basis, incognito, bringing important new people in his life to see his humble beginnings.

The traditionally poor district of East Tupelo, from which Elvis and his family hailed, was later renamed Presley Heights. The land set aside for a youth center ultimately became Presley Park: this is where the Elvis Presley Birthplace museum is located.

Tupelo holds an Elvis Presley Festival every year in June. In 2006, the town re-enacted the homecoming event to commemorate its 50th anniversary.

For more detailed information on Elvis' performances in Tupelo, see under Mississippi.

TUPELO HOMES

Elvis and his twin brother Jesse Garon were born at their family home, a shotgun shack on the dairy farm where Vernon was working, located at 306 Old Saltillo Road, East Tupelo (since renamed Elvis Presley Drive). Vernon built the wood-framed house himself, after taking out a $180 loan. The property was designated a state historical site by the Mississippi Department of Archives and History on January 8, 1978.

ABOVE: Elvis' birthplace in Tupelo. Mississippi. BELOW: Elvis as a young boy growing up in Tupelo.

Though there is no doubt about the house where Elvis first lived, the family's poverty-fuelled peregrinations over the following years remain a source of speculation. The probable succession of Presley homes are as follows:

When Vernon was in jail, Gladys took Elvis to live with her cousin Frank Richards and his family not far away at 510½ Maple Street, in East Tupelo.

They moved in with Vester and Clettes Presley and their baby Patsy at their Reese Street home in 1940-41.

In 1942, the Presleys rented a small apartment at 904 Kelly Street.

In 1945, the family moved into a four-room house on Berry Street, East Tupelo, which Vernon bought from Orville Bean. Before the year was out the family had to relinquish the property as they could not keep up with payments.

There followed temporary rented accommodations in North Commerce Street in 1946, and Mulberry Alley in Tupelo, before the family moved to 1010 N. Green St (now Elvis Presley Circle) in the Shake Rag area, which at that time was set aside for "colored" families. They shared their last home in Tupelo, not far from a slaughterhouse, with other members of the Presley clan. The house boasted the mod con of an indoor bathroom—a relative luxury at a time.

TUPELO ELVIS SITES

The town is home to the Elvis Birthplace and Museum (306 Elvis Presley Drive). The most visited attraction in Mississippi initially opened to the public in 1971, after it was founded by Virginia Boyd. An annual 100,000 visitors come to town every year to see Elvis' birthplace. Elvis' friend Janelle McComb donated her collection to the Elvis Presley Museum. The museum underwent a major renovation and reopened on Elvis' birthday in 2007. Every year admission is free on the King's birthday. Sid Shaw ruffled some feathers when he claimed that the Elvis home in Tupelo is not the original shotgun shack, but was moved to the present site.

Tupelo has renamed a number of streets and erected monuments to its favorite son. It also boasts the Elvis Presley Memorial Chapel, which was built in Elvis Presley Park after Elvis' lifelong friend Janelle McComb helped to raise $800,000 for the purpose. The chapel and meditation center were dedicated on August 17, 1979, in a ceremony attended by 4,000 people, including Colonel Tom Parker and Kathy Westmoreland. A new Tupelo Elvis Presley fan club was launched in 2006, on what would have been Elvis' 71st birthday.

Another major site is the Tupelo Hardware Store (at the time, Booth's Hardware), where Elvis bought his first guitar.

ELVIS SAID AT THE FAIRGROUNDS BETWEEN PERFORMANCES IN 1956: "Last time I was here, I didn't have a nickel to get in."

HAROLD LOYD (COUSIN): "East Tupelo, Mississippi, was just nothin', a white spot in the road.... It was very small, and a few people owned the better part of it. It was hard to get work unless you wanted to work in the fields."

D.J. FONTANA: "He always wanted to do good, but especially in his hometown."

Book:
Early Elvis: The Tupelo Years, by Bill E. Burk, Propwash Publishing, 1994.

Documentary:
The Homecoming: Tupelo Welcomes Elvis Home, by Roy Turner and Jim Palmer.

DVD/book package:
Tupelo's Own Elvis Presley (produced by Joseph Pirzada, book and DVD written by Roy Turner, Memphis Recording Service, 2007), contains live footage of six songs and audio from both shows.

TRACK LISTING:
AFTERNOON SHOW
1. Heartbreak Hotel
2. Long Tall Sally
3. Presentation of the key to the city
4. I Was The One
5. I Want You, I Need You , I Love You
6. Announcement
7. I Got A Woman
8. Don't Be Cruel
9. Ready Teddy
10. Love Me Tender
11. Hound Dog

EVENING SHOW
12. Love Me Tender
13. I Was The One
14. I Got A Woman
15. Dialogue
16. Don't Be Cruel
17. Blue Suede Shoes
18. Dialogue
19. Baby, Let's Play House
20. Hound Dog
21. Dialogue

FACING PAGE, AND ABOVE: Elvis performing a concert in the city of his birth, Tupelo, Mississippi (1956).

ABOVE: Elvis relaxes after concert in Tupelo, Mississippi (1956). FACING PAGE: With his parents.

"TURN AROUND, LOOK AT ME"

Elvis added a line or two of Glen Campbell's first hit from 1961 (written by Jerry Capeheart) to his concert song list a few times in the Seventies. Performances are on bootlegs including *Suzie Q* and *In Dreams Of Yesterday*.

"TURN YOUR EYES UPON JESUS"

Elvis ran through this hymn on March 31, 1972 during rehearsals filmed for the *Elvis On Tour* concert documentary. The track wasn't officially released until the *Amazing Grace* gospel compilation in 1994. Written by Helen Lemmell and Jeremiah Clarke in 1918, the hymn was originally titled "O Soul Are You Weary And Troubled." Elvis' version has since appeared on gospel-themed compilation *Peace In The Valley*.

TUTT, RONNIE

Dallas-born Tutt was Elvis' drummer in the TCB band from 1969 to 1977. He was brought in on the recommendation of his pal, original band pianist Larry Muhoberac. Tutt has said that he won the job over the better-known drummers who auditioned at the same time because he kept up eye contact with Elvis while he sang.

Tutt had appeared on the same bill as Elvis way back in 1955, as part of Western Swing band in Dallas, though in his childhood years he was known for his tap dancing rather than his drumming prowess.

For Elvis' second month-long stint in Las Vegas in January 1970, Tutt was replaced by Bob Lanning.

Tutt pulled out of the band for the first tour in 1976 (he was replaced a few times by Sweet Inspirations drummer Jerome "Stump" Monroe) but returned for the remainder of the year. He left again just a few dates before the end of what turned out to be Elvis' last ever tour in June 1977 for family reasons; this last time he was replaced by Larry Londin.

After Elvis, Tutt drummed for star performers including Johnny Cash, Barbra Streisand, Neil Diamond (with whom he worked with for more than two decades), The Beach Boys, The Carpenters, Elvis Costello and Billy Joel. He has also performed as a singer.

RONNIE TUTT: "If I had to narrow it down, the greatest music influences on my life would be Elvis Presley, Jerry Garcia and Neil Diamond. Elvis for the flashy, explosive, slightly out of control, style of playing that he brought out in me that mirrored his performance and personality

RONNIE TUTT: "I emulated and accented everything that he did just instinctively. Every move, almost like a glorified stripper! And he loved that."

"TUTTI FRUTTI"

Elvis performed Little Richard's trademark song at the Louisiana Hayride in December 1955, and reprised the song on two separate appearances on his first national TV booking, the Dorsey brothers' "Stage Show," on February 4 and 18, 1956.

Little Richard's own version, recorded in 1955, was his breakthrough hit. Little Richard's exuberant recording made it to #2 on the *Billboard* R&B chart, and went on to sell over three million copies. As was the fate of many black artists at this time, his sales were eclipsed by a cover released by a white singer (Pat Boone) soon afterwards. The song was originally titled "Wop-Bop-

A-Loo-Bop" and featured far more risquéÈ lyrics, before songstress Dorothy LaBostrie offered a new title and less leading words.

RCA released Elvis' version as the B-side to "Blue Suede Shoes" in late August 1956; he had recorded it in January 31 that year at the RCA Studios in New York. Elvis' version came out about the same time as Pat Boone's cover, but failed to chart. Nevertheless, RCA got plenty of mileage out of the song: it did treble duty for Elvis, appearing on his first ever EPs and on debut album *Elvis Presley*.

Elvis' "Tutti Frutti" has since appeared on *Elvis '56*, *The King Of Rock And Roll*, *Elvis Rock* and the FTD version of *Elvis Presley*. A *Golden Celebration* features recordings from Elvis' "Stage Show" performances.

TV APPEARANCES

The still-new medium of television was Elvis' springboard from regional to national fame. As Jack Clement succinctly puts it, " 'The Dorsey Show', 'The Ed Sullivan Show', 'The Steve Allen Show', they were very powerful because everybody was watching, and the public didn't have all these other choices like they do today."

As early as January 1955, Tom Diskin tried to drum up TV bookings for Elvis through the WLS Artist Bureau, in the (well-founded) belief that with his good looks he'd be a winner on the new mass medium. Early attempts to place Elvis on "Arthur Godfrey's Talent Scouts" foundered as much on Elvis' acne problems as a lack of musical appreciation. An initial approach by manager Bob Neal through DJ Bill Randle to the "Ed Sullivan Show" never made it past the audition stage. Years later, Elvis told a Las Vegas audience that he was also turned down by Ted Mack for his "Original Amateur Hour."

Before he obtained that first, all-important national exposure, Elvis made brief regional appearances on a telecast of a Louisiana Hayride show on March 5, 1955 (on KWKH), a show telecast from the Grand Prize Saturday Night Jamboree at the Eagle's Nest in Houston that same month (on KPRC), and also in 1955, an appearance on "The Roy Orbison Show," broadcast locally in Odessa, Texas, on May 31, 1955 on KOSA. Rumors have circulated that Elvis was also interviewed on the Town and Country Jubilee around this time (WMAL TV Washington), and that he might have appeared on a local TV station in Waco, hosted by Jimmy Thomason, on March 18, 1955.

DJ Bill Randle's contacts finally came through (or the Colonel's succeeded where Randle's failed) when Elvis finally landed six slots on the "Stage Show." The soon to be national #1 entertainer made his national television debut on Jimmy and Tommy Dorsey's "Stage Show," broadcast by CBS at 8 p.m. on January 28, 1956. Once competitor TV companies saw what this young singer did for the show's ratings, the offers came in thick and fast.

Elvis' appearance on the "Milton Berle Show" in April 1956 was his first in color. On June 20, 1956, Elvis appeared on local Memphis show "Top Ten Dance Party," hosted by Wink Martindale on WHBQ-TV, where his pal DJ Dewey Phillips had a slot—Elvis needed to get a dispensation from the Colonel, which he did because it was to promote a charity event.

The next month, Elvis made a guest appearance on the "Steve Allen Show" from New York, uncharacteristically dressed in a tux. That same night Elvis made a second TV appearance via a telephone interview for "Hy Gardner Calling!"

In September 1956, word spread across the nation to Elvis uninitiates when the new singing phenomenon was featured on the *TV Guide* cover for the first time.

Elvis' three bookings on the "Ed Sullivan Show," from the summer of 1956 to early 1957, were proof that he had arrived at the top table of the entertainment business. By this time, he knew what was expected of him and was more "professional" and less prone to nervous tics. His first appearance on the top-rated show in the land was minus the genial host, who was convalescing from injuries sustained in a car accident.

On the last day of 1956, Elvis did pal Dewey Phillips a favor by appearing on his new Memphis TV show, "Phillips' Pop Shop" for a quick interview. Late in 1956 and early in 1957, Elvis also made promotional appearances on TV shows in Louisville, KY and Toronto, Canada..

By 1957, Colonel Parker was focusing on the big rather than the small screen and basically embargoed Elvis' TV appearances. With Elvis a household name by now, Parker was keen to cherry-pick the moment for Elvis next to appear on the small screen. William Morris agent Harry Kalcheim wholeheartedly agreed. He wrote to the Colonel: "Because of the fact that he is not shown too often on TV, and there is great curiosity about him so that when he does appear he is sure to attract." The one exception to the Colonel's embargo was Elvis' broadcast contribution to a driver education campaign on the WKNO station in Memphis in September 1957.

RCA, however, were keen to get Elvis to appear on an NBC special. The Colonel fobbed them off, and then wrote to Elvis (while he was working on *Jailhouse Rock*), saying: "They have told me everything under the sun how good this would be for you for exposure... but I turned them all down with respect to our motion picture for reasons I know are best for us. I told them that our next TV show for any sponsor we do would be $50,000 as I want to do one or two TV shows this year, and with a set-up like we would blast the whole country with . . ." Within a month, the Colonel hiked the price to $75,000, at which point he achieved his aim of pricing Elvis out of the TV market altogether.

Elvis' only other appearances on TV in the Fifties were fictional, in art-mirrors-life interludes in *Jailhouse Rock*: his character Vince Everett is "discovered" in a talent show broadcast from the penitentiary, and later does the movie's iconic dance scene for the TV cameras.

Elvis' TV hiatus did not end until the conclusion of his time in the army in 1960. The "Frank Sinatra Show" offered Elvis a record fee and an opportunity to show America the new, cleaned-up, mainstream image the Colonel was keen to promote. The show might not have happened at all if Parker had succeeded in his original intent: he tried to set up a closed-circuit event to mark Elvis' return with a concert broadcast around the country, and was close to finalizing the project before Paramount raised objections.

In 1964, Colonel Parker briefly considered Elvis taking a starring role in a TV series adapted from his 1964 movie *Kissin' Cousins*. After rejecting this, the Colonel kept the small screen at arm's length until Elvis' slew of long-term, multi-picture deals with movie studios had begun to peter out and his lackluster soundtrack albums were threatening to kill off what remained of his musical career.

In 1967, the Colonel approached NBC Vice President Tom Sarnoff about putting on a Christmas Special Elvis show. Unbeknownst to the Colonel, during the development process Elvis would meet director Steve Binder, who persuaded the star to use the opportunity to showcase his achievements. The Colonel being the Colonel, the TV special also had a feature film attached as part of the deal. Tom Sarnoff announced the NBC TV Special, titled simply *Elvis*, in January 1968. Elvis was paid a quarter of a million dollars for his first TV appearance in 8 years. However, including his fee for the movie and extras, NBC actually wrote a check for $1 million.

Elvis' NBC Special—before long renamed Elvis' "Comeback" Special—resurrected his career and earned the network its best viewing figures for the entire year, despite an unfavorable slot on a Tuesday evening more than three weeks before Christmas. The William Morris Agency was immediately inundated with requests for Elvis to appear on TV; Colonel Parker once again turned the faucet shut, preferring to send his boy back out on stage in Las Vegas.

The Colonel only turned to TV twice more during Elvis' lifetime, both times to try and give his career a late-bloom boost. The 1973 *Aloha from Hawaii* Special was the first ever worldwide satellite broadcast, watched by a larger audience than the first moon landing four years earlier. Friends and many fans consider this show the last time that Elvis succeeded in truly rising to meet a significant professional challenge.

Before his death, Elvis signed a contract for a one-hour show on CBS—his third and final TV Special—filmed during what turned out to be his last ever tour. The show, *Elvis in Concert*, was broadcast two months after Elvis died.

Elvis' death prompted more extensive media coverage than any celebrity before him. For the first time in history, an entertainer's demise was the lead item on the majority of TV news networks around the globe. Ever since, every significant anniversary of Elvis' birth and death triggers a flurry of TV tributes and Elvis features.

Audio recordings of Elvis' many of Fifties TV performances came out on the box set *A Golden Celebration* in 1984 (re-released in 1998). A selection of Elvis' Fifties TV appearances came out in 2007 on *Elvis #1 Hit Performances / Elvis 30 #1 Hits DVD*.

For more information on Elvis TV shows, look under the relevant entries in this encyclopedia.

For TV shows in which an Elvis-like character has featured, *see* MOVIES AND ACTORS WHO HAVE PORTRAYED ELVIS OR ELVIS-BASED CHARACTERS.

ELVIS' TV APPEARANCES

- *Aloha from Hawaii*
- CBS Special (*Elvis in Concert*)
- "Ed Sullivan Show"
- "Frank Sinatra Show"
- "Hy Gardner Calling!"
- "Milton Berle Show"
- "Phillips' Pop Shop" with Dewey Phillips
- NBC TV Special (*Elvis*)
- "Stage Show"
- "Steve Allen Show"
- "Top Ten Dance Party"

ELVIS' TV WATCHING HABITS

Elvis was big into TV. He had multiple sets installed in his den downstairs at Graceland, and when he was on the road, he'd have the TV on the whole time to keep him company. He had 14 TV sets throughout Graceland (though some reports put the number at 16 at the time of his death). In the basement, he regularly watched three screens at once, though he only had the sound up on one of them. He also sometimes left a TV on with the sound down and a record playing.

Elvis' legendary propensity for shooting out TVs is exaggerated, though he was capable of dispatching a bullet into a TV set if somebody he sincerely disliked came on; if adjusting the vertical hold failed to fix a bad picture, the TV might also be silenced permanently, and replaced with a new set.

Elvis had two RCA TVs mounted in his bedroom ceiling, and another set at the end of his bed. He would switch the audio from one channel to another. When he wanted to go to sleep, he wouldn't necessarily turn the set off, just hit the mute button.

He had a member of his entourage go out and buy a TV set while he was recording at Stax so that he could watch Monday night football—he left it behind at the end of the session.

When in hospital in the Seventies, Elvis spent the day watching quiz shows, and the nights plugged in to the maternal ward monitors. He fitted Graceland out with closed-circuit monitors in 1971, and at times whiled away the hours watching what was going on from his bedroom, in his own private antecedent to Big Brother. Graceland staff knew that at any moment their employer might be looking over their shoulder at what they were doing.

TV SHOWS ELVIS WATCHED

With his multiple screens at Graceland, Elvis could consume a whole lotta programming.

Priscilla remembers that he loved watching "Laugh-In," "The Untouchables," "The Wild, Wild West," "Road Runner" and "The Tonight Show" (until Johnny Carson made a wisecrack about Elvis being "fat and forty"). Joe Esposito remembers that he loved a show called "The Millionaire," where somebody was given a million dollars.

Charlie Hodge says that as well as sport, Elvis was into comedies like "I Love Lucy" and "The Beverly Hillbillies." He often watched "Shindig" in the Sixties, and later worked with a number of artists who played on the show, including James Burton, Glen D. Hardin, and vocal group The Blossoms.

In the Seventies, Elvis was a great fan of Monday Night Football. He also liked "Hee Haw" (it's rumored he would have appeared on the show if he hadn't been sure that Colonel Parker would have said no), "The Flip Wilson Show," "The Jeffersons" and "Happy Days." Not surprisingly, given his interest in karate, he also liked to watch David Carradine in "Kung Fu."

Maid Nancy Rooks remembers Elvis' favorite shows as "Kojak," "The Wild, Wild West" and "Hawaii Five-0." He also watched game shows like "The Match Game," and on the weekends, local gospel shows.

CHARLIE HODGE: "Elvis could be a TV junkie. He had a TV set in every room at Graceland and four in the TV Room so he could watch all channels."

PRISCILLA: "He despised entering a quiet room, and soon I too adopted the habit of automatically turning on the TV whenever I walked into a room."

DR. NICHOPOULOS: "Elvis shot so many sets that it was a little standing joke that there was a TV graveyard in the back of his house."

"TWEEDLEE DEE"

Elvis sang this LaVern Baker love song (written by Winfield Scott) at many live shows in 1955 and 1956, after Baker took it to #14 on the *Billboard* Top 100 (and Georgia Gibbs took it to #2). In early 1955, Elvis told Waylon Jennings that this was slated to be his next single.

Sometimes titled "Tweedle Dee," the first official release of Elvis covering the song did not come until *Elvis: The First Live Recordings* in 1984, followed in the Nineties by *The King Of Rock 'N' Roll* anthology, *Sunrise* and the 2006 version of *The Complete Sun Sessions*. It's also on any self-respecting Louisiana Hayride compilation album, and on *Memphis Recording Service*.

"TWELFTH OF NEVER, THE"

Elvis' rehearsal of this Jerry Livingston / Paul Francis Webster composition (based on old English folk tune "I Gave My Love A Cherry") prior to his August 1974 Las Vegas engagement was recorded by photographer Ed Bonja but never released in Elvis' lifetime.

It made its first official outing on the *Walk A Mile In My Shoes* anthology. A year earlier than the rehearsal, Elvis had considered the song for the *Aloha From Hawaii* concert song list, but may have dropped it because Donny Osmond had released a cover that made it into the top ten. The song had previously been a big hit for Johnny Mathis in 1956. A version with overdubs by David Briggs has appeared on bootleg *From Sunset Blvd. to Paradise Road*.

TWENTIETH CENTURY-FOX

Elvis had only just signed for Paramount when Colonel Parker invoked an option in his Paramount contract allowing Elvis to make one film per year with another studio. Through the William Morris Agency, in mid-August 1956, 20th Century-Fox stepped in to sign a three-picture deal with Elvis, starting on $100,000, with co-star billing, plus an option for two more films, with Elvis' fee rising to $200,000 for the final picture. At the end of August 1956, Elvis went to Hollywood to live his dream of making a movie, *Love Me Tender*.

When Elvis returned from the Army in 1960, Fox put him in two dramatic pictures in an attempt to let him flex his acting muscles. The Colonel insisted on the studio shoehorning some songs into the pictures, so that the movies would follow his hitherto winning formula of cross-promoting Elvis' music sales and box office efforts. Fox executive Charles Einfield was discouraged that Parker was "more interested in selling records than he is building a motion picture career for Presley." The Colonel also exerted pressure on the director of final Fox film *Wild in the Country* to cut down on shooting time in order to contain costs. Neither of these movies generated the returns of Elvis' straightforward musical romps, a factor that the Colonel considered proof of his strategy to keep Elvis out of challenging dramatic roles.

The hyphenated studio was founded in 1935 when Fox and Twentieth Century merged. The company became part of the Murdoch empire in 1984.

MOVIES ELVIS MADE WITH TWENTIETH CENTURY-FOX:

Love Me Tender (1956)
Flaming Star (1960)
Wild in the Country (1961)

"TWENTY DAYS AND TWENTY NIGHTS"

Elvis recorded this Ben Weisman / Clive Westlake weepie on June 4, 1970 for release on *That's The Way It Is*, the first song laid down in the mammoth 6-day session at RCA's Studio B in Nashville.

It may be found on Seventies anthology *Walk A Mile In My Shoes*. An alternate is on the *That's The Way It Is* Special Edition release; a pared-down alternate studio take features on 2002 FTD release *The Nashville Marathon*. Elvis can also be heard singing a rehearsal version on FTD release *One Night In Vegas*.

TWIN

See PRESLEY, JESSE GARON

2001: A SPACE ODYSSEY THEME

See "ALSO SPRACH ZARATHUSTRA"

TYLER, JUDY
(B. JUDITH MAE HESS, 1933-1957)

Elvis' costar in *Jailhouse Rock* died in a car accident just a few days after she completed shooting on the movie, and just weeks after marrying her second husband, actor Gregory LaFayette.

Tyler had made her entertainment debut as a princess on the "Howdy Doody" show on TV; she had also worked as a chorus line dancer. Before her premature death, she appeared to be on a fast-track to leading lady status, winning a place on the cover of *Time* magazine for her performance in Broadway musical *Pipe Dream*.

Elvis was devastated by the news of her death. It has been reported that he could not bring himself to watch the movie afterwards. Kenny Baker marked her passing by recording a song for her: "Goodbye Little Star."

ELVIS SAID: "Nothing has hurt me as bad in my life."

ABOVE: Elvis with Judy Tyler his co-star of *Jailhouse Rock*.

LEFT: French film poster for *Jailhouse Rock*.

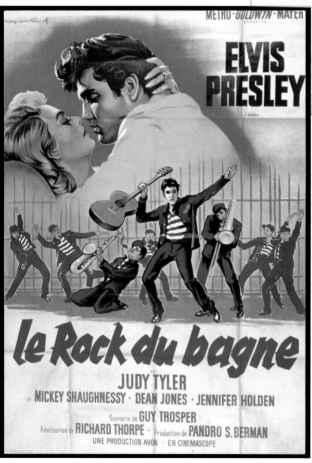

U

UFOs

Elvis and UFOs are not as outlandish a combination as they may at first appear. The subset of people who believe that we are not alone on this planet includes a healthy number of people who also believe that Elvis' death was faked; if they were regular readers of the now defunct tabloid Weekly World News, they may even believe that Elvis was abducted by aliens.

Pseudonymous author Richard Daniel has suggested that Elvis and Gladys were kidnapped by aliens. Author Michael C. Luckman writes that when Elvis was born, a mysterious blue UFO streaked across the sky, and claims that Elvis sighted a number of UFOs in his lifetime. Elvis and members of the Memphis Mafia are reported to have witnessed unidentified flying objects over Memphis and Los Angeles.

A more terrestrial link between Elvis and UFOs is the involvement of Roswell documentary maker Ray Santilli in the reputed purchase of rights to the never-seen early Elvis performance in the documentary movie *The Pied Piper of Cleveland*.

Books:
The Elvis-UFO Connection, by Richard Daniel, Castle Rock Enterprises, 1987.
Alien Rock: The Rock 'n' Roll Extraterrestrial Connection, by Michael C. Luckman, Pocket Books, 2005.

ULTIMATE GOSPEL

A 2004 single-disc BMG gospel compilation.

TRACK LISTING:
1. How Great Thou Art
2. So High
3. Amazing Grace
4. Crying In The Chapel
5. You'll Never Walk Alone
6. Swing Down, Sweet Chariot
7. Milky White Way
8. His Hand In Mine
9. I Believe In The Man In The Sky
10. Where Could I Go But To The Lord
11. If The Lord Wasn't Walking By My Side
12. Run On
13. He Touched Me
14. Bosom Of Abraham
15. Lead Me, Guide Me
16. Joshua Fit The Battle
17. If We Never Meet Again
18. I, John
19. Reach Out To Jesus
20. Who Am I?
21. Help Me
22. Miracle Of The Rosary
23. Take My Hand, Precious Lord
24. Peace In The Valley

A 2007 re-issue includes "In My Father's House (Are Many Mansions)" and "An Evening Prayer," but lacks "Miracle Of The Rosary."

"UNCHAINED MELODY"

A song that seems to hit the top of the charts every decade or so – only "White Christmas" has been a top-five hit for more artists. In the mid-Fifties, after featuring on the movie soundtrack of *Unchained*, the song was a hit for Les Baxter, Al Hibbler, Roy Hamilton and June Valli. The Righteous Brothers took it to the top five in 1965, and then higher still when their version was included on the soundtrack of *Ghost* in 1990. Over the years, Elvis associates Boots Randolph and the Sweet Inspirations—among many others—have also had a crack at the tune.

A live Elvis performance of this song was recorded on April 24, 1977 in Ann Arbor, Michigan (he hits all the high notes) and was released on the *Moody Blue* album, after the addition of some overdubbed instrumentation. RCA released another live performance from June 21, 1977 as Elvis' first posthumous single, in February 1978, with "Softly As I Leave You" on the B-Side. The highest it climbed was #6 on the Country chart.

Though Elvis only performed the song during the final six months of his life, when he started into the tune, to his own solo piano accompaniment, it was an immediate highpoint of the show, right before perennial closer "Can't Help Falling In Love."

Elvis' "Unchained Melody" has since been reissued on *Always On My Mind*, *Elvis Aron Presley, The Great Performances, Walk A Mile In My Shoes, Love Elvis* and *Elvis Live*.

Alternate live recordings have appeared on FTD albums *New Year's Eve* and *Unchained Melody*; a late performance may be found on FTD issue *Spring Tours '77*.

The song was written by Alex North and Hy Zaret.

UNCHAINED MELODY

A 2007 FTD release, the bulk of which comes from Elvis' February 20, 1977 show in Charlotte, North Carolina.

TRACK LISTING:
1. Love Me
2. Fairytale
3. You Gave Me A Mountain
4. Jailhouse Rock
5. O Sole Mio / It's Now Or Never
6. Little Sister
7. Teddy Bear / Don't Be Cruel
8. My Way
9. Moody Blue (Intro)
10. How Great Thou Art
11. Hurt
12. Hound Dog
13. Unchained Melody
14. Can't Help Falling In Love
15. Moody Blue
16. Blueberry Hill
17. Love Letters
18. Where No One Stands Alone
19. Release Me
20. Tryin' To Get To You
21. Reconsider Baby
22. Why Me Lord

"UNCLE PEN"

A song Elvis may or may not have recorded at Sun, though he did sing it in at shows during his first couple of years on the road. The 1951 original, written by Bill Monroe, was about his uncle Pendleton Vanderver. Rumors have circulated that Sam Phillips readied the song for release in 1955 (and even that it was released locally in upstate New York); it was also said to be ready for bootleg release in 1967. The Elvis world still waits.

UNITED ARTISTS

Elvis first signed to this studio in the fall of 1960, when Colonel Parker struck a $500,000 two-movie deal which included fully half of any profits. After *Follow that Dream* and *Kid Galahad*, in late 1964 the Colonel made a second two-picture deal, this time for $650,000 per movie.

Elvis laid down some of his later soundtrack albums at the UA Recorders studio (6050 Sunset Boulevard).

The United Artists studio was originally founded by actors Charlie Chaplin, Mary Pickford, Douglas Fairbanks and director D.W. Griffith in 1919, in a successful attempt to shift the balance of power towards movie talent. The studio was acquired by MGM in 1981.

MOVIES ELVIS MADE WITH UA

- *Follow That Dream* (1962)
- *Kid Galahad* (1962)
- *Frankie and Johnny* (1966)
- *Clambake* (1967)

UNITED KINGDOM

See ENGLAND and SCOTLAND

UNIVERSAL PICTURES

Elvis made his final feature film at Universal in 1969, in a co-production with NBC.

MOVIES ELVIS MADE WITH UNIVERSAL

- *Change of Habit* (1969)

UNSURPASSED MASTERS

In 1993, this four-volume set of live and studio recordings plus interviews came out on the unofficial Yellow Dog label.

In the 2000s, the title was used for a copious unofficial release on the Cool Romeo label: four multi-disc box sets of alternate spanning Elvis' whole career.

"UNTIL IT'S TIME FOR YOU TO GO"

Elvis' version of Buffy Sainte-Marie's ballad was laid down at a recording session in Nashville on May 17, 1971. On release in January 1972, with "We Can Make The Morning" on the B-side, Elvis' single sold close to 300,000 copies but failed to rise above #40 in the charts. It did make it to #5 in the UK.

The song made its album debut on *Elvis Now* that same year, when it was one of Elvis' concert favorites; he sang it in 1972 documentary *Elvis on Tour*. He still took on the tune in later years, but much less frequently. The original recording has since appeared on *Walk A Mile In My Shoes* and *Hitstory* (European edition).

Though she wrote the song in 1965, it was not until 1970 that Sainte-Marie released her own version. Since then, it has been much covered by singers including Barbra Streisand, Cher, Neil Diamond and Janis Joplin.

Follow That Dream (1962) United Artists.

Alternates from Elvis' original session have appeared on *Today Tomorrow & Forever*. A slightly faster version that Elvis attempted a month later in Nashville did not officially appear until 1996 release *Essential Elvis Vol. 4*. Further alternates from the later studio session are on FTD release *I Sing All Kinds*.

Live versions have subsequently appeared on *An Afternoon In The Garden*, *The Live Greatest Hits*, *Elvis: Close Up* and on FTD releases *An American Trilogy* and *Summer Festival*. A rehearsal from two months prior to Elvis' first recording of the song surfaced in the 2000s on FTD disc *Elvis 6363 Sunset*.

"UNTIL THEN"

Elvis' concert performance of this Stuart Hamblen song from 1958 appeared on Czech release *Slippin' n' Slidin'*, as sung with the Stamps in 1976. Some sources say that on certain bootlegs, the song is erroneously titled "God Calls Me Home."

"UP ABOVE MY HEAD"

This traditional hymn—a hit for Sister Rosetta Tharpe in 1947, and before her for the Southern Sons in 1941—was part of the spiritual medley that Elvis recorded for his 1968 NBC TV Special on June 22, 1968 at Western Recorders. Orchestra director W. Earl Brown took the writing credit.

Elvis' performance was first released on the original tie-in *Elvis NBC TV Special* LP. As part of the gospel medley, it has since appeared on *Memories: The '68 Comeback Special* and the *Peace in the Valley* anthology. An alternate take from the studio session is on FTD release *Let Yourself Go*.

"U.S. MALE"

When Elvis recorded his countrified version of this Jerry Reed talking blues track in Nashville on January 16, 1968, the songwriter (credited under his real name Jerry Hubbard) was one of the musicians playing at the session, though the song was only added to the session roster after Elvis went through all the pre-prepared material that night.

On single release in late February 1968, paired with *Stay Away, Joe* movie soundtrack song "Stay Away," "U.S. Male" climbed to #28 in the charts. Over the course of nine weeks, it sold almost half a million copies—better than any Elvis single for three years.

The song's debut album release came on Camden budget issue *Almost In Love*. Since then, it has been reissued on *Double Dynamite*, *Elvis' Golden Records Vol. 5*, *From Nashville To Memphis*, *Tomorrow Is A Long Time* and *Hitstory* (European Edition).

Alternate takes have come out on *Today Tomorrow &Forever*, *Elvis: Close Up* and on FTD release *So High*.

USS ARIZONA

In late 1960, it was announced that Elvis would be adding his contribution to fundraising efforts for a memorial to this warship, first commissioned in 1916 and sunk on December 7, 1941, in the attack on Pearl Harbor that prompted the US to join hostilities in the Second World War. Colonel Parker realized that he could kill two birds with one stone and have Elvis give a benefit concert while he was in Hawaii filming *Blue Hawaii*. Elvis performed at the Bloch Arena on March 26, 1961.

Plans for a monument were originally authorized by Congress in 1958. The monument was officially opened on Mary 30, 1962. Elvis' concert raised $62,000 towards the total $500,000 cost.

A recording of the press conference was released in 1976 on collectors' album *Elvis: A Legendary Performer, Vol. 2*.

Five years after his concert, when he was back on the island shooting *Paradise, Hawaiian Style*, Elvis and the Colonel laid a wreath of carnations, one for each of the 1,177 navy men who perished in the attack on Pearl Harbor.

Elvis planned to show new girlfriend Ginger Alden the monument on their vacation in early 1977, but had to cancel because of eye problems.

USS POTOMAC

In 1964, Elvis purchased Franklin Delano Roosevelt's former presidential yacht and donated it as a charitable gift to St. Jude's Hospital in Memphis. The converted coastguard cutter had served the US president as his "Floating White House" from 1936 to 1945.

St. Jude's sold the boat a month after Elvis donated it (for $10,000 more than Elvis paid). For the next decade and a half, the boat had a less than illustrious time: at one stage it was involved in a drug smuggling ring, and it even sank in 1980. Since then, the 165-foot boat has been salvaged, restored and opened to the public as a National Historic Landmark in Oakland, CA.

USS GENERAL RANDALL

The ship that took Elvis and fourteen hundred other soldiers to Bremerhaven, Germany, left Brooklyn on September 22, 1958 and arrived at its destination on October 1. Elvis shared a cabin with Charlie Hodge.

The *General George M. Randall*—named after civil war hero General George Randall—entered service during the last year of WWII. The vessel transported troops to the Far East, and later served in the Korean War. Capable of carrying 5,000 soldiers, the *USS General Randall* was decommissioned from the Navy in 1961 and scrapped in 1975. The ship made a movie cameo in 1956 picture *Away All Boats*.

UTAH

- Salt Lake City

Elvis played the Salt Palace on the closing night of his 12-date November 1971 tour (November 16). Elvis closed out his early summer 1974 at the same venue (on July 2).

Elvis with Michael Curtiz and Hal Wallis on the set of *King Creole*, 1953.

V

VACATIONS

In the Fifties, Elvis toured so incessantly that he spent his rare vacations at home with his folks in Memphis rather than away. He toured, recorded and toured some more for two years before he finally had a chance to spend some down time in Biloxi, and later Miami, in the summer of 1956. In Biloxi, he went deep sea fishing with his girlfriend June and her parents, and brought his own folks down too.

In 1957, after a string of inane questions from journalists, Elvis told a reporter that his ideal holiday destination would be Africa.

While serving in the Army in Germany, Elvis made side trips to other German cities and Paris.

Back in the US after 1960, Elvis' vacation destinations tended to be places he either visited for work (Florida and Hawaii for movie location shooting), or places where the Colonel had contacts (Palm Springs, the Bahamas). In the days when he shuttled between Memphis and LA by road, either in his motor home or his refurbished Greyhound bus, Elvis often stopped off in Las Vegas—always a favorite weekend destination when he was living in LA, as was Palm Springs—or in Albuquerque, Amarillo and other spots along the way.

The first time that Elvis and Priscilla went away on vacation—with the entourage in tow, of course—apart from her rare inclusion on a location shoot in Arizona, was six years after she moved to Memphis. The destination was Elvis' top vacation spot: Hawaii.

In the fall of 1969, Elvis and Priscilla, Vernon and Dee and entourage pals Joe Esposito, Gee Gee Gambill, Jerry Schilling and their wives had such a great time away in Hawaii that they planned to continue the trip in Europe, after stopping off in Memphis to pick up passports. The Colonel put the kibosh on this idea by persuading Elvis that his European fans, who had been clamoring for an Elvis tour for so long, would be horribly disappointed if his trip was solely for pleasure. The Colonel's recommendation of the Bahamas—the only vacation Elvis took outside the United States, to Paradise Island—turned into a damp squib because of torrential rain.

In later years, Elvis went on winter holidays. He stayed at Aspen and Vail, Colorado: with a ski mask on, nobody knew who he was as he scooted around on a snowmobile. Briefly, he flirted with the idea of buying a house in Vail.

Without a doubt, Hawaii was his favorite destination. Elvis overnighted in hotels there for the additional security they offered, but he tended to spend the days at a beach house that Joe Esposito rented.

In 1972, at his Madison Square Garden press conference, for the umpteenth time Elvis declared that he'd love to go to Europe and to Japan, and that apart from his time in the service he had never been overseas.

See also International Travel, and individual travel destinations.

LARRY GELLER: "I don't think he knew what a vacation was."

VALENTINE GIFT FOR YOU, A

A 1985 BMG release to commemorate what would have been Elvis' 50th birthday. Red vinyl was an insufficient lure—the album failed to make it into the LP chart top 150.

TRACK LISTING:
1. Are You Lonesome Tonight?
2. I Need Somebody To Lean On
3. Young And Beautiful
4. Playing For Keeps
5. Tell Me Why
6. Give Me The Right
7. It Feels So Right
8. I Was The One
9. Fever
10. Tomorrow Is A Long Time
11. Love Letters
12. Fame And Fortune
13. Can't Help Falling In Love

VALENTINO, RUDOLPH
(B. RODOLFO ALFONSO RAFFAELO PIERRE FILIBERT DI VALENTINA D'ANTONGUOLLA GUGLIELMI, 1895-1926)

The only male heart-throb of the Twentieth century to rival Elvis triggered mass hysteria among female fans and public displays of sexual desire at a time when such displays among women were strictly taboo, Rudolph Valentino was the original "Latin Lover."

Born in Castellaneta, Southern Italy on May 6, 1895, Valentino dropped out of a military academy and emigrated to New York as a 17-year-old, where he made ends meet by washing dishes, dancing the tango and, according to some biographers, petty theft and dubious money-making stratagems. After moving to Los Angeles, he got his on screen break in The Four Horsemen of the Apocalypse (1921), and then went on to land his most famous role, in The Sheik, a year later. The first smoldering, passionate male to woo American women from the silver screen, Valentino was targeted by self-proclaimed defenders of decency as a lewd and dangerous influence on the nation's morals.

Unlike Elvis, Valentino dug in his heels with Paramount studio executives and took time out from his film career because he did not like the kind of material he was being offered. Valentino was at the height of his fame, with new film The Son of the Sheik just out, when he suffered a perforated ulcer and died unexpectedly, aged just 31.

As many as a hundred thousand delirious fans viewed Valentino's coffin after his untimely death. For many years, devotees clung to the belief that he had faked his death and begun a new life incognito. A number of women could not cope with his death at all and committed suicide.

According to Priscilla, Elvis believed he resembled the Twenties heart throb, at least in profile. In Valentino, Elvis found one of the few people with whom he could identify. Elvis played a Valentino-like role in 1965 movie Harum Scarum. He was reputedly offered a role in a Seventies stage play about America's original heartthrob.

VELVET, JIMMY
(B. Jimmy Tennant, 1939)

Jimmy Velvet met Elvis as a teenager, when Elvis visited teacher/songwriter Mae Boren Axton in Florida. Velvet has said that in the Fifties he was part of Elvis' extended entourage in Memphis, and occasionally elsewhere when Elvis was filming.

Velvet remained a friend of Vernon's after Elvis' death. Vernon authorized him to open the first Elvis Museum across Highway 51 from Graceland. For twenty years, after starting out with a traveling show Velvet ran Elvis museums showcasing what he billed as the world's biggest collector of Elvis memorabilia. At one stage Velvet operated a chain of four Elvis museums. He sold off his collection in the Nineties.

Among other things, Elvis gave Velvet his Mercedes 600 limousine (though Lamar Fike has also said that he got that car); at least one of these vehicles went up for auction in early 2007.

As a kid, Velvet was a regular opening act for a number of Fifties rock 'n' rollers. He had hits in the Sixties with "We Belong Together" and "It's Almost Tomorrow,"

Book:
Inside the Dream: The Jimmy Velvet Story, by Jimmy Velvet, Velvet-Roese LLC, 2007.

VINCENT, GENE
(B. Vincent Eugene Craddock, 1935-1971)

Gene Vincent found instant success when he recorded "Be-Bop-A-Lula" in early 1956, with his band The Blue Caps. So similar was his sound to Elvis—Capitol had hired him as their answer to the Elvis sensation—that when Elvis' band members Scotty and Bill first heard the song on the radio, they thought that Elvis had snuck off to record it without them. Capitol completed their work with Vincent by giving him a song that aped recent Elvis release "Money Honey," including plenty of Sun-like slapback echo.

Born in Norfolk, Virginia on February 11, 1935, Vincent was an unlikely candidate for rockabilly legend, as he had suffered a bad motorcycle accident while serving in Korea that left him with a very strong limp.

Elvis and his band bumped into Vincent in New York in the summer of 1956. When Elvis complimented Vincent on his record, the other singer blurted out that he hadn't been trying to copy Elvis at all. Whether he deliberately copied Elvis' style or not, he certainly followed Elvis' early career path by using backing singers the Jordanaires, and by landing a slot on the "Ed Sullivan Show." Vincent also made it into the movies—a Vincent performance features in early rock 'n' roll flick The Girl Can't Help It.

Vincent never equaled the success of his debut song in the States, though he did achieve another million-seller in 1957 with "Lotta Lovin'." His career shifted to Europe, particularly the UK, where he became the original poster boy for the rock 'n' roll black leather look. While in the UK, Vincent survived a further vehicle accident, in which fellow-rocker Eddie Cochran died.

Vincent was one of the original inductees into the Rockabilly Hall of Fame; he's also in the Rock 'n' Roll Hall of Fame.

"VINO, DINER Y AMOR"

A latin-flavored Elvis on this January 22 1963 Radio Recorders recording for the Fun in Acapulco soundtrack and LP, written by Sid Tepper and Roy C. Bennett.

The song has since put in appearances on the Nineties Double Features soundtrack reissue, Elvis Sings Sid Tepper and Roy C. Bennett, and the FTD Fun in Acapulco release.

VIOLENCE

Elvis grew up in the tougher parts of Tupelo and Memphis, where rough and tumble was a way of life for kids, despite his mother Gladys trying to step in on her son's behalf. The fact that Elvis' parents were almost constantly on the move also meant that young Elvis was frequently a target of intimidation. As a result, Elvis had to learn how to handle himself in a fight. Relative Annie Cloyd Presley recalls young Elvis even breaking another boy's hip during a wrestling scuffle. Some biographers have also detailed violence within Elvis' family and kin, involving not just his many cousins but alcohol-fired violent rows between his parents.

When Elvis was 13, he hit a fellow usher at the cinema where he was working because he had ratted on the candy counter girl who was passing Elvis free candy.

At High School, Elvis had the temerity to look and dress differently, attracting taunts, teases and occasional fisticuffs. School friend Evan "Buzzy" Forbes said: ". . . He wasn't overly muscular . . . but if it came to a scrap, someone would have had a surprise coming. Elvis had real good, quick reflexes; I've never known him to lose a scrap, and I've seen him in quite a few." On one occasion in 1952 when things got out of hand and some school kids were intent on forcibly cutting off Elvis' long hair, Red West stepped in to protect Elvis in an act of bravado that, after Elvis became famous, turned into a job for life.

Almost as soon as he began performing, Elvis attracted a barrage of jealousy and aggression from disgruntled boyfriends. On an early tour at the Red River Arsenal near Texarkana, Merle Kilgore remembers a corporal busting out of the venue and landing Elvis a punch that sent him down two flights of stairs. True to his nickname at that time, "Hillbilly Cat" Elvis landed on his feet, then went back up and knocked the guy down. When some sergeants came out to break up the fight, the corporal explained that he'd smacked Elvis because of the effect the singer had had on his wife. Around this time, Elvis once or twice took a slug from a guy who was pretending to be waiting in line for an autograph; it became clear that Elvis needed full time security around him, for which he enlisted the help of some of his cousins and pal Red West.

In 1955, when on tour with Faron Young, Elvis asked the singer about his stunt fighting experiences in Hollywood. After Young taught Elvis some moves, the two of them had a fake fight during a football game that looked sufficiently real for Young to receive some disapproving mail afterwards. When Elvis heard about this later on, he almost died laughing.

In 1956, Elvis was accosted a number of times. In Memphis, a gas station attendant started an altercation, and ended up being arrested by the police; in Toledo, Ohio a man was driven to revenge when he found a photo of Elvis in his wife's pocketbook.

Elvis' handiness in a fight filtered through to his on-screen persona. From *Loving You* onwards, the propensity for the characters Elvis played to get into a fight—often to defend a woman's honor—became one of the main drivers of his movie plots. Indeed, fisticuffs and later karate were a recurring motif throughout Elvis' feature film career.

In March 1957, Elvis resorted to a six-page telegram to resolve an altercation with a young marine named Herschel Nixon, who had accused Elvis of insulting his wife. In the missive, Elvis explained the pressure he was under: "Many times there have been people who came up to me and stick out their hands to shake hands with me and they hit me or I have had guys to come up and ask me for autographs and hit me and then take off for no reason at all." Not unreasonably, Elvis failed to mention that he politely and unfailingly obliged young women who asked him

for a kiss, or for an autograph on their chests or thighs . . . a trick he was still happy to perform in the Seventies, when recipients reputedly included Shirley Bassey.

Sporadic acts of vandalism were committed by disaffected teenagers in places where Elvis concerts were banned or radio stations refused to air his songs. There were also threats of violence aplenty to Elvis from so-called god-fearing communities: in the Fifties, an effigy of Elvis was hanged in Nashville. Elvis' property and cars were vandalized, and he was of course attacked by gangs of female fans on more than one occasion.

In Texas during his Army basic training, one day some local toughs tracked Elvis down to his friend Eddie Fadal's house, armed with baseball bats and ready for a fight. Elvis walked out to face them, disarmed them with his charm, and a short while later the toughs were on their way home with his autograph.

Elvis liked to roughhouse with his friends. He arranged firework wars at Graceland every Christmas, and had rambunctious times skating with pals at the Rollerdrome in Memphis, resulting in various injuries including a black eye. Mock fights and feats of karate prowess were a regular feature of Elvis' movie shoots, both on-screen and between scenes.

In her memoir, Priscilla recalls a typically paradoxical Elvis moment one day when they were driving home from the mellow Self-Realization Fellowship. Elvis ordered the limousine to pull over when he saw a fight at a gas station. He leapt out, challenged one of the men to take up his problem with him, and then as a warning, launched a karate kick that jettisoned a packet of cigarettes out of the guy's pocket.

Elvis suffered a credible death threat in Vegas in 1970, not long after the Charles Manson killings, and significantly stepped up his security. In February 1973, when four guys rushed him on stage at the Hilton Hotel, he pushed one of the over-enthusiastic fans back into the crowd and told the audience, "I'm sorry ladies and gentlemen...I'm sorry I didn't break his goddammed neck is what I'm sorry about. . . . If he wants to shake my hand, that's fine. If he wants to get tough, I'll whoop his ass!" After the event, Elvis was convinced that the men had been sent to do him harm by Priscilla's beau of the time, karate champion Mike Stone. Entourage members tell of Elvis brandishing an M-16 rifle and asking Red and Sonny West to go to LA and kill Stone, or else contract someone to do the job. Marty Lacker told Alanna Nash that Red West made inquiries and actually found somebody who was prepared to do the hit for a cut-price rate (because it was Elvis). Red West waited to tell Elvis, hoping that he would lose interest—which is exactly what he did. Lacker characterized the four men as "South American porno dealers" who had jumped on stage to get Elvis' autograph.

A number of incidents took place in the Seventies involving rough handling by Elvis' bodyguards. In September 1973, Red West and two other members of Elvis' entourage were accused of beating up Kaijo Peter Pajarinen, who had been invited backstage as one of Elvis' guests. The fracas resulted in a law suit. Property developer Edward Ashley launched a $6 million law suit in 1974, after he claimed that Elvis' entourage beat him up following a show at Del Webb's Sahara Tahoe.

In June 1977, Elvis backhanded Charlie Hodge, a little the worse for drink, when he heard him complain that Elvis hadn't given him a new car, as he had just given Larry Geller and Kathy Westmoreland. This was apparently the first time that Elvis had ever done such a thing to a member of his entourage. In his final months alive, Elvis once again intervened to break up a fight at a gas station, where two guys were threatening the attendant. They were so shocked to see Elvis settle into a karate stance that they backed off.

Elvis told his step-brothers, the Stanley boys, never to back down from a fight because they would regret it for the rest of their lives.

See also ASSASSINATION ATTEMPTS, KARATE, THREATS.

ELVIS SAID IN 1957: "I have talked my way out of trouble so many times that I couldn't even count them not because I was afraid but just because I was always the type of person that I never did believe in fighting and all that kind of stuff unless I thought it was absolutely necessary."

ELVIS ALSO SAID IN 1957: "I can take ridicule and slander, and I've been called names... right in my face and everything.... But I've had a few guys that tried to take a swing at me and naturally you can't just stand there. You have to do something."

LAMAR FIKE: ." . . The Smith family was just wilder than goats. By God, they were tough! Tougher even than the Presleys, and they were violent people."

JIMMY VELVET: "Elvis could easily get into a fight with someone if they embarrassed him or if they were trying to cause a problem. He wasn't afraid of anything."

"VIOLET"

Elvis sings this 15-second paean to NYU to the same tune as "Aura Lee" ("Love Me Tender") in *The Trouble With Girls*. The recording took place at United Artist Recorders on October 23, 1968. The song (by Dueker and Lohstroh) obtained its first official release—after years of being available only on bootleg—on the *Double Features* series release for the movie, as part of a college medley from the film.

VIRGINIA

- Danville
Elvis played the Danville Fairgrounds on September 20, 1955.

- Hampton Roads
Elvis played the Coliseum on April 9, 1972 (filmed for *Elvis on Tour*). He was there again on March 11, 1974, on July 31 and on August 1, 1976.

- Newport News
Elvis had to add an extra late-night show to accommodate the fans who were left outside the Paramount Theater for his earlier show on February 13, 1956.

- Norfolk
Elvis did two shows on May 15, 1955 at the Auditorium. He came back for more on September 11 and 12, 1955 as part of the Hank Snow Jamboree, jointly topping the bill with Mr. Snow and supported by Cowboy Copas and gospel singers the Louvin Brothers. Elvis played the Monticello Auditorium on February 12, 1956. He didn't return until July 20, 1975, when he played at Scope.

- Richmond
Elvis was at the Mosque Theater on May 16, 1955. He played shows at the WRVA Theater on September 18 and 19, 1955. On November 29, 1955, Elvis was part of a Hank Snow All-Star Jamboree entertainment package during a Philip Morris Employees Night at the Mosque Theater.

On February 5, 1956 Elvis began a three-week tour as the headliner (following Ernest Tubb's boy Justin Tubb, the Louvin Brothers and the Carter Sisters) at the Mosque Theater. He played the venue again on March 22, 1956, and then on June 30, 1956, the day before his "The Steve Allen Show" appearance.

Elvis returned to the Coliseum on April 10, 1972 (filmed for *Elvis on Tour*), and was there again on March 12, 1974. He returned by popular demand for a further show on that same tour on March 18, 1974. On June 29, 1976, Elvis played his last ever date at the Coliseum.

- Roanoke

Elvis' show on May 18, 1955 was at the American Legion Auditorium, which was also the venue for his September 15, 1955 performance. He played the Civic Center on April 11, 1972. The Civic Center next hosted Elvis on March 10, 1974 and August 2, 1976.

"VIVA LAS VEGAS"

Written by Doc Pomus and Mort Shuman, the high-tempo title track to the film was released as the B-side to single "What'd I Say?" in April 1964. The single release claimed #29 on the charts. Elvis recorded the song at Radio Recorders on July 10, 1963.

The song languished as an unused back catalogue item until it appeared on the *Worldwide 50 Gold Award Hits Vol. 1* anthology in 1970, followed by *Elvis in Hollywood*, *This is Elvis*, *Elvis Sings Mort Shuman & Doc Pomus* and the *Double Features* issue for the movie. It has enjoyed greater exposure over the last decade or two, appearing on a large number of hits packages such as *Command Performances*, the CD reissue of *Elvis' Gold Records Vol. 4*, *Elvis 2nd to None*, *Hitstory*, *Elvis Movies*, *Elvis at the Movies*, *The Essential Elvis Presley*, and the 2007 BMG release titled *Viva Las Vegas*.

Alternate takes have come thick and fast on FTD releases since 2000, notably on *Silver Screen Stereo* and on the 2003 FTD *Viva Las Vegas* release. The original demo is on *Elvis Chante Mort Shuman & Doc Pomus* and FTD release *Writing For The King*.

Over the years, the song has been covered by groups as disparate as the Dead Kennedys, Bruce Springsteen and ZZ Top. For many years, it has served as the unofficial theme tune for Sin City. Elvis' rare live performances of the song at the start of his first engagement at the International Hotel have not appeared on record.

VIVA LAS VEGAS (EP)

Released in May 1964, this EP contained four songs from the movie, including a solo Elvis version of "Today, Tomorrow and Forever" (a duet with Ann-Margret in the picture), but not, strangely enough, the movie's title track. It sold just 150,000 copies on initial release, barely scraping a #92 on the *Billboard* Hot 100.

TRACK LISTING:
1. If You Think I Don't Need You
2. I Need Somebody To Lean On
3. C'mon Everybody
4. Today, Tomorrow And Forever

VIVA LAS VEGAS (LP)

The *Double Feature* release paired with Roustabout (on release, the *Viva Las Vegas* movie soundtrack originally only originally appeared on EP).

TRACK LISTING:
1. Viva Las Vegas
2. If You Think I Don't Need You

3. If You Need Somebody To Lean On
4. You're The Boss
5. What'd I Say
6. Do The Vega
7. C'mon Everybody
8. The Lady Loves Me
9. Night Life
10. Today, Tomorrow And Forever
11. Yellow Rose Of Texas / The Eyes Of Texas
12. Santa Lucia
13. Roustabout
14. Little Egypt
15. Poison Ivy League
16. Hard Knocks
17. It's A Wonderful World
18. Big Love, Big Heartaches
19. One Track Heart
20. It's Carnival Time
21. Carny Town
22. There's A Brand New Day On The Horizon
23. Wheels On My Heels

In 2003, FTD brought out a *Viva Las Vegas* soundtrack issue full of alternates and extras, accompanied by a booklet of photos and anecdotes about the movie.

TRACK LISTING:
1. Viva Las Vegas
2. What'd I Say
3. If You Think I Don't Need You
4. I Need Somebody To Lean On
5. C'mon Everybody
6. Today, Tomorrow & Forever
7. Santa Lucia
8. Do The Vega
9. Night Life
10. Yellow Rose Of Texas / Eyes Of Texas
11. The Lady Loves Me (w. Ann-Margret)
12. You're The Boss (w. Ann-Margret)
13. Today, Tomorrow And Forever (w. Ann-Margret)
14. Viva Las Vegas
15. Night Life
16. C'mon Everybody
17. I Need Somebody To Lean On
18. The Lady Loves Me (w. Ann Margret)
19. You're The Boss (w. Ann Margret)
20. Today, Tomorrow And Forever
21. What'd I Say
22. If You Think I Don't Need You
23. C'mon Everybody
24. Do The Vega
25. The Climb

VIVA LAS VEGAS

BMG released this live Elvis album in 2007.

TRACK LISTING:
DISC 1:
1. Viva Las Vegas
2. See See Rider
3. The Wonder Of You
4. Polk Salad Annie
5. Release Me
6. Let It Be Me
7. I Just Can't Help Believin'
8. Walk A Mile In My Shoes
9. Bridge Over Troubled Water
10. Patch It Up
11. You Don't Have To Say You Love Me
12. You've Lost That Lovin' Feeling
13. An American Trilogy
14. Never Been To Spain
15. You Gave Me A Mountain
16. The Impossible Dream

A second CD available outside the US featured a previously unreleased Las Vegas show from August 21, 1969.

DISC 2:
1. Blue Suede Shoes
2. I Got A Woman
3. All Shook Up
4. Love Me Tender
5. Jailhouse Rock / Don't Be Cruel
6. Heartbreak Hotel
7. Hound Dog
8. Memories
9. Mystery Train / Tiger Man
10. Monologue / Life story
11. Baby What You Want Me To Do
12. Runaway
13. Are You Lonesome Tonight?
14. Yesterday / Hey Jude
15. Introductions
16. In The Ghetto
17. Suspicious Minds
18. What'd I Say
19. Can't Help Falling In Love

VIVA LAS VEGAS

An association with one of the U.S.'s most internationally-famous towns, and fizzing on- (and off)-screen chemistry with co-star Ann-Margret, made *Viva Las Vegas* Elvis' biggest grossing movie and has assured it more TV reruns than most of his celluloid output.

Shooting lasted almost two months, from July 15 to September 11, 1963. Elvis did location shots on familiar territory: the Sahara Hotel, where he usually stayed on his frequent visits to town, plus the Flamingo Hotel pool, McCarran Airport, a gymnasium at the University of Nevada, Lake Mead Marina, and the drag racing strip at Henderson, Nevada. Externals were also shot at the Hoover Dam, Henderson and Railroad Pass, all in Nevada. The wedding scene was shot at the Church of the West.

Elvis made sure that Priscilla, freshly arrived in America to live with him at Graceland, did not come out to L.A. or Las Vegas to spoil his fun with co-star Ann-Margret, who was one of the major loves of his life. As friend and actor Lance LeGault says, "When they did those numbers together, it was great; they were playing and having fun... It was all up on the screen."

Putative titles before release included *Mister Will You Marry Me*, *The Lady Loves Me*, *The Only Girl in Town* and *That Magic Touch*. Before shooting, gossip columnists mistakenly touted Sandra Dee and Frank Sinatra Jr. for possible roles in the movie.

In some chronicles, Elvis is said to have complained when he watched the rushes and saw that Ann-Margret had all the close-ups. It seems that director George Sidney was so taken with his leading lady that he shot more footage of her than of his headline star; the director has since gone on record to say that he did this to redress the skewed balance in Elvis' previous movies, in which Elvis but none of his love interests had close-ups. It is uncertain whether Elvis really begrudged Ann-Margret the screen time; beyond a doubt, the Colonel issued a stern rebuke to the director, and went some way to redressing the balance back in Elvis' favor in post-production.

Elvis and Ann-Margret recorded three duets, only one of which ("The Lady Loves Me") made it into the finished movie. They were cut from the soundtrack album as part of Colonel Parker's campaign to ensure that this Elvis vehicle did not become a shared vehicle. Three tracks ended up not being used in the movie: "Night Life," "Do The Vega" and the sultry "You're The Boss." Ann-Margret sang solo on "My Rival" and "Appreciation," while the Jubilee Four performed "The Climb."

The studio had to weather concerns about the raciness of some of the dance scenes in the movie. The Legion of Decency expressed its opprobrium, particularly when the movie was scheduled for an Easter release. The film was actually banned on the island of Gozo, off Malta.

Though *Viva Las Vegas* did not make it into the top-ten grosser list for 1964, it did better business than Beatles film *A Hard Day's Night*, and earned more than $4.5 million in 1964 alone. Ultimately, the movie went on to become the highest grossing of all Elvis' movies, taking over $9 million in the US and internationally— though *Blue Hawaii* initially took $11 million. However, the fact that this big musical came in significantly over budget was a major concern to the Colonel; the higher the budget, the less he and Elvis could expect from their customary profit sharing arrangements. For Elvis' next movie, the Colonel picked a cheap quickie, *Kissin' Cousins*, which actually came out two months before *Viva Las Vegas* had its initial release.

Elvis' performance was rewarded with a third prize in the 1965 Laurel Awards for best male musical performance (as was co-star Ann-Margret). The movie was runner-up in the same Awards for best musical.

For international release, the film was retitled *Love in Las Vegas*, principally to avoid confusion with 1956 Oscar-nominated picture *Meet Me in Las Vegas* (which had been released in the UK as *Viva Las Vegas*). This was one of very few Elvis movies to make its world premiere outside the US.

Book:
Inside Viva Las Vegas, Elvis Unlimited, 2007.

CREDITS:
MGM, Color.
Length: 85 minutes
Release date: June 17, 1964

TAGLINES:
Elvis is at the wheel but Ann-Margret drives him wild!
It's that "go-go" guy and that "bye-bye" gal in the fun capital of the world!

Directed by: George Sidney
Produced by: Jack Cummings, George Sidney

Written by: Sally Benson
Music by: George Stoll
Cinematography by: Joseph Biroc
Film Editing by: John McSweeney
Art Direction by: Edward Carfagno, George W. Davis
Set Decoration by: Henry Grace, George R. Nelson
Costume Design by: Don Feld

CAST:

Elvis Presley	Lucky Jackson
Ann-Margret	Rusty Martin
Cesare Danova	Count Elmo Mancini
William Demarest	Mr. Martin
Nicky Blair	Shorty Fansworth
The Jubilee Four	Themselves
Robert Aiken	Driver
Holly Bane	Man
Larry Barton	Son of the Lone Star State
John Burnside	Son of the Lone Star State
Carl Carlson	Juggler
Ruth Carlson	Juggler
Regina Carrol	Dancer
Jack Carter	Himself
Taggart Casey	Guard
George Cisar	Manager of 'Swingers'
Howard Curtis	Starter
Roy Engel	Mr Baker
Harry Fleer	Son of the Lone Star State
Alan Fordney	Race announcer
Teri Garr	Showgirl
Barnaby Hale	Mechanic
Claude Hall	Son of the Lone Star State
Alean 'Bambi' Hamilton	Showgirl
John Hart	Casino patron
Connie Hermida	Waitress #1
Pete Kellett	Extra
Larry Kent	Race official
Ingeborg Kjeldsen	Showgirl
George Klein	Extra
Lance LeGault	Son of the Lone Star State
Brad Logan	Guard
Kent McCord	Extra
Rick Murray	Delivery boy
Bob Nash	Big Gus Olson
Beverly Powers	Showgirl
Eddie Quillan	Master of Ceremonies
Francis Ravel	Francois
Christopher Riordan	Dancer
'Reb' Sawitz	Extra
Kay Sutton	Showgirl
Ivan Triesault	Head captain
Red West	Son of the Lone Star State
Robert Williams	Swanson

ADDITIONAL CREW:

Sydney Guilaroff	hair stylist
William Tuttle	makeup supervisor
Milton Feldman	assistant director
Otto Lang	second unit director
Lou Watt	second assistant director
Franklin Milton	recording supervisor
Lee Faulkner	stunts
Max Balchowsky	stunts
Robert Jon Carlson	stunt driver
Lance LeGault	stunts
Carey Loftin	stunts
Harvey Parry	stunts
Dale Van Sickel	stunts
The Forté Four	music performers: "The Ride"
David Winters	choreographer

Plot:
Elvis is race car driver Lucky Jackson. True to his name, Lucky wins sufficiently big in Vegas for him and trusty sidekick/mechanic Shorty Farnsworth (played by Nicky Blair) to enter the Las Vegas Grand Prix.

A chance encounter with Italian race driver Count Elmo Mancini (played by Cesare Danova) leads to an offer Lucky can and does refuse: to get rid of the other racers, leaving the way clear for the Count's Ferrari to win the race.

A beautiful pair of legs belonging to Rusty Martin (Ann-Margret) prove to be in need of

mechanical assistance. The car is too easy for the Count to fix as far as Lucky is concerned, and doesn't give him sufficient opportunity to turn on the charm.

After Rusty drives off, assuming that the mystery beauty is a showgirl, both men scour Las Vegas clubs and casinos to try and find her. Luckily for Lucky, she turns out to be a swim instructor at the very hotel where he's staying. Seduction ensues by way of song, closely followed by a disastrous plunge into the pool, which causes Lucky's all-important race money to go literally down the drain.

Lucky and Shorty are forced to take on work as waiters at the hotel to pay off their bill, and as such are eligible for the annual employees' talent competition. Lucky ties for first prize with Rusty, then wins on a coin toss, only to discover that first prize is not, as he believed, $2,500 in cash, but an all-in honeymoon vacation. Rusty may have been even more disappointed with the second prize: a pool table.

Bang goes the money Lucky needs to buy a new engine for the Las Vegas Grand Prix. In extremis, Rusty's father (played by William Demarest) comes through. Behind the wheel at last, Lucky aces the race and there's nothing left to do except head off on honeymoon with Rusty and live happily ever after.

Songs: "Viva Las Vegas," "The Yellow Rose Of Texas"/"The Eyes Of Texas," "The Lady Loves Me," "C'mon Everybody," "Today Tomorrow And Forever," "What'd I Say," "Santa Lucia," "If You Think I Don't Love You", "I Need Somebody To Lean On"

DVD:
Viva Las Vegas Deluxe Edition (2007)

VOICE

When Elvis first walked in to the Memphis Recording Service to cut a vanity acetate, Sun Studio secretary Marion Keisker asked him whom he sounded like. Elvis famously responded, "I don't sound like nobody." In Elvis' case, this wasn't an idle boast.

The looks, the originality, being in the right place at the right time, all these factors might explain how Elvis became a star but they do little to reveal how he remained so successful for so long, and was able to record so many different genres of music. The answer to that conundrum is his voice: a combination of natural instinct, self-taught ability, a keen ear and, above all, his unique ability to fill his songs brimful with emotion and, particularly in his early years, sexual charge. Greil Marcus defines Elvis' voice on "Good Rockin' Tonight" as "raw, pleasing and pushing, full of indescribably sexual asides . . ." Operatic soprano Kiri Te Kanawa told an interviewer that the greatest voice she ever heard was the young Elvis Presley.

Over the years, Elvis' voice has been favorably compared to Dean Martin and Mario Lanza; it has been lauded as a finely-tuned instrument of hillbilly, gospel of all hues, and Delta blues. But perhaps Elvis' most singular talent was his ability to mix up styles within the very same song, singing country as blues, blues as country, gospel as ballad, popular music as opera, and on through a practically endless set of permutations.

There can be little doubt that Elvis inherited his voice from his father Vernon. Gladys was a good singer too, known for her alto voice. They sang together before Elvis was born; Elvis joined in too as soon as he was able. Elvis' famous squeaky-voiced debut in church as a two-year-old was when he squirmed out of his parents' clutch and joined the choir up on stage. By five or six years old, he was invited up regularly to sing with the choir. While he was growing up, Elvis and his

Elvis as Lucky Jackson in the 1964 film *Viva Las Vegas*.

folks often sang for their own pleasure, at a time when making one's own entertainment was a widely-practiced art.

In his heyday, Elvis' vocal range spanned two and a half octaves (some commentators claim he could manage three, an uncommonly large interval). When he was at Sun, Elvis tended to stay at the top of this range. Music critic and voice expert Henry Pleasants considered Elvis' best octave to be the middle one, in a span that ran from baritone low G to tenor high B, and through to D flat via falsetto. Pleasants was highly impressed not just by Elvis' range, but by the variety of vocal color he could produce.

Notably, Elvis sang in a Southern accent. Until Elvis, Southern accents had been confined to regional success. Elaine Dundy suggests that the major innovation in Elvis' voice was that it carried the sound of "strings," as opposed to the "horns" of popular predecessors Frank Sinatra, Bing Crosby and Louis Armstrong. Another way to define the particular—though much mimicked—quality of Elvis' voice is that it was coated in soul.

For a man who used his voice so fluently and to such great accomplishment—Elvis was an early proponent of melismatic singing, prolonging a syllable over multiple notes. "We-e-e-e-llllll . . ."—it may surprise some fans to learn that Elvis' speaking voice, even as an adult, had a slight stutter to it. He would sometimes stumble over words beginning with a "w" or an "i" if he became nervous—he can be heard stuttering slightly in movies *Wild in the Country* and *Kissin' Cousins*.

When fame was his, Elvis was mustard keen to pay his debts to his favorite singers by telling interviewers who he liked and listened to during his formative years. He also said that he developed his unique singing style as "just experimenting around and singing with the other kids and having a good time."

Elvis was naturally drawn to bass voices. His favorite singers in the gospel groups he grew up listening to were almost all bass singers, including Jimmy Jones of the Golden Gate Quartet and J. D. Sumner of the Stamps. Every now and then, Elvis would try out the lower reaches of his range, particularly on spirituals such as "So High." In the studio, Elvis sometimes called over the bass singer to "double" his voice on the low notes, using the same microphone so that the bass boost couldn't be edited out during mixing; he also used this trick sometimes on stage in his final years on stage, singing a song or two with bass singer Larry Strickland.

With his gospel upbringing, Elvis loved the power and harmonies of choral singing. Almost all of the battles Elvis had with RCA over the final mixes of his records were because he wanted his voice to be part of a sound tapestry with his backing singers, rather than pushed up front, which is what the record label wanted to do.

It seems remarkable now that Elvis' early detractors belittled his vocal talents. After his first appearance on "The Milton Berle Show" *New York Times* critic Jack Gould famously declared, "Mr Presley has no discernible singing ability."

It is a widely-held opinion among Elvis experts that the two years he spent out of the limelight on Army service gave him an unheralded opportunity to develop his vocal talents. Able to sing for his own pleasure and try out demanding new material, Elvis added composure and confidence to his already impressive natural abilities. Immediately after his return to the States in 1960, Elvis assayed the vocally-demanding song "It's Now Or Never." Enrico Caruso's version of the original Neapolitan song "O Sole Mio" had been one of his mother Gladys's favorites. Another English adaptation of a Neapolitan classic that Elvis sang that year, "Surrender," required him to learn a projection technique in the studio from Jordanaire Ray Walker, so that he could hit the final high note.

At that very same recording session, Elvis laid down his debut gospel album, *His Hand In Mine*. This album is a prime example of Elvis' new sweet-voiced style, which showcased a much more finely-tuned control of vibrato.

Perhaps surprisingly, Elvis disliked hearing his own records played at Graceland. If a visiting fan put one on, Elvis would give them a withering look until they took it off again.

Elvis' long detour into a sweet-voiced style concluded in 1968, when on his NBC TV Special he was singing to resurrect his career. The rough-edged, gritty urgency in his voice won him new fans, and assured his existing fans that he was still ready to rock 'n' roll. He gave so much when he recorded "If I Can Dream" in the studio that he finished the song a spent heap on the floor. On the TV show, he pushed his voice to the limit: it almost breaks on many of the tracks in the live and the arena segments. Gone, after a decade, were the mannerisms of his Fifties output, and the vocal tricks and embellishments that had sustained him through the Sixties.

Elvis' more powerful vocal delivery for his Comeback Special was ideally suited to the rock and R 'n' B he recorded soon after the NBC Special aired, at American Studio in Memphis—for many fans, Elvis at his mature best. It was also a clarion call to promoters around the country that he was ready to return to live performing.

In the Seventies, as Elvis' health deteriorated, his voice suffered. His studio trick of chewing on ice cubes to preserve his voice was no longer enough. In his efforts to deliver the kind of performances his fans expected, Elvis resorted to a talismanic faith in a heavy regimen of prescription drugs, health remedies and injections; before going on stage he'd take what he referred to as his "voice shot" of herbal remedies, and sometimes have drops put directly on his vocal cords.

In 1973, critics described his voice during his appearance at Stateline (Tahoe) as "flabby" and "weak." It certainly had less range, with Elvis seeming to prefer the lower reaches of his range. The songs he recorded that summer at Stax studio saw him resorting to a lounge singer's tremolo rather than the vocal power that had so thrilled concertgoers across the nation just a year or two earlier.

On the rare occasions when Elvis could be coaxed into the studio in his final years alive, he raced through his material, nailing the songs in two or three takes as opposed to lavishing however many dozens he needed to get the optimal sound as he pictured it. People he worked with during these years remark on how accomplished he was, and how quickly he mastered new material. Nevertheless, producer Felton Jarvis would sometimes inveigle Elvis into doing new takes by asking one of the musicians to own up to a non-existent mistake, and ask to do the song over. As David Briggs says, "Nobody had the balls to tell him, 'You could sing that better.'"

By 1976, for the most part Elvis voice was not as versatile and resilient as it been, and he had to give up on a couple of songs at recording sessions at Graceland, or lower the key to make the high notes.

And yet Elvis was still delivering live shows where his voice had the same strength as ever. When he was in the mood—or when he wanted to impress a new young lady in his life—he could still cram the emotion into his gospel favorites and big stage numbers. He was firing up crowds of fans right up to his final tour, as preserved for posterity on CBS's live documentary for *Elvis in Concert*.

Decades after his death, Elvis' voice continues to draw plaudits. In 2007, *Q* magazine named Elvis' the greatest voice of all time, followed by Aretha Franklin, Frank Sinatra, Otis Redding and John Lennon.

Elvis said in 1956: "My voice is God's will, not mine."

Elvis said in 1957: "I have never thought I had a good voice, I just, well, I enjoyed what I'm doing. I put my heart, soul and body into it . . . I guess one of the reasons that people have liked it is because it was a little different."

Elvis said: "I first realized I could sing at two years of age. I found myself singing, I was singing and people would listen to me around the housing project where I lived. I was about eight years old and they entered me in a talent show. I wore glasses, no music, and I won, I think it was fifth place. I got a whipping the same day, my mother whipped me for something. Destroyed my ego completely. But I'd sing in church with my mother and father and when I was about ten years old they gave me a choice between a guitar and a bicycle, so I took the guitar and I watched people and I learned to play it a little bit, but I'd never sing in public. I was very shy about it, you know. In the 11th grade in school they entered me in another talent show. Nobody knew I sang, I wasn't popular in school, I wasn't dating anybody. Anyway, I came out and did my two songs and I heard people kinda rumbling and whispering. It was amazing how popular I became in school after that."

ELVIS SAID IN 1972: "I vocalize every day, and practice if I'm working or not."

ELVIS SAID IN 1974: "I sing from down in the gut, the shoe soles."

SCOTTY MOORE: "He had a feel for rhythm in his voice. He could hear a song and he knew what he could do with a song. And nobody else could do it."

JERRY LEIBER: "He had an incredible, attractive instrument that worked in many registers. He could falsetto like Little Richard. He could sing. The equipment was outstanding. His ear was uncanny. His sense of timing was second to none."

HENRY PLEASANTS: "He is a naturally assimilative stylist with a multiplicity of voices—in fact, Elvis' is an extraordinary voice, or many voices."

NORBERT PUTNAM: "Elvis could do everything, from a very quiet sensual moan and groan to a high-panic scream, and was willing to do it within the context of a three-minute song, with no inhibitions whatsoever.... He was far and away the greatest purveyor of emotion in a song—and I have worked with two thousand singers."

JERRY SCHEFF: "Elvis was a true musician, a true vocalist. When he sang, I really believe the lyrics went through his mind, through his heart and then came out his mouth."

GREGORY SANDOWS: "What is more important about Elvis Presley is not his vocal range, nor how high or low it extends, but where its center of gravity is. By that measure, Elvis was all at once a tenor, a baritone and a bass, the most unusual voice I've ever heard."

LAMAR FIKE: "Elvis used his voice like a muscle. He'd warm it up, and get it into position, and do it."

JERRY WEXLER: "Presley's registration, the breadth of his tone, listening to some of his records, you'd think you were listening to an opera singer. But . . . it's an opera singer with a deep connection to the blues."

WAYNE JACKSON: "I loved Elvis' singing. He was a powerful soul singer. Elvis had a real love affair with his voice. That's what it takes. You have to really love your own voice."

PETER GURALNICK: "When he sang... he held back nothing; that was when he offered himself up exactly as he was, whole and without calculation."

MYRNA SMITH: "His voice was a lot more remarkable than it ever came off on record, and his vocal pitch was much better than it came off on record. He was just a much better singer than could ever be captured . . . Some great singers' voices are just too big. Elvis was like that."

Elvis and "The Voice," Frank Sinatra.

IAN GILLAN: "Elvis' voice was unique. Like so many others, he had natural, technical ability, but there was something in the humanity of his voice, and his delivery. . . . He was the greatest singer that ever lived."

LARRY STRICKLAND: "He would drop down an octave, and it was my job to match tones with him and sing along with him, fill it out down there. . . . He would never have had to let the audience know that it wasn't really him; but every night after our song, Elvis would walk over and point to me . . ."

WILLIAM BUCKLEY, JR.: "Elvis Presley had the most beautiful singing voice of any human being on earth."

JOE ESPOSITO: "He just knew that people loved him when he sang . . . When Elvis sings, you just feel better."

CHARLIE HODGE: "Elvis had a three octave range which is a fantastic range for an untrained singer. Let me tell you Elvis never had a singing lesson in his life."

CHIPS MOMAN: "Presley was a great singer . . . He could sell a song."

B.B. KING: "His phraseology, his way of looking at a song, was as unique as Sinatra's."

PHIL SPECTOR: "He can do anything with his voice. He can sing anything you want him to, anyway you tell him. The unquestionable King of Rock 'n' Roll.

VOICE (BACKING BAND)

Elvis invited this Nashville group quartet headed by Sherill Nielsen (or Donnie Sumner, according to some sources) to Las Vegas in the summer of 1973, with the intention of presenting them to Tom Jones, who was looking for a backing group to hire for his upcoming Vegas act. When it transpired that Tom Jones couldn't use them, Elvis liked Donnie Sumner (formerly of the Stamps), Sherill Nielsen (ex-Imperials) and Tim Baty so much that he took them on himself as his own personal back-up singers. Elvis famously drew up a contract on the spot for $100,000 on a screed of toilet paper. He then called Vernon and told him, "Daddy, I just want you to know I've finally got my own group." When the Colonel heard of this extravagance, he did his best to talk Elvis out of it, or at least get him to cut back on the promised payment. Elvis wouldn't hear of it: his word was his word.

Already well-supported on stage by a number of top backing groups, more than anything Elvis paid Voice for the luxury of having a group of talented singers with whom he could sing in private when he felt the urge. They also had the chance to open Elvis' Las Vegas shows on a regular basis.

It was Elvis who picked the name Voice, after drawing inspiration from the title of a one-off journal put out by pal Larry Geller. The full name of the *New Age Voice* was too long to fit onto the marquee in Las Vegas, so Elvis shortened it.

Before joining up with Elvis, the gospel quartet had been known as the "Tennessee Rangers."

In the fall of 1973, Voice backed Elvis on the two tracks he recorded at home in Palm Springs: "I Miss You" and "Are You Sincere."

Members of Voice contributed tracks to Elvis' December 1973 Stax recording session, where they were joined by pianist Per Erik "Pete" Hallin (who also took over from original member Sherill Nielsen on Elvis' March 1974 tour). Keyboard player Tony Brown joined the group for Elvis' fall 1974 tour. Elvis flew Voice out to Palm Springs and Graceland for some home singing during Thanksgiving and Christmas that year. Voice were the only back-up singers Elvis took along to his March 1975 recording session in LA. By the end of 1975, Voice had dropped out of the Elvis orbit.

Voice reunited in 2006 to produce two new CDs, *Remembering Elvis at Christmas* and *Voice Sings Elvis' Favorite Gospel Songs.*

TONY BROWN: "We were like Elvis' private musicians, you might say . . . If he wanted to sing some old hymns, he wanted a group to sing harmony with him. That was our job."

A rare and wonderful candid of Elvis and his legendary manager Colonel Tom Parker.

W

WALD, JERRY
(B. JEROME IRVING WALD, 1911-1962)

In a successful career spanning three decades, this sometime screenwriter and much-lauded producer was nominated for four Academy Awards, including Hollywood classics *Mildred Pierce* (1945) and *Treasure of the Sierra Madre* (1947). In 1960, Wald produced Elvis in *Wild in the Country*, one of Elvis' most dramatic roles.

WALKER, RAY
(B. RAY CLINTON WALKER, 1934)

Mississippi-born Jordanaire Ray Walker joined the group in 1958 and walked straight in to a rare duet with Elvis in Nashville that June, combining his bass voice with Elvis on "(Now And Then There's) A Fool Such As I." In a quirk of fate, Walker had been reprimanded in his previous job as a teacher for playing Elvis records to the kids in his class.

Walker began his career in a college quartet whose members included Pat Boone. He has sung with the Jordanaires ever since joining; he has also found time to work as a deputy sheriff in Nashville.

RAY WALKER: "There was just an aura about him— you knew he was around—and he was one of the most impressive people I have ever met in my life."

"WALK A MILE IN MY SHOES"

On February 19, 1970 Elvis sang this Joe South hit during a concert that RCA recorded for live album *On Stage*. On its original release in 2969, Joe South had taken his song to #12 in the *Billboard* Hot 100; Willie Hightower also had an R&B hit with the song the year that Elvis performed it live.

Elvis' version has since graced the eponymous *Walk A Mile In My Shoes* anthology, *Elvis Live*, and the *Viva Las Vegas* 2007 release.

Though Elvis sang the song only a limited number of times in 1970, several different performances have made it onto disc: three are on *Live In Las Vegas*; one is on *That's The Way It Is— Special Edition, Today Tomorrow & Forever*, and FTD releases *Polk Salad Annie* and *Writing For The King*.

WALK A MILE IN MY SHOES: THE ESSENTIAL 70S MASTERS

A 1995 5-disc collectors' album of Elvis' output from his last seven years, featuring various rarities.

TRACK LISTING:
DISC: 1   THE SINGLES
1. The Wonder Of You
2. I've Lost You
3. The Next Step Is Love
4. You Don't Have To Say You Love Me
5. Patch It Up
6. I Really Don't Want To Know
7. There Goes My Everything
8. Rags To Riches
9. Where Did They Go, Lord
10. Life
11. I'm Leavin'
12. Heart Of Rome
13. It's Only Love
14. The Sound Of Your Cry
15. I Just Can't Help Believin'
16. How The Web Was Woven
17. Until It's Time For You To Go
18. We Can Make The Morning
19. An American Trilogy
20. The First Time Ever I Saw Your Face
21. Burning Love
22. It's A Matter Of Time
23. Separate Ways

DISC: 2   THE SINGLES
1. Always On My Mind
2. Fool
3. Steamroller Blues
4. Raised On Rock
5. For Ol' Times Sake
6. I've Got A Thing About You Baby
7. Take Good Care Of Her
8. If You Talk In Your Sleep
9. Promised Land
10. It's Midnight
11. My Boy
12. Loving Arms
13. T-R-O-U-B-L-E
14. Mr. Songman
15. Bringin' It Back
16. Pieces Of My Life
17. Green, Green Grass Of Home
18. Thinking About You
19. Hurt
20. For The Heart
21. Moody Blue
22. She Thinks I Still Care
23. Way Down
24. Pledging My Love

DISC: 3   STUDIO HIGHLIGHTS 70/71
1. Twenty Days And Twenty Nights
2. I Was Born About Ten Thousand Years Ago
3. The Fool
4. A Hundred Years From Now (jam)
5. Little Cabin On The Hill
6. Cindy, Cindy
7. Bridge Over Troubled Water
8. Got My Mojo Working / Keep Your Hands Off Of It
9. It's Your Baby, You Rock It
10. Stranger In The Crowd
11. Mary In The Morning
12. It Ain't No Big Thing (But It's Growing)
13. Just Pretend
14. Faded Love (Unedited version)
15. Tomorrow Never Comes (False start version)
16. Make The World Go Away
17. Funny How Time Slips Away
18. I Washed My Hands In Muddy Water (Long version)
19. Snowbird
20. Whole Lotta Shakin' Goin' On
21. Amazing Grace (alternate take)
22. (That's What You Get) For Lovin' Me
23. Lady Madonna (jam)

DISC: 4   STUDIO HIGHLIGHTS 71/76
1. Merry Christmas Baby
2. I Shall Be Released (jam)
3. Don't Think Twice, It's All Right (Jam edit)
4. It's Still Here (Unedited version)
5. I'll Take You Home Again Kathleen (Undubbed version)
6. I Will Be True
7. My Way (Master)
8. For The Good Times (Master)
9. Just A Little Bit
10. It's Different Now
11. Are You Sincere
12. I Got A Feelin' In My Body
13. You Asked Me To
14. Good Time Charlie's Got The Blues
15. Talk About The Good Times
16. Tiger Man
17. I Can Help
18. Susan When She Tried
19. Shake A Hand
20. She Thinks I Still Care (alternate take)
21. Danny Boy
22. Love Coming Down
23. He'll Have To Go

DISC: 5   THE ELVIS PRESLEY SHOW
1. See See Rider
2. Men with broken hearts (Recitation)
3. Walk A Mile In My Shoes
4. Polk Salad Annie
5. Let It Be Me
6. Proud Mary
7. Something
8. You've Lost That Lovin' Feelin'
9. Heartbreak Hotel
10. I Was The One
11. One Night
12. Never Been To Spain
13. You Gave Me A Mountain
14. It's Impossible
15. A Big Hunk O' Love
16. It's Over
17. The Impossible Dream
18. Reconsider Baby
19. I'll Remember You
20. I'm So Lonesome I Could Cry
21. Suspicious Minds
22. Unchained Melody
23. The Twelfth Of Never (rehearsal)
24. Softly As I Leave You (rehearsal)
25. Alla' En El Rancho Grande (rehearsal)
26. Froggy Went A Courtin' (rehearsal)
27. Stranger In My Own Home Town (rehearsal)

"WALK THAT LONESOME ROAD"

J.D. Sumner and the Stamps sang this traditional gospel song at a number of Elvis shows in the Seventies. It has never had an official release but can be found on bootlegs.

"WALK WITH ME"

Seventies concertgoers were sometimes given a chance to hear Shaun Nielsen sing this song in concert—another bootleg-only treat.

"WALLS HAVE EARS, THE"

A Mediterranean-inspired Roy C. Bennett / Bob Roberts *Girls! Girls! Girls!* soundtrack song that Elvis recorded in Nashville on March 27, 1962 for the movie and tie-in LP. The track later appeared on the *Double Features* release for the movie, and on French issue *Elvis Chante Sid Tepper & Roy C. Bennett*.

WALLIS, HAL B.
(B. HAROLD BRENT WALLIS, 1898-1986)

Hal Wallis produced over 300 movies in a career that spanned five decades, including all-time classics *Little Caesar, Casablanca* and *The Rose Tattoo*. For the most part, he worked with New York lawyer business partner Joe Hazen.

Wallis and Joe Hazan first tried to sign Elvis in early 1956, after watching him make his national TV debut on "Stage Show." The Colonel stalled to begin with, but started negotiating after Wallis traveled to Las Vegas to see Elvis' live performances that spring.

It was Hal Wallis, working for Paramount Studios, who set up Elvis' first Hollywood screen test in March 1956, through William Morris agent Harry Kalcheim. Though he theoretically had first call on Elvis, Wallis did not have a script ready for his newest signing. Twentieth Century-Fox stepped in, clinched a deal with the William Morris Agency, and lined Elvis up to appear in *The Reno Brothers*, which before release was retitled *Loving Me Tender*. Wallis soon started putting Elvis in his own movies, and went on to produce nine Elvis vehicles in total.

Born in Chicago on September 14, 1898, Wallis worked his way up through the movie business. He began by managing a movie theater, and had established himself as a studio manager at Warner Bros. by the end of the Twenties. The hundreds of films he produced include all-time Hollywood classic Oscar-winners *Casablanca* (1942) and *The Adventures of Robin Hood* (1938). After going independent, Wallis's output extended to *Gunfight at the O.K. Corral* (1957), *Becket* (1964) and *Barefoot in the Park* (1967). Along the way, he gave major breaks to future top stars Kirk Douglas and Burt Lancaster. During his long career, he accrued 15 Oscar nominations and a pair of Golden Globe awards.

Wallis soon found the Colonel to be a formidable counterparty, ready to negotiate improved conditions for Elvis at Paramount at every opportunity. By late 1958, Elvis was contracted to earn almost ten times the amount stipulated in his initial deal. Wallis and Parker discussed potential roles for Elvis on his return from military service in Germany. Parker was keen to shoot a movie in Hawaii; Wallis liked the idea of Elvis as a gypsy foundling. In the end they agreed that the best plan was to use Elvis' service in the army as the theme of his first movie back. In the summer of 1959, Wallis went out to Germany to visit Elvis and start shooting location footage and background material for what was to become *G.I. Blues*—none of this footage actually made it into the final cut.

After Elvis' first post-Services movie, Wallis was reputedly keen on putting his star into more meaty fare at Paramount. However, the relatively poor box office returns on the more dramatic movies that Elvis made in 1960 for Twentieth Century-Fox persuaded Wallis that the Colonel's plan to follow his hitherto winning formula was the right course of action. In late 1960, Wallis declined to match a spectacular half-million dollar two-picture deal that Colonel Parker negotiated for Elvis with United Artists, only to cave in a few months later to an improved Paramount contract.

After the runaway success of *Blue Hawaii* in 1961, which grossed a staggering $11 million, Wallis no longer had any doubts that Elvis would best serve Paramount's interests as a wholesome entertainer. This effectively put paid to his original plan, which was to line Elvis up as a successor to rebellious Fifties teen icons James Dean and Marlon Brando. Wallis also resigned himself to competing with the never-ending side-projects that the Colonel arranged with other studios, content that in 1963, Elvis was the seventh-highest grossing star in the business.

On seeing an early completed version of *Viva Las Vegas*, Wallis wrote to Colonel Parker to warn him that his protégé was looking pudgy and jowly, and that his hair looked fake. Wallis concluded: "I will appreciate it if you will have a talk with Elvis, as this is a very serious concern both for us and for him, as it could have a very detrimental effect on his entire career."

Candid photograph of Elvis with co-star Debra Paget on the set of *Love Me Tender* 1956, produced by Hal Wallis.

In 1964, Elvis became insensed at an interview that Wallis gave while he was finishing work on *Roustabout*. Confirming Elvis' worst fears that his acting career had been sacrificed on the altar of commercial interests, Wallis declared: "In order to do the artistic pictures it is necessary to make the commercially-successful Presley pictures. But that doesn't mean a Presley picture can't have quality too." According to Jerry Schilling, Elvis challenged Wallis the next time that he saw him on set, and asked him point blank when he would get to do his own *Becket*—a Wallis-produced Oscar-winning picture starring Richard Burton and Peter O'Toole. Elvis' rebellion came too late; by this time, the next career move for Elvis in Hollywood was the out-and-out quickie.

The long-standing business relationship between Wallis and the Colonel unraveled after *Easy Come, Easy Go*. Before beginning work on the movie, not for the first time Wallis raised his concerns with the Colonel about the shape Elvis was in, noting that the star's hair was too puffed up and wig-like.

Wallis was reputedly ready to offer Priscilla a movie contract while she was still with Elvis—according to Red West, when Elvis got wind of this, he kept her away from the studio. Wallis considered working with Elvis again in the late Sixties, when he put him forward for Western *True Grit*, opposite John Wayne, one of many intriguing film projects that failed to come Elvis' way. It seems that Elvis had no hard feelings: he dedicated a performance of "Can't Help Falling In Love" to Hal Wallis in 1971.

It has been claimed that soon after Elvis' death, Wallis and Vernon discussed the possibility of making a movie about Elvis, tentatively titled *The Elvis Presley Years*.

French director Laurent Preyale made a 26-minute documentary "Elvis Presley and Hal Wallis" for TV in 2003. Wallis also featured in 2004 documentary *Elvis: The Echo Will Never Die.*

ALLAN WEISS: "Hal Wallis had an eye. He signed people before they got famous. Sign them to a long contract, and then he wouldn't have to pay them very much. But what an eye. He had seen Elvis and he made the test."

HAL WALLIS: "There was something about his eyes . . . an expressive face, a new personality, that I knew was definitely star material for the screen."

HAL WALLIS: "We didn't sign Elvis as a second Jimmy Dean. We signed him as a number one Elvis Presley."

WAR

The name that Elvis gave to the pitched firework battles he regularly held in the Graceland grounds over the Christmas and July 4th holidays. All the guys put on leather jackets and then fired off a carload of Roman candles at one another until the stockpile ran out. The games inevitably ended in injuries and, on rare occasions, mild fire damage to the property.

WARD, BILLY AND THE DOMINOS

This highly influential early-Fifties R&B group, fronted first by lead singer Clyde McPhatter and then Jackie Wilson, was one of Elvis' favorites. When Elvis was trying to impress Sam Phillips at Sun, one of the songs he auditioned with was "Harbor Lights," which Billy Ward and the Dominoes had covered three years earlier.

Bandleader Billy Ward was actually one Robert Williams, born in L.A. in 1921. A musical prodigy, singer, pianist and composer, in 1950 Williams formed Billy Ward and the Dominoes, an all-black quartet that drew on the singers' gospel backgrounds to make compelling, leading-edge R&B music right at the start of the rock 'n' roll era. Their 1951 hit "Sixty Minute Men" lays claim to being the first R&B track to cross over to the national pop charts.

Ward, who had previously risen through the ranks in the Army, was known as a hard task master. Ultimately, he lost many members of the band, including star singer Clyde McPhatter, because of his tough regime (and his refusal to hand on royalties to his singers). With multiple personnel changes, the group remained a force in the R&B and pop charts through the Fifties, and continued to perform until the mid-Sixties.

In 1970, Elvis covered the group's 1953 hit "Rags To Riches."

WARREN, CHARLES MARQUIS
(1912-1990)

Western specialist Warren wrote, directed and produced some of the most famous Westerns on TV including "Gunsmoke," "Rawhide" and "The Virginian." The last movie he wrote and directed was *Charro!* (1969), one of Elvis' final features.

WASHINGTON

- Seattle

Elvis performed a half-hour show to 15,000 fans at Sick's Stadium on September 1, 1957.

Elvis and his entourage friends spent ten days in Seattle in September 1962, shooting location footage for *It Happened at the World's Fair.* The next time he performed in town was on November 12, 1970, when he played the Coliseum. He was back, at the Center Arena, on April 29, 1973, and performed a final show at the Coliseum on April 26, 1976.

- Spokane

Elvis played the Memorial Stadium here on August 30, 1957. He next played two shows at the Coliseum on April 28, 1973. He returned for one more on April 27, 1976.

- Tacoma

Elvis performed an afternoon show at the Lincoln Bowl on September 1, 1957, before hot-footing it to Seattle for an evening show.

WASHINGTON, DC

Elvis' one and only capital performance was at the SS Mount Vernon, on the Country Music Cruise promoted by DJ Connie B. Gay on March 23, 1956.

He traveled to the nation's capital in December 1970, at a time when Vernon and Priscilla had been giving him a hard time about his lavish spending. Elvis had enough and left Graceland without telling anyone where he was going, not even his entourage pals. Washington DC offered the lure of girlfriend Joyce Bova, but the trip soon turned into a quest to add the badge he coveted most to his police collection: the Federal Bureau of Narcotics and Dangerous Drugs. Elvis being Elvis, when he was turned down by the bureau, he finagled a meeting with President Richard M. Nixon and ultimately got what he wanted.

After initially touching down in Washington, Elvis had a change of heart and got on a plane to LA to pick up a friendly face in Jerry Schilling. He then arranged to return to Washington and meet Sonny West there . . . En route to Washington DC the second time, he met Senator George Murphy and on airline headed notepaper wrote a letter to President Richard Nixon offering his services to help the government stamp out the use of illegal drugs.

Once in town, Elvis dropped off the letter at the White House gates, and then tried and failed

to get a meeting with BNDD Director John Ingersoll. Deputy Director John Finlator did meet him, but refused to buck protocol and give Elvis the badge he so coveted. Elvis was disappointed but not disconsolate, especially when he received a call from the White House instructing him that he could indeed meet President Nixon if he made it to at the White House within the hour. Behind closed doors, the rocker and the President found common ground. Nixon was sufficiently impressed with the patriotic young singer that he ensured he got the badge he wanted.

After completing his business dealings, Elvis then dedicated himself to catching up with Washington-based girlfriend Joyce Bova. Immediately after Christmas 1970, Elvis flew back to Washington with eight pals to visit the headquarters of the National Sheriffs Association at the FBI—one of Elvis' fellow travelers was ex-sheriff Bill Morris.

ELVIS DAY MOTIONS IN WASHINGTON

Over the years, joint resolutions have been submitted by US Representatives Barbara Mikulski (with fan Patricia Ann Emanuele), Harold Ford, Sr. and Glenn Anderson to designate January 8 as "Elvis Presley Day." Thus far, at national level nothing has been achieved, though the holiday has already been adopted by many states. An internet petition to the US Congress for an official "Elvis Presley Day" was launched by fans to mark Elvis' 70th birthday.

WATERS, MUDDY
(B. MCKINLEY MORGANFIELD, 1915-1983)

Born on April 4, 1915, in Rolling Fork, Mississippi, this rhythm and blues pioneer would have been remembered under a very different name if his grandmother hadn't given him the nickname "Muddy Waters" for his boyhood habit of messing around in a local muddy creek.

Though he was born and bred in the Mississippi Delta, Waters became the face and sound of Chicago Blues after he moved to the City of Big Shoulders in 1943. An accomplished harmonica player, he made his name playing blues guitar in the tradition of Robert Johnson and Son House.

Waters registered his first hit with "I Feel Like Going Home," after his slide guitar and growling delivery had earned him a recording contract with Chess Records. The hits came thick and fast for Waters through the early Fifties, with "Rollin' Stone" (the title of which inspired a certain English combo in the Sixties), "Mannish Boy" (an answer to Bo Diddley's "I'm A Man," which itself borrowed heavily on Waters' trademark blues riff), "Hoochie Coochie Man" and "Champagne And Reefer." Waters' star began to fade as rock 'n' roll gradually took over the market. Nevertheless, he continued to be revered as a living connection to the blues roots of modern music.

Elvis recorded Waters' classic R&B track "Got My Mojo Working" in 1970.

PETER GURALNICK: "Contemporary Chicago blues starts, and in some ways may very well end, with Muddy Waters."

"WAY DOWN"

One of just four tracks recorded at a short-lived Graceland recording session on October 29, 1976, this Layng Martine Jr. soft rocker was the

A-side to the final single of Elvis' life, released in June 1977 with "Pledging My Love" J.D. Sumner provides the lowest lows, an outlandish double low C on the song.

Elvis' death just two months later propelled the single to almost a million sales on first release: it peaked at #18 in the Hot 100, and made it to #1 on the Country chart. In the UK, "Way Down" stayed at #1 for five weeks.

"Way Down" also featured on Elvis' final album release, *Moody Blue*, in July 1977. A version without overdubs was released soon after Elvis' death on *Our Memories of Elvis Vol. 2*. Since then, the track has appeared on *Elvis' Gold Records Vol. 5*, *Walk A Mile In My Shoes*, *ELV1S 30 #1 Hits* and *Hitstory*.

Platinum: A Life In Music offers an alternate studio take, which may also be found on *ELV1S 30 #1 Hits Deluxe Edition* and FTD release *The Jungle Room Session.* Layng Martine Jr. sings the song on FTD issue *Writing For The King.*

WAY IT WAS, THE

A 2001 FTD release providing extended coverage of the background and genesis of the shows filmed for the concert documentary *Elvis: That's The Way It Is*, including a 96-page booklet.

TRACK LISTING:
1. Words
2. The Next Step Is Love
3. Ghost Riders In The Sky
4. Love Me
5. That's All Right (Mama)
6. I Got A Woman
7. I've Lost You
8. I Can't Stop Loving You
9. Just Pretend
10. Words
11. I Just Can't Help Believin'
12. Something
13. Polk Salad Annie
14. Mary In The Morning
15. You've Lost That Lovin' Feelin'
16. Sweet Caroline
17. Hound Dog
18. Heartbreak Hotel
19. Don't Be Cruel
20. Blue Suede Shoes
21. You Don't Have To Say You Love Me
22. Mystery Train / Tiger Man
23. The Wonder Of You
24. One Night
25. All Shook Up

WAYNE, JOHN
(B. MARION MICHAEL MORRISON, 1907-1979)

Wayne was long a favorite actor of Elvis'. In the late Sixties, Elvis was briefly in the frame to star opposite him in *True Grit*, the 1969 movie for which Wayne finally won an Oscar.

John Wayne saw Elvis perform in Las Vegas in 1976; "Duke" was one of the stars expected to attend Elvis' funeral the following year.

Born in Winterset, Iowa on May 26, 1907, Wayne began his long, illustrious acting career in low-budget cowboy movies. He achieved star billing in John Ford's *Stagecoach* (1939). All in all, Wayne acted in over 250 movies, notably *The Searchers* (1956), a film much-loved by top directors, and *Rio Bravo* (1958). Wayne was known as an iconic American patriot and a symbol of conservative American values. Not long before he died, Wayne was awarded the Congressional Gold Medal, inscribed simply "John Wayne, American." Like Elvis, Wayne has been commemorated on a U.S. Mail postage stamp.

WAYNE, SID
(1922-1991)

New-York born composer Sid Wayne was a regular provider of soundtrack material for Elvis, writing 35 songs that featured in the majority of his Sixties movies. Wayne worked with a wide range of partners: Sherman Edwards, Dolores Fuller, Fred Karger, Jerry Livingston, Armando Manzanero, Bix Reichner, Abner Silver and Ben Weisman.

"WE CALL ON HIM"

The B-side to "You'll Never Walk Alone," released in late March 1968, just in time for Easter, made it onto Elvis' 1971 You'll Never Walk Alone budget gospel LP. Elvis recorded the Fred Karger / Ben Weisman / Sid Wayne arrangement on September 11, 1967 in Nashville.

It later came out on the Amazing Grace and Peace in the Valley gospel anthologies, not to mention on Christmas Peace. Alternate versions have appeared on Today Tomorrow & Forever and on FTD issues So High and Easter Special.

"WE CAN MAKE THE MORNING"

Recorded by Elvis in Nashville on May 20, 1971, this country/pop number, written by Jay Ramsey, was released as the B-side to "Until It's Time For You To Go" in early 1972, before its album release on Elvis Now.

The song has since appeared on the Walk A Mile In My Shoes anthology.

"WEAR MY RING AROUND YOUR NECK"

Elvis recorded this Bert Carroll / Russell Moody song on February 1, 1958 at Radio Recorders. By the start of April it was in the stores as a single with B-side "Doncha' Think It's Time." It raced up to #3 in the charts, and easily sold a million.

Soon after, it came out on the Touch of Gold Vol. 2 EP and on the Elvis' Golden Records Vol. 2 LP, as RCA tried to get maximum mileage out of the scant material they had to tide them over until Elvis returned from serving his country overseas in Germany.

Later album outings include Worldwide 50 Gold Award Hits Vol. 1, The King Of Rock 'n' Roll, Artist Of The Century, Elvis 2nd To None, Hitstory and Elvis Rock.

The song was revived as a single in 1983, serving as the B-side to "I Was The One."

An undubbed take from the studio session has appeared on Essential Elvis Vol. 3 (which also features the originally released version) and on FTD re-issue 50,000,000 Elvis Fans Can't Be Wrong (Elvis' Golden Records Vol. 2). The Gus Coletti demo that Elvis initially heard is on FTD release Writing For The King.

"WEARIN' THAT LOVED ON LOOK"

Recorded at Chips Moman's American Studio on January 14, 1969, this belter opened the From Elvis in Memphis album released in May that year. Elvis delivers the Dallas Frazier / A.L. Owens song with plenty of gusto, though he had to take a break during recording to recover from laryngitis (one of two alternates on 2001 FTD album

The Memphis Session dutifully records his voice wearing out).

Later outings for the song include The Memphis Record, the From Nashville To Memphis anthology and Suspicious Minds: The Memphis 1969 Anthology.

Dallas Frazier sings his demo version on FTD release Writing For The King.

WECHT, CYRIL DR.
(B. 1931)

The Coroner and forensic pathologist has spoken to the media about Elvis' death, and his belief that the autopsy was faked. Wecht has been a consultant on many high profile deaths; he is perhaps best known for his opposition to the Warren Commission's findings regarding the assassination of John F. Kennedy. In 2006, Wecht was indicted for fraudulent behavior incompatible with his office.

WEDDING

Elvis and Priscilla's wedding, in Las Vegas on May 1, 1967, was the culmination of an operation of almost military precision organized by the Colonel, who ensured that at least until the press conference called soon afterwards, no interlopers (and scant few of Elvis' long-time entourage) were actually present at the ceremony. Just a few months earlier, Elvis had told Larry Geller that he wanted him to be one of his best men; Geller wasn't even invited. Red West didn't speak to Elvis for months after he was barred from the ceremony because, as he was told, there was insufficient room.

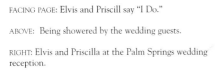

FACING PAGE: Elvis and Priscill say "I Do."

ABOVE: Being showered by the wedding guests.

RIGHT: Elvis and Priscilla at the Palm Springs wedding reception.

In the dead of night Elvis, his family, members of the entourage with him in California (but not those who were in Memphis at that time), George Klein and jeweler Harry Levitch flew to Las Vegas by chartered private plane. At 3:30 a.m., Elvis and Priscilla got their marriage license from the courthouse in Clark County. The ceremony itself took place at 11:45 a.m. in the second-floor suite of the Aladdin Hotel, owned by the Colonel's pal Milton Prell. The man who married Elvis and Priscilla in an 8-minute ceremony was Nevada Supreme Court Judge David Zenoff, a friend of Milton Prell's. Elvis' two best men were Joe Esposito and Marty Lacker. For her maid of honor, Priscilla chose her sister Michelle. By all accounts, Priscilla was far more nervous than Elvis. The groom wore a black suit made to measure by MGM tailor Lambert Marks; the bride was in a chiffon dress with a six-foot train that she had bought in an LA bridal wear store—she went gown shopping in a blonde wig, and gave her name as Mrs. Hodge.

A press conference was held immediately the ceremony. Many members of the press were still camped out in front of Elvis' Palm Springs house, aware that something was in the offing but unsure what or where. After the brief press conference, Elvis and Priscilla held a small reception, during which they cut their five-foot high, six-tier wedding cake decorated with pink and white roses.

They went off for a brief honeymoon in Palm Springs, and then held a Memphis wedding reception at Graceland for friends, family and employees. At this reception, they dressed in their wedding finery, listened to live accordion music from Tony Barrasso, and then headed off the Circle G ranch, where bride and groom at last had some (relatively) quiet time together to get to know one another as Mr. and Mrs. Elvis Presley, in the unconventional honeymoon setting of a double-wide trailer.

Elvis and Priscilla celebrated their first anniversary with a party at their LA home, catered by the Deli Restaurant on La Cienega Boulevard. The marriage lasted for five years; they were legally separated on July 26, 1972.

ELVIS WEDDING

Las Vegas is home to "A Elvis Chapel," where an Elvis impersonator sings to the newly-wedded. This is just one of several Las Vegas facilities that offer Elvis-themed wedding services.

Less well-known is that couples can also exchange vows at the Elvis Presley Memorial Chapel in Tupelo.

PRISCILLA: "Elvis and I followed the Colonel's plan, but as we raced through the day we both thought that if we had it to do over again, we would have given ourselves more time. We were particularly upset at the way our friends and relatives ended up being shuffled around . . . I wish I'd had the strength then to say, 'Wait a minute, this is our wedding . . .'"

JUDGE ZENOFF: "I was simply amazed at the boy's modesty. He was low-key, handsome as a picture, very respectful, and very intense."

JOE ESPOSITO: "They were Mr and Mrs Elvis Presley. Priscilla was thrilled; she was grinning from ear to ear, but still she was sorta in shock, to tell you the truth. I think she was really nervous. It was probably a big relief to her when it was over."

WEIGHT

It was Elvis' unfortunate lot to be the butt of weight jokes when illness caused him to puff up in his final years—a cruel fate for a man who, for the vast majority of his adult life, was known for his good looks. Elvis' ideal weight was 170 to 180 pounds, though his irregular hours and unhealthy food predilections ensured a life of yo-yo weight increases and dieting.

Elvis was a skinny kid at a time when being thin was a mark of poverty, not fashion. During periods of his childhood, his family barely had enough food to eat; perhaps it is less than surprising that when Elvis was surrounded by plenty, he indulged with unalloyed gusto. Already as a young adult, Elvis had to watch what he ate if he did not want to put on weight. His incessant touring, binge eating and topsy-turvy schedule were all a danger to his weight. When Elvis was working less or bored, as he was during his stint in Germany during his Army years, he resorted to comfort eating and put on weight.

In a 1956 radio interview, Elvis declared his weight was 153 pounds when he started singing. Priscilla wrote in her memoir that Elvis' normal weight was 170 pounds. Fan club members received information that Elvis weighed 160 pounds.

In 1958, director Michael Curtiz made a point of asking Elvis to lose a few pounds before they started shooting King Creole.

By the time Elvis enlisted into the army, he was up to 182 pounds. One of the first things he did in Germany was get one of his Memphis pals to send out alfalfa pills, after he heard that that they promoted slimming. Gladys, when she was alive, had been a big believer in slimming pills; Elvis always liked the idea of a quick fix that would not impinge upon his appetites for unhealthful down-home cooking.

Elvis emerged from his two years' Army service back down at 170 pounds, not because of the alfalfa but as a result of hard Army maneuvers and a steady intake of (then-legal) Dexedrine. In early 1961, Paramount producer Hal Wallis told Colonel Parker that he was worried about Elvis' shape, seeing as he would be baring his body to the cameras for Blue Hawaii. Elvis is less than a lean fighting machine as a boxer in Kid Galahad, which he shot in late 1961.

In mid-1962, Elvis declared that he weighed 174 pounds, and that he watched his diet by trying to eat healthily and avoid binge eating—proof that he was sufficiently self-aware to know his demons.

By the end of 1963, Wallis was increasingly worried that Elvis had let himself go too far to play the lean hero in his next movie, Roustabout, and wrote to the Colonel to do something about the situation. RCA also took precautions against Elvis' chubbiness by using two year-old photographs for the cover of the Paradise, Hawaiian Style soundtrack. Many of the stills on his records from this period portray him looking decidedly puffy.

Elvis' extra girth in the mid-Sixties was a sign of his dissatisfaction with being locked into contracts and having to churn out two or three movies a year. Entourage members recall that when a movie wrapped, Elvis often went on a comfort eating binge; they also ascribe his weight fluctuations to increased intake of drug consumption.

Elvis put on significant weight in 1967, when he owned and used the Circle G ranch. Friends recall Elvis riding round the range with a big plastic bag of hamburger buns to much on. According to Priscilla, Elvis put on weight not because of too many sausages and beans, but because of how much he loathed the script for his upcoming movie, Clambake. He was also finally about to marry Priscilla, an event that he had successfully postponed for the best part of decade. In the end, Elvis' Clambake costumes had to be let out, despite Elvis shedding some of his 200-pound bulk with the aid of diet pills.

In 1968, a Time magazine article unfavorably noted that "his cheeks are now so plump that he looks like a kid blowing gum." However, a fit and slimmed-down Elvis emerged from his next movie, Live a Little, Love a Little, and retained his lean look all the way through to 1970. Coinciding with a period of great musical endeavor and success, Elvis was back to practically the weight he had been as an aspiring young singer. Sonny West describes Elvis during this period as "trim as a 21 year-old." The 1968 NBC TV Special and Elvis' return to live performing required Herculean amounts of energy, and evidently generated sufficient satisfaction to banish food bingeing.

By 1971, Elvis was once more at risk of bulking up, and once more the press opened fire. One reviewer found him, on opening night in Las Vegas, looking, "drawn, tired and noticeably heavier." Typically, Elvis was happy to crack a joke, recommending his "Polk Salad Annie" routine for weight loss from the International Hotel stage. By late January 1972, Elvis had slimmed down again, only to balloon up again before the summer.

Until the final years of his life, Elvis had a remarkable ability to lose weight for an upcoming TV performance, movie or tour (especially when the producer or director du jour told him that he needed to slim down—it would only ever be somebody outside the entourage who had the courage to do so). Elvis shed 25 pounds in the run-up to his 1973 live satellite concert performance, Aloha From Hawaii, after producer Marty Pasetta advised him to do so. Rather than blow up at the impertinence of the request, Elvis thanked him for his honesty and dropped the weight—Sonny West has said that Elvis weighed in at 165 pounds when he did the show; Lamar Fike remembers 175 to 180 pounds—through a combination of diet pills and workouts. Peter Guralnick writes that to slim down, Elvis limited his calorie intake to just 500 per day, and took "special injections" said to include as an active ingredient the "urine of a pregnant woman."

Elvis was a lifelong believer in quick-fix fad diets. Over the years, he tried things like eating only no-calorie Jell-O, wrapping himself in Saran Wrap, and wearing a sweat suit. He once went on an all-liquid diet that further exacerbated his underlying health problems.

Four months after the Aloha From Hawaii performance, when Elvis played a residency at Del Webb's Sahara in Tahoe in May 1973, critics characterized him as thirty pounds overweight, "puffy, white-faced and blinking against the light."

In 1974, Elvis brushed off newspaper claims that he had a paunch by saying that he had been appearing on stage in a bullet-proof vest. In private, he was uneasy with his weight, puffiness and ill-health from late 1974 on—he hit 191. pounds that year—because he feared that his fans would not accept him like this.

Occasional bingeing aside, Elvis' weight gain in the final years of his life was the result of multiple medical issues: the cortisone he took to boost his adrenal glands left him looking puffy; a sluggish colon caused bloating; and the ongoing ravages of his regular regime of prescription medication including water retention.

By the beginning of 1975, Elvis was joking about his weight on stage. He told a Las Vegas audience in March 1975, "You should have seen me a month ago, I looked like Mama Cass!" When he was heavier, Elvis further taxed his body with his on-stage moves and gyrations, despite the recommendation of personal physician Dr. Nichopoulos to take it easy.

Elvis generally regained his fitness as his tours progressed, when he no longer had the discipline to crash diet before heading off on tour. There

Elvis in the late 1970s, filling out the Aztec outfit.

were times, however, when Elvis just gave up, refused to be measured and didn't want to know what his weight was. His clothes would have to be altered in secret to accommodate the extra weight, and woe betide anybody who dared to call him fat: not long before Elvis had Vernon fire Red West, the long-time bodyguard had mentioned to Charlie Hodge after a show that Elvis looked fat.

Elvis desperately tried to slim down in advance of his June 1977 tour, which was due to be filmed by CBS as *Elvis in Concert*. Despite going on a drastic liquid diet consisting of protein shakes, he was not completely successful. At his heaviest, Elvis is reputed to have hit 250 pounds. Elvis returned to a liquid diet during the final weeks of his life, as he attempted to slim down for the start of the tour that would have began the day after he died.

BILLY SMITH: "Away from Hollywood . . ., he ate like a stevedore."

LAMAR FIKE: "Elvis hated his weight."

DR. NICHOPOULOS: "He couldn't hang in there and discipline himself to do what it took to get his weight down to where he really wanted it."

BILL BELEW: "Toward the end, Elvis was like a lot of the women that I dealt with when they start fluctuating in their weight. They really didn't want to be measured because they really didn't want to know the truth."

ED PARKER: "Regardless of his weight, his fans loved him. They didn't care if he just sat and did nothing else but sing."

WEINTRAUB, JERRY
(B. 1937)

A concert promoter who worked with Colonel Parker in the Seventies, after having a dream that he would organize an Elvis concert at Madison Square Garden. Persistence paid off for Weintraub when after a year of pestering Colonel Parker, the Colonel stopped stonewalling and told him he could indeed run Elvis tours, provided that he could raise $1 million in 24 hours. Weintraub says that after pulling out all the stops and managing to bring a check to the Colonel, he waved it away—it was a test, not a requirement. The Colonel magnanimously shared the merchandising money he made that night in Vegas.

Weintraub had started out as a talent agent before going into concert management and, in the Seventies, movie production. Among other movies, he produced *Diner* (1982) the *Karate Kid* series, and the 2001 *Ocean's Eleven* remake, as well as many TV specials.

WEISBART, DAVID
(1915-1967)

Producer of Elvis movies *Love Me Tender*, *Flaming Star*, *Follow That Dream* and *Kid Galahad* for 20th Century-Fox, Weisbart's other notable movies include *Rebel Without a Cause* (1955) and *Valley of the Dolls* (1967). Prior to becoming the youngest producer at Warner Brothers in 1952, Weisbart cut his teeth as an editor, winning an Academy Award nomination for *Johnny Belinda* (1948).

WEISMAN, BEN
(1921-2007)

Hill & Range songwriter Ben Weisman has writing credits on more Elvis songs than any other, including six movie title tracks, for a total of 57

songs. Elvis nicknamed him "the mad professor."

The first song Weisman penned for Elvis was "First In Line" in 1956. Weisman first met Elvis at Paramount in early 1957, where Elvis was laying down Weisman song "Got A Lot O' Livin' to Do." Over the years, Weisman wrote with a number of partners, including Fred Wise and Sid Wayne. Weisman had a credit on every single one of the songs on Elvis' final feature film, *Change of Habit* (1969).

A trained concert pianist, Weisman started out writing for Dean Martin. He went on to compose for artists including Johnny Mathis, Dusty Springfield and Barbra Streisand.

In 1988, Weisman wrote the music for *Concerto For Elvis* (see Theater).

WEISS, ALLAN

Allan Weiss met Elvis when he did his screen test with Paramount in 1956. Weiss more or less monopolized the screenplay franchise for Elvis' Paramount films in the Sixties, from *Blue Hawaii* (1961) through *Girls! Girls! Girls!* to *Fun in Acapulco*, *Roustabout*, *Paradise Hawaiian Style* and *Easy Come, Easy Go* (1967).

He received a Writers' Guild nomination for *Roustabout* in 1964 with co-writer Anthony Lawrence (who also worked with Weiss on *Roustabout*, *Paradise Hawaiian Style* and *Easy Come, Easy Go*). Prior to working in the film business, Weiss was a reporter. He only wrote one non-Elvis movie during his screenwriting career.

ALLAN WEISS: "Wallis kept the screenplays shallow. I was asked to create a believable framework for twelve songs and lots of girls."

WELCH, LESTER
(1905-1985)

The Trouble with Girls (1969) was the final picture Welch produced, and Elvis' last with MGM.

WELCH, RAQUEL
(B. JO RAQUEL TEJADA, 1940)

The future sex siren's first speaking role in a movie was in Elvis' 1964 flick Roustabout. At the time, she was a young hopeful with two kids in tow who was thrilled to meet her childhood heart-throb. Welch appeared in an early scene in the movie, as a college girl who arrives at the café where Elvis is singing.

In 1966, Welch starred in cult sci-fi classic *Fantastic Voyage*, before cornering the market for fantasy cave girls in *One Million Years B.C.*. By the early Seventies, she had made a string of films in Europe and turned producer in an effort to break out of the typecast roles she was being offered. Welch began performing in Vegas too: Elvis dropped in after one show, and she was disappointed to see what bad shape he was in. Welch carried on working on stage through the Eighties. She also acted on TV, winning a Golden Globe nomination for *Right to Die* in 1987.

"WELCOME TO MY WORLD"

Elvis sang this song during his *Aloha From Hawaii Via Satellite* performance on January 14, 1973. The song was written by Ray Winkler and John Hathcock, and had been a Country chart #2 for Jim Reeves in 1963.

Elvis' "Welcome To My World" came out on the tie-in *Aloha* LP, and featured as the title track to the *Welcome to My World* album in 1977. It has since been reissued on *Elvis Aron Presley*, *The Country Side of Elvis* and *Elvis By The Presleys*.

A version of the song that Elvis recorded during the January 12, 1973 rehearsals for the *Aloha* show has appeared on *The Alternate Aloha*.

WELCOME TO MY WORLD

This March 1977 album relied for the most part on previously-released country songs, and consequently rose no higher than #44 on the charts. The record received an unforeseen boost after Elvis' death, and went on to become a steady seller, ultimately making it to platinum status. Unusually, the album art featured a painting rather than a photo of Elvis.

TRACK LISTING:
1. Welcome To My World
2. Help Me Make It Through The Night
3. Release Me (And Let Me Love Again)
4. I Really Don't Want To Know
5. For The Good Times
6. Make The World Go Away
7. Gentle On My Mind
8. I'm So Lonesome I Could Cry
9. Your Cheatin' Heart
10. I Can't Stop Loving You

WELD, TUESDAY
(B. SUSAN KER WELD, 1943)

Elvis' co-star *Wild in the Country* (1961) was also a love interest offset. Reportedly, Colonel Parker warned Elvis from pursuing a long-term relationship with her, as he thought her bad-girl image would tarnish his reputation.

Born in New York City on August 27, 1943, Weld had been a child model and stage actress before she scored her movie debut in 1956 music extravaganza *Rock, Rock, Rock* (in which she mentions Elvis by name). Her rise to fame was via a role in TV comedy "The Many Loves of Dobie Gills."

After acting opposite Elvis, Weld turned down the title role in *Lolita* (1962), one of many seminal Sixties movies which, for one reason or another, she declined. Weld later married British comic actor Dudley Moore. In 1988 movie *Heartbreak Hotel*, Weld played a mother so enthralled with Elvis that her son kidnaps the singer.

"WE'LL BE TOGETHER"

Elvis backed by a Spanish chorus (courtesy of The Amigos), recorded on March 26, 1962 at Radio Recorders for *Girls! Girls! Girls!* and credited to Charles O'Curran and Dudley Brooks.

"We'll Be Together" has enjoyed very few reprises. Apart from the *Girls! Girls! Girls!* LP, re-releases are limited to *Burning Love And Hits From His Movies Vol. 2*.

Outtakes have appeared on FTD releases *Out In Hollywood* and *Girls! Girls! Girls!*.

"WE'RE COMIN' IN LOADED"

Elvis cut this Otis Blackwell / Winfield Scott song at Radio Recorders with soul and spirit on March 26, 1962 for the *Girls! Girls! Girls!* movie and soundtrack LP.

Tuesday Weld and Elvis in *Wild in the Country*.

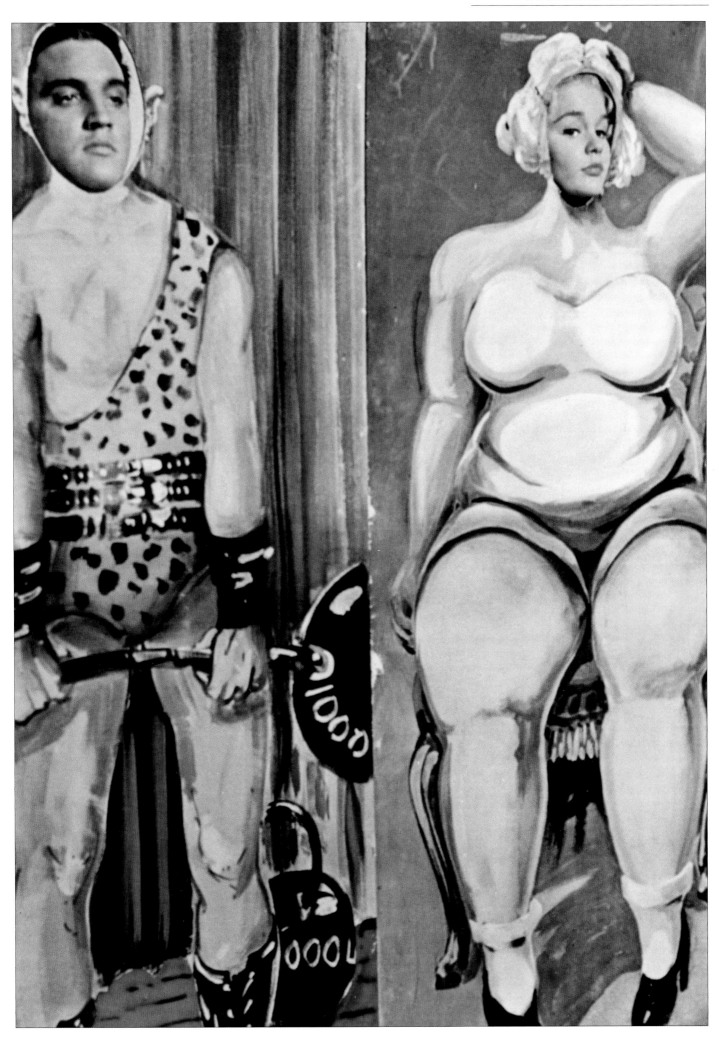

"WE'RE GONNA MOVE"

On August 24, 1956, Elvis recorded this blues / gospel fusion piece (credited to Elvis and Vera Matson, but actually composed by Ken Darby) at Radio Recorders. Based on the Southern Sons' 1941 song "There's A Leak In This Old Building," "We're Gonna Move" turned out to be Elvis' first ever movie tune, and earned a berth on the *Love Me Tender* EP.

A debut album release (an alternative mix) came on *A Date with Elvis*, followed in time by *Worldwide Gold Award Hits Vol. 2* and *The Essential Elvis Vol. 1*.

Alternative takes have appeared on posthumous album releases *The King Of Rock 'N' Roll* (which also has the original studio version) and the 1997 *Jailhouse Rock* re-issue.

WERTHEIMER, AL
(B. 1930)

Wertheimer photographed Elvis at the very start of his career, shadowing him for four months after RCA hired him to document the life of the label's newest star. Wertheimer was by Elvis' side during tumultuous times in the spring and summer of 1956: Elvis was becoming a household name on TV, recording some of his biggest hits, and criss-crossing the country to perform for his fans.

No other photographer before or after had anything like Wertheimer's access to Elvis. The many thousands of dramatic black and white photos that the German-born photographer took are among the most candid and revealing of Elvis Presley's lifetime.

Wertheimer described Elvis as "unafraid and uncaring, oblivious to the invasion of my camera." He also photographed Elvis in 1958. Wertheimer's store of Elvis photos lay untouched until Elvis' death in 1977, since when they have appeared in books that for many fans are among the favorites in their collection.

ALFRED WERTHEIMER: "Elvis was the perfect subject. He was never temperamental or shied away from the camera."

Books:
Elvis '56: In the Beginning, by Alfred Wertheimer and Gregory Martinelli, Macmillan, 1979.
Elvis at 21, New York to Memphis, by Alfred Wertheimer, Insight, 2006.
Elvis: A King in the Making, by Alfred Wertheimer (reissue of *Elvis '56*), Carlton Publishing, 2007.

WEST, MAE
(B. MARY JANE WEST, 1893 -1980)

Since first making a name for herself in vaudeville as "The Baby Vamp," Mae West made sass her trademark. So racy was her on-screen patter in her early films that the Motion Picture Production Code tried to stamp out her innuendo. Despite (or maybe because of) their efforts, West became the highest paid woman in the US in the Thirties. Increasingly, she turning her hand to writing her own material so that she could carry on being lewd without the censors noticing. Over her entire career, West only starred in 12 movies, though she also kept up a long and successful stage career.

The inimitable Mae West turned down the part of the circus owner in Elvis movie *Roustabout*, reputedly because she felt the role was too "downbeat." She did tell Paramount that she would consider working with Elvis in future.

In the Seventies, West recorded a rock album that included covers of some Elvis tracks.

WEST, RED
(B. ROBERT GENE WEST, 1936)

Like Elvis, Robert "Red" Gene West was an alumnus of Humes High School, where he was a year behind Elvis. Their friendship was cemented on the day that the well-built West stepped in to save Elvis from a beating outside school, and then later intervened to rescue Elvis from some kids in the washroom who were about to shear off his long locks. In his memoir, West comments, "That year 1952 put me in a role as Elvis' protector. It wasn't a role I looked for, it just happened that way."

Until 1976, West served as Elvis' driver, bodyguard and friend. A musician as well as a proven fighter, West could read music and play the trumpet; he also wrote a number of songs for Elvis and others. West was Elvis' karate sparring partner— his martial arts name was "Dragon"—and he appeared in no fewer than sixteen of Elvis' movies, often as a guy who fought with Elvis. On other productions, he served as Elvis' double. The first time he had a speaking role was as Elvis' brother in *Wild in the Country*.

After high school, West went to Jones Junior College on a football scholarship, and made it all the way to the Junior Rosebowl in Pasadena. He was also a Golden Gloves boxer.

West was drafted in to help drive Elvis and band members Scotty Moore and Bill Black round the deep South in 1955 and 1956, and keep his pal company on social outings such as the 25th wedding anniversary of Jim Ed and Maxine Brown's parents. West also regularly accompanied Elvis on planes as he shuttled around the South from tour to tour. Gradually, his role as a driver mutated into serving as a physical buffer between Elvis and the jealous guys whose girlfriends went crazy for the boy with the sideburns.

West traveled with Elvis to New York for his first TV engagements in 1956. Later that year, West took offence after Vernon advised Elvis not to take West with him to Hollywood when he first went to work there that August on *The Reno Brothers*—Vernon was concerned after West was involved in a fight while with Elvis at the Memphis Fairgrounds. West signed up to the Marines. He was posted to the Mediterranean, and then back in Virginia. As soon as he was out of the Marines, West traveled with Elvis to Germany for his 18-month Army tour of duty, though he returned home earlier than Elvis because he found life a little dull (or because he had too many fights at the local Beck's Beer Bar in Bad Nauheim, according to some tellers of the story).

In 1958, West's long-standing friendship with Elvis was cemented in grief: his father Newton Thomas West died exactly the same day as Elvis' mother Gladys. Amazingly, Elvis managed to pull himself out of his own despair to attend West's father's funeral the day after he buried Gladys. West recollects, "I was never closer to any man in my life than that day."

West broke his elbow when working as Elvis' double on cowboy movie *Flaming Star* in the summer of 1960, a production on which he had already survived Elvis lassoing him on the gallop.

Though Elvis' name is on the song, West penned Elvis "That's Someone You Never Forget," which Elvis recorded in June 1961 (Elvis suggested the title). At recording sessions, West sometimes served as Elvis' impromptu "conductor," using his music-reading skills to cue Elvis up on vocals. The day after Elvis recorded "That's Someone You Never Forget," he threw a party to celebrate Red West's wedding to Elvis' secretary Pat Boyd. Elvis would have been best man, if he

had managed to get to the wedding in time; instead, Joe Esposito stepped in at the last minute. Elvis hired out the Memphis Fairground to celebrate the event, and then took West off with him to Florida to work on his next movie, *Follow That Dream*.

In the Sixties, West spent much of his time in Los Angeles, living away from the rest of the gang, as he forged a career for himself in Hollywood. He kept Elvis company on his own productions; he both appeared in and wrote a song for *Viva Las Vegas*. He also continued to write songs, not just for Elvis but for Pat Boone and Ricky Nelson among others.

In early 1966, West hired an unknown guitarist called Glen Campbell to play on demos of his songs. In June that year, West doubled for Elvis at a recording session in Nashville, laying down guide tracks because Elvis was unable to attend. One of the songs at that session was West's own song, "If Every Day Was like Christmas." Elvis later overdubbed his vocals over West's.

In 1967, West was so offended at not being invited to Elvis' wedding ceremony that he spent the next couple of years out of the Elvis loop, preferring stunt work in Hollywood on shows such as "The Wild Wild West" to working for his old friend.

Elvis called West in August 1970 and flew him out to Las Vegas as an additional bodyguard after he received a credible death threat. In 1971, Elvis recorded two more Red West compositions for his Christmas album, *Elvis Sings The Wonderful World of Christmas*. West wrote "Separate Ways" for Elvis soon after his break-up with Priscilla (and also tipped Elvis to "Always On My Mind" for his March 1972 recording session). It was often the case that the songs West wrote were tailored to reflect Elvis' emotional state at the time.

In 1973, it was West whom Elvis asked, in a drug-fuelled rage, to take out a contract on Priscilla's then boyfriend, karate champion Mike Stone. In his memoir, West writes that after putting Elvis off as long as possible in the hope that he would come to his senses, West made some calls and found somebody prepared to do the deed. Fortunately, Elvis realized the folly of the project and decided to call it off.

West and two other members of the entourage were named in a lawsuit after some rough handling of a man called Kaijo Peter Pajarinen, who had been a guest of Elvis' in Las Vegas in the summer of 1973—just one of a number of legal actions brought against Elvis' bodyguards in the mid-Seventies. In 1973 and 1974, Elvis founded the Tennessee Karate Institute, and put West in charge of the operation.

Two decades of working for Elvis came to an end on July 13, 1976, when Vernon Presley fired Red West, his cousin Sonny, and karate expert Dave Hebler. Vernon informed them they were being let go because of the money they were costing in lawsuits. Soon after this, Red, Sonny and Hebler sat down and wrote the book that lifted the lid on the seedier aspects of Elvis' life, *Elvis: What Happened?*

It has been speculated that Elvis' original intention was to hire back the bodyguards after a couple of weeks; it was common for him to fire entourage members and then take them back when he felt they had learned their lesson. Other people close to Elvis claim that Elvis' real reason for jettisoning Red and Sonny West was that they were the only members of his entourage who had the guts to tell him that he had to do something about his drug addiction or he would wind up killing himself.

Red West said just this to Elvis in a 1976 phone call. Elvis had called West to try and head off publication of the book, and express his sorrow that things had come to this pass. Elvis retorted, "You worried about me so much that you turned around and tried to hurt me." In the

Elvis on the set of *Follow That Dream* with Red West (CENTER).

phone call, which West taped, Elvis also said, "You do whatever you have to do. I just want you and Pat to know I'm still here," one of many times during the conversation when he expressed his concern for the Wests and said that he wanted to do whatever he could for them. However, alternate transcripts of the taped call have been published in which West told Elvis that there was no need to worry about the book as they were writing "the good stuff." The book was published just two weeks before Elvis died in 1977. For many Elvis fans, this was the ultimate betrayal of their hero. The Wests have always maintained that they wrote the book as a warning, in what turned out to be a vain attempt to get Elvis to pull out of his nosedive.

West's Hollywood career has been long and successful, including appearances in *The Legend of Grizzly Adams* (1990) and *Natural Born Killers* (1994). In all, he has worked on over 75 productions, including Sundance Film Festival winner *Forty Shades of Blue*. More recently, he set up a drama school in Bartlett, Tennessee.

RED WEST: "I have never forgotten the face of Mrs Presley sitting there and saying to me 'Red, you look after my boy'."

RED WEST: "Elvis could bring out the best in me, and he sure as hell could bring out the worst."

RED WEST: "A lot of what went on was as much our fault as it was his because we would indulge him like a child."

RED WEST: "I love the guy."

RED WEST: "Music has been my life . . . I might have been wrestling with a music score in a studio rather than with some half-drunk or mad gal who was trying to throw her panties at Elvis."

DAVID STANLEY: "[Elvis] knew the only conscience left was those two guys; therefore, I think he fabricated an excuse to get them out of his life. He wasn't gonna listen to anybody else anymore. I believe that's why Elvis let Red and Sonny go."

Book:
Elvis: What Happened?, by Red West, Sonny West, Sonny, Dave Hebler, and Steve Dunleavy, Ballantine Books (1977).

WEST, SONNY
(B. Delbert West, 1938)

Elvis met Red West's cousin Sonny in early 1958 at the Rainbow Rollerdrome in Memphis—Elvis had been hiring the venue all week to party with friends before leaving for his Army service in Germany. They already knew one another by sight from Humes High School, where West was a few years behind (he was born on July 5, 1938). West had seen Elvis in action in 1956 at a concert in Tucson, where he was stationed with the Air Force.

Sonny West joined the entourage after Elvis returned from the Army—because he was dating

Patsy Presley, according to Lamar Fike—and was part of the crew that had such a good time in Los Angeles when Elvis shifted his focus to the movies. Like Elvis, Sonny had grown up in a government-funded housing estate in Memphis; when Elvis asked if he wanted to come and work for him, he had no qualms about giving up his job repairing washing machines at Ace Appliance. Sonny West lived at Graceland when he was working for Elvis. His karate nickname, chosen by Elvis, was "Eagle."

In 1960, Sonny West picked up a small role in *Wild in the Country*. Not long afterwards, he fell out with Elvis after a row in which Elvis is said to have hit him, after Sonny accused Elvis of stealing his girlfriend and of being despotic. To make up, Elvis arranged for Sonny to get into the screen extras guild, which normally had quite a waiting list. Sonny returned to the fold in time to work as a stuntman on Elvis' 1962 production *Kid Galahad*.

Elvis insisted on giving Sonny a Cadillac convertible in 1965, after West had an accident on a motorbike that Elvis had given him. When Sonny refused the gift because Elvis was always giving, Elvis took him to one side and explained, "Sonny, you're giving when you don't know you're giving. I put a lot on you guys, and I know it, but you handle it and you take care of things and you get it done. This is just a little way of mine that I can show you how much I appreciate it."

West continued to work on and off with Elvis, while also attempting to build a career in Hollywood beyond the stunt and bit-part roles he had on Elvis' movies, the biggest of which was in

Stay Away, Joe. In the Seventies, he featured in Elvis' concert documentaries *Elvis: That's The Way It Is* and *Elvis on Tour*.

With many years' experience serving as Elvis' bodyguard, Sonny West was a natural choice as Elvis' security chief when he returned to touring in 1970. Elvis gave Sonny a Mercedes Benz at Christmas 1970 as a wedding gift when he married his fiancée Judy Jordan. Elvis was Sonny's best man, and hosted Sonny's wedding party at Graceland. Just before Christmas that year, Sonny accompanied Elvis to Washington for his spontaneous meeting with President Nixon. West and his new wife moved in to Elvis' new Monovale Drive home in Los Angeles because Elvis wanted the reassurance of live-in security in the wake of the Manson murders.

Sonny dieted with Elvis to help get into shape for his history-making *Aloha From Hawaii* live satellite TV broadcast.

Elvis gave Sonny a new Cadillac Eldorado in 1973, after a particularly harrowing time during which Elvis (briefly) split from the Colonel—one of five cars, two motorbikes and plenty of jewelry that Elvis is said to have gifted him over the years. In 1974, Sonny was seconded to work for Colonel Parker, doing advance work and organizing security before Elvis jetted in to perform his shows. Sonny was also on duty ferrying Lisa Maria back and forth to Los Angeles

Sonny West lived at Graceland with his wife and child until the day in the summer of 1976 when he got a phone call from Vernon Presley, informing him that he was being let go. West has said that when he was fired, he felt shock and then anger. Up until the moment they were fired, they had been prepared to take a bullet for Elvis. Reputedly, Elvis wanted to fire the Wests with a settlement that would have tided them over for a few months, and then hire them back. Vernon had other ideas: he gave the Wests just three days' notice and a week's salary.

Sonny teamed up with Red and fellow firee Dave Hebler to work on a bare-all book about their time with Elvis. At the time, the book was regarded by many fans as the ultimate betrayal of Elvis. However, Sonny and Red have always said that the book was a last-ditch attempt to rouse Elvis from his dangerous reliance on prescription drugs. The book came out just two weeks Elvis died; Sonny and Red were understandably contrite in interviews soon after Elvis' death.

In later years, West has said that he and his cousin were fired because they were methodically cutting off Elvis' supply of prescription medicines, in one case by roughing up a backing-group singer who had been obtaining prescriptions in his own name and then passing them on to Elvis.

Sonny West played himself in 1980 TV biopic *This Is Elvis*. More recently, he featured in the *Elvis by the Presleys* documentary. He has raised Arabian horses, produced a movie, worked in talent booking, and been a DJ. He has also put on a touring show in which he talks about his time with Elvis.

West published a memoir about his experiences with Elvis to coincide with the thirtieth anniversary of Elvis' death. At the time of writing, he was working on a DVD of his touring show.

SONNY WEST: "When I started to work for him . . . I looked at him as a 'worldly' big brother, showing me what life was all about. But near the end of our time together, I felt like I was the big brother, looking out for my little brother."

Books:
Elvis: What Happened?, by Red West, Sonny West, Dave Hebler, and Steve Dunleavy, Ballantine Books (1977).
Elvis: Still Taking Care of Business, by Sonny West and Marshall Terrill, Triumph Books, 2007.

WEST VIRGINIA

- Charleston

Elvis and the TCB band played three shows at the Civic Center on July 11 and 12, 1975. He returned for an afternoon and evening show on July 24, 1976.

WESTERN RECORDERS

Elvis first laid down tracks at this Hollywood studio, located at 6000 W. Sunset Boulevard, in March 1968, with arranger Billy Strange and his favorite LA session musicians, for *Live a Little, Love a Little* and RCA. He returned there in June 1968 to pre-record numbers for his NBC Special TV appearance, this time with Bones Howe running the production side of things. Most of the same musicians were there, plus back-up singers the Blossoms. First on the track list that day was Elvis' impassioned Guitar Man medley.

"WESTERN UNION"

A Sid Tepper / Roy C. Bennett reworking of "Return To Sender" that Elvis recorded in Nashville on May 27, 1963, only for it to languish in the vaults until it came out as a "bonus" on the 1968 *Speedway* soundtrack LP.

"Western Union" did not make it onto the *Double Features* soundtrack reissue in the Nineties, but it is on *Elvis Chante Sid Tepper & Roy C. Bennett, For The Asking* and the *From Nashville To Memphis* anthology.

An alternate take found its way onto FTD release *Studio B: Nashville Outtakes*.

WESTMORELAND, KATHY
(B. 1945)

This soprano singer began singing with Elvis in Las Vegas in the summer of 1970, when she took over from singer Millie Kirkham, who herself was standing in for recently-departed Sweet Inspiration Cissy Houston. Initially hired for just two weeks, classically-trained Westmoreland established herself as a fixture for the rest of Elvis' performing life.

Elvis introduced her during shows as "the little girl with the beautiful high voice," or "the voice of an angel." In private, he nicknamed her "Minnie Mouse." They became intimate soon after she joined the band; Elvis, who hated sleeping alone, could count on Kathy's presence if he had nobody else to keep him company through the night.

Elvis called Westmoreland forward to sing solo at times when he thought the audience was a little too rowdy, knowing that the angelic quality in her voice would be more effective at calming the crowd than heavy-handed security.

Born in Texarkana, Arkansas on August 10, 1945, Kathy was the daughter of entertainers. Her father Bresee Gibbons Westmoreland was an opera singer who often worked on MGM productions; her mother Connie was a ballerina. Kathy commenced her performing career at high school in a comedy hillbilly act with Steve Martin. She joined an opera company, sang with The Sandpipers, and then began working as a session singer.

At a couple of shows in 1975, Elvis introduced Kathy on stage with a disparaging remark that she would "take affection from anybody, anyplace, anytime. In fact, she gets it from the whole band." This was soon after he found out that she was romantically involved with a fellow backing singer. Though Kathy complained to Tom Diskin,

Elvis continued with his on-stage comments, causing Kathy and two of the Sweet Inspirations to walk off during a show in Norfolk, Virginia. She refused to perform for one show, but was persuaded to return.

Elvis rewarded Westmoreland for her years of service with various vehicular gifts, including a Lincoln Mark V in June 1977. She also earned a recording contract with the Colonel in the Seventies.

At Elvis' funeral, Kathy sang "My Heavenly Father," a song that she had previously sung as an interlude during Elvis' stage performances.

Kathy has continued to perform ever since. She may be seen in all of Elvis' Seventies concert documentaries and TV extravaganzas (barring *Elvis: That's The Way It Is*). She also recorded for the soundtrack to 1979 Elvis TV biopic *Elvis*.

Her 1987 memoir includes a heartfelt defense of Elvis during his final years. In the book, she details the many medical conditions from which he was suffering (a heart condition, bone cancer, anemia and seizures), and lauds his ability to continue performing for his fans despite the knowledge that he was dying. In the mid-2000s, Kathy was planning to bring out a revised and updated version of the book. She has also brought out a DVD of her Elvis experiences.

KATHY WESTMORELAND: "After the very first show that I saw . . . I was just in awe of his talent."

KATHY WESTMORELAND: "Everybody who was associated with him had this feeling that we were all somehow meant to be together."

LARRY GELLER: "Of all the women Elvis ever knew, spiritually speaking, Kathy was the most attuned to him."

Book:
Elvis and Kathy, by Kathy Westmoreland and William G. Quinn, published by Glendale House Publishing, 1987.

WETHERINGTON, "BIG CHIEF" JIM
(B. JAMES STEPHEN WETHERINGTON, 1922-1973)

The bass singer for the gospel group the Statesmen was one of Elvis' favorite performers when he was growing up. "Big Chief," as he was nicknamed for his Indian heritage, had a crowd-pleasing move of making his legs tremble and shake. Elvis adopted this self-same technique at his first major concert, at Memphis's Overton Park Shell on July 30, 1954. He later claimed that his leg shook involuntarily because he was so nervous.

Wetherington began his career with the Sunny South Quartet. He moved on to the Melody Masters, where he met another Elvis favorite, Jake Hess. He joined the Statesman in 1949, and sang with the group for 24 years.

"WHAT A FRIEND WE HAVE IN JESUS"

Elvis covered this gospel song—actually an 1855 poem by Joseph M. Scriven, put to music a decade later by Charles Crozat Converse—during his Las Vegas show on August 28, 1973. A recording exists on bootleg *Take These Chains From My Heart* and other unofficial releases. "What A Friend We Have In Jesus" was one of Grandma Minnie Mae's favorite songs; it later made a very brief cameo in 1981 biopic *This Is Elvis*.

"WHAT A WONDERFUL LIFE"

An upbeat Sid Wayne / Jerry Livingston song from the *Follow That Dream* soundtrack and EP that Elvis recorded in Nashville on July 2, 1961. The opening song for the movie—at one stage it was a title song candidate—did not receive its album debut until 1971 budget LP *I Got Lucky*. It has since appeared on the Nineties *Double Features* series.

An alternate version spliced from the first two takes earned a release on *Collectors Gold* in 1991; additional alternates appeared on 2004 FTD release *Follow That Dream*.

"WHAT EVERY WOMAN LIVES FOR"

A late-vintage Doc Pomus / Mort Shuman soundtrack song that Elvis recorded at Radio Recorders on May 14, 1965 for *Frankie and Johnny*, after the band had laid down the instrumentals the previous day.

Later releases may be found on *Elvis Sings Mort Shuman & Doc Pomus*, the *Double Features* re-release, and FTD reissue *Frankie and Johnny*.

"WHAT NOW MY LOVE"

Elvis included this potboiler—an English adaptation of a French original titled "Et Maintenant," which had been a hit for Jane Morgan in 1962—in live shows from August 1972 (it's on 2005 FTD release *Summer Festival*). The song was part of his Aloha From Hawaii Via Satellite performance, and was on the tie-in LP. In concert, Elvis sometimes performed it in a spoken-word version; it remained a show regular through 1973.

Live versions have since appeared on *The Alternate Aloha*, *The Country Side Of Elvis*, *Elvis Live*, and FTD concert releases *Summer Festival*, *Takin' Tahoe Tonight!* and *Closing Night*.

An early sing-a-long recording of Elvis and pals taking on the Carl Sigman English adaptation of the tune (originally written by Pierre Delanoe and Gilbert Bécaud) has surfaced from Graceland in 1966 to appear on *The Home Recordings* and *In A Private Moment*. Before Elvis, "What Now My Love" was a mid-Sixties hit for Al Martino, Herb Alpert, and Sonny and Cher.

"WHAT NOW, WHAT NEXT, WHERE TO"

Written by Don Robertson and Hal Blair, this song was turned down by Johnny Cash before Elvis recorded it in Nashville on May 5, 1963. Elvis' version remained under wraps until it emerged as a bonus track on the 1967 *Double Trouble* soundtrack LP.

It has since appeared on *Separate Ways*, *For The Asking*, *From Nashville to Memphis*, and FTD release *Double Trouble*.

"WHAT'D I SAY?"

Elvis recorded this Ray Charles track on August 30, 1963 at Radio Recorders, when it was added at the last minute to the soundtrack of *Viva Las Vegas*. In the movie Elvis is dressed in canary yellow as he sings the song to an appreciative Ann-Margret.

"What'd I Say?" was Ray Charles' first million-selling single in 1959, after the R & B #1 crossed over to reach #6 in the *Billboard* Hot 100.

Elvis' version was released as a single in late April 1964, just two weeks after "Kiss Me Quick," Elvis' worst-selling single in a decade. "What'd I Say" did significantly better: backed with B-side track "Viva Las Vegas," the song made it to #21 on the charts, and earned gold record status.

The original recording has since appeared on compilation album *Elvis' Gold Records Vol. 4*, *Command Performances*, the *Double Features* issue for the movie, the FTD 2000s updated soundtrack reissue, and *Elvis at the Movies*.

Elvis performed the song at his opening Las Vegas engagement in August 1969—at one stage, it was in the running for selection as his closing track. Versions from that first Las Vegas season have appeared on disc on *Elvis: Greatest Hits Vol. 1*, *Collectors Gold*, *Live In Las Vegas*, *Today Tomorrow & Forever*, and 2007 title *Viva Las Vegas*.

Following a layoff, he reprised the song live in 1975, after which it remained something of a concert regular. A version is on Elvis' final concert documentary and album *Elvis in Concert*. It's also to be found on FTD releases *Elvis At The International*, *Big Boss Man*, *Tucson '76* and *New Year's Eve*.

The original studio master of Elvis' September 1967 "Guitar Man" recording includes an excerpt of "What'd I Say" at the end, though this wasn't released until the *From Nashville to Memphis* anthology in 1993.

A rehearsal version from July 1970, in preparation for concert documentary *Elvis: That's The Way It Is*, appeared on 1997 release *Platinum: A Life In Music*.

The opening two takes from the 1963 studio session are on the FTD *Viva Las Vegas* release.

"WHAT'S SHE REALLY LIKE"

Elvis recorded this Sid Wayne / Abner Silver song for the *G.I. Blues* soundtrack on April 28, 1960 at RCA's Hollywood studios. In the movie Elvis only sings an excerpt.

The track came out on the original *G.I. Blues* LP. Alternates have appeared on *The EP Collection Vol. 2*, and on more recent *G.I. Blues* soundtrack CDs.

"WHEELS ON MY HEELS"

Elvis recorded this feelgood *Roustabout* song—written by Sid Tepper and Roy C. Bennett—on March 3, 1964 at Radio Recorders. It came out on the soundtrack LP, and subsequently on the *Double Features* reissue for the movie, and on *Elvis Chante Sid Tepper & Roy C. Bennett*.

"WHEN GOD DIPS HIS LOVE IN MY HEART"

Elvis, Carl Perkins and Jerry Lee Lewis sing a line or two of this traditional country gospel—a hit for a long line of artists including Red Foley and Hank Williams—during the legendary *Million Dollar Quartet* session at Sun Studio on December 4, 1956. Recordings are to be found on all of the Million Dollar releases.

"WHEN I'M OVER YOU"

Elvis cut this Shirl Milete track in Nashville on June 7, 1970. It found its way onto the *Love Letters From Elvis* LP the following year. It has since appeared on *That's The Way It Is—Special Edition*.

"WHEN IRISH EYES ARE SMILING"

Elvis slipped a line or two of this show tune into a number of studio recording sessions (at the end of "I Got Stung" in June 1958, released on *Essential Elvis Vol. 3*; at the end of "What'd I Say" on the FTD *Viva Las Vegas* release; and on "Too Much Monkey Business" on FTD album *So High*). Trivia fans know that neither Chauncey Olcott nor George Graff Jr., who wrote the song, were Irish; nor was Ernest Ball who wrote the tune.

"WHEN IT RAINS, IT REALLY POURS"

Sam Phillips had planned for this to be Elvis' sixth Sun single. He finally got Elvis into the studio in November 1955 for what turned out to be his last official Sun session. Legend has it that while Elvis was still in the studio, the call came through that his contract was being bought out by RCA, so it wasn't worth finishing off the session. Some Elvis discologists believe that Elvis actually recorded this song in July that year. The in-house rocker had been a hit for William Robert "Billy The Kid" Emerson, who was on the Sun roster at the same time as Elvis.

On February 24, 1957, Elvis finally recorded a completed version of the song at Radio Recorders studio in Los Angeles for RCA. Release of this version was also delayed. It didn't come out until the 1965 *Elvis For Everyone* album. It has since appeared on *Reconsider Baby*, *The King of Rock 'n' Roll* anthology (which also features the Sun version), the 1997 reissue of *Loving You*, the FTD *Loving You* issue and *Elvis Sings The Blues*.

Elvis' original Sun recording went with him to RCA but did not see release until 1983, when it appeared as the first track on *Elvis: A Legendary Performer Vol. 4*. Since then, it has graced *Sunrise*, *Elvis at Sun* and *Elvis R 'n' B*. Alternates from the Sun session have seen release on *A Golden Celebration* and *The Complete Sun Sessions*.

A dressing room rehearsal from June 24, 1968, before Elvis' NBC TV Special, was a popular bootleg prior to making an official debut on *Memories: The '68 Comeback Special* and FTD disc *Let Yourself Go*.

"WHEN MY BLUE MOON TURNS TO GOLD AGAIN"

Elvis recorded this Wiley Walker / Gene Sullivan composition on September 2, 1956 at Radio Recorders for release on his second album, *Elvis*. The songwriters had previously brought out the track in 1941; it was later covered (among others) by Tex Ritter. Airplay of Elvis' version propelled it to #27 on the Top 100 singles chart following release on the *Elvis Vol. 1* EP. This version has since appeared on *Worldwide 50 Gold Award Hits Vol. 2*, *The King Of Rock And Roll* and *Great Country Songs*.

Elvis performed the song on his final Ed Sullivan Show performance (released years later on *A Golden Celebration*).

He rehearsed the song and sang it during recordings for the NBC TV Special in June 1968, though it did not make it into the final show. Rehearsals have seen the light of day on bootlegs and on FTD releases *Burbank '68* and *Let Yourself Go*. Versions from the June 27, 1968 tapings have appeared on *Platinum: A Life In Music*, *Memories: The '68 Comeback Special* and *Tiger Man* (the later performance).

Very occasionally, Elvis sang the song live in the Seventies. One such example is on bootleg *Suzie Q*.

"When The Saints Go Marchin' In"

Elvis left multiple recordings of this classic spiritual track, starting on December 4, 1956 at the Sun Studio *Million Dollar Quartet* session, available in recent decades on a variety of MDQ releases.

Almost a decade later, on May 12, 1965 at Radio Recorders, Elvis recorded a brass-heavy version for the *Frankie & Johnny* soundtrack, in a medley with "Down By The Riverside"— this time, Bill Giant, Bernie Baum and Florence Kaye claimed the songwriting credit. After the soundtrack LP, this version has done the rounds on *Elvis Sings Hits from His Movies*, and on the *Double Features* and FTD releases for the movie.

A 1956 home recording from Audubon Drive, in which Elvis' voice is drowned out by other pals, has appeared on *Platinum: A Life in Music*, *The Home* Recordings, and the *Peace In The Valley* gospel anthology—which, incidentally, features all three versions.

"When The Snow Is On The Roses"

Elvis covered this 1967 Ed Ames hit in concert in Las Vegas on August 24, 1970 (there are conflicting reports as to whether he sang the song to his own piano accompaniment or not). The moment was immortalized on the *Live In Las Vegas* box set, after years of being available on bootleg only.

The song was originally a German ditty titled "Der Weg Ins Land Der Liebe," by Ernst Bader and Larry Kusik; James Last and Eddie Snyder provided the English words. Before Elvis covered the song, it had been sung by Ed Ames and Kris Kristofferson.

"When The Swallows Come Back To Capistrano"

Elvis sang this song at home, probably in 1960, and is said to have essayed it live when he returned to performing. It was released on *In A Private Moment* and on bootlegs. Written by Leon Rene, the song was a Forties hit for the Ink Spots and the Glenn Miller Orchestra, before being covered in the Fifties by Billy Ward & The Dominoes and later Pat Boone.

"Where Could I Go But To The Lord"

Elvis is at his most mellisonant in this gospel classic, written by James B. Coats in 1940 (and a hit for Red Foley in 1951), when he recorded it in Nashville on May 28, 1966 for release on his *How Great Thou Art* LP. This recording has since appeared on gospel anthologies *Amazing Grace*, *Peace In The Valley* and *Ultimate Gospel*.

In 1968, Elvis kicked off the rock / gospel medley in his *NBC TV Special* with the song. The version used in the show was recorded on June 21. It also made it into the original gospel medley on tie-in album *Elvis*. Since then, it has reappeared as part of the gospel medley on *Memories: The '68 Comeback Special*, the *Peace In The Valley* gospel anthology and *Today Tomorrow & Forever*. A prior rehearsal version is on FTD release *Let Yourself Go*.

"Where Did They Go, Lord"

Elvis recorded this Dallas Frazier / A.L. Owens song in Nashville on September 22, 1970. It was released as the B-side to "Rags To Riches" in February 1971. The track did not qualify for album release until after Elvis' death, when it appeared on the *He Walks Beside Me* LP. Since then, it has come out on Nineties anthology *Walk A Mile In My Shoes*, and on the 2000 issue of *Elvis Country*. Alternate takes may be found on *Essential Elvis Vol. 4* and FTD release *The Nashville Marathon*.

"Where Do I Go From Here"

Elvis recorded this soul-searching Paul Williams country track on March 27, 1972 at RCA's Hollywood facility. The song first came out on the 1973 *Elvis (The Fool Album)* release.

Later outings are the 1999 *Burning Love* issue. Alternates may be found on *Today Tomorrow & Forever* and FTD release *6363 Sunset*.

"Where Do You Come From"

Elvis is in melancholy mood at the piano on this Ruth Batchelor / Bob Roberts song from the *Girls! Girls! Girls!* soundtrack, laid down at Radio Recorders on March 27, 1962.

"Where Do You Come From" first came out as the B-Side to "Return to Sender" in October 1962. The song failed to catch alight, barely charting at #99, while the flip side just missed out on top spot. The song had a run-out on the *Girls! Girls! Girls!* soundtrack, since when it has appeared officially on *Worldwide 50 Gold Award Hits Vol. 1* and the *Double Features* re-release for the movie.

Alternates are on FTD releases *Out In Hollywood* and *Girls! Girls! Girls!*.

"Where No One Stands Alone"

Elvis recorded this 1955 Mosie Lister song (initially written for The Ink Spots) at Studio B early on the morning of May 26, 1966 for his gospel album *How Great Thou Art*. It has since appeared on *Elvis in Nashville*, gospel anthologies *Amazing Grace* and *Peace in the Valley*, and festive album *Christmas Peace*.

Over a decade later, Elvis pulled up the song from the depths of his memory and performed it to his own piano accompaniment in Montgomery, Alabama on February 1977, six months before he died. For many years the performance was a much sought-after bootleg; latterly, it was released on FTD live album *Unchained Melody*.

"Whiffenpoof Song, The"

Elvis sang a snatch of this song (the theme song for a Yale *a cappella* society of the same name, credited to Tod Galloway, Meade Minnigerode and George Pomeroy) on October 23, 1968 as part of a college medley for *The Trouble with Girls*. The song did not warrant a record release until the Double Features compilation for *Live A Little, Love A Little, Love a Little / Charro! / The Trouble With Girls / Change of Habit* in 1995. Bing Crosby, Count Basie and Perry Como all had hits with the song previously.

"Whistling Tune, A"

This mellifluous Sherman Edwards / Hal David song from *Kid Galahad* was recorded by Elvis in Nashville on October 26, 1961. It first appeared on the *Kid Galahad* EP, before earning an LP debut on 1971 budget release *C'mon Everybody*. It has since appeared on the *Double Features* issue for Kid Galahad.

An earlier recording, made on July 7 that year for inclusion in previous film *Follow That Dream*, lacked Ray Walker's whistled intro. This version appeared on 1991 issue *Collectors' Gold*. Outtakes are available on the 2004 FTD releases for both movies.

White, Tony Joe
(b. 1943)

Born in Goodwill, Louisiana on July 23, 1943, part-Cherokee Tony Joe White began his recording career at Monument records with top ten hit "Polk Salad Annie." Elvis incorporated the song into his act when he returned to performing in 1969 and it immediately became a popular stage favorite.

Elvis flew White—nicknamed "The Swamp Fox"—to Las Vegas to watch him cover his song. Elvis later recorded White compositions "I Got A Thing About You Baby," "For Ol' Times Sake" and (briefly, on *Elvis on Tour*) "Rainy Night In Georgia."

Though White's recording career in the States was brief, he built a strong following in Europe after playing the Isle of Wight festival in 1970. White spent more time writing than performing in the Eighties, a decade when he toured Europe with Eric Clapton and Joe Cocker, as well as writing for Tina Turner. He enjoyed new-found success in the States in the 2000s.

TONY JOE WHITE: "Elvis always felt like Polk Salad Annie was his life story. He'd been around it all his life—he knew what I was talking about. We were brought up pretty much the same way."

"White Christmas"

This evergreen festive season song, written by Irving Berlin and first sung by Bing Crosby in 1942 movie *Holiday Inn*, made it onto *Elvis' Christmas Album* and *Christmas With Elvis* EP after he recorded it at Radio Recorders on September 6, 1957. Until it was overtaken in the Nineties by Elton John's reworked tribute to Princess Diana "Candle In The Wind," Bing Crosby's version of this song was the biggest-selling recording in history, estimated to have sold over 125 million copies worldwide.

Elvis' playfully starts off the song slow, but he is simply unable to keep his rocking instincts in check the whole way through. Irving Berlin was so irked by Elvis' intuitive interpretation of the song that he wrote to radio stations asking them not to play it.—curious conduct from a man who originally wrote the song with a lead-in verse that was a New Yorker's satirical tilt at his adopted home town of Los Angeles.

The toned-down version of the song won the Best Song Oscar for Bing Crosby, and returned to the *Billboard* charts every single year for two decades. Crosby even had to re-record the song in 1947 because the original master had worn out from so many repeat pressings. Since Crosby, the song has been covered by hundreds of artists, from Frank Sinatra to Ernest Tubb and the Drifters (who had a #2 R&B hit with it in 1954), The Beach Boys, Stiff Little Fingers and more.

Elvis' version is a regular on any of his Christmas-themed offerings, including *Blue Christmas*, *If Every Day Was Like Christmas*, *Christmas Peace*, the 2005 box set *Christmas With Elvis*, and

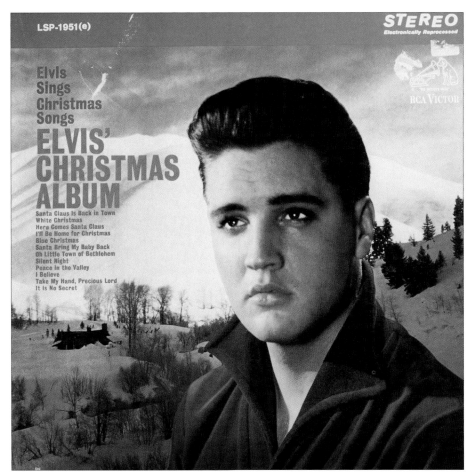

"White Christmas" was included in *Elvis' Christmas Album*.

Elvis Christmas. It has also appeared on Fifties anthology *The King of Rock And Roll*.

An instrumental version from his *Million Dollar Quartet* jam at Sun Studios on December 4, 1956 is on MDQ releases.

WHITMAN, SLIM
(B. OTIS DEWEY WHITMAN, JR., 1924)

Long-standing country star Slim Whitman was a regular at the Louisiana Hayride during Elvis' formative listening years. He was also one of the first of Elvis' heroes with whom the budding singer shared a bill: Whitman headlined a Bob Neal-promoted Overton Park Shell show on July 30, 1954, the first time that Elvis played in front of an audience numbering in the thousands. At another show, Whitman lent Elvis his rhinestone jacket to go on stage because Elvis arrived at the venue with his own stage clothes dirty.

Born in Tampa, Florida on January 20, 1924, Whitman learned to play guitar in the Navy during World War II, modeling himself on Jimmie Rodgers. He had a crack at playing minor league baseball, but decided that what he wanted to do was sing. "America's Favorite Folksinger" got his break in 1948, when Colonel Tom Parker brokered him a contract with RCA, leading to the release of his first single (and later theme song) "I'm Casting My Lasso Towards the Sky," and soon afterwards, a regular slot at the Louisiana Hayride. Whitman's breakthrough single was a version of Bob Nolan's "Love Song Of The Waterfall," after which he ran up a string of top-10 country hits just as Elvis was first beginning to make a name for himself.

Whitman joined the Grand Ole Opry in 1957, after his single "Rose Marie" spent 11 weeks at the top of the British charts (a record bettered only by three artists before or after). Also in 1957, Whitman recorded "(Now And Then There's) A Fool Such As I," which Elvis recorded the following year. Elvis later covered "I'll Take You Home Again, Kathleen" and "Tomorrow Never Comes," both of which Whitman also sang.

For much of the Sixties, Whitman was more popular in the UK than in the US. In 1979, his greatest hits record became the biggest-selling TV-promoted album ever.

"WHO AM I?"

Written by Charles Rusty Goodman, Elvis recorded this gospel tune at American Studio on February 22, 1969, at the very end of his landmark sessions there.

The song first appeared on 1971 gospel album *You'll Never Walk Alone*. Since then, it has featured on *He Walks Beside Me*, *The Memphis Record*, *From Nashville To Memphis*, *Suspicious Minds: The Memphis 1969 Anthology*, CD reissues of *His Hand in Mine*, and gospel anthologies *Peace In The Valley* and *Ultimate Gospel*.

"WHO ARE YOU? (WHO AM I?)"

Not an answer record but a Sid Wayne and Ben Weisman ballad that Elvis laid down at Radio Recorders on June 20, 1967 for *Speedway*. The track first appeared on the soundtrack LP. Since then, it has had an outing on the *Double Features* release for *Speedway*.

"WHO NEEDS MONEY?"

Randy Starr for one, which is why he wrote this song for Elvis to record for Clambake in Nashville on February 22, 1967 (featuring vocals by Ray Walker, though in the movie the other voice is mimed by actor Will Hutchins).

"Who Needs Money?" first appeared on the soundtrack LP. More recently, it has come out on the *Double Features* and FTD re-releases for the movie.

"WHO'S SORRY NOW?"

Elvis and girlfriend Anita Wood sang this song—first recorded by The Happy Six in 1923—at Eddie Fadal's home in Waco, Texas, in May 1958, where Elvis was doing his Army training. Written by Ted Snyder, Bert Kalmar and Harry Ruby, Connie Francis had had a top five hit with the song. Elvis' version of the song has appeared on unofficial release *Forever Young, Forever Beautiful*.

"WHOLE LOTTA SHAKIN' GOIN' ON"

A mild hit for Big Maybelle when she first recorded it in 1955, "Whole Lotta Shakin' Goin' On" became a multi-million-selling smash for Jerry Lee Lewis on Sun Records in 1957, when it made it to #3 in the *Billboard* Top 100 and topped both the Country and the Rhythm and Blues charts. The song was written by Dave "Curly" Williams and Sunny David (a pseudonym used by Roy Hall).

Elvis got round to recording a country rock version of this song in Nashville on September 22, 1970, for inclusion on his *Elvis Country LP*. This version has since appeared on the *Walk A Mile In My Shoes* anthology.

He performed the song live as early as his first Las Vegas season. By the summer of 1971, it was a prime mixer in his oldies medleys. The first live Elvis performance of the song to make it out of a performance environment was the *Aloha From Hawaii Via Satellite* broadcast in 1973, and the accompanying LP. A year later, the song made it onto *Elvis Recorded Live On Stage In Memphis*—in all likelihood, this was the final time that he performed the song.

Other live outings preserved on record include the FTD version of *Elvis Recorded Live On Stage In Memphis*, and FTD live releases *Takin' Tahoe Tonight!*, *Closing Night* and *I Found My Thrill*.

Essential Elvis Vol. 4 offered the entire unedited Nashville studio track, rather than the truncated album version; neither version features a horn interlude that was recorded but never added.

"WHY ME LORD"

A million-selling Kris Kristofferson country gospel classic that Elvis performed in March 1974 at the concert released as *Elvis Recorded Live on Stage in Memphis*. Elvis added the song (originally titled "Why Me?") to his repertoire early in the year, after he and the Stamps spontaneously sang it one night on stage. The *Elvis Recorded Live on Stage in Memphis* recording has since appeared on gospel anthologies *Amazing Grace* and *Peace In The Valley*.

"Why Me Lord" remained a concert regular through 1975, and still made occasional Elvis concert cameos up to his final performances. Further live releases are on *Elvis Aron Presley*, *Live In Las Vegas*, and on FTD releases *Elvis Recorded Live On Stage In Memphis*, *Live In L.A.*, *It's Midnight*, *Dixieland Rocks* and *Unchained Melody*.

WIGGINGTON, CHUCK

This Dallas-born bass player backed Elvis in Tupelo in September 1957, when regular bass player Bill Black was in dispute with Elvis and his management team.

WILBANKS, JANIE

A Mississippi beauty introduced by George Klein to Elvis in 1958 en route from Texas to his Army posting in Germany. Wilbanks went out to Germany to stay with Elvis for a week in early 1959, during a trip to visit her uncle, who was an Army chaplain in Germany.

"WILD IN THE COUNTRY"

Elvis recorded this movie title song at Radio Recorders on November 7, 1960. Written by Hugo Peretti, Luigi Creatore and George Weiss, the track was released as a single six weeks before the movie premiered, as the B-Side to "I Feel So Bad." "Wild In The Country" only made it to #26 on the *Billboard* Hot 100 during its five-week sojourn (though it climbed as high as #4 on the UK charts).

The song subsequently appeared on *Worldwide Gold Award Hits, Vol. 2, Elvis In Hollywood*, the *Double Features* issue for the movie, *Command Performances, The Country Side Of Elvis, Hitstory* and *Elvis Movies*. It's also on later CD releases of *Elvis' Golden Records Vol. 3*.

Alternate takes have come out on the 1980 *Elvis Aron Presley* anthology, and more recently on *Elvis: Close Up* and FTD issue *Out In Hollywood*.

WILD IN THE COUNTRY

Producer Jerry Wald had been looking for the right star for this movie for years. When Elvis landed the part, it proved to be the final opportunity to flex his acting muscles before being consigned to formulaic film fare for almost the whole decade.

Elvis arrived in LA to start work on his third and final 20th Century-Fox production on November 6, 1960. The script, by well-regarded playwright Clifford Odets, was adapted from J. R. Salamanca's novel *The Lost Country*. The screenplay ended up being heavily rewritten by director Phillip Dunne, after Odets was jettisoned from the project. Principal photography was complete by January, but then Elvis was called back in early February to reshoot the ending.

Initially conceived as a straight, non-musical movie, four songs were shoehorned into the script at the Colonel's insistence before principal shooting began. Studio head Spyros Skouras also weighed in to insist that the movie showcase Elvis' singing talents. More simple ballads than commercial Elvis releases, the Colonel nevertheless managed to get two of the songs onto upcoming RCA singles. For a while, the movie was known by the working title *Lonely Man* and *Forget Me Never*, both songs that were dropped from the movie before release.

Location shooting took place in Napa Valley, California and at the 20th Century Ranch near Hollywood. Other locations were the Victorian Ink House, St. Helena, and UCLA (for the college shots).

The character Elvis played in the movie is a writer, not an artist as in the original novel. Elvis has a record-breaking three love interests in this movie: a good girl, a bad girl and an older woman. The ending was reshot after negative audience reaction to Hope Lange's character killing herself.

Simone Signoret turned down the Hope Lange role, according to some sources because the pay was not sufficient. Actress Millie Perkins, who played Elvis' good girlfriend in the movie, many years later played Gladys Presley in a 1990 mini-TV series titled *Elvis*.

The movie premiered in Memphis on June 15, 1961; Elvis did not make the screening (some sources state that it was the only one of his movies whose premiere he actually attended).

CREDITS:
Twentieth Century-Fox, Color
Length: 114 minutes
Release date: June 22, 1961

TAGLINE:
Singing and loving as never before!
Giving his heart to three girls!
Elvis Presley sings of love to Hope Lange,
   Tuesday Weld, Millie Perkins

Directed by: Philip Dunne
Produced by: Jerry Wald, Peter Nelson (associate
   producer)
Written by: J.R. Salamanca (novel), Clifford Odets
Music by: Kenyon Hopkins, Bennie Benjamin,
   Sol Marcus
Cinematography by: William C. Mellor
Film Editing by: Dorothy Spencer
Art Direction by: Preston Ames, Jack Martin Smith
Set Decoration by: Stuart A. Reiss, Walter M. Scott
Costume Design by: Don Feld

CAST:
Elvis Presley	Glenn Tyler
Hope Lange	Irene Sperry
Tuesday Weld	Noreen Braxton
Millie Perkins	Betty Lee Parsons
Rafer Johnson	Davis (Macy's butler)
John Ireland	Phil Macy
Gary Lockwood	Cliff Macy
William Mims	Uncle Rolfe Braxton
Raymond Greenleaf	Dr. Underwood
Christina Crawford	Monica George (Cliff Macy's date)
Robin Raymond	Flossie (Phil Macy's secretary)
Mark Bailey	Sheriff
Charles Arnt	Mr. Parsons
Walter Baldwin	Mr. Spangler
Joe Butham	Mr. Dace
Pat Buttram	Mr. Longstreet (mechanic)
Harry Carter	Bartender
Linden Chiles	Doctor
Will Corry	Willie Dace
Ruby Goodwin	Sarah (Irene's maid)
James W. Horan	Juror
Mike Lally	Huckster
Doreen Lang	Mrs. Parsons
Hans Moebus	Conductor
Elisha "Bitsy" Mott	State trooper
Alan Napier	Prof. Joe B. Larson
Jack Orrison	Dr. Creston (coroner)
Jason Robards Sr.	Judge Parker
Harry Shannon	Sam Tyler (Glenn's father)
Frankie Silver	Woman in booth
Red West	Hank Tyler (Glenn's brother)

ADDITIONAL CREW:
Ben Nye	makeup artist
Helen Turpin	hair stylist
Joseph E. Rickards	assistant director
Alfred Bruzlin	sound
Warren B. Delaplain	sound
Edward B. Powell	orchestrator
Nancy Sharp	wardrobe
Homer Plannette	gaffer
Clyde Taylor	gaffer

Plot:
Elvis plays bright, god-fearing, short-tempered Glenn Tyler, who at the start of the movie seriously injures his drunken brother Hank (played by Red West). Caught by police after running

off—he thinks that he has killed his brother—Glenn is sent for examination by psychiatrist Irene Sperry (played by Hope Lange).

The local town court releases him and Glenn ges to work at the plant owned by his Uncle Phil Macy (played by John Ireland). He moves into his Uncle Ralph's house, after his father wants nothing more to do with him. At Ralph's, he is cornered by his sexpot cousin Noreen (played by Tuesday Weld). Childhood sweetheart Betty Lee Parsons (played by Millie Perkins) is not pleased with this development.

At his probation meeting with psychiatric consultant Sperry, Glenn pours out his anger against his ne'er-do-well father and drunken brother, and explains how he wanted to save his mother, who died when he was just nine. At his next meeting with Sperry, Glenn lets it slip that he wants to be a writer. Sperry is so impressed by one of his short stories that she intercedes to help him get into college. Meanwhile, Noreen keeps up her seduction routine, and comes close to winning her cousin away from Betty Lee. Together, and drunk, they harass Irene Sperry, who hands him his story back.

In another bout of violence, Glenn attacks his Uncle Ralph for trying to dupe him into marrying his daughter Noreen. Faithful girlfriend Betty Lee advises against flight. With Irene's help, he beats the rap against his Uncle Ralph's accusations. Irene tries once again to get Glenn into college, and then Glenn tells her that he's in love with her. He is not dissuaded by her insistence that this kind of feeling is common in a therapist/patient relationship. Tempted as she may be, Irene resists his charms. To escape this romantic entanglement, she agrees to a longstanding marriage proposal from Glenn's Uncle Phil.

In a rage, Glenn runs off with Noreen, though he still has time to pick a fight with gloating cousin Cliff (played by Gary Lockwood). Alas, Cliff dies, more from a heart condition than the mauling. Once more back in court, Phil prosecutes his nephew, carefully concealing his son's heart condition from the court... until Irene attempts to kill herself. Glenn goes to her bedside, declares his love, and then heads off to college, with a letter from Irene that his short story is soon to be published.

Songs: "Wild In The Country," "I Slipped I Stumbled I Fell," "In My Way," "Husky Dusky Day"

Elvis as Glenn Tyler in 1961's *Wild in the Country*.

WILKINSON, JOHN R.
(B. 1945)

Rhythm guitarist Wilkinson was drafted into Elvis' TCB Band for the opening engagement at the International Hotel in 1969. He worked with Elvis right up to the end in 1977.

Born in Washington, D.C. on July 3, 1945, Wilkinson grew up in Springfield, Missouri where he was something of a musical prodigy and very much an Elvis fan. Wilkinson had actually met Elvis in 1956, backstage before a show in his hometown. They chatted for an hour and Wilkinson, a precocious 11-year-old, told Elvis that he could play guitar better than him. Elvis gave the kid a chance to prove it. As the boy was leaving, Elvis told him that he knew one day they'd meet again.

Elvis' prophecy came true multiple times. He met Wilkinson again as a kid, and once more in 1965, when Wilkinson was a regular RCA studio musician. In 1969, out of the blue Elvis called Wilkinson to ask him if he wanted to join the band he was putting together, after catching sight of the guitarist on a local Los Angeles TV show. At that time, Wilkinson had his own group, "The Good Times Singers," who were signed to RCA. He had also been part of the Kingston Trio, and had worked on sessions by folk revival artists Gordon Lightfoot and Peter, Paul and Mary.

Elvis sometimes flew Wilkinson out from LA to Graceland so that they could play together. Wilkinson has described himself as a "part-time bodyguard and full-time friend."

After playing more than eleven hundred shows with Elvis, Wilkinson left the music business and worked in the defense industry. He suffered a stroke in the late Eighties. Since then, he has returned to performing as a singer.

Book:

My *Life Before, During and After Elvis Presley,* by John Wilkinson and Nick Moretti, BookSurge Pub., 2006.

WILL

Elvis made his will in March 1977, less than six months before he died. He made provisions to support Vernon, his Grandma and Lisa Marie, who was his sole heir, and named Vernon as his executor. The Will was witnessed by Charlie Hodge, girlfriend Ginger Alden, and Ann Smith. Elvis also made provisions to any relatives who, in Vernon's estimation, were adjudged to be in dire need.

Like so much in his life, Elvis' will has attracted some controversy. Over the years, Elvis had told friends and girlfriends that he had made arrangements in his will to take care of them. Cousin Billy Smith later publicly claimed that the will was a fake, and did not reflect the handwritten version he had witnessed Elvis write, which contained a number of specific bequests to friends and family. Billy Smith recalls that the will Elvis signed was 17 pages long, not 13 pages as publicly released. Claims have been made that Vernon either couldn't or wouldn't make good on Elvis' bequests to people outside his immediate family. Billy Smith has also suggested that Vernon altered Gladys's will. Author Patrick Lacy has also questioned the handwriting on Elvis' revised will.

Under the terms of his will, Lisa Marie was not to receive her inheritance until her 25th birthday. Priscilla Presley took over responsibility for this bequest following Vernon's death in 1979—in the intervening year, Vernon had appointed her as an executor.

Hope Lange, Elvis and Colonel Tom Parker on the set of *Wild in the Country,* ca 1960.

MARTY LACKER: "Elvis trusted certain people. He would sometimes just tell them what he wanted. Same thing with his last will and testament. He told his father what he wanted in the will, and he trusted his father to put it in there."

LAST WILL AND TESTAMENT OF ELVIS A. PRESLEY, DECEASED, FILED AUGUST 22, 1977

LAST WILL AND TESTAMENT OF ELVIS PRESLEY

I, Elvis A. Presley, a resident and citizen of Shelby County, Tennessee, being of sound mind and disposing memory, do hereby make, publish and declare this instrument to be my last will and testament, hereby revoking any and all wills and codicils by me at any time heretofore made.

ITEM I—DEBTS, EXPENSES AND TAXES

I direct my Executor, hereinafter named, to pay all of my matured debts and my funeral expenses, as well as the costs and expenses of the administration of my estate, as soon after my death as practicable. I further direct that all estate, inheritance, transfer and succession taxes which are payable by reason of my death, whether or not with respect to property passing under this will, be paid out of my residuary estate; and I hereby waive on behalf of my estate any right to recover from any person any part of such taxes so paid. My Executor, in his sole discretion, may pay from my domiciliary estate all or any portion of the costs of ancillary administration and similar proceedings in other jurisdictions.

ITEM II—INSTRUCTIONS CONCERNING PERSONAL PROPERTY: ENJOYMENT IN SPECIE

I anticipate that included as a part of my property and estate at the time of my death will be tangible personal property of various kinds, characters and values, including trophies and other items accumulated by me during my professional career. I hereby specifically instruct all concerned that my Executor, herein appointed, shall have complete freedom and discretion as to disposal of any and all such property so long as he shall act in good faith and in the best interest of my estate and my beneficiaries, and his discretion so exercised shall not be subject to question by anyone whomsoever.

I hereby expressly authorize my Executor and my Trustee, respectively and successively, to permit any beneficiary of any and all trusts created hereunder to enjoy in specie the use or benefit of any household goods, chattels, or other tangible personal property (exclusive of choses in action, cash, stocks, bonds or other securities) which either my Executor or my Trustees may receive in kind, and my Executor and my Trustees shall not be liable for any consumption, damage, injury to or loss of any tangible property so used, nor shall the beneficiaries of any trusts hereunder or their executors or administrators be liable for any consumption, damage, injury to or loss of any tangible personal property so used.

ITEM III—REAL ESTATE

If I am the owner of any real estate at the time of my death, I instruct and empower my Executor and my Trustee (as the case may be) to hold such real estate for investment, or to sell same, or any portion thereof, as my Executor or my Trustee (as the case may be) shall in his sole judgment determine to be for the best interest of my estate and the beneficiaries thereof.

ITEM IV—RESIDUARY TRUST

After payment of all debts, expenses and taxes as directed under Item I hereof, I give, devise, and bequeath all the rest, residue, and remainder of my estate, including all lapsed legacies and devises, and any property over which I have a power of appointment, to my Trustee, hereinafter named, in trust for the following purposes:

(a) The Trustee is directed to take, hold, manage, invest and reinvest the corpus of the trust and to collect the income therefrom in accordance with the rights, powers, duties, authority and discretion hereinafter set forth. The Trustee is directed to pay all the expenses, taxes and costs incurred in the management of the trust estate out of the income thereof.

(b) After payment of all expenses, taxes and costs incurred in the management of the trust estate, the Trustee is authorized to accumulate the net income or to pay or apply so much of the net income and such portion of the principal at any time and from time to time to time for the health, education, support, comfortable maintenance and welfare of: (1) My daughter, Lisa Marie Presley, and any other lawful issue I might have, (2) my grandmother, Minnie Mae Presley, (3) my father, Vernon E. Presley, and (4) such other relatives of mine living at the time of my death who in the absolute discretion of my Trustees are in need of emergency assistance for any of the above mentioned purposes and the Trustee is able to make such distribution without affecting the ability of the trust to meet the present needs of the first three numbered categories of beneficiaries herein mentioned or to meet the reasonably expected future needs of the first three classes of beneficiaries herein mentioned. Any decision of the Trustee as to whether or not distribution shall be made, and also as to the amount of such distribution, to any of the persons described hereunder shall be final and conclusive and not subject to question by any legatee or beneficiary hereunder.

(c) Upon the death of my Father, Vernon E. Presley, the Trustee is instructed to make no further distributions to the fourth category of beneficiaries and such beneficiaries shall cease to have any interest whatsoever in this trust.

(d) Upon the death of both my said father and my said grandmother, the Trustee is directed to divide the Residuary Trust into separate and equal trusts, creating one such equal trust for each of my lawful children then surviving and one such equal trust for the living issue collectively, if any, of any deceased child of mine. The share, if any, for the issue of any such deceased child, shall immediately vest in such issue in equal shares but shall be subject to the provisions of Item V herein. Separate books and records shall be kept for each trust, but it shall not be necessary that a physical division of the assets be made as to each trust.

The Trustee may from time to time distribute the whole or any part of the net income or principal from each of the aforesaid trusts as the Trustee, in its uncontrolled discretion, considers necessary or desirable to provide for the comfortable support, education, maintenance, benefit and general welfare of each of my children. Such distributions may be made directly to such beneficiary or to any person standing in the place of a parent or to the guardian of the person of such beneficiary and without responsibility on my Trustee to see to the application of any such distributions and in making such distributions, the Trustee shall take into account all other sources of funds known by the Trustee to be available for each respective beneficiary for such purpose.

(e) As each of my respective children attains the age of twenty-five (25) years and provided that both my father and my grandmother then be deceased, the trust created hereunder for such child shall terminate, and all the remainder of the assets then contained in said trust shall be distributed to such child so attaining the age of twenty-five (25) years outright and free of further trust.

(f) If any of my children for whose benefit a trust has been created hereunder should die before attaining the age of twenty-five (25) years,

then the trust created for such child shall terminate on his death, and all remaining assets then contained in said trust shall be distributed outright and free of further trust and in equal shares to the surviving issue of such deceased child but subject to the provisions of Item V herein; but if there be no such surviving issue, then to the brothers and sisters of such deceased child in equal shares, the issue of any other deceased child being entitled collectively to their deceased parent's share. Nevertheless, if any distribution otherwise becomes payable outright and free of trust under the provisions of this paragraph (f) of the Item IV of my will to a beneficiary for whom the Trustee is then administering a trust for the benefit of such beneficiary under provisions of this last will and testament, such distribution shall not be paid outright to such beneficiary but shall be added to and become a part of the trust so being administered for such beneficiary by the Trustee.

ITEM V—DISTRIBUTION TO MINOR CHILDREN

If any share of corpus of any trust established under this will becomes distributable outright and free of trust to any beneficiary before said beneficiary has attained the age of eighteen (18) years, then said share shall immediately vest in said beneficiary, but the Trustee shall retain possession of such share during the period in which such beneficiary is under the age of eighteen (18) years, and, in the meantime, shall use and expend so much of the income and principal of each share as the Trustee deems necessary and desirable for the care, support, and education of such beneficiary, and any income not so expended shall be added to the principal. The Trustee shall have with respect to each share so retained all the power and discretion had with respect to such trust generally.

ITEM VI—ALTERNATE DISTRIBUTEES

In the event that all of my descendants should be deceased at any time prior to the time for the termination of the trusts provided for herein, then in such event all of my estate and all the assets of every trust to be created hereunder (as the case may be) shall then distributed outright in equal shares to my heirs at law per stripes.

ITEM VII—UNENFORCEABLE PROVISIONS

If any provisions of this will are unenforceable, the remaining provisions shall, nevertheless, be carried into effect.

ITEM VIII—LIFE INSURANCE

If my estate is the beneficiary of any life insurance on my life at the time of my death, I direct that the proceeds therefrom will be used by my Executor in payment of the debts, expenses and taxes listed in Item I of this will, to the extent deemed advisable by the Executor. All such proceeds not so used are to be used by my Executor for the purpose of satisfying the devises and bequests contained in Item IV herein.

ITEM IX—SPENDTHRIFT PROVISION

I direct that the interest of any beneficiary in principal or income of any trust created hereunder shall not be subject to claims of creditors or others, nor to legal process, and may not be voluntarily or involuntarily alienated or encumbered except as herein provided. Any bequests contained herein for any female shall be for her sole and separate use, free from the debts, contracts and control of any husband she may ever have.

ITEM X—PROCEEDS FROM PERSONAL SERVICES

All sums paid after my death (either to my estate or to any of the trusts created hereunder) and resulting from personal services rendered by me during my lifetime, including, but not limited

Vernon Presley leaving probate court, August 22, 1977, after filing Elvis' will.

to, royalties of all nature, concerts, motion picture contracts, and personal appearances shall be considered to be income, notwithstanding the provisions of estate and trust law to the contrary.

ITEM XI—EXECUTOR AND TRUSTEE

I appoint as Executor of this, my last will and testament, and as Trustee of every trust required to be created hereunder, my said father.

I hereby direct that my said father shall be entitled by his last will and testament, duly probated, to appoint a successor Executor of my estate, as well as a successor Trustee or successor Trustees of all the trusts to be created under my last will and testament.

If, for any reason, my said father be unable to serve or to continue to serve as Executor and/or as Trustee, or if he be deceased and shall not have appointed a successor Executor or Trustee, by virtue of his last will and testament as stated above, then I appoint National Bank of Commerce, Memphis, Tennessee, or its successor or the institution with which it may merge, as successor Executor and/or as successor Trustee of all trusts required to be established hereunder.

None of the appointees named hereunder, including any appointment made by virtue of the last will and testament of my said father, shall be required to furnish any bond or security for performance of the respective fiduciary duties required hereunder, notwithstanding any rule of law to the contrary.

ITEM XII—POWERS, DUTIES, PRIVILEGES AND IMMUNITIES OF THE TRUSTEE

Except as otherwise stated expressly to the contrary herein, I give and grant to the said Trustee (and to the duly appointed successor Trustee when acting as such) the power to do everything he deems advisable with respect to the administration of each trust required to be established under this, my last will and testament, even though such powers would not be authorized or appropriate for the Trustee under statutory or other rules of law. By way of illustration and not in limitation of the generality of the foregoing grant of power and authority of the Trustee, I give and grant to him plenary power as follows:

(a) To exercise all those powers authorized to fiduciaries under the provisions of the Tennessee Code Annotated, Sections 35-616 to 35-618, inclusive, including any amendments thereto in effect at the time of my death, and the same are expressly referred to and incorporated herein by reference.

(b) Plenary power is granted to the Trustee, not only to relieve him from seeking judicial instruction, but to the extent that the Trustee deems it to be prudent, to encourage determinations freely to be made in favor of persons who are the current income beneficiaries. In such instances the rights of all subsequent beneficiaries are subordinate, and the Trustee shall not be answerable to any subsequent beneficiary for anything done or omitted in favor of a current income beneficiary, but no current income beneficiary may compel any such favorable or preferential treatment. Without in anywise minimizing or impairing the scope of this declaration of intent, it includes investment policy, exercise of discretionary power to pay or apply principal and income, and determination principal and income questions;

(c) It shall be lawful for the Trustee to apply any sum that is payable to or for the benefit of a minor (or any other person who in the judgment of the Trustee, is incapable of making proper disposition thereof) by payments in discharge of the costs and expenses of educating, maintaining and supporting said beneficiary, or to make payment to anyone with whom said beneficiary resides or who has the care or custody of the beneficiary, temporarily or permanently, all without intervention of any guardian or like fiduciary. The receipt of anyone to whom payment is so authorized to be

made shall be a complete discharge of the Trustee without obligation on his part to see to the further application thereof, and without regard to other resources that the beneficiary may have, or the duty of any other person to support the beneficiary;

(d) In dealing with the Trustee, no grantee, pledgee, vendee, mortgagee, lessee or other transferee of the trust properties, or any part thereof, shall be bound to inquire with respect to the purpose or necessity of any such disposition or to see to the application of any consideration therefore paid to the Trustee.

ITEM XIII—CONCERNING THE TRUSTEE AND THE EXECUTOR

(a) If at any time the Trustee shall have reasonable doubt as to his power, authority or duty in the administration of any trust herein created, it shall be lawful for the Trustee to obtain the advice and counsel of reputable legal counsel without resorting to the courts for instructions; and the Trustee shall be fully absolved from all liability and damage or detriment to the various trust estates or any beneficiary thereunder by reason of anything done, suffered or omitted pursuant to advice of said counsel given and obtained in good faith, provided that nothing contained herein shall be construed to prohibit or prevent the Trustee in all proper cases from applying to a court of competent jurisdiction for instructions in the administration of the trust assets in lieu of obtaining advice of counsel.

(b) In managing, investing, and controlling the various trust estates, the Trustee shall exercise the judgment and care under the circumstances then prevailing, which men of prudence, discretion and judgment exercise in the management of their own affairs, not in regard to speculation, but in regard to the permanent disposition of their funds, considering the probable income as well as the probable safety of their capital, and, in addition, the purchasing power of income distribution to beneficiaries.

(c) My Trustee (as well as my Executor) shall be entitled to reasonable and adequate compensation for the fiduciary services rendered by him.

(d) My Executor and his successor Executor shall have the same rights, privileges, powers and immunities herein granted to my Trustee wherever appropriate.

(e) In referring to any fiduciary hereunder, for purposes of construction, masculine pronouns may include a corporate fiduciary and neutral pronouns may include an individual fiduciary.

ITEM XIV—LAW AGAINST PERPETUITIES

(a) Having in mind the rule against perpetuities, I direct that (notwithstanding anything contained to the contrary in this last will and testament) each trust created under this will (except such trusts as have heretofore vested in compliance with such rule or law) shall end, unless sooner terminated under other provisions of this will, twenty-one (21) years after the death of the last survivor of such of the beneficiaries hereunder as are living at the time of my death; and thereupon that the property held in trust shall be distributed free of all trust to the persons then entitled to receive the income and/or principal therefrom, in the proportion in which they are then entitled to receive such income.

(b) Notwithstanding anything else contained in this will to the contrary, I direct that if any distribution under this will becomes payable to a person for whom the Trustee is then administering a trust created hereunder for the benefit of such person, such distribution shall be made to such trust and not to the beneficiary outright, and the funds so passing to such trust shall become a part thereof as corpus and be administered and distributed to the same extent and purpose as if such funds had been a part of such a trust at its inception.

ITEM XV—PAYMENT OF ESTATE AND INHERITANCE TAXES

Notwithstanding the provisions of Item X herein, I authorize my Executor to use such sums received by my estate after my death and resulting from my personal services as identified in Item X as he deems necessary and advisable in order to pay the taxes referred to in Item I of my said will.

In WITNESS WHEREOF, I, the said ELVIS A. PRESLEY, do hereunto set my hand and seal in the presence of two (2) competent witnesses, and in their presence do publish and declare this instrument to be my Last Will and Testament, this 3 day of March, 1977.

[Signed by Elvis A. Presley]
ELVIS A. PRESLEY

The foregoing instrument, consisting of this and eleven (11) preceding typewritten pages, was signed, sealed, published and declared by ELVIS A. PRESLEY, the Testator, to be his Last Will and Testament, in our presence, and we, at his request and in his presence and in the presence of each other, have hereunto subscribed our names as witnesses, this 3 day of March, 1977, at Memphis, Tennessee.

[Signed by Ginger Alden]
Ginger Alden residing at 4152 Royal Crest Place

[Signed by Charles F. Hodge]
Charles F. Hodge residing at 3764 Elvis Presley Blvd.

[Signed by Ann Dewey Smith]
Ann Dewey Smith residing at 2237 Court Avenue.

State of Tennessee
County of Shelby

Ginger Alden, Charles F. Hodge, and Ann Dewey Smith, after being first duly sworn, make oath or affirm that the foregoing Last Will and Testament was signed by ELVIS A. PRESLEY and for and at the time acknowledged, published and declared by him to his Last Will and Testament, in the sight and presence of us, the undersigned, who at his request and in his sight and presence, and in the sight and presence of each other, have subscribed our names as attesting witnesses on the 3 day of March, 1977, and we further make oath or affirm that the Testator was of sound mind and disposing memory and not acting under fraud, menace or undue influence of any person, and was more than eighteen (18) years of age; and that each of the attesting witnesses is more than eighteen (18) years of age.

[Signed by Ginger Alden]
Ginger Alden

[Signed by Charles F. Hodge]
Charles F. Hodge

[Signed by Ann Dewey Smith]
Ann Dewey Smith

SWORN TO AND SUBSCRIBED before me this 3 day of March, 1977.
Drayton Beecher Smith II Notary Public

My commission expires:
August 8, 1979

Admitted to probate and Ordered Recorded August 22, 1977
Joseph W. Evans, Judge

Recorded August 22, 1977
B.J. Dunavant, Clerk
By: Jan Scott, D.C.

WILLIAM MORRIS AGENCY

Founded in 1898, this venerable talent agency represents clients in every branch of the entertainment business and has become the largest talent agency in the world. In the Fifties and Sixties, the agency represented a veritable who's who of showbiz, from Frank Sinatra to Elvis Presley, Marilyn Monroe, Katherine Hepburn, Jack Lemmon, Walter Matthau and Steve McQueen. In the Sixties, it became a music industry titan with the Rolling Stones, Beach Boys and Sonny & Cher on its books, as well as building up a thriving literary business.

In early 1955, one of the first things that Colonel Tom Parker did when he was pursuing Elvis was to get his contacts at the Agency to help organize bookings and map out the young singer's future career. Even before the Colonel had any official remit to manage Elvis, he was telling agent Harry Kalcheim how well his new client was suited to TV and to a career in the movies.

Elvis' first national TV slot, on "Stage Show," was arranged through a competing agency; according to some sources, it was Bill Randle rather than the Colonel who set up the debut performance. Parker and the William Morris Agency then got into gear and alerted Hollywood agencies about Elvis' upcoming TV appearance so that they could see his potential for themselves.

Elvis signed an exclusive representation contract with the Agency on January 31, 1956. The agreement gave the Colonel approval of all contracts offered to Elvis. Remarkably, it appears that the deal with William Morris was verbal—a gentleman's agreement between the Colonel and the studio head.

After quickly procuring Elvis a screen test and deal with Paramount Studios, William Morris agents landed Elvis a two-week stint in Las Vegas at the New Frontier Hotel, in the belief that this high-profile exposure would rapidly spread his renown beyond his home market. It turned out that Las Vegas wasn't ready for Elvis: what had initially started as a month-long engagement was reduced to two weeks.

Parker was reputedly livid with the agency for underselling his boy on his first movie contract: Elvis received $25,000 for his first picture, less than his co-stars were getting. The Colonel spent the next decade raising Elvis' earnings on a film-by-film basis.

Then-agency head Abe Lastfogel, who had already worked with Parker in the past, personally intervened to clinch a three-movie deal with 20th Century-Fox to run alongside the Paramount commitment.

Though Elvis brought in a 10% commission to the agency, as a client he had little or no direct contact with William Morris. Colonel Parker, on the other hand, was at his power-wielding best in his relations with William Morris. For years, he had a number of assistants on from the Agency to help out at his various offices. Alanna Nash writes that the Colonel expended a great deal of time and energy in humiliating people at the Agency through pranks and tricks.

WILLIAMS, HANK
(B. HIRAM KING "HANK" WILLIAMS, 1923-1953)

Honky Tonk phenomenon Hank Williams was the first superstar of Country. He had a meteoric career that was cruelly cut short by a drugs overdose in 1953, when he was just 29.

Born near Mount Olive, Alabama on September 17, 1923, Williams grew up in a family of poor Baptist sharecroppers. Like Elvis, Williams had his first singing experiences in church. Elvis' life has rather more parallels with Williams' than fans

might have wanted: in addition to a premature death hastened by excessive use of pharmaceuticals, Williams' family was marshaled by a strong mother; the first time that Williams played the Grand Ole Opry in 1949, he was forced to keep singing "Lovesick Blues" over and over due to popular acclaim, much like Dewey Phillips had to spin Elvis' first single umpteen times to satisfy clamoring fans.

Williams got his break playing on Montgomery, Alabama radio station WSFA while still a teenager. Soon afterwards, he put together his band, the Drifting Cowboys. After a spell writing songs for others, Williams' recording career blossomed and he moved to the Louisiana Hayride, before progressing to the Grand Ole Opry. In 1951, Williams' "Cold, Cold Heart" was the top song on the Country charts for almost a whole year. His fame spread beyond a Country audience when Tony Bennett made a pop chart cover of the song. However, his penchant for drink and drugs soon led to cancellation of his Grand Ole Opry contract. After Williams died of a heart attack triggered by substance abuse, more than 20,000 people attended his funeral, including most of the country music business.

Elvis was briefly in line to star in a Hank Williams biopic in 1961, before the Colonel decided to shelve the project (or Williams' wife objected to Elvis overshadowing the subject of the picture, depending on accounts).

Elvis covered William's "Your Cheatin' Heart" in 1958 and "I'm So Lonesome I Could Cry" during his Aloha From Hawaii performance and album. He frequently sang Hank Williams songs for pleasure at home with pals—"I Can't Help It" is one that has made it onto disc. Elvis occasionally covered Williams' songs "Jambalaya" and "Take These Chains From My Heart" on stage in the Seventies. Other trademark Williams songs that Elvis might have enjoyed at home include "Move It On Over" and "Hey, Good Lookin'."

Williams was an original inductee to the Country Music Hall of Fame in 1961. Both his son (Hank Williams, Jr.) and grandson (Hank Williams III) have followed in his footsteps and become country music singers.

JOHNNY CASH: "Hank Williams is like a Cadillac. He'll always be the standard for comparison."

WILLS, BOB
(B. JAMES ROBERT WILLS, 1905-1975)

In October 1955, Elvis took in a Houston performance by the fiddle-playing "King of Western Swing." Wills' best-known period was when he worked with the band The Texas Playboys through the Forties, though he continued to perform into the Sixties. He was inducted into the Country Hall of Music in 1968.

Elvis recorded Wills song "Faded Love." He also sang "San Antonio Rose" at home and occasionally live.

WILSON, BRIAN
(B. 1942)

Elvis met the driving force behind the Beach Boys and once-renowned recluse Wilson in March 1975, when both of them were recording at RCA's Sunset Boulevard facilities. According to Wilson's autobiography, the encounter ended abruptly when Wilson made an unexpected karate move on Elvis a second time, after Elvis had already asked him not to do so.

WILSON, JACKIE "SONNY"
(B. JACK LEROY WILSON, 1934-1984)

Jackie Wilson got his break singing with Billy Ward & the Dominoes in 1953, after seminal lead singer Clyde McPhatter left to form his own group, the Drifters. So explosive was Wilson's stage presence that he earned the epithet "Mr. Excitement"; a few years later, Wilson was being promoted as "the Black Elvis."

In Las Vegas in November 1956, Elvis went to watch Wilson perform with Billy Ward and his Dominoes four (by some accounts six) times. Elvis was so impressed with the singer's power and attack that he tried it out on his own songs in late December 1956, when he jammed with fellow Sun artists Carl Perkins, Jerry Lee Lewis and Johnny Cash in what became known as the Million Dollar Quartet session. At the time, Elvis told his pals that while Wilson was covering "Don't Be Cruel," ". . . he got much better, and boy much better than that record of mine. Man, he was cutting it . . . I was under the table when he got through singing."

Wilson was born in Detroit, Michigan on June 9, 1934. A former Golden Gloves boxer, he launched into a solo singing career after gaining fame with Billy Ward and the Dominoes. In 1957, he made it to the upper echelons of the Billboard Top 100 with Berry Gordy-penned hits "Reet Petite" and "Lonely Teardrops." Music historians consider Wilson to be an important precursor to the emergence of Soul for the way he combined R & B with more pop-styled arrangements.

Elvis finally met the "Black Elvis" in Los Angeles in 1966, a couple of years after his top-5 hit "Baby Workout," and five years after Wilson was shot by a jealous female. The occasion was when Elvis took in Wilson's show at The Trip on Sunset Boulevard. As they chatted afterwards, Wilson shared a diet trick: swallow salt tablets, drink plenty of water and then do something physical—like a show—and sweat the weight off.

The two singers got on so well that Elvis invited Wilson to visit him on the MGM lot. Wilson carried around the autographed photo Elvis gave him that day for the rest of his life. They remained friends until Wilson's heart attack in 1975, after which he went into an irreversible coma that lasted almost 9 years. Elvis wired his fellow-singer some money (reputedly $30,000) to help with his the medical bills.

"WILLOW WEEP FOR ME"

A song written in the early Thirties by Ann Ronell, which Elvis is reputed to have sung during a spontaneous performance at the Lido in Paris during his 1959 visit.

"WINGS OF AN ANGEL (THE PRISONER'S SONG)"

Elvis gave this song a studio run-through early in the morning of January 17, 1968 that never saw official release due to some colorful language. The bootleggers at Angel Records sprung it from the vaults in 1993. The song, known as "The Prisoner's Song," was a huge hit for Vernon Dalhart back in 1924. Written by Guy Massey, it has the distinction of being the first ever million-selling country record.

WINGS OF AN ANGEL

Not one but two unofficial Elvis releases, both from 1993: one on Angel Records, the other on German Records, both of studio outtakes.

"WINTER WONDERLAND"

Elvis gave this Christmas classic (written by Richard Smith and Felix Bernard in the mid-Thirties) a country rock treatment when he laid it down in Nashville on May 16, 1971, for initial release on *Elvis Sings The Wonderful World Of Christmas*.

Elvis' version of the song has since appeared on Yule compilations including *Blue Christmas*, *If Every Day Was Like Christmas*, *Christmas Peace* and *Elvis Christmas*.

WINTERS, SHELLEY
(B. SHIRLEY SCHRIFT,, 1922-2006)

The two-time Oscar winner played Gladys Presley in 1979 biopic *Elvis*. She attended some of Elvis' Las Vegas shows in the Seventies too. Winters' most famous on-screen roles include *A Place in the Sun* (1951), *The Diary of Anne Frank* (1959) and *The Poseidon Adventure* (1972).

WISCONSIN

- Green Bay
Elvis was at the Brown County Veterans Memorial Coliseum on April 28, 1977.

- LaCrosse
Elvis played the Mary B. Sawyer Auditorium on May 14, 1956. He incurred the wrath of a former Army Intelligence Officer for signing autographs on female fans' thighs and bellies.

- Madison
Elvis played the Dane County Coliseum on October 19, 1976. He returned for one of his last ever shows, on June 24, 1977.

- Milwaukee
Elvis and the TCB band appeared at the Milwaukee Auditorium Arena on June 14 and 15, 1972. They played the Arena on June 28, 1974 (bootlegged on *In Dreams Of Yesterday*), and then again on April 27, 1977.

"WISDOM OF THE AGES"

Bill Giant, Bernie Baum and Florence Kaye get the credit for this *Harum Scarum* song that Elvis recorded in Nashville on February 25, 1965. It failed to survive through to the finished movie, but found a berth on the LP soundtrack.

Appearances since the film have been limited to the *Double Features* reissue and the FTD *Harum Scarum* release, which also offers an alternate take.

WISE, FRED
(1915-1966)

A regular on several songwriting teams that churned out songs for Elvis, predominantly for his Sixties movies. He would no doubt have upped his tally of Elvis songs if he had not died midway through the decade.

In partnership with Elvis regulars Randy Starr and Ben Weisman (and occasionally with Claude Demetrius, Norman Blagman, Dick Manning, Jack Lloyd and Dolores Fuller), Wise earned credits on close to thirty Elvis originals. Non-Elvis hits for the lyricist include "A—You're Adorable," which he wrote with Buddy Kaye.

Elvis on stage in Green Bay, Wisconsin April 28, 1977.

"WITCHCRAFT"

Elvis recorded the B-side to "Bossa Nova Baby" on May 26, 1963 in Nashville. On release in October 1963, the hi-energy track made it to #32 in the *Billboard* singles charts. Written by Dave Bartholomew and Pearl King and initially a 1955 R&B hit for the Spiders, "Witchcraft" made its Elvis album debut on *Elvis' Gold Records Vol. 4*. It has since appeared on *Worldwide Gold Award Hits Vol. 2*, *For The Asking*, and *From Nashville To Memphis*.

The first take from the session appeared many years later on *Collectors Gold*; a further alternate has since come out on *Today Tomorrow & Forever*.

Elvis sang the famous Sinatra song (written by Carolyn Leigh and Cy Coleman) of the same name in a duet recorded on March 1960 for *The Welcome Home Elvis* Show, while The Voice sang "Love Me Tender." This curio of a double-icon duet is on *From Nashville To Memphis*.

"WITH A SONG IN MY HEART"

Elvis recorded this Rodgers and Hart standard in May 1965 during the Radio Recorders session for the *Frankie & Johnny* soundtrack, though it was never officially released. It does appear on unofficial record *Real Fun On Stage . . . And In The Studio* and on an eponymously-titled bootleg.

"WITHOUT A SONG"

Elvis recited lyrics from this song—originally recorded by Paul Whiteman back in 1930—as part of his acceptance speech to the Jaycees in January 1971. The song was written in 1929 for the musical "Great Day" by Billy Rose, Edward Eliscu and Vincent Youmans, though Elvis' indefatigable memory for music would more likely have been triggered by Roy Hamilton's 1955 version (or by Perry Como's 1970 cover).

"WITHOUT HIM"

Elvis recorded this Mylon LeFevre gospel song for the *How Great Thou Art* album in Nashville on May 27, 1966. Elvis gospel fans have since found it on gospel anthologies *Amazing Grace* and *Peace In The Valley*; it is also on *Christmas Peace*.

Alternates have appeared this millennium on *Elvis: Close Up* and FTD release *So High*.

"WITHOUT LOVE (THERE IS NOTHING)"

Elvis recorded this 1957 Clyde McPhatter powerhouse ballad (written by Danny Small) at American Studio in Memphis on January 23, 1969. It received its initial issue on the *From Memphis To Vegas—From Vegas To Memphis* and *Back in Memphis* albums soon afterwards. Tom Jones took the song into the top 5 the following year with his single version.

Later Elvis releases include *The Memphis Record*, *From Nashville To Memphis* and *Suspicious Minds: The Memphis 1969 Anthology*.

Official alternate takes have appeared on *Suspicious Minds: The Memphis 1969 Anthology* and FTD release *The Memphis Sessions*.

"WITHOUT YOU"

Elvis auditioned for Sun Records in June 1954 with this ballad that Sam Phillips had purchased through Nashville publisher Red Wortham. Written by a prison inmate, Phillips needed to find a singer for the song. On Marion Keisker's suggestion, he called in Elvis to see if he might be the one. Elvis did not impress with this particular tune, but he did enough for the calback at which he came up with his idiosyncratic reworking of "That's All Right (Mama)."

Elvis was all set to sing a Leiber and Stoller song of this same name for movie *Loving You*, before it was dropped.

"WOLF CALL"

Elvis recorded this track for *Girl Happy* on June 12, 1964 at Radio Recorders—another Bill Giant / Bernie Baum / Florence Kaye quickie. After appearing on the soundtrack LP, it has resurfaced on *Double Features: Girl Happy/ Harum Scarum* and the FTD *Girl Happy* release.

"WOMAN WITHOUT LOVE"

Elvis laid down this Jerry Chesnut country track in the early hours of March 12, 1975 in Nashville for one of his final albums, *Today*. The song had first been released in 1968 by singers Johnny Darrell and Bob Luman.

Later releases of Elvis' version are confined to compilations such as *Love Songs*. It's on the 2005 FTD version of *Today* too, alongside the undubbed session mix.

WOMEN

Biographers concur that from his earliest years, Elvis preferred the company of girls to boys. The strong figure at home during his upbringing was his mother; as a boy among boys, he was frequently a target for teasing.

Girls—and later millions of women—were captivated by a quality in Elvis that Pamela Clarke Keogh defines as "an aching kind of vulnerability, an unspecified yearning."

The school kid who dressed strange and had trouble getting a date discovered after his performance at the Humes High School annual show in 1953 that he had suddenly become quite a catch. Within a year and a half, he needed paid security to stay safe among his wilder, more emboldened female admirers.

As long as his life wasn't in danger, Elvis was happy to give female fans the time of day and more. Dozens of pretty fans had the thrill of being invited up to Elvis' Audubon Drive home, Graceland, and his Los Angeles rented homes in the Sixties to hang out and have a good time. By way of example, junior high school girls Heidi Heissen, Gloria Mowel and Frances Forbes were regular visitors to Audubon Drive where they stayed up late, played with make-up, and had pillow fights and tickle battles. According to women who have kissed and told, if and when things became sexual, Elvis' behavior was more sophomoric than predatory.

Elvis historians concur that apart from a few circumscribed periods of sexual promiscuity, Elvis was just as happy to be in female company as to have sex. More or less up until he was drafted in 1958, Elvis was a steadfast and loyal to his main Memphis girlfriend—first teen sweetheart Dixie Locke, then Anita Wood—provided that he was in Memphis. Out on the road, he not surprisingly indulged in his newfound powers of attraction. He also stepped up his conquests during his otherwise lonely Army years.

Elvis was raised to be a Southern gentleman by a Southern Mama. From his earliest girl-friends, Elvis assumed that getting married was a pre-requisite for full sexual intercourse. His life-long habit of scrupulous gentlemanly politeness to the fair sex was yet another weapon in his armament of seduction: he always responded to women with "yes ma'am" or "no ma'am;" throughout his life, he would get up when a woman walked into the room; and he would be displeased if one of his entourage cussed when women were present.

Under his personal moral code, Elvis was appalled if he found out that one of his pals was seeing a divorced woman or, heaven forbid, a married woman. Despite his own freewheeling attitude, for Elvis, purity in a woman was a virtue above all others, hence his predilection for younger, sexually-inexperienced women. As a rule, he did not have sex with women who had given birth: more than one girlfriend was given her marching orders when Elvis found out that she had had a child; after Lisa Marie was born, Elvis was sexually uninterested in Priscilla for many months.

In the Fifties and the Sixties, Elvis was attracted to a definite type: young, petite, discreet, long-haired, and inevitably beautiful. Priscilla and others have recounted how, as young women, they were perfect blank canvases for Elvis to mold. Priscilla says in her memoir that she took up ballet after Elvis mentioned that he liked women dancers' bodies; she learned French because he liked the sound of the language; and she began learning karate to be able to share his hobby. Years later, after they were divorced, she might find herself put onto the phone to one of Elvis' new girlfriends in order to school her on Elvis' likes and dislikes.

In the mid-Sixties, Elvis was faced with a stark choice between a more independent type of woman, soul-mate Ann-Margret, and live-in fiancée Priscilla. Ann-Margret lost out on the grounds that Priscilla was better marriageable material, because she could be expected to stay home and raise children, whereas Ann-Margret made it clear that like Elvis, she wanted to pursue her career.

In differences of opinion with Priscilla, Elvis sometimes reminded her that he belonged to the stronger sex and she to the weaker. A common strand in many Elvis' movies sees him defending downtrodden women—in half a dozen movies, Elvis' character gets into a fight to save a woman's honor, protect her virtue or mete out physical justice to a woman-beater.

Many of Elvis' girlfriends noted a similar trajectory in their relationships with him: enchantment at his little-boy vulnerability, surprise at his genuine interest in them, amazement that they had been chosen, disappointment that they were not the only one, and then the gradual realization that staying with Elvis longterm meant following him in everything he wanted, being there when he called, disappearing when he wanted the space to pursue other interests or women, and listening to his life philosophy and views on the world. Seventies girlfriends could also expect to do a whole lot of mothering and nursing.

In feminist circles, Elvis has not been viewed exclusively as an example of male domination or sexual predation. Some feminist authors argue that Elvis' enormous sex appeal had a liberating effect on female sexuality, while his androgynousness—not dissimilar to Twenties heartthrob Rudolph Valentino—was a sign of more typically female physical and emotional characteristics.

See also GIRLFRIENDS.

ELVIS SAID IN 1962: "I look for a lot of things now that I wouldn't have looked for . . . a sense of humor, their taste for different things . . . their understanding of me and my way of thinking."

ELVIS SAID IN 1974: "Oh Lord, I love 'em . . . you can't live without 'em."

ELVIS SCRIBBLED IN THE MARGINS OF A BOOK: "To have a true soul mate who seeks the same spiritual level as ones self."

PRISCILLA: "Fidelity was very important to him, especially on the woman's part."

JIMMIE RODGERS SNOW: "I just think he wanted them around, it was a sense of insecurity, I guess, because I don't think he was a user. He just loved women, and I think they knew that."

BILLY SMITH: "Elvis related to women more than he did men. He had very few male friends in early childhood."

LAMAR FIKE: "He didn't like women speaking out. . . . That's one reason he liked teenage girls. They weren't a threat."

ARLENE COGAN: "Elvis was crazy about females . . . he really liked all women. He loved to flirt. There was certainly a lot of different women in his life."

LAMAR FIKE: "Elvis' thing with women was they had to baby him and take care of him. Because his mother raised him that way. I've never seen anybody who could bring out the basic instincts in a woman like he could."

PATTI PAGE: "Every woman wanted him to be either her son or her lover."

PRISCILLA: "His role with me was that of lover and father, and with neither could he let down his guard and become fallible or truly intimate. I longed for that, and as a woman, I needed it."

MARY HANCOCK HINDS: "The birth of women's liberation is recorded on the emotionally contorted faces of Elvis' young female audiences who are in the process of tearing down the ancient rules of feminine deportment."

BILLY SMITH: "Elvis thought that women were more trustworthy than men. But he never found exactly what he was looking for in a woman."

PRISCILLA: "He had a little-boy quality that could bring out the mother instinct in any woman, a beguiling way of seeming utterly dependent."

Books:
The Girls' Guide to Elvis: The Clothes, The Hair, The Women, and More!, by Kim Adelman, Broadway, 2002.

"WONDER OF YOU, THE"

Elvis first sang this 1959 Ray Peterson ballad in Las Vegas in February 1970, after clearing with Peterson that he didn't mind. Peterson replied, "You don't have to ask permission; you're Elvis Presley!," to which Elvis modestly quipped, "Yes, I do. You're Ray Peterson." The song was composed by Baker Knight, who initially wrote it with Perry Como in mind.

RCA released a live recording of Elvis' February 19, 1970 performance of the song at the International Hotel. Elvis' inaugural "live" single came out April 1970 with "Mama Liked The Roses" on the flip side. The single sold almost a million copies during a 12-week period, but only just snuck into the US top ten. In the UK, it claimed the top spot for six whole weeks.

The track graced the *On Stage* album in the year it was recorded, since when it has been tracklisted on *Worldwide Gold Award Hits Vol. 2*, *Greatest Hits Vol. 1*, *Walk A Mile In My Shoes*, *Artist Of The Century*, *ELV1S 30 #1 Hits*, *Hitstory*, *Love Elvis*, and on the 2007 versions of *The Essential Elvis Presley* and *Viva Las Vegas*.

Elvis, with long-time girlfriend Anita Wood, at the Alabama Fair in Tupelo (1957).

As an Elvis concert regular in 1970 and 1974/75, there are plenty of official alternate live versions to choose from, in addition to a slew of bootlegs. From 1970, it's on *Platinum—A Life In Music*, *That's The Way It Is—Special Edition* (with video on DVD release *Elvis #1 Hit Performances*), *Live In Las Vegas* and *The Live Greatest Hits*. It's also on FTD releases *Polk Salad Annie* (which also features a rehearsal version) and *The Way It Was*.

Late vintage performances are to be found on *Elvis Aron Presley*, *Elvis Live*, and on FTD discs *It's Midnight*, *Big Boss Man* and *Dixieland Rocks*.

"WONDERFUL WORLD"

A song with the same title but nothing else in common with the Louis Armstrong standard . . . Elvis picked this song, crafted originally by UK songwriting duo Guy Fletcher and Doug Flett for Cliff Richard's entry in the 1968 Eurovision song contest, for *Live a Little, Love a Little*. Elvis laid it down at Western Recorders on March 7, 1968, a scant three months before his 1968 Comeback Special.

The song made its vinyl debut on *Singer Presents Elvis Singing Flaming Star and Others*, followed closely by *Elvis Sings Flaming Star*. Since then, appearances have been restricted to the *Double Features* issue for the movie, *Elvis Inspirational*, and CD reissues of the original albums.

Alternates may be found on *Today Tomorrow & Forever* and FTD release *Out In Hollywood*.

"WONDERFUL WORLD OF CHRISTMAS, THE"

A Charles Tobias / Albert T. Frisch composition that Elvis recorded on May 16, 1971 in Nashville that lent its title to the album *Elvis Sings The Wonderful World Of Christmas*.

It has since added festive cheer to albums *If Every Day Was Like Christmas*, *Elvis Christmas* and *Christmas Peace*.

"WONDERS YOU PERFORM, THE"

An instrumental to which Elvis failed to record a vocal during his July 1973 sessions at Stax, finally released into the world on the 2007 FTD version of *Raised on Rock*. Tammy Wynette had taken the Jerry Chesnut song to the top 5 of the Country chart in 1970.

WOOD, ANITA
(B. 1939)

The most commonly-told version of how Elvis met Anita Wood, a 19-year-old blond beauty queen and aspiring entertainer who was Elvis' first serious girlfriend after becoming a star, is through pal George Klein, who introduced them in July 1957. She was not a particular Elvis fan, though as a DJ on WHHM she knew his music, and had watched him perform on "The Ed Sullivan Show."

Anita and Elvis in Waco, Texas, ca 1958.

Anita's recollection of the meeting is that Elvis asked Lamar Fike to call her up after seeing her on "Top Ten Dance Party," a Saturday show on local Memphis TV, hosted by Wink Martindale. To Lamar's shock, Anita said that she couldn't meet Elvis as she already had a date that evening, and she refused to break it on principle. A week later, Fike called again, and soon after Elvis went round to her house. Anita also knew entourage member Cliff Gleaves, who was from her home town of Jackson, Tennessee.

Anita shared her first date with Elvis with three entourage pals. They went to a drive-in for a few dozen hamburgers. She accepted Elvis' invitation to go back to Graceland for a personal tour, but up in his bedroom she refused to let him "get to first base." Elvis arranged for her to be taken home. On subsequent dates, they would drive around town, hang out at Graceland, or go out to the Memphian Theater, the Fairgrounds or the skating rink. They would also sometimes drive around town incognito on one of Elvis' motorbikes—sometimes to Tupelo—or in his Chevy panel truck.

When they started dating, Anita won a small role in a Hollywood film as a prize for a beauty contest. Though she landed a seven-year contract with Paramount, she walked away from a possible movie career because Elvis wanted her in Memphis, and that was more important to her than stardom.

Elvis gave Anita Wood a diamond and sapphire ring not long after they started dating. He bought her a 1956 Ford just before he left for his Army service. When he was on basic training, Anita stayed at the home of Sergeant Bill Norwood and his wife on base, so that Elvis could visit in the evenings and on weekends. Later they met up on weekends at the home of Eddie Fadal, a friend in Waco.

When Elvis was on furlough from the Army in 1958, Wood had to be in New York to work on the Andy Williams show. However, she remembers this time as the most "normal" part of their relationship; she would fly out to be with him in Texas on weekends, and they would sit around planning their future just like any couple of Army sweethearts.

Elvis was Anita's first boyfriend, and she fell head over heels in love. Elvis was smitten by "Little" or "Little Bit," as he called her—he sometimes also referred to her as Annie. He told her that he never had and never would love anyone like her. Ma Gladys used to sit around with Anita fantasizing about a future when she and Elvis would be married and they would have a little boy.

Anita was all set to visit Elvis after he moved into a private house at Bad Nauheim, until the Colonel scuppered the plan because he feared that the press would view her arrival as a sign that she and Elvis were to be married. Instead, they spoke on the phone and exchanged letters. In one of his love letters, Elvis promised that when the time came to marry, Anita was the one. He advised her to "trust me and keep yourself clean and wholesome because that is the big thing that can determine our lives and happiness together." In another letter, Elvis described himself as "a lonely little boy 5000 miles away," dreaming of a future when they would be married and have lots of little Elvises.

Elvis gave Anita a guitar with inlaid gold letters reading "To Little, from EP" for Christmas 1958, and a French poodle called Littlebit for Christmas 1959. By this time he had met Priscilla Beaulieu, and spent that festive season with her. That didn't stop him from declaring his unwavering and undying love to Anita in letters at the end of 1959.

Anita and Elvis met again on March 7, 1960, on the very first evening that Elvis was back in Memphis after two years away. Wood dyed her hair the same shade of black as Elvis', and received a diamond necklace from her beau. She continued to be his Memphis girl, and continued to stay out of the limelight so that the press did not get wind of how serious their relationship was. She also carried on making records for Sun (including an Elvis-themed tune titled "I'll Wait Forever") and other labels.

Elvis and Anita stayed together through to 1962, when she found a love letter from Priscilla and challenged Elvis about this other woman—until this point, Elvis had told her that Priscilla was just a kid and unimportant to him. The next day, Anita Wood left California for Graceland to challenge Elvis, who persuaded her that there really was nothing to it. A short while later, however, Anita overheard Elvis talking to Vernon about how hard it was for him to choose between the two women in his life. Anita told Elvis that she'd save him the trouble of making the choice by leaving. There were tears all round: for Anita, for Elvis, even for Vernon, who told Anita that he hoped that one day she would return. Elvis' parting words were, "I pray to God I'm doing the right thing here by letting you go."

In an August 1962 public statement, Anita Wood said that she had made her decision because Elvis was not ready to settle down. She did not say that two months earlier, Elvis had spent two weeks shepherding young Priscilla Beaulieu around the delights of Las Vegas.

In 1964, Wood married NFL tight end Johnny Brewer, whose first glimpse of her had been on a night that she walked into the Memphian Theater with Elvis. They had three children, and she has spent many years teaching school in Vicksburg, Mississippi.

Elvis and Anita met again in the Seventies, when she attended one of his Las Vegas shows. Afterwards, backstage, they chatted for an hour. At one point, Elvis ventured the doubt that they had made a mistake. Anita's wise response was that they had done the right thing, because now each of them had their beloved children.

ANITA WOOD SAID: ." . . One reason we got along so good together . . . I wasn't a big fan of his when I met him. And I didn't just fall at his feet, you know . . . I learned to know him. And I fell in love with him. Elvis the man, not Elvis the star."

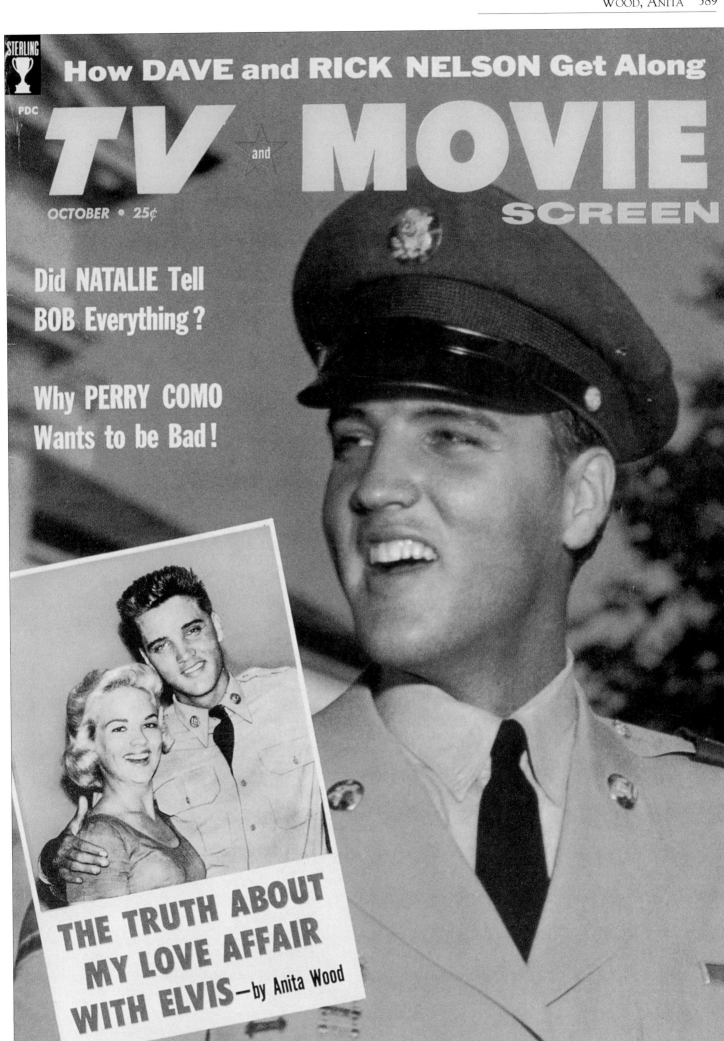

STERLING
PDC

How DAVE and RICK NELSON Get Along

TV and MOVIE SCREEN

OCTOBER • 25¢

Did NATALIE Tell
BOB Everything?

Why PERRY COMO
Wants to be Bad!

THE TRUTH ABOUT
MY LOVE AFFAIR
WITH ELVIS—by Anita Wood

Book:
Elvis: Word for Word, by Jerry Osbourne, published by Harmony, 2000, contains transcripts of Elvis' letters to Anita Wood.

WOOD, BOBBY
(B. 1941)

Keyboard player Bobby Wood knew Elvis from way back in Memphis, when he and his future wife were invited along to one of Elvis' Fairground nights. Even earlier, he had glimpsed Elvis when his family traipsed over to the Memphis Recording Service to use Sam Phillips' cheap recording facilities.

Wood hooked up with Elvis for his famous American Studio sessions in 1969, as part of Chips Moman's house band. During the session, Elvis covered "If I'm A Fool," which had been a hit for Wood back in 1964, before his solo career was curtailed by a serious car accident.

Wood next worked with Elvis at Stax in 1973, on sessions that produced "Promised Land" and "I Got A Thing About You Baby." The previous year, he had been unable to take up Elvis' invitation to go on tour with him.

Bobby Wood has worked with a roll-call of Country greats, and played keyboards for Garth Brooks since he first rose to prominence in the late Eighties. He is also an accomplished songwriter and producer.

WOOD, NATALIE
(B. NATALIA NIKOLAEVNA ZAKHARENKO, 1938-1961)

Child actress Natalie Wood grew up to become one of Hollywood's hottest stars. Famed as a Hollywood "bad girl," she scooped an Oscar nomination aged just 17 for her work in *Rebel Without a Cause* (1955).

Elvis dated Natalie Wood in the fall of 1956. She dropped in on his September 1956 recording session in LA, and accompanied him back to Memphis to meet his folks. Elvis even took her to see the place in Tupelo where he was born and spent his formative years—a pilgrimage he reserved only for special friends. When asked how serious their liaison was likely to become, Wood replied: "Elvis was the only real boy I have ever met . . . But we are both career mindful and at this time we both are committed to our film contracts."

Born in San Francisco, CA on July 20, 1938, before she was ten Wood was nationally known for her performance in *Miracle on 34th Street* (1947). She followed cult movie *Rebel Without a Cause* with another cult picture, opposite John Wayne in *The Searchers* (1956). In the Sixties, she starred in *West Side Story*, and was nominated for Oscars in 1961 and 1963.

Rumors have circulated about the intensity of Elvis and Natalie's brief relationship. Reputedly, Elvis wanted to marry her, but Gladys liked neither her nor her wild-girl ways. Lamar Fike remembers Natalie Wood threatening to jump from the window at the Beverly Wilshire hotel over Elvis. A year after they split up, Wood married fellow actor Robert Wagner, the first of her two marriages to the actor. She went on to make close to sixty movies and TV films, before drowning off Catalina Island aged 43.

"WOODEN HEART"

At his April 28, 1960 session for G.I. Blues at RCA's Hollywood studios, Elvis recorded this Fred Wise, Ben Weisman and Kay Twomey adaptation of traditional German song "Muss I Denn." German-born band leader Bert Kaempfert also helped out in the linguistic conversion from the original Swabian dialect.

Elvis' version made its vinyl debut on the original *G.I. Blues* soundtrack LP. "Wooden Heart" came out as a single in the UK, where it made it to #1 and became one of Elvis' longest selling hits. Naturally, in Germany the song sold like hotcakes in whatever form it was released. In the US, RCA held back until late 1964, when the song came out as the B-side to "Blue Christmas." The label tried again a year later, releasing it as the B-side to "Puppet On A String." Neither time did "Wooden Heart" make it into the *Billboard* Hot 100, partly because Joe Dowell's #1 cover from 1961—the reason that RCA held off releasing the song as a single in the first place—was still fresh in people's minds.

Elvis' "Wooden Heart" has since appeared on *Elvis Sings For Children (And Grown Ups Too)*, *Worldwide 50 Gold Award Hits Vol. 1*, CD reissues of *Elvis' Golden Records Vol. 3*, *Command Performances*, *Elvis Sings For Kids*, the 1997 *G.I. Blues* Deluxe Edition release, *ELVIS 30 #1 Hits*, *Hitstory* and sundry other hits collections.

Alternate takes from the 1960 studio session have surfaced on *Elvis: A Legendary Performer Vol. 4*, *Forever in Love* and *Elvis: Close Up*.

Elvis sang the song live very occasionally towards the end of his career. One rare live foray is on FTD release *Dinner At Eight*.

WOODSON, CRAIG

This L.A.-based bongo artist appeared behind his drums in *Girl Happy* and *Viva Las Vegas*, before becoming a pioneer in world music and ethnomusicography.

WOODWARD, FRED

A Memphis police inspector who, until he died of a heart attack in 1960 aged 46, had been Elvis' friend on the force. Woodward was initially assigned to look after Elvis' personal security in 1956.

"WORDS"

Elvis included this 1967 ballad written by Gibb brothers Barry, Maurice and Robin (aka the Bee Gees) at his opening Las Vegas engagement in August 1969. The first Elvis recording to make it onto vinyl was released on *From Memphis To Vegas* and sister album *In Person*. This performance, recorded on August 25, 1969, has since appeared on *Platinum: A Life In Music*.

Though Elvis only sang "Words" a handful of times, it is amply represented in his discography. Another 1969 performance is on FTD release *Writing For The King*. Footage of Elvis rehearsing and performing the song in July 1970 features in concert documentary *Elvis: That's The Way It Is*. "Words" did not make it onto the original tie-in album, but it is on the 2000 *That's The Way It Is* Special Edition release. Elvis rehearsing the song is on FTD release *The Way It Was*. A further rehearsal and concert performance are to be found on FTD release *One Night In Vegas*.

"WORKING ON THE BUILDING"

Elvis recorded this W. O. Hoyle / Lillian Bowles spiritual at Studio B in Nashville as people were going to work on the morning of October 31, 1960, at the end of an all-night session that generated enough material for inaugural gospel album *His Hand In Mine*.

Elvis likely first heard this song at his mother's knee—her favorite group the Blackwood Brothers recorded it when Elvis was just two. Back-up group The Jordanaires had also done well with this number over the years, which may be why they suggested it to round off a productive night's work.

The song has made later sorties onto *Elvis in Nashville* and gospel anthologies *Amazing Grace* and *Peace In The Valley*, in addition to one or two spiritual-themed releases.

Alternate takes have appeared on *Elvis: Close Up* and on FTD releases *Fame And Fortune* and *His Hand In Mine*.

"WORLD OF OUR OWN, A"

Bill Giant, Bernie Baum and Florence Kaye wrote this undemanding ballad for Elvis to record at Radio Recorders on September 22, 1962, to shoehorn into *It Happened at the World's Fair*.

Repeat issues are limited to the *Double Features* and FTD release for the movie.

WORLDWIDE 50 GOLD AWARD HITS VOLS. 1 AND 2

The first volume of this four-LP set, released in August 1970, was a very early Elvis hits package that included the majority of his hits to date, and followed the criteria of selling over a million copies on original release. This collectors' release shifted 150,000 copies and achieved #45 on the LP chart, where it stayed for 22 weeks in late 1970 and early 1971. It was back in the charts for a further 14 weeks (rising to #83) after Elvis' death. Since its original issue, the collection has amassed double platinum sales.

Elvis in 1956 with Nick Adams and Natalie Wood

TRACK LISTING:
VOL. 1
1. Heartbreak Hotel
2. I Was The One
3. I Want You, I Need You, I Love You
4. Don't Be Cruel
5. Hound Dog
6. Love Me Tender
7. Any Way You Want Me
8. Too Much
9. Playing For Keeps
10. All Shook Up
11. That's When Your Heartaches Begin
12. Loving You
13. (Let Me Be Your) Teddy Bear
14. Jailhouse Rock
15. Treat Me Nice
16. I Beg Of You
17. Don't
18. Wear My Ring Around Your Neck
19. Hard Headed Woman
20. I Got Stung
21. (Now And Then There's) A Fool Such As I
22. A Big Hunk O'Love
23. Stuck On You
24. A Mess Of Blues
25. It's Now Or Never
26. I Gotta Know
27. Are You Lonesome Tonight?
28. Surrender
29. I Feel So Bad
30. Little Sister
31. Can't Help Falling In Love
32. Rock-A-Hula Baby
33. Anything That's Part Of You
34. Good Luck Charm
35. She's Not You
36. Return To Sender
37. Where Do You Come From
38. One Broken Heart For Sale
39. (You're The) Devil In Disguise
40. Bossa Nova Baby
41. Kissin' Cousins
42. Viva Las Vegas
43. Ain't That Loving You Baby
44. Wooden Heart
45. Crying In The Chapel
46. If I Can Dream
47. In The Ghetto
48. Suspicious Minds
49. Don't Cry, Daddy
50. Kentucky Rain
51. Excerpts from "Elvis Sails" interview

NB: CD versions have a slightly revised track line-up.

Volume two, titled *The Other Sides—Worldwide Gold Award Hits Vol. 2*, came out in August 1971. Mainly B-sides this time round, the four-LP set sold just 50,000 copies, and managed a peak of just #120 during its seven weeks in the charts, despite the inducement in each package of a tiny piece of a white suit that Elvis had worn in the movie *Clambake*.

TRACK LISTING:
VOL. 2
1. Puppet On A String
2. Witchcraft
3. Trouble
4. Poor Boy
5. I Want To Be Free
6. Doncha' Think It's Time
7. Young Dreams
8. The Next Step Is Love
9. You Don't Have To Say You Love Me
10. Paralyzed
11. My Wish Came True
12. When My Blue Moon Turns To Gold Again
13. Lonesome Cowboy
14. My Baby Left Me
15. It Hurts Me

16. I Need Your Love Tonight
17. Tell Me Why
18. Please Don't Drag That String Around
19. Young And Beautiful
20. Hot Dog
21. New Orleans
22. We're Gonna Move
23. Crawfish
24. King Creole
25. I Believe In The Man In The Sky
26. Dixieland Rock
27. The Wonder Of You
28. They Remind Me Too Much Of You
29. Mean Woman Blues
30. Lonely Man
31. Any Day Now
32. Don't Ask Me Why
33. (Marie's The Name) His Latest Flame
34. I Really Don't Want To Know
35. (You're So Square) Baby I Don't Care
36. I've Lost You
37. Let Me
38. Love Me
39. Got A Lot O' Livin' To Do
40. Fame And Fortune
41. Rip It Up
42. There Goes My Everything
43. Lover Doll
44. One Night
45. Just Tell Her Jim Said Hello
46. Ask Me
47. Patch It Up
48. As Long As I Have You
49. You'll Think Of Me
50. Wild In The Country

"WRITE TO ME FROM NAPLES"

Elvis took on this Dean Martin hit at Graceland in 1966. Elvis' interpretation of the Alex Alstone / Jimmy Kennedy track was not released until 1984 collectors' set. *A Golden Celebration*. It has since appeared on *The Home Recordings*.

WRITING

The criticism sometimes leveled at Elvis—that he wasn't of surpassing greatness because he didn't write his own material—misses the point that he had a vocal instrument of immense power and charge. When Elvis started singing, the music business was strictly demarcated into people who wrote songs and people who sang them. This was only breached in the early Sixties, by the folk revival and new groups like The Beatles.

What Elvis did write was countless thousands of autographs . . . as did the secretaries and entourage members schooled in his graphic ways.

In later years, entourage members confirm that Elvis entertained idle thoughts about writing an autobiography, to reveal to the world some truths about Elvis the private man.

Yet Elvis was a writer: he penned an article for the second-ever issue of *Rod Builder and Customizer*, titled "Rock 'n' Roll 'n' Drag," for the September 1956 issue.

As a letter writer, Elvis was inconstant. He restricted his efforts to long-distance love letters to girlfriend Anita Wood during his time away in Germany, and the occasional handwritten missive to particular deserving fans.

His most regular written outlet was scribbling diligently in the margins of books he found interesting, or jotting down thoughts on pieces of paper. One such note—fished out of the trash after a hotel stay in December 1976—served as the inspiration for Wayne Newton's song "The (Elvis) Letter."

ELVIS SCRIBBLED IN 1976: "I feel so alone sometimes. The night is quiet for me. I'd love to be able to sleep. I am glad that everyone is gone now. I'll probably not rest. I have no need for all this. Help me, Lord"

BILLY SMITH: "Elvis wrote maybe a dozen letters his whole life."

WRITING FOR THE KING

A 2006 FTD book/CD package containing interviews with over a hundred Elvis songwriters and exhaustive information about his songs. The first disc is of 1969/1970/1972 Elvis performances, the second is of song demos.

TRACK LISTING:
DISC ONE:
1. Blue Suede Shoes
2. I Got A Woman
3. All Shook Up
4. Love Me Tender
5. Jailhouse Rock / Don't Be Cruel
6. Heartbreak Hotel
7. Hound Dog
8. Words
9. Yesterday / Hey Jude
10. In The Ghetto
11. Don't Cry, Daddy
12. Polk Salad Annie
13. Kentucky Rain
14. Walk A Mile In My Shoes
15. Something
16. You've Lost That Lovin' Feelin'
17. I Just Can't Help Believin'
18. Never Been To Spain
19. Love Me
20. (Let Me Be Your) Teddy Bear / Don't Be Cruel
21. A Big Hunk O' Love
22. Suspicious Minds
23. Can't Help Falling In Love

DISC TWO:
1. Heartbreak Hotel (Singer: Glenn Reeves)
2. (Let Me Be Your) Teddy Bear (Singer: Otis Blackwell)
3. Don't Ask Me Why (Singer: Jimmy Breedlove)
4. Hard Headed Woman (Singer: Jimmy Breedlove)
5. Trouble (Singer: Unknown)
6. Wear My Ring Around Your Neck (Singer: Gus Coletti)
7. Pocketful Of Rainbows (Singer: Jimmy Breedlove)
8. No More (Singer: Don Robertson)
9. (Marie's The Name) His Latest Flame (Singer: Mort Shuman)
10. Good Luck Charm (Singer: Robert Moseley)
11. Devil In Disguise (Singer: Bill Giant)
12. Viva Las Vegas (Singer: Mort Shuman)
13. C'mon Everybody (Singer: Bob Johnston)
14. Kissin' Cousins (Singer: Malcolm Dodd)
15. My Desert Serenade (Singer: Kenny Karen)
16. Could I Fall In Love (Singer: Malcolm Dodd)
17. The Love Machine (Singer: Gerald Nelson)
18. Clambake (Singer: Winfield Scott)
19. Wearin' That Loved On Look (Singer: Dallas Frazier)
20. I've Lost You (Singer: Peter Lee Sterling)
21. The Next Step Is Love (Singer: Paul Evans)
22. Mary In The Morning (Singer: Johnny Cymbal)
23. Burning Love (Singer: Dennis Linde)
24. T-R-O-U-B-L-E (Singer: Jerry Chesnut)
25. Raised On Rock (Singer: Mark James)
26. Way Down (Singer: Layng Martine Jr.)

WYNETTE, TAMMY
(B. VIRGINIA WYNETTE PUGH, 1942-1998)

The "First Lady of Country Music" took in an Elvis show when she was just 14 at Tupelo, in September 1956, at his homecoming concert.

Wynette worked her way up to the top of the country music tree from inauspicious beginnings. She earned money picking cotton, brought up her kids as a single mother, and trained as a beautician in Birmingham, Alabama. All in all she scored twenty country #1s, including her huge 1968 chart-toppers "D-I-V-O-R-C-E" and "Stand By Your Man."

Y

YARNALL, CELESTE
(B. 1944)

An actress and businesswoman who starred opposite Elvis in late-period movie *Live a Little, Love a Little*. During her long acting career, Yarnall has also worked opposite stars Paul Newman, Jack Lemmon and Jerry Lewis, and was the love interest of "Chekhov" in the original "Star Trek." In recent years, she has been a regular at Elvis commemorative events. She runs several businesses, including a line of pet nutrition products

"YELLOW ROSE OF TEXAS"

Elvis recorded a medley of this song (credited to Fred Wise and Randy Starr in this adaptation) with "The Eyes Of Texas" on July 10, 1963 at Radio Recorders for *Viva Las Vegas*.

The marching song has a history that dates back at least to the 1850s. During the Civil War, it was known under the name "The Gallant Hood Of Texas," in homage to General John Hood. In more modern times, the song was a #1 hit for Mitch Miller in 1955.

Elvis' version first appeared on vinyl as part of 1968 compilation *Singer Presents Elvis Singing Flaming Star and Others*. Since then, it has reappeared on *Double Dynamite*, the *Viva Las Vegas* FTD release, and not a great deal else.

"YESTERDAY"

Elvis' contribution to the estimated three thousand covers of this Lennon/McCartney track—generally believed to be the most covered song of all time—was a month of live performances in Las Vegas in August 1969. His performance an August 25, 1969 made it onto the *On Stage* album. Though he actually sang it in a medley with "Hey Jude," the second song went unreleased until the new millennium.

Other performances from that August are on *Elvis Aron Presley*, *Live In Las Vegas* (with "Hey Jude"), and the 2007 BMG *Viva Las Vegas* release (also with "Hey Jude"). FTD releases from the same engagement that feature the Beatles classic are *Writing For The King*, *Elvis At The International* and *All Shook Up* (once again with "Hey Jude").

An Elvis rehearsal from 1970 came out three decades later on *That's The Way It Is—Special Edition*.

Paul McCartney's original was a 1965 #1 hit in the US.

YOGA

Like many people approaching the life landmark of thirty, Elvis entered a phase of reflection and introspection. In 1965, hairdresser and new friend Larry Geller introduced Elvis to Kriya yoga, a form of meditation and physical exercise popularized by Paramahansa Yogananda in his book *Autobiography of a Yogi*, which was practiced at the Self-Realization Fellowship in California. Elvis was said to be very impressed when he learned that Yogananda's body had not suffered decay after his death.

Kriya yoga descends from the most ancient texts of the Hindu religion. The central pursuit of Kriya is to unleash the body's energies by working with the breath. The practice requires disciples to follow the guidance of a guru; initiation takes place after a year-long program of daily meditation and exercises. Elvis tried to persuade Self-Realization Fellowship leader Sri Daya Mata to initiate him early; after she refused, he gradually lost interest in the practice. Years later, however, he managed to persuade Larry Geller to reveal a rite usually taught only to initiates.

On the movie *Easy Come, Easy Go*, when Elvis sang throwaway ditty "Yoga Is As Yoga Does," Larry Geller recounts that Elvis stormed off the set in a rage because he believed that the Colonel had deliberately included a song that belittled a practice that he took very seriously.

YOGANANDA, PARAMAHANSA
(B. MUKUNDA LAL GHOSH 1893-1952)

Yogananda was one of the first Indians to bring yoga and Indian spirituality to the US in 1920, founding the Self-Realization Fellowship, which he later moved to LA. Paramahansa is an honorary name, meaning "supreme swan." The central tenet of the guru's teachings is that people must have direct experience of truth, rather than simply and blindly follow a belief. He believed that everything we see is God's "cosmic movie show"—a view that resonated strongly with Elvis.

YOGANANDA: "We are all part of the One Spirit. When you experience the true meaning of religion, which is to know God, you will realize that He is your Self, and that He exists equally and impartially in all beings."

"YOGA IS AS YOGA DOES"

This song from *Easy Come, Easy Go* was recorded at the Paramount soundstage on September 29, 1966. Written by Gerald Nelson and Fred Burch, the duet with actress Elsa Lanchester pokes fun at yoga—a discipline that Elvis was serious about. A candidate for Elvis' ten silliest songs, "Yoga Is As Yoga Does" first came out on the movie soundtrack EP, and has since reappeared on *I Got Lucky*, the *Double Features* issue for the movie, and on the 2007 FTD soundtrack re-release (which has alternates).

"YOU ASKED ME TO"

Elvis recorded this Waylon Jennings country hit (co-written with Billy Joe Shaver) at Stax studios on December 11, 1973, originally for release on his *Promised Land* album. It has since appeared on *Walk A Mile In My Shoes*, *Great Country Songs* and *The Country Side Of Elvis*.

Felton Jarvis's 1980 remix of Elvis' Stax recording came out on the *Guitar Man* album and made it to #8 on the Country chart as a single (with "Loving Arms") in 1981, matching the performance of the Jennings original.

Outtakes are on *Essential Elvis Vol. 5* and FTD's *Made in Memphis*. FTD release *Too Much Monkey Business* features a reworked version from the *Guitar Man* remix sessions.

"YOU BELONG TO MY HEART"

Elvis strummed his way through this Dora Luz hit from 1944 during the *Million Dollar Quartet* session in December 1956. The song was written by Ray Gilbert and Augustin Lara, under Spanish title "Solamente Una Vez." In addition to the various MDQ releases, Elvis' dulcet rendition is also represented on *Today Tomorrow & Forever*.

"YOU BETTER RUN"

Elvis sang bass to Charlie Hodge's lead on this traditional gospel song during rehearsals on March 31, 1972 at RCA's Studio C in Hollywood, when Elvis was preparing for upcoming shows and the *Elvis on Tour* documentary. The rehearsal's first public release didn't take place until many years after Elvis' death, when it appeared on gospel compilations *Peace in the Valley* and *Amazing Grace*. Elvis performed the song live in a medley with "Bosom Of Abraham" in July 1975 and March 1977.

"YOU CAN HAVE HER (I DON'T WANT HER)"

Elvis sang this 1961 Roy Hamilton hit, written by William Cook, in concert on May 11, 1974. It appeared on bootleg releases including *Suzie Q* and *Slippin' 'n' Slidin' With Elvis* prior to an official release on FTD CD *Live in L.A.*

"YOU CAN'T SAY NO IN ACAPULCO"

Sid Feller, Dorothy Fuller and Lee Morris penned this track that Elvis cut at Radio Recorders on January 23, 1963 for the *Fun in Acapulco* soundtrack.

Later releases are on the *Fun in Acapulco Double Features* and FTD issues (which also features multiple outtakes).

"YOU DO SOMETHING TO ME"

Elvis sang a line of this Cole Porter song in concert in 1975. It's on bootleg *On A April's Fool Day, Vol. 2*.

"You Don't Have To Say You Love Me"

Elvis laid down his version of this 1966 #4 Dusty Springfield hit at RCA's Nashville studio on June 6, 1970. Released as a single with "Patch It Up" on the B-side in October 1970, it sold an initial 800,000 copies, peaking at #11 in the Hot 100 over its ten week stay, and rising to #1 on the Easy Listening chart. This studio version has since appeared on *Worldwide Gold Award Hits Vol. 2*, *Elvis' Golden Records Vol. 5*, *Walk A Mile In My Shoes*, *Platinum—A Life In Music*, *Artist Of The Century*, *Elvis 2nd To None*, *Hitstory* and *Love Elvis*. A sole studio alternate has come out officially, take 2 on *Essential Elvis Vol. 4*.

The song started life in Italian as "Io che non vivo piu d'un ora senza te," written by Pino Donnagio and Vito Pallavicini and a huge success for Donnagio at the 1963 San Remo Song Festival. At Dusty Springfield's request, Vicki Wickham and Simon Napier-Bell wrote English lyrics to the tune.

Elvis performed the song regularly on stage from 1970 to 1975. It features in the *That's The Way It Is* documentary and at his 1972 Madison Square Garden shows. On disc, it came out on the *That's The Way It Is* tie-in album (and later, from this period, on *That's The Way It Is— Special Edition* and on FTD issues *One Night In Vegas* and *The Way It Was*). An early Vegas version more recently featured on the 2007 *Viva Las Vegas* title.

As well as the *Elvis As Recorded At Madison Square Garden* live album, 1972 vintage performances are on *An Afternoon In The Garden*, *The Live Greatest Hits* and on FTD releases *The Impossible Dream* and *Summer Festival*. Mid-Seventies versions can be found on FTD releases *Big Boss Man* and *Dixieland Rocks*.

"You Don't Know Me"

Elvis' version of Eddy Arnold's mid-Fifties Country hit, written by Arnold and Cindy Walker, came out as the B-side to "Big Boss Man" less than three weeks after Elvis recorded it in Nashville on September 11, 1967.

Elvis' "You Don't Know Me" rose no higher than #44 on the *Billboard* Hot 100; Ray Charles had taken it to #2 in 1962.

The ballad was on the *Clambake* LP. It was later released on *Elvis Sings Hits from His Movies*, *From Nashville To Memphis*, *Command Performances*, the *Double Features* issue for the movie, *Tomorrow Is A Long Time*, *The Country Side Of Elvis* and sundry romantic-themed hits packages.

An earlier recording of the song, laid down on February 21, 1967 at Studio B, to which strings were added, made it into the movie. This version did not officially appear on record until the *Clambake* Double Features release in 1994. Alternates may be found on FTD releases *So High* (from the second session) and *Clambake* (from the first). A further alternate is on *Today Tomorrow & Forever*.

Elvis performed the song live at least once during his summer 1970 season.

"You Gave Me A Mountain"

Elvis added this big Marty Robbins number to his live shows in early 1972, in the immediate aftermath of Priscilla walking out of his life. He sang it during his live shows that year and regularly ever after. It was on *Elvis on Tour* in 1972, *Aloha From Hawaii Via Satellite* in January 1973, and it's on his final video appearance, *Elvis In Concert*.

Frankie Laine had a gold record hit with the song in 1969, doing better than the version released around the same time by songwriter Robbins.

Various live Elvis performances have surfaced over the years on *Elvis Aron Presley*, *Always On My Mind*, *The Alternate Aloha*, *Walk A Mile In My Shoes*, *Burning Love*, *Live In Las Vegas*, *The Country Side Of Elvis*, *Elvis: Close Up*, *Elvis Live* and the 2007 *Viva Las Vegas*.

It's also on FTD live releases *An American Trilogy*, *Closing Night*, *It's Midnight*, *Dragonheart*, *Southern Nights*, *Takin' Tahoe Tonight!*, *Dinner At Eight*, *Tucson '76*, *New Year's Eve* and *Unchained Melody*.

"You Gotta Stop"

Elvis laid down this melodramatic Bill Giant / Bernie Baum/ Florence Kaye track for the movie *Easy Come Easy Go* (and the tie-in EP) on September 29, 1966, at the Paramount sound stage, after Red West gave a last minute tweak to the lyrics.

Later official releases are restricted to budget Camden album *I Got Lucky* in 1971, the *Double Features* release in the Nineties, and the 2007 FTD re-release (which includes an instrumental-only version).

"You'll Be Gone"

One of the exclusive cohort of songs on which Elvis has a writing credit, and one of even fewer on which Elvis actually did some of the writing, with pals Red West and Charlie Hodge. Hodge came up with the Spanish melody to replace the original plan, which was use the instrumental line from Cole Porter's "Begin The Beguine."

Elvis recorded the song in Nashville on March 18, 1962. It remained on hold until it was released as the B-side to "Do the Clam," from the *Girl Happy* soundtrack, in early 1965—when it failed to break into the Hot 100.

The song has since appeared on *From Nashville To Memphis*, later CD releases of *Pot Luck*, and the FTD *Girl Happy* re-release.

Alternates are on *Elvis By The Presleys* and FTD issues *Studio B: Nashville Outtakes*, *Long Lonely Highway* and *Pot Luck*.

"You'll Never Walk Alone"

A 1954 R & B #1 for Roy Hamilton, and long one of Elvis' all-time favorite tunes, Elvis finally recorded this Richard Rodgers / Oscar Hammerstein-penned spiritual in Nashville on September 11, 1967. He played the piano himself at what started out as a jam and ended as a passionate Elvis gospel classic.

"You'll Never Walk Alone" was initially a show tune for 1945 musical *Carousel*, before being covered, among others, by Judy Garland, Gerry and the Pacemakers, and many of Elvis' favorite gospel singers. The song was adopted by UK soccer team Liverpool as their club tune.

RCA first released Elvis' performance with "We Call On Him" on the B-side in March 1968, during the fallow period for record sales before Elvis' 1968 Comeback Special. Consequently, it only made it to #90 in the charts, selling a meager 50,000 copies. Despite the lack of popular acclaim, Elvis' song was nominated for a Best Sacred Performance Grammy, a prize that was won that year by Elvis favorite Jake Hess.

In 1971, "You'll Never Walk Alone" served as the title track to an Elvis gospel compilation that over the years has racked up enough sales to war-rant triple Platinum status. It has since graced *Double Dynamite*, *Greatest Hits Vol. 1*, CD versions of *His Hand in Mine*, and gospel anthologies *Amazing Grace*, *Peace In The Valley*, *Ultimate Gospel* and *Elvis Inspirational*. The song was also re-released as a single in 1982 (with "There Goes My Everything").

Alternate takes have appeared on *Platinum: A Life In Music* and FTD album *So High*.

Rumors have circulated that Elvis recorded this song in his first flush at Sun; he may also have had a stab at it in the studio in late 1960. Fortunate Seventies show fans witnessed poignant performances at which Elvis sang to his own piano accompaniment.

You'll Never Walk Alone (LP)

RCA released this album of previously-available spirituals (plus "Who Am I?") in March 1971 on its Camden label. Though never charting higher than #69, and only selling 200,000 copies on its initial release, it has sold fifteen times as much as a back catalogue item.

TRACK LISTING:

1. You'll Never Walk Alone
2. Who Am I?
3. Let Us Pray
4. Peace In The Valley
5. We Call On Him
6. I Believe
7. It Is No Secret
8. Sing You Children
9. Take My Hand, Precious Lord

The album was re-released in 2006.

"You'll Think of Me"

Elvis recorded this Mort Shuman song on January 14, 1969 at American Studio, initially for release as the B-side of "Suspicious Minds."

In short order it appeared on upcoming Elvis albums *From Vegas to Memphis*, *Back In Memphis*, and then *Worldwide Gold Award Hits Vol. 2*. In later years it has come out on *Elvis Sings Mort Shuman & Doc Pomus*, *From Nashville To Memphis*, later CD issues of *From Elvis In Memphis* and *Suspicious Minds: The Memphis 1969 Anthology*.

Alternate takes are on *Suspicious Minds: The Memphis 1969 Anthology* and FTD releases *The Memphis Sessions* and *Made in Memphis*.

"Young And Beautiful"

Elvis recorded no fewer than four different versions of this track, written by Abner Silver and Aaron Schroeder, for *Jailhouse Rock* at Radio Recorders on April 30, 1957.

He laid down one version for the *Jailhouse Rock* EP, one for the movie (released years later on *The King Of Rock & Roll*), one for the finale (once again, released years later, on *Essential Elvis Vol. 1*), and the so-called "Florita Club" version (even later for this one to gain an official release, on *Elvis: Close Up*).

The song has since come out on *Worldwide Gold Award Hits Vol. 2* and *A Valentine Gift For You*. Various alternate versions and outtakes have been leaking out since the late Fifties, starting with *A Date With Elvis*, and followed over the years by *I Was The One*, *The King Of Rock & Roll*, *Today Tomorrow & Forever* and *Elvis: Close Up*. Multiple alternates grace the forty-year anniversary *Jailhouse Rock* CD release; another alternate is on FTD release *Flashback*.

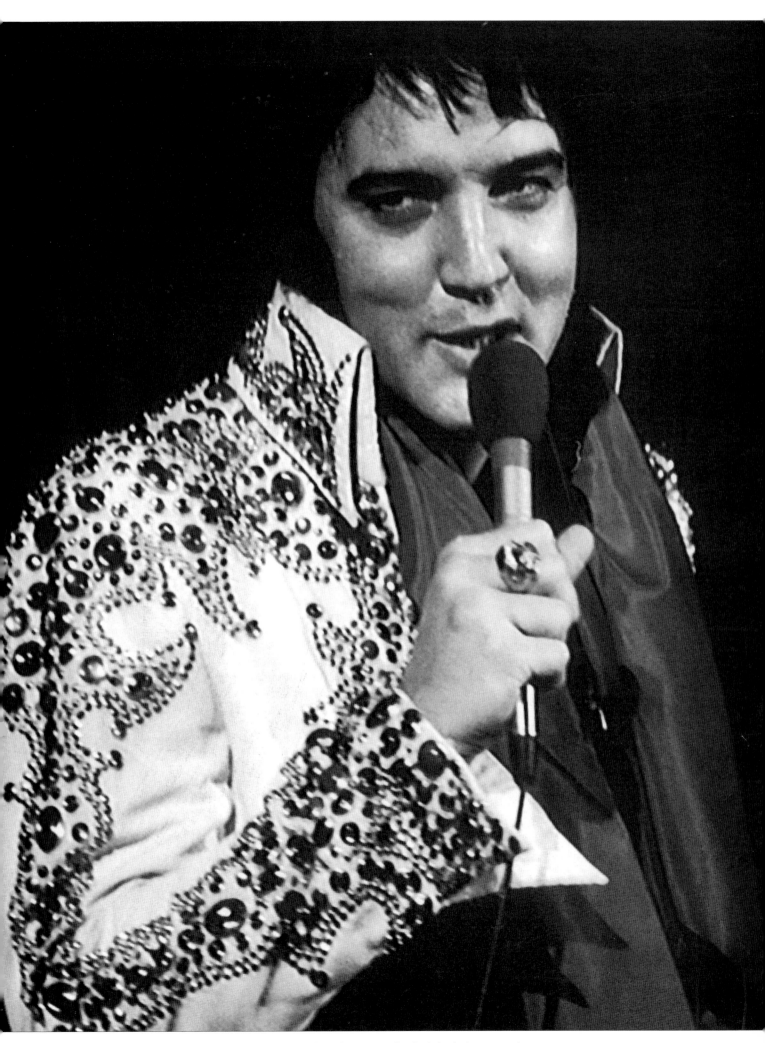

Elvis in concert Memphis Tennessee 1974. This performance was Elvis' first before his hometown audience
since his Memphis charity performance at the beginning of the swinging 60's.

Elvis with Gig Young in *Kid Galahad*, 1962.

Very, very occasionally Elvis pulled this song out of the hat on stage in the Seventies, on at least one occasion in a medley with "Wooden Heart." With the exception of a rehearsal on FTD's 2004 release *Elvis On Tour—The Rehearsals*, bootlegs have cornered the live market so far.

YOUNG, CHIP

This Atlanta-born guitarist worked with Elvis in Nashville at Felton Jarvis-produced sessions from 1966 right through to 1971. He was also involved in Elvis' last recordings session at Graceland in 1976. In 1980, he teamed up with Jarvis again for the *Guitar Man* reorchestration of Elvis material.

"YOUNG DREAMS"

Elvis laid down this Martin Kalmanoff / Aaron Schroeder composition at Radio Recorders on January 23, 1958 for the *King Creole* soundtrack and associated EP and LP.

Later outings are limited to *Worldwide Gold Award Hits Vol. 2, The King Of Rock & Roll* anthology and *King Creole* album reissues.

YOUNG, FARON
(1932-1996)

Faron Young first saw Elvis perform when the boy from Memphis was a raw rookie at the foot of the bill and Young was headlining. Before long, Young was happy to let the relative unknown take top billing—he willingly asked promoters to give him an earlier slot, because after Elvis had

done with the audience, they wouldn't listen to anyone else.

Born in Shreveport, Louisiana on February 25, 1932, in the early Fifties Young became the leading exponent of honky tonk after Hank William's untimely death. Young started out at his local venue, the Louisiana Hayride, where he teamed up with Webb Pierce. By the early Fifties, he was a regular at the Opry. He racked up top ten Country through the rest of the decade and much of the Sixties. Like Elvis, the "Hillbilly Heart Throb" had his early career interrupted by a spell in the Army; unlike Elvis, he opted for Special Services and sang for the troops rather than serving as an ordinary soldier. When the Colonel took on Elvis as a client, he was trying to get Young established in Hollywood through Hank Snow Attractions. Young became something of a fixture on TV, and acted in half a dozen movies in the mid-Fifties.

Young's best-selling song, "If You Ain't Lovin' ," came out a few months after Elvis released his debut single "That's All Right (Mama)." Young penned "Is It So Strange," a song he wrote specifically for Elvis that sounded much like Elvis' beloved Ink Spots, but then decided to release it himself after a disagreement with Elvis' management over publishing rights. Elvis eventually covered the song in 1957.

Young's career was still going strong well into the Eighties. He was inducted into the Country Music Hall of Fame in 2000, four years after taking his own life after a bout of serious illness.

YOUNG, GIG
(B. BYRON ELSWORTH BARR, 1913-1978)

This actor played the sly boxing trainer opposite Elvis in *Kid Galahad* (1962). Young was nominated for two Oscars (*Come Fill The Cup*, 1951 and *Teacher's Pet*, 1958), before winning a gong as best

supporting actor in *They Shoot Horses, Don't They?* (1969). After winning his Oscar, his career went into a decline and he believed that he was a victim of the so-called "Oscar curse." Heavy drinking had something to do with it too: in the mid-Seventies, he was replaced at the last minute by Gene Wilder in *Blazing Saddles*, and also lost the role as Charlie in TV's "Charlie's Angels"

At the time he was working on *Kid Galahad*, Young was married to actress Elizabeth Montgomery, latterly of "Bewitched" fame.

Young's fourth wife, Elaine, helped Elvis find a house to rent in LA. His fifth wife, German actress Kim Schmidt, was killed in 1978, and Young was found dead nearby after taking his own life, the gun still in his hand.

"YOUNG LOVE"

Elvis covered this 1956 Ric Cartey / Carolyn Joyner rockabilly love song in rehearsals for the 1968 NBC TV Special. In early 1957, Tab Hunter and Sonny James were respectively #1 and #2 in the *Billboard* Top 100 with this song. It has since been covered by artists including Frankie Avalon, Connie Smith and Donny Osmond.

For years, Elvis' "Young Love" was only available on bootlegs such as *The Complete Dressing Room Session*. It finally received an official release in 2006 on FTD issue *Let Yourself Go*, in a medley with "Blue Moon" and "Oh Happy Day."

YOUNG, REGGIE
(B. 1936)

A Memphis-born guitarist (and rare master of the electric sitar) who worked with Elvis at American